Notable Americans:
What They Did, from 1620 to the Present

Related Titles Published by Gale Research Company

American Diaries—This two-volume work is a chronologically arranged annotated bibliography of published American diaries and journals written from 1492 to 1980. Entries include full bibliographic information and are extensively annotated, indicating such information as historic events, modes of travel, diary's emphasis, religious affiliation, personal names, background on the diarist, and more.

Biography Almanac—This three-volume set covers about 25,000 famous and infamous newsmakers from Biblical times to the present. Volumes one and two are arranged alphabetically and provide brief biographical data together with citations to biographical sketches appearing in over 300 widely held sources. Volume three is an index volume that lists the biographical subjects chronologically by day of month for birth and death, geographically by places of birth and death, and alphabetically by occupation.

Biography and Genealogy Master Index—The eight-volume second edition, published in 1980, and its 1981 through 1987 annual supplements contain over 6 million citations to biographical articles appearing in more than 1,000 who's whos and other works of collective biography, including historical as well as present-day men and women of note.

Contemporary Newsmakers—Four quarterly issues furnish up-to-date biographical profiles on people in the news. Covering all fields, from business and international affairs to entertainment and the arts, the articles feature photographs of individuals along with biographical and career data. Each year's issues of *Contemporary Newsmakers* are cumulated annually into a hardbound volume.

In Black and White—This work identifies over 15,000 notable blacks in America, Africa, and elsewhere and the magazines, books, and newspapers in which information about them may be found. Entries provide full name, birth and/or death dates, occupation, and a list of publications containing more information. An interedition supplement providing new and updated entries for about 7,000 notable blacks is also available.

Notable Americans:
What They Did, from 1620 to the Present

Chronological and Organizational Listings of Leaders in
Government, the Military, Business, Labor, Religion,
Education, Cultural Organizations, Philanthropy, and
National Associations, Including Recipients of
Significant Awards and Honors

FOURTH EDITION

Linda S. Hubbard,
Editor

(Third Edition was titled *Notable Names in American History*)

GALE RESEARCH COMPANY • BOOK TOWER • DETROIT, MICHIGAN 48226

T 23860

Editor: Linda S. Hubbard
Assistant Editors: Connielou Crawford, Owen O'Donnell
Contributing Editors: Roger Hubbard, Jack Radike, Robert C. Thomas

Production Manager: Mary Beth Trimper
Production Assistant: Anthony J. Scolaro
Art Director: Arthur Chartow

Special thanks to members of the New York editorial staff, *Contemporary Authors* staff, and *Encyclopedia of Associations* research staff for their assistance in the preparation of this edition.

Library of Congress Cataloging-in-Publication Data

Notable Americans.

"Chronological and organizational listings of leaders in government, the military, business, labor, religion, education, cultural organizations, philanthropy, and national associations, including recipient of significant awards and honors."
Rev. ed. of: Notable names in American history. 3d ed. of White's conspectus of American biography. 1973.
Includes indexes.
1. United States—Biography. I. Hubbard, Linda S. II. Notable names in American history.
E176.N89   1988   920'.073   87-32671
ISBN 0-8103-2534-9

Computerized photocomposition by
Sterling Software
Riverdale, Maryland
Printed in the United States

Contents

Continues . . .

Preface

"Who were the delegates to the Constitutional Convention?" "How many electoral votes did Thomas E. Dewey receive when he ran against Harry S Truman in the 1948 presidential election?" "After the passage of the Civil Rights Act of 1964, which congressional delegates, governors, and mayors of leading cities took office throughout the South to implement this legislation?" "Who headed the U.S. Military Assistance Command, Vietnam?" "Who has represented the United States as ambassador to Japan?" "How many individuals have served as president of Harvard University since its founding?" "Who succeeded Ronald Reagan as president of the Screen Actors Guild?" "To whom has the American Institute of Architects given its Gold Medal?"

All these questions and thousands more are quickly and easily answered by *Notable Americans: What They Did, from 1620 to the Present*. Providing ready access to a wealth of facts, *Notable Americans* offers a single, convenient source of chronological and organizational listings of leaders in government, the military, business, labor, religion, education, cultural organizations, philanthropy, and national associations, from colonial times to the present, including recipients of significant awards and honors. In nineteen subject-oriented sections, *Notable Americans* lists the names of over forty-two thousand noteworthy individuals who have shaped the history of the United States from its earliest days through 1986. Students and teachers, writers and editors, librarians and researchers will find it a handy ready-reference tool that quickly furnishes names needed to answer a single query or to serve as a starting point for more in-depth research.

Previous Editions

This is the fourth edition of a work first published in 1906 under the title *The Conspectus of American Biography*, which was a companion to the *National Cyclopaedia of American Biography*. The *Conspectus* provided lists similar to those in this volume and referred users to sketches in *National Cyclopaedia* for details on the listees. Subsequent editions—*White's Conspectus of American Biography* (1937) and *Notable Names in American History* (1973)—refined the contents, eliminating some lists and adding others, and brought the entire work up to date. References to entries in the *National Cyclopaedia of American Biography* were not included in the third edition nor in this one.

About This Edition

The primary goals of the editors in preparing this edition have been to improve access to the contents and to bring it up to date through 1986. Page design in each chapter has been thoroughly reviewed and refined, and a new Organization Index added to improve accessibility. The updating has involved extensive research in countless published sources, supplemented by numerous letters and telephone calls to track down unpublished information. In those few instances where information through 1986 was impossible to obtain prior to going to press, the most up-to-date information available is provided.

During the fourteen years since the last edition was published, many of the institutions listed in *Notable Americans* have changed their names, as well as their leaders. Listings appear under the current institution names, but in such sections as those on colleges (Section XII), museums (Section XIV), and corporations (Section XVI), brief historical notes record the previous names as well. The dramatic changes in the American economy over the past decade are reflected in the corporate section (Section XVI), which has undergone the most substantial revision of any section in this edition. The third edition included companies with assets or sales of one billion dollars or more; this edition lists only those with assets or sales of three billion dollars or more, with the result that nine previously listed companies have been dropped but over sixty have been added.

The citations for U.S. diplomatic representatives to foreign nations in Section IX also reflect changes, such as the United States establishing relations with newly independent nations. Cross-references in this section assist in tracing political and geographic changes; for example, the entry for U.S. representatives to Germany refers users to similar entries for Prussia, the Federal Republic of Germany, and the German Democratic Republic, as well as lists representatives to the unified nation. In the section on laureates (Section XIX), a few discontinued awards and local honors have been eliminated; and in Section XIV a number of new museums—the International Center of Photography and the Museum of Broadcasting, for example—have been added. Similar additions and refinements will be made in future editions.

Contents and Arrangement

The wealth of information available in *Notable Americans*—from the names of the signers of the Mayflower Compact in 1620 to the recipients of the Academy of American Poets Fellowship through 1986—is clearly presented in the following nineteen sections:

The Colonial Era—Cites signers of important documents, delegates to principal convocations, and governing officials.

U.S. Government: Executive Branch—Lists presidents and vice presidents as well as presidential and vice presidential candidates from the first election in 1789 through the most recent in 1984. A listing of all first ladies is also included.

Cabinets—Information on cabinet members from 1789 to the present is provided in two convenient arrangements—by presidential term, and by department.

U.S. Government: Legislative Branch—Presents the First to Ninety-Ninth Congresses in chronological order and alphabetically lists the state delegations for each. Members of the Senate and House of Representatives, along with their political affiliations, are clearly indicated for each state.

U.S. Government: Judicial Branch—Identifies, in chronological order, chief justices and associate justices of the Supreme Court. Also included are U.S. Court of Appeals justices for the eleven federal court circuits and the District of Columbia as well as justices serving seven other special federal courts, such as the U.S. Court of International Trade.

States of the Union—In a new, more legible and compact format, the governors, senators, and chief justices of the state court systems are listed chronologically for each state.

The Confederacy—Notes government leaders, congressional members, and battlefield commanders of the Confererate States of America, 1861-1865.

The Military—Provides names of hundreds of individuals who have played a major role in U.S. military history. Included in this section are secretaries of defense and the services, chairmen of the Joint Chiefs of Staff, and commanders of the armed forces, from the revolutionary period through the Vietnam era.

Diplomatic Representatives of the United States—Identifies every foreign country with which the United States has established official relations, from 1790 to the present, and chronologically lists the heads of U.S. delegations to those countries.

Federal Agency Chiefs—Highlights the heads of forty current and former government bureaus and agencies, including the Central Intelligence Agency, Environmental Protection Agency, Federal Reserve System, and Small Business Administration.

Chief Executives of U.S. Cities—Organized alphabetically by state and then by city, this section cites mayors and other chief executives of seventy-eight cities that are state capitals, have populations over five hundred thousand, or have numbered among America's ten most populous since 1800.

College and University Presidents—Covers the chief executives of more than three hundred leading colleges and universities throughout the United States.

Foundation Presidents—Identifies the heads of one hundred important foundations, including the Solomon R. Guggenheim Foundation, Ford Foundation, and Twentieth Century Fund.

Museum and Art Gallery Directors—Highlights the directors of over one hundred thirty museums and art galleries, from the Museum of Science and Industry in Chicago to such outstanding local galleries as the Albright-Knox Art Gallery in Buffalo.

Religious Leaders—Lists the cardinals, archbishops, bishops, moderators, and presidents of major religious groups in the United States, from the 1780's to the present. Included are the Protestant Episcopal Church, Roman Catholic Church, Presbyterian Church, and other major denominations, as well as founders of U.S. religious sects, societies, and movements.

Corporate Executives—Presents the presidents, board chairmen, and/or chief executive officers of U.S. corporations, banks, insurance companies, and public utilities with assets or sales in excess of three billion dollars. Over two hundred corporations are listed, from Abbott Laboratories to Xerox Corp.

Labor Leaders—Notes the presidents of sixty unions, including those for steelworkers, longshoremen, teachers, actors, typographers, and musicians.

Association Executives—Presidents or executive directors of one hundred twenty national learned, scientific, technical, professional, and fraternal organizations are identified, among them the American Bar Association, American Institute of Chemists, Boy Scouts of America, and National Conference of Christians and Jews.

Laureates—Presents a listing of Americans who have been recognized for outstanding achievements in the arts, sciences, and humanities, and for contributions to the betterment of mankind. Over one hundred awards and honors are covered, including the Bollingen Prize, Presidential Medal of Freedom, and Spirit of St. Louis Medal.

Two Indexes Aid Users

To best serve the needs of a wide variety of users, the information contained in *Notable Americans* is readily accessible through two indexes.

Personal Name Index—Each mention of every name in this edition is cited in the Personal Name Index along with the accompanying page number on which the name can be located. Thus with the assistance of the fifty-five thousand citations in this index, a user can trace Dwight D. Eisenhower's career, for example, from the military positions he held during World War II, to his tenure as president of Columbia University from 1948 to 1952, and then on to his term of office as America's thirty-fourth president. The Personal Name Index also guides users to citations of the top civilian honors Eisenhower received. (Since variant forms of a name sometimes occur—for example, with or without a middle initial or such suffixes as "Jr."—users should check possible variations in the Personal Name Index to make a thorough search for a given individual.)

Organization Index—A new feature in this edition, the more than twenty-two hundred citations in the Organization Index eliminate the need to spend valuable time paging through one or more sections to locate a specific institution or group. Every major heading for corporations, government branches and agencies, cities and states, military units, associations, foundations, awards, museums, universities, religious groups, and historical events is listed in this index. And numerous name reversals further assist users in quickly pinpointing information. The entry for "Signers of the Declaration of Independence," for example, is indexed under "Signers" and "Declaration," and the citation for the "Isabella Stewart Gardner Museum" can be located either under "Isabella"" or "Gardner."

Acknowledgments

We wish to thank the many people at government agencies, corporate offices, and various other organizations who assisted us by providing updated information to include in this edition of *Notable Americans*.

A number of Gale Research Company people have also contributed guidance, research assistance, and editorial suggestions to improve this edition. Faced with a daunting variety of lists and countless requests for design changes, art director Arthur Chartow still managed to create coherent page designs that make needed information faster to locate and easier to interpret and the book as a whole more compact. (The 563 text pages in this edition contain fourteen years' worth of information not included in the 612 text pages of the previous edition.) Senior editor Annie Brewer suggested numerous valuable resources utilized in the earliest stages of research for this edition. Thanks to senior editor Denise Allard, we were able to draw on the archives of Gale's *Encyclopedia of Associations* to update Section XVIII, with the help of research assistant David T. Reid. Another *Encyclopedia of Associations* staff member, research supervisor Jack Radike, joined senior editor Robert C. Thomas as our military advisors on Section VIII. And senior editor Linda Metzger monitored proofreading of several sections by her staff members—Marilyn K. Basel, Sharon Malinowski, Michael Mueller, and Joanne M. Peters. The Organization Index reflects the work of Roger Hubbard, who also provided research assistance. Tom Bachmann, June Barnett, Sharon Gamboa, and Bettina Versaci of our New York editorial staff chased down details, input data, proofread, and checked typeset pages. The bulk of the research for material newly added to this edition was done by Connielou Crawford and Owen O'Donnell, whose persistence and care show throughout the book. Finally, the indefatigable Chris Nasso contributed at every level, from overall philosophy to punctuation in the index.

Suggestions Are Welcome

If users would like to suggest additional categories of information to be included in future editions of *Notable Americans,* they are encouraged to send these suggestions to the editor. Other comments are also most welcome and should be addressed to: The Editor, *Notable Americans,* 150 East 50th Street, New York, NY 10022.

Notable Americans:
What They Did, from 1620 to the Present

I

The Colonial Era

The Colonial Era

Signers of important documents, delegates to principal convocations, and colonial state officials from the year of the Mayflower Compact to 1789.

Signers of the Mayflower Compact

(Dec. 21, 1620)

John Alden
Isaac Allerton
John Allerton
John Billington
William Bradford
William Brewster
Richard Britteridge
Peter Brown
John Carver
James Chilton
Richard Clarke
Francis Cooke
John Crackston
Edward Doty
Francis Eaton
Thomas English
Moses Fletcher
Edward Fuller
Samuel Fuller
Richard Gardiner
John Goodman
Stephen Hopkins
John Howland
Edward Lister
Edmund Margeson
Christopher Martin
William Mullins
Degory Priest
John Ridgedale
Thomas Rogers
George Soule
Myles Standish
Edward Tilley
John Tilley
Thomas Tinker
John Turner
Richard Warren
William White
Thomas Williams
Edward Winslow
Gilbert Winslow

Delegates to the First Colonial Congress

(New York, NY, 1690)

Etienne Delancey (NY)
Nathan Gold (CT)
Jacob Leisler (NY)

William Pitkin (CT)
Samuel Sewall (MA)
William Stoughton (MA)
John Wolley (Plymouth)

Delegates to the Second Colonial Congress

(Albany, NY, 1754)

Theodore Atkinson (NH)
Abraham Barnes (MD)
John Chambers (NY)
John Chandler (MA)
James Delancey (NY)
Benjamin Franklin (PA)
Stephen Hopkins (RI)
Martin Howard, Jr. (RI)
Sir William Johnson (NY)
Joseph Murray (NY)
Isaac Norris (PA)
Oliver Partridge (MA)
John Penn (PA)
Richard Peters (PA)
William Pitkin (CT)
Henry Sherburne, Jr. (NH)
William Smith (NY)
Benjamin Tasker (MD)
Meshech Weare (NH)
Samuel Welles (MA)
Richard Wibird (NH)
Elisha Williams (CT)
Roger Wolcott (CT)
John Worthington (MA)

Delegates to the Stamp Act Congress

(New York, NY, 1765)

William Bayard (NY)
Joseph Borden (NJ)
Metcalf Bowler (RI)
George Bryan (PA)
John Cruger (NY)
John Dickinson (PA)
Eliphalet Dyer (CT)
Hendrick Fisher (NJ)
Christopher Gadsden (SC)
William S. Johnson (CT)
Leonard Lispenard (NY)
Philip Livingston (NY)
Robert R. Livingston (NY)

Thomas Lynch (SC)
Thomas McKean (DE)
John Merton (PA)
William Murdock (MD)
Robert Ogden (NJ)
James Otis (MA)
Oliver Partridge (MA)
Thomas Ringgold (MD)
Caesar Rodney (DE)
David Rowland (CT)
Timothy Ruggles (MA)
John Rutledge (SC)
Edward Tilghman (MD)
Henry Ward (RI)

Signers of the Declaration of Independence

(July 4, 1776)

Connecticut

Samuel Huntington
Roger Sherman
William Williams
Oliver Wolcott

Delaware

Thomas McKean
George Read
Caesar Rodney

Georgia

Button Gwinnett
Lyman Hall
George Walton

Maryland

Charles Carroll
 of Carrollton
Samuel Chase
William Paca
Thomas Stone

Massachusetts

John Adams
Samuel Adams

Elbridge Gerry
John Hancock
Robert Treat Paine

New Hampshire

Josiah Bartlett
Matthew Thornton
William Whipple

New Jersey

Abraham Clark
John Hart
Francis Hopkinson
Richard Stockton
John Witherspoon

New York

William Floyd
Francis Lewis
Philip Livingston
Lewis Morris

North Carolina

Joseph Hewes
William Hooper
John Penn

Pennsylvania

George Clymer
Benjamin Franklin
Robert Morris
John Morton
George Ross
Benjamin Rush
James Smith
George Taylor
James Wilson

Rhode Island

William Ellery
Stephen Hopkins

South Carolina

Thomas Heyward, Jr.
Thomas Lynch, Jr.
Arthur Middleton
Edward Rutledge

1

Virginia

Carter Braxton
Benjamin Harrison
Thomas Jefferson
Francis Lightfoot Lee
Richard Henry Lee
Thomas Nelson, Jr.
George Wythe

Members of the Committee That Prepared the Articles of Confederation

(1776)

Samuel Adams (MA)
Josiah Bartlett (NH)
John Dickinson (Chairman; PA)
Button Gwinnett (GA)
Joseph Hewes (NC)
Stephen Hopkins (RI)
Francis Hopkinson (NJ)
Robert R. Livingston (NY)
Thomas McKean (DE)
Thomas Nelson, Jr. (VA)
Edward Rutledge (SC)
Roger Sherman (CT)
Thomas Stone (MD)

Signers of the Articles of Confederation

(Adopted Nov. 15, 1777)

Connecticut

Andrew Adams
Titus Hosmer
Samuel Huntington
Roger Sherman
Oliver Wolcott

Delaware

John Dickinson
Thomas McKean
Nicholas Van Dyke

Georgia

Edward Langworthy
Edward Telfair
George Walton

Maryland

Daniel Carroll
John Hanson

Massachusetts

Samuel Adams
Francis Dana
Elbridge Gerry
John Hancock
Samuel Holten
James Lovell

New Hampshire

Josiah Bartlett
John Wentworth

New Jersey

Nathaniel Scudder
John Witherspoon

New York

James Duane
William Duer
Francis Lewis
Gouverneur Morris

North Carolina

Cornelius Harnett
John Penn
John Williams

Pennsylvania

William Clingan
Joseph Reed
Daniel Roberdeau
Jonathan Bayard Smith

Rhode Island

John Collins
William Ellery
Henry Marchant

South Carolina

William Henry Drayton
Thomas Heyward, Jr.
Richard Hutson
Henry Laurens
John Mathews

Virginia

John Banister
John Harvie
Francis Lightfoot Lee
Richard Henry Lee

Delegates to the Constitutional Convention

(Philadelphia, 1787)

Connecticut

Oliver Ellsworth
William S. Johnson
Roger Sherman

Delaware

Richard Bassett
Gunning Bedford, Jr.
Jacob Broom
John Dickinson
George Read

Georgia

Abraham Baldwin
William Few
William Houston
Nathaniel Pendleton
William Pierce
George Walton

Maryland

Daniel Carroll
Daniel Jenifer
James McHenry
Luther Martin
John Francis Mercer

Massachusetts

Francis Dana

Elbridge Gerry
Nathaniel Gorham
Rufus King
Caleb Strong

New Hampshire

John Langdon
John Pickering

New Jersey

David Brearley
Abraham Clark
Jonathan Dayton
William C. Houston
William Livingston
John Neilson
William Paterson

New York

Alexander Hamilton
John Lansing, Jr.
Robert Yates

North Carolina

Willliam Blount
William R. Davie
Alexander Martin
Richard D. Spaight
Hugh Williamson

Pennsylvania

George Clymer
Thomas Fitzsimons
Benjamin Franklin
Jared Ingersoll
Thomas Mifflin
Gouverneur Morris
Robert Morris
James Wilson

South Carolina

Pierce Butler
Charles Pinckney
Charles C. Pinckney
John Rutledge

Virginia

John Blair
James Madison
Edmund Randolph
George Washington
George Wythe

Presidents of the Continental Congresses

(The First Continental Congress met in Philadelphia from 1774 to 1775 and the Second Continental Congress in various locations from 1775 to 1781. The Third Continental Congress, more commonly referred to as the Congress of the Confederation, met from 1781 to 1789.)

Elected	Presidents	Elected	Presidents
Sept. 5, 1774	Peyton Randolph (VA)	Nov. 5, 1781	John Hanson (MD)
Oct. 22, 1774	Henry Middleton (SC)	Nov. 5, 1781	Elias Boudinot (NJ)
May 10, 1775	Peyton Randolph (VA)	Nov. 3, 1783	Thomas Mifflin (PA)
May 24, 1775	John Hancock (MA)	Nov. 30, 1784	Richard Henry Lee (VA)
Nov. 1, 1777	Henry Laurens (SC)	Nov. 23, 1785	John Hancock (MA)
Dec. 10, 1778	John Jay (NY)	June 6, 1786	Nathaniel Gorham (MA)
Sept. 28, 1779	Samuel Huntington (CT)	Feb. 2, 1787	Arthur St. Clair (PA)
July 10, 1781	Thomas McKean (DE)	Jan. 22, 1788	Cyrus Griffin (VA)

Delegates to the Continental Congresses

(Years indicate terms of service.)

Connecticut

1777-80	Andrew Adams
1781-82	Andrew Adams
1784-88	Joseph P. Cook
1774-76	Silas Deane
1774-79	Eliphalet Dyer
1780-83	Eliphalet Dyer
1787-88	Pierrepont Edwards
1777-84	Oliver Ellsworth
1783-86	William Hillhouse
1775-76	Titus Hosmer
1777-79	Titus Hosmer
1780-84	Benjamin Huntington
1787-88	Benjamin Huntington
1776-84	Samuel Huntington
1784-87	William S. Johnson
1778	Richard Law
1783-84	Richard Law
1781-84	Stephen M. Mitchell
1785-86	Stephen M. Mitchell
1787-88	Stephen M. Mitchell
1778-83	Jesse Root
1774-84	Roger Sherman
1778-79	Joseph Spencer
1782-84	Jedediah Strong
1774-75	Jonathan Sturges
1785-86	John Treadwell
1774-75	Joseph Trumbull
1783-84	James Wadsworth
1785-86	James Wadsworth
1787-88	Jeremiah Wadsworth
1776-78	William Williams
1783-84	William Williams
1775-78	Oliver Wolcott
1780-84	Oliver Wolcott

Delaware

1786-87	Gunning Bedford
1783-85	Gunning Bedford, Jr.
1776-77	John Dickinson
1779-80	John Dickinson
1782-83	Philemon Dickinson
1776-77	John Evans
1787-88	Dyre Kearney
1782-84	Eleazer McComb
1774-76	Thomas McKean
1778-83	Thomas McKean
1786-88	Nathaniel Mitchell
1785-86	John Patten
1785-86	William Peery
1774-77	George Read
1774-76	Caesar Rodney
1777-78	Caesar Rodney
1782-84	Caesar Rodney
1781-83	Thomas Rodney
1785-87	Thomas Rodney
1777-78	James Sykes
1783-85	James Tilton
1777-82	Nicholas Van Dyke
1784-86	John Vining
1782-83	Samuel Wharton

Georgia

1785-88	Abraham Baldwin
1776-78	Nathan Brownson
1776-78	Archibald Bulloch
1778-80	Joseph Caly
1780-82	William Few
1785-88	William Few
1784-86	William Gibbons
1776-77	Button Gwinnett
1785-86	John Habersham
1775-77	Lyman Hall
1775-77	John Houston
1784-87	William Houston
1780-81	Richard Howley
1775-76	Noble W. Jones
1781-83	Noble W. Jones
1777-79	Edward Langworthy
1786-87	William Pierce
1777-79	Edward Telfair
1780-83	Edward Telfair
1776-79	George Walton
1780-81	George Walton
1777-79	Joseph Wood
1775	John J. Zubly

Maryland

1775-77	Robert Alexander
1778-80	William Carmichael
1776-77	Charles Carroll
1776-77	Charles Carroll of Carrollton
1780-84	Daniel Carroll
1783-84	Jeremiah T. Chase
1774-78	Samuel Chase
1784-85	Samuel Chase
1787-88	Benjamin Contee
1778-80	James Forbes
1786-87	Uriah Forrest
1774-75	Robert Goldsborough
1775	John Hall
1783-84	John Hall
1780-83	John Hanson
1785-87	William Harrison, Jr.
1782-84	William Hemsley
1778-81	John Henry
1784-87	John Henry
1784-87	William Hindman
1787-88	John E. Howard
1778-82	Daniel Jenifer
1774-77	Thomas Johnson
1783-84	Thomas S. Lee
1783-84	Edward Lloyd
1783-86	James McHenry
1784-85	Luther Martin
1774-79	William Paca
1778-81	George Plater
1781-82	Richard Potts
1785-87	Nathaniel Ramsay
1785-86	Richard Ridgely
1775-76	John Rogers
1786-87	David Ross
1776-78	Benjamin Rumsey
1784-85	Gustavus Scott
1787-88	Joshua Seney
1777-78	William Smith
1775-79	Thomas Stone
1784-85	Thomas Stone
1774-77	Matthew Tilghman
1781-82	Turbutt Wright

Massachusetts

1774-78	John Adams
1774-82	Samuel Adams
1774-76	Thomas Cushing
1776-78	Francis Dana
1784	Francis Dana
1785-88	Nathan Dane
1776-85	Elbridge Gerry
1782-85	Elbridge Gerry
1782-83	Nathaniel Gorham
1785-87	Nathaniel Gorham
1775-80	John Hancock
1785-86	John Hancock
1782-83	Stephen Higginson
1778-80	Samuel Holten
1782-83	Samuel Holten
1784-85	Samuel Holten
1782	Jonathan Jackson
1784-87	Rufus King
1776-82	James Lovell
1782-83	John Lowell
1780-84	Samuel Osgood
1787-88	Samuel A. Otis
1774-78	Robert Treat Paine
1779-82	George Partridge
1783-85	George Partridge
1785-88	Theodore Sedgwick
1782	James Sullivan
1787	George Thacher
1780-81	Artemas Ward

New Hampshire

1775-78	Josiah Bartlett
1783-84	Jonathan Blanchard
1787	Jonathan Blanchard
1774-75	Nathaniel Folsom
1777-78	Nathaniel Folsom
1779-80	Nathaniel Folsom
1783-85	Abiel Foster
1777-79	George Frost
1782-83	John Taylor Gilman
1768-89	Nicholas Gilman
1775-77	John Langdon
1786-87	John Langdon
1779-80	Woodbury Langdon
1780-83	Samuel Livermore
1785-86	Samuel Livermore
1784-86	Pierse Long
1779-80	Nathaniel Peabody
1774-75	John Sullivan
1780-81	John Sullivan
1776-78	Matthew Thornton
1778-79	John Wentworth, Jr.
1776-79	William Whipple
1782-83	Phillips White
1787-88	Paine Wingate

New Jersey

1783-85	John Beatty
1777-78	Elias Boudinot
1781-83	Elias Boudinot
1780-81	William Burnet
1784-87	Lambert Cadwalader
1776-78	Abraham Clark
1779-83	Abraham Clark
1786-89	Abraham Clark
1781-84	Silas Condict
1776	John Cooper
1774-76	Stephen Crane
1787-88	Jonathan Dayton
1774-75	John De Hart
1776	John De Hart
1783-85	Samuel Dick
1776-78	Jonathan Elmer
1781-84	Jonathan Elmer
1787-88	Jonathan Elmer
1778-80	John Fell

1778-79	Frederick Freling-huysen
1782-83	Frederick Freling-huysen
1776	John Hart
1776	Francis Hopkinson
1785-86	Josiah Hornblower
1779-82	William C. Houston
1784-85	William C. Houston
1774-75	James Kinsey
1774-76	William Livingston
1786-87	James Schureman
1777-79	Nathaniel Scudder
1776-77	Jonathan D. Sergeant
1774-76	Richard Smith
1783-84	John Stevens
1784-85	Charles Stewart
1776	Richard Stockton
1785-86	John Symmes
1776-79	John Witherspoon
1780-81	John Witherspoon
1782	John Witherspoon

New York

1774-76	John Alsop
1784-85	Egbert Benson
1786-88	Egbert Benson
1775	Simon Boerum
1775-77	George Clinton
1783-85	Charles DeWitt
1774-84	James Duane
1777-78	William Duer
1774-77	William Floyd
1778-83	William Floyd
1787-88	Leonard Ganesvoort
1788-89	David Ghelston
1782-83	Alexander Hamilton
1787-88	Alexander Hamilton
1774-75	John Haring
1785-88	John Haring
1774-77	John Jay
1778-79	John Jay
1784-88	John Lansing, Jr.
1785-86	John Laurance
1774-79	Francis Lewis
1779-83	Ezra L'Hommedieu
1787-88	Ezra L'Hommedieu
1774-78	Philip Livingston
1775-77	Robert R. Livingston
1779-81	Robert R. Livingston
1784-85	Walter Livingston
1774-75	Isaac Low
1777-80	Gouverneur Morris
1775-77	Lewis Morris
1781-82	Alexander McDougall
1784-85	Alexander McDougall
1784-85	Ephraim Paine
1788-89	Philip Pell
1784-86	Zephaniah Platt
1775-77	Philip Schuyler
1778-81	Philip Schuyler
1780-83	John Morin Scott
1785-88	Melancthon Smith
1774-76	Henry Wisner
1787-88	Abraham Yates

1785-87	Peter W. Yates

North Carolina

1787	John B. Ashe
1786-87	Timothy Bloodworth
1782-83	William Blount
1786-87	William Blount
1777-81	Thomas Burke
1787-88	Robert Burton
1774-76	Richard Caswell
1784	William Cumming
1777-80	Cornelius Harnett
1781-84	Benjamin Hawkins
1786-87	Benjamin Hawkins
1774-77	Joseph Hewes
1779	Joseph Hewes
1778-81	Whitmil Hill
1774-77	William Hooper
1780-82	Samuel Johnston
1779-80	Allen Jones
1780-81	Willie Jones
1782-84	Abner Nash
1785-86	Abner Nash
1775-76	John Penn
1777-80	John Penn
1779-82	William Sharpe
1784-85	John Sitgreaves
1783-85	Richard D. Spaight
1787-88	John Swan
1786-88	James White
1778-79	John Williams
1782-85	Hugh Williamson
1787-88	Hugh Williamson

Pennsylvania

1775-76	Andrew Allen
1778-80	John Armstrong
1787-88	John Armstrong
1778-82	Samuel J. Atlee
1785-87	John B. Bayard
1774-76	Edward Biddle
1778-79	Edward Biddle
1787-88	William Bingham
1785-86	Matthew Clarkson
1777-79	William Clingan
1776-78	George Clymer
1780-83	George Clymer
1787-88	Tench Coxe
1774-76	John Dickinson
1782-83	Thomas Fitzsimons
1775-76	Benjamin Franklin
1774-75	Joseph Galloway
1784-85	Joseph Gardner
1784-85	Edward Hand
1784-86	William Henry
1774-76	Charles Humphreys
1780-81	Jared Ingersoll
1786-88	William Irvine
1785-86	David Jackson
1779-80	James McClene
1780-81	Timothy Matlack
1787-88	Samuel Meredith
1774-76	Thomas Mifflin

1782-84	Thomas Mifflin
1783-84	Joseph Montgomery
1783-84	Cadwalader Morris
1776-78	Robert Morris
1774-77	John Morton
1778-80	Frederick A. C. Muhlenberg
1782-83	Richard Peters, Jr.
1785-87	Charles Pettit
1777-78	Joseph Reed
1787-89	James R. Reid
1774-75	Samuel Rhoads
1777-79	Daniel Roberdeau
1774-77	George Ross
1776-77	Benjamin Rush
1785-87	Arthur St. Clair
1778-80	James Searle
1778-80	William Shippen
1776-78	James Smith
1777-78	Jonathan B. Smith
1780-82	Thomas Smith
1776-77	George Taylor
1775-76	Thomas Willing
1775-76	James Wilson
1782-83	James Wilson
1785-87	James Wilson
1779-83	Henry Wynkoop

Rhode Island

1782-84	Jonathan Arnold
1787-89	Peleg Arnold
1778-83	John Collins
1780-83	Ezekiel Cornell
1776-81	William Ellery
1783-85	William Ellery
1789	John Gardiner
1788-89	Sylvester Gardiner
1787-89	Jonathan J. Hazard
1774-80	Stephen Hopkins
1782-85	David Howell
1785-86	James Manning
1777-80	Henry Marchant
1783-84	Henry Marchant
1785-86	Nathan Miller
1780-82	Daniel Mowry, Jr.
1780-82	James M. Varnum
1786-87	James M. Varnum
1774-76	Samuel Ward

South Carolina

1788-89	Robert Barnwell
1780-82	Thomas Bee
1783-85	Richard Beresford
1784-87	John Bull
1787-88	Pierce Butler
1778-79	William H. Drayton
1781-82	Nicholas Eveleigh
1774-76	Christopher Gadsen
1782-83	John L. Gervais
1776-78	Thomas Heyward, Jr.
1786-88	Daniel Huger
1778-79	Richard Hutson
1782-83	Ralph Izard

1785-87	John Kean
1780-81	Francis Kinloch
1777-80	Henry Laurens
1774-76	Thomas Lynch, Sr.
1776-77	Thomas Lynch, Jr.
1778-82	John Mathews
1776-78	Arthur Middleton
1781-83	Arthur Middleton
1774-76	Henry Middleton
1780-82	Isaac Motte
1786-88	John Parker
1777-78	Charles Pinckney
1784-87	Charles Pinckney
1782-84	David Ramsay
1785-86	David Ramsay
1783-85	Jacob Read
1774-77	Edward Rutledge
1774-77	John Rutledge
1782-83	John Rutledge
1777-78	Paul Trapier
1787-88	Thomas T. Tucker

Virginia

1778-80	Thomas Adams
1778-79	John Banister
1774-75	Richard Bland
1780-83	Theodorick Bland
1775-76	Carter Braxton
1787-88	John Brown
1785-86	Edward Carrington
1788-89	John Dawson
1779-80	William Fitzhugh
1779-81	William Fleming
1784-87	William Grayson
1778-81	Cyrus Griffin
1787-88	Cyrus Griffin
1783-85	Samuel Hardy
1774-78	Benjamin Harrison
1777-79	John Harvie
1780-81	James Henry
1774-76	Patrick Henry
1775-76	Thomas Jefferson
1783-85	Thomas Jefferson
1777-78	Joseph Jones
1780-83	Joseph Jones
1781-84	Arthur Lee
1775-79	Francis Lightfoot Lee
1785-88	Henry Lee
1774-80	Richard Henry Lee
1784-87	Richard Henry Lee
1780-83	James Madison
1786-88	James Madison
1779-80	James Mercer
1782-85	John F. Mercer
1783-86	James Monroe
1775-77	Thomas Nelson, Jr.
1779-80	Thomas Nelson, Jr.
1777	Mann Page
1774-75	Edmund Pendleton
1779-82	Edmund Randolph
1774-75	Peyton Randolph
1778-82	Meriwether Smith
1774-75	George Washington
1775-77	George Wythe

Colonial Governors

Connecticut

1639	John Haynes
1640	Edward Hopkins
1641	John Haynes
1642	George Wyllys
1643	John Haynes
1644	Edward Hopkins
1645	John Haynes
1646	Edward Hopkins
1647	John Haynes
1648	Edward Hopkins
1649	John Haynes
1650	Edward Hopkins
1651	John Haynes
1652	Edward Hopkins
1653	John Haynes
1654	Edward Hopkins
1655	Thomas Welles
1656	John Webster
1657	John Winthrop, Jr.
1658	Thomas Welles
1659	John Winthrop, Jr.
1676	William Leete
1683	Robert Treat
1687	Edmund Andros
1689	Robert Treat
1698	Fitz-John Winthrop
1708	Gurdon Saltonstall
1725	Joseph Talcott
1741	Jonathan Law
1750	Roger Wolcott
1754	Thomas Fitch
1766	William Pitkin
1769	Jonathan Trumbull
1784	Matthew Griswold
1786	Samuel Huntington

Delaware

1776	John McKinly
1778	Caesar Rodney
1782	John Dickinson
1783	Nicholas Van Dyke
1786	Thomas Collins

Georgia

1733	James E. Oglethorpe
1743	William Stephens
1750	Henry Parker
1754	John Reynolds
1757	Henry Ellis
1760	James Wright
1776	Archibald Bulloch
1777	Button Gwinnett
1777	John A. Treutlen
1778	John Houston
1779	George Walton
1779	James Wright
1782	John Martin
1783	Lyman Hall
1784	John Houston
1785	Samuel Elbert
1786	Edward Telfair
1787	George Mathews
1788	George Handley

Maryland

1634	Leonard Calvert
1647	Thomas Green
1649	William Stone
1654	Commissioners
1657	Josias Fendall
1660	Philip Calvert
1661	Charles Calvert
1676	Thomas Notley
1680	Charles Calvert
1684	William Joseph
1688	Protestant Associators
1691	Lionel Copley
1694	Francis Nicholson
1699	Nathaniel Blackistone
1701	Thomas Tench
1703	John Seymour
1709	Edward Lloyd
1714	John Hart
1720	Charles Calvert
1727	Benedict L. Calvert
1731	Samuel Ogle
1732	Charles Calvert
1733	Samuel Ogle
1742	Thomas Bladen
1747	Samuel Ogle
1752	Benjamin Tasker
1753	Horatio Sharpe
1769	Robert Eden
1776	Convention of the Council of Safety
1777	Thomas Johnson
1779	Thomas S. Lee
1782	William Paca
1785	William Smallwood
1788	John E. Howard

Massachusetts

Plymouth Colony

1620	John Carver
1621	William Bradford
1633	Edward Winslow
1634	Thomas Prince
1635	William Bradford
1636	Edward Winslow
1637	William Bradford
1638	Thomas Prince
1639	William Bradford
1644	Edward Winslow
1645	William Bradford
1657	Thomas Prince
1673	Josiah Winslow
1681	Thomas Hinckley
1686	Edmund Andros
1689	Thomas Hinckley

Massachusetts Bay Colony

1629	John Endicott
1630	John Winthrop
1634	Thomas Dudley
1635	John Haynes
1636	Henry Vane
1637	John Winthrop
1640	Thomas Dudley
1641	Richard Bellingham
1642	John Winthrop
1644	John Endicott
1645	Thomas Dudley
1646	John Winthrop
1649	John Endicott
1650	Thomas Dudley
1651	John Endicott
1654	Richard Bellingham
1655	John Endicott
1665	Richard Bellingham
1673	John Leverett
1679	Simon Bradstreet
1686	Joseph Dudley

1687	Edmund Andros
1689	Simon Bradstreet
1692	William Phips
1694	William Stoughton
1699	Richard Coote
1700	William Stoughton
1701	Council
1702	Joseph Dudley
1715	William Tailer (Acting)
1716	Samuel Shute
1723	William Dummer (Acting)
1728	William Burnet
1729	William Dummer (Acting)
1730	William Tailer
1730	Jonathan Belcher
1741	William Shirley
1749	Spencer Phipps
1753	William Shirley
1756	Spencer Phipps
1757	Thomas Pownall
1760	Francis Bernard
1769	Thomas Hutchinson
1774	Thomas Gage
1775	Council

Commonwealth of Massachusetts

1780	John Hancock
1785	James Bowdoin
1787	John Hancock

New Hampshire

1679	John Cutts
1681	Richard Waldron
1682	Edward Cranfield
1685	Walter Barefoot
1686	Joseph Dudley
1687	Edmund Andros
1690	Simon Bradstreet
1692	Samuel Allen
1699	Richard Coote
1702	Joseph Dudley
1716	Samuel Shute
1728	William Burnet
1729	Jonathan Belcher
1741	Benning Wentworth
1767	John Wentworth
1775	Matthew Thornton
1767	Meshech Weare
1785	John Langdon
1786	John Sullivan
1788	John Langdon

New Jersey

1702	Edward Hyde
1708	John Lovelace
1710	Robert Hunter
1720	William Burnet
1728	John Montgomerie
1731	Lewis Morris
1732	William Crosby
1736	John Hamilton
1738	Lewis Morris
1746	John Hamilton
1746	John Reading
1747	Jonathan Belcher
1757	John Reading
1758	Francis Bernard
1760	Thomas Boone
1761	Josiah Hardy
1763	William Franklin

1776	William Livingston

New York

New Amsterdam

1624	Cornelius J. Mey
1625	William Verhulst
1626	Peter Minuit
1633	Wouter Van Twiller
1638	William Kieft
1647	Peter Stuyvesant

New York

1664	Richard Nicolls
1668	Francis Lovelace
1673	Anthony Colve
1674	Edmund Andros
1683	Thomas Dongan
1688	Francis Nicholson
1689	Jacob Leisler
1691	Henry Slaughter
1691	Richard Ingoldsby
1692	Benjamin Fletcher
1698	Richard Coote
1702	Edward Hyde
1708	John Lovelace
1709	Richard Ingoldsby (Acting)
1710	Gerardus Beekman
1710	Robert Hunter
1719	Peter Schuyler (Acting)
1720	William Burnet
1728	John Montgomerie
1731	Rip Van Dam
1732	William Crosby
1736	George Clarke
1743	George Clinton
1753	Danvers Osborne
1753	James Delancey
1755	Charles Hardy
1760	Cadwallader Colden
1761	Robert Monckton
1761	Cadwallader Colden
1765	Henry Moore
1769	Cadwallader Colden
1770	John Murray
1771	William Tryon
1777	George Clinton

North Carolina

1663	William Drummond
1667	Samuel Stephens
1670	Peter Carteret
1673	John Jenkins
1676	Thomas Eastchurch
1677	Thomas Miller
1677	John Culpeper
1678	Seth Sothell
1679	John Harvey
1679	John Jenkins
1682	Seth Sothell
1689	Philip Ludwell
1691	Thomas Jarvis
1694	John Archdale
1694	John Harvey
1699	Henderson Walker
1704	Robert Daniel
1705	Thomas Cary
1706	William Glover
1708	Thomas Cary
1710	Edward Hyde
1712	Thomas Pollock

1714	Charles Eden	1647	John Coggeshall	1682	Joseph Morton	1609	George Percy

1714 Charles Eden
1722 Thomas Pollock
1722 William Reed
1724 George Burrington
1725 Richard Everard
1731 George Burrington
1734 Gabriel Johnston
1752 Nathaniel Rice
1752 Matthew Rowan
1754 Arthur Dobbs
1765 William Tryon
1771 Josiah Martin
1776 Richard Caswell
1779 Abner Nash
1781 Thomas Burke
1782 Alexander Martin
1784 Richard Caswell
1787 Samuel Johnston

Pennsylvania

1681 William Markham
1682 William Penn
1684 Thomas Lloyd
1688 Five Commissioners
1688 John Blackwell
1690 Thomas Lloyd
1691 William Markham
1693 Benjamin Fletcher
1695 William Markham
1699 William Penn
1701 Andrew Hamilton
1703 Edward Shippen
1704 John Evans
1709 Charles Gookin
1717 William Keith
1726 Patrick Gordon
1736 James Logan
1738 George Thomas
1747 Anthony Palmer
1748 James Hamilton
1754 Robert Hunter Morris
1756 William Denny
1759 James Hamilton
1763 John Penn
1771 Richard Penn
1773 John Penn
1776 Thomas Wharton
1778 George Ryan
1778 Joseph Reed
1781 William Moore
1782 John Dickinson
1785 Benjamin Franklin
1788 Thomas Mifflin

Rhode Island

1640 William Coddington

1647 John Coggeshall
1648 Jeremy Clarke
1649 Roger Williams (Acting)
1649 John Smith
1650 Nicholas Easton
1651 William Coddington
1652 John Smith
1653 Gregory Dexter
1654 Nicholas Easton
1654 Roger Williams
1657 Benedict Arnold
1660 William Brenton
1662 Benedict Arnold
1666 William Brenton
1669 Benedict Arnold
1672 Nicholas Easton
1674 William Coddington
1676 Walter Clarke
1677 Benedict Arnold
1678 William Coddington
1678 John Cranston
1680 Peleg Sanford
1683 William Coddington, Jr.
1685 Henry Bull
1686 Walter Clarke
1686 Charter suspended
1689 John Coggeshall, Jr.
1690 Henry Bull
1690 John Easton
1695 Caleb Carr
1696 Walter Clarke
1698 Samuel Cranston
1727 Joseph Jenckes
1732 William Wanton
1733 John Wanton
1740 Richard Ward
1743 William Greene
1745 Gideon Wanton
1746 William Greene
1747 Gideon Wanton
1748 William Greene
1755 Stephen Hopkins
1757 William Greene
1758 Stephen Hopkins
1762 Samuel Ward
1763 Stephen Hopkins
1765 Samuel Ward
1767 Stephen Hopkins
1768 Josias Lyndon
1769 Joseph Wanton
1775 Nicholas Cooke
1778 William Greene
1786 John Collins

South Carolina

1669 William Sayle
1672 John Yeamans
1674 Joseph West

1682 Joseph Morton
1684 Sir Richard Kyrle
1684 Robert Quarry
1685 Joseph West
1685 Joseph Morton
1686 James Colleton
1689 Thomas Smith
1690 John Sothell
1691 Philip Ludwell
1693 Thomas Smith
1694 Joseph Blake
1695 John Archdale
1696 Joseph Blake
1700 James Moore
1703 Nathaniel Johnson
1708 Edward Tynte
1709 Robert Gibbes
1712 Charles Craven
1716 Robert Daniel
1717 Robert Johnson
1719 James Moore
1721 Francis Nicholson
1725 Arthur Middleton
1731 Robert Johnson
1735 Thomas Broughton
1737 William Bull
1743 James Glen
1756 William H. Lyttleton
1760 William Bull
1761 Thomas Boone
1764 William Bull
1766 Charles G. Montagu
1768 William Bull
1768 Charles G. Montagu
1769 William Bull
1771 Charles G. Montagu
1773 William Bull
1775 William Campbell
1776 John Rutledge
1778 Rawlins Lowndes
1779 John Rutledge
1782 John Mathews
1783 Benjamin Guerrard
1785 William Moultrie
1787 Thomas Pinckney

Vermont

1778 Thomas Chittenden
1789 Moses Robinson
1790 Thomas Chittenden

Virginia

1607 Edward M. Wingfield
1607 John Ratcliffe
1608 John Smith

1609 George Percy
1610 Thomas Gates
1611 George Percy
1611 Thomas Dale
1611 Thomas Gates
1614 Thomas Dale
1616 George Yeardley
1617 Samuel Argall
1619 George Yeardley
1621 Francis Wyatt
1626 George Yeardley
1627 Francis West
1629 John Pott
1630 John Harvey
1635 John West
1636 John Harvey
1639 Francis Wyatt
1642 William Berkeley
1644 Richard Kemp
1645 William Berkeley
1652 Richard Bennett
1655 Edward Digges
1657 Samuel Matthews
1660 William Berkeley
1661 Francis Moryson
1662 William Berkeley
1677 Herbert Jeffreys
1678 Henry Chichley
1680 Thomas Colepepper
1683 Nicholas Spencer
1684 Francis Howard
1688 Nathaniel Bacon
1690 Francis Nicholson
1693 Edmund Andros
1698 Francis Nicholson
1705 Edward Nott
1706 Edmund Jennings
1710 Alexander Spotswood
1722 Hugh Drysdale
1726 Robert Carter
1727 William Gooch
1740 James Blair
1741 William Gooch
1749 John Robinson
1749 Thomas Lee
1750 Lewis Burwell
1751 Robert Dinwiddie
1758 John Blair
1758 Francis Fauquier
1768 John Blair
1768 Norborne Berkeley
1770 William Nelson
1771 John Murray
1776 Patrick Henry
1779 Thomas Jefferson
1781 Thomas Nelson, Jr.
1782 Benjamin Harrison
1784 Patrick Henry
1786 Edmund Randolph
1788 Beverly Randolph

Colonial Chief Justices

Connecticut

1711 Gurdon Saltonstall
1712 Nathan Gold
1713 William Pitkin
1714 Nathan Gold
1723 Peter Burr
1725 Jonathan Law
1741 Roger Wolcott
1750 Thomas Fitch
1754 William Pitkin
1766 Jonathan Trumbull
1769 Matthew Griswold
1784 Samuel Huntington
1785 Richard Law

Delaware

1776 William Killen

Maryland

1778 Benjamin Rumsey

Massachusetts

Massachusetts Bay Colony

1692 William Stoughton
1701 Waitsill Winthrop
1702 Isaac Addington
1708 Waitsill Winthrop
1718 Samuel Sewall
1729 Benjamin Lynde
1745 Paul Dudley
1753 Stephen Sewall
1761 Thomas Hutchinson
1769 Benjamin Lynde
1772 Peter Oliver
1775 John Adams
1777 William Cushing

Commonwealth of Massachusetts

1780 William Cushing

New Jersey

1702 Roger Mompesson
1709 Thomas Gordon
1710 David Jamison
1723 William Trent
1724 Robert L. Hooper
1728 Thomas Farmer
1738 Robert Hunter Morris
1758 William Aynsley
1764 Charles Read
1764 Frederick Smyth
1777 Robert Morris
1779 David Brearley

New York

1691 Joseph Dudley
1692 William Smith
1700 Stephanus Van Cortlandt
1701 Abraham DePeyster
1701 William Attwood
1702 William Smith
1703 John Bridges
1704 Roger Mompesson
1715 Lewis Morris
1733 James Delancey
1761 Benjamin Pratt
1763 Daniel Horsmanden
1777 John Jay
1789 Richard Morris

Pennsylvania

1778 Thomas McKean

Rhode Island

1747 Gideon Cornell
1749 Joshua Babcock
1751 Stephen Hopkins
1755 Francis Willett
1755 Stephen Hopkins
1756 John Gardner
1761 Samuel Ward
1762 Jeremiah Niles
1763 Joshua Babcock
1764 John Cole
1765 Joseph Russell
1767 James Helm
1768 Joseph Russell
1769 James Helm
1770 Stephen Hopkins
1776 Metcalf Bowler
1777 William Greene
1778 Shearjashub Bourne
1781 Jabez Bowen
1781 Paul Mumford
1785 William Ellery
1786 Paul Mumford
1788 Othniel Gorton

South Carolina

1779 William H. Drayton

Vermont

1778 Moses Robinson
1782 Paul Spooner
1784 Moses Robinson
1785 Nathaniel Chipman

Virginia

(President, Court of Appeals)

1779 Edmund Pendleton

II

U.S. Government: Executive Branch

Presidents of the United States

	Name and State	Inaug-uration	Politics	Religion	Birth Date	Death Date	Burial Place
1.	George Washington (VA)	1789	Fed.	Episcopalian	Feb. 22, 1732	Dec. 14, 1799	Mount Vernon, VA
2.	John Adams (MA)	1797	Fed.	Unitarian	Oct. 30, 1735	July 4, 1826	Quincy, MA
3.	Thomas Jefferson (VA)	1801	Dem-Rep	Unitarian	Apr. 13, 1743	July 4, 1826	Charlottesville, VA
4.	James Madison (VA)	1809	Dem-Rep	Episcopalian	Mar. 16, 1751	June 28, 1836	Montpelier Station, VA
5.	James Monroe (VA)	1817	Dem-Rep	Episcopalian	Apr. 28, 1758	June 4, 1831	Richmond, VA
6.	John Quincy Adams (MA)	1825	Dem-Rep	Unitarian	July 11, 1767	Feb. 23, 1848	Quincy, MA
7.	Andrew Jackson (TN)	1829	Dem.	Presbyterian	Mar. 15, 1767	June 8, 1845	Nashville, TN
8.	Martin Van Buren (NY)	1837	Dem.	Dutch Reformed	Dec. 5, 1782	July 24, 1862	Kinderhook, NY
9.	William Henry Harrison (OH)	1841	Whig	Episcopalian	Feb. 9, 1773	Apr. 4, 1841	North Bend, OH
10.	John Tyler (VA)	1841	Whig	Episcopalian	Mar. 29, 1790	Jan. 18, 1862	Richmond, VA
11.	James K. Polk (TN)	1845	Dem.	Presbyterian	Nov. 1, 1795	Jan. 15, 1849	Nashville, TN
12.	Zachary Taylor (LA)	1849	Whig	Episcopalian	Nov. 24, 1784	July 9, 1850	Louisville, KY
13.	Millard Fillmore (NY)	1850	Whig	Episcopalian	Jan. 7, 1800	Mar. 8, 1874	Buffalo, NY
14.	Franklin Pierce (NH)	1853	Dem.	Episcopalian	Nov. 23, 1804	Oct. 8, 1869	Concord, NH
15.	James Buchanan (PA)	1857	Dem.	Presbyterian	Apr. 23, 1791	June 1, 1868	Lancaster, PA
16.	Abraham Lincoln (IL)	1861	Rep.	Unaffiliated	Feb. 12, 1809	Apr. 15, 1865	Springfield, IL
17.	Andrew Johnson (TN)	1865	Dem.	Methodist	Dec. 29, 1808	July 31, 1875	Greenville, TN
18.	Ulysses S. Grant (OH)	1869	Rep.	Methodist	Apr. 27, 1822	July 23, 1885	New York, NY
19.	Rutherford B. Hayes (OH)	1877	Rep.	Methodist	Oct. 4, 1822	Jan. 17, 1893	Fremont, OH
20.	James A. Garfield (OH)	1881	Rep.	Disciples of Christ	Nov. 19, 1831	Sept. 19, 1881	Cleveland, OH
21.	Chester A. Arthur (NY)	1881	Rep.	Episcopalian	Oct. 5, 1830	Nov. 18, 1886	Albany, NY
22.	Grover Cleveland (NY)	1885	Dem.	Presbyterian	Mar. 18, 1837	June 24, 1908	Princeton, NJ
23.	Benjamin Harrison (IN)	1889	Rep.	Presbyterian	Aug. 20, 1833	Mar. 13, 1901	Indianapolis, IN
24.	Grover Cleveland (NY)	1893	Dem.	Presbyterian	Mar. 18, 1837	June 24, 1908	Princeton, NJ
25.	William McKinley (OH)	1897	Rep.	Methodist	Jan. 29, 1843	Sept. 14, 1901	Canton, OH
26.	Theodore Roosevelt (NY)	1901	Rep.	Dutch Reformed	Oct. 27, 1858	Jan. 6, 1919	Oyster Bay, NY
27.	William Howard Taft (OH)	1909	Rep.	Unitarian	Sept. 15, 1857	Mar. 8, 1930	Arlington, VA
28.	Woodrow Wilson (NJ)	1913	Dem.	Presbyterian	Dec. 28, 1856	Feb. 3, 1924	Washington, DC
29.	Warren G. Harding (OH)	1921	Rep.	Presbyterian	Nov. 2, 1865	Aug. 1, 1923	Marion, OH
30.	Calvin Coolidge (MA)	1923	Rep.	Congregationalist	July 4, 1872	Jan. 5, 1933	Plymouth, MA
31.	Herbert Hoover (CA)	1929	Rep.	Society of Friends	Aug. 10, 1874	Oct. 20, 1964	West Branch, IA
32.	Franklin D. Roosevelt (NY)	1933	Dem.	Episcoplian	Jan. 30, 1882	Apr. 12, 1945	Hyde Park, NY
33.	Harry S Truman (MO)	1945	Dem.	Baptist	May 8, 1884	Dec. 26, 1972	Independence, MO
34.	Dwight D. Eisenhower (KS)	1953	Rep.	Presbyterian	Oct. 14, 1890	Mar. 28, 1969	Abilene, KS
35.	John F. Kennedy (MA)	1961	Dem.	Catholic	May 29, 1917	Nov. 22, 1963	Arlington, VA
36.	Lyndon B. Johnson (TX)	1963	Dem.	Disciples of Christ	Aug. 27, 1908	Jan. 22, 1973	Johnson City, TX
37.	Richard M. Nixon (CA)	1969	Rep.	Society of Friends	Jan. 9, 1913		
38.	Gerald R. Ford (MI)	1974	Rep.	Episcopalian	July 14, 1913		
39.	James Earl (Jimmy) Carter (GA)	1977	Dem.	Baptist	Oct. 1, 1924		
40.	Ronald Reagan (CA)	1981	Rep.	Christian	Feb. 6, 1911		

Vice Presidents of the United States

	Name and State	Term	President	Politics	Birth Date	Death Date
1.	John Adams (MA)	1789-1797	Washington	Fed.	Oct. 30, 1735	July 4, 1826
2.	Thomas Jefferson (VA)	1797-1801	Adams	Dem-Rep	Apr. 13, 1743	July 4, 1826
3.	Aaron Burr (NY)	1801-1805	Jefferson	Dem-Rep	Feb. 6, 1756	Sept. 14, 1836
4.	George Clinton (NY)	1805-1812	Jefferson, Madison	Dem-Rep	July 26, 1739	Apr. 20, 1812
5.	Elbridge Gerry (MA)	1813-1814	Madison	Dem-Rep	July 17, 1744	Nov. 23, 1814
6.	Daniel D. Tompkins (NY)	1817-1825	Monroe	Dem-Rep	June 21, 1774	June 11, 1825
7.	John C. Calhoun (SC)	1825-1832	J.Q. Adams, Jackson	Dem.	Mar. 18, 1782	Mar. 31, 1850
8.	Martin Van Buren (NY)	1833-1837	Jackson	Dem.	Dec. 5, 1782	July 24, 1862
9.	Richard M. Johnson (KY)	1837-1841	Van Buren	Dem.	Oct. 17, 1781	Nov. 19, 1850
10.	John Tyler (VA)	1841	W.H. Harrison	Whig	Mar. 29, 1790	Jan. 18, 1862
11.	George M. Dallas (PA)	1845-1849	Polk	Dem.	July 10, 1792	Nov. 31, 1864
12.	Millard Fillmore (NY)	1849-1850	Taylor	Whig	Jan. 7, 1800	Mar. 8, 1874
13.	William R. King (AL)	1853	Pierce	Dem.	Apr. 7, 1786	Apr. 18, 1853
14.	John C. Breckinridge (KY)	1857-1816	Buchanan	Dem.	Jan. 21, 1821	May 17, 1875
15.	Hannibal Hamlin (ME)	1861-1865	Lincoln	Rep.	Aug. 27, 1809	July 4, 1891
16.	Andrew Johnson (TN)	1865	Lincoln	Dem.	Dec. 29, 1808	July 31, 1875
17.	Schuyler Colfax (IN)	1869-1873	Grant	Rep.	Mar. 23, 1823	Jan. 13, 1885
18.	Henry Wilson (MA)	1873-1875	Grant	Rep.	Feb. 16, 1812	Nov. 22, 1875
19.	William A. Wheeler (NY)	1877-1881	Hayes	Rep.	June 19, 1819	June 4, 1887
20.	Chester A. Arthur (NY)	1881	Garfield	Rep.	Oct. 5, 1830	Nov. 18, 1886
21.	Thomas A. Hendricks (IN)	1885	Cleveland	Dem.	Sept. 7, 1819	Nov. 25, 1885
22.	Levi P. Morton (NY)	1889-1893	B. Harrison	Rep.	May 16, 1824	May 16, 1920
23.	Adlai E. Stevenson (IL)	1893-1897	Cleveland	Dem.	Oct. 23, 1835	June 14, 1914
24.	Garret A. Hobart (NJ)	1897-1899	McKinley	Rep.	June 3, 1844	Nov. 21, 1899
25.	Theodore Roosevelt (NY)	1901	McKinley	Rep.	Oct. 27, 1858	Jan. 16, 1919
26.	Charles W. Fairbanks (IN)	1905-1909	T. Roosevelt	Rep.	May 11, 1852	June 4, 1918
27.	James S. Sherman (NY)	1909-1912	Taft	Rep.	Oct. 24, 1855	Oct. 30, 1912
28.	Thomas R. Marshall (IN)	1913-1921	Wilson	Dem.	Mar. 14, 1854	June 1, 1925
29.	Calvin Coolidge (MA)	1921-1923	Harding	Rep.	July 4, 1872	Jan. 5, 1933
30.	Charles G. Dawes (IL)	1925-1929	Coolidge	Rep.	Aug. 27, 1865	Apr. 23, 1951
31.	Charles Curtis (KS)	1929-1933	Hoover	Rep.	Jan. 25, 1860	Feb. 8, 1936
32.	John Nance Garner (TX)	1933-1941	F.D. Roosevelt	Dem.	Nov. 22, 1868	Nov. 7, 1967
33.	Henry A. Wallace (IA)	1941-1945	F.D. Roosevelt	Dem.	Oct. 7, 1888	Nov. 18, 1965
34.	Harry S Truman (MO)	1945	F.D. Roosevelt	Dem.	May 8, 1884	Dec. 26, 1972
35.	Alben W. Barkley (KY)	1949-1953	Truman	Dem.	Nov. 24, 1877	Apr. 30, 1956
36.	Richard M. Nixon (CA)	1953-1961	Eisenhower	Rep.	Jan. 9, 1913	
37.	Lyndon B. Johnson (TX)	1961-1963	Kennedy	Dem.	Aug. 27, 1908	Jan. 22, 1973
38.	Hubert H. Humphrey (MN)	1965-1969	L.B. Johnson	Dem.	May 27, 1911	Jan. 13, 1978
39.	Spiro T. Agnew (MD)	1969-1973	Nixon	Rep.	Nov. 9, 1918	
40.	Gerald R. Ford (MI)	1973-1974	Nixon	Rep.	July 14, 1913	
41.	Nelson Rockefeller (NY)	1974-1977	Ford	Rep.	July 8, 1908	Jan. 27, 1979

	Name and State	Term	President	Politics	Birth Date	Death Date
42.	Walter F. Mondale (MN)	1977-1981	Carter	Dem.	Jan. 5, 1928	
43.	George Bush (TX)	1981-	Reagan	Rep.	June 12, 1924	

Presidential and Vice Presidential Candidates

(Until 1804 each elector voted for two candidates for President. The one who received the largest number of votes was declared President, and the one who received the next largest number of votes was declared Vice President.)

1789 Election

Candidates	Party	Electoral Votes
George Washington		69
John Adams		34
John Jay		9
Robert H. Harrison		6
John Rutledge		6
John Hancock		4
George Clinton		3
Samuel Huntington		2
John Milton		2
John Armstrong		1
Benjamin Lincoln		1
Edward Telfair		1

1792 Election

Candidates	Party	Electoral Votes
George Washington	Federalist	132
John Adams	Federalist	77
George Clinton	Anti-Federalist	50
Thomas Jefferson	Anti-Federalist	4
Aaron Burr	Anti-Federalist	1

1796 Election

Candidates	Party	Electoral Votes
John Adams	Federalist	71
Thomas Jefferson	Dem-Rep	68
Thomas Pinckney	Federalist	59
Aaron Burr	Dem-Rep	30
Samuel Adams		15
Oliver Ellsworth		11
George Clinton		7
John Jay		5
James Iredell		3
John Henry		2
Samuel Johnston		2
George Washington	Federalist	2
Charles C. Pinckney		1

1800 Election

Candidates	Party	Electoral Votes
Thomas Jefferson	Dem-Rep	73
Aaron Burr	Dem-Rep	73
John Adams	Federalist	65
Charles C. Pinckney	Federalist	64
John Jay	Federalist	1

1804 Election

Presidential Candidates	Party	Electoral Votes
Thomas Jefferson	Dem-Rep	162
Charles C. Pinckney	Federalist	14

Vice Presidential Candidates	Party	Electoral Votes
George Clinton	Dem-Rep	162
Rufus King	Federalist	14

1808 Election

Presidential Candidates	Party	Electoral Votes
James Madison	Dem-Rep	122
Charles C. Pinckney	Federalist	47
George Clinton	Dem-Rep	6

Vice Presidential Candidates	Party	Electoral Votes
George Clinton	Dem-Rep	113
Rufus King	Federalist	47
John Langdon		9
James Madison	Dem-Rep	3
James Monroe	Dem-Rep	3

1812 Election

Presidential Candidates	Party	Electoral Votes
James Madison	Dem-Rep	128
De Witt Clinton	Federalist	89

Vice Presidential Candidates	Party	Electoral Votes
Elbridge Gerry	Dem-Rep	131
Jared Ingersoll	Federalist	86

1816 Election

Presidential Candidates	Party	Electoral Votes
James Monroe	Dem-Rep	231
Rufus King	Federalist	34

Vice Presidential Candidates	Party	Electoral Votes
Daniel D. Tompkins	Dem-Rep	183
John E. Howard	Federalist	22
James Ross		5
John Marshall	Federalist	4
Robert G. Harper		3

1820 Election

Presidential Candidates	Party	Electoral Votes
James Monroe	Dem-Rep	231
John Quincy Adams	Dem-Rep	1

Vice Presidential Candidates	Party	Electoral Votes
Daniel D. Tompkins	Dem-Rep	218
Richard Stockton		8
Daniel Rodney		4
Robert G. Harper		1
Richard Rush		1

1824 Election

Presidential Candidates	Party	Electoral Votes
Andrew Jackson		99
John Quincy Adams		84
William H. Crawford		41
Henry Clay		37

Vice Presidential Candidates	Party	Electoral Votes
John C. Calhoun		182
Nathan Sanford		30
Nathaniel Macon		24
Andrew Jackson		13
Martin Van Buren		9
Henry Clay		2

1828 Election

Presidential Candidates	Party	Electoral Votes
Andrew Jackson	Democrat	178
John Quincy Adams	Republican	83

Vice Presidential Candidates	Party	Electoral Votes
John C. Calhoun	Democrat	171
Richard Rush	Republican	83
William Smith		7

1832 Election

Presidential Candidates	Party	Electoral Votes
Andrew Jackson	Democrat	219
Henry Clay	Republican	49
John Floyd		11
William Wirt	Anti-Masonic	7

Vice Presidential Candidates	Party	Electoral Votes
Martin Van Buren	Democrat	189
John Sergeant	Republican	49
William Wilkins		30
Henry Lee		11
Amos Ellmaker	Anti-Masonic	7

1836 Election

Presidential Candidates	Party	Electoral Votes
Martin Van Buren	Democrat	170
William Henry Harrison	Whig	73
Hugh L. White	Whig	26
Daniel Webster	Whig	14
Willie P. Mangum		11

Vice Presidential Candidates	Party	Electoral Votes
Richard M. Johnson	Democrat	147
Francis Granger	Whig	77
John Tyler	Whig	47
William Smith		23

1840 Election

Presidential Candidates	Party	Electoral Votes
William H. Harrison	Whig	234
Martin Van Buren	Democrat	60

Vice Presidential Candidates	Party	Electoral Votes
John Tyler	Whig	234
Richard M. Johnson	Democrat	48
Littleton W. Tazewell		11
James K. Polk	Democrat	1

1844 Election

Presidential Candidates	Party	Electoral Votes
James K. Polk	Democrat	170
Henry Clay	Whig	105

Vice Presidential Candidates	Party	Electoral Votes
George M. Dallas	Democrat	170
Theodore Frelinghuysen	Republican	105

1848 Election

Presidential Candidates	Party	Electoral Votes
Zachary Taylor	Whig	163
Lewis Cass	Democrat	127

Vice Presidential Candidates	Party	Electoral Votes
Millard Fillmore	Whig	163
William O. Butler	Democrat	127

1852 Election

Presidential Candidates	Party	Electoral Votes
Franklin Pierce	Democrat	254
Winfield Scott	Whig	42

Vice Presidential Candidates	Party	Electoral Votes
William R. King	Democrat	254
William A. Graham	Whig	42

1856 Election

Presidential Candidates	Party	Electoral Votes
James Buchanan	Democrat	174
John C. Fremont	Republican	114
Millard Fillmore	American	8

Vice Presidential Candidates	Party	Electoral Votes
John C. Breckinridge	Democrat	174
William L. Dayton	Republican	14
Andrew J. Donelson	American	8

1860 Election

Presidential Candidates	Party	Electoral Votes
Abraham Lincoln	Republican	180
John C. Breckinridge	Democrat	72
John Bell	Unionist	39
Stephen A. Douglas	Democrat	12

Vice Presidential Candidates	Party	Electoral Votes
Hannibal Hamlin	Republican	180
Joseph Lane	Democrat	72
Edward Everett	Unionist	39
Herschel V. Johnson	Democrat	12

1864 Election

Presidential Candidates	Party	Electoral Votes
Abraham Lincoln	Unionist	212
George B. McClellan	Democrat	21

Vice Presidential Candidates	Party	Electoral Votes
Andrew Johnson	Unionist	212
George H. Pendleton	Democrat	21

1868 Election

Presidential Candidates	Party	Electoral Votes
Ulysses S. Grant	Republican	214
Horatio Seymour	Democrat	80

Vice Presidential Candidates	Party	Electoral Votes
Schuyler Colfax	Republican	214
Francis P. Blair, Jr.	Democrat	80

1872 Election

Presidential Candidates	Party	Electoral Votes
Ulysses S. Grant	Republican	286
Horace Greeley	Dem., Liberal	8
Thomas A. Hendricks	Democrat	42
B. Gratz Brown	Dem., Liberal	18
Charles J. Jenkins	Democrat	2
David Davis	Democrat	1

Vice Presidential Candidates	Party	Electoral Votes
Henry Wilson	Republican	286
B. Gratz Brown	Dem., Liberal	47
George W. Julian		5
Alfred H. Colquitt		5
John M. Palmer		3
Thomas E. Bramlette		3
Nathaniel P. Banks		1
William S. Groesbeck		1
Willis B. Machen		1

1876 Election

Presidential Candidates	Party	Electoral Votes
Rutherford B. Hayes	Republican	185
Samuel J. Tilden	Democrat	184
Peter Cooper	Greenbeck	

Vice Presidential Candidates	Party	Electoral Votes
William A. Wheeler	Republican	185
Thomas A. Hendricks	Democrat	184
Samuel F. Cary	Greenback	

1880 Election

Presidential Candidates	Party	Electoral Votes
James A. Garfield	Republican	214
Winfield S. Hancock	Democrat	155
James B. Weaver	Greenback	

Vice Presidential Candidates	Party	Electoral Votes
Chester A. Arthur	Republican	214
William H. English	Democrat	155
B. J. Chambers	Greenback	

1884 Election

Presidential Candidates	Party	Electoral Votes
Grover Cleveland	Democrat	219
James G. Blaine	Republican	182
Benjamin F. Butler	Greenback	
John P. St. John	Prohibitionist	

Vice Presidential Candidates	Party	Electoral Votes
Thomas A. Hendricks	Democrat	219
John A. Logan	Republican	182
A. M. West	Greenback	
William Daniel	Prohibitionist	

1888 Election

Presidential Candidates	Party	Electoral Votes
Benjamin Harrison	Republican	233
Grover Cleveland	Democrat	168
Clinton B. Fisk	Prohibitionist	
Alson J. Streeter	Union-Labor	

Vice Presidential Candidates	Party	Electoral Votes
Levi P. Morton	Republican	233

Vice Presidential Candidates	Party	Electoral Votes
Allen Thurman	Democrat	168
John A. Brooks	Prohibitionist	
Charles E. Cunningham	Union-Labor	

1892 Election

Presidential Candidates	Party	Electoral Votes
Grover Cleveland	Democrat	277
Benjamin Harrison	Republican	145
James B. Weaver	People's	22
John Bidwell	Prohibitionist	

Vice Presidential Candidates	Party	Electoral Votes
Adlai E. Stevenson	Democrat	277
Whitelaw Reid	Republican	145
James G. Field	People's	22
James B. Cranfill	Prohibitionist	

1896 Election

Presidential Candidates	Party	Electoral Votes
William McKinley	Republican	271
William Jennings Bryan	Dem., People's	176
John M. Palmer	Democrat	
Joshua Levering	Prohibitionist	

Vice Presidential Candidates	Party	Electoral Votes
Garret A. Hobart	Republican	271
Arthur Sewall	Democrat	149
Thomas E. Watson	People's	27
Simon B. Buckner	Democrat	
Hale Johnson	Prohibitionist	

1900 Election

Presidential Candidates	Party	Electoral Votes
William McKinley	Republican	292
William Jennings Bryan	Dem., People's	155
John G. Wolley	Prohibitionist	
Eugene V. Debs	Socialist	

Vice Presidential Candidates	Party	Electoral Votes
Theodore Roosevelt	Republican	292
Adlai E. Stevenson	Democrat	155
Henry B. Metcalf	Prohibitionist	
Job Harriman	Socialist	

1904 Election

Presidential Candidates	Party	Electoral Votes
Theodore Roosevelt	Republican	336
Alton B. Parker	Democrat	140
Eugene V. Debs	Socialist	
Silas C. Swallow	Prohibitionist	
Thomas E. Watson	People's	

Vice Presidential Candidates	Party	Electoral Votes
Charles W. Fairbanks	Republican	336

Vice Presidential Candidates	Party	Electoral Votes
Henry G. Davis	Democrat	140
Benjamin Hanford	Socialist	
George W. Carroll	Prohibitionist	
Thomas H. Tibbles	People's	

1908 Election

Presidential Candidates	Party	Electoral Votes
William Howard Taft	Republican	321
William Jennings Bryan	Democrat	162
Eugene V. Debs	Socialist	
Eugene W. Chafin	Prohibitionist	

Vice Presidential Candidates	Party	Electoral Votes
James S. Sherman	Republican	321
John W. Kern	Democrat	162
Benjamin Hanford	Socialist	
Aaron S. Watkins	Prohibitionist	

1912 Election

Presidential Candidates	Party	Electoral Votes
Woodrow Wilson	Democrat	435
Theodore Roosevelt	Progressive	88
William Howard Taft	Republican	8
Eugene V. Debs	Socialist	
Eugene W. Chafin	Prohibitionist	

Vice Presidential Candidates	Party	Electoral Votes
Thomas R. Marshall	Democrat	435
Hiram W. Johnson	Progressive	88
Nicholas Murray Butler	Republican	8
Emil Seidel	Socialist	
Aaron S. Watkins	Prohibitionist	

1916 Election

Presidential Candidates	Party	Electoral Votes
Woodrow Wilson	Democrat	277
Charles Evans Hughes	Republican	254
A. L. Benson	Socialist	
J. Frank Hanly	Prohibitionist	

Vice Presidential Candidates	Party	Electoral Votes
Thomas R. Marshall	Democrat	277
Charles W. Fairbanks	Republican	254
G. R. Kirkpatrick	Socialist	
Ira Landrith	Prohibitionist	

1920 Election

Presidential Candidates	Party	Electoral Votes
Warren G. Harding	Republican	404
James M. Cox	Democrat	127
Eugene V. Debs	Socialist	
P. P. Christensen	Farm-Labor	
Aaron S. Watkins	Prohibitionist	

Vice Presidential Candidates	Party	Electoral Votes
Calvin Coolidge	Republican	404
Franklin D. Roosevelt	Democrat	127
Seymour Stedman	Socialist	
Max S. Hayes	Farm-Labor	
D. Leigh Colvin	Prohibitionist	

1924 Election

Presidential Candidates	Party	Electoral Votes
Calvin Coolidge	Republican	382
John W. Davis	Democrat	136
Robert M. La Follette	Progressive	13

Vice Presidential Candidates	Party	Electoral Votes
Charles G. Dawes	Republican	382
Charles W. Bryan	Democrat	136
Burton K. Wheeler	Progressive	13

1928 Election

Presidential Candidates	Party	Electoral Votes
Herbert Hoover	Republican	444
Alfred E. Smith	Democrat	87

Vice Presidential Candidates	Party	Electoral Votes
Charles Curtis	Republican	444
Joseph T. Robinson	Democrat	87

1932 Election

Presidential Candidates	Party	Electoral Votes
Franklin D. Roosevelt	Democrat	472
Herbert Hoover	Republican	59

Vice Presidential Candidates	Party	Electoral Votes
John Nance Garner	Democrat	472
Charles Curtis	Republican	59

1936 Election

Presidential Candidates	Party	Electoral Votes
Franklin D. Roosevelt	Democrat	523
Alfred M. Landon	Republican	8

Vice Presidential Candidates	Party	Electoral Votes
John Nance Garner	Democrat	523
Frank Knox	Republican	8

1940 Election

Presidential Candidates	Party	Electoral Votes
Franklin D. Roosevelt	Democrat	449
Wendell L. Willkie	Republican	82

Vice Presidential Candidates	Party	Electoral Votes
Henry A. Wallace	Democrat	449
Charles L. McNary	Republican	82

1944 Election

Presidential Candidates	Party	Electoral Votes
Franklin D. Roosevelt	Democrat	432
Thomas E. Dewey	Republican	99

Vice Presidential Candidates	Party	Electoral Votes
Harry S Truman	Democrat	432
John W. Bricker	Republican	99

1948 Election

Presidential Candidates	Party	Electoral Votes
Harry S Truman	Democrat	303
Thomas E. Dewey	Republican	189
J. Strom Thurmond	States' Rights Dem.	39
Henry A. Wallace	Progressive	

Vice Presidential Candidates	Party	Electoral Votes
Alben W. Barkley	Democrat	303
Earl Warren	Republican	189
Fielding L. Wright	States' Rights Dem.	39
Glen Taylor	Progressive	

1952 Election

Presidential Candidates	Party	Electoral Votes
Dwight D. Eisenhower	Republican	442
Adlai E. Stevenson	Democrat	89

Vice Presidential Candidates	Party	Electoral Votes
Richard M. Nixon	Republican	442
John J. Sparkman	Democrat	89

1956 Election

Presidential Candidates	Party	Electoral Votes
Dwight D. Eisenhower	Republican	457
Adlai E. Stevenson	Democrat	73
Walter B. Jones		1

Vice Presidential Candidates	Party	Electoral Votes
Richard M. Nixon	Republican	457
Estes Kefauver	Democrat	73

1960 Election

Presidential Candidates	Party	Electoral Votes
John F. Kennedy	Democrat	303
Richard M. Nixon	Republican	219
Harry F. Byrd		15

Vice Presidential Candidates	Party	Electoral Votes
Lyndon B. Johnson	Democrat	303
Henry Cabot Lodge	Republican	219

1964 Election

Presidential Candidates	Party	Electoral Votes
Lyndon B. Johnson	Democrat	486
Barry M. Goldwater	Republican	52

Vice Presidential Candidates	Party	Electoral Votes
Hubert H. Humphrey	Democrat	486
William E. Miller	Republican	52

1968 Election

Presidential Candidates	Party	Electoral Votes
Richard M. Nixon	Republican	301
Hubert H. Humphrey	Democrat	191
George C. Wallace		

Vice Presidential Candidates	Party	Electoral Votes
Spiro T. Agnew	Republican	301
Edmund S. Muskie	Democrat	191
Curtis E. LeMay	Amer. Independent	46

1972 Election

Presidential Candidates	Party	Electoral Votes
Richard M. Nixon	Republican	520
George S. McGovern	Democrat	17
John Hospers	Libertarian	1

Vice Presidential Candidates	Party	Electoral Votes
Spiro T. Agnew	Republican	520
R. Sargent Shriver	Democrat	17

1976 Election

Presidential Candidates	Party	Electoral Votes
James Earl (Jimmy) Carter	Democrat	297
Gerald R. Ford	Republican	240
Ronald Reagan		1

Vice Presidential Candidates	Party	Electoral Votes
Walter F. Mondale	Democrat	297
Robert J. Dole	Republican	240

1980 Election

Presidential Candidates	Party	Electoral Votes
Ronald Reagan	Republican	489
James Earl (Jimmy) Carter	Democrat	49

Vice Presidential Candidates	Party	Electoral Votes
George Bush	Republican	489
Walter F. Mondale	Democrat	49

1984 Election

Presidential Candidates	Party	Electoral Votes
Ronald Reagan	Republican	525
Walter F. Mondale	Democrat	13

Vice Presidential Candidates	Party	Electoral Votes
George Bush	Republican	525
Geraldine A. Ferraro	Democrat	13

First Ladies of the United States

The President's first lady may be his wife or, if he is not married, any other woman he chooses to be the official hostess.

Name	Dates	President	Relationship
Martha (Dandridge) Custis	1789-1797	George Washington	wife
Abigail Smith	1797-1801	John Adams	wife
Martha (Wayles) Skelton	1801-1809	Thomas Jefferson	wife
Dolly [Dorothea] (Payne) Todd	1809-1817	James Madison	wife
Elizabeth Kortwright	1817-1825	James Monroe	wife
Louisa Catherine Johnson	1825-1829	John Quincy Adams	wife
Rachel (Donelson) Robards	1829-1837	Andrew Jackson	wife
Hanna Hoes	1837-1841	Martin Van Buren	wife
Anna Tuthill Symmes	1841	William Henry Harrison	wife
Letitia Christian	1841-1842	John Tyler	wife
Priscilla Cooper Tyler	1842-1844	John Tyler	daughter-in-law
Julia Gardiner	1844-1845	John Tyler	wife
Sarah Childress	1845-1849	James Knox Polk	wife
Margaret Mackall Smith	1849-1850	Zachary Taylor	wife
Abigail Powers	1850-1853	Millard Fillmore	wife
Janes Means Appleton	1853-1857	Franklin Pierce	wife
Harriet Lane	1857-1861	James Buchanan	niece
Mary Ann Todd	1861-1865	Abraham Lincoln	wife
Eliza McCardle	1865-1869	Andrew Johnson	wife
Julia Boggs Dent	1869-1877	Ulysses S. Grant	wife
Lucy Ware Webb	1877-1881	Rutherford B. Hayes	wife
Lucretia Randolph	1881	James A. Garfield	wife
Ellen Lewis Herndon	1881-1885	Chester A. Arthur	wife
Frances Folsom	1885-1889	Grover Cleveland	wife
Caroline Lavinia Scott	1889-1892	Benjamin Harrison	wife
Mary Scott [Lord] Dimmock	1892-1893	Benjamin Harrison	wife
Frances Folsom	1893-1897	Grover Cleveland	wife
Ida Saxton	1897-1901	William McKinley	wife
Edith Kermit Carow	1901-1909	Theodore Roosevelt	wife
Helen Herron	1909-1913	William Howard Taft	wife
Ellen Louise Axson	1913-1914	Woodrow Wilson	wife
Helen Woodrow Bones	1914-1915	Woodrow Wilson	cousin
Edith Bolling Galt	1915-1921	Woodrow Wilson	wife
Florence (Kling) DeWolfe	1921-1923	Warren G. Harding	wife
Grace Goodhue	1923-1929	Calvin Coolidge	wife
Lou Henry	1929-1933	Herbert C. Hoover	wife
Eleanor Roosevelt	1933-1945	Franklin Delano Roosevelt	wife
Bess [Elizabeth Virginia] Wallace	1945-1953	Harry S Truman	wife
Mamie Geneva Doud	1953-1961	Dwight David Eisenhower	wife
Jacqueline Lee Bouvier	1961-1963	John F. Kennedy	wife
Lady Bird [Claudia Alta] Taylor	1963-1969	Lyndon B. Johnson	wife
Thelma Catherine Patricia Ryan	1969-1974	Richard M. Nixon	wife
Betty [Elizabeth] Bloomer	1974-1977	Gerald R. Ford	wife
Rosalynn Smith	1977-1981	James Earl (Jimmy) Carter	wife
Nancy Davis	1981-	Ronald Reagan	wife

III
Cabinets

Cabinet Members by Presidential Term

Years in parentheses indicate tenure of officer; where no years are given, tenure coincides with Presidential term.

1st Presidential Term, 1789-1793

President: George Washington

Vice President: John Adams

Secretary of State: Thomas Jefferson (1790-1793)

Secretary of the Treasury: Alexander Hamilton

Secretary of War: Henry Knox

Attorney General: Edmund Randolph (1790-1793)

2nd Presidential Term, 1793-1797

President: George Washington

Vice President: John Adams

Secretary of State: Thomas Jefferson (1793-1794), Edmund Randolph (1794-1795), Timothy Pickering (1795-1797)

Secretary of the Treasury: Alexander Hamilton (1793-1795), Oliver Wolcott, Jr. (1795-1797)

Secretary of War: Henry Knox (1793-1795), Timothy Pickering (1795), James McHenry (1796-1797)

Attorney General: Edmund Randolph (1793-1794), William Bradford (1794-1795), Charles Lee (1795-1797)

3rd Presidential Term, 1797-1801

President: John Adams

Vice President: Thomas Jefferson

Secretary of State: Timothy Pickering (1797-1800), John Marshall (1800-1801)

Secretary of the Treasury: Oliver Wolcott, Jr. (1797-1801), Samuel Dexter (1801)

Secretary of War: James McHenry (1797-1800), Samuel Dexter (1800)

Attorney General: Charles Lee

Secretary of the Navy: Benjamin Stoddert (1798-1801)

4th Presidential Term, 1801-1805

President: Thomas Jefferson

Vice President: Aaron Burr

Secretary of State: John Marshall (1801), James Madison (1801-1805)

Secretary of the Treasury: Samuel Dexter (1801), Albert Gallatin (1801-1805)

Secretary of War: Henry Dearborn

Attorney General: Levi Lincoln

Secretary of the Navy: Benjamin Stoddert (1801), Robert Smith (1801-1805)

5th Presidential Term, 1805-1809

President: Thomas Jefferson

Vice President: George Clinton

Secretary of State: James Madison

Secretary of the Treasury: Albert Gallatin

Secretary of War: Henry Dearborn

Attorney General: John Breckenridge (1805-1806), Caesar A. Rodney (1807-1809)

Secretary of the Navy: Robert Smith

6th Presidential Term, 1809-1813

President: James Madison

Vice President: George Clinton (1809-1812)

Secretary of State: Robert Smith (1809-1811), James Monroe (1811-1813)

Secretary of the Treasury: Albert Gallatin

Secretary of War: William Eustis (1809-1812), John Armstrong (1813)

Attorney General: Caesar A. Rodney (1809-1811), William Pinkney (1811-1813)

Secretary of the Navy: Robert Smith (1809), Paul Hamilton (1809-1812), William Jones (1813)

7th Presidential Term, 1813-1817

President: James Madison

Vice President: Elbridge Gerry (1813-1814)

Secretary of State: James Monroe

Secretary of the Treasury: Albert Gallatin (1813-1814), George W. Campbell (1814), Alexander J. Dallas (1814-1816), William H. Crawford (1816-1817)

Secretary of War: John Armstrong (1813-1814), James Monroe (1814-1815), William H. Crawford (1815-1816)

Attorney General: William Pinkney (1813-1814), Richard Rush (1814-1817)

Secretary of the Navy: William Jones (1813-1814), Benjamin W. Crowninshield (1814-1817)

8th Presidential Term, 1817-1821

President: James Monroe

Vice President: Daniel D. Tompkins

Secretary of State: John Quincy Adams

Secretary of the Treasury: William H. Crawford

Secretary of War: John C. Calhoun

Attorney General: Richard Rush (1817), William Wirt (1817-1821)

Secretary of the Navy: Benjamin W. Crowninshield (1817-1818), Smith Thompson (1818-1821)

9th Presidential Term, 1821-1825

President: James Monroe

Vice President: Daniel D. Tompkins

Secretary of State: John Quincy Adams

Secretary of the Treasury: William H. Crawford

Secretary of War: John C. Calhoun

Attorney General: William Wirt

Secretary of the Navy: Smith Thompson (1821-1823), Samuel L. Southard (1823-1825)

10th Presidential Term, 1825-1829

President: John Quincy Adams

Vice President: John C. Calhoun

Secretary of State: Henry Clay

Secretary of the Treasury: Richard Rush

Secretary of War: James Barbour (1825-1828), Peter B. Porter (1828-1829)

Attorney General: William Wirt

Secretary of the Navy: Samuel L. Southard

11th Presidential Term, 1829-1833

President: Andrew Jackson

Vice President: John C. Calhoun (1829-1832)

Secretary of State: Martin Van Buren (1829-1831), Edward Livingston (1831-1833)

Secretary of the Treasury: Samuel D. Ingham (1829-1831), Louis McLane (1831-1833)

Secretary of War: John H. Eaton (1829-1831), Lewis Cass (1831-1833)

Attorney General: John M. Berrien (1829-1831), Roger B. Taney (1831-1833)

Postmaster General: William T. Barry

Secretary of the Navy: John Branch (1829-1831), Levi Woodbury (1831-1833)

12th Presidential Term, 1833-1837

President: Andrew Jackson

Vice President: Martin Van Buren

Secretary of State: Edward Livingston (1833), Louis McLane (1833-1834), John Forsyth (1834-1837)

Secretary of the Treasury: Louis McLane (1833), William Duane (1833), Roger B. Taney (1833-1834), Levi Woodbury (1834-1837)

Secretary of War: Lewis Cass (1833-1836), Benjamin F. Butler (1836-1837)

Attorney General: Roger B. Taney (1833), Benjamin F. Butler (1833-1837)

Postmaster General: William T. Barry (1833-1835), Amos Kendall (1835-1837)

Secretary of the Navy: Levi Woodbury (1833-1834), Mahlon Dickerson (1834-1837)

13th Presidential Term, 1837-1841

President: Martin Van Buren

Vice President: Richard M. Johnson

Secretary of State: John Forsyth

Secretary of the Treasury: Levi Woodbury

Secretary of War: Benjamin F. Butler (1837), Joel R. Poinsett (1837-1841)

Attorney General: Benjamin F. Butler (1837-1838), Felix Grundy (1838-1840), Henry D. Gilpin (1840-1841)

Postmaster General: Amos Kendall (1837-1840), John M. Niles (1840-1841)

Secretary of the Navy: Mahlon Dickerson (1837-1838), James K. Paulding (1838-1841)

14th Presidential Term, 1841-1845

President: William Henry Harrison (1841), John Tyler (1841-1845)

Vice President: John Tyler (1841)

Secretary of State: Daniel Webster (1841-1843), Abel P. Upshur (1843-1844), John C. Calhoun (1844-1845)

Secretary of the Treasury: Thomas Ewing (1841), Walter Forward (1841-1843), John C. Spencer (1843-1844), George M. Bibb (1844-1845)

Secretary of War: John Bell (1841), John C. Spencer (1841-1843), James M. Porter (1843-1844), William Wilkins (1844-1845)

Attorney General: John J. Crittenden (1841), Hugh S. Legare (1841-1843), John Nelson (1843-1845)

Postmaster General: Francis Granger (1841), Charles A. Wickliffe (1841-1845)

Secretary of the Navy: George E. Badger (1841), Abel P. Upshur (1841-1843), David Henshaw (1843-1844), John Y. Mason (1844-1845)

15th Presidential Term, 1845-1849

President: James K. Polk

Vice President: George M. Dallas

Secretary of State: John C. Calhoun (1845), James Buchanan (1845-1849)

Secretary of the Treasury: George M. Bibb (1845), Robert J. Walker (1845-1849)

Secretary of War: William Wilkins (1845), William L. Marcy (1845-1849)

Attorney General: John Nelson (1845), John Y. Mason (1845-1846), Nathan Clifford (1846-1848), Isaac Toucey (1848-1849)

Postmaster General: Charles A. Wickliffe (1845), Cave Johnson (1845-1849)

Secretary of the Navy: John Y. Mason (1845), George Bancroft (1845-1846), John Y. Mason (1846-1849)

16th Presidential Term, 1849-1853

President: Zachary Taylor (1849-1850), Millard Fillmore (1850-1853)

Vice President: Millard Fillmore (1849-1850)

Secretary of State: James Buchanan (1848), John M. Clayton (1849-1850), Daniel Webster (1850-1852), Edward Everett (1852-1853)

Secretary of the Treasury: Robert J. Walker (1849), William M. Meredith (1849-1850), Thomas Corwin (1850-1853)

Secretary of War: William L. Marcy (1849), George W. Crawford (1849-1850), Charles M. Conrad (1850-1853)

Attorney General: Isaac Toucey (1849), Reverdy Johnson (1849-1850), John J. Crittenden (1850-1853)

Postmaster General: Cave Johnson (1849), Jacob Collamer (1849-1850), Nathan K. Hall (1850-1852), Samuel D. Hubbard (1852-1853)

Secretary of the Navy: John Y. Mason (1849), William B. Preston (1849-1850), William A. Graham (1850-1852), John P. Kennedy (1852-1853)

Secretary of the Interior: Thomas Ewing (1849-1850), Thomas M. T. McKennan (1850), Alexander H. H. Stuart (1850-1853)

17th Presidential Term, 1853-1857

President: Franklin Pierce

Vice President: William R. King (1853)

Secretary of State: William L. Marcy

Secretary of the Treasury: Thomas Corwin (1853), James Guthrie (1853-1857)

Secretary of War: Charles M. Conrad (1853), Jefferson Davis (1853-1857)

Attorney General: John J. Crittenden (1853), Caleb Cushing (1853-1857)

Postmaster General: Samuel D. Hubbard (1853), James Campbell (1853-1857)

Secretary of the Navy: John P. Kennedy (1853), James C. Dobbin (1853-1857)

Secretary of the Interior: Alexander H. H. Stuart (1853), Robert McClelland (1853-1857)

18th Presidential Term, 1857-1861

President: James Buchanan

Vice President: John C. Breckinridge

Secretary of State: William L. Marcy (1857), Lewis Cass (1857-1860), Jeremiah S. Black (1860-1861)

Secretary of the Treasury: James Guthrie (1857), Howell Cobb (1857-1860), Philip F. Thomas (1860-1861), John A. Dix (1861)

Secretary of War: John B. Floyd (1857-1861), Joseph Holt (1861)

Attorney General: Caleb Cushing (1857), Jeremiah S. Black (1857-1860), Edwin M. Stanton (1860-1861)

Postmaster General: James Campbell (1857), Aaron V. Brown (1857-1859), Joseph Holt (1859-1860), Horatio King (1861)

Secretary of the Navy: James C. Dobbin (1857), Isaac Toucey (1857-1861)

Secretary of the Interior: Robert McClelland (1857), Jacob Thompson (1857-1861)

19th Presidential Term, 1861-1865

President: Abraham Lincoln

Vice President: Hannibal Hamlin

Secretary of State: Jeremiah S. Black (1861), William H. Seward (1861-1865)

Secretary of the Treasury: John A. Dix (1861), Salmon P. Chase (1861-1864), William P. Fessenden (1864-1865)

Secretary of War: Joseph Holt (1861), Simon Cameron (1861-1862), Edwin M. Stanton (1862-1865)

Attorney General: Edwin M. Stanton (1861), Edward Bates (1861-1864), James Speed (1864-1865)

Postmaster General: Horatio King (1861), Montgomery Blair (1861-1864), William Dennison (1864-1865)

Secretary of the Navy: Isaac Toucey (1861), Gideon Welles (1861-1865)

Secretary of the Interior: Caleb B. Smith (1861-1863), John P. Usher (1863-1865)

20th Presidential Term, 1865-1869

President: Abraham Lincoln (1865), Andrew Johnson (1865-1869)

Vice President: Andrew Johnson (1865)

Secretary of State: William H. Seward

Secretary of the Treasury: Hugh McCulloch

Secretary of War: Edwin M. Stanton (1865-1868), John M. Schofield (1868-1869)

Attorney General: James Speed (1865-1866), Henry Stanbery (1866-1868), William M. Evarts (1868-1869)

Postmaster General: William Dennison (1865-1866), Alexander W. Randall (1866-1869)

Secretary of the Navy: Gideon Welles (1865-1869)

Secretary of the Interior: John P. Usher (1865), James Harlan (1865-1866), Orville H. Browning (1866-1869)

21st Presidential Term, 1869-1873

President: Ulysses S. Grant

Vice President: Schuyler Colfax

Secretary of State: William H. Seward (1869), Elihu B. Washburne (1869), Hamilton Fish (1869-1873)

Secretary of the Treasury: Hugh McCulloch (1869), George S. Boutwell (1869-1873)

Secretary of War: John M. Schoffield (1869), John A. Rawlins (1869), William W. Belknap (1869-1873)

Attorney General: William M. Evarts (1869), Ebenezer R. Hoar (1869-1870), Amos T. Akerman (1870-1871), George H. Williams (1871-1873)

Postmaster General: John A. J. Creswell

Secretary of the Navy: Adolph E. Borie (1869), George M. Robeson (1869-1873)

Secretary of the Interior: Jacob D. Cox (1869-1870), Columbus Delano (1870-1873)

22nd Presidential Term, 1873-1877

President: Ulysses S. Grant

Vice President: Henry Wilson 1873-1875

Secretary of State: Hamilton Fish

Secretary of the Treasury: George S. Boutwell (1873-1874), Benjamin H. Bristow (1874-1876), Lot M. Morrill (1876-1877)

Secretary of War: William W. Belknap (1873-1876), James D. Cameron (1876-1877)

Attorney General: George H. Williams (1873-1875), Edwards Pierrepont (1875-1876), Alphonso Taft (1876-1877)

Postmaster General: John A. J. Creswell (1873-1874), James W. Marshall (1874), Marshall Jewell (1874-1876), James N. Tyner (1876-1877)

Secretary of the Navy: George M. Robeson

Secretary of the Interior: Columbus Delano (1873-1875), Zachariah Chandler (1875-1877)

23rd Presidential Term, 1877-1881

President: Rutherford B. Hayes

Vice President: William A. Wheeler

Secretary of State: Hamilton Fish (1877), William M. Evarts (1877-1881)

Secretary of the Treasury: Lot M. Morrill (1877), John Sherman (1877-1881)

Secretary of War: James D. Cameron (1877), George W. McCrary (1877-1879), Alexander Ramsey (1879-1881)

Attorney General: Alphonso Taft (1877), Charles Devens (1877-1881)

Postmaster General: James N. Tyner (1877), David M. Key (1877-1880), Horace Maynard (1880-1881)

Secretary of the Navy: George M. Robeson (1877), Richard W. Thompson (1877-1880), Nathan Goff, Jr. (1881)

Secretary of the Interior: Zachariah Chandler (1877), Carl Schurz (1877-1881)

24th Presidential Term, 1881-1885

President: James A. Garfield (1881), Chester A. Arthur (1881-1885)

Vice President: Chester A. Arthur (1881)

Secretary of State: William M. Evarts (1881), James G. Blaine (1881), Frederick T. Frelinghuysen (1881-1885)

Secretary of the Treasury: William Windom (1881), Charles J. Folger (1881-1884), Walter Q. Gresham (1884), Hugh McCulloch (1884-1885)

Secretary of War: Alexander Ramsey (1881), Robert T. Lincoln (1881-1885)

Attorney General: Charles Devens (1881), Wayne McVeagh (1881), Benjamin H. Brewster (1881-1885)

Postmaster General: Horace Maynard (1881), Thomas L. James (1881), Timothy O. Howe (1881-1883), Walter Q. Gresham (1883-1884), Frank Hatton (1884-1885)

Secretary of the Navy: Nathan Goff, Jr. (1881), William H. Hunt (1881-1882), William E. Chandler (1882-1885)

Secretary of the Interior: Carl Schurz (1881), Samuel J. Kirkwood (1881-1882), Henry M. Teller (1882-1885)

25th Presidential Term, 1885-1889

President: Grover Cleveland

Vice President: Thomas A. Hendricks (1885)

Secretary of State: Frederick T. Frelinghuysen (1885), Thomas F. Bayard (1885-1889)

Secretary of the Treasury: Hugh McCulloch (1885), Daniel Manning (1885-1887), Charles S. Fairchild (1887-1889)

Secretary of War: Robert T. Lincoln (1885), William C. Endicott (1885-1889)

Attorney General: Benjamin H. Brewster (1885), Augustus H. Garland (1885-1889)

Postmaster General: Frank Hatton (1885), William F. Vilas (1885-1888), Don M. Dickinson (1888-1889)

Secretary of the Navy: William E. Chandler (1885), William C. Whitney (1885-1889)

Secretary of the Interior: Lucius Q. C. Lamar (1885-1888), William F. Vilas (1888-1889)

Secretary of Agriculture: Norman J. Colman (1889)

26th Presidential Term, 1889-1893

President: Benjamin Harrison

Vice President: Levi P. Morton

Secretary of State: Thomas F. Bayard (1889), James G. Blaine (1889-1892), John W. Foster (1892-1893)

Secretary of the Treasury: Charles S. Fairchild (1889), William Windom (1889-1891), Charles Foster (1891-1893)

Secretary of War: William C. Endicott (1889), Redfield Proctor (1889-1891), Stephen B. Elkins (1891-1893)

Attorney General: Augustus H. Garland (1889), William H. H. Miller (1889-1893)

Postmaster General: Don M. Dickinson (1889), John Wanamaker (1889-1893)

Secretary of the Navy: William C. Whitney (1889), Benjamin F. Tracy (1889-1893)

Secretary of the Interior: William F. Vilas (1889), John W. Noble (1889-1893)

Secretary of Agriculture: Norman J. Colman (1889), Jeremiah M. Rusk (1889-1893)

27th Presidential Term, 1893-1897

President: Grover Cleveland

Vice President: Adlai E. Stevenson

Secretary of State: Walter Q. Gresham (1893-1895), Richard Olney (1895-1897)

Secretary of the Treasury: Charles Foster (1893), John G. Carlisle (1893-1897)

Secretary of War: Stephen B. Elkins (1893), Daniel S. Lamont (1893-1897)

Attorney General: William H. H. Miller (1893), Richard Olney (1893-1895), Judson Harmon (1895-1897)

Postmaster General: John Wanamaker (1897), Wilson S. Bissell (1893-1895), William L. Wilson (1895-1897)

Secretary of the Navy: Benjamin F. Tracy (1893), Hilary A. Herbert (1893-1897)

Secretary of the Interior: John W. Noble (1893), Hoke Smith (1893-1896), David R. Francis (1897-1897)

Secretary of Agriculture: Jeremiah M. Rusk (1893), J. Sterling Morton (1893-1897)

28th Presidential Term, 1897-1901

President: William McKinley

Vice President: Garrett A. Hobart (1897-1899)

Secretary of State: Richard Olney (1897), John Sherman (1897-1898), William R. Day (1898), John M. Hay (1898-1901)

Secretary of the Treasury: John G. Carlisle (1897), Lyman J. Gage (1897-1901)

Secretary of War: Daniel S. Lamont (1897), Russell A. Alger (1897-1899), Elihu Root (1899-1901)

Attorney General: Judson Harmon (1897), Joseph McKenna (1897-1898), John W. Griggs (1891-1901)

Postmaster General: William L. Wilson (1897), James A. Gary (1897-1898), Charles E. Smith (1898-1901)

Secretary of the Navy: Hilary A. Herbert (1897), John D. Long (1897-1901)

Secretary of the Interior: David R. Francis (1897), Cornelius N. Bliss (1897-1898), Ethan A. Hitchcock (1898-1901)

Secretary of Agriculture: J. Sterling Morton (1897), James Wilson (1897-1901)

29th Presidential Term, 1901-1905

President: William McKinley (1901), Theodore Roosevelt (1901-1905)

Vice President: Theodore Roosevelt (1901)

Secretary of State: John M. Hay (1901-1905)

Secretary of the Treasury: Lyman J. Gage (1901-1902), Leslie M. Shaw (1902-1905)

Secretary of War: Elihu Root (1901-1904), William Howard Taft (1904-1905)

Attorney General: John W. Griggs (1901), Philander C. Knox (1901-1904), William H. Moody (1904-1905)

Postmaster General: Charles E. Smith (1901-1902), Henry C. Payne (1902-1904), Robert J. Wynne (1904-1905)

Secretary of the Navy: John D. Long (1901-1902), William H. Moody (1902-1904), Paul Morton (1904-1905)

Secretary of the Interior: Ethan A. Hitchcock

Secretary of Agriculture: James Wilson

Secretary of Commerce and Labor: George B. Cortelyou (1903-1904), Victor H. Metcalf (1904-1905)

30th Presidential Term, 1905-1909

President: Theodore Roosevelt

Vice President: Charles W. Fairbanks

Secretary of State: John M. Hay (1905), Elihu Root (1905-1909), Robert Bacon (1909)

Secretary of the Treasury: Leslie M. Shaw (1905-1907), George B. Cortelyou (1907-1909)

Secretary of War: William Howard Taft (1905-1908), Luke E. Wright (1908-1909)

Attorney General: William H. Moody (1906), Charles J. Bonaparte (1906-1909)

Postmaster General: Robert J. Wynne (1905), George B. Cortelyou (1905-1907), George von L. Meyer (1907-1909)

Secretary of the Navy: Paul Morton (1905), Charles J. Bonaparte (1905-1906), Victor H. Metcalf (1906-1908), Truman H. Newberry (1908-1909)

Secretary of the Interior: Ethan A. Hitchcock (1905-1907), James R. Garfield (1907-1909)

Secretary of Agriculture: James Wilson

Secretary of Commerce and Labor: Victor H. Metcalf (1905-1906), Oscar S. Straus (1906-1909)

31st Presidential Term, 1909-1913

President: William Howard Taft

Vice President: James S. Sherman (1909-1912)

Secretary of State: Robert Bacon (1909), Philander C. Knox (1909-1913)

Secretary of the Treasury: George B. Cortelyou (1909), Franklin MacVeagh (1909-1913)

Secretary of War: Luke E. Wright (1909), Jacob M. Dickinson (1909-1911), Henry L. Stimson (1911-1913)

Attorney General: Charles J. Bonaparte (1909), George W. Wickersham (1909-1913)

Postmaster General: George von L. Meyer (1909), Frank H. Hitchcock (1909-1913)

Secretary of the Navy: Truman H. Newberry (1909), George von L. Meyer (1909-1913)

Secretary of the Interior: James R. Garfield (1909), Richard A. Ballinger (1909-1911), Walter L. Fisher (1911-1913)

Secretary of Agriculture: James Wilson (1909-1913)

Secretary of Commerce and Labor: Oscar S. Straus (1909), Charles Nagel (1909-1913)

32nd Presidential Term, 1913-1917

President: Woodrow Wilson

Vice President: Thomas R. Marshall

Secretary of State: Philander C. Knox (1913), William Jennings Bryan (1913-1915), Robert Lansing (1915-1917)

Secretary of the Treasury: Franklin MacVeagh (1913), Lindley M. Garrison (1913-1916), Newton D. Baker (1916-1917)

Attorney General: George W. Wickersham (1913), James C. McReynolds (1913-1914), Thomas W. Gregory (1914-1917)

Postmaster General: Frank H. Hitchcock (1913), Albert S. Burleson (1913-1917)

Secretary of the Navy: George von L. Meyer (1913), Josephus Daniels (1913-1917)

Secretary of the Interior: Walter L. Fisher (1913), Franklin K. Lane (1913-1917)

Secretary of Agriculture: James Wilson (1913), David F. Houston (1913-1917)

Secretary of Commerce: Charles Nagel (1913), William C. Redfield (1913-1917)

Secretary of Labor: Charles Nagel (1913), William B. Wilson (1913-1917)

33rd Presidential Term, 1917-1921

President: Woodrow Wilson

Vice President: Thomas R. Marshall

Secretary of State: Robert Lansing (1917-1920), Bainbridge Colby (1920-1921)

Secretary of the Treasury: William Gibbs McAdoo (1917-1918), Carter Glass (1918-1920), David F. Houston (1920-1921)

Secretary of War: Newton D. Baker (1917-1921)

Attorney General: Thomas W. Gregory (1917-1919), A. Mitchell Palmer (1919-1921)

Postmaster General: Albert S. Burleson

Secretary of the Navy: Josephus Daniels

Secretary of the Interior: Franklin K. Lane (1917-1920), John B. Payne (1920-1921)

Secretary of Agriculture: David F. Houston (1917-1920), Edwin T. Meredith (1920-1921)

Secretary of Commerce: William C. Redfield (1917-1919), Joshua W. Alexander (1919-1921)

Secretary of Labor: William B. Wilson (1917-1921)

34th Presidential Term, 1921-1925

President: Warren G. Harding (1921-1923), Calvin Coolidge (1923-1925)

Vice President: Calvin Coolidge (1921-1923)

Secretary of State: Bainbridge Colby (1921), Charles Evans Hughes (1921-1925)

Secretary of the Treasury: David F. Houston (1921), Andrew W. Mellon (1921-1925)

Secretary of War: Newton D. Baker (1921), John W. Weeks (1921-1925)

Attorney General: A. Mitchell Palmer (1921), Harry M. Daugherty (1921-1924), Harlan F. Stone (1924-1925)

Postmaster General: Albert S. Burleson (1921), Will H. Hays (1921-1922), Hubert Work (1922-1923), Harry S. New (1923-1925)

Secretary of the Navy: Josephus Daniels (1921), Edwin Denby (1921-1924), Curtis D. Wilbur (1924-1925)

Secretary of the Interior: John B. Payne (1921), Albert F. Gall (1921-1923), Hubert Work (1923-1925)

Secretary of Agriculture: Edwin T. Meredith (1921), Henry C. Wallace (1921-1924), Howard M. Gore (1924-1925)

Secretary of Commerce: Joshua W. Alexander (1921), Herbert Hoover (1921-1925)

Secretary of Labor: William B. Wilson (1921), James J. Davis (1921-1925)

35th Presidential Term, 1925-1929

President: Calvin Coolidge

Vice President: Charles G. Dawes

Secretary of State: Charles Evans Hughes (1925), Frank B. Kellogg (1925-1929)

Secretary of the Treasury: Andrew W. Mellon

Secretary of War: John W. Weeks (1925), Dwight F. Davis (1925-1929)

Attorney General: John G. Sargent

Postmaster General: Harry S. New

Secretary of the Navy: Curtis D. Wilbur

Secretary of the Interior: Hubert Work (1925-1928), Roy O. West (1929)

Secretary of Agriculture: Howard M. Gore (1925), William M. Hardine (1925-1929)

Secretary of Commerce: Herbert Hoover (1925-1928), William F. Whiting (1928-1929)

Secretary of Labor: James J. Davis

36th Presidential Term, 1929-1933

President: Herbert Hoover

Vice President: Charles Curtis

Secretary of State: Frank B. Kellogg (1929), Henry L. Stimson (1929-1933)

Secretary of the Treasury: Andrew W. Mellon (1929-1932), Ogden L. Mills (1932-1933)

Secretary of War: Dwight F. Davis (1929), James W. Good (1929), Patrick J. Hurley (1929-1933)

Attorney General: John G. Sargent (1929), William D. Mitchell (1929-1933)

Postmaster General: Harry S. New (1929), Walter F. Brown (1929-1933)

Secretary of the Navy: Curtis D. Wilbur (1929), Charles Francis Adams (1929-1933)

Secretary of the Interior: Roy O. West (1929), Ray L. Wilbur (1929-1933)

Secretary of Agriculture: William M. Hardine (1929), Arthur M. Hyde (1929-1933)

Secretary of Commerce: William F. Whiting (1929), Robert P. Lamont (1929-1932), Roy D. Chapman (1932-1933)

Secretary of Labor: James J. Davis (1929-1930), William N. Doak (1930-1933)

37th Presidential Term, 1933-1937

President: Franklin D. Roosevelt

Vice President: John Nance Garner

Secretary of State: Cordell Hull

Secretary of the Treasury: William H. Woodin (1933-1934), Henry Morgenthau, Jr. (1934-1937)

Secretary of War: George H. Dern (1933-1936)

Attorney General: Homer S. Cummings

Postmaster General: James A. Farley

Secretary of the Navy: Claude A. Swanson

Secretary of the Interior: Harold L. Ickes

Secretary of Agriculture: Henry Wallace

Secretary of Commerce: Daniel C. Roper

Secretary of Labor: Frances Perkins

38th Presidential Term, 1937-1941

President: Franklin D. Roosevelt

Vice President: John Nance Garner

Secretary of State: Cordell Hull

Secretary of the Treasury: Henry Morgenthau, Jr.

Secretary of War: Harry H. Woodring (1937-1940), Henry L. Stimson (1940-1941)

Attorney General: Homer S. Cummings (1937-1939), Frank Murphy (1939-1940), Robert H. Jackson (1940-1941)

Postmaster General: James A. Farley (1937-1940), Frank C. Walker (1940-1941)

Secretary of the Navy: Claude A. Swanson (1937-1939), Charles Edison (1940), Frank Knox (1940-1941)

Secretary of the Interior: Harold L. Ickes

Secretary of Agriculture: Henry A. Wallace (1937-1940), Claude R. Wickard (1940-1941)

Secretary of Commerce: Daniel C. Roper (1937-1938), Harry L. Hopkins (1939-1940), Jesse H. Jones (1940-1941)

Secretary of Labor: Frances Perkins

39th Presidential Term, 1941-1945

President: Franklin D. Roosevelt

Vice President: Henry A. Wallace

Secretary of State: Cordell Hull (1941-1944), Edward R. Stettinius, Jr. (1944-1945)

Secretary of the Treasury: Henry Morgenthau, Jr.

Secretary of War: Henry L. Stimson

Attorney General: Robert H. Jackson (1941), Francis Biddle (1941-1945)

Postmaster General: Frank C. Walker

Secretary of the Navy: Frank Knox (1941-1944), James V. Forrestal (1944-1945)

Secretary of the Interior: Harold L. Ickes

Secretary of Agriculture: Claude R. Wickard

Secretary of Commerce: Jesse H. Jones

Secretary of Labor: Frances Perkins

40th Presidential Term, 1945-1949

President: Franklin D. Roosevelt (1945), Harry S Truman (1945-1949)

Vice President: Harry S Truman (1945)

Secretary of State: Edward R. Stettinius, Jr. (1945), James F. Byrnes (1945-1947), George C. Marshall (1947-1949)

Secretary of Defense: James V. Forrestal (1947-1949)

Secretary of the Treasury: Henry Morgenthau, Jr. (1945), Fred M. Vinson (1945-1946), John W. Snyder (1946-1949)

Secretary of War: Henry L. Stimson (1945), Robert P. Patterson (1945-1947), Kenneth C. Royall (1947)

Attorney General: Francis Biddle (1945), Tom C. Clark (1945-1949)

Postmaster General: Frank C. Walker (1945), Robert E. Hannegan (1945-1947), Jesse M. Donaldson (1947-1949)

Secretary of the Navy: James V. Forrestal (1945-1947)

Secretary of the Interior: Harold L. Ickes (1945-1946), Julius A. Krug (1946-1949)

Secretary of Agriculture: Claude R. Wickard (1945), Clinton P. Anderson (1945-1948), Charles F. Brannan (1948-1949)

Secretary of Commerce: Jesse H. Jones (1945), Henry A. Wallace (1945-1946), W. Averell Harriman (1947-1948), Charles Sawyer (1948-1949)

Secretary of Labor: Frances Perkins (1945), Lewis B. Schwellenbach (1945-1948), Maurice J. Tobin (1948-1949)

41st Presidential Term, 1949-1953

President: Harry S Truman

Vice President: Alben W. Barkley

Secretary of State: Dean G. Acheson

Secretary of the Treasury: John W. Snyder

Secretary of Defense: James V. Forrestal (1949), Louis A. Johnson (1949-1950), George C. Marshall (1950-1951), Robert A. Lovett (1951-1953)

Attorney General: Tom C. Clark (1949), J. Howard McGrath (1949-1952), James P. McGranery (1952-1953)

Postmaster General: Jesse M. Donaldson

Secretary of the Interior: Julius A. Krug (1949), Oscar L. Chapman (1950-1953)

Secretary of Agriculture: Charles F. Brannan

Secretary of Commerce: Charles Sawyer

Secretary of Labor: Maurice J. Tobin

42nd Presidential Term, 1953-1957

President: Dwight D. Eisenhower

Vice President: Richard M. Nixon

Secretary of State: John Foster Dulles

Secretary of the Treasury: George M. Humphrey

Secretary of Defense: Charles E. Wilson

Attorney General: Herbert Brownell, Jr.

Postmaster General: Arthur E. Summerfield

Secretary of the Interior: Douglas McKay (1953-1956), Frederick A. Seaton (1956-1957)

Secretary of Agriculture: Ezra Taft Benson

Secretary of Commerce: Sinclair Weeks

Secretary of Labor: Martin P. Durkin (1953), James P. Mitchell (1954-1957)

Secretary of Health, Education, and Welfare: Oveta Culp Hobby (1953-1955), Marion B. Folsom (1955-1957)

43rd Presidential Term, 1957-1961

President: Dwight D. Eisenhower

Vice President: Richard M. Nixon

Secretary of State: John Foster Dulles (1957-1959), Christian A. Herter (1959-1961)

Secretary of the Treasury: George M. Humphrey (1957), Robert B. Anderson (1957-1961)

Secretary of Defense: Charles E. Wilson (1957), Neil H. McElroy (1957-1960), Thomas S. Gates, Jr. (1960-1961)

Attorney General: Herbert Brownell, Jr. (1957), William P. Rogers (1958-1961)

Postmaster General: Arthur E. Summerfield

Secretary of the Interior: Frederick A. Seaton

Secretary of Agriculture: Ezra Taft Benson

Secretary of Commerce: Sinclair Weeks (1957-1958), Lewis L. Strauss (1958-1959), Frederick H. Mueller (1959-1961)

Secretary of Labor: James P. Mitchell

Secretary of Health, Education, and Welfare: Marion B. Folsom (1957-1958), Arthur S. Flemming (1958-1961)

44th Presidential Term, 1961-1965

President: John F. Kennedy (1961-1963), Lyndon B. Johnson (1963-1965)

Vice President: Lyndon B. Johnson (1961-1963)

Secretary of State: Dean Rusk

Secretary of the Treasury: C. Douglas Dillon

Secretary of Defense: Robert S. McNamara

Attorney General: Robert F. Kennedy

Postmaster General: J. Edward Day (1961-1963), John A. Gronouski (1963-1965)

Secretary of the Interior: Stewart L. Udall

Secretary of Agriculture: Orville L. Freeman

Secretary of Commerce: Luther H. Hodges

Secretary of Labor: Arthur J. Goldberg (1961-1962), W. Willard Wirtz (1962-1965)

Secretary of Health, Education, and Welfare: Abraham A. Ribicoff (1961-1962), Anthony J. Celebrezze (1962-1965)

45th Presidential Term, 1965-1969

President: Lyndon B. Johnson

Vice President: Hubert H. Humphrey

Secretary of State: Dean Rusk

Secretary of the Treasury: Henry H. Fowler (1965-1968), Joseph W. Barr (1968-1969)

Secretary of Defense: Robert S. McNamara (1965-1968), Clark M. Clifford (1968-1969)

Attorney General: Nicholas de B. Katzenbach (1965-1967), Ramsey Clark (1967-1969)

Postmaster General: Lawrence F. O'Brien (1965-1968), M. Marvin Watson (1968-1969)

Secretary of the Interior: Stewart L. Udall

Secretary of Agriculture: Orville L. Freeman

Secretary of Commerce: John T. Connor (1965-1967), Alexander B. Trowbridge (1967-1968), Cyrus R. Smith (1968-1969)

Secretary of Labor: W. Willard Wirtz

Secretary of Health, Education, and Welfare: John W. Gardner (1965-1968), Wilbur J. Cohen (1968-1969)

Secretary of Housing and Urban Development: Robert C. Weaver (1966-1968), Robert C. Wood (1968-1969)

Secretary of Transportation: Alan S. Boyd (1966-1969)

46th Presidential Term, 1969-1973

President: Richard M. Nixon

Vice President: Spiro T. Agnew

Secretary of State: William P. Rogers

Secretary of the Treasury: David M. Kennedy (1969-1971), John B. Connally (1971-1972), George P. Shultz (1972-1973)

Secretary of Defense: Melvin R. Laird

Attorney General: John N. Mitchell (1969-1972), Richard G. Kleindienst (1972-1973)

Postmaster General: Winton M. Blount (1969-1971)

Secretary of the Interior: Walter J. Hickel (1969-1971), Rogers C. B. Morton (1971-1973)

Secretary of Agriculture: Clifford M. Hardin (1969-1971), Earl L. Butz (1971-1973)

Secretary of Commerce: Maurice H. Stans (1969-1972), Peter G. Peterson (1972-1973)

Secretary of Labor: George P. Shultz (1969-1970), James D. Hodgson (1970-1973)

Secretary of Health, Education, and Welfare: Robert H. Finch (1969-1970), Elliot L. Richardson (1970-1973)

Secretary of Housing and Urban Development: George W. Romney

Secretary of Transportation: John A. Volpe

47th Presidential Term, 1973-1977

President: Richard M. Nixon (1973-1974), Gerald R. Ford (1974-1977)

Vice President: Spiro T. Agnew (1973), Gerald R. Ford (1973-1974), Nelson Rockefeller (1974-1977)

Secretary of State: William P. Rogers (1973), Henry A. Kissinger (1973-1977)

Secretary of the Treasury: George P. Shultz (1973-1974), William E. Simon (1974-1977)

Secretary of Defense: Elliot L. Richardson (1973), James R. Schlesinger (1973-1975), Donald H. Rumsfeld (1975-1977)

Attorney General: Richard G. Kleindienst (1973), Elliot L. Richardson (1973-1974), William B. Saxbe (1974-1975), Edward H. Levi (1975-1977)

Secretary of the Interior: Rogers C. B. Morton (1973-1975), Stanley K. Hathaway (1975), Thomas S. Kleppe (1975-1977)

Secretary of Agriculture: Earl L. Butz (1973-1976), John Knebel (1976-1977)

Secretary of Commerce: Frederick B. Dent (1973-1975), Rogers C. B. Morton (1975-1976), Elliot L. Richardson (1976-1977)

Secretary of Labor: Peter J. Brennan (1973-1975), John T. Dunlop (1975-1976), William J. Usery, Jr. (1976-1977)

Secretary of Health, Education, and Welfare: Caspar W. Weinberger (1973-1975), F. David Mathews (1975-1977)

Secretary of Housing and Urban Development: James T. Lynn (1973-1975), Carla A. Hills (1975-1977)

Secretary of Transportation: Claude S. Brinegar (1973-1975), William T. Coleman, Jr. (1975-1977)

48th Presidential Term, 1977-1981

President: James Earl (Jimmy) Carter

Vice President: Walter F. Mondale

Secretary of State: Cyrus R. Vance (1977-1980), Edmund S. Muskie (1980-1981)

Secretary of the Treasury: W. Michael Blumenthal (1977-1979), G. William Miller (1979-1981)

Secretary of Defense: Harold Brown

Attorney General: Griffin B. Bell (1977-1979), Benjamin R. Civiletti (1979-1981)

Secretary of the Interior: Cecil D. Andrus

Secretary of Agriculture: Bob S. Bergland

Secretary of Commerce: Juanita M. Kreps (1977-1979), Philip M. Klutznick (1979-1981)

Secretary of Labor: F. Ray Marshall

Secretary of Health and Human Services (Secretary of Health, Education, and Welfare until 1979.): Joseph A. Califano, Jr. (1977-1979), Patricia Roberts Harris (1979-1981)

Secretary of Housing and Urban Development: Patricia Roberts Harris (1977-1979), Moon Landrieu (1979-1981)

Secretary of Transportation: Brock Adams (1977-1979), Neil E. Goldschmidt (1979-1981)

Secretary of Energy: James R. Schlesinger (1977-1979), Charles W. Duncan, Jr. (1979-1981)

Secretary of Education: Shirley Mount Hufstedler (1979-1981)

49th Presidential Term, 1981-1985

President: Ronald Reagan

Vice President: George Bush

Secretary of State: Alexander M. Haig, Jr. (1981-1982), George P. Shultz (1982-1985)

Secretary of the Treasury: Donald T. Regan

Secretary of Defense: Caspar W. Weinberger

Attorney General: William French Smith

Secretary of the Interior: James G. Watt (1981-1983), William P. Clark (1983-1985)

Secretary of Agriculture: John R. Block

Secretary of Commerce: Malcolm Baldrige

Secretary of Labor: Raymond J. Donovan (1981-1985), William E. Brock (1985)

Secretary of Health and Human Services: Richard S. Schweiker (1981-1983), Margaret M. Heckler (1983-1985)

Secretary of Housing and Urban Development: Samuel R. Pierce, Jr.

Secretary of Transportation: Andrew L. Lewis, Jr. (1981-1983), Elizabeth H. Dole (1983-1985)

Secretary of Energy: James B. Edwards (1981-1983), Donald P. Hodel (1983-1985)

Secretary of Education: T. H. Bell (1981-1985), William J. Bennett (1985)

50th Presidential Term, 1985-1989

President: Ronald Reagan

Vice President: George Bush

Secretary of State: George P. Shultz

Secretary of the Treasury: James A. Baker, III

Secretary of Defense: Caspar W. Weinberger

Attorney General: Edwin Meese, 3rd

Secretary of the Interior: Donald P. Hodel

Secretary of Agriculture: John R. Block

Secretary of Commerce: Malcolm Baldrige

Secretary of Labor: William E. Brock

Secretary of Health and Human Services: Margaret M. Heckler (1983-1985), Otis R. Bowen

Secretary of Housing and Urban Development: Andrew L. Lewis, Jr.

Secretary of Energy: John S. Herrington

Secretary of Education: William J. Bennett

Cabinet Members by Department

First date indicates year department was established.

Secretaries of State

Years in Office	Name and State	Presidential Terms
1790-1794	Thomas Jefferson (VA)	Washington 1, 2
1794-1795	Edmund Randolph (VA)	Washington 2
1795-1800	Timothy Pickering (PA)	Washington 2, J. Adams
1800-1801	John Marshall (VA)	J. Adams
1801-1809	James Madison (VA)	Jefferson 1, 2
1809-1811	Robert Smith (MD)	Madison 1
1811-1817	James Monroe (VA)	Madison 1, 2
1817-1825	John Quincy Adams (MA)	Monroe 1, 2
1825-1829	Henry Clay (KY)	J. Q. Adams
1829-1831	Martin Van Buren (NY)	Jackson 1
1831-1833	Edward Livingston (LA)	Jackson 1, 2
1833-1834	Louis McLane (DE)	Jackson 2
1834-1841	John Forsyth (GA)	Jackson 2, Van Buren
1841-1843	Daniel Webster (MA)	W. H. Harrison, Tyler
1843-1844	Abel P. Upshur (MA)	Tyler
1844-1845	John C. Calhoun (VA)	Tyler, Polk
1845-1849	James Buchanan (PA)	Polk, Taylor
1849-1850	John M. Clayton (DE)	Taylor, Fillmore
1850-1852	Daniel Webster (MA)	Fillmore
1852-1853	Edward Everett (MA)	Fillmore
1853-1857	William L. Marcy (NY)	Pierce, Buchanan
1857-1860	Lewis Cass (MI)	Buchanan
1860-1861	Jeremiah S. Black (PA)	Buchanan, Lincoln 1
1861-1869	William H. Seward (NY)	Lincoln 1, 2, A. Johnson, Grant 1
1869	Elihu B. Washburne (IL)	Grant 1
1869-1877	Hamilton Fish (NY)	Grant 1, 2, Hayes
1877-1881	William M. Evarts (NY)	Hayes, Garfield
1881	James G. Blaine (ME)	Garfield, Arthur
1881-1885	Frederick T. Frelinghuysen (NJ)	Arthur, Cleveland 1
1885-1889	Thomas F. Bayard (DE)	Cleveland 1, B. Harrison
1889-1892	James G. Blaine (ME)	B. Harrison
1892-1893	John W. Foster (IN)	B. Harrison
1893-1895	Walter Q. Gresham (IL)	Cleveland 2
1895-1897	Richard Olney (MA)	Cleveland 2, McKinley 1
1897-1898	John Sherman (OH)	McKinley 1
1898	William R. Day (OH)	McKinley 1
1898-1905	John M. Hay (DC)	McKinley 1, 2, T. Roosevelt 1, 2
1905-1909	Elihu Root (NY)	T. Roosevelt 2
1909	Robert Bacon (NY)	T. Roosevelt 2, Taft
1909-1913	Philander C. Knox (PA)	Taft, Wilson 1
1913-1915	William Jennings Bryan (NE)	Wilson 1
1915-1920	Robert Lansing (NY)	Wilson 1, 2
1920-1921	Bainbridge Colby (NY)	Wilson 2, Harding
1921-1925	Charles Evans Hughes (NY)	Harding, Coolidge 1, 2
1925-1929	Frank B. Kellogg (MN)	Coolidge 2, Hoover
1929-1933	Henry L. Stimson (NY)	Hoover
1933-1944	Cordell Hull (TN)	F. D. Roosevelt 1, 2, 3
1944-1945	Edward R. Stettinius, Jr. (VA)	F. D. Roosevelt 3, 4, Truman 1
1945-1947	James F. Byrnes (SC)	Truman 1
1947-1949	George C. Marshall (PA)	Truman 1
1949-1953	Dean G. Acheson (CT)	Truman 2
1953-1959	John Foster Dulles (NY)	Eisenhower 1, 2
1959-1961	Christian A. Herter (MA)	Eisenhower 2
1961-1969	Dean Rusk (GA)	Kennedy, L. B. Johnson 1, 2
1969-1973	William P. Rogers (NY)	Nixon 1, 2
1973-1977	Henry A. Kissinger (MA)	Nixon 2, Ford
1977-1980	Cyrus R. Vance (NY)	Carter
1980-1981	Edmund S. Muskie (ME)	Carter
1981-1982	Alexander M. Haig, Jr. (CT)	Reagan 1
1982-	George P. Shultz (CA)	Reagan 1, 2

Secretaries of the Treasury

Years in Office	Name and State	Presidential Terms
1789-1795	Alexander Hamilton (NY)	Washington 1, 2
1795-1801	Oliver Wolcott, Jr. (CT)	Washington 2, J. Adams
1801	Samuel Dexter (MA)	J. Adams, Jefferson 1
1801-1814	Albert Gallatin (PA)	Jefferson 1, 2, Madison 1, 2
1814	George W. Campbell (TN)	Madison 2
1814-1816	Alexander J. Dallas (PA)	Madison 2
1816-1825	William H. Crawford (GA)	Madison 2, Monroe 1, 2
1825-1828	Richard Rush (PA)	J. Q. Adams
1829-1831	Samuel D. Ingham (PA)	Jackson 1
1831-1833	Louis McLane (DE)	Jackson 1, 2
1833	William J. Duane (PA)	Jackson 2
1833	Roger B. Taney (MD)	Jackson 2
1834-1841	Levi Woodbury (NH)	Jackson 2, Van Buren
1841	Thomas Ewing (OH)	W. H. Harrison, Tyler
1841-1843	Walter Forward (PA)	Tyler
1843-1844	John C. Spencer (NY)	Tyler
1844-1845	George M. Bibb (KY)	Tyler, Polk
1845-1849	Robert J. Walker (MS)	Polk, Taylor
1849-1850	William M. Meredith (PA)	Taylor, Fillmore
1850-1853	Thomas Corwin (OH)	Fillmore, Pierce
1853-1857	James Guthrie (KY)	Pierce, Buchanan
1857-1860	Howell Cobb (GA)	Buchanan
1860-1861	Philip F. Thomas (MD)	Buchanan
1861	John A. Dix (NY)	Buchanan, Lincoln 1
1861-1864	Salmon P. Chase (OH)	Lincoln 1
1864-1865	William P. Fessenden (ME)	Lincoln 1
1865-1869	Hugh McCulloch (IN)	Lincoln 2, A. Johnson, Grant 1
1869-1873	George S. Boutwell (MA)	Grant 1, 2
1873-1874	William A. Richardson (MA)	Grant 2
1874-1876	Benjamin H. Bristow (KY)	Grant 2

Years in Office	Name and State	Presidential Terms
1876-1877	Lot M. Morrill (ME)	Grant 2, Hayes
1877-1881	John Sherman (OH)	Hayes
1881	William Windom (MN)	Garfield, Arthur
1881-1884	Charles J. Folger (NY)	Arthur
1884	Walter Q. Gresham (IN)	Arthur
1884-1885	Hugh McCulloch (IN)	Arthur, Cleveland 1
1885-1887	Daniel Manning (NY)	Cleveland
1887-1889	Charles S. Fairchild (NY)	Cleveland 1, B. Harrison
1889-1891	William Windom (MN)	B. Harrison
1891-1893	Charles Foster (OH)	B. Harrison, Cleveland 2
1893-1897	John G. Carlisle (KY)	Cleveland 2, McKinley 1
1897-1902	Lyman J. Gage (IL)	McKinley 1, 2, T. Roosevelt 1
1902-1907	Leslie M. Shaw (IA)	T. Roosevelt 1, 2
1907-1909	George B. Cortelyou (NY)	T. Roosevelt 2, Taft
1909-1913	Franklin MacVeagh (IL)	Taft, Wilson 1
1913-1918	William Gibbs McAdoo (NY)	Wilson 1, 2
1918-1920	Carter Glass (VA)	Wilson 2
1920-1921	David F. Houston (MO)	Wilson 2, Harding
1921-1932	Andrew W. Mellon (PA)	Harding, Coolidge 1, 2, Hoover
1932-1933	Ogden L. Mills (NY)	Hoover
1933-1934	William H. Woodin (NY)	F. D. Roosevelt 1
1934-1945	Henry Morgenthau, Jr. (NY)	F. D. Roosevelt 1, 2, 3, 4, Truman
1945-1946	Frederick M. Vinson (KY)	Truman 1
1946-1953	John W. Snyder (MO)	Truman 1, 2
1953-1957	George M. Humphrey (OH)	Eisenhower 1, 2
1957-1961	Robert B. Anderson (CT)	Eisenhower 2
1961-1965	C. Douglas Dillon (NJ)	Kennedy, L. B. Johnson 1
1968-1969	Joseph W. Barr (IN)	L. B. Johnson 2
1969-1971	David M. Kennedy (IL)	Nixon 1
1971-1972	John B. Connally (TX)	Nixon 1
1972-1973	George P. Shultz (CA)	Nixon 1, 2
1974-1977	William E. Simon (NJ)	Nixon 2, Ford
1977-1979	W. Michael Blumenthal (MI)	Carter
1979-1981	G. William Miller (RI)	Carter
1981-1985	Donald T. Regan (NY)	Reagan 1
1985-	James A. Baker, III (TX)	Reagan 2

Secretaries of War

Years in Office	Name and State	Presidential Terms
1789-1795	Henry Knox (MA)	Washington 1, 2
1795	Timothy Pickering (PA)	Washington 2
1796-1800	James McHenry (MD)	Washington 2, J. Adams
1800-1801	Samuel Dexter (MA)	J. Adams
1801-1809	Henry Dearborn (MA)	Jefferson 1, 2
1809-1812	William Eustis (MA)	Madison 1
1813-1814	John Armstrong (NY)	Madison 1, 2
1814-1815	James Monroe (VA)	Madison 2
1815-1816	William H. Crawford (GA)	Madison 2
1817-1825	John C. Calhoun (SC)	Monroe 1, 2
1825-1828	James Barbour (VA)	J. Q. Adams
1828-1829	Peter B. Porter (NY)	J. Q. Adams
1829-1831	John H. Eaton (TN)	Jackson 1
1831-1836	Lewis Cass (OH)	Jackson 1, 2
1837	Benjamin F. Butler (NY)	Jackson 2, Van Buren
1837-1841	Joel R. Poinsett (SC)	Van Buren
1841	John Bell (TN)	W. H. Harrison, Tyler
1841-1843	John C. Spencer (NY)	Tyler
1843-1844	James M. Porter (PA)	Tyler
1844-1845	William Wilkins (PA)	Tyler, Polk
1845-1849	William L. Marcy (NY)	Polk, Taylor

Years in Office	Name and State	Presidential Terms
1849-1850	George W. Crawford (GA)	Taylor, Fillmore
1850-1853	Charles M. Conrad (LA)	Fillmore, Pierce
1853-1857	Jefferson Davis (MS)	Pierce
1857-1861	John B. Floyd (VA)	Buchanan
1861	Joseph Holt (KY)	Buchanan, Lincoln 1
1861-1862	Simon Cameron (PA)	Lincoln 1
1862-1868	Edwin M. Stanton (PA)	Lincoln 1, 2, A. Johnson
1868-1869	John M. Schoefield (IL)	Grant 1
1869-1876	William W. Belknap (IA)	Grant 1, 2
1876	Alphonso Taft (OH)	Grant 2
1876-1877	James D. Cameron (PA)	Grant 2, Hayes
1877-1879	George W. McCrary (IA)	Hayes
1879-1881	Alexander Ramsey (MN)	Hayes, Garfield
1881-1885	Robert T. Lincoln (IL)	Garfield, Arthur, Cleveland 1
1885-1889	William C. Endicott (MA)	Garfield, Arthur, Cleveland 1
1889-1891	Redfield Proctor (VT)	Cleveland 1, B. Harrison
1891-1893	Stephen B. Elkins (WV)	B. Harrison, Cleveland 2
1893-1897	Daniel S. Lamont (NY)	Cleveland 2, McKinley 1
1897-1899	Russell A. Alger (MI)	McKinley 1
1899-1904	Elihu Root (NY)	McKinley 1, 2, T. Roosevelt 1
1904-1908	William Howard Taft (OH)	T. Roosevelt 1, 2
1908-1909	Luke E. Wright (TN)	T. Roosevelt 2, Taft
1909-1911	Jacob M. Dickinson (TN)	Taft
1911-1913	Henry L. Stimson (NY)	Taft, Wilson 1
1913-1916	Lindley M. Garrison (NJ)	Wilson 1
1916-1921	Newton D. Baker (OH)	Wilson 1, 2, Harding
1921-1925	John W. Weeks (MA)	Harding, Coolidge 1, 2
1925-1929	Dwight F. Davis (MO)	Coolidge 2, Hoover
1929	James W. Good (IL)	Hoover
1929-1933	Patrick J. Hurley (OK)	Hoover
1933-1936	George H. Dern (UT)	F. D. Roosevelt 1
1937-1940	Harry H. Woodring (KS)	F. D. Roosevelt 2
1940-1945	Henry L. Stimson (NY)	F. D. Roosevelt 2, 3, 4, Truman 1
1945-1947	Robert P. Patterson (NY)	Truman 1
1947	Kenneth C. Royall (NC)	Truman 1

(Became part of the Department of Defense under the National Security Act of 1947.)

Attorneys General

Years in Office	Name and State	Presidential Terms
1790-1794	Edmund Randolph (VA)	Washington 1, 2
1794-1795	William Bradford (PA)	Washington 2
1795-1801	Charles Lee (VA)	Washington 2, J. Adams
1801-1804	Levi Lincoln (MA)	Jefferson 1
1805-1806	John Breckenridge (KY)	Jefferson 2
1807-1811	Caesar A. Rodney (DE)	Jefferson 2, Madison 1
1811-1814	William Pinkney (MD)	Madison 1, 2
1814-1817	Richard Rush (PA)	Madison 2, Monroe 1
1817-1829	William Wirt (VA)	Monroe 1, 2, J. Q. Adams
1829-1831	John M. Berrien (GA)	Jackson 1
1831-1833	Roger B. Taney (MD)	Jackson 1, 2
1833-1838	Benjamin F. Butler (NY)	Jackson 2, Van Buren
1838-1840	Felix Grundy (TN)	Van Buren
1840-1841	Henry D. Gilpin (PA)	Van Buren
1841	John J. Crittenden (KY)	W. H. Harrison, Tyler
1841-1843	Hugh S. Legare (SC)	Tyler
1843-1845	John Nelson (MD)	Tyler, Polk

Years in Office	Name and State	Presidential Terms
1845-1846	John Y. Mason (VA)	Polk
1846-1848	Nathan Clifford (ME)	Polk
1848-1849	Isaac Toucey (CT)	Polk, Taylor
1849-1850	Reverdy Johnson (MD)	Taylor, Fillmore
1850-1853	John J. Crittenden (KY)	Fillmore, Pierce
1853-1857	Caleb Cushing (MA)	Pierce, Buchanan
1857-1860	Jeremiah S. Black (PA)	Buchanan
1860-1861	Edwin M. Stanton (PA)	Buchanan, Lincoln 1
1861-1864	Edward Bates (MO)	Lincoln 1
1864-1866	James Speed (KY)	Lincoln 1, 2, A. Johnson
1866-1868	Henry Stanbery (OH)	A. Johnson
1868-1869	William M. Evarts (NY)	A. Johnson, Grant 1
1869-1870	Ebenezer R. Hoar (MA)	Grant 1
1870-1871	Amos T. Akerman (GA)	Grant 1
1871-1875	George H. Williams (OR)	Grant 1, 2
1875-1876	Edwards Pierrepont (NY)	Grant 2
1876-1877	Alphonso Taft (OH)	Grant 2, Hayes
1877-1881	Charles Devens (MA)	Hayes, Garfield
1881	Wayne MacVeagh (PA)	Garfield, Arthur
1881-1885	Benjamin H. Brewster (PA)	Arthur, Cleveland
1885-1889	Augustus H. Garland (AR)	Cleveland 1, B. Harrison
1889-1893	William H. H. Miller (IN)	B. Harrison, Cleveland 2
1893-1895	Richard Olney (MA)	Cleveland 2
1895-1897	Judson Harmon (CA)	McKinley 1
1898-1901	John W. Griggs (NJ)	McKinley 1, 2
1901-1904	Philander C. Knox (PA)	McKinley 2, T. Roosevelt 1
1904-1906	William H. Moody (MA)	T. Roosevelt 1, 2
1906-1909	Charles J. Bonaparte (MD)	T. Roosevelt, Taft
1909-1913	George W. Wickersham (NY)	Taft, Wilson 1
1913-1914	James C. McReynolds (TN)	Wilson 1
1914-1919	Thomas W. Gregory (TX)	Wilson 1, 2
1919-1921	A. Mitchell Palmer (PA)	Wilson 2, Harding
1921-1924	Harry M. Daugherty (OH)	Harding, Coolidge 1
1924-1925	Harlan F. Stone (NY)	Coolidge 1
1925-1929	John G. Sargent (VT)	Coolidge 2, Hoover
1929-1933	William D. Mitchell (MN)	Hoover
1933-1939	Homer S. Cummings (CT)	F. D. Roosevelt 1, 2
1939-1940	Frank Murphy (MI)	F. D. Roosevelt 2
1940-1941	Robert H. Jackson (NY)	F. D. Roosevelt 2, 3
1941-1945	Francis Biddle (PA)	F. D. Roosevelt 3, 4, Truman
1945-1949	Tom C. Clark (TX)	Truman 1, 2
1949-1952	J. Howard McGrath (RI)	Truman 2
1952-1953	James P. McGranery (PA)	Truman 2
1953-1957	Herbert Brownell, Jr. (NY)	Eisenhower 1, 2
1958-1961	William P. Rogers (NY)	Eisenhower 2
1961-1965	Robert F. Kennedy (MA)	Kennedy, L. B. Johnson 1
1965-1967	Nicholas de B. Katzenbach (NJ)	L. B. Johnson 2
1967-1969	Ramsey Clark (TX)	L. B. Johnson 2
1969-1972	John N. Mitchell (NY)	Nixon 1
1972-1973	Richard G. Kleindienst (AZ)	Nixon 1, 2
1973-1974	Elliot L. Richardson (MA)	Nixon 2
1974-1975	William B. Saxbe (OH)	Nixon 2, Ford
1975-1977	Edward H. Levi (IL)	Ford
1977-1979	Griffin B. Bell (GA)	Carter
1979-1981	Benjamin R. Civiletti (NY)	Carter
1981-1985	William French Smith (CA)	Reagan 1
1985-	Edwin Meese, III (CA)	Reagan 2

Secretaries of the Navy

Years in Office	Name and State	Presidential Terms
1798-1801	Benjamin Stoddert (MD)	J. Adams, Jefferson 1
1801-1809	Robert Smith (MD)	Jefferson 1, 2, Madison 1
1809-1812	Paul Hamilton (SC)	Madison 1
1813-1814	William Jones (PA)	Madison 1, 2
1814-1818	Benjamin W. Crowninshield (MA)	Madison 2, Monroe 1
1818-1823	Smith Thompson (NY)	Monroe 1, 2
1823-1829	Samuel L. Southard (NJ)	Monroe 2, J. Q. Adams
1829-1831	John Branch (NC)	Jackson 1
1831-1834	Levi Woodbury (NH)	Jackson 1, 2
1834-1838	Mahlon Dickerson (NJ)	Jackson 2, Van Buren
1838-1841	James K. Paulding (NY)	Van Buren
1841	George E. Badger (NC)	W. H. Harrison, Tyler
1841-1843	Abel P. Upshur (VA)	Tyler
1843-1844	David Henshaw (MA)	Tyler
1844	Thomas W. Gilmer (VA)	Tyler
1844-1845	John Y. Mason (VA)	Tyler, Polk
1845-1846	George Bancroft (MA)	Polk
1846-1849	John Y. Mason (VA)	Polk, Taylor
1849-1850	William B. Preston (VA)	Taylor, Fillmore
1850-1852	William A. Graham (NC)	Fillmore
1852-1853	John P. Kennedy (MD)	Fillmore, Pierce
1853-1857	James C. Dobbin (NC)	Pierce, Buchanan
1857-1861	Isaac Toucey (CT)	Buchanan, Lincoln 1
1861-1869	Gideon Welles (CT)	Lincoln 1, 2, A. Johnson
1869	Adolph E. Borie (PA)	Grant 1
1869-1877	George M. Robeson (NJ)	Grant 1, 2, Hayes
1877-1880	Richard W. Thompson (IN)	Hayes
1881	Nathan Goff, Jr. (WV)	Hayes, Garfield
1881-1882	William H. Hunt (LA)	Garfield, Arthur
1882-1885	William E. Chandler (NH)	Arthur, Cleveland 1
1885-1889	William C. Whitney (NY)	Cleveland 1, B. Harrison
1889-1893	Benjamin F. Tracy (NY)	B. Harrison, Cleveland 2
1893-1897	Hilary A. Herbert (AL)	Cleveland 2, McKinley 1
1897-1902	John D. Long (MA)	McKinley 1, 2, T. Roosevelt
1902-1904	William H. Moody (MA)	T. Roosevelt 1
1904-1905	Paul Morton (IL)	T. Roosevelt 2
1905-1906	Charles J. Bonaparte (MD)	T. Roosevelt 2
1906-1908	Victor H. Metcalf (CA)	T. Roosevelt 2
1908-1909	Truman H. Newberry (MI)	T. Roosevelt 2, Taft
1909-1913	George von L. Meyer (MA)	Taft, Wilson 1
1913-1921	Josephus Daniels (NC)	Wilson 1, 2, Harding
1921-1924	Edwin Denby (MI)	Harding, Coolidge 1
1924-1929	Curtis D. Wilbur (CA)	Coolidge 1, 2, Hoover
1929-1933	Charles Francis Adams (MA)	Hoover
1933-1939	Claude A. Swanson (VA)	F. D. Roosevelt 1, 2
1940	Charles Edison (NJ)	F. D. Roosevelt 2
1940-1944	Frank Knox (IL)	F. D. Roosevelt 2, 3
1944-1947	James V. Forrestal (NY)	F. D. Roosevelt 3, 4, Truman 1

(Became part of the Department of Defense under the National Security Act of 1947.)

Postmasters General

Years in Office	Name and State	Presidential Terms
1829-1835	William T. Barry (KY)	Jackson 1, 2
1835-1840	Amos Kendall (KY)	Jackson 2, Van Buren
1840-1841	John M. Niles (CT)	Van Buren
1841	Francis Granger (NY)	W. H. Harrison, Tyler
1841-1845	Charles A. Wickliffe (KY)	Tyler, Polk
1845-1849	Cave Johnson (TN)	Polk, Taylor

Years in Office	Name and State	Presidential Terms
1849-1850	Jacob Collamer (VT)	Taylor, Fillmore
1850-1852	Nathan K. Hall (NY)	Fillmore
1852-1853	Samuel D. Hubbard (CT)	Fillmore, Pierce
1853-1857	James Campbell (PA)	Pierce, Buchanan
1857-1859	Aaron V. Brown (TN)	Buchanan
1859-1861	Joseph Holt (KY)	Buchanan
1861	Horatio King (ME)	Buchanan, Lincoln 1
1861-1864	Montgomery Blair (DC)	Lincoln 1
1864-1866	William Dennison (OH)	Lincoln 1, 2, A. Johnson
1866-1869	Alexander W. Randall (WI)	A. Johnson
1869-1874	John A. J. Creswell (MD)	Grant 1, 2
1874	James W. Marshall (VA)	Grant 2
1874-1876	Marshall Jewell (CT)	Grant 2
1876-1877	James N. Tyner (IN)	Grant 2, Hayes
1877-1880	David M. Key (TN)	Hayes
1880-1881	Horace Maynard (TN)	Hayes, Garfield
1881	Thomas L. James (NY)	Garfield, Arthur
1881-1883	Timothy O. Howe (WI)	Arthur
1883-1884	Walter Q. Gresham (IN)	Arthur
1884-1885	Frank Hatton (IA)	Arthur, Cleveland 1
1885-1888	William F. Vilas (WI)	Cleveland 1
1888-1889	Don M. Dickinson (MI)	Cleveland 1, B. Harrison
1889-1893	John Wanamaker (PA)	B. Harrison, Cleveland 2
1893-1895	Wilson S. Bissell (NY)	Cleveland 2
1895-1897	William L. Wilson (WV)	Cleveland 2, McKinley 1
1897-1898	James A. Gary (MD)	McKinley 1
1898-1902	Charles E. Smith (PA)	McKinley 1, 2, T. Roosevelt 1
1902-1904	Henry C. Payne (WI)	T. Roosevelt 1
1904-1905	Robert J. Wynne (PA)	T. Roosevelt 1, 2
1905-1907	George B. Cortelyou (NY)	T. Roosevelt 2
1907-1909	George von L. Meyer (MA)	T. Roosevelt 2, Taft
1909-1913	Frank H. Hitchcock (MA)	Taft, Wilson 1
1913-1921	Albert S. Burleson (TX)	Wilson 1, 2, Harding
1921-1922	Will H. Hays (IN)	Harding
1922-1923	Hubert Work (CO)	Harding
1923-1929	Harry S. New (IN)	Harding, Coolidge 1, 2, Hoover
1929-1933	Walter F. Brown (OH)	Hoover
1933-1940	James A. Farley (NY)	F. D. Roosevelt 1, 2
1940-1945	Frank C. Walker (PA)	F. D. Roosevelt 2, 3, 4, Truman 1
1945-1947	Robert E. Hannegan (MO)	Truman 1
1947-1953	Jesse M. Donaldson (MO)	Truman 1, 2
1953-1961	Arthur E. Summerfield (MI)	Eisenhower 1, 2
1961-1963	J. Edward Day (IL)	Kennedy
1963-1965	John A. Gronouski (WI)	Kennedy, L. B. Johnson 1
1965-1968	Lawrence F. O'Brien (MA)	L. B. Johnson 2
1968-1969	W. Marvin Watson (TX)	L. B. Johnson 2
1969-1971	Winton M. Blount (AL)	Nixon 1

(Became an independent federal agency under Postal Reorganization Act of 1970.)

Secretaries of the Interior

Years in Office	Name and State	Presidential Terms
1849-1850	Thomas Ewing (OH)	Taylor, Fillmore
1850	Thomas M. T. McKennan (PA)	Fillmore
1850-1853	Alexander H. H. Stuart (VA)	Fillmore, Pierce
1853-1857	Robert McClelland (MI)	Pierce, Buchanan
1857-1861	Jacob Thompson (MS)	Buchanan
1861-1863	Caleb B. Smith (IN)	Lincoln 1
1863-1865	John P. Usher (IN)	Lincoln 1, 2, A. Johnson

Years in Office	Name and State	Presidential Terms
1865-1866	James Harlan (IA)	A. Johnson
1866-1869	Orville H. Browning (IL)	A. Johnson
1869-1870	Jacob D. Cox (OH)	Grant 1
1870-1875	Columbus Delano (OH)	Grant 1, 2
1875-1877	Zachariah Chandler (MI)	Grant 2, Hayes
1877-1881	Carl Schurz (MO)	Hayes, Garfield
1881-1882	Samuel J. Kirkwood (IA)	Garfield, Arthur
1882-1885	Henry M. Teller (CO)	Arthur
1885-1888	Lucius Q. C. Lamar (MS)	Cleveland 1
1888-1889	William F. Vilas (WI)	Cleveland 1, B. Harrison
1889-1893	John W. Noble (MO)	B. Harrison, Cleveland 2
1893-1896	Hoke Smith (GA)	Cleveland 2
1896-1897	David R. Francis (MO)	Cleveland 2, McKinley 1
1897-1898	Cornelius N. Bliss (NY)	McKinley 1
1898-1907	Ethan A. Hitchcock (MO)	McKinley 1, 2, T. Roosevelt 1, 2
1907-1909	James R. Garfield (OH)	T. Roosevelt 2, Taft
1909-1911	Richard A. Ballinger (WA)	Taft
1911-1913	Walter L. Fisher (IL)	Taft, Wilson 1
1913-1920	Franklin K. Lane (CA)	Wilson 1, 2
1920-1921	John B. Payne (IL)	Wilson 2, Harding
1921-1923	Albert B. Fall (NM)	Harding
1923-1928	Hubert Work (CO)	Harding, Coolidge 1, 2
1929	Roy O. West (IL)	Coolidge 2, Hoover
1929-1933	Ray L. Wilbur (CA)	Hoover
1933-1946	Harold L. Ickes (IA)	F. D. Roosevelt 1, 2, 3, Truman 1
1946-1949	Julius A. Krug (WI)	Truman 1, 2
1950-1953	Oscar L. Chapman (CO)	Truman 2
1953-1956	Douglas McKay (OR)	Eisenhower 1
1956-1961	Frederick A. Seaton (NE)	Eisenhower 1, 2
1961-1969	Stewart L. Udall (AZ)	Kennedy, L. B. Johnson 1, 2
1969-1970	Walter J. Hickel (AK)	Nixon 1
1970-1975	Rogers C. B. Morton (MD)	Nixon 1, 2, Ford
1975	Stanley K. Hathaway (WY)	Ford
1975-1977	Thomas S. Kleppe (ND)	Ford
1977-1981	Cecil D. Andrus (ID)	Carter
1981-1983	James G. Watt (CO)	Reagan 1
1983-1985	William P. Clark (CA)	Reagan 1
1985-	Donald P. Hodel (OR)	Reagan 2

Secretaries of Agriculture

Years in Office	Name and State	Presidential Terms
1889	Norman J. Colman (MO)	Cleveland 1, B. Harrison
1889-1893	Jeremiah M. Rusk (WI)	B. Harrison, Cleveland
1893-1897	J. Sterling Morton (NE)	Cleveland 2, McKinley 1
1897-1913	James Wilson (IA)	McKinley 1, 2, T. Roosevelt 1, 2, Taft, Wilson 1
1913-1920	David F. Houston (MO)	Wilson 1, 2
1920-1921	Edwin T. Meredith (IA)	Wilson 2, Harding
1921-1924	Henry C. Wallace (IA)	Harding, Coolidge 1
1924-1925	Howard M. Gore (WV)	Coolidge 1, 2
1925-1929	William M. Jardine (KS)	Coolidge 2, Hoover
1929-1940	Arthur M. Hyde (IA)	F. D. Roosevelt 1, 2
1940-1945	Claude R. Wickard (IN)	F. D. Roosevelt 2, 3, 4, Truman 1
1945-1948	Clinton P. Anderson (NM)	Truman 1
1948-1953	Charles F. Brannan (CO)	Truman 1, 2
1953-1961	Ezra Taft Benson (UT)	Eisenhower 1, 2
1961-1969	Orville L. Freeman (MN)	Kennedy, L. B. Johnson 1, 2
1969-1971	Clifford M. Hardin (IN)	Nixon 1
1971-1976	Earl L. Butz (IN)	Nixon 1, 2, Ford

Years in Office	Name and State	Presidential Terms
1976-1977	John Knebel (VA)	Ford
1977-1981	Bob S. Bergland (MN)	Carter
1981-	John R. Block (IL)	Reagan 1, 2

Secretaries of Commerce and Labor

Years in Office	Name and State	Presidential Terms
1903-1904	George B. Cortelyou (NY)	T. Roosevelt 1
1904-1906	Victor H. Metcalf (CA)	T. Roosevelt 1, 2
1906-1909	Oscar S. Straus (NY)	T. Roosevelt 2, Taft
1909-1913	Charles Nagel (MO)	Taft

(Became separate departments in 1913.)

Secretaries of Labor

Years in Office	Name and State	Presidential Terms
1913-1921	William B. Wilson (PA)	Wilson 1, 2, Harding
1921-1930	James J. Davis (PA)	Harding, Coolidge 1, 2, Hoover
1930-1933	William N. Diak (VA)	Hoover
1933-1945	Frances Perkins (NY)	F. D. Roosevelt 1, 2, 3, 4, Truman
1945-1948	Lewis B. Schwellenbach (WA)	Truman 1
1948-1953	Maurice J. Tobin (MA)	Truman 1, 2
1953	Martin P. Durkin (IL)	Eisenhower 1
1954-1961	James P. Mitchell (NJ)	Eisenhower 1, 2
1961-1962	Arthur J. Goldberg (IL)	Kennedy
1962-1969	W. Willard Wirtz (IL)	Kennedy, L. B. Johnson 1, 2
1969-1970	George P. Shultz (CA)	Nixon 1
1970-1973	James D. Hodgson (CA)	Nixon 1
1973-1975	Peter J. Brennan	Nixon 2, Ford
1975-1976	John T. Dunlop (MA)	Ford
1976-1977	William J. Usery, Jr. (GA)	Ford
1977-1981	F. Ray Marshall (LA)	Carter
1981-1985	Raymond J. Donovan (NJ)	Reagan 1
1985-	William E. Brock (DC)	Reagan 1, 2

Secretaries of Commerce

Years in Office	Name and State	Presidential Terms
1913-1919	William C. Redfield (NY)	Wilson 1, 2
1919-1921	Joshua W. Alexander (MO)	Wilson 2, Harding
1921-1928	Herbert C. Hoover (CA)	Harding, Coolidge 1, 2
1928-1929	William F. Whiting (MA)	Coolidge 2, Hoover
1929-1932	Robert P. Lamont (IL)	Hoover
1932-1933	Roy D. Chapin (MI)	Hoover
1933-1938	Daniel C. Roper (SC)	F. D. Roosevelt 1, 2
1939-1940	Harry L. Hopkins (NY)	F. D. Roosevelt 2
1940-1945	Jesse H. Jones (TX)	F. D. Roosevelt 2, 3, 4
1945-1946	Henry A. Wallace (IA)	F. D. Roosevelt 4, Truman 1
1947-1948	W. Averell Harriman (NY)	Truman 1
1948-1953	Charles Sawyer (OH)	Truman 1, 2
1953-1958	Sinclair Weeks (MA)	Eisenhower 1, 2
1958-1959	Lewis L. Strauss (NY)	Eisenhower 2
1959-1961	Frederick H. Mueller (MI)	Eisenhower 2
1961-1965	Luther H. Hodges (NC)	Kennedy, L. B. Johnson 1
1965-1967	John T. Connor (NJ)	L. B. Johnson 2
1967-1968	Alexander Trowbridge (NJ)	L. B. Johnson 2
1968-1969	Cyrus R. Smith (NY)	L. B. Johnson 2
1969-1972	Maurice H. Stans (MN)	Nixon 1
1972-1973	Peter G. Peterson (IL)	Nixon 1
1973-1975	Frederick B. Dent (SC)	Nixon 2, Ford
1975-1976	Rogers C. B. Morton (MD)	Ford
1976-1977	Elliot L. Richardson (MA)	Ford
1977-1979	Juanita M. Kreps (VA)	Carter
1979-1981	Philip M. Klutznick (IL)	Carter
1981-1987	Malcolm Baldrige (CT)	Reagan 1, 2

Secretaries of Defense

(The Department of Defense was created in 1947 by consolidation of the Departments of the Navy and War into a single executive department. See Section VIII: The Military, for Secretaries of the Services.)

Years in Office	Name and State	Presidential Terms
1947-1949	James V. Forrestal (NY)	Truman 1, 2
1949-1950	Louis A. Johnson (WV)	Truman 2
1950-1951	George C. Marshall (PA)	Truman 2
1951-1953	Robert A. Lovett (NY)	Truman 2
1953-1957	Charles E. Wilson (MI)	Eisenhower 1, 2
1957-1960	Neil H. McElroy (OH)	Eisenhower 2
1960-1961	Thomas S. Gates, Jr. (PA)	Eisenhower 2
1961-1968	Robert S. McNamara (MI)	Kennedy, L. B. Johnson 1, 2
1968-1969	Clark M. Clifford (MD)	L. B. Johnson 2
1969-1973	Melvin R. Laird (WI)	Nixon 1
1973	Elliot L. Richardson (MA)	Nixon 2
1973-1975	James R. Schlesinger (VA)	Nixon 2, Ford
1975-1977	Donald H. Rumsfeld (IL)	Ford
1977-1981	Harold Brown (NY)	Carter
1981-	Caspar W. Weinberger (CA)	Reagan 1, 2

Secretaries of Health, Education, and Welfare

Years in Office	Name and State	Presidential Terms
1953-1955	Oveta Culp Hobby (TX)	Eisenhower 1
1955-1958	Marion B. Folsom (NY)	Eisenhower 1, 2
1958-1961	Arthur S. Flemming (OH)	Eisenhower 1
1961-1962	Abraham A. Ribicoff (CT)	Kennedy
1962-1965	Anthony J. Celebrezze (OH)	Kennedy, L. B. Johnson 1
1965-1969	John W. Gardner (NY)	L. B. Johnson
1968-1969	Wilbur J. Cohen (MI)	L. B. Johnson 2
1969-1970	Robert H. Finch (CA)	Nixon 1
1970-1973	Elliot Richardson (MA)	Nixon 1
1973-1975	Caspar W. Weinberger (CA)	Nixon 2, Ford
1975-1977	F. David Mathews (AL)	Ford
1977-1979	Joseph A. Califano, Jr. (NY)	Carter
1979	Patricia Roberts Harris (DC)	Carter

(Department of Health and Human Services and Department of Education separated in 1979.)

Secretaries of Housing and Urban Development

Years in Office	Name and State	Presidential Terms
1966-1968	Robert C. Weaver (WA)	L. B. Johnson 2
1968-1969	Robert C. Wood (MA)	L. B. Johnson 2
1969-1973	George W. Romney (MI)	Nixon 1
1973-1975	James T. Lynn (OH)	Nixon 2, Ford
1975-1977	Carla A. Hills (CA)	Ford
1977-1979	Patricia Roberts Harris (DC)	Carter
1979-1981	Moon Landrieu (LA)	Carter
1981-	Samuel R. Pierce, Jr. (NY)	Reagan 1, 2

Secretaries of Transportation

Years in Office	Name and State	Presidential Terms
1966-1969	Alan S. Boyd (FL)	L. B. Johnson 2
1969-1973	John A. Volpe (MA)	Nixon 1
1973-1975	Claude S. Brinegar (CA)	Nixon 2, Ford
1975-1977	William T. Coleman, Jr. (PA)	Ford
1977-1979	Brock Adams (WA)	Carter
1979-1981	Neil E. Goldschmidt (OR)	Carter
1981-1983	Andrew L. Lewis, Jr. (PA)	Reagan 1
1983-	Elizabeth H. Dole (NC)	Reagan 1, 2

Secretaries of Energy

Years in Office	Name and State	Presidential Terms
1977-1979	James R. Schlesinger (VA)	Carter
1979-1981	Charles W. Duncan, Jr. (WY)	Carter
1981-1983	James B. Edwards (SC)	Reagan 1
1983-1985	Donald P. Hodel (OR)	Reagan 1
1985-	John S. Herrington (LA)	Reagan 2

Secretaries of Health and Human Services

Years in Office	Name and State	Presidential Terms
1979-1981	Patricia Roberts Harris (DC)	Carter
1981-1983	Richard S. Schweiker (PA)	Reagan 1
1983-1985	Margaret M. Heckler (MA)	Reagan 1, 2
1985-	Otis R. Bowen (IN)	Reagan 2

Secretaries of Education

Years in Office	Name and State	Presidential Terms
1979-1981	Shirley Mount Hufstedler (CA)	Carter
1981-1985	T. H. Bell (UT)	Reagan 1
1985-	William J. Bennett (NC)	Reagan 1, 2

IV
U.S. Government: Legislative Branch

This section presents Congresses in chronological order, from First through Ninety-Ninth. For each one, state delegations are listed alphabetically. If a member served less than a full term, one of the following abbreviations appears after the surname:

"r."   followed by a month and year indicates the date of resignation, retirement, or removal from office

"d."   indicates year of death while in office

"ta."   with date(s) indicates the year(s) of a temporary appointment

"s."   indicates the year the member was seated, if other than the first year of the Congress

Political party affiliations are given in parentheses after the members' surnames. It was not uncommon for members of early Congresses to be independent, in which case no affiliation is noted. The following abbreviations are used in this item:

AF	Anti-Federalist
Amer	American
Con	Conservative
D	Democrat (Includes factions of the Democratic Party such as Union Democrats, Free-Soil Democracts, and Jacksonian Democrats. Also includes Jeffersonian Republicans, the precursor of the Democratic Party.)
F	Federalist
FS	Free-Soiler
Lib	Liberal
NR	National Republican
Null-D	Nullification Democrat
Pop	Populist
R	Republican (Includes Union Republicans)
SRD	States Rights Democrat
SRW	States Rights Whig
Un	Unionist
W	Whig

Members of the Senate and House of Representatives

First Congress

(Mar. 4, 1789, to
Mar. 3, 1791)

President of the Senate: John
Adams
*President Pro Tempore of the
Senate:* John Langdon
*Speaker of the House of
Representatives:* Frederick A.
C. Muhlenberg

Connecticut

Senators

Oliver Ellsworth (F)
William S. Johnson

Representatives

Benjamin Huntington
Roger Sherman
Jonathan Sturges (F)
Jonathan Trumbull (F)
Jeremiah Wadsworth (F)

Delaware

Senators

Richard Bassett (F)
George Read (F)

Representatives

John Vining

Georgia

Senators

William Few (D)
James Gunn

Representatives

Abraham Baldwin (F)
James Jackson (D)
George Mathews

Maryland

Senators

Charles Carroll of Carrollton
(F)
John Henry (D)

Representatives

Daniel Carroll (F)
Benjamin Contee
George Gale
Joshua Seney
William Smith (F)
Michael J. Stone

Massachusetts

Senators

Tristram Dalton
Caleb Strong (F)

Representatives

Fisher Ames (F)
Elbridge Gerry (AF)
Benjamin Goodhue (F)
Jonathan Grout (D)
George Leonard
George Partridge r. Aug. 1790
Theodore Sedgwick (F)
George Thacher (F)

New Hampshire

Senators

John Langdon (D)
Paine Wingate (F)

Representatives

Abiel Foster (F)
Nicholas Gilman (F)
Samuel Livermore

New Jersey

Senators

Philemon Dickinson s. 1790
Jonathan Elmer (F)
William Paterson (F) r. Nov.
1790

Representatives

Elias Boudinot (F)
Lambert Cadwalader
James Schureman (F)
Thomas Sinnickson (F)

New York

Senators

Rufus King (F)

Philip Schuyler (F)

Representatives

Egbert Benson
William Floyd
John Hathorn (F)
John Laurance (F)
Peter Silvester
Jeremiah Van Rensselaer

North Carolina

Senators

Benjamin Hawkins (F)
Samuel Johnston (F)

Representatives

John Ashe (F)
Timothy Bloodworth (F)
John Sevier (D)
John Steele (F)
Hugh Williamson (F)

Pennsylvania

Senators

William Maclay (D)
Robert Morris (F)

Representatives

George Clymer (F)
Thomas Fitzsimons (F)
Thomas Hartley (F)
Daniel Hiester (F)
Frederick A. C. Muhlenberg (F)
John Peter G. Muhlenberg (D)
Thomas Scott
Henry Wynkoop

Rhode Island

Senators

Theodore Foster (Law & Order)
Joseph Stanton, Jr. (D)

Representatives

Benjamin Bourn (F)

South Carolina

Senators

Pierce Butler (D)
Ralph Izard

Representatives

Aedanus Burke
Daniel Huger
William L. Smith (F)
Thomas Sumter (D)
Thomas T. Tucker (F)

Virginia

Senators

William Grayson (AF) d. Mar.
1790
Richard Henry Lee (AF)
James Monroe (D) s. 1790
John Walker s. 1790

Representatives

Theodorick Bland d. 1790
John Brown
Isaac Coles
William B. Giles (AF) s. 1790
Samuel Griffin
Richard Bland Lee (F)
James Madison (D)
Andrew Moore (F)
John Page (D)
Josiah Parker (AF)
Alexander White (F)

Second Congress

(Mar. 4, 1791, to
Mar. 3, 1793)

President of the Senate: John
Adams
*Presidents Pro Tempore of the
Senate:* Richard Henry Lee;
John Langdon
*Speaker of the House of
Representatives:* Jonathan
Trumbull

Connecticut

Senators

Oliver Ellsworth (F)
William S. Johnson r. Mar.
1791
Roger Sherman

Representatives

James Hillhouse (F)
Amasa Learned
Jonathan Sturges (F)
Jonathan Trumbull (F)

Jeremiah Wadsworth (F)

Delaware

Senators

Richard Bassett (F)
George Read (F)

Representatives

John Vining

Georgia

Senators

William Few (D)
James Gunn

Representatives

Abraham Baldwin (F)
John Milledge s. 1792
Anthony Wayne r. 1792
Francis Willis

Kentucky

Senators

John Brown
John Edwards

Representatives

Christopher Greenup
Alexander D. Orr

Maryland

Senators

Charles Carroll of Carrollton (F)
    r. Nov. 1792
John Henry (D)
Richard Potts (F) s. 1793

Representatives

William Hindman (F) s. 1793
Philip Key (F)
John F. Mercer (D) s. 1792
William Vans Murray (F)
William Pinkney r. Nov. 1791
Joshua Seney r. May 1792
Upton Sheredine (D)
Samuel Sterett (AF)

Massachusetts

Senators

George Cabot (F)
Caleb Strong (F)

Representatives

Fisher Ames (F)
Shearjashub Bourne
Elbridge Gerry (AF)
Benjamin Goodhue (F)
Theodore Sedgwick (F)
George Thacher (F)
Artemas Ward (F)

New Hampshire

Senators

John Langdon (D)
Paine Wingate (D)

Representatives

Nicholas Gilman (F)
Samuel Livermore (F)
Jeremiah Smith (F)

New Jersey

Senators

Philemon Dickinson
John Rutherfurd (F)

Representatives

Elias Boudinot (F)
Abraham Clark
Jonathan Dayton (F)
Aaron Kitchell (D)

New York

Senators

Aaron Burr (D)
Rufus King (F)

Representatives

Egbert Benson (F)
James Gordon (F)
John Laurance (F)
Cornelius C. Schoonmaker
Peter Silvester (F)
Thomas Tredwell

North Carolina

Senators

Benjamin Hawkins (F)
Samuel Johnston (F)

Representatives

John Ashe (F)
William Grove (F)
Nathaniel Macon (D)
John Steele (F)
Hugh Williamson (F)

Pennsylvania

Senators

Robert Morris (F)
Vacant

Representatives

William Findley (D)
Thomas Fitzsimons (F)
Andrew Gregg (D)
Thomas Hartley (F)
Daniel Hiester (F)
Israel Jacobs
John W. Kittera (F)
Frederick A. C. Muhlenberg (F)

Rhode Island

Senators

Theodore Foster (Law & Order)
Joseph Stanton, Jr. (D)

Representatives

Benjamin Bourn (F)

South Carolina

Senators

Pierce Butler (D)
Ralph Izard

Representatives

Robert Barnwell (F)
Daniel Huger
William L. Smith (F)
Thomas Sumter (D)
Thomas T. Tucker (F)

Vermont

Senators

Stephen R. Bradley (D)
Moses Robinson (D)

Representatives

Nathaniel Niles (D)
Israel Smith (D)

Virginia

Senators

Richard Henry Lee (AF) r.
    Oct. 1792
James Monroe (D)
John Taylor (D)

Representatives

John Brown
William B. Giles (AF)
Samuel Griffin
Richard Bland Lee (F)
James Madison (D)
Andrew Moore (F)
John Page (D)
Josiah Parker (AF)
Abraham B. Venable
Alexander White (F)

Third Congress

(Mar. 4, 1793, to
Mar. 3, 1795)

President of the Senate: John
    Adams
*Presidents Pro Tempore of the
    Senate:* Ralph Izard; Henry
    Tazewell
*Speaker of the House of
    Representatives:* Frederick A.
    C. Muhlenberg

Connecticut

Senators

Oliver Ellsworth (F)
Stephen M. Mitchell (F)
Roger Sherman d. July 1793

Representatives

Joshua Coit (F)
James Hillhouse (F)
Amasa Learned (F)
Zephaniah Swift (F)
Uriah Tracy (F)
Jonathan Trumbull (F)
Jeremiah Wadsworth (F)

Delaware

Senators

Henry Latimer s. 1795
George Read (F) r. Sept. 1793
John Vining

Representatives

Henry Latimer
John Patten

Georgia

Senators

James Gunn
James Jackson (D)

Representatives

Abraham Baldwin (F)
Thomas P. Carnes

Kentucky

Senators

John Brown
John Edwards

Representatives

Christopher Greenup
Alexander D. Orr

Maryland

Senators

John Henry (D)
Richard Potts (F)

Representatives

Gabriel Christie (D)
George Dent (D)
Gabriel Duvall (D) s. 1794
Benjamin Edwards s. 1795
Uriah Forest r. Nov. 1794
William Hindman (F)
John F. Mercer r. Apr. 1794
William Vans Murray (F)
Samuel Smith (D)
Thomas Sprigg

Massachusetts

Senators

George Cabot (F)
Caleb Strong (F)

Representatives

Fisher Ames (F)
Shearjashub Bourne
David Cobb (F)
Peleg Coffin, Jr.
Henry Dearborn (D)
Samuel Dexter (F)
Dwight Foster (F)
Benjamin Goodhue (F)
Samuel Holten (AF)
William Lyman (D)
Theodore Sedgwick (F)
George Thacher (F)
Peleg Wadsworth (F)
Artemas Ward (F)

New Hampshire

Senators

John Langdon (D)
Samuel Livermore

Representatives

Nicholas Gilman
John S. Sherburne
Jeremiah Smith (F)
Paine Wingate (F)

New Jersey

Senators

Frederick Frelinghuysen (F)
John Rutherfurd (F)

Representatives

John Beatty
Elias Boudinot (F)
Lambert Cadwalader
Abraham Clark d. Sept. 1794
Jonathan Dayton (F)
Aaron Kitchell (D) s. 1795

New York

Senators

Aaron Burr (D)
Rufus King (F)

Representatives

Theodorus Bailey (D)
Ezekiel Gilbert
James Gordon (F)
Henry Glen
Silas Talbot (F)
Thomas Tredwell
John E. Van Alen (F)
Philip Van Cortlandt (D)
Peter Van Gaasbeck (AF)
John Watts

North Carolina

Senators

Benjamin Hawkins (F)
Alexander Martin (F)

Representatives

Thomas Blount (D)
William J. Dawson
James Gillespie
William B. Grove (F)
Matthew Locke (D)
Joseph McDowell
Nathaniel Macon (D)
Alexander Mebane
Benjamin Williams
Joseph Winston

Pennsylvania

Senators

Albert Gallatin (D) r. Feb.
  1794
Robert Morris (F)
James Ross (F) s. 1794

Representatives

James Armstrong (F)
William Findley (D)
Thomas Fitzsimons (F)
Andrew Gregg (F)
Thomas Hartley (F)
Daniel Hiester (F)
William Irvine
John W. Kittera (F)
William Montgomery
Frederick A. C. Muhlenberg (F)
John Peter G. Muhlenberg (D)
Thomas Scott
John Smilie (D)

Rhode Island

Senators

William Bradford
Theodore Foster (Law & Order)

Representatives

Benjamin Bourn (F)
Francis Malbone (F)

South Carolina

Senators

Pierce Butler (D)
Ralph Izard

Representatives

Lemuel Benton (D)
Alexander Gillon d. Oct. 1794
Robert G. Harper (F) s. 1795
John Hunter (F)
Andrew Pickens (D)
William L. Smith (F)
Richard Winn

Vermont

Senators

Stephen R. Bradley (D)
Moses Robinson (D)

Representatives

Nathaniel Niles (D)
Israel Smith (D)

Virginia

Senators

Stevens T. Mason (D) s. 1795
James Monroe (D) r. May 1794
John Taylor (D) r. May 1794
Henry Tazewell s. 1794

Representatives

Isaac Coles
Thomas Claiborne
William B. Giles (AF)
Samuel Griffin
George Hancock (D)
Carter B. Harrison
John Heath (D)
Richard Bland Lee (F)
James Madison (D)
Andrew Moore (F)
Joseph Neville
Anthony New (D)
John Nicholas (D)
John Page (D)
Josiah Parker (AF)
Francis Preston
Robert Rutherford
Abraham B. Venable
Francis Walker

Fourth Congress

(Mar. 4, 1795, to
Mar. 3, 1797)

President of the Senate: John
  Adams
*Presidents Pro Tempore of the
  Senate:* Henry Tazewell;
  Samuel Livermore; William
  Bingham
*Speaker of the House of
  Representatives:* Jonathan
  Dayton

Connecticut

Senators

Oliver Ellsworth (F) r. Mar.
  1796
James Hillhouse (F) s. 1796
Uriah Tracy (F) s. 1796
Jonathan Trumbull (F) r. June
  1796

Representatives

Joshua Coit (F)
Samuel W. Dana (F) s. 1797
James Davenport s. 1796
Chauncey Goodrich (F)
Roger Griswold (F)

James Hillhouse (F) r. 1796
Nathaniel Smith (F)
Zephaniah Swift (F)
Uriah Tracy (F) r. Oct. 1796

Delaware

Senators

Henry Latimer
John Vining

Representatives

John Patten

Georgia

Senators

James Gunn
James Jackson (D) r. 1795
Josiah Tattnall s. 1796
George Walton ta. 1795

Representatives

Abraham Baldwin (F)
John Milledge

Kentucky

Senators

John Brown
Humphrey Marshall (F)

Representatives

Christopher Greenup
Alexander D. Orr

Maryland

Senators

John Henry (D)
John E. Howard (F) s. 1796
Richard Potts (F) r. Oct. 1796

Representatives

Gabriel Christie
Jeremiah Crabb (D) r. 1796
William Craik (D) s. 1796
George Dent (D)
Gabriel Duvall (D) r. Mar.
  1796
William Hindman (F)
William Vans Murray (F)
Samuel Smith (D)
Richard Sprigg, Jr. s. 1796
Thomas Sprigg

Massachusetts

Senators

George Cabot (F) r. June 1796
Benjamin Goodhue (F) s. 1796
Theodore Sedgwick (F) s. 1796
Caleb Strong (F) r. June 1796

Representatives

Fisher Ames (F)

Theophilus Bradbury (F)
Henry Dearborn (D)
Dwight Foster (F)
Nathaniel Freeman, Jr.
Benjamin Goodhue (F) r. June 1796
George Leonard
Samuel Lyman
William Lyman (D)
John Reed (F)
Theodore Sedgwick (F) r. June 1796
Samuel Sweall s. 1796
Thomson J. Skinner (D) s. 1797
George Thacher (F)
Joseph B. Varnum (AF)
Peleg Wadsworth

New Hampshire

Senators

John Langdon (D)
Samuel Livermore

Representatives

Abiel Foster (F)
Nicholas Gilman (F)
John S. Sherburne
Jeremiah Smith (F)

New Jersey

Senators

Frederick Frelinghuysen (F) r. Nov. 1796
John Rutherfurd (F)
Richard Stockton (F) s. 1796

Representatives

Jonathan Dayton (F)
Thomas Henderson (F)
Aaron Kitchell (D)
Isaac Smith (F)
Mark Thomson (F)

New York

Senators

Aaron Burr (D)
Rufus King (F) r. May 1796
John Laurance (F) s. 1796

Representatives

Theodorus Bailey (D)
William Cooper (F)
Ezekiel Gilbert
Henry Glen
John Hathorn (F)
Jonathan N. Havens (D)
Edward Livingston (D)
John E. Van Alen (F)
Philip Van Cortlandt (D)
John Williams

North Carolina

Senators

Timothy Bloodworth
Alexander Martin (F)

Representatives

Thomas Blount (D)
Nathan Bryan
Dempsey Burges
Jesse Franklin
James Gillespie
William B. Grove (F)
James Holland
Matthew Locke (D)
Nathaniel Macon (D)
William F. Strudwick s. 1796
Absalom Tatom r. June 1796

Pennsylvania

Senators

William Bingham
James Ross (F)

Representatives

David Bard
George Ege s. 1796
William Findley (D)
Albert Gallatin (D)
Andrew Gregg (F)
Thomas Hartley (F)
Daniel Hiester (F) r. July 1796
John W. Kittera (F)
Samuel Maclay (F)
Frederick A. C. Muhlenberg (F)
John Richards
Samuel Sitgreaves (F)
John Swanwick (D)
Richard Thomas (F)

Rhode Island

Senators

William Bradford
Theodore Foster (Law & Order)

Representatives

Benjamin Bourn (F) r. 1796
Francis Malbone (F)
Elisha R. Potter (F) s. 1796

South Carolina

Senators

Pierce Butler (D) r. Oct. 1796
John Hunter (F) s. 1797
Jacob Read (F)

Representatives

Lemuel Benton (D)
Samuel Earle
Wade Hampton (D)
Robert G. Harper (F)
William L. Smith (F)
Richard Winn

Tennessee

Senators

William Blount
William Cocke

Representatives

Andrew Jackson (D)

Vermont

Senators

Elijah Paine (F)
Moses Robinson (D) r. Oct. 1796
Isaac Tichenor (F) s. 1796

Representatives

Daniel Buck (F)
Israel Smith (D)

Virginia

Senators

Stevens T. Mason (D)
Henry Tazewell

Representatives

Richard Brent
Samuel J. Cabell (D)
Thomas Claiborne
John Clopton (D)
Isaac Coles
William B. Giles (AF)
George Hancock (D)
Carter B. Harrison
John Heath
George Jackson
James Madison (D)
Andrew Moore (F)
Anthony New (D)
John Nicholas (D)
John Page (D)
Josiah Parker (AF)
Francis Preston
Robert Rutherford
Abraham B. Venable

Fifth Congress

(Mar. 4, 1797, to
Mar. 3, 1799)

President of the Senate: Thomas Jefferson
Presidents Pro Tempore of the Senate: William Bradford; Jacob Read; Theodore Sedgwick; John Laurance; James Ross
Speaker of the House of Representatives: Jonathan Dayton

Connecticut

Senators

James Hillhouse (F)
Uriah Tracy (F)

Representatives

John Allen (F)
Jonathan Brace (F) s. 1798
Joshua Coit (F) d. Sept. 1798
Samuel W. Dana (F)

James Davenport d. Aug. 1797
William Edmond
Chauncey Goodrich (F)
Roger Griswold (F)
Nathaniel Smith (F)

Delaware

Senators

Joshua Claton s. 1798; d. Aug. 1798
Henry Latimer
John Vining r. Jan. 1798
William H. Wells s. 1799

Representatives

James A. Bayard, Sr. (F)

Georgia

Senators

James Gunn
Josiah Tattnall

Representatives

Abraham Baldwin (F)
John Milledge

Kentucky

Senators

John Brown
Humphrey Marshall (F)

Representatives

Thomas T. Davis
John Fowler

Maryland

Senators

John Henry (D) r. Dec. 1797
John E. Howard (F)
James Lloyd (D) s. 1798

Representatives

George Baer, Jr. (F)
William Craik
John Dennis (F)
George Dent (D)
William Hindman (F)
William Matthews
Samuel Smith
Richard Sprigg, Jr.

Massachusetts

Senators

Benjamin Goodhue (F)
Theodore Sedgwick (F)

Representatives

Bailey Bartlett (F)
Theophilus Bradbury (F) r. July 1797
Stephen Bullock (F)

Dwight Foster (F)
Nathaniel Freeman, Jr.
Samuel Lyman
Harrison G. Otis (F)
Isaac Parker
John Reed (F)
Samuel Sewall
William Shepard
Thomson J. Skinner (D)
George Thacher (F)
Joseph B. Varnum (AF)
Peleg Wadsworth

New Hampshire

Senators

John Langdon (D)
Samuel Livermore

Representatives

Abiel Foster (F)
Jonathan Freeman (F)
William Gordon
Jeremiah Smith (F) r. July 1797
Peleg Sprague

New Jersey

Senators

Franklin Davenport s. 1798
John Rutherfurd (F) r. Nov.
  1798
Richard Stockton (F)

Representatives

Jonathan Dayton (F)
James H. Imlay
James Schureman (F)
Thomas Sinnickson (F)
Mark Thomson (F)

New York

Senators

John S. Hobart s. 1798; r. Apr.
  1798
John Laurance (F)
William North (F) ta. 1798
Philip Schuyler (F) r. Jan. 1798
James Watson (D) s. 1798

Representatives

David Brooks
James Cochran
Lucas C. Elmendorf (D)
Henry Glen
Jonathan N. Havens (D)
Hezekiah L. Hosmer
Edward Livingston (D)
John E. Van Alen (F)
Philip Van Cortlandt (D)
John Williams

North Carolina

Senators

Timothy Bloodworth
Alexander Martin (F)

Representatives

Thomas Blount (D)
Nathan Bryan d. June 1798
Dempsey Burges
James Gillespie
William B. Grove (F)
Matthew Locke (D)
Joseph McDowell
Nathaniel Macon (D)
Richard D. Spaight (D) s. 1798
Richard Stanford (D)
Robert Williams

Pennsylvania

Senators

William Bingham
James Ross (F)

Representatives

David Bard
Robert Brown (D) s. 1798
John Chapman (F)
George Ege r. Oct. 1797
William Findley (D)
Albert Gallatin (D)
Andrew Gregg (F)
John A. Hanna (AF)
Thomas Hartley (F)
Joseph Hiester (F)
John W. Kittera (F)
Blair McClenachan
Samuel Sitgreaves (F) r. 1798
John Swanwick (D) d. Aug.
  1798
Richard Thomas (F)
Robert Waln (F) s. 1798

Rhode Island

Senators

William Bradford r. Oct. 1797
Theodore Foster (Law & Order)
Ray Greene

Representatives

Christopher G. Champlin (F)
Elisha R. Potter (F) r. 1797
Thomas Tillinghast

South Carolina

Senators

John Hunter (F) r. Nov. 1798
Charles Pinckney (D) s. 1799
Jacob Read (F)

Representatives

Lemuel Benton (D)
Robert G. Harper (F)
Thomas Pinckney (F)
John Rutledge, Jr. (F)
William Smith (D)
William L. Smith (F) r. July
  1797
Thomas Sumter (D)

Tennessee

Senators

Joseph Anderson
William Blount r. July 1797
William Cocke ta. 1797
Andrew Jackson (D) r. 1798
Daniel Smith (D) ta. 1798

Representatives

William C. C. Claiborne

Vermont

Senators

Nathaniel Chipman (F)
Elijah Paine (F)
Isaac Tichenor (F) r. Oct. 1797

Representatives

Matthew Lyon (AF)
Lewis R. Morris (F)

Virginia

Senators

Stevens T. Mason (D)
Henry Tazewell d. Jan. 1799

Representatives

Richard Brent
Samuel J. Cabell (D)
Thomas Claiborne
Matthew Clay (D)
John Clopton (D)
John Dawson (D)
Joseph Eggleston s. 1798
Thomas Evans
William B. Giles (AF) r. Oct.
  1798
Carter B. Harrison
David Holmes
Walter Jones (D)
James Machir
Daniel Morgan (F)
Anthony New (D)
John Nicholas (D)
Josiah Parker (AF)
Abram Trigg
John Trigg
Abraham B. Venable

Sixth Congress

(Mar. 4, 1799, to
Mar. 3, 1801)

President of the Senate: Thomas
  Jefferson
*Presidents Pro Tempore of the
  Senate:* Samuel Livermore;
  Uriah Tracy; John E.
  Howard; James Hillhouse
*Speaker of the House of
  Representatives:* Theodore
  Sedgwick

Connecticut

Senators

James Hillhouse (F)
Uriah Tracy (F)

Representatives

Jonathan Brace (F) r. 1800
Samuel W. Dana (F)
John Davenport (F)
William Edmond (F)
Chauncey Goodrich (R)
Elizur Goodrich (F)
Roger Griswold (F)
John C. Smith (F) s. 1800

Delaware

Senators

Henry Latimer r. Feb. 1801
William H. Wells
Samuel White (F) s. 1801

Representatives

James A. Bayard, Sr. (F)

Georgia

Senators

Abraham Baldwin (F)
James Gunn

Representatives

James Jones (D)
Benjamin Taliaferro

Kentucky

Senators

John Brown
Humphrey Marshall (F)

Representatives

Thomas T. Davis
John Fowler

Maryland

Senators

William Hindman (F) s. 1800
John E. Howard (F)
James Lloyd (D) r. Dec. 1800

Representatives

George Baer, Jr. (F)
Gabriel Christie
William Craik
John Dennis (F)
George Dent (D)
Joseph H. Nicholson (D)
Samuel Smith (D)
John C. Thomas (F)

45

Massachusetts

Senators

Samuel Dexter (F) r. May 1800
Dwight Foster (F) s. 1800
Benjamin Goodhue (F) r. Nov. 1800
Jonathan Mason (F) s. 1800

Representatives

Bailey Bartlett (F)
Phanuel Bishop
Dwight Foster (F) r. June 1800
Silas Lee (F)
Levi Lincoln (D)
Samuel Lyman r. Nov. 1800
Ebenezer Mattoon (F) s. 1801
Harrison G. Otis (F)
Nathan Read (F) s. 1800
John Reed (F)
Theodore Sedgwick (F)
Samuel Sewall r. Jan. 1800
William Shepard (F)
George Thacher (F)
Joseph B. Varnum (AF)
Peleg Wadsworth
Lemuel Williams

New Hampshire

Senators

John Langdon (D)
Samuel Livermore

Representatives

Abiel Foster (F)
Jonathan Freeman (F)
William Gordon r. June 1800
James Sheafe (F)
Samuel Tenney s. 1800

New Jersey

Senators

Jonathan Dayton (F)
Aaron Ogden (F) s. 1801
James Schureman (F) r. Feb. 1801

Representatives

John Condit (D)
Franklin Davenport
James H. Imlay
Aaron Kitchell (D)
James Linn (D)

New York

Senators

John Armstrong s. 1801
John Laurance (F) r. Aug. 1800
Gouverneur Morris (F) s. 1800
James Watson (D) r. Mar. 1800

Representatives

Theodorus Bailey (D)
John Bird (D)
William Cooper (F)
Lucas C. Elmendorf (D)

Henry Glen
Jonathan N. Havens (D) d. Oct. 1799
Edward Livingston (D)
Jonas Platt (F)
John Smith (D) s. 1800
John Thompson (D)
Philip Van Cortlandt (D)

North Carolina

Senators

Timothy Bloodworth
Jesse Franklin (D)

Representatives

Willis Alston (D)
Joseph Dickson (F)
William B. Grove (F)
Archibald Henderson (F)
William H. Hill (F)
Nathaniel Macon (D)
Richard D. Spaight (D)
Richard Stanford (D)
David Stone (D)
Robert Williams

Pennsylvania

Senators

William Bingham
James Ross (F)

Representatives

Robert Brown (D)
Albert Gallatin (D)
Andrew Gregg (F)
John A. Hanna (AF)
Thomas Hartley (F) d. Dec. 1800
Joseph Hiester (F)
John W. Kittera (F)
Michael Leib (D)
John Peter G. Muhlenberg (D)
John Smilie (D)
John Stewart (D) s. 1801
Richard Thomas (F)
Robert Waln (F)
Henry Woods

Rhode Island

Senators

Theodore Foster (Law & Order)
Ray Greene

Representatives

John Brown (F)
Christopher G. Champlin

South Carolina

Senators

Charles Pinckney (D)
Jacob Read (F)

Representatives

Robert Harper (F)
Benjamin Huger

Abraham Nott (F)
Thomas Pinckney (F)
John Rutledge, Jr. (F)
Thomas Sumter (D)

Tennessee

Senators

Joseph Anderson
William Cocke

Representatives

William C. C. Claiborne (D)

Vermont

Senators

Nathaniel Chipman (F)
Elijah Paine (F)

Representatives

Matthew Lyon (AF)
Lewis R. Morris (F)

Virginia

Senators

Stevens T. Mason (D)
Wilson C. Nicholas (D)

Representatives

Samuel J. Cabell (D)
Matthew Clay (D)
John Dawson (D)
Joseph Eggleston (D)
Thomas Evans
Samuel Goode
Edwin Gray
David Holmes
George Jackson
Henry Lee (F)
John Marshall (F) r. June 1800
Anthony New (D)
John Nicholas (D)
Robert Page (F)
Josiah Parker (AF)
Levin Powell (F)
John Randolph (SRD)
Littleton W. Tazewell (D) s. 1800
Abram Trigg
John Trigg

Seventh Congress

(Mar. 4, 1801, to
Mar. 3, 1803)

President of the Senate: Aaron Burr
Presidents Pro Tempore of the Senate: Abraham Baldwin; Stephen R. Bradley
Speaker of the House of Representatives: Nathaniel Macon

Connecticut

Senators

James Hillhouse (F)
Uriah Tracy (F)

Representatives

Samuel W. Dana (F)
John Davenport (F)
Calvin Goddard (F)
Roger Griswold (F)
Elias Perkins (F)
John C. Smith (F)
Benjamin Tallmadge (F)

Delaware

Senators

William H. Wells (F)
Samuel White (F)

Representatives

James A. Bayard, Sr. (F)

Georgia

Senators

Abraham Baldwin (F)
James Jackson (D)

Representatives

Peter Early s. 1803
David Meriwether (D) s. 1802
John Milledge r. May 1802
Benjamin Taliaferro r. 1802

Kentucky

Senators

John Breckinridge (D)
John Brown

Representatives

Thomas T. Davis
John Fowler

Maryland

Senators

William Hindman (F) ta. 1801
John E. Howard (F)
Robert Wright (D)

Representatives

John Archer (D)
Walter Bowie (D) s. 1802
John Campbell (F)
John Dennis (F)
Daniel Hiester
Joseph H. Nicholson (D)
Thomas Plater
Samuel Smith (D)
Richard Sprigg, Jr. r. Feb. 1802

Massachusetts

Senators

Dwight Foster (F) r. Mar. 1803
Jonathan Mason (F)

Representatives

John Bacon (D)
Phanuel Bishop
Manasseh Cutler (F)
Richard Cutts (D)
William Eustis (D)
Seth Hastings (F) s. 1802
Silas Lee (F) r. Aug. 1801
Levi Lincoln (D) r. 1801
Ebenezer Mattoon (F)
Nathan Read (F)
William Shepard
Josiah Smith
Samuel Thatcher
Joseph B. Varnum (AF)
Peleg Wadsworth
Lemuel Williams

New Hampshire

Senators

Samuel Livermore r. June 1801
Simeon Olcott (F)
William Plumer (F) s. 1802
James Sheafe (F) r. Jan. 1802

Representatives

Abiel Foster (F)
Samuel Hunt s. 1802
Joseph Pierce r. 1802
Samuel Tenney
George B. Upham

New Jersey

Senators

Jonathan Dayton (F)
Aaron Ogden (F)

Representatives

John Condit (D)
Ebenezer Elmer (D)
William Helms (D)
James Mott (D)
Henry Southard (D)

New York

Senators

John Armstrong (D) r. Feb.
1802
De Witt Clinton (D) s. 1802
Gouverneur Morris (F)

Representatives

Theodorus Bailey (D)
John Bird (D) r. July 1801
Lucas C. Elmendorf (D)
Samuel L. Mitchill (D)
Thomas Morris (D)
John Smith (D)
David Thomas (D)
Thomas Tillotson r. Aug. 1801

Philip Van Cortlandt (D)
John P. Van Ness (D)
Killian K. Van Rensselaer (D)
Benjamin Walker (D)

North Carolina

Senators

Jesse Franklin (D)
David Stone (D)

Representatives

Willis Alston (D)
William B. Grove (F)
Archibald Henderson (F)
William H. Hill (F)
James Holland (AF)
Charles Johnson
Nathaniel Macon (D)
Richard Stanford (D)
John Stanly
Robert Williams
Thomas Wynns (F) s. 1802

Pennsylvania

Senators

George Logan (D)
John Peter G. Muhlenberg (D)
r. June 1801
James Ross (F)

Representatives

Thomas Boude (F)
Robert Brown (D)
Andrew Gregg (F)
John A. Hanna (AF)
Joseph Hemphill (F)
Joseph Hiester (F)
William Hoge (F)
William Jones (D)
Michael Leib (D)
John Smilie (D)
John Stewart (D)
Isaac Van Horne (D)
Henry Woods

Rhode Island

Senators

Christopher Ellery (D)
Theodore Foster (Law & Order)
Ray Greene r. Mar. 1801

Representatives

Joseph Stanton, Jr. (D)
Thomas Tillinghast

South Carolina

Senators

Pierce Butler (D)
John E. Colhoun (D) d. Oct.
1802
Charles Pinckney (D) r. 1801
Thomas Sumter (D)

Representatives

William Butler (AF)

Benjamin Huger
Thomas Lowndes (F)
Thomas Moore
John Rutledge, Jr. (F)
Thomas Sumter (D) r. Dec.
1801
Richard Winn (D) s. 1803

Tennessee

Senators

Joseph Anderson
William Cocke

Representatives

William Dickson

Vermont

Senators

Stephen R. Bradley (D)
Nathaniel Chipman (F)
Elijah Paine (F) r. Sept. 1801

Representatives

Lewis R. Morris (F)
Israel Smith (D)

Virginia

Senators

Stevens T. Mason (D)
Wilson C. Nicholas (D)

Representatives

Richard Brent
Samuel J. Cabell (D)
Thomas Claiborne
Matthew Clay (D)
John Clopton (D)
John Dawson (D)
William B. Giles (D)
Edwin Gray
David Holmes
George Jackson
Anthony New (D)
Thomas Newton, Jr. (D)
John Randolph (SDR)
John Smith
John Stratton
John Taliaferro (D)
Philip R. Thompson (D)
Abram Trigg
John Trigg

Eighth Congress

(Mar. 4, 1803, to
Mar. 3, 1805)

President of the Senate: Aaron
Burr
*Presidents Pro Tempore of the
Senate:* John Brown; Jesse
Franklin; Joseph Anderson
*Speaker of the House of
Representatives:* Nathaniel
Macon

Connecticut

Senators

James Hillhouse (F)
Uriah Tracy (F)

Representatives

Simeon Baldwin (F)
Samuel W. Dana (F)
John Davenport (F)
Calvin Goodard (F)
Roger Griswold (F)
John C. Smith (F)
Benjamin Tallmadge (F)

Delaware

Senators

James A. Bayard, Sr. (F) s.
1805
William H. Wells r. Nov. 1804
Samuel White (F)

Representatives

Caesar A. Rodney (D)

Georgia

Senators

Abraham Baldwin (F)
James Jackson (D)

Representatives

Joseph Bryan (D)
Peter Early
Samuel Hammond
David Meriwether (D)

Kentucky

Senators

John Breckinridge (D)
John Brown

Representatives

George M. Bedinger
John Boyle (D)
John Fowler
Matthew Lyon (AF)
Thomas Sandford (D)
Matthew Walton (D)

Maryland

Senators

Samuel Smith (D)
Robert Wright (D)

Representatives

John Archer (D)
Walter Bowie (D)
John Campbell (F)
John Dennis (F)
Daniel Hiester d. Mar. 1804
William McCreery
Nicholas R. Moore (D)

Roger Nelson (D) s. 1804
Joseph H. Nicholson (D)
Thomas Plater

Massachusetts

Senators

John Quincy Adams (F)
Timothy Pickering (F)

Representatives

Phanuel Bishop
Jacob Crowninshield (D)
Manasseh Cutler (F)
Richard Cutts (D)
Thomas Dwight (F)
William Eustis (D)
Seth Hastings (F)
Simon Larned s. 1804
Nahum Mitchell (F)
Ebenezer Seaver (D)
Thomson J. Skinner (D) r. Aug. 1804
William Stedman (F)
Samuel Taggart (F)
Samuel Thatcher (D)
Joseph B. Varnum (AF)
Peleg Wadsworth
Lemuel Williams

New Hampshire

Senators

Simeon Olcott (F)
William Plumer (F)

Representatives

Silas Betton
Clifton Clagett
David Hough
Samuel Hunt
Samuel Tenney

New Jersey

Senators

John Condit (D)
Jonathan Dayton (F)

Representatives

Adam Boyd (D)
Ebenezer Elmer (D)
William Helms (D)
James Mott (D)
James Sloan (D)
Henry Southard (D)

New York

Senators

John Armstrong ta. 1803-04
Theodorus Bailey (D) r. 1804
De Witt Clinton (D) r. Nov. 1803
Samuel L. Mitchill (D) s. 1804
John Smith (D) s. 1804

Representatives

Isaac Bloom d. Apr. 1803

George Clinton, Jr. (D) s. 1805
Gaylord Griswold (F)
Josiah Hasbrouck
Henry W. Livingston
Andrew McCord
Samuel L. Mitchill (D) r. Nov. 1804
Beriah Palmer
John Paterson
Oliver Phelps (D)
Samuel Riker s. 1804
Erastus Root (D)
Thomas Sammons (D)
Joshua Sands
John Smith (D) r. Feb. 1804
David Thomas (D)
George Tibbits (F)
Philip Van Cortlandt (D)
Killian K. Van Rensselaer (D)
Daniel C. Verplanck (F)

North Carolina

Senators

Jesse Franklin (D)
David Stone (D)

Representatives

Nathaniel Alexander
Willis Alston (D)
William Blackledge (D)
James Gillespie d. Jan. 1805
James Holland (AF)
William Kennedy (F)
Nathaniel Macon (D)
Samuel D. Purviance (F)
Richard Stanford (D)
Marmaduke Williams (D)
Joseph Winston (D)
Thomas Wynns (D)

Ohio

Senators

John Smith (D)
Thomas Worthington (D)

Representatives

Jeremiah Morrow

Pennsylvania

Senators

George Logan (D)
Samuel Maclay

Representatives

Isaac Anderson (D)
David Bard
Robert Brown (D)
Joseph Clay
Frederick Conrad (D)
William Findley (D)
Andrew Gregg (F)
John A. Hanna (AF)
Joseph Hiester
John Hoge (D) s. 1804
William Hoge (F) r. Oct. 1804
Michael Leib (D)
John B. C. Lucas (D)
John Rea (D)
Jacob Richards (D)

John Smilie
John Stewart (D)
Isaac Van Horne (D)
John Whitehill

Rhode Island

Senators

Christopher Ellery (D)
Benjamin Howland (D) s. 1804
Samuel J. Potter d. Oct. 1804

Representatives

Nehemiah Knight (AF)
Joseph Stanton, Jr. (D)

South Carolina

Senators

Pierce Butler r. Nov. 1804
John Gaillard (D) s. 1805
Thomas Sumter (D)

Representatives

William Butler (AF)
Levi Casey
John B. Earle
Wade Hampton (D)
Benjamin Huger
Thomas Lowndes (F)
Thomas Moore
Richard Winn (D)

Tennessee

Senators

Joseph Anderson
William Cocke

Representatives

George W. Campbell (D)
William Dickson
John Rhea (D)

Vermont

Senators

Stephen R. Bradley (D)
Israel Smith (D)

Representatives

William Chamberlain (F)
Martin Chittenden
James Elliott (F)
Gideon Olin (D)

Virginia

Senators

William B. Giles (D) s. 1804
Stevens T. Mason (D) d. May 1803
Andrew Moore s. 1804
Wilson C. Nicholas (D) r. May 1804
John Taylor (D) ta. 1803
Abraham B. Venable r. 1804

Representatives

Thomas Claiborne
Christopher Clark (D) s. 1804
Matthew Clay (D)
John Clopton (D)
John Dawson (D)
John W. Eppes (D)
Peterson Goodwyn (D)
Edwin Gray
Thomas Griffin
David Holmes (D)
John G. Jackson (D)
Walter Jones (D)
Joseph Lewis, Jr. (F)
Thomas Lewis r. Mar. 1804
Andrew Moore s. 1804; r. Nov. 1804
Anthony New (D)
Thomas Newton, Jr. (D)
John Randolph (SRD)
Thomas M. Randolph (D)
John Smith (D)
James Stephenson (F)
Philip R. Thompson (D)
Abram Trigg
John Trigg d. June 1804
Alexander Wilson

Ninth Congress

(Mar. 4, 1805, to
Mar. 3, 1807)

President of the Senate: George Clinton
President Pro Tempore of the Senate: Samuel Smith
Speaker of the House of Representatives: Nathaniel Macon

Connecticut

Senators

James Hillhouse (F)
Uriah Tracy (F)

Representatives

Samuel W. Dana (F)
John Davenport (F)
Theodore Dwight (F) s. 1806
Jonathan O. Moseley (F)
Timothy Pitkin (F)
John C. Smith (F) r. 1806
Lewis B. Struges (F)
Benjamin Tallmadge (F)

Delaware

Senators

James A. Bayard, Sr. (F)
Samuel White (F)

Representatives

James M. Broom (F)

Georgia

Senators

Abraham Baldwin (F)

James Jackson (D) d. Mar.
1806
John Milledge s. 1806

Representatives

William W. Bibb (D) s. 1807
Joseph Bryan (D) r. 1806
Peter Early
Cowles Mead r. Dec. 1805
David Meriwether (D)
Dennis Smelt s. 1806
Thomas Spalding r. 1806

Kentucky

Senators

John Adair (D) r. Nov. 1806
John Breckinridge (D) r. Aug.
1805
Henry Clay s. 1806
Buckner Thruston

Representatives

George M. Bedinger
John Boyle (D)
John Fowler
Matthew Lyon (AF)
Thomas Sandford (D)
Matthew Walton (D)

Maryland

Senators

Philip Reed s. 1806
Samuel Smith (D)
Robert Wright (D) r. 1806

Representatives

John Archer
John Campbell
Leonard Covington
Charles Goldsborough
Edward Lloyd s. 1806
William McCreery
Patrick Magruder
Nicholas R. Moore
Roger Nelson
Joseph H. Nicholson r. Mar.
1806

Massachusetts

Senators

John Quincy Adams (F)
Timothy Pickering (F)

Representatives

Joseph Barker (D)
Barnabas Bidwell
Phanuel Bishop
John Chandler
Orchard Cook
Jacob Crowninshield (D)
Richard Cutts (D)
William Ely (F)
Isaiah L. Green
Seth Hastings (F)
Jeremiah Nelson (F)
Josiah Quincy (F)
Ebenezer Seaver (D)
William Stedman (F)

Samuel Taggart (F)
Joseph B. Varnum (AF)
Peleg Wadsworth

New Hampshire

Senators

Nicholas Gilman (D)
William Plumer (F)

Representatives

Silas Betton
Caleb Ellis
David Hough
Samuel Tenney
Thomas W. Thompson

New Jersey

Senators

John Condit (D)
Aaron Kitchell (D)

Representatives

Ezra Darby (D)
Ebenezer Elmer (D)
William Helms (D)
John Lambert (D)
James Sloan
Henry Southard (D)

New York

Senators

Samuel L. Mitchill (D)
John Smith (D)

Representatives

John Blake, Jr.
George Clinton, Jr. (D)
Silas Halsey (D)
Henry W. Livingston
Josiah Masters (D)
Gurdon S. Mumford (F)
John Russell
Peter Sailly (D)
Thomas Sammons (D)
Martin G. Schuneman (D)
David Thomas (D)
Uri Tracy (D)
Philip Van Cortlandt (D)
Killian K. Van Rensselaer (D)
Daniel C. Verplanck (F)
Eliphalet Wickes
Nathan Williams (D)

North Carolina

Senators

David Stone r. Feb. 1807
James Turner

Representatives

Evan S. Alexander s. 1806
Nathaniel Alexander r. Nov.
1805
Willis Alston (D)
William Blackledge (D)
Thomas Blount (D)

James Holland (AF)
Thomas Kenan (D)
Duncan McFarlan
Nathaniel Macon (D)
Richard Stanford (D)
Marmaduke Williams (D)
Joseph Winston (D)
Thomas Wynns (F)

Ohio

Senators

John Smith (D)
Thomas Worthington (D)

Representatives

Jeremiah Morrow (D)

Pennsylvania

Senators

George Logan (D)
Samuel Maclay

Representatives

Isaac Anderson (D)
David Bard
Robert Brown (D)
Joseph Clay
Frederick Conrad (F)
William Findley (D)
Andrew Gregg (F)
John Hamilton (D)
John A. Hanna (AF) d. July
1805
James Kelly
Michael Leib (D) r. Feb. 1806
Christian Lower (D) d. Dec.
1806
John B. C. Lucas (D) r. 1805
John Porter s. 1806
John Pugh (D)
John Rea (D)
Jacob Richards (D)
John Smilie (D)
Samuel Smith s. 1805
John Whitehill
Robert Whitehill s. 1805

Rhode Island

Senators

James Fenner (D)
Benjamin Howland (D)

Representatives

Nehemiah Knight (AF)
Joseph Stanton, Jr. (D)

South Carolina

Senators

John Gaillard (D)
Thomas Sumter (D)

Representatives

William Butler (AF)
Levi Casey d. Feb. 1807
Elias Earle (D)

Robert Marion
Thomas Moore
O'Brien Smith
David R. Williams (D)
Richard Winn

Tennessee

Senators

Joseph Anderson
Daniel Smith (D)

Representatives

George W. Campbell (D)
William Dickson
John Rhea (D)

Vermont

Senators

Stephen R. Bradley (D)
Israel Smith (D)

Representatives

Martin Chittenden
James Elliott (F)
James Fisk (D)
Gideon Olin (D)

Virginia

Senators

William B. Giles (D)
Andrew Moore

Representatives

Burwell Bassett
William A. Burwell (D) s. 1806
John Claiborne
Christopher Clark (D) r. July
1806
Matthew Clay (D)
John Clopton (D)
John Dawson (D)
John W. Eppes (D)
James M. Garnett (D)
Peterson Goodwyn (D)
Edwin Gray
David Holmes (D)
John G. Jackson (D)
Walter Jones (D)
Joseph Lewis, Jr. (F)
John Morrow
Thomas Newton, Jr. (D)
John Randolph (SRD)
Thomas M. Randolph (D)
John Smith
Philip R. Thompson (D)
Abram Trigg
Alexander Wilson

Tenth Congress

(Mar. 4, 1807, to
Mar. 3, 1809)

President of the Senate: George
Clinton

Presidents Pro Tempore of the Senate: Samuel Smith; Stephen R. Bradley; John Milledge

Speaker of the House of Representatives: Joseph B. Varnum

Connecticut

Senators

Chauncey Goodrich (F)
James Hillhouse (F)
Uriah Tracy (F) d. July 1807

Representatives

Epaphroditus Champion (F)
Samuel W. Dana (F)
John Davenport (F)
Jonathan O. Moseley (F)
Timothy Pitkin (F)
Lewis B. Sturges (F)
Benjamin Tallmadge (F)

Delaware

Senators

James A. Bayard, Sr.
Samuel White (F)

Representatives

James M. Broom (F) r. 1807
Nicholas Van Dyke (F)

Georgia

Senators

Abraham Baldwin (F) d. Mar. 1807
William H. Crawford
George Jones ta. 1807
John Milledge

Representatives

William W. Bibb (D)
Howell Cobb
Dennis Smelt
George M. Troup

Kentucky

Senators

John Pope (D)
Buckner Thruston (D)

Representatives

John Boyle (D)
Joseph Desha (D)
Benjamin Howard
Richard M. Johnson
Matthew Lyon (AF)
John Rowan

Maryland

Senators

Philip Reed

Samuel Smith (D)

Representatives

John Campbell (F)
Charles Goldsborough (F)
Philip B. Key (F)
Edward Lloyd (D)
William McCreery
John Montgomery (D)
Nicholas R. Moore (D)
Roger Nelson (D)
Archibald Van Horne

Massachusetts

Senators

John Quincy Adams (F) r. June 1808
James Lloyd (F) s. 1808
Timothy Pickering (F)

Representatives

Ezekiel Bacon (D)
Joseph Barker (D)
Barnabas Bidwell r. July 1807
John Chandler
Orchard Cook
Jacob Crowninshield (D) d. Apr. 1808
Richard Cutts (D)
Josiah Dean
William Ely (F)
Isaiah L. Green
Daniel Ilsley
Edward S. Livermore (F)
Josiah Quincy
Ebenezer Seaver (D)
William Stedman (F)
Joseph Story s. 1808
Samuel Taggart (F)
Jabez Upham (F)
Joseph B. Varnum (AF)

New Hampshire

Senators

Nicholas Gilman (D)
Nahum Parker

Representatives

Peter Carleton
Daniel M. Durell
Francis Gardner
Jedediah K. Smith
Clement Storer

New Jersey

Senators

John Condit
Aaron Kitchell

Representatives

Adam Boyd (D)
Ezra Darby (D) d. Jan. 1808
William Helms (D)
John Lambert (D)
Thomas Newbold (D)
James Sloan
Henry Southard (D)

New York

Senators

Samuel L. Mitchill (D)
John Smith (D)

Representatives

John Blake, Jr.
George Clinton, Jr. (D)
Barent Gardenier
John Harris
Reuben Humphrey
William Kirkpatrick (D)
Josiah Masters (D)
Gurdon S. Mumford (F)
Samuel Riker
John Russell
Peter Swart
David Thomas r. May 1808
John Thompson
James I. Van Alen
Philip Van Cortlandt (D)
Killian K. Van Rensselaer (D)
Daniel C. Verplanck (F)
Nathan Wilson s. 1808

North Carolina

Senators

Jesse Franklin
James Turner

Representatives

Evan S. Alexander
Willis Alston (D)
William Blackledge (D)
Thomas Blount (D)
John Culpepper (F)
Meshack Franklin
James Holland (AF)
Thomas Kenan (D)
Nathaniel Macon (D)
Lemuel Sawyer
Richard Stanford (D)
Marmaduke Williams (D)

Ohio

Senators

Return J. Meigs, Jr. s. 1809
John Smith (D) r. Apr. 1808
Edward Tiffin r. Mar. 1809

Representatives

Jeremiah Morrow (D)

Pennsylvania

Senators

Andrew Gregg (F)
Michael Leib (D) s. 1809
Samuel Maclay r. Jan. 1809

Representatives

David Bard
Robert Brown (D)
Joseph Clay r. 1808
William Findley (D)
John Heister

William Hoge (F)
Robert Jenkins
James Kelly
William Milnor (F)
Daniel Montgomery, Jr. (D)
John Porter
John Pugh (D)
John Rea (D)
Jacob Richards (D)
Matthias Richards
Benjamin Say s. 1808
John Smilie (D)
Samuel Smith
Robert Whitehill

Rhode Island

Senators

James Fenner (D) r. 1807
Benjamin Howland (D)
Elisha Mathewson (D) s. 1807

Representatives

Nehemiah Knight (AF) d. June 1808
Richard Jackson, Jr. s. 1808
Isaac Wilbur

South Carolina

Senators

John Gaillard (D)
Thomas Sumter (D)

Representatives

Lemuel J. Alston
William Butler (AF)
Joseph Calhoun (D)
Robert Marion
Thomas Moore
John Taylor
David R. Williams (D)
Richard Winn (D)

Tennessee

Senators

Joseph Anderson
Daniel Smith (D)

Representatives

George W. Campbell (D)
John Rhea (D)
Jesse Wharton

Vermont

Senators

Stephen R. Bradley (D)
Jonathan Robinson
Israel Smith (D) r. Oct. 1807

Representatives

Martin Chittenden
James Elliott (F)
James Fisk (D)
Samuel Shaw (D) s. 1808
James Witherell r. May 1808

Virginia

Senators

William B. Giles (D)
Andrew Moore

Representatives

Burwell Bassett (D)
William A. Burwell (D)
John Claiborne d. Oct. 1808
Matthew Clay (D)
John Clopton (D)
John Dawson (D)
John W. Eppes (D)
James M. Garnett (D)
Thomas Gholson, Jr. s. 1808
Peterson Goodwyn (D)
Edwin Gray
David Holmes (D)
John G. Jackson (D)
Walter Jones (D)
Joseph Lewis, Jr. (F)
John Love (D)
John Morrow
Thomas Newton, Jr. (D)
Wilson C. Nicholas (D)
John Randolph
John Smith (D)
Abram Trigg
Alexander Wilson

Eleventh Congress

(Mar. 4, 1809, to
Mar. 3, 1811)

President of the Senate: George
Clinton
*Presidents Pro Tempore of the
Senate:* Andrew Gregg; John
Gaillard; John Pope
*Speaker of the House of
Representatives:* Joseph B.
Varnum

Connecticut

Senators

Samuel W. Dana (F) s. 1810
Chauncey Goodrich (F)
James Hillhouse (F) r. June
1810

Representatives

Epaphroditus Champion (F)
Samuel W. Dana (F) r. May
1810
John Davenport (F)
Ebenezer Huntington s. 1810
Jonathan O. Moseley (F)
Timothy Pitkin (F)
Lewis B. Sturges (F)
Benjamin Tallmadge (F)

Delaware

Senators

James A. Bayard, Sr. d. Nov.
1809
Outerbridge Horsey (F) s. 1810
Samuel White (F)

Representatives

Nicholas Van Dyke (F)

Georgia

Senators

William H. Crawford
John Milledge r. Nov. 1809
Charles Tait

Representatives

William W. Bibb (D)
Howell Cobb
Dennis Smelt
George M. Troup

Kentucky

Senators

Henry Clay s. 1810
John Pope (D)
Buckner Thruston (D) r. Dec.
1809

Representatives

William T. Barry (D) s. 1810
Henry Crist
Joseph Desha (D)
Benjamin Howard r. Apr. 1810
Richard M. Johnson (D)
Matthew Lyon (AF)
Samuel McKee (D)

Maryland

Senators

Philip Reed
Samuel Smith (D)

Representatives

John Brown (D) r. 1810
John Campbell
Charles Goldsborough (F)
Philip B. Key (F)
Alexander McKim (D)
John Montgomery (D)
Nicholas R. Moore (D)
Roger Nelson (D) r. May 1810
Samuel Ringgold s. 1810
Archibald Van Horne
Robert Wright (D) s. 1810

Massachusetts

Senators

James Lloyd (F)
Timothy Pickering

Representatives

Joseph Allen (F) s. 1810
Ezekiel Bacon (D)
William Baylies (D) r. June
1809
Abijah Bigelow (F) s. 1810
Orchard Cook
Richard Cutts (D)
William Ely (F)
Barzillai Gannett (D)

Gideon Gardner (F)
Edward S. Livermore (F)
Benjamin Pickman, Jr.
Josiah Quincy
Ebenezer Seaver (D)
William Stedman (F) r. July
1809
Samuel Taggart (F)
Charles Turner, Jr.
Jabez Upham r. 1810
Joseph B. Varnum (AF)
Laban Wheaton
Ezekiel Whitman

New Hampshire

Senators

Charles Cutts s. 1810
Nicholas Gilman (D)
Nahum Parker r. June 1810

Representatives

Daniel Blaisdell (F)
John C. Chamberlain (F)
William Hale (F)
Nathaniel A. Haven (F)
James Wilson

New Jersey

Senators

John Condit
Aaron Kitchell (D) r. Mar.
1809
John Lambert (D)

Representatives

Adam Boyd (D)
James Cox (D) d. Sept. 1810
William Helms (D)
Jacob Hufty (D)
Thomas Newbold (D)
John A. Scudder (D) s. 1810
Henry Southard

New York

Senators

Obadiah German (D)
John Smith (D)

Representatives

William Denning r. 1809
James Emott (F)
Jonathan Fisk (D)
Barent Gardenier
Thomas R. Gold (F)
Herman Knickerbocker (F)
Robert L. Livingston (F)
Vincent Mathews (F)
Samuel L. Mitchill (D)
Gurdon S. Mumford (F)
John Nicholson (D)
Peter B. Porter (D)
Erastus Root (D)
Ebenezer Sage (D)
Thomas Sammons (D)
John Thompson
Uri Tracy (D)
Killian K. Van Rensselaer (D)

North Carolina

Senators

Jesse Franklin
James Turner (D)

Representatives

Willis Alston (D)
James Cochran (D)
Meshack Franklin
James Holland (AF)
Thomas Kenan (D)
William Kennedy (F)
Archibald McBryde (D)
Nathaniel Macon (D)
Joseph Pearson (F)
Lemuel Sawyer (D)
Richard Stanford
John Stanly

Ohio

Senators

Alexander Campbell s. 1810
Stanley Griswold r. Jan. 1810
Return J. Meigs, Jr. (D) r. May
1810
Thomas Worthington (D) s.
1811

Representatives

Jeremiah Morrow (D)

Pennsylvania

Senators

Andrew Gregg (F)
Michael Leib (D)

Representatives

William Anderson (D)
David Bard
Robert Brown
William Crawford (D)
William Findley (D)
Daniel Hiester
Robert Jenkins (D)
Aaron Lyle (D)
William Milnor (F)
John Porter
John Rea (D)
Matthias Richards
John Ross
Benjamin Say r. June 1809
Adam Seybert (D)
John Smilie
George Smith
Samuel Smith
Robert Whitehill

Rhode Island

Senators

Christopher G. Champlin s.
1810
Francis Malbone d. June 1809
Elisha Mathewson (D)

Representatives

Richard Jackson, Jr. (F)
Elisha R. Potter (F)

South Caroliina

Senators

John Gaillard (D)
Thomas Sumter (D) r. 1810
John Taylor s. 1810

Representatives

Lemuel J. Alston
William Butler
Joseph Calhoun
Langdon Cheves (D) s. 1811
Robert Marion r. Dec. 1810
Thomas Moore
John Taylor
Richard Winn (D)
Robert Witherspoon

Tennessee

Senators

Joseph Anderson
Daniel Smith r. Mar. 1809
Jenkin Whiteside

Representatives

Pleasant M. Miller
John Rhea (D)
Robert Weakley

Vermont

Senators

Stephen R. Bradley
Jonathan Robinson

Representatives

William Chamberlain (F)
Martin Chittenden
Jonathan H. Hubbard (F)
Samuel Shaw (D)

Virginia

Senators

Richard Brent
William B. Giles (D)

Representatives

Burwell Bassett (D)
James Breckinridge (F)
William A. Burwell (D)
Matthew Clay (D)
John Clopton (D)
John Dawson (D)
John W. Eppes (D)
David S. Garland
Thomas Gholson, Jr.
Peterson Goodwyn (D)
Edwin Gray
John G. Jackson (D) r. Sept. 1810
Walter Jones (D)
Joseph Lewis, Jr. (F)

John Love (D)
William McKinley (D) s. 1810
Thomas Newton, Jr. (D)
Wilson C. Nicholas r. Nov. 1809
John Randolph (SRD)
John Roane (D)
Daniel Sheffey (F)
John Smith (D)
James Stephenson (F)
Jacob Swoope

Twelfth Congress

(Mar. 4, 1811, to
Mar. 3, 1813)

President of the Senate: George Clinton
President Pro Tempore of the Senate: William H. Crawford
Speaker of the House of Representatives: Henry Clay

Connecticut

Senators

Samuel W. Dana (F)
Chauncey Goodrich (F)

Representatives

Epaphroditus Champion (F)
John Davenport (F)
Lyman Law (F)
Jonathan O. Moseley (F)
Timothy Pitkin (F)
Lewis B. Sturges (F)
Benjamin Tallmadge (F)

Delaware

Senators

James A. Bayard, Sr. r. Mar. 1813
Outerbridge Horsey (F)

Representatives

Henry M. Ridgeley (F)

Georgia

Senators

William H. Crawford
Charles Tait (D)

Representatives

William Barnett (SRD) s. 1812
William W. Bibb (D)
Howell Cobb r. 1812
Bolling Hall (D)
George M. Troup (D)

Kentucky

Senators

George M. Bibb
John Pope (D)

Representatives

Henry Clay
Joseph Desha (D)
Richard M. Johnson (D)
Samuel McKee (D)
Anthony New (D)
Stephen Ormsby (D)

Louisiana

Senators

James Brown s. 1813
Allan B. Magruder (D)
Thomas Posey ta. 1812

Representatives

Thomas B. Robertson (D)

Maryland

Senators

Philip Reed
Samuel Smith (D)

Representatives

Stevenson Archer (D)
Charles Goldsborough (F)
Joseph Kent (F)
Philip B. Key (F)
Peter Little (F)
Alexander McKim (D)
John Montgomery (D) r. Apr. 1811
Samuel Ringgold (D)
Philip Stuart (F)
Robert Wright (D)

Massachusetts

Senators

James Lloyd (F)
Joseph B. Varnum (AF)

Representatives

Ezekiel Bacon (D)
Abijah Bigelow (F)
Elijah Brigham (F)
Francis Carr (D) s. 1812
Richard Cutts (D)
William Ely (F)
Barzillai Gannett (D) r. 1812
Isaiah L. Green
Josiah Quincy (F)
William Reed (F)
William M. Richardson (F) s. 1812
Ebenezer Seaver (D)
Samuel Taggart (F)
Peleg Tallman
Charles Turner, Jr.
Joseph B. Varnum r. June 1811
Laban Wheaton
Leonard White
William Widgery

New Hampshire

Senators

Charles Cutts

Nicholas Gilman (D)

Representatives

Josiah Bartlett, Jr.
Samuel Dinsmoor (D)
Obed Hall (D)
John A. Harper (D)
George Sullivan

New Jersey

Senators

John Condit
John Lambert (D)

Representatives

Adam Boyd (D)
Lewis Condict (AF)
Jacob Huffy (D)
George C. Maxwell
James Morgan (F)
Thomas Newbold (D)

New York

Senators

Obadiah German (D)
John Smith

Representatives

Daniel Avery (D)
Harmanus Bleecker (F)
Thomas B. Cooke (D)
James Emott (F)
Asa Fitch (F)
Thomas R. Gold (F)
Thomas P. Grosvenor (F) r. 1813
Robert L. Livingston (F) r. May 1812
Arunah Metcalf (D)
Samuel L. Mitchill (D)
William Paulding, Jr. (D)
Benjamin Pond (D)
Peter B. Porter (D)
Ebenezer Sage (D)
Thomas Sammons (D)
Silas Stow
Uri Tracy (D)
Pierre Van Cortlandt, Jr.

North Carolina

Senators

Jesse Franklin
James Turner (D)

Representatives

Willis Alston (D)
William Blackledge (D)
Thomas Blount (D) d. Feb. 1812
James Cochran
Meshack Franklin
William Kennedy (F) s. 1813
William R. King (D)
Archibald McBryde (D)
Nathaniel Macon (D)
Joseph Pearson (F)
Israel Pickens (D)
Lemuel Sawyer (D)

Richard Stanford

Ohio

Senators

Alexander Campbell
Thomas Worthington (D)

Representatives

Jeremiah Morrow (D)

Pennsylvania

Senators

Andrew Gregg
Michael Leib (D)

Representatives

William Anderson
David Bard
Robert Brown
William Crawford (D)
Roger Davis (D)
William Findley (D)
John M. Hyneman (D)
Abner Lacock (D)
Joseph Lefever (D)
Aaron Lyle (D)
James Milnor (F)
William Piper
Jonathan Roberts (F)
William Rodman (D)
Adam Seybert (D)
John Smilie d. Dec. 1812
George Smith
Robert Whitehill

Rhode Island

Senators

Christopher G. Champlin r.
Oct. 1811
Jeremiah B. Howell (F)
William Hunter (F)

Representatives

Richard Jackson, Jr. (F)
Elisha R. Potter (F)

South Carolina

Senators

John Gaillard (D)
John Taylor (D)

Representatives

William Butler
John C. Calhoun (D)
Langdon Cheves
Elias Earle (D)
William Lowndes (D)
Thomas Moore
David R. Williams (D)
Richard Winn

Tennessee

Senators

Joseph Anderson
George W. Campbell (D)
Jenkin Whiteside r. Oct. 1811

Representatives

Felix Grundy (D)
John Rhea (D)
John Sevier (D)

Vermont

Senators

Stephen R. Bradley
Jonathan Robinson

Representatives

Martin Chittenden
James Fisk (D)
Samuel Shaw (D)
William Strong

Virginia

Senators

Richard Brent
William B. Giles (D)

Representatives

John Baker (F)
Burwell Bassett (D)
James Breckinridge (F)
William A. Burwell (D)
Matthew Clay (D)
John Clopton (D)
John Dawson (D)
Thomas Gholson, Jr.
Peterson Goodwyn (D)
Edwin Gray
Aylett Hawes (D)
John P. Hungerford (D) r. Nov.
1811
Joseph Lewis, Jr. (F)
William McCoy (D)
Hugh Nelson (D)
Thomas Newton, Jr. (D)
James Pleasants (D)
John Randolph (SRD)
John Roane (D)
Daniel Sheffey (F)
John Smith (D)
John Taliaferro (D)
Thomas Wilson

Thirteenth Congress

(Mar. 4, 1813, to
Mar. 3, 1815)

President of the Senate: Elbridge
Gerry
*Presidents Pro Tempore of the
Senate:* Joseph B. Varnum;
John Gaillard
*Speakers of the House of
Representatives:* Henry Clay;
Langdon Cheves

Connecticut

Senators

David Daggett
Samuel W. Dana (F)
Chauncey Goodrich (F) r. May
1813

Representatives

Epaphroditus Champion (F)
John Davenport (F)
Lyman Law (F)
Jonathan O. Moseley (F)
Timothy Pitkin (F)
Lewis B. Sturges (F)
Benjamin Tallmadge (F)

Delaware

Senators

Outerbridge Horsey (F)
William H. Wells

Representatives

Thomas Cooper (F)
Henry M. Ridgeley (F)

Georgia

Senators

William W. Bibb (D)
William B. Bulloch (D) ta. 1813
William H. Crawford r. Mar.
1813
Charles Tait (D)

Representatives

William Barnett (SRD)
William W. Bibb (D) r. Nov.
1813
Alfred Cuthbert (D) s. 1814
John Forsyth (D)
Bolling Hall (D)
Thomas Telfair (D)
George M. Troup (D)

Kentucky

Senators

William T. Barry (D) s. 1815
George M. Bibb r. Aug. 1814
Jesse Bledsoe r. Dec. 1814
Isham Talbot s. 1815
George Walker r. 1814

Representatives

James Clark (D)
Henry Clay r. Jan. 1814
Joseph Desha (D)
William P. Duval (D)
Joseph H. Hawkins (F) s. 1814
Samuel Hopkins (D)
Richard M. Johnson (D)
Samuel McKee (D)
Thomas Montgomery (D)
Stephen Ormsby (D)
Solomon P. Sharp (D)

Louisiana

Senators

James Brown
Eligius Fromentin

Representatives

Thomas B. Robertson (D)

Maryland

Senators

Robert H. Goldsborough (F)
Samuel Smith (D)

Representatives

Stevenson Archer (D)
Charles Goldsborough (F)
Alexander C. Hanson (F)
Joseph Kent (D)
Alexander McKim (D)
Nicholas R. Moore (D)
Samuel Ringgold (D)
Philip Stuart (F)
Robert Wright (D)

Massachusetts

Senators

Christopher Gore (F) s. May
1813
James Lloyd (F) r. May 1813
Joseph B. Varnum (AF)

Representatives

William Baylies
Abijah Bigelow (F)
George Bradbury (F)
Elijah Brigham (F)
Samuel Dana (D) s. 1814
Samuel Davis (F)
Daniel Dewey (W) r. Feb. 1814
Levi Hubbard (D)
John W. Hulbert (F) s. 1814
William Ely (F)
Cyrus King (F)
James Parker (D)
Timothy Pickering (F)
John Reed (F)
William Reed (F)
William M. Richardson (F) r.
Apr. 1814
Nathaniel Ruggles (F)
Samuel Taggart (F)
Artemas Ward, Jr.
Laban Wheaton
John Wilson
Abiel Wood

New Hampshire

Senators

Charles Cutts
Nicholas Gilman (D) d. May
1814
Jeremiah Mason (F)
Thomas W. Thompson s. 1814

Representatives

Bradbury Cilley (F)
William Hale
Samuel Smith
Roger Vose (F)
Daniel Webster (F)
Jeduthun Wilcox (F)

New Jersey

Senators

John Condit
John Lambert (D)

Representatives

Thomas Bines (D) s. 1814
Lewis Condict (AF)
William Coxe, Jr. (F)
Jacob Hufty (D) d. May 1814
James Schureman (F)
Richard Stockton
Thomas Ward (D)

New York

Senators

Obadiah German (D)
Rufus King

Representatives

Daniel Avery (D)
Egbert Benson r. Aug. 1813
John M. Bowers r. Dec. 1813
Alexander Boyd
Oliver C. Comstock (D)
Peter Denoyelles
Jonathan Fisk (F)
James Geddes
Thomas P. Grosvenor (F)
Abraham J. Hasbrouck (D)
Samuel M. Hopkins
Nathaniel W. Howell
William Irving (D) s. 1814
Moss Kent (F)
John Lefferts (D)
John Lovett (F)
Jacob Markell (F)
Morris S. Miller (F)
Hosea Moffitt (F)
Thomas J. Oakley (F)
Jothan Post, Jr. (F)
Ebenezer Sage (D)
Samuel Sherwood
Zebulon R. Shipherd (F)
William S. Smith
John W. Taylor (D)
Joel Thompson
Isaac Williams, Jr.
Elisha J. Winter

North Carolina

Senators

David Stone
James Turner

Representatives

Willis Alston (D)
John Culpepper (F)
Peter Forney (D)
Meshack Franklin (D)

William Gaston (F)
William Kennedy (F)
William R. King (D)
Nathaniel Macon (D)
William H. Murfree (D)
Joseph Pearson (F)
Israel Pickens (D)
Richard Stanford
Bartlett Yancy

Ohio

Senators

Joseph Kerr (D) s. 1814
Jeremiah Morrow (D)
Thomas Worthington (D) r.
   Dec. 1814

Representatives

John Alexander (D)
Reasin Beall (W) r. June 1814
James Caldwell (D)
David Clendenin s. 1814
William Creighton, Jr. (D)
James Kilbourne (D)
John McLean (D)

Pennsylvania

Senators

Abner Lacock (D)
Michael Leib (D) r. Feb. 1814
Jonathan Roberts s. 1814

Representatives

William Anderson
David Bard
Robert Brown
John Conard (D)
William Crawford (D)
Edward Crouch (D)
Roger Davis (D)
William Findley (D)
Hugh Glasgow
John Gloninger r. Aug. 1813
Isaac Griffin (D)
Samuel Henderson (F) s. 1814
John M. Hyneman (D) r. Aug.
   1813
Charles J. Ingersoll (D)
Samuel D. Ingham (D)
Jared Irwin (D)
Aaron Lyle (D)
William Piper
John Rea (D)
Jonathan Roberts (D) r. Feb.
   1814
Adam Seybert
Amos Slaymaker s. 1814
Isaac Smith
Adamson Tannehill
Daniel Udree (D)
James Whitehill r. Sept. 1814
Robert Whitehill d. Apr. 1813
Thomas Wilson (D)

Rhode Island

Senators

Jeremiah B. Howell
William Hunter

Representatives

Richard Jackson, Jr. (F)
Elisha R. Potter (F)

South Carolina

Senators

John Gaillard (D)
John Taylor (D)

Representatives

John C. Calhoun (D)
John J. Chappell (D)
Langdon Cheves (D)
Elias Earle (D)
David R. Evans (D)
Samuel Farrow (D)
Theodore Gourdin (D)
John Kershaw (D)
William Lowndes (D)

Tennessee

Senators

Joseph Anderson
George W. Campbell (D) r.
   Feb. 1814
Jesse Wharton s. 1814

Representatives

John H. Bowen (D)
Newton Cannon s. 1814
Felix Grundy (D) r. 1814
Thomas K. Harris (D)
Parry W. Humphreys (D)
John Rhea (D)
John Sevier (D)

Vermont

Senators

Dudley Chase (D)
Jonathan Robinson

Representatives

William C. Bradley (D)
Ezra Butler (D)
James Fisk (D)
Charles Rich (D)
Richard Skinner (D)
William Strong

Virginia

Senators

James Barbour s. 1815
Richard Brent d. Dec. 1814
William B. Giles (D) r. Mar.
   1815

Representatives

Philip P. Barbour (D) s. 1814
Thomas M. Bayly (D)
James Breckinridge (F)
William A. Burwell (D)
Hugh Caperton (F)
John Clopton (D)
John Dawson (D) d. Mar. 1814

John W. Eppes (D)
Thomas Gholson, Jr.
Peterson Goodwyn (D)
Aylett Hawes (D)
John P. Hungerford (D)
John G. Jackson (D)
James Johnson (D)
John Kerr (D)
Joseph Lewis, Jr. (F)
William McCoy (D)
Hugh Nelson (D)
Thomas Newton, Jr. (D)
James Pleasants (D)
John Roane (D)
Daniel Sheffey (F)
John Smith (D)
Francis White

Fourteenth Congress

(Mar. 4, 1815, to
Mar. 3, 1817)

President of the Senate: Vacant
*President Pro Tempore of the
   Senate:* John Gaillard
*Speaker of the House of
   Representatives:* Henry Clay

Connecticut

Senators

David Daggett (F)
Samuel W. Dana (F)

Representatives

Epaphroditus Champion (F)
John Davenport (F)
Lyman Law (F)
Jonathan O. Moseley (F)
Timothy Pitkin (F)
Lewis B. Sturges (F)
Benjamin Tallmadge (F)

Delaware

Senators

Outerbridge Horsey (F)
William H. Wells

Representatives

Thomas Clayton (F)
Thomas Cooper (F)

Georgia

Senators

William W. Bibb (D) r. Nov.
   1816
Charles Tait (D)
George M. Troup (SRD) s.
   1816

Representatives

Zadock Cook s. 1817
Alfred Cuthbert (D) r. Nov.
   1816
John Forsyth (D)

Bolling Hall (D)
Wilson Lumpkin (D)
Thomas Telfair (D)
Richard Wilde (D)

Indiana

Senators

James Noble
Waller Taylor (D)

Representatives

William Hendricks (D)

Kentucky

Senators

William T. Barry r. May 1816
Martin D. Hardin (D) s. 1816
Isham Talbot

Representatives

James Clark (D) r. 1816
Henry Clay
Joseph Desha (D)
Thomas Fletcher s. 1816
Benjamin Hardin (W)
Richard M. Johnson (D)
Samuel McKee (D)
Alney McLean
Stephen Ormsby (D)
Solomon P. Sharp (D)
Micah Taul (D)

Louisiana

Senators

James Brown
Eligius Fromentin

Representatives

Thomas B. Robertson (D)

Maryland

Senators

Robert H. Goldsborough (F)
Alexander C. Hanson (F) s. 1817
Robert G. Harper (F) r. Dec. 1816

Representatives

Stevenson Archer (D)
George Baer, Jr.
Charles Goldsborough (F)
Alexander C. Hanson (F) r. 1816
John C. Herbert (F)
Peter Little (D) s. 1816
Nicholas R. Moore (D) r. 1815
George Peter (D) s. 1816
William Pinkney r. Apr. 1816
Samuel Smith (D) s. 1816
Philip Stuart (F)
Robert Wright (D)

Massachusetts

Senators

Eli P. Ashmun s. 1816
Christopher Gore r. May 1816
Joseph B. Varnum

Representatives

Benjamin Adams (F) s. 1816
William Baylies
George Bradbury (F)
Elijah Brigham (F) d. Feb. 1816
Benjamin Brown
James Carr
Samuel S. Conner
John W. Hulbert (F)
Cyrus King (F)
Elijah H. Mills (F)
Jeremiah Nelson (F)
Albion K. Parris (D)
Timothy Pickering (F)
John Reed (F)
Thomas Rice
Nathaniel Ruggles (F)
Asahel Stearns (F)
Solomon Strong (F)
Samuel Taggart (F)
Artemas Ward, Jr. (F)
Laban Wheaton (F)

New Hampshire

Senators

Jeremiah Mason (F)
Thomas W. Thompson

Representatives

Charles H. Atherton (F)
Bradbury Cilley (F)
William Hale (F)
Roger Vose (F)
Daniel Webster (F)
Jeduthun Wilcox (F)

New Jersey

Senators

John Condit
James J. Wilson (D)

Representatives

Ezra Baker
Ephraim Bateman (D)
Benjamin Bennet
Lewis Condict (AF)
Henry Southard (D)
Thomas Ward (D)

New York

Senators

Rufus King (F)
Nathan Sanford (D)

Representatives

John Adams r. Dec. 1815
Asa Adgate (D)
Daniel Avery (D) s. 1816
Samuel R. Betts (D)

James Birdsall (D)
Victory Birdseye (W)
Micah Brooks
Daniel Cady (F)
Archibald S. Clarke s. 1816
Oliver C. Comstock (D)
Henry Crocheron (D)
Jonathan Fisk r. Mar. 1815
Thomas R. Gold (F)
Thomas P. Grosvenor (F)
Jabez D. Hammond (D)
William Irving (D)
Moss Kent (F)
John Lovett (F)
Hosea Moffitt (F)
Peter B. Porter (D) r. Jan. 1816
Erastus Root (D)
John Savage (D)
Abraham H. Schenck (D)
John W. Taylor (D)
Enos T. Throop (D) r. June 1816
George Townsend (D)
Jonathan Ward (D)
Peter H. Wendover (D)
James W. Wilkin (D)
Westel Willoughby, Jr. (D)
John B. Yates (D)

North Carolina

Senators

Nathaniel Macon (D)
Montfort Stokes (D) s. 1816
James Turner r. Nov. 1816

Representatives

Joseph H. Bryan
James W. Clark (D)
John Culpepper (F)
Samuel Dickens s. 1816
Weldon N. Edwards (D) s. 1816
Daniel M. Forney
William Gaston (F)
Charles Hooks (D) s. 1816
William R. King (D) r. Nov. 1816
William C. Love (D)
Nathaniel Macon (D) r. Dec. 1815
William H. Murfree (D)
Israel Pickens (D)
Richard Stanford d. Apr. 1816
Lewis Williams
Bartlett Yancy

Ohio

Senators

Jeremiah Morrow (D)
Benjamin Ruggles (D)

Representatives

John Alexander (D)
James Caldwell (D)
David Clendenin
William Creighton, Jr. (D)
William Henry Harrison (W) s. 1816
James Kilbourne (D)
John McLean (D) r. 1816

Pennsylvania

Senators

Abner Lacock (D)
Jonathan Roberts (D)

Representatives

David Bard d. Mar. 1815
Thomas Burnside s. 1816
William Crawford (D)
William Darlington (D)
Amos Ellmaker r. July 1815
William Findley (D)
Hugh Glasgow
Isaac Griffin (D)
John Hahn (D)
Joseph Hiester (F)
Joseph Hopkinson (F)
Samuel D. Ingham (D)
Jared Irwin (D)
Aaron Lyle (D)
William Maclay
William P. Maclay (D) s. 1816
William Milnor (F)
William Piper
John Ross
John Sergeant (F)
Thomas Smith (F)
James M. Wallace
John Whiteside (D)
Jonathan Williams d. May 1815
Thomas Wilson (D)
William Wilson

Rhode Island

Senators

Jeremiah B. Howell (F)
William Hunter (F)

Representatives

John L. Boss, Jr.
James B. Mason (F)

South Carolina

Senators

John Gaillard (D)
William Smith (D) s. 1817
John Taylor (D) r. Nov. 1816

Representatives

John C. Calhoun (D)
John J. Chappell (D)
Benjamin Huger
William Lowndes (D)
William Mayrant r. Oct. 1816
Henry Middleton (D)
Stephen D. Miller (D) s. 1817
Thomas Moore
John Taylor
William Woodward

Tennessee

Senators

George W. Campbell
Jesse Wharton ta. 1815
John Williams

Representatives

William G. Blount (D) s. 1816
Newton Cannon (D)
Bennett H. Henderson
Samuel Powell
James B. Reynolds (D)
John Sevier (D) d. Sept. 1815
Isaac Thomas (D)

Vermont

Senators

Dudley Chase (D)
Isaac Tichenor (F)

Representatives

Daniel Chipman (F) r. May
1816
Luther Jewett (F)
Chauncey Langdon (F)
Asa Lyon (F)
Charles Marsh (F)
John Noyes (F)

Virginia

Senators

James Barbour (SRD)
Armistead T. Mason (D)

Representatives

Philip P. Barbour (D)
Burwell Bassett (D)
James Breckinridge (F)
William A. Burwell (D)
Matthew Clay d. May 1815
John Clopton (D) d. Sept. 1816
Peterson Goodwyn (D)
Thomas Gholson, Jr. d. July
1816
Aylett Hawes (D)
John P. Hungerford (D)
John G. Jackson (D)
James Johnson (D)
John Kerr (D) s. 1815
Joseph Lewis, Jr. (F)
William McCoy (D)
Hugh Nelson (D)
Thomas M. Nelson (D) s. 1816
Thomas Newton, Jr. (D)
James Pleasants (D)
John Randolph (SRD)
William H. Roane (D)
Daniel Sheffey (F)
Ballard Smith
Magnus Tate
Henry St. George Tucker (D)
John Tyler (D) s. 1816

Fifteenth Congress

(Mar. 4, 1817, to
Mar. 3, 1819)

President of the Senate: Daniel
D. Tompkins
*Presidents Pro Tempore of the
Senate:* John Gaillard; James
Barbour
*Speaker of the House of
Representatives:* Henry Clay

Connecticut

Senators

David Daggert (F)
Samuel W. Dana (F)

Representatives

Sylvester Gilbert s. 1818
Uriel Holmes (F) r. 1818
Ebenezer Huntington (W)
Jonathan O. Moseley (F)
Timothy Pitkin (F)
Samuel B. Sherwood (F)
Nathaniel Terry
Thomas S. Williams

Delaware

Senators

Outerbridge Horsey (F)
Nicholas Van Dyke (F)

Representatives

Willard Hall (D)
Louis McLane (D)

Georgia

Senators

John Forsyth (D) s. 1818
Charles Tait
George M. Troup (SRD) r.
Sept. 1818

Representatives

Joel Abbot (D)
Thomas W. Cobb
Zadock Cook
Joel Crawford (D)
John Forsyth (D) r. Nov. 1818
Robert R. Reid (D) s. 1819
William Terrell (D)

Illinois

Senators

Ninian Edwards (D) s. 1818
Jesse B. Thomas s. 1818

Representatives

John McLean s. 1818

Indiana

Senators

James Noble
Waller Taylor (D)

Representatives

William Hendricks (D)

Kentucky

Senators

John J. Crittenden r. Mar. 1819
Isham Talbot

Representatives

Richard C. Anderson, Jr.
Henry Clay
Joseph Desha (D)
Richard M. Johnson (D)
Anthony New (D)
Tunstall Quarles (D)
George Robertson (W)
Thomas Speed
David Trimble (D)
David Walker

Louisiana

Senators

William C. C. Claiborne (D) d.
Nov. 1817
Eligius Fromentin
Henry Johnson s. 1818

Representatives

Thomas Butler s. 1818
Thomas B. Robertson (D) r.
Apr. 1818

Maryland

Senators

Robert H. Goldsborough (F)
Alexander C. Hanson (F)

Representatives

Thomas Bayly (D)
Thomas Culbreth (D)
John C. Herbert (F)
Peter Little (D)
George Peter (D)
Philip Reed
Samuel Ringgold (D)
Samuel Smith (D)
Philip Stuart (F)

Massachusetts

Senators

Eli P. Ashmun r. May 1818
Prentiss Mellen s. 1818
Harrison Gray Otis

Representatives

Benjamin Adams (F)
Samuel C. Allen
Walter Folger, Jr. (D)
Timothy Fuller (D)
Joshua Gage (D)
John Holmes (D)
Enoch Lincoln s. 1818
Jonathan Mason (F)
Elijah H. Mills (F)
Marcus Morton (D)
Jeremiah Nelson (F)
Benjamin Orr (F)

Albion K. Parris (D) r. Feb.
1818
Thomas Rice
Nathaniel Ruggles (F)
Zabdiel Sampson (D)
Henry Shaw (F)
Nathaniel Silsbee (D)
Solomon Strong (F)
Ezekiel Whitman
John Wilson

Mississippi

Senators

Walter Leake (D)
Thomas H. Williams

Representatives

George Poindexter

New Hampshire

Senators

Jeremiah Mason (F) r. June
1817
David L. Morril (D)
Clement Storer

Representatives

Josiah Butler (D)
Clifton Clagett (D)
Salma Hale (D)
Arthur Livermore (D)
John F. Parrott (D)
Nathaniel Upham (D)

New Jersey

Senators

Mahlon Dickerson (D)
James J. Wilson (D)

Representatives

Ephraim Bateman (D)
Benjamin Bennet (D)
Joseph Bloomfield (D)
Charles Kinsey
John Linn
Henry Southard (D)

New York

Senators

Rufus King (F)
Nathan Sanford (D)

Representatives

Oliver C. Comstock (D)
Daniel Cruger (D)
John P. Cushman (D)
John R. Drake
Benjamin Ellicott (D)
Josiah Hasbrouck
John Herkimer (D)
Thomas H. Hubbard (D)
William Irving (D)
Dorrance Kirtland
Thomas Lawyer
David A. Ogden (F)

John Palmer (D)
James Porter (D)
John Savage (D)
Philip J. Schuyler
Tredwell Scudder
John C. Spencer
Henry R. Storrs (F)
James Tallmadge, Jr. (D)
John W. Taylor (D)
Caleb Tompkins
George Townsend (D)
Peter H. Wendover (D)
Rensselaer Westerlo (F)
James W. Wilkin (D)
Isaac Williams, Jr. (D)

North Carolina

Senators

Nathaniel Macon (D)
Montfort Stokes (D)

Representatives

Joseph H. Bryan (D)
William Davidson (F) s. 1818
Weldon N. Edwards (D)
Charles Fisher (D) s. 1819
Daniel M. Forney r. 1818
Thomas H. Hall (D)
George Mumford (D) d. Dec. 1818
James Owen (D)
Lemuel Sawyer (D)
Thomas Settle (D)
Jesse Slocumb (F)
James S. Smith (D)
James Stewart s. 1818
Felix Walker (D)
Lewis Williams

Ohio

Senators

Jeremiah Morrow (D)
Benjamin Ruggles (D)

Representatives

Levi Barber
Philemon Beecher (F)
John W. Campbell (D)
William Henry Harrison (W)
Samuel Herrick (D)
Peter Hitchcock

Pennsylvania

Senators

Abner Lacock (D)
Jonathan Roberts (D)

Representatives

William Anderson
Henry Baldwin (F)
Andrew Boden
Isaac Darlington (F)
Joseph Hiester (F)
Joseph Hopkinson (F)
Jacob Hostetter (D) s. 1818
Samuel D. Ingham (D) r. July 1818
William Maclay
William P. Maclay (D)

David Marchand
Robert Moore
Samuel Moore (D) s. 1818
John Murray
Alexander Ogle (D)
Thomas Patterson (D)
Levi Pawling (D)
John Ross r. Feb. 1818
Thomas J. Rogers (D) s. 1818
John Sergeant (F)
Adam Seybert (D)
Jacob Spangler r. Apr. 1818
Christian Tarr
James M. Wallace
John Whiteside (D)
William Wilson

Rhode Island

Senators

James Burrill, Jr.
William Hunter (F)

Representatives

John L. Boss, Jr.
James B. Mason (F)

South Carolina

Senators

John Gaillard (D)
William Smith (D)

Representatives

Joseph Bellinger (D)
John C. Calhoun (D) r. Nov. 1817
Elias Earle (D)
James Ervin (D)
William Lowndes (D)
Henry Middleton (D)
Stephen D. Miller (D)
Wilson Nesbitt (D)
Eldred Simkins (D) s. 1818
Starling Tucker

Tennessee

Senators

George W. Campbell (D) r. Apr. 1818
John H. Eaton (D) s. 1818
John Williams

Representatives

William G. Blount (D)
Thomas Claiborne (D)
Samuel Hogg (D)
Francis Jones
George W. L. Marr
John Rhea (D)

Vermont

Senators

Dudley Chase (D) r. Nov. 1817
James Fisk (D) r. Jan. 1818
William A. Palmer (D) s. 1818
Isaac Tichenor (F)

Representatives

Heman Allen (D) r. Apr. 1818
Samuel C. Crafts
William Hunter (R)
Orsamus C. Merrill (D)
Charles Rich (D)
Mark Richards (D)

Virginia

Senators

James Barbour (SRD)
John W. Eppes (D)

Representatives

Archibald Austin (D)
William Lee Ball (D)
Philip P. Barbour (D)
Burwell Bassett (D)
William A. Burwell (D)
Edward Colston (F)
John Floyd (D)
Robert S. Garnett (D)
Peterson Goodwyn d. Feb. 1818
James Johnson (D)
William J. Lewis (D)
William McCoy (D)
Charles F. Mercer (D)
Hugh Nelson (D)
Thomas M. Nelson (D)
Thomas Newton, Jr. (D)
John Pegram s. 1818
James Pindall (D)
James Pleasants (D)
Ballard Smith
Alexander Smyth
George F. Strother (D)
Henry St. George Tucker (D)
John Tyler (D)

Sixteenth Congress

(Mar. 4, 1819, to
Mar. 3, 1821)

President of the Senate: Daniel D. Tompkins
Presidents Pro Tempore of the Senate: James Barbour; John Gaillard
Speakers of the House of Representatives: Henry Clay; John W. Taylor

Alabama

Senators

John W. Walker (D)
William R. King (D)

Representatives

John Crowell

Connecticut

Senators

Samuel W. Dana (F)
James Lanman (D)

Representatives

Henry W. Edwards (D)
Samuel A. Foote
Jonathan O. Moseley (F)
Elisha Phelps (D)
John Russ (D)
James Stevens (D)
Gideon Tomlinson (D)

Delaware

Senators

Outerbridge Horsey (F)
Nicholas Van Dyke (F)

Representatives

Willard Hall (D)
Louis McLane (D)

Georgia

Senators

John Elliott
Freeman Walker (D)

Representatives

Joel Abbot (D)
Thomas W. Cobb
Joel Crawford (D)
John A. Cuthbert (D)
Robert R. Reid (D)
William Terrell (D)

Illinois

Senators

Ninian Edwards (D)
Jesse B. Thomas

Representatives

Daniel P. Cook

Indiana

Senators

James Nobel
Waller Taylor (D)

Representatives

William Hendricks (D)

Kentucky

Senators

Richard M. Johnson (D) s. 1820
William Logan (D) r. May 1820
Isham Talbot s. 1820

Representatives

Richard C. Anderson, Jr.
William Brown
Henry Clay
Benjamin Hardin

Francis Johnson (D) s. 1820
Alney McLean
Thomas Metcalfe (D)
Thomas Montgomery (D) s. 1820
Tunstall Quarles (D) r. June 1820
George Robertson (W)
David Trimble (D)
David Walker d. Mar. 1820

Louisiana

Senators

James Brown
Henry Johnson

Represratives

Thomas Butler

Maine

Senators

John Chandler (D) s. 1820
John Holmes s. 1820

Representatives

Joseph Dane (F) s. 1820

Maryland

Senators

Alexander C. Hanson (F) d. Apr. 1819
Edward Lloyd (D)
William Pinkney s. 1820

Representatives

Stevenson Archer (D)
Thomas Bayly (D)
Thomas Culbreth (D)
Joseph Kent (D)
Peter Little (D)
Raphael Neale
Samuel Ringgold (D)
Samuel Smith (D)
Henry R. Warfield (F)

Massachusetts

Senators

Prentiss Mellen r. May 1820
Elijah H. Mills (F) s. 1820
Harrison Gray Otis (F)

Representatives

Benjamin Adams (F)
Samuel C. Allen
Joshua Cushman (D)
Edward Dowse (D) r. May 1820
William Eustis s. 1820
Walter Folger, Jr. (F)
Timothy Fuller (D)
Benjamin Gorham s. 1820
Mark L. Hill
Aaron Hobart (D) s. 1820
John Holmes (D) r. Mar. 1820
Jonas Kendall (F)

Martin Kinsley
Samuel Lathrop (F)
Enoch Lincoln
Jonathan Mason (F) r. May 1820
Marcus Morton (D)
Jeremiah Nelson (F)
James Parker (D)
Zabdiel Sampson (D) r. July 1820
Henry Shaw (F)
Nathaniel Silsbee (D)
Ezekiel Whitman

Mississippi

Senators

David Holmes (D) s. 1820
Walter Leake (D) r. May 1820
Thomas H. Williams (D)

Representatives

Christopher Rankin (D)

New Hampshire

Senators

David L. Morril (D)
John F. Parrott (D)

Representatives

Joseph Buffum, Jr. (D)
Josiah Butler (D)
Clifton Clagett
Arthur Livermore (D)
William Plumer, Jr. (D)
Nathaniel Upham (D)

New Jersey

Senators

Mahlon Dickerson (D)
Samuel L. Southard s. 1821
James J. Wilson (D) r. Jan. 1821

Representatives

Ephraim Bateman (D)
Joseph Bloomfield (D)
John Condit r. Nov. 1819
Charles Kinsey s. 1820
John Linn d. Jan. 1821
Bernard Smith
Henry Southard (D)

New York

Senators

Rufus King (F)
Nathan Sanford (D)

Representatives

Nathaniel Allen
Caleb Baker
Walter Case
Robert Clark (D)
Jacob H. De Witt (D)
John D. Dickinson (F)
John Fay (D)

William D. Ford (D)
Ezra C. Gross (D)
James Guyon, Jr. (F) s. 1820
Aaron Hackley, Jr.
George Hall (D)
Joseph S. Lyman
Henry Meigs (D)
Robert Monell (D)
Hermanus Peek
Nathaniel Pitcher (D)
Jonathan Richmond
Henry R. Storrs (F)
Randall S. Street
James Strong (F)
John W. Taylor (D)
Caleb Tompkins
Albert H. Tracy (D)
Solomon Van Rensselaer (F)
Peter H. Wendover (D)
Silas Wood (D)

North Carolina

Senators

Nathaniel Macon (D)
Montfort Stokes (D)

Representatives

William S. Blackledge (D) s. 1821
Hutchins G. Burton
John Culpepper (F)
William Davidson (F)
Weldon N. Edwards (D)
Charles Fisher (D)
Thomas H. Hall (D)
Charles Hooks (D)
Lemuel Sawyer (D)
Thomas Settle (D)
Jesse Slocumb (F) d. Dec. 1820
James S. Smith (D)
Felix Walker (D)
Lewis Williams

Ohio

Senators

Benjamin Ruggles (D)
William A. Trimble

Representatives

Philemon Beecher (F)
Henry Brush
John W. Campbell (D)
Samuel Herrick (D)
Thomas R. Ross (D)
John Sloane (W)

Pennsylvania

Senators

Walter Lowrie (D)
Jonathan Roberts

Representatives

Henry Baldwin (F)
Andrew Boden
William Darlington (D)
George Denison (D)
Samuel Edwards (F)
Thomas Forrest
David Fullerton r. May 1820

Samuel Gross (D)
Joseph Hemphill (E)
Jacob Hibshman
Joseph Hiester r. Dec. 1820
Jacob Hostetter (D)
Thomas G. McCullough s. 1820
William P. Maclay (D)
David Marchand
Robert Moore
Samuel Moore (D)
John Murray
Thomas Patterson (D)
Robert Philson
Thomas J. Rogers (D)
John Sergeant (F)
Christian Tarr
Daniel Udree (D) s. 1821
James M. Wallace

Rhode Island

Senators

James Burrill, Jr. d. Dec. 1820
William Hunter (F)
Nehemiah R. Knight (AF) s. 1821

Representatives

Samuel Eddy (D)
Nathaniel Hazard (D) d. Dec. 1820

South Carolina

Senators

John Gaillard (D)
William Smith (D)

Representatives

Joseph Brevard (W)
Elias Earle (D)
James Ervin (D)
William Lowndes (D)
John McCreary
James Overstreet
Charles Pinckney (D)
Eldred Simkins (D)
Starling Tucker

Tennessee

Senators

John H. Eaton (D)
John Williams

Representatives

Robert Allen (D)
Henry H. Bryan
Newton Cannon (D)
John Cocke
Francis Jones
John Rhea (D)

Vermont

Senators

William A. Palmer (D)
Isaac Tichenor (F)

Representatives

Samuel C. Crafts
Rollin C. Mallary s. 1820
Ezra Meech (D)
Orsamus C. Merrill (D) r. Jan. 1820
Charles Rich (D)
Mark Richards (D)
William Strong

Virginia

Senators

James Barbour (SR)
John W. Eppes r. Dec. 1819
James Pleasants (D)

Representatives

Mark Alexander (D)
William S. Archer s. 1820
William Lee Ball (D)
Philip P. Barbour (D)
William A. Burwell (D) d. Feb. 1821
John Floyd (D)
Robert S. Garnett (D)
John C. Gray s. 1820
Edward B. Jackson s. 1820
James Johnson (D) r. Feb. 1820
James Jones (D)
William McCoy (D)
Charles F. Mercer (D)
Thomas L. Moore s. 1820
Hugh Nelson (D)
Thomas Newton, Jr. (D)
Severn E. Parker (D)
James Pindall (F) r. July 1820
James Pleasants (D) r. Dec. 1819
John Randolph (SRD)
Ballard Smith
Alexander Smyth
George F. Strother (D) r. Feb. 1820
George Tucker (D)
John Tyler (D)
Thomas Van Swearingen
Jared Williams (D)

Seventeenth Congress

(Mar. 9, 1821, to
Mar. 3, 1823)

President of the Senate: Daniel
D. Tompkins
*President Pro Tempore of the
Senate:* John Gaillard
*Speaker of the House of
Representatives:* Philip P.
Barbour

Alabama

Senators

William Kelly (D) s. 1823
William R. King (D)
John W. Walker (D) r. Dec. 1823

Representatives

Gabriel Moore

Connecticut

Senators

Elijah Boardman (D)
James Lanman (D)

Representatives

Noyes Barber (D)
Daniel Burrows (D)
Henry W. Edwards (D)
John Russ (D)
Ansel Sterling
Ebenezer Stoddard
Gideon Tomlinson (D)

Delaware

Senators

Caesar A. Rodney (D) s. 1822
Nicholas Van Dyke (F)

Representatives

Louis McLane (D)
Caesar A. Rodney (D) r. Jan. 1822
Daniel Rodney (F) s. 1822

Georgia

Senators

John Elliott
Freeman Walker (D) r. Aug. 1821
Nicholas Ware

Representatives

Joel Abbott (D)
Alfred Cuthbert (D)
George R. Gilmer (D)
Robert R. Reid (D)
Edward F. Tattnall (D)
Wiley Thompson (D)

Illinois

Senators

Ninian Edwards (D)
Jesse B. Thomas

Representatives

Daniel P. Cook

Indiana

Senators

James Noble
Waller Taylor (D)

Representatives

William Hendricks r. 1821
Jonathan Jennings s. 1822

Kentucky

Senators

Richard M. Johnson (D)
Isham Talbot

Representatives

James D. Breckinridge s. 1822
Wingfield Bullock d. Oct. 1821
Benjamin Hardin
Francis Johnson (D)
John T. Johnson (D)
Thomas Metcalfe (D)
Thomas Montgomery (D)
Anthony New (D)
George Robertson r. 1821
John S. Smith (D)
David Trimble (D)
Samuel H. Woodson

Louisiana

Senators

James Brown
Henry Johnson

Representatives

Josiah S. Johnston (D)

Maine

Senators

John Chandler (D)
John Holmes (D)

Representatives

Joshua Cushman (D)
Joseph Dane (F)
Mark Harris s. 1822
Ebenezer Herrick
Mark L. Hill
Enoch Lincoln
Ezekiel Whitman r. June 1822
William D. Williamson (D)

Maryland

Senators

Edward Lloyd (D)
William Pinkney d. Feb. 1822
Samuel Smith (D) s. 1822

Representatives

Thomas Bayly (D)
Jeremiah Cosden r. Mar. 1822
Joseph Kent (D)
Peter Little (D)
Isaac McKim (D) s. 1823
Raphael Neale
John Nelson (D)
Philip Reed s. 1822
Samuel Smith (D) r. Dec. 1822
Henry R. Warfield (F)
Robert Wright (D)

Massachusetts

Senators

James Lloyd (F) s. 1822
Elijah H. Mills (F)
Harrison Gray Otis (F) r. May 1822

Representatives

Samuel C. Allen
Gideon Barstow (D)
Francis Baylies
Lewis Bigelow
Henry W. Dwight
William Eustis (D)
Timothy Fuller (D)
Benjamin Gorham
Aaron Hobart (D)
Samuel Lathrop (F)
Jeremiah Nelson (F)
John Reed
Jonathan Russell (D)

Mississippi

Senators

David Holmes (D)
Thomas H. Williams (D)

Representatives

Christopher Rankin (D)

Missouri

Senators

David Barton
Thomas H. Benton (D)

Representatives

John Scott

New Hampshire

Senators

David L. Morril (D)
John F. Parrott (D)

Representatives

Josiah Butler (D)
Matthew Harvey (D)
Aaron Matson
William Plumer, Jr. (D)
Nathaniel Upham (D)
Thomas Whipple, Jr.

New Jersey

Senators

Mahlon Dickerson (D)
Samuel L. Southard (D)

Representatives

Ephraim Bateman (D)
George Cassedy (D)
Lewis Condict (AF)
George Holcombe (D)

James Matlack
Samuel Swan

New York

Senators

Rufus King (F)
Martin Van Buren (D)

Representatives

Charles Borland, Jr.
Churchill C. Cambreleng (D)
Samuel Campbell
Cadwallader D. Colden (D)
Alfred Conkling
John D. Dickinson (F)
John Gebhard
James Hawkes
Thomas H. Hubbard (D)
Joseph Kirkland
Elisha Litchfield (D)
Richard McCarty (D)
John J. Morgan (D)
Walter Patterson
Jeremiah H. Pierson (F)
Nathaniel Pitcher (D)
William B. Rochester (D)
Charles H. Ruggles
Elijah Spencer (D)
Micah Sterling (F)
John W. Taylor
Albert H. Tracy (D)
Selah Tuthill d. Sept. 1821
Solomon Van Rensselaer (F) r.
    Jan. 1822
Stephen Van Rensselaer (F) s.
    1822
William W. Van Wyck (D)
Reuben H. Walworth (D)
Silas Wood (D)
David Woodcock (D)

North Carolina

Senators

Nathaniel Macon (D)
Montfort Stokes (D)

Representatives

William S. Blackledge (D)
Hutchins G. Burton
Henry W. Connor (D)
Josiah Crudup
Weldon N. Edwards (D)
Thomas H. Hall (D)
Charles Hooks (D)
John Long
Archibald McNeill
Romulus M. Saunders (D)
Lemuel Sawyer (D)
Felix Walker (D)
Lewis Williams

Ohio

Senators

Ethan Allen Brown (D) s. 1822
Benjamin Ruggles (D)
William A. Trimble d. Dec.
    1821

Representatives

Levi Barber
John W. Campbell (D)
David Chambers
Thomas R. Ross (D)
John Sloane
Joseph Vance (D)

Pennsylvania

Senators

William Findlay (D)
Walter Lowrie (D)

Representatives

Henry Baldwin (F) r. May 1822
John Brown
James Buchanan (F)
William Darlington (D)
George Denison (D)
Samuel Edwards (F)
Patrick Farrelly (D)
John Findlay (D)
Thomas Forrest s. 1822
Walter Forward (D) s. 1822
Samuel Gross (D)
Joseph Hemphill (F)
Samuel D. Ingham (D) s. 1822
James McSherry
William Milnor (F) r. May
    1822
James S. Mitchell (D)
Samuel Moore (D) r. May 1822
Thomas Murray, Jr. (D)
Thomas Patterson (D)
John Phillips (F)
George Plumer (D)
Thomas J. Rogers (D)
John Sergeant (F)
Andrew Stewart
John Todd
Daniel Udree (D) s. 1822
Ludwig Worman (F) d. Oct.
    1822

Rhode Island

Senators

James DeWolf (D)
Nehemiah R. Knight (AF)

Representatives

Job Durfee (D)
Samuel Eddy (D)

South Carolina

Senators

John Gaillard (D)
William Smith (D)

Representatives

James Blair (D) r. May 1822
John Carter s. 1822
Joseph Gist (D)
Andrew R. Govan s. 1822
James Hamilton, Jr. (SRD) s.
    1823
William Lowndes (D) r. May
    1822
George McDuffie (D)

Thomas R. Mitchell
James Overstreet d. May 1822
Joel R. Poinsett (D)
Starling Tucker
John Wilson

Tennessee

Senators

John H. Eaton (D)
John Williams (D)

Representatives

Robert Allen (D)
Newton Cannon (D)
John Cocke
Francis Jones
John Rhea (D)

Vermont

Senators

William A. Palmer (D)
Horatio Seymour (D)

Representatives

Samuel C. Crafts (D)
Elias Keyes (R)
Rollin C. Mallary (D)
John Mattocks
Charles Rich (D)
Phineas White (D)

Virginia

Senators

James Barbour
James Pleasants (D) r. Dec.
    1822
John Taylor (D) s. 1822

Representatives

Mark Alexander (D)
William S. Archer (D)
William Lee Ball (D)
Philip P. Barbour (D)
Burwell Bassett (D)
John Floyd (D)
Robert S. Garnett (D)
Edward B. Jackson (D)
James Jones (D)
Jabez Leftwich
William McCoy (D)
Charles F. Mercer (D)
Thomas L. Moore (D)
Hugh Nelson (D) r. Jan. 1823
Thomas Newton, Jr. (D)
John Randolph (SRD)
Arthur Smith
William Smith
Alexander Smyth
James Stephenson (F) s. 1822
Andrew Stevenson (D)
George Tucker (D)
Thomas Van Swearingen d.
    Aug. 1822
Jared Williams (D)

Eighteenth Congress

(Mar. 4, 1823, to
Mar. 3, 1825)

President of the Senate: Daniel
    D. Tompkins
*President Pro Tempore of the
    Senate:* John Gaillard
*Speaker of the House of
    Representatives:* Henry Clay

Alabama

Senators

William Kelly (D)
William R. King (D)

Representatives

John McKee
Gabriel Moore
George W. Owen

Connecticut

Senators

Elijah Boardman (D) d. Oct.
    1823
Henry W. Edwards (D)
James Lanman (D)

Representatives

Noyes Barber (D)
Samuel A. Foote (AF)
Ansel Sterling
Ebenezer Stoddard
Gideon Tomlinson (D)
Lemuel Whitman (D)

Delaware

Senators

Thomas Clayton s. 1824
Nicholas Van Dyke (F)

Representatives

Louis McLane (D)

Georgia

Senators

Thomas W. Cobb s. 1824
John Elliott
Nicholas Ware d. Sept. 1824

Representatives

Joel Abbot (D)
George Cary
Thomas W. Cobb r. Dec. 1824
Alfred Cuthbert (D)
John Forsyth (D)
Edward F. Tattnall (D)
Wiley Thompson (D)
Richard H. Wilde (D)

Illinois

Senators

Ninian Edwards (D) r. Mar.
1824
John McLean (D) s. 1824
Jesse B. Thomas

Representatives

Daniel P. Cook

Indiana

Senators

James Nobel
Waller Taylor (D)

Representatives

Jacob Call s. 1824
Jonathan Jennings (D)
William Prince d. Sept. 1824
John Test (D)

Kentucky

Senators

Richard M. Johnson (D)
Isham Talbot

Representatives

Richard A. Buckner (D)
Henry Clay
Robert P. Henry (D)
Francis Johnson (D)
John T. Johnson (D)
Robert P. Letcher (D)
Thomas Metcalfe (D)
Thomas P. Moore (D)
Philip Thompson
David Trimble (D)
David White
Charles A. Wickliffe (D)

Louisiana

Senators

Dominique Bouligny s. 1824
James Brown r. Dec. 1823
Henry Johnson r. May 1824
Josiah S. Johnston (D) s. 1824

Representatives

William L. Brent
Henry H. Gurley
Edward Livingston (D)

Maine

Senators

John Chandler (D)
John Holmes (D)

Representatives

William Burleigh (D)
Joshua Cushman (D)
Ebenezer Herrick

David Kidder
Enoch Lincoln
Stephen Longfellow (F)
Jeremiah O'Brien (D)

Maryland

Senators

Edward Lloyd (D)
Samuel Smith (D)

Representatives

William Heyward, Jr. (D)
Joseph Kent (D)
John Lee (D)
Peter Little (D)
Isaac McKim (D)
George E. Mitchell (D)
Raphael Neale
John S. Spence (D)
Henry R. Warfield (F)

Massachusetts

Senators

James Lloyd (F)
Elijah H. Mills (F)

Representatives

Samuel C. Allen
John Bailey s. 1824
Francis Baylies
Benjamin W. Crowninshield (D)
Henry W. Dwight
Timothy Fuller (D)
Aaron Hobart (D)
Samuel Lathrop (F)
John Locke
Jeremiah Nelson (F)
John Reed
Jonas Sibley (D)
Daniel Webster (F)

Mississippi

Senators

David Holmes (D)
Thomas H. Williams (D)

Representatives

Christopher Rankin (D)

Missouri

Senators

David Barton
Thomas H. Benton (D)

Representatives

John Scott

New Hampshire

Senators

Samuel Bell
John F. Parrott (D)

Representatives

Ichabod Bartlett (D)
Matthew Harvey (D)
Arthur Livermore (D)
Aaron Matson
William Plumer, Jr. (D)
Thomas Whipple, Jr.

New Jersey

Senators

Mahlon Dickerson (D)
Joseph McIlvaine (D)

Representatives

George Cassedy (D)
Lewis Condict (AF)
Daniel Garrison (D)
George Holcombe (D)
James Matlack
Samuel Swan

New York

Senators

Rufus King (F)
Martin Van Buren (D)

Representatives

Parmenio Adams s. 1824
John W. Cady
Churchill C. Cambreleng (D)
Lot Clark
Ela Collins (D)
Hector Craig (D)
Rowland Day (D)
Justin Dwinell
Lewis Eaton
Charles A. Foote (D)
Joel Frost
Moses Hayden
John Herkimer (D)
James L. Hogeboom
Lemuel Jenkins (D)
Samuel Lawrence (D)
Elisha Litchfield (D)
Henry C. Martindale (D)
Dudley Marvin (D)
John J. Morgan (D)
John Richards
Robert S. Rose (D)
Peter Sharpe
Henry R. Storrs (F)
James Strong (F)
John W. Taylor (D)
Egbert Ten Eyck
Albert H. Tracy (D)
Jacob Tyson
Stephen Van Rensselaer (F)
William W. Van Wyck (D)
Isaac Williams, Jr. (D)
Isaac Wilson r. Jan. 1824
Silas Wood (D)

North Carolina

Senators

John Branch (D)
Nathaniel Macon (D)

Representatives

Hutchins G. Burton r. Mar.
1824
Henry W. Connor (D)
John Culpepper (F)
Weldon N. Edwards (D)
Alfred M. Gatlin (D)
Thomas H. Hall (D)
Charles Hooks (D)
John Long
Willie P. Mangum
George Outlaw (D) s. 1825
Romulus M. Saunders (D)
Richard D. Spaight, Jr. (D)
Robert B. Vance (D)
Lewis Williams

Ohio

Senators

Ethan Allen Brown (D)
Benjamin Ruggles (D)

Representatives

Mordecai Bartley
Philemon Beecher (F)
John W. Campbell (D)
James W. Gazlay (D)
Duncan McArthur (D)
William McLean
John Patterson (D)
Thomas R. Ross (D)
John Sloane
Joseph Vance (D)
Samuel F. Vinton
Elisha Whittlesey
William Wilson (D)
John C. Wright (D)

Pennsylvania

Senators

William Findlay (D)
Walter Lowrie (D)

Representatives

James Allison, Jr.
Samuel Breck (F)
John Brown
James Buchanan (F)
Samuel Edwards (F)
William C. Ellis (F)
Patrick Farrelly (D)
John Findlay (D)
Walter Forward (D)
Robert Harris
Joseph Hemphill (F)
Samuel D. Ingham (D)
George Kremer
Samuel McKean (D)
Philip S. Markley (D)
Daniel H. Miller (D)
James S. Mitchell (D)
Thomas Patterson (D)
George Plumer (D)
Thomas J. Rogers r. Apr. 1824
Andrew Stewart
John Todd (D) r. 1824
Alexander Thomson s. 1824
Daniel Udree (D)
Isaac Wayne
Henry Wilson (D)
James Wilson
George Wolf (D) s. 1824

Rhode Island

Senators

James DeWolf (D)
Nehemiah R. Knight (AF)

Representatives

Job Durfee (D)
Samuel Eddy (D)

South Carolina

Senators

John Gaillard (D)
Robert Y. Hayne (D)

Representatives

Robert B. Campbell
John Carter
Joseph Gist (D)
Andrew R. Govan
James Hamilton, Jr. (SRD)
George McDuffie (D)
Joel R. Poinsett (D)
Starling Tucker
John Wilson

Tennessee

Senators

John H. Eaton (D)
Andrew Jackson

Representatives

Adam R. Alexander (F)
Robert Allen (D)
John Blair (D)
John Cocke
Sam Houston   (D)
Jacob C. Isacks
James B. Reynolds (D)
James T. Sandford
James Standifer

Vermont

Senators

William A. Palmer (D)
Horatio Seymour (D)

Representatives

William C. Bradley (D)
Daniel A. A. Buck (D)
Samuel C. Crafts
Rollin C. Mallary
Henry Olin (D) s. 1824
Charles Rich (D) d. Oct. 1824

Virginia

Senators

James Barbour
John Taylor d. Aug. 1824
Littleton W. Tazewell (D) s. 1824

Representatives

Mark Alexander (D)
William S. Archer
William Lee Ball(D) d. Feb. 1824
John S. Barbour (SRD)
Philip P. Barbour (SRD)
Burwell Bassett (D)
John Floyd (D)
Robert S. Garnett (D)
Joseph Johnson (D)
Jabez Leftwich
William McCoy (D)
Charles F. Mercer (D)
Thomas Newton, Jr. (D)
John Randolph (SRD)
William C. Rives (D)
Arthur Smith
William Smith
Alexander Smyth
James Stephenson (F)
Andrew Stephenson (D)
John Taliaferro (D) s. 1824
George Tucker (D)
Jared Williams (D)

Nineteenth Congress

(Mar. 4, 1825, to
Mar. 3, 1827)

President of the Senate: John C. Calhoun
Presidents Pro Tempore of the Senate: John Gaillard; Nathaniel Macon
Speaker of the House of Representatives: John W. Taylor

Alabama

Senators

Henry H. Chambers (D) d. Jan. 1826
William R. King (D)
John McKinley (D) s. 1826
Israel Pickens (D) ta. 1826

Representatives

John McKee
Gabriel Moore
George W. Owen

Connecticut

Senators

Henry W. Edwards (D)
Calvin Willey

Representatives

John Baldwin
Noyes Barber (D)
Ralph I. Ingersoll (D)
Orange Merwin
Elisha Phelps (D)
Gideon Tomlinson (D)

Delaware

Senators

Thomas Clayton
Henry M. Ridgeley (F) s. 1827
Daniel Rodney (F) ta. 1826
Nicholas Van Dyke (F) d. May 1826

Representatives

Louis McLane (D) r. 1825

Georgia

Senators

John M. Berrien (D)
Thomas W. Cobb

Representatives

George Cary
Alfred Cuthbert (D)
John Forsyth (D)
Charles E. Haynes (D)
James Meriwether
Edward F. Tattnall
Wiley Thompson (D)

Illinois

Senators

Elias K. Kane (D)
Jesse B. Thomas

Representatives

Daniel P. Cook

Indiana

Senators

William Hendricks (D)
James Noble

Representatives

Ratliff Boon (D)
Jonathan Jennings (D)
John Test (D)

Kentucky

Senators

Richard M. Johnson (D)
John Rowan (D)

Representatives

Richard A. Buckner (AF)
James Clark (D)
John F. Henry s. 1826
Robert P. Henry (D) d. Aug. 1826
Francis Johnson (D)
James Johnson (D) d. Aug. 1826
Joseph Lecompte (D)
Robert P. Letcher (D)
Robert McHatton (D) s. 1826
Thomas Metcalfe (D)

(Kentucky cont.)

Thomas P. Moore (D)
David Trimble (D)
Charles A. Wickliffe (D)
William S. Young (D)

Louisiana

Senators

Dominique Bouligny (D)
Josiah S. Johnston (D)

Representatives

William L. Brent
Henry H. Gurley
Edward Livingston (D)

Maine

Senators

John Chandler (D)
John Holmes (D)

Representatives

John Anderson (D)
William Burleigh (D)
Ebenezer Herrick
David Kidder
Enoch Lincoln r. Jan. 1826
Jeremiah O'Brien (D)
James W. Ripley (D) s. 1826
Peleg Sprague

Maryland

Senators

Ezekiel F. Chambers s. 1826
Edward Lloyd (D) r. Jan. 1826
Samuel Smith (D)

Representatives

John Barney (F)
Clement Dorsey
Joseph Kent (D) r. Jan. 1826
John L. Kerr
Peter Little (D)
Robert N. Martin (D)
George E. Mitchell (D)
George Peter (D)
John C. Weems (D) s. 1826
Thomas C. Worthington (D)

Massachusetts

Senators

James Lloyd (F) r. Jan. 1826
Elijah H. Mills (F)
Nathaniel Silsbee (D) s. 1826

Representatives

Samuel C. Allen
John Bailey
Francis Baylies
Benjamin W. Crowninshield (D)
John Davis (NR)
Henry W. Dwight
Edward Everett (MR)
Aaron Hobart (D)
Samuel Lathrop (F)
John Locke

John Reed
John Varnum (F)
Daniel Webster (F)

Mississippi

Senators

Powhatan Ellis (D) ta. 1825
David Holmes (R) r. Sept. 1825
Thomas B. Reed (D) s. 1826
Thomas H. Williams (D)

Representatives

William Haile s. 1826
Christopher Rankin (D) r. Mar.
1826

Missouri

Senators

David Barton
Thomas H. Benton (D)

Representatives

John Scott

New Hampshire

Senators

Samuel Bell
Levi Woodbury

Representatives

Ichabod Bartlett (D)
Titus Brown
Nehemiah Eastman (D)
Jonathan Harvey
Joseph Healy (D)
Thomas Whipple, Jr.

New Jersey

Senators

Ephraim Bateman (D) s. 1826
Mahlon Dickerson (D)
Joseph McIlvaine d. Aug. 1826

Representatives

George Cassedy (D)
Lewis Condict (AF)
Daniel Garrison (D)
George Holcombe (D)
Samuel Swan
Ebenezer Tucker

New York

Senators

Nathan Sanford (D) s. 1826
Martin Van Buren (D)

Representatives

Parmenio Adams
William G. Angel (D)
Henry Ashley
Luther Badger

Churchill C. Cambreleng (D)
William Dietz (D)
Nicoll Fosdick
Daniel G. Garnsey (D)
John Hallock, Jr. (D)
Abraham B. Hasbrouck (NR)
Moses Hayden
Michael Hoffman (D)
Daniel Hugunin, Jr.
Charles Humphrey (D)
Jeromus Johnson (D)
Charles Kellogg
William McManus
Henry Markell (D)
Henry C. Martindale (D)
Dudley Marvin (D)
John Miller
Timothy H. Porter
Robert S. Rose
Henry H. Ross
Joshua Sands
Henry R. Storrs (F)
James Strong (F)
John W. Taylor (D)
Egbert Ten Eyck r. Dec. 1825
Stephen Van Rensselaer (F)
Gulian C. Verplanck (D)
Aaron Ward (D)
Bartow White
Elias Whitmore (D)
Silas Wood (D)

North Carolina

Senators

John Branch (D)
Nathaniel Macon (D)

Representatives

Willis Alston (D)
Daniel L. Barringer (D) s. 1826
John H. Bryan (D)
Samuel P. Carson (D)
Henry W. Connor (D)
Weldon N. Edwards (D)
Richard Hines (D)
Gabriel Holmes
John Long
Archibald McNeill
Willie P. Mangum r. Mar. 1826
Romulus M. Saunders (D)
Lemuel Sawyer (D)
Lewis Williams

Ohio

Senators

William Henry Harrison
Benjamin Ruggles (D)

Representatives

Mordecai Bartley (NR)
Philemon Beecher (F)
John W. Campbell (D)
James Findlay (D)
David Jennings r. May 1826
William McLean
Thomas Shannon (D) s. 1826
John Sloane
John Thomson (D)
Joseph Vance (D)
Samuel F. Vinton
Elisha Whittlesey
William Wilson (D)
John Woods

John C. Wright (D)

Pennsylvania

Senators

William Findlay (D)
William Marks (D)

Representatives

William Addams (D)
James Allison, Jr. r. 1825
James Buchanan (D)
Samuel Edwards (F)
Patrick Farrelly (D) d. Jan.
1826
John Findlay (D)
Chauncey Forward (D) s. 1826
Robert Harris
Joseph Hemphill (F) r. 1826
Samuel D. Ingham (D)
Thomas Kittera (F) s. 1826
Jacob Krebs (D) s. 1826
George Kremer
Joseph Lawrence
Samuel McKean (D)
Philip S. Markley (D)
Daniel H. Miller (D)
Charles Miner (F)
James S. Mitchell (D)
John Mitchell (D)
Robert Orr, Jr. (D)
George Plumer (D)
Thomas H. Sill
James S. Stevenson (D)
Andrew Stewart (D)
Alexander Thomson r. May
1826
Espy Van Horne (D)
Henry Wilson (D) d. Aug. 1826
James Wilson (D)
George Wolf (D)
John Wurts (NR)

Rhode Island

Senators

James DeWolf r. Oct. 1825
Nehemiah R. Knight (AF)
Asher Robbins

Representatives

Tristam Burges (F)
Dutee J. Pearce (D)

South Carolina

Senators

John Gaillard (D) d. Feb. 1826
William Harper (D) s. 1826
Robert Y. Hayne (D) s. 1826
William Smith (D)

Representatives

John Carter (D)
William Drayton (D)
Joseph Gist (D)
Andrew R. Govan (D)
James Hamilton, Jr. (SRD)
George McDuffie (D)
Thomas R. Mitchell (D)
Joel R. Poinsett (D) r. Mar.
1825

Starling Tucker
John Wilson

Tennessee

Senators

John H. Eaton (D)
Andrew Jackson r. Oct. 1825
Hugh L. White

Representatives

Adam R. Alexander (F)
Robert Allen (D)
John Blair (D)
John Cocke
Sam Houston (D)
Jacob C. Isacks
John H. Marable (NR)
James C. Mitchell
James K. Polk (D)

Vermont

Senators

Dudley Chase (D)
Horatio Seymour (D)

Representatives

William C. Bradley (D)
Rollin C. Mallary
John Mattocks
Ezra Meech (D)
George E. Wales

Virginia

Senators

James Barbour r. Mar. 1825
John Randolph (SRD)
Littleton W. Tazewell (D)

Representatives

Mark Alexander (D)
William S. Archer (D)
William Armstrong (D)
John S. Barbour (SRD)
Burwell Bassett (D)
Nathaniel H. Claiborne (F)
George W. Crump (D) s. 1826
Thomas Davenport (F)
Benjamin Estil
John Floyd (D)
Robert S. Garnett (D)
Joseph Johnson (D)
William McCoy (D)
Charles F. Mercer (D)
Thomas Newton, Jr. (D)
Alfred H. Powell
John Randolph (SRD) r. Dec.
1825
William C. Rives (D)
William Smith
Andrew Stevenson (D)
John Taliaferro (D)
Robert Taylor
James Trezvant

Twentieth Congress

(Mar. 4, 1827, to
Mar. 3, 1829)

President of the Senate: John C.
Calhoun
*President Pro Tempore of the
Senate:* Samuel Smith
*Speaker of the House of
Representatives:* Andrew
Stevenson

Alabama

Senators

William R. King (D)
John McKinley (D)

Representatives

John McKee
Gabriel Moore
George W. Owen

Connecticut

Senators

Samuel A. Foote
Calvin Willey (D)

Representatives

John Baldwin
Noyes Barber (D)
Ralph I. Ingersoll (D)
Orange Merwin
Elisha Phelps (D)
David Plant (NR)

Delaware

Senators

Louis McLane (D)
Henry M. Ridgeley (F)

Representatives

Kensey Johns, Jr. (F)

Georgia

Senators

John M. Berrien (D)
Thomas W. Cobb r. 1828
Oliver H. Prince s. 1828

Representatives

John Floyd
John Forsyth (D) r. Nov. 1827
Tomlinson Fort (D)
George R. Gilmer
Charles E. Haynes (D)
Wilson Lumpkin (D)
Edward F. Tattnall r. 1827
Richard H. Wilde (D) s. 1828
Wiley Thompson (D)

Illinois

Senators

Elias K. Kane (D)
Jesse B. Thomas

Representatives

Joseph Duncan (D)

Indiana

Senators

William Hendricks (D)
James Noble

Representatives

Thomas H. Blake
Jonathan Jennings (D)
Oliver H. Smith

Kentucky

Senators

Richard M. Johnson (D)
John Rowan (D)

Representatives

Richard A. Buckner (D)
John Chambers s. 1828
Thomas Chilton s. 1828
James Clark (D)
Henry Daniel (D)
Joseph Lecompte (D)
Robert P. Letcher (D)
Chittenden Lyon (D)
Robert McHatton (D)
Thomas Metcalfe r. June 1828
Thomas P. Moore (D)
Charles A. Wickliffe (D)
Joel Yancey (D)
William S. Young (D) d. Sept.
1827

Louisiana

Senators

Dominique Bouligny
Josiah S. Johnson (D)

Representatives

William L. Brent
Henry H. Gurley
Edward Livingston (D)

Maine

Senators

John Chandler (D)
John Holmes (D) s. 1829
Albion K. Parris (D) r. Aug.
1828

Representatives

John Anderson (D)
Samuel Butman
Rufus McIntire (D)

Jeremiah O'Brien (D)
James W. Ripley (D)
Peleg Sprague
Joseph F. Wingate (D)

Maryland

Senators

Ezekiel F. Chambers
Samuel Smith (D)

Representatives

John Barney (F)
Clement Dorsey
Levin Gale
John L. Kerr
Peter Little (D)
Michael C. Sprigg (D)
George C. Washington
John C. Weems (D)
Ephraim K. Wilson (D)

Massachusetts

Senators

Nathaniel Silsbee (D)
Daniel Webster (F)

Representatives

Samuel C. Allen
John Bailey
Isaac C. Bates (D)
Benjamin W. Crowninshield (D)
John Davis (NR)
Henry W. Dwight
Edward Everett (NR)
Benjamin Gorham (D)
James L. Hodges
John Locke
John Reed
Joseph Richardson
John Varnum (F)

Mississippi

Senators

Powhatan Ellis (D)
Thomas H. Williams (D)

Representatives

William Haile r. Sept. 1828
Thomas Hinds s. 1828

Missouri

Senators

David Barton
Thomas H. Benton (D)

Representatives

Edward Bates

New Hampshire

Senators

Samuel Bell
Levi Woodbury (D)

Representatives

David Barker, Jr.
Ichabod Bartlett (D)
Titus Brown
Jonathan Harvey
Joseph Healy (D)
Thomas Whipple, Jr.

New Jersey

Senators

Ephraim Bateman (D) r. Jan.
1829
Mahlon Dickerson (D)

Representatives

Lewis Condict (AF)
George Holcombe (D) d. Jan.
1828
Isaac Pierson
James F. Randolph s. 1828
Thomas Sinnickson s. 1828
Samuel Swan
Hedge Thompson d. July 1828
Ebenezer Tucker

New York

Senators

Charles E. Dudley (D) s. 1829
Nathan Sanford (D)
Martin Van Buren (D) r. Dec.
1829

Representatives

Daniel D. Barnard
George O. Belden (D)
Rudolph Bunner (D)
Churchill C. Cambreleng (D)
Samuel Chase (D)
John C. Clark (D)
John I. DeGraff (D)
John D. Dickinson (D)
Jonas Earll, Jr. (D)
Daniel G. Garnsey (D)
Nathaniel Garrow (D)
John Hallock, Jr. (D)
Selah R. Hobbie (D)
Michael Hoffman (D)
Jeromus Johnson (D)
Richard Keese (D)
John Magee (D)
Henry Markell (D)
Henry C. Martindale (D)
Dudley Marvin (D)
John Maynard
Thomas J. Oakley (D)
Henry R. Storrs (F)
John G. Stower (D)
James Strong (D)
Thomas Taber (D) s. 1828
John W. Taylor (D)
Phineas L. Tracy
Stephen Van Rensselaer (F)
Gulian C. Verplanck (D)
Aaron Ward (D)
John J. Wood (D)
Silas Wood (D)
David Woodcock (D)
Silas Wright, Jr. (D) r. Feb.
1829

North Carolina

Senators

John Branch (D)
James Iredell (D) s. 1828
Nathaniel Macon (D) r. Feb.
1828

Representatives

Willis Alston (D)
Daniel L. Barringer (D)
John H. Bryan (D)
Samuel P. Carson (D)
Henry W. Connor (D)
John Culpepper (F)
Thomas H. Hall (D)
Gabriel Holmes (D)
John Long (W)
Lemuel Sawyer (D)
Augustine H. Shepperd (D)
Daniel Turner (D)
Lewis Williams

Ohio

Senators

Jacob Burnet (F) s. 1828
William Henry Harrison r. May
1828
Benjamin Ruggles (D)

Representatives

Mordecai Bartley (NR)
Philemon Beecher (F)
William Creighton, Jr. r. 1828
John Davenport (D)
James Findlay (D)
William McLean
Francis S. Muhlenberg (NR) s.
1828
William Russell (D)
John Sloane (D)
William Stanbery (D)
Joseph Vance (D)
Samuel F. Vinton (D)
Elisha Whittlesey
William Wilson (D) d. June
1827
John Woods (D)
John C. Wright (D)

Pennsylvania

Senators

Isaac D. Barnard (F)
William Marks (D)

Representatives

William Addams (D)
Samuel Anderson
Stephen Barlow (D)
James Buchanan (F)
Richard Coulter (D)
Chauncey Forward (D)
Joseph Fry, Jr. (D)
Innis Green (D)
Samuel D. Ingham (D)
Adam King (D)
George Kremer (D)
Joseph Lawrence
Samuel McKean (D)
Daniel H. Miller (D)

Charles Miner (F)
John Mitchell (D)
Robert Orr, Jr. (D)
William Ramsey (D)
John Sergeant (F)
John B. Sterigere (D)
James S. Stevenson (D)
Andrew Stewart (D)
Joel B. Sutherland (D)
Espy Van Horne (D)
James Wilson (D)
George Wolf (D)

Rhode Island

Senators

Nehemiah R. Knight (AF)
Asher Robbins

Representatives

Tristam Burges (F)
Dutee J. Pearce (D)

South Carolina

Senators

Robert Y. Hayne (D)
William Smith (D)

Representatives

John Carter (D)
Warren R. Davis (SRD)
William Drayton (D)
James Hamilton, Jr. (SRD)
George McDuffie (D)
William D. Martin (D)
Thomas R. Mitchell
William T. Nuckolls
Starling Tucker

Tennessee

Senators

John H. Eaton (D)
Hugh L. White

Representatives

John Bell (D)
John Blair (D)
David Crockett (D)
Robert Desha
Jacob C. Isacks (D)
Pryor Lea (D)
John H. Marable (NR)
James C. Mitchell
James K. Polk (D)

Vermont

Senators

Dudley Chase (D)
Horatio Seymour (D)

Representatives

Daniel A. A. Buck (D)
Jonathan Hunt (NR)
Rollin C. Mallary
Benjamin Swift (F)
George E. Wales

Virginia

Senators

Littleton W. Tazewell (D)
John Tyler (D)

Representatives

Mark Alexander (D)
Robert Allen (D)
William S. Archer (D)
William Armstrong (D)
John S. Barbour (SRD)
Philip P. Barbour (D)
Burwell Bassett (D)
Nathaniel H. Claiborne
Thomas Davenport (F)
John Floyd (D)
Isaac Leffler
William McCoy (D)
Lewis Maxwell (NR)
Charles F. Mercer (D)
Thomas Newton, Jr. (D)
John Randolph (SRD)
William C. Rives (D)
John Roane (D)
Alexander Smyth
Andrew Stevenson (D)
John Taliaferro (D)
James Trezvant

Twenty-First Congress

(Mar. 4, 1829, to
Mar. 3, 1831)

President of the Senate: John C.
Calhoun
*President Pro Tempore of the
Senate:* Samuel Smith
*Speaker of the House of
Representatives:* Andrew
Stevenson

Alabama

Senators

William R. King (D)
John McKinley (D)

Representatives

Robert E. B. Baylor (D)
Clement Comer Clay (D)
Dixon H. Lewis (SRD)

Connecticut

Senators

Samuel A. Foote (D)
Calvin Willey (D)

Representatives

Noyes Barber (D)
William W. Ellsworth
Jabez W. Huntington
Ralph I. Ingersoll (D)
William L. Storrs
Ebenezer Young

Delaware

Senators

John M. Clayton
Louis McLane (D) r. Apr. 1829
Arnold Naudain s. 1830

Representatives

Kensey Johns, Jr. (F)

Georgia

Senators

John M. Berrien (D) r. Mar.
1829
John Forsyth (D)
George M. Troup (SRD)

Representatives

Thomas F. Foster (D)
Charles E. Haynes (D)
Henry G. Lamar (D)
Wilson Lumpkin (D)
Wiley Thompson (D)
James M. Wayne (D)
Richard H. Wilde (D)

Illinois

Senators

David J. Baker (D) s. 1830
Elias K. Kane (D)
John McLean d. Oct. 1830
John M. Robinson (D) s. 1831

Representatives

Joseph Duncan (D)

Indiana

Senators

William Hendricks (D)
James Noble d. Feb. 1831

Representatives

Ratliff Boon (D)
Jonathan Jennings (D)
John Test

Kentucky

Senators

George M. Bibb
John Rowan (D)

Representatives

Thomas Chilton (D)
James Clark (D)
Nicholas D. Coleman (D)
Henry Daniel (D)
Nathan Gaither (D)
Richard M. Johnson (D)
John Kincaid (D)
Joseph Lecompte (D)
Robert P. Letcher (D)
Chittenden Lyon (D)

Charles A. Wickliffe (D)
Joel Yancey (D)

Louisiana

Senators

Josiah S. Johnston (D)
Edward Livingston (D)

Representatives

Henry H. Gurley (D)
Walter H. Overton (D)
Edward D. White

Maine

Senators

John Holmes (D)
Peleg Sprague (NR)

Representatives

John Anderson (D)
Samuel Butman
George Evans
Cornelius Holland (D) s. 1830
Leonard Jarvis (D)
Rufus McIntire (D)
James W. Ripley (D) r. Mar.
 1830
Joseph F. Wingate (D)

Maryland

Senators

Ezekiel F. Chambers (D)
Samuel Smith (D)

Representatives

Elias Brown (W)
Clement Dorsey
Benjamin C. Howard (D)
George E. Mitchell (D)
Benedict J. Semmes (D)
Richard Spencer (D)
Michael C. Sprigg (D)
George C. Washington (D)
Ephraim K. Wilson (D)

Massachusetts

Senators

Nathaniel Silsbee (D)
Daniel Webster

Representatives

John Bailey
Isaac C. Bates
Benjamin W. Crowninshield (D)
John Davis (NR)
Henry W. Dwight
Edward Everett (NR)
Benjamin Gorham
George Grennell, Jr.
James L. Hodges
Joseph G. Kendall
John Reed
Joseph Richardson
John Varnum

Mississippi

Senators

Robert H. Adams (D) d. Nov.
 1830
Powhatan Ellis (D)
George Poindexter s. 1830
Thomas B. Reed (D) d. Nov.
 1820

Representatives

Thomas Hinds (D)

Missouri

Senators

David Barton
Thomas H. Benton (D)

Representatives

Spencer D. Pettis (D)

New Hampshire

Senators

Samuel Bell
Levi Woodbury (D)

Representatives

John Brodhead (D)
Thomas Chandler (D)
Joseph Hammons (D)
Jonathan Harvey
Henry Hubbard (D)
John W. Weeks

New Jersey

Senators

Mahlon Dickerson (D)
Theodore Frelinghuysen (D)

Representatives

Lewis Condict (AF)
Richard M. Cooper
Thomas H. Hughes (W)
Isaac Pierson
James F. Randolph
Samuel Swan

New York

Senators

Charles E. Dudley (D)
Nathan Sanford (D)

Representatives

William G. Angel (D)
Benedict Arnold
Thomas Beekman
Abraham Bockee (D)
Peter I. Borst (D)
Churchill C. Cambreleng (D)
Timothy Childs
Henry B. Cowles
Hector Craig (D) r. July 1830

Jacob Crocheron (D)
Charles G. DeWitt (D)
John D. Dickinson
Samuel W. Eager (NR) s. 1830
Jonas Earll, Jr. (D)
Isaac Finch (D)
George Fisher r. Feb. 1830
Jehiel H. Halsey (D)
Joseph Hawkins (D)
Michael Hoffman (D)
Perkins King
James Lent (D)
John Magee (D)
Henry C. Martindale (D)
Thomas Maxwell (D)
Robert Monell (D) r. Feb. 1831
Ebenezer F. Norton (D)
Gershom Powers (D)
Robert S. Rose
Jonah Sanford s. 1830
Ambrose Spencer
James Strong (F)
Henry R. Storrs
John W. Taylor (D)
Phineas L. Tracy
Gulian C. Verplanck (D)
Campbell P. White (D)

North Carolina

Senators

John Branch (D) r. Mar. 1829
Bedford Brown (D)
James Iredell (D)

Representatives

Willis Alston (D)
Daniel L. Barringer (D)
Samuel P. Carson (D)
Henry W. Connor (D)
Edmund Deberry
Edward B. Dudley (NR)
Thomas H. Hall (D)
Robert Potter (D)
Abraham Rencher (NR)
William B. Shepard (NR)
Augustine H. Shepperd (D)
Jesse Speight
Lewis Williams

Ohio

Senators

Jacob Burnet (F)
Benjamin Ruggles (D)

Representatives

Mordecai Bartley
Joseph H. Crane
William Creighton, Jr. (D)
James Findlay (D)
William W. Irvin (D)
William Kennon, Sr. (D)
Humphrey H. Leavitt (D) s.
 1830
William Russell (D)
James Shields (D)
William Stanbery (D)
John Thomson (D)
Joseph Vance (D)
Samuel F. Vinton
Elisha Whittlesey

Pennsylvania

Senators

Isaac D. Barnard (F)
William Marks (D)

Representatives

James Buchanan (F)
Richard Coulter
Thomas H. Crawford (D)
Harmar Denny (Anti-Mason)
Joshua Evans, Jr. (D)
James Ford (D)
Chauncey Forward (D)
Joseph Fry, Jr. (D)
John Gilmore (D)
Innis Green (D)
Joseph Hemphill (D)
Peter Ihrie, Jr. (D)
Thomas Irwin (D)
Adam King (D)
George C. Leiper (D)
William McCreery (D)
Alem Marr (D)
Daniel H. Miller (D)
Henry A. P. Muhlenberg (D)
William Ramsey (D)
John Scott
Thomas H. Sill
Samuel A. Smith (D)
Philander Stephens (D)
John B. Sterigere (D)
Joel B. Sutherland (D)

Rhode Island

Senators

Nehemiah R. Knight (AF)
Asher Robbins

Representatives

Tristam Burges (F)
Dutee J. Pearce (D)

South Carolina

Senators

Robert Y. Hayne (D)
William Smith (D)

Representatives

Robert W. Barnwell (D)
James Blair (D)
John Campbell (SRW)
Warren R. Davis (SRD)
William Drayton (D)
George McDuffie (D)
William D. Martin (D)
William T. Nuckolls
Starling Tucker

Tennessee

Senators

John H. Eaton (D) r. Mar.
 1829
Felix Grundy (D)
Hugh L. White (D)

Representatives

John Bell (D)
John Blair (D)
David Crockett (D)
Robert Desha
Jacob C. Isacks
Cave Johnson (D)
Pryor Lea (D)
James K. Polk (D)
James Standifer (W)

Vermont

Senators

Dudley Chase (D)
Horatio Seymour (D)

Representatives

William Cahoon (Anti-Mason)
Horace Everett (W)
Jonathan Hunt (NR)
Rollin C. Mallary
Benjamin Swift (F)

Virginia

Senators

Littleton W. Tazewell
John Tyler (D)

Representatives

Mark Alexander (D)
Robert Allen (D)
William S. Archer
William Armstrong (D)
John S. Barbour (SRD)
Philip P. Barbour (D) r. Oct.
  1830
Thomas T. Bouldin (D)
Nathaniel H. Claiborne
Richard Coke, Jr. (D)
Robert Craig (D)
Thomas Davenport (F)
Philip Doddridge
Joseph Draper s. Dec. 1830
William F. Gordon (D) s. Jan.
  1830
George Loyall (D)
William McCoy (D)
Lewis Maxwell (NR)
Charles F. Mercer (D)
Thomas Newton, Jr. (D) r.
  Mar. 1830
John M. Patton (D) s. 1830
John Roane (D)
William C. Rives (D) r. 1829
Alexander Smyth d. Apr. 1830
Andrew Stevenson (D)
John Taliaferro (D)
James Trezvant

Twenty-Second Congress

(Mar. 4, 1831, to
Mar. 3, 1833)

President of the Senate: John C.
  Calhoun

*Presidents Pro Tempore of the
  Senate:* Littleton W. Tazewell;
  Hugh L. White
*Speaker of the House of
  Representatives:* Andrew
  Stevenson

Alabama

Senators

William R. King (D)
Gabriel Moore

Representatives

Clement Comer Clay (D)
Dixon H. Lewis (SRD)
Samuel W. Mardis (D)

Connecticut

Senators

Samuel A. Foote
Gideon Tomlinson

Representatives

Noyes Barber (D)
William W. Ellsworth
Jabez W. Huntington
Ralph I. Ingersoll (D)
William L. Storrs
Ebenezer Young

Delaware

Senators

John M. Clayton (W)
Arnold Naudain

Representatives

John J. Mulligan (W)

Georgia

Senators

John Forsyth (D)
George M. Troup (SRD)

Representatives

Augustin S. Clayton (SRD) s.
  1832
Thomas F. Foster (D)
Henry G. Lamar (D)
Daniel Newnan (SRD)
Wiley Thompson (D)
James M. Wayne (D)
Richard H. Wilde (D)

Illinois

Senators

Elias K. Kane (D)
John M. Robinson (D)

Representatives

Joseph Duncan (D)

Indiana

Senators

Robert Hanna
William Hendricks (D)
John Tipton (D) s. 1832

Representatives

Ratliff Boon (D)
John Carr (D)
Jonathan McCarty

Kentucky

Senators

George M. Bibb
Henry Clay (W)

Representatives

John Adair (D)
Chilton Allan (D)
Henry Daniel (D)
Nathan Gaither (D)
Albert G. Hawes (D)
Richard M. Johnson (D)
Joseph Lecompte (D)
Robert P. Letcher
Chittenden Lyon (D)
Thomas A. Marshall
Christopher Tompkins
Charles A. Wickliffe (D)

Louisiana

Senators

Josiah S. Johnson (D)
Edward Livingston (D) r. May
  1831
George A. Waggaman (NR) s.
  1832

Representatives

Henry A. Bullard
Philemon Thomas (D)
Edward D. White

Maine

Senators

John Holmes (D)
Peleg Sprague (NR)

Representatives

John Anderson (D)
James Bates (D)
George Evans (NR)
Cornelius Holland (D)
Leonard Jarvis (D)
Edward Kavanagh (D)
Rufus McIntire (D)

Maryland

Senators

Ezekiel F. Chambers
Samuel Smith (D)

Representatives

Benjamin C. Howard (D)
Daniel Jenifer
John L. Kerr
George E. Mitchell (D) d. June
  1832
Benedict J. Semmes (D)
Charles S. Sewall s. 1832
John S. Spence (D)
Francis Thomas (D)
George C. Washington
John T. H. Worthington (D)

Massachusetts

Senators

Nathaniel Silsbee (D)
Daniel Webster

Representatives

John Quincy Adams
Nathan Appleton
Isaac C. Bates
George N. Briggs
Rufus Choate
John Davis (NR)
Henry A. S. Dearborn
Edward Everett (NR)
George Grennell, Jr.
James L. Hodges
Joseph G. Kendall
Jeremiah Nelson (F)
John Reed

Mississippi

Senators

John Black s. 1832
Powhatan Ellis (D) r. July 1832
George Poindexter

Representatives

Franklin E. Plummer

Missouri

Senators

Thomas H. Benton (D)
Alexander Buckner

Representatives

William H. Ashley

New Hampshire

Senators

Samuel Bell
Isaac Hill

Representatives

John Brodhead (D)
Thomas Chandler (D)
Joseph Hammons (D)
Joseph M. Harper (D)
Henry Hubbard (D)
John W. Weeks

New Jersey

Senators

Mahlon Dickerson (D)
Theodore Frelinghuysen (D)

Representatives

Lewis Condict (AF)
Silas Condit (D)
Richard M. Cooper
Thomas H. Hughes (W)
James F. Randolph
Isaac Southard (D)

New York

Senators

Charles E. Dudley (D)
William L. Marcy (D) r. Jan.
   1833
Silas Wright, Jr. (D) s. 1833

Representatives

William G. Angel (D)
William Babcock
Gamaliel H. Barstow (NR)
Samuel Beardsley (D)
John T. Bergen (D)
Joseph Bouck (D)
John C. Brodhead (C)
Churchill C. Cambreleng (D)
John A. Collier (D)
Bates Cooke (Anti-Mason)
Charles Dayan (D)
John Dickson
Ulysses F. Doubleday (D)
Michael Hoffman (D)
William Hogan (D)
Freeborn G. Jewett (D)
John King (D)
Gerrit Y. Lansing (D)
James Lent d. Feb. 1833
Edmund H. Pendelton (D)
Job Pierson (D)
Nathaniel Pitcher (D)
Edward C. Reed (D)
Erastus Root (D)
Nathan Soule
John W. Taylor (D)
Phineas L. Tracy
Gulian C. Verplanck (D)
Aaron Ward (D)
Daniel Wardwell
Grattan H. Wheeler
Campbell P. White (D)
Frederick Whittlesey
Samuel J. Wilkin (D)

North Carolina

Senators

Bedford Brown (D)
Willie P. Mangum (D)

Representatives

Daniel L. Barringer (D)
Lauchlin Bethune (D)
John Branch (D)
Samuel P. Carson (D)
Henry W. Connor (D)
Thomas H. Hall (D)
Micajah T. Hawkins (D)

James I. McKay (D)
Robert Potter (D)
Abraham Rencher (D)
William B. Shepard (NR)
Augustine H. Sheppard (D)
Jesse Speight
Lewis Williams

Ohio

Senators

Thomas Ewing
Benjamin Ruggles (D)

Representatives

Eleutheors Cooke
Thomas Corwin
Joseph H. Crane
William Creighton, Jr. (D)
James Findlay (D)
William W. Irvin (D)
William Kennon, Sr. (D)
Humphrey H. Leavitt (D)
William Russell (D)
William Stanbery (D)
John Thomson (D)
Joseph Vance (D)
Samuel F. Vinton (D)
Elisha Whittlesey

Pennsylvania

Senators

Isaac D. Barnard (F) r. Dec.
   1831
George M. Dallas (D)
William Wilkins (D, Anti-
   Mason)

Representatives

Robert Allison
John Banks
John C. Bucher (D)
George Burd
Richard Coulter (D)
Thomas H. Crawford (D)
Harmar Denny (Anti-Mason)
Lewis Dewart (D)
Joshua Evans, Jr. (D)
James Ford (D)
John Gilmore (D)
William Hiester (D)
Henry Horn (D)
Peter Ihrie, Jr. (D)
Adam King (D)
Henry King (D)
Robert McCoy (D)
Thomas M. T. McKennan
Joel K. Mann (D)
Henry A. P. Muhlenberg (D)
David Potts, Jr.
Samuel A. Smith (D)
Philander Stephens (D)
Andrew Stewart (D)
Joel B. Sutherland (D)
John G. Watmough

Rhode Island

Senators

Nehemiah R. Knight (AF)
Asher Robbins

Representatives

Tristam Burges (F)
Dutee J. Pearce (D)

South Carolina

Senators

John C. Calhoun (D) s. 1833
Robert Y. Hayne (D) r. Dec.
   1832
Stephen D. Miller (D) r. Mar.
   1833

Representatives

Robert W. Barnwell (D)
James Blair (D)
Warren R. Davis (SRD)
William Drayton (D)
John M. Felder (D)
John K. Griffin (SRW)
George McDuffie (D)
Thomas R. Mitchell
William T. Nuckolls

Tennessee

Senators

Felix Grundy (D)
Hugh L. White (D)

Representatives

Thomas D. Arnold
John Bell
John Blair (D)
William Fitzgerald (D)
William Hall (D)
Jacob C. Isacks
Cave Johnson (D)
James K. Polk (D)
James Standifer

Vermont

Senators

Samuel Prentiss
Horatio Seymour (D)

Representatives

Heman Allen
William Cahoon (Anti-Mason)
Horace Everett
Hiland Hall s. 1833
Jonathan Hunt (NR) d. 1832
William Slade (W)

Virginia

Senators

William C. Rives (D) s. 1833
Littleton W. Tazewell r. July
   1832
John Tyler (D)

Representatives

Mark Alexander (D)
Robert Allen (D)
William S. Archer
William Armstrong (D)

John S. Barbour (SRD)
Thomas T. Bouldin (D)
Joseph W. Chinn (D)
Nathaniel H. Claiborne (D)
Richard Coke, Jr. (D)
Robert Craig (D)
Thomas Davenport (F)
Philip Doddridge d. Nov. 1832
Joseph Draper s. 1832
William F. Gordon (D)
Joseph Johnson (D) s. 1833
Charles C. Johnston (SRD) d.
   June 1832
William McCoy (D)
John Y. Mason (D)
Lewis Maxwell (NR)
Charles F. Mercer (D)
Thomas Newton, Jr. (D)
John M. Patton (D)
John J. Roane (D)
Andrew Stevenson (D)

Twenty-Third Congress

(Mar. 4, 1833, to
Mar. 3, 1835)

President of the Senate: Martin
   Van Buren
*Presidents Pro Tempore of the
   Senate:* Hugh L. White;
   George Poindexter; John
   Tyler
*Speakers of the House of
   Representatives:* Andrew
   Stevenson; John Bell

Alabama

Senators

William R. King (D)
Gabriel Moore

Representatives

Clement Comer Clay
Dixon H. Lewis (SRD)
John McKinley (D)
Samuel W. Mardis (D)
John Murphy (D)

Connecticut

Senators

Náthan Smith (W)
Gideon Tomlinson (D)

Representatives

Noyes Barber (D)
William W. Ellsworth (W) r.
   July 1834
Samuel A. Foote (W) r. 1834
Jabez W. Huntington r. 1834
Phineas Miner (W) s. 1834
Joseph Trumbull (W) s. 1834
Samuel Tweedy (W)
Ebenezer Young

Delaware

Senators

John M. Clayton (W)
Arnold Naudain

Representatives

John J. Milligan (W)

Georgia

Senators

Alfred Cuthbert (D) s. 1835
John Fortsyth (D) r. June 1834
John P. King (D)
George M. Troup r. Nov. 1833

Representatives

Augustin S. Clayton (SRD)
John Coffee (D)
Thomas F. Foster (D)
Roger L. Gamble (W)
George R. Gilmer (D)
Seaborn Jones (D)
William Schley (D)
James M. Wayne (D) r. Jan.
1835
Richard H. Wilde (D)

Illinois

Senators

Elias K. Kane (D)
John M. Robinson (D)

Representatives

Zadoc Casey (D)
Joseph Duncan (D) r. Sept.
1834
William L. May (D) s. 1834
John Reynolds (D) s. 1834
Charles Slade (D) d. July 1834

Indiana

Senators

William Hendricks (D)
John Tipton (D)

Representatives

Ratliff Boon (D)
John Carr (D)
John Ewing (W)
Edward A. Hannegan (D)
George L. Kinnard (D)
Amos Lane (D)
Jonathan McCarty (W)

Kentucky

Senators

George M. Bibb
Henry Clay (W)

Representatives

Chilton Allan (D)

Martin Beaty (W)
Thomas Chilton (W)
Amos Davis (W)
Benjamin Hardin (W)
Albert G. Hawes (D)
Richard M. Johnson (D)
Robert P. Letcher (W) s. 1834
James Love
Chittenden Lyon (D)
Thomas A. Marshall (W)
Patrick H. Pope
Christopher Tompkins

Louisiana

Senators

Josiah S. Johnston (D) d. May
1833
Alexander Porter (W) s. 1834
George A. Waggaman (D)

Representatives

Henry A. Bullard (W) r. Jan.
1834
Rice Garland (W) s. 1834
Henry Johnson (W) s. 1834
Philemon Thomas (D)
Edward D. White r. Nov. 1834

Maine

Senators

John Ruggles (D) s. 1835
Ether Shepley (D)
Peleg Sprague (NR) r. Jan.
1834

Representatives

George Evans
Joseph Hall (D)
Leonard Jarvis (D)
Edward Kavanagh (D)
Rufus McIntire (D)
Moses Mason, Jr. (D)
Gorham Parks (D)
Francis O. J. Smith (D)

Maryland

Senators

Ezekiel F. Chambers (W) r.
1834
Robert H. Goldsborough (W) s.
1835
Joseph Kent (NR)

Reprsentatives

Richard B. Carmichael (D)
Littleton P. Dennis (W) d. Apr.
1834
James P. Heath (D)
William Cost Johnson (W)
Isaac McKim (D)
John N. Steele (W) s. 1834
John T. Stoddert (D)
Francis Thomas (D)
James Turner (D)

Massachusetts

Senators

Nathaniel Silsbee (D)
Daniel Webster

Representatives

John Quincy Adams (W)
Isaac C. Bates
William Baylies
George N. Briggs (W)
Rufus Choate (W) r. June 1834
John Davis (NR) r. Jan. 1834
Edward Everett (NR)
Benjamin Gorham
George Grennell, Jr.
William Jackson (W)
Levi Lincoln s. Mar. 1835
Gayton P. Osgood (D)
Stephen C. Phillips (W) s. 1834
John Reed (W)

Mississippi

Senators

John Black (W)
George Poindexter

Representatives

Harry Cage
Franklin E. Plummer

Missouri

Senators

Thomas H. Benton (D)
Alexander Buckner d. June
1833
Lewis F. Linn (D)

Representatives

William H. Ashley (W)
John Bull (W)

New Hampshire

Senators

Samuel Bell
Isaac Hill (D)

Representatives

Benning M. Bean (D)
Robert Burns (D)
Joseph M. Harper (D)
Henry Hubbard (D)
Franklin Pierce (D)

New Jersey

Senators

Theodore Frelinghuysen (D)
Samuel L. Southard (W)

Representatives

Philemon Dickerson (D)
Samuel Fowler (D)

Thomas Lee
James Parker (D)
Ferdinand S. Schenck (D)
William N. Shinn (D)

New York

Senators

Nathaniel P. Tallmadge (D)
Silas Wright, Jr. (D)

Representatives

John Adams (D)
Samuel Beardsley (D)
Abraham Bockee (D)
Charles Bodle (D)
John W. Brown (D)
Churchill C. Cambreleng (D)
Samuel Clark (D)
John Craker (D)
John Cramer (D)
Rowland Day (D)
John Dickson (W)
Charles G. Ferris (D) s. 1834
Millard Fillmore (W)
Philo C. Fuller (W)
William K. Fuller (D)
Ranson H. Gillett (D)
Nicoll Halsey (D)
Gideon Hard (D)
Samuel G. Hathaway (D)
Abner Hazeltine (W)
Edward Howell (D)
Abel Huntington (D)
Noadiah Johnson (D)
Gerrit Y. Lansing (D)
Cornelius W. Lawrence (D) r.
May 1834
George W. Lay (W)
Charles McVean (D)
Abijah Mann, Jr. (D)
Henry C. Martindale
Henry Mitchell (D)
John J. Morgan (D) s. 1834
Sherman Page (D)
Job Pierson (D)
Dudley Selden (D) r. July 1834
William Taylor (D)
Joel Turrill (D)
Aaron Vanderpoel (D)
Isaac B. Van Houten (D)
Aaron Ward (D)
Daniel Wardwell (D)
Reuben Whallon (D)
Campbell P. White (D)
Frederick Whittlesey

North Carolina

Senators

Bedford Brown (D)
Willie P. Mangum (D)

Representatives

Daniel L. Barringer (D)
Jesse A. Bynum (D)
Henry W. Connor (D)
Edmund Deberry (W)
James Graham
Thomas H. Hall (D)
Micajah T. Hawkins (D)
James I. McKay (D)
Abraham Rencher (D)
William B. Shepard
Augustine H. Shepperd (D)

Jesse Speight
Lewis Williams

Ohio

Senators

Thomas Ewing (W)
Thomas Morris (D)

Representatives

William Allen (D)
James M. Bell (D)
John Chaney (D)
Thomas Corwin (W)
Joseph H. Crane (W)
Thomas L. Hamer (D)
Benjamin Jones (D)
Daniel Kilgore (D) s. 1834
Humphrey H. Leavitt (D) r.
July 1834
Robert T. Lytle (D) r. Mar.
1834
Jeremiah McLene (D)
Robert Mitchell (D)
William Patterson (D)
Jonathan Sloane (W)
David Spangler (W)
John Thomson (D)
Joseph Vance (D)
Samuel F. Vinton (W)
Taylor Webster (D)
Elisha Whittlesey

Pennsylvania

Senators

James Buchanan (D) s. 1834
Samuel McKean (D)
William Wilkins (D) r. June
1834

Representatives

Joseph B. Anthony (D)
John Banks (W)
Charles A. Barnitz (W)
Andrew Beaumont (D)
Horace Binney (W)
George Burd
George Chambers (W)
William Clark (W)
Richard Coutler (D)
Edward Darlington (W)
Harmar Denny (Anti-Mason)
John Galbraith (D)
James Harper (D)
Samuel S. Harrison (D)
Joseph Henderson
William Hiester (W)
Henry King (D)
John Laporte
Thomas M. T. McKennan (W)
Joel K. Mann (D)
Jesse Miller (D)
Henry A. P. Muhlenberg (D)
David Potts, Jr. (W)
Robert Ramsey (W)
Andrew Stewart (D)
Joel B. Sutherland (D)
David D. Wagener (D)
John G. Watmough

Rhode Island

Senators

Nehemiah R. Knight (AF)
Asher Robbins (W)

Representatives

Tristam Burges (F)
Dutee J. Pearce (D)

South Carolina

Senators

John C. Calhoun (D)
William C. Preston (Null)

Representatives

James Blair (D) d. Apr. 1834
Robert B. Campbell (Null-D) s.
1834
William K. Clowney (Null-D)
Warren R. Davis (SRD) d. Jan.
1835
John M. Felder (D)
William J. Grayson (W)
John K. Griffin (SRW)
George McDuffie (D) r. 1834
Richard I. Manning (D) s. 1834
Francis W. Pickens (Null-D) s.
1834
Henry L. Pinckney (D)

Tennessee

Senators

Felix Grundy (D)
Hugh L. White (D)

Representatives

John Bell (W)
John Blair (D)
Samuel Bunch (W)
David Crockett (W)
David W. Dickinson (D)
William C. Dunlap (D)
John B. Forester (D)
William M. Inge (D)
Cave Johnson (D)
Luke Lea (D)
Balie Peyton (W)
James K. Polk (D)
James Standifer (W)

Vermont

Senators

Samuel Prentiss (W)
Benjamin Swift (F)

Representatives

Herman Allen (W)
Benjamin F. Deming (W) d.
July 1834
Horace Everett (W)
Hiland Hall (W)
Henry F. Janes (W) s. 1834
William Slade (W)

Virginia

Senators

Benjamin W. Leigh (W) s. 1834
William C. Rives (D) r. Feb.
1834
John Tyler (W)

Representatives

John J. Allen (W)
William S. Archer
James M. H. Beale (D)
James W. Bouldin (D) s. 1834
Thomas T. Bouldin (D) d. Feb.
1834
Joseph W. Chinn (D)
Nathaniel H. Claiborne
Thomas Davenport (F)
John H. Fulton (W)
James H. Gholson (D)
William F. Gordon (D)
George Loyall (D)
Edward Lucas (D)
William McComas (W)
Samuel McDowell (W)
Samuel M. Moore (W)
John Y. Mason (D)
Charles F. Mercer (D)
John M. Patton (D)
John Randolph d. May 1833
John Robertson (W) s. 1834
Andrew Stevenson (D) r. June
1834
William P. Taylor (W)
Edgar C. Wilson (W)
Henry A. Wise (D)

Twenty-Fourth Congress

(Mar. 4, 1835, to
Mar. 3, 1837)

President of the Senate: Martin
Van Buren
*President Pro Tempore of the
Senate:* William R. King
*Speaker of the House of
Representatives:* James K.
Polk

Alabama

Senators

William R. King (D)
Gabriel Moore

Representatives

Reuben Chapman (D)
Joab Lawler (W)
Dixon H. Lewis (SRD)
Francis S. Lyon (W)
Joshua L. Martin (D)

Arkansas

Senators

William S. Fulton (D) s. 1836
Ambrose H. Sevier (D) s. 1836

Representatives

Archibald Yell (D) s. 1836

Connecticut

Senators

John M. Niles (D)
Nathan Smith (W) d. Dec. 1835
Gideon Tomlinson (D)

Representatives

Elisha Haley (D)
Orrin Holt (D) s. 1836
Samuel Ingham (D)
Andrew T. Judson (D) r. July
1836
Lancelot Phelps (D)
Isaac Toucey (D)
Thomas T. Whittlesey (D) s.
1836
Zalmon Wildman (D) d. Dec.
1835

Delaware

Senators

Richard H. Bayard (W) s. 1836
John M. Clayton (W) r. Dec.
1836
Thomas Clayton (W) s. 1837
Arnold Naudain r. June 1836

Representatives

John J. Milligan (W)

Georgia

Senators

Alfred Cuthbert (D)
John P. King (D)

Representatives

Julius C. Alford (SRW) s. 1837
Jesse F. Cleveland (D)
John Coffee (D) d. Sept. 1836
William C. Dawson (SRW) s.
1836
Thomas Glascock (D)
Seaton Grantland (Un)
Charles E. Haynes (D)
Hopkins Holsey (D)
Jabez Y. Jackson (D)
George W. Owens (Un)
John W. A. Sanford (D) r. July
1835
William Schley (D) r. July 1835
James C. Terrell (D) r. July
1835
George W. B. Towns (D) r.
Sept. 1836

Illinois

Senators

William L. D. Ewing (D) s.
1836
Elias K. Kane (D) d. Dec.
1835
John M. Robinson (D)

Representatives

Zadoc Casey (D)
William L. May (D)
John Reynolds (D)

Indiana

Senators

William Hendricks (D)
John Tipton (D)

Representatives

Ratliff Boon (D)
John Carr (D)
John W. Davis (D)
Edward A. Hannegan (D)
William Herod (W) s. 1837
George L. Kinnard (D) d. Nov. 1836
Amos Lane (D)
Jonathan McCarty (W)

Kentucky

Senators

Henry Clay (W)
John J. Crittenden

Representatives

Chilton Allan (D)
Linn Boyd (D)
John Calhoon (W)
John Chambers (W)
Richard French (D)
William J. Graves (W)
Benjamin Hardin (W)
James Harlan (W)
Albert G. Hawes (D)
Richard M. Johnson (D)
John White (W)
Sherrod Williams (W)
Joseph R. Underwood (W)

Louisiana

Senators

Alexander Mouton (D) s. 1837
Robert C. Nicholas (D) s. 1836
Alexander Porter (W) r. Jan. 1837

Representatives

Rice Garland (W)
Henry Johnson (W)
Eleazar W. Ripley (D)

Maine

Senators

Judah Dana (D) s. 1836
John Ruggles (D)
Ether Shepley (D) r. Mar. 1836

Representatives

Jeremiah Bailey (S)
George Evans (W)
John Fairfield (D)
Joseph Hall (D)

Leonard Jarvis (D)
Moses Mason, Jr. (D)
Gorham Parks (D)
Francis O. J. Smith (D)

Maryland

Senators

Robert H. Goldsborough
Joseph Kent (NR)
John S. Spence (D)

Representatives

Benjamin C. Howard (D)
Daniel Jenifer (R)
Isaac McKim (D)
James A. Pearce (W)
John N. Steele (W)
Francis Thomas (D)
James Turner (D)
George C. Washington (W)

Massachusetts

Senators

John Davis (W)
Daniel Webster

Representatives

John Quincy Adams (W)
Nathaniel B. Borden (W)
George N. Briggs (W)
William B. Calhoun (W)
Caleb Cushing (W)
George Grennell, Jr. (W)
Samuel Hoar
William Jackson (W)
Abbott Lawrence (W)
Levi Lawrence (W)
Stephen C. Phillips (W)
John Reed (W)

Mississippi

Senators

John Black (W)
Robert J. Walker (D)

Representatives

John F. H. Claiborne (D)
David Dickson (D) d. 1836
Samuel J. Gholson (D) s. 1837

Missouri

Senators

Thomas H. Benton (D)
Lewis F. Linn (D)

Representatives

William H. Ashley (W)
Albert G. Harrison (D)

New Hampshire

Senators

Isaac Hill (D) r. May 1836

Henry Hubbard (D)
John Page (D) s. 1836

Representatives

Benning M. Bean (D)
Robert Burns (D)
Samuel Cushman (D)
Franklin Pierce (D)
Joseph Weeks (D)

New Jersey

Senators

Samuel L. Southard (W)
Garret D. Wall (D)

Representatives

William Chetwood (D) s. 1836
Philemon Dickerson (D) r. Nov. 1836
Samuel Fowler (D)
Thomas Lee (D)
James Parker (D)
Ferdinand S. Schenck (D)
William N. Shinn (D)

New York

Senators

Nathaniel P. Tallmadge (D)
Silas Wright, Jr. (D)

Representatives

Samuel Barton (D)
Samuel Beardsley (D) r. Mar. 1836
Abraham Bockee (D)
Matthias J. Bovee (D)
John W. Brown (D)
Churchill C. Cambreleng (D)
Graham H. Chapin (D)
Timothy Childs (W)
John Cramer (D)
Ulysses F. Doubleday (D)
Valentine Efner (D)
Dudley Farlin (D)
Philo C. Fuller (W) r. Sept. 1836
William K. Fuller (D)
Ranson H. Gillet (D)
Francis Granger (W)
Gideon Hard (D)
Abner Hazeltine (W)
Hiram P. Hunt (W)
Abel Huntington (D)
Gerrit Y. Lansing (D)
George W. Lay (W)
Gideon Lee (D)
Joshua Lee (D)
Stephen B. Leonard (D)
Thomas C. Love (W)
John McKeon (D)
Abijah Mann, Jr. (D)
William Mason (D)
Rutger B. Miller (D) s. 1836
Ely Moore (D)
Sherman Page (D)
Joseph Reynolds (D)
David A. Russell (W)
William Seymour (D)
Nicholas Sickles (D)
William Taylor (D)
Joel Turrill (D)
Aaron Vanderpoel (D)

Aaron Ward (D)
Daniel Wardwell (NB)
John Young (W) s. 1836

North Carolina

Senators

Bedford Brown (D)
Willie P. Mangum (W) r. Nov. 1836
Robert Strange (D) s. 1836

Representatives

Jesse A. Bynum (D)
Henry W. Connor (D)
Edmund Deberry (W)
James Graham s. 1836
Micajah T. Hawkins (D)
James I. McKay (D)
William Montgomery (D)
Ebenezer Pettigrew (W)
Abraham Rencher (D)
William B. Shepard (NR)
Augustine H. Shepperd (D)
Jesse Speight
Lewis Williams

Ohio

Senators

Thomas Ewing (W)
Thomas Morris (D)

Representatives

William K. Bond (W)
John Chaney (D)
Thomas Corwin (W)
Joseph H. Crane (W)
Thomas L. Hamer (D)
Elias Howell (D)
Benjamin Jones (D)
William Kennon, Sr. (D)
Daniel Kilgore (D)
Jeremiah McLene (D)
Samson Mason (W)
William Patterson (D)
Jonathan Sloane (W)
David Spangler (W)
Bellamy Storer (W)
John Thomson (D)
Samuel F. Vinton (W)
Taylor Webster (D)
Elisha Whittlesey (W)

Pennsylvania

Senators

James Buchanan (D)
Samuel McKean (D)

Representatives

Joseph B. Anthony (D)
Michael W. Ash (D)
John Banks (W) r. 1836
Andrew Baumont (D)
James Black (D) s. 1836
Andrew Buchanan (D)
George Chambers (W)
William Clark (W)
Edward Darlington (W)
Harmar Denny (Anti-Mason)
Jacob Fry, Jr. (D)

John Galbraith (D)
James Harper (D)
Samuel S. Harrison (D)
Joseph Henderson
William Hiester (W)
Edward B. Hubley (D)
Joseph R. Ingersoll (W)
John Klingensmith, Jr. (D)
John Laporte
Henry Logan (D)
Thomas M. T. McKennan (W)
Job Mann (D)
Jesse Miller (D) r. Oct. 1836
Mathias Morris (W)
Henry A. P. Muhlenberg (D)
John J. Pearson (W) s. 1836
David Potts, Jr. (W)
Joel B. Sutherland (D)
David D. Wagener

Rhode Island

Senators

Nehemiah R. Knight (D)
Asher Robbins (W)

Representatives

Dutee J. Pearce (D)
William Sprague (W)

South Carolina

Senators

John C. Calhoun (D)
William C. Preston (Null-D)

Representatives

Robert B. Campbell (W)
Franklin H. Elmore (SRD) s. 1836
William J. Grayson (W)
John K. Griffin (SRW)
James H. Hammond (SRD) r. Feb. 1836
Richard I. Manning (D) d. May 1836
Francis W. Pickens (Null-D)
Henry L. Pinckney (D)
John P. Richardson (SRD) s. 1836
James Rogers (D)
Waddy Thompson, Jr. (W)

Tennessee

Senators

Felix Grundy (D)
Hugh L. White (D)

Representatives

John Bell (W)
Samuel Bunch (W)
William B. Carter (W)
William C. Dunlap (D)
John B. Forester
Adam Huntsman (D)
Cave Johnson (D)
Luke Lea (D)
Abram P. Maury (W)
Balie Peyton (W)
James K. Polk (D)
Ebenezer J. Shields (W)

James Standifer (W)

Vermont

Senators

Samuel Prentiss (W)
Benjamin Swift (F)

Representatives

Heman Allen (W)
Horace Everett (W)
Hiland Hall (W)
Henry F. Janes (W)
William Slade (W)

Virginia

Senators

Benjamin W. Leigh (W) r. July 1836
Richard E. Parker (D) s. 1836
William C. Rives (D) s. 1836
John Tyler (W) r. Feb. 1836

Representatives

James M. H. Beale (D)
James W. Bouldin (D)
Nathaniel H. Claiborne
Walter Coles (D)
Robert Craig (D)
George C. Dromgoole (D)
James Garland (D)
George W. Hopkins (D)
Joseph Johnson (D)
John W. Jones (D)
George Loyall (D)
Edward Lucas (D)
William McComas (W)
John Y. Mason (D) r. Jan. 1837
Charles F. Mercer (D)
William S. Morgan (D)
John M. Patton (D)
John Roane (D)
John Robertson (W)
John Taliaferro (W)
Henry A. Wise (D)

Twenty-Fifth Congress

(Mar. 4, 1837, to
Mar. 3, 1839)

President of the Senate: Richard
  M. Johnson
*President Pro Tempore of the
  Senate:* William R. King
*Speaker of the House of
  Representatives:* James K.
  Polk

Alabama

Senators

Clement Comer Clay (D)
William R. King (D)

Representatives

Reuben Chapman (D)
George W. Crabb (W) s. 1838
Joab Lawler (W) d. May 1838
Dixon H. Lewis (SRD)
Francis S. Lyon (W)
Joshua L. Martin (D)

Arkansas

Senators

William S. Fulton (D)
Ambrose H. Sevier (D)

Representatives

Archibald Yell (D)

Connecticut

Senators

John M. Niles (D)
Perry Smith (D)

Representatives

Elisha Haley (D)
Orrin Holt (D)
Samuel Ingham (D)
Lancelot Phelps (D)
Isaac Toucey (D)
Thomas T. Whittlesey

Delaware

Senators

Richard H. Bayard (W)
Thomas Clayton (W)

Representatives

John J. Milligan (W)

Georgia

Senators

Alfred Cuthbert(D)
John P. King (D) r. Nov. 1837
Wilson Lumpkin (D)

Representatives

Jesse F. Cleveland (D)
William C. Dawson (SRW)
Thomas Glascock (D)
Seaton Grantland (Un)
Charles E. Haynes (D)
Hopkins Holsey (D)
Jabez Y. Jackson (D)
George W. Owens (Un)
George W. B. Towns (D)

Illinois

Senators

John M. Robinson (D)
Richard M. Young (D)

Representatives

Zadoc Casey (D)
William L. May (D)
Adam W. Snyder (D)

Indiana

Senators

Oliver H. Smith (W)
John Tipton. (D)

Representatives

Ratliff Boon (D)
George H. Dunn (W)
John Ewing (W)
William Graham (W)
William Herod (W)
James Rariden (W)
Albert S. White (W)

Kentucky

Senators

Henry Clay (W)
John J. Crittenden

Representatives

John Calhoon (W)
John Chambers (W)
William J. Graves (W)
James Harlan (W)
Richard Hawes (W)
Richard H. Menifee (W)
John L. Murray (D)
John Pope (D)
Edward Rumsey (W)
William W. Southgate (W)
Joseph R. Underwood (W)
John White (W)
Sherrod Williams (W)

Louisiana

Senators

Alexander Mouton (D)
Robert C. Nicholas (D)

Representatives

Rice Garland (W)
Henry Johnson (W)
Eleazar W. Ripley (D)

Maine

Senators

John Ruggles (D)
Reuel Williams (D)

Representatives

Hugh J. Anderson (D)
Timothy J. Carter (D) d. Mar. 1838
Jonathan Cilley (D) d. Feb. 1838
Thomas Davee (D)
George Evans (W)
John Fairfield (D) r. Dec. 1838
Joseph C. Noyes (W)

Virgil D. Parris (SRD) s. 1838
Edward Robinson (W) s. 1838
Francis O. J. Smith (D)

Maryland

Senators

Joseph Kent (NR) d. Nov. 1837
William D. Merrick (W) s.
  1838
John S. Spence (D)

Representatives

John Dennis (W)
Benjamin C. Howard (D)
Daniel Jenifer
William Cost Johnson (W)
John P. Kennedy (W) s. 1838
Isaac McKim (D) d. Apr. 1838
James A. Pearce (W)
Francis Thomas (D)
John T. H. Worthington (D)

Massachusetts

Senators

John Davis (W)
Daniel Webster (W)

Representatives

John Quincy Adams (W)
Nathaniel B. Borden (W)
George N. Briggs (W)
William B. Calhoun (W)
Caleb Cushing (W)
Richard Fletcher (W)
George Grennell, Jr.
William S. Hastings (D)
Levi Lincoln (W)
William Parmenter (D)
Stephen C. Phillips (W) r. Sept.
  1838
John Reed (W)
Leverett Saltonstall (W) s. 1838

Michigan

Senators

Lucius Lyon (D)
John Norvell (D)

Representatives

Isaac E. Crary (D)

Mississippi

Senators

John Black (W) r. Jan. 1838
James F. Trotter (D) ta. 1838
Robert J. Walker (D)
Thomas H. Williams (D) s.
  1838

Representatives

John F. H. Claiborne (D)
Samuel J. Gholson (D)
Sergeant S. Prentiss (W) s. 1838
Thomas J. Word (W) s. 1838

Missouri

Senators

Thomas H. Benton (D)
Lewis F. Linn (D)

Representatives

Albert G. Harrison (D)
John Miller (D)

New Hampshire

Senators

Henry Hubbard (D)
Franklin Pierce (D)

Representatives

Charles G. Atherton (D)
Samuel Cushman (D)
James Farrington (D)
Joseph Weeks (D)
Jared W. Williams (D)

New Jersey

Senators

Samuel L. Southward (W)
Garret D. Wall (D)

Representatives

John B. Aycrigg (W)
William Halstead (W)
John P. B. Maxwell (W)
Joseph F. Randolph (W)
Charles C. Stratton (W)
Thomas Jones Yorke (W)

New York

Senators

Nathaniel P. Tallmadge (D)
Silas Wright, Jr. (D)

Representatives

John T. Andrews (D)
Cyrus Beers s. 1838
Bennett Bicknell (D)
Samuel Birdsall (D)
John C. Brodhead (D)
Isaac H. Bronson (D)
Andrew D. W. Bruyn (D) d.
  July 1838
Churchill C. Cambreleng (D)
Timothy Childs (W)
John C. Clark (D)
Edward Curtis (W)
John I. DeGraff (D)
John Edwards (D)
Millard Fillmore (W)
Henry A. Foster (D)
Albert Gallup (D)
Abraham P. Grant (D)
Hiram Gray (D)
J. Ogden Hoffman (W)
Thomas B. Jackson (D)
Nathaniel Jones (D)
Gouverneur Kemble (D)
Arphaxed Loomis (D)
Robert McClellan (D)

Richard P. Marvin (W)
Charles F. Mitchell (W)
Ely Moore (D)
William H. Noble (D)
John Palmer (D)
Amasa J. Parker (D)
William Patterson (W) d. Aug.
  1838
Luther C. Peck (W)
Zadock Pratt (D)
John H. Prentiss (D)
Harvey Putnam (W) s. 1838
David A. Russell (W)
Mark H. Sibley (W)
James B. Spencer (D)
William Taylor (D)
Obadiah Titus (D)
Henry Vail (D)
Abraham Vanderveer (D)

North Carolina

Senators

Bedford Brown (D)
Robert Strange (D)

Representatives

Jesse A. Bynum (D)
Henry W. Connor (D)
Edmund Deberry (W)
James Graham
Micajah T. Hawkins (D)
James I. McKay (D)
William Montgomery (D)
Abraham Rencher (D)
Samuel T. Sawyer (D)
Charles B. Shepard (D)
Augustine H. Shepperd (D)
Edward Stanly (W)
Lewis Williams

Ohio

Senators

William Allen (D)
Thomas Morris

Representatives

James Alexander, Jr. (D)
John W. Allen (W)
William K. Bond (W)
John Chaney (D)
Charles D. Coffin (W)
Thomas Corwin (W)
Alexander Duncan (W)
Joshua R. Giddings (W) s. 1838
Patrick G. Goode (W)
Thomas L. Hamer (D)
Alexander Harper (W)
William H. Hunter (D)
Daniel Kilgore (D) r. July 1838
Daniel P. Leadbetter (D)
Andrew W. Loomis (W) r. Oct.
  1838
Samson Mason
Calvary Morris (W)
Joseph Ridgway (W)
Matthias Shepler (D)
Henry Swearingen (D) s. 1838
Taylor Webster (D)
Elisha Whittlesey (W) r. July
  1838

Pennsylvania

Senators

James Buchanan (D)
Samuel McKean (D)

Representatives

William Beatty (D)
Richard Biddle (W)
Andrew Buchanan (D)
Edward Darlington (Anti-
  Mason)
Edward Davies (W)
Jacob Fry, Jr. (D)
Robert H. Hammond (D)
Francis J. Harper (D) r. Mar.
  1837
Thomas Henry (W)
Edward B. Hubley (D)
George M. Keim (D) s. 1838
John Klingensmith, Jr. (D)
Henry Logan (D)
Charles McClure (D)
Thomas M. T. McKennan (W)
Mathias Morris (W)
Samuel W. Morris (D)
Henry A. P. Muhlenberg (D) r.
  Feb. 1838
Charles Ogle (W)
Charles Naylor (W)
Lemuel Paynter (D)
David Petrikin (D)
Arnold Plumer (D)
William W. Potter (D)
David Potts, Jr. (W)
Luther Reily (D)
John Sergeant (F)
Daniel Sheffer (D)
George W. Toland (W)
David D. Wagener (D)

Rhode Island

Senators

Nehemiah R. Knight (AF)
Asher Robbins (W)

Representatives

Robert B. Cranston (W)
Joseph L. Tillinghast (W)

South Carolina

Senators

John C. Calhoun (D)
William C. Preston (Null-D)

Representatives

John Campbell (SRD)
William K. Clowney (SRD)
Franklin H. Elmore (SRD)
John D. Griffin (SRW)
Hugh S. Legare
Francis W. Pickens (Null-D)
R. Barnwell Rhett (D)
John P. Richardson (SRD)
Waddy Thompson, Jr. (W)

Tennessee

Senators

Ephraim H. Foster (W) s. 1838
Felix Grundy (D) r. July 1838
Hugh L. White (D)

Representatives

John Bell (W)
William B. Campbell (W)
William B. Carter (W)
Richard Cheatham (W)
John W. Crockett (W)
Abraham McClellan (D)
Abram P. Maury (W)
James K. Polk (D)
Ebenezer J. Shields (W)
James Standifer (W) d. Aug.
  1837
William Stone (W)
Hopkins L. Turney (D)
Christopher H. Williams (W)
Joseph L. Williams (W)

Vermont

Senators

Samuel Prentiss (W)
Benjamin Swift (F)

Representatives

Heman Allen (W)
Horace Everett (W)
Isaac Fletcher (D)
Hiland Hall (W)
William Slade (W)

Virginia

Senators

Richard E. Parker (D) r. Mar.
  1837
William C. Rives (D)
William H. Roane (D) s. 1837

Representatives

Linn Banks (D) s. 1838
Andrew Beirne (D)
James W. Bouldin (D)
Walter Coles (D)
Robert Craig (D)
George C. Dromgoole (D)
James Garland (D)
George W. Hopkins (D)
Robert M. T. Hunter (D)
Joseph Johnson (D)
John W. Jones (D)
Francis Mallory (D)
James M. Mason (D)
Charles F. Mercer (D)
William S. Morgan (D)
John M. Patton (D) r. 1838
Isaac S. Pennybacker (D)
Francis E. Rives (D)
John Robertson (W)
Archibald Stuart (W)
John Taliaferro (W)
Henry A. Wise (W)

Twenty-Sixth Congress

(Mar. 4, 1839, to
Mar. 3, 1841)

President of the Senate: Richard
  M. Johnson
*President Pro Tempore of the
  Senate:* William R. King
*Speaker of the House of
  Representatives:* Robert M. T.
  Hunter

Alabama

Senators

Clement Comer Clay (D)
William R. King (D)

Representatives

Reuben Chapman (D)
George W. Crabb (W)
James Dellet (W)
David Hubbard (SRD)
Dixon H. Lewis (SRD)

Arkansas

Senators

William S. Fulton (D)
Ambrose H. Sevier (D)

Representatives

Edward Cross (D)

Connecticut

Senators

Thaddeus Betts (W) d. Apr.
  1840
Jabez W. Huntington (W) s.
  1840
Perry Smith (D)

Representatives

William W. Boardman (W) s.
  1840
John H. Brockway (W)
Thomas B. Osborne (W)
Truman Smith (W)
William L. Storrs (W) r. June
  1840
Joseph Trumbull (W)
Thomas W. Williams (W)

Delaware

Senators

Richard H. Bayard (W)
Thomas Clayton (W)

Representatives

Thomas Robinson, Jr. (D)

Georgia

Senators

Alfred Cuthbert (D)
Wilson Lumpkin (D)

Representatives

Julius C. Alford (W)
Edward J. Black (SRW)
Walter T. Colquitt (SRW) r.
  July 1840
Mark A. Cooper (SRW)
William C. Dawson (SRW)
Richard W. Habersham (D)
Hines Holt (W) s. 1841
Thomas B. King (W)
Eugenius A. Nisbet (W)
Lott Warren (W)

Illinois

Senators

John M. Robinson (D)
Richard M. Young (D)

Representatives

Zadoc Casey (D)
John Reynolds (D)
John T. Stuart (W)

Indiana

Senators

Oliver H. Smith (W)
Albert S. White (W)

Representatives

John Carr (D)
John W. Davis (D)
Tilghman A. Howard (D) r.
  Aug. 1840
Henry S. Lane (W) s. Dec.
  1840
George H. Proffit (W)
James Rariden (W)
Thomas Smith (D)
William W. Wick (D)

Kentucky

Senators

Henry Clay (W)
John J. Crittenden

Representatives

Simeon H. Anderson (W) d.
  Aug. 1840
Landaff W. Andrews (W)
Linn Boyd (D)
William O. Butler (D)
Garrett Davis (W)
William J. Graves (W)
Willis Green (W)
Richard Hawes (W)
John Pope (W)
John B. Thompson (W) s. 1840
Philip Triplett (W)
John White (W)
Sherrod Williams (W)

Joseph R. Underwood (W)

Louisiana

Senators

Alexander Mouton (D)
Robert C. Nicholas (D)

Representatives

Thomas W. Chinn (W)
Rice Garland (W) r. July 1840
John Moore (W) s. 1840
Edward D. White (W)

Maine

Senators

John Ruggles (D)
Reuel Williams (D)

Representatives

Hugh J. Anderson (D)
Nathan Clifford (D)
Thomas Davee (D)
George Evans (W)
Joshua A. Lowell (D)
Virgil D. Parris (SRD)
Benjamin Randall (W)
Albert Smith (D)

Maryland

Senators

John J. Kerr (W) s. 1841
William D. Merrick (W)
John S. Spence (D) d. Oct.
  1840

Representatives

James Carroll (D)
John Dennis (W)
Solomon Hillen, Jr. (D)
Daniel Jenifer (R)
William Cost Johnson (W)
Francis Thomas (D)
Philip F. Thomas (D)
John T. H. Worthington (D)

Massachusetts

Senators

Isaac C. Bates (W) s. 1841
Rufus Choate (W) s. 1841
John Davis (W) r. Jan. 1841
Daniel Webster (W) r. Feb.
  1841

Representatives

John Quincy Adams (W)
Osmyn Baker (W) s. 1840
George N. Briggs (W)
William B. Calhoun (W)
Caleb Cushing (W)
William S. Hastings (D)
Abbott Lawrence (W) r. Sept.
  1840
Levi Lincoln (W)
William Parmenter (D)
John Reed (W)

Leverett Saltonstall (W)
Henry Williams (D)
Robert C. Winthrop (W) s.
1840

Michigan

Senators

John Norvell (D)
Augustus S. Porter (W)

Representatives

Isaac E. Crary (D)

Mississippi

Senators

John Henderson (W)
Robert J. Walker (D)

Representatives

Albert G. Brown (D)
Jacob Thompson (D)

Missouri

Senators

Thomas H. Benton (D)
Lewis F. Linn (D)

Representatives

Albert G. Harrison (D) d. Sept.
  1839
John Jameson (D)
John Miller (D)

New Hampshire

Senators

Henry Hubbard (D)
Franklin Pierce (D)

Representatives

Charles G. Atherton (D)
Edmund Burke (D)
Ira A. Eastman (D)
Tristram Shaw (D)
Jared W. Williams (D)

New Jersey

Senators

Samuel L. Southard (W)
Garret D. Wall (D)

Representatives

William R. Cooper (D)
Philemon Dickerson (D)
Joseph Kille (D)
Joseph F. Randolph (W)
Daniel B. Ryall (D)
Peter D. Vroom (D)

New York

Senators

Nathaniel P. Tallmadge (D)
Silas Wright, Jr. (D)

Representatives

Judson Allen (D)
Daniel D. Barnard (W)
David P. Brewster (D)
Anson Brown (W) d. June 1840
Thomas C. Chittenden (W)
John C. Clark (W)
Edward Curtis (W)
Amasa Dana (D)
James DeLa Montanya (D)
Nicholas B. Doe (W) s. 1840
Andrew W. Doig (D)
Nehemiah H. Earll (D)
John Ely (D)
Millard Fillmore (W)
John Fine (D)
John G. Floyd (D)
Seth M. Gates (W)
Francis Granger (W)
Moses H. Grinnell (W)
Augustus C. Hand (D)
Ogden J. Hoffman (W)
Hiram P. Hunt (W)
Thomas B. Jackson (D)
Charles Johnston (W)
Nathaniel Jones (D)
Gouverneur Kemble (D)
Thomas Kempshall (W)
Stephen B. Leonard (D)
Meredith Mallory (D)
Richard P. Marvin (W)
Charles F. Mitchell (W)
James Monroe (W)
Christopher Morgan (W)
Rufus Palen (W)
Luther C. Peck (W)
John H. Prentiss (D)
Edward Rogers (D)
David A. Russell (W)
Theron R. Strong (D)
Aaron Vanderpoel (D)
Peter J. Wagner (W)

North Carolina

Senators

Bedford Brown (D) r. Nov.
  1840
William A. Graham (W) s.
  1840
Willie P. Mangum (W)
Robert Strange (D) r. Nov.
  1840

Representatives

Jesse A. Bynum (D)
Henry W. Connor (D)
Edmund Deberry (W)
Charles Fisher (D)
James Craham (D)
Micajah T. Hawkins (D)
John Hill (D)
James I. McKay (D)
William Montgomery (D)
Kenneth Rayner (W)
Charles B. Shepard (D)
Edward Stanly (W)
Lewis Williams

Ohio

Senators

William Allen (D)
Benjamin Tappan (D)

Representatives

John W. Allen (W)
William K. Bond (W)
Thomas Corwin (W) r. May
  1840
William Doan (D)
Alexander Duncan (W)
Joshua R. Giddings (W)
Patrick G. Goode (W)
John Hastings (D)
Daniel P. Leadbetter (D)
Samson Mason (W)
William Medill (D)
Calvary Morris (W)
Jeremiah Morrow (W) s. 1840
Isaac Parrish (D)
Joseph Ridgway (W)
David A. Starkweather (D)
Henry Swearingen (D)
George Sweeny (D)
Jonathan Taylor (D)
John B. Weller (D)

Pennsylvania

Senators

James Buchanan (D)
Daniel Sturgeon (D) s. 1840

Representatives

William Beatty (D)
Richard Biddle (W) r. 1840
Henry M. Brackenridge (W) s.
  1840
James Cooper (W)
Edward Davies (W)
John Davis (D)
John Edwards (W)
Joseph Fornance (D)
John Galbraith (D)
James Gerry (D)
Robert H. Hammond (D)
Thomas Henry (W)
Enos Hook (D)
Francis James (W)
George M. Keim (D)
Isaac Leet (D)
Charles McClure (D) s. 1840
George McCulloch (D)
Albert G. Marchand (D)
Samuel W. Morris (D)
Charles Naylor (W)
Peter Newhard (D)
Charles Ogle (W)
Lemuel Paynter (D)
David Petrikin (D)
William S. Ramsey (D) d. Oct.
  1840
John Sergeant (F)
William Simonton (W)
George W. Toland (W)
David D. Wagener (D)

Rhode Island

Senators

Nathan F. Dixon (W)

Nehemiah R. Knight (D)

Representatives

Robert B. Cranston (W)
Joseph L. Tillinghast (W)

South Carolina

Senators

John C. Calhoun (D)
William C. Preston (Null-D)

Representatives

Sampson H. Butler (D)
John Campbell (SRD)
John K. Griffin (SRW)
Isaac E. Holmes (D)
Francis W. Pickens (Null-D)
R. Barnwell Rhett (D)
James Rogers (D)
Thomas D. Sumter (D)
Waddy Thompson, Jr. (W)

Tennessee

Senators

Alexander Anderson (D) s. 1840
Felix Grundy (D) d. Dec. 1840
Alfred O. P. Nicholson (D) s.
  1841
Hugh L. White (D) r. Jan.
  1840

Representatives

John Bell (W)
Julius W. Blackwell (D)
Aaron V. Brown (D)
William B. Campbell (W)
William B. Carter (W)
John W. Crockett (W)
Meredith P. Gentry (W)
Cave Johnson (D)
Abraham McClellan (D)
Harvey M. Watterson (D)
Christopher H. Williams (W)
Joseph L. Williams (S)
Hopkins L. Turney (D)

Vermont

Senators

Samuel S. Phelps (W)
Samuel Prentiss (W)

Representatives

Horace Everett (W)
Isaac Fletcher (D)
Hiland Hall (W)
William Slade (W)
John Smith (D)

Virginia

Senators

William C. Rives (D)
William H. Roane (D)

Representatives

Linn Banks (D)
Andrew Beirne (D)
John M. Botts (W)
Walter Coles (D)
Robert Craig (D)
George C. Dromgoole (D)
James Garland (D)
William L. Goggin (W)
John Hill (W)
Joel Holleman (D) r. 1840
George W. Hopkins (D)
Robert M. T. Hunter (D)
Joseph Johnson (D)
John W. Jones (D)
William Lucas (D)
William M. McCarty (W) s. 1840
Francis Mallory (W) s. 1841
Charles F. Mercer (D) r. Dec. 1839
Francis E. Rives (D)
Green B. Samuels (D)
Lewis Steenrod (D)
John Taliaferro (W)
Henry W. Wise (W)

Twenty-Seventh Congress

(Mar. 4, 1841, to
Mar. 3, 1843)

President of the Senate: John Tyler
Presidents Pro Tempore of the Senate: William R. King; Samuel L. Southard; Willie P. Mangum
Speaker of the House of Representatives: John White

Alabama

Senators

Arthur P. Bagby (D)
Clement Comer Clay (D) r. Nov. 1841
William R. King (D)

Representatives

Reuben Chapman (D)
George S. Houston (D)
Dixon H. Lewis (SRD)
William W. Payne (D)
Benjamin G. Shields (W)

Arkansas

Senators

William S. Fulton (D)
Ambrose H. Sevier (D)

Representatives

Edward Cross (D)

Connecticut

Senators

Jabez W. Huntington (W)
Perry Smith (D)

Representatives

William W. Boardman (W)
John H. Brockway (W)
Thomas B. Osborne (W)
Truman Smith (W)
Joseph Trumbull (W)
Thomas W. Williams (W)

Delaware

Senators

Richard H. Bayard (W)
Thomas Clayton (W)

Representatives

George B. Rodney (W)

Georgia

Senators

John M. Berrien (D)
Alfred Cuthbert (D)

Representatives

Julius C. Alford (W) r. 1841
Edward J. Black (SRW) s. 1842
Walter T. Colquitt (D) s. 1842
Mark A. Cooper (SRW) s. 1842
George W. Crawford (W)
William C. Dawson (SRW) r. Nov. 1841
Thomas F. Foster (D)
Roger L. Gamble (W)
Richard W. Habersham (D)
Thomas B. King (W)
James A. Meriwether (W)
Eugenius A. Nisbet (W) r. 1841
Lott Warren (W)

Illinois

Senators

Samuel McRoberts (D)
Richard M. Young (D)

Representatives

Zadoc Casey (D)
John Reynolds (D)
John T. Stuart (W)

Indiana

Senators

Oliver H. Smith (W)
Albert S. White (W)

Representatives

James H. Cravens (W)
Andrew Kennedy (D)
Henry S. Lane (W)

George H. Proffit (W)
Richard W. Thompson (W)
David Wallace (W)
Joseph L. White (W)

Kentucky

Senators

Henry Clay (W) r. Mar. 1842
John J. Crittenden (Un) s. 1842
James T. Morehead (W)

Representatives

Landaff W. Andrews (W)
Linn Boyd (D)
William O. Butler (D)
Garrett Davis (W)
Willis Green (W)
Thomas F. Marshall
Bryan Y. Owsley (W)
John Pope (D)
James C. Sprigg (W)
John B. Thompson (W)
Philip Triplett (W)
Joseph R. Underwood (W)
John White (W)

Louisiana

Senators

Alexander Barrow (W)
Charles M. Conrad (W) s. 1842
Alexander Mouton (D) r. Mar. 1842

Representatives

John B. Dawson (D)
John Moore (W)
Edward D. White (W)

Maine

Senators

George Evans (W)
John Fairfield (D) s. 1843
Reuel Williams (D) r. Feb. 1843

Representatives

Elisha H. Allen (W)
David Bronson (W)
Nathan Clifford (D)
William P. Fessenden (W)
Nathaniel S. Littlefield (D)
Joshua A. Lowell (D)
Alfred Marshall (D)
Benjamin Randall (W)

Maryland

Senators

John L. Kerr (W)
William D. Merrick (W)

Representatives

William Cost Johnson (W)
Isaac D. Jones (W)
John P. Kennedy (W)
John T. Mason (D)

James A. Pearce (W)
Alexander Randall (W)
Charles S. Sewall s. 1843
Augustus R. Sollers (W)
James W. Williams (D) d. Dec. 1842

Massachusetts

Senators

Isaac C. Bates (W)
Rufus Choate (W)

Representatives

John Quincy Adams (W)
Nathan Appleton (W) s. 1842
Osmyn Baker (W)
Nathaniel B. Borden (W)
George N. Briggs (W)
Barker Burnell (W)
William B. Calhoun (W)
Caleb Cushing (W)
William S. Hastings (D) d. June 1842
Charles Hudson (W)
William Parmenter (D)
Leverett Saltonstall (W)
Robert C. Winthrop (W)

Michigan

Senators

Augustus S. Porter (W)
William Woodbridge (W, D)

Representatives

Jacob M. Howard (W)

Mississippi

Senators

John Henderson (W)
Robert J. Walker (D)

Representatives

William M. Gwin (D)
Jacob Thompson (D)

Missouri

Senators

Thomas H. Benton (D)
Lewis F. Linn (D)

Representatives

John C. Edwards (D)
John Miller (D)

New Hampshire

Senators

Franklin Pierce (D) r. Feb. 1842
Leonard Wilcox s. 1842
Levi Woodbury (D)

Representatives

Charles G. Atherton (D)
Edmund Burke (D)
Ira A. Eastman (D)
John R. Reding (D)
Tristram Shaw

New Jersey

Senators

William L. Dayton (W) s. 1842
Jacob W. Miller (W)
Samuel L. Southard (W) d.
June 1842

Representatives

John B. Aycrigg (W)
William Halstead (W)
John P. B. Maxwell (W)
Joseph F. Randolph (W)
Charles C. Stratton (W)
Thomas Jones Yorke (W)

New York

Senators

Nathaniel P. Tallmadge (D)
Silas Wright, Jr. (D)

Representatives

Alfred Babcock (W)
Daniel D. Barnard (W)
Victory Birdseye(W)
Bernard Blair (W)
Samuel S. Bowne (D)
David P. Brewster (D)
Timothy Childs (W)
Thomas C. Chittenden (W)
John C. Clark (W)
Staley N. Clarke (W)
James G. Clinton (D)
Richard D. Davis (D)
Andrew W. Doig (D)
Joseph Egbert (D)
Charles G. Ferris (D)
Millard Fillmore (W)
Charles A. Floyd (D)
John G. Floyd (D)
A. Lawrence Foster (W)
Seth M. Gates (W)
Samuel Gordon (D)
Francis Granger (W) r. Mar.
1841
John Greig (W)
Hiram P. Hunt (W)
Jacob Houck, Jr. (D)
Archibald L. Linn (W)
Robert McClellan (D)
John McKeon (D)
John Maynard (W)
Christopher Morgan (W)
William M. Oliver (D)
Samuel Partridge (D)
Lewis Riggs (D)
James I. Roosevelt (D)
John Sanford (D)
Thomas A. Tomlinson (W)
John Van Buren (D)
Henry B. Van Rensselaer (W)
Aaron Ward (D)
Fernando Wood (D)
John Young (W)

North Carolina

Senators

William A. Graham (W)
Willie P. Mangum (W)

Representatives

Archibald H. Arrington (D)
Greene W. Caldwell (D)
John R. J. Daniel (D)
Edmund Deberry (W)
James Graham
James I. MacKay (D)
Anderson Mitchell (W) s. 1842
Kenneth Rayner (W)
Abraham Rencher (D)
Romulus M. Saunders (D)
Augustine H. Shepperd (W)
Edward Stanly (W)
William H. Washington
Lewis Williams d. Feb. 1842

Ohio

Senators

William Allen (D)
Benjamin Tappan (D)

Representatives

Sherlock J. Andrews (W)
Benjamin S. Cowen (W)
Ezra Dean (D)
William Doan (D)
Joshua R. Giddings (W)
Patrick G. Goode (W)
John Hastings (D)
Samson Mason (W)
James Mathews (D)
Joshua Mathiot (W)
William Medill (D)
Calvary Morris (W)
Jeremiah Morrow (W)
Nathaniel G. Pendleton (W)
Joseph Ridgway (W)
William Russell (W)
George Sweeny (D)
Samuel Stokely (W)
John B. Weller (D)

Pennsylvania

Senators

James Buchanan (D)
Daniel Sturgeon (D)

Representatives

Henry W. Beeson (D) s. 1841
Benjamin A. Bedlack (D)
Henry Black (W) d. Nov. 1841
Charles Brown (D)
Jeremiah Brown (W)
James Cooper (W)
Davis Dimock, Jr. (D) d. 1842
John Edwards (W)
Joseph Fornance (D)
James Gerry (D)
Amos Gustine (D)
Thomas Henry (W)
Enos Hook (D) r. Apr. 1842
Charles J. Ingersoll (D)
Joseph R. Ingersoll (W)
James Irvin (W)

William W. Irvin (W)
William Jack (D)
Francis James (W)
George M. Keim (D)
Joseph Lawrence (W) d. Apr.
1842
Thomas M. T. McKennan (W)
s. 1842
Albert G. Marchand (D)
Peter Newhard (D)
Arnold Plumer (D)
Robert Ramsey (W)
Almon H. Read (D) s. 1842
James W. Russell (W) s. 1842
John Sergeant (F) r. Sept. 1841
William Simonton (W)
John Snyder
George W. Toland (W)
John Westbrook (D)

Rhode Island

Senators

Nathan F. Dixon (W) d. Jan.
1842
James F. Simmons (W)
William Sprague (W) s. 1842

Representatives

Robert B. Cranston (W)
Joseph L. Tillinghast (W)

South Carolina

Senators

John C. Calhoun (D) r. Mar.
1843
George McDuffie (D) s. 1843
William C. Preston (Null-D) r.
Nov. 1842

Representatives

Sampson H. Butler (D) r. Sept.
1842
William Butler (W)
Patrick C. Caldwell (SRD)
John Campbell (SRD)
Isaac E. Holmes (D)
Francis W. Pickens (Null-D)
R. Barnwell Rhett (D)
James Rogers (D)
Thomas D. Sumter (D)
Samuel W. Trotti (D) s. Dec.
1842

Tennessee

Senators

Alfred O. P. Nicholson (D) r.
Feb. 1842
Vacant

Representatives

Thomas D. Arnold (W)
Aaron V. Brown (D)
Milton Brown (W)
William B. Campbell (W)
Robert L. Caruthers (W)
Meredith P. Gentry (W)
Cave Johnson (D)
Abraham McClellan (D)
Hopkins L. Turney (D)

Harvey M. Watterson (D)
Christopher H. Williams (W)
Joseph L. Williams (W)

Vermont

Senators

Samuel C. Crafts (W) s. 1842
Samuel S. Phelps (W)
Samuel Prentiss (W) r. Apr.
1842

Representatives

Horace Everett (W)
Hiland Hall (W)
John Mattocks (W)
William Salde (W)
Augustus Young (W)

Virginia

Senators

William S. Archer (W)
William C. Rives (W)

Representatives

Linn Banks (D) r. Dec. 1841
Richard W. Bartin (W)
John W. Botts (W)
George B. Cary (D)
Walter Coles (D)
Thomas W. Gilmer (W)
William L. Goggin (W)
William O. Goode (D)
William A. Harris (D)
Samuel L. Hays (D)
George W. Hopkins (D)
Edmund W. Hubard (D)
Robert M. T. Hunter (D)
John W. Jones (D)
Francis Mallory (W)
Cuthbert Powell (W)
William Smith (D) s. 1841
Lewis Steenrod (D)
Alexander H. H. Stuart (W)
George W. Summers (W)
John Taliaferro (W)
Henry A. Wise (W)

Twenty-Eighth Congress

(Mar. 4, 1843, to
Mar. 3, 1845)

President of the Senate: John
Tyler
*President Pro Tempore of the
Senate:* Willie P. Mangum
*Speaker of the House of
Representatives:* John W.
Jones

Alabama

Senators

Arthur P. Bagby (D)
William R. King (D) r. Apr.
1844
Dixon H. Lewis (D) s. 1844

Representatives

James E. Belser (D)
Reuben Chapman (D)
James Dellet (W)
George S. Houston (D)
Dixon H. Lewis (SRD) r. Apr. 1844
Felix G. McConnell (D)
William W. Payne (D)
William L. Yancey (D) s. 1844

Arkansas

Senators

Chester Ashley (D) s. 1844
William S. Fulton (D) d. Aug. 1844
Ambrose H. Sevier (D)

Representatives

Edward Cross (D)

Connecticut

Senators

Jabez W. Huntington (W)
John M. Niles (D)

Representatives

George S. Catlin (D)
Thomas H. Seymour (D)
Samuel Simons (D)
John Stewart (D)

Delaware

Senators

Richard H. Bayard (W)
Thomas Clayton (W)

Representatives

George B. Rodney (W)

Georgia

Senators

John M. Berrien (W)
Walter T. Colquitt (D)

Representatives

Edward J. Balck (SRW)
Absalom H. Chappell (SRW)
Duncan L. Clinch (W) s. 1844
Howell Cobb (D)
Mark A. Cooper (SRW) r. June 1843
Hugh A. Haralson (D)
John B. Lamar (D) r. July 1843
John H. Lumpkin (D)
John Millen (D) d. Oct. 1943
Alexander H. Stephens (W)
Williams H. Stiles (D)

Illinois

Senators

Sidney Breese (D)
Samuel McRoberts (D) d. Mar. 1843
James Semple (D) s. Dec. 1843

Representatives

Stephen A. Douglas (D)
Orlando B. Ficklin (D)
John J. Hardin (W)
Joseph P. Hoge (D)
John A. McClernand (D)
Robert Smith (D)
John Wentworth (D)

Indiana

Senators

Edward A. Hannegan (D)
Albert S. White (W)

Representatives

William J. Brown (D)
John W. Davis (D)
Thomas J. Henley (D)
Andrew Kennedy (D)
Robert D. Owen (D)
John Pettit (D)
Samuel C. Sample (W)
Caleb B. Smith (W)
Thomas Smith (D)
Joseph A. Wright (D)

Kentucky

Senators

John J. Crittenden (W)
James T. Morehead (W)

Representatives

Linn Boyd (D)
George A. Caldwell (D)
Garrett Davis (W)
Richard French (D)
Willis Green (W)
Henry Grider (W)
James W. Stone (D)
William P. Thomasson (W)
John W. Tibbatts (D)
John White (W)

Louisiana

Senators

Alexander Barrow (W)
Henry Johnson (W) s. 1844

Representatives

Pierre E. J. B. Bossier (D) d. Apr. 1844
John B. Dawson (D)
Alcee L. La Branche (D)
Isaac E. Morse (D) s. 1844
John Slidell (SRD)

Maine

Senators

George Evans (W)
John Fairfield (D)

Representatives

Shepard Cary (D) s. 1844
Robert P. Dunlap (D)
Hannibal Hamlin (D)
Joshua Herrick (D)
Freeman H. Morse (W)
Luther Severance (W)
Benjamin White (D) s. 1844

Maryland

Senators

William D. Merrick (W)
James A. Pearce (W)

Representatives

Francis Brengle (W)
John M. S. Causin (W)
John P. Kennedy (W)
Jacob A. Preston (W)
Thomas A. Spence (W)
John Wethered

Massachusetts

Senators

Isaac C. Bates (W)
Rufus Choate (W)

Representatives

Amos Abbott (W)
John Quincy Adams (W)
Osmyn Baker (W)
Barker Burnell (W) d. 1843
Joseph Grinnell (W)
Charles Hudson (W)
Daniel P. King (W)
William Parmenter (D)
Julius Rockwell (W)
Henry Williams (D)
Robert C. Winthrop (W)

Michigan

Senators

Augustus S. Porter (W)
William Woodbridge (W, D)

Representatives

James B. Hunt (D)
Lucius Lyon (D)
Robert McClelland (D)

Mississippi

Senators

John Henderson (W)
Robert J. Walker (D)

Representatives

William H. Hammett (D)
Robert W. Roberts (D)
Jacob Thompson (D)
Tilghman M. Tucker (D)

Missouri

Senators

David R. Atchison (W)
Thomas H. Benton (D)
Lewis F. Linn (D) d. Oct. 1843

Representatives

Gustavus M. Bower (D)
James B. Bowlin (D)
John Jameson (D)
James M. Hughes (D)
James H. Relfe (D)

New Hampshire

Senators

Charles G. Atherton (D)
Levi Woodbury (D)

Representatives

Edmund Burke (D)
John P. Hale (D)
Moses Norris, Jr. (D)
John R. Reding (D)

New Jersey

Senators

William L. Dayton (W)
Jacob W. Miller (W)

Representatives

Lucius Q. C. Elmer (D)
Isaac G. Farlee
Littleton Kirkpatrick (D)
George Sykes (D)
William Wright (W)

New York

Senators

Daniel S. Dickinson (D) s. 1844
John A. Dix (D) s. 1845
Henry A. Foster (D) ta. 1844
Nathaniel P. Tallmadge (D) r. June 1844
Silas Wright, Jr. (D) r. Nov. 1844

Representatives

Joseph H. Anderson (D)
Daniel D. Barnard (W)
Samuel Beardsley (D) r. Mar. 1844
Charles S. Benton (D)
Levi D. Carpenter (D) s. 1844
Charles H. Carroll (W)
Jeremiah E. Cary (D)
James G. Clinton (D)
Amasa Dana (D)
Richard D. Davis (D)

Chesselden Ellis (D)
Hamilton Fish (W)
Byram Green
William S. Hubbell (D)
Orville Hungerford (D)
Washington Hunt (W)
Preston King (D)
Moses G. Leonard (D)
William B. Maclay (D)
William A. Moseley (W)
Henry C. Murphy (D)
Thomas J. Patterson (W)
J. Phillips Phoenix (W)
Zadock Pratt (D)
Smith M. Purdy (D)
George Rathbun (D)
Orville Robinson (D)
Charles Rogers (W)
Jeremiah Russell (D)
David L. Seymour (D)
Albert Smith
Lemuel Stetson (D)
Selah B. Strong (D)
Asher Tyler (W)
Horace Wheaton (D)

North Carolina

Senators

William H. Haywood, Jr. (D)
Willie P. Mangum (W)

Representatives

Archibald H. Arrington (D)
Daniel M. Barringer (W)
Thomas L. Clingman (W)
John R. J. Daniel (D)
Edmund Deberry (W)
James I. McKay (D)
Kenneth Rayner (W)
David S. Reid (D)
Romulus M. Saunders (D)

Ohio

Senators

William Allen (D)
Benjamin Tappan (D)

Representatives

Jacob Brinkerhoff (D)
Ezra Dean (D)
Alexander Duncan (W)
Elias Florence (W)
Joshua R. Giddings (W)
Edward S. Hamlin (W) s. 1844
Alexander Harper (W)
Perley B. Johnson (W)
William C. McCauslen (D)
Joseph J. McDowell (D)
James Mathews (D)
Heman A. Moore (D) d. Apr.
  1844
Joseph Morris (D)
Emery D. Potter (D)
Henry St. John (D)
Robert C. Schenck (W)
Alfred P. Stone (D) s. 1844
Daniel R. Tilden (W)
Joseph Vance (W)
John I. Vanmeter (W)
Samuel F. Vinton (W)
John B. Weller (D)

Pennsylvania

Senators

James Buchanan (D)
Daniel Sturgeon (D)

Representatives

Benjamin A. Bidlack (D)
James Black (D)
Richard Brodhead (D)
Jeremiah Brown (W)
Joseph Buffington (D)
Cornelius Darragh (W) s. 1844
John Dickey (W)
Henry D. Foster (D)
Henry Frick (W) d. Mar. 1844
George Fuller (D) s. 1844
Samuel Hays (D)
Charles J. Ingersoll (D)
Joseph R. Ingersoll (W)
James Irvin (W)
Michael H. Jenks (W)
Abraham R. McIlvaine (W)
Edward Joy Morris (W)
Henry Nes
James Pollock (W) s. 1844
Alexander Ramsey (W)
Almon H. Read (D) d. June
  1844
Charles M. Reed (D)
John Ritter (D)
John T. Smith (D)
Andrew Stewart (W)
William Wilkins (D) r. Feb.
  1844
Jacob S. Yost (D)

Rhode Island

Senators

John B. Francis (Law & Order)
  s. 1844
James F. Simmons (W)
William Sprague (W) r. Jan.
  1844

Representatives

Henry Y. Cranston (W)
Elisha R. Potter, Jr. (W)

South Carolina

Senators

Daniel E. Huger (SRD)
George McDuffie (D)

Representatives

James A. Balck (D)
Armistead Burt (D)
John Campbell (SRD)
Isaac E. Holmes (D)
R. Barnwell Rhett (D)
Richard F. Simpson (D)
Joseph A. Woodward (D)

Tennessee

Senators

Ephraim H. Foster (W)
Spencer Jarnagin (W)

Representatives

John B. Ashe (W)
Julius W. Blackwell (D)
Aaron V. Brown (D)
Milton Brown (W)
Alvan Cullom (D)
David W. Dickinson (W)
Andrew Johnson (D)
Cave Johnson (D)
George W. Jones (D)
Joseph H. Peyton (W)
William T. Senter (W)

Vermont

Senators

Samuel S. Phelps (W)
William Upham (W)

Representatives

Jacob Collamer (W)
Paul Dillingham, Jr. (D)
Solomon Foot (W)
George F. Marsh (W)

Virginia

Senators

William S. Archer (W)
William C. Rives (W)

Representatives

Archibald Atkinson (D)
Thomas H. Bayly (SRD) s.
  1844
Augustus A. Chapman (D)
Samuel Chilton (W)
Walter Coles (D)
George C. Dromgoole (D)
Thomas W. Gilmer (W) r. Feb.
  1844
William L. Goggin (W) s. 1844
George W. Hopkins (D)
Edmund W. Hubard (D)
John W. Jones (D)
William Lucas (D)
Willoughby Newton (W)
Lewis Steenrod (D)
George W. Summers (W)
William Taylor (D)
Henry A. Wise (D) r. Feb.
  1844

Twenty-Ninth Congress

(Mar. 4, 1845, to
Mar. 3, 1847)

President of the Senate: George
  M. Dallas
*Presidents Pro Tempore of the
  Senate:* Ambrose H. Sevier;
  David R. Atchison
*Speaker of the House of
  Representatives:* John W.
  Davis

Alabama

Senators

Arthur P. Bagby (D)
Dixon H. Lewis (D)

Representatives

Franklin W. Bowdon (D) s.
  1846
Reuben Chapman (D)
James L. Cottrell (D) s. 1846
Edmund S. Dargan (D)
Henry W. Hilliard (W)
George S. Houston (D)
Felix G. McConnell (D) d.
  Sept. 1846
William W. Payne (D)
William L. Yancey (D) r. Sept.
  1846

Arkansas

Senators

Chester Ashley (D)
Ambrose H. Sevier (D)

Representatives

Thomas W. Newton (W) s.
  1847
Archibald Yell (D) r. July 1846

Connecticut

Senators

Jabez W. Huntington (W)
John M. Niles (D)

Representatives

James Dixon (W)
Samuel D. Hubbard (W)
John A. Rockwell (W)
Truman Smith (W)

Delaware

Senators

John M. Clayton (W)
Thomas Clayton (W)

Representatives

John W. Houston

Florida

Senators

James D. Westcott, Jr. (D)
David Levy Yulee

Representatives

William H. Brockenbrough (D)
  s. 1846
Edward C. Cabell (W) r. Jan.
  1846

Georgia

Senators

John M. Berrien (W)
Walter T. Colquitt (D)

Representatives

Howell Cobb (D)
Hugh A. Haralson (D)
Seaborn Jones (D)
Thomas B. King (W)
John H. Lumpkin (D)
Alexander H. Stephens (D)
Robert Toombs (SRD)
George W. B. Towns (D) s.
1846

Illinois

Senators

Sidney Breese (D)
James Semple (D)

Representatives

Edward D. Baker (W) r. Dec.
1846
Stephen A. Douglas (D)
Orlando B. Ficklin (D)
John Henry (W) s. 1847
Joseph P. Hoge (D)
John A. McClernand (D)
Robert Smith (D)
John Wentworth (D)

Indiana

Senators

Jesse D. Bright (D)
Edward A. Hannegan (D)

Representatives

Charles W. Cathcart (D)
John W. Davis (D)
Thomas J. Henley (D)
Andrew Kennedy (D)
Edward W. McGaughey (W)
Robert D. Owen (D)
John Pettit (D)
Caleb B. Smith (W)
Thomas Smith (D)
William W. Wick (D)

Iowa

Senators

Vacant

Representatives

S. Clinton Hastings (D) s. 1846
Shepherd Leffler (D) s. 1846

Kentucky

Senators

John J. Crittenden
James T. Morehead (W)

Representatives

Joshua F. Bell (W)
Linn Boyd (D)
Garrett Davis (W)
Henry Grider (W)
John H. McHenry (W)
John P. Martin (D)
William P. Thomasson (W)
John W. Tibbatts (D)
Andrew Trumbo (W)
Bryan R. Young (D)

Louisiana

Senators

Alexander Barrow (W) d. Dec.
1846
Henry Johnson (W)
Pierre Soule s. 1847

Representatives

John H. Harmanson (D)
Emile LaSere (D) s. 1846
Isaac E. Morse (D)
John Slidell (SRD) r. Nov. 1845
Bannon G. Thibodeaux

Maine

Senators

George Evans (W)
John Fairfield (D)

Representatives

Robert P. Dunlap (D)
Hannibal Hamlin (D)
John D. McCrate (D)
Cullen Sawtelle (D)
John F. Scammon (D)
Luther Severance (W)
Hezekiah Williams (D)

Maryland

Senators

Reverdy Johnson (W)
James A. Pearce (W)

Representatives

John G. Chapman (W)
Albert Constable (D)
William F. Giles (D)
Thomas W. Ligon (D)
Edward H. C. Long (W)
Thomas J. Perry (D)

Massachusetts

Senators

Isaac C. Bates (W) d. Mar.
1845
John Davis (W) s. 1845
Daniel Webster (W)

Representatives

Amos Abbott (W)
John Quincy Adams (W)
George Ashmun (W)

Joseph Grinnell (W)
Artemas Hale (W)
Charles Hudson (W)
Daniel P. King (W)
Julius Rockwell (W)
Benjamin Thompson (W)
Robert C. Winthrop (W)

Michigan

Senators

Lewis Cass (D)
William Woodbridge (W, D)

Representatives

John S. Chipman (D)
James B. Hunt (D)
Robert McClelland (D)

Mississippi

Senators

Joseph W. Chalmers (D) s.
1845
Jesse Speight (D)
Robert J. Walker (D) r. Mar.
1845

Representatives

Stephen Adams (D)
Jefferson Davis (D) r. June
1846
Henry T. Ellett (D) s. 1847
Robert W. Roberts (D)
Jacob Thompson (D)

Missouri

Senators

David R. Atchison (W)
Thomas H. Benton (D)

Representatives

James B. Bowlin (D)
William McDaniel (D) s. 1846
Sterling Price (D) r. Aug. 1846
John S. Phelps (D)
James H. Relfe (D)
Leonard H. Sims (D)

New Hampshire

Senators

Charles G. Atherton (D)
Joseph Cilley (D) s. 1846
Benning W. Jenness (D) ta.
1845
Levi Woodbury (D) r. Nov.
1845

Representatives

James H. Johnson
Mace Moulton (D)
Moses Norris, Jr. (D)

New Jersey

Senators

William L. Dayton (W)
Jacob W. Miller (W)

Representatives

Joseph E. Edsall (D)
James G. Hampton (W)
John Runk (W)
George Sykes (D) s. 1845
Samuel G. Wright
William Wright (W)

New York

Senators

Daniel S. Dickinson (D)
John A. Dix (D)

Representatives

Joseph H. Anderson (D)
Charles S. Benton (D)
William W. Campbell (Amer.)
Charles H. Carroll (D)
John F. Collin (D)
Erastus D. Culver (W)
John De Mott (D)
Samuel S. Ellsworth (D)
Charles Goodyear (D)
Samuel Gordon (D)
Martin Grover (D)
Richard P. Herrick (W) d. June
1846
Elias B. Holmes (W)
William J. Hough (D)
Orville Hungerford (D)
Washington Hunt (W)
Timothy Jenkins (D)
Preston King (D)
John W. Lawrence (D)
Abner Lewis (W)
William B. Maclay (D)
William S. Miller
William A. Moseley (W)
Archibald C. Niven (D)
George Rathbun (D)
Thomas C. Ripley s. 1846
Joseph Russell (D)
Henry J. Seaman (Amer)
Albert Smith (R)
Stephen Strong (D)
Horace Wheaton (D)
Hugh White
Bradford R. Wood (D)
Thomas M. Woodruff (D)
William W. Woodworth (D)

North Carolina

Senators

George E. Badger (W) s. 1846
William H. Haywood, Jr. (D) r.
July 1846
Willie P. Mangum (W)

Representatives

Daniel M. Barringer (W)
Asa Biggs (D)
Henry S. Clark (D)
John R. J. Daniel (D)
James C. Dobbin (D)

Alfred Dockery (W)
James Graham (W)
James I. McKay (D)
David S. Reid (D)

Ohio

Senators

William Allen (D)
Thomas Corwin (W)

Representatives

Jacob Brinkerhoff (D)
John D. Cummins (D)
Francis A. Cunningham (D)
Columbus Delano (W)
James J. Faran (D)
George Fries (D)
Joshua R. Giddings (W)
Alexander Harper (W)
Joseph J. McDowell (D)
Joseph Morris (D)
Isaac Parrish (D)
Augustus L. Perrill (D)
Joseph M. Root (W)
William Sawyer (D)
Robert C. Schenck (W)
Henry St. John (D)
David A. Starkweather (D)
Allen G. Thurman (D)
Daniel R. Tilden (W)
Joseph Vance (W)
Samuel F. Vinton (W)

Pennsylvania

Senators

James Buchanan (D) r. Mar.
1845
Simon Cameron (D) s. Mar.
1845
Daniel Sturgeon (D)

Representatives

James Black (D)
John Blanchard (W)
Richard Brodhead (D)
Joseph Buffington (W)
John H. Campbell (W)
Cornelius Darragh (W)
Jacob Erdman (D)
John H. Ewing (W)
Henry D. Foster (D)
William S. Garvin (D)
Charles J. Ingersoll (D)
Joseph R. Ingersoll (W)
Owen D. Leib (D)
Lewis C. Levin (Amer.)
Moses McClean (D)
Abraham R. McIlvaine (W)
James Pollock (W)
Alexander Ramsey (W)
John Ritter (D)
Andrew Stewart (W)
John Strohm (W)
James Thompson (W)
David Wilmot (D)
Jacob S. Yost (D)

Rhode Island

Senators

Albert C. Greene (W)

James F. Simmons (W)

Representatives

Lemuel H. Arnold (W)
Henry Y. Cranston (W)

South Carolina

Senators

Andrew P. Butler (SRD) s.
1846
John C. Calhoun (D) s. 1846
George McDuffie (D) r. Aug.
1846

Representatives

James A. Black (D)
Armistead Burt (D)
Isaac E. Holmes (D)
R. Barnwell Rhett (D)
Richard F. Simpson (D)
Alexander D. Sims (D)
Joseph A. Woodward (D)

Tennessee

Senators

Spencer Jarnagin (W)
Hopkins L. Turney (D)

Representatives

Milton Brown (W)
Lucien B. Chase (D)
William M. Cocke (D)
John H. Crozier (W)
Alvan Cullom (D)
Edwin H. Ewing (W) s. 1846
Meredith P. Gentry (W)
Andrew Johnson (D)
George W. Jones (D)
Barclay Martin (D)
Joseph H. Peyton (W) d. Nov.
1845
Frederick P. Stanton (D)

Texas

Senators

Sam Houston (D) s. 1846
Thomas J. Rusk (D) s. 1846

Representatives

David S. Kaufman (D) s. 1846
Timothy Pilsbury (D) s. 1846

Vermont

Senators

Samuel S. Phelps (W)
William Upham (W)

Representatives

Jacob Collamer (W)
Paul Dillingham, Jr. (D)
Solomon Foot (W)
George P. Marsh (W)

Virginia

Senators

William S. Archer (W)
James M. Mason (D) s. 1847
Isaac S. Pennybacker (D) d.
Jan. 1847

Representatives

Archibald Atkinson (D)
Thomas H. Bayly (SRD)
Henry Bedinger (D)
William G. Brown (D)
Augustus A. Chapman (D)
George C. Dromgoole (D)
George W. Hopkins (D)
Edmund W. Hubard (D)
Robert M. T. Hunter (D)
Joseph Johnson (D)
Shelton F. Leake (D)
James McDowell (D) s. 1846
John S. Pendleton (W)
James A. Seddon (D)
William Taylor (D) d. Jan.
1847
William M. Tredway (D)

Thirtieth Congress

(Mar. 4, 1847, to
Mar. 3, 1849)

President of the Senate: George
M. Dallas
*President Pro Tempore of the
Senate:* David R. Atchison
*Speaker of the House of
Representatives:* Robert C.
Winthrop

Alabama

Senators

Arthur P. Bagby (D) r. June
1848
Benjamin Fitzpatrick (SRD) s.
1848
William R. King (D) s. 1848
Dixon H. Lewis (D) d. Oct.
1848

Representatives

Franklin W. Bowdon (D)
Williamson R. W. Cobb (D)
John Gayle (W)
Sampson W. Harris (D)
Henry W. Hilliard (W)
George S. Houston (D)
Samuel W. Inge (D)

Arkansas

Senators

Chester Ashley (D) d. Apr.
1848
Solon Borland (D) s. 1848
William K. Sebastian (D) s.
1848
Ambrose H. Sevier (D) r. Mar.
1848

Representatives

Robert W. Johnson (D)

Connecticut

Senators

Roger S. Baldwin (W) s. 1847
Jabez W. Huntington (W) d.
Nov. 1847
John M. Niles (D)

Representatives

James Dixon (W)
Samuel D. Hubbard (W)
John A. Rockwell (W)
Truman Smith (W)

Delaware

Senators

John M. Clayton (W) r. Feb.
1849
Presley Spruance (W)
John Wales s. 1849

Representatives

John W. Houston (W)

Florida

Senators

James D. Westcott, Jr. (D)
David Levy Yulee

Representatives

Edward C. Cabell (W)

Georgia

Senators

John M. Berrien (W)
Walter T. Colquitt (D) r. Feb.
1848
Herschel V. Johnson (D) s.
1848

Representatives

Howell Cobb (D)
Hugh A. Haralson (D)
Alfred Iverson (D)
John W. Jones (W)
Thomas B. King (W)
John H. Lumpkin (D)
Alexander H. Stephens (D)
Robert Toombs (SRD)

Illinois

Senators

Sidney Breese (D)
Stephen A. Douglas (D)

Representatives

Orlando B. Ficklin (D)

Abraham Lincoln (W)
John A. McClernand (D)
William A. Richardson (D)
Robert Smith (D)
Thomas J. Turner (D)
John Wentworth (D)

Indiana

Senators

Jesse D. Bright (D)
Edward A. Hannegan (D)

Representatives

Charles W. Cathcart (D)
George G. Dunn (W)
Elisha Embree (W)
Thomas J. Henley (D)
John Petit (D)
John L. Robinson (D)
William Rockhill (D)
Caleb B. Smith (W)
Richard W. Thompson (W)
William W. Wick (D)

Iowa

Senators

Augustus C. Dodge (D)
George W. Jones

Representatives

Shepherd Leffler (D)
William Thompson (D)

Kentucky

Senators

John J. Crittenden r. June 1848
Thomas Metcalfe (D) s. 1848
Joseph R. Underwood (W)

Representatives

Green Adams (W)
Linn Boyd (D)
Aylett Buckner (W)
Beverly L. Clarke (D)
W. Garnett Duncan (W)
Richard French (D)
John P. Gaines (W)
Charles S. Morehead (W)
Samuel O. Peyton (D)
John B. Thompson (W)

Louisiana

Senators

Solomon W. Downs (D)
Henry Johnson (W)

Representatives

John H. Harmanson (D)
Emile La Sere (D)
Isaac E. Morse (D)
Bannon G. Thibodeaux

Maine

Senators

James W. Bradbury (D)
John Fairfield (D) d. Dec. 1847
Hannibal Hamlin (D) s. 1848
Wyman B. S. Moor (D) ta. 1848

Representatives

Hiram Belcher (W)
Asa W. H. Clapp (D)
Franklin Clark (D)
David Hammons (D)
Ephraim K. Smart (D)
James S. Wiley (D)
Hezekiah Williams (D)

Maryland

Senators

Reverdy Johnson (W)
James A. Pearce (W)

Representatives

John G. Chapman (W)
John W. Crisfield (W)
Alexander Evans (W)
Thomas W. Ligon (D)
Robert M. McLane (D)
J. Dixon Roman (W)

Massachusetts

Senators

John Davis (W)
Daniel Webster (W)

Representatives

Amos Abbott (W)
John Quincy Adams (W) d. Feb. 1848
George Ashmun (W)
Joseph Grinnell (W)
Artemas Hale (W)
Charles Hudson (W)
Daniel P. King (W)
Horace Mann (W) s. 1848
John G. Palfrey (W)
Julius Rockwell (W)
Robert C. Winthrop (W)

Michigan

Senators

Lewis Cass (D) r. May 1848
Alpheus Felch (D)
Thomas Fitzgerald (D) s. June 1848

Representatives

Kinsley S. Bingham (D)
Edward Bradley (D)
Robert McClelland (D)
Charles E. Stuart (D)

Mississippi

Senators

Jefferson Davis (D) s. Aug. 1847
Henry S. Foote (Un)
Jesse Speight (D) d. May 1847

Representatives

Albert G. Brown (D)
Winfield S. Featherston (D)
Jacob Thompson (D)
Patrick W. Thompkins (W)

Missouri

Senators

David R. Atchison (W)
Thomas H. Benton (D)

Representatives

James B. Bowlin (D)
James S. Green (D)
Williard P. Hall (D)
John Jameson (D)
John S. Phelps (D)

New Hampshire

Senators

Charles G. Atherton (D)
John P. Hales (Anti-Slavery)

Representatives

James H. Johnson
Charles H. Peaslee (D)
Amos Tuck
James Wilson (W)

New Jersey

Senators

William L. Dayton (W)
Jacob W. Miller (W)

Representatives

Joseph E. Edsall (D)
Dudley S. Gregory (W)
James G. Hampton (W)
William A. Newell (W)
John Van Dyke (W)

New York

Senators

Daniel S. Dickinson (D)
John A. Dix (D)

Representatives

Ausburn Birdsall (D)
Esbon Blackmar (W) s. 1848
William Collins (D)
Harmon S. Conger (W)
William Duer (W)
Daniel Gott (W)
Horace Greeley (W) s. 1848

Nathan K. Hall (W)
John M. Holley (W) d. Mar. 1848
Elias B. Holmes (W)
Washington Hunt (W)
David S. Jackson (D) r. Apr. 1848
Timothy Jenkins (D)
Orlando Kellogg (W)
Sidney Lawrence (D)
William T. Lawrence (D)
Frederick W. Lord (W)
William B. Maclay (D)
Dudley Marvin (W)
Joseph Mullin (W)
Henry C. Murphy (D)
William Nelson (W)
Henry Nicoll (D)
George Petrie
Harvey Putnam (W)
Gideon Reynolds (W)
Robert L. Rose (W)
David Rumsey, Jr. (W)
Daniel B. St. John (W)
Eliakim Sherrill (W)
Peter H. Silvester (W)
John I. Slingerland
George A. Starkweather (D)
Frederick A. Tallmadge (W)
Cornelius Warren (W)
Hugh White

North Carolina

Senators

George E. Badger (W)
Willie P. Mangum (W)

Representatives

Daniel M. Barringer (W)
Nathaniel Boyden
Thomas L. Clingman (W)
John R. J. Daniel (D)
Richard S. Donnell (W)
James I. McKay (D)
David Outlaw (W)
Augustine H. Shepperd (W)
Abraham W. Venable (D)

Ohio

Senators

William Allen (D)
Thomas Corwin (W)

Representatives

Richard S. Canby (W)
John Crowell (W)
John D. Cummins (D)
Rodolphus Dickinson (D)
Daniel Duncan (W)
Thomas O. Edward (W)
Nathan Evans (W)
James J. Faran (D)
David Fisher (W)
George Fries (D)
Joshua R. Giddings (W)
William Kennon, Jr. (D)
Samuel Lahm (D)
John K. Miller (D)
Jonathan D. Morris (D)
Thomas Ritchey (D)
Joseph M. Root (W)
William Sawyer (D)
Robert C. Schenck (W)

John L. Taylor (W)
Samuel F. Vinton (W)

Pennsylvania

Senators

Simon Cameron (D)
Daniel Sturgeon (D)

Representatives

John Blanchgard (W)
Jasper E. Brady (W)
Samuel A. Bridges (D) s. 1848
Richard Brodhead (D)
Charles Brown (D)
Chester P. Butler (W)
John Dickey (W)
George N. Eckert (W)
John W. Farrelly (W)
John Freedley (W)
Moses Hampton (W)
John W. Hornbeck (W) d. Jan. 1848
Charles J. Ingersoll (D)
Joseph R. Ingersoll (W)
Alexander Irvin (W)
Lewis C. Levin (Amer)
Abraham R. McIlvaine (W)
Job Mann (D)
Henry Nes
James Pollock (W)
Andrew Stewart (W)
John Strong (D)
James Thompson (W)
David Wilmot (D)

Rhode Island

Senators

John H. Clarke (W)
Albert C. Greene (W)

Representatives

Robert B. Cranston (W)
Benjamin B. Thurston (D)

South Carolina

Senators

Andrew P. Butler (SRD)
John C. Calhoun (D)

Representatives

James A. Black (D) d. Apr. 1848
Armistead Burt (D)
Isaac E. Holmes (D)
John McQueen (D)
R. Barnwell Rhett (D)
Richard F. Simpson (D)
Alexander D. Sims (D) d. Nov. 1848
Daniel Wallace (W) s. 1848
Joseph A. Woodward (D)

Tennessee

Senators

John Bell (W)
Hopkins L. Turney (D)

Representatives

Washington Barrow (W)
Lucien B. Chase (D)
William M. Cocke (D)
John H. Crozier (W)
Meredith P. Gentry (W)
William T. Haskell (W)
Hugh L. W. Hill (D)
Andrew Johnson (D)
George W. Jones (D)
Frederick P. Stanton (D)
James H. Thomas (D)

Texas

Senators

Sam Houston (D)
Thomas J. Rusk (D)

Representatives

David S. Kaufman (D)
Timothy Pilsbury (D)

Vermont

Senators

Samuel S. Phelps (W)
William Upham (W)

Representatives

Jacob Collamer (W)
William Henry (W)
George P. Marsh (W)
Lucius B. Peck (D)

Virginia

Senators

Robert M. T. Hunter (D)
James M. Mason (D)

Representatives

Archibald Atkinson (D)
Thomas H. Bayly (SRD)
Richard Lee T. Beale (D)
Henry Bedinger (D)
Thomas S. Bocock (D)
John M. Botts (W)
William G. Brown (D)
George C. Dromgoole (D) d. Apr. 1847
Thomas S. Flournoy (W)
Andrew S. Fulton (W)
William L. Goggin (W)
James McDowell (D)
Richard K. Meade (D)
John S. Pendleton (W)
William B. Preston (W)
Robert A. Thompson (D)

Wisconsin

Senators

Henry Dodge (D) s. 1848
Isaac P. Walker (D) s. 1848

Representatives

Mason C. Darling (D) s. 1848

William P. Lynde (D) s. 1848

Thirty-First Congress

(Mar. 4, 1849, to
Mar. 3, 1851)

President of the Senate: Millard Fillmore
Presidents Pro Tempore of the Senate: David R. Atchison; William R. King
Speaker of the House of Representatives: Howell Cobb

Alabama

Senators

Jeremiah Clemens (D)
Benjamin Fitzpatrick (SRD) r. Dec. 1849
William R. King (D)

Representatives

William J. Alston (W)
Franklin W. Bowdon (D)
Williamson R. W. Cobb (D)
Sampson W. Harris (D)
Henry W. Hilliard (W)
David Hubbard (SRD)
Samuel W. Inge (D)

Arkansas

Senators

Solon Borland (D)
William K. Sebastian (D)

Representatives

Robert W. Johnson (D)

California

Senators

John C. Fremont (D) s. 1850
William M. Gwin (D) s. 1850

Representatives

Edward Gilbert (D) s. 1850
George W. Wright s. 1850

Connecticut

Senators

Roger S. Baldwin (W)
Truman Smith (W)

Representatives

Walter Booth (Free-Soiler)
Thomas B. Butler (W)
Chauncey F. Cleveland (D)
Loren P. Waldo (D)

Delaware

Senators

Presley Spruance (W)
John Wales

Representatives

John W. Houston (W)

Florida

Senators

Jackson Morton (W)
David Levy Yulee (W)

Representatives

Edward C. Cabell (W)

Georgia

Senators

John M. Berrien (W)
William C. Dawson (SRW)

Representatives

Howell Cobb (D)
Thomas C. Hackett (D)
Hugh A. Haralson (D)
Joseph W. Jackson (D) s. 1850
Thomas B. King (W) r. 1850
Allen F. Owen (W)
Alexander H. Stephens (D)
Robert Toombs (SRD)
Marshall J. Wellborn (D)

Illinois

Senators

Stephen A. Douglas (D)
James Shields (D)

Representatives

Edward D. Baker
William H. Bissell (D)
Thomas L. Harris (D)
John A. McClernand (D)
William A. Richardson (D)
John Wentworth (D)
Timothy R. Young (D)

Indiana

Senators

Jesse D. Bright (D)
James Whitcomb (D)

Representatives

Nathaniel Albertson (D)
William J. Brown (D)
Cyrus L. Dunham (D)
Graham N. Fitch (D)
Willis A. Gorman (D)
Andrew J. Harlan (D)
George W. Julian (Free-Soiler)
Joseph E. McDonald (D)
Edward W. McGaughey (W)

John L. Robinson (D)

Iowa

Senators

Augustus C. Dodge (D)
George W. Jones (D)

Representatives

Shepherd Leffler (D)
Daniel F. Miller (W) s. 1850
William Thompson (D) r. June 1850

Kentucky

Senators

Henry Clay (W)
Joseph R. Underwood (W)

Representatives

Daniel Breck (W)
Linn Boyd (D)
George A. Caldwell (D)
James L. Johnson (W)
Finis E. McLean (W)
Humphrey Marshall (W)
John C. Mason (D)
Charles S. Morehead (W)
Richard H. Stanton (D)
John B. Thompson (W)

Louisiana

Senators

Solomon W. Downs (D)
Pierre Soule (SRD)

Representatives

Henry A. Bullard (W) s. 1850
Charles M. Conrad (W) r. Aug. 1850
John H. Harmanson (D) d. Oct. 1850
Emile LaSere (D)
Isaac E. Morse (D)
Alexander G. Penn (D) s. 1850

Maine

Senators

James W. Bradbury (D)
Hannibal Hamlin (D)

Representatives

Thomas J. D. Fuller (D)
Elbridge Gerry (D)
Rufus K. Goodenow (W)
Nathaniel S. Littlefield (D)
John Otis (W)
Cullen Sawtelle (D)
Charles Stetson (D)

Maryland

Senators

Reverdy Johnson (W) r. Mar. 1849
James A. Pearce (W)
Thomas G. Pratt (W) s. 1850
David Stewart (W) ta. 1849

Representatives

Richard J. Bowie (W)
Alexander Evans (W)
William T. Hamilton (D)
Edward Hammond (D)
John B. Kerr (W)
Robert M. McLane (D)

Massachusetts

Senators

John Davis (W)
Robert Rantoul, Jr. (D) s. 1851
Daniel Webster (W) r. July 1850
Robert C. Winthrop (W) ta. 1850

Representatives

Charles Allen (Free-Soiler)
George Ashmun (W)
James H. Duncan (W)
Samuel A. Eliot (W) s. 1850
Orin Fowler (W)
Joseph Grinnell (W)
Daniel P. King (W) d. July 1850
Horace Mann (W)
Julius Rockwell (W)
Robert C. Winthrop (W) r. July 1850

Michigan

Senators

Lewis Cass (D)
Alpheus Felch (D)

Representatives

Kinsley S. Bingham (D)
Alexander W. Buel (D)
William Sprague (W)

Mississippi

Senators

Jefferson Davis (D)
Henry S. Foote (Un)

Representatives

Albert G. Brown (D)
Winfield S. Featherston (D)
William McWillie (D)
Jacob Thompson (D)

Missouri

Senators

David R. Atchison (W)
Thomas H. Benton (D)

Representatives

William V. Bay (D)
James B. Bowlin (D)
James S. Green (D)
Willard P. Hall (D)
John S. Phelps (D)

New Hampshire

Senators

John P. Hale (Anti-Slavery)
Moses Norris, Jr. (D)

Representatives

Harry Hibbard (D)
George W. Morrison (D) s. 1850
Charles H. Peaslee (D)
Amos Tuck
James Wilson (W) r. Sept. 1850

New Jersey

Senators

William L. Dayton (W)
Jacob W. Miller (W)

Representatives

Andrew K. Hay (W)
James G. King (W)
William A. Newell (W)
John Van Dyke (W)
Isaac Wildrick (D)

New York

Senators

Daniel S. Dickinson (D)
William H. Seward (W)

Representatives

Henry P. Alexander (W)
George R. Andrews (W)
Henry Bennett (W)
David A. Bokee (W)
George Briggs (W)
James Brooks (W)
Lorenzo Burrows (W)
Charles E. Clarke (W)
Harmon S. Conger (W)
William Duer (W)
Daniel Gott (W)
Herman D. Gould (W)
Ransom Halloway (W)
William T. Jackson (W)
John A. King (W)
Preston King (D)
Thomas McKissock (W)
Orsamus B. Matteson (W)
William Nelson (W)
J. Phillips Phoenix (W)
Harvey Putnam (W)
Gideon Reynolds (W)

Elijah Risley (W)
Robert L. Rose (W)
David Rumsey, Jr. (W)
William A. Sackett (W)
Abraham M. Schermerhorn (W)
John L. Schoolcraft (W)
Peter H. Silvester (W)
Elbridge G. Spaulding (W)
John R. Thurman (W)
Walter Underhill (W)
Hiram Walden (D)
Hugh White

North Carolina

Senators

George E. Badger (W)
Willie P. Mangum (W)

Representatives

William S. Ashe (D)
Joseph P. Caldwell (W)
Thomas L. Clingman (W)
John R. J. Daniel (D)
Edmund Deberry (W)
David Outlaw (W)
Augustine H. Shepperd (W)
Edward Stanly (W)
Abraham W. Venable (D)

Ohio

Senators

Salmon P. Chase (D)
Thomas Corwin (W) r. July 1850
Thomas Ewing (W) s. 1850

Representatives

John Bell (W) s. 1851
Joseph Cable (D)
Lewis D. Campbell (W)
David K. Cartter (D)
Moses B. Corwin (W)
John Crowell (W)
Rodolphus Dickinson d. Mar. 1849
David T. Disney (D)
Nathan Evans (W)
Joshua R. Giddings (W)
Moses Hoagland (D)
William F. Hunter (W)
John K. Miller (D)
Jonathan D. Morris (D)
Edson B. Olds (D)
Emery D. Potter (D)
Joseph M. Root (W)
Robert C. Schenck (W)
Charles Sweetser (D)
John L. Taylor (W)
Samuel F. Vinton (W)
William A. Whittlesey (D)
Amos E. Wood (D) d. Nov. 1850

Pennsylvania

Senators

James Cooper (W)
Daniel Sturgeon (D)

Representatives

John Brisbin (W) s. 1851
Chester P. Butler (W) d. Oct. 1850
Samuel Calvin (W)
Joseph Casey (W)
Joseph R. Chandler (W)
Joel B. Danner (D) s. 1850
Jesse C. Dickey (W)
Milo M. Dimmick (D)
John Freedley (W)
Alfred Gilmore (D)
Moses Hampton (W)
John W. Howe (W)
Lewis C. Levin (Amer)
James X. McLanahan (D)
Job Mann (D)
Henry D. Moore (W)
Henry Nes d. Sept. 1850
Andrew J. Ogle (W)
Charles W. Pitman (W)
Robert R. Reed (W)
John Robbins, Jr. (D)
Thomas Ross (D)
Thaddeus Stevens (W)
William Strong (D)
James Thompson (W)
David Wilmot (D)

Rhode Island

Senators

John H. Clarke (W)
Albert C. Greene (W)

Representatives

Nathan F. Dixon (W)
George G. King (W)

South Carolina

Senators

Robert W. Barnwell (D) ta. 1850
Andrew P. Butler (SRD)
John C. Calhoun (D) d. Mar. 1850
Franklin H. Elmore (D) s. d. 1850
R. Barnwell Rhett (D) s. 1851

Representatives

Armistead Burt (D)
William F. Colcock (D)
Isaac E. Holmes (D)
John McQueen (D)
James L. Orr (D)
Daniel Wallace (D)
Joseph A. Woodward (D)

Tennessee

Senators

John Bell (W)
Hopkins L. Turney (D)

Representatives

Josiah M. Anderson (W)
Andrew Ewing (D)
Meredith P. Gentry (W)
Isham G. Harris (W)

Andrew Johnson (D)
George W. Jones (D)
John H. Savage (D)
Frederick P. Stanton (D)
James H. Thomas (D)
Albert G. Watkins (W)
Christopher H. Williams (W)

Texas

Senators

Sam Houston (D)
Thomas J. Rusk (D)

Representatives

Volney E. Howard (D)
David S. Kaufman (D) d. Jan. 1851

Vermont

Senators

Samuel S. Phelps (W)
William Upham (W)

Representatives

William Hebard (W)
William Henry (W)
George P. Marsh (W) r. 1849
James Meacham (W)
Lucius B. Peck (D)

Virginia

Senators

Robert M. T. Hunter (D)
James M. Mason (D)

Representatives

Thomas H. Averett (D)
Thomas H. Bayly (SRD)
James M. H. Beale (D)
Thomas S. Bocock (D)
Henry A. Edmundson (D)
Thomas S. Haymond (W)
Alexander R. Holladay (D)
James McDowell (D)
Fayette McMullen (D)
Richard K. Meade (D)
John S. Millson (D)
Jeremiah Morton (W)
Alexander Newman (D) d. Sept. 1849
Richard Parker (D)
Paulus Powell (D)
James A. Seddon (D)

Wisconsin

Senators

Henry Dodge (D)
Isaac P. Walker (D)

Representatives

Orsamus Cole (W)
James D. Doty (Free-Soiler)
Charles Durkee (Free-Soiler)

Thirty-Second Congress

(Mar. 4, 1851, to
Mar. 3, 1853)

President of the Senate: Millard Fillmore
Presidents Pro Tempore of the Senate: William R. King; David R. Atchison
Speaker of the House of Representatives: Linn Boyd

Alabama

Senators

Jeremiah Clemens (D)
Benjamin Fitzpatrick (SRD) s. 1853
William R. King (D) r. Dec. 1852

Representatives

James Abercrombie (W)
John Bragg (SRD)
Williamson R. W. Cobb (D)
Sampson W. Harris (D)
George W. Houston (D)
William R. Smith (W)
Alexander White (W)

Arkansas

Senators

Solon Borland (D)
William K. Sebastian (D)

Representatives

Robert W. Johnson (D)

California

Senators

William M. Gwin (D)
John B. Weller (D) s. 1852

Representatives

Joseph W. McCorkle (D)
Edward C. Marshall (D)

Connecticut

Senators

Truman Smith (W)
Isaac Toucey (D) s. 1852

Representatives

Charles Chapman (W)
Chauncey F. Cleveland (D)
Colin M. Ingersoll (D)
Origen S. Seymour (D)

Delaware

Senators

James A. Baryard (D)
Presley Spruance (W)

Representatives

George R. Riddle (D)

Florida

Senators

Stephen R. Mallory (D)
Jackson Morton (W)

Representatives

Edward C. Cabell (W)

Georgia

Senators

John M. Berrien (W) r. May 1852
Robert M. Charlton s. 1852
William C. Dawson (SRW)

Representatives

David J. Bailey (SRD)
Elijah W. Chastain (D)
Junius Hillyer (D)
Joseph W. Jackson (D)
James Johnson (D)
Charles Murphey (D)
Alexander H. Stephens (D)
Robert Toombs (SRD)

Illinois

Senators

Stephen A. Douglas (D)
James Shields (D)

Representatives

Willis Allen (D)
William H. Bissell (D)
Thompson Campbell (D)
Orlando B. Ficklin (D)
Richard S. Molony (D)
William A. Richardson (D)
Richard Yates (W)

Indiana

Senators

Jesse D. Bright (D)
Charles W. Cathcart (D) ta. 1852
John Pettit (D) s. 1853
James Whitcomb (D) d. Oct. 1852

Representatives

Samuel Brenton (W)
John G. Davis (D)
Cyrus L. Dunham (D)
Graham N. Fitch (D)

Willis A. Gorman (D)
Thomas A. Hendricks (D)
James Lockhart (D)
Daniel Mace (D)
Samuel W. Parker (W)
John L. Robinson (D)

Iowa

Senators

Augustus C. Dodge (D)
George W. Jones (D)

Representatives

Lincoln Clark (D)
Bernhart Henn (D)

Kentucky

Senators

Henry Clay (W) d. June 1852
Archibald Dixon (W) s. 1852
David Meriwether (D) ta. 1852
Joseph R. Underwood (W)

Representatives

John C. Breckinridge (D)
Linn Boyd (D)
Presley U. Ewing (W)
Benjamin E. Grey (W)
Humphrey Marshall (W) r.
  Aug. 1852
John C. Mason (D)
William Preston (W) s. 1852
Richard H. Stanton (D)
James W. Stone (D)
William T. Ward (W)
Addison White (W)

Louisiana

Senators

Solomon W. Downs (D)
Pierre Soule (SRD)

Representatives

J. Aristide Landry (D)
John Moore (W)
Alexander G. Penn (D)
Louis St. Martin (D)

Maine

Senators

James W. Bradbury (D)
Hannibal Hamlin (D)

Representatives

Charles Andrews (D) d. Apr.
  1852
John Appleton (D)
Thomas J. D. Fuller (D)
Robert Goodenow (W)
Moses Macdonald (D)
Isaac Reed (W) s. 1852
Ephraim K. Smart (D)
Israel Washburn, Jr. (W)

Maryland

Senators

James A. Pearce (W)
Thomas G. Pratt (W)

Representatives

Richard J. Bowie (W)
Joseph S. Cottman (W)
Alexander Evans (W)
William T. Hamilton (D)
Edward Hammond (D)
Thomas Yates Walsh (W)

Massachusetts

Senators

John Davis (W)
Charles Sumner (D)

Representatives

Charles Allen (Free-Soiler)
William Appleton (W)
George T. Davis (W)
James H. Duncan (W)
Francis B. Fay (W) s. 1852
Orin Fowler (W) d. Dec. 1852
John Z. Goodrich (W)
Edward P. Little (D) s. 1852
Horace Mann (W)
Robert Rantoul, Jr. (D) d. Aug.
  1852
Lorenzo Sabine (W)
Zeno Scudder (W)
Benjamin Thompson (W) d.
  Sept. 1852

Michigan

Senators

Lewis Cass (D)
Alpheus Felch (D)

Representatives

James L. Conger (W)
Ebenezer J. Penniman (W)
Charles E. Stuart (D)

Mississippi

Senators

Stephen Adams (D) s. 1852
Walker Brooke (W) s. 1852
Jefferson Davis (D) r. Sept.
  1851
Henry S. Foote (Un) r. Jan.
  1852
John J. McRae (D) ta. 1852

Representatives

Albert G. Brown (D)
John D. Freeman (Un)
Benjamin D. Nabers (Un)
John A. Wilcox (W)

Missouri

Senators

David R. Atchison (W)
Henry S. Geyer (D)

Representatives

John F. Darby (W)
Willard P. Hall (D)
John G. Miller (W)
John S. Phelps (D)
Gilchrist Porter (W)

New Hampshire

Senators

John P. Hale (Anti-Slavery)
Moses Norris, Jr. (D)

Representatives

Harry Hibbard (D)
Charles H. Peaslee (D)
Jared Perkins (W)
Amos Tuck

New Jersey

Senators

Jacob W. Miller (W)
Robert F. Stockton (D)

Representatives

George H. Brown (W)
Rodman M. Price (D)
Charles Skelton (D)
Nathan T. Stratton (D)
Isaac Wildrick (D)

New York

Senators

Hamilton Fish (W)
William H. Seward (W)

Representatives

Leander Babrock (D)
Henry Bennett (W)
Obadiah Bowne (W)
John H. Boyd (W)
George Briggs (W)
James Brooks (W)
Alexander H. Buell (D) d. Jan.
  1853
Lorenzo Burrows (W)
Gilbert Dean (D)
John G. Floyd (D)
Emanuel B. Hart (D)
Augustus P. Hascall (W)
Solomon G. Haven (W)
J. H. Hobart Haws (W)
Jerediah Horsford (W)
Thomas Y. Howe, Jr. (D)
Willard Ives (D)
Timothy Jenkins (D)
Daniel T. Jones (D)
Preston King (D)
Frederick S. Martin (W)
William Murray (D)
Reuben Robie (D)

Joseph Russell (D)
William A. Sackett (W)
Abraham M. Schermerghorn
  (W)
John L. Schoolcraft (W)
Marius Schoonmaker (W)
David L. Seymour (D)
William W. Snow (D)
Abraham P. Stephens
Josiah Sutherland (D)
Henry S. Walbridge (W)
John Wells (W)

North Carolina

Senators

George E. Badger (W)
Willie P. Mangum (W)

Representatives

William S. Ashe (D)
Joseph P. Caldwell (W)
Thomas L. Clingman (W)
John R. J. Daniel (D)
Alfred Dockery (W)
James T. Morehead (W)
David Outlaw (W)
Edward Stanly (W)
Abraham W. Venable (D)

Ohio

Senators

Salmon P. Chase (D)
Benjamin F. Wade (W)

Representatives

Nelson Barrere (W)
Hiram Bell (W)
George H. Busby (D)
Joseph Cable (D)
Lewis D. Campbell (W)
David K. Cartter (D)
David T. Disney (D)
Alfred P. Edgerton (D)
James M. Gaylord
Joshua R. Giddings (W)
Frederick W. Green (D)
Alexander Harper (W)
William F. Hunter (W)
John Johnson
Eben Newton (W)
Edson B. Olds (D)
Benjamin Stanton (W)
Charles Sweetser (D),
John L. Taylor (W)
Norton S. Townshend (D)
John Welch (W)

Pennsylvania

Senators

Richard Brodhead (D)
James Cooper (W)

Representatives

John Allison (W)
Thomas M. Bibignaus (W)
Joseph R. Chandler (W)
Carlton B. Curtis (D)
John L. Dawson (D)
Milo M. Dimmick (D)

Thomas B. Florence (D)
Henry M. Fuller (W)
James Gamble (D)
Alfred Gilmore (D)
Galusha A. Grow (D)
John W. Howe (W)
Thomas M. Howe (W)
J. Glancy Jones (D)
Joseph H. Kuhns (W)
William H. Kurtz (D)
James X. McLanahan (D)
John McNair (D)
Henry D. Moore (W)
John A. Morrison (D)
Andrew Parker (D)
John Robbins, Jr. (D)
Thomas Ross (D)
Thaddeus Stevens (W)

Rhode Island

Senators

John H. Clark (W)
Charles T. James (D)

Representatives

George G. King (W)
Benjamin B. Thurston (D)

South Carolina

Senators

Andrew P. Butler (SRD)
William F. DeSaussure (D) s. 1852
R. Barnwell Rhett (D) r. May 1852

Representatives

William Aiken (D)
Armistead Burt (D)
William F. Colcock (D)
John McQueen (D)
James L. Orr (D)
Daniel Wallace (W)
Joseph A. Woodward (D)

Tennessee

Senators

John Bell (W)
James C. Jones (W)

Representatives

William M. Churchwell (D)
William Cullom (W)
Meredith P. Gentry (W)
Isham G. Harris (D)
Andrew Johnson (D)
George W. Jones (D)
William H. Polk (D)
John H. Savage (D)
Frederick P. Stanton (D)
Albert G. Watkins (W)
Christopher H. Williams (W)

Texas

Senators

Sam Houston (D)

Thomas J. Rusk (D)

Representatives

Volney E. Howard (D)
Richardson Scurry (D)

Vermont

Senators

Solomon Foot
Samuel S. Phelps (W) s. 1853
William Upham (W) d. Jan. 1853

Representatives

Thomas Barlett, Jr. (D)
William Hebard (W)
James Meacham (W)
Ahiman L. Miner (W)

Virginia

Senators

Robert M. T. Hunter (D)
James M. Mason (D)

Representatives

Thomas H. Averett (D)
Thomas H. Bayly (SRD)
James M. H. Beale (D)
Thomas S. Bocock (D)
John S. Caskie (D)
Sherrard Clemens (D) s. 1852
Henry A. Edmundson (D)
Charles J. Faulkner (D)
Alexander R. Holladay (D)
John Letcher (D)
Fayette McMullen (D)
Richard K. Meade (D)
John S. Millson (D)
Paulus Powell (D)
James F. Strother (W)
George W. Thompson (D) r. July 1852

Wisconsin

Senators

Henry Dodge (D)
Isaac P. Walker (D)

Representatives

James D. Doty (Free-Soiler)
Charles Durkee (Free-Soiler)
Ben C. Eastman (D)

Thirty-Third Congresss

(Mar. 4, 1853, to
Mar. 3, 1855)

President of the Senate: William R. King
Presidents Pro Tempore of the Senate: David R. Atchison; Lewis Cass; Jesse D. Bright

Speaker of the House of Representatives: Linn Boyd

Alabama

Senators

Clement Claiborne Clay (D)
Benjamin Fitzpatrick (SRD)

Representatives

James Abercrombie (W)
Williamson R. W. Cobb (D)
James F. Dowdell (SRD)
Sampson W. Harris (D)
George S. Houston (D)
Philip Phillips (D)
William R. Smith (W)

Arkansas

Senators

Solon Borland (D) r. Apr. 1853
Robert W. Johnson (D) s. 1853
William K. Sebastian (D)

Representatives

Alfred B. Greenwood (D)
Edward A. Warren (D)

California

Senators

William M. Gwin (D)
John B. Weller (D)

Representatives

Milton S. Latham (D)
James A. McDougall (D)

Connecticut

Senators

Francis Gillette (W) s. 1854
Truman Smith (W) r. May 1854
Isaac Toucey (D)

Representatives

Nathan Belcher (D)
Colin M. Ingeroll (D)
James T. Pratt (D)
Origen S. Seymour (D)

Delaware

Senators

James A. Bayard (D)
John M. Clayton (W)

Representatives

George R. Riddle (D)

Florida

Senators

Stephen R. Mallory (D)
Jackson Morton (W)

Representatives

Augustus E. Maxwell (D)

Georgia

Senators

William C. Dawson (SRW)
Robert Toombs (SRD)

Representatives

David J. Bailey (SRD)
Elijah W. Chastain (D)
Alfred H. Colquitt (D)
William B. W. Dent (D)
Junius Hilyer (D)
David A. Reese (W)
James L. Seward (D)
Alexander H. Stephens (D)

Illinois

Senators

Stephen A. Douglas (D)
James Shields (D)

Representatives

James C. Allen (D)
Willis Allen (D)
William H. Bissell (D)
James Knox (W)
Jesse O. Norton
William A. Richardson (D)
Elihu B. Washburne (W)
John Wentworth (D)
Richard Yates (W)

Indiana

Senators

Jesse D. Bright (D)
John Pettit (D)

Representatives

Ebenezer M. Chamberlain (D)
John G. Davis (D)
Cyrus L. Dunham (D)
Norman Eddy (D)
William H. English (D)
Andrew J. Harlan (D)
Thomas A. Hendricks (D)
James H. Lane (D)
Daniel Mace (D)
Smith Miller (D)
Samuel W. Parker (W)

Iowa

Senators

Augustus C. Dodge (D)
George W. Jones (D)

Representatives

John P. Cook (W)
Bernhart Henn (D)

Kentucky

Senators

Archibald Dixon (W)
John B. Thompson (W)

Representatives

Linn Boyd (D)
John C. Breckinridge (D)
Francis M. Bristow (W) s. 1854
James S. Chrisman (D)
Leander M. Cox (W)
John M. Elliott (D)
Presley U. Ewing (W) d. Sept. 1854
Benjamin E. Grey (W)
Clement S. Hill (D)
William Preston (W)
Richard H. Stanton (D)

Louisiana

Senators

Judah P. Benjamin (W)
John Slidell (SRD) s. 1853
Pierre Soule (SRD) r. 1853

Representatives

William Dunbar (D)
Theodore G. Hunt (W)
Roland Jones (D)
John Perkins, Jr. (D)

Maine

Senators

William P. Fessenden (W) s. 1854
Hannibal Hamlin (D)

Representatives

Samuel P. Benson (W)
E. Wilder Farley (W)
Thomas J. D. Fuller (D)
Moses Macdonald (D)
Samuel Mayall (D)
Israel Washburn, Jr. (W)

Maryland

Senators

James A. Peare (W)
Thomas G. Pratt (W)

Representatives

John R. Franklin (W)
William T. Hamilton (D)
Henry May (D)
Jacob Shower
Augustus R. Sollers (W)
Joshua Van Sant (D)

Massachusetts

Senators

Edward Everett (R) r. June 1854
Julius Rockwell (R) ta. 1854
Charles Summers (D)
Henry Wilson (Free-Soiler) s. 1855

Representatives

William Appleton (W)
Nathaniel P. Banks (D)
Samuel L. Crocker (W)
Alexander De Witt (Amer)
Edward Dickinson (W)
J. Wiley Edmunds (W)
Thomas D. Eliot s. 1854
John Z. Goodrich (W)
Zeno Scudder (W) r. Mar. 1854
Charles W. Upham (W)
Samuel H. Walley (W)
Tappan Wentworth (W)

Michigan

Senators

Lewis Cass (D)
Charles E. Stuart (D)

Representatives

Samuel Clark (D)
David A. Noble (D)
Hester L. Stevens (D)
David Stuart (D)

Mississippi

Senators

Stephen Adams (D)
Albert G. Brown (D) s. 1854

Representatives

William Barksdale (SRD)
William T. S. Barry (D)
Wiley P. Harris (D)
Otho R. Singleton (D)
Daniel B. Wright (D)

Missouri

Senators

David R. Atchison (W)
Henry S. Geyer (D)

Representatives

Thomas H. Benton (D)
Samuel Caruthers (W)
Alfred W. Lamb (D)
James J. Lindley (W)
John G. Miller (W)
Mordecai Oliver (W)
John S. Phelps (D)

New Hampshire

Senators

Charles G. Atherton (D) d. Nov. 1853
Moses Norris, Jr. (D) d. Jan. 1855
John S. Wells (D) s. 1855
Jared W. Williams (D) s. 1853

Representatives

Harry Hibbard (D)
George W. Kittredge (D)
George W. Morrison (D)

New Jersey

Senators

John R. Thomson (D)
William Wright (D)

Representatives

Samuel Lilly (D)
Alexander C. M. Pennington (W)
Charles Skelton (D)
Nathan T. Stratton (D)
George Vail (D)

New York

Senators

Hamilton Fish (W)
William H. Seward (W)

Representatives

Henry Bennet (W)
Davis Carpenter (W)
George W. Chase (W)
Thomas W. Cumming (D)
Francis B. Cutting (D)
Gilbert Dean (D) r. July 1854
Reuben E. Fenton
Thomas T. Flager (D)
Henry C. Goodwin s. 1854
George Hastings (D)
Solomon G. Haven (W)
Charles Hughes (D)
Daniel T. Jones (D)
Caleb Lyon (D)
Orsamus B. Matteson (W)
James Maurice (D)
Edwin B. Morgan (D)
William Murray (D)
Andrew Oliver (D)
Jared V. Peck (D)
Rufus W. Peckham (D)
Bishop Perkins (D)
Benjamin Pringle (W)
Peter Rowe (D)
Russell Sage (W)
George A. Simmons (W)
Gerrit Smith (Abolitionist) r. Aug. 1854
John J. Taylor (D)
Isaac Teller (D) s. 1854
William M. Tweed (D)
Hiram Walbridge (D)
William A. Walker (D)
Mike Walsh (D)
Theodore R. Westbrook (D)
John Wheeler (D)

North Carolina

Senators

George E. Badger (W)
David S. Reid (D) s. 1854

Representatives

William S. Ashe (D)
Thomas L. Clingman (W)
F. Burton Craige (D)
John Kerr, Jr. (W)
Richard C. Puryear (W)
Sion H. Rogers (W)
Thomas Ruffin (D)
Henry M. Shaw (D)

Ohio

Senators

Salmon P. Chase (D)
Benjamin F. Wade (W)

Representatives

Edward Ball (W)
George Bliss (D)
Lewis D. Campbell (W)
Moses B. Corwin (W)
David T. Disney (D)
Alfred P. Edgerton (D)
Andrew Ellison (D)
Joshua R. Giddings (W)
Frederick W. Green (D)
Aaron Harlan (W)
John Scott Harrison (W)
Harvey H. Johnson (D)
William D. Lindsley (D)
Matthias H. Nichols (W)
Edson B. Olds (D)
Thomas Ritchey (D)
William R. Sapp (W)
Wilson Shannon (D)
Andrew Stuart (D)
John L. Taylor (W)
Edward Wade (W)

Pennsylvania

Senators

Richard Brodhead (D)
James Cooper (W)

Representatives

Samuel A. Bridges (D)
Joseph R. Chandler (W)
Carlton B. Curtis (D)
John L. Dawson (D)
John Dick (W)
Augustus Drum (D)
William Everhart (W)
Thomas B. Florence (D)
James Gamble (D)
Galusha A. Grow (D)
Isaac E. Hiester (W)
Thomas M. Howe (W)
J. Glancy Jones (D) s. 1854
William H. Kurtz (D)
John McCulloch (W)
John McNair (D)
Ner Middelswarth (W)
Henry A. Muhlenberg (D) d. Jan. 1854
Asa Packer (D)

David Ritchie
John Robbins, Jr. (D)
Samuel L. Russell (W)
Christian M. Straub (D)
Michael C. Trout (D)
William H. White (D)
Hendrick B. Wright (D)

Rhode Island

Senators

Philip Allen (D)
Charles T. James (D)

Representatives

Thomas Davis (D)
Benjamin B. Thruston (D)

South Carolina

Senators

Andrew P. Butler (SRD)
Josiah J. Evans (SRD)

Representatives

William Aiken (D)
William W. Boyce (SRD)
Preston S. Brooks (SRD)
Laurence M. Keitt (D)
John McQueen
James L. Orr (D)

Tennessee

Senators

John Bell (W)
James C. Jones (W)

Representatives

Robert M. Bugg (W)
William M. Churchwell (D)
William Cullom (W)
Emerson Ethridge (W)
George W. Jones (D)
Charles Ready (W)
Samuel A. Smith (D)
Frederick P. Stanton (D)
Nathaniel G. Taylor (W) s. 1854
Felix K. Zollicoffer (SRW)

Texas

Senators

Sam Houston (D)
Thomas J. Rusk (D)

Representatives

Peter H. Bell (D)
George W. Smyth

Vermont

Senators

Lawrence Brainerd (W) s. 1854
Solomon Foot

Samuel S. Phelps (W) r. Mar. 1854

Representatives

James Meacham (W)
Alvah Sabin (W)
Andrew Tracy (W)

Virginia

Senators

Robert M. T. Hunter (D)
James M. Mason (D)

Representatives

Thomas H. Bayly (SRD)
Thomas S. Bocock (D)
John S. Caskie (D)
Henry A. Edmundson (D)
Charles J. Faulkner (D)
William O. Goode (D)
Zedekiah Kidwell (D)
John Letcher (D)
Charles S. Lewis (D) s. 1854
Fayette McMullen (D)
John S. Millson (D)
Paulus Powell (D)
William Smith (D)
John F. Sondgrass d. June 1854

Wisconsin

Senators

Henry Dodge (D)
Isaac P. Walker (D)

Representatives

Ben C. Eastman (D)
John B. Macy (D)
Daniel Wells, Jr. (D)

Thirty-Fourth Congress

(Mar. 4, 1855, to Mar. 3, 1857)

President of the Senate: Vacant
Presidents Pro Tempore of the Senate: Jesse D. Bright; Charles E. Stuart; James M. Mason
Speaker of the House of Representatives: Nathaniel P. Banks

Alabama

Senators

Clement Claiborne Clay (D)
Benjamin Fitzptrick (SRD)

Representatives

Williamson R. W. Cobb (D)
James F. Dowdell (SRD)
Sampson W. Harris (D)
George S. Houston (D)
Eli S. Shorter (D)

William R. Smith (Amer)
Percy Walker (Amer)

Arkansas

Senators

Robert W. Johnson (D)
William K. Sebastian (D)

Representatives

Alfred B. Greenwood (SRD)
Albert Rust (D)

California

Senators

William M. Gwin (D) s. 1857
John B. Weller (D)

Representatives

James W. Denver (D)
Philemon T. Herbert (D)

Connecticut

Senators

Lafayette S. Foster (R)
Isaac Toucey (D)

Representatives

Ezra Clark, Jr. (Amer)
Sidney Dean (Amer)
William W. Welch (Amer)
John Woodruff (Amer)

Delaware

Senators

Martin W. Bates (D) s. 1857
James A. Bayard (D)
John M. Clayton (W) d. Nov. 1856
Joseph P. Comegys (W) s. 1856

Representatives

Elisha D. Cullen (Amer)

Florida

Senators

Stephen R. Malory (D)
David Levy Yulee (D)

Representatives

Augustus E. Maxwell (D)

Georgia

Senators

Alfred Iverson (D)
Robert Toombs (SRD)

Representatives

Martin J. Crawford (D)
Howell Cobb (D)
Nathaniel G. Foster (Amer)
John H. Lumpkin (D)
James L. Seward (D)
Alexander H. Stephens (D)
Robert P. Trippe (W)
Hiram Warner (D)

Illinois

Senators

Stephen A. Douglas (D)
Lyman Trumbull (R)

Representatives

James C. Allen (D) s. 1856
Jacob C. Davis (D) s. 1856
Thomas L. Harris (D)
James Knox (W)
Samuel S. Marshall (D)
James L. D. Morrison (D) s. 1856
Jesse O. Norton
William A. Richardson (D) r. Aug. 1856
Elihu B. Washburne (W)
James H. Woodworth

Indiana

Senators

Jesse D. Bright (D)
Graham N. Fitch (D) s. 1857

Representatives

Lucien Barbour (Free-Soiler)
Samuel Brenton (W)
Schuyler Colfax (R)
William Cumback
George G. Dunn
William H. English (D)
David P. Holloway (People's Party)
Daniel Mace (D)
Smith Miller (D)
John U. Pettit (R)
Harvey D. Scott

Iowa

Senators

James Harlan (W) s. 1857
George W. Jones (D)

Representatives

Augustus Hall (D)
James Thorington (W)

Kentucky

Senators

John J. Crittenden (Un)
John B. Thompson (W)

Representatives

Henry C. Burnett (D)

John P. Campbell, Jr. (Amer)
Leander M. Cox (Amer)
John M. Elliott (D)
Joshua H. Jewett (D)
Alexander K. Marshall (Amer)
Humphrey Marshall (Amer)
Samuel F. Swope (Amer)
Albert G. Talbott (D)
Warner L. Underwood (Amer)

Louisiana

Senators

Judah P. Benjamin (W)
John Slidell (SRD)

Representatives

Thomas G. Davidson (D)
George Eustis, Jr. (Amer)
John M. Sandidge (D)
Miles Taylor (D)

Maine

Senators

William P. Fessenden (W)
Hannibal Hamlin (D) r. Jan.
1857
Amos Nourse s. 1857

Representatives

Samuel P. Benson
Thomas J. D. Fuller (D)
Ebenezer Knowlton
John J. Perry
Israel Washburn, Jr.
John M. Wood

Maryland

Senators

James A. Pearch (W)
Thomas G. Pratt (W)

Representatives

Thomas F. Bowie (D)
H. Winter Davis (Amer)
J. Morrison Harris (Amer)
Henry W. Hoffman (Amer)
James B. Ricaud (Amer)
James A. Stewart (D)

Massachusetts

Senators

Charles Sumner
Henry Wilson (Free-Soiler)

Representatives

Nathaniel P. Banks (Amer)
James Buffinton (Amer)
Anson Burlingame (Amer)
Calvin C. Chaffee (Amer)
Linus B. Comins (Amer)
Timothy Davis (Amer)
William S. Damrell (Amer)
Alexander De Witt (Amer)
Robert B. Hall (Amer)
Chauncey L. Knapp (Amer)

Mark Trafton (Amer)

Michigan

Senators

Lewis Cass (D)
Charles E. Stuart (D)

Representatives

William A. Howard
George W. Peck (D)
David S. Walbridge
Henry Waldron

Mississippi

Senators

Stephen Adams (D)
Albert G. Brown (D)

Representatives

William Barksdale (SRD)
Hendley S. Bennett (D)
William A. Lake (W)
John A. Quitman (D)
Daniel B. Wright (D)

Missouri

Senators

Henry S. Geyer (D)
James S. Green (D) s. 1857

Representatives

Thomas P. Aker (Amer) s.
1856
Samuel Caruthers (W)
Luther M. Kennett (Amer)
James J. Lindley (W)
Mordecai Oliver (W)
John S. Phelps (D)
Gilchrist Porter (W)

New Hampshire

Senators

James Bell (W)
John P. Hale

Representatives

Aaron H. Cragin (Amer)
James Pike (Amer)
Mason W. Tappan (R)

New Jersey

Senators

John R. Thompson (D)
William Wright (D)

Representatives

James Bishop (W)
Isaiah D. Clawson (W)
Alexander C. M. Pennington
(W)
George R. Robbins (W)

George Vail (D)

New York

Senators

Hamilton Fish (W)
William H. Seward (R)

Representatives

Henry Bennett (W)
Bayard Clarke (Amer)
Samuel Dickson (W)
Edward Dodd (W)
Francis S. Edwards (Amer) r.
Feb. 1857
Thomas T. Flagler (W)
William A. Gilbert (W) r. Feb.
1857
Amos P. Granger (W)
Solomon G. Haven (W)
Thomas R. Horton (W)
Jonas A. Hughston (W)
John Kelly (D)
William H. Kelsey (W)
Rufus H. King (W)
Andrew Z. McCarty (W)
Orsamus B. Matteson (W) r.
Feb. 1857
Killian Miller (W)
Edwin B. Morgan (D)
Ambrose S. Murray (W)
Andrew Oliver (D)
John M. Parker (W)
Guy R. Pelton (W)
Benjamin Pringle (W)
Russell Sage (W)
George A. Simmons (W)
Francis E. Spinner (D)
James S. T. Stranahan (W)
William W. Valk (Amer)
Abram Wakeman (W)
John Wheeler (D)
Thomas R. Whitney (Amer)
John Williams (D)

North Carolina

Senators

Asa Biggs (D)
David S. Reid (D)

Representatives

Lawrence O'B. Branch (D)
Thomas L. Clingman (W)
F. Burton Craige (D)
Robert T. Paine (Amer)
Richard C. Puryear (W)
Edwin G. Reade (Amer)
Thomas Ruffin (D)
Warren Winslow (D)

Ohio

Senators

George E. Pugh (D)
Benjamin F. Wade (W)

Representatives

Charles J. Albright (W)
Edward Ball (W)
John A. Bingham
Philemon Bliss

Lewis D. Campbell (W)
Timothy C. Day
Jonas R. Emrie
Samuel Galloway
Joshua R. Giddings (W)
Aaron Harlan (W)
John Scott Harison (W)
Valentine B. Horton (W)
Benjamin F. Leiter
Oscar F. Moore
Richard Mott
Matthias H. Nichols
William R. Sapp (W)
John Sherman (W)
Benjamin Stanton (W)
Edward Wade (W)
Cooper K. Watson (Free-Soiler)

Pennsylvania

Senators

William Bigler (D) s. 1856
Richard Brodhead (D)

Representatives

John Allison (W)
David Barclay (D)
Samuel C. Bradshaw (W)
Jacob Broom
John Cadwalader (D)
James H. Campbell (W)
John Covode (W)
John Dick
John R. Edie (W)
Thomas B. Florence (D)
Henry M. Fuller (W)
Galusha A. Grow (D)
John Hickman (D)
J. Glancy Jones (D)
Jonathan Knight (W)
John C. Kunkel (W)
William Millward (W)
Asa Packer (D)
John J. Pearce (W)
Samuel A. Purviance (W)
David Ritchie
Anthony E. Roberts (W)
David F. Robison (W)
Lemuel Todd
Job R. Tyson (W)

Rhode Island

Senators

Philip Allen (D)
Charles T. James (D)

Representatives

Nathaniel B. Durfee (Amer)
Benjamin B. Thurston (D)

South Carolina

Senators

Andrew P. Butler (SRD)
Josiah J. Evans (SRD)

Representatives

William Aiken (D)
William W. Boyce (SRD)
Preston S. Brooks (SRD) d.
Jan. 1857

Laurence M. Keitt (D)
John McQueen (D)
James L. Orr (D)

Tennessee

Senators

John Bell (W)
James C. Jones (W)

Representatives

Emerson Ethridge (W)
George W. Jones (D)
Charles Ready (W)
Thomas Rivers (Amer)
John H. Savage
Samuel A. Smith (D)
William H. Sneed (Amer)
Albert G. Watkins (D)
John V. Wright (D)
Felix K. Zollicoffer (SRW)

Texas

Senators

Sam Houston (D)
Thomas J. Rusk (D)

Representatives

Peter H. Bell (D)
Lemuel D. Evans (Amer)

Vermont

Senators

Jacob Collamer (R)
Solomon Foot (R)

Representatives

George T. Hodges
James Meacham (W) d. Aug.
    1856
Justin S. Morrill (W)
Alvah Sabin (W)

Virginia

Senators

Robert M. T. Hunter (D)
James M. Mason (D)

Representatives

Thomas H. Bayly (SRD) d.
    June 1856
Thomas S. Bocock (D)
John S. Carlile (Amer)
John S. Caskie (D)
Henry A. Edmundson (D)
Charles J. Faulkner (D)
Muscoe R. H. Garnett (D) s.
    1856
William O. Goode (D)
Zedekiah Kidwell (D)
John Letcher (D)
Fayette McMullen (D)
John S. Milson (D)
Paulus Powell (D)
William Smith (D)

Wisconsin

Senators

Henry Dodge (D)
Charles Durkee

Representatives

Charles Billingshurst
Cadwallader C. Washburn
Daniel Wells, Jr. (D)

Thirty-Fifth Congress

(Mar. 4, 1857, to
Mar. 3, 1859)

President of the Senate: John C.
    Breckinridge
*Presidents Pro Tempore of the
    Senate:* James M. Mason;
    Thomas J. Rusk; Benjamin
    Fitzpatrick
*Speaker of the House of
    Representatives:* James L. Orr

Alabama

Senators

Clement Claiborne Clay (D)
Benjamin Fitzpatrick (SRD)

Representatives

Williamson R. W. Cobb (D)
Jabez L. M. Curry (SRD)
James F. Dowdell (SRD)
George S. Houston (D)
Sydenham Moore (D)
Eli S. Shorter (D)
James A. Stallworth (D)

Arkansas

Senators

Robert W. Johnson (D)
William K. Sebastian (D)

Representatives

Alfred B. Greenwood (D)
Edward A. Warren (D)

California

Senators

David C. Broderick (D)
William M. Gwin (D)

Representatives

Joseph C. McKibbin (D)
Charles L. Scott (D)

Connecticut

Senators

James Dixon (R)
Lafayette S. Foster (R)

Representatives

Samuel Arnold (D)
William D. Bishop (D)
Ezra Clark, Jr. (R)
Sidney Dean (R)

Delaware

Senators

Martin W. Bates (D)
James A. Bayard (D)

Representatives

William G. Whiteley (D)

Florida

Senators

Stephen R. Mallory (D)
David Levy Yulee (D)

Representatives

George S. Hawkins (D)

Georgia

Senators

Alfred Iverson (D)
Robert Toombs (SRD)

Representatives

Martin J. Crawford (D)
Lucius J. Gartrell (D)
Joshua Hill (Amer)
James Jackson (D)
James L. Seward (D)
Alexander H. Stephens (D)
Robert P. Trippe (W)
Augustus R. Wright (D)

Illinois

Senators

Stephen A. Douglas (D)
Lyman Trumbull (R)

Representatives

John F. Farnsworth (R)
Thomas L. Harris (D) d. Nov.
    1858
Charles D. Hodges (D) s. 1859
William Kellogg (D)
Owen Lovejoy (R)
Samuel S. Marshal (D)
Isaac N. Morris (D)
Aaron Shaw (D)
Robert Smith (D)
Elihu B. Washburne (W)

Indiana

Senators

Jesse D. Bright (D)
Graham N. Fitch (D)

Representatives

Samuel Brenton (W) d. Mar.
    1857
Charles Case (D)
Schuyler Colfax (R)
John G. Davis (D)
William H. English
James B. Foley (D)
James M. Gregg (D)
James Hughes (D)
David Kilgore (R)
James Lockhart (D) d. Sept.
    1857
William E. Niblack (D)
John U. Pettit (R)
James Wilson (R)

Iowa

Senators

James Harlan (R)
George W. Jones (D)

Representatives

Samuel R. Curtis (R)
Timothy Davis (W)

Kentucky

Senators

John J. Crittenden (Un)
John B. Thompson (W)

Representatives

Henry C. Burnett (D)
James B. Clay (D)
John M. Elliott (D)
Joshua H. Jewett (D)
Humphrey Marshall (Amer)
John C. Mason (D)
Samuel O. Peyton (D)
John W. Stevenson (D)
Albert G. Talbott (D)
Warner L. Underwood (Amer)

Louisiana

Senators

Judah P. Benjamin (W)
John Slidell (SRD)

Representatives

Thomas G. Davison (D)
George Eustis, Jr. (Amer)
John M. Sandidge (D)
Miles Taylor (D)

Maine

Senators

William P. Fessenden (W)

Hannibal Hamlin (D)

Representatives

Nehemiah Abbott (R)
Stephen C. Foster (R)
Charles J. Gilman (R)
Freeman H. Morse (R)
Israel Washburn, Jr. (R)
John M. Wood (R)

Maryland

Senators

Anthony Kennedy (Un)
James A. Pearce (W)

Representatives

Thomas F. Bowie (D)
H. Winter Davis (R)
J. Morrison Harris (Amer)
Jacob M. Kunkel (D)
James B. Ricaud (Amer)
James A. Stewart (D)

Massachusetts

Senators

Charles Sumner (R)
Henry Wilson (Free-Soiler)

Representatives

Nathaniel P. Banks (R) r. Dec. 1857
James Buffunton (R)
Anson Burlingame (Amer)
Calvin C. Chaffee (Amer)
Linus B. Comins (R)
William S. Damrell (R)
Timothy Davis (R)
Henry L. Dawes
Daniel W. Gooch (R) s. 1858
Robert B. Hall (R)
Chauncey L. Knapp
Eli Thayer (R)

Michigan

Senators

Zachariah Chandler (R)
Charles E. Stuart (D)

Representatives

William A. Howard (R)
DeWitt C. Leach (R)
David S. Walbridge (R)
Henry Waldron (R)

Minnesota

Senators

Henry M. Rice (D) s. 1858
James Shields s. 1858

Representatives

James M. Cavanaugh (D)
William W. Phelps (D)

Mississippi

Senators

Albert G. Brown (D)
Jefferson Davis (D)

Representatives

William Barksdale (SRD)
Reuben Davis (D)
Lucius Q. C. Lamar (D)
John J. McRae (SRD) s. 1858
John A. Quitman (D) d. July 1858
Otho R. Singleton

Missouri

Senators

James S. Green (D)
Trusten Polk (D)

Representatives

Thomas L. Anderson (Amer)
Francis P. Blair, Jr. (Free-Soiler)
Samuel Caruthers (D)
John B. Clark (D)
James Craig (D)
John S. Phelps (D)
Samuel H. Woodson (Amer)

New Hampshire

Senators

James Bell (W) d. May 1857
Daniel Clark (R)
John P. Hale

Representatives

Aaron H. Cragin (R)
James Pike (Amer)
Mason W. Tappan (R)

New Jersey

Senators

John R. Thomson (D)
William Wright (D)

Representatives

Garnett B. Adrain (D)
Isaiah D. Clawson (W)
John Huyler (D)
George R. Robbins (W)
Jacob R. Wortendyke (D)

New York

Senators

Preston King (R)
William H. Seward (R)

Representatives

Samuel G. Andrews (R)
Thomas J. Barr (D) s. 1859
Henry Bennett (W)

Silas M. Burroughs (R)
Horace F. Clark (D)
Clark B. Cochrane (R)
John Cochrane (SRD)
Erastus Corning (D)
Edward Dodd (W)
Reuben E. Genton (R)
Henry C. Goodwin (R)
Amos P. Granger (W)
John B. Haskin (D)
Israel T. Hatch (D)
Charles B. Hoard (R)
John Kelly (D) r. Dec. 1858
William H. Kelsey (W)
William B. Maclay (D)
Orsamus B. Matteson (W)
Edwin B. Morgan (R)
Oliver A. Morse (R)
Ambrose S. Murray (R)
Abram B. Olin (R)
George W. Palmer (R)
John M. Parker (R)
Emory B. Pottle (R)
William F. Russell (D)
John A. Searing (D)
Judson W. Sherman (R)
Daniel E. Sickles (D)
Francis E. Spinner (R)
George Taylor (D)
John Thompson (R)
Elijah Ward (D)

North Carolina

Senators

Asa Biggs (D) r. May 1858
Thomas L. Clingman (D) s. 1858
David S. Reid (D)

Representatives

Lawrence O. B. Branch (D)
Thomas L. Clingman (W) r. May 1858
F. Burton Craige (D)
John A. Gilmer (Amer)
Thomas Ruffin (D)
Alfred M. Scales (D)
Henry M. Shaw (D)
Zebulon B. Vance (D) s. Dec. 1858
Warren Winslow (D)

Ohio

Senators

George E. Pugh (D)
Benjamin F. Wade (R)

Representatives

John A. Bingham (R)
Philemon Bliss (R)
Joseph Burns (D)
Lewis D. Campbell (W) r. May 1858
Joseph R. Cockerill (D)
Samuel S. Cox (D)
Joshua R. Giddings (W)
William S. Groesbeck (D)
Lawrence W. Hall (D)
Aaron Harlan (W)
Valentine B. Horton (W)
William Lawrence (R)
Benjamin F. Leiter (R)
Joseph Miller (D)

Richard Mott (R)
Matthias H. Nichols (R)
George H. Pendleton (D)
John Sherman (R)
Benjamin Stanton (W)
Cydnor B. Tompkins (R)
Clement L. Vallandigham (D) s. 1858
Edward Wade (R)

Oregon

Senators

Joseph Lane (D) s. 1859
Delazon Smith (D) s. 1859

Representatives

La Fayette Grover (D) s. 1859

Pennsylvania

Senators

William Bigler (D)
Simon Cameron (D)

Representatives

John A. Ahl (D)
Henry Chapman (D)
John Covode (R)
William L. Dewart (D)
John Dick (R)
William H. Dimmick (D)
John R. Edie (R)
Thomas B. Florence (D)
James L. Gillis (D)
Galusha A. Grow (R)
John Hickman (D)
J. Glancy Jones (D) r. Oct. 1858
Owen Jones (D)
William H. Keim (D) s. 1858
John C. Kunkel (W)
James Landy (D)
Paul Leidy (D)
William Montgomery (D)
Edward Joy Morris (W)
Henry M. Phillips (D)
Samuel A. Purviance (W)
Wilson Reilly (D)
David Ritchie (R)
Anthony E. Roberts (W)
William Stewart (R)
Allison White (D)

Rhode Island

Senators

Philip Allen (D)
James F. Simmons

Representatives

William D. Brayton (R)
Nathaniel B. Durfee (R)

South Carolina

Senators

Andrew P. Butler (SRD) d. May 1857

James Chesnut, Jr. (SRD) s. 1859
Josiah J. Evans (SRD) d. May 1858
James H. Hammond (SRD) s. 1857
Arthur P. Hayne (D) ta. 1858

Representatives

Milledge L. Bonham (SRD)
William W. Boyce (SRD)
Laurence M. Keitt (D)
W. Porcher Miles (D)
John McQueen (D)
James L. Orr (D)

Tennessee

Senators

John Bell (W)
Andrew Johnson (D)

Representatives

John D. C. Atkins (D)
William T. Avery (D)
George W. Jones (D)
Horace Maynard (Amer)
Charles Ready (W)
John H. Savage (D)
Samuel A. Smith (D)
Albert G. Watkins (D)
John V. Wright (D)
Felix K. Zollicoffer (SRW)

Texas

Senators

J. Pinckney Henderson ta. 1857
Sam Houston (D)
Thomas J. Rusk (D) d. July 1857
Matthias Ward (D) s. 1858

Representatives

Guy M. Bryan (D)
John H. Reagan (D)

Vermont

Senators

Jacob Collamer (R)
Solomon Foot (R)

Representatives

Justin S. Morrill (W)
Homer E. Royce (R)
Eliakim P. Walton (R)

Virginia

Senators

Robert M. T. Hunter (D)
James M. Mason (D)

Representatives

Thomas S. Bocock (D)
John S. Caskie (D)
Sherrard Clemens (D)

Henry A. Edmundson (D)
Charles J. Faulkner (D)
Muscoe R. H. Garnett (D)
William O. Goode (D)
George W. Hopkins (D)
Albert G. Jenkins (D)
John Letcher (D)
John S. Milson (D)
Paulus Powell (D)
William Smith (D)

Wisconsin

Senators

James R. Doolittle (R)
Charles Durkee (R)

Representatives

Charles Billinghurst (R)
John F. Potter (R)
Cadwallader C. Washburn (R)

Thirty-Sixth Congress

(Mar. 4, 1859, to
Mar. 3, 1861)

President of the Senate: John C. Breckinridge
Presidents Pro Tempore of the Senate: Benjamin Fitzpatrick; Jesse D. Bright; Solomon Foot
Speaker of the House of Representatives: William Pennington

Alabama

Senators

Clement Claiborne Clay (D)
Benjamin Fitzpatrick (SRD)

Representatives

David Clopton (SRD)
Williamson R. W. Cobb (D) r. Jan. 1861
Jabez L. M. Curry (SRD)
George S. Houston (D)
Sydenham Moore (D)
James L. Pugh (D)
James A. Stallworth (D)

Arkansas

Senators

Robert W. Johnson (D)
William K. Sebastian (D)

Representatives

Thomas C. Hindman (D)
Albert Rust (D)

California

Senators

William M. Gwin (D)
David C. Broderick (D) d. Sept. 1859
Henry P. Haun (D) ta. 1859
Milton S. Latham (D) s. 1860

Representatives

John C. Burch (D)
Charles L. Scott (D)

Connecticut

Senators

James Dixon (R)
Lafayette S. Foster (R)

Representatives

Alfred A. Burnaham (R)
Orris S. Ferry (R)
Dwight Loomis (R)
John Woodruff (Amer)

Delaware

Senators

James A. Bayard (D)
Willard Saulsbury (D)

Representatives

William G. Whiteley (D)

Florida

Senators

Stephen R. Mallory (D)
David Levy Yulee (D)

Representatives

George S. Hawkins (D)

Georgia

Senators

Alfred Iverson (D) r. Jan. 1861
Robert Toombs (SRD) r. Feb. 1861

Representatives

Martin J. Crawford (D)
Lucius J. Gartrell (D)
Thomas Hardeman, Jr. (D)
Joshua Hill (Amer) r. Jan. 1861
James Jackson (D)
John J. Jones (D)
Peter E. Love (D)
John W. H. Underwood (D)

Illinois

Senators

Stephen A. Douglas (D)

Lyman Trumbull (R)

Representatives

John F. Farnsworth (R)
Philip B. Fouke (D)
William Kellogg (R)
John A. Logan (D)
Owen Lovejoy (R)
John A. McClernand (D)
Isaac N. Morris (D)
James C. Robinson (D)
Elihu B. Washburne (W)

Indiana

Senators

Jesse D. Bright (D)
Graham N. Fitch (D)

Representatives

Charles Case (D)
Schuyler Colfax (R)
John G. Davis (D)
William McK. Dunn (R)
William H. English (D)
William S. Holman (D)
David Kilgore (R)
William E. Niblack (D)
John U. Pettit (R)
Albert G. Porter (R)
James Wilson (R)

Iowa

Senators

James W. Grimes (R)
James Harlan (F)

Representatives

Samuel R. Curtis (R)
William Vandever (R)

Kansas

Senators

Vacant
Vacant

Representatives

Martin F. Conway (R)

Kentucky

Senators

John J. Crittenden (Un)
Lazarus W. Powell (D)

Representatives

Green Adams (Amer)
William C. Anderson (Amer)
Francis M. Bristow (W)
John Y. Brown (D)
Henry C. Burnett (D)
Robert Mallory (D)
Laban T. Moore (Amer)
Samuel O. Peyton (D)
William E. Simms (D)
John W. Stevenson (D)

Louisiana

Senators

Judah P. Benjamin (W)
John Slidell (SRD)

Representatives

John E. Bouligny (Amer)
Thomas G. Davidson (D)
John M. Landrum (D)
Miles Taylor (D)

Maine

Senators

William P. Fessenden (W)
Hannibal Hamlin (D) r. Jan. 1861
Lot M. Morrill (R) s. 1861

Respresentatives

Stephen Coburn (R) s. 1861
Stephen C. Foster (R)
Ezra B. French (R)
Freeman H. Morse (R)
John J. Perry (R)
Daniel E. Somes (R)
Israel Washburn, Jr. (R) r. Jan. 1861

Maryland

Senators

Anthony Kennedy (Un)
James A. Pearce (W)

Representatives

H. Winter Davis (R)
J. Morrison Harris (Amer)
George W. Hughes (D)
Jacob M. Kunkel (D)
James A. Stewart (D)
Edwin H. Webster (R)

Massachusetts

Senators

Charles Sumner (R)
Henry Wilson

Representatives

Charles Francis Adams (R)
John B. Alley (R)
James Buffinton (R)
Anson Burlingame (R)
Henry L. Dawes (R)
Charles Delano (R)
Thomas D. Eliot (R)
Daniel W. Gooch (R)
Alexander H. Rice (R)
Eli Thayer (R)
Charles R. Train (R)

Michigan

Senators

Kinsley S. Bingham (R)

Zachariah Chandler (R)

Representatives

George B. Cooper (D) r. May 1860
William A. Howard (R) s. 1860
Francis W. Kellogg (R)
De Witt C. Leach (R)
Henry Waldron (R)

Minnesota

Senators

Henry M. Rice (D)
Morton S. Wilkinson (R)

Representatives

Cyrus Aldrich (R)
William Windom (R)

Mississippi

Senators

Albert G. Brown (D)
Jefferson Davis (D)

Representatives

William Barksdale (SRD)
Reuben Davis (D)
Lucius Q. C. Lamar (D) r. Dec. 1860
John J. McRae (SRD)
Otho R. Singleton (D)

Missouri

Senators

James S. Green (D)
Trusten Polk (D)

Representatives

Thomas L. Anderson (D)
John R. Barret (D)
Francis P. Blair, Jr. (Free-Soiler)
John B. Clark (D)
James Craig (D)
John W. Noell (D)
John S. Phelps (D)
Samuel H. Woodson (Amer)

New Hampshire

Senators

Daniel Clark (R)
John P. Hale

Representatives

Thomas M. Edwards (R)
Gilman Marston (R)
Mason W. Tappan (R)

New Jersey

Senators

John C. Ten Eyck (R)
John R. Thomson (D)

Representatives

Garnett B. Adrain (D)
John T. Nixon (R)
William Pennington (W)
Jetur R. Riggs (D)
John L. N. Stratton (R)

New York

Senators

Preston King (R)
William H. Seward (R)

Representatives

Thomas J. Barr (D)
Charles L. Beale (R)
George Briggs (Amer)
Silas M. Burroughs (R) d. June 1860
Martin Butterfield (R)
Luther C. Carter (R)
Horace F. Clark (D)
Clark B. Cochrane (R)
John Cochrane (SRD)
Roscoe Conkling
R. Holland Duell (R)
Alfred Ely (R)
Reuben E. Fenton (R)
Augustus Frank (R)
James H. Graham (R)
John B. Haskin (D)
Charles B. Hoard (R)
James Humphrey (R)
William Irvine (R)
William S. Kenyon (R)
M. Lindley Lee (R)
James B. McKean (R)
William B. Maclay (D)
Abram B. Olin (R)
George W. Palmer (R)
Emory B. Pottle (R)
Edwin R. Reynolds (R) s. 1860
John H. Reynolds (R)
Charles B. Sedgwick (R)
Daniel E. Sickles (D)
Elbridge G. Spaulding (Un)
Francis E. Spinner (R)
Charles H. Van Wyck (R)
Alfred Wells (R)

North Carolina

Senators

Thomas Bragg (D)
Thomas L. Clingman (D)

Representatives

Lawrence O'B. Branch (D)
F. Burton Craige (D)
John A. Gilmer (Amer)
James M. Leach (W)
Thomas Ruffin (D)
William N. H. Smith (D)
Zebulon B. Vance (D)
Warren Winslow (D)

Ohio

Senators

George E. Pugh (D)
Benjamin F. Wade (R)

Representatives

William Allen (D)
James M. Ashley (R)
John A. Bingham (R)
Harrison G. O. Blake (R)
John Carey (R)
Thomas Corwin (R)
Samuel S. Cox (D)
Sidney Edgerton (R)
John A. Gurley (R)
William Helmick (R)
William Howard (D)
John Hutchins (R)
Charles D. Martin (D)
George H. Pendleton (D)
John Sherman (R)
Benjamin Stanton (R)
Thomas C. Theaker (R)
Cydnor B. Tompkins (R)
Carey A. Trimble (R)
Clement L. Vallandigham (D)
Edward Wade (R)

Oregon

Senators

Edward D. Baker (R)
Joseph Lane (D)

Representatives

Lansing Stout (D)

Pennsylvania

Senators

William Bigler (D)
Simon Cameron (D)

Representatives

Elijah Babbitt (Un)
Samuel S. Blair (R)
James H. Campbell (W)
John Covode (R)
William H. Dimmick (D)
Thomas B. Florence (D)
Galusha A. Grow (R)
James T. Hale (R)
Chapin Hall (R)
John Hickman (R)
Benjamin F. Junkin (R)
John W. Killinger (R)
Henry C. Longnecker (R)
Jacob K. McKenty (D) s. 1860
Robert McKnight (R)
Edward McPherson (R)
William Millward (W)
William Montgomery (D)
James K. Moorhead (R)
Edward Joy Morris (W)
John Schwartz (D) d. June 1860
George W. Scranton (R)
Thaddeus Stevens (R)
William Stewart (R)
John P. Verree (R)
John Wood (R)

Rhode Island

Senators

Henry B. Anthony (R)
James F. Simmons (W)

Representatives

Christopher Robinson (Amer)
William D. Brayton (R)

South Carolina

Senators

James Chesnut, Jr. (SRD)
James H. Hammond (SRD)

Representatives

John D. Ashmore (D)
Milledge L. Bonham (SRD)
William W. Boyce (SRD)
Laurence M. Keitt (D)
W. Porcher Miles (D)
John McQueen (D)

Tennessee

Senators

Andrew Johnson (D)
Alfred O. P. Nicholson (D) r.
  Mar. 1861

Representatives

William T. Avery (D)
Reese B. Brabson (D)
Emerson Etheridge (W)
Robert H. Hatton (Amer)
Horace Maynard (Amer)
Thomas A. R. Nelson (Un)
James M. Quarles (W)
William B. Stokes (W)
James H. Thomas (D)
John V. Wright (D)

Texas

Senators

John Hemphill (SRD)
Matthias Ward (D)
Louis T. Wigfall (D) s. 1859

Representatives

Andrew J. Hamilton (D)
John H. Reagan (D)

Vermont

Senators

Jacob Collamer (R)
Solomon Foot (R)

Representatives

Justin S. Morrill (W)
Homer E. Royce (R)
Eliakim P. Walton (R)

Virginia

Senators

Robert M. T. Hunter (D)
James M. Mason (D)

Representatives

Thomas S. Bocock (D)
Alexander R. Boteler (Amer)
Sherrard Clemens (D)
Daniel C. DeJarnette (D)
Henry A. Edmundson (D)
Muscoe R. H. Garnett (D)
William O. Goode (D) d. July
  1859
John T. Harris (D)
Albert G. Jenkins (D)
Shelton F. Leake (D)
Elbert S. Martin (Amer)
John S. Millson (D)
Roger A. Pryor (D)
William Smith (D)

Wisconsin

Senators

James R. Doolittle (R)
Charles Durkee (R)

Representatives

Charles H. Larrabee (D)
John F. Potter (R)
Cadwallader C. Washburn (R)

Thirty-Seventh Congress

(Mar. 4, 1861, to
Mar. 3, 1863)

President of the Senate:
  Hannibal Hamlin
President Pro Tempore of the
  Senate: Solomon Foot
Speaker of the House of
  Representatives: Galusha A.
  Grow

Alabama

Senators

Clement Claiborne Clay (D) r.
  Mar. 1861
Vacant

Representaives

Vacant

Arkansas

Senators

Charles B. Mitchel (D) r. July
  1861
William K. Sebastian (D) r.
  July 1861

Representatives

Vacant

California

Senators

Milton S. Latham (D)
James A. McDougall (D)

Representatives

Frederick F. Low (R)
Timothy G. Phelps (R)
Aaron A. Sargent (R)

Connecticut

Senators

James Dixon (R)
Lafayette S. Foster (R)

Representatives

Alfred A. Burnham (R)
James E. English (D)
Dwight Loomis (R)
George C. Woodruff (D)

Delaware

Senators

James A. Bayard (D)
Willard Saulsbury (D)

Representatives

George P. Fisher (R)

Florida

Senators

Stephen R. Mallory (D) r. Mar.
  1861
Vacant

Representatives

Vacant

Georgia

Senators

Vacant

Representatives

Vacant

Illinois

Senators

Orville H. Browning (R) ta.
  1861
Stephen A. Douglas (D) d. June
  1861
William A. Richardson (D) s.
  1863
Lyman Trumbull (R)

Representatives

William J. Allen (D) s. 1862

Isaac N. Arnold (R)
Philip B. Fouke (D)
William Kellogg (R)
Anthony L. Knapp (D)
John A. Logan (D) r. Apr.
  1862
Owen Lovejoy (R)
John A. McClernand (D) r.
  Oct. 1861
William A. Richardson (D)
James C. Robinson (D)
Elihu B. Washburne (W)
Joseph A. Wright (D) s. 1862

Indiana

Senators

Jesse D. Bright (D) r. Feb.
  1862
Henry S. Lane (R)
David Turpie (D) ta. 1862
Joseph A. Wright (D) s. 1862

Representatives

Schuyler Colfax (R)
James A. Cravens (D)
William McK. Dunn (R)
William S. Holman (D)
George W. Julian (R)
John Law (D)
William Mitchell (R)
Albert G. Porter (R)
John P. C. Shanks (R)
Daniel W. Voorhees (D)
Albert S. White (R)

Iowa

Senators

James W. Grimes (R)
James Harlan (R)

Representatives

Samuel R. Curtis (R) r. Aug.
  1861
William Vandever (R)
James F. Wilson (R)

Kansas

Senators

James H. Lane (R)
Samuel C. Pomeroy (R)

Representatives

Martin F. Conway (R)

Kentucky

Senators

John C. Breckinridge (D) r.
  Dec. 1861
Garrett Davis (W) s. 1861
Lazarus W. Powell (R)

Representatives

Henry C. Burnett (D) r. Dec.
  1861
Samuel L. Casey (R) s. 1862

John J. Crittenden (Un)
George W. Dunlap (Un)
Henry Grider (W)
Aaron Harding (Un)
James S. Jackson (Un) r. Dec. 1861
Robert Mallory (D)
John W. Menzies (Un)
William H. Wadsworth (Un)
Charles A. Wickliffe (Un)
George H. Yeaman (Un) s. 1862

Louisiana

Senators

Judah P. Benjamin (W) r. Mar. 1861
Vacant

Representatives

Benjamin F. Flanders (Un) s. 1862
Michael Hahn (Un) s. 1863

Maine

Senators

William P. Fessenden (W)
Lot M. Morrill (R)

Representatives

Thomas A. D. Fessenden (R) s. 1862
Samuel C. Fessenden (R)
John N. Goodwin (R)
Anson P. Morrill (R)
Frederick A. Pike (R)
John H. Rice (R)
Charles W. Walton (R) r. May 1862

Maryland

Senators

Thomas H. Hicks (R) s. 1863
Anthony Kennedy (Un)
James A. Pearce (W) d. Dec. 1862

Representatives

Charles B. Calvert (D)
John W. Crisfield (Un)
Cornelius L. L. Leary (Un)
Henry May (D)
Francis Thomas (R)
Edwin H. Webster (R)

Massachusetts

Senators

Charles Sumner (R)
Henry Wilson

Representatives

Charles Francis Adams (R) r. May 1861
John B. Alley (R)

William Appleton (W) r. Sept. 1861
Goldsmith F. Bailey (R) d. May 1862
James Buffinton (R)
Henry L. Dawes (R)
Charles Delano (R)
Thomas D. Eliot (R)
Daniel W. Gooch (R)
Samuel Hooper (R)
Alexander H. Rice (R)
Benjamin F. Thomas (Un)
Charles R. Train (R)
Amasa Walker (R) s. 1862

Michigan

Senators

Kinsley S. Bingham (R) d. Oct. 1861
Zachariah Chandler (R)
Jacob M. Howard (R) s. 1862

Representatives

Fernando C. Beaman (R)
Bradley F. Granger (D)
Francis W. Kellogg (R)
Rowland E. Trowbridge (R)

Minnesota

Senators

Henry M. Rice (D)
Morton S. Wilkinson (R)

Representatives

Cyrus Aldrich (R)
William Windom

Mississippi

Senators

Vacant

Representatives

Vacant

Missouri

Senators

John B. Henderson (D) s. 1862
Waldo P. Johnson (D) r. Jan. 1862
Trusten Polk (D) r. Jan. 1862
Robert Wilson (Un) ta. 1862

Representatives

Francis P. Blair, Jr. (Free-Soiler) r. July 1862
John B. Clark (D) r. July 1861
William A. Hall (D) s. 1862
John W. Noell (D)
Elijah H. Norton (D)
John S. Phelps (D)
Thomas L. Price s. 1862
John W. Reid (D) r. Dec. 1862
James S. Rollins

New Hampshire

Senators

Daniel Clark (R)
John P. Hale (R)

Representatives

Thomas M. Edwards (R)
Gilman Marston (R)
Edward H. Rollins (R)

New Jersey

Senators

Richard S. Field (R) ta. 1862
John R. Thomson (D) d. Sept. 1862
John C. Ten Eyck (R)
James W. Wall (D) s. 1863

Representatives

George T. Cobb (D)
John T. Nixon (R)
Nehemiah Perry (Un)
William G. Steele (D)
John L. N. Stratton (R)

New York

Senators

Ira Harris (R)
Preston King (R)

Representatives

Stephen Baker
Jacob P. Chamberlain (R)
Ambrose W. Clark (R)
Frederick A. Conkling (R)
Roscoe Conkling (R)
Erastus Corning (D)
Isaac C. Delaplaine (D)
Alexander S. Diven (R)
R. Holland Duell (R)
Alfred Ely (R)
Reuben E. Fenton (R)
Richard Franchot (R)
Augustus Frank (R)
Edward Haight (D)
James E. Kerrigan (D)
William E. Lansing (R)
James B. McKean (R)
Moses F. Odell (D)
Abram B. Olin (R)
Theodore M. Pomeroy (R)
Charles B. Sedgwick (R)
Socrates N. Sherman (R)
Edward H. Smith (D)
Elbridge G. Spaulding (Un)
John B. Steele (D)
Burt Van Horn (R)
Robert B. Van Valkenburgh (R)
Charles H. Van Wyck (R)
Chauncey Vibbard (D)
William Wall (R)
Elijah Ward (D)
William A. Wheeler (R)
Benjamin Wood (D)

North Carolina

Senators

Thomas Bragg (D) r. Mar. 1861
Thomas L. Clingman (D) r. Mar. 1861

Representatives

Vacant

Ohio

Senators

Salmon P. Chase (D) r. Mar. 1861
John Sherman (R) s. 1861
Benjamin F. Wade (R)

Representatives

William Allen (D)
James M. Ashley (R)
John A. Bingham (R)
Harrison G. O. Blake (R)
Thomas Corwin (R) r. Mar. 1861
Samuel S. Cox (D)
William P. Cutler (R)
Sidney Edgerton (R)
John A. Gurley (R)
Richard A. Harrison (D) s. 1861
Valentine B. Horton (R)
John Hutchins (R)
James R. Morris (D)
Warren P. Noble (D)
Robert H. Nugen (D)
George H. Pendleton (D)
Albert G. Riddle (R)
Samuel Shellabarger (R)
John Sherman (R) r. Mar. 1861
Carey A. Trimble (R)
Clement L. Vallandigham (D)
Chilton A. White (D)
Samuel T. Worcester (R) s. 1861

Oregon

Senators

Edward D. Baker (R) d. Oct. 1861
Benjamin F. Harding (R) s. 1862
James W. Nesmith (D)
Benjamin Stark (D) ta. 1862

Representatives

George K. Shiel (D)
Andrew J. Thayer (D) r. July 1861

Pennsylvania

Senators

Simon Cameron (R) r. Mar. 1861
Edgar Cowan (R)
David Wilmot (R) s. 1861

Representatives

Sydenham E. Ancona (D)
Elijah Babbit (R)
Joseph Bailey (D)
Charles J. Biddle (D)
Samuel S. Blair (R)
James H. Campbell
Thomas B. Cooper (D) d. Apr.
  1862
John Covode (R)
William M. Davis (R)
Galusha A. Grow (R)
James T. Hale (R)
John Hickman (R)
Philip Johnson (R)
William D. Kelley (R)
John W. Killinger (R)
Jesse Lazear (D)
William E. Lehman (D)
Robert McKnight (R)
Edward McPherson (R)
James K. Moorhead (R)
Edward J. Morris (W) r. June
  1861
John Patton (R)
George W. Scranton (R) d.
  Mar. 1861
John D. Stiles (D) s. 1862
Thaddeus Stevens (R)
John P. Verree (R)
John W. Wallace (R)
Hendrick B. Wright (D)

Rhode Island

Senators

Henry B. Anthony (R)
Samuel G. Arnold (R) s. 1862
James F. Simmons (W) r. Aug.
  1862

Representatives

George H. Browne (D)
William P. Sheffield (R)

South Carolina

Senators

James Chesnut, Jr. (SRD) r.
  July 1861
Vacant

Representatives

Vacant

Tennessee

Senators

Andrew Johnson (D) r. Mar.
  1862
Alfred O.P. Nicholson r. July
  1861

Representatives

George W. Bridges (Un) s. 1863
Andrew J. Clements (Un) s.
  1862
Horace Maynard (Amer)

Texas

Senators

John Hemphill (SRD) r. Mar.
  1861
Louis Wigfall (D) r. Mar. 1861

Representatives

Vacant

Vermont

Senators

Jacob Collamer (R)
Solomon Foot (R)

Representatives

Portus Baxter (R)
Justin S. Morrill (W)
Eliakim P. Walton (R)

Virginia

Senators

John S. Carlile (Un)
Robert M. T. Hunter r. Mar.
  1861
James M. Mason (D) r. Mar.
  1861
Waitman T. Willey

Representatives

Jacob B. Blair (Un)
William G. Brown (Un)
John S. Carlile (Amer) r. July
  1861
Lewis McKenzie (Un) s. 1863
Joseph E. Segar (Un)
Charles H. Upton (R)
Kellian V. Whaley (R)

Wisconsin

Senators

James R. Doolittle (R)
Timothy O. Howe (R)

Representatives

Luther Hanchett (R) d. Nov.
  1862
Walter D. McIndoe (R) s. 1863
John F. Potter (R)
A. Scott Sloan (R)

Thirty-Eighth Congress

(Mar. 4, 1863, to
Mar. 3, 1865)

President of the Senate:
  Hannibal Hamlin
*Presidents Pro Tempore of the
  Senate:* Solomon Foot; Daniel
  Clark

*Speaker of the House of
  Representatives:* Schuyler
  Colfax

Alabama

Senators

Vacant

Representatives

Vacant

Arkansas

Senators

Vacant

Representatives

Vacant

California

Senators

John Conness (D)
James A. McDougall (D)

Representatives

Cornelius Cole (R)
William Higby (R)
Thomas B. Shannon (R)

Connecticut

Senators

James Dixon (R)
Lafayette S. Foster (R)

Representatives

Augustus Brandegee (R)
Henry C. Deming (R)
James E. English (D)
John H. Hubbard (R)

Delaware

Senators

James A. Bayard (D) r. Jan.
  1864
George R. Riddle (D) s. 1864
Willard Saulsbury (D)

Representatives

Nathaniel B. Smithers (R)

Florida

Senators

Vacant

Representatives

Vacant

Georgia

Senators

Vacant

Representatives

Vacant

Illinois

Senators

William A. Richardson (D)
Lyman Trumbull (R)

Representatives

James C. Allen (D)
William J. Allen (D)
Isaac N. Arnold (R)
John R. Eden (D)
John F. Farnsworth (R)
Charles M. Harris (D)
Ebon C. Ingersoll (R) s. 1864
Anthony L. Knapp (D)
Owen Lovejoy (R) d. Mar. 1864
William R. Morrison (D)
Jesse O. Norton (R)
James C. Robinson (D)
Lewis W. Ross (D)
John T. Stuart (D)
Elihu B. Washburne (W)

Indiana

Senators

Thomas A. Hendricks (D)
Henry S. Lane (R)

Representatives

Schuyler Colfax (R)
James A. Cravens (D)
Ebenezer Dumont (Un)
Joseph K. Edgerton (D)
Henry W. Harrington (D)
William S. Holman (D)
George W. Julian (R)
John Law (D)
James F. McDowell (D)
Godlove S. Orth (R)
Daniel W. Voorhees (D)

Iowa

Senators

James W. Grimes (R)
James Harlan (R)

Representatives

William B. Allison (R)
Josiah B. Grinnell (R)
Asahel W. Hubbard (R)
John A. Kasson (R)
Hiram Price (R)
James F. Wilson (R)

Kansas

Senators

James H. Lane (R)
Samuel C. Pomeroy (R)

Representatives

A. Carter Wilder

Kentucky

Senators

Garrett Davis (W)
Lazarus W. Powell (D)

Representatives

Lucien Anderson (Un)
Brutus J. Clay (Un)
Henry Grider (W)
Aaron Harding (Un)
Robert Mallory (D)
William H. Randall (R)
Green C. Smith
William H. Wadsworth (Un)
George H. Yeaman (Un)

Louisiana

Senators

Vacant

Representatives

Vacant

Maine

Senators

Nathan A. Farwell (R) s. 1864
William P. Fessenden (W) r.
    July 1864
Lot M. Morrill (R)

Representatives

James G. Blaine (R)
Sidney Perham (R)
Frederick A. Pike (R)
John H. Rice (R)
Lorenzo D. M. Sweat (D)

Maryland

Senators

Thomas H. Hicks (R) d. Feb.
    1865
Reverdy Johnson (D)

Representatives

John A. J. Creswell (R)
H. Winter Davis (Un)
Benjamin G. Harris (D)
Francis Thomas (Un)
Edwin H. Webster (R)

Massachusetts

Senators

Charles Sumner (R)
Henry Wilson

Representatives

John B. Alley (R)
Oakes Ames (R)
John D. Baldwin (R)
George S. Boutwell (R)
Henry L. Dawes (R)
Thomas D. Eliot (R)
Daniel W. Gooch (R)
Samuel Hooper (R)
Alexander H. Rice (R)
William B. Washburn (R)

Michigan

Senators

Zachariah Chandler (R)
Jacob M. Howard (R)

Representatives

Augustus C. Baldwin (D)
Fernando C. Beaman (R)
John F. Driggs (R)
Francis W. Kellogg (R)
John W. Longyear (R)
Charles Upson (R)

Minnesota

Senators

Alexander Ramsey (R)
Morton S. Wilkinson (R)

Representatives

Ignatius Donnelly (R)
William Windom (R)

Mississippi

Senators

Vacant

Representatives

Vacant

Missouri

Senators

B. Gratz Brown (D) s. 1863
John B. Henderson (D)
Robert Wilson (Un) r. 1863

Representatives

Francis P. Blair, Jr. (Free-Soiler) r.
    June 1864
Henry T. Blow (R)
Sempronius H. Boyd
    (Emancipationist)
William A. H. Hall (D)
Austin A. King (D)
Samuel Knox (R) s. 1864

Benjamin F. Loan
    (Emancipationist)
Joseph W. McClurg
    (Emancipationist)
John W. Noell (D) d. Mar.
    1863
James S. Rollins (Con)
John G. Scott (D)

Nevada

Senators

James W Nye (R) s. 1865
William M. Stewart (R) s. 1865

Representatives

Henry G. Worthington (R) s.
    1864

New Hampshire

Senators

Daniel Clark (R)
John P. Hale (R)

Representatives

Daniel March (D)
James W. Patterson (R)
Edward H. Rollins (R)

New Jersey

Senators

John C. Ten Eyck (R)
William Wright (D)

Representatives

George Middleton (D)
Nehemiah Perry (Un)
Andrew J. Rogers (D)
John F. Starr (R)
William G. Steele (D)

New York

Senators

Ira Harris (R)
Edwin D. Morgan (R)

Representatives

James Brooks (D)
John W. Chanler (D)
Ambrose W. Clark (R)
Freeman Clarke (R)
Thomas T. Davis (Un)
Reuben E. Fenton (R) r. Dec.
    1864
Augustus Frank (R)
John Ganson (D)
John A. Griswold (D)
Anson Herrick (D)
Giles W. Hotchkiss (R)
Calvin T. Hulburd (R)
Martin Kalbfleisch (D)
Orlando Kellogg (R)
Francis Kernan (D)
De Witt C. Littlejohn (R)
James M. Marvin (Un)
Samuel F. Miller (R)

Daniel Morris (R)
Homer A. Nelson (D)
Moses F. Odell (D)
Theodore M. Pomeroy (R)
John V. L. Pruyn (D)
William Radford (D)
Henry G. Stebbins (D) r. Oct.
    1864
John B. Steele (D)
Dwight Townsend (D) s. 1864
Robert B. Van Valkenburgh (R)
Elijah Ward (D)
Charles H. Winfield (D)
Benjamin Wood (D)
Fernando Wood (D)

North Carolina

Senators

Vacant

Representatives

Vacant

Ohio

Senators

John Sherman (R)
Benjamin F. Wade (R)

Representatives

James M. Ashley (R)
George Bliss (D)
Samuel S. Cox (D)
Ephraim R. Eckley (R)
William E. Finck (D)
James A. Garfield (R)
Wells A. Hutchins (D)
William Johnston (D)
Francis C. Le Blond (D)
Alexander Long (D)
John F. McKinney (D)
James R. Morris (D)
Warren P. Noble (D)
John O'Neill (D)
George H. Pendleton (D)
Robert C. Schenck (D)
Rufus P. Spalding (D)
Chilton A. White (D)
Joseph W. White (D)

Oregon

Senators

Benjamin F. Harding (R)
James W. Nesmith (D)

Representatives

John R. McBride (R)

Pennsylvania

Senators

Charles R. Buckalew (D)
Edgar Cowan (R)

Representatives

Sydenham E. Ancona (D)
Joseph Bailey (D)

John M. Broomall (R)
Alexander H. Coffroth (D)
John L. Dawson (D)
Charles Denison (D)
James T. Hale (R)
Philip Johnson (R)
William D. Kelley (R)
Jesse Lazear (D)
Archibald McAllister (D)
William H. Miller (D)
James K. Moorhead (R)
Amos Myers (R)
Leonard Myers (R)
Charles O'Neill (R)
Samuel J. Randall (D)
Glenni W. Scofield (R)
Thaddeus Stevens (R)
John D. Stiles (D)
Myer Strouse (D)
M. Russell Thayer (R)
Henry W. Tracy (R)
Thomas Williams (R)

Rhode Island

Senators

Henry B. Anthony (R)
William Sprague

Representatives

Nathan F. Dixon (R)
Thomas A. Jenckes (R)

South Carolina

Senators

Vacant

Representatives

Vacant

Tennessee

Senators

Vacant

Representatives

Vacant

Texas

Senators

Vacant

Representatives

Vacant

Vermont

Senators

Jacob Collamer (R)
Solomon Foot (R)

Representatives

Portus Baxter (R)
Justin S. Morrill

Frederick E. Woodbridge (R)

Virginia

Senators

John S. Carlile (Un)
Lemuel J. Bowden (R) d. Jan.
1864

Represenatives

Vacant

West Virginia

Senators

Peter G. Van Winkle (Un)
Waitman T. Willey (R)

Representatives

Jacob B. Blair (R)
William G. Brown (Un)
Kellian V. Whaley (R)

Wisconsin

Senators

James R. Doolittle (R)
Timothy O. Howe (R)

Representatives

James S. Brown (D)
Amasa Cobb (R)
Charles A. Eldridge (D)
Walter D. McIndoe (R)
Ithamar C. Sloan (R)
Ezra Wheeler (D)

Thirty-Ninth Congress

(Mar. 4, 1865, to
Mar. 3, 1867)

President of the Senate: Andrew
Johnson
*Presidents Pro Tempore of the
Senate:* Lafayette S. Foster;
Benjamin F. Wade
*Speaker of the House of
Representatives:* Schuyler
Colfax

Alabama

Senators

Vacant

Representatives

Vacant

Arkansas

Senators

Vacant

Representatives

Vacant

California

Senators

James A. McDougall (D)
John Conness (R)

Representatives

John Bidwell (Un)
William Higby (R)
Donald C. McRuer (R)

Connecticut

Senators

James Dixon (R)
Lafayette S. Foster (R)

Representatives

Augustus Brandegee (R)
Henry C. Deming (R)
John H. Hubbard (R)
Samuel L. Warner (R)

Delaware

Senators

George R. Riddle (D)
Willard Saulsbury (D)

Representatives

John A. Nicholson (D)

Florida

Senators

Vacant

Representatives

Vacant

Georgia

Senators

Vacant

Representatives

Vacant

Illinois

Senators

Lyman Trumbull (R)
Richard Yates (R)

Representatives

Jehu Baker (R)
Henry P. H. Bromwell (R)
Burton C. Cook (R)

Shelby M. Cullom (R)
John F. Farnsworth (R)
Abner C. Harding (R)
Ebon C. Ingeroll (R)
Andrew J. Kuykendall (R)
Samuel S. Marshall (D)
Samuel W. Moulton (D)
Lewis W. Ross (D)
Anthony Thornton (D)
Elihu B. Washburne (W)
John Wentworth (R)

Indiana

Senators

Thomas A. Hendricks (D)
Henry S. Lane (R)

Representatives

Schuyler Colfax (R)
Joseph H. Defrees (R)
Ebenezer Dumont (Un)
John H. Farquhar (R)
Ralph Hill (R)
George W. Julian (R)
Michael C. Kerr (D)
William E. Niblack (D)
Godlove S. Orth (R)
Thomas N. Stillwell (R)
Daniel W. Voorhees (D) r. Feb.
1866
Henry D. Washburn (R) s.
1866

Iowa

Senators

James W. Grimes (R)
James Harlan (R) r. May 1865
Samuel J Kirkwood (R) s. 1866

Representatives

William B. Allison (R)
Josiah B. Grinnell (R)
Asahel W. Hubbard (R)
John A. Kasson (R)
Hiram Price (R)
James F. Wilson (R)

Kansas

Senators

James H. Lane (R) d. July
1866
Samuel C. Pomeroy (R)
Edmund G. Ross (R) s. 1866

Representatives

Sidney Clarke (R)

Kentucky

Senators

Garrett Davis (W)
James Guthrie (D)

Representatives

Henry Grider (W) d. Sept. 1866
Aaron Harding (D)

Elijah Hise (D) s. 1866
Samuel McKee (R)
William H. Randall (R)
Burwell C. Ritter (Con)
Lovell H. Rousseau (R)
George S. Shanklin (D)
Green C. Smith (Un) r. 1866
Lawrence S. Trimble (D)
Andrew H. Ward

Louisiana

Senators

Vacant

Representatives

Vacant

Maine

Senators

William P. Fessenden (W)
Lot M. Morrill (R)

Representatives

James G. Blaine (R)
John Lynch (R)
Sidney Perham (R)
Frederick A. Pike (R)
John H. Rice (R)

Maryland

Senators

John A. J. Creswell (R)
Reverdy Johnson (D)

Representatives

Benjamin G. Harris (D)
Hiram McCullough (D)
Charles E. Phelps (Con)
Francis Thomas (R)
John L. Thomas, Jr. (R)
Edwin H. Webster r. July 1865

Massachusetts

Senators

Charles Sumner (R)
Henry Wilson

Representatives

John B. Alley (R)
Oakes Ames (R)
John D. Baldwin (R)
Nathaniel P. Banks (R)
George S. Boutwell (R)
Henry L. Dawes (R)
Thomas D. Eliot (R)
Samuel Hooper (R)
Alexander H. Rice (R)
William B. Washburn (R)

Michigan

Senators

Zachariah Chandler (R)

Jacob M. Howard (R)

Representatives

Fernando C. Beaman (R)
John F. Driggs (R)
Thomas W. Ferry (R)
John W. Longyear (R)
Rowland E. Trowbridge (R)
Charles Upson (R)

Minnesota

Senators

Daniel S. Norton (Con)
Alexander Ramsey (R)

Representatives

Ignatius Donnelly (R)
William Windom (R)

Mississippi

Senators

Vacant

Representatives

Vacant

Missouri

Senators

B. Gratz Brown (D)
John B. Henderson (D)

Representatives

George W. Anderson (R)
John F. Benjamin (R)
Henry T. Blow (R)
John Hogan (D)
John R. Kelso (Radical)
Benjamin F. Loan
 (Emancipationist)
Joseph W. McClurg (Radical)
Thomas E. Noel (D)
Robert T. Van Horn (R)

Nebraska

Senators

John M. Thayer (R) s. 1867
Thomas W. Tipton (R) s. 1867

Representatives

Turner M. Marquette (R) s.
 1867

Nevada

Senators

James W. Nye (R)
William M. Stewart (R)

Representatives

Delos R. Ashley (R)

New Hampshire

Senators

Aaron H. Cragin (Amer)
Daniel Clark (R) r. July 1866
George G. Fogg (R) s. 1866

Representatives

Gilman Marston (R)
James W. Patterson (R)
Edward H. Rollins (R)

New Jersey

Senators

Alexander G. Cattell (R) s.
 1866
Frederick T. Frelinghuysen (R)
 s. 1866
John P. Stockton (D) r. 1866
William Wright (D) d. Nov.
 1866

Representatives

William A. Newell (R)
Andrew J. Rogers (D) r. Mar.
 1866
Charles Sitgreaves (D)
John F. Starr (R)
Edwin R. V. Wright (D) s.
 1866

New York

Senators

Ira Harris (R)
Edwin D. Morgan (R)

Representatives

Teunis G. Bergen (D)
James Brooks (D) r. Apr. 1866
John W. Chanler (D)
Roscoe Conkling (R) r. Mar.
 1867
William A. Darling (R)
Thomas T. Davis (Un)
William E. Dodge (R) s. 1866
Charles Goodyear (D)
John A. Griswold (D)
Robert S. Hale (R) s. 1866
Roswell Hart (R)
Sidney T. Holmes (R)
Giles W. Hotchkiss (R)
Demas Hubbard, Jr. (R)
Edwin N. Hubbell (R)
Calvin T. Hulburd (R)
James Humphrey (R) d. June
 1866
James M. Humphrey (D)
John W. Hunter s. 1866
Morgan Jones (D)
Orlando Kellogg (R) d. Aug.
 1865
John H. Ketcham (R)
Addison H. Laflin (R)
James M Marvin (Un)
Daniel Morris (D)
Theodore M. Pomeroy (R)
William Radford (D)
Henry J. Raymond (R)
Stephen Taber (D)
Nelson Taylor (D)

Henry Van Aernam (R)
Burt Van Horn (R)
Hamilton Ward (R)
Charles H. Winfield (D)

North Carolina

Senators

Vacant

Representatives

Vacant

Ohio

Senators

John Sherman (R)
Benjamin F. Wade (R)

Representatives

James M. Ashley (R)
John A. Bingham (R)
Ralph P. Buckland (R)
Hezekiah S. Bundy (R)
Reader W. Clarke (R)
Columbus Delano (R)
Ephraim R. Eckley (R)
Benjamin Eggleston (R)
William E. Finck (D)
James A. Garfield (R)
Rutherford B. Hayes (R)
James R. Hubbell (R)
William Lawrence (R)
Francis C. Le Blond (D)
Tobias A. Plants (R)
Robert C. Schenck (R)
Samuel Shellabarger (R)
Rufus P. Spaulding (D)
Martin Welker (R)

Oregon

Senators

James W. Nesmith (D)
George H. Williams (R)

Representatives

James H. Henderson (R)

Pennsylvania

Senators

Charles R. Buckalew (D)
Edgar Cowan (R)

Representatives

Sydenham E. Ancona (D)
Abraham A. Barker (R)
Benjamin M. Boyer (D)
John M. Broomall (R)
Alexander H. Coffroth (D) r.
 July 1866
Charles V. Culver (R)
John L. Dawson (D)
Charles Denison (D)
Adam J. Glossbrenner (D)
Philip Johnson (D) d. Jan. 1867
William D. Kelley (R)
William H. Koontz (R) s. 1866

George V. Lawrence (W)
Ulysses Mercur (R)
George F. Miller (R)
James K. Moorhead (R)
Leonard Myers (R)
Charles O'Neill (R)
Samuel J. Randall (D)
Glenni W. Scofield (R)
Thaddeus Stevens (R)
Myer Stouse (D)
M. Russell Thayer (R)
Thomas Williams (R)
Stephen F. Wilson (R)

Rhode Island

Senators

Henry B. Anthony (R)
William Sprague (R)

Representatives

Nathan F. Dixon (R)
Thomas A. Jenckes (R)

South Carolina

Senators

Vacant

Representatives

Vacant

Tennessee

Senators

Joseph S. Fowler (R) s. 1866
David T. Patterson (D) s. 1866

Representatives

Samuel M. Arnell (R) s. 1866
William B. Campbell (D) s. 1866
Edmund Cooper (Con) s. 1866
Isaac R. Hawkins (R) s. 1866
John W. Leftwich (D) s. 1866
Horace Maynard (R) s. 1866
William B. Stokes (R) s. 1866
Nathaniel G. Taylor s. 1866

Texas
Vacant

Senators

Vacant

Representatives

Vermont

Senators

George F. Edmunds (R) s. 1866
Solomon Foot (R) d. Mar. 1866
Jacob Collamer (R) d. Nov. 1865
Luke P. Poland (R) s. 1865

Representatives

Portus Baxter (R)
Justin S. Morrill
Frederick E. Woodbridge (R)

Virginia

Senators

Vacant

Representatives

Vacant

West Virginia

Senators

Peter G. Van Winkle (Un)
Waitman T. Willey (R)

Representatives

Chester D. Hubbard (R)
George R. Latham (R)
Kellian V. Whaley (R)

Wisconsin

Senators

James R. Doolittle (R)
Timothy O. Howe (R)

Representatives

Amasa Cobb (R)
Charles A. Eldridge (D)
Walter D. McIndoe (R)
Halbert E. Paine (R)
Philetus Sawyer (R)
Ithamar C. Sloan (R)

Fortieth Congress

(Mar. 4, 1867, to
Mar. 3, 1869)

President of the Senate: Vacant
President Pro Tempore of the Senate: Benjamin F. Wade
Speakers of the House of Representatives: Schuyler Colfax; Theodore M. Pomeroy

Alabama

Senators

George E. Spencer (R) s. 1868
Willard Warner (R) s. 1868

Representatives

Charles W. Buckley (R) s. 1868
John B. Callis (R) s. 1868
Thomas Haughey (R) s. 1868
Francis W. Kellogg (R) s. 1868
Benjamin W. Norris (R) s. 1868

Arkansas

Senators

Alexander McDonald (R) s. 1868
Benjamin F. Rice (R) s. 1868

Representatives

Thomas Boles (R) s. 1868
James T. Elliott (R) s. 1868
James Hinds (R) s. 1868
Logan H. Roots (R) s. 1868

California

Senators

Cornelius Cole (R)
John Conness (R)

Representatives

Samuel B. Axtell (D) s. 1867
William Higby (R) s. 1867
James A. Johnson (D) s. 1867

Connecticut

Senators

James Dixon (R)
Orris S. Ferry (R)

Representatives

William H. Barnum (D)
Julius Hotchkiss (R)
Richard D. Hubbard (D)
Henry H. Starkweather (R)

Delaware

Senators

James A. Baynard (D)
George R. Riddle (D) d. Mar. 1867
Willard Saulsbury (D)

Representatives

John A. Nicholson (D)

Florida

Senators

Thomas W. Osborn (R) s. 1868
Adonijah S. Welch (R) s. 1868

Representatives

Charles M. Hamilton (R) s. 1868

Georgia

Senators

Vacant

Representatives

Joseph W. Clift (R) s. 1868
William P. Edwards (R) s. 1868
Samuel F. Gove (R) s. 1868
Charles H. Prince (R) s. 1868
Nelson Tift (D) s. 1868
Pierce M. B. Young (D) s. 1868

Illinois

Senators

Lyman Trumbull (R)
Richard Yates (R)

Representatives

Jehu Baker (R)
Henry P. H. Bromwell (R)
Albert G. Burr (D)
Burton C. Cook (R)
Shelby M. Cullom (R)
John F. Farnsworth (R)
Abner C. Harding (R)
Ebon C. Ingersoll (R)
Norman B. Judd (R)
Samuel S. Marshall (D)
Green B. Raum (R)
Lewis W. Ross (D)
Elihu B. Washburne (W)

Indiana

Senators

Thomas A. Hendricks (D)
Oliver H. P. T. Morton (R)

Representatives

John Coburn (R)
Schuyler Colfax (R)
William S. Holman (D)
Morton C. Hunter (R)
George W. Julian (R)
Michael C. Kerr (D)
William E. Niblack (D)
Godlove S. Orth (R)
John P. C. Shanks (R)
Henry D. Washburn (R)
William Williams (R)

Iowa

Senators

James W. Grimes (R)
James Harlan (R)

Representatives

William B. Allison (R)
Grenville M. Dodge (R)
Asahel W. Hubbard (R)
William Loughridge (R)
Hiram P. Rice (R)
James R. Wilson (R)

Kansas

Senators

Samuel C. Pomeroy (R)
Edmund G. Ross (D)

Representatives

Sidney Clarke (R)

Kentucky

Senators

Garrett Davis (W)
James Guthrie (D) r. Feb. 1868
Thomas C. McCreery (D) s.
1868

Representatives

George M. Adams (D)
James B. Beck (D)
Jacob S. Golladay (D)
Asa P. Grover (D)
Thomas L. Jones (D)
J. Proctor Knott (D)
Samuel McKee (R) s. 1868
Lawrence S. Trimble (D) s.
1868

Louisiana

Senators

John S. Harris (R) s. 1868
William P. Kellogg (R)

Representatives

W. Jasper Blackburn (R) s.
1868
James Mann (D) d. 1868
Joseph P. Newsham (R) s. 1868
J. Hale Sypher (R) s. 1868
Michel Vidal (R) s. 1868

Maine

Senators

William P. Fessenden (W)
Lot M. Morrill (R)

Representatives

James G. Blaine (R)
John Lynch (R)
Sidney Perham (R)
John A. Peters (R)
Frederick A. Pike (R)

Maryland

Senators

Reverdy Johnson (D) r. July
1868
George Vickers (D) s. 1868
William P. Whyte (D) s. 1868

Representatives

Stevenson Archer (D)
Hiram McCullough (D)
Charles E. Phelps (Con)
Frederick Stone (D)
Francis Thomas (R)

Massachusetts

Senators

Charles Sumner (R)
Henry Wilson (Free-Soiler)

Representatives

Oakes Ames
John D. Baldwin (R)
Nathaniel P. Banks (R)
George S. Boutwell (R)
Benjamin F. Butler (R)
Henry L. Dawes (R)
Thomas D. Eliot (R)
Samuel Hooper (R)
Ginery Twichell (R)
William B. Washburn (R)

Michigan

Senators

Zachariah Chandler (R)
Jacob M. Howard (R)

Representatives

Fernando C. Beaman (R)
Austin Blair (R)
John F. Driggs (R)
Thomas W. Ferry (R)
Rowland E. Trowbridge (R)
Charles Upson (R)

Minnesota

Senators

Daniel S. Norton (Con)
Alexander Ramsey (R)

Representatives

William Windom (R)
Ignatius Donnelly (R)

Mississippi

Senators

Vacant

Representatives

Vacant

Missouri

Senators

Charles D. Drake (R)
John B. Henderson (D)

Representatives

George W. Anderson (R)
John F. Benjamin (R)
Joseph J. Gravely (R)
Joseph W. McClurg (Radical) r.
1868
Benjamin F. Loan (Radical)
James R. McCormick (D)
Carman A. Newcomb (R)

Thomas E. Noell (Radical) d.
Oct. 1867
William A. Pile (R)
John H. Stover s. 1868
Robert T. Van Horn (R)

Nebraska

Senators

John M. Thayer (R)
Thomas W. Tipton (R)

Representatives

John Taffe (R)

Nevada

Senators

James W. Nye (R)
William M. Stewart (R)

Representatives

Delos R. Ashley (R)

New Hampshire

Senators

Aaron H. Cragin (Amer)
James W. Patterson (R)

Representatives

Jacob Benton (R)
Jacob H. Ela (R)
Aaron F. Stevens (R)

New Jersey

Senators

Alexander G. Cattell (R)
Frederick T. Frelinghuysen (R)

Representatives

Charles Haight (D)
George A. Halsey (R)
John Hill (R)
William Moore (R)
Charles Sitgreaves (D)

New York

Senators

Roscoe Conkling (R)
Edwin D. Morgan (R)

Representatives

Alexander H. Bailey (R)
Demas Barnes (D)
James Brooks (D)
John W. Chanler (D)
John C. Churchill (R)
Thomas Cornell (R)
Orange Ferriss (R)
William C. Fields (R)
John Fox (D)
John A. Griswold (R)
Calvin T. Hulburd (R)

James M. Humphrey (D)
William H. Kelsey (R)
John H. Ketcham (R)
Addison H. Laflin (R)
William S. Lincoln (R)
Dennis McCarthy (R)
James M. Marvin (Un)
John Morrissey (D)
Theodore M. Pomeroy (R)
John V. L. Pruyn (D)
William H. Robertson (R)
William E. Robinson (D)
Lewis Selye
Thomas E. Stewart
Stephen Taber (D)
Henry Van Aernam (R)
Burt Van Horn (R)
Charles H. Van Wyck (R)
Hamilton Ward (R)
Fernando Wood (D)

North Carolina

Senators

Joseph C. Abbott (R) s. 1868
John Pool s. 1868

Representatives

Nathaniel Boyden (R) s. 1868
John T. Deweese (D) s. 1868
Oliver H. Dockery (R) s. 1868
John R. French (R) s. 1868
David Heaton (R) s. 1868
Alexander H. Jones (R) s. 1868
Israel G. Lash (R) s. 1868

Ohio

Senators

Benjamin F. Wade (R)
John Sherman (R)

Representatives

James M. Ashley (R)
John Beatty (R) s. 1868
John A. Bingham (R)
Ralph P. Buckland (R)
Samuel F. Cary (R)
Reader W. Clarke (R)
Columbus Delano (R) s. 1868
Ephraim R. Eckley (R)
Benjamin Eggleston (R)
James A. Garfield (R)
Cornelius S. Hamilton (R) d.
Dec. 1867
Rutherford B. Hayes (R) r. July
1867
William Lawrence (R)
George W. Morgan (D) r. Jun.
1868
William Mungen (D)
Tobias A. Plants (R)
Robert C. Schenck (R)
Samuel Shellabarger (R)
Rufus P. Spalding (D)
Philadelph Van Trump (D)
Martin Welker (R)
John T. Wilson (R)

Oregon

Senators

Henry W. Corbett (R)

George H. Williams (R)

Representatives

Rufus Mallory (R)

Pennsylvania

Senators

Charles R. Buckalew (D)
Simon Cameron (R)

Representatives

Benjamin M. Boyer (D)
John M. Broomall (R)
Henry L. Cake (R)
John Covode (R)
Charles Denison (D) d. June
1867
Oliver J. Dickey (R) s. 1868
Darwin A. Finney (R) d. Aug.
1868
J. Lawrence Getz (D)
Adam J. Glossbrenner (D)
William D. Kelley (R)
William H. Koontz (R)
George V. Lawrence (W)
Ulysses Mercur (R)
George F. Miller (R)
James K. Moorhead
Daniel J. Morrell (R)
Leonard Myers (R)
Charles O'Neill (R)
S. Newton Pettis (R) s. 1868
Samuel J. Randall (D)
Glenni W. Scofield (R)
Thaddeus Stevens (R) d. Aug.
1868
Caleb N. Taylor (R)
Daniel M. Van Auken (D)
Thomas Williams (R)
Stephen F. Wilson (R)
George W. Woodward (D)

Rhode Island

Senators

Henry B. Anthony (R)
William Sprague (R)

Representatives

Nathan F. Dixon (R)
Thomas A. Jenckes (R)

South Carolina

Senators

Thomas J. Robertson (R) s.
1868
Frederick A. Sawyer (R) s.
1868

Representatives

Christopher C. Bowen (R) s.
1868
M. Simeon Corley (R) s. 1868
James H. Goss (R) s. 1868
B. Frank Whittemore (R) s.
1868

Tennessee

Senators

Joseph S. Fowler (R)
David T. Patterson (D)

Representatives

Samuel M. Arnell (R) s. 1868
Roderick R. Butler (R) s. 1868
Isaac R. Hawkins (R) s. 1868
Horace Maynard (R) s. 1868
James Mullins (R) s. 1868
David A. Nunn (R) s. 1868
William B. Stokes (R) s. 1868
John Trimble (R) s. 1868

Texas

Senators

Vacant

Representatives

Vacant

Vermont

Senators

George F. Edmunds (R)
Justin S. Morrill (R)

Representatives

Luke P. Poland (R)
Worthington C. Smith (R)
Frederick E. Woodbridge (R)

Virginia

Senators

Vacant

Representatives

Vacant

West Virginia

Senators

Peter G. Van Winkle (Un)
Waitman T. Willey (R)

Representatives

Chester D. Hubbard (R)
Bethuel M. Kitchen (R)
Daniel H. Polsley (R)

Wisconsin

Senators

James R. Doolittle (R)
Timothy O. Howe (R)

Representatives

Charles A. Eldredge (D)
Amasa Cobb (R)

Benjamin F. Hopkins (R)
Halbert E. Paine (R)
Philetus Sawyer (R)
Cadwallader C. Washburn (R)

Forty-First Congress

(Mar. 4, 1869, to
Mar. 3, 1871)

President of the Senate: Schuyler
Colfax
*President Pro Tempore of the
Senate:* Henry B. Anthony
*Speaker of the House of
Representatives:* James G.
Blaine

Alabama

Senators

George E. Spencer (R)
Willard Warner (R)

Representatives

Alfred E. Buck (R)
Charles W. Buckley (R)
Peter M. Dox (D)
Charles Hays (R)
Robert S. Heflin (R)
William C. Sherrod (D)

Arkansas

Senators

Alexander McDonald (R)
Benjamin F. Rice (R)

Representatives

Thomas Boles (R)
Anthony A. C. Rogers (D)
Logan H. Roots (R)

California

Senators

Eugene Casserly (D)
Cornelius Cole (R)

Representatives

Samuel B. Axtell (D)
James A. Johnson (D)
Aaron A. Sargent (R)

Connecticut

Senators

William A. Buckingham (R)
Orris S. Ferry (R)

Representatives

William H. Barnum (D)
Stephen W. Kellogg (R)
Henry H. Starkweather (R)
Julius L. Strong (R)

Delaware

Senators

Thomas F. Bayard (D)
Willard Saulsbury (D)

Representatives

Benjamin T. Biggs (D)

Florida

Senators

Thomas W. Osborn (R)
Abijah Gilbert (R)

Representatives

Charles M. Hamilton (R)

Georgia

Senators

Joshua Hill (R) s. 1871
Homer V. M. Miller (D) s.
1871

Representatives

Marion Bethune (R) s. 1871
Stephen A. Corker (D) s. 1871
Jefferson F. Long (R) s. 1871
William W. Paine (D) s. 1871
William P. Price (D) s. 1871
Richard H. Whiteley (R) s.
1871
Pierce M. B. Young (D) s.
1871

Illinois

Senators

Lyman Trumbull (R)
Richard Yates (R)

Representatives

Horatio C. Burchard (R)
Albert G. Burr (D)
Burton C. Cook (R)
John M. Crebs (D)
Shelby M. Cullom (R)
John F. Farnsworth (R)
John B. Hawley (R)
John B. Hay (R)
Ebon C. Ingersoll (R)
Norman B. Judd (R)
Thompson W. McNeely (D)
Samuel S. Marshall (D)
Jesse H. Moore (R)

Indiana

Senators

Oliver H. P. T. Morton (R)
Daniel D. Pratt (R)

Representatives

John Coburn (R)
William S. Holman (R)

George W. Julian (R)
Michael C. Kerr (D)
William E. Niblack (D)
Godlove S. Orth (R)
Jasper Packard (R)
John P. C. Shanks (R)
James N. Tyner (R)
Daniel W. Voorhees (D)
William Williams (R)

Iowa

Senators

James W. Grimes (R) r. Dec. 1869
James Harlan (R)
James B. Howell (R) s. 1870

Representatives

William B. Allison (R)
William Loughridge (R)
George W. McCrary (R)
Frank W. Palmer (R)
Charles Pomeroy (R)
William Smyth (R) d. Sept. 1870
William P. Wolf (R) s. 1870

Kansas

Senators

Samuel C. Pomeroy (R)
Edmund G. Ross (D)

Representatives

Sidney Clarke (R)

Kentucky

Senators

Garrett Davis (D)
Thomas C. McCreery (D)

Representatives

George M. Adams (D)
James B. Beck (D)
Jacob S. Golladay (D) r. Feb. 1870
Thomas L. Jones (D)
J. Proctor Knott (D)
Joseph H. Lewis (D) s. 1870
John M. Rice (D)
William N. Sweeney (D)
Lawrence S. Trimble (D)
Boyd Winchester (D)

Louisiana

Senators

John S. Harris (R)
William P. Kellogg (R)

Representatives

Chester B. Darrall (R) s. 1870
Frank Morey (R) s. 1870
Joseph P. Newsham (R) s. 1870
Lionel A. Sheldon (R)
J. Hale Sypher (R) s. 1870

Maine

Senators

William P. Fessenden d. Sept. 1869
Hannibal Hamlin (R)
Lot M. Morrill (R) s. Dec. 1869

Representatives

James G. Blaine (R)
Eugene Hale (R)
John Lynch (R)
Samuel P. Morrill (R)
John A. Peters (R)

Maryland

Senators

William T. Hamilton (D)
George Vickers (D)

Representatives

Stevenson Archer (D)
Samuel Hambleton (D)
Patrick Hamill (D)
Frederick Stone (D)
Thomas Swann (D)

Massachusetts

Senators

Charles Sumner (R)
Henry Wilson

Representatives

Oakes Ames (R)
Nathaniel P. Banks (R)
George S. Boutwell (R) r. Mar. 1869
George M. Brooks (R)
James Buffinton (R)
Benjamin F. Butler (R)
Henry L. Dawes (R)
George F. Hoar (R)
Samuel Hooper (R)
Ginery Twichell (R)
William B. Washburn (R)

Michigan

Senators

Zachariah Chandler (R)
Jacob M. Howard (R)

Representatives

Fernando C. Beaman (R)
Austin Blair (R)
Omar D. Conger (R)
Thomas W. Ferry (R)
Randolph Strickland (R)
William L. Stoughton (R)

Minnesota

Senators

Daniel S. Norton (Con) d. July 1870
Alexander Ramsey (R)
Ozora P. Stearns (R) s. 1871
William Windom (R) ta. 1870

Representatives

Morton S. Wilkinson (R)
Eugene M. Wilson (D)

Mississippi

Senators

Adelbert Ames (R) s. 1870
Hiram R. Revels (R) s. 1870

Representatives

Henry W. Barry (R) s. 1870
George E. Harris (R) s. 1870
George C. McKee (R) s. 1870
Joseph L. Morphis (R) s. 1870
Legrand W. Perce (R) s. 1870

Missouri

Senators

Francis P. Blair, Jr. (D) s. 1871
Charles D. Drake (R) r. Dec. 1870
Daniel T. Jewett (R) s. 1871
Carl Schurz (R)

Representatives

Joel F. Asper (R)
John F. Benjamin (R)
Sempronius H. Boyd
Samuel S. Burdett (R)
David P. Dyer (R)
Gustavus A. Finkelnburg (R)
James R. McCormick (D)
Robert T. Van Horn (R)
Erastus Wells (D)

Nebraska

Senators

John M. Thayer (R)
Thomas W. Tipton (D)

Representatives

John Taffe (R)

Nevada

Senators

William M. Stewart (R)
James W. Nye (R)

Representatives

Thomas Fitch (R)

New Hampshire

Senators

Aaron H. Cragin (Amer)
James W. Patterson (R)

Represenatatives

Jacob Benton (R)
Jacob H. Ela (R)
Aaron F. Stevens (R)

New Jersey

Senators

Alexander G. Catell (R)
John P. Stockton (D)

Representatives

John T. Bird (D)
Orestes Cleveland (D)
Charles Haight (D)
John Hill (R)
William Moore (R)

New York

Senators

Roscoe Conkling (R)
Reuben E. Fenton (R)

Representatives

Alexander H. Bailey (R)
David S. Bennett (R)
James Brooks (D)
Hervey C. Calkin (D)
John C. Churchill (R)
George W. Cowles (R)
Samuel S. Cox (D)
Noah Davis (R) r. July 1870
Orange Ferriss (R)
John Fisher (R)
John Fox (D)
George W. Greene (D) r. Feb. 1870
John A. Griswold (D)
Charles H. Holmes (R) s. 1870
Giles W. Hotchkiss (R)
William H. Kelsey (R)
John H. Ketcham (R)
Charles Knapp (R)
Addison H. Laflin (R)
Stephen L. Mayham (D)
Dennis McCarthy (R)
John Morrissey (D)
Clarkson N. Potter (D)
Henry A. Reeves (D)
Stephen Sanford (R)
John G. Schumaker (D)
Porter Sheldon (R)
Henry W. Slocum (D)
Adolphus H. Tanner (R)
Charles H. Van Wyck (R) s. 1870
Hamilton Ward (R)
William A. Wheeler (R)
Fernando Wood (D)

North Carolina

Senators

Joseph C. Abbott (R)
John Pool

Representatives

Clinton L. Cobb (R)
John T. Deweese (D) r. Feb.
  1870
Joseph Dixon (R) s. 1870
Oliver H. Dockery (R)
David Heaton (R) d. June 1870
Alexander H. Jones (R)
Israel G. Lash (R)
John Manning, Jr. (D) s. 1870
Francis E. Shober (D)

Ohio

Senators

John Sherman (R)
Allen G. Thurman (D)

Representatives

Jacob A. Ambler (R)
John Beatty (R)
John A. Bingham (R)
Edward F. Dickinson (D)
James A. Garfield (R)
Truman H. Hoag (D) d. Feb.
  1870
William Lawrence (R)
Eliakim H. Moore (R)
George W. Morgan (D)
William Mungen (D)
Erasmus D. Peck (R) s. 1870
Robert C. Schenck (R) r. Jan.
  1871
John A. Smith (R)
Job E. Stevenson (R)
Peter W. Strader (D)
William H. Upson (R)
Philadelph Van Trump (D)
Martin Welker (R)
John T. Wilson (R)
James J. Winans (R)

Oregon

Senators

Henry W. Corbett (R)
George H. Williams (R)

Representatives

Joseph S. Smith (D)

Pennsylvania

Senators

Simon Cameron (R)
John Scott (R)

Representatives

William H. Armstrong (R)
Henry L. Cake (R)
John Cessna (R)
John Covode (R) s. 1870 d.
  Jan. 1871

Oliver J. Dickey (R)
Joseph B. Donley (R)
J. Lawrence Getz (D)
Calvin W. Gilfillan (R)
Richard J. Haldeman (D)
William D. Kelley (R)
Ulysses Mercur (R)
John Moffet (D) r. Apr. 1869
Daniel J. Morrell (R)
Leonard Myers (R)
James S. Negley (R)
Charles O'Neill (R)
John B. Packer (R)
Darwin Phelps (R)
Samuel J. Randall (D)
John R. Reading (R) r. Apr.
  1870
Glenni W. Scofield (R)
John D. Stiles (D)
Caleb N. Taylor (R) s. 1870
Washington Townsend (R)
Daniel M. Van Auken (D)
George W. Woodward (D)

Rhode Island

Senators

Henry B. Anthony (R)
William Sprague (R)

Representatives

Nathan F. Dixon (R)
Thomas A. Jenckes (R)

South Carolina

Senators

Thomas J. Robertson (R)
Frederick A. Sawyer (R)

Representatives

Christopher C. Bowen (R)
Solomon L. Hoge (R)
Joseph H. Rainey (R) s. 1870
Alexander S. Wallace (R) s.
  1870
B. Frank Whittemore (R) r.
  Feb. 1870

Tennessee

Senators

William G. Brownlow (R)
Joseph S. Fowler (R)

Representatives

Samuel M. Arnell (R)
Roderick R. Butler (R)
Isaac R. Hawkins (R)
Horace Maynard (R)
William F. Prosser (R)
William J. Smith (R)
William B. Stokes (R)
Lewis Tillman (R)

Texas

Senators

James W. Flanagan (R) s. 1870

Morgan C. Hamilton (R) s.
  1870

Representatives

William T. Clark (R) s. 1870
John C. Conner (D) s. 1870
Edward Degener (R) s. 1870
George W. Whitmore (R) s.
  1870

Vermont

Senators

George F. Edmunds (R)
Justin S. Morrill (R)

Representative

Luke P. Poland (R)
Worthington C. Smith (R)
Charles W. Willard (R)

Virginia

Senators

John W. Johnston (Con) s.
  1870
John F. Lewis (R) s. 1870

Representatives

Richard S. Ayer (R) s. 1870
George W. Booker (Con) s.
  1870
Richard T. W. Duke (Con) s.
  1870
James King Gibson (D) s. 1870
Lewis McKenzie (Un) s. 1870
William Milnes, Jr. (Con) s.
  1870
James H. Platt, Jr. (R) s. 1870
Charles H. Porter (R) s. 1870
Robert Ridgway (Con) d. 1870

West Virginia

Senators

Arthur I. Boreman (R)
Waitman T. Willey (R)

Representatives

Isaac H. Duval (R)
James C. McGrew (R)
John S. Witcher (R)

Wisconsin

Senators

Matthew H. Carpenter (R)
Timothy O. Howe (R)

Representatives

David Atwood (R) s. 1870
Amasa Cobb (R)
Charles A. Eldredge (D)
Benjamin F. Hopkins (R) d.
  1870
Halbert E. Paine (R)
Philetus Sawyer (R)
Cadwallader C. Washburn (R)

Forty-Second Congress

(Mar. 4, 1871, to
Mar. 3, 1873)

President of the Senate: Schuyler
  Colfax
*President Pro Tempore of the
  Senate:* Henry B. Anthony
*Speaker of the House of
  Representatives:* James G.
  Blaine

Alabama

Senators

George T. Goldthwaite (D) s.
  1872
George E. Spencer (R)

Representatives

Charles W. Buckley (R)
Peter M. Dox (D)
William A. Handley s. 1872
Charles Hays (R)
Joseph H. Stloss (D)
Benjamin S. Turner (R)

Arkansas

Senators

Powell Clayton (R)
Benjamin F. Rice (R)

Representatives

Thomas Boles (R) s. 1872
John Edwards (R) r. Feb. 1872
James M. Hanks (D)
Oliver P. Snyder (R)

California

Senators

Eugene Casserly (D)
Cornelius Cole (R)

Representatives

John M. Coghlan (R)
Sherman O. Houghton (R)
Aaron A. Sargent (R)

Connecticut

Senators

William A. Buckingham (R)
Orris S. Ferry (R)

Representatives

William H. Barnum (D)
Joseph R. Hawley (R) s. Dec.
  1872
Stephen W. Kellogg (R)
Henry H. Starkweather (R)
Julius L. Strong (R) d. Sept.
  1872

Delaware

Senators

Thomas F. Bayard (D)
Eli Saulsbury (D)

Representatives

Benjamin T. Biggs (D)

Florida

Senators

Abijah Gilbert (R)
Thomas W. Osborn (R)

Representatives

Silas L. Niblack (D) s. 1873
Josiah T. Walls (R) r. Jan.
1873

Georgia

Senators

Joshua Hill (R)
Thomas M. Norwood (D)

Representatives

Erasmus W. Beck (D) s. 1872
John S. Bigby (R)
Dudley M. DuBose (D)
Archibald T. MacIntyre (D)
William P. Price (D)
Thomas J. Speer (R) d. Aug.
1872
Richard H. Whiteley (R)
Pierce M. B. Young

Illinois

Senators

John A. Logan (R)
Lyman Trumbull (R)

Representatives

John L. Beveridge (R) r. Jan.
1873
Horatio C. Burchard (R)
Burton C. Cook (R) r. Aug.
1871
John M. Crebs (D)
John F. Farnsworth (R)
Charles B. Farwell (R)
John B. Hawley (R)
John B. Hay (R)
Thompson W. McNeely (D)
Samuel S. Marshall (D)
Jesse H. Moore (D)
Edward Y. Rice (R)
James C. Robinson (D)
Henry Snapp (R)
Bradford N. Stevens (D)

Indiana

Senators

Oliver H. P. T. Morton (R)
Daniel D. Pratt (D)

Representatives

John Coburn (R)
William S. Holman (D)
Michael C. Kerr (D)
Mahlon D. Manson (D)
William E. Niblack (D)
Jasper Packard (R)
John P. C. Shanks (R)
James N. Tyner (R)
Daniel W. Voorhees (D)
William Williams (R)
Jeremiah M. Wilson (R)

Iowa

Senators

James Harlan (R)
George G. Wright (R)

Representatives

Aylett R. Cotton (R)
William G. Donnan (R)
George W. McCrary (R)
Jackson Orr (R)
Frank W. Palmer (R)
Madison M. Walden (R)

Kansas

Senators

Alexander Caldwell (R)
Samuel C. Pomeroy (R)

Representatives

David P. Lowe (R)

Kentucky

Senators

Garrett Davis (D) d. Sept. 1872
Willis B. Machen (D) s. 1872
John W. Stevenson (D)

Representatives

George M. Adams (D)
William E. Arthur (D)
James B. Beck (D)
Edward Crossland (D)
Joseph H. Lewis (D)
Henry D. McHenry (D)
William B. Read (D)
John M. Rice (D)
Boyd Winchester (D)

Louisiana

Senators

William P. Kellogg (R) r. Nov.
1872
J. Rodman West (R)

Representatives

Aleck Boarman (Lib) s. 1872
Chester B. Darrall (R)
James McCleery (D) d. Nov.
1871
Frank Morey (R)
Lionel A. Sheldon (R)

J. Hale Sypher (R)

Maine

Senators

Hannibal Hamlin (R)
Lot M. Morrill (R)

Representatives

James G. Blaine (R)
William P. Frye (R)
Eugene Hale (R)
John Lynch (R)
John A. Peters (R)

Maryland

Senators

William T. Hamilton (D)
George Vickers (D)

Representatives

Stevenson Archer (D)
Samuel Hambleton (D)
William M. Merrick (D)
John Ritchie (D)
Thomas Swann (D)

Massachusetts

Senators

Charles Sumner (R)
Henry Wilson r. Mar. 1873

Representatives

Oakes Ames (R)
Nathaniel P. Banks (R)
George M. Brooks (R) r. May
1872
James Buffinton (R)
Benjamin F. Butler (R)
Alvah Crocker (R) s. 1872
Henry L. Dawes
Constantine C. Esty (R) s. 1872
George F. Hoar (R)
Samuel Hooper (R)
Ginery Twichell (R)
William B. Washburn (R) r.
Dec. 1871

Michigan

Senators

Zachariah Chandler (R)
Thomas W. Ferry (R)

Representatives

Austin Blair (R)
Omar D. Conger (R)
Wilder D. Foster (R)
William L. Stoughton (R)
Jabez G. Sutherland (D)
Henry Waldron (R)

Minnesota

Senators

Alexander Ramsey (R)
William Windom (R)

Representatives

John T. Averill (R)
Mark H. Dunnell (R)

Mississippi

Senators

James L. Alcorn (R)
Adelbert Ames (R)

Representatives

Henry W. Barry (R)
George E. Harris (R)
George C. McKee (R)
Joseph L. Morphis (R)
Legrand W. Perce (R)

Missouri

Senators

Francis P. Blair, Jr. (D)
Carl Schurz (R)

Representatives

James G. Blair (D)
Samuel S. Burdett (R)
Abram Comingo (D)
Gustavus A. Finkelnburg (R)
Harrison E. Havens (R)
Andrew King (D)
James R. McCormick (D)
Isaac C. Parker (R)
Erastus Wells (D)

Nebraska

Senators

Phineas W. Hitchcock (R)
Thomas W. Tipton (D)

Representatives

John Taffe (R)

Nevada

Senators

William M. Stewart (R)
James W. Nye (R)

Representatives

Charles W. Kendall (D)

New Hampshire

Senators

Aaron H. Cragin (Amer)
James W. Patterson (R)

Representatives

Samuel N. Bell (D)
Ellery A. Hibbard (D)
Hosea W. Parker (D)

New Jersey

Senators

Frederick T. Frelinghuysen (R)
John P. Stockton (D)

Representatives

John T. Bird (D)
Samuel C. Forker (D)
George A. Halsey (R)
John W. Hazelton (R)
John Hill (R)

New York

Senators

Roscoe Conkling (R)
Reuben E. Fenton (R)

Representatives

James Brooks (D)
John M. Carroll (D)
Freeman Clarke (R)
Samuel S. Cox (D)
R. Holland Duell (R)
Smith Ely, Jr. (D)
Milo Goodrich (R)
John H. Ketcham (R)
Thomas Kinsella (D)
William H. Lamport (R)
William E. Lansing (R)
Clinton L. Merriam (R)
Eli Perry (D)
Clarkson N. Potter (D)
Elizur H. Prindle (R)
Ellis H. Roberts (R)
William R. Roberts (D)
John Rogers (D)
Robert B. Roosevelt (D)
Charles St. John (R)
John E. Seeley (R)
Walter L. Sessions (R)
Henry W. Slocum (D)
H. Boardman Smith (R)
Dwight Townsend (D)
Joseph H. Tuthill (D)
Seth Wakeman (R)
Joseph M. Warren (D)
William A. Wheeler (R)
William Williams (R)
Fernando Wood (D)

North Carolina

Senators

John Pool
Matt W. Ransom (D) s. 1872

Representatives

Clinton L. Cobb (R)
James C. Harper (Con)
James M. Leach (Con)
Sion H. Rogers (D) s. 1872
Francis E. Shober (D)
Charles R. Thomas (R)
Alfred M. Waddell (D)

Ohio

Senators

John Sherman (R)
Allen G. Thurman (D)

Representatives

Jacob A. Ambler (R)
John Beatty (R)
John A. Bingham (R)
Lewis D. Campbell (D)
Ozro J. Dodds (D) s. 1872
Charles Foster (R)
James A. Garfield (R)
Charles N. Lamison (D)
John F. McKinney (D)
James Monroe (R)
George W. Morgan (D)
Erasmus D. Peck (R)
Aaron F. Perry (R) r. 1872
Samuel Shellabarger
John A. Smith (R)
William P. Sprague (R)
Job E. Stevenson (R)
William H. Upson (R)
Philadelph Van Trump (D)
John T. Wilson (R)

Oregon

Senators

Henry W. Corbett (R)
James K. Kelly (D)

Representatives

James H. Slater (D)

Pennsylvania

Senators

Simon Cameron (R)
John Scott (R)

Representatives

Ephraim L. Acker (R)
Frank C. Bunnell s. 1873
John V. Creely (R)
Oliver J. Dickey (R)
Henry D. Foster (D)
J. Lawrence Getz (D)
Samuel Griffith (D)
Richard J. Haldeman (D)
Alfred C. Harmer (R)
William D. Kelley (R)
John W. Killinger (R)
William McClelland (D)
Ebenezer McJunkin (R)
Ulysses Mercur (R) r. Dec. 1872
Benjamin F. Meyers (D)
Leonard Myers (R)
James S. Negley (R)
John B. Packer (R)
Samuel J. Randall (D)
Glenni W. Scofield (R)
Henry Sherwood (D)
Lazarus D. Schoemaker (R)
R. Milton Speer (D)
John B. Storm (D)
Washington Townsend (R)

Rhode Island

Senators

Henry B. Anthony (R)
William Sprague (R)

Representatives

Benjamin T. Eames (R)
James M. Pendleton (R)

South Carolina

Senators

Thomas J. Robertson (R)
Frederick A. Sawyer (R)

Representatives

Robert C. De Large (R) r. Jan. 1873
Robert B. Elliott (R)
Joseph H. Rainey (R)
Alexander S. Wallace (R)

Tennessee

Senators

William G. Brownlow (R)
Henry Cooper (D)

Representatives

John M. Bright (D)
Roderick R. Butler (R)
Robert P. Caldwell (D)
Abraham E. Garrett
Edward I. Golladay (D)
Horace Maynard (R)
William W. Vaughan (D)
Washington C. Whitthorne (D)

Texas

Senators

James W. Flanagan (R)
Morgan C. Hamilton (R)

Representative

William T. Clark (R) s. 1872
John C. Conner (D)
De Witt C. Giddings (D) s. 1872
John Hancock (D)
William S. Herndon (D)

Vermont

Senators

George F. Edmunds (R)
Justin S. Morrill (R)

Representatives

Luke P. Poland (R)
Worthington C. Smith (R)
Charles W. Willard (R)

Virginia

Senators

John W. Johnston (Con)
John F. Lewis (R)

Representatives

Elliott M. Braxton (D)
John Critcher (Con)
Richard T. W. Duke (Con)
John T. Harris (D)
James H. Platt, Jr. (R)
Charles H. Porter (R)
William H. H. Stowell (R)
William Terry (Con)

West Virginia

Senators

Arthur I. Boreman (R)
Henry G. Davis (D)

Representatives

John J. Davis (D)
Frank Hereford (D)
James C. McGrew (R)

Wisconsin

Senators

Matthew H. Carpenter (R)
Timothy O. Howe (R)

Representatives

J. Allen Barber (R)
Charles A. Eldredge (D)
Gerry W. Hazelton (R)
Alexander Mitchell (D)
Jeremiah M. Rusk (R)
Philetus Sawyer (R)

Forty-Third Congress

(Mar. 4, 1873, to
Mar. 3, 1875)

President of the Senate: Henry Wilson
Presidents Pro Tempore of the Senate: Matthew H. Carpenter; Henry B. Anthony
Speaker of the House of Representatives: James G. Blaine

Alabama

Senators

George T. Goldthwaite (D)
George E. Spencer (R)

Representatives

Frederick G. Bromberg (D)
John H. Caldwell (D)
Charles Hays (R)

Charles Pelham (R)
James T. Rapier (R)
Joseph H. Sloss (D)

Arkansas

Sentors

Powell Clayton (R)
Stephen W. Dorsey (R)

Representatives

Thomas M. Gunter (D) s. 1874
Asa Hodges (R) s. 1874
Oliver P. Snyder (R)
William W. Wilshire (R) r.
   June 1874

California

Senators

Eugene Casserly (D) r. Nov.
   1873
John S. Hager (D) s. 1874
Aaron A. Sargent (R)

Representatives

Charles Clayton (R)
Sherman O. Houghton (R)
John K. Luttrell (D)
Horace F. Page (R)

Connecticut

Senators

William A. Buckingham (R) d.
   1875
William W. Eaton (D) s. 1875
Orris S. Ferry (R)

Representatives

William H. Barnum (D)
Joseph R. Hawley (R)
Stephen W. Kellogg (R)
Henry H. Starkweather (R)

Delaware

Senators

Thomas F. Bayard (D)
Eli Saulsbury (D)

Representatives

James R. Lofland (R)

Florida

Senators

Simon B. Conover (R)
Abijah Gilbert (R)

Representatives

William J. Purman (R) r. Jan.
   1875
Josiah T. Walls (R)

Georgia

Senators

John B. Gordon (D)
Thomas M. Norwood (D)

Representatives

Hiram P. Bell (D)
James H. Blount (D)
Philip Cook (D)
James C. Freeman (D)
Henry R. Harris (D)
Morgan Rawls (D) r. Mar.
   1874
Andrew Sloan (R) s. 1874
Alexander H. Stephens (D) s.
   1874
Richard H. Whiteley (R)
Pierce M. B. Young (D)

Illinois

Senators

John A. Logan (R)
Richard J. Oglesby (R)

Representatives

Granville Barrere (R)
Horatio C. Burchard (R)
Joseph G. Cannon (R)
Bernard G. Caulfield (D) s.
   1875
Isaac Clements (R)
Franklin Corwin (R)
John R. Eden (D)
Charles B. Farwell (R)
Greenbury L. Fort (R)
John B. Hawley (R)
Stephen A. Hurlbut (R)
Robert M. Knapp (D)
John McNulta (R)
Samuel S. Marshall (D)
James S. Martin (D)
William R. Morrison (D)
William H. Ray (R)
John B. Rice (D) d. 1874
James C. Robinson (D)
Jasper D. Ward (D)

Indiana

Senators

Oliver H. P. T. Morton (R)
Daniel D. Pratt (R)

Representatives

Thomas J. Cason (D)
John Coburn (D)
William S. Holman (D)
Morton C. Hunter (R)
William E. Niblack (D)
Godlove S. Orth (R)
Jasper Packard (R)
John P. C. Shanks (R)
Henry B. Sayler (D)
James N. Tyner (R)
Jeremiah M. Wilson (R)
William Williams (R)
Simeon K. Wolfe (D)

Iowa

Senators

William B. Allison (R)
George G. Wright (R)

Representatives

Aylett R. Cotton (R)
William G. Donnan (R)
John A. Kasson (R)
William Loughridge (R)
George W. McCrary (R)
James W. McDill (R)
Henry O. Pratt (R)
Jackson Orr (R)
James Wilson (R)

Kansas

Senators

Alexander Caldwell (R) r. Mar.
   1873
Robert Crozier (R) ta. 1873
James M. Harvey (R) s. 1874
John J. Ingalls (R)

Representatives

Stephen A. Cobb (R)
David P. Lowe (R)
William A. Phillips (R)

Kentucky

Senators

Thomas C. McCreery (D)
John W. Stevenson (D)

Representatives

George M. Adams (D)
William E. Arthur (D)
James B. Beck (D)
John Y. Brown (D)
Edward Crossland (D)
Milton J. Durham (D)
Charles W. Milliken (D)
William B. Read (D)
Elisha D. Standiford (D)
John D. Young (D)

Louisiana

Senators

J. Rodman West (R)
Vacant

Representatives

Chester B. Darrall (R)
Effingham Lawrence (D) s.
   1875
Frank Morey (R)
Lionel A. Sheldon (R)
George A. Sheridan (Lib) s.
   1875
George L. Smith (R)
J. Hale Sypher (R)

Maine

Senators

Hannibal Hamlin (R)
Lot M. Morrill (R)

Representatives

James G. Blaine (R)
John H. Burleigh (R)
William P. Frye (R)
Eugene Hale (R)
Samuel Hersey (R) d. Feb. 1875

Maryland

Senators

George R. Dennis (D)
William T. Hamilton (D)

Representatives

William J. Albert (R)
Stevenson Archer (D)
Lloyd Lowndes, Jr. (R)
William J. O'Brien (D)
Thomas Swann (D)
Ephraim K. Wilson (D)

Massachusetts

Senators

George S. Boutwell (R)
Charles Sumner (R) d. Mar.
   1874
William B. Washburn (R) s.
   1874

Representatives

James Buffinton (R)
Benjamin F. Butler (R)
Alvah Crocker (R) d. Dec.
   1874
Henry L. Dawes (R)
Daniel W. Gooch (R)
Benjamin W. Harris (R)
Ebenezer R. Hoar (R)
George F. Hoar (R)
Samuel Hooper (R) d. Feb.
   1875
Henry L. Pierce (R)
Charles A. Stevens
William Whiting (R) d. June
   1873
John M. S. Williams (R)

Michigan

Senators

Zachariah Chandler (R)
Thomas W. Ferry (R)

Representatives

Josiah W. Begole (R)
Nathan B. Bradley (R)
Julius C. Burrows (R)
Omar D. Conger (R)
Moses W. Field (R)
Jay A. Hubbell (R)
Henry Waldron (R)
William B. Williams (R)

Minnesota

Senators

Alexander Ramsey (R)
William Windom (R)

Representatives

John T. Averill (R)
Mark H. Dunnell (R)
Horace B. Strait (R)

Mississippi

Senators

James L. Alcorn (R)
Adelbert Ames (R) r. Jan. 1874
Henry R. Pease (R) s. 1874

Representatives

Henry W. Barry (R)
Albert R. Howe (R)
Lucius Q. C. Lamar (D)
John R. Lynch (R)
George C. McKee (R)
Jason Niles (R)

Missouri

Senators

Lewis V. Bogy (D)
Carl Schurz (R)

Representatives

Richard P. Bland (D)
Aylett H. Buckner (D)
John B. Clark, Jr. (D)
Abram Comingo (D)
Thomas T. Crittenden (D)
John M. Glover (D)
Robert A. Hatcher (D)
Harrison E. Havens (R)
Ira B. Hyde (R)
Isaac C. Parker (R)
Edwin O. Stanard (R)
William H. Stone (D)
Erastus Wells (D)

Nebraska

Senators

Phileas W. Hitchcock (R)
Thomas W. Tipton (R)

Representatives

Lorenzo Crounse (R)

Nevada

Senators

William M. Stewart (R)
John P. Jones (R)

Representatives

Charles W. Kendall (D)

New Hampshire

Senators

Aaron H. Cragin (Amer)
Bainbridge Wadleigh (R)

Representatives

Hosea W. Parker (D)
Austin F. Pike (R)
William B. Small (R)

New Jersey

Senators

Frederick T. Frelinghuysen (R)
John P. Stockton (D)

Representatives

Amos Clark, Jr. (R)
Samuel A. Dobbins (R)
Robert Hamilton (D)
John W. Hazelton (R)
William W. Phelps (R)
Isaac W. Scudder (R)
Marcus L. Ward (R)

New York

Senators

Roscoe Conkling (R)
Reuben E. Fenton (R)

Representatives

Lyman K. Bass (R)
James Brooks (D) d. Apr. 1873
Simeon B. Chittenden (R) s. 1874
Freeman Clarke (R)
Samuel S. Cox (D)
Thomas J. Creamer (R)
Philip S. Crooke (R)
David M. De Witt (D)
R. Holland Duell (R)
Robert S. Hale (R)
Henry H. Hathorn (R)
George G. Hoskins (R)
William H. Lamport (R)
William E. Lansing (R)
John D. Lawson (R)
Clinton MacDougall (R)
David B. Mellish (R) d. May 1874
Clinton L. Merriam (R)
Eli Perry (D)
Thomas C. Platt (R)
Clarkson N. Potter (D)
Ellis H. Roberts (R)
William R. Roberts (D)
Charles St. John (R)
Richard Schell (D) s. 1874
John G. Schumaker (D)
Henry J. Scudder (R)
Walter L. Sessions
James S. Smart (R)
H. Boardman Smith (R)
Lyman Tremain (R)
William A. Wheeler (R)
John O. Whitehouse (D)
David Wilber (R)
Fernando Wood (D)
Stewart L. Woodford (R) r. 1874

North Carolina

Senators

Augustus S. Merrimon
Matt W. Ransom (D)

Representatives

Thomas S. Ashe (Con)
Clinton L. Cobb (R)
James M. Leach (Con)
William M. Robbins (D)
William A. Smith (R)
Charles R. Thomas (R)
Robert B. Vance (D)
Alfred M. Waddell (D)

Ohio

Senators

John Sherman
Allen G. Thurman (D)

Representatives

Henry B. Banning (D)
John Berry (D)
Hezekiah S. Bundy (R)
Lorenzo Danford (R)
William E. Finck (D) s. 1874
Charles Foster (R)
James A. Garfield (R)
Lewis B. Gunckel (R)
Hugh J. Jewett (D) r. June 1874
Charles N. Lamison (D)
William Lawrence (R)
James Monroe (R)
Lawrence T. Neal (D)
Richard C. Parsons (R)
James W. Robinson (R)
Milton Sayler (D)
Isaac R. Sherwood (R)
John Q. Smith (R)
Milton I. Southard (D)
William P. Sprague (R)
Laurin D. Woodworth (D)

Oregon

Senators

James K. Kelly (D)
John H. Mitchell (R)

Representatives

James W. Nesmith (D)
Joseph G. Wilson (R) d. July 1873

Pennsylvania

Senators

Simon Cameron (R)
John Scott (R)

Representatives

Charles Albright (R)
James S. Biery (R)
John Cessna (R)
Hiester Clymer (D)
Carlton B. Curtis (R)
Alfred C. Harmer (R)
William D. Kelley (R)
John W. Killinger (D)
Ebenezer McJunkin (R) r. Jan. 1875
John A. Magee (D)
William S. Moore (D)
Leonard Myers (R)
James S. Negley (R)
Charles O'Neill (R)
John B. Packer (R)
Samuel J. Randall (D)
Hiram L. Richmond (R)
Sobieski Ross (R)
Glenni W. Scofield (R)
Lazarus D. Shoemaker (R)
A. Herr Smith (R)
R. Milton Speer (D)
John B. Storm (D)
James D. Strawbridge (R)
Alexander W. Taylor (R)
John M. Thompson (R) s. 1875
Lemuel Todd (R)
Washington Townsend (R)

Rhode Island

Senators

Henry B. Anthony (R)
William Sprague (R)

Representatives

Benjamin T. Eames (R)
James M. Pendleton (R)

South Carolina

Senators

John J. Patterson (R)
Thomas J. Robertson (R)

Representatives

Richard H. Cain (R)
Lewis C. Carpenter (R) s. 1874
Robert B. Elliott (R) r. Nov. 1874
Joseph H. Rainey (R)
Alonzo J. Ransier (R)
Alexander S. Wallace (R)

Tennessee

Senators

William G. Brownlow (R)
Henry Cooper (D)

Representatives

John D. C. Atlins (D)
John M. Bright (D)
Roderick R. Butler (R)
William Crutchfield (R)
Horace H. Harrison (R)
Barbour Lewis (R)
Horace Maynard (R)
David A. Nunn (R)
Jacob M. Thornburgh (R)
Washington C. Whitthorne (D)

Texas

Senators

James W. Flanagan (R)
Morgan C. Hamilton (R)

Representatives

De Witt C. Giddings (D)
John Hancock (D)
William S. Herndon (D)
William P. McLean (D)
Roger Q. Mills (D)
Asa H. Willie (D)

Vermont

Senators

George F. Edmunds (R)
Justin S. Morrill (R)

Representatives

George W. Hendee (R)
Luke P. Poland (R)
Charles W. Willard (R)

Virginia

Senators

John W. Johnston (Con)
John F. Lewis (R)

Representatives

Rees T. Bowen (Con)
Alexander M. Davis r. Mar.
1874
John T. Harris (D)
Eppa Hunton (D)
James H. Platt, Jr. (R)
James B. Sener (R)
J. Amber Smith (R)
William H. H. Stowell (R)
Christopher Y. Thomas (R) s.
1874
Thomas Whitehead (Con)

West Virginia

Senators

Arthur I. Boreman (R)
Henry G. Davis (D)

Representatives

John J. Davis (D) s. 1874
John M. Hagans (R) s. 1874
Frank Hereford (D)

Wisconsin

Senators

Matthew H. Carpenter (R)
Timothy O. Howe (R)

Representatives

J. Allen Barber (R)
Charles A. Eldredge (D)
Gerry W. Hazelton (R)

Alexander S. McDill (R)
Alexander Mitchell (R)
Jeremiah M. Rusk (R)
Philetus Sawyer (R)
Charles G. Williams (R)

Forty-Fourth Congress

(Mar. 4, 1875, to
Mar. 3, 1877)

President of the Senate: Henry
Wilson
*President Pro Tempore of the
Senate:* Thomas W. Ferry
*Speakers of the House of
Representatives:* Michael C.
Kerr; Samuel J. Randall

Alabama

Senators

George T. Goldthwaite (D)
George E. Spencer (R)

Representatives

Taul Bradford (D)
John H. Caldwell (D)
William H. Forney (D)
Jeremiah Haralson (R)
Charles Hays (R)
Goldsmith W. Hewitt (D)
Burwell B. Lewis (D)
Jeremiah N. Williams (D)

Arkansas

Senators

Powell Clayton (R)
Stephen W. Dorsey (R)

Representatives

Lucien C. Gause (D)
Thomas M. Gunter (D)
William F. Slemons (D)
William W. Wilshire (R)

California

Senators

Newton Booth (Anti-
Monopolist)
Aaron A. Sargent (R)

Representatives

John K. Luttrell (D)
Horace F. Page (R)
William A. Piper (D)
Peter D. Wigginton (D)

Colorado

Senators

Jerome B. Chaffee (R) s. 1876
Henry M. Teller (R) s. 1876

Representatives

James B. Belford (R) s. 1877

Connecticut

Senators

William H. Barnum (D) s. 1876
William W. Eaton (D)
James E. English (D) ta. 1875
Orris S. Ferry (R, D) d. Nov.
1875

Representatives

William H. Barnum (D) r. May
1876
George M. Landers (D)
James Phelps (D)
Henry H. Starkweather (R) d.
Jan. 1876
John T. Wait (R) s. 1876
Levi Warner (D) s. 1876

Delaware

Senators

Thomas F. Bayard (D)
Eli Saulsbury (D)

Representatives

James Williams (D)

Florida

Senators

Simon B. Conover (R)
Charles W. Jones (D)

Representatives

Jesse J. Finley (D) s. 1876
William J. Purman (R)
Josiah T. Walls (R) r. Apr.
1876

Georgia

Senators

John B. Gordon (D)
Thomas M. Norwood (D)

Representatives

James H. Blount (D)
Milton A. Candler (D)
Philip Cook (D)
William H. Felton (D)
Henry R. Harris (D)
Julian Hartridge (D)
Benjamin H. Hill (D)
William E. Smith (D)
Alexander H. Stephens (D)

Illinois

Senators

John A. Logan (R)
Richard J. Oglesby (R)

Representatives

William B. Anderson (D)
John C. Bagby (R)
Horatio C. Burchard (R)
Alexander Campbell
Joseph G. Cannon (R)
Bernard G. Caulfield (D)
John R. Eden (D)
Charles B. Farwell (R) r. May
1876
Greenbury L. Fort (R)
Carter H. Harrison (D)
William Hartzell (D)
Thomas J. Henderson (R)
Stephen A. Hurlbut (R)
John V. Le Moyne (R) s. 1876
William R. Morrison (D)
William A. J. Sparks (D)
William M. Springer (D)
Adlai E. Stevenson (D)
Richard H. Whiting (R)
Scott Wike (D)

Indiana

Senators

Joseph E. McDonald (D)
Oliver H. P. T. Morton (R)

Representatives

John H. Baker (R)
Nathan T. Carr (D) s. 1876
Thomas J. Cason (R)
James L. Evans (R)
Benoni S. Fuller (D)
Andrew H. Hamilton (D)
William S. Haymond (D)
William S. Holman (D)
Andrew Humphreys (D) s. 1876
Morton C. Hunter (R)
Michael C. Kerr (D) d. Aug.
1876
Franklin Landers (D)
Jeptha D. New (D)
Milton S. Robinson (R)
James D. Williams (D) r. Dec.
1876

Iowa

Senators

William B. Allison (R)
George G. Wright (R)

Representatives

Lucien L. Ainsworth (Anti-
Monopolist)
John A. Kasson (R)
George W. McCrary (R)
James W. McDill (R)
S. Addison Oliver (R)
Henry O. Pratt (R)
Ezekiel S. Sampson (R)
John Q. Tufts (R)
James Wilson (R)

Kansas

Senators

James M. Harvey (R)
John J. Ingalls (R)

Representatives

William R. Brown (R)
John R. Goodin (D)
William A. Phillips (R)

Kentucky

Senators

Thomas C. McCreery (D)
John W. Stevenson (D)

Representatives

Joseph C. S. Blackburn (D)
Andrew R. Boone (D)
John Y. Brown (D)
John B. Clarke (D)
Milton J. Durham (D)
Thomas L. Jones (D)
J. Proctor Knott (D)
Charles W. Milliken (D)
Edward Y. Parsons (D) d. July 1876
Henry Watterson (D) s. 1876
John D. White (R)

Louisiana

Senators

James B. Eustis (D) s. 1876
J. Rodman West (R)

Representatives

Chester B. Darrall (R)
E. John Ellis (D)
Randall L. Gibson (D)
William M. Levy (D)
Frank Morey (R) r. June 1876
Charles E. Nash (R)
William B. Spencer (D) s. 1876
    r. Jan. 1877

Maine

Senators

James G. Blaine (R) s. 1876
Hannibal Hamlin (R)
Lot M. Morrill (R) r. July 1876

Representatives

James G. Blaine (R) r. July 1876
John H. Burleigh (R)
Edwin Flye (R) s. 1876
William P. Frye (R)
Eugene Hale (R)
Harris M. Plaisted (R)

Maryland

Senators

George R. Dennis (D)
William P. Whyte (D)

Representatives

Eli J. Henkle (D)
William J. O'Brien (D)
Charles B. Roberts (D)
Thomas Swann (D)

Philip F. Thomas (D)
William Walsh (D)

Massachusetts

Senators

George S. Boutwell (R)
Henry L. Dawes (R)

Representatives

Josiah G. Abbott (D) s. 1876
Nathaniel P. Banks (R)
Chester W. Chapin (D)
William W. Crapo (R)
Rufus S. Frost (R) r. July 1876
Benjamin W. Harris (R)
George F. Hoar (R)
Henry L. Pierce (R)
Julius H. Seelye
John K. Tarbox (D)
Charles P. Thompson (D)
William W. Warren (D)

Michigan

Senators

Issac P. Christiancy (R)
Thomas W. Ferry (R)

Representatives

Nathan B. Bradley (R)
Omar D. Conger (R)
George H. Durand (D)
Jay A. Hubbell (R)
Allen Potter
Henry Waldron (R)
George Willard (R)
Alpheus S. Williams (D)
William B. Williams (R)

Minnesota

Senators

Samuel J. R. McMillan (R)
William Windom (R)

Representatives

Mark H. Dunnell (R)
William S. King (R)
Horace B. Strait (R)

Mississippi

Senators

James L. Alcorn (R)
Blanche K. Bruce (R)

Representatives

Charles E. Hooker (D)
Lucius Q. C. Lamar (D)
John R. Lynch (R)
Hernando D. Money (D)
Otho R. Singleton (D)
G. Wiley Wells (R)

Missouri

Senators

Lewis V. Bogy (D)
Francis M. Cockrell (D)

Representatives

Richard P. Bland (D)
Aylett H. Buckner (D)
John B. Clark, Jr. (D)
Rezin A. DeBolt (D)
Benjamin J. Franklin (D)
John M. Glover (D)
Robert A. Hatcher (D)
Edward C. Kehr (D)
Charles H. Morgan (D)
John F. Philips (D)
David Rea (D)
William H. Stone (D)
Erastus Wells (D)

Nebraska

Senators

Phineas W. Hitchock
Algernon S. Paddock (R)

Representatives

Lorenzo Crounse (R)

Nevada

Senators

John P. Jones (R)
William Sharon (R)

Representatives

William Woodburn (R)

New Hampshire

Senators

Aaron H. Cragin (Amer)
Bainbridge Wadleigh (R)

Representatives

Samuel N. Bell (D)
Henry W. Blair (R)
Frank Jones (D)

New Jersey

Senators

Frederick T. Frelinghuysen (R)
Theodore F. Randolph (D)

Representatives

Samuel A. Dobbins (R)
Augustus W. Cutler (D)
Robert Hamilton (D)
Augustus A. Hardenbergh (D)
Miles Ross (D)
Clement H. Sinnickson (R)
Frederick H. Teese (D)

New York

Senators

Roscoe Conkling (R)
Francis Kernan (D)

Representatives

Charles H. Adams (R)
George A. Bagley (R)
John H. Bagley, Jr. (D)
William H. Baker (R)
Lyman K. Bass (R)
George M. Beebe (D)
Archibald M. Bliss (D)
Simeon B. Chittendin (R)
Samuel S. Cox (D)
John M. Davy (R)
Smith Ely, Jr. (D) r. Dec. 1876
David Dudley Field (D) s. 1877
Henry H. Hathorn (R)
Abram S. Hewitt (D)
George G. Hoskins (R)
Elbridge G. Lapham (R)
Elias W. Leavenworth (R)
Scott Lord (D)
Clinton D. MacDougall (R)
Edwin R. Meade (D)
Henry B. Metcalfe (D)
Samuel F. Miller (R)
Nelson I. Norton (R)
N. Holmes Odell (D)
Thomas C. Platt (R)
John G. Schumaker (D)
Martin I. Townsend (R)
Charles C. B. Walker (D)
Elijah Ward (D)
William A. Wheeler (R)
John O. Whitehouse (D)
Andrew Williams (R)
Benjamin A. Willis
Fernando Wood (D)

North Carolina

Senators

Matt W. Ransom (D)
Augustus S. Merrimon (D)

Representatives

Thomas A. Ashe (D)
Joseph J. Davis (D)
John A. Hyman (R)
William M. Robbins (D)
Alfred M. Scales (D)
Robert B. Vance (D)
Alfred M. Waddell (D)
Jesse J. Yeates (D)

Ohio

Senators

John Sherman (R)
Allen G. Thurman (D)

Representatives

Henry B. Banning (D)
Jacob P. Cowan
Lorenzo Danford (R)
Charles Foster (R)
James Garfield (R)
Frank H. Hurd (D)
William Lawrence (R)

John A. McMahon (D)
James Monroe (R)
Lawrence T. Neal (D)
Henry B. Payne (D)
Earley F. Poppleton (D)
Americus V. Rice (D)
John S. Savage (D)
Milton Sayler (D)
Milton I. Southard (D)
John L. Vance (D)
Nelson H. Van Vorhes (R)
Ansel T. Walling (D)
Laurin D. Woodworth (R)

Oregon

Senators

James K. Kelly (D)
John H. Mitchell (R)

Representatives

George A. LaDow (D) d. May 1875
La Fayette Lane (D)

Pennsylvania

Senators

Simon Cameron (R)
William A. Wallace (D)

Representatives

Hiester Clymer (D)
Alexander G. Cochran (D)
Francis D. Collins (D)
Albert G. Egbert (D)
Chapman Freeman (R)
James H. Hopkins (D)
George A. Jenks (D)
William D. Kelley (R)
Winthrop W. Ketchum (R) r. July 1876
Levi A. Mackey (D)
Levi Maish (D)
William Mutchler (D)
Charles O'Neill (R)
John B. Packer (R)
Joseph Powell (D)
Samuel J. Randall (D)
James B. Reilly (D)
John Reilly (D)
John Robbins (R)
Sobieski Ross (R)
James Sheakley (D)
A. Herr Smith (R)
William H. Stanton (D) s. 1876
William S. Stenger (D)
Washington Townsend (R)
Jacob Turney (D)
John W. Wallace (R)
Alan Wood, Jr. (R)

Rhode Island

Senators

Henry B. Anthony (R)
Ambrose E. Burnside (R)

Representatives

Latimer W. Ballou (R)
Benjamin T. Eames (R)

South Carolina

Senators

John J. Patterson (R)
Thomas J. Robertson (R)

Representatives

Charles W. Buttz (R)
Solomon L. Hoge (R)
Edmund W. M. Mackey (R) r. July 1876
Joseph H. Rainey (R)
Robert Smalls (R)
Alexander S. Wallace (R)

Tennessee

Senators

James E. Bailey (D) s. 1877
Henry Cooper (D)
Andrew Johnson (D) d. July 1875
David M. Key (D) ta. 1875

Representatives

John D. C. Atkins (D)
John M. Bright (D)
William P. Caldwell (D)
George G. Dibrell (D)
John F. House (D)
William McFarland (D)
Haywood Y. Riddle (D) s. 1876
Jacob M. Thornburgh (R)
Washington C. Whitthorne (D)
H. Casey Young (D)

Texas

Senators

Morgan C. Hamilton (R)
Samuel B. Maxey (D)

Representatives

David B. Culberson (D)
John Hancock (D)
Roger Q. Mills (D)
John H. Reagan (D)
Gustave Schleicher (D)
James W. Throckmorton (D)

Vermont

Senators

George F. Edmunds (R)
Justin S. Morrill (R)

Representatives

Dudley C. Denison (R)
George W. Hendee (R)
Charles H. Joyce (R)

Virginia

Senators

John W. Johnston (Con)
Robert E. Withers (Con)

Representatives

George C. Cabell (D)
Beverly B. Douglas (Con)
John Goode, Jr. (D)
John T. Harris (D)
Eppa Hunton (D)
William H. H. Stowell (R)
William Terry (Con)
John R. Tucker (D)
Gilbert C. Walker (Con)

West Virginia

Senators

Allen T. Caperton (D) d. July 1876
Henry G. Davis (D)
Frank Hereford (D) s. 1877
Samuel Price ta. 1876

Representatives

Charles J. Faulkner (D)
Frank Hereford (D) r. Jan. 1877
Benjamin Wilson (D)

Wisconsin

Senators

Angus Cameron (R)
Timothy O. Howe (R)

Representatives

Samuel D. Burchard (D)
Lucien B. Caswell (R)
George W. Cate (D)
Alanson M. Kimball (R)
William P. Lynde (D)
Henry S. Magoon (R)
Jeremiah M. Rusk (R)
Charles G. Williams (R)

Forty-Fifth Congress

(Mar. 4, 1877, to Mar. 3, 1879)

President of the Senate: William A. Wheeler
President Pro Tempore of the Senate: Thomas W. Ferry
Speaker of the House of Representatives: Samuel J. Randall

Alabama

Senators

John T. Morgan (D)
George E. Spencer (R)

Representatives

William H. Forney (D)
William W. Garth (D)
Hilary A. Herbert (D)
Goldsmith W. Hewitt (D)
James T. Jones (D)
Robert F. Ligon (D)
Charles M. Shelley (D)
Jeremiah N. Williams (D)

Arkansas

Senators

Stephen W. Dorsey (R)
Augustus H. Garland (D)

Representatives

Jordan E. Cravens (D)
Lucien C. Gause (D)
Thomas M. Gunter (D)
William F. Slemons (D)

California

Senators

Newton Booth (Anti-Monopolist)
Aaron A. Sargent (R)

Representatives

Horace Davis (R)
John K. Luttrell (D)
Romualdo Pacheco (R) r. Feb. 1878
Horace F. Page (R)
Peter D. Wigginton (D) s. 1878

Colorado

Senators

Jerome B. Chaffee (R)
Henry M. Teller (R)

Representatives

James B. Belford (R) r. Dec. 1877
Thomas M. Patterson (D)

Connecticut

Senators

William H. Barnum (D)
William W. Eaton (D)

Representatives

George M. Landers (D)
James Phelps (D)
John T. Wait (R)
Levi Warner (D)

Delaware

Senators

Thomas F. Bayard (D)
Eli Saulsbury (D)

Representatives

James Williams (D)

Florida

Senators

Simon B. Conover (R)
Charles W. Jones (D)

Representatives

Horatio Bisbee, Jr. (R) r. Feb. 1879
Robert H. M. Davidson (D)
Jesse J. Finley (D) s. 1879

Georgia

Senators

John B. Gordon (D)
Benjamin H. Hill (D)

Representatives

Hiram P. Bell (D)
James H. Blount (D)
Milton A. Candler (D)
Philip Cook (D)
William H. Felton (D)
William B. Fleming (D) s. 1879
Henry R. Harris (D)
Julian Hartridge (D) d. Jan. 1879
William E. Smith (D)
Alexander H. Stephens

Illinois

Senators

David Davis (R)
Richard J. Oglesby (R)

Representatives

William Aldrich (R)
Thomas A. Boyd (R)
Lorenzo Brentano (R)
Horatio C. Burchard (R)
Joseph G. Cannon (R)
John R. Eden (D)
Greenbury L. Fort (R)
Carter H. Harrison (R)
William Hartzell (D)
Philip C. Hayes (R)
Thomas J. Henderson (R)
Robert M. Knapp (D)
William Lathrop (R)
Benjamin F. Marsh (R)
William R. Morrison (D)
William A. J. Sparks (D)
William M. Springer (D)
Thomas F. Tipton (R)
Richard W. Townshend (D)

Indiana

Senators

Joseph E. McDonald (D)
Oliver H. P. T. Morton (R) d. 1877
Daniel W. Voorhees (D)

Representatives

John H. Baker (R)
George A. Bicknell (D)

Thomas M. Browne (R)
William H. Calkins (R)
Thomas R. Cobb (D)
Benoni S. Fuller (D)
James L. Evans (R)
Andrew H. Hamilton (D)
John Hanna (R)
Morton C. Hunter (R)
Milton S. Robinson (R)
Leonidas Sexton (R)
Michael D. White (R)

Iowa

Senators

William B. Allison (R)
Samuel J. Kirkwood (R)

Representatives

Theodore W. Burdick (R)
Rush Clark (R)
Henry J. B. Cummings (R)
Nathaniel C. Deering (R)
S. Addison Oliver (R)
Hiram Price (R)
Ezekiel S. Sampson (R)
William F. Sapp (R)
Joseph C. Stone (R)

Kansas

Senators

John J. Ingalls (R)
Preston B. Plumb (R)

Representatives

Dudley C. Haskell (R)
William A. Phillips (R)
Thomas Ryan (R)

Kentucky

Senators

James B. Beck (D)
Thomas C. McCreery (D)

Representatives

Joseph C. S. Blackburn (D)
Andrew R. Boone (D)
John W. Caldwell (D)
John G. Carlisle (D)
John B. Clarke (D)
Milton J. Durham (D)
J. Proctor Knott (D)
James A. McKenzie (D)
Thomas Turner (D)
Albert S. Willis (D)

Louisiana

Senators

James B. Eustis (D)
William P. Kellogg (R)

Representatives

Joseph H. Acklen (D) s. 1878
Chester B. Darrall (R) r. 1878
Joseph B. Elam (D)
E. John Ellis (D)

Randall L. Gibson (D)
John E. Leonard (R) d. 1878
Edward W. Robertson (D)
John S. Young (D) s. 1878

Maine

Senators

James G. Blaine (R)
Hannibal Hamlin (R)

Representatives

William P. Frye (R)
Eugene Hale (R)
Stephen D. Lindsey (R)
Llewellyn Powers (R)
Thomas B. Reed (R)

Maryland

Senators

George R. Dennis (D)
William P. Whyte (D)

Representatives

Eli J. Henkle (D)
Daniel M. Henry (D)
William Kinnel (D)
Charles B. Roberts (D)
Thomas Swann (D)
William Walsh (D)

Massachusetts

Senators

Henry L. Dawes (R)
George F. Hoar (R)

Representatives

Nathaniel P. Banks (R)
Benjamin F. Butler (R)
William Claflin (R)
William W. Crapo (R)
Benjamin Dean (D) s. 1878
Walbridge A. Field (R) r. Mar. 1878
Benjamin W. Harris (R)
George B. Loring (R)
Leopold Morse (D)
Amasa Norcross (R)
William W. Rice (R)
George D. Robinson (R)

Michigan

Senators

Thomas W. Ferry (R)
Isaac P. Christiancy (R) r. Feb. 1879

Representatives

Mark S. Brewer (R)
Omar D. Conger (R)
Charles C. Ellsworth (R)
Jay A. Hubbell (R)
Edwin W. Keightley (R)
Jonas H. McGowan (R)
John W. Stone (R)

Alpheus S. Williams (D) d. 1878
Edwin Willits (R)

Minnesota

Senators

Samuel J. R. McMillan (R)
William Windom (R)

Representatives

Mark H. Dunnell (R)
Jacob H. Stewart (R)
Horace B. Strait (R)

Mississippi

Senators

Blanche K. Bruce (R)
Lucius Q. C. Lamar (D)

Representatives

James R. Chalmers (D)
Charles E. Hooker (D)
Vannoy H. Manning (D)
Hernando D. Money (D)
Henry L. Muldrow (D)
Otho R. Singleton (D)

Missouri

Senators

David H. Armstrong (D) d. Sept. 1877
Lewis V. Bogy (D) d. Sept. 1877
Francis M. Cockrell (D)
James Shields (D) ta. 1877

Representatives

Richard P. Bland (D)
Aylett H. Buckner (D)
John B. Clark, Jr. (D)
Nathan Cole (R)
Thomas T. Crittenden (D)
Benjamin J. Franklin (D)
John M. Glover (D)
Robert A. Hatcher (D)
Anthony Ittner (R)
Lyne S. Metcalfe (R)
Charles H. Morgan (D)
Henry M. Pollard (R)
David Rea (D)

Nebraska

Senators

Algernon S. Paddock (R)
Alvin Saunders (R)

Representatives

Thomas J. Majors (R) s. 1878
Frank Welch (R) d. 1878

Nevada

Senators

John P. Jones (R)
William Sharon (R)

Representatives

Thomas Wren (R)

New Hampshire

Senators

Edward H. Rollins (R)
Bainbridge Wadleigh (R)

Representatives

Henry W. Blair (R)
James F. Briggs (R)
Frank Jones (D)

New Jersey

Senators

John R. McPherson (D)
Theodore F. Randolph (D)

Representatives

Alvah A. Clark (D)
Augustus W. Cutler (D)
Augustus A. Hardenbergh (D)
Thomas B. Peddie (R)
John H. Pugh (R)
Miles Ross (D)
Clement H. Sinnickson (R)

New York

Senators

Roscoe Conkling (R)
Francis Kernan (D)

Representatives

William J. Bacon (R)
George A. Bagley (R)
John M. Bailey (R) s. 1878
William H. Baker (R)
George M. Beebe (D)
Charles B. Benedict (D)
Archibald M. Bliss (D)
Solomon Bundy (R)
John H. Camp (R)
Simeon B. Chittenden (R)
James W. Covert (D)
Samuel S. Cox (D)
Jeremiah W. Dwight (R)
Anthony Eickhoff (D)
E. Kirke Hart (D)
Abram S. Hewitt (D)
Frank Hiscock (R)
John N. Hungerford (R)
Amaziah B. James (R)
John H. Ketcham (R)
Elbridge G. Lapham (R)
Daniel N. Lockwood (D)
Anson G. McCook (R)
Stephen L. Mayham (D)
Nicholas Muller (D)
George W. Patterson (R)
Clarkson N. Potter (D)

Terence J. Quinn (D) d. June 1878
John H. Starin (R)
Martin I. Townsend (R)
William D. Veeder (D)
Andrew Williams (R)
Benjamin A. Willis (D)
Fernando Wood (D)

North Carolina

Senators

Augustus S. Merrimon (D)
Matt W. Ransom (D)

Representatives

Curtis H. Brogden (R)
Joseph J. Davis (D)
William M. Robbins (D)
Alfred M. Scales (D)
Walter L. Steele (D)
Robert B. Vance (D)
Alfred M. Waddell (D)
Jesse J. Yeates (D)

Ohio

Senators

Stanley Matthews (R)
Allen G. Thurman (D)

Representatives

Henry B. Banning (D)
Jacob D. Cox (R)
Lorenzo Danford (R)
Henry L. Dickey (D)
Thomas Ewing (D)
Ebenezer B. Finley (D)
Charles Foster (R)
Mills Gardner (R)
James A. Garfield (R)
John S. Jones (R)
J. Warren Keifer (R)
William McKinley, Jr. (R)
John A. McMahon (D)
James Monroe (R)
Henry S. Neal (R)
Americus V. Rice (D)
Milton Sayler (D)
Milton I. Southard (D)
Amos Townsend (R)
Nelson H. Van Vorhes (R)

Oregon

Senators

La Fayette Grover (D)
John H. Mitchell (R)

Representatives

Richard Williams (R)

Pennsylvania

Senators

J. Donald Cameron (R) s. 1877
Simon Cameron (R) r. 1877
William A. Wallace (D)

Representatives

Thomas M. Bayne (R)
Samuel A. Bridges (D)
Jacob M. Campbell (R)
Hiester Clymer (D)
Francis D. Collins (D)
Russell Errett (R)
I. Newton Evans (R)
Chapman Freeman (R)
Alfred C. Harmer (R)
William D. Kelley (R)
John W. Killinger (R)
Levi A. Mackey (D)
Levi Maish (D)
John I. Mitchell (R)
Charles O'Neill (R)
Edward Overton, Jr. (R)
Samuel J. Randall (D)
James B. Reilly (D)
William S. Shallenberger (R)
A. Herr Smith (R)
William S. Stenger (D)
John M. Thompson (R)
Jacob Turney (D)
William Ward (R)
Lewis F. Watson (R)
Harry White (R)
Hendrick B. Wright (D)

Rhode Island

Senators

Henry B. Anthony (R)
Ambrose E. Burnside (R)

Respresentatives

Latimer W. Ballou (R)
Benjamin T. Eames (R)

South Carolina

Senators

Matthew C. Butler (D)
John J. Patterson (R)

Representatives

D. Wyatt Aiken (D)
Richard H. Cain (D)
John H. Evins (D)
Joseph H. Rainey (R)
Robert Smalls (R)

Tennessee

Senators

James E. Bailey (D)
Isham G. Harris (D)

Representatives

John D. C. Atkins (D)
John M. Bright (D)
William P. Caldwell (D)
George G. Dibrell (D)
John F. House (D)
James H. Randolph (R)
Haywood Y. Riddle (D)
Jacob M. Thornburgh (R)
Washington C. Whitthorne (D)
H. Casey Yound (D)

Texas

Senators

Richard Coke (D)
Samuel B. Maxey (D)

Representatives

David B. culberson (D)
De Witt C. Giddings (D)
Roger Q. Mills (D)
John H. Reagan (D)
Gustave Schleicher (D) d. Jan. 1879
James W. Throckmorton (D)

Vermont

Senators

George F. Edmunds (R)
Justin S. Morrill (R)

Representatives

Dudley C. Denison (R)
George W. Hendee (R)
Charles H. Joyce (R)

Virginia

Senators

John W. Johnston (Con)
Robert E. Withers (Con)

Representatives

Richard Lee T. Beale (D) s. 1879
George C. Cabell (D)
Beverly B. Douglas (D) d. 1878
John Goode, Jr. (Con)
John T. Harris (D)
Eppa Hunton (D)
Joseph Jorgensen (R)
Auburn L. Pridemore (D)
John R. Tucker (D)
Gilbert C. Walker (Con)

West Virginia

Senators

Henry G. Davis (D)
Frank Hereford (D)

Representatives

John E. Kenna (D)
Benjamin F. Martin (D)
Benjamin Wilson (D)

Wisconsin

Senators

Angus Cameron (R)
Timothy O. Howe (R)

Representatives

Gabriel Bouck (D)
Edward S. Bragg (D)
Lucien B. Caswell (R)

George C. Hazelton (R)
Herman L. Humphrey (R)
William P. Lynde (D)
Thaddeus C. Pound (R)
Charles G. Williams (R)

Forty-Sixth Congress

(Mar. 4, 1879, to
Mar. 3, 1881)

President of the Senate: William
A. Wheeler
*President Pro Tempore of the
Senate:* Allen G. Thurman
*Speaker of the House of
Representatives:* Samuel J.
Randall

Alabama

Senators

George S. Houston (D) d. 1879
John T. Morgan (D)
Luke Pryor (D) ta. 1880
James L. Pugh (D) s. 1880

Representatives

Newton N. Clements s. 1880
William H. Forney (D)
Hilary A. Herbert (D)
Thomas H. Herndon (D)
Burwell B. Lewis (D) r. Oct.
1880
William M. Lowe (D)
William J. Samford (D)
Charles M. Shelley (D)
Thomas Williams (D)

Arkansas

Senators

Augustus H. Garland (D)
James D. Walker (D)

Representatives

Jordan E. Cravens (D)
Poindexter Dunn (D)
Thomas M. Gunter (D)
William F. Slemons (D)

California

Senators

Newton Booth (Anti-
Monopolist)
James T. Farley (R)

Representatives

Campbell P. Berry (R)
Horace Davis (R)
Romualdo Pacheco (R)
Horace F. Page (R)

Colorado

Senators

Henry M. Teller (R)
Nathaniel P. Hill (R)

Representatives

James B. Belford (R)

Connecticut

Senators

William W. Eaton (D)
Orville H. Platt (R)

Representatives

Joseph R. Hawley (R)
Frederick Miles (R)
James Phelps (D)
John T. Wait (R)

Delaware

Senators

Thomas F. Bayard (D)
Eli Saulsbury (D)

Representatives

Edward L. Martin (D)

Florida

Senators

Wilkinson Call (D)
Charles W. Jones (D)

Representatives

Horatio Bisbee, Jr. (R) s. 1881
Robert H. M. Davidson (D)
Noble A. Hull (D) r. Jan. 1881

Georgia

Senators

Joseph E. Brown (D) s. 1880
John B. Gordon (D) r. May
1880
Benjamin H. Hill (D)

Representatives

James H. Blount (D)
Philip Cook (D)
William H. Felton (D)
Nathaniel J. Hammond (D)
John C. Nicholls (D)
Henry Persons (D)
William E. Smith (D)
Emory Speer (D)
Alexander H. Stephens (D)

Illinois

Senators

David Davis (R)

John A. Logan (R)

Representatives

William Aldrich (R)
Hiram Barber, Jr. (R)
Thomas A. Boyd (R)
Joseph G. Cannon (R)
George R. Davis (R)
Albert P. Forsythe (R)
Greenbury L. Fort (R)
Robert M. A. Hawk (R)
Philip C. Hayes (R)
Thomas J. Henderson (R)
Benjamin F. Marsh (R)
William R. Morrison (D)
John C. Sherwin (R)
James W. Singleton (D)
William A. J. Sparks (D)
William M. Springer (D)
Adlai E. Stevenson (D)
John R. Thomas (R)
Richard W. Townshend (D)

Indiana

Senators

Joseph E. McDonald (D)
Daniel W. Voorhees (D)

Representatives

John H. Baker (R)
George A. Bicknell (D)
Thomas M. Browne (R)
William H. Calkins (R)
Thomas R. Cobb (D)
Walpole G. Colerick (D)
Calvin Cowgill (R)
Gilbert De La Matyr (D)
William Heilman (R)
Abraham J. Hostetler (D)
William R. Myers (D)
Jeptha D. New (D)
Godlove S. Orth (R)

Iowa

Senators

William B. Allison (R)
Samuel J. Kirkwood (R)

Representatives

Cyrus C. Carpenter (R)
Rush Clark (R) d. Apr. 1879
Nathaniel C. Deering (R)
Edward H. Gillette (Greenback)
Moses A. McCoid (R)
Hiram Price (R)
William F. Sapp (R)
William G. Thompson (R)
Thomas Updegraff (R)
James B. Weaver (Greenback)

Kansas

Senators

John J. Ingalls (R)
Preston B. Plumb (R)

Representatives

John A. Anderson (R)
Dudley C. Haskell (R)

Thomas Ryan (R)

Kentucky

Senators

James B. Beck (D)
John W. Williams (D)

Representatives

Joseph C. S. Blackburn (D)
John W. Caldwell (D)
John G. Carlisle (D)
J. Proctor Knott (D)
James A. McKenzie (D)
Elijah C. Phister (D)
Philip B. Thompson, Jr. (D)
Oscar Turner (D)
Thomas Turner (D)
Albert S. Willis (D)

Louisiana

Senators

William P. Kellogg (R)
Benjamin F. Jonas (D)

Representatives

Joseph H. Acklen (D)
Joseph B. Elam (D)
E. John Ellis (D)
Randall L. Gibson (D)
J. Floyd King (D)
Edward W. Robertson (D)

Maine

Senators

James G. Blaine (R)
Hannibal Hamlin (R)

Representatives

William P. Frye (R)
George W. Ladd (Greenback,
D)
Stephen D. Lindsey (R)
Thompson H. Murch
(Greenback)
Thomas B. Reed (R)

Maryland

Senators

James B. Groome (D)
William P. Whyte (D)

Representatives

Eli J. Henkle (D)
Daniel M. Henry (D)
William Kimmel (D)
Robert M. McLane (D)
J. Fred C. Talbott (D)
Milton G. Urner (R)

Massachusetts

Senators

Henry L. Dawes (R)

George F. Hoar (R)

Representatives

Selwyn Z. Bowman (R)
William Claflin (R)
William W. Crapo (R)
Walbridge A. Field (R)
Benjamin W. Harris (R)
George B. Loring (R)
Leopold Morse (D)
Amasa Norcross (R)
William W. Rice (R)
George D. Robinson (R)
William A. Russell (R)

Michigan

Senators

Henry P. Baldwin (R) s. 1879
Zachariah Chandler (R) d. 1879
Thomas W. Ferry (R)

Representatives

Mark S. Brewer (R)
Julius C. Burrows (R)
Omar D. Conger (R) r. Mar. 1879
Roswell G. Horr (R)
Jay A. Hubbell (R)
Jonas H. McGowan (R)
John S. Newberry (R)
John W. Stone (R)
Edwin Willits (R)

Minnesota

Senators

Samuel J. R. McMillan (R)
William Windom (R)

Representatives

Mark H. Dunnell (R)
Henry Poehler (D)
William D. Washburn (R)

Mississippi

Senators

Blanche K. Bruce (R)
Lucius Q. C. Lamar (D)

Representatives

James R. Chalmers (D)
Charles E. Hooker (D)
Vannoy H. Manning (D)
Hernando D. Money (D)
Henry L. Muldrow (D)
Otho R. Singleton (D)

Missouri

Senators

Francis M. Cockrell (D)
George G. Vest (D)

Representatives

Richard P. Bland (D)
Aylett H. Buckner (D)

Martin L. Clardy (D)
John B. Clark, Jr. (D)
Lowndes H. Davis (D)
Nicholas Ford (R)
Richard G. Frost (D)
William H. Hatch (D)
Alfred M. Lay (D) d. 1879
John F. Philips (D) s. 1880
Gideon F. Rothwell (D)
Samuel L. Sawyer (D)
James R. Waddill (D)
Erastus Wells (D)

Nebraska

Senators

Algernon S. Paddock (R)
Alvin Saunders (R)

Representatives

Edward K. Valentine (R)

Nevada

Senators

John P. Jones (R)
William Sharon (R)

Representatives

Rollin M. Daggett (R)

New Hampshire

Senators

Charles H. Bell (R) ta. 1879
Henry W. Blair (R) s. 1879
Edward H. Rollins (R)

Representatives

James F. Briggs (R)
Evarts W. Farr (D) d. Nov. 1880
Joshua G. Hall (R)
Ossian Ray (R) s. 1881

New Jersey

Senators

John R. McPherson (D)
Theodore F. Randolph (D)

Representatives

John L. Blake (R)
Lewis A. Brigham (R)
Alvah A. Clark (D)
George M. Robeson (R)
Miles Ross (D)
Hezekiah B. Smith (D)
Charles H. Voorhis (R)

New York

Senators

Roscoe Conkling (R)
Francis Kernan (D)

Representatives

John M. Bailey (R)
Archibald M. Bliss (D)
John H. Camp (R)
Simeon B. Chittenden (R)
James W. Covert (D)
Samuel S. Cox (D)
Richard Crowley (R)
Jeremiah W. Dwight (R)
Edwin Einstein (R)
John W. Ferdon (R)
John Hammond (R)
Frank Hiscock (R)
Waldo Hutchins (D)
Amaziah B. James (R)
John H. Ketcham (R)
Elbridge G. Lapham (R)
William Lounsbery (D)
Anson G. McCook (R)
Joseph Mason (R)
Warner Miller (R)
Levi P. Morton (R)
Nicholas Muller (D)
James O'Brien (D)
Daniel O'Reilly (D)
Ray V. Pierce (R) r. 1880
Cyrus D. Prescott (R)
David P. Richardson (R)
Jonathan Scoville (D) s. 1880
John H. Starin (R)
Henry Van Aernam (R)
John Van Voorhis (R)
David Wilber (R)
Fernando Wood (D) d. Feb. 1881
Walter A. Wood (R)

North Carolina

Senators

Matt W. Ransom (D)
Zebulon B. Vance (D)

Representatives

Robert F. Armfield (D)
Joseph J. Davis (D)
William H. Kitchin (D)
Joseph J. Martin (R) r. Jan. 1881
Daniel L. Russell (R)
Alfred M. Scales (D)
Walter L. Steele (D)
Robert B. Vance (D)
Jesse J. Yeates (D) s. 1881

Ohio

Senators

George H. Pendleton (D)
Allen G. Thurman (D)

Representatives

Gibson Atherton (D)
Benjamin Butterworth (R)
George L. Converse (D)
Henry L. Dickey (D)
Thomas Ewing (D)
Ebenezer B. Finley (D)
James A. Garfield (R) r. Nov. 1880
George W. Geddes (D)
William D. Hill (D)
Frank H. Hurd (D)
J. Warren Keifer (R)

Benjamin LeFevre (D)
William McKinley, Jr. (R)
John A. McMahon (D)
James Monroe (R)
Henry S. Neal (R)
Ezra B. Taylor (R) s. 1880
Amos Townsend (R)
Jonathan T. Updegraff (R)
Adoniram J. Warner (D)
Thomas L. Young (R)

Oregon

Senators

La Fayette Grover (D)
James H. Slater (D)

Representatives

John Whiteaker (D)

Pennsylvania

Senators

J. Donald Cameron (R)
William A. Wallace (D)

Representatives

Reuben K. Bachman (D)
Thomas M. Bayne (R)
Frank E. Beltzhoover (D)
Henry H. Bingham (R)
Hiester Clymer (D)
Alexander H. Coffroth (D)
Samuel B. Dick (R)
Russell Errett (R)
Horatio G. Fisher (R)
William Godshalk (R)
Alfred C. Harmer (R)
William D. Kelley (R)
John W. Killinger (R)
Robert Klotz (D)
John I. Mitchell (R)
Charles O'Neill (R)
James H. Osmer (R)
Edward Overton, Jr. (R)
Samuel J. Randall (D)
John W. Ryon (D)
William S. Shallenberger (R)
A. Herr Smith (R)
William Ward (R)
Harry White (R)
Morgan R. Wise (D)
Hendrick B. Wright (D)
Seth H. Yocum (R)

Rhode Island

Senators

Henry B. Anthony (R)
Ambrose E. Burnside (R)

Representatives

Nelson W. Aldrich (D)
Latimer W. Ballou (R)

South Carolina

Senators

Matthew C. Butler (D)
Wade Hampton (D)

Representatives

D. Wyatt Aiken (D)
John H. Evins (D)
Michael P. O'Connor (D)
John S. Richardson (D)
George D. Tillman (D)

Tennessee

Senators

James E. Bailey (D)
Isham G. Harris (D)

Representatives

John D. C. Atkins (D)
John M. Bright (D)
George G. Dibrell (D)
Leonidas C. Houk (R)
John F. House (D)
Benton McMillin (D)
Charles B. Simonton (D)
Robert L. Taylor (D)
Washington C. Whitthorne (D)
H. Casey Young (D)

Texas

Senators

Richard Coke (D)
Samuel B. Maxey (D)

Representatives

David B. Culberson (D)
George W. Jones (Greenback)
Roger Q. Mills (D)
John H. Reagan (D)
Christopher C. Upson (D)
Olin Wellborn (D)

Vermont

Senators

George F. Edmunds (R)
Justin S. Morrill (R)

Representatives

Bradley Barlow (R)
Charles H. Joyce (R)
James M. Tyler (R)

Virginia

Senators

John W. Jonston (C)
Robert E. Withers (C)

Representatives

Richard Lee T. Beale (D)
George C. Cabell (D)
John Goode, Jr. (D)
John T. Harris (D)
Eppa Hunton (D)
Joseph E. Johnston (D)
Joseph Jorgensen (R)
James B. Richmond (D)
John R. Tucker (D)

West Virginia

Senators

Henry G. Davis (D)
Frank Hereford (D)

Representatives

John E. Kenna (D)
Benjamin F. Martin (D)
Benjamin Wilson (D)

Wisconsin

Senators

Angus Cameron (R)
Matthew H. Carpenter (R) d.
  Feb. 1881

Representatives

Gabriel Bouck (D)
Edward S. Bragg (D)
Lucien B. Caswell (R)
Peter V. Deuster (D)
George C. Hazelton (R)
Herman L. Humprhrey (R)
Thaddeus C. Pound (R)
Charles G. Williams (R)

Forty-Seventh Congress

(Mar. 4, 1881, to
Mar. 3, 1883)

President of the Senate: Chester
A. Arthur
*Presidents Pro Tempore of the
Senate:* Thomas F. Bayard;
David Davis; George F.
Edmunds
*Speaker of the House of
Representatives:* J. Warren
Keifer

Alabama

Senators

John T. Morgan (D)
James L. Pugh (D)

Representatives

William H. Forney (D)
Hilary A. Herbert (D)
Thomas H. Herndon (D)
Goldsmith W. Hewitt (D)
William M. Lowe (D) d. 1882
William C. Oates (D)
Charles M. Shelley (D)
Joseph Wheeler (D)
Thomas Williams (D)

Arkansas

Senators

Augustus H. Garland (D)
James D. Walker (D)

Representatives

Poindexter Dunn (D)
Jordan E. Cravens (D)
Thomas M. Gunter (D)
James K. Jones (D)

California

Senators

James T. Farley (R)
John F. Miller (R)

Representatives

Campbell P. Berry (R)
Romualdo Pacheco (R)
Horace F. Page (R)
William S. Rosecrans (D)

Colorado

Senators

George M. Chilcott (R) ta.
  1882
Nathaniel P. Hill (R)
Horace A. W. Tabor (R) s.
  1883
Henry M. Teller (R) r. Apr.
  1882

Representatives

James B. Belford (R)

Connecticut

Senators

Joseph R. Hawley (R)
Orville H. Platt (R)

Representatives

John R. Buck (R)
Frederick Miles (R)
James Phelps (D)
John T. Wait (R)

Delaware

Senators

Thomas F. Bayard (D)
Eli Saulsbury (D)

Representatives

Edward L. Martin (D)

Florida

Senators

Wilkinson Call (D)
Charles W. Jones (D)

Representatives

Horatio Bisbee, Jr. (R) s. 1882
Robert H. M. Davidson (D)
Jesse J. Finley (D) r. June 1882

Georgia

Senators

M. Pope Barrow (D) s. 1882
Joseph E. Brown (D)
Benjamin H. Hill (D) d. 1882

Representatives

George R. Black (D)
James H. Blount (D)
Hugh Buchanan (D)
Judson C. Clements (D)
Philip Cook (D)
Nathaniel J. Hammond (D)
Seaborn Reese (D) s. 1882
Emory Speer (D)
Alexander H. Stephens (D) r.
  Nov. 1882
Henry G. Turner (D)

Illinois

Senators

David Davis (R)
John A. Logan (R)

Representatives

William Aldrich (R)
Joseph G. Cannon (R)
William Cullen (R)
George R. Davis (R)
Charles B. Farwell (R)
Robert M. A. Hawk (R) d.
  June 1882
Thomas J. Henderson (R)
Robert R. Hitt (R) s. 1882
John H. Lewis (R)
Benjamin F. Marsh (R)
William R. Morrison (D)
Samuel W. Moulton (D)
Lewis E. Payson (R)
John C. Sherwin (R)
James W. Singleton (D)
Dietrich C. Smith (R)
William A. J. Sparks (D)
William M. Springer (D)
John R. Thomas (R)
Richard W. Townshend (D)

Indiana

Senators

Benjamin Harrison (R)
Daniel W. Voorhees (D)

Representatives

Thomas M. Browne (R)
William H. Calkins (R)
Thomas R. Cobb (D)
Walpole G. Colerick (D)
Mark L. DeMotte (R)
Charles T. Doxey (R) s. 1883
William Heilman (R)
William S. Holman (D)
Courtland C. Matson (D)
Godlove S. Orth (R) d. Dec.
  1882
Stanton J. Peelle (R)
Robert B. F. Pierce (R)
George W. Steele (R)
Strother M. Stockslager (D)

Iowa

Senators

William B. Allison (R)
Samuel J. Kirkwood (R) r.
   Mar. 1881
James W. McDill (R) s. 1881

Representatives

Cyrus C. Carpenter (R)
Marsena E. Cutts (R)
Nathaniel C. Deering (R)
Sewall S. Farwell (R)
William P. Hepburn (R)
John A. Kasson (R)
Moses A. McCoid (R)
William G. Thompson (R)
Thomas Updegraff (R)

Kansas

Senators

John J. Ingalls (R)
Preston B. Plumb (R)

Representatives

John A. Anderson (R)
Dudley C. Haskell (R)
Thomas Ryan (R)

Kentucky

Senators

James B. Beck (D)
John S. Williams (D)

Representatives

Joseph C. S. Blackburn (D)
John W. Caldwell (D)
John G. Carlisle (D)
J. Proctor Knott (D)
James A. McKenzie (D)
Elijah C. Phister (D)
Philip B. Thompson, Jr. (D)
Oscar Turner (D)
John D. White (R)
Albert S. Willis (D)

Louisiana

Senators

Benjamin F. Jonas (D)
William P. Kellogg (R)

Representatives

Newton C. Blanchard (D)
Chester B. Darrall (R)
E. John Ellis (D)
Randall L. Gibson (D)
J. Floyd King (D)
Edward W. Robertson (D)

Maine

Senators

James G. Blaine (R) r. Mar.
   1881

William P. Frye (R) s. 1881
Eugene Hale (R)

Representatives

Nelson Dingley, Jr. (R)
William P. Frye (R) r. Mar.
   1881
George W. Ladd (Greenback,
   D)
Stephen D. Lindsey (R)
Thompson H. Murch
   (Greenback)
Thomas B. Reed (R)

Maryland

Senators

Arthur P. Gorman (D)
James B. Groome (D)

Representatives

Andrew G. Chapman (D)
George W. Covington (D)
Fetter S. Hoblitzell (D)
Robert M. McLane (D)
J. Fred C. Talbott (D)
Milton G. Urner (R)

Massachusetts

Senators

Henry L. Dawes (R)
George F. Hoar (R)

Representatives

Selwyn Z. Bowman (R)
John W. Candler (R)
William W. Crapo (R)
Benjamin W. Harris (R)
Leopold Morse (D)
Amasa Norcross (R)
Ambrose A. Ranney (R)
William W. Rice (R)
George D. Robinson (R)
William A. Russell (R)
Eben F. Stone (R)

Michigan

Senators

Omar D. Conger (R)
Thomas W. Ferry (R)

Representatives

Julius C. Burrows (R)
Roswell G. Horr (R)
Jay A. Hubbell (R)
Edward S. Lacey (R)
Henry W. Lord (R)
John T. Rich (R)
Oliver L. Spaulding (R)
George W. Webber (R)
Edwin Willits (R)

Minnesota

Senators

Alonzo J. Edgerton (R) ta.
   1881

Samuel J. R. McMillan (R)
William Windom (R) r. Mar.
   1881

Representatives

Mark H. Dunnell (R)
Horace B. Strait (R)
William D. Washburn (R)

Mississippi

Senators

James Z. George (D)
Lucius Q. C. Lamar (D)

Representatives

James R. Chalmers (D) r. Apr.
   1882
Charles E. Hooker (D)
John R. Lynch (R) s. 1882
Vannoy H. Manning (D)
Hernando D. Money (D)
Henry L. Muldrow (D)
Otho R. Singleton (D)

Missouri

Senators

Francis M. Cockrell (D)
George G. Vest (D)

Representatives

Thomas Allen (D) d. Apr. 1882
Richard P. Bland (D)
Aylett H. Buckner (D)
Joseph H. Burrows (Greenback)
Martin L. Clardy (D)
John B. Clark, Jr. (D)
Lowndes H. Davis (D)
Nicholas Ford (D)
Richard G. Frost (D)
William H. Hatch (D)
Ira S. Hazeltone (Greenback)
James H. McLean (R) s. 1882
Theron M. Rice (Greenback)
Robert T. Van Horn (R)

Nebraska

Senators

Alvin Saunders (R)
Charles H. Van Wyck (R)

Representatives

Edward K. Valentine (R)

Nevada

Senators

James G. Fair (D)
John P. Jones (R)

Representatives

George W. Cassidy (D)

New Hampshire

Senators

Henry W. Blair (R)
Edward H. Rollins (R)

Representatives

James F. Briggs (R)
Joshua G. Hall (R)
Ossian Ray (R)

New Jersey

Senators

John R. McPherson (D)
William J. Sewell (R)

Representatives

J. Hart Brewer (R)
Augustus A. Hardenbergh (D)
Henry S. Harris (D)
John Hill (R)
Phineas Jones (R)
George M. Robeson (R)
Miles Ross (D)

New York

Senators

Elbridge G. Lapham (R)
Warner Miller (R)

Representatives

Lewis Beach (D)
Perry Belmont (D)
Archibald M. Bliss (D)
John H. Camp (R)
Thomas Cornell (R)
Samuel S. Cox (D)
Richard Crowley (R)
P. Henry Dugro (D)
Jeremiah W. Dwight (R)
Roswell P. Flower (D)
John Hammond (R)
John Hardy (D)
Abram S. Hewitt (D)
Frank Hiscock (R)
Waldo Hutchins (D)
Ferris Jacobs (R)
John Ketcham (R)
Elbridge G. Lapham (R) r.
   1881
Anson G. McCook (R)
Joseph Mason (R)
Warner Miller (R) r. July 1881
Levi P. Morton (R) r. Mar.
   1881
Michael N. Nolan (D)
Abraham X. Parker (R)
Cyrus D. Prescott (R)
David P. Richardson (R)
William E. Robinson (D)
Jonathan Scoville (D)
Charles R. Skinner (R)
J. Hyatt Smith (R,D)
Henry Van Aernam (R)
John Van Voorhis (R)
James W. Wadsworth (R)
George West (R)
Benjamin Wood (D)
Walter A. Wood (R)

North Carolina

Senators

Matt W. Ransom (D)
Zebulon B. Vance (D)

Representatives

Robert F. Armfield (D)
William R. Cox (D)
Clement Dowd (D)
Orlando Hubbs (R)
Louis C. Latham (D)
Alfred M. Scales (D)
John W. Shackelford (D) d.
  1883
Robert B. Vance (D)

Ohio

Senators

George H. Pendleton (D)
John Sherman (R)

Representatives

Gibson Atherton (D)
Benjamin Butterworth (R)
George L. Converse (D)
Rufus R. Dawes (R)
George W. Geddes (D)
J. Warren Keifer (R)
John P. Leedom (D)
Benjamin LeFevre (D)
Addison S. McClure (R)
William McKinley, Jr. (R)
Henry L. Morey (R)
Henry S. Neal (R)
John B. Rice (R)
James M. Ritchie (R)
James S. Robinson (R)
Emanuel Shultz (R)
Ezra B. Taylor (R)
Joseph D. Taylor (R) s. 1883
Amos Townsend (R)
Jonathan T. Updegraff (R) d.
  Nov. 1882
Thomas L. Young (R)

Oregon

Senators

La Fayette Grover (D)
James H. Slater (D)

Representatives

Melvin C. George (R)

Pennsylvania

Senators

J. Donald Cameron (R)
John I. Mitchell (R)

Representatives

Samuel F. Barr (R)
Thomas M. Bayne (R)
Frank E. Beltzhoover (D)
Henry H. Bingham (R)
Charles N. Brumm
  (Greenback,R)

Jacob M. Campbell (R)
Andrew G. Curtin (D)
Daniel Ermentrout (D)
Russell Errett (R)
Horatio G. Fisher (R)
William Godshalk (R)
Alfred C. Harmer (R)
Cornelius C. Jadwin (R)
William D. Kelley (R)
Robert Klotz (D)
Samuel H. Miller (R)
James Mosgrove (Greenback, D)
William Mutchler (D)
Charles O'Neill (R)
Samuel J. Randall (D)
Joseph A. Scranton (R)
William S. Shallenberger (R)
A. Herr Smith (R)
Robert J. C. Walker (R)
William Ward (R)
Lewis F. Watson (R)
Morgan R. Wise (D)

Rhode Island

Senators

Nelson W. Aldrich (R) s. 1881
Henry B. Anthony (R)
Ambrose E. Burnside (R) d.
  Sept. 1881

Representatives

Nelson W. Aldrich (R) r. Oct.
  1881
Jonathan Chace (R)
Henry J. Spooner (R)

South Carolina

Senators

Matthew C. Butler (D)
Wade Hampton (D)

Representatives

D. Wyatt Aiken (D)
Samuel Dibble (D) r. May 1882
John H. Evins (D)
Edmund W. M. Mackey (D) s.
  1882
Michael P. O'Connor (D) d.
  Apr. 1881
John S. Richardson (D)
Robert Smalls (R) s. 1882
George D. Tillman (D) r. July
  1882

Tennessee

Senators

Isham G. Harris (D)
Howell E. Jackson (D)

Representatives

John D. C. Atkins (D)
George G. Dibrell (D)
Leonidas C. Houk (R)
John F. House (D)
Benton McMillin (D)
William R. Moore (R)
Augustus H. Pettibone (R)
Charles B. Simonton (D)
Richard Warner (D)

Washington C. Whitthorne (D)

Texas

Senators

Richard Coke (D)
Samuel B. Maxey (D)

Representatives

David B. Culberson (D)
George W. Jones (Greenback)
Roger Q. Mills (D)
John H. Reagan (D)
Christopher C. Upson (D)
Olin Wellborn (D)

Vermont

Senators

George F. Edmunds (R)
Justin S. Morrill (R)

Representatives

William W. Grout (R)
Charles H. Joyce (R)
James M. Tyler (R)

Virginia

Senators

John W. Johnston (D)
William Mahone (Readjuster)

Representatives

John S. Barbour (D)
George C. Cabell (D)
John F. Dezendorf (R)
Abram Fulkerson (Readjuster)
George T. Garrison (D)
Joseph Jorgensen (R)
John Paul (Readjuster)
John R. Tucker (D)
George D. Wise (D)

West Virginia

Senators

Johnson N. Camden (D)
Henry G. Davis (D)

Representatives

John B. Hoge (D)
Benjamin Wilson (D)

Wisconsin

Senators

Angus Cameron (R)
Philetus Sawyer (R)

Representatives

Edward S. Bragg (D)
Lucien B. Caswell (R)
Peter V. Deuster (D)
Richard W. Guenther (R)
George C. Hazelton (R)

Herman L. Humphrey (R)
Thaddeus C. Pound (R)
Charles G. Williams (R)

Forty-Eighth Congress
(Mar. 4, 1883, to
Mar. 3, 1885)

President of the Senate: Vacant
*President Pro Tempore of the
  Senate:* George F. Edmunds
*Speaker of the House of
  Representatives:* John G.
  Carlisle

Alabama

Senators

John T. Morgan (D)
James L. Pugh (D)

Representatives

George H. Craig (R) s. 1885
William H. Forney (D)
Hilary A. Herbert (D)
Goldsmith W. Hewitt (D)
James T. Jones (D)
William C. Oates (D)
Luke Pryor (D)
Charles M. Shelley (D) r. Jan.
  1885
Thomas Williams (D)

Arkansas

Senators

Augustus H. Garland (D)
James D. Walker (D)

Representatives

Clifton R. Breckinridge (D)
Poindexter Dunn (D)
James K. Jones (D) r. Feb.
  1885
Samuel W. Peel (D)
John H. Rogers (D)

California

Senators

James T. Farley (R)
John F. Miller (R)

Representatives

James H. Budd (D)
Joh R. Glascock (D)
Barclay Henley (D)
William S. Rosecrans (D)
Charles A. Sumner (D)
Pleasant B. Tully (D)

Colorado

Senators

Thomas M. Bowen (R)

Nathaniel P. Hill (R)

Representatives

James B. Belford (R)

Connecticut

Senators

Joseph R. Hawley (R)
Orville H. Platt (R)

Representatives

William W. Eaton (D)
Charles L. Mitchell (D)
Edward W. Seymour (D)
John T. Wait (R)

Delaware

Senators

Thomas F. Bayard (D)
Eli Saulsbury (D)

Representatives

Charles B. Lore (D)

Florida

Senators

Wilkinson Call (D)
Charles W. Jones (D)

Representatives

Horatio Bisbee, Jr. (R)
Robert H. M. Davidson (D)

Georgia

Senators

Joseph E. Brown (D)
Alfred H. Colquitt (D)

Representatives

James H. Blount (D)
Hugh Buchanan (D)
Allen D. Candler (D)
Judson C. Clements (D)
Charles F. Crisp (D)
Nathaniel J. Hammond (D)
Thomas Hardeman (D)
John C. Nicholls (D)
Seaborn Reese (D)
Henry G. Turner (D)

Illinois

Senators

Shelby M. Cullom (R)
John A. Logan (R)

Representatives

George E. Adams (R)
Joseph G. Cannon (R)
William Cullen (R)

George R. Davis (R)
Ransom W. Dunham (R)
Reuben Ellwood (R)
John F. Finerty (D)
Thomas J. Henderson (R)
Robert R. Hitt (R)
William R. Morrison (D)
Samuel W. Moulton (D)
William H. Neece (D)
Lewis E. Payson (R)
James M. Riggs (D)
Jonathan H. Rowell (R)
Aaron Shaw (D)
William M. Springer (D)
John R. Thomas (R)
Richard W. Townshend (D)
Nicholas E. Worthington (D)

Indiana

Senators

Benjamin Harrison (R)
Daniel W. Voorhees (D)

Representatives

Thomas M. Browne (R)
William H. Calkins (R) r. Oct.
  1884
Thomas R. Cobb (D)
William E. English (D) s. 1884
William S. Holman (D)
John J. Kleiner (D)
John E. Lamb (D)
Robert Lowry (D)
Courtland C. Matson (D)
Stanton J. Peelle (R) r. May
  1884
Benjamin F. Shively (D) s. 1884
George W. Steele (R)
Strother M. Stockslager (D)
Thomas B. Ward (D)
Thomas J. Wood (D)

Iowa

Senators

William B. Allison (R)
James F. Wilson (R)

Representatives

John C. Cook (D)
Benjamin T. Frederick (D) s.
  1885
David B. Henderson (R)
William P. Hepburn (R)
Adoniram J. Holmes (R)
John A. Kasson (R) r. July
  1884
Moses A. McCoid (R)
Jeremiah H. Murphy (D)
William H. M. Pusey (D)
Hiram Y. Smith (R) s. 1884
Isaac S. Struble (R)
Luman H. Weller (D)
James Wilson (R) r. Mar. 1885

Kansas

Senators

John J. Ingalls (R)
Preston B. Plumb (R)

Representatives

John A. Anderson (R)
Edward H. Funston (R) s. 1884
Lewis Hanback (R)
Dudley C. Haskell (R) d. Dec.
  1883
Edmund N. Morrill (R)
Bishop W. Perkins (R)
Samuel R. Peters (R)
Thomas Ryan (R)

Kentucky

Senators

James B. Beck (D)
John S. Williams (D)

Representatives

Joseph C. S. Blackburn (D)
John G. Carlisle (D)
James F. Clay (D)
William W. Culbertson (R)
John E. Halsell (D)
Thomas A. Robertson (D)
Philip B. Thompson, Jr. (D)
Oscar Turner (D)
John D. White (R)
Albert S. Willis (D)
Frank L. Wolford (D)

Louisiana

Senators

Randall L. Gibson (D)
Benjamin F. Jonas (D)

Representatives

Newton C. Blanchard (D)
E. John Ellis (D)
Carleton Hunt (D)
William P. Kellogg (R)
J. Floyd King (D)
Edward T. Lewis (D)

Maine

Senators

William P. Frye (R)
Eugene Hale (R)

Representatives

Charles A. Boutelle (R)
Nelson Dingley, Jr. (R)
Seth L. Milliken (R)
Thomas B. Reed (R)

Maryland

Senators

Arthur P. Gorman (D)
James B. Groome (D)

Representatives

George W. Covington (D)
John V. L. Findlay (D)
Fetter S. Hoblitzell (D)
Hart B. Holton (R)
Louis E. McComas (R)

J. Fred C. Talbott (D)

Massachusetts

Senators

Henry L. Dawes (R)
George F. Hoar (R)

Representatives

Patrick A. Collins (D)
Robert T. Davis (R)
John D. Long (R)
Henry B. Lovering (D)
Theodore Lyman
Leopold Morse (D)
Ambrose A. Ranney (R)
William W. Rice (R)
George D. Robinson (R) r. Jan.
  1884
Francis W. Rockwell (R) s. Jan.
  1884
William A. Russell (R)
Eben F. Stone (R)
William Whiting (R)

Michigan

Senators

Omar D. Conger (R)
Thomas W. Palmer (R)

Representatives

Edward Breitung (R)
Ezra C. Carleton (D)
Byron M. Cutcheon (R)
Nathaniel B. Eldredge (D)
Herschel H. Hatch (R)
Roswell G. Horr (R)
Julius Houseman (D)
Edward S. Lacey (R)
William C. Maybury (D)
Edwin B. Winans (D)
George L. Yaple (Un)

Minnesota

Senators

Samuel J. R. McMillan (R)
Dwight M. Sabin (R)

Representatives

Knute Nelson (R)
Horace B. Strait (R)
James B. Wakefield (R)
William D. Washburn (R)
Milo White (R)

Mississippi

Senators

James Z. George (D)
Lucius Q. C. Lamar (D)

Representatives

Ethelbert Barksdale (D)
James R. Chalmers s. 1884
Elza Jeffords (D)
Hernando D. Money (D)
Henry L. Muldrow (D)

Otho R. Singleton (D)
Henry S. Van Eaton (D)

Missouri

Senators

Francis M. Cockrell (D)
George G. Vest (D)

Representatives

Armstead M. Alexander (D)
Richard P. Bland (D)
James O. Broadhead (D)
Aylett H. Buckner (D)
James N. Burnes (D)
Martin L. Clardy (D)
John Cosgrove (D)
Lowndes H. Davis (D)
Alexander M. Dockery (D)
Robert W. Fyan (D)
Alexander Graves (D)
William H. Hatch (D)
Charles H. Morgan (D)
John J. O'Neill (D)

Nebraska

Senators

Charles F. Manderson (R)
Charles H. Van Wyck (R)

Representatives

James Laird (R)
Edward K. Valentine (R)
Archibald J. Weaver (R)

Nevada

Senators

James G. Fair (D)
John P. Jones (R)

Representatives

George W. Cassidy (D)

New Hampshire

Senators

Henry W. Blair (R)
Austin F. Pike (R)

Representatives

Martin A. Haynes (R)
Ossian Ray (R)

New Jersey

Senators

John R. McPherson (D)
William J. Sewell (R)

Representatives

J. Hart Brewer (D)
Thomas M. Ferrell (D)
William H. F. Fiedler (D)
Benjamin F. Howey (R)

John Kean (R)
William McAdoo (D)
William W. Phelps (R)

New York

Senators

Elbridge G. Lapham (R)
Warner Miller (R)

Representatives

John J. Adams (D)
John Arnot, Jr. (D)
John H. Bagley, Jr. (D)
Lewis Beach (D)
Perry Belmont (D)
Francis B. Brewer (R)
Henry G. Burleigh (R)
Felix Campbell (D)
Samuel S. Cox (D)
William Dorsheimer (D)
Halbert S. Greenleaf (D)
John Hardy (D)
Abram S. Hewitt (D)
Frank Hiscock (R)
Waldo Hutchins (D)
Darwin R. James (R)
Frederick A. Johnson
John H. Ketcham (R)
Stephen C. Millard (R)
Nicholas Muller (R)
Newton W. Nutting (R)
Abraham X. Parker (R)
Sereno E. Payne (R)
Orlando B. Potter (D)
George W. Ray (R)
William E. Robinson (D)
William F. Rogers (D)
Charles R. Skinner (R)
Henry W. Slocum (D)
John T. Spriggs (D)
Robert S. Stevens (D)
Thomas J. Van Alstyne (D)
James W. Wadsworth (R)
Edward Wemple (D)

North Carolina

Senators

Matt W. Ransom (D)
Zebulon B. Vance (D)

Representatives

Risden T. Bennett (D)
William R. Cox (D)
Clement Dowd (D)
Wharton J. Green (D)
James E. O'Hara (R)
Walter F. Pool (R) d. Aug.
  1883
James W. Reid (D) s. 1885
Alfred M. Scales (D) r. Dec.
  1884
Thomas G. Skinner (D)
Tyre York (D)
Robert B. Vance (D)

Ohio

Senators

George H. Pendleton (D)
John Sherman (R)

Representatives

James E. Campbell (D) s. 1884
George L. Converse (D)
John F. Follett (D)
Martin A. Foran (D)
George W. Geddes (D)
Alphonso Hart (R)
William D. Hill (D)
Frank H. Hurd (D)
Isaac M. Jordan (D)
J. Warren Keifer (R)
Benjamin LeFevre (D)
John W. McCormick (R)
William McKinley, Jr. (R) r.
  May 1884
Henry L. Morey (R) r. June
  1884
Robert M. Murray (D)
David R. Paige (D)
James S. Robinson (R) r. Jan.
  1885
George E. Seney (D)
Ezra B. Taylor (R)
Joseph D. Taylor (R)
Jonathan H. Wallace (D) s.
  1884
Adoniram J. Warner (D)
Beriah Wilkins (D)

Oregon

Senators

Joseph N. Dolph (R)
James H. Slater (D)

Representatives

Melvin C. George (R)

Pennsylvania

Senators

J. Donald Cameron (R)
John I. Mitchell (R)

Representatives

Louis E. Atkinson (R)
Samuel F. Barr (R)
Thomas M. Bayne (R)
Henry H. Bingham (R)
Charles E. Boyle (D)
Samuel M. Brainerd (R)
William W. Brown (R)
Charles N. Brumm (Greenback)
Jacob M. Campbell (R)
Daniel W. Connolly (D)
Andrew G. Curtin (D)
William A. Duncan (D)
Mortimer F. Elliott (D)
Daniel Ermentrout (D)
I. Newton Evans (R)
James S. Everhart (R)
Alfred C. Harmer (R)
James H. Hopkins (D)
William D. Kelley (R)
George V. Lawrence (R)
Samuel H. Miller (R)
William Mutchler (D)
Charles O'Neill (R)
John D. Patton (D)
George A. Post (D)
Samuel J. Randall (R)
A. Herr Smith (R)
John B. Storm (D)
John A. Swope (D) s. 1885

Rhode Island

Senators

Nelson W. Aldrich (R)
Henry B. Anthony (R) d. Sept.
  1884
Jonathan Chace (R) s. 1885
William P. Sheffield (R) ta.
  1884

Representatives

Jonathan Chace (R) r. Jan.
  1885
Nathan F. Dixon (R) s. 1885
Henry J. Spooner (R)

South Carolina

Senators

Matthew C. Butler (D)
Wade Hampton (D)

Representatives

D. Wyatt Aiken (D)
John Bratton (D) s. 1884
George W. Dargan (D)
Samuel Dibble (D)
John H. Evins (D) d. Oct. 1884
John J. Hemphill (D)
Edmund W. M. Mackey (R) d.
  Jan. 1884
Robert Smalls (R)
George D. Tillman (D)

Tennessee

Senators

Isham G. Harris (D)
Howell E. Jackson (D)

Representatives

John G. Ballentine (D)
Andrew J. Caldwell (D)
George G. Dibrell (D)
Leonidas C. Houk (R)
Benton McMillin (D)
Augustus H. Pettibone (R)
Rice A. Pierce (D)
John M. Taylor (D)
Richard Warner (D)
H. Casey Young (D)

Texas

Senators

Richard Coke (D)
Samuel B. Maxey (D)

Representatives

David B. Culberson (D)
John Hancock (D)
James H. Jones (D)
Samuel W. T. Lanham (D)
James F. Miller (D)
Roger Q. Mills (D)
Thomas P. Ochiltree (D)
John H. Reagan (D)
Charles Stewart (D)
James W. Throckmorton (D)

Olin Wellborn (D)

Vermont

Senators

George F. Edmunds (R)
Justin S. Morrill (R)

Representatives

Luke P. Poland (R)
John W. Stewart (R)

Virginia

Senators

William Mahone (Readjuster)
Harrison H. Riddleberger
  (Readjuster)

Representatives

John S. Barbour (D)
Henry Bowen (Readjuster)
George C. Cabell (D)
George T. Garrison s. 1884
Benjamin S. Hooper (D)
Harry Libbey (R)
Robert M. Mayo (Readjuster) r.
  1884
Charles T. O'Ferrall (D) s.
  1884
John R. Tucker (D)
George D. Wise (D)
John S. Wise

West Virginia

Senators

Johnson N. Camden (D)
John E. Kenna (D)

Representatives

Eustace Gibson (D)
Nathan Goff (R)
Charles P. Snyder (D)
William L. Wilson (D)

Wisconsin

Senators

Angus Cameron (R)
Philetus Sawyer (R)

Representatives

Peter V. Deuster (D)
Richard W. Guenther (R)
Burr W. Jones (D)
William T. Price (R)
Joseph Rankin (D)
Isaac Stephenson (R)
Daniel H. Sumner (D)
John Winans (D)
Gilbert M. Woodward (D)

Forty-Ninth Congress

(Mar. 4, 1885, to
Mar. 3, 1887)

President of the Senate: Thomas
  A. Hendricks
*Presidents Pro Tempore of the
  Senate:* John Sherman; John
  J. Ingalls
*Speaker of the House of
  Representatives:* John G.
  Carlisle

Alabama

Senators

John T. Morgan (D)
James L. Pugh (D)

Representatives

Alexander C. Davidson (D)
William H. Forney (D)
Hilary A. Herbert (D)
James T. Jones (D)
John M. Martin (D)
William C. Oates (D)
Thomas W. Sadler (D)
Joseph Wheeler (D)

Arkansas

Senators

James H. Berry (D) s. 1885
Augustus H. Garland (D) r.
  Mar. 1885
James K. Jones (D)

Representatives

Clifton R. Breckinridge (D)
Poindexter Dunn (D)
Thomas C. McRae (D)
Samuel W. Peel (D)
John H. Rogers (D)

California

Senators

George Hearst (D) ta. 1886
John F. Miller (R) d. Mar.
  1886
Leland Stanford (R)
Abram P. Williams (R) s. 1886

Representatives

Charles N. Felton (R)
Barclay Henley (D)
James A. Louttit (R)
Joseph McKenna (R)
Henry H. Markham (R)
William W. Morrow (R)

Colorado

Senators

Thomas M. Bowen (R)
Henry M. Teller (R)

Representatives

George G. Symes (R)

Connecticut

Senators

Joseph R. Hawley (R)
Orville H. Platt (R)

Representatives

John R. Buck (R)
Charles L. Mitchell (D)
Edward W. Seymour (D)
John T. Wait (R)

Delaware

Senators

Thomas F. Bayard (D) r. Mar.
  1885
George Gray (D) s. 1885
Eli Saulsbury (D)

Representatives

Charles B. Lore (D)

Florida

Senators

Wilkinson Call (D)
Charles W. Jones (D)

Representatives

Robert H. M. Davidson (D)
Charles Dougherty (D)

Georgia

Senators

Joseph E. Brown (D)
Alfred H. Colquitt (D)

Representatives

George T. Barnes (D)
James H. Blount (D)
Allen D. Candler (D)
Judson C. Clements (D)
Charles F. Crisp (D)
Nathaniel J. Hammond (D)
Henry R. Harris (D)
Thomas M. Norwood (D)
Seaborn Reese (D)
Henry G. Turner (D)

Illinois

Senators

Shelby M. Cullom (R)
Charles B. Farwell (R) s. Jan.
  1887
John A. Logan (R) d. Dec.
  1886

Representatives

George E. Adams (R)
Joseph G. Cannon (R)
Ransom W. Dunham (R)
John R. Eden (D)
Reuben Ellwood (R) d. 1887
Thomas J. Henderson (R)
Robert R. Hitt (R)
Albert J. Hopkins (R)
Silas Z. Landes (D)
Frank Lawler (D)
William R. Morrison (D)
William H. Neece (D)
Lewis E. Payson (R)
Ralph Plumb (R)
James M. Riggs (D)
Jonathan H. Rowell (R)
William H. Springer (D)
John R. Thomas (R)
Richard W. Townshend (D)
James H. Ward (D)
Nicholas E. Worthington (D)

Indiana

Senators

Benjamin Harrison (R)
Daniel W. Voorhees (D)

Representatives

Thomas M. Browne (R)
William D. Bynum (D)
Thomas R. Cobb (D)
George Ford (D)
William S. Holman (D)
Jonas G. Howard (D)
James T. Johnston (R)
John J. Kleiner (D)
Robert Lowry (D)
Courtland C. Matson (D)
William D. Owen (R)
George W. Steele (R)
Thomas B. Ward (D)

Iowa

Senators

William B. Allison (R)
James F. Wilson (R)

Representatives

Edwin H. Conger (R)
Benjamin T. Frederick (D)
William E. Fuller (R)
Benton J. Hall (D)
David B. Henderson (R)
William P. Hepburn (R)
Adoniram J. Holmes (R)
Joseph Lyman (R)
Jeremiah H. Murphy (D)
Isaac S. Struble (R)
James B. Weaver (Greenback)

Kansas

Senators

John J. Ingalls (R)
Preston B. Plumb (R)

Representatives

John A. Anderson (R)

Edward H. Funston (R)
Lewis Hanback (R)
Edmund N. Morrill (R)
Bishop W. Perkins (R)
Samuel R. Peters (R)
Thomas Ryan (R)

Kentucky

Senators

James B. Beck (D)
Joseph C. S. Blackburn (D)

Representatives

William C. P. Breckinridge (D)
John G. Carlisle (D)
John E. Halsell (D)
Polk Laffoon (D)
James B. McCreary (D)
Thomas A. Robertson (D)
William J. Stone (D)
William P. Taulbee (D)
William H. Wadsworth (R)
Albert S. Willis (D)
Frank L. Wolford (D)

Louisiana

Senators

James B. Eustis (D)
Randall L. Gibson (D)

Representatives

Newton C. Blanchard (D)
Edward J. Gay (D)
Michael Hahn (R) d. Mar. 1886
Alfred B. Irion (D)
J. Floyd King (D)
Louis St. Martin (D)
Nathaniel D. Wallace (D) s. 1886

Maine

Senators

William P. Frye (R)
Eugene Hale (R)

Representatives

Charles A. Boutelle (R)
Nelson Dingley, Jr. (R)
Seth L. Milliken (R)
Thomas B. Reed (R)

Maryland

Senators

Arthur P. Gorman (D)
Ephraim K. Wilson (D)

Representatives

William H. Cole (D) d. July 1886
Barnes Compton (D)
John V. L. Dindlay (D)
Charles H. Gibson (D)
Louis E. McComas (R)
Harry W. Rusk (D) s. 1886
Frank T. Shaw (D)

Massachusetts

Senators

Henry L. Dawes (R)
George F. Hoar (R)

Representatives

Charles H. Allen (R)
Patrick A. Collins (D)
Robert T. Davis (R)
Frederick D. Ely (R)
Edward D. Hayden (R)
John D. Long (R)
Henry B. Lovering (D)
Ambrose A. Ranney (R)
William W. Rice (R)
Francis W. Rockwell (R)
Eben F. Stone (R)
William Whiting (R)

Michigan

Senators

Omar D. Conger (R)
Thomas W. Palmer (R)

Representatives

Julius C. Burrows (R)
Ezra C. Carleton (D)
Charles C. Comstock (D)
Byron M. Cutcheon (R)
Nathaniel B. Eldredge (D)
Spencer O. Fisher (D)
William C. Maybury (D)
Seth C. Moffatt (R)
James O'Donnell (R)
Timothy E. Tarsney (D)
Edwin B. Winans (D)

Minnesota

Senators

Samuel J. R. McMillan (R)
Dwight M. Sabin (R)

Representatives

John B. Gilfillan (R)
Knute Nelson (R)
Horace B. Strait (R)
James B. Wakefield (R)
Milo White (R)

Mississippi

Senators

James Z. George (D)
Lucius Q. C. Lamar (D) r. Mar. 1885
Edward C. Walthall (D) s. 1885

Representatives

John M. Allen (D)
Ethelbert Barksdale (D)
Frederick G. Barry (D)
Thomas C. Catchings (D)
James B. Morgan (D)
Otho R. Singleton (D)
Henry S. Van Eaton (D)

Missouri

Senators

Francis M. Cockrell (D)
George G. Vest (D)

Representatives

Richard P. Bland (D)
James N. Burnes (D)
Martin L. Clardy (D)
William Dawson (D)
Alexander M. Dockery (D)
John M. Glover (D)
John B. Hale (D)
William H. Hatch (D)
John T. Heard (D)
John E. Hutton (D)
John J. O'Neill (D)
William J. Stone (D)
William H. Wade (R)
William Warner (R)

Nebraska

Senators

Charles F. Manderson (R)
Charles H. Van Wyck (R)

Representatives

George W. E. Dorsey (R)
James Laird (R)
Archibald J. Weaver (R)

Nevada

Senators

James G. Fair (D)
John P. Jones (R)

Representatives

William Woodburn (R)

New Hampshire

Senators

Henry W. Blair (R)
Person C. Cheney (R) s. 1886
Austin F. Pike (R) d. Oct. 1886

Representatives

Martin A. Haynes (R)
Jacob H. Gallinger (R)

New Jersey

Senators

John R. McPherson (D)
William J. Sewell (R)

Representatives

James Buchanan (R)
Robert S. Green (D) r. Jan. 1887
George Hires (R)
Herman Lehlbach (R)
William McAdoo (D)

William W. Phelps (R)
James N. Pidcock (D)

New York

Senators

William M. Evarts (R)
Warner Miller (R)

Representatives

John J. Adams (D)
John Arnot, Jr. (D) d. Nov. 1886
Henry Bacon (D) s. 1886
Charles S. Baker (R)
Lewis Beach (D) d. Aug. 1886
Perry Belmont (D)
Archibald M. Bliss (D)
Henry G. Burleigh (R)
Felix Campbell (D)
Timothy J. Campbell (D)
Ira Davenport (R)
Abraham Dowdney (D) d. Dec. 1886
John M. Farquhar (R)
Abram S. Hewitt (D) r. Dec. 1886
Frank Hiscock (R)
Darwin R. James (R)
Frederick A. Johnson
John H. Ketcham (R)
James G. Lindsley (R)
Peter P. Mahoney (D)
Truman A. Merriman (D)
Stephen C. Millard (R)
Nicholas Muller (D)
Abraham X. Parker (R)
Sereno E. Payne (R)
John S. Pindar (D)
Joseph Pulitzer (D) r. Apr. 1886
John G. Sawyer (R)
Walter L. Sessions (R)
William G. Stahlnecker (D)
John T. Spriggs (R)
John Swinburne (R)
Egbert L. Viele (D)
John B. Weber (R)
George West (R)

North Carolina

Senators

Matt W. Ransom (D)
Zebulon B. Vance (D)

Representatives

Risden T. Bennett (D)
William H. H. Cowles (D)
William R. Cox (D)
Wharton J. Green (D)
John S. Henderson (D)
Thomas D. Johnston (D)
James E. O'Hara (R)
James W. Reid (D) r. Nov. 1886
Thomas G. Skinner (D)

Ohio

Senators

Henry B. Payne (D)
John Sherman (R)

Representatives

Charles M. Anderson (D)
Charles E. Brown (R)
Benjamin Butterworth (R)
James E. Campbell (D)
William C. Cooper (R)
William W. Ellsberry (D)
Martin A. Foran (D)
George W. Geddes (D)
Charles H. Grosvenor (R)
William D. Hill (D)
Benjamin Le Fevre (D)
John Little (R)
William McKinley, Jr. (R)
Joseph H. Outhwaite (D)
Jacob Romeis (R)
George E. Seney (D)
Ezra B. Taylor (R)
Isaac H. Taylor (R)
Albert C. Thompson (R)
Adoniram J. Warner (D)
Beriah Wilkins (D)

Oregon

Senators

Joseph N. Dolph (R)
John H. Mitchell (R)

Representatives

Binger Hermann (R)

Pennsylvania

Senators

J. Donald Cameron (R)
John I. Mitchell (R)

Representatives

Louis E. Atkinson (R)
Thomas M. Bayne (R)
Henry H. Bingham (R)
Franklin Bound (R)
Charles E. Boyle (D)
William W. Brown (R)
Charles N. Brumm (Greenback)
Frank C. Bunnell (R)
Jacob M. Campbell (R)
Andrew G. Curtin (D)
Daniel Ermentrout (D)
I. Newton Evans (R)
James B. Everhart (R)
George W. Fleeger (R)
Alfred C. Harmer (R)
John A. Hiestand (R)
Oscar L. Jackson (R)
William D. Kelley (R)
James S. Negley (R)
Charles O'Neill (R)
Edwin S. Osborne (R)
Samuel J. Randall (D)
William L. Scott (D)
Joseph A. Scranton (R)
William H. Sowden (D)
John B. Storm (D)
John A. Swope (D)
Alexander C. White (R)

Rhode Island

Senators

Nelson W. Aldrich (R)

Jonathan Chace (R)

Representatives

Charles H. Page (D) s. 1887
William A. Pirce (R) r. Jan. 1887
Henry J. Spooner (R)

South Carolina

Senators

Matthew C. Butler (D)
Wade Hampton (D)

Representatives

D. Wyatt Aiken (D)
George W. Dargan (D)
Samuel Dibble (D)
John J. Hemphill (D)
William H. Perry (D)
Robert Smalls (R)
George D. Tilman (R)

Tennessee

Senators

Isham G. Harris (D)
Howell E. Jackson (D) r. Apr. 1886
Washington C. Whitthorne (D) s. 1886

Representatives

John G. Ballentine (D)
Andrew J. Caldwell (D)
Presley T. Glass (D)
Leonidas C. Houk (R)
Benton McMillin (D)
John R. Neal (D)
Augustus H. Pettibone (R)
James D. Richardson (D)
John M. Taylor (D)
Zachary Taylor (R)

Texas

Senators

Richard Coke (D)
Samuel B. Maxey (D)

Representatives

William H. Crain (D)
David B. Culberson (D)
James H. Jones (D)
Samuel W. T. Lanham (D)
James F. Miller (D)
Roger Q. Mills (D)
John H. Reagan (D)
Joseph D. Sayers (D)
Charles Stewart (D)
James W. Throckmorton (D)
Olin Wellborn (D)

Vermont

Senators

George F. Edmunds (R)
Justin S. Morrill (R)

Representatives

William W. Grout (R)
John W. Stewart (R)

Virginia

Senators

William Mahone (Readjuster)
Harrison H. Riddleberger (Readjuster)

Representatives

John S. Barbour (D)
James D. Brady (R)
George C. Cabell (D)
Thomas Croxton (D)
John W. Daniel (D)
Harry Libbey (R)
Charles T. O'Ferrall (D)
Connally F. Trigg (D)
John R. Tucker (D)
George D. Wise (D)

West Virginia

Senators

Johnson N. Camden (D)
John E. Kenna (D)

Representatives

Eustace Gibson (D)
Nathan Goff (R)
Charles P. Snyder (D)
William L. Wilson (D)

Wisconsin

Senators

Philetus Sawyer (R)
John C. Spooner (R)

Representatives

Edward S. Bragg (D)
Lucien B. Caswell (R)
Richard W. Guenther (R)
Thomas R. Hudd (D) s. 1886
Robert M. La Follette (R)
Hugh H. Price (R) s. 1887
William T. Price (R) d. Dec. 1886
Joseph Rankin (D) d. Jan. 1886
Isaac Stephenson (R)
Ormsby B. Thomas (R)
Isaac W. Van Schaick (R)

Fiftieth Congress

(Mar. 4, 1887, to
Mar. 3, 1889)

President of the Senate: Vacant
President Pro Tempore of the Senate: John J. Ingalls
Speaker of the House of Representatives: John G. Carlisle

Alabama

Senators

John T. Morgan (D)
James L. Pugh (D)

Representatives

John H. Bankhead (D)
James E. Cobb
Alexander C. Davidson (D)
William H. Forney (D)
Hilary A. Herbert (D)
James T. Jones (D)
William C. Oates (D)
Joseph Wheeler (D)

Arkansas

Senators

James H. Berry (D)
James K. Jones (D)

Representatives

Clifton R. Breckinridge (D)
Poindexter Dunn (D)
Thomas C. McRae (D)
Samuel W. Peel (D)
John H. Rogers (D)

California

Senators

George Hearst (D)
Leland Stanford (R)

Representatives

Marion Biggs (D)
Charles N. Felton (R)
Joseph McKenna (R)
William W. Morrow (R)
Thomas L. Thompson (D)
William Vandever (R)

Colorado

Senators

Thomas M. Bowen (R)
Henry M. Teller (R)

Representatives

George G. Symes (R)

Connecticut

Senators

Joseph R. Hawley (R)
Orville H. Platt (R)

Representatives

Carlos French (D)
Miles T. Granger (D)
Charles A. Russell (R)
Robert J. Vance (D)

Delaware

Senators

George Gray (D)
Eli Saulsbury (D)

Representatives

John B. Penington (D)

Florida

Senators

Wilkinson Call (D)
Samuel Pasco (D)

Representatives

Robert H. M. Davidson (D)
Charles Dougherty (D)

Georgia

Senators

Joseph E. Brown (D)
Alfred H. Colquitt (D)

Representatives

George T. Barnes (D)
James H. Blount (D)
Allen D. Candler (D)
Henry H. Carlton (D)
Judson C. Clements (D)
Charles F. Crisp (D)
Thomas W. Grimes (D)
Thomas M. Norwood (D)
John D. Stewart (D)
Henry G. Turner (D)

Illinois

Senators

Shelby M. Cullom (R)
Charles B. Farwell (R)

Representatives

George E. Adams (R)
George A. Anderson (D)
Jehu Baker (R)
Joseph G. Cannon (R)
Ransom W. Dunham (R)
William H. Gest (R)
Thomas J. Henderson (R)
Robert R. Hitt (R)
Albert J. Hopkins (R)
Silas Z. Landes (D)
Edward Lane (D)
Frank Lawler (D)
William E. Mason (R)
Lewis E. Payson (R)
Ralph Plumb (R)
Philip S. Post (R)
Jonathan H. Rowell (R)
William M. Springer (D)
John R. Thomas (R)
Richard W. Townshend (D)

Indiana

Senators

David Turpie (D)
Daniel W. Voorhess (D)

Representatives

Thomas M. Browne (R)
William D. Bynum (D)
Joseph B. Cheadle (R)
William S. Holman (D)
Alvin P. Hovey (R) r. Jan. 1889
Jonas G. Howard (D)
James T. Johnston (R)
Courtland C. Matson (D)
John H. O'Neall (D)
William D. Owen (R)
Francis B. Posey (R) s. 1889
Benjamin F. Shively (D)
George W. Steele (R)
James B. White

Iowa

Senators

William B. Allison (R)
James F. Wilson (R)

Representatives

Albert R. Anderson (R)
Edwin H. Conger (R)
William E. Fuller (R)
John H. Gear (R)
Walter L. Hayes (D)
David B. Henderson (R)
Adoniram J. Holmes (R)
Daniel Kerr (R)
Joseph Lyman (R)
Isaac S. Struble (R)
James B. Weaver (Democratic-Greenback Laborite)

Kansas

Senators

John J. Ingalls (R)
Preston B. Plumb (R)

Representatives

John A. Anderson (R)
Edward H. Funston (R)
Edmund N. Morrill (R)
Bishop W. Perkins (R)
Samuel R. Peters (R)
Thomas Ryan (R)
Erastus J. Turner (R)

Kentucky

Senators

James B. Beck (D)
Joseph C. S. Blackburn (D)

Representatives

William C. P. Breckinridge (D)
John G. Carlisle (D)
Asher G. Caruth (D)
Hugh F. Finley (R)

W. Godfrey Hunter (R)
Polk Laffoon (D)
James B. McCreary (D)
Alexander B. Montgomery (D)
William J. Stone (D)
William P. Taulbee (D)
George M. Thomas (R)

Louisiana

Senators

James B. Eustis (D)
Randall L. Gibson (D)

Representatives

Newton C. Blanchard (D)
Edward J. Gay (D)
Matthew D. Lagan (D)
Cherubusco Newton (D)
Samuel M. Robertson (D)
Theodore S. Wilkinson (D)

Maine

Senators

William P. Frye (R)
Eugene Hale (R)

Representatives

Charles A. Boutelle (R)
Nelson Dingley, Jr. (R)
Seth L. Milliken (R)
Thomas B. Reed (R)

Maryland

Senators

Arthur P. Gorman (D)
Ephraim K. Wilson (D)

Representatives

Barnes Compton (D)
Charles H. Gibson (D)
Louis E. McComas (R)
Isidor Rayner (D)
Harry W. Rusk (D)
Frank T. Shaw (D)

Massachusetts

Senators

Henry L. Dawes (R)
George F. Hoar (R)

Representatives

Charles H. Allen (R)
Edward Burnett (D)
William Cogswell (R)
Patrick A. Collins (D)
Robert T. Davis (R)
Edward D. Hayden (R)
Henry Cabot Lodge (R)
John D. Long (R)
Leopold Morse (D)
Francis W. Rockwell (R)
John E. Russell (D)
William Whiting (R)

Michigan

Senators

Thomas W. Palmer (R)
Francis B. Stockbridge (R)

Representatives

Edward P. Allen (R)
Mark S. Brewer (R)
Julius C. Burrows (R)
J. Logan Chipman (D)
Byron M. Cutcheon (R)
Spencer O. Fisher (D)
Melbourne H. Ford (D)
Seth C. Moffatt (R) d. Dec. 1887
James O'Donnell (R)
Henry W. Seymour (R) s. 1888
Timothy E. Tarsney (D)
Justin R. Whiting (Greenback, D)

Minnesota

Senators

Cushman K. Davis (R)
Dwight M. Sabin (R)

Representatives

John Lind (R)
John L. MacDonald (D)
Knute Nelson (R)
Edmund Rice (D)
Thomas Wilson (D)

Mississippi

Senators

James Z. George (D)
Edward C. Walthall (D)

Representatives

John M. Allen (D)
Chapman L. Anderson (D)
Frederick G. Barry (D)
Thomas C. Catchings (D)
Charles E. Hooker (D)
James B. Morgan (D)
Thomas R. Stockdale (D)

Missouri

Senators

Francis M. Cockrell (D)
George G. Vest (D)

Representatives

Richard P. Bland (D)
Charles F. Booher (D) s. 1889
James N. Burnes (D)
Martin L. Clardy (D)
Alexander M. Dockery (D)
John M. Glover (D)
William H. Hatch (D)
John T. Heard (D)
John E. Hutton (D)
Charles H. Mansur (D)
John J. O'Neill (D)
William J. Stone (D)

William H. Wade (R)
James P. Walker (D)
William Warner (R)

Nebraska

Senators

Charles F. Manderson (R)
Algernon S. Paddock (R)

Representatives

George W. E. Dorsey (R)
James Laird (R)
John A. McShane (D)

Nevada

Senators

John P. Jones (R)
William M. Stewart (R)

Representatives

William Woodburn (R)

New Hampshire

Senators

Henry W. Blair (R)
William E. Chandler (R)

Representatives

Jacob H. Gallinger (R)
Luther F. McKinney (D)

New Jersey

Senators

Rufus Blodgett (D)
John R. McPherson (D)

Representatives

James Buchanan (R)
George Hires (R)
John Kean (R)
Herman Lehlbach (R)
William McAdoo (D)
William W. Phelps (R)
James N. Pidcock (D)

New York

Senators

William M. Evarts (R)
Frank Hiscock (R)

Representatives

Henry Bacon (D)
Charles S. Baker (R)
James J. Belden (R)
Perry Belmont (D) r. Dec. 1888
Archibald M. Bliss (D)
Lloyd S. Bryce (D)
Felix Campbell (D)
Timothy J. Campbell (D)
W. Bourke Cockran (D)
Samuel S. Cox (D)

Amos J. Cummings (D)
Ira Davenport (R)
Milton De Lano (R)
John M. Farquhar (R)
Ashbel P. Fitch (R)
Thomas S. Flood (R)
Edward W. Greenman (D)
Stephen T. Hopkins (R)
John H. Ketcham (R)
William G. Laidlaw (R)
Peter P. Mahoney (D)
Truman A. Merriman (D)
John H. Moffitt (R)
Newton W. Nutting (R)
Abraham X. Parker (R)
John G. Sawyer (R)
James S. Sherman (R)
Francis B. Spinola (D)
William G. Stahlnecker (D)
Charles Tracey (D)
John B. Weber (R)
George West (R)
Stephen V. White (R)
David Wilber (R)

North Carolina

Senators

Matt W. Ransom (D)
Zebulon B. Vance (D)

Representatives

John M. Brower (R)
William H. H. Cowles (D)
John S. Henderson (D)
Thomas D. Johnston (D)
Louis C. Latham (D)
Charles W. McClammy (D)
John Nichols
Alfred Rowland (D)
Furnifold McL. Simmons (D)

Ohio

Senators

Henry B. Payne (D)
John Sherman (R)

Representatives

Melvin M. Boothman (R)
Charles E. Brown (R)
Benjamin Butterworth (R)
James E. Campbell (D)
William C. Cooper (R)
George W. Crouse (R)
Martin A. Foran (D)
Charles H. Grosvenor (R)
Robert P. Kennedy (R)
William McKinley, Jr. (R)
Joseph H. Outhwaite (D)
Jacob J. Pugsley (R)
Jacob Romeis (R)
George E. Seney (D)
Ezra B. Taylor (R)
Joseph D. Taylor (R)
Albert C. Thompson (R)
Charles P. Wickham (R)
Beriah Wilkins (D)
Elihu S. Williams (R)
Samuel S. Yoder (D)

Oregon

Senators

Joseph N. Dolph (R)
John H. Mitchell (R)

Representatives

Binger Hermann (R)

Pennsylvania

Senators

J. Donald Cameron (R)
Matthew S. Quay (R)

Representatives

Louis E. Atkinson (R)
Thomas M. Bayne (R)
Henry H. Bingham (R)
Franklin Bound (R)
Charles N. Brumm (Greenback)
Charles R. Buckalew (D)
Frank C. Bunnell (R)
John Dalzell (R)
Smedley Darlington (R)
Daniel Ermentrout (D)
Norman Hall (D)
Alfred C. Harmer (R)
John A. Hiestand (R)
Oscar L. Jackson (R)
William D. Kelley (R)
John Lynch (R)
Henry C. McCormick (R)
Welty McCullogh (R)
James T. Maffett (R)
Levi Maish (D)
Charles O'Neill (R)
Edwin S. Osborne (R)
John Patton (R)
Samuel J. Randall (D)
William L. Scott (D)
Edward Scull (R)
William H. Sowden (D)
Robert M. Yardley (R)

Rhode Island

Senators

Nelson W. Aldrich (R)
Jonathan Chace (R)

Representatives

Warren O. Arnold (R)
Henry J. Spooner (R)

South Carolina

Senators

Matthew C. Butler (D)
Wade Hampton (D)

Representatives

James S. Cothran (D)
George W. Dargan (D)
Samuel Dibble (D)
William Elliott (D)
John J. Hemphill (D)
William H. Perry (D)
George D. Tillman (D)

Tennessee

Senators

William B. Bate (D)
Isham G. Harris (D)

Representatives

Roderick R. Butler (R)
Benjamin A. Enloe (D)
Presley T. Glass (D)
Leonidas C. Houk (R)
Benton McMillin (D)
John R. Neal (D)
James Phelan (D)
James D. Richardson (D)
Joseph E. Washington (D)
Washington C. Whitthorne (D)

Texas

Senators

Richard Coke (D)
John H. Reagan (D)

Representatives

Jo Abbott (D)
William H. Crain (D)
David B. Culberson (D)
Silas Hare (D)
Constantine B. Kilgore (D)
Samuel W. T. Lanham (D)
William H. Martin (D)
Roger Q. Mills (D)
Littleton W. Moore (D)
Joseph D. Sayers (D)
Charles Stewart (D)

Vermont

Senators

George F. Edmunds (R)
Justin S. Morrill (R)

Representatives

William W. Grout (R)
John W. Stewart (R)

Virginia

Senators

John W. Daniel (D)
Harrison H. Riddleberger
  (Readjuster)

Representatives

George E. Bowden (R)
Henry Bowen (R)
John R. Brown (R)
Thomas H. B. Browne (R)
William E. Gaines (R)
Samuel I. Hopkins (D)
William H. F. Lee (D)
Charles T. O'Ferrall (D)
George D. Wise (D)
Jacob Yost (R)

West Virginia

Senators

Charles J. Faulkner (D)
John E. Kenna (D)

Representatives

Charles E. Hogg (D)
Nathan Goff (R)
Charles P. Snyder (D)
William L. Wilson (D)

Wisconsin

Senators

Philetus Sawyer (R)
John C. Spooner (R)

Representatives

Lucien B. Caswell (R)
Charles B. Clark (R)
Richard W. Guenther (R)
Nils P. Haugen (R) s. 1888
Thomas R. Hudd (D)
Robert M. La Follette (R)
Henry Smith (People's Party)
Isaac Stephenson (R)
Ormsby B. Thomas (R)

Fifty-First Congress

(Mar. 4, 1889, to
Mar. 3, 1891)

President of the Senate: Levi P. Morton
Presidents Pro Tempore of the Senate: John J. Ingalls; Charles F. Manderson
Speaker of the House of Representatives: Thomas B. Reed

Alabama

Senators

John T. Morgan (D)
James L. Pugh (D)

Representatives

John H. Bankhead (D)
Richard H. Clarke (R)
James E. Cobb
William H. Forney (D)
Hilary A. Herbert (D)
John V. McDuffie (R) s. 1890
William C. Oates (D)
Louis W. Turpin (D) r. June 1890
Joseph Wheeler (D)

Arkansas

Senators

James H. Berry (D)
James K. Jones (D)

Representatives

Clifton R. Breckinridge (D)
William H. Cate (D) r. Mar. 1890
Lewis P. Featherstone (Laborite) s. 1890
Thomas C. McRae (D)
Samuel W. Peel (D)
John H. Rogers (D)

California

Senators

George Hearst (D)
Leland Stanford (R)

Representatives

Marion Biggs (D)
Thomas J. Clunie (D)
John J. De Haven (R) r. Oct. 1890
Thomas J. Geary (D) s. 1890
Joseph McKenna (R)
William W. Morrow (R)
William Vandever (R)

Colorado

Senators

Henry M. Teller (R)
Edward O. Wolcott (R)

Representatives

Hosea Townsend (R)

Connecticut

Senators

Joseph R. Hawley (R)
Orville H. Platt (R)

Representatives

Frederick Miles (R)
Charles A. Russell (R)
William E. Simonds (R)
Washington F. Willcox (D)

Delaware

Senators

George Gray (D)
Anthony Higgins (R)

Representatives

John B. Penington (D)

Florida

Senators

Wilkinson Call (D)
Samuel Pasco (D)

Representatives

Robert Bullock (D)

Robert H. M. Davidson (D)

Georgia

Senators

Joseph E. Brown (D)
Alfred H. Colquitt (D)

Representatives

George T. Barnes (D)
James H. Blount (D)
Allen D. Candler (D)
Henry H. Carlton (D)
Judson C. Clements (D)
Charles F. Crisp (D)
Thomas W. Grimes (D)
Rufus E. Lester (D)
John D. Stewart (D)
Henry G. Turner (D)

Idaho

Senators

William J. McConnell (R) s. 1891
George L. Shoup (R) s. 1890

Representatives

Willis Sweet (R) s. 1890

Illinois

Senators

Shelby M. Cullom (R)
Charles B. Farwell (R)

Representatives

George E. Adams (R)
Joseph G. Cannon (R)
George W. Fithian (D)
William S. Forman (D)
William H. Gest (R)
Thomas J. Henderson (R)
Charles A. Hill (R)
Robert H. Hitt (R)
Albert J. Hopkins (R)
Edward Lane (D)
Frank Lawler (D)
William E. Mason (R)
Lewis E. Payson (R)
Philip S. Post (R)
Jonathan H. Rowell (R)
George W. Smith (R)
William M. Springer (D)
Abner Taylor (R)
Scott Wike (D)
James R. Williams (R)

Indiana

Senators

David Turpie (D)
Daniel W. Voorhees (D)

Representatives

Elijah V. Brookshire (D)
Jason B. Brown (D)
Thomas M. Browne (R)
William D. Bynum (D)

Joseph B. Cheadle (R)
George W. Cooper (D)
William S. Holman (D)
Charles A. O. McClellan (D)
Augustus N. Martin (D)
John H. O'Neall (D)
William D. Owen (R)
William F. Parrett (D)
Benjamin F. Shively (D)

Iowa

Senators

William B. Allison (R)
James F. Wilson (R)

Representatives

Edwin H. Conger (R) r. Oct. 1890
Jonathan P. Dolliver (R)
James P. Flick (R)
John H. Gear (R)
Walter I. Hayes (D)
Edward R. Hays (R) s. 1890
David B. Henderson (R)
Daniel Kerr (R)
John F. Lacey (R)
Joseph R. Reed (R)
Isaac S. Struble (R)
Joseph H. Sweney (R)

Kansas

Senators

John J. Ingalls (R)
Preston B. Plumb (R)

Representatives

John A. Anderson (R)
Edward H. Funston (R)
Harrison Kelley (R)
Edmund N. Morrill (R)
Samuel R. Peters (R)
Bishop W. Perkins (R)
Erastus J. Turner (R)

Kentucky

Senators

James B. Beck (D) d. May 1890
Joseph C. S. Blackburn (D)
John G. Carlisle (D) s. 1890

Representatives

William C. P. Breckinridge (D)
John G. Carlisle (D) r. May 1890
Asher G. Caruth (D)
William W. Dickerson (D) s. June 1890
William T. Ellis (D)
Hugh F. Finley (R)
Isaac H. Goodnight (D)
James B. McCreary (D)
Alexander B. Montgomery (D)
Thomas H. Paynter (D)
William J. Stone (D)
John H. Wilson (R)

Louisiana

Senators

James B. Eustis (D)
Randall L. Gibson (D)

Representatives

Newton C. Blanchard (D)
Charles J. Boatner (D)
Hamilton D. Coleman (R)
Andrew Price (D)
Samuel M. Robertson (D)
Theodore S. Wilkinson (D)

Maine

Senators

William P. Frye (R)
Eugene Hale (R)

Representatives

Charles A. Boutelle (R)
Nelson Dingley, Jr. (R)
Seth L. Milliken (R)
Thomas B. Reed (R)

Maryland

Senators

Arthur P. Gorman (D)
Ephraim K. Wilson (D) d. Feb. 1890

Representatives

Barnes Compton (D) r. May 1890
Charles H. Gibson (D)
Louis E. McComas (R)
Sydney E. Mudd (R) s. 1890
Harry W. Rusk (D)
Henry Stockbridge (R)
Herman Strump (D)

Massachusetts

Senators

Henry L. Dawes (R)
George F. Hoar (R)

Representatives

John F. Andrew (D)
Nathaniel P. Banks (R)
John W. Candler (R)
William Cogswell (R)
Frederic T. Greenhalge (R)
Henry Cabot Lodge (R)
Elijah A. Morse (R)
Joseph H. O'Neil (D)
Charles S. Randall (R)
Francis W. Rockwell (R)
Joseph H. Walker (R)
Rodney Wallace (R)

Michigan

Senators

James McMillan (R)

Francis B. Stockbridge (R)

Representatives

Edward P. Allen (R)
Charles E. Belknap (R)
Aaron T. Bliss (R)
Mark S. Brewer (R)
Julius C. Burrows (R)
J. Logan Chipman (D)
Byron M. Cutcheon (R)
James O'Donnell (R)
Samuel M. Stephenson (R)
Frank W. Wheeler (R)
Justin R. Whiting (D)

Minnesota

Senators

Cushman K. Davis (R)
William D. Washburn (R)

Representatives

Solomon G. Comstock (R)
Mark H. Dunnell (R)
Darwin S. Hall (R)
John Lind (R)
Samuel P. Snider (R)

Mississippi

Senators

James Z. George (D)
Edward C. Walthall (D)

Representatives

John M. Allen (D)
Chapman L. Anderson (D)
Thomas C. Catchings (D)
Charles E. Hooker (D)
Clarke Lewis (D)
James B. Morgan (D)
Thomas R. Stockdale (D)

Missouri

Senators

Francis M. Cockrell (D)
George G. Vest (D)

Representatives

Richard P. Bland (D)
Alexander M. Dockery (D)
Nathan Frank (R)
William H. Hatch (D)
John T. Heard (D)
William M. Kinsey (R)
Charles H. Mansur (D)
Frederick G. Niedringhaus (R)
Richard H. Norton (D)
William J. Stone (D)
John C. Tarsney (D)
William H. Wade (R)
James P. Walker (D) d. July 1890
Robert H. Whitelaw (D) s. 1890
Robert P. C. Wilson (D)

Montana

Senators

Thomas C. Powers (R) s. 1890
Wilbur F. Sanders (R) s. 1890

Representatives

Thomas H. Carter (R)

Nebraska

Senators

Charles F. Manderson (R)
Algernon S. Paddock (R)

Representatives

William J. Connell (R)
George W. E. Dorsey (R)
Gilbert L. Laws (R)

Nevada

Senators

John P. Jones (R)
William M. Stewart (R)

Representatives

Horace F. Bartine (R)

New Hampshire

Senators

Henry W. Blair (R)
William E. Chandler (R)

Representatives

Alonzo Nute (R)
Orren C. Moore (R)

New Jersey

Senators

Rufus Blodgett (D)
John R. McPherson (D)

Representatives

Charles D. Beckwith (R)
Christopher A. Bergen (R)
James Buchanan (R)
Samuel Fowler (D)
Jacob A. Geissenhainer (D)
Herman Lehlbach (R)
William McAdoo (D)

New York

Senators

William M. Evarts (R)
Frank Hiscock (R)

Representatives

Charles S. Baker (R)
James J. Belden (R)

Felix Campbell (D)
John M. Clancy (D)
James W. Covert (D)
Amos J. Cummings (D)
Milton De Lano (R)
Edward J. Dunphy (D)
John M. Farquhar (R)
Ashbel P. Fitch (D)
Thomas S. Flood (R)
Roswell P. Flower (D)
John H. Ketcham (R)
Charles J. Knapp (R)
William G. Laidlaw (R)
Frederick Lansing (R)
John H. McCarthy (D)
Thomas F. Magner (D)
John H. Moffitt (R)
Sereno E. Payne (R)
John S. Pindar (D) s. 1890
John A. Quackenbush (R)
John Quinn (D)
John Raines (R)
John Sanford (R)
John G. Sawyer (R)
James S. Sherman (R)
Francis B. Spinola (D)
William G. Stahlnecker (D)
Moses D. Stivers (R)
Charles Tracey (D)
Charles H. Turner (D)
William C. Wallace (R)
David Wilber (R) d. Apr. 1890
John McC. Wiley (D)

North Carolina

Senators

Matt W. Ransom (D)
Zebulon B. Vance (D)

Representatives

John M. Brower (R)
Benjamin H. Bunn (D)
Henry P. Cheatham (R)
William H. H. Cowles (D)
Hamilton G. Ewart (R)
John S. Henderson (D)
Charles W. McClammy (D)
Alfred Rowland (D)
Thomas G. Skinner (D)

North Dakota

Senators

Lyman R. Casey (R)
Gilbert A. Pierce (R)

Representatives

Henry C. Hansbrough (R)

Ohio

Senators

Henry B. Payne (D)
John Sherman (R)

Representatives

Melvin M. Boothman (R)
Theodore E. Burton (R)
Benjamin Butterworth (R)
John A. Caldwell (R)
William C. Cooper (R)

Charles H. Grosvenor (R)
William E. Haynes (D)
Robert P. Kennedy (R)
William McKinley, Jr. (R)
Henry L. Morey (R)
Joseph H. Outhwaite (D)
James W. Owens (D)
Jacob J. Pugsley (R)
George E. Seney (D)
Martin L. Smyser (R)
Ezra B. Taylor (R)
Joseph D. Taylor (R)
Albert C. Thompson (R)
Charles P. Wickham (D)
Elihu S. Williams (R)
Samuel S. Yoder (D)

Oregon

Senators

Joseph N. Dolph (R)
John H. Mitchell (R)

Representatives

Binger Hermann (R)

Pennsylvania

Senators

J. Donald Cameron (R)
Matthew S. Quay (R)

Representatives

Louis E. Atkinson (R)
Thomas M. Bayne (R)
Henry H. Bingham (R)
Marriott Brosius (R)
David B. Brunner (D)
Charles R. Buckalew (D)
Samuel A. Craig (R)
William C. Culbertson (R)
John Dalzell (R)
Smedley Darlington (R)
Alfred C. Harmer (R)
William D. Kelley (R) d. 1890
James Kerr (D)
Henry C. McCormick (R)
Levi Maish (D)
William Mutchler (D)
Charles O'Neill (R)
Edwin S. Osborne (R)
Samuel J. Randall (D) d. 1890
Joseph W. Ray (D)
James B. Reilly (D)
John E. Reyburn (R) s. 1890
John W. Rife (R)
Joseph A. Scranton (R)
Edward Scull (R)
Charles W. Stone (R) s. 1890
Charles C. Townsend (R)
Richard Vaux (R) s. 1890
Lewis F. Watson (R) d. Aug.
  1890
Myron B. Wright (R)
Robert M. Yardley (R)

Rhode Island

Senators

Nelson W. Aldrich (R)
Jonathan Chace (R) r. Apr.
  1889
Nathan F. Dixon (R) s. 1889

Representatives

Warren O. Arnold (R)
Henry J. Spooner (R)

South Carolina

Senators

Matthew C. Butler (D)
Wade Hampton (D)

Representatives

James S. Cothran (D)
George W. Dargan (D)
Samuel Dibble (D)
William Elliott (D) r. Sept.
  1890
John J. Hemphill (D)
Thomas E. Miller (R) s. 1890
William H. Perry (D)
George D. Tillman (D)

South Dakota

Senators

Richard F. Pettigrew (R)
Gideon C. Moody (R)

Representatives

Oscar S. Gifford (R)
John A. Pickler (R)

Tennessee

Senators

William B. Bate (D)
Isham G. Harris (D)

Representatives

Benjamin A. Enloe (D)
H. Clay Evans (R)
Leonidas C. Houk (R)
Benton McMillin (D)
James Phelan (D) d. Jan. 1891
Rice A. Pierce (D)
James D. Richardson (D)
Alfred A. Taylor (R)
Joseph E. Washington (D)
Washington C. Witthorne (D)

Texas

Senators

Richard Coke (D)
John H. Reagan (D)

Representatives

Jo Abbott (D)
William H. Crain (D)
David B. Culberson (D)
Silas Hare (D)
Constantine B. Kilgore (D)
Samuel W. T. Lanham (D)
William H. Martin (D)
Roger Q. Mills (D)
Littleton W. Moore (D)
Joseph D. Sayers (D)
Charles Stewart (D)

Vermont

Senators

George F. Edmunds (R)
Justin S. Morrill (R)

Representatives

William W. Grout (R)
John W. Stewart (R)

Virginia

Senators

John S. Barbour (D)
John W. Daniel (D)

Representatives

George E. Bowden (R)
Thomas H. B. Browne (R)
John A. Buchanan (D)
Paul C. Edmunds (D)
John M. Langston (R) s. 1890
William H. F. Lee (D)
Posey G. Lester (D)
Charles T. O'Ferrall (D)
Henry St. George Tucker (D)
Edward C. Venable (D) r. Sept.
  1890
Edmund Waddill, Jr. (R) s.
  1890
George D. Wise (R) r. Apr.
  1890

Washington

Senators

John B. Allen (R)
Watson C. Squire (R)

Representatives

John Wilson (R)

West Virginia

Senators

Charles J. Faulkner (D)
John E. Kenna (D)

Representatives

John D. Alderson (D)
George W. Atkinson (R) s.
  1890
J. Monroe Jackson (D) r. Feb.
  1890
John O. Pendleton (D) r. Feb.
  1890
Charles B. Smith (R) s. 1890
William L. Wilson (D)

Wisconsin

Senators

Philetus Sawyer (R)
John C. Spooner (R)

Representatives

Charles Barwig (D)
George H. Brickner (D)
Lucien B. Caswell (R)
Charles B. Clark (R)
Nils P. Haugen (R)
Robert M. La Follette (R)
Myron H. McCord (D)
Ormsby B. Thomas (R)
Isaac W. Van Schaick (R)

Wyoming

Senators

Joseph M. Carey (R) s. 1890
Francis E. Warren (R) s. 1890

Representatives

Clarence D. Clark (R) s. 1890

Fifty-Second Congress

(Mar. 4, 1891, to
Mar. 3, 1893)

President of the Senate: Levi P.
  Morton
*President Pro Tempore of the
  Senate:* Charles F. Manderson
*Speaker of the House of
  Representatives:* Charles F.
  Crisp

Alabama

Senators

John T. Morgan (D)
James L. Pugh (D)

Representatives

John H. Bankhead (D)
Richard H. Clarke (R)
James E. Cobb
William H. Forney (D)
Hilary A. Herbert (D)
William C. Oates (D)
Louis W. Turpin (D)
Joseph Wheeler (D)

Arkansas

Senators

James H. Berry (D)
James K. Jones (D)

Representatives

Clifton R. Breckinridge (D)
William H. Cate (D)
Thomas C. McRae
Samuel W. Peel (D)
William L. Terry (D)

California

Senators

Charles N. Felton (R)
Leland Stanford (R)

Representatives

William W. Bowers (R)
Anthony Caminetti (D)
John T. Cutting (R)
Thomas J. Geary (D)
Samuel G. Hilborn (R) s. 1892
Eugene F. Loud (R)
Joseph McKenna (R) r. Mar.
 1892

Colorado

Senators

Henry M. Teller (R)
Edward O. Wolcott (R)

Representatives

Hosea Townsend (R)

Connecticut

Senators

Joseph R. Hawley (R)
Orville H. Platt (R)

Representatives

Robert E. DeForest (D)
Charles A. Russell (R)
Lewis Sperry (D)
Washington F. Willcox (D)

Delaware

Senators

George Gray (D)
Anthony Higgins (R)

Representatives

John W. Causey (D)

Florida

Senators

Wilkinson Call (D)
Samuel Pasco (D)

Representatives

Robert Bullock (D)
Stephen R. Mallory (D)

Georgia

Senators

Alfred H. Colquitt (D)
John B. Gordon (D)

Representatives

James H. Blount (D)
Charles F. Crisp (D)
Robert W. Everett (D)
Thomas G. Lawson (D)
Rufus E. Lester (D)
Leonidas F. Livingston (D)
Charles L. Moses (D)
Henry G. Turner (D)
Thomas E. Watson (Pop)
Thomas E. Winn (D)

Idaho

Senators

Fred T. Dubois (R)
George L. Shoup (R)

Representatives

Willis Sweet (R)

Illinois

Senators

Shelby M. Cullom (R)
John M. Palmer (D)

Representatives

Samuel T. Busey (D)
Benjamin T. Cable (D)
Allan C. Durborow, Jr. (D)
George W. Fithian (D)
William S. Forman (D)
Thomas J. Henderson (R)
Robert R. Hitt (R)
Albert J. Hopkins (R)
Edward Lane (D)
Lawrence E. McGann (D)
Walter C. Newberry (D)
Philip S. Post (R)
Owen Scott (D)
George W. Smith (R)
Herman W. Snow (D)
William M. Springer (D)
Lewis Steward (D)
Abner Taylor (R)
Scott Wike (D)
James R. Williams (D)

Indiana

Senators

Daniel W. Voorhees (D)
David Turpie (D)

Representatives

John L. Bretz (D)
Elijah V. Brookshire (D)
Jason B. Brown (D)
William D. Bynum (D)
George W. Cooper (D)
William S. Holman (D)
Henry U. Johnson (R)
Charles A. O. McClellan (D)
Augustus N. Martin (D)
William F. Parrett (D)
David H. Patton (D)
Benjamin F. Shively (D)
Daniel W. Waugh (R)

Iowa

Senators

William B. Allison (R)
James F. Wilson (R)

Representatives

Thomas Bowman (D)
Walter H. Butler (D)
Jonathan P. Dolliver (R)
James P. Flick (R)
John T. Hamilton (D)
Walter I. Hayes (D)
David B. Henderson (R)
John A. T. Hull (R)
George D. Perkins (R)
John J. Seerley (D)
Frederick E. White (D)

Kansas

Senators

William A. Peffer (Pop)
Bishop W. Perkins (R) s. 1892
Preston B. Plumb (R) d. 1892

Representatives

William Baker (People's Party)
Case Broderick (R)
Benjamin H. Clover (Farmer's
 Alliance)
John Davis (People's Party)
Edward H. Funston (R)
John G. Otis (People's Party)
Jeremiah Simpson (Pop)

Kentucky

Senators

Joseph C. S. Blackburn (D)
John G. Carlisle (D) r. Feb.
 1893

Representatives

William C. P. Breckinridge (D)
Asher G. Caruth (D)
William W. Dickerson (D)
William T. Ellis (D)
Isaac H. Goodnight (D)
John W. Kendall (D) d. Mar.
 1892
Joseph M. Kendall (D) s. 1892
James B. McCreary (D)
Alexander B. Montgomery (D)
Thomas H. Paynter (D)
William J. Stone (D)
John H. Wilson (R)

Louisiana

Senators

Donelson Caffery (D) s. 1893
Randall L. Gibson (D) d. Dec.
 1892
Edward D. White (D)

Representatives

Newton C. Blanchard (D)
Charles J. Boatner (D)

Matthew D. Lagan (D)
Adolph Meyer (D)
Andrew Price (D)
Samuel M. Robertson (D)

Maine

Senators

William P. Fyre (R)
Eugene Hale (R)

Representatives

Charles A. Boutelle (R)
Nelson Dingley, Jr. (R)
Seth L. Milliken (R)
Thomas B. Reed (R)

Maryland

Senators

Charles H. Gibson (D)
Arthur P. Gorman (D)

Representatives

John B. Brown (D) s. 1892
Barnes Compton (D)
William M. McKaig (D)
Henry Page (D) r. Sept. 1892
Isidor Rayner (D)
Harry W. Rusk (D)
Herman Stump (D)

Massachusetts

Senators

Henry L. Dawes (R)
George F. Hoar (R)

Representatives

John F. Andrew (D)
William Cogswell (R)
Frederick S. Coolidge (D)
John C. Crosby (D)
Sherman Hoar (D)
Henry Cabot Lodge (R) r. Mar.
 1893
Elijah A. Morse (R)
Joseph H. O'Neil (D)
Charles S. Randall (R)
Moses T. Stevens (D)
Joseph H. Walker (R)
George F. Williams (D)

Michigan

Senators

James McMillan (R)
Francis B. Stockbridge (R)

Representatives

Charles E. Belknap (R)
Julius C. Burrows (R)
J. Logan Chipman (D)
Melbourne H. Ford (D) d. Apr.
 1891
James S. Gorman (D)
James O'Donnell (R)
Samuel M. Stephenson (R)
Byron G. Stout (D)

Thomas A. E. Weadock (D)
Harrison H. Wheeler (R)
Justin R. Whiting (Greenback, D)
Henry M. Youmans (D)

Minnesota

Senators

Cushman K. Davis (R)
William D. Washburn (R)

Representatives

James N. Castle (D)
Osee M. Hall (D)
Kittel Halvorson (Farmer's Alliance)
William H. Harries (D)
John Lind (R)

Mississippi

Senators

James Z. George (D)
Edward C. Walthall (D)

Representatives

John M. Allen (D)
Joseph H. Beeman (D)
Thomas C. Catchings (D)
Charles E. Hooker (D)
John C. Kyle (D)
Clarke Lewis (D)
Thomas R. Stockdale (D)

Missouri

Senators

Francis M. Cockrell (D)
George G. Vest (D)

Representatives

Marshall Arnold (D)
Richard P. Bland (D)
Samuel Byrns (D)
Seth W. Cobb (D)
David A. De Armond (D)
Alexander M. Dockery (D)
Robert W. Fyan (D)
William H. Hatch (D)
John T. Heard (D)
Charles H. Mansur (D)
Richard H. Norton (D)
John J. O'Neill (D)
John C. Tarsney (D)
Robert P. C. Wilson (D)

Montana

Senators

Thomas C. Power (R)
Wilbur F. Sanders (R)

Representatives

William W. Dixon (D)

Nebraska

Senators

Charles F. Manderson (R)
Algernon S. Paddock (R)

Representatives

William Jennings Bryan (D)
Omer M. Kem (Pop)
William A. McKeighan (D)

Nevada

Senators

John P. Jones (R)
William M. Stewart (R)

Representatives

Horace F. Bartine (R)

New Hampshire

Senators

William E. Chandler (R)
Jacob H. Gallinger (R)

Representatives

Warren F. Daniell (D)
Luther F. McKinney (D)

New Jersey

Senators

Rufus Blodgett (D)
John R. McPherson (D)

Representatives

Christopher A. Bergen (R)
James Buchanan (R)
Cornelius A. Cadmus (D)
Thomas D. English (D)
Samuel Fowler (D)
Jacob A. Geissenhainer (D)
Edward F. McDonald (D) d. Nov. 1892

New York

Senators

David B. Hill (D) s. 1892
Frank Hiscock (R)

Representatives

Henry Bacon (D)
James J. Belden (R)
Henry W. Bentley (D)
Thomas L. Bunting (D)
Timothy J. Campbell (D)
Alfred C. Chapin (D) r. Nov. 1892
John M. Clancy (D)
W. Bourke Cockran (D)
William J. Coombs (D)
James W. Covert (D)
Isaac N. Cox (D)
Amos J. Cummings (D)

Newton M. Curtis (R)
Edward J. Dunphy (D)
John R. Fellows (D)
Ashbel P. Fitch (D)
Halbert S. Greenleaf (D)
Warren B. Hooker (R)
John H. Ketcham (R)
Joseph J. Little (D)
Daniel N. Lockwood (D)
Thomas F. Magner (D)
Sereno E. Payne (R)
John A. Quackenbush (R)
John Raines (R)
George W. Ray (R)
Hosea H. Rockwell (D)
John Sanford (R)
William G. Stahlnecker (D)
Charles Tracey (D)
George Van Horn (D)
James W. Wadsworth (D)
J. De Witt Warner (D)
John M. Wever (R)

North Carolina

Senators

Matt W. Ransom (D)
Zebulon B. Vance (D)

Representatives

Sydenham B. Alexander (D)
William A. B. Branch (D)
Benjamin H. Bunn (D)
Henry P. Cheatham (R)
William H. H. Cowles (D)
William T. Crawford (D)
Benjamin F. Grady (D)
John S. Henderson (D)
Archibald H. A. Williams (D)

North Dakota

Senators

Lyman R. Casey (R)
Henry C. Hansbrough (R)

Representatives

Martin N. Johnson (R)

Ohio

Senators

Calvin S. Brice (D)
John Sherman (R)

Representatives

John A. Caldwell (R)
Robert E. Doan (R)
Dennis D. Donovan (D)
James Irvine Dungan (D)
William H. Enochs (D)
Martin K. Gantz (D)
Darius D. Hare (D)
Michael D. Harter (D)
William E. Haynes (D)
George W. Houk (D)
Tom L. Johnson (D)
Fernando C. Layton (D)
Lewis P. Ohliger (D) s. 1892
Joseph H. Outhwaite (D)
James W. Owens (D)
John M. Pattison (D)

Albert J. Pearson (D)
Bellamy Storer (R)
Ezra B. Taylor (R)
Joseph D. Taylor (R)
Vincent A. Taylor (R)
John G. Warwick (D)

Oregon

Senators

Joseph N. Dolph (R)
John H. Mitchell (R)

Representatives

Binger Hermann (R)

Pennsylvania

Senators

J. Donald Cameron (R)
Matthew S. Quay (R)

Representatives

Lemuel Amerman (D)
Louis E. Atkinson (R)
Frank E. Beltzhoover (D)
Henry H. Bingham (R)
Marriott Brosius (R)
David B. Brunner (D)
Alexander K. Craig (D) d. 1892
John Dalzell (R)
Eugene P. Gillespie (D)
Matthew Griswold (R)
Edwin Hallowell (D)
Alfred C. Harmer (R)
Albert C. Hopkins (R)
George F. Huff (R)
George F. Kribbs (D)
William McAleer (D)
William Mutchler (D)
Charles O'Neill (R)
James B. Reilly (D)
John E. Reyburn (R)
John W. Rife (R)
John B. Robinson (R)
Edward Scull (R)
George W. Shonk (R)
William A. Sipe (D) s. 1892
Andrew Stewart (R) r. Feb. 1892
Charles W. Stone (R)
William A. Stone (R)
Simon P. Wolverton (D)
Myron B. Wright (R)

Rhode Island

Senators

Nelson W. Aldrich (R)
Nathan F. Dixon (R)

Representatives

Oscar Lapham (D)
Charles H. Page (D)

South Carolina

Senators

Matthew C. Butler (D)
John L. M. Irby (D)

Representatives

William H. Brawley (D)
William Elliott (D)
John J. Hemphill (D)
George Johnstone (D)
John I. McLaurin (D) s. 1892
George W. Shell (D)
Eli T. Stackhouse (D) d. June 1892
George D. Tillman (D)

South Dakota

Senators

James H. Kyle
Richard F. Pettigrew (R)

Representatives

John R. Gamble (R) d. Aug. 1891
John L. Jolley (R)
John A. Pickler (R)

Tennessee

Senators

William B. Bate (D)
Isham G. Harris (D)

Representatives

Nicholas N. Cox (D)
Benjamin A. Enloe (D)
John C. Houk (R)
Benton McMillin (D)
Josiah Patterson (D)
Rice A. Pierce (D)
James D. Richardson (D)
Henry C. Snodgrass (D)
Alfred A. Taylor (R)
Joseph E. Washington (D)

Texas

Senators

Horace Chilton (D) ta. 1891
Richard Coke (D)
Roger Q. Mills (D) s. 1892
John H. Reagan (D) r. 1891

Representatives

Jo Abbott (D)
Edwin Le Roy Antony (D) s. 1892
Joseph W. Bailey (D)
William H. Crain (D)
David B. Culberson (D)
Constantine B. Kilgore (D)
Samuel W. T. Lanham (D)
John B. Long (D)
Roger Q. Mills (D) r. Mar. 1892
Littleton W. Moore (D)
Joseph D. Sayers (D)
Charles Stewart (D)

Vermont

Senators

George F. Edmunds (R) r. Nov. 1891
Justin S. Morrill (R)
Redfield Proctor (R) s. 1891

Representatives

William W. Grout (R)
H. Henry Powers (R)

Virginia

Senators

John S. Barbour (D) d. May 1892
John W. Daniel (D)
Eppa Hunton (D) s. 1892

Representatives

John A. Buchanan (D)
Paul C. Edmunds (D)
James F. Epes (D)
William A. Jones (D)
John W. Lawson (D)
Posey G. Lester (D)
Elisha E. Meredith (D)
Charles T. O'Ferrall (D)
Henry St. George Tucker (D)
George D. Wise (D)

Washington

Senators

John B. Allen (R)
Watson C. Squire (R)

Representatives

John L. Wilson (R)

West Virginia

Senators

Johnson N. Camden (D) s. 1893
Charles J. Faulkner (D)
John E. Kenna (D) s. Jan. 1893

Representatives

John D. Alderson (D)
James Capehart (D)
John O. Pendleton (D)
William L. Wilson (D)

Wisconsin

Senators

Philetus Sawyer (R)
William F. Vilas (D)

Representatives

Clinton Babbitt (D)
Charles Barwig (D)
George H. Brickner (D)
Allen R. Bushnell (D)

Frank P. Coburn (D)
Nils P. Haugen (R)
Thomas Lynch (D)
Lucas M. Miller (D)
John L. Mitchell (D)

Wyoming

Senators

Joseph M. Carey (R)
Francis E. Warren (R)

Representatives

Clarence D. Clark (R)

Fifty-Third Congress

(Mar. 4, 1893, to Mar. 3, 1895)

President of the Senate: Adlai E. Stevenson
Presidents Pro Tempore of the Senate: Charles F. Manderson; Isham G. Harris; Matt W. Ransom
Speaker of the House of Representatives: Charles F. Crisp

Alabama

Senators

John T. Morgan (D)
James L. Pugh (D)

Representatives

John H. Bankhead (D)
Richard H. Clarke (D)
James E. Cobb
William H. Denson (D)
George P. Harrison (D) s. 1894
William C. Oates (D) r. Nov. 1894
Gaston A. Robbins (D)
Jesse F. Stallings (D)
Louis W. Turpin (D)
Joseph Wheeler (D)

Arkansas

Senators

James H. Berry (D)
James K. Jones (D)

Representatives

Clifton R. Breckinridge (D) r. Aug. 1894
Hugh A. Dinsmore (D)
John S. Little (D) s. 1894
Philip D. McCulloch, Jr. (D)
Thomas C. McRae (D)
Robert Neill (D)
William L. Terry (D)

California

Senators

George C. Perkins (R) s. 1893
Leland Stanford (R) d. 1893
Stephen M. White (D)

Representatives

William W. Bowers (R)
Anthony Caminetti (D)
Marion Cannon (People's Party)
Warren B. English (D) s. 1894
Thomas L. Geary (D)
Samuel G. Hilborn (R) r. Apr. 1894
Eugene F. Loud (R)
James G. Maguire (D)

Colorado

Senators

Henry M. Teller (R)
Edward O. Wolcott (R)

Representatives

John C. Bell (D)
Lafayette Pence (D)

Connecticut

Senators

Joseph R. Hawley (R)
Orville H. Platt (R)

Representatives

Robert E. DeForest (D)
James P. Pigott (D)
Charles A. Russell (R)
Lewis Sperry (D)

Delaware

Senators

George Gray (D)
Anthony Higgins (R)

Representatives

John W. Causey (D)

Florida

Senators

Wilkinson Call (D)
Samuel Pasco (D)

Representatives

Charles M. Cooper (D)
Stephen R. Mallory (D)

Georgia

Senators

Alfred H. Colquitt (D) d. Mar. 1894

John B. Gordon (D)
Patrick Walsh (D) s. 1894

Representatives

James C. C. Black (D)
Thomas B. Cabaniss (D)
Charles F. Crisp (D)
Thomas G. Lawson (D)
Rufus E. Lester (D)
Leonidas F. Livingston (D)
John W. Maddox (D)
Charles L. Moses (D)
Benjamin E. Russell (D)
Farish C. Tate (D)
Henry G. Turner (D)

Idaho

Senators

Fred T. Dubois (R)
George L. Shoup (R)

Representatives

Willis Sweet (R)

Illinois

Senators

Shelby M. Cullom (R)
John M. Palmer (R)

Representatives

J. Frank Aldrich (R)
John C. Black (D) r. Jan. 1895
Joseph G. Cannon (R)
Robert A. Childs (R)
Allan C. Durborow, Jr. (D)
George W. Fithian (D)
William S. Forman (D)
Benjamin F. Funk (R)
Julius Golozier (D)
Thomas J. Henderson (R)
Robert R. Hitt (R)
Albert J. Hopkins (R)
Andrew J. Hunter (D)
Edward Lane (D)
John J. McDannold (D)
Lawrence E. McGann (D)
Benjamin F. Marsh (R)
Philip S. Post (R) d. Jan. 1895
George W. Smith (R)
William M. Springer (D)
Hamilton K. Wheeler (R)
James R. Williams (D)

Indiana

Senators

David Turpie (D)
Daniel W. Voorhees (D)

Representatives

John L. Bretz (D)
Elijah V. Brookshire (D)
Jason B. Brown (D)
William D. Bynum (D)
Charles G. Conn (D)
George W. Cooper (D)
Thomas Hammond (D)
William S. Holman (D)
Henry U. Johnson (R)

William F. McNagny (D)
Augustus N. Martin (D)
Arthur H. Taylor (D)
Daniel W. Waugh (R)

Iowa

Senators

William B. Allison (R)
James F. Wilson (R)

Representatives

Robert G. Cousins (R)
Jonathan P. Dolliver (R)
John H. Gear (R)
Alva L. Hager (R)
Walter I. Hayes (D)
David B. Henderson (R)
William P. Hepburn (R)
John A. T. Hull (R)
John F. Lacey (R)
George D. Perkins (R)
Thomas Updegraff (R)

Kansas

Senators

John Martin (D)
William A. Peffer (Pop)

Representatives

William Baker (People's Party)
Case Broderick (R)
Charles Curtis (R)
John Davis (People's Party)
Edward H. Funston r. Aug. 1894
William A. Harris (Pop)
Thomas J. Hudson (Progressive)
Horace L. Moore (D) s. 1894
Jeremiah Simpson (Progressive)

Kentucky

Senators

Joseph C. S. Blackburn (D)
William Lindsay (D)

Representatives

Silas Adams (R)
William M. Beckner (D) s. 1894
Albert S. Berry (D)
William C. P. Breckinridge (D)
Asher G. Caruth (D)
William T. Ellis (D)
Isaac H. Goodnight (D)
Marcus C. Lisle (D) d. July 1894
James B. McCreary (D)
Alexander B. Montgomery (D)
Thomas H. Paynter (D) r. Jan. 1895
William J. Stone (D)

Louisiana

Senators

Newton C. Blanchard (D) s. 1894

Donelson Caffery (D)
Edward D. White (D) r. Mar. 1894

Representatives

Newton C. Blanchard (R) r. Mar. 1894
Charles J. Boatner (D)
Robert C. Davey (D)
Adolph Meyer (D)
Henry W. Ogden (D) s. 1894
Andrew Price (D)
Samuel M. Robertson (D)

Maine

Senators

William P. Frye (R)
Eugene Hale (R)

Representatives

Charles A. Boutelle (R)
Nelson Dingley, Jr. (R)
Seth L. Milliken (R)
Thomas B. Reed (R)

Maryland

Senators

Charles H. Gibson (D)
Arthur P. Gorman (D)

Representatives

Robert F. Bratton (D)
Charles E. Coffin (R) s. 1894
Barnes Compton (D) r. May 1894
W. Laird Henry (D) s. 1894
William M. McKaig (D)
Isidor Rayner (D)
Harry W. Rusk (D)
J. Fred C. Talbott (D)

Massachusetts

Senators

George F. Hoar (R)
Henry Cabot Lodge (R)

Representatives

Lewis D. Apsley (R)
William Cogswell (R)
William F. Draper (R)
William Everett (D)
Frederick H. Gillett (R)
Samuel W. McCall (R)
Michael J. McEttrick (D)
Elijah A. Morse (R)
Joseph H. O'Neill (D)
Charles S. Randall (R)
Moses T. Stevens (D)
Joseph H. Walker (R)
Ashley B. Wright (R)

Michigan

Senators

Julius C. Burrows (R) s. 1895
James McMillan (R)

Francis B. Stockbridge (R) d. Apr. 1894
John Patton, Jr. (R) ta. 1894

Representatives

David D. Aitken (R)
John Avery (R)
Julius C. Burrows (R) r. 1895
J. Logan Chipman (D) d. Aug. 1893
James S. Gorman (D)
Levi T. Griffin (D)
William S. Linton (R)
John W. Moon (R)
George F. Richardson (D)
Samuel M. Stephenson (R)
Henry F. Thomas (R)
Thomas A. E. Weadock (D)
Justin R. Whiting (Greenback)

Minnesota

Senators

Cushman K. Davis (R)
William D. Washburn (R)

Representatives

Melvin R. Baldwin (D)
Haldor E. Boen (People's Party)
Loren Fletcher (R)
Osee M. Hall (D)
Andrew R. Kiefer (R)
James T. McCleary (R)
James A. Tawney (R)

Mississippi

Senators

James Z. George (D)
Anselm J. McLaurin (D) s. 1894
Edward C. Walthall (D) r. Jan. 1894

Representatives

John M. Allen (D)
Thomas C. Catchings (D)
Charles E. Hooker (D)
John C. Kyle (D)
Hernando D. Money (D)
Thomas R. Stockdale (D)
John Sharp Williams (D)

Missouri

Senators

Francis M. Cockrell (D)
George G. Vest (D)

Representatives

Marshall Arnold (D)
Richard Bartholdt (R)
Richard P. Bland (D)
Daniel D. Burns (D)
Champ Clark (D)
Seth W. Cobb (D)
David A. De Armond (D)
Alexander M. Dockery (D)
Robert W. Fyan (D)
Uriel S. Hall (D)
William H. Hatch (D)

John T. Heard (D)
Charles F. Joy (R) r. Apr. 1894
Charles H. Morgan (D)
John J. O'Neill (D) s. 1894
John C. Tarsney (D)

Montana

Senators

Lee Mantle (R)
Thomas C. Power (R)

Representatives

Charles S. Hartman (R)

Nebraska

Senators

William V. Allen (Pop)
Charles F. Manderson (R)

Representatives

William Jennings Bryan (D)
Eugene J. Hainer (R)
Omer M. Kem (Pop)
William McKeighan
George D. Meiklejohn (R)
David H. Mercer (R)

Nevada

Senators

John P. Jones (R)
William M. Stewart (R)

Representatives

Francis G. Newlands (D)

New Hampshire

Senators

William E. Chandler (R)
Jacob H. Gallinger (R)

Representatives

Henry M. Baker (R)
Henry W. Blair (R)

New Jersey

Senators

John R. McPherson (D)
James Smith, Jr. (D)

Representatives

Cornelius A. Cadmus (D)
Johnston Cornish (D)
John T. Dunn (D)
Thomas D. English (D)
George B. Fielder (D)
John J. Gardner (D)
Jacob A. Geissenhainer (D)
Henry C. Loudenslager (R)

New York

Senators

David B. Hill (D)
Edward Murphy, Jr. (D)

Representatives

Franklin Bartlett (D)
James J. Belden (R)
Timothy J. Campbell (D)
Charles A. Chickering (R)
John M. Clancy (D)
W. Bourke Cockran (D)
William J. Coombs (D)
James W. Covert (D)
Amos J. Cummings (D) r. Nov. 1893
Newton M. Curtis (R)
Charles Daniels (R)
Edward J. Dunphy (D)
John R. Fellows (D) r. Dec. 1893
Ashbel P. Fitch (D) r. Dec. 1893
Charles W. Gillet (R)
John H. Graham (D)
Charles D. Haines (D)
Joseph C. Hendrix (D)
Warren B. Hooker (R)
Jacob Le Fever (R)
Daniel N. Lockweed (D)
Thomas F. Magner (D)
Francis Marvin (R)
Sereno E. Payne (R)
Lemuel E. Quigg (R) s. 1894
George W. Ray (R)
William Ryan (D)
Simon J. Schermerhorn (D)
James S. Sherman (R)
Daniel E. Sickles (D)
Isidor Straus (D) s. 1894
Charles Tracey (D)
John Van Voorhis (R)
James W. Wadsworth (R)
J. De Witt Warner (D)
John M. Wever (R)

North Carolina

Senators

Thomas J. Jarvis (D) ta. 1894
Jeter C. Pritchard (R) s. 1895
Matt W. Ransom (D)
Zebulon B. Vance (D) d. Apr. 1894

Representatives

Sydenham B. Alexander (D)
William H. Bower (D)
William A. B. Branch (D)
Benjamin H. Bunn (D)
William T. Crawford (D)
Benjamin F. Grady (D)
John S. Henderson (D)
Thomas Settle (R)
Frederick A. Woodard (D)

North Dakota

Senators

Henry C. Hansbrough (R)
William N. Roach (D)

Representatives

Martin N. Johnson (R)

Ohio

Senators

Calvin S. Brice (D)
John Sherman (R)

Representatives

Jacob H. Bromwell (R) s. 1894
Hezekiah S. Bundy (R)
John A. Caldwell (R) r. May 1894
Dennis D. Donovan (D)
Charles H. Grosvenor (R)
Darius D. Hare (D)
Michael D. Harter (D)
George W. Houk (D) d. Feb. 1894
George W. Hulick (R)
George P. Ikirt (D)
Tom L. Johnson (D)
Fernando C. Layton (D)
Stephen A. Northway (R)
Joseph H. Outhwaite (D)
Albert J. Pearson (D)
James A. D. Richards (D)
Bryon F. Ritchie (D)
Paul J. Sorg (D) s. 1894
Bellamy Storer (R)
Luther M. Strong (R)
Henry C. Van Voorhis (R)
William J. White (R)
George W. Wilson (R)

Oregon

Senators

Joseph N. Dolph (R)
John H. Mitchell (R)

Representatives

William R. Ellis (R)
Binger Hermann (R)

Pennsylvania

Senators

J. Donald Cameron (R)
Matthew S. Quay (R)

Representatives

Robert Adams, Jr. (R) s. 1894
Frank E. Beltzhoover (D)
Henry H. Bingham (R)
Marriott Brosius (R)
John Dalzell (R)
Constantine J. Erdman (D)
Galusha A. Grow (R) s. 1894
Alfred C. Harmer (R)
Daniel B. Heiner (R)
Josiah D. Hicks (R)
William H. Hines (D)
Albert C. Hopkins (R)
Edwin J. Jorden (R) s. 1895
George F. Kribbs (D)
William Lilly (R) d. Dec. 1893
William McAleer (D)
Alexander McDowell (R)
Thaddeus M. Mahon (R)

Howard Mutchler (D)
Charles O'Neill (R) d. Nov. 1893
Thomas W. Phillips (R)
James B. Reilly (D)
John E. Reyburn (R)
John B. Robinson (R)
Joseph A. Scranton (R)
Joseph C. Sibley (D)
William A. Sipe (D)
Charles W. Stone (R)
William A. Stone (R)
Irving P. Wanger (R)
Simon P. Wolverton (D)
Ephraim M. Woomer (R)
Myron B. Wright (R) d. Nov. 1894

Rhode Island

Senators

Nelson W. Aldrich (R)
Nathan F. Dixon (R)

Representatives

Oscar Lapham (D)
Charles H. Page (D)

South Carolina

Senators

Matthew C. Butler (D)
John L. M. Irby (D)

Representatives

William H. Brawley (D) r. Feb. 1894
James F. Izlar (D) s. 1894
Asbury C. Latimer (D)
John L. McLaurin (D)
George W. Murray (R)
George W. Shell (D)
Thomas J. Strait (D)
W. Jasper Talbert (D)

South Dakota

Senators

James H. Kyle (R)
Richard F. Pettigrew (R)

Representatives

William V. Lucas (R)
John A. Pickler (R)

Tennessee

Senators

William B. Bate (D)
Isham G. Harris (D)

Representatives

Nicholas N. Cox (D)
Benjamin A. Enloe (D)
John C. Houk (R)
James C. McDearmon (D)
Benton McMillin (D)
Josiah Patterson (D)
James D. Richardson (D)

Henry C. Snodgrass (D)
Alfred A. Taylor (R)
Joseph E. Washington (D)

Texas

Senators

Richard Coke (D)
Robert Q. Mills (D)

Representatives

Jo Abbott (D)
Joseph W. Bailey (D)
Charles K. Bell (D)
Jeremiah V. Cockrell (D)
Samuel B. Cooper (D)
William H. Crain (D)
David B. Culberson (D)
Walter Gresham (D)
Joseph C. Hutcheson (D)
Constantine B. Kilgore (D)
Thomas M. Paschal (D)
George C. Pendleton (D)
Joseph D. Sayers (D)

Vermont

Senators

Justin S. Morrill (R)
Redfield Proctor (R)

Representatives

William W. Grout (R)
H. Henry Powers (R)

Virginia

Senators

John W. Daniel (D)
Eppa Hunton (D)

Representatives

Paul C. Edmunds (D)
James F. Epes (D)
William A. Jones (D)
James W. Marshall (D)
Elisha E. Meredith (D)
Charles T. O'Ferrall (D) r. Dec.
  1893
Claude A. Swanson (D)
Henry St. George Tucker (D)
Smith S. Turner (D) s. 1894
D. Gardiner Tyler (D)
George D. Wise (D)

Washington

Senators

Watson C. Squire (R)
John L. Wilson (R) s. 1895

Representatives

William H. Doolittle (R)
John L. Wilson (R) r. Feb.
  1895

West Virginia

Senators

Johnson N. Camden (D)
Charles J. Faulkner (D)

Representatives

John D. Alderson (D)
James Capehart (D)
John O. Pendleton (D)
William L. Wilson (D)

Wisconsin

Senators

John L. Mitchell (D)
William F. Vilas (D)

Representatives

Joseph W. Babcock (R)
Lyman E. Barnes (D)
Charles Barwig (D)
George H. Brickner (D)
Henry Allen Cooper (R)
Michael Griffin (R) s. 1894
Nils P. Haugen (R)
Thomas Lynch (D)
George B. Shaw (R) d. Aug.
  1894
Peter J. Somers (D)
Owen A. Wells (D)

Wyoming

Senators

Joseph M. Carey (R)
Clarence D. Clark (R) s. 1895

Representatives

Henry A. Coffeen (D)

Fifty-Fourth Congress

(Mar. 4, 1895, to
Mar. 3, 1897)

President of the Senate: Adlai
  E. Stevenson
*President Pro Tempore of the
  Senate:* William P. Frye
*Speaker of the House of
  Representatives:* Thomas B.
  Reed

Alabama

Senators

John T. Morgan (D)
James L. Pugh (D)

Representatives

Truman H. Aldrich (R) s. 1896
William F. Aldrich (R) s. 1896
John H. Bankhead (D)
Richard H. Clarke (D)

James E. Cobb r. Apr. 1896
Albert T. Goodwyn (D) s. 1896
George P. Harrison (D)
Milford W. Howard (Pop)
Gaston A. Robbins (D) r. Mar.
  1896
Jesse F. Stallings (D)
Oscar W. Underwood (D) r.
  1896
Joseph Wheeler (D)

Arkansas

Senators

James H. Berry (D)
James K. Jones (D)

Representatives

Hugh A. Dinsmore (D)
John S. Little (D)
Philip D. McCulloch, Jr. (D)
Thomas C McRae (D)
Robert Neill (D)
William L. Terry (D)

California

Senators

George C. Perkins (R)
Stephen M. White (D)

Representatives

John A. Barham (R)
William W. Bowers (R)
Samuel G. Hillborn (R)
Grove L. Johnson (R)
Eugene F. Loud (R)
James McLachlan (R)
James G. Maguire (D)

Colorado

Senators

Henry M. Teller (R)
Edward O. Wolcott (R)

Representatives

John C. Bell (D)
John F. Shafroth (R)

Connecticut

Senators

Joseph R. Hawley (R)
Orville H. Platt (R)

Representatives

E. Stevens Henry (R)
Ebenezer J. Hill (R)
Charles A. Russell (R)
Nehemiah D. Sperry (R)

Delaware

Senators

George Gray (D)

Richard R. Kennedy (D) s.
  1897

Representatives

Jonathan S. Willis (R)

Florida

Senators

Wilkinson Call (D)
Samuel Pasco (D)

Representatives

Charles M. Cooper (D)
Stephen M. Sparkman (D)

Georgia

Senators

Augustus O. Bacon (D)
John B. Gordon (D)

Representatives

Charles L. Bartlett (D)
James C. C. Black (D)
Charles F. Crisp (D) d. Oct.
  1896
Charles R. Crisp (D) s. 1896
Thomas G. Lawson (D)
Rufus E. Lester (D)
Leonidas F. Livingston (D)
John W. Maddox (D)
Charles L. Moses (D)
Benjamin E. Russell (D)
Farish C. Tate (D)
Henry G. Turner (D)

Idaho

Senators

Fred T. Dubois (R)
George L. Shoup (R)

Representatives

Edgar Wilson (R)

Illinois

Senators

Shelby M. Cullom (R)
John McA. Palmer (D)

Representatives

J. Frank Aldrich (R)
Hugh R. Belknap (R)
Orlando Burrell (R)
Joseph G. Cannon (R)
James A. Connolly (R)
Edward D. Cooke (R)
Finis E. Downing (R) r. June
  1896
George E. Foss (R)
Joseph V. Graff (R)
William F. L. Hadley (R)
Robert R. Hitt (R)
Albert J. Hopkins (R)
William Lorimer (R)

Lawrence E. McGann (D) r.
 Dec. 1895
Benjamin F. Marsh (R)
Everett J. Murphy (R)
George W. Prince (R)
Walter Reeves (R)
John I. Rinaker (R) s. 1896
George W. Smith (R)
Vespasian Warner (R)
George E. White (R)
Benson Wood (R)
Charles W. Woodman (R)

Indiana

Senators

David Turpie (D)
Daniel W. Voorhees (D)

Representatives

George W. Faris (R)
J. Frank Hanly (R)
Alexander M. Hardy (R)
Jethro A. Hatch (R)
James A. Hemenway (R)
Charles L. Henry (R)
Henry U. Johnson (R)
Jacob D. Leighty (R)
Jesse Overstreet (R)
Lemuel W. Royse (R)
George W. Steele (R)
Robert J. Tracewell (R)
James E. Watson (R)

Iowa

Senators

William B. Allison (R)
John H. Gear (R)

Representatives

Samuel M. Clark (R)
Robert G. Cousins (R)
George M. Curtis (R)
Jonathan P. Dolliver (R)
Alva L. Hager (R)
David B. Henderson (R)
William P. Hepburn (R)
John A. T. Hull (R)
John F. Lacey (R)
George D. Perkins (R)
Thomas Updegraff (R)

Kansas

Senators

Lucien Baker (R)
William A. Peffer (Pop)

Representatives

William Baker (People's Party)
Richard W. Blue (R)
Case Broderick (R)
William A. Calderhead (R)
Charles Curtis (R)
Snyder S. Kirkpatrick (R)
Chester I. Long (R)
Orrin L. Miller (R)

Kentucky

Senators

Joseph C. S. Blackburn (D)
William Lindsay (D)

Representatives

Albert S. Berry (D)
John D. Clardy (D)
David G. Colson (R)
Walter Evans (R)
John K. Hendrick (D)
Nathan T. Hopkins (R) s. 1897
W. Godfrey Hunter (R)
Joseph M. Kendall (D) r. Feb.
 1897
John W. Lewis (R)
James B. McCreary (D)
William C. Owens (D)
Samuel J. Pugh

Louisiana

Senators

Newton C. Blanchard (D)
Donelson Caffery (D)

Representatives

Charles J. Boatner (D)
Charles F. Buck (D)
Adolph Meyer (D)
Henry W. Ogden (D)
Andrew Price (D)
Samuel M. Robertson (D)

Maine

Senators

William P. Frye (R)
Eugene Hale (R)

Representatives

Charles A. Boutelle (R)
Nelson Dingley, Jr. (R)
Seth L. Milliken (R)
Thomas B. Reed (R)

Maryland

Senators

Charles H. Gibson (D)
Arthur P. Gorman (D)

Representatives

William B. Baker (R)
Charles E. Coffin (R)
John K. Cowen (D)
Joshua W. Miles (D)
Harry W. Rusk (D)
George L. Wellington (R)

Massachusetts

Senators

George F. Hoar (R)
Henry Cabot Lodge (R)

Representatives

Lewis D. Apsley (R)
Harrison H. Atwood (R)
William E. Barrett (R)
William F. Draper (R)
John F. Fitzgerald (D)
Frederick H. Gillett (R)
William S. Knox (R)
Samuel W. McCall (R)
William H. Moody (R)
Elijah A. Morse (R)
John Simpkins (R)
Joseph H. Walker (R)
Ashley B. Wright (R)

Michigan

Senators

Julius C. Burrows (R)
James McMillan (R)

Representatives

David D. Aiken (R)
John Avery (R)
Roswell P. Bishop (R)
John B. Corliss (R)
Rousseau O. Crump (R)
William S. Linton (R)
Alfred Milnes (R)
William Alden Smith (R)
Horace G. Snover (R)
George Spalding (R)
Samuel M. Stephenson (R)
Henry F. Thomas (R)

Minnesota

Senators

Cushman K. Davis (R)
Knute Nelson (R)

Representatives

Frank M. Eddy (R)
Loren Fletcher (R)
Joel P. Heatwole (R)
Andrew R. Keifer (R)
James T. McCleary (R)
James A. Tawney (R)
Charles A. Towne (R)

Mississippi

Senators

James Z. George (D)
Edward C. Walthall (D)

Representatives

John M. Allen (D)
Thomas C. Catchings (D)
Walter McK. Denny (D)
John C. Kyle (D)
Hernando D. Money (D)
James G. Spencer (D)
John Sharp Williams (D)

Missouri

Senators

Francis M. Cockrell (D)

George G. Vest (D)

Representatives

Richard Bartholdt (R)
Charles G. Burton (R)
Charles N. Clark (R)
Seth W. Cobb (D)
George C. Crowther (R)
David A. De Armond (D)
Alexander M. Dockery (D)
Uriel S. Hall (D)
Joel D. Hubbard (R)
Charles F. Joy (R)
Norman A. Mozley (R)
John H. Raney (R)
John C. Tarsney (D)
John P. Tracey (R)
William M. Treloar (R)
Robert T. Van Horn (R)

Montana

Senators

Thomas H. Carter (R)
Lee Mantle (R)

Representatives

Charles S. Hartman (R)

Nebraska

Senators

William V. Allen (Pop)
John M. Thurston (R)

Representatives

William E. Andrews (R)
Eugene J. Hainer (R)
Omer M. Kem (Pop)
George D. Meiklejohn (R)
David H. Mercer (R)
Jesse B. Strode (R)

Nevada

Senators

John P. Jones (R)
William M. Stewart (R)

Representatives

Francis G. Newlands (D)

New Hampshire

Senators

William E. Chandler (R)
Jacob H. Gallinger (R)

Representatives

Henry M. Baker (R)
Cyrus A. Sulloway (R)

New Jersey

Senators

William J. Sewell (R)

James J. Sewell, Jr. (R)

Representatives

Charles N. Fowler (R)
John J. Gardner (D)
Benjamin F. Howell (R)
Henry C. Loudenslager (R)
Thomas McEwan, Jr. (R)
Richard W. Parker (R)
Mahlon Pitney (R)
James F. Stewart (R)

New York

Senators

David B. Hill (D)
Edward Murphy, Jr. (D)

Representatives

Franklin Bartlett (D)
Charles G. Bennett (R)
Frank S. Black (R) r. Jan. 1897
Henry C. Brewster (R)
Charles A. Chickering (R)
Amos J. Cummings (D)
Newton M. Curtis (R)
Charles Daniels (R)
Benjamin L. Fairchild (R)
Israel F. Fischer (R)
Wallace T. Foote, Jr. (R)
Charles W. Gillet (R)
Warren B. Hooker (R)
James R. Howe (R)
Denis M. Hurley (R)
Jacob Le Fever (R)
Philip B. Low (R)
George B. McClellan (D)
Richard C. McCormick (R)
Rowland B. Mahany (R)
Henry Clay Miner (D)
John M. Mitchell (R) s. June 1896
Benjamin B. Odell, Jr. (R)
Sereno E. Payne (R)
Theodore L. Poole (R)
Lemuel E. Quigg (R)
George W. Ray (R)
Richard C. Shannon (R)
James S. Sherman (R)
George N. Southwick (R)
William Sulzer (D)
James W. Wadsworth (R)
James J. Walsh (D) r. June 1896
David F. Wilber (R)
Francis H. Wilson (R)

North Carolina

Senators

Marion Butler (Pop)
Jeter C. Pritchard (R)

Representatives

Romulus Z. Linney (R)
James A. Lockhart (D)
Charles H. Martin (Pop) s. 1896
Richmond Pearson (R)
Thomas Settle (R)
John G. Shaw (D)
Alonzo C. Shuford (Pop)
Harry Skinner (Pop)
William F. Strowd (Pop)

Frederick A. Woodard (D)

North Dakota

Senators

Henry C. Hansbroug (R)
William N. Roach (D)

Representatives

Martin N. Johnson (R)

Ohio

Senators

Calvin S. Brice (D)
John Sherman (D)

Representatives

Clifton B. Beach (R)
Jacob H. Bromwell (R)
Theodore E. Burton (R)
Lorenzo Danford (R)
Francis B. De Witt (R)
Lucien J. Fenton (R)
Charles H. Grosvenor (R)
Stephen R. Harris (R)
George W. Hulick (R)
Winfield S. Kerr (R)
Fernando C. Layton (D)
Addison S. McClure (R)
Stephen A. Northway (R)
Paul J. Sorg (D)
James H. Southard (R)
Luther M. Strong (R)
Charles P. Taft (R)
Robert W. Tayler (R)
Henry C. Van Voorhis (R)
David K. Watson (R)
George W. Wilson (R)

Oregon

Senators

George W. McBride (R)
John H. Mitchell (R)

Representatives

William R. Ellis (R)
Binger Hermann (R)

Pennsylvania

Senators

J. Donald Cameron (R)
Matthew S. Quay (R)

Representatives

Ernest F. Acheson (R)
Robert Adams, Jr. (R)
William C. Arnold (R)
Henry H. Bingham (R)
Marriott Brosius (R)
Charles N. Brumm (R)
James H. Codding (R)
John Dalzell (R)
Constantine J. Erdman (D)
Matthew Griswold (R)
Galusha A. Grow (R)
Frederick Halterman (R)

Alfred C. Harmer (R)
Joseph J. Hart (D)
Daniel B. Heiner (R)
Josiah D. Hicks (R)
George F. Huff (R)
Monroe H. Kulp (R)
John Leisenring (R)
Fred C. Leonard (R)
Thaddeus M. Mahon (R)
Thomas W. Phillips (R)
John E. Reyburn (R)
John B. Robinson (R)
Joseph A. Scranton (R)
James A. Stahle (R)
Charles W. Stone (R)
William A. Stone (R)
Irving P. Wanger (R)
Ephraim M. Woomer (R)

Rhode Island

Senators

Nelson W. Aldrich (R)
George P. Wetmore (R)

Representatives

Warren O. Arnold (R)
Melville Bull (R)

South Carolina

Senators

John L. M. Irby (D)
Benjamin R. Tillman (D)

Representatives

William Elliott (D) r. June 1896
Asbury C. Latimer (D)
John L. McLaurin (D)
George W. Murray (R) s. 1896
J. William Stokes (D) s. 1896
Thomas J. Strait (Alliance D)
W. Jasper Talbert (D)
Stanyarne Wilson (D)

South Dakota

Senators

James H. Kyle (R)
Richard F. Pettigrew (R)

Representatives

Robert J. Gamble (R)
John A. Pickler (R)

Tennessee

Senators

William B. Bate (D)
Isham G. Harris (D)

Representatives

William C. Anderson (R)
Foster V. Brown (R)
Nicholas N. Cox (D)
Henry R. Gibson (R)
John E. McCall (R)
James C. McDearmon (D)
Benton McMillin (D)

Josiah Patterson (D)
James D. Richardson (D)
Joseph E. Washington (D)

Texas

Senators

Horace Chilton (D)
Roger Q. Mills (D)

Representatives

Jo Abbott (D)
Joseph W. Bailey (D)
Charles K. Bell (D)
Jeremiah V. Cockrell (D)
Samuel L. Cooper (D)
William H. Crain (D) d. Feb. 1896
Miles Crowley (D)
David B. Culberson (D)
Joseph C. Hutcheson (D)
Rudolph Kleberg (D) s. 1896
George H. Noonan (R)
George C. Pendleton (D)
Joseph D. Sayers (D)
Charles H. Yoakum (D)

Utah

Senators

Arthur Brown (R) s. 1896
Frank J. Cannon (R) s. 1896

Representatives

Clarence E. Allen (R) s. 1896

Vermont

Senators

Justin S. Morrill (R)
Redfield Proctor (R)

Representatives

William W. Grout (R)
H. Henry Powers (R)

Virginia

Senators

John W. Daniel (D)
Thomas S. Martin (D)

Representatives

Tazewell Ellett (D)
William A. Jones (D)
William R. McKenney (D) r. May 1896
Elisha E. Meredith (D)
Peter J. Otey (D)
Claude A. Swanson (D)
Robert T. Thorp (R) s. 1896
Henry St. George Tucker (D)
Smith S. Turner (D)
D. Gardiner Tyler (D)
James A. Walker (R)

Washington

Senators

Watson C. Squire (R)
John L. Wilson (R)

Representatives

William H. Doolittle (R)
Samuel C. Hyde (R)

West Virginia

Senators

Stephen B. Elkins (R)
Charles J. Faulkner (D)

Representatives

Alston G. Dayton (R)
Blackburn B. Dovener (R)
James H. Huling (R)
Warren Miller (R)

Wisconsin

Senators

John L. Mitchell (R)
William F. Vilas (D)

Representatives

Joseph W. Babcock (R)
Samuel S. Barney (R)
Samuel A. Cook (R)
Henry A. Cooper (R)
Michael Griffin (R)
John J. Jenkins (R)
Edward S. Minor (R)
Theobald Otjen (R)
Edward Sauerhering (R)
Alexander Stewart (R)

Wyoming

Senators

Clarence D. Clark (R)
Francis E. Warren (R)

Representatives

Frank W. Mondell (R)

Fifty-Fifth Congress

(Mar. 4, 1897, to
Mar. 3, 1899)

President of the Senate: Garret
A. Hobart
*President Pro Tempore of the
Senate:* William P. Frye
*Speaker of the House of
Representatives:* Thomas B.
Reed

Alabama

Senators

John T. Morgan (D)
Edmund W. Pettus (D)

Representatives

William F. Aldrich (R) s. 1898
John H. Bankhead (D)
Willis Brewer (D)
Henry D. Clayton (D)
Milford W. Howard (Pop)
Thomas S. Plowman (D) r. Feb.
1898
Jesse F. Stallings (D)
George W. Taylor (D)
Oscar W. Underwood (D)
Joseph Wheeler (D)

Arkansas

Senators

James H. Berry (D)
James K. Jones (D)

Representatives

Stephen Brundidge, Jr. (D)
Hugh A. Dinsmore (D)
John S. Little (D)
Philip D. McCulloch, Jr. (D)
Thomas C. McRae (D)
William L. Terry (D)

California

Senators

George C. Perkins (R)
Stephen M. White (D)

Representatives

John A. Barham (R)
Charles A. Barlow (D)
Curtis H. Castle (D)
Marion De Vries (D)
Samuel G. Hilborn (R)
Eugene F. Loud (R)
James G. Maguire (D)

Colorado

Senators

Henry M. Teller (R)
Edward O. Wolcott (R)

Representatives

John C. Bell (D)
John F. Shafroth (D)

Connecticut

Senators

Joseph R. Hawley (R)
Orville H. Platt (R)

Representatives

E. Stevens Henry (R)
Ebenezer J. Hill (R)
Charles A. Russell (R)
Nehemiah D. Sperry (R)

Delaware

Senators

George Gray (D)
Richard R. Kenney (D)

Representatives

Levin I. Handy (D)

Florida

Senators

Samuel Pasco (D)
Stephen R. Mallory (D)

Representatives

Robert W. Davis (D)
Stephen M. Sparkman (D)

Georgia

Senators

Augustus O. Bacon (D)
Alexander S. Clay (D)

Representatives

William C. Adamson (D)
Charles L. Bartlett (D)
William G. Brantley (D)
William H. Fleming (D)
James M. Griggs (D)
William M. Howard (D)
Rufus E. Lester (D)
Elijah B. Lewis (D)
Leonidas F. Livingston (D)
John W. Maddox (D)
Farish C. Tate (D)

Idaho

Senators

Henry Heitfeld (D)
George L. Shoup (R)

Representatives

James Gunn (P)

Illinois

Senators

Shelby M. Cullom (R)
William E. Mason (R)

Representatives

Jehu Baker (Fusion)
Hugh R. Belknap (R)
Henry S. Boutell (R)
James R. Campbell (D)
Joseph G. Cannon (R)
James A. Connolly (R)
Edward D. Cooke (R) d. June
1897
George E. Foss (R)
Joseph V. Graff (R)
William H. Hinrichsen (D)
Robert R. Hitt (R)
Albert J. Hopkins (R)
Andrew J. Hunter (D)
Thomas M. Jett (D)
William Lorimer (R)
James R. Mann (R)
Benjamin F. Marsh (R)
Daniel W. Mills (R)
George W. Prince (R)
Walter Reeves (R)
George W. Smith (R)
Vespasian Warner (R)
George E. White (R)

Indiana

Senators

Charles W. Fairbanks (R)
David Turpie (D)

Representatives

Edgar D. Crumpacker (R)
George W. Faris (R)
Francis M. Griffith (D)
James A. Hemenway (R)
Charles L. Henry (R)
William S. Holman (D) d. Apr.
1897
Henry U. Johnson (R)
Charles B. Landis (R)
Robert W. Miers (D)
Jesse Overstreet (R)
James M. Robinson (D)
Lemuel W. Royse (R)
George W. Steele (R)
William T. Zenor (D)

Iowa

Senators

William B. Allison (R)
John H. Gear (R)

Representatives

Samuel M. Clark (R)
Robert G. Cousins (R)
George M. Curtis (R)
Jonathan P. Dolliver (R)
Alva L. Hager (R)
David B. Henderson (R)
William P. Hepburn (R)
John A. T. Hull (R)
John F. Lacey (R)
George D. Perkins (R)
Thomas Updegraff (R)

Kansas

Senators

Lucien Baker (R)
William A. Harris (D)

Representatives

Jeremiah D. Botkin (Fusion)
Case Broderick (R)
Charles Curtis (R)
Nelson B. McCormick (Pop)
Mason S. Peters (D)
Edwin R. Ridgely (People's)

Jeremiah Simpson (Pop)
William D. Vincent (Pop)

Kentucky

Senators

William J. DeBoe (R)
William Lindsay (D)

Representatives

Albert S. Berry (D)
John D. Clardy (D)
David G. Colson (R)
George M. Davison (R)
Walter Evans (R)
Thomas Y. Fitzpatrick (D)
Samuel J. Pugh (R)
John S. Rhea (D)
Evan E. Settle (D)
David H. Smith (D)
Charles K. Wheeler (D)

Louisiana

Senators

Donelson Caffery (D)
Samuel D. McEnery (D)

Representatives

Samuel T. Baird (D)
Robert F. Broussard (D)
Robert C. Davey (D)
Adolph Meyer (D)
Henry W. Ogden (D)
Samuel M. Robertson (D)

Maine

Senators

William P. Frye (R)
Eugene Hale (R)

Representatives

Charles A. Boutelle (R)
Edwin C. Burleigh (R)
Nelson Dingley, Jr. (R) d. Jan.
  1899
Seth L. Milliken (R) d. Apr.
  1897
Thomas B. Reed (R)

Maryland

Senators

Arthur P. Gorman (D)
George L. Wellington (D)

Representatives

William B. Baker (R)
Isaac A. Barber (R)
William S. Booze (R)
John McDonald (R)
William W. McIntire (R)
Sydney E. Mudd (R)

Massachusetts

Senators

George F. Hoar (R)
Henry Cabot Lodge (R)

Representatives

William E. Barrett (R)
Samuel J. Barrows (R)
John F. Fitzgerald (D)
Frederick H. Gillett (R)
William S. Greene (R) s. 1898
William S. Knox (R)
George P. Lawrence (R)
William C. Lovering (R)
Samuel W. McCall (R)
William H. Moody (R)
John Simpkins (R) d. Mar.
  1898
Charles F. Sprague (R)
Joseph H. Walker (R)
George W. Weymouth (R)
Ashley B. Wright (R) d. Aug.
  1897

Michigan

Senators

Julius C. Burrows (R)
James McMillan (R)

Representatives

Roswell P. Bishop (R)
Ferdinand Brucker (D)
John B. Corliss (R)
Rousseau O. Crump (R)
Edward L. Hamilton (R)
William S. Mesick (R)
Carlos D. Shelden (R)
Samuel W. Smith (R)
William Alden Smith (R)
Horace G. Snover (R)
George Spalding (R)
Albert M. Todd

Minnesota

Senators

Cushman K. Davis (R)
Knute Nelson (R)

Representatives

Frank M. Eddy (R)
Loren Fletcher (R)
Joel P. Heatwole (R)
James T. McCleary (R)
R. Page W. Morris (R)
James A. Tawney (R)
Frederick C. Stevens (R)

Mississippi

Senators

James Z. George (D) d. Aug.
  1897
Hernando D. Money (D) s.
  1897
Edward C. Walthall (D) d.
  Apr. 1898
William V. Sullivan (D) s. 1898

Representatives

John M. Allen (D)
Thomas C. Catchings (D)
Andrew F. Fox (D)
Patrick Henry (D)
William F. Love (D) d. Oct.
  1898
Frank A. McLain (D) s. 1898
Thomas Spight (D) s. 1898
William V. Sullivan (D) r. May
  1898
John Sharp Williams (D)

Missouri

Senators

Francis M. Cockrell (D)
George G. Vest (D)

Representatives

Richard Bartholdt (R)
Maecenas E. Benton (D)
Richard P. Bland (D)
Robert N. Bodine (D)
Champ Clark (D)
Charles F. Cochran (D)
James Cooney (D)
William S. Cowherd (D)
David A. De Armond (D)
Alexander M. Dockery (D)
Charles F. Joy (R)
James T. Lloyd (D)
Charles E. Pearce (R)
Edward Robb (D)
Willard D. Vandiver (D)

Montana

Senators

Thomas H. Carter (R)
Lee Mantle (R)

Representatives

Charles S. Hartman (R)

Nebraska

Senators

William V. Allen (Pop)
John M. Thurston (R)

Representatives

William L. Greene (Pop)
Samuel Maxwell (Fusion)
David H. Mercer (R)
William L. Stark (D)
Jesse B. Strode (R)
Roderick D. Sutherland (Pop)

Nevada

Senators

John P. Jones (R)
William M. Stewart (R)

Representatives

Francis G. Newlands (D)

New Hampshire

Senators

William E. Chandler (R)
Jacob H. Gallinger (R)

Representatives

Frank G. Clarke (R)
Cyrus A. Sulloway (R)

New Jersey

Senators

William J. Sewell (R)
James Smith, Jr. (D)

Representatives

Charles N. Fowler (R)
John J. Gardner (D)
Benjamin F. Howell (R)
Henry C. Loudenslager (R)
Thomas McEwan, Jr. (R)
Richard W. Parker (R)
Mahlon Pitney (R) r. Jan. 1899
James F. Stewart (R)

New York

Senators

Edward Murphy, Jr. (D)
Thomas C. Platt (R)

Representatives

De Alva S. Alexander (R)
James J. Belden (R)
Joseph M. Belford (R)
Charles G. Bennett (R)
Thomas J. Bradley (D)
Henry C. Brewster (R)
Charles A. Chickering (R)
Aaron V. S. Cochrane (R)
Amos Cummings (D)
Edmund H. Driggs (D)
Israel F. Fischer (R)
Wallace T. Foote, Jr. (R)
Charles W. Gillet (R)
Warren B. Hooker (R) r. Nov.
  1898
James R. Howe (R)
Denis M. Hurley (R) d. Feb.
  1898
John H. Ketcham (R)
Lucius N. Littauer (R)
Philip B. Low (R)
George B. McClellan (D)
Rowland B. Mahany (R)
John M. Mitchell (R)
Benjamin B. Odell, Jr. (R)
Sereno E. Payne (R)
Lemuel E. Quigg (R)
George W. Ray (R)
Richard C. Shannon (R)
James S. Sherman (R)
George N. Southwick (R)
William Sulzer (D)
John H. G. Vehslage (D)
James W. Wadsworth (R)
William L. Ward (R)
David F. Wilber (R)
Francis H. Wilson (R) r. Sept
  1897

North Carolina

Senators

Marion Butler (Pop)
Jeter C. Pritchard (R)

Representatives

John E. Fowler (Pop)
William W. Kitchin (D)
Romulus Z. Linney (R)
Charles H. Martin (Pop)
Richmond Pearson (R)
Alonzo C. Shuford (Pop)
Harry Skinner (Pop)
William F. Strowd (Pop)
George H. White (R)

North Dakota

Senators

Henry C. Hansbrough (R)
William N. Roach (D)

Representatives

Martin N. Johnson (R)

Ohio

Senators

Joseph B. Foraker (R)
Marcus A. Hanna (R)

Representatives

Clifton B. Beach (R)
John L. Brenner (D)
Jacob H. Bromwell (R)
Seth W. Brown (R)
Theodore E. Burton (R)
Lorenzo Danford (R)
Charles W. F. Dick (R) s. 1898
Lucien J. Fenton (R)
Charles H. Grosvenor (R)
Winfield S. Kerr (R)
John J. Lentz (D)
Archibald Lybrand (R)
John A. McDowell (D)
George A. Marshall (D)
David Meekison (D)
Stephen A. Northway (R) d. Sept. 1898
James A. Norton (D)
William B. Shattuc (R)
James H. Southard (R)
Robert W. Tayler (R)
Henry C. Van Voorhis (R)
Walter L. Weaver (R)

Oregon

Senators

George W. McBride (R)
Joseph Simon (R) s. 1898

Representatives

William R. Ellis (R)
Thomas H. Tongue (R)

Pennsylvania

Senators

Matthew S. Quay (R)
Boies Penrose (R)

Representatives

Ernest F. Acheson (R)
Robert Adams, Jr. (R)
William C. Arnold (R)
George J. Benner (D)
Henry H. Bingham (R)
Marriott Brosius (R)
Charles N. Brumm (R)
Thomas S. Butler (R)
James H. Codding (R)
William Connell (R)
John Dalzell (R)
Samuel A. Davenport (R)
Daniel Ermentrout (D)
William H. Graham (R) s. 1898
Galusha A. Grow (R)
Alfred C. Harmer (R)
Josiah D. Hicks (R)
William S. Kirkpatrick (R)
Monroe H. Kulp (R)
William McAleer (D)
Thaddeus M. Mahon (R)
Marlin E. Olmsted (R)
Horace B. Packer (R)
Edward E. Robbins (R)
Joseph B. Showalter (R)
Charles W. Stone (R)
William A. Stone (R) r. Nov. 1898
John C. Sturtevant (R)
Irving P. Wanger (R)
Morgan B. Williams (R)
James R. Young (R)

Rhode Island

Senators

Nelson W. Aldrich (R)
George P. Wetmore (R)

Representatives

Melville Bull (R)
Adin B. Capron (R)

South Carolina

Senators

Joseph H. Earle (D) d. May 1897
John L. McLaurin (D) s. 1897
Benjamin R. Tillman (D)

Representatives

William Elliott (D)
Asbury C. Latimer (D)
John L. McLaurin (D) r. May 1897
James Norton (D)
J. William Stokes (D)
Thomas J. Strait (Alliance D)
W. Jasper Talbert (D)
Stanyarne Wilson (D)

South Dakota

Senators

James H. Kyle
Richard F. Pettigrew (R)

Representatives

John E. Kelley (D)
Freeman Knowles (Pop)

Tennessee

Senators

William B. Bate (D)
Isham G. Harris (D) d. July 1897
Thomas B. Turley (D) s. 1897

Representatives

Walter P. Brownlow (R)
Edward W. Carmack (D)
Nicholas N. Cox (D)
John W. Gaines (D)
Henry R. Gibson (R)
Benton McMillin (D) r. Jan. 1899
John A. Moon (D)
Rice A. Pierce (D)
James D. Richardson (D)
Thetus W. Sims (D)

Texas

Senators

Horace Chilton (D)
Roger Q. Mills (D)

Representatives

Joseph W. Bailey (D)
Thomas H. Ball (D)
Robert E. Burke (D)
Samuel B. Cooper (D)
John W. Cranford (D)
Reese C. De Graffenreid (D)
Robert B. Hawley (R)
Robert L. Henry (D)
Rudolph Kleberg (D)
Samuel W. T. Lanham (D)
Joseph D. Sayers (D) r. Jan. 1899
James L. Slayden (D)
John H. Stephens (D)

Utah

Senators

Frank J. Cannon (R)
Joseph L. Rawlins (D)

Representatives

William H. King (D)

Vermont

Senators

Justin S. Morrill (R) d. Dec. 1898

Redfield Proctor (R)
Jonathan Ross (R) s. 1899

Representatives

William W. Grout (R)
H. Henry Powers (R)

Virginia

Senators

John W. Daniel (D)
Thomas S. Martin (D)

Representatives

Sydney P. Epes (D) r. Mar. 1898
James Hay (D)
William A. Jones (D)
John Lamb (D)
Peter J. Otey (D)
John F. Rixey (D)
Claude A. Swanson (D)
Robert T. Thorp (R) s. 1898
James A. Walker (D)
Richard A. Wise (R) s. 1898
Jacob Yost (R)
William A. Young (D) r. Apr. 1898

Washington

Senators

George Turner (Fusion)
John L. Wilson (R)

Representatives

William C. Jones (R)
James Hamilton Lewis (D)

West Virginia

Senators

Stephen B. Elkins (R)
Charles J. Faulkner (D)

Representatives

Alston G. Dayton (R)
Charles P. Dorr (R)
Blackburn B. Dovener (R)
Warren Miller (R)

Wisconsin

Senators

John L. Mitchell (D)
John C. Spooner (R)

Representatives

Joseph W. Babcock (R)
Samuel S. Barney (R)
Henry Allen Cooper (R)
James H. Davidson (R)
Michael Griffin (R)
John J. Jenkins (R)
Edward S. Minor (R)
Theobald Otjen (R)
Edward Sauerhering (R)
Alexander Stewart (R)

Wyoming

Senators

Clarence D. Clark (R)
Francis E. Warren (R)

Representatives

John E. Osborne (D)

Fifty-Sixth Congress

(Mar. 4, 1899, to
Mar. 3, 1901)

President of the Senate: Garret
A. Hobart
*President Pro Tempore of the
Senate:* William P. Frye
*Speaker of the House of
Representatives:* David B.
Henderson

Alabama

Senators

John T. Morgan (D)
Edmund W. Pettus (D)

Representatives

William F. Aldrich (R)
John H. Bankhead (D)
Willis Brewer (D)
John L. Burnett (D)
Henry D. Clayton (D)
William Richardson (D) s. 1900
Gaston A. Robbins (D) r. Mar.
1900
Jesse F. Stallings (D)
George W. Taylor (D)
Oscar W. Underwood (D)
Joseph Wheeler (D) r. Apr.
1900

Arkansas

Senators

James K. Jones (D)
James H. Berry (D)

Representatives

Stephen Brundidge, Jr. (D)
Hugh A. Dinsmore (D)
John S. Little (D)
Philip D. McCulloch, Jr. (D)
Thomas C. McRae (D)
William L. Terry (D)

California

Senators

Thomas R. Bard (R)
George C. Perkins (R)

Representatives

John A. Barham (R)

Marion De Vries (D) r. Aug.
1900
Julius Kahn (R)
Eugene F. Loud (R)
Victor H. Metcalf (R)
James C. Needham (R)
Russell J. Waters (R)
Samuel D. Woods (R) s. 1900

Colorado

Senators

Henry M. Teller (R)
Edward O. Wolcott (R)

Representatives

John C. Bell (D)
John F. Shafroth (D)

Connecticut

Senators

Joseph R. Hawley (R)
Orville H. Platt (R)

Representatives

E. Stevens Henry (R)
Ebenezer J. Hill (R)
Charles A. Russell (R)
Nehemiah D. Sperry (R)

Delaware

Senators

Richard R. Kenney (D)
Vacant

Representatives

John H. Hoffecker (R) d. June
1900
Walter O. Hoffecker (R)

Florida

Senators

Stephen R. Mallory (D)
Samuel Pasco (D) ta. 1899
James P. Taliaferro (D) s. Dec.
1899

Representatives

Robert W. Davis (D)
Stephen M. Sparkman (D)

Georgia

Senators

Augustus O. Bacon (D)
Alexander S. Clay (D)

Representatives

William C. Adamson (D)
Charles L. Barlett (D)
William G. Brantley (D)
William H. Fleming (D)
James M. Griggs (D)

William M. Howard (D)
Rufus E. Lester (D)
Elijah B. Lewis (D)
Leonidas F. Livingston (D)
John W. Maddox (R)
Farish C. Tate (D)

Idaho

Senators

Henry Heitfeld (Pop)
George L. Shoup (R)

Representatives

Edgar Wilson (R)

Illinois

Senators

Shelby M. Cullom (R)
William E. Mason (R)

Representatives

Henry S. Boutell (R)
Ben F. Caldwell (D)
Joseph G. Cannon (R)
Joseph B. Crowley (D)
Thomas Cusack (D)
George E. Foss (R)
George P. Foster (D)
Joseph V. Graff (R)
Robert R. Hitt (R)
Albert J. Hopkins (R)
Thomas M. Jett (D)
William Lorimer (R)
James R. Mann (R)
Benjamin F. Marsh (R)
Edward T. Noonan (D)
George W. Prince (R)
Walter Reeves (R)
William A. Rodenberg (R)
George W. Smith (R)
Vespasian Warner (R)
James R. Williams (D)
William E. Williams (D)

Indiana

Senators

Albert J. Beveridge (R)
Charles W. Fairbanks (R)

Representatives

Abraham L. Brick (R)
George W. Cromer (R)
Edgar D. Crumpacker (R)
George W. Faris (R)
Francis M. Griffith (D)
James A. Hemenway (R)
Charles B. Landis (R)
Robert W. Miers (D)
Jesse Overstreet (R)
James M. Robinson (D)
George W. Steele (R)
James E. Watson (R)
William T. Zenor (D)

Iowa

Senators

William B. Allison (R)
Jonathan P. Dolliver (R) s.
1900
John H. Gear (R) d. July 1900

Representatives

James P. Conner (R) s. 1900
Robert G. Cousins (R)
Jonathan P. Dolliver (R) r.
Aug. 1900
Gilbert N. Haugen (R)
Thomas Hedge (R)
David B. Henderson (R)
William P. Hepburn (R)
John A. T. Hull (R)
John F. Lacey (R)
Joseph R. Lane (R)
Smith McPherson (R) r. 1900
Walter I. Smith (R) s. 1900
Lot Thomas (R)

Kansas

Senators

Lucien Baker (R)
William A. Harris (D)

Representatives

Willis J. Bailey (R)
Justin D. Browersock (R)
William A. Calderhead (R)
Charles Curtis (R)
Chester I. Long (R)
James M. Miller (R)
William A. Reeder (R)
Edwin R. Ridgely (D)

Kentucky

Senators

William J. DeBoe (R)
William Lindsay (D)

Representatives

Henry D. Allen (D)
Albert S. Berry (D)
Vincent S. Boreing (R)
Thomas Y. Fitzpatrick (D)
June W. Gayle (D)
George G. Gilbert (D)
Samuel J. Pugh (R)
John S. Rhea (D-P)
David H. Smith (D)
Oscar Turner (D)
Charles K. Wheeler (D)

Louisiana

Senators

Donelson Caffrey (D)
Samuel D. McEnery (D)

Representatives

Phanor Breazeale (D)
Robert F. Broussard (D)
Robert C. Davey (D)

Adolph Meyer (D)
Joseph E. Ransdell (D)
Samuel M. Robertson (D)

Maine

Senators

William P. Frye (R)
Eugene Hale (R)

Representatives

Amos L. Allen (R)
Charles A. Boutelle (R)
Edwin C. Burleigh (R)
Charles E. Littlefield (R)

Maryland

Senators

Louis E. McComas (R)
George L. Wellington (D)

Representatives

William B. Baker (R)
James W. Denny (D)
Josiah L. Kerr (R) s. 1900
Sydney E. Mudd (R)
George A. Pearre (R)
John Walter Smith (D) r. Jan. 1900
Frank C. Wachter (R)

Massachusetts

Senators

George F. Hoar (R)
Henry Cabot Lodge (R)

Representatives

John F. Fitzgerald (D)
Frederick H. Gillett (R)
William S. Greene (R)
William S. Knox (R)
George P. Lawrence (R)
William C. Lovering (R)
Samuel W. McCall (R)
William H. Moody (R)
Henry F. Naphen (D)
Ernest W. Roberts (R)
Charles F. Sprague (R)
John R. Thayer (D)
George W. Weymouth (R)

Michigan

Senators

Julius C. Burrows (R)
James McMillan (R)

Representatives

Roswell P. Bishop (R)
John B. Corliss (R)
Rousseau O. Crump (R)
Joseph W. Fordney (R)
Washington Gardner (R)
Edward L. Hamilton (R)
William S. Mesick (R)
Carlos D. Shelden (R)
Henry C. Smith (R)

Samuel W. Smith (R)
William Alden Smith (R)
Edgar Weeks (R)

Minnesota

Senators

Moses E. Clapp (R) s. 1901
Cushman K. Davis (R) d. Nov. 1900
Knute Nelson (R)
Charles A. Towne (D) ta. 1900

Representatives

Frank M. Eddy (R)
Loren Fletcher (R)
Joel P. Heatwole (R)
James T. McCleary (R)
R. Page W. Morris (R)
Frederick C. Stevens (R)
James A. Tawney (R)

Mississippi

Senators

Hernando D. Money (D)
William V. Sullivan (D)

Representatives

John M. Allen (D)
Thomas C. Catchings (D)
Andrew F. Fox (D)
Patrick Henry (D)
Frank A. McLain (D)
Thomas Spight (D)
John Sharp Williams (D)

Missouri

Senators

Francis M. Cockrell (D)
George G. Vest (D)

Representatives

Richard Bartholdt (R)
Maecenas E. Benton (D)
Champ Clark (D)
Charles F. Cochran (D)
James Cooney (D)
William S. Cowherd (D)
David A. De Armond (D)
John Dougherty (D)
Charles F. Joy
James T. Lloyd (D)
Charles E. Pearce (R)
Edward Robb (D)
William W. Rucker (D)
Dorsey W. Shackleford (D)
Willard D. Vandiver (D)

Montana

Senators

Thomas H. Carter (R)
William A. Clark (D) r. May 1900

Representatives

Albert J. Campbell (D)

Nebraska

Senators

William V. Allen (Pop)
John M. Thurston (R)

Representatives

Elmer J. Burkett (R)
David H. Mercer (R)
William Neville (Pop)
John S. Robinson (D)
William L. Stark (D)
Roderick D. Sutherland (Pop)

Nevada

Senators

John P. Jones (R)
William M. Stewart (R)

Representatives

Francis G. Newlands (D)

New Hampshire

Senators

William E. Chandler (R)
Jacob H. Gallinger (R)

Representatives

Frank G. Clarke (R) d. Jan. 1901
Cyrus A. Sulloway (R)

New Jersey

Senators

John Kean (R)
William J. Sewell (R)

Representatives

William D. Daly (D) d. July 1900
Charles N. Fowler (R)
John J. Gardner (R)
Benjamin F. Howell (R)
Henry C. Loudenslager (R)
Allan L. McDermott (D) s. 1900
Richard W. Parker (R)
Joshua S. Salmon (D)
James F. Stewart (R)

New York

Senators

Chauncey M. Depew (R)
Thomas C. Platt (R)

Representatives

De Alva S. Alexander (R)
Thomas J. Bradley (D)
William A. Chanler (D)
Charles A. Chickering (R)
Bertram T. Clayton (D)
Aaron V. S. Cochrane (R)

Amos J. Cummings (D)
Edmund H. Driggs (D)
Michael E. Driscoll (R)
Louis W. Emerson (R)
John J. Fitzgerald (D)
Charles W. Gillet (R)
Martin H. Glynn (D)
John H. Ketcham (R)
Jefferson M. Levy (D)
Lucius N. Littauer (R)
George B. McClellan (D)
Mitchell May (D)
Nicholas Muller (D)
James M. E. O'Grady (R)
Sereno E. Payne (R)
George W. Ray (R)
Daniel J. Riordan (D)
Jacob Ruppert, Jr. (D)
William H. Ryan (D)
Townsend Scudder (D)
Albert D. Shaw (R) s. 1900
James S. Sherman (R)
John K. Stewart (R)
William Sulzer (D)
Arthur S. Thompkins (R)
John Q. Underhill (D)
Edward B. Vreeland (R)
James W. Wadsworth (R)
Frank E. Wilson (D)

North Carolina

Senators

Marion Butler (Pop)
Jeter C. Pritchard (R)

Representatives

John W. Atwater (Pop)
John D. Bellamy (D)
William T. Crawford (D) r. May 1900
William W. Kitchin (D)
Theodore F. Kluttz (D)
Romulus Z. Linney (R)
Richmond Pearson (R) s. 1900
John H. Small (D)
Charles R. Thomas (D)
George H. White (R)

North Dakota

Senators

Henry C. Hansbrough (R)
Porter J. McCumber (R)

Representatives

Burleigh F. Spalding (R)

Ohio

Senators

Joseph B. Foraker (R)
Marcus A. Hanna (R)

Representatives

John L. Brenner (D)
Jacob H. Bromwell (R)
Seth W. Brown (R)
Theodore E. Burton (R)
Charles W. F. Dick (R)
Joseph J. Gill (R)
Robert B. Gordon (D)

Charles H. Grosvenor (R)
Winfield S. Kerr (R)
John J. Lentz (D)
Archibald Lybrand (R)
John A. McDowell (D)
David Meekison (D)
Stephen Morgan (R)
James A. Norton (D)
Fremont O. Phillips (R)
William B. Shattuc (R)
James H. Southard (R)
Robert W. Tayler (R)
Henry C. Van Voorhis (R)
Walter L. Weaver (R)

Oregon

Senators

George W. McBride (R)
Joseph Simon (R)

Representatives

Malcolm A. Moody (R)
Thomas H. Tongue (R)

Pennsylvania

Senators

Boies Penrose (R)
Matthew S. Quay (R)

Representatives

Ernest F. Acheson (R)
Robert Adams, Jr. (R)
Laird H. Barber (D)
Henry H. Bingham (R)
Marriott Brosius (R)
Thomas S. Butler (R)
William Connell (R)
John Dalzell (R)
Samuel A. Davenport (R)
Stanley W. Davenport (D)
Athelston Gaston (D)
William H. Graham (R)
Henry D. Green (D)
Galusha A. Grow (R)
James K. P. Hall (D)
Alfred C. Harmer (R) d. Mar.
  1900
Summers M. Jack (R)
William McAleer (D)
Thaddeus M. Mahon (R)
Edward de V. Morrell (R) s.
  1900
Marlin E. Olmsted (R)
Horace B. Packer (R)
Rufus K. Polk (D)
James W. Ryan (D)
Joseph B. Showalter (R)
Joseph C. Sibley (D)
Joseph E. Thropp (R)
Irving P. Wanger (R)
Charles F. Wright (R)
James R. Young (R)
Edward Ziegler (D)

Rhode Island

Senators

Nelson W. Aldrich (R)
George P. Wetmore (R)

Representatives

Melville Bull (R)
Adin B. Capron (R)

South Carolina

Senators

John L. McLaurin (D)
Benjamin R. Tillman (D)

Representatives

William Elliott (D)
David E. Finley (D)
Asbury C. Latimer (D)
James Norton (D)
J. William Stokes (D)
W. Jasper Talbert (D)
Stanyarne Wilson (D)

South Dakota

Senators

James H. Kyle
Richard F. Pettigrew (R)

Representatives

Charles H. Burke (R)
Robert J. Gamble (R)

Tennessee

Senators

William B. Bate (D)
Thomas B. Turley (D)

Representatives

Walter P. Brownlow (R)
Edward W. Carmack (D)
Nicholas N. Cox (D)
John W. Gaines (D)
Henry R. Gibson (R)
John A. Moon (D)
Rice A. Pierce (D)
James D. Richardson (D)
Thetus W. Sims (D)
Charles E. Snodgrass (D)

Texas

Senators

Horace Chilton (D)
Charles A. Culberson (D)

Representatives

Joseph W. Bailey (D)
Thomas H. Ball (D)
Robert E. Burke (D)
Albert S. Burleson (D)
Samuel B. Cooper (D)
Reese C. DeGraffenreid (D)
Robert B. Hawley (R)
Robert L. Henry (D)
Rudolph Kleberg (D)
Samuel W. T. Lanham (D)
John L. Sheppard (D)
James L. Slayden (D)
John H. Stephens (D)

Utah

Senators

Thomas Kearns (R) s. 1901
Joseph L. Rawlins (D)

Representatives

William H. King (D) s. 1900

Vermont

Senators

William P. Dillingham (R) s.
  1900
Redfield Proctor (R)
Jonathan Ross (R) ta. 1899

Representatives

William W. Grout (R)
H. Henry Powers (R)

Virginia

Senators

John W. Daniel (D)
Thomas S. Martin (D)

Representatives

Sydney P. Epes (D) d. Mar.
  1900
James Hay (D)
William A. Jones (D)
John Lamb (D)
Francis R. Lassiter (D) s. 1900
Peter J. Otey (D)
Julian M. Quarles (D)
William F. Rhea (D)
John F. Rixey (D)
Claude A. Swanson (D)
Richard A. Wise (R) d. 1900
William A. Young (D) r. Mar.
  1900

Washington

Senators

Addison G. Foster (R)
George Turner (Fusion)

Representatives

Francis W. Cushman (R)
Wesley L. Jones (R)

West Virginia

Senators

Stephen B. Elkins (R)
Nathan B. Scott (R)

Representatives

Alston G. Dayton (R)
Blackburn B. Dovener (R)
Romeo H. Freer (R)
David E. Johnson (D)

Wisconsin

Senators

Joseph V. Quarles (R)
John C. Spooner (R)

Representatives

Joseph W. Babcock (R)
Samuel S. Barney (R)
Henry A. Cooper (R)
Herman B. Dahle (R)
James H. Davidson (R)
John J. Esch (R)
John J. Jenkins (R)
Edward S. Minor (R)
Theobald Otjen (R)
Alexander Stewart (R)

Wyoming

Senators

Clarence D. Clark (R)
Francis E. Warren (R)

Representatives

Frank W. Mondell (R)

Fifty-Seventh Congress

(Mar. 4, 1901, to
Mar. 3, 1903)

President of the Senate:
  Theodore Roosevelt
*President Pro Tempore of the
  Senate:* William P. Frye
*Speaker of the House of
  Representatives:* David B.
  Henderson

Alabama

Senators

John T. Morgan (D)
Edmund W. Pettus (D)

Representatives

John H. Bankhead (D)
Sydney J. Bowie (D)
John L. Burnett (D)
Henry D. Clayton (D)
William Richardson (D)
George W. Taylor (D)
Charles W. Thompson (D)
Oscar W. Underwood (D)
Ariosto A. Wiley (D)

Arkansas

Senators

James H. Berry (D)
James K. Jones (D)

Representatives

Stephen Brundidge, Jr. (D)

Hugh A. Dinsmore (D)
John S. Little (D)
Philip D. McCulloch, Jr. (D)
Thomas C. McRae (D)
Charles C. Reid (D)

California

Senators

Thomas R. Bard (R)
George C. Perkins (R)

Representatives

Frank L. Coombs (R)
Julius Kahn (R)
Eugene F. Loud (R)
James McLachlan (R)
Victor H. Metcalf (R)
James C. Needham (R)
Samuel D. Woods (R)

Colorado

Senators

Henry M. Teller (R)
Thomas M. Patterson (D)

Representatives

John C. Bell (D)
John F. Shafroth (D)

Connecticut

Senators

Joseph R. Hawley (R)
Orville H. Platt (R)

Representatives

Frank B. Brandegee (R) s. 1902
E. Stevens Henry (R)
Ebenezer J. Hill (R)
Charles A. Russell (R) d. Oct.
   1902
Nehemiah D. Sperry (R)

Delaware

Senators

J. Frank Allee (R) s. 1903
L. Heisler Ball (R) s. 1903

Representatives

L. Heisler Ball (R) r. March
   1903

Florida

Senators

Stephen R. Mallory (D)
James P. Taliaferro (D)

Representatives

Robert W. Davis (D)
Stephen M. Sparkman (D)

Georgia

Senators

Augustus O. Bacon (D)
Alexander S. Clay (D)

Representatives

William C. Adamson (D)
Charles L. Bartlett (D)
William G. Brantley (D)
William H. Fleming (D)
James M. Griggs (D)
William M. Howard (D)
Rufus E. Lester (D)
Elijah B. Lewis (D)
Leonidas F. Livingston (D)
John W. Maddox (D)
Farish C. Tate (D)

Idaho

Senators

Fred Dubois (R)
Henry Heitfeld (Pop)

Representatives

Thomas L. Glenn (Pop)

Illinois

Senators

Shelby M. Cullom (R)
William E. Mason (R)

Representatives

Henry S. Boutell (R)
Ben F. Caldwell (D)
Joseph G. Cannon (R)
Joseph B. Crowley (D)
John J. Feely (D)
George E. Foss (R)
George P. Foster (D)
Joseph V. Graff (R)
Robert R. Hitt (R)
Albert J. Hopkins (R)
Thomas M. Jett (D)
Fredrick J. Kern (D)
James McAndrews (D)
William F. Mahoney (D)
James R. Mann (R)
J. Ross Mickey (D)
George W. Prince (R)
Walter Reeves (R)
Thomas J. Selby (D)
George W. Smith (R)
Vespasian Warner (R)
James R. Williams (D)

Indiana

Senators

Albert J. Beveridge (R)
Charles W. Fairbanks (R)

Representatives

Abraham L. Brick (R)
George W. Cromer (R)
Edgar D. Crumpacker (R)
Francis M. Griffith (D)

James A. Hemenway (R)
Elias S. Holliday (R)
Charles B. Landis (R)
Robert W. Miers (D)
Jesse Overstreet (R)
James M. Robinson (D)
George W. Steele (R)
James E. Watson (R)
William T. Zenor (D)

Iowa

Senators

William B. Allison (R)
Jonathan P. Dolliver (R)

Representatives

James P. Conner (R)
Robert G. Cousins (R)
Gilbert N. Haugen (R)
Thomas Hedge (R)
David B. Henderson (R)
William P. Hepburn (R)
John A. T. Hull (R)
John F. Lacey (R)
John N. W. Rumple (R) d. Jan.
   1903
Walter I. Smith (R)
Lot Thomas (R)

Kansas

Senators

Joseph R. Burton (R)
William A. Harris (D)

Representatives

Justin D. Bowersock (R)
William A. Calderhead (R)
Charles Curtis (R)
Alfred M. Jackson (D)
Chester I. Long (R)
James M. Miller (R)
William A. Reeder (R)

Kentucky

Senators

Joseph C. S. Blackburn (D)
William J. Deboe (R)

Representatives

Henry D. Allen (D)
Vincent Boreing (R)
George G. Gilbert (D)
Daniel L. Gooch (D)
Harvey S. Irwin (R)
James N. Kehoe (D)
J. McKenzie Moss (R) s. 1902
John S. Rhea (D, Pop)
David H. Smith (D)
South Trimble (D)
Charles K. Wheeler (D)
James B. White (D)

Louisiana

Senators

Murphy J. Foster (D)
Samuel D. McEnery (D)

Representatives

Phanor Breazeale (D)
Robert F. Broussard (D)
Robert C. Davey (D)
Adolph Meyer (D)
Joseph E. Ransdell (D)
Samuel M. Robertson (D)

Maine

Senators

William P. Frye (R)
Eugene Hale (R)

Representatives

Amos L. Allen (R)
Edwin C. Burleigh (R)
Charles E. Littlefield (R)
Llewellyn Powers (R)

Maryland

Senators

George L. Wellington (D)
Louis E. McComas (R)

Representatives

Albert A. Blakeney (R)
William H. Jackson (R)
Sydney E. Mudd (R)
George A. Pearre (R)
Charles R. Schirm (R)
Frank C. Wachter (R)

Massachusetts

Senators

George F. Hoar (R)
Henry Cabot Lodge (R)

Representatives

Joseph A. Conry (D)
Augustus P. Gardner (R) s.
   1902
Frederick H. Gillett (R)
William S. Greene (R)
William S. Knox (R)
George P. Lawrence (R)
William C. Lovering (R)
Samuel W. McCall (R)
William H. Moody (R) r. May
   1902
Henry F. Naphen (D)
Samuel L. Powers (R)
Ernest W. Roberts (R)
John R. Thayer (D)
Charles Q. Tirrell (R)

Michigan

Senators

Russell A. Alger (R) s. 1902
Julius C. Burrows (R)
James McMillan (R) d. Aug.
   1902

Representatives

Henry H. Aplin (R)

Roswell P. Bishop (R)
John B. Corliss (R)
Archibald B. Darragh (R)
Joseph W. Fordney (R)
Washington Gardner (R)
Edward L. Hamilton (R)
Carlos D. Shelden (R)
Henry C. Smith (R)
Samuel W. Smith (R)
William Alden Smith (R)
Edgar Weeks (R)

Minnesota

Senators

Moses E. Clapp (R) s. 1903
Knute Nelson (R)

Representatives

Frank M. Eddy (R)
Loren Fletcher (R)
Joel P. Heatwole (R)
James T. McCleary (R)
R. Page W. Morris (R)
Frederick C. Stevens (R)
James A. Tawney (R)

Mississippi

Senators

Anselm J. McLaurin (D)
Hernando D. Money (D)

Representatives

Ezekiel S. Candler, Jr. (D)
Andrew F. Fox (D)
Patrick Henry (D)
Charles E. Hooker (D)
Frank A. McLain (D)
Thomas Spight (D)
John Sharp Williams (D)

Missouri

Senators

Francis M. Cockrell (D)
George G. Vest (D)

Representatives

Richard Bartholdt (R)
Maecenas E. Benton (D)
James J. Butler (D) s. 1902
Champ Clark (D)
Charles F. Cochran (D)
James Cooney (D)
William S. Cowherd (D)
David A. DeArmond (D)
John Dougherty (D)
Charles F. Joy (R)
James T. Lloyd (D)
Edward Robb (D)
William W. Rucker (D)
Dorsey W. Shackleford (D)
Willard D. Vandiver (D)
George C. R. Wagoner (R) s.
  1903

Montana

Senators

William A. Clark (D)
Paris Gibson (D)

Representatives

Caldwell Edwards (D, Pop)

Nebraska

Senators

William V. Allen (Pop) r. 1901
Charles H. Dietrich (R) s. 1901
Joseph H. Millard (R)

Representatives

Elmer J. Burkett (D)
David H. Mercer (R)
William Neville (Pop)
John S. Robinson (D)
Ashton C. Shallenberger (D)
William L. Stark (D)

Nevada

Senators

John P. Jones (R)
William M. Stewart (R)

Representatives

Francis G. Newlands (D)

New Hampshire

Senators

Henry E. Burnham (R)
Jacob H. Gallinger (R)

Representatives

Frank D. Currier (R)
Cyrus A. Sulloway (R)

New Jersey

Senators

John F. Dryden (R)
John Kean (R)
William J. Sewell (R) d. Dec.
  1901

Representatives

DeWitt C. Flanagan (D) s.
  1903
Charles N. Fowler (R)
John J. Gardner (R)
Benjamin F. Howell (R)
Henry C. Loudenslager (R)
Allan L. McDermott (D)
Richard W. Parker (R)
Joshua S. Salmon (D) d. May
  1902
James F. Stewart (R)

New York

Senators

Chauncey M. Depew (R)
Thomas C. Platt (R)

Representatives

De Alva S. Alexander (R)
Oliver H. P. Belmont (D)
Henry Bristow (R)
Thomas J. Creamer (D)
Amos J. Cummings (D) d. May
  1902
William H. Douglas (R)
William H. Draper (R)
Michael E. Driscoll (R)
John W. Dwight (R) s. 1902
Louis W. Emerson (R)
John J. Fitzgerald (D)
Charles W. Gillet (R)
Henry M. Goldfogle
Harry A. Hanbury (R)
John H. Ketcham (R)
Charles L. Knapp (R)
Montague Lessler (R) s. 1902
George H. Lindsay (D)
Lucius N. Littauer (R)
George B. McClellan (D)
Nicholas Muller (D) r. Dec.
  1902
Sereno E. Payne (D)
James B. Perkins (R)
Cornelius A. Pugsley (D)
George W. Ray (R) r. Sept.
  1902
Jacob Ruppert, Jr. (D)
William H. Ryan (D)
James S. Sherman (R)
George N. Southwick (R)
John K. Stewart (R)
Frederic Storm (R)
William Sulzer (D)
Edward Swann (D) s. 1902
Arthur S. Tompkins (R)
Edward B. Vreeland (R)
James W. Wadsworth (R)
Frank E. Wilson (R)

North Carolina

Senators

Jeter C. Pritchard (R)
Furnifold McL. Simmons (D)

Representaitves

John D. Bellamy (D)
Edmond S. Blackburn (R)
Claude Kitchin (D)
William W. Kitchin (D)
Theodore F. Kluttz (D)
James M. Moody (R) d. Feb.
  1903
Edward W. Pou (D)
John H. Small (D)
Charles R. Thomas (D)

North Dakota

Senators

Henry C. Hansbrough (R)
Porter J. McCumber (R)

Representatives

Thomas F. Marshall (R)

Ohio

Senators

Joseph B. Foraker (R)
Marcus A. Hanna (R)

Representatives

Jacob A. Beidler (R)
Jacob H. Bromwell (R)
Theodore E. Burton (R)
John W. Cassingham (D)
Charles W. F. Dick (R)
Joseph J. Gill (R)
Robert B. Gordon (D)
Charles H. Grosvenor (R)
Charles Q. Hildebrant (R)
Thomas B. Kyle (R)
Stephen Morgan (R)
Robert M. Nevin (R)
James A. Norton (D)
William B. Shattuc (R)
William W. Skiles (R)
John S. Snook (R)
James H. Southard (R)
Robert W. Tayler (R)
Emmett Tompkins (R)
Henry C. Van Voorhis (R)
William R. Warnock (R)

Oregon

Senators

John H. Mitchell (R)
Joseph Simon (R)

Representatives

Malcolm A. Moody (R)
Thomas H. Tongue (R) d. Jan.
  1903

Pennsylvania

Senators

Boies Penrose (R)
Matthew S. Quay (R)

Representatives

Ernest F. Acheson (R)
Robert Adams, Jr. (R)
Arthur L. Bates (R)
Alexander Billmeyer (D) s. 1902
Henry H. Bingham (R)
Henry Burk (R)
Thomas S. Butler (R)
Henry B. Cassel (R)
William Connell (R)
John Dalzell (R)
Elias Deemer (R)
Alvin Evans (R)
Robert H. Foerderer (R)
William H. Graham (R)
Henry D. Green (D)
Galusha A. Grow (R)
James K. P. Hall (D) r. Nov.
  1902
Summers M. Jack (R)
Robert J. Lewis (R)
Thaddeus M. Mahon (R)

Edward de V. Morrell (R)
Howard Mutchler (D)
Martin E. Olmsted (R)
Henry W. Palmer (R)
George R. Patterson (R)
Rufus K. Polk (D) d. Mar.
1902
Joseph B. Showalter (R)
Joseph C. Sibley (R)
Irving P. Wanger (R)
Charles F. Wright (R)
James R. Young (R)

Rhode Island

Senators

Nelson W. Aldrich (R)
George P. Wetmore (R)

Representatives

Melville Bull (R)
Adin B. Capron (R)

South Carolina

Senators

John L. McLaurin (D)
Benjamin R. Tillman (D)

Representatives

William Elliott (D)
David E. Finley (D)
Joseph T. Johnson (D)
Asbury C. Latimer (D)
Asbury F. Lever (D)
Robert B. Scarborough (D)
William J. Talbert (D)

South Dakota

Senators

Robert J. Gamble (R)
Alfred B. Kittredge (R) s. 1901
James H. Kyle d. July 1901

Representatives

Charles H. Burke (R)
Eben W. Martin (R)

Tennessee

Senators

William B. Bate (D)
Edward W. Carmack (D)

Representatives

Walter P. Brownlow (R)
John W. Gaines (D)
Henry R. Gibson (R)
John A. Moon (D)
Lemuel P. Padgett (D)
Malcolm R. Patterson (D)
Rice A. Pierce (D)
James D. Richardson (D)
Thetus W. Sims (D)
Charles E. Snodgrass (D)

Texas

Senators

Joseph W. Bailey (D)
Charles A. Culberson (D)

Representatives

Thomas H. Ball (D)
George F. Burgess (D)
Albert S. Burleson (D)
Samuel B. Cooper (D)
Reese C. De Graffenreid (D) d.
Aug. 1902
Robert L. Henry (D)
Rudolph Kleberg (D)
Samuel W. T. Lanham (D) r.
Jan. 1903
Choice B. Randell (D)
Gordon J. Russell (D) s. 1902
John L. Sheppard (D) d. Oct.
1902
Morris Sheppard (D) s. 1902
James L. Slayden (D)
John H. Stephens (D)
Dudley G. Wooten (D)

Utah

Senators

Joseph L. Rawlins (D)
Thomas Kearns (R)

Representatives

George Sutherland (R)

Vermont

Senators

William P. Dillingham (R)
Redfield Proctor (R)

Representatives

David J. Foster (R)
Kittredge Haskins (R)

Virginia

Senators

John W. Daniels (D)
Thomas S. Martin (D)

Representatives

Henry D. Flood (D)
Carter Glass (D) s. 1902
James Hay (D)
William A. Jones (D)
John Lamb (D)
Francis R. Lassiter (D)
Harry L. Maynard (D)
Peter J. Otey (D) d. May 1902
William F. Rhea (D)
John F. Rixey (D)
Claude A. Swanson (D)

Washington

Senators

Addison G. Foster (R)
George Turner (Fusion)

Representatives

Francis W. Cushman (R)
Wesley L. Jones (R)

West Virginia

Senators

Stephen B. Elkins (R)
Nathan B. Scott (R)

Representatives

Alston G. Dayton (R)
Blackburn B. Dovener (R)
Joseph H. Gaines (R)
James A. Hughes (R)

Wisconsin

Senators

Joseph V. Quarles (R)
John C. Spooner (R)

Representatives

Joseph W. Babcock (R)
Samuel S. Barney (R)
Webster E. Brown (R)
Henry A. Cooper (R)
Herman B. Dahle (R)
James H. Davidson (R)
John J. Esch (R)
John J. Jenkins (R)
Edward S. Minor (R)
Theobald Otjen (R)

Wyoming

Senators

Clarence D. Clark (R)
Francis E. Warren (R)

Representatives

Frank W. Mondell (R)

Fifty-Eighth Congress

(Mar. 4, 1903, to
Mar. 3, 1905)

President of the Senate: Vacant
*President Pro Tempore of the
Senate:* William P. Frye
*Speaker of the House of
Representatives:* Joseph G.
Cannon

Alabama

Senators

John T. Morgan (D)
Edmund W. Pettus (D)

Representatives

John H. Bankhead (D)
Sydney J. Bowie (D)
John L. Burnett (D)
Henry D. Clayton (D)
J. Thomas Heflin (D) s. 1904
William Richardson (D)
George W. Taylor (D)
Charles W. Thompson (D) d.
Mar. 1904
Oscar W. Underwood (D)
Ariosto A. Wiley (D)

Arkansas

Senators

James H. Berry (D)
James P. Clark (D)

Representatives

Stephen Brundidge, Jr. (D)
Hugh A. Dinsmore (D)
John S. Little (D)
Robert B. Macon (D)
Charles C. Reid (D)
Joseph T. Robinson (D)
Robert M. Wallace (D)

California

Senators

Thomas R. Bard (R)
George C. Perkins (R)

Representatives

Theodore A. Bell (D)
Milton J. Daniels (R)
James N. Gillett (R)
Joseph R. Knowland (R) s.
1904
Edward J. Livernash (Union
Labor)
James McLachlan (R)
Victor H. Metcalf (R) r. July
1904
James C. Needham (R)
William J. Wynn (Union Labor)

Colorado

Senators

Thomas M. Patterson (D)
Henry M. Teller (D)

Representatives

Robert W. Bonynge (R) s. 1904
Franklin E. Brooks (R)
Herschel M. Hogg (R)
John F. Shafroth (D) r. Feb.
1904

Connecticut

Senators

Orville H. Platt (R)
Joseph R. Hawley (R)

Representatives

Frank B. Brandegee (R)
E. Stevens Henry (R)
Ebenezer J. Hill (R)
George L. Lilley (R)
Nehemiah D. Sperry (R)

Delaware

Senators

J. Frank Allee (R)
L. Heisler Ball (R)

Representatives

Henry A. Houston (D)

Florida

Senators

Stephen R. Mallory (D)
James P. Taliaferro (D)

Representatives

Robert W. Davis (D)
William B. Lamar (D)
Stephen M. Sparkman (D)

Georgia

Senators

Augustus O. Bacon (D)
Alexander S. Clay (D)

Representatives

William C. Adamson (D)
Charles L. Bartlett (D)
William G. Brantley (D)
James M. Griggs (D)
Thomas W. Hardwick (D)
William M. Howard (D)
Rufus E. Lester (D)
Elijah B. Lewis (D)
Leonidas F. Livingston (D)
John W. Maddox (D)
Farish C. Tate (D)

Idaho

Senators

Fred T. Dubois (D)
Weldon B. Heyburn (R)

Representatives

Burton L. French (R)

Illinois

Senators

Shelby M. Cullom (R)
Albert J. Hopkins (R)

Representatives

Henry S. Boutell (R)
Ben F. Caldwell (D)
Joseph G. Cannon (R)
Joseph B. Crowley (D)
Martin Emerich (D)
George E. Foss (R)
George P. Foster (D)
Charles E. Fuller (R)
Joseph V. Graff (R)
Robert R. Hitt (R)
Philip Knopf (R)
William Lorimer (R)
James McAndrews (D)
William F. Mahoney (D) d.
  Dec. 1904
James R. Mann (R)
Benjamin F. Marsh (R)
George W. Prince (R)
Henry T. Rainey (D)
William A. Rodenberg (R)
George W. Smith (R)
Howard M. Snapp (R)
John A. Sterling (R)
Vespasian Warner (R)
James R. Williams (D)
William W. Wilson (R)

Indiana

Senators

Albert J. Beveridge (R)
Charles W. Fairbanks (R)

Representatives

Abraham L. Brick (R)
George W. Cromer (R)
Edgar D. Crumpacker (R)
Francis M. Griffith (D)
James A. Hemenway (R) (R)
Elias S. Holliday (R)
Charles B. Landis (R)
Frederick Landis (R)
Robert W. Miers (D)
Jesse Overstreet (R)
James M. Robinson (D)
James E. Watson (R)
William T. Zenor (D)

Iowa

Senators

William B. Allison (R)
Jonathan P. Dolliver (R)

Representatives

Benjamin P. Birdsall (R)
James P. Conner (R)
Robert G. Cousins (R)
Gilbert N. Haugen (R)
Thomas Hedge (R)
William P. Hepburn (R)
John A. T. Hull (R)
John F. Lacey (R)
Walter I. Smith (R)
Lot Thomas (R)

Martin J. Wade (D)

Kansas

Senators

Joseph R. Burton (R)
Chester I. Long (R)

Representatives

Justin D. Bowersock (R)
William A. Calderhead (R)
Philip P. Campbell (R)
Charles Curtis (R)
James M. Miller (R)
Victor Murdock (R)
William A. Reeder (R)
Charles F. Scott (R)

Kentucky

Senators

Joseph C. S. Blackburn (D)
James B. McCreary (D)

Representatives

George G. Gilbert (D)
Daniel L. Gooch (D)
Frank A. Hopkins (D)
W. Godfrey Hunter (R)
Ollie M. James (R)
James N. Kehoe (D)
John S. Rhea (D, Pop)
J. Swagar Sherley (D)
David H. Smith (D)
Augustus O. Stanley (D)
South Trimble (D)

Louisiana

Senators

Murphy J. Foster (D)
Samuel D. McEnery (D)

Representatives

Phanor Breazeale (D)
Robert F. Broussard (D)
Robert C. Davey (D)
Adolph Meyer (D)
Arsene P. Pujo (D)
Joseph E. Ransdell (D)
Samuel M. Robertson (D)

Maine

Senators

William P. Frye (R)
Eugene Hale (R)

Representatives

Amos L. Allen (R)
Edwin C. Burleigh (R)
Charles E. Littlefield (R)
Llewellyn Powers (R)

Maryland

Senators

Arthur P. Gorman (D)
Louis E. McComas (R)

Representatives

James W. Denny (D)
William H. Jackson (R)
Sydney E. Mudd (R)
George A. Pearre (R)
J. Fred C. Talbott (D)
Frank C. Wachter (R)

Massachusetts

Senators

W. Murray Crane (R) s. 1904
George F. Hoar (R) d. Sept.
  1904
Henry Cabot Lodge (R)

Representatives

Butler Ames (R)
Augustus P. Gardner (R)
Frederick H. Gillett (R)
William S. Greene (R)
John A. Keliher (D)
George P. Lawrence (R)
William C. Lovering (R)
Samuel W. McCall (R)
William S. McNary (D)
Samuel L. Powers (R)
Ernest W. Roberts (R)
John A. Sullivan (D)
John R. Thayer (D)
Charles Q. Tirrell (R)

Michigan

Senators

Russell A. Alger (R)
Julius C. Burrows (R)

Representatives

Roswell P. Bishop (R)
Archibald B. Darragh (R)
Joseph W. Fordney (R)
Washington Gardner (R)
Edward L. Hamilton (R)
George A. Loud (R)
Alfred Lucking (D)
Henry McMorran (R)
Samuel W. Smith (R)
William Alden Smith (R)
Charles E. Townsend (R)
H. Olin Young (R)

Minnesota

Senators

Moses E. Clapp (R)
Knute Nelson (R)

Representatives

J. Adam Bede (R)
Clarence B. Buckman (R)
Charles R. Davis (R)
John Lind (D)

James T. McCleary (R)
Halvor Steenerson (R)
Frederick C. Stevens (R)
James A. Tawney (R)
Andrew J. Volstead (R)

Mississippi

Senators

Anselm J. McLaurin (D)
Hernando D. Money (D)

Representatives

Eaton J. Bowers (D)
Adam M. Byrd (D)
Ezekiel S. Candler, Jr. (D)
Wilson S. Hill (D)
Benjamin G. Humphreys (D)
Frank A. McLain (D)
Thomas Spight (D)
John Sharp Williams (D)

Missouri

Senators

Francis M. Cockrell (D)
William J. Stone (D)

Representatives

Richard Bartholdt (R)
Maecenas E. Benton (D)
James J. Butler (D)
Champ Clark (D)
Charles F. Cochran (D)
William S. Cowherd (D)
David A. De Armond (D)
John Dougherty (D)
Courtney W. Hamlin (D)
John T. Hunt (D)
J. Robert Lamar (D)
James T. Lloyd (D)
Edward Robb (D)
Willaim W. Rucker (D)
Dorsey W. Shackleford (D)
Willard D. Vandiver (D)

Montana

Senators

William A. Clark (D)
Paris Gibson (D)

Representatives

Joseph M. Dixon (R)

Nebraska

Senators

Charles H. Dietrich (R)
Joseph H. Millard (R)

Representatives

Elmer J. Burkett (D)
Edmund H. Hinshaw (R)
Gilbert M. Hitchcock (D)
Moses P. Kinkaid (R)
John J. McCarthy (R)
George W. Norris (R)

Nevada

Senators

Francis G. Newlands (D)
William M. Stewart (R)

Representatives

Clarence D. Van Duzer (D)

New Hampshire

Senators

Henry E. Burnham (R)
Jacob H. Gallinger (R)

Representatives

Frank D. Currier (R)
Cyrus A. Sulloway (R)

New Jersey

Senators

John F. Dryden (R)
John Kean (R)

Representatives

Allan Benny (D)
Charles N. Fowler (R)
John J. Gardner (D)
Benjamin F. Howell (R)
William Hughes (D)
William M. Lanning (R) r. June
   1904
Henry C. Loudenslager (R)
Allan L. McDermott (D)
Richard W. Parker (R)
William H. Wiley (R)
Ira W. Wood (R) s. 1904

New York

Senators

Chauncey M. Depew (R)
Thomas C. Platt (R)

Representatives

De Alva S. Alexander (R)
Robert Baker (D)
Edward M. Bassett (D)
Thomas W. Bradley (R)
W. Bourke Cockran (D) s. Mar.
   1904
William H. Douglas (R)
William H. Draper (R)
Michael E. Driscoll (R)
Charles T. Dunwell (R)
John W. Dwight (R)
John J. Fitzgerald (D)
William H. Flack (R)
Charles W. Gillet (R)
Henry M. Goldfogle (D)
Joseph A. Goulden (D)
Francis B. Harrison (D)
William Randolph Hearst (D)
John H. Ketcham (R)
Charles L. Knapp (R)
George H. Lindsay (D)
Lucius N. Littauer (R)

George B. McClellan (D) r.
   Dec. 1903
Norton P. Otis (R) d. Feb.
   1905
Sereno E. Payne (R)
James B. Perkins (R)
Ira E. Rider (D)
Jacob Ruppert, Jr. (D)
William H. Ryan (D)
Townsend Scudder (D)
James S. Sherman (R)
Francis E. Shober (D)
George J. Smith (R)
George N. Southwick (R)
Timothy D. Sullivan (D)
William Sulzer (D)
Edward B. Vreeland (R)
James W. Wadsworth (R)
Frank E. Wilson (D)

North Carolina

Senators

Lee S. Overman (D)
Furnifold McL. Simmons (D)

Representatives

James M. Gudger, Jr. (D)
Claude Kitchin (D)
William W. Kitchin (D)
Theodore F. Kluttz (D)
Robert N. Page (D)
Gilbert B. Patterson (D)
Edward W. Pou (D)
John H. Small (D)
Charles R. Thomas (D)
Edwin Y. Webb (D)

North Dakota

Senators

Henry C. Hansbrough (R)
Porter J. McCumber (R)

Representatives

Thomas F. Marshall (R)
Burleigh F. Spalding (R)

Ohio

Senators

Charles W. F. Dick (R) s. 1904
Joseph B. Foraker (R)
Marcus A. Hanna (R) d. Feb.
   1904

Representatives

De Witt C. Badger (D)
Jacob A. Beidler (R)
Theodore E. Burton (R)
John W. Cassingham (D)
Charles W. F. Dick (R) r. Mar.
   1904
Harvey C. Garber (D)
Herman P. Goebel (R)
Charles H. Grosvenor (R)
Charles Q. Hildebrandt (R)
Amos H. Jackson (R)
James Kennedy (R)
Thomas B. Kyle (R)
Nicholas Longworth (R)
Stephen Morgan (R)

Robert M. Nevin (R)
William W. Skiles (R) d. Jan.
   1904
John S. Snook (D)
James H. Southard (R)
William A. Thomas (R) s. 1904
Henry C. Van Voorhis (R)
William R. Warnock (R)
Amos R. Webber (R) s. 1904
Capell L. Weems (R)

Oregon

Senators

Charles W. Fulton (R)
John H. Mitchell (R)

Representatives

Binger Hermann (R)
John N. Williamson (R)

Pennsylvania

Senators

Philander C. Knox (R) s. 1905
Boies Penrose (R)
Matthew S. Quay (R) d. May
   1904

Representatives

Ernest F. Acheson (R)
Robert Adams, Jr. (R)
Arthur L. Bates (R)
Henry H. Bingham (R)
James W. Brown (R)
Henry Burk (R) d. Dec. 1903
Thomas S. Butler (R)
Henry B. Cassel (R)
George A. Castor (R) s. 1904
William Connell (R) s. 1904
Allen F. Cooper (R)
John Dalzell (R)
Elias Deemer (R)
Charles H. Dickerman (D)
Solomon R. Dresser (R)
Alvin Evans (R)
George Howell (R) r. Nov.
   1903
George F. Huff (R)
Marcus C. L. Kline (D)
Daniel F. Lafean (R)
George D. McCreary (R)
Thaddeus M. Mahon (R)
Reuben O. Moon (R)
Edward de V. Morrell (R)
Marlin E. Olmsted (R)
Henry W. Palmer (R)
George R. Patterson (R)
Henry Kirke Porter
George Shiras (R)
Joseph H. Shull (D)
Joseph C. Sibley (R)
William O. Smith (R)
Irving P. Wanger (R)
Charles F. Wright (R)

Rhode Island

Senators

Nelson W. Aldrich (R)
George P. Wetmore (R)

Representatives

Adin B. Capron (R)
Daniel L. D. Granger (D)

South Carolina

Senators

Asbury C. Latimer (D)
Benjamin R. Tillman (D)

Representatives

Wyatt Aiken (D)
George W. Croft (D) d. Mar. 1904
Theodore G. Croft (D) s. 1904
David E. Finley (D)
Joseph T. Johnson (D)
George S. Legare (D)
Asbury F. Lever (D)
Robert B. Scarborough (D)

South Dakota

Senators

Robert J. Gamble (R)
Alfred B. Kittredge (R)

Representatives

Charles H. Burke (R)
Eben W. Martin (R)

Tennessee

Senators

William B. Bate (D)
Edward W. Carmack (D)

Representatives

Walter P. Brownlow (R)
Morgan C. Fitzpatrick (D)
John W. Gaines (D)
Henry R. Gibson (R)
John A. Moon (D)
Lemuel P. Padgett (D)
Malcolm R. Patterson (D)
Rice A. Pierce (D)
James D. Richardson (D)
Thetus W. Sims (D)

Texas

Senators

Joseph W. Bailey (D)
Charles A. Culberson (D)

Representatives

Thomas H. Ball (D) r. Nov. 1903
Jack Beall (D)
George F. Burgess (D)
Albert S. Burleson (D)
Samuel B. Cooper (D)
Scott Field (D)
John Nance Garner (D)
Oscar W. Gillespie (D)
Alexander W. Gregg (D)
Robert L. Henry (D)
John M. Pickney (D)

Choice B. Randell (D)
Gordon J. Russell (D)
Morris Sheppard (D)
James L. Slayden (D)
William R. Smith (D)
John H. Stephens (D)

Utah

Senators

Thomas Kearns (R)
Reed Smoot (R)

Representatives

Joseph Howell (R)

Vermont

Senators

William P. Dillingham (R)
Redfield Proctor (R)

Representatives

David J. Foster (R)
Kittredge Haskins (R)

Virginia

Senators

John W. Daniel (D)
Thomas S. Martin (D)

Representatives

Henry D. Flood (D)
Carter Glass (D)
James Hay (D)
William A. Jones (D)
John Lamb (D)
Harry L. Maynard (D)
John F. Rixey (D)
Campbell Slemp (R)
Robert G. Southall (D)
Claude A. Swanson (D)

Washington

Senators

Levi Ankeny (R)
Addison G. Foster (R)

Representatives

Francis W. Cushman (R)
William E. Humphrey (R)
Wesley L. Jones (R)

West Virginia

Senators

Stephen B. Elkins (R)
Nathan B. Scott (R)

Representatives

Alston G. Dayton (R)
Blackburn B. Dovener (R)
Joseph H. Gaines (R)
James A. Hughes (R)

Harry C. Woodyard (R)

Wisconsin

Senators

Joseph V. Quarles (R)
John C. Spooner (R)

Representatives

Henry C. Adams (R)
Joseph W. Babcock (R)
Webster E. Brown (R)
Henry A. Cooper (R)
James H. Davidson (R)
John J. Esch (R)
John J. Jenkins (R)
Edward S. Minor (R)
Theobald Otjen (R)
William H. Stafford (R)
Charles H. Weisse (D)

Wyoming

Senators

Clarence D. Clark (R)
Francis E. Warren (R)

Representatives

Frank W. Mondell (R)

Fifty-Ninth Congress

(Mar. 4, 1905, to Mar. 3, 1907)

President of the Senate: Charles W. Fairbanks
President Pro Tempore of the Senate: William P. Frye
Speaker of the House of Representatives: Joseph G. Cannon

Alabama

Senators

John T. Morgan (D)
Edmund W. Pettus (D)

Representatives

John H. Bankhead (D)
Sydney J. Bowie (D)
John L. Burnett (D)
Henry D. Clayton (D)
J. Thomas Heflin (D)
William Richardson (D)
George W. Taylor (D)
Oscar W. Underwood (D)
Ariosto A. Wiley (D)

Arkansas

Senators

James H. Berry (D)
James P. Clark (D)

Representatives

Stephen Brundidge, Jr. (D)
John C. Floyd (D)
John S. Little (D)
Robert B. Macon (D)
Charles C. Reid (D)
Joseph T. Robinson (D)
Robert M. Wallace (D)

California

Senators

Frank P. Flint (R)
George C. Perkins (R)

Representatives

William F. Englebright (R) s. 1907
James S. Gillett r. Nov. 1906
Everis A. Hayes (R)
Julius Kahn (R)
Joseph R. Knowland (R)
Duncan E. McKinlay (R)
James McLachlan (R)
James C. Needham (R)
Sylvester C. Smith (R)

Colorado

Senators

Thomas M. Patterson (D)
Henry M. Teller (D)

Representatives

Robert W. Bonynge (R)
Franklin E. Brooks (R)
Herschel M. Hogg (R)

Connecticut

Senators

Frank B. Brandegee (R) s. 1905
Morgan G. Bulkeley (R)
Orville H. Platt (R) d. Apr. 1905

Representatives

E. Stevens Henry (R)
Edwin W. Higgins (R)
Ebenezer J. Hill (R)
George L. Lilley (R)
Nehemiah D. Sperry (R)

Delaware

Senators

J. Frank Allee (R)
Henry A. Du Pont (R) s. 1906

Representatives

Hiram R. Burton (R)

Florida

Senators

Stephen R. Mallory (D)

James P. Taliaferro (D)

Representatives

Frank Clark (R)
William B. Lamar (D)
Stephen M. Sparkman (D)

Georgia

Senators

Augustus O. Bacon (D)
Alexander S. Clay (D)

Representatives

William C. Adamson (D)
Charles L. Bartlett (D)
Thomas M. Bell (D)
William G. Brantley (D)
James M. Griggs (D)
Thomas W. Hardwick (D)
William M. Howard (D)
Gordon Lee (D)
Rufus E. Lester (D) d. June
1906
Elijah B. Lewis (D)
Leonidas F. Livingston (D)
James W. Overstreet (D) s.
1906

Idaho

Senators

Fred T. Dubois (D)
Weldon B. Heyburn (R)

Representatives

Burton L. French (R)

Illinois

Senators

Shelby M. Cullom (R)
Albert J. Hopkins (R)

Representatives

Henry S. Boutell (R)
Joseph G. Cannon (R)
Pleasant T. Chapman (R)
Frank S. Dickson (R)
George E. Foss (R)
Charles E. Fuller (R)
Joseph V. Graff (R)
Robert R. Hitt (R) d. Sept.
1906
Philip Knopf (R)
William Lorimer (R)
Frank O. Lowden (R) s. 1906
Charles McGavin (R)
William B. McKinley (R)
James McKinney (R)
Martin B. Madden (R)
James R. Mann (R)
Anthony Michalek (R) s. 1906
George W. Prince (R)
Henry T. Rainey (R)
Zeno J. Rives (R)
William A. Rodenberg (R)
George W. Smith (R)
Howard M. Snapp (R)
John A. Sterling (R)
Charles S. Wharton (R)

William W. Wilson (R)

Indiana

Senators

Albert J. Beveridge (R)
James A. Hemenway (R)

Representatives

Abraham L. Brick (R)
John C. Chaney (R)
George W. Cromer (R)
Edgar D. Crumpacker (R)
Lincoln Dixon (D)
John H. Foster (R)
Newton W. Gilbert (R) r. Nov.
1906
Clarence C. Gilhams (R) s.
1906
Elias S. Holliday (R)
Charles B. Landis (R)
Frederick Landis (R)
Jesse Overstreet (R)
James E. Watson (R)
William T. Zenor (D)

Iowa

Senators

William B. Allison (R)
Jonathan P. Dolliver (R)

Representatives

Benjamin P. Birdsall (R)
James P. Conner (R)
Robert G. Cousins (R)
Albert F. Dawson (R)
Gilbert N. Haugen (R)
Thomas Hedge (R)
William P. Hepburn (R)
Elbert H. Hubbard (R)
John A. T. Hull (R)
John F. Lacey (R)
Walter I. Smith (R)

Kansas

Senators

Alfred W. Benson (R) ta. 1906
Joseph R. Burton (R) r. June
1906
Charles Curtis (R) s. 1907
Chester I. Long (R)

Representatives

Justin D. Bowersock (R)
William A. Calderhead (R)
Philip P. Campbell (R)
Charles Curtis (R) r. Jan. 1907
James M. Miller (R)
Victor Murdock (R)
William A. Reeder (R)
Charles F. Scott (R)

Kentucky

Senators

Joseph C. S. Blackburn (D)
James B. McCreary (D)

Representatives

Joseph B. Bennett (R)
Don C. Edwards (R)
George G. Gilbert (D)
Frank A. Hopkins (D)
Ollie M. James (D)
James M. Richardson (D)
Joseph L. Rhinock (D)
J. Swagar Sherley (D)
David H. Smith (D)
Augustus O. Stanley (D)
South Trimble (D)

Louisiana

Senators

Murphy J. Foster (D)
Samuel D. McEnery (D)

Representatives

Robert F. Broussard (D)
Robert C. Davey (D)
Adolph Meyer (D)
Arsene P. Pujo (D)
Joseph E. Ransdell (D)
Samuel M. Robertson (D)
John T. Watkins (D)

Maine

Senators

William P. Frye (R)
Eugene Hale (R)

Representatives

Amos L. Allen (R)
Edwin C. Burleigh (R)
Charles E. Littlefield (R)
Llewellyn Powers (R)

Maryland

Senators

Arthur P. Gorman (D) d. June
1906
Isidor Rayner (D)
William P. Whyte (D) s. 1906

Representatives

John Gill, Jr. (D)
Sydney E. Mudd (R)
George A. Pearre (R)
Thomas A. Smith (D)
J. Fred C. Talbott (D)
Frank C. Wachter (R)

Massachusetts

Senators

W. Murray Crane (R)
Henry Cabot Lodge (R)

Representative

Butler Ames (R)
Augustus P. Gardner (R)
Frederick H. Gillett (R)
William S. Greene (R)

Rockwood Hoar (R) d. Nov.
1906
John A. Keliher (D)
George P. Lawrence (R)
William C. Lovering (R)
Samuel W. McCall (R)
William S. McNary (D)
Ernest W. Roberts (R)
John A. Sullivan (D)
Charles Q. Tirrell (R)
Charles G. Washburn (R) s.
1907
John W. Weeks (R)

Michigan

Senators

Russell A. Alger (R) d. Jan.
1907
Julius C. Burrows (R)
William Alden Smith (R) s.
1907

Representatives

Roswell P. Bishop (R)
Archibald B. Darragh (R)
Edwin Denby (R)
Joseph W. Fordney (R)
Washington Gardner (R)
Edward L. Hamilton (R)
George A. Loud (R)
Henry McMorran (R)
Samuel W. Smith (R)
William Alden Smith (R) r.
Feb. 1907
Charles E. Townsend (R)
H. Olin Young (R)

Minnesota

Senators

Moses E. Clapp (R)
Knute Nelson (R)

Representatives

J. Adam Bede (R)
Clarence B. Buckman (R)
Charles R. Davis (R)
Loren Fletcher (R)
James T. McCleary (R)
Halvor Steenerson (R)
Frederick C. Stevens (R)
James A. Tawney (R)
Andrew J. Volstead (R)

Mississippi

Senators

Hernando D. Money (D)
Anselm J. McLaurin (D)

Representatives

Eaton J. Bowers (D)
Adam M Byrd (D)
Ezekiel S. Candler, Jr. (D)
Wilson S. Hill (D)
Benjamin G. Humphreys (D)
Frank A. McLain (D)
Thomas Spight (D)
John Sharp Williams (D)

Missouri

Senators

William J. Stone (D)
William Warner (R)

Representatives

Richard Bartholdt (R)
Champ Clark (D)
Harry M. Coudrey (R) s. 1906
David A. De Armond (D)
Edgar C. Ellis (R)
Frank B. Fulkerson (R)
John T. Hunt (D)
Frank B. Klepper (R)
James T. Lloyd (D)
Arthur P. Murphy (R)
Marion E. Rhodes (R)
William W. Rucker (D)
Dorsey W. Shackleford (D)
Cassius M. Shartel (R)
William T. Tyndall (R)
John Welborn (R)
Ernest E. Wood (D) r. June
 1906

Montana

Senators

Thomas H. Carter (R)
William A. Clark (D)

Representatives

Joseph M. Dixon (R)

Nebraska

Senators

Elmer J. Burkett (R)
Joseph H. Millard (R)

Representatives

Edmund H. Hinshaw (R)
John L. Kennedy (R)
Moses P. Kinkaid (R)
John J. McCarthy (R)
George W. Norris (R)
Ernest M. Pollard (R)

Nevada

Senators

Francis G. Newlands (D)
George S. Nixon (R)

Representatives

Clarence D. Van Duzer (D)

New Hampshire

Senators

Henry E. Burnham (R)
Jacob H. Gallinger (R)

Representatives

Frank D. Currier (R)

Cyrus A. Sulloway (R)

New Jersey

Senators

John F. Dryden (R)
John Kean (R)

Representatives

Henry C. Allen (R)
Charles N. Fowler (R)
John J. Gardner (D)
Benjamin F. Howell (R)
Henry C. Loudenslager (R)
Allan L. McDermott (D)
Richard W. Parker (R)
Marshall Van Winkle (R)
William H. Wiley (R)
Ira W. Wood (R)

New York

Senators

Chauncey M. Depew (R)
Thomas C. Platt (R)

Representatives

De Alva S. Alexander (R)
John E. Andrus (R)
William S. Bennett (R)
Thomas W. Bradley (R)
William M. Calder (R)
W. Bourke Cockran (D)
William W. Cocks (R)
William H. Draper (R)
Michael E. Driscoll (R)
Charles T. Dunwell (R)
John W. Dwight (R)
J. Sloat Fassett (R)
John J. Fitzgerald (D)
William H. Flack (R) d. Feb.
 1907
Henry M. Goldfogle (D)
Joseph A. Goulden (D)
William Randolph Hearst (D)
John H. Ketcham (R) d. Nov.
 1906
Charles L. Knapp (R)
Charles B. Law (R)
Frank J. Le Fevre (R)
George H. Lindsay (D)
Lucius N. Littauer (R)
J. Van Vechten Olcott (R)
Herbert Parsons (R)
Sereno E. Payne (R)
James B. Perkins (R)
Daniel B. Perkins (R)
Daniel J. Riordan (D) s. 1906
Jacob Ruppert, Jr. (D)
William H. Ryan (D)
James S. Sherman (R)
George N. Southwick (R)
Timothy D. Sullivan (D)
William Sulzer (D)
Charles A. Towne (D)
Edward B. Vreeland (R)
James W. Wadsworth (R)
George E. Waldo (R)

North Carolina

Senators

Lee S. Overman (D)

Furnifold McL. Simmons (D)

Representatives

Edmond Blackburn (D)
James M. Gudger, Jr. (D)
Claude Kitchin (D)
William W. Kitchin (D)
Robert N. Page (D)
Gilbert B. Patterson (D)
Edward W. Pou (D)
John H. Small (D)
Charles R. Thomas (D)
Edwin Y. Webb (D)

North Dakota

Senators

Henry C. Hansbrough (R)
Porter J. McCumber (R)

Representatives

Asle J. Gronna (R)
Thomas F. Marshall (R)

Ohio

Senators

Charles W. F. Dick (R)
Joseph B. Foraker (R)

Representatives

Henry T. Bannon (R)
Jacob A. Beidler (R)
Theodore E. Burton (R)
William W. Campbell (R)
Ralph D. Cole (R)
Beman G. Dawes (R)
Harvey C. Garber (D)
Herman P. Goebel (R)
Charles H. Grosvenor (R)
J. Warren Keifer (R)
James Kennedy (R)
Nicholas Longworth (R)
Grant E. Mouser (R)
Robert M. Nevin (R)
Thomas E. Scroggy (R)
Martin L. Smyser (R)
James H. Southard (R)
Edward L. Taylor, Jr. (R)
William A. Thomas (R)
Amos R. Webber (R)
Capell L. Weems (R)

Oregon

Senators

Charles W. Fulton (R)
John M. Gearin (D) ta. 1906
John H. Mitchell (R) d. Dec.
 1905
Frederick W. Mulkey (R) s.
 1907

Representatives

Binger Hermann (R)

Pennsylvania

Senators

Philander C. Knox (R)
Boies Penrose (R)

Representatives

Ernest F. Acheson (R)
Robert Adams, Jr. (R) d. June
 1906
Andrew J. Barchfeld (R)
Arthur L. Bates (R)
Henry H. Bingham (R)
Charles N. Brumm (R) s. 1906
James F. Burke (R)
Thomas S. Butler (R)
Henry B. Cassel (R)
George A. Castor (R) d. Feb.
 1906
Allen F. Cooper (R)
Thomas H. Dale (R)
John Dalzell (R)
Elias Deemer (R)
Solomon R. Dresser (R)
William H. Graham (R)
George F. Huff (R)
Marcus C. L. Kline (D)
Daniel F. Lafean (R)
Mial E. Lilley (R)
George D. McCreary (R)
Thaddeus M. Mahon (R)
Reuben O. Moon (R)
J. Hampton Moore (R) s. Dec.
 1906
Edward de V. Morrell (R)
Marlin E. Olmsted (R)
Henry W. Palmer (R)
George R. Patterson (R) d.
 March 1906
John E. Reyburn (R) s. 1906
John M. Reynolds (R)
Edmund W. Samuel (R)
Gustav A. Schneebeli (R)
Joseph C. Sibley (R)
William O. Smith (R)
Irving P. Wanger (R)

Rhode Island

Senators

Nelson W. Aldrich (R)
George P. Wetmore (R)

Representatives

Adin B. Capron (R)
Daniel L. D. Granger (D)

South Carolina

Senators

Asbury C. Latimer (D)
Benjamin R. Tillman (D)

Representatives

Wyatt Aiken (D)
J. Edwin Ellerbe (D)
David E. Finley (D)
Joseph T. Johnson (D)
George S. Legare (D)
Asbury F. Lever (D)
James O. Patterson (D)

South Dakota

Senators

Robert J. Gamble (R)
Alfred B. Kittredge (R)

Representatives

Charles H. Burke (R)
Eben W. Martin (R)

Tennessee

Senators

Edward W. Carmack (D)
James B. Frazier (D)

Representatives

Walter P. Brownlow (R)
Mounce G. Butler (D)
Finis J. Garrett (D)
John W. Gaines (D)
Nathan W. Hale (R)
William C. Houston (D)
John A. Moon (D)
Lemuel P. Padgett (D)
Malcolm R. Patterson (D) r.
Nov. 1906
Thetus W. Sims (D)

Texas

Senators

Charles A. Culberson (D)
Joseph W. Bailey (D)

Representatives

Jack Beall (D)
Moses L. Broocks (D)
George F. Burgess (D)
Albert S. Burleson (D)
Scott Field (D)
John Nance Garner (D)
Oscar W. Gillespie (D)
Alexander W. Gregg (D)
Robert L. Henry (D)
John M. Moore (D)
Choice B. Randell (D)
Gordon J. Russell (D)
Morris Sheppard (D)
James L. Slayden (D)
William R. Smith (D)
John H. Stephens (D)

Utah

Senators

Reed Smoot (R)
George Sutherland (R)

Representatives

Joseph Howell (R)

Vermont

Senators

William P. Dillingham (R)
Redfield Proctor (R)

Representatives

David J. Foster (R)
Kittredge Haskins (R)

Virginia

Senators

John W. Daniel (D)
Thomas S. Martin (D)

Representatives

Henry D. Flood (D)
Carter Glass (D)
James Hay (D)
William A. Jones (D)
John Lamb (D)
Harry L. Maynard (D)
John F. Rixey (D) d. Feb. 1907
Edward W. Saunders (D) s.
1906
Campbell Slemp (R)
Robert G. Southall (D)
Claude A. Swanson (D) r. Jan.
1906

Washington

Senators

Levi Ankeny (R)
Samuel H. Piles (R)

Representatives

Francis W. Cushman (R)
William E. Humphrey (R)
Wesley L. Jones (R)

West Virginia

Senators

Stephen B. Elkins (R)
Nathan B. Scott (R)

Representatives

Thomas B. Davis (D)
Alston G. Dayton (R) r. Mar.
1905
Blackburn B. Dovener (R)
Joseph H. Gaines (R)
James A. Hughes (R)
Harry C. Woodyard (R)

Wisconsin

Senators

Robert M. La Follette (R)
John C. Spooner (R)

Representatives

Henry C. Adams (R) d. July
1906
Joseph W. Babcock (R)
Webster E. Brown (R)
Henry A. Cooper (R)
James H. Davidson (R)
John J. Esch (R)
John J. Jenkins (R)
Edward S. Minor (R)
John M. Nelson (R) s. 1906

Theobald Otjen (R)
William H. Stafford (R)
Charles H. Weisse (D)

Wyoming

Senators

Clarence D. Clark (R)
Francis E. Warren (R)

Representatives

Frank W. Mondell (R)

Sixtieth Congress

(Mar. 4, 1907, to
Mar. 3, 1909)

President of the Senate: Charles
W. Fairbanks
*President Pro Tempore of the
Senate:* William P. Frye
*Speaker of the House of
Representatives:* Joseph G.
Cannon

Alabama

Senators

John H. Bankhead (D) s. 1907
Joseph F. Johnston (D)
John T. Morgan (D) d. June
1907
Edmund W. Pettus (D) d. July
1907

Representatives

John L. Burnett (D)
Henry D. Clayton (D)
William B. Craig (D)
J. Thomas Heflin (D)
Richmond P. Hobson (D)
William Richardson (D)
George W. Taylor (D)
Oscar W. Underwood (D)
Ariosto A. Wiley (D) d. June
1908
Oliver C. Wiley (D) s. 1908

Arkansas

Senators

James P. Clarke (D)
Jeff Davis (D)

Representatives

Stephen Brundidge, Jr. (D)
William B. Cravens (D)
John C. Floyd (D)
Robert B. Macon (D)
Charles C. Reid (D)
Joseph T. Robinson (D)
Robert M. Wallace (D)

California

Senators

Frank P. Flint (R)

George C. Perkins (R)

Representatives

William F. Englebright (R)
Everis A. Hayes (R)
Julius Kahn (R)
Joseph R. Knowland (R)
Duncan E. McKinlay (R)
James McLachlan (R)
James C. Needham (R)
Sylvester C. Smith (R)

Colorado

Senators

Simon Guggenheim (R)
Henry M. Teller (D)

Representatives

Robert W. Bonynge (R)
George W. Cook (R)
Warren A. Haggott (R)

Connecticut

Senators

Morgan G. Bulkeley (R)
Frank B. Brandegee (R)

Representatives

E. Stevens Henry (R)
Edwin W. Higgins (R)
Ebenezer J. Hill (R)
George L. Lilley (R)
Nehemiah D. Sperry (R)

Delaware

Senators

Henry A. Du Pont (R)
Harry A. Richardson (R)

Representatives

Hiram R. Burton (R)

Florida

Senators

William J. Bryan (D) ta. 1908
Stephen R. Mallory (D) d. Dec.
1908
William H. Milton (D) s. 1908
James P. Taliaferro (D)

Representatives

Frank Clark (D)
William B. Lamar (D)
Stephen M Sparkman (D)

Georgia

Senators

Augustus O. Bacon (D)
Alexander S. Clay (D)

Representatives

William C. Adamson (D)
Charles L. Bartlett (D)
Thomas M. Bell (D)
William G. Brantley (D)
Charles G. Edwards (D)
James M. Griggs (D)
Thomas W. Hardwick (D)
William M. Howard (D)
Gordon Lee (D)
Elijah B. Lewis (D)
Leonidas F. Livingston (D)

Idaho

Senators

William E. Borah (R)
Weldon B. Heyburn (R)

Representatives

Burton L. French (R)

Illinois

Senators

Shelby M. Cullom (R)
Albert J. Hopkins (R)

Representatives

Henry S. Boutell (R)
Ben Franklin Caldwell (D)
Joseph G. Cannon (R)
Pleasant T. Chapman (R)
George E. Foss (R)
Martin D. Foster (D)
Charles E. Fuller (R)
Joseph V. Graff (R)
Philip Knopf (R)
William Lorimer (R)
Frank O. Lowden (R)
James T. McDermott (D)
Charles McGavin (R)
William B. McKinley (R)
James McKinney (R)
Martin B. Madden (R)
James R. Mann (R)
George W. Prince (R)
Henry T. Rainey (D)
William A. Rodenberg (R)
Adolph J. Sabath (D)
Howard M. Snapp (R)
John A. Sterling (R)
Napoleon B. Thistlewood (R) s.
  1908
William W. Wilson (R)

Indiana

Senators

Albert J. Beveridge (R)
James A. Hemenway (R)

Representatives

John A. M. Adair (D)
Henry A. Barnhart (D) s. 1908
Abraham L. Brick (R) d. Apr.
  1908
John C. Chaney (R)
William E. Cox (D)
Edgar D. Crumpacker (R)
Lincoln Dixon (D)

John H. Foster (R)
Clarence C. Gilhams (R)
Elias S. Holliday (R)
Charles B. Landis (R)
Jesse Overstreet (R)
George W. Rauch (D)
James E. Watson (R)

Iowa

Senators

William B. Allison (R) d. Aug.
  1908
Albert B. Cummins (R) s. 1908
Jonathan P. Dolliver (R)

Representatives

Benjamin P. Birdsall (R)
James P. Conner (R)
Robert G. Cousins (R)
Albert F. Dawson (R)
Daniel W. Hamilton (D)
Gilbert N. Haugen (R)
William P. Hepburn (R)
Elbert H. Hubbard (R)
John A. T. Hull (R)
Charles A. Kennedy (R)
Walter I. Smith (R)

Kansas

Senators

Charles Curtis (R)
Chester I. Long (R)

Representatives

Daniel R. Anthony, Jr. (R)
William A. Calderhead (R)
Philip P. Campbell (R)
Edmond H. Madison (R)
James M. Miller (R)
Victor Murdock (R)
William A. Reeder (R)
Charles F. Scott (R)

Kentucky

Senators

James B. McCreary (D)
Thomas H. Paynter (D)

Representatives

Joseph B. Bennett (R)
Don C. Edwards (R)
Harvey Helm (D)
Addison D. James (R)
Ollie M. James (D)
Ben Johnson (D)
William P. Kimball (D)
John W. Langley (R)
Joseph L. Rhinock (D)
J. Swagar Sherley (D)
Augustus O. Stanley (D)

Louisiana

Senators

Murphy J. Foster (D)
Samuel D. McEnery (D)

Representatives

Robert F. Broussard (D)
Robert C. Davey (D) d. Dec.
  1908
Albert Estopinal (D) s. 1908
George K. Favrot (D)
Adolph Meyer (D) d. Mar.
  1908
Arsene P. Pujo (D)
Joseph E. Ransdell (D)
John T. Watkins (D)

Maine

Senators

William P. Frye (R)
Eugene Hale (R)

Representatives

Amos L. Allen (R)
Edwin C. Burleigh (R)
Frank E. Guernsey (R) s. 1908
Charles E. Littlefield (R) r.
  Sept. 1908
Llewellyn Powers (R) d. July
  1908
John P. Swasey (R) s. 1908

Maryland

Senators

Isidor Rayner (D)
John Walter Smith (D) s. 1908
William P. Whyte (D) d. Mar.
  1908

Representatives

John Gill, Jr. (D)
William H. Jackson (R)
Sydney E. Mudd (R)
George A. Pearre (R)
J. Fred C. Talbott (D)
Harry B. Wolf (D)

Massachusetts

Senators

W. Murray Crane (R)
Henry Cabot Lodge (R)

Representatives

Butler Ames (R)
Augustus P. Gardner (R)
Frederick H. Gillett (R)
William S. Greene (R)
John A. Keliher (D)
George P. Lawrence (R)
William C. Lovering (R)
Samuel W. McCall (R)
Joseph F. O'Connell (D)
Andrew J. Peters (D)
Ernest W. Roberts (R)
Charles Q. Tirrell (R)
Charles G. Washburn (R)
John W. Weeks (R)

Michigan

Senators

Julius C. Burrows (R)
William Alden Smith (R)

Representatives

Archibald B. Darragh (R)
Edwin Denby (R)
Gerrit J. Diekema (R)
Joseph W. Fordney (R)
Washington Gardner (R)
Edward L. Hamilton (R)
George A. Loud (R)
James C. McLaughlin (R)
Henry McMorran (R)
Samuel W. Smith (R)
Charles E. Townsend (R)
H. Olin Young (R)

Minnesota

Senators

Moses E. Clapp (R)
Knute Nelson (R)

Representatives

J. Adam Bede (R)
Charles R. Davis (R)
Winfield S. Hammond (D)
Charles A. Lindbergh (R)
Frank M. Nye (R)
Halvor Steenerson (R)
Frederick C. Stevens (R)
James A. Tawney (R)
Andrew J. Volstead (R)

Mississippi

Senators

Anselm J. McLaurin (D)
Hernando D. Money (D)

Representatives

Eaton J. Bowers (D)
Adam M. Byrd (D)
Ezekiel S. Candler, Jr. (D)
Wilson S. Hill (D)
Benjamin G. Humphreys (D)
Frank A. McLain (D)
Thomas Spight (D)
John Sharp Williams (D)

Missouri

Senators

William J. Stone (D)
William Warner (R)

Representatives

Joshua W. Alexander (D)
Richard Bartholdt (R)
Charles F. Booher (D)
Henry S. Caulfield (R)
Champ Clark (D)
Harry M. Coudrey (R)
David A. De Armond (D)
Edgar C. Ellis (R)
Thomas Hackney (D)

Courtney W. Hamlin (D)
J. Robert Lamar (D)
James T. Lloyd (D)
William W. Rucker (D)
Joseph J. Russell (D)
Dorsey W. Shackleford (D)
Madison R. Smith (D)

Montana

Senators

Thomas H. Carter (R)
Joseph M. Dixon (R)

Representatives

Charles N. Pray (R)

Nebraska

Senators

Elmer J. Burkett (R)
Norris Brown (R)

Representatives

John F. Boyd (R)
Edmund H. Hinshaw (R)
Gilbert M. Hitchcock (D)
Moses P. Kinkaid (R)
George W. Norris (R)
Ernest M. Pollard (R)

Nevada

Senators

Francis G. Newlands (D)
George S. Nixon (R)

Representatives

George A. Bartlett (D)

New Hampshire

Senators

Henry E. Burnham (R)
Jacob H. Gallinger (R)

Representatives

Frank D. Currier (R)
Cyrus A. Sulloway (R)

New Jersey

Senators

Frank O. Briggs (R)
John Kean (R)

Representatives

Charles N. Fowler (R)
John J. Gardner (D)
James A. Hamill (D)
Benjamin F. Howell (R)
William Hughes (D)
Eugene W. Leake (D)
Henry C. Loudenslager (R)
Richard W. Parker (R)
Le Gage Pratt (D)

Ira W. Wood (R)

New York

Senators

Chauncey M. Depew (R)
Thomas C. Platt (R)

Representatives

De Alva S. Alexander (R)
John E. Andrus (R)
William S. Bennet (R)
Thomas W. Bradley (R)
William M. Calder (R)
W. Bourke Cochran (D)
William W. Cocks (R)
William H. Draper (R)
Michael E. Driscoll (R)
Charles T. Dunwell (R) d. June 1908
Cyrus Durey (R)
John W. Dwight (R)
George W. Fairchild (R)
J. Sloat Fassett (R)
John J. Fitzgerald (D)
Otto G. Foelker (R) s. 1908
Charles V. Fornes (D)
Henry M. Goldfogle (D)
Joseph A. Goulden (D)
Francis B. Harrison (D)
Charles L. Knapp (R)
Charles L. Law (R)
George H. Lindsay (D)
Samuel McMillan (R)
George R. Malby (R)
J. Van Vechten Olcott (R)
Herbert Parsons (R)
Sereno E. Payne (R)
James B. Perkins (R)
Peter A. Porter (R,D)
Daniel J. Riordan (D)
William H. Ryan (D)
James S. Sherman (R)
George N. Southwick (R)
William Sulzer (D)
Edward B. Vreeland (R)
George E. Waldo (R)
William Willett, Jr. (D)

North Carolina

Senators

Furnifold McL. Simmons (D)
Lee S. Overman (D)

Representatives

William T. Crawford (D)
Hannibal L. Godwin (D)
Richard N. Hackett (D)
Claude Kitchin (D)
William W. Kitchin (D) r. Jan. 1909
Robert N. Page (D)
Edward W. Pou (D)
John H. Small (D)
Charles R. Thomas (D)
Edwin Y. Webb (D)

North Dakota

Senators

Henry C. Hansbrough (R)
Porter J. McCumber (R)

Representatives

Asle J. Gronna (R)
Thomas F. Marshall (R)

Ohio

Senators

Charles W. F. Dick (R)
Joseph B. Foraker (R)

Representatives

Timothy T. Ansberry (D)
William A. Ashbrook (R)
Henry T. Bannon (R)
Theodore E. Burton (R)
Ralph D. Cole (R)
Beman G. Dawes (R)
Matthew R. Denver (D)
Albert Douglas (R)
Herman P. Goebel (R)
J. Eugene Harding (R)
L. Paul Howland (R)
J. Warren Keifer (R)
James Kennedy (R)
J. Ford Laning (R)
Nicholas Longworth (R)
Grant E. Mouser (R)
Isaac R. Sherwood (D)
Edward L. Taylor (R)
William A. Thomas (R)
William E. Tou Velle (D)
Capell L. Weems (R)

Oklahoma

Senators

Thomas P. Gore (D)
Robert L. Owen (D)

Representatives

Charles D. Carter (D)
James S. Davenport (D)
Scott Ferris (D)
Elmer L. Fulton (D)
Bird S. McGuire (R)

Oregon

Senators

Jonathan Bourne, Jr. (R)
Charles W. Fulton (R)

Representatives

William R. Ellis (R)
Willis C. Hawley (R)

Pennsylvania

Senators

Philander C. Knox (R)
Boies Penrose (R)

Representatives

Ernest F. Acheson (R)
Charles F. Barclay (R)
Andrew J. Barchfeld (R)
Arthur L. Bates (R)
Joseph G. Beale (R)

Henry H. Bingham (R)
J. Davis Brodhead (D)
Charles N. Brumm (R) r. Jan. 1909
James F. Burke (R)
Thomas S. Butler (R)
Henry B. Cassel (R)
Joel Cook (R)
Allen F. Cooper (R)
John Dalzell (R)
Benjamin K. Focht (R)
William W. Foulkrod (R)
William H. Graham (R)
George F. Huff (R)
George W. Kipp (D)
Daniel F. Lafean (R)
John T. Lenahan (D)
George D. McCreary (R)
John G. McHenry (D)
Reuben O. Moon (R)
J. Hampton Moore (R)
Thomas D. Nicholls (D)
Marlin E. Olmsted (R)
John M. Reynolds (R)
John H. Rothermel (D)
Irving P. Wanger (R)
Nelson P. Wheeler (R)
William B. Wilson (D)

Rhode Island

Senators

Nelson W. Aldrich (R)
George P. Wetmore (R)

Representatives

Adin B. Capron (R)
Daniel L. D. Granger (D) d. Feb. 1909

South Carolina

Senators

Frank B. Gary (D) s. 1908
Asbury C. Latimer (D) d. Feb. 1908
Benjamin R. Tillman (D)

Representatives

Wyatt Aiken (D)
J. Edwin Ellerbe (D)
David E. Finley (D)
Joseph T. Johnson (D)
George S. Legare (D)
Asbury F. Lever (D)
James O. Patterson (D)

South Dakota

Senators

Robert J. Gamble (R)
Alfred B. Kittredge (R)

Representatives

Philo Hall (R)
Eben W. Martin (R)
William H. Parker (R)

Tennessee

Senators

James B. Frazier (D)
Robert L. Taylor (D)

Representatives

Walter P. Brownlow (R)
John W. Gaines (D)
Finis J. Garrett (D)
George W. Gordon (D)
Nathan W. Hale (R)
William C. Houston (D)
Cordell Hull (D)
John A. Moon (D)
Lemuel P. Padgett (D)
Thetus W. Sims (D)

Texas

Senators

Charles A. Culberson (D)
Joseph W. Bailey (D)

Representatives

Jack Beall (D)
George F. Burgess (D)
Albert S. Burleson (D)
Samuel B. Cooper (D)
John Nance Garner (D)
Oscar W. Gillespie (D)
Alexander W. Gregg (D)
Rufus Hardy (D)
Robert L. Henry (D)
John M. Moore (D)
Choice B. Randell (D)
Gordon J. Russell (D)
Morris Sheppard (D)
James L. Slayden (D)
William R. Smith (D)
John H. Stephens (D)

Utah

Senators

Reed Smoot (R)
George Sutherland (R)

Representatives

Joseph Howell (R)

Vermont

Senators

William P. Dillingham (R)
Carroll S. Page (R) s. 1908
Redfield Proctor (R) d. Mar.
   1908
John W. Stewart (R) ta. 1908

Representatives

David J. Foster (R)
Kittredge Haskins (R)

Virginia

Senators

John W. Daniel (D)
Thomas S. Martin (D)

Representatives

Charles C. Carlin (D)
Henry D. Flood (D)
Carter Glass (D)
James Hay (D)
William A. Jones (D)
John Lamb (D)
Francis R. Lassiter (D)
Harry L. Maynard (D)
Edward W. Saunders (D)
C. Bascom Slemp (R) s. 1908

Washington

Senators

Levi Ankeny (R)
Samuel H. Piles (R)

Representatives

Francis W. Cushman (R)
William E. Humphrey (R)
Wesley L. Jones (R)

West Virginia

Senators

Stephen B. Elkins (R)
Nathan B. Scott (R)

Representatives

Joseph H. Gaines (R)
William P. Hubbard (R)
James A. Hughes (R)
George C. Sturgiss (R)
Harry C. Woodyard (R)

Wisconsin

Senators

Robert M. La Follette (R)
John C. Spooner (R) r. Apr.
   1907
Isaac Stephenson (R) s. 1907

Representatives

William J. Cary (R)
Henry A. Cooper (R)
James H. Davidson (R)
John J. Esch (R)
John J. Jenkins (R)
Gustav Kustermann (R)
Elmer A. Morse (R)
James W. Murphy (D)
John M. Nelson (R)
William H. Stafford (R)
Charles H. Weisse (D)

Wyoming

Senators

Clarence D. Clark (R)

Francis E. Warren (R)

Representatives

Frank W. Mondell (R)

Sixty-First Congress

(Mar. 4, 1908, to
Mar. 3, 1911)

President of the Senate: James
   S. Sherman
*President Pro Tempore of the
   Senate:* William P. Frye
*Speaker of the House of
   Representatives:* Joseph G.
   Cannon

Alabama

Senators

John H. Bankhead (D)
Joseph F. Johnston (D)

Representatives

John L. Burnett (D)
Henry D. Clayton (D)
William B. Craig (D)
S. Hubert Dent, Jr. (D)
J. Thomas Heflin (D)
Richmond P. Hobson (D)
William Richardson (D)
George W. Taylor (D)
Oscar W. Underwood (D)

Arkansas

Senators

James P. Clarke (D)
Jeff Davis (D)

Representatives

William B. Cravens (D)
John C. Floyd (D)
Robert B. Macon (D)
William A. Oldfield (D)
Joseph T. Robinson (D)
Charles C. Reid (D)
Robert M. Wallace (D)

California

Senators

Frank P. Flint (R)
George C. Perkins (R)

Representatives

William F. Englebright (R)
Everis A. Hayes (R)
Julius Kahn (R)
Joseph R. Knowland (R)
Duncan E. McKinlay (R)
James McLachlan (R)
James C. Needham (R)
Sylvester C. Smith (R)

Colorado

Senators

Simon Guggenheim (R)
Charles J. Hughes, Jr. (D) d.
   Jan. 1911

Representatives

John A. Martin (D)
Atterson W. Rucker (D)
Edward T. Taylor (D)

Connecticut

Senators

Frank B. Brandegee (R)
Morgan G. Bulkeley (R)

Representatives

E. Stevens Henry (R)
Edwin W. Higgins (R)
Ebenezer J. Hill (R)
Nehemiah D. Sperry (R)
John Q. Tilson (R)

Delaware

Senators

Henry A. Du Pont (R)
Harry A. Richardson (R)

Representatives

William H. Herald (R)

Florida

Senators

Duncan U. Fletcher (D)
James P. Taliaferro (D)

Representatives

Frank Clark (D)
Dannitte H. Mays (D)
Stephen M Sparkman (D)

Georgia

Senators

Augustus O. Bacon (D)
Alexander S. Clay (D) d. Nov.
   1910
Joseph M. Terrell (D) s. 1910

Representatives

William C. Adamson (D)
Charles L. Bartlett (D)
Thomas M. Bell (D)
William G. Brantley (D)
Charles G. Edwards (D)
James M. Griggs (D) d. Jan.
   1910
Thomas W. Hardwick (D)
William M. Howard (D)
Dudley M. Hughes (D)
Gordon Lee (D)
Leonidas F. Livingston (D)

Seaborn A. Roddenbery (D) s.
1910

Idaho

Senators

William E. Borah (R)
Weldon B. Heyburn (R)

Representatives

Thomas R. Hamer (R)

Illinois

Senators

Shelby M. Cullom (R)
William Lorimer (R)

Representatives

Henry S. Boutell (R)
Joseph G. Cannon (R)
Pleasant T. Chapman (R)
George E. Foss (R)
Martin D. Foster (R)
Charles E. Fuller (R)
Thomas Gallagher (D)
Joseph V. Graff (R)
James M. Graham (D)
William Lorimer (R) r. June
1909
Frank O. Lowden (R)
Frederick Lundin (R)
James T. McDermott (D)
William B. McKinley (R)
James McKinney (R)
Martin B. Madden (R)
James R. Mann (R)
William J. Moxley (R) r. June
1909
George W. Prince (R)
Henry T. Rainey (D)
William A. Rodenberg (R)
Adolph J. Sabath (D)
Howard M. Snapp (R)
John A. Sterling (R)
Napoleon B. Thistlewood (R)
William W. Wilson (R)

Indiana

Senators

Albert J. Beveridge (R)
Benjamin F. Shively (D)

Representatives

John A. M. Adair (D)
William O. Barnard (R)
Henry A. Barnhart (D)
John W. Boehne (D)
Cyrus Cline (D)
William E. Cox (D)
Edgar D. Crumpacker (R)
William A. Cullop (D)
Lincoln Dixon (D)
Charles A. Korbly (D)
Martin A. Morrison (D)
Ralph W. Moss (D)
George W. Rauch (D)

Iowa

Senators

Albert B. Cummins (R)
Jonathan P. Dolliver (R) d.
Oct. 1910
Lafayette Young (R) ta. 1910

Representatives

Albert F. Dawson (R)
James W. Good (R)
Gilbert N. Haugen (R)
Elbert H. Hubbard (R)
John A. T. Hull (R)
William D. Jamieson (D)
Nathan E. Kendall (R)
Charles A. Kennedy (R)
Charles E. Pickett (R)
Walter I. Smith (R)
Frank P. Woods (R)

Kansas

Senators

Joseph L. Bristow (R)
Charles Curtis (R)

Representatives

Daniel R. Anthony, Jr. (R)
William A. Calderhead (R)
Philip P. Campbell (R)
Edmond H. Madison (R)
James M. Miller (R)
Victor Murdock (R)
William A. Reeder (R)
Charles F. Scott (R)

Kentucky

Senators

William O. Bradley (R)
Thomas H. Paynter (D)

Representatives

Joseph B. Bennett (R)
James C. Cantrill (D)
Don C. Edwards (R)
Harvey Helm (D)
Ollie M. James (D)
Ben Johnson (D)
John W. Langley (R)
Joseph L. Rhinock (D)
J. Swagar Sherley (D)
Augustus O. Stanley (D)
Robert Y. Thomas, Jr. (D)

Louisiana

Senators

Murphy J. Foster (D)
Samuel D. McEnery (D) d.
June 1910
John R. Thorton (D) s. 1910

Representatives

Robert F. Broussard (D)
H. Garland Dupre (D) s. 1910
Albert Estopinal (D)

Samuel L. Gilmore (D) d. July
1910
Arsene P. Pujo (D)
Joseph E. Ransdell (D)
John T. Watkins (D)
Robert C. Wickliffe (D)

Maine

Senators

William P. Frye (R)
Eugene Hale (R)

Representatives

Amos L. Allen (R) d. Feb.
1911
Edwin C. Burleigh (R)
Frank E. Guernsey (R)
John P. Swasey (R)

Maryland

Senators

Isidor Rayner (D)
John Walter Smith (D)

Representatives

J. Harry Covington (D)
John Gill, Jr. (D)
John Kronmiller (R)
Sydney E. Mudd (R)
George A. Pearre (R)
J. Fred C. Talbott (D)

Massachusetts

Senators

W. Murray Crane (R)
Henry Cabot Lodge (R)

Representatives

Butler Ames (R)
Eugene N. Foss (D) s. 1910
Augustus P. Gardner (R)
Frederick H. Gillett (R)
William S. Greene (R)
John A. Keliher (D)
George P. Lawrence (R)
William C. Lovering (R) d.
Feb. 1910
Samuel W. McCall (R)
John J. Mitchell (D) s. 1910
Joseph F. O'Connell (D)
Andrew J. Peters (D)
Ernest W. Roberts (R)
Charles Q. Tirrell (R) d. July
1910
Charles G. Washburn (R)
John W. Weeks (R)

Michigan

Senators

Julius C. Burrows (R)
William Alden Smith (R)

Representatives

Edwin Denby (R)
Gerrit J. Diekema (R)

Francis H. Dodds (R)
Joseph W. Fordney (R)
Washington Gardner (R)
Edward L. Hamilton (R)
George A. Loud (R)
James C. MCLaughlin (R)
Henry McMorran (R)
Samuel W. Smith (R)
Charles E. Townsend (R)
H. Olin Young (R)

Minnesota

Senators

Moses E. Clapp (R)
Knute Nelson (R)

Representatives

Charles R. Davis (R)
Winfield S. Hammond (D)
Charles A. Lindbergh (R)
Clarence B. Miller (R)
Frank M. Nye (R)
Halvor Steenerson (R)
Frederick C. Stevens (R)
James A. Tawney (R)
Andrew J. Volstead (R)

Mississippi

Senators

James Gordon (D) ta. 1910
Anselm J. McLaurin (D) d.
Dec. 1909
Hernando D. Money (D)
Le Roy Percy (D) s. 1910

Representatives

Eaton J. Bowers (D)
Adam M. Byrd (D)
Ezekiel S. Candler, Jr. (D)
James W. Collier (D)
William A. Dickson (D)
Benjamin G. Humphreys (D)
Thomas U. Sisson (D)
Thomas Spight (D)

Missouri

Senators

William J. Stone (D)
William Warner (R)

Representatives

Joshua W. Alexander (D)
Richard Bartholdt (R)
Charles F. Booher (D)
William P. Borland (D)
Champ Clark (D)
Harry M. Coudrey (R)
Charles A. Crow (R)
David A. De Armond (D) d.
Nov. 1909
Clement C. Dickinson (D) s.
1910
Politte Elvins (R)
Patrick F. Gill (D)
Courtney W. Hamlin (D)
James T. Lloyd (D)
Charles H. Morgan (R)
Arthur P. Murphy (R)
William W. Rucker (D)

Dorsey W. Shackleford (D)

Montana

Senators

Thomas H. Carter (R)
Joseph M. Dixon (R)

Representatives

Charles N. Pray (R)

Nebraska

Senators

Norris Brown (R)
Elmer J. Burkett (R)

Representatives

Edmund H. Hinshaw (R)
Gilbert M. Hitchcock (D)
Moses P. Kinkaid (R)
James P. Latta (D)
John A. Maguire (D)
George W. Norris (R)

Nevada

Senators

Francis G. Newlands (D)
George S. Nixon (R)

Representatives

George A. Bartlett (D)

New Hampshire

Senators

Henry E. Burnham (R)
Jacob H. Gallinger (R)

Representatives

Frank D. Currier (R)
Cyrus A. Sulloway (R)

New Jersey

Senators

Frank O. Briggs (R)
John Kean (R)

Representatives

Charles N. Fowler (R)
John J. Gardner (D)
James A. Hamill (D)
Benjamin F. Howell (R)
William Hughes (D)
Eugene F. Kinkead (D)
Henry C. Loudenslager (R)
Richard W. Parker (R)
William H. Wiley (R)
Ira W. Wood (R)

New York

Senators

Chauncey M. Depew (R)
Elihu Root (R)

Representatives

De Alva S. Alexander (R)
John E. Andrus (R)
William S. Bennett (R)
Thomas W. Bradley (R)
William M. Calder (R)
William W. Cocks (R)
Michael F. Conry (D)
William H. Draper (R)
Daniel A. Driscoll (D)
Michael E. Driscoll (R)
Cyrus Durey (R)
John W. Dwight (R)
George W. Fairchild (R)
J. Sloat Fassett (R)
Hamilton Fish (R)
John J. Fitzgerald (D)
Otto G. Foelker (R)
Charles V. Fornes (D)
Henry M. Goldfogle (D)
Joseph A. Goulden (D)
Francis B. Harrison (D)
James S. Havens (D) s. 1910
Charles L. Knapp (R)
Charles B. Law (R)
George H. Lindsay (D)
George R. Malby (R)
Charles S. Millington (R)
J. Van Vechten Olcott (R)
Herbert Parsons (R)
Sereno E. Payne (R)
James B. Perkins (R) d. Mar. 1910
Daniel J. Riordan (D)
James S. Simmons (R)
George N. Southwick (R)
William Sulzer (D)
Edward B. Vreeland (R)
William Willett, Jr. (D)
Richard Young (R)

North Carolina

Senators

Lee S. Overman (D)
Furnifold McL. Simmons (D)

Representatives

Charles H. Cowles (R)
Hannibal L. Godwin (D)
John G. Grant (R)
Claude Kitchin (D)
John M. Morehead (R)
Robert N. Page (D)
Edward W. Pou (D)
John H. Small (D)
Charles R. Thomas (D)
Edwin Y. Webb (D)

North Dakota

Senators

Asle J. Gronna (R) s. 1911
Martin N. Johnson (R) d. Oct. 1909
Porter J. McCumber (R)
William E. Purcell (D) ta. 1910

Fountain L. Thompson (D) r. Jan. 1910

Representatives

Asle J. Gronna (R) r. 1911
Louis B. Hanna (R)

Ohio

Senators

Theodore E. Burton (R)
Charles W. F. Dick (R)

Representatives

Carl C. Anderson (D)
Timothy T. Ansberry (D)
William A. Ashbrook (D)
James H. Cassidy (R)
Ralph D. Cole (R)
James M. Cox (D)
Matthew R. Denver (D)
Albert Douglas (R)
Herman P. Goebel (R)
David A. Hollingsworth (R)
L. Paul Howland (R)
Adna R. Johnson (R)
James Joyce (R)
J. Warren Keifer (R)
James Kennedy (R)
Nicholas Longworth (R)
William G. Sharp (D)
Isaac R. Sherwood (D)
Edward L. Taylor, Jr. (R)
William A. Thomas (R)
William E. Tou Velle (D)

Oklahoma

Senators

Thomas P. Gore (D)
Robert L. Owen (D)

Representatives

Charles D. Carter (D)
Charles E. Creager (R)
Scott Ferris (D)
Bird S. McGuire (R)
Dick T. Morgan (R)

Oregon

Senators

Jonathan Bourne, Jr. (R)
George E. Chamberlain (D)

Representatives

William R. Ellis (R)
Willis C. Hawley (R)

Pennsylvania

Senators

George T. Oliver (R)
Boies Penrose (R)

Representatives

Andrew J. Barchfeld (R)
Charles F. Barclay (R)

Arthur L. Bates (R)
Henry H. Bingham (R)
James F. Burke (R)
Thomas S. Butler (R)
Joel Cook (R)
Allen F. Cooper (R)
John Dalzell (R)
Benjamin K. Focht (R)
William W. Foulkrod (R) d. Nov. 1910
Alfred B. Garner (R)
William H. Graham (R)
William W. Griest (R)
George F. Huff (R)
Daniel F. Lafean (R)
Jonathan N. Langham (R)
George D. McCreary (R)
John G. McHenry (D)
Reuben O. Moon (R)
J. Hampton Moore (R)
Thomas D. Nicholls (D)
Marlin E. Olmsted (R)
A. Mitchell Palmer (D)
Henry W. Palmer (R)
Charles C. Pratt (R)
John M. Reynolds (R)
John H. Rothermel (D)
John K. Tener (R)
Irving P. Wanger (R)
Nelson P. Wheeler (R)
William B. Wilson (D)

Rhode Island

Senators

Nelson W. Aldrich (R)
George P. Wetmore (R)

Representatives

Adin B. Capron (R)
William P. Sheffield (R)

South Carolina

Senators

Ellison D. Smith (D)
Benjamin R. Tillman (D)

Representatives

Wyatt Aiken (D)
J. Edwin Ellerbe (D)
David E. Finley (D)
Joseph T. Johnson (D)
George S. Legare (D)
Asbury F. Lever (D)
James O. Patterson (D)

South Dakota

Senators

Coe I. Crawford (R)
Robert J. Gamble (R)

Representatives

Charles H. Burke (R)
Eben W. Martin (R)

Tennessee

Senators

James B. Frazier (D)
Robert L. Taylor (D)

Representatives

Richard W. Austin (R)
Walter P. Brownlow (R) d. July 1910
Joseph W. Byrns (D)
Finis J. Garrett (D)
George W. Gordon (D)
William C. Houston (D)
Cordell Hull (D)
Zachary D. Massey (R) s. 1910
John A. Moon (D)
Lemuel P. Padgett (D)
Thetus W. Sims (D)

Texas

Senators

Joseph W. Bailey (D)
Charles A. Culberson (D)

Representatives

Jack Beall (D)
George F. Burgess (D)
Albert A. Burleson (D)
Martin Dies (D)
John Nance Garner (D)
Oscar W. Gillespie (D)
Alexander W. Gregg (D)
Rufus Hardy (D)
Robert L. Henry (D)
Robert M. Lively (D) s. 1910
John M. Moore (D)
Choice B. Randell (D)
Gordon J. Russell (D) r. June 1910
Morris Sheppard (D)
James L. Slayden (D)
William R. Smith (D)
John H. Stephens (D)

Utah

Senators

Reed Smoot (R)
George Sutherland (R)

Representatives

Joseph Howell (R)

Vermont

Senators

William P. Dillingham (R)
Carroll S. Page (R)

Representatives

David J. Foster (R)
Frank Plumley (R)

Virginia

Senators

John W. Daniel (D) d. June 1910
Thomas S. Martin (D)
Claude A. Swanson (D) s. 1910

Representatives

Charles C. Carlin (D)
Henry D. Flood (D)
Carter Glass (D)
James Hay (D)
William A. Jones (D)
John Lamb (D)
Francis R. Lassiter (D) d. Oct. 1909
Harry L. Maynard (D)
Edward W. Saunders (D)
C. Bascom Slemp (R)
Robert Turnbull (D) s. 1910

Washington

Senators

Wesley L. Jones (R)
Samuel H. Piles (R)

Representatives

Francis W. Cushman (R) d. July 1909
William E. Humphrey (R)
William W. McCredie (R)
Miles Poindexter (R)

West Virginia

Senators

Stephen B. Elkins (R) d. Jan. 1911
Davis Elkins (R) ta. 1911
Nathan B. Scott (R)
Clarence W. Watson (D) s. 1911

Representatives

Joseph H. Gaines (R)
William P. Hubbard (R)
James A. Hughes (R)
George C. Sturgiss (R)
Harry C. Woodyard (R)

Wisconsin

Senators

Robert M. La Follette (R)
Isaac Stephenson (R)

Representatives

William J. Cary (R)
Henry A. Cooper (R)
James H. Davidson (R)
John J. Esch (R)
Arthur W. Kopp (R)
Gustav Kustermann (R)
Irvine L. Lenroot (R)
Elmer A. Morse (R)
John M. Nelson (R)
William H. Stafford (R)

Charles H. Weisse (D)

Wyoming

Senators

Clarence D. Clark (R)
Francis E. Warren (R)

Representatives

Frank W. Mondell (R)

Sixty-Second Congress

(Mar. 4, 1911, to Mar. 3, 1913)

President of the Senate: James S. Sherman
Presidents Pro Tempore of the Senate: William P. Frye; Charles Curtis; Augustus O. Bacon; Jacob H. Gallinger; Henry Cabot Lodge; Frank B. Brandegee
Speaker of the House of Representatives: Champ Clark

Alabama

Senators

John H. Bankhead (D)
Joseph F. Johnston (D)

Representatives

Fred L. Blackmon (D)
John L. Burnett (D)
Henry D. Clayton (D)
S. Hubert Dent, Jr. (D)
J. Thomas Heflin (D)
Richmond P. Hobson (D)
William Richardson (D)
George W. Taylor (D)
Oscar W. Underwood (D)

Arizona

Senators

Henry F. Ashurst (D) s. 1912
Marcus A. Smith (D) s. 1912

Representatives

Carl Hayden (D) s. 1912

Arkansas

Senators

James P. Clarke (D)
Jeff Davis (D) d. Jan. 1913
John N. Heiskell (D) ta. 1913
William M. Kavanaugh (D) ş. 1913

Representatives

William B. Cravens (D)
John C. Floyd (D)

William S. Goodwin (D)
Henderson M. Jacoway (D)
Robert B. Macon (D)
William A. Oldfield (D)
Joseph T. Robinson (D) r. Jan. 1913
Samuel M. Taylor (D) s. 1913

California

Senators

George C. Perkins (R)
John D. Works (R)

Representativs

Everis A. Hayes (R)
Julius Kahn (R)
William Kent (R)
Joseph R. Knowland (R)
James C. Needham (R)
John E. Raker (D)
Sylvester C. Smith (R) d. Jan. 1913
William D. Stephens (R)

Colorado

Senators

Simon Guggenheim (R)
Charles S. Thomas (D) s. 1913

Representatives

John A. Martin (D)
Atterson W. Rucker (D)
Edward T. Taylor (D)

Connecticut

Senators

Frank B. Brandegee (R)
George P. McLean (R)

Representatives

E. Stevens Henry (R)
Edwin W. Higgins (R)
Ebenezer J. Hill (R)
Thomas L. Reilly (D)
John Q. Tilson (R)

Delaware

Senators

Henry A. Du Pont (R)
Harry A. Richardson (R)

Representatives

William H. Heald (R)

Florida

Senators

Nathan P. Bryan (D)
Duncan U. Fletcher (D)

Representatives

Frank Clark (D)

Dannitte H. Mays (D)
Stephen M. Sparkman (D)

Georgia

Senators

Augustus O. Bacon (D)
Hoke Smith (D) s. 1911
Joseph M. Terrell (D) r. July
  1911

Representatives

William C. Adamson (D)
Charles L. Bartlett (D)
Thomas M. Bell (D)
William G. Brantley (D)
Charles G. Edwards (D)
Thomas W. Hardwick (D)
William S. Howard (D)
Dudley M. Hughes (D)
Gordon Lee (D)
Seaborn A. Roddenbery (D)
Samuel J. Tribble (D)

Idaho

Senators

William E. Borah (R)
James H. Brady (R) s. 1913
Weldon B. Heyburn (R) d. Oct.
  1911
Kirtland I. Perky (D) ta. 1912

Representatives

Burton L. French (R)

Illinois

Senators

Shelby M. Cullom (R)
William Lorimer (R) r. July
  1912

Representatives

Frank Buchanan (D)
Joseph G. Cannon (R)
Ira C. Copley (R)
Lynden Evans (D)
George E. Foss (R)
Martin D. Foster (D)
H. Robert Fowler (D)
Charles E. Fuller (R)
Thomas Gallagher (D)
James M. Graham (D)
James T. McDermott (D)
John C. McKenzie (R)
William B. McKinley (R)
James McKinney (R)
Martin B. Madden (R)
James R. Mann (R)
George W. Prince (R)
Henry T. Rainey (D)
William A. Rodenberg (R)
Adolph J. Sabath (D)
Edmund J. Stack (D)
John A. Sterling (R)
Claudius U. Stone (D)
Napoleon B. Thistlewood (R)
William W. Wilson (R)

Indiana

Senators

John W. Kern (D)
Benjamin F. Shively (D)

Representatives

John A. M. Adair (D)
Henry A. Barnhart (D)
John W. Boehne (D)
Cyrus Cline (D)
William E. Cox (D)
Edgar D. Crumpacker (R)
William A. Cullop (D)
Lincoln Dixon (D)
Finly H. Gray (D)
Charles A. Korbly (D)
Martin A. Morrison (D)
Ralph W. Moss (D)
George W. Rauch (D)

Iowa

Senators

Albert B. Cummins (R)
William S. Kenyon (R)

Representatives

James W. Good (R)
William R. Green (R)
Gilbert N. Haugen (R)
Elbert H. Hubbard (R) d. June
  1912
Nathan E. Kendall (R)
Charles A. Kennedy (R)
Irvin S. Pepper (D)
Charles E. Pickett (R)
Solomon F. Prouty (R)
George C. Scott (R) s. 1912
Walter I. Smith (R) r. Mar.
  1911
Horace M. Towner (R)
Frank P. Woods (R)

Kansas

Senators

Joseph L. Bristow (R)
Charles Curtis (R)

Representatives

Daniel R. Anthony, Jr. (R)
Philip P. Campbell (R)
Fred S. Jackson (R)
Edmond H. Madison (R) d.
  Sept. 1911
Alexander C. Mitchell (R) d.
  July 1911
Victor Murdock (R)
George A. Neeley (D) s. 1912
Rollin R. Rees (R)
Joseph Taggert (D)
Isaac D. Young (R)

Kentucky

Senators

William O. Bradley (R)
Thomas H. Paynter (D)

Representatives

James C. Cantrill (D)
William J. Fields (D)
Harvey Helm (D)
Ollie M. James (D)
Ben Johnson (D)
John W. Langley (R)
Caleb Powers (R)
Arthur B. Rouse (D)
J. Swagar Sherley (D)
Augustus O. Stanley (D)
Robert Y. Thomas, Jr. (D)

Louisiana

Senators

Murphy J. Foster (D)
John R. Thornton (D)

Representatives

Robert F. Broussard (D)
H. Garland Dupre (D)
Albert Estopinal (D)
Lewis L. Morgan (D) s. 1912
Arsene P. Pujo (D)
Joseph E. Ransdell (D)
John T. Watkins (D)
Robert C. Wickliffe (D) d. June
  1912

Maine

Senators

William P. Frye (R) d. Aug.
  1911
Obadiah Gardner (D) s. 1911
Charles F. Johnson (D)

Representatives

Samuel W. Gould (D)
Frank E. Guernsey (R)
Asher C. Hinds (R)
Daniel J. McGillicuddy (D)

Maryland

Senators

William P. Jackson (R) ta. 1912
Isidor Rayner (D) d. Nov. 1912
John Walter Smith (D)

Representatives

J. Harry Covington (D)
George Konig (D)
David J. Lewis (D)
J. Charles Linthicum (D)
Thomas Parran (R)
J. Fred C. Talbott (D)

Massachusetts

Senators

W. Murray Crane (R)
Henry Cabot Lodge (R)

Representatives

Butler Ames (R)
James M. Curley (D)

Augustus P. Gardner (R)
Frederick H. Gillett (R)
William S. Greene (R)
Robert O. Harris (R)
George P. Lawrence (R)
Samuel W. McCall (R)
William F. Murray (D)
Andrew J. Peters (D)
Ernest W. Roberts (R)
John A. Thayer (D)
John W. Weeks (R)
William H. Wilder (R)

Michigan

Senators

William Alden Smith (R)
Charles E. Townsend (R)

Representatives

Francis H. Dodds (R)
Frank E. Doremus (D)
Joseph W. Fordney (R)
Edward L. Hamilton (R)
George A. Loud (R)
James C. McLaughlin (R)
Henry McMorran (R)
John M. C. Smith (R)
Samuel W. Smith (R)
Edwin F. Sweet (D)
William W. Wedemeyer (R) d.
  Jan. 1913
H. Olin Young (R)

Minnesota

Senators

Moses E. Clapp (R)
Knute Nelson (R)

Representatives

Sydney Anderson (R)
Charles R. Davis (R)
Winfield S. Hammond (D)
Charles A. Lindbergh (R)
Clarence B. Miller (R)
Frank M. Nye (R)
Halvor Steenerson (R)
Frederick C. Stevens (R)
Andrew J. Volstead (R)

Mississippi

Senators

LeRoy Percy (D)
John Sharp Williams (D)

Representatives

Ezekiel S. Candler, Jr. (D)
James W. Collier (D)
William A. Dickson (D)
Pat Harrison (D)
Benjamin G. Humphreys (D)
Thomas U. Sisson (D)
Hubert D. Stephens (D)
Samuel A. Witherspoon (D)

Missouri

Senators

James A. Reed (D)
William J. Stone (D)

Representatives

Joshua W. Alexander (D)
Richard Bartholdt (R)
Charles F. Booher (D)
William P. Borland (D)
Theron E. Catlin (R) r. Aug.
  1912
Champ Clark (D)
James A. Daugherty (D)
Clement C. Dickinson (D)
Leonidas C. Dyer (R)
Patrick F. Gill (D) s. 1912
Courtney H. Hamlin (D)
Walter L. Hensley (D)
James T. Lloyd (D)
Thomas L. Rubey (D)
William W. Rucker (D)
Joseph J. Russell (D)
Dorsey W. Shackleford (D)

Montana

Senators

Joseph M. Dixon (R)
Henry L. Myers (D)

Representatives

Charles N. Pray (R)

Nebraska

Senators

Norris Brown (R)
Gilbert M. Hitchcock (D)

Representatives

Moses P. Kinkaid (R)
James P. Latta (D) d. Sept.
  1911
Charles O. Lobeck (D)
John A. Maguire (D)
George W. Norris (R)
Charles H. Sloan (R)
Daniel V. Stephens (D)

Nevada

Senators

William A. Massey (R) ta. 1912
Francis G. Newlands (D)
George S. Nixon (R) d. June
  1912
Key Pittman (D) s. 1913

Representatives

Edwin E. Roberts (R)

New Hampshire

Senators

Henry E. Burnham (R)

Jacob H. Gallinger (R)

Representatives

Frank D. Currier (R)
Cyrus A. Sulloway (R)

New Jersey

Senators

Frank O. Briggs (R)
James E. Martine (D)

Representatives

William J. Browning (R)
John J. Gardner (D)
James A. Hamill (D)
Archibald C. Hart (D) s. 1912
William Hughes (D) r. Sept.
  1912
Eugene F. Kinkead (D)
Henry C. Loudenslager (R) d.
  Aug. 1911
Walter I. McCoy (D)
Thomas J. Scully (D)
Edward W. Townsend (D)
William E. Tuttle, Jr. (D)
Ira W. Wood (R)

New Mexico

Senators

Thomas B. Catron (R) s. 1912
Albert B. Fall (R) s. 1912

Representatives

George Curry (R) s. 1912
Harvey B. Fergusson (D) s.
  1912

New York

Senators

James A. O'Gorman (D)
Elihu Root (R)

Representatives

Theron Akin (R)
John E. Andrus (R)
Steven B. Ayers (D)
Thomas W. Bradley (R)
William M. Calder (R)
Richard E. Connell (D) d. Oct.
  1912
Michael F. Conry (D)
Henry G. Danforth (R)
Henry S. De Forest (R)
William H. Draper (R)
Daniel A. Driscoll (D)
Michael E. Driscoll (R)
John W. Dwight (R)
George W. Fairchild (R)
John J. Fitzgerald (D)
Charles V. Fornes (D)
Henry George, Jr. (D)
Henry M. Goldfogle (D)
Francis B. Harrison (D)
John J. Kindred (D)
Jefferson M. Levy (D)
George H. Lindsay (D)
Martin W. Littleton (D)
James P. Maher (D)

George R. Malby (D) d. July
  1912
Edwin A. Merritt, Jr. (R) s.
  1912
Luther W. Mott (R)
Thomas G. Patten (D)
Sereno E. Payne (R)
William C. Redfield (D)
Daniel J. Riordan (D)
James S. Simmons (R)
Charles B. Smith (D)
William Sulzer (D) r. 1912
Charles A. Talcott (D)
Edwin S. Underhill (D)
Edward B. Vreeland (R)
Frank E. Wilson (D)

North Carolina

Senators

Lee S. Overman (D)
Furnifold McL. Simmons (D)

Representatives

Robert L. Doughton (D)
John M. Faison (D)
Hannibal L. Godwin (D)
James M. Gudger, Jr. (D)
Claude Kitchin (D)
Robert N. Page (D)
Edward W. Pou (D)
John H. Small (D)
Charles M. Stedman (D)
Edwin Y. Webb (D)

North Dakota

Senators

Asle J. Gronna (R)
Porter J. McCumber (R)

Representatives

Louis B. Hanna (R) r. Jan.
  1913
Henry T. Helgesen (R)

Ohio

Senators

Theodore E. Burton (R)
Atlee Pomerene (D)

Representatives

Alfred G. Allen (D)
Carl C. Anderson (D) d. Oct.
  1912
Timothy T. Ansberry (D)
William A. Ashbrook (D)
Ellsworth R. Bathrick (D)
Robert J. Bulkley (D)
Horatio C. Claypool (D)
James M. Cox (D) r. Jan. 1913
Matthew R. Denver (D)
William B. Francis (D)
J. Henry Goeke (D)
L. Paul Howland (R)
Nicholas Longworth (R)
James D. Post (D)
William G. Sharp (D)
Isaac R. Sherwood (D)
Robert M. Switzer (R)
Edward L. Taylor, Jr. (R)

John J. Whitacre (D)
George White (D)
Frank B. Willis (R)

Oklahoma

Senators

Thomas P. Gore (D)
Robert L. Owen (D)

Representatives

Charles D. Carter (D)
James S. Davenport (D)
Scott Ferris (D)
Bird S. McGuire (R)
Dick T. Morgan (R)

Oregon

Senators

Jonathan Bourne, Jr. (R)
George E. Chamberlain (D)

Representatives

Willis C. Hawley (R)
Abraham W. Lafferty (R)

Pennsylvania

Senators

George T. Oliver (R)
Boies Penrose (R)

Representatives

William D. B. Ainey (R)
Andrew J. Barchfeld (R)
Arthur L. Bates (R)
Henry H. Bingham (R) d. Mar.
  1912
Charles C. Bowman (R) r. Dec.
  1912
James F. Burke (R)
Thomas S. Butler (R)
Thomas S. Crago (R)
John Dalzell (R)
Robert E. Diffenderfer (D)
Michael Donohoe (D)
John R. Farr (R)
Benjamin K. Focht (R)
Curtis H. Gregg (D)
William W. Griest (R)
Jesse L. Hartman (R)
George W. Kipp (D) d. July
  1911
Daniel F. Lafean (R)
Jonathan N. Langham (R)
Robert E. Lee (D)
George D. McCreary (D)
John G. McHenry (D) d. Dec.
  1912
Charles Matthews (R)
Reuben O. Moon (R)
J. Hampton Moore (R)
Marlin E. Olmsted (R)
A. Mitchell Palmer (D)
Charles E. Patton (R)
Stephen G. Porter (R)
William S. Reyburn (R)
John H. Rothermel (D)
Peter M. Speer (R)
William S. Vare (R) s. 1912
William B. Wilson (D)

Rhode Island

Senators

Henry F. Lippitt (R)
George P. Wetmore (R)

Representatives

George F. O'Shaunessy (D)
George H. Utter (R) d. Nov.
 1912

South Carolina

Senators

Ellison D. Smith (D)
Benjamin R. Tillman (D)

Representatives

Wyatt Aiken (D)
James F. Byrnes (D)
J. Edwin Ellerbe (D)
David E. Finley (D)
Joseph T. Johnson (D)
George S. Legare (D) d. Jan.
 1913
Asbury F. Lever (D)

South Dakota

Senators

Coe I. Crawford (R)
Robert J. Gamble (R)

Representatives

Charles H. Burke (R)
Eben W. Martin (R)

Tennessee

Senators

Luke Lea (D)
Newell Sanders (R) ta. 1912
Robert L. Taylor (D) d. Mar.
 1912
William R. Webb (D) s. 1913

Representatives

Richard W. Austin (R)
Joseph W. Byrns (D)
Finis J. Garrett (D)
George W. Gordon (D) d. Aug.
 1911
William C. Houston (D)
Cordell Hull (D)
Kenneth D. McKellar (D)
John A. Moon (D)
Lemuel P. Padgett (D)
Sam R. Sells (R)
Thetus W. Sims (D)

Texas

Senators

Joseph W. Bailey (D) r. Jan.
 1913
Charles A. Culberson (D)

Rienzi M. Johnston (D) ta.
 1913
Morris Sheppard (D) s. 1913

Representatives

Jack Beall (D)
George F. Burgess (D)
Albert S. Burleson (D)
Oscar Callaway (D)
Martin Dies (D)
John Nance Garner (D)
Alexander W. Gregg (D)
Rufus Hardy (D)
Robert L. Henry (D)
John M. Moore (D)
Choice B. Randell (D)
Morris Sheppard (D) r. Feb.
 1913
James L. Slayden (D)
William R. Smith (D)
John H. Stephens (D)
James Young (D)

Utah

Senators

Reed Smoot (R)
George Sutherland (R)

Representatives

Joseph Howell (R)

Vermont

Senators

William P. Dillingham (R)
Carroll S. Page (R)

Representatives

David J. Foster (R) d. Mar.
 1912
Frank L. Greene (R) s. 1912
Frank Plumley (R)

Virginia

Senators

Thomas S. Martin (D)
Claude A. Swanson (D)

Representatives

Charles C. Carlin (D)
Henry D. Flood (D)
Carter Glass (D)
James Hay (D)
Edward E. Holland (D)
William A. Jones (D)
John Lamb (D)
Edward W. Saunders (D)
C. Bascom Slemp (R)
Robert Turnbull (D)

Washington

Senators

Wesley L. Jones (R)
Miles Poindexter (R)

Representatives

William E. Humphrey (R)
William L. La Follette (R)
Stanton Warburton (R)

West Virginia

Senators

William E. Chilton (D)
Clarence W. Watson (D)

Representatives

William G. Brown, Jr. (D)
John W. Davis (D)
John M. Hamilton (D)
James A. Hughes (R)
Adam B. Littlepage (D)

Wisconsin

Senators

Robert M. La Follette (R)
Isaac Stephenson (R)

Representatives

Victor L. Berger (Socialist)
Michael E. Burke (D)
William J. Cary (R)
Henry A. Cooper (R)
James H. Davidson (R)
John J. Esch (R)
Thomas F. Konop (D)
Arthur W. Kopp (R)
Irvine L. Lenroot (R)
Elmer A. Morse (R)
John M. Nelson (R)

Wyoming

Senators

Clarence D. Clark (R)
Francis E. Warren (R)

Representatives

Frank W. Mondell (R)

Sixty-Third Congress

(Mar. 4, 1913, to
Mar. 3, 1915)

President of the Senate: Thomas
 R. Marshall
*President Pro Tempore of the
 Senate:* James P. Clarke
*Speaker of the House of
 Representatives:* Champ Clark

Alabama

Senators

John H. Bankhead (D)
Joseph F. Johnston (D) d. Aug.
 1913
Frank S. White (D) s. 1914

Representatives

John W. Abercrombie (D)
Fred L. Blackmon (D)
John L. Burnett (D)
Henry D. Clayton (D) r. May
 1914
S. Hubert Dent, Jr. (D)
Christopher C. Harris (D) s.
 1914
J. Thomas Heflin (D)
Richmond P. Hobson (D)
William O. Mulkey (D) s. 1914
William Richardson (D) d. Mar.
 1914
George W. Taylor (D)
Oscar W. Underwood (D)

Arizona

Senators

Henry F. Ashurst (D)
Marcus A. Smith (D)

Representatives

Carl Hayden (D)

Arkansas

Senators

James P. Clarke (D)
Joseph T. Robinson (D)

Representatives

Thaddeus H. Caraway (D)
John C. Floyd (D)
William S. Goodwin (D)
Henderson M. Jacoway (D)
William A. Oldfield (D)
Samuel M. Taylor (D)
Otis Wingo (D)

California

Senators

George C. Perkins (R)
John D. Works (R)

Representatives

Charles W. Bell (R)
Denver S. Church (D)
Charles F. Curry (R)
Everis A. Hayes (R)
Julius Kahn (R)
William Kettner (D)
William Kent
Joseph R. Knowland (R)
John I. Nolan (R)
John E. Raker (D)
William D. Stephens (R)

Colorado

Senators

Charles S. Thomas (D)
John F. Shafroth (D)

Representatives

Edward Keating (D)

George J. Kindel (D)
Harry H. Seldomridge (D)
Edward T. Taylor (D)

Connecticut

Senators

Frank B. Brandegee (R)
George P. McLean (R)

Representatives

Jeremiah Donovan (D)
William Kennedy (D)
Augustine Lonergan (D)
Bryan F. Mahan (D)
Thomas L. Reilly (D)

Delaware

Senators

Henry A. Du Pont (R)
Willard Saulsbury (D)

Representatives

Frank Brockson (D)

Florida

Senators

Nathan P. Bryan (D)
Duncan U. Fletcher (D)

Representatives

Frank Clark (D)
Claude L'Engle (D)
Stephen M. Sparkman (D)
Emmett Wilson (D)

Georgia

Senators

Augustus O. Bacon (D) d. Feb.
1914
Thomas W. Hardwick (D) s.
1914
Hoke Smith (D)
William S. West (D) ta. 1914

Representatives

William C. Adamson (D)
Charles L. Bartlett (D)
Thomas M. Bell (D)
Charles R. Crisp (D)
Charles G. Edwards (D)
Thomas W. Hardwick (D) r.
Nov. 1914
William S. Howard (D)
Dudley M. Hughes (D)
Gordon Lee (D)
Frank Park (D)
Seaborn A. Roddenbery (D) d.
Sept. 1913
Samuel J. Tribble (D)
Carl Vinson (D) s. 1914
John R. Walker (D)

Idaho

Senators

William E. Borah (R)
James H. Brady (R)

Representatives

Burton L. French (R)
Addison T. Smith (R)

Illinois

Senators

James H. Lewis (D)
Lawrence Y. Sherman (R)

Representatives

William N. Baltz (D)
Charles M. Borchers (D)
Fred A. Britten (R)
Frank Buchanan (D)
Ira C. Copley (R)
Louis FitzHenry (D)
Martin D. Foster (D)
H. Robert Fowler (D)
Thomas Gallagher (D)
George E. Gorman (D)
James M. Graham (D)
Robert P. Hill (D)
William H. Hinebaugh
(Progressive)
Stephen Hoxworth (D)
James McAndrews (D)
James T. McDermott (D) s.
1914
John C. McKenzie (R)
Martin B. Madden (R)
James R. Mann (R)
Frank T. O'Hair (D)
Henry T. Rainey (D)
Adolph J. Sabath (D)
Claudius U. Stone (D)
Lawrence B. Stringer (D)
Clyde H. Tavenner (D)
Charles M. Thomson (R)
William E. Williams (D)

Indiana

Senators

John W. Kern (D)
Benjamin F. Shively (D)

Representatives

John A. M. Adair (D)
Henry A. Barnhart (D)
Cyrus Cline (D)
William E. Cox (D)
William A. Cullop (D)
Lincoln Dixon (D)
Finly H. Gray (D)
Charles A. Korbly (D)
Charles Lieb (D)
Martin A. Morrison (D)
Ralph W. Moss (D)
John B. Peterson (D)
George W. Rauch (D)

Iowa

Senators

Albert B. Cummins (R)
William S. Kenyon (R)

Representatives

Maurice Connolly (D)
James W. Good (R)
William R. Green (R)
Gilbert N. Haugen (R)
Charles A. Kennedy (R)
Sanford Kirkpatrick (D)
Irvin S. Pepper (D) d. Dec.
1913
Solomon F. Prouty (R)
George C. Scott (R)
Horace M. Towner (R)
Henry Vollmer (D) s. 1914
Frank P. Woods (R)

Kansas

Senators

Joseph L. Bristow (R)
William H. Thompson (D)

Representatives

Daniel R. Anthony, Jr. (R)
Philip P. Campbell (R)
John R. Connelly (D)
Dudley Doolittle (D)
Guy T. Helvering (D)
Victor Murdock (R)
George A. Neeley (D)
Joseph Taggart (D)

Kentucky

Senators

William O. Bradley (R) d. May
1914
Johnson N. Camden (D) s.
1914
Ollie M. James (D)

Representatives

Alben W. Barkley (D)
James C. Cantrill (D)
William J. Fields (D)
Harvey Helm (D)
Ben Johnson (D)
John W. Langley (R)
Caleb Powers (R)
Arthur B. Rouse (D)
J. Swagar Sherley (D)
Augustus O. Stanley (D)
Robert Y. Thomas, Jr. (D)

Louisiana

Senators

Joseph E. Ransdell (D)
John R. Thornton (D)

Representatives

James B. Aswell (D)
Robert F. Broussard (D)
H. Garland Dupre

J. Walter Elder (D)
Albert Estopinal (D)
Ladislas Lazaro (D)
Lewis L. Morgan (D)
John T. Watkins (D)

Maine

Senators

Edwin C. Burleigh (R)
Charles F. Johnson (D)

Representatives

Forrest Goodwin (R) d. May
1913
Frank E. Guernsey (R)
Asher C. Hinds (R)
Daniel J. McGillicuddy (D)
John A. Peters (R)

Maryland

Senators

William P. Jackson (R) r. 1914
Blair Lee (D) s. 1914
John Walter Smith (D)

Representatives

Charles P. Coady (D)
J. Harry Covington (D) r. Sept.
1914
George Konig (D) d. May 1913
David J. Lewis (D)
J. Charles Linthicum (D)
Jesse D. Price (D) s. 1914
Frank O. Smith (D)
J. Fred C. Talbott (D)

Massachusetts

Senators

Henry Cabot Lodge (R)
John W. Weeks (R)

Representatives

James M. Curley (D) r. Feb.
1914
Frederick S. Deitrick (D)
James A. Gallivan (D) s. 1914
Augustus P. Gardner (R)
Frederick H. Gillett (R)
Edward Gilmore (D)
William S. Greene (R)
John J. Mitchell (D)
William F. Murray (D) r. Sept.
1914
Calvin D. Paige (R)
Andrew J. Peters (D) r. Aug.
1914
Michael F. Phelan (D)
Ernest W. Roberts (R)
John Jacob Rogers (R)
Thomas C. Thatcher (D)
Allen T. Treadway (R)
William H. Wilder (R) d. Sept.
1913
Samuel E. Winslow (R)

Michigan

Senators

William Alden Smith (R)
Charles E. Townsend (R)

Representatives

Samuel W. Beakes (D)
Louis C. Cramton (R)
Frank E. Doremus (D)
Joseph W. Fordney (R)
Edward L. Hamilton (R)
Patrick H. Kelley (R)
Francis O. Lindquist (R)
William J. MacDonald
  (Progressive)
James C. McLaughlin (R)
Carl E. Mapes (R)
John. M. C. Smith (R)
Samuel W. Smith (R)
Roy O. Woodruff (R)
H. Olin Young (R) r. May
  1913

Minnesota

Senators

Moses E. Clapp (R)
Knute Nelson (R)

Representatives

Sydney Anderson (R)
Charles R. Davis (R)
Winfield S. Hammond (D) r.
  1915
Charles A. Lindbergh (R)
James Manahan (R)
Clarence B. Miller (R)
George R. Smith (R)
Halvor Steenerson (R)
Frederick C. Stevens (R)
Andrew J. Volstead (R)

Mississippi

Senators

James K. Vardaman (D)
John Sharp Williams (D)

Representatives

Ezekiel S. Candler, Jr. (D)
James W. Collier
Pat Harrison (D)
Benjamin G. Humphreys (D)
Percy E. Quin (D)
Thomas U. Sisson (D)
Hubert D. Stephens (D)
Samuel A. Witherspoon (D)

Missouri

Senators

James A. Reed (D)
William J. Stone (D)

Representatives

Joshua W. Alexander (D)
Richard Bartholdt (R)
Charles F. Booher (D)

William P. Borland (D)
Champ Clark (D)
Perl D. Decker (D)
Clement C. Dickinson (D)
Leonidas C. Dyer (R) r. June
  1914
Michael J. Gill (D) s. 1914
Courtney W. Hamlin (D)
Walter L. Hensley (D)
William L. Igoe (D)
James T. Lloyd (D)
Thomas L. Rubey (D)
William W. Rucker (D)
Joseph J. Russell (D)
Dorsey W. Shackleford (D)

Montana

Senators

Henry L. Myers (D)
Thomas J. Walsh (D)

Representatives

John M. Evans (D)
John Stout (D)

Nebraska

Senators

Gilbert M. Hitchcock (D)
George W. Norris (R)

Representatives

Silas R. Barton (R)
Moses P. Kinkaid (R)
Charles O. Lobeck (D)
John A. Maguire (D)
Charles H. Sloan (R)
Daniel V. Stephens (D)

Nevada

Senators

Francis G. Newlands (D)
Key Pittman (D)

Representatives

Edwin E. Roberts (R)

New Hampshire

Senators

Jacob H. Gallinger (R)
Henry F. Hollis (D)

Representatives

Eugene E. Reed (D)
Raymond B. Stevens (D)

New Jersey

Senators

William Hughes (D)
James E. Martine (D)

Representatives

J. Thompson Baker (D)
Robert G. Bremner (D) d. Feb.
  1914
William J. Browning (R)
Dow H. Drukker (R) s. 1914
John J. Eagan (D)
James A. Hamill (D)
Archibald C. Hart (D)
Eugene F. Kinkead (D) r. Feb.
  1915
Walter I. McCoy (D) r. Oct.
  1914
Lewis J. Martin (D) d. May
  1913
Richard W. Parker (R) s. 1914
Thomas J. Scully (D)
Edward W. Townsend (D)
William E. Tuttle, Jr. (D)
Allan B. Walsh (D)

New Mexico

Senators

Thomas B. Catron (R)
Albert B. Fall (R)

Representatives

Harvey B. Fergusson (D)

New York

Senators

James A. O'Gorman (D)
Elihu Root (R)

Representatives

Lathrop Brown (D)
Henry Bruckner (D)
William M. Calder (R)
Jacob A. Cantor (D)
John F. Carew (D)
Walter M. Chandler
  (Progressive)
John R. Clancy (D)
Michael F. Conry (D)
Harry H. Dale (D)
Henry G. Danforth (R)
Peter J. Dooling (D)
Daniel A. Driscoll (D)
Thomas B. Dunn (R)
George W. Fairchild (R)
John J. Fitzgerald (D)
Henry George, Jr. (D)
Robert H. Gittins (D)
Henry M. Goldfogle (D)
Joseph A. Goulden (D)
Daniel J. Griffin (D)
Charles M. Hamilton (R)
Francis B. Harrison (D) r. Sept.
  1913
Jefferson M. Levy (D)
George W. Loft (D)
George McClellan (D)
James P. Maher (D)
Edwin A. Merritt, Jr. (R) d.
  Dec. 1914
Herman A. Metz (D)
Luther W. Mott (R)
James H. O'Brien (D)
Woodson R. Oglesby (D)
Denis O'Leary (D) r. Dec. 1914
James S. Parker (R)
Thomas G. Patten (D)

Sereno E. Payne (R) d. Dec.
  1914
Edmund Platt (R)
Daniel J. Riordan (D)
Charles B. Smith (D)
Timothy D. Sullivan (D) d.
  Aug. 1913
Charles A. Talcott (D)
Benjamin I. Taylor (D)
Peter G. Ten Eyck (D)
Edwin S. Underhill (D)
Samuel Wallin (R)
Frank E. Wilson (D)

North Carolina

Senators

Lee S. Overman (D)
Furnifold McL. Simmons (D)

Representatives

Robert L. Doughton (D)
John M. Faison (D)
Hannibal L. Godwin (D)
James M. Gudger, Jr. (D)
Claude Kitchin (D)
Robert N. Page (D)
Edward W. Pou (D)
John H. Small (D)
Charles M. Stedman (D)
Edwin Y. Webb (D)

North Dakota

Senators

Asle J. Gronna (R)
Porter J. McCumber (R)

Representatives

Henry T. Helgesen (R)
Patrick D. Norton (R)
George M. Young (R)

Ohio

Senators

Theodore E. Burton (R)
Atlee Pomerene (D)

Representatives

Alfred G. Allen (D)
Timothy T. Ansberry (D) r.
  Jan. 1915
William A. Ashbrook (D)
Ellsworth R. Bathrick (D)
Stanley E. Bowdle (D)
Clement L. Brumbaugh (D)
Robert J. Bulkley (D)
Horatio C. Claypool (D)
Robert Crosser (D)
Simeon D. Fess (R)
William B. Francis (D)
Warren Gard (D)
J. Henry Goeke (D)
William Gordon (D)
John A. Key (D)
James D. Post (D)
William G. Sharp (D) r. July
  1914
Isaac R. Sherwood (D)
Robert M. Switzer (R)
John J. Whitacre (D)

George White (D)
Frank B. Willis (R) r. Jan.
1915

Oklahoma

Senators

Thomas P. Gore (D)
Robert L. Owen (D)

Representatives

Charles D. Carter (D)
James S. Davenport (D)
Scott Ferris (D)
Bird S. McGuire (R)
Dick T. Morgan (R)
William H. Murray (D)
Joseph B. Thompson (D)
Claude Weaver (D)

Oregon

Senators

George E. Chamberlain (D)
Harry Lane (D)

Representatives

Willis C. Hawley (R)
Abraham W. Lafferty (R)
Nicholas J. Sinnott (R)

Pennsylvania

Senators

George T. Oliver (R)
Boies Penrose (R)

Representatives

William D. B. Ainey (R)
Warren W. Bailey (D)
Andrew J. Barchfeld (R)
Andrew F. Brodbeck (D)
James F. Burke (R)
Thomas S. Butler (R)
Wooda N. Carr (D)
John J. Casey (D)
Frank L. Dershem (D)
Robert E. Diffenderfer (D)
Michael Donohoe (D)
George W. Edmonds (R)
John R. Farr (R)
George S. Graham (R)
William W. Griest (R)
Willis J. Hulings (Progressive)
Abraham L. Keister (R)
M. Clyde Kelly (R)
Edgar R. Kiess (R)
Aaron S. Kreider (R)
Jonathan N. Langham (R)
Robert E. Lee (D)
John V. Lesher (D)
Fred E. Lewis (R)
J. Washington Logue (D)
J. Hampton Moore (R)
John M. Morin (R)
A. Mitchell Palmer (D)
Charles E. Patton (R)
Stephen G. Porter (R)
John H. Rothermel (D)
Arthur R. Rupley (Progressive)
Milton W. Shreve (R)
Henry W. Temple (R)

William S. Vare (R)
Anderson H. Walters (R)

Rhode Island

Senators

Le Baron B. Colt (R)
Henry F. Lippitt (R)

Representatives

Peter G. Gerry (D)
Ambrose Kennedy (R)
George F. O'Shaunessy (D)

South Carolina

Senators

Ellison D. Smith (D)
Benjamin R. Tillman (D)

Representatives

Wyatt Aiken (D)
James F. Byrnes (D)
David E. Finley (D)
Joseph T. Johnson (D)
Asbury F. Lever (D)
J. Willard Ragsdale (D)
Richard S. Whaley (D)

South Dakota

Senators

Coe I. Crawford (R)
Thomas Sterling (R)

Representatives

Charles H. Burke (R)
Charles H. Dillon (R)
Eben W. Martin (R)

Tennessee

Senators

Luke Lea (D)
John K. Shields (D)

Representatives

Richard W. Austin (R)
Joseph W. Byrns (D)
Finis J. Garrett (D)
William C. Houston (D)
Cordell Hull (D)
Kenneth D. McKellar (D)
John A. Moon (D)
Lemuel P. Padgett (D)
Sam R. Sells (R)
Thetus W. Sims (D)

Texas

Senators

Charles A. Culberson (D)
Morris Sheppard (D)

Representatives

Jack Beall (D)

James P. Buchanan (D)
George F. Burgess (D)
Albert S. Burleson (D) r. Mar.
1913
Oscar Callaway (D)
Martin Dies (D)
Joe H. Eagle (D)
John Nance Garner (D)
Daniel E. Garrett (D)
Alexander W. Gregg (D)
Rufus Hardy (D)
Robert L. Henry (D)
Sam Rayburn (D)
James L. Slayden (D)
William R. Smith (D)
John H. Stephens (D)
Hatton W. Sumners (D)
Horace W. Vaughan (D)
James Young (D)

Utah

Senators

Reed Smoot (R)
George Sutherland (R)

Representatives

Joseph Howell (R)
Jacob Johnson (R)

Vermont

Senators

William P. Dillingham (R)
Carroll S. Page (R)

Representatives

Frank L. Greene (R)
Frank Plumley (R)

Virginia

Senators

Thomas S. Martin (D)
Claude A. Swanson (D)

Representatives

Charles C. Carlin (D)
Henry D. Flood (D)
Carter Glass (D)
James Hay (D)
Edward E. Holland (D)
William A. Jones (D)
Andrew J. Montague (D)
Edward W. Saunders (D)
C. Bascom Slemp (D)
Walter A. Watson (D)

Washington

Senators

Wesley L. Jones (R)
Miles Poindexter (R)

Representatives

James W. Bryan (R)
Jacob A. Falconer (Progressive)
William E. Humphrey (R)
Albert Johnson (R)

William L. La Follette (R)

West Virginia

Senators

William E. Chilton (D)
Nathan Goff (R)

Representatives

Samuel B. Avis (R)
William G. Brown, Jr. (D)
John W. Davis (D) r. Aug.
1913
James A. Hughes (R)
Hunter H. Moss, Jr. (R)
Matthew M. Neely (D)
Howard Sutherland (R)

Wisconsin

Senators

Robert M. La Follette (R)
Isaac Stephenson (R)

Representatives

Edward E. Browne (R)
Michael E. Burke (D)
William J. Cary (R)
Henry A. Cooper (R)
John J. Esch (R)
James A. Frear (R)
Thomas F. Konop (D)
Irvine L. Lenroot (R)
John M. Nelson (R)
Michael K. Reilly (D)
William H. Stafford (R)

Wyoming

Senators

Clarence D. Clark (R)
Francis E. Warren (R)

Representatives

Frank W. Mondell (R)

Sixty-Fourth Congress

(Mar. 4, 1915, to
Mar. 3, 1917)

President of the Senate: Thomas
R. Marshall
*Presidents Pro Tempore of the
Senate:* James P. Clarke;
Willard Saulsbury
*Speaker of the House of
Representatives:* Champ Clark

Alabama

Senators

John H. Bankhead (D)
Oscar W. Underwood (D)

Representatives

John W. Abercrombie (D)
Edward B. Almon (D)
Fred L. Blackmon (D)
John L. Burnett (D)
S. Hubert Dent, Jr. (D)
Oscar L. Gray (D)
J. Thomas Heflin (D)
George Huddleston (D)
William B. Oliver (D)
Henry B. Steagall (D)

Arizona

Senators

Henry F. Ashurst (D)
Marcus A. Smith (D)

Representatives

Carl Hayden (D)

Arkansas

Senators

James P. Clarke (D) d. Oct.
   1916
William F. Kirby (D) s. 1916
Joseph T. Robinson (D)

Representatives

Thaddeus H. Caraway (D)
William S. Goodwin (D)
Henderson M. Jacoway (D)
William A. Oldfield (D)
Samuel M. Taylor (D)
John N. Tillman (D)
Otis Wingo (D)

California

Senators

James D. Phelan (D)
John D. Works (R)

Representatives

H. Stanley Benedict (R) s. 1916
Denver S. Church (D)
Charles F. Curry (R)
John A. Elston (R)
Everis A. Hayes (R)
Julius Kahn (R)
William Kent
William Kettner (D)
John I. Nolan (R)
John E. Raker (D)
Charles H. Randall (D)
William D. Stephens (R) r. July
   1916

Colorado

Senators

John F. Shafroth (D)
Charles S. Thomas (D)

Representatives

Benjamin C. Hilliard (D)
Edward Keating (D)

Edward T. Taylor (D)
Charles B. Timberlake (R)

Connecticut

Senators

Frank B. Brandegee (R)
George P. McLean (R)

Representatives

Richard P. Freeman (R)
James P. Glynn (R)
Ebenezer J. Hill (R)
P. Davis Oakey (R)
John Q. Tilson (R)

Delaware

Senators

Henry A. Du Pont (R)
Willard Saulsbury (D)

Representatives

Thomas W. Miller (R)

Florida

Senators

Nathan P. Bryan (D)
Duncan U. Fletcher (D)

Representatives

Frank Clark (D)
William J. Sears (D)
Stephen M. Sparkman (D)
Emmett Wilson (D)

Georgia

Senators

Thomas W. Hardwick (D)
Hoke Smith (D)

Representatives

William C. Adamson (D)
Thomas M. Bell (D)
Charles R. Crisp (D)
Charles G. Edwards (D)
William S. Howard (D)
Dudley M. Hughes (D)
Gordon Lee (D)
Frank Park (D)
Tinsley W. Rucker (D) s. 1917
Samuel J. Tribble (D) d. Dec.
   1916
Carl Vinson (D)
John R. Walker (D)
James W. Wise (D)

Idaho

Senators

William E. Borah (R)
James H. Brady (R)

Representatives

Robert M. McCracken (R)
Addison T. Smith (R)

Illinois

Senators

James H. Lewis (D)
Lawrence Y. Sherman (R)

Representatives

Fred A. Britten (R)
Frank Buchanan (D)
Joseph G. Cannon (R)
Burnett M. Chiperfield (R)
Ira C. Copley (R)
Edward E. Denison (R)
George E. Foss (R)
Martin D. Foster (D)
Charles E. Fuller (R)
Thomas Gallagher (D)
Edward J. King (R)
James McAndrews (D)
James T. McDermott (D)
John C. McKenzie (R)
William B. McKinley (R)
Martin B. Madden (R)
James R. Mann (R)
Henry T. Rainey (D)
William A. Rodenberg (R)
Adolph J. Sabath (D)
John A. Sterling (R)
Claudius U. Stone (D)
Clyde H. Tavenner (D)
Loren E. Wheeler (R)
Thomas S. Williams (R)
William E. Williams (D)
William W. Wilson (R)

Indiana

Senators

John W. Kern (D)
Benjamin F. Shively (D) d.
   Mar. 1916
Thomas Taggart (D) ta. 1916
James E. Watson (R) s. 1916

Representatives

John A. M. Adair (D)
Henry A. Barnart (D)
Cyrus Cline (D)
William E. Cox (D)
William A. Cullop (D)
Lincoln Dixon (D)
Finly H. Gray (D)
Charles Lieb (D)
Merrill Moores (R)
Martin A. Morrison (D)
Ralph W. Moss (D)
George W. Rauch (D)
William R. Wood (R)

Iowa

Senators

Albert B. Cummins (R)
William S. Kenyon (R)

Representatives

Cassius C. Dowell (R)

James W. Good (R)
William R. Green (R)
Gilbert N. Haugen (R)
Harry E. Hull (R)
Charles A. Kennedy (R)
C. William Ramseyer (R)
Thomas J. Steele (D)
Burton E. Sweet (R)
Horace M. Towner (R)
Frank P. Woods (R)

Kansas

Senators

Charles Curtis (R)
William H. Thompson (D)

Representatives

Daniel R. Anthony, Jr. (R)
William A. Ayers (D)
Philip P. Campbell (R)
John R. Connelly (D)
Dudley Doolittle (D)
Guy T. Helvering (D)
Jouett Shouse (D)
Joseph Taggart (D)

Kentucky

Senators

John C. W. Beckham   (D)
Ollie M. James (D)

Representatives

Alben W. Barkley (D)
James C. Cantrill (D)
William J. Fields (D)
Harvey Helm (D)
Ben Johnson (D)
David H. Kincheloe (D)
John W. Langley (R)
Caleb Powers (R)
Arthur B. Rouse (D)
J. Swagar Sherley (D)
Robert Y. Thomas, Jr. (D)

Louisiana

Senators

Robert F. Broussard (D)
Joseph E. Ransdell (D)

Representatives

James B. Aswell (D)
H. Garland Dupre (D)
Albert Estopinal (D)
Ladislas Lazaro (D)
Whitmell P. Martin
   (Progressive)
Lewis L. Morgan (D)
John T. Watkins (D)
Riley J. Wilson (D)

Maine

Senators

Edwin C. Burleigh (R) d. June
   1916
Bert M. Fernald (R) s. 1916
Charles F. Johnson (D)

Representatives

Frank E. Guernsey (R)
Asher C. Hinds (R)
Daniel J. McGillicuddy (D)
John A. Peters (R)

Maryland

Senators

Blair Lee (D)
John Walter Smith (D)

Representatives

Charles P. Coady (D)
David J. Lewis (D)
J. Charles Linthicum (D)
Sydney E. Mudd (R)
Jesse D. Price (D)
J. Fred C. Talbott (D)

Massachusetts

Senators

Henry Cabot Lodge (R)
John W. Weeks (R)

Representatives

William H. Carter (R)
Frederick W. Dallinger (R)
James A. Gallivan (D)
Augustus P. Gardner (R)
Frederick H. Gillett (R)
William S. Greene (R)
Richard Olney (D)
Calvin D. Paige (R)
Michael F. Phelan (D)
Ernest W. Roberts (R)
John Jacob Rogers (R)
Peter F. Tague (D)
George H. Tinkham (R)
Allen T. Treadway (R)
Joseph Walsh (R)
Samuel E. Winslow (R)

Michigan

Senators

William Alden Smith (R)
Charles E. Townsend (R)

Representatives

Samuel W. Beakes (D)
Louis C. Cramton (R)
Frank E. Doremus (D)
Joseph W. Fordney (R)
Edward L. Hamilton (R)
W. Frank James (R)
Patrick H. Kelley (R)
George A. Loud (R)
James C. McLaughlin (R)
Carl E. Mapes (R)
Charles A. Nichols (R)
Frank D. Scott (R)
John M. C. Smith (R)

Minnesota

Senators

Moses E. Clapp (R)

Knute Nelson (R)

Representatives

Sydney Anderson (R)
Charles R. Davis (R)
Franklin F. Ellsworth (R)
Charles A. Lindbergh (R)
Clarence B. Miller (R)
Thomas D. Schall (R)
George R. Smith (R)
Halvor Steenerson (R)
Carl C. Van Dyke (D)
Andrew J. Volstead (R)

Mississippi

Senators

James K. Vardaman (D)
John Sharp Williams (D)

Representatives

Ezekiel S. Candler, Jr. (D)
James W. Collier (D)
Pat Harrison (D)
Benjamin G. Humphreys (D)
Percy E. Quin (D)
Thomas U. Sisson (D)
Hubert D. Stephens (D)
William W. Venable (D) s. 1916
Samuel A. Witherspoon (D) d.
   Nov. 1915

Missouri

Senators

James A. Reed (D)
William J. Stone (D)

Representatives

Joshua W. Alexander (D)
Charles F. Booher (D)
William P. Borland (D)
Champ Clark (D)
Perl D. Decker (D)
Clement C. Dickinson (D)
Leonidas C. Dyer (R)
Courtney W. Hamlin (D)
Walter L. Hensley (D)
William L. Igoe (D)
James T. Lloyd (D)
Jacob E. Meeker (R)
Thomas L. Rubey (D)
William L. Rucker (D)
Joseph J. Russell (D)
Dorsey W. Shackleford (D)

Montana

Senators

Henry L. Myers (D)
Thomas J. Walsh (D)

Representatives

John M. Evans (D)
Tom Stout (D)

Nebraska

Senators

Gilbert M. Hitchcock (D)
George W. Norris (R)

Representatives

Moses P. Kinkaid (R)
Charles O. Lobeck (D)
C. Frank Reavis (R)
Ashton C. Shallenberger (D)
Charles H. Sloan (R)
Daniel V. Stephens (D)

Nevada

Senators

Francis G. Newlands (D)
Key Pittman (D)

Representatives

Edwin E. Roberts (R)

New Hampshire

Senators

Jacob H. Gallinger (R)
Henry F. Hollis (D)

Representatives

Cyrus A. Sulloway (R)
Edward H. Wason (R)

New Jersey

Senators

James E. Martine (D)
William Hughes (D)

Representatives

Isaac Bacharach (R)
William J. Browning (R)
John H. Capstick (R)
Dow H. Drukker (R)
John J. Eagan (D)
Edward W. Gray (R)
James A. Hamill (D)
Archibald C. Hart (D)
Elijah C. Hutchinson (R)
Frederick R. Lehlbach (R)
Richard W. Parker (R)
Thomas J. Scully (D)

New Mexico

Senators

Thomas B. Catron (R)
Albert B. Fall (R)

Representatives

Benigno C. Hernandez (R)

New York

Senators

James A. O'Gorman (D)
James W. Wadsworth, Jr. (R)

Representatives

William S. Bennet (R)
Henry Bruckner (D)
Charles P. Caldwell (D)
John F. Carew (D)
Walter M. Chandler
   (Progressive)
William B. Charles (R)
Michael F. Conry (D) d. Mar.
   1917
Harry H. Dale (D)
Henry G. Danforth (R)
S. Wallace Dempsey (R)
Peter J. Dooling (D)
Daniel A. Driscoll (D)
Thomas B. Dunn (R)
George W. Fairchild (R)
Michael F. Farley (D)
John J. Fitzgerald (D)
Joseph V. Flynn (D)
Norman J. Gould (R)
Joseph A. Goulden (D)
Daniel J. Griffin (D)
Charles M. Hamilton (R)
Reuben L. Haskell (R)
Frederick C. Hicks (R)
G. Murray Hulbert (D)
James W. Husted (R)
George W. Loft (D)
Meyer London (Socialist)
Walter W. Magee (R)
James P. Maher (D)
Luther W. Mott (R)
Woodson R. Oglesby (D)
James S. Parker (D)
Thomas G. Patten (D)
Edmund Platt (R)
Harry H. Pratt (R)
Daniel J. Riordan (D)
Frederick W. Rowe (R)
Rollin B. Sanford (R)
Isaac Siegel (R)
Charles B. Smith (D)
Bertrand H. Snell (R)
Homer P. Snyder (R)
Oscar W. Swift (R)
Charles B. Ward (R)

North Carolina

Senators

Lee S. Overman (D)
Furnifold McL. Simmons (D)

Representatives

James J. Britt (R)
Robert L. Doughton (D)
Hannibal L. Godwin (D)
George E. Hood (D)
Claude Kitchin (D)
Robert N. Page (D)
Edward W. Pou (D)
John H. Small (D)
Charles M. Stedman (D)
Edwin Y. Webb (D)

North Dakota

Senators

Asle J. Gronna (R)
Porter J. McCumber (R)

Representatives

Henry T. Helgesen (R)
Patrick D. Norton (R)
George M. Young (R)

Ohio

Senators

Warren G. Harding (R)
Atlee Pomerene (D)

Representatives

Alfred G. Allen (D)
William A. Ashbrook (D)
Clement L. Brumbaugh (D)
John G. Cooper (R)
Robert Crosser (D)
Henry I. Emerson (R)
Simeon D. Fess (R)
Warren Gard (D)
William Gordon (D)
David A. Hollingsworth (R)
Charles C. Kearns (R)
John A. Key (D)
Nicholas Longworth (R)
Roscoe C. McCulloch (R)
Nelson E. Matthews (R)
William C. Mooney (R)
Arthur W. Overmyer (D)
Edwin D. Ricketts (R)
J. Edward Russell (R)
Isaac R. Sherwood (D)
Robert M. Switzer (R)
Seward H. Williams (R)

Oklahoma

Senators

Thomas P. Gore (D)
Robert L. Owen (D)

Representatives

Charles D. Carter (D)
James S. Davenport (D)
Scott Ferris (D)
William W. Hastings (D)
James V. McClintic (D)
Dick T. Morgan (R)
William H. Murray (D)
Joseph B. Thompson (D)

Oregon

Senators

George E. Chamberlain (D)
Harry Lane (D)

Representatives

Willis C. Hawley (R)
Clifton N. McArthur (R)
Nicholas J. Sinnott (R)

Pennsylvania

Senators

George T. Oliver (R)
Boies Penrose (R)

Representatives

Warren W. Bailey (D)
Andrew J. Barchfeld (R)
C. William Beales (R)
Thomas S. Butler (R)
John J. Casey (D)
William H. Coleman (R)
Peter E. Costello (R)
Thomas S. Crago (R)
George P. Darrow (R)
Arthur G. Dewalt (D)
George W. Edmonds (R)
John R. Farr (R)
Benjamin K. Focht (R)
Mahlon M. Garland (R)
George S. Graham (R)
William W. Griest (R)
Robert D. Heaton (R)
Robert F. Hopwood (R)
Abraham L. Keister (R)
Edgar R. Kiess (R)
Aaron S. Kreider (R)
Daniel F. Lafean (R)
John V. Lesher (D)
Michael Liebel, Jr. (D)
Louis T. McFadden (R)
Samuel H. Miller (R)
J. Hampton Moore (R)
John M. Morin (R)
S. Taylor North (R)
Stephen G. Porter (R)
Charles H. Rowland (R)
John R. K. Scott (R)
Henry J. Steele (D)
Henry W. Temple (R)
William S. Vare (R)
Henry W. Watson (R)

Rhode Island

Senators

LeBaron B. Colt (R)
Henry F. Lippitt (R)

Representatives

Ambrose Kennedy (R)
George F. O'Shaunessy (D)
Walter R. Stiness (R)

South Carolina

Senators

Ellison D. Smith (D)
Benjamin R. Tillman (D)

Representatives

Wyatt Aiken (D)
James F. Byrnes (D)
David E. Finley (D) d. Jan.
   1917
Joseph T. Johnson (D)
Asbury F. Lever (D)
Paul G. McCorkle (D) s. 1917
Samuel J. Nicholls (D)
J. Willard Ragsdale (D)
Richard S. Whaley (D)

South Dakota

Senators

Edwin S. Johnson (D)
Thomas Sterling (R)

Representatives

Charles H. Dillon (R)
Harry L. Gandy (D)
Royal C. Johnson (R)

Tennessee

Senators

Luke Lea (D)
John K. Shields (D)

Representatives

Richard W. Austin (R)
Joseph W. Byrns (D)
Finis J. Garrett (D)
William C. Houston (D)
Cordell Hull (D)
Kenneth D. McKellar (D)
John A. Moon (D)
Lemuel P. Padgett (D)
Sam R. Sells (R)
Thetus W. Sims (D)

Texas

Senators

Charles A. Culberson (D)
Morris Sheppard (D)

Representatives

Eugene Black (D)
James P. Buchanan (D)
George F. Burgess (D)
Oscar Callaway (D)
James H. Davis (D)
Martin Dies (D)
Joe H. Eagle (D)
John Nance Garner (D)
Alexander W. Gregg (D)
Rufus Hardy (D)
Robert L. Henry (D)
Jeff McLemore (D)
Sam Rayburn (D)
James L. Slayden (D)
William R. Smith (D)
John H. Stephens (D)
Hatton W. Sumners (D)
James Young (D)

Utah

Senators

Reed Smoot (R)
George Sutherland (R)

Representatives

Joseph Howell (R)
James H. Mays (D)

Vermont

Senators

William P. Dillingham (R)
Carroll S. Page (R)

Representatives

Porter H. Dale (R)
Frank L. Greene (R)

Virginia

Senators

Thomas S. Martin (D)
Claude A. Swanson (D)

Representatives

Charles C. Carlin (D)
Henry D. Flood (D)
Carter Glass (D)
Thomas W. Harrison (D) s.
   1916
James Hay (D) r. Oct. 1916
Edward E. Holland (D)
William A. Jones (D)
Andrew J. Montague (D)
Edward W. Saunders (D)
C. Bascom Slemp (D)
Walter A. Watson (D)

Washington

Senators

Wesley L. Jones (R)
Miles Poindexter (R)

Representatives

Clarence C. Dill (D)
Lindley H. Hadley (R)
William E. Humphrey (R)
Albert Johnson (R)
William L. La Follette (R)

West Virginia

Senators

William E. Chilton (D)
Nathan Goff (R)

Representatives

George M. Bowers (R) s. 1916
William G. Brown, Jr. (D) d.
   Mar. 1916
Edward Cooper (R)
Adam B. Littlepage (D)
Hunter H. Moss, Jr. (R) d.
   July 1916
Matthew M. Neely (D)
Howard Sutherland (R)
Harry C. Woodyard (R) s. 1916

Wisconsin

Senators

Paul O. Husting (D)
Robert M. La Follette (R)

Representatives

Edward E. Browne (R)
Michael E. Burke (D)
William J. Cary (R)
Henry A. Cooper (R)
John J. Esch (R)
James A. Frear (R)
Thomas F. Konop (D)
Irvine L. Lenroot (R)
John M. Nelson (R)
Michael K. Reilly (D)
William H. Stafford (R)

Wyoming

Senators

Clarence D. Clark (R)
Francis E. Warren (R)

Representatives

Frank W. Mondell (R)

Sixty-Fifth Congress

(Mar. 4, 1917, to
Mar. 3, 1919)

President of the Senate: Thomas
R. Marshall
*President Pro Tempore of the
Senate:* Willard Saulsbury
*Speaker of the House of
Representatives:* Champ Clark

Alabama

Senators

John H. Bankhead (D)
Oscar W. Underwood (D)

Representatives

Edward B. Almon (D)
William B. Bankhead (D)
Fred L. Backmon (D)
John L. Burnett (D)
S. Hubert Dent, Jr. (D)
Oscar L. Gray (D)
J. Thomas Heflin (D)
George Huddleston (D)
William B. Oliver (D)
Henry B. Steagall (D)

Arizona

Senators

Henry F. Ashurst (D)
Marcus A. Smith (D)

Representatives

Carl Hayden (D)

Arkansas

Senators

William F. Kirby (D)

Joseph T. Robinson (D)

Representatives

Thaddeus H. Caraway (D)
William S. Goodwin (D)
Henderson M. Jacoway (D)
William A. Oldfield (D)
Samuel M. Taylor (D)
John N. Tillman (D)
Otis Wingo (D)

California

Senators

Hiram W. Johnson (R)
James D. Phelan (D)

Representatives

Denver S. Church (D)
Charles F. Curry (R)
John A. Elston (R)
Everis A. Hayes (R)
Julius Kahn (R)
William Kettner (D)
Clarence F. Lea (D)
John I. Nolan (R)
Henry Z. Osborne (R)
John E. Raker (D)
Charles H. Randall (R)

Colorado

Senators

John F. Shafroth (D)
Charles S. Thomas (D)

Representatives

Benjamin C. Hilliard (D)
Edward Keating (D)
Edward T. Taylor (D)
Charles B. Timberlake (R)

Connecticut

Senators

Frank B. Brandegee (R)
George P. McLean (R)

Representatives

Richard P. Freeman (R)
James P. Glynn (R)
Ebenezer J. Hill (R) d. Sept.
1917
Augustine Lonergan (D)
Schuyler Merritt (R) s. 1917
John Q. Tilson (R)

Delaware

Senators

Willard Saulsbury (D)
Josiah O. Wolcott (D)

Representtives

Albert F. Polk (D)

Florida

Senators

Duncan U. Fletcher (D)
Park Trammell (D)

Representatives

Frank Clark (D)
Herbert J. Drane (D)
J. Walter Kehoe (D)
William J. Sears (D)

Georgia

Senators

Thomas W. Hardwick (D)
Hoke Smith (D)

Representatives

William C. Adamson (D) r.
Dec. 1917
Thomas M. Bell (D)
Charles H. Brand (D)
Charles R. Crisp (D)
William S. Howard (D)
William W. Larsen (D)
Gordon Lee (D)
James W. Overstreet (D)
Frank Park (D)
Carl Vinson (D)
John R. Walker (D)
James W. Wise (D)
William C. Wright (D) s. 1918

Idaho

Senators

William E. Borah (R)
James H. Brady (R) d. Jan.
1918
John F. Nugent (D) s. 1918

Representatives

Burton L. French (R)
Addison T. Smith (R)

Illinois

Senators

James H. Lewis (D)
Lawrence Y. Sherman (R)

Representatives

Fred A. Britten (R)
Joseph G. Cannon (R)
Ira C. Copley (R)
Edward E. Denison (R)
George E. Foss (R)
Martin D. Foster (D)
Charles E. Fuller (R)
Thomas Gallagher (D)
William J. Graham (R)
Clifford Ireland (R)
Niels Juul (R)
Edward J. King (R)
James McAndrews (D)
Medill McCormick (R)
John C. McKenzie (R)
William B. McKinley (R)

Martin B. Madden (R)
James R. Mann (R)
Charles Martin (D) d. Oct.
1917
William E. Mason (R)
Henry T. Rainey (D)
John W. Rainey (D) s. 1918
William A. Rodenberg (R)
Adolph J. Sabath (D)
John A. Sterling (R) d. Oct.
1918
Loren E. Wheeler (R)
Thomas S. Williams (R)
William W. Wilson (R)

Indiana

Senators

Harry S. New (R)
James E. Watson (R)

Representatives

Henry A. Barnhart (D)
Oscar E. Bland (R)
Daniel W. Comstock (R) d.
May 1917
William E. Cox (D)
George K. Denton (D)
Lincoln Dixon (D)
Richard N. Elliott (R)
Louis W. Fairfield (R)
Milton Kraus (R)
Merrill Moores (R)
Fred S. Purnell (R)
Everett Sanders (R)
Albert H. Vestal (R)
William R. Wood (R)

Iowa

Senators

Albert B. Cummins (R)
William S. Kenyon (R)

Representatives

Cassius C. Dowell (R)
William R. Green (R)
James W. Good (R)
Gilbert N. Haugen (R)
Harry E. Hull (R)
Charles A. Kennedy (R)
C. William Ramseyer (R)
George C. Scott (R)
Burton E. Sweet (R)
Horace M. Towner (R)
Frank P. Woods (R)

Kansas

Senators

Charles Curtis (R)
William H. Thompson (D)

Representatives

Daniel R. Anthony, Jr. (R)
William A. Ayres (D)
Philip P. Campbell (R)
John R. Connelly (D)
Dudley Doolittle (D)
Guy T. Helvering (D)
Edward C. Little (R)
Jouett Shouse (D)

Kentucky

Senators

John C. W. Beckham (D)
Ollie M. James (D) d. Aug.
  1918
George B. Martin (D) s. 1918

Representatives

Alben W. Barkley (D)
James C. Cantrill (D)
William J. Fields (D)
Harvey Helm (D)
Ben Johnson (D)
David H. Kincheloe (D)
John W. Langley (R)
Caleb Powers (R)
Arthur B. Rouse (D)
J. Swagar Sherley (D)
Robert Y. Thomas, Jr. (D)

Louisiana

Senators

Robert F. Broussard (D) d.
  Apr. 1918
Edward J. Gay (D) s. 1918
Walter Guion (D) ta. 1918
Joseph E. Ransdell (D)

Representatives

James B. Aswell (D)
H. Garland Dupre (D)
Albert Estopinal (D)
Ladislas Lazaro (D)
Whitmell P. Martin
  (Progressive)
Jared Sanders (D)
John T. Watkins (D)
Riley J. Wilson (D)

Maine

Senators

Bert M. Fernald (R)
Frederick Hale (R)

Representatives

Louis B. Goodall (R)
Ira G. Hersey (R)
John A. Peters (R)
Wallace H. White, Jr. (R)

Maryland

Senators

Joseph I. France (R)
John Walter Smith (D)

Representatives

Carville D. Benson (D) s. 1918
Charles P. Coady (D)
J. Charles Linthicum (D)
Sydney E. Mudd (R)
Jesse D. Price (D)
J. Fred C. Talbott (D) d. Oct.
  1918
Frederick N. Zihlman (R)

Massachusetts

Senators

Henry Cabot Lodge (R)
John W. Weeks (R)

Representatives

William H. Carter (R)
Frederick W. Dallinger (R)
Alvan T. Fuller (R)
James A. Gallivan (D)
Augustus P. Gardner (R) r.
  May 1917
Frederick H. Gillett (R)
William S. Greene (R)
Willfred W. Lufkin (R)
Richard Olney (D)
Calvin D. Paige (R)
Michael F. Phelan (D)
John Jacob Rogers (R)
Peter F. Tague (D)
George H. Tinkham (R)
Allen T. Treadway (R)
Joseph Walsh (R)
Samuel E. Winslow (R)

Michigan

Senators

William Alden Smith (R)
Charles E. Townsend (R)

Representatives

Mark R. Bacon (R) r. Dec.
  1917
Samuel W. Beakes (D)
Louis C. Cramton (R)
Gilbert A. Currie (R)
Frank E. Doremus (D)
Joseph W. Fordney (R)
Edward J. Hamilton (R)
W. Frank James (R)
Patrick H. Kelley (R)
James C. McLaughlin (R)
Carl E. Mapes (R)
Charles A. Nichols (R)
Frank D. Scott (R)
John M. C. Smith (R)

Minnesota

Senators

Frank B. Kellogg (R)
Knute Nelson (R)

Representatives

Sydney Anderson (R)
Charles R. Davis (R)
Frank F. Ellsworth (R)
Harold Knutson (R)
Ernest Lundeen (R)
Clarence B. Miller (R)
Thomas D. Schall (R)
Halvor Steenerson (R)
Carl C. Van Dyke (D)
Andrew J. Volstead (R)

Mississippi

Senators

James K. Vardaman (D)
John Sharp Williams (D)

Representatives

Ezekiel S. Candler, Jr. (D)
James W. Collier (D)
Pat Harrison (D)
Benjamin G. Humphreys (D)
Percy E. Quin (D)
Thomas U. Sisson (D)
Hubert D. Stephens (D)
William W. Venable (D)

Missouri

Senators

James A. Reed (D)
Selden P. Spencer (R) s. 1918
William J. Stone (D) d. Apr.
  1918
Xenophon P. Wilfley (D) ta.
  1918

Representatives

Joshua W. Alexander (D)
Charles F. Booher (D)
William P. Borland (D) d. Feb.
  1919
Champ Clark (D)
Perl D. Decker (D)
Clement C. Dickinson (D)
Leonidas C. Dyer (R)
Frederick Essen (R) s. Nov.
  1918
Courtney W. Hamlin (D)
Walter L. Hensley (D)
William L. Igoe (D)
Jacob E. Meeker (R) d. Oct.
  1918
Milton A. Romjue (D)
Thomas L. Rubey (D)
William W. Rucker (D)
Joseph J. Russell (D)
Dorsey W. Shackleford (D)

Montana

Senators

Henry L. Myers (D)
Thomas J. Walsh (D)

Representatives

John M. Evans (D)
Jeannette Rankin (R)

Nebraska

Senators

Gilbert M. Hitchcock (D)
George W. Norris (R)

Representatives

Moses P. Kinkaid (R)
Charles O. Lobeck (D)
C. Frank Reavis (R)
Ashton C. Shallenberger (D)

Charles H. Sloan (R)
Daniel V. Stephens (D)

Nevada

Senators

Charles B. Henderson (D) s.
  1918
Francis G. Newlands (D) d.
  Dec. 1917
Key Pittman (D)

Representatives

Edwin E. Roberts (R)

New Hampshire

Senators

Irving W. Drew (R) ta. 1918
Jacob H. Gallinger (R) d. Aug.
  1918
Henry F. Hollis (D)
George H. Moses (R) s. 1918

Representatives

Sherman E. Burroughs (R)
Cyrus A. Sulloway (R)
Edward H. Wason (R)

New Jersey

Senators

David Baird (R) s. 1918
Joseph S. Frelinghuysen (R)
William Hughes (D) d. Mar.
  1917

Representatives

Isaac Bacharach (R)
William F. Birch (R) s. Nov.
  1918
William J. Browning (R)
John H. Capstick (R) d. Mar.
  1918
Dow H. Drukker (R)
John J. Eagan (D)
Edward W. Gray (R)
James A. Hamill (D)
Elijah C. Hutchinson (R)
Frederick R. Lehlbach (R)
Richard W. Parker (R)
John R. Ramsey (R)
Thomas J. Scully (D)

New Mexico

Senators

Albert B. Fall (R)
Andrieus A. Jones (D)

Representatives

William B. Walton (D)

New York

Senators

William M. Calder (R)

James W. Wadsworth, Jr. (R)

Representatives

Henry Bruckner (D) r. Dec. 1917
Charles P. Caldwell (D)
John F. Carew (D)
Walter M. Chandler (Progressive)
William E. Cleary (D) s. 1918
Harry H. Dale (D)
John J. Delaney (D) s. 1918
S. Wallace Dempsey (R)
Jerome F. Donovan (D) s. 1918
Peter J. Dooling (D)
Thomas B. Dunn (R)
Benjamin L. Fairchild (R)
George W. Fairchild (R)
John J. Fitzgerald (D) r. Dec. 1917
Joseph V. Flynn (D)
George B. Francis (R)
Norman J. Gould (R)
Anthony J. Griffin (D) s. 1918
Daniel J. Griffin (D) r. Dec. 1917
Charles M. Hamilton (R)
Reuben L. Haskell (R)
Frederick C. Hicks (R)
G. Murray Hulbert (D) r. Jan. 1918
James W. Husted (R)
Fiorello H. LaGuardia (R)
Meyer London (Socialist)
George R. Lunn (D)
Walter W. Magee (R)
James P. Maher (D)
Luther W. Mott (R)
Daniel C. Oliver (D)
James S. Parker (R)
Edmund Platt (R)
Harry H. Pratt (R)
Daniel J. Riordan (D)
Frederick W. Rowe (R)
Archie D. Sanders (R)
Rollin B. Sanford (R)
Isaac Siegel (R)
Charles B. Smith (D)
Thomas F. Smith (D)
Bertrand H. Snell (R)
Homer P. Snyder (R)
Christopher D. Sullivan (D)
Oscar W. Swift (R)
William F. Waldo (R)
Charles B. Ward (R)

North Carolina

Senators

Lee S. Overman (D)
Furnifold McL. Simmons (D)

Representatives

James J. Britt (D) s. 1919
Robert L. Doughton (D)
Hannibal L. Godwin (D)
George E. Hood (D)
Claude Kitchin (D)
Edward W. Pou (D)
Leonidas D. Robinson (D)
John H. Small (D)
Charles M. Stedman (D)
Zebulon Weaver (D)
Edwin Y. Webb (D)

North Dakota

Senators

Asle J. Groona (R)
Porter J. McCumber (R)

Representatives

John M. Baer (R) s. 1917
Henry T. Helgesen (R) d. Apr. 1917
Patrick D. Norton (R)
George M. Young (R)

Ohio

Senators

Warren G. Harding (R)
Atlee Pomerene (D)

Representatives

William A. Ashbrook (D)
Ellsworth R. Bathrick (D) d. Dec. 1917
Clement L. Brumbaugh (D)
Horatio C. Claypool (D)
John G. Cooper (D)
Robert Crosser (D)
Martin L. Davey (D) s. 1918
Henry I. Emerson (R)
Simeon D. Fess (R)
Warren Gard (D)
William Gordon (D)
Victor Heintz (R)
David A. Hollingsworth (R)
Charles C. Kearns (R)
John A. Key (D)
Nicholas Longworth (R)
Roscoe C. McCulloch (R)
Arthur W. Overmyer (D)
Isaac R. Sherwood (D)
John S. Snook (D)
Robert M. Switzer (R)
Benjamin F. Welty (D)
George White (D)

Oklahoma

Senators

Thomas P. Gore (D)
Robert L. Owen (D)

Representatives

Charles D. Carter (D)
Thomas A. Chandler (R)
Scott Ferris (D)
William W. Hastings (D)
James V. McClintic (D)
Thomas D. McKeown (D)
Dick T. Morgon (D)
Joseph B. Thompson (D)

Oregon

Senators

George E. Chamberlain (D)
Harry Lane (D) d. May 1917
Charles L. McNary (R) s. 1918

Representatives

Willis C. Hawley (R)
Clifton N. McArthur (R)
Nicholas J. Sinnott (R)

Pennsylvania

Senators

Philander C. Knox (R)
Boies Penrose (R)

Representatives

Earl H. Beshlin (D)
Andrew R. Brodbeck (D)
Thomas S. Butler (R)
Guy E. Campbell (R)
Henry A. Clark (R)
Peter E. Costello (R)
Thomas S. Crago (R)
George P. Darrow (R)
Arthur G. Dewalt (D)
George W. Edmonds (R)
John R. Farr (R)
Benjamin K. Focht (R)
Mahlon M. Garland (R)
George S. Graham (R)
William W. Griest (R)
Robert D. Heaton (R)
M. Clyde Kelly (R)
Edgar R. Kiess (R)
Aaron S. Kreider (R)
John V. Lesher (D)
Louis T. McFadden (R)
Joseph McLaughlin (R)
J. Hampton Moore (R)
John M. Morin (R)
Stephen G. Porter (R)
Edward E. Robbins (R)
John M. Rose (D)
Charles H. Rowland (R)
John R. K. Scott (R)
Henry J. Steele (D)
Bruce F. Sterling (D)
Nathan L. Strong (R)
Henry W. Temple (R)
Thomas W. Templeton (R)
William S. Vare (R)
Henry W. Watson (R)

Rhode Island

Senators

LeBaron B. Colt (R)
Peter G. Gerry (D)

Representatives

Ambrose Kennedy (R)
George F. O'Shaunessy (D)
Walter R. Stiness (R)

South Carolina

Senators

Christie Benet (D) ta. 1918
William P. Pollock (D) s. 1918
Ellison D. Smith (D)
Benjamin R. Tillman (D) d. July 1918

Representatives

James F. Byrnes (D)

Fred H. Dominick (D)
Asbury F. Lever (D)
Samuel J. Nicholls (D)
J. Willard Ragsdale (D)
William F. Stevenson (D)
Richard S. Whaley (D)

South Dakota

Senators

Edwin S. Johnson (D)
Thomas Sterling (R)

Representatives

Charles H. Dillon (R)
Harry L. Gandy (D)
Royal C. Johnson (R)

Tennessee

Senators

Kenneth D. McKellar (D)
John K. Shields (D)

Representatives

Richard W. Austin (R)
Joseph W. Byrns (D)
Hubert F. Fisher (D)
Finis J. Garrett (D)
William C. Houston (D)
Cordell Hull (D)
John A. Moon (D)
Lemuel P. Padgett (D)
Sam R. Sells (D)
Thetus W. Sims (D)

Texas

Senators

Charles A. Culberson (D)
Morris Sheppard (D)

Representatives

Eugene Black (D)
Thomas L. Blanton (D)
James P. Buchanan (D)
Tom T. Connally (D)
Martin Dies (D)
Joe H. Eagle (D)
John Nance Garner (D)
Daniel E. Garrett (D)
Alexander W. Gregg (D)
Rufus Hardy (D)
Marvin Jones (D)
A. Jeff McLemore (D)
Joseph J. Mansfield (D)
Sam Rayburn (D)
James L. Slayden (D)
Hatton W. Sumners (D)
James C. Wilson (D)
James Young (D)

Utah

Senators

William H. King (D)
Reed Smoot (R)

Representatives

James H. Mays (D)
Milton H. Welling (D)

Vermont

Senators

William P. Dillingham (R)
Carroll S. Page (R)

Representatives

Porter H. Dale (R)
Frank L. Greene (R)

Virginia

Senators

Thomas S. Martin (D)
Claude A. Swanson (R)

Representatives

Schuyler Otis Bland (D) s. 1918
Charles C. Carlin (D)
Henry D. Flood (D)
Carter Glass (D) r. Dec. 1918
Thomas W. Harrison (D)
Edward E. Holland (D)
William A. Jones (D) d. Apr. 1918
Andrew J. Montague (D)
Edward W. Saunders (D)
C. Bascom Slemp (D)
Walter A. Watson (D)
James P. Woods (D)

Washington

Senators

Wesley L. Jones (R)
Miles Poindexter (R)

Representatives

Clarence C. Dill (D)
Lindley H. Hadley (R)
Albert Johnson (R)
William L. La Follette (R)
John F. Miller (R)

West Virginia

Senators

Nathan Goff (R)
Howard Sutherland (R)

Representatives

George M. Bowers (R)
Edward Cooper (R)
Adam B. Littlepage (D)
Matthew M. Neely (D)
Stuart F. Reed (R)
Harry C. Woodyard (R)

Wisconsin

Senators

Paul O. Husting (D) d. Oct. 1917
Robert M. La Follette (R)
Irvine L. Lenroot (R) s. 1918

Representatives

Edward E. Browne (R)
William J. Cary (R)
David G. Classon (R)
Henry A. Cooper (R)
James H. Davidson d. Aug. 1918
John J. Esch (R)
James A. Frear (R)
Florian Lampbert (R) s. 1918
Irvine L. Lenroot (R) r. Apr. 1918
Adolphus P. Nelson (R) s. 1918
John M. Nelson (R)
William H. Stafford (R)
Edward Voigt (R)

Wyoming

Senators

John B. Kendrick (D)
Francis E. Warren (R)

Representatives

Frank W. Mondell (R)

Sixty-Sixth Congress

(Mar. 4, 1919, to
Mar. 3, 1921)

President of the Senate: Thomas R. Marshall
President Pro Tempore of the Senate: Albert B. Cummins
Speaker of the House of Representatives: Frederick H. Gillett

Alabama

Senators

John H. Bankhead (D) d. 1920
Braxton B. Comer (D) ta. 1920
J. Thomas Heflin (D) s. 1920
Oscar W. Underwood (D)

Representatives

Edward B. Almon (D)
William B. Bankhead (D)
Fred L. Blackmon (D)
William B. Bowling (D) s. 1920
S. Hubert Dent, Jr. (D)
J. Thomas Heflin (D) r. Nov. 1920
George Huddleston (D)
John McDuffie (D)
William B. Oliver (D)
Lilius B. Rainey (D)
Henry B. Steagall (D)

Arizona

Senators

Henry F. Ashurst (D)
Marcus A. Smith (D)

Representatives

Carl Hayden (D)

Arkansas

Senators

William F. Kirby (D)
Joseph T. Robinson (D)

Representatives

Thaddeus H. Caraway (D)
William S. Goodwin (D)
Henderson M. Jacoway (D)
William A. Oldfield (D)
Samuel M. Taylor (D)
John N. Tillman (D)
Otis Wingo (D)

California

Senators

Hiram W. Johnson (R)
James D. Phelan (D)

Representatives

Henry E. Barbour (R)
Charles F. Curry (R)
John A. Elston (R)
Hugh S. Hersman (D)
Julius Kahn (R)
William Kettner (D)
Clarence F. Lea (D)
John I. Nolan (R)
Henry Z. Osborne (R)
John E. Raker (D)
Charles H. Randall (R)

Colorado

Senators

Lawrence C. Phipps (R)
Charles S. Thomas (D)

Representatives

Guy U. Hardy (R)
Edward T. Taylor (D)
Charles B. Timberlake (R)
William N. Vaile (R)

Connecticut

Senators

Frank B. Brandegee (R)
George P. McLean (R)

Representatives

Richard P. Freeman (R)
James P. Glynn (R)
Augustine Lonergan (D)
Schuyler Merritt (R)

John Q. Tilson (R)

Delaware

Senators

L. Heisler Ball (R)
Josiah O. Wolcott (D)

Representatives

Caleb R. Layton (R)

Florida

Senators

Duncan U. Fletcher (D)
Park Trammell (D)

Representatives

Frank Clark (D)
Herbert J. Drane (D)
William J. Sears (D)
John H. Smithwick (D)

Georgia

Senators

William J. Harris (D)
Hoke Smith (D)

Representatives

Thomas M. Bell (D)
Charles H. Brand (D)
Charles R. Crisp (D)
William C. Lankford (D)
William W. Larsen (D)
Gordon Lee (D)
James W. Overstreet (D)
Frank Park (D)
William D. Upshaw (D)
Carl Vinson (D)
James W. Wise (D)
William C. Wright (D)

Idaho

Senators

William E. Borah (R)
Frank R. Gooding (R) s. 1921
John F. Nugent (D) r. Jan. 1921

Representatives

Burton L. French (R)
Addison T. Sith (R)

Illinois

Senators

Medill McCormick (R)
Lawrence Y. Sherman (R)

Representatives

Fred A. Britten (R)
Edwin B. Brooks (R)
Joseph G. Cannon (R)
Carl R. Chindblom (R)

Ira C. Copley (R)
Edward E. Denison (R)
Charles E. Fuller (R)
Thomas Gallagher (D)
William J. Graham (R)
Clifford Ireland (R)
Niels Juul (R)
Edward J. King (R)
James McAndrews (D)
John C. McKenzie (R)
William B. McKinley (R)
Martin B. Madden (R)
James R. Mann (R)
William E. Mason (R)
John W. Rainey (D)
William A. Rodenberg (R)
Adolph J. Sabath (D)
Frank L. Smith (R)
Loren E. Wheeler (R)
Thomas S. Williams (R)
William W. Wilson (R)
Richard Yates (R)

Indiana

Senators

Harry S. New (R)
James E. Watson (R)

Representatives

John S. Benham (R)
Oscar E. Bland (R)
James W. Dunbar (R)
Richard N. Elliott (R)
Louis W. Fairfield (R)
Andrew J. Hickey (R)
Milton Kraus (R)
Oscar R. Luhring (R)
Merrill Moores (R)
Fred S. Purnell (R)
Everett Sanders (R)
Albert H. Vestal (R)
William R. Wood (R)

Iowa

Senators

Albert B. Cummins (R)
William S. Kenyon (R)

Representatives

William D. Boies (R)
Lester J. Dickinson (R)
Cassius C. Dowell (R)
James W. Good (R)
William R. Green (R)
Gilbert N. Haugen (R)
Harry E. Hull (R)
Charles A. Kennedy (R)
C. William Ramseyer (R)
Burton E. Sweet (R)
Horace M. Towner (R)

Kansas

Senators

Arthur Capper (R)
Charles Curtis (R)

Representatives

Daniel R. Anthony, Jr. (R)
William A. Ayres (D)

Philip P. Campbell (R)
Homer Hoch (R)
Edward C. Little (R)
James G. Strong (R)
Jasper N. Tincher (R)
Hays B. White (R)

Kentucky

Senators

John C. W. Beckham (D)
Augustus O. Stanley (D)

Representatives

Alben W. Barkley (D)
James C. Cantrill (D)
William J. Fields (D)
Ben Johnson (D)
David H. Kincheloe (D)
John W. Langley (R)
Charles F. Ogden (R)
John M. Robsion (R)
Arthur B. Rouse (D)
King Swope (R)
Robert Y. Thomas, Jr. (D)

Louisiana

Senators

Edward J. Gay (D)
Joseph E. Ransdell (D)

Representatives

James B. Aswell (D)
H. Garland Dupre (D)
Ladislas Lazaro (D)
Whitmell P. Martin (D)
James O'Connor (D)
Jared Y. Sanders (D)
John T. Watkins (D)
Riley J. Wilson (D)

Maine

Senators

Bert M. Fernald (R)
Frederick Hale (R)

Representatives

Louis B. Goodall (R)
Ira G. Hersey (R)
John A. Peters (R)
Wallace H. White, Jr. (R)

Maryland

Senators

Joseph I. France (R)
John Walter Smith (D)

Representatives

William N. Andrews (R)
Carville D. Benson (D)
Charles P. Coady (D)
J. Charles Linthicum (D)
Sydney E. Mudd (R)
Frederick N. Zihlman (R)

Massachusetts

Senators

Henry Cabot Lodge (R)
David I. Walsh (D)

Representatives

Frederick W. Dallinger (R)
John F. Fitzgerald (D) r. Oct. 1919
Alvan T. Fuller (R) r. Jan. 1921
James A. Gallivan (D)
Frederick H. Gillett (R)
William S. Greene (R)
Robert Luce (R)
Willfred W. Lufkin (R)
Richard Olney (D)
Calvin D. Paige (R)
Michael F. Phelan (D)
John Jacob Rogers (R)
Peter F. Tague (D)
George H. Tinkham (R)
Allen T. Treadway (R)
Joseph Walsh (R)
Samuel E. Winslow (R)

Michigan

Senators

Truman H. Newberry (R)
Charles E. Townsend (R)

Representatives

Louis C. Cramton (R)
Gilbert A. Currie (R)
Frank E. Doremus (D)
Joseph W. Fordney (R)
Edward L. Hamilton (R)
W. Frank James (R)
Patrick H. Kelley (R)
James C. McLaughlin (R)
Clarence J. McLeod (R) s. 1920
Carl E. Mapes (R)
Earl C. Michener (R)
Charles A. Nichols (R) d. Apr. 1920
Frank D. Scott (R)
John M. C. Smith (R)

Minnesota

Senators

Frank B. Kellogg (R)
Knute Nelson (R)

Representatives

Sydney Anderson (R)
William L. Carss (D)
Charles R. Davis (R)
Franklin F. Ellsworth (R)
Oscar E. Keller (R)
Harold Knutson (R)
Walter H. Newton (R)
Thomas D. Schall (R)
Halvor Steenerson (R)
Carl C. Van Dyke (R) d. May 1919
Andrew J. Volstead (R)

Mississippi

Senators

Pat Harrison (D)
John Sharp Williams (D)

Representatives

Ezekiel S. Candler, Jr. (D)
James W. Collier (D)
Benjamin G. Humphreys (D)
Paul B. Johnson (D)
Percy E. Quin (D)
Thomas U. Sisson (D)
Hubert D. Stephens (D)
William W. Venable (D)

Missouri

Senators

James A. Reed (D)
Selden P. Spencer (R)

Representatives

Joshua W. Alexander (D) r. Dec. 1919
William T. Bland (D)
Charles F. Booher (D) d. Jan. 1921
Champ Clark (D) d. Mar. 1921
Clement C. Dickinson (D)
Leonidas C. Dyer (R)
Edward D. Hays (R)
William L. Igoe (D)
Isaac V. McPherson (R)
Samuel C. Major (D)
Jacob L. Milligan (D) s. 1920
William L. Nelson (D)
Cleveland A. Newton (R)
Marion E. Rhodes (R)
Milton A. Romjue (D)
Thomas L. Rubey (D)
William W. Rucker (D)

Montana

Senators

Henry L. Myers (D)
Thomas J. Walsh (D)

Representatives

John M. Evans (D)
Carl W. Riddick (R)

Nebraska

Senators

Gilbert M. Hitchcock (D)
George W. Norris (R)

Representatives

William E. Andrews (R)
Robert E. Evans (R)
Albert W. Jefferis (R)
Moses P. Kinkaid (R)
Melvin O. McLaughlin (R)
C. Frank Reavis (R)

172

Nevada

Senators

Charles B. Henderson (D)
Key Pittman (D)

Representatives

Charles R. Evans (D)

New Hampshire

Senators

Henry W. Keyes (R)
George H. Moses (R)

Representatives

Sherman E. Burroughs (R)
Edward H. Wason (R)

New Jersey

Senators

Walter E. Edge (R)
Joseph S. Frelinghuysen (R)

Representatives

Ernest R. Ackerman (R)
Isaac Bacharach (R)
William J. Browning (R) d.
  Mar. 1920
John J. Eagan (D)
James A. Hamill (D)
Elijah C. Hutchinson (R)
Frederick R. Lehlbach (R)
Cornelius A. McGlennon (D)
Daniel F. Minahan (D)
Francis F. Patterson, Jr. (R) s.
  1920
Amos H. Radcliffe (R)
John R. Ramsey (D)
Thomas J. Scully (D)

New Mexico

Senators

Albert B. Fall (R)
Andrieus A. Jones (D)

Representatives

Benigno C. Hernandez (R)

New York

Senators

William M. Calder (R)
James W. Wadsworth, Jr. (R)

Representatives

Charles P. Caldwell (D)
John F. Carew (D)
William E. Cleary (D)
Frank Crowther (R)
Thomas H. Cullen (D)
S. Wallace Dempsey (R)
Jerome F. Donovan (D)
Peter J. Dooling (D)

Thomas B. Dunn (R)
Hamilton Fish, Jr. (R) s. Dec.
  1920
James V. Ganly (D)
Henry M. Goldfogle (D)
Norman J. Gould (R)
Anthony J. Griffin (D)
Reuben L. Haskell (R) r. Dec.
  1919
Frederick C. Hicks (R)
William H. Hill (R)
Alanson B. Houghton (R)
James W. Husted (R)
John B. Johnston (D)
Fiorello H. LaGuardia (R) r.
  Dec. 1919
John MacCrate (R) r. Dec.
  1920
Clarence MacGregor (R)
Richard F. McKiniry (D)
Walter W. Magee (R)
James P. Maher (D)
James M. Mead (D)
Luther W. Mott (R)
David J. O'Connell (D)
James S. Parker (R)
Herbert Claiborne Pell (D)
Nathan D. Perlman (R) s. Dec.
  1920
Edmund Platt (R) r. June 1920
Daniel A. Reed (R)
Daniel J. Riordan (D)
Joseph Rowan (D)
Frederick W. Rowe (R)
Archie D. Sanders (R)
Rollin B. Sanford (R)
Isaac Siegel (R)
Thomas F. Smith (D)
Bertrand H. Snell (R)
Homer P. Snyder (R)
Christopher D. Sullivan (D)
Lester D. Volk (R) s. 1920
Charles B. Ward (R)

North Carolina

Senators

Lee S. Overman (D)
Furnifold M. Simmons (D)

Representatives

Samuel M. Brinson (D)
Robert L. Doughton (D)
Hannibal L. Godwin (D)
Clyde R. Hoey (D) s. 1920
Claude Kitchin (D)
Edward W. Pou (D)
Leonidas D. Robinson (D)
John H. Small (D)
Charles M. Stedman (D)
Zebulon Weaver (D)
Edwin Y. Webb (D) r. Nov.
  1919

North Dakota

Senators

Asle J. Gronna (R)
Porter J. McCumber (R)

Representatives

John M. Baer (R)
James H. Sinclair (R)
George M. Young (R)

Ohio

Senators

Warren G. Harding (R) r. Jan.
  1921
Atlee Pomerene (D)
Frank B. Willis (R) s. 1921

Representatives

William A. Ashbrook (D)
John J. Babka (D)
James T. Begg (R)
Clement L. Brumbaugh (D)
R. Clint Cole (R)
John G. Cooper (R)
Martin L. Davey (D)
Henry I. Emerson (R)
Simeon D. Fess (R)
Israel M. Foster (R)
Warren Gard (D)
Charles C. Kearns (R)
Nicholas Longworth (R)
Roscoe C. McCulloch (R)
Charles A. Mooney (D)
C. Ellis Moore (R)
B. Frank Murphy (R)
Edwin D. Ricketts (R)
Isaac R. Sherwood (D)
Ambrose E. B. Stephens (R)
Charles J. Thompson (R)
Benjamin F. Welty (D)

Oklahoma

Senators

Thomas P. Gore (D)
Robert L. Owen (D)

Representatives

Charles D. Carter (D)
Scott Ferris (D)
John W. Harreld (R) s. 1919
William W. Hastings (D)
Everette B. Howard (D)
James V. McClintic (D)
Thomas D. McKeown (D)
Dick T. Morgan (R) d. June
  1920
Charles Swindall (R) s. 1920
Joseph B. Thompson (D) d.
  Sept. 1919

Oregon

Senators

George E. Chamberlain (D)
Charles L. McNary (R)

Representatives

Willis C. Hawley (R)
Clifton N. McArthur (R)
Nicholas J. Sinnott (R)

Pennsylvania

Senators

Philander C. Knox (R)
Boies Penrose (R)

Representatives

Edward S. Brooks (R)
William J. Burke (R)
Thomas S. Butler (R)
Guy E. Campbell (D)
John J. Casey (D)
Peter E. Costello (R)
Thomas S. Crago (R)
George P. Darrow (R)
Arthur G. Dewalt (D)
George W. Edmonds (R)
John R. Farr (R) s. 1921
Benjamin K. Focht (R)
Mahlon M. Garland (R) d.
  Nov. 1920
George S. Graham (R)
William W. Griest (R)
Willis J. Hulings (R)
Evan J. Jones (R)
M. Clyde Kelly (R)
Samuel A. Kendall (R)
Edgar R. Kiess (R)
Aaron S. Kreider (R)
John V. Lesher (D)
Louis T. McFadden (R)
Patrick McLane (D)
J. Hampton Moore (R) r. Jan.
  1920
John M. Morin (R)
Stephen G. Porter (R)
Harry C. Ransley (R) s. 1920
John Reber (R)
John M. Rose (R)
Milton W. Shreve (R)
Henry J. Steele (D)
Nathan L. Strong (R)
Henry W. Temple (R)
William S. Vare (R)
Anderson H. Walters (R)
Henry W. Watson (R)
John H. Wilson (D) s. 1919

Rhode Island

Senators

LeBaron B. Colt (R)
Peter G. Gerry (D)

Representatives

Clark Burdick (R)
Ambrose Kennedy (R)
Walter R. Stiness (R)

South Carolina

Senators

Nathaniel B. Dial (D)
Ellison D. Smith (D)

Representatives

James. F. Byrnes (D)
Fred H. Dominick (D)
Asbury F. Lever (D) r. Aug.
  1919
Edward C. Mann (D)
Samuel J. Nicholls (D)
J. Willard Ragsdale (D) d. July
  1919
William F. Stevenson (D)
Philip H. Stoll (D) s. 1919
Richard S. Whaley (D)

South Dakota

Senators

Edwin S. Johnson (D)
Thomas Sterling (R)

Representatives

Charles A. Christopherson (R)
Harry L. Gandy (D)
Royal C. Johnson (R)

Tennessee

Senators

Kenneth D. McKellar (D)
John K. Shields (D)

Representatives

Joseph W. Byrns (D)
Ewin L. Davis (D)
Hubert F. Fisher (D)
Finis J. Garrett (D)
Cordell Hull (D)
John A. Moon (D)
Lemuel P. Padgett (D)
Sam R. Sells (R)
Thetus W. Sims (D)
J. Will Taylor (R)

Texas

Senators

Charles A. Culberson (D)
Morris Sheppard (D)

Representatives

Carlos Bee (D)
Eugene Black (D)
Thomas L. Blanton (D)
John C. Box (D)
Clay Stone Briggs (D)
James P. Buchanan (D)
Tom T. Connally (D)
Joe H. Eagle (D)
John Nance Garner (D)
Rufus Hardy (D)
Claude B. Hudspeth (D)
Marvin Jones (D)
Fritz G. Lanham (D)
Joseph J. Mansfield (D)
Lucian W. Parrish (D)
Sam Rayburn (D)
Hatton W. Sumners (D)
James Young (D)

Utah

Senators

William H. King (D)
Reed Smoot (R)

Representatives

James H. Mays (D)
Milton H. Welling (D)

Vermont

Senators

William P. Dillingham (R)
Carroll S. Page (R)

Representatives

Porter H. Dale (R)
Frank L. Greene (R)

Virginia

Senators

Carter Glass (D) s. 1920
Thomas S. Martin (D) d. Nov.
  1919
Claude A. Swanson (D)

Representatives

Schuyler Otis Bland (D)
Patrick H. Drewry (D) s. 1920
Henry D. Flood (D)
Thomas W. Harrison (D)
Edward E. Holland (D)
Rorer A. James (D) s. 1920
Andrew J. Montague (D)
R. Walton Moore (D)
Edward W. Saunders (D) r.
  Feb. 1920
C. Bascom Slemp (D)
Walter A. Watson (D) d. Dec.
  1919
James P. Woods (D)

Washington

Senators

Wesley L. Jones (R)
Miles Poindexter (R)

Representatives

Lindley H. Hadley (R)
Albert Johnson (R)
John F. Miller (R)
John W. Summers (R)
Stanley J. Webster (R)

West Virginia

Senators

Davis Elkins (R)
Howard Sutherland (R)

Representatives

George M. Bowers (R)
Leonard S. Echols (R)
Wells Goodykoontz (R)
Matthew M. Neely (D)
Stuart F. Reed (R)
Harry C. Woodyard (R)

Wisconsin

Senators

Robert M. La Follette (R)
Irvine L. Lenroot (R)

Representatives

Edward E. Browne (R)
David G. Classon (R)
John J. Esch (R)
James A. Frear (R)
John C. Kleczka (R)
Florian Lampert (R)
James G. Monahan (R)
Adolphus P. Nelson (R)
Clifford E. Randall (R)
Edward Voigt (R)

Wyoming

Senators

John B. Kendrick (D)
Francis E. Warren (R)

Representatives

Frank W. Mondell (R)

Sixty-Seventh Congress

(Mar. 4, 1921, to
Mar. 3, 1923)

President of the Senate: Calvin
  Coolidge
*President Pro Tempore of the
  Senate:* Albert B. Cummins
*Speaker of the House of
  Representatives:* Frederick H.
  Gillett

Alabama

Senators

J. Thomas Heflin (D)
Oscar W. Underwood (D)

Representatives

Edward B. Almon (D)
William B. Bankhead (D)
William B. Bowling (D)
George Huddleston (D)
Lamar Jeffers (D)
John McDuffie (D)
William B. Oliver (D)
Lilius B. Rainey (D)
Henry B. Steagall (D)
John R. Tyson (D)

Arizona

Senators

Henry F. Ashurst (D)
Ralph H. Cameron (R)

Representatives

Carl Hayden (D)

Arkansas

Senators

Thaddeus H. Caraway (D)

Joseph T. Robinson (D)

Representatives

William J. Driver (D)
Henderson M. Jacoway (D)
William A. Oldfield (D)
Tilman B. Parks (D)
Chester W. Taylor (D)
Samuel M. Taylor (D) d. Sept.
  1921
John N. Tillman (D)
Otis Wingo (D)

California

Senators

Hiram W. Johnson (R)
Samuel M. Shortridge (R)

Representatives

Henry E. Barbour (R)
Charles F. Curry (R)
John A. Elston (R) d. Dec.
  1921
Arthur M. Free (R)
Julius Kahn (R)
Clarence F. Lea (D, R)
Walter F. Lineberger (R)
James H. MacLafferty (R) s.
  1922
Mae E. Nolan (R)
John I. Nolan (R) d. Nov. 1922
Henry Z. Osborne (R) d. Feb.
  1923
John E. Raker (D)
Philip D. Swing (R)

Colorado

Senators

Samuel D. Nicholson (R)
Lawrence C. Phipps (R)

Representatives

Guy U. Hardy (R)
Edward T. Taylor (D)
Charles B. Timberlake (R)
William N. Vaile (R)

Connecticut

Senators

Frank B. Brandegee (R)
George P. McLean (R)

Representatives

E. Hart Fenn (R)
Richard P. Freeman (R)
James P. Glynn (R)
Schuyler Merritt (R)
John Q. Tilson (R)

Delaware

Senators

L. Heisler Ball (R)
Thomas F. Bayard, Jr. (D) s.
  1922

T. Coleman Du Pont (R) ta.
1921
Josiah O. Wolcott (D) r. July
1921

Representatives

Caleb R. Layton (R)

Florida

Senators

Duncan U. Fletcher (D)
Park Trammell (D)

Representatives

Frank Clark (D)
Herbert J. Drane (D)
William J. Sears (D)
John H. Smithwick (D)

Georgia

Senators

Walter F. George (D) s. 1922
William J. Harris (D)
Thomas E. Watson (D) d. Sept.
1922

Representatives

Thomas M. Bell (D)
Charles H. Brand (D)
Charles R. Crisp (D)
William C. Lankford (D)
William W. Larsen (D)
Gordon Lee (D)
James W. Overstreet (D)
Frank Park (D)
William D. Upshaw (D)
Carl Vinson (D)
James W. Wise (D)
William C. Wright (D)

Idaho

Senators

William E. Borah (R)
Frank R. Gooding (R)

Representatives

Burton L. French (R)
Addison T. Smith (R)

Illinois

Senators

Medill McCormick (R)
William B. McKinley (R)

Representatives

Fred A. Britten (R)
Edwin B. Brooks (R)
Joseph G. Cannon (R)
Carl R. Chindblom (R)
Ira C. Copley (R)
Edward E. Denison (R)
Charles E. Fuller (R)
Frank H. Funk (R)
John J. Gorman (R)

William J. Graham (R)
Winnefred S. M. Huck (R) s.
1922
Clifford Ireland (R)
Edward J. King (R)
Stanley H. Kunz (D)
John C. McKenzie (R)
Martin B. Madden (R)
James R. Mann (R) d. Nov.
1922
William E. Mason (R) d. June
1921
M. Alfred Michaelson (R)
Allen F. Moore (R)
John W. Rainey (D)
William A. Rodenberg (R)
Adolph J. Sabath (D)
Guy L. Shaw (R)
Elliott W. Sproul (R)
Loren E. Wheeler (R)
Thomas S. Williams (R)
Richard Yates (R)

Indiana

Senators

Harry S. New (R)
James E. Watson (R)

Representatives

John S. Benham (R)
Oscar E. Bland (R)
James W. Dunbar (R)
Richard N. Elliott (R)
Louis W. Fairfield (R)
Andrew J. Hickey (R)
Milton Kraus (R)
Oscar R. Luhring (R)
Merrill Moores (R)
Fred S. Purnell (R)
Everett Sanders (R)
Albert H. Vestal (R)
William R. Wood (R)

Iowa

Senators

Smith W. Brookhart (R) s.
1922
Albert B. Cummins (R)
William S. Kenyon (R) r. Feb.
1922
Charles A. Rawson (R) ta. 1922

Representatives

William D. Boies (R)
Cyrenus Cole (R)
Lester J. Dickinson (R)
Cassius C. Dowell (R)
James W. Good r. June 1921
William R. Green (R)
Gilbert N. Haugen (R)
Harry E. Hull (R)
William F. Kopp (R)
C. William Ramseyer (R)
Burton E. Sweet (R)
Horace M. Towner (R)

Kansas

Senators

Arthur Capper (R)
Charles Curtis (R)

Representatives

Daniel R. Anthony, Jr. (R)
Richard E. Bird (R)
Philip P. Campbell (R)
Homer Hoch (R)
Edward C. Little (R)
James G. Strong (R)
Jasper N. Tincher (R)
Hays B. White (R)

Kentucky

Senators

Richard P. Ernst (R)
Augustus O. Stanley (D)

Representatives

Alben W. Barkley (D)
James C. Cantrill (D)
William J. Fields (D)
Ralph Gilbert (D)
Ben Johnson (D)
David H. Kincheloe (D)
John W. Langley (R)
Charles F. Ogden (R)
John M. Robsion (R)
Arthur B. Rouse (D)
Robert Y. Thomas, Jr. (D)

Louisiana

Senators

Edwin S. Broussard (D)
Joseph E. Ransdell (D)

Representatives

James B. Aswell (D)
H. Garland Dupre (D)
George K. Favrot (D)
Ladislas Lazaro (D)
Whitmell P. Martin (D)
James O'Connor (D)
John N. Sandlin (D)
Riley J. Wilson (D)

Maine

Senators

Bert M. Fernald (R)
Frederick Hale (R)

Representatives

Carroll L. Beedy (R)
Ira G. Hersey (R)
John E. Nelson (R) s. 1922
John A. Peters (R) r. Jan. 1922
Wallace H. White, Jr. (R)

Maryland

Senators

Joseph I. France (R)
Ovington E. Weller (R)

Representatives

Albert A. Blakeney (R)
T. Alan Goldsborough (D)
John P. Hill (R)

J. Charles Linthicum (D)
Sydney E. Mudd (R)
Frederick N. Zihlman (R)

Massachusetts

Senators

Henry Cabot Lodge (R)
David I. Walsh (R)

Representatives

A. Piatt Andrew, Jr. (R)
Frederick W. Dallinger (R)
Louis A. Frothingham (R)
James A. Gallivan (D)
Charles L. Gifford (R) s. 1922
Frederick H. Gillett (R)
William S. Greene (R)
Robert Luce (R)
Willfred W. Lufkin (R) r. June
1921
Robert S. Maloney (R)
Calvin D. Paige (R)
John Jacob Rogers (R)
Peter F. Tague (D)
George H. Tinkham (R)
Allen T. Treadway (R)
Charles L. Underhill (R)
Joseph Walsh (R) r. Aug. 1922
Samuel E. Winslow (R)

Michigan

Senators

James Couzens (R) s. 1922
Truman H. Newberry (R) r.
Nov. 1922
Charles E. Townsend (R)

Representatives

Vincent M. Brennan (R)
George P. Codd (R)
Louis C. Cramton (R)
Joseph W. Fordney (R)
W. Frank James (R)
Patrick H. Kelley (R)
John C. Ketcham (R)
James C. McLaughlin (R)
Carl E. Mapes (R)
Earl C. Michener (R)
Frank D. Scott (R)
John M. C. Smith (R)
Roy O. Woodruff (R)

Minnesota

Senators

Frank B. Kellogg (R)
Knute Nelson (R)

Representatives

Sydney Anderson (R)
Frank Clague (R)
Charles R. Davis (R)
Oscar E. Keller (R)
Harold Knutson (R)
Oscar J. Larson (R)
Walter H. Newton (R)
Thomas D. Schall (R)
Halvor Steenerson (R)
Andrew J. Volstead (R)

Mississippi

Senators

Pat Harrison (D)
John Sharp Williams (D)

Representatives

James W. Collier (D)
Ross A. Collins (D)
Benjamin G. Humphreys (D)
Paul B. Johnson (D)
Bill G. Lowrey (D)
Percy E. Quin (D)
John E. Rankin (D)
Thomas U. Sisson (D)

Missouri

Senators

James A. Reed (D)
Selden P. Spencer (R)

Representatives

William O. Atkeson (R)
Leonidas C. Dyer (R)
Edgar C. Ellis (R)
Charles L. Faust (R)
Harry B. Hawes (D)
Edward D. Hays (R)
Theodore W. Hukriede (R)
Henry F. Lawrence (R)
Isaac V. McPherson (R)
Frank C. Millspaugh (R) r. Dec. 1922
Cleveland A. Newton (R)
Roscoe C. Patterson (R)
Marion E. Rhodes (R)
Sidney C. Roach (R)
William W. Rucker (D)
Samuel A. Shelton (R)

Montana

Senators

Henry L. Myers (D)
Thomas J. Walsh (D)

Representatives

Washington J. McCormick (R)
Carl W. Riddick (R)

Nebraska

Senators

Gilbert M. Hitchcock (D)
George W. Norris (R)

Representatives

William E. Andrews (R)
Robert E. Evans (R)
Augustin R. Humphrey (R) s. 1922
Albert W. Jefferis (R)
Moses P. Kinkaid (R) d. July 1922
Melvin O. McLaughlin (R)
C. Frank Reavis (R) r. June 1922
Roy H. Thorpe (R) s. 1922

Nevada

Senators

Tasker L. Oddie (R)
Key Pittman (D)

Representatives

Samuel S. Arentz (R)

New Hampshire

Senators

Henry W. Keyes (R)
George H. Moses (R)

Representatives

Sherman E. Burroughs (R)
Edward H. Wason (R)

New Jersey

Senators

Walter E. Edge (R)
Joseph S. Frelinghuysen (R)

Representatives

Ernest R. Ackerman (R)
T. Frank Appleby (R)
Isaac Bacharach (R)
Elijah C. Hutchinson (R)
Frederick R. Lehlbach (R)
Charles F. X. O'Brien (D)
Archibald E. Olpp (R)
Richard W. Parker (R)
Francis F. Patterson, Jr. (R)
Randolph Perkins (R)
Amos H. Radcliffe (R)
Herbert W. Taylor (R)

New Mexico

Senators

Holm O. Bursom (R)
Andrieus A. Jones (D)

Representatives

Nestor Montoya (R) d. Jan. 1923

New York

Senators

William M. Calder (R)
James W. Wadsworth, Jr. (R)

Representatives

Martin C. Ansorge (R)
Charles G. Bond (R)
John F. Carew (D)
Walter M. Chandler (R)
John D. Clarke (R)
W. Bourke Cockran (D) d. Mar. 1923
Frank Crowther (R)
Thomas H. Cullen (D)
S. Wallace Dempsey (R)

Thomas B. Dunn (R)
Benjamin L. Fairchild (R)
Hamilton Fish, Jr. (R)
Norman J. Gould (R)
Anthony J. Griffin (D)
Lewis Henry (R)
Frederick C. Hicks (R)
Michael J. Hogan (R)
Alanson B. Houghton (R) r. Feb. 1922
James W. Husted (R)
John J. Kindred (D)
John Kissel (R)
Ardolph L. Kline (R)
Warren I. Lee (R)
Meyer London (Socialist)
Clarence MacGregor (R)
Walter W. Magee (R)
James M. Mead (D)
Ogden L. Mills (R)
Luther W. Mott (R)
James S. Parker (R)
Nathan D. Perlman (R)
Andrew N. Petersen (R)
Daniel A. Reed (R)
Daniel J. Riordan (D)
Albert B. Rossdale (R)
Thomas J. Ryan (R)
Archie D. Sanders (R)
Isaac Siegel (R)
Bertrand H. Snell (R)
Homer P. Snyder (R)
Christopher D. Sullivan (D)
Peter G. Ten Eyck (D)
Lester D. Volk (R)
Charles B. Ward (R)

North Carolina

Senators

Lee S. Overman (D)
Furnifold M. Simmons (D)

Representatives

Charles L. Abernethy (D) s. 1922
Samuel M. Brinson (D) d. Apr. 1922
Alfred L. Bulwinkle (D)
Robert L. Doughton (D)
William C. Hammer (D)
Claude Kitchin (D)
Homer L. Lyon (D)
Edward W. Pou (D)
Charles M. Stedman (D)
Hallett S. Ward (D)
Zebulon Weaver (D)

North Dakota

Senators

Edwin F. Ladd (R)
Porter J. McCumber (R)

Representatives

Olger B. Burtness (R)
James H. Sinclair (R)
George M. Young (R)

Ohio

Senators

Atlee Pomerene (D)

Frank B. Willis (R)

Representatives

James T. Begg (R)
Theodore E. Burton (R)
John L. Cable (R)
William W. Chalmers (R)
R. Clint Cole (R)
John G. Cooper (R)
Simeon D. Fess (R)
Roy G. Fitzgerald (R)
Israel M. Foster (R)
Harry C. Gahn (R)
Joseph H. Himes (R)
Charles C. Kearns (R)
Charles L. Knight (R)
Nicholas Longworth (R)
C. Ellis Moore (R)
William M. Morgan (R)
B. Frank Murphy (R)
Miner G. Norton (R)
Edwin D. Ricketts (R)
John C. Speaks (R)
Ambrose E. B. Stephens (R)
Charles J. Thompson (R)

Oklahoma

Senators

John W. Harreld (R)
Robert L. Owen (D)

Representatives

Charles D. Carter (D)
Thomas A. Chandler (R)
Lorraine M. Gensman (R)
Manuel Herrick (R)
James V. McClintic (D)
Joseph C. Pringey (R)
Alice M. Robertson (R)
Fletcher B. Swank (D)

Oregon

Senators

Charles L. McNary (R)
Robert N. Stanfield (R)

Representatives

Willis C. Hawley (R)
Clifton N. McArthur (R)
Nicholas J. Sinnott (R)

Pennsylvania

Senators

William E. Crow (R) ta. 1921-1922
Philander C. Knox (R) d. Oct. 1921
Boies Penrose (R) d. Dec. 1921
George Wharton Pepper (R) s. 1922
David A. Reed (R) s. 1922

Representatives

Harris J. Bixler (R)
Edward S. Brooks (R)
William J. Burke (R)
Thomas S. Butler (R)
Guy E. Campbell (R)

Charles R. Connell (R) d. Sept. 1922
James J. Connolly (R)
Clarence D. Coughlin (R)
Thomas S. Crago (R)
George P. Darrow (R)
George W. Edmonds (R)
Benjamin K. Focht (R)
Fred B. Gernerd (R)
George S. Graham (R)
William W. Griest (R)
Evan J. Jones (R)
M. Clyde Kelly (R)
Samuel A. Kendall (R)
Edgar R. Kiess (R)
William H. Kirkpatrick (R)
I. Clinton Kline (R)
Aaron S. Kreider (R)
Louis T. McFadden (R)
Joseph McLaughlin (R)
John M. Morin (R)
Stephen G. Porter (R)
Harry C. Ransley (R)
John Reber (R)
John M. Rose (R)
Milton W. Shreve (R)
Nathan L. Strong (R)
Henry W. Temple (R)
William S. Vare (R)
Anderson H. Walters (R)
Henry W. Watson (R)
Adam M. Wyant (R)

Rhode Island

Senators

LeBaron B. Colt (R)
Peter G. Gerry (D)

Representatives

Clark Burdick (R)
Ambrose Kennedy (R)
Walter R. Stiness (R)

South Carolina

Senators

Nathaniel B. Dial (D)
Ellison D. Smith (D)

Representatives

James F. Byrnes (D)
Fred H. Dominick (D)
Hampton P. Fulmer (D)
W. Turner Logan (D)
John J. McSwain (D)
William F. Stevenson (D)
Philip H. Stoll (D)

South Dakota

Senators

Peter Norbeck (R)
Thomas Sterling (R)

Representatives

Charles A. Christopherson (R)
Royal C. Johnson (R)
William Williamson (R)

Tennessee

Senators

Kenneth D. McKellar (D)
John K. Shields (D)

Representatives

Joseph E. Brown (R)
Joseph W. Byrns (D)
Wynne F. Clouse (R)
Ewin L. Davis (D)
Hubert F. Fisher (D)
Finis J. Garrett (D)
Lemuel P. Padgett (D) d. Aug. 1922
B. Carroll Reece (R)
Lon A. Scott (R)
J. Will Taylor (R)
Clarence W. Turner (D) s. 1922

Texas

Senators

Charles A. Culberson (D)
Morris Sheppard (D)

Representatives

Eugene Black (D)
Thomas L. Blanton (D)
John C. Box (D)
Clay Stone Briggs (D)
James P. Buchanan (D)
Tom T. Connally (D)
John Nance Garner (D)
Daniel E. Garrett (D)
Rufus Hardy (D)
Claude B. Hudspeth (D)
Marvin Jones (D)
Fritz G. Lanham (D)
Joseph J. Mansfield (D)
Lucian W. Parrish (D)
Sam Rayburn (D)
Morgan G. Sanders (D)
Hatton W. Sumners (D)
Guinn Williams (D) s. 1922
Harry M. Wurzbach (R)

Utah

Senators

William H. King (D)
Reed Smoot (R)

Representatives

Don B. Colton (R)
Elmer O. Leatherwood (R)

Vermont

Senators

William P. Dillingham (R)
Carroll S. Page (R)

Representatives

Porter H. Dale (R)
Frank L. Greene (R)

Virginia

Senators

Carter Glass (D)
Claude A. Swanson (D)

Representatives

Schuyler Otis Bland (D)
Joseph T. Deal (D)
Patrick H. Drewry (D)
Henry D. Flood (D) d. Dec. 1921
Thomas W. Harrison (D) r. Dec. 1922
James M. Hooker (D)
Rorer A. James (D) d. Aug. 1921
R. Walton Moore (D)
Andrew J. Montague (D)
John Paul (R) s. 1922
C. Bascom Slemp (D)
Henry St. George Tucker (D) s. 1922
James P. Woods (D)

Washington

Senators

Wesley L. Jones (R)
Miles Poindexter (R)

Representatives

Lindley H. Hadley (R)
Albert Johnson (R)
John F. Miller (R)
John W. Summers (R)
J. Stanley Webster (R)

West Virginia

Senators

Davis Elkins (R)
Howard Sutherland (R)

Representatives

George M. Bowers (R)
Leonard S. Echols (R)
Wells Goodykoontz (R)
Stuart F. Reed (R)
Benjamin L. Rosenbloom (R)
Harry C. Woodyard (R)

Wisconsin

Senators

Robert M. La Follette (R)
Irvine L. Lenroot (R)

Representatives

Joseph D. Beck (R)
Edward E. Browne (R)
David G. Classon (R)
Henry A. Cooper (R)
James A. Frear (R)
John C. Kleczka (R)
Florian Lampert (R)
Adolphus P. Nelson (R)
John M. Nelson (R)
William H. Stafford (R)

Edward Voigt (R)

Wyoming

Senators

John B. Kendrick (D)
Francis E. Warren (R)

Representatives

Frank W. Mondell (R)

Sixty-Eighth Congress

(Mar. 4, 1923, to Mar. 3, 1925)

President of the Senate: Calvin Coolidge
President Pro Tempore of the Senate: Albert B. Cummins
Speaker of the House of Representatives: Frederick H. Gillett

Alabama

Senators

J. Thomas Heflin (D)
Oscar W. Underwood (D)

Representatives

Miles C. Allgood (D)
Edward B. Almon (D)
William B. Bankhead (D)
William B. Bowling (D)
Lister Hill (D)
George Huddleston (D)
Lamar Jeffers (D)
John McDuffie (D)
William B. Oliver (D)
Henry B. Steagall (D)

Arizona

Senators

Henry F. Ashurst (D)
Ralph H. Cameron (R)

Representatives

Carl Hayden (D)

Arkansas

Senators

Thaddeus H. Caraway (D)
Joseph T. Robinson (D)

Representatives

William J. Driver (D)
William A. Oldfield (D)
Tilman B. Parks (D)
Heartsill Ragon (D)
James B. Reed (D)
John N. Tillman (D)
Otis Wingo (D)

California

Senators

Hiram W. Johnson (R)
Samuel M. Shortridge (R)

Representatives

Henry E. Barbour (R)
Charles F. Curry (R)
John D. Fredericks (R)
Arthur M. Free (R)
Clarence F. Lea (D, R)
Walter F. Lineberger (R)
James H. MacLafferty (R)
Mae E. Nolan (R)
John E. Raker (D)
Philip D. Swing (R)

Colorado

Senators

Alva B. Adams (D) ta. 1923
Rice W. Means (R) s. 1924
Samuel D. Nicholson (R) d. Mar. 1923
Lawrence C. Phipps (R)

Representatives

Guy U. Hardy (R)
Edward T. Taylor (D)
Charles B. Timberlake (R)
William N. Vaile (R)

Connecticut

Senators

Hiram Bingham (R) s. 1925
Frank B. Brandegee (R) d. Oct. 1924
George P. McLean (R)

Representatives

E. Hart Fenn (R)
Richard P. Freeman (R)
Schuyler Merritt (R)
Patrick B. O'Sullivan (D)
John Q. Tilson (R)

Delaware

Senators

L. Heisler Ball (R)
Thomas F. Bayard, Jr. (D)

Representatives

William H. Boyce (D)

Florida

Senators

Duncan U. Fletcher (D)
Park Trammell (D)

Representatives

Frank Clark (D)
Herbert J. Drane (D)

William J. Sears (D)
John H. Smithwick (D)

Georgia

Senators

Walter F. George (D)
William J. Harris (D)

Representatives

Thomas M. Bell (D)
Charles H. Brand (D)
Charles R. Crisp (D)
William C. Lankford (D)
William W. Larsen (D)
Gordon Lee (D)
R. Lee Moore (D)
Frank Park (D)
William D. Upshaw (D)
Carl Vinson (D)
William C. Wright (D)

Idaho

Senators

William E. Borah (R)
Frank R. Gooding (R)

Representatives

Burton L. French (R)
Addison T. Smith (R)

Illinois

Senators

Charles S. Deneen (R) s. 1925
Medill McCormick (R) d. Feb. 1925
William B. McKinley (R)

Representatives

William W. Arnold (D)
Fred A. Britten (R)
James R. Buckley (D)
Carl R. Chindblom (R)
Edward E. Denison (R)
Thomas A. Doyle (D)
Charles E. Fuller (R)
Frank H. Funk (R)
William J. Graham (R) r. June 1924
William P. Holaday (R)
Morton D. Hull (R)
William E. Hull (R)
Edward J. King (R)
Stanley H. Kunz (D)
John C. McKenzie (R)
Martin B. Madden (R)
J. Earl Major (D)
M. Alfred Michaelson (R)
Edward E. Miller (R)
Allen F. Moore (R)
Henry T. Rainey (D)
Henry R. Rathbone (R)
Frank R. Reid (R)
Adolph J. Sabath (D)
Elliott W. Sproul (R)
Thomas S. Williams (R)
Richard Yates (R)

Indiana

Senators

Samuel M. Ralston (D)
James E. Watson (R)

Representatives

Harry C. Canfield (D)
Samuel E. Cook (D)
Richard N. Elliott (R)
Louis W. Fairfield (R)
Frank Gardner (D)
Arthur H. Greenwood (D)
Andrew J. Hickey (R)
Merrill Moores (R)
Fred S. Purnell (R)
Everett Sanders (R)
Albert H. Vestal (R)
William E. Wilson (D)
William R. Wood (R)

Iowa

Senators

Smith W. Brookhart (R)
Albert B. Cummins (R)

Representatives

William D. Boies (R)
Cyrenus Cole (R)
Lester J. Dickinson (R)
Cassius C. Dowell (R)
Hiram K. Evans (R)
William R. Green (R)
Gilbert N. Haugen (R)
Harry E. Hull (R)
William F. Kopp (R)
C. William Ramseyer (R)
Thomas J. B. Robinson (R)

Kansas

Senators

Arthur Capper (R)
Charles Curtis (R)

Representatives

Daniel R. Anthony, Jr. (R)
William A. Ayres (D)
Ulysses S. Guyer (R) s. 1924
Homer Hoch (R)
Edward C. Little (R) d. June 1924
William H. Sproul (R)
James G. Strong (R)
Jasper N. Tincher (R)
Hays B. White (R)

Kentucky

Senators

Richard P. Ernst (R)
Augustus O. Stanley (D)

Representatives

Alben W. Barkley (D)
William J. Fields (D) r. Dec. 1923
Ralph Gilbert (D)

Ben Johnson (D)
David H. Kincheloe (D)
John W. Langley (R)
Joseph W. Morris (D)
John M. Robsion (R)
Arthur B. Rouse (D)
Maurice H. Thatcher (R)
Robert Y. Thomas, Jr. (D)
Fred M. Vinson (D) s. 1924

Louisiana

Senators

Edwin S. Broussard (D)
Joseph E. Ransdell (D)

Representatives

James B. Aswell (D)
H. Garland Dupre (D) d. Feb. 1924
George K. Favrot (D)
Ladislas Lazaro (D)
Whitmell P. Martin (D)
James O'Connor (D)
John N. Sandlin (D)
J. Zach Spearing (D) s. 1924
Riley J. Wilson (D)

Maine

Senators

Bert M. Fernald (R)
Frederick Hale (R)

Representatives

Carroll L. Beedy (R)
Ira G. Hersey (R)
John E. Nelson (R)
Wallace H. White, Jr. (R)

Maryland

Senators

William Cabell Bruce (D)
Ovington E. Weller (R)

Representatives

Stephen W. Gambrill (D) s. 1924
T. Alan Goldsborough (D)
John Philip Hill (R)
J. Charles Linthicum (D)
Sydney E. Mudd (R) d. Oct. 1924
Millard E. Tydings (D)
Frederick N. Zihlman (R)

Massachusetts

Senators

William M. Butler (R) s. 1924
Henry Cabot Lodge (R) d. Nov. 1924
David I. Walsh (D)

Representatives

A. Piatt Andrew, Jr. (R)
William P. Connery, Jr. (D)
Frederick W. Dallinger (R)

Louis A. Frothingham (R)
James A. Gallivan (D)
Charles L. Gifford (R)
Frederick H. Gillett (R)
William S. Greene (R) d. Sept. 1924
Robert M. Leach (R) s. 1924
Robert Luce (R)
Calvin D. Paige (R)
John Jacob Rogers (R)
Peter F. Tague (D)
George H. Tinkham (R)
Allen T. Treadway (R)
Charles L. Underhill (R)
Samuel E. Winslow (R)

Michigan

Senators

James Couzens (R)
Woodbridge N. Ferris (D)

Representatives

Robert H. Clancy (D)
Louis C. Cramton (R)
Grant M. Hudson (R)
W. Frank James (R)
John C. Ketcham (R)
James C. McLaughlin (R)
Clarence J. McLeod (R)
Carl E. Mapes (R)
Earl C. Michener (R)
Frank D. Scott (R)
Bird J. Vincent (R)
Arthur B. Williams (R)
Roy O. Woodruff (R)

Minnesota

Senators

Magnus Johnson (Farm-Labor)
Henrik Shipstead (Farm-Labor)

Representatives

Sydney Anderson (R)
Frank Clague (R)
Charles R. Davis (R)
Oscar E. Keller (R)
Harold Knutson (R)
Ole J. Kvale (R)
Oscar J. Larson (R)
Walter H. Newton (R)
Thomas D. Schall (R)
Knud Wefald (Farm-Labor)

Mississippi

Senators

Pat Harrison (D)
Hubert D. Stephens (D)

Representatives

T. Jeff Busby (D)
James W. Collier (D)
Ross A. Collins (D)
William Y. Humphreys (D)
Bill G. Lowrey (D)
Percy E. Quin (D)
John E. Rankin (D)
T. Webber Wilson (D)

Missouri

Senators

James A. Reed (D)
Selden P. Spencer (R)

Representatives

Clarence Cannon (D)
Clement C. Dickinson (D)
Leonidas C. Dyer (R)
Charles L. Faust (R)
James F. Fulbright (D)
Harry B. Hawes (D)
Henry L. Jost (D)
Ralph F. Lozier (D)
Samuel C. Major (D)
Joe J. Manlove (R)
Jacob L. Milligan (D)
Cleveland A. Newton (R)
Sidney C. Roach (R)
Milton A. Romjue (D)
Thomas L. Rubey (D)
J. Scott Wolff (D)

Montana

Senators

Thomas J. Walsh (D)
Burton K. Wheeler (D)

Representatives

John M. Evans (D)
Scott Leavitt (R)

Nebraska

Senators

Robert B. Howell (R)
George W. Norris (R)

Representatives

Edgar Howard (D)
Melvin O. McLaughlin (R)
John H. Morehead (D)
Willis G. Sears (R)
Ashton C. Shallenberger (D)
Robert G. Simmons (R)

Nevada

Senators

Tasker L. Oddie (R)
Key Pittman (D)

Representatives

Charles L. Richards (D)

New Hampshire

Senators

Henry W. Keyes (R)
George H. Moses (R)

Representatives

William N. Rogers (D)
Edward H. Wason (R)

New Jersey

Senators

Walter E. Edge (R)
Edward I. Edwards (D)

Representatives

Ernest R. Ackerman (R)
Isaac Bacharach (R)
Charles Browne (D)
John J. Eagan (D)
Elmer H. Geran (D)
Frederick R. Lehlbach (R)
Frank J. McNulty (D)
Daniel F. Minahan (D)
Charles F. X. O'Brien (D)
Francis F. Patterson, Jr. (R)
Randolph Perkins (R)
George N. Seger (R)

New Mexico

Senators

Holm O. Bursum (R)
Andrieus A. Jones (D)

Representatives

John Morrow (D)

New York

Senators

Royal S. Copeland (D)
James W. Wadsworth, Jr. (R)

Representatives

Robert L. Bacon (R)
Loring M. Black, Jr. (D)
Sol Bloom (D)
John J. Boylan (D)
John F. Carew (D)
Emanuel Celler (D)
John D. Clarke (R)
William E. Cleary (D)
Parker Corning (D)
Frank Crowther (R)
Thomas H. Cullen (D)
S. Wallace Dempsey (R)
Samuel Dickstein (D)
Benjamin L. Fairchild (R)
Hamilton Fish, Jr. (R)
Anthony J. Griffin (D)
Meyer Jacobstein (D)
John J. Kindred (D)
Fiorello H. LaGuardia (R)
George W. Lindsay (D)
Clarence MacGregor (R)
Walter W. Magee (R)
James M. Mead (D)
Ogden L. Mills (R)
David J. O'Connell (D)
John J. O'Connor (D)
Frank Oliver (D)
James S. Parker (R)
Nathan D. Perlman (R)
Anning S. Prall (D)
John F. Quayle (D)
Daniel A. Reed (R)
Archie D. Sanders (R)
Bertrand H. Snell (R)
Homer P. Snyder (R)
Gale H. Stalker (R)

Charles I. Stengle (D)
Christopher D. Sullivan (D)
Thaddeus C. Sweet (R)
John Taber (R)
J. Mayhew Wainwright (R)
Charles B. Ward (R)
Royal H. Weller (D)

North Carolina

Senators

Lee S. Overman (D)
Furnifold M. Simmons (D)

Representatives

Charles L. Abernethy (D)
Alfred L. Bulwinkle (D)
Robert L. Doughton (D)
William C. Hammer (D)
John H. Kerr (D)
Homer L. Lyon (D)
Edward W. Pou (D)
Charles M. Stedman (D)
Hallett S. Ward (D)
Zebulon Weaver (D)

North Dakota

Senators

Lynn J. Frazier (R)
Edwin F. Ladd (R)

Representatives

Olger B. Burtness (R)
Thomas Hall (D) s. 1924
James H. Sinclair (R)
George M. Young (R) r. Sept. 1924

Ohio

Senators

Simeon D. Fess (R)
Frank B. Willis (R)

Representatives

James T. Begg (R)
Charles Brand (R)
Theodore E. Burton (R)
John L. Cable (R)
R. Clint Cole (R)
John G. Cooper (R)
Robert Crosser (D)
Martin L. Davey (D)
Roy G. Fitzgerald (R)
Israel M. Foster (R)
Charles C. Kearns (R)
Nicholas Longworth (R)
John McSweeney (D)
Charles A. Mooney (D)
C. Ellis Moore (R)
William M. Morgan (R)
B. Frank Murphy (R)
Isaac R. Sherwood (D)
John C. Speaks (R)
Ambrose E. B. Stephens (R)
Charles J. Thompson (R)
Mell G. Underwood (D)

Oklahoma

Senators

John W. Harreld (R)
Robert L. Owen (D)

Representatives

Charles D. Carter (D)
Milton C. Garber (R)
William W. Hastings (D)
Everette B. Howard (D)
James V. McClintic (D)
Thomas D. McKeown (D)
Fletcher B. Swank (D)
J. W. Elmer Thomas (D)

Oregon

Senators

Charles L. McNary (R)
Robert N. Stanfield (R)

Representatives

Willis C. Hawley (R)
Nicholas J. Sinnott (R)
Elton Watkins (D)

Pennsylvania

Senators

George Wharton Pepper (R)
David A. Reed (R)

Representatives

Edward M. Beers (R)
Harris J. Bixler (R)
George F. Brumm (R)
Thomas S. Butler (R)
Guy E. Campbell (R)
John J. Casey (D)
James J. Connolly (R)
William M. Croll (D)
Herbert W. Cummings (D)
George P. Darrow (R)
George W. Edmonds (R)
Samuel F. Glatfelter (D)
George S. Graham (R)
William W. Griest (R)
M. Clyde Kelly (R)
Samuel A. Kendall (R)
Everett Kent (D)
Edgar R. Kiess (R)
J. Banks Kurtz (R)
Louis T. McFadden (R)
James M. Magee (R)
John M. Morin (R)
Thomas W. Phillips, Jr. (R)
Stephen G. Porter (R)
Harry C. Ransley (R)
Milton W. Shreve (R)
Frank C. Sites (D)
Nathan L. Strong (R)
William I. Swoope (R)
Henry W. Temple (R)
William S. Vare (R)
Laurence H. Watres (R)
Henry W. Watson (R)
George A. Welsh (R)
George M. Wertz (R)
Adam M. Wyant (R)

Rhode Island

Senators

LeBaron B. Colt (R) d. Aug.
  1924
Peter G. Gerry (D)
Jesse H. Metcalf (R) s. 1924

Representatives

Richard S. Aldrich (R)
Clark Burdick (R)
Jeremiah E. O'Connell (D)

South Carolina

Senators

Nathaniel B. Dial (D)
Ellison D. Smith (D)

Representatives

James F. Byrnes (D)
Fred H. Dominick (D)
Hampton P. Fulmer (D)
Allard H. Gasque (D)
W. Turner Logan (D)
John J. McSwain (D)
William F. Stevenson (D)

South Dakota

Senators

Peter Norbeck (R)
Thomas Sterling (R)

Representatives

Charles A. Christopherson (R)
Royal C. Johnson (R)
William Williamson (R)

Tennessee

Senators

Kenneth D. McKellar (D)
John K. Shields (D)

Representatives

Gordon Browing (D)
Joseph W. Byrns (D)
Ewin L. Davis (D)
Hubert F. Fisher (D)
Finis J. Garrett (D)
Cordell Hull (D)
Sam D. McReynolds (D)
B. Carroll Reece (R)
William C. Salmon (D)
J. Will Taylor (R)

Texas

Senators

Earle B. Mayfield (D)
Morris Sheppard (D)

Representatives

Eugene Black (D)
Thomas L. Blanton (D)

John C. Box (D)
Clay Stone Briggs (D)
James P. Buchanan (R)
Tom T. Connally (D)
John Nance Garner (D)
Daniel E. Garrett (D)
Claude B. Hudspeth (D)
Luther A. Johnson (D)
Marvin Jones (D)
Fritz G. Lanham (D)
Joseph J. Mansfield (D)
Sam Rayburn (D)
Morgan G. Sanders (D)
Hatton W. Sumners (D)
Guinn Williams (D)
Harry M. Wurzbach (R)

Utah

Senators

William H. King (D)
Reed Smoot (R)

Representatives

Don B. Colton (R)
Elmer O. Leatherwood (R)

Vermont

Senators

Porter H. Dale (R)
Frank L. Greene (R)

Representatives

Frederick G. Fleetwood (R)
Ernest W. Gibson (R)

Virginia

Senators

Carter Glass (D)
Claude A. Swanson (D)

Representatives

Schuyler Otis Bland (D)
Joseph T. Deal (D)
Patrick H. Drewry (D)
Thomas W. Harrison (D)
James M. Hooker (D)
Andrew J. Montague (D)
R. Walton Moore (D)
George C. Peery (D)
Henry St. George Tucker (D)
Clifton A. Woodrum (D)

Washington

Senators

Clarence C. Dill (D)
Wesley L. Jones (R)

Representatives

Lindley H. Hadley (R)
Samuel B. Hill (D)
Albert Johnson (R)
John F. Miller (R)
John W. Summers (R)

West Virginia

Senators

Davis Elkins (R)
Matthew M. Neeley (D)

Representatives

Robert E. L. Allen (D)
George W. Johnson (D)
Thomas J. Lilly (D)
Stuart F. Reed (R)
Benjamin L. Rosenbloom (R)
J. Alfred Taylor (D)

Wisconsin

Senators

Robert M. La Follette (R)
Irvine L. Lenroot (R)

Representatives

Joseph D. Beck (R)
Victor L. Berger (Socialist)
Edward E. Browne (R)
Henry A. Cooper (R)
James A. Frear (R)
Florian Lampert (R)
John M. Nelson (R)
Hubert H. Peavey (R)
John C. Schafer (R)
George J. Schneider
  (Progressive)
Edward Voigt (R)

Wyoming

Senators

John B. Kendrick (D)
Francis E. Warren (R)

Representatives

Charles E. Winter (R)

Sixty-Ninth Congress

(Mar. 4, 1925, to
Mar. 3, 1927)

President of the Senate: Charles
  G. Dawes
*Presidents Pro Tempore of the
  Senate:* Albert B. Cummins;
  George H. Moses
*Speaker of the House of
  Representatives:* Nicholas
  Longworth

Alabama

Senators

J. Thomas Heflin (D)
Oscar W. Underwood (D)

Representatives

Miles C. Allgood (D)

Edward B. Almon (D)
William B. Bankhead (D)
William B. Bowling (D)
Lister Hill (D)
George Huddleston (D)
Lamar Jeffers (D)
John McDuffie (D)
William B. Oliver (D)
Henry B. Steagall (D)

Arizona

Senators

Henry F. Ashurst (D)
Ralph H. Cameron (R)

Representatives

Carl Hayden (D)

Arkansas

Senators

Thaddeus H. Caraway (D)
Joseph T. Robinson (D)

Representatives

William J. Driver (D)
William A. Oldfield (D)
Tilman B. Parks (D)
Heartsill Ragon (D)
James B. Reed (D)
John N. Tillman (D)
Otis Wingo (D)

California

Senators

Hiram W. Johnson (R)
Samuel M. Shortridge (R)

Representatives

Henry E. Barbour (R)
Albert E. Carter (R)
Charles F. Curry (R)
Harry L. Englebright (R) s. 1926
Lawrence J. Flaherty (R) d. June 1926
John D. Fredericks (R)
Arthur M. Free (R)
Florence Prag Kahn (R)
Clarence F. Lea (D, R)
Walter F. Lineberger (R)
Philip D. Swing (R)
Richard J. Welch (R) s. 1926

Colorado

Senators

Lawrence C. Phipps (R)
Rice W. Means (R)

Representatives

Guy U. Hardy (R)
Edward T. Taylor (D)
Charles B. Timberlake (R)
William N. Vaile (R)

Connecticut

Senators

Hiram Bingham (R)
George P. McLean (R)

Representatives

E. Hart Fenn (R)
Richard P. Freeman (R)
James P. Glynn (R)
Schuyler Merritt (R)
John Q. Tilson (R)

Delaware

Senators

Thomas F. Bayard (D)
T. Coleman Du Pont (R)

Representatives

Robert G. Houston (R)

Florida

Senators

Duncan U. Fletcher (D)
Park Trammell (D)

Representatives

Herbert J. Drane (D)
Robert A. Green (D)
William J. Sears (D)
John H. Smithwick (D)

Georgia

Senators

Walter F. George (D)
William J. Harris (D)

Representatives

Thomas M. Bell (D)
Charles H. Brand (D)
Edward E. Cox (D)
Charles R. Crisp (D)
Charles G. Edwards (D)
William C. Lankford (D)
William W. Larsen (D)
Gordon Lee (D)
Samuel Rutherford (D)
William D. Upshaw (D)
Carl Vinson (D)
William C. Wright (D)

Idaho

Senators

William E. Borah (R)
Frank R. Gooding (R)

Representatives

Burton L. French (R)
Addison T. Smith (R)

Illinois

Senators

Charles S. Deneen (R)
William B. McKinley (R) d. Dec. 1926

Representatives

Charles Adkins (R)
John C. Allen (R)
William W. Arnold (D)
Fred A. Britten (R)
Carl R. Chindblom (R)
Edward E. Denison (R)
Thomas A. Doyle (R)
Charles E. Fuller (R) d. June 1926
Frank H. Funk (R)
John J. Gorman (R)
William P. Holaday (R)
Morton D. Hull (R)
William E. Hull (R)
Edward M. Irwin (R)
William R. Johnson (R)
Edward J. King (R)
Stanley H. Kunz (D)
Martin B. Madden (R)
M. Alfred Michaelson (R)
Henry T. Rainey (D)
Henry R. Rathbone (R)
Frank R. Reid (R)
Adolph J. Sabath (D)
Elliott W. Sproul (R)
Loren E. Wheeler (R)
Thomas S. Williams (R)
Richard Yates (R)

Indiana

Senators

Arthur R. Robinson (R)
James E. Watson (R)

Representatives

Harry C. Canfield (D)
Richard N. Elliott (R)
Frank Gardner (D)
Arthur H. Greenwood (D)
Albert R. Hall (R)
Andrew J. Hickey (R)
David Hogg (R)
Noble J. Johnson (R)
Fred S. Purnell (R)
Harry E. Rowbottom (R)
Ralph E. Updike (R)
Albert H. Vestal (R)
William R. Wood (R)

Iowa

Senators

Smith W. Brookhart (R) r. Apr. 1926
Albert B. Cummins (R) d. July 1926
Daniel F. Steck (D) s. 1926
David W. Stewart (R) s. 1926

Representatives

William D. Boies (R)
Cyrenus Cole (R)
Lester J. Dickinson (R)

Cassius C. Dowell (R)
William R. Green (R)
Gilbert N. Haugen (R)
William F. Kopp (R)
F. Dickinson Letts (R)
C. William Ramseyer (R)
Thomas J. B. Robinson (R)
Lloyd Thurston (R)

Kansas

Senators

Arthur Capper (R)
Charles Curtis (R)

Representatives

Daniel R. Anthony, Jr. (R)
William A. Ayres (D)
Homer Hoch (R)
Chauncey B. Little (D)
William H. Sproul (R)
James G. Strong (R)
Jasper N. Tincher (R)
Hays B. White (R)

Kentucky

Senators

Richard P. Ernst (R)
Frederic M. Sackett (R)

Representatives

Alben W. Barkley (D)
Virgil M. Chapman (D)
Ralph Gilbert (D)
Ben Johnson (D)
David H. Kincheloe (D)
Andrew J. Kirk (R)
John W. Moore (D)
John M. Robsion (R)
Arthur B. Rouse (D)
Maurice H. Thatcher (R)
Fred M. Vinson (D)

Louisiana

Senators

Edwin S. Broussard (D)
Joseph E. Ransdell (D)

Representatives

James B. Aswell (D)
Bolivar E. Kemp (D)
Ladislas Lazaro (D)
Whitmell P. Martin (D)
James O'Connor (D)
John N. Sandlin (D)
J. Zack Spearing (D)
Riley J. Wilson (D)

Maine

Senators

Bert M. Fernald (R) d. Aug. 1926
Arthur R. Gould (R) s. 1926
Frederick Hale (R)

Maryland

Senators

William Cabell Bruce (D)
Ovington E. Weller (R)

Representatives

Stephen W. Gambrill (D)
T. Alan Goldsborough (D)
John P. Hill (R)
J. Charles Linthicum (D)
Millard E. Tydings (D)
Frederick N. Zihlman (R)

Massachusetts

Senators

William M. Butler (R)
Frederick H. Gillett (R)
David I. Walsh (D) s. 1926

Representatives

A. Piatt Andrew, Jr. (R)
Henry L. Bowles (R)
William P. Connery, Jr. (D)
Frederick W. Dallinger (D) s. 1926
John J. Douglas (D)
Frank H. Foss (R)
Louis A. Frothingham (R)
James A. Gallivan (D)
Charles L. Gifford (R)
Robert Luce (R)
Joseph W. Martin, Jr. (R)
Edith Nourse Rogers (R)
George R. Stobbs (R)
Harry I. Thayer (R) d. Mar. 1926
George H. Tinkham (R)
Allen T. Treadway (R)
Charles L. Underhill (R)

Michigan

Senators

James Couzens (R)
Woodbridge N. Ferris (D)

Representatives

Louis C. Cramton (R)
Joseph L. Hooper (R)
Grant M. Hudson (R)
W. Frank James (R)
John C. Ketcham (R)
James C. McLaughlin (R)
Clarence J. McLeod (R)
Carl E. Mapes (R)
Earl C. Michener (R)
Frank D. Scott (R)
John B. Sosnowski (R)
Bird J. Vincent (R)
Roy O. Woodruff (R)

Representatives

Carroll L. Beedy (R)
Ira G. Hersey (R)
John E. Nelson (R)
Wallace H. White, Jr. (R)

Minnesota

Senators

Thomas D. Schall (R)
Henrik Shipstead (Farm-Labor)

Representatives

August H. Andresen (R)
William L. Carss (Farm-Labor)
Frank Clague (R)
Allen J. Furlow (R)
Godfrey G. Goodwin (R)
Oscar E. Keller (R)
Harold Knutson (R)
Ole J. Kvale (Farm-Labor)
Walter H. Newton (R)
Knud Wefald (Farm-Labor)

Mississippi

Senators

Pat Harrison (D)
Hubert D. Stephens (D)

Representatives

T. Jeff Busby (D)
James W. Collier (D)
Ross A. Collins (D)
Bill G. Lowrey (D)
Percy E. Quin (D)
John E. Rankin (D)
William M. Whittington (D)
T. Webber Wilson (D)

Missouri

Senators

Harry B. Hawes (D) s. 1926
James A. Reed (D)
George H. Williams (R) ta. 1925

Representatives

Ralph E. Bailey (R)
Clarence Cannon (D)
John J. Cochran (D) s. 1926
Clement C. Dickinson (D)
Leonidas C. Dyer (R)
Edgar C. Ellis (R)
Charles L. Faust (R)
Harry B. Hawes (D) r. Oct. 1926
Charles E. Kiefner (R)
Ralph F. Lozier (D)
Samuel C. Major (D)
Joe J. Manlove (R)
Jacob L. Milligan (D)
William L. Nelson (D)
Cleveland A. Newton (R)
Milton A. Romjue (D)
Thomas L. Rubey (D)

Montana

Senators

Thomas J. Walsh (D)
Burton K. Wheeler (D)

Representatives

John M. Evans (D)
Scott Leavitt (R)

Nebraska

Senators

Robert B. Howell (R)
George W. Norris (R)

Representatives

Edgar Howard (D)
Melvin O. McLaughlin (R)
John H. Morehead (D)
Willis G. Sears (R)
Ashton C. Shallenberger (D)
Robert G. Simmons (R)

Nevada

Senators

Tasker L. Oddie (R)
Key Pittman (D)

Representatives

Samuel S. Arentz (R)

New Hampshire

Senators

Henry W. Keyes (R)
George H. Moses (R)

Representatives

Fletcher Hale (R)
Edward H. Wason (R)

New Jersey

Senators

Walter E. Edge (R)
Edward I. Edwards (D)

Representatives

Ernest R. Ackerman (R)
Stewart H. Appleby (R)
Oscar L. Auf Der Heide (D)
Isaac Bacharach (R)
Charles A. Eaton (R)
Franklin W. Fort (R)
Frederick R. Lehlbach (R)
Mary T. Norton (D)
Francis F. Patterson, Jr. (R)
Randolph Perkins (R)
George N. Seger (R)
Herbert W. Taylor (R)

New Mexico

Senators

Sam G. Bratton (D)
Andrieus A. Jones (D)

Representatives

John Morrow (D)

New York

Senators

Royal S. Copeland (D)
James W. Wadsworth, Jr. (R)

Representatives

Robert L. Bacon (R)
Loring M. Black, Jr. (D)
Sol Bloom (D)
John J. Boylan (D)
John F. Carew (D)
Emanuel Celler (D)
William E. Cleary (D)
Parker Corning (D)
Frank Crowther (R)
Thomas H. Cullen (D)
Frederick M. Davenport (R)
S. Wallace Dempsey (R)
Samuel Dickstein (D)
Benjamin L. Fairchild (R)
Hamilton Fish, Jr. (R)
Anthony J. Griffin (D)
Meyer Jacobstein (D)
John J. Kindred (D)
Fiorello H. LaGuardia (Socialist)
George W. Lindsay (D)
Clarence MacGregor (R)
Walter W. Magee (R)
James M. Mead (D)
Ogden L. Mills (R)
David I. O'Connell (D)
John J. O'Connor (D)
Frank Oliver (D)
James S. Parker (R)
Nathan D. Perlman (R)
Anning S. Prall (D)
Harcourt J. Pratt (R)
John F. Quayle (D)
Daniel A. Reed (R)
Archie D. Sanders (R)
Bertrand H. Snell (R)
Andrew L. Somers (D)
Gale H. Stalker (R)
Christopher D. Sullivan (D)
Thaddeus C. Sweet (R)
John Taber (R)
Harold S. Tolley (R)
J. Mayhew Wainwright (R)
Royal H. Weller (D)

North Carolina

Senators

Lee S. Overman (D)
Furnifold M. Simmons (D)

Representatives

Charles L. Abernethy (D)
Alfred L. Bulwinkle (D)
Robert L. Doughton (D)
William C. Hammer (D)
John H. Kerr (D)
Homer L. Lyon (D)
Edward W. Pou (D)
Charles M. Stedman (D)
Lindsay C. Warren (D)
Zebulon Weaver (D)

North Dakota

Senators

Lynn J. Frazier (R)
Gerald P. Nye (R)

Representatives

Olger B. Burtness (R)
Thomas Hall (R)
James H. Sinclair (R)

Ohio

Senators

Simeon D. Fess (R)
Frank B. Willis (R)

Representatives

James T. Begg (R)
Charles Brand (R)
Theodore E. Burton (R)
William W. Chalmers (R)
John G. Cooper (R)
Robert Crosser (D)
Martin L. Davey (D)
Roy G. Fitzgerald (R)
William T. Fitzgerald (R)
Thomas B. Fletcher (D)
Thomas A. Jenkins (R)
Charles C. Kearns (R)
Nicholas Longworth (R)
John McSweeney (D)
Charles A. Mooney (D)
C. Ellis Moore (R)
William M. Morgan (R)
B. Frank Murphy (R)
John C. Speaks (R)
Ambrose E. B. Stephens
Charles J. Thompson (R)
Mell G. Underwood (D)

Oklahoma

Senators

John W. Harreld (R)
William B. Pine (R)

Representatives

Charles D. Carter (D)
Milton C. Garber (R)
William W. Hastings (D)
James V. McClintic (D)
Thomas D. McKeown (D)
Samuel J. Montgomery (R)
Fletcher B. Swank (D)
J. W. Elmer Thomas (D)

Oregon

Senators

Charles L. McNary (R)
Robert N. Stanfield (R)

Representatives

Maurice E. Crumpacker (R)
Willis C. Hawley (R)
Nicholas J. Sinnott (R)

Pennsylvania

Senators

George Wharton Pepper (R)
David A. Reed (R)

Representatives

Edward M. Beers (R)
Harris J. Bixler (R)
George F. Brumm (R)
Thomas S. Butler (R)
Guy E. Campbell (R)
Edmund N. Carpenter (R)
James J. Connolly (R)
William R. Coyle (R)
George P. Darrow (R)
Charles J. Esterly (R)
Benjamin M. Golder (R)
George S. Graham (R)
William W. Griest (R)
M. Clyde Kelly (R)
Samuel A. Kendall (R)
Edgar R. Kiess (R)
J. Banks Kurtz (R)
Louis T. McFadden (R)
James M. Magee (R)
Frederick W. Magrady (R)
Franklin Menges (R)
John M. Morin (R)
Thomas W. Phillips, Jr. (R)
Stephen G. Porter (R)
Harry C. Ransley (R)
Milton W. Shreve (R)
Nathan L. Strong (R)
Joshua W. Swartz (R)
William I. Swoope (R)
Henry W. Temple (R)
William S. Vare (R)
Anderson H. Walters
Laurence H. Watres (R)
Henry W. Watson (R)
George A. Welsh (R)
Adam M. Wyant (R)

Rhode Island

Senators

Peter G. Gerry (D)
Jesse H. Metcalf (R)

Representatives

Richard S. Aldrich (R)
Clark Burdick (R)
Jeremiah E. O'Connell (D)

South Carolina

Senators

Coleman L. Blease (D)
Ellison D. Smith (D)

Representatives

Fred H. Dominick (D)
Hampton P. Fulmer (D)
Allard H. Gasque (D)
Butler B. Hare (D)
Thomas S. McMillan (D)
John J. McSwain (D)
William F. Stevenson (D)

South Dakota

Senators

William H. McMaster (R)
Peter Norbeck (R)

Representatives

Charles A. Christopherson (R)
Royal C. Johnson (R)
William Williamson (R)

Tennessee

Senators

Kenneth D. McKellar (D)
Lawrence D. Tyson (D)

Representatives

Gordon Browing (D)
Joseph W. Byrns (D)
Ewin L. Davis (D)
Edward E. Eslick (D)
Hubert F. Fisher (D)
Finis J. Garrett (D)
Cordell Hull (D)
Sam D. McReynolds (D)
B. Carroll Reece (R)
J. Will Taylor (R)

Texas

Senators

Earle B. Mayfield (D)
Morris Sheppard (D)

Representatives

Eugene Black (D)
Thomas L. Blanton (D)
John C. Box (D)
Clay Stone Briggs (D)
James P. Buchanan (D)
Tom T. Connally (D)
John Nance Garner (D)
Daniel E. Garrett (D)
Claude B. Hudspeth (D)
Luther A. Johnson (D)
Marvin Jones (D)
Fritz G. Lanham (D)
Joseph J. Mansfield (D)
Sam Rayburn (D)
Morgan G. Sanders (D)
Hatton W. Sumners (D)
Guinn Williams (D)
Harry M. Wurzbach (D)

Utah

Senators

William H. King (D)
Reed Smoot (R)

Representatives

Don B. Colton (R)
Elmer O. Leatherwood (R)

Vermont

Senators

Porter H. Dale (R)
Frank L. Greene (R)

Representatives

Elbert S. Brigham (R)
Ernest W. Gibson (R)

Virginia

Senators

Carter Glass (D)
Claude A. Swanson (D)

Representatives

Schuyler Otis Bland (D)
Joseph T. Deal (D)
Patrick H. Drewry (D)
Thomas W. Harrison (D)
Andrew J. Montague (D)
R. Walton Moore (D)
George C. Peery (D)
Henry St. George Tucker (D)
Joseph Whitehead (D)
Clifton A. Woodrum (D)

Washington

Senators

Clarence C. Dill (D)
Wesley L. Jones (R)

Representatives

Lindley H. Hadley (R)
Samuel B. Hill (D)
Albert Johnson (R)
John F. Miller (R)
John W. Summers (R)

West Virginia

Senators

Guy D. Goff (R)
Matthew M. Neely (D)

Representatives

Carl G. Bachmann (R)
Frank L. Bowman (R)
James F. Strother (R)
J. Alfred Taylor (D)
John M. Wolverton (R)
Harry C. Woodyard (R)

Wisconsin

Senators

Robert M. La Follette (R) d.
  June 1925
Robert M. La Follette, Jr.
  (Progressive) s. 1925
Irvine L. Lenroot (R)

Representatives

Joseph D. Beck (R)

Victor L. Berger (Socialist)
Edward E. Browne (R)
Henry A. Cooper (R)
James A. Frear (R)
Hubert H. Peavey (R)
Florian Lampert (R)
John M. Nelson (R)
John C. Schafer (R)
George J. Schneider
  (Progressive)
Edward Voigt (R)

Wyoming

Senators

John B. Kendrick (D)
Francis E. Warren (R)

Representatives

Charles E. Winter (R)

Seventieth Congress

(Mar. 4, 1927, to
Mar. 3, 1929)

President of the Senate: Charles
  G. Dawes
*President Pro Tempore of the
  Senate:* George H. Moses
*Speaker of the House of
  Representatives:* Nicholas
  Longworth

Alabama

Senators

Hugo L. Black (D)
J. Thomas Heflin (D)

Representatives

Miles C. Allgood (D)
Edward B. Almon (D)
William B. Bankhead (D)
William B. Bowling (D) r. Aug.
  1928
Lister Hill (D)
George Huddleston (D)
Lamar Jeffers (D)
John McDuffie (D)
William B. Oliver (D)
LaFayette L. Patterson (D) s.
  1928
Henry B. Steagall (D)

Arizona

Senators

Henry F. Ashurst (D)
Carl Hayden (D)

Representatives

Lewis W. Douglas (D)

Arkansas

Senators

Joseph T. Robinson (D)
Thaddeus H. Caraway (D)

Representatives

William J. Driver (D)
Pearl Peden Oldfield (D) s.
  1929
William A. Oldfield (D) d.
  Nov. 1928
Tilman B. Parks (D)
Heartsill Ragon (D)
James B. Reed (D)
John N. Tillman (D)
Otis R. Wingo (D)

California

Senators

Hiram W. Johnson (R)
Samuel M. Shortridge (R)

Representatives

Henry E. Barbour (R)
Albert E. Carter (R)
Joe Crail (R)
Charles F. Curry (R)
Harry L. Englebright (R)
William E. Evans (R)
Arthur M. Free (R)
Florence Prag Kahn (R)
Clarence F. Lea (D, R)
Philip D. Swing (R)
Richard J. Welch (R)

Colorado

Senators

Lawrence C. Phipps (R)
Charles W. Waterman (R)

Representatives

Guy U. Hardy (R)
Edward T. Taylor (D)
Charles B. Timberlake (R)
S. Harrison White (D)

Connecticut

Senators

Hiram Bingham (R)
George P. McLean (R)

Representatives

E. Hart Fenn (R)
Richard P. Freeman (R)
James P. Glynn (R)
Schuyler Merritt (R)
John Q. Tilson (R)

Delaware

Senators

Thomas F. Bayard, Jr. (D)

T. Coleman Du Pont (R) r.
  Dec. 1928
Daniel O. Hastings (R) s. 1928

Representatives

Robert G. Houston (R)

Florida

Senators

Duncan U. Fletcher (D)
Park Trammell (D)

Representatives

Herbert J. Drane (D)
Robert A. Green (D)
William J. Sears (D)
Thomas A. Yon (D)

Georgia

Senators

Walter F. George (D)
William J. Harris (D)

Representatives

Thomas M. Bell (D)
Charles H. Brand (D)
Edward E. Cox (D)
Charles R. Crisp (D)
Charles G. Edwards (D)
William C. Lankford (D)
William W. Larsen (D)
Samuel Rutherford (D)
Leslie J. Steele (D)
Malcolm C. Tarver (D)
Carl Vinson (D)
William C. Wright (D)

Idaho

Senators

William E. Borah (R)
Frank R. Gooding (R) d. June
  1928
John Thomas (R) s. 1928

Representatives

Burton L. French (R)
Addison T. Smith (R)

Illinois

Senators

Charles S. Deneen (R)
Otis F. Glenn (R) s. 1928
Frank L. Smith (R) r. Feb.
  1928

Representatives

Charles Adkins (R)
John C. Allen (R)
William W. Arnold (D)
Fred A. Britten (R)
John T. Buckbee (R)
Carl R. Chindblom (R)
Edward E. Denison (R)
Thomas A. Doyle (D)

Homer W. Hall (R)
William P. Holaday (R)
Morton D. Hull (R)
William E. Hull (R)
James T. Igoe (D)
Edward M. Irwin (R)
William R. Johnson (R)
Edward J. King (R)
Stanley H. Kunz (D)
Martin B. Madden (R) d. Apr.
  1928
J. Earl Major (D)
M. Alfred Michaelson (R)
Henry T. Rainey (D)
Henry R. Rathbone (R) d. July
  1928
Frank R. Reid (R)
Adolph J. Sabath (D)
Elliott W. Sproul (R)
Thomas S. Williams (R)
Richard Yates (R)

Indiana

Senators

Arthur R. Robinson (R)
James E. Watson (R)

Representatives

Harry C. Canfield (D)
Richard N. Elliott (R)
Frank Gardner (D)
Arthur H. Greenwood (R)
Albert R. Hall (R)
Andrew J. Hickey (R)
David Hogg (R)
Noble J. Johnson (R)
Fred S. Purnell (R)
Harry E. Rowbottom (R)
Ralph E. Updike (R)
Albert H. Vestal (R)
William R. Wood (R)

Iowa

Senators

Smith W. Brookhart (D)
Daniel F. Steck (D)

Representatives

William D. Boies (R)
Cyrenus Cole (R)
Lester J. Dickinson (R)
Cassius C. Dowell (R)
William R. Green (R) r. Mar.
  1928
Gilbert N. Haugen (R)
William F. Kopp (R)
F. Dickinson Letts (R)
C. William Ramseyer (R)
Thomas J. B. Robinson (R)
Lloyd Thurston (R)
Earl W. Vincent (R) s. 1928

Kansas

Senators

Arthur Capper (R)
Charles Curtis (R) s. 1928

Representatives

Daniel R. Anthony, Jr. (R)

William A. Ayres (D)
Homer Hoch (R)
Ulysses S. Guyer (R)
Clifford R. Hope (R)
William H. Sproul (R)
James G. Strong (R)
Hays B. White (R)

Kentucky

Senators

Alben W. Barkley (D)
Frederic M. Sackett (R)

Representatives

Virgil M. Chapman (D)
Ralph Gilbert (D)
William V. Gregory (D)
David H. Kincheloe (D)
Katherine Langley (R)
Henry D. Moorman (D)
John W. Moore (D)
John M. Robsion (R)
Maurice H. Thatcher (R)
Fred M. Vinson (D)
Orie S. Ware (D)

Louisiana

Senators

Edwin S. Broussard (D)
Joseph E. Ransdell (D)

Representatives

James B. Aswell (D)
Rene L. DeRouen (D)
Bolivar E. Kemp (D)
Whitmell P. Martin (D)
James O'Connor (D)
John N. Sandlin (D)
J. Zack Spearing (D)
Riley J. Wilson (D)

Maine

Senators

Arthur R. Gould (R)
Frederick Hale (R)

Representatives

Carroll L. Beedy (R)
Ira G. Hersey (R)
John E. Nelson (R)
Wallace H. White, Jr. (R)

Maryland

Senators

William Cabell Bruce (D)
Millard E. Tydings (D)

Representatives

William P. Cole, Jr. (D)
Stephen W. Gambrill (D)
T. Alan Goldsborough (D)
J. Charles Linthicum (D)
Vincent L. Palmisano (D)
Frederick N. Zihlman (R)

Massachusetts

Senators

Frederick H. Gillett (R)
David I. Walsh (D)

Representatives

A. Piatt Andrew, Jr. (R)
Henry L. Bowles (D)
William P. Connery, Jr. (D)
Frederick W. Dallinger (D)
John J. Douglass (D)
Frank H. Foss (R)
Louis A. Frothingham (R) d.
   Aug. 1928
James A. Gallivan (D) d. Apr.
   1928
Charles L. Gifford (D)
Robert Luce (R)
John W. McCormack (D) s.
   1928
Joseph W. Martin, Jr. (R)
Edith Nourse Rogers (R)
George R. Stobbs (R)
George H. Tinkham (R)
Allen T. Treadway (R)
Charles L. Underhill (R)
Richard B. Wigglesworth (R) s.
   1928

Michigan

Senators

James Couzens (R)
Woodbridge N. Ferris (D) d.
   Mar. 1928
Arthur H. Vandenberg (R) s.
   1928

Representatives

Frank P. Bohn (R)
Robert H. Clancy (D)
Louis C. Cramton (R)
Joseph L. Hooper (R)
Grant M. Hudson (R)
W. Frank James (R)
John C. Ketcham (R)
James C. McLaughlin (R)
Clarence J. McLeod (R)
Carl E. Mapes (R)
Earl C. Michener (R)
Bird J. Vincent (R)
Roy O. Woodruff (R)

Minnesota

Senators

Thomas D. Schall (R)
Henrik Shipstead (Farm-Labor)

Representatives

August H. Andresen (R)
William L. Carss (Farm-Labor)
Frank Clague (R)
Allen J. Furlow (R)
Godfrey G. Goodwin (R)
Harold Knutson (R)
Ole J. Kvale (Farm-Labor)
Melvin J. Maas (R)
Walter H. Newton (R)
Conrad G. Selvig (R)

Mississippi

Senators

Pat Harrison (D)
Hubert D. Stephens (D)

Representatives

T. Jeff Busby (D)
James W. Collier (D)
Ross A. Collins (D)
Bill G. Lowrey (D)
Percy E. Quin (D)
John E. Rankin (D)
William W. Whittington (D)
T. Webber Wilson (D)

Missouri

Senators

Harry B. Hawes (D)
James A. Reed (D)

Representatives

Clarence Cannon (D)
John J. Cochran (D)
George H. Combs (D)
Clement C. Dickinson (D)
Leonidas C. Dyer (R)
Charles L. Faust (R) d. Dec.
   1928
James F. Fulbright (D)
David W. Hopkins (R) s. 1929
Ralph F. Lozier (D)
Samuel C. Major (D)
Joe J. Manlove (R)
Jacob L. Milligan (D)
William L. Nelson (D)
Henry F. Niedringhaus (R)
Milton A. Romjue (D)
Thomas L. Rubey (D) d. Nov.
   1928
Clyde Williams (D)

Montana

Senators

Thomas J. Walsh (D)
Burton K. Wheeler (D)

Representatives

John M. Evans (D)
Scott Leavitt (R)

Nebraska

Senators

Robert B. Howell (R)
George W. Norris (R)

Representatives

Edgar Howard (D)
John H. Morehead (D)
John N. Norton (D)
Willis G. Sears (R)
Ashton C. Shallenberger (D)
Robert G. Simmons (R)

Nevada

Senators

Tasker L. Oddie (R)
Key Pittman (D)

Representatives

Samuel S. Arentz (R)

New Hampshire

Senators

Henry W. Keyes (R)
George H. Moses (R)

Representatives

Fletcher Hale (R)
Edward H. Wason (R)

New Jersey

Senators

Walter E. Edge (R)
Edward I. Edwards (D)

Representatives

Ernest R. Ackerman (R)
Oscar L. Auf Der Heide (D)
Isaac Bacharach (R)
Charles A. Eaton (R)
Franklin W. Fort (R)
Harold G. Hoffman (R)
Frederick R. Lehlbach (R)
Paul J. Moore (D)
Mary T. Norton (D)
Randolph Perkins (R)
George N. Seger (R)
Charles A. Wolverton (R)

New Mexico

Senators

Sam G. Bratton (D)
Bronson M. Cutting (R) ta.
   1928
Andrieus A. Jones (D) d. Dec.
   1927
Octaviano A. Larrazolo (R) s.
   1928

Representatives

John Morrow (D)

New York

Senators

Royal S. Copeland (D)
Robert F. Wagner (D)

Representatives

Robert L. Bacon (R)
Loring M. Black, Jr. (D)
Sol Bloom (D)
John J. Boylan (D)
John F. Carew (D)
Patrick J. Carley (D)

Emanuel Celler (D)
John D. Clarke (R)
William W. Cohen (D)
Parker Corning (D)
Frank Crowther (R)
Francis D. Culkin (R) s. 1928
Thomas H. Cullen (D)
Frederick M. Davenport (R)
S. Wallace Dempsey (R)
Samuel Dickstein (D)
Hamilton Fish, Jr. (R)
James M. Fitzpatrick (D)
Anthony J. Griffin (D)
Clarence E. Hancock (R)
Meyer Jacobstein (D)
John J. Kindred (D)
Fiorello H. LaGuardia (R)
Goerge W. Lindsay (D)
Clarence MacGregor (R) r. Dec. 1928
James M. Mead (D)
David J. O'Connell (D)
John J. O'Connor (D)
Frank Oliver (D)
James S. Parker (R)
Anning S. Prall (D)
Harcourt J. Pratt (R)
John F. Quayle (D)
Daniel A. Reed (R)
Archie D. Sanders (R)
William I. Sirovich (D)
Bertrand H. Snell (R)
Andrew L. Somers (D)
Gale H. Stalker (R)
Christopher D. Sullivan (D)
Thaddeus C. Sweet (R) d. May 1928
John Tabor (R)
J. Mayhew Wainwright (R)
Royal H. Weller (D) d. Mar. 1929

North Carolina

Senators

Lee S. Overman (D)
Furnifold M. Simmons (D)

Representatives

Charles L. Abernethy (D)
Alfred L. Bulwinkle (D)
Robert L. Doughton (D)
William C. Hammer (D)
John H. Kerr (D)
Homer L. Lyon (D)
Edward W. Pou (D)
Charles M. Stedman (D)
Lindsay C. Warren (D)
Zebulon Weaver (D)

North Dakota

Senators

Lynn Frazier (R)
Gerald P. Nye (R)

Representatives

Olger B. Burtness (R)
Thomas Hall (R)
James H. Sinclair (R)

Ohio

Senators

Frank B. Willis (R) d. Mar. 1928
Cyrus Locher (D) ta. 1928
Theodore E. Burton (R) s. 1928
Simeon D. Fess (R)

Representatives

James T. Berg (R)
Charles Brand (R)
Theodore E. Burton (R) r. Dec. 1928
William W. Chalmers (R)
John G. Cooper (R)
Robert Crosser (D)
Martin L. Davey (D)
Roy G. Fitzgerald (R)
William T. Fitzgerald (R)
Thomas B. Fletcher (D)
Thomas A. Jenkins (R)
Charles C. Kearns (R)
Nicholas Longworth (R)
John McSweeney (D)
Charles A. Mooney (D)
C. Ellis Moore (R)
William M. Morgan (R)
B. Frank Murphy (R)
John C. Speaks (R)
Charles Tatgenhorst, Jr. (R)
Charles J. Thompson (R)
Mell G. Underwood (D)

Oklahoma

Senators

William B. Pine (R)
J. W. Elmer Thomas (D)

Representatives

Wilburn Cartwright (D)
Milton C. Garber (R)
William W. Hastings (D)
Everett B. Howard (D)
Jed Johnson (D)
James V. McClintic (D)
Thomas D. McKeown (D)
Fletcher B. Swank (D)

Oregon

Senators

Charles L. McNary (R)
Frederick Steiwer (R)

Representatives

Robert R. Butler (R) s. 1928
Willis C. Hawley (R)
Franklin F. Korell (R)
Nicholas J. Sinnott (R) r. May 1928

Pennsylvania

Senators

David A. Reed (R)
William S. Vare (R)

Representatives

James M. Beck (R)
Edward M. Beers (R)
Robert G. Bushong (R)
Thomas S. Butler (R) d. May 1928
Guy E. Campbell (R)
John J. Casey (D)
J. Mitchell Chase (R)
Thomas C. Cochran (R)
James J. Connolly (R)
George P. Darrow (R)
Isaac H. Doutrich (R)
Harry A. Estep (R)
Benjamin M. Golder (R)
George S. Graham (R)
William W. Griest (R)
M. Clyde Kelly (R)
Samuel A. Kendall (R)
Everett Kent (R)
Edgar R. Kiess (R)
J. Banks Kurtz (R)
J. Russell Leech (R)
Louis T. McFadden (R)
Frederick W. Magrady (R)
Franklin Menges (R)
John M. Morin (R)
Cyrus M. Palmer (R)
Stephen G. Porter (R)
Harry C. Ransley (R)
Milton W. Shreve (R)
Nathan L. Strong (R)
J. Howard Swick (R)
Henry W. Temple (R)
Laurence H. Watres (R)
Henry W. Watson (R)
George A. Welsh (R)
James Wolfenden (R) s. 1928
Adam M. Wyant (R)

Rhode Island

Senators

Peter G. Gerry (D)
Jesse H. Metcalf (R)

Representatives

Richard S. Aldrich (R)
Clark Burdick (R)
Louis Monast (R)

South Carolina

Senators

Coleman L. Blease (D)
Ellison D. Smith (D)

Representatives

Fred H. Dominick (D)
Hampton P. Fulmer (D)
Allard H. Gasque (D)
Butler B. Hare (D)
Thomas S. McMillan (D)
John J. McSwain (D)
William F. Stevenson (D)

South Dakota

Senators

William H. McMaster (R)
Peter Norbeck (R)

Representatives

Charles A. Christopherson (R)
Royal C. Johnson (R)
William Williamson (R)

Tennessee

Senators

Kenneth D. McKellar (D)
Lawrence D. Tyson (D)

Representatives

Gordon Browning (D)
Joseph W. Byrns (D)
Ewin L. Davis (D)
Edward E. Eslick (D)
Hubert F. Fisher (D)
Finis J. Garrett (D)
Cordell Hull (D)
Sam D. McReynolds (D)
B. Carroll Reece (R)
J. Will Taylor (R)

Texas

Senators

Earle B. Mayfield (D)
Morris Sheppard (D)

Representatives

Eugene Black (D)
Thomas L. Blanton (D)
John C. Box (D)
Clay Stone Briggs (D)
James P. Buchanan (D)
Tom T. Connally (D)
John Nance Garner (D)
Daniel E. Garrett (D)
Claude B. Hudspeth (D)
Luther A. Johnson (D)
Marvin Jones (D)
Fritz G. Lanham (D)
Joseph J. Mansfield (D)
Sam Rayburn (D)
Morgan G. Sanders (D)
Hatton W. Sumners (D)
Guinn Williams (D)
Harry M. Wurzbach (D)

Utah

Senators

William H. King (D)
Reed Smoot (R)

Representatives

Don B. Colton (R)
Elmer O. Leatherwood (R)

Vermont

Senators

Porter H. Dale (R)
Frank L. Greene (R)

Representatives

Elbert S. Brigham (R)
Ernest W. Gibson (R)

Virginia

Senators

Carter Glass (D)
Claude A. Swanson (D)

Representatives

Schuyler Otis Bland (D)
Joseph T. Deal (D)
Patrick H. Drewry (D)
Thomas W. Harrison (D)
Andrew J. Montague (D)
R. Walton Moore (D)
George C. Peery (D)
Henry St. George Tucker (D)
Joseph Whitehead (D)
Clifton A. Woodrum (D)

Washington

Senators

Clarence C. Dill (D)
Wesley L. Jones (R)

Representatives

Lindley H. Hadley (R)
Samuel B. Hill (D)
Albert Johnson (R)
John F. Miller (R)
John W. Summers (R)

West Virginia

Senators

Guy D. Goff (R)
Matthew M. Neely (D)

Representatives

Carl G. Bachmann (R)
Frank L. Bowman (R)
Edward T. England (R)
James A. Hughes (R)
William S. O'Brien (D)
James F. Strother (R)

Wisconsin

Senators

John J. Blaine (R)
Robert M. La Follette, Jr.
(Progressive)

Representatives

Victor L. Berger (Socialist)
Joseph D. Beck (R)
Edward E. Browne (R)
Henry A. Cooper (R)
James A. Frear (R)
Charles A. Kading (R)
Florian Lampert (R)
John M. Nelson (R)
Hubert H. Peavey (R)
John C. Schafer (R)
George J. Schneider
(Progressive)

Wyoming

Senators

John B. Kendrick (D)
Francis E. Warren (R)

Representatives

Charles E. Winter (R)

Seventy-First Congress

(Mar. 4, 1929, to
Mar. 3, 1931)

President of the Senate: Charles
Curtis
*President Pro Tempore of the
Senate:* George H. Moses
*Speaker of the House of
Representatives:* Nicholas
Longworth

Alabama

Senators

Hugo L. Black (D)
J. Thomas Heflin (D)

Representatives

Miles C. Allgood (D)
Edward B. Almon (D)
William B. Bankhead (D)
Lister Hill (D)
George Huddleston (D)
Lamar Jeffers (D)
John McDuffie (D)
William B. Oliver (D)
LaFayette L. Patterson (D)
Henry B. Steagall (D)

Arizona

Senators

Henry F. Ashurst (D)
Carl Hayden (D)

Representatives

Lewis W. Douglas (D)

Arkansas

Senators

Thaddeus H. Caraway (D)
Joseph T. Robinson (D)

Representatives

William J. Driver (D)
Claude A. Fuller (D)
David D. Glover (D)
Pearl Peden Oldfield (D)
Tilman B. Parks (D)
Heartsill Ragon (D)
Effiegene (Locke) Wingo (D) s.
1930
Otis Wingo (D) d. Oct. 1930

California

Senators

Hiram W. Johnson (R)
Samuel M. Shortridge (R)

Representatives

Henry E. Barbour (R)
Albert E. Carter (R)
Joe Crail (R)
Charles F. Curry (R) d. Oct.
1930
Harry L. Englebright (R)
William E. Evans (R)
Arthur M. Free (R)
Florence Prag Kahn (R)
Clarence F. Lea (D, R)
Philip D. Swing (R)
Richard J. Welch (R)

Colorado

Senators

Lawrence C. Phipps (R)
Charles W. Waterman (R)

Representatives

William R. Eaton (R)
Guy U. Hardy (R)
Edward T. Taylor (D)
Charles B. Timberlake (R)

Connecticut

Senators

Hiram Bingham (R)
Frederic C. Walcott (R)

Representatives

E. Hart Fenn (R)
Richard P. Freeman (R)
James P. Glynn (R) d. Mar.
1930
Edward W. Goss (R) s. 1930
Schuyler Merritt (R)
John Q. Tilson (R)

Delaware

Senators

Daniel O. Hastings (R)
John G. Townsend, Jr. (R)

Representatives

Robert G. Houston (R)

Florida

Senators

Duncan U. Fletcher (D)
Park Trammell (D)

Representatives

Herbert J. Drane (D)
Robert A. Green (D)
Ruth Bryan Owen (D)

Thomas A. Yon (D)

Georgia

Senators

Walter F. George (D)
William J. Harris (D)

Representatives

Thomas M. Bell (D)
Charles H. Brand (D)
Edward E. Cox (D)
Charles R. Crisp (D)
Charles G. Edwards (D)
William C. Lankford (D)
William W. Larsen (D)
Robert C. Ramspeck (D)
Samuel Rutherford (D)
Leslie J. Steele (D) d. July 1929
Malcolm C. Tarver (D)
Carl Vinson (D)
William C. Wright (D)

Idaho

Senators

William E. Borah (R)
John Thomas (R)

Representatives

Burton L. French (R)
Addison T. Smith (R)

Illinois

Senators

Charles S. Deneen (R)
Otis F. Glenn (R)

Representatives

Charles Adkins (R)
John C. Allen (R)
William W. Arnold (D)
Fred A. Britten (R)
John T. Buckbee (R)
Carl R. Chindblom (R)
Burnett M. Chiperfield (R) s.
1930
Edward E. Denison (R)
Oscar DePriest (R)
Thomas A. Doyle (D)
Homer W. Hall (R)
William P. Holaday (R)
Morton D. Hull (R)
William E. Hull (R)
James T. Igoe (D)
Edward M. Irwin (R)
William R. Johnson (R)
Stanley H. Kunz (D)
Ruth H. McCormick (R)
M. Alfred Michaelson (R)
Claude V. Parsons (D) s. 1930
Henry T. Rainey (D)
Frank M. Ramey (R)
Frank R. Reid (R)
Adolph J. Sabath (D)
Elliott W. Sproul (R)
Thomas S. Williams (R) r. Nov.
1929
Richard Yates (R)

Indiana

Senators

Arthur R. Robinson (R)
James E. Watson (R)

Representatives

Harry C. Canfield (D)
James W. Dunbar (R)
Richard N. Elliott (R)
Arthur H. Greenwood (D)
Albert R. Hall (R)
Andrew J. Hickey (R)
David Hogg (R)
Noble J. Johnson (R)
Louis L. Ludlow (D)
Fred S. Purnell (R)
Harry E. Rowbottom (R)
Albert H. Vestal (R)
William R. Wood (R)

Iowa

Senators

Smith W. Brookhart (R)
Daniel F. Steck (D)

Representatives

Ed H. Campbell (R)
Cyrenus Cole (R)
Lester J. Dickinson (R)
Cassius C. Dowell (R)
Gilbert N. Haugen (R)
William F. Kopp (R)
F. Dickinson Letts (R)
C. William Ramseyer (R)
Thomas J. B. Robinson (R)
Charles E. Swanson (R)
Lloyd Thurston (R)

Kansas

Senators

Henry J. Allen (R) ta. 1929
Arthur Capper (R)
George McGill (D) s. 1930

Representatives

William A. Ayres (D)
Ulysses S. Guyer (R)
Homer Hoch (R)
Clifford R. Hope (R)
William P. Lambertson (R)
Charles I. Sparks (R)
William H. Sproul (R)
James G. Strong (R)

Kentucky

Senators

Alben W. Barkley (D)
John M. Robsion (R) ta. 1930
Frederic M. Sackett (R) r. Jan.
 1930
Ben M. Williamson (D) s. 1930

Representatives

Robert E. Lee Blackburn (R)
John D. Craddock (R)

John L. Dorsey, Jr. (D) s. 1930
Charles Finley (R) s. 1930
William V. Gregory (D)
Elva R. Kendall (R)
David H. Kincheloe (D) r. Oct.
 1930
Katherine Langley (R)
John W. Moore (D)
J. Lincoln Newhall (R)
John M. Robsion (R) r. Jan.
 1930
Maurice H. Thatcher (R)
Lewis L. Walker (R)

Louisiana

Senators

Edwin S. Broussard (D)
Joseph E. Ransdell (D)

Representatives

James B. Aswell (D)
Rene L. DeRouen (D)
Bolivar E. Kemp (D)
Numa F. Montet (D)
James O'Connor (D)
John N. Sandlin (D)
J. Zach Spearing (D)
Riley J. Wilson (D)

Maine

Senators

Arthur R. Gould (R)
Frederick Hale (R)

Representatives

Carroll L. Beedy (R)
John E. Nelson (R)
Donald F. Snow (R)
Wallace H. White, Jr. (R)

Maryland

Senators

Phillips Lee Goldsborough (R)
Millard E. Tydings (D)

Representatives

Linwood L. Clark (R)
Stephen W. Gambrill (D)
T. Alan Goldsborough (D)
J. Charles Linthicum (D)
Vincent L. Palmisano (D)
Frederick N. Zihlman (R)

Massachusetts

Senators

Frederick H. Gillett (R)
David I. Walsh (D)

Representatives

A. Piatt Andrew, Jr. (R)
William P. Connery, Jr. (D)
Frederick W. Dallinger (R)
John J. Douglass (D)
Frank H. Foss (R)
Charles L. Gifford (R)

William J. Granfield (D) s.
 1930
William K. Kaynor (R) d. Dec.
 1929
Robert Luce (R)
John W. McCormack (D)
Joseph W. Martin, Jr. (R)
Edith Nourse Rogers (R)
George R. Stobbs (R)
George H. Tinkham (R)
Allen T. Treadway (R)
Charles L. Underhill (R)
Richard B. Wigglesworth (R)

Michigan

Senators

James Couzens (R)
Arthur H. Vandenburg (R)

Representatives

Frank P. Bohn (R)
Robert H. Clancy (D)
Louis C. Cramton (R)
Joseph L. Hooper (R)
Grant M. Hudson (R)
W. Frank James (R)
John C. Ketcham (R)
James C. McLaughlin (R)
Clarence J. McLeod (R)
Carl E. Mapes (R)
Earl C. Michener (R)
Bird J. Vincent (R)
Roy O. Woodruff (R)

Minnesota

Senators

Thomas D. Schall (R)
Henrik Shipstead (Farm-Labor)

Representatives

August H. Andresen (R)
Victor Christgau (R)
Frank Clague (R)
Godfrey G. Goodwin (R)
Harold Knutson (R)
Ole J. Kvale (Farm-Labor) d.
 Sept. 1929
Melvin J. Maas (R)
Walter H. Newton (R) r. June
 1929
William I. Nolan (R)
William A. Pittenger (R)
Conrad G. Selvig (R)

Mississippi

Senators

Pat Harrison (D)
Hubert D. Stephens (D)

Representatives

T. Jefferson Busby (D)
James W. Collier (D)
Ross A. Collins (D)
Wall Doxey (D)
Robert S. Hall (D)
Percy E. Quinn (D)
John E. Rankin (D)
William M. Whittington (D)

Missouri

Senators

Harry B. Hawes (D)
Roscoe C. Patterson (R)

Representatives

Clarence Cannon (D)
John J. Cochran (D)
Leonidas C. Dyer (R)
Edgar C. Ellis (R)
Thomas J. Halsey (R)
David W. Hopkins (R)
Rowland L. Johnston (R)
Charles E. Kiefner (R)
Ralph F. Lozier (D)
Joe J. Manlove (R)
Jacob L. Milligan (D)
William L. Nelson (D)
Henry F. Niedringhaus (R)
John W. Palmer (R)
Milton A. Romjue (D)
Dewey Short (R)

Montana

Senators

Thomas J. Walsh (D)
Burton K. Wheeler (D)

Representatives

John M. Evans (D)
Scott Leavitt (R)

Nebraska

Senators

Robert B. Howell (R)
George W. Norris (R)

Representatives

Edgar Howard (D)
Fred G. Johnson (R)
John H. Morehead (D)
Willis G. Sears (R)
Robert G. Simmons (R)
Charles H. Sloan (R)

Nevada

Senators

Tasker L. Oddie (R)
Key Pittman (D)

Representatives

Samuel S. Arentz (R)

New Hampshire

Senators

Henry W. Keyes (R)
George H. Moses (R)

Representatives

Fletcher Hale (R)
Edward H. Wason (R)

New Jersey

Senators

David Baird, Jr. (R) ta. 1929
Walter E. Edge (R) r. Nov. 1929
Hamilton F. Kean (R)
Dwight W. Morrow (R) s. 1930

Representatives

Ernest R. Ackerman (R)
Oscar L. Auf Der Heide (D)
Isaac Bacharach (R)
Charles A. Eaton (R)
Franklin W. Fort (R)
Fred A. Hartley, Jr. (R)
Harold G. Hoffman (R)
Frederick R. Lehlbach (R)
Mary T. Norton (D)
Randolph Perkins (R)
George N. Seger (R)
Charles A. Wolverton (R)

New Mexico

Senators

Sam G. Bratton (D)
Bronson M. Cutting (R)

Representatives

Albert G. Simms (R)

New York

Senators

Royal S. Copeland (D)
Robert F. Wagner (D)

Representatives

Robert L. Bacon (R)
Loring M. Black, Jr. (D)
Sol Bloom (D)
John J. Boylan (D)
William F. Brunner (D)
John F. Carew (D) r. Dec. 1929
Patrick J. Carley (D)
Emanuel Celler (D)
John D. Clarke (R)
Edmund F. Cooke (R)
Parker Corning (D)
Frank Crowther (R)
Francis D. Culkin (R)
Thomas H. Cullen (D)
Frederick M. Davenport (R)
S. Wallace Dempsey (R)
Samuel Dickstein (D)
Hamilton Fish, Jr. (R)
James M. Fitzpatrick (D)
Joseph A. Gavagan (D)
Anthony J. Griffin (D)
Clarence E. Hancock (R)
Martin J. Kennedy (D) s. 1930
Fiorello H. LaGuardia (R)
George W. Lindsay (D)
James M. Mead (D)
David J. O'Connell (D) d. Dec. 1930
John J. O'Connor (D)
Frank Oliver (D)
James S. Parker (R)
Anning S. Prall (D)

Harcourt J. Pratt (R)
Ruth S. B. Pratt (R)
John F. Quayle (D) d. Nov. 1930
Daniel A Reed (R)
Archie D. Sanders (R)
William I. Sirovich (D)
Bertrand H. Snell (R)
Andrew L. Somers (D)
Gale H. Stalker (R)
Christopher D. Sullivan (D)
John Taber (R)
J. Mayhew Wainwright (R)
James L. Whitley (R)

North Carolina

Senators

Cameron A. Morrison (D) s. 1930
Lee S. Overman (D) d. Dec. 1930
Furnifold M. Simmons (D)

Representatives

Charles L. Abernethy (D)
J. Bayard Clark (D)
Roert L. Doughton (D)
William C. Hammer (D) d. Sept. 1930
Franklin W. Hancock, Jr. (D)
Hinton James (D)
Chares A. Jonas (R)
John H. Kerr (D)
Edward W. Pou (D)
George M. Pritchard (R)
Charles M. Stedman (D)
Lindsay C. Warren (D)

North Dakota

Senators

Lynn J. Frazier (R)
Gerald P. Nye (R)

Representatives

Olger B. Burtness (R)
Thomas Hall (R)
James H. Sinclair (R)

Ohio

Senators

Robert J. Bulkley (D) s. 1930
Theodore E. Burton (R) d. Oct. 1929
Simeon D. Fess (R)
Roscoe C. McCulloch (R) ta. 1929

Representatives

Joseph E. Baird (R)
Chester C. Bolton (R)
Charles Brand (R)
John L. Cable (R)
William W. Chalmers (R)
John G. Cooper (R)
Robert Crosser (D)
Roy G. Fitzgerald (R)
William E. Hess (R)
Thomas A. Jenkins (R)
Charles C. Kearns (R)

Nicholas Longworth (R)
Charles B. McClintock (R)
Charles A. Mooney (D)
C. Ellis Moore (R)
William M. Morgan (R)
Grant E. Mouser, Jr. (R)
B. Frank Murphy (R)
Francis Seiberling (R)
John C. Speaks (R)
Charles J. Thompson (R)
Mell G. Underwood (R)

Oklahoma

Senators

William B. Pine (R)
J. W. Elmer Thomas (D)

Representatives

Wilburn Cartwright (D)
Milton C. Garber (R)
William W. Hastings (D)
Jed Johnson (D)
James V. McClintic (D)
Thomas D. McKeown (D)
Charles O'Connor (R)
Ulysses S. Stone (R)

Oregon

Senators

Charles L. McNary (R)
Frederick Steiwer (R)

Representatives

Robert R. Butler (R)
Willis C. Hawley (R)
Franklin F. Korell (R)

Pennsylvania

Senators

James J. Davis (R) s. 1930
Joseph R. Grundy (R) ta. 1929
David A. Reed (R)

Representatives

James M. Beck (R)
Edward M. Beers (R)
George F. Brumm (R)
Guy E. Campbell (R)
John J. Casey (D) d. May 1929
J. Mitchell Chase (R)
Thomas C. Cochran (R)
James J. Connolly (R)
William R. Coyle (R)
George P. Darrow (R)
Isaac H. Doutrich (R)
Edmund F. Erk (R) s. 1930
Harry A. Estep (R)
Charles J. Esterly (R)
Benjamin Golder (R)
George S. Graham (R)
William W. Griest (R) d. Dec. 1929
M. Clyde Kelly (R)
Samuel A. Kendall (R)
Edgar R. Kiess (R) d. July 1930
J. Roland Kinzer (R) s. 1930
J. Banks Kurtz (R)
J. Russell Leech (R)

Louis T. McFadden (R)
Frederick W. Magrady (R)
Franklin Menges (R)
Stephen G. Porter (R) d. June 1930
Harry C. Ransley (R)
Robert F. Rich (R) s. 1930
Milton W. Shreve (R)
Nathan L. Strong (R)
Patrick J. Sullivan (R)
J. Howard Swick (R)
Henry W. Temple (R)
C. Murray Turpin (R)
Laurence H. Watres (R)
Henry W. Watson (R)
George A. Welsh (R)
James Wolfenden (R)
Adam M. Wyant (R)

Rhode Island

Senators

Felix Hebert (R)
Jesse H. Metcalf (R)

Representatives

Richard S. Aldrich (R)
Clark Burdick (R)
Francis B. Condon (D) s. 1930
Jeremiah E. O'Connell (D) r. May 1930

South Carolina

Senators

Coleman L. Blease (D)
Ellison D. Smith (D)

Representatives

Fred H. Dominick (D)
Hampton P. Fulmer (D)
Allard H. Gasque (D)
Butler B. Hare (D)
Thomas S. McMillan (D)
John J. McSwain (D)
William F. Stevenson (D)

South Dakota

Senators

William H. McMaster (R)
Peter Norbeck (R)

Representatives

Charles A. Christopherson (R)
Royal C. Johnson (R)
William Williamson (R)

Tennessee

Senators

William E. Brock (D) s. 1929
Kenneth D. McKellar (D)
Lawrence D. Tyson (D) d. Aug. 1929

Representatives

Gordon Browning (D)
Joseph W. Byrns (D)

Jere Cooper (D)
Ewin L. Davis (D)
Edward E. Eslick (D)
Hubert F. Fisher (D)
Cordell Hull (D)
Sam D. McReynolds (D)
B. Carroll Reece (R)
J. Will Taylor (R)

Texas

Senators

Tom T. Connally (D)
Morris Sheppard (D)

Representatives

John C. Box (D)
Clay Stone Briggs (D)
Thomas L. Blanton (D)
James P. Buchanan (D)
Oliver H. Cross (D)
John Nance Garner (D)
Daniel E. Garrett (D)
Claude B. Hudspeth (D)
Luther A. Johnson (D)
Marvin Jones (D)
Fritz G. Lanham (D)
Robert Q. Lee (D) d. Apr. 1930
Augustus McCloskey (D) r. Feb. 1930
Joseph J. Mansfield (D)
Wright Patman (D)
Sam Rayburn (D)
Morgan G. Sanders (D)
Hatton W. Sumners (D)
Guinn Williams (D)
Harry M. Wurzbach (D)

Utah

Senators

William H. King (D)
Reed Smoot (R)

Representatives

Don B. Colton (R)
Elmer O. Leatherwood (R) d. Dec. 1929
Frederick C. Loofbourow (R) s. 1930

Vermont

Senators

Porter H. Dale (R)
Frank L. Greene (R) d. Dec. 1930
Frank C. Partridge (R) ta. Jan. 1931

Representatives

Elbert S. Brigham (R)
Ernest W. Gibson (R)

Virginia

Senators

Carter Glass (D)
Claude A. Swanson (D)

Representatives

Schuyler Otis Bland (D)
Patrick H. Drewry (D)
Jacob A. Garber (R)
Menalcus Lankford (R)
Andrew J. Montague (D)
R. Walton Moore (D)
Joseph C. Shaffer (R)
Henry St. George Tucker (D)
Joseph Whitehead (D)
Clifton A. Woodrum (D)

Washington

Senators

Clarence C. Dill (D)
Wesley L. Jones (R)

Representatives

Lindley H. Hadley (R)
Samuel B. Hill (D)
Albert Johnson (R)
John F. Miller (R)
John W. Summers (R)

West Virginia

Senators

Guy D. Goff (R)
Henry D. Hatfield (R)

Representatives

Carl G. Bachmann (R)
Frank L. Bowman (R)
Robert L. Hogg (R) s. 1930
James A. Hughes (R) d. Mar. 1930
Hugh I. Shott (R)
Joe L. Smith (D)
John M. Wolverton (R)

Wisconsin

Senators

John J. Blaine (R)
Robert M. La Follette, Jr. (Progressive)

Representatives

Edward E. Browne (R)
Henry A. Cooper (R) d. Mar. 1931
James A. Frear (R)
Merlin Hull (R)
Charles A. Kading (R)
Florian Lampert (R) d. July 1930
John M. Nelson (R)
Hubert H. Peavey (R)
Michael K. Reilly (D) s. 1930
John C. Schafer (R)
George J. Schneider (Progressive)
William H. Stafford (R)

Wyoming

Senators

Robert D. Carey (R) s. 1930

John B. Kendrick (D)
Patrick J. Sullivan (R) ta. 1929
Francis E. Warren (R) d. Nov. 1929

Representatives

Vincent M. Carter (R)

Seventy-Second Congress

(Mar. 4, 1931, to Mar. 3, 1933)

President of the Senate: Charles Curtis
President Pro Tempore of the Senate: George H. Moses
Speaker of the House of Representatives: John Nance Garner

Alabama

Senators

John H. Bankhead, II (D)
Hugo L. Black (D)

Representatives

Miles C. Allgood (D)
Edward B. Almon (D)
William B. Bankhead (D)
Lister Hill (D)
George Huddleston (D)
Lamar Jeffers (D)
John McDuffie (D)
William B. Oliver (D)
LaFayette L. Patterson (D)
Henry B. Steagall (D)

Arizona

Senators

Henry F. Ashurst (D)
Carl Hayden (D)

Representatives

Lewis W. Douglas (D)

Arkansas

Senators

Hattie W. Caraway (D) s. 1931
Thaddeus H. Caraway (D) d. Oct. 1931
Joseph T. Robinson (D)

Representatives

William J. Driver (D)
Claude A. Fuller (D)
David D. Glover (D)
John E. Miller (D)
Tilman B. Parks (D)
Heartsill Ragon (D)
Effiegene (Locke) Wingo (D)

California

Senators

Hiram W. Johnson (R)
Samuel M. Shortridge (R)

Representatives

Henry E. Barbour (R)
Albert E. Carter (R)
Joe Crail (R)
Charles F. Curry, Jr. (R)
Harry L. Englebright (R)
William E. Evans (R)
Arthur M. Free (R)
Florence Prag Kahn (R)
Clarence F. Lea (D, R)
Philip D. Swing (R)
Richard J. Welch (R)

Colorado

Senators

Edward P. Costigan (D)
Karl C. Schuyler (R) s. 1932
Walter Walker (D) ta. 1932
Charles W. Waterman (R) d. Aug. 1932

Representatives

William R. Eaton (R)
Guy U. Hardy (R)
Edward T. Taylor (D)
Charles B. Timberlake (R)

Connecticut

Senators

Hiram Bingham (R)
Frederic C. Walcott (R)

Representatives

Richard P. Freeman (R)
Edward W. Goss (R)
Augustine Lonergan (D)
William L. Tierney (D)
John Q. Tilson (R) r. Dec. 1932

Delaware

Senators

Daniel O. Hastings (R)
John G. Townsend, Jr. (R)

Representatives

Robert G. Houston (R)

Florida

Senators

Duncan U. Fletcher (D)
Park Trammell (D)

Representatives

Herbert J. Drane (D)
Robert A. Green (D)

Ruth Bryan Owen (D)
Thomas A. Yon (D)

Georgia

Senators

John S. Cohen (D) ta. 1932
Walter F. George (D)
William J. Harris (D) d. Apr.
 1932
Richard B. Russell (D) s. 1933

Representatives

Charles H. Brand (D)
Bryant T. Castellow (D) s. 1932
Edward E. Cox (D)
Charles R. Crisp (D) r. Oct.
 1932
William C. Lankford (D)
William W. Larsen (D)
W. Carlton Mobley (D) s. Mar.
 1932
Homer C. Parker (D)
Robert C. Ramspeck (D)
Samuel Rutherford (D) d. Feb.
 1932
Malcolm C. Tarver (D)
Carl Vinson (D)
John S. Wood (D)
William C. Wright (D)

Idaho

Senators

William E. Borah (R)
John Thomas (R)

Representatives

Burton L. French (R)
Addison T. Smith (R)

Illinois

Senators

Otis F. Glenn (R)
J. Hamilton Lewis (D)

Representatives

Charles Adkins (R)
John C. Allen (R)
William W. Arnold (D)
Harry P. Beam (D)
Fred A. Britten (R)
John T. Buckbee (R)
Carl R. Chindblom (R)
Burnett M. Chiperfield (R)
Oscar DePriest (R)
William Dieterich (D)
Peter C. Granata (R) r. Apr.
 1932
Homer W. Hall (R)
William P. Holaday (R)
Morton D. Hull (R)
William E. Hulol (R)
James T. Igoe (D)
William R. Johnson (R)
Charles A. Karch (D) d. Nov.
 1932
Kent E. Keller (D)
Edward A. Kelly (D)
Stanley H. Kunz (D) s. 1932
J. Earl Major (D)

Claude V. Parsons (D)
Henry T. Rainey (D)
Frank R. Reid (D)
Adolph J. Sabath (D)
Leonard W. Schuetz (D)
Richard Yates (R)

Indiana

Senators

Arthur R. Robinson (R)
James E. Watson (R)

Representatives

John W. Boehne, Jr. (D)
Harry C. Canfield (D)
Eugene B. Crowe (D)
Courtland C. Gillen (D)
Arthur H. Greenwood (D)
Glenn Griswold (D0
David Hogg (R)
William H. Larrabee (D)
Louis J. Ludlow (D)
Samuel B. Pettengill (D)
Fred S. Purnell (R)
Albert H. Vestal (R) d. Apr.
 1932
William R. Wood (R)

Iowa

Senators

Smith W. Brookhart (R)
Lester J. Dickinson (R)

Representatives

Ed H. Campbell (R)
Cyrenus Cole (R)
Cassius C. Dowell (R)
Fred C. Gilchrist (R)
Gilbert N. Haugen (R)
Bernhard M. Jacobsen (D)
William F. Kopp (R)
C. William Ramseyer (R)
Thomas J. B. Robinson (R)
Charles E. Swanson (R)
Lloyd Thurston (R)

Kansas

Senators

Arthur Capper (R)
George McGill (D)

Representatives

William A. Ayres (D)
Ulysses S. Guyer (R)
Homer Hoch (R)
Clifford R. Hope (R)
William P. Lambertson (R)
Harold C. McGugin (R)
Charles I. Sparks (R)
James G. Strong (R)

Kentucky

Senators

Alben W. Barkley (D)
Marvel M. Logan (D)

Representatives

Cap R. Garden (D)
Glover H. Cary (D)
Virgil M. Chapman (D)
Charles Finley (R)
Ralph Gilbert (D)
William V. Gregory (D)
Andrew J. May (D)
John W. Moore (D)
Brent Spence (D)
Maurice H. Thatcher (R)
Fred M. Vinson (D)

Louisiana

Senators

Edwin S. Broussard (D)
Huey P. Long (D) s. 1932

Representatives

Rene L. DeRouen (D)
Joachim O. Fernandez (D)
Bolivar E. Kemp (D)
Paul H. Maloney (D)
Numa F. Montet (D)
John H. Overton (D)
John N. Sandlin (D)
Riley J. Wilson (D)

Maine

Senators

Frederick Hale (R)
Wallace H. White, Jr. (R)

Representatives

Carroll L. Beedy (R)
John E. Nelson (R)
Donald B. Patridge (R)
Donald F. Snow (R)

Maryland

Senators

Phillips Lee Goldsborough (R)
Millard E. Tydings (D)

Representatives

William P. Cole, Jr. (D)
Stephen W. Gambrill (D)
T. Alan Goldsborough (D)
Ambrose J. Kennedy (D) s.
 1932
David J. Lewis (D)
J. Charles Linthicum (D) d.
 Oct. 1932
Vincent L. Palmisano (D)

Massachusetts

Senators

Marcus A. Coolidge (D)
David I. Walsh (D)

Representatives

A. Piatt Andrew, Jr. (R)
William P. Connery, Jr. (D)

Frederick W. Dallinger (D) r.
 Oct. 1932
John J. Douglass (D)
Frank H. Foss (R)
Charles L. Gifford (R)
William J. Granfield (D)
Pehr G. Holmes (R)
Robert Luce (R)
John W. McCormack (D)
Joseph W. Martin, Jr. (R)
Edith Nourse Rogers (R)
George H. Tinkham (R)
Allen T. Treadway (R)
Charles L. Underhill (R)
Richard B. Wigglesworth (R)

Michigan

Senators

James Couzens (R)
Arthur H. Vandenberg (R)

Representatives

Frank P. Bohn (R)
Robert H. Clancy (D)
Michael J. Hart (D)
Joseph L. Hooper (R)
W. Frank James (R)
John C. Ketcham (R)
James C. McLaughlin (R) d.
 Nov. 1932
Clarence J. McLeod (R)
Carl E. Mapes (R)
Earl C. Michener (R)
Seymour H. Person (R)
Jesse P. Wolcott (R)
Roy O. Woodruff (R)

Minnesota

Senators

Thomas D. Schall (R)
Henrik Shipstead (Farm-Labor)

Representatives

August H. Andresen (R)
Victor Christgau (R)
Frank Clague (R)
Godfrey G. Goodwin (R) d.
 Feb. 1933
Harold Knutson (R)
Paul J. Kvale (Farm-Labor)
Melvin J. Maas (R)
William I. Nolan (R)
William A. Pittenger (R)
Conrad G. Selvig (R)

Mississippi

Senators

Pat Harrison (D)
Hubert D. Stephens (D)

Representatives

T. Jeff Busby (D)
James W. Collier (D)
Ross A. Collins (D)
Wall Doxey (D)
Lawrence R. Ellzey (D) s. 1932
Robert S. Hall (D)
Percy E. Quin (D) d. Feb. 1932
John E. Rankin (D)

William M. Whittington (D)

Missouri

Senators

Bennett Champ Clark (D) s. 1933
Harry B. Hawes (D) r. Feb. 1933
Roscoe C. Patterson (R)

Representatives

William E. Barton (D)
Clarence Cannon (D)
John J. Cochran (D)
Clement C. Dickinson (D)
Leonidas C. Dyer (R)
James F. Fulbright (D)
David W. Hopkins (R)
Robert D. Johnson (D)
Ralph F. Lozier (D)
Joe J. Manlove (R)
Jacob L. Milligan (D)
William L. Nelson (D)
Henry F. Niedringhaus (R)
Milton A. Romjue (D)
Joseph B. Shannon (D)
Clyde Williams (D)

Montana

Senators

Thomas J. Walsh (D) d. Mar. 1933
Burton K. Wheeler (D)

Representatives

John M. Evans (D)
Scott Leavitt (R)

Nebraska

Senators

Robert B. Howell (R)
George W. Norris (R)

Representatives

H. Malcolm Baldrige (R)
Edgar Howard (D)
John H. Morehead (D)
John N. Norton (D)
Ashton C. Shallenberger (D)
Robert G. Simmons (R)

Nevada

Senators

Tasker L. Oddie (R)
Key Pittman (D)

Representatives

Samuel S. Arentz (R)

New Hampshire

Senators

Henry W. Keyes (R)

George H. Moses (R)

Representatives

William N. Rogers (D) s. 1932
Edward H. Wason (R)

New Jersey

Senators

W. Warren Barbour (R) s. 1931
Hamilton F. Kean (R)
Dwight W. Morrow (R) d. Oct. 1931

Representatives

Oscar L. Auf Der Heide (D)
Isaac Bacharach (R)
Peter A. Cavicchia (R)
Charles A. Eaton (R)
Fred A. Hartley, Jr. (R)
Frederick R. Lehlbach (R)
Mary T. Norton (D)
Randolph Perkins (R)
George N. Seger (R)
Percy H. Stewart (D)
William H. Sutphin (D)
Charles A. Wolverton (R)

New Mexico

Senators

Sam G. Bratton (D)
Bronson M. Cutting (R)

Representatives

Dennis Chavez (D)

New York

Senators

Royal S. Copeland (D)
Robert F. Wagner (D)

Representatives

Walter G. Andrews (R)
Robert L. Bacon (R)
Loring M. Black, Jr. (D)
Sol Bloom (D)
John J. Boylan (D)
William F. Brunner (D)
Patrick J. Carley (D)
Emanuel Celler (D)
John D. Clarke (R)
Edmund F. Cooke (R)
Parker Corning (D)
Frank Crowther (R)
Francis D. Culkin (R)
Thomas H. Cullen (D)
Frederick M. Davenport (R)
John J. Delaney (D)
Samuel Dickstein (D)
Hamilton Fish, Jr. (R)
James M. Fitzpatrick (D)
Joseph A. Gavagan (D)
Anthony J. Griffin (D)
Clarence E. Hancock (R)
Martin J. Kennedy (D)
Fiorello H. Laguardia (R)
George W. Lindsay (D)
James M. Mead (D)
Charles D. MIllard (R)

John J. O'Connor (D)
Frank Oliver (D)
James S. Parker (R)
Anning S. Prall (R)
Harcourt J. Pratt (R)
Ruth S. B. Pratt (R)
Daniel A. Reed (R)
Stephen A. Rudd (D)
Archie D. Sanders (R)
William I. Sirovich (D)
Bertrand H. Snell (R)
Andrew L. Somers (D)
Gale H. Stalker (R)
Christopher D. Sullivan (D)
John Taber (R)
James L. Whitley (R)

North Carolina

Senators

Josiah W. Bailey (D)
Cameron A. Morrison (D) ta. 1931
Robert R. Reynolds (D) s. 1932

Representatives

Charles L. Abernethy (D)
Alfred L. Bulwinkle (D)
J. Bayard Clark (D)
Robert L. Doughton (D)
Franklin W. Hancock, Jr. (D)
John H. Kerr (D)
J. Walter Lambeth (D)
Edward W. Pou (D)
Lindsay C. Warren (D)
Zebulon Weaver (D)

North Dakota

Senators

Lynn J. Frazier (R)
Gerald P. Nye (R)

Representatives

Olger B. Burtness (R)
Thomas Hall (R)
James H. Sinclair (R)

Ohio

Senators

Robert J. Bulkley (D)
Simeon D. Fess (R)

Representatives

Chester C. Bolton (R)
Charles Brand (R)
John L. Cable (R)
John G. Cooper (R)
Robert Crosser (D)
William L. Fiesinger (D)
Byron B. Harlan (D)
William E. Hess (R)
John B. Hollister (R)
Thomas A. Jenkins (R)
Frank C. Kniffin (D)
Arthur P. Lamneck (D)
Charles B. McClintock (R)
C. Ellis Moore (R)
Grant E. Mouser, Jr. (R)
B. Frank Murphy (R)
James G. Polk (D)

Francis Seiberling (R)
Martin L. Sweeney (D)
Mell G. Underwood (D)
Charles West (D)
Wilbur M. White (R)

Oklahoma

Senators

Thomas P. Gore (D)
J. W. Elmer Thomas (D)

Representatives

Wilburn Cartwright (D)
Wesley E. Disney (D)
Milton C. Garber (R)
William W. Hastings (D)
Jed Johnson (D)
James V. McClintic (D)
Thomas D. McKeown (D)
Fletcher B. Swank (D)

Oregon

Senators

Charles L. McNary (R)
Frederick Steiwer (R)

Representatives

Robert R. Butler (R) d. Jan. 1933
Willis C. Hawley (R)
Charles H. Martin (D)

Pennsylvania

Senators

James J. Davis (R)
David A. Reed (R)

Representatives

James M. Beck (R)
Edward M. Beers (R) d. Apr. 1932
Joseph F. Biddle (R) s. Dec. 1932
Patrick J. Boland (D)
George F. Brumm (R)
Guy E. Campbell (R)
J. Mitchell Chase (R)
Thomas C. Cochran (R)
James J. Connolly (R)
William R. Coyle (R)
George P. Darrow (R)
Robert L. Davis (R)
Isaac H. Doutrich (R)
Edmund F. Erk (R)
Harry A. Estep (R)
Benjamin M. Golder (R)
Harry L. Haines (R)
M. Clyde Kelly (R)
Samuel A. Kendall (R) d. Jan. 1933
J. Roland Kinzer (R)
J. Banks Kurtz (R)
J. Russell Leech (R) r. Jan. 1932
Norton L. Lichtenwalner (D)
Louis T. McFadden (R)
Frederick W. Magrady (R)
Harry C. Ransley (R)
Robert F. Rich (R)

Milton W. Shreve (R)
Edward L. Stokes (R)
Nathan L. Strong (R)
Howard W. Stull (R) s. 1932
Patrick J. Sullivan (R)
J. Howard Swick (R)
Henry W. Temple (R)
C. Murray Turpin (R)
Henry W. Watson (R)
George A. Welsh (R) r. May 1932
James Wolfenden (R)
Adam M. Wyant (R)

Rhode Island

Senators

Felix Hebert (R)
Jesse H. Metcalf (R)

Representatives

Richard S. Aldrich (R)
Clark Burdick (R)
Francis B. Condon (D)

South Carolina

Senators

James F. Byrnes (D)
Ellison D. Smith (D)

Representatives

Fred H. Dominick (D)
Hampton P. Fulmer (D)
Allard H. Gasque (D)
Butler B. Hare (D)
Thomas S. McMillan (D)
John J. McSwain (D)
William F. Stevenson (D)

South Dakota

Senators

William J. Bulow (D)
Peter Norbeck (R)

Representatives

Charles A. Christopherson (R)
Royal C. Johnson (R)
William Williamson (R)

Tennessee

Senators

Cordell Hull (D)
Kenneth D. McKellar (D)

Representatives

Gordon Browning (D)
Joseph W. Byrns (D)
Jere Cooper (D)
Edward H. Crump (D)
Ewin L. Davis (D)
Edward E. Eslick (D) d. June 1932
Willa M. B. Eslick (D) s. 1932
Oscar B. Lovette (R)
Sam D. McReynolds (D)
John R. Mitchell (D)

J. Will Taylor (R)

Texas

Senators

Tom T. Connally (D)
Morris Sheppard (D)

Representatives

Thomas L. Blanton (D)
Clay Stone Briggs (D)
James P. Buchanan (D)
Oliver H. Cross (D)
Martin Dies, Jr. (D)
Joe H. Eagle (D) s. 1933
John Nance Garner (D)
Daniel E. Garrett (D) d. Dec. 1932
Luther A. Johnson (D)
Marvin Jones (D)
Richard M. Kleberg (D) s. 1931
Fritz G. Lanham (D)
Joseph J. Mansfield (D)
Wright Patman (D)
Sam Rayburn (D)
Morgan G. Sanders (D)
Hatton W. Sumners (D)
R. Ewing Thomason (D)
Guinn Williams (D)

Utah

Senators

William H. King (D)
Reed Smoot (R)

Representatives

Don B. Colton (R)
Frederick C. Loofbourow (R)

Vermont

Senators

Warren R. Austin (R) s. 1931
Porter H. Dale (R)
Frank C. Partridge (R) ta. 1931

Representatives

Ernest W. Gibson (R)
John E. Weeks (R)

Virginia

Senators

Carter Glass (D)
Claude A. Swanson (D)

Representatives

Schuyler Otis Bland (D)
Thomas G. Burch (D)
Patrick H. Drewry (D)
John W. Fishburne (D)
John W. Flannagan, Jr. (D)
Joel W. Flood s. 1932
Menalcus Lankford (R)
Andrew J. Montague (D)
Howard W. Smith (D)
Henry St. George Tucker (D) d. July 1932

Clifton A. Woodrum (D)

Washington

Senators

Clarence C. Dill (D)
Elijah S. Grammer (R) s. 1932
Wesley L. Jones (R) d. Nov. 1932

Representatives

Lindley H. Hadley (R)
Samuel B. Hill (D)
Ralph A. Horr (R)
Albert Johnson (R)
John W. Summers (R)

West Virginia

Senators

Henry D. Hatfield (R)
Matthew M. Neely (D)

Representatives

Carl G. Bachmann (R)
Frank L. Bowman (R)
Robert L. Hogg (R)
Lynn S. Hornor (D)
Hugh I. Shott (R)
Joe L. Smith (D)

Wisconsin

Senators

John J. Blaine (R)
Robert M. La Follette, Jr. (R)

Representatives

Thomas R. Amlie (R)
Gerald J. Boileau (R)
James A. Frear (R)
Charles A. Kading (R)
John M. Nelson (R)
Hubert H. Peavey (R)
Michael K. Reilly (D)
John C. Shafer (R)
George J. Schneider (Progressive)
William H. Stafford (R)
Gardner R. Withrow (R)

Wyoming

Senators

Robert D. Carey (R)
John B. Kendrick (D)

Representatives

Vincent M. Carter (R)

Seventy-Third Congress

(Mar. 4, 1933, to Jan. 3, 1935)

President of the Senate: John Nance Garner
President Pro Tempore of the Senate: Key Pittman
Speaker of the House of Representatives: Henry T. Rainey

Alabama

Senators

Hugo L. Black (D)
John H. Bankhead, II (D)

Representatives

Miles C. Allgood (D)
Edward B. Almon (D) d. June 1933
William B. Bankhead (D)
Archibald H. Carmichael (D) s. 1934
Lister Hill (R)
George Huddleston (D)
Lamar Jeffers (D)
John McDuffie (D)
William B. Oliver (D)
Henry B. Steagall (D)

Arizona

Senators

Henry F. Ashurst (D)
Carl Hayden (D)

Representatives

Isabella S. Greenway (D) s. 1934

Arkansas

Senators

Hattie W. Caraway (D)
Joseph T. Robinson (D)

Representatives

William B. Cravens (D)
William J. Driver (D)
Claude A. Fuller (D)
David D. Glover (D)
John E. Miller (D)
Tilman B. Parks (D)
Heartsill Ragon (D) r. June 1933
David D. Terry (D) s. 1934

California

Senators

Hiram W. Johnson (R)
William Gibbs McAdoo (D)

Representatives

Frank H. Buck (D)
John H. Burke (D)
George Burnham (D)
Albert E. Carter (R)
Denver S. Church (D)
Charles J. Colden (D)
Samuel L. Collins (R)
John F. Dockweiler (D)
Ralph R. Eltse (R)
Harry L. Englebright (R)
William E. Evans (R)
Thomas F. Ford (D)
John H. Hoeppel (D)
Florence Prag Kahn (R)
Charles Kramer (D)
Clarence F. Lea (D, R)
John J. McGrath (D)
Henry E. Stubbs (D)
William I. Traeger (R)
Richard J. Welch (R)

Colorado

Senators

Alva B. Adams (D)
Edward P. Costigan (D)

Representatives

Fred Cummings (D)
Lawrence Lewis (D)
John A. Martin (D)
Edward T. Taylor (D)

Connecticut

Senators

Augustine Lonergan (D)
Frederic C. Walcott (R)

Representatives

Charles M. Bakewell (R)
Edward W. Goss (R)
William L. Higgins (R)
Herman P. Kopplemann (D)
Francis T. Maloney (D)
Schuyler Merritt (R)

Delaware

Senators

Daniel O. Hastings (R)
John G. Townsend, Jr. (R)

Representatives

Wilbur L. Adams (D)

Florida

Senators

Duncan U. Fletcher (D)
Park Trammell (D)

Representatives

Millard F. Caldwell (D)
Robert A. Green (D)
J. Hardin Peterson (D)
William J. Sears (D)

J. Mark Wilcox (D)

Georgia

Senators

Walter F. George (D)
Richard B. Russell (D)

Representatives

Charles H. Brand (D) d. May
  1933
Paul Brown (D) s. 1934
Bryant T. Castellow (D)
Edward E. Cox (D)
Braswell D. Deen (D)
Emmett M. Owen (D)
Homer C. Parker (D)
Robert C. Ramspeck (D)
Malcolm C. Tarver (D)
Carl Vinson (D)
John S. Wood (D)

Idaho

Senators

William E. Borah (R)
James P. Pope (D)

Representatives

Thomas C. Coffin (D) d. June
  1934
Compton I. White (D)

Illinois

Senators

William H. Dieterich (D)
H. Hamilton Lewis (D)

Representatives

J. Leroy Adair (D)
Leo E. Allen (R)
William W. Arnold (D)
Harry P. Beam (D)
Martin A. Brennan (D)
Fred A. Britten (R)
John T. Buckbee (R)
Oscar DePriest (R)
Everett M. Dirksen (R)
Donald C. Dobbins (D)
Frank Gillespie (D)
Kent E. Keller (D)
Edward A. Kelly (D)
Leo Kocialkowski (D)
J. Earl Major (D) r. Oct. 1933
James A. Meeks (D)
Patrick H. Moynihan (R)
Walter Nesbit (D)
Thomas J. O'Brien (D)
Claude V. Parsons (D)
Henry T. Rainey (D) d. Aug.
  1934
Frank R. Reid (R)
Adolph J. Sabath (D)
Edwin M. Schaefer (D)
Leonard W. Schuetz (D)
James J. Simpson, Jr. (R)
Chester C. Thompson (D)

Indiana

Senators

Arthur R. Robinson (R)
Frederick Van Nuys (D)

Representatives

John W. Boehne, Jr. (D)
Eugene B. Crowe (D)
George R. Durgan (D)
James I. Farley (D)
Finly H. Gray (D)
Arthur H. Greenwood (D)
Glenn Griswold (D)
Virginia Ellis Jenckes (D)
William H. Larrabee (D)
Louis L. Ludlow (D)
Samuel B. Pettengill (D)
William T. Schulte (D)

Iowa

Senators

Lester J. Dickinson (R)
Richard L. Murphy (D)

Representatives

Fred Biermann (D)
Cassius C. Dowell (R)
Edward C. Eicher (D)
Fred C. Gilchrist (R)
Guy M. Gillette (D)
Bernhard M. Jacobsen (D)
Lloyd Thurston (R)
Otha D. Wearin (D)
Albert C. Willford (D)

Kansas

Senators

Arthur Capper (R)
George McGill (D)

Representatives

William A. Ayres (D) r. Aug.
  1934
William R. Carpenter (D)
Ulysses S. Guyer (R)
Clifford R. Hope (R)
William P. Lambertson (R)
Kathryn O'Loughlin McCarthy
  (D)
Harold McGugin (R)

Kentucky

Senators

Alben W. Barkley (D)
Marvel M. Logan (D)

Representatives

John Y. Brown (D)
Cap R. Carden (D)
Glover H. Cary (D)
Virgil M. Chapman (D)
William V. Gregory (D)
Finley Hamilton (D)
Andrew J. May (D)
Brent Spence (D)

Fred M. Vinson (D)

Louisiana

Senators

Huey P. Long (D)
John H. Overton (D)

Representatives

Cleveland Dear (D)
Rene L. DeRouen (D)
Joachim O. Fernandez (D)
Bolivar E. Kemp (D) d. June
  1933
Paul H. Maloney (D)
Numa F. Montet (D)
Jared Y. Sanders, Jr. (D) s.
  1934
John N. Sandlin (D)
Riley J. Wilson (D)

Maine

Senators

Frederick Hale (R)
Wallace H. White, Jr. (R)

Representatives

Carroll L. Beedy (R)
Edward C. Moran, Jr. (R)
John G. Utterback (D)

Maryland

Senators

Phillips Lee Goldsborough (R)
Millard E. Tydings (D)

Representatives

William P. Cole, Jr. (D)
Stephen W. Gambrill (D)
T. Alan Goldsborough (D)
Ambrose J. Kennedy (D)
David J. Lewis (D)
Vincent L. Palmisano (D)

Massachusetts

Senators

Marcus A. Coolidge (D)
David I. Walsh (D)

Representatives

A. Piatt Andrew, Jr. (R)
William P. Connery, Jr. (D)
John J. Douglass (D)
Frank H. Foss (R)
Charles L. Gifford (R)
William J. Granfield (D)
Arthur D. Healey (D)
Pehr G. Holmes (R)
Robert Luce (R)
John W. McCormack (D)
Joseph W. Martin, Jr. (R)
Edith Nourse Rogers (R)
George H. Tinkham (R)
Allen T. Treadway (R)
Richard B. Wigglesworth (R)

Michigan

Senators

James Couzens (R)
Arthur H. Vandenberg (R)

Representatives

Prentiss M. Brown (R)
Claude E. Cady (D)
John D. Dingell (D)
George A. Dondero (R)
George E. Foulkes (D)
Michael J. Hart (D)
Joseph L. Hooper (R) d. Feb.
   1934
W. Frank James (R)
John C. Lehr (D)
John Lesinski (D)
Clarence J. McLeod (R)
Carl E. Mapes (R)
Harry W. Musselwhite (D)
George G. Sadowksi (D)
Carl M. Weideman (D)
Jesse P. Wolcott (R)
Roy O. Woodruff (R)

Minnesota

Senators

Thomas D. Schall (R)
Henrik Shipstead (Farm-Labor)

Representatives

Henry Arens (Farm-Labor)
Ray P. Chase (R)
Theodore Christianson (R)
Einar Hoidale (D)
Magnus Johnson (Farm-Labor)
Harold Knutson (R)
Paul J. Kvale (Farm-Labor)
Ernest Lundeen (Farm-Labor)
Francis H. Shoemaker (Farm-
   Labor)

Mississippi

Senators

Pat Harrison (D)
Hubert D. Stephens (D)

Representatives

T. Jeff Busby (D)
Wall Doxey (D)
Lawrence R. Ellzey (D)
Ross A. Collins (D)
William M. Colmer (D)
John E. Rankin (D)
William M. Whittington (D)

Missouri

Senators

Bennett Champ Clark (D)
Roscoe C. Patterson (R)

Representatives

Clarence Cannon (D)
James R. Claiborne (D)
John J. Cochran (D)

Clement C. Dickinson (D)
Richard M. Duncan (D)
Frank H. Lee (D)
Ralph F. Lozier (D)
Jacob L. Milligan (D)
Milton A. Romjue(D)
James E. Ruffin (D)
Joseph B. Shannon (D)
Clyde Williams (D)
Reuben T. Wood (D)

Montana

Senators

John E. Erickson (D) ta. 1933-
   1934
James E. Murray (D) s. 1935
Burton K. Wheeler (D)

Representatives

Roy E. Ayers (D)
Joseph P. Monaghan (D)

Nebraska

Senators

Robert B. Howell (R) d. Mar.
   1933
Richard C. Hunter (D) s. 1934
George W. Norris (R)
William H. Thompson ta. 1933-
   1934

Representatives

Edward R. Burke (D)
Terry M. Carpenter (D)
Edgar Howard (D)
John M. Morehead (D)
Ashton C. Shallenberger (D)

Nevada

Senators

Patrick A. McCarran (D)
Key Pittman (D)

Representatives

James G. Scrugham (D)

New Hampshire

Senators

Fred H. Brown (D)
Henry W. Keyes (R)

Representatives

William N. Rogers (D)
Charles W. Tobey (R)

New Jersey

Senators

W. Warren Barbour (R)
Hamilton F. Kean (R)

Representatives

Oscar L. Auf Der Heide (D)
Isaac Bacharach (R)
Peter A. Cavicchia (R)
Charles A. Eaton (R)
Fred A. Hartley, Jr. (R)
Edward A. Kenney (D)
Frederick R. Lehlbach (R)
Donald H. McLean (R)
Mary T. Norton (D)
Randolph Perkins (R)
D. Lane Powers (R)
George N. Seger (R)
William H. Sutphin (D)
Charles A. Wolverton (R)

New Mexico

Senators

Sam G. Bratton (D) r. June
   1933
Bronson M. Cutting (R)
Carl A. Hatch (D) s. 1934

Representatives

Dennis Chavez (D)

New York

Senators

Royal S. Copeland (D)
Robert F. Wagner (D)

Representatives

Walter G. Andrews (R)
Robert L. Bacon (R)
Alfred F. Beiter (D)
Loring M. Black, Jr. (D)
Sol Bloom (D)
John J. Boyland (D)
William F. Brunner (D)
Patrick J. Carley (D)
Emanuel Celler (D)
John D. Clarke (R) d. 1934
Marian W. Clarke (R) s. 1934
Parker Corning (D)
Frank Crowther (R)
Francis D. Culkin (R)
Thomas Cullen (D)
John J. Delaney (D)
Samuel Dickstein (D)
Hamilton Fish, Jr. (D)
John Fitzgibbons (D)
James M. Fitzpatrick (D)
Joseph A. Gavagan (D)
Philip A. Goodwin (R)
Anthony J. Griffin (D)
Clarence E. Hancock (R)
Martin J. Kennedy (D)
James J. Lanzetta (D)
George W. Lindsay (D)
James M. Mead (D)
Charles D. Millard (R)
John J. O'Connor (D)
Frank Oliver (D) r. June 1934
James S. Parker (R) d. Dec.
   1933
Theodore A. Peyser (D)
Anning S. Prall (D)
Daniel A. Reed (R)
Stephen A. Rudd (D)
William I. Sirovich (D)
Fred J. Sisson (D)
Bertrand H. Snell (R)

Andrew L. Somers (D)
Gale H. Stalker (R)
Elmer E. Studley (D)
Christopher D. Sullivan (D)
John Taber (R)
William D. Thomas (R) s. 1934
James W. Wadsworth, Jr. (R)
James L. Whitley (R)

North Carolina

Senators

Josiah W. Bailey (D)
Robert R. Reynolds (D)

Representatives

Charles L. Abernethy (D)
Alfred L. Bulwinkle (D)
J. Bayard Clark (D)
Harold D. Cooley (D) s. 1934
Robert L. Doughton (D)
Franklin W. Hancock, Jr. (D)
John H. Kerr (D)
J. Walter Lambeth (D)
Edward W. Pou (D) d. Apr.
   1934
William B. Umstead (D)
Lindsay C. Warren (D)
Zebulon Weaver (D)

North Dakota

Senators

Lynn J. Frazier (R)
Gerald P. Nye (R)

Representatives

William Lemke (R)
James H. Sinclair (R)

Ohio

Senators

Robert J. Bulkley (D)
Simeon D. Fess (R)

Representatives

Chester C. Bolton (R)
John G. Cooper (R)
Robert Crosser (D)
Warren J. Duffey (D)
William L. Fiesinger (D)
Thomas B. Fletcher (D)
Byron B. Harlan (D)
Dow W. Harter (D)
William E. Hess (R)
John B. Hollister (R)
Lawrence E. Imhoff (D)
Thomas A. Jenkins (R)
Frank L. Kloeb (D)
Frank C. Kniffin (D)
Arthur P. Lamneck (D)
Leroy T. Marshall (R)
James G. Polk (D)
Robert T. Secrest (D)
Martin L. Sweeney (D)
William R. Thom (D)
Charles V. Truax (D)
Mell G. Underwood (D)
Charles West (D)
Stephen M. Young (D)

Oklahoma

Senators

Thomas P. Gore (D)
J. W. Elmer Thomas (D)

Representatives

Wilburn Cartwright (D)
Wesley E. Disney (D)
William W. Hastings (D)
Jed Johnson (D)
James V. McClintic (D)
Thomas D. McKeown (D)
Ernest W. Marland (D)
Will Rogers (D)
Fletcher B. Swank (D)

Oregon

Senators

Charles L. McNary (R)
Frederick Steiwer (R)

Representatives

Charles H. Martin (D)
James W. Mott (R)
Walter M. Pierce (D)

Pennsylvania

Senators

James J. Davis (R)
David A. Reed (R)

Representatives

James M. Beck (R) r. Sept.
   1934
William M. Berlin (D)
Patrick J. Boland (D)
J. Twing Brooks (D)
George F. Brumm (R) d. May
   1934
Thomas C. Cochran (R)
James J. Connolly (R)
Charles N. Crosby (D)
George P. Darrow (R)
J. William Ditter (R)
Isaac H. Doutrich (R)
Matthew A. Dunn (D)
George W. Edmonds (R)
Henry Ellenbogen (D)
Charles I. Faddis (D)
Benjamin K. Focht (R)
Oliver W. Frey (D) s. 1934
Harry L. Haines (D)
M. Clyde Kelly (R)
J. Roland Kinzer (R)
J. Banks Kurtz (R)
Louis T. McFadden (R)
Michael J. Muldowney (R)
Harry C. Ransley (R)
Robert F. Rich (R)
William E. Richardson (D)
J. Buell Snyder (D)
Edward L. Stokes (R)
Nathan L. Strong (R)
J. Howard Swick (R)
C. Murray Turpin (R)
Alfred M. Waldron (R)
Francis E. Walter (D)
Henry W. Watson (R) d. Aug.
   1933

James Wolfenden (R)

Rhode Island

Senators

Felix Hebert (R)
Jesse H. Metcalf (R)

Representatives

Francis B. Condon (D)
John M. O'Connell (D)

South Carolina

Senators

James F. Byrnes (D)
Ellison D. Smith (D)

Representatives

Hampton P. Fulmer (D)
Allard H. Gasque (D)
Thomas S. McMillan (D)
John J. McSwain (D)
James P. Richards (D)
John C. Taylor (D)

South Dakota

Senators

William J. Bulow (D)
Peter Norbeck (R)

Representatives

Fred H. Hildebrandt (D)
Theodore B. Werner (D)

Tennessee

Senators

Nathan L. Bachman (D)
Kenneth D. McKellar (D)

Representatives

Gordon Browning (D)
Joseph W. Byrns (D)
Jere Cooper (D)
Edward H. Crump (D)
Sam D. McReynolds (D)
John R. Mitchell (D)
B. Carroll Reece (R)
J. Will Taylor (R)
Clarence W. Turner (D)

Texas

Senators

Tom T. Connally (D)
Morris Sheppard (D)

Representatives

Joseph W. Bailey, Jr. (D)
Thomas L. Blanton (D)
Clay Stone Briggs (D)
James P. Buchanan (D)
Oliver H. Cross (D)
Martin Dies, Jr. (D)

Joe H. Eagle (D)
Luther A. Johnson (D)
Marvin Jones (D)
Richard M. Kleberg (D)
Fritz G. Lanham (D)
William D. McFarlane (D)
Joseph J. Mansfield (D)
Wright Patman (D)
Sam Rayburn (D)
Morgan G. Sanders (D)
Sterling P. Strong (D)
Hatton W. Sumners (D)
George B. Terrell (D)
R. Ewing Thomason (D)
Clark W. Thompson (D)
Milton H. West (D)

Utah

Senators

William H. King (D)
Elbert D. Thomas (D)

Representatives

Abe Murdock (D)
J. W. Robinson (D)

Vermont

Senators

Warren R. Austin (R)
Porter H. Dale (R) d. Oct.
   1933
Ernest W. Gibson (R) s. 1934

Representatives

Ernest W. Gibson (R) r. Oct.
   1933
Charles A. Plumley (R) s. 1934

Virginia

Senators

Harry F. Byrd (D)
Carter Glass (D)

Representatives

Schuyler Otis Bland (D)
Thomas G. Burch (D)
Colgate W. Darden, Jr. (D)
Patrick H. Drewry (D)
John W. Flannagan, Jr. (D)
Andrew J. Montague (D)
A. Willis Robertson (D)
Howard W. Smith (D)
Clifton A. Woodrum (D)

Washington

Senators

Homer T. Bone (D)
Clarence C. Dill (D)

Representatives

Knute Hill (D)
Samuel B. Hill (D)
Wesley Lloyd (D)
Martin F. Smith (D)
Monrad C. Wallgren (D)

Marion A. Zioncheck (D)

West Virginia

Senators

Henry D. Hatfield (R)
Matthew M. Neely (D)

Representatives

Andrew Edmiston (D) s. 1934
Lynn S. Hornor (D) d. Sept.
   1933
George W. Johnson (D)
John Kee (D)
Robert L. Ramsay (D)
Jennings Randolph (D)
Joe L. Smith (D)

Wisconsin

Senators

F. Ryan Duffy (D)
Robert M. La Follette, Jr.
   (Progressive)

Representatives

George W. Blanchard (R)
Gerald J. Boileau (R)
Raymond J. Cannon (D)
James A. Frear (R)
Charles W. Henney (D)
James F. Hughes (D)
Thomas O'Malley (D)
Hubert H. Peavey (R)
Michael K. Reilly (D)
Gardner R. Withrow (R)

Wyoming

Senators

Robert D. Carey (R)
John B. Kendrick (D) d. Nov.
   1933
Joseph C. O'Mahoney (D) s.
   1934

Representatives

Vincent M. Carter (R)

Seventy-Fourth Congress

(Jan. 3, 1935, to
Jan. 3, 1937)

President of the Senate: John
   Nance Garner
*President Pro Tempore of the
   Senate:* Key Pittman
*Speakers of the House of
   Representatives:* Joseph W.
   Byrns; William B. Bankhead

Alabama

Senators

John H. Bankhead, II (D)

Hugo L. Black (D)

Representatives

William B. Bankhead (D)
Frank W. Boykin (D)
Archibald H. Carmichael (D)
Lister Hill (D)
Sam Hobbs (D)
George Huddleston (D)
John McDuffie (D) r. Mar.
 1935
William B. Oliver (D)
Joe Starnes (D)
Henry B. Steagall (D)

Arizona

Senators

Henry F. Ashurst (D)
Carl Hayden (D)

Representatives

Isabella S. Greenway (D)

Arkansas

Senators

Hattie W. Caraway (D)

Representatives

William B. Cravens (D)
William J. Driver (D)
Claude A. Fuller (D)
John L. McClellan (D)
John E. Miller (D)
Tilman B. Parks (D)
David D. Terry (D)

California

Senators

Hiram W. Johnson (R)
William Gibbs McAdoo (D)

Representatives

Frank H. Buck (D)
George Burnham (R)
Albert E. Carter (R)
Charles J. Colden (D)
Samuel L. Collins (R)
John M. Costello (D)
John F. Dockweiler (D)
Harry L. Englebright (R)
Thomas F. Ford (D)
Bertrand W. Gearhart (R)
John H. Hoeppel (D)
Florence Prag Kahn (R)
Charles Kramer (D)
Clarence F. Lea (D, R)
John J. McGrath (D)
John S. McGroarty (D)
Byron N. Scott (D)
Henry E. Stubbs (D)
John H. Tolan (D)
Richard J. Welch (R)

Colorado

Senators

Alva B. Adams (D)
Edward P. Costigan (D)

Representatives

Fred Cummings (D)
Lawrence Lewis (D)
John A. Martin (D)
Edward T. Taylor (D)

Connecticut

Senators

Augustine Lonergan (D)
Francis T. Maloney (D)

Representatives

William M. Citron (D)
William L. Higgins (R)
Herman P. Kopplemann (D)
Schuyler Merritt (R)
James A. Shanley (D)
J. Joseph Smith (D)

Delaware

Senators

Daniel O. Hastings (R)
John G. Townsend, Jr. (R)

Representatives

John G. Stewart (R)

Florida

Senators

Charles O. Andrews (D) s. 1937
Duncan U. Fletcher (D) d. June
 1936
William L. Hill (D) ta. July
 1936
Scott Loftin (D) ta. May 1936
Claude D. Pepper (D) s. 1937
Park Trammell (D) d. May
 1936

Representatives

Millard F. Caldwell (D)
Robert A. Green (D)
J. Hardin Peterson (D)
William J. Sears (D)
J. Mark Wilcox (D)

Georgia

Senators

Walter F. George (D)
Richard B. Russell (D)

Representatives

Paul Brown (D)
Bryant T. Castellow (D)
Edward E. Cox (D)
Braswell D. Deen (D)

Emmett M. Owen (D)
Hugh Peterson (D)
Robert Ramspeck (D)
Malcolm C. Tarver (D)
Carl Vinson (D)
B. Frank Whelchel (D)

Idaho

Senators

William E. Borah (R)
James P. Pope (D)

Representatives

D. Worth Clark (D)
Compton I. White (D)

Illinois

Senators

William H. Dieterich (D)
J. Hamilton Lewis (D)

Representatives

J. Leroy Adair (D)
Leo E. Allen (R)
Leslie C. Arends (R)
William W. Arnold (D) r. Sept.
 1935
Harry P. Beam (D)
Martin A. Brennan (D)
John T. Buckbee (R) d. Apr.
 1936
Ralph E. Church (R)
Everett M. Dirksen (R)
Donald C. Dobbins (D)
Michael L. Igoe (D) r. June
 1935
Kent E. Keller (D)
Edward A. Kelly (D)
Leo Kocialkowski (D)
Scott W. Lucas (D)
James McAndrews (D)
Raymond S. McKeough (D)
Harry H. Mason (D)
James A. Meeks (D)
Arthur W. Mitchell (D)
Thomas J. O'Brien (D)
Claude V. Parsons (D)
Chauncey W. Reed (R)
Adolph J. Sabath (D)
Edwin M. Schaefer (D)
Leonard W. Schuetz (D)
Chester C. Thompson (D)

Indiana

Senators

Sherman Minton (D)
Frederick Van Nuys (D)

Representatives

John W. Boehne, Jr. (D)
Eugene B. Crowe (D)
James I. Farley (D)
Finly H. Gray (D)
Arthur H. Greenwood (D)
Glenn Griswold (D)
Charles A. Halleck (R)
Virginia E. Jenckes (D)
William H. Larrabee (D)
Louis Ludlow (D)

Samuel B. Pettengill (D)
William T. Schulte (D)

Iowa

Senators

Lester J. Dickinson (R)
Guy M. Gillette (D) s. 1936
Richard L. Murphy (D) d. July
 1936

Representatives

Fred Biermann (D)
Edward C. Eicher (D)
Fred C. Gilchrist (R)
Guy M. Gillette (D) r. Nov.
 1936
John W. Gwynne (R)
Bernhard M. Jacobsen (D) d.
 June 1936
Lloyd Thurston (R)
Hubert Utterback (D)
Otha D. Wearin (D)

Kansas

Senators

Arthur Capper (R)
George McGill (D)

Representatives

Frank Carlson (R)
William R. Carpenter (D)
Ulysses Guyer (R)
Clifford R. Hope (R)
John M. Houston (D)
William P. Lambertson (R)
Edward W. Patterson (D)

Kentucky

Senators

Alben W. Barkley (D)
Marvel M. Logan (D)

Representatives

Cap R. Carden (D) d. June
 1935
Glover H. Cary (D) d. Dec.
 1936
Virgil M. Chapman (D)
Edward W. Creal (D) s. Oct.
 1936
William V. Gregory (D)
Andrew J. May (D)
Emmet O'Neal (D)
John M. Robsion (R)
Brent Spence (D)
Fred M. Vinson (D)

Louisiana

Senators

Huey P. Long (D) d. Sept.
 1935
Rose McConnell Long (D) s.
 1936
John H. Overton (D)

Representatives

Cleveland Dear (D)
Rene L. DeRouen (D)
Joachim O. Fernandez (D)
Paul H. Maloney (D)
Numa F. Montet (D)
Jared Y. Sanders, Jr. (D)
John N. Sandlin (D)
Riley J. Wilson (D)

Maine

Senators

Frederick Hale (R)
Wallace H. White, Jr. (R)

Representatives

Ralph O. Brewster (R)
Simon M. Hamlin (D)
Edward C. Moran, Jr. (R)

Maryland

Senators

George L. Radcliffe (D)
Millard E. Tydings (D)

Representatives

William P. Cole, Jr. (D)
Stephen W. Gambrill (D)
T. Alan Goldsborough (D)
Ambrose J. Kennedy (D)
David J. Lewis (D)
Vincent L. Palmisano (D)

Massachusetts

Senators

Marcus A. Coolidge (D)
David I. Walsh (D)

Representatives

A. Piatt Andrew, Jr. (R) d.
June 1936
Joseph E. Casey (D)
William P. Connery, Jr. (D)
Charles L. Gifford (R)
William J. Granfield (D)
Arthur D. Healey (D)
John P. Higgins (D)
Pehr G. Holmes (R)
John W. McCormack (D)
Joseph W. Martin, Jr. (R)
Edith Nourse Rogers (R)
Richard M. Russell (D)
George H. Tinkham (R)
Allen T. Treadway (R)
Richard B. Wigglesworth (R)

Michigan

Senators

Prentiss M. Brown (D) ta. Nov.
1936
James Couzens (R) d. Oct. 1936
Arthur H. Vandenberg (R)

Representatives

William W. Blackney (R)
Prentiss M. Brown (D) r. Nov.
1936
Fred L. Crawford (R)
John D. Dingell (D)
George A. Dondero (R)
Albert J. Engel (R)
Clare E. Hoffman (R)
Frank E. Hook (D)
Henry M. Kimball (R) d. Oct.
1935
John Lesinski (D)
Clarence J. McLeod (R)
Verner W. Main (R) s. 1936
Carl E. Mapes (R)
Earl C. Michener (R)
Louis C. Rabaut (D)
George G. Sadowski (D)
Jesse P. Wolcott (R)
Roy O. Woodruff (R)

Minnesota

Senators

Elmer A. Benson (Farm-Labor)
ta. Jan. 1936
Guy V. Howard (R) s. 1936
Thomas D. Schall (R) d. Dec.
1935
Henrik Shipstead (Farm-Labor)

Representatives

August H. Andresen (R)
Richard T. Buckler (Farm-
Labor)
Theodore Christianson (R)
Harold Knutson (R)
Paul J. Kvale (Farm-Labor)
Ernest Lundeen (Farm-Labor)
Melvin J. Maas (R)
William A. Pittenger (R)
Elmer J. Ryan (D)

Mississippi

Senators

Theodore G. Bilbo (D)
Pat Harrison (D)

Representatives

William M. Colmer (D)
Wall Doxey (D)
Aubert C. Dunn (D)
Aaron L. Ford (D)
Dan R. McGehee (D)
John E. Rankin (D)
William M. Whittington (D)

Missouri

Senators

Bennett Champ Clark (D)
Harry S Truman (D)

Representatives

C. Jasper Bell (D)
Clarence Cannon (D)
James R. Claiborne (D)
John J. Cochran (D)
Richard M. Duncan (D)

Thomas C. Hennings, Jr. (D)
William L. Nelson (D)
MIlton A. Romjue (D)
Joseph B. Shannon (D)
Dewey Short (R)
Clyde Williams (D)
Reuben T. Wood (D)
Orville Zimmerman (D)

Montana

Senators

James E. Murray (D)
Burton K. Wheeler (D)

Representatives

Roy E. Ayers (D)
Joseph P. Monaghan (D)

Nebraska

Senators

Edward R. Burke (D)
George W. Norris (R)

Representatives

Charles G. Binderup (D)
Harry B. Coffee (D)
Henry C. Luckey (D)
Charles F. McLaughlin (D)
Karl Stefan (R)

Nevada

Senators

Patrick A. McCarran (D)
Key Pittman (D)

Representatives

James G. Scrugham (D)

New Hampshire

Senators

Fred H. Brown (D)
Henry W. Keyes (R)

Representatives

William N. Rogers (D)
Charles W. Tobey (R)

New Jersey

Senators

W. Warren Barbour (R)
A. Harry Moore (D)

Representatives

Isaac Bacharach (R)
Peter A. Cavicchia (R)
Charles A. Eaton (R)
Edward J. Hart (D)
Fred A. Hartley, Jr. (R)
Edward A. Kenney (D)
Frederick R. Lehlbach (R)
Donald H. McLean (R)

Mary T. Norton (D)
Randolph Perkins (R) d. May
1936
D. Lane Powers (R)
George N. Seger (R)
William H. Sutphin (D)
Charles A. Wolverton (R)

New Mexico

Senators

Dennis Chavez (D)
Bronson M. Cutting (R) d. May
1935
Carl A. Hatch (D)

Representatives

John J. Dempsey (D)

New York

Senators

Royal S. Copeland (D)
Robert F. Wagner (D)

Representatives

Walter G. Andrews (R)
Robert L. Bacon (R)
William B. Barry (D) s. 1936
Alfred F. Beiter (D)
Sol Bloom (D)
John J. Boylan (D)
William F. Brunner (D) r. Sept.
1935
Charles A. Buckley (D)
Emanuel Celler (D)
W. Sterling Cole (R)
Parker Corning (D)
Frank Crowther (R)
Francis D. Culkin (R)
Thomas H. Cullen (D)
Edward W. Curley (D) s. 1936
John J. Delaney (D)
Samuel Dickstein (D)
James P. B. Duffy (D)
Marcellus H. Evans (D)
Hamilton Fish, Jr. (R)
James M. Fitzpatrick (D)
Joseph A. Gavagan (D)
Philip A. Goodwin (R)
Anthony J. Griffin (D) d. Jan.
1935
Clarence E. Hancock (R)
Martin J. Kennedy (D)
Bert Lord (R)
Vito Marcantonio (R)
James M. Mead (D)
Matthew J. Merritt (D)
Charles D. Millard (R)
John J. O'Connor (D)
Caroline O'Day (D)
James A. O'Leary (D)
Theodore A. Peyser (D)
Joseph L. Pfeifer (D)
Daniel A. Reed (R)
Stephen A. Rudd (D) d. Mar.
1936
William I. Sirovich (D)
Fred J. Sisson (D)
Bertrand H. Snell (R)
Andrew L. Somers (D)
Christopher D. Sullivan (D)
John Taber (R)
William D. Thomas (R) d. May
1936

Richard J. Tonry (D)
James W. Wadsworth, Jr. (R)

North Carolina

Senators

Josiah W. Bailey (D)
Robert R. Reynolds (D)

Representatives

Graham A. Barden (D)
Alfred L. Bulwinkle (D)
J. Bayard Clark (D)
Harold D. Cooley (D)
Robert L. Doughton (D)
Franklin W. Hancock, Jr. (D)
John H. Kerr (D)
J. Walter Lambeth (D)
William B. Umstead (D)
Lindsay C. Warren (D)
Zebulon Weaver (D)

North Dakota

Senators

Lynn J. Frazier (R)
Gerald P. Nye (R)

Representatives

Usher L. Burdick (D)
William Lemke (R)

Ohio

Senators

Robert J. Bulkley (D)
A. Victor Donahey (D)

Representatives

William A. Ashbrook (D)
Chester C. Bolton (R)
John G. Cooper (R)
Robert Crosser (D)
Warren J. Duffey (D) d. July 1936
Daniel S. Earhart (D) s. 1936
William L. Fiesinger (D)
Thomas B. Fletcher (D)
Peter F. Hammond (D) s. 1936
Byron B. Harlan (D)
Dow W. Harter (D)
William E. Hess (R)
John B. Hollister (R)
Lawrence E. Imhoff (D)
Thomas A. Jenkins (R)
Frank L. Kloeb (D)
Frank C. Kniffin (D)
Arthur P. Lamneck (D)
Leroy T. Marshall (R)
James G. Polk (D)
Robert T. Secrest (D)
Martin L. Sweeney (D)
William R. Thom (D)
Charles V. Truax (D) d. Aug. 1935
Mell G. Underwood (D) r. Apr. 1936
Stephen M. Young (D)

Oklahoma

Senators

J. W. Elmer Thomas (D)
Thomas P. Gore (D)

Representatives

Wilburn Cartwright (D)
Wesley E. Disney (D)
Phil Ferguson (D)
P. L. Gassaway (D)
Jed Johnson (D)
Josh Lee (D)
Sam C. Massingale (D)
Jack Nichols (D)
Will Rogers (D)

Oregon

Senators

Charles L. McNary (R)
Frederick Steiwer (R)

Representatives

William A. Ekwall (R)
James W. Mott (R)
Walter M. Pierce (D)

Pennsylvania

Senators

James J. Davis (R)
Joseph F. Guffey (D)

Representatives

William M. Berlin (D)
Patrick J. Boland (D)
J. Twing Brooks (D)
Charles N. Crosby (D)
J. Burrwood Daly (D)
George P. Darrow (R)
C. Elmer Dietrich (D)
J. William Ditter (R)
Frank J. G. Dorsey (D)
Isaac H. Doutrich (R)
D. J. Driscoll (D)
Matthew A. Dunn (D)
Charles R. Eckert (D)
Henry Ellenbogen (D)
Charles I. Faddis (D)
Clare G. Fenerty (R)
Benjamin K. Focht (R)
Oliver W. Frey (D)
James H. Gildea (D)
Don Gingery (D)
Joseph Gray (D)
Harry L. Haines (D)
J. Roland Kinzer (R)
Theodore L. Moritz (D)
James L. Quinn (D)
Harry C. Ransley (R)
Robert F. Rich (R)
William E. Richardson (D)
J. Buell Snyder (D)
Michael J. Stack (D)
C. Murray Turpin (R)
Francis E. Walter (D)
William H. Wilson (R)
James Wolfenden (R)

Rhode Island

Senators

Peter G. Gerry (D)
Jesse H. Metcalf (R)

Representatives

Francis B. Condon (D) r. Jan. 1935
John M. O'Connell (D)
Charles F. Risk (R)

South Carolina

Senators

James F. Byrnes (D)
Ellison D. Smith (D)

Representatives

Hampton P. Fulmer (D)
Allard H. Gasque (D)
Thomas S. McMillan (D)
John J. McSwain (D) d. Aug. 1936
G. Heyward Mahon, Jr. (D) s. 1936
James P. Richards (D)
John C. Taylor (D)

South Dakota

Senators

William J. Bulow (D)
Herbert E. Hitchcock (D) ta. Jan. 1937
Peter Norbeck (D) d. Dec. 1936

Representatives

Fred H. Hildebrandt (D)
Theodore B. Werner (D)

Tennessee

Senators

Nathan L. Bachman (D)
Kenneth D. McKellar (D)

Representatives

Joseph W. Byrns (D) d. June 1936
Walter Chandler (D)
Jere Cooper (D)
Sam D. McReynolds (D)
John R. Mitchell (D)
Herron Pearson (D)
B. Carroll Reece (R)
J. Will Taylor (D)
Clarence W. Turner (D)

Texas

Senators

Tom T. Connally (D)
Morris Sheppard (D)

Representatives

Thomas L. Blanton (D)
James P. Buchanan (D)
Oliver H. Cross (D)
Martin Dies, Jr. (D)
Joe H. Eagle (D)
Luther A. Johnson (D)
Marvin Jones (D)
Richard M. Kleberg (D)
Fritz G. Lanham (D)
William D. McFarlane (D)
George H. Mahon (D)
Joseph J. Mansfield (D)
Maury Maverick (D)
Wright Patman (D)
Nat Patton (D)
Sam Rayburn (D)
Morgan G. Sanders (D)
Charles L. South (D)
Hatton W. Sumners (D)
R. Ewing Thomason (D)
Milton H. West (D)

Utah

Senators

William H. King (D)
Elbert D. Thomas (D)

Representatives

Abe Murdock (D)
J. W. Robinson (D)

Vermont

Senators

Warren R. Austin (R)
Ernest W. Gibson (R)

Representatives

Charles A. Plumley (R)

Virginia

Senators

Harry F. Byrd (D)
Carter Glass (D)

Representatives

Schuyler Otis Bland (D)
Thomas G. Burch (D)
Colgate W. Darden, Jr. (D)
Patrick H. Drewry (D)
John W. Flannagan, Jr. (D)
Andrew J. Montague (D)
A. Willis Robertson (D)
Howard W. Smith (D)
Clifton A. Woodrum (D)

Washington

Senators

Homer T. Bone (D)
Lewis B. Schwellenbach (D)

Representatives

Knute Hill (D)

Samuel B. Hill (D) r. June 1936
Wesley Lloyd (D) d. Jan. 1936
Martin F. Smith (D)
Monrad C. Wallgren (D)
Marion A. Zioncheck (D) d. Aug. 1936

West Virginia

Senators

Rush D. Holt (D)
Matthew M. Neely (D)

Representatives

Andrew Edmiston (D)
George W. Johnson (D)
John Kee (D)
Robert L. Ramsay (D)
Jennings Randolph (D)
Joe L. Smith (D)

Wisconsin

Senators

F. Ryan Duffy (D)
Robert M. La Follette, Jr. (Progressive)

Representatives

Thomas R. Amlie (Progressive)
Gerald J. Boileau (R)
Raymond J. Cannon (D)
Bernard J. Gehrmann (Progressive)
Merlin Hull (Progressive)
Thomas O'Malley (D)
Michael K. Reilly (D)
Harry Sauthoff (Progressive)
George J. Schneider (Progressive)
Gardner R. Withrow (Progressive)

Wyoming

Senators

Robert D. Carey (R)
Joseph C. O'Mahoney (D)

Representatives

Paul R. Greever (D)

Seventy-Fifth Congress

(Jan. 3, 1937, to Jan. 3, 1939)

President of the Senate: John Nance Garner
President Pro Tempore of the Senate: Key Pittman
Speaker of the House of Representatives: William B. Bankhead

Alabama

Senators

John H. Bankhead, II (D)
Hugo L. Black (D) r. Aug. 1937
Dixie Bibb Graves (D) ta. 1937
Lister Hill (D) s. 1938

Representatives

William B. Bankhead (D)
Frank W. Boykin (D)
George M. Grant (D) s. 1938
Lister Hill (D) r. Jan. 1938
Sam Hobbs (D)
Pete Jarman (D)
Luther Patrick (D)
John J. Sparkman (D)
Joe Starnes (D)
Henry B. Steagall (D)

Arizona

Senators

Henry F. Ashurst (D)
Carl Hayden (D)

Representatives

John R. Murdock (D)

Arkansas

Senators

Hattie W. Caraway (D)
John E. Miller (D)
Joseph T. Robinson (D) d. July 1937

Representatives

William B. Cravens (D)
William J. Driver (D)
Claude A. Fuller (D)
Wade H. Kitchens (D)
John L. McClellan (D)
John E. Miller (D) r. Nov. 1937
David D. Terry (D)

California

Senators

Hiram W. Johnson (R)
William Gibbs McAdoo (D) r. Nov. 1938
Thomas M. Storke (D) s. 1938

Representatives

Frank H. Buck (D)
Albert E. Carter (R)
Charles J. Colden (D) d. Apr. 1938
John M. Costello (D)
John F. Dockweiler (D)
Alfred J. Elliott (D)
Harry L. Englebright (R)
Thomas F. Ford (D)
Bertrand W. Gearhart (R)
Franck R. Havenner (Progressive)

Edouard V. M. Izac (D)
Charles Kramer (D)
Clarence F. Lea (D, R)
John J. McGrath (D)
John S. McGroarty (D)
Byron N. Scott (D)
Harry R. Sheppard (D)
Henry E. Stubbs (D) d. Feb. 1937
John H. Tolan (D)
H. Jerry Voorhis (D)
Richard J. Welch (R)

Colorado

Senators

Alva B. Adams (D)
Edwin C. Johnson (D)

Representatives

Fred Cummings (D)
Lawrence Lewis (D)
John A. Martin (D)
Edward T. Taylor (D)

Connecticut

Senators

Augustine Lonergan (D)
Francis T. Maloney (D)

Representatives

William M. Citron (D)
William J. Fitzgerald (D)
Herman P. Kopplemann (D)
Alfred N. Phillips, Jr. (D)
James A. Shanley (D)
J. Joseph Smith (D)

Delaware

Senators

James H. Hughes (D)
John G. Townsend, Jr. (R)

Representatives

William F. Allen (D)

Florida

Senators

Charles O. Andrews (D)
Claude D. Pepper (D)

Representatives

Millard F. Caldwell (D)
Robert A. Green (D)
Joe Hendricks (D)
J. Hardin Peterson (D)
J. Mark Wilcox (D)

Georgia

Senators

Walter F. George (D)
Richard B. Russell (D)

Representatives

Paul Brown (D)
Edward E. Cox (D)
Braswell D. Deen (D)
Emmett M. Owen (D)
Stephen Pace (D)
Hugh Peterson (D)
Robert Ramspeck (D)
Malcolm C. Tarver (D)
Carl Vinson (D)
B. Frank Whelchel (D)

Idaho

Senators

William E. Borah (R)
James P. Pope (D)

Representatives

D. Worth Clark (D)
Compton I. White (D)

Illinois

Senators

William H. Dieterich (D)
J. Hamilton Lewis (D)

Representatives

Leo E. Allen (R)
Leslie C. Arends (R)
Laurence F. Arnold (D)
Harry P. Beam (D)
Lewis L. Boyer (D)
Edwin V. Champion (D)
Ralph E. Church (R)
Everett M. Dirksen (R)
Frank W. Fries (D)
Kent E. Keller (D)
Edward A. Kelly (D)
Leo Kocialkowski (D)
Lewis M. Long (D)
Scott W. Lucas (D)
James McAndrews (D)
Raymond S. McKeough (D)
Noah M. Mason (R)
James A. Meeks (D)
Arthur W. Mitchell (D)
Thomas J. O'Brien (D)
Claude V. Parsons (D)
Chauncey W. Reed (R)
Hugh M. Rigney (D)
Adolph J. Sabath (D)
Edwin M. Schaefer (D)
Leonard W. Schuetz (D)
Chester C. Thompson (D)

Indiana

Senators

Sherman Minton (D)
Frederick Van Nuys (D)

Representatives

John W. Boehne, Jr. (D)
Eugene B. Crowe (D)
James I. Farley (D)
Finly H. Gray (D)
Arthur H. Greenwood (D)
Glenn Griswold (D)
Charles A. Halleck (R)

Virginia Ellis Jenckes (D)
William H. Larrabee (D)
Louis Ludlow (D)
Samuel B. Pettengill (D)
William T. Schulte (D)

Iowa

Senators

Guy M. Gillette (D)
Clyde L. Herring (D)

Representatives

Fred Biermann (D)
Cassius C. Dowell (R)
Edward C. Eicher (D) r. Dec.
1938
Fred C. Gilchrist (R)
John W. Gwynne (R)
Vincent F. Harrington (D)
William S. Jacobsen (D)
Lloyd Thurston (R)
Otha D. Wearin (D)

Kansas

Senators

Arthur Capper (R)
George McGill (D)

Representatives

Frank Carlson (R)
Ulysses S. Guyer (R)
Clifford R. Hope (R)
John M. Houston (D)
William P. Lambertson (R)
Edward W. Patterson (D)
Edward H. Rees (R)

Kentucky

Senators

Alben W. Barkley (D)
Marvel M. Logan (D)

Representatives

Joe B. Bates (D) s. 1938
Virgil M. Chapman (D)
Edward W. Creal (D)
Noble J. Gregory (D)
Andrew J. May (D)
Emmet O'Neal (D)
John M. Robsion (R)
Brent Spence (D)
Beverly M. Vincent (D)
Fred M. Vinson (D) r. May
1938

Louisiana

Senators

Allen J. Ellender (D)
John H. Overton (D)

Representatives

A. Leonard Allen (D)
Overton Brooks (D)
Rene L. De Rouen (D)
Joachim O. Fernandez (D)

John K. Griffith (D)
Paul H. Maloney (D)
Newt V. Mills (D)
Robert L. Mouton (D)

Maine

Senators

Frederick Hale (R)
Wallace H. White, Jr. (R)

Representatives

Ralph O. Brewster (R)
James C. Oliver (R)
Clyde H. Smith (R)

Maryland

Senators

George L. Radcliffe (D)
Millard E. Tydings (D)

Representatives

William P. Cole, Jr. (D)
Stephen W. Gambrill (D)
T. Alan Goldsborough (D)
Ambrose J. Kennedy (D)
David J. Lewis (D)
Vincent L. Palmisano (D)

Massachusetts

Senators

Henry Cabot Lodge, Jr. (R)
David I. Walsh (D)

Representatives

George J. Bates (R)
Joseph E. Casey (D)
Charles R. Clason (R)
Lawrence J. Connery (D)
William P. Connery, Jr. (D) d.
June 1937
Thomas A. Flaherty (D) s.
1938
Charles L. Gifford (R)
Arthur D. Healey (D)
John P. Higgins (D) r. Sept.
1937
Pehr G. Holmes (R)
Robert Luce (R)
John W. McCormack (D)
Joseph W. Martin, Jr. (R)
Edith Nourse Rogers (R)
George H. Tinkham (R)
Allen T. Treadway (R)
Richard B. Wigglesworth (R)

Michigan

Senators

Prentiss M. Brown (D)
Arthur H. Vandenberg (R)

Representatives

Fred L. Crawford (R)
John D. Dingell (D)
George A. Dondero (R)
Albert J. Engel (R)

Clare E. Hoffman (R)
Frank E. Hook (D)
John Lesinski (D)
John Luecke (D)
Carl E. Mapes (R)
Earl C. Michener (R)
George D. O'Brien (D)
Louis C. Rabaut (D)
George G. Sadowski (D)
Paul W. Shafer (R)
Andrew J. Transue (D)
Jesse P. Wolcott (R)
Roy O. Woodruff (R)

Minnesota

Senators

Ernest Lundeen (Farm-Labor)
Henrik Shipstead (Farm-Labor)

Representatives

August H. Andresen (R)
John T. Bernard (Farm-Labor)
Richard T. Buckler (Farm-
Labor)
Dewey W. Johnson (Farm-
Labor)
Harold Knutson (R)
Paul J. Kvale (Farm-Labor)
Melvin J. Maas (R)
Elmer J. Ryan (D)
Henry G. Teigan (Farm-Labor)

Mississippi

Senators

Theodore G. Bilbo (D)
Pat Harrison (D)

Representatives

Ross A. Collins (D)
William M. Colmer (D)
Wall Doxey (D)
Aaron L. Ford (D)
Dan R. McGehee (D)
John E. Rankin (D)
William M. Whittington (D)

Missouri

Senators

Bennett Champ Clark (D)
Harry S Truman (D)

Representatives

C. Arthur Anderson (D)
C. Jasper Bell (D)
Clarence Cannon (D)
John J. Cochran (D)
Richard M. Duncan (D)
Thomas C. Hennings, Jr. (D)
William L. Nelson (D)
Milton A. Romjue (D)
Joseph B. Shannon (D)
Dewey Short (R)
Clyde Williams (D)
Reuben T. Wood (D)
Orville Zimmerman (D)

Montana

Senators

James E. Murray (D)
Burton K. Wheeler (D)

Representatives

Jerry J. O'Connell (D)
James F. O'Connor (D)

Nebraska

Senators

Edward R. Burke (D)
George W. Norris (R)

Representatives

Charles G. Binderup (D)
Harry B. Coffee (D)
Henry C. Luckey (D)
Charles F. McLaughlin (D)
Karl Stefan (R)

Nevada

Senators

Patrick A. McCarran (D)
Key Pittman (D)

Representatives

James G. Scrugham (D)

New Hampshire

Senators

H. Styles Bridges (R)
Fred H. Brown (D)

Representatives

Arthur B. Jenks (R) r. June
1938
Alphonse Roy (D) s. 1938
Charles W. Tobey (R)

New Jersey

Senators

W. Warren Barbour (R) s. 1939
John Milton (R) ta. 1938
A. Harry Moore (D) r. Jan.
1938
William H. Smathers (D)

Representatives

Charles A. Eaton (R)
Edward J. Hart (D)
Fred A. Hartley, Jr. (R)
Edward A. Kenney (D)
Donald H. McLean (R)
Mary T. Norton (D)
Edward L. O'Neill (D)
D. Lane Powers (R)
George N. Seger (R)
William H. Sutphin (D)
J. Parnell Thomas (R)
Frank W. Towey, Jr. (D)

Elmer H. Wene (D)
Charles A. Wolverton (R)

New Mexico

Senators

Dennis Chavez (D)
Carl A. Hatch (D)

Representatives

John J. Dempsey (D)

New York

Senators

Royal S. Copeland (D)
James M. Mead (D) s. 1939
Robert F. Wagner (D)

Representatives

Walter G. Andrews (R)
Robert L. Bacon (R) d. Sept.
 1938
William B. Barry (D)
Bruce Barton (R)
Alfred F. Beiter (D)
Sol Bloom (D)
John J. Boylan (D) d. Oct.
 1938
Charles A. Buckley (D)
William T. Byrne (D)
Emanuel Celler (D)
E. Harold Cluett (R)
W. Sterling Cole (R)
Frank Crowther (R)
Francis D. Culkin (R)
Thomas H. Cullen (D)
Edward W. Curley (D)
John J. Delaney (D)
Samuel Dickstein (D)
Fred J. Douglas (R)
Marcellus H. Evans (D)
Hamilton Fish, Jr. (R)
James M. Fitzpatrick (D)
Ralph A. Gamble (R)
Joseph A. Gavagan (D)
Philip A. Goodwin (R) d. June
 1937
Clarence E. Hancock (R)
George B. Kelly (D)
Martin J. Kennedy (D)
Eugene J. Keogh (D)
James J. Lanzetta (D)
Bert Lord (R)
James M. Mead (D) r. Dec.
 1938
Matthew J. Merritt (D)
Charles D. Millard (R) r. Sept.
 1937
John J. O'Connor (D)
Caroline O'Day (D)
James A. O'Leary (D)
Donald L. O'Toole (D)
Theodore A. Peyser (D) d.
 Aug. 1937
Joseph L. Pfeifer (D)
Daniel A. Reed (R)
Lewis K. Rockefeller (R)
William I. Sirovich (D)
Bertrand H. Snell(R)
Andrew L. Somers (D)
Christopher D. Sullivan (D)
John Taber (R)
James W. Wadsworth, Jr. (R)

North Carolina

Senators

Josiah W. Bailey (D)
Robert R. Reynolds (D)

Representatives

Graham A. Barden (D)
Alfred L. Bulwinkle (D)
J. Bayard Clark (D)
Harold D. Cooley (D)
Robert L. Doughton (D)
Franklin W. Hancock, Jr. (D)
John H. Kerr (D)
J. Walter Lambeth (D)
William B. Umstead (D)
Lindsay C. Warren (D)
Zebulon Weaver (D)

North Dakota

Senators

Lynn J. Frazier (R)
Gerald P. Nye (R)

Representative

Usher L. Burdick (R)
William Lemke (R)

Ohio

Senators

Robert J. Bulkley (D)
A. Victor Donahey (D)

Representatives

Walter H. Albaugh (R) s. 1938
Arthur W. Aleshire (D)
William A. Ashbrook (D)
Herbert S. Bigelow (D)
Harold K Claypool (D)
Robert Crosser (D)
Joseph A. Dixon (D)
Anthony A. Fleger (D)
Thomas B. Fletcher (D)
Byron B. Harlan (D)
Dow W. Harter (D)
John F. Hunter (D)
Lawrence E. Imhoff (D)
Thomas A. Jenkins (R)
Michael J. Kirwan (D)
Frank L. Kloeb (D) r. Aug.
 1937
Frank C. Kniffin (D)
Arthur P. Lamneck (D)
John McSweeney (D)
Harold G. Mosier (D)
James G. Polk (D)
Robert T. Secrest (D)
Martin L. Sweeney (D)
William R Thom (D)
Dudley A. White (R)

Oklahoma

Senators

Josh Lee (D)
J. W. Elmer Thomas (D)

Representatives

Lyle H. Boren (D)
Wilburn Cartwright (D)
Wesley E. Disney (D)
Phil Ferguson (D)
Robert P. Hill (D) d. Oct. 1937
Jed Johnson (D)
Sam C. Massingale (D)
Jack Nichols (D)
Will Rogers (D)
Gomer Smith (D) s. 1938

Oregon

Senators

Alexander G. Barry (R) s. 1938
Charles L. McNary (R)
Alfred E. Reames (D) ta. 1938
Frederick Steiwer (R) r. Jan.
 1938

Representatives

Nan Wood Honeyman (D)
James W. Mott (R)
Walter M. Pierce (D)

Pennsylvania

Senators

James J. Davis (R)
Joseph F. Guffey (D)

Representatives

Robert G. Allen (D)
Patrick J. Boland (D)
Michael J. Bradley (D)
Charles N. Crosby (D)
J. Burrwood Daly (D)
George P. Darrow (R)
Peter J. DeMuth (D)
J. William Ditter (R)
Frank J. G. Dorsey (D)
Ira W. Drew (D)
Matthew A. Dunn (D)
Herman P. Eberharter (D)
Charles R. Eckert (D)
Henry Ellenbogen (D) r. Jan.
 1938
Charles I. Faddis (D)
J. Harold Flannery (D)
Benjamin K. Focht (R) d.
 March. 1937
Oliver W. Frey (D)
James H. Gildea (D)
Don Gingery (D)
Joseph Gray (D)
Harry L. Haines (D)
Benjamin Jarrett (R)
J. Roland Kinzer (R)
James P. McGranery (D)
Guy L. Moser (D)
James L. Quinn (D)
Robert F. Rich (R)
Albert G. Rutherford (R)
Leon Sacks (D)
Richard M. Simpson (R)
J. Buell Snyder (D)
Michael J. Stack (D)
Guy J. Swope (D)
Francis E. Walter (D)
James Wolfenden (R)

Rhode Island

Senators

Peter G. Gerry (D)
Theodore F. Green (D)

Representatives

Aime J. Forand (D)
John M. O'Connell (D)

South Carolina

Senators

James F. Byrnes (D)
Ellison D. Smith (D)

Representatives

Hampton P. Fulmer (D)
Allard H. Gasque (D) d. June
 1938
Bessie H. Gasque (D) s. 1938
Thomas S. McMillan (D)
G. Heyward Mahon, Jr. (D)
James P. Richards (D)
John C. Taylor (D)

South Dakota

Senators

William J. Bulow (D)
Herbert E. Hitchcock (D) ta.
 1938
Gladys Pyle (R) s. 1938

Representatives

Francis H. Case (R)
Fred H. Hildebrandt (D)

Tennessee

Senators

Nathan L. Bachman (D) d.
 Apr. 1937
George L. Berry (D) ta. 1937-
 1938
Kenneth D. McKellar (D)
A. Tom Stewart (D) s. 1938

Representatives

Richard M. Atkinson (D)
Walter Chandler (D)
Jere Cooper (D)
Sam D. McReynolds (D)
John R. Mitchell (D)
Herron C. Pearson (D)
B. Carroll Reece (R)
J. Will Taylor (R)
Clarence W. Turner (D)

Texas

Senators

Tom T. Connally (D)
Morris Sheppard (D)

Representatives

James P. Buchanan (D) d. Feb. 1937
Martin Dies, Jr. (D)
Clyde L. Garrett (D)
Luther A. Johnson (D)
Lyndon B. Johnson (D)
Marvin Jones (D)
Richard M. Kleberg (D)
Fritz G. Lanham (D)
William D. McFarlane (D)
George H. Mahon (D)
Joseph J. Mansfield (D)
Maury Maverick (D)
Wright Patman (D)
Nat Patton (D)
William R. Poage (D)
Sam Rayburn (D)
Morgan G. Sanders (D)
Charles L. South (D)
Hatton W. Sumners (D)
Albert Thomas (D)
R. Ewing Thomason (D)
Milton H. West (D)

Utah

Senators

William H. King (D)
Elbert D. Thomas (D)

Representatives

Abe Murdock (D)
J. W. Robinson (D)

Vermont

Senators

Warren R. Austin (R)
Ernest W. Gibson (R)

Representatives

Charles A. Plumley (R)

Virginia

Senators

Harry F. Byrd (D)
Carter Glass (D)

Representatives

Schuyler Otis Bland (D)
Thomas G. Burch (D)
Patrick H. Drewry (D)
Norman R. Hamilton (D)
John W. Flannagan, Jr. (D)
Andrew J. Montague (D) d. Jan. 1937
A. Willis Robertson (D)
Dave E. Satterfield, Jr. (D) s. 1937
Howard W. Smith (D)
Clifton A. Woodrum (D)

Washington

Senators

Homer T. Bone (D)
Lewis B. Schwellenbach (D)

Representatives

John M. Coffee (D)
Knute Hill (D)
Charles H. Leavy (D)
Warren G. Magnuson (D)
Martin F. Smith (D)
Monrad C. Wallgren (D)

West Virginia

Senators

Rush D. Holt (D)
Matthew M. Neely (D)

Representatives

Andrew Edmiston (D)
George W. Johnson (D)
John Kee (D)
Robert L. Ramsay (D)
Jennings Randolph (D)
Joe L. Smith (D)

Wisconsin

Senators

F. Ryan Duffy (D)
Robert M. La Follette, Jr. (Progressive)

Representatives

Thomas R. Amlie (Progressive)
Gerald J. Boileau (R)
Raymond J. Cannon (D)
Bernard J. Gehrmann (Progressive)
Merlin Hull (Progressive)
Thomas O'Malley (D)
Michael K. Reilly (D)
Harry Sauthoff (Progressive)
George J. Schneider (Progressive)
Gardner R. Withrow (Progressive)

Wyoming

Senators

Joseph C. O'Mahoney (D)
H. H. Schwartz (D)

Representatives

Paul R. Greever (D)

Seventy-Sixth Congress

(Jan. 3, 1939, to Jan. 3, 1941)

President of the Senate: John Nance Garner
Presidents Pro Tempore of the Senate: Key Pittman; William King
Speakers of the House of Representatives: William B. Bankhead; Sam Rayburn

Alabama

Senators

John H. Bankhead, II (D)
Lister Hill (D)

Representatives

William B. Bankhead (D) d. Sept. 1940
Frank W. Boykin (D)
George M. Grant (D)
Sam Hobbs (D)
Pete Jarman (D)
Luther Patrick (D)
Joe Starnes (D)
John J. Sparkman (D)
Henry B. Steagall (D)
Zadoc L. Weatherford (D) s. 1940

Arizona

Senators

Henry F. Ashurst (D)
Carl Hayden (D)

Representatives

John R. Murdock (D)

Arkansas

Senators

Hattie W. Caraway (D)
John E. Miller (D)

Representatives

Fadjo Cravens (D)
William B. Cravens (D) d. Jan. 1939
Clyde T. Ellis (D)
Ezekiel C. Gathings (D)
Wade H. Kitchens (D)
Wilbur D. Mills (D)
William F. Norrell (D)
David D. Terry (D)

California

Senators

Sheridan Downey (D)
Hiram W. Johnson (R)

Representatives

John Z. Anderson (R)
Frank H. Buck (D)
Albert E. Carter (R)
John M. Costello (D)
Thomas M. Eaton (R) d. Sept. 1939
Alfred J. Elliott (D)
Harry L. Englebright (R)
Leland M. Ford (R)
Bertrand W. Gearhart (R)
Lee E. Geyer (D)
Franck R. Havenner (D)
Carl Hinshaw (R)
Edouard V. M. Izac (D)
Charles Kramer (D)
Clarence F. Lea (D)

Harry R. Sheppard (D, R)
John H. Tolan (D)
H. Jerry Voorhis (D)
Richard J. Welch (R)

Colorado

Senators

Alva B. Adams (D)
Edwin C. Johnson (D)

Representatives

William E. Burney (D) s. 1940
Fred Cummings (D)
Lawrence Lewis (D)
John A. Martin (D) d. Sept. 1939
Edward T. Taylor (D)

Connecticut

Senators

John A. Danaher (R)
Francis T. Maloney (D)

Representatives

Albert E. Austin (R)
Thomas R. Ball (R)
William J. Miller (R)
Boleslaus J. Monkiewicz (R)
James A. Shanley (D)
J. Joseph Smith (D)

Delaware

Senators

James H. Hughes (D)
John G. Townsend, Jr. (R)

Representatives

George S. Williams (R)

Florida

Senators

Charles O. Andrews (D)
Claude D. Pepper (R)

Representatives

Millard F. Caldwell (D)
Arthur P. Cannon (D)
Robert A. Green (D)
Joe Hendricks (D)
J. Hardin Peterson (D)

Georgia

Senators

Walter F. George (D)
Richard B. Russell (D)

Representatives

Paul Brown (D)
A. Sidney Camp (D)
Edward E. Cox (D)
Florence R. Gibbs (D) s. 1940

W. Benjamin Gibbs (D) d. Aug. 1940
Emmett M. Owen (D) d. June 1939
Stephen Pace (D)
Hugh Peterson (D)
Robert Ramspeck (D)
Malcolm C. Tarver (D)
Carl Vinson (D)
B. Frank Whelchel (D)

Idaho

Senators

William E. Borah (R) d. Jan. 1940
D. Worth Clark (D)
John Thomas (R) s. 1940

Representatives

Henry C. Dworshak (R)
Compton I. White (D)

Illinois

Senators

C. Wayland Brooks (R) s. 1940
J. Hamilton Lewis (D) d. Apr. 1939
Scott W. Lucas (D)
James M. Slattery (D) ta. 1939-1940

Representatives

Leo E. Allen (R)
Leslie C. Arends (R)
Laurence F. Arnold (D)
James M. Barnes (D)
Harry P. Beam (D)
Robert B. Chiperfield (R)
Ralph E. Church (R)
Everett M. Dirksen (R)
Frank W. Fries (D)
Anton J. Johnson (R)
Kent E. Keller (D)
Edward A. Kelly (D)
Leo Kocialkowski (D)
James McAndrews (D)
Raymond S. McKeough (D)
Anton F. Maciejewski (D)
John C. Martin (D)
Noah M. Mason (R)
Arthur W. Mitchell (D)
Claude V. Parsons (D)
Chauncey W. Reed (R)
Adolph J. Sabath (D)
Edwin M. Schaefer (D)
Leonard W. Schuetz (D)
Thomas V. Smith (D)
Jessie Sumner (R)
William H. Wheat (R)

Indiana

Senators

Sherman Minton (D)
Frederick Van Nuys (D)

Representatives

John W. Boehne, Jr. (D)
Eugene B. Crowe (D)
George W. Gillie (R)

Robert A. Grant (R)
Charles A. Halleck (R)
Forest A. Harness (R)
Noble J. Johnson (R)
Gerald W. Landis (R)
William H. Larrabee (D)
Louis Ludlow (D)
William T. Schulte (D)
Raymond S. Springer (R)

Iowa

Senators

Guy M. Gillette (D)
Clyde L. Herring (D)

Representatives

Cassius C. Dowell (R) d. Feb. 1940
Fred C. Gilchrist (R)
Robert K. Goodwin (R) s. 1940
John W. Gwynne (R)
Vincent F. Harrington (D)
William S. Jacobsen (D)
Ben F. Jensen (R)
Karl M. LeCompte (R)
Thomas E. Martin (R)
Henry O. TAlle (R)

Kansas

Senators

Arthur Capper (R)
Clyde M. Reed (R)

Representatives

Frank Carlson (R)
Ulysses S. Guyer (R)
Clifford R. Hope (R)
John M. Houston (D)
William P. Lambertson (R)
Edward H. Rees (R)
Thomas D. Winter (R)

Kentucky

Senators

Alben W. Barkley (D)
Albert B. Chandler (D)
Marvel M. Logan (D) d. Oct. 1939

Representatives

Joe B. Bates (D)
Virgil M. Chapman (D)
Edward W. Creal (D)
Noble J. Gregory (D)
Andrew J. May (D)
Emmet O'Neal (D)
John M. Robsion (R)
Brent Spence (D)
Beverly M. Vincent (D)

Louisiana

Senators

Allen J. Ellender (D)
John H. Overton (D)

Representatives

A. Leonard Allen (D)
Overton Brooks (D)
Rene L. De Rouen (D)
Joachim O. Fernandez (D)
John K. Griffith (D)
Paul H. Maloney (D) r. Dec. 1940
Newt V. Mills (D)
Robert L. Mouton (D)

Maine

Senators

Frederick Hale (R)
Wallace H. White, Jr. (R)

Representatives

Ralph O. Brewster (R)
James C. Oliver (R)
Clyde H. Smith (R) d. Apr. 1940
Margaret Chase Smith (R) s. 1940

Maryland

Senators

George L. Radcliffe (D)
Millard E. Tydings (D)

Representatives

William D. Byron (D)
William P. Cole, Jr. (D)
Thomas D'Alesandro, Jr. (D)
T. Alan Goldsborough (D) r. Apr. 1939
Ambrose J. Kennedy (D)
Lansdale G. Sasscer (D)
David J. Ward (D)

Massachusetts

Senators

Henry Cabot Lodge, Jr. (R)
David I. Walsh (D)

Representatives

George J. Bates (R)
Joseph E. Casey (D)
Charles R. Clason (R)
Lawrence J. Connery (D)
Thomas A. Flaherty (D)
Charles L. Gifford (R)
Arthur D. Healey (D)
Pehr G. Holmes (R)
Robert Luce (R)
John W. McCormack (D)
Joseph W. Martin, Jr. (R)
Edith Nourse Rogers (R)
George H. Tinkham (R)
Allen T. Treadway (R)
Richard B. Wigglesworth (R)

Michigan

Senators

Prentiss M. Brown (D)
Arthur H. Vandenberg (R)

Representatives

William W. Blackney (R)
Frederick V. Bradley (R)
Fred L. Crawford (R)
John D. Dingell (D)
George A. Dondero (R)
Albert J. Engel (R)
Clare E. Hoffman (R)
Frank E. Hook (D)
Bartel J. Jonkman (R) s. 1940
John Lesinski (D)
Clarence J. McLeod
Carl E. Mapes (R) d. Apr. 1939
Earl C. Michener (R)
Louis C. Rabaut (D)
Paul W. Shafer (R)
Rudolph G. Tenerowicz (D)
Jesse P. Wolcott (R)
Roy O. Woodruff (R)

Minnesota

Senators

Joseph H. Ball s. 1940
Henrik Shipstead (R)
Ernest Lundeen (Farm-Labor) d. Aug. 1940

Representatives

John G. Alexander (R)
H. Carl Andersen (R)
August H. Andresen (R)
Richard T. Buckler (Farm-Labor)
Harold Knutson (R)
Melvin J. Maas (R)
William A. Pittenger (R)
Elmer J. Ryan (D)
Oscar Youngdahl (R)

Mississippi

Senators

Theodore G. Bilbo (D)
Pat Harrison (D)

Representatives

Ross A. Collins (D)
William M. Colmer (D)
Wall Doxey (D)
Aaron L. Ford (D)
Dan R. McGehee (D)
John E. Rankin (D)
William M. Whittington (D)

Missouri

Senators

Bennett Champ Clark (D)
Harry S Truman (D)

Representatives

C. Arthur Anderson (D)
C. Jasper Bell (D)
Clarence Cannon (D)
John J. Cochran (D)
Richard M. Duncan (D)
Thomas C. Hennings, Jr. (D) r. Dec. 1940
William L. Nelson (D)

Milton A. Romjue (D)
Joseph B. Shannon (D)
Dewey Short (R)
Clyde Williams (D)
Reuben T. Wood (D)
Orville Zimmerman (D)

Montana

Senators

James E. Murray (D)
Burton K. Wheeler (D)

Representatives

James F. O'Connor (D)
Jacob Thorkelson (R)

Nebraska

Senators

Edward R. Burke (D)
George W. Norris (R)

Representatives

Harry B. Coffee (D)
Carl T. Curtis (R)
George H. Heinke (R) d. Jan.
  1940
Charles F. McLaughlin (D)
Karl Stefan (R)
John H. Sweet (R) s. 1940

Nevada

Senators

Berkeley L. Bunker (D) s. 1940
Patrick A. McCarran (D)
Key Pittman (D) d. Nov. 1940

Representatives

James G. Scrugham (D)

New Hampshire

Senators

H. Styles Bridges (R)
Charles W. Tobey (R)

Representatives

Arthur B. Jenks (R)
Foster Stearns (R)

New Jersey

Senators

W. Warren Barbour (R)
William H. Smathers (D)

Representatives

Charles A. Eaton (R)
Edward J. Hart (D)
Fred A. Hartley, Jr. (R)
Walter S. Jeffries (R)
Robert W. Kean (R)
Donald H. McLean (R)
Mary T. Norton (D)

Frank C. Osmers, Jr. (R)
D. Lane Powers (R)
George N. Seger (R) d. Aug.
  1940
William H. Sutphin (D)
J. Parnell Thomas (R)
Albert L. Vreeland (R)
Charles A. Wolverton (R)

New Mexico

Senators

Dennis Chavez (D)
Carl A. Hatch (D)

Representatives

John J. Dempsey (D)

New York

Senators

James M. Mead (D)
Robert F. Wagner (D)

Representatives

Walter G. Andrews (R)
William B. Barry (D)
Bruce Barton (R)
Sol Bloom (D)
Charles A. Buckley (D)
William T. Byrne (D)
Emanuel Celler (D)
E. Harold Cluett (R)
W. Sterling Cole (R)
Frank Crowther (R)
Francis D. Culkin (R)
Thomas H. Cullen (D)
Edward W. Curley (D) d. Jan.
  1940
John J. Delaney (D)
Samuel Dickstein (D)
Fred J. Douglas (R)
M. Michael Edelstein (D) s.
  1940
Marcellus H. Evans (D)
James H. Fay (D)
Hamilton Fish, Jr. (R)
James M. Fitzpatrick (D)
Ralph A. Gamble (R)
Joseph A. Gavagan (D)
Edwin A. Hall (R) s. 1940
Leonard W. Hall (R)
Clarence E. Hancock (R)
J. Francis Harter (R)
Martin J. Kennedy (D)
Michael J. Kennedy (D)
Eugene J. Keogh (D)
Clarence E. Kilburn (R) s. 1940
Bert Lord (R) d. May 1939
Walter A. Lynch (D) s. 1940
Vito Marcantonio (Amer.
  Labor)
Matthew J. Merritt (D)
Joseph J. O'Brien (R)
Caroline O'Day (D)
James A. O'Leary (D)
Donald L. O'Toole (D)
Wallace E. Pierce (R) d. Jan.
  1940
Joseph L. Pfeifer (D)
Daniel A. Reed (R)
Lewis K. Rockefeller (R)
Pius L. Schwert (D)
William I. Sirovich (D) d. Dec.
  1939

Andrew L. Somers (D)
Christopher D. Sullivan (D)
John Tabor (R)
James W. Wadsworth, Jr. (R)

North Carolina

Senators

Josiah W. Bailey (D)
Robert R. Reynolds (D)

Representatives

Graham A. Barden (D)
Herbert C. Bonner (D) s. 1940
Alfred L. Bulwinkle (D)
William O. Burgin (D)
J. Bayard Clark (D)
Harold D. Cooley (D)
Robert L. Doughton (D)
Carl T. Durham (D)
Alonzo D. Folger (D)
John H. Kerr (D)
Lindsay C. Warren (D) r. Oct.
  1940
Zebulon Weaver (D)

North Dakota

Senators

Lynn J. Frazier (R)
Gerald P. Nye (R)

Representatives

Usher L. Burdick (R)
William Lemke (R)

Ohio

Senators

A. Victor Donahey (D)
Robert A. Taft (R)

Representatives

William A. Ashbrook (D) d.
  Jan. 1940
George H. Bender (R)
Chester C. Bolton (R) d. Oct.
  1939
Frances P. Bolton (R) s. 1940
Clarence J. Brown (R)
Harold K. Claypool (D)
Cliff Clevenger (R)
Robert Crosser (D)
Charles H. Elston (R)
Dow W. Harter (D)
William E. Hess (R)
John F. Hunter (D)
Thomas A. Jenkins (R)
Robert F. Jones (R)
Michael J. Kirwan (D)
Earl R. Lewis (R)
J. Harry McGregor (R) s. 1940
Lycurgus L. Marshall (R)
James G. Polk (D)
Harry N. Routzohn (R)
James Seccombe (R)
Robert T. Secrest (D)
Frederick C. Smith (R)
Martin L. Sweeney (D)
John M. Vorys (R)
Dudley A. White (R)

Oklahoma

Senators

Josh Lee (D)
J. W. Elmer Thomas (D)

Representatives

Lyle H. Boren (D)
Wilburn Cartwright (D)
Wesley E. Disney (D)
Phil Ferguson (D)
Jed Johnson (D)
Sam C. Massingale (D)
A. S. Mike Monroney (D)
Jack Nichols (D)
Will Rogers (D)

Oregon

Senators

Rufus C. Holman (R)
Charles L. McNary (R)

Representatives

Homer D. Angell (R)
James W. Mott (R)
Walter M. Pierce (D)

Pennsylvania

Senators

James J. Davis (R)
Joseph F. Guffey (D)

Representatives

Robert G. Allen (D)
Patrick J. Boland (D)
Michael J. Bradley (D)
Robert J. Corbett (R)
J. Burrwood Daly (D) d. Mar.
  1939
George P. Darrow (R)
J. William Ditter (R)
Matthew A. Dunn (D)
Herman P. Eberharter (D)
Charles I. Faddis (D)
Ivor D. Fenton (R)
J. Harold Flannery (D)
Fred C. Garner (D)
Charles L. Gerlach (R)
Louis E. Graham (R)
Chester H. Gross (R)
Benjamin Jarrett (R)
J. Roland Kinzer (R)
John C. Kunkel (R)
Joseph A. McArdle (D)
John R. McDowell (R)
James P. McGranery (D)
Guy L. Moser (D)
Francis J. Myers (D)
Robert F. Rich (R)
Robert L. Rodgers (R)
Albert G. Rutherford (R)
Leon Sacks (D)
John E. Sheridan (D) s. 1940
Richard M. Simpson (R)
J. Buell Snyder (D)
Harve Tibbott (R)
James E. Van Zandt (R)
Francis E. Walter (D)
James Wolfenden (R)

Rhode Island

Senators

Peter G. Gerry (D)
Theodore F. Green (D)

Representatives

Charles F. Risk (R)
Harry Sandager (R)

South Carolina

Senators

James F. Byrnes (D)
Ellison D. Smith (D)

Representatives

Joseph R. Bryson (D)
Hampton P. Fulmer (D)
Butler B. Hare (D)
Clara Gooding McMillan (D) s.
1940
John L. McMillan (D)
Thomas S. McMillan (D) d.
Sept. 1939
James P. Richards (D)

South Dakota

Senators

William J. Bulow (D)
J. Chandler Gurney (R)

Representatives

Francis H. Case (R)
Karl E. Mundt (R)

Tennessee

Senators

Kenneth D. McKellar (D)
A. Tom Stewart (D)

Representatives

Joseph W. Byrns, Jr. (D)
Walter Chandler (D) r. Jan.
1940
Jere Cooper (D)
Wirt Courtney (D)
Clifford Davis (D) s. 1940
Albert A. Gore (D)
John Jennings, Jr. (R) s. 1940
Estes Kefauver (D)
Sam D. McReynolds (D) d.
July 1939
Herron Pearson (D)
B. Carroll Reece (R)
J. Will Taylor (R) d. Nov. 1939
Clarence W. Turner (D) d.
Mar. 1939

Texas

Senators

Tom T. Connally (D)
Morris Sheppard (D)

Representatives

Lindley Beckworth (D)
Martin Dies, Jr. (D)
Clyde L. Garrett (D)
Ed Gossett (D)
Luther A. Johnson (D)
Lyndon B. Johnson (D)
Marvin Jones (D) r. Nov. 1940
Paul J. Kilday (D)
Richard M. Kleberg (D)
Fritz G. Lanham (D)
George H. Mahon (D)
Joseph J. Mansfield (D)
Wright Patman (D)
Nat Patton (D)
William R. Poage (D)
Sam Rayburn (D)
Charles L. South (D)
Hatton W. Sumners (D)
Albert Thomas (D)
R. Ewing Thomason (D)
Milton H. West (D)

Utah

Senators

William H. King (D)
Elbert D. Thomas (D)

Representatives

Abe Murdock (D)
J. W. Robinson (D)

Vermont

Senators

Warren R. Austin (R)
Ernest W. Gibson (R) d. June
1940
Ernest W. Gibson, Jr. (R) s.
1940

Representatives

Charles A. Plumley (R)

Virginia

Senators

Harry F. Byrd (D)
Carter Glass (D)

Representatives

Schuyler Otis Bland (D)
Thomas G. Burch (D)
Colgate W. Darden, Jr. (D)
Patrick H. Drewry (D)
John W. Flannagan, Jr. (D)
A. Willis Robertson (D)
Dave E. Satterfield, Jr. (D)
Howard W. Smith (D)
Clifton A. Woodrum (D)

Washington

Senators

Homer T. Bone (D)
Lewis B. Schwellenbach (D) r.
Dec. 1940

Monrad C. Wallgren (D) s.
1940

Representatives

John M. Coffee (D)
Knute Hill (D)
Charles H. Leavy (D)
Warren G. Magnuson (D)
Martin F. Smith (D)
Monrad C. Wallgren (D) r.
Dec. 1940

West Virginia

Senators

Rush D. Holt (D)
Matthew M. Neely (D)

Representatives

Andrew Edmiston (D)
George W. Johnson (D)
John Kee (D)
Jennings Randolph (D)
Andrew C. Schiffler (R)
Joe L. Smith (D)

Wisconsin

Senators

Robert M. La Follette, Jr.
(Progressive)
Alexander Wiley (R)

Representatives

Stephen Bolles (R)
Bernard J. Gehrmann
(Progressive)
Harry W. Griswold (R)
Charles Hawks, Jr. (R)
Merlin Hull (R)
Joshua L. Johns (R)
Frank B. Keefe (R)
Reid F. Murray (R)
John C. Schafer (R)
Lewis D. Thill (R)

Wyoming

Senators

Joseph C. O'Mahoney (D)
H. H. Schwartz (D)

Representatives

Frank O. Horton (R)

Seventy-Seventh Congress

(Jan. 3, 1941, to
Jan. 3, 1943)

Presidents of the Senate: John
Nance Garner; Henry A.
Wallace
*Presidents Pro Tempore of the
Senate:* Pat Harrison; Carter
Glass

*Speaker of the House of
Representatives:* Sam Rayburn

Alabama

Senators

John H. Bankhead, II (D)
Lister Hill (D)

Representatives

Walter W. Bankhead (D) r.
Feb. 1941
Frank W. Boykin (D)
George M. Grant (D)
Sam Hobbs (D)
Pete Jarman (D)
Carter Manasco (D)
Luther Patrick (D)
John J. Sparkman (D)
Joe Starnes (D)
Henry B. Steagall (D)

Arizona

Senators

Carl Hayden (D)
Ernest W. McFarland (D)

Representatives

John R. Murdock (D)

Arkansas

Senators

Hattie W. Caraway (D)
John E. Miller (D) r. Mar.
1941
George L. Spencer (D)

Representatives

Fadjo Cravens (D)
Clyde T. Ellis (D)
Ezekiel C. Gathings (D)
Oren Harris (D)
Wilbur D. Mills (D)
William F. Norrell (D)
David D. Terry (D)

California

Senators

Sheridan Downey (D)
Hiram W. Johnson (R)

Representatives

John Z. Anderson (R)
Frank H. Buck (D) d. Sept.
1942
Albert E. Carter (R)
John M. Costello (D)
Alfred J. Elliott (D)
Harry L. Englebright (R)
Leland M. Ford (R)
Thomas F. Ford (D)
Bertrand W. Gearhart (R)
Lee E. Geyer (D) d. Oct. 1941
Carl Hinshaw (R)
Edouard V. M. Izac (D)
Ward Johnson (R)

Cecil R. King (D) s. 1942
Charles Kramer (D)
Clarence F. Lea (D, R)
Thomas Rolph (R)
Harry R. Sheppard (D)
John H. Tolan (D)
H. Jerry Voorhis (D)
Richard J. Welch (R)

Colorado

Senators

Alva B. Adams (D) d. Dec.
  1941
Edwin C. Johnson (D)
Eugene D. Millikin (R) s. 1942

Representatives

J. Edgar Chenoweth (D)
William S. Hill (R)
Lawrence Lewis (D)
Robert F. Rockwell (R)
Edward T. Taylor (D) d. Sept.
  1941

Connecticut

Senators

John A. Danaher (R)
Francis T. Maloney (D)

Representatives

LeRoy D. Downs (D)
William J. Fitzgerald (D)
Herman P. Kopplemann (D)
Lucien J. Maciora (D)
James A. Shanley (D)
J. Joseph Smith (D) r. Nov.
  1942
Joseph E. Talbot (R) s. 1942

Delaware

Senators

James H. Hughes (D)
James M. Tunnell (D)

Representatives

Philip A. Traynor (D)

Florida

Senators

Charles O. Andrews (D)
Claude D. Pepper (D)

Representatives

Arthur P. Cannon (D)
Robert A. Green (D)
Joe Hendricks (D)
J. Hardin Peterson (D)
Robert L. F. Sikes (D)

Georgia

Senators

Walter F. George (D)

Richard B. Russell (D)

Representatives

Paul Brown (D)
A. Sidney Camp (D)
Edward E. Cox (D)
John S. Gibson (D)
Stephen Pace (D)
Hugh Peterson (D)
Robert Ramspeck (D)
Malcolm C. Tarver (D)
Carl Vinson (D)
B. Frank Whelchel (D)

Idaho

Senators

D. Worth Clark (D)
John Thomas (R)

Representatives

Henry C. Dworshak (R)
Compton I. White (D)

Illinois

Senators

C. Wayland Brooks (R)
Scott W. Lucas (D)

Representatives

Leo E. Allen (R)
Leslie C. Arends (R)
Laurence F. Arnold (D)
James M. Barnes (D)
Harry P. Beam (D) r. Dec.
  1942
Cecil W. Bishop (R)
Robert B. Chiperfield (R)
Stephen A. Day (R)
Charles S. Dewey (R)
Everett M. Dirksen (R)
James V. Heidinger (R)
Evan Howell (R)
Anton J. Johnson (R)
Edward A. Kelly (D)
Leo Kocialkowski (D)
Raymond S. McKeough (D)
Anton F. Maciejewski (D) r.
  Dec. 1942
Noah M. Mason (R)
Arthur W. Mitchell (D)
George A. Paddock (R)
Chauncey W. Reed (R)
Adolph J. Sabath (D)
Edwin M. Schaefer (D)
Leonard W. Schuetz (D)
William G. Stratton (R)
Jessie Sumner (R)
William H. Wheat (R)

Indiana

Senators

Frederick Van Nuys (D)
Raymond E. Willis (R)

Representatives

John W. Boehne, Jr. (D)
George W. Gillie (R)
Robert A. Grant (R)

Charles A. Halleck (R)
Forest A. Harness (R)
Noble J. Johnson (R)
Gerald W. Landis (R)
William H. Larrabee (D)
Louis Ludlow (D)
William T. Schulte (D)
Raymond S. Springer (R)
Earl Wilson (R)

Iowa

Senators

Guy M. Gillette (D)
Clyde L. Herring (D)

Representatives

Paul Cunningham (R)
Fred C. Gilchrist (R)
John W. Gwynne (R)
Vincent F. Harrington (D) r.
  Sept. 1942
William S. Jacobsen (D)
Ben F. Jensen (R)
Karl M. LeCompte (R)
Thomas E. Martin (R)
Harry E. Narey (R) s. 1942
Henry O. Talle (R)

Kansas

Senators

Arthur Capper (R)
Clyde M. Reed (R)

Representatives

Frank Carlson (R)
Ulysses S. Guyer (R)
Clifford R. Hope (R)
John M. Houston (D)
William P. Lambertson (R)
Edward H. Rees (R)
Thomas D. Winter (R)

Kentucky

Senators

Alben W. Barkley (D)
Albert B. Chandler (D)

Representatives

Joe B. Bates (D)
Virgil M. Chapman (D)
Edward W. Creal (D)
Noble J. Gregory (D)
Andrew J. May (D)
Emmet O'Neal (D)
John M. Robsion (R)
Brent Spence (D)
Beverly M. Vincent (D)

Louisiana

Senators

Allen J. Ellender (D)
John H. Overton (D)

Representatives

A. Leonard Allen (D)

T. Hale Boggs (D)
Overton Brooks (D)
James Domengeaux (D)
F. Edward Hebert (D)
Newt V. Mills (D)
Vance Plauche (D)
Jared Y. Sanders, Jr. (D)

Maine

Senators

Ralph O. Brewster (R)
Wallace H. White, Jr. (R)

Representatives

Frank Fellows (R)
James C. Oliver (R)
Margaret Chase Smith (R)

Maryland

Senators

George L. Radcliffe (D)
Millard E. Tydings (D)

Representatives

Katharine E. Byron (D)
William D. Byron (D) d. Feb.
  1941
William P. Cole, Jr. (D) r. Oct.
  1942
Thomas D'Alesandro, Jr. (D)
John A. Meyer (D)
Lansdale G. Sasscer (D)
David J. Ward (D)

Massachusetts

Senators

Henry Cabot Lodge, Jr. (R)
David I. Walsh (D)

Representatives

George J. Bates (R)
Joseph E. Casey (D)
Charles R. Clason (R)
Lawrence J. Connery (D) d.
  Oct. 1941
Thomas H. Eliot (D)
Thomas A. Flaherty (D)
Charles L. Gifford (R)
Arthur D. Healey (D) r. Aug.
  1942
Pehr G. Holmes (R)
Thomas J. Lane (D) s. 1942
John W. McCormack (D)
Joseph W. Martin, Jr. (R)
Edith Nourse Rogers (R)
George H. Tinkham (R)
Allen T. Treadway (R)
Richard B. Wigglesworth (R)

Michigan

Senators

Prentiss M. Brown (D)
Arthur H. Vandenberg (R)

Representatives

William W. Blackney (R)
Frederick V. Bradley (R)
Fred L. Crawford (R)
John D. Dingell (D)
George A. Dondero (R)
Albert J. Engel (R)
Clare E. Hoffman (R)
Frank E. Hook (D)
Bartel J. Jonkman (R)
John Lesinski (D)
Earl C. Michener (R)
George D. O'Brien (D)
Louis C. Rabaut (D)
Paul W. Shafer (R)
Rudolph G. Tenerowicz (D)
Jesse P. Wolcott (R)
Roy O. Woodruff (R)

Minnesota

Senators

Joseph H. Ball (R) ta. 1941-
1942
Arthur E. Nelson (R) s. 1942
Henrik Shipstead (R)

Representatives

H. Carl Andersen (R)
August H. Andresen (R)
Richard T. Buckler (Farm-
Labor)
Richard P. Gale (R)
Harold Knutson (R)
Melvin J. Maas (R)
Joseph P. O'Hara (R)
William A. Pittenger (R)
Oscar Youngdahl (R)

Mississippi

Senators

Theodore G. Bilbo (D)
Wall Doxey (D)
James O. Eastland (D) ta. 1941
Pat Harrison (D) d. June 1941

Representatives

Ross A. Collins (D)
William M. Colmer (D)
Wall Doxey (D) r. Sept. 1941
Aaron L. Ford (D)
Dan R. McGehee (D)
John E. Rankin (D)
Jamie L. Whitten (D)
William R. Whittingham (D)

Missouri

Senators

Bennett Champ Clark (D)
Harry S Truman (D)

Representatives

C. Jasper Bell (D)
Philip A. Bennett (R) d. Dec.
1942
Clarence Cannon (D)
John J. Cochran (D)
Richard M. Duncan (D)
William L. Nelson (D)

Walter C. Ploeser (R)
Milton A. Romjue (D)
Joseph B. Shannon (D)
Dewey Short (R)
John B. Sullivan (D)
Clyde Williams (D)
Orville Zimmerman (D)

Montana

Senators

James E. Murray (D)
Burton K. Wheeler (D)

Representatives

James F. O'Connor (D)
Jeannette Rankin (R)

Nebraska

Senators

Hugh A. Butler (R)
George W. Norris (R)

Representatives

Harry B. Coffee (D)
Oren S. Copeland (R)
Carl T. Curtis (R)
Charles F. McLaughlin (D)
Karl Stefan (R)

Nevada

Senators

Berkeley L. Bunker (R) ta.
1941-1942
Patrick A. McCarran (D)
James G. Scrugham (D) s. 1942

Representatives

James G. Scrugham (D)

New Hampshire

Senators

H. Styles Bridges (R)
Charles W. Tobey (R)

Representatives

Arthur B. Jenks (R)
Foster Stearns (R)

New Jersey

Senators

W. Warren Barbour (R)
William H. Smathers (D)

Representatives

Gordon Canfield (R)
Charles A. Eaton (R)
Edward J. Hart (D)
Fred A. Hartley, Jr. (R)
Robert W. Kean (R)
Donald H. McLean (R)
Mary T. Norton (D)

Frank C. Osmers, Jr. (R)
D. Lane Powers (R)
William H. Sutphin (D)
J. Parnell Thomas (R)
Albert L. Vreeland (R)
Elmer H. Wene (D)
Charles A. Wolverton (R)

New Mexico

Senators

Dennis Chavez (D)
Carl A. Hatch (D)

Representatives

Clinton P. Anderson (D)

New York

Senators

James M. Mead (D)
Robert F. Wagner (D)

Representatives

Walter G. Andrews (R)
William B. Barry (D)
Joseph C. Baldwin (R)
Alfred F. Beiter (D)
Sol Bloom (D)
Charles A. Buckley (D)
John C. Butler (R)
William T. Byrne (D)
Louis J. Capozzoli (D)
Emanuel Celler (D)
E. Harold Cluett (R)
W. Sterling Cole (R)
Frank Crowther (R)
Francis D. Culkin (R)
Thomas H. Cullen (D)
John J. Delaney (D)
Samuel Dickstein (D)
Fred J. Douglas (R)
M. Michael Edelstein (D) d.
June 1941
Hamilton Fish, Jr. (R)
James M. Fitzpatrick (D)
Ralph A. Gamble (R)
Joseph A. Gavagan (D)
Edwin A. Hall (R)
Leonard W. Hall (R)
Clarence E. Hancock (R)
James J. Heffernan (D)
Martin J. Kennedy (D)
Michael J. Kennedy (D)
Eugene J. Keogh (D)
Clarence E. Kilburn (R)
Arthur G. Klein (D)
Walter A. Lynch (D)
Vito Marcantonio (Amer.
Labor)
Matthew J. Merritt (D)
Joseph J. O'Brien (R)
Caroline O. Day (D)
James A. O'Leary (D)
Donald L. O'Toole (D)
Joseph L. Pfeifer (D)
William T. Pheiffer (R)
Daniel A. Reed (R)
Lewis K. Rockefeller (R)
Pius L. Schwert (D) d. Mar.
1941
Kenneth F. Simpson (R) d. Jan.
1941
Andrew L. Somers (D)
John Taber (R)

James W. Wadsworth, Jr. (R)

North Carolina

Senators

Josiah W. Bailey (D)
Robert R. Reynolds (D)

Representatives

Graham A. Barden (D)
Herbert C. Bonner (D)
Alfred L. Bulwinkle (D)
William O. Burgin (D)
J. Bayard Clark (D)
Harold D. Cooley (D)
Robert L. Doughton (D)
Carl T. Durham (D)
Alonzo D. Folger (D) d. Apr.
1941
John H. Folger (D)
John H. Kerr (D)
Zebulon Weaver (D)

North Dakota

Senators

Gerald P. Nye (R)
William Langer (R)

Representatives

Usher L. Burdick (R)
Charles R. Robertson (R)

Ohio

Senators

Harold H. Burton (R)
Robert A. Taft (R)

Representatives

Albert D. Baumhart, Jr. (R) r.
Sept. 1942
George H. Bender (R)
Frances P. Bolton (R)
Clarence J. Brown (R)
Cliff Clevenger (R)
Harold K. Claypool (D)
Robert Crosser (D)
Jacob E. Davis (D)
Charles H. Elston (R)
Dow W. Harter (D)
William E. Hess (R)
Greg J. Holbrock (D)
John F. Hunter (D)
Lawrence E. Imhoff (D)
Thomas A. Jenkins (R)
Robert F. Jones (R)
Michael J. Kirwan (D)
J. Harry McGregor (R)
Robert T. Secrest (D) r. Aug.
1942
Frederick C. Smith (R)
Martin L. Sweeney (D)
William R. Thom (D)
John M. Vorys (R)
Stephen M. Young (D)

Oklahoma

Senators

Josh Lee (D)
J. W. Elmer Thomas (D)

Representatives

Lyle H. Boren (D)
Wilburn Cartwright (D)
Wesley E. Disney (D)
Jed Johnson (D)
Sam C. Massingale (D) d. Jan.
 1941
A. S. Mike Monroney (D)
Jack Nichols (D)
Ross Rizley (R)
Will Rogers (D)
Victor Wickersham (D)

Oregon

Senators

Rufus C. Holman (R)
Charles L. McNary (R)

Representatives

Homer D. Angell (R)
James W. Mott (R)
Walter M. Pierce (D)

Pennsylvania

Senators

James J. Davis (R)
Joseph F. Guffey (D)

Representatives

Michael J. Bradley (D)
Patrick J. Boland (D) d. May
 1942
Veronica Boland (D)
J. William Ditter (R)
Herman P. Eberharter (D)
Charles I. Faddis (D) r. Dec.
 1942
Ivor D. Fenton (R)
J. Harold Flannery (D) r. Jan.
 1942
Charles L. Gerlach (R)
Wilson D. Gillette (R) s. 1941
Louis E. Graham (R)
Harry L. Haines (D)
Elmer J. Holland (D) s. 1942
Benjamin Jarrett (R)
Augustine B. Kelley (D)
J. Roland Kinzer (R)
John C. Kunkel (R)
Joseph A. McArdle (D) r. Jan.
 1942
James P. McGranery (D)
Thomas B. Miller (R)
Guy L. Moser (D)
Francis J. Myers (D)
Robert F. Rich (R)
Robert L. Rodgers (R)
Albert G. Rutherford (R) d.
 Aug. 1941
Leon Sacks (D)
Thomas E. Scanlon (D)
Hugh D. Scott, Jr. (R)
John E. Sheridan (D)
Richard M. Simpson (R)

Francis R. Smith (D)
J. Buell Snyder (D)
Harve Tibbott (R)
James E. Van Zandt (R)
Francis E. Walter (D)
Samuel A. Weiss (D)
James A. Wright (D)
James Wolfenden (R)

Rhode Island

Senators

Peter G. Gerry (D)
Theodore F. Green (D)

Representatives

John E. Fogarty (D)
Aime J. Forand (D)

South Carolina

Senators

James F. Byrnes (D) r. July
 1941
Burnet R. Maybank (D)
Roger C. Peace (D) ta. 1941
Ellison D. Smith (D)

Representatives

Joseph R. Bryson (D)
Hampton P. Fulmer (D)
Butler B. Hare (D)
John L. McMillan (D)
James P. Richards (D)
L. Mendel Rivers (D)

South Dakota

Senators

William J. Bulow (D)
J. Chandler Gurney (R)

Representatives

Francis H. Case (R)
Karl E. Mundt (R)

Tennessee

Senators

Kenneth D. McKellar (D)
A. Tom Stewart (D)

Representatives

Jere Cooper (D)
Wirt Courtney (D)
Clifford Davis (D)
Albert A. Gore (D)
John Jennings, Jr. (R)
Estes Kefauver (D)
Herron Pearson (D)
J. Percy Priest (D)
B. Carroll Reece (R)

Texas

Senators

Tom T. Connally (D)

W. Lee O'Daniel (D)
Morris Sheppard (D) d. Apr.
 1941

Representatives

Lindley Beckworth (D)
Martin Dies, Jr. (D)
Ed Gossett (D)
Luther A. Johnson (D)
Lyndon B. Johnson (D)
Paul J. Kilday (D)
Richard M. Kleberg (D)
Fritz G. Lanham (D)
George H. Mahon (D)
Joseph J. Mansfield (D)
Wright Patman (D)
Nat Patton (D)
William R. Poage (D)
Sam Rayburn (D)
Sam M. Russell (D)
Charles L. South (D)
Hatton W. Sumners (D)
Albert Thomas (D)
R. Ewing Thomason (D)
Milton H. West (D)
Eugene Worley (D)

Utah

Senators

Abe Murdock (D)
Elbert D. Thomas (D)

Representatives

Walter K. Granger (D)
J. W. Robinson (D)

Vermont

Senators

George D. Aiken (R)
Warren R. Austin (R)

Representatives

Charles A. Plumley (R)

Virginia

Senators

Harry F. Byrd (D)
Carter Glass (D)

Representatives

Schuyler Otis Bland (D)
Thomas G. Burch (D)
Colgate W. Darden, Jr. (D) r.
 Mar. 1941
Patrick H. Drewry (D)
John W. Flannagan, Jr. (D)
Winder R. Harris (D)
A. Willis Robertson (D)
Dave E. Satterfield, Jr. (D)
Howard W. Smith (D)
Clifton A. Woodrum (D)

Washington

Senators

Homer T. Bone (D)

Monrad C. Wallgren (D)

Representatives

John M. Coffee (D)
Knute Hill (D)
Henry M. Jackson (D)
Charles H. Leavy (D) r. Aug.
 1942
Warren G. Magnuson (D)
Martin F. Smith (D)

West Virginia

Senators

Harley M. Kilgore (D)
Matthew M. Neely (D) r. Jan.
 1941
Joseph Rosier (D) ta. 1941
Hugh I. Shott (R) s. 1942

Representatives

Andrew Edmiston (D)
George W. Johnson (D)
John Kee (D)
Robert L. Ramsay (D)
Jennings Randolph (D)
Joe L. Smith (D)

Wisconsin

Senators

Robert M. La Follette, Jr.
 (Progressive)
Alexander Wiley (R)

Representatives

Stephen Bolles (R) d. July 1941
Bernard J. Gehrmann
 (Progressive)
Merlin Hull (R)
Joshua L. Johns (R)
Frank B. Keefe (R)
Reid F. Murray (R)
Harry Sauthoff (Progressive)
Lawrence H. Smith (R)
William H. Stevenson (R)
Lewis D. Thill (R)
Thaddeus F. B. Wasielewski (D)

Wyoming

Senators

Joseph C. O'Mahoney (D)
H. H. Schwartz (D)

Representatives

John J. McIntyre (D)

Seventy-Eighth Congress

(Jan. 3, 1943, to
Jan. 3, 1945)

President of the Senate: Henry
 A. Wallace
*President Pro Tempore of the
 Senate:* Carter Glass

Speaker of the House of Representatives: Sam Rayburn

Alabama

Senators

John H. Bankhead, II (D)
Lister Hill (D)

Representatives

George W. Andrews (D) s.
1944
Frank W. Boykin (D)
George M. Grant (D)
Sam Hobbs (D)
Pete Jarman (D)
Carter Manasco (D)
John P. Newsome (D)
John J. Sparkman (D)
Joe Starnes (D)
Henry B. Steagall (D) d. Nov.
1943

Arizona

Senators

Carl Hayden (D)
Ernest W. McFarland (D)

Representatives

Richard F. Harless (D)
John R. Murdock (D)

Arkansas

Senators

Hattie W. Caraway (D)
John L. McClellan (D)

Representatives

Fadjo Cravens (D)
J. William Fulbright (D)
Ezekiel C. Gathings (D)
Oren Harris (D)
Brooks Hays (D)
Wilbur D. Mills (D)
William F. Norrell (D)

California

Senators

Sheridan Downey (D)
Hiram W. Johnson (R)

Representatives

John Z. Anderson (R)
Albert E. Carter (R)
John M. Costello (D)
Alfred J. Elliott (D)
Clair Engle (D)
Harry L. Englebright (R)
Thomas F. Ford (D)
Bertrand W. Gearhart (R)
Carl Hinshaw (R)
Chet Holifield (D)
Edouard V. M. Izac (D)
Leroy Johnson (R)
Ward Johnson (R)
Cecil R. King (D)

Clarence F. Lea (D, R)
George E. Outland (D)
John Phillips (R)
Norris Poulson (R)
Will Rogers, Jr. (D)
Thomas Rolph (R)
Harry R. Sheppard (D)
John H. Tolan (D)
H. Jerry Voorhis (D)
Richard J. Welch (R)

Colorado

Senators

Edwin C. Johnson (D)
Eugene D. Millikin (R)

Representatives

J. Edgar Chenoweth (D)
Dean M. Gillespie (R)
William S. Hill (R)
Lawrence Lewis (D)
Robert F. Rockwell (R)

Connecticut

Senators

John A. Danaher (R)
Francis T. Maloney (D)

Representatives

Ranulf Compton (R)
Clare Boothe Luce (R)
John D. McWilliams (R)
William J. Miller (R)
Boleslaus J. Monkiewicz (R)
Joseph E. Talbot (R)

Delaware

Senators

C. Douglass Buck (R)
James M. Tunnell (D)

Representatives

Earle D. Willey (R)

Florida

Senators

Charles O. Andrews (D)
Claude D. Pepper (D)

Representatives

Arthur P. Cannon (D)
Robert A. Green (D)
Joe Hendricks (D)
J. Hardin Peterson (D)
Emory H. Price (D)
Robert L. F. Sikes (D)

Georgia

Senators

Walter F. George (D)
Richard B. Russell (D)

Representatives

Paul Brown (D)
A. Sidney Camp (D)
Edward E. Cox (D)
John S. Gibson (D)
Stephen Pace (D)
Hugh Peterson (D)
Robert Ramspeck (D)
Malcolm C. Tarver (D)
Carl Vinson (D)
B. Frank Whelchel (D)

Idaho

Senators

D. Worth Clark (D)
John Thomas (R)

Representatives

Henry C. Dworshak (R)
Compton I. White (D)

Illinois

Senators

C. Wayland Brooks (R)
Scott W. Lucas (D)

Representatives

Leo E. Allen (R)
Leslie C. Arends (R)
Cecil W. Bishop (R)
Fred E. Busbey (R)
Robert B. Chiperfield (R)
Ralph E. Church (R)
William L. Dawson (D)
Stephen A. Day (R)
Charles S. Dewey (R)
Everett M. Dirksen (R)
Martin Gorski (D)
Thomas S. Gordon (D)
James V. Heidinger (R)
Evan Howell (R)
Anton J. Johnson (R)
Calvin D. Johnson (R)
Rolla C. McMillen (R) s. 1944
Noah M. Mason (R)
Thomas J. O'Brien (D)
Chauncey W. Reed (R)
William A. Rowan (D)
Adolph J. Sabath (D)
Leonard W. Schuetz (D) d.
Feb. 1944
Sidney E. Simpson (R)
Jessie Sumner (R)
Charles W. Vursell (R)
William H. Wheat (R) d. Jan.
1944

Indiana

Senators

Samuel D. Jackson (D) ta. 1944
William E. Jenner (R) s. 1944
Frederick Van Nuys (D) d. Jan.
1944
Raymond E. Willis (R)

Representatives

George W. Gillie (R)
Robert A. Grant (R)

Charles A. Halleck (R)
Forest A. Harness (R)
Noble J. Johnson (R)
Charles M. LaFollette (R)
Gerald W. Landis (R)
Louis Ludlow (D)
Ray J. Madden (D)
Earl Wilson (R)
Raymond S. Springer (R)

Iowa

Senators

Guy M. Gillette (D)
George A. Wilson (R)

Representatives

Paul Cunningham (R)
Fred C. Gilchrist (R)
John W. Gwynne (R)
Charles B. Hoeven (R)
Ben F. Jensen (R)
Karl M. LeCompte (R)
Thomas E. Martin (R)
Henry O. Talle (R)

Kansas

Senators

Arthur Capper (R)
Clyde M. Reed (R)

Representatives

Frank Carlson (R)
Ulysses S. Guyer (R) d. June
1943
Clifford R. Hope (R)
William P. Lambertson (R)
Edward H. Rees (R)
Errett P. Scrivner (R)
Thomas D. Winter (R)

Kentucky

Senators

Alben W. Barkley (D)
Albert B. Chandler (D)

Representatives

Joe B. Bates (D)
Chester O. Carrier (R)
Virgil M. Chapman (D)
Edward W. Creal (D) d. Oct.
1943
Noble J. Gregory (D)
Andrew J. May (D)
Emmet O'Neal (D)
John M. Robsion (R)
Brent Spence (D)
Beverly M. Vincent (D)

Louisiana

Senators

John H. Overton (D)
Allen J. Ellender (D)

Representatives

A. Leonard Allen (D)

Overton Brooks (D)
James Domengeaux (D) r. Apr. 1944
F. Edward Hebert (D)
Henry D. Larcade, Jr. (D)
Charles E. McKenzie (D)
Paul H. Maloney (D)
James H. Morrison (D)

Maine

Senators

Ralph O. Brewster (R)
Wallace H. White, Jr. (R)

Representatives

Frank Fellows (R)
Robert Hale (R)
Margaret Chase Smith (R)

Maryland

Senators

George L. Radcliffe (D)
Millard E. Tydings (D)

Representatives

H. Streett Baldwin (D)
J. Glenn Beall (R)
Thomas D'Alesandro, Jr. (D)
Daniel Ellison (R)
Lansdale G. Sasscer (D)
David J. Ward (D)

Massachusetts

Senators

Henry Cabot Lodge, Jr. (R) r. Feb. 1944
David I. Walsh (D)
Sinclair Weeks (R) s. 1944

Representatives

George J. Bates (R)
Charles R. Clason (R)
James M. Curley (D)
Charles L. Gifford (R)
Angier L. Goodwin (R)
Christian A. Herter (R)
Pehr G. Holmes (R)
Thomas J. Lane (D)
John W. McCormack (D)
Joseph W. Martin, Jr. (R)
Philip J. Philbin (D)
Edith Nourse Rogers (R)
Allen T. Treadway (R)
Richard B. Wigglesworth (R)

Michigan

Senators

Homer Ferguson (R)
Arthur H. Vandenberg (R)

Representatives

John B. Bennett (R)
William W. Blackney (R)
Frederick V. Bradley (R)
Fred L. Crawford (R)

John D. Dingell (D)
George A. Dondero (R)
Albert J. Engel (R)
Clare E. Hoffman (R)
Bartel J. Jonkman (R)
John Lesinski (D)
Earl C. Michener (R)
George D. O'Brien (D)
Louis C. Rabaut (D)
George G. Sadowski (D)
Paul W. Shafer (R)
Jesse P. Wolcott (R)
Roy O. Woodruff (R)

Minnesota

Senators

Joseph H. Ball (R)
Henrik Shipstead (R)

Representatives

H. Carl Andersen (R)
August H. Andresen (R)
Richard P. Gale (R)
Harold C. Hagen (Farm-Labor)
Walter H. Judd (R)
Harold Knutson (R)
Melvin J. Maas (R)
Joseph P. O'Hara (R)
William A. Pittenger (R)

Mississippi

Senators

Theodore G. Bilbo (D)
James O. Eastland (D)

Representatives

Thomas G. Abernethy (D)
William M. Colmer (D)
Dan R. McGehee (D)
John E. Rankin (D)
W. Arthur Winstead (D)
Jamie L. Whitten (D)
William M. Whittington (D)

Missouri

Senators

Bennett Champ Clark (D)
Harry S Truman (D)

Representatives

Samuel W. Arnold (R)
C. Jasper Bell (D)
Marion T. Bennett (R)
Clarence Cannon (D)
John J. Cochran (D)
William C. Cole (R)
William P. Elmer (R)
Louis E. Miller (R)
Walter C. Ploeser (R)
Max Schwabe (R)
Dewey Short (R)
Roger C. Slaughter (D)
Orville Zimmerman (D)

Montana

Senators

James E. Murray (D)
Burton K. Wheeler (D)

Representatives

Mike Mansfield (D)
James F. O'Connor (D)

Nebraska

Senators

Hugh A. Butler (R)
Kenneth S. Wherry (R)

Representatives

Howard H. Buffett (R)
Carl T. Curtis (R)
Arthur L. Miller (R)
Karl Stefan (R)

Nevada

Senators

Patrick A. McCarran (D)
James G. Scrugham (D)

Representatives

Maurice J. Sullivan (D)

New Hampshire

Senators

H. Styles Bridges (R)
Charles W. Tobey (R)

Representatives

Chester E. Merrow (R)
Foster Stearns (R)

New Jersey

Senators

W. Warren Barbour (R) d. Nov. 1943
Albert W. Hawkes (R)
H. Alexander Smith (R) s. 1944
Arthur Walsh (D) ta. 1943-1944

Representatives

James C. Auchincloss (R)
Gordon Canfield (R)
Charles A. Eaton (R)
Edward J. Hart (D)
Fred A. Hartley, Jr. (R)
Robert W. Kean (R)
Donald H. McLean (R)
Mary T. Norton (D)
D. Lane Powers (R)
Frank L. Sundstrom (R)
J. Parnell Thomas (R)
Harry L. Towe (R)
Elmer H. Wene (D)
Charles A. Wolverton (R)

New Mexico

Senators

Dennis Chavez (D)
Carl A. Hatch (D)

Representatives

Clinton P. Anderson (D)
Antonio M. Fernandez (D)

New York

Senators

James M. Mead (D)
Robert F. Wagner (D)

Representatives

Walter G. Andrews (R)
Joseph C. Baldwin (R)
William B. Barry (D)
Sol Bloom (D)
Ellsworth B. Buck (R) s. 1944
Charles A. Buckley (D)
Thomas F. Burchill (D)
John C. Butler (R)
William T. Byrne (D)
Emanuel Celler (D)
Louis J. Capozzoli (D)
W. Sterling Cole (R)
Francis D. Culkin (R) d. Aug. 1943
Thomas H. Cullen (D) d. Mar. 1944
John J. Delaney (D)
Samuel Dickstein (D)
Fred J. Douglas (R)
James H. Fay (D)
Hamilton Fish, Jr. (R)
James M. Fitzpatrick (D)
Hadwen C. Fuller (R) s. 1943
Ralph A. Gamble (R)
Joseph A. Gavagan (D) r. Dec. 1943
Edwin A. Hall (R)
Leonard W. Hall (R)
Clarence E. Hancock (R)
James J. Heffernan (D)
Bernard W. Kearney (R)
Martin J. Kennedy (D)
Eugene J. Keogh (D)
Clarence E. Kilburn (R)
Arthur G. Klein (D)
Jay LeFevre (R)
Walter A. Lynch (D)
Vito Marcantonio (Amer. Labor)
Matthew J. Merritt (D)
Joseph Mruk (R)
Joseph J. O'Brien (R)
James A. O'Leary (R) d. Mar. 1944
Donald L. O'Toole (D)
Joseph L. Pfeifer (D)
Daniel A. Reed (R)
John J. Rooney (D) s. 1944
Andrew L. Somers (D)
Winifred C. Stanley (R)
John Taber (R)
Dean P. Taylor (R)
James H. Torrens (D) s. 1944
James W. Wadsworth, Jr. (R)

North Carolina

Senators

Josiah W. Bailey (D)
Robert R. Reynolds (D)

Representatives

Graham A. Barden (D)
Herbert C. Bonner (D)
Alfred L. Bulwinkle (D)
William O. Burgin (D)
J. Bayard Clark (D)
Harold D. Cooley (D)
Robert L. Doughton (D)
Carl T. Durham (D)
John H. Folger (D)
John H. Kerr (D)
Cameron Morrison (D)
Zebulon Weaver (D)

North Dakota

Senators

William Langer (R)
Gerald P. Nye (R)

Representatives

Usher L. Burdick (R)
William Lemke (R)

Ohio

Senators

Harold H. Burton (R)
Robert A. Taft (R)

Representatives

George H. Bender (R)
Frances P. Bolton (R)
Walter E. Brehm (R)
Clarence J. Brown (R)
Henderson H. Carson (R)
Cliff Clevenger (R)
Robert Crosser (D)
Charles H. Elston (R)
Michael A. Feighan (D)
Percy W. Griffiths (R)
William E. Hess (R)
Harry P. Jeffrey (R)
Thomas A. Jenkins (R)
Robert F. Jones (R)
Michael J. Kirwan (D)
Earl R. Lewis (R)
Edward O. McCowen (R)
J. Harry McGregor (R)
Homer A. Ramey (R)
Ed Rowe (R)
Frederick C. Smith (R)
John M. Vorys (R)
Alvin F. Weichel (R)

Oklahoma

Senators

Edward H. Moore (R)
J. W. Elmer Thomas (D)

Representatives

Lyle H. Boren (D)

Wesley E. Disney (D)
Jed Johnson (D)
A. S. Mike Monroney (D)
Jack Nichols (D) r. July 1943
Ross Rizley (R)
Paul Stewart (D)
William G. Stigler (D) s. 1944
Victor Wickersham (D)

Oregon

Senators

Guy Cordon (R) s. 1944
Rufus C. Holman (R)
Charles L. McNary (R) d. Feb.
1944

Representatives

Homer D. Angell (R)
Harris Ellsworth (R)
James W. Mott (R)
Lowell Stockman (R)

Pennsylvania

Senators

James J. Davis (R)
Joseph F. Guffey (D)

Representatives

Michael J. Bradley (D)
D. Emmert Brumbaugh (R)
J. William Ditter (R) d. Nov.
1943
Herman P. Eberharter (D)
Ivor D. Fenton (R)
Grant Furlong (D)
James Gallagher (R)
Leon H. Gavin (R)
Charles L. Gerlach (R)
Wilson D. Gillette (R)
Louis E. Graham (R)
Chester H. Gross (R)
Daniel K. Hoch (D)
Augustine B. Kelley (D)
J. Roland Kinzer (R)
John C. Kunkel (R)
Samuel K. McConnell (R) s.
1944
James P. McGranery (D) r.
Nov. 1943
Thomas B. Miller (R)
John W. Murphy (D)
Francis J. Myers (D)
C. Frederick Pracht (R)
Joseph M. Pratt (R) s. 1944
Robert L. Rodgers (R)
Thomas E. Scanlon (D)
Hugh D. Scott, Jr. (R)
John E. Sheridan (D)
Richard M. Simpson (R)
J. Buell Snyder (D)
Harve Tibbott (R)
William I. Troutman (R) r. Jan.
1945
James E. Van Zandt (R) r.
Sept. 1943
Francis E. Walter (D)
Samuel A. Weiss (D)
James Wolfenden (R)
James A. Wright (D)

Rhode Island

Senators

Peter G. Gerry (D)
Theodore F. Green (D)

Representatives

John E. Fogarty (D) r. Dec.
1944
Aime J. Forand (D)

South Carolina

Senators

Wilton E. Hall (D) s. 1944
Burnet R. Maybank (D)
Ellison D. Smith (D) d. Nov.
1944

Representatives

Joseph R. Bryson (D)
Hampton P. Fulmer (D) d. Oct.
1944
Willa L. Fulmer (D) s. 1944
Butler B. Hare (D)
John L. McMillan (D)
James P. Richards (D)
L. Mendel Rivers (D)

South Dakota

Senators

Harlan J. Bushfield (R)
J. Chandler Gurney (R)

Representatives

Francis H. Case (R)
Karl E. Mundt (R)

Tennessee

Senators

Kenneth D. McKellar (D)
A. Tom Stewart (D)

Representatives

Jere Cooper (D)
Wirt Courtney (D)
Clifford Davis (D)
Albert A. Gore (D)
John Jennings, Jr. (R)
Estes Kefauver (D)
Jim Nance McCord (D)
Thomas J. Murray (D)
J. Percy Priest (D)
B. Carroll Reece (R)

Texas

Senators

Tom T. Connally (D)
W. Lee O'Daniel (D)

Representatives

Lindley Beckworth (D)
Martin Dies, Jr. (D)

O. Clark Fisher (D)
Ed Gossett (D)
Luther A. Johnson (D)
Lyndon B. Johnson (D)
Paul J. Kilday (D)
Richard M. Kleberg (D)
Fritz G. Lanham (D)
George H. Mahon (D)
Joseph J. Mansfield (D)
Wright Patman (D)
Nat Patton (D)
William R. Poage (D)
Sam Rayburn (D)
Sam M. Russell (D)
Hatton W. Sumners (D)
Albert Thomas (D)
R. Ewing Thomason (D)
Milton H. West (D)
Eugene Worley (D)

Utah

Senators

Abe Murdock (D)
Elbert D. Thomas (D)

Representatives

Walter K. Granger (D)
J. W. Robinson (D)

Vermont

Senators

George D. Aiken (R)
Warren R. Austin (R)

Representatives

Charles A. Plumley (R)

Virginia

Senators

Harry F. Byrd (D)
Carter Glass (D)

Representatives

Schuyler Otis Bland (D)
Thomas G. Burch (D)
Ralph H. Daughton (D)
Patrick H. Drewry (D)
John W. Flannagan, Jr. (D)
Winder R. Harris (D)
A. Willis Robertson (D)
Dave E. Satterfield, Jr. (D)
Howard W. Smith (D)
Clifton A. Woodrum (D)

Washington

Senators

Homer T. Bone (D)
Warren G. Magnuson (D) s.
1944
Monrad C. Wallgren (D)

Representatives

John M. Coffee (D)
Hal Holmes (R)
Walter F. Horan (R)

Henry M. Jackson (D)
Warren G. Magnuson (D)
Fred Norman (R)

West Virginia

Senators

Harley M. Kilgore (D)
Chapman Revercomb (R)

Representatives

Hubert S. Ellis (R)
John Kee (D)
Jennings Randolph (D)
Edward G. Rohrbough (R)
Andrew C. Schiffler (R)
Joe L. Smith (D)

Wisconsin

Senators

Robert M. La Follette, Jr.
  (Progressive)
Alexander Wiley (R)

Representatives

LaVern R. Dilweg (D)
Merlin Hull (R)
Frank B. Keefe (R)
Howard J. McMurray (D)
Reid F. Murray (R)
Alvin E. O'Konski (R)
Harry Sauthoff (Progressive)
Lawrence H. Smith (R)
William H. Stevenson (R)
Thaddeus F. B. Wasielewski (D)

Wyoming

Senators

Joseph C. O'Mahoney (D)
Edward V. Robertson (R)

Representatives

Frank A. Barrett (R)

Seventy-Ninth Congress

(Jan. 3, 1945, to
Jan. 3, 1947)

President of the Senate: Harry
  S Truman
*President Pro Tempore of the
  Senate:* Kenneth D. McKellar
*Speaker of the House of
  Representatives:* Sam Rayburn

Alabama

Senators

John H. Bankhead, II (D) d.
  Nov. 1946
Lister Hill (D)
John J. Sparkman (D) s. 1946
George R. Swift ta. 1946

Representatives

George W. Andrews (D)
Frank W. Boykin (D)
George M. Grant (D)
Sam Hobbs (D)
Pete Jarman (D)
Carter Manasco (D)
Luther Patrick (D)
Albert Rains (D)
John J. Sparkman (D) r. Nov.
  1946

Arizona

Senators

Carl Hayden (D)
Ernest W. McFarland (D)

Representatives

Richard F. Harless (D)
John R. Murdock (D)

Arkansas

Senators

J. William Fulbright (D)
John L. McClellan (D)

Representatives

Fadjo Cravens (D)
Ezekiel C. Gathings (D)
Oren Harris (D)
Brooks Hays (D)
Wilbur D. Mills (D)
William F. Norrell (D)
James W. Trimble (D)

California

Senators

Sheridan Downey (D)
Hiram W. Johnson (R) d. Aug.
  1945
William F. Knowland (R)

Representatives

John Z. Anderson (R)
Helen Gahagan Douglas (D)
Clyde G. Doyle (D)
Alfred J. Elliot (D)
Clair Engle (D)
Bertrand W. Gearhart (R)
Franck R. Havenner (D)
Ned R. Healy (D)
Carl Hinshaw (R)
Chet Holifield (D)
Edouard V. M. Izac (D)
Leroy Johnson (R)
Cecil R. King (D)
Clarence F. Lea (D, R)
Gordon L. McDonough (R)
George P. Miller (D)
George E. Outland (D)
Ellis E. Patterson (D)
John Phillips (R)
Harry R. Sheppard (D)
John H. Tolan (D)
H. Jerry Voorhis (D)
Richard J. Welch (R)

Colorado

Senators

Edwin C. Johnson (D)
Eugene D. Millikin (R)

Representatives

J. Edgar Chenoweth (D)
Dean M. Gillespie (R)
William S. Hill (R)
Robert F. Rockwell (R)

Connecticut

Senators

Thomas C. Hart (R)
Brien McMahon (D)
Francis T. Maloney (D) d. Jan.
  1945

Representatives

James P. Geelan (D)
Herman P. Kopplemann (D)
Clare Boothe Luce (R)
Joseph F. Ryter (D)
Joseph E. Talbot (R)
Chase Going Woodhouse (D)

Delaware

Senators

C. Douglass Buck (R)
James M. Tunnell (D)

Representatives

Philip A. Traynor (D)

Florida

Senators

Charles O. Andrews (D) d.
  Sept. 1946
Spessard L. Holland (D) s. 1946
Claude D. Pepper (D)

Representatives

Arthur P. Cannon (D)
Joe Hendricks (D)
J. Hardin Peterson (D)
Emory H. Price (D)
Dwight L. Rogers (D)
Robert L. F. Sikes (D)

Georgia

Senators

Walter F. George (D)
Richard B. Russell (D)

Representatives

Paul Brown (D)
A. Sidney Camp (D)
Edward E. Cox (D)
Helen Douglas Mankin (D) s.
  1946
John S. Gibson (D)

Stephen Pace (D)
Hugh Peterson (D)
Robert Ramspeck (D) r. Dec.
  1945
Malcolm C. Tarver (D)
Carl Vinson (D)
John S. Wood (D)

Idaho

Senators

Charles C. Gossett (D) ta. 1945
Glen H. Taylor (D)
John Thomas (R) d. Nov. 1945

Representatives

Henry C. Dworshak (R)
Compton I. White (D)

Illinois

Senators

C. Wayland Brooks (R)
Scott W. Lucas (D)

Representatives

Leo E. Allen (R)
Leslie C. Arends (R)
Cecil W. Bishop (R)
Robert B. Chiperfield (R)
Ralph E. Church (R)
Roy Clippinger (R)
William L. Dawson (D)
Everett M. Dirksen (R)
Emily Taft Douglas (D)
Thomas S. Gordon (D)
Martin Gorski (D)
James V. Heidinger (R)
Evan Howell (R)
Anton J. Johnson (R)
Edward A. Kelly (D)
William W. Link (D)
Rolla C. McMillen (R)
Noah M. Mason (R)
Thomas J. O'Brien (D)
Melvin Price (D)
Chauncey W. Reed (R)
Alexander J. Resa (D)
William A. Rowan (D)
Adolph J. Sabath (D)
Sidney E. Simpson (R)
Jessie Sumner (R)
Charles W. Vursell (R)

Indiana

Senators

Homer E. Capehart (R)
Raymond E. Willis (R)

Representatives

George W. Gillie (R)
Robert A. Grant (R)
Charles A. Halleck (R)
Forest A. Harness (R)
Noble J. Johnson (R)
Charles M. LaFollette (R)
Gerald W. Landis (R)
Louis Ludlow (D)
Ray J. Madden (D)
Raymond S. Springer (R)
Earl Wilson (R)

Iowa

Senators

Bourke B. Hickenlooper (R)
George A. Wilson (R)

Representatives

Paul Cummingham (R)
James I. Dolliver (R)
John W. Gwynne (R)
Charles B. Hoeven (R)
Ben F. Jensen (R)
Karl M. LeCompte (R)
Thomas E. Martin (R)
Henry O. Talle (R)

Kansas

Senators

Arthur Capper (R)
Clyde M. Reed (R)

Representatives

Frank Carlson (R)
Albert M. Cole (R)
Clifford R. Hope (R)
Edward H. Rees (R)
Errett P. Scrivner (R)
Thomas D. Winter (R)

Kentucky

Senators

Alben W. Barkley (D)
Albert B. Chandler (D) r. Nov.
1945
William A. Stanfill (R) ta.
1945-1946

Representatives

Joe B. Bates (D)
Virgil M. Chapman (D)
Frank L. Chelf (D)
Earle C. Clements (D)
Noble J. Gregory (D)
Andrew J. May (D)
Emmet O'Neal (D)
John M. Robsion (R)
Brent Spence (D)

Louisiana

Senators

Allen J. Ellender (D)
John H. Overton (D)

Representatives

A. Leonard Allen (D)
Overton Brooks (D)
James Domengeaux (D)
F. Edward Hebert (D)
Henry D. Larcade, Jr. (D)
Charles E. McKenzie (D)
James H. Morrison (D)

Maine

Senators

Ralph O. Brewster (R)
Wallace H. White, Jr. (R)

Representatives

Frank Fellows (R)
Robert Hale (R)
Margaret Chase Smith (R)

Maryland

Senators

George L. Radcliffe (D)
Millard E. Tydings (D)

Representatives

H. Streett Baldwin (D)
J. Glenn Beall (R)
Thomas D'Alesandro Jr. (D)
George H. Fallon (D)
Dudley G. Roe (D)
Lansdale G. Sasscer (D)

Massachusetts

Senators

Leverett Saltonstall (R)
David I. Walsh (D)

Representatives

George J. Bates (R)
Charles R. Clason (R)
James M. Curley (D)
Charles L. Gifford (R)
Angier L. Goodwin (R)
Christian A. Herter (R)
John W. Heselton (R)
Pehr G. Holmes (R)
Thomas J. Lane (D)
John W. McCormack (D)
Joseph W. Martin, Jr. (R)
Philip J. Philbin (D)
Edith Nourse Rogers (R)
Richard B. Wigglesworth (R)

Michigan

Senators

Homer Ferguson (R)
Arthur H. Vandenberg (R)

Representatives

William W. Blackney (R)
Frederick V. Bradley (R)
Fred L. Crawford (R)
John D. Dingell (D)
George A. Dondero (R)
Albert J. Engel (R)
Clare E. Hoffman (R)
Frank E. Hook (D)
Bartel J. Jonkman (R)
John Lesinski (D)
Earl C. Michener (R)
George D. O'Brien (D)
Louis C. Rabaut (D)
George G. Sadowski (D)
Paul W. Shafer (R)

Jesse P. Wolcott (R)
Roy O. Woodruff (R)

Minnesota

Senators

Joseph H. Ball (R)
Henrik Shipstead (R)

Representatives

H. Carl Andersen (R)
August H. Andresen (R)
William J. Gallagher (D) d.
Aug. 1946
Harold C. Hagen (R)
Walter H. Judd (R)
Harold Knutson (R)
Joseph P. O'Hara (R)
William A. Pittenger (R)
Frank T. Starkey (D)

Mississippi

Senators

Theodore G. Bilbo (D)
James O. Eastland (D)

Representatives

Thomas G. Abernethy (D)
William M. Colmer (D)
Dan R. McGehee (D)
John E. Rankin (D)
Jamie L. Whitten (D)
William M. Whittington (D)
W. Arthur Winstead (D)

Missouri

Senators

Frank P. Briggs (D)
Forrest C. Donnell (R)
Harry S Truman (D) r. Jan.
1945

Representatives

Samuel W. Arnold (R)
C. Jasper Bell (D)
Marion T. Bennett (R)
Clarence Cannon (D)
Albert S. J. Carnahan (D)
John J. Cochran (D)
William C. Cole (R)
Walter C. Ploeser (R)
Max Schwabe (R)
Dewey Short (R)
Roger C. Slaughter (D)
John B. Sullivan (D)
Orville Zimmerman (D)

Montana

Senators

James E. Murray (D)
Burton K. Wheeler (D)

Representatives

Wesley A. D'Ewart (R)
Mike Mansfield (D)

James F. O'Connor (D) d. Jan.
1945

Nebraska

Senators

Hugh A. Butler (R)
Kenneth S. Wherry (R)

Representatives

Howard H. Buffett (R)
Carl T. Curtis (R)
Arthur L. Miller (R)
Karl Stefan (R)

Nevada

Senators

Edward P. Carville (D)
Patrick A. McCarran (D)
James G. Scrugham (D) d. June
1945

Representatives

Berkeley L. Bunker (D)

New Hampshire

Senators

H. Styles Bridges (R)
Charles W. Tobey (R)

Representatives

Sherman Adams (R)
Chester E. Merrow (R)

New Jersey

Senators

Albert W. Hawkes (R)
H. Alexander Smith (R)

Representatives

James C. Auchincloss (R)
Gordon Canfield (R)
Clifford P. Case (R)
Charles A. Eaton (R)
T. Millet Hand (R)
Edward J. Hart (D)
Fred A. Hartley, Jr. (R)
Robert W. Kean (R)
Frank A. Mathews, Jr. (R)
Mary T. Norton (D)
D. Lane Powers (R) r. Aug.
1945
Frank L. Sundstrom (R)
J. Parnell Thomas (R)
Harry L. Towe (R)
Charles A. Wolverton (R)

New Mexico

Senators

Dennis Chavez (D)
Carl A. Hatch (D)

Representatives

Clinton P. Anderson (D)
Antonio M. Fernandez (D)

New York

Senators

James M. Mead (D)
Robert F. Wagner (D)

Representatives

Walter G. Andrews (R)
Joseph C. Baldwin (R)
William B. Barry (D) d. Oct.
  1946
Augustus W. Bennet (R)
Sol Bloom (D)
Ellsworth B. Buck (R)
Charles A. Buckley (D)
John C. Butler (R)
William T. Byrne (D)
Emanuel Celler (D)
W. Sterling Cole (R)
James J. Delaney (D)
John J. Delaney (D)
Samuel Dickstein (D) r. Dec.
  1945
Edward J. Elsaesser (R)
Hadwen C. Fuller (R)
Ralph A. Gamble (R)
Ralph W. Gwinn (R)
Edwin A. Hall (R)
Leonard W. Hall (R)
Clarence E. Hancock (R)
James J. Heffernan (D)
Bernard W. Kearney (R)
Eugene J. Keogh (D)
Clarence E. Kilburn (R)
Arthur G. Klein (D) s. 1946
Henry J. Latham (R)
Jay LeFevre (R)
Walter A. Lynch (D)
Vito Marcantonio (Amer.
  Labor)
Donald L. O'Toole (D)
Joseph L. Pfeifer (D)
Adam Clayton Powell, Jr. (D)
Peter A. Quinn (D)
Benjamin J. Rabin (D)
Leo F. Rayfiel (D)
Daniel A. Reed (R)
James A. Roe (D)
George F. Rogers (D)
John J. Rooney (D)
Edgar A. Sharp (R)
Andrew L. Somers (D)
John Taber (R)
Dean P. Taylor (R)
James H. Torrens (D)
James W. Wadsworth, Jr. (R)

North Carolina

Senators

Josiah W. Bailey (D) d. Dec.
  1946
Clyde R. Hoey (D)

Representatives

Graham A. Barden (D)
Herbert C. Bonner (D)
Alfred L. Bulwinkle (D)
William O. Burgin (D) d. Apr.
  1946

J. Bayard Clark (D)
Harold D. Cooley (D)
Robert L. Doughton (D)
Carl T. Durham (D)
John H. Folger (D)
Joe W. Ervin (D) d. Dec. 1945
Sam J. Ervin, Jr. (D)
John H. Kerr (D)
Eliza Jane Pratt (D) s. 1946
Zebulon Weaver (D)

North Dakota

Senators

William Langer (R)
John Moses (D) d. Mar. 1945
Milton R. Young (R)

Representatives

William Lemke (R)
Charles R. Robertson (R)

Ohio

Senators

Harold H. Burton (R) r. Sept.
  1945
James W. Huffman (D) ta.
  1945-1946
Kingsley A. Taft (R) s. 1946
Robert A. Taft (R)

Representatives

George H. Bender (R)
Frances P. Bolton (R)
Walter E. Brehm (R)
Clarence J. Brown (R)
Cliff Clevenger (R)
Robert Crosser (D)
Charles H. Elston (R)
Michael A. Feighan (D)
Edward J. Gardner (D)
Percy W. Griffiths (R)
William E. Hess (R)
Walter B. Huber (D)
Thomas A. Jenkins (R)
Robert F. Jones (R)
Michael J. Kirwan (D)
Earl R. Lewis (R)
Edward O. McCowen (R)
J. Harry McGregor (R)
Homer A. Ramey (R)
Frederick C. Smith (R)
William R. Thom (D)
John M. Vorys (R)
Alvin F. Weichel (R)

Oklahoma

Senators

Edward H. Moore (R)
J. W. Elmer Thomas (D)

Representatives

Lyle H. Boren (D)
Jed Johnson (D)
A. S. Mike Monroney (D)
Ross Rizley (R)
George B. Schwabe (R)
Paul Stewart (D)
William G. Stigler (D)
Victor Wickersham (D)

Oregon

Senators

Guy Gordon (R)
Wayne L. Morse (R)

Representatives

Homer D. Angell (R)
Harris Ellsworth (R)
James W. Mott (R)
A. Walter Norblad, Jr. (R)
Lowell Stockman (R)

Pennsylvania

Senators

Joseph F. Guffey (D)
Francis J. Myers (D)

Representatives

William A. Barrett (D)
Michael J. Bradley (D)
D. Emmert Brumbaugh (R)
Frank Buchanan (D) s. 1946
Howard E. Campbell (R)
Robert J. Corbett (R)
Herman P. Eberharter (D)
Ivor D. Fenton (R)
Daniel J. Flood (D)
James G. Fulton (R)
Leon H. Gavin (R)
Charles L. Gerlach (R)
Wilson D. Gillette (R)
Louis E. Graham (R)
William T. Granahan (D)
William J. Green, Jr. (D)
Chester H. Gross (R)
Daniel K. Hoch (D)
Carl H. Hoffman (R) s. 1946
Augustine B. Kelley (D)
J. Roland Kinzer (R)
John C. Kunkel (R)
Samuel K. McConnell, Jr. (R)
Herbert J. McGlinchey (D)
Thomas E. Morgan (D)
John W. Murphy (D) r. July
  1946
Robert F. Rich (R)
Robert L. Rodgers (R)
John E. Sheridan (D)
Richard M. Simpson (R)
J. Buell Snyder (D) d. Feb.
  1946
Harve Tibbott (R)
Francis E. Walter (D)
Samuel A. Weiss (D) r. Jan.
  1946
James Wolfenden (R)

Rhode Island

Senators

Peter G. Gerry (D)
Theodore F. Green (D)

Representatives

John E. Fogarty (D)
Aime J. Forand (D)

South Carolina

Senators

Olin D. Johnston (D)
Burnet R. Maybank (D)

Representatives

Joseph R. Bryson (D)
Butler B. Hare (D)
John L. McMillan (D)
James P. Richards (D)
John J. Riley (D)
L. Mendel Rivers (D)

South Dakota

Sentors

Harlan J. Bushfield (R)
J. Chandler Gurney (R)

Representatives

Francis H. Case (R)
Karl E. Mundt (R)

Tennessee

Senators

Kenneth D. McKellar (D)
A. Tom Stewart (D)

Representatives

Jere Cooper (D)
Wirt Courtney (D)
Clifford Davis (D)
Harold H. Earthman (D)
Albert A. Gore (D)
John Jennings, Jr. (R)
Estes Kefauver (D)
Thomas J. Murray (D)
J. Percy Priest (D)
B. Carroll Reece (R)

Texas

Senators

Tom T. Connally (D)
W. Lee O'Daniel (D)

Representatives

Lindley Beckworth (D)
Jesse M. Combs (D)
O. Clark Fisher (D)
Ed Gossett (D)
Luther A. Johnson (D) r. July
  1946
Lyndon B. Johnson (D)
Paul J. Kilday (D)
Fritz G. Lanham (D)
John E. Lyle, Jr. (D)
George H. Mahon (D)
Joseph J. Mansfield (D)
Wright Patman (D)
Tom Pickett (D)
William R. Poage (D)
Sam Rayburn (D)
Sam M. Russell (D)
Hatton W. Sumners (D)
Albert Thomas (D)
R. Ewing Thomason (D)

Milton H. West (D)
Eugene Worley (D)

Utah

Senators

Abe Murdock (D)
Elbert D. Thomas (D)

Representatives

Walter K. Granger (D)
J. W. Robinson (D)

Vermont

Senators

George D. Aiken (R)
Warren R. Austin (R) r. Aug.
1945
Ralph E. Flanders (R) ta. 1946

Representatives

Charles A. Plumley (R)

Virginia

Senators

Thomas G. Burch (D) ta. 1946
Harry F. Byrd (D)
Carter Glass (D) d. May 1946

Representatives

J. Lindsay Almond, Jr. (D) s.
1946
Schuyler Otis Bland (D)
Thomas G. Burch (D) r. May
1946
Ralph H. Daughton (D)
Patrick H. Drewry (D)
John W. Flannagan, Jr. (D)
J. Vaughan Gary s. 1945
A. Willis Robertson (D) r. Nov.
1946
Dave E. Satterfield, Jr. (D) r.
Nov. 1945
Howard W. Smith (D)
Clifton A. Woodrum (D) r.
1945

Washington

Senators

Warren G. Magnuson (D)
Hugh B. Mitchell (D) s. 1945

Representatives

John M. Coffee (D)
Hugh DeLacy (D)
Hal Holmes (R)
Walter F. Horan (R)
Henry M. Jackson (D)
Charles R. Savage (D)

West Virginina

Senators

Harley M. Kilgore (D)

Chapman Revercomb (R)

Representatives

Cleveland M. Bailey (D)
Hubert S. Ellis (R)
Erland H. Hedrick (D)
John Kee (D)
Matthew M. Neeley (D)
Jennings Randolph (D)

Wisconsin

Senators

Robert M. LaFollette, Jr.
(Progressive)
Alexander Wiley (R)

Representatives

Andrew J. Biemiller (D)
John W. Byrnes (R)
Robert K. Henry (R) d. Nov.
1946
Merlin Hull (R)
Frank B. Keefe (R)
Reid F. Murray (R)
Alvin E. O'Konski (R)
Lawrence H. Smith (R)
William H. Stevenson (R)
Thaddeus F. B. Wasielewski (D)

Wyoming

Senators

Joseph C. O'Mahoney (D)
Edward V. Robertson (R)

Representatives

Frank A. Barrett (R)

Eightieth Congress

(Jan. 3, 1947, to
Jan. 3, 1949)

President of the Senate: Vacant
*President Pro Tempore of the
Senate:* Arthur H. Vandenberg
*Speaker of the House of
Representatives:* Joseph W.
Martin, Jr.

Alabama

Senators

Lister Hill (D)
John J. Sparkman (D)

Representatives

George W. Andrews (D)
Laurie C. Battle (D)
Frank W. Boykin (D)
George M. Grant (D)
Sam Hobbs (D)
Pete Jarman (D)
Robert E. Jones, Jr. (D)
Carter Manasco (D)
Albert Rains (D)

Arizona

Senators

Carl Hayden (D)
Ernest W. McFarland (D)

Representatives

Richard F. Harless (D)
John R. Murdock (D)

Arkansas

Senators

J. William Fulbright (D)
John L. McClellan (D)

Representatives

Fadjo Cravens (D)
Ezekiel C. Gathings (D)
Oren Harris (D)
Brooks Hays (D)
Wilbur D. Mills (D)
William F. Norrell (D)
James W. Trimble (D)

California

Senators

Sheridan Downey (D)
William F. Knowland (R)

Representatives

John J. Allen, Jr. (R)
John Z. Anderson (R)
Willis W. Bradley (R)
Ernest K. Bramblett (R)
Helen Gahagan Douglas (D)
Alfred J. Elliott (D)
Clair Engle (D)
Charles K. Fletcher (R)
Bertrand W. Gearhart (R)
Franck R. Havenner (D)
Carl Hinshaw (R)
Chet Holifield (D)
Donald L. Jackson (R)
Leroy Johnson (R)
Cecil R. King (D)
Clarence F. Lea (D, R)
Gordon L. McDonough (R)
George P. Miller (D)
Richard M. Nixon (R)
John Phillips (R)
Norris Poulson (R)
Harry R. Sheppard (D)
Richard J. Welch (R)

Colorado

Senators

Edwin C. Johnson (D)
Eugene D. Millikin (R)

Representatives

John A. Carroll (D)
J. Edgar Chenoweth (R)
William S. Hill (R)
Robert F. Rockwell (R)

Connecticut

Senators

Raymond E. Baldwin (R)
Brien McMahon (D)

Representations

Ellsworth B. Foote (R)
John Davis Lodge (R)
William J. Miller (R)
James T. Patterson (R)
Antoni N. Sadlak (R)
Horace Seely-Brown, Jr. (R)

Delaware

Senators

C. Douglass Buck (R)
John J. Williams (R)

Representatives

J. Caleb Boggs (R)

Florida

Senators

Spessard L. Holland (D)
Claude D. Pepper (D)

Representatives

Joe Hendricks (D)
J. Hardin Peterson (D)
Emory H. Price (D)
Dwight L. Rogers (D)
Robert L. F. Sikes (D)
George A. Smathers (D)

Georgia

Senators

Walter F. George (D)
Richard B. Russell (D)

Representatives

Paul Brown (D)
A. Sidney Camp (D)
Edward E. Cox (D)
James C. Davis (D)
Henderson L. Lanham (D)
Stephen Pace (D)
Prince H. Preston, Jr. (D)
Carl Vinson (D)
William M. Wheeler (D)
John S. Wood (D)

Idaho

Senators

Henry C. Dworshak (R)
Glen H. Taylor (D)

Representatives

Abe McGregor Goff (R)
John C. Sanborn (R)

Illinois

Senators

C. Wayland Brooks (R)
Scott W. Lucas (D)

Representatives

Leo E. Allen (R)
Leslie C. Arends (R)
Cecil W. Bishop (R)
Fred E. Busbey (R)
Robert B. Chiperfield (R)
Ralph E. Church (R)
Roy Clippinger (R)
William L. Dawson (D)
Everett M. Dirksen (R)
Thomas S. Gordon (D)
Martin Gorski (D)
Evan Howell (R) r. Oct. 1947
Edward H. Jenison (R)
Anton J. Johnson (R)
Rolla C. McMillen (R)
Noah M. Mason (R)
Thomas J. O'Brien (D)
Thomas L. Owens (R) d. June 1948
Melvin Price (D)
Chauncey W. Reed (R)
Adolph J. Sabath (D)
Sidney E. Simpson (R)
William G. Stratton (R)
Robert J. Twyman (R)
Richard B. Vail (R)
Charles W. Vursell (R)

Indiana

Senators

Homer E. Capehart (R)
William E. Jenner (R)

Representatives

George W. Gillie (R)
Robert A. Grant (R)
Charles A. Halleck (R)
Forest A. Harness (R)
Ralph Harvey (R)
Noble J. Johnson (R) r. July 1948
Gerald W. Landis (R)
Louis Ludlow (D)
Ray J. Madden (D)
Edward A. Mitchell (R)
Raymond S. Springer (R) d. Aug. 1947
Earl Wilson (R)

Iowa

Senators

Bourke B. Hickenlooper (R)
George A. Wilson (R)

Representatives

Paul Cunningham (R)
James I. Dolliver (R)
John W. Gwynne (R)
Charles B. Hoeven (R)
Ben F. Jensen (R)
Karl M. LeCompte (R)
Thomas E. Martin (R)
Henry O. Talle (R)

Kansas

Senators

Arthur Capper (R)
Clyde M. Reed (R)

Representatives

Albert M. Cole (R)
Clifford R. Hope (R)
Herbert A. Meyer (R)
Edward H. Rees (R)
Errett P. Scrivner (R)
Wint Smith (R)

Kentucky

Senators

Alben W. Barkley (D)
John Sherman Cooper (R)

Representatives

Joe B. Bates (D)
Virgin M. Chapman (D)
Frank L. Chelf (D)
Earle C. Clements (D) r. Jan. 1948
Noble J. Gregory (D)
William Lewis (R) s. 1948
W. Howes Meade (R)
Thruston B. Morton (R)
John M. Robsion (R) d. Feb. 1948
Brent Spence (D)
John A. Whitaker (R) s. 1948

Louisiana

Senators

Allen J. Ellender (D)
William C. Feazel (D) ta. 1948
Russell B. Long (D) s. 1948
John H. Overton (D) d. May 1948

Representatives

A. Leonard Allen (D)
T. Hale Boggs (D)
Overton Brooks (D)
James Domengeaux (D)
F. Edward Hebert (D)
Henry D. Larcade, Jr. (D)
James H. Morrison (D)
Otto E. Passman (D)

Maine

Senators

Wallace H. White, Jr. (R)
Ralph O. Brewster (R)

Representatives

Frank Fellows (R)
Robert Hale (R)
Margaret Chase Smith (R)

Maryland

Senators

Millard E. Tydings (D)
Herbert R. O'Conor (D)

Representatives

J. Glenn Beall (R)
Thomas D'Alesandro, Jr. (D) r. May 1947
George H. Fallon (R)
Edward A. Garmatz (D)
Hugh A. Meade (D)
Edward T. Miller (R)
Lansdale G. Sasscer (D)

Massachusetts

Senators

Leverett Saltonstall (R)
Henry Cabot Lodge, Jr. (R)

Representatives

George J. Bates (R)
Charles R. Clason (R)
Harold D. Donohue (D)
Charles L. Gifford (R) d. Aug. 1947
Angier L. Goodwin (R)
Christian A. Herter (R)
John W. Heselton (R)
John F. Kennedy (D)
Thomas J. Lane (D)
John W. McCormack (D)
Joseph W. Martin, Jr. (R)
Donald W. Nicholson (R)
Philip J. Philbin (D)
Edith Nourse Rogers (R)
Richard B. Wigglesworth (R)

Michigan

Senators

Arthur H. Vandenberg (R)
Homer Ferguson (R)

Representatives

John B. Bennett (R)
William W. Blackney (R)
Frederick V. Bradley (R) d. May 1947
Howard A. Coffin (R)
Fred L. Crawford (R)
John D. Dingell (D)
George A. Dondero (R)
Albert J. Engel (R)
Clare E. Hoffman (R)
Bartel J. Jonkman (R)
John Lesinski (D)
Earl C. Michener (R)
Charles E. Potter (R)
George G. Sadowski (D)
Paul W. Shafer (R)
Jesse P. Wolcott (R)
Roy O. Woodruff (R)
Harold F. Youngblood (R)

Minnesota

Senators

Joseph H. Ball (R)
Edward J. Thye (R)

Representatives

H. Carl Andersen (R)
August H. Andresen (R)
John A. Blatnik (D)
Edward J. Devitt (R)
Harold C. Hagen (R)
Walter H. Judd (R)
Harold Knutson (R)
George E. MacKinnon (R)
Joseph P. O'Hara (R)

Mississippi

Senators

Theodore G. Bilbo (D) d. Aug. 1947
James O. Eastland (D)
John C. Stennis (D)

Representatives

Thomas G. Abernethy (D)
William M. Colmer (D)
John E. Rankin (D)
Jamie L. Whitten (D)
William M. Whittington (D)
John Bell Williams (D)
W. Arthur Winstead (D)

Missouri

Senators

Forrest C. Donnell (R)
James P. Kem (R)

Representatives

Samuel W. Arnold (R)
Claude I. Bakewell (R)
Parke M. Banta (R)
C. Jasper Bell (D)
Marion T. Bennett (R)
Clarence Cannon (D)
William C. Cole (R)
Paul C. Jones (D) s. 1948
Frank M. Karsten (D)
Walter C. Ploeser (R)
Albert L. Reeves, Jr. (R)
Max Schwabe (R)
Dewey Short (R)
Orville Zimmerman (D) d. Apr. 1948

Montana

Senators

Zales N. Ecton (R)
James E. Murray (D)

Representatives

Wesley A. D'Ewart (R)
Mike Mansfield (D)

Nebraska

Senators

Hugh A. Butler (R)
Kenneth S. Wherry (R)

Representatives

Howard H. Buffett (R)
Carl T. Curtis (R)
Arthur L. Miller (R)
Karl Stefan (R)

Nevada

Senators

George W. Malone (R)
Patrick A. McCarran (D)

Representatives

Charles H. Russell (R)

New Hampshire

Senators

H. Styles Bridges (R)
Charles W. Tobey (R)

Representatives

Norris Cotton (R)
Chester E. Merrow (R)

New Jersey

Senators

Albert W. Hawkes (R)
H. Alexander Smith (R)

Representatives

James C. Auchincloss (R)
Gordon Canfield (R)
Clifford P. Case (R)
Charles A. Eaton (R)
T. Millet Hand (R)
Edward J. Hart (D)
Fred A. Hartley, Jr. (R)
Robert W. Kean (R)
Frank A. Mathews, Jr. (R)
Mary T. Norton (D)
Frank L. Sundstrom (R)
J. Parnell Thomas (R)
Harry L. Towe (R)
Charles A. Wolverton (R)

New Mexico

Senators

Dennis Chavez (D)
Carl A. Hatch (D)

Representatives

Antonio M. Fernandez (D)
Georgia L. Lusk (D)

New York

Senators

Irving M. Ives (R)
Robert F. Wagner (D)

Representatives

Walter G. Andrews (R)
Sol Bloom (D)
Ellsworth B. Buck (R)
Charles A. Buckley (D)
John C. Butler (R)
William T. Byrne (D)
Emanuel Celler (D)
W. Sterling Cole (R)
Frederic R. Coudert, Jr. (R)
John J. Delaney (D) d. Nov.
   1948
Edward J. Elsaesser (R)
Hadwen C. Fuller (R)
Ralph A. Gamble (R)
Ralph W. Gwinn (R)
Edwin A. Hall (R)
Leonard W. Hall (R)
James J. Heffernan (D)
Leo Isacson (Amer. Labor) s.
   1948
Jacob K. Javits (R)
Bernard W. Kearney (R)
Kenneth B. Keating (R)
Eugene J. Keogh (D)
Clarence E. Kilburn (R)
Arthur G. Klein (D)
Henry J. Latham (R)
Jay LeFevre (R)
Walter A. Lynch (D)
Gregory McMahon (R)
W. Kingsland Macy (R)
Vito Marcantonio (Amer.
   Labor)
Abraham J. Multer (D)
Robert J. Nodar, Jr. (R)
Donald L. O'Toole (D)
Joseph L. Pfeifer (D)
David M. Potts (R)
Adam Clayton Powell, Jr. (D)
Benjamin J. Rabin (D) r. Dec.
   1947
Leo F. Rayfiel (D) r. Sept.
   1947
Daniel A. Reed (R)
R. Walter Riehlman (R)
John J. Rooney (D)
Robert T. Ross (R)
Katharine St. George (R)
Andrew L. Somers (D)
John Taber (R)
Dean P. Taylor (R)
James W. Wadsworth, Jr. (R)

North Carolina

Senators

J. Melville Broughton (D) s.
   1948
Clyde R. Hoey (D)
William B. Umstead (D) ta.
   1947-1948

Representatives

Graham A. Barden (D)
Herbert C. Bonner (D)
Alfred L. Bulwinkle (D)
J. Bayard Clark (D)
Harold D. Cooley (D)

Charles B. Deane (D)
Robert L. Doughton (D)
Carl T. Durham (D)
John H. Folger (D)
Hamilton C. Jones (D)
John H. Kerr (D)
Monroe M. Redden (D)

North Dakota

Senators

William Langer (R)
Milton R. Young (R)

Representatives

William Lemke (R)
Charles R. Robertson (R)

Ohio

Senators

John W. Bricker (R)
Robert A. Taft (R)

Representatives

George H. Bender (R)
Frances P. Bolton (R)
Walter E. Brehm (R)
Clarence J. Brown (R)
Raymond H. Burke (R)
Henderson H. Carson (R)
Cliff Clevenger (R)
Robert Crosser (D)
Charles H. Elston (R)
Michael A. Feighan (D)
William E. Hess (R)
Walter B. Huber (D)
Percy W. Griffiths (R)
Thomas A. Jenkins (R)
Robert F. Jones (R) r. Sept.
   1497
Michael J. Kirwan (D)
Earl R. Lewis (R)
Edward O. McCowen (R)
William M. McCulloch (R)
J. Harry McGregor (R)
Homer A. Ramey (R)
Frederick C. Smith (R)
John M. Vorys (R)
Alvin F. Weichel (R)

Oklahoma

Senators

Edward H. Moore (R)
J. W. Elmer Thomas (D)

Representatives

Carl Albert (D)
Glen D. Johnson (D)
A. S. Mike Monroney (D)
Toby Morris (D)
Preston E. Peden (D)
Ross Rizley (R)
George B. Schwabe (R)
William G. Stigler (D)

Oregon

Senators

Guy Cordon (R)
Wayne L. Morse (R)

Representatives

Homer D. Angell (R)
Harris Ellsworth (R)
A. Walter Norblad, Jr. (R)
Lowell Stockman (R)

Pennsylvania

Senators

Edward Martin (R)
Francis J. Myers (D)

Representatives

Frank Buchanan (D)
E. Wallace Chadwick (R)
Robert J. Corbett (R)
William J. Crow (R)
Paul B. Dague (R)
Herman P. Eberharter (D)
Ivor D. Fenton (R)
James G. Fulton (R)
James Gallagher (R)
Leon H. Gavin (R)
Charles L. Gerlach (R) d. May
   1947
Wilson D. Gillette (R)
Louis E. Graham (R)
Chester H. Gross (R)
Mitchell Jenkins (R)
Carroll D. Kearns (R)
Augustine B. Kelley (D)
John C. Kunkel (R)
Franklin H. Lichtenwalter (R)
Samuel K. McConnell, Jr. (R)
John R. McDowell (R)
Robert N. McGarvey (R)
Franklin J. Maloney (R)
Thomas E. Morgan (D)
Frederick A. Muhlenberg (R)
Robert F. Rich (R)
George W. Sarbacher, Jr. (R)
James P. Scoblick (R)
Hardie Scott (R)
Hugh D. Scott, Jr. (R)
Richard M. Simpson (R)
Harve Tibbott (R)
James E. Van Zandt (R)
Francis E. Walter (D)

Rhode Island

Senators

Theodore F. Green (D)
J. Howard McGrath (D)

Representatives

John E. Fogarty (D)
Aime J. Forand (D)

South Carolina

Senators

Olin D. Johnston (D)
Burnet R. Maybank (D)

Representatives

Joseph R. Bryson (D)
W. J. Bryan Dorn (D)
John L. McMillan (D)
James P. Richards (D)
John J. Riley (D)
L. Mendel Rivers (D)

South Dakota

Senators

Harlan J. Bushfield (R) d. Sept.
1948
J. Chandler Gurney (R)
Karl E. Mundt (R) s. 1948

Representatives

Francis H. Case (R)
Karl E. Mundt (R) r. Dec.
1948

Tennessee

Senators

Kenneth D. McKellar (D)
A. Tom Stewart (D)

Representatives

Jere Cooper (D)
Wirt Courtney (D)
Clifford Davis (D)
Joe L. Evins (D)
Albert A. Gore (D)
John Jennings, Jr. (R)
Estes Kefauver (D)
Thomas J. Murray (D)
Dayton E. Phillips (R)
J. Percy Priest (D)

Texas

Senators

Tom T. Connally (D)
W. Lee O'Daniel (D)

Representatives

Lindley Beckworth (D)
Lloyd M. Bentsen, Jr. (D) s.
1948
Omar T. Burleson (D)
Jesse M. Combs (D)
O. Clark Fisher (D)
Ed Gossett (D)
Lyndon B. Johnson (D)
Paul J. Kilday (D)
Wingate H. Lucas (D)
John E. Lyle, Jr. (D)
George H. Mahon (D)
Joseph J. Mansfield (D) d. July
1947
Wright Patman (D)
Tom Pickett (D)
William R. Poage (D)
Sam Rayburn (D)
Kenneth M. Regan (D)
Olin E. Teague (D)
Albert Thomas (D)
R. Ewing Thomason (D) r. July
1947
Clark W. Thompson (D)

Milton H. West (D) d. Oct.
1948
J. Frank Wilson (D)
Eugene Worley (D)

Utah

Senators

Elbert D. Thomas (D)
Arthur V. Watkins (R)

Representatives

William A. Dawson (R)
Walter K. Granger (D)

Vermont

Senators

George D. Aiken (R)
Ralph E. Flanders (R)

Representatives

Charles A. Plumley (R)

Virginia

Senators

Harry F. Byrd (D)
A. Willis Robertson (D)

Representatives

Watkins M. Abbitt (D) s. 1948
J. Lindsay Almond, Jr. (D) r.
Apr. 1948
Schuyler Otis Bland (D)
Clarence G. Burton (D) s. 1948
Patrick H. Drewry (D) d. Dec.
1947
John W. Flannagan, Jr. (D)
J. Vaughan Gary (D)
Porter Hardy, Jr. (D)
Burr P. Harrison (D)
Howard W. Smith (D)
Thomas B. Stanley (D)

Washington

Senators

Harry P. Cain (R)
Warren G. Magnuson (D)

Representatives

Hal Holmes (R)
Walter F. Horan (R)
Henry M. Jackson (D)
Home R. Jones (R)
Russell V. Mack (R)
Fred B. Norman (R) d. Apr.
1947
Thor C. Tollefson (R)

West Virginia

Senators

Harley M. Kilgore (D)
Chapman Revercomb (R)

Representatives

Hubert S. Ellis (R)
Erland H. Hedrick (D)
John Kee (D)
Francis J. Love (R)
Edward G. Rohrbough (R)
Melvin C. Snyder (R)

Wisconsin

Senators

Joseph R. McCarthy (R)
Alexander Wiley (R)

Representatives

John C. Brophy (R)
John W. Byrnes (R)
Glenn R. Davis (R)
Merlin Hull (R)
Frank B. Keefe (R)
Charles J. Kersten (R)
Reid F. Murray (R)
Alvin E. O'Konski (R)
Lawrence H. Smith (R)
William H. Stevenson (R)

Wyoming

Senators

Joseph C. O'Mahoney (D)
Edward V. Robertson (R)

Representatives

Frank A. Barrett (R)

Eighty-First Congress

(Jan. 3, 1949, to
Jan. 3, 1951)

President of the Senate: Alben
W. Barkley
*President Pro Tempore of the
Senate:* Kenneth D. McKellar
*Speaker of the House of
Representatives:* Sam Rayburn

Alabama

Senators

Lister Hill (D)
John J. Sparkman (D)

Representatives

George W. Andrews (D)
Laurie C. Battle (D)
Frank W. Boykin (D)
Edward deGraffenried (D)
Carl A. Elliott (D)
George M. Grant (D)
Sam Hobbs (D)
Robert E. Jones, Jr. (D)
Albert Rains (D)

Arizona

Senators

Carl Hayden (D)
Ernest W. McFarland (D)

Representatives

John R. Murdock (D)
Harold A. Patten (D)

Arkansas

Senators

J. William Fulbright (D)
John L. McClellan (D)

Representatives

Ezekiel C. Gathings (D)
Oren Harris (D)
Brooks Hays (D)
Wilbur D. Mills (D)
William F. Norrell (D)
Boyd Tackett (D)
James W. Trimble (D)

California

Senators

Sheridan Downey (D) r. Nov.
1950
William F. Knowland (R)
Richard M. Nixon (R) s. 1950

Representatives

John J. Allen, Jr. (R)
John Z. Anderson (R)
Ernest K. Bramblett (R)
Helen Gahagan Douglas (D)
Clyde G. Doyle (D)
Clair Engle (D)
Franck R. Havenner (D)
Carl Hinshaw (R)
Chet Holifield (D)
Donald L. Jackson (R)
Leroy Johnson (R)
Cecil R. King (D)
Gordon L. McDonough (R)
Clinton D. McKinnon (D)
George P. Miller (D)
Richard M. Nixon (R) r. Nov.
1950
John Phillips (R)
Norris Poulson (R)
Hubert B. Scudder (R)
John F. Shelley (D) s. 1950
Harry R. Sheppard (D)
Richard J. Welch (R) d. Sept.
1949
Thomas H. Werdel (R)
Cecil F. White (D)

Colorado

Senators

Edwin C. Johnson (D)
Eugene D. Millikin (R)

Representatives

Wayne N. Aspinall (D)

John A. Carroll (D)
William S. Hill (R)
John H. Marsalis (D)

Connecticut

Senators

Raymond E. Baldwin (R) r.
Dec. 1949
William Benton (D) s. 1950
Brien McMahon (D)

Representatives

John Davis Lodge (R)
John A. McGuire (D)
James T. Patterson (R)
Abraham A. Ribicoff (D)
Antoni N. Sadlak (R)
Chase Going Woodhouse (D)

Delaware

Senators

J. Allen Frear, Jr. (D)
John J. Williams (R)

Representatives

J. Caleb Boggs (R)

Florida

Senators

Spessard L. Holland (D)
Claude D. Pepper (D)

Representatives

Charles E. Bennett (D)
Albert S. Herlong, Jr. (D)
J. Hardin Peterson (D)
Dwight L Rogers (D)
Robert L. F. Sikes (D)
George A. Smathers (D)

Georgia

Senators

Walter F. George (D)
Richard B. Russell (D)

Representatives

Paul Brown (D)
A. Sidney Camp (D)
Edward E. Cox (D)
James C. Davis (D)
Henderson L. Lanham (D)
Stephen Pace (D)
Prince H. Preston, Jr. (D)
Carl Vinson (D)
William M. Wheeler (D)
John S. Wood (D)

Idaho

Senators

Henry C. Dworshak (R)
Bert H. Miller (D) d. Oct. 1949
Glen H. Taylor (D)

Representatives

John C. Sanborn (R)
Compton I. White (D)

Illinois

Senators

Paul H. Douglas (D)
Scott W. Lucas (D)

Representatives

Leo E. Allen (R)
Leslie C. Arends (R)
Cecil W. Bishop (R)
James V. Buckley (D)
Chester A. Chesney (D)
Robert B. Chiperfield (R)
Ralph E. Church (R) d. Mar.
1950
William L. Dawson (D)
Thomas S. Gordon (D)
Martin Gorski (D) d. Dec. 1949
Richard W. Hoffman (R)
Edward H. Jenison (R)
Edgar A. Jonas (R)
Neil J. Linehan (D)
Rolla C. McMillen (R)
Peter F. Mack, Jr. (D)
Noah M. Mason (R)
Thomas J. O'Brien (D)
Barratt O'Hara (D)
Melvin Price (D)
Chauncey W. Reed (R)
Adolph J. Sabath (D)
Sidney E. Simpson (R)
Harold H. Velde (R)
Charles W. Vursell (R)
Sidney R. Yates (D)

Indiana

Senators

Homer E. Capehart (R)
William E. Jenner (R)

Representatives

Thurman C. Crook (D)
Winfield K. Denton (D)
Charles A. Halleck (R)
Cecil M. Harden (R)
Ralph Harvey (R)
Andrews Jacobs, Sr. (D)
Edward H. Kruse, Jr. (D)
Ray J. Madden (D)
James E. Noland (D)
John R. Walsh (D)
Earl Wilson (R)

Iowa

Senators

Guy M. Gillette (D)
Bourke B. Hickenlooper (R)

Representatives

Paul Cunningham (R)
James I. Dolliver (R)
Harold R. Gross (R)
Charles B. Hoeven (R)
Ben F. Jensen (R)
Karl M. LeCompte (R)

Thomas E. Martin (R)
Henry O. Talle (R)

Kansas

Senators

Frank Carlson (R) s. 1950
Harry Darby (R) ta. 1950
Clyde M. Reed (R) d. Nov.
1949
Andrew F. Schoeppel (R)

Representatives

Albert M. Cole (R)
Myron V. George (R) s. 1950
Clifford R. Hope (R)
Herbert A. Meyer (R) d. Oct.
1950
Edward H. Rees (R)
Errett P. Scrivner (R)
Wint Smith (R)

Kentucky

Senators

Alben W. Barkley (D) r. Jan.
1949
Virgil M. Chapman (D)
Earle C. Clements (D) s. 1950
Garrett L. Withers (D) ta. 1949

Representatives

Joe B. Bates (D)
Frank L. Chelf (D)
James S. Golden (R)
Noble J. Gregory (D)
Thruston B. Morton (R)
Carl D. Perkins (D)
Brent Spence (D)
Thomas R. Underwood (D)
John A. Whitaker (D)

Louisiana

Senators

Allen J. Ellender, Sr. (D)
Russell B. Long (D)

Representatives

A. Leonard Allen (D)
T. Hale Boggs (D)
Overton Brooks (D)
F. Edward Hebert (D)
Henry D. Larcade, Jr. (D)
James H. Morrison (D)
Otto E. Passman (D)
Edwin E. Willis (D)

Maine

Senators

Ralph O. Brewster (R)
Margaret Chase Smith (R)

Representatives

Frank Fellows (R)
Robert Hale (R)
Charles P. Nelson (R)

Maryland

Senators

Herbert R. O'Conor (D)
Millard E. Tydings (D)

Representatives

J. Glenn Beall (R)
William P. Bolton (D)
George H. Fallon (D)
Edward A. Garmatz (D)
Edward T. Miller (R)
Lansdale G. Sasscer (D)

Massachusetts

Senators

Henry Cabot Lodge, Jr. (R)
Leverett Saltonstall (R)

Representatives

George J. Bates (R) d. Nov.
1949
William H. Bates (R) s. 1950
Harold D. Donohue (D)
Foster Frucolo (D)
Angier L. Goodwin (R)
Christian A. Herter (R)
John W. Heselton (R)
John F. Kennedy (D)
Thomas J. Lane (D)
John W. McCormack (D)
Joseph W. Martin, Jr. (R)
Donald W. Nicholson (R)
Philip J. Philbin (D)
Edith Nourse Rogers (R)
Richard B. Wigglesworth (R)

Michigan

Senators

Homer Ferguson (R)
Arthur H. Vandenberg (R)

Representatives

John B. Bennett (R)
William W. Blackney (R)
Fred L. Crawford (R)
John D. Dingell (R)
George A. Dondero (R)
Albert J. Engel (R)
Gerald R. Ford, Jr. (R)
Clare E. Hoffman (R)
John Lesinski (D) d. May 1950
Earl C. Michener (R)
George D. O'Brien (D)
Charles E. Potter (R)
Louis C. Rabaut (D)
George G. Sadowski (D)
Paul W. Shafer (R)
Jesse P. Wolcott (R)
Roy O. Woodruff (R)

Minnesota

Senators

Hubert H. Humphrey (D)
Edward J. Thye (R)

Representatives

H. Carl Andersen (R)
August H. Andresen (R)
John A. Blatnik (D)
Harold C. Hagen (R)
Walter H. Judd (R)
Eugene J. McCarthy (D)
Fred Marshall (D)
Joseph P. O'Hara (R)
Roy W. Wier (D)

Mississippi

Senators

James O. Eastland (D)
John C. Stennis (D)

Representatives

Thomas G. Abernethy (D)
William M. Colmer (D)
John E. Rankin (D)
Jamie L. Whitten (D)
William M. Whittington (D)
John Bell Williams (D)
W. Arthur Winstead (D)

Missouri

Senators

Forrest C. Donnell (R)
James P. Kem (R)

Representatives

Richard W. Bolling (D)
Clarence Cannon (D)
Albert S. J. Carnahan (D)
George H. Christopher (D)
Theodore L. Irving (D)
Paul C. Jones (D)
Raymond W. Karst (D)
Frank M. Karsten (D)
Clare Magee (D)
Morgan M. Moulder (D)
Dewey Short (R)
John B. Sullivan (D)
Philip J. Welch (D)

Montana

Senators

Zales N. Ecton (R)
James E. Murray (D)

Representatives

Wesley A. D'Ewart (R)
Mike Mansfield (D)

Nebraska

Senators

Hugh A. Butler (R)
Kenneth S. Wherry (R)

Representatives

Carl T. Curtis (R)
Arthur L. Miller (R)
Eugene D. O'Sullivan (D)
Karl Stefan (R)

Nevada

Senators

Patrick A. McCarran (D)
George W. Malone (R)

Representatives

Walter S. Baring (D)

New Hampshire

Senators

H. Styles Bridges (R)
Charles W. Tobey (R)

Representatives

Norris Cotton (R)
Chester E. Merrow (R)

New Jersey

Senators

Robert C. Hendrickson (R)
H. Alexander Smith (R)

Representatives

Hugh J. Addonizio (D)
James C. Auchincloss (R)
Gordon Canfield (R)
Clifford P. Case (R)
Charles A. Eaton (R)
T. Millet Hand (R)
Edward J. Hart (D)
Charles R. Howell (D)
Robert W. Kean (R)
Mary T. Norton (D)
Peter W. Rodino, Jr. (D)
J. Parnell Thomas (R) r. Jan. 1950
Harry L. Towe (R)
William B. Widnall (R) s. 1950
Charles A. Wolverton (R)

New Mexico

Senators

Clinton P. Anderson (D)
Dennis Chavez (D)

Representatives

Antonio M. Fernandez (D)
John E. Miles (D)

New York

Senators

John Foster Dulles (R) ta. 1950
Irving M. Ives (R)
Herbert H. Lehman (D) s. 1950
Robert F. Wagner (D) r. June 1949

Representatives

Sol Bloom (D) d. Mar. 1949
Charles A. Buckley (D)
William T. Byrne (D)
Emanuel Celler (D)
L. Gary Clemente (D)
W. Sterling Cole (R)
Frederic R. Coudert, Jr. (R)
John C. Davies (D)
James J. Delaney (D)
Isidore Dollinger (D)
Ralph A. Gamble (R)
Chester C. Gorski (D)
Ralph W. Gwinn (R)
Edwin A. Hall (R)
Leonard W. Hall (R)
James J. Heffernan (D)
Louis B. Heller (D)
Jacob K. Javits (R)
Bernard W. Kearney (R)
Kenneth B. Keating (R)
Edna F. Kelly (D)
Eugene J. Keogh (D)
Clarence E. Kilburn (R)
Arthur G. Klein (D)
Henry J. Latham (R)
Jay LeFevre (R)
Walter A. Lynch (D)
Christopher C. McGrath (D)
W. Kingsland Macy (R)
Vito Marcantonio (Amer. Labor)
Abraham J. Multer (D)
James J. Murphy (D)
Donald L. O'Toole (D)
Joseph L. Pfeifer (D)
William L. Pfeiffer (R)
Adam Clayton Powell, Jr. (D)
T. Vincent Quinn (D)
Daniel A. Reed (R)
R. Walter Riehlman (R)
John J. Rooney (D)
Franklin D. Roosevelt, Jr. (D)
Katharine St. George (R)
Andrew L. Somers (D) d. Apr. 1949
John Taber (R)
Anthony F. Tauriello (D)
Dean P. Taylor (R)
James W. Wadsworth, Jr. (R)

North Carolina

Senators

J. Melville Broughton (D) d. Mar. 1949
Frank P. Graham (D) ta. 1949-1950
Clyde R. Hoey (D)
Willis Smith (D) s. 1950

Representatives

Graham A. Barden (D)
Herbert C. Bonner (D)
Alfred L. Bulwinkle (D) d. Aug. 1950
F. Ertel Carlyle (D)
Richard T. Chatham (D)
Harold D. Cooley (D)
Charles B. Deane (D)
Robert L. Doughton (D)
Carl T. Durham (D)
John H. Kerr (D)
Hamilton C. Jones (D)
Woodrow W. Jones (D) s. 1950
Monroe M. Redden (D)

North Dakota

Senators

William Langer (R)
Milton R. Young (R)

Representatives

Usher L. Burdick (R)
William Lemke (R) d. May 1950

Ohio

Senators

John W. Bricker (R)
Robert A. Taft (R)

Representatives

Frances P. Bolton (R)
Edward F. Breen (D)
Walter E. Brehm (R)
Clarence J. Brown (R)
Thomas H. Burke (D)
Cliff Clevenger (R)
Robert Crosser (D)
Charles H. Elston (R)
Michael A. Feighan (D)
Wayne L. Hays (D)
Walter B. Huber (D)
Thomas A. Jenkins (R)
Michael J. Kirwan (D)
William M. McCulloch (R)
J. Harry McGregor (R)
John McSweeney (D)
James G. Polk (D)
Robert T. Secrest (D)
Frederick C. Smith (R)
John M. Vorys (R)
Earl T. Wagner (D)
Alvin F. Weichel (R)
Stephen M. Young (D)

Oklahoma

Senators

Robert S. Kerr (D)
J. W. Elmer Thomas (D)

Representatives

Carl Albert (D)
William F. Gilmer (D)
A. S. Mike Monroney (D)
Toby Morris (D)
Thomas J. Steed (D)
William G. Stigler (D)
Victor E. Wickersham (D)
George H. Wilson (D)

Oregon

Senators

Guy Cordon (R)
Wayne L. Morse (R)

Representatives

Homer D. Angell (R)
Harris Ellsworth (R)
A. Walter Norblad, Jr. (R)
Lowell Stockman (R)

Pennsylvania

Senators

Edward Martin (R)
Francis J. Myers (D)

Representatives

William A. Barrett (D)
Frank Buchanan (D)
Anthony Cavalcante (D)
Earl Chudoff (D)
Robert L. Coffey, Jr. (D)
Robert J. Corbett (R)
Paul B. Dague (R)
Harry J. Davenport (D)
Herman P. Eberharter (D)
Ivor D. Fenton (R)
Daniel J. Flood (D)
James G. Fulton (R)
Leon H. Gavin (R)
Wilson D. Gillette (R)
Louis E. Graham (R)
William T. Granahan (D)
William J. Green, Jr. (D)
Benjamin F. James (R)
Carroll D. Kearns (R)
Augustine B. Kelley (D)
John C. Kunkel (R)
Franklin H. Lichtenwalter (R)
James F. Lind (D)
Samuel K. McConnell, Jr. (R)
Thomas E. Morgan (D)
Harry P. O'Neill (D)
George M. Rhodes (D)
Robert F. Rich (R)
John P. Saylor (R)
Hardie Scott (D)
Hugh D. Scott, Jr. (D)
Richard M. Simpson (R)
James E. Van Zandt (R)
Francis E. Walter (D)

Rhode Island

Senators

Theodore F. Green (D)
Edward L. Leahy (D) ta. 1949-
  1950
J. Howard McGrath (D) r.
  Aug. 1949
John O. Pastore (D) s. 1950

Representatives

John E. Fogarty (D)
Aime J. Forand (D)

South Carolina

Senators

Olin D. Johnston (D)
Burnet R. Maybank (D)

Representatives

Joseph R. Bryson (D)
James B. Hare (D)
John L. McMillan (D)
James P. Richards (D)
L. Mendel Rivers (D)
Hugo S. Sims, Jr. (D)

South Dakota

Senators

J. Chandler Gurney (R)
Karl E. Mundt (R)

Representatives

Francis H. Case (R)
Harold O. Lovre (R)

Tennessee

Senators

Estes Kefauver (D)
Kenneth D. McKellar (D)

Representatives

Jere Cooper (D)
Clifford Davis (D)
Joseph L. Evins (D)
James B. Frazier, Jr. (D)
Albert A. Gore (D)
John Jennings, Jr. (R)
Thomas J. Murray (D)
Dayton E. Phillips (R)
J. Percy Priest (D)
James P. Sutton (D)

Texas

Senators

Tom T. Connally (D)
Lyndon B. Johnson (D)

Representatives

Lindley Beckworth (D)
Lloyd M. Bentsen, Jr. (D)
Omar T. Burleson (D)
Jesse M. Combs (D)
O. Clark Fisher (D)
Ed Gossett (D)
Ben H. Guill (D) s. 1950
Paul J. Kilday (D)
Wingate H. Lucas (D)
John E. Lyle, Jr. (D)
George H. Mahon (D)
Wright Patman (D)
Tom Pickett (D)
William R. Poage (D)
Sam Rayburn (D)
Kenneth M. Regan (D)
Olin E. Teague (D)
Albert Thomas (D)
Clark W. Thompson (D)
W. Homer Thornberry (D)
J. Frank Wilson (D)
Eugene Worley (D) r. Apr.
  1950

Utah

Senators

Elbert D. Thomas (D)
Arthur V. Watkins (R)

Representatives

Reva Z. B. Bosone (D)
Walter K. Granger (D)

Vermont

Senators

George D. Aiken (R)
Ralph E. Flanders (R)

Representatives

Charles A. Plumley (R)

Virginia

Senators

Harry F. Byrd (D)
A. Willis Robertson (D)

Representatives

Watkins M. Abbitt (D)
Schuyler Otis Bland (D) d. Feb.
  1950
Clarence G. Burton (D)
Thomas B. Fugate (D)
J. Vaughan Gary (D)
Porter Hardy, Jr. (D)
Burr P. Harrison (D)
Edward J. Robeson, Jr. (D) s.
  1950
Howard W. Smith (D)
Thomas B. Stanley (D)

Washington

Senators

Harry P. Cain (D)
Warren G. Magnuson (D)

Representatives

Hal Holmes (R)
Walter F. Horan (R)
Henry M. Jackson (D)
Russell V. Mack (R)
Hugh B. Mitchell (D)
Thor C. Tollefson (R)

West Virginia

Senators

Harley M. Kilgore (D)
Matthew M. Neely

Representatives

Cleveland M. Bailey (D)
Maurice G. Burnside (D)
Erland H. Hedrick (D)
John Kee (D)
Robert L. Ramsey (D)
Harley O. Staggers (D)

Wisconsin

Senators

Joseph R. McCarthy (R)
Alexander Wiley (R)

Representatives

Andrew J. Biemiller (D)
John W. Byrnes (R)

Glenn R. Davis (R)
Merlin Hull (R)
Frank B. Keefe (R)
Reid F. Murray (R)
Alvin E. O'Konski (R)
Lawrence H. Smith (R)
Gardner R. Wilthrow (R)
Clement J. Zablocki (D)

Wyoming

Senators

Lester C. Hunt (D)
Joseph C. O'Mahoney (D)

Representatives

Frank A. Barrett (R)

Eighty-Second Congress

(Jan. 3, 1951, to
Jan. 3, 1953)

President of the Senate: Alben
  W. Barkley
*President Pro Tempore of the
  Senate:* Kenneth D. McKellar
*Speaker of the House of
  Representatives:* Sam Rayburn

Alabama

Senators

Lister Hill (D)
John J. Sparkman (D)

Representatives

George W. Andrews (D)
Laurie C. Battle (D)
Frank W. Boykin (D)
Edward deGraffenreid (D)
Carl A. Elliott (D)
George M. Grant (D)
Robert E. Jones, Jr. (D)
Albert Rains (D)
Kenneth A. Roberts (D)

Arizona

Senators

Carl Heyden (D)
Ernest W. McFarland (D)

Representatives

John R. Murdock (D)
Harold A. Patten (D)

Arkansas

Senators

J. William Fulbright (D)
John L. McClellan (D)

Representatives

Ezekiel C. Gathings (D)

Oren Harris (D)
Brooks Hays (D)
Wilbur D. Mills (D)
William F. Norrell (D)
Boyd Tackett (D)
James W. Trimble (D)

California

Senators

William F. Knowland (R)
Richard M. Nixon (R)

Representatives

John J. Allen, Jr. (R)
John Z. Anderson (R)
Ernest K. Bramblett (R)
Clyde G. Doyle (R)
Clair Engle (D)
Franck R. Havenner (D)
Patrick J. Hillings (R)
Carl Hinshaw (R)
Chet Holifield (D)
Allan O. Hunter (R)
Donald L. Jackson (R)
Leroy Johnson (R)
Cecil R. King (D)
Gordon L. McDonough (R)
Clinton D. McKinnon (D)
George P. Miller (D)
John Phillips (R)
Norris Poulson (R)
Hubert B. Scudder (R)
John F. Shelley (D)
Harry R. Sheppard (D)
Thomas H. Werdel (R)
Samuel W. Yorty (D)

Colorado

Senators

Edwin C. Johnson (D)
Eugene D. Millikin (R)

Representatives

Wayne N. Aspinall (D)
J. Edgar Chenoweth (R)
William S. Hill (R)
Byron G. Rogers (D)

Connecticut

Senators

William Benton (D)
Brien McMahon (D) d. July
1952

Representatives

John A. McGuire (D)
Albert P. Morano (R)
James T. Patterson (R)
Abraham A. Ribicoff (D)
Antoni N. Sadlak (R)
Horace Seely-Brown, Jr. (R)

Delaware

Senators

J. Allen Frear, Jr. (D)
John J. Williams (R)

Representatives

J. Caleb Boggs (R)

Florida

Senators

Spessard L. Holland (D)
George A. Smathers (D)

Representatives

Charles E. Bennett (D)
Albert S. Herlong, Jr. (D)
William C. Lantaff (D)
Chester B. McMullen (D)
Dwight L. Rogers (D)
Robert L. F. Sikes (D)

Georgia

Senators

Walter F. George (D)
Richard B. Russell (D)

Representatives

Paul Brown (D)
A. Sidney Camp (D)
Edward E. Cox (D) d. Dec.
1952
James C. Davis (D)
Elijah L. Forrester (D)
Henderson L. Lanham (D)
Prince H. Preston, Jr. (D)
Carl Vinson (D)
William M. Wheeler (D)
John S. Wood (D)

Idaho

Senators

Henry C. Dworshak (R)
Herman Welker (R)

Representatives

Hamer H. Budge (R)
John T. Wood (R)

Illinois

Senators

Everett M. Dirksen (D)
Paul H. Douglas (D)

Representatives

Leo E. Allen (R)
Leslie C. Arends (R)
Cecil W. Bishop (R)
Fred E. Busbey (R)
Robert B. Chiperfield (R)
Marguerite Stitt Church (R)
William L. Dawson (D)
Thomas S. Gordon (D)
Richard W. Hoffman (R)
Edward H. Jenison (R)
Edgar A. Jonas (R)
John C. Kluczynski (D)
William E. McVey (R)
Peter F. Mack, Jr. (D)
Noah M. Mason (R)

Thomas J. O'Brien (D)
Melvin Price (D)
Chauncey W. Reed (R)
Adolph J. Sabath (D) d. Nov.
1952
Timothy P. Sheehan (R)
Sidney E. Simpson (R)
William L. Springer (R)
Richard B. Vail (R)
Harold H. Velde (R)
Charles W. Vursell (R)
Sidney Yates (D)

Indiana

Senators

Homer E. Capehart (R)
William E. Jenner (R)

Representatives

E. Ross Adair (R)
William G. Bray (R)
John V. Beamer (R)
Charles B. Brownson (R)
Shepard J. Crumpacker, Jr. (R)
Winfield K. Denton (D)
Charles A. Halleck (R)
Cecil M. Harden (R)
Ralph Harvey (R)
Ray J. Madden (D)
Earl Wilson (R)

Iowa

Senators

Guy M. Gillette (D)
Bourke B. Hickenlooper (R)

Representatives

Paul Cunningham (R)
James I. Dolliver (R)
Harold R. Gross (R)
Charles B. Hoeven (R)
Ben F. Jensen (R)
Karl M. LeCompte (R)
Thomas E. Martin (R)
Henry O. Talle (R)

Kansas

Senators

Frank Carlson (R)
Andrew F. Schoeppel (R)

Representatives

Albert M. Cole (R)
Myron V. George (R)
Clifford R. Hope (R)
Edward H. Rees (R)
Errett P. Scrivner (R)
Wint Smith (R)

Kentucky

Senators

Virgil M. Chapman (D) d. Mar.
1951
Earle C. Clements (D)
Thomas R. Underwood (D)

Representatives

Joe B. Bates (D)
Frank L. Chelf (D)
Noble J. Gregory (D)
James S. Golden (R)
Thruston B. Morton (R)
Carl D. Perkins (D)
Brent Spence (D)
Thomas R. Underwood (D) r.
Mar. 1951
John C. Watts (D)
John A. Whitaker (D) d. Dec.
1951

Louisiana

Senators

Allen J. Ellender, Sr. (D)
Russell B. Long (D)

Representatives

A. Leonard Allen (D)
T. Hale Boggs (D)
Overton Brooks (D)
F. Edward Hebert (D)
Henry D. Larcade, Jr. (D)
James H. Morrison (D)
Otto E. Passman (D)
Edwin E. Willis (D)

Maine

Senators

Ralph O. Brewster (R)
Margaret Chase Smith (R)

Representatives

Frank Fellows (R) d. Aug. 1951
Robert Hale (R)
Clifford G. McIntire (R) s.
1952
Charles P. Nelson (R)

Maryland

Senators

John Marshall Butler (R)
Herbert R. O'Conor (D)

Representatives

J. Glenn Beall (R)
James P. S. Devereux (R)
George H. Fallon (D)
Edward A. Garmatz (D)
Edward T. Miller (R)
Lansdale G. Sasscer (D)

Massachusetts

Senators

Henry Cabot Lodge, Jr. (R)
Leverett Saltonstall (R)

Representatives

William H. Bates (R)
Harold D. Donohue (D)
Foster Furcolo (D) r. Sept.
1952

Angier L. Goodwin (R)
Christian A. Herter (R)
John W. Heselton (R)
John F. Kennedy (D)
Thomas J. Lane (D)
John W. McCormack (D)
Joseph W. Martin, Jr. (R)
Donald W. Nicholson (R)
Philip J. Philbin (D)
Edith Nourse Rogers (R)
Richard B. Wigglesworth (R)

Michigan

Senators

Homer Ferguson (R)
Arthur Blair Moody (D)
Arthur H. Vandenberg (R) d.
  Apr. 1951

Representatives

John B. Bennett (R)
William W. Blackney (R)
Fred L. Crawford (R)
John D. Dingell (D)
George A. Dondero (R)
Gerald R. Ford, Jr. (R)
Clare E. Hoffman (R)
John Lesinski, Jr. (D)
Thaddeus M. Machrowicz (D)
George Meader (R)
George D. O'Brien (D)
Charles E. Potter (R) r. Nov.
  1952
Louis C. Rabaut (D)
Paul W. Shafer (R)
Ruth Thompson (R)
Jesse P. Wolcott (R)
Roy O. Woodruff (R)

Minnesota

Senators

Hubert H. Humphrey (D)
Edward J. Thye (R)

Representatives

H. Carl Andersen (R)
August H. Andresen (R)
John A. Blatnik (D)
Harold C. Hagen (R)
Walter H. Judd (R)
Eugene J. McCarthy (D)
Fred Marshall
Joseph P. O'Hara (R)
Roy W. Wier (D)

Mississippi

Senators

James O. Eastland (D)
John C. Stennis (D)

Representatives

Thomas G. Abernethy (D)
William M. Colmer (D)
John E. Rankin (D)
Frank E. Smith (D)
Jamie L. Whitten (D)
John Bell Williams (D)
W. Arthur Winstead (D)

Missouri

Senators

Thomas C. Hennings, Jr. (D)
James P. Kem (R)

Representatives

Orland K. Armstrong (R)
Claude I. Bakewell (R)
Richard W. Bolling (D)
Clarence Cannon (D)
Albert S. J. Carnahan (D)
Thomas B. Curtis (R)
Theodore L. Irving (D)
Paul C. Jones (D)
Frank M. Karsten (D)
Clare Magee (D)
Morgan M. Moulder (D)
Dewey Short (R)
John B. Sullivan (D) d. Jan.
  1951
Philip J. Welch (D)

Montana

Senators

Zales N. Ecton (R)
James E. Murray (D)

Representatives

Wesley A. D'Ewart (R)
Mike Mansfield (D)

Nebraska

Senators

Hugh A. Butler (R)
Frederick A. Seaton (R) s. 1952
Kenneth S. Wherry (R) d. Nov.
  1951

Represenatives

Howard H. Buffett (R)
Carl T. Curtis (R)
Robert D. Harrison (R) s. 1952
Arthur L. Miller (R)
Karl Stefan (R) d. Oct. 1951

Nevada

Senators

Patrick A. McCarran (D)
George W. Malone (R)

Representatives

Walter S. Baring (D)

New Hampshire

Senators

H. Styles Bridges (R)
Charles W. Tobey (R)

Representatives

Norris Cotton (R)
Chester E. Merrow (R)

New Jersey

Senators

Robert C. Hendrickson (R)
H. Alexander Smith (R)

Representatives

Hugh J. Addonizio (D)
James C. Auchincloss (R)
Gordon Canfield (R)
Clifford P. Case (R)
Charles A. Eaton (R)
T. Millet Hand (R)
Edward J. Hart (D)
Charles R. Howell (D)
Robert W. Kean (R)
Frank C. Osmers, Jr. (R) s.
  1952
Peter W. Rodino, Jr. (D)
Alfred D. Sieminski (D)
Harry L. Towe (R) r. Sept.
  1951
William B. Widnall (R)
Charles A. Wolverton (R)

New Mexico

Senators

Clinton P. Anderson (D)
Dennis Chavez (D)

Representatives

John J. Dempsey (D)
Antonio M. Fernandez (D)

New York

Senators

Irving M. Ives (R)
Herbert H. Lehman (D)

Representatives

Victor L. Anfuso (D)
Charles A. Buckley (D)
John C. Butler (R)
William T. Byrne (D) d. Jan.
  1952
Emanuel Celler (D)
L. Gary Clemente (D)
W. Sterling Cole (R)
Frederic R. Coudert, Jr. (R)
James J. Delaney (D)
Isidore Dollinger (D)
James G. Donovan (D,R,L)
Sidney A. Fine (D)
Ralph A. Gamble (R)
Ernest Greenwood (D)
Ralph W. Gwinn (R)
Edwin A. Hall (R)
Leonard W. Hall (R)
James J. Heffernan (D)
Louis B. Heller (D)
Jacob K. Javits (R)
Bernard W. Kearney (R)
Kenneth B. Keating (R)
Edna F. Kelly (D)
Eugene J. Keogh (D)
Clarence E. Kilburn (R)
Arthur G. Klein (D)
Henry J. Latham (R)
Christopher C. McGrath (D)
William E. Miller (R)

Abraham J. Multer (D)
James J. Murphy (D)
Leo W. O'Brien (D) s. 1952
Donald L. O'Toole (D)
Harold C. Ostertag (R)
Adam Clayton Powell, Jr. (D)
T. Vincent Quinn (D) r. Dec.
  1951
Edmund P. Radwan (R)
Daniel A. Reed (R)
R. Walter Riehlman (R)
John J. Rooney (D)
Franklin D. Roosevelt, Jr. (D)
Robert T. Ross (R) s. 1952
Katharine St. George (R)
John Taber (R)
Dean P. Taylor (R)
J. Ernest Wharton (R)
William R. Williams (R)

North Carolina

Senators

Clyde R. Hoey (D)
Willis Smith (D)

Representatives

Graham A. Barden (D)
Herbert C. Bonner (D)
F. Ertel Carlyle (D)
Richard T. Chatham (D)
Harold D. Cooley (D)
Charles B. Deane (D)
Robert L. Doughton (D)
Carl T. Durham (D)
Hamilton C. Jones (D)
Woodrow W. Jones (D)
John H. Kerr (D)
Monroe M. Redden (D)

North Dakota

Senators

William Langer (R)
Milton R. Young (R)

Representatives

Fred G. Aandahl (R)
Usher L. Burdick (R)

Ohio

Senators

John W. Bricker (R)
Robert A. Taft (R)

Representatives

William H. Ayres (R)
George H. Bender (R)
Jackson E. Betts (R)
Frances P. Bolton (R)
Frank T. Bow (R)
Edward F. Breen (D) r. Oct.
  1951
Walter E. Brehm (R)
Clarence J. Brown (R)
Cliff Clevenger (R)
Robert Crosser (D)
Charles H. Elston (R)
Michael A. Feighan (D)
Wayne L. Hays (D)
William E. Hess (R)

Thomas A. Jenkins (R)
Michael J. Kirwan (D)
J. Harry McGregor (R)
William M. McCulloch (R)
James G. Polk (D)
Henry F. Reams
Paul F. Schenck (R) s. 1952
Robert T. Secrest (D)
John M. Vorys (R)
Alvin F. Weichel (R)

Oklahoma

Senators

Robert S. Kerr (D)
A. S. Mike Monroney (D)

Representatives

Carl Albert (D)
Page H. Belcher (R)
John Jarman (D)
Toby Morris (D)
George B. Schwabe (R) d. Apr.
  1952
Thomas J. Steed (D)
William G. Stigler (D) d. Aug.
  1952
Victor E. Wickersham (D)

Oregon

Senators

Guy Gordon (R)
Wayne L. Morse (R)

Representatives

Homer D. Angell (R)
Harris Ellsworth (R)
A. Walter Norblad, Jr. (R)
Lowell Stockman (R)

Pennsylvania

Senators

James H. Duff (R)
Edward Martin (D)

Representatives

William A. Barrett (D)
Frank B. Buchanan (D) d. Apr.
  1951
Vera D. Buchanan (D)
Alvin R. Bush (R)
Joseph L. Carrigg (R) s. 1952
Robert J. Corbett (D)
Earl Chudoff (D)
Paul B. Dague (R)
Harmar J. Denny, Jr. (D)
Herman P. Eberharter (D)
Ivor D. Fenton (R)
Daniel J. Flood (D)
James G. Fulton (R)
Leon H. Gavin (R)
Wilson D. Gillette (R) d. Aug.
  1951
Louis E. Graham (R)
William T. Granahan (D)
William J. Green, Jr. (D)
Benjamin F. James (R)
Carroll D. Kearns (R)
Augustine B. Kelley (D)
Karl C. King (R) s. 1952

James F. Lind (D)
Samuel K. McConnell, Jr. (R)
Thomas E. Morgan (D)
Walter M. Mumma (R)
Harry P. O'Neill (D)
George M. Rhodes (D)
John P. Saylor (R)
Hardie Scott (R)
Hugh D. Scott, Jr. (R)
Richard M. Simpson (R)
Edward L. Sittler, Jr. (R)
James E. Van Zandt (R)
Albert C. Vaughn (R) d. Sept.
  1951
Francis E. Walter (D)

Rhode Island

Senators

Theodore F. Green (D)
John O. Pastore (D)

Representatives

John E. Fogarty (D)
Aime J. Forand (D)

South Carolina

Senators

Olin D. Johnston (D)
Burnet R. Maybank (D)

Representatives

Joseph R. Bryson (D)
W. J. Bryan Dorn (D)
John L. McMillan (D)
James P. Richards (D)
John J. Riley (D)
L. Mendel Rivers (D)

South Dakota

Senators

Francis H. Case (R)
Karl E. Mundt (R)

Representatives

Ellis Y. Berry (R)
Harold O. Lovre (R)

Tennessee

Senators

Estes Kefauver (D)
Kenneth D. McKellar (D)

Representatives

Howard H. Baker (R)
Jere Cooper (D)
Clifford Davis (D)
Joseph L. Evins (D)
James B. Frazier, Jr. (D)
Albert A. Gore (D)
Thomas J. Murray (D)
J. Percy Priest (D)
B. Carroll Reece (D)
James P. Sutton (D)

Texas

Senators

Tom T. Connally (D)
Lyndon B. Johnson (D)

Representatives

Lindley Beckworth (D)
Lloyd M. Bentsen, Jr. (D)
Omar T. Burleson (D)
Jesse M. Combs (D)
O. Clark Fisher (D)
Ed Gossett (D) r. July 1951
Frank N. Ikard (D)
Paul J. Kilday (D)
Wingate H. Lucas (D)
John E. Lyle, Jr. (D)
George H. Mahon (D)
Wright Patman (D)
Tom Pickett (D) r. June 1952
William R. Poage (D)
Sam Rayburn (D)
Kenneth M. Regan (D)
Walter E. Rogers (D)
Olin E. Teague (D)
Albert Thomas (D)
Clark W. Thompson (D)
W. Homer Thornberry (D)
J. Frank Wilson (D)

Utah

Senators

Wallace F. Bennett (R)
Arthur V. Watkins (R)

Representatives

Reva Z. B. Bosone (D)
Walter K. Granger (D)

Vermont

Senators

George D. Aiken (R)
Ralph E. Flanders (R)

Representatives

Winston L. Prouty (R)

Virginia

Senators

Harry F. Byrd (D)
A. Willis Robertson (D)

Representatives

Watkins M. Abbitt (D)
Clarence G. Burton (D)
Thomas B. Fugate (D)
J. Vaughan Gary (D)
Porter Hardy, Jr. (D)
Burr P. Harrison (D)
Edward J. Robeson, Jr. (D)
Howard W. Smith (D)
Thomas B. Stanley (D)

Washington

Senators

Harry P. Cain (D)
Warren G. Magnuson (D)

Representatives

Hal Holmes (R)
Walter F. Horan (R)
Henry M. Jackson (D)
Russell V. Mack (R)
Hugh B. Mitchell (D)
Thor C. Tollefson (R)

West Virginia

Senators

Harley M. Kilgore (D)
Matthew M. Neely (D)

Representatives

Cleveland M. Bailey (D)
Maurice G. Burnside (D)
Erland H. Hedrick (D)
John Kee (D) d. May 1951
Maude Elizabeth Kee (D)
Robert L. Ramsay (D)
Harley O. Staggers (D)

Wisconsin

Senators

Joseph R. McCarthy (R)
Alexander Wiley (R)

Representatives

John W. Byrnes (R)
Glenn R. Davis (R)
Merlin Hull (R)
Charles J. Kersten (R)
Reid F. Murray (R) d. Apr.
  1952
Alvin E. O'Konski (R)
William K. Van Pelt (R)
Lawrence H. Smith (R)
Gardner R. Withrow (R)
Clement J. Zablocki (D)

Wyoming

Senators

Lester C. Hunt (D)
Joseph C. O'Mahoney (D)

Representatives

William H. Harrison (R)

Eighty-Third Congress

(Jan. 3, 1953, to
Jan. 3, 1955)

President of the Senate: Richard
  M. Nixon

*President Pro Tempore of the
    Senate:* H. Styles Bridges
*Speaker of the House of
    Representatives:* Joseph W.
    Martin, Jr.

Alabama

Senators

Lister Hill (D)
John J. Sparkman (D)

Representatives

George W. Andrews (D)
Laurie C. Battle (D)
Frank W. Boykin (D)
Carl A. Elliott (D)
George M. Grant (D)
Robert E. Jones, Jr. (D)
Albert Rains (D)
Kenneth A. Roberts (D)
Armistead I. Selden, Jr. (D)

Arizona

Senators

Barry M. Goldwater (D)
Carl Hayden (D)

Representatives

Harold A. Patten (D)
John J. Rhodes (R)

Arkansas

Senators

J. William Fulbright (D)
John L. McClellan (D)

Representatives

Ezekiel C. Gathings (D)
Oren Harris (D)
Brooks Hays (D)
Wilbur D. Mills (D)
William F. Norell (D)
James W. Trimble (D)

California

Senators

William F. Knowland (R)
Thomas H. Kuchel (R)

Representatives

John J. Allen, Jr. (R)
Ernest K. Bramblett (R)
Robert L. Condon (D)
Clyde G. Doyle (D)
Clair Engle (D)
Charles S. Gubser (R)
Harlan F. Hagan (D)
Edgar W. Hiestand (R)
Patrick J. Hillings (R)
Carl Hinshaw (R)
Chet Holifield (D)
Joseph F. Holt (R)
Craig Hosmer (R)
Allan O. Hunter (R)
Donald L. Jackson (R)

Leroy Johnson (R)
Cecil R. King (D)
Glenard P. Lipscomb (R) s.
    1954
Gordon L. McDonough (R)
William S. Malliard (R)
George P. Miller (D)
John E. Moss, Jr. (D)
John Phillips (R)
Norris Poulson (R) r. June
    1953
Hubert B. Scudder (R)
John F. Shelley (D)
Harry R. Sheppard (D)
James B. Utt (R)
Robert C. Wilson (R)
Samuel W. Yorty (D)
J. Arthur Younger (R)

Colorado

Senators

Edwin C. Johnson (D)
Eugene D. Millikin (R)

Representatives

Wayne N. Aspinall (D)
J. Edgar Chenoweth (R)
William S. Hill (R)
Byron G. Rogers (R)

Connecticut

Senators

Prescott S. Bush (R)
William A. Purtell (R)

Representatives

Albert W. Cretella (R)
Thomas J. Dodd (D)
Albert P. Morano (R)
James T. Patterson (R)
Antoni N. Sadlak (R)
Horace Seely-Brown, Jr. (R)

Delaware

Senators

John J. Williams (R)
J. Allen Frear, Jr. (D)

Representatives

Herbert B. Warburton (R)

Florida

Senators

Spessard L. Holland (D)
George A. Smathers (D)

Representatives

Charles E. Bennett (D)
Courtney W. Campbell (D)
James A. Haley (D)
Albert S. Herlong, Jr. (D)
William C. Lantaff (D)
Donald R. Matthews (D)
Dwight L. Rogers (D) d. Dec.
    1954

Robert L. F. Sikes (D)

Georgia

Senators

Walter F. George (D)
Richard B. Russell (D)

Representatives

Paul Brown (D)
A. Sidney Camp (D) d. July
    1954
James C. Davis (D)
Elijah L. Forrester (D)
Phillip M. Landrum (D)
Henderson L. Lanham (D)
John L. Pilcher (D)
Prince H. Preston, Jr. (D)
Carl Vinson (D)
William M. Wheeler (D)

Idaho

Senators

Henry C. Dworshak (R)
Herman Welker (R)

Representatives

Hamer H. Budge (R)
Gracie B. Pfost (D)

Illinois

Senators

Everett M. Dirksen (R)
Paul H. Douglas (D)

Representatives

Leo E. Allen (R)
Leslie C. Arends (R)
Cecil W. Bishop (R)
Fred E. Busbey (R)
Robert B. Chiperfield (R)
Marguerite Stitt Church (R)
William L. Dawson (D)
Thomas S. Gordon (D)
Richard W. Hoffman (R)
Edgar A. Jonas (R)
John C. Kluczynski (D)
William E. McVey (R)
Peter F. Mack, Jr. (D)
Noah M. Mason (R)
Thomas J. O'Brien (D)
Barratt O'Hara (D)
Melvin Price (D)
Chauncey W. Reed (R)
Timothy P. Sheehan (R)
Sidney E. Simpson (R)
William L. Springer (R)
Harold H. Velde (R)
Charles W. Vursell (R)
Sidney R. Yates (D)

Indiana

Senators

Homer E. Capehart (R)
William E. Jenner (R)

Representatives

E. Ross Adair (R)
John V. Beamer (R)
William G. Bray (R)
Charles B. Brownson (R)
Shepard J. Crumpacker, Jr. (R)
Charles A. Halleck (R)
Cecil M. Harden (R)
Ralph Harvey (R)
Ray J. Madden (D)
D. Bailey Merrill (R)
Earl Wilson (R)

Iowa

Senators

Guy M. Gillette (D)
Bourke B. Hickenlooper (R)

Representatives

Paul Cunningham (R)
James I. Dolliver (R)
Harold R. Gross (R)
Charles B. Hoeven (R)
Ben F. Jensen (R)
Karl M. LeCompte (R)
Thomas E. Martin (R)
Henry O. Talle (R)

Kansas

Senators

Frank Carlson (R)
Andrew F. Schoeppel (R)

Representatives

Myron V. George (R)
Clifford R. Hope (R)
Howard S. Miller (D)
Edward H. Rees (R)
Errett P. Scrivner (R)
Wint Smith (R)

Kentucky

Senators

Earle C. Clements (D)
John Sherman Cooper (R)

Representatives

Frank L. Chelf (D)
James S. Golden (R)
Noble J. Gregory (D)
William H. Natcher (D) s. 1954
Carl D. Perkins (D)
John M. Robsion, Jr. (R)
Brent Spence (D)
John C. Watts (D)
Garrett L. Withers (D) d. April
    1953

Louisiana

Senators

Allen J. Ellender, Sr. (D)
Russell B. Long (D)

Representatives

T. Hale Boggs (D)
Overton Brooks (D)
F. Edward Hebert (D)
George S. Long (D)
James H. Morrison (D)
Otto E. Passman (D)
T. Ashton Thompson (D)
Edwin E. Willis (D)

Maine

Senators

Frederick G. Payne (R)
Margaret Chase Smith (R)

Representatives

Robert Hale (R)
Clifford G. McIntire (R)
Charles P. Nelson (R)

Maryland

Senators

J. Glenn Beall (R)
John Marshall Butler (R)

Representatives

James P. S. Devereux (R)
George H. Fallon (D)
Samuel N. Friedel (D)
Edward A. Garmatz (D)
DeWitt S. Syde (R)
Edward T. Miller (R)
Frank Small, Jr. (R)

Massachusetts

Senators

John F. Kennedy (D)
Leverett Saltonstall (R)

Representatives

William H. Bates (R)
Edward P. Boland (D)
Laurence Curtis (R)
Harold D. Donohue (D)
Angier L. Goodwin (R)
John W. Heselton (R)
Thomas J. Lane (D)
John W. McCormack (D)
Joseph W. Martin, Jr. (R)
Donald W. Nicholson (R)
Thomas P. O'Neill, Jr. (D)
Philip J. Philbin (D)
Edith Nourse Rogers (R)
Richard B. Wigglesworth (R)

Michigan

Senators

Homer Ferguson (R)
Charles E. Potter (R)

Representatives

John B. Bennett (R)
Alvin M. Bentley (R)
Elford A. Cederberg (R)

Kit F. Clardy (R)
John D. Dingell (D)
George A. Dondero (R)
Gerald R. Ford, Jr. (R)
Clare E. Hoffman (R)
Victor A. Knox (R)
John Lesinski, Jr. (D)
Thaddeus M. Machrowicz (D)
George Meader (R)
Charles G. Oakman (R)
George D. O'Brien (D)
Louis C. Rabaut (D)
Paul W. Shafer (R) d. Aug.
    1954
Ruth Thompson (R)
Jesse P. Wolcott (R)

Minnesota

Senators

Hubert H. Humphrey (D)
Edward J. Thye (R)

Representatives

H. Carl Andersen (R)
August H. Andresen (R)
John A. Blatnik (D)
Harold C. Hagen (R)
Walter H. Judd (R)
Eugene J. McCarthy (D)
Fred Marshall (D)
Joseph P. O'Hara (R)
Roy W. Wier (D)

Mississippi

Senators

James O. Eastland (D)
John C. Stennis (D)

Representatives

Thomas G. Abernethy (D)
William M. Colmer (D)
Frank E. Smith (D)
Jamie L. Whitten (D)
John Bell Williams (D)
W. Arthur Winstead (D)

Missouri

Senators

Thomas C. Hennings, Jr. (D)
Stuart Symington (D)

Representatives

Richard W. Bolling (D)
Clarence Cannon (D)
Albert S. J. Carnahan (D)
William C. Cole (R)
Thomas B. Curtis (R)
Jeffrey P. Hillelson (R)
Paul C. Jones (D)
Frank M. Karsten (D)
Morgan M. Moulder (D)
Dewey Short (R)
Leonor Kretzer Sullivan (D)

Montana

Senators

Mike Mansfield (D)
James E. Murray (D)

Representatives

Wesley A. D'Ewart (R)
Lee Metcalf (D)

Nebraska

Senators

Hazel H. Abel (R) s. 1954, r.
    Dec. 1954
Eva K. Bowring (R) ta. 1954
Hugh A. Butler (R) d. July
    1954
Dwight P. Griswold (R) d.
    Apr. 1954
Roman L. Hruska (R) s. 1954
Sam W. Reynolds (R) ta. 1954

Representatives

Carl T. Curtis (R)
Robert D. Harrison (R)
Roman L. Hruska (R) r. Nov.
    1954
Arthur L. Miller (R)

Nevada

Senators

Alan H. Bible (D) s. 1954
Ernest S. Brown (R) ta. 1954
Patrick A. McCarran (D) d.
    Sept. 1954
George W. Malone (R)

Representatives

Clifton Young (R)

New Hampshire

Senators

H. Styles Bridges (R)
Norris Cotton (R) s. 1954
Charles W. Tobey (R) d. July
    1953
Robert W. Upton (R) ta. 1954

Representatives

Norris Cotton (R) r. Nov. 1954
Chester E. Merrow (R)

New Jersey

Senators

Robert C. Hendrickson (R)
H. Alexander Smith (R)

Representatives

Hugh J. Addonizio (D)
James C. Auchincloss (R)
Gordon Canfield (R)

Clifford P. Case (R) r. Aug.
    1953
Peter H. B. Frelinghuysen, Jr.
    (R)
T. Millet Hand (R)
Edward J. Hart (D)
Charles R. Howell (D)
Robert W. Kean (R)
Frank C. Osmers, Jr. (R)
Peter W. Rodino, Jr. (D)
Alfred D. Sieminski (D)
William B. Widnall (R)
Harrison A. Williams, Jr. (D) s.
    1954
Charles A. Wolverton (R)

New Mexico

Senators

Clinton P. Anderson (D)
Dennis Chavez (D)

Representatives

John J. Dempsey (D)
Antonio M. Fernandez (D)

New York

Senators

Irving M. Ives (R)
Herbert H. Lehman (D)

Representatives

Frank J. Becker (R)
Albert H. Bosch (R)
Charles A. Buckley (D)
Emanuel Celler (D)
W. Sterling Cole (R)
Frederic R. Coudert, Jr. (R)
James J. Delaney (D)
Steven B. Derounian (R)
Isidore Dollinger (D)
James G. Donovan (D)
Francis E. Dorn (R)
Sidney A. Fine (D)
Paul A. Fino (R)
Ralph A. Gamble (R)
Ralph W. Gwinn (R)
Louis B. Heller (D) r. July
    1954
Lester Holtzman (D)
Jacob K. Javits (R)
Bernard W. Kearney (R)
Kenneth B. Keating (R)
Edna F. Kelly (D)
Eugene J. Keogh (D)
Clarence E. Kilburn (R)
Arthur G. Klein (D)
Henry J. Latham (R)
William E. Miller (R)
Abraham J. Multer (D)
Leo W. O'Brien (D)
Harold C. Ostertag (R)
John R. Pillion (R)
Adam Clayton Powell, Jr. (D)
Edmund P. Radwan (R)
John H. Ray (R)
Daniel A. Reed (R)
R. Walter Riehlman (R)
John J. Rooney (D)
Franklin D. Roosevelt, Jr. (D)
Katharine St. George (R)
John Taber (R)
Dean P. Taylor (R)
Stuyvesant Wainright, II (R)

J. Ernest Wharton (R)
William R. Williams (R)

North Carolina

Senators

Sam J. Ervin, Jr. (D) s. 1954
Clyde R. Hoey (D) d. May
1954
Alton A. Lennon (D) ta. 1953
W. Kerr Scott (D) s. 1954
Willis Smith (D) d. June 1953

Representatives

Hugh Q. Alexander (D)
Graham A. Barden (D)
Herbert C. Bonner (D)
F. Ertel Carlyle (D)
Richard T. Chatham (D)
Harold D. Cooley (D)
Charles B. Deane (D)
Carl T. Durham (D)
Lawrence H. Fountain (D)
Charles R. Jonas (R)
Woodrow W. Jones (D)
George A. Shuford (D)

North Dakota

Senators

William Langer (R)
Milton R. Young (R)

Representatives

Usher L. Burdick (R)
Otto Krueger (R)

Ohio

Senators

John W. Bricker (R)
Thomas A. Burke (D) ta. 1954
Robert A. Taft (R) d. July
1953

Representatives

William H. Ayers (R)
George H. Bender (R) r. Dec.
1954
Jackson E. Betts (R)
Frances P. Bolton (R)
Oliver P. Bolton (R)
Frank T. Bow (R)
Clarence J. Brown (R)
Cliff Clevenger (R)
Robert Crosser (D)
Michael A. Feighan (D)
Wayne L. Hays (D)
William E. Hess (R)
Thomas A. Jenkins (R)
Michael J. Kirwan (D)
William M. McCulloch (R)
J. Harry McGregor (R)
James G. Polk (D)
Henry F. Reams (I)
Paul F. Schenck (R)
Gordon H. Scherer (R)
Robert T. Secrest (D) r. Sept.
1954
John M. Vorys (R)
Alvin F. Weichel (R)

Oklahoma

Senators

Robert S. Kerr (D)
A. S. Mike Monroney (D)

Representatives

Carl Albert (D)
Page H. Belcher (R)
Edmond Emondson (D)
John Jarman (D)
Thomas J. Steed (D)
Victor E. Wickersham (D)

Oregon

Senators

Guy Cordon (R)
Wayne L. Morse (R)

Representatives

Homer D. Angell (R)
Samuel H. Coon (R)
Harris Ellsworth (R)
A. Walter Norblad, Jr. (R)

Pennsylvania

Senators

James H. Duff (R)
Edward Martin (D)

Representatives

William A. Barrett (D)
Edward J. Bonin (R)
Vera D. Buchanan (D)
Alvin R. Bush (R)
James A. Byrne (D)
Joseph L. Carrigg (R)
Earl Chudoff (D)
Robert J. Corbett (R)
Paul B. Dague (R)
Herman P. Eberharter (D)
Ivor D. Fenton (R)
James G. Fulton (R)
Leon H. Gavin (R)
Louis E. Graham (R)
William T. Granahan (D)
William J. Green, Jr. (D)
Benjamin F. James (R)
Carroll D. Kearns (R)
Augustine B. Kelly (D)
Karl C. King (R)
Samuel K. McConnell, Jr. (R)
Thomas E. Morgan (D)
Walter M. Mumma (R)
George M. Rhodes (D)
John P. Saylor (R)
Hugh D. Scott, Jr. (D)
Richard M. Simpson (R)
S. Walter Stauffer (R)
James E. Van Zandt (R)
Francis E. Walter (D)

Rhode Island

Senators

Theodore F. Green (D)
John O. Pastore (D)

Representatives

John E. Fogarty (D)
Aime J. Forand (D)

South Carolina

Senators

Charles E. Daniel (D) s. 1954
Olin D. Johnston (D)
Burnet R. Maybank (D) d.
Sept. 1954

Representatives

Robert T. Ashmore (D)
Joseph R. Bryson (D) d. Mar.
1953
W. J. Bryan Dorn (D)
John L. McMillan (D)
James P. Richards (D)
John J. Riley (D)
L. Mendel Rivers (D)

South Dakota

Senators

Francis H. Case (R)
Karl E. Mundt (R)

Representatives

Ellis Y. Berry (R)
Harold O. Lovre (R)

Tennessee

Senators

Albert A. Gore (D)
Estes Kefauver (D)

Representatives

Howard H. Baker (R)
Jere Cooper (D)
Clifford Davis (D)
Joseph L. Evins (D)
James B. Frazier, Jr. (D)
Thomas J. Murray (D)
J. Percy Priest (D)
B. Carroll Reece (R)
James P. Sutton (D)

Texas

Senators

M. Price Daniel (D)
Lyndon B. Johnson (D)

Representatives

Lloyd M. Bentsen, Jr. (D)
Jack B. Brooks (D)
Omar T. Burleson (D)
Martin Dies, Jr. (D)
John V. Dowdy (D)
O. Clark Fisher (D)
Brady P. Gentry (D)
Frank N. Ikard (D)
Paul J. Kilday (D)
Wingate H. Lucas (D)
John E. Lyle, Jr. (D)
George H. Mahon (D)

Wright Patman (D)
William R. Poage (D)
Sam Rayburn (D)
Kenneth M. Regan (D)
Walter E. Rogers (D)
Olin E. Teague (D)
Albert Thomas (D)
Clark W. Thompson (D)
W. Homer Thornberry (D)
J. Frank Wilson (D)

Utah

Senators

Wallace F. Bennett (R)
Arthur V. Watkins (R)

Representatives

William A. Dawson (R)
Douglas R. Stringfellow (R)

Vermont

Senators

George D. Aiken (R)
Ralph E. Flanders (R)

Representatives

Winston L. Prouty (R)

Virginia

Senators

Harry F. Byrd (D)
A. Willis Robertson (D)

Representatives

Watkins M. Abbitt (D)
Joel T. Broyhill (R)
J. Vaughan Gary (D)
Porter Hardy, Jr. (D)
Burr P. Harrison (D)
Richard H. Poff (R)
Edward J. Robeson, Jr. (D)
Howard W. Smith (D)
Thomas B. Stanley (D) r. Feb.
1953
William M. Tuck (D)
William C. Wampler (R)

Washington

Senators

Henry M. Jackson (D)
Warren G. Magnuson (D)

Representatives

Hal Holmes (R)
Walter F. Horan (R)
Russell V. Mack (R)
Donald H. Magnuson (D)
Thomas M. Pelly (R)
Thor C. Tollefson (R)
Alfred J. Westland (R)

West Virginia

Senators

Harley M. Kilgore (D)
Matthew M. Neely (D)

Representatives

Cleveland M. Bailey (D)
Robert C. Byrd (D)
Maude Elizabeth Kee (D)
Robert H. Mollohan (D)
William E. Neal (R)
Harley O. Staggers (D)

Wisconsin

Senators

Joseph R. McCarthy (R)
Alexander Wiley (R)

Representatives

John W. Byrnes (R)
Glenn R. Davis (R)
Merlin Hull (R) d. May 1953
Lester R. Johnson (D) s. 1954
Charles J. Kersten (R)
Melvin R. Laird (R)
Alvin E. O'Konski (R)
Lawrence H. Smith (R)
William K. Van Pelt (R)
Gardner R. Withrow (R)
Clement J. Zablocki (D)

Wyoming

Senators

Lester C. Hunt (D) d. June
  1954
Edward D. Crippa (R) ta. 1954
Joseph C. O'Mahoney (D) s.
  1954
Frank A. Barrett (R)

Representatives

William H. Harrison (R)

Eighty-Fourth Congress

(Jan. 3, 1955, to
Jan. 3, 1957)

President of the Senate: Richard
  M. Nixon
*President Pro Tempore of the
  Senate:* Walter F. George
*Speaker of the House of
  Representatives:* Sam Rayburn

Alabama

Senators

Lister Hill (D)
John J. Sparkman (D)

Representatives

George W. Andrews (D)
Frank W. Boykin (D)
Carl A. Elliott (D)
George M. Grant (D)
George Huddleston, Jr. (D)
Robert E. Jones, Jr. (D)
Albert Rains (D)
Kenneth A. Roberts (D)
Armistead I. Selden, Jr. (D)

Arizona

Senators

Barry M. Goldwater (D)
Carl Hayden (D)

Representatives

John J. Rhodes (R)
Stewart L. Udall (D)

Arkansas

Senators

J. William Fulbright (D)
John L. McClellan (D)

Representatives

Ezekiel C. Gathings (D)
Oren Harris (D)
Brooks Hays (D)
Wilbur D. Mills (D)
William F. Norrell (D)
James W. Trimble (D)

California

Senators

William F. Knowland (R)
Thomas H. Kuchel (R)

Representatives

John J. Allen, Jr. (R)
John F. Baldwin, Jr. (R)
Clyde G. Doyle (D)
Clair Engle (D)
Charles S. Gubser (R)
Harlan F. Hagen (D)
Patrick J. Hillings (R)
Edgar W. Hiestand (R)
Carl Hinshaw (R)
Chet Holifield (D)
Joseph F. Holt (R)
Craig Hosmer (R)
Donald L. Jackson (R)
Leroy Johnson (R)
Cecil R. King (D)
Glenard P. Lipscomb (R)
Gordon L. McDonough (R)
William S. Mailliard (R)
George P. Miller (D)
John E. Moss, Jr. (D)
John Phillips (R)
James Roosevelt (D)
Hubert B. Scudder (R)
John F. Shelley (D)
Harry R. Sheppard (D)
Bernice F. Sisk (D)
Charles M. Teague (R)
James B. Utt (R)
Robert C. Wilson (R)

J. Arthur Younger (R)

Colorado

Senators

Gordon L. Allott (R)
Eugene D. Millikin (R)

Representatives

Wayne N. Aspinall (D)
J. Edgar Chenoweth (R)
William S. Hill (R)
Byron G. Rogers (D)

Connecticut

Senators

Prescott S. Bush (R)
William A. Purtell (R)

Representatives

Albert W. Cretella (R)
Thomas J. Dodd (D)
Albert P. Morano (R)
James T. Patterson (R)
Antoni N. Sadlak (R)
Horace Seely-Brown, Jr. (R)

Delaware

Senators

J. Allen Frear, Jr. (D)
John J. Williams (R)

Representatives

Harris B. McDowell, Jr. (D)

Florida

Senators

Spessard L. Holland (D)
George A. Smathers (D)

Representatives

Charles E. Bennett (D)
William C. Cramer (R)
Dante B. Fascell (D)
James A. Haley (D)
Albert S. Herlong, Jr. (D)
Donald R. Matthews (D)
Paul G. Rogers (D)
Robert L. F. Sikes (D)

Georgia

Senators

Walter F. George (D)
Richard B. Russell (D)

Representatives

Iris F. Blitch (D)
Paul Brown (D)
James C. Davis (D)
Elijah L. Forrester (D)
John J. Flynt, Jr. (D)
Phillip M. Landrum (D)

Henderson L. Lanham (D)
John L. Pilcher (D)
Prince H. Preston, Jr. (D)
Carl Vinson (D)

Idaho

Senators

Henry C. Dworshak (R)
Herman Welker (R)

Representatives

Hamer H. Budge (R)
Gracie B. Pfost (D)

Illinois

Senators

Everett M. Dirksen (R)
Paul H. Douglas (D)

Representatives

Leo E. Allen (R)
Leslie C. Arends (R)
James B. Bowler (D)
Charles A. Boyle (D)
Robert B. Chiperfield (R)
Marguerite Stitt Church (R)
William L. Dawson (D)
Thomas S. Gordon (D)
Kenneth J. Gray (D)
Richard W. Hoffman (R)
John C. Kluczynski (D)
William E. McVey (R)
Peter F. Mack, Jr. (R)
Noah M. Mason (R)
James C. Murray (D)
Thomas J. O'Brien (D)
Barratt O'Hara (D)
Melvin Price (D)
Chauncey W. Reed (R) d. Feb.
  1956
Timothy P. Sheehan (R)
Sidney E. Simpson (R)
William L. Springer (R)
Harold H. Velde (R)
Charles W. Vursell (R)
Sidney R. Yates (D)

Indiana

Senators

Homer E. Capehart (R)
William E. Jenner (R)

Representatives

E. Ross Adair (R)
John V. Beamer (R)
William G. Bray (R)
Charles B. Brownson (R)
Shepard J. Crumpacker, Jr. (R)
Winfield K. Denton (D)
Charles A. Halleck (R)
Cecil M. Harden (R)
Ralph Harvey (R)
Ray J. Madden (D)
Earl Wilson (R)

Iowa

Senators

Bourke B. Hickenlooper (R)
Thomas E. Martin (R)

Representatives

Paul Cummingham (R)
James I. Dolliver (R)
Harold R. Gross (R)
Charles B. Hoeven (R)
Ben F. Jensen (R)
Karl M. LeCompte (R)
Frederick D. Schwengel (R)
Henry O. Talle (R)

Kansas

Senators

Frank Carlson (R)
Andrew F. Schoeppel (R)

Representatives

William H. Avery (R)
Myron V. George (R)
Clifford R. Hope (R)
Edward H. Rees (R)
Errett P. Scrivner (R)
Wint Smith (R)

Kentucky

Senators

Alben W. Barkley (D) d. Apr.
1956
Earle C. Clements (D)
John Sherman Cooper (R) s.
1957
Robert Humphreys (R) ta. 1956

Representatives

Frank L. Chelf (D)
Noble J. Gregory (D)
William H. Natcher (D)
Carl D. Perkins (D)
John M. Robsion, Jr. (R)
Eugene Siler (R)
Brent Spence (D)
John C. Watts (D)

Louisiana

Senators

Allen J. Ellender, Sr. (D)
Russell B. Long (D)

Representatives

T. Hale Boggs (D)
Overton Brooks (D)
F. Edward Hebert (D)
George S. Long (D)
James H. Morrison (D)
Otto E. Passman (D)
T. Ashton Thompson (D)
Edwin E. Willis (D)

Maine

Senators

Frederick G. Payne (R)
Margaret Chase Smith (R)

Representatives

Robert Hale (R)
Clifford G. McIntire (R)
Charles P. Nelson (R)

Maryland

Senators

J. Glenn Beall (R)
John Marshall Butler (R)

Representatives

James P. S. Devereux (R)
George H. Fallon (D)
Samuel N. Friedel (D)
Edward A. Garmatz (D)
DeWitt S. Hyde (R)
Richard E. Lankford (D)
Edward T. Miller (R)

Massachusetts

Senators

John F. Kennedy (D)
Leverett Saltonstall (R)

Representatives

William H. Bates (R)
Edward P. Boland (D)
Laurence Curtis (R)
Harold D. Donohue (D)
John W. Heselton (R)
Thomas J. Lane (D)
John W. McCormack (D)
Torbert H. Macdonald (D)
Joseph W. Martin, Jr. (R)
Donald W. Nicholson (R)
Thomas P. O'Neill, Jr. (D)
Philip J. Philbin (D)
Edith Nourse Rogers (R)
Richard B. Wigglesworth (R)

Michigan

Senators

Patrick V. McNamara (D)
Charles E. Potter (R)

Representatives

John B. Bennett (R)
Alvin M. Bentley (R)
Elford A. Cederberg (R)
Charles C. Diggs, Jr. (D)
John D. Dingell (D) d. Sept.
1955
John D. Dingell, Jr. (D) s.
1956
George A. Dondero (R)
Gerald R. Ford, Jr. (R)
Martha W. Griffiths (R)
Don Hayworth (D)
Clare E. Hoffman (R)
August E. Johansen (R)

Victor A. Knox (R)
John Lesinski, Jr. (D)
Thaddeus M. Machrowicz (D)
George Meader (R)
Louis C. Rabaut (D)
Ruth Thompson (R)
Jesse P. Wolcott (R)

Minnesota

Senators

Hubert H. Humphrey (D)
Edward J. Thye (R)

Representatives

H. Carl Anderson (R)
August H. Andresen (R)
John A. Blatnik (D)
Walter H. Judd (R)
Coya G. Knutson (R)
Eugene J. McCarthy (D)
Fred Marshall (D)
Joseph P. O'Hara (R)
Roy W. Wier (D)

Mississippi

Senators

James O. Eastland (D)
John C. Stennis (D)

Representatives

Thomas G. Abernethy (D)
William M. Colmer (D)
Frank E. Smith (D)
Jamie L. Whitten (D)
John Bell Williams (D)
W. Arthur Winstead (D)

Missouri

Senators

Thomas C. Hennings, Jr. (D)
Stuart Symington (D)

Representatives

Richard W. Bolling (D)
Clarence Cannon (D)
Albert S. J. Carnahan (D)
George H. Christopher (D)
Thomas B. Curtis (R)
William R. Hull, Jr. (D)
Paul C. Jones (D)
Frank M. Karsten (D)
Morgan M. Moulder (D)
Dewey Short (R)
Leonor Kretzer Sullivan (D)

Montana

Senators

Mike Mansfield (D)
James E. Murray (D)

Representatives

Orvin B. Fjare (R)
Lee Metcalf (D)

Nebraska

Senators

Carl T. Curtis (R)
Roman L. Hruska (R)

Representatives

Jackson B. Chase (R)
Robert D. Harrison (R)
Arthur L. Miller (R)
Phillip H. Weaver (R)

Nevada

Senators

Alan H. Bible (D)
George W. Malone (R)

Representatives

Clifton Young (R)

New Hampshire

Senators

H. Styles Bridges (R)
Norris Cotton (R)

Representatives

Perkins Bass (R)
Chester E. Merrow (R)

New Jersey

Senators

Clifford P. Case (R)
H. Alexander Smith (R)

Representatives

Hugh J. Addonizio (D)
James C. Auchincloss (R)
Gordon Canfield (R)
Peter H. B. Frelinghuysen, Jr.
(R)
T. Millet Hand (R) d. Dec.
1956
Robert W. Kean (R)
Frank C. Osmers, Jr. (R)
Peter W. Rodino, Jr. (D)
Alfred D. Sieminski (D)
Frank Thompson, Jr. (D)
T. James Tumulty (D)
William B. Widnall (R)
Harrison A. Williams, Jr. (D)
Charles A. Wolverton (R)

New Mexico

Senators

Clinton P. Anderson (D)
Dennis Chavez (D)

Representatives

John J. Dempsey (D)
Antonio M. Fernandez (D) d.
Nov. 1956

New York

Senators

Irving M. Ives (R)
Herbert H. Lehman (D)

Representatives

Victor L. Anfuso (D)
Frank J. Becker (R)
Albert H. Bosch (R)
Charles A. Buckley (D)
Emanuel Celler (D)
W. Sterling Cole (R)
Frederic R. Coudert, Jr. (R)
Irwin D. Davidson (D)
James J. Delaney (D)
Steven B. Derounian (R)
Isidore Dollinger (D)
James G. Donovan (D)
Francis E. Dorn (R)
Sidney A. Fine (D) r. Jan. 1956
Paul A. Fino (R)
Ralph A. Gamble (R)
Ralph W. Gwinn (R)
James C. Healey (D) s. 1956
Lester Holtzman (D)
Bernard W. Kearney (R)
Kenneth B. Keating (R)
Edna F. Kelly (D)
Eugene J. Keogh (D)
Clarence E. Kilburn (R)
Arthur G. Klein (D)
Henry J. Latham (R)
William E. Miller (R)
Abraham J. Multer (D)
Leo W. O'Brien (D)
Harold C. Ostertag (R)
John R. Pillion (R)
Adam Clayton Powell, Jr. (D)
Edmund P. Radwan (R)
John H. Ray (R)
Daniel A. Reed (R)
R. Walter Riehlman (R)
John J. Rooney (D)
Katharine St. George (R)
John Taber (R)
Dean P. Taylor (R)
Stuyvesant Wainwright (R)
J. Ernest Wharton (R)
William R. Williams (R)
Herbert Zelenko (D)

North Carolina

Senators

Sam J. Ervin, Jr. (D)
W. Kerr Scott (D)

Representatives

Hugh Q. Alexander (D)
Graham A. Barden (D)
Herbert C. Bonner (D)
F. Ertel Carlyle (D)
Richard T. Chatham (D)
Harold D. Cooley (D)
Charles B. Deane (D)
Carl T. Durham (D)
Lawrence H. Fountain (D)
Charles R. Jonas (R)
Woodrow W. Jones (D)
George A. Shuford (D)

North Dakota

Senators

William Langer (R)
Milton R. Young (R)

Representatives

Usher L. Burdick (R)
Otto Krueger (R)

Ohio

Senators

George H. Bender (R)
John W. Bricker (R)

Representatives

Thomas L. Ashley (D)
William H. Ayres (R)
Albert D. Baumhart, Jr. (R)
Jackson E. Betts (R)
Frances P. Bolton (R)
Oliver P. Bolton (R)
Frank T. Bow (R)
Clarence J. Brown (R)
Cliff Clevenger (R)
Michael A. Feighan (D)
Wayne L. Hays (D)
John E. Henderson (R)
William E. Hess (R)
Thomas A. Jenkins (R)
Michael J. Kirwan (D)
William M. McCulloch (R)
J. Harry McGregor (R)
William E. Minshall (R)
James G. Polk (D)
Paul F. Schenck (R)
Gordon H. Scherer (R)
Charles A. Vanik (D)
John M. Vorys (R)

Oklahoma

Senators

Robert S. Kerr (D)
A. S. Mike Monroney (D)

Representatives

Carl Albert (D)
Page H. Belcher (R)
Edmond Edmondson (D)
John Jarman (D)
Thomas J. Steed (D)
Victor E. Wickersham (D)

Oregon

Senators

Wayne L. Morse (D)
Richard L. Neuberger (D)

Representatives

Samuel H. Coon (R)
Harris Ellsworth (R)
Edith S. Green (D)
A. Walter Norblad (R)

Pennsylvania

Senators

James H. Duff (R)
Edward Martin (D)

Representatives

William A. Barrett (D)
Vera D. Buchanan (D) d. Nov. 1955
Alvin R. Bush (R)
James A. Byrne (D)
Joseph L. Carrigg (R)
Earl Chudoff (D)
Frank M. Clark (D)
Robert J. Corbett (R)
Paul B. Dague (R)
Herman P. Eberharter (D)
Ivor D. Fenton (R)
Daniel J. Flood (D)
James G. Fulton (R)
Leon H. Gavin (R)
William T. Granahan (D) d. May 1956
William J. Green, Jr. (D)
Elmer J. Holland (D) s. 1956
Benjamin F. James (R)
Carroll D. Kearns (R)
Augustine B. Kelley (D)
Karl C. King (R)
Samuel K. McConnell, Jr. (R)
Thomas E. Morgan (D)
Walter M. Mumma (R)
James M. Quigley (D)
George M. Rhodes (D)
John P. Saylor (R)
Hugh D. Scott, Jr. (R)
Richard M. Simpson (R)
James E. Van Zandt (R)
Francis E. Walter (D)

Rhode Island

Senators

Theodore F. Green (D)
John O. Pastore (D)

Representatives

John E. Fogarty (D)
Aime J. Forand (D)

South Carolina

Senators

Olin D. Johnston (D)
J. Strom Thurmond (D) r. Apr. 1956
Thomas A. Woffard (D) s. 1956

Representatives

Robert T. Ashmore (D)
W. J. Bryan Dorn (D)
John L. McMillan (D)
James P. Richards (D)
John J. Riley (D)
L. Mendel Rivers (D)

South Dakota

Senators

Francis H. Case (R)
Karl E. Mundt (R)

Representatives

Ellis Y. Berry (R)
Harold O. Lovre (R)

Tennessee

Senators

Albert A. Gore (D)
Estes Kefauver (D)

Representatives

Howard H. Baker (R)
Ross Bass (D)
Jere Cooper (D)
Clifford Davis (D)
Joseph L. Evins (D)
James B. Frazier, Jr. (D)
Thomas J. Murray (D)
J. Percy Priest (D) d. Oct. 1956
B. Carroll Reece (R)

Texas

Senators

M. Price Daniel (D)
Lyndon B. Johnson (D)

Representatives

Bruce R. Alger (R)
John J. Bell (D)
Jack B. Brooks (D)
Omar T. Burleson (D)
Martin Dies, Jr. (D)
John V. Dowdy (D)
O. Clark Fisher (D)
Brady P. Gentry (D)
Frank N. Ikard (D)
Paul J. Kilday (D)
Joe M. Kilgore (D)
George H. Mahon (D)
Wright Patman (D)
William R. Poage (D)
Sam Rayburn (D)
Walter E. Rogers (D)
J. T. Rutherford (D)
Olin E. Teague (D)
Albert Thomas
Clark W. Thompson (D)
W. Homer Thornberry (D)
James C. Wright, Jr. (D)

Utah

Senators

Wallace F. Bennett (R)
Arthur V. Watkins (R)

Representatives

William A. Dawson (R)
Henry A. Dixon (R)

Vermont

Senators

George D. Aiken (R)
Ralph E. Flanders (R)

Representatives

Winston L. Prouty (R)

Virginia

Senators

Harry F. Byrd (D)
A. Willis Robertson (D)

Representatives

Watkins M. Abbitt (D)
Joel T. Broyhill (R)
J. Vaughan Gary (D)
Porter Hardy, Jr. (D)
Burr P. Harrison (D)
William P. Jennings (D)
Richard H. Poff (R)
Edward J. Robeson, Jr. (D)
Howard W. Smith (D)
William M. Tuck (D)

Washington

Senators

Henry M. Jackson (D)
Warren G. Magnuson (D)

Representatives

Hal Holmes (R)
Walter F. Horan (R)
Russ V. Mack (R)
Donald H. Magnuson (D)
Thomas M. Pelly (R)
Thor C. Tollefson (R)
Alfred J. Westland (R)

West Virginia

Senators

Harley M. Kilgore (D) d. Feb.
 1956
William R. Laird, III (D) ta.
 1956
Matthew M. Neely (D)
Chapman Revercomb (R) s.
 1957

Representatives

Cleveland M. Bailey (D)
Maurice G. Burnside (D)
Robert C. Byrd (D)
Maude Elizabeth Kee (D)
Robert H. Mollohan (D)
Harley O. Staggers (D)

Wisconsin

Senators

Joseph R. McCarthy (R)
Alexander Wiley (R)

Representatives

John W. Byrnes (R)
Glenn R. Davis (R)
Lester R. Johnson (D)
Melvin R. Laird (R)
Alvin E. O'Konski (R)
Henry S. Reuss (D)
Lawrence H. Smith (R)
William K. Van Pelt (R)
Gardner R. Withrow (R)
Clement J. Zablocki (D)

Wyoming

Senators

Frank A. Barrett (R)
Joseph C. O'Mahoney (D)

Representatives

E. Keith Thomson (R)

Eighty-Fifth Congress

(Jan. 3, 1957, to
Jan. 3, 1959)

President of the Senate: Richard
 M. Nixon
*President Pro Tempore of the
 Senate:* Carl Hayden
*Speaker of the House of
 Representatives:* Sam Rayburn

Alabama

Senators

Lister Hill (D)
John J. Sparkman (D)

Representatives

George W. Andrews (D)
Frank W. Boykin (D)
Carl A. Elliott (D)
George M. Grant (D)
George Huddleston, Jr. (D)
Robert E. Jones, Jr. (D)
Albert Rains (D)
Kenneth A. Roberts (D)
Armistead I. Selden, Jr. (D)

Arizona

Senators

Barry M. Goldwater (R)
Carl Hayden (D)

Representatives

John J. Rhodes (R)
Stewart L. Udall (D)

Arkansas

Senators

J. William Fulbright (D)
John L. McClellan (D)

Representatives

Ezekiel C. Gathings (D)
Oren Harris (D)
Brooks Hays (D)
Wilbur D. Mills (D)
William F. Norrell (D)
James W. Trimble (D)

California

Senators

William F. Knowland (R)
Thomas H. Kuchel (R)

Representatives

John J. Allen, Jr. (R)
John F. Baldwin, Jr. (R)
Clyde G. Doyle (D)
Clair Engle (D)
Charles S. Gubser (R)
Harlan F. Hagen (D)
Edgar W. Hiestand (R)
Patrick J. Hillings (R)
Chet Holifield (D)
Joseph F. Holt (R)
Craig Hosmer (R)
Donald L. Jackson (R)
Cecil R. King (D)
Glenard P. Lipscomb (R)
Gordon L. McDonough (R)
John J. McFall (D)
William S. Mailliard (R)
George P. Miller (D)
John E. Moss, Jr. (D)
James Roosevelt (D)
Dalip S. Saund (D)
Hubert B. Scudder (R)
John F. Shelley (D)
Harry R. Sheppard (D)
Bernice F. Sisk (D)
H. Allen Smith (R)
Charles M. Teague (R)
James B. Utt (R)
Robert C. Wilson (R)
J. Arthur Younger (R)

Colorado

Senators

Gordon L. Allott (R)
John A. Carroll (D)

Representatives

Wayne N. Aspinall (D)
J. Edgar Chenoweth (R)
William S. Hill (R)
Byron G. Rogers (D)

Connecticut

Senators

Prescott S. Bush (R)
William A. Purtell (R)

Representatives

Albert W. Cretella (R)
Edwin H. May, Jr. (D)
Albert P. Morano (R)
James T. Patterson (R)
Antoni N. Sadlak (R)
Horace Seely-Brown, Jr. (R)

Delaware

Senators

J. Allen Frear, Jr. (D)
John J. Williams (R)

Representatives

Harry G. Haskell, Jr. (R)

Florida

Senators

Spessard L. Holland (D)
George A. Smathers (D)

Representatives

Charles E. Bennett (D)
William C. Cramer (R)
Dante B. Fascell (D)
James A. Haley (D)
Albert S. Herlong, Jr. (D)
Donald R. Matthews (D)
Paul G. Rogers (D)
Robert L. F. Sikes (D)

Georgia

Senators

Richard B. Russell (D)
Herman E. Talmadge (D)

Representatives

Iris F. Blitch (D)
Paul Brown (D)
James C. Davis (D)
John James Flynt, Jr. (D)
Elijah L. Forrester (D)
Phillip M. Landrum (D)
Henderson L. Lanham (D) d.
 Nov. 1957
Harlan E. Mitchell (D) s. 1958
John L. Pilcher (D)
Prince H. Preston, Jr. (D)
Carl Vinson (D)

Idaho

Senators

Frank Church (D)
Henry C. Dworshak (R)

Representatives

Hamer H. Budge (R)
Gracie B. Pfost (D)

Illinois

Senators

Everett M. Dirksen (R)
Paul H. Douglas (D)

Representatives

Leo E. Allen (R)
Leslie C. Arends (R)
James B. Bowler (D) d. July
 1957

Charles A. Boyle (D)
Emmett F. Byrne (R)
Robert B. Chiperfield (R)
Marguerite Stitt Church (R)
Harold R. Collier (R)
William L. Dawson (D)
Kenneth J. Gray (D)
Thomas S. Gordon (D)
Russell W. Keeney (R) d. Jan.
  1958
John C. Kluczynski (D)
Roland V. Libonati (D) s. 1958
William E. McVey (R) d. Aug.
  1958
Peter F. Mack, Jr. (D)
Noah M. Mason (R)
Robert H. Michel (R)
Melvin Price (D)
Thomas J. O'Brien (D)
Barratt O'Hara (D)
Timothy P. Sheehan (R)
Sidney E. Simpson (R) d. Oct.
  1958
William L. Springer (R)
Charles W. Vursell (R)
Sidney R. Yates (D)

Indiana

Senators

Homer E. Capehart (R)
William E. Jenner (R)

Representatives

E. Ross Adair (R)
John V. Beamer (R)
William G. Bray (R)
Charles B. Brownson (R)
Winfield K. Denton (D)
Charles A. Halleck (R)
Cecil M. Harden (R)
Ralph Harvey (R)
Ray J. Madden (D)
F. Jay Nimtz (R)
Earl Wilson (R)

Iowa

Senators

Bourke B. Hickenlooper (R)
Thomas E. Martin (R)

Representatives

Merwin Coad (D)
Paul Cunningham (R)
Harold R. Gross (R)
Charles B. Hoeven (R)
Ben F. Jensen (R)
Karl M. LeCompte (R)
Frederick D. Schwengel (R)
Henry O. Talle (R)

Kansas

Senators

Frank Carlson (R)
Andrew F. Schoeppel (R)

Representatives

William H. Avery (R)
J. Floyd Breeding (D)
Myron V. George (R)

Edward H. Rees (R)
Errett P. Scrivner (R)
Wint Smith (R)

Kentucky

Senators

John Sherman Cooper (R)
Thruston B. Morton (R)

Representatives

Frank L. Chelf (D)
Noble J. Gregory (D)
William H. Natcher (D)
Carl D. Perkins (D)
John M. Robsion, Jr. (R)
Eugene Siler (R)
Brent Spence (D)
John C. Watts (D)

Louisiana

Senators

Allen J. Ellender (D)
Russell B. Long (D)

Representatives

T. Hale Boggs (D)
Overton Brooks (D)
F. Edward Hebert (D)
George S. Long (D) d. Mar.
  1958
James H. Morrison (D)
Otto E. Passman (D)
T. Ashton Thompson (D)
Edwin E. Willis (D)

Maine

Senators

Frederick G. Payne (R)
Margaret Chase Smith (R)

Representatives

Frank M. Coffin (R)
Robert Hale (R)
Clifford G. McIntire (R)

Maryland

Senators

J. Glenn Beall (R)
John Marshall Butler (R)

Representatives

James P. S. Devereux (R)
George H. Fallon (D)
Samuel N. Friedel (D)
Edward A. Garmatz (D)
DeWitt S. Hyde (R)
Richard E. Lankford (D)
Edward T. Miller (R)

Massachusetts

Senators

John F. Kennedy (D)

Leverett Saltonstall (R)

Representatives

William H. Bates (R)
Edward P. Boland (D)
Laurence Curtis (R)
Harold D. Donohue (D)
John W. Heselton (R)
Thomas J. Lane (D)
John W. McCormack (D)
Torbert H. Macdonald (D)
Joseph W. Martin, Jr. (R)
Donald W. Nicholson (R)
Thomas P. O'Neill, Jr. (D)
Philip J. Philbin (D)
Edith Nourse Rogers (R)
Richard B. Wigglesworth(R) r.
  Nov. 1958

Michigan

Senators

Patrick V. McNamara (D)
Charles E. Potter (R)

Representatives

John B. Bennett (R)
Alvin M. Bentley (R)
William S. Broomfield (R)
Elford A. Cederberg (R)
Charles E. Chamberlain (R)
Charles C. Diggs, Jr. (D)
John D. Dingell, Jr. (D)
Gerald R. Ford, Jr. (R)
Robert P. Griffin (R)
Martha W. Griffiths (R)
Clare E. Hoffman (R)
August E. Johansen (R)
Victor A. Knox (R)
John Lesinski, Jr. (D)
Robert J. McIntosh (R)
Thaddeus M. Machrowicz (D)
George Meader (R)
Louis C. Rabaut (D)

Minnesota

Senators

Hubert H. Humphrey (D)
Edward J. Thye (R)

Representatives

H. Carl Andersen (R)
August H. Andresen (R) d. Jan.
  1958
John A. Blatnik (D)
Walter H. Judd (R)
Coya G. Knutson (R)
Eugene J. McCarthy (D)
Fred Marshall (D)
Joseph P. O'Hara (R)
Albert H. Quie (R) s. 1958
Roy W. Wier (D)

Mississippi

Senators

James O. Eastland (D)
John C. Stennis (D)

Representatives

Thomas G. Abernethy (D)
William M. Colmer (D)
Frank E. Smith (D)
Jamie L. Whitten (D)
John Bell Williams (D)
W. Arthur Winstead (D)

Missouri

Senators

Thomas C. Hennings, Jr. (D)
Stuart Symington (D)

Representatives

Richard W. Bolling (D)
Charles H. Brown (D)
Clarence Cannon (D)
Albert S. J. Carnahan (D)
George H. Christopher (D)
Thomas B. Curtis (D)
William R. Hull, Jr. (D)
Paul C. Jones (D)
Frank M. Karsten (D)
Morgan M. Moulder (D)
Leonor Kretzer Sullivan (D)

Montana

Senators

Mike Mansfield (D)
James E. Murray (D)

Representatives

LeRoy H. Anderson (D)
Lee Metcalf (D)

Nebraska

Senators

Carl T. Curtis (R)
Roman L. Hruska (R)

Representatives

Glenn C. Cunningham (R)
Robert D. Harrison (R)
Arthur L. Miller (R)
Phillip H. Weaver (R)

Nevada

Senators

Alan H. Bible (D)
George W. Malone (R)

Representatives

Walter S. Baring (D)

New Hampshire

Senators

H. Styles Bridges (R)
Norris Cotton (R)

Representatives

Perkins Bass (R)
Chester E. Merrow (R)

New Jersey

Senators

Clifford P. Case (R)
H. Alexander Smith (R)

Representatives

Hugh J. Addonizio (D)
James C. Auchincloss (R)
Gordon Canfield (R)
Vincent J. Dellay (R)
Florence P. Dwyer (R)
Peter H. B. Frelinghuysen, Jr. (R)
Milton W. Glenn (R) s. 1958
Robert W. Kean (R)
Frank C. Osmers, Jr. (R)
Peter W. Rodino, Jr. (D)
Alfred D. Sieminski (D)
Frank Thompson, Jr. (D)
William B. Widnall (R)
Charles A. Wolverton (R)

New Mexico

Senators

Clinton P. Anderson (D)
Dennis Chavez (D)

Representatives

John J. Dempsey (R) d. Mar. 1958
Joseph M. Montoya (D) s. 1957

New York

Senators

Irving M. Ives (R)
Jacob K. Javits (R)

Representatives

Victor L. Anfuso (D)
Frank J. Becker (R)
Albert H. Bosch (R)
Charles A. Buckley (D)
Emanuel Celler (D)
W. Sterling Cole (R) r. Dec. 1957
Frederic R. Coudert, Jr. (R)
James J. Delaney (D)
Steven B. Derounian (R)
Isidore Dollinger (D)
Edwin B. Dooley (R)
Francis E. Dorn (R)
Leonard Farbstein (D)
Paul A. Fino (R)
Ralph W. Gwinn (R)
James C. Healey (D)
Lester Holtzman (D)
Bernard W. Kearney (R)
Kenneth B. Keating (R)
Edna F. Kelly (D)
Eugene J. Keogh (D)
Clarence E. Kilburn (R)
Henry J. Latham (R)
William E. Miller (R)
Abraham J. Multer (D)

Leo W. O'Brien (D)
Harold C. Ostertag (R)
John R. Pillion (R)
Adam Clayton Powell, Jr. (D)
Edmund P. Radwan (R)
John H. Ray (R)
Daniel A. Reed (R)
R. Walter Riehlman (R)
Howard W. Robison (R) s. 1958
John J. Rooney (D)
Katharine St. George (R)
Alfred E. Santangelo (D)
John Taber (R)
Dean P. Taylor (R)
Ludwig Teller (D)
Stuyvesant Wainwright (R)
J. Ernest Wharton (R)
William R. Williams (R)
Herbert Zelenko (D)

North Carolina

Senators

Sam J. Ervin, Jr. (D)
B. Everett Jordan (D) s. 1958
W. Kerr Scott (D) d. Apr. 1958

Representatives

Hugh Q. Alexander (D)
Graham A. Barden (D)
Herbert C. Booner (D)
Harold D. Cooley (D)
Carl T. Durham (D)
Lawrence H. Fountain (D)
Charles R. Jonas (R)
A. Paul Kitchin (D)
Alton A. Lennon (D)
Ralph J. Scott (D)
George A. Shuford (D)
Basil L. Whitener (D)

North Dakota

Senators

William Langer (R)
Milton R. Young (R)

Representatives

Usher L. Burdick (R)
Otto Krueger (R)

Ohio

Senators

John W. Bricker (R)
Frank J. Lausche (D)

Representatives

William H. Ayres (R)
Thomas L. Ashley (D)
Albert D. Baumhart, Jr. (R)
Jackson E. Betts (R)
Frances P. Bolton (R)
Frank T. Bow (R)
Clarence J. Brown (R)
Cliff Clevenger (R)
David S. Dennison (R)
Michael A. Feighan (D)
Wayne L. Hays (D)
John E. Henderson (R)

William E. Hess (R)
Thomas A. Jenkins (R)
Michael J. Kirwan (D)
William M. McCulloch (R)
J. Harry McGregor (R) d. Oct. 1958
William E. Minshall (R)
James G. Polk (D)
Paul F. Schenck (R)
Gordon H. Scherer (R)
Charles A. Vanik (D)
John M. Vorys (R)

Oklahoma

Senators

Robert S. Kerr (D)
A. S. Mike Monroney (D)

Representatives

Carl Albert (D)
Page H. Belcher (R)
Edmond Edmondson (D)
John Jarman (D)
Toby Morris (D)
Thomas J. Steed (D)

Oregon

Senators

Wayne L. Morse (D)
Richard L. Neuberger (D)

Representatives

Edith Green (D)
A. Walter Norblad (R)
Charles O. Porter (D)
Albert C. Ullman (D)

Pennsylvania

Senators

Joseph S. Clark (D)
Edward Martin (D)

Representatives

William A. Barrett (D)
Alvin R. Bush (R)
James A. Byrne (D)
Joseph L. Carrigg (R)
Earl Chudoff (D) r. Jan. 1958
Frank M. Clark (D)
Robert J. Corbett (R)
Willard S. Curtin (R)
Paul B. Dague (R)
John H. Dent (D) s. 1958
Herman P. Eberharter (D) d. Sept. 1958
Ivor D. Fenton (R)
Daniel J. Flood (D)
James G. Fulton (R)
Leon H. Gavin (R)
Kathryn E. Granahan (D)
William J. Green, Jr. (D)
Elmer J. Holland (D)
Benjamin F. James (R)
Carroll D. Kearns (R)
Augustine B. Kelley (D) d. Nov. 1957
John A. LaFore, Jr. (R) s. 1958
Samuel K. McConnell, Jr. (R) r. Sept. 1957

Thomas E. Morgan (D)
Walter M. Mumma (R)
Robert N. C. Nix (D) s. 1958
George M. Rhodes (D)
John P. Saylor (R)
Hugh D. Scott, Jr. (R)
Richard M. Simpson (R)
S. Walter Stauffer (R)
James E. Van Zandt (R)
Francis E. Walter (D)

Rhode Island

Senators

Theodore F. Green (D)
John O. Pastore (D)

Representatives

John E. Fogarty (D)
Aime J. Forand (D)

South Carolina

Senators

Olin D. Johnston (D)
J. Strom Thurmond (D)

Representatives

Robert T. Ashmore (D)
W. J. Bryan Dorn (D)
Robert W. Hemphill (D)
John L. McMillan (D)
John J. Riley (D)
L. Mendel Rivers (D)

South Dakota

Senators

Francis H. Case (R)
Karl E. Mundt (R)

Representatives

Ellis Y. Berry (R)
George S. McGovern (D)

Tennessee

Senators

Albert A. Gore (D)
Estes Kefauver (D)

Representatives

Howard H. Baker (R)
Ross Bass (D)
Jere Cooper (D) d. Dec. 1957
Clifford Davis (D)
Robert A. Everett (D) s. 1958
Joseph L. Evins (D)
James B. Frazier, Jr. (D)
J. Carlton Loser (D)
Thomas J. Murray (D)
B. Carroll Reece (R)

Texas

Senators

William A. Blakley (D) ta. 1957

M. Price Daniel (D) r. Jan. 1957
Lyndon B. Johnson (D)
Ralph W. Yarborough (D)

Representatives

Bruce R. Alger (R)
Lindley G. Beckworth (D)
Jack B. Brooks (D)
Omar T. Burleson (D)
Martin Dies, Jr. (D)
John V. Dowdy (D)
O. Clark Fisher (D)
Frank N. Ikard (D)
Paul J. Kilday (D)
Joe M. Kilgore (D)
George H. Mahon (D)
Wright Patman (D)
William R. Poage (D)
Sam Rayburn (D)
Walter E. Rogers (D)
J. T. Rutherford (D)
Olin E. Teague (D)
Albert Thomas (D)
Clark W. Thompson (D)
W. Homer Thornberry (D)
James C. Wright, Jr. (D)
John A. Young (D)

Utah

Senators

Wallace F. Bennett (R)
Arthur V. Watkins (R)

Representatives

William A. Dawson (R)
Henry A. Dixon (R)

Vermont

Senators

George D. Aiken (R)
Ralph E. Flanders (R)

Representatives

Winston L. Prouty (R)

Virginia

Senators

Harry F. Byrd (D)
A. Willis Robertson (D)

Representatives

Watkins M. Abbitt (D)
Joel T. Broyhill (D)
J. Vaughan Gary (D)
Porter Hardy, Jr. (D)
Burr P. Harrison (D)
William P. Jennings (D)
Richard H. Poff (R)
Edward J. Robeson, Jr. (D)
Howard W. Smith (D)
William M. Tuck (D)

Washington

Senators

Henry M. Jackson (D)
Warren G. Magnuson (D)

Representatives

Hal Holmes (R)
Walter F. Horan (R)
Russell V. Mack (R)
Donald H. Magnuson (D)
Thomas M. Pelly (R)
Thor C. Tollefson (R)
Alfred J. Westland (R)

West Virginia

Senators

John D. Hoblitzell, Jr. (R) ta. 1958
Matthew M. Neely (D) d. Jan. 1958
Jennings Randolph (D) s. 1959
Chapman Revercomb (R)

Representatives

Cleveland M. Bailey (D)
Robert C. Byrd (D)
Maude Elizabeth Kee (D)
Arch A. Moore, Jr. (R)
William F. Neal (R)
Harley O. Staggers (D)

Wisconsin

Senators

Alexander Wiley (R)
Joseph R. McCarthy (R) d. May 1957
William Proxmire (D)

Representatives

John W. Byrnes (R)
Lester R. Johnson (D)
Melvin R. Laird (R)
Alvin E. O'Konski (R)
Henry S. Reuss (D)
Lawrence H. Smith (R) d. Jan. 1958
Donald E. Tewes (R)
William K. VanPelt (R)
Gardner R. Withrow (R)
Clement J. Zablocki (D)

Wyoming

Senators

Frank A. Barrett (R)
Joseph C. O'Mahoney (D)

Representatives

E. Keith Thomson (R)

Eighty-Sixth Congress

(Jan. 3, 1959, to Jan. 3, 1961)

President of the Senate: Richard M. Nixon
President Pro Tempore of the Senate: Carl Hayden
Speaker of the House of Representatives: Sam Rayburn

Alabama

Senators

Lister Hill (D)
John J. Sparkman (D)

Representatives

George W. Andrews (D)
Frank W. Boykin (D)
Carl A. Elliott (D)
George M. Grant (D)
George Huddleston, Jr. (D)
Robert E. Jones, Jr. (D)
Albert Rains (D)
Kenneth A. Roberts (D)
Armistead I. Selden, Jr. (D)

Alaska

Senators

Edward L. Bartlett (D)
Ernest Gruening (D)

Representatives

Ralph J. Rivers (D)

Arizona

Senators

Barry M. Goldwater (R)
Carl Hayden (D)

Representatives

John J. Rhodes (D)
Stewart L. Udall (D)

Arkansas

Senators

J. William Fulbright (D)
John L. McClellan (D)

Representatives

T. Dale Alford (D)
Ezekiel C. Gathings (D)
Oren Harris (D)
Wilbur D. Mills (D)
William F. Norrell (D)
James W. Trimble (D)

California

Senators

Clair Engle (D)
Thomas H. Kuchel (R)

Representatives

John F. Baldwin, Jr. (R)
Jeffery Cohelan (D)
Clyde G. Doyle (D)
Charles S. Gubser (R)
Harlan F. Hagen (D)
Edgar W. Hiestand (R)
Chet Holifield (D)
Joseph F. Holt (R)
Craig Hosmer (R)
Donald L. Jackson (R)
Harold T. Johnson (D)
George A. Kasem (D)
Cecil R. King (D)
Glenard P. Lipscomb (R)
Gordon L. McDonough (R)
John J. McFall (D)
William S. Mailliard (R)
Clement W. Miller (D)
George P. Miller (D)
John E. Moss, Jr. (D)
James Roosevelt (D)
Dalip S. Saund (D)
John F. Shelley (D)
Harry R. Sheppard (D)
Bernice F. Sisk (D)
H. Allen Smith (R)
Charles M. Teague (R)
James B. Utt (R)
Robert C. Wilson (R)
J. Arthur Younger (R)

Colorado

Senators

Gordon L. Allott (R)
John A. Carroll (D)

Representatives

Wayne N. Aspinall (D)
J. Edgar Chenoweth (R)
Byron L. Johnson (D)
Byron G. Rogers (D)

Connecticut

Senators

Prescott S. Bush (R)
Thomas J. Dodd (D)

Representatives

Chester B. Bowles (D)
Emilio Q. Daddario (D)
Robert N. Giaimo (D)
Donald J. Irwin (D)
Frank Kowalski (D)
John S. Monagan (D)

Delaware

Senators

J. Allen Frear, Jr. (D)
John J. Williams (R)

Representatives

Harris B. McDowell, Jr. (D)

Florida

Senators

Spessard L. Holland (D)
George A. Smathers (D)

Representatives

Charles E. Bennett (D)
William C. Cramer (R)
Dante B. Fascell (D)
James A. Haley (D)
Albert S. Herlong, Jr. (D)
Donald R. Matthews (D)
Paul G. Rogers (D)
Robert L. F. Sikes (D)

Georgia

Senators

Richard B. Russell (D)
Herman E. Talmadge (D)

Representatives

Iris F. Blitch (D)
Paul Brown (D)
James C. Davis (D)
John J. Flynt, Jr. (D)
Elijah L. Forrester (D)
Phillip M. Landrum (D)
Harlan E. Mitchell (D)
John L. Pilcher (D)
Prince H. Preston, Jr. (D)
Carl Vinson (D)

Hawaii

Senators

Hiram L. Fong (R)
Oren E. Long (D)

Representatives

Daniel K. Inouye (D)

Idaho

Senators

Frank Church (D)
Henry C. Dworshak (R)

Representatives

Hamer H. Budge (R)
Gracie B. Pfost (D)

Illinois

Senators

Everett M. Dirksen (R)
Paul H. Douglas (D)

Representatives

Leo E. Allen (R)

Leslie C. Arends (R)
Charles A. Boyle (D) d. Nov. 1959
Robert B. Chiperfield (R)
Marguerite Stitt Church (R)
Harold R. Collier (R)
William L. Dawson (D)
Edward J. Derwinski (R)
Kenneth J. Gray (D)
Elmer J. Hoffman (R)
John C. Kluczynski (D)
Roland V. Libonati (D)
Peter F. Mack, Jr. (D)
Noah M. Mason (R)
Robert H. Michel (R)
William T. Murphy (D)
Thomas J. O'Brien (D)
Barratt O'Hara (D)
Melvin Price (D)
Roman C. Pucinski (D)
Daniel D. Rostenkowski (D)
George E. Shipley (D)
Edna Oakes Simpson (R)
William L. Springer (R)
Sidney R. Yates (D)

Indiana

Senators

Homer E. Capehart (R)
Vance Hartke (D)

Representatives

E. Ross Adair (R)
Joseph W. Barr (D)
John Brademas (D)
William G. Bray (R)
Winfield K. Denton (D)
Charles A. Halleck (R)
Randall S. Harmon (D)
Earl L. Hogan (D)
Ray J. Madden (D)
J. Edward Roush (D)
Fred Wampler (D)

Iowa

Senators

Bourke B. Hickenlooper (R)
Thomas E. Martin (R)

Representatives

Steven V. Carter (D) d. Nov. 1959
Merwin Coad (D)
Harold R. Gross (R)
Charles B. Hoeven (R)
Ben F. Jensen (R)
John H. Kyl (R) s. 1960
Frederick D. Schwengel (R)
Neal Smith (D)
Leonard G. Wolf (D)

Kansas

Senators

Frank Carlson (R)
Andrew F. Schoeppel (R)

Representatives

William H. Avery (R)
J. Floyd Breeding (D)

Newell A. George (D)
Denver D. Hargis (D)
Edward H. Rees (R)
Wint Smith (R)

Kentucky

Senators

John Sherman Cooper (R)
Thruston B. Morton (R)

Representatives

Frank W. Burke (D)
Frank L. Chelf (D)
William H. Natcher (D)
Carl D. Perkins (D)
Eugene Siler (R)
Brent Spence (D)
Frank A. Stubblefield (D)
John C. Watts (D)

Louisiana

Senators

Allen J. Ellender (D)
Russell B. Long (D)

Representatives

T. Hale Boggs (D)
Overton Brooks (D)
F. Edward Hebert (D)
Harold B. McSween (D)
James H. Morrison (D)
Otto E. Passman (D)
T. Ashton Thompson (D)
Edwin E. Willis (D)

Maine

Senators

Edmund S. Muskie (D)
Margaret Chase Smith (R)

Representatives

Frank M. Coffin (R)
Clifford G. McIntire (R)
James C. Oliver (D)

Maryland

Senators

J. Glenn Beall (R)
John Marshall Butler (R)

Representatives

Daniel B. Brewster (D)
George H. Fallon (D)
Edward A. Garmatz (D)
John R. Foley (D)
Samuel N. Friedel (D)
Thomas F. Johnson (D)
Richard E. Lankford (D)

Massachusetts

Senators

John F. Kennedy (D) r. Dec. 1960
Leverett Saltonstall (R)

Representatives

William H. Bates (R)
Edward P. Boland (D)
James A. Burke (D)
Silvio O. Conte (R)
Laurence Curtis (R)
Harold D. Donohue (D)
Hastings Keith (R)
Thomas J. Lane (D)
John W. McCormack (D)
Torbert H. Macdonald (D)
Joseph W. Martin, Jr. (R)
Thomas P. O'Neill, Jr. (D)
Philip J. Philbin (D)
Edith Nourse Rogers (R) d. Sept. 1960

Michigan

Senators

Philip A. Hart (D)
Patrick V. McNamara (D)

Representatives

John B. Bennett (R)
Alvin M. Bentley (R)
William S. Broomfield (R)
Elford A. Cederberg (R)
Charles E. Chamberlain (R)
Charles C. Diggs, Jr. (D)
John D. Dingell, Jr. (D)
Gerald R. Ford, Jr. (R)
Robert P. Griffin (R)
Martha W. Griffiths (D)
Clare E. Hoffman (R)
August E. Johansen (R)
Victor A. Knox (R)
John Lesinski, Jr. (D)
Thaddeus M. Machrowicz (D)
George Meader (R)
James G. O'Hara (D)
Louis C. Rabaut (D)

Minnesota

Senators

Hubert H. Humphrey (D)
Eugene J. McCarthy (D)

Representatives

H. Carl Andersen (R)
John A. Blatnik (D)
Walter H. Judd (R)
Joseph E. Karth (D)
Odin Langen (R)
Fred Marshall (D)
Ancher Nelsen (R)
Albert H. Quie (R)
Roy W. Wier (D)

Mississippi

Senators

James O. Eastland (D)
John C. Stennis (D)

Representatives

Thomas G. Abernethy (D)
William M. Colmer (D)
Frank E. Smith (D)
Jamie L. Whitten (D)
John Bell Williams (D)
W. Arthur Winstead (D)

Missouri

Senators

Thomas C. Hennings, Jr. (D) d.
    Sept. 1960
Edward V. Long (D) s. 1960
Stuart Symington (D)

Representatives

Richard W. Bolling (D)
Charles H. Brown (D)
Clarence Cannon (D)
Albert S. J. Carnahan (D)
George H. Christopher (D) d.
    Jan. 1959
Thomas B. Curtis (R)
William R. Hull, Jr. (D)
Paul C. Jones (D)
Frank M. Karsten (D)
Morgan M. Moulder (D)
William J. Randall (D)
Leonor Kretzer Sullivan (D)

Montana

Senators

Mike Mansfield (D)
James E. Murray (D)

Representatives

LeRoy H. Anderson (D)
Lee Metcalf (D)

Nebraska

Senators

Carl T. Curtis (R)
Roman L. Hruska (R)

Representatives

Lawrence Brock (D)
Glenn C. Cunningham (R)
Donald F. McGinley (D)
Phillip H. Weaver (R)

Nevada

Senators

Alan H. Bible (D)
Howard W. Cannon (D)

Representative

Walter S. Baring (D)

New Hampshire

Senators

H. Styles Bridges (R)
Norris Cotton (R)

Representatives

Perkins Bass (R)
Chester E. Merrow (R)

New Jersey

Senators

Clifford P. Case (R)
Harrison A. Williams, Jr. (D)

Representatives

Hugh J. Addonizio (D)
James C. Auchincloss (R)
William T. Cahill (R)
Gordon Canfield (R)
Dominick V. Daniels (D)
Florence P. Dwyer (R)
Peter H. B. Frelinghuysen, Jr.
    (R)
Cornelius E. Gallagher (D)
Milton W. Glenn (R)
Frank C. Osmers, Jr. (R)
Peter W. Rodino, Jr. (D)
Frank Thompson, Jr. (D)
George M. Wallhauser (R)
William B. Widnall (R)

New Mexico

Senators

Clinton P. Anderson (D)
Dennis Chavez (D)

Representatives

Joseph M. Montoya (D)
Thomas G. Morris (D)

New York

Senators

Jacob K. Javits (R)
Kenneth B. Keating (R)

Representatives

Victor L. Anfuso (D)
Robert R. Barry (R)
Frank J. Becker (R)
Albert H. Bosch (R)
Charles A. Buckley (D)
Emanuel Celler (D)
James J. Delaney (D)
Steven B. Derounian (R)
Isidore Dollinger (D) r. Dec.
    1959
Edwin B. Dooley (R)
Francis E. Dorn (R)
Thaddeus J. Dulski (D)
Leonard Farbstein (D)
Paul A. Fino (R)

Jacob H. Gilbert (D) s. 1960
Charles E. Goodell (R)
Seymour Halpern (R)
James C. Healey (D)
Lester Holtzman (D)
Edna F. Kelly (D)
Eugene J. Keogh (D)
Clarence E. Kilburn (R)
John V. Kindsay (R)
William E. Miller (R)
Abraham J. Multer (D)
Leo W. O'Brien (D)
Harold C. Ostertag (R)
John R. Pillion (R)
Alexander Pirnie (R)
Adam Clayton Powell, Jr. (D)
John H. Ray (R)
Daniel A. Reed (R) d. Feb.
    1959
R. Walter Riehlman (R)
Howard W. Robison (R)
John J. Rooney (D)
Katharine St. George (R)
Alfred E. Santangelo (D)
Samuel S. Stratton (D)
John Tabor (R)
Dean P. Taylor (R)
Ludwig Teller (D)
Stuyvesant Wainwright (R)
Jessica McCullough Weis (R)
J. Ernest Wharton (R)
Herbert Zelenko (D)

North Carolina

Senators

Sam J. Ervin, Jr. (D)
B. Everett Jordan (D)

Representatives

Hugh Q. Alexander (D)
Graham A. Barden (D)
Herbert C. Bonner (D)
Harold D. Cooley (D)
Carl T. Durham (D)
Lawrence H. Fountain (D)
David M. Hall (D) d. Jan. 1960
Charles R. Jonas (R)
A. Paul Kitchin (D)
Alton A. Lennon (D)
Ralph J. Scott (D)
Roy A. Taylor (D) s. 1960
Basil L. Whitener (D)

North Dakota

Senators

Quentin N. Burdick (D) s. 1960
C. Norman Brunsdale (R) ta.
    1960
William Langer (R) d. Nov.
    1959
Milton R. Young (R)

Representatives

Quentin N. Burdick (D) r. Aug.
    1960
Don L. Short (R)

Ohio

Senators

Frank J. Lausche (D)

Stephen M. Young (D)

Representatives

Thomas L. Ashley (D)
William H. Ayres (R)
Albert D. Baumhart, Jr. (R)
Jackson E. Betts (R)
Frances P. Bolton (R)
Frank T. Bow (R)
Clarence J. Brown (R)
Robert E. Cook (D)
Samuel L. Devine (R)
Michael A. Feighan (D)
Wayne L. Hays (D)
John E. Henderson (R)
William E. Hess (R)
Michael J. Kirwan (D)
Delbert L. Latta (R)
Robert W. Levering (D)
William M. McCulloch (R)
William E. Minshall (R)
Walter H. Moeller (D)
James G. Polk (D) d. Apr.
    1959
Paul F. Schenck (R)
Gordon H. Scherer (R)
Charles A. Vanik (D)

Oklahoma

Senators

Robert S. Kerr (D)
A. S. Mike Monroney (D)

Representatives

Carl Albert (D)
Page H. Belcher (R)
Edmond Edmondson (D)
John Jarman (D)
Toby Morris (D)
Thomas J. Steed (D)

Oregon

Senators

Hall S. Lusk (D) ta. 1960
Wayne L. Morse (D)
Richard L. Neuberger (D) d.
    Mar. 1960

Representatives

Edith S. Green (D)
A. Walter Norblad (R)
Charles O. Porter (D)
Albert C. Ullman (D)

Pennsylvania

Senators

Joseph S. Clark (D)
Hugh D. Scott, Jr. (R)

Representatives

William A. Barrett (D)
Alvin R. Bush (R) d. Nov.
    1959
James A. Byrne (D)
Frank M. Clark (D)
Robert J. Corbett (R)
Willard S. Curtin (R)
Paul B. Dague (R)

John H. Dent (D)
Douglas H. Elliott (R) s. 1960,
    d. June 1960
Ivor D. Fenton (R)
Daniel J. Flood (D)
James G. Fulton (R)
Leon H. Gavin (R)
Kathryn E. Granahan (D)
William J. Green, Jr. (D)
Elmer J. Holland (D)
Carroll D. Kearns (R)
John A. Lafore, Jr. (R)
William H. Milliken, Jr. (R)
William S. Moorhead (D)
Thomas E. Morgan (D)
Walter M. Mumma (R)
Robert N. C. Nix (D)
Stanley A. Prokop (D)
James M. Quigley (D)
George M. Rhodes (D)
John P. Saylor (R)
Herman T. Schneebeli (R) s.
    1960
Richard M. Simpson (R) d.
    Jan. 1960
Herman Toll (D)
James E. Van Zandt (R)
Francis E. Walter (D)

Rhode Island

Senators

Theodore F. Green (D)
John O. Pastore (D)

Representatives

John E. Fogarty (D)
Aime J. Forand (D)

South Carolina

Senators

Olin D. Johnston (D)
J. Strom Thurmond (D)

Representatives

Robert T. Ashmore (D)
W. J. Bryan Dorn (D)
Robert W. Hemphill (D)
John L. McMillan (D)
John J. Riley (D)
L. Mendel Rivers (D)

South Dakota

Senators

Francis H. Case (R)
Karl E. Mundt (R)

Representatives

Ellis Y. Berry (R)
George S. McGovern (D)

Tennessee

Senators

Albert A. Gore (D)
Estes Kefauver (D)

Representatives

Howard H. Baker (R)
Ross Bass (D)
Clifford Davis (D)
Robert A. Everett (D)
Joseph L. Evins (D)
James B. Frazier, Jr. (D)
J. Carlton Loser (D)
Thomas J. Murray (D)
B. Carroll Reece (R)

Texas

Senators

Lyndon B. Johnson (D)
Ralph W. Yarborough (D)

Representatives

Bruce R. Alger (R)
Lindley G. Beckworth (D)
Jack B. Brooks (D)
Omar T. Burleson (D)
Robert R. Casey (D)
John V. Dowdy (D)
O. Clark Fisher (D)
Frank N. Ikard (D)
Paul J. Kilday (D)
Joe M. Kilgore (D)
George H. Mahon (D)
Wright Patman (D)
William R. Poage (D)
Sam Rayburn (D)
Walter E. Rogers (D)
J. T. Rutherford (D)
Olin E. Teague (D)
Albert Thomas (D)
Clark W. Thompson (D)
W. Homer Thornberry (D)
James C. Wright, Jr. (D)
John A. Young (D)

Utah

Senators

Wallace F. Bennett (R)
Frank E. Moss (D)

Representatives

Henry Aldous Dixon (R)
David S. King (D)

Vermont

Senators

George D. Aiken (R)
Winston L. Prouty (R)

Representatives

William H. Meyer (D)

Virginia

Senators

Harry F. Byrd (D)
A. Willis Robertson (D)

Representatives

Watkins M. Abbitt (D)

Joel T. Broyhill (D)
Thomas N. Downing (D)
J. Vaughan Gary (D)
Porter Hardy, Jr. (D)
Burr P. Harrison (D)
William P. Jennings (D)
Richard H. Poff (R)
Howard W. Smith (D)
William M. Tuck (D)

Washington

Senators

Henry M. Jackson (D)
Warren G. Magnuson (D)

Representatives

Walter F. Horan (R)
Russell V. Mack (R) d. Mar.
    1960
Donald H. Magnuson (D)
Catherine D. May (R)
Thomas M. Pelly (R)
Thor C. Tollefson (R)
Alfred J. Westland (R)

West Virginia

Senators

Robert C. Byrd (D)
Jennings Randolph (D)

Representatives

Cleveland M. Bailey (D)
Kenneth Hechler (D)
Maude Elizabeth Kee (D)
Arch A. Moore, Jr. (R)
John M. Slack, Jr. (D)
Harley O. Staggers (D)

Wisconsin

Senators

William Proxmire (D)
Alexander Wiley (R)

Representatives

John W. Byrnes (R)
Gerald T. Flynn (D)
Lester R. Johnson (D)
Robert W. Kastenmeier (D)
Melvin R. Laird (R)
Alvin E. O'Konski (R)
Henry S. Reuss (D)
William K. Van Pelt (R)
Gardner R. Withrow (R)
Clement J. Zablocki (D)

Wyoming

Senators

Gale W. McGee (D)
Joseph C. O'Mahoney (D)

Representatives

E. Keith Thompson (R) d.
    Nov. 1960

Eighty-Seventh Congress

(Jan. 3, 1961, to
Jan. 3, 1963)

Presidents of the Senate:
    Richard M. Nixon; Lyndon
    B. Johnson
*President Pro Tempore of the
    Senate:* Carl Hayden
*Speakers of the House of
    Representatives:* Sam Rayburn;
    John W. McCormack

Alabama

Senators

Lister Hill (D)
John J. Sparkman (D)

Representatives

George W. Andrews (D)
Frank W. Boykin (D)
Carl Elliott (D)
George M. Grant (D)
George Huddleston, Jr. (D)
Robert E. Jones, Jr. (D)
Albert Raines (D)
Kenneth A. Roberts (D)
Armistead I. Selden, Jr. (D)

Alaska

Senators

Edward L. Bartlett (D)
Ernest Gruening (D)

Representatives

Ralph J. Rivers (D)

Arizona

Senators

Barry M. Goldwater (R)
Carl Hayden (D)

Representatives

John J. Rhodes (R)
Morris K. Udall (D)

Arkansas

Senators

J. William Fulbright (D)
John L. McClellan (D)

Representatives

T. Dale Alford (D)
Ezekiel C. Gathings (D)
Oren Harris (D)
Wilbur D. Mills (D)
Catherine D. Norrell (D)
James W. Trimble (D)

California

Senators

Clair Engle (D)
Thomas H. Kuchel (R)

Representatives

John F. Baldwin, Jr. (R)
Alphonzo Bell (R)
Jeffery Cohelan (D)
James C. Corman (D)
Clyde G. Doyle (D)
Charles S. Gubser (R)
Harlan F. Hagen (D)
Edgar W. Hiestand (R)
Chet Holifield (D)
Craig Hosmer (R)
Harold T. Johnson (D)
Cecil R. King (D)
Glenard P. Lipscomb (R)
Gordon L. McDonough (R)
John J. McFall (D)
William S. Mailliard (R)
Clement W. Miller (D) d. Oct. 1962
George P. Miller (D)
John E. Moss, Jr. (D)
James Roosevelt (D)
John H. Rousselot (R)
Dalip S. Saund (D)
John F. Shelley (D)
Harry R. Sheppard (D)
Bernice F. Sisk (D)
H. Allen Smith (R)
Charles M. Teague (R)
James B. Utt (R)
Robert C. Wilson (R)
J. Arthur Younger (R)

Colorado

Senators

Gordon L. Allott (R)
John A. Carroll (D)

Representatives

Wayne N. Aspinall (D)
J. Edgar Chenoweth (R)
Peter H. Dominick (R)
Byron G. Rogers (D)

Connecticut

Senators

Prescott S. Bush (R)
Thomas J. Dodd (D)

Representatives

Emilio Q. Daddario (D)
Robert N. Giaimo (D)
Frank Kowalski (D)
John S. Monagan (D)
Horace Seely-Brown, Jr. (R)
Abner W. Sibal (R)

Delaware

Senators

J. Caleb Boggs (R)
John J. Williams (R)

Representatives

Harris B. McDowell, Jr. (D)

Florida

Senators

Spessard L. Holland (D)
George A. Smathers (D)

Representatives

Charles E. Bennett (D)
William C. Cramer (R)
Dante B. Fascell (D)
James A. Haley (D)
Albert S. Herlong, Jr. (D)
Donald R. Matthews (D)
Paul G. Rogers (D)
Robert L. F. Sikes (D)

Georgia

Senators

Richard B. Russell (D)
Herman E. Talmadge (D)

Representatives

Iris F. Blitch (D)
James C. Davis (D)
John W. Davis (D)
John J. Flynt, Jr. (D)
Elijah L. Forrester (D)
G. Elliott Hagan (D)
Phillip M. Landrum (D)
John L. Pilcher (D)
Robert G. Stephens (D)
Carl Vinson (D)

Hawaii

Senators

Hiram L. Fong (R)
Oren E. Long (D)

Representatives

Daniel K. Inouye

Idaho

Senators

Frank Church (D)
Henry C. Dworshak (R) d. July 1962
Len B. Jordan (R) s. 1962

Representatives

Ralph R. Harding (D)
Gracie Pfost (D)

Illinois

Senators

Everett M. Dirksen (R)
Paul H. Douglas (D)

Representatives

John B. Anderson (R)
Leslie C. Arends (R)
Robert B. Chiperfield (R)
Marguerite Stitt Church (R)
Harold R. Collier (R)
William L. Dawson (D)
Edward J. Derwinski (R)
Paul Findley (R)
Edward R. Finnegan (D)
Kenneth J. Gray (D)
Elmer J. Hoffman (R)
John C. Kluczynski (D)
Roland V. Libonati (D)
Peter F. Mack, Jr. (D)
Noah M. Mason (R)
Robert H. Michel (R)
William T. Murphy (D)
Thomas J. O'Brien (D)
Barratt O'Hara (D)
Melvin Price (D)
Roman C. Pucinski (D)
Dan Rostenkowski (D)
George E. Shipley (D)
William L. Springer (R)
Sidney R. Yates (D)

Indiana

Senators

Homer E. Capehart (R)
Vance Hartke (D)

Representatives

E. Ross Adair (R)
John Brademas (D)
William G. Bray (R)
Donald C. Bruce (R)
Winfield K. Denton (D)
Charles A. Halleck (R)
Ralph Harvey (R)
Ray J. Madden (D)
Richard L. Roudebush (R)
J. Edward Roush (D)
Earl Wilson (R)

Iowa

Senators

Bourke B. Hickenlooper (R)
Jack R. Miller (R)

Representatives

James E. Bromwell (R)
Merwin Coad (D)
Harold R. Gross (R)
Charles B. Hoeven (R)
Ben F. Jensen (R)
John H. Kyl (R)
Frederick D. Schwengel (R)
Neal Smith (D)

Kansas

Senators

Frank Carlson (R)
James B. Pearson (R) s. 1962
Andrew F. Schoeppel (R) d. Jan. 1962

Representatives

William H. Avery (R)
J. Floyd Breeding (D)
Bob Dole (R)
Robert F. Ellsworth (R)
Walter L. McVey (R)
Garner E. Shriver (R)

Kentucky

Senators

John Sherman Cooper (R)
Thruston B. Morton (R)

Representatives

Frank W. Burke (D)
Frank L. Chelf (D)
William H. Natcher (D)
Carl D. Perkins (D)
Eugene Siler (R)
Brent Spence (D)
Frank A. Stubblefield (D)
John C. Watts (D)

Louisiana

Senators

Allen J. Ellender (D)
Russell B. Long (D)

Representatives

T. Hale Boggs (D)
Overton Brooks (D) d. Sept. 1961
F. Edward Herbert (D)
Harold B. McSween (D)
James H. Morrison (D)
Otto E. Passman (D)
T. Ashton Thompson (D)
Joe D. Waggonner, Jr. (R) s. 1962
Edwin E. Willis (D)

Maine

Senators

Edmund S. Muskie (D)
Margaret Chase Smith (R)

Representatives

Peter A. Garland (R)
Clifford G. McIntire (R)
Stanley R. Tupper (R)

Maryland

Senators

J. Glenn Beall (R)
John Marshall Butler (R)

Representatives

Daniel B. Brewster (D)
George H. Fallon (D)
Samuel N. Friedel (D)
Edward A. Garmatz (D)
Thomas F. Johnson (D)
Richard E. Lankford (D)
Charles McC. Mathias, Jr. (R)

Massachusetts

Senators

Edward M. Kennedy (D) s. 1962
Leverett Saltonstall (R)
Benjamin A. Smith 2d (D) ta. 1961

Representatives

William H. Bates (R)
Edward P. Boland (D)
James A. Burke (D)
Silvio O. Conte (R)
Laurence Curtis (R)
Harold D. Donahue (D)
Hastings Keith (R)
Thomas J. Lane (D)
John W. McCormack (D)
Torbert H. Macdonald (D)
Joseph W. Martin, Jr. (R)
F. Bradford Morse (R)
Thomas P. O'Neill, Jr. (D)
Philip J. Philbin (D)

Michigan

Senators

Philip A. Hart (D)
Patrick V. McNamara (D)

Representatives

John B. Bennett (R)
William S. Broomfield (R)
Elford A. Cederberg (R)
Charles E. Chamberlain (R)
Charles C. Diggs, Jr. (D)
John D. Dingell (D)
Gerald R. Ford, Jr. (R)
Robert P. Griffin (R)
Martha W. Griffiths (D)
James Harvey (R)
Clare E. Hoffman (R)
August E. Johansen (R)
Victor A. Knox (R)
John Lesinski (D)
Thaddeus M. Machrowicz (D) r. Sept. 1961
George Meader (R)
Lucien N. Nedzi (D) s. 1962
James G. O'Hara (D)
Louis C. Rabaut (D) d. Nov. 1961
Harold M. Ryan (D) s. 1962

Minnesota

Senators

Hubert H. Humphrey (D)
Eugene J. McCarthy (D)

Representatives

H. Carl Andersen (R)
John A. Blatnik (D)
Walter H. Judd (R)
Joseph E. Karth (D)
Odin Langen (R)
Clark MacGregor (R)
Fred Marshall (D)
Ancher Nelsen (R)
Albert H. Quie (R)

Mississippi

Senators

James O. Eastland (D)
John C. Stennis (D)

Representatives

Thomas G. Abernethy (D)
William M. Colmer (D)
Frank E. Smith (D) r. Nov. 1962
Jamie L. Whitten (D)
John Bell Williams (D)
W. Arthur Winstead (D)

Missouri

Senators

Stuart Symington (D)
Edward V. Long (D)

Representatives

Richard W. Bolling (D)
Clarence Cannon (D)
Thomas B. Curtis (R)
Durward G. Hall (R)
William R. Hull, Jr. (D)
Richard H. Ichord (D)
Paul C. Jones (D)
Frank M. Karsten (D)
Leonor Kretzer Sullivan (D)
Morgan M. Moulder (D)
William J. Randall (D)

Montana

Senators

Mike Mansfield (D)
Lee Metcalf (D)

Representatives

James F. Battin (R)
Arnold Olsen (D)

Nebraska

Senators

Carl T. Curtis (R)
Roman L. Hruska (R)

Representatives

Ralph F. Beermann (R)
Glenn C. Cunningham (R)
David T. Martin (R)
Phillip H. Weaver (R)

Nevada

Senators

Alan Bible (D)
Howard W. Cannon (D)

Representatives

Walter S. Baring (D)

New Hampshire

Senators

Styles Bridges (R) d. Nov. 1961
Norris Cotton (R)
Maurice J. Murphy, Jr. (R) ta. 1962

Reprsentatives

Perkins Bass (R)
Chester E. Merrow (R)

New Jersey

Senators

Clifford P. Case (R)
Harrison A. Williams, Jr. (D)

Representatives

Hugh J. Addonizio (D) r. June 1962
James C. Auchincloss (R)
William T. Cahill (R)
Dominick V. Daniels (D)
Florence P. Dwyer (R)
Peter H. B. Frelinghuysen, Jr. (R)
Cornelius E. Gallagher (D)
Milton W. Glenn (R)
Charles S. Joelson (D)
Frank C. Osmers, Jr. (R)
Peter W. Rodino, Jr. (D)
Frank Thompson, Jr. (D)
George M. Wallhauser (R)
William B. Widnall (R)

New Mexico

Senators

Clinton P. Anderson (D)
Dennis Chavez (D) d. Nov. 1962

Representatives

Joseph M. Montoya (D)
Thomas G. Morris (D)

New York

Senators

Jacob K. Javits (R)
Kenneth B. Keating (R)

Representatives

Joseph P. Addabbo (D)
Victor L. Anfuso (D)
Robert R. Barry (R)
Frank J. Becker (R)
Charles A. Buckley (D)
Hugh L. Carey (D)
Emanuel Celler (D)
James J. Delaney (D)
Steven B. Derounian (R)
Edwin B. Dooley (R)
Thaddeus J. Dulski (D)
Leonard Farbstein (D)
Paul A. Fino (R)
Jacob H. Gilbert (D)
Charles E. Goodell (R)

Seymour Halpern (R)
James C. Healey (D)
Lester Holtzman (D) r. Dec. 1961
Edna F. Kelly (D)
Eugene J. Keogh (D)
Clarence E. Kilburn (R)
Carleton J. King (R)
John V. Lindsay (R)
William E. Miller (R)
Abraham J. Multer (D)
Leo W. O'Brien (D)
Harold C. Ostertag (R)
Otis G. Pike (D)
John R. Pillion (R)
Alexander Pirnie (R)
Adam Clayton Powell (D)
John H. Ray (R)
R. Walter Riehlman (R)
Howard W. Robison (R)
John J. Rooney (D)
Benjamin S. Rosenthal (D) s. 1962
William F. Ryan (D)
Katharine St. George (R)
Alfred E. Santangelo (D)
Samuel S. Stratton (D)
John Taber (R)
Jessica McCullough Weis (R)
J. Ernest Wharton (R)
Herbert Zelenko (D)

North Carolina

Senators

Sam J. Ervin, Jr. (D)
B. Everett Jordan (D)

Representatives

Hugh Q. Alexander (D)
Herbert C. Bonner (D)
Harold D. Cooley (D)
Lawrence H. Fountain (D)
David N. Henderson (D)
Charles R. Jonas (R)
A. Paul Kitchin (D)
Horace R. Kornegay (D)
Alton A. Lennon (D)
Ralph J. Scott (D)
Roy A. Taylor (D)
Basil L. Whitener (D)

North Dakota

Senators

Quentin N. Burdick (D)
Milton R. Young (R)

Representatives

Hjalmar C. Nygaard (R)
Don L. Short (R)

Ohio

Senators

Frank J. Lausche (D)
Stephen M. Young (D)

Representatives

John M. Ashbrook (R)
Thomas L. Ashley (D)
William H. Ayres (R)

Jackson E. Betts (R)
Frances P. Bolton (R)
Frank T. Bow (R)
Clarence J. Brown (R)
Donald D. Clancy (R)
Robert E. Cook (D) r. Dec. 1962
Samuel L. Devine (R)
Michael A. Feighan (D)
William H. Harsha, Jr. (R)
Wayne L. Hays (D)
Michael J. Kirwan (D)
Delbert L. Latta (R)
William M. McCulloch (R)
William E. Minshall, Jr. (R)
Walter H. Moeller (D)
Tom V. Moorehead (R)
Charles A. Mosher (R)
Paul F. Schenck (R)
Gordon H. Scherer (R)
Charles A. Vanik (D)

Oklahoma

Senators

Robert S. Kerr (D) d. Jan. 1963
A. S. Mike Monroney (D)

Representatives

Carl Albert (D)
Page H. Belcher (R)
Edmond Edmondson (R)
John Jarman (R)
Thomas J. Steed (D)
Victor Wickersham (D)

Oregon

Senators

Wayne L. Morse (D)
Maurine B. Neuberger (D)

Representatives

Edwin R. Durno (R)
Edith Green (D)
A. Walter Norblad, Jr. (R)
Al Ullman (D)

Pennsylvania

Senators

Joseph S. Clark (D)
Hugh Scott (R)

Representatives

William A. Barrett (D)
James A. Byrne (D)
Frank M. Clark (D)
Robert J. Corbett (R)
Willard S. Curtin (R)
Paul B. Dague (R)
John H. Dent (D)
Ivor D. Fenton (R)
Daniel J. Flood (D)
James G. Fulton (R)
Leon H. Gavin (R)
George A. Goodling (R)
Kathryn E. Granahan (D)
William J. Green, Jr. (D)
Elmer J. Holland (D)
Carroll D. Kearns (R)

John C. Kunkel (R)
William H. Milliken, Jr. (R)
William S. Moorhead (D)
Thomas E. Morgan (D)
Robert N. C. Nix (D)
George M. Rhodes (D)
John P. Saylor (R)
Herman T. Schneebeli (R)
Richard S. Schweiker (R)
William W. Scranton (R)
Herman Toll (D)
Francis E. Walter (D)
J. Irving Whalley (R)
James E. Van Zandt (R)

Rhode Island

Senators

John O. Pastore (D)
Claiborne Pell (D)

Representatives

John E. Fogarty (D)
Fernand J. St. Germain (D)

South Carolina

Senators

Olin D. Johnston (D)
J. Strom Thurmond (D)

Representatives

Robert T. Ashmore (D)
W. J. Bryan Dorn (D)
Robert W. Hemphill (D)
John L. McMillan (D)
John J. Riley (D) d. Jan. 1962
Corrinne B. Riley (D) s. 1962
L. Mendel Rivers (D)

South Dakota

Senators

Joseph H. Bottum (R) s. 1962
Francis Case (R) d. June 1962
Karl E. Mundt (R)

Representatives

Ellis Y. Berry (R)
Benjamin Reifel (R)

Tennessee

Senators

Albert A. Gore (D)
Estes Kefauver (D)

Representatives

Howard H. Baker (R)
Ross Bass (D)
Clifford Davis (D)
Robert A. Everett (D)
Joe L. Evins (D)
James B. Frazier, Jr. (D)
J. Carlton Loser (D)
Thomas J. Murray (D)
B. Carroll Reece (R) d. Mar. 1961
Louise G. Reece (R)

Texas

Senators

William A. Blakley (D) ta. 1961
John G. Tower (R)
Ralph W. Yarborough (D)

Representatives

Bruce R. Alger (R)
Lindley G. Beckworth (D)
Jack B. Brooks (D)
Omar Burleson (D)
Robert R. Casey (D)
John Dowdy (D)
O. Clark Fisher (D)
Henry B. Gonzalez (D) s. 1962
Frank Ikard (D) r. Dec. 1961
Paul J. Kilday (D) r. Sept. 1961
Joe M. Kilgore (D)
George H. Mahon (D)
Wright Patman (D)
William R. Poage (D)
Graham Purcell, Jr. (D) s. 1962
Sam Rayburn (D) d. Nov. 1961
H. Ray Roberts (D) s. 1962
Walter E. Rogers (D)
J. T. Rutherford (D)
Olin E. Teague (D)
Albert Thomas (D)
Clark W. Thompson (D)
W. Homer Thornberry (D)
James C. Wright, Jr. (D)
John A. Young (D)

Utah

Senators

Wallace F. Bennett (R)
Frank E. Moss (D)

Representatives

David S. King (D)
M. Blaine Peterson (D)

Vermont

Senators

George D. Aiken (R)
Winston L. Prouty (R)

Representatives

Robert T. Stafford (R)

Virginia

Senators

Harry F. Byrd (D)
A. Willis Robertson (D)

Representatives

Watkins M. Abbitt (D)
Joel T. Broyhill (R)
Thomas N. Downing (D)
J. Vaughan Gary (D)
Porter Hardy, Jr. (D)
Burr P. Harrison (D)
William P. Jennings (D)
Richard H. Poff (R)

Howard W. Smith (D)
William M. Tuck (D)

Washington

Senators

Henry M. Jackson (D)
Warren G. Magnuson (D)

Representatives

Julia Butler Hansen (D)
Walter F. Horan (R)
Donald H. Magnuson (D)
Catherine D. May (R)
Thomas M. Pelly (R)
Thor C. Tollefson (R)
Alfred J. Westland (R)

West Virginia

Senators

Robert C. Byrd (D)
Jennings Randolph (D)

Representatives

Cleveland M. Bailey (D)
Kenneth Hechler (D)
Maude Elizabeth Kee (D)
Arch A. Moore, Jr. (R)
John M. Slack, Jr. (D)
Harley O. Staggers (D)

Wisconsin

Senators

William Proxmire (D)
Alexander Wiley (R)

Representatives

John W. Byrnes (R)
Lester R. Johnson (D)
Robert W. Kastenmeier (D)
Melvin R. Laird (R)
Alvin E. O'Konski (R)
Henry S. Reuss (D)
Henry C. Schadeberg (R)
Vernon W. Thompson (R)
William K. Van Pelt (R)
Clement J. Zablocki (D)

Wyoming

Senators

John J. Hickey (D)
Gale W. McGee (D)

Representatives

William H. Harrison (R)

Eighty-Eighth Congress

(Jan. 3, 1963, to
Jan. 3, 1965)

President of the Senate: Lyndon
B. Johnson
*President Pro Tempore of the
Senate:* Carl Hayden
*Speaker of the House of
Representatives:* John W.
McCormack

Alabama

Senators

Lister Hill (D)
John J. Sparkman (D)

Representatives

George W. Andrews (D)
Carl Elliott (D)
George M. Grant (D)
George Huddleston, Jr. (D)
Robert E. Jones, Jr. (D)
Albert Rains (D)
Kenneth A. Roberts (D)
Armistead I. Selden, Jr. (D)

Alaska

Senators

Edward L. Bartlett (D)
Ernest Gruening (D)

Representatives

Ralph J. Rivers (D)

Arizona

Senators

Barry M. Goldwater (R)
Carl Hayden (D)

Representatives

John J. Rhodes (R)
George F. Senner, Jr. (D)
Morris K. Udall (D)

Arkansas

Senators

J. William Fulbright (D)
John L. McClellan (D)

Representatives

Ezekiel C. Gathings (D)
Oren Harris (D)
Wilbur D. Mills (D)
James W. Trimble (D)

California

Senators

Clair Engle (D) d. July 1964
Thomas H. Kuchel (R)
Pierre Salinger (D) ta. 1964

Representatives

John F. Baldwin, Jr. (R)
Alphonzo Bell (R)
George E. Brown, Jr. (D)
Everett G. Burkhalter (D)
Phillip Burton (D) s. 1964
Ronald B. Cameron (D)
Don H. Clausen (R)
Del Clawson (R) s. 1963
Jeffery Cohelan (D)
James C. Corman (D)
Clyde G. Doyle (D) d. Mar.
  1963
Don Edwards (D)
Charles S. Gubser (R)
Harlan F. Hagen (D)
Richard T. Hanna (D)
Augustus F. Hawkins (D)
Chet Holifield (D)
Craig Hosmer (R)
Harold T. Johnson (D)
Cecil R. King (D)
Robert L. Leggett (D)
Glenard P. Lipscomb (R)
John J. McFall (D)
William S. Mailliard (R)
Pat M. Martin (R)
George P. Miller (D)
John E. Moss, Jr. (D)
James Roosevelt (D)
Edward R. Roybal (D)
John F. Shelley (D) r. Jan.
  1964
Harry R. Sheppard (D)
Bernice F. Sisk (D)
H. Allen Smith (R)
Burt L. Talcott (R)
Charles M. Teague (R)
James B. Utt (R)
Lionel Van Derrlin (D)
Charles H. Wilson (D)
Robert C. Wilson (R)
J. Arthur Younger (R)

Colorado

Senators

Gordon L. Allott (R)
Peter H. Dominick (R)

Representatives

Wayne N. Aspinall (D)
Donald G. Brotzman (R)
J. Edgar Chenoweth (R)
Byron G. Rogers (D)

Connecticut

Senators

Thomas J. Dodd (D)
Abraham A. Ribicoff (D)

Representatives

Emilio Q. Daddario (D)
Robert N. Giaimo (D)

Bernard F. Grabowski (D)
John S. Monagan (D)
William L. St. Onge (D)
Abner W. Sibal (R)

Delaware

Senators

J. Caleb Boggs (R)
John J. Williams (R)

Representatives

Harris B. McDowell, Jr. (D)

Florida

Senators

Spessard L. Holland (D)
George A. Smathers (D)

Representatives

Charles E. Bennett (D)
William C. Cramer (R)
Dante B. Fascell (D)
Don Fuqua (D)
Sam M. Gibbons (D)
Edward J. Gurney (R)
James A. Haley (D)
Albert S. Herlong, Jr. (D)
Donald R. Matthews (D)
Claude D. Pepper (D)
Paul G. Rogers (D)
Robert L. F. Sikes (D)

Georgia

Senators

Richard B. Russell (D)
Herman E. Talmadge (D)

Representatives

John W. Davis (D)
John J. Flynt, Jr. (D)
E. L. Forrester (D)
G. Elliott Hagan (D)
Phillip M. Landrum (D)
John L. Pilcher (D)
Robert G. Stephens, Jr. (D)
J. Russell Tuten (D)
Carl Vinson (D)
Charles L. Weltner (R)

Hawaii

Senators

Hiram L. Fong (R)
Daniel K. Inouye (D)

Representatives

Thomas P. Gill (D)
Spark M. Matsunaga (R)

Idaho

Senators

Frank Church (D)
Len B. Jordan (R)

Representatives

Ralph R. Harding (D)
Compton I. White, Jr. (D)

Illinois

Senators

Everett M. Dirksen (R)
Paul H. Douglas (D)

Representatives

John B. Anderson (R)
Leslie C. Arends (R)
Harold R. Collier (R)
William L. Dawson (D)
Edward J. Derwinski (R)
Paul Findley (R)
Edward R. Finnegan (D) r.
  Dec. 1964
Kenneth J. Gray (D)
Elmer J. Hoffman (R)
John C. Kluczynski (D) d. Apr.
  1964
Roland V. Libonati (D)
Robert McClory (R)
Robert T. McLoskey (R)
Robert H. Michel (R)
William T. Murphy (D)
Thomas J. O'Brien (D)
Barratt O'Hara (D)
Melvin Price (D)
Roman C. Pucinski (D)
Charlotte T. Reid (R)
Daniel Rostenkowski (D)
Donald Rumsfeld (R)
George E. Shipley (D)
William L. Springer (R)

Indiana

Senators

Birch Bayh (D)
Vance Hartke (D)

Representatives

E. Ross Adair (R)
William G. Bray (R)
John Brademas (D)
Donald C. Bruce (R)
Winfield K. Denton (D)
Charles A. Halleck (R)
Ralph Harvey (R)
Ray J. Madden (D)
Richard L. Roudebush (R)
J. Edward Roush (D)
Earl Wilson (R)

Iowa

Senators

Bourke B. Hickenlooper (R)
Jack R. Miller (R)

Representatives

James E. Bromwell (R)
Harold R. Gross (R)
Charles B. Hoeven (R)
Ben F. Jensen (R)
John H. Kyl (R)
Frederick D. Schwengel (R)
Neal Smith (D)

Kansas

Senators

Frank Carlson (R)
James B. Pearson (R)

Representatives

William H. Avery (R)
Robert J. Dole (R)
Robert F. Ellsworth (R)
Garner E. Shriver (R)
Joe Skubitz (R)

Kentucky

Senators

John Sherman Cooper (R)
Thruston B. Morton (R)

Representatives

Frank L. Chelf (D)
William H. Natcher (D)
Carl D. Perkins (D)
Eugene Siler (R)
M. G. (Gene) Snyder (R)
Frank A. Subblefield (D)
John C. Watts (D)

Louisiana

Senators

Allen J. Ellender (D)
Russell B. Long (D)

Representatives

T. Hale Boggs (D)
F. Edward Hebert (D)
Gillis W. Long (D)
James H. Morrison (D)
Otto E. Passman (D)
T. Ashton Thompson (D)
Joe D. Waggonner, Jr. (D)
Edwin E. Willis (D)

Maine

Senators

Edmund S. Muskie (R)
Margaret Chase Smith (R)

Representatives

Clifford G. McIntire (R)
Stanley R. Tupper (R)

Maryland

Senators

J. Glenn Beall (R)
Daniel B. Brewster (D)

Representatives

George H. Fallon (D)
Samuel N. Friedel (D)
Edward A. Garmatz (D)
Richard E. Lankford (D)
Clarence D. Long (D)

Charles McC. Mathias, Jr. (R)
Rogers C. B. Morton (R)
Carlton R. Sickles (D)

Massachusetts

Senators

Edward M. Kennedy (D)
Leverett Saltonstall (R)

Representatives

William H. Bates (R)
Edward P. Boland (D)
James A. Burke (D)
Silvio O. Conte (R)
Harold D. Donohue (D)
Hastings Keith (R)
John W. McCormack (D)
Torbert H. Macdonald (D)
Joseph W. Martin, Jr. (R)
F. Bradford Morse (R)
Thomas P. O'Neill, Jr. (D)
Philip J. Philbin (D)

Michigan

Senators

Philip A. Hart (D)
Patrick V. McNamara (D)

Representatives

John B. Bennett (R) d. Aug. 1964
William S. Broomfield (R)
Elford A. Cederberg (R)
Charles E. Chamberlain (R)
Charles C. Diggs, Jr. (D)
John D. Dingell, Jr. (D)
Gerald R. Ford, Jr. (R)
Robert P. Griffin (R)
Martha W. Griffiths (D)
James Harvey (R)
Edward Hutchinson (R)
August E. Johansen (R)
Victor A. Knox (R)
John Lesinski (D)
George Meader (R)
Lucien N. Nedzi (D)
James G. O'Hara (D)
Harold M. Ryan (D)
Neil Staebler (D)

Minnesota

Senators

Hubert H. Humphrey (D)
Eugene J. McCarthy (D)

Representatives

John A. Blatnik (D)
Donald M. Fraser (D)
Joseph E. Karth (D)
Odin Langen (R)
Clark MacGregor (R)
Ancher Nelsen (R)
Alec G. Olson (D)
Albert H. Quie (R)

Mississippi

Senators

James O. Eastland (D)
John C. Stennis (D)

Representatives

Thomas G. Abernethy (D)
William M. Colmer (D)
Jamie L. Whitten (D)
John Bell Williams (D)
W. Arthur Winstead (D)

Missouri

Senators

Edward V. Long (D)
Stuart Symington (D)

Representatives

Richard W. Bolling (D)
Clarence Cannon (D) d. May 1964
Thomas B. Curtis (R)
Durward G. Hall (R)
William R. Hull, Jr. (D)
William L. Hungate (D) s. 1964
Richard H. Ichord (D)
Paul C. Jones (D)
Frank M. Karsten (D)
William J. Randall (D)
Leonor Kretzer Sullivan (D)

Montana

Senators

Mike Mansfield (D)
Lee Metcalf (F)

Representatives

James F. Battin (R)
Arnold Olsen (D)

Nebraska

Senators

Carl T. Curtis (R)
Roman L. Hruska (R)

Representatives

Ralph F. Beermann (R)
Glenn C. Cunningham (R)
David T. Martin (R)

Nevada

Senators

Alan Bible (D)
Howard W. Cannon (D)

Representatives

Walter S. Baring (D)

New Hampshire

Senators

Norris Cotton (R)
Thomas J. McIntyre (D)

Representatives

James C. Cleveland (D)
Louis C. Wyman (R)

New Jersey

Senators

Clifford P. Case (R)
Harrison A. Williams, Jr. (D)

Representatives

James C. Auchincloss (R)
William T. Cahill (R)
Dominick V. Daniels (D)
Florence P. Dwyer (R)
Peter H. B. Frelinghuysen, Jr. (R)
Cornelius E. Gallagher (D)
Milton W. Glenn (R)
Charles S. Joelson (D)
Joseph G. Minish (D)
Frank C. Osmers, Jr. (R)
Edward J. Patten (D)
Peter W. Rodino, Jr. (D)
Frank Thompson, Jr. (D)
George M. Wallhauser (R)
William B. Widnall (R)

New Mexico

Senators

Clinton P. Anderson (D)
Edwin L. Mechem (R)

Representatives

Joseph M. Montoya (D) r. Nov. 1964
Thomas G. Morris (D)

New York

Senators

Jacob K. Javits (R)
Kenneth B. Keating (R)

Representatives

Joseph P. Addabbo (R)
Robert R. Barry (R)
Frank J. Becker (R)
Charles A. Buckley (D)
Hugh L. Carey (D)
Emanuel Celler (D)
James J. Delaney (D)
Steven B. Derounian (R)
Thaddeus J. Dulski (D)
Leonard Farbstein (D)
Paul A. Fino (R)
Jacob H. Gilbert (D)
Charles E. Goodell (R)
James R. Grover, Jr. (R)
Seymour Halpern (R)
James C. Healey (D)
Frank J. Horton (R)

Edna F. Kelly (D)
Eugene J. Keogh (D)
Clarence E. Kilburn (R)
Carleton J. King (R)
John V. Lindsay (R)
William E. Miller (R)
Abraham J. Multer (D)
John M. Murphy (D)
Leo W. O'Brien (D)
Harold C. Ostertag (R)
Otis G. Pike (D)
John R. Pillion (R)
Alexander Pirnie (R)
Adam Clayton Powell (D)
Ogden R. Reid (R)
Walter R. Riehlman (R)
Howard W. Robison (R)
John J. Rooney (D)
Benjamin S. Rosenthal (D)
William F. Ryan (D)
Katharine St. George (R)
Samuel S. Stratton (D)
J. Ernest Wharton (R)
John W. Wydler (R)

North Carolina

Senators

Sam J. Ervin, Jr. (D)
B. Everett Jordan (D)

Representatives

Herbert C. Bonner (D)
James T. Broyhill (R)
Harold D. Cooley (D)
L. H. Fountain (D)
David N. Henderson (D)
Charles R. Jonas (R)
Horace R. Kornegay (D)
Alton A. Lennon (D)
Ralph J. Scott (D)
Roy A. Taylor (D)
Basil L. Whitener (D)

North Dakota

Senators

Quentin N. Burdick (D)
Milton R. Young (R)

Representatives

Mark Andrews (R)
Hjalmar C. Nygaard (R) d. July
  1963
Don L. Short (R)

Ohio

Senators

Frank J. Lausche (D)
Stephen M. Young (D)

Representatives

Homer E. Abele (R)
John M. Ashbrook (R)
Thomas L. Ashley (D)
William H. Ayres (R)
Jackson E. Betts (R)
Frances P. Bolton (R)
Oliver P. Bolton (R)
Frank T. Bow (R)
Clarence J. Brown (R)

Donald D. Clancy (R)
Samuel L. Divine (R)
Michael A. Feighan (D)
William H. Harsha, Jr. (R)
Wayne L. Hays (D)
Michael J. Kirwan (D)
Delbert L. Latta (R)
William M. McCulloch (R)
William E. Minshall (R)
Charles A. Mosher (R)
Carl W. Rich (R)
Paul F. Schenck (R)
Robert T. Secrest (D)
Robert Taft, Jr. (R)
Charles A. Vanik (D)

Oklahoma

Senators

J. Howard Edmondson (D) ta.
  1963
Fred R. Harris (D) s. 1964
A. S. Mike Monroney (D)

Representatives

Carl Albert (D)
Page H. Belcher (R)
Edmond Edmondson (D)
John Jarman (D)
Thomas J. Steed (D)
Victor Wickersham (D)

Oregon

Senators

Wayne Morse (D)
Maurine B. Neuberger (D)

Representatives

Robert B. Duncan (D)
Edith Green (D)
A. Walter Norblad (R) d. Sept.
  1964
Al Ullman (D)

Pennsylvania

Senators

Joseph S. Clark (D)
Hugh Scott (R)

Representatives

William A. Barrett (D)
James A. Byrne (D)
Frank M. Clark (D)
Robert J. Corbett (R)
Willard S. Curtin (R)
Paul B. Dague (R)
John H. Dent (D)
Daniel J. Flood (D)
James G. Fulton (R)
Leon H. Gavin (R) d. Sept.
  1963
George A. Goodling (R)
William J. Green (D) s. 1964
William J. Green, Jr. (D) d.
  Dec. 1963
Elmer J. Holland (D)
Albert W. Johnson (R)
John C. Kunkel (R)
Joseph M. McDade (R)
William H. Milliken (R)

William S. Moorhead (D)
Thomas E. Morgan (D)
Robert N. C. Nix (D)
George M. Rhodes (D)
Fred B. Rooney (D)
John P. Saylor (R)
Herman T. Schneebeli (R)
Richard S. Schweiker (R)
Herman Toll (D)
Francis E. Walter (D) d. May
  1963
James D. Weaver (R)
J. Irving Whalley (R)

Rhode Island

Senators

John O. Pastore (D)
Claiborne Pell (D)

Representatives

John E. Fogarty (D)
Fernand J. St. Germain (D)

South Carolina

Senators

Olin D. Johnston (D)
J. Strom Thurmond (D)

Representatives

Robert T. Ashmore (D)
W. J. Bryan Dorn (D)
Robert W. Hemphill (D) r.
  May 1964
John L. McMillan (D)
L. Mendel Rivers (D)
Albert W. Watson (D)

South Dakota

Senators

George McGovern (D)
Karl E. Mundt (R)

Representatives

Ellis Y. Berry (R)
Benjamin Reifel (R)

Tennessee

Senators

Albert Gore (D)
Estes Kefauver (D) d. Aug.
  1963
Herbert S. Walters (D) ta. 1963

Representatives

Howard H. Baker (R) d. Jan.
  1964
Irene Bailey Baker (R) s. 1964
Ross Bass (D)
William E. Brock, III (R)
Clifford Davis (D)
Robert A. Everett (D)
Joe L. Evins (D)
Richard H. Fulton (D)
Thomas J. Murray (D)
James H. Quillen (R)

Texas

Senators

John G. Tower (R)
Ralph W. Yarborough (D)

Representatives

Bruce R. Alger (R)
Lindley G. Beckworth (D)
Jack B. Brooks (D)
Omar Burleson (D)
Robert R. Casey (D)
John V. Dowdy (D)
O. Clark Fisher (D)
Edgar F. Forman (R)
Henry B. Gonzalez (D)
Joe M. Kilgore (D)
George H. Mahon (D)
Wright Patman (D)
J. J. Pickle (D)
William R. Poage (D)
Joe R. Pool (D)
Graham Purcell (D)
H. Ray Roberts (D)
Walter E. Rogers (D)
Olin E. Teague (D)
Albert Thomas (D)
Clark W. Thompson (D)
W. Homer Thornberry (D) r.
  Dec. 1963
James C. Wright, Jr. (D)
John A. Young (D)

Utah

Senators

Wallace F. Bennett (R)
Frank E. Moss (D)

Representatives

Laurence J. Burton (R)
Sherman P. Lloyd (R)

Vermont

Senators

George D. Aiken (R)
Winston L. Prouty (R)

Representatives

Robert T. Stafford (R)

Virginia

Senators

Harry F. Byrd (D)
A. Willis Robertson (D)

Representatives

Watkins M. Abbitt (D)
Joel T. Broyhill (R)
Thomas N. Downing (D)
J. Vaughan Gary (D)
Porter Hardy, Jr. (D)
William P. Jennings (D)
John O. Marsh, Jr. (D)
Richard H. Poff (R)
Howard W. Smith (D)
William M. Tuck (D)

Washington

Senators

Henry M. Jackson (D)
Warren G. Magnuson (D)

Representatives

Julia Butler Hansen (D)
Walter F. Horan (R)
Catherine May (R)
Thomas M. Pelly (R)
Bill Stinson (R)
Thor C. Tollefson (R)
Alfred J. Westland (R)

West Virginia

Senators

Robert C. Byrd (D)
Jennings Randolph (D)

Representatives

Kenneth Hechler (D)
Maude Elizabeth Kee (D)
Arch A. Moore, Jr. (R)
John M. Slack, Jr. (D)
Harley O. Staggers (D)

Wisconsin

Senators

Gaylord A. Nelson (D)
William Proxmire (D)

Representatives

John W. Byrnes (R)
Lester R. Johnson (D)
Robert W. Kastenmeier (D)
Melvin R. Laird (R)
Alvin E. O'Konski (R)
Henry S. Reuss (D)
Henry C. Schadeberg (R)
Vernon W. Thomson (R)
William K. Van Pelt (R)
Clement J. Zablocki (D)

Wyoming

Senators

Gale W. McGee (D)
Milward L. Simpson (R)

Representatives

William H. Harrison (R)

Eighty-Ninth Congress

(Jan. 3, 1965, to
Jan. 3, 1967)

President of the Senate: Hubert
H. Humphrey
*President Pro Tempore of the
Senate:* Carl Hayden

*Speaker of the House of
Representatives:* John W.
McCormack

Alabama

Senators

Lister Hill (D)
John J. Sparkman (D)

Representatives

George W. Andrews (D)
Glenn Andrews (R)
John H. Buchanan, Jr. (R)
William L. Dickinson (R)
Jack Edwards (R)
Robert E. Jones, Jr. (D)
James D. Martin (R)
Armistead I. Selden, Jr. (D)

Alaska

Senators

Edward L. Bartlett (D)
Ernest Gruening (D)

Representatives

Ralph J. Rivers (D)

Arizona

Senators

Paul J. Fannin (R)
Carl Hayden (D)

Representatives

John J. Rhodes (R)
George F. Senner, Jr. (D)
Morris K. Udall (D)

Arkansas

Senators

J. William Fulbright (D)
John L. McClellan (D)

Representatives

Ezekiel C. Gathings (D)
Oren Harris (D) r. Feb. 1966
Wilbur D. Mills (D)
James W. Trimble (D)

California

Senators

Thomas H. Kuchel (R)
George L. Murphy (R)

Representatives

John F. Baldwin, Jr. (R) d.
Mar. 1966
Alphonzo Bell (R)
George E. Brown, Jr. (D)
Phillip Burton (D)
Ronald B. Cameron (D)
Don H. Clausen (R)

Del Clawson (R)
Jeffery Cohelan (D)
James C. Corman (D)
Ken W. Dyal (D)
Don Edwards (D)
Charles S. Gubser (R)
Harlan F. Hagen (D)
Richard T. Hanna (D)
Augustus F. Hawkins (D)
Chet Holifield (D)
Craig Hosmer (R)
Harold T. Johnson (D)
Cecil R. King (D)
Robert L. Leggett (D)
Glenard P. Lipscomb (R)
John J. McFall (D)
William S. Mailliard (R)
George P. Miller (D)
John E. Moss, Jr. (D)
Thomas M. Rees (D) s. 1966
Ed Reinecke (R)
James Roosevelt (D) r. Sept.
1965
Edward R. Roybal (D)
Bernice F. Sisk (D)
H. Allen Smith (R)
Burt L. Talcott (R)
Charles M. Teague (R)
John V. Tunney (D)
James B. Utt (R)
Lionel Van Deerlin (D)
Jerome R. Waldie (D) s. 1966
Charles H. Wilson (D)
Robert C. Wilson (R)
J. Arthur Younger (R)

Colorado

Senators

Gordon L. Allott (R)
Peter H. Dominick (R)

Representatives

Wayne N. Aspinall (D)
Frank E. Evans (D)
Roy H. McVicker (D)
Byron G. Rogers (D)

Connecticut

Senators

Thomas J. Dodd (D)
Abraham A. Ribicoff (D)

Representatives

Emilio Q. Daddario (D)
Robert N. Giaimo (D)
Bernard F. Grabowski (D)
Donald J. Irwin (D)
John S. Monagan (D)
William L. St. Onge (D)

Delaware

Senators

J. Caleb Boggs (R)
John J. Williams (R)

Representatives

Harris B. McDowell, Jr. (D)

Florida

Senators

Spessard L. Holland (D)
George A. Smathers (D)

Representatives

Charles E. Bennett (D)
William C. Cramer (R)
Dante B. Fascell (D)
Don Fuqua (D)
Sam M. Gibbons (D)
Edward J. Gurney (R)
James A. Haley (D)
Albert S. Herlong, Jr. (D)
Donald R. Matthews (D)
Claude D. Pepper (D)
Paul G. Rogers (D)
Robert L. F. Sikes (D)

Georgia

Senators

Richard B. Russell (D)
Herman E. Talmadge (D)

Representatives

Howard H. Callaway (R)
John W. Davis (D)
John J. Flynt, Jr. (D)
G. Elliott Hagan (D)
Phillip M. Landrum (D)
James A. Mackay (D)
Maston O'Neal, Jr. (D)
Robert G. Stephens, Jr. (R)
J. Russell Tuten (D)
Charles L. Weitner (D)

Hawaii

Senators

Hiram L. Fong (R)
Daniel K. Inouye (D)

Representatives

Spark M. Matsunaga (D)
Patsy T. Mink (D)

Idaho

Senators

Frank Church (D)
Len B. Jordan (R)

Representatives

George V. Hansen (R)
Compton I. White, Jr. (D)

Illinois

Senators

Everett M. Dirksen (R)
Paul H. Douglas (D)

Representatives

John B. Anderson (R)

Frank Annunzio (D)
Leslie C. Arends (R)
Harold R. Collier (R)
William L. Dawson (R)
Edward J. Derwinski (R)
John N. Erlenborn (R)
Paul Findley (R)
Kenneth J. Gray (D)
John C. Kluczynski (D)
Robert McClory (R)
Robert H. Michel (R)
William T. Murphy (D)
Barratt O'Hara (D)
Melvin Price (D)
Roman C. Pucinski (R)
Charlotte T. Reid (R)
Daniel J. Ronan (D)
Dan Rostenkowski (D)
Donald Rumsfeld (R)
Gale Schisler (D)
George E. Shipley (D)
William L. Springer (R)
Sidney R. Yates (D)

Indiana

Senators

Birch Bayh (D)
Vance Hartke (D)

Representatives

E. Ross Adair (R)
John Brademas (D)
William G. Bray (R)
Winfield K. Denton (D)
Charles A. Halleck (R)
Lee H. Hamilton (D)
Ralph Harvey (R)
Andrew Jacobs, Jr. (D)
Ray J. Madden (D)
Richard L. Roudebush (R)
J. Edward Roush (D)

Iowa

Senators

Bourke B. Hickenlooper (R)
Jack R. Miller (R)

Representatives

Bert A. Bandstra (D)
John C. Culver (D)
Stanley L. Greigg (D)
Harold R. Gross (R)
John R. Hansen (D)
John R. Schmidhauser (D)
Neal Smith (D)

Kansas

Senators

Frank Carlson (R)
James B. Pearson (R)

Representatives

Robert J. Dole (R)
Robert F. Ellsworth (R)
Chester L. Mize (R)
Garner E. Shriver (R)
Joe Skubitz (R)

Kentucky

Senators

John Sherman Cooper (R)
Thruston B. Morton (R)

Representatives

Tim Lee Carter (R)
Frank L. Chelf (D)
Charles P. Farnsley (D)
William H. Natcher (D)
Carl D. Perkins (D)
Frank A. Stubblefield (D)
John C. Watts (D)

Louisiana

Senators

Allen J. Ellender (D)
Russell B. Long (D)

Representatives

T. Hale Boggs (D)
Edwin W. Edwards (D) s. 1965
F. Edward Hebert (D)
Speedy O. Long (D)
James H. Morrison (D)
Otto E. Passman (D)
T. Ashton Thompson (D) d.
    July 1965
Joe D. Waggonner, Jr. (D)
Edwin E. Willis (D)

Maine

Senators

Edmund S. Muskie (D)
Margaret Chase Smith (R)

Representatives

William D. Hathaway (D)
Stanley R. Tupper (R)

Maryland

Senators

Daniel B. Brewster (D)
Joseph D. Tydings (D)

Representatives

George H. Fallon (D)
Samuel N. Friedel (D)
Edward A. Garmatz (D)
Clarence D. Long (D)
Rogers C. B. Morton (R)
Hervey G. Machen (D)
Charles McC. Mathias, Jr. (R)
Carlton R. Sickles (D)

Massachusetts

Senators

Edward M. Kennedy (D)
Leverett Saltonstall (R)

Representatives

William H. Bates (R)
Edward P. Boland (D)
James A. Burke (D)
Silvio O. Conte (R)
Harold D. Donohue (D)
Hastings Keith (R)
John W. McCormack (D)
Torbert H. Macdonald (D)
Joseph W. Martin, Jr. (R)
F. Bradford Morse (R)
Thomas P. O'Neill, Jr. (D)
Philip J. Philbin (D)

Michigan

Senators

Robert P. Griffin (R) s. 1966
Philip A. Hart (D)
Patrick V. McNamara (D) d.
    Apr. 1966

Representatives

William S. Broomfield (R)
Elford A. Cederberg (R)
Charles E. Chamberlain (R)
Raymond F. Clevenger (D)
John Conyers, Jr. (D)
Charles C. Diggs, Jr. (R)
John D. Dingell, Jr. (D)
Billie S. Farnum (D)
Gerald R. Ford, Jr. (R)
William D. Ford (D)
Robert P. Griffin (R) r. May
    1966
Martha W. Griffiths (D)
James Harvey (R)
Edward Hutchinson (R)
John C. Mackie (D)
Lucien N. Nedzi (D)
James G. O'Hara (D)
Paul H. Todd, Jr. (D)
Weston E. Vivian (D)

Minnesota

Senators

Eugene J. McCarthy (D)
Walter F. Mondale (D)

Representatives

John A. Blatnik (D)
Donald M. Fraser (D)
Joseph E. Karth (D)
Odin Langen (R)
Clark MacGregor (R)
Ancher Nelsen (R)
Alec G. Olson (D)
Albert H. Quie (R)

Mississippi

Senators

James O. Eastland (D)
John C. Stennis (D)

Representatives

Thomas G. Abernethy (D)
William M. Colmer (D)
Prentiss Walker (R)
Jamie L. Whitten (D)

John Bell Williams (D)

Missouri

Senators

Stuart Symington (D)
Edward V. Long (D)

Representatives

Richard W. Bolling (D)
Thomas B. Curtis (R)
Durward G. Hall (R)
William R. Hull, Jr. (D)
William L. Hungate (D)
Richard H. Ichord (D)
Paul C. Jones (D)
Frank M. Karsten (D)
William J. Randall (D)
Leonor Kretzer Sullivan (D)

Montana

Senators

Mike Mansfield (D)
Lee Metcalf (D)

Representatives

James F. Battin (R)
Arnold Olsen (D)

Nebraska

Senators

Carl T. Curtis (R)
Roman L. Hurska (R)

Representatives

Clair A. Callan (D)
Glenn C. Cunningham (R)
David T. Martin (R)

Nevada

Senators

Alan Bible (D)
Howard W. Cannon (D)

Representatives

Walter S. Baring (D)

New Hampshire

Senators

Norris Cotton (R)
Thomas J. McIntyre (D)

Representatives

James C. Cleveland (R)
J. Oliva Huot (D)

New Jersey

Senators

Clifford P. Case (R)

Harrison A. Williams, Jr. (D)

Representatives

William T. Cahill (R)
Dominick V. Daniels (D)
Florence P. Dwyer (R)
Peter H. B. Frelinghuysen, Jr. (R)
Cornelius E. Gallagher (D)
Henry Helstoski (D)
James J. Howard (D)
Charles S. Joelson (D)
Paul J. Krebs (D)
Thomas C. McGrath, Jr. (D)
Joseph G. Minish (D)
Edward J. Patten (D)
Peter W. Rodino, Jr. (D)
Frank Thompson, Jr. (D)
William B. Widnall (R)

New Mexico

Senators

Clinton P. Anderson (D)
Joseph M. Montoya (D)

Representatives

Thomas G. Morris (D)
E. S. Johnny Walker (D)

New York

Senators

Jacob K. Javits (R)
Robert F. Kennedy (D)

Representatives

Joseph P. Addabbo (D)
Jonathan B. Bingham (D)
Hugh L. Carey (D)
Emanuel Celler (D)
Barber B. Conable, Jr. (R)
James J. Delaney (D)
John G. Dow (D)
Thaddeus J. Dulski (D)
Leonard Farbstein (D)
Paul A. Fino (R)
Jacob H. Gilbert (D)
Charles E. Goodell (R)
James R. Grover, Jr. (R)
Seymour Halpern (R)
James M. Hanley (D)
Frank J. Horton (R)
Edna F. Kelly (D)
Eugene J. Keogh (D)
Carleton J. King (R)
Theodore Kupferman (R) s. 1966
John V. Lindsay (R) r. Dec. 1965
Richard D. McCarthy (D)
Robert C. McEwen (R)
Abraham J. Multer (D)
John M. Murphy (D)
Leo W. O'Brien (D)
Richard L. Ottinger (D)
Otis G. Pike (D)
Alexander Pirnie (R)
Adam Clayton Powell (D)
Ogden R. Reid (R)
Joseph Y. Resnick (D)
Howard W. Robison (R)
John J. Rooney (D)
Benjamin S. Rosenthal (D)

William F. Ryan (D)
James H. Scheuer (D)
Henry P. Smith, III (R)
Samuel S. Stratton (D)
Herbert Tenzer (D)
Lester L. Wolff (D)
John W. Wydler (R)

North Carolina

Senators

Sam J. Ervin, Jr. (D)
B. Everett Jordan (D)

Representatives

Herbert C. Bonner (D) d. Nov. 1965
James T. Broyhill (R)
Harold D. Cooley (D)
Lawrence H. Fountain (D)
David N. Henderson (D)
Charles R. Jonas (R)
Walter B. Jones (D) s. 1966
Horace R. Kornegay (D)
Alton A. Lennon (D)
Ralph J. Scott (D)
Roy A. Taylor (D)
Basil L. Whitener (D)

North Dakota

Senators

Quentin N. Burdick (D)
Milton R. Young (R)

Representatives

Mark Andrews (R)
Rolland Redlin (D)

Ohio

Senators

Frank J. Lausche (D)
Stephen M. Young (D)

Representatives

John M. Ashbrook (R)
Thomas L. Ashley (D)
William H. Ayres (R)
Jackson E. Betts (R)
Frances P. Bolton (R)
Frank T. Bow (R)
Clarence J. Brown (R) d. Aug. 1965
Clarence J. Brown, Jr. (R) s. 1966
Donald D. Clancy (R)
Samuel L. Devine (R)
Michael A. Feighan (D)
John J. Gilligan (D)
William H. Harsha, Jr. (R)
Wayne L. Hays (D)
Michael J. Kirwan (D)
Delbert L. Latta (R)
Rodney M. Love (D)
William M. McCulloch (R)
William E. Minshall (R)
Walter H. Moeller (D)
Charles A. Mosher (R)
Robert T. Secrest (D)
J. William Stanton (R)
Robert E. Sweeney (D)

Charles A. Vanik (D)

Oklahoma

Senators

Fred R. Harris (D)
A. S. Mike Monroney (D)

Representatives

Carl Albert (D)
Page H. Belcher (R)
Edmond Edmondson (D)
John Jarman (D)
Jed Johnson, Jr. (D)
Thomas J. Steed (D)

Oregon

Senators

Wayne Morse (D)
Maurine B. Neuberger (D)

Representatives

Robert B. Duncan (D)
Edith Green (D)
Wendell Wyatt (R)
Albert C. Ullman (D)

Pennsylvania

Senators

Joseph S. Clark (D)
Hugh Scott (R)

Representatives

William A. Barrett (D)
James A. Byrne (D)
Frank M. Clark (D)
Robert J. Corbett (R)
N. Neiman Craley, Jr. (D)
Willard S. Curtin (R)
Paul B. Dague (R)
John H. Dent (D)
Daniel J. Flood (D)
James G. Fulton (R)
William J. Green (D)
Elmer J. Holland (D)
Albert W. Johnson (R)
John C. Kunkel (R)
Joseph M. McDade (R)
William S. Moorhead (D)
Thomas E. Morgan (D)
Robert N. C. Nix (D)
George M. Rhodes (D)
Fred B. Rooney (D)
John P. Saylor (R)
Herman T. Schneebeli (R)
Richard S. Schweiker (R)
Herman Toll (D)
Joseph P. Vigorito (D)
G. Robert Watkins (R)
J. Irving Whalley (R)

Rhode Island

Senators

John O. Pastore (D)
Claiborne Pell (D)

Representatives

John E. Fogarty (D)
Fernand J. St. Germain (D)

South Carolina

Senators

Olin D. Johnston (D) d. Apr. 1965
Donald S. Russell (D) s. 1965
J. Strom Thurmond (R)

Representatives

Robert T. Ashmore (D)
W. J. Bryan Dorn (D)
Tom S. Gettys (D)
John L. McMillan (D)
L. Mendel Rivers (D)
Albert W. Watson (R) r. 1965

South Dakota

Senators

George McGovern (D)
Karl E. Mundt (R)

Representatives

Ellis Y. Berry (R)
Benjamin Reifel (R)

Tennessee

Senators

Ross Bass (D)
Albert A. Gore (D)

Representatives

William R. Anderson (D)
William E. Brock, III (R)
John J. Duncan (R)
Robert A. Everett (D)
Joe L. Evins (D)
Richard H. Fulton (D)
George W. Grider (D)
Thomas J. Murray (D)
James H. Quillen (R)

Texas

Senators

John G. Tower (R)
Ralph W. Yarborough (D)

Representatives

Lindley G. Beckworth (D)
Jack B. Brooks (D)
Omar T. Burleson (D)
Earle Cabell (D)
Robert R. Casey (D)
Eligio de la Garza, II (D)
John V. Dowdy (D)
O. Clark Fisher (D)
Henry B. Gonzalez (D)
George H. Mahon (D)
Wright Patman (D)
J. J. Pickle (D)
William R. Poage (D)
Joe R. Pool (D)

Graham Purcell (D)
H. Ray Roberts (D)
Walter E. Rogers (D)
Olin E. Teague (D)
Albert Thomas (D) d. 1965
Lera Thomas (D) s. 1966
Clark W. Thompson (D)
Richard C. White (D)
James C. Wright, Jr. (D)
John A. Young (D)

Utah

Senators

Wallace F. Bennett (R)
Frank E. Moss (D)

Representatives

Laurence J. Burton (R)
David S. King (D)

Vermont

Senators

George D. Aiken (R)
Winston L. Prouty (R)

Representatives

Robert T. Stafford (R)

Virginia

Senators

Harry F. Byrd (D) r. Nov.
1965
Harry F. Byrd, Jr. (D)
A. Willis Robertson (D)

Representatives

Watkins M. Abbitt (D)
Joel T. Broyhill (R)
Thomas N. Downing (D)
Porter Hardy, Jr. (D)
William P. Jennings (D)
John O. Marsh, Jr. (D)
Richard H. Poff (R)
David E. Satterfield, III (D)
Howard W. Smith (D)
William M. Tuck (D)

Washington

Senators

Henry M. Jackson (D)
Warren G. Magnuson (D)

Representatives

Brock Adams (D)
Thomas S. Foley (D)
Julia Butler Hansen (D)
Floyd V. Hicks (D)
Catherine May (R)
Lloyd Meeds (D)
Thomas M. Pelly (R)

West Virginia

Senators

Robert C. Byrd (D)
Jennings Randolph (D)

Representatives

Kenneth Hechler (D)
James Kee (D)
Arch A. Moore, Jr. (R)
John M. Slack, Jr. (D)
Harley O. Staggers (D)

Wisconsin

Senators

Gaylord A. Nelson (D)
William Proxmire (D)

Representatives

John W. Byrnes (R)
Glenn R. Davis (R)
Robert W. Kastenmeier (D)
Melvin R. Laird (R)
Alvin E. O'Konski (R)
John A. Race (D)
Henry S. Reuss (D)
Lynn E. Stalbaum (D)
Vernon W. Thomson (R)
Clement J. Zablocki (D)

Wyoming

Senators

Gale W. McGee (D)
Milward L. Simpson (R)

Representatives

Teno Roncalio (D)

Ninetieth Congress

(Jan. 3, 1967, to
Jan. 3, 1969)

President of the Senate: Hubert
H. Humphrey
*President Pro Tempore of the
Senate:* Carl Hayden
*Speaker of the House of
Representatives:* John W.
McCormack

Alabama

Senators

Lister Hill (D)
John J. Sparkman (D)

Representatives

George W. Andrews (D)
Tom Bevill (D)
John H. Buchanan, Jr. (R)
William L. Dickinson (R)
Jack Edwards (R)
Robert E. Jones, Jr. (D)
William Nichols (D)

Armistead I. Selden, Jr. (D)

Alaska

Senators

Edward L. Bartlett (D) d. Dec.
1968
Ernest Gruening (D)

Representatives

Howard W. Pollock (R)

Arizona

Senators

Carl Hayden (D)
Paul J. Fannin (R)

Representatives

John J. Rhodes (R)
Sam Steiger (R)
Morris K. Udall (D)

Arkansas

Senators

J. William Fulbright (D)
John L. McClellan (D)

Representatives

Ezekiel C. Gathings (D)
John P. Hammerschmidt (R)
Wilbur D. Mills (D)
David H. Pryor (D)

California

Senators

Thomas H. Kuchel (R)
George Murphy (R)

Representatives

Alphonzo Bell (R)
George E. Brown, Jr. (D)
Phillip Burton (D)
Don H. Clausen (R)
Del Clawson (R)
Jeffery Cohelan (D)
James C. Corman (D)
Don Edwards (D)
Charles S. Gubser (R)
Richard T. Hanna (D)
Augustus F. Hawkins (D)
Chet Holifield (D)
Craig Hosmer (R)
Harold T. Johnson (D)
Cecil R. King (D)
Robert L. Leggett (D)
Glenard P. Lipscomb (R)
Paul N. McCloskey, Jr. (R)
John J. McFall (D)
William S. Mailliard (R)
Robert B. Mathias (R)
George P. Miller (D)
John E. Moss, Jr. (D)
Jerry L. Pettis (R)
Thomas M. Rees (D)
Ed Reinecke (R)
Edward R. Roybal (D)

Bernice F. Sisk (D)
H. Allen Smith (R)
Burt L. Talcott (R)
Charles M. Teague (R)
John V. Tunney (D)
James B. Utt (R)
Lionel Van Deerlin (D)
Jerome R. Waldie (D)
Charles E. Wiggins (R)
Charles H. Wilson (D)
Robert C. Wilson (R)
J. Arthur Younger (R) d. June
1967

Colorado

Senators

Gordon L. Allott (R)
Peter H. Dominick (R)

Representatives

Wayne N. Aspinall (D)
Donald G. Brotzman (R)
Frank E. Evans (D)
Byron G. Rogers (D)

Connecticut

Senators

Thomas J. Dodd (D)
Abraham A. Ribicoff (D)

Representatives

Emilio Q. Daddario (D)
Robert N. Giaimo (D)
Donald J. Irwin (D)
Thomas J. Meskill (R)
John S. Monagan (D)
William L. St. Onge (D)

Delaware

Senators

J. Caleb Boggs (R)
John J. Williams (R)

Representatives

William V. Roth, Jr. (R)

Florida

Senators

Spessard L. Holland (D)
George A. Smathers (D)

Representatives

Charles E. Bennett (D)
J. Herbert Burke (R)
William C. Cramer (R)
Dante B. Fascell (D)
Don Fuqua (D)
Sam M. Gibbons (D)
Edward J. Gurney (R)
James A. Haley (D)
Albert S. Herlong, Jr. (D)
Claude D. Pepper (D)
Paul G. Rogers (D)
Robert L. F. Sikes (D)

Georgia

Senators

Richard B. Russell (D)
Herman E. Talmadge (D)

Representatives

Benjamin B. Blackburn (R)
Jack T. Brinkley (D)
John W. Davis (D)
John J. Flynt, Jr. (D)
G. Elliott Hagan (D)
Phillip M. Landrum (D)
Maston O'Neal (D)
Robert G. Stephens, Jr. (D)
Williamson S. Stuckey, Jr. (D)
Fletcher Thompson (R)

Hawaii

Senators

Hiram L. Fong (R)
Daniel K. Inouye (D)

Representatives

Spark M. Matsunaga (D)
Patsy T. Mink (D)

Idaho

Senators

Frank Church (D)
Len B. Jordan (R)

Representatives

George V. F. Hansen (R)
James A. McClure (R)

Illinois

Senators

Everett M. Dirksen (R)
Charles H. Percy (R)

Representatives

John B. Anderson (R)
Frank Annunzio (D)
Leslie C. Arends (R)
Harold R. Collier (R)
William L. Dawson (D)
Edward J. Derwinski (R)
John N. Erlenborn (R)
Paul Findley (R)
Kenneth J. Gray (D)
John C. Kluczynski (D)
Robert McClory (R)
Robert H. Michel (R)
William T. Murphy (D)
Barratt O'Hara (D)
Melvin Price (D)
Roman C. Pucinski (D)
Thomas F. Railsback (R)
Charlotte T. Reid (R)
Daniel J. Ronan (D)
Dan Rostenkowski (D)
Donald Rumsfeld (R)
George E. Shipley (D)
William L. Springer (R)
Sidney R. Yates (D)

Indiana

Senators

Birch Bayh (D)
Vance Hartke (D)

Representatives

E. Ross Adair (R)
John Brademas (D)
William G. Bray (R)
Charles A. Halleck (R)
Lee H. Hamilton (D)
Andrew Jacobs, Jr. (D)
Ray J. Madden (D)
John T. Myers (R)
Richard L. Roudebush (R)
J. Edward Roush (D)
Roger H. Zion (R)

Iowa

Senators

Bourke B. Hickenlooper (R)
Jack R. Miller (R)

Representatives

John C. Culver (D)
Harold R. Gross (R)
John H. Kyl (R)
Wiley Mayne (R)
William J. Scherle (R)
Fred Schwengel (R)
Neal Smith (D)

Kansas

Senators

Frank Carlson (R)
James B. Pearson (R)

Representatives

Robert J. Dole (R)
Chester L. Mize (R)
Garner E. Shriver (R)
Joe Skubitz (R)
Larry Winn, Jr. (R)

Kentucky

Senators

John Sherman Cooper (R)
Thruston B. Morton (R)

Representatives

Tim Lee Carter (R)
William O. Cowger (R)
William H. Natcher (D)
Carl D. Perkins (D)
M. G. (Gene) Snyder (R)
Frank A. Stubblefield (D)
John C. Watts (D)

Louisiana

Senators

Allen J. Ellender (D)
Russell B. Long (D)

Representatives

T. Hale Boggs (D)
Edwin W. Edwards (D)
F. Edward Hebert (D)
Speedy O. Long (D)
Otto E. Passman (D)
John R. Rarick (D)
Joe D. Waggonner, Jr. (D)
Edwin E. Willis (D)

Maine

Senators

Edmund S. Muskie (D)
Margaret Chase Smith (R)

Representatives

William D. Hathaway (D)
Peter N. Kyros (D)

Maryland

Senators

Daniel B. Brewster (D)
Joseph D. Tydings (D)

Representatives

George H. Fallon (D)
Samuel N. Friedel (D)
Edward A. Garmatz (D)
Gilbert Gude (R)
Clarence D. Long (D)
Hervey G. Machen (D)
Charles McC. Mathias, Jr. (R)
Rogers C. B. Morton (R)

Massachusetts

Senators

Edward W. Brooke (R)
Edward M. Kennedy (D)

Representatives

William H. Bates (R)
Edward P. Boland (D)
James A. Burke (D)
Silvio O. Conte (R)
Harold D. Donohue (D)
Margaret M. Heckler (R)
Hastings Keith (R)
John W. McCormack (D)
Torbert H. Macdonald (D)
F. Bradford Morse (R)
Thomas P. O'Neill, Jr. (D)
Philip J. Philbin (D)

Michigan

Senators

Robert P. Griffin (R)
Philip A. Hart (D)

Representatives

William S. Broomfield (R)
Garry E. Brown (R)
Elford A. Cederberg (R)
Charles E. Chamberlain (R)
John Conyers, Jr. (D)
Charles C. Diggs, Jr. (D)
John D. Dingell, Jr. (D)
Marvin L. Esch (R)
Gerald R. Ford, Jr. (R)
William D. Ford (D)
Martha W. Griffiths (D)
James Harvey (R)
Edward Hutchinson (R)
Jack H. McDonald (R)
Lucien N. Nedzi (D)
James G. O'Hara (D)
Donald W. Riegle, Jr. (R)
Philip E. Ruppe (R)
Guy Vander Jagt (R)

Minnesota

Senators

Eugene J. McCarthy (D)
Walter F. Mondale (D)

Representatives

John A. Blatnik (D)
Donald M. Fraser (D)
Joseph E. Karth (D)
Odin Langen (R)
Clark MacGregor (R)
Ancher Nelsen (R)
Albert H. Quie (R)
John M. Zwach (R)

Mississippi

Senators

James O. Eastland (D)
John C. Stennis (D)

Representatives

Thomas G. Abernethy (D)
William M. Colmer (D)
Charles H. Griffin (D) s. 1968
Gillespie V. Montgomery (D)
Jamie L. Whitten (D)
John Bell Williams (D) r. Jan.
  1968

Missouri

Senators

Edward V. Long (D)
Stuart Symington (D)

Representatives

Richard W. Bolling (D)
Thomas B. Curtis (R)
Durward G. Hall (R)
William R. Hull, Jr. (D)
William L. Hungate (D)
Richard H. Ichord (D)
Paul C. Jones (D)
Frank M. Karsten (D)
William J. Randall (D)
Leonor Kretzer Sullivan (D)

Montana

Senators

Mike Mansfield (D)
Lee Metcalf (D)

Representatives

James F. Battin (R)
Arnold Olsen (D)

Nebraska

Senators

Carl T. Curtis (R)
Roman L. Hruska (R)

Representatives

Glenn C. Cunningham (R)
Robert V. Denney (R)
David T. Martin (R)

Nevada

Senators

Alan Bible (D)
Howard W. Cannon (D)

Representatives

Walter S. Baring (D)

New Hampshire

Senators

Norris Cotton (R)
Thomas J. McIntyre (D)

Representatives

James C. Cleveland (R)
Louis C. Wyman (R)

New Jersey

Senators

Clifford P. Case (R)
Harrison A. Williams, Jr. (D)

Representatives

William T. Cahill (R)
Dominick V. Daniels (D)
Florence P. Dwyer (R)
Peter H. B. Frelinghuysen, Jr. (R)
Cornelius E. Gallagher (D)
Henry Helstoski (D)
James J. Howard (D)
John E. Hunt (R)
Charles S. Joelson (D)
Joseph G. Minish (D)
Edward J. Patten (D)
Peter W. Rodino, Jr. (D)
Charles W. Sandman, Jr. (R)
Frank Thompson, Jr. (D)
William B. Widnall (R)

New Mexico

Senators

Clinton P. Anderson (D)
Joseph M. Montoya (D)

Representatives

Thomas G. Morris (D)
E. S. Johnny Walker (D)

New York

Senators

Charles E. Goodell (R) s. 1968
Jacob K. Javits (R)
Robert F. Kennedy (D) d. June 1968

Representatives

Joseph P. Addabbo (D)
Jonathan B. Bingham (D)
Frank J. Brasco (D)
Daniel E. Button (R)
Hugh L. Carey (D)
Emanuel Celler (D)
Barber B. Conable, Jr. (R)
James J. Delaney (D)
John G. Dow (D)
Thaddeus J. Dulski (D)
Leonard Farbstein (D)
Paul A. Fino (R)
Jacob H. Gilbert (D)
Charles E. Goodell (R)
James R. Grover, Jr. (R)
Seymour Halpern (R)
James M. Hanley (D)
Frank J. Horton (R)
Edna F. Kelly (D)
Carleton J. King (R)
Theodore R. Kupferman (R)
Richard D. McCarthy (D)
Robert C. McEwen (R)
Abraham J. Multer (D) r. Dec. 1967
John M. Murphy (D)
Richard L. Ottinger (D)
Otis G. Pike (D)
Alexander Pirnie (R)
Bertram L. Podell (D) s. 1968
Adam Clayton Powell (D)
Ogden R. Reid (R)
Joseph Y. Resnick (D)
Howard W. Robison (R)
John J. Rooney (D)
Benjamin S. Rosenthal (D)
William F. Ryan (D)
James H. Scheuer (D)
Henry P. Smith, III (R)
Samuel S. Stratton (D)
Herbert Tenzer (D)
Lester L. Wolff (D)
John W. Wydler (R)

North Carolina

Senators

Sam J. Ervin, Jr. (D)
B. Everett Jordan (D)

Representatives

James T. Broyhill (R)
Lawrence H. Fountain (D)
Nick Galifianakis (D)
James C. Gardner (R)
David N. Henderson (D)
Charles R. Jonas (R)
Walter B. Jones (D)
Horace R. Kornegay (D)
Alton A. Lennon (D)
Roy A. Taylor (D)

Basil L. Whitener (D)

North Dakota

Senators

Quentin N. Burdick (D)
Milton R. Young (R)

Representatives

Mark Andrews (R)
Thomas S. Kleppe (R)

Ohio

Senators

Frank J. Lausche (D)
Stephen M. Young (D)

Representatives

John M. Ashbrook (R)
Thomas L. Ashley (D)
William H. Ayres (R)
Jackson E. Betts (R)
Frances P. Bolton (R)
Frank T. Bow (R)
Clarence J. Brown, Jr. (R)
Donald D. Clancy (R)
Samuel L. Devine (R)
Michael A. Feighan (D)
William H. Harsha, Jr. (R)
Wayne L. Hays (D)
Michael J. Kirwan (D)
Delbert L. Latta (R)
Donald E. Lukens (R)
William M. McCulloch (R)
Clarence E. Miller (R)
William E. Minshall (R)
Charles A. Mosher (R)
J. William Stanton (R)
Robert Taft, Jr. (R)
Charles A. Vanik (D)
Charles W. Whalen, Jr. (R)
Chalmers P. Wylie (R)

Oklahoma

Senators

Fred R. Harris (D)
A. S. Mike Monroney (D)

Representatives

Carl Albert (D)
Page H. Belcher (R)
Edmond Edmondson (D)
John Jarman (D)
James V. Smith (R)
Thomas J. Steed (D)

Oregon

Senators

Mark O. Hatfield (R)
Wayne Morse (D)

Representatives

John R. Dellenback (R)
Edith Green (D)
Albert C. Ullman (D)
Wendell Wyatt (R)

Pennsylvania

Senators

Joseph S. Clark (D)
Hugh Scott (R)

Representatives

William A. Barrett (D)
Edward G. Biester, Jr. (R)
James A. Byrne (D)
Frank M. Clark (D)
Robert J. Corbett (R)
John H. Dent (D)
Joshua Eilberg (D)
Edwin D. Eshleman (R)
Daniel J. Flood (D)
James G. Fulton (R)
George A. Goodling (R)
William J. Green (D)
Elmer J. Holland (D) d. Aug. 1968
Albert W. Johnson (R)
Joseph M. McDade (R)
William S. Moorhead (D)
Thomas E. Morgan (D)
Robert N. C. Nix (R)
George M. Rhodes (D)
Fred B. Rooney (D)
John P. Saylor (R)
Herman T. Schneebeli (R)
Richard S. Schweiker (R)
Joseph P. Vigorito (D)
G. Robert Watkins (R)
J. Irving Whalley (R)
Lawrence G. Williams (R)

Rhode Island

Senators

John O. Pastore (D)
Claiborne Pell (D)

Representatives

Fernand J. St. Germain (D)
Robert O. Tiernan (D)

South Carolina

Senators

Ernest F. Hollings (D)
J. Strom Thurmond (R)

Representatives

Robert T. Ashmore (D)
W. J. Bryan Dorn (D)
Tom S. Gettys (D)
John L. McMillan (D)
L. Mendel Rivers (D)
Albert W. Watson (R)

South Dakota

Senators

George S. McGovern (D)
Karl E. Mundt (R)

Representatives

Ellis Y. Berry (R)
Benjamin Reifel (R)

Tennessee

Senators

Howard H. Baker, Jr. (R)
Albert Gore (D)

Representatives

William R. Anderson (D)
L. Ray Blanton (D)
William E. Brock, III (R)
John J. Duncan (R)
Robert A. Everett (D)
Joe L. Evins (D)
Richard H. Fulton (D)
Dan H. Kuykendall (R)
James H. Quillen (R)

Texas

Senators

John G. Tower (R)
Ralph W. Yarborough (D)

Representatives

Jack B. Brooks (D)
Omar T. Burleson (D)
George Bush (D)
Earle Cabell (D)
Robert R. Casey (D)
James M. Collins (D) s. 1968
Eligio de la Garza, II (D)
John V. Dowdy (D)
Robert C. Eckhardt (D)
O. Clark Fisher (D)
Henry B. Gonzalez (D)
Abraham Kazen, Jr. (D)
George H. Mahon (D)
Wright Patman (D)
J. J. Pickle (D)
William R. Poage (D)
Joe R. Pool (D) d. July 1968
Robert D. Price (R)
Graham Purcell (D)
H. Ray Roberts (D)
Olin E. Teague (D)
Richard C. White (D)
James C. Wright, Jr. (D)
John A. Young (D)

Utah

Senators

Wallace F. Bennett (R)
Frank E. Moss (D)

Representatives

Laurence J. Burton (R)
Sherman P. Lloyd (R)

Vermont

Senators

George D. Aiken (R)
Winston L. Prouty (R)

Representatives

Robert T. Stafford (R)

Virginia

Senators

Harry F. Byrd, Jr. (D)
William B. Spong, Jr. (D)

Representatives

Watkins M. Abbitt (D)
Joel T. Broyhill (R)
Thomas N. Downing (D)
Porter Hardy, Jr. (D)
John O. Marsh, Jr. (D)
Richard H. Poff (R)
David E. Satterfield, III (D)
William L. Scott (R)
William M. Tuck (D)
William C. Wampler (R)

Washington

Senators

Henry M. Jackson (D)
Warren G. Magnuson (D)

Representatives

Brock Adams (D)
Thomas S. Foley (D)
Julia Butler Hansen (D)
Floyd V. Hicks (D)
Catherine May (R)
Lloyd Meeds (D)
Thomas M. Pelly (R)

West Virginia

Senators

Robert C. Byrd (D)
Jennings Randolph (D)

Representatives

Kenneth Hechler (D)
James Kee (D)
Arch A. Moore, Jr. (R)
John M. Slack, Jr. (D)
Harley O. Staggers (D)

Wisconsin

Senators

Gaylord A. Nelson (D)
William Proxmire (D)

Representatives

John W. Byrnes (R)
Glenn R. Davis (R)
Robert W. Kastenmeier (R)
Melvin R. Laird (R)
Alvin E. O'Konski (R)
Henry S. Reuss (D)
Henry C. Schadeberg (R)
William A. Steiger (R)
Vernon W. Thomson (R)
Clement J. Zablocki (D)

Wyoming

Senators

Gale W. McGee (D)
Clifford P. Hansen (R)

Representatives

William H. Harrison

Ninety-First Congress

(Jan. 3, 1969, to
Jan. 3, 1971)

President of the Senate: Spiro T.
Agnew
*President Pro Tempore of the
Senate:* Richard B. Russell
*Speaker of the House of
Representatives:* John W.
McCormack

Alabama

Senators

James B. Allen (D)
John J. Sparkman (D)

Representatives

George W. Andrews (D)
Tom Bevill (D)
John H. Buchanan, Jr. (R)
William L. Dickinson (R)
Jack Edwards (R)
Walter Flowers (D)
Robert E. Jones, Jr. (D)
William Nichols (D)

Alaska

Senators

Mike Gravel (D)
Ted Stevens (R)

Representatives

Howard W. Pollock (R)

Arizona

Senators

Paul J. Fannin (R)
Barry M. Goldwater (R)

Representatives

John J. Rhodes (R)
Sam Steiger (R)
Morris K. Udall (D)

Arkansas

Senators

J. William Fulbright (D)
John L. McClellan (D)

Representatives

Bill Alexander (D)
John P. Hammerschmidt (R)
Wilbur D. Mills (D)
David H. Pryor (D)

California

Senators

Alan Cranston (D)
George Murphy (R)

Representatives

Glenn M. Anderson (D)
Alphonzo Bell (R)
George E. Brown, Jr. (D)
Phillip Burton (D)
Don H. Clausen (R)
Del Clawson (R)
Jeffery Cohelan (D)
James C. Corman (D)
Don Edwards (D)
Barry Goldwater, Jr. (R)
Charles S. Gubser (R)
Richard T. Hanna (D)
Augustus F. Hawkins (D)
Chet Holifield (D)
Craig Hosmer (R)
Harold T. Johnson (D)
Robert L. Leggett (D)
Glenard P. Lipscomb (R) d.
Feb. 1970
Paul N. McCloskey, Jr. (R)
John J. McFall (D)
William S. Mailliard (R)
Robert B. Mathias (R)
George P. Miller (D)
John E. Moss, Jr. (D)
Jerry L. Pettis (R)
Thomas M. Rees (D)
John H. Rousselot (R) s. 1970
Edward R. Roybal (D)
John G. Schmitz (R) s. 1970
Bernice F. Sisk (D)
H. Allen Smith (R)
Burt L. Talcott (R)
Charles M. Teague (R)
John V. Tunney (D)
James B. Utt (R) d. Mar. 1970
Lionel Van Deerlin (D)
Jerome R. Waldie (D)
Charles E. Wiggins (R)
Charles H. Wilson (D)
Robert C. Wilson (R)

Colorado

Senators

Gordon L. Allott (R)
Peter H. Dominick (R)

Representatives

Wayne N. Aspinall (D)
Donald G. Brotzman (R)
Frank E. Evans (D)
Byron G. Rogers (D)

Connecticut

Senators

Thomas J. Dodd (D)
Abraham A. Ribicoff (D)

Representatives

Emilio Q. Daddario (D)
Robert N. Giaimo (D)
Thomas J. Meskill (R)
John S. Monagan (D)
William L. St. Onge (D) d.
 May 1970
Robert H. Steele (R) s. 1970
Lowell P. Weicker, Jr. (R)

Delaware

Senators

J. Caleb Boggs (R)
John J. Williams (R)

Representatives

William V. Roth, Jr. (R)

Florida

Senators

Edward J. Gurney (R)
Spessard L. Holland (D)

Representatives

Charles E. Bennett (D)
J. Herbert Burke (R)
Bill Chappell, Jr. (D)
William C. Cramer (R)
Dante B. Fascell (D)
Louis Frey, Jr. (R)
Don Fuqua (D)
Sam M. Gibbons (D)
James A. Haley (D)
Claude D. Pepper (D)
Paul G. Rogers (D)
Robert L. F. Sikes (D)

Georgia

Senators

Richard B. Russell (D)
Herman E. Talmadge (D)

Representatives

Benjamin B. Blackburn (R)
Jack Brinkley (D)
John W. Davis (D)
John J. Flynt, Jr. (D)
G. Elliott Hagan (D)
Phillip M. Landrum (D)
Maston O'Neal (D)
Robert G. Stephens, Jr. (D)
William S. Stuckey, Jr. (D)
Fletcher Thompson (R)

Hawaii

Senators

Hiram L. Fong (R)
Daniel K. Inouye (D)

Representatives

Spark M. Matsunaga (D)
Patsy T. Mink (D)

Idaho

Senators

Frank Church (D)
Len B. Jordan (R)

Representatives

Orval Hansen (R)
James A. McClure (R)

Illinois

Senators

Everett M. Dirksen (R) d. Sept.
 1969
Charles H. Percy (R)
Ralph T. Smith (R) ta. 1969
Adlai E. Stevenson, III (D) s.
 1970

Representatives

John B. Anderson (R)
Frank Annunzio (D)
Leslie C. Arends (R)
Harold R. Collier (R)
George W. Collins (D) s. 1970
Philip M. Crane (R)
William L. Dawson (D) d. Sept.
 1970
Edward J. Derwinski (R)
John N. Erlenborn (R)
Paul Findley (R)
Kenneth J. Gray (D)
John C. Kluczynski (D)
Robert McClory (R)
Robert H. Michel (R)
Abner J. Mikva (D)
William T. Murphy (D)
Melvin Price (D)
Roman C. Pucinski (D)
Thomas F. Railsback (R)
Charlotte T. Reid (R)
Daniel J. Ronan (D) d. Aug.
 1969
Dan Rostenkowski (D)
Donald Rumsfeld (R) r. May
 1969
George E. Shipley (D)
William L. Springer (R)
Sidney R. Yates (D)

Indiana

Senators

Birch Bayh (D)
Vance Hartke (D)

Representatives

E. Ross Adair (R)
John Brademas (D)
William G. Bray (R)
David W. Dennis (R)
Lee H. Hamilton (D)
Andrew Jacobs, Jr. (D)
Earl F. Landgrebe (R)
Ray J. Madden (D)
John T. Myers (R)
Richard L. Roudebush (R)
Roger H. Zion (R)

Iowa

Senators

Harold E. Hughes (D)
Jack R. Miller (R)

Representatives

John C. Culver (D)
Harold R. Gross (R)
John H. Kyl (R)
Wiley Mayne (R)
William J. Scherle (R)
Fred Schwengel (R)
Neal Smith (D)

Kansas

Senators

Robert J. Dole (R)
James B. Pearson (R)

Representatives

Chester L. Mize (R)
Keith G. Sebelius (R)
Garner E. Shriver (R)
Joe Skubitz (R)
Larry Winn, Jr. (R)

Kentucky

Senators

Marlow W. Cook (R)
John Sherman Cooper (R)

Representatives

Tim Lee Carter (R)
William O. Cowger (R)
William H. Natcher (D)
Carl D. Perkins (D)
M. G. (Gene) Snyder (R)
Frank A. Stubblefield (D)
John C. Watts (D)

Louisiana

Senators

Allen J. Ellender (D)
Russell B. Long (D)

Representatives

T. Hale Boggs (D)
Patrick T. Caffery (D)
Edwin W. Edwards (D)
F. Edward Hebert (D)
Speedy O. Long (D)
Otto E. Passman (D)
John R. Rarick (D)
Joe D. Waggoner, Jr. (D)

Maine

Senators

Edmund S. Muskie (D)
Margaret Chase Smith (R)

Representatives

William D. Hathaway (D)
Peter N. Kyros (D)

Maryland

Senators

Charles McC. Mathias, Jr. (D)
Joseph D. Tydings (D)

Representatives

J. Glenn Beall, Jr. (R)
George H. Fallon (D)
Samuel N. Friedel (D)
Edward A. Garmatz (R)
Gilbert Gude (R)
Lawrence J. Hogan (R)
Clarence D. Long (D)
Rogers C. B. Morton (R)

Massachusetts

Senators

Edward W. Brooke (R)
Edward M. Kennedy (D)

Representatives

William H. Bates (R) d. June
 1969
Edward P. Boland (D)
James A. Burke (D)
Silvio O. Conte (R)
Harold D. Donohue (D)
Michael J. Harrington (D) s.
 1969
Margaret M. Heckler (R)
Hastings Keith (R)
John W. McCormack (D)
Torbert H. Macdonald (D)
F. Bradford Morse (R)
Thomas P. O'Neill, Jr. (D)
Philip J. Philbin (D)

Michigan

Senators

Robert P. Griffin (R)
Philip A. Hart (D)

Representatives

William S. Broomfield (R)
Garry E. Brown (R)
Elford A. Cederberg (R)
Charles E. Chamberlain (R)
John Conyers, Jr. (D)
Charles C. Diggs, Jr. (D)
John D. Dingell, Jr. (D)
Marvin L Esch (R)
Gerald R. Ford, Jr. (R)
William D. Ford (D)
Martha W. Griffiths (D)
James Harvey (R)
Edward Hutchinson (R)
Jack H. McDonald (R)
Lucien N. Nedzi (D)
James G. O'Hara (D)
Donald W. Riegle, Jr. (R)
Philip E. Ruppe (R)
Guy Vander Jagt (R)

Minnesota

Senators

Eugene J. McCarthy (D)
Walter F. Mondale (D)

Representatives

John A. Blatnik (D)
Donald M. Fraser (D)
Joseph E. Karth (D)
Odin Langen (R)
Clark MacGregor (R)
Ancher Nelsen (R)
Albert H. Quie (R)
John M. Zwach (R)

Mississippi

Senators

James O. Eastland (D)
John C. Stennis (D)

Representatives

Thomas G. Abernethy (D)
William M. Colmer (D)
Charles H. Griffin (D)
Gillespie V. Montgomery (D)
Jamie L. Whitten (D)

Missouri

Senators

Thomas F. Eagleton (D)
Stuart Symington (D)

Representatives

Richard W. Bolling (D)
Bill D. Burlison (D)
William L. Clay (D)
Durward G. Hall (R)
William R. Hull, Jr. (D)
William L. Hungate (D)
Richard H. Ichord (D)
William J. Randall (D)
Leonor Kretzer Sullivan (D)
James W. Symington (D)

Montana

Senators

Mike Mansfield (D)
Lee Metcalf (D)

Representatives

James F. Battin (R) r. Feb. 1969
John Melcher (D)
Arnold Olsen (D)

Nebraska

Senators

Carl T. Curtis (R)
Roman L. Hruska (R)

Representatives

Glenn C. Cunningham (R)
Robert V. Denney (R)
David T. Martin (R)

Nevada

Senators

Alan Bible (D)
Howard W. Cannon (D)

Representatives

Walter S. Baring (D)

New Hampshire

Senators

Norris Cotton (R)
Thomas J. McIntyre (D)

Representatives

James C. Cleveland (R)
Louis C. Wyman (R)

New Jersey

Senators

Clifford P. Case (R)
Harrison A. Williams, Jr. (D)

Representatives

William T. Cahill (R) r. Jan. 1970
Dominick V. Daniels (D)
Florence P. Dwyer (R)
Edwin B. Forsythe (R) s. 1970
Peter H. B. Frelinghuysen, Jr. (R)
Cornelius E. Gallagher (D)
Henry Helstoski (D)
James J. Howard (D)
John E. Hunt (R)
Charles S. Joelson (D) r. Sept. 1969
Joseph G. Minish (D)
Edward J. Patten (D)
Peter W. Rodino, Jr. (D)
Robert A. Roe (D)
Charles W. Sandman, Jr. (D)
William B. Widnall (R)

New Mexico

Senators

Clinton P. Anderson (D)
Joseph M. Montoya (D)

Representatives

Edgar F. Foreman (R)
Manuel Lujan, Jr. (R)

New York

Senators

Charles E. Goodell (R)
Jacob K. Javits (R)

Representatives

Joseph P. Addabbo (D)
Mario Biaggi (D)
Jonathan B. Bingham (D)
Frank J. Brasco (D)
Daniel E. Button (R)
Hugh L. Carey (D)
Emanuel Celler (D)
Shirley Chisholm (D)
Barber B. Conable, Jr. (R)
James J. Delaney (D)
Thaddeus J. Dulski (D)
Leonard Farbstein (D)
Hamilton Fish, Jr. (R)
Jacob H. Gilbert (D)
James R. Grover, Jr. (R)
Seymour Halpern (R)
James M. Hanley (D)
James F. Hastings (R)
Frank J. Horton (R)
Carleton J. King (R)
Edward I. Koch (D)
Allard K. Lowenstein (D)
Richard D. McCarthy (D)
Robert C. McEwen (R)
Martin B. McKneally (R)
John M. Murphy (D)
Richard L. Ottinger (D)
Otis G. Pike (D)
Alexander Pirnie (R)
Bertram L. Podell (D)
Adam Clayton Powell (D)
Ogden R. Reid (R)
Howard W. Robison (R)
John J. Rooney (D)
Benjamin S. Rosenthal (D)
William F. Ryan (D)
James H. Scheuer (D)
Henry P. Smith, III (R)
Samuel S. Stratton (D)
Lester L. Wolff (D)
John W. Wydler (R)

North Carolina

Senators

Sam J. Ervin, Jr. (D)
B. Everett Jordan (D)

Representatives

James T. Broyhill (R)
Lawrence H. Fountain (D)
Nick Galifianakis (D)
David N. Henderson (D)
Charles R. Jonas (R)
Walter B. Jones (D)
Alton A. Lennon (D)
Wilmer D. Mizell (R)
Richardson Preyer (D)
Earl B. Ruth (R)
Roy A. Taylor (D)

North Dakota

Senators

Quentin N. Burdick (D)
Milton R. Young (R)

Representatives

Mark Andrews (R)
Thomas S. Kleppe (R)

Ohio

Senators

William B. Saxbe (R)
Stephen M. Young (D)

Representatives

John M. Ashbrook (R)
Thomas L. Ashley (D)
William H. Ayres (R)
Jackson E. Betts (R)
Frank T. Bow (R)
Clarence J. Brown, Jr. (R)
Charles J. Carney (D) s. 1970
Donald D. Clancy (R)
Samuel L. Devine (R)
Michael A. Feighan (R)
William H. Harsha, Jr. (R)
Wayne L. Hays (D)
Michael J. Kirwan (D) d. July 1970
Delbert L. Latta (R)
Donald E. Lukens (R)
William M. McCulloch (R)
Clarence E. Miller (R)
William E. Minshall (R)
Charles A. Mosher (R)
J. William Stanton (R)
Louis Stokes (D)
Robert Taft, Jr. (R)
Charles A. Vanik (D)
Charles W. Whalen, Jr. (R)
Chalmers P. Wylie (R)

Oklahoma

Senators

Henry L. Bellmon (R)
Fred R. Harris (D)

Representatives

Carl Albert (D)
Page H. Belcher (R)
John N. Camp (R)
Edmond Edmondson (D)
John Jarman (D)
Thomas J. Steed (D)

Oregon

Senators

Mark O. Hatfield (R)
Robert W. Packwood (R)

Representatives

John R. Dellenback (R)
Edith Green (D)
Albert C. Ullman (D)
Wendell Wyatt (R)

Pennsylvania

Senators

Richard S. Schweiker (R)
Hugh Scott (R)

Representatives

William A. Barrett (D)
Edward G. Biester, Jr. (R)

James A. Byrne (D)
Frank M. Clark (D)
Robert J. Corbett (R)
R. Lawrence Coughlin (R)
John H. Dent (D)
Joshua Eilberg (D)
Edwin D. Eshleman (R)
Daniel J. Flood (D)
James G. Fulton (R)
Joseph M. Gaydos (D)
George A. Goodling (R)
William J. Green (D)
Albert W. Johnson (R)
Joseph M. McDade (R)
William S. Moorhead (D)
Thomas E. Morgan (D)
Robert N. C. Nix (D)
Fred B. Rooney (D)
John P. Saylor (R)
Herman T. Schneebeli (R)
Joseph P. Vigorito (D)
John H. Ware, III (R) s. 1970
G. Robert Watkins (R) d. Aug. 1970
J. Irving Whalley (R)
Lawrence G. Williams (R)
Gus Yatron (D)

Rhode Island

Senators

John O. Pastore (D)
Claiborne Pell (D)

Representatives

Fernand J. St. Germain (D)
Robert O. Tiernan (D)

South Carolina

Senators

Ernest F. Hollings (D)
J. Strom Thurmond (R)

Representatives

W. J. Bryan Dorn (D)
Tom S. Gettys (D)
John L. McMillan (D)
James R. Mann (D)
L. Mendel Rivers (D) d. Dec. 1970
Albert W. Watson (R)

South Dakota

Senators

George McGovern (D)
Karl E. Mundt (R)

Representatives

Ellis Y. Berry (R)
Benjamin Reifel (R)

Tennessee

Senators

Howard H. Baker, Jr. (R)
Albert Gore (D)

Representatives

William R. Anderson (D)
L. Ray Blanton (D)
William E. Brock, III (R)
John J. Duncan (R)
Joe L. Evins (D)
Richard H. Fulton (D)
Ed Jones (D)
Dan H. Kuykendall (R)
James H. Quillen (R)

Texas

Senators

John G. Tower (R)
Ralph W. Yarborough (D)

Representatives

Jack B. Brooks (D)
Omar T. Burleson (D)
George Bush (R)
Earle Cabell (D)
Robert R. Casey (D)
James M. Collins (R)
Eligio de la Garza, II (D)
John V. Dowdy (D)
Robert C. Eckhardt (D)
O. Clark Fisher (D)
Henry B. Gonzalez (D)
Abraham Kazen, Jr. (D)
George H. Mahon (D)
Wright Patman (D)
J. J. Pickle (D)
William R. Poage (D)
Robert D. Price (R)
Graham Purcell (D)
H. Ray Roberts (D)
Olin E. Teague (D)
Richard C. White (D)
James C. Wright, Jr. (D)
John A. Young (D)

Utah

Senators

Wallace F. Bennett (R)
Frank E. Moss (R)

Representatives

Laurence J. Burton (R)
Sherman P. Lloyd (R)

Vermont

Senators

George D. Aiken (R)
Winston L. Prouty (R)

Representatives

Robert T. Stafford (R)

Virginia

Senators

Harry F. Byrd, Jr. (D)
William B. Spong, Jr. (D)

Representatives

Watkins M. Abbitt (D)
Joel T. Broyhill (R)
W. C. (Dan) Daniel (D)
Thomas N. Downing (D)
John O. Marsh, Jr. (D)
Richard H. Poff (R)
David E. Satterfield, III (D)
William L. Scott (R)
William C. Wampler (R)
G. William Whitehurst (R)

Washington

Senators

Henry M. Jackson (D)
Warren G. Magnuson (D)

Representatives

Brock Adams (D)
Thomas S. Foley (D)
Julia Butler Hansen (D)
Floyd V. Hicks (D)
Catherine May (R)
Lloyd Meeds (D)
Thomas M. Pelly (R)

West Virginia

Senators

Robert C. Byrd (D)
Jennings Randolph (D)

Representatives

Kenneth Hechler (D)
James Kee (D)
Robert H. Mollohan (D)
John M. Slack, Jr. (D)
Harley O. Staggers (D)

Wisconsin

Senators

Gaylord Nelson (D)
William Proxmire (D)

Representatives

John W. Byrnes (R)
Glenn R. Davis (R)
Robert W. Kastenmeier (D)
David R. Obey (D)
Alvin E. O'Konski (R)
Henry S. Reuss (D)
Henry C. Schadeberg (R)
William A. Steiger (R)
Vernon W. Thomson (R)
Clement J. Zablocki (D)

Wyoming

Senators

Clifford P. Hansen (R)
Gale W. McGee (D)

Representatives

John Wold (R)

Ninety-Second Congress

(Jan. 3, 1971, to
Jan. 3, 1973)

President of the Senate: Spiro T. Agnew
President Pro Tempore of the Senate: Allen J. Ellender
Speaker of the House of Representatives: Carl Albert

Alabama

Senators

James B. Allen (D)
John J. Sparkman (D)

Representatives

Elizabeth Andrews (D) s. Apr. 1972
George Andrews (D) d. 1972
Tom Bevill (D)
John H. Buchanan, Jr. (R)
William L. Dickinson (R)
Jack Edwards (R)
Walter Flowers (D)
Robert E. Jones (D)
William Nichols (D)

Alaska

Senators

Mike Gravel (D)
Ted Stevens (R)

Representatives

Nick Begich (D)

Arizona

Senators

Paul J. Fannin (R)
Barry M. Goldwater (R)

Representatives

John J. Rhodes (R)
Sam Steiger (R)
Morris K. Udall (D)

Arkansas

Senators

J. William Fulbright (D)
John L. McClellan (D)

Representatives

Bill Alexander, Jr. (D)
John P. Hammerschmidt (R)
Wilbur D. Mills (D)
David H. Pryor (D)

California

Senators

Alan Cranston (D)
John V. Tunney (D)

Representatives

Glenn M. Anderson (D)
Alphonzo Bell (R)
Phillip Burton (D)
Don H. Clausen (R)
Del M. Clawson (R)
James C. Corman (D)
George E. Danielson (D)
Ronald V. Dellums (D)
Don Edwards (D)
Barry M. Goldwater, Jr. (R)
Charles S. Gubser (R)
Richard T. Hanna (D)
Augustus F. Hawkins (D)
Chet Holifield (D)
Craig Hosmer (R)
Harold T. Johnson (D)
Robert L. Leggett (D)
Paul N. McCloskey, Jr. (R)
John J. McFall (D)
William S. Mailliard (R)
Robert B. Mathias (R)
George P. Miller (D)
John E. Moss (D)
Jerry L. Pettis (R)
Thomas M. Rees (D)
John H. Rousselot (R)
Edward R. Roybal (D)
John G. Schmitz (R)
Bernice F. Sisk (D)
H. Allen Smith (R)
Burt L. Talcott (R)
Charles M. Teague (R)
Lionel Van Deerlin (D)
Victor V. Veysey (R)
Jerome R. Waldie (D)
Robert C. Wilson (R)
Charles H. Wilson (D)
Charles E. Wiggins (R)

Colorado

Senators

Gordon L. Allott (R)
Peter H. Dominick (R)

Representatives

Wayne N. Aspinall (D)
Donald G. Brotzman (R)
Frank E. Evans (D)
James D. McKevitt (R)

Connecticut

Senators

Abraham A. Ribicoff (D)
Lowell P. Weicker, Jr. (R)

Representatives

William R. Cotter (D)
Robert N. Giaimo (D)
Ella T. Grasso (D)
Stewart B. McKinney (R)
John S. Monagan (D)
Robert H. Steele (R)

Delaware

Senators

J. Caleb Boggs (R)
William V. Roth, Jr. (R)

Representatives

Pierre S. duPont, IV (R)

Florida

Senators

Lawton M. Chiles, Jr. (D)
Edward J. Gurney (R)

Representatives

Charles E. Bennett (D)
J. Herbert Burke (R)
William V. Chappell, Jr. (D)
Dante B. Fascell (D)
Louis Frey, Jr. (R)
Don Fuqua (D)
Sam M. Gibbons (D)
James A. Haley (D)
Claude D. Pepper (D)
Paul G. Rogers (D)
Robert L. F. Sikes (D)
C. W. Bill Young (R)

Georgia

Senators

David H. Gambrell (D)
Herman E. Talmadge (D)

Representatives

Benjamin B. Blackburn (R)
Jack T. Brinkley (D)
John W. Davis (D)
John J. Flynt, Jr. (D)
G. Elliott Hagan (D)
Phillip M. Landrum (D)
M. Dawson Mathis (D)
Robert G. Stephens, Jr. (D)
William S. Stuckey, Jr.
Fletcher Thompson (R)

Hawaii

Senators

Hiram L. Fong (R)
Daniel K. Inouye (D)

Representatives

Spark M. Matsunaga (D)
Patsy T. Mink (D)

Idaho

Senators

Frank Church (D)
Len B. Jordan (R)

Representatives

Orval Hansen (R)
James A. McClure (R)

Illinois

Senators

Charles H. Percy (R)
Adlai E. Stevenson, III (D)

Representatives

John B. Anderson (R)
Frank Annunzio (D)
Leslie C. Arends (R)
Harold R. Collier (R)
George W. Collins (D)
Philip M. Crane (R)
Edward J. Derwinski (R)
John N. Erlenborn (R)
Paul Findley (R)
Kenneth J. Gray (D)
John C. Kluczynski (D)
Robert McClory (R)
Ralph H. Metcalfe (D)
Robert H. Michel (R)
Abner J. Mikva (D)
Morgan F. Murphy (D)
C. Melvin Price (D)
Roman C. Pucinski (D)
Thomas F. Railsback (R)
Charlotte T. Reid (R) r. Oct.
 1971
Dan Rostenkowski (D)
George E. Shipley (D)
William L. Springer (R)
Sidney R. Yates

Indiana

Senators

Birch Bayh (D)
Vance Hartke (D)

Representatives

John Brademas (D)
William G. Bray (R)
David W. Dennis (R)
Lee H. Hamilton (D)
Elwood H. Hillis (R)
Andrew Jacobs, Jr. (D)
Earl F. Landgrebe (R)
Ray J. Madden (D)
John T. Myers (R)
J. Edward Roush (D)
Roger H. Zion (R)

Iowa

Senators

Harold E. Hughes (D)
Jack R. Miller (R)

Representatives

John C. Culver (D)
Harold R. Gross (R)
John H. Kyl (R)
Wiley Mayne (R)
William J. Scherle (R)
Fred Schwengel (R)
Neal Smith (D)

Kansas

Senators

Robert J. Dole (R)
James B. Pearson (R)

Representatives

William R. Roy (D)
Keith G. Sebelius (R)
Garner E. Shriver (R)
Joe Skubitz (R)
Larry Winn, Jr. (R)

Kentucky

Senators

Marlow W. Cook (R)
John Sherman Cooper (R)

Representatives

Tim Lee Carter (R)
William O. Cowger (R) d. Oct.
 1971
William P. Curlin, Jr. (D)
Romano L. Mazzoli (D)
William H. Natcher (D)
Carl D. Perkins (D)
M. Gene Snyder (R)
Frank A. Stubblefield (D)
John C. Watts (D) d. Sept.
 1971

Louisiana

Senators

Allen J. Ellender (D) d. July
 1972
Russell B. Long (D)

Representatives

T. Hale Boggs (D)
Patrick T. Caffery (D)
Edwin W. Edwards (D)
F. Edward Hebert (D)
Speedy O. Long (D)
Otto E. Passman (D)
John R. Rarick (D)
Joe D. Waggonner, Jr. (D)

Maine

Senators

Edmund S. Muskie (D)
Margaret Chase Smith (R)

Representatives

William D. Hathaway (D)
Peter N. Kyros (D)

Maryland

Senators

J. Glenn Beall, Jr. (R)
Charles McC. Mathias, Jr. (R)

Representatives

Goodloe E. Byron (D)
Edward A. Garmatz (D)
Gilbert Gude (R)
Lawrence J. Hogan (R)
Clarence D. Long (D)
William O. Mills (R)
Parren J. Mitchell (D)
Paul S. Sarbanes (D)

Massachusetts

Senators

Edward W. Brooke (R)
Edward M. Kennedy (D)

Representatives

James A. Burke (D)
Edward P. Boland (D)
Silvio O. Conte (R)
Harold D. Donohue (D)
Robert F. Drinan (D)
Michael J. Harrington (D)
Margaret M. Heckler (R)
Louise Day Hicks (D)
Hastings Keith (R)
Torbert H. Macdonald (D)
F. Bradford Morse (R)
Thomas P. O'Neill, Jr. (D)

Michigan

Senators

Robert P. Griffin (R)
Philip A. Hart (D)

Representatives

William S. Broomfield (R)
Garry E. Brown (R)
Elford A. Cederberg (R)
Charles E. Chamberlain (R)
John Conyers, Jr. (D)
Charles C. Diggs, Jr. (D)
John D. Dingell (D)
Marvin L. Esch (R)
Gerald R. Ford, Jr. (R)
William D. Ford (D)
Martha W. Griffiths (D)
James Harvey (R)
Edward Hutchinson (R)
Jack H. McDonald (R)
Lucien N. Nedzi (D)
James G. O'Hara (D)
Donald W. Riegle, Jr. (R)
Philip E. Ruppe (R)
Guy Vander Jagt (R)

Minnesota

Senators

Hubert H. Humphrey (D)
Walter F. Mondale (D)

Representatives

Bob Bergland (D)
John A. Blatnik (D)
Donald M. Fraser (D)
Bill Frenzel (R)
Joseph E. Karth (D)
Ancher Nelsen (R)
Albert H. Quie (R)

John M. Zwach (R)

Mississippi

Senators

James O. Eastland (D)
John C. Stennis (D)

Representatives

Thomas G. Abernethy (D)
William M. Colmer (D)
Charles H. Griffin (D)
Gillespie V. Montgomery (D)
Jamie L. Whitten (D)

Missouri

Senators

Thomas F. Eagleton (D)
Stuart Symington (D)

Representatives

Richard Bolling (D)
Bill D. Burlison (D)
William L. Clay (D)
Durward G. Hall (R)
W. R. Hull, Jr. (D)
William L. Hungate (D)
Richard H. Ichord (D)
William J. Randall (R)
Leonor Kretzer Sullivan (D)
James W. Symington (D)

Montana

Senators

Mike Mansfield (D)
Lee Metcalf (D)

Representatives

John Melcher (D)
Richard G. Shoup (R)

Nebraska

Senators

Carl T. Curtis (R)
Roman L. Hruska (R)

Representatives

John Y. McCollister (R)
David T. Martin (R)
Charles Thone (R)

Nevada

Senators

Alan Bible (D)
Howard W. Cannon (D)

Representatives

Walter S. Baring (D)

New Hampshire

Senators

Norris Cotton (R)
Thomas J. McIntyre (D)

Representatives

James C. Cleveland (R)
Louis C. Wyman (R)

New Jersey

Senators

Clifford P. Case (R)
Harrison A. Williams, Jr. (D)

Representatives

Dominick V. Daniels (D)
Florence P. Dwyer (R)
Edwin B. Forsythe (R)
Peter H. B. Frelinghuysen, Jr. (R)
Cornelius E. Gallagher (D)
Henry Helstoski (D)
James J. Howard (D)
John E. Hunt (R)
Joseph G. Minish (D)
Edward J. Patten (D)
Peter W. Rodino, Jr. (D)
Robert A. Roe (D)
Charles W. Sandman, Jr. (R)
Frank Thompson, Jr. (D)
William B. Widnall (R)

New Mexico

Senators

Clinton P. Anderson (D)
Joseph M. Montoya (D)

Representatives

Manuel Lujan, Jr. (R)
Harold Runnels (D)

New York

Senators

James L. Buckley (Con-R)
Jacob K. Javits (R)

Representatives

Bella S. Abzug (D)
Joseph P. Addabbo (D)
Herman Badillo (D)
Mario Biaggi (D)
Jonathan B. Bingham (D)
Frank J. Brasco (D)
Hugh L. Carey (D)
Emanuel Celler (D)
Shirley Chisholm (D)
Barber B. Conable, Jr. (R)
James J. Delaney (D)
John G. Dow (D)
Thaddeus J. Dulski (D)
Hamilton Fish, Jr. (R)
James R. Grover, Jr. (R)
Seymour Halpern (R)
James M. Hanley (D)
James F. Hastings (R)

Frank Horton (R)
Jack F. Kemp (R)
Carleton J. King (R)
Edward I. Koch (D)
Norman F. Lent (R)
Robert C. McEwen (R)
John M. Murphy (D)
Peter A. Peyser (R)
Otis G. Pike (D)
Alexander Pirnie (R)
Bertram L. Podell (D)
Charles B. Rangel (D)
Ogden R. Reid (D)
Howard W. Robison (R)
John J. Rooney (D)
Benjamin S. Rosenthal (D)
William F. Ryan (D) d. Sept. 1972
James H. Scheuer (D)
Henry P. Smith, III (R)
Samuel S. Stratton (D)
John H. Terry (R)
Lester L. Wolff (D)
John W. Wydler (R)

North Carolina

Senators

Sam J. Ervin, Jr. (D)
B. Everett Jordan (D)

Representatives

James T. Broyhill (R)
Lawrence H. Fountain (D)
Nick Galifianakis (D)
David N. Henderson (D)
Charles R. Jonas (R)
Walter B. Jones (D)
Alton A. Lennon (D)
Wilmer D. Mizell (R)
L. Richardson Preyer (D)
Earl B. Ruth (R)
Roy A. Taylor (D)

North Dakota

Senators

Quentin N. Burdick (D)
Milton R. Young (R)

Representatives

Mark Andrews (R)
Arthur A. Link (D)

Ohio

Senators

William B. Saxbe (R)
Robert Taft, Jr. (R)

Representatives

John M. Ashbrook (R)
Thomas L. Ashley (D)
Jackson E. Betts (R)
Frank T. Bow (R)
Clarence J. Brown, Jr. (R)
Charles J. Carney (D)
Donald D. Clancy (R)
Samuel L. Devine (R)
William H. Harsha, Jr. (R)
Wayne L. Hays (D)
William J. Keating (R)

Delbert L. Latta (R)
William M. McCulloch (R)
Clarence E. Miller (R)
William E. Minshall (R)
Charles A. Mosher (R)
Walter E. Powell (R)
John F. Seiberling (D)
J. William Stanton (R)
James V. Stanton (D)
Louis Stokes (D)
Charles A. Vanik (D)
Charles W. Whalen, Jr. (R)
Chalmers P. Wylie (R)

Oklahoma

Senators

Henry L. Bellmon (R)
Fred R. Harris (D)

Representatives

Carl Albert (D)
Page H. Belcher (R)
John N. Camp (R)
Edmond Edmondson (D)
John Jarman (D)
Thomas J. Steed (D)

Oregon

Senators

Mark O. Hatfield (R)
Robert Packwood (R)

Representatives

John Dellenbach (R)
Edith Green (D)
Al Ullman (D)
Wendel Wyatt (R)

Pennsylvania

Senators

Richard S. Schweiker (R)
Hugh Scott (R)

Representatives

William A. Barrett (D)
Edward G. Biester, Jr. (R)
James A. Byrne (D)
Frank M. Clark (D)
Robert J. Corbett (R) d. Apr. 1971
R. Lawrence Coughlin (R)
John H. Dent (D)
Joshua Eilberg (D)
Edwin D. Eshleman (R)
Daniel J. Flood (D)
James G. Fulton (R) d. Oct. 1971
Joseph M. Gaydos (D)
George A. Goodling (R)
William J. Green (D)
H. John Heinz, III (R)
Albert W. Johnson (R)
Joseph M. McDade (R)
William S. Moorhead (D)
Thomas E. Morgan (D)
Robert N. C. Nix (D)
Fred B. Rooney (D)
John P. Saylor (R)
Herman T. Schneebeli (R)

Joseph P. Vigorito (D)
John H. Ware, III (R)
J. Irving Whalley (R)
Lawrence G. Williams (R)
Gus Yatron (D)

Rhode Island

Senators

John O. Pastore (D)
Claiborne Pell (D)

Representatives

Fernand J. St. Germain (D)
Robert O. Tiernan (D)

South Carolina

Senators

Ernest F. Hollings (D)
J. Strom Thurmond (R)

Representatives

Mendel J. Davis (D)
W. J. Bryan Dorn (D)
Tom S. Gettys (D)
John L. McMillan (D)
James R. Mann (D)
Floyd D. Spence (R)

South Dakota

Senators

George McGovern (D)
Karl E. Mundt (R)

Representatives

James G. Abourezk (D)
Frank E. Denholm (D)

Tennessee

Senators

Howard H. Baker, Jr. (R)
William E. Brock, III (R)

Representatives

William R. Anderson (D)
LaMar Baker (R)
L. Ray Blanton (D)
John J. Duncan (R)
Joe L. Evins (D)
Richard H. Fulton (D)
Ed Jones (D)
Dan H. Kuykendall (R)
James H. Quillen (R)

Texas

Senators

Lloyd M. Bentsen, Jr. (D)
John G. Tower (R)

Representatives

Bill Archer (D)
Jack B. Brooks (D)

Omar T. Burleson (D)
Earle Cabell (D)
Robert R. Casey (D)
James M. Collins (R)
Eligio de la Garza, II (D)
John V. Dowdy (D)
Robert C. Eckhardt (E)
O. Clark Fisher (D)
Henry B. Gonzalez (D)
Abraham Kazen, Jr. (D)
George H. Mahon (D)
Wright Patman (D)
J. J. Pickle (D)
William R. Poage (D)
Robert D. Price (R)
Graham Purcell (D)
Ray Roberts (R)
Olin E. Teague (D)
Richard C. White (D)
James C. Wright, Jr. (D)
John Young (D)

Utah

Senators

Wallace F. Bennett (R)
Frank E. Moss (D)

Representatives

Sherman P. Lloyd (R)
K. Gunn McKay (D)

Vermont

Senators

George D. Aiken (R)
Winston L. Prouty (R) d. Sept. 1971
Robert T. Stafford (R)

Representatives

Robert T. Stafford (R) r. Sept. 1971

Virginia

Senators

Harry F. Byrd, Jr. (Independent)
William B. Spong, Jr. (D)

Representatives

Watkins M. Abbitt (D)
Joel T. Broyhill (R)
W. C. (Dan) Daniel (D)
Thomas N. Downing (D)
Richard H. Poff (R)
J. Kenneth Robinson (R)
David E. Satterfield, III (D)
William L. Scott (R)
William C. Wampler (R)
G. William Whitehurst (R)

Washington

Senators

Henry M. Jackson (D)
Warren G. Magnuson (D)

Representatives

Brock Adams (D)
Thomas S. Foley (D)
Julia Butler Hansen (D)
Floyd V. Hicks (D)
Mike McCormack (D)
Lloyd Meeds (D)
Thomas M. Pelly (R)

West Virginia

Senators

Robert C. Byrd (D)
Jennings Randolph (D)

Representatives

Kenneth Hechler (D)
James Kee (D)
Robert H. Mollohan (D)
John M. Slack, Jr. (D)
Harley O. Staggers (D)

Wisconsin

Senators

Gaylord Nelson (D)
William Proxmire (D)

Representatives

Les Aspin (D)
John W. Byrnes (R)
Glenn R. Davis (R)
Robert W. Kastenmeier (D)
David R. Obey (D)
Alvin E. O'Konski (R)
Henry S. Reuss (D)
William A. Steiger (R)
Vernon W. Thomson (R)
Clement J. Zablocki (D)

Wyoming

Senators

Clifford P. Hansen (R)
Gale W. McGee (D)

Representatives

Teno Roncalio (D)

Ninety-Third Congress

(Jan. 3, 1973, to
Jan. 3, 1975)

President of the Senate: Spiro T. Agnew
Speaker of the House of Representatives: Carl Albert

Alabama

Senators

James B. Allen (D)
John J. Sparkman (D)

Representatives

Tom Bevill (D)
John H. Buchanan, Jr. (R)
William L. Dickinson (R)
Jack Edwards (D)
Walter Flowers (D)
Robert E. Jones (D)
William Nichols (D)

Alaska

Senators

Mike Gravel (D)
Ted Stevens (R)

Representatives

Vacant

Arizona

Senators

Paul J. Fannin (R)
Barry M. Goldwater (R)

Representatives

John B. Conlan (R)
John J. Rhodes (R)
Sam Steiger (R)
Morris K. Udall (D)

Arkansas

Senators

J. William Fulbright (D)
John L. McClellan (D)

Representatives

William V. Alexander, Jr. (D)
John P. Hammerschmidt (R)
Wilbur D. Mills (D)
Ray Thornton (D)

California

Senators

Alan Cranston (D)
John V. Tunney (D)

Representatives

Glenn M. Anderson (D)
Alphonzo Bell (R)
George E. Brown, Jr. (D)
Clair W. Burgener (R)
Yvonne Brathwaite Burke (D)
Phillip Burton (D)
Don H. Clausen (R)
Del M. Clawson (R)
James C. Corman (D)
George E. Danielson (D)
Ronald V. Dellums (D)
Don Edwards (D)
Barry M. Goldwater, Jr. (R)
Charles S. Gubser (R)
Richard T. Hanna (D)
Augustus F. Hawkins (D)
Andrew J. Hinshaw (R)
Chet Holifield (D)
Craig Hosmer (R)

Harold T. Johnson (D)
William M. Ketchum (R)
Robert L. Leggett (D)
Paul N. McCloskey, Jr. (R)
John J. McFall (D)
William S. Mailliard (R)
Robert B. Mathias (R)
Carlos J. Moorhead (R)
John E. Moss (D)
Jerry L. Pettis (R)
Thomas M. Rees (D)
John H. Rousselot (R)
Edward R. Roybal (D)
Leo J. Ryan (D)
Bernice F. Sisk (D)
Fortney H. Stark (D)
Burt L. Talcott (R)
Charles M. Teague (R)
Lionel Van Deerlin (D)
Victor V. Veysey (R)
Jerome R. Waldie (D)
Charles E. Wiggins (R)
Charles H. Wilson (D)
Robert C. Wilson (R)

Colorado

Senators

Peter H. Dominick (R)
Floyd K. Haskell (D)

Representatives

William L. Armstrong (R)
Donald G. Brotzman (R)
Frank E. Evans (D)
James P. Johnson (R)
Patricia Schroeder (D)

Connecticut

Senators

Abraham A. Ribicoff (D)
Lowell P. Weicker, Jr. (R)

Representatives

William R. Cotter (D)
Robert N. Giaimo (D)
Ella T. Grasso (D)
Stewart B. McKinney (R)
Ronald A. Sarsin (R)
Robert H. Steele (R)

Delaware

Senators

Joseph R. Biden, Jr. (D)
William V. Roth, Jr. (R)

Representatives

Pierre S. duPont, IV (R)

Florida

Senators

Lawton M. Chiles, Jr. (D)
Edward J. Gurney (R)

Representatives

Louis A. (Skip) Bafalis (R)

Charles E. Bennett (D)
J. Herbert Burke (R)
William V. Chappell, Jr. (D)
Dante B. Fascell (D)
Louis Frey, Jr. (R)
Don Fuqua (D)
Sam M. Gibbons (D)
William D. Gunter, Jr. (D)
James Haley (D)
William Lehman (D)
Claude D. Pepper (D)
Paul G. Rogers (D)
Robert L. F. Sikes (D)
C. W. (Bill) Young (R)

Georgia

Senators

Sam Nunn (D)
Herman E. Talmadge (D)

Representatives

Benjamin B. Blackburn (R)
Jack T. Brinkley (D)
John W. David (D)
Ronald B. Ginn (D)
John J. Flynt, Jr. (D)
Phillip M. Landrum (D)
M. Dawson Mathis (D)
Robert G. Stephens, Jr. (D)
William S. Stuckey, Jr. (D)
Andrew Young (D)

Hawaii

Senators

Hiram L. Fong (R)
Daniel K. Inouye (D)

Representatives

Spark M. Matsunaga (D)
Patsy T. Mink (D)

Idaho

Senators

Frank Church (D)
James A. McClure (R)

Representatives

Orval Hansen (R)
Steven D. Symms (R)

Illinois

Senators

Charles H. Percy (R)
Adlai E. Stevenson, III (D)

Representatives

John B. Anderson (R)
Frank Annunzio (D)
Leslie C. Arends (R)
Harold R. Collier (R)
George W. Collins (D)
Philip M. Crane (R)
Edward J. Derwinski (R)
John N. Erlenborn (R)
Paul Findley (R)

Kenneth J. Gray (D)
Robert P. Hanrahan (R)
John C. Kluczynski (D)
Robert McClory (R)
Edward R. Madigan (R)
Ralph H. Metcalfe (D)
Robert H. Michel (R)
Morgan F. Murphy (D)
George M. O'Brien (R)
C. Melvin Price (D)
Thomas F. Railsback (R)
Dan Rostenkowski (D)
George E. Shipley (D)
Sidney R. Yates (D)
Samuel H. Young (R)

Indiana

Senators

Birch Bayh (D)
Vance Hartke (D)

Representatives

John Brademas (D)
William G. Bray (R)
David W. Dennis (R)
Lee H. Hamilton (D)
Elwood H. Hillis (R)
William H. Hudnut, III (R)
Earl F. Landgrebe (R)
Ray J. Madden (D)
John T. Myers (R)
J. Edward Roush (D)
Roger H. Zion (R)

Iowa

Senators

Richard Clark (D)
Harold E. Hughes (D)

Representatives

John C. Culver (D)
Harold R. Gross (R)
Wiley Mayne (R)
Edward Mezvinsky (D)
William J. Scherle (R)
Neal Smith (D)

Kansas

Senators

Robert J. Dole (R)
James B. Pearson (R)

Representatives

William R. Roy (D)
Keith G. Sebelius (R)
Garner E. Shriver (R)
Joe Skubitz (R)
Larry Winn, Jr. (R)

Kentucky

Senators

Marlow W. Cook (R)
Walter Huddleston (R)

Representatives

John B. Breckinridge (D)
Tim Lee Carter (R)
Romano L. Mazzoli (D)
William H. Natcher (D)
Carl D. Perkins (D)
M. Gene Snyder (R)
Frank A. Stubblefield (D)

Louisiana

Senators

J. Bennett Johnston, Jr. (D)
Russell B. Long (D)

Representatives

John B. Breaux (D)
F. Edward Hebert (D)
Gillis W. Long (D)
Otto E. Passman (D)
John R. Rarick (D)
David C. Treen (R)
Joe D. Waggonner, Jr. (D)

Maine

Senators

William B. Hathaway (D)
Edmund S. Muskie (D)

Representatives

William S. Cohen (R)
Peter N. Kyros (D)

Maryland

Senators

J. Glenn Beall, Jr. (R)
Charles McC. Mathias, Jr. (R)

Representatives

Goodloe E. Bryon (D)
Gilbert Gude (R)
Lawrence J. Hogan (R)
Marjorie S. Holt (R)
Clarence D. Long (D)
William O. Mills (R)
Parren J. Mitchell (D)
Paul S. Sarbanes (D)

Massachusetts

Senators

Edward W. Brooke (R)
Edward M. Kennedy (D)

Representatives

James A. Burke (D)
Edward P. Boland (D)
Silvio O. Conte (R)
Paul W. Cronin (R)
Harold D. Donohue (D)
Robert F. Drinan (D)
Michael J. Harrington (D)
Margaret M. Heckler (R)
Torbert H. Macdonald (D)
John J. Moakley
Thomas P. O'Neill, Jr. (D)

Gerry E. Studds (D)

Michigan

Senators

Robert P. Griffin (R)
Philip A. Hart (D)

Representatives

William S. Broomfield (R)
Garry E. Brown (R)
Elford A. Cederberg (R)
Charles E. Chamberlain (R)
John Conyers, Jr. (D)
Charles C. Diggs, Jr. (D)
John D. Dingell (D)
Marvin L. Esch (R)
Gerald R. Ford, Jr. (D)
William D. Ford (D)
Martha W. Griffiths (D)
James Harvey (R)
Robert J. Huber (R)
Edward Hutchinson (R)
Lucien N. Nedzi (D)
James G. O'Hara (D)
Donald W. Riegle, Jr. (R)
Philip E. Ruppe (R)
Guy Vander Jagt (R)

Minnesota

Senators

Hubert H. Humphrey (D)
Walter F. Mondale (D)

Representatives

Bob Bergland (D)
John A. Blatnik (D)
Donald M. Fraser (D)
Bill Frenzel (R)
Joseph E. Karth (D)
Ancher Nelsen (R)
Albert H. Quie (R)
John M. Zwach (R)

Mississippi

Senators

James O. Eastland (D)
John C. Stennis (D)

Representatives

David R. Bowen (D)
Thad Cochran (R)
Trent Lott (R)
Gillespie V. Montgomery (D)
Jamie L. Whitten (D)

Missouri

Senators

Thomas F. Eagleton (D)
Stuart Symington (D)

Representatives

Richard Bolling (D)
Bill D. Burlison (D)
William L. Clay (D)
William L. Hungate (D)

Richard H. Ichord (D)
Jerry Litton (D)
William J. Randall (R)
Leonor Kretzer Sullivan (D)
James W. Symington (D)
Gene Taylor (R)

Montana

Senators

Mike Mansfield (D)
Lee Metcalf (D)

Representatives

John Melcher (D)
Richard G. Shoup (R)

Nebraska

Senators

Carl T. Curtis (R)
Roman L. Hruska (R)

Representatives

John Y. McCollister (R)
David T. Martin (R)
Charles Thone (R)

Nevada

Senators

Alan Bible (D)
Howard W. Cannon (D)

Representatives

David Powell (R)

New Hampshire

Senators

Norris Cotton (R)
Thomas J. McIntyre (D)

Representatives

James C. Cleveland (R)
Louis C. Wyman (R)

New Jersey

Senators

Clifford P. Case (R)
Harrison A. Williams, Jr. (D)

Representatives

Dominick V. Daniels (D)
Edwin B. Forsythe (R)
Peter H. B. Frelinghuysen, Jr.
(R)
Henry Helstoski (D)
James J. Howard (D)
John E. Hunt (R)
Joseph J. Maraziti (R)
Joseph G. Minish (D)
Edward J. Patten (D)
Matthew J. Rinaldo (R)
Peter W. Rodino, Jr. (D)

Robert A. Roe (D)
Charles W. Sandman, Jr. (R)
Frank Thompson, Jr. (D)
William B. Widnall (R)

New Mexico

Senators

Peter V. Domenici (R)
Joseph M. Montoya (D)

Representatives

Manuel Lujan, Jr. (R)
Harold Runnels (D)

New York

Senators

James L. Buckley (Con-R)
Jacob K. Javits (R)

Representatives

Bella S. Abzug (D)
Joseph P. Addabbo (D)
Herman Badillo (D)
Mario Biaggi (D)
Jonathan B. Bingham (D)
Frank J. Brasco (D)
Hugh L. Carey (D)
Shirley Chisholm (D)
Barber B. Conable, Jr. (R)
James J. Delaney (D)
Thaddeus J. Dulski (D)
Hamilton Fish, Jr. (R)
Benjamin A. Gilman (R)
James R. Grover, Jr. (R)
James M. Hanley (D)
James F. Hastings (R)
Elizabeth Holtzman (D)
Frank J. Horton (R)
Jack F. Kemp (R)
Carleton J. King (R)
Edward I. Koch (D)
Norman F. Lent (R)
Robert C. McEwen (R)
Donald J. Mitchell (R)
John M. Murphy (D)
Peter A. Peyser (R)
Otis G. Pike (D)
Bertram L. Podell (D)
Charles B. Rangel (D)
Ogden R. Reid (D)
Howard W. Robison (R)
Angelo D. Roncallo (R)
John J. Rooney (D)
Benjamin S. Rosenthal (D)
Henry P. Smith, III (R)
Samuel S. Stratton (D)
William F. Walsh (R)
Lester L. Wolff (D)
John W. Wydler (R)

North Carolina

Senators

Sam J. Ervin, Jr. (D)
Jesse A. Helms (R)

Representatives

Ike F. Andrews (D)
James T. Broyhill (R)
L. H. Fountain (D)

David N. Henderson (D)
Walter B. Jones (D)
James G. Martin (R)
Wilmer D. Mizell (R)
L. Richardson Preyer (D)
Charles G. Rose, III (D)
Earl B. Ruth (R)
Roy A. Taylor (D)

North Dakota

Senators

Quentin N. Burdick (D)
Milton R. Young (R)

Representatives

Mark Andrews (R)

Ohio

Senators

William B. Saxbe (R)
Robert Taft, Jr. (R)

Representatives

John M. Ashbrook (R)
Thomas L. Ashley (D)
Clarence J. Brown (R)
Charles J. Carney (D)
Donald D. Clancy (R)
Samuel L. Devine (R)
Tennyson Guyer (R)
William H. Harsha, Jr. (R)
Wayne L. Hays (D)
William J. Keating (R)
Delbert L. Latta (R)
Clarence E. Miller (R)
William E. Minshall (R)
Charles A. Mosher (R)
Walter E. Powell (R)
Ralph S. Regula (R)
John F. Seiberling (D)
J. William Stanton (R)
James V. Stanton (D)
Louis Stokes (D)
Charles A. Vanik (D)
Charles W. Whalen, Jr. (R)
Chalmers P. Wylie (R)

Oklahoma

Senators

Dewey F. Bartlett (R)
Henry L. Bellmon (R)

Representatives

Carl Albert (D)
John N. Camp (R)
John Jarman (D)
James R. Jones (D)
Clem R. McSpadden (D)
Tom Steed (D)

Oregon

Senators

Mark O. Hatfield (R)
Robert W. Packwood (R)

Representatives

John Dellenback (R)
Edith Green (D)
Al Ullman (D)
Wendell Wyatt (R)

Pennsylvania

Senators

Richard S. Schweiker (R)
Hugh Scott (R)

Representatives

William A. Barrett (D)
Edward G. Biester, Jr. (R)
Frank M. Clark (D)
R. Lawrence Coughlin (R)
John H. Dent (D)
Joshua Eilberg (D)
Edwin D. Eshleman (R)
Daniel J. Flood (D)
Joseph M. Gaydos (D)
George A. Gooding (R)
William J. Green (D)
H. John Heinz, III (R)
Albert W. Johnson (R)
Joseph M. McDade (R)
William S. Moorhead (D)
Thomas E. Morgan (D)
Robert N. C. Nix (D)
Fred B. Rooney (D)
John P. Saylor (R)
Herman T. Schneebeli (R)
E. G. Shuster (R)
Joseph P. Vigorito (D)
John H. Ware (R)
Lawrence G. Williams (R)
Gus Yatron (D)

Rhode Island

Senators

John O. Pastore (D)
Claiborne Pell (D)

Representatives

Fernand J. St. Germain (D)
Robert O. Tiernan (D)

South Carolina

Senators

Ernest F. Hollings (D)
J. Strom Thurmond (R)

Representatives

Mendel J. Davis (D)
W. J. Bryan Dorn (D)
Tom S. Gettys (D)
James R. Mann (D)
Floyd D. Spence (R)
Edward L. Young (R)

South Dakota

Senators

James G. Abourezk (D)
George McGovern (D)

Representatives

James Abdnor (R)
Frank E. Denholm (D)

Tennessee

Senators

Howard H. Baker, Jr. (R)
William E. Brock, III (R)

Representatives

LaMar Baker (R)
Robin L. Beard, Jr. (R)
John J. Duncan (R)
Joe L. Evins (D)
Richard H. Fulton (D)
Ed Jones (D)
Dan H. Kuykendall (R)
James H. Quillen (R)

Texas

Senators

Lloyd M. Bentsen, Jr. (D)
John G. Tower (R)

Representatives

Bill Archer (R)
Jack B. Brooks (D)
Omar T. Burleson (D)
Robert R. Casey (D)
James M. Collins (R)
Eligio de la Garza, II (D)
Robert C. Eckhardt (D)
O. Clark Fisher (D)
Henry B. Gonzalez (D)
Barbara Jordan (D)
Abraham Kazen, Jr. (D)
George H. Mahon (D)
Dale Milford (D)
Wright Patman (D)
J. J. Pickle (D)
William R. Poage (D)
Robert D. Price (R)
Ray Roberts (D)
Alan Steelman (R)
Olin E. Teague (D)
Richard C. White (D)
Charles Wilson (D)
James C. Wright, Jr. (D)
John Young (D)

Utah

Senators

Wallace F. Bennett (R)
Frank E. Moss (D)

Representatives

K. Gunn McKay (D)
D. Wayne Owens (D)

Vermont

Senators

George D. Aiken (R)
Robert T. Stafford (R)

Representatives

Richard W. Mallary (R)

Virginia

Senators

Harry F. Byrd, Jr.
William L. Scott (R)

Representatives

Joel T. Broyhill (R)
M. Caldwell Butler (R)
Robert W. Daniel, Jr. (R)
W. C. (Dan) Daniel (D)
Thomas N. Downing (D)
Stanford E. Parris (R)
J. Kenneth Robinson (R)
David E. Satterfield, III (D)
William C. Wampler (R)
G. William Whitehurst (R)

Washington

Senators

Henry M. Jackson (D)
Warren G. Magnuson (D)

Representatives

Brock Adams (D)
Thomas S. Foley (D)
Julia Butler Hansen (D)
John Hempelmann (D)
Floyd V. Hicks (D)
Mike McCormack (D)
Lloyd Meeds (D)

West Virginia

Senators

Robert C. Byrd (D)
Jennings Randolph (D)

Representatives

Kenneth Hechler (D)
Robert H. Mollohan (D)
John Slack (D)
Harley O. Staggers (D)

Wisconsin

Senators

Gaylord Nelson (D)
William Proxmire (D)

Representatives

Les Aspin (D)
Glenn R. Davis (R)
Harold V. Froehlich (R)
Robert W. Kastenmeier (D)
David R. Obey (D)
Henry S. Reuss (D)
William A. Steiger (R)
Vernon W. Thomson (R)
Clement J. Zablocki (D)

Wyoming

Senators

Clifford P. Hansen (R)
Gale W. McGee (D)

Representatives

Teno Roncalio (D)

Ninety-Fourth Congress

(Jan. 3, 1975, to
Jan. 3, 1977)

President of the Senate: Nelson Rockefeller
Speaker of the House of Representatives: Carl Albert

Alabama

Senators

James B. Allen (D)
John J. Sparkman (D)

Representatives

Tom Bevill (D)
John H. Buchanan, Jr. (R)
William L. Dickinson (R)
Jack Edwards (R)
Robert E. Jones (D)
William Nichols (D)

Alaska

Senators

Mike Gravel (D)
Theodore F. Stevens (R)

Representatives

Donald E. Young (R)

Arizona

Senators

Paul J. Fannin (R)
Barry M. Goldwater (R)

Representatives

John B. Conlan (R)
John J. Rhodes (R)
Sam Stelger (R)
Morris K. Udall (D)

Arkansas

Senators

Dale Bumpers (D)
John L. McClellan (D)

Representatives

William V. Alexander, Jr. (D)

John P. Hammerschmidt (R)
Wilbur D. Mills (D)
Ray Thornton (D)

California

Senators

Alan Cranston (D)
John V. Tunney (D)

Representatives

Glenn M. Anderson (D)
Alphonzo Bell (R)
George E. Brown, Jr. (D)
Clair W. Burgener (R)
Yvonne Brathwaite Burke (D)
John Burton (D)
Phillip Burton (D)
Don H. Clausen (R)
Del M. Clawson (R)
James C. Corman (D)
George E. Danielson (D)
Ronald V. Dellums (D)
Don Edwards (D)
B. F. Fisk (D)
Barry Goldwater, Jr. (R)
Mark W. Hannaford (D)
Augustus F. Hawkins (D)
Andrew Hinshaw (R)
Harold T. Johnson (D)
William M. Ketchum (R)
John Krebs (D)
Robert J. Lagomarsino (R)
Robert L. Leggett (D)
James F. Lloyd (D)
John J. McFall (D)
George Miller (D)
Norman Y. Mineta (D)
Carlos J. Moorhead (R)
John E. Moss (D)
Jerry M. Patterson (D)
Jerry L. Pettis (R)
Thomas M. Rees (D)
John Rousselot (R)
Edward R. Roybal (D)
Leo J. Ryan (D)
Fortney H. Stark (D)
Burt L. Talcott (R)
Lionel Van Deerlin (D)
Henry A. Waxman (D)
Charles E. Wiggins (R)
Bob C. Wilson (R)
Charles H. Wilson (D)

Colorado

Senators

Gary Hart (D)
Floyd K. Haskell (D)

Representatives

William L. Armstrong (R)
Frank E. Evans (D)
James P. Johnson (R)
Patricia Schroeder (D)
Timothy E. Wirth (D)

Connecticut

Senators

Abraham A. Ribicoff (D)
Lowell P. Weicker, Jr. (R)

Representatives

William R. Cotter (D)
Christopher J. Dodd (D)
Robert Giaimo (D)
Stewart B. McKinney (R)
Anthony T. Moffett (D)
Ronald A. Sarasin (R)

Delaware

Senators

Joseph R. Biden, Jr. (D)
William V. Roth, Jr. (R)

Representatives

Pierre S. duPont, IV (R)

Florida

Senators

Lawton M. Chiles, Jr. (D)
Richard Stone (D)

Representatives

Louis A. (Skip) Bafalis (R)
Charles E. Bennett (D)
J. Herbert Burke (R)
William V. Chappell, Jr. (D)
Dante B. Fascell (D)
Louis Frey, Jr. (R)
Don Fuqua (D)
Sam M. Gibbons (D)
James A. Haley (D)
Richard Kelly (R)
William Lehman (D)
Claude D. Pepper (D)
Paul G. Rogers (D)
Robert L. F. Sikes (D)
C. W. Bill Young (R)

Georgia

Senators

Sam Nunn (D)
Herman E. Talmadge (D)

Representatives

Jack T. Brinkley (D)
John J. Flynt, Jr. (D)
Ronald B. (Bo) Ginn (D)
Phillip M. Landrum (D)
Elliott H. Levitas (D)
M. Dawson Mathis (D)
Larry McDonald (D)
Robert G. Stephens, Jr. (D)
William S. Stuckey, Jr. (D)
Andrew Young (D)

Hawaii

Senators

Hiram L. Fong (R)
Daniel K. Inouye (D)

Representatives

Spark M. Matsunaga (D)
Patsy Takemoto Mink (D)

Idaho

Senators

Frank Church (D)
James A. McClure (R)

Representatives

George Hansen (R)
Steven D. Symms (R)

Illinois

Senators

Charles H. Percy (R)
Adlai E. Stevenson, III (D)

Representatives

John B. Anderson (R)
Frank Annunzio (D)
Cardiss Collins (D)
Philip M. Crane (R)
Edward J. Derwinski (R)
John N. Erlenborn (R)
Paul Findley (R)
Tim L. Hall (D)
Henry J. Hyde (R)
John C. Kluczynski (D)
Edward R. Madigan (R)
Ralph H. Metcalfe (D)
Robert McClory (R)
Robert H. Michel (R)
Abner J. Mikua (D)
Morgan F. Murphy (D)
George M. O'Brien (R)
C. Melvin Price (D)
Thomas F. Railsback (R)
Daniel D. Rostenkowski (D)
Martin A. Russo (D)
George E. Shipley (D)
Paul Simon (D)
Sidney R. Yates (D)

Indiana

Senators

Birch Bayh (D)
Vance Hartke (D)

Representatives

John Brademas (D)
David W. Evans (D)
Floyd J. Fithian (D)
Lee H. Hamilton (D)
Philip H. Hayes (D)
Elwood H. Hillis (R)
Andrew Jacobs, Jr. (D)
Ray J. Madden (D)
John T. Myers (R)
J. Edward Roush (D)
Philip R. Sharp (D)

Iowa

Senators

Richard Clark (D)
John C. Culver (D)

Representatives

Berkley Bedell (D)

Michael T. Blouin (D)
Charles E. Grassley (R)
Tom Harkin (D)
Edward Mezvinsky (D)
Neal Smith (D)

Kansas

Senators

Robert J. Dole (R)
James B. Pearson (R)

Representatives

Martha Keys (D)
Keith G. Sebelius (R)
Garner E. Shriver (R)
Joe Skubitz (R)
Larry Winn, Jr. (R)

Kentucky

Senators

Wendell H. Ford (D)
Walter Huddleston (D)

Representatives

John B. Breckinridge (D)
Tim Lee Carter (R)
Carroll Hubbard, Jr. (D)
Romano L. Mazzoli (D)
William H. Natcher (D)
Carl D. Perkins (D)
Marion Gene Snyder (R)

Louisiana

Senators

J. Bennett Johnston, Jr. (D)
Russell B. Long (D)

Representatives

Lindy Boggs (D)
John B. Breaux (D)
F. Edward Hebert (D)
Gillis W. Long (D)
W. Henson Moore (R)
Otto E. Passman (D)
David C. Treen (R)
Joe D. Waggoner, Jr. (D)

Maine

Senators

William D. Hathaway (D)
Edmund S. Muskie (D)

Representatives

William S. Cohen (R)
David F. Emery (R)

Maryland

Senators

J. Glenn Beall, Jr. (R)
Charles McC. Mathias, Jr. (R)

Representatives

Robert E. Bauman (R)
Goodloe E. Byron (D)
Gilbert Gude (R)
Marjorie S. Holt (R)
Clarence D. Long (D)
Parren J. Mitchell (D)
Paul S. Sarbanes (D)
Gladys Noon Spellman (D)

Massachusetts

Senators

Edward W. Brooke (R)
Edward M. Kennedy (D)

Representatives

Edward P. Boland (D)
James A. Burke (D)
Silvio O. Conte (R)
Robert F. Drinan (D)
Joseph D. Early (D)
Michael J. Harrington (D)
Margaret M. Heckler (R)
John J. Moakley (D)
Thomas P. O'Neill, Jr. (D)
Torbert H. MacDonald (D)
Gerry E. Studds (D)
Paul E. Tsongas (D)

Michigan

Senators

Robert P. Griffin (R)
Philip A. Hart (D)

Representatives

James J. Blanchard (D)
William M. Brodhead (D)
William S. Broomfield (R)
Garry E. Brown (R)
M. Robert Carr (D)
Elford A. Cederberg (R)
John Conyers, Jr. (D)
Charles C. Diggs, Jr. (D)
John D. Dingell (D)
Marvin L. Esch (R)
William D. Ford (D)
Edward Hutchinson (R)
Lucien N. Nedzi (D)
James G. O'Hara (D)
Donald W. Riegle, Jr. (D)
Philip E. Ruppe (R)
Bob Traxler (D)
Guy A. Vander Jagt (R)
Richard F. Vander Veen (D)

Minnesota

Senators

Hubert Humphrey (D)
Walter F. Mondale (D)

Representatives

Bob Bergland (D)
Donald Fraser (D)
William E. Frenzel (R)
Thomas M. Hagedorn (R)
Joseph E. Karth (D)
Richard Nolan (D)
James L. Oberstar (D)

Albert H. Quie (R)

Mississippi

Senators

James O. Eastland (D)
John Stennis (D)

Representatives

David R. Bowen (D)
Thad Cochran (R)
Trent Lott (R)
Gillespie V. Montgomery (D)
Jamie L. Whitten (D)

Missouri

Senators

Thomas F. Eagleton (D)
Stuart Symington (D)

Representatives

Richard Bolling (D)
Bill D. Burlison (D)
William L. Clay (D)
William L. Hungate (D)
Richard H. Ichord (D)
Jerry Litton (D)
William J. Randall (D)
Leonor K. Sullivan (D)
James W. Symington (D)
Gene Taylor (R)

Montana

Senators

Michael J. Mansfield (D)
Lee Metcalf (D)

Representatives

Max S. Baucher (D)
John Melcher (D)

Nebraska

Senators

Carl T. Curtis (R)
Roman L. Hruska (R)

Representatives

John Y. McCollister (R)
Virginia Smith (R)
Charles Thone (R)

Nevada

Senators

Howard W. Cannon (D)
Paul Laxalt (R)

Representatives

James D. Santini (D)

New Hampshire

Senators

Thomas J. McIntyre (D)
Louis C. Wyman (R)

Representatives

James C. Cleveland (R)
Norman E. D'Amours (D)

New Jersey

Senators

Clifford P. Case (R)
Harrison A. Williams, Jr. (D)

Representatives

Dominick V. Daniels (D)
Millicent Fenwick (R)
James J. Florio (D)
Edwin B. Forsythe (R)
Henry Helstoski (D)
James J. Howard (D)
William J. Hughes (D)
Andrew Maguire (D)
Helen S. Meyner (D)
Joseph G. Minish (D)
Edward J. Patten (D)
Matthew J. Rinaldo (R)
Peter W. Rodino, Jr. (D)
Robert A. Roe (D)
Frank Thompson, Jr. (D)

New Mexico

Senators

Pete V. Domenici (R)
Joseph M. Montoya (D)

Representatives

Manuel Lujan, Jr. (R)
Harold Runnels (D)

New York

Senators

James L. Buckley (Con.)
Jacob K. Javits (R)

Representatives

Bella S. Abzug (D)
Joseph P. Addabbo (D)
Jerome A. Ambro, Jr. (D)
Herman Badillo (D)
Mario Biaggi (D)
Jonathan B. Bingham (D)
Shirley A. Chisholm (D)
Barber B. Conable, Jr. (R)
James J. Delaney (D)
Thomas J. Downey (D)
Hamilton Fish, Jr. (R)
Benjamin A. Gilman (R)
James M. Hanley (D)
James F. Hastings (R)
Elizabeth Holtzman (D)
Frank Horton (R)
Jack F. Kemp (R)
Edward I. Koch (D)
John J. LaFalce (D)

Norman F. Lent (R)
Robert C. McEwen (R)
Matthew F. McHugh (D)
Donald J. Mitchell (R)
John M. Murphy (D)
Henry J. Nowak (D)
Richard L. Ottinger (D)
Edward W. Pattison (D)
Peter A. Peyser (R)
Otis G. Pike (D)
Charles B. Rangel (D)
Frederick W. Richmond (D)
Benjamin S. Rosenthal (D)
James H. Scheuer (D)
Stephen J. Solarz (D)
Samuel S. Stratton (D)
William F. Walsh (R)
Lester L. Wolff (D)
John W. Wydler (R)
Leo C. Zeferetti (D)

North Carolina

Senators

Jesse A. Helms (R)
Robert Morgan (D)

Representatives

Ike F. Andrew (D)
James T. Broyhill (R)
L. H. Fountain (D)
W. G. Hefner (D)
David N. Henderson (R)
Walter B. Jones (D)
James G. Martin (R)
Stephen L. Neal (D)
L. Richardson Preyer (D)
Charles G. Rose, III (D)
Roy A. Taylor (D)

North Dakota

Senators

Quentin N. Burdick (D)
William L. Guy (D)

Representatives

Mark Andrews (R)

Ohio

Senators

John Glenn (D)
Robert Taft, Jr. (R)

Representatives

John M. Ashbrook (R)
Thomas L. Ashley (D)
Clarence J. Brown (R)
Charles J. Carney (D)
Donald D. Clancy (R)
Samuel L. Devine (R)
Willis D. Gradison, Jr. (R)
Tennyson Guyer (R)
William H. Harsha (R)
Wayne L. Hays (D)
Thomas N. Kindness (R)
Delbert L. Latta (R)
Clarence E. Miller (R)
Charles A. Moser (R)
Ronald M. Mottl (D)
Ralph S. Regula (R)

John F. Seiberling (D)
James V. Stanton (D)
J. William Stanton (R)
Louis Stokes (D)
Charles A. Vanik (D)
Charles W. Whalen, Jr. (R)
Chalmers P. Wylie (R)

Oklahoma

Senators

Dewey F. Bartlett (R)
Henry L. Bellmon (R)

Representatives

Carl Albert (D)
Glenn English (D)
John Jarman (D)
James R. Jones (D)
Theodore M. Risenhoover (D)
Tom Steed (D)

Oregon

Senators

Mark O. Hatfield (R)
Robert W. Packwood (R)

Representatives

Les AuCoin (D)
Robert Duncan (D)
Al Ullman (D)
James Weaver (D)

Pennsylvania

Senators

Richard S. Schweiker (R)
Hugh Scott (R)

Representatives

William A. Barrett (D)
Edward G. Biester, Jr. (R)
R. Lawrence Coughlin (R)
John H. Dent (D)
Robert W. Edgar (D)
Joshua Eilberg (D)
Edwin D. Eshleman (R)
Daniel J. Flood (D)
Joseph M. Gaydos (D)
William F. Goodling (R)
William J. Green (D)
H. John Heinz, III (R)
Albert W. Johnson (R)
Joseph M. McDade (R)
William S. Moorhead (D)
Thomas E. Morgan (D)
John P. Murtha (D)
Gary A. Myers (R)
Robert N. C. Nix (D)
Fred B. Rooney (D)
Herman T. Schneebeli (R)
Richard T. Schulze (R)
E. G. Shuster (R)
Joseph P. Vigorito (D)
Gus Yatron (D)

Rhode Island

Senators

John O. Pastore (D)
Claiborne Pell (D)

Representatives

Edward P. Beard (D)
Fernand J. St. Germain (D)

South Carolina

Senators

Ernest F. Hollings (D)
Strom Thurmond (R)

Representatives

Mendel J. Davis (D)
Butler Derrick (D)
Kenneth L. Holland (D)
John W. Jenrette, Jr. (D)
James R. Mann (D)
Floyd D. Spence (R)

South Dakota

Senators

James G. Abourezk (D)
George McGovern (D)

Representatives

James Abdnor (R)
Larry Pressler (R)

Tennessee

Senators

Howard H. Baker, Jr. (R)
William E. Brock, III (R)

Representatives

Robin L. Beard, Jr. (R)
John J. Duncan (R)
Joe L. Evins (D)
Harold E. Ford (D)
Richard H. Fulton (D)
Ed Jones (D)

Texas

Senators

Lloyd M. Bentsen, Jr. (D)
John G. Tower (R)

Representatives

William R. Archer, Jr. (R)
Jack Brooks (D)
Omar T. Burleson (D)
Robert R. Casey (D)
James M. Collins (R)
Eligio de la Garza, II (D)
Robert C. Eckhardt (D)
Henry B. Gonzalez (D)
Jack E. Hightower (D)
Barbara Jordan (D)
Abraham Kazen, Jr. (D)

Robert Krueger (D)
George H. Mahon (D)
Dale Milford (D)
Wright Patman (D)
J. J. Pickle (D)
William R. Poage (D)
Ray Roberts (D)
Alan Steelman (R)
Olin E. Teague (D)
Richard C. White (D)
Charles Wilson (D)
James C. Wright, Jr. (D)
John Young (D)

Utah

Senators

Edwin J. (Jake) Garn (R)
Frank E. Moss (D)

Representatives

Allen T. Howe (D)
K. Gunn McKay (D)

Vermont

Senators

Patrick J. Leahy (D)
Robert T. Stafford (R)

Representatives

James M. Jeffords (R)

Virginia

Senators

Harry F. Byrd, Jr. (Ind.)
William L. Scott (R)

Representatives

M. Caldwell Butler (R)
Robert W. Daniel, Jr. (R)
W. D. Daniel (D)
Thomas N. Downing (D)
Joseph L. Fisher (D)
Herbert E. Harris, II (D)
J. Kenneth Robinson (R)
David E. Satterfield, III (D)
William C. Wampler (R)
G. William Whitehurst (R)

Washington

Senators

Henry M. Jackson (D)
Warren G. Magnuson (D)

Representatives

Brock Adams (D)
Don L. Bonker (D)
Thomas S. Foley (D)
Floyd V. Hicks (D)
Mike McCormack (D)
Lloyd Meeds (D)
Joel Pritchard (R)

West Virginia

Senators

Robert C. Byrd (D)
Jennings Randolph (D)

Representatives

Ken Hechler (D)
Robert H. Mollohan (D)
John M. Slack (D)
Harley O. Staggers (D)

Wisconsin

Senators

Gaylord A. Nelson (D)
William Proxmire (D)

Representatives

Les Aspin (D)
Alvin Baldus (D)
Robert J. Cornell (D)
Robert W. Kasten, Jr. (R)
Robert W. Kastenmeier (D)
David R. Obey (D)
Henry S. Reuss (D)
William A. Steiger (R)
Clement J. Zablocki (D)

Wyoming

Senators

Clifford P. Hansen (R)
Gale W. McGee (D)

Representatives

Teno Roncalio (D)

Ninety-Fifth Congress

(Jan. 3, 1977, to
Jan. 3, 1979)

President of the Senate: Walter
  F. Mondale
*Speaker of the House of
  Representatives:* Thomas P.
  O'Neill, Jr.

Alabama

Senators

James B. Allen (D)
John J. Sparkman (D)

Representatives

Tom Bevill (D)
John H. Buchanan, Jr. (R)
William L. Dickinson (R)
Jack Edwards (R)
Ronnie G. Flippo (D)
Walter Flowers (D)
William Nichols (D)

Alaska

Senators

Mike Gravel (D)
Theodore F. Stevens (R)

Representatives

Don Young (R)

Arizona

Senators

Dennis DeConcini (D)
Barry M. Goldwater (R)

Representatives

John J. Rhodes (R)
Eldon Rudd (R)
Bob Stump (D)
Morris K. Udall (D)

Arkansas

Senators

Dale Bumpers (D)
John L. McClellan (D)

Representatives

William V. Alexander, Jr. (D)
John P. Hammerschmidt (R)
Ray Thornton (D)
Jim G. Tucker, Jr. (D)

California

Senators

Alan Cranston (D)
Sam I. Hayakawa (R)

Representatives

Glenn M. Anderson (D)
Robert E. Badham (R)
Anthony C. Beilenson (D)
George E. Brown, Jr. (D)
Clair W. Burgener (R)
Yvonne Brathwaite Burke (D)
John L. Burton (D)
Phillip Burton (D)
Del M. Clawson (R)
Don H. Clausen (R)
James C. Corman (D)
George E. Danielson (D)
Ronald V. Dellums (D)
Robert K. Dornan (R)
Don Edwards (D)
Barry Goldwater, Jr. (R)
Mark W. Hannaford (D)
Augustus F. Hawkins (D)
Harold T. Johnson (D)
William M. Ketchum (R)
John Krebs (D)
Robert J. Lagomarsino (R)
Robert L. Leggett (D)
James F. Lloyd (D)
Paul N. McCloskey, Jr. (R)
John J. McFall (D)
George Miller (D)
Norman Y. Mineta (D)
Carlos J. Moorhead (R)

John E. Moss (D)
Leon E. Panetta (D)
Jerry Patterson (D)
Shirley N. Pettis (R)
John H. Rousselot (R)
Edward R. Roybal (D)
Leo J. Ryan (D)
Bernice F. Sisk (D)
Fortney H. Stark (D)
Lionel Van Deerlin (D)
Henry A. Waxman (D)
Charles E. Wiggins (R)
Charles H. Wilson (D)
Robert C. Wilson (R)

Colorado

Senators

Gary Hart (D)
Floyd K. Haskell (D)

Representatives

William L. Armstrong (R)
Frank E. Evans (D)
James P. Johnson (R)
Patricia Schroeder (D)
Timothy E. Wirth (D)

Connecticut

Senators

Abraham A. Ribicoff (D)
Lowell P. Weicker, Jr. (R)

Representatives

William R. Cotter (D)
Christopher J. Dodd (D)
Robert N. Giaimo (D)
Stewart B. McKinney (R)
Anthony T. Moffett (D)
Ronald A. Sarasin (R)

Delaware

Senators

Joseph R. Biden, Jr. (D)
William V. Roth, Jr. (R)

Representatives

Thomas B. Evans, Jr. (R)

Florida

Senators

Lawton M. Chiles, Jr. (D)
Richard Stone (D)

Representatives

Louis A. (Skip) Bafalis (R)
Charles E. Bennett (D)
J. Herbert Burke (R)
William V. Chappell, Jr. (D)
Dante B. Fascell (D)
Louis Frey, Jr. (R)
Don Fuqua (D)
Sam M. Gibbons (D)
Andrew P. Ireland (D)
Richard Kelly (R)
William Lehman (D)

Claude D. Pepper (D)
Paul G. Rogers (D)
Robert L. F. Sikes (D)
C. W. Bill Young (R)

Georgia

Senators

Sam Nunn (D)
Herman E. Talmadge (D)

Representatives

Druie D. (Doug) Barnard, Jr.
  (D)
Jack T. Brinkley (D)
Billy Lee Evans (D)
John J. Flynt, Jr. (D)
Ronald B. (Bo) Ginn (D)
Edgar L. Jenkins (D)
Elliott H. Levitas (D)
Dawson Mathis (D)
Larry P. McDonald (D)
Andrew Young (D)

Hawaii

Senators

Daniel K. Inouye (D)
Spark M. Matsunaga (D)

Representatives

Daniel K. Akaka (D)
Cecil L. Heftel (D)

Idaho

Senators

Frank Church (D)
James A. McClure (R)

Representatives

George Hansen (R)
Steven D. Symms (R)

Illinois

Senators

Charles H. Percy (R)
Adlai E. Stevenson, III (D)

Representatives

John B. Anderson (R)
Frank Annunzio (D)
Cardiss Collins (D)
Tom Corcoran (R)
Philip M. Crane (R)
Edward J. Derwinski (R)
John N. Erlenborn (R)
John G. Fary (D)
Paul Findley (R)
Henry J. Hyde (R)
Robert McClory (R)
Edward R. Madigan (R)
Ralph H. Metcalfe (D)
Robert H. Michel (R)
Abner J. Mikva (D)
Morgan F. Murphy (D)
George M. O'Brien (R)
C. Melvin Price (D)

Thomas F. Railsback (R)
Daniel D. Rostenkowski (D)
Martin A. Russo (D)
George E. Shipley (D)
Paul Simon (D)
Sidney R. Yates (D)

Indiana

Senators

Birch Bayh (D)
Richard G. Lugar (R)

Representatives

Adam Benjamin, Jr. (D)
John Brademas (D)
David L. Cornwell (D)
David W. Evans (D)
Floyd J. Fithian (D)
Lee H. Hamilton (D)
Elwood H. Hillis (R)
Andrew Jacobs, Jr. (D)
John T. Myers (R)
J. Danforth Quayle (R)
Philip R. Sharp (D)

Iowa

Senators

Richard Clark (D)
John C. Culver (D)

Representatives

Berkley Bedell (D)
Michael T. Blouin (D)
Charles E. Grassley (R)
Tom Harkin (D)
James A. S. Leach (R)
Neal Smith (D)

Kansas

Senators

Robert J. Dole (R)
James B. Pearson (R)

Representatives

Daniel R. Glickman (D)
Martha Keys (D)
Keith G. Sebelius (R)
Joe Skubitz (R)
Larry Winn, Jr. (R)

Kentucky

Senators

Wendell H. Ford (D)
Walter Huddleston (D)

Representatives

John B. Breckinridge (D)
Tim Lee Carter (R)
Caroll Hubbard, Jr. (D)
Romano L. Mazzoli (D)
William H. Natcher (D)
Carl D. Perkins (D)
M. Gene Snyder (R)

Louisiana

Senators

J. Bennett Johnston, Jr. (D)
Russell B. Long (D)

Representatives

Lindy Boggs (D)
John B. Breaux (D)
Thomas J. (Jerry) Huckaby (D)
Robert L. Livingston (R)
Gillis W. Long (D)
W. Henson Moore (R)
David C. Treen (R)
Joe D. Waggonner, Jr. (D)

Maine

Senators

William D. Hathaway (D)
Edmund S. Muskie (D)

Representatives

William S. Cohen (R)
David F. Emery (R)

Maryland

Senators

Charles McC. Mathias, Jr. (R)
Paul S. Sarbanes (D)

Representatives

Robert E. Bauman (R)
Goodloe E. Byron (D)
Marjorie S. Holt (R)
Clarence D. Long (D)
Barbara A. Mikulski (D)
Parren J. Mitchell (D)
Gladys Noon Spellman (D)
Newton I. Steers, Jr. (R)

Massachusetts

Senators

Edward W. Brooke (R)
Edward M. Kennedy (D)

Representatives

Edward P. Boland (D)
James A. Burke (D)
Silvio O. Conte (R)
Robert F. Drinan (D)
Joseph D. Early (D)
Michael J. Harrington (D)
Margaret M. Heckler (R)
Edward J. Markey (D)
John J. Moakley (D)
Thomas P. O'Neill, Jr. (D)
Gerry E. Studds (D)
Paul E. Tsongas (D)

Michigan

Senators

Robert P. Griffin (R)
Donald W. Riegle, Jr. (D)

Representatives

James J. Blanchard (D)
David E. Bonior (D)
William M. Brodhead (D)
William S. Broomfield (R)
Garry E. Brown (R)
M. Robert Carr (D)
Elford A. Cederberg (R)
John Conyers, Jr. (D)
Charles C. Diggs, Jr. (D)
John D. Dingell (D)
William D. Ford (D)
Dale E. Kildee (D)
Lucien N. Nedzi (D)
Carl D. Pursell (R)
Philip E. Ruppe (R)
Harold S. Sawyers (R)
David A. Stockman (R)
Bob Traxler (D)
Guy A. Vander Jagt (R)

Minnesota

Senators

Wendell R. Anderson (D)
Hubert H. Humphrey (D)

Representatives

Donald M. Fraser (D)
William E. Frenzel (R)
Thomas M. Hagedorn (R)
Richard Nolan (D)
James L. Oberstar (D)
Albert H. Quie (R)
Arlan Strangeland (R)
Bruce F. Vento (D)

Mississippi

Senators

James O. Eastland (D)
John C. Stennis (D)

Representatives

David R. Bowen (D)
Thad Cochran (R)
Trent Lott (R)
G. V. Montgomery (D)
Jamie L. Whitten (D)

Missouri

Senators

John C. Danforth (R)
Thomas F. Eagleton (D)

Representatives

Richard Bolling (D)
Bill D. Burlison (D)
William L. Clay (D)
E. Thomas Coleman (R)
Richard A. Gephardt (D)
Richard H. Ichord (D)
Ike N. Skelton, Jr. (D)
Gene Taylor (R)
Harold L. Volkmer (D)
Robert A. Young (D)

Montana

Senators

John Melcher (D)
Lee Metcalf (D)

Representatives

Max Baucus (D)
Ronald C. Marlenee (R)

Nebraska

Senators

Carl T. Curtis (R)
Edward Zorinsky (D)

Representatives

John J. Cavanaugh (D)
Virginia Smith (R)
Charles Thone (R)

Nevada

Senators

Howard W. Cannon (D)
Paul Laxalt (R)

Representatives

James D. Santini (D)

New Hampshire

Senators

John A. Durkin (D)
Thomas J. McIntyre (D)

Representatives

Norman E. D'Amours (D)
James C. Cleveland (R)

New Jersey

Senators

Clifford P. Case (R)
Harrison A. Williams, Jr. (D)

Representatives

Millicent H. Fenwick (R)
James J. Florio (D)
Harold C. Hollenbeck (R)
Edwin B. Forsythe (R)
James J. Howard (D)
William J. Hughes (D)
Joseph A. LeFante (D)
Andrew Maguire (D)
Helen S. Meyner (D)
Joseph G. Minish (D)
Edward J. Patten (D)
Matthew J. Rinaldo (R)
Peter W. Rodino, Jr. (D)
Robert A. Roe (D)
Frank Thompson, Jr. (D)

New Mexico

Senators

Pete V. Domenici (R)
Harrison Schmitt (R)

Representatives

Manuel Lujan, Jr. (R)
Harold Runnels (D)

New York

Senators

Jacob K. Javits (R)
Daniel P. Moynihan (D)

Representatives

Joseph P. Addabbo (D)
Jerome A. Ambro, Jr. (D)
Herman Badillo (D)
Mario Braggi (D)
Jonathan B. Bingham (D)
Bruce F. Caputo (R)
Shirley Chisholm (D)
Barber B. Conable, Jr. (R)
James J. Delaney (D)
Thomas J. Downey (D)
Hamilton Fish, Jr. (R)
Benjamin A. Gilman (R)
James M. Hanley (D)
Elizabeth Holtzman (D)
Frank J. Horton (R)
Jack F. Kemp (R)
Edward I. Koch (D)
John J. LaFalce (D)
Norman F. Lent (R)
Stanley N. Lundine (D)
Robert C. McEwen (R)
Matthew F. McHugh (R)
Donald J. Mitchell (R)
John M. Murphy (D)
Henry J. Nowak (D)
Richard L. Ottinger (D)
Edward W. Pattison (D)
Otis G. Pike (D)
Charles B. Rangel (D)
Frederick W. Richmond (D)
Benjamin S. Rosenthal (D)
James H. Scheuer (D)
Stephen J. Solarz (D)
Samuel S. Stratton (D)
William F. Walsh (R)
Theodore S. Weiss (D)
Lester L. Wolff (D)
John W. Wydler (R)
Leo C. Zeferetti (D)

North Carolina

Senators

Jesse A. Helms (R)
Robert Morgan (D)

Representatives

Ike F. Andrews (D)
James T. Broyhill (R)
L. H. Fountain (D)
Lamar Gudger (D)
W. G. Hefner (D)
Walter B. Jones (D)
James G. Martin (R)
Stephen L. Neal (D)

L. Richardson Preyer (D)
Charles G. Rose (D)
Charles Whitley (D)

North Dakota

Senators

Quentin N. Burdick (D)
Milton R. Young (R)

Representatives

Mark Andrews (R)

Ohio

Senators

John Glenn (D)
Howard M. Metzenbaum (D)

Representatives

Douglas Applegate (D)
John M. Ashbrook (R)
Thomas L. Ashley (D)
Clarence J. Brown (R)
Charles J. Carney (D)
Samuel L. Devine (R)
Willis D. Gradison, Jr. (R)
Tennyson Guyer (R)
William H. Harsha (R)
Thomas N. Kindness (R)
Delbert L. Latta (R)
Thomas A. Luken (D)
Clarence E. Miller (R)
Ronald M. Mottl (D)
Mary Rose Oakar (D)
Donald J. Pease (D)
Ralph S. Regula (R)
John F. Seiberling (D)
J. William Stanton (R)
Louis Stokes (D)
Charles A. Vanik (D)
Charles W. Whalen, Jr. (R)
Chalmers P. Wylie (R)

Oklahoma

Senators

Dewey F. Bartlett (R)
Henry L. Bellmon (R)

Representatives

Marvin H. (Mickey) Edwards
  (R)
Glenn English (D)
James R. Jones (D)
Theodore M. Risenhoover (D)
Tom Steed (D)
Wes Watkins (D)

Oregon

Senators

Mark O. Hatfield (R)
Robert W. Packwood (R)

Representatives

Les AuCoin (D)
Robert B. Duncan (D)
Al Ullman (D)

James Weaver (D)

Pennsylvania

Senators

H. John Heinz, III (R)
Richard S. Schweiker (R)

Representatives

Joseph S. Ammerman (D)
R. Lawrence Coughlin (R)
John H. Dent (D)
Robert W. Edgar (D)
Joshua Eilberg (D)
Allen E. Ertel (D)
Daniel J. Flood (D)
Joseph M. Gaydos (D)
William F. Goodling (R)
Peter H. Kostmayer (D)
Raymond F. Lederer (D)
Joseph M. McDade (R)
Marc L. Marks (R)
William S. Moorhead (D)
Austin J. Murphy (D)
John P. Murtha (D)
Gary A. Myers (R)
Michael O. Myers (D)
Robert N. C. Nix (D)
Fred B. Rooney (D)
Richard T. Schulze (R)
Bud Shuster (R)
Douglas Walgren (D)
Robert S. Walker (R)
Gus Yatron (D)

Rhode Island

Senators

John H. Chafee (R)
Claiborne Pell (D)

Representatives

Edward P. Beard (D)
Fernand J. St. Germain (D)

South Carolina

Senators

Ernest F. Hollings (D)
Strom Thurmond (R)

Representatives

Mendel J. Davis (D)
Butler C. Derrick (D)
Kenneth L. Holland (D)
John W. Jenrette, Jr. (D)
James R. Mann (D)
Floyd D. Spence (R)

South Dakota

Senators

James G. Abourezk (D)
George McGovern (D)

Representatives

James Abdnor (R)
Larry Pressler (R)

Tennessee

Senators

Howard H. Baker, Jr. (R)
James R. Sasser (D)

Representatives

Clifford Allen (D)
Robin L. Beard, Jr. (R)
John J. Duncan (R)
Harold E. Ford (D)
Albert Gore, Jr. (D)
Ed Jones (D)
Marilyn Lloyd (D)
James H. Quillen (R)

Texas

Senators

Lloyd M. Bentsen, Jr. (D)
John G. Tower (R)

Representatives

William R. Archer (R)
Jack B. Brooks (D)
Omar T. Burleson (D)
James M. Collins (R)
Robert C. Eckhardt (D)
Eligio de la Garza (D)
Henry B. Gonzalez (D)
Sam B. Hall, Jr. (D)
Jack E. Hightower (D)
Barbara Jordan (D)
Abraham Kazen, Jr. (D)
Robert Krueger (D)
George H. Mahon (D)
Jim Mattox (D)
Dale Milford (D)
Ron Paul (R)
J. J. Pickle (D)
William R. Poage (D)
Ray Roberts (D)
Olin E. Teague (D)
Richard C. White (D)
Charles Wilson (D)
James C. Wright, Jr. (D)
John Young (D)

Utah

Senators

Edwin J. (Jake) Garn (R)
Orrin G. Hatch (R)

Representatives

K. Gunn McKay (D)
David D. Marriott (R)

Vermont

Senators

Patrick J. Leahy (D)
Robert T. Stafford (R)

Representatives

James M. Jeffords (R)

266

Virginia

Senators

Harry F. Byrd, Jr. (Ind.)
William L. Scott (R)

Representatives

M. Caldwell Butler (R)
Robert W. Daniel, Jr. (R)
W. C. Daniel (D)
Joseph L. Fisher (D)
Herbert E. Harris, II (D)
J. Kenneth Robinson (R)
David E. Satterfield, III (D)
Paul S. Trible, Jr. (R)
William C. Wampler (R)
G. William Whitehurst (R)

Washington

Senators

Henry M. Jackson (D)
Warren G. Magnuson (D)

Representatives

Brock Adams (D)
Don L. Bonker (D)
Norman D. Dicks (D)
Thomas S. Foley (D)
Mike McCormack (D)
Lloyd Meeds (D)
Joel Pritchard (R)

West Virginia

Senators

Robert C. Byrd (D)
Jennings Randolph (D)

Representatives

Robert H. Mollohan (D)
Nick J. Rahall, II (D)
John M. Slack (D)
Harley O. Staggers (D)

Wisconsin

Senators

Gaylord A. Nelson (D)
William Proxmire (D)

Representatives

Les Aspin (D)
Alvin J. Baldus (D)
Robert J. Cornell (D)
Robert W. Kasten, Jr. (R)
Robert W. Kastenmeier (D)
David R. Obey (D)
Henry S. Reuss (D)
William A. Steiger (R)
Clement J. Zablocki (D)

Wyoming

Senators

Clifford P. Hansen (R)
Malcolm Wallop (R)

Representatives

Teno Roncalio (D)

Ninety-Sixth Congress

(Jan. 3, 1979, to
Jan. 3, 1981)

President of the Senate: Walter
 F. Mondale
*Speaker of the House of
 Representatives:* Thomas P.
 O'Neill, Jr.

Alabama

Senators

Howell Heflin (D)
Donald Stewart (D)

Representatives

Tom Bevill (D)
John H. Buchanan, Jr. (R)
William L. Dickinson (R)
Jack Edwards (R)
Ronnie G. Flippo (D)
William Nichols (D)
Richard C. Shelby (D)

Alaska

Senators

Mike Gravel (D)
Theodore F. Stevens (R)

Representatives

Donald E. Young (R)

Arizona

Senators

Dennis DeConcini (D)
Barry M. Goldwater (R)

Representatives

John J. Rhodes (R)
Eldon Rudd (R)
Bob Stump (D)
Morris K. Udall (D)

Arkansas

Senators

Dale Bumpers (D)
David Pryor (D)

Representatives

William V. Alexander, Jr. (D)
Beryl Anthony, Jr. (D)
Edwin R. Bethune, Jr. (R)
John P. Hammerschmidt (R)

California

Senators

Alan Cranston (D)
Sam I. Hayakawa (R)

Representatives

Glenn M. Anderson (D)
Robert E. Badham (R)
Anthony C. Beilenson (D)
George E. Brown, Jr. (D)
Clair W. Burgener (R)
John L. Burton (D)
Phillip Burton (D)
Don H. Clausen (R)
Tony Coelho (D)
James C. Corman (D)
George E. Danielson (D)
William E. Dannemeyer (R)
Ronald V. Dellums (D)
Julian C. Dixon (D)
Robert K. Dornan (R)
Don Edwards (D)
Victor H. Fazio (D)
Barry M. Goldwater, Jr. (R)
Wayne Grisham (R)
Augustus F. Hawkins (D)
Harold T. Johnson (D)
Robert J. Lagomarsino (R)
Jerry Lewis (R)
James F. Lloyd (D)
Daniel E. Lungren (R)
Paul N. McCloskey, Jr. (R)
Robert T. Matsui (D)
George Miller (D)
Norman Y. Mineta (D)
Carlos J. Moorhead (R)
Leon E. Panetta (D)
Charles Pashayan, Jr. (R)
Jerry M. Patterson (D)
John H. Rousselot (R)
Edward R. Roybal (D)
Leo J. Ryan (D)
Norman D. Shumway (R)
Fortney H. Stark, Jr. (D)
William M. Thomas (R)
Lionel Van Deerlin (D)
Henry A. Waxman (D)
Charles H. Wilson (D)
Robert C. Wilson (R)

Colorado

Senators

William L. Armstrong (R)
Gary Hart (D)

Representatives

James P. Johnson (R)
Ray P. Kogovsek (D)
Ken Kramer (R)
Patricia Schroeder (D)
Timothy E. Wirth (D)

Connecticut

Senators

Abraham A. Ribicoff (D)
Lowell P. Weicker, Jr. (R)

Representatives

William R. Cotter (D)

Christopher J. Dodd (D)
Robert N. Giaimo (D)
Stewart B. McKinney (R)
Anthony T. Moffett (D)
William R. Ratchford (D)

Delaware

Senators

Joseph R. Biden, Jr. (D)
William V. Roth, Jr. (R)

Representatives

Thomas B. Evans, Jr. (R)

Florida

Senators

Lawton M. Chiles (D)
Richard Stone (D)

Representatives

Louis A. (Skip) Bafalis (R)
Charles E. Bennett (D)
William V. Chappell, Jr. (D)
Dante B. Fascell (D)
Don Fuqua (D)
Sam M. Gibbons (D)
Earl D. Hutto (D)
Andrew P. Ireland (D)
Richard Kelly (R)
William Lehman (D)
Daniel A. Mica (D)
C. William (Bill) Nelson (D)
Claude D. Pepper (D)
Edward J. Stack (D)
C. W. Bill Young (R)

Georgia

Senators

Sam Nunn (D)
Herman E. Talmadge (D)

Representatives

Druie D. (Doug) Barnard, Jr.
 (D)
Jack T. Brinkley (D)
Billy Lee Evans D)
Wyche Fowler, Jr. (D)
Newton L. Gingrich (R)
Ronald B. (Bo) Ginn (D)
Edgar L. Jenkins (D)
Elliott H. Levitas (D)
M. Dawson Mathis (D)
Larry P. McDonald (D)

Hawaii

Senators

Daniel K. Inouye (D)
Spark M. Matsunaga (D)

Representatives

Daniel K. Akaka (D)
Cecil Heftel (D)

Idaho

Senators

Frank Church (D)
James A. McClure (R)

Representatives

George Hansen (R)
Steven D. Symms (R)

Illinois

Senators

Charles H. Percy (R)
Adlai E. Stevenson, III (D)

Representatives

John B. Anderson (R)
Frank Annunzio (D)
Cardiss Collins (D)
Tom Corcoran (R)
Daniel B. Crane (R)
Philip M. Crane (R)
Edward J. Derwinski (R)
John N. Erlenborn (R)
John G. Fary (D)
Paul Findley (R)
Henry J. Hyde (R)
Robert M. McClory (R)
Edward R. Madigan (R)
Robert H. Michel (R)
Abner J. Mikva (D)
Morgan F. Murphy (D)
George M. O'Brien (R)
C. Melvin Price (D)
Thomas F. Railsback (R)
Daniel D. Rostenkowski (D)
Martin A. Russo (D)
Paul Simon (D)
Bennett M. Stewart (D)
Sidney R. Yates (D)

Indiana

Senators

Birch Bayh (D)
Richard G. Lugar (R)

Representatives

Adam Benjamin, Jr. (D)
John Brademas (D)
H. Joel Deckard (R)
David W. Evans (D)
Floyd J. Fithian (D)
Lee H. Hamilton (D)
Elwood H. Hillis (R)
Andrew Jacobs, Jr. (D)
John T. Myers (R)
J. Danforth Quayle (R)
Philip R. Sharp (D)

Iowa

Senators

John C. Culver (D)
Roger W. Jepsen (R)

Representatives

Berkley Bedell (D)

Charles E. Grassley (R)
Tom Harkin (D)
James A. S. Leach (R)
Neal Smith (D)
Thomas J. Tauke (R)

Kansas

Senators

Robert J. Dole (R)
Nancy Landon Kassebaum (R)

Representatives

Daniel R. Glickman (D)
James E. Jeffries (R)
Keith G. Sebelius (R)
Larry Winn, Jr. (R)
Robert R. Whittaker (R)

Kentucky

Senators

Wendell H. Ford (D)
Walter D. Huddleston (D)

Representatives

Tim Lee Carter (R)
Larry J. Hopkins (R)
Carroll Hubbard, Jr. (D)
Romano L. Mazzoli (D)
William Natcher (D)
Carl D. Perkins (D)
M. Gene Snyder (R)

Louisiana

Senators

J. Bennett Johnston, Jr. (D)
Russell B. Long (D)

Representatives

Lindy Boggs (D)
John B. Breaux (D)
Thomas J. (Jerry) Huckaby (D)
Claude Leach (D)
Robert L. Livingston (R)
Gillis W. Long (D)
W. Henson Moore (R)
David C. Treen (R)

Maine

Senators

William S. Cohen (R)
Edmund S. Muskie (D)

Representatives

David F. Emery (R)
Olympia J. Snowe (R)

Maryland

Senators

Charles McC. Mathias, Jr. (R)
Paul S. Sarbanes (D)

Representatives

Michael D. Barnes (D)
Robert E. Bauman (R)
Beverly B. Byron (D)
Marjorie S. Holt (R)
Clarence D. Long (D)
Barbara A. Mikulski (D)
Parren J. Mitchell (D)
Gladys Noon Spellman (D)

Massachusetts

Senators

Edward M. Kennedy (D)
Paul E. Tsongas (D)

Representatives

Edward P. Boland (D)
Silvio O. Conte (R)
Brian J. Donnelly (D)
Robert F. Drinan (D)
Joseph D. Early (D)
Margaret M. Heckler (R)
Edward J. Markey (D)
Nicholas Mavroules (D)
John J. Moakley (D)
Thomas P. O'Neill, Jr. (D)
James M. Shannon (D)
Gerry E. Studds (D)

Michigan

Senators

Carl Levin (D)
Donald W. Riegle, Jr. (D)

Representatives

Donald J. Albosta (D)
James J. Blanchard (D)
David E. Bonior (D)
William M. Brodhead (D)
William S. Broomfield (R)
M. Robert Carr (D)
John Conyers, Jr. (D)
Robert W. Davis (R)
Charles C. Diggs, Jr. (D)
John D. Dingell (D)
William D. Ford (D)
Dale E. Kildee (D)
Lucien N. Nedzi (D)
Carl D. Pursell (R)
Harold S. Sawyer (R)
David A. Stockman (R)
Bob Traxler (D)
Guy Vander Jagt (R)
Howard Wolpe (D)

Minnesota

Senators

Rudolph E. Boschwitz (R)
David Durenberger (R)

Representatives

Arlen Erdahl (R)
William E. Frenzel (R)
Thomas M. Hagedorn (R)
Richard Nolan (D)
James L. Oberstar (D)
Martin O. Sabo (D)
Arlan Strangeland (R)

Bruce F. Vento (D)

Mississippi

Senators

Thad Cochran (R)
John C. Stennis (D)

Representatives

David R. Bowen (D)
Jon C. Hinson (R)
Trent Lott (R)
Gillespie V. Montgomery (D)
Jamie L. Whitten (D)

Missouri

Senators

John C. Danforth (R)
Thomas F. Eagleton (D)

Representatives

Richard Bolling (D)
Bill D. Burlison (D)
William L. Clay (D)
E. Thomas Coleman (R)
Richard A. Gephardt (D)
Richard H. Ichord (D)
Ike N. Skelton, Jr. (D)
Gene Taylor (R)
Harold L. Volkmer (D)
Robert A. Young (D)

Montana

Senators

Max Baucus (D)
John Melcher (D)

Representatives

Ronald C. Marlenee (R)
Pat Williams (D)

Nebraska

Senators

J. James Exon (D)
Edward Zorinsky (D)

Representatives

Douglas K. Bereuter (R)
John J. Cavanaugh (D)
Virginia Smith (R)

Nevada

Senators

Howard W. Cannon (D)
Paul Laxalt (R)

Representatives

James D. Santini (D)

New Hampshire

Senators

John A. Durkin (D)
Gordon J. Humphrey (R)

Representatives

James C. Cleveland (R)
Norman E. D'Amours (D)

New Jersey

Senators

Bill Bradley (D)
Harrison A. Williams, Jr. (D)

Representatives

James A. Courter (R)
Millicent H. Fenwick (R)
James J. Florio (D)
Edwin B. Forsythe (R)
Frank J. Guarini (D)
Harold C. Hollenbeck (R)
James J. Howard (D)
William J. Hughes (D)
Andrew Maguire (D)
Joseph G. Minish (D)
Edward J. Patten (D)
Matthew J. Rinaldo (R)
Peter W. Rodino, Jr. (D)
Robert A. Roe (D)
Frank Thompson, Jr. (D)

New Mexico

Senators

Pete V. Domenici (R)
Harrison Schmitt (R)

Representatives

Manuel Lujan, Jr. (R)
Harold Runnels (D)

New York

Senators

Jacob K. Javits (R)
Daniel P. Moynihan (D)

Representatives

Joseph P. Addabbo (D)
Jerome A. Ambro, Jr. (D)
Mario Biaggi (D)
Jonathan B. Bingham (D)
William Carney (R)
Shirley Chisholm (D)
Barber B. Conable (R)
Thomas J. Downey (D)
Geraldine A. Ferraro (D)
Hamilton Fish, Jr. (R)
Robert Garcia (D)
Benjamin A. Gilman (R)
S. William Green (R)
James M. Hanley (D)
Elizabeth Holtzman (D)
Frank J. Horton (D)
Jack F. Kemp (R)
John J. LaFalce (D)
Gary A. Lee (R)

Norman F. Lent (R)
Stanley N. Lundine (D)
Robert C. McEwen (R)
Matthew F. McHugh (D)
Donald J. Mitchell (R)
John M. Murphy (D)
Henry J. Nowak (D)
Richard L. Ottinger (D)
Peter A. Peyser (D)
Charles B. Rangel (D)
Frederick W. Richmond (D)
Benjamin S. Rosenthal (D)
James H. Scheuer (D)
Stephen J. Solarz (D)
Gerald B. H. Solomon (R)
Samuel S. Stratton (D)
Ted S. Weiss (D)
Lester L. Wolff (D)
John W. Wydler (R)
Leo C. Zeferetti (D)

North Carolina

Senators

Jesse A. Helms (R)
Robert Morgan (D)

Representatives

Ike F. Andrews (D)
James T. Broyhill (R)
L. H. Fountain (D)
Lamar Gudger (D)
W. G. (Bill) Hefner (D)
Walter B. Jones (D)
James G. Martin (R)
Stephen L. Neal (D)
L. Richardson Preyer (D)
Charles G. Rose (D)
Charles Whitly (D)

North Dakota

Senators

Quentin N. Burdick (D)
Milton R. Young (R)

Representatives

Mark Andrews (R)

Ohio

Senators

John Glenn (D)
Howard M. Metzenbaum (D)

Representatives

Douglas Applegate (D)
John M. Ashbrook (R)
Thomas L. Ashley (D)
Clarence J. Brown (R)
Samuel L. Devine (R)
Willis D. Gradison, Jr. (R)
Tennyson Guyer (R)
Tony P. Hall (D)
William H. Harsha (R)
Thomas N. Kindness (R)
Delbert L. Latta (R)
Thomas A. Luken (D)
Clarence E. Miller (R)
Ronald M. Mottl (D)
Mary Rose Oakar (D)
Donald J. Pease (D)

Ralph S. Regula (R)
John F. Seiberling (D)
J. William Stanton (R)
Louis Stokes (D)
Charles A. Vanik (D)
Lyle Williams (R)
Chalmers P. Wylie (R)

Oklahoma

Senators

Henry L. Bellmon (R)
David L. Boren (D)

Representatives

Marvin H. (Mickey) Edward (R)
Glenn English (D)
James R. Jones (D)
Tom Steed (D)
Michael L. Synar (D)
Wesley W. Watkins (D)

Oregon

Senators

Mark O. Hatfield (R)
Robert W. Packwood (R)

Representatives

Les AuCoin (D)
Robert B. Duncan (D)
Al Ullman (D)
James Weaver (D)

Pennsylvania

Senators

H. John Heinz, III (R)
Richard S. Schweiker (R)

Representatives

Eugene V. Atkinson (D)
Donald A. Bailey (D)
William F. Clinger, Jr. (R)
R. Lawrence Coughlin (R)
Charles F. Dougherty (R)
Robert W. Edgar (D)
Allen E. Ertel (D)
Daniel J. Flood (D)
Joseph M. Gaydos (D)
William F. Goodling (R)
William H. Gray, III (D)
Peter H. Kostmayer (D)
Raymond F. Lederer (D)
Joseph M. McDade (R)
Marc L. Marks (R)
William S. Moorhead (D)
Austin J. Murphy (D)
John P. Murtha (D)
Michael Myers (D)
Donald L. Ritter (R)
Richard T. Schulze (R)
Bud Shuster (R)
Doug Walgren (D)
Robert S. Walker (R)
Gus Yatron (D)

Rhode Island

Senators

John H. Chafee (R)
Claiborne Pell (D)

Representatives

Edward P. Beard (D)
Fernand J. St. Germain (D)

South Carolina

Senators

Ernest F. Hollings (D)
Strom Thurmond (R)

Representatives

Carroll A. Campbell, Jr. (R)
Mendel J. Davis (D)
Butler Derrick (D)
Kenneth L. Holland (D)
John W. Jenrette, Jr. (D)
Floyd D. Spence (R)

South Dakota

Senators

George McGovern (D)
Larry Pressler (R)

Representatives

James Abdnor (R)
Thomas A. Daschle (D)

Tennessee

Senators

Howard H. Baker, Jr. (R)
James R. Sasser (D)

Representatives

Robin L. Beard, Jr. (R)
William H. Boner (D)
John J. Duncan (R)
Harold E. Ford (D)
Albert Gore, Jr. (D)
Ed Jones (D)
Marilyn Lloyd (D)
James H. Quillen (R)

Texas

Senators

Lloyd M. Bentsen, Jr. (D)
John G. Tower (R)

Representatives

William R. Archer (R)
Jack B. Brooks (D)
James M. Collins (R)
Eligio de la Garza (D)
Robert C. Eckhardt (D)
Martin Frost (D)
Henry B. Gonzalez (D)
William P. Gramm (D)
Sam B. Hall, Jr. (D)

Kent Hance (D)
Jack E. Hightower (D)
Abraham Kazen, Jr. (D)
Marvin Leath (D)
George T. Leland (D)
Thomas G. Loeffler (R)
James A. Mattox (D)
Ronald E. Paul (R)
James J. Pickle (D)
Ray Roberts (D)
Charles W. Stenholm (D)
Richard C. White (D)
Charles Wilson (D)
James C. Wright, Jr. (D)
Joe Wyatt, Jr. (D)

Utah

Senators

Edwin J. (Jake) Garn (R)
Orrin G. Hatch (R)

Representatives

David D. Marriott (R)
Gunn McKay (D)

Vermont

Senators

Patrick J. Leahy (D)
Robert T. Stafford (R)

Representatives

James M. Jeffords (R)

Virginia

Senators

Harry F. Byrd, Jr. (Ind.)
John W. Warner (R)

Representatives

M. Caldwell Butler (R)
W. C. (Dan) Daniel (D)
Robert W. Daniel, Jr. (R)
Joseph L. Fisher (D)
Herbert E. Harris, II (D)
J. Kenneth Robinson (R)
David E. Satterfield (D)
Paul S. Trible, Jr. (R)
William C. Wampler (R)
G. William Whitehurst (R)

Washington

Senators

Henry M. Jackson (D)
Warren G. Magnuson (D)

Representatives

Don L. Bonker (D)
Norman D. Dicks (D)
Thomas S. Foley (D)
Michael E. Lowry (D)
Mike McCormack (D)
Joel Pritchard (R)
Allan B. Swift (D)

West Virginia

Senators

Robert C. Byrd (D)
Jennings Randolph (D)

Representatives

Robert H. Mollohan (D)
Nick J. Rahall, II (D)
John M. Slack (D)
Harley O. Staggers (D)

Wisconsin

Senators

Gaylord A. Nelson (D)
William Proxmire (D)

Representatives

Les Aspin (D)
Alvin Baldus (D)
Robert W. Kastenmeier (D)
David R. Obey (D)
Henry S. Reuss (D)
Toby Roth (R)
F. James Sensenbrenner, Jr. (R)
William A. Steiger (R)
Clement J. Zablocki (D)

Wyoming

Senators

Alan K. Simpson (R)
Malcolm Wallop (R)

Representatives

Richard B. Cheney (R)

Ninety-Seventh Congress

(Jan. 3, 1981, to
Jan. 3, 1983)

President of the Senate: George
  Bush
*Speaker of the House of
  Representatives:* Thomas P.
  O'Neill, Jr.

Alabama

Senators

Jeremiah Denton (R)
Howell Heflin (D)

Representatives

Tom Bevill (D)
William L. Dickinson (R)
Jack Edwards (R)
Ronnie G. Flippo (D)
William Nichols (D)
Richard C. Shelby (D)
Albert L. Smith, Jr. (R)

Alaska

Senators

Frank H. Murkowski (R)
Theodore F. Stevens (R)

Representatives

Donald E. Young (R)

Arizona

Senators

Dennis DeConcini (D)
Barry M. Goldwater (R)

Representatives

John J. Rhodes (R)
Eldon Rudd (R)
Bob Stump (D)
Morris K. Udall (D)

Arkansas

Senators

Dale Bumpers (D)
David Pryor (D)

Representatives

William V. Alexander, Jr. (D)
Beryl Anthony, Jr. (D)
Edwin R. Bethune, Jr. (R)
John P. Hammerschmidt (R)

California

Senators

Alan Cranston (D)
Sam I. Hayakawa (R)

Representatives

Glenn M. Anderson (D)
Robert E. Badham (R)
Anthony C. Beilenson (D)
George E. Brown, Jr. (D)
Clair W. Burgener (R)
John L. Burton (D)
Phillip Burton (D)
Gene Chappie (R)
Don H. Clausen (R)
Tony Coelho (D)
George E. Danielson (D)
William E. Dannemeyer (R)
Ronald V. Dellums (D)
Julian C. Dixon (D)
Robert K. Dornan (R)
David Dreier (R)
Mervyn M. Dymally (D)
Don Edwards (D)
Victor H. Fazio (D)
Bobbi Fiedler (R)
Barry M. Goldwater, Jr. (R)
Wayne Grisham (R)
Augustus F. Hawkins (D)
Duncan Hunter (R)
Robert J. Lagomarsino (R)
Tom Lantos (D)
Jerry Lewis (R)
Bill Lowry (R)
Daniel E. Lungren (R)

Paul N. McCloskey, Jr. (R)
Robert T. Matsui (D)
George Miller (D)
Norman Y. Mineta (D)
Carlos J. Moorhead (R)
Leon E. Panetta (D)
Charles Pashayan, Jr. (R)
Jerry M. Patterson (D)
John H. Rousselot (R)
Edward R. Roybal (D)
Norman D. Shumway (R)
Fortney H. Stark (D)
William N. Thomas (R)
Henry A. Waxman (D)

Colorado

Senators

William L. Armstrong (R)
Gary Hart (D)

Representatives

Hank Brown (R)
Ray P. Kogovsek (D)
Ken Kramer (R)
Patricia Schroeder (D)
Timothy E. Wirth (D)

Connecticut

Senators

Christopher J. Dodd (D)
Lowell P. Weicker, Jr. (R)

Representatives

William R. Cotter (D)
Lawrence J. DeNardis (R)
Samuel Gejdenson (D)
Stewart B. McKinney (R)
Anthony T. Moffett (D)
William R. Ratchford (D)

Delaware

Senators

Joseph R. Biden, Jr. (D)
William V. Roth, Jr. (D)

Representatives

Thomas B. Evans, Jr. (R)

Florida

Senators

Lawton M. Chiles, Jr. (D)
Paula Hawkins (R)

Representatives

Louis A. (Skip) Bafalis (R)
Charles E. Bennett (D)
William V. Chappell, Jr. (D)
Dante B. Fascell (D)
Don Fuqua (D)
Sam M. Gibbons (D)
Earl Hutto (D)
Andrew P. Ireland (D)
William Lehman (D)
Bill McCollum (R)
Daniel A. Mica (D)

C. William (Bill) Nelson (D)
Claude D. Pepper (D)
E. Clay Shaw (R)
C. W. Bill Young (R)

Georgia

Senators

Mack F. Mattingly (R)
Sam Nunn (D)

Representatives

Druie D. (Doug) Barnard, Jr.
 (D)
Jack T. Brinkley (D)
Billy Lee Evans (D)
Wyche Fowler, Jr. (D)
Newt Gingrich (R)
Ronald B. (Bo) Ginn (D)
Charles Hatcher (D)
Edgar L. Jenkins (D)
Elliott H. Levitas (D)
Larry P. McDonald (D)

Hawaii

Senators

Daniel K. Inouye (D)
Spark M. Matsunaga (D)

Representatives

Daniel K. Akaka (D)
Cecil Heftel (D)

Idaho

Senators

James A. McClure (R)
Steven D. Symms (R)

Representatives

Larry E. Craig (R)
George Hansen (R)

Illinois

Senators

Alan J. Dixon (D)
Charles H. Percy (R)

Representatives

Frank Annunzio (D)
Cardiss Collins (D)
Tom Corcoran (R)
Daniel B. Crane (R)
Philip M. Crane (R)
Edward J. Denwinski (R)
John N. Erlenborn (R)
John G. Fary (D)
Paul Findley (R)
Henry J. Hyde (R)
Robert McClory (R)
Edward R. Madigan (R)
Lynn Martin (R)
Robert H. Michel (R)
George M. O'Brien (R)
John E. Porter (R)
C. Melvin Price (D)
Thomas F. Railsback (R)

Daniel D. Rostenkowski (D)
Marty Russo (D)
Augustus Savage (D)
Paul Simon (D)
Harold Washington (D)
Sidney R. Yates (D)

Indiana

Senators

Richard G. Lugar (R)
Dan Quayle (R)

Representatives

Adam Benjamin, Jr. (D)
Daniel R. Coats (R)
Joel Deckard (R)
David W. Evans (D)
Floyd J. Fithian (D)
Lee H. Hamilton (D)
John P. Hiler (R)
Elwood H. Hillis (R)
Andrew Jacobs, Jr. (D)
John T. Myers (R)
Philip R. Sharp (D)

Iowa

Senators

Charles E. Grassley (R)
Roger W. Jepsen (R)

Representatives

Berkley Bedell (D)
Cooper Evans (R)
Tom Harkin (D)
James A. S. Leach (R)
Neal Smith (D)
Thomas J. Tauke (R)

Kansas

Senators

Robert J. Dole (R)
Nancy Landon Kassebaum (R)

Representatives

Daniel R. Glickman (D)
James E. Jeffries (R)
C. Patrick Roberts (R)
Larry Winn, Jr. (R)
Robert R. Whittaker (R)

Kentucky

Senators

Wendell H. Ford (D)
Walter D. Huddleston (D)

Representatives

Larry J. Hopkins (R)
Carroll Hubbard, Jr. (D)
Romano L. Mazzoli (D)
William H. Natcher (D)
Carl D. Perkins (D)
Harold Rogers (R)
M. Gene Snyder (R)

Louisiana

Senators

J. Bennett Johnston (D)
Russell B. Long (D)

Representatives

Lindy Boggs (D)
John B. Breaux (D)
Thomas J. (Jerry) Huckaby (D)
Robert L. Livingston (R)
Gillis W. Long (D)
W. Henson Moore (R)
Buddy Roemer (D)
W. J. (Billy) Tauzin (D)

Maine

Senators

William S. Cohen (R)
George J. Mitchell (D)

Representatives

David F. Emery (R)
Olympia J. Snowe (R)

Maryland

Senators

Charles McC. Mathias, Jr. (R)
Paul S. Sarbanes (D)

Representatives

Michael D. Barnes (D)
Beverly B. Byron (D)
Roy Dyson (D)
Marjorie S. Holt (R)
Steny H. Hoyer (D)
Clarence D. Long (D)
Barbara A. Mikulski (D)
Parren J. Mitchell (D)

Massachusetts

Senators

Edward M. Kennedy (D)
Paul E. Tsongas (D)

Representatives

Edward P. Boland (D)
Silvio O. Conte (R)
Brian J. Donnelly (D)
Joseph D. Early (D)
Barney Frank (D)
Margaret M. Heckler (R)
Edward J. Markey (D)
Nicholas Mavroules (D)
John J. Moakley (D)
Thomas P. O'Neill, Jr. (D)
James M. Shannon (D)
Gerry E. Studds (D)

Michigan

Senators

Carl Levin (D)
Donald W. Riegle, Jr. (D)

Representatives

Donald J. Albosta (D)
James J. Blanchard (D)
David E. Bonior (D)
William M. Brodhead (D)
William S. Broomfield (R)
John Conyers, Jr. (D)
George W. Crockett, Jr. (D)
Robert W. Davis (R)
John D. Dingell (D)
James W. Dunn (R)
William D. Ford (D)
Dennis M. Hertel (D)
Dale E. Kildee (D)
Carl D. Pursell (R)
Howard S. Sawyer (R)
Mark D. Siljander (R)
Bob Traxler (D)
Guy Vander Jagt (R)
Howard Wolpe (D)

Minnesota

Senators

David Durenberger (R)
Rudolph E. Boschwitz (R)

Representatives

Arlen Erdahl (R)
William E. Frenzel (R)
Thomas M. Hagedorn (R)
James L. Oberstar (D)
Martin O. Sabo (D)
Arlan Strangeland (R)
Bruce F. Vento (D)
Vin Weber (R)

Mississippi

Senators

Thad Cochran (R)
John C. Stennis (D)

Representatives

David R. Bowen (D)
Jon Hinson (R)
Trent Lott (R)
Gillespie V. Montgomery (D)
Jamie L. Whitten (D)

Missouri

Senators

John C. Danforth (R)
Thomas F. Eagleton (D)

Representatives

Wendell Bailey (R)
Richard Bolling (D)
William L. Clay (D)
E. Thomas Coleman (R)
Bill Emerson (R)
Richard A. Gephardt (D)
Ike N. Skelton, Jr. (D)
Gene Taylor (D)
Harold L. Volkmer (D)
Robert A. Young (D)

Montana

Senators

Max Baucus (D)
John Melcher (D)

Representatives

Ronald C. Marlenee (R)
Pat Williams (D)

Nebraska

Senators

J. James Exon (D)
Edward Zorinsky (D)

Representatives

Douglas K. Bereuter (R)
Harold (Hal) Daub, Jr. (R)
Virginia Smith (R)

Nevada

Senators

Howard W. Cannon (D)
Paul Laxalt (R)

Representatives

James D. Santini (D)

New Hampshire

Senators

Gordon J. Humphrey (R)
Warren Rudman (R)

Representatives

Norman E. D'Amours (D)
Judd A. Gregg (R)

New Jersey

Senators

Bill Bradley (D)
Harrison A. Williams, Jr. (D)

Representatives

James A. Courter (R)
Bernard J. Dwyer (D)
Millicent Fenwick (R)
James J. Florio (D)
Edwin B. Forsythe (R)
Frank J. Guarini (D)
Harold C. Hollenbeck (R)
James J. Howard (D)
William J. Hughes (D)
Joseph G. Minish (D)
Matthew J. Rinaldo (R)
Peter W. Rodino, Jr. (D)
Robert A. Roe (D)
Marge Roukema (R)
Christopher H. Smith (R)

New Mexico

Senators

Pete V. Domenici (R)
Harrison Schmitt (R)

Representatives

Manuel Lujan, Jr. (R)
Joseph R. Skeen (R)

New York

Senators

Alphonse M. D'Amato (R)
Daniel P. Moynihan (D)

Representatives

Joseph P. Addabbo (D)
Mario Biaggi (D)
Jonathan B. Bingham (D)
Gregory W. Carman (R)
William Carney (R)
Shirley Chisholm (D)
Barber B. Conable, Jr. (R)
Thomas J. Downey (D)
Geraldine A. Ferraro (D)
Hamilton Fish, Jr. (R)
Robert Garcia (D)
Benjamin A. Gilman (R)
Bill Green (R)
Frank J. Horton (R)
Jack F. Kemp (R)
John J. LaFalce (D)
John LeBoutillier (R)
Gary A. Lee (R)
Norman F. Lent (R)
Stanley N. Lundine (D)
Raymond J. McGrath (R)
Matthew F. McHugh (D)
David O'B. Martin (R)
Donald J. Mitchell (R)
Guy V. Molinari (R)
Henry J. Nowak (D)
Richard L. Ottinger (D)
Peter A. Peyser (D)
Charles B. Rangel (D)
Frederick W. Richmond (D)
Benjamin S. Rosenthal (D)
James H. Scheuer (D)
Charles E. Schumer (D)
Stephen J. Solarz (D)
Gerald B. H. Solomon (R)
Samuel S. Stratton (D)
Theodore Weiss (D)
George C. Wortley (R)
Leo C. Zeferetti (D)

North Carolina

Senators

John P. East (R)
Jesse A. Helms (R)

Representatives

Ike F. Andrews (D)
James T. Broyhill (R)
L. H. Fountain (D)
W. G. Hefner (D)
William M. Hendon (R)
Eugene Johnston (R)
Walter B. Jones (D)
James G. Martin (R)

Stephen L. Neal (D)
Charles G. Rose (D)
Charles O. Whitley (D)

North Dakota

Senators

Mark Andrews (R)
Quentin N. Burdick (D)

Representatives

Byron L. Dorgan (D)

Ohio

Senators

John Glenn (D)
Howard M. Metzenbaum (D)

Representatives

Douglas Applegate (D)
John M. Ashbrook (R)
Clarence J. Brown (R)
Dennis E. Eckart (D)
Willis D. Gradison, Jr. (R)
Tennyson Guyer (R)
Tony P. Hall (D)
Thomas N. Kindness (R)
Delbert L. Latta (R)
Thomas A. Luken (D)
Bob McEwen (R)
Clarence E. Miller (R)
Ronald M. Mottl (D)
Mary Rose Oakar (D)
Donald J. Pease (D)
Ralph S. Regula (R)
John F. Seiberling (D)
Robert N. Shamansky (D)
J. William Stanton (R)
Louis Stokes (D)
Edward F. Weber (R)
Lyle Williams (R)
Chalmers P. Wylie (R)

Oklahoma

Senators

David L. Boren (D)
Don Nickles (R)

Representatives

Marvin H. (Mickey) Edwards (R)
Glenn English (D)
James R. Jones (D)
Dave McCurdy (D)
Michael L. Synar (D)
Wesley W. Watkins (D)

Oregon

Senators

Mark O. Hatfield (R)
Robert W. Packwood (R)

Representatives

Les AuCoin (D)
Denny Smith (R)
James Weaver (D)

Ronald L. Wyden (D)

Pennsylvania

Senators

H. John Heinz, III (R)
Arlen Specter (R)

Representatives

Eugene V. Atkinson (D)
Donald A. Bailey (D)
William F. Clinger, Jr. (R)
R. Lawrence Coughlin (R)
James K. Coyne (R)
William J. Coyne (D)
Charles F. Dougherty (R)
Robert W. Edgar (D)
Allen E. Ertel (D)
Thomas M. Foglietta (Ind.)
Joseph M. Gaydos (D)
William F. Goodling (R)
William H. Gray, III (D)
Raymond F. Lederer (D)
Joseph M. McDade (R)
Marc L. Marks (R)
Austin J. Murphy (D)
John P. Murtha (D)
James L. Nelligan (R)
Donald L. Ritter (R)
Richard T. Schulze (R)
Bud Shuster (R)
Doug Walgren (D)
Robert S. Walker (R)
Gus Yatron (D)

Rhode Island

Senators

John H. Chafee (R)
Claiborne Pell (D)

Representatives

Fernand J. St. Germain (D)
Claudine Schneider (R)

South Carolina

Senators

Ernest F. Hollings (D)
Strom Thurmond (R)

Representatives

Carroll A. Campbell, Jr. (R)
Butler Derrick (D)
Thomas F. Harnett (R)
Kenneth L. Holland (D)
John L. Napier (R)
Floyd D. Spence (R)

South Dakota

Senators

James Abdnor (R)
Larry Pressler (R)

Representatives

Thomas A. Daschle (D)
Clint Roberts (R)

Tennessee

Senators

Howard H. Baker, Jr. (R)
James R. Sasser (D)

Representatives

Robin L. Beard, Jr. (R)
William H. Boner (D)
Marilyn Lloyd Bouquard (D)
John J. Duncan (R)
Harold E. Ford (D)
Albert Gore, Jr. (D)
Ed Jones (D)
James H. Quillen (R)

Texas

Senators

Lloyd M. Benton, Jr. (D)
John G. Tower (R)

Representatives

William R. Archer (R)
Jack B. Brooks (D)
James M. Collins (R)
Eligio de la Garza (D)
Jack M. Fields, Jr. (R)
Martin Frost (D)
Henry B. Gonzalez (D)
William P. Gramm (D)
Ralph M. Hall (D)
Sam B. Hall, Jr. (D)
Kent Hance (D)
Jack E. Hightower (D)
Abraham Kazen, Jr. (D)
Marvin Leath (D)
George T. (Mickey) Leland (D)
Thomas G. Loeffler (R)
James A. Mattox (D)
William N. Patman (D)
Ronald E. Paul (R)
J. J. Pickle (D)
Charles W. Stenholm (D)
Richard C. White (D)
Charles Wilson (D)
James C. Wright (D)

Utah

Senators

Edwin J. (Jake) Garn (R)
Orrin G. Hatch (R)

Representatives

James V. Hansen (R)
David D. Marriott (R)

Vermont

Senators

Patrick J. Leahy (D)
Robert T. Stafford (R)

Representatives

James M. Jeffords (R)

Virginia

Senators

Harry F. Byrd, Jr. (Ind.)
John W. Warner (R)

Representatives

Thomas J. Bliley, Jr. (R)
M. Caldwell Butler (R)
Dan Daniel (D)
Robert W. Daniel, Jr. (R)
Stanford E. Parris (R)
J. Kenneth Robinson (R)
Paul S. Trible, Jr. (R)
William C. Wampler (R)
G. William Whitehurst (R)
Frank R. Wolf (R)

Washington

Senators

Slade Gorton (R)
Henry M. Jackson (D)

Representatives

Don L. Bonker (D)
Norman D. Dicks (D)
Thomas S. Foley (D)
Michael E. Lowry (D)
Sid Morrison (R)
Joel Pritchard (R)
Allan B. Swift (D)

West Virginia

Senators

Robert C. Byrd (D)
Jennings Randolph (D)

Representatives

Cleve Benedict (R)
Robert H. Mollohan (D)
Nick J. Rahall (D)
David M. (Mick) Staton (R)

Wisconsin

Senators

Robert W. Kasten, Jr. (R)
William Proxmire (D)

Representatives

Les Aspin (D)
Steven Gunderson (R)
Robert W. Kastenmeier (D)
David R. Obey (D)
Thomas E. Petri (R)
Henry S. Reuss (D)
Toby Roth (R)
F. James Sensenbrenner, Jr. (R)
Clement J. Zablocki (D)

Wyoming

Senators

Alan K. Simpson (R)
Malcolm Wallop (R)

Representatives

Richard B. Cheney (R)

Ninety-Eighth Congress

(Jan. 3, 1983, to
Jan. 3, 1985)

President of the Senate: George Bush
Speaker of the House of Representatives: Thomas P. O'Neill, Jr.

Alabama

Senators

Jeremiah Denton (R)
Howell Heflin (D)

Representatives

Tom Bevill (D)
William L. Dickinson (R)
Jack Edwards (R)
Ben Erdreich (D)
Ronnie G. Flippo (D)
William Nichols (D)
Richard C. Shelby (D)

Alaska

Senators

Frank H. Murkowski (R)
Theodore F. Stevens (R)

Representatives

Donald E. Young (R)

Arizona

Senators

Dennis DeConcini (D)
Barry M. Goldwater (D)

Representatives

John McCain (R)
James F. McNulty, Jr. (D)
Eldon Rudd (R)
Bob Stump (D)
Morris K. Udall (D)

Arkansas

Senators

Dale Bumpers (D)
David Pryor (D)

Representatives

William V. Alexander, Jr. (D)
Beryl Anthony, Jr. (D)
Edwin R. Bethune, Jr. (R)
John P. Hammerschmidt (R)

California

Senators

Alan Cranston (D)
Pete Wilson (R)

Representatives

Glenn M. Anderson (D)
Roy Archer (D)
Robert E. Badham (R)
Jim Bates (D)
Anthony C. Beilenson (D)
Howard L. Berman (D)
Douglas H. Bosco (D)
Barbara Boxer (D)
George E. Brown, Jr. (D)
Sala Burton (D)
Gene Chappie (R)
Tony Coelho (D)
William E. Dannemeyer (R)
Ronald V. Dellums (D)
Julian C. Dixon (D)
David Dreier (R)
Mervyn M. Dymally (D)
Don Edwards (D)
Victor H. Fazio (D)
Bobbi Fiedler (R)
Augustus F. Hawkins (D)
Duncan Hunter (R)
Robert J. Lagomarsino (R)
Tom Lantos (D)
Richard Lehman (D)
Meldon E. Levine (D)
Jerry Lewis (R)
Bill Lowery (R)
Daniel E. Lungren (R)
Alfred A. McCandless (R)
Matthew G. Martinez (D)
Robert T. Matsui (D)
George Miller (D)
Norman Y. Mineta (D)
Carlos J. Moorhead (R)
Leon E. Panetta (D)
Charles Pashayan, Jr. (R)
Jerry M. Patterson (D)
Edward R. Roybal (D)
Norman D. Shumway (R)
Fortney H. Stark (D)
William M. Thomas (R)
Esteban Torres (D)
Henry A. Waxman (D)
Edwin V. Zschau (R)

Colorado

Senators

William L. Armstrong (R)
Gary Hart (D)

Representatives

Hank Brown (R)
Ray P. Kogovsek (D)
Ken Kramer (R)
Paricia Schroeder (D)
Jack Swigert (R)
Timothy E. Wirth (D)

Connecticut

Senators

Christopher J. Dodd (D)
Lowell P. Weicker, Jr. (R)

Representatives

Samuel Gejdenson (D)
Nancy L. Johnson (R)
Barbara B. Kennelly (D)
Stewart B. McKinney (R)
Bruce A. Morrison (D)
William R. Ratchford (D)

Delaware

Senators

Joseph R. Biden, Jr. (D)
William V. Roth, Jr. (R)

Representatives

Thomas R. Carper (D)

Florida

Senators

Lawton M. Chiles, Jr. (D)
Paula Hawkins (R)

Representatives

Charles E. Bennett (D)
Michael Bilirakis (R)
William V. Chappell, Jr. (D)
Dante B. Fascell (D)
Don Fuqua (D)
Sam M. Gibbons (D)
Earl Hutto (D)
Andrew P. Ireland (D)
William Lehman (D)
Thomas F. Lewis (R)
Bill McCollum (R)
Connie Mack (R)
Kenneth H. MacKay (D)
Daniel A. Mica (D)
C. William (Bill) Nelson (D)
Claude D. Pepper (D)
Clay Shaw, Jr. (R)
Larry Smith (D)
C. W. Bill Young (R)

Georgia

Senators

Mack F. Mattingly (R)
Sam Nunn (D)

Representatives

Druie D. (Doug) Barnard, Jr. (D)
Wyche Fowler, Jr. (D)
Newt Gingrich (R)
Charles Hatcher (D)
Edgar L. Jenkins (D)
Elliott H. Levitas (D)
Larry P. McDonald (D)
Richard Roy (D)
J. Roy Rowland (D)
Lindsay Thomas (D)

Hawaii

Senators

Daniel K. Inouye (D)
Spark M. Matsunaga (D)

Representatives

Daniel K. Akaka (D)
Cecil Heftel (D)

Idaho

Senators

James A. McClure (R)
Steven D. Symms (R)

Representatives

Larry E. Craig (R)
George Hansen (R)

Illinois

Senators

Alan J. Dixon (D)
Charles H. Percy (R)

Representatives

Frank Annunzio (D)
Cardiss Collins (D)
Tom Corcoran (R)
Daniel B. Crane (R)
Philip M. Crane (R)
Richard J. Durbin (D)
John N. Erlenborn (R)
Lane Evans (D)
Henry J. Hyde (R)
William O. Lipinski (D)
Edward R. Madigan (R)
Lynn Martin (R)
Robert H. Michel (R)
George M. O'Brien (R)
John E. Porter (R)
C. Melvin Price (D)
Daniel D. Rostenkowski (D)
Marty Russo (D)
Augustus Savage (D)
Paul Simon (D)
Harold Washington (D)
Hidney R. Yates (D)

Indiana

Senators

Richard G. Lugar (R)
Dan Quayle (R)

Representatives

Dan L. Burton (R)
Daniel R. Coats (R)
Katie Hall (D)
Lee H. Hamilton (D)
John Hiler (R)
Elwood H. Hillis (R)
Andrew Jacobs, Jr. (D)
Francis X. McCloskey (D)
John T. Myers (R)
Philip R. Sharp (D)

Iowa

Senators

Charles E. Grassley (R)
Roger W. Jepsen (R)

Representatives

Berkley Bedell (D)
Cooper Evans (R)
Tom Harkin (D)
James A. S. Leach (R)
Neal Smith (D)
Thomas J. Tauke (R)

Kansas

Senators

Robert J. Dole (R)
Nancy Landon Kassebaum (R)

Representatives

Daniel R. Glickman (D)
C. Patrick Roberts (R)
James E. Slattery (D)
Robert R. Whittaker (R)
Larry Winn, Jr. (R)

Kentucky

Senators

Wendell H. Ford (D)
Walter D. Huddleston (D)

Representatives

Larry J. Hopkins (R)
Carroll Hubbard, Jr. (D)
Romano L. Mazzoli (D)
William H. Natcher (D)
Carl D. Perkins (D)
Harold Rogers (R)

Louisiana

Senators

J. Bennett Johnston (D)
Russell B. Long (D)

Representatives

Lindy Boggs (D)
John B. Breaux (D)
Thomas J. (Jerry) Huckaby (D)
Robert L. Livingston (R)
Gillis W. Long (D)
W. Henson Moore (R)
Buddy Roemer (D)
W. J. Tauzin (D)

Maine

Senators

William S. Cohen (R)
George J. Mitchell (D)

Representatives

John R. McKernan, Jr. (R)
Olympia J. Snowe (R)

Maryland

Senators

Charles McC. Mathias, Jr. (R)
Paul S. Sarbanes (D)

Representatives

Michael D. Barnes (D)
Beverly B. Byron (D)
Roy Dyson (D)
Marjorie S. Holt (R)
Steny H. Hoyer (D)
Clarence D. Long (D)
Barbara A. Mikulski (D)
Parren J. Mitchell (D)

Massachusetts

Senators

Edward M. Kennedy (D)
Paul E. Tsongas (D)

Representatives

Edward P. Boland (D)
Silvio O. Conte (R)
Brian J. Donnelly (D)
Joseph D. Early (D)
Barney Frank (D)
Edward J. Markey (D)
Nicholas Mavroules (D)
John J. (Joe) Moakley (D)
Thomas P. O'Neill, Jr. (D)
James M. Shannon (D)
Gerry E. Studds (D)

Michigan

Senators

Carl Levin (D)
Donald W. Riegle, Jr. (D)

Representatives

Donald J. Albosta (D)
David E. Bonior (D)
William S. Broomfield (R)
M. Robert Carr (D)
John Conyers, Jr. (D)
George W. Crockett, Jr. (D)
Robert W. Davis (R)
John D. Dingell (D)
William D. Ford (D)
Dennis M. Hertel (D)
Dale E. Kildee (D)
Sander Levin (D)
Carl D. Pursell (R)
Harold S. Sawyer (R)
Mark D. Siljander (R)
Bob Traxler (D)
Guy Traxler (D)
Guy Vander Jagt (R)
Howard Wolpe (D)

Minnesota

Senators

Rudolph E. Boschwitz (R)
David Durenberger (R)

Representatives

William E. Frenzel (R)
James L. Oberstar (D)
Timothy J. Penny (D)
Martin O. Sabo (D)
Gerry Sikorski (D)
Arlan Strangeland (D)
Bruce F. Vento (D)
Vin Weber (R)

Mississippi

Senators

Thad Cochran (R)
John C. Stennis (D)

Representatives

Wayne Dowdy (D)
Webb Franklin (R)
Trent Lott (R)
Gillespie V. Montgomery (D)
Jamie L. Whitten (D)

Missouri

Senators

John C. Danforth (R)
Thomas F. Eagleton (D)

Representatives

William L. Clay (D)
E. Thomas Coleman (R)
Bill Emerson (R)
Richard A. Gephardt (D)
Ike N. Skelton, Jr. (D)
Gene Taylor (R)
Harold L. Volkmer (D)
Alan Wheat (D)
Robert A. Young (D)

Montana

Senators

Max Baucus (D)
John Melcher (D)

Representatives

Ronald C. Marlenee (R)
Pat Williams (D)

Nebraska

Senators

J. James Exon (D)
Edward Zorinsky (D)

Representatives

Douglas K. Bereuter (R)
Harold (Hal) Daub, Jr. (R)
Virginia Smith (R)

Nevada

Senators

Chic Hecht (R)
Paul Laxalt (R)

Representatives

Harry Reid (D)
Barbara Vucanovich (R)

New Hampshire

Senators

Gordon J. Humphrey (R)
Warren Rudman (R)

Representatives

Norman E. D'Amours (D)
Judd Gregg (R)

New Jersey

Senators

Bill Bradley (D)
Frank R. Lautenberg (D)

Representatives

James A. Courter (R)
Bernard J. Dwyer (D)
James J. Florio (D)
Edwin B. Forsythe (R)
Frank J. Guarini (D)
James J. Howard (D)
William J. Hughes (D)
Joseph G. Minish (D)
Matthew J. Rinaldo (R)
Peter W. Rodino, Jr. (D)
Robert A. Roe (D)
Marge Roukema (R)
Christopher H. Smith (R)
Robert G. Torricelli (D)

New Mexico

Senators

Jeff Bingaman (D)
Pete V. Domenici (R)

Representatives

Manuel Lujan, Jr. (R)
Bill Richardson (D)
Joseph R. Skeen (R)

New York

Senators

Alphonse M. D'Amato (R)
Daniel P. Moynihan (D)

Representatives

Joseph P. Addabbo (D)
Mario Biaggi (D)
Sherwood L. Boehlert (R)
William Carney (R)
Barber B. Conable, Jr. (R)
Thomas J. Downey (D)
Geraldine A. Ferraro (D)
Hamilton Fish, Jr. (R)
Robert Garcia (D)
Benjamin A. Gilman (R)
Bill Green (R)
Frank J. Horton (R)
Jack F. Kemp (R)
John J. LaFalce (D)
Norman F. Lent (R)
Stanley N. Lundine (D)
Raymond J. McGrath (R)
Matthew F. McHugh (D)
David O'B. Martin (R)

Guy V. Molinari (R)
Robert J. Mrazek (D)
Henry J. Nowak (D)
Richard L. Ottinger (D)
Major R. Owens (D)
Charles B. Rangel (D)
Benjamin S. Rosenthal (D)
James H. Scheuer (D)
Charles E. Schumer (D)
Stephen J. Solarz (D)
Gerald B. H. Solomon (R)
Samuel S. Stratton (D)
Edolphus Towns (D)
Theodore Weiss (D)
George C. Wortley (R)

North Carolina

Senators

John P. East (R)
Jesse A. Helms (R)

Representatives

Ike F. Andrews (D)
Charles R. Britt (D)
James T. Broyhill (R)
James M. Clarke (D)
W. G. Hefner (D)
Walter B. Jones (D)
James G. Martin (R)
Stephen L. Neal (D)
Charles G. Rose, III (D)
I. T. Valentine, Jr. (D)
Charles O. Whitley (D)

North Dakota

Senators

Mark Andrews (R)
Quentin N. Burdick (D)

Representatives

Byron L. Dorgan (D)

Ohio

Senators

John Glenn (D)
Howard M. Metzenbaum (D)

Representatives

Douglas Applegate (D)
Michael Dewine (R)
Dennis E. Eckart (D)
Edward F. Feighan (D)
Willis D. (Bill) Gradison, Jr. (R)
Tony P. Hall (D)
Marcy Kaptur (D)
John R. Kasich (R)
Thomas N. Kindness (R)
Delbert L. Latta (R)
Thomas A. Luken (D)
Bob McEwen (R)
Clarence E. Miller (R)
Mary Rose Oakar (D)
Michael Oxley (R)
Donald J. Pease (D)
Ralph S. Regula (R)
John F. Seiberling (D)
Louis Stokes (D)
Lyle Williams (R)

Chalmers P. Wylie (R)

Oklahoma

Senators

David L. Boren (D)
Don Nickles (R)

Representatives

Marvin H. (Mickey) Edwards (R)
Glenn English (D)
James R. Jones (D)
Dave McCurdy (D)
Michael L. (Mike) Synar (D)
Wesley W. Watkins (D)

Oregon

Senators

Mark O. Hatfield (R)
Robert W. Packwood (R)

Representatives

Les AuCoin (D)
Bob Smith (R)
Denny Smith (R)
James Weaver (D)

Pennsylvania

Senators

John Heinz (R)
Arlen Specter (R)

Representatives

Robert A. Borski (D)
William F. Clinger, Jr. (R)
R. Lawrence Coughlin (R)
William J. Coyne (D)
Robert W. Edgar (D)
Thomas M. Foglietta (D)
Joseph M. Gaydos (D)
George W. Gekas (R)
William F. Goodling (R)
William H. Gray, III (D)
Frank Harrison (D)
Joseph P. Kolter (D)
Peter H. Kostmayer (D)
Joseph M. McDade (R)
Austin J. Murphy (D)
John P. Murtha (D)
Thomas J. Ridge (R)
Donald L. Ritter (R)
Richard T. Schulze (R)
Bud Shuster (R)
Doug Walgren (D)
Robert S. Walker (R)
Gus Yatron (D)

Rhode Island

Senators

John H. Chafee (R)
Claiborne Pell (D)

Representatives

Fernand J. St. Germain (D)
Claudine Schneider (R)

South Carolina

Senators

Ernest F. Hollings (D)
Strom Thurmond (R)

Representatives

Carroll A. Campbell, Jr. (R)
Butler Derrick (D)
Thomas F. Harnett (R)
Floyd D. Spence (R)
John Spratt (D)
Robert M. Tallon, Jr. (D)

South Dakota

Senators

James Abdnor (R)
Larry Pressler (R)

Representatives

Thomas A. Daschle (D)

Tennessee

Senators

Howard H. Baker, Jr. (R)
James R. Sasser (D)

Representatives

William H. Boner (D)
Marilyn Lloyd Bouquard (D)
James H. S. Cooper (D)
John J. Duncan (R)
Harold E. Ford (D)
Albert Gore, Jr. (D)
Ed Jones (D)
James H. Quillen (R)
Donald K. Sunquist (R)

Texas

Senators

Lloyd M. Bentsen, Jr. (D)
John G. Tower (R)

Representatives

Michael A. Andrew (D)
William R. Archer (R)
Steve Bartlett (R)
Jack B. Brooks (D)
John Bryant (D)
Ronald Coleman (D)
Eligio de la Garza (D)
Jack M. Fields, Jr. (R)
Martin Frost (D)
Henry B. Gonzalez (D)
William P. Gramm (D)
Ralph M. Hall (D)
Sam B. Hall, Jr. (D)
Kent Hance (D)
Jack E. Hightower (D)
Abraham Kazen, Jr. (D)
Marvin Leath (D)
George T. (Mickey) Leland (D)
Thomas G. Loeffler (R)
Solomon P. Ortiz (D)
William N. Patman (D)
Ronald E. Paul (R)

J. J. Pickle (D)
Charles W. Stenholm (D)
Tom Vandergriff (D)
Charles Wilson (D)
James C. Wright (D)

Utah

Senators

Edwin J. Garn (R)
Orrin G. Hatch (R)

Representatives

James V. Hansen (R)
David D. Marriott (R)
Howard C. Nielson (R)

Vermont

Senators

Patrick J. Leahy (D)
Robert T. Stafford (R)

Representatives

James M. Jeffords (R)

Virginia

Senators

Paul S. Trible, Jr. (R)
John J. Warner (R)

Representatives

Herbert Bateman (R)
Thomas J. Bliley, Jr. (R)
Frederick Boucher (D)
Dan Daniel (D)
James Olin (D)
Stanford E. Parris (R)
J. Kenneth Robinson (R)
Norman Sisisky (D)
G. William Whitehurst (R)
Frank R. Wolf (R)

Washington

Senators

Slade Gorton (R)
Henry M. Jackson (D)

Representatives

Don L. Bonker (D)
Rodney Chandler (R)
Norman D. Dicks (D)
Thomas S. Foley (D)
Michael E. Lowry (D)
Sid Morrison (R)
Joel Pritchard (R)
Allan B. Swift (D)

West Virginia

Senators

Robert C. Byrd (D)
Jennings Randolph (D)

Representatives

Alan B. Mollohan (D)
Nick J. Rahall, II (D)
Harley O. Staggers, Jr. (D)
Robert E. Wise, Jr. (D)

Wisconsin

Senators

Robert W. Kasten, Jr. (R)
William Proxmire (D)

Representatives

Les Aspin (D)
Steven Gunderson (R)
Robert Kastenmeier (D)
James P. Moody (D)
David R. Obey (D)
Thomas E. Petri (R)
Toby Roth (R)
F. James Sensenbrenner, Jr. (R)

Wyoming

Senators

Alan K. Simpson (R)
Malcolm Wallop (R)

Representatives

Richard B. Cheney (R)

Ninety-Ninth Congress

(Jan. 3, 1985, to
Jan. 3, 1987)

President of the Senate: George
  Bush
*Speaker of the House of
  Representatives:* Thomas P.
  O'Neill, Jr.

Alabama

Senators

Jeremiah Denton (R)
Howell Heflin (D)

Representatives

Tom Bevill (D)
H. L. (Sonny) Callahan (R)
William L. Dickinson (R)
Ben Erdreich (D)
Ronnie G. Flippo (D)
William Nichols (D)
Richard C. Shelby (D)

Alaska

Senators

Frank Murkowski (R)
Theodore F. Stevens (R)

Representatives

Donald E. Young (R)

Arizona

Senators

Dennis DeConcini (D)
Barry M. Goldwater (R)

Representatives

John McCain (R)
James T. Kolbe (R)
Eldon Rudd (R)
Bob Stump (R)
Morris K. Udall (D)

Arkansas

Senators

Dale Bumpers (D)
David Pryor (D)

Representatives

William V. Alexander, Jr. (D)
Beryl Anthony, Jr. (D)
John P. Hammerschmidt (R)
Tommy F. Robinson (D)

California

Senators

Alan Cranston (D)
Pete Wilson (R)

Representatives

Glenn M. Anderson (D)
Robert E. Badham (R)
Jim Bates (D)
Anthony C. Bellenson (D)
Howard L. Berman (D)
Douglas H. Bosco (D)
Barbara Boxer (D)
George E. Brown, Jr. (D)
Sala Burton (D)
Gene Chappie (R)
Tony Coelho (D)
William E. Dannemeyer (R)
Ronald V. Dellums (D)
Julian C. Dixon (D)
Robert K. Dornan (R)
David Dreier (R)
Mervyn M. Dymally (D)
Don Edwards (D)
Victor H. Fazio (D)
Bobbi Fiedler (R)
Augustus F. Hawkins (D)
Duncan Hunter (R)
Robert J. Lagomarsino (R)
Tom Lantos (D)
Richard H. Lehman (D)
Meldon E. Levine (D)
Jerry Lewis (R)
Bill Lowery (R)
Daniel E. Lungren (R)
Alfred A. McCandless (R)
Matthew G. Martinez (D)
Robert T. Matsui (D)
George Miller (D)
Norman Y. Mineta (D)
Calos J. Moorhead (R)
Ron Packard (R)

Leon E. Panetta (D)
Charles Pashayan, Jr. (R)
Edward R. Roybal (D)
Norman Shumway (R)
Fortney H. Stark (D)
William M. Thomas (R)
Esteban E. Torres (D)
Henry A. Waxman (D)
Edwin V. Zschau (R)

Colorado

Senators

William L. Armstrong (R)
Gary Hart (D)

Representatives

Hank Brown (R)
Ken Kramer (R)
Daniel Schaefer (R)
Patricia Schroeder (D)
Michael L. Strang (R)
Timothy E. Wirth (D)

Connecticut

Senators

Christopher J. Dodd (D)
Lowell P. Weicker, Jr. (R)

Representatives

Samuel Gejdenson (D)
Nancy L. Johnson (R)
Barbara B. Kennelly (D)
Stewart B. McKinney (R)
Bruce A. Morrison (D)
John G. Rowland (R)

Delaware

Senators

Joseph R. Biden, Jr. (D)
William V. Roth, Jr. (R)

Representatives

Thomas R. Carper (D)

Florida

Senators

Lawton M. Chiles, Jr. (D)
Paula Hawkins (R)

Representatives

Charles E. Bennett (D)
Michael Bilirakis (R)
William V. Chappell, Jr. (D)
Dante B. Fascell (D)
Don Fuqua (D)
Sam M. Gibbons (D)
Earl Hutto (D)
Andrew P. Ireland (R)
William Lehman (D)
Thomas F. Lewis (R)
Bill McCollum (R)
Connie Mack (R)
Kenneth H. MacKay (D)
Daniel A. Mica (D)
C. William Nelson (D)

Claude D. Pepper (D)
Clay Shaw, Jr. (R)
Larry Smith (D)
C. W. Bill Young (R)

Georgia

Senators

Mack F. Mattingly (R)
Sam Nunn (D)

Representatives

Druie D. (Doug) Barnard, Jr. (D)
George Darden (D)
Wyche Fowler, Jr. (D)
Newt Gingrich (R)
Charles Hatcher (D)
Edgar L. Jenkins (D)
Richard Ray (D)
J. Roy Rowland (D)
Patrick Swindall (R)
Lindsay Thomas (D)

Hawaii

Senators

Daniel K. Inouye (D)
Spark M. Matsunaga (D)

Representatives

Daniel K. Akaka (D)
Cecil Heftel (D)

Idaho

Senators

James A. McClure (R)
Steven D. Symms (R)

Representatives

Larry E. Craig (R)
Richard Stallings (D)

Illinois

Senators

Alan J. Dixon (D)
Paul Simon (D)

Representatives

Frank Annunzio (D)
Terry Bruce (D)
Cardiss Collins (D)
Philip M. Crane (R)
Richard J. Durbin (D)
Lane Evans (D)
Harris Fawell (R)
Kenneth J. Gray (D)
John Grotberg (R)
Charles Hayes (D)
Henry J. Hyde (R)
William O. Lipinski (D)
Edward R. Madigan (R)
Lynn Martin (R)
Robert H. Michel (R)
George M. O'Brien (R)
John E. Porter (R)
Melvin Price (D)

Daniel D. Rostenkowski (D)
Marty Russo (D)
Augustus Savage (D)
Sidney R. Yates (D)

Indiana

Senators

Richard G. Lugar (R)
Dan Quayle (R)

Representatives

Dan L. Burton (R)
Daniel R. Coats (R)
Lee H. Hamilton (D)
John Hiler (R)
Elwood H. Hillis (R)
Andrew Jacobs, Jr. (D)
Richard McIntyre (R)
John T. Myers (R)
Philip R. Sharp (D)
Peter Vicloskey (D)

Iowa

Senators

Charles E. Grassley (R)
Tom Harkin (D)

Representatives

Berkley Bedell (D)
Cooper Evans (R)
James A. S. Leach (R)
James Lightfoot (R)
Neal Smith (D)
Thomas J. Tauke (R)

Kansas

Senators

Robert J. Dole (R)
Nancy Landon Kassebaum (R)

Representatives

Daniel R. Glickman (D)
Jan Myers (R)
C. Patrick Roberts (R)
James E. Slattery (D)
Robert R. Whittaker (R)

Kentucky

Senators

Wendell H. Ford (D)
Addison M. McConnell (R)

Representatives

Larry J. Hopkin (R)
Carroll Hubbard, Jr.(D)
Romano L. Mazzoli (D)
William H. Natcher (D)
Carl D. Perkins (D)
Harold Rogers (R)
M. Gene Snyder (R)

Louisiana

Senators

J. Bennett Johnston (D)
Russell B. Long (D)

Representatives

Lindy Boggs (D)
John B. Breaux (D)
Thomas J. (Jerry) Huckaby (D)
Robert L. Livingston (R)
Cathy Long (D)
W. Henson Moore (R)
Buddy Roemer (D)
W. J. Tauzin (D)

Maine

Senators

William S. Cohen (R)
George J. Mitchell (D)

Representatives

John R. McKernan, Jr. (R)
Olympia J. Snowe (R)

Maryland

Senators

Charles McC. Mathias, Jr. (R)
Paul S. Sarbanes (D)

Representatives

Michael D. Barnes (D)
Helen D. Bentley (R)
Beverly B. Byron (D)
Roy Dyson (D)
Marjorie S. Holt (R)
Steny H. Hoyer (D)
Barbara A. Mikulski (D)
Parren J. Mitchell (D)

Massachusetts

Senators

Edward M. Kennedy (D)
John Kerry (D)

Representatives

Chester Atkins (D)
Edward P. Boland (D)
Silvio O. Conte (R)
Brian J. Donnelly (D)
Joseph D. Early (D)
Barney Frank (D)
Edward J. Markey (D)
Nicholas Mavroules (D)
John J. Moakley (D)
Thomas P. O'Neill, Jr. (D)
Gerry E. Studds (D)

Michigan

Senators

Carl Levin (D)
Donald W. Riegle, Jr. (D)

Representatives

David E. Bonior (D)
William S. Broomfield (R)
M. Robert Carr (D)
John Conyers, Jr. (D)
George W. Crockett, Jr. (D)
Robert W. Davis (R)
John D. Dingell (D)
William D. Ford (D)
Paul Henry (R)
Dennis M. Hertel (D)
Dale E. Kildee (D)
Sander Levin (D)
Carl D. Pursell (R)
Bill Schuette (R)
Mark D. Siljander (R)
Bob Traxler (D)
Guy Vander Jagt (R)
Howard Wolpe (D)

Minnesota

Senators

Rudolph E. Boschwitz (R)
David Durenberger (R)

Representatives

William E. Frenzel (R)
James L. Oberstar (D)
Timothy J. Penny (D)
Martin O. Sabo (D)
Gerry Sikorski (D)
Arlan Strangeland (R)
Bruce F. Vento (D)
Vin Weber (R)

Mississippi

Senators

Thad Cochran (R)
John C. Stennis (D)

Representatives

Wayne Dowdy (D)
Webb Franklin (R)
Trent Lott (R)
Gillespie V. Montgomery (D)
Jamie L. Whitten (D)

Missouri

Senators

John C. Danforth (R)
Thomas F. Eagleton (D)

Representatives

William L. Clay (D)
E. Thomas Coleman (R)
Bill Emerson (R)
Richard A. Gephardt (D)
Ike N. Skelton, Jr. (D)
Gene Taylor (R)
Harold L. Volkmer (D)
Alan Wheat (D)
Robert A. Young (D)

Montana

Senators

Max Baucus (D)
John Melcher (D)

Representatives

Ronald C. Marlenee (R)
Pat Williams (D)

Nebraska

Senators

J. James Exon (D)
Edward Zorinsky (D)

Representatives

Douglas K. Bereuter (R)
Harold (Hal) Daub, Jr. (R)
Virginia Smith (R)

Nevada

Senators

Chic Hecht (R)
Paul Laxalt (R)

Representatives

Harry Reid (D)
Barbara Vucanovich (R)

New Hampshire

Senators

Gordon J. Humphrey (R)
Warren Rudman (R)

Representatives

Judd A. Gregg (R)
Robert C. Smith (R)

New Jersey

Senators

Bill Bradley (D)
Frank R. Lautenberg (D)

Representatives

James A. Courter (R)
Bernard J. Dwyer (D)
James J. Florio (D)
Dean Gallo (R)
Frank J. Guarini (D)
James J. Howard (D)
William J. Hughes (D)
Matthew J. Rinaldo (R)
Peter W. Rodino, Jr. (D)
Robert A. Roe (D)
Marge Roukema (R)
H. James Saxton (R)
Christopher H. Smith (R)
Robert G. Torricelli (D)

New Mexico

Senators

Jeff Bingaman (D)
Pete V. Domenici (R)

Representatives

Manuel Lujan, Jr. (R)
Bill Richardson (D)
Joseph R. Skeen (R)

New York

Senators

Alphonse D'Amato (R)
Daniel P. Moynihan (D)

Representatives

Gary Ackerman (D)
Joseph P. Addabbo (D)
Mario Biaggi (D)
Sherwood L. Boehlert (R)
William Carney (R)
Joseph J. DioGuardi (R)
Thomas J. Downey (D)
Fred J. Eckert (R)
Hamilton Fish, Jr. (R)
Robert Garcia (D)
Benjamin A. Gilman (R)
Bill Green (R)
Frank Horton (R)
Jack F. Kemp (R)
John J. LaFalce (D)
Norman F. Lent (R)
Stanley N. Lundine (D)
Raymond J. McGrath (R)
Matthew F. McHugh (D)
Thomas Manton (D)
David O'B. Martin (R)
Guy V. Molinari (R)
Robert J. Mrazek (D)
Henry J. Nowak (D)
Major R. Owens (D)
Charles B. Rangel (D)
James H. Scheuer (D)
Charles E. Schumer (D)
Stephen J. Solarz (D)
Gerald B. H. Solomon (R)
Samuel S. Stratton (D)
Edolphus Towns (D)
Theodore Weiss (D)
George C. Wortley (R)

North Carolina

Senators

John P. East (R)
Jesse Helms (R)

Representatives

James T. Broyhill (R)
William Cobey, Jr. (R)
J. Howard Coble (R)
W. G. Hefner (D)
William M. Hendon (R)
Walter B. Jones (D)
Alex McMillan (R)
Stephen L. Neal (D)
Charles G. Rose, III (D)
I. T. Valentine, Jr. (D)
Charles O. Whitley (D)

North Dakota

Senators

Mark Andrews (R)
Quentin N. Burdick (D)

Representatives

Byron L. Dorgan (D)

Ohio

Senators

John Glenn (D)
Howard M. Metzenbaum (D)

Representatives

Douglas Applegate (D)
Michael Dewine (R)
Dennis E. Eckart (D)
Edward F. Feighan (D)
Willis D. Gradison (R)
Tony P. Hall (D)
Marcy Kaptur (D)
John R. Kasich (R)
Thomas N. Kindness (R)
Delbert L. Latta (R)
Thomas A. Luken (D)
Bob McEwen (R)
Clarence E. Miller (R)
Mary Rose Oakar (D)
Michael Oxley (R)
Donald J. Pease (D)
Ralph S. Regula (R)
John F. Seiberling (D)
Louis Stokes (D)
James Traficant (D)
Chalmers P. Wylie (R)

Oklahoma

Senators

David L. Boren (D)
Don Nickles (R)

Representatives

Marvin H. (Mickey) Edwards
(R)
Glenn English (D)
James R. Jones (D)
Dave McCurdy (D)
Michael L. Synar (D)
Wesley W. Watkins (D)

Oregon

Senators

Mark O. Hatfield (R)
Robert W. Packwood (R)

Representatives

Les AuCoin (D)
Bob Smith (R)
Denny Smith (R)
James Weaver (D)
Ronald L. Wyden (D)

Pennsylvania

Senators

John Heinz (R)
Arlen Specter (R)

Representatives

Robert A. Borski (D)
William F. Clinger, Jr. (R)
Lawrence Coughlin (R)
William J. Coyne (D)
Robert W. Edgar (D)
Thomas M. Foglietta (D)
Joseph M. Gaydos (D)
George W. Gekas (R)
William F. Goodling (R)
William H. Gray, III (D)
Paul Kanjorski (D)
Joseph P. Kolter (D)
Peter H. Kostmayer (D)
Joseph M. McDade (R)
Austin J. Murphy (D)
John P. Murtha (D)
Thomas J. Ridge (R)
Donald L. Ritter (R)
Richard T. Schulze (R)
Bud Shuster (R)
Doug Walgren (D)
Robert S. Walker (R)
Gus Yatron (D)

Rhode Island

Senators

John H. Chafee (R)
Claiborne Pell (D)

Representatives

Fernand J. St. Germain (D)
Claudine Schneider (R)

South Carolina

Senators

Ernest F. Hollings (D)
Strom Thurmond (R)

Representatives

Carroll A. Campbell, Jr. (R)
Butler Derrick (D)
Thomas F. Harnett (R)
Floyd Spence (R)
John Spratt (D)
Robert M. Tallon, Jr. (D)

South Dakota

Senators

James Abdnor (R)
Larry Pressler (R)

Representatives

Thomas A. Daschle (D)

Tennessee

Senators

Albert Gore, Jr. (D)
James R. Sasser (D)

Representatives

William H. Boner (D)
James H. S. Cooper (D)
John J. Duncan (R)
Harold E. Ford (D)
Barton J. Gordon (D)
Ed Jones (D)
Marilyn Lloyd (D)
James H. Quillen (R)
Donald K. Sundquist (R)

Texas

Senators

Lloyd M. Bentsen, Jr. (D)
Phil Gramm (R)

Representatives

Michael A. Andrews (D)
William R. Archer (R)
Richard K. Armey (R)
Steve Bartlett (R)
Joe L. Barton (R)
Beau Boulter (R)
Jack B. Brooks (D)
John Bryant (D)
Albert Bustamente (D)
Ronald Coleman (D)
Larry E. Combest (R)
Eligio de la Garza (D)
Thomas D. DeLay (R)
Jack M. Fields, Jr. (R)
Martin Frost (D)
Henry B. Gonzalez (D)
Ralph M. Hall (D)
Sam B. Hall, Jr. (D)
Marvin Leath (D)
George T. (Mickey) Leland (D)
Thomas G. Loeffler (R)

Solomon P. Ortiz (D)
J. J. Pickle (D)
Charles W. Stenholm (D)
David McC. Sweeney (R)
Charles Wilson (D)
James C. Wright (D)

Utah

Senators

Edwin J. Garn (R)
Orrin G. Hatch (R)

Representatives

James V. Hansen (R)
David D. Monson (R)
Howard C. Nielson (R)

Vermont

Senators

Patrick J. Leahy (D)
Robert T. Stafford (R)

Representatives

James M. Jeffords (R)

Virginia

Senators

Paul S. Trible, Jr. (R)
John W. Warner (R)

Representatives

Herbert Bateman (R)
Thomas J. Bliley, Jr. (R)
Frederick Boucher (D)
Dan Daniel (D)
James Olin (D)
Stanford E. Parris (R)
Norman Sisisky (D)
French D. Slaughter, Jr. (R)
G. William Whitehurst (R)
Frank R. Wolf (R)

Washington

Senators

Daniel J. Evans (R)
Slade Gorton (R)

Representatives

Don L. Bonker (D)
Rodney Chandler (R)
Norman D. Dicks (D)
Thomas S. Foley (D)
Michael E. Lowry (D)
John Miller (R)
Sid Morrison (R)
Allan B. Swift (D)

West Virginia

Senators

Robert C. Byrd (D)
John D. Rockefeller, IV (D)

Representatives

Alan B. Mollohan (D)
Nick J. Rahall, II (D)
Harley O. Staggers, Jr. (D)
Robert E. Wise, Jr. (D)

Wisconsin

Senators

Robert W. Kasten, Jr. (R)
William Proxmire (D)

Representatives

Les Aspin (D)
Steven Gunderson (R)
Robert Kastenmeier (D)
Gerald D. Kleczka (D)
James P. Moody (D)
David R. Obey (D)
Thomas E. Petri (R)
Toby Roth (R)
F. James Sensenbrenner, Jr. (R)

Wyoming

Senators

Alan K. Simpson (R)
Malcolm Wallop (R)

Representatives

Richard B. Cheney (R)

V

U.S. Government: Judicial Branch

Justices of the Supreme Court of the United States

Chief Justices

1789-1795	John Jay
1795	John Rutledge
1796-1800	Oliver Ellsworth
1801-1835	John Marshall
1836-1864	Roger B. Taney
1864-1873	Salmon P. Chase
1874-1888	Morrison R. Waite
1888-1910	Melville W. Fuller
1910-1921	Edward D. White
1921-1930	William Howard Taft
1930-1941	Charles Evans Hughes
1941-1946	Harlan F. Stone
1946-1953	Fred M. Vinson
1953-1969	Earl Warren
1969-1986	Warren E. Burger
1986-	William H. Rehnquist

Associate Justices

1789-1791	John Rutledge
1789-1810	William Cushing
1789-1798	James Wilson
1789-1796	John Blair
1790-1799	James Iredell
1791-1793	Thomas Johnson
1793-1806	William Paterson
1796-1811	Samuel Chase
1789-1829	Bushrod Washington
1799-1804	Alfred Moore
1804-1834	William Johnson
1806-1823	Henry B. Livingston
1807-1826	Thomas Todd
1811-1836	Gabriel Duval
1811-1845	Joseph Story
1823-1843	Smith Thompson
1826-1828	Robert Trimble
1829-1861	John McLean
1830-1844	Henry Baldwin
1835-1867	James M. Wayne
1836-1841	Philip P. Barbour
1837-1865	John Catron
1837-1852	John McKinley
1841-1860	Peter V. Daniel
1845-1872	Samuel Nelson
1845-1851	Levi Woodbury
1846-1870	Robert C. Grier
1851-1857	Benjamin R. Curtis
1853-1861	John A. Campbell
1858-1881	Nathan Clifford
1862-1881	Noah H. Swayne
1862-1890	Samuel F. Miller
1862-1877	David Davis
1863-1897	Stephen J. Field
1870-1880	William Strong
1870-1892	Joseph P. Bradley
1872-1882	Ward Hunt
1877-1911	John M. Harlan
1880-1887	William B. Woods
1881-1889	Stanley Matthews
1881-1902	Horace Gray
1882-1893	Samuel Blatchford
1888-1893	Lucius Q. C. Lamar
1889-1910	David J. Brewer
1890-1906	Henry B. Brown
1892-1903	George Shiras, Jr.
1893-1895	Howell E. Jackson
1894-1910	Edward D. White
1895-1909	Rufus W. Peckham
1898-1925	Joseph McKenna
1902-1932	Oliver Wendell Holmes
1903-1922	William R. Day
1906-1910	William H. Moody
1910-1914	Horace H. Lurton
1910-1916	Charles Evans Hughes
1910-1937	Willis Van Devanter
1910-1916	Joseph R. Lamar
1912-1922	Mahlon Pitney
1914-1941	James C. McReynolds
1916-1939	Louis D. Brandeis
1916-1922	John H. Clarke
1922-1938	George Sutherland
1922-1939	Pierce Butler
1923-1930	Edward T. Sanford
1925-1941	Harlan F. Stone
1930-1945	Owen J. Roberts
1932-1938	Benjamin N. Cardozo
1937-1971	Hugo L. Black
1938-1957	Stanley F. Reed
1939-1962	Felix Frankfurter
1939-1975	William O. Douglas
1940-1949	Frank Murphy
1941-1942	James F. Byrnes
1941-1954	Robert H. Jackson
1943-1949	Wiley B. Rutledge
1945-1958	Harold H. Burton
1945-1967	Tom C. Clark
1949-1956	Sherman Minton
1955-1971	John Marshall Harlan
1956-	William J. Brennan, Jr.
1957-1962	Charles E. Whittaker
1959-1981	Potter Stewart
1962-	Byron R. White
1962-1965	Arthur J. Goldberg
1965-1969	Abe Fortas
1967-	Thurgood Marshall
1970-	Harry A. Blackmun
1971-1987	Lewis F. Powell, Jr.
1971-1986	William H. Rehnquist
1975-	John Paul Stevens
1981-	Sandra Day O'Connor
1986-	Antonin Scalia

Justices of the Circuit Courts of Appeals and Other High Court Judges

U.S. Court of Appeals for the First Circuit

Boston, MA

1891-1913	LeBaron B. Colt
1892-1917	William L. Putnam
1905-1911	Francis C. Lowell
1911-1912	William Schofield
1912-1918	Frederic Dodge
1913-1939	George H. Bingham
1917-1929	Charles F. Johnson
1918-1931	George W. Anderson
1929-1940	Scott Wilson
1932-1939	James M. Morton, Jr.
1939-1959	Calvert Magruder
1940-1950	John C. Mahoney
1941-1964	Peter Woodbury
1951-1965	John P. Hartigan
1959-	Bailey Aldrich
1965-1980	Edward M. McEntee
1965-	Frank M. Coffin
1972-	Levin Hicks Campbell
1977-	Hugh Henry Bownes
1980-	Stephen Gerald Breyer
1985-	Juan R. Torruella

U.S. Court of Appeals for the Second Circuit

New York, NY

1882-1906	William J. Wallace
1888-1915	E. Henry LaCombe
1892-1902	Nathaniel Shipman
1902-1907	William K. Townsend
1902-1917	Alfred C. Coxe
1908-1923	Henry G. Ward
1908-1913	Walter C. Noyes
1913-1927	Henry W. Rogers
1916-1927	Charles M. Hough
1916-1939	Martin T. Manton
1921-1924	Julius M. Mayer
1924-1961	Learned Hand
1924-1939	Julian W. Mack
1926-1974	Thomas W. Swan
1927-1953	Augustus N. Hand
1929-1969	Harrie Brigham Chase
1939-1964	Charles E. Clark
1939-1940	Robert P. Patterson
1941-1957	Jerome N. Frank
1951-	Harold R. Medina
1953-1964	Carroll C. Hincks
1954-1955	John M. Harlan
1955-	J. Edward Lumbard
1955-1983	Sterry R. Waterman
1957-1982	Leonard P. Moore
1959-	Henry J. Friendly
1960-1980	J. Joseph Smith
1961-	Irving R. Kaufman
1961-1965	Thurgood Marshall
1961-1980	Paul R. Hays
1964-1979	Robert P. Anderson
1966-	Wilfred Feinberg

1971-	Walter T. Mansfield
1971-	James L. Oakes
1971-1980	William H. Mulligan
1971-	William H. Timbers
1974-1979	Murray Irwin Gurfein
1974-	Ellsworth A. Van Graafeiland
1975-	Thomas J. Meskill
1979-	Jon O. Newman
1979-	Amalya Lyle Kearse
1981-	Richard J. Cardamone
1981-	Lawrence W. Pierce
1982-	Ralph K. Winter, Jr.
1982-	George C. Pratt
1985-	Roger J. Miner
1985-	Frank X. Altimari

U.S. Court of Appeals for the Third Circuit

Philadelphia, PA

1869-1891	William McKennan
1891-1906	Marcus W. Acheson
1892-1909	George M. Dallas
1899-1914	George Gray
1906-1938	Joseph Buffington
1909-1912	William M. Lanning
1911-1913	Robert W. Archbald
1912-1919	John B. McPherson
1914-1941	Victor B. Woolley
1919-1920	Thomas G. Haight
1920-1941	John W. Davis
1931-1938	Joseph W. Thompson
1937-1978	John Biggs, Jr.
1938-	Albert B. Maris
1938-1943	William Clark
1939-1940	Francis Biddle
1939-1944	Charles A. Jones
1940-1962	Herbert F. Goodrich
1943-1976	Gerald McLaughlin
1945-1949	John J. O'Connell
1946-1976	Harry E. Kalodner
1949-1975	William H. Hastie
1950-1977	Austin L. Staley
1959-1961	Philip Forman
1961-1966	J. Cullen Ganey
1961-1968	William F. Smith
1964-1971	Abraham L. Freedman
1966-	Collins J. Seitz
1967-	Francis L. Van Dusen
1968-	Ruggero J. Aldisert
1968-1970	David Stahl
1969-	John J. Gibbons
1969-	Arlin M. Adams
1970-	Max Rosenn
1971-	James Hunter, III
1971-1972	James Rosen
1973-	Joseph F. Weis, Jr.
1973-	Leonard I. Garth
1977-	A. Leon Higginbotham, Jr.
1979-	Dolores Korman Sloviter
1981-	Edward R. Becker
1985-	Walter K. Stapleton
1985-	Carol Los Mansmann

U.S. Court of Appeals for the Fourth Circuit

Richmond, VA

1892-1913	Nathan Goff
1893-1904	Charles H. Simonton
1904-1921	Jeter C. Pritchard
1910-1923	Martin A. Knapp
1913-1925	Charles A. Woods
1921-1931	Edmund Waddill, Jr.
1922-1927	John C. Rose
1925-1958	John J. Parker
1927-1939	Elliott Northcott
1931-1955	Morris A. Soper
1939-1956	Armistead M. Dobie
1956-1972	Simon E. Sobeloff
1957-	Clement F. Haynsworth, Jr.
1959-1982	Herbert S. Boreman
1961-1983	Albert V. Bryan
1961-1967	J. Spencer Bell
1966-	Harrison L. Winter
1966-1976	J. Braxton Craven, Jr.
1967-	John D. Butzner, Jr.
1971-	Donald S. Russell
1971-	John A. Field, Jr.
1972-	H. Emory Widener, Jr.
1976-	Kenneth K. Hall
1978-	James Dickson Phillips, Jr.
1979-	Francis D. Murnaghan, Jr.
1979-	James M. Sprouse
1980-	Sam J. Ervin, III
1981-	Robert F. Chapman
1984-	James Harvie Wilkinson, III
1985-	Emory Sneeden

U.S. Court of Appeals for the Fifth Circuit

New Orleans, LA

1891-1919	Don A. Pardee
1892-1916	Andrew P. McCormick
1899-1914	David D. Shelby
1914-1936	Richard W. Walker
1917-1919	Robert L. Batts
1920-1935	Nathan P. Bryan
1920-1925	Alexander C. King
1925-1942	Rufus E. Foster
1931-1949	Samuel H. Sibley
1931-1957	Joseph C. Hutcheson, Jr.
1936-1961	Edwin R. Holmes
1939-1951	Leon P. McCord
1944-1951	Curtis L. Waller
1944-1949	Elmo P. Lee, Sr.
1949-1966	Wayne G. Borah
1949-1956	Robert L. Russell
1951-1955	Louie W. Strum
1951-1981	Richard T. Rives
1955-1980	Elbert P. Tuttle
1955	John R. Brown
1956-1963	Ben F. Cameron
1956-1980	Warren L. Jones
1958-	John M. Wisdom

1962-1981	Walter P. Gewin
1961-1975	Griffin B. Bell
1965-1983	James P. Coleman
1966-	Homer Thornberry
1966-1981	Robert A. Ainsworth, Jr.
1967-	Irving L. Goldberg
1966-1981	John C. Godbold
1967-1981	David W. Dyer
1968-1981	Bryan Simpson
1968-1969	Claude F. Clayton
1969-1981	Lewis R. Morgan
1969-1970	G. Harrold Carswell
1969-	Charles Clark
1970-	Joe M. Ingraham
1971-1981	Paul H. Roney
1973-	Thomas Gibbs Gee
1975-1980	Gerald B. Tjoflat
1976-1981	James C. Hill
1976-1981	Peter T. Fay
1977-1981	Robert S. Vance
1977-	Alvin B. Rubin
1979-1981	Robert L. Anderson, III
1979-	Thomas M. Reavley
1979-1981	Thomas A. Clark
1979-	Henry A. Politz
1979-1981	Joseph W. Hatchett
1979-	Carolyn D. Randall
1979-1981	Albert John Henderson
1979-	Albert Tate, Jr.
1979-1981	Frank M. Johnson, Jr.
1979-	Samuel D. Johnson
1979-1981	Phyllis A. Kravitch
1979-	Reynaldo G. Garza
1980-	Jerre S. Williams
1981-	William L. Garwood
1982-	E. Grady Jolly
1982-	Patrick E. Higginbotham
1983-	W. Eugene Davis
1984-	Robert Madden Hill
1985-	Edith Hollan Jones

U.S. Court of Appeals for the Sixth Circuit

Cincinnati, OH

1891-1893	Howell E. Jackson
1892-1900	William Howard Taft
1893-1909	Horace H. Lurton
1899-1903	William R. Day
1900-1911	Henry F. Severns
1903-1909	John K. Richards
1909-1919	John W. Warrington
1910-1930	Loyal E. Knappen
1911-1931	Arthur C. Denison
1919-1928	Maurice H. Donahue
1925-1938	Charles H. Morrman
1928-1951	Xenophon Hicks
1928-1933	Smith Hickenlooper
1932-1958	Charles C. Simons
1934-1959	Florence E. Allen
1938-1940	Elwood Hamilton
1939-1941	Herschel W. Arant
1940-1962	John D. Martin
1941-1976	Thomas F. McAllister
1945-1965	Shackelford Miller, Jr.
1954-1958	Potter Stewart
1959-	Lester L. Cecil
1959-	Paul C. Weick
1960-1975	Clifford O'Sullivan
1963-	Harry Phillips
1963-	George Edwards
1965-	Anthony J. Celebrezze
1966-	John W. Peck
1966-1976	Wade H. McCree, Jr.
1967-1970	Bert T. Combs
1969-1970	Henry L. Brooks
1970-1975	William E. Miller
1971-1972	W. Wallace Kent
1972-	Pierce Lively

1973-	Albert J. Engel
1977-	Damon J. Keith
1977-	Gilbert S. Merritt
1979-	Bailey Brown
1979-	Cornelia G. Kennedy
1979-	Boyce F. Martin, Jr.
1979-	Nathaniel R. Jones
1982-	Leroy J. Contie, Jr.
1982-	Robert B. Krupansky
1982-	Harry W. Wellford
1985-	H. Ted Milburn
1985-	Ralph B. Guy, Jr.
1985-	James L. Ryan
1985-	David A. Nelson

U.S. Court of Appeals for the Seventh Circuit

Chicago, IL

1891-1893	Walter Q. Gresham
1892-1901	William A. Woods
1893-1905	James G. Jenkins
1895-1898	John W. Showalter
1899-1911	Peter S. Grosscup
1902-1924	Francis E. Baker
1905-1918	Christian C. Kohlsaat
1905-1915	William H. Seaman
1915-1936	Samuel Alschuler
1916-1948	Evan A. Evans
1919-1930	George T. Page
1925-1929	Albert B. Anderson
1929-1948	William M. Sparks
1933-1935	Louis FitzHenry
1937-1956	J. Earl Major
1937-1941	Walter E. Treanor
1939-1952	Otto Kerner
1941-1949	Sherman Minton
1949-1966	F. Ryan Duffy
1949-1959	Philip J. Finnegan
1949-1958	Walter C. Lindley
1949-1957	H. Nathan Swaim
1954-1968	Elmer J. Schnackenberg
1957-1969	John S. Hastings
1957-1959	W. Lynn Parkinson
1958-1967	Win G. Knoch
1959-1970	Lathan Castle
1961-1974	Roger J. Kiley
1961-	Luther M. Swygert
1966-	Thomas E. Fairchild
1966-	Walter J. Cummings
1968-1973	Otto Kerner
1970-	Wilbur F. Pell, Jr.
1970-1975	John P. Stevens
1971-1982	Robert A. Sprecher
1974-1979	Philip Willis Tone
1975-	William J. Bauer
1976-	Harlington Wood, Jr.
1979-	Richard D. Cudahy
1981-	Richard A. Posner
1981-	Jesse E. Eschbach
1982-	John L Coffey
1984-	Joel M. Flaum
1985-	Frank Easterbrook
1985-	Kenneth F. Ripple

U.S. Court of Appeals for the Eighth Circuit

St. Louis, MO

1891-1903	Henry C. Caldwell
1892-1928	Walter H. Sanborn
1894-1905	Amos M. Thayer
1903-1910	Willis VanDevanter
1903-1921	William C. Hook
1905-1916	Elmer B. Adams
1911-1922	John E. Carland

1911-1922	Walter I. Smith
1916-1947	Kimbrough Stone
1921-1929	Robert E. Lewis
1922-1933	William S. Kenyon
1925-1931	Wilbur F. Booth
1925-1933	Arba S. Van Valkenburgh
1928-1933	John H. Cotteral
1929-1960	Archibald K. Gardner
1932-1959	John B. Sanborn
1933-1961	Joseph W. Woodrough
1935-1936	Charles B. Faris
1935-1954	Seth Thomas
1940-1965	Harvey M. Johnsen
1942-1953	Walter G. Riddick
1947-1955	John C. Collet
1954-1968	Charles J. Vogel
1954-1971	Martin D. Van Oosterhout
1956-1957	Charles E. Whittaker
1958-1980	Marion C. Matthes
1961-1965	Albert A. Ridge
1963-1981	Pat Mehaffy
1965-	Floyd R. Gibson
1966-	Donald P. Lay
1966-	Gerald W. Heaney
1968-	Myron H. Bright
1971-1982	Roy Laverne Stephenson
1971-	Donald R. Ross
1973-1977	William Hedgcock Webster
1975-	J. Smith Henley
1978-	Theodore McMillan
1980-	Richard S. Arnold
1982-	John R. Gibson
1982-	George C. Fagg
1983-	Pasco M. Bowman, II
1985-	Roger L. Wollman

U.S. Court of Appeals for the Ninth Circuit

San Francisco, CA

1891	Lorenzo Sawyer
1892-1896	Joseph McKenna
1892-1931	William B. Gilbert
1895-1925	Erskine M. Ross
1897-1923	William W. Morrow
1911-1928	William H. Hunt
1923-1936	Frank H. Rudkin
1925-1926	Wallace McCamant
1927-1930	Frank S. Dietrich
1929-1945	Curtis D. Wilbur
1931-1934	William H. Sawtelle
1933-1948	Francis A. Garrecht
1935-1957	William Denman
1935-1953	Clifton Mathews
1935-1943	Bert E. Haney
1937-1965	Albert Lee Stephens
1937-1962	William Healy
1944-1956	Homer T. Bone
1945-1956	William E. Orr
1949-1969	Walter L. Pope
1954-1958	Dal M. Lemmon
1954-1959	James A. Fee
1954-	Richard H. Chambers
1956-	Stanley N. Barnes
1956-1974	Frederick G. Hamley
1958-1973	Oliver D. Hamlin
1958-1972	Gilbert H. Jertberg
1959-	Charles M. Merrill
1959-	M. Oliver Koelsch
1961-	James R. Browning
1961-	Ben C. Duniway
1964-1983	Walter Ely
1967-1979	James M. Carter
1968-1979	Shirley M. Hufstedler
1969-	Eugene A. Wright
1969-	John F. Kilkenny
1969-1983	Ozell M. Trask
1971-	Herbert Y. C. Choy
1971-	Alfred T. Goodwin

1972-	J. Clifford Wallace
1973-	Joseph T. Sneed, III
1975-	Anthony M. Kennedy
1976-	J. Blaine Anderson
1977-	Procter Hug, Jr.
1977-	Thomas Tang
1979-	Otto R. Skopil, Jr.
1979-	Mary Murphy Schroeder
1979-	Betty B. Fletcher
1979-	Jerome Farris
1979-	Harry Pregerson
1979-	Arthur L. Alarcon
1979-	Cecil F. Poole
1979-	Warren J. Ferguson
1979-	Dorothy W. Nelson
1980-	William C. Canby, Jr.
1980-	Robert Boochever
1980-	William A. Norris
1980-	Stephen Reinhardt
1984-	Robert R. Beezer
1984-	Cynthia Holcomb Hall
1984-	Charles E. Wiggins
1985-	Melvin Brunetti
1985-	David R. Thompson
1985-	Alex Kozinski
1985-	John T. Noonan, Jr.

U.S. Court of Appeals for the Tenth Circuit

Denver, CO

1929-1940	Robert E. Lewis
1929-1933	John H. Cotteral
1929-	Orie L. Phillips
1929-1937	George T. McDermott
1933-1963	Sam G. Bratton
1937-1939	Robert Lee Williams
1939-1972	Walter Huxman
1940-1975	Alfred P. Murrah
1949-1983	John C. Pickett
1956-1983	David T. Lewis
1957-	Jean S. Breitenstein
1961-	Delmas C. Hill
1962-	Oliver Seth
1966-1970	John J. Hickey
1968-	William J. Holloway, Jr.
1970-	Robert H. McWilliams
1971-	James E. Barrett
1971-	William E. Doyle
1977-	Monroe G. McKay
1977-	James K. Logan
1979-	Stephanie K. Seymour
1985-	John P. Moore
1985-	Stephen Hale Anderson
1985-	Bobby R. Baldock
1985-	Deanell Reece Tacha

U.S. Court of Appeals for the Eleventh Circuit

Atlanta, GA

1981-1982	Richard T. Rives
1981-	Elbert P. Tuttle
1981-	Warren L. Jones
1981-	John C. Godbold
1981-	David W. Dyer
1981-	Bryan Simpson
1981-	Lewis R. Morgan
1981-	Paul H. Roney
1981-	Gerald B. Tjoflat
1981-	James C. Hill
1981-	Peter T. Fay
1981-	Robert S. Vance
1981-	Phyllis A. Kravitch
1981-	Frank M. Johnson, Jr.
1981-	Albert J. Henderson

1981-	Joseph W. Hatchett
1981-	Robert L. Anderson, III
1981-	Thomas A. Clark
1986-	James L. Edmondson

U.S. Court of Appeals for the District of Columbia

1919-1937	Josiah A. Van Orsdel
1919-1938	Charles H. Robb
1919-1924	Constantine J. Smyth
1923-1927	James F. Smith
1923-1929	Orion M. Barber
1923-1938	George E. Martin
1924-1929	Charles S. Hatfield
1924-1929	Oscar E. Bland
1925-1929	William J. Graham
1928-1929	Finis J. Garrett
1932-1935	William Hitz
1932-1948	D. Lawrence Grover
1936-1955	Harold M. Stephens
1937-1945	Justin Miller
1938-1943	Fred M. Vinson
1938-1969	Henry W. Edgerton
1940-1945	Wiley B. Rutledge, Jr.
1944-1945	Thurman W. Arnold
1946-1954	Bennett C. Clark
1946-1965	Wilbur K. Miller
1946-1971	E. Barrett Prettyman
1948-1953	James M. Proctor
1949-1970	George T. Washington
1950-	David L. Bazelon
1951-1979	Charles Fahy
1954-	John A. Danaher
1954-1977	Walter M. Bastian
1957-1970	Warren E. Burger
1962-	J. Skelly Wright
1963-	Carl McGowan
1965-	Edward A. Tamm
1965-1979	Harold Leventhal
1966-	Spottswood W. Robinson, III
1969-	George E. MacKinnon
1969-	Roger Robb
1970-	Malcolm R. Wilkey
1979-	Patricia M. Wald
1979-	Abner J. Mikva
1980-	Harry T. Edwards
1980-	Ruth Bader Ginsburg
1982-	Robert H. Bork
1982-1986	Antonin Scalia
1984-	Kenneth W. Starr
1985-	Laurence H. Silberman
1985-	James L. Buckley

U.S. Court of Appeals for the Federal Circuit

1982	Don N. Laramore
1982-	Giles S. Rich
1982-	Oscar H. Davis
1982-1986	J. Lindsay Almond, Jr.
1982	Wilson Cowen
1982-1983	Philip Nichols, Jr.
1982	Byron G. Skelton
1982-1985	Phillip B. Baldwin
1982-	Howard T. Markey
1982-1986	Shiro Kashiwa
1982-1986	Marion T. Bennett
1982-1985	Jack R. Miller
1982-	Daniel M. Friedman
1982-	Edward S. Smith
1982-	Helen W. Nies
1984-	Pauline Newman
1984-	Jean Galloway Bissell
1985-	Glenn L. Archer, Jr.
1987-	H. Robert Mayer

U.S. Claims Court

1982-1984	Alex Kozinski
1982-1983	Joseph V. Colaianni
1982-1986	Kenneth R. Harkins
1982-1983	Roald A. Hogenson
1982-1987	Thomas J. Lydon
1982-	James F. Merow
1982-1986	Philip R. Miller
1982-1987	Robert M. M. Seto
1982-1984	Louis Spector
1982-	John P. Wiese
1982-1984	George Willi
1982-1986	Harry E. Wood
1982-1987	Judith Ann Yannello
1982-	Robert J. Yock
1982-	Reginald W. Gibson
1982-	Lawrence S. Margolis
1982-1987	H. Robert Mayer
1983-	Christine Cook Nettesheim
1983-	Moody R. Tidwell, III
1982-1987	Mastin G. White
1985-	Loren A. Smith
1986-	Marian Blank Horn
1986-	Eric Brugginck
1986-	John Napier
1987-	Bohdan A. Futey
1987-	Roger B. Andewelt
1987-	Wilkes C. Robinson

U.S. Court of Claims

1855-1858	John J. Gilchrist
1855-1859	Isaac N. Blackford
1855-1861	George P. Scarburgh
1858-1877	Edward G. Loring
1860-1865	James Hughes
1861-1870	Joseph Casey
1863-1868	David Wilmot
1863-1878	Ebenezer Peck
1865-1896	Charles C. Nott
1868-1874	Samuel Milligan
1870-1885	Charles D. Drake
1874-1896	William A. Richardson
1877-1881	J.C. Bancroft Davis
1878-1881	William H. Hunt
1881-1892	Glenni W. Scofield
1882-1883	J.C. Bancroft Davis
1883-1905	Lawrence Weldon
1885-1902	John Davis
1892-1913	Stanton J. Peelle
1896-1906	Charles C. Nott
1897-1915	Charles B. Howry
1903-1905	Francis M. Wright
1905-1939	Fenton W. Booth
1905-1916	George W. Atkinson
1906-1919	Samuel S. Barney
1913-1928	Edward K. Campbell
1915-1926	George E. Downey
1916-1928	James Hay
1919-1930	Samuel J. Grahamn
1926-1929	McKenzie Moss
1928-1940	William R. Green
1928-1958	Benjamin H. Littleton
1930-1947	Richard S. Whaley
1939-1964	Samuel Whitaker
1940-1964	Marvin Jones
1941-1961	J. Warren Madden
1947-1953	Evan Howell
1954-1981	Don N. Laramore
1960-1976	James R. Durfee
1962-1981	Oscar H. Davis
1964-1981	Wilson Cowen
1964-1972	Linton M. Collins
1966-1981	Byron Skelton
1966-1981	Philip Nichols, Jr.
1971-1981	Shiro Kashiwa
1971-1981	Robert Lowe Kunzig
1972-1981	Marion Tinsley Bennett

1978-1981	Daniel Mortimer Friedman
1978-1981	Edward Samuel Smith
1980-1981	Wilson Cowen
1980-1981	Oscar H. Davis
1980-1981	Don N. Laramore

Superseded by U.S. Claims Court in 1982.

U.S. Court of Customs and Patent Appeals

1910-1920	Robert M. Montgomery
1910-1911	William H. Hunt
1910-1928	Orion M. Barber
1910-1922	Marion DeVries
1910-1928	James F. Smith
1911-1924	George E. Martin
1923-1947	Oscar E. Bland
1923-1950	Charles S. Hatfield
1924-1927	William J. Graham
1929-1955	Finis J. Garrett
1929-1944	Irvine L. Lenroot
1937-1952	Joseph R. Jackson
1944-1962	Ambrose O'Connell
1948-1959	Noble J. Johnson
1950-1974	Eugene Worley
1952-1957	William P. Cole, Jr.
1956-1982	Giles S. Rich
1958-1966	I. Jack Martin
1959-1968	Arthur M. Smith
1962-1982	J. Lindsay Almond, Jr.
1968-1982	Philip E. Baldwin
1969-1982	Donald E. Lane
1972-1982	Howard T. Markey
1973-1982	Jack Richard Miller
1980-1982	Helen Wilson Nies
1980-1982	Giles S. Rich

Superseded by U.S. Court of Appeals for the Federal Circuit in 1982.

U.S. Court of International Trade

1980-	Paul P. Rao
1980-	Morgan Ford
1980-1981	Scovel Richardson
1980-1984	Frederick Landis
1980-	James L. Watson
1980-1982	Herbert N. Maletz
1980-	Edward D. Re

1980-	Samuel M. Rosenstein
1980-1984	Bernard Newman
1980-1984	Nils A. Boe
1983-	Gregory W. Carman
1983-	Jane A. Restani
1984-	Dominick L. DiCarlo
1985-	Thomas J. Aquilano
1986-	Nicholas Tsoucalas

U.S. Customs Court

1926-1932	Israel F. Fischer
1926-1927	William B. Howell
1926-1930	Byron S. Waite
1926-1939	Charles M. McClelland
1926-1939	Jerry B. Sullivan
1926-1942	George S. Brown
1926-1928	William C. Adamson
1926-1931	George E. Weller
1926-1932	George M. Young
1928-1955	Genevieve R. Cline
1928-1949	William J. Tilson
1931-1948	David H. Kincheloe
1931-1941	Walter H. Evans
1932-1942	Frederick W. Dallinger
1933-1946	William J. Keefe
1940-1944	Thomas J. Walker
1940-1969	Webster J. Oliver
1942-1952	William P. Cole
1942-1957	William A. Ekwall
1943-1974	Charles D. Lawrence
1945-1962	Irvin C. Mollison
1947-1963	Jed Johnson
1948-1979	Paul R. Rao
1949-1979	Morgan Ford
1954-1975	David J. Wilson
1955-1974	Mary H. Donlon
1957-1979	Scovel Richardson
1964-1966	Philip Nichols, Jr.
1965-1979	Frederick Landis
1966-1978	James L. Watson
1967-1968	Lindley Beckworth
1967-1979	Herbert N. Maletz
1968-1979	Samuel M. Rosenstein
1968-1979	Bernard Newman
1968-1979	Edward D. Re
1971-1979	Nils A. Boe

Superseded by U.S. Court of International Trade.

U.S. Emergency Court of Appeals

1943-1962	Albert B. Maris
1943-1962	Calvert Magruder
1943-1958	Bolitha J. Laws
1945-1962	Thomas F. McAllister
1944-1958	Walter C. Lindley

U.S. Temporary Emergency Court of Appeals

1972-1983	Edward A. Tamm
1972-1979	James M. Carter
1972-1976	William H. Hastie
1972-1978	Robert P. Anderson
1972-	A. Sherman Christensen
1972-1976	Martin D. Van Oosterhout
1972-	Joe Ewing Estes
1972-1982	Frank M. Johnson, Jr.
1972-1976	John S. Hastings
1976-	Joe MacDonald Ingraham
1977-1979	Herbert P. Sorg
1972-	William J. Jameson
1976-	Robert A. Grant
1977-	William H. Becker
1977-	Alfonso J. Zirpoli
1977-1981	Walter P. Gewin
1977-	Dudley B. Bonsal
1977-	John K. Regan
1977-1985	Walter E. Hoffman
1978-1985	Frederick B. Lacey
1979-	Charles M. Metzner
1979-	Lewis R. Morgan
1979-1983	Earl R. Larson
1979-1986	John W. Peck
1979-	Ben C. Duniway
1980-	Edward T. Gignoux
1981-1983	Adrian A. Spears
1980-	Wesley E. Brown
1980-1982	Stanley A. Weigel
1981-1983	Robert W. Hemphill
1981-	Robert E. Maxwell
1980-	Sam C. Pointer
1981-1987	J. Skelly Wright
1982-	Reynaldo G. Garza
1982-	Thomas J. MacBride
1982-1983	Fred Daugherty
1982-1985	Walter Early Craig
1982-	Homer Thornberry
1982-1985	Ray McNichols
1982-	Morey L. Sear

VI

States of the Union

States of the Union

Chronological lists of the governors, U.S. senators, and chief justices of the state court systems for all the states. Political affiliations are noted for governors and senators serving since 1973, when the third edition of this book was published.

Alabama

Governors

1819	William W. Bibb
1820	Thomas Bibb
1821-1824	Israel Pickens
1825-1828	John Murphy
1829-1830	Gabriel Moore
1831	Samuel B. Moore
1831-1834	John Gayle
1835-1836	Clement Comer Clay
1837-1840	Arthur P. Bagby
1841-1844	Benjamin Fitzpatrick
1845-1846	Joshua L. Martin
1847-1848	Reuben Chapman
1849-1852	Henry W. Collier
1853-1856	John A. Winston
1857-1860	Andrew B. Moore
1861-1862	John G. Shorter
1863-1864	Thomas H. Watts
1865	Lewis E. Parsons
1865-1867	Robert M. Patton
1868-1869	William H. Smith
1870-1871	Robert B. Lindsay
1872-1873	David P. Lewis
1874-1877	George S. Houston
1878-1881	Rufus W. Cobb
1882-1885	Edward A. O'Neal
1886-1889	Thomas Seay
1890-1893	Thomas G. Jones
1894-1895	William C. Oates
1896-1899	Joseph F. Johnston
1900-1902	William J. Samford
1903-1906	William D. Jelks
1907-1910	Braxton B. Comer
1911-1914	Emmet O'Neal
1915-1918	Charles Henderson
1919-1922	Thomas E. Kilby
1923-1926	William W. Brandon
1927-1930	David Bibb Graves
1931-1934	Benjamin M. Miller
1935-1938	David Bibb Graves
1939-1942	Frank M. Dixon
1943-1946	Chauncey Sparks
1947-1950	James E. Folsom
1951-1954	Gordon Persons
1955-1958	James E. Folsom
1959-1962	John M. Patterson
1963-1966	George C. Wallace
1967	Lurleen B. Wallace
1968-1970	Albert P. Brewer
1971-1978	George C. Wallace (D)
1979-1982	Forrest James (D)
1983-1986	George C. Wallace (D)
1987-	Guy Hunt (R)

Senators

1819-1822	John W. Walker
1819-1843	William R. King
1823-1824	William Kelly
1825	Henry H. Chambers
1826	Israel Pickens
1826-1830	John McKinley
1831-1836	Gabriel Moore
1837-1840	Clement Comer Clay
1841-1847	Arthur P. Bagby
1844-1847	Dixon H. Lewis
1848	Benjamin Fitzpatrick
1848-1852	William R. King
1849-1852	Jeremiah Clemens
1853-1860	Benjamin Fitzpatrick
1853-1860	Clement Claiborne Clay
1860-1867	Vacant
1868-1871	Willard Warner
1868-1878	George E. Spencer
1872-1876	George T. Goldthwaite
1877-1906	John T. Morgan
1879	George S. Houston
1880	Luke Pryor
1880-1896	James L. Pugh
1897-1906	Edmund W. Pettus
1907-1913	Joseph F. Johnston
1907-1919	John H. Bankhead
1914	Frank S. White
1915-1926	Oscar W. Underwood
1920	Braxton B. Comer
1920-1930	J. Thomas Heflin
1927-1936	Hugo L. Black
1931-1945	John H. Bankhead, II
1937	Dixie Bibb Graves
1938-1968	Lister Hill
1946	George R. Swift
1947-1979	John J. Sparkman (D)
1969-1978	James B. Allen (D)
1978-	Howell Heflin (D)
1979-1981	Donald Stewart (D)
1981-1987	Jeremiah Denton (R)
1987-	Richard C. Shelby (R)

Chief Justices

1820-1822	Clement Comer Clay
1823-1834	Abner Lipscomb
1835	Reuben Saffold
1836	Henry Hitchcock
1837	Arthur F. Hopkins
1837-1848	Henry W. Collier
1849-1851	Edmund S. Dargan
1852-1855	William P. Chilton
1856	George T. Goldthwaite
1857-1858	Samuel F. Rice
1859-1864	Abram J. Walker
1865-1872	Elijah W. Peck
1873	Thomas M. Peters
1874-1883	Robert C. Brickell
1884-1893	George W. Stone
1894-1897	Robert C. Brickell
1898-1905	Thomas N. McClellan
1906	Samuel D. Weakley
1907-1908	John R. Tyson
1909-1913	James R. Dowdell
1914-1939	John C. Anderson
1940-1950	Lucien D. Gardner
1951-1970	J. Ed Livingston
1971-1976	Howell T. Heflin
1977-	Clement C. Torbert, Jr.

Alaska

Governors

1959-1966	William A. Egan
1967-1968	Walter J. Hickel
1969-1970	Keith J. Miller
1971-1974	William A. Egan (D)
1975-1982	Jay S. Hammond (R)
1983-1986	William Sheffield (D)
1987-	Steve Cowper (D)

Senators

1959-1968	Edward L. Bartlett
1959-1968	Ernest Gruening
1969-	Theodore F. Stevens (R)
1969-1980	Mike (Maurice R.) Gravel (D)
1981-	Frank H. Murkowski (R)

Chief Justices

1959-1969	Buell A. Nesbett
1970-1971	George F. Boney
1972-1974	Jay A. Rabinowitz
1975-1977	Robert Boochever
1978-1983	Jay A. Rabinowitz
1984-1985	Edmond W. Burke
1986-	Jay A. Rabinowitz

Arizona

Governors

1912-1918	George W. P. Hunt
1919-1922	Thomas E. Campbell
1923-1928	George W. P. Hunt
1929-1930	John C. Phillips
1931-1932	George W. P. Hunt
1933-1935	Benjamin B. Moeur
1936-1937	R. C. Stanford
1938-1939	R. T. Jones
1940-1947	Sidney P. Osborn
1948-1949	Dan E. Garvey
1950-1953	Howard Pyle
1954-1957	Ernest W. McFarland
1958-1963	Paul J. Fannin
1964-1965	Samuel P. Goddard
1966-1974	Jack Williams (R)
1975-1977	Raul Castro (D)

1978-1986	Bruce E. Babbitt (D)
1987-	Evan Mecham (R)

Senators

1912-1920	Marcus A. Smith
1912-1940	Henry F. Ashurst
1921-1926	Ralph H. Cameron
1927-1968	Carl T. Hayden
1941-1952	Ernest W. McFarland
1953-1964	Barry M. Goldwater
1965-1976	Paul J. Fannin (R)
1969-1986	Barry M. Goldwater (R)
1977-	Dennis DeConcini (D)
1987-	John McCain (R)

Chief Justices

Justices of the Supreme Court serve on a rotating basis as Chief Presiding Judge.

Arkansas

Governors

1836-1839	James S. Conway
1840-1843	Archibald Yell
1844	Samuel Adams (Acting)
1844-1848	Thomas S. Drew
1849	Richard C. Byrd (Acting)
1849-1850	John S. Roane
1851	John R. Hampton (Acting)
1852-1859	Elias N. Conway
1860-1861	Henry M. Rector
1862	Thomas Fletcher (Acting)
1862-1863	Harris Flanagin
1864-1867	Isaac Murphy
1868-1870	Powell Clayton
1871-1872	Ozro A. Hadley (Acting)
1873	Elisha Baxter
1874-1876	Augustus H. Garland
1877-1880	William R. Miller
1881-1882	Thomas J. Churchill
1883-1884	James H. Berry
1885-1888	Simon P. Hughes
1889-1891	James P. Eagle
1892	William M. Fishback
1893-1894	Clay Sloan (Acting)
1895-1896	James P. Clarke
1897-1900	Daniel W. Jones
1901-1906	Jeff Davis
1907	John S. Little
1907-1908	Xenophon Pindall
1909-1912	George W. Donaghey
1913	Joseph T. Robinson
1913-1916	George W. Hays
1917-1920	Charles H. Brough
1921-1924	Thomas C. McRae
1925-1926	Thomas J. Terral
1927	John E. Martineau
1928-1932	Harvey Parnell
1933-1936	J. Marion Futrell
1937-1940	Carl E. Bailey
1941-1944	Homer M. Adkins
1945-1948	Ben Laney
1949-1952	Sid McMath
1953-1954	Francis Cherry
1955-1966	Orville Faubus
1967-1970	Winthrop Rockefeller
1971-1974	Dale Bumpers (D)
1975-1978	David Pryor (D)
1979-1980	William Clinton (D)
1981-1982	Frank White (R)
1983-	William Clinton (D)

Senators

1836-1843	William S. Fulton
1836-1847	Ambrose H. Sevier
1844-1847	Chester Ashley
1848-1852	Solon Borland
1848-1860	William K. Sebastian
1853-1860	Robert W. Johnson
1861	Charles B. Mitchell
1861-1867	Vacant
1862-1867	Vacant
1868-1870	Alexander McDonald
1868-1872	Benjamin F. Rice
1871-1876	Powell Clayton
1873-1878	Stephen W. Dorsey
1877-1884	Augustus H. Garland
1879-1884	James D. Walker
1885-1902	James K. Jones
1885-1906	James H. Berry
1903-1915	James P. Clarke
1907-1912	Jeff Davis
1913-1936	Joseph T. Robinson
1916-1920	William F. Kirby
1921-1931	Thaddeus H. Caraway
1932-1944	Hattie W. Caraway
1937-1940	John E. Miller
1941-1942	George L. Spencer
1943-1976	John C. McClellan (D)
1945-1974	J. William Fulbright (D)
1975-	Dale Bumpers (D)
1977-	David Pryor (D)

Chief Justices

1836-1844	Daniel Ringo
1845-1852	Thomas Johnson
1853-1854	George C. Watkins
1855-1863	Elbert H. English
1864-1865	Elisha Baxter
1866-1867	David Walker
1868-1870	William W. Wilshire
1871-1873	John McClure
1874-1883	Elbert H. English
1884-1891	Sterling R. Cockrill
1892-1903	Henry G. Bunn
1904-1908	Joseph M. Hill
1909-1926	Edgar A. McCulloch
1927-1931	Jesse C. Hart
1932-1936	C. E. Johnson
1937-1954	Griffin Smith
1955-1956	Lee Seamster
1957-1980	Carleton Harris
1981-1984	Richard B. Adkisson
1985-	Jack W. Holt, Jr.

California

Governors

1849-1850	Peter H. Burnett
1851	John McDougall
1852-1855	John Bigler
1856-1857	James N. Johnson
1858-1859	John B. Weller
1860	Milton S. Latham
1860-1861	John G. Downey
1862	Leland Stanford
1863-1866	Frederick F. Low
1867-1870	Henry H. Haight
1871-1874	Newton Booth
1875	Romualdo Pacheco
1875-1879	William Irwin
1880-1882	George C. Perkins
1883-1886	George Stoneman
1887	Washington Bartlett

1887-1890	Robert W. Waterman
1891-1894	Henry H. Markham
1895-1898	James H. Budd
1899-1902	Henry T. Gage
1903-1906	George C. Pardee
1907-1910	James N. Gillett
1911-1916	Hiram W. Johnson
1917-1922	William D. Stephens
1923-1926	Friend W. Richardson
1927-1930	Clement C. Young
1931-1933	James Rolph, Jr.
1934-1938	Frank F. Merriam
1939-1942	Culbert L. Olson
1943-1952	Earl Warren
1953-1959	Goodwin J. Knight
1959-1967	Edmund G. Brown
1967-1974	Ronald Reagan (R)
1975-1982	Edmund G. Brown (D)
1983-	George Deukmejian (R)

Senators

1850-1851	John C. Fremont
1850-1854	William M. Gwin
1852-1856	John B. Weller
1855-1856	Vacant
1857-1858	David C. Broderick
1857-1860	William M. Gwin
1859	Henry P. Haun
1860-1862	Milton S. Latham
1861-1866	James A. McDougall
1863-1868	John Conness
1867-1872	Cornelius Cole
1869-1872	Eugene Casserly
1873-1874	John S. Hager
1873-1878	Aaron A. Sargent
1875-1880	Newton Booth
1879-1884	James T. Farley
1881-1885	John F. Miller
1885-1892	Leland Stanford
1886	George Hearst
1886	Abram P. Williams
1887-1890	George Hearst
1891-1892	Charles N. Felton
1893-1899	Stephen M. White
1893-1914	George C. Perkins
1900-1904	Thomas R. Bard
1905-1910	Frank P. Flint
1911-1916	John D. Works
1915-1920	James D. Phelan
1917-1944	Hiram W. Johnson
1921-1932	Samuel M. Shortridge
1933-1937	William Gibbs McAdoo
1938	Thomas M. Storke
1939-1949	Sheridan Downey
1945-1958	William F. Knowland
1950-1952	Richard M. Nixon
1953-1968	Thomas H. Kuchel
1959-1963	Clair Engle
1964	Pierre Salinger
1965-1970	George Murphy
1969-	Alan Cranston (D)
1971-1977	John V. Tunney (D)
1978-1982	Sam I. Hayakawa (R)
1983-	Pete Wilson (R)

Chief Justices

1849-1851	S. Clinton Hastings
1852	Henry A. Lyons
1853-1856	Hugh C. Murray
1857-1858	David S. Terry
1859-1862	Stephen J. Field
1863	Edwin B. Crocker
1864-1869	Silas W. Sanderson
1870-1871	Jackson Temple
1872-1879	Addison C. Niles
1880-1886	Robert F. Morrison

1887-1888	Niles Searls
1888-1913	William H. Beatty
1914	Matt I. Sullivan
1915-1920	Frank M. Angellotti
1921-1922	Lucien Shaw
1923	Curtis D. Wilbur
1924-1925	Louis W. Myers
1926-1939	William H. Waste
1940-1963	Phil S. Gibson
1964-1969	Roger J. Traynor
1970-1976	Donald R. Wright
1977-	Rose Elizabeth Bird

Colorado

Governors

1876-1878	John L. Routt
1879-1882	Frederick W. Pitkin
1883-1884	James B. Grant
1885-1886	Benjamin H. Eaton
1887-1888	Alva Adams
1889-1890	Job A. Cooper
1891-1892	John L. Routt
1893-1894	Davis H. Waite
1895-1896	Albert W. McIntire
1897-1898	Alva Adams
1899-1900	Charles S. Thomas
1901-1902	James B. Orman
1903-1904	James H. Peabody
1905	Alva Adams
1905	James H. Peabody
1905-1906	Jesse F. McDonald
1907-1908	Henry A. Buchtel
1909-1912	John F. Shafroth
1913-1914	Elias M. Ammons
1915-1916	George A. Carlson
1917-1918	Julius C. Gunter
1919-1922	Oliver H. Shoup
1923-1924	William E. Sweet
1925-1926	Clarence J. Morley
1927-1932	William H. Adams
1933-1936	Edwin C. Johnson
1937	Ray H. Talbot
1937-1938	Teller Ammons
1939-1942	Ralph L. Carr
1943-1946	John C. Vivian
1947-1949	William L. Knous
1950	Walter W. Johnson
1951-1954	Dan Thornton
1955-1956	Edwin C. Johnson
1957-1962	Stephen L. R. McNichols
1963-1974	John A. Love (R)
1975-1986	Richard D. Lamm (D)
1987-	Roy Romer (D)

Senators

1876-1878	Jerome B. Chaffee
1876-1881	Henry M. Teller
1879-1884	Nathaniel P. Hill
1882	George M. Chilcott
1883	Horace A. W. Tabor
1883-1888	Thomas A. Bowen
1885-1908	Henry M. Teller
1889-1900	Edward O. Wolcott
1901-1906	Thomas M. Patterson
1907-1912	Simon Guggenheim
1909-1910	Charles J. Hughes, Jr.
1911-1912	Vacant
1913-1918	John F. Shafroth
1913-1920	Charles S. Thomas
1919-1930	Lawrence C. Phipps
1921-1922	Samuel D. Nicholson
1923	Alva B. Adams
1924-1926	Rice W. Means

1927-1931	Charles W. Waterman
1931-1936	Edward P. Costigan
1932	Karl C. Schuyler
1933-1941	Alva B. Adams
1937-1954	Edwin C. Johnson
1942-1956	Eugene D. Millikin
1955-1972	Gordon L. Allott
1957-1962	John A. Carroll
1963-1974	Peter H. Dominick (R)
1973-1978	Floyd K. Haskell (D)
1975-1986	Gary Hart (D)
1979-	William L. Armstrong (R)
1987-	Timothy E. Wirth (D)

Chief Justices

1876	Moses Hallett
1877-1879	Henry C. Thatcher
1880-1882	Samuel H. Elbert
1883-1888	William E. Beck
1889-1892	Joseph C. Helm
1893-1897	Charles D. Hayt
1898-1903	John Campbell
1904-1906	William H. Gabbert
1907-1909	Robert W. Steele
1910-1912	John Campbell
1913-1914	George W. Musser
1915	William H. Gabbert
1916-1917	S. Harrison White
1918	William A. Hill
1919-1920	James A. Garrigues
1921-1922	Tully Scott
1923-1924	James H. Teller
1925-1926	George W. Allen
1927	Haslett P. Burke
1928	John H. Dennison
1929-1930	Greeley W. Whitford
1931-1934	John T. Adams
1935	Charles C. Butler
1936	John Campbell
1937-1938	Haslett P. Burke
1939	Benjamin C. Hilliard
1940	Francis E. Bouck
1941-1944	John C. Young
1945	Norris C. Bakke
1946	William L. Knous
1947-1948	Haslett P. Burke
1949-1950	Benjamin C. Hilliard
1951	William S. Jackson
1952-1954	Mortimer Stone
1955-1956	Wilbur M. Alter
1957	O. Otto Moore
1958	E. V. Holland
1959	Francis J. Knauss
1960	Leonard B. Sutton
1961	Frank H. Hall
1962	Edward C. Day
1963	Albert T. Frantz
1964	Robert H. McWilliams
1965	Edward E. Pringle
1966	Leonard B. Sutton
1967-1968	O. Otto Moore
1969	Robert H. McWilliams
1970-1978	Edward E. Pringle
1979-1982	Paul V. Hodges
1983-1985	William H. Erickson
1986-	Joseph R. Quinn

Connecticut

Governors

1789-1795	Samuel Huntington
1796	Oliver Wolcott
1797-1808	Jonathan Trumbull, II
1809-1810	John Treadwell

1811-1812	Roger Griswold
1813-1816	John C. Smith
1817-1826	Oliver Wolcott, Jr.
1827-1830	Gideon Tomlinson
1831-1832	John S. Peters
1833	Henry W. Edwards
1834	Samuel A. Foote
1835-1837	Henry W. Edwards
1838-1841	William W. Ellsworth
1842-1843	Chauncey F. Cleveland
1844-1845	Roger S. Baldwin
1846	Isaac Toucey
1847-1848	Clark Bissell
1849	Joseph Trumbull
1850-1852	Thomas H. Seymour
1853	Charles H. Pond
1854	Henry Dutton
1855-1856	William T. Minor
1857	Alexander H. Holley
1858-1865	William A. Buckingham
1866	Joseph R. Hawley
1867-1868	James E. English
1869	Marshall Jewell
1870	James E. English
1871-1872	Marshall Jewell
1873-1876	Charles R. Ingersoll
1877-1878	Richard D. Hubbard
1879-1880	Charles B. Andrews
1881-1882	Hobart B. Bigelow
1883-1884	Thomas M. Waller
1885-1886	Henry B. Harrison
1887-1888	Phineas C. Lounsbury
1889-1892	Morgan G. Bulkeley
1893-1894	Luzon B. Morris
1895-1896	Owen V. Coffin
1897-1898	Lorrin A. Cooke
1899-1900	George E. Lounsbury
1901-1902	George P. McLean
1903-1904	Abiram Chamberlain
1905-1906	Henry Roberts
1907-1908	Rollins S. Woodruff
1909	George L. Lilley
1909-1910	Frank B. Weeks
1911-1914	Simeon E. Baldwin
1915-1920	Marcus H. Holcomb
1921-1922	Everett J. Lake
1923-1924	Charles A. Templeton
1925-1930	John H. Trumbull
1931-1938	Wilbur L. Cross
1939-1940	Raymond E. Baldwin
1941-1942	Robert E. Hurley
1943-1945	Raymond E. Baldwin
1946	Wilbert Snow
1947	James L. McConaughy
1948	James C. Shannon
1949-1950	Chester Bowles
1951-1954	John D. Lodge
1955-1960	Abraham Ribicoff
1961-1970	John Dempsey
1971-1974	Thomas Meskill (R)
1975-1980	Ella T. Grasso (D)
1981-	William A. O'Neill (D)

Senators

1789-1790	William S. Johnson
1789-1795	Oliver Ellsworth
1791-1792	Roger Sherman
1793-1794	Stephen M. Mitchell
1795	Jonathan Trumbull
1796-1806	Uriah Tracy
1796-1809	James Hillhouse
1807-1812	Chauncey Goodrich
1810-1820	Samuel W. Dana
1813-1818	David Daggett
1819-1824	James Lanman
1821-1822	Elijah Boardman
1823-1826	Henry W. Edwards
1825-1830	Calvin Willey
1827-1832	Samuel A. Foote

1831-1836	Gideon Tomlinson
1833-1834	Nathan Smith
1835-1838	John M. Niles
1837-1842	Perry Smith
1839	Thaddeus Betts
1840-1846	Jabez W. Huntington
1843-1848	John M. Niles
1847-1851	Roger S. Baldwin
1849-1853	Truman Smith
1852-1856	Isaac Toucey
1854	Francis Gillette
1855-1866	Lafayette S. Foster
1857-1868	James Dixon
1867-1874	Orris S. Ferry
1869-1874	William A. Buckingham
1875	James E. English
1875-1880	William W. Eaton
1876-1878	William H. Barnum
1879-1904	Orville H. Platt
1881-1904	Joseph R. Hawley
1905-1910	Morgan G. Bulkeley
1905-1923	Frank B. Brandegee
1911-1928	George P. McLean
1924-1932	Hiram Bingham
1929-1934	Frederic C. Walcott
1933-1944	Augustine Lonergan
1935-1938	Francis T. Maloney
1939-1944	John A. Danaher
1945	Thomas C. Hart
1945-1951	J. Brien McMahon
1946-1948	Raymond E. Baldwin
1949-1952	William Benton
1952	William A. Purtell
1953-1958	William A. Purtell
1953-1962	Prescott S. Bush
1959-1969	Thomas J. Dodd
1963-1980	Abraham Ribicoff (D)
1970-	Lowell P. Weicker, Jr. (R)
1981-	Christopher J. Dodd (D)

Chief Justices

1789-1792	Eliphalet Dyer
1793-1797	Andrew Adams
1798-1806	Jesse Root
1807-1813	Stephen M. Mitchell
1814	Tapping Reeve
1815-1818	Zephaniah Swift
1819-1832	Stephen T. Hosmer
1833	David Daggett
1834-1846	Thomas S. Williams
1847-1853	Samuel Church
1854-1856	Henry M. Waite
1857-1860	William L. Storrs
1861-1869	Joel Hinman
1870-1872	Thomas B. Butler
1873	Origen S. Seymour
1874-1888	John D. Park
1889-1900	Charles B. Andrews
1901-1906	David Torrance
1907-1909	Simeon E. Baldwin
1910-1912	Frederick B. Hall
1913-1919	Samuel O. Prentice
1920-1929	George W. Wheeler
1930-1949	William M. Maltbie
1950-1952	Allyn M. Brown
1953-1956	Ernest A. Inglis
1957	Patrick B. O'Sullivan
1957	Kenneth Wynne
1958	Edward J. Daly
1959-1962	Raymond E. Baldwin
1963-1969	John H. King
1970	Howard W. Alcorn
1971-1978	Charles S. House
1979-1980	John P. Cotter
1981-1983	John A. Speziale
1984-	Ellen Ash Peters

Delaware

Governors

1789-1795	Joshua Clayton
1796	Gunning Bedford
1797-1798	Daniel Rogers (Acting)
1799-1800	Richard Bassett
1801	James Sykes (Acting)
1802-1804	David Hall
1805-1807	Nathaniel Mitchell
1808-1810	George Truitt
1811-1813	Joseph Haslet
1814-1816	Daniel Rodney
1817-1819	John Clark
1820	Jacob Stout (Acting)
1821	John Collins
1822	Caleb Rodney (Acting)
1823	Joseph Haslet
1824-1826	Samuel Paynter
1827-1829	Charles Polk
1830-1832	David Hazzard
1833-1835	Caleb P. Bennett
1836	Charles Polk (Acting)
1837-1840	Cornelius P. Comegys
1841-1844	William B. Cooper
1845	Thomas Stockton
1846	William Temple (Acting)
1847-1850	William Tharp
1851-1854	William H. H. Ross
1855-1858	Peter F. Causey
1859-1962	William Burton
1863-1864	William Cannon
1865-1870	Gove Saulsbury
1871-1874	James Ponder
1875-1878	John P. Cochran
1879-1882	John W. Hall
1883-1886	Charles C. Stockley
1887-1890	Benjamin T. Biggs
1891-1894	Robert J. Reynolds
1895-1896	Joshua H. Marvil
1897-1900	Elbe W. Tunnell
1901-1904	John Hunn
1905-1908	Preston Lea
1909-1912	Simeon S. Pennewill
1913-1916	Charles R. Miller
1917-1920	John G. Townsend, Jr.
1921-1924	William D. Denney
1925-1928	Robert P. Robinson
1929-1936	C. Douglass Buck
1937-1940	Richard C. McMullen
1941-1948	Walter W. Bacon
1949-1952	Elbert N. Carvel
1953-1959	J. Caleb Boggs
1960	David P. Buckson
1961-1964	Elbert N. Carvel
1965-1968	Charles L. Terry, Jr.
1969-1972	Russell W. Peterson (R)
1973-1976	Sherman W. Tribbitt (D)
1977-1984	Pierre S. duPont, IV (R)
1985-	Michael N. Castle (R)

Senators

1789-1792	Richard Bassett
1789-1792	George Read
1793-1794	Vacant
1793-1797	John Vining
1795-1800	Henry Latimer
1798	Joshua Clayton
1799-1803	William H. Wells
1801-1809	Samuel White
1804-1812	James A. Bayard, Sr.
1810-1821	Outerbridge Horsey
1813-1816	William H. Wells
1817-1825	Nicholas Van Dyke
1822-1823	Caesar A. Rodney

1824-1826	Thomas Clayton
1826	Daniel Rodney
1827-1828	Louis McLane
1827-1829	Henry M. Ridgely
1829-1836	John M. Clayton
1830-1835	Arnold Naudain
1836-1838	Richard H. Bayard
1837-1846	Thomas Clayton
1839-1840	Vacant
1841-1844	Richard H. Bayard
1845-1848	John M. Clayton
1847-1852	Presley Spruance
1849-1850	John Wales
1851-1863	James A. Bayard, Jr.
1853-1855	John M. Clayton
1856	Joseph P. Comegys
1857-1858	Martin W. Bates
1859-1870	Willard Saulsbury, Sr.
1864-1866	George R. Riddle
1867-1868	James A. Bayard, Jr.
1869-1884	Thomas F. Bayard
1871-1888	Eli Saulsbury
1885-1898	George Gray
1889-1894	Anthony Higgins
1895-1896	Vacant
1897-1900	Richard R. Kenney
1899-1902	Vacant
1901-1902	Vacant
1903-1904	L. Heisler Ball
1903-1906	J. Frank Allee
1905-1916	Henry A. duPont
1907-1912	Harry A. Richardson
1913-1918	Willard Saulsbury, Jr.
1917-1920	Josiah O. Wolcott
1919-1924	L. Heisler Ball
1921	T. Coleman duPont
1922-1928	Thomas F. Bayard, Jr.
1925-1927	T. Coleman duPont
1928-1936	Daniel O. Hastings
1929-1940	John G. Townsend, Jr.
1937-1942	James H. Hughes
1941-1946	James M. Tunnell
1943-1948	C. Douglass Buck
1947-1970	John J. Williams
1949-1960	J. Allen Frear, Jr.
1961-1972	J. Caleb Boggs (R)
1971-	William V. Roth, Jr. (R)
1973-	Joseph R. Biden, Jr. (D)

Chief Justices

(Chancellors until 1951.)

1793-1800	William Killen
1801-1829	Nicholas Ridgely
1830-1831	Kensey Johns
1832-1856	Kensey Johns, Jr.
1857-1864	Samuel M. Harrington
1865-1872	Daniel M. Bates
1873-1891	Willard Saulsbury
1892-1894	James L. Wolcott
1895-1908	John R. Nicholson
1909-1920	Charles M. Curtis
1921-1937	Josiah O. Wolcott
1938-1949	William W. Harrington
1950	Daniel F. Wolcott
1951-1962	Clarence A. Southerland
1963	Charles L. Terry, Jr.
1964-1972	Daniel F. Wolcott
1973-1984	Daniel L. Herrmann
1985-	Andrew D. Christie

Florida

Governors

1845-1848	William D. Moseley

1849-1852	Thomas Brown
1853-1856	James E. Broome
1857-1860	Madison S. Perry
1861-1864	John Milton
1865	William Marvin
1866-1867	David S. Walker
1868-1872	Harrison Reed
1873	Ossian B. Hart
1874-1876	Marcellus L. Stearns
1877-1880	George F. Drew
1881-1884	William D. Bloxham
1885-1888	Edward A. Perry
1889-1892	Francis P. Fleming
1893-1896	Henry L. Mitchell
1897-1900	William D. Bloxham
1901-1904	William S. Jennings
1905-1908	Napoleon B. Broward
1909-1912	Albert W. Gilchrist
1913-1916	Park Trammell
1917-1921	Sidney J. Catts
1921-1924	Cary A. Hardee
1925-1928	John W. Martin
1929-1932	Doyle E. Carlton
1933-1936	David Scholtz
1937-1940	Fred P. Cone
1941-1944	Spessard L. Holland
1945-1948	Millard F. Caldwell
1949-1952	Fuller Warren
1953	Dan McCarty
1953-1954	Charley E. Johns
1955-1960	Leroy Collins
1961-1964	Farris Bryant
1965-1966	Haydon Burns
1967-1970	Claude R. Kirk
1971-1978	Reubin Askew (D)
1979-1986	Robert Graham (D)
1987-	Bob Martinez (R)

Senators

1845-1848	James D. Westcott, Jr.
1845-1850	David Levy Yulee
1849-1854	Jackson Morton
1851-1860	Stephen R. Mallory
1855-1860	David Levy Yulee
1861-1867	Vacant
1868	Adonijah S. Welch
1868-1872	Thomas W. Osborn
1869-1874	Abijah Gilbert
1873-1878	Simon B. Conover
1875-1886	Charles W. Jones
1879-1886	Wilkinson Call
1887-1898	Samuel Pasco
1897-1906	Stephen R. Mallory, Jr.
1899-1910	James P. Taliaferro
1907	William J. Bryan
1908	William H. Milton
1909-1935	Duncan U. Fletcher
1911-1916	Nathan P. Bryan
1917-1935	Park Trammell
1936	William L. Hill
1936	Scott M. Loftin
1936-1945	Charles O. Andrews
1936-1950	Claude D. Pepper
1946-1970	Spessard L. Holland
1951-1968	George A. Smathers
1969-1974	Edward J. Gurney (R)
1971-	Lawton M. Chiles, Jr. (D)
1975-1980	Richard Stone (D)
1981-1986	Paula Hawkins (R)
1987-	Robert Graham (D)

Chief Justices

1846-1850	Thomas Douglas
1851-1852	Walker Anderson
1853	Benjamin D. Wright
1854-1859	Thomas Baltzell

1860-1867	Charles H. Dupont
1868-1884	Edwin M. Randall
1885-1886	George G. McWhorter
1887-1888	Augustus E. Maxwell
1889-1893	George P. Raney
1894	Benjamin S. Liddon
1895-1896	Milton H. Mabry
1897-1904	Robert F. Taylor
1905-1908	Thomas M. Shackleford
1909-1910	James B. Whitfield

Hereafter justices of Supreme Court serve on a rotating basis as Chief Presiding Judge.

Georgia

Governors

1789	George Walton
1789-1792	Edward Telfair
1793-1795	George Mathews
1796-1797	Jared Irwin
1798-1800	James Jackson
1801	David Emanuel
1801	Josiah Tattnall
1802-1805	John Milledge
1806-1808	Jared Irwin
1809-1812	David B. Mitchell
1813-1814	Peter Early
1815-1816	David B. Mitchell
1817-1818	William Rabun
1819-1822	John Clark
1823-1826	George M. Troup
1827-1828	John Forsyth
1829-1830	George R. Gilmer
1831-1834	Wilson Lumpkin
1835-1836	William Schley
1837-1838	George R. Gilmer
1839-1842	Charles J. McDonald
1843-1846	George W. Crawford
1847-1850	George W. Towns
1851-1852	Howell Cobb
1853-1856	Herschel V. Johnson
1857-1864	Joseph E. Brown
1865	James Johnson
1865-1867	Charles J. Jenkins
1868	Thomas H. Ruger
1868-1869	Rufus B. Bullock
1871-1872	Benjamin Conley
1872-1876	Joseph M. Smith
1877-1881	Alfred H. Colquitt
1882	Alexander H. Stephens
1883-1886	Henry D. McDaniel
1886-1889	John B. Gordon
1890-1893	William J. Northen
1894-1897	William Y. Atkinson
1898-1901	Allen D. Candler
1902-1906	Joseph M. Terrell
1907-1908	Hoke Smith
1909-1910	Joseph M. Brown
1911	Hoke Smith
1912	Joseph M. Brown
1913-1914	John M. Slaton
1915-1916	Nathaniel E. Harris
1917-1920	Hugh M. Dorsey
1921-1922	Thomas W. Hardwick
1923-1926	Clifford Walker
1927-1930	Lamartine G. Hardman
1931-1932	Richard B. Russell
1933-1936	Eugene Talmadge
1937-1940	Eurith D. Rivers
1941-1942	Eugene Talmadge
1943-1946	Ellis G. Arnall
1947	Melvin E. Thompson
1948-1954	Herman E. Talmadge
1955-1958	S. Marvin Griffin

1959-1962	Samuel E. Vandiver, Jr.
1963-1966	Carl E. Sanders
1967-1970	Lester Maddox
1971-1974	James Earl (Jimmy) Carter (D)
1975-1982	George Busbee (D)
1983-	Joe F. Harris (D)

Senators

1789-1792	William Few
1789-1800	James Gunn
1793-1794	James Jackson
1795	George Walton
1796-1798	Josiah Tattnall
1799-1806	Abraham Baldwin
1801-1805	James Jackson
1806-1808	John Milledge
1807	George Jones
1807-1812	William H. Crawford
1809-1818	Charles Tait
1813	William B. Bulloch
1813	William W. Bibb
1816-1817	George M. Troup
1818	John Forsyth
1819-1820	Freeman Walker
1819-1824	John Elliott
1821-1823	Nicholas Ware
1824-1827	Thomas W. Cobb
1825-1828	John M. Berrien
1828	Oliver H. Prince
1829-1832	George M. Troup
1829-1834	John Forsyth
1833-1836	John P. King
1835-1842	Alfred Cuthbert
1841-1851	John M. Berrien
1843-1847	Walter T. Colquitt
1848	Herschel V. Johnson
1849-1854	William C. Dawson
1852	Robert M. Charlton
1853-1860	Robert Toombs
1855-1860	Alfred Iverson
1861-1869	Vacant
1871	Homer V. M. Willer
1871-1872	Joshua Hill
1871-1876	Thomas M. Norwood
1873-1879	John B. Gordon
1877-1881	Benjamin H. Hill
1880-1890	Joseph E. Brown
1882	M. Pope Barrow
1883-1893	Alfred H. Colquitt
1891-1896	John B. Gordon
1894	Patrick Walsh
1895-1913	Augustus O. Bacon
1897-1909	Alexander S. Clay
1910	Joseph M. Terrell
1911-1920	Hoke Smith
1914	William S. West
1914-1918	Thomas W. Hardwick
1919-1931	William J. Harris
1921	Thomas E. Watson
1922-1956	Walter F. George
1932	John S. Cohen
1933-1970	Richard B. Russell, Jr.
1957-1980	Herman E. Talmadge
1971-1972	David H. Gambrell
1973-	Sam Nunn (D)
1981-1986	Mack Mattingly (R)
1987-	Wycke Fowler (D)

Chief Justices

(Office of Chief Justice was created in 1866.)

1866	Joseph H. Lumpkin
1867	Hiram Warner
1868-1869	Joseph E. Brown

1871-1872	Osborne A. Lochrane
1872-1879	Hiram Warner
1880-1886	James Jackson
1887-1893	Logan E. Bleckley
1894-1904	Thomas J. Simmons
1905-1922	William H. Fish
1923-1937	Richard B. Russell
1938-1942	Charles S. Reid
1943-1946	Reason C. Bell
1947	William F. Jenkins
1948-1968	William H. Duckworth
1969-1972	Bond Almand
1973	Carlton Mobley
1974	Benning M. Grice
1975-1981	Horace E. Nichols
1982-1983	Robert N. Jordan
1984-	Harold N. Hill, Jr.

Hawaii

Governors

1959-1961	William F. Quinn
1962-1974	John A. Burns (D)
1975-1986	George R. Ariyoshi (D)
1987-	John Waihee (D)

Senators

1959-1962	Oren E. Long
1959-1976	Hiram L. Fong (R)
1963-	Daniel K. Inouye (D)
1977-	Spark M. Matsunaga (D)

Chief Justices

1959-1965	Wilfred C. Tsukiyama
1966-1982	William S. Richardson
1983-	Herman T. F. Lum

Idaho

Governors

1890	George L. Shoup
1890-1892	Norman B. Willey
1893-1896	William J. McConnell
1897-1900	Frank Steunenberg
1901-1902	Frank W. Hunt
1903-1904	John T. Morrison
1905-1908	Frank R. Gooding
1909-1910	James H. Brady
1911-1912	James H. Hawley
1913-1914	John M. Haines
1915-1918	Moses Alexander
1919-1922	David W. Davis
1923-1926	Charles C. Moore
1927-1930	H. Clarence Baldridge
1931-1936	C. Ben Ross
1937-1938	Barzilla W. Clark
1939-1940	C. A. Bottolfsen
1941-1942	Charles A. Clark
1943-1944	C. A. Bottolfsen
1945-1946	Charles C. Gossett
1947-1950	C. A. Robins
1951-1954	Len B. Jordan
1955-1966	Robert E. Smylie
1967-1970	Don Samuelson
1971-1977	Cecil D. Andrus' (D)
1978-1986	John V. Evans (D)

1987-	Cecil D. Andrus (D)

Senators

1890	William J. McConnell
1890-1900	George L. Shoup
1891-1896	Fred T. Dubois
1897-1902	Henry Heitfeld
1901-1906	Fred T. Dubois
1903-1911	Weldon B. Heyburn
1907-1939	William E. Borah
1912	Kirtland I. Perky
1913-1917	James H. Brady
1918-1920	John F. Negent
1921-1927	Frank R. Gooding
1928-1932	John Thomas
1933-1938	James P. Pope
1939-1944	D. Worth Clark
1940-1944	John Thomas
1945-1946	Charles C. Gossett
1945-1950	Glen H. Taylor
1947-1948	Henry C. Dworshak
1949	Bert H. Miller
1949-1962	Henry C. Dworshak
1951-1956	Herman Welker
1957-1981	Frank F. Church (D)
1963-1972	Len B. Jordan (R)
1973-	James A. McClure (R)
1981-	Steven D. Symms (R)

Chief Justices

Justices of the Supreme Court serve on a rotating basis as Chief Presiding Judge.

Illinois

Governors

1822-1825	Edward Coles
1826-1829	Ninian Edwards
1830-1833	John Reynolds
1834-1837	Joseph Duncan
1838-1841	Thomas Carlin
1842-1845	Thomas Ford
1846-1852	Augustus C. French
1853-1856	Joel A. Matteson
1857-1859	William H. Bissell
1860	John Wood (Acting)
1861-1864	Richard Yates
1865-1868	Richard J. Oglesby
1869-1872	John M. Palmer
1873	Richard J. Oglesby
1873-1876	John L. Beveridge
1877-1882	Shelby M. Cullom
1883-1884	John M. Hamilton
1885-1888	Richard J. Oglesby
1889-1892	Joseph W. Fifer
1893-1896	John P. Altgeld
1897-1900	John R. Tanner
1901-1904	Richard Yates
1905-1912	Charles S. Deneen
1913-1916	Edward F. Dunne
1917-1920	Frank O. Lowden
1921-1928	Len Small
1929-1932	Louis L. Emmerson
1933-1939	Henry Horner
1940	John H. Stelle
1941-1948	Dwight H. Green
1949-1952	Adlai E. Stevenson
1953-1960	William G. Stratton
1961-1967	Otto Kerner
1968	Samuel H. Shapiro
1969-1972	Richard B. Ogilvie

1973-1975	Daniel Walker (D)
1976-	James R. Thompson (R)

Senators

1824	John McLean
1825-1834	Elias K. Kane
1829	John McLean
1830	David J. Baker
1830-1840	John M. Robinson
1835-1836	William L. D. Ewing
1837-1842	Richard M. Young
1841-1842	Samuel McRoberts
1843-1846	James Semple
1843-1848	Sidney Breese
1847-1860	Stephen A. Douglas
1849-1854	James Shields
1855-1872	Lyman Trumbull
1861-1862	Orville H. Browning
1863-1864	William A. Richardson
1865-1870	Richard Yates
1871-1876	John A. Logan
1873-1878	Richard J. Oglesby
1877-1882	David Davis
1879-1886	John A. Logan
1883-1912	Shelby M. Cullom
1887-1890	Charles B. Farwell
1891-1896	John M. Palmer
1897-1902	William E. Mason
1903-1908	Albert J. Hopkins
1909-1911	William Lorimer
1912	Vacant
1913-1918	J. Hamilton Lewis
1913-1920	Lawrence Y. Sherman
1919-1924	Medill McCormick
1921-1925	William B. McKinley
1925-1930	Charles S. Deneen
1926-1927	Vacant
1928-1932	Otis F. Glenn
1931-1938	J. Hamilton Lewis
1933-1938	William H. Dieterich
1939	James M. Slattery
1939-1950	Scott W. Lucas
1940-1948	C. Wayland Brooks
1949-1966	Paul H. Douglas
1951-1968	Everett M. Dirksen
1967-1984	Charles H. Percy
1969-1970	Ralph T. Smith (R)
1971-1980	Adlai E. Stevenson, III (D)
1981-	Alan J. Dixon (D)
1985-	Paul Simon (D)

Chief Justices

1822-1824	Thomas Reynolds
1825-1847	William Wilson
1848-1854	Samuel H. Treat
1855	Onias C. Skinner
1856	Walter B. Scates
1857	Sidney Breese
1858-1863	John D. Caton
1864-1866	Pinkney H. Walker
1867-1869	Sidney Breese
1870-1873	Charles B. Lawrence

Hereafter Justices of the Supreme Court served on a rotating basis as Chief Presiding Judge.

Indiana

Governors

1816-1821	Jonathan Jennings

1822	Ratliff Boon
1822-1824	William Hendricks
1825-1830	James B. Ray
1831-1836	Noah Noble
1837-1839	David Wallace
1840-1842	Samuel Bigger
1843-1847	James Whitcomb
1848	Paris C. Dunning
1849-1856	Joseph A. Wright
1857-1859	Ashbel P. Willard
1860	Abram A. Hammond
1861	Henry S. Lane
1861-1866	Oliver H. P. T. Morton
1867-1872	Conrad Baker
1873-1876	Thomas A. Hendricks
1877-1879	James D. Williams
1880	Isaac P. Gray
1881-1884	Albert G. Porter
1885-1888	Isaac P. Gray
1889-1890	Alvin P. Hovey
1891-1892	Ira J. Chase
1893-1896	Claude Matthews
1897-1900	James A. Mount
1901-1904	Winfield T. Durbin
1905-1908	J. Frank Hanly
1909-1912	Thomas R. Marshall
1913-1916	Samuel M. Ralston
1917-1920	James P. Goodrich
1921-1923	Warren T. McCray
1924	Emmet F. Branch
1925-1928	Ed Jackson
1929-1932	Harry G. Leslie
1933-1936	Paul V. McNutt
1937-1940	H. Clifford Townsend
1941-1944	Henry F. Schricker
1945-1948	Ralph E. Gates
1949-1952	Henry F. Schricker
1953-1956	George Craig
1957-1960	Harold W. Handley
1961-1964	Matthew E. Welsh
1965-1968	Roger D. Branigin
1969-1972	Edgar Whitcomb
1973-1980	Otis R. Bowen (R)
1981-	Robert D. Orr (R)

Senators

1816-1824	Waller Taylor
1816-1830	James Noble
1825-1836	William Hendricks
1831	Robert Hanna
1832-1838	John Tipton
1837-1842	Oliver H. Smith
1839-1844	Albert S. White
1843-1848	Edward A. Hannegan
1845-1861	Jesse D. Bright
1849-1851	James Whitcomb
1852	Charles W. Cathcart
1853-1855	John Pettit
1856	Vacant
1857-1860	Graham N. Fitch
1861-1866	Henry S. Lane
1862	Joseph A. Wright
1863	David Turpie
1863-1868	Thomas A. Hendricks
1867-1876	Oliver H. P. T. Morton
1869-1874	Daniel D. Pratt
1875-1880	Joseph E. McDonald
1877-1896	Daniel W. Voorhees
1881-1886	Benjamin Harrison
1887-1898	David Turpie
1897-1904	Charles W. Fairbanks
1899-1910	Albert J. Beveridge
1905-1908	James A. Hemenway
1909-1915	Benjamin F. Shively
1911-1916	John W. Kern
1916	Thomas Taggard
1916-1932	James E. Watson
1917-1922	Harry S. New
1923-1924	Samuel M. Ralston

1925-1934	Arthur R. Robinson
1933-1943	Frederick Van Nuys
1935-1940	Sherman Minton
1941-1946	Raymond E. Willis
1944	Samuel D. Jackson
1944	William E. Jenner
1945-1962	Homer E. Capehart
1947-1958	William E. Jenner
1959-1976	Vance Hartke (D)
1963-1980	Birch Bayh (D)
1977-	Richard G. Lugar (R)
1981-	Dan Quayle (R)

Chief Justices

Justices of the Supreme Court serve on a rotating basis as Chief Presiding Judge.

Iowa

Governors

1846-1849	Ansel Briggs
1850-1853	Stephen Hempstead
1854-1857	James W. Grimes
1858-1859	Ralph P. Lowe
1860-1863	Samuel J. Kirkwood
1864-1867	William M. Stone
1868-1871	Samuel Merrill
1872-1875	Cyrus C. Carpenter
1876	Samuel J. Kirkwood
1877	Joshua G. Newbold
1878-1881	John H. Gear
1882-1885	Buren R. Sherman
1886-1889	William Larrabee
1890-1893	Horace Boies
1894-1895	Frank D. Jackson
1896-1897	Francis M. Drake
1898-1901	Leslie M. Shaw
1902-1908	Albert B. Cummins
1909-1912	Beryl F. Carroll
1913-1916	George W. Clarke
1917-1920	William L. Harding
1921-1924	Nathan E. Kendall
1925-1930	John Hammill
1931-1932	Dan W. Turner
1933-1936	Clyde L Herring
1937-1938	Nelson G. Kraschel
1939-1942	George A. Wilson
1943-1944	Bourke B. Hickenlooper
1945-1948	Robert D. Blue
1949-1953	William S. Beardsley
1954	Leo Elthon
1955-1956	Leo A. Hoegh
1957-1960	Herschel C. Loveless
1961-1962	Norman A. Erbe
1963-1968	Harold E. Hughes
1969	Robert D. Fulton (Acting)
1969-1982	Robert D. Ray (R)
1983-	Terry Branstad (R)

Senators

1848-1854	Augustus C. Dodge
1848-1854	George W. Jones
1855-1856	Vacant
1855-1858	Vacant
1857-1865	James Harlan
1859-1869	James W. Grimes
1866	Samuel J. Kirkwood
1867-1872	James Harlan
1870	James B. Howell
1871-1876	George G. Wright
1873-1907	William B. Allison

1877-1880	Samuel J. Kirkwood
1881-1882	James W. McDill
1883-1894	James F. Wilson
1895-1899	John H. Gear
1900-1909	Jonathan P. Dolliver
1908-1925	Albert B. Cummins
1910	Lafayette Young
1911-1921	William S. Kenyon
1922	Charles A. Rawson
1922-1925	Smith W. Brookhart
1926	David W. Stewart
1926-1930	Daniel F. Steck
1927-1932	Smith W. Brookhart
1931-1936	Lester J. Dickinson
1933-1935	Richard L. Murphy
1936-1944	Guy M. Gillette
1937-1942	Clyde L. Herring
1943-1948	George A. Wilson
1945-1968	Bourke B. Hickenlooper
1949-1954	Guy M. Gillette
1955-1960	Thomas E. Martin
1961-1972	Jack R. Miller
1969-1974	Harold E. Hughes (D)
1973-1978	Richard Clark (D)
1979-1984	Roger W. Jepson (R)
1981-	Charles E. Grassky (R)
1985-	Tom Harkin (D)

Chief Justices

Justices of the Supreme Court serve on a rotating basis as Chief Presiding Judge.

Kansas

Governors

1861-1862	Charles Robinson
1863-1864	Thomas Carney
1865-1867	Samuel J. Crawford
1868	Nehemiah Greene
1869-1872	James M. Harvey
1873-1876	Thomas A. Osborn
1877-1878	George T. Anthony
1879-1882	John P. St. John
1883-1884	George W. Glick
1885-1888	John A. Martin
1889-1892	Lyman U. Humphrey
1893-1894	Lorenzo D. Lewelling
1895-1896	Edmund N. Morill
1897-1898	John W. Leedy
1899-1902	William E. Stanley
1903-1904	Willis J. Bailey
1905-1908	Edward W. Hoch
1909-1912	Walter R. Stubbs
1913-1914	George H. Hodges
1915-1918	Arthur Capper
1919-1922	Henry J. Allen
1923-1924	Jonathan M. Davis
1925-1928	Ben S. Paulen
1929-1930	Clyde M. Reed
1931-1932	Harry H. Woodring
1933-1936	Alf M. Landon
1937-1938	Walter A. Huxman
1939-1942	Payne H. Ratner
1943-1946	Andrew F. Schoeppel
1947-1949	Frank Carlson
1950	Frank L. Hagaman
1951-1954	Edward F. Arn
1955-1956	Fred Hall
1957	John McCuish
1957-1960	George Docking
1961-1964	John Anderson, Jr.
1965-1966	William H. Avery
1967-1974	Robert B. Docking (D)
1975-1978	Robert F. Bennett (R)

1979-1986	John Carlin (D)
1987-	Mike Hayden (R)

Senators

1861-1865	James H. Lane
1861-1872	Samuel C. Pomeroy
1866-1870	Edmund G. Ross
1871-1872	Alexander Caldwell
1873	Robert Crozier
1873-1890	John J. Ingalls
1874-1876	James M. Harvey
1877-1891	Preston B. Plumb
1891-1896	William A. Peffer
1892	Bishop W. Perkins
1893-1894	John A. Martin
1895-1900	Lucien Baker
1897-1902	William A. Harris
1901-1905	Joseph R. Burton
1903-1908	Chester I. Long
1906	Alfred W. Benson
1907-1912	Charles Curtis
1909-1918	Joseph L. Bristow
1919-1938	Arthur Capper
1929	Henry J. Allen
1930-1948	George McGill
1939-1948	Clyde M. Reed
1949	Harry Darby
1949-1962	Andrew F. Schoeppel
1950-1968	Frank Carlson
1963-1978	James B. Pearson (R)
1969-	Robert J. Dole (R)
1979-	Nancy Landon Kassebaum (R)

Chief Justices

1861	Thomas Ewing
1862-1863	Nelson Cobb
1864-1866	Robert Crozier
1867-1876	Samuel A. Kingman
1877-1894	Albert H. Horton
1895-1896	David Martin
1897-1902	Frank Doster
1903-1934	William A. Johnston
1935-1936	Rousseau A. Burch
1937-1944	John S. Dawson
1945-1955	William W. Harvey
1956	William A. Smith
1957	Walter G. Thiele
1957-1965	Jay S. Parker
1966-1971	Robert T. Price
1972-1977	Harold R. Fatzer
1978-	Alfred G. Schroeder

Kentucky

Governors

1792-1795	Isaac Shelby
1796-1803	James Garrard
1804-1807	Christopher Greenup
1808-1811	Charles Scott
1812-1815	Isaac Shelby
1816	George Madison
1816-1819	Gabriel Slaughter
1820-1823	John Adair
1824-1827	Joseph Desha
1828-1831	Thomas Metcalfe
1832-1833	John Breathitt
1834-1835	James T. Morehead
1836-1838	James Clark
1839	Charles A. Wickliffe
1840-1843	Robert P. Letcher

1844-1847	William Owsley
1848-1849	John J. Crittenden
1850	John L. Helm
1851-1854	Lazarus W. Powell
1855-1858	Charles S. Morehead
1859-1861	Beriah Magoffin
1862	James F. Robinson
1863-1866	Thomas E. Bramlette
1867	John L. Helm
1867-1870	John W. Stevenson
1871-1874	Preston H. Leslie
1875-1878	James B. McCreary
1879-1882	Luke P. Blackburn
1883-1886	J. Proctor Knott
1887-1890	Simon B. Buckner
1891-1894	John Y. Brown
1895-1898	William O. Bradley
1899	William S. Taylor
1900	William Goebel
1900-1906	John C. W. Beckham
1907-1910	Augustus E. Willson
1911-1914	James B. McCreary
1915-1918	Augustus O. Stanley
1919	James D. Black
1919-1922	Edwin P. Morrow
1923-1926	William J. Fields
1927-1930	Flem D. Sampson
1931-1934	Ruby Laffoon
1935-1938	Albert B. Chandler
1939-1942	Keen Johnson
1943-1946	Simeon S. Willis
1947-1949	Earle C. Clements
1950-1954	Lawrence W. Wetherby
1955-1958	Albert B. Chandler
1959-1962	Bert T. Combs
1963-1966	Edward T. Breathitt
1967-1970	Louis B. Nunn
1971-1975	Wendell H. Ford (D)
1976-1980	Julian Carroll (D)
1981-1984	John Y. Brown, Jr. (D)
1985-	Martha L. Collins (D)

Senators

1792-1794	John Edwards
1792-1804	John Brown
1795-1800	Humphrey Marshall
1801-1804	John Breckinridge
1805	John Adair
1805-1809	Buckner Thruston
1806	Henry Clay
1807-1812	John Pope
1810	Henry Clay
1811-1813	George M. Bibb
1813	Jesse Bledsoe
1814	George Walker
1814-1815	William T. Barry
1815-1818	Isham Talbot
1816	Martin D. Hardin
1817-1818	John J. Crittenden
1819	William Logan
1819-1828	Richard M. Johnson
1820-1824	Isham Talbot
1825-1830	John Rowan
1829-1834	George M. Bibb
1831-1841	Henry Clay
1835-1840	John J. Crittenden
1841-1847	James T. Morehead
1842-1846	John J. Crittenden
1847-1852	Joseph R. Underwood
1848	Thomas Metcalfe
1849-1851	Henry Clay
1852-1854	Archibald Dixon
1853-1858	John B. Thompson
1855-1860	John J. Crittenden
1859-1864	Lazarus W. Powell
1861	John C. Breckinridge
1861-1871	Garrett Davis
1865-1867	James Guthrie
1868-1870	Thomas C. McCreery

1871-1876	John W. Stevenson
1872	Willis B. Machen
1873-1878	Thomas C. McCreery
1877-1889	James B. Beck
1879-1884	John S. Williams
1885-1896	Joseph C. S. Blackburn
1890-1892	John G. Carlisle
1893-1900	William Lindsay
1897-1902	William J. Deboe
1901-1906	Joseph C. S. Blackburn
1903-1908	James B. McCreary
1907-1912	Thomas H. Paynter
1909-1913	William O. Bradley
1913-1917	Ollie M. James
1914	Johnson N. Camden, Jr.
1915-1920	John C. W. Beckham
1918	George B. Martin
1919-1924	Augustus O. Stanley
1921-1926	Richard P. Ernst
1925-1929	Frederic M. Sackett
1927-1948	Alben W. Barkley
1930	John M. Robsion
1930	Ben M. Williamson
1931-1938	Marvel M. Logan
1939-1944	Albert B. Chandler
1945	William A. Stanfill
1946-1948	John Sherman Cooper
1949	Garrett L. Withers
1949-1950	Virgil M. Chapman
1950-1956	Earle C. Clements
1951	Thomas R. Underwood
1952-1954	John Sherman Cooper
1955	Alben W. Barkley
1956	Robert Humphreys
1956-1972	John Sherman Cooper
1957-1968	Thruston B. Morton
1969-1974	Marlow W. Cook (R)
1973-1984	Walter D. Huddleston (D)
1975-	Wendell H. Ford (D)
1985-	Mitch McConnell (R)

Chief Justices

1792	Harry Innes
1792-1805	George Muter
1806	Thomas Todd
1807	Felix Grundy
1808	Ninian Edwards
1809	George M. Bibb
1810-1826	John Boyle
1827-1828	George M. Bibb
1829-1842	George Robertson
1843-1846	Ephraim M. Ewing
1847-1851	Thomas A. Marshall

Hereafter members of the Court of Appeals served on a rotating basis as Chief Presiding Judge.

Louisiana

Governors

1812-1815	William C. C. Claiborne
1816-1819	Jacques P. Villere
1820-1823	Thomas B. Robertson
1824-1827	Henry Johnson
1828	Pierre Derbigny
1829	Armand Beauvais
1830	Jacques Dupre
1831-1834	Andre B. Roman
1835-1838	Edward D. White
1839-1842	Andre B. Roman
1843-1845	Alexander Mouton
1846-1849	Isaac Johnson
1850-1852	Joseph M. Walker

1853-1855	Paul O. Hebert
1856-1859	Robert C. Wickliffe
1860-1861	Thomas O. Moore
1862-1863	George F. Shepley
1864	Henry W. Allen
1864	Michael Hahn
1865-1866	James M. Wells
1867	Benjamin F. Flanders
1868	Joshua Baker
1868-1871	Henry C. Warmoth
1872	P. B. S. Pinchback (Acting)
1873-1876	William P. Kellogg
1877-1879	Francis T. Nicholls
1880	Louis A. Wiltz
1881-1887	Samuel D. McEnery
1888-1891	Francis T. Nicholls
1892-1899	Murphy J. Foster
1900-1903	William W. Heard
1904-1907	Newton C. Blanchard
1908-1911	Jared Y. Sanders
1912-1915	Luther E. Hall
1916-1919	Ruffin G. Pleasant
1920-1923	John M. Parker
1924-1925	Henry L. Fuqua
1926-1927	Oramel H. Simpson
1928-1931	Huey P. Long
1932-1935	Oscar K. Allen
1936	James A. Noe
1936-1938	Richard W. Leche
1939	Earl K. Long
1940-1943	Sam Houston Jones
1944-1947	James H. Davis
1948-1951	Earl K. Long
1952-1955	Robert F. Kennon
1956-1959	Earl K. Long
1960-1963	James H. Davis
1964-1971	John J. McKeithen
1972-1979	Edwin W. Edwards (D)
1980-1983	David C. Treen (R)
1984-	Edwin W. Edwards (D)

Senators

1812	Allen B. Magruder
1812	Thomas Posey
1813-1816	James Brown
1813-1818	Eligius Fromentin
1817	William C. C. Claiborne
1818-1823	Henry Johnson
1819-1823	James Brown
1824-1828	Dominique Bouligny
1824-1832	Josiah S. Johnston
1829-1830	Edward Livingston
1831-1834	George A. Waggaman
1833-1836	Alexander Porter
1835	Vacant
1836-1840	Robert C. Nicholas
1837-1841	Alexander Mouton
1841-1842	Alexander Barrow
1842-1848	Charles M. Conrad
1843	Vacant
1844-1846	Henry Johnson
1847	Pierre Soule
1847-1852	Solomon W. Downs
1849-1852	Pierre Soule
1853-1860	John Slidell
1853-1860	Judah P. Benjamin
1861-1868	Vacant
1868-1870	John S. Harris
1868-1871	William P. Kellogg
1871-1876	J. Rodman West
1872-1875	Vacant
1876-1878	James B. Eustis
1877-1882	William P. Kellogg
1879-1884	Benjamin F. Jonas
1883-1891	Randall L. Gibson
1885-1890	James B. Eustis
1891-1893	Edward D. White
1892-1900	Donelson Caffery
1894-1896	Newton C. Blanchard

1897-1909	Samuel D. McEnery
1901-1912	Murphy J. Foster
1910-1914	John R. Thornton
1913-1930	Joseph E. Ransdell
1915-1917	Robert F. Broussard
1918	Walter Guion
1918-1920	Edward J. Gay
1921-1932	Edwin S. Broussard
1931	Vacant
1932-1934	Huey P. Long
1933-1947	John H. Overton
1935	Vacant
1936	Rose McConnell Long
1937-1972	Allen J. Ellender
1948	William C. Feazel
1948-1986	Russell B. Long (D)
1973-	J. Bennett Johnston, Jr. (D)
1987-	John B. Breaux (D)

Chief Justices

1813-1835	George Mathews
1836-1845	Francois X. Martin
1846-1852	George Eustis
1853-1854	Thomas Slidell
1855-1864	Edwin T. Merrick
1865-1868	William B. Hyman
1868-1876	John T. Ludeling
1877-1879	Thomas C. Manning
1880-1891	Edward E. Bermudez
1892-1903	Francis T. Nicholls
1904-1913	Joseph A. Breaux
1914-1921	Frank A. Monroe
1922	Olivier O. Provosty
1922-1948	Charles A. O'Neill
1949-1969	John B. Fournet
1970	Joe B. Hamiter
1971-1972	E. Howard McCaleb
1973-1978	Joe W. Sanders
1979-1980	Frank W. Summers
1981-	John A. Dixon, Jr.

Maine

Governors

1820	William King
1821	William D. Williamson
1822-1826	Albion K. Parris
1827-1828	Enoch Lincoln
1829	Nathan Cutler
1830	Jonathan G. Hunton
1831-1833	Samuel E. Smith
1834-1837	Robert P. Dunlap
1838	Edward Kent
1839	John Fairfield
1840	Edward Kent
1841-1842	John Fairfield
1843	Edward Kavanagh
1844-1846	Hugh H. Anderson
1847-1849	John W. Dana
1850-1852	John Hubbard
1853-1854	William G. Crosby
1855	Anson P. Morrill
1856	Samuel Wells
1857	Hannibal Hamlin
1857	Joseph H. Williams
1858-1860	Lot M. Morrill
1861-1862	Israel Washburn, Jr.
1863	Abner Coburn
1864-1866	Samuel Cony
1867-1870	Joshua L. Chamberlain
1871-1873	Sidney Perham
1874-1875	Nelson Dingley, Jr.
1876-1878	Seldon Connor
1879	Alonzo Garcelon

1880	Daniel F. Davis
1881-1882	Harris M. Plaisted
1883-1886	Frederick Robie
1887	Joseph R. Bodwell
1887-1888	Sebastian S. Marble
1889-1892	Edwin C. Burleigh
1893-1896	Henry B. Cleaves
1897-1900	Llewellyn Powers
1901-1904	John F. Hill
1905-1908	William T. Cobb
1909-1910	Bert M. Fernald
1911-1912	Frederick W. Plaisted
1913-1914	William T. Haines
1915-1916	Oakley C. Curtis
1917-1920	Carl E. Milliken
1921	Frederick H. Parkhurst
1921-1924	Percival P. Baxter
1925-1928	Ralph O. Brewster
1929-1932	William T. Gardiner
1933-1936	Louis J. Brann
1937-1940	Lewis O. Barrows
1941-1944	Sumner Sewall
1945-1948	Horace A. Hildreth
1949-1951	Frederick G. Payne
1952-1954	Burton M. Cross
1955-1958	Edmund S. Muskie
1959	Robert N. Haskell
1959	Clinton A. Clauson
1960-1966	John H. Reed
1967-1974	Kenneth M. Curtis (D)
1975-1978	James Longley (Ind.)
1979-1986	Joseph E. Brennan (D)
1987-	John McKernan (R)

Senators

1820-1826	John Holmes
1820-1828	John Chandler
1827	Albion K. Parris
1828	Vacant
1929-1832	John Holmes
1829-1834	Peleg Sprague
1833-1835	Ether Shepley
1835-1840	John Ruggles
1836	Judah Dana
1837-1842	Reuel Williams
1841-1846	George Evans
1843-1847	John Fairfield
1847-1852	James W. Bradbury
1848	Wyman B. S. Moor
1848-1856	Hannibal Hamlin
1853	Vacant
1854-1863	William P. Fessenden
1857	Amos Nourse
1857-1860	Hannibal Hamlin
1861-1868	Lot M. Morrill
1864	Nathan A. Farwell
1865-1868	William P. Fessenden
1869-1875	Lot M. Morrill
1869-1880	Hannibal Hamlin
1876-1880	James G. Blaine
1881-1910	William P. Frye
1881-1910	Eugene Hale
1911-1912	Obadiah Gardner
1911-1916	Charles F. Johnson
1913-1915	Edwin C. Burleigh
1916-1925	Bert M. Fernald
1917-1940	Frederick Hale
1926-1930	Arthur R. Gould
1931-1948	Wallace H. White, Jr.
1941-1951	Ralph O. Brewster
1949-1972	Margaret Chase Smith
1952-1958	Frederick G. Payne
1959-1980	Edmund S. Muskie (D)
1973-1978	William D. Hathaway (D)
1979-	William S. Cohen (R)
1981-	George J. Mitchell (D)

Chief Justices

1820-1833	Prentiss Mellen
1834-1840	Nathan Weston
1841-1847	Ezekiel Whitman
1848-1854	Ether Shepley
1855-1861	John S. Tenney
1862-1882	John Appleton
1883-1899	John A. Peters
1900-1905	Andrew P. Wiswell
1906-1910	Lucilius A. Emery
1911-1912	William P. Whitehouse
1913-1916	Albert R. Savage
1917-1924	Leslie C. Cornish
1925-1928	Scott Wilson
1929	Luere B. Deasy
1930-1934	William R. Pattangall
1935-1938	Charles J. Dunn
1939	Charles P. Barnes
1940-1948	Guy H. Sturgis
1949-1952	Harold H. Murchie
1953	Edward F. Merrill
1954-1956	Raymond Fellows
1957-1969	Robert B. Williamson
1970-1976	Armand A. Dufresne, Jr.
1977-	Vincent L. McKusick

Maryland

Governors

1789-1790	John E. Howard
1791	George Plater
1792-1793	Thomas S. Lee
1794-1796	John H. Stone
1797	John Henry
1798-1800	Benjamin Ogle
1801-1802	John F. Mercer
1803-1805	Robert Bowie
1806-1808	Robert Wright
1809-1810	Edward Lloyd
1811	Robert Bowie
1812-1814	Levin Winder
1815-1817	Charles C. Ridgely
1818	Charles Goldsborough
1819-1821	Samuel Sprigg
1822-1825	Samuel Stevens, Jr.
1826-1827	Joseph Kent
1828	Daniel Martin
1829	Thomas K. Carroll
1830	Daniel Martin
1831-1832	George Howard
1833-1834	James Thomas
1835-1837	Thomas W. Veazey
1838-1840	William Grason
1841-1843	Francis Thomas
1844-1846	Thomas G. Pratt
1847-1849	Philip F. Thomas
1850-1853	Enoch L. Lowe
1854-1857	Thomas W. Ligon
1858-1861	Thomas H. Hicks
1862-1864	Augustus W. Bradford
1865-1868	Thomas Swann
1869-1871	Oden Bowie
1872-1873	William P. Whyte
1874-1875	James B. Groome
1876-1879	John L. Carroll
1880-1883	William T. Hamilton
1884	Robert M. McLane
1885-1887	Henry Lloyd
1888-1891	Elihu E. Jackson
1892-1895	Frank Brown
1896-1899	Lloyd Lowndes
1900-1903	John W. Smith
1904-1907	Edwin Warfield
1908-1911	Austin L. Crothers
1912-1915	Phillips L. Goldsborough

1916-1920	Emerson C. Harrington
1920-1934	Albert C. Ritchie
1935-1938	Harry W. Nice
1939-1946	Herbert R. O'Conor
1947-1950	William P. Lane, Jr.
1951-1958	Theodore R. McKeldin
1959-1966	J. Millard Tawes
1967-1968	Spiro T. Agnew
1969-1977	Marvin Mandel (D)
1978	Blair Lee, III (D)
1979-1986	Harold Hughes (D)
1987-	William D. Schaefer (D)

Senators

1789-1792	Charles Carroll
1789-1796	John Henry
1793-1795	Richard Potts
1796-1802	John E. Howard
1797-1799	James Lloyd
1800	William Hindman
1801-1805	Robert Wright
1803-1814	Samuel Smith
1806-1812	Philip Reed
1813-1818	Robert H. Goldsborough
1815	Vacant
1816	Robert G. Harper
1816-1818	Alexander C. Hanson
1819	Vacant
1819-1821	William Pinkney
1819-1825	Edward Lloyd
1822-1832	Samuel Smith
1826-1834	Ezekiel F. Chambers
1833-1837	Joseph Kent
1835	Robert H. Goldsborough
1836-1840	John S. Spence
1838-1844	William D. Merrick
1841-1842	John L. Kerr
1843-1861	James A. Pearce
1845-1848	Reverdy Johnson
1849	David Stewart
1850-1856	Thomas G. Pratt
1857-1862	Anthony Kennedy
1862-1864	Thomas H. Hicks
1863-1867	Reverdy Johnson
1865-1866	John A. J. Creswell
1867	Vacant
1868	William P. Whyte
1868-1872	George Vickers
1869-1874	William T. Hamilton
1873-1878	George R. Dennis
1875-1880	William P. Whyte
1879-1884	James B. Groome
1881-1898	Arthur P. Gorman
1885-1890	Ephraim K. Wilson
1891-1896	Charles H. Gibson
1897-1902	George L. Wellington
1899-1904	Louis E. McComas
1903-1905	Arthur P. Gorman
1905-1911	Isidor Rayner
1906-1907	William P. Whyte
1908-1920	John W. Smith
1912-1913	William P. Jackson
1914-1916	Blair Lee
1917-1922	Joseph I. France
1921-1926	Ovington E. Weller
1923-1928	William Cabell Bruce
1927-1950	Millard E. Tydings
1928-1934	Phillips L. Goldsborough
1935-1946	George L. Radcliffe
1947-1952	Herbert R. O'Conor
1951-1962	John M. Butler
1953-1964	J. Glenn Beall
1963-1968	Daniel B. Brewster
1965-1970	Joseph D. Tydings
1969-1986	Charles McC. Mathias (R)
1971-1976	J. Glenn Beall, Jr. (R)
1977-	Paul S. Sarbanes (D)
1987-	Barbara A. Mikulski (D)

Chief Justices

1789-1805	Benjamin Rumsey
1806-1824	Jeremiah T. Chase
1825-1843	John Buchanan
1844-1847	Stevenson Archer
1848-1850	Thomas B. Dorsey
1851-1860	John C. LeGrand
1861-1866	Richard J. Bowie
1867-1882	James L. Bartol
1883-1892	Richard H. Alvey
1893-1895	John M. Robinson
1896-1906	James McSherry
1907-1923	A. Hunter Boyd
1924-1942	Carroll T. Bond
1943	D. Lindley Stoan
1944-1951	Ogle Marbury
1952	Charles Markell
1952-1953	Simon E. Sobeloff
1954-1963	Frederick W. Brune
1964	William L. Henderson
1964-1965	Stedman Prescott
1966-1971	Hall Hammond
1972-	Robert C. Murphy

Massachusetts

Governors

1789-1793	John Hancock
1794-1796	Samuel Adams
1797-1799	Increase Sumner
1800-1806	Caleb Strong
1807-1808	James Sullivan
1809	Christopher Gore
1810-1811	Elbridge Gerry
1812-1815	Caleb Strong
1816-1822	John Brooks
1823-1824	William Eustis
1825-1833	Levi Lincoln
1834-1835	John Davis
1836-1839	Edward Everett
1840	Marcus Morton
1841-1842	John Davis
1843	Marcus Morton
1844-1850	George N. Briggs
1851-1852	George S. Boutwell
1853	John H. Clifford
1854	Emory Washburn
1855	Henry J. Gardner
1858-1860	Nathaniel P. Banks
1861-1865	John A. Andrew
1866-1868	Alexander H. Bullock
1869-1871	William Claflin
1872-1874	William B. Washburn
1875	William Gaston
1876-1878	Alexander H. Rice
1879	Thomas Talbot
1880-1882	John D. Long
1883	Benjamin F. Butler
1884-1886	George D. Robinson
1887-1889	Oliver Ames
1890	John Q. A. Brackett
1891-1893	William E. Russell
1894-1895	Frederic T. Greenhalge
1896-1899	Roger Wolcott
1900-1902	Winthrop M. Crane
1903-1904	John L. Bates
1905	William L. Douglas
1906-1908	Curtis Guild, Jr.
1909-1910	Eben S. Draper
1911-1913	Eugene N. Foss
1914-1915	David I. Walsh
1916-1918	Samuel W. McCall
1919-1920	Calvin Coolidge
1921-1924	Channing H. Cox
1925-1928	Alvan T. Fuller

1929-1930	Frank G. Allen
1931-1934	Joseph B. Ely
1935-1936	James M. Curley
1937-1938	Charles F. Hurley
1939-1944	Leverett Saltonstall
1945-1946	Maurice J. Tobin
1947-1948	Robert F. Bradford
1949-1952	Paul A. Dever
1953-1956	Christian A. Herter
1957-1960	Foster Furcolo
1961-1962	John A. Volpe
1963-1964	Endicott Peabody
1965-1969	John A. Volpe
1970-1974	Francis W. Sargent (R)
1975-1978	Michael S. Dukakis (D)
1979-1982	Edward J. King (D)
1983-	Michael S. Dukakis (D)

Senators

1789-1790	Tristram Dalton
1789-1795	Caleb Strong
1791-1795	George Cabot
1796-1798	Theodore Sedgwick
1796-1799	Benjamin Goodhue
1799	Samuel Dexter
1800-1802	Jonathan Mason
1800-1802	Dwight Foster
1803-1807	John Quincy Adams
1803-1810	Timothy Pickering
1808-1812	James Lloyd
1811-1816	Joseph B. Varnum
1813-1815	Christopher Gore
1816-1817	Eli P. Ashmun
1817-1821	Harrison G. Otis
1818-1819	Prentiss Mellen
1820-1826	Elijah H. Mills
1822-1825	James Lloyd
1826-1834	Nathaniel Silsbee
1827-1840	Daniel Webster
1835-1840	John Davis
1841-1844	Rufus Choate
1841-1844	Isaac C. Bates
1845-1849	Daniel Webster
1845-1852	John Davis
1850	Robert C. Winthrop
1851	Robert Rantoul, Jr.
1851-1873	Charles Sumner
1853	Edward Everett
1854	Julius Rockwell
1855-1872	Henry Wilson
1873-1876	George S. Boutwell
1874	William B. Washburn
1875-1892	Henry L. Dawes
1877-1903	George F. Hoar
1893-1924	Henry Cabot Lodge
1904-1912	Winthrop M. Crane
1913-1918	John W. Weeks
1919-1924	David I. Walsh
1924-1925	William M. Butler
1925-1930	Frederick H. Gillett
1926-1946	David I. Walsh
1931-1936	Marcus A. Coolidge
1937-1943	Henry Cabot Lodge, Jr.
1944	Sinclair Weeks
1945-1966	Leverett Saltonstall
1947-1952	Henry Cabot Lodge, Jr.
1953-1960	John F. Kennedy
1961-1962	Benjamin A. Smith
1963-	Edward M. Kennedy (D)
1967-1978	Edward W. Brooke (R)
1979-1984	Paul E. Tsongas (D)
1985-	John Kerry (D)

Chief Justices

1789-1790	Nathaniel P. Sargeant
1791-1805	Francis Dana
1806-1812	Theophilus Parsons
1813	Samuel Sewall
1814-1829	Isaac Parker
1830-1859	Lemuel Shaw
1860-1867	George T. Bigelow
1868-1872	Reuben A. Chapman
1873-1881	Horace Gray
1882-1889	Marcus Morton
1890-1898	Walbridge A. Field
1899-1902	Oliver Wendell Holmes
1903-1910	Marcus P. Knowlton
1911-1937	Arthur P. Rugg
1938-1946	Fred T. Field
1947-1955	Stanley E. Qua
1956-1969	Raymond S. Wilkins
1970-1975	G. Joseph Tauro
1976-	Edward F. Hennessey

Michigan

Governors

1837-1839	Stevens T. Mason
1840	William Woodbridge
1841	James W. Gordon
1842-1845	John S. Barry
1846	Alpheus Felch
1847	William L. Greenly
1848-1849	Epaphroditus Ransom
1850-1851	John S. Barry
1852	Robert McClelland
1853-1854	Andrew Parsons
1855-1858	Kinsley S. Bingham
1859-1860	Moses Wisner
1861-1864	Austin Blair
1865-1868	Henry H. Crapo
1869-1872	Henry P. Baldwin
1873-1876	John J. Bagley
1877-1880	Charles M. Croswell
1881-1882	David H. Jerome
1883-1884	Josiah W. Begole
1885-1886	Russell A. Alger
1887-1890	Cyrus G. Luce
1891-1892	Edwin B. Winans
1893-1896	John T. Rich
1897-1900	Hazen S. Pingree
1901-1904	Aaron T. Bliss
1905-1910	Frederick M. Warner
1911-1912	Chase S. Osborn
1913-1916	Woodbridge N. Ferris
1917-1920	Albert E. Sleeper
1921-1926	Alexander J. Groesbeck
1927-1930	Fred W. Green
1931-1932	Wilber M. Brucker
1933-1934	William A. Comstock
1935-1936	Frank D. Fitzgerald
1937-1938	Frank D. Murphy
1939	Frank D. Fitzgerald
1939-1940	Lauren D. Dickinson
1941-1942	Murray D. Van Wagoner
1943-1946	Harry F. Kelly
1947-1948	Kim Sigler
1949-1960	G. Mennen Williams
1961-1962	John B. Swainson
1963-1968	George Romney
1969-1982	William G. Milliken (R)
1983-	James J. Blanchard (D)

Senators

1837-1838	Lucius Lyon
1837-1840	John Norvell
1839	Vacant
1840-1844	Augustus S. Porter
1841-1846	William Woodbridge
1845-1847	Lewis Cass
1847-1852	Alpheus Felch
1848	Thomas Fitzgerald
1849-1856	Lewis Cass
1853-1858	Charles E. Stuart
1857-1874	Zachariah Chandler
1859-1861	Kinsley S. Bingham
1862-1870	Jacob M. Howard
1871-1882	Thomas W. Ferry
1875-1878	Isaac P. Christiancy
1879	Zachariah Chandler
1879-1880	Henry P. Baldwin
1881-1886	Omar D. Conger
1883-1888	Thomas W. Palmer
1887-1893	Francis B. Stockbridge
1889-1901	James McMillan
1894	John Patton, Jr.
1895-1910	Julius C. Burrows
1902-1906	Russell A. Alger
1907-1918	William S. Smith
1911-1921	Charles E. Townsend
1919-1935	Truman H. Newberry
1922	James Couzens
1923-1927	Woodbridge N. Ferris
1928-1951	Arthur H. Vandenberg
1936-1942	Prentiss M. Brown
1943-1954	Homer Ferguson
1951	Arthur E. B. Moody
1952-1958	Charles E. Potter
1955-1966	Patrick V. McNamara
1959-1976	Philip A. Hart (D)
1967-1978	Robert P. Griffin (R)
1977-	Donald W. Riegle, Jr. (D)
1979-	Carl Levin (D)

Chief Justices

Justices of the Supreme Court serve on a rotating basis as Chief Presiding Judge.

Minnesota

Governors

1858-1859	Henry J. Sibley
1860-1862	Alexander Ramsey
1863	H. A. Swift
1864-1865	Stephen Miller
1866-1869	William R. Marshall
1870-1873	Horace Austin
1874-1875	Cushman K. Davis
1876-1881	John S. Pillsbury
1882-1886	Lucius F. Hubbard
1887-1888	Andrew R. McGill
1889-1892	William R. Merriam
1893-1894	Knute Nelson
1895-1898	David M. Clough
1899-1900	John Lind
1901-1904	Samuel R. Van Sant
1905-1908	John A. Johnson
1909-1914	Adolph O. Eberhart
1915	Winfield S. Hammond
1915-1920	Joseph A. A. Burnquist
1921-1924	Jacob A. O. Preus
1925-1930	Theodore Christianson
1931-1935	Floyd B. Olson
1936	Hjalmar Peterson
1937-1938	Elmer A. Benson
1939-1942	Harold E. Stassen
1943-1946	Edward J. Thye
1947-1950	Luther W. Youngdahl
1951-1954	C. Elmer Anderson
1955-1960	Orville L. Freeman
1961-1962	Elmer L. Andersen
1963-1966	Karl F. Rolvaag
1967-1970	Harold LeVander
1971-1977	Wendell R. Anderson (D)

1978	Rudy Perpich (D)
1979-1982	Albert H. Quie (R)
1983-	Rudy Perpich (D)

Senators

1858	James Shields
1858-1862	Henry M. Rice
1859-1864	Morton S. Wilkinson
1863-1874	Alexander Ramsey
1865-1869	Daniel S. Norton
1870	William Windom
1871	Ozora P. Stearns
1871-1880	William Windom
1875-1886	Samuel J. R. McMillan
1881	Alonzo J. Edgerton
1881-1882	William Windom
1883-1888	Dwight M. Sabin
1887-1899	Cushman K. Davis
1889-1894	William D. Washburn
1895-1922	Knute Nelson
1900	Charles A. Towne
1901-1916	Moses E. Clapp
1917-1922	Frank B. Kellogg
1923-1924	Magnus Johnson
1923-1946	Henrik Shipstead
1925-1934	Thomas D. Schall
1935	Elmer A. Benson
1936	Guy V. Howard
1937-1939	Ernest Lundeen
1940-1941	Joseph H. Ball
1942	Arthur E. Nelson
1943-1948	Joseph H. Ball
1947-1958	Edward J. Thye
1949-1964	Hubert H. Humphrey
1959-1970	Eugene J. McCarthy
1965-1975	Walter F. Mondale (D)
1971-1978	Hubert H. Humphrey (D)
1976-1978	Wendell R. Anderson (D)
1979-	David Durenberger (R)
1979-	Rudolph E. Boschwitz (R)

Chief Justices

1858-1864	Lafayette Emmett
1865-1868	Thomas Wilson
1869	James Gilfillan
1870-1873	Christopher G. Ripley
1874	Samuel J. R. McMillan
1875-1894	James Gilfillan
1895-1912	Charles N. Start
1913-1922	Calvin L. Brown
1923-1932	Samuel B. Wilson
1933-1936	John P. Devaney
1937-1943	Henry M. Gallagher
1944-1952	Charles Loring
1953-1961	Roger L. Dell
1962-1973	Oscar R. Knutson
1974-1980	Robert J. Sheran
1981-	Douglas K. Amdahl

Mississippi

Governors

1817-1819	David Holmes
1820-1821	George Poindexter
1822-1824	Walter Leake
1825	Gerald C. Brandon (Acting)
1826	David Holmes
1827-1831	Gerard C. Brandon
1832	Abram M. Scott
1833-1834	Hiram G. Runnels
1835	John A. Quitman (Acting)

1836-1837	Charles Lynch
1838-1841	Alexander G. McNutt
1842-1843	Tilghman M. Tucker
1844-1847	Albert G. Brown
1848-1849	Joseph W. Matthews
1850	John A. Quitman
1851	John I. Guion
1851	James Whitfield
1852-1853	Henry S. Foote
1854	John J. Pettus
1854-1856	John I. McRae
1857-1858	William McWillie
1859-1862	John J. Pettus
1863-1864	Charles Clark
1865-1867	Benjamin G. Humphreys
1868-1869	Adelbert Ames
1870	James L. Alcorn
1871-1873	Ridgley C. Powers (Acting)
1874-1875	Adelbert Ames
1876-1881	John M. Stone (Acting)
1882-1889	Robert Lowry
1890-1895	John M. Stone
1896-1899	Anselm J. McLaurin
1900-1903	Andrew H. Longino
1904-1907	James K. Vardaman
1908-1911	Edmund F. Noel
1912-1915	Earl L. Brewer
1916-1919	Theodore G. Bilbo
1920-1923	Lee M. Russell
1924-1926	Henry L. Whitfield
1927	Dennis Murphree
1928-1931	Theodore G. Bilbo
1932-1935	Martin S. Conner
1936-1939	Hugh White
1940-1942	Paul B. Johnson
1943	Dennis Murphree
1944-1945	Thomas L. Bailey
1946-1951	Fielding L. Wright
1952-1955	Hugh L. White
1956-1959	James P. Coleman
1960-1963	Ross R. Barnett
1964-1967	Paul B. Johnson
1968-1971	John Bell Williams
1972-1975	William L. Waller (D)
1976-1979	Charles C. Finch (D)
1980-1983	William Winter (D)
1984-	William A. Allain (D)

Senators

1817-1819	Walter Leake
1817-1828	Thomas H. Williams
1820-1824	David Holmes
1825	Powhatan Ellis
1826	Thomas B. Reed
1827-1831	Powhatan Ellis
1829	Thomas B. Reed
1830	Robert H. Adams
1830-1834	George Poindexter
1832-1837	John Black
1835-1844	Robert J. Walker
1838	James F. Trotter
1838	Thomas H. Williams
1839-1844	John Henderson
1845-1846	Jesse Speight
1845-1846	Joseph W. Chalmers
1847-1850	Jefferson Davis
1847-1851	Henry S. Foote
1851	John J. McRae
1852	Walker Brooke
1852-1856	Stephen Adams
1853	Vacant
1854-1860	Albert G. Brown
1857-1860	Jefferson Davis
1861-1869	Vacant
1870	Hiram R. Revels
1870-1873	Adelbert Adams
1871-1876	James L. Alcorn
1874	Henry R. Pease
1875-1880	Blanche K. Bruce

1877-1884	Lucius Q. C. Lamar
1881-1896	James Z. George
1885-1893	Edward C. Walthall
1894	Anselm J. McLaurin
1895-1897	Edward C. Walthall
1897-1910	Hernando D. Money
1898-1900	William V. Sullivan
1901-1908	Anselm J. McLaurin
1909	James Gordon
1910-1912	LeRoy Percy
1911-1922	John S. Williams
1913-1918	James. K. Vardaman
1919-1940	Byron P. Harrison
1923-1934	Hubert D. Stephens
1935-1946	Theodore G. Bilbo
1941	James O. Eastland
1941-1942	Wall Doxey
1943-1978	James O. Eastland (D)
1947-	John C. Stennis (D)
1979-	Thad Cochran (R)

Chief Justices

1833-1850	William L. Sharkey
1851-1863	Cotesworth P. Smith
1864-1867	Alexander H. Handy
1868-1869	Thomas G. Shackleford
1870-1875	Ephraim G. Peyton
1876-1877	Horatio F. Simrall
1878-1879	James Z. George
1880-1893	Josiah A. P. Campbell
1894-1895	Tim E. Cooper
1896-1899	Thomas H. Woods
1900-1909	Albert H. Whitfield
1910-1911	Robert B. Mayes
1912-1947	Sydney Smith
1948	Virgil Griffith
1949-1963	Harvey McGehee
1964-1965	Percy M. Lee
1966-1971	William N. Ethridge, Jr.
1972	Robert G. Gillesple
1977	Neville Patterson

Missouri

Governors

1821-1823	Alexander McNair
1824-1825	Frederick Bates
1826-1831	John Miller
1832-1835	Daniel Dunklin
1836-1839	Lilburn W. Boggs
1840-1843	Thomas Reynolds
1844-1847	John C. Edwards
1848-1852	Austin A. King
1853-1856	Sterling Price
1857	Trusten Polk
1857	Hancock Jackson
1857-1860	Robert M. Stewart
1861	Claiborne F. Jackson
1861-1863	Hamilton R. Gamble
1864	Willard P. Hall (Acting)
1865-1868	Thomas C. Fletcher
1869-1870	Joseph W. McClurg
1871-1872	B. Gratz Brown
1873-1874	Silas Woodson
1875-1876	Clarles H. Hardin
1877-1880	John S. Phelps
1881-1884	Thomas T. Crittenden
1885-1886	John S. Marmaduke
1887-1888	Allen P. Morehouse
1889-1892	David R. Francis
1893-1896	William J. Stone
1897-1900	Lon V. Stephens
1901-1904	Alexander M. Dockery
1905-1908	Joseph W. Folk

1909-1912	Herbert S. Hadley
1913-1916	Elliott W. Major
1917-1920	Frederick D. Gardner
1921-1924	Arthur M. Hyde
1925-1928	Sam A. Baker
1929-1932	Henry S. Caulfield
1933-1936	Guy B. Park
1937-1940	Lloyd Crow Stark
1941-1944	Forrest C. Donnell
1945-1948	Phil M. Donnelly
1949-1952	Forrest Smith
1953-1956	Phil M. Donnelly
1957-1960	James T. Blair, Jr.
1961-1964	John M. Dalton
1965-1972	Warren E. Hearnes
1973-1976	Christopher S. Bond (R)
1977-1980	Joseph P. Teasdale (D)
1981-1984	Christopher S. Bond (R)
1985-	John D. Ashcroft (R)

Senators

1821-1830	David Barton
1821-1850	Thomas H. Benton
1831-1832	Alexander Buckner
1833-1842	Lewis F. Linn
1843-1854	David R. Atchison
1851-1856	Henry S. Geyer
1855-1856	Vacant
1857-1860	James S. Green
1857-1861	Trusten Polk
1861	Waldo P. Johnson
1862	Robert Wilson
1862-1868	John B. Henderson
1863-1866	B. Gratz Brown
1867-1869	Charles D. Drake
1869-1874	Carl Schurz
1870	Daniel T. Jewett
1871-1872	Francis P. Blair, Jr.
1873-1876	Lewis V. Bogy
1875-1904	Francis M. Cockrell
1877-1878	David H. Armstrong
1879	James Shields
1879-1902	George G. Vest
1903-1917	William J. Stone
1905-1918	William Warner
1911-1928	James A. Reed
1918	Xenophon P. Wilfley
1918-1924	Seldon P. Spencer
1925	George H. Williams
1926-1932	Harry B. Hawes
1929-1934	Roscoe C. Patterson
1933-1944	Bennett Champ Clark
1935-1944	Harry S Truman
1945-1946	Frank P. Briggs
1945-1950	Forrest C. Donnell
1947-1952	James P. Kem
1951-1959	Thomas C. Hennings, Jr.
1953-1976	W. Stuart Symington (D)
1960-1968	Edward V. Long
1969-1986	Thomas F. Eagleton (D)
1977-	John C. Danforth (R)
1987-	Christopher S. Bond (R)

Chief Justices

1821-1839	Matthias McGirk
1840-1844	George Tompkins
1845-1850	William B. Napton
1851-1853	Hamilton R. Gamble
1854-1861	William Scott
1862-1864	Barton Bates
1865-1875	David Wagner
1876-1882	Thomas A. Sherwood
1883-1884	Warwick Hough
1885-1886	John W. Henry
1887-1888	Elijah H. Norton
1889-1890	Robert D. Ray

1891-1892	Thomas A. Sherwood
1893-1896	Francis M. Black
1897	Shepard Barclay
1898-1900	James B. Gantt
1901-1902	Gavon D. Burgess
1903-1904	Waltour M. Robinson
1905-1906	Theodore Brace
1907-1908	James B. Gantt
1909-1912	Leroy B. Valliant
1913-1914	Henry Lamm
1915	Archelaus M. Woodson
1916-1917	Waller W. Graves
1918	Henry W. Bond
1919-1921	Robert F. Walker
1922	James T. Blair
1922-1923	Archelaus M. Woodson

Hereafter justices of the Supreme Court serve on a rotating basis as Chief Presiding Judge.

Montana

Governors

1889-1892	Joseph K. Toole
1893-1896	John E. Rickards
1897-1900	Robert B. Smith
1901-1907	Joseph K. Toole
1908-1912	Edwin L. Norris
1913-1920	Samuel V. Stewart
1921-1924	Joseph M. Dixon
1925-1932	John E. Erickson
1933-1934	Frank H. Cooney
1935-1936	Elmer Holt
1937-1940	Roy E. Ayers
1941-1948	Sam C. Ford
1949-1952	John W. Bonner
1953-1960	J. Hugo Aronson
1961	Donald G. Nutter
1962-1968	Tim Babcock
1969-1972	Forrest H. Anderson
1973-1980	Thomas L. Judge (D)
1981-	Ted Schwinden (D)

Senators

1890-1892	Wilbur F. Sanders
1890-1894	Thomas C. Power
1893-1894	Vacant
1895-1898	Lee Mantle
1895-1900	Thomas H. Carter
1899	William A. Clark
1900	Vacant
1901-1904	Paris Gibson
1901-1906	William A. Clark
1905-1910	Thomas H. Carter
1907-1912	Joseph M. Dixon
1911-1922	Henry L. Myers
1913-1932	Thomas J. Walsh
1923-1946	Burton K. Wheeler
1933	John E. Erickson
1934-1960	James E. Murray
1947-1952	Zales N. Ecton
1953-1976	Mike Mansfield (D)
1961-1978	Lee Metcalf (D)
1977-	John Melcher (D)
1979-	Max Baucus (D)

Chief Justices

1889-1892	Henry N. Blake
1893-1897	William Y. Pemberton
1898-1921	Theodore Brantly

1922-1934	Llewllyn L. Callaway
1935-1937	W. B. Sands
1938	O. F. Goddard
1939-1945	Howard A. Johnson
1946	Carl Lindquist
1947-1956	Hugh Adair
1957-1976	James T. Harrison
1977	Paul G. Hatfield
1978-1985	Frank I. Haswell
1986-	Jean Turnage

Nebraska

Governors

1867-1870	David Butler
1871-1872	William H. James
1873-1874	Robert W. Furnas
1875-1878	Silas Garber
1879-1882	Albinus Nance
1883-1886	James W. Dawes
1887-1890	John M. Thayer
1891	James E. Boyd
1891	John M. Thayer
1892	James E. Boyd
1893-1894	Lorenzo Crounse
1895-1898	Silas A. Holcomb
1899-1900	William A. Poynter
1901	Charles H. Dietrich
1901-1902	Ezra P. Savage
1903-1906	John H. Mickey
1907-1908	George L. Sheldon
1909-1910	Ashton C. Shallenberger
1911-1912	Chester H. Aldrich
1913-1916	John H. Morehead
1917-1918	Keith Neville
1919-1922	Samuel R. McKelvie
1923-1924	Charles W. Bryan
1925-1928	Adam McMullen
1929-1930	Arthur J. Weaver
1931-1934	Charles W. Bryan
1935-1940	Robert L. Cochran
1941-1946	Dwight Griswold
1947-1952	Val Peterson
1953-1954	Robert B. Crosby
1955-1958	Victor E. Anderson
1959	Ralph G. Brooks
1960	Dwight W. Burney
1961-1966	Frank B. Morrison
1967-1970	Norbert T. Tiemann
1971-1978	J. James Exon (D)
1979-1982	Charles Thone (R)
1983-1985	Robert Kerrey (D)
1987-	Kay Orr (R)

Senators

1867-1870	John M. Thayer
1867-1874	Thomas W. Tipton
1871-1876	Phineas W. Hitchcock
1875-1880	Algernon S. Paddock
1877-1882	Alvin Saunders
1881-1886	Charles H. Van Wyck
1883-1894	Charles F. Manderson
1887-1892	Algernon S. Paddock
1893-1898	William V. Allen
1895-1900	John M. Thurston
1899	Monroe L. Hayward
1899-1900	William V. Allen
1901-1904	Charles H. Dietrich
1901-1906	Joseph H. Millard
1905-1910	Elmer J. Burkett
1907-1912	Norris Brown
1911-1922	Gilbert M. Hitchcock
1913-1942	George W. Norris
1923-1932	Robert B. Howell

1933	William H. Thompson
1934	Richard C. Hunter
1935-1940	Edward R. Burke
1941-1953	Hugh A. Butler
1943-1950	Kenneth S. Wherry
1951	Frederick A. Seaton
1952-1953	Dwight P. Griswold
1954	Eva K. Bowring
1954	Sam W. Reynolds
1954	Hazel H. Abel
1954-1977	Roman L. Hruska (R)
1955-1978	Carl T. Curtis (R)
1977	John Y. McCollister (R)
1977-	Edward Zorinsky (D)
1979-	J. James Exon (D)

Chief Justices

1867-1872	Oliver P. Mason
1873-1877	George B. Lake
1878	Daniel Gantt
1878-1881	Samuel Maxwell
1882-1883	George B. Lake
1884-1885	Amasa Cobb
1886-1887	Samuel Maxwell
1888-1889	Manoah B. Reese
1890-1891	Amasa Cobb
1892-1893	Samuel Maxwell
1894-1895	Theophilus L. Norval
1896-1897	A. M. Post
1898-1899	T. O. C. Harrison
1900-1901	Theophilus L. Norval
1902-1903	John L. Sullivan
1904-1905	Silas A. Holcomb
1906-1907	Samuel H. Sedgwick
1908	John B. Barnes
1908-1914	Manoah B. Reese
1915	Conrad Hollenbeck
1915	Jacob Fawcett
1915-1926	Andrew M. Morrissey
1927-1938	Charles A. Goss
1939-1962	Robert G. Simmons
1963-1977	Paul W. White
1978-	Norman M. Krivosha

Nevada

Governors

1864-1870	Henry G. Blasdel
1871-1878	Lewis R. Bradley
1879-1882	John H. Kinkead
1883-1886	Jewett W. Adams
1887-1889	Charles C. Stevenson
1890	Frank Bell
1891-1894	Roswell K. Colcord
1895	John S. Jones
1896-1902	Reinhold Sadler
1903-1907	John Sparks
1908-1910	Denver S. Dickerson
1911-1914	Tasker L. Oddie
1915-1922	Emmet D. Boyle
1923-1926	James G. Scrugham
1927-1933	Frederick B. Balzar
1934	Morley Griswold
1935-1938	Richard Kirman
1939-1945	Edward P. Carville
1946-1950	Vail M. Pittman
1951-1958	Charles H. Russell
1959-1966	Grant Sawyer
1967-1970	Paul Laxalt
1971-1978	Mike O'Callaghan (D)
1979-1982	Robert List (R)
1983-	Richard Bryan (D)

Senators

1864-1872	James W. Nye
1864-1874	William M. Stewart
1873-1902	John P. Jones
1875-1880	William Sharon
1881-1886	James G. Fair
1887-1904	William M. Stewart
1903-1917	Francis G. Newlands
1905-1911	George S. Nixon
1912	William A. Massey
1913-1939	Key Pittman
1918-1920	Charles B. Henderson
1921-1932	Tasker L. Oddie
1933-1953	Patrick A. McCarran
1940-1941	Berkeley L. Bunker
1942-1944	James G. Scrugham
1945-1946	Edward P. Carville
1947-1958	George W. Malone
1954	Ernest Brown
1954-1974	Alan H. Bible (D)
1959-1982	Howard W. Cannon (D)
1975-1986	Paul Laxalt (R)
1983-	Chic Hecht (R)
1987-	Harry M. Reid (D)

Chief Justices

Justices of the Supreme Court serve on a rotating basis as Chief Presiding Judge.

New Hampshire

Governors

1789	John Sullivan
1790-1793	Josiah Bartlett
1794-1804	John T. Gilman
1805-1808	John Langdon
1809	Jeremiah Smith
1810-1811	John Langdon
1812	William Plumer
1813-1815	John T. Gilman
1816-1818	William Plumer
1819-1822	Samuel Bell
1823	Levi Woodbury
1824-1826	David L. Morrill
1827	Benjamin Pierce
1828	John Bell
1829	Benjamin Pierce
1830	Matthew Harvey
1831-1833	Samuel Dinsmoor
1834-1835	William Badger
1836-1838	Isaac Hill
1839-1841	John Page
1842-1843	Henry Hubbard
1844-1845	John H. Steele
1846	Anthony Colby
1847-1848	Jared W. Williams
1849-1851	Samuel Dinsmoor
1852-1853	Noah Martin
1854	Nathaniel B. Baker
1855-1856	Ralph Metcalf
1857-1858	William Haile
1859-1860	Ichabod Goodwin
1861-1862	Nathaniel S. Berry
1863-1864	Joseph A. Gilmore
1865-1866	Frederick Smyth
1867-1868	Walter Harriman
1869-1870	Onslow Stearns
1871	James A. Weston
1872-1873	Ezekiel A. Straw
1874	James A. Weston
1875-1876	Person C. Cheney
1877-1878	Benjamin F. Prescott

1879-1880	Natt Head
1881-1882	Charles H. Bell
1883-1884	Samuel W. Hale
1885-1886	Moody Currier
1887-1888	Charles H. Sawyer
1889-1890	David H. Goodell
1891-1892	Hiram A. Tuttle
1893-1894	John B. Smith
1895-1896	Charles A. Busiel
1897-1898	George A. Ramsdell
1899-1900	Frank W. Rollins
1901-1902	Chester B. Jordan
1903-1904	Nahum J. Bachelder
1905-1906	John McLane
1907-1908	Charles M. Floyd
1909-1910	Henry B. Quinby
1911-1912	Robert P. Bass
1913-1914	Samuel D. Felker
1915-1916	Rolland H. Spaulding
1917-1918	Henry W. Keyes
1919-1920	John H. Bartlett
1921-1922	Albert O. Brown
1923-1924	Fred H. Brown
1925-1926	John G. Winant
1927-1928	Huntley N. Spaulding
1929-1930	Charles W. Tobey
1931-1934	John G. Winant
1935-1936	H. Styles Bridges
1937-1940	Francis P. Murphy
1941-1944	Robert O. Blood
1945-1948	Charles M. Dale
1949-1952	Sherman Adams
1953-1954	Hugh Gregg
1955-1958	Lane Dwinell
1959-1962	Wesley Powell
1963-1968	John W. King
1969-1972	Walter Peterson (R)
1973-1978	Meldrim Thompson, Jr. (R)
1979-1982	Hugh J. Gallen (D)
1983-	John H. Sununu (R)

Senators

1789-1792	Paine Wingate
1789-1800	John Langdon
1793-1800	Samuel Livermore
1801	James Sheafe
1801-1804	Simeon Olcott
1802-1806	William Plumer
1805-1813	Nicholas Gilman
1807-1809	Nahum Parker
1810-1812	Charles Cutts
1813-1816	Jeremiah Mason
1814-1816	Thomas W. Thompson
1817-1818	Clement Storer
1817-1822	David L. Morril
1819-1824	John F. Parrott
1823-1834	Samuel Bell
1825-1830	Levi Woodbury
1831-1835	Isaac Hill
1835-1840	Henry Hubbard
1836	John Page
1837-1841	Franklin Pierce
1841-1844	Levi Woodbury
1842	Leonard Wilcox
1843-1848	Charles G. Atherton
1845	Benning W. Jenness
1846	Joseph Cilley
1847-1852	John P. Hale
1849-1854	Moses Norris, Jr.
1853-1854	Jared W. Williams
1855	John S. Wells
1855-1856	James Bell
1855-1864	John P. Hale
1857-1865	Daniel Clark
1865-1876	Aaron H. Cragin
1866	George G. Fogg
1867-1872	James W. Patterson
1873-1878	Bainbridge Wadleigh
1877-1882	Edward H. Rollins

1879	Charles H. Bell
1879-1890	Henry W. Blair
1883-1885	Austin F. Pike
1886	Person C. Cheney
1887-1888	William E. Chandler
1889	Gilman Marston
1889-1900	William E. Chandler
1891-1917	Jacob H. Gallinger
1901-1912	Henry E. Burnham
1913-1918	Henry F. Hollis
1918	Irving W. Drew
1918-1932	George H. Moses
1919-1937	Henry W. Keyes
1933-1938	Fred H. Brown
1937-1961	H. Styles Bridges
1939-1952	Charles W. Tobey
1953	Robert W. Upton
1954-1975	Norris Cotton
1962	Maurice J. Murphy, Jr.
1963-1978	Thomas J. McIntyre (D)
1975-1976	Louis C. Wyman (R)
1976-1980	John A. Durkin (D)
1979-	Gordon J. Humphrey (R)
1981-	Warren Rudman (R)

Chief Justices

1789	Josiah Bartlett
1790-1794	John Pickering
1795-1801	Simeon Olcott
1802-1808	Jeremiah Smith
1809-1812	Arthur Livermore
1813-1815	Jeremiah Smith
1816-1837	William M. Richardson
1838-1847	Joel Parker
1848-1854	John J. Gilchrist
1855	Andrew S. Woods
1855-1858	Ira Perley
1859-1863	Samuel Bell
1864-1868	Ira Perley
1869-1872	Henry A. Bellows
1873	Jonathan E. Sargent
1874-1875	Edmund L. Cushing
1876-1895	Charles Doe
1896-1897	Alonzo P. Carpenter
1898	Lewis W. Clark
1898-1901	Isaac N. Blodgett
1902-1923	Frank N. Parsons
1924-1933	Robert J. Peaslee
1934-1942	John E. Allen
1943-1945	Thomas L. Marble
1946-1948	Oliver W. Branch
1949-1951	Francis W. Johnston
1952-1978	Frank R. Kenison
1979	William A. Grimes
1980-	John W. King

New Jersey

Governors

1789	William Livingston
1790-1792	William Paterson
1793-1800	Richard Howell
1801	Joseph Bloomfield
1802	John Lambert (Acting)
1803-1811	Joseph Bloomfield
1812	Aaron Ogden
1813-1814	William S. Pennington
1815-1816	Mahlon Dickerson
1817-1828	Isaac H. Williamson
1829-1831	Peter D. Vroom
1832	Samuel L. Southard
1833	Elias P. Seeley
1833-1835	Peter D. Vroom
1836	Philemon Dickerson

1837-1842	William Pennington
1843	Daniel Haines
1844-1847	Charles C. Stratton
1848-1850	Daniel Haines
1851-1853	George F. Fort
1854-1856	Rodman M. Price
1857-1859	William A. Newell
1860-1862	Charles S. Olden
1863-1865	Joel Parker
1866-1868	Marcus L. Ward
1869-1871	Theodore F. Randolph
1872-1874	Joel Parker
1875-1877	Joseph D. Bedle
1878-1880	George B. McClellan
1881-1883	George C. Ludlow
1884-1886	Leon Abbett
1887-1889	Robert S. Green
1890-1892	Leon Abbett
1893-1895	George T. Werts
1896-1897	John W. Griggs
1898	David O. Watkins
1899-1901	Foster M. Voorhees
1902-1904	Franklin Murphy
1905-1907	Edward C. Stokes
1908-1910	John F. Fort
1911-1912	Woodrow Wilson
1913	Leon Taylor (Acting)
1914-1916	James F. Fielder
1917-1918	Walter E. Edge
1919	William N. Runyon (Acting)
1920-1922	Edward I. Edwards
1923-1925	George S. Silzer
1926-1928	A. Harry Moore
1929-1931	Morgan F. Larson
1932-1934	A. Harry Moore
1935-1937	Harold G. Hoffman
1938-1940	A. Harry Moore
1941-1943	Charles Edison
1944-1946	Walter E. Edge
1947-1953	Alfred E. Driscoll
1954-1961	Robert B. Meyner
1962-1969	Richard J. Hughes
1970-1974	William T. Cahill (R)
1975-1982	Brendan T. Byrne (D)
1983-	Thomas H. Kean (R)

Senators

1789	William Patterson
1789-1790	Jonathan Elmer
1790-1792	Philemon Dickinson
1791-1797	John Rutherfurd
1793-1795	Frederick Frelinghuysen
1796-1798	Richard Stockton
1798	Franklin Davenport
1799-1800	James Schureman
1799-1804	Jonathan Dayton
1801-1802	Aaron Ogden
1803-1808	John Condit
1805-1808	Aaron Kitchell
1809-1814	John Lambert
1809-1816	John Condit
1815-1820	James J. Wilson
1817-1828	Mahlon Dickerson
1821-1822	Samuel L. Southard
1823-1825	Joseph McIlvaine
1826-1828	Ephraim Bateman
1829-1832	Mahlon Dickerson
1829-1834	Theodore Frelinghuysen
1833-1841	Samuel L. Southard
1835-1840	Garret D. Wall
1841-1852	Jacob W. Miller
1842-1850	William L. Dayton
1851-1852	Robert F. Stockton
1853-1858	William Wright
1853-1861	John R. Thomson
1859-1864	John C. Ten Eyck
1862	Richard S. Field
1863	James W. Wall
1863-1865	William Wright

1865	John P. Stockton
1866-1868	Frederick T. Frelinghuysen
1866-1870	Alexander G. Cattell
1869-1874	John P. Stockton
1871-1876	Frederick T. Frelinghuysen
1875-1880	Theodore F. Randolph
1877-1894	John R. McPherson
1881-1886	William J. Sewell
1887-1892	Rufus Blodgett
1893-1898	James Smith, Jr.
1895-1901	William J. Sewell
1899-1910	John Kean
1902-1906	John F. Dryden
1907-1912	Frank O. Briggs
1911-1916	James E. Martine
1913-1917	William Hughes
1917-1922	Joseph S. Frelinghuysen
1918	David Baird
1919-1928	Walter E. Edge
1923-1928	Edward I. Edwards
1929	David Baird, Jr.
1929-1934	Hamilton F. Kean
1930	Dwight W. Morrow
1931-1936	W. Warren Barbour
1935-1937	A. Harry Moore
1937-1942	William H. Smathers
1938	John Milton
1938-1942	W. Warren Barbour
1943	Arthur Walsh
1943-1948	Albert W. Hawkes
1944-1958	H. Alexander Smith
1949-1954	Robert C. Hendrickson
1955-1978	Clifford P. Case (R)
1959-1982	Harrison A. Williams, Jr. (D)
1979-	Bill Bradley (D)
1983-	Frank. R. Lautenberg (D)

Chief Justices

1789-1802	James Kinsey
1803-1823	Andrew Kirkpatrick
1824-1831	Charles Ewing
1832-1845	Joseph C. Hornblower
1846-1860	Henry W. Green
1861-1863	Edward W. Whelpley
1864-1896	Mercer Beasley
1897-1899	William J. Magie
1900	David A. Depue
1901-1932	William S. Gummere
1933-1945	Thomas J. Brogan
1946-1947	Clarence E. Case
1948-1956	Arthur T. Vanderbilt
1957-1973	Joseph T. Weintraub
1974-1978	Richard J. Hughes
1979-	Robert N. Wilentz

New Mexico

Governors

1912-1916	William C. McDonald
1917	Ezequiel C. DeBaca
1917-1918	Washington E. Lindsey
1919-1920	Octaviano A. Larrazolo
1921-1922	Merritt C. Mechem
1923-1924	James F. Hinkle
1925-1926	Arthur T. Hannett
1927-1930	Richard C. Dillon
1931-1932	Arthur Seligman
1933-1934	Andy W. Hockenhull
1935-1938	Clyde Tingley
1939-1942	John E. Miles
1943-1946	John J. Dempsey
1947-1950	Thomas J. Mabry
1951-1954	Edwin L. Mechem
1955-1956	John F. Simms

1957-1958	Edwin L. Mechem
1959-1960	John Burroughs
1961	Edwin L. Mechem
1962	Tom Bolack
1963-1966	Jack M. Campbell
1967-1970	David F. Cargo
1971-1974	Bruce King (D)
1975-1978	Jerry Apodaca (D)
1979-1982	Bruce King (D)
1983-1986	Toney Anaya (D)
1987-	Garrey Carruthers (R)

Senators

1912-1916	Thomas B. Catron
1912-1920	Albert B. Fall
1917-1926	Andrieus A. Jones
1921-1924	Holm O. Bursum
1925-1932	Sam G. Bratton
1927	Bronson M. Cutting
1928	Octaviano A. Larrazolo
1929-1934	Bronson M. Cutting
1933-1948	Carl A. Hatch
1935-1962	Dennis Chavez
1949-1972	Clinton P. Anderson
1963-1964	Edwin L. Mechem
1965-1976	Joseph M. Montoya (D)
1973-	Peter V. Domenici (R)
1977-1982	Harrison Schmitt (R)
1983-	Jeff Bingaman (D)

Chief Justices

Justices of the Supreme Court serve on a rotating basis as Chief Presiding Judge.

New York

Governors

1789-1794	George Clinton
1795-1800	John Jay
1801-1803	George Clinton
1804-1806	Morgan Lewis
1807-1816	Daniel D. Tompkins
1817	John Taylor
1817-1822	DeWitt Clinton
1823-1824	Joseph C. Yates
1825-1827	DeWitt Clinton
1828	Nathaniel Pitcher
1829	Martin Van Buren
1829-1832	Enos T. Throop
1833-1838	William L. Marcy
1839-1842	William H. Seward
1843-1844	William C. Bouck
1845-1846	Silas Wright, Jr.
1847-1848	John Young
1849-1950	Hamilton Fish
1851-1852	Washington Hunt
1853-1854	Horatio Seymour
1855-1856	Myron H. Clark
1857-1858	John A. King
1859-1862	Edwin D. Morgan
1863-1864	Horatio Seymour
1865-1868	Reuben E. Fenton
1869-1872	John T. Hoffman
1873-1874	John A. Dix
1875-1876	Samuel J. Tilden
1877-1879	Lucius Robinson
1880-1882	Alonzo B. Cornell
1883-1884	Grover Cleveland
1885-1891	David B. Hill
1892-1894	Roswell P. Flower
1895-1896	Levi P. Morton

1897-1898	Frank S. Black
1899-1900	Theodore Roosevelt
1901-1904	Benjamin B. Odell, Jr.
1905-1906	Frank W. Higgins
1907-1909	Charles Evans Hughes
1910	Horace White
1911-1912	John Alden Dix
1913	William Sulzer
1914	Martin H. Glynn
1915-1918	Charles S. Whitman
1919-1920	Alfred E. Smith
1921-1922	Nathan L. Miller
1923-1928	Alfred E. Smith
1929-1932	Franklin D. Roosevelt
1933-1941	Herbert H. Lehman
1942	Charles Poletti
1943-1954	Thomas E. Dewey
1955-1958	W. Averell Harriman
1959-1974	Nelson Rockefeller (R)
1974	Malcolm Wilson (R)
1975-1982	Hugh L. Carey (D)
1983-	Mario Cuomo (D)

Senators

1789-1790	Philip J. Schuyler
1789-1795	Rufus King
1791-1796	Aaron Burr
1796-1799	John Laurance
1797	Philip J. Schuyler
1798	John S. Hobart
1798	William North
1798-1799	James Watson
1800-1801	John Armstrong
1800-1802	Gouverneur Morris
1802	De Witt Clinton
1803	John Armstrong
1803	Theodorus Bailey
1804-1808	Samuel L. Mitchill
1804-1812	John Smith
1809-1814	Obadiah German
1813-1824	Rufus King
1815-1820	Nathan Sanford
1821-1828	Martin Van Buren
1825	Vacant
1826-1830	Nathan Sanford
1829-1832	Charles E. Dudley
1831-1832	William L. Marcy
1833-1843	Silas Wright, Jr.
1833-1843	Nathaniel P. Tallmadge
1844	Henry A. Foster
1844-1850	Daniel S. Dickinson
1845-1848	John A. Dix
1849-1860	William H. Seward
1851-1856	Hamilton Fish
1857-1862	Preston King
1861-1866	Ira Harris
1863-1868	Edwin D. Morgan
1867-1880	Roscoe Conkling
1869-1874	Reuben E. Fenton
1875-1880	Francis Kernan
1881	Thomas C. Platt
1881-1884	Elbridge G. Lapham
1881-1886	Warner Miller
1885-1891	William M. Evarts
1887-1892	Frank Hiscock
1892-1896	David B. Hill
1893-1898	Edward Murphy, Jr.
1897-1908	Thomas C. Platt
1899-1910	Chauncey M. Depew
1909-1914	Elihu Root
1911-1916	James A. O'Gorman
1915-1926	James W. Wadsworth, Jr.
1917-1922	William M. Calder
1923-1937	Royal S. Copeland
1927-1948	Robert F. Wagner, Sr.
1938	Vacant
1939-1946	James M. Mead
1947-1958	Irving M. Ives
1949	John Foster Dulles

1949-1956	Herbert H. Lehman
1957-1980	Jacob K. Javits (R)
1959-1964	Kenneth B. Keating
1965-1967	Robert F. Kennedy
1968-1970	Charles E. Goodell
1971-1976	James L. Buckley (R)
1977-	Daniel P. Moynihan (D)
1981-	Alphonse M. D'Amato (R)

Chief Justices

1789	Richard Morris
1790-1797	Robert Yates
1798-1800	John Lansing, Jr.
1801-1803	Morgan Lewis
1804-1813	James Kent
1814-1818	Smith Thompson
1819-1822	Ambrose Spencer
1823-1836	John Savage
1837-1844	Samuel Nelson
1845-1846	Greene C. Bronson
1847	Samuel Beardsley
1847-1849	Freeborn G. Jewett
1850	Greene C. Bronson
1851-1853	Charles H. Ruggles
1854-1855	Addison Gardiner
1856-1857	Hiram Denio
1858-1859	Alexander S. Johnson
1860-1861	George F. Comstock
1862	Samuel L. Selden
1862-1865	Hiram Denio
1866-1867	Henry E. Davies
1868-1869	Ward Hunt
1870	Robert Earl
1870-1879	Sanford E. Church
1880	Charles J. Folger
1881	Charles Andrews
1882-1891	William C. Ruger
1892-1896	Robert Earl
1897-1903	Alton B. Parker
1904-1912	Edgar M. Cullen
1913-1916	Willard Bartlett
1917-1925	Frank Hiscock
1926-1931	Benjamin N. Cardozo
1932-1934	Cuthbert W. Pound
1935-1938	Frederick E. Crane
1939-1944	Irving Lehman
1945-1952	John A. Loughran
1953	Edmund H. Lewis
1954-1958	Albert Conway
1959-1965	Charles S. Desmond
1966-1973	Stanley Fuld
1974-1978	Charles D. Breitel
1979-1984	Lawrence H. Cooke
1985-	Sol Wachtler

North Carolina

Governors

1789-1791	Alexander Martin
1792-1794	Richard D. Spaight
1795-1797	Samuel Ashe
1798	William R. Davie
1799-1801	Benjamin Williams
1802-1804	James Turner
1805-1806	Nathaniel Alexander
1807	Benjamin Williams
1808-1809	David Stone
1810	Benjamin Smith
1811-1813	William Hawkins
1814-1816	William Miller
1817-1819	John Branch
1820	Jesse Franklin
1821-1823	Gabriel Holmes
1824-1826	Hutchins G. Burton

1827	James Iredell, Jr.
1828-1829	John Owen
1830-1831	Montfort Stokes
1832-1834	David L. Swain
1835	Richard D. Spaight
1836-1840	Edward B. Dudley
1841-1844	John M. Morehead
1845-1848	William A. Graham
1849-1850	Charles Manly
1851-1853	David S. Reid
1854	Warren Winslow (Acting)
1855-1858	Thomas Bragg
1859-1860	John W. Ellis
1861	Henry T. Clark
1862-1864	Zebulon B. Vance
1865-1867	Jonathan Worth
1868-1870	William W. Holden
1871-1873	Tod R. Caldwell
1874-1876	Curtis H. Brogden
1877-1878	Zebulon B. Vance
1879-1884	Thomas J. Jarvis
1885-1888	Alfred M. Scales
1889-1890	Daniel G. Fowle
1891-1892	Thomas M. Holt
1893-1896	Elias Carr
1897-1900	Daniel L. Russell
1901-1904	Charles B. Aycock
1905-1908	Robert B. Glenn
1909-1912	William W. Kitchin
1913-1916	Locke Craig
1917-1920	Thomas W. Bickett
1921-1924	Cameron Morrison
1925-1928	Angus W. McLean
1929-1932	O. Max Gardner
1933-1936	John C. B. Ehringhaus
1937-1940	Clyde R. Hoey
1941-1944	J. Melville Broughton
1945-1948	R. Gregg Cherry
1949-1952	W. Kerr Scott
1953	William B. Umstead
1954-1960	Luther H. Hodges
1961-1964	Terry Sanford
1965-1968	Daniel K. Moore
1969-1972	Robert W. Scott
1973-1976	James E. Holshouser (R)
1977-1984	James B. Hunt, Jr. (D)
1985-	James G. Martin (R)

Senators

1789-1792	Samuel Johnston
1789-1794	Benjamin Hawkins
1793-1798	Alexander Martin
1795-1800	Timothy Bloodworth
1799-1804	Jesse Franklin
1801-1806	David Stone
1805-1815	James Turner
1807-1812	Jesse Franklin
1813-1814	David Stone
1815-1822	Nathaniel Macon
1816-1828	Montfort Stokes
1823-1827	John Branch
1828-1830	James Iredell
1829-1839	Bedford Brown
1831-1835	Willie P. Mangum
1836-1839	Robert Strange
1840-1842	William A. Graham
1840-1852	Willie P. Mangum
1843-1845	William H. Haywood, Jr.
1846-1854	George E. Badger
1853	Vacant
1854-1858	David S. Reid
1855-1857	Asa Biggs
1858-1860	Thomas L. Clingman
1859-1860	Thomas Bragg
1861-1867	Vacant
1868-1871	Joseph C. Abbott
1868-1872	John Pool
1872-1894	Matt W. Ransom
1873-1878	Augustus S. Merrimon

1879-1893	Zebulon B. Vance
1894	Thomas J. Jarvis
1895-1900	Marion Butler
1895-1902	Jeter C. Pritchard
1901-1930	Furnifold M. Simmons
1903-1929	Lee S. Overman
1930-1931	Cameron Morrison
1931-1945	Josiah W. Bailey
1932-1944	Robert R. Reynolds
1945-1953	Clyde R. Hoey
1946-1947	William B. Umstead
1948	J. Melville Broughton
1949	Frank P. Graham
1950-1952	Willis Smith
1953	Alton A. Lennon
1954-1957	W. Kerr Scott
1954-1975	Samuel J. Ervin, Jr. (D)
1958-1972	B. Everett Jordan (D)
1973-	Jesse A. Helms (R)
1975-1981	Robert Morgan (D)
1981-1986	John P. East (R)
1987-	Terry Sanford (D)

Chief Justices

1809-1828	John L. Taylor
1829-1832	Leonard Henderson
1833-1851	Thomas Ruffin
1852-1857	Frederick Nash
1858-1877	Richmond M. Pearson
1878-1888	William N. H. Smith
1889-1891	Augustus S. Merrimon
1892-1894	James E. Shepherd
1895-1900	William T. Faircloth
1901-1902	David M. Furches
1903-1923	Walter Clark
1924-1925	William A. Hoke
1925-1950	Walter P. Stacy
1951-1953	William A. Devin
1954-1955	M. V. Barnhill
1956-1961	J. Wallace Winborne
1962-1965	Emery B. Denny
1966-1971	R. Hunt Parker
1972-1975	William H. Bobbitt
1976-1978	Susie M. Sharp
1979-	Joseph W. Branch

North Dakota

Governors

1889-1890	John Miller
1891-1892	Andrew H. Burke
1893-1894	Eli C. D. Shortridge
1895-1896	Roger Allen
1897	Frank A. Briggs
1898	Joseph M. Devine
1899-1900	Frederick B. Fancher
1901-1904	Frank White
1905-1906	Elmore Y. Sarles
1907-1912	John Burke
1913-1916	Louis B. Hanna
1917-1920	Lynn J. Frazier
1921-1924	Ragnvald A. Nestos
1925-1927	Arthur G. Sorlie
1928	Walter Maddock
1929-1932	George F. Shafer
1933	William Langer
1934	Ole H. Olson
1935	Thomas H. Moodie
1935-1936	Walter Welford
1937-1938	William Langer
1939-1944	John Moses
1945-1950	Fred Aandahl
1951-1956	C. Norman Brunsdale
1957-1960	John E. Davis

1961-1972	William L. Guy (D)
1973-1980	Arthur A. Link (D)
1981-1984	Allen I. Olsen (R)
1985-	George A. Sinner (D)

Senators

1889-1892	Lyman R. Casey
1889-1908	Gilbert A. Pierce
1893-1898	William N. Roach
1899-1922	Porter J. McCumber
1909	Martin N. Johnson
1909	Fountain L. Thompson
1910	William E. Purcell
1911-1920	Asle J. Gronna
1921-1924	Edwin F. Ladd
1923-1940	Lynn J. Frazier
1925-1944	Gerald P. Nye
1941-1958	William Langer
1945	John Moses
1945-1980	Milton R. Young (R)
1959	C. Norman Brunsdale
1960-	Quentin N. Burdick (D)
1981-1986	Mark Andrews (R)
1987-	Kent Conrad (D)

Chief Justices

Justices of the Supreme Court serve on a rotating basis as Chief Presiding Judge.

Ohio

Governors

1803-1806	Edward Tiffin
1807	Thomas Kirker
1808-1809	Samuel Huntington
1810-1813	Return J. Meigs, Jr.
1814	Othneil Looker (Acting)
1814-1817	Thomas Worthington
1818-1821	Ethan A. Brown
1822-1825	Jeremiah Morrow
1826-1829	Allen Trimble
1830-1831	Duncan McArthur
1832-1835	Robert Lucas
1836-1837	Joseph Vance
1838-1839	Wilson Shannon
1840-1841	Thomas Corwin
1842-1843	Wilson Shannon
1844	Thomas W. Bartley (Acting)
1845	Mordecai Bartley
1846-1848	William Bebb
1849	Seabury Ford
1850-1852	Reuben Wood
1853-1856	William Medill
1856-1859	Salmon P. Chase
1860-1861	William Dennison
1862-1863	David Tod
1864-1865	John Brough
1866-1867	Jacob D. Cox
1868-1871	Rutherford B. Hayes
1872-1873	Edward F. Noyes
1874-1875	William Allen
1876	Rutherford B. Hayes
1877	Thomas L. Young
1878-1879	Richard M. Bishop
1880-1883	Charles Foster
1884-1885	George Hoadly
1886-1889	Joseph B. Foraker
1890-1891	James E. Campbell
1892-1895	William McKinley
1896-1899	Asa S. Bushnell
1900-1903	George K. Nash

1904-1905	Myron T. Herrick
1906	John M. Pattison
1906-1908	Andrew L. Harris
1909-1912	Judson Harmon
1913-1914	James M. Cox
1915-1916	Frank B. Willis
1917-1920	James M. Cox
1921-1922	Harry L. Davis
1923-1928	A. Victor Donahey
1929-1930	Myers Y. Cooper
1931-1934	George White
1935-1938	Martin L. Davey
1939-1944	John W. Bricker
1945-1946	Frank J. Lausche
1947-1948	Thomas J. Herbert
1949-1956	Frank J. Lausche
1957-1958	C. William O'Neill
1959-1962	Michael V. DiSalle
1963-1970	James A. Rhodes
1971-1974	John J. Gilligan (D)
1975-1982	James A. Rhodes (R)
1983-	Richard F. Celeste (D)

Senators

1803-1806	Thomas Worthington
1803-1807	John Smith
1807-1808	Edward Tiffin
1808-1809	Return J. Meigs, Jr.
1809	Stanley Griswold
1809-1812	Alexander Campbell
1810-1813	Thomas Worthington
1813-1819	Jeremiah Morrow
1814	Joseph Kerr
1815-1832	Benjamin Ruggles
1819-1821	William A. Trimble
1822-1824	Ethan A. Brown
1825-1827	William Henry Harrison
1828-1830	Jacob Burnet
1831-1836	Thomas Ewing
1833-1838	Thomas Morris
1837-1848	William Allen
1839-1844	Benjamin Tappan
1845-1849	Thomas Corwin
1849-1854	Salmon P. Chase
1850	Thomas Ewing
1851-1868	Benjamin F. Wade
1855-1860	George E. Pugh
1861	Salmon P. Chase
1861-1876	John Sherman
1869-1880	Allen G. Thurman
1877-1878	Stanley Matthews
1879-1884	George H. Pendleton
1881-1896	John Sherman
1885-1890	Henry B. Payne
1891-1896	Calvin S. Brice
1897-1903	Marcus A. Hanna
1897-1908	Joseph B. Foraker
1904-1910	Charles W. F. Dick
1909-1914	Theodore E. Burton
1911-1922	Atlee Pomerene
1915-1920	Warren G. Harding
1921-1927	Frank B. Willis
1923-1934	Simeon D. Fess
1928	Cyrus Locher
1928	Theodore E. Burton
1929	Roscoe C. McCulloch
1930-1938	Robert J. Bulkley
1935-1940	A. Victor Donahey
1939-1952	Robert A. Taft
1941-1944	Harold H. Burton
1945	James W. Huffman
1946	Kingsley A. Taft
1947-1958	John W. Bricker
1953	Thomas A. Burke
1954-1956	George H. Bender
1957-1968	Frank J. Lausche
1959-1970	Stephen M. Young
1969-1974	William B. Saxbe (R)
1971-1976	Robert Taft, Jr. (R)

1975-	John Glenn (D)
1977-	Howard M. Metzenbaum (D)

Chief Justices

1803-1807	Samuel Huntington
1808-1809	William Sprigg
1810-1814	Thomas Scott
1815-1817	Ethan A. Brown
1818-1820	Jessup N. Couch
1821-1828	Calvin Pease
1829-1832	Peter Hitchcock
1833-1834	Joshua Collett
1835-1844	Ebenezer Lane
1845-1846	Reuben Wood
1847	Matthew Birchard
1848-1851	Peter Hitchcock
1852-1854	William B. Caldwell
1855-1856	Rufus P. Ranney
1857	Thomas W. Bartley
1858	Joseph R. Swan
1859-1870	Jacob Brinkerhoff
1871	Josiah Scott
1872	John Welch
1873	William White
1874	Luther Day
1875-1876	George Rex
1877	John Welch
1878	William White
1879	William J. Gilmore
1880	George W. McIlvaine
1881	Washington W. Boynton
1882	John W. Okey
1883	William White
1884	Selwyn N. Owen
1885	George W. McIlvaine
1886-1888	Selwyn N. Owen
1889-1890	Thaddeus A. Minshall
1891	Marshall J. Williams
1892	William T. Spear
1893	Joseph P. Bradbury
1894	Franklin Dickman
1895	Thaddeus A. Minshall
1896	Marshall J. Williams
1897	Jacob Burket
1898	William T. Spear
1899	Joseph P. Bradbury
1900	John A. Shauck
1901	Thaddeus A. Minshall
1902-1904	Jacob Burket
1905	William Z. Davis
1906-1907	John A. Shauck
1908	James L. Price
1909	William B. Crew
1910	Augustus N. Summers
1911	William T. Spear
1912	William Z. Davis
1913	John A. Shauck
1913-1920	Hugh L. Nichols
1921-1932	Carrington T. Marshall
1933-1962	Carl V. Weygandt
1963-1969	Kingsley A. Taft
1970-1977	C. William O'Neill
1978-	Frank D. Celebrezze

Oklahoma

Governors

1907-1910	Charles N. Haskell
1911-1914	Lee Cruce
1915-1918	Robert L. Williams
1919-1922	James B. A. Robertson
1923	James C. Walton
1923-1926	Martin E. Trapp
1927-1928	Henry S. Johnston

1929-1930	William J. Holloway
1931-1934	William H. Murray
1935-1938	Ernest W. Marland
1939-1942	Leon C. Phillips
1943-1946	Robert S. Kerr
1947-1950	Roy J. Turner
1951-1954	Johnston Murray
1955-1958	Raymond S. Gary
1959-1963	J. Howard Edmondson
1963-1966	Henry L. Bellmon
1967-1970	Dewey F. Bartlett
1971-1974	David Hall (D)
1975-1978	David L. Boren (D)
1979-1986	George Nigh (D)
1987-	Henry Bellmon (R)

Senators

1907-1918	Robert L. Owen
1907-1920	Thomas P. Gore
1919-1924	Summers Hardy
1921-1926	John W. Harreld
1925-1929	William B. Pine
1927-1950	J. W. Elmer Thomas
1930-1936	Thomas P. Gore
1937-1942	Josh Lee
1943-1948	Edward H. Moore
1949-1962	Robert S. Kerr
1951-1968	A. S. Mike Monroney
1963-1964	J. Howard Edmondson
1965-1972	Fred R. Harris (D)
1969-1980	Henry L. Bellmon (R)
1973-1978	Dewey F. Bartlett (R)
1979-	David L. Boren (D)
1981-	Don Nickles (R)

Chief Justices

1907-1908	Robert L. Williams
1909	Matthew J. Kane
1910	Jesse J. Dunn
1911-1912	John B. Turner
1913	Samuel W. Hayes
1914-1916	Matthew J. Kane
1917-1919	John F. Sharp
1919	Thomas H. Owen
1920	Robert M. Rainey
1921-1922	John B. Harrison
1923	John H. Pitchford
1923	John T. Johnson
1924	Neal E. McNeill
1925-1926	George M. Nicholson
1927-1928	Fred P. Branson
1929-1930	Charles W. Mason
1931-1932	E. F. Lester
1933-1934	Fletcher Riley
1935-1936	Edwin R. McNeill
1937-1938	Monroe Osborn
1939-1940	Wayne W. Bayless
1941-1942	Earl Welch
1943-1944	N. S. Corn
1945-1946	Thomas L. Gibson
1947-1948	Thurman S. Hurst
1949-1950	Denver N. Davison
1951-1952	Ben Arnold
1953-1954	Harry L. S. Halley
1955-1956	N. B. Johnson
1957-1958	Earl Welch
1959-1960	Denver M. Davison
1961-1962	Ben T. Williams
1963-1964	W. H. Blackbird
1965-1966	Harry L. S. Halley
1967-1968	Floyd L. Jackson
1969-1970	Pat Irwin
1971-1972	William A. Berry
1973-1975	Denver N. Davison
1976	Ben T. Williams
1977-1979	Ralph B. Hodges

1980	Robert B. Lavender
1981-1982	Pat Irwin
1983-1985	Don Barnes
1986-	Robert D. Sims

Oregon

Governors

1859-1861	John Whiteaker
1862-1865	Addison C. Gibbs
1866-1869	George L. Woods
1870-1876	LaFayette Grover
1877	Stephen F. Chadwick
1878-1881	William W. Thayer
1882-1886	Zenas F. Moody
1887-1894	Sylvester Pennoyer
1895-1898	William P. Lord
1899-1902	Theodore T. Geer
1903-1908	George E. Chamberlain
1909	Frank W. Benson
1910	Jay R. Bowerman (Acting)
1911-1914	Oswald West
1915-1918	James Withycombe
1919-1922	Ben W. Olcott
1923-1926	Walter M. Pierce
1927-1928	Isaac L. Patterson
1929-1930	Albin W. Norblad
1931-1934	Julius Meier
1935-1938	Charles H. Martin
1939-1942	Charles A. Sprague
1943-1946	Earl Snell
1947-1948	John H. Hall
1949-1951	Douglas McKay
1952-1955	Paul L. Patterson
1956	Elmo Smith
1957-1958	Robert D. Holmes
1959-1966	Mark O. Hatfield
1967-1974	Tom McCall (R)
1975-1978	Robert Straub (D)
1979-1986	Victor Atiyeh (R)
1987-	Neil Goldschmidt (D)

Senators

1859	Delazon Smith
1859-1860	Joseph Lane
1860	Edward D. Baker
1861	Benjamin Stark
1861-1866	James W. Nesmith
1862-1864	Benjamin F. Harding
1865-1870	George H. Williams
1867-1872	Henry W. Corbett
1871-1876	James K. Kelly
1873-1878	John H. Mitchell
1877-1882	LaFayette Grover
1879-1884	James H. Slater
1883-1894	Joseph N. Dolph
1885	Vacant
1885-1896	John H. Mitchell
1895-1900	George W. McBride
1897	Vacant
1898-1902	Joseph Simon
1901-1904	John H. Mitchell
1903-1908	Charles W. Fulton
1905-1906	John M. Gearin
1907	Frederick W. Mulkey
1907-1912	Jonathan Bourne, Jr.
1909-1920	George E. Chamberlain
1913-1916	Harry Lane
1917-1943	Charles L. McNary
1921-1926	Robert N. Stanfield
1927-1937	Frederick Steiwer
1938	Alfred E. Reames
1939-1944	Rufus C. Holman
1944-1954	Guy Cordon

1945-1968	Wayne L. Morse
1955-1959	Richard L. Neuberger
1960	Hall S. Lusk
1961-1966	Maurine B. Neuberger
1967-	Mark O. Hatfield (R)
1969-	Robert W. Packwood (R)

Chief Justices

Justices of the Supreme Court serve on a rotating basis as Chief Presiding Judge.

Pennsylvania

Governors

1789-1798	Thomas Mifflin
1799-1807	Thomas McKean
1808-1816	Simon Snyder
1817-1819	William Findlay
1820-1822	Joseph Hiester
1823-1828	John A. Schulze
1829-1834	George Wolf
1835-1838	Joseph Ritner
1839-1844	David R. Porter
1845-1847	Francis R. Shunk
1848-1851	William F. Johnston
1852-1854	William Bigler
1855-1857	James Pollock
1858-1860	William F. Packer
1861-1866	Andrew G. Curtin
1867-1872	John W. Geary
1873-1878	John F. Hartranft
1879-1882	Henry M. Hoyt
1883-1886	Robert E. Pattison
1887-1890	James A. Beaver
1891-1894	Robert E. Pattison
1895-1898	Daniel H. Hastings
1899-1902	William A. Stone
1903-1906	Samuel W. Pennypacker
1907-1910	Edwin S. Stuart
1911-1914	John K. Tener
1915-1918	Martin G. Brumbaugh
1919-1923	William C. Sproul
1923-1926	Gifford Pinchot
1927-1930	John S. Fischer
1931-1934	Gifford Pinchot
1935-1938	George H. Earle
1939-1942	Arthur H. James
1943-1947	Edward Martin
1947-1950	James H. Duff
1951-1954	John S. Fine
1955-1958	George M. Leader
1959-1962	David L. Lawrence
1963-1966	William W. Scranton
1967-1970	Raymond P. Shafer
1971-1978	Milton J. Shapp (D)
1979-1986	Richard Thornburgh (R)
1987-	Robert Casey (D)

Senators

1789-1790	William Maclay
1789-1794	Robert Morris
1791-1792	Vacant
1793	Albert Gallatin
1794-1802	James Ross
1795-1800	William Bingham
1801	John Peter G. Muhlenberg
1801-1806	George Logan
1803-1808	Samuel Maclay
1807-1812	Andrew Gregg
1809-1813	Michael Leib
1813-1818	Abner Lacock

1814-1820	Jonathan Roberts
1819-1824	Walter Lowrie
1821-1826	William Findlay
1825-1830	William Marks
1827-1830	Isaac D. Barnard
1831-1832	George M. Dallas
1831-1833	William Wilkins
1833-1898	Samuel McKean
1834-1844	James Buchanan
1839	Vacant
1840-1850	Daniel Sturgeon
1845-1848	Simon Cameron
1849-1854	James Cooper
1851-1856	Richard Brodhead
1855	Vacant
1856-1860	William Bigler
1857-1860	Simon Cameron
1861-1862	David Wilmot
1861-1866	Edgar Cowan
1863-1868	Charles R. Buckalew
1867-1876	Simon Cameron
1869-1874	John Scott
1875-1880	William A. Wallace
1877-1896	J. Donald Cameron
1881-1886	John I. Mitchell
1887-1898	Matthew S. Quay
1897-1921	Boies Penrose
1899-1900	Vacant
1901-1903	Matthew S. Quay
1904-1908	Philander C. Knox
1909-1916	George T. Oliver
1917-1920	Philander C. Knox
1921	William E. Crow
1922-1926	George W. Pepper
1922-1934	David A. Reed
1927-1928	William S. Vare
1929	Joseph R. Grundy
1930-1944	James J. Davis
1935-1946	Joseph F. Guffey
1945-1950	Francis J. Myers
1947-1958	Edward Martin
1951-1956	James H. Duff
1957-1968	Joseph S. Clark
1959-1976	Hugh D. Scott, Jr. (R)
1969-1980	Richard S. Schweiker (R)
1977-	H. John Heinz, III (R)
1981-	Arlen Specter (R)

Chief Justices

1789-1798	Thomas McKean
1799-1805	Edward Shippen
1806-1826	William Tilghman
1827-1850	John B. Gibson
1851-1853	Jeremiah S. Black
1854-1856	Ellis Lewis
1857-1862	Walter H. Lowrie
1863-1866	George W. Woodward
1867-1871	James Thompson
1872	John M. Read
1873-1878	Daniel Agnew
1879-1882	George Sharswood
1883-1886	Ulysses Mercur
1887-1888	Isaac G. Gordon
1889-1892	Edward M. Paxson
1893-1898	James P. Sterett
1899	Henry Green
1900-1902	J. Brewster McCollum
1903-1909	James T. Mitchell
1910-1914	D. Newlin Fell
1915-1920	J. Hay Brown
1921-1929	Robert Von Moschzisker
1930-1935	Robert S. Frazer
1936-1939	John W. Kephart
1940-1942	William I. Schaffer
1943-1949	George Maxey
1950-1951	James B. Drew
1952-1955	Horace Stern
1956-1960	Charles A. Jones
1961-1971	John C. Bell, Jr.

1972	Robert N. C. Nix, Jr.
1973-1976	Benjamin R. Jones
1977-1980	Michael J. Eagen
1981-1983	Henry X. O'Brien
1984-	Robert N. C. Nix, Jr.

Rhode Island

Governors

1789	John Collins
1790-1804	Arthur Fenner
1805	Henry Smith (Acting)
1806	Isaac Wilbour (Acting)
1807-1810	James Fenner
1811-1816	William Jones
1817-1820	Nehemiah R. Knight
1821-1823	William C. Gibbs
1824-1830	James Fenner
1831-1832	Lemuel H. Arnold
1833-1837	John B. Francis
1838	William Sprague
1839-1842	Samuel W. King
1843-1844	James Fenner
1845	Charles Jackson
1846	Byron Diman
1847-1848	Elisha Harris
1849-1850	Henry B. Anthony
1851-1852	Philip Allen
1853	Francis M. Dimond
1854-1856	William W. Hoppin
1857-1858	Elisha Dyer
1859	Thomas G. Turner
1860-1862	William Sprague
1863-1865	James Y. Smith
1866-1868	Ambrose E. Burnside
1869-1872	Seth Padelford
1873-1874	Henry Howard
1875-1876	Henry Lippitt
1877-1879	Charles C. Van Zandt
1880-1882	Alfred H. Littlefield
1883-1884	Augustus O. Bourn
1885-1886	George P. Wetmore
1887	John W. Davis
1888	Royal C. Taft
1889	Herbert W. Ladd
1890	John W. Davis
1891	Herbert W. Ladd
1892-1894	Daniel R. Brown
1895-1896	Charles W. Lippitt
1897-1899	Elisha Dyer
1900	William Gregory
1901-1902	Charles D. Kimball
1903-1904	Lucius F. C. Garvin
1905-1906	George H. Utter
1907-1908	James H. Higgins
1909-1914	Aram J. Pothier
1915-1920	R. Livingston Beeckman
1921-1922	Emery J. San Souci
1923-1924	William S. Flynn
1925-1927	Aram J. Pothier
1928-1932	Norman S. Case
1933-1936	Theodore F. Green
1937-1938	Robert E. Quinn
1939-1940	William H. Vanderbilt
1941-1944	J. Howard McGrath
1945-1949	John O. Pastore
1950	John S. McKiernan
1951-1958	Dennis J. Roberts
1959-1960	Christopher Del Sesto
1961-1962	John A. Notte, Jr.
1963-1968	John H. Chafee
1969-1972	Frank Licht
1973-1976	Philip W. Noel (D)
1977-1984	J. Joseph Garrahy (D)
1985-	Edward DiPrete (R)

Senators

1790-1792	Joseph Stanton, Jr.
1790-1802	Theodore Foster
1793-1796	William Bradford
1797-1800	Ray Greene
1801-1804	Christopher Ellery
1803	Samuel J. Potter
1804-1808	Benjamin Howland
1805-1806	James Fenner
1807-1810	Elisha Mathewson
1809	Francis Malbone
1809-1810	Christopher G. Champlin
1811-1816	Jeremiah B. Howell
1811-1820	William Hunter
1817-1820	James Burrill, Jr.
1821-1824	James De Wolf
1821-1840	Nehemiah R. Knight
1825-1838	Asher Robbins
1839-1841	Nathan F. Dixon
1841-1846	James F. Simmons
1842-1843	William Sprague
1844	John B. Francis
1845-1850	Albert C. Greene
1847-1852	John H. Clarke
1851-1856	Charles T. James
1853-1858	Philip Allen
1857-1861	James F. Simmons
1859-1883	Henry B. Anthony
1862	Samuel G. Arnold
1863-1874	William Sprague
1875-1880	Ambrose E. Burnside
1881-1910	Nelson W. Aldrich
1884	William P. Sheffield
1885-1888	Jonathan Chace
1889-1894	Nathan F. Dixon
1895-1906	George P. Wetmore
1907	Vacant
1908-1912	George P. Wetmore
1911-1916	Henry F. Lippitt
1913-1923	LeBaron B. Colt
1917-1928	Peter G. Gerry
1924-1936	Jesse H. Metcalf
1929-1934	Felix E. Hebert
1935-1946	Peter G. Gerry
1937-1960	Theodore F. Green
1947-1948	J. Howard McGrath
1949	Edward L. Leahy
1950-1976	John O. Pastore (D)
1961-	Claiborne Pell (D)
1977-	John H. Chafee (R)

Chief Justices

1789	Othniel Gorton
1790-1794	Daniel Owen
1795-1808	Peleg Arnold
1809	Thomas Arnold
1810-1811	Peleg Arnold
1812-1815	Daniel Lyman
1816	James Burrill, Jr.
1817	Tristam Burges
1818	James Fenner
1819-1826	Isaac Wilbour
1827-1834	Samuel Eddy
1835-1847	Job Durfee
1848-1853	Richard W. Greene
1854-1855	William R. Staples
1856-1865	Samuel Ames
1866-1867	Charles S. Bradley
1868-1874	George A. Brayton
1875-1890	Thomas Durfee
1891-1899	Charles Matteson
1900-1902	John H. Stiness
1903-1904	Pardon E. Tillinghast
1905-1908	William W. Douglas
1909-1912	Edward C. Dubois
1913-1916	Clarke H. Johnson
1917-1919	Christopher F. Parkhurst

1920-1928	William H. Sweetland
1929-1934	Charles F. Stearns
1935-1957	Edmund W. Flynn
1958-1965	Francis B. Condon
1966-1975	Thomas H. Roberts
1976-	Joseph A. Bevilacqua

South Carolina

Governors

1789-1791	Charles Pinckney
1792-1793	Arnoldus Vanderhorst
1794-1795	William Moultrie
1796-1797	Charles Pinckney
1798-1799	Edward Rutledge
1800-1801	John Drayton
1802-1803	James R. Richardson
1804-1805	Paul Hamilton
1806-1807	Charles Pinckney
1808-1809	John Drayton
1810-1811	Henry Middleton
1812-1813	Joseph Alston
1814-1815	David R. Williams
1816-1817	Andrew Pickens
1818-1819	John Geddes
1820-1821	Thomas Bennett
1822-1823	John L. Wilson
1824-1825	Richard I. Manning
1826-1827	John Taylor
1828-1829	Stephen D. Miller
1830-1831	James Hamilton
1832-1833	Robert Y. Hayne
1834-1835	George McDuffie
1836-1837	Pierce M. Butler
1838-1839	Patrick Noble
1840-1841	John P. Richardson
1842-1843	James H. Hammond
1844-1845	William Aiken
1846-1847	David Johnson
1848-1849	Whitemarsh B. Seabrook
1850-1851	John H. Means
1852-1853	John L. Manning
1854-1855	James H. Adams
1856-1857	Robert F. W. Allston
1858-1859	William H. Gist
1860-1861	Francis W. Pickens
1862-1863	Milledge L. Bonham
1864	Andrew G. Magrath
1865	Benjamin F. Perry
1866-1867	James L. Orr
1868-1871	Robert K. Scott
1872-1873	Franklin J. Moses
1874-1875	Daniel H. Chamberlain
1876-1877	Wade Hampton
1878-1879	William D. Simpson
1880	Thomas B. Jeter
1880-1881	Johnson Hagood
1882-1885	Hugh S. Thompson
1886	John C. Sheppard
1886-1889	John P. Richardson
1890-1893	Benjamin R. Tillman
1894-1895	John G. Evans
1896-1898	William H. Ellerbe
1899-1902	Miles B. McSweeney
1903-1906	Duncan C. Heyward
1907-1910	Martin F. Ansel
1911-1914	Coleman L. Blease
1915-1918	Richard I. Manning
1919-1922	Robert A. Cooper
1923-1926	Thomas G. McLeod
1927-1930	John G. Richards
1931-1934	Irbra C. Blackwood
1935-1938	Olin D. Johnston
1939-1940	Burnet R. Maybank
1941	J. E. Harley
1942	R. M. Jefferies

1943-1944	Olin D. Johnston
1945-1946	Ransome J. Williams
1947-1950	J. Strom Thurmond
1951-1954	James F. Byrnes
1955-1958	George Bell Timmerman, Jr.
1959-1962	Ernest F. Hollings
1963-1964	Donald S. Russell
1965-1970	Robert E. McNair
1971-1974	John C. West (D)
1975-1978	James B. Edwards (R)
1979-1986	Richard W. Riley (D)
1987-	Carroll Campbell (R)

Senators

1789-1794	Ralph Izard
1789-1795	Pierce Butler
1795-1800	Jacob Read
1796-1797	John Hunter
1798-1800	Charles Pinckney
1801	John E. Colhoun
1801-1809	Thomas Sumter
1802-1803	Pierce Butler
1804-1825	John Gaillard
1810-1815	John Taylor
1816-1822	William Smith
1823-1831	Robert Y. Hayne
1826	William Harper
1826-1830	William Smith
1831-1832	Stephen D. Miller
1832-1842	John C. Calhoun
1833-1841	William C. Preston
1842-1845	George McDuffie
1843-1844	Daniel E. Huger
1845-1849	John C. Calhoun
1846-1856	Andrew P. Butler
1850	Franklin H. Elmore
1850	Robert W. Barnwell
1850-1851	R. Barnwell Rhett
1852	William F. De Saussure
1853-1857	Josiah J. Evans
1857-1859	James H. Hammond
1858	Authur P. Hayne
1858-1859	James Chesnut, Jr.
1860-1867	Vacant
1868-1872	Frederick A. Sawyer
1868-1876	Thomas J. Robertson
1873-1878	John J. Patterson
1877-1894	Matthew C. Butler
1879-1890	Wade Hampton
1891-1896	John L. M. Irby
1895-1917	Benjamin R. Tillman
1897	Joseph H. Earle
1897-1902	John L. McLaurin
1903-1907	Asbury C. Latimer
1908	Frank B. Gary
1909-1943	Ellison D. Smith
1918	Christie Benet
1918	William P. Pollock
1919-1924	Nathaniel B. Dial
1925-1930	Coleman L. Blease
1931-1940	James F. Byrnes
1941	Roger C. Peace
1941-1953	Burnet R. Maybank
1944	Wilton E. Hall
1945-1964	Olin D. Johnston
1954	Charles E. Daniel
1955	J. Strom Thurmond
1956	Thomas A. Wofford
1957-	J. Strom Thurmond (R)
1965-1966	Donald S. Russell
1967-	Ernest F. Hollings (D)

Chief Justices

1789-1790	William H. Drayton
1791-1794	John Rutledge
1795-1859	None

1860-1864	John B. O'Neall
1865-1876	Benjamin F. Dunkin
1877-1878	Ammiel J. Willard
1879-1898	William D. Simpson
1899-1902	Henry McIver
1903-1908	Young J. Pope
1909-1911	Ira B. Jones
1912-1925	Eugene B. Gary
1926-1930	Richard C. Watts
1931-1934	Eugene S. Blease
1935-1939	John G. Stabler
1940-1943	Milledge Bonham
1944-1955	D. Gordon Baker
1956-1960	Taylor H. Stukes
1961-1965	Claude A. Taylor
1966-1975	Joseph R. Moss
1976	James W. Lewis
1986-	Julius Ness

South Dakota

Governors

1889-1892	Arthur C. Mellette
1893-1896	Charles H. Sheldon
1897-1900	Andrew E. Lee
1901-1904	Charles N. Herreid
1905-1906	Samuel H. Elrod
1907-1908	Corie I. Crawford
1909-1912	Robert S. Vessey
1913-1916	Frank M. Byrne
1917-1920	Peter Norbeck
1921-1924	William H. McMaster
1925-1926	Carl Gunderson
1927-1930	William J. Bulow
1931-1932	Warren E. Green
1933-1936	Tom Berry
1937-1938	Leslie Jensen
1939-1942	Harlan J. Bushfield
1943-1946	M. Q. Sharpe
1947-1950	George T. Mickelson
1951-1954	Sigurd Anderson
1955-1958	Joe Foss
1959-1960	Ralph Herseth
1961-1964	Archie Gubbrud
1965-1968	Nils A. Boe
1969-1970	Frank L. Farrar
1971-1978	Richard F. Kneip (D)
1979-1986	William J. Janklow (R)
1987-	George Mickelson (R)

Senators

1889-1890	Gideon C. Moody
1889-1900	Richard F. Pettigrew
1891-1900	James H. Kyle
1901-1908	Alfred B. Kittredge
1901-1912	Robert J. Gamble
1909-1914	Coe I. Crawford
1913-1924	Thomas Sterling
1915-1920	Edwin S. Johnson
1921-1936	Peter Norbeck
1925-1930	William H. McMaster
1931-1942	William J. Bulow
1937	Herbert E. Hitchcock
1938	Gladys Pyle
1939-1950	J. Chandler Gurney
1943-1946	Harlan J. Bushfield
1947-1972	Karl E. Mundt
1951-1961	Francis H. Case
1962	Joseph J. Bottum
1963-1980	George S. McGovern (D)
1973-1979	James Abourezk (D)
1979-	Larry Pressler (R)
1981-1986	James Abdnor (R)
1987-	Thomas A. Daschle (D)

Chief Justices

Justices of the Supreme Court serve on a rotating basis as Chief Presiding Judge.

Tennessee

Governors

1796-1800	John Sevier
1801-1802	Archibald Roane
1803-1808	John Sevier
1809-1814	Willie Blount
1815-1820	Joseph McMinn
1821-1826	William Carroll
1827-1828	Sam Houston
1829	William Hall
1829-1834	William Carroll
1835-1838	Newton Cannon
1839-1840	James K. Polk
1841-1844	James C. Jones
1845-1846	Aaron V. Brown
1847-1848	Neil S. Brown
1849-1850	William Trousdale
1851-1852	William B. Campbell
1853-1856	Andrew Johnson
1857-1861	Isham G. Harris
1862-1864	Andrew Johnson
1865-1868	William G. Brownlow
1869-1870	DeWitt C. Senter
1871-1874	John C. Brown
1875-1878	James D. Porter
1879-1880	Albert S. Marks
1881-1882	Alvin Hawkins
1883-1886	William B. Bate
1887-1890	Robert L. Taylor
1891-1892	John P. Buchanan
1893-1896	Peter Turney
1897-1898	Robert L. Taylor
1899-1902	Benton McMillin
1903-1904	James B. Frazier
1905-1906	John I. Cox
1907-1910	Malcolm R. Petterson
1911-1914	Ben W. Hooper
1915-1918	Thomas C. Rye
1919-1920	Albert H. Roberts
1921-1922	Alfred A. Taylor
1923-1926	Austin Peay
1927-1932	Henry H. Horton
1933-1936	Hill McAlister
1937-1938	Gordon Browning
1939-1944	Prentice Cooper
1945-1948	Jim McCord
1949-1952	Gordon Browning
1953-1958	Frank Clement
1959-1962	Buford Ellington
1963-1965	Frank Clement
1967-1970	Buford Ellington
1971-1974	Winfield Dunn (R)
1975-1978	Ray Blanton (D)
1979-1986	Lamar Alexander (R)
1987-	Ned McWherter (D)

Senators

1796	William Blount
1796	William Cocke
1797	Andrew Jackson
1797-1814	Joseph Anderson
1798	Daniel Smith
1799-1804	William Cocke
1805-1808	Daniel Smith
1809-1810	Jenkin Whiteside
1811-1813	George W. Campbell
1814	Jesse Wharton

1815-1817	George W. Campbell
1815-1822	John Williams
1818-1828	John H. Eaton
1823-1824	Andrew Jackson
1825-1839	Hugh L. White
1829-1837	Felix Grundy
1838-1839	Ephraim H. Foster
1839	Felix Grundy
1840	Alexander Anderson
1840-1842	Alfred O. P. Nicholson
1841-1842	None
1843-1844	Ephraim H. Foster
1843-1846	Spencer Jarnagin
1845-1850	Hopkins L. Turney
1847-1858	John Bell
1851-1856	James C. Jones
1857-1862	Andrew Johnson
1859-1862	Alfred O. P. Nicholson
1863-1865	None
1866-1868	David T. Patterson
1866-1870	Joseph S. Fowler
1869-1874	William G. Brownlow
1871-1876	Henry Cooper
1875	Andrew Johnson
1875-1876	David M. Key
1877-1880	James E. Bailey
1877-1896	Isham G. Harris
1881-1885	Howell E. Jackson
1886	Washington C. Whitthorne
1887-1904	William B. Bate
1897-1900	Thomas B. Turley
1901-1906	Edward W. Carmack
1905-1910	James B. Frazier
1907-1911	Robert L. Taylor
1911-1916	Luke Lea
1912	Newell Sanders
1913	William R. Webb
1913-1924	John K. Shields
1917-1952	Kenneth D. McKellar
1925-1928	Lawrence D. Tyson
1929-1930	William E. Brock
1931-1932	Cordell Hull
1933-1936	Nathan L. Bachman
1937	George L. Berry
1938	None
1939-1948	A. Tom Stewart
1949-1963	Estes Kefauver
1953-1970	Albert A. Gore
1964	Herbert S. Walters
1964-1965	Ross Bass
1967-1984	Howard H. Baker, Jr. (R)
1971-1976	William E. Brock, III (R)
1977-	James R. Sasser (D)
1985-	Albert Gore, Jr. (D)

Chief Justices

1831-1834	John Catron
1835-1869	None
1870-1875	Alfred O. P. Nicholson
1876-1885	James W. Deaderick
1886-1892	Peter Turney
1893	Horace H. Lurton
1893	Benjamin J. Lea
1894-1901	David L. Snodgrass
1902-1909	William D. Beard
1910-1912	John K. Shields
1913-1917	Matt M. Neil
1918-1922	Dick L. Lansden
1923-1946	Grafton Green
1947	Alex W. Chambliss
1947-1959	A. B. Neil
1960-1962	Alan M. Prewitt
1963-1968	Hamilton S. Burnett
1969-1973	Ross W. Dyer
1974-1976	William H. D. Fones
1977-1979	Joseph W. Henry
1980-1981	Ray L. Brock, Jr.
1982-1984	William H. D. Fones
1985-	Ray L. Brock, Jr.

Texas

Governors

1846	James P. Henderson
1847-1848	George T. Wood
1849-1852	Peter H. Bell
1853	J. W. Henderson (Acting)
1853-1856	Elisha M. Pease
1857-1858	Hardin R. Runnels
1859-1860	Sam Houston
1861	Edward Clark (Acting)
1861-1862	Francis R. Lubbock
1863-1864	Pendleton Murrah
1865	Andrew J. Hamilton
1866	James W. Throckmorton
1867-1869	Elisha M. Pease
1870-1873	Edmund J. Davis
1874-1875	Richard Coke
1876-1878	Richard B. Hubbard
1879-1882	Oran M. Roberts
1883-1886	John Ireland
1887-1890	Lawrence S. Ross
1891-1894	James S. Hogg
1895-1898	Charles A. Culberson
1899-1902	Joseph D. Sayers
1903-1906	Samuel W. T. Lanham
1907-1910	Thomas M. Campbell
1911-1914	Oscar B. Colquitt
1915-1916	James E. Ferguson
1917-1920	William P. Hobby
1921-1924	Pat M. Neff
1925-1926	Miriam A. Ferguson
1927-1930	Dan Moody
1931-1932	Ross S. Sterling
1933-1934	Miriam A. Ferguson
1935-1938	James V. Allred
1939-1940	W. Lee O'Daniel
1941-1946	Coke R. Stevenson
1947-1948	Beauford H. Jester
1949-1956	Allan Shivers
1957-1962	M. Price Daniel
1963-1968	John B. Connally
1969-1972	Preston Smith
1973-1978	Dolph Briscoe (D)
1979-1982	William P. Clements, Jr. (R)
1983-1986	Mark White, Jr. (D)
1987-	William P. Clements, Jr. (R)

Senators

1846-1856	Thomas J. Rusk
1846-1858	Sam Houston
1857	James P. Henderson
1858	Matthias Ward
1859-1860	Louis T. Wigfall
1859-1860	John Hemphill
1861-1869	None
1870-1874	James W. Flanagan
1870-1876	Morgan C. Hamilton
1875-1886	Samuel B. Maxey
1877-1894	Richard Coke
1887-1890	John H. Reagan
1891	Horace Chilton
1892-1898	Roger Q. Mills
1895-1900	Horace Chilton
1899-1922	Charles A. Culberson
1901-1912	Joseph W. Bailey
1913	Rienzi M. Johnston
1913-1940	Morris Sheppard
1923-1928	Earle B. Mayfield
1929-1952	Tom T. Connally
1941-1948	W. Lee O'Daniel
1949-1960	Lyndon B. Johnson
1953-1956	M. Price Daniel
1957	William A. Blakley
1957-1970	Ralph W. Yarborough
1961	William A. Blakley

1961-1984	John G. Tower (R)
1971-	Lloyd M. Bentsen, Jr. (D)
1985-	Phil Gramm (R)

Chief Justices

1846-1857	John Hemphill
1858-1863	Royal T. Wheeler
1864-1865	Oran M. Roberts
1866	George F. Moore
1867-1869	Amos Morrill
1870-1872	Lemuel D. Evans
1873	Wesley Ogden
1874-1877	Oran M. Roberts
1878-1880	George F. Moore
1881	Robert S. Gould
1882-1887	Asa H. Willie
1888-1893	John W. Stayton
1894-1910	Reuben R. Gaines
1911-1914	Thomas J. Brown
1915-1920	Nelson Phillips
1921-1939	Calvin M. Cureton
1940	W. F. Moore
1941-1947	James P. Alexander
1948-1960	J. E. Hickman
1961-1972	Robert W. Calvert
1973-1981	Joe R. Greenhill
1982-1984	Jack Pope
1985-	John L. Hill

Utah

Governors

1896-1904	Heber M. Wells
1905-1908	John C. Cutler
1909-1916	William Spry
1917-1920	Simon Bamberger
1921-1924	Charles R. Mabey
1925-1932	George H. Dern
1933-1940	Henry H. Blood
1941-1948	Herbert B. Maw
1949-1956	J. Bracken Lee
1957-1964	George D. Clyde
1965-1976	Calvin L. Rampton (D)
1977-1984	Scott M. Matheson (D)
1985-	Norman Bangerter (R)

Senators

1896	Arthur Brown
1896-1898	Frank J. Cannon
1897-1902	Joseph L. Rawlins
1899-1900	Vacant
1901-1904	Thomas Kearns
1903-1932	Reed Smoot
1905-1916	George Sutherland
1917-1940	William H. King
1933-1950	Elbert D. Thomas
1941-1946	Abe Murdock
1947-1958	Arthur V. Watkins
1951-1974	Wallace F. Bennett (R)
1959-1976	Frank E. Moss (D)
1975-	Edwin J. Garn (R)
1977-	Orrin G. Hatch (R)

Chief Justices

Justices of the Supreme Court serve on a rotating basis as Chief Presiding Judge.

Vermont

Governors

1791-1796	Thomas Chittenden
1797	Paul Brigham
1797-1806	Isaac Tichenor
1807	Israel Smith
1808	Isaac Tichenor
1809-1812	Jonas Galusha
1813-1814	Martin Chittenden
1815-1819	Jonas Galusha
1820-1822	Richard Skinner
1823-1825	Cornelius P. Van Ness
1826-1827	Ezra Butler
1828-1830	Samuel C. Crafts
1831-1834	William A. Palmer
1835-1840	Silas H. Jenison
1841-1842	Charles Paine
1843	John Mattocks
1844-1845	William Slade
1846-1848	Horace Eaton
1849	Carlos Coolidge
1850-1851	Charles K. Williams
1852	Erastus Fairbanks
1853	John S. Robinson
1854-1855	Stephen Royce
1856-1857	Ryland Fletcher
1858-1859	Hiland Hall
1860	Erastus Fairbanks
1860	Hiland Hall
1861-1862	Frederick Holbrook
1863-1864	John G. Smith
1865-1866	Paul Dillingham, Jr.
1867-1868	John B. Page
1869	Peter T. Washburn
1870	George W. Hendee
1870-1871	John W. Stewart
1872-1873	Julius Converse
1874-1875	Asahel Peck
1876-1877	Horace Fairbanks
1878-1879	Redfield Proctor
1880-1881	Roswell Farnham
1882-1883	John L. Barstow
1884-1885	Samuel E. Pingree
1886-1887	Ebenezer J. Ormsbee
1888-1889	William P. Dillingham
1890-1891	Carrol S. Page
1892-1893	Levi K. Fuller
1894-1895	Urban A. Woodbury
1896-1897	Josiah Grout
1898-1899	Edward C. Smith
1900-1901	William W. Stickney
1902-1903	John G. McCullough
1904-1905	Charles J. Bell
1906-1907	Fletcher D. Proctor
1908-1909	George H. Prouty
1910-1911	John A. Mead
1912-1914	Allen M. Fletcher
1915-1916	Charles W. Gates
1917-1918	Horace F. Graham
1919-1920	Percival W. Clement
1921-1922	James Hartness
1923-1924	Redfield Proctor
1925-1926	Franklin S. Billings
1927-1930	John E. Weeks
1931-1934	Stanley C. Wilson
1935-1936	Charles M. Smith
1937-1940	George D. Aiken
1941-1944	William H. Wills
1945-1946	Mortimer R. Proctor
1947-1949	Ernest W. Gibson, Jr.
1950	Harold J. Arthur
1951-1954	Lee E. Emerson
1955-1958	Joseph B. Johnson
1959-1960	Robert T. Stafford
1961-1962	F. Ray Keyser, Jr.
1963-1968	Philip H. Hoff
1969-1972	Deane C. Davis
1973-1976	Thomas Salmon (D)
1977-1984	Richard A. Snelling (R)
1985-	Madeleine Kunin (D)

Senators

1791-1794	Stephen R. Bradley
1791-1795	Moses Robinson
1795-1800	Elijah Paine
1796	Isaac Tichenor
1797-1802	Nathaniel Chipman
1801-1812	Stephen R. Bradley
1803-1806	Israel Smith
1807-1814	Jonathan Robinson
1813-1816	Dudley Chase
1815-1820	Isaac Tichenor
1817	James Fisk
1818-1824	William A. Palmer
1821-1832	Horatio Seymour
1825-1830	Dudley Chase
1831-1841	Samuel Prentiss
1833-1838	Benjamin Swift
1839-1850	Samuel S. Phelps
1842	Samuel C. Crafts
1843-1852	William Upham
1851-1865	Solomon Foot
1853	Samuel S. Phelps
1854	Lawrence Brainerd
1855-1864	Jacob Collamer
1865-1866	Luke P. Poland
1866-1890	George F. Edmunds
1867-1898	Justin S. Morrill
1891-1907	Redfield Proctor
1899	Jonathan Ross
1900-1922	William P. Dillingham
1908	John W. Stewart
1908-1922	Carroll S. Page
1923-1929	Frank L. Greene
1923-1932	Porter H. Dale
1930	Frank C. Partridge
1931-1945	Warren R. Austin
1933-1939	Ernest W. Gibson
1940	Ernest W. Gibson, Jr.
1941-1974	George D. Aiken (R)
1946-1958	Ralph E. Flanders
1959-1970	Winston L. Prouty (R)
1971-	Robert T. Stafford (R)
1975-	Patrick J. Leahy (D)

Chief Justices

1791-1793	Samuel Knight
1794-1795	Isaac Tichenor
1796	Nathaniel Chipman
1797	Israel Smith
1798-1800	Enoch Woodbridge
1801-1806	Jonathan Robinson
1807-1812	Royall Tyler
1813-1814	Nathaniel Chipman
1815-1816	Asa Aldis
1817-1820	Dudley Chase
1821-1822	Cornelius P. Van Ness
1823-1828	Richard Skinner
1829	Samuel Prentiss
1830-1832	Titus Hutchinson
1833-1845	Charles K. Williams
1846-1851	Stephen Royce
1852-1859	Isaac F. Redfield
1860-1864	Luke P. Poland
1865-1881	John Pierpoint
1882-1889	Homer E. Royce
1890-1897	Jonathan Ross
1898-1901	Russell S. Taft
1902-1912	John W. Rowell
1913-1914	George M. Powers
1915-1916	Loveland Munson
1917-1928	John H. Watson
1929-1937	George M. Powers
1938-1948	Sherman R. Moulton
1949-1954	John C. Sherburne
1955-1957	Olin M. Jeffords
1958	Walter H. Cleary
1959-1962	Benjamin N. Hulburd
1963-1971	James S. Holden
1972-1973	Percival L. Shangraw
1974-1982	Albert W. Barney, Jr.
1983-1984	Franklin S. Billings, Jr.
1985-	Frederic W. Allen

Virginia

Governors

1789-1790	Beverly Randolph
1791-1793	Henry Lee
1794-1795	Robert Brooke
1796-1798	James Wood
1799-1801	James Monroe
1802-1804	John Page
1805-1807	William H. Cabell
1808-1810	John Tyler
1811	James Monroe
1811	George W. Smith
1812-1813	James Barbour
1814-1815	Wilson C. Nicholas
1816-1818	James P. Preston
1819-1821	Thomas M. Randolph
1822-1824	James Pleasants
1825-1826	John Tyler
1827-1829	William B. Giles
1830-1833	John Floyd
1834-1835	Littleton W. Tazewell
1836	Wyndham Robertson
1837-1839	David Campbell
1840	Thomas W. Gilmer
1841	John Rutherford
1842	John M. Gregory
1843-1845	James McDowell
1846-1848	William Smith
1849-1851	John B. Floyd
1852-1855	Joseph Johnson
1856-1859	Henry A. Wise
1860-1863	John Letcher
1864	William Smith
1865-1867	Francis H. Pierpont
1868	Henry H. Wells
1869-1873	Gilbert C. Walker
1874-1877	James L. Kemper
1878-1881	Frederick W. M. Holliday
1882-1885	William E. Cameron
1886-1889	Fitzhugh Lee
1890-1893	Philip W. McKinney
1894-1897	Charles T. O'Ferrall
1898-1901	J. Hoge Tyler
1902-1905	Andrew J. Montague
1906-1909	Claude A. Swanson
1910-1913	William H. Mann
1914-1917	Henry C. Stuart
1918-1921	Westmoreland Davis
1922-1925	E. Lee Trinkle
1926-1929	Harry F. Byrd
1930-1933	John G. Pollard
1934-1937	George C. Peery
1938-1941	James H. Price
1942-1945	Colgate W. Darden, Jr.
1946-1949	William M. Tuck
1950-1953	John S. Battle
1954-1957	Thomas B. Stanley
1958-1961	J. Lindsay Almond, Jr.
1962-1965	Albertis S. Harrison, Jr.
1966-1969	Mills E. Godwin, Jr.
1970-1973	Linwood Holton (R)
1974-1977	Mills E. Godwin, Jr. (R)
1978-1981	John N. Dalton (R)
1982-1985	Charles S. Robb (D)
1986-	Gerald L. Baliles (D)

Senators

1789	William Grayson
1789-1791	Richard Henry Lee
1790	John Walker
1790-1793	James Monroe
1792-1793	John Taylor
1794-1798	Henry Tazewell
1794-1802	Stevens T. Mason
1799-1803	Wilson C. Nicholas
1803	John Taylor
1803	Abraham B. Venable
1804-1808	Andrew Moore
1804-1815	William B. Giles
1809-1814	Richard Brent
1815-1824	James Barbour
1816	Armistead T. Mason
1817-1818	John W. Eppes
1819-1821	James Pleasants
1822-1823	John Taylor
1824-1831	Littleton W. Tazewell
1825-1826	John Randolph
1827-1835	John Tyler
1832-1833	William C. Rives
1834-1835	Benjamin W. Leigh
1836	Richard E. Parker
1836-1844	William C. Rives
1837-1840	William H. Roane
1841-1846	William S. Archer
1845-1846	Isaac S. Pennybacker
1847-1860	Robert M. T. Hunter
1847-1860	James M. Mason
1861-1862	Waitman T. Willey
1861-1864	John S. Carlile
1863-1864	Lemuel J. Bowden
1865-1869	Vacant
1870-1874	John F. Lewis
1870-1882	John W. Johnston
1875-1880	Robert E. Withers
1881-1886	William Mahone
1883-1888	Harrison H. Riddleberger
1887-1909	John W. Daniel
1889-1891	John S. Barbour
1892-1894	Eppa Hunton
1895-1919	Thomas S. Martin
1920-1945	Carter Glass
1933-1964	Harry F. Byrd
1946	Thomas G. Burch
1947-1966	A. Willis Robertson
1965-1982	Harry F. Byrd, Jr.
1967-1972	William B. Spong, Jr. (D)
1973-1978	William L. Scott (R)
1979-	John W. Warner (R)
1983-	Paul S. Trible, Jr. (R)

Chief Justices

1788-1803	Edmund Pendleton
1804-1809	Peter Lyons
1810-1823	William F. Fleming
1824-1830	Francis T. Brooke
1831-1841	Henry St. George Tucker
1842-1851	William H. Cabell
1852-1865	John J. Allen
1866-1881	Richard C. L. Moncure
1882-1893	Lunsford L. Lewis
1894-1915	James Keith
1916	Richard H. Cardwell
1916	George M. Harrison
1917-1919	Stafford G. White
1920-1923	Joseph L. Kelly
1924	Frederick W. Sims
1925-1930	Robert R. Prentis
1931-1945	Preston W. Campbell
1946	Henry W. Holt
1947-1957	Edward W. Hudgins
1958-1968	John W. Eggleston
1969-1973	Harold F. Snead
1974-1980	Lawrence W. I'Anson

1981-	Harry L. Carrico

Washington

Governors

1889-1892	Elisha P. Ferry
1893-1896	John H. McGraw
1897-1900	John R. Rogers
1901-1904	Henry McBride
1905-1908	Albert E. Mead
1909	Samuel G. Cosgrove
1909-1912	Marion E. Hay
1913-1918	Ernest Lister
1919-1924	Louis F. Hart
1925-1932	Roland H. Hartley
1933-1940	Clarence D. Martin
1941-1944	Arthur B. Langlie
1945-1948	Monrad C. Wallgren
1949-1956	Arthur B. Langlie
1957-1964	Albert D. Rosellini
1965-1976	Daniel J. Evans (R)
1977-1980	Dixy Lee Ray (D)
1981-1984	John Spellman (R)
1985-	Booth Gardner (D)

Senators

1889-1892	John B. Allen
1889-1896	Watson C. Squire
1893-1894	Vacant
1895-1898	John L. Wilson
1897-1902	George Turner
1899-1904	Addison G. Foster
1903-1908	Levi Ankeny
1905-1910	Samuel H. Piles
1909-1931	Wesley L. Jones
1911-1922	Miles Poindexter
1923-1934	Clarence C. Dill
1932	Elijah S. Grammer
1933-1943	Homer T. Bone
1935-1939	Lewis B. Schwellenbach
1940-1944	Monrad C. Wallgren
1944-1980	Warren G. Magnuson (D)
1945-1946	Hugh B. Mitchell
1946-1952	Harry P. Cain
1953-1983	Henry M. Jackson (D)
1981-1986	Slade Gorton (R)
1983-	Daniel J. Evans (R)
1987-	Brock Adams (D)

Chief Justices

1889-1892	Thomas J. Anders
1893-1894	Ralph O. Dunbar
1895-1896	John P. Hoyt
1897-1898	Elmon Scott
1899	Merritt J. Gordon
1900	Ralph O. Dunbar
1901-1902	James B. Reavis
1903-1904	Mark A. Fullerton
1905-1906	Wallace Mount
1907-1908	Hiram E. Hadley
1909-1910	Frank H. Rudkin
1911-1912	Ralph O. Dunbar
1913-1914	Herman D. Crow
1915-1916	George E. Morris
1917	Overton G. Ellis
1918	John F. Main
1919-1920	Stephen J. Chadwick
1921-1922	Emmett N. Parker
1923-1924	John F. Main
1925	Warren W. Tolman
1926	John F. Main
1927	Kenneth Mackintosh

1928	Mark A. Fullerton
1929-1930	John R. Mitchell
1931-1932	Warren W. Tolman
1933-1934	Walter B. Beals
1935-1936	William J. Millard
1937-1938	William J. Steinert
1939-1940	Bruce Blake
1941-1942	John S. Robinson
1943-1944	George B. Simpson
1945	Walter B. Beals
1946	Samuel M. Driver
1947-1948	Joseph A. Mallery
1949	Clyde G. Jeffers
1949-1950	George B. Simpson
1951-1952	E. W. Schwellenbach
1953-1954	Thomas E. Grady
1955-1956	Frederick G. Hamley
1957-1958	Matthew W. Hill
1959-1960	Frank P. Weaver
1961-1962	Robert C. Finley
1963-1964	Richard B. Ott
1965-1966	Hugh J. Rosellini
1967-1968	Robert C. Finley
1969-1970	Robert T. Hunter
1971-1972	Orris L. Hamilton
1973-1975	Frank Hale
1976	Charles F. Stafford
1977-1978	Charles T. Wright
1979-1980	Robert F. Utter
1981-1984	Robert F. Brachtenbach
1985-	James M. Dolliver

West Virginia

Governors

1863-1868	Arthur I. Boreman
1869	Daniel D. T. Farnsworth
1869-1870	William E. Stevenson
1871-1876	John J. Jacob
1877-1880	Henry M. Mathews
1881-1884	Jacob B. Jackson
1885-1889	Emanuel W. Wilson
1890-1892	Aretas B. Fleming
1893-1896	William A. MacCorkle
1897-1900	George W. Atkinson
1901-1904	Albert B. White
1905-1908	William M. O. Dawson
1909-1912	William E. Glasscock
1913-1916	Henry D. Hatfield
1917-1920	John J. Cornwell
1921-1924	Ephraim F. Morgan
1925-1928	Howard M. Gore
1929-1932	William G. Conley
1933-1936	Herman G. Kump
1937-1940	Homer A. Holt
1941-1944	Matthew M. Neely
1945-1948	Clarence W. Meadows
1949-1952	Okey L. Patteson
1953-1956	William C. Marland
1957-1960	Cecil Underwood
1961-1964	William W. Barron
1965-1968	Hulett C. Smith
1969-1976	Arch A. Moore, Jr. (R)
1977-1984	John D. Rockefeller, IV (D)
1985-	Arch A. Moore, Jr. (R)

Senators

1863-1868	Peter G. Van Winkle
1863-1870	Waitman T. Willey
1869-1874	Arthur I. Boreman
1871-1882	Henry G. Davis
1875	Allen T. Caperton
1876	Samuel Price
1877-1880	Frank Hereford

1881-1886	Johnson N. Camden
1883-1892	John E. Kenna
1887-1898	Charles J. Faulkner
1893-1894	Johnson N. Camden
1895-1910	Stephen B. Elkins
1899-1910	Nathan B. Scott
1911	Davis Elkins
1911-1916	William E. Chilton
1911-1912	Clarence W. Watson
1913-1918	Nathan Goff
1917-1922	Howard Sutherland
1919-1924	Davis Elkins
1923-1928	Matthew M. Neely
1925-1930	Guy D. Goff
1929-1934	Henry Hatfield
1931-1940	Matthew M. Neely
1935-1940	Rush D. Holt
1941	Joseph Rosier
1941-1955	Harley M. Kilgore
1942	Hugh Ike Shott
1943-1948	Chapman Revercomb
1949-1957	Matthew M. Neely
1956	William R. Laird
1957-1958	Chapman Revercomb
1958	John D. Hoblitzell, Jr.
1959-1984	Jennings Randolph (D)
1959-	Robert C. Byrd (D)
1985-	John D. Rockefeller, IV (D)

Chief Justices

Justices of the Supreme Court serve on a rotating basis as Chief Presiding Judge.

Wisconsin

Governors

1848-1851	Nelson Dewey
1852-1853	Leonard J. Farwell
1954-1955	William A. Barstow
1856	Arthur MacArthur
1956-1857	Coles Bashford
1858-1861	Alexander W. Randall
1862	Louis P. Harvey
1862-1863	Edward Salomon
1864-1865	James T. Lewis
1866-1871	Lucius Fairchild
1872-1873	Cadwallader Washburn
1874-1875	William R. Taylor
1876-1877	Harrison Ludington
1878-1881	William E. Smith
1882-1888	Jeremiah M. Rusk
1889-1890	William D. Hoard
1891-1894	George W. Peck
1895-1896	William H. Upham
1897-1900	Edward Scofield
1901-1904	Robert M. La Follette
1905-1910	James O. Davidson
1911-1914	Francis E. McGovern
1915-1920	Emanuel L. Philipp
1921-1926	John J. Blaine
1927-1928	Fred R. Zimmerman
1929-1930	Walter J. Kohler
1931-1932	Philip F. La Follette
1933-1934	Albert G. Schmedeman
1935-1938	Philip F. La Follette
1939-1942	Julius P. Heil
1943-1946	Walter S. Goodland
1947-1950	Oscar Rennebohm
1951-1956	Walter J. Kohler, Jr.
1957-1958	Vernon W. Thomson
1959-1962	Gaylord A. Nelson
1963-1964	John W. Reynolds
1965-1970	Warren P. Knowles
1971-1978	Patrick J. Lucey (D)

1979-1982	Lee Dreyfus (R)
1983-1986	Anthony S. Earl (D)
1987-	Tommy G. Thompson (R)

Senators

1848-1854	Isaac P. Walker
1848-1856	Henry Dodge
1855-1860	Charles Durkee
1857-1868	James R. Doolittle
1861-1878	Timothy O. Howe
1869-1874	Matthew H. Carpenter
1875-1880	Angus Cameron
1879-1880	Matthew H. Carpenter
1881-1884	Angus Cameron
1881-1892	Philetus Sawyer
1885-1890	John C. Spooner
1891-1896	William F. Vilas
1893-1898	John L. Mitchell
1897-1906	John C. Spooner
1899-1905	Joseph V. Quarles
1906-1924	Robert M. La Follette
1907-1914	Isaac Stephenson
1915-1917	Paul O. Husting
1918-1926	Irvine L. Lenroot
1925-1946	Robert M. La Follette, Jr.
1927-1932	John J. Blaine
1933-1938	F. Ryan Duffy
1939-1960	Alexander Wiley
1947-1956	Joseph R. McCarthy
1957-	William Proxmire (D)
1961-1980	Gaylord A. Nelson (D)
1981-	Robert W. Kasten, Jr. (R)

Chief Justices

1848-1852	Alexander W. Stow
1853-1858	Edward V. Whiton
1859-1873	Luther S. Dixon
1874-1879	Edward G. Ryan
1880-1891	Orsamus Cole
1892-1893	William P. Lyon
1894	Harlow S. Orton
1895-1906	John P. Cassoday
1907-1919	John B. Winslow
1920-1921	Robert C. Siebecker
1922-1928	Aad J. Vinje
1929-1949	Marvin B. Rosenberry
1950-1953	Oscar M. Fritz
1954-1956	Edward T. Fairchild
1957-1961	John E. Martin
1962	Grover L. Broadfoot
1962-1963	Timothy Brown
1964-1967	George R. Currie
1968-1975	E. Harold Hallows
1976	Horace W. Wilkie
1977-1982	Bruce F. Beilfuss
1983-	Nathan S. Hefferman

Wyoming

Governors

1890	Francis E. Warren
1890-1892	Amos W. Barber
1893-1894	John E. Osborne
1895-1898	William A. Richards
1899-1902	DeForest Richards
1903-1904	Fenimore Chatterton
1905-1910	Bryant B. Brooks
1911-1914	Joseph M. Carey
1915-1916	John B. Kendrick
1917-1918	Frank L. Houx
1919-1922	Robert D. Carey

1923	William B. Ross
1924	Frank Lucas
1925-1926	Nellie T. Ross
1927-1930	Frank C. Emerson
1931-1932	Alonzo M. Clark
1933-1938	Leslie A. Miller
1939-1942	Nels H. Smith
1943-1948	Lester C. Hunt
1949-1950	Arthur G. Crane (Acting)
1951-1952	Frank A. Barrett
1953-1954	C. J. Rogers
1955-1958	Milward L. Simpson
1959-1960	John J. Hickey
1961-1962	Jack R. Gage
1963-1966	Clifford P. Hansen
1967-1974	Stanley K. Hathaway (R)
1975-1986	Ed Herschler (D)
1987-	Mike Sullivan (D)

Senators

1890-1892	Francis E. Warren
1890-1894	Joseph M. Carey
1893-1894	Vacant
1895-1916	Clarence D. Clark
1895-1928	Francis E. Warren
1917-1933	John B. Kendrick
1929	Patrick J. Sullivan
1930-1936	Robert D. Carey
1934-1952	Joseph C. O'Mahoney
1937-1942	Harry H. Schwartz
1943-1948	Edward V. Robertson
1949-1953	Lester C. Hunt
1953-1958	Frank A. Barrett
1954	Edward D. Crippa
1954-1960	Joseph C. O'Mahoney
1959-1976	Gale W. McGee (D)
1961-1962	John J. Hickey
1963-1966	Milward L. Simpson
1967-1979	Clifford P. Hansen (R)
1977-	Malcolm Wallop (R)
1979-	Alan K. Simpson (R)

Chief Justices

1890	Willis Van Devanter
1890-1896	Herman V. S. Groesbeck
1897	Asbury B. Conway
1897-1902	Charles N. Potter
1903-1904	Samuel T. Corn
1905	Jesse Knight
1905-1910	Charles N. Potter
1911-1912	Cyrus Beard
1913-1914	Richard H. Scott
1915-1918	Charles N. Potter
1919	Cyrus Beard
1920-1926	Charles N. Potter
1927-1930	Fred H. Blume
1931-1936	Ralph Kimball
1937-1938	Fred H. Blume
1939-1942	William A. Riner
1943-1944	Ralph Kimball
1945-1946	Fred H. Blume
1947-1950	William A. Riner
1951-1952	Ralph Kimball
1953-1954	Fred H. Blume
1955-1956	William A. Riner
1957-1962	Fred H. Blume
1963-1966	Glenn Parker
1967-1968	Harry S. Harnsberger
1969-1970	Norman B. Gray
1971-1972	John J. McIntyre
1973-1975	Glenn Parker
1976-1979	Rodney M. Guthrie
1980	John F. Raper
1981-1982	Robert R. Rose, Jr.
1983-1985	John J. Rooney
1986-	Richard V. Thomas

VII
The Confederacy

Confederate Government Leaders

Executive Branch

President: Jefferson Davis (1861-1865)

Vice President: Alexander H. Stephens (1861-1865)

Secretary of State: Robert Toombs (1861), Robert M. T. Hunter (1861-62), William M. Browne (Acting, 1862), Judah P. Benjamin (1862-65)

Attorney General: Judah P. Benjamin (1861), Thomas Bragg (1861), Thomas H. Watts (1862-63), Wade Keyes (Acting) (1863-64), George Davis (1864-65)

Secretary of the Treasury: Christopher G. Memminger (1861-64), George A. Trenholm (1864-65)

Secretary of the Navy: Stephen R. Mallory (1861-65)

Postmaster General: John H. Reagan (1861-65)

Secretary of War: Leroy P. Walker (1861), Judah P. Benjamin (1861-62), George W. Randolph (1862), James A. Seddon (1862-65), John C. Breckinridge (1865)

Delegates to the Constitutional Convention

(Montgomery, AL, Feb. 4-9, 1861)

President: Howell Cobb (GA)
Secretary: Johnson J. Hooper (AL)

Alabama

William P. Chilton
Jabez L. M. Curry
Thomas M. Fearn
S. L. Hale
Johnson J. Hooper
David P. Lewis
Colin J. McRae
John G. Shorter
Robert H. Smith
Richard W. Walker

Florida

J. Patton Anderson
Jackson Morton
James B. Owens

Georgia

Frank S. Barton
Howell Cobb
Thomas R. R. Cobb
Martin J. Crawford
Benjamin H. Hill
Augustus H. Kenan
Eugenius A. Nisbet
Alexander Stephens
Robert Toombs
August R. Wright

Louisiana

Charles M. Conrad
A. DeCluet
Duncan F. Kenner
Henry Marshall
John Perkins, Jr.
Edward Sparrow

Mississippi

William T. Barry
Walker Brooks
Josiah A. P. Campbell
Alexander M. Clayton
Wiley P. Harris
James T. Harrison
W. T. Wilson

South Carolina

Robert W. Barnwell
W. W. Boyce
L. M. Reitt
Christopher G. Memminger
William P. Miles
James Chestnut
Robert B. Rhett
Thomas J. Withers

Delegates to Provisional Congress

(Montgomery, AL, Feb. 4, 1861 to Feb. 17, 1862)

Alabama

William P. Dhilton
Jabez L. M. Curry
Nicholas Davis
Thomas M. Fearn
Stephen F. Hale
David P. Lewis
Colin J. McRae
Cornelius Robinson
John Gill Shorter
Robert H. Smith
Richard W. Walker

Arkansas

Augustus H. Garland
Robert W. Johnson
Albert Rust
Hugh F. Thomason
W. W. Watkins

Florida

J. Patton Anderson
Jackson Morton
James B. Owens
John P. Sanderson
George T. Ward

Georgia

Nathan Bass
Francis S. Bartow
Howell Cobb
Thomas R. R. Cobb
Martin J. Crawford
Thomas M. Foreman
Augustus H. Kenan
Eugenius A. Nisbet
Alexander H. Stephens
Robert Toombs
Augustus R. Wright

Kentucky

Henry C. Burnett
Theodore L. Burnett
John M. Elliott
George W. Ewing
L. H. Ford
George B. Hodge
Thomas Johnson
Thomas Monroe
John J. Thomas
Daniel P. White

Louisiana

Alexander D. Clouet
Charles M. Conrad
Duncan F. Kenner
Henry Marshall
John Perkins, Jr.

Mississippi

William S. Barry
Alexander B. Bradford
Walker Brooke

J. A. P. Campbell
Alexander M. Clayton
Wiley P. Harris
James T. Harrison
John A. Orr
William S. Wilson

Missouri

Casper W. Bell
John B. Clark
Aaron H. Conrow
Thomas A. Harris
Robert L. Y. Peyton
George G. Vest

North Carolina

W. W. Avery
Burton Craige
George Davis
A. T. Davidson
Thomas D. McDowell
John P. Morehead
R. C. Puryear
Thomas Ruffin
W. N. H. Smith
A. W. Venable

South Carolina

Robert W. Barnwell
William W. Boyce
James Chesnut, Jr.
Lawrence M. Keitt
Charles G. Memminger
W. Porcher Miles
James L. Orr
R. Barnwell Rhett, Sr.
Thomas J. Withers

Tennessee

John D. C. Atkins
Robert L. Caruthers
David M. Currin
W. H. DeWitt
John F. House
Thomas M. Jones

Texas

John Gregg
John Hemphill
William B. Ochiltree
William S. Oldham
John H. Reagan
Thomas N. Waul
Louis T. Wigfall

Virginia

Thomas S. Bocock
Alexander R. Boteler
John W. Brockenbrough
Robert M. T. Hunter
Robert Johnson
W. H. MacFarland
James M. Mason
Walter Preston
William B. Preston

Roger A. Pryor
William C. Rives
Charles W. Russell
Robert E. Scott
James A. Seddon
Waller R. Staples
John Tyler

First Congress

(Montgomery, AL, Feb. 18,
1862 to Feb. 17, 1864)

Alabama

Senators

Clement Claiborne Clay
Robert Jemison, Jr.
William L. Yancey

Representatives

William P. Chilton
David Clopton
Jabez L. M. Curry
E. S. Dargan
Thomas J. Foster
Francis L. Lyon
James L. Pugh
John R. Ralls
William R. Smith

Arkansas

Senators

Robert W. Johnson
Charles B. Mitchell

Representatives

Felix I. Batson
Augustus H. Garland
Thomas B. Hanly
Grandison D. Royston

Florida

Senators

Augustus E. Maxwell
James M. Baker

Representatives

James B. Dawkins
Robert B. Hilton
John M. Martin

Georgia

Senators

Benjamin H. Hill
Herschel V. Johnson
John W. Lewis

Representatives

William W. Clark
Lucius J. Gartrell
Julian Hartridge
Hines Holt
Porter Ingram
Augustus H. Kenan
David W. Lewis
Charles J. Munnerlyn
Hardy Strickland

Robert P. Trippe
Augustus R. Wright

Kentucky

Senators

Henry C. Burnett
William E. Simms

Representatives

Robert J. Breckinridge
Horatio W. Bruce
John W. Crockett
John M. Elliott
George W. Ewing
Willis B. Machen
James W. Moore

Louisiana

Senators

Thomas J. Semmes
Edward Sparrow

Representatives

Ely M. Bruce
Theodore L. Burnett
James S. Chrisman
George B. Hodge

Mississippi

Senators

Albert G. Brown
James Phelan

Representatives

Ethelbert Barksdale
Henry C. Chambers
J. W. Clapp
Reuben Davis
William D. Holder
John J. McRae
Otho R. Singleton
Israel Welsh

Missouri

Senators

John B. Clark
Waldo P. Johnson
Robert L. Y. Peyton

Representatives

Casper W. Bell
Aaron H. Conrow
William M. Cook
Thomas W. Freeman
Thomas A. Harris
George G. Vest

North Carolina

Senators

George Davis
William T. Dortch
Edwin G. Reade

Representatives

Archibald H. Arrington
Thomas S. Ashe

Robert R. Bridgers
A. T. Davidson
Burgess S. Gaither
Owen R. Kenan
William Lander
J. R. McLean
W. N. H. Smith

South Carolina

Senators

Robert W. Barnwell
James L. Orr

Representatives

Lewis M. Ayer
Milledge L. Bonham
William W. Boyce
James Farrow
John McQueen
W. Porcher Miles
William D. Simpson

Tennessee

Senators

Landon C. Haynes
Gustavus A. Henry

Representatives

John D. C. Atkins
David M. Currin
Henry S. Foote
E. L. Gardenhier
Meredith P. Gentry
Joseph B. Heiskell
George W. Jones
Thomas Menees
William G. Swan
William H. Tibbs
John V. Wright

Texas

Senators

William S. Oldham
Louis T. Wigfall

Representatives

M. D. Graham
Peter W. Gray
Caleb C. Herbert
Frank B. Sexton
John A. Wilcox

Virginia

Senators

Allen T. Caperton
Robert M. T. Hunter
William B. Preston

Representatives

John B. Baldwin
Thomas S. Bocock
Alexander R. Boteler
John R. Chambliss
Charles F. Collier
Daniel C. De Jarnette
David Funsten
Muscoe R. Garnett
John Goode, Jr.
James P. Holcombe

Albert G. Jenkins
Robert Johnson
James Lyons
Samuel A. Miller
Walter Preston
Roger A. Pryor
Charles W. Russell
William Smith
Waller R. Staples

Second Congress

(Richmond, VA, May 2, 1864
to Mar. 18, 1865)

Alabama

Senators

Robert Jemison, Jr.
Richard W. Walker

Representatives

William P. Chilton
David Clopton
M. H. Cruikshank
James S. Dickinson
Thomas J. Foster
Francis S. Lyon
James L. Pugh
William R. Smith

Arkansas

Senators

Augustus H. Garland
Robert W. Johnson
Charles B. Mitchell

Representatives

Felix I. Batson
David W. Carroll
Augustus H. Garland
Rufus H. Garland
Thomas B. Hanley

Florida

Senators

James E. Baker
Augustus E. Maxwell

Representatives

Robert B. Hilton
S. St. George Rogers

Georgia

Senators

Benjamin H. Hill
Herschel V. Johnson

Representatives

Warren Akin
Clifford Anderson
Hiram P. Bell
Mark H. Blandford
Joseph H. Echols
Julian Hartridge
George N. Lester
John T. Shewmake
James M. Smith
William E. Smith

Kentucky

Senators

Henry C. Burnett
William E. Simms

Representatives

Benjamin F. Bradley
Ely M. Bruce
Horatio W. Bruce
Theodore L. Burnett
James S. Chrisman
John M. Elliott
George W. Ewing
Willis B. Machen
Humphrey Marshall
James W. Moore
Henry E. Read
George W. Triplett

Louisiana

Senators

Thomas J. Semmes
Edward Sparrow

Representatives

Charles M. Conrad
Lucien J. Dupre
Henry Gray
Benjamin L. Hodge
Duncan F. Kenner
John Perkins, Jr.
Charles J. Villere

Mississippi

Senators

Albert G. Brown

John W. C. Watson

Representatives

Ethelbert Barksdale
Henry C. Chambers
William D. Holder
John T. Lampkin
John A. Orr
Otho R. Singleton
Israel Welsh

Missouri

Senators

Waldo P. Johnson
George G. Vest

Representatives

John B. Clark
Aaron H. Conrow
Robert A. Hatcher
R. L. Norton
Thomas L. Snead
George G. Vest
Peter S. Wilkes

North Carolina

Senators

William A. Graham
William T. Dortch

Representatives

Robert R. Bridges
Thomas C. Fuller
Burgess S. Gaither
John A. Gilmer
James M. Leach
James T. Leach
George W. Logan
James G. Ramsey
W. N. H. Smith
Josiah Turner

South Carolina

Senators

Robert W. Barnwell
James L. Orr

Representatives

Lewis M. Ayer
William W. Boyce
James Farrow
W. Porcher Miles
William D. Simpson
James H. Witherspoon

Tennessee

Senators

Landon C. Haynes
Gustavus A. Henry

Representatives

John D. C. Atkins
Michael W. Cluskey
Arthur S. Colyar
David M. Currin
Henry S. Foote
Joseph B. Heiskell
Edwin A. Keeble
James McCallum
Thomas Menees
John P. Murray
William G. Swan
John V. Wright

Texas

Senators

William S. Oldham
Louis T. Wigfall

Representatives

John R. Baylor
A. M. Branch
Stephen H. Darden
Caleb C. Herbert
Simpson H. Morgan
Frank B. Sexton

Virginia

Senators

Allen T. Caperton
Robert M. T. Hunter

Representatives

John B. Baldwin
Thomas S. Bocock
Daniel C. De Jarnette
David Funsten
Thomas S. Gholson
John Goode, Jr.
Frederick W. M. Holliday
Robert Johnston
Fayette McMullen
Samuel A. Miller
Robert L. Montague
William C. Rives
Charles W. Russell
Waller R. Staples
Robert L. Whitfield
William C. Wickham

Confederate Battlefield Commanders

First Battle of Bull Run, or Manassas
(July 21, 1861)

Army of the Shenandoah	Joseph E. Johnston
Army of the Potomac	Pierre G. T. Beauregard

Battle of Shiloh
(April 6-7, 1862)

Army of the Mississippi	Albert S. Johnston
I Corps	Leonidas Polk
First Division	Charles Clark
	Alexander P. Stewart
Second Division	Benjamin F. Cheatham
II Corps	Braxton Bragg
First Division	Daniel Ruggles
Second Division	Jones M. Withers
III Corps	William J. Hardee
Reserve Corps	John C. Breckinridge

Battle of Seven Pines, or Fair Oaks
(May 31-June 1, 1862)

Army of Northern Virginia	Joseph E. Johnston
	Robert E. Lee
Right Wing	James Longstreet
Longstreet's Division	Richard H. Anderson
Hill's Division	Daniel H. Hill
Huger's Division	Benjamin Huger
Left Wing	Gustavus W. Smith
Smith's Division	William H. C. Whiting

Seven Days' Battles
(June 25-July 1, 1862)

Army of Northern Virginia	Robert E. Lee
Jackson's Corps	Thomas J. ("Stonewall") Jackson
Whiting's Division	William H. C. Whiting
Third Division	Richard S. Ewell
Hill's Division	Daniel H. Hill
Magruder's Corps	John B. Magruder
Jones' Division	David R. Jones
McLaws' Division	Lafayette McLaws
Longstreet Corps	James Longstreet
Hill's Division	Ambrose P. Hill
Holmes' Division	Theophilus H. Holmes
Cavalry	James E. B. ("Jeb") Stuart
Reserve Artillery	William N. Pendleton

Second Battle of Bull Run, or Manassas
(Aug. 29-30, 1862)

Army of Northern Virginia	Robert E. Lee
Right Wing	James Longstreet
Anderson's Division	Richard H. Anderson
Jones' Division	David R. Jones
Wilcox's Division	Cadmus M. Wilcox
Hood's Division	John B. Hood

Kemper's Division	James L. Kemper
Left Wing	Thomas J. ("Stonewall") Jackson
First Division	William B. Taliaferro
Second (Light) Division	Ambrose P. Hill
Third Division	Richard S. Ewell
Cavalry Division	James E. B. ("Jeb") Stuart

Battle of Antietam
(Sept. 17, 1862)

Army of Northern Virginia	Robert E. Lee
Longstreet's Corps	James Longstreet
McLaws' Division	Lafayette McLaws
Anderson's Division	Richard H. Anderson
Jones' Division	David R. Jones
Walker's Division	John C. Walker
Hood's Division	John B. Hood
Jackson's Corps	Thomas J. ("Stonewall") Jackson
Ewell's Division	A. R. Lawton
Light Division	Ambrose P. Hill
Jackson's Division	John R. Jones
Hill's Division	Daniel H. Hill
Cavalry	James E. B. ("Jeb") Stuart
Reserve Artillery	William N. Pendleton

Battle of Corinth
(Oct. 3-4, 1862)

Army of West Tennessee	Earl Van Dorn
Price's Corps	Sterling Price
First Division	Louis Hebert
Maury's Division	Dabney H. Maury
District of the Mississippi	
First Division	Mansfield Lovell

Battle of Fredericksburg
(Dec. 13, 1862)

Army of Northern Virginia	Robert E. Lee
I Corps	James Longstreet
McLaws' Division	Lafayette McLaws
Anderson's Division	Richard H. Anderson
Pickett's Division	George E. Pickett
Hood's Division	John B. Hood
Ransom's Division	Robert Ransom
II Corps	Thomas J. ("Stonewall") Jackson
Hill's Division	Daniel H. Hill
Light Division	Ambrose P. Hill
Ewell's Division	Jubal A. Early
Jackson's Division	William B. Taliaferro
Reserve Artillery	William N. Pendleton
Cavalry	James E. B. ("Jeb") Stuart

Battle of Stones River, or Murfreesboro
(Dec. 31, 1862 - Jan. 2, 1863)

Army of Tennessee	Braxton Bragg
Polk's Corps	Leonidas Polk

First Division	Benjamin F. Cheatham
Second Division	Jones M. Withers
Hardee's Corps	William J. Hardee
First Division	John C. Breckinridge
Second Division	Patrick R. Cleburne
McCown's Division	John P. McCown
Cavalry	Joseph Wheller

Battle of Chancellorsville

(May 2-4, 1863)

Army of Northern Virginia	Robert E. Lee
I Corps	James Longstreet
McLaws' Division	Lafayette McLaws
Anderson's Division	Richard H. Anderson
II Corps	Thomas J. ("Stonewall") Jackson
Light Division	Ambrose P. Hill
D. H. Hill's Division	Robert E. Rodes
	S. D. Ramseur
Early's Division	Jubal A. Early
Trimble's Division	R. E. Colston
Cavalry	James E. B. ("Jeb") Stuart

Vicksburg Campaign

(May 1 - July 4, 1863)

Commanders	John C. Pemberton
	Joseph E. Johnston
First Division	William W. Loring
Stevenson's Division	Carter L. Stevenson
Forney's Division	John H. Forney
Smith's Division	Martin L. Smith
Bowen's Division	John S. Bowen

Battle of Gettysburg

(July 1-3, 1863)

Army of Northern Virginia	Robert E. Lee
I Corps	James Longstreet
McLaws' Division	Lafayette McLaws
Pickett's Division	George E. Pickett
Hood's Division	John B. Hood
II Corps	Richard S. Ewell
Early's Division	Jubal A. Early
Johnson's Division	Edward Johnson
Rodes' Division	Robert E. Rodes
III Corps	Ambrose P. Hill
Anderson's Division	Richard H. Anderson
Heth's Division	Henry Heth
Pender's Division	William D. Pender
Cavalry	James E. B. ("Jeb") Stuart

Battle of Chickamauga

(Sept. 19-20, 1863)

Army of Tennessee	Braxton Bragg
Right Wing (Polk's Corps)	Leonidas Polk
Cheatham's Division	Benjamin F. Cheatham
Hindman's Division	Thomas C. Hindman
Hill's Corps	Daniel H. Hill
Cleburne's Division	Patrick R. Cleburne
Breckinridge's Division	John C. Breckinridge
Reserve Corps	William H. T. Walker
Walker's Division	States R. Gist
Liddell's Division	St. John R. Liddell
Left Wing	James Longstreet
Buckner's Corps	Simon B. Buckner
Stewart's Division	Alexander P. Stewart
Preston's Division	William Preston
Johnson's Division	Bushrod R. Johnson
Longstreet's Corps	John B. Hood
McLaws' Division	Lafayette McLaws
Hood's Division	John B. Hood

Wheeler's Cavalry Corps	Joseph Wheeler
Wharton's Division	John A. Wharton
Martin's Division	Will T. Martin
Forrest's Corps	Nathan B. Forrest
Armstrong's Division	Frank C. Armstrong
Pegram's Division	John Pegram

Battle of Chattanooga

(Nov. 23-25, 1863)

Commander	Braxton Bragg
Hardee's Corps	William J. Hardee
Cheatham's Division	John K. Jackson
Stevenson's Division	Carter L. Stevenson
Cleburne's Division	Patrick R. Cleburne
Walker's Division	States R. Gist
Breckinridge's Corps	John C. Breckinridge
Hindman's Division	J. Patton Anderson
Breckinridge's Division	William B. Bate
Stewart's Division	Alexander P. Stewart

Battle of the Wilderness and Spottsylvania Court House

(May 5-21, 1864)

Army of Northern Virginia	Robert E. Lee
I Corps	James Longstreet
	Richard H. Anderson
Kershaw's Division	Joseph B. Kershaw
Field's Division	Charles W. Field
Artillery	Edward P. Alexander
II Corps	Richard S. Ewell
	Jubal A. Early
Early's Division	Jubal A. Early
Johnson's Division	Edward Johnson
Rode's Division	Robert E. Rodes
Artillery	Armistead L. Long
III Corps	Ambrose P. Hill
Anderson's Division	Richard H. Anderson
Heth's Division	Henry Heth
Wilcox's Division	Cadmus M. Wilcox
Artillery	R. Lindsay Walker
Cavalry Corps	James E. B. ("Jeb") Stuart
Hampton's Division	Wade Hampton
Fitz-Lee's Division	Fitzhugh Lee
W. H. F. Lee's Division	William H. F. Lee

Atlanta Campaign

(May 3 - Sept. 8, 1864)

Army of Tennessee	Joseph E. Johnston
	John B. Hood
Cheatham's Division	Benjamin F. Cheatham
Cleburne's Division	Patrick R. Cleburne
	Mark B. Lowrey
Walker's Division	William H. T. Walker
Bate's Division	William B. Bate
	John C. Brown
Hood's Corps	John B. Hood
	Carter L. Stevenson
	Benjamin F. Cheatham
	Stephen D. Lee
Hindman's Division	Thomas C. Hindman
Stevenson's Division	Carter L. Stevenson
Stewart's Division	Alexander P. Stewart
Cavalry Corps	Joseph Wheeler
Martin's Division	Will T. Martin
Kelly's Division	John H. Kelly
Humes' Division	William Y. C. Humes
Roddey's Command	Philip D. Roddey
Army of the Mississippi	
Polk's Corps	Leonidas Polk
	William W. Loring
	Alexander P. Stewart

Loring's Division	Benjamin F. Cheatham	Cheatham's Corps	Benjamin F. Cheatham
	William W. Loring	Brown's Division	John C. Brown
	Winfield S. Featherston	Cleburne's Division	J. A. Smith
French's Division	Samuel G. French	Bate's Division	William B. Bate
Cantey's Division	James Cantey	Cavalry Division	James R. Chalmers
	Edward C. Walthall		
Cavalry Division	William H. Jackson		
Georgia Militia			
First Division	G. A. Smith		

Campaign of the Carolinas

(Feb. - Mar., 1865)

Battle of Nashville

(Dec. 15-16, 1864)

Army of Tennessee	John B. Hood	Army of Tennessee	Joseph E. Johnson
Lee's Corps	Stephen D. Lee	Hardee's Corps	William J. Hardee
Johnson's Division	Edward Johnson	Hoke's Division	R. F. Hoke
Stevenson's Division	Carter L. Stevenson	Cheatham's Division	Benjamin F. Cheatham
Clayton's Division	Henry D. Clayton	Stewart's Corps	Alexander P. Stewart
Stewart's Corps	Alexander P. Stewart	Loring's Division	William W. Loring
Loring's Division	William W. Loring	Anderson's Division	J. Patton Anderson
French's Division	Samuel G. French	Walthall's Division	Edward C. Walthall
Walthall's Division	Edward C. Walthall	Lee's Corps	Stephen D. Lee
		Hill's Division	Daniel H. Hill
		Stevenson's Division	Carter L. Stevenson
		Cavalry	Wade Hampton

Confederate Naval Commanders

Charleston Squadron

| 1862 | Duncan N. Ingraham |
| 1863 | John R. Tucker |

Galveston Squadron

| 1861 | Willian N. Hunter |
| 1863 | Joseph N. Barney |

James River Squadron

1861	Samuel Barron
1861	William F. Lynch
1862	Franklin Buchanan
1862	Josiah Tatnall
1862	Samuel Barron
1863	French Forrest
1864	John K. Mitchell

| 1865 | Raphael Semmes |

Mississippi River Squadron

1861	Lawrence Rousseau
1861	George N. Hollins
1862	John K. Mitchell
1862	William F. Lynch

Mobile Squadron

1862	Victor M. Randolph
1862	Franklin Buchanan
1864	Ebenezer Farrand

North Carolina Squadron

| 1862 | William F. Lynch |

| 1864 | Robert F. Pinkney |

Red River Squadron

| 1863 | Thomas R. Brent |
| 1863 | Jonathan H. Carter |

Savannah River Squadron

1861	Josiah Tatnall
1863	Richard L. Page
1863	William A. Webb
1863	William W. Hunter

Naval Forces in Europe

| 1862-1864 | Samuel Barron |

VIII
The Military

This section includes the following subdivisions:

Secretaries of Defense and the Services
   and Chairmen of the Joint Chiefs of Staff

U.S. Army
   Chiefs of Staff
   U.S. Army General Staff
   U.S. Army Special Staff
   U.S. Army Major Field Commanders
   U.S. Army Commanders

Army Commanders During Wartime
   Revolutionary War
   War of 1812
   Civil War
   Spanish American War
   First World War
   Second World War
   Korean Conflict
   Vietnam Conflict

U.S. Air Force

U.S. Navy
   Chiefs of Naval Operations
   U.S. Marine Corps
   U.S. Navy Fleet Commanders
   U.S. Navy Bureau Chiefs
   Naval Commanders During Wartime
      Revolutionary War
      War of 1812
      Civil War
      Spanish American War
      First World War

Colleges of the Armed Forces

Secretaries of Defense and the Services and Chairmen of the Joint Chiefs of Staff

Secretaries of Defense

Years in Office	Name and State	Presidential Terms
1947-1949	James V. Forrestal (NY)	Truman 1, 2
1949-1950	Louis A. Johnson (WV)	Truman 2
1950-1951	George C. Marshall (PA)	Truman 2
1951-1953	Robert A. Lovett (NY)	Truman 2
1953-1957	Charles E. Wilson (MI)	Eisenhower 1, 2
1957-1960	Neil H. McElroy (OH)	Eisenhower 2
1960-1961	Thomas S. Gates, Jr. (PA)	Eisenhower 2
1961-1968	Robert S. McNamara (MI)	Kennedy L. B. Johnson 1, 2
1968-1969	Clark M. Clifford (MD)	L. B. Johnson 2
1969-1973	Melvin R. Laird (WI)	Nixon 1
1973	Elliot L. Richardson (MA)	Nixon 2
1973-1975	James R. Schlesinger (VA)	Nixon 2, Ford
1975-1977	Donald H. Rumsfeld (IL)	Ford
1977-1981	Harold Brown (NY)	Carter
1981-	Caspar W. Weinberger (CA)	Reagan 1, 2

Deputy Secretaries of Defense

1949	Stephen T. Early
1950	Robert A. Lovett
1951	William C. Foster
1953	Roger M. Kyes
1953	Robert B. Anderson
1955	Reuben B. Robertson, Jr.
1957	Donald A. Quarles
1959	Thomas S. Gates, Jr.
1959	James H. Douglas, Jr.
1961	Roswell L. Gilpatric
1964	Cyrus R. Vance
1967	Paul H. Nitze
1969	David Packard
1972	Kenneth Rush
1973	William P. Clements, Jr.
1977	Charles W. Duncan, Jr.
1979	W. Graham Claytor
1981	Frank C. Carlucci
1982	W. Paul Thayer
1984	William Howard Taft, IV

Secretaries of the U.S. Army, Navy, and Air Force

(Not members of the cabinet.)

Army

1947	Kenneth C. Royall
1949	Gordon Gray
1950	Frank Pace, Jr.
1953	Robert T. Stevens
1955	Wilber M. Brucker
1961	Elvis J. Stahr, Jr.
1962	Cyrus R. Vance
1964	Stephen Ailes
1965	Stanley R. Resor
1971	Robert F. Froehlke
1973	Howard H. Callaway
1975	Martin R. Hoffman
1977	Clifford L. Alexander, Jr.
1981	John O. Marsh, Jr.

Navy

1947	John L. Sullivan
1949	Francis P. Matthews
1951	Dan A. Kimball
1953	Robert B. Anderson
1954	Charles S. Thomas
1957	Thomas S. Gates, Jr.
1958	William B. Franke
1958	John B. Connally, Jr.
1961	Fred Korth
1963	Paul H. Nitze
1967	Paul R. Ignatius
1969	John H. Chaffee
1972	John W. Warner
1974	J. William Middendorf, II
1977	W. Graham Claytor
1979	Edward Hidalgo
1981	John F. Lehman, Jr.
1987	James H. Webb, Jr.

Air Force

1947	W. Stuart Symington
1950	Thomas K. Finletter
1953	Harold E. Talbot
1955	Donald A. Quarles
1957	James H. Douglas, Jr.
1959	Dudley C. Sharpe
1961	Eugene M. Zuckert
1965	Harold Brown
1969	Robert C. Seamans, Jr.
1973	John L. McLucas
1976	Thomas C. Reed
1977	John C. Stetson
1981	Verne Orr
1985	Russell A. Rourke

Chairmen of the Joint Chiefs of Staff

(Chiefs of Staff listed separately under respective services.)

Aug.	1949	Omar N. Bradley
Aug.	1953	Arthur W. Radford
Aug.	1957	Nathan F. Twining
Oct.	1960	Lyman L. Lemnitzer
Oct.	1962	Maxwell D. Taylor
July	1964	Earle G. Wheeler
July	1970	Thomas H. Moorer
June	1974	George S. Brown
July	1978	David C. Jones
June	1982	John W. Vessey, Jr.
Oct.	1985	William J. Crowe, Jr.

Joint Staff, Joint Chiefs of Staff

Directors

1947	Alfred M. Gruenther
1949	Arthur C. Davis
1951	Charles P. Cabell
1953	Frank F. Everest
1954	Lemuel Mathewson
1956	Bernard L. Austin
1958	Oliver S. Picher
1960	Earle G. Wheeler
1962	Herbert D. Riley
1964	David A. Burchinal
1966	Andrew J. Goodpaster
1967	Berton E. Spivy, Jr.
1968	Nels C. Johnson
1970	John W. Vogt, Jr.
1972	George M. Seignious, II
1975	Harry D. Train, II
1977	Patrick Hannifin
1979	John A. Wickham, Jr.
1980	Thor Hanson
1982	James E. Dalton
1984	Jack N. Merritt
1986	Powell F. Carter, Jr.

U.S. Army

Chiefs of Staff

(Until 1903 known as Commanders of the Army.)

June	1775	George Washington
Dec.	1783	Henry Knox
June	1784	John Doughty
Aug.	1784	Josiah Harmer
Mar.	1791	Arthur St. Clair
Apr.	1792	Anthony Wayne
Dec.	1796	James Wilkinson
July	1798	George Washington
Dec.	1799	Alexander Hamilton
June	1800	James Wilkinson
Jan.	1812	Henry Dearborn
June	1815	Jacob Brown
May	1828	Alexander Macomb
July	1841	Winfield Scott
Nov.	1816	George B. McClellan
July	1862	Henry W. Halleck
Mar.	1864	Ulysses S. Grant
Mar.	1869	William T. Sherman
Nov.	1883	Philip H. Sheridan
Aug.	1888	John M. Schofield
Oct.	1895	Nelson A. Miles
Aug.	1903	Samuel B. M. Young
Jan.	1904	Adna R. Chaffee
Jan.	1906	John C. Bates
Apr.	1906	J. Franklin Bell
Apr.	1910	Leonard Wood
Apr.	1914	William W. Witherspoon
Nov.	1914	Hugh L. Scott
Sept.	1917	Tasker H. Bliss
May	1918	Peyton C. March
July	1921	John J. Pershing
Sept.	1924	John L. Hines
Nov.	1926	Charles P. Summerall
Nov.	1930	Douglas MacArthur
Oct.	1935	Malin Craig
Sept.	1939	George C. Marshall
Nov.	1945	Dwight D. Eisenhower
Feb.	1948	Omar N. Bradley
Aug.	1949	J. Lawton Collins
Aug.	1953	Matthew B. Ridgway
June	1955	Maxwell D. Taylor
July	1959	Lyman L. Lemnitzer
Sept.	1960	George H. Decker
Oct.	1962	Earle G. Wheeler
July	1964	Harold K. Johnson
July	1968	William C. Westmoreland
June	1972	Creighton W. Abrams, Jr.
Oct.	1974	Frederick C. Weyand
Oct.	1976	Bernard W. Rogers
June	1979	Edward C. Meyer
July	1983	John A. Wickham

U.S. Army General Staff

Deputy Chiefs of Staff for Personnel

(Until 1956 known as G-1 — Personnel and Administration.)

Sept.	1921	James H. McRae
Sept.	1922	Charles H. Martin
May	1925	Campbell King
May	1929	Albert J. Bowley
Oct.	1931	Andrew Moses
Nov.	1935	Harry E. Knight
Sept.	1937	Lorenzo D. Gasser
Oct.	1939	William E. Shedd
Feb.	1941	Wade H. Haislip
Jan.	1942	John H. Hilldring
July	1942	Donald Wilson
Sept.	1942	Miller G. White
Aug.	1944	Stephen G. Henry
Oct.	1945	Willard S. Paul
Jan.	1949	Edward H. Brooks
June	1951	Clovis E. Byers (Acting)
July	1951	Anthony C. McAuliffe
Mar.	1953	Robert N. Young
Apr.	1955	Donald P. Booth
Jan.	1956	Walter L. Weibel
Dec.	1956	Donald P. Booth
Mar.	1958	James F. Collins
Mar.	1961	Russell L. Vittrup
May	1963	James L. Richardson, Jr.
July	1965	James K. Woolnough
June	1967	Albert O. Connor
Aug.	1969	Walter T. Kerwin, Jr.
	1973	Bernard W. Rogers
	1976	Harold G. Moore
	1977	Dewitt C. Smith, Jr.
	1979	Robert G. Yerks
	1982	Maxwell R. Thurman
	1983	Robert M. Elton

Assistant Chiefs of Staff for Intelligence

(Until 1956 known as G-2 — Intelligence.)

May	1917	Ralph H. Van Deman
June	1918	Marlborough Churchill
Sept.	1920	Dennis E. Nolan
Sept.	1921	Stuart Heintzelman
Nov.	1922	William K. Naylor
July	1924	James H. Reeves
May	1927	Stanley H. Ford
Jan.	1931	Alfred T. Smith
Feb.	1935	Harry E. Knight
Nov.	1935	Francis H. Lincoln
July	1937	E. R. Warner McCabe
Apr.	1940	Sherman Miles

Feb.	1942	Raymond E. Lee
May	1942	George V. Strong
Feb.	1944	Clayton L. Bissell
Jan.	1946	Hoyt S. Vandenberg
June	1946	Stephen J. Chamberlin
Nov.	1948	Stafford L. Irwin
Sept.	1950	Alexander R. Bolling
Sept.	1952	Richard C. Partridge
Nov.	1953	Arthur G. Trudeau
Aug.	1955	Ridgely Gaither
July	1956	Robert A. Schow
Oct.	1958	John M. Willens
Oct.	1961	Alvah R. Fitch
Dec.	1963	Edgar C. Doleman
Aug.	1965	John J. Davis
Nov.	1966	William P. Yarborough
	1969	J. A. McChristian
	1971	Phillip B. Davidson, Jr.
	1973	William E. Potts
	1975	Harold R. Aaron
	1977	Edmund R. Thompson
	1982	William E. Odom
	1986	Sidney T. Weinstein

Deputy Chiefs of Staff for Operations and Plans

(From 1921 to 1949 known as Chiefs of Plans and Operations Division — G-3; from 1949 to 1955 G-3 was known as Deputy Chief of Staff/Operations; from 1955 to 1974 known as Deputy Chiefs of Staff for Military Operations.)

Sept.	1921	Briant H. Wells
Dec.	1923	Stuart Heintzelman
July	1924	Leroy Eltinge
July	1925	Harry A. Smith
Sept.	1927	George S. Simonds
Sept.	1931	Joseph P. Tracy
Sept.	1932	Charles E. Kilbourne
Mar.	1935	Stanley D. Embick
May	1936	Walter Krueger
July	1938	George C. Marshall
Oct.	1938	George V. Strong
Dec.	1940	Leonard T. Gerow
Feb.	1942	Dwight D. Eisenhower
June	1942	Thomas T. Handy
Oct.	1944	John E. Hull
June	1946	Lauris Norstad
Oct.	1947	Albert C. Wedemeyer
Nov.	1948	Ray T. Maddocks
1949-1955		See Chiefs of Organization and Training
Oct.	1955	Clyde D. Eddleman
May	1958	James E. Moore
Oct.	1959	John C. Oakes
Jan.	1961	Barksdale Hamlett
Mar.	1962	Edwin H. J. Carns
May	1962	Theodore W. Parker
May	1963	Harold K. Johnson
July	1964	Bruce Palmer, Jr.
Apr.	1965	Vernon P. Mock

Aug.	1966	Harry J. Lemley, Jr.
Aug.	1969	Richard G. Stilwell
	1973	Donald H. Cowles
	1975	John W. Vessey, Jr.
	1977	Edward C. Meyer
	1980	Glenn K. Otis
	1982	William R. Richardson
	1983	Fred K. Mahaffey
	1986	Carl E. Vuono

Chiefs of Organization and Training — G-3

(From 1949 to 1955 known as Deputy Chiefs of Staff/Operations; see Deputy Chiefs of Staff for Operations and Plans for later Chiefs.)

Sept.	1921	William Lassiter
Dec.	1923	Hugh A. Drum
Apr.	1926	Malin Craig
Apr.	1927	Frank Parker
July	1929	Edward L. King
Feb.	1932	Edgar T. Collins
July	1933	John H. Hughes
Apr.	1937	George P. Tyner
Mar.	1938	R. M. Beck
Aug.	1939	F. M. Andrews
Nov.	1940	Harry L. Twaddle
Apr.	1941	Harry J. Malony
Apr.	1941	Harry L. Twaddle
Mar.	1942	Harold R. Bull
May	1942	Idwal H. Edwards
May	1943	Ray E. Porter
Feb.	1945	Idwal H. Edwards
July	1946	Charles P. Hall
Nov.	1948	Harold R. Bull
May	1949	Clift Andrus
Mar.	1950	Charles L. Bolte
Feb.	1951	Maxwell D. Taylor
Sept.	1951	Reuben E. Jenkins
Sept.	1952	Clyde D. Eddleman
Mar.	1954	James M. Gavin
Mar.	1955	Paul D. Adams
July	1955	Paul D. Harkins

Deputy Chiefs of Staff for Logistics

(Until 1955 known as G-4 — Logistics.)

Dec.	1917	George W. Goethals
Feb.	1918	P. E. Pierce
Apr.	1918	George W. Goethals
Mar.	1919	George W. Burr
Sept.	1920	William M. Wright
Sept.	1921	William D. Connor
Nov.	1922	Stuart Heintzelman
Dec.	1923	Dennis E. Nolan
Dec.	1924	Fox Conner
Mar.	1926	Briant H. Wells
May	1927	E. E. Booth
Jan.	1931	R. E. Callan
Feb.	1935	C. S. Lincoln
June	1956	George R. Spalding
Apr.	1937	George P. Tyner
Aug.	1940	Eugene Reybold (Acting)
Nov.	1941	Brehon B. Somervell
Mar.	1942	Raymond G. Moses
Sept.	1943	Russell L. Maxwell
Mar.	1946	Stanley L. Scott (Acting)
June	1946	LeRoy Lutes
Jan.	1948	Henry S. Aurand
Mar.	1949	Thomas B. Larkin
Mar.	1953	Williston B. Palmer
Apr.	1955	Carter B. Magruder
June	1959	Robert W. Colglazier, Jr.
July	1964	Lawrence J. Lincoln, Jr.

June	1967	Jean E. Engler
Sept.	1969	Joseph M. Heiser, Jr.
	1973	Fred Kornet, Jr.
	1976	Jack C. Fuson
	1977	Eivind H. Johansen
	1980	Arthur J. Gregg
	1982	Richard H. Thompson
	1985	Benjamin F. Register, Jr.

Chiefs of Research, Development, and Acquisition

(Until 1974 known as Chiefs of Research and Development.)

1956	James M. Gavin
1958	Arthur G. Trudeau
1962	Dwight E. Beach
1963	William W. Dick, Jr.
1966	Austin W. Betts
1969	W. C. Gribble, Jr.
1974	John R. Deane, Jr.
1975	Howard H. Cooksey
1978	Donald R. Keith
1982	James H. Merryman
1985	Louis C. Wagner, Jr.

Directors of the Women's Army Corps

(Abolished in 1978.)

1943	Oveta Culp Hobby
1945	Westray Battle Boyce
1947	Mary A. Hallaren
1953	Irene O. Galloway
1957	Mary L. Milligan
1962	Emily C. Gorman
1966	Elizabeth P. Hoisington
1971	Mildred C. Bailey
1975	Mary E. Clarke (to Sept. 1978)

U.S. Army Special Staff

Adjutants General

June	1775	Horatio Gates
June	1776	Joseph Reed
Jan.	1777	Arthur St. Clair (Acting)
Feb.	1777	George Weedon (Acting)
Apr.	1777	Morgan Connor
June	1777	Timothy Pickering
Jan.	1778	Alexander Scammel
Jan.	1781	Edward Hand
Nov.	1783	William North
Oct.	1787	Ebenezer Denny (Acting)
Nov.	1790	John Pratt
Sept.	1791	Winthrop Sargent
Nov.	1791	Ebenezer Denny (Acting)
Mar.	1792	Henry DeButts (Acting)
Feb.	1793	Michael Rudolph (Acting)
July	1793	Edward Butler (Acting)
May	1794	John Mills (Acting)
Feb.	1796	Jonathan Haskell (Acting)
Aug.	1796	Edward Butler (Acting)
Feb.	1797	Thomas H. Cushing (Acting)
July	1798	William North
June	1800	Thomas H. Cushing
Apr.	1807	A. Y. Nicholl
Apr.	1812	Alexander Macomb
July	1812	Thomas H. Cushing
Mar.	1813	Zebulon M. Pike
May	1814	William H. Winder
Nov.	1814	Daniel Parker

Aug.	1821	James Gadsden
May	1822	C. J. Nourse (Acting)
Mar.	1825	Roger Jones
July	1852	Samuel Cooper
Mar.	1861	Lorenzo Thomas
Feb.	1869	E. D. Townsend
June	1880	R. C. Drum
June	1889	J. C. Kelton
Nov.	1893	G. D. Ruggles
Sept.	1897	Samuel Breck
Feb.	1898	Henry C. Corbin
Apr.	1904	Fred C. Ainsworth
Feb.	1912	William P. Hall
Aug.	1912	George Andrews
Aug.	1914	Henry P. McCain
Sept.	1918	Peter C. Harris
Sept.	1922	Robert C. Davis
July	1927	Lutz Wahl
Dec.	1928	Charles H. Bridges
Feb.	1933	James F. McKinley
Nov.	1935	Edgar T. Conley
May	1938	Emory S. Adams
Mar.	1942	James A. Ulio
July	1945	Edward F. Witsell (Acting)
Feb.	1946	Edward F. Witsell
July	1951	William E. Bergin (Acting)
July	1951	William E. Bergin
June	1954	John A. Klein
Jan.	1957	Herbert M. Jones
Nov.	1958	Robert V. Lee
Oct.	1961	Joe C. Lambert
July	1966	Kenneth J. Wickham
Sept.	1970	Verne L. Bowers
	1975	Paul T. Smith
	1977	James C. Pennington
	1982	Robert M. Joyce
	1985	Donald J. Delandro
	1986	Robert L. Dilworth

Commanders, Army Air Corps

(Reorganized as separate service in 1947.)

1918	Charles T. Menoher
1921	Mason M. Patrick
1927	James E. Fechet
1931	Benjamin D. Foulois
1935	Oscar Westover
1938	Henry H. Arnold

Chiefs of Artillery

(Reorganized as Coast Artillery in 1908.)

Feb.	1903	Wallace F. Randolph
Jan.	1904	John P. Story
June	1905	Samuel M. Mills
Oct.	1906	Arthur Murray

Chiefs of Cavalry

July	1920	Willard A. Holbrook
July	1924	Malin Craig
Mar.	1926	Herbert B. Crosby
Mar.	1930	Guy V. Henry
Mar.	1934	Leon B. Kromer
Mar.	1938	John K. Herr (to Mar. 1942)

Chiefs of Chaplains

1920	John T. Axton
1927	Edmund P. Easterbrook
1929	Julian E. Yates
1933	Alva J. Brasted

1937 William R. Arnold
1945 Luther D. Miller
1949 Roy H. Parker
1952 Ivan L. Bennett
1954 Patrick J. Ryan
1958 Frank A. Tobey
1962 Charles E. Brown, Jr.
1967 Francis L. Sampson
1971 Gerhardt W. Hyatt
1976 Orris E. Kelly
1980 Kermit D. Johnson
1983 Patrick J. Hessian

Chiefs of Chemical Corps

(Until 1946 known as Chemical Warfare Service.)

July 1918 William L. Sibert
July 1920 Amos A. Fries
Mar. 1929 Harry L. Gilchrist
May 1933 Claude E. Brigham
May 1937 Walter C. Baker
May 1941 William N. Porter
Nov. 1945 Alden H. Waitt
Oct. 1949 Anthony C. McAuliffe
June 1951 Egbert F. Bullene
May 1954 William M. Creasy
Sept. 1958 Marshall Stubbs (to July 1962)

Chiefs of Coast Artillery

July 1908 Arthur Murray
Mar. 1911 Erasmus M. Weaver
May 1918 Frank W. Coe
Mar. 1926 Andrew Hero, Jr.
Mar. 1930 John W. Gulick
Mar. 1934 William F. Hase
Jan. 1935 Harry L. Steele
Apr. 1936 Archibald H. Sutherland
Apr. 1940 Joseph A. Green (to Mar. 1942)

Chiefs of Engineers

June 1775 Richard Gridley
Aug. 1776 Rufus Putnam
July 1777 L. L. Duportail
Feb. 1795 Stephen Rochefontaine
May 1798 Henry Burbeck
July 1802 Jonathan Williams
July 1812 Joseph G. Swift
Nov. 1818 W. K. Armistead
June 1821 Alexander Macomb
May 1828 Charles Gratiat
Dec. 1838 J. G. Totten
Apr. 1864 Richard Delafield
Aug. 1866 A. A. Humphries
June 1879 Horatio G. Wright
Mar. 1884 John Newton
Oct. 1886 J. C. Duane
July 1888 T. L. Casey
May 1895 William P. Craighill
Feb. 1897 John M. Wilson
May 1901 L. Gillespie
Jan. 1904 Alexander Mackenzie
July 1908 William L. Marshall
June 1910 William H. Bixby
Aug. 1913 William T. Rossell
Oct. 1913 Dan C. Kingman
Mar. 1916 William M. Black
Jan. 1920 Lansing H. Beach
June 1924 Harry Taylor
June 1926 Edgar Jadwin
Oct. 1929 Lytle Brown

Oct. 1933 Edward M. Markham
Oct. 1937 Julian L. Schley
Oct. 1941 Eugene Reybold
Oct. 1945 Raymond A. Wheeler
Mar. 1949 Lewis A. Pick
Mar. 1953 Samuel D. Sturgis, Jr.
Oct. 1956 E. C. Itschner
Mar. 1961 Keith R. Barney (Acting)
May 1967 Walter K. Wilson, Jr.
June 1965 William F. Cassidy
Aug. 1969 Frederick J. Clarke
1974 W. C. Gribble, Jr.
1977 John W. Morris
1981 Joseph K. Bratton
1985 Elvin R. Heiberg, III

Chiefs of Field Artillery

July 1920 William J. Snow
Dec. 1927 Fred T. Austin
Mar. 1930 Harry G. Bishop
Mar. 1934 Upton Birnie, Jr.
Mar. 1938 Robert M. Danford (to Mar. 1942)

Chiefs of Infantry

July 1920 Charles S. Farnsworth
Mar. 1925 Robert H. Allen
Mar. 1929 Stephen O. Fuqua
May 1933 Edward Croft
May 1937 George A. Lynch
May 1941 Courtney H. Hodges (to Mar. 1942)

Inspectors General

Dec. 1777 Thomas Conway
May 1778 F. W. A. von Steuben
Apr. 1784 William North
Mar. 1792 Henry DeButts
Feb. 1793 Michael Rudolph
July 1793 Edward Butler
May 1794 John Mills
Feb. 1796 Jonathan Haskell
Aug. 1796 Edward Butler
Feb. 1797 Thomas H. Cushing
July 1798 Alexander Hamilton
June 1800 Thomas H. Cushing
Apr. 1807 Abimael Y. Nicoll
July 1812 Alexander Smyth
Mar. 1813 Zebulon M. Pike
May 1814 William H. Winder
Nov. 1814 Daniel Parker
June 1821 John E. Wood
June 1841 George Croghan
Jan. 1849 Sylvester Churchill
Aug. 1861 Randolph B. Marcy
Jan. 1881 Delos B. Sacket
Mar. 1885 Nelson H. Davis
Sept. 1885 Absolom Baird
Aug. 1888 Roger Jones
Jan. 1889 Joseph C. Breckinridge
Apr. 1903 Peter D. Vroom
Apr. 1903 George H. Burton
Oct. 1906 Ernest A. Garlington
Feb. 1917 John L. Chamberlain
Nov. 1912 Eli A. Helmick
Sept. 1927 William C. Rivers
Jan. 1930 Hugh A. Drum
Dec. 1931 John F. Preston
Dec. 1935 Walter L. Reed
Dec. 1939 Virgil L. Peterson
July 1945 Daniel I. Sultan
Jan. 1947 Ira T. Wyche
July 1948 Louis A. Craig

June 1952 Daniel Noce
Nov. 1954 Wayne C. Zimmerman
Feb. 1956 David A. D. Ogden
Nov. 1957 Albert Pierson
July 1959 Edward H. McDaniel
Nov. 1963 Hiram D. Ives
Oct. 1965 James A. Richardson, III
Nov. 1966 William C. Garrison
Aug. 1968 William A. Enemark
1973 Gilbert H. Woodward
1974 Herron N. Maples
1977 Marvin D. Fuller
1978 R. G. Trefry
1984 Nathaniel R. Thompson

Judge Advocates General

July 1775 William Tudor
Apr. 1777 John Lawrence
Oct. 1782 Thomas Edwards
July 1794 Campbell Smith
Mar. 1849 John F. Lee
Sept. 1862 Joseph Holt
Dec. 1875 William M. Dunn
Feb. 1881 David G. Swain
Jan. 1895 G. Norman Lieber
May 1901 George B. Davis
Feb. 1911 Enoch H. Crowder
Feb. 1923 Walter A. Bethel
Nov. 1924 John A. Hull
Nov. 1928 Edward A. Kreger
Mar. 1931 Blanton Winship
Dec. 1933 Arthur W. Brown
Dec. 1937 Allen W. Gullion
Dec. 1941 Myron C. Cramer
Dec. 1945 Thomas H. Green
Jan. 1950 Ernest M. Brannon
Jan. 1954 Eugene M. Caffey
Jan. 1957 George W. Hickman, Jr.
Dec. 1960 Charles T. Decker
Feb. 1964 Robert H. McCaw
June 1967 Kenneth J. Hodson
July 1971 George S. Prugh
1976 Wilton B. Persons, Jr.
1980 Alton H. Harvey
1982 Hugh J. Clausen
1986 Hugh R. Overholt

Chiefs of National Guard Bureau

(Until 1933 known as Militia Bureau.)

1908 Erasmus M. Weaver
1911 Robert K. Evans
1912 Albert L. Mills
1916 William A. Mann
1917 Jessie M. Carter
1918 John W. Heavey (Acting)
1919 Jessie M. Carter
1921 George C. Rickards
1925 Creed C. Hammond
1929 Ernest R. Redmond (Acting)
1929 William G. Everson
1931 George E. Leach
1935 Herold J. Weiler (Acting)
1936 John F. Williams (Acting)
1936 Albert H. Blanding
1940 John F. Williams
1946 Butler B. Miltonberger
1947 Kenneth F. Cramer
1950 Raymond H. Fleming
1953 Earl T. Ricks
1953 Edgar C. Erickson
1959 Donald W. McGowan
1964 Winston P. Wilson
1972 Francis F. Greenlief
1975 LaVerne E. Weber

1983 Emmett H. Walker

Chiefs of Ordnance

July	1812	Decius Wadsworth
June	1821	George Bomford
Mar.	1848	George Talcott
July	1851	Henry K. Craig
Apr.	1861	James W. Ripley
Sept.	1863	George D. Ramsay
Sept.	1864	Alexander B. Dyer
June	1874	Stephen V. Benet
June	1891	Daniel W. Flagler
Apr.	1899	Adelbert R. Buffington
Nov.	1901	William Crozier
July	1918	Clarence C. Williams
June	1930	Samuel Hof
June	1934	William H. Tschappat
June	1938	Charles M. Wesson
June	1942	Levin H. Campbell
June	1946	Everett S. Hughes
Nov.	1949	Elbert L. Ford
Nov.	1953	Emerson L. Cummings
Feb.	1958	John H. Hinrichs
May	1962	Horace F. Bigelow (to July 1962)

Provost Marshals General

July	1941	Allen W. Gullion
June	1944	Archer L. Lerch
Dec.	1945	Blackshear M. Bryan
Apr.	1948	Edwin P. Parker, Jr.
Feb.	1953	William H. Maglin
Nov.	1957	Haydon L. Boatner
Oct.	1960	Ralph J. Butchers
June	1964	Carl C. Turner
	1969	K. W. Gustafson
	1970	Lloyd B. Ramsey (to 1974)

Quartermasters General

Aug.	1775	Thomas Mifflin
June	1776	Stephen Moylan
Sept.	1776	Thomas Mifflin
Mar.	1778	Nathaniel Greene
Aug.	1780	Timothy Pickering
Mar.	1791	Samuel Hodgson
Apr.	1792	James O'Hara
June	1796	John Wilkins, Jr.
Apr.	1812	Morgan Lewis
Mar.	1813	Robert Swartwout
Apr.	1816	James Mullaney
Apr.	1816	George Gibson
May	1818	Thomas S. Jesup
June	1860	Joseph E. Johnston
May	1861	Montgomery C. Meigs
Feb.	1882	Daniel H. Rucker
Feb.	1882	Rufus Ingalls
July	1883	Samuel B. Holabird
June	1890	Richard N. Batchelder
Aug.	1896	Charles G. Sawtelle
Feb.	1897	George H. Weeks
Feb.	1898	Marshall I. Ludington
Apr.	1903	Charles F. Humphrey
July	1907	James B. Aleshire
Sept.	1916	Henry G. Sharpe
July	1918	Harry L. Rogers
Aug.	1922	William H. Hart
Jan.	1926	B. Franklin Cheatham
Feb.	1930	John L. DeWitt
Feb.	1934	Louis H. Bash
Apr.	1936	Henry Gibbins
Apr.	1940	Edmund B. Gregory
Feb.	1946	Thomas B. Larkin
Mar.	1949	Herman Feldman

Oct.	1951	George A. Horkan
Feb.	1954	Kester L. Hastings
June	1957	Andrew T. McNamara
June	1961	Webster Anderson (to July 1962)

Chiefs of the U.S. Army Reserve

Mar.	1927	David L. Stone
July	1930	Charles D. Herron
July	1935	Edwin S. Hartshorn
Sept.	1938	Charles F. Thompson
June	1940	John H. Hester
June	1941	Frank E. Lowe
Sept.	1942	Edward W. Smith
Oct.	1945	Edward S. Bres
June	1948	Wendell Westover
Nov.	1949	George E. Butler (Acting)
Jan.	1950	James B. Cress
Aug.	1950	George E. Butler (Acting)
Feb.	1951	Hugh M. Milton, II
Nov.	1953	Philip F. Lindeman
Aug.	1957	Ralph A. Palladino
July	1959	Frederick M. Warren
Aug.	1963	William J. Sutton
June	1970	J. Milnor Roberts, Jr.
	1976	J. Henry Mohr
	1980	William R. Berkman

Chief Signal Officers

June	1860	Albert J. Myer
Oct.	1863	William J. L. Nicodemus
Dec.	1864	Albert J. Myer
Dec.	1880	William B. Hazen
Mar.	1887	Adolphus W. Greely
Feb.	1906	James Allen
Mar.	1913	George P. Scriven
Feb.	1917	George O. Squier
Jan.	1924	Charles M. Saltzman
Jan.	1928	George S. Gibbs
July	1931	Irving J. Carr
Jan.	1935	James B. Allison
Oct.	1937	Joseph O. Mauborgne
Oct.	1941	Dawson Olmstead
July	1943	Harry C. Ingles
Apr.	1947	Spencer B. Akin
May	1951	George I. Back
May	1955	James D. O'Connell
Apr.	1959	Ralph T. Nelson
June	1962	Earle F. Cook
June	1963	David P. Gibbs (to July 1966)

Surgeons General

July	1775	Benjamin Church
Oct.	1775	John Morgan
Apr.	1777	William Shippen, Jr.
Jan.	1781	John Cochran
July	1798	James Craik
June	1813	James Tilton
Apr.	1818	Joseph Lovell
Nov.	1836	Thomas Lawson
May	1861	Clement A. Finley
Apr.	1862	William A. Hammond
Aug.	1864	Joseph K. Barnes
July	1882	Charles H. Crane
Nov.	1883	Robert Murray
Nov.	1886	John Moore
Aug.	1890	Jedediah H. Baxter
Dec.	1890	Charles Sutherland
May	1893	George M. Sternberg
June	1902	William H. Forwood
Sept.	1902	Robert M. O'Reilly
Jan.	1909	George H. Torney

Jan.	1914	William C. Gorgas
Oct.	1918	Merritte W. Ireland
June	1931	Robert U. Patterson
June	1935	Charles R. Reynolds
June	1939	James C. Magee
June	1943	Norman T. Kirk
June	1947	Raymond W. Bliss
June	1951	George E. Armstrong
June	1955	Silas B. Hays
May	1959	Leonard D. Heaton
Oct.	1969	Hal B. Jennings, Jr.
	1974	Richard R. Taylor
	1977	Charles C. Pixley
	1982	Bernard T. Mittemeyer
	1985	Quinn H. Becker

U.S. Army Major Field Commanders

Commanders, Army Ground Forces

Mar.	1942	Lesley J. McNair
July	1944	Ben Lear
Jan.	1945	Joseph W. Stilwell
July	1945	Jacob L. Devers (to Mar. 1948)

Commanding Generals, U.S. Army Forces Command

(Until 1973 known as Continental Army Command.)

Feb.	1955	John E. Dahlquist
Mar.	1956	Willard G. Wyman
Aug.	1958	Bruce C. Clarke
Sept.	1960	Herbert B. Powell
Jan.	1963	John K. Waters
Feb.	1964	Hugh Harris
Feb.	1965	Paul L. Freeman, Jr.
June	1967	James K. Woolnough
Nov.	1970	Ralph E. Haines, Jr.
	1973	W. T. Kerwin, Jr.
	1975	Bernard W. Rogers
	1976	Frederick J. Kroesen
	1979	Robert M. Shoemaker
	1982	Richard E. Cavazos
	1985	Robert W. Sennewald

Commanders-in-Chief, U.S. Army, Europe

May	1945	Dwight D. Eisenhower
Nov.	1945	George S. Patton, Jr.
Nov.	1945	Joseph T. McNarney
Mar.	1947	Lucius D. Clay
May	1949	Clarence R. Huebner
Sept.	1949	Thomas T. Handy
Aug.	1952	Manton S. Eddy
Apr.	1953	Charles L. Bolte
Sept.	1953	William M. Hoge
Feb.	1955	Anthony C. McAuliffe
May	1956	Henry I. Hodes
Mar.	1959	Clyde D. Eddleman
Oct.	1960	Bruce C. Clarke
Apr.	1962	Paul L. Freeman, Jr.
Feb.	1965	Andrew P. O'Meara
May	1967	James H. Polk
May	1971	Michael S. Davison
	1976	George J. Blanchard

1979	Frederick J. Kroesen	
1983	Glenn K. Otis	

Commanders, Supreme Headquarters Allied Powers in Europe (SHAPE)

Feb.	1951	Dwight D. Eisenhower
May	1952	Matthew B. Ridgway
Aug.	1953	Alfred M. Gruenther
Nov.	1956	Lauris Norstad
Dec.	1962	Lyman L. Lemnitzer (to 1969)

Commanders-in-Chief, United Nations Command

July	1950	Douglas MacArthur
Apr.	1951	Matthew B. Ridgway
May	1952	Mark W. Clark
Oct.	1953	John E. Hull
Apr.	1955	Maxwell D. Taylor
June	1955	Lyman L. Lemitzer
July	1957	George H. Decker
June	1959	Carter B. Magruder
June	1961	Guy S. Meloy, Jr.
July	1963	Hamilton H. Howze
June	1965	Dwight E. Beach
Aug.	1966	Charles H. Bonesteel, Jr. (to 1969)

Commanders-in-Chief, U.S. Army, Pacific

	1909	W. S. Schuyler
	1911	M. M. Macomb
	1913	Frederick Funston
	1914	M. M. Macomb
	1914	N. H. Carter
	1915	John P. Wisser
	1916	Robert K. Evans
	1916	Frederick S. Strong
	1917	Charles G. Treat
	1917	John P. Wisser
	1918	Augustus P. Blocksom
	1918	J. W. Heard
	1919	J. C. Hodges, Jr.
	1919	Charles G. Morton
Aug.	1921	Charles P. Summerall
Aug.	1924	Charles T. Menoher
Jan.	1925	Edward M. Lewis
Aug.	1927	William R. Smith
Jan.	1928	Fox Conner
Aug.	1930	Edwin B. Winans
Oct.	1930	William Lassiter
Sept.	1931	Briant H. Wells
Sept.	1934	Halstead Dorey
Mar.	1935	Hugh A. Drum
July	1937	Andrew Moses
Mar.	1938	Charles D. Herron
Feb.	1941	Walter Short
Dec.	1941	Delos C. Emmons
June	1943	Robert C. Richardson
Mar.	1946	George F. Moore
July	1946	John E. Hull
Feb.	1949	Floyd L. Parks
Apr.	1949	Henry S. Aurand
Sept.	1952	John W. O'Daniel
June	1954	Clark L. Ruffner
Dec.	1954	Bruce C. Clarke
July	1956	Blackshear M. Bryan
July	1957	Isaac D. White
Apr.	1961	Carter B. Magruder
Apr.	1962	James F. Collins

Feb.	1964	John K. Waters
Aug.	1966	Dwight E. Beach
Oct.	1970	William B. Rosson
	1973	Frederick C. Weyand
	1974	Donald V. Bennett (to 1975)

Commanders-in-Chief, U.S. Army Forces in Far East

July	1941	Douglas MacArthur
Mar.	1951	Matthew B. Ridgway
May	1952	Mark W. Clark
Oct.	1953	John E. Hull
Dec.	1954	Maxwell D. Taylor
Mar.	1955	Lyman L. Lemnitzer
July	1955	Isaac D. White (to June 1957)

Commanding Generals, U.S. Army Training and Doctrine Command

(Until 1973 known as Combat Developments Command.)

June	1962	John P. Daley
Aug.	1963	Dwight E. Beach
May	1965	Ben Harrell
June	1967	Harry W. O. Kinnard
Jan.	1970	George I. Forsythe
Oct.	1970	John Norton
	1973	William E. Dupuy
	1977	Donn A. Starry
	1982	Glenn K. Otis
	1983	William R. Richardson

Commanding Generals, U.S. Army Western Command

1980	Herbert E. Wolff
1981	Eugene P. Forrester
1983	James M. Lee

Commanding Generals, Air Defense Command

Apr.	1957	Stanley R. Mickelson
Oct.	1957	Charles E. Hart
July	1960	Robert J. Wood
Aug.	1962	William W. Dick, Jr.
Aug.	1963	Charles B. Duff
July	1966	Robert Hackett
	1969	G. V. Underwood
Apr.	1971	Richard T. Cassidy
	1973	Raymond L. Shoemaker (to 1974)

U.S. Army Commanders

First Army

July	1918	John J. Pershing
Oct.	1918	Hunter Liggett (to Apr. 1919)
Nov.	1938	Hugh A. Drum
Jan.	1944	Omar N. Bradley
Aug.	1944	Courtney H. Hodges
Feb.	1949	Roscoe B. Woodruff
Mar.	1949	Walter Bedell Smith
Nov.	1950	Willis D. Crittenberger

Jan.	1953	Withers A. Burress
Dec.	1954	Thomas W. Herren
Aug.	1957	Blackshear M. Bryan
Feb.	1960	Edward J. O'Neill
Mar.	1962	Garrison H. Davidson
Apr.	1964	Robert W. Porter, Jr.
Feb.	1965	Thomas W. Dunn
Dec.	1965	William F. Train
May	1967	Jonathan O. Seaman
Mar.	1971	Claire E. Hutchin
	1974	James G. Kalergis
	1976	Jeffrey G. Smith
	1979	John F. Forrest
	1982	Donald E. Rosenblum
	1985	Charles D. Franklin

Second Army

(Merged with First U.S. Army, Jan. 1966; reactivated in 1984.)

Oct.	1918	Robert L. Bullard (to Apr. 1919)
Oct.	1940	Ben Lear
Apr.	1943	Lloyd R. Fredendall
Apr.	1946	William H. Simpson
Sept.	1946	Albert C. Wedemeyer
Oct.	1947	John T. Lewis
Jan.	1948	Leonard T. Gerow
Aug.	1950	James A. Van Fleet
June	1951	Edward H. Brooks
Sept.	1953	Floyd L. Parks
Apr.	1956	Charles E. Hart
Oct.	1957	George W. Read, Jr.
July	1960	Ridgely Gaither
Apr.	1962	John S. Upham, Jr.
June	1964	William F. Train
	1984	Charles P. Graham
	1986	Johnny J. Johnston

Third Army

(Deactivated in 1973; reactivated in 1982.)

Nov.	1918	Joseph T. Dickman (to July 1919)
Oct.	1936	George Van Horne Moseley
Oct.	1939	Stanley D. Embick
Oct.	1940	Herbert J. Brees
May	1941	Walter Krueger
Feb.	1943	Courtney H. Hodges
Jan.	1944	George S. Patton, Jr.
Oct.	1945	Lucien K. Truscott, Jr.
Apr.	1946	Geoffrey Keyes
Jan.	1947	Ernest N. Harmon
Mar.	1947	Oscar W. Griswold
Apr.	1947	Edward H. Brooks
June	1947	Alvan C. Gillem, Jr.
Sept.	1950	John R. Hodge
May	1952	William A. Beiderlinden
Aug.	1952	Alexander R. Bolling
Aug.	1955	Thomas F. Hickey
May	1958	Clark L. Ruffner
Feb.	1960	Herbert B. Powell
Oct.	1960	Paul D. Adams
Oct.	1961	Thomas J. H. Trapnell
Nov.	1962	Hamilton H. Howze (Acting)
Dec.	1962	Albert Watson, II
July	1964	Charles W. G. Rich
June	1965	Louis W. Truman
July	1967	John L. Throckmorton
Aug.	1969	Albert O. Connor
	1972	Melvin Zais (to 1973)
	1982	Marion C. Ross
	1984	William J. Livesey
	1985	Theodore G. Jones, Jr.

Fourth Army

Aug.	1932	Johnson Hagood
Oct.	1936	George S. Simonds
May	1938	Albert J. Bowley
Dec.	1939	John H. DeWitt
Oct.	1943	William H. Simpson
Apr.	1944	John P. Lucas
July	1945	Alexander M. Patch, Jr.
Oct.	1945	John P. Lucas
June	1946	Jonathan M. Wainwright
Sept.	1947	Thomas T. Handy
Aug.	1949	Andrew D. Bruce
Oct.	1949	LeRoy Lutes
Feb.	1952	Hobart R. Gay
Feb.	1952	William M. Hoge
Mar.	1953	John E. Dahlquist
June	1953	Haydon L. Boatner
Sept.	1953	Isaac D. White
June	1955	Samuel T. Williams
Oct.	1955	John H. Collier
Oct.	1958	Guy S. Meloy, Jr.
Sept.	1959	Edward T. Williams
Feb.	1961	Donald P. Booth
Feb.	1962	Paul H. Jark
July	1964	Robert W. Colglazier, Jr.
Jan.	1966	Thomas W. Dunn
Jan.	1967	Lawrence J. Lincoln, Jr.
July	1968	Harry H. Critz (to July 1971)

Fifth Army

Jan.	1943	Mark W. Clark
Dec.	1944	Lucien K. Truscott, Jr.
June	1946	Walton H. Walker
Oct.	1948	Stephen J. Chamberlin
Jan.	1952	Albert C. Smith
July	1952	William B. Kean
Oct.	1954	Hobart R. Gay
Aug.	1955	Philip D. Ginder
Nov.	1955	William H. Arnold
Jan.	1961	Emerson L. Cummings
May	1962	John K. Waters

Jan.	1963	Charles G. Dodge
Mar.	1966	John H. Michaelis
June	1969	Vernon P. Mock
Sept.	1970	G. V. Underwood, Jr.
Sept.	1971	Patrick F. Cassidy
	1973	John J. Hennessey
	1975	Allen M. Burdett, Jr.
	1978	William B. Caldwell, III
	1980	John R. McGiffert, II
	1982	Edward A. Partain
	1985	Louis C. Menetrey

Sixth Army

Feb.	1943	Walter Krueger
Mar.	1946	Joseph W. Stilwell
Oct.	1946	George P. Hays
June	1947	Mark W. Clark
Oct.	1949	Albert C. Wedemeyer
Aug.	1951	Joseph M. Swing
Mar.	1954	Willard G. Wyman
July	1955	Robert N. Young
Oct.	1957	Lemuel Mathewson
Jan.	1958	Robert L. Howze
Mar.	1958	Charles D. Palmer
Aug.	1959	Robert N. Cannon
Aug.	1961	John T. Ryan, Jr.
July	1963	Frederic J. Brown
July	1965	James T. Richardson, Jr.
June	1967	Ben Harrell
June	1968	Stanley R. Larsen
June	1971	Alexander D. Surles, Jr.
	1973	Richard G. Stilwell
	1974	Elvy B. Roberts
	1975	Edward M. Flanagan, Jr.
	1978	Eugene P. Forrester
	1981	Charles M. Hall
	1983	David E. Grange, Jr.
	1984	Robert Arter
	1986	Frederick F. Woerner, Jr.

Seventh Army

July	1943	George S. Patton, Jr.

Jan.	1944	Mark W. Clark
Mar.	1944	Alexander M. Patch, Jr.
June	1945	Wade H. Haislip
Sept.	1945	Geoffrey Keyes
June	1946	Oscar W. Griswald
Jan.	1951	Manton S. Eddy
Sept.	1952	Charles L. Bolte
Mar.	1953	William M. Hoge
Oct.	1953	Anthony C. McAuliffe
Jan.	1955	Henry I. Hodes
Apr.	1956	Bruce C. Clarke
June	1958	Clyde D. Eddleman
Mar.	1959	Francis W. Farrell
June	1960	Garrison H. Davidson
Mar.	1962	John C. Oakes
Dec.	1962	Hugh P. Harris
Feb.	1964	William W. Quinn
Feb.	1966	Theodore J. Conway (to Oct. 1966)

Eighth Army

(Deactivated in 1969; reactivated in 1974.)

Sept.	1944	Robert L. Eichelberger
Sept.	1948	Walton H. Walker
Dec.	1950	Matthew B. Ridgway
Apr.	1951	James A. Van Fleet
Feb.	1953	Maxwell D. Taylor
Mar.	1955	Lyman L. Lemnitzer
June	1955	Thomas F. Hickey (Acting)
July	1955	Isaac D. White
July	1957	George H. Decker
July	1959	Carter B. Magruder
Aug.	1961	Guy S. Meloy, Jr.
Aug.	1963	Hamilton H. Howze
July	1965	Dwight E. Beach
Sept.	1966	Charles H. Bonesteel, III (to Sept. 1969)
	1974	Richard G. Stilwell
	1977	John W. Vessey, Jr.
	1980	John A. Wickham, Jr.
	1982	Robert W. Sennewald
	1985	William J. Livesey

Army Commanders During Wartime

Revolutionary War

Commander-in-Chief

George Washington

Commanding Generals

John Armstrong
Benedict Arnold
John Ashe
George Rogers Clark
George Clinton
James Clinton
Thomas Conway
Philemon Dickinson
David Forman
John Glover
Nathaniel Greene
John Hancock
Edward Hand
William Heath
Nicholas Herkimer
Robert Howe
Isaac Huger
William Irvine
Henry Knox
Robert Lawson
Charles Lee
Benjamin Lincoln
Solomon Lovell
Alexander McDougall
Lauchlin McIntosh
Francis Marion
William Maxwell
Thomas Mifflin
Richard Montgomery
Daniel Morgan
Peter Muhlenberg
Francis Nash
John Nixon
Samuel Parsons
John Patterson
Earl Hugh Percy
Andrew Pickens
Timothy Pickering
Seth Pomeroy
Enoch Poor
Israel Putnam
Griffith Rutherford
Arthur St. Clair
Philip Schuyler
Charles Scott
Gold Silliman
William Smallwood
Joseph Spencer
Adam Stephen

John Sullivan
Jethro Sumner
Thomas Sumter
John Thomas
Robert van Renssalaer
James Varnum
Artemas Ward
David Waterbury, Jr.
Anthony Wayne
George Wheedon
Andrew Williamson
William Woodford
David Wooster

War of 1812

Commanding Generals

Isaac Brock
Jacob Brown
Henry Dearborn
Wade Hampton
William Henry Harrison
William Hull
Andrew Jackson
Zebulon Pike
Winfield Scott
Alexander Smyth
Stephen van Renssalaer
James Wilkinson

Civil War

Union Army Commanders

Generals-in-Chief of the Armies

Apr.	1861	Winfield Scott (to Nov. 1861)
Nov.	1861	George B. McClellan (to Mar. 1862)
July	1862	Henry W. Halleck (to Mar. 1864)
Mar.	1864	Ulysses S. Grant (to Apr. 1865)

Army of the Potomac

Aug.	1861	George B. McClellan
Nov.	1862	Ambrose E. Burnside
Jan.	1863	Joseph Hooker
June	1863	George G. Meade

Army of the Ohio

Nov.	1861	Don Carlos Buell

Aug.	1862	Horatio G. Wright
Mar.	1863	Ambrose E. Burnside
Dec.	1863	John G. Foster
Feb.	1864	John M. Schofield

Army of the Southwest

Dec.	1861	Samuel R. Curtis
Sept.	1862	Eugene A. Carr
Oct.	1862	Willis A. Gorman

Army of the Mississippi

Feb.	1862	John Pope
June	1862	William S. Rosecrans

Army of the Mountain Department

Mar.	1862	John C. Fremont (to June 1862)

Army of the Cumberland

Oct.	1862	William S. Rosecrans
Oct.	1863	George H. Thomas

Army of the Frontier

Oct.	1862	John M. Schofield
Mar.	1863	Francis J. Herron

Army of the Tennessee

Oct.	1862	Ulysses S. Grant
Oct.	1863	William T. Sherman
Mar.	1864	James B. McPherson
July	1864	Oliver O. Howard

Army of the James

Nov.	1862	Benjamin F. Butler (to Dec. 1864)

Army of West Virginia

June	1863	B. F. Kelley
Mar.	1864	Franz Sigel
May	1864	David Hunter
Aug.	1864	George Crook

Army of the Shenandoah

Aug.	1864	Philip H. Sheridan
Feb.	1865	Alfred T. A. Torbert

Army of Georgia

Nov.	1864	Henry W. Slocum

Union Battlefield Commanders

First Battle of Bull Run, or Manassas

(July 21, 1861)

Commander	Irvin McDowell
First Division	Daniel Tyler
Second Division	David Hunter
Third Division	Samuel P. Heintzelman
Fourth Division	Theodore Runyon
Fifth Division	D. S. Miles

Battle of Shiloh

(Apr. 6-7, 1862)

Army of the Tennessee	Ulysses S. Grant
First Division	John A. McClernand
Second Division	William H. L. Wallace
Third Division	Lew Wallace
Fourth Division	Stephen A. Hurlbut
Fifth Division	William T. Sherman
Sixth Division	Benjamin M. Prentiss
Army of the Ohio	Don Carlos Buell
Second Division	Alexander M. McCook
Fourth Division	William Nelson
Fifth Division	Thomas L. Crittenden
Sixth Division	Thomas J. Wood

Battle of Seven Pines, or Fair Oaks

(May 31-June 1, 1862)

Army of the Potomac	George B. McClellan
II Corps	Edwin V. Sumner
First Division	Israel B. Richardson
Second Division	John Sedgwick
III Corps	Samuel P. Heintzelman
Second Division	Joseph Hooker
Third Division	Philip Kearny
IV Corps	Erasmus D. Keyes
First Division	Darius N. Couch
Second Division	Silas Casey

Seven Days' Battles

(June 25-July 1, 1862)

Army of the Potomac	George B. McClellan
II Corps	Edwin V. Sumner
First Division	Israel B. Richardson
Second Division	John Sedgwick
III Corps	Samuel P. Heintzelman
Second Division	Joseph Hooker
Third Division	Philip Kearny
IV Corps	Erasmus D. Keyes
First Division	Darius N. Couch
Second Division	John J. Peck
V Corps	Fitz-John Porter
First Division	George W. Morell
Second Division	George Sykes
Third Division	George A. McCall
VI Corps	William B. Franklin
First Division	Henry W. Slocum
Second Division	William F. Smith

Second Battle of Bull Run, or Manassas

(Aug. 29-30, 1862)

Army of Virginia	John Pope
I Corps	Franz Sigel
First Division	Robert C. Schenck
Second Division	Adolph von Steinwehr
Third Division	Carl Schurz
II Corps	Nathaniel P. Banks
First Division	Alpheus S. Williams
Second Division	George S. Greene

III Corps	Irvin McDowell
First Division	Rufus King, Abner Doubleday
Second Division	James B. Ricketts
Reynolds Division	John F. Reynolds
Reserve Corps	Samuel D. Sturgis
Army of the Potomac	George B. McClellan
III Corps	Samuel P. Heintzelman
First Division	Philip Kearny
Second Division	Joseph Hooker
V Corps	Fitz-John Porter
First Division	George W. Morell
Second Division	George Sykes
IX Corps	Jesse L. Reno
First Division	Isaac I. Stevens, Benjamin C. Christ

Battle of Antietam

(Sept. 17, 1862)

Army of the Potomac	George B. McClellan
I Corps	Joseph Hooker
First Division	Abner Doubleday
Second Division	James B. Ricketts
Third Division	George G. Meade
II Corps	Edwin V. Sumner
First Division	Israel B. Richardson
Second Division	John Sedgwick
Third Division	William H. French
IV Corps	
First Division	Darius N. Couch
V Corps	Fitz-John Porter
Second Division	George Sykes
VI Corps	William B. Franklin
First Division	Henry W. Slocum
Second Division	William F. Smith
IX Corps	Ambrose E. Burnside
First Division	Orlando B. Willcox
Second Division	Samuel D. Sturgis
Third Division	Isaac P. Rodman
Kanawha Division	Jacob D. Cox

Battle of Corinth

(Oct. 3-4, 1862)

Army of the Mississippi	William S. Rosecrans
Second Division	David S. Stanley
Third Division	Charles S. Hamilton
Cavalry	John K. Mizner
District of West Tennessee	
Second Division	Thomas A. Davies
Sixth Division	Thomas J. McKean

Battle of Fredericksburg

(Dec. 13, 1862)

Army of the Potomac	Ambrose E. Burnside
I Corps	Joseph Hooker
First Division	Abner Doubleday
Second Division	James B. Ricketts
Third Division	George G. Meade
II Corps	Edwin V. Sumner
First Division	Israel B. Richardson
Second Division	John Sedgwick
Third Division	William H. French
IV Corps	
First Division	Darius N. Couch
V Corps	Fitz-John Porter
First Division	George W. Morell
Second Division	George Sykes
VI Corps	William B. Franklin
First Division	Henry W. Slocum
Second Division	William F. Smith
IX Corps	Ambrose E. Burnside
First Division	Orlando B. Willcox
Second Division	Samuel D. Sturgis
Third Division	Isaac P. Rodman
Kanawha Division	Jacob D. Cox
Right Grand Division	Edwin V. Sumner

II Corps	Darius N. Couch
First Division	Winfield S. Hancock
Second Division	Oliver O. Howard
Third Division	William H. French
IX Corps	Orlando B. Willcox
First Division	William W. Burns
Second Division	Samuel D. Sturgis
Third Division	George W. Getty
Cavalry Division	Alfred Pleasanton
Center Grand Division	Joseph Hooker
III Corps	George Stoneman
First Division	D. B. Binney
Second Division	Daniel E. Sickles
Third Division	Amiel W. Whipple
V Corps	Daniel Butterfield
First Division	Charles Griffin
Second Division	George Sykes
Third Division	Andrew A. Humphreys
Left Grand Division	William B. Franklin
I Corps	John F. Reynolds
First Division	Abner Doubleday
Second Division	John Gibbon
Third Division	George G. Meade
VI Corps	William F. Smith
First Division	William T. H. Brooks
Second Division	Albion P. Howe
Third Division	John Newton

Battle of Stones River, or Murfreesboro

(Dec. 31, 1862-Jan. 2, 1863)

Army of the Cumberland	William S. Rosecrans
Right Wing	Alexander M. McCook
First Division	Jefferson C. Davis
Second Division	Richard W. Johnson
Third Division	Philip H. Sheridan
Center Wing	George H. Thomas
First Division	Lovell H. Rousseau
Second Division	James S. Negley
Third Division	M. B. Walker
Left Wing	Thomas L. Crittenden
First Division	Thomas J. Wood
Second Division	John M. Palmer
Third Division	H. P. Van Cleve
Cavalry	David S. Stanley
Cavalry Division	John Kennett

Battle of Chancellorsville

(May 2-4, 1863)

Army of the Potomac	Joseph Hooker
I Corps	John F. Reynolds
First Division	James S. Wadsworth
Second Division	John C. Robinson
Third Division	Abner Doubleday
II Corps	Darius N. Couch
First Division	Winfield S. Hancock
Second Division	John Gibbon
Third Division	William H. French
III Corps	Daniel E. Sickles
First Division	David B. Birney
Second Division	Hiram G. Berry, Joseph B. Carr
Third Division	Amiel W. Whipple, Charles K. Graham
V Corps	George G. Meade
First Division	Charles Griffin
Second Division	George Sykes
VI Corps	John Sedgwick
First Division	William T. H. Brooks
Second Division	Albion P. Howe
Third Division	John Newton
Light Division	Hiram Burnham
XI Corps	Oliver O. Howard
First Division	Charles Devens
Second Division	Adolph von Steinwehr
Third Division	Carl Schurz
XII Corps	Henry W. Slocum
First Division	Alpheus S. Williams

Second Division	John W. Geary
Cavalry Corps	George Stoneman
First Division	Alfred Pleasanton
Second Division	William W. Averell
Third Division	David M. Gregg

Vicksburg Campaign

(May 1-July 4, 1863)

Army of the Tennessee	Ulysses S. Grant
IX Corps	John G. Parke
First Division	Thomas Welsh
Second Division	Robert B. Potter
XIII Corps	John A. McClernand, Edward O. C. Ord
Ninth Division	Peter J. Osterhaus
Tenth Division	Andrew J. Smith
Twelfth Division	Alvin P. Hovey
Fourteenth Division	Eugene A. Carr
XV Corps	William T. Sherman
First Division	Frederick Steele
Second Division	Francis P. Blair, Jr.
Third Division	James M. Tuttle
XVI Corps	Cadwallader C. Washburn
First Division	William S. Smith
Fourth Division	J. C. Lauman
Provisional Division	Nathan Kimball
XVII Corps	James B. McPherson
Third Division	John A. Logan
Sixth Division	John McArthur
Seventh Division	Marcellus M. Crocker, J. F. Quimby, John E. Smith
Herron's Division	Francis J. Herron

Battle of Gettysburg

(July 1-3, 1863)

Army of the Potomac	
I Corps	George G. Meade, John F. Reynolds, Abner Doubleday, John Newton
First Division	James S. Wadsworth
Second Division	John C. Robinson
Third Division	T. A. Rowley
II Corps	Winfield S. Hancock, John Gibbon
First Division	John C. Caldwell
Second Division	John Gibbon
Third Division	Alexander Hayes
III Corps	Daniel E. Sickles
First Division	David B. Birney
Second Division	Andrew A. Humphreys
V Corps	George Sykes
First Division	James Barnes
Second Division	Romeyn B. Ayres
Third Division	Samuel W. Crawford
VI Corps	John Sedgwick
First Division	Horatio G. Wright
Second Division	Albion P. Howe
Third Division	John Newton
XI Corps	Oliver O. Howard
First Division	Francis C. Barlow
Second Division	Adolph von Steinwehr
Third Division	Carl Schurz
XII Corps	Henry W. Slocum
First Division	Alpheus S. Williams
Second Division	John W. Geary
Cavalry Corps	Alfred Pleasanton
First Division	John Buford
Second Division	David M. Gregg
Third Division	Judson Kilpatrick

Battle of Chickamauga

(Sept. 19-20, 1863)

Army of the Cumberland	William S. Rosecrans
XIV Corps	George H. Thomas
First Division	Absolom Baird

Second Division	James S. Negley
Third Division	John M. Brannan
Fourth Division	Joseph J. Reynolds
XX Corps	Alexander M. McCook
First Division	Jefferson C. Davis
Second Division	Richard W. Johnson
Third Division	Philip H. Sheridan
XXI Corps	Thomas L. Crittenden
First Division	Thomas J. Wood
Second Division	John M. Palmer
Third Division	H. P. Van Cleve
Reserve Corps	Gordon Granger
First Division	James B. Steedman
Cavalry Corps	Robert B. Mitchell
First Division	Edward M. McCook
Second Division	George Crook

Battle of Chattanooga

(Nov. 23-25, 1863)

Union Forces	Ulysses S. Grant
Army of the Cumberland	George H. Thomas
IV Corps	Gordon Granger
First Division	Charles Cruft
Second Division	Philip H. Sheridan
Third Division	Thomas J. Wood
XIV Corps	John M. Palmer
First Division	Richard W. Johnson
Second Division	Jefferson C. Davis
Third Division	Absolom Baird
Army of the Tennessee	William T. Sherman
XV Corps	Francis P. Blair, Jr.
First Division	Peter J. Osterhaus
Second Division	Mathew C. Smith
Fourth Division	Hugh Ewing
XVII Corps	John E. Smith
Second Division	John E. Smith
XI Corps	Oliver O. Howard
Second Division	Adolph von Steinwehr
Third Division	Carl Schurz
XII Corps	Joseph Hooker

Battles of Wilderness and Spottsylvania Court House

(May 5-21, 1864)

Union Forces	Ulysses S. Grant
Army of the Potomac	George G. Meade
II Corps	Winfield S. Hancock
First Division	Francis C. Barlow
Second Division	John Gibbon
Third Division	David B. Birney
Fourth Division	Gershom Mott
V Corps	Gouverneur K. Warren
First Division	Charles Griffin
Second Division	John C. Robinson
Third Division	Samuel W. Crawford
Fourth Division	James S. Wadsworth
VI Corps	John Sedgwick
First Division	Horatio G. Wright
Second Division	George W. Getty
Third Division	James B. Ricketts
IX Corps	Ambrose E. Burnside
First Division	Thomas G. Stevenson
Second Division	Robert B. Potter
Third Division	Orlando B. Willcox
Fourth Division	Edward Ferrero
Cavalry Corps	Philip H. Sheridan
First Division	Alfred T. A. Torbert
Second Division	David M. Gregg
Third Division	James H. Wilson

Atlanta Campaign

(May 3-Sept. 8, 1864)

Union Forces	William T. Sherman
Army of the Cumberland	George H. Thomas
IV Corps	Oliver O. Howard, David S. Stanley

First Division	David S. Stanley, William Grose, Nathan Kimball
Second Division	John Newton
Third Division	Thomas J. Wood
XIV Corps	John M. Palmer, Richard W. Johnson, Jefferson C. Davis
First Division	Richard W. Johnson, John H. King, William P. Carlin
Second Division	Jefferson C. Davis, J. D. Morgan
Third Division	Absolom Baird
XX Corps	Joseph Hooker, Alpheus S. Williams, Henry W. Slocum
First Division	Alpheus S. Williams, J. F. Knipe
Second Division	John W. Geary
Third Division	Daniel Butterfield
Cavalry Corps	W. D. Elliott
First Division	Edward M. McCook
Second Division	Kenner Garrard
Third Division	Judson Kilpatrick
Army of the Tennessee	James B. McPherson, John A. Logan, Oliver O. Howard
XV Corps	John A. Logan, Martin L. Smith
First Division	Peter J. Osterhaus, C. R. Woods
Second Division	Martin L. Smith, J. M. J. Lightburn, William B. Hazen
Fourth Division	William Harrow
XVI Corps	Grenville M. Dodge, Thomas E. G. Ransom
Second Division	Thomas W. Sweeney, Elliott W. Rice, John M. Corse
Fourth Division	James C. Veatch, John W. Fuller, Thomas E. G. Ransom
XVII Corps	Francis P. Blair, Jr.
Third Division	Mortimer D. Leggett, C. R. Woods
Fourth Division	Walter Q. Gresham, William Hall, G. A. Smith
Army of the Ohio	John M. Schofield
XXIII Corps	John M. Schofield
First Division	Alvin P. Hovey
Third Division	Jacob D. Cox
Cavalry Division	George Stoneman

Battle of Nashville

(Dec. 15-16, 1864)

Union Forces	George H. Thomas
IV Corps	Thomas J. Wood
First Division	Nathan Kimball
Second Division	Washington L. Elliott
Third Division	Samuel Beatty
XXIII Corps	John M. Schofield
Second Division	Darius N. Couch
Third Division	Jacob D. Cox
Garrison of Nashville	John F. Miller
Cavalry Corps	James H. Wilson
Fifth Division	Edward Hatch
Sixth Division	Richard W. Johnson
Seventh Division	J. F. Knipe

Campaign of the Carolinas

(Feb.-Mar. 1865)

Army of the Tennessee	Oliver O. Howard
XV Corps	John A. Logan
First Division	Charles R. Woods
Second Division	William B. Hazen
Third Division	John E. Smith
Fourth Division	John M. Course
XVII Corps	Francis P. Blair, Jr.
First Division	Joseph A. Mower, Manning F. Force
Third Division	Mortimer D. Leggett
Fourth Division	Giles A. Smith
Army of Georgia	Henry W. Slocum
XIV Corps	Jefferson C. Davis
First Division	William P. Carlin, George P. Buell
Second Division	James D. Morgan
Third Division	Absolom Baird

XX Corps	Alpheus S. Williams		First Division	Henry W. Birge
First Division	Nathaniel J. Jackson		Second Division	Adelbert Ames
Second Division	Alpheus S. Williams, John W.		Third Division	Charles J. Paine
	Geary		XXIII Corps	Jacob D. Cox
Third Division	William T. Ward		First Division	Thomas H. Ruger
Cavalry Corps			Second Division	Nathaniel C. McLean, Orlando H.
Third Division	Judson Kilpatrick			Moore, Joseph A. Cooper
Army of the Ohio	John M. Schofield		Third Division	James W. Reilly, Samuel P. Carter
X Corps	Alfred H. Terry			

Spanish American War

Philippines Expeditionary Force

1898   Wesley Merritt

Cuban Expeditionary Force

1898   William Shafter

First World War

Commanders

American Expeditionary Forces

1917-1918   John J. Pershing

I Corps

Jan.	1918	Hunter Liggett
Oct.	1918	Joseph T. Dickman
Nov.	1918	William M. Wright

II Corps

June	1918	George W. Read

III Corps

June	1918	William M. Wright
July	1918	Robert L. Bullard
Oct.	1918	John L. Hines

IV Corps

Aug.	1918	Joseph T. Dickman
Oct.	1918	Charles H. Muir

V Corps

July	1917	William M. Wright
Aug.	1918	George H. Cameron
Oct.	1918	Charles P. Summerall

VI Corps

Aug.	1918	Omar Bundy
Oct.	1918	Charles T. Ballou
Nov.	1918	Charles T. Menoher

VII Corps

Aug.	1918	William M. Wright
Sept.	1918	Omar Bundy
Nov.	1918	William G. Haan

VIII Corps

Nov.	1918	Henry T. Allen

IX Corps

Nov.	1918	Adelbert Cronkhite

Northeastern Department

May	1917	Clarence R. Edwards
Sept.	1917	John A. Johnston
May	1918	John W. Ruckman
July	1918	William Crozier
Dec.	1918	Clarence R. Edwards

Eastern Department

Apr.	1917	Leonard Wood
May	1917	J. Franklin Bell
Aug.	1917	Eli D. Hoyle
Jan.	1918	William A. Mann
Aug.	1918	J. Franklin Bell
Jan.	1919	Thomas H. Barry
Oct.	1919	Robert L. Bullard

Southeastern Department

May	1917	Leonard Wood
Aug.	1917	William P. Duvall
Jan.	1918	William L. Sibert
June	1918	Henry G. Sharpe

Central Department

Apr.	1917	Thomas H. Barry
Aug.	1917	William H. Carter
Mar.	1918	Thomas H. Barry
Jan.	1919	Leonard Wood

Southern Department

Apr.	1917	John J. Pershing
Aug.	1917	John W. Ruckman
May	1918	Willard A. Holbrook
Sept.	1918	De Rosey C. Cabell
Aug.	1919	Joseph T. Dickman

Western Department

Apr.	1917	J. Franklin Bell
May	1917	Hunter Liggett
Sept.	1917	Arthur Murray
May	1918	Charles G. Treat
June	1918	John F. Morrison
July	1919	Hunter Liggett

Panama Canal Department

July	1917	Edward H. Plummer
Aug.	1917	Adelbert Cronkhite
Feb.	1918	Richard M. Blatchford
Apr.	1919	Chase W. Kennedy

Philippine Department

Apr.	1917	Charles J. Bailey
Aug.	1918	Henry A. Greene
Feb.	1919	Francis H. French

Hawaiian Department

Apr.	1917	Frederick S. Strong
Sept.	1917	John P. Wisser
May	1918	Augustus P. Blocksom
Mar.	1919	Henry C. Hodges, Jr.
July	1919	Charles G. Morton

Second World War

Army Group Commanders

(Army commanders listed earlier in this Section.)

1st Army Group

Oct.	1943	Omar N. Bradley (to July 1944)

6th Army Group

Aug.	1944	Jacob L. Devers (to June 1945)

12th Army Group

July	1944	Omar N. Bradley (to July 1945)

15th Army Group

Dec.	1944	Mark W. Clark (to July 1945)

Field Commanders

Airborne Command

Mar.	1942	William C. Lee
Aug.	1942	Elbridge G. Chapman
Nov.	1943	Les Donovan
Jan.	1944	Josiah T. Dalbey
Sept.	1945	Anthony C. McAuliffe (to June 1946)

Allied Expeditionary Force, Supreme Headquarters (SHAEF)

Feb.	1944	Dwight D. Eisenhower (to July 1945)

Antiaircraft Command

Mar.	1942	Joseph A. Green
Oct.	1944	Frank C. McConnell
Feb.	1945	George R. Meyer (to Oct. 1945)

Armored Force

Aug.	1941	Jacob L. Devers

May 1943 Alvan C. Gillem, Jr.
Dec. 1943 Charles L. Scott (to Oct. 1945)

Army Ground Forces

Mar. 1942 Lesley J. McNair
July 1944 Ben Lear
Jan. 1945 Joseph W. Stilwell
July 1945 Jacob L. Devers (to Dec. 1947)

Caribbean Defense Command

Sept. 1941 F. M. Andrews
Nov. 1942 G. H. Brett

Central Defense Command

July 1941 Ben Lear
July 1943 Lloyd R. Fredendall (to Jan. 1944)

Central Pacific Area

Aug. 1943 Robert C. Richardson, Jr. (to Mar. 1946)

China Theater

Oct. 1944 Albert C. Wedemeyer (to May 1946)

China-Burma-India Theater

(See also India-Burma Theater.)

Mar. 1942 Joseph W. Stilwell
Apr. 1943 Raymond A. Wheeler
June 1943 Joseph W. Stilwell (to Oct. 1944)

Eastern Defense Command

Dec. 1941 Hugh A. Drum
Oct. 1943 George Grunert
Aug. 1945 Kennet P. Lord (to Feb. 1946)

European Theater of Operations

June 1942 Dwight D. Eisenhower
Feb. 1943 William S. Key
May 1943 Jacob L. Devers
Jan. 1944 Dwight D. Eisenhower (to Nov. 1945)

Far East

July 1941 Douglas MacArthur
Mar. 1942 Jonathan Wainwright (to June 1942)

General Headquarters, U.S. Army (GHQ)

July 1940 George C. Marshall (to Mar. 1942)

India-Burma Theater

(See also China-Burma-India Theater.)

Oct. 1944 Daniel I. Sultan
June 1945 Raymond A. Wheeler
Sept. 1945 Thomas A. Terry (to Feb. 1946)

Mediterranean Theater of Operations

Nov. 1944 Joseph T. McNarney

Dec. 1945 John C. H. Lee (to Sept. 1947)

Middle East Forces

June 1942 Russell L. Maxwell
Nov. 1942 Frank L. Andrews
Jan. 1943 Lewis H. Brereton
Sept. 1943 Ralph Royce
Mar. 1944 Benjamin F. Giles (to Mar. 1945)

Military District of Washington

May 1942 John T. Lewis
Sept. 1944 Charles F. Thompson

North African Theater of Operations

Feb. 1943 Dwight D. Eisenhower
Jan. 1944 Jacob L. Devers (to Oct. 1944)

Pacific Theater of Operations

Apr. 1942 Douglas MacArthur (to Dec. 1946)

Persian Gulf Command

Oct. 1942 Donald H. Connolly
Dec. 1944 Donald P. Booth
Aug. 1945 George A. M. Anderson (to Oct. 1945)

South Atlantic Forces

Nov. 1942 Robert L. Walsh
May 1944 Ralph H. Wooten (to Oct. 1945)

Southern Defense Command

May 1941 Walter Krueger
Feb. 1943 Courtney H. Hodges
Jan. 1944 Henry C. Pratt (to Oct. 1944)

Western Defense Command

Mar. 1941 John L. DeWitt
Sept. 1943 Delos C. Emmons
June 1944 Charles H. Bonesteel
Dec. 1944 Henry C. Pratt (to Nov. 1945)

Commanders, Army Air Forces

First Air Force

Dec. 1941 Arnold N. Krogstad
Mar. 1942 Follett Bradley
July 1942 James E. Chaney
Apr. 1943 Ralph Royce
Sept. 1943 Frank O. Hunter
July 1944 Caleb V. Haynes
Sept. 1944 Frank O. Hunter
Oct. 1945 Robert W. Douglass, Jr.

Second Air Force

Dec. 1941 John B. Brooks
Feb. 1942 Frederick L. Martin
May 1942 Robert Olds
Feb. 1943 Davenport Johnson
July 1953 Eugene Eubank
Sept. 1943 St. Clair Streett
Jan. 1944 Uzal G. Ent
Oct. 1944 Robert B. Williams

Third Air Force

Oct. 1941 Walter H. Frank
June 1942 Carlyle H. Wash
Dec. 1942 St. Clair Streett
Sept. 1943 Westside T. Larson
May 1945 Thomas W. Blackburn
July 1945 Lewis H. Brereton

Fourth Air Force

Jan. 1941 Jacob E. Fickel
Apr. 1942 George C. Kenney
July 1942 Barney M. Giles
Mar. 1943 William E. Kepner
July 1944 James E. Parker
May 1945 Edward M. Morris
July 1945 Willis H. Hale

Fifth Air Force

Nov. 1941 Lewis H. Brereton
Feb. 1942 George H. Brett
Sept. 1942 George C. Kenney
June 1944 Ennis C. Whitehead

Sixth Air Force

Sept. 1941 Davenport Johnson
Nov. 1942 Hubert R. Harmon
Nov. 1943 Ralph H. Wooten
May 1944 Edgar P. Sorenson
Sept. 1944 William O. Butler
July 1945 Earl H. DeFord

Seventh Air Force

Dec. 1941 Clarence L. Tinker
June 1942 Willis H. Hale
Apr. 1944 Robert W. Douglass, Jr.
June 1945 Thomas D. White

Eighth Air Force

Jan. 1942 Asa N. Duncan
May 1942 Carl A. Spaatz
Dec. 1942 Ira C. Eaker
Jan. 1944 James H. Doolittle
Sept. 1945 Earle E. Partridge

Ninth Air Force

June 1942 Lewis H. Brereton
Aug. 1944 Hoyt S. Vandenberg
May 1945 Otto P. Weyland
Aug. 1945 William E. Kepner

Tenth Air Force

Mar. 1942 Lewis H. Brereton
June 1942 Earl L. Naiden
Aug. 1942 Clayton L. Bissell
Aug. 1943 Howard C. Davidson
Aug. 1945 Albert F. Hegenberger

Eleventh Air Force

Mar. 1942 William O. Butler
Sept. 1943 Davenport Johnson
July 1945 John B. Brooks
Nov. 1945 Edmund C. Lynch

Thirteenth Air Force

Jan. 1943 Nathan F. Twining
Jan. 1944 Hubert R. Harmon
June 1944 St. Clair Streett
Feb. 1945 Paul B. Wurtsmith

Fourteenth Air Force

Mar. 1943 Claire L. Chennault
Aug. 1945 Charles B. Stone

Fifteenth Air Force

Nov. 1943 James H. Doolittle
Jan. 1944 Nathan F. Twining
May 1945 James A. Mollison

Twentieth Air Force

Apr. 1944 Henry A. Arnold
Aug. 1945 Nathan F. Twining
Oct. 1945 James E. Parker

Corps Commanders

I Corps

Oct. 1940 Charles F. Thompson
June 1942 Robert L. Eichelberger
Aug. 1944 Innis P. Swift

II Corps

Aug. 1941 Lloyd R. Fredendall
July 1942 Mark W. Clark
Oct. 1942 Lloyd R. Fredendall
Mar. 1943 George S. Patton, Jr.
Apr. 1943 Omar N. Bradley
Sept. 1943 Geoffrey Keyes

III Corps

July 1941 Joseph W. Stilwell
Dec. 1941 Walter K. Wilson
Apr. 1942 John P. Lucas
June 1943 Harold R. Bull
Oct. 1943 John Milikin
Mar. 1945 James A. Van Fleet

IV Corps

Oct. 1941 Jay L. Benedict
July 1942 Oscar W. Griswold
Apr. 1943 Alexander M. Patch, Jr.
Mar. 1944 Willis D. Crittenberger

V Corps

Jan. 1942 William S. Key
May 1942 Russell P. Hartle
July 1943 Leonard T. Gerow
Jan. 1945 Clarence R. Huebner

VI Corps

Dec. 1941 George Grunert
Apr. 1942 Ernest J. Dawley
Sept. 1943 John P. Lucas
Feb. 1944 Lucien K. Truscott, Jr.
Oct. 1944 Edward H. Brooks
June 1945 William H. H. Morris, Jr.

VII Corps

Aug. 1941 Robert C. Richardson, Jr.
May 1943 Roscoe B. Woodruff
Mar. 1944 J. Lawton Collins
Aug. 1945 Alvan C. Gillem, Jr.

VIII Corps

Dec. 1943 Emil F. Reinhardt
Mar. 1944 Troy H. Middleton

IX Corps

Oct. 1940 Kenyon A. Joyce
Apr. 1942 Charles H. White
Mar. 1944 Emil F. Reinhardt
Sept. 1944 Charles W. Ryder

X Corps

May 1942 Courtney H. Hodges
Mar. 1943 Jonathan W. Anderson
Aug. 1944 Franklin C. Sibert

XI Corps

June 1942 Lloyd R. Fredendall
Oct. 1942 Charles P. Hall

XII Corps

Sept. 1942 William H. Simpson
Oct. 1943 Gilbert R. Cook
Aug. 1944 Manton S. Eddy
Apr. 1945 Stafford L. Irwin

XIII Corps

Dec. 1942 Emil F. Reinhardt
Dec. 1943 Alvan C. Gillem, Jr.

XIV Corps

Jan. 1943 Alexander M. Patch, Jr.
Apr. 1943 Oscar W. Griswold

XV Corps

Feb. 1943 Wade H. Haislip
June 1945 Walter M. Robertson

XVI Corps

Jan. 1944 John B. Anderson

XVIII Corps

Oct. 1943 William H. H. Morris, Jr.
Sept. 1944 Matthew B. Ridgway

XIX Corps

Oct. 1943 Willis D. Crittenberger
Mar. 1944 Charles H. Corlett
Nov. 1944 Raymond S. McLain

XX Corps

Oct. 1943 Walton H. Walker
May 1945 Louis A. Craig

XXI Corps

Dec. 1943 Frank W. Milburn

XXII Corps

Jan. 1944 Henry Terrell, Jr.
Jan. 1945 Ernest N. Harmon

XXIII Corps

Jan. 1944 Louis A. Craig
Sept. 1944 James I. Muir
Dec. 1944 Jesmond Balmer
Feb. 1945 James A. Van Fleet
Mar. 1945 Hugh J. Gaffey

XXIV Corps

Apr. 1944 John R. Hodge

XXXVI Corps

July 1944 Jonathan W. Anderson
Jan. 1945 Charles H. Corlett

I Armored Corps

Apr. 1941 Charles L. Scott
Jan. 1942 George S. Patton, Jr. (to July 1943)

III Armored Corps

Sept. 1942 Willis D. Crittenberger (to Oct. 1943)

IV Armored Corps

Sept. 1942 Walton H. Walker (to Oct. 1943)

Division Commanders

1st Infantry Division

Feb. 1941 Donald Cubbison
Aug. 1942 Terry Allen
July 1943 Clarence R. Huebner
Dec. 1944 Clift Andrus

2nd Infantry Division

Nov. 1941 John C. H. Lee
May 1942 Walter M. Robertson
June 1945 William K. Harrison, Jr.

3rd Infantry Division

Sept. 1941 John P. Lucas
Mar. 1942 Jonathan W. Anderson
Mar. 1943 Lucien K. Truscott, Jr.
Feb. 1944 John W. O'Daniel
July 1945 William R. Schmidt

4th Infantry Division

Dec. 1941 Terry Allen
Jan. 1942 Fred C. Wallace
July 1942 Raymond O. Barton
Dec. 1944 Harold W. Blakeley

5th Infantry Division

Aug. 1941 Cortlandt Parker
June 1943 Stafford L. Irwin
Apr. 1945 Albert E. Brown

6th Infantry Division

Jan. 1941 Clarence S. Ridley
Sept. 1942 Durward S. Wilson
Oct. 1942 Franklin C. Sibert
Aug. 1944 Edwin D. Patrick
Mar. 1945 Charles E. Hurdis

7th Infantry Division

Aug. 1941 Charles H. White
Oct. 1942 Albert E. Brown
May 1943 Eugene M. Landrum
July 1943 Archibald V. Arnold
Sept. 1943 Charles H. Corlett
Feb. 1944 Archibald V. Arnold

8th Infantry Division

Apr. 1941 James P. Marley
Aug. 1942 Paul E. Peabody
Feb. 1943 William C. McMahon

July 1944 Donald A. Stroh
Dec. 1944 William G. Weaver
Feb. 1945 Bryant E. Moore

9th Infantry Division

Aug. 1941 Rene E. D. Hoyle
Aug. 1942 Manton S. Eddy
Aug. 1944 Louis A. Craig
May 1945 Jesse A. Ladd

10th Infantry Division

Nov. 1944 George P. Hays

23rd Infantry Division

May 1942 Alexander M. Patch, Jr.
Jan. 1943 Edmund B. Sebree
May 1943 John R. Hodge
Apr. 1944 Robert B. McClure
Nov. 1944 William H. Arnold

24th Infantry Division

Oct. 1941 Durward S. Wilson
Aug. 1942 Frederick A. Irving
Nov. 1944 Roscoe B. Woodruff

25th Infantry Division

Oct. 1941 Maxwell Murray
May 1942 L. Lawton Collins
Jan. 1944 Charles L. Mullins, Jr.

26th Infantry Division

Jan. 1940 Robert W. Eckfeldt
Aug. 1943 Willard S. Paul
June 1945 Harlan N. Hartness
July 1945 Stanley E. Reinhart

27th Infantry Division

Nov. 1941 Ralph M. Pennell
Nov. 1942 Ralph C. Smith
June 1944 George W. Griner, Jr.

28th Infantry Division

Jan. 1942 J. Garsche Ord
June 1942 Omar N. Bradley
Jan. 1943 Lloyd D. Brown
Aug. 1944 Norman D. Cota

29th Infantry Division

Feb. 1942 Leonard T. Gerow
July 1943 Charles H. Gerhardt

30th Infantry Division

Dec. 1940 Henry D. Russell
May 1942 William H. Simpson
Sept. 1942 Leland S. Hobbs

31st Infantry Division

Nov. 1940 John C. Persons
Sept. 1944 Clarence A. Martin

32nd Infantry Division

Feb. 1942 Edwin F. Harding
Dec. 1942 Frayne Baker
Mar. 1943 William H. Gill

33rd Infantry Division

Mar. 1941 Samuel T. Lawton
May 1942 Frank C. Mahin

Aug. 1942 John Millikin
Oct. 1943 Percy W. Clarkson

34th Infantry Division

Aug. 1941 Russell P. Hartle
May 1942 Charles W. Ryder
July 1944 Charles L. Bolte

35th Infantry Division

Oct. 1941 William H. Simpson
May 1942 Maxwell Murray
Jan. 1943 Paul W. Baade

36th Infantry Division

Sept. 1941 Fred L. Walker
July 1944 John E. Dahlquist

37th Infantry Division

Dec. 1940 Robert S. Beightler

38th Infantry Division

Apr. 1941 Daniel I. Sultan
Apr. 1942 Henry L. L. Jones
Feb. 1945 William C. Chase

40th Infantry Division

Sept. 1941 Ernest J. Dawley
Apr. 1942 Rapp Brush
July 1945 Donald J. Myers

41st Infantry Division

Dec. 1941 Horace H. Fuller
June 1944 Jens A. Doe

42nd Infantry Division

July 1943 Henry J. Collins

43rd Infantry Division

Aug. 1941 John H. Hester
Aug. 1943 Leonard F. Wing

44th Infantry Division

Aug. 1941 James I. Muir
Aug. 1944 Robert L. Spragins
Jan. 1945 William F. Dean

45th Infantry Division

Sept. 1940 William S. Key
Oct. 1942 Troy H. Middleton
Dec. 1943 William W. Eagles
Dec. 1944 Robert T. Frederick

63rd Infantry Division

June 1943 Louis E. Hibbs

65th Infantry Division

Aug. 1943 Stanley E. Reinhart

66th Infantry Division

Apr. 1943 Herman F. Kramer

69th Infantry Division

May 1943 Charles L. Bolte
Sept. 1944 Emil F. Reinhardt

70th Infantry Division

June 1943 John E. Dahlquist
July 1944 Allison J. Barnett
July 1945 Thomas W. Herren

71st Infantry Division

July 1943 Robert L. Spragins
Oct. 1944 Eugene M. Landrum
Nov. 1944 Willard G. Wyman

75th Infantry Division

Apr. 1943 Willard S. Paul
Aug. 1943 Fay B. Prickett
Jan. 1945 Ray E. Porter
June 1945 Arthur A. White

76th Infantry Division

June 1942 Emil F. Reinhardt
Dec. 1942 William R. Schmidt
Aug. 1945 Henry C. Evans

77th Infantry Division

Mar. 1942 Robert L. Eichelberger
June 1942 Roscoe B. Woodruff
May 1943 Andrew D. Bruce

78th Infantry Division

1942 Edwin P. Parker, Jr.

79th Infantry Division

June 1942 Ira T. Wyche
May 1945 LeRoy H. Watson

80th Infantry Division

July 1942 Joseph D. Patch
Mar. 1943 Horace L. McBride

81st Infantry Division

June 1942 Gustave H. Franke
Aug. 1942 Paul J. Mueller

83rd Infantry Division

Aug. 1942 Frank W. Milburn
Jan. 1944 Robert C. Macon

84th Infantry Division

June 1944 Alexander R. Bolling

85th Infantry Division

May 1942 Wade H. Haislip
Feb. 1943 John B. Coulter

86th Infantry Division

Dec. 1942 Alexander E. Anderson
Jan. 1943 Harris M. Melasky

87th Infantry Division

Dec. 1942 Percy W. Clarkson
Oct. 1943 Eugene M. Landrum
Apr. 1944 Frank L. Culin, Jr.

88th Infantry Division

July 1942 John E. Sloan
Sept. 1944 Paul W. Kendall
July 1945 James C. Fry

89th Infantry Division

July	1942	William H. Gill
Feb.	1943	Thomas D. Finley

90th Infantry Division

Mar.	1942	Henry Terrell, Jr.
Jan.	1944	Jay W. Mackelvie
July	1944	Eugene M. Landrum
Aug.	1944	Raymond S. McLain
Oct.	1944	James A. Van Fleet
Feb.	1945	Lowell W. Rooks
Mar.	1945	Herbert L. Earnest

91st Infantry Division

Aug.	1942	Charles H. Gerhardt
July	1943	William G. Livesay

92nd Infantry Division

Oct.	1942	Edward M. Almond
Aug.	1945	John E. Weed

93rd Infantry Division

May	1942	Charles P. Hall
Oct.	1942	Fred W. Miller
May	1943	Raymond G. Lehman
Aug.	1944	Harry H. Johnson

94th Infantry Division

Sept.	1942	Harry J. Maloney
June	1945	Louis J. Fortier
Aug.	1945	Allison J. Barnett

95th Infantry Division

July	1942	Harry L. Twaddle

96th Infantry Division

Aug.	1942	James L. Bradley

97th Infantry Division

Feb.	1943	Louis A. Craig
Jan.	1944	Milton B. Halsey

98th Infantry Division

Sept.	1942	Paul L. Ransom
Nov.	1943	George W. Griner, Jr.
July	1944	Ralph C. Smith
Nov.	1944	Arthur M. Harper

99th Infantry Division

Nov.	1942	Thompson Lawrence
July	1943	Walter F. Lauer
Aug.	1945	Frederick H. Black

100th Infantry Division

Nov.	1942	Withers A. Burress

102nd Infantry Division

Sept.	1942	John B. Anderson
Jan.	1944	Frank A. Keating

103rd Infantry Division

Nov.	1942	Charles C. Haffner, Jr.
Jan.	1945	Anthony C. McAuliffe
Aug.	1945	John N. Robinson

104th Infantry Division

June	1942	Gilbert R. Cook
Oct.	1943	Terry Allen

106th Infantry Division

Mar.	1943	Alan W. Jones
Dec.	1944	Herbert T. Perrin
Feb.	1945	Donald A. Stroh
Aug.	1945	Francis A. Woolfley

Americal Infantry Division

May	1942	Alexander M. Patch, Jr.
Jan.	1943	Edmund B. Sebree
May	1943	John R. Hodge
Apr.	1944	Robert McClure
Nov.	1944	William H. Arnold

1st Armored Division

July	1940	Bruce Magruder
Mar.	1942	Orlando Ward
Apr.	1943	Ernest N. Harmon
July	1944	Vernon E. Prichard

2nd Armored Division

July	1940	George S. Patton, Jr.
Feb.	1942	Willis D. Crittenberger
July	1942	Ernest N. Harmon
May	1943	Hugh J. Gaffey
Apr.	1944	Edward H. Brooks
Sept.	1944	Ernest N. Harmon
Jan.	1945	Isaac D. White
May	1945	John H. Collier
Aug.	1945	John M. Devine

3rd Armored Division

Apr.	1941	Alvan C. Gillem, Jr.
Jan.	1942	Walton H. Walker
Aug.	1942	Leroy H. Watson
Aug.	1944	Maurice Rose
Mar.	1945	Doyle O. Hickey
June	1945	Truman E. Boudinot
July	1945	Robert W. Grow

4th Armored Division

Apr.	1941	Henry W. Baird
May	1942	J. S. Wood
Dec.	1944	Hugh J. Gaffey
Mar.	1945	William M. Hoge
June	1945	Bruce C. Clarke
July	1945	W. Lyn Roberts

5th Armored Division

Oct.	1941	Jack W. Heard
Mar.	1943	Lunsford E. Oliver
June	1945	Morrill Ross

6th Armored Division

Feb.	1942	William H. H. Morris, Jr.
May	1943	Robert W. Grow
Apr.	1945	George W. Read, Jr.

7th Armored Division

Mar.	1942	Lindsay M. Silvester
Nov.	1944	Robert W. Hasbrouck

8th Armored Division

Apr.	1942	William M. Grimes
Oct.	1944	John M. Devine
Aug.	1945	Charles F. Colson

9th Armored Division

June	1942	Geoffrey Keyes
Oct.	1942	John W. Leonard

10th Armored Division

July	1942	Paul W. Newgarden
July	1944	William H. H. Morris, Jr.
May	1945	Fay B. Prickett

11th Armored Division

Aug.	1942	Edward H. Brooks
Mar.	1944	Charles S. Kilburn
Mar.	1945	Holmes E. Dager

12th Armored Division

Sept.	1942	Carlos Brewer
Aug.	1944	Douglass T. Greene
Sept.	1944	Roderick R. Allen
July	1945	Willard A. Holbrook, Jr.

13th Armored Division

Oct.	1942	John B. Wogan
Apr.	1945	John Millikin

14th Armored Division

Nov.	1942	Vernon E. Prichard
July	1944	Albert C. Smith

16th Armored Division

July	1943	Douglass T. Greene
Sept.	1944	John L. Pierce

20th Armored Division

Feb.	1943	Stephen G. Henry
Oct.	1943	Roderick R. Allen
Sept.	1944	Orlando Ward
Aug.	1945	John W. Leonard

11th Airborne Division

Feb.	1943	Joseph M. Swing

13th Airborne Division

Aug.	1943	George W. Griner, Jr.
Nov.	1943	Elbridge G. Chapman, Jr.

17th Airborne Division

Apr.	1943	William M. Miley

82nd Airborne Division

Mar.	1942	Omar N. Bradley
June	1942	Matthew B. Ridgway
Aug.	1944	James M. Gavin

101st Airborne Division

Aug.	1942	William C. Lee
Mar.	1944	Maxwell D. Taylor

1st Cavalry Division

Apr.	1941	Innis P. Swift
Aug.	1944	Verne D. Mudge
Feb.	1945	Hugh F. T. Hoffman

10th Mountain Division

July	1943	Lloyd E. Jones
Nov.	1944	George P. Hays

Korean Conflict

Commanders-in-Chief, United Nations Command

July 1950 Douglas MacArthur
Apr. 1951 Matthew B. Ridgway
May 1952 Mark W. Clark

U.S. Army Commanders

U.S. Forces in Korea

(In late July 1950 command of the U.S. forces was assumed by the Commander, U.S. Eighth Army.)

July 1950 William F. Dean

U.S. Eighth Army

July 1950 Walton H. Walker
Dec. 1950 Matthew B. Ridgway
Apr. 1951 James A. Van Fleet
Feb. 1953 Maxwell D. Taylor

I Corps

Sept. 1950 Frank W. Milburn
July 1951 John W. O'Daniel
June 1952 Paul W. Kendall
Mar. 1953 Bruce C. Clarke

IX Corps

Sept. 1950 John B. Coulter
Feb. 1951 Bryant E. Moore
Feb. 1951 William M. Hoge
Nov. 1951 Willard E. Wyman
July 1952 Reuben E. Jenkins

X Corps

Sept. 1950 Edward M. Almond
July 1951 Clovis E. Byers
Nov. 1951 Williston B. Palmer
Aug. 1952 Isaac D. White

1st Cavalry Division

July 1950 Hobart R. Gay
Feb. 1951 Charles D. Palmer
June 1951 Thomas L. Harrold

2nd Infantry Division

Aug. 1950 Lawrence B. Keiser
Dec. 1950 Robert B. McClure
Jan. 1951 Clark L. Ruffner
Oct. 1951 James C. Fry

3rd Infantry Division

Nov. 1950 Robert H. Soule
Oct. 1951 Thomas J. Cross
May 1952 Robert L. Dulaney
Oct. 1952 George W. Smythe

24th Infantry Division

July 1950 John H. Church
Feb. 1951 Blackshear M. Bryan
Nov. 1951 Henry I. Hodes
Feb. 1952 Charles L. Dasher

25th Infantry Division

July 1950 William B. Kena
Mar. 1951 Joseph S. Bradley
July 1951 Ira P. Swift

40th Infantry Division

Sept. 1950 Daniel H. Hudelson
June 1952 Joseph P. Cleland

45th Infantry Division

May 1952 David L. Ruffner
Mar. 1953 P. D. Ginder

Vietnam Conflict

U.S. Military Assistance Command, Vietnam (MACV)

Commanders

Feb. 1962 Paul D. Harkins
June 1964 William C. Westmoreland
July 1968 Creighton W. Abrams
June 1972 Frederick C. Weyand

Deputy Commanders

Jan. 1964 William C. Westmoreland
Aug. 1964 John L. Throckmorton
Nov. 1965 John A. Heintges
June 1967 Creighton W. Abrams
July 1968 Andrew J. Goodpaster
May 1969 William B. Rosson
Apr. 1970 Frederick C. Weyand
May 1972 John W. Vogt, Jr. (USAF)

U.S. Army, Vietnam (USARV)

Commanders

July 1965 William C. Westmoreland
July 1968 Creighton W. Abrams

Deputy Commanders

July 1965 John Norton
Jan. 1966 Jean E. Engler
July 1967 Bruce Palmer, Jr.
June 1968 Frank T. Milden
July 1970 William J. McCaffrey
Sept. 1972 Morgan G. Roseborough

I Field Force, Vietnam (I FFV)

Sept. 1965 Stanley R. Larsen
Mar. 1968 William R. Peers
Mar. 1969 Charles A. Corcoran
Mar. 1970 Arthur S. Collins, Jr.
Jan. 1971 Charles P. Brown

II Field Force, Vietnam (II FFV)

Mar. 1966 Jonathan O. Seaman
Mar. 1967 Bruce Palmer, Jr.
July 1967 Frederick C. Weyand
Aug. 1968 Walter T. Kerwin, Jr.
Apr. 1969 Julian J. Ewell
Apr. 1970 Michael S. Davison

XXIV Corps

Mar. 1968 William B. Rosson
July 1968 Richard G. Stilwell

June 1969 Melvin Zais
June 1970 James W. Sutherland, Jr.
June 1971 Welborn G. Dolvin

1st Cavalry Division

July 1965 Harry W. B. Kinnard
May 1966 John Norton
Apr. 1967 John J. Tolson, III
July 1968 George I. Forsythe
May 1969 Elvy B. Roberts
May 1970 George W. Casey
July 1970 George W. Putnam, Jr.

3rd Brigade, 1st Cavalry Division

Apr. 1971 Jonathan R. Burton
Dec. 1971 James F. Hamlet

1st Infantry Division

Oct. 1965 Jonathan O. Seaman
Mar. 1966 William E. Dupuy
Feb. 1967 John H. Hay, Jr.
Mar. 1968 Keith L. Ware
Sept. 1968 Orwin C. Talbott
Aug. 1969 Albert E. Milloy
Mar. 1970 John Q. Herrion

4th Infantry Division

Aug. 1966 David O. Byars
Sept. 1966 Arthur S. Collins, Jr.
Jan. 1967 William R. Peers
Jan. 1968 Charles P. Stone
Nov. 1968 Donn R. Pepke
Nov. 1969 Glenn D. Walker
July 1970 William A. Burke

1st Brigade, 5th Infantry Division

July 1968 Richard J. Glikes
Oct. 1968 James M. Gibson
June 1969 John L. Osteen, Jr.
Apr. 1970 William A. Burke
July 1970 John G. Hill, Jr.
May 1971 Harold H. Dunwoody

9th Infantry Division

Dec. 1966 George S. Eckhardt
June 1967 George G. O'Connor
Feb. 1968 Julian J. Ewell
Apr. 1969 Harris W. Hollis

3rd Brigade, 9th Infantry Division

Sept. 1969 Andrew J. Gatsis
Mar. 1970 Walworth F. Williams

23rd Infantry Division (Americal)

Sept. 1967 Samuel W. Koster
June 1968 Charles M. Gettys
June 1969 Lloyd B. Ramsey
Mar. 1970 Albert E. Milloy
Nov. 1970 James L. Baldwin
July 1971 Frederick J. Kroesen, Jr.

25th Infantry Division

Jan. 1966 Frederick C. Weyand
Mar. 1967 John C. F. Tillson, III
Aug. 1967 Fillmore K. Mearns
Aug. 1968 Ellis W. Williamson
Sept. 1969 Harris W. Hollis
Apr. 1970 Edward Bautz, Jr.

2nd Brigade, 25th Infantry Division

Dec. 1970 Joseph R. Ulatoski

3rd Brigade, 82nd Airborne Division

Feb.	1968	Alex R. Bolling, Jr.
Dec.	1968	George W. Dickerson

101st Airborne Division

Dec.	1967	Olinto M. Barsanti
July	1968	Melvin Zais
May	1969	John M. Wright, Jr.
May	1970	John J. Hennessey
Feb.	1971	Thomas M. Tarpley

1st Brigade, 101st Airborne Division

Aug.	1965	Joseph D. Mitchell
Sept.	1965	James S. Timothy
Jan.	1966	Willard Pearson
Feb.	1967	Salve H. Matheson

Task Force Oregon

Apr.	1967	William B. Rosson
June	1967	Richard T. Knowles

11th Infantry Brigade

Dec.	1967	Andy A. Lipscomb

Mar.	1968	Oran K. Henderson
Oct.	1968	John W. Donalson
Mar.	1969	Jack L. Treadwell
Sept.	1969	Hugh F. T. Hoffman
Mar.	1970	Kendrick B. Barlow
Sept.	1970	John L. Insani

173rd Airborne Brigade

May	1965	Ellis W. Williamson
Feb.	1966	Paul F. Smith
Dec.	1966	John R. Deane, Jr.
Aug.	1967	Leo H. Schweiter
Apr.	1968	Richard J. Allen
Dec.	1968	John W. Barnes
Aug.	1969	Hubert S. Cunningham
Aug.	1970	Elmer R. Ochs
Jan.	1971	Jack MacFarlane

196th Infantry Brigade

Aug.	1966	Francis Conaty
Aug.	1966	Edward H. deSaussure, Jr.
Sept.	1966	Francis Conaty
Nov.	1966	Richard T. Knowles
May	1967	Frank H. Linnell
Nov.	1967	Louis Gelling
June	1968	Frederick J. Kroesen, Jr.

May	1969	Thomas H. Tackaberry
Nov.	1969	James M. Lee
May	1970	Edwin L. Kennedy
Nov.	1970	William S. Hathaway
June	1971	Rutland D. Beard, Jr.
Nov.	1971	Joseph P. McDonough

198th Infantry Brigade

Oct.	1967	J. R. Waldie
June	1968	Charles B. Thomas
Dec.	1968	Robert B. Tully
May	1969	Jere D. Whittington
Nov.	1969	Joseph G. Clemons
July	1970	William R. Richardson
Mar.	1971	Charles R. Smith

199th Infantry Brigade

Dec.	1966	Charles W. Ryder, Jr.
Mar.	1967	John F. Freund
Sept.	1967	Robert C. Forbes
May	1968	Franklin M. Davis, Jr.
Aug.	1968	Frederic E. Davison
May	1969	Warren K. Bennett
Nov.	1969	William R. Bond
Apr.	1970	Robert W. Selton
July	1970	Joseph E. Collins

U.S. Air Force

Chiefs of Staff

Sept.	1947	Carl A. Spaatz
Apr.	1948	Hoyt S. Vandenberg
June	1953	Nathan F. Twining
July	1957	Thomas D. White
June	1961	Curtis E. LeMay
Feb.	1965	John P. McConnell
Aug.	1969	John D. Ryan
July	1973	George S. Brown
June	1974	David C. Jones
July	1978	Lew Allen, Jr.
July	1982	Charles A. Gabriel
July	1986	Larry D. Welch

Vice Chiefs of Staff

1947	Hoyt S. Vandenberg
1948	Muir S. Fairchild
1950	Lauris Norstad (Acting)
1950	Nathan F. Twining
1953	Thomas D. White
1957	Curtis E. LeMay
1961	Frederic H. Smith, Jr.
1962	William F. McKee
1964	John P. McConnell
1965	William H. Blanchard
1966	Bruce K. Holloway
1968	John D. Ryan
1969	John C. Meyer
1972	Horace M. Wade
1974	Richard H. Ellis
1976	William V. McBride
1977	Lew Allen, Jr.
1978	James A. Hill
1980	Robert C. Mathis
1982	Jerome F. O'Malley
1984	Larry D. Welch
1986	John L. Piotrowski

Logistics Commanders

1947	Joseph T. McNarney
1949	Benjamin W. Chidlaw
1951	Edwin W. Rawlings
1959	Samuel E. Anderson
1961	William F. McKee
1962	Mark E. Bradley, Jr.
1965	Kenneth B. Hobson
1967	Thomas P. Gerrity
1968	Jack G. Merrell
1971	Jack J. Catton
1974	William V. McBride
1976	Felix M. Rogers
1978	Bryce Poe, II
1981	James P. McMullins
1984	Earl T. O'Loughlin

Military Airlift Commanders

1948	Laurence S. Kuter
1951	Joseph Smith
1958	William H. Tunner
1960	Joe W. Kelly
1964	Howell M. Estes, Jr.
1969	Jack J. Catton
1973	Paul K. Carlton
1977	William G. Moore
1980	Robert E. Huyser
1982	James R. Allen
1984	Thomas M. Ryan, Jr.
1986	Duane H. Cassidy

Strategic Air Commanders

1946	George C. Kenney
1948	Curtis E. LeMay
1957	Thomas S. Power
1964	John D. Ryan
1967	Joseph J. Nazzaro
1968	Bruce K. Holloway
1972	John C. Meyer
1974	Russell E. Dougherty
1977	Richard H. Ellis
1981	Bennie L. Davis
1985	Larry D. Welch

Systems Commanders

(Until 1961 known as Air Research Development Command.)

1950	David M. Schlatter
1951	Earle E. Partridge
1953	Donald R. Putt
1954	Thomas S. Power
1957	Samuel E. Anderson
1959	John W. Sessums, Jr.
1959	Bernard A. Schreiver
1966	James Ferguson
1970	George S. Brown
1973	Samuel C. Phillips
1975	William J. Evans
1978	Alton D. Slay
1981	Robert T. Marsh
1984	Lawrence A. Skantze

Tactical Air Commanders

1946	Elwood R. Quesada
1948	Robert M. Lee
1950	Glenn D. Barcus
1951	John K. Cannon
1954	Otto P. Weyland
1959	Frank F. Everest
1961	Walter C. Sweeney, Jr.
1965	Gabriel P. Disosway
1968	William W. Momyer
1973	Robert J. Dixon
1978	Wilbur L. Creech
1983	Robert D. Russ

Commanders-in-Chief, North American Air Defense Command

1957	Earle E. Partridge
1959	Laurence S. Kuter
1962	John K. Gerhart
1965	Dean C. Strother
1966	Raymond J. Reeves
1969	Seth J. McKee

Commanders, Pacific Air Forces

1946	Ennis C. Whitehead
1949	George E. Stratemeyer
1951	Otto P. Weyland
1954	Earle E. Partridge
1955	Laurence S. Kuter
1959	Emmett O'Donnell, Jr.
1963	Jacob E. Smart
1964	Hunter Harris
1967	John D. Ryan
1968	Joseph J. Nazzaro
1971	Lucius D. Clay, Jr.
1974	Louis L. Wilson, Jr.
1977	James A. Hill
1978	James D. Hughs
1981	Arnold W. Blackwell
1984	Robert W. Bazley

Commanders, U.S. Air Forces in Europe

1947	Curtis E. LeMay
1948	John K. Cannon
1950	Lauris Norstad
1953	William H. Tunner
1957	Frank F. Everest
1959	Frederic H. Smith, Jr.
1961	Truman H. Landon
1963	Gabriel P. Disosway
1965	Bruce K. Holloway
1966	Maurice A. Preston
1968	Horace M. Wade
1969	Joseph R. Holzapple
1971	David C. Jones
1974	John W. Vogt, Jr.
1976	Richard H. Ellis
1977	William J. Evans
1979	John W. Pauly
1981	Charles A. Gabriel
1982	Billy M. Minter
1985	Charles C. Donnelly, Jr.

U.S. Navy

Chiefs of Naval Operations

May	1915	William Benson
Nov.	1919	Robert E. Coontz
July	1923	Edward W. Eberle
Nov.	1927	Charles F. Hughes
Sept.	1930	William V. Pratt
July	1933	William H. Standley
Jan.	1937	William D. Leahy
Aug.	1939	Harold R. Stark
Mar.	1942	Ernest J. King
Dec.	1945	Chester W. Nimitz
Dec.	1947	Louis E. Denfeld
Nov.	1949	Forrest P. Sherman
Aug.	1951	William M. Fechteler
Aug.	1953	Robert B. Carney
Aug.	1955	Arleigh A. Burke
Aug.	1961	George W. Anderson, Jr.
Aug.	1963	David L. McDonald
Aug.	1967	Thomas H. Moorer
July	1970	Elmo R. Zumwalt, Jr.
July	1974	James L. Holloway, III
July	1978	Thomas B. Hayward
July	1982	James D. Watkins
July	1986	Carlisle A. H. Trost

Assistant Chiefs of Naval Operations (Intelligence)

(Formerly known as Office of Naval Intelligence.)

1915	James Oliver
1917	Roger Welles
1919	Albert P. Niblack
1921	Luke McNamee
1923	Henry H. Hough
1925	W. W. Galbraith
1926	A. J. Hepburn
1928	A. W. Johnson
1930	H. A. Baldridge
1931	Hayne Ellis
1934	W. D. Puleston
1937	Ralston S. Holmes
1939	W. S. Anderson
1941	Alan G. Kirk
1941	T. S. Wilkinson
1943	H. C. Train
1944	R. E. Schuirmann
1945	Hewlett Thebaud
1946	T. B. Inglis
1949	Felix Johnson
1952	Richard F. Stout
1953	Carl Espe
1956	Lawrence H. Frost
1961	V. L. Lowrance
1963	R. L. Taylor
1967	Eugene B. Fluckey
1968	Frederick J. Harlfinger
1971	Earl F. Rectanus

1974	Bobby R. Inman
1976	D. P. Harvey
1978	Sumner Shapiro
1982	John L. Butts
1985	W. O. Studeman

U.S. Navy Judge Advocates General

1880	William B. Remey
1892	Samuel C. Lemly
1904	Samuel W. B. Diehl
1907	Edward H. Campbell
1909	Robert L. Russell
1913	Ridley McLean
1917	William C. Watts
1918	George R. Clark
1921	Julian L. Latimer
1925	Edward H. Campbell
1929	David F. Seller
1931	Orrin G. Murfin
1934	Claude C. Block
1936	Gilbert J. Rowcliff
1938	Walter B. Woodson
1943	Thomas L. Gatch
1945	Oswald S. Colclough
1948	George L. Russell
1952	Ira H. Nunn
1956	Chester Ward
1960	W. C. Mott
1964	W. A. Hearn
1968	Joseph B. McDevitt
1971	Merlin H. Staring
1974	Horace B. Robertson Jr.
1976	William O. Miller
1978	C. E. McDowell
1980	J. S. Jenkins
1982	J. J. McHugh
1985	Thomas E. Flynn

U.S. Navy Surgeons General

1869	William M. Wood
1871	J. M. Foltz
1872	Joseph C. Palmer
1873	Joseph Beale
1877	William Grier
1878	J. Winthrop Taylor
1879	P. S. Wales
1884	Francis M. Gunnell
1888	J. M. Browne
1893	J. R. Tryon
1897	William K. Van Reypen
1902	Presley M. Rixley
1910	Charles F. Stokes
1914	W. C. Braisted
1920	E. R. Stitt
1928	C. E. Riggs
1933	Percival S. Rossiter
1938	Ross T. McIntyre
1946	Clifford A. Swanson

1951	Herbert L. Pugh
1955	Bartholomew W. Hogan
1961	Edward C. Kenney
1965	R. B. Brown
1969	George M. Davis
1972	D. L. Custis
1976	Willard P. Arentzen
1980	J. William Cox
1982	Lewis H. Seaton

Commanders-in-Chief, Pacific (CINPAC)

1949	Arthur W. Radford
1953	Felix B. Stump
1958	Harry D. Felt
1964	Ulysses S. G. Sharp
1968	John S. McCain, Jr.
1972	Noel Gayler
1976	Maurice F. Weisner
1979	Robert L. J. Long
1983	William J. Crowe
1985	Ronald J. Hays

Commanders, U.S. Naval Forces in Europe

(Includes predecessor commands.)

1940	Robert L. Ghormley
1942	Harold R. Stark
1945	H. Kent Hewitt
1946	Richard L. Connolly
1950	Robert B. Carney
1952	Jerauld Wright
1954	John H. Cassady
1956	Walter F. Boone
1958	James L. Holloway, Jr.
1959	Robert L. Dennison
1960	Harold P. Smith
1963	Charles D. Griffin
1965	John S. Thach
1967	John S. McCain, Jr.
1968	Waldemar F. Wendt
1971	William F. Bringle
1973	Worth H. Bagley
1974	Harold E. Shear
1975	David H. Bagley
1977	John P. Moorer
1980	Ronald J. Hays
1983	William N. Small
1985	Lee Baggett, Jr.
1986	A. S. Moreau, Jr.

U.S. Marine Corps

Commandants

1798	William S. Burrows

1804	Franklin Wharton
1819	Anthony Gale
1820	Archibald Henderson
1859	John Harris
1864	Jacob Zeilin
1876	Charles G. McCawley
1891	Charles Heywood
1903	George F. Elliott
1911	William P. Biddle
1914	George Barnett
1920	John A. Lejeune
1929	Wendell C. Neville
1930	Ben H. Fuller
1934	John H. Russell
1936	Thomas Holcomb
1944	Alexander A. Vandegrift
1948	Clifton B. Cates
1952	Lemuel C. Shepherd
1956	Randolph M. Pate
1960	David M. Shoup
1964	Wallace M. Greene, Jr.
1968	Leonard F. Chapman, Jr.
1972	Robert E. Cushman
1975	Louis H. Wilson, Jr.
1979	Robert H. Barrow
1983	Paul X. Kelley

U.S. Navy Fleet Commanders

Pacific Fleet

1941	Husband E. Kimmell
1942	Chester W. Nimitz
1945	Raymond A. Spruance
1946	John H. Towers
1947	Louis E. Denfeld
1948	Dewitt C. Ramsey
1949	Arthur W. Radford
1953	Felix B. Stump
1958	Herbert G. Hopwood
1960	John H. Sides
1963	Ulysses S. G. Sharp
1964	Thomas H. Moorer
1965	Roy L. Johnson
1967	John J. Hyland
1970	Bernard A. Clarey
1973	Maurice F. Weisner
1976	Thomas B. Hayward
1978	D. C. Davis
1981	James D. Watkins
1982	Sylvester R. Foley
1985	John A. Lyons, Jr.

Atlantic Fleet

Feb.	1941	Ernest J. King
Dec.	1941	Royal E. Ingersoll
Nov.	1944	Jonas H. Ingram
Sept.	1946	Marc A. Mitscher
Feb.	1947	William H. P. Blandy
Feb.	1950	William M. Fechteler
Aug.	1951	Lynde D. McCormick
Apr.	1954	Jerauld Wright
Feb.	1960	Robert L. Dennison
Apr.	1963	Harold P. Smith
Apr.	1965	Thomas H. Moorer
June	1967	Ephraim P. Holmes
Sept.	1970	Charles K. Duncan
	1972	Ralph W. Cousins
	1975	Isaac C. Kidd, Jr.
	1978	Harry D. Train, II
	1982	Wesley L. McDonald
	1985	Carlisle A. H. Trost
	1986	Frank B. Kelso, II

First Fleet

(Deactivated in 1973.)

Aug.	1943	Raymond A. Spruance
Nov.	1945	John H. Towers
Jan.	1946	Frederick C. Sherman
Sept.	1946	Alfred E. Montgomery
Aug.	1947	George D. Murray
Aug.	1948	Laurence T. Du Bose
Jan.	1949	Gerald F. Bogan
July	1951	Ralph A. Ofstie
July	1952	Joseph J. Clark
Oct.	1952	Harold M. Martin
Sept.	1953	William K. Phillips
Aug.	1955	Herbert G. Hopwood
June	1956	Robert L. Dennison
Aug.	1958	Ruthven E. Libby
Apr.	1960	Ulysses S. G. Sharp
July	1960	Charles L. Melson
May	1962	Robert T. S. Keith
Dec.	1963	Paul D. Stroop
Jan.	1964	Ephraim P. Holmes
July	1964	Lawson P. Ramage
July	1966	Bernard F. Roeder
Sept.	1969	Isaac C. Kidd, Jr.
Aug.	1970	Raymond E. Peet
Aug.	1972	James F. Calvert (to Feb. 1973)

Second Fleet

Mar.	1946	Marc A. Mitscher
Aug.	1946	Joseph A. E. Hindman
Mar.	1947	Arthur W. Radford
Feb.	1948	Donald B. Duncan
June	1950	Robert B. Carney
Sept.	1950	Matthias B. Gardner
Apr.	1951	Felix B. Stump
June	1953	Thomas S. Combs
Apr.	1954	Edmund T. Wooldridge
June	1955	Charles Wellborn, Jr.
July	1957	Robert B. Pirie
May	1958	Bernard L. Austin
Mar.	1959	William R. Smedberg, III
Jan.	1960	Harold T. Deutermann
Feb.	1961	Claude V. Ricketts
Sept.	1961	John M. Taylor
Oct.	1962	Alfred G. Ward
Aug.	1963	Charles B. Martell
Apr.	1964	Kleber S. Masterson
Aug.	1966	Bernard A. Clarey
May	1967	Charles K. Duncan
Apr.	1968	Benedict J. Semmes, Jr.
Sept.	1970	Gerald E. Miller
	1971	Vincent P. dePoix
Aug.	1972	Douglas C. Plate
Dec.	1972	John G. Finnegan
June	1974	Stansfield Turner
	1975	John J. Shanahan, Jr.
	1985	Charles R. Larson

Third Fleet

(Reactivated in 1973.)

Aug.	1973	Means Johnston, Jr.
Nov.	1973	William T. Rapp
	1974	James H. Doyle
	1975	Robert P. Coogan
	1976	Samuel L. Gravely, Jr.
	1986	Diego E. Hernandez

Sixth Fleet

June	1946	Bernard H. Bieri

Feb.	1948	Forrest P. Sherman
Nov.	1949	John J. Ballentine
Mar.	1951	Matthias B. Gardner
May	1952	John H. Cassady
Mar.	1954	Thomas S. Combs
Mar.	1955	Ralph A. Ofstie
Apr.	1956	Harry D. Felt
Aug.	1956	Charles R. Brown
Sept.	1958	Clarence E. Ekstrom
Sept.	1959	George W. Anderson, Jr.
July	1961	David L. McDonald
Mar.	1963	William E. Gentner, Jr.
June	1964	William E. Ellis
May	1966	Frederick L. Ashworth
Apr.	1967	William I. Martin
Aug.	1968	David C. Richardson
Aug.	1970	Isaac C. Kidd, Jr.
Dec.	1972	Daniel J. Murphy
Mar.	1971	Gerald E. Miller
Dec.	1972	Daniel J. Murphy
	1974	Frederick C. Turner
Aug.	1976	Harry D. Train, II
	1978	James D. Watkins
	1986	Kendall E. Moranville

Seventh Fleet

1942	Herbert F. Leary
1942	Arthur S. Carpenter
1943	Thomas C. Kinkaid
1946	Charles M. Cooke, Jr.
1948	Oscar C. Badger
1949	Russell S. Berkey
1950	Arthur D. Struble
1951	Harold M. Martin
1952	Joseph J. Clark
1953	Alfred M. Pride
1955	Stuart H. Ingersoll
1957	Wallace M. Beakeley
1958	Frederick N. Kivette
1960	Charles D. Griffin
1961	William A. Schoech
1962	Thomas H. Moorer
1964	Roy L. Johnson
1965	Paul P. Blackburn, Jr.
1965	John J. Hyland
1967	William F. Bringle
1970	Maurice F. Weisner
1972	James L. Holloway, III
1973	George Steel
1975	Thomas B. Hayward
1976	Robert B. Baldwin
1980	Carlisle A. H. Trost
1986	Paul B. Miller

U.S. Navy Bureau Chiefs

Naval Air Systems Command

(Bureau of Aeronautics until 1959 when it combined with the Bureau of Ordnance to form the Bureau of Naval Weapons; present Command established in 1966.)

1921	William A. Moffett
1933	Ernest J. King
1936	A. B. Cook
1939	John H. Towers
1942	J. S. McCain
1943	Dewitt C. Ramsey
1945	H. B. Sallada
1947	Alfred M. Pride
1951	Thomas S. Combs
1953	Appolo Soucer
1955	James S. Russell

1957	Robert E. Dixon
1959	Paul D. Stroop
1962	K. S. Masterson
1964	Wellington T. Hines
1964	Allen M. Shinn
1966	Robert L. Townsend
1969	T. J. Walker
1971	T. R. McClellan
1973	Kent L. Lee
1976	F. S. Petersen
1979	E. R. Seymour
1982	James B. Busey
1985	J. B. Wilkinson

Bureau of Engineering

(In 1940 combined with the Bureau of Construction and Repair to become the Bureau of Ships.)

1862	Benjamin F. Isherwood
1870	J. W. King
1874	W. W. Wood
1878	W. H. Shock
1884	Charles H. Loring
1888	George W. Melville
1903	C. W. Rae
1908	John K. Barton
1909	Hutch I. Cone
1913	Robert S. Griffin
1921	John K. Robison
1925	John Halligan, Jr.
1928	H. E. Yarnell
1931	Samuel M. Robinson
1935	H. G. Bowen
1939	Samuel M. Robinson

Bureau of Naval Personnel

(Bureau of Navigation until 1942.)

1862	Charles Henry Davis
1865	Percival Drayton
1865	David D. Porter
1865	T. A. Jenkins
1869	James Alden
1871	Daniel Ammen
1878	William D. Whiting
1881	John D. G. Walker
1889	Francis M. Ramsay
1897	A. S. Crowninshield
1902	Henry Clay Taylor
1904	George A. Converse
1907	Willard H. Brownson
1908	John E. Pillsbury
1909	William P. Potter
1909	R. F. Nicholson
1912	Philip Andrews
1913	Victor Blue
1916	Leigh C. Palmer
1918	Victor Blue
1919	Thomas Washington
1923	Andrew T. Long
1924	William R. Shoemaker
1927	Richard H. Leigh
1930	Frank B. Upham
1933	William D. Leahy
1935	Adolphus Andrews
1938	James O. Richardson
1939	Chester W. Nimitz
1941	Randall Jacobs
1945	Louis E. Denfeld
1947	Thomas L. Sprague
1949	John W. Roper
1951	Laurance T. Debose
1953	James L. Holloway, Jr.
1958	H. Page Smith

1960	William R. Smedberg
1964	B. J. Semmes, Jr.
1967	Charles K. Duncan
1970	D. Henry Guinn
1972	David H. Bagley
1975	James D. Watkins
1978	Robert B. Baldwin
1980	L. W. Zech, Jr.
1982	W. P. Lawrence
1985	D. L. Carlson

Naval Facilities Engineering Command

(Bureau of Yards and Docks until 1966.)

1842	Lewis Warrington
1846	Joseph Smith
1869	Daniel Ammen
1871	C. R. P. Rodgers
1874	John Howell
1878	Richard L. Law
1881	Edward T. Nichols
1885	David B. Harmony
1889	George B. White
1890	Norman H. Farquhar
1894	Edmund O. Matthews
1898	Mordecai T. Endicott
1907	R. C. Hollyday
1912	Homer R. Stanford
1916	Frederic R. Harris
1918	Charles W. Parks
1921	Luther E. Gregory
1929	Archibald L. Parsons
1933	Norman M. Smith
1937	Ben Moreell
1945	John J. Manning
1949	Joseph F. Jelley, Jr.
1953	John R. Perry
1955	Robert H. Meade
1959	Eugene J. Peltier
1962	P. Corradi
1965	A. C. Husband
1970	W. M. Enger
1972	A. R. Marschall
1977	D. G. Iselin
1980	W. M. Zobel
1984	John P. Jones, Jr.

Office of Acquisition Support

(Office of Naval Material until 1984.)

1942	Samuel M. Robinson
1946	Ben Moreell
1947	Edward L. Cochrane
1948	Arthur C. Miles
1950	E. D. Foster
1951	Albert G. Noble
1952	Charles W. Fox
1954	John Gingrich
1955	M. L. Royar
1956	Edward W. Clexton
1962	G. F. Beardsley
1963	William A. Schoech
1965	Ignatius J. Galantin
1970	Jackson D. Arnold
1971	Isaac C. Kidd, Jr.
1975	F. H. Michaelis
1978	A. J. Whittle, Jr.
1981	J. G. Williams, Jr.
1983	Steven A. White
1984	Richard A. Miller (to 1985)

Naval Ordnance Systems Command

(Bureau of Ordnance until 1960 when it combined with Bureau of Aeronautics to form the Bureau of Naval Weapons; present Command established in 1966.)

1842	William M. Crane
1846	Lewis Warrington
1851	Charles Morris
1856	Duncan N. Ingraham
1860	George A. Magruder
1861	Andrew A. Harwood
1862	John A. Dahlgren
1863	Henry Augustus Wise
1868	John A. Dahlgren
1869	Augustus Ludlow Case
1873	William N. Jeffers
1881	Montgomery Sicard
1890	William M. Folger
1893	William T. Sampson
1897	Charles O'Neil
1904	George A. Converse
1904	Newton E. Mason
1911	Nathan C. Twining
1913	Joseph Strauss
1916	Ralph Earle
1920	Charles B. McVay, Jr.
1923	Claude C. Bloch
1927	William D. Leahy
1931	Edgar B. Larimer
1934	Harold R. Stark
1937	William R. Furlong
1941	William H. P. Blandy
1943	George F. Hussey, Jr.
1947	Albert G. Noble
1950	Malcolm F. Schoeppel
1954	Frederic S. Withington
1958	Paul D. Stroop
1966	Arthur R. Gralla
1970	M. W. Woods
1972	R. E. Spreen (to 1973)

Naval Sea Systems Command

(Bureau of Construction and Repairs until 1940; combined with Bureau of Engineering to form Bureau of Ships, 1940-1966; Naval Ship Systems Command until 1973.)

1842	David Conner
1843	Beverly Kennon
1844	Charles Morris
1847	Charles W. Skinner
1852	William B. Shubrick
1853	Samuel Hartt
1853	John Lenthall
1872	Isaiah Hanscom
1878	J. W. Easby
1882	Theodore D. Wilson
1894	Philip Hichborn
1901	F. T. Bowles
1903	W. L. Capps
1910	Richard M. Watt
1914	David W. Taylor
1922	John D. Beuret
1929	Geroge H. Rock
1933	Emory S. Land
1937	William G. DuBose
1939	Alexander H. Van Keuren
1940	Samuel M. Robinson
1942	Alexander H. Van Keuren
1942	Edward L. Cochrane
1946	Earle W. Mills
1949	David H. Clark
1951	Homer N. Wallin
1953	Wilson D. Leggett, Jr.

1955	Albert G. Mumma	
1959	Ralph K. James	
1963	William A. Brockett	
1966	Edward J. Fahy	
1970	N. Sonenshein	
1972	Robert C. Gooding	
1976	C. R. Bryan	
1979	Earl B. Fowler	
1985	W. Rowden	

Naval Commanders During Wartime

(Through the First World War.)

Revolutionary War

Commander-in-Chief

Esek Hopkins

Commodores

John P. Hazlewood
John Paul Jones
Dudley Saltonstall

War of 1812

Commodores

Isaac Chauncey

Stephen Decatur
Thomas Macdonough
Oliver H. Perry
David Porter

Civil War

Gunboat Squadron, Western Waters

1861	George W. Rodgers
1861	Andrew H. Foote
1862	Charles H. Davis

Mississippi Squadron

1862	David D. Porter
1864	Samuel P. Lee

North Atlantic Blockading Squadron

1861	Silas H. Strigham
1861	Louis M. Goldsborough
1862	Samuel P. Lee
1864	David D. Porter

South Atlantic Blockading Squadron

1861	Samuel F. DuPont
1863	John A. Dahlgren

West Gulf Blockading Squadron

1862	David G. Farragut
1864	James S. Palmer
1865	Henry K. Thatcher

West Indies Squadron

1862	Charles Wilkes
1863	James L. Lardner

Spanish American War

Asiatic Squadron

1898	George Dewey

Atlantic Fleet

1898	William Sampson

First World War

U.S. Naval Forces in Europe

1917	William S. Simms (to 1919)

Atlantic Fleet

1916	Harry T. Mayo
1919	Henry B. Wilson

Pacific Fleet

1916	William Caperton

Asiatic Fleet

1917	Austin Knight
1918	William Rogers

Colleges of the Armed Forces

See Section XII: College and University Presidents for Commandants of Service Academies.

Armed Forces Staff College

Commandants

Aug. 1946 Delos C. Emmons
June 1948 John L. Hall, Jr.
July 1951 Andrew D. Bruce
July 1954 David M. Schlatter
July 1957 Charles Wellborn, Jr.
Mar. 1960 Thomas J. Sands
May 1960 John S. Upham, Jr.
Apr. 1962 Robert Wienecke
July 1963 J. Stanley Holtoner
June 1965 Lawrence R. Daspit
Oct. 1967 Frank W. Norris
1970 James F. Kirkendall
1973 Jeremiah A. Denton, Jr.
1977 L. Gordon Hill, Jr.
1980 Robert B. Tanguy
1982 T. G. Darling
1984 K. A. Jolemore

Army War College

Presidents

July 1902 Samuel B. M. Young
Aug. 1903 Tasker H. Bliss
June 1905 W. W. Wotherspoon (Acting)
Dec. 1905 Thomas H. Barry
Feb. 1907 W. W. Wotherspoon (Acting)
Oct. 1907 W. W. Wotherspoon
June 1909 Tasker H. Bliss
Dec. 1909 W. W. Wotherspoon
Feb. 1912 Albert L. Mills
Sept. 1912 William Crozier
July 1913 Hunter Liggett
Apr. 1914 M. M. Macomb
Feb. 1917 Joseph E. Kuhn
June 1919 James W. McAndrew
July 1921 E. F. McGlachlin, Jr.
July 1923 Hanson E. Ely
Dec. 1927 William D. Connor
May 1932 George S. Simonds
Feb. 1935 Malin Craig
Oct. 1935 Walter S. Grant
June 1937 John L. DeWitt
Dec. 1939 Philip B. Peyton
Apr. 1950 Joseph M. Swing
Aug. 1951 Edward M. Almond
Dec. 1952 Verdi B. Barnes (Acting)
Apr. 1953 James E. Moore
Feb. 1955 Thomas W. Dunn (Acting)
May 1955 Clyde D. Eddleman
Oct. 1955 Max S. Johnson
Mar. 1959 William P. Ennis, Jr.
July 1960 Thomas W. Dunn
Apr. 1962 William F. Train
June 1964 Eugene A. Salet
Sept. 1967 William J. McCaffrey

National Defense University

(Formed in Jan. 1976 to supervise the National War College and the Industrial College of the Armed Forces.)

Presidents

1976 M. G. Bayne
1977 Robert G. Gard, Jr.
1981 John S. Pustay
1984 Richard D. Lawrence

U.S. Army National War College

Commandants

1947 Harry W. Hill
1949 Harold R. Bull
1953 Howard A. Craig
1956 Edmund F. Wooldridge
1959 Thomas L. Harrold
1961 Francis H. Griswold
1964 Fitzhugh Lee
1967 Andrew J. Goodpaster
1970 John B. McPherson
1973 M. G. Bayne
1976 James S. Murphy
1977 Harrison Lobdell, Jr.
1979 John C. Barrow
1981 L. E. Surut
1983 Perry M. Smith

Army Command and General Staff College

Commandants

Nov. 1881 Elwell S. Otil
June 1885 Thomas H. Ruger
May 1886 Alexander M. McCook
Aug. 1890 Edwin F. Townsend
Oct. 1894 Hamilton S. Hawkins
Sept. 1902 C. W. Miner
July 1903 J. Franklin Bell
Aug. 1906 C. B. Hall
Apr. 1908 John F. Morrison (Acting)
Aug. 1908 Frederick Funston
Jan. 1911 R. D. Potts
Feb. 1913 William P. Burnham (Acting)
Sept. 1914 Henry A. Greene
Aug. 1916 Eben Swift
Nov. 1916 James W. McAndrew
July 1917 William A. Shunk
July 1919 Charles H. Muir
Aug. 1920 Lucius R. Holbrook

Sept. 1920 Hugh A. Drum
Aug. 1921 Hanson E. Ely
July 1923 Harry A. Smith
July 1925 Edward L. King
July 1929 Stuart Heintzelman
Feb. 1935 Herbert J. Brees
June 1936 Charles M. Bundel
Apr. 1939 Lesley J. McNair
Oct. 1940 Edmund L. Gruber
June 1941 Horace H. Fuller
Mar. 1942 Karl Truesdell
Nov. 1945 Leonard T. Gerow
Jan. 1948 Manton S. Eddy
July 1950 Harlan N. Hartness (Acting)
Oct. 1950 Horace L. McBride
Mar. 1952 Henry I. Hodes
Mar. 1954 Charles E. Beauchamp (Acting)
July 1954 Garrison H. Davidson
July 1956 Lionel C. McGarr
July 1960 Harold K. Johnson
Feb. 1963 Harry J. Lemley, Jr.
Aug. 1966 Michael S. Davison

U.S. Army Industrial College of the Armed Forces

1924 Harley B. Ferguson
1928 William P. Wooten
1929 Irving J. Carr
1930 William A. McCain
1934 Harry B. Jordan
1938 Francis H. Miles, Jr.
1940 John E. Lewis
1941 Frank Whitehead
1944 Donald Armstrong
1946 Edward B. McKinley
1948 Arthur W. Vanaman
1952 Wesley M. Hague
1955 Robert P. Hollis
1957 George W. Mundy
1961 Rufus E. Rose
1964 August Schomburg
1967 Leighton I. Davis
1969 John S. Hardy
1971 John V. Smith
1973 Walther J. Woolwine
1975 Theodore Antonelli
1978 John E. Ralph
1980 J. E. Dalton
1982 R. E. Narmi
1984 C. D. Dean

Naval War College

Presidents

1884 Stephen B. Luce

1886 Alfred T. Mahan	1922 Clarence S. Williams	1953 Thomas H. Robbins, Jr.
1889 Casper F. Goodrich	1925 William V. Pratt	1954 Lynde D. McCormick
1892 Alfred T. Mahan	1927 Joel R. P. Pringle	1956 Thomas H. Robbins, Jr.
1893 Henry C. Taylor	1930 Harris Lanning	1957 Stuart H. Ingersoll
1896 Casper F. Goodrich	1933 Luke McNamee	1960 Bernard L. Austin
1898 Charles H. Stockton	1934 Edward C. Kalbfus	1964 Charles L. Melson
1900 French E. Chadwick	1937 Charles P. Snyder	1966 John T. Hayward
1903 Charles S. Sperry	1939 Edward C. Kalbfus	1968 Richard G. Colbert
1906 John P. Merrell	1942 William S. Pye	1971 Benedict J. Semmes, Jr.
1909 Raymond P. Rodgers	1946 Raymond A. Spruance	1972 Stansfield Turner
1911 William L. Rodgers	1948 Allen E. Smith (Acting)	1974 Julien J. LeBourgeois
1913 Austin M. Knight	1948 Donald B. Beary	1977 James B. Stockdale
1917 William S. Sims	1950 Richard L. Connolly	1984 James E. Service

IX

Diplomatic Representatives of the United States

Diplomatic Representatives of the United States

A complete listing of heads of U.S. delegations to foreign countries since 1790. Note: The abbreviation EEMP stands for Envoy Extraordinary and Minister Plenipotentiary.

Abyssinia

(See Ethiopia for later representation.)

Ministers

1908-1909	Hoffman Philip
1909-1911	Vacant
1911	Legation closed

Afghanistan

EEMP

1935-1936	William H. Hornibrook
1937-1940	Vacant
1940-1942	Louis G. Dreyfus, Jr.
1942-1945	Cornelius Van H. Engert
1945-1948	Ely E. Palmer

Ambassadors

1948-1949	Ely E. Palmer
1949-1951	Louis G. Dreyfus, Jr.
1951-1952	George R. Merrell
1952-1956	Angus Ward
1956-1959	Sheldon T. Mills
1959-1962	Henry A. Bryoade
1962-1965	John M. Steeves
1966-1973	Robert G. Neumann
1973-1978	Theodore L. Eliot, Jr.
1978-1979	Adolph Dubs
1979-1986	Vacant

Albania

EEMP

1922-1925	Ulysses Grant-Smith
1925-1929	Charles C. Hart
1930-1933	Herman Bernstein
1933-1934	Post Wheeler
1935-1939	Hugh G. Grant
1939	Legation closed

Algeria

Ambassadors

1962-1965	William J. Porter
1965-1967	John D. Jernigan
1967-1974	Embassy closed
1974-1977	Richard B. Parker
1977-1980	Ulric St. Clair Haynes, Jr.
1981-1984	Michael H. Newlin
1985-	L. Craig Johnstone

Antigua and Baruda

Ambassadors

1981-1984	Milan D. Bish
1984-	Thomas H. Anderson, Jr.

Arab Republic of Egypt

(See Egypt and United Arab Republic for earlier representation.)

Ambassadors

1974-1979	Herman F. Eilts
1979-1983	Alfred L. Atherton
1984-1986	Nicholas A. Veliotes
1986-	Frank G. Wisner, II

Argentina

Ministers Plenipotentiary

1823-1824	Caesar A. Rodney

Charges d'Affaires

1825-1831	John M. Forbes
1832-1843	Francis Baylies
1844-1846	William Brent, Jr.
1846-1851	William A. Harris
1851-1854	John S. Pendleton

Ministers

1854-1858	James A. Peden
1858-1859	Benjamin C. Yancey
1859-1861	John F. Cushman
1861-1862	Robert M. Palmer
1862-1866	Robert C. Kirk
1866-1868	Alexander Asboth
1868-1869	Henry G. Worthington
1869-1871	Robert C. Kirk
1872-1874	Julius White
1874-1885	Thomas O. Osborn
1885-1887	Bayless W. Hanna

EEMP

1887-1889	Bayless W. Hanna
1889-1894	John R. G. Pitkin
1894-1899	William I. Buchanan
1899-1903	William P. Lord
1903-1904	John Barrett
1904-1907	Arthur M. Beaupre
1907-1909	Spencer F. Eddy
1909-1911	Charles H. Sherrill
1911	John R. Carter
1911-1914	John W. Garrett

Ambassadors

1914-1921	Frederic J. Stimson
1921-1924	John W. Riddle
1924-1927	Peter A. Jay
1927-1933	Robert W. Bliss
1933-1939	Alexander W. Weddell
1939-1944	Norman Armour
1945	Spruille Braden
1946-1947	George S. Messersmith
1947-1949	James M. Bruce
1949-1950	Stanton Griffis
1951-1952	Ellsworth Bunker
1952-1956	Albert F. Nufer
1956-1960	Willard L. Beaulac
1960-1961	Roy R. Rubottom, Jr.
1962-1964	Robert McClintock
1964-1967	Edwin M. Martin
1968-1969	Carter L. Burgess
1969-1973	John Davis Lodge
1973-1977	Robert C. Hill
1977-1980	Raul H. Castro
1980-1983	Harry W. Shlaudeman
1984-1986	Frank V. Ortiz, Jr.
1986-	Theodore Gildred

Australia

EEMP

1940-1941	Clarence E. Hauss
1941-1946	Nelson T. Johnson

Ambassadors

1946-1948	Robert Butler
1948-1949	Myron M. Cowen
1949-1953	Peter Jarman
1953-1956	Amos J. Peasley
1956	Douglas M. Moffat
1957-1961	William J. Sebald
1962-1964	William C. Battle
1965-1968	Edward A. Clark
1968-1969	William H. Crook
1969-1973	Walter L. Rice
1973-1975	Marshall Green
1976-1977	James W. Hargrove
1977-1981	Philip H. Alston, Jr.
1981-1985	Robert D. Nesen
1986-	Frank V. Ortiz, Jr.

Austria

(Austria-Hungary 1868-1919; see also Hungary.)

EEMP

1838-1840	Henry A. P. Muhlenberg
1841-1845	Daniel Jenifer

Charges d'Affaires

1845-1849	William H. Stiles
1849-1850	James W. Webb
1850-1852	Charles J. McCurdy
1852-1853	Thomas M. Foote
1853-1854	Henry R. Jackson

Ministers

1854-1858	Henry R. Jackson
1858-1861	J. Glancy Jones

EEMP

1861-1867	J. Lothrop Motley
1868-1869	Henry M. Watts
1869-1875	John Jay
1875-1876	Godlove S. Orth
1876-1877	Edward F. Beale
1877-1882	John A. Kasson
1882-1884	Alphonso Taft
1884-1885	John M. Francis
1887-1889	Alexander R. Lawton
1889-1893	Frederick D. Grant
1893-1897	Bartlett Tripp
1897-1899	Charlemagne Tower
1899-1901	Addison C. Harris
1901-1902	Robert S. McCormick

Ambassadors

1902-1906	Bellamy Storer
1906-1909	Charles S. Francis
1909-1913	Richard C. Kerens
1913-1917	Frederic C. Penfield
1917-1919	Embassy closed

Commissioners

1919-1920	Albert Halstead
1920-1921	Arthur H. Frazier

Charges d'Affaires

1921-1922	Arthur H. Frazier

EEMP

1922-1930	Albert H. Washburn
1930-1933	Gilchrist B. Stockton
1933-1934	George H. Earle
1934-1937	George S. Messersmith
1937-1938	Grenville T. Emmet
1939-1946	Legation closed
1946-1950	John G. Erhardt
1950-1952	Walter J. Donnelly

Ambassadors

1952-1957	Llewellyn E. Thompson
1957-1962	H. Freeman Matthews
1962-1967	James W. Riddleberger
1967-1969	Douglas MacArthur, II
1969-1975	John P. Humes
1975-1977	Wiley T. Buchanan, Jr.
1977-1980	Milton A. Wolf
1980-1981	Philip M. Kaiser
1981-1982	Theodore E. Cummings
1983-1985	Helene A. von Damm-Guertler
1986-	Ronald S. Lauder

Bahamas

Ambassadors

1973-1974	Ronald I. Spiers

1974-1976	Seymour Weiss
1976-1977	Jack B. Olson
1977-1981	William B. Schwartz
1982	Vacant
1983-	Lev E. Dobriansky

Bahrain

Ambassadors

1971-1974	William A. Stoltzfus, Jr.
1974-1976	Joseph W. Twinam
1976-1978	Wat T. Cluverius, IV
1979-1980	Robert H. Pelletreau, Jr.
1980-1983	Peter A. Sutherland
1984-	Donald C. Leidel

Bangladesh

Ambassadors

1972	Herman F. Eilts
1972-1974	Vacant
1974-1976	Davis Eugene Boster
1976-1977	Edward E. Masters
1978-1981	David T. Schneider
1981-1984	Jane Abell Coon
1984-	Howard B. Schaffer

Barbados

Charges d'Affaires

1965-1967	George Dolgin

Ambassadors

1967-1969	Frederic R. Mann
1969-1974	Eileen R. Donovan
1974-1977	Theodore R. Britton, Jr.
1977-1979	Frank V. Ortiz, Jr.
1979-1981	Sally A. Shelton
1981-1984	Milan D. Bish
1984-	Thomas H. Anderson, Jr.

Belgium

Charges d'Affaires

1832-1836	Hugh S. Legare
1837-1842	Virgil Maxcy
1842-1844	Henry W. Hillhard
1844-1851	Thomas C. Clemson
1850-1853	Richard H. Bayard
1853-1856	John J. Seibels
1858-1861	Elisha Y. Fair
1861-1869	Henry S. Sanford
1869-1875	J. Russell Jones
1876-1877	Ayres P. Merrill
1878-1880	William C. Goodloe
1880-1882	James O. Putnam
1882-1885	Nicholas Fish
1885-1888	Lambert Tree

EEMP

1888-1889	John G. Parkhurst
1889-1893	Edwin E. Terrell
1893-1897	James S. Ewing
1897-1899	Bellamy Storer
1899-1905	Lawrence Townsend
1905-1909	Henry L. Wilson
1909-1911	Charles P. Bryan

1911-1912	Larz Anderson
1912-1913	Theodore Marburg
1913-1922	Brand Whitlock

Ambassadors

1922-1924	Henry P. Fletcher
1924-1927	William Phillips
1927-1933	Hugh S. Gibson
1933-1937	Dave H. Morris
1937-1938	Hugh S. Gibson
1938-1940	Joseph E. Davies
1940	John Cudahy
1941-1943	Anthony J. Drexel Biddle, Jr.
1944-1945	Charles Sawyer
1946-1949	Alan G. Kirk
1949-1952	Robert D. Murphy
1952-1953	Myron M. Cowen
1953-1957	Frederick M. Alger, Jr.
1957-1959	John C. Folger
1959-1961	William A. M. Burden
1961-1965	Douglas MacArthur, II
1965-1969	Ridgway B. Knight
1969-1972	John S. D. Eisenhower
1972-1974	Robert Strausz-Hupe
1974-1977	Leonard Kimball Firestone
1977-1981	Anne C. Chambers
1981-1983	Charles H. Price, II
1984-	Geoffrey Swaebe

Belize

Ambassadors

1983-1985	Malcolm R. Barneby
1985-	Vacant

Benin

(See Dahomey for earlier representation.)

Ambassadors

1976-1983	Vacant
1984-	George E. Moose

Bolivia

Charges d'Affaires

1848-1849	John Appleton
1849-1851	Alexander K. McClung
1852-1853	Horace H. Miller

Ministers

1853-1858	John W. Dana
1859-1861	John C. Smith, Jr.
1861-1863	David K. Cartter
1863-1867	Allen A. Hall
1868-1869	John W. Caldwell
1869-1873	Leopold Markbreit
1873-1874	John T. Croxton
1874-1877	Robert M. Reynolds
1878-1880	S. Newton Pettis
1880-1882	Charles Adams
1882-1883	George Maney
1883-1885	Richard Gibbs
1885-1887	William A. Seay
1887-1890	S. S. Carlisle

EEMP

1890-1892	Thomas H. Anderson
1892-1894	Frederick J. Grant

1894-1897	Thomas Moonlight
1897-1902	George Herbert Bridgman
1902-1908	William B. Sorsby
1908-1910	James F. Stutesman
1910-1913	Horace G. Knowles
1913-1918	John D. O'Rear
1919-1921	S. Abbot Maginnis
1921-1928	Jesse S. Cottrell
1928-1929	David E. Kaufman
1929-1930	Evan E. Young
1930-1933	Edward F. Feely
1933-1936	Fay A. Des Portes
1936-1937	R. Henry Norweb
1937-1939	Robert G. Caldwell
1939-1941	Douglas Jenkins

Ambassadors

1942-1944	Pierre de L. Boal
1944-1946	Walter Thurston
1946-1949	Joseph Flack
1949-1951	Irving Florman
1951-1954	Edward J. Sparks
1954-1957	Gerald A. Drew
1957-1959	Philip W. Bonsal
1959-1961	Carl W. Strom
1961-1963	Ben S. Stephansky
1963-1968	Douglas Henderson
1968-1969	Raul H. Castro
1969-1973	Ernest V. Siracusa
1973-1977	William Perry Stedman, Jr.
1977-1980	Paul M. Boeker
1980	Marvin Weissman
1980-1982	Embassy closed
1982-1985	Edwin G. Corr
1985-	Edward M. Rowell

Botswana

Ambassadors

1970-1971	W. Kennedy Cromwell, III
1971-1974	Charles J. Nelson
1974-1976	David B. Bolen
1976-1979	Donald R. Norland
1979-1982	Horace G. Dawson, Jr.
1983-1985	Theodore C. Maino
1986-	Natale H. Bellocchi

Brazil

Charges d'Affaires

1825-1827	Condy Raquet
1827-1830	William Tudor
1830-1834	Ethan A. Brown
1834-1841	William Hunter

EEMP

1841-1843	William Hunter
1843-1844	George H. Proffit
1844-1847	Henry A. Wise
1847-1851	David Tod
1851-1853	Robert C. Schenck
1853-1857	William Trousdale
1857-1861	Richard K. Meade
1861-1869	James W. Webb
1869-1871	Henry T. Blow
1871-1877	James R. Partridge
1877-1881	Henry W. Hilliard
1881-1885	Thomas A. Osborn
1885-1890	Thomas J. Jarvis
1890-1893	Edwin H. Conger
1893-1898	Thomas L. Thompson
1898-1902	Charles P. Bryan
1902-1905	David E. Thompson

Ambassadors

1905-1907	Lloyd C. Griscom
1907-1912	Irving B. Dudley
1912-1933	Edwin V. Morgan
1933-1937	Hugh S. Gibson
1937-1944	Jefferson Caffery
1945-1946	Adolf A. Berle, Jr.
1946-1948	William D. Pawley
1948-1953	Herschel V. Johnson
1953-1955	James S. Kemper
1955-1956	James C. Dunn
1956-1959	Ellis O. Briggs
1959-1961	John M. Cabot
1961-1966	Lincoln Gordon
1966-1969	John W. Tuthill
1969-1970	C. Burke Elbrick
1970-1973	William M. Rountree
1973-1978	John Hugh Crimmins
1978-1981	Robert M. Sayre
1981-1983	Langhorne A. Motley
1984-	Diego C. Asencio

Brunei

Ambassadors

1984-	Barrington King

Bulgaria

Agents

1901-1903	Charles M. Dickinson
1903-1907	John B. Jackson
1907-1909	Horace G. Knowles
1909	John R. Carter

EEMP

1910	John R. Carter
1911	John B. Jackson
1913-1919	Charles J. Vopicka
1921-1928	Charles S. Wilson
1928-1929	H. F. Arthur Schoenfeld
1930-1933	Henry W. Shoemaker
1933-1937	Frederick A. Sterling
1937-1939	Ray Atherton
1940-1941	George H. Earle
1941-1947	Legation closed
1947-1950	Donald R. Heath
1950-1960	Legation closed
1960-1962	Edward Page, Jr.
1962-1965	Eugenie Anderson
1965-1966	Nathaniel Davis

Ambassadors

1966-1970	John McSweeney
1970-1973	Horace G. Torbert, Jr.
1974-1977	Martin F. Herz
1977-1979	Raymond L. Garthoff
1979-1981	Jack Richard Perry
1981-1984	Robert L. Barry
1985-	Melvyn Levitsky

Burkina-Faso

(See Upper Volta for earlier representation.)

Ambassadors

1984-	Leonardo Neher

Burma

Ambassadors

1947-1949	J. Klahr Huddle
1950-1952	David McK. Key
1952-1954	William J. Sebald
1955-1957	Joseph C. Satterthwaite
1957-1959	Walter P. McConaughy
1959-1961	William P. Snow
1961-1963	John S. Everton
1963-1968	Henry A. Byroade
1968-1971	Arthur W. Hummel, Jr.
1971-1973	Edwin M. Martin
1974-1977	David L. Osborn
1977-1979	Maurice D. Bean
1979-1983	Patricia M. Byrne
1984-	Daniel A. O'Donohue

Burundi

EEMP

1962-1966	Donald A. Dumont

Ambassadors

1968-1969	George W. Renchard
1969-1972	Thomas P. Melady
1972-1974	Robert L. Yost
1974-1977	David E. Mark
1978-1980	Thomas J. Corcoran
1980-1983	Frances D. Cook
1983-	James R. Bullington

Cambodia

(See Khmer Republic for later representation.)

EEMP

1950-1952	Donald R. Heath

Ambassadors

1952	Donald R. Heath
1952-1956	Robert McClintock
1956-1959	Carl W. Strom
1959-1962	William C. Trimble
1962-1964	Philip D. Sprouse
1964-1965	Randolph A. Kidder
1965-1969	Embassy closed

Charges d'Affaires

1969-1970	Lloyd M. Rives

Cameroon

Ambassadors

1960-1966	Leland Barrows
1967-1969	Robert L. Payton
1969-1972	Lewis Hoffacker
1972-1975	C. Robert Moore
1975-1977	Herbert J. Spiro
1977-1980	Mabel M. Smythe
1980-1983	Hume A. Horan
1983-	Myles R. Frechette

Canada

EEMP

1927-1929	William Phillips
1930-1932	Hanford MacNider
1933-1935	Warren D. Robbins
1935-1937	Norman Armour
1939	Daniel C. Roper
1940	James H. R. Cromwell
1940-1943	Jay Pierrepont Moffat
1943	Ray Atherton

Ambassadors

1944-1948	Ray Atherton
1948-1950	Laurence A. Steinhardt
1950-1952	Stanley Woodward
1953-1956	R. Douglas Stuart
1956-1958	Livingston T. Merchant
1958-1960	Richard B. Wigglesworth
1961-1962	Livingston T. Merchant
1962-1968	W. Walton Butterworth
1968-1969	Harold F. Linder
1969-1974	Adolph W. Schmidt
1974-1975	William J. Porter
1975-1979	Thomas O. Enders
1979-1981	Kenneth M. Curtis
1981-1985	Paul Heron Robinson, Jr.
1985-	Thomas M. T. Niles

Central African Republic

Ambassadors

1960-1961	W. Wendell Blancke
1961-1963	John H. Burns
1963-1967	Claude G. Ross
1967-1970	Geoffrey W. Lewis
1970-1972	Melvin L. Manfull
1973-1975	William N. Dale
1976-1978	Anthony C. E. Quainton
1978-1979	Goodwin Cooke
1979-1981	Vacant
1981-1983	Arthur H. Woodruff
1984-	Edmund T. DeJarnette

Ceylon

(See Republic of Sri Lanka for later representation.)

Ambassadors

1948-1949	Felix Cole
1949-1953	Joseph C. Satterthwaite
1953-1957	Philip K. Crowe
1957-1958	Maxwell H. Gluck
1958-1959	Lampton Berry
1959-1961	Bernard A. Gufler
1961-1964	Frances E. Willis
1964-1967	Cecil B. Lyon
1967-1970	Andrew V. Corry
1970-1972	Robert Strausz-Hupe
1972-	Christopher Van Hollen

Chad

Ambassadors

1960-1961	W. Wendell Blancke
1961-1962	John A. Calhoun
1963-1967	Brewster H. Morris
1967-1969	Sheldon B. Vance
1969-1972	Terence A. Todman

1972-1974	Edward W. Mulcahy
1974-1976	Edward S. Little
1976-1979	William G. Bradford
1979-1980	Donald R. Norland
1980-1982	Embassy closed
1982-1983	Vacant
1983-1985	Jay P. Moffat
1985-	John Blane

Chile

Ministers Plenipotentiary

1823-1827	Heman Allen

Charges d'Affaires

1828-1829	Samuel Larned
1830-1833	John Hamm
1834-1842	Richard Pollard
1842-1844	John S. Pendleton
1844-1847	William Crump
1847-1849	Seth Barton

EEMP

1849-1853	Balie Peyton
1854-1857	David A. Starkweather
1857-1861	John Bigler
1861-1866	Thomas H. Nelson
1866-1870	Judson Kilpatrick
1870-1873	Joseph P. Root
1873-1877	Cornelius A. Logan
1877-1882	Thomas A. Osborn
1882-1885	Cornelius A. Logan
1885-1889	William R. Roberts
1889-1893	Patrick Egan
1893-1894	James D. Porter
1894-1897	Edward H. Strobel
1897-1905	Henry L. Wilson
1905-1909	John Hicks
1909-1916	Henry P. Fletcher

Ambassadors

1916-1921	Joseph H. Shea
1921-1928	William M. Collier
1928-1933	William S. Culbertson
1933-1935	Hal H. Sevier
1935-1938	Hoffman Philip
1938-1939	Norman Armour
1939-1953	Claude G. Bowers
1953-1956	Willard L. Beaulac
1956-1958	Cecil B. Lyon
1958-1961	Walter Howe
1961	Robert F. Woodward
1961-1964	Charles W. Cole
1964-1967	Ralph A. Dungan
1967-1971	Edward M. Korry
1971-1973	Nathaniel Davis
1973-1977	David H. Popper
1977-1982	George W. Landau
1982-1985	James D. Theberge
1985-	Harry G. Barnes, Jr.

China

(See People's Republic of China and Republic of China for later representation.)

Commissioners

1843-1845	Caleb Cushing
1846-1847	Alexander H. Everett
1848-1850	John W. Davis
1851-1852	Thomas A. R. Nelson
1852-1854	Humphrey Marshall

1854-1857	Robert M. McLane

EEMP

1857-1858	William B. Reed
1858-1860	John E. Ward
1861-1867	Anson Burlingame
1868-1869	J. Ross Browne
1869-1874	Frederick F. Low
1874-1876	Benjamin P. Avery
1876-1880	George F. Seward
1880-1882	James B. Angell
1882-1885	J. Russel Young
1885-1898	Charles Denby
1898-1905	Edwin H. Conger
1905-1909	William W. Rockhill
1909-1913	William J. Calhoun
1913-1919	Paul S. Reinsch
1920-1921	Charles R. Crane
1921-1924	Jacob G. Schurman
1925-1929	John Van A. MacMurray
1929-1935	Nelson T. Johnson

Ambassadors

1935-1941	Nelson T. Johnson
1941-1944	Clarence E. Gauss
1944-1945	Patrick J. Hurley
1946-1950	J. Leighton Stuart

Ministers

(to China on Taiwan)

1950-1953	Karl L. Rankin

Ambassadors

(to China on Taiwan)

1953-1957	Karl L. Rankin
1958-1962	Everett F. Drumwright
1962-1963	Alan G. Kirk
1963-1966	Jerauld Wright
1966-1974	Walter P. McConaughy

Colombia

Ministers Plenipotentiary

1823-1826	Richard C. Anderson, Jr.
1826-1829	William Henry Harrison
1829-1833	Thomas P. Moore

Charges d'Affaires

1833-1837	Robert B. McAfee
1837-1842	James Semple
1842-1844	William M. Blackford
1845-1849	Benjamin A. Bidlack
1849-1850	Thomas M. Foote
1851-1853	Yelverton P. King
1853-1854	James S. Green

Ministers

1854-1857	James B. Bowlin
1859-1861	George W. Jones
1861-1867	Allan A. Burton
1867-1869	Peter J. Sullivan
1869-1872	Stephen A. Hurlbut
1873-1876	William L. Scruggs
1878-1882	Ernest Dichman
1882-1886	William L. Scruggs

EEMP

1886-1889	Dabney H. Maury

1889-1893	John T. Abbott
1893-1897	Luther F. McKinney
1897-1903	Charles B. Hart
1903-1904	Arthur M. Beaupre
1904-1905	William W. Russell
1905-1907	John Barrett
1907-1909	Thomas C. Dawson
1909-1911	Elliott Northcott
1911-1913	James T. DuBois
1913-1916	Thaddeus A. Thomson
1917-1922	Hoffman Philip
1922-1928	Samuel H. Piles
1928-1933	Jefferson Caffery
1933-1934	Sheldon Whitehouse
1934-1937	William Dawson
1938-1939	Spruille Braden

Ambassadors

1939-1942	Spruille Braden
1942-1944	Arthur Bliss Lane
1944-1947	John C. Wiley
1947-1951	Willard L. Beaulac
1951-1953	Capus M. Waynick
1953-1955	Rudolph E. Schoenfeld
1955-1957	Philip W. Bonsal
1957-1959	John M. Cabot
1959-1961	Dempster McIntosh
1961-1964	Fulton Freeman
1964-1966	Covey T. Oliver
1966-1969	Reynold E. Carlson
1969-1970	Jack H. Vaughn
1970-1973	Leonard J. Saccio
1973-1976	Viron P. Vaky
1976-1977	Phillip V. Sanchez
1977-1980	Diego C. Asencio
1980-1983	Thomas D. Boyatt
1983-1985	Lewis A. Tambs
1985-	Charles A. Gillespie, Jr.

Comoros

Ambassadors

1986-	Robert B. Keating

Costa Rica

Special Envoys

1852	Robert M. Walsh

EEMP

1853-1854	Solon Borland

Ministers

1858-1859	Mirabeau B. Lamar
1859-1861	Alexander Dimitry
1861-1867	Charles N. Riotte
1867-1868	Albert G. Lawrence
1868-1873	Jacob B. Blair
1873-1879	George Williamson
1879-1882	Cornelius A. Logan

EEMP

1882-1891	Henry C. Hall
1891-1893	Richard C. Shannon
1893-1897	Lewis Baker
1897-1911	William M. Merry
1911-1913	Lewis Einstein
1913-1919	Edward J. Hale
1922-1929	Roy T. Davis
1929-1930	H. F. Arthur Schoenfeld
1930-1933	Charles C. Eberhardt

1933-1937	Leo R. Sack
1937-1941	William H. Hornibrook
1941-1942	Arthur Bliss Lane
1942-1943	Robert M. Scotten

Ambassadors

1943-1944	Fay A. Des Portes
1944-1947	Hallett Johnson
1947	Walter J. Donnelly
1947-1949	Nathaniel Davis
1949-1950	Joseph Flack
1951-1953	Philip B. Fleming
1953-1954	Robert C. Hill
1954-1958	Robert F. Woodward
1958-1961	Whiting Willauer
1961-1967	Raymond Telles
1967-1969	Clarence A. Boonstra
1970-1972	Walter C. Ploeser
1972-1974	Viron P. Vaky
1974-1977	Terence A. Todman
1977-1980	Marvin Weissman
1980-1983	Francis J. McNeil
1983-1985	Curtin Winsor, Jr.
1985-	Lewis A. Tambs

Cuba

EEMP

1902-1905	Herbert G. Squiers
1905-1909	Edwin V. Morgan
1909-1911	John B. Jackson
1911-1913	Arthur M. Beaupre
1913-1919	William E. Gonzales
1919-1922	Boaz W. Long

Ambassadors

1923-1927	Enoch H. Crowder
1927-1929	Nobel B. Judah
1929-1933	Harry F. Guggenheim
1933-1934	Sumner Welles
1934-1937	Jefferson Caffery
1937-1940	J. Butler Wright
1940-1941	George S. Messersmith
1941-1945	Spruille Braden
1945-1948	R. Henry Norweb
1948-1951	Robert Butler
1951-1953	Willard L. Beaulac
1953-1957	Arthur Gardner
1957-1959	Earl E. T. Smith
1959-1960	Philip W. Bonsal
1961	Embassy closed

Cyprus

Ambassadors

1960-1964	Fraser Wilkins
1964-1969	Taylor G. Belcher
1969-1973	David H. Popper
1973-1974	Robert J. McCloskey
1974	Rodger P. Davies
1974-1978	William R. Crawford
1978-1981	Galen L. Stone
1981-1984	Raymond C. Ewing
1984-	Richard W. Boehm

Czechoslovakia

EEMP

1919-1921	Richard Crane
1921-1930	Lewis Einstein

1930-1932	Abraham C. Ratshesky
1933-1934	Francis White
1934-1937	J. Butler Wright
1937-1939	Wilbur J. Carr
1939	Legation closed
1941-1945	Legation in London
1941-1943	Anthony J. Drexel Biddle, Jr.

Ambassadors

1943-1944	Anthony J. Drexel Biddle, Jr.
1944-1948	Laurence A. Steinhardt
1948-1949	Joseph E. Jacobs
1949-1952	Ellis O. Briggs
1952-1953	George Wadsworth
1953-1958	U. Alexis Johnson
1958-1960	John M. Allison
1960-1961	Christian M. Ravndal
1961-1962	Edward T. Wailes
1962-1966	Outerbridge Horsey
1966-1969	Jacob D. Beam
1969-1972	Malcolm Toon
1972-1975	Albert W. Sherer, Jr.
1976-1978	Thomas R. Byrne
1979-1980	Francis J. Meehan
1981-1983	Jack F. Matlock, Jr.
1984-	William H. Luers

Dahomey

(See Benin for later representation.)

Ambassadors

1960-1961	R. Borden Reams
1961-1964	Robinson McIlvaine
1964-1969	Clinton E. Knox
1969-1972	Matthew J. Lorram, Jr.
1972-1974	Robert Anderson
1974-1976	James B. Engle

Democratic Republic of the Congo

(Kinshasa; see Zaire for later representation.)

Ambassadors

1960-1961	Clare H. Timberlake
1961-1964	Edmund A. Gullion
1964-1967	G. McMurtrie Godley
1967-1969	Robert H. McBride
1969-1974	Sheldon B. Vance

Denmark

Special Ministers

1811-1812	George W. Irving

Charges d'Affaires

1827-1835	Henry Wheaton
1835-1841	Jonathan F. Woodside
1841-1842	Isaac Rand Jackson
1843-1847	William W. Irwin
1847-1849	Robert P. Flennikan
1849-1851	Walter Forward
1852-1853	Miller Grieve
1853-1854	Henry Bedinger

Ministers

1854-1858	Henry Bedinger
1858-1861	James M. Buchanan
1861-1865	Bradford R. Wood

1865-1870	George H. Yeaman
1870-1876	M. J. Cramer
1882-1883	J. P. Wickersham
1883-1885	Wickham Hoffman
1885-1890	Rasmus B. Anderson

EEMP

1890-1893	Clark E. Carr
1893-1897	John E. Risley
1897-1905	Laurits S. Swenson
1905-1907	Thomas J. O'Brien
1907-1918	Maurice F. Egan
1919-1921	Norman Hapgood
1921-1926	John D. Prince
1926-1930	H. Percival Dodge
1930-1931	Ralph H. Booth
1931-1933	Frederick W. B. Coleman
1933-1936	Ruth Bryan Owen
1937-1939	Alvin M. Owsley
1939-1945	Ray Atherton
1945-1946	Michael B. Davis
1946-1947	Josiah Marvel, Jr.

Ambassadors

1947-1949	Josiah Marvel, Jr.
1949-1952	Eugenie Anderson
1953-1957	Robert D. Coe
1957-1961	Val Peterson
1961-1964	William M. Blair, Jr.
1964-1968	Katherine E. White
1968-1969	Angier Biddle Duke
1969-1971	Guilford Dudley, Jr.
1971-1972	Fred J. Russell
1973-1975	Philip K. Crowe
1975-1978	John Gunther Dean
1978-1981	Warren D. Manshel
1981-1983	John L. Loeb, Jr.
1984-	Terence A. Todman

Djibouti

Charges d'Affaires

1977-1980	Walter S. Clarke

Ambassadors

1980-1982	Jerrold M. North
1983-1985	Alvin P. Adams, Jr.
1985-	John P. Ferriter

Dominica

Ambassadors

1979-1981	Sally A. Shelton
1981	Milan D. Bish
1981	Embassy closed

Dominican Republic

(Santo Domingo 1883-1895.)

Charges d'Affaires

1883-1885	John M. Langston
1885-1891	John E. W. Thompson
1891-1893	John S. Durgan
1893-1897	Henry M. Smythe
1897-1904	William F. Powell

Ministers

1904-1907	Thomas C. Dawson
1907-1909	Fenton R. McCreery
1909-1910	Horace G. Knowles
1910-1913	William W. Russell

EEMP

1913-1915	James M. Sullivan
1915-1925	William W. Russell
1925-1929	Evan E. Young
1929-1931	Charles B. Curtis
1931-1937	H. F. Arthur Schoenfeld
1937-1940	R. Henry Norweb
1940-1942	Robert M. Scotten
1942-1943	Avra M. Warren

Ambassadors

1943-1944	Avra M. Warren
1944-1945	Ellis O. Briggs
1945-1946	Joseph M. McGurk
1946-1948	George H. Butler
1948-1952	Ralph H. Ackerman
1952-1953	Phelps Phelps
1953-1957	William T. Pheiffer
1957-1960	Joseph S. Farland
1962-1964	John Bartlow Martin
1964-1966	W. Tapley Bennett, Jr.
1966-1969	John H. Crimmins
1969-1973	Francis E. Meloy, Jr.
1973-1978	Robert A. Hurwitch
1978-1982	Robert L. Yost
1982-1985	Robert Anderson
1985-	Lowell C. Kilday

Ecuador

Special Agents

1844	Delazon Smith

Charges d'Affaires

1848-1849	Vanbrugh Livingston
1849-1850	John T. Van Allen
1850-1853	Courtland Cushing
1853-1854	Philo White

Ministers

1854-1858	Philo White
1858-1861	Charles R. Buckalew
1861-1866	Frederick Hassaurek
1866-1867	William T. Coggeshall
1869-1875	E. Rumsey Wing
1875-1892	Christian Willweber

EEMP

1892-1893	Rowland B. Mahany
1895-1897	James D. Tillman
1897-1905	Archibald J. Sampson
1905-1907	Joseph W. J. Lee
1907-1911	Williams C. Fox
1911-1912	Evan E. Young
1913-1922	Charles S. Hartman
1922-1930	Gerhard A. Bading
1930-1934	William Dawson
1934-1938	Antonio C. Gonzalez
1938-1942	Boaz W. Long

Ambassadors

1942-1943	Boaz W. Long
1943-1947	Robert M. Scotten
1947-1950	John F. Simmons

1951-1953	Paul C. Daniels
1954-1956	Sheldon T. Mills
1956-1960	Christian Ravndal
1960-1965	Maurice M. Bernbaum
1965-1968	Wymberley D. Coerr
1968-1970	Edson O. Sessions
1970-1973	Findley Burns, Jr.
1973-1976	Robert C. Brewster
1976-1978	Richard J. Bloomfield
1978-1982	Raymond E. Gonzalez
1983-1985	Samuel F. Hart
1985-	Fernando E. Rondon

Egypt

(See United Arab Republic and Arab Republic of Egypt for later representation.)

Agents

1893-1897	Frederic C. Penfield
1897-1899	Thomas S. Harrison
1899-1903	John G. Long
1903-1905	John W. Riddle
1905-1909	Lewis M. Iddings
1909-1913	Peter A. Jay
1913-1916	Olney Arnold
1917-1921	Hampson Gary
1921-1922	J. Morton Howell

EEMP

1922-1927	J. Morton Howell
1928-1930	Franklin M. Gunther
1930-1933	William M. Jardine
1933-1941	Bert Fish
1941-1944	Alexander C. Kirk
1944-1946	S. Pinkney Tuck

Ambassadors

1946-1948	S. Pinkney Tuck
1948-1949	Stanton Griffis
1949-1955	Jefferson Caffery
1955-1956	Henry A. Bryoade
1956-1958	Raymond A. Hare

El Salvador

(See Salvador for earlier representation.)

EEMP

1929-1931	Warren D. Robbins
1931-1933	Charles B. Curtis
1934-1937	Frank P. Corrigan
1937-1942	Robert Frazer
1942-1943	Walter Thurston

Ambassadors

1943-1944	Walter Thurston
1944-1947	John F. Simmons
1947-1949	Albert F. Nufer
1949-1952	George P. Shaw
1952-1953	Angier Biddle Duke
1953-1954	Michael J. McDermott
1954-1955	Robert C. Hill
1955-1957	Thomas C. Mann
1957-1961	Thorsten V. Kalijarvi
1961-1964	Murat W. Williams
1964-1968	Raul H. Castro
1968-1971	William G. Bowdler
1971-1973	Henry E. Catto, Jr.
1974-1976	James F. Campbell
1976-1977	Ignacio E. Lozano, Jr.
1977-1980	Frank J. Devine

1980-1981	Robert E. White
1981-1983	Deane R. Hinton
1983-1985	Thomas R. Pickering
1985-	Edwin G. Corr

Equatorial Guinea

Ambassadors

1968-1969	Albert W. Sherer, Jr.
1969-1972	Lewis Hoffacker
1972-1975	C. Robert Moore
1975-1976	Herbert J. Spiro
1977-1979	Vacant
1979-1980	Mable Murphy Smythe
1980-1981	Hume A. Horan
1981-1984	Alan M. Hardy
1985-	Francis S. Ruddy

Estonia

EEMP

1922-1931	Frederick W. B. Coleman
1931-1933	Robert P. Skinner
1933-1936	John Van A. MacMurray
1936-1937	Arthur Bliss Lane
1937-1938	Frederick A. Sterling
1938-1941	John C. Wiley
1941	Legation closed

Ethiopia

(See Abyssinia for earlier representation.)

Ministers

1927-1934	Addison E. Southard
1936-1937	Cornelius Van H. Engert
1937-1943	Legation closed
1943-1944	John K. Caldwell

EEMP

1944-1945	John K. Caldwell
1945-1947	Felix Cole
1947-1949	George R. Merrell

Ambassadors

1949-1951	George R. Merrell
1951-1952	J. Rives Childs
1953-1957	Joseph Simonson
1957-1960	Don C. Bliss
1960-1963	Arthur L. Richards
1963-1966	Edward M. Korry
1966-1967	Robert Donhauser
1967-1971	William O. Hall
1971-1974	E. Ross Adair
1975-1976	Arthur W. Hummel
1977	Vacant
1978-1980	Frederic L. Chapin
1981-1982	Vacant
1983-1985	David A. Korn
1985-	Vacant

Federal Republic of Germany

(See Germany for earlier representation.)

U.S. High Commissioners

1949-1952	John J. McCloy

1952-1953	Walter J. Donnelly
1953-1955	James B. Conant

Ambassadors

1955-1957	James B. Conant
1957-1959	David K. E. Bruce
1959-1963	Walter C. Dowling
1963-1968	George C. McGhee
1968-1969	Henry Cabot Lodge
1969-1972	Kenneth Rush
1972-1976	Martin J. Hillenbrand
1976-1981	Walter J. Stoessel, Jr.
1981-1985	Arthur F. Burns
1985-	Richard R. Burt

Federation of Central America

Charges d'Affaires

1825-1826	John Williams
1827-1828	William B. Rochester
1833-1839	Charles G. DeWitt

Special Diplomatic Agents

1839-1840	John L. Stephens
1841-1842	William S. Murphy

Fiji

Ambassadors

1972	Kenneth Franzheim, II
1973	Vacant
1974-1978	Armistead I. Selden, Jr.
1978-1980	John P. Condon
1980-1981	William Bodde, Jr.
1982-1984	Fred J. Eckert
1985-1986	C. Edward Dillery

Finland

EEMP

1921-1924	Charles L. Kagey
1925	John B. Stetson, Jr.
1925-1930	Alfred J. Pearson
1930-1933	Edward E. Brodie
1933-1937	Edward Albright
1937-1944	H. F. Arthur Schoenfeld
1945-1947	Maxwell M. Hamilton
1947-1950	Avra M. Warren
1950-1952	John M. Cabot
1952-1955	Jack McFall

Ambassadors

1955-1959	John D. Hickerson
1959-1960	Edson O. Sessions
1961-1963	Bernard A. Gufler
1963-1964	Carl T. Rowan
1964-1969	Tyler Thompson
1969-1973	Val Peterson
1973-1975	V. John Krehbiel
1975-1977	Mark Evans Austad
1977-1980	Rozanne L. Ridgway
1980-1981	James E. Goodby
1981-1985	Keith F. Nyborg
1986-	Rockwell A. Schnabel

France

Charges d'Affaires

1790-1792	William Short

Ministers Plenipotentiary

1792-1794	Gouverneur Morris
1794-1796	James Monroe

EEMP

1797-1798	Elbridge Gerry
1799-1800	Oliver Ellsworth
1799-1800	William V. Murray
1799-1800	William R. Davie
1801-1804	Robert B. Livingston
1804-1810	James Monroe

Ministers Plenipotentiary

1810-1811	Jonathan Russell
1811-1812	Joel Barlow
1813-1815	William H. Crawford

EEMP

1815-1823	Albert Gallatin
1823-1829	James Brown
1829-1832	William C. Rives

Charges d'Affaires

1833	Leavitt Harris

EEMP

1833-1835	Edward Livingston
1836-1842	Lewis Call
1844-1846	William R. King
1847-1849	Richard Rush
1849-1853	William C. Rives
1853-1859	John Y. Mason
1860-1861	Charles J. Faulkner
1861-1864	William L. Dayton
1865-1866	John Bigelow
1866-1869	John A. Dix
1869-1877	Elihu B. Washburne
1877-1881	Edward F. Noyes
1881-1885	Levi P. Morton
1885-1892	Robert M. McLane
1892-1893	T. Jefferson Coolidge

Ambassadors

1893-1897	James B. Eustis
1897-1905	Robert S. McCormick
1906-1909	Henry White
1909-1912	Robert Bacon
1912-1914	Myron T. Herrick
1914-1919	William G. Sharp
1919-1921	Hugh C. Wallace
1921-1929	Myron T. Herrick
1929-1933	Walter E. Edge
1933-1936	Jesse I. Straus
1936-1940	William C. Bullitt
1940-1942	William D. Leahy
1942-1944	Embassy Closed
1944-1949	Jefferson Caffery
1949-1952	David K. E. Bruce
1952-1953	James C. Dunn
1953-1957	C. Douglas Dillon
1957-1961	Amory Houghton
1961-1962	James M. Gavin
1962-1968	Charles E. Bohlen
1968-1970	R. Sargent Shriver, Jr.
1970-1972	Arthur K. Watson
1973-1974	John N. Irwin, II
1974-1977	Kenneth Rush

1977-1981	Arthur A. Hartman
1981-1985	Evan G. Galbraith
1985-	Joe M. Rodgers

Gabon

Ambassadors

1960-1961	W. Wendell Blancke
1961-1965	Charles F. Darlington
1965-1969	David M. Bane
1969-1970	Richard Funkhouser
1970-1975	John A. McKesson, III
1975-1977	Andrew L. Steigman
1978-1981	Arthur T. Tienken
1981-1984	Francis T. McNamara
1984-	Larry C. Williamson

Gambia

Ambassadors

1965-1966	Mercer Cook
1966-1967	William R. Rivkin
1967-1970	L. Dean Brown
1970-1973	G. Edward Clark
1973-1977	O. Rudolph Aggrey
1977-1980	Herman J. Cohen
1980-1982	Larry G. Piper
1983-1984	Vacant
1984-	Robert T. Hennemeyer

German Democratic Republic

(See Germany for earlier representation.)

Ambassadors

1974-1976	John Sherman Cooper
1977-1980	David B. Bolen
1980-1982	Herbert S. Okun
1983-1985	Rozanne L. Ridgway
1985-	Francis J. Meehan

Germany

(See also Prussia; see Federal Republic of Germany and German Democratic Republic for later representation.)

EEMP

1871-1874	George Bancroft
1875-1876	J. C. Bancroft Davis
1879-1882	Andrew D. White
1882-1884	Aaron A. Sargent
1884-1885	John A. Kasson
1885-1889	George H. Pendleton
1889-1893	William W. Phelps
1893-1894	Theodore Runyon

Ambassadors

1894-1896	Theodore Runyon
1896-1897	Edwin F. Uhl
1897-1902	Andrew D. White
1902-1908	Charlemagne Tower
1908-1911	David Hill
1911-1913	John G. A. Leishman
1913-1917	James W. Gerard
1917-1922	Embassy closed
1922-1925	Alanson B. Houghton
1925-1930	Jacob G. Shurman
1930-1933	Frederic M. Sackett, Jr.

1933-1938	William E. Dodd
1938-1939	Hugh R. Wilson
1939-1941	Vacant
1941-1949	Embassy closed

U. S. Political Advisors

1945-1949	Robert D. Murphy

Ghana

Charges d'Affaires

1957	Donald W. Lamm

Ambassadors

1957-1960	Wilson C. Flake
1960-1962	Francis H. Russell
1962-1965	William P. Mahoney, Jr.
1966-1968	Franklin H. Williams
1968-1971	Thomas W. McElhiney
1971-1974	Fred L. Hadsel
1974-1976	Shirley Temple Black
1976-1979	Robert P. Smith
1979-1983	Thomas W. M. Smith
1983-	Robert E. Fritts

Great Britain

Ministers Plenipotentiary

1792-1796	Thomas Pinckney

Envoys Extraordinary

1794-1795	John Jay

Ministers Plenipotentiary

1796-1803	Rufus King
1803-1807	James Monroe
1806-1811	William Pinkney

Commissioners

1806-1807	James Monroe
1806-1811	William Pinkney

Charges d'Affaires

1811-1812	Jonathan Russell
1812-1814	Relations suspended

Ministers Plenipotentiary and Envoys

1814	John Quincy Adams
1814	James A. Bayard
1814	Henry Clay
1814	Jonathan Russell
1814	Albert Gallatin

EEMP

1815-1817	John Quincy Adams
1817-1825	Richard Rush
1825-1826	Rufus King
1826-1827	Albert Gallatin
1828-1829	James Barbour
1829-1831	Louis McLane
1831-1832	Martin Van Buren

Charges d'Affaires

1832-1836	Aaron Vail

EEMP

1836-1841	Andrew Stevenson
1841-1845	Edward Everett
1845-1846	Louis McLane
1846-1849	George Bancroft
1849-1852	Abbott Lawrence
1852-1853	Joseph R. Ingersoll
1853-1856	James Buchanan
1856-1861	George M. Dallas
1861-1868	Charles Francis Adams
1868-1869	Reverdy Johnson
1869-1870	J. Lothrop Motley
1870-1876	Robert C. Schenck
1876-1877	Edwards Pierrepont
1877-1879	John S. Welsh
1880-1885	James Russell Lowell
1885-1889	Edward J. Phelps
1889-1893	Robert T. Lincoln

Ambassadors

1893-1897	Thomas F. Bayard
1897-1899	John Hay
1899-1905	Joseph H. Choate
1905-1913	Whitelaw Reid
1913-1918	Walter H. Page
1918-1921	John W. Davis
1921-1923	George Harvey
1923-1925	Frank B. Kellogg
1925-1929	Alanson B. Houghton
1929-1932	Charles G. Dawes
1932-1933	Andrew W. Mellon
1933-1938	Robert W. Bingham
1938-1940	Joseph P. Kennedy
1941-1946	John G. Winant
1946	W. Averell Harriman
1947-1950	Lewis W. Douglas
1950-1953	Walter S. Gifford
1953-1957	Winthrop W. Aldrich
1957-1961	John Hay Whitney
1961-1969	David K. E. Bruce
1969-1974	Walter H. Annenberg
1975-1976	Elliot L. Richardson
1976-1977	Ann Legendre Armstrong
1977-1981	Kingman Brewster, Jr.
1981-1983	John J. Louis, Jr.
1984-	Charles H. Price

Greece

Ministers

1868-1871	Charles K. Tuckerman
1871-1873	John M. Francis
1873-1882	John M. Read, Jr.
1882-1885	Eugene Schuyler
1885-1892	J. Walker Fearn
1892-1893	Truxtun Beale

EEMP

1893-1897	Eben Alexander
1897-1899	William W. Rockhill
1899-1900	Arthur S. Hardy
1900-1902	Charles S. Francis
1902-1907	John B. Jackson
1907-1909	Richmond Pearson
1909-1912	George H. Moses
1912-1913	Jacob G. Schurman
1914-1921	Garrett Droppers
1924-1926	Irwin B. Laughlin
1926-1931	Robert P. Skinner
1933-1941	Lincoln MacVeagh
1941-1942	Anthony J. Drexel Biddle, Jr.

Ambassadors

1942-1943	Anthony J. Drexel Biddle, Jr.

1943	Alexander C. Kirk
1943-1948	Lincoln MacVeagh
1948-1950	Henry F. Grady
1950-1953	John E. Peurifoy
1953-1956	Cavendish W. Cannon
1956-1957	George V. Allen
1958-1959	James W. Riddleberger
1959-1961	Ellis O. Briggs
1961-1965	Henry R. Labouisse
1965-1969	Phillips Talbot
1969-1974	Henry J. Tasca
1974-1977	Jack B. Kubisch
1977-1978	Vacant
1978-1981	Robert J. McCloskey
1981-1985	Monteagle Stearns
1985-	Robert V. Keeley

Grenada

Ambassadors

1974-1977	Theodore R. Britton, Jr.
1977-1979	Frank V. Ortiz, Jr.
1979-1981	Sally A. Shelton
1982-1983	Vacant

Charges d'Affaires

1984-1985	Loren E. Lawrence
1985-	Roy L. Haverkamp

Guatemala

Charges d'Affaires

1848-1849	Elijah Hise
1849-1850	E. George Squier

Ministers

1853-1854	Solon Borland
1854-1858	John L. Marling
1858-1860	Beverly L. Clarke
1861-1864	Elisha O. Crosby
1865-1869	FitzHenry Warren
1869-1872	Silas A. Hudson
1873-1879	George Williamson
1879-1882	Cornelius A. Logan

EEMP

1882-1891	Henry C. Hall
1891-1893	Romualdo Pacheco
1893-1896	Pierce M. B. Young
1896-1897	Macgrane Coxe
1897-1902	W. Godfrey Hunter
1902-1907	Leslie Combs
1907-1908	Joseph W. J. Lee
1908-1909	William Heimke
1909-1910	William F. Sands
1910-1913	R. S. Reynolds Hitt
1913-1919	William H. Leavell
1919-1921	Benton McMillin
1921-1922	Roy T. Davis
1922-1929	Arthur H. Geissler
1929-1933	Sheldon Whitehouse
1933-1936	Matthew E. Hanna
1936-1943	Fay A. Des Portes
1943-1945	Boaz W. Long
1945-1948	Edwin J. Kyle
1948-1951	Richard C. Patterson, Jr.
1951-1953	Rudolf E. Schoenfeld
1953-1954	John E. Peurifoy
1954-1955	Norman Armour
1955-1958	Edward J. Sparks
1958-1959	Lester D. Mallory
1959-1961	John J. Muccio

1961-1965	John O. Bell
1965-1967	John G. Mein
1967-1968	Max V. Krebs
1968-1971	Nathaniel Davis
1971-1973	William G. Bowdler
1973-1976	Francis E. Meloy, Jr.
1976-1979	Davis E. Boster
1979-1980	Frank V. Ortiz, Jr.
1981-1984	Frederic L. Chapin
1984-	Alberto M. Piedra

Guinea

Ambassadors

1959-1961	John H. Morrow
1961-1963	William Attwood
1963-1966	James I. Loeb
1966-1969	Robinson McIlvaine
1970-1972	Albert W. Sherer, Jr.
1972-1975	Terrence A. Todman
1975-1977	William C. Harrop
1977-1980	Oliver S. Crosby
1980-1983	Allen Clayton Davis
1983-	James D. Rosenthal

Guinea-Bissau

Ambassadors

1976-1977	Melissa F. Wells
1977-1980	Edward Marks
1980-1983	Peter J. DeVos
1983-1984	Wesley W. Eagan, Jr.
1985-	Vacant

Guyana

Ambassadors

1964-1969	Delmar R. Carlson
1969-1974	Spencer M. King
1974-1976	Max V. Krebs
1977-1979	John R. Burke
1979-1981	George B. Roberts, Jr.
1981-1983	Gerald B. Thomas

Haiti

Commissioners

1862-1865	Benjamin F. Whidden
1865-1866	H. E. Peck

Ministers

1866-1867	H. E. Peck
1868-1869	Gideon H. Hollister
1869-1877	Ebenezer D. Bassett
1877-1885	John M. Langston
1885-1891	John E. W. Thompson
1891-1893	John S. Durham
1893-1897	Henry M. Smythe

EEMP

1897-1905	William F. Powell
1905-1913	Henry W. Furniss
1913-1914	Madison R. Smith
1914-1925	Arthur Bailly-Blanchard
1930-1932	Dana G. Munro
1932-1935	Norman Armour
1935-1937	George A. Gordon

1937-1940	Ferdinand L. Mayer
1940-1943	John C. White

Ambassadors

1943-1944	John C. White
1944-1946	Orme Wilson
1946-1948	Harold H. Tittmann, Jr.
1948-1951	William E. De Courcy
1951-1953	Howard K. Travers
1953-1957	Roy T. Davis
1957-1960	Gerald A. Drew
1960-1961	Robert Newbegin
1961-1963	Raymond L. Thurston
1963-1967	Benson E. L. Timmons, III
1967-1969	Claude G. Ross
1969-1973	Clinton E. Knox
1973-1977	Heyward Isham
1977-1980	William B. Jones
1980-1981	Henry L. Kimelman
1981-1983	Ernest Preeg
1984-	Clayton E. McManaway, Jr.

Hawaiian Islands

Commissioners

1843-1846	George Brown
1846-1849	Anthony Ten Eyck
1849	Charles Eames
1850-1853	Luther Severence
1853-1858	David L. Gregg
1858-1861	James W. Borden
1861-1863	Thomas J. Dryer

Ministers

1863-1866	James McBride
1866-1868	Edward M. McCook
1869-1877	Henry A. Pierce
1877	James M. Comly
1877-1885	Rollin M. Daggett
1885-1890	George W. Merrill

EEMP

1890-1893	John L. Stevens
1893	James H. Blount
1893-1896	Albert S. Willis
1897	Harold M. Sewall

Holy See

(See Papal States for earlier representation.)

Ambassadors

1984-	William A. Wilson

Honduras

EEMP

1853-1854	Solon Borland

Ministers

1858-1860	Beverly L. Clarke
1862-1863	James R. Partridge
1863-1866	Thomas H. Clay
1866-1869	Richard H. Rousseau
1869-1873	Henry Baxter
1873-1879	George Williamson
1879-1882	Cornelius A. Logan

EEMP

1882-1891	Henry C. Hall
1891-1893	Romualdo Pacheco
1893-1896	Pierce M. B. Young
1896-1897	Macgrane Coxe
1897-1902	W. Godfrey Hunter
1902-1907	Leslie Combs
1907-1908	H. Percival Dodge
1908-1909	William B. Sorsby
1909-1911	Fenton R. McCreery
1911-1913	Charles D. White
1913-1918	John Ewing
1918-1921	T. Sambola Jones
1921-1925	Franklin E. Morales
1925-1929	George T. Summerlin
1929-1934	Julius G. Lay
1935-1937	Leo J. Keena
1937-1943	John D. Erwin

Ambassadors

1943-1947	John D. Erwin
1947	Paul C. Daniels
1947-1950	Herbert S. Bursley
1951-1954	John D. Erwin
1954-1958	Whiting Willauer
1958-1960	Robert Newbegin
1960-1965	Charles R. Burrows
1965-1969	Joseph J. Jova
1969-1973	Hewson A. Ryan
1973-1976	Philip V. Sanchez
1976-1977	Ralph E. Becker
1977-1980	Mari-Luci Jarimillo
1980-1981	Jack R. Binns
1981-1985	John D. Negroponte
1985-	John A. Ferch

Hungary

EEMP

1922-1927	Theodore Brentano
1927-1930	J. Butler Wright
1930-1933	Nicholas Roosevelt
1933-1941	John F. Montgomery
1941	Herbert Claiborne Pell
1941-1945	Legation closed
1945-1947	H. F. Arthur Schoenfeld
1947-1949	Selden Chapin
1949-1951	Nathaniel P. Davis
1951-1956	Christian M. Ravndal
1956-1957	Edward T. Wailes
1957-1967	Vacant

Ambassadors

1967-1969	Martin J. Hillenbrand
1969-1973	Alfred Puhan
1973-1975	Richard F. Pedersen
1975-1976	Eugene V. McAuliffe
1977-1980	Philip M. Kaiser
1980-1983	Harry E. Bergold, Jr.

Iceland

EEMP

1941-1942	Lincoln MacVeagh
1942-1944	Leland B. Morris
1944-1946	Louis G. Dreyfus, Jr.
1948-1949	Richard P. Butrick
1949-1954	Edward B. Lawson
1954-1955	John J. Muccio

Ambassadors

1955-1959	John J. Muccio
1960-1961	Tyler Thompson
1961-1967	James K. Penfield
1967-1969	Karl F. Rolvaag
1969-1972	Luther J. Replogle
1972-1976	Frederick Irving
1976-1978	James J. Blake
1978-1981	Richard A. Ericson, Jr.
1981-1985	Marshall Brement
1985-	Nicholas Ruwe

India

Charges d'Affaires

1946-1947	George R. Merrell

Ambassadors

1947-1948	Henry F. Grady
1948-1951	Loy W. Henderson
1951-1953	Chester Bowles
1953-1955	George V. Allen
1955-1956	John Sherman Cooper
1956-1961	Ellsworth Bunker
1961-1963	John Kenneth Galbraith
1963-1969	Chester Bowles
1969-1972	Kenneth B. Keating
1973-1975	Daniel P. Moynihan
1975-1976	William B. Saxbe
1977-1980	Robert F. Goheen
1981-1985	Harry G. Barnes, Jr.
1985-	John Gunther Dean

Indonesia

Ambassadors

1949-1953	H. Merle Cochran
1953-1957	Hugh S. Cumming, Jr.
1957-1958	John M. Allison
1958-1965	Howard P. Jones
1965-1969	Marshall Green
1969-1974	Francis J. Galbraith
1973-1977	David D. Newsom
1977-1981	Edward E. Masters
1982	Vacant
1983-1985	John H. Holdridge
1986-	Paul D. Wolfowitz

Iran

(See Persia for earlier representation.)

EEMP

1935-1936	William H. Hornibrook
1936-1939	Vacant
1939-1944	Louis G. Dreyfus, Jr.

Ambassadors

1944-1945	Leland B. Morris
1945-1946	Wallace Murray
1946-1948	George V. Allen
1948-1950	John C. Wiley
1950-1951	Henry F. Grady
1951-1955	Loy W. Henderson
1955-1958	Selden Chapin
1959-1961	Edward T. Wailes
1961-1965	Julius C. Holmes
1965-1969	Armin H. Meyer
1969-1972	Douglas MacArthur, II

1972-1973	Joseph S. Farland
1973-1977	Richard Helms
1977-1979	William H. Sullivan
1979-1980	Vacant
1980	Embassy closed

Iraq

Charges d'Affaires

1931-1932	Alexander K. Sloan

Ministers

1932-1942	Paul Knabenshue
1942-1943	Thomas M. Wilson

EEMP

1943-1945	Loy W. Henderson
1946	Lowell C. Pinkerton

Ambassadors

1946-1948	George Wadsworth
1948-1952	Edward S. Crocker, II
1952-1954	Burton Y. Berry
1954-1958	Waldemar J. Gallman
1958-1962	John D. Jernegan
1963-1967	Robert C. Strong
1967-1985	Embassy closed

Charges d'Affaires

1985-	David G. Newton

Ireland

(Irish Free State 1927-1937.)

EEMP

1927-1933	Frederick A. Sterling
1933-1934	W. W. McDowell
1935-1937	Alvin M. Owsley
1937-1940	John Cudahy
1940-1947	David Gray
1947-1950	George A. Garrett

Ambassadors

1950-1951	George A. Garrett
1951-1953	Francis P. Matthews
1953-1957	William Howard Taft, III
1957-1961	Scott McLeod
1961-1962	Edward G. Stockdale
1962-1964	Matthew H. McCloskey
1965-1968	Raymond R. Guest
1968-1969	Leo J. Sheridan
1969-1975	John D. J. Moore
1975-1977	Walter J. P. Curley, Jr.
1977-1981	William V. Shannon
1982-1983	Peter H. Dailey
1984-1985	Robert F. Kane
1986-	Margaret M. Heckler

Israel

Ambassadors

1948-1951	James G. McDonald
1951-1954	Monnett B. Davis
1954-1959	Edward B. Lawson
1959-1961	Ogden R. Reid
1961-1973	Walworth Barbour

1973-1975	Kenneth B. Keating
1975-1976	Malcolm Toon
1977-1985	Samuel L. Lewis
1985-	Thomas R. Pickering

Italy

(See Papal States, Sardinia, Sicily for earlier representation.)

EEMP

1861-1882	George P. Marsh
1882-1885	William W. Astor
1885-1889	John B. Stallo
1889-1892	Albert G. Porter
1892-1893	William Potter

Ambassadors

1893-1897	Wayne MacVeagh
1897-1900	William F. Draker
1900-1905	George V. L. Mayer
1905-1906	Henry White
1906-1909	Lloyd C. Griscom
1909-1911	John G. A. Leishman
1911-1913	Thomas J. O'Brien
1913-1919	Thomas N. Page
1921-1924	Richard W. Child
1924-1929	Henry P. Fletcher
1929-1933	John W. Garrett
1933-1936	Breckinridge Long
1936-1941	William Phillips
1941-1944	Embassy closed
1944-1946	Alexander C. Kirk
1946-1952	William C. Dunn
1952-1953	Ellsworth Bunker
1953-1956	Clare Boothe Luce
1956-1960	James D. Zellerbach
1961-1968	G. Frederick Reinhardt
1968-1969	H. Gardner Ackley
1969-1973	Graham A. Martin
1973-1977	John A. Volpe
1977-1981	Richard N. Gardner
1981-	Maxwell M. Rabb

Ivory Coast

Ambassadors

1960-1962	R. Borden Reams
1962-1965	James W. Wine
1965-1969	George A. Morgan
1969-1974	John F. Root
1974-1976	Robert S. Smith
1976-1979	Monteagle Stearns
1979-1983	Nancy V. Rawls
1984-	Robert H. Miller

Jamaica

Ambassadors

1962-1964	William C. Doherty
1965-1967	Wilson T. M. Beale, Jr.
1967-1969	Walter N. Tobriner
1969-1973	Vincent de Roulet
1974-1977	Sumner Gerard
1977-1978	Frederick Irving
1979-1982	Loren E. Lawrence
1983-1985	William A. Hewitt
1986-	Michael G. Sotirhos

Japan

Commissioners General

1855-1859	Townsend Harris

Ministers

1862-1865	Robert H. Pruyn
1866-1869	Robert B. Van Valkenburgh
1869-1870	Charles E. DeLong

EEMP

1870-1873	Charles E. DeLong
1873-1885	John A. Bingham
1885-1892	Richard B. Hubbard
1892-1893	Frank L. Coombs
1893-1897	Edwin Dun
1897-1902	Alfred E. Buck
1902-1906	Lloyd C. Griscom

Ambassadors

1906-1907	Luke E. Wright
1907-1911	Thomas J. O'Brien
1911-1913	Charles P. Bryan
1913-1917	George W. Guthrie
1917-1921	Roland S. Morris
1921-1923	Charles B. Warren
1923-1924	Cyrus E. Woods
1924-1925	Edgar A. Bancroft
1925-1929	Charles MacVeagh
1929-1930	William R. Castle, Jr.
1930-1932	W. Cameron Forbes
1932-1941	Joseph C. Grew
1941-1945	Embassy closed

Political Advisors

1945-1952	William J. Sebald

Ambassadors

1952-1953	Robert D. Murphy
1953-1956	John M. Allison
1956-1961	Douglas MacArthur, II
1961-1966	Edwin O. Reischauer
1966-1969	U. Alexis Johnson
1969-1972	Armin H. Meyer
1972-1973	Robert Stephen Ingersoll
1974-1977	James D. Hodgson
1977-	Michael J. Mansfield

Jordan

EEMP

1950-1952	Gerald A. Drew
1952	Joseph C. Green

Ambassadors

1952-1953	Joseph C. Green
1953-1958	Lester deWitt Mallory
1959-1961	Sheldon T. Mills
1961-1964	William B. Macomber, Jr.
1964-1966	Robert G. Barnes
1966-1967	Findley Burns, Jr.
1967-1970	Harrison M. Symmes
1970-1973	L. Dean Brown
1974-1978	Thomas R. Pickering
1978-1981	Nicholas A. Veliotes
1981-1984	Richard N. Viets
1984-	Paul H. Boeker

Kenya

Ambassadors

1964-1966	William Attwood
1966-1969	Glenn W. Ferguson
1969-1973	Robinson McIlvaine
1973-1977	Anthony D. Marshall
1977-1980	Wilbert J. LeMelle
1980-1983	William C. Harrop
1984-	Gerald E. Thomas

Khmer Republic

(See Cambodia for earlier representation.)

Ambassadors

1970-1973	Emory C. Swank
1974-1975	John Gunther Dean
1975	Embassy closed

Kiribati

Ambassadors

1980-1981	William Bodde, Jr.
1982	Fred J. Eckert
1982	Embassy closed

Korea

(See Republic of Korea for later representation.)

EEMP

1883-1885	Lucius H. Foote

Ministers

1887-1890	Hugh A. Dinsmore
1890-1894	Augustine Heard
1894-1897	John M. B. Sill
1897-1905	Horace N. Allen

EEMP

1905	Edwin V. Morgan
1905-1945	Annexed by Japan

Kuwait

Ambassadors

1961-1963	Parker T. Hart
1963-1969	Howard R. Cottam
1969-1971	John P. Walsh
1971-1976	William A. Stoltzfus, Jr.
1976-1979	Frank E. Maestrone
1979-1983	Francois M. Dickman
1984-	Anthony C. Quainton

Laos

EEMP

1950-1954	Donald R. Heath
1954-1955	Charles W. Yost

Ambassadors

1955-1956	Charles W. Yost
1956-1958	J. Graham Parsons
1958-1960	Horace H. Smith
1960-1962	Winthrop G. Brown
1962-1964	Leonard Unger
1964-1969	William H. Sullivan
1969-1973	G. McMurtrie Godley
1973-1975	Charles S. Whitehouse

Charges d'Affaires

1975-1978	Thomas J. Corcoran
1978-1979	George B. Roberts
1979-1982	Leo J. Moser
1982-1983	William W. Thomas, Jr.
1984-	Theresa A. Tull

Latvia

EEMP

1922-1931	Frederick W. B. Coleman
1931-1933	Robert P. Skinner
1933-1936	John Van A. MacMurray
1936-1937	Arthur Bliss Lane
1937-1938	Frederick A. Sterling
1938-1941	John C. Wiley
1941	Legation closed

Lebanon

Diplomatic Agents

1942-1944	George Wadsworth

EEMP

1944-1946	George Wadsworth
1946-1951	Lowell C. Pinkerton
1951-1953	Harold B. Minor

Ambassadors

1951-1953	Harold B. Minor
1953-1954	Raymond A. Hare
1955-1957	Donald R. Heath
1957-1961	Robert M. McClintock
1961-1965	Armin H. Meyer
1965-1970	Dwight J. Porter
1970-1974	William B. Buffum
1974-1976	G. McMurtrie Godley
1976	Francis E. Meloy, Jr.
1977-1978	Richard B. Parker
1978-1981	John Gunther Dean
1981-1983	Robert Sherwood Dillon
1984-	Reginald Bartholomew

Lesotho

Ambassadors

1971-1974	Charles J. Nelson
1974-1976	David J. Bolen
1976-1979	Donald R. Norland
1979-1981	John R. Clingerman
1982-1983	Keith Lapham Brown
1984-	S. L. Abbott

Liberia

Commissioners

1863-1866	Abraham Hanson

Ministers

1866-1870	Jahn Seys
1871-1878	J. Milton Turner
1878-1885	John H. Smyth
1888-1892	Ezekiel Smith
1892-1893	William D. McCoy
1895-1898	William H. Heard
1898-1902	Owen L. W. Smith
1902-1903	J. R. A. Crossland
1903-1910	Ernest Lyon
1910-1913	William D. Crum
1913-1914	George W. Buckner
1915-1917	James L. Curtis
1918-1921	Joseph L. Johnson
1921-1926	Solomon P. Hood
1927-1929	William T. Francis
1930-1933	Charles E. Mitchell

EEMP

1935-1946	Lester A. Walton
1946-1948	Raphael O. Lanier
1948-1949	Edward R. Dudley

Ambassadors

1949-1953	Edward R. Dudley
1953-1955	Jesse D. Locker
1955-1959	Richard Lee Jones
1959-1962	Elbert G. Mathews
1962-1965	Charles E. Rhetts
1965-1969	Ben H. Brown, Jr.
1969-1972	Samuel Z. Westerfield, Jr.
1972-1975	Melvin L. Manfull
1976-1979	W. Beverly Carter, Jr.
1979-1981	Robert P. Smith
1981-1985	William Lacy Swing
1985-	Edward J. Perkins

Libya

(Also known as Libyan Arab Republic.)

EEMP

1952-1954	Henry S. Villard

Ambassadors

1954-1958	John L. Tappin
1958-1963	J. Wesley Jones
1963-1965	E. Allen Lightner
1965-1969	David D. Newsom
1969-1972	Joseph Palmer, II

Charges d'Affaires

1972-1973	Harold G. Josif
1973-1974	Robert A. Stein
1975-1978	Robert Carle
1978-1980	William L. Eagleton
1980	Embassy closed

Lithuania

EEMP

1922-1931	Frederick W. B. Coleman
1931-1933	Robert B. Skinner

1933-1936	John Van A. MacMurray
1936-1937	Arthur Bliss Lane
1937-1940	Owen J. C. Norem
1941	Legation closed

Luxembourg

EEMP

1903-1905	Stanford Newel
1905-1908	David J. Hill
1908-1911	Arthur M. Beaupre
1911-1913	Lloyd Bryce
1913-1917	Henry Van Dyke
1917-1919	John W. Garrett
1920-1922	William Phillips
1923-1924	Henry P. Fletcher
1924-1927	William Phillips
1927-1933	Hugh S. Gibson
1933-1937	Dave H. Morris
1937-1938	Hugh S. Gibson
1938-1940	Joseph E. Davies
1940	John Cudahy
1941-1943	Jay Pierrepont Moffat
1943-1944	Ray Atherton

Charges d'Affaires

1944	Rudolph E. Schoenfeld

Ambassadors

1944-1945	Charles Sawyer

EEMP

1946-1949	Alan G. Kirk
1949-1953	Perle Mesta
1953-1957	Wiley T. Buchanan, Jr.
1957-1960	Vinton Chapin

Ambassadors

1960-1961	A. Burke Summers
1961-1962	James W. Wine
1962-1965	William R. Rivkin
1965-1967	Patricia R. Harris
1967-1969	George J. Feldman
1969-1972	Kingdon Gould, Jr.
1973-1976	Ruth Lewis Farkas
1976-1977	Rosemary L. Ginn
1977-1981	James G. Lowenstein
1981-1985	John E. Dolibois
1986-	Jean B. S. Gerard

Madagascar

(See Malagasy for earlier representation.)

Ambassadors

1970-1972	Anthony D. Marshall
1972-1975	Joseph A. Mendenhall
1975-1980	Vacant
1980-1983	Fernando E. Rondon
1983-	Robert B. Keating

Malagasy

(See Madagascar for later representation.)

Ambassadors

1960-1962	Frederic P. Bartlett
1962-1966	C. Vaughan Ferguson

1967-1969   David S. King

Malawi

Ambassadors

1964-1966	Sam P. Gilstrap
1966-1970	Marshall P. Jones
1970-1974	William C. Burdett
1974-1978	Robert A. Stevenson
1978-1980	Harold E. Horan
1981-1984	John A. Burroughs
1984-	Weston Adams

Malaysia

(Federation of Malaya 1957-1963.)

1957-1961	Homer M. Byington, Jr.
1961-1964	Charles F. Baldwin
1964-1969	James K. Bell
1969-1973	Jack W. Lydman
1973-1977	Francis T. Underhill, Jr.
1977-1980	Robert H. Miller
1980-1981	Barbara M. Watson
1981-1983	Ronald DeWayne Palmer
1984-	Thomas P. Shoesmith

Maldives

Ambassadors

1965-1967	Cecil B. Lyon
1969-1970	Andrew V. Corry
1970-1971	Robert Strausz-Hupe
1972-1976	Christopher Van Hollen
1976-1977	John H. Reed
1978-1979	W. Howard Wriggins
1979-1980	Donald R. Toussaint
1981	John Hathaway Reed
1981	Embassy closed

Mali

Ambassadors

1960-1961	Thomas K. Wright
1961-1964	William J. Handley
1965-1968	C. Robert Moore
1968-1970	G. Edward Clark
1970-1973	Robert O. Blake
1973-1976	Ralph J. McGuire
1976-1979	Patricia M. Byrne
1979-1981	Anne F. Holloway
1981-1984	Parker W. Borg
1984-	Robert J. Ryan, Jr.

Malta

Ambassadors

1965-1967	George J. Feldman
1967-1969	Hugh H. Smythe
1969-1972	John C. Pritzlaff, Jr.
1972-1974	John I. Getz
1974-1976	Robert P. Smith
1976-1979	Lowell Bruce Laingen
1979-1981	Joan M. Clark
1982-1985	James M. Rentschler
1985-	Gary L. Matthews

Mauritania

Ambassadors

1960-1961	Henry S. Villard
1961-1964	Philip M. Kaiser
1965-1967	Geoffrey W. Lewis
1967-1970	Embassy closed
1970-1971	Vacant
1971-1974	Richard W. Murphy
1975-1977	Holsey G. Handyside
1977-1980	E. Gregory Kryza
1980-1982	Vacant
1983-1985	Edward L. Peck
1985-	Robert L. Pugh

Mauritius

Ambassadors

1968-1969	David S. King
1970-1973	William D. Brewer
1974-1976	Philip W. Manhard
1976-1978	Robert V. Keeley
1978-1980	Samuel R. Gammon, III
1980-1983	Robert C. F. Gordon
1984-	George R. Andrews

Mexico

EEMP

1825-1829	Joel R. Poinsett

Charges d'Affaires

1829-1836	Anthony Butler
1836	Powhatan Ellis
1836-1839	Legation closed

EEMP

1839-1842	Powhatan Ellis
1842-1844	Waddy Thompson, Jr.
1844-1845	Wilson Shannon
1845-1847	Legation closed

Commissioners

1847-1848	Nicholas P. Trist

EEMP

1848	Ambrose H. Sevier
1848-1849	Nathan Clifford
1849-1852	Robert P. Latcher
1852-1853	Alfred Conkling
1853-1856	James Godsden
1856-1858	John Forsyth
1859-1860	Robert M. McLane
1860-1861	John B. Weller
1861-1864	Thomas Corwin
1864-1868	Vacant
1868-1869	William S. Rosecrans
1869-1873	Thomas H. Nelson
1873-1880	John W. Foster
1880-1886	P. H. Morgan
1886-1887	Thomas C. Manning
1888-1889	Edward S. Bragg
1889-1893	Thomas Ryan
1893-1895	Issac P. Gray
1895-1897	Matt W. Ransom
1897-1898	Powell Clayton

Ambassadors

1898-1905	Powell Clayton
1905-1906	Edwin H. Conger
1906-1909	David E. Thompson
1909-1912	Henry L. Wilson
1912-1916	Vacant
1916-1921	Henry P. Fletcher
1921-1923	Vacant
1924	Charles B. Warren
1924-1927	James R. Sheffield
1927-1930	Dwight W. Morrow
1930-1933	J. Reuben Clark, Jr.
1933-1941	Josephus Daniels
1941-1946	George S. Messersmith
1946-1950	Walter Thurston
1950-1953	William O'Dwyer
1953-1957	Francis White
1957-1960	Robert C. Hill
1961-1964	Thomas C. Mann
1964-1969	Fulton Freeman
1969-1974	Robert H. McBride
1973-1977	Joseph J. Jova
1977-1979	Patrick J. Lucey
1980-1981	Julian Nava
1981-	John A. Gavin

Montenegro

(See Yugoslavia for later representation.)

EEMP

1905-1907	John B. Jackson
1907-1909	Richmond Pearson
1909-1912	George H. Moses
1912-1913	Jacob G. Schurman
1914-1920	Garrett Droppers
1920	Edward Capps

Morocco

EEMP

1905-1909	Samuel R. Gummere
1909-1910	H. Percival Dodge
1910-1912	Fred W. Carpenter
1912-1917	Vacant

Agents

1917-1922	Maxwell Blake
1922-1924	Joseph M. Denning

Diplomatic Agents

1925-1940	Maxwell Blake
1940-1941	John C. White
1941-1945	Vacant
1945-1947	Paul H. Alling
1947-1951	Edwin A. Plitt
1951-1953	John Carter Vincent
1953-1955	Joseph C. Satterthwaite
1955-1956	Julius C. Holmes

Charges d'Affaires

1956	William J. Porter

Ambassadors

1956-1958	Cavendish W. Cannon
1958-1961	Charles W. Yost
1961-1962	Philip W. Bonsal
1962-1964	John H. Ferguson
1965-1969	Henry J. Tasca
1970-1973	Stuart W. Rockwell

1973-1976	Robert G. Neumann
1976-1978	Robert Anderson
1978-1979	Richard B. Parker
1979-1981	Angier Biddle Duke
1981-1985	Joseph V. Reed, Jr.
1985-	Thomas A. Nassif

Mozambique

Ambassadors

1976-1980	William A. D. Pree
1981-1983	Vacant
1984-	Peter Jon DeVos

Nauru

Ambassadors

1974-1975	Marshall Green
1976-1977	James W. Hargrove
1979-1981	Philip H. Alston, Jr.
1981	Robert D. Nesen
1981	Embassy closed

Nepal

EEMP

1948-1951	Loy W. Henderson

Ambassadors

1951-1953	Chester Bowles
1953-1955	George V. Allen
1955-1959	John Sherman Cooper
1956-1959	Ellsworth Bunker
1959-1966	Henry E. Stebbins
1966-1973	Carol C. Laise
1973-1976	William I. Cargo
1976-1977	Marquita M. Maytag
1977-1980	L. Douglas Heck
1980-1981	Philip R. Trimble
1981-1984	Carleton S. Coon
1984-	Leon J. Weil

Netherlands

Ministers

1792-1794	William Short
1794-1797	John Quincy Adams
1797-1801	William V. Murray

EEMP

1814-1818	William Eustis

Charges d'Affaires

1818-1824	Alexander H. Everett
1825-1829	Christopher Hughes, Jr.

EEMP

1829-1831	William P. Preble

Charges d'Affaires

1831-1839	Auguste Davezac
1839-1842	Harmanus Bleecker
1842-1845	Christopher Hughes
1845-1850	Auguste Davezac

1850-1853	George Folsom
1853-1854	August Belmont

Ministers

1854-1857	August Belmont
1857-1861	Henry C. Murphy
1861-1866	James S. Pike
1866-1870	Hugh Ewing
1870-1875	Charles T. Gorham
1875-1876	Francis B. Stockbridge
1876-1882	James Birney
1882-1885	William L. Dayton, Jr.
1885-1888	Issac Bell, Jr.

EEMP

1888-1889	Robert B. Roosevelt
1889-1893	Samuel R. Thayer
1893-1897	William E. Quinby
1897-1905	Stanford Newel
1905-1908	David J. Hill
1908-1911	Arthur M. Beaupre
1911-1913	Lloyd Bryce
1913-1917	Henry Van Dyke
1917-1919	John W. Garrett
1920-1922	William Phillips
1923-1929	Richard M. Tobin
1929-1931	Gerrit J. Diekema
1931-1934	Laurits S. Swenson
1934-1937	Grenville T. Emmet
1937-1941	George A. Gordon
1941-1942	Anthony J. Drexel Biddle, Jr.

Ambassadors

1942-1943	Anthony J. Drexel Biddle, Jr.
1944-1947	Stanley K. Hornbeck
1947-1949	Herman B. Baruch
1949-1953	Selden Chapin
1953-1957	H. Freeman Matthews
1957-1961	Philip Young
1961-1964	John S. Rice
1965-1969	William R. Tyler
1969-1973	J. William Middendorf, II
1973-1976	Kingdon Gould, Jr.
1976-1978	Robert J. McCloskey
1978-1981	Geri M. Joseph
1981-1983	William J. Dyess
1983-	L. Paul Bremer, III

New Zealand

EEMP

1942-1943	Patrick J. Hurley
1943	William C. Burdett
1944-1945	Kenneth S. Patton
1945-1947	Avra M. Warren

Ambassadors

1947-1955	Robert M. Scotten
1955-1956	Robert C. Hendrickson
1957-1960	Francis H. Russell
1961-1963	Anthony B. Akers
1963-1967	Herbert B. Powell
1967-1969	John F. Henning
1969-1972	Kenneth Franzheim, II
1972-1974	Vacant
1974-1979	Armistead I. Seldon, Jr.
1979-1981	Anne C. Martindell
1981-1985	H. Monroe Browne
1986-	Paul M. Cleveland

Nicaragua

Charges d'Affaires

1851-1853	John B. Kerr

Ministers

1854-1856	John H. Wheeler
1858-1859	Mirabeau B. Lamar
1859-1861	Alexander Dimitry
1861-1862	Andrew B. Dickinson
1862-1863	Thomas H. Clay
1863-1869	Andrew B. Dickinson
1869-1873	Charles N. Riotte
1873-1879	George Williamson
1879-1882	Cornelius A. Logan

EEMP

1882-1891	Henry C. Hall
1891-1893	Richard C. Shannon
1893-1897	Lewis Bader
1897-1908	William L. Merry
1908-1909	John G. Coolidge
1909-1911	Vacant
1911	Elliott Northcott
1911-1913	George T. Weitzel
1913-1921	Benjamin L. Jefferson
1921-1925	John E. Ramer
1925-1929	Charles C. Eberhardt
1929-1933	Matthew E. Hanna
1933-1936	Arthur Bliss Lane
1936-1938	Boaz W. Long
1938-1941	Meredith Nicholson
1941-1942	Pierre de L. Boal
1942-1943	James B. Stewart

Ambassadors

1943-1945	James B. Stewart
1945-1947	Fletcher Warren
1948-1949	George P. Shaw
1949-1951	Capus M. Waynick
1951-1961	Thomas E. Whelan
1961-1967	Aaron S. Brown
1967-1970	Kennedy M. Crockett
1970-1975	Turner B. Shelton
1975-1977	James D. Theberge
1977-1979	Mauricio Solaun
1979-1981	Lawrence A. Pezzullo
1982-1984	Anthony C. E. Quainton
1984-	Harry E. Bergold, Jr.

Niger

Ambassadors

1960-1961	R. Borden Reams
1961-1964	Mercer Cook
1964-1968	Robert J. Ryan
1968-1969	Samuel C. Adams, Jr.
1970-1973	Roswell D. McClelland
1974-1976	L. Douglas Heck
1976-1979	Charles A. James
1979-1981	James K. Bishop
1982-1985	William Robert Casey, Jr.
1985-	Richard W. Bogosian

Nigeria

Ambassadors

1960-1964	Joseph Palmer, II
1964-1969	Elbert G. Mathews
1969-1971	William C. Trueheart
1971-1975	John E. Reinhardt

1975-1979	Donald B. Easum
1979-1981	Stephen Low
1981-1983	Thomas R. Pickering
1984-1986	Thomas W. M. Smith
1986-	Vacant

Norway

(See Sweden for earlier representation.)

EEMP

1906-1911	Herbert H. D. Peirce
1911-1913	Laurits S. Swenson
1913-1921	Albert G. Schmedeman
1921-1930	Laurits S. Swenson
1930-1935	Hoffman Philip
1935-1937	Anthony J. Drexel Biddle, Jr.
1937-1941	Florence Jaffray Harriman
1941-1942	Anthony J. Drexel Biddle, Jr.

Ambassadors

1942-1943	Anthony J. Drexel Biddle, Jr.
1944-1946	Lithgow Osborne
1946-1953	Charles U. Bay
1953-1957	L. Corrin Strong
1957-1961	Frances E. Willis
1961-1964	Clifton R. Wharton
1964-1969	Margaret J. Tibbetts
1969-1973	Philip K. Crowe
1973-1976	Thomas R. Byrne
1976-1977	William A. Anders
1977-1979	Louis A. Lerner
1979-1981	Sidney Anders Rand
1981-1984	Mark Evans Austad
1985-	Robert D. Stuart

Oman

Ambassadors

1972-1974	William A. Stoltzfus, Jr.
1974-1978	William D. Wolle
1978-1981	Marshall W. Wiley
1981-1985	John R. Countryman
1985-	George C. Montgomery

Pakistan

Ambassadors

1947-1949	Paul H. Alling
1949	H. Merle Cochran
1949-1953	Avra M. Warren
1953-1957	Horace A. Hildreth
1957-1959	James M. Langley
1959-1962	William M. Rountree
1962-1966	Walter P. McConaughy
1966-1967	Eugene M. Locke
1967-1969	Benjamin H. Olgeert, Jr.
1969-1972	Joseph S. Farland
1973-1977	Henry A. Byroade
1977-1981	Arthur W. Hummel, Jr.
1981-1983	Robert I. Spiers
1984-	Deane R. Hinton

Panama

EEMP

1903-1904	William L. Buchanan
1904-1905	John Barrett
1905-1906	Charles E. Magoon

1906-1909	Herbert G. Squiers
1909-1910	R. S. Reynolds Hitt
1910-1911	Thomas C. Dawson
1911-1913	H. Percival Dodge
1913-1921	William J. Price
1921-1929	John G. South
1929-1933	Roy T. Davis
1933-1934	Antonio C. Gonzalez
1934-1937	George T. Summerlin
1937-1939	Frank P. Corrigan

Ambassadors

1939-1941	William Dawson
1941-1943	Edwin C. Wilson
1944-1945	Avra M. Warren
1945-1948	Frank T. Hines
1948-1951	Monnett B. Davis
1951-1953	John C. Wiley
1953-1955	Selden Chapin
1955-1960	Julian F. Harrington
1960-1963	Joseph S. Farland
1964-1965	Jack H. Vaughn
1965-1969	Charles W. Adair, Jr.
1969-1972	Robert M. Sayre
1972	Frank T. Bow
1973	Vacant
1974-1978	William J. Jorden
1978-1982	Ambler H. Moss, Jr.
1983-1986	Everett E. Briggs
1986-	Arthur H. Davis

Papal States

(See Italy and Holy See for later representation.)

Charges d'Affaires

1848	J. L. Martin
1848-1854	Lewis Cass, Jr.

Ministers

1854-1858	Lewis Cass, Jr.
1858-1861	John P. Stockton
1861-1862	Alexander W. Randall
1862-1863	Richard M. Blatchford
1863-1867	Rufus King

Papua New Guinea

Ambassadors

1975-1979	Mary S. Olmsted
1979-1981	Harvey J. Feldman
1981-1984	M. Virginia Shafer
1984-	Paul F. Gardner

Paraguay

Commissioners

1858-1859	James B. Bowlin
1858-1859	Charles A. Washburn

Ministers

1863-1868	Charles A. Washburn
1868-1869	Martin T. McMahon
1870-1873	John L. Stevens
1874-1876	John C. Caldwell

Charges d'Affaires

1876-1882	John C. Caldwell
1882-1885	William Williams
1885-1890	John E. Bacon

EEMP

1890-1894	George Maney
1894-1897	Granville Stuart
1897-1905	William R. Finch
1905-1909	Edward C. O'Brien
1909-1911	Edwin V. Morgan
1911-1914	Nicolay A. Grevstad
1914-1922	Daniel F. Mooney
1922-1924	William J. O'Toole
1925-1929	George L. Kreeck
1929-1933	Post Wheeler
1933-1935	Meredith Nicholson
1935-1941	Findley B. Howard
1941-1942	Wesley Frost

Ambassadors

1942-1944	Wesley Frost
1944-1947	Willard L. Beaulac
1947-1950	Fletcher Warren
1950-1952	Howard H. Tewksbury
1952-1954	George P. Shaw
1954-1957	Arthur A. Ageton
1957-1959	Walter C. Ploeser
1959-1960	Harry F. Stimpson, Jr.
1961-1967	William P. Snow
1967-1969	Benigno C. Hernandez
1969-1972	J. Raymond Ylitalo
1972-1977	George W. Landau
1977-1980	Robert E. White
1980-1982	Lyle F. Lane
1982-1985	Arthur H. Davis, Jr.
1986-	Clyde D. Taylor

People's Republic of China

(See China for earlier representation; see also Republic of China.)

Ambassadors

1979-1981	Leonard F. Woodcock
1981-1985	Arthur W. Hummel, Jr.
1986-	Winston Lord

People's Republic of the Congo

(Brazzaville)

Ambassadors

1960-1964	W. Wendell Blancke
1964-1965	Henry L. Koren
1965-1977	Embassy closed
1979-1981	William L. Swing
1981-1984	Kenneth Lee Brown
1984-	Alan W. Lukens

Persia

(See Iran for later representation.)

Ministers

1883-1886	S. C. W. Benjamin
1886-1892	E. Spencer Pratt
1892-1893	Watson R. Sperry
1893-1897	Alexander McDonald

1897-1899	Arthur S. Hardy
1899-1901	Herbert W. Bowen
1901-1902	Lloyd C. Griscom
1902-1905	Richmond Pearson

EEMP

1905-1907	Richmond Pearson
1907-1909	John B. Jackson
1909-1914	Charles W. Russell
1914-1921	John L. Caldwell
1921-1924	Joseph S. Kornfeld
1925-1929	Hoffman Philip
1929-1933	Charles C. Hart
1933-1935	William H. Hornibrook

Peru

Charges d'Affaires

1826-1828	James Cooley
1828-1837	Samuel Larned
1836-1838	James B. Thornton
1838-1845	J. C. Pickett
1844-1845	John A. Bryan
1845-1847	Albert G. Jewett
1847-1853	John Randolph Clay

EEMP

1853-1860	John Randolph Clay
1861-1865	Christopher Robinson
1865-1870	Alvin P. Hovey
1871-1872	Thomas Settle
1872-1875	Francis Thomas
1875-1879	Richard Gibbs
1879-1882	Isaac B. Christiancy
1883-1885	Seth L. Phelps
1885-1889	Charles W. Buck
1889-1893	John Hicks
1893-1897	James A. McKenzie
1897-1906	Irving B. Dudley
1906-1911	Leslie Combs
1911-1913	H. Clay Howard
1913-1919	Benton McMillin

Ambassadors

1919-1921	William E. Gonzales
1923-1928	Miles Poindexter
1928-1930	Alexander P. Moore
1930-1937	Fred M. Dearing
1937-1939	Laurence A. Steinhardt
1940-1944	R. Henry Norweb
1944-1945	John Campbell White
1945-1946	William D. Pawley
1946-1948	Prentice Cooper
1948-1955	Harold H. Tittmann, Jr.
1955-1956	Ellis O. Briggs
1956-1960	Theodore C. Achilles
1960-1961	Selden Chapin
1961-1962	James Loeb
1962-1969	J. Wesley Jones
1969-1974	Taylor G. Belcher
1974-1977	Robert W. Dean
1977-1980	Harry W. Shlaudeman
1980-1981	Edwin G. Corr
1981-1983	Frank V. Ortiz, Jr.
1984-	David C. Jordan

Philippines

Ambassadors

1946-1947	Paul V. McNutt
1947-1949	Emmet O'Neal
1949-1951	Myron M. Cowen

1952-1955	Raymond A. Spruance
1955-1956	Homer Ferguson
1956	Albert F. Nufer
1957-1959	Charles E. Bohlen
1959-1961	John D. Hickerson
1961-1964	William E. Stevenson
1964-1967	William M. Blair, Jr.
1968-1969	G. Mennen Williams
1969-1973	Henry A. Byroade
1973-1977	William H. Sullivan
1977-1978	David D. Newsom
1978-1981	Richard W. Murphy
1982-1984	Michael Hayden Armacost
1984-	Stephen W. Bosworth

Poland

EEMP

1919-1924	Hugh S. Gibson
1924-1925	Alfred J. Pearson
1925-1930	John B. Stetson, Jr.

Ambassadors

1930-1932	John N. Willys
1932-1933	F. Lammot Belin
1933-1937	John Cudahy
1937-1943	Anthony J. Drexel Biddle, Jr.
1944-1947	Arthur Bliss Lane
1947-1948	Stanton Griffis
1948-1950	Waldemar J. Gallman
1950-1955	Joseph Flack
1955-1957	Joseph E. Jacobs
1957-1962	Jacob D. Beam
1962-1965	John M. Cabot
1965-1968	John A. Gronouski
1968-1972	Walter J. Stoessel, Jr.
1972-1978	Richard T. Davies
1978-1980	William E. Schaufele, Jr.
1980-1983	Francis J. Meehan

Charges d'Affaires

1983	Herbert E. Wilgis, Jr.
1984-	John R. Davis, Jr.

Portugal

Ministers Plenipotentiary

1791-1797	David Humphreys
1797-1801	William L. Smith
1801-1809	Vacant
1809-1819	Thomas Sumter, Jr.
1819-1820	John Graham
1822-1824	Henry Dearborn

Charges d'Affaires

1825-1834	Thomas L. L. Brent
1835-1841	Edward Kavanagh
1841-1844	Washington Barrow
1843-1847	Abraham Rencher
1847-1849	George W. Hopkins
1849-1850	John B. Clay
1850-1854	Charles B. Haddock

Ministers

1854-1858	John L. O'Sullivan
1858-1861	George W. Morgan
1861-1869	James E. Harvey
1869	Samuel Shellabarger
1870-1874	Charles H. Lewis
1874-1882	Benjamin Moran
1882-1884	John M. Francis

1884-1885	Lewis Richmond
1885-1890	E. P. C. Lewis
1890-1893	George S. Batcheller
1893	Gilbert A. Pierce

EEMP

1893-1897	George W. Caruth
1897-1899	Lawrence Townsend
1899-1901	John N. Irwin
1901-1903	Francis B. Loomis
1903-1909	Charles P. Bryan
1909-1911	Henry T. Gage
1911	Edwin V. Morgan
1912-1913	Cyrus E. Woods
1913-1922	Thomas H. Birch
1922-1929	Fred M. Dearing
1929-1933	John G. South
1933-1937	Robert G. Caldwell
1937-1941	Herbert Claiborne Pell
1941-1943	Bert Fish
1943-1945	R. Henry Norweb

Ambassadors

1945-1947	Herman B. Baruch
1947-1948	John C. Wiley
1948-1952	Lincoln MacVeagh
1952-1953	Cavendish W. Cannon
1953-1954	M. Robert Guggenheim
1955-1958	James C. H. Bonbright
1958-1963	C. Burke Elbrick
1963-1966	George W. Anderson, Jr.
1966-1969	W. Tapley Bennett, Jr.
1969-1973	Ridgway B. Knight
1973-1975	Stuart Nash Scott
1974-1978	Frank C. Carlucci
1978-1982	Richard J. Bloomfield
1983-1985	H. Allen Holmes
1985-	Frank Shakespeare

Prussia

Ministers Plenipotentiary

1797-1801	John Quincy Adams

Charges d'Affaires

1835-1837	Henry Wheaton

EEMP

1846-1849	Andrew J. Donelson
1849-1850	Edward A. Hannegan
1850-1853	Daniel D. Barnard
1853-1857	Peter D. Vroom
1857-1861	Joseph A. Wright
1861-1865	Norman B. Judd
1865-1867	Joseph A. Wright
1867-1871	George Bancroft

Qatar

Ambassadors

1971-1974	William A. Stoltzfus, Jr.
1974-1977	Robert P. Paganelli
1977-1980	Andrew I. Killgore
1980-1983	Charles E. Marthinsen
1984-1985	Charles F. Dunbar
1986-	Joseph Ghougassian

Republic of Cape Verde

Ambassadors

1976-1977	Melissa F. Wells
1977-1980	Edward Marks
1980-1983	Peter J. DeVos
1983-	John M. Yates

Republic of China

(See China for earlier representation; see also People's Republic of China.)

Ambassadors

1974-1978	Leonard Unger
1978	Embassy closed

Republic of Korea

(See Korea for earlier representation.)

Ambassadors

1949-1952	John J. Muccio
1952-1955	Ellis O. Briggs
1955	William S. B. Lacy
1956-1959	Walter C. Dowling
1959-1961	Walter P. McConaughy
1961-1964	Samuel D. Berger
1964-1967	Winthrop G. Brown
1967-1971	William J. Porter
1971-1974	Philip C. Habib
1974-1978	Richard L. Sneider
1978-1981	William H. Gleysteen, Jr.
1981-	Richard L. Walker

Republic of South Africa

(See Union of South Africa for earlier representation.)

Ambassadors

1961-1965	Joseph C. Satterthwaite
1965-1970	William M. Rountree
1970-1975	John G. Hurd
1975-1978	William G. Bowdler
1978-1981	William S. Edmondson
1982-	Herman W. Nickel

Republic of Sri Lanka

(See Ceylon for earlier representation.)

Ambassadors

1972-1976	Christopher Van Hollen
1976-1977	John H. Read
1977-1979	W. Howard Wriggins
1979-1982	Donald R. Toussaint
1982-1985	John Hathaway Reed
1986-	James W. Spain

Republic of Texas

Charges d'Affaires

1837-1840	Alcee La Branche
1841-1843	George H. Hood

1841-1843	Joseph Eve
1843-1844	William S. Murphy
1844	Tilghman A. Howard
1844-1845	Andrew J. Donelson

Romania

Ministers

1882-1885	Eugene Schuyler
1885-1889	J. Walker Fearn
1889-1892	A. Landon Snowden
1892-1893	Truxtun Beale

EEMP

1893-1897	Eben Alexander
1897-1899	William W. Rockhill
1899-1900	Arthur S. Hardy
1900-1902	Charles S. Francis
1902-1905	John B. Jackson
1905-1907	John W. Riddle
1907-1909	Horace G. Knowles
1909-1911	John R. Carter
1911-1913	John B. Jackson
1913-1921	Charles J. Vopicka
1921-1925	Peter A. Jay
1925-1928	William S. Culbertson
1928-1933	Charles S. Wilson
1933-1935	Alvin M. Owsley
1935-1937	Leland Harrison
1937-1941	Franklin M. Gunther
1941-1947	Legation closed
1947-1951	Rudolf E. Schoenfeld
1953-1955	Harold Shantz
1955-1958	Robert H. Thayer
1958-1961	Clifton R. Wharton
1961-1965	William A. Crawford

Ambassadors

1965-1969	Richard H. Davis
1969-1973	Leonard C. Meeker
1973-1977	Harry G. Barnes, Jr.
1977-1981	O. Rudolph Aggrey
1981-1985	David B. Funderburk
1986-	Roger Kirk

Russia

(See Union of Soviet Socialist Republics for later representation.)

Ministers Plenipotentiary

1809-1814	John Quincy Adams

Charges d'Affaires

1814-1817	Leavitt Harris

EEMP

1816-1818	William Pinkney
1818-1820	George W. Campbell
1820-1830	Henry Middleton
1830	John Randolph
1832-1833	James Buchanan
1834-1835	William Wilkins

Charges d'Affaires

1836-1837	John Randolph Clay

EEMP

1837-1839	George M. Sallas

1840-1841	Churchill C. Cambreleng
1841-1846	Charles S. Todd
1846-1848	Ralph J. Ingersoll
1848-1849	Arthur P. Bagby
1850-1853	Neil S. Brown
1853-1858	Thomas H. Seymour
1858-1860	Francis W. Pickens
1860-1861	John Appleton
1861-1862	Cassius M. Clay
1862	Simon Cameron
1863-1869	Cassius M. Clay
1869-1872	Andrew G. Curtin
1872-1873	James L. Orr
1873-1875	Marshall Jewell
1875-1877	George H. Boker
1877-1879	E. W. Stoughton
1880-1882	John W. Foster
1882-1884	William H. Hunt
1884-1885	Alphonso Taft
1885-1888	George V. N. Lothrop
1888-1892	Lambert Tree
1892-1894	Andrew D. White
1894-1897	Clifton R. Breckinridge
1897-1899	Ethan A. Hitchcock

Ambassadors

1899-1902	Charlemagne Tower
1902-1905	Robert S. McCormick
1905-1906	George V. L. Meyer
1906-1909	John W. Riddle
1909-1911	William W. Rockhill
1911-1913	Curtis Gould
1914-1916	George T. Marye
1916-1921	David R. Francis

Rwanda

Ambassadors

1963-1966	Charles D. Withers
1966-1971	Leo G. Cyr
1971-1973	Robert F. Corrigan
1974-1976	Robert E. Fritts
1976-1979	T. Frank Crigler
1979-1982	Harry R. Melone, Jr.
1983-1985	John Blane
1986-	John E. Upston

St. Lucia

Ambassadors

1979-1981	Sally A. Shelton
1981-	Milan D. Bish

St. Vincent and the Grenadines

Ambassadors

1981	Milan D. Bish

Salvador

(See El Salvador for later representation.)

EEMP

1853-1854	Solon Borland

Ministers

1863-1866	James R. Partridge

1866-1869	Alpheus S. Williams
1869-1871	Alfred T. A. Torbert
1871-1873	Thomas Biddle
1873-1879	George Williamson
1879-1882	Cornelius A. Logan

EEMP

1882-1891	Henry C. Hall
1891-1893	Richard C. Shannon
1893-1897	Lewis Baker
1897-1906	William L. Merry
1907-1909	H. Percival Dodge
1909-1914	William Heimke
1914-1919	Boaz W. Long
1921-1925	Montgomery Schuyler
1926-1928	Jefferson Caffery
1928-1929	Warren D. Robbins

Sao Tome and Principe

Ambassadors

1975-1977	Andrew L. Steigman
1978-1981	Arthur T. Tienken
1981-1984	Francis T. McNamara
1984-	Larry C. Williamson

Sardinia

Charges d'Affaires

1840-1841	H. Gold Rogers
1841-1843	Ambrose Baber
1843-1848	Robert Wickliffe, Jr.
1848-1850	Nathaniel Niles
1850-1853	William B. Kinney
1853	John M. Daniel

Ministers

1854-1861	John M. Daniel

Saudi Arabia

EEMP

1939-1941	Bert Fish
1941-1943	Alexander C. Kirk
1943-1944	James S. Moose, Jr.
1944-1946	William A. Eddy
1946-1949	J. Rives Childs

Ambassadors

1949-1950	J. Rives Childs
1950-1953	Raymond A. Hare
1953-1957	George Wadsworth
1957-1961	Donald R. Heath
1961-1966	Parker T. Hart
1966-1970	Herman F. Eilts
1970-1973	Nicholas G. Thacher
1973-1975	James E. Akins
1975-1977	William J. Porter
1977-1981	John C. West
1981	Robert G. Neumann
1981-1983	Richard W. Murphy
1984-	Walter L. Cutler

Senegal

Ambassadors

1960-1961	Henry S. Villard
1961-1964	Philip M. Kaiser
1964-1966	Mercer Cook
1966-1967	William R. Rivkin
1967-1970	L. Dean Brown
1970-1973	G. Edward Clark
1973-1977	O. Rudolph Aggrey
1977-1980	Herman J. Cohen
1980-1981	Walter C. Carrington
1981-1985	Charles W. Bray, III
1985-	Lannon Walker

Serbia

(See Yugoslavia for later representation.)

Ministers

1882-1885	Eugene Schuyler
1885-1890	J. Walker Fearn
1890-1893	Truxtun Beale

EEMP

1893-1897	Eben Alexander
1897-1899	William W. Rockhill
1899-1900	Arthur S. Hardy
1900-1902	Charles S. Francis
1902-1905	John B. Jackson
1905-1907	John W. Riddle
1907-1909	Horace G. Knowles
1909-1911	John R. Carter
1911-1913	John B. Jackson
1913-1919	Charles J. Vopicka
1919-1926	H. Percival Dodge
1926-1929	John D. Prince

Seychelles

Ambassadors

1976-1977	Anthony D. Marshall
1977-1980	Wilbert J. LeMelle
1980-1982	William C. Harrop
1983-1985	David J. Fischer
1985-	Irvin Hicks

Siam

(See Thailand for later representation.)

Ministers

1882-1886	J. A. Halderman
1886-1890	Jacob T. Child
1890-1894	Sempronius H. Boyd
1894-1898	John Barrett
1898-1903	Hamilton King

EEMP

1903-1912	Hamilton King
1912-1913	Fred W. Carpenter
1915-1916	William H. Hornibrook
1917-1918	George P. Ingersoll
1921-1925	Edward E. Brodie
1925-1926	William W. Russell
1927-1930	Harold O. Mackenzie
1930-1933	David E. Kaufman
1933-1937	James M. Baker

Sicily

(See Italy for later representation.)

Ministers Plenipotentiary

1816	William Pinkney

Charges d'Affaires

1831-1832	John Nelson
1838-1842	Enos T. Throop
1841-1845	William Boulware
1845-1847	William H. Polk
1848-1850	John Rowan
1849	Thomas W. Chinn
1850-1853	Edward J. Morris
1853-1854	Robert D. Owen

Ministers

1854-1858	Robert D. Owen
1858-1860	Joseph R. Chandler

Sierra Leone

Ambassadors

1961-1963	A. S. J. Carnahan
1964-1967	Andrew V. Corry
1967-1972	Robert G. Miner
1972-1974	Clinton L. Olson
1974-1977	Michael A. Samuels
1977-1980	John A. Linehan, Jr.
1980-1983	Theresa A. Healy
1983-	Arthur W. Lewis

Singapore

Ambassadors

1966-1969	Francis J. Galbraith
1969-1972	Charles T. Cross
1972-1975	Edwin M. Cronk
1975-1978	John H. Holdridge
1978-1980	Richard F. Kniep
1980-1984	Harry E. T. Thayer
1985-	J. Stapleton Roy

Solomon Islands

Ambassadors

1978-1979	Mary S. Olmsted
1979-1981	Harvey J. Feldman
1981	M. Virginia Schafer

Somalia

Ambassadors

1960-1962	Andrew G. Lynch
1962-1965	Horace G. Torbert, Jr.
1965-1968	Raymond L. Thurston
1969-1971	Fred L. Hadsel
1972-1973	Matthew J. Looram, Jr.
1973-1975	Roger Kirk
1975-1978	John L. Loughran
1978-1982	Donald K. Petterson
1983-1984	Robert B. Oakley
1985-	Peter S. Bridges

Southern Yemen

Charges d'Affaires

1967-1969	William Eagleton, Jr.
1969	Embassy closed

Spain

Charges d'Affaires

1790-1794	William Carmichael

Ministers

1794-1795	William Short

Envoys Extraordinary

1794-1795	Thomas Pinckney

Ministers Plenipotentiary

1796-1801	David Humphreys
1801-1805	Charles Pinckney
1805-1808	James Bowdoin
1808-1814	Vacant
1814-1819	George W. Erving
1819-1823	John Forsyth
1823-1825	Hugh Nelson

EEMP

1825-1829	Alexander H. Everett
1829-1836	Cornelius P. Van Ness
1836-1840	John H. Eaton

Charges d'Affaires

1840-1842	Aaron Vail

EEMP

1842-1846	Washington Irving
1846-1849	Romulus M. Saunders
1849-1853	Daniel M. Barringer
1853-1855	Pierre Soule
1855-1858	Augustus C. Dodge
1858-1861	William Preston
1861-1862	Carl Schurz
1862-1864	Gustavus Koerner
1865-1869	John P. Hale
1869-1873	Daniel E. Sickles
1874-1877	Caleb Cushing
1877-1880	James Russell Lowell
1880-1881	Lucius Fairchild
1881-1883	Hannibal Hamlin
1883-1885	John W. Foster
1885-1888	Jabez L. M. Curry
1888-1892	Perry Belmont
1892-1893	A. Landon Snowden
1893-1897	Hannis Taylor
1897-1898	Stewart L. Woodford
1899-1902	Bellamy Storer
1902-1905	Arthur S. Hardy
1905-1909	William M. Collier
1909-1913	Henry C. Ide

Ambassadors

1913-1921	Joseph E. Willard
1921-1923	Cyrus E. Woods
1923-1925	Alexander P. Moore
1925-1929	Ogden H. Hammond
1929-1933	Irwin B. Laughlin
1933-1939	Claude G. Bowers
1939-1942	Alexander W. Weddell
1942-1944	Carlton J. H. Hayes

1944-1945	Norman Armour
1945-1951	Vacant
1951-1952	Stanton Griffis
1952-1953	Lincoln MacVeagh
1953-1955	James C. Dunn
1955-1961	John Davis Lodge
1961	Anthony J. Drexel Biddle, Jr.
1962-1965	Robert F. Woodward
1965-1968	Angier Biddle Duke
1968-1969	Robert F. Wagner
1969-1972	Robert C. Hill
1972-1974	Horacio Rivero
1975-1978	Wells Stabler
1978-1983	Terence A. Todman
1983-	Thomas O. Enders

Sudan

Ambassadors

1956-1958	Lowell C. Pinkerton
1958-1962	James S. Moose, Jr.
1962-1965	William M. Rountree
1965-1967	William H. Weatherby
1967-1972	Embassy closed
1972-1973	Cleo A. Noel, Jr.
1973-1977	William D. Brewer
1977-1980	Donald C. Bergus
1980-1983	C. William Kontos
1983-	Hume A. Horan

Suriname

Ambassadors

1976-1978	J. Owen Zurhellen, Jr.
1978-1980	Nancy Ostrander
1980-1982	John J. Crowley, Jr.
1982-1984	Robert W. Duemling
1985-	Robert E. Barbour

Swaziland

1971-1974	Charles J. Nelson
1974-1976	David B. Bolen
1976-1979	Donald R. Norland
1979-1982	Richard C. Matheron
1982-1984	Robert H. Phinny
1985-	Harvey F. Nelson, Jr.

Sweden

(Sweden and Norway 1797-1905.)

Commissioners

1798	John Quincy Adams

Ministers Plenipotentiary

1814-1818	Jonathan Russell

Charges d'Affaires

1819-1825	Christopher Hughes
1826-1830	John J. Appleton
1830-1841	Christopher Hughes
1842-1845	George W. Lay
1845-1849	Henry W. Ellsworth
1849-1854	Francis Schroeder

Ministers

1854-1857	Francis Schroeder
1857-1861	Benjamin F. Angel
1861-1864	Jacob S. Haldeman
1864-1867	James H. Campbell
1867-1869	Joseph J. Bartlett
1869-1877	Christopher C. Andrews
1877-1883	John L. Stevens
1883-1885	William W. Thomas, Jr.
1885-1889	Rufus Magee

EEMP

1889-1894	William W. Thomas, Jr.
1894-1897	Thomas B. Ferguson
1897-1905	William W. Thomas, Jr.
1905-1914	Charles H. Graves
1914-1923	Ira N. Morris
1923-1927	Robert W. Bliss
1927-1929	Leland Harrison
1930-1933	John M. Morehead
1933-1937	Laurence A. Steinhardt
1937-1938	Fred M. Dearing
1938-1941	Frederick A. Sterling
1941-1946	Herschel V. Johnson
1946-1947	Louis G. Dreyfus, Jr.

Ambassadors

1947-1950	H. Freeman Matthews
1951-1954	W. Walton Butterworth
1954-1957	John M. Cabot
1957-1958	Francis White
1958-1961	James C. H. Bonbright
1961-1967	J. Graham Parsons
1967-1969	William W. Heath
1970-1972	Jerome H. Holland
1972-1974	Vacant
1974-1976	Robert Strausz-Hupe
1976-1977	David S. Smith
1977-1980	Rodney O. Kennedy-Minott
1981-1985	Franklin F. Forsberg
1986-	Gregory J. Newell

Switzerland

Ministers

1853-1861	Theodore S. Fay
1861-1865	George G. Fogg
1865-1869	George Harrington
1869-1876	Horace Rublee

Charges d'Affaires

1876-1877	Horace Rublee
1877-1882	Nicholas Fish

Ministers

1882-1885	Michael J. Cramer
1885-1890	Boyd Winchester

EEMP

1890-1892	John D. Washburn, Jr.
1892-1893	Person C. Cheney
1893-1895	James O. Broadhead
1895-1897	John L. Peak
1897-1900	John G. A. Leishman
1900-1902	Arthur S. Hardy
1903-1905	David J. Hill
1905-1909	Brutus J. Clay
1909-1911	Laurits S. Swenson
1911-1913	Henry S. Bortell
1913-1921	Pleasant A. Stovall
1921-1924	Joseph C. Grew
1924-1927	Hugh S. Gibson

1927-1937	Hugh R. Wilson
1937-1947	Leland Harrison
1947-1951	John Carter Vincent
1951-1953	Richard C. Patterson
1953	Frances E. Willis

Ambassadors

1953-1957	Frances E. Willis
1957-1961	Henry J. Taylor
1961-1963	Robert M. McKinney
1963-1966	W. True Davis, Jr.
1966-1969	John S. Hayes
1969-1975	Shelby Davis
1975	Peter H. Dominick
1975-1977	Nathaniel Davis
1977-1979	Marvin L. Warner
1979-1981	Richard D. Vine
1981-1983	Faith Ryan Whittlesey
1983-1985	John D. Lodge
1985-	Faith Ryan Whittlesey

Syria

(Syrian Arab Republic 1958-1967.)

EEMP

1942-1946	George Wadsworth
1947	Paul H. Alling
1947-1950	James H. Keeley, Jr.
1950-1952	Cavendish W. Cannon

Ambassadors

1952-1957	James S. Moose, Jr.
1957-1958	Charles W. Yost
1958-1961	Vacant
1961-1965	Ridgway B. Knight
1965-1967	Hugh H. Smythe
1967-1974	Embassy closed
1974-1978	Richard W. Murphy
1978-1981	Talcott W. Seelye
1981-1984	Robert P. Paganelli
1985-	William L. Eagleton, Jr.

Tanzania

(Tanganyika 1962-1964.)

Ambassadors

1962-1965	William Leonhart
1965-1969	John H. Burns
1969-1972	Claude G. Ross
1972-1975	W. Beverly Carter, Jr.
1975-1979	James W. Spain
1979-1981	Richard N. Viets
1981-1984	David C. Miller, Jr.
1984-	John W. Shirley

Thailand

(See Siam for earlier representation.)

EEMP

1939-1940	Edwin L. Neville
1940-1941	Hugh G. Grant
1941-1942	Willys R. Peck
1942-1946	Legation closed
1946	Edwin F. Stanton

Ambassadors

1947-1953	Edwin F. Stanton
1953-1954	William J. Donovan
1954-1955	John E. Peurifoy
1955-1958	Max W. Bishop
1958-1961	U. Alexis Johnson
1961-1963	Kenneth T. Young
1963-1967	Graham A. Martin
1967-1973	Leonard Unger
1973-1975	William R. Kintner
1975-1978	Charles S. Whitehouse
1978-1981	Morton I. Abramowitz
1981-1985	John Gunther Dean
1985-	William A. Brown

Togo

Ambassadors

1960-1961	Leland Barrows
1961-1964	Leon B. Poullada
1964-1967	William Witman, II
1967-1970	Albert W. Sherer, Jr.
1970-1974	Dwight Dickinson
1974-1976	Nancy V. Rawls
1976-1978	Ronald D. Palmer
1978-1981	Marilyn P. Johnson
1982-1984	Howard K. Walker
1984-	Owen W. Roberts

Trinidad and Tobago

Ambassadors

1962-1967	Robert G. Miner
1967-1969	William A. Costello
1969-1972	J. Fife Symington, Jr.
1972-1973	Anthony D. Marshall
1973-1975	Lloyd I. Miller
1976-1977	Albert B. Fay
1977-1979	Richard K. Fox, Jr.
1979-1981	Irving G. Cheslaw
1981-1984	Melvin H. Evans
1985-	Sheldon J. Krys

Tunisia

Ambassadors

1956-1959	G. Lewis Jones
1959-1962	Walter N. Walmsley, Jr.
1962-1969	Francis H. Russell
1969-1972	John A. Calhoun
1972-1976	Talcott W. Seelye
1976-1979	Edward W. Mulcahy
1979-1981	Stephen W. Bosworth
1981-1984	Walter L. Cutler
1985-	Peter Sebastian

Turkey

Charges d'Affaires

| 1831-1839 | David Porter |

Ministers

1839-1843	David Porter
1843-1849	Dabney S. Carr
1849-1853	George P. Marsh
1853-1857	Carroll Spence
1858-1861	James Williams

1861-1870	Edward J. Morris
1870-1871	Wayne MacVeagh
1871-1875	George H. Boker
1875-1880	Horace Maynard
1880-1882	James Longstreet

EEMP

1882-1885	Lew Wallace
1887-1889	Oscar S. Straus
1889-1892	Solomon Hirsch
1892-1893	David P. Thompson
1893-1897	Alexander W. Terrell
1897-1898	James B. Angell
1898-1900	Oscar S. Straus
1900-1906	John G. A. Leishman

Ambassadors

1906-1909	John G. A. Leishman
1909-1911	Oscar S. Straus
1911-1913	William W. Rockhill
1913-1916	Henry Morgenthau
1916-1917	Abram I. Elkus
1927-1932	Joseph C. Grew
1932-1933	Charles H. Sherrill
1933-1936	Robert P. Skinner
1936-1942	John Van A. MacMurray
1942-1944	Laurence A. Steinhardt
1945-1948	Edwin C. Wilson
1948-1951	George Wadsworth
1951-1953	George C. McGhee
1953-1956	Avra M. Warren
1956-1960	Fletcher Warren
1961-1965	Raymond A. Hare
1965-1968	Parker T. Hart
1968-1969	Robert W. Komer
1969-1973	William J. Handley
1973-1977	William B. Macomber, Jr.
1977-1980	Ronald I. Spiers
1980-1981	James W. Spain
1981-	Robert Strausz-Hupe

Tuvalu

Ambassadors

1979-1980	John P. Condon
1980-1981	William Bodde, Jr.
1982-1984	Fred J. Eckert
1985-	C. Edward Dillery

Uganda

Ambassadors

1963-1966	Olcott H. Deming
1966-1969	Henry E. Stebbins
1970-1972	Clarence C. Ferguson, Jr.
1972-1973	Thomas Patrick Melady
1973-1979	Embassy closed
1980-1983	Gordon R. Beyer
1983-1985	Allen C. Davis
1986-	Robert G. Houdek

Union of South Africa

(See Republic of South Africa for later representation.)

Ministers

| 1929-1937 | Ralph J. Totten |

EEMP

1937-1942	Leo J. Keena
1942-1943	Lincoln MacVeagh
1944-1948	Thomas Holcomb
1948-1949	North Winship

Ambassadors

1949-1950	North Winship
1950-1951	John G. Erhardt
1951-1954	Waldemar J. Gallman
1954-1956	Edward T. Wailes
1956-1959	Henry A. Myronde
1959-1961	Philip K. Crowe

Union of Soviet Socialist Republics

(See Russia for earlier representation.)

Ambassadors

1933-1936	William C. Bullitt
1936-1938	Joseph E. Davies
1939-1942	Laurence A. Steinhardt
1942-1943	William H. Standley
1943-1946	W. Averell Harriman
1946-1949	Walter Bedell Smith
1949-1952	Alan G. Kirk
1952-1953	George F. Kennan
1953-1957	Charles E. Bohlen
1957-1962	Llewellyn E. Thompson
1962-1967	Foy D. Kohler
1967-1969	Llewellyn E. Thompson
1969-1973	Jacob D. Beam
1973-1976	Walter J. Stoessel, Jr.
1976-1979	Malcolm Toon
1979-1981	Thomas J. Watson, Jr.
1981-	Arthur A. Hartman

United Arab Emirates

Ambassadors

1972-1974	William A. Stoltzfus, Jr.
1974-1976	Michael Sterner
1976-1979	Francois Dickman
1979-1981	William D. Wolle
1982-	G. Quincy Lumsden, Jr.

United Arab Republic

(See Egypt and Syria for earlier representation; see Arab Republic of Egypt for later representation.)

Ambassadors

1958-1960	Raymond A. Hare
1960-1961	G. Frederick Reinhardt
1961-1964	John S. Badeau
1964-1967	Lucius D. Battle
1967	Richard H. Nolte
1967	Embassy closed

Upper Volta

(See Burkina-Faso for later representation.)

Ambassadors

1960-1961	R. Borden Reams

1961-1966	Thomas S. Estes
1966-1969	Elliott P. Skinner
1969-1971	William E. Schaufele, Jr.
1971-1974	Donald B. Easum
1974-1978	Pierre R. Graham
1978-1980	Thomas D. Boyatt
1981-1984	Julius Waring Walker

Uruguay

Ministers

1867-1868	Alexander Asboth
1869-1870	Henry G. Worthington
1869-1870	Robert C. Kirk
1870-1873	John L. Stevens
1874-1876	John C. Caldwell

Charges d'Affaires

1876-1882	John C. Caldwell
1882-1885	William Williams
1885-1890	John E. Bacon

EEMP

1890-1894	George Maney
1894-1897	Granville Stuart
1897-1905	William R. Finch
1905-1909	Edward C. O'Brien
1909-1911	Edwin V. Morgan
1911-1915	Nicolay A. Grevstad
1915-1921	Robert E. Jeffrey
1922-1925	Hoffman Philip
1925-1929	Ulysses Grant-Smith
1929-1930	Leland Harrison
1930-1934	J. Butler Wright
1934-1937	Julius G. Lay
1937-1939	William Dawson
1939-1941	Edwin C. Wilson

Ambassadors

1941-1946	William Dawson
1946-1947	Joseph F. McGurk
1947-1949	Ellis O. Briggs
1949-1951	Christian M. Ravndal
1951-1953	Edward L. Roddan
1953-1956	Dempster McIntosh
1956-1958	Jefferson Patterson
1958-1961	Robert F. Woodward
1961-1962	Edward J. Sparks
1962-1965	Wymberley D. Coerr
1965-1967	Henry A. Hoyt
1968-1969	Robert M. Sayre
1969-1972	Charles W. Adair
1973-1977	Ernest V. Siracusa
1977-1979	Lawrence A. Pezzullo
1979-1980	Lyle F. Lane
1980-1981	Vacant
1981-1985	Thomas Aranda, Jr.
1986-	Malcolm R. Wilkey

Venezuela

Charges d'Affaires

1835-1840	John G. A. Williamson
1841-1844	Allen A. Hall
1844-1845	Vespasian Ellis
1845-1850	Benjamin G. Shields
1850-1853	Isaac N. Steele
1854	Charles Eames

Ministers

1854-1858	Charles Eames

1858-1861	Edward A. Turpin
1861-1862	Henry T. Blow
1862-1866	Erastus D. Culver
1866-1867	James Wilson
1867-1868	Thomas N. Stillwell
1869-1870	James R. Partridge
1870-1874	William A. Pile
1874-1878	Thomas Russell
1878-1885	Jehu Baker
1885-1889	Charles L. Scott

EEMP

1889-1893	William L. Scruggs
1893-1894	Frank C. Partridge
1894-1895	Seneca Haselton
1895-1897	Allen Thomas
1897-1901	Francis B. Loomis
1901-1905	Herbert W. Bowen
1905-1909	William W. Russell
1910-1911	John W. Garrett
1911-1913	Elliott Northcott
1913-1921	Preston McGoodwin
1921-1929	Willis C. Cook
1929-1934	George T. Summerlin
1935-1938	Meredith Nicholson
1938-1939	Antonio C. Gonzales

Ambassadors

1939-1947	Frank P. Corrigan
1947-1950	Walter J. Donnelly
1950-1951	Norman Armour
1951-1956	Fletcher Warren
1956-1957	Dempster McIntosh
1958-1961	Edward J. Sparks
1961-1962	Teodoro Moscoso
1962-1964	C. Allan Stewart
1965-1969	Maurice M. Bernbaum
1970-1975	Robert McClintock
1975-1976	Harry W. Shlaudeman
1976-1978	Viron P. Vaky
1978-1982	William H. Luers
1982-1985	George W. Landau
1986-	Otto J. Reich

Vietnam

(Republic of Vietnam after 1954.)

Charges d'Affaires

1949-1950	Edmund A. Gullion

EEMP

1950-1952	Donald R. Heath

Ambassadors

1952-1955	Donald R. Heath
1955-1957	G. Frederick Reinhardt
1957-1961	Elbridge Durbrow
1961-1963	Frederick E. Nolting, Jr.
1963-1964	Henry Cabot Lodge
1964-1965	Maxwell D. Taylor
1965-1967	Henry Cabot Lodge
1967-1973	Ellsworth Bunker
1973-1975	Graham A. Martin
1975	Embassy closed

Western Samoa

Ambassadors

1971-1972	Kenneth Franzheim, II
1973	Vacant

1974-1979	Armistead I. Selden, Jr.
1979-1981	Anne C. Martindell
1981	H. Monroe Browne
1981	Embassy closed

Yemen

(See Southern Yemen and Yemen Arab Republic for later representation.)

EEMP

1946-1950	J. Rives Childs
1950-1953	Raymond A. Hare
1953-1957	George Wadsworth
1957-1959	Donald R. Heath
1959-1960	Raymond A. Hare
1960-1961	G. Frederick Reinhardt
1961-1962	Parker T. Hart
1963-1967	Vacant
1967	Embassy closed

Yemen Arab Republic

(See Yemen for earlier representation.)

Ambassadors

1972-1974	William R. Crawford
1974-1978	Thomas J. Scotes
1978-1981	George M. Lane

1981-1984	David E. Zweifeln
1985-	William A. Rugh

Yugoslavia

(See Montenegro and Serbia for earlier representation.)

EEMP

1929-1933	John D. Prince
1933-1937	Charles S. Wilson
1937-1941	Arthur Bliss Lane
1941-1942	Anthony J. Drexel Biddle, Jr.

Ambassadors

1942-1943	Anthony J. Drexel Biddle, Jr.
1943-1944	Lincoln MacVeagh
1944-1947	Richard C. Patterson, Jr.
1947-1949	Cavendish W. Cannon
1949-1953	George V. Allen
1953-1957	James W. Riddleberger
1957-1961	Karl L. Rankin
1961-1963	George F. Kennan
1964-1969	C. Burke Elbrick
1969-1971	William Leonhart
1971-1975	Malcolm Toon
1975-1976	Laurence H. Silberman
1977-1981	Lawrence S. Eagleburger
1981-1985	David Anderson
1985-	John D. Scanlon

Zaire

(See Democratic Republic of the Congo for earlier representation.)

1974-1975	Deane R. Hinton
1975-1979	Walter L. Cutler
1979-1982	Robert B. Oakley
1983-1984	Peter D. Constable
1984-	Brandon H. Grove, Jr.

Zambia

Ambassadors

1965-1969	Robert C. Good
1969-1972	Oliver L. Troxel, Jr.
1972-1976	Jean M. Wilkowski
1976-1979	Stephen Low
1979-1982	Frank G. Wisner, II
1982-1985	Nicholas Platt
1985-	Paul J. Hare

Zimbabwe

Ambassadors

1980-1984	Robert V. Keeley
1984-	David C. Miller

X
Federal Agency Chiefs

Federal Agency Chiefs

Agency for International Development

Administrators

1961 Fowler Hamilton
1962 David E. Bell
1966 William S. Gaud
1969 John A. Hannah
1973 Daniel Parker
1977 John J. Gilligan
1978 Robert H. Nooter (Acting)
1979 Douglas J. Bennet, Jr.
1981 M. Peter McPherson

(Predecessor agencies)

Economic Cooperation Administration

Administrators

1948 Paul G. Hoffman
1950 William C. Foster

Technical Cooperation Administration

Administrators

1950 Henry G. Bennett
1952 Stanley Andrews

Mutual Security Agency

Directors

1951 W. Averell Harriman
1953 Harold E. Stassen

Foreign Operations Administration

Directors

1953 Harold E. Stassen

International Cooperation Administration

Directors

1955 John B. Hollister
1957 James H. Smith, Jr.
1959 James W. Riddleberger
1961 Henry R. Labouisse

Atomic Energy Commission

(Abolished in 1974; some powers assumed by Nuclear Regulatory Commission.)

Chairmen

1946 David E. Lilienthal
1950 Sumner T. Pike (Acting)
1950 Gordon Dean
1953 Lewis L. Strauss
1958 John A. McCone
1961 Glenn T. Seaborg
1971 James R. Schlesinger
1973 Dixy Lee Ray

Central Intelligence Agency

Directors

1947 Roscoe H. Millenkoetter
1950 Walter Bedell Smith
1953 Allen Dulles
1961 John A. McCone
1965 William A. Radford
1966 Richard M. Helms
1973 Vernon A. Walters (Acting)
1973 William E. Colby
1976 George Bush
1977 Stansfield Turner
1981 William J. Casey

Drug Enforcement Agency

Administrators

1973 John R. Bartels, Jr.
1976 Peter B. Bensinger
1982 Francis M. Mullen, Jr.
1985 John C. Lawn

Environmental Protection Agency

Administrators

1970 William D. Ruckelshaus
1973 Robert W. Fri (Acting)
1973 Russell E. Train
1977 Douglas M. Costle
1981 Ann McGill Gorsuch
1983 William D. Ruckelshaus
1985 Lee M. Thomas

Export-Import Bank of the United States

Presidents

1934 George N. Peek
1935 Jesse H. Jones
1936 Warren L. Pierson
1945 Wayne C. Taylor
1946 William McChesney Martin, Jr.
1949 Herbert E. Gaston
1953 Glen E. Edgerton
1955 Samuel C. Waugh
1961 Harold F. Linder
1969 Henry Kearns
1974 William J. Casey
1976 Stephen M. DuBrul, Jr.
1977 John L. Moore, Jr.
1981 Margaret W. Kahliff (Acting)
1982 William H. Draper, III
1986 John A. Bohn, Jr.

Federal Communications Commission

Chairmen

1934 Eugene O. Sykes
1935 Anning S. Prall
1937 Frank R. McNinch
1939 James L. Fly
1944 Paul A. Porter
1946 Charles R. Denny
1947 Wayne Coy
1952 Paul A. Walker
1953 Rosel H. Hyde
1954 George C. McConnaughey
1957 John C. Doerfer
1960 Frederick W. Ford
1961 Newton N. Minow
1963 E. William Henry
1966 Rosel H. Hyde
1969 Dean Burch
1974 Richard E. Wiley
1977 Charles D. Ferris
1981 Mark S. Fowler

Federal Home Loan Bank Board

Chairmen

1932 Franklin W. Fort
1933 William F. Stevenson
1933 John H. Fahey
1947 William K. Divers
1953 Walter W. McAllister

1956 Albert J. Robertson
1961 Joseph P. McMurray
1963 John E. Horne
1968 Robert L. Rand (Acting)
1969 Preston Martin
1973 Thomas P. Bomar
1976 Garth Marston
1977 Robert H. McKinney
1979 Jay Janis
1981 Richard T. Pratt
1983 Edwin J. Gray

Federal Maritime Commission

Chairmen

1961 James L. Pimper (Acting)
1961 Thomas E. Stakem, Jr.
1963 John Harllee
1969 Helen Delich Bentley
1976 Karl E. Bakke
1978 Richard J. Daschbach
1981 Leslie L. Kanuk
1982 Alan Green, Jr.
1985 Edward V. Hickey, Jr.

Federal Mediation and Conciliation Service

(U.S. Conciliation Service until 1947.)

Directors

1917 Hugh L. Kerwin
1937 John R. Steelman
1944 Howard T. Colvin (Acting)
1945 Edgar L. Warren
1947 Cyrus S. Ching
1952 David L. Cole
1953 Clyde M. Mills (Acting)
1953 Whitley P. McCoy
1955 Joseph F. Finnegan
1961 William E. Sinkin
1969 J. Curtis Counts
1973 W. J. Usery, Jr.
1976 James F. Scearce
1977 Wayne L. Horvitz
1981 Kenneth E. Moffett
1982 Kay McMurray

Federal Power Commission

(Abolished in 1977; see Department of Energy in Cabinets section.)

Chairmen

1930 George O. Smith
1933 Frank R. McNinch
1939 Clyde L. Seavey
1940 Leland Olds
1944 Basil Manly
1945 Leland Olds
1947 Nelson Lee Smith
1950 Mon C. Wallgren
1952 Thomas C. Buchanan
1953 Jerome K. Kuykendall
1961 Joseph C. Swidler
1966 Lee C. White
1969 John N. Nassikas
1975 Richard L. Dunham

Federal Reserve System

Chairmen

1914 Charles S. Hamlin
1916 W. P. G. Harding
1923 Daniel R. Crissinger
1927 Roy A. Young
1930 Eugene Meyer
1933 Eugene R. Black
1934 Marriner S. Eccles
1948 Thomas B. McCabe
1951 William McChesney Martin, Jr.
1970 Arthur F. Burns
1978 G. William Miller
1979 Paul A. Volcker

Geological Survey

Directors

1879 Clarence King
1881 John W. Powell
1894 Charles D. Walcott
1907 George O. Smith
1931 Walter C. Mendenhall
1943 William E. Wrather
1956 Thomas B. Nolan
1965 William T. Pecora
1971 Vincent E. McKelvey
1978 William Menard
1981 Dallas L. Peck

Government Printing Office

Public Printers

1861 John D. Defrees
1866 Cornelius Wendell
1867 John D. Defrees
1869 Almon M. Clapp
1877 John D. Defrees
1882 Sterling P. Rounds
1886 Thomas B. Benedict
1889 Frank W. Palmer
1894 Thomas B. Benedict
1897 Frank W. Palmer
1905 Charles A. Stillings

1908 Samuel B. Donnelly
1913 Cornelius Ford
1921 George H. Carter
1934 Augustus E. Geigengack
1948 John J. Deviny
1953 Raymond Blattenberger
1961 James L. Harrison
1971 Adolphus N. Spence, II
1973 Thomas F. McCormick
1978 John J. Boyle
1980 Samuel L. Saylor (Acting)
1982 Danford L. Sawyer, Jr.
1984 William J. Barrett (Acting)
1985 Ralph E. Kinnickell, Jr.

Immigration and Naturalization Service

(Formed by consolidation of Bureau of Immigration and Bureau of Naturalization in 1933.)

Commissioners

1933 Daniel W. MacCormack
1937 James L. Houghteling
1940 Lemuel B. Schofield
1942 Earl G. Harrison
1945 Ugo Carusi
1947 Watson B. Miller
1951 Argyle R. Mackey
1954 Joseph M. Swing
1962 Raymond F. Farrell
1973 James F. Greene (Acting)
1974 Leonard F. Chapman, Jr.
1978 Leonel J. Castillo
1980 David Crosland (Acting)
1982 Alan C. Nelson

Internal Revenue Service

Commissioners

1862 George S. Boutwell
1863 Joseph J. Lewis
1865 William Orton
1865 Edward A. Rollins
1869 Columbus Delano
1871 Alfred Pleasonton
1871 John W. Douglass
1875 Daniel D. Pratt
1876 Green B. Raum
1883 Walter Evans
1885 Joseph S. Miller
1889 John W. Mason
1893 Joseph S. Miller
1896 W. St. John Forman
1898 Nathan B. Scott
1899 George W. Wilson
1900 John W. Yerkes
1907 John G. Capers
1909 Royal E. Cabell
1913 William H. Osborn
1917 Daniel C. Roper
1920 William M. Williams
1921 David H. Blair
1929 Robert H. Lucas
1930 David Burnet
1933 Guy T. Helevering
1943 Robert E. Hannegan
1944 Joseph D. Nunan, Jr.
1947 George J. Schoeneman
1951 John B. Dunlap
1953 T. Coleman Andrews
1955 Russell C. Harrington

1958 Dana Latham
1961 Mortimer M. Caplin
1965 Sheldon S. Cohen
1969 Randolph W. Thrower
1971 Johnnie M. Walters
1973 Donald C. Alexander
1977 Jerome Kurtz
1981 Roscoe L. Egger, Jr.

Library of Congress

Librarians

1802 John James Beckley
1807 Patrick Magruder
1815 George Watterston
1829 John S. Meehan
1861 John G. Stephenson
1864 Ainsworth R. Spofford
1897 John R. Young
1899 Herbert Putnam
1939 Archibald MacLeish
1945 Luther H. Evans
1954 Lawrence Q. Mumford
1974 John G. Lorenz (Acting)
1975 Daniel J. Boorstin

Merit Systems Protection Board

(U.S. Civil Service Commission until 1978.)

Presidents

1883 Dorman B. Eaton
1885 Alfred P. Edgerton
1886 Charles Lyman
1893 John R. Proctor
1904 John C. Black
1906 John A. McIlhenny
1919 Martin A. Morrison
1921 John H. Bartlett
1923 William C. Deming
1930 Thomas E. Campbell
1933 Harry B. Mitchell

Chairmen

1949 Harry B. Mitchell
1951 Robert Ramspeck
1953 Philip Young
1957 Harris Ellsworth
1959 Roger W. Jones
1961 John W. Macy, Jr.
1969 Robert E. Hampton
1977 Georgiana H. Sheldon (Acting)
1978 Alan K. Campbell
1979 Ruth T. Prokop
1981 Herbert E. Ellingwood
1986 Maria L. Johnson (Acting)

National Aeronautics and Space Administration

Administrators

1958 T. Keith Glennan
1961 James E. Webb
1968 Thomas O. Paine
1971 James C. Fletcher
1977 Robert A. Frosch

1980 Alan M. Lovelace (Acting)
1981 James M. Beggs
1986 James C. Fletcher

National Mediation Board

Chairmen

1934 William M. Leiserson
1936 James W. Carmalt
1937 Otto S. Beyer
1939 George A. Cook
1941 David J. Lewis
1942 William M. Leiserson
1944 Harry H. Schwartz
1946 Frank P. Douglass
1948 Francis A. O'Neill, Jr.
1950 John Thad Scott, Jr.
1951 Leverett Edwards
1952 Francis A. O'Neill, Jr.
1955 Leverett Edwards
1956 Robert O. Boyd
1957 Francis A. O'Neill, Jr.
1958 Leverett Edwards
1959 Robert O. Boyd
1960 Francis A. O'Neill, Jr.
1961 Leverett Edwards
1963 Francis A. O'Neill, Jr.
1964 Howard G. Gamser
1965 Leverett Edwards
1966 Francis A. O'Neill, Jr.
1967 Howard G. Gamser
1968 Leverett Edwards
1969 Francis A. O'Neill, Jr.
1970 George S. Ives
1972 David H. Stowe
1975 Kay McMurray
1978 George S. Ives
1979 David H. Stowe
1980 Robert O. Harris
1981 George S. Ives
1982 Robert O. Harris
1983 Walter C. Wallace
1984 Helen M. Witt
1985 Walter C. Wallace
1986 Charles L. Woods

National Park Service

Directors

1921 Stephen T. Mather
1929 Horace M. Albright
1933 Arno Cammerer
1940 Newton B. Drury
1951 Arthur E. Demaray
1951 Conrad L. Wirth
1964 George B. Hartzog, Jr.
1973 Ronald H. Walker
1975 Gary E. Everhardt
1978 William J. Whalen
1981 Russell E. Dickenson
1985 Mary Lou Grier (Acting)
1986 William Penn Mott, Jr.

National Science Foundation

Directors

1951 Alan T. Waterman
1963 Leland J. Haworth
1969 William D. McElroy
1972 H. Guyford Stever

1977	Richard C. Atkinson
1980	Lewis M. Branscomb
1985	Roland W. Schmitt

National Security Agency/Central Security Service

(National Security Agency until 1974.)

Directors

1951	Ralph J. Canine
1956	John A. Samford
1960	Laurence H. Frost
1962	Gordon A. Blake
1965	Marshall S. Carter
1969	Noel Gayler
1973	Samuel Phillips
1974	Lew Allen, Jr.
1977	Bobby R. Inman
1981	Ernest Graves
1982	Lincoln D. Faurer
1985	William E. Odom

Nuclear Regulatory Commission

Chairmen

1975	William A. Anders
1976	Marcus A. Rowden
1977	Joseph M. Hendrie
1980	John F. Ahearne
1981	Joseph M. Hendrie
1982	Nunzio J. Pallidino
1986	Lando W. Zech, Jr.

Office of Education

(Superseded by Department of Education in 1979; see Cabinets section.)

Commissioners

1867	Henry Barnard
1870	John Eaton
1886	N. H. R. Dawson
1889	William T. Harris
1906	Elmer E. Brown
1911	Philander P. Claxton
1921	John J. Tigert
1929	William J. Cooper
1933	George F. Zook
1934	John W. Studebaker
1949	Earl J. McGrath
1953	Lee M. Thurston
1953	Samuel M. Brownell
1956	Lawrence G. Derthick
1961	Sterling M. McMurrin
1962	Francis Keppel
1966	Harold Howe, II
1969	John Ottina
1974	Terrell H. Bell
1977	Ernest L. Boyer

Office of Human Development Services

(Office of Economic Opportunity until 1975; Community Services Administration until 1976; Public Services Administration until 1977.)

Directors

1964	Sargent Shriver
1968	R. Bertrand Harding (Acting)
1969	Donald Rumsfeld
1970	Frank Carlucci
1971	Philip Sanchez
1973	Alvin J. Arnett (Acting)
1974	Bert Gallegos
1976	Samuel R. Martinez
1977	Graciela Olivarez

Assistant Secretaries

1981	Dorcas R. Hardy

Office of Management and Budget

(Bureau of the Budget until 1970.)

Directors

1921	Charles G. Dawes
1922	Herbert M. Lord
1929	J. Clawson Roop
1933	Lewis W. Douglas
1934	Daniel W. Bell
1939	Harold D. Smith
1946	James E. Webb
1949	Frank Pace
1950	Frederick J. Lawton
1953	Joseph M. Dodge
1954	Rowland R. Hughes
1956	Percival F. Brundage
1958	Maurice H. Stans
1961	David E. Bell
1962	Kermit Gordon
1965	Charles L. Schultze
1968	Charles J. Zwick
1969	Robert P. Mayo
1970	George P. Shultz
1973	Roy L. Ash
1975	James T. Lynn
1977	Bert Lance
1978	James T. McIntyre, Jr.
1981	David A. Stockman
1985	James C. Miller, III

Office of the Treasury

Treasurers

1775	Michael Hillegas
1789	Samuel Meredith
1801	Thomas T. Tucker
1828	Wilbur Clark
1829	John Campbell
1839	William Selden
1850	John Sloan
1853	Samuel Casey
1860	William C. Price
1861	F. E. Spinner
1875	John C. New
1876	A. U. Wyman
1877	James Gilfillan

1883	A. U. Wyman
1885	Conrad N. Jordan
1887	James W. Hyatt
1889	J. N. Huston
1891	Enos H. Nebecker
1893	D. N. Morgan
1897	Ellis H. Roberts
1905	Charles H. Treat
1909	Lee McClung
1912	Carmi A. Thompson
1913	John Burke
1921	Frank White
1928	H. T. Tate
1929	W. O. Woods
1933	W. A. Julian
1949	Georgia Neese Clark
1953	Ivy Baker Priest
1961	Elizabeth Rudel Smith
1963	Kathryn O'Hay Granahan
1966	William T. Howell (Acting)
1969	Dorothy Andrews Kabis
1971	Romana Acosta Banuelos
1974	Francine I. Neff
1978	Azie Taylor Morton
1981	Angela Buchanan
1983	Katherine D. Ortega

Patent and Trademark Office

(Patent Office until 1975.)

Commissioners

1836	Henry L. Ellsworth
1845	Edmund Burke
1849	Thomas Ewbank
1852	Silas H. Hodges
1853	Charles Mason
1857	Joseph Holt
1859	William D. Bishop
1860	Philip F. Thomas
1861	David P. Holloway
1865	Thomas C. Theaker
1868	Elisha Foote
1869	Samuel S. Fisher
1871	Mortimer D. Leggett
1875	John M. Thacher
1875	Robert H. Duell
1877	Ellis Spear
1878	Halbert E. Paine
1880	Edgar M. Marble
1883	Benjamin Butterworth
1885	Martin V. B. Montgomery
1887	Benton J. Hall
1889	Charles E. Mitchell
1891	William E. Simonds
1893	John S. Seymour
1897	Benjamin Butterworth
1898	Charles H. Duell
1901	Frederick I. Allen
1907	Edward B. Moore
1913	Thomas Ewing
1917	James T. Newton
1920	Robert F. Whitehead
1921	Thomas E. Robertson
1933	Conway P. Coe
1945	Casper W. Ooms
1947	Lawrence C. Kingsland
1949	John A. Marzall
1953	Robert C. Watson
1961	David L. Ladd
1964	Edward J. Brenner
1969	William E. Schuyler, Jr.
1971	Robert Gottschalk
1974	C. Marshall Dann

1978	Lutrelle F. Parker (Acting)
1979	Donald W. Banner
1980	Sidney Diamond
1981	Gerald J. Mossinghoff
1985	Donald J. Quigg

Public Health Service

Surgeons General

1871	John M. Woodworth
1879	John B. Hammond
1891	Walter Wyman
1912	Rupert Blue
1920	Hugh S. Cumming
1936	Thomas Parran
1948	Leonard A. Scheele
1956	Leroy E. Burney
1961	Luther L. Terry
1965	William H. Stewart
1969	Jesse L. Steinfeld
1978	Julius B. Richmond
1982	C. Everett Koop

Securities and Exchange Commission

Chairmen

1934	Joseph P. Kennedy
1935	James M. Landis
1937	William O. Douglas
1939	Jerome N. Frank
1941	Edward C. Eicher
1942	Ganson Purcell
1946	James J. Caffrey
1948	Edmond M. Hanrahan
1949	Harry A. McDonald
1952	Donald C. Cook
1953	Ralph H. Demmler
1955	J. Sinclair Armstrong
1957	Edward N. Gadsby
1961	William L. Cary
1964	Manuel F. Cohen
1969	Hamer H. Budge
1971	William J. Casey
1973	Ray Garrett, Jr.
1975	Roderick M. Hills
1977	Harold M. Williams
1981	John S. R. Shad

Selective Service System

Directors

1940	Clarence A. Dykstra
1941	Lewis B. Hershey
1970	Curtis W. Tarr
1972	Byron V. Pepitone
1978	Robert E. Shuck (Acting)
1980	Bernard D. Rostker
1981	Thomas K. Turnage
1986	Wilfred Ebel

Small Business Administration

Administrators

1953	William D. Mitchell
1954	Wendell B. Barnes
1959	Philip McCallum

1961	John E. Horne					

1961 John E. Horne
1963 Eugene P. Foley
1966 Bernard L. Boutin
1967 Robert C. Moot
1968 Howard J. Samuels
1969 Hilary J. Sandoval, Jr.
1971 Thomas S. Kleppe
1976 Mitchell P. Kobelinski
1977 A. Vernon Weaver, Jr.
1981 Michael Cardenas
1982 James C. Sanders
1986 Charles L. Heatherly

Social Security Administration

(Social Security Board until 1946.)

Chairmen

1935 John G. Winant
1937 Arthur J. Altmeyer

Commissioners

1946 Arthur J. Altmeyer
1953 John W. Tramburg
1954 Charles I. Schottland
1959 William L. Mitchell
1962 Robert M. Ball
1973 Arthur E. Hess (Acting)
1974 James B. Cardwell
1977 Don I. Wortman (Acting)
1978 Stanford G. Ross
1980 William J. Driver
1981 John A. Svahn
1984 Martha A. McSteen (Acting)

Tennessee Valley Authority

Chairmen

1933 Arthur E. Morgan
1938 Harcourt A. Morgan
1941 David E. Lilienthal
1946 Gordon R. Clapp
1954 Herbert D. Vogel
1962 Aubrey J. Wagner
1977 S. David Freeman
1981 Charles H. Dean, Jr.

U.S. Coast Guard

Commandants

1915 Ellsworth P. Bertholf
1919 William E. Reynolds
1924 Frederick C. Billard
1932 Harry G. Hamlet
1936 Russell R. Waesche
1946 Joseph F. Farley
1950 Merlin O'Neill
1954 Alfred C. Richmond
1962 Edwin J. Roland
1966 Willard J. Smith
1970 Chester R. Bender
1974 Owen W. Siler
1978 John B. Hayes
1982 James S. Gracey
1986 Paul A. Yost

U.S. Customs Service

(Bureau of Customs until 1973.)

Commissioners

1927 Ernest W. Camp

1929 Francis X. A. Eble
1933 James H. Moyle
1939 Basil Harris
1940 William R. Johnson
1949 Frank Dow
1954 Ralph Kelly
1961 Philip Nichols, Jr.
1965 Lester Johnson
1969 Myles J. Ambrose
1973 Vernon D. Acree
1977 Robert E. Chasen
1980 William T. Archey (Acting)
1981 William von Raab

U.S. Information Agency

Directors

1953 Theodore Streibert
1956 Arthur Larson
1957 George V. Allen
1961 Edward R. Murrow
1964 Carl Rowan
1965 Leonard H. Marks
1969 Frank Shakespeare
1973 James Keogh
1977 John E. Reinhardt
1980 John W. Shirley (Acting)
1981 Charles Z. Wick

U.S. International Trade Commission

(U.S. Tariff Commission until 1974.)

Chairmen

1917 Frank W. Taussig
1920 Thomas W. Page

1922 Thomas O. Marvin
1930 Edgar B. Brossard
1930 Henry P. Fletcher
1931 Robert L. O'Brien
1937 Raymond B. Stevens
1942 Oscar B. Ryder
1953 Edgar B. Brossard
1959 Joseph E. Talbot
1961 Ben Dorfman
1966 Paul Kaplowitz
1967 Stanley D. Metzger
1969 Glenn W. Sutton
1971 Chester L. Mize
1971 Catherine Bedell
1975 Will E. Leonard, Jr.
1977 Daniel Minchew
1979 Joseph O. Parker
1980 Bill Alberger
1982 Alfred E. Eckes, Jr.
1985 Paula Stern

U.S. Postal Service

(Temporarily established as a branch of the Treasury Department in 1789; Postmaster General was a Cabinet member 1829-1970, see section III; reorganized as an independent federal agency in 1970.)

Postmasters General

1789 Samuel Osgood
1791 Timothy Pickering
1795 Joseph Habersham
1801 Gideon Granger
1814 Return J. Meigs, Jr.
1823 John McLean
1971 Edwin T. Klassen
1975 Benjamin F. Bailar
1978 William F. Bolger
1985 Paul N. Carlin
1986 Albert V. Casey

XI

Chief Executives of U.S. Cities

Chief Executives of U.S. Cities

A listing of mayors and other chief executives of cities that are state capitals, have populations over 500,000, or have been among the ten most populous in any census since 1800.

Alabama

Montgomery

1819 William Graham
1821 W. E. Benson
1824 John Gindrat
1825 William Cook
1826 John Edmondson
1827 Francis McGehee
1827 Andrew Dexter
1828 William Sayre
1828 F. Bugbee
1829 John Edmondson
1830 William Sayre
1831 B. Gordon
1832 J. Wyman
1833 John Lambert
1833 Isaac Tinker
1834 M. B. Tatum
1835 John H. Thorington
1836 F. Bugbee
1837 G. D. Shortridge
1838 J. Hutchinson
1838 Samuel D. Holt
1839 Jack Thorington
1841 Hardy Herbert
1842 Perez Coleman
1847 Nimrod E. Benson
1848 Edwin B. Harris
1850 Robert T. Davis
1851 Thomas Welch
1852 Samuel D. Holt
1853 Charles R. Hansford
1860 Andrew J. Noble
1862 J. T. Johnson
1864 Walter L. Coleman
1868 Thomas O. Glasscock
1870 H. E. Faber
1876 M. L. Moses
1881 J. B. Gaston
1885 W. S. Reese
1890 Edward A. Graham
1891 John H. Crommelin
1895 John H. Clisby
1900 E. B. Joseph
1903 Thomas H. Carr
1905 C. P. McIntyre
1905 W. M. Teague
1909 Gaston Gunter
1910 W. A. Gunter
1915 W. T. Robertson
1920 W. A. Gunter
1940 Cyrus B. Brown
1944 David E. Dunn
1946 John L. Goodwyn
1951 W. A. Gayle
1960 Earl D. James
1973 Jim Robinson
1979 Emory Folmar

Alaska

Juneau

1900 A. K. Delaney
1901 George F. Forrest
1902 O. H. Adsit
1903 P. H. Adsit
1904 George F. Forrest
1905 John F. Maloney
1906 H. T. Tripp
1907 George F. Forrest
1908 Emery Valentine
1912 Harry Bishop
1913 Charles W. Carter
1914 John Reck
1916 B. D. Stewart
1917 Emery Valentine
1919 E. L. Gray
1920 R. E. Robertson
1923 I. Goldstein
1925 J. J. Connors
1927 Thomas B. Judson
1933 I. Goldstein
1937 Thomas B. Judson
1938 Harry I. Lucas
1944 A. B. Hayes
1945 Ernest Parsons
1946 Waino Hendrickson
1953 Bert F. McDowell
1955 M. L. MacSpadden
1959 Lauris S. Parker
1961 A. W. Boddy
1961 Wayne Johnson
1962 Lauris S. Parker
1967 Timothy O'Day
1968 Joseph L. George
1969 Joseph A. McLean
1973 William R. Macomber
1976 Virginia Kline
1979 W. D. (Bill) Overstreet
1983 Fran Ulmer

Arizona

Phoenix

1881 John T. Alsop
1882 Francis T. Shaw
1883 De Forest Porter
1884 George F. Coats
1885 E. Ganz
1886 De Forest Porter
1888 A. Leonard Meyer
1889 George F. Coats
1890 T. N. E. McGlasson
1891 Joseph Campbell
1893 P. J. Cole
1894 J. O. Monihan
1895 R. S. Rossin
1895 R. Allyn Lewis
1896 F. B. Moss
1896 J. D. Monihan
1897 J. C. Adams
1898 C. J. Dyer
1899 E. Ganz
1901 Walter Talbot
1903 Walter Bennett
1904 John T. Dunlop
1905 F. B. Moss
1906 R. H. Greene (Acting)
1906 L. W. Coggins (Acting)
1909 Lloyd B. Christy
1914 George U. Young
1916 Peter Corpstein
1920 Willis H. Plunkett
1922 L. L. Harmon
1923 Louis B. Whitney
1925 Frank A. Jefferson
1928 F. J. Paddock
1930 Franklin D. Lane
1932 F. J. Paddock
1934 Joseph S. Jenckes
1936 John H. Udall
1938 Walter J. Thalheimer
1940 Reed Shupe
1942 Newell Stewart
1944 J. R. Fleming
1946 Ray Busey
1948 Nicholas Udall
1952 Hohen Foster
1954 Frank Murphy
1956 Jack Williams
1960 Sam Mardian
1964 Milton H. Graham
1970 John D. Driggs
1974 Timothy A. Barrow
1976 Margaret T. Hance
1984 Terry Goddard

Arkansas

Little Rock

1835 James Pitcher
1838 Jesse Brown
1840 S. H. Webb
1842 John Widgery
1844 William Brown, Sr.
1845 Lambert J. Reardon
1847 R. L. Dodge
1848 S. H. Webb
1849 Roswell Beebe
1850 D. J. Baldwin
1851 John E. Knight
1852 A. J. Hutt
1854 Thomas D. Merrick
1855 C. P. Bertrand
1857 William E. Ashley
1859 Gordon N. Peay
1861 William E. Ashley
1863 Vacant
1866 J. J. McAlmont
1867 J. W. Hopkins
1868 John Wassell
1869 A. K. Hartman
1871 J. G. Botsford
1871 Robert F. Catterson
1873 Frederick Kramer
1875 John G. Fletcher
1881 Frederick Kramer
1887 William G. Whipple
1891 H. L. Fletcher
1893 M. G. Hall
1895 James A. Woodson
1900 W. R. Duley
1903 W. E. Lenon
1908 John H. Hollis
1911 Charles E. Taylor
1919 Ben D. Brickhouse
1925 Charles E. Moyer
1929 Pat L. Robinson
1931 Horace A. Knowlton
1935 Richard E. Overman
1939 J. V. Satterfield, Jr.
1941 Charles E. Moyer
1945 Dan T. Sprick
1947 Sam M. Wassell
1952 Pratt C. Remmell
1956 Woodrow W. Mann
1958 Werner C. Knoop
1963 Byron R. Morse
1965 Harold Henson
1967 Martin Borchert
1969 Haco Boyd
1971 George E. Wimberly
1973 William H. Walters
1975 George E. Wimberly
1977 Donald L. Mehlburger
1979 Webster L. Hubbell
1981 Charles Bussey
1983 J. W. Benafield
1985 Thomas A. Prince

California

Los Angeles

1850 Alpheus P. Hodges
1851 Benjamin D. Wilson
1852 John G. Nichols
1853 Antonio F. Coronel
1854 Stephen C. Foster
1855 Thomas Foster
1856 Stephen C. Foster
1856 John G. Nichols
1859 Damien Marchessault
1860 Henry Mellus
1861 Damien Marchessault
1865 Jose Mascarel
1866 Cristobal Aguilar
1868 Joel H. Turner
1871 Cristobal Aguilar
1872 James R. Toberman
1874 Prudent Beaudry
1876 Frederick A. MacDougall
1878 James R. Toberman

1882 Cameron E. Thom	**San Diego**	1976 George Moscone	1868 William M. Clayton
1884 Edward F. Spence		1978 Dianne Feinstein	1869 Baxter B. Stiles
1886 William H. Workman	1850 Joshua H. Bean		1871 John Harper
1888 John Bryson	1851 David B. Kurtz		1872 Joseph E. Bates
1889 Henry T. Hazard	1852 George P. Tebbetts	**San Jose**	1873 Francis M. Case
1892 Thomas E. Rowan	1887 W. J. Hunsaker		1874 William J. Barker
1894 Frank Rader	1889 Douglas Gunn	1850 Josiah Belden	1876 Richard G. Buckingham
1896 Meredith P. Snyder	1891 Matthew Sherman	1851 Thomas W. White	1877 Baxter B. Stiles
1898 Fred Eaton	1893 William H. Carlson	1854 O. H. Allen	1878 Richard Sopris
1900 Meredith P. Snyder	1897 D. C. Reed	1855 S. O. Houghton	1881 Robert Morris
1904 Owen C. McAleer	1899 Edwin M. Capps	1856 Lawrence Archer	1883 John L. Routt
1906 Arthur C. Harper	1901 Frank P. Frary	1856 John M. Murphy	1885 Joseph E. Bates
1909 William D. Stephens	1905 John L. Sehon	1857 R. G. Moody	1887 William S. Lee
1909 George Alexander	1907 John F. Forward, Jr.	1858 P. O. Miner	1889 Wolfe Londoner
1913 Henry R. Rose	1909 Grant Conard	1859 Thomas Fallon	1891 Platt Rogers
1915 Charles E. Sebastian	1911 James E. Wadham	1860 R. B. Buckner	1893 Marion D. Van Horn
1916 Frederick T. Woodman	1913 Charles F. O'Neall	1861 Joseph W. Johnson	1895 Thomas S. McMurry
1919 Meredith P. Snyder	1915 Edwin M. Capps	1863 J. A. Quimby	1899 Henry V. Johnson
1921 George E. Cryer	1917 Louis J. Wilde	1868 M. Leavenworth	1901 Robert R. Wright
1929 John C. Porter	1921 John L. Bacon	1870 Adolph Pfister	1904 Robert W. Speer
1933 Frank L. Shaw	1927 Harry C. Clark	1873 Bernard D. Murphy	1912 Henry J. Arnold
1938 Fletcher Bowron	1931 Walter W. Austin	1877 George B. McKee	1912 James M. Perkins
1853 Norris Poulson	1932 John F. Forward, Jr.	1879 Lawrence Archer	1 William H. Sharpley
1961 Sam Yorty	1934 Rutherford B. Irones	1880 Bernard D. Murphy	1 Robert W. Speer
1973 Thomas Bradley	1935 Percy J. Benbough	1882 C. J. Martin	1918 William F. R. Mills
	1942 Howard B. Bard	1884 C. T. Settle	1919 Dewey C. Bailey
	1943 Harley E. Knox	1886 C. W. Breyfogle	1923 Benjamin F. Stapleton
Sacramento	1951 John D. Butler	1888 Samuel W. Boring	1931 George D. Begole
	1955 Charles C. Dail	1890 S. M. Rucker	1935 Benjamin F. Stapleton
1849 A. M. Winn	1963 Frank E. Curran	1892 H. E. Schilling	1947 James Q. Newton
1850 Hardin Bigelow	1971 Pete Wilson	1894 Paul P. Austin	1955 Will F. Nicholson
1850 Horace Smith	1983 Roger A. Hedgecock	1896 Valentine Koch	1959 Richard Y. Batterton
1851 James R. Hardenberg		1898 C. J. Martin	1963 Thomas G. Currigan
1852 C. I. Hutchinson		1902 George D. Worswick	1969 William H. McNichols,
1853 James R. Hardenberg	**San Francisco**	1906 H. D. Mathews	Jr.
1854 R. P. Johnson		1908 Charles W. Davison	1983 Federico Pena
1855 James L. English	*Alcaldes*	1912 Thomas Monahan	
1856 B. B. Redding		1914 F. R. Husted	
1857 J. P. Dyer	1846 Washington A. Bartlett	1916 Elmer E. Chase	**Connecticut**
1858 H. L. Nichols	1847 G. Hyde Bryant	1918 Charles M. O'Brien	
1859 W. Shattuck	1848 J. Townsend	1920 Albert C. Jayet	**Hartford**
1863 C. H. Swift	1848 T. M. Leavenworth	1922 M. E. Arnerich	
1872 Christopher Green	1849 John W. Geary	1924 Joseph T. Brooks	1784 Thomas Seymour
1878 Jabez Turner		1926 Dan W. Gray	1812 Chauncey Goodrich
1881 John Q. Brown	*Mayors*	1928 Fred Doerr	1815 Jonathan Brace
1887 Eugene J. Gregory		1930 W. L. Biebrach	1824 Nathaniel Terry
1889 W. D. Comstock	1850 John W. Geary	1932 A. M. Meyer	1831 Thomas S. Williams
1893 B. U. Steinman	1851 Charles J. Brenham	1934 Charles Bishop	1835 Henry L. Ellsworth
1896 C. H. Hubbard	1852 Steven R. Harris	1936 Richard French	1835 Jared Griswold
1898 William Land	1853 Cornelius K. Garrison	1938 Clyde L. Fischer	1835 Jeremy Hoadley
1900 George H. Clark	1854 Stephen P. Webb	1940 Harry A. Young	1836 Henry Hudson
1904 W. J. Hassett	1855 James Van Ness	1944 Dr. Earl Campbell	1840 Thomas K. Brace
1906 M. R. Beard	1856 Ephraim W. Burr	1945 Ernest Renzel	1843 Amos M. Collins
1908 Clinton I. White	1859 Henry F. Teschemacher	1946 Albert Ruffo	1847 Philip Ripley
1910 M. R. Beard	1863 Henry P. Coon	1948 Fred Watson	1851 Ebenezer Flower
1912 M. J. Burke	1867 Frank McCoppin	1950 Clark L. Bradley	1853 William J. Hamersley
1915 G. C. Simmons	1869 Thomas H. Selby	1952 Parker Hathaway	1854 Henry C. Deming
1917 D. W. Carmichael	1871 William Alvord	1954 George Starbird	1858 Timothy M. Allyn
1919 John Q. Brown	1873 James Otis	1956 Robert Doerr	1860 Henry C. Deming
1920 Charles A. Bliss	1875 George Hewston	1958 Louis Solari	1862 Charles Benton
1921 Albert Alkus	1875 Andrew J. Bryant	1960 Paul Moore	1862 William J. Hamersley
1926 A. E. Goddard	1879 Isaac S. Kalloch	1962 Robert Welch	1864 Allyn S. Stillman
1928 R. E. Conley	1881 Maurice C. Blake	1964 Joseph L. Pace, M.D.	1866 Charles R. Chapman
1929 Martin I. Welsh	1883 Washington Bartlett	1966 Ronald R. James	1872 Henry C. Robinson
1930 C. H. S. Bidwell	1887 Edward B. Pond	1971 Norman Y. Mineta	1874 Joseph H. Sprague
1934 Thomas P. Scollan	1891 George H. Sanderson	1974 Janet Gray Hayes	1878 George G. Sumner
1935 Arthur D. Ferguson	1893 Levi R. Ellert	1983 Thomas McEnery	1880 Morgan G. Bulkeley
1938 Tom B. Monk	1895 Adolph Sutro		1888 John G. Root
1946 George L. Klumpp	1897 James D. Phelan		1890 Henry C. Dwight
1948 Belle Cooledge	1902 Eugene E. Schmitz	**Colorado**	1892 William W. Hyde
1950 Bert E. Geisreiter	1907 Charles Boxton		1894 Leverett Brainard
1952 Leslie E. Wood	1907 Edward R. Taylor	**Denver**	1896 Miles B. Preston
1953 W. A. Hicks	1910 Patrick H. McCarthy		1900 Alexander Harbison
1954 H. H. Hendren	1912 James Rolph, Jr.	1859 John C. Moore	1902 Ignatius A. Sullivan
1956 Clarence L. Azevedo	1931 Angelo J. Rossi	1861 Charles A. Cook	1904 William F. Henney
1960 James B. McKinney	1944 Roger D. Lapham	1863 Amos Steck	1908 Edward W. Hooker
1966 Walter Christensen	1948 Elmer E. Robinson	1864 Hiram J. Brendlinger	1910 Edward L. Smith
1968 Richard H. Marriott	1956 George Christopher	1865 George T. Clark	1912 Louis R. Cheney
1975 Phillip Isenberg	1964 John F. Shelley	1866 Milton M. DeLano	1914 Joseph H. Lawler
1983 Anna N. Rudin	1968 Joseph L. Alioto		

1916	Frank A. Hagarty
1918	Richard J. Kinsella
1920	Newton C. Brainard
1922	Richard J. Kinsella
1924	Norman C. Stevens
1928	Walter E. Batterson
1931	William J. Rankin
1933	Joseph W. Beach
1935	John A. Pilgard
1935	Thomas J. Spellacy
1943	Dennis P. O'Connor
1943	William H. Mortensen
1945	Cornelius A. Moylan
1947	Edward N. Allen
1948	Cyril Coleman
1951	Joseph V. Cronin
1953	Dominick J. DeLucco
1955	Joseph V. Cronin
1957	James H. Kinsella
1960	Dominick J. DeLucco
1961	William E. Glynn
1965	George B. Kinsella
1967	Antonina P. Uccello
1971	George A. Athanson
1983	Thirman L. Milner

District of Columbia

Washington

Mayors

1802	Robert Brent
1812	Daniel Rapine
1813	James Blake
1817	Benjamin G. Orr
1819	Samuel N. Smallwood
1822	Thomas Carberry
1824	Samuel N. Smallwood
1824	Roger C. Weightman
1827	Joseph Gales, Jr.
1830	John P. Van Ness
1834	William A. Bradley
1836	Peter Force
1840	William W. Seaton
1850	Walter Lenox
1852	John W. Maury
1854	John T. Towers
1856	William B. Magruder
1858	James G. Berrett
1861	Richard Wallach
1868	Sayles J. Bowen
1870	Matthew G. Emery
1871	Vacant

Presidents of the Board of Commissioners

1878	Seth L. Phelps
1879	Josiah Dent
1882	Joseph R. West
1885	James B. Edmonds
1886	William B. Webb
1889	John W. Douglass
1893	John W. Ross
1898	John B. Wright
1900	Henry B. F. Macfarland
1910	C. Hugo Rudolph
1913	Oliver P. Newman
1917	Louis Brownlow
1920	Charles W. Kutz (Acting)
1920	John T. Hendrick
1921	C. Hugo Rudolph
1926	Proctor L. Dougherty
1930	Luther H. Reichelderfer

1933	Melvin C. Hazen
1941	John R. Young
1952	F. Joseph Donohue
1953	Samuel Spencer
1956	Robert E. McLaughlin
1961	Walter N. Tobriner

Commissioners (Mayors)

1967	Walter E. Washington
1979	Marion S. Barry

Florida

Jacksonville

1865	Halstead H. Hoeg
1866	Holmes Steele
1867	John Clark
1868	Edward Hopkins
1870	Peter Jones
1873	J. C. Greeley
1874	Peter Jones
1876	Luther McConihe
1877	W. Stokes Boyd
1878	Luther McConihe
1879	Peter Jones
1880	J. Ramsey Dey
1881	Morris A. Dzialynski
1883	W. McLaws Dancy
1885	M. C. Rice
1886	Patrick McQuaid
1887	J. Q. Burbridge
1887	C. B. Smith
1889	Patrick McQuaid
1891	Henry Robinson
1893	Duncan U. Fletcher
1895	William M. Bostwick
1897	Raymond D. Knight
1899	J. E. T. Bowden
1901	Duncan U. Fletcher
1903	George M. Nolan
1906	William H. Baker
1907	William H. Sebring
1909	William S. Jordan
1913	Van C. Swearingen
1915	J. E. T. Bowden
1916	John W. Martin
1923	John T. Alsop, Jr.
1937	George C. Blume
1941	John T. Alsop, Jr.
1945	C. Frank Whitehead
1949	Haydon Burns
1965	Louis Ritter
1967	Hans Tanzler, Jr.
1979	Jake Godbold

Tallahassee

1826	Charles Haire
1827	David Ochiltree
1828	John Y. Gary
1830	Leslie A. Thompson
1831	Charles Austin
1832	Leslie A. Thompson
1834	Robert J. Hackley
1835	William Wilson
1835	Charles Haire
1835	William Hilliard
1836	John Rea
1837	William P. Gorman
1838	William Hilliard
1839	R. F. Ker
1840	Leslie A. Thompson
1841	Francis Epps
1845	James A. Berthelot

1846	Simon Towle
1847	James Kirksey
1848	F. H. Flagg
1849	Thomas J. Perkins
1850	D. P. Hogue
1852	David S. Walker
1853	Richard Hayward
1854	Thomas Hayward
1856	Francis Epps
1858	D. P. Hogue
1861	P. T. Pearce
1866	Francis Epps
1867	D. P. Hogue
1869	T. P. Tatum
1871	C. E. Dyke
1872	C. H. Edwards
1875	David S. Walker, Jr.
1876	Samuel Walker
1877	Jesse T. Bernard
1878	David S. Walker, Jr.
1880	Henry Bernreuter
1881	Edward Lewis
1882	John W. Nash
1883	Edward Lewis
1884	Charles C. Pearce
1886	George W. Walker
1887	A. J. Fish
1888	R. B. Gorman
1890	R. B. Carpenter
1895	Jesse T. Bernard
1897	R. A. Shino
1898	R. B. Gorman
1903	William L. Moor
1905	John W. Henderson
1906	F. C. Gilmore
1907	W. M. McIntosh, Jr.
1908	F. C. Gilmore
1909	Francis B. Winthrop
1910	D. M. Lowry
1918	J. R. McDaniel
1919	Guyte P. McCord
1922	A. P. McCaskill
1923	Guyte P. McCord
1923	B. A. Meginniss
1928	W. Theodore Proctor
1930	G. E. Lewis
1931	Frank D. Moor
1931	W. Theodore Proctor
1931	W. L. Marshall
1934	J. L. Fain
1935	L. A. Wesson
1936	H. J. Yaeger
1937	L. A. Wesson
1938	J. R. Jinks
1939	S. A. Wahnish
1940	F. C. Moor
1940	S. A. Wahnish
1941	Charles S. Ausley
1942	Jack W. Simmons
1943	A. R. Richardson
1944	Charles S. Ausley
1945	Ralph E. Proctor
1946	Fred S. Winterle
1947	George I. Martin
1948	Fred N. Lowry
1949	Robert C. Parker
1951	W. H. Cates
1952	B. A. Ragsdale
1953	William T. Mayo
1954	H. G. Easterwood
1954	H. C. Summitt
1955	J. T. Williams
1956	Fred S. Winterle
1956	John Y. Humphress
1957	J. W. Cordell
1958	Davis H. Atkinson
1959	Hugh E. Williams, Jr.
1960	George S. Taff
1961	J. W. Cordell
1962	Davis H. Atkinson
1963	Sam E. Teague, Jr.

1964	Hugh E. Williams, Jr.
1965	George S. Taff
1966	W. H. Cates
1966	John A. Rudd,, Sr.
1967	Gene Berkowitz
1967	Spurgeon Camp
1968	W. H. Cates
1968	George S. Taff
1969	Lee A. Everhart
1970	Spurgeon Camp
1971	Gene Berkowitz
1972	James R. Ford
1973	Joan Heggen
1974	John R. Jones
1976	James R. Ford
1977	Neal D. Sapp
1979	Sheldon A. Hilaman
1980	Hurley W. Rudd
1982	James R. Ford
1983	Carol Bellamy
1984	Kent Spriggs
1985	Hurley Rudd

Georgia

Atlanta

1848	Moses W. Formwalt
1849	Benjamin F. Bomar
1850	Willis Buell
1851	Jonathan Norcross
1852	Thomas F. Gibbs
1853	John F. Mims
1853	William Markham
1854	William M. Butt
1855	Allison Nelson
1855	John Glen
1856	William Ezzard
1858	Luther J. Glenn
1860	William Ezzard
1861	Jard I. Whitaker
1861	Thomas F. Lowe
1862	James M. Calhoun
1866	James E. Williams
1869	William H. Hulsey
1870	William Ezzard
1871	Dennis F. Hammond
1872	John H. James
1873	Cicero C. Hammock
1874	S. B. Spencer
1875	Cicero C. Hammock
1877	Nedom L. Angier
1879	William L. Calhoun
1881	James W. English
1883	John B. Goodwin
1885	George Hillyer
1887	John T. Cooper
1889	John T. Glenn
1891	William A. Hemphill
1893	John B. Goodwin
1895	Porter King
1897	Charles A. Collier
1899	James G. Woodward
1901	Livingston Mims
1903	Evan P. Howell
1905	James G. Woodward
1907	W. R. Joyner
1909	Robert F. Maddox
1911	Courtland S. Winn
1913	James G. Woodward
1917	Asa G. Candler
1919	James L. Key
1923	Walter A. Sims
1927	Isaac N. Ragsdale
1931	James L. Key
1937	William B. Hartsfield
1941	Roy LeCraw
1943	William B. Hartsfield

1962 Ivan Allen, Jr.
1970 Sam Massell
1973 Maynard H. Jackson
1981 Andrew Young

Hawaii

Honolulu

1909 Joseph J. Fern
1915 John C. Lane
1917 Joseph J. Fern
1920 John H. Wilson
1927 Charles N. Arnold
1929 John H. Wilson
1931 George Fred Wright
1938 Charles S. Crane
1941 Lester Petrie
1947 John H. Wilson
1955 Neal S. Blaisdell
1969 Frank F. Fasi
1980 Eileen Anderson
1984 Frank F. Fasi

Idaho

Boise

1867 H. E. Prickett
1868 Thomas B. Hart
1869 Charles Himrod
1872 George H. Twitchell
1874 John Lemp
1876 T. E. Logan
1879 Charles Himrod
1880 Cy Jacobs
1881 C. P. Bilderback
1883 J. A. Pinney
1885 Sol Hasbrook
1886 J. W. Huston
1887 Peter J. Pefley
1889 J. A. Pinney
1892 Peter Sonna
1895 W. E. Pierce
1897 Moses Alexander
1899 J. H. Richards
1901 Moses Alexander
1903 James H. Hawley
1906 J. A. Pinney
1907 John M. Haines
1909 J. T. Pence
1911 Harry K. Fritchman
1912 Arthur Hodges
1915 Jeremiah W. Robinson
1916 S. H. Hays
1919 Ern G. Eagleson
1921 Eugene B. Sherman
1925 Ern G. Eagleson
1927 Walter F. Hansen
1929 J. P. Pope
1931 Ross Cady
1933 J. J. McCue
1935 Byron E. Hyatt
1936 J. L. Edlefsen
1939 James L. Straight
1941 H. Westerman Whillock
1942 Austin A. Walker
1945 Sam S. Griffin
1946 H. Westerman Whillock
1947 Potter P. Howard
1951 Russell E. Edlefsen
1959 Robert Day
1961 Eugene W. Shellworth
1965 Jay S. Amyx
1974 Richard R. Eardlay

1985 Dirk Kempthorne

Illinois

Chicago

1837 William B. Ogden
1838 Buckner S. Morris
1839 Benjamin W. Raymond
1840 Alexander Loyd
1841 Francis C. Sherman
1842 Benjamin W. Raymond
1843 Augustus Garrett
1844 Alson S. Sherman
1845 Augustus Garrett
1846 John P. Chapin
1847 James Curtiss
1848 James H. Woodworth
1850 James Curtiss
1851 Walter S. Gurnee
1853 Charles M. Gray
1854 Isaac L. Milliken
1855 Levi D. Boone
1856 Thomas Dyer
1857 John Wentworth
1858 John C. Haines
1860 John Wentworth
1861 Julian S. Rumsey
1862 Francis C. Sherman
1865 John B. Rice
1869 Roswell B. Mason
1871 Joseph Medill
1873 Harvey D. Colvin
1876 Monroe Heath
1879 Carter H. Harrison, Sr.
1887 John A. Roche
1889 De Witt C. Cregier
1891 Hempstead Washburne
1893 Carter H. Harrison, Sr.
1893 George B. Swift
1893 John P. Hopkins
1895 George B. Swift
1897 Carter H. Harrison, Jr.
1905 Edward F. Dunne
1907 Fred A. Busse
1911 Carter H. Harrison, Jr.
1915 William H. Thompson
1923 William E. Dever
1927 William H. Thompson
1931 Anton J. Cermak
1933 Frank J. Corr (Acting)
1933 Edward J. Kelly
1947 Martin H. Kennelly
1955 Richard J. Daley
1975 Michael A. Bilandic
1979 Jane M. Byrne
1983 Harold Washington

Springfield

1840 Benjamin S. Clements
1841 William L. May
1842 Daniel B. Campbell
1843 Daniel B. Hill
1844 Andrew McCormick
1845 James C. Conkling
1846 Eli Cook
1849 John Calhoun
1852 William Lavely
1853 Josiah Francis
1854 William H. Herndon
1855 John Cook
1856 John W. Priest
1859 William Jayne
1860 Goyn A. Sutton
1861 George L. Huntington
1863 John W. Smith

1864 John S. Vredenburgh
1865 John J. Dennis
1866 John S. Bradford
1867 Norman M. Broadwell
1868 William E. Shutt
1869 Norman M. Broadwell
1870 John W. Priest
1871 John W. Smith
1873 Charles E. Hay
1874 Obed Lewis
1875 Charles E. Hay
1876 William Jayne
1878 John A. Vincent
1879 R. L. McGuire
1880 Horace C. Irwin
1881 John McCreery
1882 A. N. J. Crook
1883 John McCreery
1885 James M. Garland
1887 Charles E. Hay
1891 Rheuna D. Lawrence
1894 Frank Kramer
1896 Marion U. Woodruff
1898 Loren E. Wheeler
1901 John L. Phillips
1903 Harry H. Devereux
1907 David S. Griffiths
1907 Roy R. Reece
1909 John S. Schnepp
1915 Charles T. Baumann
1923 Samuel Bullard
1926 J. Emil Smith
1930 Hal M. Smith
1931 John W. Kapp, Jr.
1947 Harry Eielson
1951 John E. MacWherter
1955 Nelson O. Howarth
1959 Lester E. Collins
1963 Nelson O. Howarth
1971 William C. Telford
1979 J. Michael Houston

Indiana

Indianapolis

1847 Samuel Henderson
1849 Horatio C. Newcomb
1851 Caleb Scudder
1854 James McCready
1856 Henry F. West
1856 Charles G. Covlin
1856 William J. Wallace
1858 Samuel D. Maxwell
1863 John Caven
1867 Daniel McCauley
1873 James L. Mitchell
1875 John Caven
1881 Daniel W. Grubbs
1884 John L. McMaster
1886 Caleb S. Denny
1890 Thomas L. Sullivan
1893 Caleb S. Denny
1895 Thomas Taggart
1901 Charles A. Bookwalter
1903 John W. Holtzman
1906 Charles A. Bookwalter
1910 Samuel L. Shank
1913 Harry R. Wallace
1914 Joseph E. Bell
1918 Charles W. Jewett
1922 Samuel L. Shank
1926 John L. Duvall
1927 L. Ert Slack
1930 Reginald H. Sullivan
1935 John W. Kern, Jr.
1937 Walter C. Boetcher
1939 Reginald H. Sullivan

1943 Robert Tyndall
1947 George L. Denny
1948 Al G. Feeney
1950 Phillip L. Bayt, Jr.
1951 Christian J. Emhardt
1952 Alex M. Clark
1956 Phillip L. Bayt, Jr.
1959 Charles Boswell
1962 Albert Losche
1964 John J. Barton
1968 Richard G. Lugar
1975 William Hudnut

Iowa

Des Moines

1852 Thompson Bird
1853 B. Luce
1854 L. P. Sherman
1855 B. Granger
1856 W. DeFord
1857 C. W. Nash
1857 W. H. McHenry
1858 H. E. Lamereaux
1859 R. L. Tidrick
1860 P. H. W. Latshaw
1861 Ira Cook
1861 W. S. Barnes
1862 Thomas Cavenaugh
1863 W. H. Leas
1865 G. W. Cleveland
1868 S. F. Spofford
1869 J. H. Hatch
1871 Martin Tuttle
1872 J. P. Foster
1873 G. H. Turner
1874 A. Newton
1876 G. H. Turner
1877 George Sneer
1880 W. H. Merritt
1878 George Sneer
1882 P. V. Carey
1886 J. H. Phillips
1888 W. L. Carpenter
1890 J. H. Campbell
1892 C. C. Lane
1894 Isaac L. Hillis
1896 John MacVicar
1900 J. J. Hartenbower
1902 J. M. Brenton
1904 George W. Mattern
1908 A. J. Mathis
1910 James R. Hanna
1916 John MacVicar
1918 Thomas Fairweather
1920 H. H. Barton
1922 C. M. Garver
1926 Fred H. Hunter
1928 John MacVicar
1928 E. H. Muloch
1930 Parker L. Crouch
1932 Dwight N. Lewis
1936 Joseph E. Allen
1938 Dwight N. Lewis
1938 Mark L. Conkling
1942 John MacVicar, Jr.
1948 Heck Ross
1950 A. B. Chambers
1952 Allan W. Denny
1954 Joseph Van Dresser
1956 Ray Mills
1958 Charles F. Iles
1960 Reinhold O. Carlson
1962 Charles F. Iles
1966 George C. Whitmer
1968 Thomas N. Urban, Jr.
1972 Richard E. Olson

1979 Peter Crivaro

Kansas

Topeka

1858 Loring Farnsworth
1859 Lorenzo Dow
1859 Cyrus K. Holliday
1860 Hiram W. Farnsworth
1861 Harris F. Otis
1862 N. W. Cox
1863 J. F. Cummings
1864 Samuel H. Fletcher
1865 W. W. Ross
1866 Ross Burns
1867 Cyrus K. Holliday
1868 Orin T. Welch
1869 Cyrus K. Holliday
1870 J. B. McAfee
1871 Orin T. Welch
1873 Henry Bartling
1875 Thomas J. Anderson
1877 W. H. Case
1881 Joseph C. Wilson
1883 Bradford Miller
1885 Rosswell T. Cofran
1887 D. C. Metsker
1889 Rosswell T. Cofran
1893 D. C. Jones
1893 W. Harrison
1895 Charles A. Fellows
1899 Charles J. Drew
1901 J. W. F. Hughes
1902 Albert Parker
1903 W. S. Bergundthal
1905 W. H. Davis
1907 William Green
1910 J. B. Billard
1913 Rosswell T. Cofran
1915 Jay E. House
1919 Herbert J. Corwine
1923 Earl Akers
1925 James E. Thomas
1927 W. O. Rigby
1931 Omar B. Ketchum
1935 Herbert G. Barrett
1939 John F. Scott
1941 Frank J. Warren
1951 Kenneth W. Wilke
1953 George G. Schnellbacher
1959 E. J. Camp
1963 Hal W. Gerlach
1965 Charles W. Wright, Jr.
1969 Gene C. Martin
1971 William B. McCormick
1983 Douglas Wright

Kentucky

Frankfort

1849 Phillip Swigert
1868 S. I. M. Major
1871 E. H. Taylor, Jr.
1877 William S. Chinn
1879 S. I. M. Major
1881 E. H. Taylor, Jr.
1891 Louis Mangan
1892 Richard Tobin
1894 Ira Julian
1898 W. S. Dehoney
1902 J. S. Darnell
1906 E. E. Hume
1910 James Polsgrove

1914 Joseph Rupert
1918 W. S. Rosson
1922 D. D. Smith
1926 C. T. Coleman
1930 T. E. Kenny
1934 C. T. Coleman
1938 D. D. Smith
1942 C. T. Coleman
1946 A. C. Jones
1950 C. T. Coleman
1954 Robert C. Yount
1958 John Gerard
1960 Paul Judd
1962 J. W. Flynn
1967 Farnham F. Dudgeon (Acting)
1968 Frank W. Sower
1972 Robert K. Bennett
1976 James C. Burch
1980 John R. Sower
1984 James C. Burch

Louisville

1828 John C. Bucklin
1834 John Joves
1837 Frederick A. Kaye
1841 D. L. Beatty
1844 Frederick A. Kaye
1847 William F. Vance
1850 John M. Delph
1853 James S. Speed
1855 John Barbee
1857 W. S. Pilcher
1859 T. H. Crawford
1861 John M. Delph
1863 William Kaye
1865 Phil Tomppert
1865 James S. Lithgow
1867 Phil Tomppert
1869 J. H. Bunce
1870 John G. Baxter
1873 Charles D. Jacob
1879 John G. Baxter
1882 Charles D. Jacob
1885 P. Barker Reed
1888 Charles D. Jacob
1890 William L. Lyons (Pro tem)
1891 Henry S. Tyler
1896 George D. Todd
1897 Charles P. Weaver
1901 Charles F. Grainger
1905 Paul C. Barth
1907 Robert W. Bingham
1907 James F. Grinstead
1909 W. O. Head
1913 John H. Buschmeyer
1917 George W. Smith
1921 Huston Quinn
1925 Arthur A. Will
1927 Joseph T. O'Neal
1927 William S. Harrison
1933 Neville Miller
1937 Joseph D. Scholtz
1941 Wilson W. Wyatt
1946 E. Leland Taylor
1948 Charles P. Farnsley
1953 Andrew Broaddus
1957 Bruce Hoblitzell
1961 William O. Cowger
1965 Kenneth A. Schmied
1969 Frank W. Burke
1973 Harvey Sloane
1977 William Stansbury
1981 Harvey Sloane
1985 Jerry Abramson

Louisiana

Baton Rouge

1850 John R. Dufrocq
1855 Joseph Monget
1857 Edward Cousinard
1859 James E. Elam
1862 B. F. Bryan
1865 Jordan Holt
1865 James E. Elam
1869 O. P. Skolfield
1870 James E. Elam
1872 Henry Schorten
1872 James E. Elam
1873 Henry Schorten
1876 Leon Justremski
1882 J. C. Charrotte
1883 William S. Booth
1884 G. L. Vay
1888 B. F. Bryan
1890 G. L. Vay
1894 B. F. Bryan
1896 John J. Wax
1898 Robert A. Hart
1902 Robert L. Pruyn
1903 W. H. Bynum
1910 Jules Roux
1913 Alex Grouchy, Jr.
1922 Turner Bynum
1923 W. H. Bynum
1941 Fred S. LeBlanc
1944 Powers Higginbottom
1953 Jesse L. Webb, Jr.
1956 Mrs. Jesse L. Webb, Jr.
1957 John Christian
1965 Woodrow W. Dumas
1980 Pat Screen

New Orleans

Mayors

1803 Etienne De Bore
1804 James Pitot
1805 John Watkins
1807 James J. Mather
1812 Charles Trudeau (Acting)
1812 Nicholas Girod
1815 August McCarty
1820 Joseph Roffignoc
1828 Denis Prieur
1838 Paul Bertus (Acting)
1838 Charles Benois
1840 William Freret
1844 Joseph E. Montegut
1846 Abdil D. Crossman
1854 John L. Lewis
1856 Charles M. Waterman
1858 Gerald Stith
1860 John T. Monroe

Military Mayors

1862 George F. Shepley
1862 Godfrey Weitzel
1862 Jonas H. French
1862 Godfrey Weitzel
1862 Henry C. Deming
1863 James F. Miller
1864 Stephen Hoyt
1865 Hugh Kennedy
1865 Samuel M. Quincy
1865 Hugh Kennedy
1866 George Clark
1866 John T. Monroe
1867 Edward Heath
1868 John R. Conway

1870 Benjamin F. Flanders
1872 Louis A. Wiltz
1874 Charles J. Leeds
1876 Edward Pilsbury

Mayors

1878 Isaac W. Patton
1880 Joseph A. Shakspeare
1882 W. J. Behan
1884 J. Valsin Guillotte
1888 Joseph A. Shakspeare
1892 John Fitzpatrick
1896 Walter C. Flower
1900 Paul Capdeville
1904 Martin Behrman
1920 Andrew J. McShane
1926 Arthur J. O'Keefe
1929 T. Semmes Walmsley
1936 Robert S. Maestri
1946 deLesseps S. Morrison
1961 Victor H. Schiro
1970 Moon Landrieu
1978 Ernest Morial
1986 Richard Barthelemy

Maine

Augusta

1850 Alfred Redington
1852 John A. Pettingill
1854 Samuel Cony
1855 Joseph W. Patterson
1856 Albert M. Dole
1857 James W. North
1861 Sylvanus Caldwell
1863 William T. Johnson
1864 Sylvanus Caldwell
1865 Joseph W. Patterson
1866 Sylvanus Caldwell
1867 Joseph W. Patterson
1868 Daniel Williams
1869 Samuel Titcomb
1871 Joseph J. Eveleth
1874 James W. North
1875 Daniel Cony
1876 Charles E. Nash
1880 Peleg O. Vickery
1883 Alden W. Philbrook
1884 Seth C. Whitehouse
1885 George E. Weeks
1886 George E. Macomber
1889 Samuel W. Lane
1891 John W. Chase
1893 Moses R. Leighton
1894 Charles A. Milliken
1896 Winfield S. Choate
1898 J. Manchester Haynes
1899 Samuel W. Lane
1901 Lendall Titcomb
1903 Gustavus A. Robertson
1905 Charles S. Hichborn
1906 Frederick W. Plaisted
1909 Treby Johnson
1910 Frederick W. Plaisted
1911 Reuel J. Noyes
1913 Elmer E. Newbert
1915 Blaine S. Viles
1917 Willis E. Swift
1919 Burleigh Martin
1921 Sanford L. Fogg
1923 Ernest L. McLean
1929 Robert A. Cony
1934 Frederick G. Payne
1941 Sanford L. Fogg, Jr.
1943 Levi T. Williams
1945 Sanford L. Fogg, Jr.

1947	Charles P. Nelson	1843	Richard Swann	1881	William P. Whyte	1945 John E. Kerrigan
1949	Richard B. Sanborn	1848	Abram Claude	1883	F. C. Latrobe	1946 James M. Curley
1953	Brooks Brown, Jr.	1851	Brice T. B. Worthington	1885	James Hodges	1947 John F. Hynes
1957	H. Lloyd Carey	1852	Richard R. Goodwin	1887	F. C. Latrobe	1960 John F. Collins
1960	Sylvio J. Gilbert	1853	Dennis Claude	1889	Robert C. Davidson	1968 Kevin H. White
1969	Anthony Violette	1855	Nicholas Brewer, Jr.	1891	F. C. Latrobe	1983 Raymond L. Flynn
1971	Stanley E. Sproul	1856	Richard Swann	1895	Alcaeus Hooper	
1975	David N. Elvin	1858	Joseph Brown	1897	William T. Malster	
1980	Peter G. Thompson	1859	William Harwood	1899	Thomas G. Hayes	**Salem**
1986	Charles Devaney	1860	John R. Magruder	1903	Robert M. McLane	

Maryland

Annapolis

1708	Amos Garrett
1720	Thomas Larkin
1721	Benjamin Tasker
1722	Vachel Denton
1726	Benjamin Tasker
1727	Vachel Denton
1749	John Ross
1753	Michael McNamar
1754	Benjamin Tasker
1755	John Brice
1756	Benjamin Tasker
1757	John Bullen
1758	John Ross
1759	George Stewart
1760	Michael McNamar
1761	Stephen Bordley
1762	John Brice
1763	George Stewart
1764	Daniel Dulany
1765	John Ross
1766	Walter Dulany
1767	Upton Scott
1768	Allen Quynn
1780	John Brice
1781	John Bullen
1782	James Brice
1783	Jeremiah T. Chase
1784	Nicholas Carroll
1785	Robert Couden
1786	Allen Quynn
1788	James Brice
1789	John Bullen
1790	Nicholas Carroll
1791	Robert Couden
1792	Allen Quynn
1793	John Bullen
1794	James Williams
1795	William Pinkney
1800	John Davidson
1801	James Williams
1802	Allen Quynn
1803	Samuel Ridout
1804	John Johnson
1805	James Williams
1806	Samuel Ridout
1807	Burton Whetcroft
1808	John Kelly
1809	Burton Whetcroft
1810	John Johnson
1811	Nicholas Brewer
1812	Gideon White
1813	John Randall
1814	Nicholas Brewer
1815	John Randall
1816	Nicholas Brewer
1817	John Randall
1818	Nicholas Brewer
1819	Lewis Duvall
1823	James Boyle
1825	Richard Harwood
1828	Dennis Claude
1837	John Miller
1840	Alexander C. Magruder

1864	Solomon Phillips
1865	Richard R. Goodwin
1866	Richard Swann
1867	Abram Claude
1869	Augustus Gassway
1870	John T. E. Hyde
1871	James Munroe
1875	Arthur W. Wells
1877	James H. Brown
1879	Thomas E. Martin
1883	Abram Claude
1889	James H. Brown
1893	John H. Thomas
1897	Richard Green
1899	Edwin A. Seidewitz
1901	Charles A. Dubois
1903	Samuel Jones
1905	John DeP. Douw
1907	Gordon H. Claude
1909	James F. Strange
1919	John J. Levy
1921	Samuel Jones
1923	Charles W. Smith
1925	Allen B. Howard
1927	Charles W. Smith
1929	Walter E. Quenstedt
1935	Louis N. Phipps
1939	George W. Haley
1941	William U. McCready
1949	Roscoe C. Rowe
1952	Arthur G. Ellington
1961	Joseph H. Griscom, Sr.
1965	Roger W. Moyer
1973	John C. Apostol
1981	Richard L. Hillman

Baltimore

1797	James Calhoun
1804	Thorowgood Smith
1808	Edward Johnson
1814	Vacant
1816	George Stiles
1819	Edward Johnson
1820	John Montgomery
1822	Edward Johnson
1824	John Montgomery
1826	Jacob Small
1831	William Steuart
1832	Jesse Hunt
1835	Samuel Smith
1838	Sheppard Leakin
1840	Samuel Brady
1842	Solomon Hillen, Jr.
1843	James O. Law
1844	Jacob G. Davies
1848	Elijah Stansbury
1850	J. Hanson Jerome
1852	John S. Hollins
1854	Samuel Hinks
1856	Thomas Swann
1860	George W. Brown
1861	John C. Blackburn
1862	John L. Chapman
1867	Robert T. Banks
1871	Joshua Vansant
1875	F. C. Latrobe
1877	George P. Kane
1878	F. C. Latrobe

1904	E. Clay Timanus
1907	J. Barry Mahool
1911	James H. Preston
1919	William F. Broening
1923	Howard W. Jackson
1927	William F. Broening
1931	Howard W. Jackson
1943	Theodore R. McKeldin
1947	Thomas D'Alesandro, Jr.
1959	J. Harold Grady
1962	Philip H. Goodman
1963	Theodore R. McKeldin
1967	Thomas J. D'Alesandro, III
1972	William D. Schaefer

Massachusetts

Boston

1822	John Phillips
1823	Josiah Quincy
1829	Harrison G. Otis
1832	Charles Wells
1834	Theodore Lyman, Jr.
1836	Samuel T. Armstrong
1837	Samuel A. Eliot
1840	Jonathan Chapman
1843	Martin Brimmer
1845	Thomas A. Davis
1846	Josiah Quincy, Jr.
1849	John P. Bigelow
1852	Benjamin Seaver
1854	Jerome V. C. Smith
1856	Alexander H. Rice
1858	Frederic W. Lincoln, Jr.
1861	Joseph M. Wightman
1863	Frederic W. Lincoln, Jr.
1867	Otis Norcross
1868	Nathaniel B. Shurtleff
1871	William Gaston
1873	Henry L. Pierce
1873	Leonard R. Cutter
1874	Samuel C. Cobb
1877	Frederick O. Prince
1878	Henry L. Pierce
1879	Frederick O. Prince
1882	Samuel A. Green
1883	Albert Palmer
1884	Augustus P. Martin
1885	Hugh O'Brien
1889	Thomas N. Hart
1891	Nathan Matthews, Jr.
1895	Edwin U. Curtis
1896	Josiah Quincy
1900	Thomas N. Hart
1902	Patrick A. Collins
1905	Daniel A. Whelton
1906	John F. Fitzgerald
1908	George A. Hibbard
1910	John F. Fitzgerald
1914	James M. Curley
1918	Andrew J. Peters
1922	James M. Curley
1926	Malcolm E. Nichols
1930	James M. Curley
1934	Frederick W. Mansfield
1938	Maurice J. Tobin

Salem

1836	Leverett Saltonstall
1838	Stephen C. Phillips
1842	Stephen P. Webb
1845	Joseph S. Cabot
1849	Nathaniel Silsbee, Jr.
1851	David Pingree
1852	Charles W. Upham
1853	Asahel Huntington
1854	Joseph Andrews
1856	William S. Messervy
1858	Nathaniel Silsbee, Jr.
1860	Stephen P. Webb
1863	Stephen G. Wheatland
1865	Joseph B. Osgood
1866	David Roberts
1868	William Cogswell
1870	Nathaniel Brown
1872	Samuel Calley
1873	William Cogswell
1875	Henry L. Williams
1877	Henry K. Oliver
1881	Samuel Calley
1883	William M. Hill
1885	Arthur L. Huntington
1886	John M. Raymond
1890	Robert S. Rantoul
1894	James H. Turner
1898	David P. Waters
1899	James H. Turner
1900	David M. Little
1901	John F. Hurley
1903	Joseph N. Peterson
1906	Thomas C. Pinnock
1908	John F. Hurley
1910	Arthur F. Howard
1911	Rufus D. Adams
1913	John F. Hurley
1915	Matthias J. O'Keefe
1916	Henry P. Benson
1918	Denis J. Sullivan
1924	George J. Bates
1938	Edward A. Coffey
1948	Joseph B. Harrington
1950	Francis X. Collins
1970	Samuel E. Zoll
1972	Gene Levesque
1983	Anthony V. Salvo

Michigan

Detroit

1824	John R. Williams
1826	Henry J. Hunt
1826	Jonathon Kearsley
1827	John Biddle
1829	Jonathon Kearsley
1830	John R. Williams
1831	Marshall Chapin
1832	Levi Cook
1833	Marshall Chapin
1834	C. C. Trowbridge
1834	Andrew Mack
1835	Levi Cook
1837	Henry Howard
1838	Augustus A. Porter
1839	De Garmo Jones
1840	Zina Pitcher

1842	Douglas Houghton
1843	Zina Pitcher
1844	John R. Williams
1847	James A. Van Dyke
1848	Frederick Buhl
1849	Charles Howard
1850	John LaDue
1851	Zachariah Chandler
1852	John H. Harmon
1854	Oliver M. Hyde
1855	Henry Ledyard
1856	Oliver M. Hyde
1858	John Patton
1860	Christian H. Buhl
1862	William C. Duncan
1864	Kirkland C. Barker
1866	Merrill I. Mills
1868	William W. Wheaton
1872	Hugh Moffat
1876	Alexander Lewis
1878	George C. Langdon
1880	William G. Thompson
1884	S. B. Grummond
1886	M. H. Chamberlain
1888	John Pridgeon, Jr.
1890	H. S. Pingree
1897	William Richert
1897	William C. Maybury
1905	George P. Codd
1907	William B. Thompson
1909	Philip Breitmeyer
1911	William B. Thompson
1913	Oscar B. Marx
1919	James Couzens
1922	John C. Lodge
1923	Frank E. Doremus
1924	Joseph A. Martin
1924	John C. Lodge
1924	John W. Smith
1928	John C. Lodge
1930	Charles Bowles
1930	Frank Murphy
1933	Frank Couzens
1938	Richard W. Reading
1940	Edward J. Jeffries, Jr.
1948	Eugene I. Van Antwerp
1950	Albert E. Cobo
1957	Louis C. Miriani
1962	Jerome P. Cavanagh
1970	Roman S. Gribbs
1973	Coleman A. Young

Lansing

1859	Hiram H. Smith
1860	John A. Kerr
1861	William H. Chapman
1863	Ira H. Bartholomew
1866	William H. Haze
1867	George W. Peck
1868	Cyrus Hewitt
1870	Solomon W. Wright
1871	John Robson
1872	John S. Tooker
1874	Daniel W. Buck
1876	John S. Tooker
1877	Orlando M. Barnes
1878	Joseph E. Warner
1879	William H. Van Buren
1881	John Robson
1882	Orlando F. Barnes
1884	William Donovan
1886	Daniel W. Buck
1887	Jacob F. Shultz
1888	John Crotty
1889	James M. Turner
1890	Frank B. Johnson
1892	A. O. Bement
1894	Alroy A. Wilbur

1895	James M. Turner
1896	Russell C. Ostrander
1897	Charles J. Davis
1900	James F. Hammell
1904	Hugh Lyons
1908	John S. Bennett
1912	J. G. Reutter
1918	Jacob W. Ferle
1920	Benjamin A. Kyes
1922	Jacob W. Ferle
1922	Silas S. Main
1923	Alfred H. Doughty
1927	Laird J. Troyer
1931	Peter F. Gray
1933	Max A. Templeton
1941	Arthur E. Stoppel
1941	Sam S. Hughes
1943	Ralph W. Crego
1961	Willard I. Bowerman, Jr.
1965	Max E. Murningham
1969	Gerald W. Graves
1981	Terry John McKane

Minnesota

Minneapolis

1855	H. T. Welles
1856	Alvarin Allen
1857	William W. Wales
1858	Orrin Curtis
1860	R. B. Graves
1861	O. C. Merriman
1863	E. S. Brown
1864	O. C. Merriman
1865	William W. Wales
1867	Dorilus Morrison
1867	O. C. Merriman
1868	Winthrop Young
1868	Hugh Harrison
1869	Dorilus Morrison
1869	O. C. Merriman
1869	William W. McNair
1870	Eli B. Ames
1871	E. S. Brown
1872	Eugene M. Wilson
1873	G. A. Brackett
1874	Eugene M. Wilson
1875	O. C. Merriman
1876	A. A. Ames
1877	John DeLaittre
1878	A. C. Rand
1882	A. A. Ames
1884	George A. Pillsbury
1886	A. A. Ames
1887	E. C. Babb
1890	Phillip B. Winston
1892	William H. Eustis
1894	Robert Pratt
1898	James Gray
1900	A. A. Ames
1902	J. C. Haynes
1904	D. P. Jones
1906	J. C. Haynes
1912	Wallace G. Nye
1916	Thomas Van Lear
1918	J. E. Meyers
1921	George E. Leach
1929	William F. Kunze
1931	William A. Anderson
1933	A. G. Bainbridge
1935	Thomas E. Latimer
1937	George E. Leach
1941	Marvin L. Kline
1945	Hubert H. Humphrey, Jr.
1948	Eric G. Hoyer
1957	P. Kenneth Peterson
1961	Arthur Naftalin

1968	Charles Stenvig
1973	Albert J. Hofstede
1975	Charles Stenvig
1977	Albert J. Hofstede
1979	Donald Fraser

St. Paul

1850	Thomas R. Potts
1851	Robert Kennedy
1852	Bushrod W. Lott
1854	David Olmsted
1855	Alexander Ramsey
1856	George L. Becker
1857	John B. Brisbin
1858	Norman W. Kittson
1859	Daniel A. Robertson
1860	John S. Prince
1863	John E. Warren
1864	Jacob H. Stewart
1865	John S. Prince
1867	George L. Otis
1868	Jacob H. Stewart
1869	James T. Maxfield
1870	William Lee
1872	Jacob H. Stewart
1875	James T. Maxfield
1878	William Dawson
1881	Edmund Rice
1883	Christopher D. O'Brien
1885	Edmund Rice
1887	Robert A. Smith
1892	Frederick P. Wright
1894	Robert A. Smith
1896	Frank B. Doran
1898	Andrew R. Kiefer
1900	Robert A. Smith
1908	Daniel W. Lawler
1910	Herbert P. Keller
1914	Winn Powers
1916	Vivian R. Irvin
1918	Laurence C. Hodgson
1922	Arthur E. Nelson
1926	Laurence C. Hodgson
1930	Gerhard J. Bundlie
1932	William Mahoney
1934	Mark H. Gehan
1938	William H. Fallon
1940	John J. McDonough
1948	Edward K. Delaney
1952	John E. Daubney
1954	Joseph E. Dillon
1960	George J. Vavoulis
1966	Thomas R. Byrne
1970	Charles P. McCarty
1972	Lawrence D. Cohen
1976	George Latimer

Mississippi

Jackson

1834	Thomas H. Dickson
1835	S. P. Baley
1837	John P. Oldham
1842	James H. Boyd
1844	John P. Oldham
1852	William H. Taylor
1854	Richard Fletcher
1855	James H. Boyd
1859	W. A. Purdom
1860	Richard C. Kerr
1862	Charles H. Manship
1864	D. N. Barrows
1868	Thomas H. Norton
1868	James Biddle
1868	James P. Sessions

1869	Rhesa Hatcher
1869	Joseph C. Crane
1869	F. A. Field
1869	A. Way Kelly
1869	E. W. Cabaniss
1870	Oliver Clifton
1871	Rhesa Hatcher
1872	Marion Smith
1874	John McGill
1888	William Henry
1893	L. F. Chiles
1895	Oliver Clifton
1897	Ramsey Wharton
1899	H. M. Taylor
1899	W. M. Morrison
1899	W. H. Reber
1901	William Hemingway
1905	Ramsey Wharton
1908	William Hamilton
1909	A. C. Crowder
1913	S. J. Taylor
1917	Walter Scott
1945	Leland Speed
1949	Allen C. Thompson
1969	Russell C. Davis
1977	Dale Danks

Missouri

Jefferson City

1839	Thomas L. Price
1841	John F. Hogle
1843	E. L. Edwards
1844	Jefferson T. Rogers
1846	Calvin Gunn
1847	Jefferson T. Rogers
1850	A. P. Dorris
1851	Jason Harrison
1854	Alfred Sanford
1855	Jefferson T. Rogers
1858	J. B. Gardenhire
1859	Jefferson T. Rogers
1861	H. Clay Ewing
1862	Bernard Bruns
1864	M. M. Flesh
1865	Andrew Gundellinger
1866	Sylvester W. Cox
1868	Jonathan Grimshaw
1869	Ellwood Kirby
1870	Frank Schmidt
1872	J. H. Bodine
1873	Charles F. McCarty
1874	Fred Fischer
1876	Phil E. Chappell
1877	James E. Carter
1879	A. M. Davison
1881	Sylvester W. Cox
1883	Joseph R. Edwards
1884	Fred H. Binder
1885	John G. Riddler
1888	Ashley W. Ewing
1889	Phillip Ott
1891	Arthur P. Grimshaw
1895	Edwin Silver
1899	Arthur P. Grimshaw
1901	A. C. Shoup
1903	J. P. Porth
1905	H. J. Wallau
1909	John F. Heinrichs
1911	C. W. Thomas
1917	Frank Chapman
1919	Louis S. Rephlo
1921	Paul C. Hunt
1923	C. W. Thomas
1928	Earl W. Jenkins
1931	Henry C. Asel
1933	Means R. Ray

1937 Jesse N. Owens
1947 James T. Blair, Jr.
1949 Robert E. Dorr
1950 Lawrence Lutkewitte
1951 Arthur W. Ellis
1959 C. Forrest Whaley
1963 John G. Christy
1975 Robert Hyder
1979 George Hartsfield

Kansas City

1853 William S. Gregory
1854 Johnston Lykins
1855 John Johnson
1855 Milton J. Payne
1860 George M. B. Haughs
1861 Robert T. Van Horn
1862 Milton J. Payne
1863 William Bonnifield
1864 Robert T. Van Horn
1865 Patrick Shannon
1866 Alexander L. Harris
1867 Edward H. Allen
1868 Alexander L. Harris
1869 Francis R. Long
1870 Elijah M. McGee
1871 William Warner
1872 Robert H. Hunt
1873 Edward L. Martin
1874 Smith D. Woods
1875 Turner A. Gill
1876 James W. L. Slavens
1878 George M. Shelley
1880 Charles A. Chace
1881 Daniel A. Frink
1882 Thomas B. Bullene
1883 James Gibson
1884 Leander J. Talbott
1885 John W. Moore
1886 Henry C. Kumpf
1889 Joseph J. Davenport
1890 Benjamin Holmes
1892 William S. Cowherd
1894 Webster Davis
1896 James M. Jones
1900 James A. Reed
1904 Jay H. Neff
1906 Henry M. Beardsley
1908 Thomas T. Crittenden, Jr.
1910 Darius A. Brown
1912 Henry L. Jost
1916 George H. Edwards
1918 James Cowgill
1922 Samuel B. Strother
1922 Frank H. Cromwell
1924 Albert I. Beach
1930 Bryce B. Smith
1939 Charles S. Keith
1940 John B. Gage
1946 William E. Kemp
1955 H. Roe Bartle
1963 Ilus W. Davis
1971 Charles B. Wheeler, Jr.
1979 Richard L. Berkley

St. Louis

1823 William C. Lane
1829 Daniel D. Page
1833 John W. Johnston
1835 John F. Darby
1837 William C. Lane
1840 John F. Darby
1841 John D. Daggett
1842 George Maguire
1843 John M. Wimer

1844 Bernard Pratte
1846 Peter G. Camden
1847 Bryan Mullanphy
1848 John M. Krum
1849 James G. Barry
1850 Luther M. Kennett
1853 John How
1855 Washington King
1856 John How
1857 John M. Wimer
1858 Oliver D. Filley
1861 Daniel G. Taylor
1863 Chauncey I. Filley
1864 James S. Thomas
1869 Nathan Cole
1871 Joseph Brown
1875 Arthur B. Barret
1875 James H. Britton
1876 Henry Overstolz
1881 William L. Ewing
1885 David R. Francis
1889 Edward A. Noonan
1893 Cyrus P. Walbridge
1897 Henry Ziegenhein
1901 Rolla Wells
1909 Frederick Kreismann
1913 Henry W. Kiel
1925 Victor J. Miller
1933 Bernard F. Dickmann
1941 William D. Becker
1943 Aloys P. Kaufmann
1949 Joseph M. Darst
1953 Raymond R. Tucker
1965 Alfonso J. Cervantes
1973 John Poelker
1977 James F. Conway
1981 Vincent Schoemehl

Montana

Helena

1881 John Kinna
1882 E. W. Knight
1883 T. H. Kleinschmidt
1884 W. B. Hundley
1885 James Sullivan
1886 T. H. Kleinschmidt
1887 W. L. Steele
1888 T. P. Fuller
1891 Donald Bradford
1892 T. H. Kleinschmidt
1893 John C. Curtin
1894 E. D. Weed
1895 W. L. Steele
1898 J. D. Edwards
1904 R. R. Purcell
1906 F. S. P. Lindsay
1908 J. D. Edwards
1911 Edward Horsky
1912 R. R. Purcell
1914 Lincoln Working
1916 R. R. Purcell
1918 John Dryburgh
1922 Percy Witmer
1930 George P. Arnold
1932 C. J. Bausch
1936 A. J. Roberts
1940 John J. Haytin
1946 J. R. Wine, Jr.
1950 J. R. Kaiserman
1953 Otto L. Brackman
1960 Wanna F. Thompson
1962 Robert E. Johnson
1964 John W. Schroeder
1966 David A. Lewis
1968 Darryl A. Lee
1969 David A. Lewis

1971 Stephen F. Keim
1973 Don Harriott
1975 A. W. Scribner
1977 Kathleen Ramey
1979 Rich D. Brown
1981 Russell J. Ritter

Nebraska

Lincoln

1871 W. F. Chapin
1872 E. E. Brown
1873 Robert D. Silver, Jr.
1874 Samuel W. Little
1875 Amasa Cobb
1876 Robert D. Silver, Jr.
1877 H. W. Hardy
1879 Seth P. Galey
1880 John B. Wright
1882 John Doolittle
1883 Robert E. Moore
1885 C. C. Burr
1887 Andrew J. Sawyer
1889 Robert B. Graham
1891 A. H. Weir
1895 Frank A. Graham
1899 H. J. Winnett
1903 George A. Adams
1905 Frances W. Brown
1909 Don L. Love
1911 A. H. Armstrong
1913 Frank C. Zehrung
1915 Charles W. Bryan
1917 John E. Miller
1921 Frank C. Zehrung
1927 Verne Hedge
1929 Don L. Love
1931 Frank C. Zehrung
1933 Fenton B. Fleming
1935 Charles W. Bryan
1937 Oren S. Copeland
1940 R. E. Campbell
1941 Richard O. Johnson
1943 Lloyd Marti
1947 Clarence G. Miles
1950 Victor E. Anderson
1953 Clark Jeary
1956 Bennett S. Martin
1959 Bartlett E. Boyles
1963 D. L. Tyrrell
1963 Dean H. Petersen
1965 Sam Schwartzkopf
1975 Helen Boosalis
1983 Roland Luedtke

Nevada

Reno

1931 Arnold A. Millard
1939 M. E. Norton
1941 C. B. Austin
1945 George Lind
1947 R. M. Elston
1949 Caro Pendergraft
1951 Wilbur H. Stodieck
1955 Turner Houston
1959 Harley W. Carter
1960 Turner Houston
1961 Al Autrand
1963 James Y. Robertson
1969 Eugene M. Scrivner
1971 John Edward Chism
1973 Sam Dibitonto

1975 Carl F. Bogart
1976 Bruno Menicucci
1979 Barbara Bennett
1983 Peter J. Sfemazza

New Hampshire

Concord

1853 Joseph Low
1855 Rufus Clements
1856 John Abbott
1859 Moses T. Willard
1861 Moses Humphrey
1863 Benjamin F. Gale
1865 Moses Humphrey
1866 John Abbott
1868 Lyman D. Stevens
1870 Abraham G. Jones
1872 John Kimball
1876 George A. Pillsbury
1878 Horace A. Brown
1880 George A. Cummings
1883 Edgar H. Woodman
1887 John E. Robertson
1889 Stillman Humphrey
1891 Henry W. Clapp
1893 Parsons B. Cogswell
1895 Henry Robinson
1897 Albert B. Woodworth
1899 Nathaniel Martin
1901 Harry G. Sargent
1903 Charles R. Corning
1909 Charles J. French
1916 Nathaniel W. Hobbs
1918 Charles J. French
1920 Henry E. Chamberlin
1924 Willis H. Flint
1926 Fred N. Marden
1928 Olin H. Chase
1928 Robert W. Brown
1934 John W. Storrs
1942 Charles J. McKee
1946 Charles C. Davie
1948 Charles J. McKee
1950 Shelby Walker
1954 Herbert W. Rainie
1958 Charles P. Johnson
1962 Charles C. Davie
1966 J. Herbert Quinn
1967 William P. Gove
1968 John E. Henchey (City Manager)
1970 Malcolm McLane
1976 Martin L. Gross
1982 C. David Coeyman

New Jersey

Trenton

1792 Moore Furman
1794 Aaron D. Woodruff
1797 James Ewing
1803 Joshua Wright
1806 Stacy Potts
1814 Robert McNealy
1832 Charles Burroughs
1847 Samuel R. Hamilton
1849 William C. Howell
1850 William Napton
1852 John R. Tucker
1854 William Napton
1855 William P. Sherman
1855 John R. Tucker

1856	Joseph Wood
1859	Franklin S. Mills
1861	William R. McKean
1863	Franklin S. Mills
1867	Alfred Reed
1868	William Napton
1871	John Briest
1875	Wesley Creveling
1877	Daniel R. Bodine
1879	William Rice
1881	Garret D. W. Vroom
1884	Richard A. Donnelly
1886	John Woolverton
1887	Frank A. Magowan
1889	Anthony A. Skirm
1891	Daniel J. Bechtel
1893	Joseph B. Shaw
1895	Emory N. Yard
1897	Welling G. Sickel
1899	Frank O. Briggs
1902	Frank S. Katzenbach, Jr.
1906	Frederick W. Gnichtel
1908	Walter Madden
1911	Frederick W. Donnelly
1932	George B. LaBarre
1935	William J. Connor
1939	Leo J. Rogers
1939	Edward W. Lee
1941	John A. Hartmann
1943	Andrew J. Duch
1947	Donal J. Connolly
1959	Arthur J. Holland
1966	Carmen J. Armenti
1970	Arthur J. Holland

New Mexico

Santa Fe

1891	William T. Thornton
1892	Manuel Valdez
1893	R. E. Twitchell
1894	J. H. Sloan
1895	Charles F. Easley
1896	Pedro Delgado
1897	Charles A. Spiess
1898	J. R. Hudson
1899	J. H. Sloan
1901	Amado Chaves
1902	I. Sparks
1904	A. R. Gibson
1906	Thomas B. Catron
1908	Jose D. Sena
1910	Arthur Seligman
1912	Celso Lopez
1914	William G. Sargent
1918	E. P. Davies
1920	T. Z. Winter
1922	Charles C. Closson
1924	Nathan Jaffa
1926	Edward L. Safford
1928	James C. McConnery
1932	David Chavez, Jr.
1934	William Barker
1936	Frank Andrews
1938	Alfredo Ortiz
1942	Manuel Lujan
1948	Frank S. Ortiz
1952	H. Paul Huss
1956	Leo T. Murphy
1962	Pat Hollis
1965	George A. Gonzales
1972	Joseph E. Valdes
1976	Sam Pick
1978	Arthur E. Trujillo
1982	Louis R. Montano
1986	Sam Pick

New York

Albany

1686	Pieter Schuyler
1694	Johannes Abeel
1695	Evert Bancker
1696	Dirck Ten Broeck
1698	Hendrick Hansen
1699	Pieter Van Brugh
1700	Johannes Bleecker
1701	Johannes Bleecker, Jr.
1702	Albert J. Ryckman
1703	Johannes Schuyler
1706	David Schuyler
1707	Evert Bancker
1709	Johannes Abeel
1710	Robert Livingston, Jr.
1719	Myndert Schuyler
1721	Pieter Van Brugh
1723	Myndert Schuyler
1725	Johannes Cuyler
1726	Rutger Bleecker
1729	Johannes De Peyster
1731	Johannes Hansen
1732	Johannes De Peyster
1733	Edward Holland
1741	Johannes Schuyler
1742	Cornelis Cuyler
1746	Dirck Ten Broeck
1748	Jacob C. Ten Eyck
1750	Robert Sanders
1754	Johannes Hansen
1756	Sybrant G. Van Schaick
1761	Volckert P. Douw
1770	Abraham C. Cuyler
1778	John Barclay
1779	Abraham Ten Broeck
1783	Johannes Beeckman
1786	John Lansing, Jr.
1789	Abraham Yates
1796	Abraham Ten Broeck
1799	Philip S. Van Rensselaer
1816	Elisha Jenkins
1819	Philip S. Van Rensselaer
1821	Charles E. Dudley
1824	Ambrose Spencer
1826	James Stevenson
1828	Charles E. Dudley
1829	John Townsend
1831	Francis Bloodgood
1832	John Townsend
1833	Francis Bloodgood
1834	Erastus Corning
1837	Teunis Van Vechten
1838	Jared L. Rathbone
1841	Teunis Van Vechten
1842	Barent P. Staats
1843	Friend Humphrey
1845	John K. Paige
1846	William Parmelee
1848	John Taylor
1849	Friend Humphrey
1850	Franklin Townsend
1851	Eli Perry
1854	William Parmelee
1855	Charles W. Godard
1856	Eli Perry
1860	George H. Thacher
1862	Eli Perry
1866	George H. Thacher
1868	Charles E. Bleecker
1870	George H. Thacher
1874	John G. Burch
1875	Edmund L. Judson
1876	A. Bleecker Banks
1878	Michael N. Nolan
1883	John Swinburne
1884	A. Bleecker Banks
1886	John B. Thacher

1888	Edward A. Maher
1890	James M. Manning
1894	Oren E. Wilson
1896	John B. Thacher
1898	Thomas J. Van Alstyne
1900	James H. Blessing
1902	Charles H. Gaus
1909	Henry F. Snyder
1910	James B. McEwan
1914	Joseph W. Stevens
1918	James R. Watt
1922	William S. Hackett
1926	John B. Thacher, II
1941	Herman F. Hoogkamp
1942	Erastus Corning, II
1983	Thomas M. Whalen, III

Buffalo

1832	Ebenezer Johnson
1833	Major A. Andrews
1834	Ebenezer Johnson
1835	Hiram Pratt
1836	Samuel Wilkeson
1837	Josiah Trowbridge
1837	Pierre A. Barker
1838	Ebenezer Walden
1839	Hiram Pratt
1840	Sheldon Thompson
1841	Isaac R. Harrington
1842	George W. Clinton
1843	Joseph G. Masten
1844	William Ketchum
1845	Joseph G. Masten
1846	Solomon G. Haven
1847	Elbridge G. Spaulding
1848	Orlando Allen
1849	Hiram Barton
1850	Henry K. Smith
1851	James Wadsworth
1852	Hiram Barton
1853	Eli Cook
1856	Frederick Stephens
1858	Timothy T. Lockwood
1860	Franklin A. Alberger
1862	William G. Fargo
1866	Chandler J. Wells
1870	Alexander Brush
1874	Louis P. Dayton
1876	Philip Becker
1878	Solomon Scheu
1880	Alexander Brush
1882	Grover Cleveland
1882	Marcus M. Drake
1882	Harmon S. Cutting
1883	John B. Manning
1884	Jonathan Scoville
1886	Philip Becker
1890	Charles F. Bishop
1895	Edgar B. Jewett
1898	Conrad Diehl
1902	Erastus C. Knight
1906	James N. Adam
1910	Louis P. Fuhrmann
1918	George S. Buck
1922	Frank X. Schwab
1930	Charles E. Roesch
1934	George J. Zimmerman
1938	Thomas L. Holling
1942	Joseph J. Kelly
1946	Bernard J. Dowd
1950	Joseph Mruk
1954	Steven Pankow
1958	Frank A. Sedita
1962	Chester W. Kowal
1966	Frank A. Sedita
1973	Stanley M. Makowsky
1977	James D. Griffen

New York City

1665	Thomas Willett
1666	Thomas Delavall
1667	Thomas Willett
1668	Cornelius Steenwyck
1671	Thomas Delavall
1672	Matthias Nicolls
1673	John Lawrence
1675	William Dervall
1676	Nicholas De Meyer
1677	Stephanus Van Cortlandt
1678	Thomas Delavall
1679	Francis Rombouts
1680	William Dyre
1682	Cornelius Steenwyck
1684	Gabriel Minvielle
1685	Nicholas Bayard
1686	Stephanus Van Cortlandt
1689	Peter Delanoy
1691	John Lawrence
1692	Abraham De Peyster
1694	Charles Lodwick
1695	William Merritt
1698	Johannes De Peyster
1699	David Provoost
1700	Isaac De Reimer
1701	Thomas Noell
1702	Philip French
1703	William Peartree
1707	Ebenezer Wilson
1710	Jacobus Van Cortlandt
1711	Caleb Heathcote
1714	John Johnston
1719	Jacobus Van Cortlandt
1720	Robert Walters
1725	Johannes Jansen
1726	Robert Lurting
1735	Paul Richard
1739	John Cruger
1744	Stephen Bayard
1747	Edward Holland
1757	John Cruger, Jr.
1766	Whitehead Hicks
1776	David Matthews
1784	James Duane
1789	Richard Varick
1801	Edward Livingston
1803	De Witt Clinton
1807	Marinus Willett
1808	De Witt Clinton
1810	Jacob Radcliff
1811	De Witt Clinton
1815	John Ferguson
1815	Jacob Radcliff
1818	Cadwallader D. Colden
1821	Stephen Allen
1825	William Paulding
1826	Philip Hone
1827	William Paulding
1829	Walter Bowne
1833	Gideon Lee
1834	Cornelius V. Lawrence
1837	Aaron Clark
1839	Isaac L. Varian
1841	Robert H. Morris
1844	James Harper
1845	William F. Havemeyer
1846	Andrew H. Mickle
1847	William V. Brady
1848	William F. Havemeyer
1849	Caleb S. Woodhull
1851	Ambrose C. Kingsland
1853	Jacob A. Westervelt
1855	Fernando Wood
1858	Daniel F. Tiemann
1860	Fernando Wood
1862	George Opdyke
1864	C. Godfrey Gunther
1866	John T. Hoffman
1868	T. Coman (Acting)

1869	A. Oakey Hall
1873	William F. Havemeyer
1874	S. B. H. Vance (Acting)
1875	William H. Wickham
1877	Smith Ely
1879	Edward Cooper
1881	William R. Grace
1883	Franklin Edson
1885	William R. Grace
1887	Abram S. Hewitt
1889	Hugh J. Grant
1893	Thomas F. Gilroy
1895	William L. Strong
1898	Robert A. Van Wyck
1902	Seth Low
1904	George B. McClellan
1910	William J. Gaynor
1913	Ardolph L. Kline
1914	John P. Mitchel
1918	John F. Hylan
1926	James J. Walker
1932	Joseph V. McKee
1933	John P. O'Brien
1934	Fiorello H. La Guardia
1946	William O'Dwyer
1950	Vincent R. Impellitteri
1954	Robert F. Wagner
1966	John V. Lindsay
1973	Abraham Beame
1977	Edward Koch

North Dakota

Bismarck

1885	I. P. Hunt
1887	William A. Bentley
1890	I. P. Baker
1891	William A. Bentley
1892	Edward S. Allen
1894	A. N. Leslie
1896	Edward G. Patterson
1901	W. H. Webb, Jr.
1905	F. R. Smythe
1909	E. A. Williams
1913	A. W. Lucas
1921	A. P. Lenhart
1937	Obert Olson
1939	Neil Churchill
1947	A. P. Lenhart
1950	Tom Kleppe
1954	Evan Lips
1964	E. V. Lahr
1974	Robert O. Heskin
1978	Eugene (Bus) Leary
1983	Marlan Haakenson

North Carolina

Raleigh

1880	B. C. Manly
1882	William H. Dodd
1887	Al A. Thompson
1891	Thomas Badger
1895	William M. Russ
1899	A. M. Powell
1903	James I. Johnson
1909	J. S. Wynne
1911	James I. Johnson
1921	T. B. Eldridge
1923	E. E. Culbreth
1931	George A. Iseley
1939	Graham H. Andrews
1947	P. D. Snipes

1951	James E. Briggs
1953	Fred B. Wheeler
1957	W. G. Enloe
1963	James W. Reid
1965	Travis H. Tomlinson
1969	Seby B. Jones
1971	Tom W. Bradshaw, Jr.
1973	Clarence E. Lightner
1975	J. J. Coggins
1977	Isabella W. Cannon
1979	G. Smedes York
1983	Avery C. Upchurch

Ohio

Cincinnati

1815	William Corry
1819	Isaac G. Burnet
1831	Elisha Hotchkiss
1833	Samuel W. Davies
1843	Henry E. Spencer
1851	Mark P. Taylor
1853	David T. Snelbaker
1855	James J. Faran
1857	Nicholas W. Thomas
1859	Richard M. Bishop
1861	George Hatch
1863	Leonard A. Harris
1867	Charles F. Wilstach
1869	John F. Torrence
1871	S. S. Davis
1873	George W. C. Johnston
1877	Robert M. Moore
1879	Charles Jacob
1881	William Means
1883	Thomas J. Stephens
1885	Amor Smith, Jr.
1889	John B. Mosby
1894	John A. Caldwell
1897	Gustav Tafel
1900	Julius Fleischman
1906	Edward J. Dempsey
1908	Leopold Markbreit
1909	John Galvin
1910	Louis Schwab
1912	Henry T. Hunt
1914	Frederick S. Spiegel
1916	George Puchta
1918	John Galvin
1922	George P. Carrel
1926	Murray Seasongood
1930	Russell Wilson
1938	James G. Stewart
1947	Carl W. Rich
1948	Albert D. Cash
1951	Carl W. Rich
1953	Edward N. Waldvogel
1954	Dorothy N. Dolbey
1954	Carl W. Rich
1955	Charles P. Taft
1957	Donald D. Clancy
1960	Walton Bachrach
1967	Eugene P. Ruehlmann
1971	W. David Gradison, Jr.
1972	Thomas Luken
1973	Theodore M. Berry
1975	Bobbie Sterne
1976	James T. Luken
1977	Gerald W. Springer
1980	David S. Mann
1983	Thomas B. Brush
1984	Arn Bortz
1985	Charles J. Luken

Cleveland

Mayors

1836	John W. Willey
1838	Joshua Mills
1840	Nicholas Dohrstader
1841	John W. Allen
1842	Joshua Mills
1843	Nelson Haywood
1844	Samuel Starkweather
1846	George Hoadley
1847	Joshua Hadley
1848	Lorenzo A. Kelsey
1849	Flavel Bingham
1850	William Case
1852	Abner C. Brownell
1855	William B. Castle
1857	Samuel Starkweather
1859	George B. Senter
1861	Edward S. Flint
1863	Irving U. Masters
1865	Herman A. Chapin
1867	Stephen Buher
1871	F. W. Pelton
1873	Charles W. Otis
1875	Nathan F. Payne
1877	William G. Rose
1879	P. R. Herrick
1883	John H. Farley
1885	George W. Gardner
1887	Brenton D. Babcock
1889	George W. Gardner
1891	William G. Rose
1893	Robert Blee
1895	Robert E. McKisson
1899	John H. Farley
1901	Tom L. Johnson
1910	Herman Baehr
1912	Newton D. Baker
1916	Harry L. Davis
1920	William S. FitzGerald
1921	Fred Kohler

City Managers

1923	William R. Hopkins
1930	Daniel E. Morgan

Mayors

1931	Harold H. Burton
1932	Ray T. Miller
1933	Harry L. Davis
1935	Harold H. Burton
1940	Edward Blythin
1941	Frank Lausche
1945	Thomas Burke
1953	Anthony J. Celebrezze
1962	Ralph S. Locher
1967	Carl B. Stokes
1972	Ralph J. Perk
1977	Dennis J. Kucinich
1979	George Voinovich

Columbus

1816	Jarvis Pike
1818	John Kerr
1820	Eli C. King
1823	John Longhenry
1824	William T. Martin
1827	James Robinson
1828	William Long
1833	Philo H. Olmstead
1834	John Brooks
1836	Warren Jenkins
1838	Philo H. Olmstead
1840	John G. Miller

1842	Abraham J. McDowell
1843	Smithson E. Wright
1845	Alexander Patton
1846	A. S. Decker
1847	Alexander Patton
1850	Lorenzo English
1861	Wray Thomas
1865	James G. Bull
1869	George W. Meeker
1871	James G. Bull
1875	John H. Heitman
1879	G. G. Collins
1881	George S. Peters
1883	Charles C. Walcutt
1887	Philip H. Bruck
1891	George J. Karb
1895	Cotton H. Allen
1897	Samuel L. Black
1899	Samuel J. Schwartz
1901	John H. Hinkle
1903	Robert H. Jeffrey
1906	DeWitt C. Badger
1908	Charles A. Bond
1910	George S. Marshall
1912	George J. Karb
1920	James J. Thomas
1932	Henry W. Worley
1936	Myron B. Gessaman
1940	Floyd F. Green
1944	James A. Rhodes
1953	Robert T. Ostreicher
1954	Maynard E. Sensenbrenner
1960	W. Ralston Westlake
1964	Maynard E. Sensenbrenner
1971	Tom Moody
1983	Dana Rinehart

Oklahoma

Oklahoma City

1890	W. J. Gault
1892	O. A. Mitscher
1894	Nelson Button
1896	C. G. Jones
1897	J. P. Allen
1899	Lee Van Winkle
1901	C. G. Jones
1903	Lee Van Winkle
1905	J. F. Messenbaugh
1907	Henry M. Scales
1910	Dan V. Lackey
1911	Whit M. Grant
1915	Ed Overholser
1918	Byron D. Shear
1919	J. C. Walton
1923	Mike Donnelly
1925	O. A. Cargill
1927	Walter C. Dean
1931	C. J. Blinn
1933	Tom E. McGee
1935	John Frank Martin
1939	R. A. Hefner
1947	Allen Street
1959	James H. Norick
1963	Jack S. Wilkes
1964	George H. Shirk
1967	James H. Norick
1971	Patience Latting
1983	Andrew M. Coats

Oregon

Salem

1857	Wiley Kenyon
1861	Lucien Heath
1862	E. N. Cooke
1863	H. M. Thatcher
1864	John H. Moores
1865	J. Q. Wilson
1866	John H. Moores
1869	L. S. Scott
1871	J. W. Smith
1872	Daniel Payton
1873	A. J. Monroe
1874	John G. Wright
1877	T. M. Gatch
1879	G. W. Gray
1880	T. B. Wait
1881	J. W. Crawford
1883	Andrew Kelly
1885	W. W. Skinner
1887	William M. Ramsey
1888	J. J. Murphy
1889	George Williams
1891	P. H. D'Arcy
1893	Claude Gatch
1897	J. A. Richardson
1899	Charles P. Bishop
1904	F. W. Waters
1907	G. F. Rodgers
1911	Louis Lachmund
1913	J. C. Siegmund
1914	B. L. Steeves
1915	H. O. White
1917	Walter Keyes
1919	C. E. Albin
1920	O. J. Wilson
1921	G. E. Halvorsen
1923	J. B. Giesy
1927	T. A. Livesley
1931	P. M. Gregory
1933	Douglas McKay
1935	V. E. Kuhn
1939	W. W. Chadwick
1943	I. M. Doughton
1947	Robert L. Elfstrom
1951	Alfred W. Loucks
1954	Robert White
1959	Russell F. Bonesteele
1963	Willard C. Marshall
1965	Vern W. Miller
1972	Robert E. Lindsey
1976	Kent L. Aldrich
1982	Sue Harris

Pennsylvania

Harrisburg

1860	William H. Hepner
1863	Augustus L. Roumfort
1866	Oliver Edwards
1869	William W. Hayes
1870	George B. Cole
1871	William K. Verbeke
1873	Jacob D. Boas
1875	John D. Patterson
1881	John C. Herman
1883	Simon C. Wilson
1886	Samuel W. Fleming
1887	John A. Fritchey
1893	Maurice C. Eby
1896	John D. Patterson
1899	John A. Fritchey
1902	Vance C. McCormick
1905	Edward Z. Gross
1908	Ezra S. Meals
1912	John K. Royal
1916	Ezra S. Meals
1917	William L. Gorgas
1917	Charles A. Miller
1917	William L. Gorgas
1917	J. William Bowman
1917	Daniel L. Keister
1920	George A. Hoverter
1936	John A. F. Hall
1940	Howard E. Milliken
1948	Claude R. Robins
1956	Nolan F. Ziegler
1963	Daniel J. Barry
1964	William K. McBride
1968	Albert H. Straub
1970	Harold A. Swenson
1977	Paul Doutrich
1981	Stephen Reed

Philadelphia

1691	Humphrey Morrey
1701	Edward Shippen
1703	Anthony Morris
1704	Griffith Jones
1705	Joseph Wilcox
1706	Nathan Stanbury
1707	Thomas Masters
1709	Richard Hill
1710	William Carter
1711	Samuel Preston
1712	Jonathan Dickinson
1713	George Roch
1714	Richard Hill
1717	Jonathan Dickinson
1719	William Fishbourn
1722	James Logan
1723	Clement Plumsted
1724	Isaac Norris
1725	William Hudson
1726	Charles Read
1728	Thomas Lawrence
1729	Thomas Griffiths
1731	Samuel Hasell
1733	Thomas Griffiths
1734	Thomas Lawrence
1735	William Allen
1736	Clement Plumsted
1737	Thomas Griffiths
1738	Anthony Morris
1739	Edward Roberts
1740	Samuel Hasell
1741	Clement Plumsted
1742	William Till
1743	Benjamin Shoemaker
1744	Edward Shippen
1745	James Hamilton
1746	William Atwood
1748	Charles Willing
1749	Thomas Lawrence
1750	William Plumsted
1751	Robert Strettell
1752	Benjamin Shoemaker
1753	Thomas Lawrence
1754	Charles Willing
1755	William Plumsted
1756	Atwood Shute
1758	Thomas Lawrence
1759	John Stamper
1760	Benjamin Shoemaker
1761	Jacob Duche
1762	Henry Harrison
1763	Thomas Willing
1764	Thomas Lawrence
1765	John Lawrence
1767	Isaac Jones
1769	Samuel Shoemaker
1771	John Gibson
1773	William Fisher
1774	Samuel Rhoads
1775	Samuel Powel
1790	Samuel Miles
1791	John Barclay
1792	Matthew Clarkson
1796	Hillary Baker
1798	Robert Wharton
1800	John Inskeep
1801	Matthew Lawlor
1804	John Inskeep
1806	Robert Wharton
1808	John Barker
1810	Robert Wharton
1811	Michael Keppelle
1812	John Barker
1813	John Geyer
1814	Robert Wharton
1819	James N. Barker
1820	Robert Wharton
1824	Joseph Watson
1828	George M. Dallas
1829	Benjamin W. Richards
1832	John Swift
1838	Isaac Roach
1839	John Swift
1841	John M. Scott
1844	Peter McCall
1845	John Swift
1849	Joel Jones
1850	Charles Gilpin
1853	Robert T. Conrad
1856	Richard Vaux
1858	Alexander Henry
1866	Morton McMichael
1869	Daniel M. Fox
1872	William S. Stokley
1881	Samuel G. King
1884	William B. Smith
1887	Edwin H. Fitler
1891	Edwin S. Stuart
1895	Charles F. Warwick
1899	Samuel H. Ashbridge
1903	John Weaver
1907	John E. Reyburn
1911	R. Blankenburg
1916	Thomas B. Smith
1920	J. Hampton Moore
1924	W. Freeland Kendrick
1928	Harry A. Mackey
1932	J. Hampton Moore
1936	S. Davis Wilson
1939	George Connell (Acting)
1940	Robert E. Lamberton
1941	Bernard Samuel
1952	Joseph S. Clark
1956	Richardson Dilworth
1962	James H. J. Tate
1971	Frank L. Rizzo
1980	William Green
1983	W. Wilson Goode

Pittsburgh

1816	Ebenezer Denny
1817	John Darragh
1825	J. M. Snowden
1828	M. M. Murray
1830	M. B. Laurie
1832	Samuel Pettigrew
1836	J. R. McClintock
1839	William Little
1840	William W. Irwin
1841	James Thompson
1842	Alexander Hay
1845	W. J. Howard
1846	William Kerr
1847	Gabriel Adams
1849	John Herron
1850	Joseph Barker
1851	J. B. Guthrie
1853	R. M. Rittle
1854	R. E. Voltz
1856	William Bingham
1857	H. A. Weaver
1860	George Wilson
1862	B. C. Sawyer
1864	James Lawyer
1866	W. S. McCarthy
1868	James Blackmore
1869	Gerard M. Brush
1875	William C. McCarthy
1878	Walter Lidwell
1881	Robert W. Lyons
1884	Andrew Fulton
1887	William McCallim
1890	H. J. Gourley
1893	Bernard McKenna
1896	Henry P. Ford
1899	William J. Diehl
1901	J. O. Brown
1901	A. M. Brown
1903	W. G. Hays
1906	George W. Guthrie
1909	William A. Magee
1914	Joseph G. Armstrong
1918	E. G. Babcock
1922	William A. Magee
1926	Charles H. Kline
1933	John S. Herron
1934	William McNair
1936	Cornelius Scully
1946	David L. Lawrence
1959	Thomas J. Gallagher
1959	Joseph M. Barr
1970	Peter F. Flaherty
1977	Richard S. Caliguiri

Rhode Island

Providence

1832	Samuel W. Bridgham
1841	Thomas M. Burgess
1852	Amos C. Barstow
1853	Walter R. Danforth
1854	Edward P. Knowles
1855	James Y. Smith
1857	William M. Rodman
1859	Jabez C. Knight
1864	Thomas A. Doyle
1869	George L. Clarke
1870	Thomas A. Doyle
1881	William S. Hayward
1884	Thomas A. Doyle
1886	Gilbert F. Robbins
1889	Henry R. Barker
1891	Charles S. Smith
1892	William K. Potter
1894	Frank F. Olney
1896	Edwin D. McGuinness
1898	William C. Baker
1901	Daniel L. D. Granger
1903	Augustus S. Miller
1906	Elisha Dyer
1907	Patrick J. McCarthy
1909	Henry Fletcher
1913	Joseph H. Gainer
1927	James E. Dunne
1939	John F. Collins
1941	Dennis J. Roberts
1951	Walter H. Reynolds
1964	Joseph A. Doorley, Jr.
1975	Vincent A. Cianci, Jr.
1986	Joseph Paolino, Jr.

South Carolina

Charleston

Intendants

1783 Richard Hutson
1783 Arnoldus Vander Horst
1786 John F. Grimke
1788 Rawlins Lowndes
1789 Thomas Jones
1790 Arnoldus Vander Horst
1792 John Huger
1794 John B. Holmes
1795 John Edwards
1797 Henry W. deSaussure
1799 Thomas Roper
1801 John Ward
1802 David Deas
1803 John Drayton
1804 Thomas Winstanley
1805 Charles B. Cochran
1806 John Dawson, Jr.
1808 Benjamin Boyd
1808 William Rouse
1810 Thomas McCalla
1812 Thomas Bennett
1813 Thomas Rhett Smith
1815 Elias Horry
1817 John Geddes
1819 Daniel Stevens
1820 Elias Horry
1821 James Hamilton, Jr.
1823 John Geddes
1824 Samuel Prioleau
1825 Joseph Johnson
1827 John Gadsden
1829 Henry L. Pinckney
1830 James R. Pringle
1831 Henry L. Pinckney
1833 Edward W. North

Mayors

1836 Robert W. Hayne
1837 Henry L. Pinckney
1840 Jacob F. Mintzing
1842 John Schnierle
1846 T. Leger Hutchinson
1850 John Schnierle
1852 T. Leger Hutchinson
1855 W. Porcher Miles
1857 Charles Macbeth
1865 Peter C. Gaillard
1868 Gilbert Pillsbury
1871 John A. Wagener
1873 G. I. Cunningham
1877 W. W. Sale
1879 William A. Courtenay
1887 George D. Bryan
1891 John F. Ficken
1895 J. Adger Smyth
1903 R. Goodwin Rhett
1911 John P. Grace
1915 Tristram T. Hyde
1919 John P. Grace
1923 Thomas P. Stoney
1931 Burnet R. Maybank
1938 Henry W. Lockwood
1944 E. Edward Wehman, Jr.
1947 William M. Morrison
159 J. Palmer Gaillard, Jr.
     Joseph P. Riley, Jr.

Columbia

Intendants

1806 John Taylor
1807 Abraham Nott
1807 Claiborne Clifton
1808 John Hooker
1808 Daniel Faust
1809 Simon Taylor
1810 Robert Stark
1811 Simon Taylor
1812 Daniel Faust
1815 William E. Hayne
1816 James Gregg
1817 Daniel Morgan
1818 James T. Goodwyn
1822 David J. McCord
1823 James T. Goodwyn
1824 David J. McCord
1825 James T. Goodwyn
1826 William F. deSaussure
1828 E. H. Maxcy
1830 William C. Preston
1831 William C. Clifton
1832 E. H. Maxcy
1833 M. H. DeLeon
1836 John Bryce
1838 R. W. Gibbes
1841 Benjamin T. Elmore
1841 R. H. Goodwin
1842 William M. Myers
1845 William B. Stanley
1846 Joel Stevenson
1847 Edward Sill
1850 Henry Lyons
1851 A. H. Gladden
1853 William Maybin

Mayors

1855 Edward J. Arthur
1857 James D. Tradewell
1859 Allen J. Green
1861 John H. Boatwright
1863 Thomas J. Goodwyn
1865 James G. Gibbes
1866 Theodore Start
1868 John McKenzie
1870 John Alexander
1876 John Agnew
1878 W. B. Stanley
1880 R. O'Neale
1882 John T. Rhett
1890 F. W. McMaster
1892 W. C. Fisher
1894 W. McB. Sloan
1898 T. J. Lipscomb
1900 F. S. Earle
1904 T. H. Gibbes
1908 W. S. Reamer
1910 W. H. Gibbes
1914 L. A. Griffith
1918 R. J. Blalock
1922 W. A. Coleman
1926 L. B. Owens
1941 Fred D. Marshall
1946 Frank C. Owens
1950 J. Macfie Anderson
1954 J. Clarence Dreher, Jr.
1958 Lester L. Bates
1970 John T. Campbell
1978 Kirkman Finlay, Jr.

South Dakota

Pierre

1883 Henry Blakeley
1885 P. F. McClure
1887 A. W. Johnston
1890 B. J. Templeton
1892 Louis Kehr
1894 James H. Owen
1896 J. E. Mallery
1898 Louis B. Albright
1902 A. W. Ewert
1906 Louis B. Albright
1908 L. B. Wadleigh
1909 G. H. Jaynes
1910 J. E. Mallery
1911 L. L. Stephens
1915 William Borst
1918 Joseph B. Binder
1924 J. E. Hipple
1939 Godfrey M. Roberts, Sr.
     (Acting)
1940 John B. Griffin
1955 A. E. Munck
1958 John B. Griffin
1965 Godfrey M. Roberts, Jr.
1970 Clint Gregory
1980 Grace Petersen

Tennessee

Memphis

1827 M. B. Winchester
1829 Isaac Rawlings
1831 Seth Wheatley
1832 Robert Lawrence
1833 Isaac Rawlings
1836 Enoch Banks
1837 John H. Morgan
1838 Enoch Banks
1839 Thomas Dixon
1841 William Spickernagle
1842 E. Hickman
1845 Jesse J. Finley
1846 E. Hickman
1847 Enoch Banks
1848 G. B. Locke
1849 E. Hickman
1852 A. B. Taylor
1855 A. H. Douglass
1856 T. B. Carroll
1857 R. D. Baugh
1861 John Park
1864 Thomas H. Harris
     (Acting)
1864 C. Richards (Acting)
1865 John Park
1866 William O. Lofland
1868 John W. Leftwich
1869 John Johnson
1873 John Logue
1875 John R. Flippin
1879 D. T. Porter
1881 John Overton, Jr.
1883 D. P. Hadden
1891 W. D. Bethell
1893 W. L. Clapp
1898 J. J. Williams
1906 James H. Malone
1910 Edward H. Crump
1915 George C. Love
1916 T. C. Ashcroft
1917 H. H. Litty
1918 F. L. Monteverde
1920 Rowlett Paine

1928 Watkins Overton
1939 Edward H. Crump
1940 Walter Chandler
1946 Sylvanus Polk
1947 James J. Pleasants, Jr.
1949 Watkins Overton
1953 F. T. Tobey
1955 Walter Chandler
1956 Edmund Orgill
1960 Henry Loeb III
1963 Claude A. Armour
1964 William B. Ingram, Jr.
1968 Henry Loeb II
1973 Wyeth Chandler
1983 Richard C. Hackett

Nashville

1806 Joseph Coleman
1809 Benjamin J. Bradford
1811 William Tait
1814 Joseph T. Elliston
1817 Stephen Cantrell, Jr.
1818 Felix Robertson
1819 Thomas Crutcher
1820 James Condon
1821 John P. Endin
1822 Robert B. Currey
1824 Randal McGavock
1825 Wilkins Tennehill
1827 Felix Robertson
1829 William Armstrong
1833 John M. Bass
1834 John P. Erwin
1835 William Nichol
1837 Henry Hollinsworth
1839 Charles C. Trahue
1841 Samuel V. D. Stout
1842 Thomas B. Coleman
1843 Powhattan W. Maxey
1845 John Hugh Smith
1846 John A. Goodlett
1847 Alexander Anderson
1849 John M. Lea
1850 John Hugh Smith
1853 Williamson H. Horn
1854 Robert B. Castleman
1856 Andrew Anderson
1857 John A. McEwen
1858 Randal W. McGavock
1859 S. N. Hollinsworth
1860 Richard B. Cheatham
1862 John Hugh Smith
1865 W. Matt Brown
1867 A. E. Alden
1869 Kindred J. Morris
1872 Thomas A. Kercheval
1874 Morton B. Howell
1875 Thomas A. Kercheval
1883 C. Hooper Phillips
1885 Thomas A. Kercheval
1887 C. P. McCarver
1890 William Litterer
1891 George B. Guild
1895 William McCarthy
1897 R. H. Dudley
1899 J. M. Head
1903 A. S. Williams
1905 T. O. Morris
1907 James S. Brown
1909 Hilary E. Howse
1915 Robert Ewing
1917 William Gupton
1921 Felix Z. Wilson
1922 Percy Sharpe
1923 Hilary E. Howse
1938 Thomas L. Cummings
1951 Ben West
1963 C. Beverly Briley

1975　Richard Fulton

Texas

Austin

1839	Edwin N. Waller
1851	S. G. Haynie
1852	George J. Durham
1853	Thomas W. Ward
1854	John S. Ford
1855	J. T. Cleveland
1856	E. R. Peck
1857	Thomas E. Sneed
1858	B. F. Carter
1860	James W. Smith
1863	S. G. Haynie
1865	Thomas W. Ward
1866	W. H. Carr
1867	Leander Brown
1871	John W. Glenn
1872	T. B. Wheeler
1877	J. C. De Gress
1880	L. M. Crooker
1881	W. A. Saylor
1884	J. W. Robertson
1887	Joseph Nalle
1889	John McDonald
1895	Lewis Hancock
1897	John D. McCall
1901	R. E. White
1905	W. D. Shelley
1907	F. M. Maddox
1909	A. P. Woolridge
1919	W. D. Yett
1926	P. W. McFadden
1933	Tom Miller
1949	Taylor Glass
1951	W. S. Drake, Jr.
1953	C. A. McAden
1955	Tom Miller
1961	Lester E. Palmer
1967	Harry Akin
1969	Travis LaRue
1971	Roy Butler
1975	Jeffrey M. Friedman
1977	Carole K. McClellan
1983	Ron Mullen
1985	Frank C. Cooksey

Dallas

1856	Samuel B. Pryor
1857	John M. Crockett
1858	Isaac Naylor
1858	A. D. Rice
1859	John M. Crockett
1860	J. L. Smith
1861	Thomas E. Sherwood
1862	John W. Lane
1868	Benjamin Long
1870	Henry S. Ervay
1872	Benjamin Long
1875	W. L. Cabell
1876	John D. Kerfoot
1877	W. L. Cabell
1879	J. M. Thurman
1881	John Stone
1883	W. L. Cabell
1885	John Henry Brown
1887	W. C. Conner
1895	F. P. Holland
1897	Bryan T. Barry
1898	John H. Traylor
1900	Benjamin E. Cabell
1904	Bryan T. Barry
1906	Curtis P. Smith

1907	S. J. Hay
1911	W. M. Holland
1915	Henry D. Lindsley
1917	Joe E. Lawther
1919	Frank W. Wozencraft
1921	Sawnie R. Aldredge
1923	L. Blaylock
1927	R. E. Burt
1929	J. Waddy Tate
1931	T. L. Bradford
1933	Charles E. Turner
1935	George Sergeant
1937	George A. Sprague
1939	Woodall Rogers
1947	J. R. Temple
1949	Wallace H. Savage
1951	J. B. Adoue, Jr.
1953	R. L. Thornton
1961	Earle Cabell
1964	Erik Jonsson
1971	Wes Wise
1977	Robert S. Folsom
1979	Jack W. Evans
1983	A. Starke Taylor

Houston

1838	Francis Moore, Jr.
1839	G. W. Lively
1840	Charles Bigelow
1841	John D. Andrews
1843	Francis Moore, Jr.
1844	Horace Baldwin
1845	W. W. Swain
1846	James Bailey
1847	Benjamin P. Buckner
1849	Francis Moore, Jr.
1853	Nathan Fuller
1855	James H. Stevens
1857	Cornelius Ennis
1858	Alexander McGowan
1859	William H. King
1860	Thomas Whitmarsh
1861	W. J. Hutchins
1862	T. W. House, Sr.
1863	William Andrews
1866	Horace D. Taylor
1867	Alexander McGowan
1868	Joseph R. Morris
1870	Timothy H. Scanlan
1874	James T. D. Wilson
1875	I. C. Lord
1877	James T. D. Wilson
1879	Andrew J. Burke
1880	William R. Baker
1886	Daniel C. Smith
1890	Henry Scheriffus
1892	John T. Browne
1896	Baldwin Rice
1898	Samuel H. Brashear
1901	John D. Woolford
1902	O. T. Holt
1904	Andrew L. Jackson
1905	H. Baldwin Rice
1913	Ben Campbell
1917	Joseph J. Pastoriza
1917	J. C. Hutcheson, Jr.
1918	A. E. Amerman
1921	Oscar Holcombe
1929	Walter E. Monteith
1933	Oscar Holcombe
1937	R. H. Fonville
1939	Oscar Holcombe
1941	Neal C. Pickett
1943	Otis Massey
1947	Oscar Holcombe
1953	Roy Hofheinz
1956	Oscar Holcombe
1958	Lewis Cutrer

1964	Louie Welch
1974	Fred Hofheinz
1978	James S. McConn
1981	Kathryn Whitmire

San Antonio

1837	John W. Smith
1838	Antonio Menchaca
1839	S. A. Maverick
1840	John W. Smith
1841	Juan N. Sequin
1841	Francis Gilbeau (Acting)
1842	John W. Smith
1844	Edward Dwyer
1847	S. S. Smith
1848	Charles F. King
1849	J. M. Devine
1851	J. S. McDonald
1852	C. F. King
1853	J. M. Devine
1854	John M. Carolan
1855	James R. Sweet
1856	J. M. Devine
1857	J. H. Beck (Acting)
1857	A. A. Lockwood
1858	James R. Sweet
1862	S. A. Maverick
1863	P. S. Buquor
1865	J. H. Lyons
1867	W. C. A. Thielepape
1872	S. G. Newton
1872	F. Giraud
1875	James H. French
1885	Bryan Callaghan
1892	A. I. Lockwood
1893	George Paschal
1894	Henry Elmendorf
1897	Bryan Callaghan
1899	Marshall Hicks
1903	John S. Campbell
1905	Bryan Callaghan
1912	A. H. Jones
1913	Clinton G. Brown
1917	Sam C. Bell
1921	O. B. Black
1923	John W. Tobin
1927	C. M. Chambers
1933	C. K. Quin
1939	Maury Maverick
1941	C. K. Quin
1943	Gus B. Mauerman
1947	Alfred Callaghan
1949	A. C. White
1952	Sam B. Steves
1953	A. C. White
1954	R. L. Lester
1954	R. N. White, Sr.
1955	J. Edwin Kuykendall
1961	Walter W. McAllister
1971	John Gatti
1973	Charles L. Becker
1975	Lila Cockrell
1977	Tom Parrett
1979	Lila Cockrell
1981	Henry G. Cisneros

Utah

Salt Lake City

1851	Jedediah M. Grant
1857	Abraham O. Smoot
1866	Daniel H. Wells
1876	Feramorz Little
1882	William Jennings
1884	James Sharp

1886	Francis Armstrong
1890	George M. Scott
1892	Robert N. Baskin
1896	James Glendinning
1898	John Clark
1900	Ezra Thompson
1904	Richard P. Morris
1906	Ezra Thompson
1907	John S. Bransford
1912	Samuel C. Park
1916	William M. Ferry
1920	E. A. Bock
1920	Charles C. Neslen
1928	John F. Bowman
1932	Louis Marcus
1936	E. B. Erwin
1938	John M. Wallace
1940	Ab. Jenkins
1944	Earl J. Glade
1956	Adiel F. Stewart
1960	J. Bracken Lee
1972	Jake Garn
1976	Ted Wilson
1985	Palmer DePaulis

Vermont

Montpelier

1895	George W. Wing
1896	George O. Stratton
1897	George H. Guernsey
1898	John H. Senter
1900	Joseph G. Brown
1902	James M. Boutwell
1903	Frank M. Corry
1906	James S. Haley
1908	Frank R. Dawley
1911	Smith S. Ballard
1912	James B. Estee
1914	James M. Boutwell
1917	Frank W. Mitchell
1919	Harry C. Shurtleff
1921	George L. Blanchard
1922	Dean K. Lillie
1924	George L. Edson
1926	Edward H. Deavitt
1930	Riley C. Bowers
1933	William L. McKee
1934	Perry H. Merrill
1935	James F. Ewing
1936	William H. Dyer
1938	Birney L. Hall
1939	William F. Corry
1945	Harry R. Sheridan
1947	Daughly Gould
1949	Anson F. Barber
1956	Edward F. Knapp
1959	Elbert B. Colburn
1963	Manuel Canas, Jr.
1966	Willard R. Strong
1972	Richard W. Curtis
1976	Frederic H. Bertrand
1978	Charles B. Nichols
1982	Frank O. Romano

Virginia

Norfolk

1898	C. Brooks Johnston
1901	Nathaniel Beaman
1902	E. G. Riddick
1912	Wyndham R. Mayo
1918	Albert L. Roper

1924 S. Heth Tyler
1931 E. Jeff Robertson
1932 Philip H. Mason
1933 S. L. Slover
1934 W. R. L. Taylor
1938 John A. Gurkin
1940 Joseph D. Wood
1944 James W. Reed
1946 R. D. Cooke
1949 Pretlow Darden
1950 W. F. Duckworth
1962 Roy B. Martin, Jr.
1974 Irvine B. Hill
1976 Vincent J. Thomas
1984 Joseph A. Leafe

Richmond

1782 William Foushee
1783 John Beckley
1784 Robert Mitchell
1785 John Harvie
1786 William Pennock
1787 Richard Adams, Sr.
1788 John Beckley
1789 Alexander McRoberts
1790 Robert Boyd
1790 George Nicholas
1791 John Barrett
1792 Robert Mitchell
1793 John Barrett
1794 Robert Mitchell
1795 Andrew Dunscomb
1796 Robert Mitchell
1797 James McClurg
1798 John Barrett
1799 George Nicolas
1800 James McClurg
1801 William Richardson
1802 John Foster
1803 James McClurg
1804 Robert Mitchell
1805 William DuVal
1806 Edward Carrington
1810 David Bullock
1811 Benjamin Tate
1812 Thomas Wilson
1813 Robert Greenhow
1814 Thomas Wilson
1815 Robert Gamble
1816 Thomas Wilson
1817 William H. Fitzwhylson
1818 Thomas Wilson
1819 John Adams
1826 Joseph Tate
1839 Francis Worker
1840 William Lambert
1852 Samuel Pulliam
1853 Joseph Mayo
1865 David J. Saunders
1866 Joseph Mayo
1868 George Chahoon
1868 Joseph Mayo
1870 Vacant
1871 A. M. Keiley
1876 William C. Carrington
1888 J. Taylor Ellyson
1894 Richard M. Taylor
1904 Carlton McCarthy
1908 David C. Richardson
1912 George Ainslie
1924 J. Fulmer Bright
1940 Gordon B. Ambler
1944 William C. Herbert
1946 Horace H. Edwards
1948 W. Stirling King
1950 T. Nelson Parker
1952 Edward E. Haddock
1954 Thomas P. Bryan, Jr.

1956 F. Henry Garber
1958 A. Scott Anderson
1960 Claude W. Woodward
1962 Eleanor P. Sheppard
1964 Morrill M. Crowe
1968 Phil J. Bagley, Jr.
1970 Thomas J. Bliley, Jr.
1978 Henry L. Marsh, III
1982 Roy A. West

Washington

Olympia

1873 W. W. Miller
1874 I. C. Ellis
1875 T. F. McElroy
1876 J. C. Horr
1877 John P. Judson
1878 E. N. Quinette
1880 George A. Barnes
1881 E. T. Young
1882 N. Ostrander
1884 J. S. Dobbins
1885 A. A. Phillips
1886 A. H. Chambers
1889 J. F. Gowey
1891 J. C. Horr
1892 R. G. O'Brien
1893 J. W. Robinson
1894 C. B. Mann
1896 Charles H. Ayer
1897 John Byrne
1898 George B. Lane
1899 C. S. Reinhart
1902 C. J. Lord
1904 H. G. Richardson
1905 P. H. Carlyon
1907 Thomas McLarty
1908 W. A. Hagemeyer
1909 Mitchell Harris
1912 W. L. Bridgford
1913 G. A. Mottman
1917 Jesse T. Mills
1921 C. H. Bowen
1923 George W. Draham
1925 James C. Johnson
1929 George G. Mills
1932 E. N. Steele
1934 F. B. Longaker
1941 J. T. Trullinger
1947 Ernest Mallory
1950 Ralph A. Swanson
1953 Amanda B. Smith
1960 Neil R. McKay
1969 Thomas Allen
1978 Lyle T. Watson
1982 David A. Skramstad

Seattle

1869 Henry A. Atkins
1871 John T. Jordan
1872 Corliss P. Stone
1873 Moses R. Maddocks
1873 John Collins
1874 Henry L. Yesler
1875 Bailey Gatzert
1876 Gideon A. Weed
1878 Beriah Brown
1879 Orange Jacobs
1880 L. P. Smith
1882 Henry G. Struve
1884 John Leary
1885 Henry L. Yesler
1886 William H. Shoudy
1887 Thomas T. Minor

1888 Robert Moran
1890 Harry White
1891 George W. Hall
1892 James T. Ronald
1894 Byron Phelps
1896 Frank D. Black
1896 W. D. Wood
1897 Thomas D. Humes
1904 Richard A. Ballinger
1906 William H. Moore
1908 John F. Miller
1910 Hiram C. Gill
1911 George W. Dilling
1912 George F. Cotterill
1914 Hiram C. Gill
1918 Ole Hanson
1919 C. B. Fitzgerald
1920 Hugh M. Caldwell
1922 Edwin J. Brown
1926 Bertha K. Landes
1928 Frank E. Edwards
1931 Robert H. Harlin
1932 John F. Dore
1934 Charles L. Smith
1936 John F. Dore
1938 Arthur B. Langlie
1941 John E. Carroll
1941 Earl Milliken
1942 William F. Devin
1952 Allan Pomeroy
1956 Gordon S. Clinton
1964 J. D. Braman
1969 Floyd C. Miller
1969 Wesley C. Uhlman
1978 Charles T. Royer

West Virginia

Charleston

1861 Jacob Goshorn
1865 John A. Truslow
1867 George Ritter
1869 John Williams
1870 J. W. Wingfield
1871 H. C. Dickinson
1871 John P. Hale
1872 John Williams
1873 C. P. Synder
1875 John C. Ruby
1877 C. J. Botkin
1881 R. R. Delaney
1883 J. D. Baines
1885 J. H. Huling
1887 Joseph L. Fry
1891 J. B. Pemberton
1893 E. W. Staunton
1895 J. A. de Gruyter
1899 W. Herman Smith
1900 John B. Floyd
1901 George S. Morgan
1903 C. E. Rudesill
1905 John A. Jarrett
1907 James A. Holley
1913 J. F. Bedell
1914 O. A. Petty
1915 George E. Breece
1917 G. A. MacQueen
1918 R. L. Walker
1919 Grant P. Hall
1923 William W. Wertz
1931 R. P. Devan
1935 D. Boone Dawson
1947 R. Carl Andrews
1951 J. T. Copenhaver
1959 John A. Shanklin
1967 Elmer H. Dodson
1971 John G. Hutchinson

1980 Joe F. Smith
1983 James E. Roark

Wisconsin

Madison

1856 Jairus C. Fairchild
1857 Augustus A. Bird
1858 George B. Smith
1861 Levi B. Vilas
1862 William T. Leitch
1865 Elisha W. Keyes
1867 Alden S. Sanborn
1868 David Atwood
1869 Andrew Proudfit
1871 J. B. Bowen
1872 James L. Hill
1873 J. C. Gregory
1874 Silas U. Pinney
1876 John N. Jones
1877 Harlow S. Orton
1878 George B. Smith
1879 John R. Baltzell
1880 Philip L. Spooner, Jr.
1881 James Conklin
1884 Breese J. Stevens
1885 H. N. Moulton
1887 James Conklin
1888 M. R. Doyton
1890 Robert M. Bashford
1891 William H. Rogers
1893 John Corscot
1895 Jabe Alford
1896 Albert A. Dye
1897 Mathew J. Hoven
1898 Charles E. Whelan
1899 Mathew J. Hoven
1901 Storm Bull
1902 John W. Groves
1904 W. D. Curtis
1906 Joseph C. Schubert
1912 John B. Heim
1914 A. H. Kayser
1916 George C. Sayle
1920 I. Milo Kittleson
1926 A. G. Schmedeman
1932 James R. Law
1943 F. Halsey Kraege
1947 Leonard C. Howell (City Manager)
1951 George J. Forster
1955 A. W. Bareis
1956 Ivan A. Nestingen
1961 Harold E. Hanson
1961 Henry E. Reynolds
1965 Otto Festge
1969 William D. Dyke
1973 Paul Soglin
1979 Joel Skornicka
1983 F. T. Sensenbrenner, Jr.

Milwaukee

1846 Solomon Juneau
1847 H. N. Wells
1848 Byron Kilbourn
1849 Don A. J. Upham
1851 George H. Walker
1852 Hans Crocker
1853 George H. Walker
1854 Byron Kilbourn
1855 James B. Cross
1858 William A. Prentiss
1859 Herman L. Page
1860 William P. Lynde
1861 James S. Brown

1862	Horace Chase	1912	Gerhard A. Bading	1872	M. Sloan	1913	D. W. Gill
1863	Edward O'Neill	1916	Daniel W. Hoan	1873	M. V. Boughten	1914	R. N. Lafountaine
1864	Abner Kirby	1940	Carl F. Zeidler	1874	George Cassels	1918	Edward W. Stone
1865	John J. Tallmadge	1942	John L. Bohn	1875	J. C. Whipple	1920	Ed R. Taylor
1867	Edward O'Neill	1948	Frank P. Zeidler	1876	L. R. Bresnahen	1924	Archie Allison
1870	Joseph Phillips	1960	Henry W. Maier	1877	Dwight Fisk	1926	C. W. Riner

Wyoming

Cheyenne

Mayors

1867	H. M. Hook
1868	L. Murrin
1869	W. M. Slaughter

City Council Presidents

1869	J. H. Martin
1871	Jervis Joslin

1871	Harrison Ludington		
1872	David G. Hooker		
1873	Harrison Ludington		
1876	A. A. R. Butler		
1878	John Black		
1880	Thomas H. Brown		
1882	John M. Stowell		
1884	Emil Wallber		
1888	Thomas H. Brown		
1890	George W. Peck		
1890	P. J. Somers		
1893	John C. Koch		
1896	William G. Rauschenberger		
1898	David S. Rose		
1906	Sherburn M. Becker		
1908	David S. Rose		
1910	Emil Seidel		

Mayors

1878	L. R. Bresnahen	1930	Cal Holliday
1880	F. E. Addoms	1932	J. F. Weybrecht
1881	J. M. Carey	1934	Archie Allison
1885	F. E. Warren	1940	Ed Warren
1885	A. H. Reel	1944	Ira L. Hanna
1887	C. W. Riner	1944	Bruce S. Jones
1891	L. R. Bresnahen	1946	John J. McInerney
1893	Edward F. Stahle	1948	Ben Nelson
1895	Samuel Merrill	1951	Ed Warren
1897	W. R. Schnitger	1952	R. E. Cheever
1901	J. L. Murray	1954	Val S. Christensen
1903	M. P. Keefe	1958	Worth Story
1904	D. W. Gill	1962	Bill Nation
1907	P. S. Cook	1966	Herbert Kingham
1911	L. R. Bresnahen	1968	George R. Cox
		1969	Floyd Holland
		1972	Bill Nation
		1976	Donald Erickson

XII
College and University Presidents

College and University Presidents

Lists chief executives of 314 leading educational institutions, beginning with the year in which the school became a degree-granting, four-year institution, not necessarily the year of its founding. In some instances a president's term may have begun before the institution was elevated to four-year status. Unless otherwise specified, the chief executive has the title of president.

Adelphi University

Garden City, NY

(Adelphi College until 1963.)

1896 Charles H. Levermore
1912 S. Parkes Cadman (Acting)
1915 Frank D. Blodgett
1937 Paul D. Eddy
1965 Arthur W. Brown
1967 Robert G. Olmsted (Acting)
1969 Charles Vevier
1972 Timothy W. Costello
1986 Peter Diamandopoulos

Albion College

Albion, MI

1861 Thomas H. Sinex
1864 George B. Jocelyn
1870 William B. Silber
1871 J. L. G. McKeown
1871 George B. Jocelyn
1877 Lewis R. Fiske
1898 John P. Ashley
1902 Samuel Dickie
1921 John W. Laird
1924 John L. Seaton
1945 William W. Whitehouse
1960 Louis W. Norris
1970 Bernard T. Lomas
1983 Melvin L. Vulgamore

Albright College

Reading, PA

(Central Pennsylvania College until 1902.)

1887 Aaron Gobble
1902 James D. Woodring
1908 Clellan A. Bowman (Acting)
1909 John F. Dunlap
1915 L. Clarence Hunt
1923 Clellan A. Bowman
1928 Warren F. Teel
1932 J. Warren Klein
1938 Harry V. Masters
1965 Arthur L. Schultz
1978 David G. Ruffer

Alfred University

Alfred, NY

1857 William C. Kenyon
1867 Jonathan M. Allen
1892 Alpheus B. Kenyon (Acting)
1893 Arthur E. Main
1895 Boothe C. Davis
1933 Paul E. Titsworth
1933 John N. Norwood
1945 Jack E. Walters
1948 Miles E. Drake
1967 Leland W. Miles
1974 Merle R. Rose
1979 Howard R. Neville
1982 Edward G. Coll, Jr.

Allegheny College

Meadville, PA

1815 Timothy Alden
1833 Martin Ruter
1837 Homer J. Clark
1847 John Barker
1860 George Loomis
1874 Jonathan Hamnett (Acting)
1875 Lucius Bugbee
1882 Jonathan Hamnett (Acting)
1883 David H. Wheeler
1888 Wilbur G. Williams
1889 David H. Wheeler
1893 William H. Crawford
1920 Fred W. Hixson
1924 Clarence F. Ross (Acting)
1926 James A. Beebe
1930 Clarence F. Ross (Acting)
1931 William P. Tolley
1942 John R. Schultz
1947 Chester A. Darling (Acting)
1948 Louis T. Benezet
1955 Lawrence L. Pelletier
1980 David B. Harned

American University

Washington, DC

Chancellors

1891 John F. Hurst
1902 Charles C. McCabe
1906 Wilbur L. Davidson (In charge)
1907 Franklin Hamilton

1922 Lucius C. Clark
1933 Edwin H. Hughes (Acting)
1934 Joseph M. M. Gray

Presidents

1940 E. W. Engel (Acting)
1941 Paul F. Douglass
1951 James J. Robbins (Acting)
1952 Hurst R. Anderson
1968 George H. Williams
1976 Joseph J. Sisco
1980 Richard E. Berendzen

Amherst College

Amherst, MA

1821 Zephaniah S. Moore
1823 Heman Humphrey
1845 Edward Hitchcock
1854 William A. Stearns
1876 Julius H. Seelye
1890 Merrill E. Gates
1899 George Harris
1912 Alexander Meiklejohn
1924 George D. Olds
1927 Arthur S. Pease
1932 Stanley King
1946 Charles W. Cole
1960 Calvin H. Plimpton
1971 John W. Ward
1980 G. Armour Craig
1984 Peter R. Pouncey

Antioch College

Yellow Springs, OH

1853 Horace Mann
1860 Thomas Hill
1862 Austin Craig
1862 John B. Weston (Acting)
1866 George W. Hosmer
1872 Edward Orton
1873 Samuel C. Derby (Acting)
1876 John B. Weston (Acting)
1882 Orin J. Wait
1883 Daniel A. Long
1899 William A. Bell
1902 Franklin Hooper (Acting)
1906 Simeon D. Fess
1917 George D. Black (Acting)
1919 William M. Dawson (Acting)
1921 Arthur E. Morgan
1935 Algo D. Henderson
1948 Douglas McGregor
1954 Samuel B. Gould

1959 James P. Dixon, Jr.
1976 William M. Birenbaum
1986 Alan E. Guskin

Arizona State University

Tempe, AZ

1925 Arthur J. Matthews
1930 Ralph W. Swetman
1933 Grady Gammage
1959 Harold D. Richardson (Acting)
1960 G. Homer Durham
1969 Harry K. Newburn
1971 John W. Schwada
1981 J. Russell Nelson

Auburn University

Auburn, AL

(East Alabama Male College until 1899.)

1858 William J. Sasmett
1866 James F. Dowdell
1872 Isaac T. Tichenor
1882 William L. Broun
1883 David F. Boyd
1884 William L. Broun
1902 Charles C. Thach
1919 Bennett B. Ross (Acting)
1920 Spright Dowell
1928 Bradford Knapp
1932 John J. Wilmore
1932 Bolling H. Crenshaw
1932 Luther N. Duncan
1935 Luther N. Duncan
1947 Ralph B. Draughon
1965 Harry M. Philpott
1980 H. Hanley Funderburk, Jr.
1983 Wilford S. Bailey
1984 James E. Martin

Baker University

Baldwin City, KS

1858 Werter R. Davis
1862 George W. Paddock
1864 Leonard L. Hartman
1865 John W. Locke
1866 John W. Horner
1867 Elial J. Rice
1869 John A. Simpson
1870 Patterson McNutt
1871 Robert L. Harford
1873 Samuel S. Weatherby
1874 Joseph J. Denison

1879	William H. Sweet
1886	Hillary A. Gobin
1890	William A. Quayle
1894	Lemuel H. Murlin
1911	Wilbur N. Mason
1917	Samuel A. Lough
1921	Osmon G. Markham
1922	Wallace B. Fleming
1936	Nelson P. Horn
1956	William J. Scarborough
1966	James E. Doty
1973	Neil Malicky (Acting)
1974	Jerald C. Walker
1980	Ralph M. Tanner

Ball State University

Muncie, IN

(Ball State Teachers College until 1965.)

1927	Lemuel A. Pittenger
1943	W. E. Wagoner (Acting)
1945	John R. Emens
1968	John J. Pruis
1979	Jerry M. Anderson
1981	Robert P. Bell
1984	John E. Worthen

Bard College

Annandale, NY

(St. Stephens College until 1934.)

1860	George F. Seymour
1861	Thomas Richey
1863	Robert B. Fairbairn
1899	Lawrence T. Cole
1904	Thomas R. Harris
1909	William C. Rodgers
1919	Bernard I. Bell
1933	Donald G. Tewksbury
1938	Harold Mestre
1940	Harold Gray
1948	Edward C. Fuller
1950	James H. Case, Jr.
1960	Reamer Kline
1975	Leon Botstein

Barnard College

New York, NY

Deans

1894	Emily James (Smith) Putnam
1901	Laura Drake Gill
1907	Vacant
1911	Virginia Crocheron Gildersleeve

Presidents

1947	Millicent Carey McIntosh
1962	Rosemary (Park) Anastos
1967	Martha E. Peterson
1976	Jacquelyn Phillips Mattfeld
1980	Ellen Futter

Bates College

Lewiston, ME

1863	Oren B. Cheney
1894	George C. Chase
1920	Clifton D. Gray
1944	Charles F. Phillips
1967	Thomas H. Reynolds

Baylor University

Waco, TX

1845	Henry L. Graves
1851	Rufus C. Burleson
1861	George W. Baines
1863	William C. Crane
1885	Reddin Andrews
1886	Rufus C. Burleson
1897	Vacant
1899	Oscar H. Cooper
1902	Samuel P. Brooks
1932	Pat M. Neff
1948	William R. White
1961	Abner V. McCall
1981	Herbert H. Reynolds

Beloit College

Beloit, WI

1850	Aaron L. Chapin
1886	Edward D. Eaton
1917	Melvin A. Brannon
1923	Edward D. Eaton (Acting)
1924	W. Irving Maurer
1942	W. Bradley Tyrell (Acting)
1944	Carey Croneis
1954	Harold S. Wood (Acting)
1954	Miller Upton
1976	Martha E. Peterson
1981	Roger H. Hull

Bennington College

Bennington, VT

1928	Robert D. Leigh
1941	Lewis W. Jones
1947	Frederick Burkhardt
1957	William C. Fels
1965	Edward J. Bloustein
1971	Gail T. Parker
1976	Joseph S. Iseman (Acting)
1977	Joseph S. Murphy
1982	Michael K. Hooker

Berea College

Berea, KY

1853	John G. Fee
1869	Edward Fairchild
1892	William G. Frost
1920	William J. Hutchins
1939	Francis S. Hutchins
1967	Willis D. Weatherford
1984	John B. Stephenson

Bernard M. Baruch College of the City University of New York

New York, NY

1968	Samuel F. Thomas (Acting)
1969	Robert C. Weaver
1970	Jerome B. Cohen (Acting)
1971	Clyde J. Wingfield
1977	Joel Segall

Bethany College

Bethany, WV

1840	Alexander Campbell
1866	William K. Pendleton
1887	W. H. Woolery
1889	Archibald McLean
1891	Hugh McDiarmid
1897	B. C. Hagerman
1899	J. M. Kershey
1901	Thomas E. Cramblet
1919	Cloyd Goodnight
1933	Joseph A. Serena
1934	W. H. Cramblet
1953	Perry E. Gresham
1972	Cecil H. Underwood
1975	Orville Wake (Acting)
1976	William E. Tucker
1980	Todd H. Bullard

Boston College

Chestnut Hill, MA

1863	John Bapst
1869	Robert W. Brady
1870	Robert B. Fulton
1880	Jeremiah O'Connor
1884	Edward V. Boursaud
1887	Thomas H. Stack
1887	Nicholas Russo
1888	Robert B. Fulton
1891	Edward I. Devitt
1894	Timothy Brosnahan
1898	W. J. Reid Mullan
1903	William F. Gannon
1907	Thomas I. Gasson
1914	Charles W. Lyons
1919	William Devlin
1925	James H. Dolan
1932	Louis Gallagher
1937	William J. McGarry
1939	William J. Murphy
1945	William J. Keleher
1951	Joseph R. N. Maxwell
1958	Michael P. Walsh
1968	W. Seavey Joyce
1972	T. Donald Moran

Boston University

Boston, MA

1873	William F. Warren
1903	William E. Huntington
1911	Lemuel H. Murlin
1925	W. F. Anderson
1926	Daniel L. Marsh
1951	Harold C. Case
1967	Arland F. Christ-Janer
1970	John R. Silber

Bowdoin College

Brunswick, ME

1802	Joseph McKeen
1807	Jesse Appleton
1820	William Allen
1839	Leonard Woods
1867	Samuel Harris
1871	Joshua L. Chamberlain
1885	William D. Hyde
1918	Kenneth C. M. Sills
1952	James S. Coles
1968	Athern P. Daggett (Acting)
1969	Roger Howell, Jr.
1978	Willard Enteman
1981	A. LeRoy Greason, Jr.

Bowling Green State University

Bowling Green, KY

(Bowling Green State Normal College until 1929; Bowling Green State College until 1935.)

1912	Homer B. Williams
1937	Roy E. Offenhauer
1939	Frank J. Prout
1951	Ralph W. McDonald
1961	Ralph G. Harshman
1963	William T. Jerome, III
1970	Hollis A. Moore
1981	Michael R. Ferrari, Jr.
1982	Paul J. Olscamp

Bradley University

Peoria, IL

(Bradley Polytechnic Institute until 1946.)

1897	William R. Harper
1906	Theodore C. Burgess
1925	Charles T. Wyckoff (Acting)
1925	Frederick R. Hamilton
1946	David B. Owen
1952	A. G. Haussler (Acting)
1954	Harold P. Rodes
1960	A. G. Haussler (Acting)
1961	T. W. Van Arsdale, Jr.
1971	Martin G. Abegg

Brandeis University

Waltham, MA

1948	Abram B. Sachar
1968	Morris B. Abram
1970	Charles I. Schottland
1971	Marver H. Bernstein
1983	Evelyn E. Handler

Brigham Young University

Provo, UT

(Brigham Young Academy until 1903.)

1904 George H. Brimhall
1921 Franklin S. Harris
1945 Howard S. McDonald
1951 Ernest L. Wilkinson
1972 Dallin H. Oaks
1980 Jeffrey R. Holland

Brooklyn College of the City University of New York

Brooklyn, NY

(Brooklyn College until 1961.)

1930 William A. Boylan
1939 Harry D. Gideonse
1966 Francis P. Kilcoyne
1968 Harold C. Syrett
1969 John W. Kneller
1979 Robert L. Hess

Brown University

Providence, RI

(Rhode Island College until 1804.)

1765 James Manning
1792 Jonathan Maxcy
1802 Asa Messer
1827 Francis Wayland
1855 Barnas Sears
1868 Alexis Caswell
1872 Ezekiel G. Robinson
1889 Elisha B. Andrews
1899 William H. P. Faunce
1929 Clarence A. Barbour
1937 Henry M. Wriston
1955 Barnaby C. Keeney
1966 Ray L. Heffner
1969 Merton P. Stoltz (Acting)
1970 Donald F. Hornig
1977 Howard R. Swearer

Bryn Mawr College

Bryn Mawr, PA

1885 James E. Rhoads
1894 M. Carey Thomas
1922 Marion Edwards Park
1944 Katherine E. McBride
1970 Harris L. Wofford, Jr.
1976 Mary Patterson McPherson (Acting)
1978 Mary Patterson McPherson

Bucknell University

Lewisburg, PA

(University at Lewisburg until 1886.)

1851 Howard Malcolm

1858 Justin R. Loomis
1879 David J. Hill
1889 John H. Harris
1919 Emory W. Hunt
1931 Homer P. Rainey
1935 Arnaud C. Marts (Acting)
1945 Herbert L. Spencer
1949 Horace A. Hildreth
1954 Merle M. Odgers
1964 Charles H. Watts, II
1976 George D. O'Brien
1984 Gary A. Sojka

Butler University

Indianapolis, IN

1855 John Young
1858 Samuel Hoshour
1861 Allen R. Benton
1868 Otis R. Burgess
1870 W. F. Black
1873 Otis R. Burgess
1881 Harvey W. Everest
1885 Allen R. Benton
1891 Scot Butler
1904 Winfred E. Garrison
1906 Scot Butler
1907 Thomas Carr Howe
1920 James W. Putnam
1921 Robert J. Aley
1931 Walter S. Athearn
1933 James W. Putnam
1939 Daniel S. Robinson
1942 Maurice O. Ross
1963 Alexander E. Jones
1977 Paul Stewart (Acting)
1978 John G. Johnson

California Institute of Technology

Pasadena, CA

(Throop Polytechnic Institute until 1912; Throop College of Technology until 1919.)

1891 Charles H. Keyes
1897 Walter A. Edwards
1908 James A. B. Scherer
1921 Robert A. Millikan (Chairman of the Executive Council)
1946 Lee A. DuBridge
1969 Harold Brown
1977 Robert W. Christy (Acting)
1978 Marvin L. Goldberger

California State University, Fresno

Fresno, CA

(Fresno State Normal School until 1921; Fresno State Teachers College until 1935; Fresno State College until 1972.)

1911 Charles L. McLane
1927 Frank W. Thomas
1948 Arnold E. Joyal
1964 Frederick W. Ness
1969 Karl L. Falk (Acting)

1970 Norman A. Baxter
1980 Harold H. Haak

California State University, Long Beach

Long Beach, CA

(Long Beach State College from 1950 to 1964.)

1949 P. Victor Peterson
1959 Henry Magnusen (Interim)
1959 Carl W. McIntosh
1969 Donald Simonsen (Acting)
1970 Stephen Horn

California State University, Northridge

Northridge, CA

(San Fernando Valley State College until 1972.)

1958 Ralph Prator
1968 Paul B. Blomgren (Acting)
1969 Malcolm O. Sillars (Acting)
1969 James W. Cleary

California State University, Sacramento

Sacramento, CA

(Sacramento State College until 1972.)

1947 Guy A. West
1965 F. Blair Mayne (Acting)
1965 Stephen L. Walker (Acting)
1966 Robert Johns
1969 Otto Butz (Acting)
1970 Bernard L. Hyink
1972 Glenn S. Dumke (Chancellor)
1974 James Bond
1979 W. Lloyd Johns
1984 Donald R. Gerth

California State University, San Diego

San Diego, CA

(San Diego State Teachers College until 1935; San Diego State College until 1972.)

1925 Edward L. Hardy
1935 Walter R. Hepner
1952 Malcolm A. Love
1972 Donald Walker (Acting)
1972 Brage Golding
1978 Thomas B. Day

California State University, San Francisco

San Francisco, CA

(San Francisco State College until 1972.)

1899 Frederick L. Burk
1924 Archibald B. Anderson
1927 Alexander C. Roberts
1945 J. Paul Leonard
1957 Glenn S. Dumke
1961 Frank Fenton (Acting)
1962 Paul Dodd
1966 John Summerskill
1968 S. I. Hayakawa
1974 Paul F. Romberg
1984 Chia-Wei Woo

California State University, San Jose

San Jose, CA

(San Jose State Teachers College until 1935; San Jose State College until 1972.)

1921 Willim W. Kemp
1923 Alexander R. Heron (Acting)
1923 Edwin R. Snyder
1925 Herman F. Minssen (Acting)
1925 Thomas W. MacQuarrie
1952 John T. Wahlquist
1964 Robert D. Clark
1969 Hobert W. Burns (Acting)
1970 John H. Bunzel
1978 Gail J. Fullerton

Canisius College

Buffalo, NY

1870 William Becker
1872 Henry Behrens
1876 John B. Lessmann
1877 Martin Port
1883 Theodore Van Rossum
1888 J. Ulric Heinzle
1891 John I. Zahm
1897 James A. Rockliff
1898 John B. Theis
1901 Aloysius J. Pfeil
1905 Augustine A. Miller
1913 George J. Krim
1919 Michael J. Ahern
1923 Peter Cusick
1929 Rudolph J. Eichhorn
1934 James P. Sweeney
1937 Francis A. O'Malley
1941 Timothy J. Coughlin
1947 Raymond W. Schouten
1952 Philip E. Dobson
1959 James J. McGinley
1966 James M. Demske

Capital University

Columbus, OH

1850 W. M. Reynolds
1854 C. Spielmann

1857	William F. Lehmann
1881	M. Loy
1890	C. H. Schuette
1894	William F. Stellhorn
1900	L.H. Schuh
1913	Otto Mees
1946	Harold L. Yochum
1969	Thomas H. Langevin
1980	Harvey A. Stegemoeller

Carleton College

Northfield, MN

1870	James W. Strong
1903	William H. Sallmon
1909	Donald J. Cowling
1945	Laurence M. Gould
1962	John W. Nason
1970	Howard R. Swearer
1977	Robert H. Edwards
1986	David H. Porter

Carnegie-Mellon University

Pittsburgh, PA

(Carnegie Institute of Technology until 1967.)

1912	Arthur A. Hamerschlag
1923	Thomas S. Baker
1936	Robert E. Doherty
1950	John C. Warner
1965	H. Guyford Stever
1972	Edward Schatz (Acting)
1972	Richard M. Cyert

Carroll College

Waukesha, WI

1850	John A. Savage
1863	Rensellaer B. Hammond
1864	William Alexander
1866	Walter L. Rankin
1871	Vacant
1893	Walter L. Rankin
1903	Wilbur O. Carrier
1918	Herbert P. Houghton
1921	William A. Ganfield
1940	Gerrit T. Vander Lught
1946	Nelson V. Russell
1952	Robert D. Steele
1967	John T. Middaugh
1971	Robert V. Cramer

Carson-Newman College

Jefferson City, TN

1851	William Rogers
1851	R. R. Bryan
1853	Samuel Anderson
1857	Matt Hillsman
1859	N.B. Goforth
1866	R. R. Bryan
1869	Jesse Baker
1870	N. B. Goforth
1882	B. O. Manard
1883	S. W. Tindell
1888	W. A. Montgomery
1892	J. T. Henderson
1903	M. D. Jeffries

1912	J. M. Burnett
1917	W. L. Gentry
1920	Oscar E. Sams
1927	James T. Warren
1948	Daniel H. Fite
1968	John A. Fincher
1978	J. Cordell Maddox

Case Western Reserve University

Cleveland, OH

(Formed in 1967 from the merger of Case Institute of Technology with Western Reserve University.)

1967	Robert W. Morse
1971	Louis A. Toepfer
1980	David V. Ragone

Catholic University of America

Washington, DC

1887	John J. Keane
1896	Thomas J. Conaty
1908	Denis J. O'Connell
1909	Thomas J. Shahan
1928	James H. Ryan
1936	Joseph M. Corrigan
1943	Patrick J. McCormick
1953	Bryan J. McEntegart
1957	William J. McDonald
1967	John P. Whalen
1968	Nivard Scheel
1969	Clarence C. Walton
1978	Edmund D. Pellegrino
1982	William J. Byron

City College of the City University of New York

New York, NY

(City College of New York until 1961.)

1848	Horace Webster
1869	Alexander Webb
1902	Alfred G. Compton (Acting)
1903	John H. Finley
1913	Adolph Werner (Acting)
1915	Sidney E. Mezes
1927	Frederick B. Robinson
1938	Nelson P. Mead (Acting)
1941	Harry N. Wright
1952	Buell G. Gallagher
1961	Harry N. Rivlin (Acting)
1962	Buell G. Gallagher
1969	Joseph J. Copeland (Acting)
1970	Robert E. Marshak
1980	Arthur E. Tiedemann (Acting)
1981	Bernard W. Harleston

City University of New York

New York, NY

(See also Bernard M. Baruch College; Brooklyn College; City College; Hunter College; Queens College)

Chancellors

1961	John R. Everett
1963	Albert H. Bowker
1971	Robert J. Kibbee
1982	Joseph S. Murphy

Clemson University

Clemson, SC

(Clemson Agricultural College of South Carolina until 1964.)

1890	H. A. Strode
1893	Edwin B. Craighead
1897	Henry S. Hartzog
1902	Patrick H. Mell
1910	Walter M. Riggs
1924	S. B. Earle (Acting)
1925	Enoch W. Sikes
1940	R. F. Poole
1958	Robert C. Edwards
1979	Bill Lee Atchley
1986	Max Lennon

Colby College

Waterville, ME

(Maine Literary and Theological Institution until 1821; Waterville College until 1867; Colby University until 1899.)

1818	Jeremiah Chaplin
1933	Rufus Babcock
1836	Robert E. Pattison
1839	George W. Keely (Acting)
1841	Eliphaz Fay
1843	David N. Sheldon
1854	Robert E. Pattison
1857	James T. Champlin
1873	Henry E. Robins
1882	George D. B. Pepper
1889	Albion W. Small
1892	Benaiah L. Whitman
1896	Nathaniel Butler, Jr.
1901	Charles L. White
1908	Arthur J. Roberts
1929	Franklin W. Johnson
1942	Julius S. Bixler
1960	Robert E. L. Strider, II
1979	William R. Cotter

Colgate University

Hamilton, NY

(Madison University from 1846 to 1890.)

1851	Stephen W. Taylor
1856	George W. Eaton
1868	Ebenezer Dodge
1890	Vacant

1895	George W. Smith
1897	William H. Crawshaw (Acting)
1899	George E. Merrill
1909	Elmer B. Bryan
1922	George B. Cutten
1942	Everett N. Case
1963	Vincent M. Barnett, Jr.
1969	Thomas A. Bartlett
1978	George D. Langdon, Jr.

College of the Holy Cross

Worcester, MA

1848	John Early
1851	Anthony F. Ciampi
1854	Peter J. Blenkinsop
1857	Anthony F. Ciampi
1861	James Clark
1867	Robert W. Brady
1869	Anthony F. Ciampi
1872	Joseph B. O'Hagan
1878	Edward D. Boone
1883	Robert W. Brady
1887	Samuel Cahill
1889	Michael O'Kane
1893	Edward A. McGurk
1895	John F. Lehy
1901	Joseph F. Hanselman
1906	Thomas E. Murphy
1911	Joseph N. Dinand
1918	James J. Carlin
1924	Joseph N. Dinand
1927	John M. Fox
1933	Francis J. Dolan
1939	Joseph R. N. Maxwell
1945	William J. Healy
1948	John A. O'Brien
1954	William A. Donaghy
1960	Raymond J. Swords
1970	John E. Brooks

College of William and Mary

Williamsburg, VA

1693	James Clair
1743	William Dawson
1752	William Stith
1755	Thomas Dawson
1761	William Yates
1764	James Horrocks
1771	John Camm
1777	James Madison
1812	John Bracken
1814	John A. Smith
1826	William H. Wilmer
1827	Adam Empie
1836	Thomas R. Dew
1847	Robert Saunders
1848	Benjamin S. Ewell
1849	John Johns
1854	Benjamin S. Ewell
1888	Lyon G. Tyler
1919	Julian A. C. Chandler
1934	John S. Bryan
1942	John E. Pomfret
1951	Alvin D. Chandler
1960	Davis Y. Paschall
1971	Thomas A. Graves, Jr.
1985	Paul R. Verkuil

College of Wooster
Wooster, OH

(University of Wooster until 1914.)

1870 Willis Lord
1873 Archibald A. E. Taylor
1883 Sylvester F. Scoval
1899 Louis E. Holden
1915 John Campbell White
1919 Charles F. Wishart
1944 Howard F. Lowry
1967 J. Garber Drushal
1977 Henry J. Copeland

Colorado State University
Fort Collins, CO

(State Agricultural College of Colorado until 1935; Colorado State College of Agriculture and Mechanic Arts until 1944; Colorado Agricultural and Mechanical College until 1957.)

1879 Elijah E. Edwards
1882 Charles L. Ingersoll
1892 Alston Ellis
1899 Barton O. Aylesworth
1909 Charles A. Lory
1940 Roy M. Green
1948 Isaac E. Newsom
1949 William E. Morgan
1969 Adrian R. Chamberlain
1980 C. O. Neidt
1981 Ralph E. Christoffersen
1983 Robert D. Phemister
1984 Philip E. Austin

Columbia University
New York, NY

(King's College until 1784; Columbia College until 1912.)

1754 Samuel Johnson
1763 Myles Cooper
1775 Benjamin Moore (Acting)
1781 Vacant
1787 William S. Johnson
1801 Charles H. Wharton
1801 Benjamin Moore
1811 William Harris
1829 William A. Duer
1842 Nathaniel F. Moore
1849 Charles King
1864 Frederick A. P. Barnard
1890 Seth Low
1902 Nicholas Murray Butler
1945 Frank D. Fackenthal (Acting)
1948 Dwight D. Eisenhower
1953 Grayson Kirk
1968 Andrew W. Cordier
1970 William J. McGill
1980 Michael I. Sovern

Cornell College
Mount Vernon, IA

1857 Richard W. Keeler
1859 Samuel M. Fellows

1863 William F. King
1908 James E. Harlan
1914 Hamline H. Freer (Acting)
1915 Charles W. Flint
1922 William S. Ebersole (Acting)
1923 Harlan Updegraff
1927 Herbert J. Burgstahler
1939 John B. Magee
1943 Russell D. Cole
1960 Arland F. Christ-Janer
1967 Samuel E. Stumpf
1974 Charles Cochran (Acting)
1975 Philip Secor
1984 David G. Marker

Cornell University
Ithaca, NY

1865 Andrew D. White
1885 Charles K. Adams
1892 Jacob G. Schurman
1921 Livingston Farrand
1937 Edmund E. Day
1949 Cornelis W. deKiewiet (Acting)
1951 Theodore P. Wright (Acting)
1951 Deane W. Malott
1963 James A. Perkins
1969 Dale R. Corson
1977 Frank H. T. Rhodes

Creighton University
Omaha, NE

1878 Romanus A. Shaffel
1880 Thomas H. Miles
1883 Joseph Zealand
1884 Hugh M. Finnegan
1885 Michael P. Dowling
1889 Thomas S. Fitzgerald
1891 James F. X. Hoeffer
1895 John N. X. Pahls
1908 Eugene A. Magevney
1914 Francis X. McMenamy
1919 John F. McCormick
1925 William J. Grace
1928 William H. Agnew
1931 Patrick J. Mahan
1937 Joseph P. Zuercher
1943 Thomas S. Bowdern
1945 William H. McCabe
1950 Carl M. Reinert
1962 Henry W. Linn
1969 C. J. Schneider (Acting)
1970 Joseph J. Labaj
1979 Matthew E. Creighton
1981 Michael G. Morrison

Dartmouth College
Hanover, NH

1769 Eleazar Wheelock
1779 John Wheelock
1815 Francis Brown
1820 Daniel Dana
1821 Bennett T. Tyler
1828 Nathan Lord
1863 Asa D. Smith
1877 Samuel C. Bartlett
1893 William J. Tucker
1909 Ernest F. Nichols

1916 Ernest M. Hopkins
1945 John S. Dickey
1970 John G. Kemeny
1981 David T. McLaughlin

Davidson College
Davidson, NC

1836 Robert H. Morrison
1841 Samuel Williamson
1855 Drury Lacy
1860 John L. Kirkpatrick
1866 George W. McPhail
1871 John R. Blake (Chairman of Faculty)
1877 Andrew D. Hepburn
1885 Luther McKinnon
1887 William J. Martin (Acting)
1888 John B. Shearer
1901 Henry L. Smith
1912 William J. Martin
1929 William L. Lingle
1941 John R. Cunningham
1957 Clarence J. Pietenpol (Acting)
1958 David G. Martin
1968 Frontis W. Johnston (Acting)
1968 Samuel R. Spencer, Jr.
1984 John W. Kuykendall

Denison University
Granville, OH

(Granville College from 1845 to 1856.)

1846 Silas Bailey
1852 John Pratt (Acting)
1853 Jeremiah Hall
1863 Samson Talbot
1873 Fletcher O. Marsh (Acting)
1875 Elisha B. Andrews
1879 Alfred Owen
1886 Nathan S. Burton (Acting)
1887 Galusha Anderson
1890 Daniel B. Purinton
1901 Emory W. Hunt
1912 Richard S. Colwell (Acting)
1913 Clark W. Chamberlain
1925 Bunyan Spencer (Acting)
1927 Avery A. Shaw
1940 Kenneth I. Brown
1950 Cyril F. Richards (Acting)
1951 A. Blair Knapp
1968 Parker E. Lichtenstein (Acting)
1969 Joel P. Smith
1976 Robert C. Good
1984 Andrew G. DeRocco

DePaul University
Chicago, IL

(St. Vincent's College until 1907.)

1898 Peter V. Byrne
1909 John J. Martin
1910 Francis X. McCabe

1920 Thomas F. Levan
1930 Francis V. Corcoran
1935 Michael J. O'Connell
1944 Comerford J. O'Malley
1964 John R. Cortelyou
1981 John T. Richardson

DePauw University
Greencastle, IN

(Indiana Asbury University until 1884.)

1837 Cyrus Nutt (Acting)
1839 Matthew Simpson
1848 William C. Larrabee (Acting)
1849 Lucien W. Berry
1854 Daniel Curry
1857 Cyrus Nutt (Acting)
1858 Thomas Bowman
1872 Reuben Andrus
1875 Alexander Martin
1889 John P. D. John
1895 Hillary A. Gobin
1903 Edwin H. Hughes
1909 Francis J. McConnell
1912 George W. Grose
1924 Henry B. Longden (Acting)
1925 Lemuel H. Murlin
1928 G. Bromley Oxnam
1936 Clyde E. Wildman
1951 Russell J. Humbert
1962 Glenn W. Thompson (Acting)
1963 William E. Kerstetter
1977 Richard F. Rosser
1987 Robert G. Bottoms

Dickinson College
Carlisle, PA

1784 Charles Nisbet
1804 Robert Davidson
1809 Jeremiah Atwater
1815 John McKnight
1816 College Closed
1821 John M. Mason
1824 William Neill
1830 Samuel B. How
1831 College Closed
1833 John P. Durbin
1845 Robert Emory
1848 Jesse T. Peck
1852 Charles Collins
1860 Herman M. Johnson
1868 Robert L. Dashiell
1872 James A. McCauley
1889 George E. Reed
1911 Eugene A. Noble
1914 James H. Morgan
1928 Mervin G. Filler
1931 James H. Morgan
1932 Karl T. Waugh
1933 James H. Morgan
1934 Fred P. Corson
1944 Cornelius W. Prettyman
1946 William W. Edel
1959 Gilbert Malcolm
1961 Howard L. Rubendall
1975 Samuel A. Banks

Drake University

Des Moines, IA

1881	George T. Carpenter
1894	Barton O. Aylesworth
1897	William B. Craig
1902	H. McClelland Bell
1918	Arthur Holmes
1922	Daniel W. Morehouse
1941	Henry G. Harmon
1966	Paul F. Sharp
1972	Wilbur C. Miller
1985	Michael R. Ferrari, Jr.

Drexel University

Philadelphia, PA

(Drexel Insitute of Art, Science and Industry until 1936; Drexel Institute of Technology until 1970.)

1892	James MacAlister
1913	Hollis Godfrey
1922	Kenneth G. Matheson
1932	Parke R. Kolbe
1942	George P. Rea
1944	Robert C. Disque (Acting)
1945	James Creese
1963	William W. Hagerty
1984	William S. Gaither

Duke University

Durham, NC

(Normal College until 1859; Trinity College until 1924.)

1851	Braxton Craven
1883	Marquis L. Wood
1884	Vacant
1887	John F. Crowell
1894	John C. Kilgo
1910	William P. Few
1941	Robert L. Flowers
1948	Arthur H. Edens
1960	Julian D. Hart
1963	Douglas M. Knight
1969	Barnes Woodhall (Chancellor pro tem)
1970	Terry Sanford
1985	H. Keith H. Brodie

Duquesne University

Pittsburgh, PA

(Pittsburgh Catholic College of the Holy Ghost until 1911.)

1878	Joseph Graf (Acting)
1879	W. Power
1885	John Willms
1886	John T. Murphy
1899	Martin A. Hehir
1931	J. Joseph Callahan
1940	Raymond V. Kirk
1946	Francis P. Smith
1950	Vernon F. Gallagher
1959	Henry J. McAnulty
1980	Donald S. Nesti

Earlham College

Richmond, IN

1867	Barnabas C. Hobbs
1868	Joseph Moore
1883	William P. Pinkham (Acting)
1884	Joseph J. Mills
1903	Robert L. Kelly
1917	David M. Edwards
1929	William C. Dennis
1946	Thomas E. Jones
1958	Landrum R. Bolling
1974	Franklin W. Wallin
1985	Richard J. Wood

Elmira College

Elmira, NY

1856	Augustus W. Cowles
1889	Wilson Phraner (Acting)
1890	Charles Van Norden
1893	Rufus S. Green
1896	A. Cameron MacKenzie
1915	John B. Shaw
1918	Frederick Lent
1935	W. S. A. Pott
1949	Lewis Eldred
1954	J. Ralph Murray
1976	Leonard T. Grant

Emory and Henry College

Emory, VA

1838	Charles Collins
1852	E. E. Wiley
1879	John L. Buchanan
1880	David Sullins
1885	E. Embree Hoss
1885	Thomas W. Jordan
1888	R. W. Jones
1889	James Atkins
1893	R. G. Waterhouse
1910	C. C. Weaver
1920	J. Stewart French
1922	James N. Hillman
1941	Foye G. Gibson
1956	Earl G. Hunt, Jr.
1964	Daniel G. Leidig (Acting)
1965	William C. Finch
1970	C. Glenn Mingledorff
1973	Thomas F. Chilcote
1984	Charles W. Sydnos, Jr.

Emory University

Atlanta, GA

(Emory College, in Oxford, GA, until 1915.)

1837	Ignatius A. Few
1840	Augustus B. Longstreet
1848	George F. Pierce
1854	Alexander Means
1855	James R. Thomas
1867	Luther M. Smith
1871	Osborn L. Smith
1875	Atticus G. Haygood
1884	Isaac S. Hopkins
1888	Warren A. Candler
1898	Charles E. Dowman

1902	James E. Dickey
1915	Warren A. Candler (Chancellor)
1920	Harvey W. Cox
1942	Goodrich C. White
1957	S. Walter Martin
1963	Sanford S. Atwood
1977	James T. Laney

Fairleigh Dickinson University

Rutherford, NJ

1942	Peter Sammartino
1969	J. O. Fuller
1975	Jerome M. Pollack
1982	Walter T. Savage
1984	Robert H. Donaldson

Florida Agricultural and Mechanical University

Tallahassee, FL

1901	N. B. Young
1923	W. H. A. Howard
1924	J. R. E. Lee
1944	J. B. Bragg (Acting)
1944	W. H. Gray, Jr.
1949	H. Manning Efferson (Acting)
1950	George W. Gore
1969	Benjamin L. Perry,, Jr.
1981	Walter L. Smith
1985	Frederick S. Humphries

Florida State University

Tallahassee, FL

(Florida State College from 1901 to 1905; Florida State College for Women until 1947.)

1897	Albert A. Murphree
1909	Edward Conradi
1941	Doak S. Campbell
1957	Robert M. Strozier
1960	Gordon W. Blackwell
1965	John E. Champion
1969	J. Stanley Marshall
1977	Bernard F. Sliger

Fordham University

Bronx, NY

(St. John's College until 1905.)

1841	John McCloskey
1843	John Harley
1844	James R. Bayley
1846	Augustus J. Thebaud
1851	John Larkin
1854	Remigius I. Tellier
1859	Augustus J. Thebaud
1863	Edward Doucet
1865	William Moylan
1868	Joseph Shea
1874	F. William Gockeln
1882	Patrick F. Dealy
1885	Thomas J. Campbell
1888	John Scully
1891	Thomas Gannon

1896	Thomas J. Campbell
1900	George A. Petit
1904	John J. Collins
1906	Daniel J. Quinn
1911	Thomas J. McCluskey
1915	Joseph A. Mulry
1919	Edward P. Tivnan
1924	William J. Duane
1930	Aloysius J. Hogan
1936	Robert I. Gannon
1949	Laurence J. McGinley
1963	Vincent T. O'Keefe
1965	Leo P. McLaughlin
1969	Michael P. Walsh
1972	James C. Finley
1984	Joseph A. O'Hare

Franklin and Marshall College

Lancaster, PA

(Marshall College until 1852.)

1836	Frederick A. Rauch
1841	John W. Nevin
1855	Emanuel V. Gerhart
1866	John W. Nevin
1877	Thomas G. Apple
1889	John S. Stahr
1909	Henry H. Apple
1935	John A. Schaeffer
1941	H. M. J. Klein (Acting)
1941	Theodore A. Distler
1955	William W. Hall
1956	Frederick deW. Bolman, Jr.
1962	Anthony R. Appel
1962	G. Wayne Glick (Acting)
1963	Keith Spalding
1983	James L. Powell

Furman University

Greenville, SC

1859	James C. Furman
1881	Charles Manly
1897	Andrew P. Montague
1903	Edwin McN. Poteat
1919	William J. McGlothlin
1933	Bennette E. Geer
1939	John P. Plyler
1964	Gordon W. Blackwell
1976	John E. Johns

George Washington University

Washington, DC

(Columbian College until 1873; Columbian University until 1904.)

1821	William Straughton
1827	Stephen Chapin
1843	Joel S. Bacon
1854	Joseph G. S. Binney
1859	George W. Samson
1871	James C. Welling
1894	S. H. Greene
1895	Benaiah L. Whitman
1900	S. H. Greene
1902	Charles W. Needham
1910	Charles H. Stockton
1918	William M. Collier

1921	Howard L. Hodgkins	
1923	William L. Lewis	
1927	Cloyd H. Marvin	
1959	Oswald S. Colclough	
	(Acting)	
1961	Thomas H. Carroll	
1964	Oswald S. Colclough	
	(Acting)	
1965	Lloyd H. Elliott	

Georgetown University

Washington, DC

(Georgetown College until 1815.)

1791	Robert Plunkett
1793	Robert Molyneux
1796	Louis G. du Bourg
1798	Leonard Neal
1806	Robert Molyneux
1808	Francis Neale
1809	William Matthews
1809	Francis Neale
1812	John A. Grassi
1817	Benedict J. Fenwick
1817	Anthony Kohlmann
1820	Enoch Fenwick
1822	Benedict J. Fenwick
1825	Stephen J. Dubuisson
1826	William Feiner
1829	John W. Beschter
1829	Thomas F. Mulledy
1837	William McSherry
1840	Joseph A. Lopez
1840	James Ryder
1845	Samuel Mulledy
1845	Thomas F. Mulledy
1848	James Ryder
1851	Charles H. Stonestreet
1852	Bernard A. Maguire
1858	John Early
1866	Bernard A. Maguire
1870	John Early
1873	Patrick F. Healy
1882	James A. Doonan
1888	J. Havens Richards
1898	John D. Whitney
1901	Jerome Daugherty
1905	David H. Buel
1908	Joseph J. Himmel
1912	Alphonsus J. Donlon
1918	John B. Creeden
1924	Charles W. Lyons
1928	W. Coleman Nevils
1935	Arthur A. O'Leary
1942	Lawrence C. Gorman
1949	Hunter Guthrie
1952	Edward B. Bunn
1964	Gerard J. Campbell
1969	Edwin A. Quain (Acting)
1969	Robert J. Henle
1976	Timothy S. Healy

Georgia Institute of Technology

Atlanta, GA

(Georgia School of Technology until 1948.)

1888	Isaac S. Hopkins
1896	Lyman Hall
1905	Kenneth G. Matheson
1922	Nathan P. Pratt (Acting)
1922	Marion L. Brittain
1944	Blake R. Van Leer

1956	Paul Weber (Acting)
1957	Edwin D. Harrison
1969	Vernon D. Crawford
1969	Arthur G. Hansen
1972	Joseph M. Pettit

Georgia State University

Atlanta, GA

(Georgia State College of Business Administration from 1955 to 1961; Georgia State College until 1969.)

1955	George M. Sparks
1957	Noah Langdale, Jr.

Gettysburg College

Gettysburg, PA

(Pennsylvania College of Gettysburg until 1921.)

1832	Samuel S. Shmucker
1834	Charles P. Krauth
1850	Henry L. Baugher
1868	Milton Valentine
1884	Harvey W. McKnight
1904	Samuel G. Hefelbower
1910	William A. Granville
1923	Henry W. A. Hanson
1952	Walter C. Langsam
1956	Willard S. Paul
1961	C. Arnold Hanson
1977	Charles E. Glassick

Goucher College

Towson, MD

(Woman's College of Baltimore until 1910.)

1886	William H. Hopkins
1890	John F. Goucher
1908	Eugene A. Noble
1913	William W. Guth
1930	David A. Robertson
1948	Otto F. Kraushaar
1967	Marvin B. Perry, Jr.
1973	Rhoda M. Dorsey

Grinnell College

Grinnell, IA

(Iowa College until 1909.)

1863	George F. Magoun
1884	Samuel J. Buck (Acting)
1887	George A. Gates
1900	John H. T. Main (Acting)
1902	Dan F. Bradley
1906	John H. T. Main
1931	John S. Nollen
1940	Samuel N. Stevens
1954	Rupert A. Hawk (Acting)
1955	Howard R. Bowen
1964	James H. Struss (Acting)
1965	Glenn Leggett
1975	A. Richard Turner
1981	George A. Drake

Hamilton College

Clinton, NY

1812	Azel Backus
1817	Henry Davis
1833	Sereno E. Dwight
1835	Joseph Penney
1839	Simeon North
1858	Samuel W. Fisher
1866	Samuel G. Brown
1881	Henry Darling
1892	Melancthon W. Stryker
1917	Frederick C. Ferry
1938	William H. Cowley
1945	David Worcester
1947	Thomas B. Rudd
1949	Robert W. McEwen
1967	John W. Chandler
1974	J. Martin Corovano

Hamline University

St. Paul, MN

1854	Jabez Brooks
1857	Benjamin Crary
1880	David C. John
1883	George H. Bridgman
1912	Samuel F. Kerfoot
1927	Alfred F. Hughes
1932	Henry L. Osborn (Acting)
1934	Charles N. Pace
1948	Hurst R. Anderson
1952	Walter C. Coffey (Acting)
1953	Paul H. Giddens
1968	Richard P. Bailey
1975	Jerry E. Hudson
1981	Charles J. Graham

Hampden-Sydney College

Hampden-Sydney, VA

1775	S. Stanhope Smith
1779	John B. Smith
1789	Drury Lacy
1797	Archibald Alexander
1807	William S. Reid (Acting)
1807	Moses Hoge
1821	Jonathan P. Cushing
1835	George A. Baxter (Acting)
1835	Daniel L. Carroll
1838	William Maxwell
1845	Patrick J. Sparrow
1848	Lewis W. Green
1856	Charles Martin (Acting)
1857	John M. P. Atkinson
1883	Richard McIlwaine
1904	William H. Whiting, Jr. (Acting)
1905	James G. McAllister
1908	Henry T. Graham
1917	Ashton W. McWhorter (Acting)
1919	Joseph D. Eggleston
1939	Edgar G. Gammon
1955	Joseph C. Robert
1960	Thomas E. Gilmer
1963	W. Taylor Reveley
1977	Josiah Bunting, III

Hardin-Simmons University

Abilene, TX

(Simmons College until 1925; Simmons University until 1934.)

1892	W. C. Friley
1894	George O. Thatcher
1898	O. C. Pope
1901	J. C. Hairfield
1902	Oscar H. Cooper
1909	Jefferson D. Sandefer
1940	Lucian Q. Campbell (Acting)
1940	William R. White
1943	Rupert N. Richardson
1953	Evan A. Reiff
1962	George L. Graham (Acting)
1963	James H. Landis
1966	Elwin L. Skiles
1977	Jesse C. Fletcher

Harvard University

Cambridge, MA

1640	Henry Dunster
1654	Charles Chauncy
1672	Leonard Hoar
1675	Urian Oakes
1682	John Rogers
1685	Increase Mather
1708	John Leverett
1725	Benjamin Wadsworth
1737	Edward Holyoke
1770	Samuel Locke
1774	Samuel Langdon
1781	Joseph Willard
1806	Samuel Webber
1810	John T. Kirkland
1829	Josiah Quincy
1846	Edward Everett
1849	Jared Sparks
1853	James Walker
1860	Cornelius C. Felton
1862	Thomas Hill
1869	Charles W. Eliot
1909	A. Lawrence Lowell
1933	James B. Conant
1953	Nathan M. Pusey
1971	Derek C. Bok

Haverford College

Haverford, PA

1857	Joseph G. Harlan
1857	Vacant
1863	Samuel J. Gummere
1874	Thomas Chase
1887	Isaac Sharpless
1917	William W. Comfort
1940	Felix M. Morley
1946	Gilbert F. White
1957	Hugh Borton
1967	John R. Coleman
1977	Stephen Cary (Acting)
1978	Robert B. Stevens

Heidelberg College

Tiffin, OH

1851 Emanuel V. Gerhart
1855 Moses Kieffer
1863 G. W. Aughinbaugh
1866 George W. Williard
1890 John A. Peters
1902 Charles E. Miller
1937 Clarence E. Josephson
1945 Nevin C. Harner
1948 William T. Wickham
1969 Leslie H. Fishel, Jr.
1980 William C. Cassell

Hiram College

Hiram, OH

1867 Silas E. Shepard
1868 John M. Atwater
1870 Burke A. Hinsdale
1882 Bailey S. Dean (Acting)
1883 George H. Laughlin
1887 Colman Bancroft (Acting)
1888 Ely V. Zollars
1902 James A. Beattie
1903 Edmund B. Wakefield
      (Acting)
1905 C. C. Rowlinson
1907 Miner L. Bates
1930 Kenneth I. Brown
1940 Paul H. Fall
1957 Paul F. Sharp
1964 James N. Primm
1965 Wendell G. Johnson
      (Acting)
1967 Elmer Jagow
1985 Russel Aiuto

Hobart and William Smith Colleges

Geneva, NY

(Geneva College until 1852; Hobart Free College until 1860; William Smith College founded 1908.)

1826 Jasper Adams
1828 Richard S. Mason
1835 Benjamin Hale
1858 Abner Jackson
1867 James K. Stone
1869 James Rankine
1871 Maunsell Van Renssalaer
1876 William S. Perry
1876 Robert G. Hinsdale
1884 Eliphalet N. Potter
1897 Robert E. Jones
1902 Langdon C. Stewardson
1913 Lyman P. Powell
1919 Murray Bartlett
1936 William A. Eddy
1942 John M. Potter
1947 Walter H. Durfee
1948 Alan W. Brown
1956 Horace N. Hubbs
1956 Louis M. Hirshson
1966 Albert E. Holland
1968 Beverley D. Causey, Jr.
1970 Allan A. Kuusisto
1982 Caroll W. Brewster

Hofstra University

Hempstead, NY

1937 Truesdale P. Calkins
1942 Howard Brower (Acting)
1944 John C. Adams
1964 Clifford L. Lord
1972 James Marshall
1973 Robert L. Payton
1976 James M. Shuart

Howard University

Washington, DC

1867 Charles B. Boynton
1867 Byron Sunderland
1869 Oliver O. Howard
1873 John M. Langston
      (Acting)
1875 F. W. Fairfield (Acting)
1875 Edward P. Smith
1876 F. W. Fairfield (Acting)
1877 William M. Patton
1890 Jeremiah Rankin
1903 Teunis S. Hamlin
      (Acting)
1903 John Gordon
1906 F. W. Fairfield (Acting)
1906 Wilbur Thirkfield
1912 Stephen M. Newman
1918 J. Stanley Durkee
1926 Mordecai W. Johnson
1960 James M. Nabrit, Jr.
1965 Stanton L. Wormley
      (Acting)
1969 James E. Cheek

Hunter College of the City University of New York

New York, NY

(Normal College of the City of New York until 1914; Hunter College until 1961.)

1870 Thomas Hunter
1906 Joseph A. Gillet (Acting)
1908 George S. Davis
1929 James Kieran
1933 Eugene Colligan
1940 George N. Shuster
1960 John J. Meng
1966 Mary L. Gambrell
1967 Douglas Maynard
      (Acting)
1967 Robert D. Cross
1969 F. Joachim Weyl
      (Acting)
1970 Jacqueline G. Wexler
1980 Donna E. Shalala

Illinois State University

Normal, IL

(Illinois State Normal University until 1963.)

1907 David Felmley
1930 Harry A. Brown
1933 Raymond W. Fairchild
1956 Robert G. Bone

1967 Samuel E. Braden
1970 F. R. Geigle (Acting)
1971 David K. Berlo
1973 Gene A. Budig
1977 Lloyd I. Watkins

Illinois Wesleyan University

Bloomington, IL

1855 Clinton W. Sears
1857 Oliver S. Munsell
1873 Samuel J. Fallows
1875 William H. H. Adams
1888 William H. Wilder
1898 Edgar M. Smith
1905 Francis G. Barnes
1908 Theodore Kemp
1922 William J. Davidson
1932 Harry W. McPherson
1937 Wiley G. Brooks
1939 William E. Shaw
1947 Merrill J. Holmes
1958 Lloyd M. Bertholf
1968 Robert C. Eckley

Indiana State University

Terre Haute, IN

(Indiana State Normal School until 1929; Indiana State Teachers College until 1961; Indiana State College until 1965.)

1908 William W. Parsons
1921 Linnaeus Hines
1933 Lemuel A. Pittenger
      (Acting)
1934 Ralph W. Tirey
1953 Raleigh W. Holmstedt
1965 Alan C. Rankin
1975 Richard Landini

Indiana University

Bloomington, IN

(Indiana College until 1838.)

1829 Andrew Wylie
1852 Alfred Ryors
1853 William M. Daily
1859 John H. Lathrop
1860 Cyrus Nutt
1875 Lemuel Moss
1885 David S. Jordan
1891 John M. Coulter
1893 Joseph Swain
1902 William L. Bryan
1937 Herman B. Wells
1962 Elvis J. Stahr, Jr.
1968 Joseph L. Sutton
1971 John W. Ryan

Iowa State University

Ames, IA

(Iowa Agricultural until 1898; Iowa State College of Agriculture and Mechanic Arts until 1958.)

1868 A. S. Welsh
1883 S. A. Knapp

1885 Leigh Hunt
1886 W. I. Chamberlain
1891 W. M. Beardshear
1903 A. B. Storms
1912 Raymond A. Pearson
1927 Raymond M. Hughes
1936 Charles E. Friley
1953 James H. Hilton
1965 W. Robert Parks
1986 Gordon P. Eaton

Jefferson College

(Merged with Washington College in 1866 to form Washington and Jefferson College.)

1802 John Watson
1803 James Dunlap
1812 Andrew Wylie
1817 William McMillan
1822 Matthew Brown
1845 Robert J. Breckinridge
1847 Alexander B. Brown
1857 Joseph Alden
1862 David H. Riddle

John Carroll University

Cleveland, OH

(St. Ignatius College until 1923.)

1886 John B. Neustich
1888 Henry Knappenmeyer
1893 Joseph Le Halle
1897 Godfrey V. Schulte
1902 John I. Zahm
1907 George J. Pickel
1910 John B. Furay
1915 William B. Sommerhauser
1919 Thomas J. Smith
1925 Murtha A. Boylan
1928 Benedict J. Rodman
1937 George J. Pickel (Pro
      tem)
1938 William G. Magee
1938 Edmund C. Horne
1942 Thomas J. Donnelly
1946 Frederick E. Welfle
1956 Hugh E. Dunn
1967 Joseph O. Schell
1970 Henry F. Birkenhauer
1980 Thomas P. O'Malley

Johns Hopkins University

Baltimore, MD

1875 Daniel C. Gilman
1901 Ira Remsen
1914 Frank J. Goodnow
1929 Joseph S. Ames
1935 Isaiah Bowman
1949 Detlev W. Bronk
1953 Lowell Reed
1956 Milton S. Eisenhower
1967 Lincoln Gordon
1971 Milton S. Eisenhower
1972 Steven Muller

Kalamazoo College

Kalamazoo, MI

1843	J. A. B. Stone
1864	John M. Gregory
1867	Daniel Putnam (Interim)
1868	Silas Bailey (Acting)
1868	Kendall Brooks
1883	Theodore Nelson(Acting)
1884	Kendall Brooks
1887	Monson A. Willcox
1891	Theodore Nelson
1892	A. Gaylord Slocum
1912	Herbert L. Stetson
1922	Allan Hoben
1935	Charles T. Goodsell
1936	Stewart G. Cole
1938	Paul Thompson
1948	Allen B. Stowe (Interim)
1949	John S. Everton
1953	Harold T. Smith (Interim)
1953	Weimer K. Hicks
1972	George N. Rainsford
1983	David W. Breneman

Kansas State University

Manhattan, KS

(Kansas State Agricultural College until 1931.)

1863	Joseph Denison
1873	John A. Anderson
1879	George T. Fairchild
1897	Thomas E. Will
1899	Ernest R. Nichols
1909	Henry J. Waters
1918	William M. Jardine
1925	Francis D. Farrell
1943	Milton S. Eisenhower
1950	James A. McCain
1975	Duane C. Acker
1986	Jon Wefald

Kean College

Union, NJ

(Newark State Teachers College from 1935 to 1958; Newark State College until 1973.)

1877	William N. Barringer
1896	Charles B. Gilbert
1897	William S. Willis
1928	Bertha R. Kain
1970	Nathan Weiss

Kent State University

Kent, OH

(Kent State College from 1929 to 1935.)

1928	James O. Engleman
1938	Karl C. Leebrick
1943	Raymond M. Clark (Acting)
1944	George A. Bowman

1963	Robert I. White
1971	Glenn A. Olds
1977	Brage Golding
1982	Michael Schwartz

Kenyon College

Gambier, OH

1824	Philander Chase
1831	Charles P. McIlvaine
1840	David B. Douglass
1844	Samuel Fuller (Acting)
1845	Sherlock A. Bronson
1851	Thomas M. Smith
1854	Lorin Andrews
1861	Benjamin S. Lange (Acting)
1863	Charles Short
1867	James K. Stone
1868	Eli T. Tappan
1874	Edward C. Benson (Acting)
1876	William B. Bodine
1890	Theodore Sterling
1896	William F. Peirce
1937	Gordon K. Chalmers
1956	Frank E. Bailey (Acting)
1957	F. Edward Lund
1968	William G. Caples
1975	Philip H. Jordon, Jr.

Knox College

Galesburg, IL

(Knox Manual Labor College until 1857.)

1841	Hiram H. Kellogg
1845	Jonathan Blanchard
1858	Harvey Curtis
1863	William S. Curtiss
1868	John P. Gulliver
1874	Newton Bateman
1892	John H. Finley
1900	Thomas McClelland
1918	James L. McConaughy
1925	Albert Britt
1936	Carter Davidson
1947	Lyndon O. Brown
1949	Sharvy G. Umbeck
1974	E. Inman Fox
1982	John P. McCall

Lafayette College

Easton, PA

1849	Charles W. Nassau
1850	Daniel V. McLean
1857	George W. McPhail
1863	William C. Cattell
1883	James H. M. Knox
1890	Traill Green (Acting)
1891	Ethelbert D. Warfield
1914	William S. Kirkpatrick (Acting)
1915	John H. MacCracken
1926	Donald B. Prentice (Acting)
1927	William M. Lewis
1945	Ralph C. Hutchison

1957	Guy Snavely (Interim)
1958	K. Roald Bergethon
1978	David W. Ellis

Lawrence University

Appleton, WI

(Lawrence University of Wisconsin until 1913; Lawrence College of Wisconsin until 1964.)

1853	Edward Cooke
1859	Russell Z. Mason
1865	George McK. Steele
1879	Elias D. Huntley
1883	Bradford P. Raymond
1889	Charles W. Gallagher
1893	L. Wesley Underwood (Acting)
1894	Samuel Plantz
1924	Wilson S. Naylor (Acting)
1925	Henry M. Wriston
1937	Thomas N. Barrows
1943	Ralph J. Watts (Acting)
1944	Nathan M. Pusey
1954	Douglas M. Knight
1963	Curtis W. Tarr
1969	Thomas S. Smith
1979	Richard Warch

Lehigh University

Bethlehem, PA

1866	Henry Coppee
1875	John McD. Leavitt
1880	Robert A. Lamberton
1895	Thomas M. Drown
1905	Henry S. Drinker
1920	Vacant
1922	Charles R. Richards
1935	Clement C. Williams
1944	Vacant
1946	Martin D. Whitaker
1960	Harvey A. Neville
1964	W. Deming Lewis
1982	Peter W. Likins

Lewis and Clark College

Portland, OR

(Albany College until 1942.)

1867	William J. Monteith
1868	Henry Bushnell
1879	Elbert N. Condit
1885	Joseph C. Wyckoff
1886	Earl T. Lockhard
1886	Edwin J. Thompson
1887	Elbert N. Condit
1894	Frederick G. Young
1895	Wallace H. Lee
1905	Harry M. Crooks
1915	Wallace H. Lee (Acting)
1920	Alfred M. Williams
1922	Raymond J. Baker (Acting)
1923	Clarence W. Green
1929	Thomas W. Bibb
1938	Clarence W. Greene

1941	Benjamin A. Thaxter (Acting)
1942	Morgan S. Odell
1960	John R. Howard
1981	James A. Gardner

Louisiana State University

Baton Rouge, LA

(Louisiana State Seminary of Learning until 1870.)

1859	William T. Sherman
1861	(Seminary closed)
1865	David F. Boyd
1880	William P. Johnston
1883	James W. Nicholson
1884	David F. Boyd
1887	James W. Nicholson
1896	Thomas D. Boyd
1927	Thomas W. Atkinson
1930	James M. Smith
1939	Paul M. Hebert (Acting)
1941	Campbell B. Hodges
1944	William B. Hatcher
1947	Fred C. Frey (Acting)
1947	Harold W. Stoke
1951	Troy H. Middleton
1962	John A. Hunter
1972	Martin Woodin
1973	Paul W. Murrill (Chancellor)
1981	James H. Wharton (Chancellor)

Loyola University of Chicago

Chicago, IL

(St. Ignatius College until 1909; Loyola University until 1970.)

1870	Arnold Damen
1872	Ferdinand Coosemans
1874	John De Blieck
1877	Thomas Miles
1880	Thomas O'Neill
1884	Joseph Zealand
1887	Edward A. Higgins
1891	Thomas Fitzgerald
1894	James F. X. Hoeffer
1898	John Pahls
1900	Henry Dumbach
1908	Alexander J. Burrowes
1912	John Mathery
1915	Joseph Egan
1945	James T. Hussey
1955	James F. Maguire
1970	Raymond C. Baumhart

Macalester College

St. Paul, MN

1874	Edward D. Neill
1884	Thomas A. McCurdy
1890	David J. Burrell
1892	Adam W. Ringland
1894	James Wallace

1907	Thomas M. Hodgman	
1918	Elmer A. Bess	
1924	John C. Acheson	
1939	Charles J. Turck	
1958	Harvey M. Rice	
1968	Arthur S. Flemming	
1971	James A. Robinson	
1975	C. McLarnan (Acting)	
1976	John B. Davis, Jr.	
1985	Robert M. Gavin, Jr.	

Manhattan College

Bronx, NY

1863	Patrick Murphy
1873	Paulian Fanning
1879	Anthony Byrnes
1886	Justin McMahon
1890	Anthony Byrnes
1894	Justin McMahon
1900	B. Charles Foley
1902	E. Jerome Daley
1904	Arnold E. Saunders
1907	B. Peter Tracey
1909	E. Jerome Daley
1912	Arnold E. Saunders
1918	Apelles J. Scanlon
1921	Cantidius T. Fitzsimmons
1927	Cornelius M. Hession
1932	Adelphus P. McKenzie
1938	Alexius V. Lally
1944	Bonaventure T. McGinty
1953	Augustine P. Nelan
1962	Gregory Nugent
1975	J. Stephen Sullivan

Marietta College

Marietta, OH

1835	Joel H. Linsley
1846	Henry Smith
1855	Israel W. Andrews
1885	John Eaton
1892	John W. Simpson
1896	Joseph H. Chamberlain (Acting)
1900	Alfred T. Perry
1912	Joseph Manley (Acting)
1913	George W. Hinman
1918	Jesse V. McMillan (Acting)
1919	Edward S. Parsons
1937	Harry K. Eversull
1942	Draper T. Schoonover
1945	William A. Shimer
1947	Vacant
1948	William B. Irvine
1963	Frank E. Duddy, Jr.
1973	Sherrill Cleland

Marquette University

Milwaukee, WI

(Marquette College until 1907.)

1881	Joseph Rigge
1882	Isidor Boudreaux
1884	Thomas S. Fitzgerald
1887	Stanislaus P. Lalumiere
1889	Joseph Grimmelsman
1891	Rudolph J. Meyer
1893	Leopold Bushart
1898	William B. Rogers
1900	Alexander J. Burrowes

1908	James McCabe
1911	Joseph Grimmelsman
1915	Herbert C. Noonan
1922	Albert C. Fox
1928	William M. Magee
1936	Raphael C. McCarthy
1944	Peter A. Brooks
1948	Edward J. O'Donnell
1962	William F. Kelley
1965	John P. Raynor

Massachusetts Institute of Technology

Cambridge, MA

1862	William B. Rogers
1870	John D. Runkle
1879	William B. Rogers
1881	Francis A. Walker
1897	James M. Crafts
1900	Henry S. Pritchett
1907	Arthur A. Noyes (Acting)
1909	Richard C. Maclaurin
1921	Ernest F. Nichols
1923	Samuel W. Stratton
1930	Karl T. Compton
1949	James R. Killian, Jr.
1959	Julius A. Stratton
1966	Howard W. Johnson
1971	Jerome B. Wiesner
1980	Paul E. Gray

Memphis State University

Memphis, TN

(West Tennessee State Teachers College from 1929 to 1941; Memphis State College until 1957.)

1924	John W. Brister
1939	Richard Jones
1943	Jennings B. Sanders
1946	J. Millard Smith
1960	Cecil C. Humphreys
1974	John Richardson (Acting)
1975	Billy Jones
1979	Jerry Boone (Acting)
1980	Thomas G. Carpenter

Mercer University

Macon, GA

1833	B. M. Sanders
1839	Otis Smith
1844	John L. Dagg
1854	N. M. Crawford
1866	Henry H. Tucker
1871	A. J. Battle
1890	G. A. Nunnally
1893	J. B. Gambrell
1896	P. D. Pollock
1905	Charles L. Smith
1906	Samuel Y. Jameson
1914	William L. Pickard
1918	Rufus W. Weaver
1928	Spright Dowell
1953	George B. Connell
1959	Spright Dowell (Interim)
1960	Rufus C. Harris
1979	R. Kirkby Godsey

Miami University

Oxford, OH

1824	Robert H. Bishop
1841	George Junkin
1845	Erasmus D. McMaster
1849	William C. Anderson
1854	John W. Hall
1866	Robert L. Stanton
1871	Andrew D. Hepburn
1873	(University closed)
1885	Robert W. McFarland
1888	Ethelbert D. Warfield
1891	William O. Thompson
1899	David S. Tappan
1902	Guy P. Benton
1911	Raymond M. Hughes
1928	Alfred H. Upham
1946	Ernest H. Hahne
1953	John D. Millett
1965	Phillip R. Shriver
1981	Paul G. Pearson

Michigan State University

East Lansing, MI

(State Agricultural College until 1909; Michigan Agricultural College until 1925; Michigan State College of Agriculture and Applied Science until 1955; Michigan State University of Agriculture and Applied Science until 1964.)

1857	Joseph R. Williams
1859	Lewis R. Fisk
1862	Theophilus C. Abbot
1885	Edwin Willits
1889	Oscar Clute
1893	Lewis G. Gorton
1896	Jonathan L. Snyder
1915	Frank S. Kedzie
1921	David Friday
1924	Kenyon L. Butterfield
1928	Robert S. Shaw
1941	John A. Hannah
1969	Walter Adams
1970	Clifton R. Wharton, Jr.
1979	Cecil Mackey
1986	John A. DiBiaggio

Middlebury College

Middlebury, VT

1800	Jeremiah Atwater
1809	Henry Davis
1818	Joshua Bates
1840	Benjamin Labaree
1866	Harvey D. Kitchel
1873	Vacant
1875	Calvin B. Hulbert
1880	Cyrus Hamlin
1885	Ezra Brainerd
1908	John M. Thomas
1921	Paul D. Moody
1943	Samuel S. Stratton
1963	James I. Armstrong
1975	Olin C. Robinson

Mills College

Oakland, CA

(Mills Seminary until 1877; Mills Seminary-College until 1885.)

1865	Cyrus T. Mills
1885	Homer B. Sprague
1887	C. S. Stratton
1890	Susan T. Mills
1909	Luella C. Carson
1914	Hettie B. Ege (Acting)
1916	Aurelia H. Reinhardt
1943	Lynn T. White, Jr.
1958	Mary W. Bennett (Acting)
1959	Charles E. Rothwell
1967	Robert J. Wert
1977	Barbara White
1981	Mary S. Metz

Mississippi State University

State College, MS

(A & M College until 1932; Mississippi State College until 1958.)

1880	Stephen D. Lee
1899	John M. Stone
1900	John C. Hardy
1912	George R. Hightower
1916	William H. Smith
1920	David C. Hull
1925	Buz M. Walker
1930	Hugh Critz
1934	George D. Humphrey
1945	Fred T. Mitchell
1953	Benjamin F. Hilbun
1960	Dean W. Colvard
1966	William L. Giles
1976	James D. McComas
1985	Donald W. Zacharias

Montana State University

Bozeman, MT

(Agricultural College of the State of Montana until 1911; Montana State College until 1965.)

1893	Augustus M. Ryon
1895	James Reid
1904	James M. Hamilton
1919	Alfred Atkinson
1937	August L. Strand
1942	William M. Cobleigh (Acting)
1943	Roland R. Renne
1963	Leon H. Johnson
1969	William A. Johnstone (Acting)
1970	Carl W. McIntosh
1977	William J. Tietz

Moravian College

Bethlehem, PA

(Moravian College and Theological Seminary until merger in 1954 with Moravian College for Women.)

1864	Lewis L. Kampmann
1865	R. H. Huebner
1867	Edmund A. deSchweinitz
1885	Augustus Schultze
1918	John T. Hamilton
1928	William Schwarze
1944	Raymond S. Haupert
1969	Herman E. Collier, Jr.
1986	Roger H. Martin

Morehouse College

Atlanta, GA

1871	Joseph T. Robert
1884	David F. Estes
1885	Samuel Graves
1900	George Sale
1906	John Hope
1930	Samuel H. Archer
1937	Charles D. Hubert
1940	Benjamin E. Mays
1967	Hugh M. Gloster

Mount Holyoke College

South Hadley, MA

1888	Elizabeth Blanchard (Acting)
1889	Louis F. Cowles (Acting)
1890	Elizabeth Storrs Mead
1901	Mary E. Wolley
1937	Rosewell G. Ham
1957	Richard G. Gettell
1968	Meribeth E. Cameron (Acting)
1969	David B. Truman
1978	Elizabeth Topham Kennan

Muhlenberg College

Allentown, PA

1867	Frederick A. Muhlenberg
1877	Benjamin Stadtler
1885	Theodore L. Seip
1904	John A. W. Haas
1937	Levering Tyson
1953	J. Conrad Seegers
1961	Erling N. Jensen
1969	John H. Morey
1984	Jonathan C. Messerli

Muskingum College

New Concord, OH

1837	Benjamin Waddle
1838	Samuel Wilson
1846	David A. Wallace
1848	John Milligan
1849	Samuel G. Irvine
1851	Samuel McArthur
1855	Benjamin Waddle

1861	L. B. Shryock
1865	David Paul
1879	Frank M. Spencer
1887	John D. Irons
1893	Jesse Johnson
1904	John K. Montgomery
1932	Robert N. Montgomery
1962	Glenn M. McConagha
1965	Harry S. Manley
1972	William P. Miller
1976	John A. Brown, Jr.
1978	Russell Hutchinson (Acting)
1978	Arthur J. DeJong

New Mexico State University

Las Cruces, NM

(Las Cruces College until 1889; New Mexico College of Agriculture and Mechanic Arts until 1960.)

1888	Hiram Hadley
1894	Samuel P. McCrea
1896	Cornelius T. Jordan
1899	Frederic W. Sanders
1901	Luther Foster
1908	Winfred E. Garrison
1913	George E. Ladd
1917	Austin D. Crile
1920	Robert W. Clothier
1921	Harry L. Kent
1935	Hugh M. Gardner (Acting)
1936	Ray Fife
1938	Hugh M. Milton, II
1941	John W. Branson (Acting)
1946	Hugh M. Milton, II
1947	John R. Nichols
1949	John W. Branson
1955	Roger B. Corbett
1970	Gerald W. Thomas
1984	James E. Halligan

New York University

New York, NY

(University of the City of New York until 1896.)

Chancellors

1831	James M. Mathews
1839	Theodore Frelinghuysen
1850	Vacant
1853	Isaac Ferris
1870	Howard Crosby
1882	John Hall
1891	Henry M. MacCracken
1911	Elmer E. Brown
1933	Harry W. Chase
1951	James L. Madden (Acting)
1952	Henry T. Heald

Presidents

1956	Carroll V. Newsom
1962	James M. Hester
1975	John Sawhill
1981	John Brademas

Niagara University

Niagara, NY

(Seminary of Our Lady of the Angels until 1883.)

1856	John J. Lynch
1859	John O'Reilly
1862	Thomas J. Smith
1963	Robert E. Rice
1878	Patrick V. Kavanagh
1894	Patrick S. McHale
1901	William F. Likly
1906	Perry J. Conroy
1908	Edward J. Walsh
1912	Michael A. Drennan
1917	William F. Likly
1919	William E. Katzenberger
1927	Francis J. Dodd
1929	John J. O'Byrne
1932	Joseph M. Noonan
1947	Francis L. Meade
1957	Vincent T. Swords
1964	Joseph T. Cahill
1965	Kenneth F. Slattery
1977	John G. Mahoney
1982	John G. Nugent
1984	Donald J. Harrington

North Carolina State University at Raleigh

Raleigh, NC

(University of North Carolina at Raleigh until 1965.)

1889	Alexander Q. Holladay
1899	George T. Winston
1908	Daniel H. Hall
1916	Wallace C. Riddick
1923	Eugene C. Brooks

Chancellors

1934	John W. Harrelson
1953	Carey H. Bostian
1959	John T. Caldwell
1976	Joab L. Thomas
1982	Bruce R. Poulton

North Dakota State University of Agriculture and Applied Science

Fargo, ND

(North Dakota Agricultural College until 1960.)

1890	H. E. Stockbridge
1893	J. B. Power (Acting)
1895	J. H. Worst
1916	E. F. Ladd
1921	E. S. Keene (Acting)
1921	John L. Coulter
1929	A. E. Minard (Acting)
1929	J. H. Shepperd
1937	J. C. West (Acting)
1939	F. L. Eversull
1946	J. H. Longwell
1948	Fred S. Hultz
1961	Arlon G. Hazen (Acting)
1962	H. R. Albrecht
1968	L. D. Loftsgard

North Texas State University

Denton, TX

(North Texas State Teachers College from 1923 to 1949; North Texas State College until 1961.)

1923	Robert L. Marquis
1934	W. Joseph McConnell
1951	James C. Matthews
1968	John J. Kamerick
1970	John L. Carter, Jr. (Acting)
1972	C. C. Nolen
1979	Frank E. Vandiver
1982	Alfred F. Hurley (Chancellor)

Northeastern University

Boston, MA

1940	Carl S. Ell
1959	Asa S. Knowles
1975	Kenneth G. Ryder

Northern Illinois University

DeKalb, IL

(Northern Illinois State Teachers College from 1921 to 1955; Northern Illinois State College until 1957.)

1921	J. Stanley Brown
1927	J. Clifton Brown
1929	Karl L. Adams
1949	Leslie A. Holmes
1967	Rhoten A. Smith
1973	Richard Nelson
1978	William R. Monat
1985	Clyde J. Wingfield
1987	John E. La Tourette

Northwestern University

Evanston, IL

1853	Clark T. Hinman
1854	Henry S. Noyes
1856	Randolph S. Foster
1860	Henry S. Noyes
1867	David H. Wheeler
1869	Erastus O. Haven
1872	Charles H. Fowler
1876	Oliver Marcy
1881	Joseph Cummings
1890	Henry W. Rogers
1900	Daniel Bonbright
1902	Edmund J. James
1904	Thomas F. Holgate
1906	Abram W. Harris
1916	Thomas F. Holgate
1919	Lynn H. Hough
1920	Walter D. Scott
1939	Franklyn B. Snyder
1949	J. Roscoe Miller
1970	Robert H. Strotz
1985	Arnold R. Weber

Norwich University

Northfield, VT

1819 Alden Partridge
1844 Truman B. Ransom
1847 James D. Butler
1848 Henry S. Wheaton
1850 Edward Bourns
1867 Thomas W. Walker
1869 Roger S. Howard
1871 Malcolm Douglass
1875 Josiah Swett
1876 Charles A. Curtis
1880 Charles H. Lewis
1896 Allen D. Brown
1904 Charles H. Spooner
1915 Ira L. Reeves
1920 Charles A. Plumley
1934 Porter H. Adams
1940 John M. Thomas
1944 Homer L. Dodge
1950 Ernest N. Harmon
1965 Barksdale Hamlett
1973 Loring Hart
1983 W. Russell Todd

Oberlin College

Oberlin, OH

1835 Asa Mahan
1849 Charles G. Finney
 (Acting)
1850 John Morgan (Acting)
1851 Charles G. Finney
1866 James H. Fairchild
1889 Henry M. Tenney
 (Acting)
1891 William G. Ballantine
1896 James H. Fairchild
 (Acting)
1899 John H. Barrows
1902 Henry C. King
1909 Henry M. Tenney
1911 Henry C. King
1918 Edward I. Bosworth
1920 Henry C. King
1927 Ernest H. Wilkins
1946 William E. Stevenson
1960 Robert K. Carr
1972 Robert Fuller
1975 Emil Danenberg
1982 James L. Powell (Acting)
1983 S. Frederick Starr

Occidental College

Los Angeles, CA

1887 Samuel H. Weller
1891 J. Melville McPherron
1894 Elbert N. Condit
1896 James W. Parkhill
1897 Guy W. Wadsworth
1905 William S. Young
 (Acting)
1906 John W. Baer
1916 Thomas G. Burt (Acting)
1917 Silas Evans
1920 Thomas G. Burt (Acting)
1921 Remsen Bird
1946 Arthur G. Coons
1965 Richard C. Gilman

Oglethorpe University

Atlanta, GA

1836 Carlyle P. Beman
1841 Samuel K. Talmage
1869 William M. Cunningham
1870 David Wills
1913 Thornwell Jacobs
1944 Philip Weltner
1953 James W. Bunting
1956 Donald R. Wilson
1958 Donald C. Agnew
1965 Paul R. Beall
1967 Paul K. Vonk
1975 Manning M. Pattillo, Jr.

Ohio State University

Columbus, OH

(Ohio Agricultural and Mechanical College until 1878.)

1873 Edward Orton
1881 Walter Q. Scott
1883 William H. Scott
1895 James H. Canfield
1899 William O. Thompson
1926 George W. Rightmire
1938 William McPherson
 (Acting)
1940 Howard L. Bevis
1956 Novice G. Fawcett
1972 Harold L. Enarson
1981 Edward H. Jennings

Ohio University

Athens, OH

1809 Jacob Lindly
1822 James Irvine
1824 Robert G. Wilson
1839 William H. McGuffey
1843 (University closed)
1848 Alfred Ryors
1852 Solomon Howard
1872 William H. Scott
1883 Charles W. Super
1896 Isaac Crook
1899 Charles W. Super
1901 Alston Ellis
1920 Edwin W. Chubb
 (Acting)
1921 Elmer B. Bryan
1934 Edwin W. Chubb
 (Acting)
1935 Herman G. James
1943 Walter S. Gamertsfelder
1945 John C. Baker
1961 Vernon R. Alden
1969 Claude R. Sowle
1974 Harry Crewson
1975 Charles J. Ping

Oklahoma State University

Stillwater, OK

(Oklahoma A & M College until 1957.)

1891 R. J. Barker
1894 Henry E. Alvord
1895 Edmund D. Murdaugh

1895 George E. Morrow
1899 Angelo C. Scott
1908 James H. Connell
1914 Lowry L. Lewis
1915 James W. Cantwell
1921 James B. Eskridge
1923 George Wilson
1923 Richard G. Tyler
1923 Bradford Knapp
1928 Clarence H. McElroy
1928 Henry G. Bennett
1952 Oliver S. Willham
1966 Robert B. Kamm
1977 Lawrence L. Boger

Oregon State University

Corvallis, OR

(Agricultural College of the State of Oregon until 1929; Oregon State Agricultural College until 1953; Oregon State College until 1961.)

1865 W. A. Finley
1872 B. L. Arnold
1892 John D. Letcher
1892 John M. Bloss
1896 H. B. Miller
1897 Thomas M. Gatch
1907 William J. Kerr
1932 George W. Peavy
1940 Frank L. Ballard
1941 Francois A. Gilfillan
1942 August L. Strand
1961 James H. Jensen
1969 Roy A. Young
1970 Robert W. MacVicar
1984 John V. Byrne

Pennsylvania State University

University Park, PA

(Agricultural College of Pennsylvania until 1874; Pennsylvania State College until 1953.)

1864 William H. Allen
1866 John Fraser
1868 Thomas H. Burrowes
1871 James Calder
1880 Joseph Shortlidge
1881 James Y. McKee
 (Acting)
1882 George W. Atherton
1906 James A. Beaver (Acting)
1908 Edwin E. Sparks
1920 Vacant
1921 John M. Thomas
1926 Vacant
1927 Ralph D. Hetzel
1947 James Milholland
 (Acting)
1950 Milton S. Eisenhower
1956 Eric A. Walker
1970 John W. Oswald
1983 Bryce Jordan

Polytechnic University

Brooklyn, NY

(Polytechnic Institute of Brooklyn until 1975; Polytechnic Institute of New York until 1984.)

1889 David H. Cochran
1899 Henry S. Snow (Interim)
1904 Fred W. Atkinson
1925 Parke Rexford Kolbe
1932 Charles E. Potts
 (Interim)
1933 Henry S. Rogers
1957 Ernst Weber
1969 Benjamin Adler (Interim)
1971 Arthur Grad
1973 Norman P. Auburn
 (Acting)
1973 George Bugliarello

Pomona College

Claremont, CA

1890 Cyrus G. Baldwin
1897 Franklin L. Ferguson
1901 George A. Gates
1910 James A. Blaisdell
1928 Charles K. Edmunds
1941 E. Wilson Lyon
1969 J. David Alexander

Pratt Institute

Brooklyn, NY

1937 Charles Pratt
1953 Francis H. Horn
1957 Robert Oxnam
1961 Richard H. Heindel
1967 William P. Maddox
 (Acting)
1968 James B. Donovan
1970 Henry Saltzman
1972 Richardson Pratt, Jr.

Princeton University

Princeton, NJ

(Known originally as the College of New Jersey.)

1747 Jonathan Dickinson
1747 Aaron Burr
1757 Jonathan Edwards
1759 Samuel Davies
1761 Samuel Finley
1768 John Witherspoon
1795 S. Stanhope Smith
1812 Ashbel Green
1823 James Carnahan
1854 John Maclean
1868 James McCosh
1888 Francis L. Patton
1902 Woodrow Wilson
1912 John G. Hibben
1933 Harold W. Dodds
1957 Robert F. Goheen
1971 William C. Bowen

Purdue University

West Lafayette, IN

1872	Richard Owen
1874	Abram C. Shortridge
1876	Emerson E. White
1883	James H. Smart
1900	Winthrop E. Stone
1922	Edward C. Elliott
1946	Frederick L. Hovde
1972	Arthur G. Hansen
1983	Steven C. Beering

Queens College of the City University of New York

Flushing, NY

(Queens College until 1961.)

1937	Paul Klapper
1947	Margaret V. Kiely (Acting)
1949	John J. Theobald
1956	Thomas V. Garvey (Provost)
1958	Harold W. Stoke
1965	Joseph P. McMurray
1971	Joseph S. Murphy
1978	Saul B. Cohen
1985	Shirley S. Kenny

Radcliffe College

Cambridge, MA

1882	Elizabeth C. Agassiz
1903	LeBaron R. Briggs
1923	Ada L. Comstock
1943	Wilbur K. Jordan
1960	Mary I. Bunting
1972	Matina S. Horner

Randolph-Macon College

Ashland, VA

1833	Stephen Olin
1837	Landon C. Garland
1846	William A. Smith
1866	Thomas C. Johnson
1868	James A. Duncan
1877	William W. Bennett
1886	William W. Smith
1897	John A. Kern
1899	William G. Starr
1902	Robert E. Blackwell
1938	Samuel C. Hatcher (Acting)
1939	Jesse E. Morland
1967	Luther W. White, III
1979	Ladell Payne

Rice University

Houston, TX

(Rice Institute until 1960.)
| 1961 | Kenneth S. Pitzer |

1968	Frank E. Vandiver (Acting)
1970	Norman Hackerman
1985	George E. Rupp

Roanoke College

Salem, VA

1853	David F. Bittle
1877	Thomas W. Dosh
1878	Julius D. Dreher
1904	John A. Morehead
1920	Charles J. Smith
1949	Henry S. Oberly
1963	Perry F. Kendig
1975	Norman D. Fintel

Rochester Institute of Technology

Rochester, NY

1953	Mark Ellingson
1969	Paul A. Miller
1979	M. Richard Rose

Rollins College

Winter Park, FL

1885	Edward Payson Hooker
1892	John H. Ford (Acting)
1893	Charles G. Fairchild
1895	John H. Ford (Acting)
1896	George M. Ward
1902	William F. Blackman
1916	George M. Ward (Acting)
1917	Calvin H. French
1919	George M. Ward (Acting)
1923	Robert J. Sprague
1924	William C. Weir
1925	Hamilton Holt
1949	Paul A. Wagner
1951	Hugh F. McKean
1969	Jack B. Critchfield
1978	Thaddeus Seymour

Rutgers University

New Brunswick, NJ

(Queens College until 1825; Rutgers College until 1924.)

1785	Jacob R. Hardenbergh
1791	William Linn
1794	Ira Condict
1810	John H. Livingston
1825	Philip Milledoler
1840	Abraham B. Hasbrouck
1850	Theodore Frelinghuysen
1863	William H. Campbell
1882	Merrill E. Gates
1891	Austin Scott
1906	William H. S. Demarest
1925	John M. Thomas
1971	Edward J. Bloustein

St. Bonaventure University

St. Bonaventure, NY

1874	Charles Vissani
1877	Leo DaSaracena
1880	Theophilus Pospisilik
1886	Joseph Butler
1911	Fidelis Reynolds
1916	Alexander Hickey
1920	Thomas Plassmann
1949	Juvenal Lalor
1955	Brian Lhota
1961	Francis W. Kearney
1967	Reginald Redlon
1973	D. McElrath
1975	Mathias F. Doyle

St. John's College

Annapolis, MD

1790	John McDowell
1807	Bethel Judd
1812	John McDowell
1820	Henry L. Davis
1824	William Rafferty
1831	Hector Humphreys
1857	Cleland K. Nelson
1861	(College closed)
1866	Henry Barnard
1867	James C. Welling
1870	James M. Garnett
1880	John M. Leavitt
1884	William H. Hopkins
1886	Thomas Fell
1923	Enoch B. Garey
1929	Vacant
1931	Douglas H. Gordon
1934	Amos W. W. Woodcock
1937	Stringfellow Barr
1947	John S. Kieffer
1949	Richard D. Weigle
1980	Edwin J. Delattre

St. John's University

Jamaica, NY

1870	John T. Landry
1875	Patrick M. O'Regan
1877	Andrew J. Meyer
1882	Jeremiah A. Hartnett
1897	James J. Sullivan
1901	Patrick S. McHale
1906	John W. Moore
1925	John J. Cloonan
1931	Thomas F. Ryan
1935	Edward J. Walsh
1942	William J. Mahoney
1947	John A. Flynn
1961	Edward J. Burke
1965	Joseph T. Cahill

St. Joseph's College

Philadelphia, PA

1851	Felix Barbelin
1856	James Ryder
1896	William F. Clark

1900	Cornelius Gillespie
1907	Dean T. O'Sullivan
1908	Cornelius Gillespie
1909	Charles W. Lyons
1914	Charles Davey
1917	Redmond J. Walsh
1920	Patrick F. O'Gorman
1921	Albert G. Brown
1927	William T. Tallon
1933	Thomas J. Higgins
1939	Thomas J. Love
1944	John J. Long
1950	Edward G. Jacklin
1956	J. Joseph Bluett
1962	William F. Maloney
1968	Terrence Toland
1976	Donald I. MacLean
1987	Nicholas S. Rashford

St. Lawrence University

Canton, NY

(St. Lawrence College until 1899.)

1859	John S. Lee
1868	Richmond Fisk
1872	Absalom G. Gaines
1889	Alpheus B. Hervey
1894	Vacant
1896	John C. Lee
1899	Almon Gunnison
1914	Vacant
1916	Frank A. Gallup
1919	Richard E. Sykes
1935	Laurens H. Seelye
1940	Millard H. Jencks
1945	Eugene G. Bewkes
1963	Foster S. Brown
1969	Frank P. Piskor
1981	W. Lawrence Gulik

St. Louis University

St. Louis, MO

1818	Francis Niel
1824	Edmond Saulnier
1828	Charles F. Van Quickenborne
1829	Peter J. Verhaegen
1836	John A. Elet
1840	James O. Van de Velde
1843	George A. Carrell
1847	John B. Druyts
1854	John S. Verdin
1859	Ferdinand Coosemans
1862	Thomas O'Neill
1868	Francis F. Stuntebeck
1871	Joseph Zealand
1874	Leopold Bushart
1877	Joseph E. Keller
1881	Rudolph J. Meyer
1885	Henry Moeller
1889	Edward J. Gleeson
1891	Joseph Grimmelsman
1898	James F. X. Hoeffer
1900	William B. Rogers
1907	Francis B. O'Boyle
1908	John P. Frieden
1912	Alexander J. Burrowes
1913	Bernard J. Otting
1920	William F. Robi
1936	Harry B. Crimmins
1942	Robert Kelley

1943 Patrick J. Holloran
1949 Paul C. Reinert
1974 Daniel C. O'Connell
1978 Edward Drummond
1979 Thomas R. Fitzgerald

Sarah Lawrence College

Bronxville, NY

1928 Marion Coats
1929 Constance Warren
1945 Harold Taylor
1959 Harrison Tweed
1960 Paul Ward
1965 Esther Raushenbush
1969 Charles DeCarlo
1981 Alice Stone Ilchman

Simmons College

Boston, MA

1902 Henry Lefavour
1933 Bancroft Beatley
1955 William E. Park
1970 William J. Holmes, Jr.

Skidmore College

Saratoga Springs, NY

1912 Charles H. Keyes
1925 Henry T. Moore
1957 Val H. Wilson
1965 Joseph C. Palamountain, Jr.

Smith College

Northampton, MA

1873 Laurenus Seelye
1910 Marion L. Burton
1917 William A. Neilson
1939 Elizabeth Morrow (Acting)
1940 Herbert J. Davis
1949 Benjamin F. Wright
1959 Thomas C. Mendenhall
1975 Jill Kathryn Kerr Conway
1985 Mary Maples Dunn

Southern Illinois University

Carbondale, IL

1874 Robert Allyn
1892 John Hull (Regent)
1893 Harvey W. Everest
1897 Daniel B. Parkinson
1913 Henry W. Shyrock
1935 Roscoe Pulliam
1944 Bruce W. Merwin (Interim)
1945 Chester F. Lay
1948 Delyte W. Morris

Chancellors

1970 Robert G. Layer

1972 David R. Derge
1975 Warren W. Brandt
1979 Hiram H. Lesar (Acting)
1980 Albert Somit

Southern Methodist University

Dallas, TX

1911 Robert S. Hyer
1920 Hiram A. Boaz
1923 Charles C. Selecman
1939 Umphrey Lee
1954 Willis M. Tate
1972 Paul Hardin
1974 Willis Tate (Chancellor)
1975 James H. Zumberge
1980 L. Donald Shields

Stanford University

Stanford, CA

1891 David S. Jordan
1913 John C. Branner
1915 Ray L. Wilbur
1943 Donald B. Tresidder
1949 J. E. Wallace Sterling
1968 Kenneth S. Pitzer
1970 Richard W. Lyman
1980 Donald Kennedy

State University of New York

Albany, NY

1949 Alvia C. Eurich
1952 Charles Garside (Acting)
1952 William S. Carlson
1959 Thomas H. Hamilton

Chancellors

1964 Samuel B. Gould
1970 Ernest L. Boyer
1977 J. F. Kelly (Acting)
1978 Clifton R. Wharton, Jr.

State University of New York at Albany

Albany, NY

1889 William J. Milne
1915 Abram R. Brubacher
1939 John M. Sayles
1947 Milton G. Nelson (Acting)
1949 Evan R. Collins
1969 Allan A. Kuusisto
1970 Louis T. Benezet
1976 Emmet B. Fields
1978 Vincent I. O'Leary

State University of New York at Buffalo

Buffalo, NY

(University of Buffalo until 1962.)

Chancellors

1846 Millard Fillmore
1882 Orsamus H. Marshall
1885 E. Carleton Sprague
1895 James O. Putnam
1902 Wilson S. Bissell
1905 Charles P. Norton
1922 Samuel P. Capen
1950 T. Raymond McConnell
1954 Clifford C. Furnas

Presidents

1962 Clifford C. Furnas
1966 Martin Meyerson
1970 Robert L. Ketter
1982 Steven B. Sample

Stephens College

Columbia, MO

1870 E. S. Dulin
1877 R. P. Rider
1883 T. W. Barrett
1894 Sam F. Taylor
1904 J. R. Pentuff
1905 W. B. Peeler
1910 H. N. Quisenberry
1912 James M. Wood
1947 Homer P. Rainey
1952 Thomas A. Spragens
1958 Seymour A. Smith
1975 Arland F. Christ-Janer
1983 Patsy H. Sampson

Stetson University

DeLand, FL

1885 John F. Forbes
1904 Lincoln Hulley
1934 William S. Allen
1948 J. Ollie Edmunds
1967 Paul F. Geren
1970 John E. Johns
1977 George Borders
1977 Pope A. Duncan

Susquehanna University

Selinsgrove, PA

1893 Franlin P. Manhart
1895 Jonathan R. Dimm
1899 Charles W. Heisler
1902 George W. Enders
1904 John B. Focht
1905 Charles T. Aikens
1928 G. Morris Smith
1959 Gustave W. Weber
1977 Jonathan C. Messerli
1984 Joel L. Cunningham

Swarthmore College

Swarthmore, PA

1864 Edward Parrish
1872 Edward H. Magill
1890 William H. Appleton
1891 Charles DeGarmo
1898 William W. Birdsall
1902 Joseph Swain
1921 Frank Aydelotte
1940 John W. Nason
1953 Courtney C. Smith
1969 Robert D. Cross
1973 Theodore W. Friend, III
1982 David W. Fraser

Syracuse University

Syracuse, NY

1873 Alexander Winchell
1874 Erastus O. Haven
1881 Charles N. Sims
1894 James R. Day
1922 Charles W. Flint
1936 William P. Graham
1942 William P. Tolley
1969 John E. Corbally, Jr.
1971 Melvin A. Eggers (Chancellor)
1984 Melvin A. Eggers (President)

Temple University

Philadelphia, PA

1891 Russell H. Conwell
1925 Charles E. Beury
1941 Robert L. Johnson
1959 Millard E. Gladfelter
1967 Paul R. Anderson
1973 Marvin Wachman
1982 Peter J. Liacouras

Texas A and M University

College Station, TX

1876 Thomas S. Gathright
1879 John G. James
1883 James R. Cole
1883 Hardaway H. Dinwiddie
1888 Louis M. McInnis
1890 William L. Bringhurst
1891 Lawrence S. Ross
1898 Roger H. Whitlock
1898 Lafayette L. Foster
1901 Roger H. Whitlock
1902 David F. Houston
1905 Henry H. Harrington
1908 Robert T. Milner
1913 Charles Puryear (Acting)
1914 William B. Bizzell
1925 Thomas O. Walton
1943 Frank C. Bolton (Acting)
1944 Gibb Gilchrist
1948 Frank C. Bolton
1950 Marion T. Harrington
1953 David H. Morgan
1956 David W. Williams (Acting)
1957 Marion T. Harrington
1959 James E. Rudder

1970 Alvin R. Luedecke
(Acting)
1970 Jack K. Williams
1980 Charles Samson (Acting)
1981 Frank E. Vandiver

Texas Christian University

Fort Worth, TX

(Add-Ran College until 1889; Add-Ran Christian University until 1902.)

1873 Addison Clark
1899 Vacant
1902 Ely V. Zollars
1906 Clinton Lockhart
1911 Frederick D. Kershner
1916 Edward M. Waits
1941 McGruder E. Sadler
1965 James M. Moudy
(Chancellor)
1979 William E. Tucker
(Chancellor)

Texas Tech University

Lubbock, TX

1925 Paul W. Horn
1932 Bradford Knapp
1938 Clifford B. Jones
1944 William M. Whyburn
1948 Dossie M. Wiggins
1952 Edward N. Jones
1959 Robert C. Goodwin
1966 Grover E. Murray
1976 Maurice C. Mackey
1980 Lauro F. Cavazos

Transylvania University

Lexington, KY

1794 Harry Toulmin
1796 James Moore
1804 James Blythe
1818 Horace Holley
1828 Alva Woods
1833 Benjamin O. Peers
1835 Thomas W. Coit
1838 Louis Marshall
1840 Robert Davidson
1842 Henry B. Bascom
1849 James B. Dodd
1856 Lewis W. Green
1857 (University closed)
1865 John B. Bowman
1878 Henry H. White
1880 Charles L. Loos
1897 Reuben L. Cave
1900 Alexander R. Milligan
1901 Burris A. Jenkins
1906 Thomas B. Macartney
1908 Richard H. Crossfield
1921 Thomas B. Macartney
1922 Andrew D. Harmon
1928 Thomas B. Macartney
1929 Elmer G. Campbell
1930 Arthur Braden
1938 Richard H. Crossfield
1939 Raymond F. McLain
1943 Leland A. Brown
1946 Raymond F. McLain
1951 Frank A. Rose

1957 Irvin E. Lunger
1976 William W. Kelly
1982 David G. Brown
1984 Charles L. Shearer

Trinity College

Hartford, CT

(Washington College until 1845.)

1824 Thomas C. Brownell
1831 Nathaniel S. Wheaton
1837 Silas Totten
1848 John Williams
1853 Daniel R. Goodwin
1860 Samuel Eliot
1864 John B. Kerfoot
1866 John Brocklesby (Acting)
1867 Abner Jackson
1874 Thomas R. Pynchon
1883 George W. Smith
1904 Flavel S. Luther
1915 Henry A. Perkins
(Acting)
1920 Remsen B. Ogilby
1943 Arthur H. Hughes
(Acting)
1945 G. Keith Funston
1951 Arthur H. Hughes
(Acting)
1953 Albert C. Jacobs
1968 Theodore D. Lockwood
1981 James F. English, Jr.

Trinity University

San Antonio, TX

1882 S. T. Anderson
1883 B. G. McLeskey
1886 Luther A. Johnson
1888 J. L. Dickens
1890 B. D. Cockrill
1896 Vacant
1901 Jesse Anderson
1902 L. C. Kirkes
1904 Archelaus E. Turner
1907 Samuel L. Hornbeak
1921 John H. Burma
1934 Raymond H. Leach
1937 Frank L. Wear
1942 Monroe G. Everett
1950 Marion B. Thomas
(Interim)
1951 James Laurie
1970 Gordon D. Wimpress, Jr.
1977 M. Bruce Thomas
1979 Ronald K. Calgaard

Tufts University

Medford, MA

(Tufts College until 1955.)

1853 Hosea Ballou, II
1861 John P. Marshall
(Acting)
1862 Alonzo A. Miner
1875 Elmer H. Capen
1905 Frederick W. Hamilton
1912 William L. Hooper
(Acting)
1914 Hermon C. Bumpus
1919 John A. Cousens
1937 George S. Miller (Acting)

1938 Leonard Carmichael
1953 Nils Y. Wessell
1966 Leonard C. Mead
(Acting)
1967 Burton C. Hallowell
1976 Jean Mayer

Tulane University

New Orleans, LA

(Medical College of Louisiana until 1847; University of Louisiana until 1884.)

1834 Thomas Hunt
1847 Francis L. Hawks
1850 Theodore H. McCaleb
1863 (University closed)
1865 Thomas Hunt
1867 Randell Hunt
1884 William P. Johnston
1889 William O. Rogers
(Acting)
1900 Edwin A. Alderman
1904 Edwin B. Craighead
1912 Robert Sharp
1918 Albert B. Dinwiddie
1935 Douglas S. Anderson
(Acting)
1936 Robert L. Menuet
(Acting)
1937 Rufus C. Harris
1960 Herbert E. Longenecker
1975 Sheldon Hackney
1981 Eamon M. Kelly

Tusculum College

Greeneville, TN

(Tusculum and Greeneville College from 1868 to 1912.)

1868 Stephenson Doak
1882 Jeremiah Moore
1901 Samuel A. Coile
1907 Charles O. Gray
1931 Charles A. Anderson
1942 John McSween
1944 Jere A. Moore (Acting)
1946 George K. Davies
1950 Leslie K. Patton (Acting)
1951 Raymond C. Rankin
1965 Douglas G. Trout
1968 Charles J. Ping (Acting)
1969 Andrew N. Cothran
1973 Thomas Voss
1979 Earl R. Mezoff

Tuskegee University

Tuskegee Institute, AL

(Tuskegee Normal and Industrial Institute until 1937.)

1881 Booker T. Washington
1916 Robert R. Moton
1936 Frederick D. Patterson
1953 Luther H. Foster
1981 Benjamin F. Payton

Union College

Schenectady, NY

(Union College and University until 1969.)

1795 John B. Smith
1799 Jonathan Edwards
1801 Jonathan Maxcy
1804 Eliphalet Nott
1866 Laurens P. Hickok
1869 Charles A. Aiken
1871 Eliphalet N. Potter
1884 Judson Landon (Interim)
1888 Harrison E. Webster
1894 Andrew Van V.
Raymond
1907 George Alexander
1909 Charles A. Richmond
1929 Frank P. Day
1933 Edward Ellery (Acting)
1934 Dixon R. Fox
1945 Benjamin P. Whitaker
(Acting)
1946 Carter Davidson
1965 Harold C. Martin
1974 Thomas Bonner
1978 Norman P. Auburn
(Acting)
1979 John S. Morris

United States Air Force Academy

Colorado Springs, CO

1954 Hubert R. Harmon
1956 James E. Briggs
1959 William S. Stone
1962 Robert H. Warren
1965 Thomas S. Moorman
1970 Albert P. Clark
1974 James R. Allen
1978 Robert Kelley
1984 Winfield W. Scott, Jr.

United States Coast Guard Academy

New London, CT

1877 J. A. Henriques
1883 L. G. Shepard
1887 D. B. Hodgson
1894 J. W. Congdon
1895 O. C. Hamlet
1898 D. A. Hall
1902 W. E. Reynolds
1908 J. E. Reinburg
1910 W. V. E. Jacobs
1914 Frederick C. Billard
1918 T. G. Crapster
1919 B. L. Reed
1919 W. V. E. Jacobs
1923 H. D. Hinckley
1928 Harry G. Hamlet
1932 R. Ridgley, Jr.
1935 E. D. Jones
1940 James Pine
1947 Wilfred N. Derby
1950 A. G. Hall
1954 R. J. Mauerman
1957 F. A. Leamy
1960 S. H. Evans
1962 W. J. Smith
1965 Chester R. Bender
1967 A. B. Engel

1970 J. F. Thompson
1974 William Jenkins
1978 Malcolm E. Clark
(Superintendent)
1981 Charles Larkin
(Superintendent)
1982 E. Nelson, Jr.
(Superintendent)

United States Military Academy

West Point, NY

1802 Jonathan Williams
1803 Vacant
1805 Jonathan Williams
1812 Joseph G. Swift
1815 Alden Partridge
1817 Sylvanus Thayer
1833 Rene E. DeRussy
1838 Richard Delafield
1845 Henry Brewerton
1852 Robert E. Lee
1855 John G. Barnard
1856 Richard Delafield
1861 Pierre G. T. Beauregard
1861 Richard Delafield
1861 Alexander H. Bowman
1864 Zealous B. Tower
1864 George W. Cullum
1866 Thomas G. Pitcher
1871 Thomas H. Ruger
1876 John M. Schofield
1881 Oliver O. Howard
1882 Wesley Merritt
1887 John G. Parke
1889 John M. Wilson
1893 Oswald H. Ernst
1898 Albert L. Mills
1906 Hugh L. Scott
1910 Thomas H. Barry
1912 Clarence P. Townsley
1916 John Biddle
1917 Samuel E. Tillman
1919 Douglas MacArthur
1922 Fred W. Sladen
1926 Merch B. Stewart
1927 Edwin B. Winans
1928 William R. Smith
1932 William D. Connor
1938 Jay L. Benedict
1940 Robert I. Eichelberger
1942 Frances B. Wilby
1945 Maxwell D. Taylor
1949 Bryant E. Moore
1951 Frederick A. Irving
1954 Blackshear M. Bryan
1956 Garrison H. Davidson
1960 William C. Westmoreland
1963 James B. Lampert
1966 Donald V. Bennett
1968 Samuel W. Koster
1970 William V. Knowlton
(Superintendent)
1974 Sidney B. Berry
(Superintendent)
1977 A. J. Goodpaster
(Superintendent)
1982 Winfield W. Scott, Jr.

United States Naval Academy

Annapolis, MD

1845 Franklin Buchanan

1847 George P. Upshur
1850 C. K. Stribling
1853 Louis M. Goldsborough
1857 George S. Blake
1865 David D. Porter
1869 John L. Worden
1874 C. R. P. Rodgers
1878 F. A. Parker
1879 George B. Balch
1881 C. R. P. Rodgers
1881 Francis M. Ramsay
1886 W. T. Sampson
1890 Robert L. Phythian
1894 Philip H. Cooper
1898 F. V. McNair
1900 Richard Wainwright
1902 Willard H. Brownson
1905 James H. Sands
1907 Charles J. Badger
1909 John M. Bowyer
1911 John H. Gibbons
1914 William F. Fullam
1915 Edward W. Eberle
1919 Archibald H. Scales
1921 Henry B. Wilson
1925 Louis M. Nulton
1928 Samuel S. Robison
1931 Thomas C. Hart
1934 David F. Sellers
1938 Wilson Brown
1941 Russell Willson
1942 John R. Beardall
1945 Aubrey W. Fitch
1947 James L. Holloway, Jr.
1950 Harry W. Hill
1952 C. Turner Joy
1954 Walter F. Boone
1956 William R. Smedberg, III
1958 Charles L. Melson
1960 John F. Davidson
1962 C. C. Kirkpatrick
1964 Charles S. Minter, Jr.
1965 Draper L. Kauffman
1968 Lawrence Heyworth, Jr.
1968 James Calvert
1972 William P. Mack
(Superintendent)
1975 Kinnaird R. McKee
(Superintendent)
1978 William P. Lawrence
(Superintendent)
1982 E. C. Walker
1983 Charles R. Larson
(Superintendent)

University of Akron

Akron, OH

(Buchtel College until 1913; Municipal University of Akron until 1926.)

1872 S. H. McCollester
1878 E. L. Rexford
1880 Orello Cone
1896 Charles M. Knight
(Acting)
1897 Ira A. Priest
1901 A. B. Church
1913 Parke R. Kolbe
1925 George F. Zook
1933 Hezzleton E. Simmons
1951 Norman P. Auburn
1971 Dominic J. Guzzetta
1984 William V. Muse

University of Alabama

Tuscaloosa, AL

1831 Alva Woods
1837 Basil Manly
1855 Landon C. Garland
1866 Vacant
1871 Nathaniel T. Lupton
1874 Carlos G. Smith
1878 Josiah Gorgas
1879 William S. Wyman
(Acting)
1880 B. B. Lewis
1885 William S. Wyman
(Acting)
1886 Henry D. Clayton
1890 Richard C. Jones
1897 James K. Powers
1901 William S. Wyman
1902 John W. Abercrombie
1911 William B. Saffold
1912 George H. Denny
1937 Richard C. Foster
1941 George H. Denny
1942 Raymond R. Paty
1947 Ralph E. Adams (Acting)
1948 John M. Gallalee
1953 Lee Bidgood (Acting)
1953 Oliver C. Carmichael
1957 James H. Newman
(Acting)
1958 Frank A. Rose
1969 Forrest D. Matthews
1981 Joab L. Thomas

University of Alabama at Birmingham

Birmingham, AL

(Founded 1969.)

1969 Joseph F. Volker
1977 S. Richardson Hill, Jr.

University of Alabama in Huntsville

Huntsville, AL

(Founded 1969.)

1969 Benjamin B. Graves
1978 John C. Wright

University of Arizona

Tucson, AZ

1893 Theodore B. Comstock
1895 Howard Billman
1897 Millard M. Parker
1901 Frank Y. Adams
1903 Kendric C. Babcock
1910 Andrew E. Douglass
1911 Arthur H. Wilde
1914 Rufus B. von KleinSmid
1922 Francis C. Lockwood
1922 Cloyd H. Marvin
1927 Byron Cummings
1928 Homer L. Shantz
1936 Paul S. Burgess
1937 Alfred Atkinson
1947 James B. McCormick
1951 Richard A. Harvill

1971 John P. Schaefer
1982 Henry Koffler

University of Arkansas

Fayetteville, AR

(Arkansas Industrial University until 1899.)

1871 Noah P. Gates
1873 Albert W. Bishop
1875 Noah P. Gates
1877 Daniel H. Hill
1884 George M. Edgar
1887 Edward H. Murfee
1894 John L. Buchanan
1902 Henry S. Hartzog
1905 John N. Tillman
1913 John C. Futrall
1939 J. William Fulbright
1941 Arthur M. Harding
1947 Lewis W. Jones
1951 Joe E. Covington
1952 John T. Caldwell
1959 Storm H. Whaley
1960 David W. Mullins
1974 Charles E. Bishop
1980 James E. Martin
1984 Ray Thornton

University of Bridgeport

Bridgeport, CT

(Junior College of Connecticut until 1947.)

1946 James H. Halsey
1962 Henry W. Littlefield
1971 Thurston E. Manning
1974 Leland W. Miles

University of California

Berkeley, CA

(Presidents since 1952 have presided over the statewide university system and the chancellors over the Berkeley campus.)

1868 John Le Conte (Acting)
1870 Henry Durant
1872 Daniel C. Gilman
1875 John Le Conte
1881 William T. Reid
1885 Edward S. Holden
1888 Horace Davis
1890 Martin Kellogg
1899 Benjamin I. Wheeler
1919 David P. Barrows
1923 William W. Campbell
1930 Robert G. Sproul
1958 Clark Kerr
1967 Henry R. Wellman
(Acting)
1968 Charles J. Hitch
1980 David S. Saxon
1983 David P. Gardner

Chancellors

1952 Clark Kerr
1958 Glenn T. Seaborg
1961 Edward W. Strong
1965 Roger Heyns

1971 Albert H. Bowker
1980 Ira M. Heyman

University of Chicago

Chicago, IL

1891 William R. Harper
1906 Harry P. Judson
1923 Ernest D. Burton
1925 Max Mason
1928 Frederic C. Woodward
      (Acting)
1929 Robert M. Hutchins
1951 Lawrence A. Kimpton
1960 R. W. Harrison (Acting)
1961 George W. Beadle
1968 Edward H. Levi
1975 John Wilson
1978 Hanna Holborn Cray

University of Cincinnati

Cincinnati, OH

(Cincinnati College until 1870.)

1819 Elijah Slack
1822 Philander Chase
1823 Elijah Slack (Acting)
1836 William H. McGuffey
1839 Thomas J. Biggs
1845 Vacant
1873 George H. Harper
1877 Thomas Vickers
1884 Henry T. Eddy (Acting)
1885 Jacob D. Cox
1889 Henry T. Eddy
1891 Vacant
1899 Howard Ayers
1904 Joseph E. Harry (Acting)
1904 Charles W. Dabney
1920 Frederick C. Hicks
1928 Herman Schneider
1932 Raymond Walters
1955 Walter C. Langsam
1971 Warren G. Bennis
1977 Henry R. Winkler
1984 Joseph A. Steger

University of Colorado

Boulder, CO

1877 Joseph A. Sewall
1887 Horace M. Hale
1892 James H. Baker
1914 Livingston Farrand
1919 George Norlin
1939 Robert L. Stearns
1953 Ward Darley
1956 James Q. Newton
1963 Joseph R. Smiley
1969 Eugene H. Wilson
1969 Frederick P. Thieme
1978 R. C. Rautenstraus
1980 Arnold R. Weber
1985 Harrison Shull

University of Connecticut

Storrs, CT

(Connecticut Agricultural College from 1899 to 1933; Connecticut State College until 1939.)

1898 George W. Flint
1901 Rufus W. Stimson
1908 Edwin O. Smith (Acting)
1908 Charles L. Beach
1928 Charles B. Gentry
1929 George A. Works
1930 Charles C. McCracken
1935 Charles B. Gentry
      (Acting)
1935 Albert N. Jorgensen
1962 Homer D. Babbidge, Jr.
1972 Edward V. Gant (Acting)
1973 Glenn Fergusen
1979 John A. DiBiaggio
1985 John T. Casteen, III

University of Dayton

Dayton, OH

(St. Mary's College from 1912 to 1920.)

1912 Bernard P. O'Reilly
1918 Joseph Tetzlaff
1923 Bernard P. O'Reilly
1932 Walter S. Tredtin
1938 John A. Elbert
1944 George J. Renneker
1953 Andrew L. Seebold
1959 Raymond A. Roesch
1979 Raymond L. Fitz

University of Delaware

Newark, DE

(Newark College until 1843; Delaware College until 1921.)

1834 Eliphalet W. Gilbert
1835 Richard S. Mason
1840 Eliphalet W. Gilbert
1847 James P. Wilson
1850 William A. Norton
1850 Matthew Meigs
1851 Walter S. F. Graham
1854 Daniel Kirkwood
1856 Ellis J. Newlin
1859 Vacant
1870 William H. Purnell
1885 John H. Caldwell
1888 Lewis P. Bush (Acting)
1888 Albert N. Raub
1896 George A. Harter
1914 Samuel C. Mitchell
1920 Walter Hullihen
1944 Wilbur O. Sypherd
1946 William S. Carlson
1950 John A. Perkins
1967 John W. Shirley (Acting)
1968 E. Arthur Trabant

University of Denver

Denver, CO

1880 David H. Moore
1890 William F. McDowell

1899 Henry A. Buchtel
1922 Heber R. Harper
1928 Frederick M. Hunter
1935 David S. Duncan
1941 Caleb F. Gates, Jr.
1943 Ben M. Cherrington
1946 Caleb F. Gates, Jr.
1948 James F. Price
1948 Alfred C. Nelson
1949 Albert C. Jacobs
1953 Chester M. Alter
1967 Maurice B. Mitchell
1977 Ross Pritchard
1984 Dwight M. Smith

University of Detroit

Detroit, MI

1877 John B. Miege
1880 James J. Walshe
1885 John P. Frieden
1889 Michael P. Dowling
1893 Henry A. Schaapman
1897 James D. Foley
1902 Louis Kellinger
1907 Richard D. Slevin
1911 William F. Dooley
1915 William T. Doran
1921 John P. Nichols
1932 Albert H. Poetker
1939 Charles H. Cloud
1944 William J. Millor
1949 Celestin J. Steiner
1960 Laurence V. Britt
1966 Malcolm Carron
1979 Robert A. Mitchell

University of Florida

Gainesville, FL

1904 Andrew Sledd
1909 Albert A. Murphree
1928 John J. Tigert
1947 J. Hillis Miller
1953 John S. Allen (Acting)
1955 J. Wayne Reitz
1967 Stephen C. O'Connell
1974 Robert Q. Marston
1984 Marshall M. Criser

University of Georgia

Athens, GA

1801 Josiah Meigs
1811 John Brown
1816 Robert Finley
1817 Vacant
1819 Moses Waddel
1829 Alonzo Church
1860 Andrew A. Lipscomb

Chancellors

1874 Henry H. Tucker
1878 Patrick H. Mell
1888 William E. Boggs
1899 Walter B. Hill
1906 David C. Barrow
1926 Charles M. Snelling

Presidents

1932 Steadman V. Sanford

1935 Harmon W. Caldwell
1948 Johnathan C. Rogers
1950 Omer C. Aderhold
1967 Frederick C. Davison
1987 Henry K. Stanford
      (Acting)

University of Hawaii at Manoa

Honolulu, HI

(College of Agriculture and Mechanic Arts until 1911; College of Hawaii until 1920.)

1907 Willia T. Pope (Acting)
1908 John W. Gilmore
1913 John S. Donaghho
      (Acting)
1914 Arthur L. Dean
1927 David L. Crawford
1941 Arthur R. Keller
      (Acting)
1942 Gregg M. Sinclair
1955 Paul S. Bachman
1957 Willard Wilson (Acting)
1958 Laurence H. Snyder
1963 Thomas H. Hamilton
1968 Robert W. Hiatt (Acting)
1969 Harlan Cleveland
1974 Douglas S. Yamamura
1978 Howard P. McKaughan
1979 Durward Long
1981 Marvin J. Anderson
1984 Richard S. Kosaki

University of Houston

Houston, TX

1927 Edison E. Oberholtzer
1950 W. W. Kemmerer
1953 C. F. McElhinney
      (Acting)
1954 A. D. Bruce
1956 Clanton W. Williams
1961 Philip G. Hoffman
1980 Charles E. Bishop

University of Idaho

Moscow, ID

1892 Franklin B. Gault
1898 Joseph P. Blanton
1900 James A. MacLean
1914 Melvin A. Brannon
1917 Earnest H. Lindly
1920 Alfred H. Upham
1928 Frederick J. Kelly
1930 Mervin G. Neale
1937 Harrison C. Dale
1946 Jesse E. Buchanan
1954 Donald R. Theophilus
1965 Ernest W. Hartung
1977 Richard D. Gibb

University of Illinois

Urbana, IL

1867 John M. Gregory
1880 Selim H. Peabody

1891	Thomas J. Burrill (Acting)
1894	Andrew S. Draper
1904	Edmund J. James
1920	David Kinley
1930	Harry W. Chase
1933	Arthur H. Daniels (Acting)
1934	Arthur C. Willard
1946	George D. Stoddard
1953	Lloyd Morey
1955	David D. Henry
1971	John E. Corbally, Jr.
1979	Stanley Ikenberry
1984	Thomas E. Everhart (Chancellor)

University of Iowa

Iowa City, IA

1855	Amos Dean
1859	Silas Totten
1862	Oliver Spencer
1867	Nathan R. Leonard (Pro tem)
1868	James Black
1871	George Thacher
1877	Christian W. Slagle (Acting)
1878	Josiah L. Pickard
1887	Charles A. Schaeffer
1898	Amos N. Currier (Acting)
1899	George E. MacLean
1911	John G. Bowman
1914	Thomas H. MacBride
1916	Walter A. Jessup
1934	Eugene A. Gilmore
1940	Virgil M. Hancher
1964	Howard R. Bowen
1969	Willard L. Boyd
1982	James O. Freedman

University of Kansas

Lawrence, KS

1865	Robert W. Oliver
1867	John Fraser
1875	James Marvin
1883	Joshua A. Lippincott
1889	W. C. Spangler (Acting)
1890	Francis H. Snow
1901	W. C. Spangler (Acting)
1902	Frank Strong
1920	Ernest H. Lindley
1939	Deane W. Malott
1951	John H. Nelson (Acting)
1951	Franklin D. Murphy
1960	W. Clarke Wescoe
1969	James R. Surface (Acting)
1969	E. Lawrence Chalmers, Jr. Jr. (Chancellor)
1973	Archie R. Dykes (Chancellor)
1981	Gene A. Budig (Chancellor)

University of Kentucky

Lexington, KY

(Agricultural and Mechanical College of Kentucky until 1908.)

1865	John B. Bowman (Regent)
1866	John A. Williams (Presiding Officer)
1868	Joseph D. Pickett (Presiding Officer)
1869	James K. Patterson
1910	Henry S. Barker
1917	Frank L. McVey
1940	Thomas P. Cooper (Acting)
1941	Herman L. Donovan
1956	Frank G. Dickey
1963	John W. Oswald
1968	Albert D. Kirwan
1969	Otis A. Singletary

University of Louisville

Louisville, KY

1914	Y. A. Ford
1926	George Colvin
1928	John L. Patterson (Acting)
1929	Raymond A. Kent
1943	Einar W. Jacobsen
1946	Frederick W. Stamm (Acting)
1947	John W. Taylor
1950	Eli H. Brown, III (Acting)
1951	Philip Davidson
1968	Woodrow M. Strickler
1973	James G. Miller
1981	Donald C. Swain

University of Maine

Orono, ME

(Maine State College of Agriculture and the Mechanic Arts until 1897.)

1867	Merritt C. Fernald
1871	Charles F. Allen
1879	Merritt C. Fernald
1893	Abram W. Harris
1902	George E. Fellows
1910	Robert J. Aley
1922	Clarence C. Little
1925	Harold S. Boardman
1934	Arthur A. Hauck
1958	Charles E. Crossland (Acting)
1958	Lloyd H. Elliott
1965	H. Edwin Young
1968	Winthrop C. Libby
1972	Donald McNeil (Chancellor)
1975	Howard Neville
1979	Kenneth W. Allen (Acting)
1980	Paul H. Silverman
1984	Arthur M. Johnson
1987	Dale W. Lick

University of Maryland

College Park, MD

1813	Robert Smith
1815	James Kemp
1826	Roger B. Taney
1839	Ashton Alexander
1850	John P. Kennedy
1870	Severn T. Wallis
1894	Bernard Carter
1912	Henry Stockbridge, Jr. (Acting)
1913	Thomas B. Fell
1920	Albert F. Woods
1926	Raymond A. Pearson
1935	Harry C. Byrd
1954	Wilson H. Elkins
1976	Robert L. Gluckstern
1982	John B. Slaughter

University of Massachusetts

Amherst, MA

(Massachusetts Agricultural College until 1931; Massachusetts State College until 1947.)

1866	Paul A. Chadbourne
1867	William S. Clark
1879	Charles L. Flint
1880	Levi Stockbridge
1882	Paul A. Chadbourne
1883	James C. Greenough
1886	Henry H. Goodell
1905	William P. Brooks (Acting)
1906	Kenyon L. Butterfield
1924	Edward M. Lewis
1927	Roscoe W. Thatcher
1933	Hugh P. Baker
1947	Ralph A. Van Meter
1954	Jean Paul Mather
1960	John W. Lederle
1970	Robert C. Wood
1977	Randolph W. Bromery (Chancellor)
1978	Henry Koffler (Chancellor)
1982	Joseph Duffey (Chancellor)

Boston Campus

Chancellors

1964	John W. Ryan
1968	Francis L. Broderick
1975	Carlo L. Golino
1978	Barbara Van Ummersen
1979	Robert A. Corrigan

University of Miami

Coral Gables, FL

1926	Bowman F. Ashe
1953	Jay F. W. Pearson
1962	Henry K. Stanford
1981	Edward T. Foote, II

University of Michigan

Ann Arbor, MI

1852	Henry P. Tappan
1863	Erastus O. Haven
1869	Henry S. Frieze (Acting)
1871	James B. Angell
1909	Harry B. Hutchins
1920	Marion L. Burton
1925	Clarence C. Little
1929	Alexander G. Ruthven
1951	Harlan H. Hatcher
1968	Robben W. Fleming
1979	Allan F. Smith
1980	Harold T. Shapiro

University of Minnesota

Minneapolis, MN

1869	William W. Folwell
1884	Cyrus Northrop
1911	George E. Vincent
1917	Marion L. Burton
1920	Lotus D. Coffman
1938	Guy S. Ford
1941	Walter C. Coffey
1945	James L. Morrill
1960	Owen M. Wilson
1967	Malcolm C. Moos
1974	C. Peter Magrath
1985	Kenneth H. Keller

University of Mississippi

University, MS

Chancellors

1848	George F. Holmes
1849	Albert T. Bledsoe (Acting)
1849	Augustus B. Longstreet
1856	Frederick A. P. Barnard
1860	William D. Moore (Acting)
1865	John N. Waddell
1874	John J. Wheat (Acting)
1874	Alexander P. Stewart
1886	Edward Mayes
1891	Robert B. Fulton
1906	Alfred Hume (Acting)
1907	Andrew A. Kincannon
1914	Joseph N. Powers
1924	Alfred Hume
1930	Joseph N. Powers
1930	Christopher Longest (Acting)
1932	Alfred Hume
1935	Alfred B. Butts
1942	Alfred Hume (Acting)
1946	John D. Williams
1968	Porter L. Fortune, Jr.
1984	R. Gerald Turner

University of Missouri

Columbia, MO

1841	John H. Lathrop
1849	William W. Hudson (Acting)
1850	James Shannon
1856	William W. Hudson
1859	George H. Matthews (Chairman)

1860	Benjamin B. Minor
1862	John H. Lathrop (Chairman)
1866	Daniel Read
1876	Samuel S. Laws
1889	Michael M. Fisher (Chairman)
1891	Richard H. Jesse
1908	Albert R. Hill
1921	John C. Jones
1923	Isidor Loeb (Acting)
1923	Stratton D. Brooks
1930	Walter Williams
1935	Frederick A. Middlebush
1954	Elmer Ellis
1966	John C. Weaver
1970	C. Brice Ratchford
1974	H. W. Schooling (Chancellor)
1978	Barbara S. Uehling (Chancellor)

University of Montana

Missoula, MT

(University of Montana until 1913; State University of Montana until 1935; Montana State University until 1965.)

1895	Oscar J. Craig
1908	Clyde A. Duniway
1912	Edwin B. Craighead
1915	Frederick C. Scheuch (Acting)
1917	Edward O. Sisson
1921	Charles H. Clapp
1935	Frederick C. Scheuch (Acting)
1936	George F. Simmons
1941	Ernest O. Melby
1945	James A. McCain
1950	R. H. Jesse (Acting)
1951	Carl McFarland
1958	Gordon B. Castle (Acting)
1959	Harry K. Newburn
1963	Robert Johns
1966	Robert T. Pantzer
1974	Richard C. Bowers
1981	Neil S. Bucklew
1986	James V. Koch

University of Nebraska

Lincoln, NE

1871	Allen R. Benton
1876	Edmund B. Fairfield
1882	Henry E. Hitchcock (Acting)
1884	James I. Mannatt
1889	Charles E. Bessey (Acting)
1891	James H. Canfield
1895	George E. McLean
1899	Charles E. Bessey
1900	Elisha B. Andrews
1908	Samuel Avery
1927	Edgar A. Burnett
1938	Chauncey S. Boucher
1946	Reuben G. Gustavson
1953	John K. Selleck (Acting)
1954	Clifford M. Hardin
1969	Merk Hobson (Acting)
1970	Durward B. Varner

1972	James H. Zumberge (Chancellor)
1976	Roy A. Young (Chancellor)
1981	Martin Massengale (Chancellor)

University of Nebraska at Omaha

Omaha, NE

(University of Omaha until 1930; Municipal University of Omaha until 1968.)

1908	Daniel E. Jenkins
1917	Karl F. Whetstone
1926	Walter G. James
1928	Ernest Emery
1931	Walter G. James
1931	William E. Sealock
1935	Rowland Haynes
1948	P. Milo Bail
1965	Leland Traywick
1966	Kirk E. Naylor
1972	Ronald W. Roskens (Chancellor)
1977	Delbert D. Weber (Chancellor)

University of Nevada

Reno, NV

1887	LeRoy D. Brown
1890	Stephen A. Jones
1894	Joseph E. Stubbs
1914	Archer W. Hendrick
1917	Walter E. Clark
1939	Leon W. Hartman
1944	John O. Moseley
1950	Malcolm A. Love
1952	Minard W. Stout
1958	Charles J. Armstrong
1968	N. Edd Miller
1974	Max Milam
1978	Joseph N. Crowley

University of New Hampshire

Durham, NH

(New Hampshire College of Agriculture and Mechanic Arts until 1923.)

1891	Lyman D. Stevens
1893	Charles S. Murkland
1903	Charles H. Pettee (Acting)
1903	William D. Gibbs
1912	Charles H. Pettee (Acting)
1912	Edward T. Fairchild
1917	Charles H. Pettee (Acting)
1917	Ralph D. Hetzel
1927	Edward M. Lewis
1936	Roy D. Hunter (Acting)
1937	Fred Engelhardt
1944	Roy D. Hunter (Acting)
1944	Harold W. Stoke
1948	Arthur S. Adams
1950	Robert F. Chandler, Jr.

1954	Edward D. Eddy, Jr. (Acting)
1955	Eldon L. Johnson
1962	John F. Reed (Acting)
1962	Jere A. Chase (Acting)
1963	John W. McConnell
1972	Thomas Bonner
1974	Eugene S. Mills
1979	Bruce R. Poulton
1980	Evelyn E. Handler
1984	Gordon A. Haaland

University of New Mexico

Albuquerque, NM

1892	Elias S. Stover
1897	Clarence L. Herrick
1901	William G. Tight
1909	Edward M. Gray
1912	David R. Boyd
1919	David S. Hill
1927	James F. Zimmerman
1945	John P. Wernette
1948	Thomas L. Popejoy
1968	Ferrell Heady
1976	William Davis
1984	John Perovich
1985	Tom J. Farer
1987	Gerald W. May

University of North Carolina

Chapel Hill, NC

1804	Joseph Caldwell
1812	Robert H. Chapman
1817	Joseph Caldwell
1835	David L. Swain
1868	Solomon S. Pool
1876	Kemp P. Battle
1891	George T. Winston
1896	Edwin A. Alderman
1900	Francis P. Venable
1914	Edward K. Graham
1919	Harry W. Chase
1930	Frank P. Graham
1959	Gordon Gray
1966	William C. Friday
1972	Nelson F. Taylor (Chancellor)
1980	Christopher C. Fordham, III (Chancellor)

University of North Carolina at Greensboro

Greensboro, NC

(State Normal and Industrial College until 1919; North Carolina College for Women until 1932; Women's College of the University of North Carolina until 1963.)

1892	Charles D. McIver
1906	Julius I. Foust

Chancellors

1934	Walter C. Jackson
1950	Edward K. Graham
1956	W. W. Pierson, Jr. (Acting)

1957	Gordon W. Blackwell
1961	Otis Singletary
1966	James S. Ferguson
1979	William E. Moran

University of North Dakota

Grand Forks, ND

1884	William M. Blackburn
1885	Henry Montgomery (Acting)
1887	Homer B. Sprague
1891	Webster Merrifield
1909	Frank L. McVey
1918	Thomas F. Kane
1933	John C. West
1954	George W. Starcher
1971	Thomas J. Clifford

University of Northern Iowa

Cedar Falls, IA

(Iowa State Teachers College from 1909 to 1961; State College of Iowa from 1961 to 1967.)

1903	Homer H. Seerley
1928	Orval R. Latham
1940	Malcolm Price
1950	James W. Maucker
1970	John J. Kamerick
1983	Constantine W. Curris

University of Notre Dame

South Bend, IN

1842	Edward F. Sorin
1865	Patrick Dillon
1866	William Corby
1872	August Lemmonier
1874	Patrick Colovin
1877	William Corby
1881	Thomas E. Walsh
1893	Andrew Morrissey
1905	John W. Cavanaugh
1919	James A. Burns
1922	Matthew J. Walsh
1928	Charles L. O'Donnell
1934	John F. O'Hara
1940	J. Hugh O'Donnell
1946	John J. Cavanaugh
1952	Theodore M. Hesburgh

University of Oklahoma

Norman, OK

1892	David R. Boyd
1908	Arthur G. Evans
1911	Julien C. Monnet
1912	Stratton D. Brooks
1923	James S. Buchanan
1925	William B. Bizzell
1941	Joseph A. Brandt
1944	George L. Cross
1968	John H. Hollomon
1970	Peter K. McCarter (Interim)

1971	Paul F. Sharp	1843	Heman Dyer	1951	Cornelis W. deKiewiet
1979	William S. Banowsky	1849	David H. Riddle (Acting)	1962	W. Allen Wallis
1984	Martin C. Jischke	1855	John F. McLaren	1970	Robert W. Sproull
1985	Frank E. Horton	1858	George Woods	1984	G. Dennis O'Brien

1843 Heman Dyer
1849 David H. Riddle (Acting)
1855 John F. McLaren
1858 George Woods
1880 Milton B. Goff (Acting)
1881 Henry M. MacCracken
1884 Milton B. Goff
1891 William J. Holland
1901 John A. Brashear (Acting)
1904 Samuel B. McCormick
1921 John G. Bowman
1945 Rufus H. Fitzgerald
1955 Charles B. Nutting (Acting)
1956 Edward H. Litchfield
1965 Stanton H. Crawford (Acting)
1966 David H. Kurtzman
1967 Wesley W. Posvar

University of Oregon

Eugene, OR

1876 John W. Johnson
1893 Charles H. Chapman
1899 Frank Strong
1902 Prince L. Campbell
1926 Arnold B. Hall
1932 Vacant
1934 Clarence V. Boyer
1938 Donald M. Erb
1944 Orlando J. Hollis (Acting)
1945 Harry K. Newburn
1953 Victor P. Morris (Acting)
1954 O. Meredith Wilson
1960 William C. Jones (Acting)
1961 Arthur S. Flemming
1968 Charles E. Johnson (Acting)
1969 N. Ray Hawk (Acting)
1969 Robert D. Clark
1975 William B. Boyd
1980 Paul Olum

University of Pennsylvania

Philadelphia, PA

(College of Philadelphia until 1779.)

Provosts

1754 William Smith
1779 John Ewing
1802 Vacant
1806 John McDowell
1810 John Andrews
1813 Frederick Beasley
1828 William H. DeLancey
1834 John Ludlow
1854 Henry Vethake
1860 Daniel R. Goodwin
1868 Charles J. Stille
1881 William Pepper
1894 Charles C. Harrison
1910 Edgar F. Smith
1921 Josiah H. Penniman

Presidents

1930 Thomas S. Gates
1944 George W. McClelland
1948 Harold E. Stassen
1953 Gaylord P. Harnwell
1970 Martin Meyerson
1981 F. Sheldon Hackney

University of Pittsburgh

Pittsburgh, PA

(Western University of Pennsylvania until 1908.)

1819 Robert Bruce
1835 Gilbert Morgan
1836 Robert Bruce

University of Rhode Island

Kingston, RI

(Rhode Island College of Agriculture and Mechanic Arts until 1909; Rhode Island State College until 1951.)

1892 John H. Washburn
1902 Homer J. Wheeler (Acting)
1903 Kenyon L. Butterfield
1906 Howard Edwards
1930 John Barlow (Acting)
1931 Raymond G. Bressler
1940 John Barlow (Acting)
1941 Carl R. Woodward
1958 Francis H. Horn
1967 F. Don James (Acting)
1968 Werner A. Baum
1974 Frank Newman
1983 Edward D. Eddy

University of Richmond

Richmond, VA

(Richmond College until 1920.)

1840 Robert Ryland
1866 Tiberius G. Hones
1869 Bennett Puryear (Chairman)
1885 H. H. Harris (Chairman)
1889 Bennett Puryear (Chairman)
1895 F. W. Boatwright
1946 George M. Modlin
1971 E. Bruce Heilman

University of Rochester

Rochester, NY

1850 Ira Harris (Chancellor)

Presidents

1853 Martin B. Anderson
1890 David J. Hall
1896 Samuel A. Lattimore
1898 Henry F. Burton (Acting)
1900 Rush Rhees
1935 Alan Valentine

Chancellors

1970 W. Allen Wallis

University of San Francisco

San Francisco, CA

(St. Ignatius College until 1930.)

1855 Anthony Maraschi
1862 Nicholas Congiato
1865 Burchard Villiger
1866 Nicholas Congiato
1869 Joseph Bayma
1873 Aloysius Masnata
1876 John Pinasco
1880 Robert E. Kenna
1883 Joseph Sasia
1887 Henry Imoda
1893 Edward Allen
1896 John P. Frieden
1908 Joseph Saisa
1911 Albert Trivelli
1915 Patrick Foote
1919 Pius Moore
1925 Edward Whelan
1932 William Lonergan
1934 Harold Ring
1938 William Dunne
1954 John F. X. Connolly
1963 Charles Dullea
1969 Albert R. Jonsen
1972 William C. McInnes
1977 John J. LoSchiavo

University of Santa Clara

Santa Clara, CA

(Santa Clara College until 1912.)

1851 John Nobili
1856 Nicholas Congiato
1857 Felix Cicaterri
1861 Burchard Villiger
1865 Aloysius Masnata
1868 Aloysius Varsi
1876 Aloysius Brunengo
1880 John Pinasco
1883 Robert E. Kenna
1888 John Pinasco
1893 Joseph W. Riordan
1899 Robert E. Kenna
1905 Richard A. Gleeson
1910 James P. Morrissey
1913 Walter F. Thornton
1918 Timothy L. Murphy
1921 Zacheus J. Maher
1926 Cornelius J. McCoy
1932 James J. Lyons
1935 Louis C. Rudolph
1940 Charles J. Walsh
1945 William C. Gianera
1951 Herman J. Hauck
1958 Patrick A. Donohoe
1968 Thomas D. Terry
1976 William J. Rewak

University of South Carolina

Charleston, SC

1805 Jonathan Maxcy
1821 Thomas Cooper
1833 Vacant
1835 Robert W. Barnwell
1842 Robert Henry
1846 William C. Preston
1851 James H. Thornwell
1856 Charles F. McCay
1858 Augustus B. Longstreet
1862 (University closed)
1865 Robert W. Barnwell (Chairman)
1873 Vacant
1880 W. Porcher Miles
1882 John M. McBryde
1891 James Woodrow
1897 Frank C. Woodward
1902 Benjamin M. Sloan
1909 Samuel C. Mitchell
1914 William S. Currell
1922 William D. Melton
1927 Davison M. Douglas
1932 Leonard T. Baker
1935 James R. McKissick
1945 Norman M. Smith
1952 Donald S. Russell
1957 Robert L. Sumwalt
1962 Thomas F. Jones
1975 William Patterson
1979 James B. Holderman

University of South Dakota

Vermillion, SD

1882 Ephraim M. Epstein
1883 John W. Simonds
1885 John W. Herrick
1887 Edward Olson
1890 Howard B. Grose
1891 Joseph W. Mauck
1899 Garrett Droppers
1906 Benjamin F. Gault
1914 Robert L. Slagle
1929 Herman G. James
1935 I. D. Weeks
1966 Edward Q. Moulton
1968 Richard L. Bowen
1977 Charles D. Lein
1982 Joseph M. McFadden

University of South Florida

Tampa, FL

1957 John S. Allen
1970 Harris W. Dean (Acting)
1971 Maurice C. Mackey
1977 William Smith, Jr.
1978 John Lott Brown

University of Southern California

Los Angeles, CA

1880 Marion M. Bovard
1892 Joseph P. Widney

1895	George W. White
1903	George F. Bovard
1921	Rufus B. von KleinSmid
1947	Fred D. Fagg, Jr.
1958	Norman Topping
1970	John R. Hubbard
1980	James H. Zumberge

University of Tennessee

Knoxville, TN

(Blount College until 1809; East Tennessee College until 1840; East Tennessee University until 1879.)

1794	Samuel Carrick
1809	(College closed)
1820	David A. Sherman
1825	James McBath
1827	Charles Coffin
1833	James H. Piper
1834	Joseph Estabrook
1850	William B. Reese
1853	George Cooke
1858	W. D. Carnes
1860	J. J. Ridley
1862	(University closed)
1865	Thomas W. Humes
1883	Vacant
1887	Charles W. Dabney
1904	Brown Ayres
1919	Harcourt A. Morgan
1934	James D. Hoskins
1946	C. E. Brehm
1959	Andrew D. Holt
1970	Edward J. Boling (President)
1971	Archie R. Dykes (Chancellor)
1973	John W. Prados (Acting) (Chancellor)
1973	Jack E. Reese (Chancellor)

University of Texas

Austin, TX

1895	Leslie Waggener (Interim)
1896	George T. Winston
1899	William L. Prather
1905	David F. Houston
1908	Sidney E. Mezes
1914	William J. Battle (Interim)
1916	Robert E. Vinson
1923	William S. Sutton (Interim)
1924	Walter M. W. Splawn
1927	Harry Y. Benedict
1937	John W. Calhoun (Interim)
1939	Homer P. Rainey
1944	Theophilus S. Painter
1952	James C. Dolley
1953	Logan Wilson
1960	Harry H. Ransom
1961	Joseph R. Smiley
1963	Vacant
1967	Norman Hackerman
1970	Bryce Jorden (Interim)

Chancellors

1971	Charles A. LeMaistre
1979	E. Don Walker
1984	Hans M. Mark

Presidents

1971	Stephen H. Spurr
1976	Lorene L. Rogers
1980	Peter T. Flawn
1985	William H. Cunningham

University of the Pacific

Stockton, CA

(College of the Pacific from 1911 to 1961.)

1852	Edward Bannister
1854	M. C. Briggs
1856	William J. Maclay
1857	A. S. Gibbons
1859	Edward Bannister
1867	Thomas H. Sinex
1872	A. S. Gibbons
1877	C. S. Stratton
1887	A. C. Hirst
1891	Isaac Crook
1893	W. C. Sawyer (Acting)
1894	J. N. Beard
1896	Eli McClish
1906	M. S. Cross (Acting)
1908	William W. Guth
1913	B. J. Morris
1914	John L. Seaton
1919	Tully C. Knoles
1946	Robert E. Burns
1972	Stanley McCaffrey

University of the South

Sewanee, TN

1867	Charles T. Quintard
1872	Josiah Gorgas
1878	John B. Elliott (Acting)
1879	Telfair Hodgson
1890	Thomas F. Gailor
1893	Benjamin L. Wiggins
1909	William B. Hall
1914	Albion W. Knight
1922	Benjamin F. Finney
1938	Alexander Guerry
1948	George M. Baker (Acting)
1949	Cordes B. Green
1951	Edward McCrady
1971	James J. Bennett
1978	Robert M. Ayres, Jr.

University of Toledo

Toledo, OH

(Toledo University until 1921; University of the City of Toledo until 1947.)

1909	Jerome H. Raymond
1910	Charles A. Cockayne
1914	A. Monroe Stowe
1925	John W. Dowd
1926	Ernest A. Smith
1926	Lee W. MacKinnon (Acting)
1928	Henry J. Doermann
1932	Lee W. MacKinnon (Acting)
1933	Philip C. Nash
1947	Raymond L. Carter (Acting)

1947	Wilbur W. White
1951	Asa S. Knowles
1958	William S. Carlson
1972	Glen R. Driscoll
1985	James D. McComas

University of Tulsa

Tulsa, OK

1920	James M. Gordon
1924	Franklin G. Dill (Acting)
1927	John D. Finlayson (Chancellor)
1934	Ralph L. Langenheim (Acting)
1935	Clarence I. Pontius
1958	Ben G. Henneke
1967	Eugene L. Swearingen
1968	Joseph P. Twyman

University of Utah

Salt Lake City, UT

1894	James E. Talmage
1897	Joseph R. Kingsbury
1916	John A. Widsoe
1921	George Thomas
1941	LeRoy E. Cowles
1946	A. Ray Olpin
1964	James C. Fletcher
1973	David P. Gardner
1984	Chase N. Peterson

University of Vermont

Burlington, VT

1800	Daniel C. Sanders
1815	Samuel Austin
1821	Daniel Haskel
1825	Willard Preston
1826	James Marsh
1833	John Wheeler
1849	Worthington Smith
1855	Calvin Pease
1862	Joseph Torrey
1866	James B. Angell
1871	Matthew H. Buckham
1911	Guy P. Benton
1920	Guy W. Bailey
1941	John S. Millis
1950	William S. Carlson
1952	Carl W. Borgmann
1958	John T. Fey
1965	Shannon McCune
1966	Lyman S. Rowell
1970	Edward C. Andrews, Jr.
1975	W. Patterson (Acting)
1976	Lattie F. Coor

University of Virginia

Charlottesville, VA

1825	George Tucker
1826	Robley Dunglison
1827	John T. Lomax
1828	George Tucker
1828	Robley Dunglison
1830	Robert M. Patterson
1832	George Tucker
1833	Charles Bonnycastle
1835	John A. G. Davis

1837	Gessner Harrison
1839	John A. G. Davis
1840	Gessner Harrison
1842	Henry St. George Tucker
1844	William B. Rogers
1845	Edward H. Courteney
1846	James L. Cabell
1847	Gessner Harrison
1854	Socrates Maupin
1870	Charles S. Venable
1873	James F. Harrison
1886	Charles S. Venable
1888	William M. Thornton
1896	Paul B. Barringer
1904	Edwin A. Alderman
1931	John L. Newcomb
1947	Colgate W. Darden, Jr.
1959	Edgar F. Shannon, Jr.
1974	Frank L. Hereford, Jr.
1985	Robert M. O'Neil

University of Washington

Seattle, WA

1861	Asa S. Mercer
1863	William E. Barnard
1866	George F. Whitworth
1867	University closed
1869	John H. Hall
1872	Eugene K. Hill
1874	University closed
1874	George F. Whitworth
1876	University closed
1877	Alexander J. Anderson
1882	Leonard J. Powell
1887	Thomas M. Gatch
1895	Mark W. Harrington
1897	William F. Edwards
1897	Charles F. Reeves (Acting)
1898	Frank P. Graves
1902	Thomas F. Kane
1914	Henry Landes (Acting)
1915	Henry Suzzallo
1926	David Thomson (Acting)
1927	Matthew L. Spencer
1933	Hugh Winkenwerder (Acting)
1934	Lee P. Sieg
1946	Raymond B. Allen
1952	H. P. Everest (Acting)
1952	Henry Schmitz
1958	Charles E. Odegaard
1974	John R. Hogness
1979	William P. Gerberding

University of Wisconsin

Madison, WI

1849	John H. Lathrop
1859	Henry Barnard
1861	John W. Sterling
1867	Paul A. Chadbourne
1871	John Twombly
1874	John Bascom
1887	Thomas C. Chamberlin
1892	Charles K. Adams
1901	Edward A. Birge (Acting)
1903	Charles R. Van Hise
1918	Edward A. Birge
1925	Glenn Frank
1937	George C. Sellery (Acting)
1937	Clarence A. Dykstra
1945	Edwin B. Fred

1958	Conrad A. Elvehjem
1962	Fred H. Harrington
1970	Robert L. Clodius
1971	John C. Weaver

University of Wisconsin, Eau Claire

Eau Claire, WI

(Eau Claire State Teachers College until 1951; Wisconsin State College at Eau Claire until 1964; Wisconsin State University, Eau Claire until 1971.)

1927	Harvey A. Schofield
1941	W. R. Davies
1959	Leonard Haas
1980	Mary-Emily Hannah
1985	Larry G. Schnack

University of Wisconsin, La Crosse

La Crosse, WI

(La Crosse State Teachers College until 1951; Wisconsin State College, La Crosse until 1964: Wisconsin State University, La Crosse until 1971.)

1927	George M. Snodgrass
1939	Rexford S. Mitchell
1966	Samuel G. Gates
1971	Kenneth E. Lindner
1979	W. Carl Wimberly (Acting)
1980	Noel J. Richards

University of Wisconsin, Milwaukee

Milwaukee, WI

(Wisconsin State College, Milwaukee and Milwaukee facility of University of Wisconsin Extension Division merged under this name in 1955.)

1956	J. Martin Klotsche
1973	Werner A. Baum
1980	Frank E. Horton
1985	Norma S. Rees (Acting)

University of Wisconsin, Platteville

Platteville, WI

(Platteville State Teachers College until 1951; Wisconsin State College, Platteville until 1959; Wisconsin State College and Institute of Technology, Platteville until 1964; Wisconsin State University, Platteville until 1971.)

1927	Asa M. Royce
1944	Chester O. Newlun
1958	Bjarne R. Ullsvik
1975	Warren P. Carrier
1983	William W. Chmurny

University of Wisconsin, River Falls

River Falls, WI

(River Falls State Teachers College until 1951; Wisconsin State College at River Falls until 1964; Wisconsin State University, River Falls until 1971.)

1927	Jesse H. Ames
1946	Eugene H. Kleinpell
1967	Richard J. Delorit (Interim)
1968	George R. Field
1985	Gary A. Thibodeau

University of Wisconsin, Stevens Point

Stevens Point, WI

(Central State Teachers College until 1951; Wisconsin State College until 1963; Wisconsin State University, Stevens Point until 1971.)

1927	Robert D. Baldwin
1930	Frank S. Hyer
1938	Phillip H. Falk
1939	Ernest T. Smith
1940	William C. Hansen
1962	James H. Albertson
1967	Lee S. Dreyfus
1979	Philip R. Marshall

University of Wisconsin, Superior

Superior, WI

(State Teachers College, Superior until 1952; Wisconsin State College, Superior until 1964; Wisconsin State University, Superior until 1971.)

1927	Arthur D. S. Gillett
1931	Jin D. Hill
1964	Karl W. Meyer

University of Wisconsin, Whitewater

Whitewater, WI

(Whitewater State Teachers College until 1951; Wisconsin State College, Whitewater until 1964; Wisconsin State University, Whitewater until 1971.)

1927	Frank S. Hyer
1930	Claude M. Yoder
1946	Robert C. Williams
1962	Walker W. Wyman
1967	Cord O. Wells (Acting)
1967	William L. Carter
1974	James R. Connor

University of Wyoming

Laramie, WY

1887	John W. Hoyt
1891	Albinus A. Johnson
1896	Frank P. Graves
1898	Elmer E. Smiley
1903	Charles W. Lewis
1904	Frederick M. Tisdel
1912	Clyde A. Duniway
1917	Aven Nelson
1922	Arthur G. Crane
1942	James L. Morrill
1945	John A. Hill (Acting)
1945	George D. Humphrey
1964	John T. Fey
1966	John E. King, Jr.
1967	H. T. Person
1968	William D. Carlson
1979	Edward H. Jennings
1981	Donald L. Veal

Valparaiso University

Valparaiso, IN

(Northern Indiana Normal School until 1900; Valparaiso College until 1907.)

1873	Henry B. Brown
1912	Oliver P. Kinsey (Acting)
1919	Henry K. Brown
1920	Daniel R. Hodgdon
1921	John E. Roessler
1922	Milo J. Bowman
1923	Horace M. Evans
1926	John C. Baur
1926	William H. T. Dau
1930	Oscar C. Kreinheder
1939	Walter G. Friedrich (Acting)
1940	Otto P. Kretzmann
1968	Albert G. Huegli
1978	Robert V. Schnabel

Vanderbilt University

Nashville, TN

1875	Landon C. Garland
1893	James H. Kirkland
1937	Oliver C. Carmichael
1946	Harvie Branscomb
1963	Alexander Heard (Chancellor)
1982	Joe B. Wyatt (Chancellor)

Vassar College

Poughkeepsie, NY

1861	Milo P. Jewett
1864	John H. Raymond
1878	Samuel L. Caldwell
1885	J. Ryland Kendrick (Acting)
1886	James M. Taylor
1915	Henry M. MacCracken
1946	Sarah G. Blanding
1964	Alan Simpson
1977	Virginia B. Smith
1987	Frances Daly Ferusson

Villanova University

Villanova, PA

1843	John P. O'Dwyer
1847	William Harnett
1848	John P. O'Dwyer
1850	William Harnett
1851	Patrick E. Moriarty
1855	William Harnett
1857	University closed
1865	Ambrose Mullen
1869	Patrick Stanton
1872	Thomas Galberry
1876	Thomas Middleton
1878	John Fedigan
1880	Joseph Coleman
1886	Francis Sheeran
1890	Christopher McEvoy
1894	Francis McShane
1895	Lawrence Delurey
1910	Edward G. Dohan
1917	James Dean
1920	Francis A. Driscoll
1924	Joseph A. Hickey
1925	Mortimer A. Sullivan
1926	James H. Griffin
1932	Edward V. Stanford
1944	Francis X. N. McGuire
1954	James A. Donnellon
1959	John A. Klekotka
1965	Joseph A. Flaherty
1967	Robert J. Welsh
1972	Edward McCarthy
1975	John M. Driscoll

Virginia Military Institute

Lexington, VA

1839	Francis H. Smith
1890	Scott Shipp
1907	Edward W. Nichols
1924	William H. Cocke
1929	John A. LeJeune
1937	Charles E. Kilbourne
1946	Richard J. Marshall
1952	William H. Milton, Jr.
1960	George R. E. Shell
1971	Richard L. Irby
1981	Sam S. Walker

Virginia Polytechnic Institute and State University

Blacksburg, VA

(Virginia Agricultural and Mechanical College until 1896; Virginia Agricultural and Mechanical College and Polytechnic Institute until 1944; Virginia Polytechnic Institute until 1970.)

1872	Charles L. C. Minor
1880	John L. Buchanan
1882	Thomas N. Conrad
1886	Lunsford L. Lomax
1891	John M. McBryde
1907	Paul B. Barringer
1913	Joseph D. Eggleston
1919	Julian A. Burruss
1945	John R. Hutcheson
1947	Walter S. Newman
1962	Thomas M. Hahn, Jr.
1975	William E. Lavery

Wabash College

Crawfordsville, IN

1834 Elihu W. Baldwin
1841 Charles White
1862 Joseph F. Tuttle
1892 George S. Burroughs
1899 William P. Kane
1907 George L. Mackintosh
1926 Louis B. Hopkins
1941 Frank H. Sparks
1955 Byron K. Trippet
1966 Paul W. Cook, Jr.
1969 Thaddeus Seymour
1978 Lewis S. Salter

Wake Forest University

Winston-Salem, NC

(Wake Forest College until 1967.)

1834 Samuel Wait
1845 William Hooper
1849 John B. White
1854 Washington M. Wingate
1879 Thomas H. Pritchard
1882 Vacant
1884 Charles E. Taylor
1905 William L. Poteat
1927 Francis P. Gaines
1930 Thurman D. Kitchin
1950 Harold W. Tribble
1967 James R. Scales
1983 Thomas K. Hearn, Jr.

Washburn University of Topeka

Topeka, KS

(Washburn College until 1942; Washburn Municipal University of Topeka until 1952.)

1869 H. Q. Butterfield
1871 Peter MacVicar
1896 George M. Herrick
1902 Norman Plass
1909 Frank K. Sanders
1915 Parley P. Womer
1931 Philip C. King
1942 Bryan S. Stoffer
1961 Harold E. Sponberg
1965 John W. Henderson
1981 John L. Green, Jr.

Washington and Jefferson College

Washington, PA

(Formed in 1866 by merger of Jefferson College and Washington College.)

1866 Jonathan Edwards
1869 Samuel J. Wilson (Pro tem)
1870 James I. Brownson
1870 George P. Hays
1882 James D. Moffat
1915 Frederick W. Hinitt
1915 Vacant
1918 William E. Slemmons

(Pro tem)
1919 Samuel C. Black
1922 Simon S. Baker
1932 Ralph C. Hutchison
1946 James H. Case, Jr.
1950 Boyd C. Patterson
1970 Howard J. Burnett

Washington and Lee University

Lexington, VA

(Liberty Hall Academy from 1782 to 1798; Washington Academy until 1813; Washington College until 1871.)

1782 William Graham
1797 Samuel L. Campbell
1799 George A. Baxter
1830 Louis Marshall
1834 Henry Vethake
1836 Henry Ruffner
1848 George Junkin
1865 Robert E. Lee
1871 George W. C. Lee
1897 William L. Wilson
1900 Henry St. George Tucker (Acting)
1901 George H. Denny
1911 Henry D. Campbell (Acting)
1911 John L. Campbell (Acting)
1912 Henry L. Smith
1930 Robert H. Tucker (Acting)
1930 Francis P. Gaines
1959 Fred C. Cole
1967 William W. Pusey, III (Acting)
1968 Robert E. R. Huntley
1983 John D. Wilson

Washington College

(Merged with Jefferson College in 1866 to form Washington and Jefferson College.)

1806 Matthew Brown
1817 Andrew Wylie
1828 Vacant
1830 David Elliot
1831 Davic McConaughy
1850 James Clark
1852 James I. Brownson (Pro tem)
1853 John W. Scott

Washington State University

Pullman, WA

(Washington State Agricultural College and School of Science until 1892; Agricultural College, Experiment Station, and School of Science until 1905; State College of Washington until 1959.)

1891 George X. Lilley
1892 John W. Heston
1893 Enoch A. Bryan
1916 Ernest O. Holland
1945 Wilson M. Compton
1951 William A. Pearl (Acting)
1952 C. Clement French
1966 Wallis Beasley (Acting)
1967 Glenn Terrell, Jr.
1985 Samuel H. Smith

Washington University

St. Louis, MO

1858 Joseph G. Hoyt
1862 William Chauvenet
1869 Benjamin Tweed (Acting)
1870 William G. Eliot
1887 Marshall S. Snow (Acting)
1891 Winfield S. Chaplin (Acting)
1907 Marshall S. Snow (Acting)
1908 David F. Houston
1913 Frederic A. Hall
1923 Herbert S. Hadley
1927 George R. Throop
1944 Harry B. Wallace (Acting)
1945 Arthur H. Compton
1953 Ethan A. H. Shepley
1961 Carl Tolman
1962 Thomas H. Eliot
1971 William H. Danforth

Wayne State University

Detroit, MI

(Wayne University until 1956.)

1933 Frank Cody
1942 Warren Bow
1945 David Henry
1952 Clarence Hilberry
1965 William R. Keast
1972 George Cullen
1978 Thomas N. Bonner
1982 David W. Adamany

Waynesburg College

Waynesburg, PA

1849 Joshua Loughran
1855 Jonathan P. Weethee
1858 John C. Flenniken (Acting)
1859 Alfred B. Miller
1899 J. W. McKay (Acting)
1900 Archelaus E. Turner
1904 Alvin F. Lewis
1905 J. F. Bucher
1908 William M. Hudson
1911 Henry Patton (Acting)
1912 Ezra F. Baker
1915 Herbert P. Houghton
1918 J. W. McKay
1921 Paul R. Stewart
1963 Bennett M. Rich
1974 Joseph F. Marsh, Jr.

1983 J. Thomas Mills, Jr.

Wellesley College

Wellesley, MA

1875 Ada Howard
1881 Alice Freeman
1887 Helen Shafer
1894 Julia Irvine
1899 Caroline Hazard
1911 Ellen F. Pendleton
1936 Mildred M. Horton
1949 Margaret Clapp
1966 Ruth M. Adams
1972 Barbara W. Newell
1980 Carol J. Johns (Acting)
1981 Nannerl Overholser Keohane

Wells College

Aurora, NY

1868 William W. Howard
1869 S. Irenaeus Prime
1873 Thomas C. Strong
1875 Edward S. Frisbee
1894 William E. Waters
1900 Jasper W. Freley (Acting)
1904 George M. Ward
1912 Thomas J. Preston, Jr.
1912 Robert Zabriskie (Acting)
1913 Kerr D. Macmillan
1936 William E. Weld
1946 Richard L. Greene
1950 Jerome H. Bentley
1951 Louis J. Long
1969 John D. Wilson
1976 Frances Farenthold
1980 Patti McGill Peterson

Wesleyan University

Middletown, CT

1831 Wilbur Fisk
1839 Stephen Olin
1841 Nathan Bangs
1842 Stephen Olin
1852 Augustus W. Smith
1857 Joseph Cummings
1875 Cyrus D. Foss
1880 John W. Beach
1887 John M. Van Vleck (Acting)
1889 Bradford P. Raymond
1909 William A. Shanklin
1923 Leroy A. Howland (Acting)
1925 James L. McConaughy
1943 Victor L. Butterfield
1967 Edwin D. Etherington
1970 Colin G. Campbell

West Virginia University

Morgantown, WV

1867 Alexander Martin
1875 John W. Scott (Acting)
1877 John R. Thompson
1881 Daniel B. Purinton (Acting)
1882 William L. Wilson

1883 Vacant
1885 Eli M. Turner
1893 Powell B. Reynolds
 (Acting)
1895 James L. Goodnight
1897 Robert A. Armstrong
 (Acting)
1897 Jerome H. Raymond
1901 Powell B. Reynolds
 (Acting)
1901 Daniel B. Purinton
1911 Alexander R. Whitehill
 (Acting)
1911 Thomas E. Hodges
1914 Frank B. Trotter
1928 John R. Turner
1935 Robert A. Armstrong
 (Acting)
1935 Chauncey S. Boucher
1938 Charles E. Lawall
1945 Charles T. Neff, Jr.
 (Acting)
1946 Irvin Stewart
1958 Clyde Colson (Acting)
1959 Elvis J. Stahr, Jr.
1962 Paul A. Miller
1966 Harry B. Heflin (Acting)
1967 James G. Harlow
1977 Gene A. Budig
1981 E. Gordon Gee
1985 Diane L. Reinhard
1986 Neil S. Bucklew

Western Michigan University

Kalamazoo, MI

(Western State Normal School until 1927; Western State Teachers College until 1941; Western Michigan College of Education until 1955.)

1903 Dwight B. Waldo
1936 Paul V. Sangren
1961 James W. Miller
1974 John T. Bernhard
1985 Diether H. Haenicke

Western Reserve University

Cleveland, OH

(Merged in 1967 with Case Institute of Technology to form Case Western Reserve University.)

1830 Charles B. Storrs
1834 George E. Pierce
1855 Henry L. Hitchcock
1871 Carroll Cutler
1887 Hiram C. Haydn
1890 Charles F. Thwing
1921 James D. Williamson
 (Acting)
1923 Robert E. Vinson
1933 Winfred G. Leutner
1949 John S. Millis

Westminster College

Fulton, MO

1855 Samuel S. Laws

1864 John Montgomery
1865 Michael M. Fisher
 (Acting)
1868 Nathan L. Rice
1874 Michael M. Fisher
 (Acting)
1877 Charles C. Hersman
1887 William H. Marquess
1894 Edward C Gordon
1897 John J. Rice (Acting)
1899 John H. MacCracken
1903 John J. Rice (Acting)
1904 David R. Kerr
1911 Charles B. Boving
1914 John J. Rice (Acting)
1915 Elmer E. Reed
1926 Marion E. Melvin
1933 Franc L. McCluer
1947 William W. Hall
1955 Robert L. D. Davidson
1973 Dale Purcell
1977 J. Harvey Saunders

Wichita State University

Wichita, KS

(Fairmont College from 1895 to 1926; Municipal University of Wichita until 1964.)

1895 N. J. Morrison
1908 Henry E. Thayer
1915 Walter H. Rollins
1926 John D. Finlayson
1928 H. W. Foght
1934 W. M. Jardine
1949 Harry F. Corbin
1963 Emory Lindquist
1968 Clark D. Ahlberg
1983 Warren B. Armstrong

Wilberforce University

Wilberforce, OH

1856 M. P. Gaddis
1857 James K. Parker
1858 Richard S. Rust
1863 D. A. Payne
1876 Benjamin F. Lee
1884 S. T. Mitchell
1900 J. H. Jones
1908 W. S. Scarborough
1920 J. A. Gregg
1924 G. H. Jones
1932 Charles H. Wesley
1932 R. R. Wright, Jr.
1936 D. Ormonde Walker
1941 R. R. Wright, Jr.
1942 Charles H. Wesley
1947 Charles L. Hill
1956 Rembert E. Stokes
1977 Charles E. Taylor
1984 Yvonne Walker-Taylor

Willamette University

Salem, OR

1853 Francis S. Hoyt
1860 Thomas M. Gatch
1865 Joseph H. Wythe
1867 Luther T. Woodward
1868 Nelson Rounds
1870 Thomas M. Gatch
1879 Charles E. Lambert

1880 Thomas Van Scoy
1891 George Whitaker
1893 Willis C. Hawley
1902 John Coleman
1907 Fletcher Homan
1914 George H. Alden
 (Acting)
1915 Carl G. Doney
1934 Bruce R. Baxter
1941 Carl S. Knopf
1942 George H. Smith
1969 Robert J. Fritz
1974 Robert Lisensky
1980 Jerry E. Hudson

William Jewell College

Liberty, MO

1853 Robert S. Thomas
1857 William Thompson
1868 Thomas Rambaut
1873 William R. Rothwell
1883 James G. Clark
1892 John P. Greene
1920 David J. Evans
1923 H. C. Wayman
1928 John F. Herget
1942 H. I. Hester (Interim)
1943 Walter P. Binns
1962 Minetry L. Jones
 (Interim)
1962 H. Guy Moore
1968 B. G. Olson (Interim)
1969 E. W. Holzapfel
1970 Thomas S. Field
1980 J. Gordon Kingsley

William Paterson College of New Jersey

Wayne, NJ

(Paterson State Teachers College from 1937 to 1954; Paterson State College from 1954 to 1971.)

1937 Clair S. Wightman
1954 Marion E. Shea
1966 Michael B. Gilligan
 (Acting)
1967 James J. Forcina (Acting)
1968 James K. Olsen
1973 Frank Zanfino (Acting)
1973 William J. McKeefery
1977 Seymour C. Hyman
1986 Arnold Speert

Williams College

Williamstown, MA

1793 Ebenezer Fitch
1815 Zephaniah S. Moore
1821 Edward D. Griffin
1836 Mark Hopkins
1872 Paul A. Chadbourne
1881 Franklin Carter
1901 John H. Hewitt (Acting)
1902 Henry Hopkins
1908 Harry A. Garfield
1934 Tyler Dennett
1937 James P. Baxter, III
1961 John E. Sawyer
1973 John W. Chandler
1985 Francis C. Oakley

Wittenberg University

Springfield, OH

(Wittenberg College until 1959.)

1845 Ezra Keller
1848 Michael Diehl (Acting)
1849 Samuel Sprecher
1874 John B. Helwig
1882 Samuel A. Ort
1900 John M. Ruthrauff
1902 Samuel A. Ort
1903 Charles G. Heckert
1920 Rees E. Tulloss
1949 Clarence C. Stoughton
1963 John N. Stauffer
1969 G. Kenneth Andeen
1974 William A. Kinnison

Wofford College

Spartanburg, SC

1854 William M. Wightman
1859 Albert M. Shipp
1875 James H. Carlisle
1902 Henry N. Snyder
1942 Walter K. Greene
1951 Clarence C. Norton
 (Acting)
1952 Francis P. Gaines
1957 Philip S. Covington
 (Acting)
1958 Charles F. Marsh
1968 Paul Hardin
1972 Joab M. Lesesne, Jr.

Worcester Polytechnic Institute

Worcester, MA

1868 Charles O. Thompson
1883 Homer T. Fuller
1894 Thomas C. Mendenhall
1901 Edmund A. Engler
1911 Levi L. Conant (Acting)
1913 Ira N. Hollis
1925 Ralph Earle
1939 Francis W. Roys (Acting)
1939 Wat Tyler Cluverius
1952 Francis W. Roys (Acting)
1953 Alvin E. Cormeny
1954 Francis W. Roys (Acting)
1955 Arthur B. Bronwell
1962 Harry P. Storke
1969 George W. Hazzard
1978 Edmund T. Cranch
1987 Jon C. Strauss

Xavier University

Cincinnati, OH

1831 James I. Mullon
1834 John B. Purcell
1840 John A. Elet
1847 J. E. Blox
1848 John DeBlieck
1851 George A. Carrell
1853 Isidor Boudreaux
1856 M. Oakley
1861 John Schultz
1865 W. H. Hill
1869 Thomas O'Neil

1871	Leopold Bushart
1874	Edward A. Higgins
1878	Thomas O'Neil
1879	Rudolph J. Meyer
1881	John I. Coghlan
1884	Henry Moeller
1885	Edward A. Higgins
1887	Henry Schapman
1893	Alexander J. Burrowes
1896	Michael J. O'Connor
1900	Albert A. Dierckes
1907	Joseph Grimmelsman
1911	Francis Heiermann
1916	James McCabe
1922	Hubert F. Brockman
1930	Hugo F. Sloctemyer

1934	Dennis F. Burns
1940	Celestin J. Steiner
1949	James F. Maguire
1955	Paul L. O'Connor
1972	Robert W. Mulligan
1982	Charles L. Currie

Yale University

New Haven, CT

(Collegiate School until 1718; Yale College until 1872.)

1701	Abraham Pierson (Rector)

1707	Samuel Andrew (Rector)
1719	Timothy Cutler (Rector)
1722	Vacant
1726	Elisha Williams (Rector)
1740	Thomas Clap
1766	Naphtali Daggett (Pro tem)
1778	Ezra Stiles
1795	Timothy Dwight
1817	Jeremiah Day
1846	Theodore D. Woolsey
1871	Noah Porter
1886	Timothy Dwight
1899	Arthur T. Hadley
1921	James R. Angell
1937	Charles Seymour

1950	A. Whitney Griswold
1963	Kingman Brewster, Jr.
1978	A. Bartlett Giamatti
1986	Benno C. Schmidt, Jr.

XIII
Foundation Presidents

Foundation Presidents

Allis Chalmers Foundation, Inc.

1951 W. A. Roberts
1955 R. S. Stevenson
1969 David C. Scott
1984 Wendell F. Bueche

Allstate Foundation

1952 Calvin Fentress, Jr.
1957 Judson B. Branch
1975 Archie R. Boe
1982 Donald F. Craib, Jr.

Amax Foundation, Inc.

(American Metal Climax Foundation, Inc. until 1977.)

1956 Arthur H. Bunker
1958 Thomas W. Childs
1959 Ian K. MacGregor
1964 Frank X. White
1966 Donald J. Donahue
1968 John F. Frawley
1969 Roger C. Sonnemann
1975 F. Taylor Ostrander
1983 H. A. Sawyer, Jr.
1985 Sonja B. Weill

American Can Company Foundation

1960 R. J. Sund
1965 W. C. Stolk
1966 William F. May
1980 William S. Woodside

M. D. Anderson Foundation

1936 M. D. Anderson
1939 W. B. Bates
1949 John H. Freeman
1979 Leon Jaworski
1983 Aylmer G. McNeese, Jr.
1985 Hugh Q. Buck

M. L. Annenberg Foundation

1944 Walter H. Annenberg

Vincent Astor Foundation

1949 Vincent Astor
1960 Brooke Astor

Mary Reynolds Babcock Foundation, Inc.

1953 Charles H. Babcock
1968 Katharine B. Mountcastle
1975 Jay P. Babcock
1977 Zachary T. Smith, II
1979 Kenneth F. Mountcastle, Jr.
1980 Katharine B. Mountcastle
1986 L. Richardson Preyer

George F. Baker Trust

1942 Sheridan A. Logan
1966 G. Sealy Newell
1979 Charles A. Dunn
1982 Miss Rocio Suarez

Mary Louise Curtis Bok Foundation

1932 Mary Louise Curtis Bok
1969 Cary W. Bok

Lynde and Harry Bradley Foundation, Inc.

(Allen-Bradley Foundation, Inc. until 1985.)

1942 Harry L. Bradley
1955 Louis Quarles
1967 Arloe W. Paul
1970 I. Andrew Rader

Brown Foundation, Inc. (Texas)

1951 Herman Brown
1962 George R. Brown
1979 Merrill L. Nash
1981 George R. Brown
1985 Nancy B. Negley
1986 Maconda B. O'Connor

Callaway Foundation, Inc.

1943 Fuller E. Callaway, Jr.
1949 Willis E. Howard
1952 Arthur B. Edge, Jr.
1970 Horace B. Thom
1977 J. T. Gresham

Carnegie Corporation of New York

1920 James R. Angell
1921 Henry S. Pritchett
1923 Frederick P. Keppel
1941 Walter A. Jessup
1945 Devereaux C. Josephs
1948 Charles Dollard
1955 John W. Gardner
1967 Alan Pifer
1983 David A. Hamburg

Amon G. Carter Foundation

1945 Amon G. Carter
1955 Amon G. Carter, Jr.
1982 Ruth Carter Stevenson

Chartor Foundation

1953 Aaron J. Farfel

Chrysler Corporation Fund

1953 Howard J. Pridmore
1953 George W. Troost
1956 Frank W. Misch
1967 Tom Killefer
1977 Gwain H. Gillespie
1979 W. W. Larsen
1985 James L. Tolley

Clark Foundation

1931 Edward S. Clark
1934 Stephen C. Clark
1960 Charles E. Main
1963 Stephen C. Clark, Jr.

Robert Sterling Clark Foundation, Inc.

1953 Robert Sterling Clark
1959 Francine J. M. Clark
1962 Hugo Kohlmann
1966 Eugene W. Goodwillie
1977 Winslow M. Lovejoy, Jr.

Commonwealth Fund

1918 Edward S. Harkness
1940 Malcolm P. Aldrich
1963 James Q. Newton, Jr.
1974 Carleton B. Chapman
1981 Margaret E. Mahoney

S. H. Cowell Foundation

1956 Max Thelen
1970 Max Thelen, Jr.

Crown Zellerbach Foundation

1952 James D. Zellerbach
1963 Richard G. Shephard
1981 Charles E. Stine

Cummins Engine Foundation

1954 J. Irwin Miller
1970 R. B. Stoner
1972 James A. Joseph
1979 James A. Henderson

Danforth Foundation

1951 Kenneth I. Brown
1961 Merrimon Cuninggim
1973 Gene L. Schwilck

Henry L. And Grace Doherty Charitable Foundation, Inc.

1947 Grace Doherty
1949 Helen Lee Wessel Lassen
1965 Walter L. Brown
1977 Dorothy R. McCall

1985 Walter L. Brown

Duke Endowment

1925 George V. Allen
1960 Thomas L. Perkins
1977 Richard B. Henney
1980 John F. Day

El Pomar Foundation

1937 Spencer Penrose
1939 Julie V. L. Penrose
1956 Charles L. Tutt
1961 William T. Tutt
1977 Russell T. Tutt
1983 William J. Hybl

Exxon Education Foundation

(Esso Education Foundation until 1972.)

1955 Claude L. Alexander
1959 George M. Buckingham
1971 M. M. Brisco
1972 C. C. Garvin, Jr.
1977 Stephen Stamas
1979 Robert L. Payton

Samuel S. Fels Fund

1936 Samuel S. Fels
1950 Jerome J. Rothschild
1956 Lewis M. Stevens
1963 Nochem S. Winnet

First National City Bank Foundation

1967 Carl W. Desch

Ford Foundation

1936 Edsel Ford
1943 Henry Ford II
1950 Paul G. Hoffman
1953 H. Rowan Gaither, Jr.
1956 Henry T. Heald
1966 McGeorge Bundy
1979 Franklin A. Thomas

Charles A. Frueauff Foundation, Inc.

1950 Harry D. Frueauff
1959 Lena R. Frueauff
1968 Harry D. Frueauff, Jr.

General Foods Fund, Inc.

1953 William M. Robbins
1956 L. E. Waterbury

1960 A. F. Watters
1961 L. F. Genz
1977 David M. Brush

William T. Grant Foundation, Inc.

(Grant Foundation, Inc. until 1977.)

1936 William T. Grant
1947 Perrin C. Galpin
1955 John G. Byler
1965 Douglas D. Bond
1977 Philip Sapir
1979 R. McAllister Lloyd
1980 Robert J. Haggerty

John Simon Guggenheim Memorial Foundation

1925 Simon Guggenheim
1942 Olga H. Guggenheim
1961 Henry A. Moe
1963 Gordon N. Ray
1985 Joel Conarroe

Solomon R. Guggenheim Foundation

1937 Solomon R. Guggenheim
1957 Harry F. Guggenheim
1970 Peter O. Lawson-Johnston

Charles Hayden Foundation

1937 J. Willard Hayden
1955 Edgar A. Doubleday
1968 William T. Wachenfeld

M. S. Hershey Foundation

1936 M. S. Hershey
1945 P. A. Staples
1957 C. Paul Witmer
1960 James E. Bobb
1977 John O. Hershey
1983 Susan Fowler

Houston Endowment Inc.

1953 John T. Jones, Jr.
1964 J. Howard Creekmore

Hyde and Watson Foundation

(Lillia Babbitt Hyde Foundation until 1985.)

1924 Lillia Babbitt Hyde
1939 Charles C. Harris
1959 Robert W. Parsons

1969 Robert W. Parsons, Jr.

Inland Steel-Ryerson Foundation, Inc.

1945 Edward L. Ryerson
1956 Leigh B. Block
1965 Lemuel B. Hunter
1969 Robert J. Greenebaum
1982 Otto R. Nottelmann

W. Alton Jones Foundation, Inc.

1944 W. Alton Jones
1962 Nettie M. Jones
1971 James P. Farrell
1981 Nettie M. Jones
1983 H. W. Foster
1985 Nettie M. Jones

Kalamazoo Foundation

1926 W. H. Upjohn
1929 A. B. Connable
1934 Donald S. Gilmore
1977 William J. Lawrence, Jr.

W. K. Kellogg Foundation

1930 A. C. Selmon
1930 Wendell L. Smith
1933 Stuart Pritchard
1940 George B. Darling
1943 Emory W. Morris
1970 Russell G. Mawby
1983 Robert D. Sparks

Joseph P. Kennedy Jr. Foundation

1945 Edward J. O'Leary
1946 John F. Kennedy
1953 Robert F. Kennedy
1961 Edward M. Kennedy

Charles F. Kettering Foundation

1927 Charles F. Kettering
1942 Eugene W. Kettering
1967 Richard D. Lombard
1971 Robert G. Chollar
1981 David Matthews

Kresge Foundation

1924 Paul W. Voorheis
1952 Stanley S. Kresge
1966 William H. Baldwin
1979 Alfred H. Taylor, Jr.

Samuel H. Kress Foundation

1929 Samuel H. Kress
1955 Rush H. Kress
1963 Franklin D. Murphy
1985 Marilyn Perry

Albert and Mary Lasker Foundation

1942 Albert Lasker
1952 Mary Lasker

Lilly Endowment, Inc.

1938 Josiah K. Lilly
1948 Josiah K. Lilly, Jr.
1966 Eli Lilly
1975 Eugene N. Beesley
1977 Landrum R. Bolling
1979 Thomas H. Lake
1984 James T. Morris

Lincoln Foundation, Inc.

1947 John C. Lincoln
1959 David C. Lincoln

John and Mary R. Markle Foundation

1927 John Markle
1933 J. Pierpont Morgan
1943 Thomas W. Lamont
1948 George Whitney
1960 John M. Russell
1969 Lloyd N. Morrisett

A. W. Mellon Educational and Charitable Trust

1950 Donald D. Shepard
      Administrative trustee
      from 1930
1954 Adolph W. Schmidt
1965 Theodore L. Hazlett, Jr.

Andrew W. Mellon Foundation

(Avalon Foundation until 1969.)

1954 G. Lauder Greenway
1958 Thomas Parran
1961 Charles S. Hamilton, Jr.
1974 Nathan M. Pusey
1975 John E. Sawyer

Eugene and Agnes E. Meyer Foundation

1950 Davidson Sommers

1970 Charles A. Horsky
1975 James L. Kunen
1983 James O. Gibson

Charles Stewart Mott Foundation

1926 Charles Stewart Mott
1965 Charles S. Harding Mott
1976 William S. White

NCR Foundation

(National Cash Register Foundation until 1971.)

1953 Stanley C. Allyn
1962 Robert S. Oelman
1977 William S. Anderson

Nemours Foundation

1936 Mrs. Alfred I. duPont
1970 Edward Ball

New York Community Trust

1923 Ralph Hayes
1967 Herbert B. West

New York Foundation

1909 Morris Loeb
1912 Alfred M. Heinsheimer
1930 Felix M. Warburg
1937 David M. Heyman
1967 D. John Heyman
1979 Myron S. Falk, Jr.
1981 John H. Fischer
1982 Malcolm B. Smith
1986 Barbara D. Finberg

Edward John Noble Foundation

1940 Edward John Noble
1958 Alger B. Chapman
1977 John F. Joline, III
1983 June Noble Larkin

Jessie Smith Noyes Foundation, Inc.

1947 Charles F. Noyes
1969 Edith N. Muma
1985 Dan M. Martin

Old Dominion Foundation

(Merged into Andrew W. Mellon Foundation in 1969.)

1941 Donald D. Shepard

1946 Paul Mellon
1956 Ernest Brooks, Jr.

Olin Foundation, Inc.

1938 Franklin W. Olin
1951 Charles L. Horn
1979 Carlton T. Helming
1981 William E. Simon
1983 Lawrence W. Milas

William Penn Foundation

(Haas Community Fund until 1975.)

1945 Otto Haas
1960 John C. Haas
1981 Richard K. Bennett
1982 Bernard C. Watson

Gustavus and Louise Pfeiffer Research Foundation

1942 Marvin R. Thompson
1945 Gustavus A. Pfeiffer
1951 Elmer H. Bobst
1975 Henry R. Herold
1981 Paul H. Pfeiffer

PPG Industries Foundation

1951 H. B. Higgins
1955 David G. Hill
1966 R. F. Barker
1967 J. A. Neubauer
1979 J. E. Burrell
1985 Edward J. Slack

Procter & Gamble Fund

1954 Kelly Y. Siddall
1961 Dean P. Fite
1976 W. Wallace Abbott

Public Welfare Foundation, Inc.

1951 Claudia H. Marsh
1977 Charles D. Haines
1986 Charles G. Ihrig

Reader's Digest Foundation

1938 DeWitt Wallace
1970 Paul W. Thompson
1974 Kent Rhodes
1986 George V. Grune

Research Corporation

1915 Elon H. Hooker
1922 Arthur H. Hamerschlag
1927 Howard A. Poillon
1946 Joseph W. Barker
1957 J. William Hinkley
1967 James S. Coles
1982 John P. Schaefer

Resources for the Future, Inc.

1952 Horace M. Albright
1953 Reuben G. Gustavson
1959 Joseph L. Fisher
1975 Marion Clawson (Acting)
1975 Charles J. Hitch
1979 Emery N. Castle

Smith Richardson Foundation, Inc.

1968 H. Smith Richardson, Jr.
1969 John W. Red, Jr.
1975 R. Randolph Richardson

Fannie E. Rippel Foundation

1953 Julius A. Rippel
1985 Herbert C. Englert

Rockefeller Brothers Fund

1940 Arthur W. Packard
1951 Dana S. Creel
1975 William M. Dietel

Rockefeller Foundation

1913 John D. Rockefeller, Jr.
1917 George E. Vincent
1929 Max Mason
1936 Raymond B. Fosdick
1948 Chester I. Barnard
1952 Dean Rusk
1961 J. George Harrar
1971 John H. Knowles
1979 Sterling Wortman (Acting)
1980 Richard W. Lyman

Rogoff Foundation

1938 Julius M. Rogoff
1966 Fannie Rogoff
1979 Paul R. Harmel

Rosenberg Foundation

1956 Richard E. Guggenheim
1957 Roy Sorenson
1961 Eleanor Anderson

1964 Ben C. Duniway
1965 Frederic B. Whitman
1968 Ben C. Duniway
1971 Mrs. Allan E. Charles
1977 Lewis H. Butler
1981 Leslie L. Luttgens
1982 Peter E. Haas
1983 Norvel L. Smith

S & H Foundation, Inc.

1962 William S. Beinecke
1981 Frederick A. Collins, Jr.

Russell Sage Foundation

1907 John M. Glen
1931 Shelby M. Harrison
1947 Ralph G. Hurlin (Acting)
1948 Donald Young
1964 Orville G. Brim, Jr.
1975 Hugh F. Cline
1977 Mrs. Winslow Wheeler
1979 David B. Truman
1981 Marshall A. Robinson

Sarah Mellon Scaife Foundation, Inc.

1941 Alan M. Scaife
1958 James M. Bovard
1975 Richard M. Scaife
1981 Richard M. Larry

Scriven Foundation, Inc.

(Merged with Clark Foundation in 1973.)

1937 Walter C. Flanders
1950 W. Beach Day
1961 Charles J. Nourse
1967 Paul S. Kerr

Sears-Roebuck Foundation

1941 Robert E. Wood
1954 T. B. Houser
1957 J. C. Worthy
1961 James T. Griffin
1966 William F. McCurdy
1981 Charles W. Harper
1983 Gene L. Harmon
1987 Richard M. Jones

Alfred P. Sloan Foundation

1934 Alfred P. Sloan, Jr.
1962 Everett Case
1968 Nils Y. Wessell
1979 Albert E. Rees

Elliott White Springs Foundation, Inc.

1942 Elliott White Springs
1959 H. William Close
1972 Charles A. Bundy

W. Clement & Jessie V. Stone Foundation

1958 W. Clement Stone
1970 Donna Stone Bradshaw
1977 Donna J. Stone

Aaron Straus & Lillie Straus Foundation Inc.

1926 Aaron Straus
1958 S. Meyer Barnett

Taconic Foundation, Inc.

1958 Stephen R. Currier
1967 John G. Simon

Teagle Foundation, Inc.

1944 Walter C. Teagle
1962 Frank E. Mott
1977 Mary R. Williams
1980 George T. Piercy

Timken Foundation of Canton

1934 Henry H. Timken
1942 Edith K. Timken
1948 Henry H. Timken, Jr.
1968 W. R. Timken
1981 Ward J. Timken

Turrell Fund

1935 Herbert Turrell
1947 Margaret Turrell
1948 Leon H. Johnston
1961 Sealand W. Landon
1979 Frank J. Hoenemyer

Twentieth Century Fund

1919 Edward A. Filene
1938 John H. Fahey
1951 Adolf A. Berle, Jr.
1971 James Rowe
1977 Don K. Price
1982 Peter A. A. Berle

United States Steel Foundation, Inc.

1953 Clifford F. Hood
1959 Leslie B. Worthington
1967 Edwin H. Gott
1969 Edgar B. Speer

1974 Wilbert A. Walker
1975 David M. Roderick
1981 William R. Roesch
1985 Peter B. Mulloney

William Volker Fund

1932 William Volker
1944 Harold W. Luhnow
1975 Morris A. Cox

Western Electric Fund

1953 F. W. Bierworth
1954 A. B. Goetze
1956 T. E. Shea
1957 A. P. Clow
1960 Robert D. Lilley
1962 H. G. Mehlhouse
1965 P. E. Hogin
1966 W. G. Chaffee
1975 R. F. Ehinger
1983 R. H. Selleck

Westinghouse Electric Fund

1953 Dale McFeatters
1960 H. S. Kaltenborn
1975 Erias A. Hyman
1977 Richard W. Dittmer
1981 C. M. Springer
1986 Walter A. Schratz

Whitehall Foundation, Inc.

1953 James A. Moffett, II
1985 George M. Moffett, II

Amherst H. Wilder Foundation

1910 Victor M. Watkins
1921 Charles L. Spencer
1941 Frederic R. Bigelow
1947 George W. Morgan
1957 Roger B. Shepard
1961 Julian B. Baird
1977 Robert H. Tucker
1982 Leonard H. Wilkening

Woodrow Wilson National Fellowship Foundation

1958 Hugh S. Taylor
1969 Hans Rosenhaupt

Gustav Wurzweiler Foundation, Inc.

1969 Max Gruenewald

XIV
Museum and Art Gallery Directors

Museum and Art Gallery Directors

Akron Art Museum

Akron, OH

(Akron Art Institute until 1986.)

1924 Wilbur Peat
1929 Theodore H. Pond
1931 Vacant
1945 Charles Val Clear
1949 George D. Culler
1954 Leroy Flint
1965 Paul Binai (Acting)
1966 Forrest Selvig
1968 Leroy Flint (Acting)
1969 Orrel Thompson
1974 Robert M. Doty
1978 John Coplans
1980 I. Michael Danoff
1985 Kathleen M. Monaghan

Albany Institute of History and Art

Albany, NY

1923 R. Loring Dunn
1940 John Davis Hatch, Jr.
1948 Robert C. Wheeler
1956 Janet R. MacFarlane
1966 Norman S. Rice
1986 Christine M. Miles

Albright-Knox Art Gallery

Buffalo, NY

1905 Charles M. Kurtz
1909 Cornelia B. Sage (Acting)
1910 Cornelia B. Sage Quinton
1924 William M. Hekking
1931 Gordon B. Washburn
1942 Andrew C. Ritchie
1949 Edgar C. Schenck
1955 Gordon M. Smith
1973 Robert T. Buck, Jr.
1984 Douglas G. Schultz

Allen Memorial Art Museum, Oberlin College

Oberlin, OH

1917 Clarence Ward
1941 Charles Parkhurst
1962 John R. Spencer
1972 Richard E. Spear
1983 William Olander (Acting)
1985 M. Kirby Talley, Jr.

1986 William J. Chiego

Lyman Allyn Museum

New London, CT

1932 Winslow Ames
1942 William Douglass
1950 Edgar deN. Mayhew

American Craft Museum

New York, NY

(Museum of Contemporary Crafts until 1979.)

1955 Herwin Schaefer
1956 Thomas S. Tibbs
1960 David Campbell
1963 Paul J. Smith

American Museum of Natural History

New York, NY

1869 Albert S. Bickmore
1884 Morris K. Jessup
1902 Hermon C. Bumpus
1910 Charles H. Townsend (Acting)
1911 Frederic A. Lucas
1924 George H. Sherwood
1935 Roy Chapman Andrews
1942 Albert E. Parr
1959 James A. Oliver
1969 Thomas D. Nicholson

Arizona State Museum

Tucson, AZ

1893 Herbert Brown
1914 John J. Thornber
1915 Byron Cummings
1938 Emil W. Haury
1964 Raymond H. Thompson

Arnot Art Museum

Elmira, NY

1913 Jeannette Murdock Diven
1943 Ernfred Anderson
1961 Dorotha McClurkin Masters

1964 J. R. von Reinhold-Jamesson
1965 Mary-Ellen Earl
1975 Kenneth H. Lindquist

Art Institute of Chicago

Chicago, IL

1879 William M. R. French
1914 Newton H. Carpenter
1916 George W. Eggers (Pro Tem)
1921 Robert B. Harshe
1938 Potter Palmer (Pro Tem)
1938 Daniel C. Rich
1958 John Maxon
1965 Charles C. Cunningham
1972 E. Lawrence Chalmers, Jr.

Baltimore City Life Museum

Baltimore, MD

(Peale Museum until 1984; Municipal Museum of the City of Baltimore until 1985.)

1931 Raphael Semmes
1933 Macgill James
1940 Richard C. Medford
1945 Jean Heimer (Acting)
1946 Wilbur H. Hunter
1979 Barry Dressel (Acting)
1980 Dennis K. McDaniel
1984 Nancy Brennan

Baltimore Museum of Art

Baltimore, MD

1923 Florence N. Levy
1927 Meyric C. Rogers
1929 Roland J. McKinney
1937 (Administrative Committee)
1939 Leslie Cheek, Jr.
1942 Adelym D. Breeskin
1962 Charles Parkhurst
1971 William V. Elder, III (Acting)
1972 Thomas Freudenheim
1979 Arnold L. Lehman

Bennington Museum

Bennington, VT

(Bennington Historical Museum and Art Gallery until 1953.)

1928 John Spargo
1954 Richard C. Barret
1978 Peter W. Cook
1979 William R. Best
1980 David W. Dangremond

Bernice P. Bishop Museum

Honolulu, HI

1898 William T. Brigham
1920 Herbert E. Gregory
1936 Peter H. Buck
1951 Vacant
1953 Alexander Spoehr
1962 Roland W. Force
1978 Edward C. Creutz
1985 W. Donald Duckworth

Bowdoin College Museum of Art

Brunswick, ME

1914 Henry Johnson
1918 Charles T. Burnett
1921 Henry E. Andrews
1939 Philip C. Beam
1964 Marvin S. Sadik
1967 Richard V. West
1973 R. Peter Mooz
1977 Katherine J. Watson

Brooklyn Museum

Brooklyn, NY

1899 Franklin W. Hooper
1914 William H. Fox
1934 Philip N. Youtz
1938 Laurance P. Roberts
1943 Albert N. Henrickson (Acting)
1943 Mrs. Laurance P. Roberts
1946 Charles Nagel
1955 Edgar C. Schenck
1960 Thomas S. Buechner
1971 Duncan F. Cameron
1973 Michael Kan (Acting)
1974 Michael Botwinick
1983 Robert T. Buck

Buffalo Museum of Science

Buffalo, NY

1866	Charles Linden
1873	Augustus R. Grote
1880	Charles Linden
1883	Julius Pohlman
1890	William C. Barrett
1892	Frederick K. Mixer
1900	Elizabeth J. Letson
1909	William L. Bryant
1926	Charles J. Fish
1934	Carlos E. Cummings
1951	Fred T. Hall
1970	Virginia L. Cummings
1979	Robert G. Chenhall
1981	Ernst E. Both

Butler Institute of American Art

Youngstown, OH

(Butler Art Institute until 1954.)

1919	Margaret Evans
1935	Joseph G. Butler, III
1981	Louis A. Zona

California Academy of Sciences

San Francisco, CA

1868	Robert E. C. Stearns
1868	Henry G. Bloomer
1875	Albert Kellogg
1876	W. G. W. Harford
1887	J. G. Cooper
1892	J. Z. Davis
1897	Charles A. Keeler
1902	Leverett M. Loomis
1913	Gulian P. Rixford
1914	Barton W. Evermann
1932	Carl E. Grunsky (Acting)
1934	Frank M. MacFarland (Acting)
1938	Robert C. Miller
1963	George E. Lindsay
1982	Frank H. Talbot

California Palace of the Legion of Honor

San Francisco, CA

(Became part of Fine Arts Museums of San Francisco in 1976.)

1924	Cornelia B. Sage Quinton
1931	Lloyd Rollins
1933	Walter Heil
1940	Thomas C. Howe
1968	Ian McKibbin White

Carnegie Institute Museum of Art

Pittsburgh, PA

(Department of Fine Arts, Carnegie Institute until 1963.)

1896	John W. Beatty
1922	Homer Saint-Gaudens
1950	Gordon B. Washburn
1963	Gustave von Groschwitz
1968	Leon A. Arkus
1980	John R. Lane

Carnegie Museum of Natural History, Carnegie Institute

Pittsburgh, PA

(Carnegie Institute, Carnegie Museum until 1975.)

1896	Frank H. Gerrodette
1898	William J. Holland
1922	Douglas Stewart
1926	Andrey Avinoff
1946	O. E. Jennings
1949	Wallace Richards
1954	M. Graham Netting
1976	Craig S. Black
1982	Robert M. West

Cincinnati Art Museum

Cincinnati, OH

1881	Alfred T. Goshorn
1902	Joseph H. Gest
1929	Walter H. Siple
1945	Philip R. Adams
1974	Millard F. Rogers, Jr.

Cleveland Health Education Museum

Cleveland, OH

(Cleveland Health Museum and Education Center until 1976.)

1939	Bruno Gebhard
1965	John J. Beeston
1968	Lowell F. Bernard

Cleveland Museum of Art

Cleveland, OH

1913	Frederic A. Whiting
1930	William M. Milliken
1958	Sherman E. Lee
1983	Evan H. Turner

Colorado Springs Fine Arts Center

Colorado Springs, CO

1935	Stanley Lothrop
1939	Paul Parker

1945	Mitchell A. Wilder
1953	James Byrnes
1955	Fred S. Bartlett
1974	Milo M. Naeve
1975	Arne R. Hansen
1980	Paul Piazza

Columbus Museum of Art

Columbus, OH

(Columbus Gallery of Fine Arts until 1976.)

1931	Karl S. Bolander
1934	Philip R. Adams
1946	Lee H. B. Malone
1953	Mahonri Sharp Young
1976	Budd Harris Bishop

Corcoran Gallery of Art

Washington, DC

1873	William MacLeod
1889	F. Sinclair Barbarin
1900	Frederick B. McGuire
1915	C. Powell Minnigerode
1947	Hermann W. Williams, Jr.
1968	James Harithas
1970	Walter Hopps
1972	Roy Slade
1978	Peter C. Marzio
1982	Michael Botwinick

Crocker Art Museum

Sacramento, CA

(E. B. Crocker Art Gallery until 1986.)

1885	William Jackson
1936	Harry N. Pratt
1944	Frederick P. Vickery
1950	Don R. Birrell
1954	Ernest Van Harlingen
1958	Frank W. Kent
1969	John A. Mahey
1973	Richard V. West
1983	Barbara K. Gibbs

Currier Gallery of Art

Manchester, NH

1929	Maud Briggs Knowlton
1946	Gordon M. Smith
1955	Charles E. Buckley
1965	William F. Hutton
1968	David S. Brooke
1978	Robert M. Doty

Dallas Museum of Art

Dallas, TX

(Dallas Museum of Fine Arts until 1984.)

1935	Richard F. Howard
1943	Jerry Bywaters
1964	Merrill C. Rueppel

1974	Harry S. Parker, III

Dallas Museum of Natural History

Dallas, TX

1935	Fredric W. Miller
1964	Hal P. Kirby
1979	Louis F. Gorr

Dayton Art Institute

Dayton, OH

1921	Herman Sachs
1922	Theodore H. Pond
1929	Siegfried R. Weng
1950	Esther I. Seaver
1956	Mrs. Alvin Raffel
1957	Thomas C. Colt, Jr.
1976	Bruce H. Evans

M. H. de Young Memorial Museum

San Francisco, CA

(Became part of Fine Arts Museums of San Francisco in 1976.)

Curators

1895	C. P. Wilcomb
1905	John W. Rogers
1908	Albert E. Gray
1910	George Barron
1917	William Altmann
1917	Charles Penez
1922	George Barron

Directors

1931	Lloyd Rollins
1933	Walter Heil
1961	Richard S. Rheem
1963	Jack R. McGregor
1970	Ian McKibbin White

Delaware Art Museum

Wilmington, DE

(Delaware Art Center until 1970.)

1938	Constance Moore
1957	Bruce St. John
1973	Charles L. Wyrick, Jr.
1980	Rowland P. Elzea (Acting)
1981	Robert H. Frankel
1986	Stephen T. Bruni

Denver Art Museum

Denver, CO

1919	Reginald R. Poland
1921	George W. Eggers
1927	Arnold Ronnebeck
1929	Samuel Heavenrich
1931	Anne Evans (Acting)
1931	Cyril Kay-Scott

1936 Donald J. Bear
1941 Frederick Douglas
1942 Charles Bayly, Jr. (Acting)
1944 Otto Karl Bach
1974 Thomas N. Maytham
1984 Lewis W. Story (Interim)
1985 Richard S. Teitz

Denver Museum of Natural History

Denver, CO

1910 Jessie D. Figgins
1936 Alfred M. Bailey
1970 Roy E. Coy
1975 Charles T. Crockett

Henry Francis duPont Winterthur Museum

Winterthur, DE

1951 Joseph Downs
1954 Charles F. Montgomery
1962 Edgar P. Richardson
1966 Charles van Ravenswaay
1976 James Morton Smith
1985 Thomas Ashley Graves, Jr.

Essex Institute

Salem, MA

(Formed in 1848 through merger of Essex Historical Society and Essex County Natural History Society.)

Presidents

1848 Daniel A. White
1861 Asahel Huntington
1865 Francis Peabody
1868 Henry Wheatland
1893 Edmund B. Wilson
1895 Robert S. Rantoul
1905 Francis H. Appleton
1916 William C. Endicott
1926 Alden P. White
1934 William C. Endicott
1937 Stephen W. Phillips
1956 W. Hammond Bowden
1961 Albert Goodhue

Directors

1945 Russell L. Jackson
1953 Bessom Smith Harris (Acting)
1954 Walter M. Merrill
1959 Huldah M. Smith (Acting)
1959 Dean A. Fales, Jr.
1967 David B. Little
1974 Bryant F. Tolles, Jr.
1985 Anne Farnam

William A. Farnsworth Library and Art Museum

Rockland, ME

1948 James M. Brown, III
1951 Wendell S. Hadlock
1976 Marius B. Peladeau

Field Museum of Natural History

Chicago, IL

(Columbian Museum until 1894; Field Columbian Museum until 1905; Field Museum of Natural History until 1943; Chicago Natural History Museum until 1966.)

1893 Frederick J. V. Skiff
1921 David C. Davies
1928 Stephen C. Simms
1937 Clifford C. Gregg
1942 Orr Goodson (Acting)
1945 Clifford C. Gregg
1962 E. Leland Webber
1981 Williard Boyd

Fine Arts Museums of San Francisco

San Francisco, CA

(Formed in 1976 by merger of California Palace of the Legion of Honor and M. H. deYoung Memorial Museum.)

1976 Ian McKibbin White

Robert Hull Fleming Museum

Burlington, VT

1931 Henry F. Perkins
1945 Horace B. Eldred
1954 Alan Gowans
1956 Thomas McCormick
1958 Richard Janson
1978 William C. Lipke
1980 Ildiko Heffernan

Florida State Museum

Gainesville, FL

1917 Thompson Van Hyning
1946 Nile C. Schaffer (Acting)
1952 Arnold B. Grobman
1961 J. C. Dickinson, Jr.
1979 F. Wayne King
1986 Thomas Peter Bennett

Fogg Art Museum

Cambridge, MA

1896 Charles H. Moore
1909 Edward W. Forbes
1944 Arthur Pope (Acting)
1948 John Coolidge

1968 Agnes Mongan
1974 Daniel Robbins
1976 Seymour Slive
1982 John Rosenfield (Acting)
1986 Edgar Peters Bowron

Folger Shakespeare Library

Washington, DC

1930 William A. Slade
1934 Joseph Q. Adams
1946 James G. McManaway (Acting)
1948 Louis B. Wright
1968 Philip A. Knachel (Acting)
1969 O. B. Hardison, Jr.
1984 Werner Gundersheimer

Freer Gallery of Art

Washington, DC

1920 John E. Lodge
1943 Archibald G. Wenley
1962 John A. Pope
1974 Harold P. Stern
1978 Thomas Lawton

Frick Collection

New York, NY

1931 Frederick M. Clapp
1951 Franklin M. Biebel
1964 Harry D. M. Grier
1974 Everett Fahy

Isabella Stewart Gardner Museum

Boston, MA

1900 Isabella Stewart Gardner
1924 Morris Carter
1955 George L. Stout
1970 Rollin van N. Hadley

Solomon R. Guggenheim Museum

New York, NY

(Museum of Non-Objective Art until 1953.)

1947 Hilla Rebay
1952 James Johnson Sweeney
1961 Thomas M. Messer

High Museum of Art

Atlanta, GA

1928 Roland McKinney
1929 Lewis P. Skidmore
1948 Ben Shute
1952 E. Robert Hunter
1954 Reginald Poland

1963 Gudmund Vigtel

Honolulu Academy of Arts

Honolulu, HI

1924 Frank M. Moore
1927 Catharine E. B. Cox (Acting)
1929 Kathrine McLane (Acting)
1935 Edgar C. Schenck
1947 Robert P. Griffing, Jr.
1963 James W. Foster, Jr.
1981 George R. Ellis

Hood Museum, Dartmouth College

Hanover, NH

(Hopkins Center Art Galleries until 1976; Dartmouth College Museum and Galleries until 1980.)

1930 Churchill P. Lathrop
1967 Truman H. Brackett, Jr.
1974 Jan vander Marck
1980 Richard Stucker (Acting)
1981 Richard S. Teitz
1984 Jacquelyn Baas

Hudson River Museum

Yonkers, NY

(Yonkers Museum of Sciences and Arts until 1948.)

1925 William N. Berkeley
1937 H. Armour Smith
1953 Thomas W. Voter
1969 Donald M. Halley, Jr.
1976 Richard Koshalek
1981 Peter Langlykke
1985 Rick Beard

Henry E. Huntington Library and Art Gallery

San Marino, CA

1927 Max Farrand
1941 (Executive Committee)
1948 J. E. Wallace Sterling
1949 (Executive Committee)
1951 John E. Pomfret
1966 James Thorpe
1983 Robert Middlekauff

Indianapolis Museum of Art

Indianapolis, IN

(John Herron Art Institute until 1962; Herron Museum of Art until 1968.)

1905 William H. Fox
1910 Vacant
1912 Frederic A. Whiting

1914 Harold H. Brown
1919 Vacant
1923 J. Arthur Maclean
1926 Vacant
1929 Wilbur D. Peat
1965 Carl J. Weinhardt, Jr.
1975 Robert A. Yassin

International Center of Photography

New York, NY

1974 Cornell Capa

International Museum of Photography at George Eastman House

Rochester, NY

1949 Oscar N. Solbert
1959 Beaumont Newhall
1973 Robert J. Doherty
1980 John Kuiper (Acting)
1981 Robert A. Mayer

Jewish Museum

New York, NY

1931 Paul Romanoff
1943 Alexander Marx
1947 Stephen Kayser
1962 Alan Solomon
1964 Hans van Weeren-Griek
1965 Sam Hunter
1968 Karl Katz
1971 Harriet Catlin (Interim)
1971 Joy Ungerleider (Interim)
1974 Joy G. Ungerleider-
       Mayerson
1981 Joan H. Rosenbaum

Joslyn Art Museum

Omaha, NE

1931 Paul Grumman
1946 Eugene Kingman
1969 Richard N. Gregg
1974 William A. McGonagle
1976 Laurance R. Hoagland
1978 Frederick Schmid
1979 Henry F. Robert, Jr.

Layton Art Gallery

Milwaukee, WI

(Merged with the Milwaukee Art Institute in 1957 to form the Milwaukee Art Center.)

1888 Edwin C. Eldridge
1902 George Raab
1922 Charlotte Partridge
1953 LaVera Pohl
1955 Edward H. Dwight

Long Beach Museum of Art

Long Beach, CA

(Municipal Art Center until 1957.)

1951 Samuel W. Heavenrich
1956 Edwin Castagna (Acting)
1956 Jerome Donson
1961 Frederick Black
1965 Jason D. Wong
1974 Jan Ernst Adlmann
1978 Frances Henselman
1978 Russel J. Moore
1984 Gregory Devereaux
1986 Stephen Garrett

Los Angeles County Museum of Art

Los Angeles, CA

1961 Richard F. Brown
1966 Kenneth Donahue
1980 Earl A. Powell, III

Robert H. Lowie Museum of Anthropology

Berkeley, CA

1903 Frederic W. Putnam
1908 Alfred L. Kroeber
1947 Edward W. Gifford
1955 George M. Foster
       (Acting)
1957 William Bascom
1979 James J. Deetz

Mead Art Museum

Amherst, MA

(Mead Art Building, Amherst College until 1979.)

1950 Charles H. Morgan
1969 Frank A. Trapp

Memphis Brooks Museum of Art

Memphis, TN

(Brooks Memorial Art Gallery until 1983.)

1916 Florence McIntyre
1922 Valerie Farrington
1933 Louise Bennett Clark
1962 Robert L. Shalkop
1964 Robert J. McKnight
1972 John J. Whitlock
1979 Jay Gates
1982 Douglas Hyland
1984 J. Richard Gruber

Metropolitan Museum of Art

New York, NY

1879 Louis Palma di Cesnola
1905 Caspar P. Clarke
1910 Edward Robinson
1932 Herbert E. Winlock
1940 Francis Henry Taylor
1955 James J. Rorimer
1967 Thomas P. F. Hoving
1978 Philippe de Montebello

Milwaukee Art Museum

Milwaukee, WI

(Milwaukee Art Society until 1916; Milwaukee Art Institute until 1957, when it merged with Layton Art Gallery to form Milwaukee Art Center. In 1953 director of Milwaukee Art Institute became director also of Layton Art Gallery; Milwaukee Art Center until 1983.)

1913 Dudley C. Watson
1925 John E. D. Trask
1926 Alfred G. Pelikan
1940 Marion Burnham
1941 Burton Cumming
1943 Mary Francis Coan
1946 Burton Cumming
1951 LaVera Pohl
1955 Edward H. Dwight
1963 Tracy Atkinson
1977 Gerald Nordland
1985 Christopher Goldsmith
1986 Russell Bowman

Milwaukee Public Museum

Milwaukee, WI

1883 Carl Doerflinger
1887 William M. Wheeler
1890 Henry Nehrling
1900 Henry L. Ward
1920 Samuel A. Barrett
1940 Ira Edwards
1943 Will C. McKern
1958 Albert M. Fuller (Acting)
1959 Stephan F. deBorhegyi
1960 Wallace N. MacBriar, Jr.
       (Acting)
1970 M. Kenneth Starr

Mint Museum

Charlotte, NC

(Mint Museum of Art until 1986.)

1936 Mrs. Lewis C. Burwell
1945 Joseph Hutchinson
1951 Bruce St. John
1955 Mrs. Dayrell Kortheuer
       (Acting)
1958 Robert W. Schlageter
1966 Herbert Cohen
1967 Russell Hicken
1968 Herbert Cohen (Acting)
1969 Cleve K. Scarbrough

1976 Milton J. Bloch

Montclair Art Museum

Montclair, NJ

1919 Katherine Innes
1929 Marion Haviland
1932 Mary Cooke Swartwout
1953 Kathryn E. Gamble
1980 Robert J. Koenig

Montgomery Museum of Fine Arts

Montgomery, AL

(Private museum 1930-1959.)

1959 Donald A. Winer
1962 Elizabeth Metcalf
       (Acting)
1963 Paul Chatelain
1968 David W. Chase
1973 Paul Chatelain
1974 Theodore W. James
       (Acting)
1974 Henry F. Robert, Jr.
1979 Theodore W. James
       (Acting)
1979 Philip A. Klopfenstein
1983 Ross C. Anderson

Pierpont Morgan Library

New York, NY

1905 Belle Da Costa Greene
1948 Frederick B. Adams, Jr.
1969 Charles A. Ryskamp

Munson-Williams-Proctor Institute Museum of Art

Utica, NY

1937 Arthur Derbyshire
1943 Vacant
1947 Harris K. Prior
1951 Mahonri S. Young
1953 Harris K. Prior
1957 Richard B. McLanthan
1962 Edward H. Dwight
1975 William C. Murray
1978 Paul J. Farinella

Museum of Broadcasting

New York, NY

1976 Robert Saudek
1981 Robert M. Batscha

Museum of Fine Arts

Boston, MA

1876 Charles G. Loring
1902 Edward Robinson
1907 Arthur Fairbanks
1925 Edward J. Holmes
1934 George H. Edgell

1955 Perry T. Rathbone
1974 Merrill C. Rueppel
1978 Jan Fontein

Museum of Fine Arts

Houston, TX

1924 James Chillman, Jr.
1953 Lee H. B. Malone
1959 James Chillman, Jr.
1961 James Johnson Sweeney
1969 Philippe de Montebello
1974 William C. Agee
1982 David B. Warren
     (Associate)
1982 Peter C. Marzio

Museum of Modern Art

New York, NY

1929 Alfred H. Barr, Jr.
1949 Rene d'Harnoncourt
1968 Bates Lowry
1970 John B. Hightower
1972 Richard Oldenburg

Museum of New Mexico

Santa Fe, NM

1909 Edgar L. Hewett
1947 Paul A. F. Walter
     (Acting)
1947 Sylvanus G. Morley
1948 Boaz W. Long
1956 Wayne L. Mauzy
     (Acting)
1959 Bruce T. Ellis (Acting)
1960 K. Ross Toole
1962 James T. Forrest
1964 Delmar M. Kolb
1969 George Ewing (Acting)
1969 Carlos R. Nagel
1974 George Ewing
1981 Jean M. Weber
1985 George Ewing (Interim)
1986 Thomas A. Livesay

Museum of Science and Hayden Planetarium

Boston, MA

(New England Museum of Natural History until 1950.)

1864 Samuel H. Scudder
1870 Alpheus Hyatt
1903 Charles W. Johnson
1917 Edward Wigglesworth
1939 Bradford Washburn
1980 David M. Pynchon
1981 Richard O. Howe
     (Interim)
1982 Roger L. Nichols

Museum of Science and Industry

Chicago, IL

1928 Waldemar Kaempffert
1931 John R. Van Pelt
     (Acting)
1931 Otto T. Kreusser
1937 Philip Fox
1940 Lenox R. Lohr
1950 Daniel M. MacMaster
1978 Victor J. Danilov

Museum of the American Indian, Heye Foundation

New York, NY

1916 George G. Heye
1957 Edwin K. Burnett
1960 Frederick J. Dockstader
1977 Roland W. Force

Museum of the Chicago Academy of Sciences

Chicago, IL

(Chicago Academy of Sciences until 1976; Chicago Academy of Sciences Museum of Ecology until 1986.)

Secretaries

1879 Selim H. Peabody
1892 William K. Higley
1905 Frank C. Baker
1907 Charles S. Raddin
1908 Wallace W. Atwood
1918 Charles F. Hills
1926 Nathan S. Davis, III

Directors

1928 Alfred M. Bailey
1937 Howard K. Gloyd
1958 William J. Beecher
1983 Paul G. Heltne

Museum of the City of New York

New York, NY

1926 Hardinge Scholle
1951 John W. Myer
1958 K. Ross Toole
1960 Ralph R. Miller
1970 Joseph Veach Noble
1985 Robert R. MacDonald

National Air and Space Museum

Washington, DC

1958 P. S. Hopkins
1965 S. Paul Johnston
1970 Frank A. Taylor (Acting)
1971 David Challinor (Acting)
1975 Michael Collins

1979 Noel W. Hinners
1983 Walter J. Boyne

National Gallery of Art

Washington, DC

1941 David E. Finley
1956 John Walker
1969 J. Carter Brown

National Museum of American Art

Washington, DC

(National Collection of Fine Arts until 1981.)

1920 William H. Holmes
1935 Ruel P. Tolman
1948 Thomas M. Beggs
1964 David W. Scott
1969 Robert Tyler Davis
     (Acting)
1970 Joshua C. Taylor
1981 Harry Lowe (Acting)
1982 Charles C. Eldredge

National Museum of American History

Washington, DC

(National Museum of History and Technology until 1981.)

1958 Frank A. Taylor
1964 John C. Ewers
1966 Robert P. Multhauf
1969 Daniel J. Boorstin
1975 Brooke Hindle
1979 Roger G. Kennedy

National Museum of Natural History

Washington, DC

1958 A. C. Smith
1962 T. Dale Stewart
1965 Richard S. Cowan
1972 Porter M. Kier
1979 James F. Mello (Acting)
1980 Richard S. Fiske
1986 Robert S. Hoffmann

National Portrait Gallery

Washington, DC

1964 Charles Nagel
1969 Marvin S. Sadik
1981 Harold F. Pfister
1982 Alan Fern

Natural History Museum of Los Angeles County

Los Angeles, CA

(Museum of History, Science and Art until 1928; Los Angeles Museum of History, Science, and Art until 1938; Los Angeles County Museum of History, Science, and Art until 1961; Los Angeles County Museum until 1965; Los Angeles County Museum of Natural History until 1970.)

1911 Frank S. Daggett
1920 Howard Robertson
     (Acting)
1921 William A. Bryan
1939 Roland J. McKinney
1946 James H. Breasted, Jr.
1951 C. F. Gehring (Acting)
1952 Jean Delacour
1960 C. F. Gehring (Acting)
1961 Herbert Friedmann
1970 Giles W. Mead
1979 Leon G. Arnold (Acting)
1980 William B. Lee
1982 Craig C. Black

Neville Public Museum

Green Bay, WI

1927 Arthur C. Neville
1929 Theodore Brown
1933 Henry L. Ward
1941 Earl Wright
1952 Ellis Burcaw
1958 James L. Quinn
1985 Donn P. Quigley
     (Interim)
1986 Ann L. Koski

New Britain Museum of American Art

New Britain, CT

1937 Sanford Low
1965 Charles B. Ferguson
1985 Daniel DuBois

New Jersey State Museum

Trenton, NJ

1890 Helen Perry
1918 Kathryn Greywacz
1963 Kenneth W. Prescott
1971 Leah Phyfer Sloshberg

New York State Museum

Albany, NY

(New York State Museum of Natural History until 1904; New York State Museum until 1945; New York State Museum and Science Service until 1976.)

1870 James Hall

1894	Frederick J. H. Merrill
1904	John Clarke
1926	Charles C. Adams
1943	Carl Guthe (Assistant Commissioner)
1953	William Fenton (Assistant Commissioner)
1967	John G. Broughton (Assistant Commissioner)
1970	G. Carroll Lindsay (Museum services)
1971	Hugo Jamnback (Science services)
1975	Noel C. Fritzinger (Assistant Commissioner)
1981	Patrick T. Houlihan (Assistant Commissioner)
1984	Robert Sullivan (Acting Director, Museum Services)
1984	Martin E. Sullivan (Assistant Commissioner)
1986	Richard Monheimer (Science Services)

Oakland Museum

Oakland, CA

1964	James M. Brown, III
1968	J. S. Holliday
1970	John E. Peetz
1982	Julian T. Euell

Ohio Historical Center

Columbus, OH

(Ohio Historical Society until 1971.)

Curators

1894	Warren K. Moorehead
1897	Clarence Loveberry
1898	William C. Mills

Directors

1921	William C. Mills
1928	Henry C. Shetrone
1947	Erwin C. Zepp
1965	Daniel R. Porter, III
1976	Thomas Smith
1980	William Keener (Acting)
1981	Gary C. Ness

Oriental Institute Museum, University of Chicago

Chicago, IL

(Oriental Institute until 1983.)

1919	James H. Breasted
1936	John A. Wilson
1946	Thorkild P. R. Jacobsen
1950	Carl H. Kraeling
1960	John A. Wilson
1961	Emery T. Filbey
1962	Robert McCormick Adams
1968	George R. Hughes
1974	John A. Brinkman

1982	Robert McCormick Adams
1983	Janet H. Johnson

Peabody Museum of Archaeology and Ethnology

Cambridge, MA

1866	Jeffries Wyman
1874	Asa Gray
1875	Frederic W. Putnam
1915	Charles C. Willoughby
1928	Edward Reynolds
1932	Donald Scott
1948	John O. Brew
1967	Stephen Williams
1978	C. C. Lamberg-Karlovsky

Peabody Museum of Natural History

New Haven, CT

1866	Othniel C. Marsh
1900	Charles S. Beecher
1904	Charles Schuchert
1922	Richard S. Lull
1938	Albert E. Parr
1943	Carl O. Dunbar
1959	S. Dillon Ripley
1964	Alfred W. Crompton
1970	Charles G. Sibley
1978	Keith S. Thomson
1979	Karl M. Waage
1983	Leo J. Hickey

Peabody Museum of Salem

Salem, MA

(The museum of the Salem East India Marine Society until 1867; Peabody Academy of Science until 1915.)

Superintendents

1820	Seth Bass
1825	Malthus A. Ward
1831	George Osborne
1835	Charles G. Page
1837	Henry Wheatland
1848	George D. Phippen
1855	Vacant
1957	Thomas Saul
1981	Peter Fetchko

Directors

1867	Frederic W. Putnam
1876	Alpheus S. Packard
1880	Edward S. Morse
1916	Lawrence W. Jenkins
1950	Ernest S. Dodge

Pennsylvania Academy of the Fine Arts

Philadelphia, PA

Secretaries

1805	Charles Chauncey
1805	William S. Biddle
1807	Nicholas Biddle
1813	William Smith
1817	Francis Hopkinson
1842	J. G. Morris
1843	R. Rundle Smith
1844	John Rutherford
1846	John T. Lewis
1856	John Sartain
1859	John T. Lewis
1868	John Sartain
1877	George Corliss
1891	J. D. Woodward
1892	Harrison S. Morris
1905	John E. D. Trask
1913	John A. Myers
1938	Joseph T. Fraser, Jr.

Directors

1946	Joseph T. Fraser, Jr.
1969	William B. Stevens
1970	Henry H. Hotz, Jr. (Acting)
1973	Richard J. Boyle
1983	Frank H. Goodyear, Jr.
1985	Linda Bantel

Philadelphia Museum of Art

Philadelphia, PA

(Pennsylvania Museum of Art until 1938.)

1876	William P. Pepper
1879	William W. Justice
1880	Vacant
1893	Balton Dorr
1899	William P. Pepper
1907	Edwin A. Barber
1917	Langdon Warner
1923	Samuel W. Woodhouse, Jr. (Acting)
1925	Fiske Kimball
1955	Henri Marceau
1965	Evan H. Turner
1977	Arnold Jolles (Acting)
1980	Jean Sutherland Boggs
1980	Robert Montgomery Smith

Phoenix Art Museum

Phoenix, AZ

1957	Forest M. Hinkhouse
1967	Hugh T. Broadley
1970	Goldthwaite H. Dorr, III
1974	Ronald Hickman
1982	James K. Ballinger

Portland Art Museum

Portland, OR

1909	Anna Belle Crocker (Curator)
1936	Frederick A. Sweet
1939	Robert Tyler Davis
1948	Thomas C. Colt, Jr.
1957	Max W. Sullivan
1960	Francis J. Newton
1976	Donald Jenkins

Princeton University Art Museum

Princeton, NJ

1882	Allan Marquand
1922	Frank J. Mather, Jr.
1947	Ernest T. DeWald
1960	Patrick J. Kelleher
1972	David Steadman
1973	Peter C. Bunnell
1980	Allen Rosenbaum

John and Mable Ringling Museum of Art

Sarasota, FL

1946	A. Everett Austin, Jr.
1958	Kenneth Donahue
1965	Curtis G. Coley
1974	Richard S. Carroll
1984	John P. Daniels
1986	Lawrence J. Ruggiero

Rochester Museum and Science Center

Rochester, NY

1924	Arthur C. Parker
1946	W. Stephen Thomas
1969	Alan R. Mahl
1970	Charles F. Hayes, III
1976	Richard C. Schultz

Abby Aldrich Rockefeller Folk Art Collection

Williamsburg, VA

1957	Mitchell Wilder
1958	Lucius D. Battle
1961	Mary Black
1964	Bruce Etchison
1966	Peter A. G. Brown
1971	Graham S. Hood
1974	Beatrix T. Rumford
1984	Carolyn J. Weekley

St. Louis Art Museum

St. Louis, MO

(City Art Museum of St. Louis until 1974.)

1909	Halsey C. Ives
1911	R. A. Holland

1922	Samuel L. Sherer
1928	Charles P. Davis
1929	Meyric C. Rogers
1939	James B. Musick
1940	Perry T. Rathbone
1955	Charles Nagel
1964	Charles E. Buckley
1975	James Nowell Wood
1978	James D. Burke

San Diego Museum of Art

San Diego, CA

(Fine Arts Gallery of San Diego until 1979.)

1926	Reginald R. Poland
1950	Thomas B. Robertson
1955	Warren W. Beach
1969	Henry G. Gardiner
1978	Steven L. Brezzo

San Francisco Museum of Modern Art

San Francisco, CA

(San Francisco Museum of Art until 1976.)

1935	Grace L. McCann Morley
1960	George D. Culler
1964	Clifford Peterson (Acting)
1966	Gerald Nordland
1974	Henry T. Hopkins

Santa Barbara Museum of Art

Santa Barbara, CA

1939	Donald J. Bear
1952	Ala Story
1957	James W. Foster, Jr.
1966	Thomas W. Leavitt
1968	Goldthwaite H. Dorr, III
1970	Paul C. Mills
1982	Carl B. Vance (Deputy Director)
1983	Richard V. West

Santa Barbara Museum of Natural History

Santa Barbara, CA

1916	William L. Dawson
1923	Ralph Hoffmann
1932	Harold Sidebotham
1933	Paul M. Rea
1936	Nora K. Morres (Acting)
1937	Arthur S. Coggeshall
1958	Nora K. Morres (Acting)
1959	V. L. Vanderhoff
1963	Nora K. Morres (Acting)
1965	Frederick H. Pough
1966	Nora K. Morres (Acting)
1969	Lawrence J. Pinter
1974	Dennis M. Power

Seattle Art Museum

Seattle, WA

1928	John Davis Hatch, Jr.
1930	Richard E. Fuller
1974	Willis F. Woods
1979	Bagley Wright (Acting)
1979	Arnold Jolles
1986	Bonnie Pitman-Gelles

Sheldon Memorial Art Gallery, University of Nebraska

Lincoln, NE

(University of Nebraska Galleries until 1980.)

1912	Paul Grumman
1931	Dwight Kirsch
1950	Duard Laging
1953	Norman A. Geske
1983	George Neubert

Smith College Museum of Art

Northampton, MA

1920	Alfred V. Churchill
1932	Jere Abbott
1946	Frederick C. Hartt (Acting)
1947	Edgar Schenck
1949	Henry-Russell Hitchcock
1955	Robert O. Parks
1962	Charles Chetham

Smithsonian Institution

Washington, DC

(See also Freer Gallery; National Air and Space Museum; National Collection of Fine Arts; National Museum of History and Technology; National Museum of Natural History; National Portrait Gallery; United States National Museum.)

Secretaries

1846	Joseph Henry
1878	Spencer F. Baird
1887	Samuel P. Langley
1907	Charles D. Walcott
1928	Charles G. Abbot
1945	Alexander Wetmore
1953	Leonard Carmichael
1964	S. Dillon Ripley
1984	Robert McCormick Adams

Snite Museum of Art

Notre Dame, IN

(Wightman Gallery until 1952; Art Gallery, University of Notre Dame until 1986.)

1925	Gregory Gerrer
1934	Maurice Goldblatt

1955	Anthony J. Lauck
1976	Dean A. Porter

J. B. Speed Art Museum

Louisville, KY

1927	Hattie B. Speed
1942	Catherine Grey (Acting)
1946	Paul S. Harris
1962	Addison Franklin Page
1984	Jesse G. Wright, Jr.

Staten Island Institute of Arts and Sciences

Staten Island, NY

(Staten Island Museum until 1971.)

1907	Charles L. Pollard (Curator-in-Chief)
1913	Arthur Hollick
1919	Charles W. Leng
1941	Roswell S. Coles
1951	James L. Whitehead
1962	George O. Pratt, Jr.
1978	High Rock
1980	William A. Siebenheller
1985	Richard U. Maren
1986	James Abruzzo

Taft Museum

Cincinnati, OH

1932	Walter H. Siple
1945	Philip R. Adams
1952	Katherine Hanna
1983	Ruth K. Meyer

Toledo Museum of Art

Toledo, OH

1903	George W. Stevens
1927	Blake-More Godwin
1959	Otto Wittmann
1977	Earl Roger Mandle

United States National Museum

Washington, DC

(Reorganized in 1958 to form the National Museum of History and Technology and the National Museum of Natural History.)

1850	Spencer F. Baird
1878	G. Brown Goode
1896	Charles D. Walcott
1898	Richard Rathbun
1918	William deC. Ravenel
1925	Alexander Wetmore
1948	A. Remington Kellogg

University of Colorado Museum

Boulder, CO

1902	Junius Henderson
1933	Hugo G. Rodeck
1975	Peter Robinson
1983	William W. Hay

University of Oregon Museum of Art

Eugene, OR

1929	Gertrude Bass Warner
1951	Mabel Klockars Garner (Acting)
1953	Paul S. Dull
1953	Wallace S. Baldinger
1960	James F. Colley (Acting)
1970	Richard C. Paulin

Valentine Museum

Richmond, VA

1930	Helen G. McCormack
1942	Mrs. Robert W. Claiborne
1956	Edward M. Davis
1963	Leslie D. Carter (Acting)
1966	Robert B. Mayo
1976	Jean DuVal Kane
1981	John G. Zehmer, Jr.
1985	B. Frank Jewell

Virginia Museum of Fine Arts

Richmond, VA

1936	Thomas C. Colt, Jr.
1941	Mrs. John Garland Pollard
1941	Beatrice von Keller
1945	Thomas C. Colt, Jr.
1948	Leslie Cheek, Jr.
1969	James M. Brown, III
1977	R. Peter Mooz
1981	Charles L. Reed, Jr.
1983	Bruce C. Gottwald
1985	Paul N. Perrot

Wadsworth Atheneum

Hartford, CT

1911	Frank B. Gay
1927	A. Everett Austin, Jr.
1946	Charles C. Cunningham
1966	James Elliott
1977	Tracy Atkinson

Walters Art Gallery

Baltimore, MD

1933	C. Morgan Marshall
1946	Edward S. King
1965	Richard H. Randall, Jr.
1981	Robert P. Bergman

Whitney Museum of American Art

New York, NY

1931 Juliana Force
1948 Hermon More
1958 Lloyd Goodrich
1968 John I. H. Baur
1974 Thomas N. Armstrong

Williams College Museum of Art

Williamstown, MA

1926 Karl E. Weston

1948 S. Lane Faison, Jr.
1975 Franklin W. Robinson
1979 John W. Coffey (Acting)
1980 Thomas Krens

Worcester Art Museum

Worcester, MA

1908 Philip Gentner
1917 Frederick Pratt (Acting)
1918 Raymond Henniker-
       Heaton
1926 George W. Eggers
1931 Francis Henry Taylor
1940 Charles H. Sawyer

1943 Perry Cott (Acting)
1947 George L. Stout
1955 Francis Henry Taylor
1958 Daniel C. Rich
1970 Richard S. Teitz
1982 Tom L. Freudenheim
1986 James A. Welu

Yale University Art Gallery

New Haven, CT

1869 John F. Weir
1913 William S. Kendall
1922 Everett V. Meeks

1941 John Marshall Phillips
       (Acting)
1942 Emerson Tuttle (Acting)
1945 Theodore Sizer
1946 John Marshall Phillips
1953 Lamont Moore
1957 Andrew C. Ritchie
1971 Alan Shestack
1985 Anne Coffin Hanson
       (Acting)

XV
Religious Leaders

This section includes the following subdivisions:

The Protestant Episcopal Church in the United States of America
    Succession of Bishops
    Protestant Episcopal Church Bishops by Diocese

The Roman Catholic Church in America
    Cardinals
    Roman Catholic Archbishops by Archdiocese
    Roman Catholic Bishops by Diocese

The United Methodist Church
    Bishops of the Methodist Episcopal Church
    Bishops of the Methodist Episcopal Church, South
    The Methodist Protestant Church
    Bishops of the Methodist Church
    Bishops of the Church of the United Brethren in Christ
    Bishops of the Evangelical Church (Methodist)
    Bishops of the Evangelical United Brethren Church
    Bishops of the United Methodist Church

The Presbyterian Church (U.S.A.)
    Moderators of the Presbyterian Church in the United States of America
    Moderators of the United Presbyterian Church of North America
    Moderators of the United Presbyterian Church in the United States of America
    Moderators of the Presbyterian Church (U.S.A.)

Other Major Denominations
    The United Church of Christ
    Moderators of the Congregational Christian Church
    Presidents of the Evangelical and Reformed Church
    American Baptist Churches in the U.S.A.
    Southern Baptist Convention
    The Lutheran Churches
    Presidents of the Lutheran Church—Missouri Synod
    Presidents of the United Lutheran Church
    Presidents of the Lutheran Church in America
    Presidents of the American Lutheran Church
    Christian Church (Disciples of Christ)
    The Church of Christ, Scientist
    The Church of Jesus Christ of Latter-Day Saints (Mormon)
    Union of Orthodox Hebrew Congregations of America
    Union of American Hebrew Congregations

Founders of Religious Sects, Societies, and Movements in the United States

The Protestant Episcopal Church in the United States of America

Succession of Bishops

Succession	Consecrated	Name and Diocese	Succession	Consecrated	Name and Diocese
1	1784	Samuel Seabury Connecticut	30	1834	James H. Otey Tennessee
2	1787	William White Pennsylvania	31	1835	Jackson Kemper Missouri and Indiana; Wisconsin, 1859
3	1787	Samuel Provoost New York	32	1836	Samuel A. McCoskry Michigan
4	1790	James Madison Virginia	33	1838	Leonidas Polk Arkansas, missionary; Louisiana, 1841
5	1792	John T. Claggett Maryland	34	1839	William H. DeLancey Western New York
6	1795	Robert Smith South Carolina	35	1840	Christopher E. Gadsden South Carolina
7	1797	Edward Bass Massachusetts	36	1840	William R. Whittingham Maryland
8	1797	Abraham Jarvis Connecticut	37	1841	Stephen Elliott Georgia
9	1801	Benjamin Moore New York, coadjutor; bishop, 1815	38	1841	Alfred Lee Delaware
10	1804	Samuel Parker Massachusetts	39	1842	John Johns Virginia, assistant; bishop, 1862
11	1811	John H. Hobart New York, coadjutor; bishop, 1816	40	1842	Manton Eastburn Massachusetts, coadjutor; bishop, 1843
12	1811	Alexander V. Griswold Eastern Diocese	41	1843	John P. K. Henshaw Rhode Island
13	1812	Theodore Dehon South Carolina	42	1844	Carlton Chase New Hampshire
14	1814	Richard C. Moore Virginia	43	1844	Nicholas H. Cobbs Alabama
15	1814	James Kemp Maryland, suffragan; bishop, 1816	44	1844	Cicero S. Hawks Missouri
16	1815	John Croes New Jersey	45	1844	William J. Boone Amoy (China), missionary
17	1818	Nathaniel Bowen South Carolina	46	1844	George W. Freeman Arkansas and the Southwest, missionary
18	1819	Philander Chase Ohio; Illinois, 1835	47	1844	Horatio Southgate Constantinople, missionary
19	1819	Thomas C. Brownell Connecticut	48	1845	Alonzo Potter Pennsylvania
20	1823	John S. Ravenscroft North Carolina	49	1847	George Burgess Maine
21	1827	Henry U. Onderdonk Pennsylvania, assistant; bishop, 1836	50	1849	George Upfold Indiana
22	1829	William Meade Virginia, coadjutor; bishop 1841	51	1850	William M. Green Mississippi
23	1830	William M. Stone Maryland	52	1851	John Payne Africa, missionary
24	1830	Benjamin T. Onderdonk New York	53	1851	Francis H. Rutledge Florida
25	1831	Levi S. Ives North Carolina	54	1851	John Williams Connecticut, coadjutor; bishop, 1865
26	1832	John H. Hopkins Vermont	55	1851	Henry J. Whitehouse Illinois, coadjutor; bishop, 1852
27	1832	Benjamin B. Smith Kentucky	56	1852	Jonathan M. Wainwright New York, provisional
28	1832	Charles P. McIlvaine Ohio	57	1853	Thomas F. Davis South Carolina
29	1832	George W. Doane New Jersey	58	1853	Thomas Atkinson North Carolina

Succession of Protestant Episcopal Bishops (continued)

Succession	Consecrated	Name and Diocese
59	1853	William I. Kip California, missionary; bishop, 1857
60	1854	Thomas F. Scott Oregon and Washington territory, missionary
61	1854	Henry W. Lee Iowa
62	1854	Horatio Potter New York, provisional; bishop, 1861
63	1854	Thomas M. Clark Rhode Island
64	1858	Samuel Bowman Pennsylvania, assistant
65	1859	Alexander Gregg Texas
66	1859	William H. Odenheimer New Jersey; Northern New Jersey, 1874
67	1859	Gregory T. Bedell Ohio, coadjutor; bishop, 1873
68	1859	Henry B. Whipple Minnesota
69	1859	Henry C. Lay Southwest, missionary; Arkansas, missionary; Easton, 1869
70	1860	Joseph C. Talbot Northwest, missionary; Indiana, coadjutor, 1865; bishop, 1872
71	1862	William B. Stevens Pennsylvania, coadjutor; bishop, 1865
72	1862	Richard H. Wilmer Alabama
73	1864	Thomas H. Vail Kansas
74	1865	Arthur C. Coxe Western New York, coadjutor; bishop 1865
75	1865	Charles T. Quintard Tennessee
76	1865	Robert H. Clarkson Nebraska, missionary; bishop, 1870
77	1865	George M. Randall Colorado and adjacent territory, missionary
78	1866	John B. Kerfoot Pittsburgh
79	1866	Channing M. Williams China and Japan, missionary; Yedo, 1874
80	1866	Joseph P. B. Wilmer Lousiana
81	1866	George D. Cummins Kentucky, assistant
82	1866	William E. Armitage Wisconsin, coadjutor; bishop, 1870
83	1867	Henry A. Neely Maine
84	1867	Daniel S. Tuttle Montana, Idaho and Utah, mmissionary; Missouri, 1886
85	1867	John F. Young Florida
86	1868	John W. Beckwith Georgia
87	1868	Francis McN. Whittle Virginia, coadjutor; bishop, 1876
88	1868	William H. A. Bissell Vermont
89	1868	Charles F. Robertson Missouri
90	1868	Benjamin W. Morris 2d Oregon and Washington territory; Oregon, missionary, 1880; bishop, 1889
91	1869	Abram N. Littlejohn Long Island
92	1869	William C. Doane Albany
93	1869	Frederic D. Huntington Central New York
94	1869	Ozi W. Whitaker Nevada and Arizona, missionary; Nevada, 1874; Pennsylvania, coadjutor, 1886; bishop, 1887
95	1870	Henry N. Pierce Arkansas, misionary; bishop, 1871
96	1870	William W. Niles New Hampshire
97	1870	William Pinkney Maryland, coadjutor; bishop, 1879
98	1871	William B. W. Howe South Carolina
99	1871	Mark A. deW. Howe Central Pennsylvania
100	1873	William H. Hare Niobrara, missionary
101	1873	John G. Auer Cape Palmas (Africa), missionary
102	1873	Benjamin H. Paddock Massachusetts
103	1873	Theodore B. Lyman New York, coadjutor; bishop, 1881
104	1873	John F. Spalding Colorado, missionary; bishop, 1887
105	1874	Edward R. Welles Wisconsin
106	1874	Robert W. B. Elliott West Texas, missionary
107	1874	John H. D. Wingfield Northern California, missionary
108	1874	Alexander C. Garrett Northern Texas, missionary; Dallas, 1895
109	1875	William F. Adams New Mexico and Arizona, missionary; Easton, 1887
110	1875	Thomas U. Dudley Kentucky, coadjutor; bishop, 1884
111	1875	John Scarborough New Jersey
112	1875	George DeN. Gillespie Western Michigan
113	1875	Thomas A. Jaggar Southern Ohio
114	1875	William E. McLaren Illinois; Chicago, 1883
115	1875	J. H. Hobart Brown Fond du Lac
116	1876	William S. Perry Iowa
117	1877	Charles C. Penick Cape Palmas (Africa), missionary
118	1877	Samuel I. J. Schereschewsky Shanghai, missionary
119	1878	Alexander Burgess Quincy
120	1878	George W. Peterkin West Virginia
121	1878	George F. Seymour Springfield
122	1879	Samuel S. Harris Michigan
123	1880	Thomas A. Starkey Northern New Jersey
124	1880	John N. Galleher Louisiana
125	1880	George K. Dunlop New Mexico and Arizona, missionary
126	1880	Leigh R. Brewer Montana, missionary; bishop, 1904
127	1880	John A. Paddock Washington territory, missionary; Olympia, missionary, 1892
128	1882	Cortlandt Whitehead Pittsburgh
129	1883	Hugh M. Thompson Mississippi, coadjutor; bishop, 1887

Succession	Consecrated	Name and Diocese	Succession	Consecrated	Name and Diocese
130	1883	David B. Knickerbacker Indiana	165	1893	Francis K. Brooke Oklahoma, missionary
131	1883	Henry C. Potter New York, coadjutor; bishop, 1887	166	1893	William M. Barker Western Colorado, missionary; Olympia, 1894; bishop, 1894
132	1883	Alfred M. Randolph Virginia coadjutor; bishop, Southern Virginia, 1892	167	1893	John McKim North Tokyo, missionary
133	1883	William D. Walker North Dakota, missionary; Western New York, bishop, 1897	168	1893	Frederick R. Graves Shanghai, missionary
134	1884	Alfred A. Watson East Carolina	169	1893	Ellison Capers South Carolina, coadjutor; bishop, 1894
135	1884	William J. Boone Shanghai, missionary	170	1893	Thomas F. Gailor Tennessee, coadjutor; bishop, 1898
136	1884	Nelson S. Rulison Central Pennsylvania, coadjutor; bishop, 1895	171	1893	William Lawrence Masschusetts
137	1885	William Paret Maryland	172	1893	Joseph B. Cheshire, Jr. North Carolina, coadjutor; bishop, 1893
138	1885	George Worthington Nebraska	173	1894	Arthur C. A. Hall Vermont
139	1885	Samuel D. Ferguson Liberia, missionary	174	1894	John B. Newton Virginia, coadjutor
140	1886	Edwin G. Weed Florida	175	1895	John H. White Indiana; Michigan City, 1899
141	1886	Mahlon N. Gilbert Minnesota, coadjutor	176	1895	Frank R. Millspaugh Kansas
142	1887	Elisha S. Thomas Kansas, coadjutor; bishop, 1889	177	1895	Peter T. Rowe Alaska, missionary
143	1887	Ethelbert Talbot Wyoming and Idaho, missionary; transferred to Central Pennsylvania, 1897; Bethlehem, 1908	178	1896	Lewis W. Burton Lexington
			179	1896	Joseph H. Johnson Los Angeles
144	1888	James S. Johnston West Texas, missionary; bishop, 1904	180	1896	Henry Y. Satterlee Washington
145	1888	Abiel Leonard III Nevada and Utah; Salt Lake, missionary, 1898	181	1896	Gershom M. Williams Marquette
			182	1897	James D. Morrison Duluth, missionary
146	1888	Leighton Coleman Delaware	183	1897	Chauncey B. Brewster Connecticut, coadjutor; bishop, 1899
147	1889	John M. Kendrick New Mexico and Arizona, missionary; Arizona, 1892	184	1897	Robert A. Gibson Virginia, coadjutor; bishop, 1902
148	1889	Boyd Vincent Southern Ohio, coadjutor; bishop, 1904	185	1898	William N. McVickar Rhode Island, coadjutor; bishop, 1903
149	1889	Cyrus F. Knight Milwaukee	186	1898	William M. Brown Arkansas, coadjutor; bishop, 1899
150	1889	Charles C. Grafton Fond du Lac	187	1898	Junius M. Horner Asheville, missionary; Western North Carolina, 1922
151	1889	William A. Leonard Ohio	187	1899	Lucien L. Kinsolving Southern Brazil, missionary, 1907
152	1889	Thomas F. Davies Michigan	188	1899	William H. Moreland Sacramento, missionary
153	1890	Anson R. Graves The Platte, missionary; Kearney, missionary, 1907	189	1899	Samuel C. Edsall North Dakota, missionary; Minnesota, bishop, 1901
154	1890	William F. Nichols California, coadjutor; bishop, 1893	190	1899	Theodore N. Morrison Iowa
155	1890	Edward R. Atwill West Missouri; Kansas City, 1904	191	1899	James B. Funsten Boise, missionary; Wyoming, 1907; Idaho, 1907
156	1891	Henry M. Jackson Alabama, coadjutor	192	1899	Joseph M. Francis Indiana
157	1891	Davis Sessums Louisiana, coadjutor; bishop, 1891	193	1899	Arthur L. Williams Nebraska, coadjutor; bishop, 1908
158	1891	Phillips Brooks Massachusetts	194	1899	William L. Gravatt West Virginia, coadjutor; bishop, 1916
159	1891	Isaac L. Nicholson Milwaukee	195	1900	Sidney C. Partridge Kyoto, missionary; West Missouri, 1911
160	1892	Cleland K. Nelson Georgia; Atlanta, 1907	196	1900	Robert Codman Maine
161	1892	Charles R. Hale Springfield, coadjutor	197	1900	Charles P. Anderson Chicago, coadjutor; bishop, 1905
162	1892	George H. Kinsolving Texas, coadjutor; bishop, 1893	198	1900	Robert W. Barnwell Alabama
163	1892	Lemuel H. Wells Spokane, missionary	199	1900	Reginald H. Weller Fond du Lac, coadjutor; bishop, 1912
164	1892	William C. Gray South Florida, missionary	200	1901	Frederick W. Taylor Quincy

Succession of Protestant Episcopal Bishops (continued)

Succession	Consecrated	Name and Diocese
201	1901	Cameron Mann North Dakota, missionary; South Florida, missionary, 1913; bishop, 1922
202	1901	Charles H. Brent Philippines, missionary; Western New York, bishop, 1918
203	1902	Frederick W. Keator Olympia, missionary
204	1902	Frederick Burgess Long Island
205	1902	James A. Ingle Hankow, missionary
206	1902	Alexander H. Vinton Western Massachusetts
207	1902	Charles S. Olmsted Colorado
208	1902	Alexander Mackay-Smith Pennsylvania, coadjutor; bishop, 1911
209	1902	James H. VanBuren Puerto Rico, mmissionary
210	1902	Henry B. Restarick Honolulu
211	1902	Charles T. Olmsted Central New York, coadjutor; bishop, 1904
212	1902	Charles M. Beckwith Alabama
213	1903	Sheldon M. Griswold Salina, missionary; Chicago, suffragan, 1917; bishop, 1930
214	1903	Theodore DuB. Bratton Mississippi
215	1903	Edwin S. Lines Newark
216	1904	M. Edward Fawcett Quincy
217	1904	David H. Greer New York, coadjutor; bishop, 1908
218	1904	Richard H. Nelson Albany, coadjutor; bishop, 1913
219	1904	Edward W. Osborne Springfield, coadjutor; bishop, 1906
220	1904	Robert Strange East Carolina, coadjutor; bishop, 1905
221	1904	Logan H. Roots Hankow, missionary
222	1904	Franklin S. Spalding Salt Lake, missionary (Western Colorado, 1904-07)
223	1904	Henry D. Aves Mexico, missionary
224	1904	Albion W. Knight Cuba, missionary; New Jersey, coadjutor, 1923
225	1905	Charles E. Woodcock Kentucky
226	1905	James H. Darlington Harrisburg
227	1905	Frederick F. Johnson South Dakota, assistant; missionary, 1910; Missouri, coadjutor, 1911; bishop, 1923
228	1906	Charles D. Williams Michigan
229	1906	Edward M. Parker New Hampshire, coadjutor; bishop, 1914
230	1906	John N. McCormick Western Michigan, coadjutor; bishop, 1909
231	1906	William W. Webb Milwaukee, coadjutor; bishop, 1906
232	1906	Charles Scadding Oregon
233	1906	Beverly D. Tucker Southern Virginia, coadjutor; bishop, 1918
234	1907	William A. Guerry South Carolina, coadjutor; bishop, 1908
235	1907	Robert L. Paddock Eastern Oregon, missionary
236	1907	Edward J. Knight Western Coloardo, missionary
237	1908	Henry D. Robinson Nevada, missionary
238	1908	Frederick F. Reese Georgia
239	1908	Frederick J. Kinsman Delaware
240	1909	Alfred Harding Washington, D.C.
241	1909	Nathaniel S. Thomas Wyoming, missionary
242	1909	Benjamin Brewster Western Colorado, missionary; Maine, bishop, 1916
243	1909	John G. Murray Maryland, coadjutor; bishop, 1911
244	1909	Arthur S. Lloyd Virginia, coadjutor; New York, suffragan, 1921
245	1910	George A. Beecher Kearney, missionary
246	1910	Edward A. Temple North Texas, missionary
247	1911	James DeWolf Perry Rhode Island
248	1911	Julius W. Atwood Arizona, missionary
249	1911	Theodore P. Thurston Eastern Oklahoma, missionary; combined Eastern Oklahoma and Oklahoma, 1919
250	1911	Louis C. Sanford San Joaquin, missionary
251	1911	Charles S. Burch New York, suffragan; bishop, 1919
252	1911	Rogers Israel Erie
253	1911	James R. Winchester Arkansas, coadjutor; bishop, 1912
254	1911	Thomas F. Davies Western Massachusetts
255	1911	Philip M. Rhinelander Pennsylvania, coadjutor; bishop, 1911
256	1911	Thomas J. Garland Pennsylvania, suffragan; bishop, 1924
257	1911	William E. Toll Chicago, suffragan
258	1912	Henry St. G. Tucker Kyoto, missionary; Virginia, coadjutor; 1926; bishop, 1927
259	1912	Daniel T. Huntington Anking, missionary
260	1912	George Biller, Jr. South Dakota, missionary
261	1912	Harry S. Longley Iowa, suffragan; coadjutor, 1917; bishop, 1929
262	1912	Frank A. McElwain Minnesota, suffragan; bishop, 1917
263	1913	William F. Weeks Vermont, coadjutor
264	1913	Theodore I. Reese Southern Ohio, coadjutor; bishop 1929
265	1913	Samuel G. Babcock Massachusetts, suffragan
266	1913	Charles B. Colmore Puerto Rico, missionary
267	1914	John P. Tyler North Dakota, missionary
268	1914	Frank DuMoulin Ohio, coadjutor
269	1914	Frederick B. Howden New Mexico, missionary

Succes-sion	Conse-crated	Name and Diocese	Succes-sion	Conse-crated	Name and Diocese
270	1914	William T. Capers West Texas, coadjutor; bishop, 1916	305	1920	Gouverneur F. Mosher Philippine Islands, missionary
271	1914	William C. Brown Virginia, coadjutor; bishop, 1919	306	1920	Robert C. Jett Southwestern Virginia
272	1914	William F. Faber Montana, coadjutor; bishop, 1916	307	1920	Arthur W. Moulton Utah
273	1914	George C. Hunting Nevada, missionary	308	1920	George W. Davenport Easton
274	1914	Paul Jones Utah, missionary	309	1920	William B. Stevens Los Angeles, coadjutor; bishop, 1928
275	1915	Thomas C. Darst East Carolina	310	1920	David L. Ferris Western New York, suffragan; coadjutor, 1924; bishop, 1929; Rochester, 1931
276	1915	Walter T. Sumner Oregon	311	1920	Philip Cook Delaware
277	1915	Hiram R. Hulse Cuba, missionary	312	1920	Herbert H. H. Fox Montana, suffragan; coadjutor, 1925; bishop, 1934
278	1915	Paul Matthews New Jersey	313	1920	Granville G. Bennett Duluth, coadjutor; bishop, 1922; Rhode Island, suffragan, 1939; bishop, 1946
279	1915	Herman Page Spokane, missionary; Michigan, 1923	314	1921	Robert H. Mize Salina, missionary
280	1915	George Y. Bliss Vermont, coadjutor	315	1921	Kirkman G. Finlay South Carolina, coadjutor; Upper South Carolina, bishop, 1922
281	1915	Charles Fiske Central New York, coadjutor; bishop, 1924	316	1921	William T. Manning New York
282	1915	Wilson R. Stearly Newark, suffragan; coadjutor, 1917; bishop, 1927	317	1921	Fred Ingley Colorado, coadjutor; bishop, 1938
283	1915	E. Campion Acheson Connecticut, suffragan; coadjutor, 1926; bishop, 1928	318	1921	Theophilus M. Gardiner Liberia, suffragan
284	1916	James Wise Kansas, coadjutor; bishop, 1916	319	1921	John D. LaMothe Honolulu, missionary
285	1916	Hugh L. Burleson South Dakota, missionary	320	1921	John C. Ward Erie
286	1917	Irving P. Johnson Colorado, coadjutor; bishop, 1918	321	1921	Herbert Shipman New York, suffragan
287	1917	Frank H. Touret Western Colorado, missionary; Idaho, 1919	322	1922	Edwin A. Penick North Carolina, Coadjutor; bishop, 1932
288	1917	Granville H. Sherwood Springfield	323	1922	James M. Maxon Tennessee, coadjutor; bishop, 1935
289	1917	Edwin W. Saphore Arkansas, suffragan; bishop, 1935	324	1922	William C. McDowell Alabama, coadjutor; bishop, 1928
290	1917	Arthur C. Thomson Southern Virginia, suffragan; coadjutor, 1919; bishop, 1930	325	1922	George A. Oldham Albany, coadjutor; bishop, 1929
291	1917	Harry T. Moore Dallas, coadjutor; bishop, 1924	326	1922	Charles L. Slattery Massachusetts, coadjutor; bishop, 1927
292	1917	Henry J. Mikell Atlanta	327	1922	William B. Roberts South Dakota, suffragan; bishop, 1931
293	1918	William P. Remington South Dakota, suffragan; Eastern Oregon, missionary, 1922	328	1923	Harry R. Carson Haiti, missionary
294	1918	John C. Sage Salina, missionary	329	1923	Alexander Mann Pittsburgh
295	1918	Robert LeR. Harris Marquette, coadjutor; bishop, 1919	330	1923	James E. Freeman Washington, D.C.
296	1918	Edward T. Denby Arkansas and Province of the Southwest, suffragan	331	1923	Robert E. L. Strider West Virginia, coadjutor; bishop, 1939
297	1918	Clinton S. Quin Texas, coadjutor; bishop, 1928	332	1923	Frank W. Sterrett Bethlehem, coadjutor; bishop, 1928
298	1918	Henry B. Delany North Carolina, suffragan	333	1924	Charles S. Reifsnider North Tokyo, suffragan; missionary, 1935
299	1919	William M. Green Mississippi, coadjutor; bishop, 1938	334	1924	Edward M. Cross Spokane, missionary
300	1919	Ernest V. Shayler Nebraska	335	1924	John C. White Springfield
301	1919	Troy Beatty Tennessee, coadjutor	336	1924	Edward H. Coley Central New York, suffragan; bishop, 1936
302	1919	Edward L. Parsons California, coadjutor; bishop, 1924	337	1924	Frank A. Juhan Florida
303	1919	Walter H. Overs Liberia, missionary	338	1925	Eugene C. Seaman North Texas, missionary
304	1920	James C. Morris Canal Zone, missionary; Louisiana, bishop, 1930	339	1925	Samuel B. Booth Vermont, coadjutor; bishop, 1930
			340	1925	Alfred A. Gilman Hankow, suffragan; bishop, 1937

Succession of Protestant Episcopal Bishops (continued)

Succession	Consecrated	Name and Diocese
341	1925	Warren L. Rogers Ohio, coadjutor; bishop, 1930
342	1925	Campbell Gray Northern Indiana
343	1925	Benjamin F. P. Ivins Milwaukee, coadjutor; bishop, 1933
344	1925	Simeon A. Huston Olympia
345	1925	John D. Wing South Florida, coadjutor; bishop, 1932
346	1925	Ernest M. Stires Long Island
347	1925	Robert E. Campbell Liberia, missionary
348	1925	William M. M. Thomas Southern Brazil, suffragan; missionary, 1928
349	1925	Middleton S. Barnwell Idaho, missionary; Georgia, coadjutor, 1935; bishop, 1937
350	1926	Walter Mitchell Arizona, missionary
351	1926	Frank W. Creighton Mexico, missionary; Long Island, suffragan, 1933; Michigan, coadjutor; bishop, 1939
352	1926	Shirley H. Nichols Kyoto, missionary; Salina, 1943
353	1926	John T. Dallas New Hampshire
354	1926	Edward T. Helfenstein Maryland, coadjutor; bishop, 1929
355	1927	Thomas Casady Oklahoma, missionary
356	1928	Albert S. Thomas South Carolina
357	1928	Norman S. Binsted Tohuku, missionary; Philippines, bishop, 1942
358	1929	Thomas Jenkins Nevada, missionary
359	1929	John I. B. Larned Long Island, suffragan
360	1929	Frank E. Wilson Eau Claire
361	1929	Henry P. A. Abbott Lexington
362	1929	Francis M. Taitt Pennsylvania, coadjutor; bishop, 1931
363	1929	Harwood Sturtevant Fond du Lac, coadjutor; bishop, 1933
364	1929	Elmer N. Schmuck Wyoming, missionary
365	1930	Cameron J. Davis Wetern New York, coadjutor; bishop, 1931
366	1930	Samuel H. Littell Honolulu, missionary
367	1930	Hayward S. Ablewhite Marquette
368	1930	Henry W. Hobson Southern Ohio, coadjutor; bishop, 1931
369	1930	William Scarlett Missouri, coadjutor; bishop, 1933
370	1930	Robert B. Gooden Los Angeles, suffragan
371	1930	George C. Stewart Chicago, coadjutor; bishop, 1930
372	1930	Henry K. Sherrill Massachusetts
373	1930	Frederick D. Goodwin Virginia, coadjutor; bishop, 1944
374	1930	Charles K. Gilbert New York, suffragan, bishop, 1947
375	1930	Robert M. Spencer Western Missouri
376	1930	Benjamin T. Kemerer Duluth, coadjutor; bishop, 1933; Minnesota, suffragan, 1944
377	1931	Hunter Wyatt-Brown Harrisburg
378	1931	Stephen E. Keeler Minnesota, coadjutor; bishop, 1944
379	1931	John B. Bentley Alaska, suffragan; bishop, 1943
380	1931	Efrain Salinas y Velasco Mexico, suffragan; missionary, 1934
381	1931	Frederick G. Budlong Connecticut, coadjutor; bishop, 1934
382	1931	Frederick B. Bartlett North Dakota, missionary; Idaho, missionary, 1936
383	1932	Benjamin M. Washburn Newark, coadjutor; bishop, 1935
384	1932	Ralph E. Urban New Jersey, suffragan
385	1933	A. W. Noel Porter Sacramento, coadjutor; bishop, 1933
386	1934	Robert E. Gribbin Western North Carolina
387	1934	John W. Nichols Shanghai, suffragan
388	1936	Theodore R. Ludlow Newark, suffragan
389	1936	Benjamin D. Dagwell Oregon
390	1936	Leopold Kroll Liberia, missionary
391	1936	Vedder VanDyck Vermont
392	1936	Bartel H. Reinheimer Rochester, coadjutor; bishop, 1938
393	1936	Charles Clingman Kentucky
394	1936	Lewis B. Whittemore Western Michigan, coadjutor; bishop, 1937
395	1936	Wallace J. Gardner New Jersey, coadjutor
396	1936	William L. Essex Quincy
397	1936	Winfred H. Ziegler Wyoming
398	1937	William A. Lawrence Western Massachusetts
399	1937	Harry Beal Panama and Canal Zone
400	1937	Douglass H. Atwill North Dakota
401	1937	Goodrich R. Fenner Kansas, coadjutor; bishop, 1939
402	1937	William P. Roberts Shanghai
403	1938	Robert F. Wilner Philippines, suffragan
404	1938	Raymond A. Heron Massachusetts, suffragan
405	1938	William A. Brown Southern Virginia
406	1938	Charles C. J. Carpenter Alabama
407	1938	Edmund P. Dandridge Tennessee, coadjutor; bishop, 1947
408	1938	Henry D. Philips Southwestern Virginia
409	1938	Beverly D. Tucker Ohio
410	1938	Malcolm E. Peabody Central New York, coadjutor; bishop, 1942
411	1938	Karl M. Block California, coadjutor; bishop, 1941
412	1938	Richard B. Mitchell Arkansas

Succes-sion	Conse-crated	Name and Diocese	Succes-sion	Conse-crated	Name and Diocese
413	1939	Richard A. Kirchhoffer Indianapolis	451	1945	Bravid W. Harris Liberia
414	1939	Arthur R. McKinstry Delaware	452	1945	Conrad H. Gesner South Dakota, suffragan; bishop, 1954
415	1939	A. H. Blankingship Cuba	453	1945	Donald B. Aldrich Michigan, coadjutor
416	1939	Spence Burton Haiti, suffragan; Nassau, bishop, 1942	454	1945	Reginald H. Gooden Panama Canal Zone
417	1939	John J. Gravatt Upper South Carolina	455	1945	Henry I. Louttit South Florida, suffragan; bishop, 1951
418	1939	William McClelland Easton	456	1945	Arthur B. Kinsolving, II Arizona, missionary; bishop, 1959
419	1939	Henry H. Daniels Montana	457	1945	Frederick L. Barry Albany, coadjutor; bishop, 1949
420	1939	Edwin J. Randall Chicago, suffragan	458	1945	Charles A. Mason Dallas
421	1940	Howard R. Brinker Nebraska	459	1945	Alfred L. Banyard New Jersey, suffragan; bishop, 1955
422	1940	Athalicio T. Pithan Southern Brazil, suffragan; bishop, 1950	460	1945	Thomas H. Wright East Carolina
423	1940	John L. Jackson Louisiana	461	1945	John E. Hines Texas, coadjutor; bishop, 1955
424	1940	Walter H. Gray Connecticut, coadjutor; bishop, 1951	462	1945	William R. Moody Lexington
425	1940	Lloyd R. Craighill Anking	463	1946	Richard S. M. Emrich Michigan
426	1941	Wallace E. Conkling Chicago	464	1946	Harold E. Sawyer Erie
427	1941	Oliver L. Loring Maine	465	1946	Lane W. Barton Eastern Oregon
428	1941	Noble C. Powell Maryland, coadjutor; bishop, 1944	466	1946	George H. Quarterman Northwest Texas
429	1942	James M. Stoney New Mexico and Southwest Texas, missionary, 1942; bishop, 1954	467	1946	Stephen C. Clark Utah
430	1942	Frank A. Rhea Idaho	468	1947	Norman B. Nash Massachusetts
431	1942	James P. DeWolfe Long Island	469	1947	Stephen F. Bayne, Jr. Olympia
432	1942	William F. Lewis Nevada, Olympia, 1960	470	1947	Harold L. Bowen Colorado, coadjutor; bishop, 1949
433	1942	Wiley R. Mason Virginia, suffragan	471	1947	Richard T. Loring, Jr. Springfield
434	1942	John M. Walker Atlanta	472	1947	Horace W. B. Donegan New York City, suffragan, 1947; bishop, 1950
435	1942	Oliver J. Hart Pennsylvania, coadjutor; bishop, 1943	473	1948	George P. Gunn Southern Virginia, coadjutor, 1948;
436	1942	Herman R. Page Northern Michigan			bishop, 1950
437	1943	Duncan M. Gray Mississippi	474	1948	Charles F. Hall New Hampshire
438	1943	John T. Heistand Harrisburg	475	1948	Louis C. Melcher Southern Brazil, suffragan; bishop, 1944
439	1943	Edward P. Wroth Erie	476	1948	James W. Hunter Wyoming
440	1943	Everett H. Jones West Texas	477	1948	Francis E. I. Bloy Los Angeles
441	1943	Charles A. Voegeli Haiti	478	1948	Lauriston L. Scaife Western New York
442	1944	Charles F. Boynton Puerto Rico, coadjutor; bishop, 1947	479	1948	William J. Gordon, Jr. Alaska
443	1944	Sumner F. D. Walters San Joaquin	480	1948	Russell S. Hubbard Michigan, suffragan; Spokane, bishop, 1954
444	1944	Harry S. Kennedy Honolulu; Taiwan, 1960	481	1948	Charles A. Clough Springfield
445	1944	Austin Pardue Pittsburgh	482	1948	Theodore N. Barth Tennessee, coadjutor; bishop, 1953
446	1944	Angus Dun Washington, D.C.	483	1948	Matthew G. Henry Western North Carolina
447	1944	Thomas N. Carruthers South Carolina	484	1948	Edward H. West Florida, coadjutor; bishop, 1956
448	1944	Elwood L. Haines Iowa	485	1948	Walter M. Higley Central New York, suffragan
449	1944	William W. Horstick Eau Claire	486	1949	Jonathan G. Sherman Long Island, suffragan; bishop, 1966
450	1944	James R. Mallett Northern Indiana	487	1949	Donald J. Campbell Los Angeles, suffragan

Succession of Protestant Episcopal Bishops (continued)

Succes-sion	Conse-crated	Name and Diocese
488	1949	Girault M. Jones Louisiana
489	1949	Randolph R. Claiborne, Jr. Alabama, suffragan; Atlanta, bishop, 1953
490	1949	Robert F. Gibson, Jr. Virginia, suffragan; bishop, 1961
491	1949	Joseph G. Armstrong Pennsylvania, suffragan; coadjutor, 1960; bishop, 1963
492	1949	Charles L. Street Chicago, suffragan
493	1949	Allen J. Miller Easton
494	1949	Nelson M. Burroughs Ohio, coadjutor; bishop, 1952
496	1950	Dudley S. Stark Rochester
497	1950	Edward R. Welles West Missouri
498	1950	Gordon V. Smith Iowa
499	1950	Wilburn C. Campbell West Virginia, coadjutor; bishop, 1955
500	1950	G. Francis Burrill Dallas, suffragan; Chicago, bishop, 1954
501	1950	Henry H. Shires California, suffragan
502	1951	Richard H. Baker North Carolina, coadjutor; bishop, 1959
503	1951	Arthur C. Lichtenberger Missouri, coadjutor; bishop, 1952
504	1951	Robert M. Hatch Connecticut, suffragan; Western Massachusetts, 1957
505	1951	Richard S. Watson Utah
506	1951	A. Ervine Swift Puerto Rico; South Florida, suffragan, 1969
507	1951	Richard R. Emery North Dakota
508	1951	David E. Richards Albany, suffragan
509	1951	Martin J. Bram South Florida, suffragan
510	1951	Chilton Powell Oklahoma
511	1952	John B. Walthour Atlanta
512	1952	Donald H. V. Hallock Milwaukee
513	1952	Hamilton H. Kellogg Minnesota, coadjutor; bishop, 1956
514	1952	William Crittenden Erie
515	1952	Iveson B. Noland Louisiana
516	1953	Lyman C. Ogilby Philippines, suffragan; bishop, 1957; South Dakota, coadjutor, 1967
517	1953	John S. Higgins Rhode Island, coadjutor; bishop, 1955
518	1953	Frederick J. Warnecke Bethlehem
519	1953	William H. Brady Fond du Lac, coadjutor; bishop, 1956
520	1953	Leland Stark Newark, coadjutor; bishop, 1958
521	1953	George M. Murray Alabama, suffragan; bishop, 1968
522	1953	Dudley B. McNeil Western Michigan
523	1953	William S. Thomas Pittsburgh, suffragan
524	1953	Clarence A. Cole Upper South Carolina
525	1953	Charles J. Kinsolving III New Mexico and Southwest Texas, coadjutor, 1953; bishop, 1956
526	1953	J. Brooke Mosley Delaware, coadjutor; bishop, 1955
527	1954	Charles G. Marmion Kentucky
528	1954	William H. Marmion Southwestern Virginia
529	1954	Joseph M. Harte Dallas, suffragan; Arizona, bishop, 1962
530	1954	Joseph S. Minnis Colorado
531	1954	Archie H. Crowley Michigan, suffragan
532	1954	Albert R. Stuart Georgia
533	1954	Anson P. Stokes, Jr. Massachusetts, coadjutor; bishop, 1966
534	1955	John VanderHorst Tennessee, suffragan; bishop, 1961
535	1955	Harry L. Doll Maryland, suffragan; coadjutor, 1958; bishop, 1963
536	1955	Richard E. Dicus West Texas, suffragan
537	1955	Frederick P. Goddard Texas, suffragan
538	1955	Robert R. Brown Arkansas, coadjutor; bishop, 1956
539	1956	Arnold M. Lewis Salina
540	1956	James W. F. Carman Oregon, coadjutor; bishop, 1958
541	1956	Earl M. Honaman Harrisburg
543	1956	Edward C. Turner Kansas, coadjutor; bishop, 1959
544	1956	James P. Clements Texas, suffragan
545	1956	William F. Moses South Florida, suffragan
546	1956	Chandler W. Sterling Montana, coadjutor; bishop, 1957
547	1956	Frederic C. Lawrence Massachusetts, suffragan
548	1957	Norman L. Foote Idaho
549	1957	John P. Craine Indianapolis, 1959
550	1957	Clarence R. Haden Sacramento, coadjutor; bishop, 1958
552	1958	Philip F. McNairy Minnesota, coadjutor
553	1958	John H. Esquirol Connecticut, suffragan; bishop, 1969
554	1958	Daniel Corrigan Colorado, suffragan
555	1958	James A. Pike California
556	1958	David S. Rose Southern Virginia, suffragan
557	1958	Francis W. Lickfield Quincy
558	1958	Donald Macadie Newark, suffragan
559	1958	Roger W. Blanchard Southern Ohio, coadjutor; bishop, 1959
560	1959	Edmund K. Sherrill Central Brazil
561	1959	Allen W. Brown Albany, suffragan; bishop, 1961
563	1959	George L. Cadigan Missouri

Succession	Consecrated	Name and Diocese	Succession	Consecrated	Name and Diocese
564	1959	William F. Creighton Washington, D.C., suffragan; bishop 1962	605	1964	C. Kilmer Myers Michigan, suffragan; California, bishop, 1966
565	1960	C. Richard Millard California, suffragan	606	1964	Robert C. Rusack Los Angeles, suffragan
566	1960	William G. Wright Nevada	607	1964	George R. Selway Northern Michigan
567	1960	Charles E. Bennison Western Michigan	608	1964	Francisco Reus-Froylan Puerto Rico
568	1960	Paul A. Kellogg Dominican Republic	609	1964	James Chang L. Wong Taiwan
569	1960	James S. Wetmore New York, suffragan	610	1965	George T. Masuda North Dakota
570	1960	Ivol I. Curtis Los Angeles, suffragan; Olympia, 1964	611	1965	James M. Richardson Texas
571	1960	Samuel B. Chilton Virginia, suffragan	612	1965	Hal R. Gross Oregon, suffragan
572	1960	Thomas A. Fraser, Jr. North Carolina, coadjutor; bishop, 1965	613	1966	William Davidson Western Kansas
573	1960	Robert L. Dewitt Michigan, suffragan; Pennsylvania, 1964	614	1966	Albert W. Van Duzer New Jersey, suffragan
574	1960	Edwin B. Thayer Colorado	615	1966	William F. Gates, Jr. Tennessee, suffragan
575	1961	Gray Temple South Carolina	616	1966	William P. Barnds Dallas, suffragan
576	1961	Harvey D. Butterfield Vermont	617	1966	Dean T. Stevenson Harrisburg
577	1961	Russell T. Rauscher Nebraska, coadjutor; bishop, 1962	618	1966	Robert B. Hall Virginia, coadjutor
578	1961	Charles P. Gilson Honolulu, suffragan	619	1966	George A. Taylor Easton
580	1961	Dillard H. Brown, Jr. Liberia	620	1967	Richard B. Martin Long Island, suffragan
581	1961	John M. Allin Mississippi, suffragan; bishop, 1966	621	1967	John H. Burt Ohio, suffragan; bishop, 1968
582	1961	Joseph W. Hutchens Connecticut, suffragan	622	1967	William M. Moore North Carolina, suffragan
583	1961	James L. Duncan South Florida, suffragan	623	1967	John R. Wyatt Spokane
584	1961	William L. Hargrave South Florida	624	1967	Robert R. Spears West Missouri, suffragan; Rochester, 1970
585	1962	Charles W. MacLean Long Island, suffragan	625	1967	Milton L. Wood Atlanta, suffragan
586	1962	William F. Sanders Tennessee, coadjutor	626	1967	Christopher Keller, Jr. Arkansas, coadjutor
587	1962	James W. Montgomery Chicago, suffragan; coadjutor, 1965	627	1967	William C. Frey Guatemala
588	1962	Albert A. Chambers Springfield	628	1967	Edward McNair Northern California, suffragan
589	1962	Theodore H. McCrea Dallas, suffragan	629	1967	Edwin L. Hanchett Honolulu
590	1962	John M. Burgess Massachusetts, suffragan	630	1968	Edmond Browning Okinawa
591	1963	Edward G. Longid Philippines	631	1968	Robert Appleyard Pittsburgh
592	1963	Charles B. Persell, Jr. Albany, suffragan	632	1968	Harold Robinson Western New York, coadjutor
593	1963	Cedric Earl Mills Panama Canal Zone	633	1968	Harold C. Gosnell West Texas
594	1963	George W. Barrett Rochester	634	1968	Jackson Gilliam Montana
595	1963	Frederick W. Putman, Jr. Oklahoma, suffragan	635	1968	Victor M. Rivera San Joaquin
596	1963	Walter C. Klein Northern Indiana	636	1968	Huntley A. Elebash East Carolina, suffragan
597	1963	John A. Pinckney Upper South Carolina	637	1968	Frederick B. Wolfe Maine
598	1964	Paul Moore, Jr. Washington, suffragan; New York, suffragan, 1970; bishop, 1972	638	1968	William H. Mead Delaware
601	1964	George E. Rath Newark, suffragan	639	1968	David K. Leighton Maryland, coadjutor
602	1964	Ned Cole, Jr. Central New York	640	1969	George Haynsworth Nicaragua
603	1964	David B. Reed Colombia	643	1969	William B. Spofford, Jr. Eastern Oregon
604	1964	Scott Field Bailey Texas, suffragan	644	1969	David R. Thornberry Wyoming

Succession of Protestant Episcopal Bishops (continued)

Succes-sion	Conse-crated	Name and Diocese
645	1969	Stanley H. Atkins Eau Claire, coadjutor
646	1969	George P. Reeves Georgia, coadjutor
647	1970	Philip A. Smith Virginia, suffragan
648	1970	William Folwell Florida
649	1970	Addison Hosea Lexington
650	1970	A. Donald Davies Dallas
651	1970	Walter H. Jones South Dakota
652	1970	George Browne Liberia
653	1970	Alexander D. Stewart Western Massachusetts
654	1970	Lloyd E. Gressle Bethlehem
656	1971	Clarence Hobgood Suffragan, Armed Forces
658	1971	Furman C. Stough Alabama
659	1971	John M. Krumm Southern Ohio
660	1971	Luc A. J. Garnier Haiti
661	1971	Robert P. Varley Nebraska, coadjutor
662	1971	Arthur A. Vogel West Missouri, coadjutor
663	1971	Willis R. Henton N.W. Texas, coadjutor
664	1971	John T. Walker Washington, suffragan
665	1971	E. Otis Charles Utah
666	1971	Frederick H. Belder Rhode Island, coadjutor
667	1971	H. Coleman McGehee, Jr. Michigan, coadjutor
668	1971	Morgan Porteus Connecticut, suffragan
669	1971	Richard M. Trelease, Jr. Rio Grande, New Mexico
670	1972	Harold Stephen Jones South Dakota, suffragan
671	1972	Walter C. Righter Iowa
672	1972	Morris F. Arnold Massachusetts, suffragan
673	1972	William A. Franklin San Diego
674	1972	Albert W. Hillestad Springfield, Illinois
675	1972	Lemuel B. Shirley Panama & Canal Zone
676	1972	Bennett J. Simms Atlanta
677	1972	Wesley Frensdorff Arizona
678	1972	Telesforo A. Isaac Dominican Republic
679	1972	Samuel J. Wylie Northern Michigan
680	1972	Edward Mason Turner Virgin Islands
681	1972	Hanford L. King, Jr. Idaho
682	1972	William C. R. Sheridan Northern Indiana
683	1972	Quintin E. Primo, Jr. Chicago, suffragan
684	1972	William Jackson Cox Maryland, suffragan

Succes-sion	Conse-crated	Name and Diocese
685	1973	George M. Alexander Upper South Carolina
686	1973	Anselmo Carral-Solar Texas, assistant bishop
687	1973	Robert P. Atkinson West Virginia
688	1973	John Alfred Baden Virginia, suffragan
689	1973	Charles T. Gaskell Milwaukee
690	1973	William G. Weinhauer Western North Carolina
691	1973	Donald James Parsons Quincy, Illinois
692	1973	Donald James Davis Northwestern Pennsylvania
693	1974	Matthew P. Bigliardi Oregon
694	1974	Harold Louis Wright New York, suffragan
695	1974	Wilbur Emory Hogg, Jr. Albany, New York
696	1974	Robert Shaw Kerr Vermont
697	1974	Robert M. Wolterstorff San Diego, California
698	1974	Duncan M. Gray, Jr. Mississippi
699	1974	Frank S. Cerveny Florida
700	1974	David Rea Cochran Alaska
701	1974	Emerson Paul Haynes Southwest Florida
702	1975	George Phelps Mellick Belshaw New Jersey
703	1975	Robert Campbell Witcher Long Island
704	1975	William Augustus Jones, Jr. Missouri
705	1975	William Hawley Clark Delaware
706	1975	William Arthur Dimmick Northern Michigan
707	1975	Richard Abelardo Abellon Northern Philippines
708	1975	Robert Elwin Terwilliger Dallas, suffragan
709	1976	Robert Hume Cochrane Olympia, Washington
710	1976	Robert Howard Cilley Texas, suffragan
711	1976	James Barrow Brown Louisiana
712	1976	Claude Charles Vache Southern Virginia
713	1976	John Shelby Spong Newark
714	1976	Joseph Thomas Heistand Arizona
715	1976	John Bowen Coburn Massachusetts
716	1976	Henry Irving Mayson Michigan, suffragan
717	1976	James Daniel Warner Nebraska
718	1977	Gerald Nicholas McAllister Oklahoma
719	1977	Edward Witker Jones Indiana
720	1977	Manuel Capuyan Lumpias Central Philippines
721	1977	Bobby Gordon Jones Wyoming
722	1978	Robert Marshall Anderson Minnesota
723	1978	Charles Judson Child Atlanta

Succession	Consecrated	Name and Diocese	Succession	Consecrated	Name and Diocese
724	1978	Charles Lee Burgreen Armed Forces, suffragan; Micronesia	763	1981	Clarence L. Coleridge Connecticut, suffragan
725	1978	Hugo Luis Pina Honduras	764	1981	W. Bradford Hastings Connecticut, suffragan
726	1978	John Lester Thompson III Northern California	765	1982	Armando R. Guerra-Soria Guatemala
727	1979	Leigh Allen Wallace Spokane, Washington	766	1982	Donald M. Hultstrand Springfield, Illinois
728	1979	Calvin Onderdonk Schofield, Jr. Southest Florida	767	1982	Albert Theodore Eastman Maryland, coadjutor
729	1979	Arthur Heath Light Southwest Virginia	768	1982	David B. Birney, IV Idaho
730	1979	Bernardo Merino-Botero Colombia	769	1982	Thomas K. Ray Northern Michigan
731	1979	Stanley Fillmore Hauser West Texas, suffragan	770	1982	Gordon T. Charlton, Jr. Texas, suffragan
732	1979	William Edwin Swing California	771	1982	Charles B. Morton San Diego
733	1979	William Arthur Beckham Upper South Carolina	772	1982	James Michael Mark Dyer Bethlehem, Pennsylvania
734	1979	Walter Decoster Dennis New York, suffragan	773	1983	Alex D. Dickson, Jr. Western Tennessee
735	1979	Brice Sidney Sanders East Carolina	774	1983	James R. Moodey Ohio
736	1979	Arthur Edward Walmsley Connecticut	775	1983	Elliott L. Sorge Eaton, Maryland
737	1979	William Grant Black Southern Ohio	776	1983	Donis D. Patterson Dallas
738	1980	Pui-Yeung Cheung Taiwan	777	1983	Robert Lee Omengan Longid Northern Philippines, suffragan
739	1980	David H. Lewis, Jr. Virginia, suffragan	778	1984	Harry Woolston Shipps Georgia, coadjutor
740	1980	Harold A. Hopkins, Jr. North Dakota	779	1984	James Hamilton Ottley Panama
741	1980	Robert W. Estill North Carolina	780	1984	Leopold Frade Honduras
742	1980	Roberto Martinez-Resendiz Central and South Mexico, suffragan	781	1984	Vincent King Pettit New Jersey, suffragan
743	1980	Claro Huerta-Ramos Central and South Mexico, suffragan	782	1984	David Standish Bald Albany, New York
744	1980	George N. Hunt, III Rhode Island	783	1984	Andrew Frederick Wissemann Western Massachusetts
745	1980	Rustin R. Kimsey Eastern Oregon	784	1984	William George Burrill Rochester, New York
746	1980	William L. Stevens Fond du Lac, Wisconsin	785	1984	Peter James Lee Virginia, coadjutor
747	1980	Maurice M. Benitez Texas	786	1984	Craig Berry Anderson South Dakota
748	1980	Herbert A. Donovan Arkansas	787	1984	Roger John White Milwaukee
749	1980	C. FitzSimons Allison South Carolina	788	1984	Edward Cole Chalfant Maine, coadjutor
750	1980	William C. Wantland Eau Claire, Wisconsin	789	1984	Don Adger Wimberly Lexington, Kentucky
751	1980	C. Shannon Mallory El Camino Real, California	790	1984	Howard Samuel Meeks Western Michigan, coadjutor
752	1980	Charlie Fuller McNutt, Jr. Central Pennsylvania	791	1985	Clarence Cullam Pope, Jr. Fort Worth, Texas, coadjutor
753	1980	Sam Byron Hulsey Northwest Texas	792	1985	Martiniano Garcia-Monteil Central and South Mexico, suffragan
754	1981	William H. Wolfrum Colorado, suffragan	793	1985	Sturdie Wyman Downs-Higgs Nicaragua
755	1981	Charles F. Duvall Central Gulf Coast	794	1985	Frank Tracy Griswold, III Chicago, coadjutor
756	1981	O'Kelley Whitaker Central New York	795	1985	Rogers Sanders Harris Upper South Carolina, suffragan
757	1981	John F. Ashby Western Kansas	796	1985	Frank Harris Vest, Jr. North Carolina, suffragan
758	1981	Richard F. Grein Kansas	797	1985	Oliver Bailey Garver, Jr. Los Angeles, California, suffragan
759	1981	George C. Harris Alaska	798	1985	William Franklin Carr West Virginia, suffragan
760	1981	Henry B. Hucles, III Long Island, suffragan	799	1985	George Lazenby Reynolds Tennessee
761	1981	Alden M. Hathaway Pittsburgh	800	1985	David Elliot Johnson Massachusetts, coadjutor
762	1981	Samuel Espinoza-Venegas Western Mexico			

Protestant Episcopal Church
Bishops by Diocese

Alabama

1844	Nicholas H. Cobbs
1862	Richard H. Wilmer
1900	Robert W. Barnwell
1902	Charles M. Beckwith
1928	William G. McDowell
1938	Charles C. J. Carpenter
1968	George M. Murray
1971	Furman C. Stough

Alaska

1895	Peter T. Rowe
1943	John B. Bentley
1948	William J. Gordon
1974	David E. Cochran
1981	George C. Harris

Albany, New York

1869	William C. Doane
1913	Richard H. Nelson
1929	George A. Oldham
1949	Frederick L. Barry
1961	Allen W. Brown
1974	Wilbur E. Hogg
1985	David S. Ball

Arizona

1869	Ozi W. Whitaker
1875	William F. Adams
1880	George K. Dunlop
1892	John M. Kendrick
1911	Julius W. Atwood
1926	Walter Mitchell
1945	Arthur B. Kinsolving II
1962	Joseph M. Harte
1979	Joseph T. Heistand

Arkansas

1838	Leonidas Polk
1844	George W. Freeman
1859	Henry C. Lay
1871	Henry N. Pierce
1899	William M. Brown
1912	James R. Winchester
1935	Edwin W. Saphore
1938	Richard B. Mitchell
1956	Robert R. Brown
1970	Christopher Keller, Jr.
1981	Herbert Donovan, Jr.

Asheville, North Carolina

(See Western North Carolina.)

Atlanta, Georgia

1907	Cleland K. Nelson
1917	Henry J. Mikell
1942	John M. Walker
1952	John B. Walthour

1953	Randolph R. Claiborne, Jr.
1972	Bennett J. Sims
1983	C. Judson Child, Jr.

Bethlehem, Pennsylvania

(Diocese of Central Pennsylvania until 1908.)

1871	Mark A. DeW. Howe
1895	Nelson S. Rulison
1897	Ethelbert Talbot
1928	Frank W. Sterrett
1953	Frederick J. Warnecke
1971	Lloyd E. Gressle
1983	J. Mark Dyer

California

1857	William I. Kip
1893	William F. Nichols
1924	Edward L. Parsons
1941	Karl M. Block
1958	James A. Pike
1966	C. Kilmer Myers
1980	William E. Swing

Central Florida

1970	William H. Folwell

Central Gulf Coast

1971	George M. Murray
1981	Charles F. Duvall

Central New York

1869	Frederic D. Huntington
1904	Charles T. Olmsted
1924	Charles Fiske
1936	Edward H. Coley
1942	Malcolm E. Peabody
1964	Ned Cole, Jr.
1983	O'Kelley Whitaker

Central Pennsylvania

(Diocese of Harrisburg, Pennsylvania until 1971.)

1905	James H. Darlington
1931	Hunter Wyatt-Brown
1943	John T. Heistand
1956	Earl M. Honaman
1966	Dean T. Stevenson
1982	Charlie F. McNutt

Chicago, Illinois

(Diocese of Illinois until 1883.)

1835	Philander Chase
1852	Henry J. Whitehouse

1875	William E. McLaren
1905	Charles P. Anderson
1930	Sheldon M. Griswold
1930	George C. Stewart
1941	Wallace E. Conkling
1954	G. Francis Burrill
1971	James W. Montgomery

Colorado

1865	George M. Randall
1873	John F. Spalding
1902	Charles S. Olmsted
1918	Irving P. Johnson
1938	Fred Ingley
1949	Harold L. Bowen
1955	Joseph S. Minnis
1960	Edwin B. Thayer
1973	William C. Frey

Connecticut

1784	Samuel Seabury
1797	Abraham Jarvis
1819	Thomas C. Brownell
1865	John Williams
1899	Chauncey B. Brewster
1928	E. Campion Acheson
1934	Frederick G. Budlong
1951	Walter H. Gray
1969	John H. Esquirol
1971	J. Warren Hutchens
1977	Morgan Porteus
1981	Arthur E. Walmsley

Dallas, Texas

(Diocese of Northern Texas until 1895.)

1874	Alexander C. Garrett
1924	Harry T. Moore
1945	Charles A. Mason
1970	A. Donald Davies
1983	Donis D. Patterson

Delaware

1841	Alfred Lee
1888	Leighton Coleman
1908	Frederick J. Kinsman
1920	Philip Cook
1939	Arthur R. McKinstry
1955	J. Brooke Mosley
1968	William H. Mead
1975	William Hawley Clark

Duluth, Minnesota

(Reunited with Minnesota in 1944.)

1897	James D. Morrison
1922	Granville G. Bennett
1933	Benjamin T. Kemerer

East Carolina

1884	Alfred A. Watson
1905	Robert Strange
1915	Thomas C. Darst
1945	Thomas H. Wright
1974	Huntley A. Elebash
1984	B. Sidney Sanders

East Tennessee

1985	William E. Sanders

Eastern Diocese

(Included present states of Maine, New Hampshire, Vermont, Massachusetts, and Rhode Island; discontinued in 1843.)

1811	Alexander V. Griswold

Eastern Oklahoma

(Reunited with Oklahoma in 1919.)

1911	Theodore P. Thurston

Eastern Oregon

1907	Robert L. Paddock
1922	William P. Remington
1946	Lane W. Barton
1969	William B. Spofford, Jr.
1980	Rustin R. Kimsey

Easton, Maryland

1869	Henry C. Lay
1887	William F. Adams
1920	George W. Davenport
1939	William McClelland
1949	Allen J. Miller
1966	George A. Taylor
1975	Moultrie Moore
1984	Elliott L. Sorge

Eau Claire, Wisconsin

1929	Frank E. Wilson
1944	William W. Horstick
1969	Stanley H. Atkins
1980	William C. Wantland

El Camino Real, California

1980	C. Shannon Mallory

Erie, Pennsylvania

1911	Rogers Israel
1921	John C. Ward
1943	Edward P. Wroth
1946	Harold E. Sawyer
1952	William Crittenden
1974	Donald J. Davis

Florida

1851	Francis H. Rutledge
1867	John F. Young
1886	Edwin G. Weed
1924	Frank A. Juhan
1956	Hamilton West
1975	Frank S. Cerveny

Fond du Lac, Wisconsin

1875	J. H. Hobart Brown
1889	Charles C. Grafton
1912	Reginald H. Weller
1933	Harwood Sturtevant
1956	William H. Brady
1980	William L. Stevens

Fort Worth, Texas

1983	A. Donald Davies
1986	Clarence C. Pope

Georgia

1841	Stephen Elliott
1868	John W. Beckwith
1892	Cleland K. Nelson
1908	Frederick F. Reese
1937	Middleton S. Barnwell
1954	Albert R. Stuart
1972	G. Paul Reeves
1985	Harry W. Shipps

Harrisburg, Pennsylvania

(See Central Pennsylvania.)

Hawaii

(Diocese of Honolulu until 1971.)

1902	Henry B. Restarick
1921	John D. LaMothe
1930	Samuel H. Littell
1944	Harry S. Kennedy
1967	Edwin L. Hanchett
1976	Edmond L. Browning

Idaho

1867	Daniel S. Tuttle
1887	Ethelbert Talbot
1899	James B. Funsten
1919	Frank H. Touret
1925	Middleton S. Barnwell
1936	Frederick B. Bartlett
1942	Frank A. Rhea
1957	Norman L. Foote
1972	Hanford L. King
1982	David B. Birney

Illinois

(See Chicago.)

Indiana

(See Indianapolis.)

Indianapolis, Indiana

(Diocese of Indiana until 1902.)

1835	Jackson Kemper
1849	George Upfold
1872	Joseph C. Talbot
1883	David B. Knickerbacker
1895	John H. White
1899	Joseph M. Francis
1939	Richard A. Kirchhoffer
1959	John P. Craine
1977	Edward W. Jones

Iowa

1854	Henry W. Lee
1876	William S. Perry
1899	Theodore N. Morrison
1929	Harry S. Longley
1944	Elwood L. Haines
1950	Gordon V. Smith
1972	Walter C. Righter

Kansas

1864	Thomas H. Vail
1889	Elisha S. Thomas
1895	Frank R. Millspaugh
1916	James Wise
1939	Goodrich R. Fenner
1959	Edward C. Turner
1981	Richard F. Grein

Kansas City, Missouri

(See West Missouri.)

Kearney, Nebraska

(See Western Nebraska.)

Kentucky

1832	Benjamin B. Smith
1884	Thomas U. Dudley
1905	Charles E. Woodcock
1936	Charles Clingman
1954	C. Gresham Marmion, Jr.
1975	David B. Reed

Lexington, Kentucky

1896	Lewis W. Burton
1929	Henry P. A. Abbott
1945	William R. Moody
1970	Addison Hosea
1986	Don A. Wimberley

Long Island, New York

1869	Abram N. Littlejohn
1902	Frederick Burgess
1925	Ernest M. Stires
1942	James P. DeWolfe
1966	Jonathan G. Sherman

1977	Robert Campbell Witcher

Los Angeles, California

1896	Joseph H. Johnson
1928	William B. Stevens
1948	Francis Eric Bloy
1974	Robert C. Rusack

Louisiana

1841	Leonidas Polk
1866	Joseph P. B. Wilmer
1880	John N. Galleher
1891	Davis Sessums
1930	James C. Morris
1940	John L. Jackson
1949	Girault M. Jones
1952	Iveson B. Noland
1976	James Barrow Brown

Maine

(Part of Eastern Diocese 1811-1843.)

1847	George Burgess
1867	Henry A. Neely
1900	Robert Codman
1916	Benjamin Brewster
1941	Oliver L. Loring
1968	Frederick B. Wolfe

Marquette

(See Northern Michigan.)

Maryland

1792	John T. Claggett
1816	James Kemp
1830	William M. Stone
1840	William M. Whittington
1879	William Pinkney
1885	William Paret
1911	John G. Murray
1929	Edward T. Helfenstein
1944	Noble C. Powell
1963	Harry L. Doll
1972	David Leighton, Sr.
1986	A. Theodore Eastman

Massachusetts

1797	Edward Bass
1804	Samuel Parker
1811	Alexander V. Griswold
1843	Manton Eastburn
1873	Benjamin H. Paddock
1891	Phillips Brooks
1893	William Lawrence
1927	Charles L. Slattery
1930	Henry K. Sherrill
1947	Norman B. Nash
1966	Anson B. Stokes
1970	John M. Burgess
1976	John B. Coburn

Michigan

1836	Samuel A. McCoskry
1879	Samuel S. Harris

1889	Thomas F. Davies
1906	Charles D. Williams
1923	Herman Page
1939	Frank W. Creighton
1946	Richard S. M. Emrich
1973	H. Coleman McGehee, Jr.

Michigan City, Indiana

(See Northern Indiana.)

Milwaukee, Wisconsin

(Diocese of Wisconsin until 1884.)

1859	Jackson Kemper
1870	William E. Armitage
1874	Edward R. Welles
1889	Cyrus F. Knight
1891	Isaac L. Nicholson
1906	William W. Webb
1933	Benjamin F. P. Ivins
1952	Donald H. V. Hallock
1974	Charles T. Gaskell
1985	Roger J. White

Minnesota

1859	Henry B. Whipple
1901	Samuel C. Edsall
1917	Frank A. McElwain
1944	Stephen E. Keeler
1956	Hamilton H. Kellogg
1971	Philip F. McNairy
1978	Robert M. Anderson

Mississippi

1850	William M. Green
1887	Hugh M. Thompson
1903	Theodore DuB. Bratton
1938	William M. Green
1943	Duncan M. Gray
1966	J. Maury Allin
1974	Duncan M. Gray, Jr.

Missouri

1835	Jackson Kemper
1844	Cicero S. Hawks
1868	Charles F. Robertson
1886	Daniel S. Tuttle
1923	Frederick F. Johnson
1933	William Scarlett
1952	Arthur C. Lichtenberger
1959	George L. Cadigan
1975	William Augustus Jones, Jr.

Montana

1867	Daniel S. Tuttle
1880	Leigh R. Brewer
1916	William F. Faber
1934	Herbert H. H. Fox
1939	Henry H. Daniels
1957	Chandler W. Sterling
1968	Jackson E. Gilliam

Protestant Episcopal Bishops by Diocese (continued)

Navajoland Area Mission

1980 Frederick Putman
1984 Wesley Frensdorff

Nebraska

1870 Robert *H. Clarkson
1885 George Worthington
1908 Arthur L. Williams
1919 Ernest V. Shayler
1940 Howard R. Brinker
1962 Russell T. Rauscher
1972 Robert P. Varley
1976 James Daniel Warner

Nevada

(Diocese divided between Sacramento, Northern California, and Salt Lake, 1898-1907.)

1874 Ozi W. Whitaker
1888 Abiel Leonard III
1908 Henry D. Robinson
1914 George C. Hunting
1929 Thomas Jenkins
1942 William F. Lewis
1960 William G. Wright
1972 Wesley Frensdorff

New Hampshire

(Part of Eastern Diocese, 1811-1843.)

1844 Carlton Chase
1870 William W. Niles
1914 Edward M. Parker
1926 John T. Dallas
1948 Charles F. Hall
1973 Philip A. Smith

New Jersey

1815 John Croes
1832 George W. Doane
1859 William H. Odenheimer
1875 John Scarborough
1915 Paul Matthews
1937 Wallace J. Gardner
1955 Alfred L. Banyard
1974 Albert W. Van Duzer
1983 G. P. Mellick Belshaw

New Mexico and Southwest Texas

(See Rio Grande.)

New York

1787 Samuel Provoost
1815 Benjamin Moore
1816 John H. Hobart
1830 Benjamin T. Onderdonk
1852 Jonathan M. Wainwright
      (provisional)
1854 Horatio Potter
1881 Theodore B. Lyman
1887 Henry C. Potter

1908 David H. Greer
1919 Charles S. Burch
1921 William T. Manning
1947 Charles K. Gilbert
1950 Horace W. B. Donegan
1972 Paul Moore, Jr.

Newark, New Jersey

(Diocese of Northern New Jersey until 1886.)

1874 William H. Odenheimer
1880 Thomas A. Starkey
1903 Edwin S. Lines
1927 Wilson R. Stearly
1935 Benjamin M. Washburn
1958 Leland Stark
1974 George E. Rath
1979 John Shelby Spong

Niobrara

(See South Dakota.)

North Carolina

1823 John S. Ravenscroft
1831 Levi S. Ives
1853 Thomas Atkinson
1893 Joseph B. Cheshire, Jr.
1932 Edwin A. Penick
1959 Richard H. Baker
1965 Thomas A. Fraser, Jr.
1983 Robert W. Estill

North Dakota

1883 William D. Walker
1899 Samuel C. Edsall
1901 Cameron Mann
1914 John P. Tyler
1931 Frederick B. Bartlett
1937 Douglass H. Atwill
1951 Richard R. Emery
1965 George T. Masuda
1980 Harold A. Hopkins, Jr.

North Texas

(See Northwest Texas.)

Northern California

(Diocese of Sacramento until 1961.)

1874 John H. D. Wingfield
1899 William H. Moreland
1933 A. W. Noel Porter
1958 Clarence R. Haden, Jr.
1978 John L. Thompson, III

Northern Indiana

(Diocese of Michigan City until 1925.)

1899 John H. White
1925 Campbell Gray
1944 James R. Mallett
1963 Walter C. Klein
1972 William C. R. Sheridan

Northern Michigan

(Diocese of Marquette until 1937.)

1896 Gershom M. Williams
1919 Robert LeR. Harris
1930 Hayward S. Ablewhite
1942 Herman R. Page
1964 George R. Selway
1972 Samuel J. Wylie
1975 William Arthur Dimmick
1982 Thomas K. Ray

Northern New Jersey

(See Newark.)

Northern Philippines

1972 E. G. Longid
1975 Richard A. Abellon

Northern Texas

(See Dallas.)

Northwest

(Diocese discontinued in 1865.)

1860 Joseph C. Talbot

Northwest Texas

(Diocese of North Texas until 1958.)

1910 Edward A. Temple
1925 Eugene C. Seaman
1946 George H. Quarterman
1972 Willis R. Henton
1980 Sam Byron Hulsey

Northwestern Pennsylvania

1911 Rogers Israel
1921 John C. Ward
1943 Edward P. Wroth
1946 Harold E. Sawyer
1952 William Crittenden
1974 Donald James Davis

Ohio

1819 Philander Chase
1832 Charles P. McIlvaine
1873 Gregory T. Bedell
1889 William A. Leonard
1930 Warren L. Rogers
1938 Beverly D. Tucker
1952 Nelson M. Burroughs
1968 John H. Burt
1984 James R. Moodey

Oklahoma

1893 Francis K. Brooke
1919 Theodore P. Thurston
1927 Thomas Casady
1951 Chilton Powell
1977 Gerald N. McAllister

Olympia, Washington

(Diocese of Oregon and Washington Territory until 1880; Washington Territory until 1892.)

1854 Thomas F. Scott
1868 Benjamin W. Morris
1880 John A. Paddock
1894 William M. Barker
1902 Frederick W. Keator
1925 Simeon A. Huston
1947 Stephen F. Bayne, Jr.
1960 William F. Lewis
1964 Ivol I. Curtis
1976 Robert H. Cochrane

Oregon

(Diocese of Oregon and Washington Territory until 1880.)

1854 Thomas F. Scott
1889 Benjamin W. Morris 2d
1906 Charles Scadding
1915 Walter T. Sumner
1936 Benjamin D. Dagwell
1958 James W. F. Carman
1974 Matthew P. Bigliardi

Oregon and Washington Territory

(See Olympia, Oregon.)

Panama and the Canal Zone

1920 James C. Morris
1930 Vacant
1937 Harry Beal
1945 Reginald H. Gooden
1972 Lemuel Barnett Shirley
1984 James Hamilton Ottley

Pennsylvania

1787 William White
1836 Henry U. Onderdonk
1845 Alonzo Potter
1865 William B. Stevens
1887 Ozi W. Whitaker
1911 Alexander Mackay-Smith
1911 Philip M. Rhinelander
1924 Thomas J. Garland
1931 Francis M. Taitt
1943 Oliver J. Hart
1963 Joseph G. Armstrong
1964 Robert L. DeWitt
1974 Lyman C. Ogilby

Philippines

1901 Charles H. Brent
1920 Gouverneur F. Mosher
1942 Norman S. Binsted
1957 Lyman C. Ogilby
1967 Benito C. Cabanban
1978 Manuel C. Lumpias

Pittsburgh, Pennsylvania

1866 John B. Kerfoot

460

1882 Cortlandt Whitehead	
1923 Alexander Mann	
1944 Austin Pardue	
1968 Robert B. Appleyard	
1983 Alden M. Hathaway	

The Platt

(See Western Nebraska.)

Puerto Rico

1902 James H. VanBuren
1913 Charles B. Colmore
1947 Charles F. Boynton
1951 A. Ervine Smith
1965 Francisco Reus-Froylan

Quincy, Illinois

1878 Alexander Burgess
1901 Frederick W. Taylor
1904 M. Edward Fawcett
1936 William L. Essex
1958 F. William Lickfield
1973 Donald J. Parsons

Rhode Island

(See Connecticut, Massachusetts, and Eastern Diocese for earlier bishops.)

1843 John P. K. Henshaw
1854 Thomas M. Clark
1903 William N. McVicker
1911 James DeWolf Perry
1946 Granville G. Bennett
1955 John S. Higgins
1972 Frederick H. Belden
1980 George Hunt

Rio Grande, New Mexico

(Diocese of New Mexico & Southwest Texas until 1972.)

1880 George K. Dunlop
1889 John M. Kendrick
1914 Frederick B. Howden
1942 James M. Stoney
1956 Charles J. Kinsolving, III
1972 Richard M. Trelease, Jr.

Rochester, New York

1931 David L. Ferris
1938 Bartel H. Reinheimer
1950 Dudley S. Stark
1963 George W. Barrett
1970 Robert R. Spears, Jr.
1984 William G. Burrill, Jr.

Sacramento

(See Northern California.)

Salina

(See Western Kansas.)

Salt Lake

(See Utah.)

San Diego, California

1974 Robert M. Wolterstorff
1982 C. Brinkley Morton

San Joaquin, California

1911 Louis C. Sanford
1944 Sumner F. D. Walters
1968 Victor M. Rivera

South Carolina

1795 Robert Smith
1812 Theodore Dehon
1818 Nathaniel Bowen
1840 Christopher E. Gadsden
1853 Thomas F. Davis
1871 William B. W. Howe
1894 Ellison Capers
1908 William A. Guerry
1928 Albert S. Thomas
1944 Thomas N. Carruthers
1961 Gray Temple
1982 C. FitzSimons Allison

South Dakota

(Diocese of Niobrara until 1883.)

1873 William H. Hare
1910 Frederick F. Johnson
1912 George Biller, Jr.
1916 Hugh L. Burleson
1931 William B. Roberts
1954 Conrad H. Gesner
1970 Walter H. Jones
1984 Craig B. Anderson

South Florida

(Diocese of Central Florida, Southwest Florida, and Southeast Florida after 1970.)

1892 William C. Gray
1913 Cameron Mann
1932 John D. Wing
1951 Henry I. Louttit
1961 William L. Hargrave

Southeast Florida

1970 James L. Duncan
1980 Calvin O. Schofield, Jr.

Southern Ohio

1875 Thomas A. Jaggar
1904 Boyd Vincent
1929 Theodore I. Reese
1931 Henry W. Hobson
1959 Roger W. Blanchard
1971 John M. Krumm

Southern Philippines

1972 Richard A. Abellon

Southern Virginia

1892 Alfred M. Randolph
1918 Beverly D. Tucker
1930 Arthur C. Thomson
1938 William A. Brown
1950 George P. Gunn
1971 David S. Rose
1978 Claude Charles Vache

Southwest

(Included present states of Arkansas, New Mexico, Arizona, and the Indian Territory; discontinued in 1865.)

1859 Henry C. Clay

Southwest Florida

1970 William L. Hargrave
1975 Emerson Paul Haynes

Southwestern Virginia

1920 Robert C. Jett
1938 Henry D. Phillips
1954 William H. Marmion
1979 A. Heath Light

Spokane, Washington

1892 Lemuel H. Wells
1915 Herman Page
1924 Edward M. Cross
1954 Russell S. Hubbard
1967 John R. Wyatt
1979 Leigh Allen Wallace, Jr.

Springfield, Illinois

1878 George F. Seymour
1906 Edward W. Osborne
1917 Granville H. Sherwood
1924 John C. White
1947 Richard T. Loring, Jr.
1948 Charles A. Clough
1962 Albert A. Chambers
1972 Albert W. Hillestad
1982 Donald M. Hultstrand

Tennessee

1834 James H. Otey
1865 Charles T. Quintard
1898 Thomas F. Gailor
1935 James M. Maxon
1947 Edmund P. Dendridge
1953 Theodore N. Barth
1961 John Vander Horst
1977 William E. Sanders
1985 George Lazenby Reynolds

Texas

1859 Alexander Gregg
1893 George H. Kinsolving
1928 Clinton S. Quin
1955 John E. Hines

1965 J. Milton Richardson
1980 Maurice M. Benitez

Upper South Carolina

1922 Kirkman G. Finlay
1939 John J. Gravatt
1953 Clarence A. Cole
1963 John A. Pinckney
1973 George M. Alexander
1979 William A. Beckham

Utah

(Diocese of Salt Lake, 1898-1907.)

1867 Daniel S. Tuttle
1888 Abiel Leonard III
1904 Franklin S. Spalding
1914 Paul Jones
1920 Arthur W. Moulton
1946 Stephen C. Clark
1951 Richard S. Watson
1971 E. Otis Charles

Vermont

(See Eastern Diocese for period 1811-1832.)

1832 John H. Hopkins
1868 William H. A. Bissell
1894 Arthur C. A. Hall
1930 Samuel B. Booth
1936 Vedder Van Dyck
1961 Harvey D. Butterfield
1974 Robert S. Kerr

Virginia

1790 James Madison
1814 Richard C. Moore
1841 William Meade
1862 John Johns
1876 Francis McN. Whittle
1902 Robert A. Gibson
1919 William C. Brown
1927 Henry St. G. Tucker
1944 Frederick D. Goodwin
1961 Robert F. Gibson
1974 Robert B. Hall
1985 Peter James Lee

Washington, DC

1896 Henry Y. Satterlee
1909 Alfred Harding
1923 James E. Freeman
1944 Angus Dun
1962 William F. Creighton
1977 John T. Walker

Washington Territory

(See Olympia.)

West Missouri

(Diocese of Kansas City, 1904-1911.)

1890 Edward R. Atwill
1911 Sidney C. Partridge
1930 Robert N. Spencer

461

Protestant Episcopal Bishops by Diocese (continued)

1950 Edward R. Welles
1973 Arthur Vogel

West Tennessee

1983 Alex D. Dickson

West Texas

1874 Robert W. B. Elliott
1904 James S. Johnston
1916 William T. Capers
1943 Everett H. Jones
1968 Harold C. Gosnell
1977 Scott Field Bailey

West Virginia

1878 George W. Peterkin
1916 William L. Gravatt
1939 Robert E. L. Strider
1955 Wilburn C. Campbell
1976 Robert P. Atkinson

Western Colorado

(Reunited with Colorado in 1919.)

1893 William M. Barker
1895 Abiel Leonard III
1904 Franklin S. Spalding
1907 Edward J. Knight
1909 Benjamin Brewster
1917 Frank H. Touret

Western Kansas

(Diocese of Salina until 1960.)

1903 Sheldon M. Griswold
1918 John C. Sage
1921 Robert H. Mize
1943 Shirley H. Nichols
1956 Arnold M. Lewis
1966 William Davidson
1981 John F. Ashby

Western Louisiana

1980 Willis R. Henton

Western Massachusetts

1902 Alexander H. Vinton

1911 Thomas F. Davies
1937 William A. Lawrence
1957 Robert M. Hatch
1970 Alexander D. Stewart
1985 Andrew F. Wissemann

Western Michigan

1875 George DeN. Gillespie
1909 John N. McCormick
1937 Lewis B. Wittemore
1953 Dudley B. McNeil
1960 Charles E. Bennison
1984 Howard S. Meeks

Western Nebraska

(Diocese of the Platt, 1889-1898; Laramie, 1898-1908; Kearney, 1908-1913; reunited with Nebraska, 1946.)

1890 Anson R. Graves
1910 George A. Beecher

Western New York

1839 William H. DeLancey
1865 Arthur C. Coxe
1897 William D. Walker

1918 Charles H. Brent
1929 David L. Ferris
1931 Cameron J. Davis
1948 Lauriston L. Scaife
1970 Harold B. Robinson

Western North Carolina

(Diocese of Asheville until 1922.)

1898 Junius M. Horner
1934 Robert E. Gribbin
1948 M. George Henry
1975 William G. Weinhauer

Wisconsin

(See Milwaukee.)

Wyoming

1887 Ethelbert Talbot
1907 James B. Funsten
1909 Nathaniel S. Thomas
1929 Elmer N. Schmuck
1936 Winfred H. Ziegler
1948 James W. Hunter
1969 David R. Thornberry
1977 Bob Gordon Jones

The Roman Catholic Church in America

Cardinals

Year	Name	City	Year	Name	City
1875	John McCloskey	New York, NY	1965	Lawrence Shehan	Baltimore, MD
1886	James Gibbons	Baltimore, MD	1967	Francis Brennan	(Roman Curial Official)
1911	John M. Farley	New York, NY			
1911	William H. O'Connell	Boston, MA	1967	Patrick O'Boyle	Washington, DC
1921	Dennis J. Dougherty	Philadelphia, PA	1967	John J. Krol	Philadelphia, PA
1924	George W. Mundelein	Chicago, IL	1967	John P. Cody	Chicago, IL
1924	Patrick J. Hayes	New York, NY	1969	John F. Dearden	Detroit, MI
1946	John J. Glennon	St. Louis, MO	1969	John J. Carberry	St. Louis, MO
1946	Samuel A. Stritch	Chicago, IL	1969	Terence J. Cooke	New York, NY
1946	Edward A. Mooney	Detroit, MI	1969	John J. Wright	(Roman Curial Official)
1946	Francis J. Spellman	New York, NY			
1953	James McIntyre	Los Angeles, CA	1973	Humberto S. Medeiros	Boston, MA
1958	Richard J. Cushing	Boston, MA	1973	Timothy Manning	Los Angeles, CA
1958	John F. O'Hara	Philadelphia, PA	1977	William Baum	Washington, DC
1959	Aloisius J. Muench	Fargo, ND	1983	Joseph L. Bernardin	Chicago, IL
1959	Albert G. Meyer	Chicago, IL	1985	Bernard Law	Boston, MA
1961	Joseph E. Ritter	St. Louis, MO	1985	John J. O'Connor	New York, NY

Roman Catholic Archbishops by Archdiocese

(First inauguration date also indicates year Archdiocese was created.)

Alabama

Mobile

1980   Oscar H. Lipscomb

Alaska

Anchorage

1966   Joseph T. Ryan
1976   Francis T. Hurley

California

Los Angeles

1936   John J. Cantwell
1948   James McIntyre
1970   Timothy Manning
1985   Roger M. Mahoney

San Francisco

1853   Joseph S. Alemany
1884   Patrick W. Riordan
1915   Edward J. Hanna
1935   John Mitty
1962   Joseph T. McGucken
1977   John R. Quinn

Colorado

Denver

1941   Urban J. Vehr
1967   James V. Casey

Connecticut

Hartford

1953   Henry J. O'Brien
1969   John F. Whealon

District of Columbia

Washington

1939   Michael J. Curley
1948   Patrick O'Boyle
1973   William Baum
1980   James A. Hickey

Florida

Miami

1958   Coleman F. Carroll
1977   Edward A. McCarthy

Georgia

Atlanta

1962   Paul J. Hallinan
1968   Thomas A. Donnellan

Illinois

Chicago

1880   Patrick A. Feehan
1903   James E. Quigley
1915   George W. Mundelein
1939   Samuel A. Stritch
1958   Albert G. Meyer
1965   John P. Cody
1982   Joseph L. Bernardin

Indiana

Indianapolis

1944   Joseph E. Ritter
1946   Paul C. Schulte
1970   George J. Biskup
1980   Edward T. O'Meara

Iowa

Dubuque

1893   John Hennessy

1900 John J. Keane
1911 James J. Keane
1930 Francis J. Beckman
1946 Henry P. Rohlman
1954 Leo Binz
1984 Daniel W. Kucera

Kansas

Kansas City

1952 Edward J. Hunkeler
1969 Ignatius J. Strecker

Kentucky

Louisville

1937 John A. Floersh
1967 Thomas J. McDonough
1981 Thomas C. Kelly

Louisiana

New Orleans

1850 Anthony Blanc
1861 Jean Marie Odin
1870 Napoleon J. Perche
1883 Francis X. Leray
1888 Francis A. Janssens
1897 Placide L. Chapelle
1906 James H. Blenk
1918 John W. Shaw
1935 Joseph F. Rummell
1964 John P. Cody
1965 Philip M. Hannan

Maryland

Baltimore

1808 John Carroll
1815 Leonard Neale
1817 Ambrose Marechal
1828 James Whitfield
1834 Samuel Eccleston
1851 Francis P. Kenrick
1864 Martin J. Spalding
1872 James R. Bayley
1877 James Gibbons
1921 Michael J. Curley
1947 Francis P. Keough
1961 Lawrence Shehan
1974 William D. Borders

Massachusetts

Boston

1875 John J. Williams
1907 William H. O'Connell
1944 Richard J. Cushing
1970 Humberto S. Medeiros
1985 Bernard Law

Michigan

Detroit

1937 Edward A. Mooney
1958 John F. Dearden
1981 Edmund C. Szoka

Minnesota

St. Paul

1888 John Ireland
1919 John Dowling
1931 John G. Murray
1956 William O. Brady
1962 Leo Binz
1967 Leo C. Byrne
1975 John R. Roach

Missouri

St. Louis

1847 Peter R. Kenrick
1895 John J. Kain
1903 John J. Glennon
1945 Joseph E. Ritter
1968 John J. Carberry
1980 John L. May

Nebraska

Omaha

1945 James H. Ryan
1948 Gerald T. Bergan
1969 Daniel E. Sheehan

New Jersey

Newark

1937 Thomas J. Walsh
1953 Thomas A. Boland
1974 Peter L. Gerety

New Mexico

Santa Fe

1875 John B. Lamy
1885 John B. Salpointe
1894 Placide L. Chapelle
1899 Peter Bourgade
1909 John B. Pitaval
1919 Albert T. Daeger
1933 Rudolph A. Gerken
1943 Edwin V. Byrne
1964 James P. Davis
1974 Robert F. Sanchez

New York

New York

1850 John J. Hughes
1864 John McCloskey
1885 Michael A. Corrigan
1902 John M. Farley
1919 Patrick J. Hayes
1939 Francis J. Spellman
1965 John J. Maguire
1968 Terence J. Cooke
1984 John J. O'Connor

Ohio

Cincinnati

1850 John B. Purcell
1883 William H. Elder
1904 Henry Moeller
1925 John T. McNicholas
1950 Karl J. Alter
1969 Paul F. Leibold
1972 Joseph L. Bernardin
1982 Daniel E. Pilarczyk

Oklahoma

Oklahoma City

1973 John R. Quinn

1977 Charles A. Salatka

Oregon

Portland

1846 Francis N. Blanchet
1880 Charles J. Seghers
1885 William H. Gross
1889 Alexander Christie
1926 Edward D. Howard
1966 Robert J. Dwyer
1974 Cornelius M. Power

Pennsylvania

Philadelphia

1875 James F. B. Wood
1884 Patrick J. Ryan
1911 Edmond F. Predergast
1918 Dennis J. Dougherty
1951 John F. O'Hara
1961 John J. Krol

Texas

San Antonio

1926 Jerome Drossaerts
1941 Robert E. Lucey
1969 Francis J. Furey
1979 Patrick F. Flores

Washington

Seattle

1950 Thomas A. Connolly
1975 Raymond G. Hunthausen

Wisconsin

Milwaukee

1875 John M. Henni
1881 Michael Heiss
1891 Frederick X. Katzer
1903 Sebastian G. Messmer
1930 Samuel A. Stritch
1940 Moses E. Kiley
1953 Albert G. Meyer
1959 William E. Cousins
1977 Rembert G. Weakland

Roman Catholic Bishops by Diocese

(First date indicates year in which diocese was created unless otherwise specified.)

Alabama

Birmingham

(See Mobile for earlier bishops.)

1969   Joseph G. Vath

Mobile

(Diocese of Mobile-Birmingham, 1954-1969; became archdiocese 1980.)

1829   Michael Portier
1859   John Quinlan
1884   Dominic Manucy
1885   Jeremiah O'Sullivan
1897   Edward P. Allen
1927   Thomas J. Toolen
1969   John L. May

Alaska

Fairbanks

1962   Francis D. Gleeson
1968   Robert Louis Whelan
1985   Michael Kaniecki

Juneau

1951   Dermot O'Flanagan
1970   Francis D. Hurley (auxiliary)
1971   Joseph T. Ryan
1979   Michael H. Kenny

Arizona

Phoenix

1969   Edward A. McCarthy
1977   James S. Rausch
1982   Thomas J. O'Brien

Tucson

1897   Peter Bourgade
1900   Henry Granjon
1923   Daniel J. Gercke
1960   Francis J. Green
1982   Manuel D. Moreno

Arkansas

Little Rock

1843   Andrew Byrne
1866   Edward Fitzgerald
1907   John B. Morris
1946   Albert L. Fletcher
1972   Andrew J. McDonald

California

Fresno

1967   Timothy Manning
1969   Hugh A. Donohoe
1980   Joseph J. Madera

Los Angeles

(Diocese of the Two Californias until 1850; Monterey, 1850-1859; Monterey-Los Angeles, 1859-1922; Los Angeles-San Diego, 1922-1936; became archdiocese 1936.)

1840   Francisco Garcia Diego y Moreno
1850   Joseph S. Alemany
1854   Thaddeus Amat
1878   Francis Mora
1896   George T. Montgomery
1903   Thomas J. Conaty
1917   John J. Cantwell

Monterey

(Monterey-Fresno until 1967; see Los Angeles for earlier bishops.)

1922   John J. Cantwell (apostolic administrator)
1924   John B. MacGinley
1933   Philip G. Scher
1953   Aloysius J. Wilinger
1967   Harry Anselm Clinch
1982   Thaddeus Shubsda

Oakland

1962   Floyd L. Begin
1977   John S. Cummins

Orange

1976   William R. Johnson

Sacramento

(Diocese of Grass Valley until 1886.)

1868   Eugene O'Connell
1884   Patrick Manogue
1896   Thomas L. Grace
1922   Patrick J. Keane
1929   Robert J. Armstrong
1957   Joseph T. McGucken
1962   Alden J. Bell
1979   Francis A. Quinn

San Bernardino

1978   Philip F. Straling

San Diego

1936   Charles F. Buddy
1966   Francis J. Furey
1969   Leo T. Maher

San Jose

1981   Pierre DuMaine

Santa Rosa

1962   Leo T. Maher
1969   Mark J. Hurley

Stockton

1962   Hugh A. Donohoe
1969   Merlin J. Guilfoyle
1980   Roger M. Mahony
1986   Donald W. Montrose

Colorado

Colorado Springs

1984   Richard C. Hanifen

Denver

(Became archdiocese 1941.)

1887   Joseph P. Macheboeuf
1889   Nicholas C. Matz
1917   John H. Tihen
1931   Urban J. Vehr

Pueblo

1941   Joseph C. Willging
1959   Charles A. Buswell
1980   Arthur N. Tafoya

Connecticut

Bridgeport

1953   Lawrence J. Shehan
1961   Walter W. Curtis

Hartford

(Became archdiocese 1953.)

1843   William Tyler
1850   Bernard O'Reilly
1859   Francis P. MacFarland
1876   Thomas Galberry
1879   Laurence S. McMahon
1894   Michael Tierney
1910   John J. Nilan
1934   Maurice F. McAuliffe
1945   Henry J. O'Brien

Norwich

1953   Bernard J. Flanagan
1960   Vincent J. Hines
1975   Daniel P. Reilly

Delaware

Wilmington

1868   Thomas A. Becker
1886   Alfred A. Curtis
1897   John J. Monaghan
1925   Edmond J. Fitzmaurice
1960   Michael Hyle
1968   Thomas J. Mardaga
1985   Robert E. Mulvee

Florida

Miami

(Became archdiocese 1968.)

1958   Coleman F. Carroll

Orlando

1968   William D. Borders
1974   Thomas J. Grady

Palm Beach

1984   Thomas V. Daily

Pensacola-Tallahassee

1975   Rene H. Gracida
1983   J. Keith Symons

St. Augustine

1870   Augustin Verot
1877   John Moore
1902   William J. Kenny
1914   Michael J. Curley
1922   Patrick J. Barry
1940   Joseph P. Hurley
1968   Paul F. Tanner
1979   John J. Snyder

Roman Catholic Bishops by Diocese (continued)

St. Petersburg

1968   Charles B. McLaughlin
1979   W. Thomas Larkin

Venice

1984   John J. Nevins

Georgia

Atlanta

(Part of Savannah-Atlanta, 1937-1956; became archdiocese 1962.)

1956   Francis E. Hyland
1962   Paul J. Hallinan

Savannah

(Diocese of Savannah-Atlanta, 1937-1956.)

1850   Francis X. Gartland
1854   John Barry
1861   Augustin Verot
1870   Ignatius Persico
1873   William H. Gross
1886   Thomas A. Becker
1900   Benjamin J. Keiley
1922   Michael J. Keyes
1935   Gerald P. O'Hara
1960   Thomas J. McDonough
1967   Gerard L. Frey
1973   Raymond W. Lessard

Hawaii

Honolulu

1941   James J. Sweeney
1968   John J. Scanlan
1982   Joseph A. Ferrario

Idaho

Boise

1893   Alphonse J. Glorieux
1918   Daniel M. Gorman
1928   Edward J. Kelly
1956   James J. Byrne
1962   Sylvester W. Treinen

Illinois

Belleville

1888   John Janssen
1913   Henry Althoff
1947   Albert B. Zuroweste
1976   William M. Cosgrove
1981   John N. Wurm
1984   James J. Keleher

Chicago

(Became archdiocese 1880.)

1843   William Quarter
1848   James O. Van de Velde
1854   Anthony O'Regan
1858   James Duggan

Joliet

1948   Martin D. McNamara
1966   Romeo Blanchette
1979   Joseph L. Imesch

Peoria

(Erected 1875.)

1876   John L. Spalding
1909   Edmund M. Dunne
1930   Joseph H. Schlarman
1952   William E. Cousins
1959   John Baptist Franz
1971   Edward W. O'Rourke

Rockford

1908   Peter J. Muldoon
1928   Edward F. Hoban
1943   John J. Boylan
1953   Raymond P. Hillinger
1956   Loras T. Lane
1968   Arthur J. O'Neill

Springfield

(Diocese of Quincy until 1857; Alton until 1923.)

1853   Peter R. Kenrick (apostolic administrator)
1855   Anthony O'Regan (apostolic administrator)
1857   Henry D. Juncker
1870   Peter J. Baltes
1888   James Ryan
1924   James A. Griffin
1949   William A. O'Connor
1975   Joseph A. McNichols
1984   Daniel L. Ryan

Indiana

Evansville

1944   Henry J. Grimmelsman
1966   Paul F. Leibold
1970   Francis R. Shea

Fort Wayne-South Bend

(Diocese of Fort Wayne until 1960.)

1857   John H. Luers
1872   Joseph Dwenger
1893   Joseph Rademacher
1900   Herman J. Alerding

1925   John F. Noll
1957   Leo Aloysius Pursley
1976   William E. McManus
1985   John M. D'Arcy

Gary

1957   Andrew G. Grutka
1984   Norbert F. Gaughan

Indianapolis

(Diocese of Vincennes until 1898; became archdiocese 1944.)

1834   Simon G. Brute de Remur
1839   Celestine de la Hailandiere
1847   John S. Bazin
1849   James M. de Saint-Palais
1878   Francis S. Chatard
1918   Joseph Chartrand
1934   Joseph E. Ritter

Lafayette

1944   John G. Bennett
1957   John J. Carberry
1965   Raymond J. Gallagher
1983   George A. Fulcher
1984   William L. Higi

Iowa

Davenport

1881   John McMullen
1884   Henry Cosgrove
1906   James Davis
1927   Henry P. Rohlman
1944   Ralph L. Hayes
1967   Gerald F. O'Keefe

Des Moines

1912   Austin Dowling
1919   Thomas W. Drumm
1934   Gerald T. Bergan
1948   Edward C. Daly
1965   George J. Biskup
1968   Maurice J. Dingman

Dubuque

(Became archdiocese 1893.)

1837   Peter J. M. Loras
1858   Timothy C. Smyth
1866   John Hennessy

Sioux City

1902   Philip J. Garrigan
1920   Edmond Heelan
1948   Joseph M. Mueller
1970   Frank H. Greteman
1983   Lawrence D. Soens

Kansas

Dodge City

1951   John B. Franz
1960   Marion F. Forst
1976   Eugene Gerber
1983   Stanley G. Schlarman

Kansas City

(Diocese of Leavenworth until 1891; Kansas City in Kansas 1891-1897; Leavenworth 1897-1947; became archdiocese 1952.)

1877   Michael L. Fink
1904   Thomas F. Lillis
1910   John Ward
1929   Francis Johannes
1937   Paul C. Schulte
1944   George J. Donnelly
1951   Edward J. Hunkeler

Leavenworth

(See Kansas City, Kansas.)

Salina

(Diocese of Concordia until 1944.)

1887   Richard Scannell
1891   John J. Hennessey (apostolic administrator)
1898   John F. Cunningham
1919   Francis J. Tief
1938   Frank A. Thill
1957   Frederick W. Freking
1965   Cyril J. Vogel
1980   Daniel W. Kucera
1984   George K. Fitzsimons

Wichita

(Erected 1887.)

1888   John J. Hennessy
1921   Augustus J. Schwertner
1940   Christian H. Winkelmann
1947   Mark K. Carroll
1967   David M. Maloney
1983   Eugene J. Gerber

Kentucky

Covington

1853   George A. Carrell
1870   Augustus M. Toebbe
1885   Camillus P. Maes
1916   Ferdinand Brossart
1923   Francis W. Howard
1945   William T. Mulloy
1960   Richard H. Ackerman
1979   William A. Hughes

Louisville

(Diocese of Bardstown until 1841; became archdiocese 1937.)

1808   Benedict J. Flaget
1819   John B. M. David

1833 Benedict J. Flaget
1850 Martin J. Spalding
1865 Peter J. Lavialle
1868 William G. McCloskey
1910 Denis O'Donaghue
1924 John A. Floersh

Owensboro

1937 Francis R. Cotton
1961 Henry J. Soenneker
1982 John J. McRaith

Louisiana

Alexandria-Shreveport

(Diocese of Natchitoches, 1853-1910; diocese of Alexandria until 1977.)

1853 Augustus M. Martin
1877 Francis X. Leray
1885 Anthony Durier
1904 Cornelius Van de Ven
1933 Daniel F. Desmond
1946 Charles P. Greco
1974 Lawrence P. Graves
1983 William B. Friend

Baton Rouge

1961 Robert E. Tracy
1974 Joseph V. Sullivan
1983 Stanley J. Ott

Houma-Thibodaux

1977 Warren L. Boudreaux

Lafayette

1918 Jules B. Jeanmard
1956 Maurice Schexnayder
1973 Gerard L. Frey

Lake Charles

1980 Jude Speyrer

New Orleans

(Diocese of Louisiana and the Two Floridas, 1793-1826; became archdiocese 1850.)

1827 Joseph Rosati (apostolic administrator)
1829 Leo R. De Neckere
1835 Anthony Blanc

Maine

Portland

(Erected 1853.)

1855 David W. Bacon

1875 James A. Healy
1901 William H. O'Connell
1906 Louis S. Walsh
1925 John G. Murray
1932 Joseph E. McCarthy
1955 Daniel J. Feeney
1969 Peter Leo Gerety
1974 Edward C. O'Leary

Maryland

Baltimore

(Became archdiocese 1808.)

1789 John Carroll

Massachusetts

Boston

(Became archdiocese 1875.)

1808 John L. de Cheverus
1825 Benedict J. Fenwick
1846 John J. Williams

Fall River

1904 William Stang
1907 Daniel F. Feehan
1934 James E. Cassidy
1951 James L. Connolly
1970 Daniel A. Cronin

Springfield

1870 Patrick T. O'Reilly
1892 Thomas D. Beaven
1921 Thomas M. O'Leary
1950 Christopher J. Weldon
1977 Joseph F. Maguire

Worcester

1950 John J. Wright
1959 Bernard J. Flanagan
1983 Timothy J. Harrington

Michigan

Detroit

(Became archdiocese 1937.)

1833 Frederick Rese
1841 Peter P. Lefevre (coadjutor)
1870 Caspar H. Borgess
1888 John S. Foley
1918 Michael J. Gallagher

Gaylord

1971 Edmund C. Szoka
1981 Robert J. Rose

Grand Rapids

1883 Henry J. Richter
1916 Michael J. Gallagher
1919 Edward D. Kelly
1926 Joseph G. Pinten
1941 Joseph C. Plagens
1943 Francis J. Haas
1954 Allen J. Babcock
1969 Joseph M. Breitenbeck

Kalamazoo

1971 Paul V. Donovan

Lansing

1937 Joseph H. Albers
1965 Alexander M. Zaleski
1975 Kenneth J. Povish

Marquette

(Diocese of Sainte-Marie until 1865; Sault Sainte-Marie and Marquette, 1865-1937.)

1857 Frederic Baraga
1869 Ignatius Mrak
1879 John Vertin
1899 Frederick Eis
1922 Paul J. Nussbaum
1935 Joseph C. Plagens
1941 Francis J. Magner
1947 Thomas L. Noa
1968 Charles A. Salatka
1978 Mark F. Schmitt

Saginaw

1938 William F. Murphy
1950 Stephen S. Woznicki
1969 Francis F. Reh
1980 Kenneth E. Untener

Minnesota

Crookston

1910 Timothy Corbett
1938 John H. Peschges
1945 Francis J. Schenk
1960 Laurence A. Glenn
1970 Kenneth J. Povish
1976 Victor Balke

Duluth

1889 James McGolrick
1918 John T. McNicholas
1926 Thomas A. Welch
1960 Francis J. Schenk
1969 Paul F. Anderson
1983 Robert H. Brom

New Ulm

1958 Alphonse J. Schladweiler
1976 Raymond A. Lucker

St. Cloud

1889 Otto Zardetti
1894 Martin Marty
1897 James Trobec
1915 Joseph F. Busch
1953 Peter W. Bartholome
1968 George H. Speltz

St. Paul

(Became archdiocese 1888.)

1850 Joseph Cretin
1859 Thomas L. Grace
1884 John Ireland

Winona

1889 Joseph B. Cotter
1910 Patrick R. Heffron
1928 Francis M. Kelly
1949 Edward A. Fitzgerald
1969 Loras J. Watters

Mississippi

Biloxi

1977 Joseph Howze

Jackson

(Diocese of Natchez-Jackson until 1977.)

1840 John J. Chanche
1853 James O. Van de Velde
1857 William H. Elder
1881 Francis A. Janssens
1889 Thomas Heslin
1911 John E. Gunn
1924 Richard O. Gerow
1967 Joseph B. Brunini
1984 William R. Houck

Natchez-Jackson

(See Jackson, Mississippi.)

Missouri

Jefferson City

1956 Joseph M. Marling
1969 Michael F. McAuliffe

Kansas City-St. Joseph

(Diocese of Kansas City until 1956; see also diocese of St. Joseph.)

1880 John J. Hogan
1913 Thomas F. Lillis
1938 Edwin V. O'Hara
1956 John P. Cody
1962 Charles H. Helmsing
1977 John T. Sullivan

Roman Catholic Bishops by Diocese (continued)

St. Joseph

(Incorporated into Diocese of Kansas City-St. Joseph, 1956.)

1868 John J. Hogan
1893 Maurice F. Burke
1923 Francis Gilfillan
1933 Charles H. LeBlond

St. Louis

(Became archdiocese 1847.)

1826 Joseph Rosati
1843 Peter R. Kenrick

Springfield-Cape Girardeau

1956 Charles Helmsing
1962 Ignatius J. Strecker
1970 William W. Baum
1973 Bernard Law
1984 John J. Leibrecht

Montana

Great Falls-Billings

(Diocese of Great Falls until 1982.)

1904 Mathias C. Lenihan
1930 Edwin V. O'Hara
1939 William J. Condon
1968 Eldon Bernard Schuster
1978 Thomas J. Murphy

Helena

1884 John B. Brondel
1904 John P. Carroll
1927 George J. Finnegan
1933 Ralph L. Hayes
1936 Joseph M. Gilmore
1962 Raymond G. Hunthausen
1976 Elden F. Curtiss

Nebraska

Grand Island

(Diocese of Kearney until 1917.)

1913 James A. Duffy
1932 Stanislaus V. Bona
1945 Edward J. Hunkeler
1951 John L. Paschang
1972 John J. Sullivan
1978 Lawrence J. McNamara

Lincoln

1887 Thomas Bonacum
1911 John H. Tihen
1918 Charles J. O'Reilly
1924 Francis J. Beckman
1930 Louis B. Kucera

1957 James V. Casey
1967 Glennon P. Flavin

Omaha

(Became archdiocese 1945.)

1885 James O'Connor
1891 Richard Scannell
1916 Jeremiah J. Harty
1926 Francis J. Beckman (apostolic administrator)
1928 Joseph F. Rummell
1935 James H. Ryan

Nevada

Reno-Las Vegas

(Diocese of Reno until 1976.)

1931 Thomas K. Gorman
1952 Robert J. Dwyer
1967 Joseph Green
1976 Norman F. McFarland

New Hampshire

Manchester

1884 Denis M. Bradley
1904 John B. Delaney
1907 George A. Guertin
1932 John B. Peterson
1944 Matthew F. Brady
1960 Ernest J. Primeau
1975 Odore J. Gendron

New Jersey

Camden

1937 Bartholomew J. Eustace
1957 Justin J. McCarthy
1960 Celestine J. Damiano
1968 George H. Guilfoyle

Metuchen

1982 Theodore E. McCarrick

Newark

(Became archdiocese 1937.)

1853 James R. Bayley
1873 Michael A. Corrigan
1881 Winand M. Wigger
1901 John J. O'Connor
1928 Thomas J. Walsh

Paterson

1937 Thomas H. McLaughlin
1947 Thomas A. Boland
1953 James A. McNulty
1963 James J. Navagh

1966 Lawrence B. Casey
1978 Frank J. Rodimer

Trenton

1881 Michael J. O'Farrell
1894 James A. McFaul
1918 Thomas J. Walsh
1928 John J. McMahon
1934 Moses E. Kiley
1940 William A. Griffin
1950 George W. Ahr
1980 John C. Reiss

New Mexico

Gallup

1940 Bernard T. Espelage
1969 Jerome J. Hastrich

Las Cruces

1982 Ricardo Ramirez

Santa Fe

(Became archdiocese 1875.)

1853 John B. Lamy

New York

Albany

1847 John McCloskey
1865 John J. Conroy
1877 Francis McNeirny
1894 Thomas M. A. Burke
1915 Thomas F. Cusack
1919 Edmund F. Gibbons
1954 William A. Scully
1969 Edwin B. Broderick
1977 Howard J. Hubbard

Brooklyn

1853 John Loughlin
1892 Charles E. McDonnell
1921 Thomas E. Molloy
1957 Bryan J. McEntegart
1968 Francis J. Mugavero

Buffalo

1847 John Timon
1868 Stephen V. Ryan
1897 James E. Quigley
1903 Charles H. Colton
1915 Dennis J. Dougherty
1919 William Turner
1937 John A. Duffy
1944 John F. O'Hara
1952 Joseph A. Burke
1963 James A. McNulty
1973 Edward D. Head

New York

(Became archdiocese 1850.)

1808 Richard L. Concanen
1814 John Connolly
1826 John Dubois
1842 John J. Hughes

Ogdensburg

1872 Edgar P. Wadhams
1892 Henry Gabriels
1921 Joseph H. Conroy
1939 Francis J. Monaghan
1943 Bryan J. McEntegart
1954 Walter P. Kellenberg
1957 James J. Navagh
1962 Leo R. Smith
1964 Thomas A. Donnellan
1968 Stanislaus Brzana

Rochester

1868 Bernard J. McQuaid
1909 Thomas F. Hickey
1929 John F. O'Hern
1933 Edward A. Mooney
1937 James E. Kearney
1966 Fulton J. Sheen
1969 Joseph L. Hogan
1979 Matthew H. Clark

Rockville Centre

1957 Walter P. Kellenberg
1976 John R. McGann

Syracuse

1886 Patrick A. Ludden
1912 John Grimes
1923 Daniel J. Curley
1933 James A. Duffy
1937 Walter A. Foery
1970 David F. Cunningham
1977 Frank J. Harrison

North Carolina

Charlotte

1972 Michael S. Begley
1984 John F. Donoghue

Raleigh

(Erected 1924.)

1925 William J. Hafey
1937 Eugene J. McGuinness
1945 Vincent S. Waters
1975 F. Joseph Gossman

North Dakota

Bismarck

1910   Vincent Wehrle
1940   Vincent J. Ryan
1952   Lambert A. Hoch
1956   Hilary B. Hacker
1982   John F. Kinney

Fargo

(Diocese of Jamestown until 1897.)

1889   John Shanley
1909   James O'Reilly
1935   Aloisius J. Muench
1960   Leo F. Dworchak
1970   Justin A. Driscoll
1985   James S. Sullivan

Ohio

Cincinnati

(Became archdiocese 1850.)

1822   Edward Fenwick
1833   John B. Purcell

Cleveland

1847   Amadeus Rappe
1872   Richard Gilmour
1891   Ignatius F. Horstmann
1909   John P. Farrelly
1921   Joseph Schrembs
1945   Edward F. Hoban
1966   Clarence G. Issenmann
1974   James A. Hickey
1981   Anthony M. Pilla

Columbus

1868   Sylvester H. Rosecrans
1880   John A. Watterson
1900   Henry Moeller
1904   James J. Hartley
1944   Michael J. Ready
1957   Clarence G. Issenmann
1965   John J. Carberry
1968   Clarence E. Elwell
1973   Edward J. Herrmann
1983   James A. Griffin

Steubenville

(Erected 1944.)

1945   John King Mussio
1977   Albert H. Ottenwell

Toledo

(Erected 1910.)

1911   Joseph Schrembs
1921   Samuel A. Stritch
1931   Karl J. Alter
1950   George J. Rehring
1967   John A. Donovan

1980   James R. Hoffman

Youngstown

1943   James A. McFadden
1952   Emmet M. Walsh
1968   James W. Malone

Oklahoma

Oklahoma City and Tulsa

(Diocese of Oklahoma until 1930; raised to archdiocese 1973.)

1905   Theophile Meerschaert
1924   Francis C. Kelley
1948   Eugene J. McGuinness
1958   Victor J. Reed
1973   John R. Quinn

Tulsa

1973   Bernard J. Ganter
1978   Eusebius J. Beltran

Oregon

Baker

1903   Charles J. O'Reilly
1918   Joseph F. McGrath
1950   Francis P. Leipzig
1971   Thomas J. Connolly

Pennsylvania

Allentown

1961   Joseph McShea
1983   Thomas J. Welsh

Altoona-Johnstown

(Diocese of Altoona until 1957.)

1901   Eugene A. Garvey
1920   John J. McCort
1936   Richard T. Guilfoyle
1958   Howard J. Carroll
1960   J. Carroll McCormick
1966   James J. Hogan

Erie

1853   Michael O'Connor
1854   Josue M. Young
1869   Tobias Mullen
1899   John E. Fitzmaurice
1920   John M. Gannon
1966   John F. Whealon
1969   Alfred M. Watson
1982   Michael J. Murphy

Greensburg

1951   Hugh L. Lamb
1960   William G. Connare

Harrisburg

1868   Jeremiah F. Shanahan
1888   Thomas McGovern
1899   John W. Shanahan
1916   Philip R. McDevitt
1935   George L. Leech
1971   Joseph T. Daley
1984   William Keeler

Philadelphia

(Became archdiocese 1875.)

1808   Michael F. Egan
1819   Henry Conwell
1842   Francis P. Kenrick
1852   John N. Neumann
1860   James F. B. Wood

Pittsburgh

1843   Michael O'Connor
1860   Michael Domenec
1876   John Tuigg
1889   Richard Phelan
1904   John F. R. Canevin
1921   Hugh C. Boyle
1950   John F. Dearden
1959   John J. Wright
1969   Vincent M. Leonard
1983   Anthony J. Bevilacqua

Scranton

1868   William O'Hara
1899   Michael J. Hoban
1928   Thomas C. O'Reilly
1938   William J. Hafey
1954   Jerome D. Hannan
1966   J. Carroll McCormick
1984   James C. Timlin

Rhode Island

Providence

1872   Thomas F. Henricken
1887   Matthew Harkins
1921   William A. Hickey
1934   Francis P. Keough
1948   Russell J. McVinney
1972   Louis E. Gelineau

South Carolina

Charleston

1820   John England
1843   Ignatius A. Reynolds
1857   Patrick N. Lynch
1883   Henry P. Northrop
1916   William T. Russell
1927   Emmet M. Walsh

1950   John J. Russell
1958   Paul J. Hallinan
1962   Francis F. Reh
1964   Ernest L. Unterkoefler

South Dakota

Rapid City

(Diocese of Lead until 1930.)

1902   John N. Stariha
1910   Joseph F. Busch
1916   John J. Lawler
1948   William T. McCarty
1969   Harold J. Dimmerling

Sioux Falls

1889   Martin Marty
1896   Thomas O'Gorman
1922   Bernard J. Mahoney
1939   William O'Brady
1956   Lambert A. Hoch
1978   Paul V. Dudley

Tennessee

Memphis

1971   Carroll Dozier
1983   J. Francis Stafford

Nashville

1837   Richard P. Miles
1859   James Whelan
1865   Patrick A. Feehan
1883   Joseph Rademacher
1894   Thomas S. Byrne
1924   Alphonse J. Smith
1936   William L. Adrian
1969   Joseph A. Durick
1975   James D. Niedergeses

Texas

Amarillo

1927   Rudolph A. Gerken
1934   Robert E. Lucey
1941   Laurence J. Fitzsimmons
1958   John L. Morkovsky
1963   Lawrence M. De Falco
1980   Leroy T. Matthiesen

Austin

1947   Louis Joseph Reicher
1971   Vincent M. Harris
1986   John E. McCarthy

Beaumont

1966   Vincent M. Harris
1971   Warren L. Boudreaux
1977   Bernard J. Ganter

Roman Catholic Bishops by Diocese (continued)

Brownsville

1965   Adolph Marx
1966   Humberto S. Medeiros
1971   John J. Fitzpatrick

Corpus Christi

1913   Paul J. Nussbaum
1921   Emmanuel B. Ledvina
1949   Mariano S. Garriga
1965   Thomas J. Drury
1983   Rene H. Gracida

Dallas

(Diocese of Dallas-Fort Worth, 1953-1969.)

1891   Thomas F. Brennan
1893   Edward J. Dunne
1911   Joseph P. Lynch
1954   Thomas K. Gorman
1969   Thomas Tschoepe

El Paso

1915   Anthony J. Schuler
1942   Sidney M. Metzger
1978   Patrick F. Flores
1980   Raymond J. Pena

Fort Worth

(Diocese of Dallas-Fort Worth, 1953-1969.)

1969   John J. Cassata
1981   Joseph D. Delaney

Galveston-Houston

(Diocese of Galveston until 1959.)

1847   Jean Marie Odin
1862   Claude M. Dubuis
1892   Nicholas A. Gallagher
1918   Christopher E. Byrne
1948   Wendelin J. Nold
1975   John L. Morkovsky
1985   Joseph A. Fiorenza

Lubbock

1983   Michael Sheehan

San Angelo

1961   Thomas J. Drury
1966   Thomas Tschoepe
1969   Stephen A. Leven
1979   Joseph A. Fiorenza
1985   Michael Pfeifer

San Antonio

(Became archdiocese 1926.)

1874   Anthony D. Pellicer
1881   John C. Neraz
1895   John A. Forest
1911   John W. Shaw
1918   Jerome Drossaerts

Victoria

1982   Charles V. Grahmann

Utah

Salt Lake City

1891   Lawrence Scanlan
1915   Joseph S. Glass
1926   John J. Mitty
1932   James E. Kearney
1937   Juane G. Hunt
1960   Joseph Lennox Federal
1980   William K. Weigand

Vermont

Burlington

1853   Louis J. DeGoesbriand
1892   John S. Michaud
1910   Joseph J. Rice
1938   Matthew F. Brady
1945   Edward F. Ryan
1957   Robert F. Joyce
1972   John A. Marshall

Virginia

Arlington

1974   Thomas J. Welsh
1983   John Richard Keating

Richmond

1820   Patrick Kelly
1822   Ambrose Marechal
        (apostolic administrator)
1828   James Whitfield
        (apostolic administrator)
1834   Samuel Eccleston
        (apostolic administrator)
1841   Richard V. Whelan
1850   John McGill
1872   James Gibbons
1878   John J. Keane
1889   Augustine Van de Vyver
1912   Denis J. O'Connell
1926   Andrew J. Brennan
1945   Peter L. Ireton
1958   John J. Russell
1974   Walter F. Sullivan

Washington

Seattle

(Diocese of Nesqually until 1907; became archdiocese 1951.)

1850   Augustine M. A.
        Blanchet
1879   Aegidius Junger
1896   Edward J. O'Dea
1933   Gerald Shaughnessy
1950   Thomas A. Connolly

Spokane

(Erected 1913.)

1914   Augustine F. Schinner
1927   Charles D. White
1955   Bernard J. Topel
1978   Lawrence H. Welsh

Yakima

1951   Joseph P. Dougherty
1969   Cornelius M. Power
1974   Nicolas E. Walsh
1977   William S. Skylstad

West Virginia

Wheeling-Charleston

(Diocese of Wheeling until 1974.)

1850   Richard V. Whelan
1875   John J. Kain
1894   Patrick J. Donahue
1922   John J. Swint
1962   Joseph H. Hodges

Wisconsin

Green Bay

1868   Joseph Melcher
1875   Francis X. Krautbauer
1886   Frederick X. Katzer
1892   Sebastian G. Messmer
1904   Joseph J. Fox
1915   Paul P. Rhode
1945   Stanislaus V. Bona
1968   Aloysius J. Wycislo
1984   Adam J. Maida

La Crosse

1868   Michael Heiss
1881   Kilian C. Flasch
1892   James Schwebach
1921   Alexander J. McGavick
1948   John P. Treacey
1965   Frederick W. Freking
1983   John J. Paul

Madison

1946   William P. O'Connor
1967   Cletus F. O'Donnell

Milwaukee

(Became archdiocese 1875.)

1843   John M. Henni

Superior

1905   Augustine F. Schinner
1913   Joseph M. Koudelka
1922   Joseph G. Pinten
1926   Theodore M. Reverman
1942   William P. O'Connor
1946   Albert G. Meyer
1954   Joseph Annabring
1960   George A. Hammes
1985   Raphael M. Fliss

Wyoming

Cheyenne

1887   Maurice F. Burke
1896   Thomas M. Lenihan
1902   James J. Keane
1912   Patrick A. McGovern
1951   Hubert M. Newell
1978   Joseph H. Hart

The United Methodist Church

(The Methodist Church was originally known as the Methodist Episcopal Church in America but in 1844 split into two separate churches — the Methodist Episcopal Church and the Methodist Episcopal Church, South. These churches were reunited in 1939 and joined with the Methodist Protestant Church to form the Methodist Church. The United Methodist Church came into being in 1968 as a union of the Methodist Church and the Evangelical United Brethren Church. See further notes below.)

Bishops of the Methodist Episcopal Church

1800	Richard Whatcoat
1808	William McKendree
1816	Enoch George
1816	Robert R. Roberts
1824	Elijah Hedding
1824	Joshua Soule
1832	James O. Andrew
1832	John Emory
1836	Thomas A. Morris
1836	Beverly Waugh
1841	Henry Kumler, Jr.
1844	Leonidas L. Hamline
1844	Edmund S. Janes
1845	William Hanby
1852	Edward R. Ames
1852	Osmon C. Baker
1852	Levi Scott
1852	Matthew Simpson
1858	Francis Burns
1864	Davis W. Clark
1864	Calvin Kingsley
1864	Edward Thomson
1866	John W. Roberts
1872	Edward G. Andrews
1872	Thomas Bowman
1872	Randolph S. Foster
1872	William L. Harris
1872	Gilbert Haven
1872	Stephen M. Merrill
1872	Jesse T. Peck
1872	Isaac W. Wiley
1880	Cyrus D. Foss
1880	Erastus O. Haven
1880	John F. Hurst
1880	Henry W. Warren
1884	Charles H. Fowler
1884	Willard F. Mallalieu
1884	William X. Ninde
1884	William Taylor
1884	John M. Walden
1888	Daniel A. Goodsell
1888	Isaac W. Joyce
1888	John P. Newman
1888	James M. Thoburn
1888	John H. Vincent
1890	Oscar P. Fitzgerald
1896	Earl Cranston
1896	Charles C. McCabe
1900	John W. Hamilton
1900	David H. Moore
1900	Edwin W. Parker
1900	Frank W. Warne
1902	Henry Hartzler
1904	James W. Bashford
1904	Joseph F. Berry
1904	William Burt
1904	Merriman C. Harris
1904	William F. McDowell
1904	Thomas B. Neely
1904	William F. Oldham

1904	John E. Robinson
1904	Isaiah B. Scott
1904	Henry Spellmeyer
1904	Luther B. Wilson
1908	William F. Anderson
1908	Frank M. Bristol
1908	Edwin H. Hughes
1908	Wilson S. Lewis
1908	Robert McIntyre
1908	John L. Nuelson
1908	William A. Quayle
1908	Charles W. Smith
1912	Richard J. Cooke
1912	William P. Eveland
1912	Theodore S. Henderson
1912	Frederick D. Leete
1912	Naphtali Luccock
1912	Francis J. McConnell
1912	John W. Robinson
1912	William O. Shepard
1912	Homer C. Stuntz
1912	Wilbur Thirkfield
1916	Alexander P. Camphor
1916	Franklin Hamilton
1916	Matthew S. Hughes
1916	Eben S. Johnson
1916	Adna W. Leonard
1916	Charles B. Mitchell
1916	Thomas Nicholson
1916	Herbert Welch
1920	George H. Bickley
1920	Lauriss J. Birney
1920	Edgar Blake
1920	Charles W. Burns
1920	Matthew W. Clair
1920	Frederick B. Fisher
1920	Robert E. Jones
1920	Frederick T. Keeney
1920	Charles E. Locke
1920	Charles L. Mead
1920	Ernest G. Richardson
1920	H. Lester Smith
1920	Ernest L. Waldorf
1924	Brenton T. Badley
1924	Wallace E. Brown
1924	George R. Grose
1924	Titus Lowe
1924	George A. Miller
1928	James C. Baker
1928	Edwin F. Lee
1928	Raymond J. Wade
1930	John Gowdy
1930	Chi P'ing Wang
1932	Ralph S. Cushman
1932	J. Ralph Magee
1936	Charles W. Flint
1936	Wilbur E. Hammaker
1936	G. Bromley Oxnam
1936	J. Waskom Pickett
1936	Alexander P. Shaw
1936	John M. Springer
1937	Ralph A. Ward
1938	John L. Decell
1938	Ivan Lee Holt

1938	William C. Martin
1938	William W. Peele
1938	Clare Purcell
1938	Charles C. Selecman
1938	William T. Watkins
1939	John C. Broomfield
1939	James H. Straughn

Bishops of the Methodist Episcopal Church, South

1846	William Capers
1846	Robert Paine
1854	John Early
1854	Hubbard R. Kavanaugh
1854	George F. Pierce
1866	David S. Doggett
1866	Enoch M. Marvin
1866	Holland N. McTyeire
1866	William M. Wightman
1870	John C. Keener
1882	John C. Granbery
1882	Robert K. Hargrove
1882	Linus Parker
1882	Alpheus W. Wilson
1886	William W. Duncan
1886	Charles B. Galloway
1886	Eugene R. Hendrix
1886	Joseph S. Key
1888	James N. Fitzgerald
1890	Atticus G. Haygood
1898	Warren A. Candler
1898	Henry C. Morrison
1902	E. Embree Hoss
1902	A. Coke Smith
1906	James Atkins
1906	John J. Tigert
1906	Seth Ward
1910	Collins Denny
1910	John C. Kilgo
1910	Walter R. Lambuth
1910	James H. McCoy
1910	Edwin D. Mouzon
1910	William B. Murrah
1918	William N. Ainsworth
1918	James Cannon, Jr.
1918	Urban V. W. Darlington
1918	Horace M. DuBose
1918	John F. McMurry
1918	John M. Moore
1922	William B. Beauchamp
1922	Hiram A. Boaz
1922	James E. Dickey
1922	Hoyt M. Dobbs
1922	Sam R. Hay
1930	Paul B. Kern
1930	Arthur J. Moore
1930	A. Frank Smith

The Methodist Protestant Church

There were no bishops of the Methodist Protestant Church from its organization in 1828 until 1939, when Bishops John C. Broomfield and James H. Straughn were elected to represent their church at the union from which the Methodist Church was formed.

Bishops of the Methodist Church

(Joined with the Evangelical United Brethren Church to form the United Methodist Church in 1968.)

1940	Bruce R. Baxter
1940	William A. C. Hughes
1940	Lorenzo H. King
1941	Carleton Lacy
1941	Clement D. Rockey
1941	Newell S. Booth
1944	Charles W. Brashares
1944	Robert N. Brooks
1944	Fred P. Corson
1944	Paul N. Garber
1944	Schuyler E. Garth
1944	Costen J. Harrell
1944	Lewis O. Hartman
1944	Edward W. Kelly
1944	Willis J. King
1944	W. Earl Ledden
1944	Paul E. Martin
1944	W. Angie Smith
1944	Arthur F. Wesley
1948	J. W. E. Bowen
1948	Dana Dawson
1948	Gerald H. Kennedy
1948	John W. Lord
1948	H. Clifford Northcott
1948	Glenn R. Phillips
1948	Richard C. Raines
1948	Marshall R. Reed
1948	Roy H. Short
1948	Donald H. Tippett
1948	Hazen G. Werner
1948	Lloyd C. Wicke
1949	Sante Uberto Barbieri
1950	Raymond L. Archer
1952	John W. Branscomb
1952	Matthew W. Clair, Jr.
1952	D. Stanley Coors
1952	F. Gerald Ensley
1952	A. Raymond Grant
1952	Edgar A. Love
1952	Frederick B. Newell
1952	Edwin E. Voigt
1952	H. Bascom Watts
1956	Hobart B. Amstutz

1956	Ralph E. Dodge
1956	Eugene M. Frank
1956	Nolan B. Harmon
1956	Bachman G. Hodge
1956	Prince A. Taylor, Jr.
1958	Paul M. Herrick
1960	Ralph T. Alton
1960	Kenneth W. Copeland
1960	Paul V. Galloway
1960	Edwin R. Garrison
1960	Charles F. Golden
1960	Walter C. Gum
1960	Paul Hardin, Jr.
1960	Marquis L. Harris
1960	James W. Henley
1960	Fred G. Holloway
1960	James K. Mathews
1960	W. Vernon Middleton
1960	Noah W. Moore, Jr.
1960	T. Otto Nall
1960	Everett W. Palmer
1960	W. Kenneth Pope
1960	O. Eugene Slater
1960	B. Foster Stockwell
1960	Aubrey G. Walton
1960	W. Ralph Ward
1964	H. Ellis Finger, Jr.
1964	W. Kenneth Goodson
1964	Earl G. Hunt, Jr.
1964	Francis E. Kearns
1964	Dwight H. Loder
1964	Robert F. Lundy
1964	Edward J. Pendergrass
1964	Thomas M. Pryer
1964	W. McFerrin Stowe
1964	R. Marvin Stuart
1964	James S. Thomas
1964	Lance Webb
1967	L. Scott Allen

Bishops of the Church of the United Brethren in Christ

(Joined with the Evangelical Church to form the Evangelical United Brethren Church in 1946.)

1800	Martin Boehm
1800	Philip W. Otterbein
1800	Christian Newcomer
1817	Andrew Zeller
1821	Joseph Hoffman
1825	Henry Kumler
1833	William Brown
1833	Samuel Heistand
1837	Jacob Erb
1841	John Coons
1845	Jacob Glossbrenner
1845	John Russell
1849	David Edwards
1853	Lewis Davis
1861	Jacob Markwood
1861	Daniel Shuck
1865	Jonathan Weaver

1869	John Dickson
1877	Nicholas Castle
1877	Milton Wright
1881	Ezekiel Kephart
1885	Daniel Flickinger
1889	James Hott
1893	Job Mills
1902	George Mathews
1905	William Bell
1905	Thomas Carter
1905	William Weekley
1913	Henry H. Fout
1913	Alfred T. Howard
1913	Cyrus J. Kephart
1917	William Washinger
1921	Arthur Clippinger
1925	Arthur Statton
1926	John S. Stamm
1929	Grant D. Batdorf
1929	Ira D. Warner
1941	Fred L. Dennis
1945	J. Balmer Showers

Bishops of the Evangelical Church (Methodist)

(Joined with the Church of the United Brethren in Christ to form the Evangelical United Brethren Church in 1946.)

1807	Jacob Albright
1839	John Seybert
1843	Joseph Long
1859	William Orwig
1863	John Esher
1871	Reuben Yeakel
1875	Thomas Bowman
1875	Rudolph Dubs
1891	Sylvanus Breyfogel
1891	William Horn
1896	Joseph C. Hartzell
1902	William Heil
1907	Samuel Spreng
1910	William Fouke
1910	Uriah Swengel

Bishops of the Evangelical United Brethren Church

(Formed in 1946 by a merger of the Church of the United Brethren in Christ and the Evangelical Church; joined with the Methodist Church in 1968 to form the United Methodist Church.)

1950	David T. Gregory
1954	Lyle L. Baughman
1954	Harold R. Heininger

1954	Reuben H. Mueller
1957	J. Gordon Howard
1957	Paul E. V. Shannon
1958	Hermann W. Kaebnick
1958	W. Maynard Sparks
1960	Paul W. Milhouse
1968	Paul A. Washburn

Bishops of the United Methodist Church

(Formed in 1968 by a merger of the Methodist Church and the Evangelical United Brethren Church.)

1968	Arthur J. Armstrong
1968	William R. Cannon
1968	Alsie H. Carleton
1968	Roy C. Nichols
1968	D. Frederick Wertz
1969	Paul M. Herrick
1970	L. Scott Allen
1970	Ralph T. Alton
1970	Kenneth W. Copeland
1970	F. Gerald Ensley
1970	H. Ellis Finger, Jr.
1970	Eugene M. Frank
1970	Paul V. Galloway
1970	Charles F. Golden
1970	W. Kenneth Goodson
1970	Paul Hardin, Jr.
1970	James W. Henley
1970	J. Gordon Howard
1970	Earl G. Hunt, Jr.
1970	Hermann W. Kaebnick
1970	Francis E. Kearns
1970	Gerald H. Kennedy
1970	Dwight H. Loder
1970	John Wesley Lord
1970	James K. Mathews
1970	Paul W. Milhouse
1970	Noah W. Moore
1970	Reuben H. Mueller
1970	Everett W. Palmer
1970	Edward J. Pendergrass
1970	W. Kenneth Pope
1970	Thomas M. Pryor
1970	Roy H. Short
1970	O. Eugene Slater
1970	John Owen Smith
1970	W. Maynard Sparks
1970	W. McFerrin Stowe
1970	R. Marvin Stuart
1970	Prince A. Taylor, Jr.
1970	James S. Thomas
1970	Aubrey G. Walton
1970	W. Ralph Ward
1970	Paul A. Washburn
1970	Lance Webb
1970	Lloyd C. Wicke
1973	James M. Ault

1973	Robert M. Blackburn
1973	Edward G. Carroll
1973	Wilbur W. Y. Choy
1973	Wayne K. Clymer
1973	Finis A. Crutchfield
1973	Jesse R. DeWitt
1973	Ernest T. Dixon
1973	Robert E. Goodrich
1973	Don W. Holter
1973	Joel D. McDavid
1973	Frank L. Robertson
1973	Carl J. Sanders
1973	Mack B. Stokes
1973	Jack M. Tuell
1973	Edward L. Tullis
1973	John B. Warman
1973	Melvin B. Wheatley, Jr.
1973	Joseph H. Yeakel
1977	Edsel A. Ammons
1977	Monk Bryan
1977	Kenneth W. Hicks
1977	Leroy C. Hodapp
1977	J. Chess Lovern
1977	J. Kenneth Shamblin
1977	C. Dale White
1981	George W. Bashore
1981	Edwin C. Boulton
1981	Roy C. Clark
1981	Emerson S. Colaw
1981	Paul A. Duffey
1981	William B. Grove
1981	W. T. Handy, Jr.
1981	John W. Hardt
1981	Marjorie S. Matthews
1981	Calvin D. McConnell
1981	Carlton P. Minnick, Jr.
1981	Benjamin R. Oliphant
1981	John W. Russell
1981	Louis W. Schowengerdt
1981	F. Herbert Skeete
1981	Melvin G. Talbert
1985	Woodie W. White
1985	Judith Craig
1985	Reuben P. Job
1985	David J. Lawson
1985	Forest C. Stith
1985	Felton E. May
1985	Neil L. Irons
1985	Richard B. Wilke
1985	Walter L. Underwood
1985	J. Woodrow Hearn
1985	James L. Knox
1985	R. Kern Eutsler
1985	Ernest W. Newman
1985	Robert C. Morgan
1985	Ernest A. Fitzgerald
1985	L. Bevel Jones
1985	Leontine T. C. Kelly
1985	Roy I. Sano
1986	Donald C. Cunningham
1986	Elias Galvin

472

The Presbyterian Church (U.S.A.)

(Formed in 1983 by the merger of the United Presbyterian Church in the United States of America and the Presbyterian Church in the United States. Leaders of major predecessor sects are also listed below.)

Moderators of the Presbyterian Church in the United States of America

(From 1838 to 1870 the church was divided between the Old School and the New School factions; moderators of both are listed here. Became part of the United Presbyterian Church in the United States of America in 1958.)

1789	John Witherspoon
1789	John Rodgers
1790	Robert Smith
1791	John Woodhull
1792	John King
1793	James Latta
1794	Alexander McWhorter
1795	John McKnight
1796	Robert Davidson
1797	William M. Tennent
1798	John B. Smith
1799	S. Stanhope Smith
1800	Joseph Clark
1801	Nathaniel Irwin
1802	Azel Roe
1803	James Hall
1804	James F. Armstrong
1805	James Richards
1806	Samuel Miller
1807	Archibald Alexander
1808	Philip Milledoler
1809	Drury Lacy
1810	John B. Romeyn
1811	Eliphalet Nott
1812	Andre Flinn
1813	Samuel Blachford
1814	James Inglis
1815	William Neill
1816	James Blythe
1817	Jonas Coe
1818	Jacob J. Janeway
1819	John H. Rice
1820	John McDowell
1821	William Hill
1822	Obadiah Jennings
1823	John Chester
1824	Ashbel Green
1825	Stephen N. Rowan
1826	Thomas McAuley
1827	Francis Herron
1828	Ezra S. Ely
1829	Benjamin H. Rice
1830	Ezra Fisk
1831	Nathan S. S. Beman
1832	James Hoge
1833	William A. McDowell
1834	Philip Lindsley
1835	William W. Phillips
1836	John Witherspoon
1837	David Elliott
1838	William S. Plumer
	Samuel Fisher
1839	Joshua L. Wilson
	Baxter Dickinson
1840	William M. Engles
	William Wisner
1841	Robert J. Breckenridge
1842	John T. Edgar
1843	Gardiner Spring
	Ansel D. Eddy
1844	George Junkin
1845	John M. Krebs
1846	Charles Hodge
	Samuel H. Cox
1847	James H. Thornwell
1848	Alexander T. McGill
1849	Nicholas Murray
	Philip C. Hay
1850	Aaron W. Leland
	David H. Riddle
1851	Edward P. Humphrey
	Albert Barnes
1852	John C. Lord
	William Adams
1853	John C. Young
	Diarca H. Allen
1854	Henry A. Boardman
	Thomas H. Skinner
1855	Nathan L. Rice
	William C. Wisner
1856	Francis McFarland
	Laurens P. Hickok
1857	Cortlandt Van Rensselaer
	Samuel W. Fisher
1858	William A. Scott
	Matthew L. P. Thompson
1859	William L. Breckenridge
	Robert W. Patterson
1860	John W. Yeomans
	Thornton A. Mills
1861	J. Chester Backuse
	Jonathan B. Condit
1862	Charles C. Beatty
	George Duffield
1863	John H. Morrison
	Henry B. Smith
1864	James Wood
	Thomas Brainerd
1865	John C. Lowrie
	James B. Shaw
1866	Robert L. Stanton
	Samuel M. Hopkins
1867	Phineas D. Gurley
	Henry A. Nelson
1868	George W. Musgrave
	Jonathan F. Stearns
1869	M. W. Jocobus
	Philemon H. Fowler
1870	J. Trumbull Backus
1871	Zephaniah M. Humphrey
1872	Samuel J. Niccolls
1873	Howard Crosby
1874	Samuel J. Wilson
1875	Edward D. Morris
1876	Henry J. Van Dyke
1877	James Eells
1878	Francis L. Patton
1879	Henry H. Jessup
1880	William M. Paxton
1881	Henry Darling
1882	Herrick Johnson
1883	Edwin F. Hatfield
1884	George P. Hays
1885	Elijah R. Craven
1886	David C. Marquis
1887	Joseph T. Smith
1888	Charles L. Thompson
1889	William C. Roberts
1890	William E. Moore
1891	W. Henry Green
1892	William C. Young
1893	Willis G. Craig
1894	S. A. Mutchmore
1895	Robert R. Booth
1896	John L. Withrow
1897	Sheldon Jackson
1898	Wallace Radcliffe
1899	Robert F. Sample
1900	Charles A. Dickey
1901	Henry C. Minton
1902	Henry Van Dyke
1903	Robert F. Coyle
1904	J. Addison Henry
1905	James D. Moffat
1906	Hunter Corbett
1907	William H. Roberts
1908	Baxter P. Fullerton
1909	James M. Barkley
1910	Charles Little
1911	John F. Carson
1912	Mark A. Matthews
1913	John T. Stone
1914	Maitland Alexander
1915	J. Ross Stevenson
1916	John A. Marquis
1917	J. Wilbur Chapman
1918	J. Frank Smith
1919	John W. Baer
1920	Samuel S. Palmer
1921	Henry C. Swearingen
1922	Calvin C. Hays
1923	Charles F. Wishart
1924	Clarence E. Macartney
1925	Charles R. Erdman
1926	William O. Thompson
1927	Robert E. Speer
1928	Hugh K. Walker
1929	Cleland B. McAfee
1930	Hugh T. Kerr
1931	Lewis S. Mudge
1932	Charles W. Kerr
1933	John McDowell
1934	William C. Covert
1935	Joseph A. Vance
1936	Henry B. Master
1937	William H. Foulkes
1938	Charles W. Welch
1939	Sam Higginbottom
1940	William L. Young
1941	Herbert B. Smith
1942	Stuart N. Hutchison
1943	Henry S. Coffin
1944	Roy E. Vale
1945	William B. Lampe
1946	Frederick W. Evans
1947	Wilbur LaRoe, Jr.
1948	Jesse H. Baird
1949	Clifford E. Barbour
1950	Hugh I. Evans
1951	H. Ray Anderson
1952	Hermann N. Morse
1953	John A. Mackay
1954	Ralph W. Lloyd
1955	Paul S. Wright
1956	David W. Proffitt
1957	Harold R. Martin
1958	Harold R. Martin

Moderators of the United Presbyterian Church of North America

(Became part of the United Presbyterian Church in the United States of America in 1958.)

1858	John T. Pressly
1859	Peter Bullions
1860	Joseph Clokey
1861	R. D. Harper
1862	J. T. Cooper
1863	A. Young
1864	D. A. Wallace
1865	John B. Clark
1866	David R. Kerr
1867	John B. Dales
1868	James Harper
1869	R. A. Browne
1870	T. S. Kendall
1871	R. A. McAyeal
1872	John S. Easton
1873	John Y. Scouller
1874	John G. Brown
1875	W. W. Barr
1876	James Brown
1877	Robert B. Ewing
1878	S. G. Irvine
1879	William Bruce
1880	E. T. Jeffers
1881	David W. Carson
1882	David Paul
1883	W. H. McMillan
1884	William H. French
1885	William Johnston
1886	John T. Brownlee
1887	Matthew M. Gibson
1888	William T. Meloy
1889	E. S. McKitrick
1890	Andrew Watson
1891	Thomas J. Kennedy
1892	David MacDill
1893	James Bruce
1894	John A. Wilson
1895	J. B. McMichael
1896	James White
1897	Thomas H. Hanna
1898	R. G. Ferguson
1899	William J. Robinson
1900	James P. Sankey
1901	J. A. Thompson
1902	James C. Wilson
1903	James P. Cowan
1904	James W. Witherspoon
1905	William C. Williamson
1906	J. K. McClurkin
1907	William T. Campbell
1908	James G. Carson
1909	D. A. McClenahan
1910	James D. Rankin
1911	John C. Scouller
1912	Hugh H. Bell

1913   R. M. Russell
1914   Joseph Kyle
1915   T. H. McMichael
1916   W. B. Smiley
1917   W. E. McCulloch
1918   W. M. Anderson
1919   James T. McCrory
1920   F. M. Spencer
1921   A. F. Kirkpatrick
1922   J. Kelly Giffen
1923   W. R. Sawhill
1924   Charles H. Robinson
1925   W. I. Wishart
1926   R. A. Hutchison
1927   M. G. Kyle
1928   William A. Spalding
1929   John McNaugher
1930   T. C. Atchison
1931   J. K. Montgomery
1932   Charles S. Cleland
1933   W. B. Anderson
1934   J. Alvin Orr
1935   E. C. McCown
1936   Robert W. Thompson
1937   A. R. Robinson
1938   Ralph Atkinson
1939   H. Walton Mitchell
1940   Homer B. Henderson
1941   R. L. Lanning

1942   Thomas C. Pollock
1943   W. Bruce Wilson
1944   James H. Grier
1945   James M. Ferguson
1946   Lytle R. Free
1947   Samuel A. Fulton
1948   Albert H. Baldinger
1949   Tim J. Campbell
1950   J. Lowrie Anderson
1951   W. Kyle George
1952   James L. Kelso
1953   Samuel C. Weir
1954   Albert E. Kelly
1955   George A. Long
1956   Robert W. Gibson
1957   Robert N. Montgomery
1958   Robert N. Montgomery

Moderators of the United Presbyterian Church in the United States of America

(Formed in 1958 by the merger of the Presbyterian Church in the United States of America and the United Presbyterian Church of North America. Became part of the Presbyterian Church (U.S.A.) in 1983.)

1958   Theophilus M. Taylor
1959   Arthur L. Miller
1960   Herman L. Turner
1961   Paul D. McKelvey
1962   Marshal L. Scott
1963   Silas G. Kessler
1964   Edler G. Hawkins
1965   William P. Thompson
1966   Ganse Little
1967   Eugene Smathers
1968   John C. Smith
1969   George E. Sweazey
1970   William R. Laws, Jr.
1971   Lois Stair
1972   C. Willard Heckel
1973   Clinton M. Marsh
1974   Robert C. Lamar
1975   William F. Kessecker
1976   Thelma C. D. Adair
1977   John T. Conner
1978   William P. Lytle
1979   Howard L. Rice

1980   Charles A. Hammond
1981   Robert M. Davidson
1982   James H. Costen

Moderators of the Presbyterian Church (U.S.A.)

1983   J. Randolph Taylor
1984   Harriet Nelson
1985   William H. Wilson

Other Major Denominations

The United Church of Christ

(Formed in 1957 by the merger of the Evangelical and Reformed Church with the Congregational Christian Church.)

Moderators of the Congregational Christian Church

(Formed in 1930 by the merger of the Congregational Church with the American Christian Church.)

1931	Carl S. Patton
	Frank G. Coffin
1936	Jay T. Stocking
	John V. Sees
1938	Roger W. Babson
1940	Oscar E. Maurer
1942	William E. Sweet
	John V. Sees
1944	Ferdinand Q. Blanchard
1946	Ronald Bridges
1948	Albert W. Palmer
1949	Helen Kenyon
1952	Vere V. Loper
1954	Robert Cashman
1956	Albert B. Coe
1958	George B. Hastings

Presidents of the Evangelical and Reformed Church

(Formed in 1934 by the merger of the Evangelical Synod of North America with the Reformed Church in the United States.)

1934	George W. Richards
1939	Louis W. Goebel
1954	James E. Wagner

The United Church of Christ

Presidents

1957	Fred Hoskins
1957	James E. Wagner
1961	Ben Herbster
1969	Robert V. Moss
1977	Joseph H. Evans
1978	Avery Post

Moderators

1957	Louis W. Goebel
1957	George B. Hastings
1959	Frances Kapitzky
1959	Ray E. Phillips
1961	Mrs. George E. Kahlenberg
1961	Ernst Press
1963	Donald Webber
1965	Gerhard W. Grauer
1967	Hollis F. Price
1969	Gibson I. Daniels
1969	Richard C. Pfeiffer
1973	David G. Colwell
1974	Margaret A. Haywood
1977	Robert K. Nace
1978	Milton S. Hurst
1980	Nathanael M. Guptill
1982	Helen I. Barnhill
1984	John Kreuger
1986	Kenneth P. Stewart

American Baptist Churches in the U.S.A.

(Northern Baptist Convention until 1950; American Baptist Convention until 1973.)

Presidents

1907	Charles Evans Hughes
1908	Harry P. Judson
1910	Emory W. Hunt
1912	Henry Bond
1914	Edward S. Clinch
1915	Shailer Mathews
1916	Clarence A. Barbour
1917	George W. Coleman
1918	Francis W. Ayer
1919	D. C. Shull
1920	Ernest L. Tustin
1921	Helen Barrett Montgomery
1922	Frederick E. Taylor
1923	Corwin S. Shank
1924	Carl E. Milliken
1925	Edward H. Rhoades, Jr.
1926	J. Whitcomb Brougher
1927	William C. Coleman
1928	Arthur M. Harris
1929	Alton L. Miller
1930	Albert W. Beaven
1931	Mattison B. Jones
1932	C. Oscar Johnson
1933	William S. Abernethy
1934	Avery A. Shaw
1935	James H. Franklin
1936	Herbert B. Clark
1937	Earle V. Pierce
1938	Arthur J. Hudson
1939	Elmir A. Fridell
1940	E. J. Millington
1941	William A. Elliott
1942	Joseph C. Robbins
1944	Mrs. Leslie E. Swain
1946	Edwin T. Dahlberg
1948	Sandford Fleming
1949	Mrs. Howard G. Colwell
1950	Edward H. Pruden
1951	Kenneth S. Latourette
1952	John A. Dawson
1953	Winfield Edson
1954	V. Carney Hargroves
1955	Frank A. Nelson
1956	Harry L. Dillin
1957	Clarence W. Cranford
1958	Mrs. Maurice B. Hodge
1959	Herbert Gezork
1960	C. Stanton Gallup
1961	Warner R. Cole
1962	Benjamin P. Browne
1963	Harold E. Stassen
1964	J. Lester Harnish
1965	Robert G. Torbet
1966	Carl W. Tiller
1967	L. Doward McBain
1968	C. G. Rutenber
1969	Thomas Kilgore, Jr.
1970	Roger L. Fredrikson
1971	Mrs. Marcus Rohlfs
1973	Gene E. Bartlett
1975	Peter H. Armacost
1976	Charles Z. Smith
1978	Cora Sparrowk
1980	William F. Keucher
1982	John F. Mandt
1984	Margaret Prine
1985	Walter B. Pulliam

Southern Baptist Convention

Presidents

1845	William B. Johnson
1851	R. B. C. Howell
1859	Richard Fuller
1863	Patrick H. Mell
1872	James P. Boyce
1880	Patrick H. Mell
1888	James P. Boyce
1889	Jonathan Haralson
1899	William J. Northern
1902	James P. Eagle
1905	E. W. Stephens
1908	Joshua Levering
1911	Edwin C. Dargan
1914	Lansing Burrows
1917	J. B. Gambrell
1921	Edgar Y. Mullins
1924	George W. McDaniel
1927	George W. Truett
1930	William J. McGlothlin
1933	Frederick F. Brown
1934	Monroe E. Dodd
1936	John R. Sampey
1939	Lee R. Scarborough
1941	William W. Hamilton
1944	Pat M. Neff
1947	Louie D. Newton
1949	Robert G. Lee
1952	J. D. Grey
1954	James W. Storer
1956	Casper C. Warren
1958	Brooks Hays
1960	Ramsey Pollard
1962	Herschel H. Hobbs
1964	K. Owen White
1965	W. Wayne Dehoney
1967	H. Franklin Paschall
1969	W. A. Criswell
1972	Carl E. Bates
1973	Owen Cooper
1975	Jaroy Weber
1977	James L. Sullivan
1978	Jimmy R. Allen
1980	Adrian P. Rogers
1981	Bailey E. Smith
1983	James T. Draper, Jr.
1985	Charles F. Stanley

The Lutheran Churches

Presidents of the Lutheran Church — Missouri Synod

1847	C. F. W. Walther
1850	F. C. D. Wyneken
1864	C. F. W. Walther
1878	H. C. Schwan
1899	Franz Pieper
1911	F. Pfotenhauer
1935	J. W. Behnken
1962	Oliver R. Harms
1969	Jacob A. O. Preus
1982	Ralph A. Bohlmann

Presidents of the United Lutheran Church

(Formed in 1918 by the merger of separate branches of the Evangelical Lutheran Church; became part of the Lutheran Church in America in 1962.)

1918	Frederick H. Knubel
1945	Franklin C. Fry

Presidents of the Lutheran Church in America

(Formed in 1962 by the merger of the Augustana Evangelical Lutheran Church, the Finnish Evangelical Lutheran Church of America, the American Evangelical Lutheran Church, and the United Lutheran Church.)

1962 Franklin C. Fry
1968 Robert J. Marshall
1979 James R. Crumley, Jr.

Presidents of the American Lutheran Church

(Formed in 1930 by the merger of the Buffalo, Iowa, and Ohio Synods.)

1930 C. C. Hein
1937 Emanuel Poppen
1950 Henry F. Schuh
1961 Fredrik A. Schiotz
1971 Kent Sigvart Knutson
1974 David W. Preus

Christian Church (Disciples of Christ)

Presidents

1849 D. S. Burnet
1850 Alexander Campbell
1867 D. S. Burnet
1868 Richard M. Bishop
1875 Isaac Errett
1877 William K. Pendleton
1878 A. I. Hobbs
1879 W. H. Hopson
1880 Thomas P. Haley
1881 Robert Moffett
1882 B. B. Tyler
1883 D. R. Dungan
1884 A. G. Thomas
1885 L. L. Carpenter
1886 Francis M. Drake
1887 Charles L. Loos
1888 James H. Garrison
1889 Nathaniel S. Haynes
1890 T. M. Phillips
1891 D. R. Ewing
1892 A. M. Atkinson
1893 George Darsie
1894 J. W. Allen
1895 Jabez Hall
1896 J. M. Hardin
1897 M. M. Davis
1898 F. D. Power
1899 W. R. Richardson
1900 W. K. Homan
1901 I. J. Spencer
1902 H. O. Breeden
1903 A. B. Philputt
1904 Zachary T. Sweeney
1905 E. I. Powell
1906 S. M. Copper
1907 George H. Coombs
1908 Robert A. Long
1909 Charles S. Medbury
1910 Peter Ainslie

1911 Harry D. Smith
1912 C. M. Chilton
1913 Fred A. Henry
1914 Hill M. Bell
1915 Walter M. White
1916 William F. Richardson
1917 Jesse N. Haymaker
1919 Edgar D. Jones
1920 Raphael H. Miller
1921 George A. Miller
1922 Stephen E. Fisher
1923 T. W. Grafton
1924 Abram E. Cory
1925 Jacob H. Goldner
1926 Andrew D. Harmon
1928 Edward S. Jouett
1929 Harry H. Rogers
1930 Robert A. Long
1931 L. D. Anderson
1932 Homer W. Carpenter
1933 George A. Campbell
1934 William F. Rothenburger
1935 Daniel W. Morehouse
1936 L. N. D. Wells
1937 Alonzo W. Fortune
1938 Frederick D. Kershner
1939 Roger T. Nooe
1941 Harry B. McCormick
1942 William A. Shullenberger
1944 Clarence E. Lemmon
1946 McGruder E. Sadler
1947 Hampton Adams
1948 Roy C. Snodgrass
1949 Frank E. Davison
1950 John A. Tate
1952 Marvin O. Sansbury
1953 Howard T. Wood
1954 Cleveland Kleihauer
1956 Riley B. Montgomery
1957 John Rogers
1958 Cranville T. Walker
1959 John Paul Pack
1960 Loren E. Lair
1961 Perry E. Gresham
1962 Leslie R. Smith
1963 Robert W. Burns
1964 W. A. Welsh
1966 Stephen J. England
1967 Forrest L. Richeson

Moderators

1968 Ronald E. Osborn
1969 Myron C. Cole
1971 James M. Moudy
1973 Walter D. Bingham
1975 Jean Wolfolk
1976 James A. Moak
1978 James A. Noe
1981 Thomas J. Youngblood, Jr.
1982 Joy L. Greer
1984 William E. Tucker
1986 Thomas J. Liggett

The Church of Christ, Scientist

Presidents

1892 E. J. Foster Eddy
1895 Edward P. Bates
1896 Septimus J. Hanna
1898 Albert A. Metcalf
1899 William P. McKenzie
1900 Edward P. Bates
1901 John B. Willis
1902 John W. Reeder
1903 Irving C. Tomlinson

1903 Edward P. Bates
1904 Alfred Farlow
1905 Hermann S. Hering
1906 William P. McKenzie
1906 Willis F. Gross
1907 Eugene H. Greene
1908 John Blish
1909 William P. McKenzie
1910 William D. Baldwin
1911 Clifford P. Smith
1912 James A. Neal
1912 Bliss Knapp
1913 Frederick Dixon
1914 John C. Lathrop
1915 Edward A. Merritt
1916 Calvin A. Frye
1917 William P. McKenzie
1917 William D. McCrackan
1918 Francis J. Fluno
1919 John W. Doorly
1920 Willard P. Emery
1921 Irving C. Tomlinson
1922 Albert F. Gilmore
1923 Charles E. Heitman
1924 Torrance Parker
1925 David N. McKee
1926 Archie E. Van Ostrand
1927 Ella W. Hoag
1928 Frank C. Colby
1929 William W. Davis
1930 Duncan Sinclair
1931 Robert E. Buffum
1932 Ralph O. Brewster
1933 Mary G. Ewing
1934 John M. Brewer
1935 A. Harry Bacon
1936 Frank C. Colby
1936 Elizabeth Tomlinson
1937 Clifford P. Smith
1938 Ralph H. Knapp
1939 George Shaw Cook
1940 Margaret M. G. Matters
1941 John R. Dunn
1942 Elisabeth Norwood
1943 Daisette D. S. McKenzie
1944 Paul S. Seely
1945 Myrtle Holm Smith
1946 Luther P. Cudworth
1947 Helen Chaffee Elwell
1948 Harry C. Browne
1949 Emma C. Shipman
1950 Walter S. Cross
1951 Lora C. Rathvon
1952 Robert E. Key
1953 Grace F. Cudworth
1954 William R. Knox
1955 Gertrude W. Eiseman
1956 Clifford A. Woodard
1957 Mabel E. Lucas
1958 Leonard T. Carney
1959 Kathryn F. Cook
1960 Arthur W. Eckman
1961 Mary L. G. Nay
1962 Ralph E. Wagers
1963 Helen Wood Bauman
1964 Edward Froderman
1965 Frances S. Wells
1966 Erwin D. Canham
1967 Beatrice T. Pittman
1968 Gordon V. Comer
1969 L. Ivimy Gwalter
1970 Clem W. Collins
1971 Elizabeth Glass Barlow
1972 George Nay
1973 Roy Garrett Watson
1974 Georgina Tennant
1975 Jules Cern
1976 Naomi Price
1977 James Spencer
1978 John R. Peterson
1979 Ada Reynolds Jandron
1980 Saville R. Davis

1981 Berthe S. Girardin
1982 Dorothy E. Klein
1983 James K. Kyser
1984 Zadie Hatfield
1985 Robert H. Mitchell

The Church of Jesus Christ of Latter-Day Saints (Mormon)

Presidents

1832 Joseph Smith
1847 Brigham Young
1880 John Taylor
1889 Wilford Woodruff
1898 Lorenzo Snow
1901 Joseph F. Smith
1918 Heber J. Grant
1945 George A. Smith
1951 David O. McKay
1970 Joseph Fielding Smith
1973 Harold B. Lee
1974 Spencer W. Kimball
1986 Ezra Taft Benson

Union of Orthodox Jewish Congregations of America

Presidents

1898 H. Pereira Mendes
1913 Bernard Drachman
1918 Charles H. Shapiro
1920 Julius J. Dukas
1924 Herbert S. Goldstein
1933 William Weiss
1942 Samuel Nirenstein
1949 William B. Herlands
1951 Max Etra
1954 Moses I. Feuerstein
1966 Joseph Karasick
1974 Harold Jacobs
1980 Julius Berman

Union of American Hebrew Congregations

Presidents

1873 Morris Loth
1889 Julius Freiberg
1903 Samuel Woolner
1907 Louis J. Goodman
1911 J. Walter Freiberg
1921 Charles Shohl
1925 Ludwig Vogelstein
1934 Jacob W. Mack
1937 Robert P. Goldman
1943 Adolph Rosenberg
1946 Maurice Eisendrath
1973 Alexander M. Schindler

Founders of Religious Sects, Societies, and Movements in the United States

Title	Year Founded	Founder
Abyssinian Baptist Church	1809	Thomas Paul
Adventists (Millerites)	1831	William Miller
African Methodist Episcopal Church	1816	Richard Allen
African Orthodox Church	1921	George A. McGuire
Allenites	1774	Henry Allen
Amana Society	1855	Christian Metz
Apostolic Faith	1907	Florence L. Crawford
Black Muslims	1930	Wallace D. Fard
Brethren In Christ (See Christadelphians)		
Brotherhood of the New Life	1861	Thomas L. Harris
Campbellites (See Disciples of Christ)		
Christadelphians	1847	John Thomas
Christian Catholic Church	1893	John A. Dowie
Christian and Missionary Alliance	1881	A. B. Simpson
Christians	1793	James O'Kelly
Church of Christ (Holiness)	1894	C. P. Jones
Church of Christ, Scientist	1879	Mary Baker Eddy
Church of God	1830	John Winebrenner
Disciples of Christ	1827	Alexander Campbell
Dunkards (See German Baptist Brethern)		
Ebenezer Society (See Amana Society)		
Ethical Culture Society	1876	Felix Adler
First Century Christian Fellowship	1921	Frank N. D. Buchman
Freewill Baptists	1780	Benjamin Randall
German Baptist Brethern	1728	Johann C. Beissel
Harmonists	1803	George Rapp
Hicksites	1827	Elias Hicks
Hopedale Community (See Practical Christian Republic)		
House of David	1903	Benjamin Purnell
Independent Christian Universalists	1779	John Murray
Jehovah's Witnesses	1884	Charles T. Russell
Mellannial Church (See Shakers)		
Millerites (See Adventists)		

Title	Year Founded	Founder
Moravian Church in the United States	1742	Nicholas Zinzendorf, Augustus G. Spangenberg
Nothingarians	1636	Samuel Gorton
Oneida Community	1848	John H. Noyes
Osgoodites	1848	Jacob Osgood
Oxford Movement (See First Century Christian Fellowship)		
Peace Mission	1915	George Baker (Father Divine)
Peoples Liberal Church	1917	Henry Frank
Perfectionists (See Society of Bible Communists)		
Pillar of Fire Church	1901	Alma B. White
Practical Christian Republic	1842	Adin Ballou
Quakers (See Society of Friends)		
Reformed Mennonites	1912	John Herr
River Brethren	1776	Jacob Engel
Salvation Army	1878	Ballington Booth Maud Booth
Sandemanians	1765	Robert Sandeman
Separatist Society of Zoar	1817	Joseph M. Bimeler
Shakers	1774	Ann Lee
Society of Bible Communists	1836	John H. Noyes
Society of Friends	1647	George Fox
Spiritualists	1848	Margaret Fox Kate Fox
Theosophical Society	1875	Helena P. H. Blavatsky
Thomasites (See Christadelphians)		
Unitarian Church	1787	James Freeman
Unity Movement	1914	Charles Fillmore
Universal Brotherhood and Theosophical Society	1892	Katherine Tingley
Universalists	1774	John Murray
Volunteers of America	1896	Ballington Booth Maud Booth
Wesleyan Methodist Church	1843	Orange Scott
Winebrennians (See Church of God)		
Zoarites (See Separatist Society of Zoar)		

XVI
Corporate Executives

Corporate Executives

A listing of presidents, board chairmen, and/or chief executive officers of U.S. corporations, banks, insurance companies, and public utilities with assets or sales in excess of three billion dollars.

Abbott Laboratories

North Chicago, IL

Presidents

1937	S. DeWitt Clough
1947	Rolly M. Cain
1948	Raymond E Horn
1951	Ernest H. Volwiler
1959	George R. Cain
1967	Edward J. Ledder, Jr.
1976	Robert A. Schoellhorn
1982	G. Kirk Raab

Board Chairmen

1937	Edward H. Ravenscroft
1947	S. DeWitt Clough
1953	James F. Stiles, Jr.
1959	Ernest H. Volwiler
1960	Elmer B. Vliet
1964	George R. Cain
1973	Vacant
1976	Edward J. Ledder, Jr.
1981	Robert A. Schoellhorn

Aetna Life & Casualty Co.

Hartford, CT

Presidents

1850	Eliphalet A. Bulkeley
1872	Thomas O. Enders
1879	Morgan G. Bulkeley
1922	Morgan B. Brainard
1957	Henry S. Beers
1963	Olcott D. Smith
1970	Donald M. Johnson
1976	William O. Bailey

Board Chairmen

1962	Henry S. Beers
1963	Olcott D. Smith
1972	John H. Filer
1985	James T. Lynn

Agway, Inc.

DeWitt, NY

Presidents

1965	Jonathan Davis
1971	George Steele
1981	William A. Hiller

Board Chairmen

1965	J. C. Corwith
1967	Harold G. Soper
1971	George Steele
1982	Richard Croner

Allied-Signal, Inc.

Morristown, NJ

(Formed by merger of Allied Corp. and Signal Companies.)

Board Chairmen

1985	Edward L. Hennessey, Jr.

Aluminum Company of America (ALCOA)

Pittsburgh, PA

Presidents

1888	Alfred E. Hunt
1899	Richard B. Mellon
1910	Arthur V. Davis
1928	Roy A. Hunt
1951	I. W. Wilson
1957	Frank L. Magee
1960	Lawrence Litchfield, Jr.
1963	John D. Harper
1970	W. H. Krome George
1975	William B. Renner
1981	Charles W. Parry
1983	C. Fred Fetterolf

Board Chairmen

1928	Arthur V. Davis
1957	I. W. Wilson
1960	Frank L. Magee
1963	Lawrence Litchfield, Jr.
1966	Frederick J. Close
1970	John D. Harper
1975	W. H. Krome George
1983	Charles W. Parry

Amerada Hess Corp.

New York, NY

(Formed by merger of Hess Oil with Amenada Corp. in 1969.)

Presidents

1969	A. T. Jacobsen
1972	Phillip Kramer
1986	Robert F. Wright

Board Chairmen

1969	Leon Hess
1970	Hubert W. McCollum
1972	Leon Hess

American Airlines Inc.

Dallas, TX

Presidents

1934	L. D. Seymour
1935	Cyrus R. Smith
1964	Marion Sadler
1969	George A. Spater
1974	Albert V. Casey
1980	Robert L. Crandall

Board Chairmen

1946	Cyrus R. Smith
1972	George A. Spater
1973	Cyrus R. Smith
1974	Albert V. Casey
1985	Robert L. Crandall

American Brands, Inc.

New York, NY

(Formerly American Tobacco Co.)

Presidents

1904	James B. Duke
1912	Percival S. Hill
1925	George W. Hill
1946	Vincent Riggio
1950	Paul M. Hahn
1963	Robert B. Walker
1969	Robert K. Heimann
1977	John F. Walrath
1981	Virginius B. Lougee, III

Board Chairmen

1965	Robert B. Walker
1973	Robert K. Heimann
1981	Edward W. Whittemore

American Cyanamid Co.

Wayne, NJ

Presidents

1907	Frank S. Washburn
1922	William B. Bell
1951	Raymond C. Gaugler
1952	Kenneth C. Towe
1957	Wilbur G. Malcolm

1961	Kenneth H. Klipstein
1965	John Allegaert
1967	Clifford D. Siverd
1972	James G. Affleck
1979	George J. Sella, Jr.

Board Chairmen

1957	Kenneth C. Towe
1958	Thomas L. Perkins
1961	Wilbur G. Malcolm
1967	John Allegaert
1972	Clifford D. Siverd
1976	James G. Affleck
1984	George J. Sella, Jr.

American Electric Power Co.

Columbus, OH

Presidents

1906	Willard C. Humstone
1907	Henry L. Doherty
1910	R. E. Breed
1923	George N. Tidd
1947	Philip Sporn
1961	Donald C. Cook
1971	G. V. Patterson
1979	Richard E. Disbrow

Board Chairmen

1971	Donald C. Cook
1976	W. S. White, Jr.

American Home Products Corp.

New York, NY

Presidents

1937	Harry S. Howard
1945	Knox Ide
1947	Walter Silbersack
1960	William F. Laporte
1973	John W. Culligan
1981	John R. Stafford

Board Chairmen

1936	Alvin G. Brush
1965	William F. Laporte
1981	John W. Culligan

American Motors Corp.

Southfield, MI

Presidents

1916	Charles W. Nash
1932	Earl H. McCarty
1936	George W. Mason
1954	George W. Romney
1962	Roy Abernathy
1967	William V. Luneberg
1977	Gerald C. Meyers
1978	Paul W. Tippett
1982	Jose J. Dedeurwaerer

Board Chairmen

1916	James J. Storrow
1926	Charles W. Nash
1948	George W. Mason
1954	George W. Romney
1962	Richard E. Cross
1966	Robert B. Evans
1967	Roy D. Chapin, Jr.
1978	Gerald C. Meyers
1982	Paul W. Tippett

American National Insurance Co.

Galveston, TX

Presidents

1905	William L. Moody, Jr.
1955	Mary Moody Northern
1961	William L. Vogler
1962	R. A. Furbush
1969	Phil B. Noah
1971	Glendon E. Johnson
1977	Orson C. Clay

Board Chairmen

1962	William L. Vogler
1969	R. A. Furbush
1969	Phil B. Noah
1972	Glendon E. Johnson
1986	Orson C. Clay

American Standard, Inc.

New York, NY

Presidents

1962	Joseph A. Grazier
1967	William D. Eberle
1971	William A. Marquand
1982	William B. Boyd
1986	William G. Roth

Board Chairmen

1966	Joseph A. Grazier
1969	Vacant
1980	William A. Marquand
1986	William B. Boyd

American Telephone & Telegraph Co. (AT&T)

New York, NY

Presidents

1885	Theodore N. Vail
1887	John E. Hudson
1900	Alexander Cochrane
1901	Frederick P. Fish
1907	Theodore N. Vail
1919	Harry B. Thayer
1925	Walter S. Gifford
1948	Leroy A. Wilson
1951	Cleo F. Craig
1956	Frederick R. Kappel
1961	Eugene J. McNeely
1965	Haakon I. Romnes
1967	Ben S. Gilmer
1970	Hakon I. Romnes
1972	Robert D. Lilley
1976	William L. Lindholm
1977	Charles L. Brown
1979	William M. Ellinghaus
1985	James E. Olson

Board Chairmen

1919	Theodore N. Vail
1956	Cleo F. Craig
1961	Frederick R. Kappel
1967	Hakon I. Romnes
1972	John D. DeButts
1979	Charles L. Brown
1982	Charles J. Waidelich

Ameritrust Co.

Cleveland, OH

(Cleveland Trust Co. until 1980.)

Presidents

1895	John G. W. Cowles
1903	Calvary Morris
1908	F. H. Goff
1923	Harris Creech
1941	George Gund
1962	George F. Karch
1969	Everett W. Smith
1973	M. Brock Weir
1978	Jerry V. Jarrett
1983	James D. Rode

Board Chairmen

1903	John G. W. Cowles
1908	Calvary Morris
1941	I. F. Freiberger
1962	George Gund
1966	George F. Karch
1969	Everett W. Smith
1978	M. Brock Weir
1983	Jerry V. Jarrett

Amoco Corp.

Chicago, IL
(Standard Oil of Indiana until 1985.)

Presidents

1911	William P. Cowan
1918	Lauren J. Drake
1918	William M. Burton
1927	Edward G. Seubert
1945	Alonzo W. Peake
1955	Frank O. Prior
1958	John E. Swearingen
1965	Robert C. Gunness
1974	George V. Myers
1978	Richard M. Morrow
1983	H. Laurence Fuller

Board Chairmen

1918	Robert W. Stewart
1945	Robert E. Wilson
1958	Frank O. Prior
1965	John E. Swearingen
1983	Richard M. Morrow

Anaconda Co.

Denver, CO

(See Atlantic Richfield Co. for representation after 1981.)

Presidents

1895	James B. A. Haggin
1899	Marcus Daly
1901	William Scanlon
1905	John D. Ryan
1909	Benjamin B. Thayer
1915	John D. Ryan
1918	Cornelius F. Kelly
1940	James R. Hobbins
1949	William H. Hoover
1952	Robert E. Dwyer
1956	Clyde E. Weed
1958	Charles M. Brinckerhoff
1965	C. Jay Parkinson
1969	John G. Hall
1971	John B. M. Place
1978	Louis F. Davis
1979	Ralph F. Cox

Board Chairmen

1919	John D. Ryan
1940	Cornelius F. Kelly
1955	Roy H. Glover
1958	Clyde E. Weed
1969	C. Jay Parkinson
1971	John B. M. Place
1979	Robert O. Anderson

Anheuser-Busch Companies, Inc.

St. Louis, MO

(Anheuser-Bush, Inc. until 1979.)

Presidents

1939	Adolphus Busch, III
1947	August A. Busch, Jr.
1971	Richard A. Meyer
1974	August A. Busch, III

Board Chairmen

1951	Eberhard Anheuser
1956	August A. Busch, Jr.
1977	August A. Busch, III

Archer Daniels Midland Co.

Decatur, IL

Presidents

1935	S. M. Archer
1949	Thomas L. Daniels
1960	John H. Daniels
1969	Lowell W. Andreas
1972	Donald B. Walker
1975	James R. Randall

Board Chairmen

1945	S. M. Archer
1949	Samuel Mairs
1956	Vacant
1960	Thomas L. Daniels
1966	Erwin A. Olsen
1969	John H. Daniels
1970	Dwayne O. Andreas

Armco, Inc.

Middletown, OH
(American Rolling Mill Co. until 1947; Armco Steel Corp. until 1979.)

Presidents

1900	George M. Verity
1930	Charles R. Hook
1948	W. W. Sebald
1956	Ralph L. Gray
1960	Logan T. Johnston
1965	C. William Verity, Jr.
1971	Donald E. Reichelderfer
1974	Harry Holiday
1979	Daniel C. Boone
1983	Robert E. Boni

Board Chairmen

1968	Logan T. Johnston
1971	C. William Verity, Jr.
1982	Harry Holiday
1986	Robert E. Boni

Armour & Co.

Pheonix, AZ

Presidents

1878	Philip D. Armour
1900	J. Ogden Armour
1923	F. Edson White
1931	T. George Lee
1935	Robert H. Cabell
1939	George A. Eastwood
1947	Frederick W. Specht
1957	William Wood Prince
1961	Edward W. Wilson
1965	Edward J. McAdams
1968	Charles R. Orem
1971	Jess Nicks
1975	David L. Duensing
1977	Clifton B. Cox
1978	Donald J. Shaughnessy
1980	Gerald H. Trautman
1981	John W. Teets

Board Chairmen

1923	J. Ogden Armour

1934 Frederick H. Prince	1986 George H. Babiklan
1947 George A. Eastwood	
1952 Frederick W. Specht	*Board Chairman*
1961 William Wood Prince	
1970 Gerald H. Trautman	1952 Robert H. Colley
1975 Clifton B. Cox	1964 Henderson Supplee, Jr.
1980 Gerald H. Trautman	1965 Robert O. Anderson
1981 John W. Teets	

Ashland Oil, Inc.

Russell, KY

(Ashland Refining Co. until 1943;
Ashland Oil & Refining Co. until
1971.)

Presidents

1936 Paul G. Blazer
1946 J. Howard Marshall
1952 Rexford S. Blazer
1958 Everett F. Wells
1965 Orin E. Atkins
1972 Robert E. Yancey
1982 Vacant
1986 Charles J. Luellen

Board Chairmen

1936 James L. Martin
1946 Paul G. Blazer
1958 Rexford S. Blazer
1972 Orin E. Atkins
1981 John R. Hall

Atchison, Topeka & Santa Fe Railway Co.

Chicago, IL

Presidents

1895 Edward P. Ripley
1920 William B. Storey
1933 Samuel T. Bledsoe
1939 Edward J. Engel
1944 Fred G. Gurley
1957 Ernest S. Marsh
1967 John S. Reed
1978 Lawrence Cena
1983 William J. Swartz

Board Chairmen

1916 Walter D. Hines
1920 Edward P. Ripley
1957 Fred G. Gurley
1967 Ernest S. Marsh
1973 John S. Reed
1983 J. J. Schmidt

Atlantic Richfield Co.

Los Angeles, CA

(Richfield Oil Corp. until merger
with Atlantic Refining Co. in
1966; Sinclair Oil Corp. merged
into present company in 1969;
Anaconda Co., in 1981.)

Presidents

1951 Robert H. Colley
1952 Henderson Supplee, Jr.
1964 Thornton F. Bradshaw
1981 William F. Kieschnick

Avco Corp.

Greenwich, CT

Presidents

1929 Graham B. Grosvenor
1930 Frederic G. Coburn
1932 Lucius B. Manning
1937 Victor Emanuel
1945 Irving B. Babcock
1948 Victor Emanuel
1957 Raymond A. Rich
1958 Kendrick R. Wilson, Jr.
1961 James R. Kerr
1974 George L. Hogemann
1979 Ross M. Hett
1981 Donald K. Farrar

Board Chairmen

1929 W. Averell Harriman
1932 Erritt L. Cord
1936 Lucius B. Manning
1945 Victor Emanuel
1961 Kendrick R. Wilson, Jr.
1974 James R. Kerr
1985 Beverly F. Dolan

Chief Executive Officers

1929 W. Averell Harriman
1932 Erritt L. Cord
1934 Lucius B. Manning
1937 Victor Emanuel
1960 Kendrick R. Wilson
1969 James R. Kerr

Bank of America National Trust & Savings Association

San Francisco, CA

(Bank of Italy until 1930.)

Presidents

1904 Antonio Chichizola
1905 Lorenzo Scatena
1915 A. P. Giannini
1924 James A. Bacigalupi
1929 Arnold J. Mount
1932 William F. Morrish
1934 A. P. Giannini
1936 Lawrence M. Giannini
1952 C. F. Wente
1954 S. Clark Beise
1963 R. A. Peterson
1970 Alden W. Clausen
1981 Samuel H. Armacost

Board Chairmen

1966 Louis B. Lundborg
1971 Chauncey J. Medberry
1981 Leland S. Prussia

Bank of New York

New York, NY

(Merged with New York Life Insurance & Trust Co. in 1922 and
with Empire Trust Co. in 1966.)

Presidents

1784 Alexander McDougall
1785 Jeremiah Wadsworth
1786 Isaac Roosevelt
1791 Gulian Verplanck
1799 Nicholas Gouverneur
1802 Herman LeRoy
1804 Matthew Clarkson, Jr.
1825 Charles Wilkes
1832 Cornelius Heyer
1843 John Oothout
1858 Anthony P. Halsey
1863 Charles P. Leverich
1876 Charles M. Fry
1892 E. S. Mason
1901 Herbert L. Griggs
1922 Edwin G. Merrill
1931 John C. Traphagan
1948 Albert C. Simmonds
1963 Samuel H. Wooley
1968 Elliott Averett
1974 J. Carter Bacot
1982 Peter Herrick

Board Chairmen

1948 Albert C. Simmonds
1968 Samuel H. Woolley
1974 Elliott Averett
1982 J. Carter Bacot

Bankers Trust Co.

New York, NY

Presidents

1902 Edmund C. Converse
1914 Benjamin Strong
1914 Sewart Prosser
1923 A. A. Tilney
1929 Henry J. Cochran
1931 S. Sloan Colt
1957 William H. Moore
1968 Lewis Lapham
1975 John W. Hannon, Jr.
1983 Charles S. Sanford

Board Chairmen

1956 S. Sloan Colt
1966 William H. Moore
1975 Alfred Brittain, III

BASF Corp.

Parsippany, NJ

Presidents

1985 Juergen F. Strube

Board Chairmen

1985 Juergen F. Strube

Baxter Travenol Laboratories, Inc.

Deerfield, IL

Presidents

1973 R. Douglas Petrie
1976 Vernon R. Loucks, Jr.

Board Chairmen

1973 William B. Graham
1986 Karl D. Bays

Bethlehem Steel Corp.

Bethlehem, PA

Presidents

1905 Charles M. Schwab
1916 Eugene G. Grace
1945 Arthur B. Homer
1960 Edmund F. Martin
1963 Stewart S. Cort
1970 Lewis W. Foy
1974 Frederic W. West, Jr.
1979 Richard F. Schubert
1980 Walter F. Williams

Board Chairmen

1905 Charles M. Schwab
1945 Eugene G. Grace
1960 Arthur B. Homer
1964 Edmund F. Martin
1970 Stewart S. Cort
1974 Lewis W. Foy
1980 Donald H. Trautlein
1986 Walter F. Williams

Boeing Co.

Seattle, WA

Presidents

1916 William E. Boeing
1922 E. N. Gott
1925 William E. Boeing
1926 P. G. Johnson
1933 C. L. Egtvedt
1939 P. G. Johnson
1945 William M. Allen
1968 Thornton A. Wilson
1972 Malcolm T. Stamper

Board Chairmen

1968 William A. Allen
1972 Thornton A. Wilson

Boise Cascade Corp.

Boise, ID

Presidents

1959 R. V. Hansberger
1972 John B. Fery
1978 Jon H. Miller

Board Chairmen

1959 Gilbert H. Osgood
1970 R. V. Hansberger

483

1972 Stephen B. Moser
1978 John B. Fery

Borden, Inc.

New York, NY
(Borden Co. until 1970.)

Presidents

1935 Arthur W. Milburn
1939 Theodore B. Montague
1957 Harold W. Comfort
1965 Francis R. Elliott
1967 Augustine R. Marusi
1973 Eugene J. Sullivan
1985 R. J. Ventres

Board Chairmen

1935 Albert G. Milbank
1957 Theodore G. Montague
1965 Roy D. Wooster
1967 Francis R. Elliott
1968 Augustine R. Marusi
1980 Eugene J. Sullivan

Borg-Warner Corp.

Chicago, IL

Presidents

1928 George W. Borg
1929 Charles S. Davis
1950 Roy C. Ingersoll
1956 Robert S. Ingersoll
1961 Lester G. Porter
1968 James F. Bere
1975 Robert O. Bass
1980 Jerry E. Dempsey
1983 Clarence E. Johnson

Board Chairmen

1928 Charles S. Davis
1929 George W. Borg
1950 Charles S. Davis
1955 Roy C. Ingersoll
1961 Robert S. Ingersoll
1972 James F. Bere
1973 Vacant
1975 James F. Bere

Bristol-Myers Co.

New York, NY

Presidents

1935 Henry P. Bristol
1950 Lee H. Bristol
1959 Frederic N. Schwartz
1965 Gavin K. McBain
1967 Richard L. Gelb
1977 Herman Sokol
1982 Vacant

Board Chairmen

1935 William M. Bristol
1936 Vacant
1950 Henry P. Bristol
1959 Lee H. Bristol
1965 Frederic N. Schwartz
1967 Gavin K. McBain
1977 Richard L. Gelb

Burlington Northern, Inc.

Seattle, WA
(See also Chicago, Burlington &
Quincy Railroad Co., Great
Northern Railway Co., and North-
ern Pacific Railway Co.)

Presidents

1970 Louis W. Menk
1971 Robert W. Downing
1977 Norman M. Lorentzen
1986 Richard M. Bressler

Board Chairmen

1970 John M. Budd
1971 Louis W. Menk
1982 Richard M. Bressler

Campbell Soup Co.

Camden, NJ

Presidents

1892 Joseph Campbell
1894 Arthur Dorrance
1914 John T. Dorrance
1930 Arthur C. Dorrance
1946 James McGowan, Jr.
1953 William B. Murphy
1972 Harold A. Shaub
1980 R. Gordon McGovern

Board Chairmen

1914 Arthur Dorrance
1930 George M. Dorrance
1953 James McGowan, Jr.
1956 Oliver G. Willits
1962 John T. Dorrance, Jr.

Carnation Co.

Los Angeles, CA

Presidents

1899 Elbridge A. Stuart
1932 Elbridge H. Stuart
1957 Alfred M. Ghormley
1963 H. Everett Olson
1973 Dwight L. Stuart
1983 Timm F. Crull

Board Chairmen

1932 Elbridge A. Stuart
1957 Elbridge H. Stuart
1971 H. Everett Olson

Caterpillar, Inc.

Peoria, IL
(Caterpillar Tractor Co. until
1984.)

Presidents

1925 Raymond C. Force
1930 B. C. Heacock
1941 Louis B. Neumiller
1954 Harmon S. Eberhard
1962 William Blackie
1966 William H. Franklin

1972 Lee L. Morgan
1977 Robert E. Gilmore
1985 P. Donis

Board Chairmen

1954 Louis B. Neumiller
1962 Harmon S. Eberhard
1966 William A. Blackie
1972 W. H. Franklin
1975 W. L. Naumann
1977 Lee L. Morgan
1985 George A. Schaefer

Champion International Corp.

Stamford, CT
(United States Plywood Corp. un-
til 1969; U.S. Plywood-Champion
Papers, Inc. until 1973.)

Presidents

1937 Lawrence Ottinger
1952 S. W. Antoville
1964 Gene C. Brewer
1967 Karl R. Bendetsen
1972 Thomas F. Willers
1974 Andrew C. Sigler
1980 Robert F. Longbine

Board Chairmen

1973 Thomas F. Willers
1974 E. Roger Montgomery
1979 Andrew C. Sigler

Chase Manhattan Bank

New York, NY
(Formed by merger of Chase Na-
tional Bank with Bank of the
Manhattan Co. in 1955.)

Presidents

1955 J. Stewart Baker
1956 George Champion
1961 David Rockefeller
1968 Herbert P. Patterson
1972 Willard C. Butcher
1981 Thomas G. Labreque

Board Chairmen

1955 John J. McCloy
1961 George Champion
1969 David Rockefeller
1981 Willard C. Butcher

Bank of the Manhattan Co.

Presidents

1799 Daniel Ludlow
1808 Henry Remsen
1825 John C. Costar
1829 Maltby Galston
1840 Johnathan Thompson
1847 Caleb O. Halsted
1860 James M. Morrison
1879 John S. Harberger
1880 William Henry Smith
1884 DeWitt C. Hays
1893 Stephen Baker
1927 J. Stewart Baker

1929 Park A. Rowley
1932 F. Abbot Goodhue
1948 Lawrence Marshall

Chase National Bank

Presidents

1877 Samuel C. Thompson
1884 John Thompson
1886 Henry W. Cannon
1904 A. Barton Hepburn
1911 Albert H. Wiggin
1926 John McHugh
1928 Robert L. Clarkson
1929 Charles S. McCain
1930 Winthrop W. Aldrich
1934 H. Donald Campbell
1946 Arthur W. McCain
1949 Percy J. Ebbott

Chemical Bank

New York, NY
(New York Chemical Manufactur-
ing Co. until 1844; Chemical Bank
until 1865; Chemical National
Bank until 1929; Chemical Bank &
Trust Co. until 1954; Chemical
Corn Exchange Bank until 1959;
Chemical Bank New York Trust
Co. until 1969.)

Presidents

1824 Balthazar P. Melick
1831 John Mason
1839 Isaac Jones
1844 John Quentin Jones
1878 George G. Williams
1903 William H. Porter
1910 Joseph B. Martindale
1917 Herbert K. Twitchell
1920 Percy H. Johnston
1935 Frank K. Houston
1946 N. Baxter Jackson
1947 Harold H. Helm
1956 Isaac B. Grainger
1960 William S. Renchard
1966 Howard W. McCall, Jr.
1972 Donald C. Platten
1973 Norborne Berkeley, Jr.
1981 Walter V. Shipley
1983 Robert J. Callander

Board Chairmen

1920 Herbert K. Twitchell
1929 John W. Platten
1930 Percy H. Johnston
1946 Frank K. Houston
1947 N. Baxter Jackson
1956 Harold H. Helm
1966 William S. Renchard
1973 Donald C. Platten
1983 Walter V. Shipley

Chesebrough-Pond's, Inc.

Westport, CT

Presidents

1956 Jerome A. Straka
1968 Ralph E. Ward
1984 George F. Goebeler
1986 Robert M. Phillips

Board Chairmen

1956	Arthur B. Richardson
1961	Lloyd V. Young
1962	Vacant
1969	Jerome A. Straka
1973	Vacant
1976	Ralph E. Ward

Chevron Corp.

San Francisco, CA

(Standard Oil Company of California until 1985.)

Presidents

1926	Kenneth R. Kingsbury
1937	William H. Berg
1940	Henry D. Collier
1945	R. Gwin Follis
1948	Theodore S. Petersen
1961	Otto N. Miller
1966	J. E. Gosline
1969	Harold J. Haynes
1974	John R. Gray

Board Chairmen

1945	Henry D. Collier
1949	R. Gwin Follis
1966	Otto N. Miller
1974	Harold J. Haynes
1981	George M. Keller

Chicago, Burlington & Quincy Railroad Co.

Chicago, IL

(Became part of Burlington Northern, Inc. 1970.)

Presidents

1857	John Van Nortwick
1865	James F. Joy
1871	James M. Walker
1876	Robert Harris
1878	John M. Forbes
1881	Charles E. Perkins
1901	George B. Harris
1910	Darius Miller
1914	Hale Holden
1918	Charles E. Perkins, Jr.
1920	Hale Holden
1929	Frederick E. Williamson
1932	Ralph Budd
1949	Harry C. Murphy
1965	Louis W. Menk
1966	William J. Quinn

Chrysler Corp.

Detroit, MI

(Chrysler Motors Corp. Inc. until 1935.)

Presidents

1925	Walter P. Chrysler
1936	K. T. Keller
1952	Lester L. Colbert
1962	Lynn A. Townshend
1968	V. E. Boyd
1970	John J. Riccardo
1975	Eugene A. Cafiero

1978	Lee A. Iacocca
1979	Paul J. Bergmoser
1984	Harold K. Sperlich

Board Chairmen

1925	Walter P. Chrysler
1951	Lester L. Colbert
1952	K. T. Keller
1961	Lester L. Colbert
1962	George H. Love
1967	Lynn A. Townshend
1975	John J. Riccardo
1979	Lee A. Iacocca

Citibank

New York, NY

(First National City Bank until 1975.)

Presidents

1812	Samuel Osgood
1813	William Few
1817	Peter Stagg
1825	Thomas L. Smith
1827	Isaac Wright
1832	Thomas Bloodgood
1843	Gorham A. Worth
1856	Moses Taylor
1882	Percy R. Pyne
1891	James Stillman
1909	F. A. Vanderlip
1919	James A. Stillman
1921	Charles E. Mitchell
1929	Gordon S. Rentschler
1940	William G. Brady, Jr.
1948	Howard C. Sheperd
1952	James S. Rockefeller
1959	George S. Moore
1967	Walter B. Wriston
1970	William I. Spencer

Board Chairmen

1909	James Stillman
1918	James A. Stillman
1921	Eric P. Swenson
1929	Charles E. Mitchell
1933	James H. Perkins
1940	Gordon S. Rentschler
1948	William G. Brady, Jr.
1952	Howard C. Sheperd
1959	James S. Rockefeller
1967	George S. Moore
1970	Walter B. Writson
1985	John S. Reed

Cities Service Co.

Tulsa, OK

Presidents

1910	Henry L. Doherty
1940	W. Alton Jones
1953	Burl S. Watson
1959	J. Edward Warren
1966	Charles S. Mitchell
1968	J. Edgar Heston
1981	Robert H. Chitwood

Board Chairmen

1953	W. Alton Jones
1959	Burl S. Watson
1966	John L. Burns

1968	Charles S. Mitchell
1972	Robert V. Sellers
1982	Charles J. Waidelich

Coastal Corp.

Houston, TX

(Coastal States Gas Producing Co., Inc. until 1983.)

Presidents

1955	Oscar S. Wyatt, Jr.
1971	Harry G. Fair
1974	Oscar S. Wyatt, Jr.
1976	Harry L. Blomquist, Jr.
1986	James R. Paul

Board Chairmen

1955	Oscar S. Wyatt, Jr.

Coca-Cola Co.

Atlanta, GA

Presidents

1892	Asa G. Candler
1916	Charles H. Candler
1919	Samuel C. Dobbs
1920	Charles H. Candler
1923	Robert W. Woodruff
1939	A. A. Acklin
1945	Robert W. Woodruff
1946	William J. Hobbs
1952	H. Burke Nicholson
1955	William E. Robinson
1958	Lee Talley
1962	J. Paul Austin
1971	Charles W. Duncan
1974	J. Lucian Smith
1980	Roberto C. Goizueta
1981	Donald R. Keough

Board Chairmen

1919	Charles H. Candler
1920	William C. Bradley
1939	Robert W. Woodruff
1942	Harrison Jones
1952	Robert W. Woodruff
1955	H. Burke Nicholson
1958	William E. Robinson
1961	Lee Talley
1971	J. Paul Austin
1980	Roberto C. Goizueta

Colgate-Palmolive Co.

New York, NY

(Colgate Co., 1806)

Presidents

1933	S. Bayard Colgate
1939	Edward H. Little
1954	J. H. McConnell
1956	William L. Sims, II
1958	Edward H. Little
1960	George H. Lesch
1970	David R. Foster
1975	Keith Crane
1983	Reuben Mark

Board Chairmen

1933	Charles S. Pearce
1939	S. Bayard Colgate
1954	Edward H. Little
1961	George H. Lesch
1975	David R. Foster
1980	Keith Crane
1986	Reuben Mark

Commonwealth Edison Co.

Chicago, IL

Presidents

1907	Samuel Insull
1930	Edward J. Doyle
1951	Willis Gale
1953	John W. Evers
1959	J. Harris Wood
1964	Thomas G. Ayers
1977	James J. O'Connor

Board Chairmen

1930	Samuel Insull
1932	James Simpson
1939	Charles Y. Freeman
1953	Willis Gale
1961	J. Harris Ward
1973	Thomas G. Ayers
1980	James J. O'Connor

Chief Executive Officers

1933	Charles Y. Freeman
1961	Willis Gale
1964	Morgan F. Murphy
1977	James J. O'Connor

ConAgra, Inc.

Omaha, NE

Presidents

1973	J. A. Mactier
1974	Claude I. Carter
1976	Charles M. Harper
1981	G. W. Doering
1983	Vacant

Board Chairmen

1975	Robert B. Daugherty
1978	Vacant
1981	Charles M. Harper

Connecticut Mutual Life Insurance Co.

Hartford, CT

Presidents

1846	Eliphalet A. Bulkeley
1848	James Goodwin
1866	Guy R. Phelps
1869	James Goodwin
1878	Jacob L. Greene
1905	John M. Taylor
1918	Henry S. Robinson
1926	James L. Loomis
1945	Peter M. Fraser

1955 George F. B. Smith	1941 Justin R. Whiting	1968 T. E. Kraner	1985 Boyd C. Bartlett
1956 Charles J. Zimmerman	1951 Daniel E. Karn	1970 Eugene L. Miller	
1967 Edward B. Bates	1960 James H. Campbell	1975 Robert Cizik	*Board Chairmen*
1978 Denis F. Mullane	1972 Alphonse H. Aymond		
	1975 John D. Selby	*Board Chairmen*	1964 William A. Hewitt
Board Chairmen	1985 William T. McCormick, Jr.		1982 Robert A. Hanson
		1967 Eugene L. Miller	
1978 Edward B. Bates		1980 Vacant	
	Board Chairmen	1983 Robert Cizik	

Conoco, Inc.

Wilmington, DE

(Continental Oil Co. until 1980.)

Presidents

1929 Dan Moran
1947 Leonard F. McCollum
1964 Andrew W. Tarkington
1969 John G. McLean
1977 Ralph E. Bailey

Board Chairmen

1929 Edward T. Wilson
1946 James J. Cosgrove
1963 Charles A. Perlitz, Jr.
1964 Leonard F. McCollum
1972 John G. McLean
1974 Howard W. Blauvelt
1979 Ralph E. Bailey

Consolidated Edison Company of New York, Inc.

New York, NY

(Consolidated Gas Company of New York until 1936.)

Presidents

1884 Charles Roome
1886 James W. Smith
1894 Harrison E. Gawtry
1909 George B. Cortelyou
1935 Frank W. Smith
1937 Ralph H. Tapscott
1949 Hudson R. Searing
1955 Harland C. Forbes
1957 Charles E. Eble
1966 John V. Cleary
1969 Louis H. Roddis, Jr.
1973 William W. Lapsley
1975 Arthur Hauspurg

Board Chairmen

1905 Harrison E. Gawtry
1932 Floyd L. Carlisle
1949 Ralph H. Tapscott
1955 Hudson R. Searing
1957 Harland C. Forbes
1966 Charles E. Eble
1967 Charles F. Luce
1982 Arthur Hauspurg

Consumers Power Co.

Jackson, MI

Presidents

1910 William A. Foote
1915 Bernard C. Cobb
1932 T. A. Kenney

Board Chairmen

1930 Bernard C. Cobb
1934 Wendell L. Willkie
1940 Justin R. Whiting
1960 Alphonse H. Aymond
1979 John D. Selby
1985 William T. McCormick, Jr.

Continental Illinois National Bank & Trust Co.

Chicago, IL

(Merchants' Savings, Loan & Trust Co. until 1923; Illinois Merchants' Trust Co. until 1930.)

Presidents

1857 John H. Dunham
1862 Henry Farnham
1863 Solomon A. Smith
1879 John Tyrrell
1884 John W. Doane
1898 Orson Smith
1916 Edmund D. Hulbert
1923 John J. Mitchell
1927 Eugene M. Stevens
1932 James R. Leavell
1948 Carl Birdsall
1956 David M. Kennedy
1959 Richard Aishton
1960 Tilden Cummings
1973 John H. Perkins

Board Chairmen

1930 Arthur Reynolds
1932 Stanley Field
1934 Walter J. Cummings, Sr.
1959 David M. Kennedy
1969 Donald M. Graham
1973 Roger E. Anderson
1984 William S. Ogden

Control Data Corp.

Minneapolis, MN

Presidents

1957 William C. Norris
1980 Robert M. Price

Board Chairmen

1957 William C. Norris
1986 Robert M. Price

Cooper Industries, Inc.

Houston, TX

President

1957 Eugene L. Miller

CPC International, Inc.

Englewood Cliffs, NJ

(CPC Engineering Corp. until 1971.)

Presidents

1959 Lloyd W. Pote
1969 James W. McKee, Jr.
1979 James R. Eiszner

Board Chairmen

1971 H. C. Harder
1973 Vacant
1979 James W. McKee, Jr.

Crocker National Bank

San Francisco, CA

(Crocker First National until 1956; Crocker-Anglo National until 1963; Crocker-Citizens National Bank until 1973.)

Presidents

1893 William H. Crocker
1936 W. W. Crocker
1950 Jerd F. Sullivan, Jr.
1956 Paul A. Hoover
1962 Emmett G. Solomon
1968 Joseph F. Hogan
1970 Leslie C. Peacock
1974 Thomas R. Wilcox
1975 Robert K. Wilmouth
1978 Thomas R. Wilcox
1978 John B. M. Place
1981 J. Hallam Dawson

Board Chairmen

1936 William H. Crocker
1937 James K. Moffitt
1950 W. W. Crocker
1963 Paul A. Hoover
1968 Emmett G. Solomon
1974 Thomas R. Wilcox
1980 John B. M. Place
1984 Frank V. Cahouet

Deere & Co.

Moline, IL

Presidents

1869 John Deere
1886 Charles H. Deere
1907 William Butterworth
1928 Charles Deere Wiman
1942 Burton F. Peek
1944 Charles Deere Wiman
1955 William A. Hewitt
1964 Ellwood F. Curtis
1978 Robert A. Hanson

Detroit Edison Co.

Detroit, MI

Presidents

1903 Charles W. Wetmore
1912 Alex Dow
1940 Alfred C. Marshall
1944 James W. Parker
1951 Walker L. Cisler
1964 Donald F. Kigar
1967 Edwin O. George
1970 William G. Meese
1975 John R. Hamann
1979 Walter J. McCarthy
1981 Charles M. Heidel

Board Chairmen

1944 Prentiss M. Brown
1964 Walker L. Cisler
1975 William G. Meese
1981 Walter J. McCarthy

Diamond Shamrock Corp.

Dallas, TX

Presidents

1947 Raymond F. Evans
1967 James A. Hughes
1971 C. Allison Cash
1975 William H. Bricker
1980 Allan J. Tomlinson
1984 J. L. Jackson

Board Chairmen

1954 Raymond F. Evans
1971 James A. Hughes
1975 C. Allison Cash
1979 William H. Bricker

Digital Equipment Corp.

Maynard, MA

Presidents

1962 Kenneth H. Olsen

Board Chairmen

1962 Kenneth H. Olsen

Dow Chemical Co.

Midland, MI

Presidents

1897 Albert E. Convers
1918 Herbert Dow
1930 Willard H. Dow
1949 Leland I. Doan
1962 Herbert D. Doan
1971 C. B. Branch

1976 Zoltan Merszei
1978 Paul F. Oreffice

Board Chairmen

1960 Carl A. Gerstacker
1962 Leland I. Doan
1976 C. B. Branch
1978 Zoltan Merszei
1979 Earl B. Barnes
1982 Robert W. Lundeen

Dresser Industries, Inc.

Dallas, TX

(S. R. Dresser Manufacturing Co. until 1945.)

Presidents

1905 Solomon R. Dresser
1911 Fred A. Miller
1929 H. Neil Mallon
1957 John B. O'Connor
1964 F. G. Fabian, Jr.
1965 John Lawrence
1969 Charles Kuhn
1970 John V. James
1981 James R. Brown, Jr.
1982 John J. Murphy

Board Chairmen

1905 Fred A. Miller
1929 H. Neil Mallon
1935 Fred A. Miller
1939 Vacant
1957 H. Neil Mallon
1962 John Lawrence
1976 John V. James
1983 John J. Murphy

Duke Power Co.

Charlotte, NC
(Wateree Electric Co. until 1924.)

Presidents

1917 James B. Duke
1925 George G. Allen
1949 Edward C. Marshall
1953 Norman A. Cocke
1959 William B. McGuire
1971 Carl Horn, Jr.
1976 B. B. Parker
1978 William S. Lee, III
1982 Douglas W. Booth

Board Chairmen

1949 George G. Allen
1957 William S. O. Robinson, Jr.
1961 Thomas L. Perkins
1976 Carl Horn, Jr.
1982 William S. Lee, III

E. I. du Pont de Nemours & Co.

Wilmington, DE

Presidents

1802 Eleuthere Irenee du Pont

1834 Antoine Bidermann
1837 Alfred Victor du Pont
1850 Henry du Pont
1889 Eugene du Pont
1902 T. Coleman du Pont
1915 Pierre S. du Pont
1919 Irenee du Pont
1926 Lammot du Pont
1940 Walter S. Carpenter, Jr.
1948 Crawford H. Greenewalt
1962 Lammot du Pont Copeland
1967 Charles B. McCoy
1973 Edward R. Kane
1979 Edward G. Jefferson
1981 Richard E. Heckert

Board Chairmen

1968 Lammot du Pont Copeland
1971 Charles B. McCoy
1974 Irving S. Shapiro
1981 Edward G. Jefferson
1986 Richard E. Heckert

Eastern Air Lines Inc.

Miami, FL

Presidents

1938 Edward V. Rickenbacker
1953 Thomas F. Armstrong
1959 Malcolm M. MacIntyre
1963 Floyd D. Hall
1971 Samuel L. Higgenbottom
1973 Floyd D. Hall
1975 Frank Borman
1986 Joseph B. Leonard

Board Chairmen

1953 Edward V. Rickenbacker
1969 Floyd D. Hall
1976 Frank Borman

Eastman Kodak Co.

Rochester, NY

Presidents

1884 Henry A. Strong
1919 George Eastman
1925 William G. Stuber
1934 Frank W. Lovejoy
1941 Thomas J. Hargrave
1952 Albert K. Chapman
1960 William S. Vaughn
1967 Louis K. Eilers
1970 Gerald B. Zornow
1972 Walter A. Fallon
1976 Colby H. Chandler
1983 Kay R. Whitmore

Board Chairmen

1925 George Eastman
1934 William G. Stuber
1941 Frank W. Lovejoy
1945 Perry Wilcox
1952 Thomas J. Hargrave
1962 Albert K. Chapman
1967 William S. Vaughn
1970 Louis K. Eilers
1972 Gerald B. Zornow
1976 Walter A. Fallon

1983 Colby H. Chandler

Eaton Corp.

Cleveland, OH

(Eaton Manufacturing Co. until 1968; Eaton, Yale & Towne, Inc. until 1972.)

Presidents

1923 Joseph O. Eaton
1925 Clarence I. Ochs
1952 Howard J. McGinn
1957 John C. Virden
1965 E. L. Ludvigsen
1967 E. M. de Windt
1969 William A. Mattie
1973 Paul A. Miller
1979 James R. Stover

Board Chairmen

1925 Joseph O. Eaton
1952 Clarence I. Ochs
1957 Howard J. McGinn
1958 John C. Virden
1968 E. L. Ludvigsen
1969 E. Mandell de Windt
1986 James R. Stover

Emerson Electric Co.

St. Louis, MO

(Emerson Electric Manufacturing Co. until 1954.)

Presidents

1923 Herbert I. Finch
1935 Joseph Newman
1939 W. Stuart Symington
1946 Oscar C. Schmitt
1954 William S. Snead
1954 Wallace R. Persons
1965 William L. Davis, Jr.
1970 Edward L. O'Neill
1972 Vincent T. Gorguze
1977 E. L. Keys, Jr.
1986 Charles F. Knight

Board Chairmen

1935 Herbert I. Finch
1939 W. Stuart Symington
1947 Oscar C. Schmitt
1949 Vacant
1954 William S. Snead
1965 Wallace R. Persons
1974 Charles F. Knight

Equitable Life Assurance Society of the United States

New York, NY

Presidents

1859 William C. Alexander
1874 Henry H. Hyde
1899 James M. Alexander
1905 Paul Morton
1911 William A. Day
1927 Thomas I. Parkinson
1953 Ray D. Murphy

1957 James F. Oates, Jr.
1967 J. Henry Smith
1974 Coy G. Eklund
1983 John B. Carter

Board Chairmen

1958 James F. Oates, Jr.
1969 J. Henry Smith
1971 Davidson Sommers
1974 J. Henry Smith
1975 John T. Fey
1983 Robert F. Froehlke

Exxon Corp.

New York, NY

(Standard Oil Co., New Jersey until 1973.)

Presidents

1882 Henry M. Flagler
1883 James McGee
1885 Paul Babcock, Jr.
1892 Henry M. Flagler
1899 John D. Rockefeller
1911 John D. Archbold
1916 Alfred C. Bedford
1917 Walter C. Teagle
1937 William S. Farish
1943 Ralph W. Gallagher
1944 Eugene Holman
1954 Monroe J. Rathbone
1963 Michael L. Haider
1965 J. Kenneth Jamieson
1969 Milo M. Brisco
1972 Clifton C. Garvin, Jr.
1975 Howard C. Kauffmann
1986 Lawrence G. Rawl

Board Chairmen

1917 Alfred C. Bedford
1925 George H. Jones
1933 William S. Farish
1937 Walter C. Teagle
1942 Ralph W. Gallagher
1946 Frank W. Abrams
1954 Eugene Holman
1960 Leo D. Welch
1963 M. J. Rathbone
1965 M. L. Haider
1969 J. Kenneth Jamieson
1975 Clifton C. Garvin, Jr.

Fidelity Bank

Philadelphia, PA

Presidents

1926 Henry G. Brengle
1938 Marshall M. Morgan
1948 Stanley W. Cousley
1950 Howard C. Peterson
1961 Carl K. Dellmuth
1971 Samuel H. Ballam, Jr.
1978 Raymond J. Dempsey
1984 Bernard J. Morgan

Board Chairmen

1966 Howard C. Petersen
1978 Raymond J. Dempsey
1984 Harold W. Pote

Firestone Tire & Rubber Co.

Akron, OH

Presidents

1903	Harvey S. Firestone
1935	John W. Thomas
1943	Harvey S. Firestone, Jr.
1949	Lee R. Jackson
1957	Raymond C. Firestone
1965	Earl B. Hathaway
1971	Robert D. Thomas
1972	Richard A. Riley
1976	Mario A. DiFederico
1979	John J. Nevin
1982	Leon R. Brodeur
1984	John J. Nevin

Board Chairmen

1932	Harvey S. Firestone
1939	Vacant
1943	John W. Thomas
1949	Harvey S. Firestone, Jr.
1966	Raymond C. Firestone
1976	Richard A. Riley
1981	John J. Nevin

First National Bank of Chicago

Chicago, IL

Presidents

1863	Edmun Aiken
1867	Samuel M. Nickerson
1891	Lyman J. Gage
1897	Samuel M. Nickerson
1900	James B. Forgan
1916	Frank O. Wetmore
1925	Melvin A. Traylor
1934	Edward E. Brown
1945	Bentley G. McCloud
1950	Homer J. Livingston
1960	Gaylord A. Freeman, Jr.
1962	Herbert V. Prochnow
1967	Edward F. Blettner
1969	John E. Drick
1975	Richard L. Thomas

Board Chairmen

1916	James B. Forgan
1925	Frank O. Wetmore
1945	Edward E. Brown
1960	Homer J. Livingston
1969	Gaylord A. Freeman, Jr.
1975	A. Robert Abboud
1980	Barry F. Sullivan

Chief Executive Officers

1900	James B. Forgan
1916	Frank O. Wetmore
1930	Melvin A. Traylor
1940	Edward E. Brown
1955	Homer J. Livingston
1969	Gaylord A. Freeman, Jr.
1980	Barry F. Sullivan

First Pennsylvania Banking & Trust Co.

Philadelphia, PA

Presidents

1809	Joseph Ball
1812	James Paul
1813	Samuel Hodgdon
1814	Samuel Yorke
1816	Condy Raguet
1819	Jacob Sperry
1822	Robert U. Patterson
1826	William Boyd
1827	Thomas Astley
1837	Hyman Gratz
1857	Charles Dutilh
1873	Lindley Smyth
1893	Henry N. Paul
1899	C. S. W. Packard
1934	C. S. Newhall
1938	William F. Kurtz
1952	William L. Day
1955	William F. Kelly
1965	William B. Walker
1968	John R. Bunting
1972	James F. Bodine
1977	George A. Butler
1984	Frank E. Reed

Board Chairmen

1952	William F. Kurtz
1955	William L. Day
1972	John R. Bunting
1979	George A. Butler

FMC Corp.

Chicago, IL

Presidents

1929	John D. Crummey
1940	Paul L. Davies
1956	Ernest Hart
1960	James M. Hait
1966	Jack M. Pope
1972	Robert H. Malott
1977	Raymond C. Tower

Board Chairmen

1929	William C. Anderson
1940	John D. Crummey
1956	Paul L. Davies
1966	James M. Hait
1971	Benjamin C. Carter
1973	Robert H. Malott

Ford Motor Co.

Dearborn, MI

Presidents

1903	John S. Gray
1906	Henry Ford
1919	Edsel Ford
1943	Henry Ford
1945	Henry Ford, II
1960	Robert S. McNamara
1961	John Dykstra
1963	Arjay Miller
1968	Simon E. Knudsen
1970	Lee A. Iacocca
1978	Philip Caldwell

1980	Donald E. Petersen
1985	Harold A. Poling

Board Chairmen

1960	Henry Ford, II
1980	Philip Caldwell
1985	Donald E. Petersen

GenCorp, Inc.

Akron, OH

(General Tire & Rubber Co. until 1984.)

Presidents

1915	William O'Neil
1960	Michael G. O'Neil
1982	Warren J. Hayford
1984	Michael G. O'Neil
1986	A. William Reynolds

Board Chairmen

1940	William O'Neil
1953	Vacant
1961	Thomas F. O'Neil
1981	Michael G. O'Neil

General Dynamics Corp.

St. Louis, MO

Presidents

1952	John Jay Hopkins
1957	Frank Pace, Jr.
1959	Earl D. Johnson
1962	Roger Lewis
1971	Hilliard W. Paige
1973	David S. Lewis, Jr.
1980	Oliver C. Boileau

Board Chairmen

1952	John Jay Hopkins
1959	Frank Pace, Jr.
1962	Roger Lewis
1970	David S. Lewis, Jr.
1985	Stanley C. Pace

General Electric Co.

Fairfield, CT

Presidents

1892	Charles A. Coffin
1922	Gerard Swope
1941	Charles E. Wilson
1943	Gerard Swope
1945	Charles E. Wilson
1952	Ralph J. Cordiner
1959	Robert Paxton
1962	Gerald L. Phillippe
1964	F. J. Borch

Board Chairmen

1913	Charles A. Coffin
1922	Owen D. Young
1941	Philip D. Reed
1943	Owen D. Young
1946	Philip D. Reed
1959	Ralph J. Cordiner
1964	Gerald L. Phillippe

1970	F. J. Borch
1973	Reginald H. Jones
1981	John F. Welch, Jr.

General Foods Corp.

White Plains, NY

(Postum Cereal Inc. until 1930.)

Presidents

1924	Colby M. Chester
1935	Clarence Francis
1943	Austin S. Igleheart
1954	Charles G. Mortimer
1959	Wayne C. Marks
1962	Chauncey W. Cook
1966	Arthur E. Larkin, Jr.
1972	James L. Ferguson
1977	Ross Barzelay
1981	Philip L. Smith

Board Chairmen

1923	Edward F. Hutton
1935	Colby M. Chester
1943	Clarence Francis
1954	Austin S. Igleheart
1959	Charles G. Mortimer
1966	Chauncey W. Cook
1974	James L. Ferguson

General Mills, Inc.

Minneapolis, MN

Presidents

1928	James F. Bell
1934	Donald D. Davis
1943	Harry A. Bullis
1948	Leslie N. Perrin
1952	Charles H. Bell
1961	Edwin W. Rawlings
1967	James P. McFarland
1969	James A. Summer
1973	E. Robert Kinney
1977	H. Brewster Atwater, Jr.
1985	Mark H. Willes

Board Chairmen

1934	James F. Bell
1948	Harry A. Bullis
1959	Gerald S. Kennedy
1961	Charles H. Bell
1967	Edwin W. Rawlings
1969	James P. McFarland
1977	E. Robert Kinney
1980	H. Brewster Atwater, Jr.

General Motors Corp.

Detroit, MI

Presidents

1916	Benoni Lockwood
1917	W. C. Durant
1920	Pierre S. du Pont
1923	Alfred P. Sloan, Jr.
1937	William S. Knudsen
1940	Charles E. Wilson
1953	Harlow H. Curtice
1958	John F. Gordon
1965	James M. Roche
1967	Edward N. Cole

1974	Elliott M. Estes
1981	F. James McDonald

Board Chairmen

1917	Pierre S. du Pont
1929	Lammot du Pont
1937	Alfred P. Sloan, Jr.
1956	Albert Bradley
1958	Frederic G. Donner
1967	James M. Roche
1972	Richard C. Gerstenberg
1974	Thomas A. Murphy
1981	Roger B. Smith

Georgia-Pacific Corp.

Atlanta, GA

(Georgia-Pacific Plywood & Lumber Co. until 1957.)

Presidents

1949	Owen R. Cheatham
1957	Robert B. Pamplin
1971	William H. Hunt
1972	Robert B. Pamplin
1975	Robert E. Flowerree
1976	T. Marshall Hahn, Jr.
1986	Robert A. Schumacher

Board Chairmen

1954	Owen R. Cheatham
1967	Robert B. Pamplin
1976	Robert E. Flowerree
1986	T. Marshall Hahn, Jr.

Getty Oil Co.

Los Angeles, CA

(Pacific Western Oil Corp. until 1956; acquired Tidewater Oil Co. in 1967.)

Presidents

1929	William C. McDuffie
1932	H. P. Grimm
1937	William G. Skelly
1947	D. T. Staples
1948	J. Paul Getty
1976	Harold E. Berg
1979	S. R. Petersen
1980	Robert N. Miller

Board Chairmen

1979	Harold E. Berg
1980	S. R. Petersen

Girard Co.

Bala-Cynwyd, PA

(Girard Trust Bank until 1983.)

Presidents

1939	James E. Gowen
1948	Geoffrey S. Smith
1959	George H. Brown, Jr.
1966	Stephen S. Gardner
1971	William B. Eagleson, Jr.
1981	Thomas A. Cooper

Board Chairmen

1948	James E. Gowen
1951	David E. Williams
1954	James E. Gowen
1959	Geoffrey S. Smith
1966	George H. Brown, Jr.
1971	Stephen S. Gardner
1974	William B. Eagleson, Jr.

Goodyear Tire & Rubber Co.

Akron, OH

Presidents

1898	D. E. Holl
1899	R. C. Penfield
1903	L. C. Miles
1906	Frank A. Seiberling
1921	E. G. Wilmer
1923	G. M. Stadelman
1926	Paul W. Litchfield
1940	Edwin J. Thomas
1958	Russell DeYoung
1971	Victor Holt, Jr.
1972	Charles J. Pilliod, Jr.
1974	John H. Gerstenmaier
1978	Robert E. Mercer
1982	Tom H. Barrett

Board Chairmen

1930	Paul W. Litchfield
1958	E. J. Thomas
1964	Russell DeYoung
1974	Charles J. Pilliod, Jr.
1983	Robert E. Mercer

W. R. Grace & Co.

New York, NY

Presidents

1929	D. Stewart Iglehart
1945	J. Peter Grace, Jr.
1971	Felix E. Larkin
1975	J. Peter Grace, Jr.
1981	Carl N. Graf

Board Chairmen

1932	Joseph P. Grace
1946	William G. Holloway
1956	C. E. Wilson
1957	Vacant
1968	A. S. Rupley
1971	J. Peter Grace, Jr.
1974	Felix E. Larkin
1981	J. Peter Grace, Jr.

Great Northern Railway Co.

St. Paul, MN

(Became part of Burlington Northern, Inc. in 1970.)

Presidents

1888	James J. Hill
1907	Louis W. Hill
1912	Carl R. Gray
1914	Louis W. Hill
1919	Ralph Budd
1932	William P. Kenney
1939	Frank J. Gavin
1951	John M. Budd

Grumman Corp.

Bethpage, NY

(Grumman Aircraft Engineering Corp. until 1970.)

Presidents

1939	LeRoy R. Grumman
1947	Leon A. Swirbul
1960	E. Clinton Towl
1967	L. J. Evans
1973	John C. Bierwirth
1976	Joseph G. Gavin, Jr.
1985	George M. Skurla
1986	John O'Brien

Board Chairmen

1947	LeRoy R. Grumman
1966	E. Clinton Towl
1976	John C. Bierwirth

Gulf Oil Corp.

Pittsburgh, PA

Presidents

1901	James M. Guffey
1907	Andrew W. Mellon
1908	W. L. Mellon
1931	J. Frank Drake
1948	Sidney A. Swensrud
1953	William K. Whiteford
1960	Ernest D. Brockett, Jr.
1965	Bob R. Dorsey
1972	James E. Lee
1981	Edward B. Walker, III

Board Chairmen

1960	William K. Whiteford
1965	Ernest D. Brockett, Jr.
1972	Bob R. Dorsey
1976	Jerry McAfee
1981	James E. Lee

Hanson Industries North America

Iselin, NJ

(Hanson Industries, Inc. until 1986.)

Presidents

1978	David H. Clarke

Board Chairmen

1983	Gordon White

H. J. Heinz Co.

Pittsburgh, PA

Presidents

1905	Henry J. Heinz

1915	Howard Heinz
1941	Henry J. Heinz, II
1960	Frank Armour, Jr.
1961	Frank T. Sherk
1964	Frank Armour, Jr.
1965	Edward V. Anderson
1966	R. Burt Gookin
1969	John A. Connell
1970	R. Burt Gookin
1973	Anthony J. F. O'Reilly

Board Chairmen

1907	Howard Heinz
1941	Vacant
1959	Henry J. Heinz, II

Hewlett-Packard Co.

Palo Alto, CA

Presidents

1947	David Packard
1964	William R. Hewlett
1977	John A. Young

Board Chairmen

1964	David Packard

HNG/Internorth, Inc.

Omaha, NB

(Northern Natural Gas Co. until 1981; Internorth, Inc. until 1986.)

Presidents

1930	William Chamberlain
1933	Louis E. Fischer
1936	F. H. Brooks
1939	Burt R. Bay
1950	John F. Merriam
1960	Willis A. Strauss
1976	Sam F. Segnar
1986	K. L. Lay

Board Chairmen

1930	Clement Studebaker, Jr.
1933	William Chamberlain
1936	Charles S. McCain
1938	J. D. Mortimer
1960	John F. Merriam
1966	Willis A. Strauss
1984	Sam F. Segnar

Honeywell, Inc.

Minneapolis, MN

Presidents

1927	Mark C. Honeywell
1933	Harold W. Sweatt
1952	Paul B. Wishart
1960	James H. Binger
1965	Stephen F. Keating
1974	Edson W. Spencer

Board Chairmen

1965	James H. Binger
1975	Stephen F. Keating
1978	Edson W. Spencer

Illinois Central Gulf Railroad (IC Industries)

Chicago, IL

(Formed by merger of Illinois Central with Gulf, Mobile & Ohio in 1971.)

Presidents

1851 Robert Schuyler
1853 William P. Burrall
1854 John N. A. Griswold
1855 William H. Osborn
1865 John M. Douglas
1871 John Newell
1874 Wilson G. Hunt
1875 John M. Douglas
1877 William K. Ackerman
1883 James C. Clarke
1887 Stuyvesant Fish
1906 James T. Hanrahan
1911 Charles H. Markham
1918 Charles A. Peabody
1919 Charles H. Markham
1926 Lawrence A. Downs
1938 John L. Beven
1945 Wayne A. Johnston
1966 William B. Johnson
1969 Alan S. Boyd
1977 William J. Taylor
1983 James E. Martin

Board Chairmen

1926 Charles H. Markham
1938 Lawrence A. Downs
1966 Wayne A. Johnston
1969 William B. Johnson
1972 Glen Brock
1977 Stanley E. G. Hillman
1983 Harry J. Bruce

Inland Steel Co.

Chicago, IL

Presidents

1893 Joseph E. Porter
1898 George H. Jones
1906 Charles Hart
1908 Alexis W. Thompson
1919 Philip D. Block
1941 Wilfred Sykes
1949 Clarence B. Randall
1953 Joseph L. Block
1959 John F. Smith, Jr.
1966 Frederick G. Jaicks
1971 Michael Tenenbaum
1978 Frank W. Luerssen
1984 Robert J. Darnall

Board Chairmen

1906 Alexis W. Thompson
1919 Leigh E. Block
1940 Edward L. Ryerson
1953 Clarence B. Randall
1959 Joseph L. Block
1967 Philip D. Block
1971 Frederick G. Jaicks
1983 Frank W. Luerssen

International Business Machines Corp. (IBM)

Armonk, NY

(Computer-Tabulating-Recording Co. until 1923.)

Presidents

1915 Thomas J. Watson
1949 John G. Phillips
1951 Thomas J. Watson, Jr.
1961 Albert L. Williams
1966 T. Vincent Learson
1971 Frank T. Cary
1974 John R. Opel
1983 John F. Akers

Board Chairmen

1915 George W. Fairchild
1949 Thomas J. Watson
1961 Thomas J. Watson, Jr.
1971 T. Vincent Learson
1972 Frank T. Cary
1983 John R. Opel

International Harvester Co.

Chicago, IL

Presidents

1902 Cyrus H. McCormick
1918 Harold F. McCormick
1922 Alexander Legge
1929 Herbert F. Perkins
1931 Alexander Legge
1933 Addis E. McKinstry
1935 Sydney G. McAllister
1941 Fowler McCormick
1946 John L. McCaffrey
1956 Peter V. Moulder
1957 Frank W. Jenks
1962 Harry O. Bercher
1968 Brooks McCormick
1978 Archie R. McCardle
1979 Warren J. Hayford
1982 Donald D. Lennox
1984 Neil A. Springer

Board Chairmen

1904 Charles Deering
1918 Cyrus H. McCormick
1935 Harold F. McCormick
1941 Judson F. Stone
1946 Fowler McCormick
1956 John L. McCaffrey
1968 Harry O. Bercher
1977 Brooks McCormick
1979 Archie R. McCardle
1982 Louis W. Menks
1983 Donald D. Lennox

International Paper Co.

New York, NY

Presidents

1921 Archibald R. Graustein
1937 R. J. Cullen
1944 John H. Hinman
1955 Richard C. Doanes
1962 Lamar M. Fearing

1967 Edward B. Hinman
1971 Paul A. Gorman
1974 Judson D. Hannigan
1978 Edwin A. Gee
1986 Paul H. O'Neill

Board Chairmen

1944 Richard J. Cullen
1950 Vacant
1955 John H. Hinman
1962 Richard C. Doane
1968 Vacant
1970 Frederick R. Kappel
1971 Paul A. Gorman
1974 J. Stanford Smith
1980 Edwin A. Gee
1986 John A. Georges

ITT Corp.

New York, NY

(International Telephone & Telegraph Corp. until 1984.)

Presidents

1920 Sosthenes Behn
1949 William H. Harrison
1957 Edmond H. Leavey
1959 Harold S. Geneen
1973 Francis J. Dunleavy
1977 Lyman C. Hamilton, Jr.
1980 Rand V. Araskog
1986 Edmund M. Carpenter

Board Chairmen

1947 Sosthenes Behn
1960 Edmond H. Leavey
1961 Vacant
1964 Harold S. Geneen
1980 Rand V. Araskog

John Hancock Mutual Life Insurance Co.

Boston, MA

Presidents

1862 George P. Sanger
1873 Lafayette A. Lyon
1874 George Thornton
1879 Samuel Atherton
1879 Stephen H. Rhodes
1909 Roland O. Lamb
1921 Walton L. Crocker
1936 Guy W. Cox
1945 Paul F. Clark
1957 Byron K. Elliott
1965 Clyde F. Gay
1966 Robert E. Slater
1970 Frank B. Maher
1976 J. Edwin Matz
1979 John G. McElwee
1982 E. James Morton

Board Chairmen

1945 Guy W. Cox
1948 Paul F. Clark
1963 Byron K. Elliott
1969 Robert E. Slater
1970 Gerhard D. Bleicken
1981 J. Edwin Matz
1982 John G. McElwee

Johnson & Johnson

New Brunswick, NJ

Presidents

1888 Robert W. Johnson
1910 James W. Johnson
1932 Robert W. Johnson
1938 A. R. Clapham
1942 F. A. Cosgrove (Acting)
1943 George F. Smith
1961 Robert W. Johnson, Jr.
1965 Gustav O. Leinhard
1970 Richard B. Sellars
1973 James E. Burke
1976 David R. Clare

Board Chairmen

1938 Robert W. Johnson
1963 Philip B. Hofmann
1974 Richard B. Sellars
1976 James E. Burke

Kellogg Co.

Battle Creek, MI

Presidents

1911 W. K. Kellogg
1942 Watson H. Vanderploeg
1957 Lyle C. Roll
1968 Joseph E. Lonning
1973 William E. LaMothe
1980 Walter T. Redmond
1986 Gerald D. Robinson

Board Chairmen

1937 W. K. Kellogg
1947 Vacant
1962 Lyle C. Roll
1973 Joseph E. Lonning
1980 William E. LaMothe

Kennecott Corp.

Salt Lake City, UT

(Kennecott Copper Corp. until 1982.)

Presidents

1915 Stephen Birch
1933 E. T. Stannard
1950 Charles R. Cox
1961 Frank R. Milliken
1979 William H. Wendel
1980 Glenn P. Bakken
1984 Frank Joklik

Board Chairmen

1978 Frank R. Milliken
1978 Thomas D. Barrow
1985 A. W. Whitehouse, Jr.

Kimberly-Clark Corp.

Dallas, TX

Presidents

1872 John A. Kimberly
1928 Frank J. Sensenbrenner

1942	Cola G. Parker
1953	John R. Kimberly
1959	William R. Kellett
1964	John R. Kimberly
1967	Guy M. Minard
1970	Darwin E. Smith
1972	Harry J. Sheerin
1978	Robert C. Ernest

Board Chairmen

1942	Frank J. Sensenbrenner
1953	Cola G. Parker
1955	John R. Kimberly
1970	Guy M. Minard
1972	Darwin E. Smith

Kraft Inc.

Glenview, IL

(Formerly National Dairy Products Corp.; Kraftco Corp. until 1977.)

Presidents

1923	Thomas H. McInnerney
1941	Leroy A. Van Bomel
1952	E. E. Stewart
1959	J. Huber Wetenhall
1965	Gordon Edwards
1968	William O. Beers
1974	Arthur W. Woelfle
1982	Michael A. Miles

Board Chairmen

1924	Edward E. Rieck
1925	Loton Horton
1941	Thomas H. McInnerney
1952	Leroy A. Van Bomel
1957	E. E. Stewart
1965	J. Huber Wetenhall
1968	Gordon Edwards
1972	William O. Beers
1979	John M. Richman

Chief Executive Officers

1941	Thomas H. McInnerney
1942	Leroy A. Van Bomel
1952	E. E. Stewart
1961	J. Huber Wetenhall
1966	Gordon Edwards
1972	William O. Beers
1979	John M. Richman

Eli Lilly & Co.

Indianapolis, IN

Presidents

1881	Eli Lilly
1898	Josiah K. Lilly, Sr.
1932	Eli Lilly
1949	Josiah K. Lilly, Jr.
1953	Eugene N. Beesley
1970	Burton E. Beck
1973	Richard D. Wood
1973	Thomas H. Lake
1977	Richard D. Wood

Board Chairmen

1948	Eli Lilly
1962	Josiah K. Lilly, Jr.
1966	Eli Lilly

1969	Eugene N. Beesley
1973	Richard D. Wood

Litton Industries, Inc.

Beverly Hills, CA

Presidents

1953	Charles B. Thornton
1962	Roy L. Ash
1972	Fred W. O'Green
1983	Orion L. Hoch

Board Chairmen

1957	Charles B. Thornton
1981	Fred W. O'Green

Lockheed Corp.

Calabasas, CA

(Lockheed Aircraft Corp. until 1978.)

Presidents

1932	Lloyd Stearman
1934	Robert E. Gross
1956	Courtlandt S. Gross
1961	Daniel J. Haughton
1967	A. Carl Kotchian
1976	Lawrence O. Kitchen
1986	Robert A. Fuhrman

Board Chairmen

1933	Robert E. Gross
1961	Courtlandt S. Gross
1967	Daniel J. Haughton
1976	Robert W. Haack
1977	Roy A. Anderson
1986	Lawrence O. Kitchen

Louisville & Nashville Railroad Co.

Louisville, KY

(Associated with Seaboard Coast Line Railroad in 1980; became part of CSX Corp. in 1982.)

Presidents

1851	Levin L. Shreve
1854	John L. Helm
1860	James Guthrie
1868	Russell Houston
1868	Horatio D. Newcomb
1874	Thomas Martin
1875	Elisha D. Standiford
1880	Horatio D. Newcomb
1880	Edward Green
1881	Christopher C. Baldwin
1884	Jacob S. Rogers
1884	Milton H. Smith
1886	Eckstein Norton
1891	Milton H. Smith
1921	Wible L. Mapother
1926	Whitefoord R. Cole
1934	James B. Hill
1950	John E. Tilford
1959	William H. Kendall
1972	Prime F. Osborn
1978	Richard D. Spence
1982	Richard D. Sanborn

Board Chairmen

1891	August Belmont
1903	Henry Walters
1931	Lyman Delano
1944	Frederick B. Adams
1948	A. L. M. Wiggins
1974	W. Thomas Rice
1979	Prime F. Osborn
1982	Hays T. Watkins

LTV Corp.

Dallas, TX

Presidents

1970	Clyde Skeen
1971	W. Paul Thayer
1972	Roscoe G. Haynie
1975	Raymond A. Hay

Board Chairmen

1970	James J. Ling
1972	W. Paul Thayer
1983	Raymond A. Hay

McDonnell Douglas Corp.

St. Louis, MO

(Formed by merger of McDonnell Aircraft with Douglas Aircraft in 1967.)

Presidents

1939	James S. McDonnell
1962	David S. Lewis
1970	James S. McDonnell, Jr.
1971	Sanford N. McDonnell
1980	John F. McDonnell

Board Chairmen

1962	James S. McDonnell, Jr.
1980	Sanford N. McDonnell

Manufacturers National Bank

Detroit, MI

(Manufacturers National Bank of Detroit until 1983.)

Presidents

1933	John Ballantyne
1938	Henry H. Sanger
1943	Charles A. Kanter
1949	William A. Mayberry
1959	Arthur J. Fushman
1963	Roland A. Mewhort
1969	Dean E. Richardson
1973	Louis G. Allen
1982	Gerald V. MacDonald

Board Chairmen

1943	Henry H. Sanger
1949	Charles A. Kanter
1959	William A. Mayberry
1969	Roland A. Mewhort
1973	Dean E. Richardson

Marathon Oil Co.

Findlay, OH

Presidents

1887	H. M. Ernst
1889	William P. Fleming
1892	John D. Archbold
1911	James C. Donnell
1927	Otto D. Donnell
1948	James C. Donnell, II
1972	Harold D. Hoopman
1985	William E. Swales

Board Chairmen

1972	James C. Donnell, II

Marine Midland Bank, N. A.

Buffalo, NY

Presidents

1929	George F. Rand
1942	Charles H. Diefendorf
1955	Baldwin Maull
1966	J. Fred Schoellkopf, IV
1970	Charles A. Winding
1972	Crocker Nevin
1973	Edward W. Duffy
1973	John S. Lawson
1975	Edward W. Duffy
1976	John R. Petty

Board Chairmen

1955	Charles H. Diefendorf
1966	Baldwin Maull
1968	J. Fred Schoellkopf, IV
1970	Charles A. Winding
1972	John S. Lawson
1974	Edward W. Duffy
1983	John R. Petty

Martin Marietta Corp.

Bethesda, MD

Presidents

1962	George M. Bunker
1972	J. Donald Rauth
1977	Thomas G. Pownall
1979	Frank X. Bradley
1980	Thomas G. Pownall
1983	Laurence J. Adams
1986	Norman R. Augustine

Board Chairmen

1962	Grover M. Hermann
1966	Vacant
1973	George M. Bunker
1977	J. Donald Rauth
1983	Thomas G. Pownall

Massachusetts Mutual Life Insurance Co.

Springfield, MA

Presidents

1851	Caleb Rice
1873	Ephraim W. Bond
1886	Martin V. B. Edgerly
1895	John A. Hall
1908	William W. McClench
1928	William H. Sargeant
1936	Bertrand J. Perry
1945	Alexander T. Maclean
1950	Leland J. Kalmbach
1962	Charles H. Schaaff
1968	James R. Martin
1974	William J. Clark

Board Charmen

1968	Charles H. Schaaff
1976	James R. Martin

Mead Corp.

Dayton, OH

Presidents

1930	George H. Mead
1942	Sydney Ferguson
1948	C. R. Van de Carr, Jr.
1952	H. E. Whitaker
1957	Donald F. Morris
1963	George H. Pringle
1968	James W. McSwiney
1971	Paul V. Allemang
1973	Warren L. Batts
1980	C. Green Garner
1981	Burnell R. Roberts
1983	Steven C. Mason

Board Chairmen

1937	George H. Mead
1948	Sydney Ferguson
1957	H. E. Whitaker (to 1968)
1971	James W. McSwiney
1982	Burnell R. Roberts

Merck & Co., Inc.

Rahway, NJ

Presidents

1925	George W. Merck
1951	James J. Kerrigan
1956	John T. Connor
1965	Henry W. Gadsden
1971	Antonie T. Knoppers
1974	Henry W. Gadsden
1975	John J. Horan
1978	John J. Huck
1985	P. Roy Vagelos

Board Chairmen

1927	Frederic Rosengarten
1949	George W. Merck
1959	Vannevar Bush
1964	Charles S. Garland
1971	Henry W. Gadsden
1976	John J. Horan
1985	John L. Huck

Metropolitan Life Insurance Co.

New York, NY

Presidents

1868	James R. Dow
1871	Joseph F. Knapp
1891	John R. Hegeman
1919	Haley Fiske
1929	Frederick H. Ecker
1936	Leroy A. Lincoln
1951	Charles G. Taylor, Jr.
1953	Frederic W. Ecker
1959	Cecil J. North
1963	Gilbert W. Fitzhugh
1966	Charles A. Siegfried
1969	Richard R. Shinn
1980	John J. Creedon

Board Chairmen

1936	Frederick H. Ecker
1951	Leroy A. Lincoln
1959	Frederic W. Ecker
1966	Gilbert W. Fitzhugh
1973	George P. Jenkins
1980	Richard R. Shinn
1983	Robert G. Schwartz

Minnesota Mining & Manufacturing Co. (3M)

St. Paul, MN

Presidents

1902	Henry S. Bryan
1905	Edgar B. Ober
1906	Lucius P. Ordway
1909	Edgar B. Ober
1929	William L. McKnight
1949	Richard P. Carlton
1953	Herbert P. Buetow
1963	Bert S. Cross
1966	Harry Heltzer
1970	Raymond H. Herzog
1980	John M. Pitblado
1981	James A. Thwaits

Board Chairmen

1949	William L. McKnight
1966	Bert S. Cross
1970	Harry Heltzer
1975	Raymond H. Herzog
1980	Lewis W. Lehr
1986	Allen F. Jacobson

Missouri Pacific Railroad Co.

St. Louis, MO

Presidents

1876	Cornelius K. Garrison
1979	Jay Gould
1892	George J. Gould
1911	B. F. Bush
1917	John G. Drew
1917	B. F. Bush
1918	Harry Brouner
1920	B. F. Bush
1923	L. W. Baldwin
1946	Paul J. Neff

1956	R. L. Dearmont
1961	Downing B. Jenks
1972	John H. Lloyd
1978	James W. Gessner
1982	Robert G. Flannery

Board Chairmen

1962	John T. Suggs
1968	W. C. Marbury
1971	Downing B. Jenks
1982	J. C. Kenefick
1986	A. L. Lewis, Jr.

Monsanto Co.

St. Louis, MO

Presidents

1901	John F. Queeny
1919	Gaston DuBois
1923	John F. Queeny
1928	Edgar Monsanto Queeny
1943	Charles Belknap
1945	William McN. Rand
1951	Charles A. Thomas
1960	Charles H. Sommer
1968	Edward J. Bock
1972	Charles H. Sommer
1972	John W. Hanley
1980	Richard J. Mahoney

Board Chairmen

1939	Edgar Monsanto Queeny
1960	Charles A. Thomas
1965	Edward A. O'Neal, Jr.
1968	Charles H. Sommer
1975	John W. Hanley
1984	Louis Fernandez
1986	Richard J. Mahoney

Philip Morris Companies, Inc.

New York, NY

(Philip Morris & Company Ltd., Inc. until 1955; Philip Morris, Inc. until 1986.)

Presidents

1935	Leonard B. McKittrick
1937	Otway H. Chalkley
1947	Alfred E. Lyon
1950	O. Parker McComas
1957	Joseph F. Cullman, III
1967	George Weissman
1973	Ross R. Millhiser
1978	Clifford H. Goldsmith
1985	John A. Murphy

Board Chairmen

1946	Alfred E. Lyon
1947	Otway H. Chalkley
1950	Alfred E. Lyon
1967	Joseph F. Cullman, III
1978	George Weissman
1985	Hamish Maxwell

Motorola, Inc.

Roselle, IL

Presidents

1948	Paul V. Galvin
1956	Robert W. Galvin
1965	Elmer H. Wavering
1970	William J. Weisz
1980	John F. Mitchell

Board Chairmen

1955	Paul V. Galvin
1964	Robert W. Galvin

Mutual Life Insurance Company of New York (MONY)

New York, NY

Presidents

1842	Morris Robinson
1849	Joseph B. Collins
1853	Frederick S. Winston
1885	Richard A. McCurdy
1905	Charles Peabody
1927	David F. Houston
1940	Lewis W. Douglas
1947	Alex E. Patterson
1948	Louis W. Dawson
1959	Roger Hull
1967	J. McCall Hughes
1972	James S. Bingay
1977	James E. Devitt
1978	Robert U. Shallenberger
1981	Henry S. Romaine

Board Chairmen

1950	Lewis W. Douglas
1959	Louis W. Dawson
1967	Roger Hull
1972	Richard I. Fricke
1979	James E. Devitt
1983	James A. Attwood

National Life Insurance Co.

Montpelier, VT

Presidents

1849	William C. Kittredge
1851	Julius Y. Dewey
1877	Charles Dewey
1901	James C. Houghton
1902	Joseph A. DeBoer
1916	Fred A. Howland
1937	Elbert S. Brigham
1948	Ernest M. Hopkins
1950	Deane C. Davis
1966	John T. Fey
1975	Norman L. Campbell
1977	Richard I. Fricke
1985	Frederic H. Bertrand

Board Chairmen

1937	Fred A. Howland
1950	Ernest M. Hopkins
1965	Deane C. Davis
1983	Robert S. Gillette

1985   Richard I. Fricke

Navistar International Corp.

Chicago, IL

Presidents

1984   Neil A. Springer

Board Chairmen

1983   Donald D. Lennox

NCR Corp.

Dayton, OH

(Formerly National Cash Register Co.)

Presidents

1884   John H. Patterson
1921   Frederick B. Patterson
1935   Edward A. Deeds
1940   Stanley C. Allyn
1957   Robert S. Oelman
1963   R. Stanley Laing
1972   William S. Anderson
1975   Charles E. Exley, Jr.

Board Chairmen

1931   Edward A. Deeds
1957   Stanley C. Allyn
1962   Robert S. Oelman
1974   William S. Anderson
1984   Charles E. Exley, Jr.

New England Mutual Life Insurance Co.

Boston, MA

Presidents

1843   Willard Phillips
1865   Benjamin F. Stevens
1908   Alfred D. Foster
1924   Daniel F. Appel
1929   George W. Smith
1951   O. Kelley Anderson
1966   Abram T. Collier
1974   Edward E. Phillips
1981   John A. Fibiger

Board Chairmen

1924   Alfred D. Foster
1932   George W. Smith
1964   O. Kelley Anderson
1975   Abram T. Collier
1978   Edward E. Phillips

Niagara Mohawk Power Corp.

Syracuse, NY

Presidents

1937   John L. Haley
1950   Earle J. Machold

1968   James A. O'Neill
1973   John G. Haehl, Jr.
1980   William J. Donlon

Board Chairmen

1937   Alfred H. Schoellkopf
1942   H. Edmund Machold
1968   Earle J. Machold
1980   John G. Haehl, Jr.

North American Philips Corp.

New York, NY

(North American Philips Co., Inc. until 1969, when it merged with Consolidated Electric Industries Corp.)

Presidents

1945   Pieter F. S. Otten
1947   Othon M. E. Loupart
1949   Pieter van den Berg
1969   Pieter C. Vink
1979   Cees Bruynes

Board Chairmen

1947   Pieter F. S. Otten
1949   Louis van Zelm
1953   E. Colahan
1966   Francis T. Christy
1967   Pieter van den Berg
1976   Pieter C. Vink
1986   Cees Bruynes

Northern Pacific Railway Co.

St. Paul, MN

(Became part of Burlington Northern Inc. in 1970.)

Presidents

1896   Edwin W. Winter
1897   Charles S. Mellen
1903   Howard Elliott
1913   Jule M. Hannaford
1918   Howard Elliott
1920   Jule M. Hannaford
1920   Charles Donnelly
1939   C. E. Denney
1951   Robert S. MacFarlane
1966   Louis W. Menk

Board Chairmen

1966   Robert S. MacFarlane

Northern Trust Corp.

Chicago, IL

(Northern Trust Co. until 1974; Nortrust Corp. until 1979.)

Presidents

1889   Byron L. Smith
1914   Solomon A. Smith
1963   Douglas R. Fuller
1972   E. Norman Staub
1975   Philip W. K. Sweet, Jr.
1981   Charles H. Barrow

Board Chairmen

1914   Soloman A. Smith
1963   Edward B. Smith
1979   E. Norman Staub
1981   Philip W. K. Sweet, Jr.
1984   Weston R. Christopherson

Northrop Corp.

Los Angeles, CA

(Northrop Aircraft, Inc. until 1960.)

Presidents

1940   John K. Northrop
1953   Oliver P. Echols
1955   Whitley C. Collins
1959   Thomas V. Jones
1976   Thomas O. Paine
1982   Frank W. Lynch

Board Chairmen

1940   LaMotte T. Cohu
1948   Richard W. Millar
1950   Oliver P. Echols
1955   William C. McDuffie
1963   Thomas V. Jones

Northwestern Mutual Life Insurance Co.

Milwaukee, WI

Presidents

1858   Joseph A. Sleeper
1858   Henry W. Collins
1859   Samuel S. Daggett
1869   Lester Sexton
1869   John H. Van Dyke
1874   Henry L. Palmer
1908   George C. Markham
1919   William D. Van Dyke
1932   Michael J. Cleary
1947   Edmund Fitzgerald
1958   Donald C. Slichter
1965   Robert E. Dineen
1968   Francis E. Ferguson
1980   Donald J. Schuenke

Board Chairmen

1958   Edmund Fitzgerald
1965   Donald C. Slichter
1968   Robert E. Dineen
1980   Francis E. Ferguson

Occidental Petroleum Corp.

Los Angeles, CA

Presidents

1956   Dave E. Harris
1957   Armand Hammer
1968   Thomas F. Willers
1970   William Bellano
1972   Armand Hammer
1973   Joseph E. Baird
1979   Zoltan Merszei
1980   A. Robert Abboud

Board Chairmen

1968   Armand Hammer

Owens-Corning Fiberglas Corp.

Toledo, OH

Presidents

1939   Harold Boeschenstein
1945   J. P. Levis
1946   Harold Boeschenstein
1965   Lauris Norstad
1968   John H. Thomas
1971   William W. Boeschenstein

Board Chairmen

1939   Amory Houghton
1945   William E. Levis
1946   Amory Houghton
1948   Vacant
1965   Harold Boeschenstein
1968   Lauris Norstad
1973   Vacant
1982   William W. Boeschenstein

Owens-Illinois, Inc.

Toledo, OH

Presidents

1925   W. H. Boshart
1930   W. E. Levis
1941   J. P. Levis
1950   C. R. Megowen
1961   R. H. Mulford
1968   Edwin D. Dodd
1976   Robert J. Lanigan
1979   William F. Spengler
1982   Robert J. Lanigan
1985   Joseph H. Lemieux

Board Chairmen

1925   William S. Walbridge
1928   William Ford
1941   W. E. Levis
1950   J. P. Levis
1968   Raymond H. Mulford
1976   Edwin D. Dodd
1984   Robert J. Lanigan

Pacific Lighting Corp.

Los Angeles, CA

Presidents

1886   James M. Livingston
1898   C. O. G. Miller
1940   Robert W. Miller
1956   Robert A. Hornby
1968   Paul A. Miller
1972   Joseph R. Rensch

Board Chairmen

1940   C. O. G. Miller (to 1952)
1956   Robert W. Miller (to 1967)
1972   Paul A. Miller

Pan American World Airways

New York, NY

Presidents

1927 Juan T. Trippe
1964 Harold E. Gray
1969 Najeeb E. Halaby
1971 William T. Seawell
1976 Forwood C. Wiser, Jr.
1978 Dan A. Colussy
1982 William H. Waltrip

Board Chairmen

1931 Cornelius V. Whitney
1964 Juan T. Trippe
1968 Harold E. Gray
1969 Najeeb E. Halaby
1972 William T. Seawell
1981 C. Edward Acker

Penn Mutual Life Insurance Co.

Philadelphia, PA

Presidents

1847 Daniel L. Miller
1862 James Traquair
1870 Samuel C. Huey
1886 Edward M. Needles
1897 Harry F. West
1906 George K. Johnson
1922 William A. Law
1936 William H. Kingsley
1939 John A. Stevenson
1949 Malcolm Adam
1961 Charles R. Tyson
1971 Frank K. Tarbox
1979 Robert O. Purcifull
1980 Frank K. Tarbox
1982 John E. Tait

Board Chairmen

1939 William H. Kingsley
1949 William A. Bodine
1961 Malcolm Adam
1971 Charles R. Tyson
1979 Frank K. Tarbox

J. C. Penney Co., Inc.

New York, NY

Presidents

1913 James C. Penney
1917 Earl C. Sams
1946 Albert W. Hughes
1958 William M. Batten
1964 Ray H. Jordan
1968 Cecil L. Wright
1972 Jack B. Jackson
1976 Walter J. Neppl

Board Chairmen

1917 James C. Penney
1946 Earl C. Sams
1950 James C. Penney
1958 Albert W. Hughes
1964 William M. Batten
1974 Donald V. Seibert

1983 William R. Howell

PepsiCo, Inc.

Purchase, NY
(Pepsi-Cola Co. until 1966.)

Presidents

1940 Walter S. Mack, Jr.
1942 Edward Risedorph
1945 Walter S. Mack, Jr.
1951 Alfred N. Steele
1956 Herbert L. Barnet
1963 Donald M. Kendall
1971 Andrall E. Pearson
1986 Michael H. Jordan

Board Chairmen

1952 James W. Carkner
1956 Alfred N. Steele
1960 James W. Carkner
       (Honorary Chairman)
1964 Herbert L. Barnet
1965 Herman W. Lay
1971 Donald M. Kendall
1986 D. Wayne Calloway

Pfizer, Inc.

New York, NY

Presidents

1945 George A. Anderson
1946 John L. Smith
1950 John E. McKeen
1966 John J. Powers, Jr.
1971 Edmund T. Pratt
1972 Gerald D. Laubach

Board Chairmen

1946 George A. Anderson
1950 John L. Smith
1952 John E. McKeen
1969 John J. Power, Jr.
1972 Edmund T. Pratt, Jr.

Philadelphia Electric Co.

Philadelphia, PA

Chief Executive Officers

1902 Joseph B. McCall
1924 W. H. Johnson
1928 Arthur W. Thompson
1929 John E. Zimmerman
1938 William H. Taylor
1940 John E. Zimmerman
1943 Horace P. Liversidge
1955 Roy G. Rincliffe
1971 Robert F. Gilkeson
1982 James L. Everett, III

Philadelphia National Bank

Philadelphia, PA

Presidents

1803 George Clymer

1813 David Lenox
1818 John Read
1842 Samuel F. Smith
1852 Thomas Robins
1879 Benjamin B. Comegys
1900 N. Parker Shortridge
1907 Levi L. Rue
1926 Joseph Wayne, Jr.
1941 Evan Randolph
1947 Frederick A. Potts
1964 G. Morris Dorrance, Jr.
1973 Frederick Heldring
1980 Richard S. Ravenscroft

Board Chairmen

1907 N. Parker Shortridge
1926 Levi L. Rue
1941 Joseph Wayne, Jr.
1947 J. William Hardt
1964 Frederick A. Potts
1969 John McDowell
1970 G. Morris Dorrance, Jr.

Phillips Petroleum Co.

Bartlesville, OK

Presidents

1917 Frank Phillips
1938 Kenneth S. Adams
1951 Paul Endacott
1962 Stanley Learned
1967 William W. Keeler
1968 John M. Houchin
1971 William F. Martin
1974 William C. Douce
1982 C. J. Silas
1985 Glenn A. Cox

Board Chairmen

1938 Frank Phillips
1951 Kenneth S. Adams
1968 William W. Keeler

Phoenix Insurance Co.

Hartford, CT

(Subsidiary of Travelers Corp. 1964 to 1975.)

Presidents

1854 Nathaniel H. Morgan
1855 Simeon L. Loomis
1863 Henry Kellogg
1891 D. W. C. Skilton
1913 Edward Milligan
1937 George C. Long, Jr.
1951 John A. North
1961 Jack D. Taylor
1975 Morrison H. Beach
1976 Edward B. Budd
1983 Alva O. Way
1985 Wheeler H. Hess, Jr.

Board Chairmen

1975 Roger C. Wilkins
1976 Morrison H. Beach
1982 Edward B. Budd
1985 Frank E. Walton

Phoenix Mutual Life Insurance Co.

Hartford, CT

Presidents

1851 Barzillai Hudson
1852 Benjamin E. Hale
1853 Edson Fessenden
1875 Aaron C. Goodman
1889 Jonathan B. Bunce
1904 John M. Holcombe
1924 Archibald A. Welch
1935 Arthur M. Collens
1948 Benjamin L. Holland
1961 Lyndes B. Stone
1971 Robert T. Jackson
1978 Dennis F. Hardcastle
1981 John Gummere

Board Chairmen

1978 Robert T. Jackson

Pillsbury Co.

Minneapolis, MN

Presidents

1909 Charles Stinson (V.P.)
1913 John S. Pillsbury (V.P.)
1935 Harry H. Whiting
1937 Clark Hempstead
1941 Philip W. Pillsbury
1953 Paul S. Gerot
1965 Ogburn F. Stafford
1966 Robert J. Keith
1967 Terrance Hanold
1973 James R. Peterson
1977 Winston R. Wallin
1984 John M. Stafford

Board Chairmen

1935 John S. Pillsbury
1953 Philip W. Pillsbury
1966 Paul S. Gerot
1968 Robert J. Keith
1973 William H. Spoor
1986 John M. Stafford

PPG Industries, Inc.

Pittsburgh, Pa
(Pittsburgh Plate Glass Co. until 1969.)

Presidents

1883 Edward Ford
1898 John Pitcairn
1905 William L. Clause
1916 C. W. Brown
1928 Harry S. Wherrett
1941 Robert L. Clause
1944 Harry B. Higgins
1955 David G. Hill
1966 Robinson F. Barker
1967 Joseph A. Neubauer
1976 J. Earl Burrell
1984 E. J. Slack

Board Chairmen

1898 John Pitcairn
1916 William L. Clause

1931	Clarence M. Brown
1955	Harry B. Higgins
1957	E. T. Asplundh
1966	David G. Hill
1967	Robinson F. Barker
1979	L. Stanton Williams
1985	Vincent A. Sarni

Procter & Gamble Co.

Cincinnati, OH

Presidents

1890	William A. Procter
1907	William C. Procter
1930	Richard R. Deupree
1948	Neil H. McElroy
1957	Howard J. Morgens
1971	Edward G. Harness
1974	John G. Smale
1986	John E. Pepper, Jr.

Board Chairmen

1930	William C. Procter
1948	Richard R. Deupree
1959	Neil H. McElroy
1971	Howard J. Morgens
1974	Edward G. Harness
1981	Owen B. Butler
1986	John G. Smale

Provident Mutual Life Insurance Company of Philadelphia

Philadelphia, PA

Presidents

1865	Samuel R. Shipley
1905	Asa S. Wing
1931	M. Albert Linton
1953	Thomas A. Bradshaw
1969	Edward L. Stanley
1976	John A. Miller
1984	Lester J. Rowell, Jr.

Board Chairmen

1977	Edward L. Stanley
1982	John A. Miller

Prudential Insurance Company of America

Newark, NJ

Presidents

1975	Allen L. Bassett
1979	Noah F. Blanchard
1881	John F. Dryden
1912	Forrest F. Dryden
1922	Edward D. Duffield
1938	Franklin D'Olier
1946	Carrol M. Shanks
1961	Louis R. Menagh
1962	Orville E. Beal
1969	Donald S. MacNaughton
1970	Kenneth C. Foster
1974	Robert A. Beck
1978	David J. Sherwood
1984	Joseph J. Melone

Board Chairmen

1970	Donald S. MacNaughton
1978	Robert A. Beck

Public Service Electric & Gas Co.

Newark, NJ

Presidents

1924	Thomas N. McCarter
1939	Edmund W. Wakelee
1945	George H. Blake
1954	Donald C. Luce
1965	Edwin H. Snyder
1968	Edward R. Eberle
1972	Robert I. Smith
1977	John F. Betz
1980	Harold W. Sonn
1986	E. James Ferland

Chief Executive Officers

1924	Thomas N. McCarter
1945	George H. Blake
1954	Lyle McDonald
1958	Donald C. Luce
1965	Watson F. Tait, Jr.
1968	Edwin H. Snyder
1971	Edward R. Eberle
1975	Robert I. Smith
1985	Harold W. Sonn
1986	E. James Ferland

Quaker Oats Co.

Chicago, IL

Presidents

1922	John Stuart
1943	R. Douglas Stuart
1948	Donald B. Lourie
1954	H. Earle Muzzy
1955	Donald B. Lourie
1962	Robert D. Stuart, Jr.
1976	Kenneth Mason
1979	William D. Smithburg
1983	Frank J. Morgan

Board Chairmen

1922	Henry P. Crowell
1943	John Stuart
1957	R. D. Stuart
1964	Donald B. Lourie
1971	Vacant
1976	Robert D. Stuart, Jr.
1983	William D. Smithburg

Rainier National Bank

Seattle, WA

(National Bank of Commerce of Seattle until 1975.)

Presidents

1906	Manson F. Backus
1932	Andrew Price
1948	Maxwell Carlson
1971	T. Robert Faragher
1973	G. Robert Truex, Jr.
1976	John D. Mangels

Board Chairmen

1965	Andrew Price, Jr.
1973	G. Robert Truex, Jr.
1975	T. Robert Faragher
1977	G. Robert Truex, Jr.

Ralston Purina Co.

St. Louis, MO

Presidents

1896	William H. Danforth
1932	Donald Danforth
1956	Raymond E. Rowland
1964	R. Hal Dean
1968	A. J. O'Brien
1972	Warren M. Shapleigh
1978	R. Hal Dean
1981	William P. Stiritz

Board Chairmen

1932	William H. Danforth
1956	Donald Danforth
1964	Raymond E. Rowland
1968	R. Hal Dean
1981	William P. Stiritz

Raytheon Co.

Lexington, MA

Presidents

1948	Charles F. Adams
1964	Thomas L. Phillips
1975	D. Brainerd Holmes

Board Chairmen

1964	Charles F. Adams
1975	Thomas L. Phillips

RCA Corp.

New York, NY

(Radio Corporation of America until 1971.)

Presidents

1919	Edward J. Nally
1923	James G. Harbord
1930	David Sarnoff
1949	Frank M. Folsom
1957	John L. Burns
1961	Elmer W. Engstrom
1966	Robert W. Sarnoff
1971	Anthony L. Conrad
1976	Edgar H. Griffiths
1980	Maurice R. Valente
1985	Robert R. Frederick

Board Chairmen

1919	Owen D. Young
1930	James G. Harbord
1947	David Sarnoff
1966	Elmer W. Engstrom
1971	Robert W. Sarnoff
1980	Edgar H. Griffiths
1981	Thornton F. Bradshaw

Reynolds Metals Co.

Richmond, VA

(Formerly Reynolds Aluminum Co.)

Presidents

1928	Richard S. Reynolds, Sr.
1948	Richard S. Reynolds, Jr.
1963	Joseph H. McConnell
1971	Richard S. Reynolds, Jr.
1975	George M. Walters
1978	John E. Blomquist
1983	William O. Bourke

Board Chairmen

1948	Richard S. Reynolds, Sr.
1963	Richard S. Reynolds, Jr.
1976	David P. Reynolds

R. J. Reynolds Tobacco Co.

Winston-Salem, NC

(Became a subsidiary of R. J. Reynolds Industries in 1970.)

Presidents

1911	Richard J. Reynolds
1918	William N. Reynolds
1924	Bowman Gray
1931	S. Clay Williams
1934	James A. Gray
1946	James W. Glenn
1948	John C. Whitaker
1952	Edward A. Darr
1957	Bowman Gray, Jr.
1959	F. G. Carter
1960	Alexander H. Galloway
1970	William S. Smith, Jr.
1972	Colin Stokes
1972	William D. Hobbs
1973	J. Paul Sticht
1974	William D. Hobbs
1977	Morgan V. Hunter
1980	Edward A. Horrigan, Jr.
1981	Gerald H. Long

Board Chairmen

1924	William N. Reynolds
1931	Bowman Gray
1935	S. Clay Williams
1949	James A. Gray
1952	John C. Whitaker
1959	Bowman Gray, Jr.
1969	Alexander H. Galloway
1970	Colin Stokes
1972	William S. Smith, Jr.
1973	Colin Stokes
1974	William D. Hobbs
1980	Edward A. Horrigan, Jr.

Rockwell International Corp.

Pittsburgh, PA

(North American Rockwell Corp. until 1973; merged with Rockwell Manufacturing Co.)

Presidents

1928	Clement M. Keys

1931	Thomas A. Morgan
1934	James H. Kindelberger
1948	John L. Atwood
1970	Robert Anderson
1979	Donald R. Beall

Board Chairmen

1928	Clement M. Keys
1931	Harold E. Talbot
1932	George N. Armsby
1933	Ernest R. Breech
1942	Henry H. Hogan
1948	James H. Kindelberger
1962	John L. Atwood
1967	Willard F. Rockwell, Jr.
1979	Robert Anderson

St. Regis Paper Co.

Stamford, CT

(Became part of Champion International Corp. in 1984.)

Presidents

1899	George E. Dodge
1901	George W. Knowlton, Jr.
1908	Gordon H. P. Gould
1916	Floyd L. Carlisle
1934	Roy K. Furguson
1957	William R. Adams
1971	William E. Caldwell, Jr.
1973	William R. Haselton
1981	Edward J. McMahon

Board Chairmen

1971	William R. Adams
1972	George J. Kneeland
1981	William R. Haselton

Scott Paper Co.

Philadelphia, PA

Presidents

1900	Arthur H. Scott
1927	Thomas B. McCabe
1962	Harrison F. Dunning
1968	Charles D. Dickey, Jr.
1971	G. Willing Pepper
1973	Charles D. Dickey, Jr.
1979	Morgan V. Hunter
1980	Philip E. Lippencott

Board Chairmen

1962	Thomas B. McCabe
1968	Harrison F. Dunning
1973	Charles D. Dickey, Jr.
1985	Philip E. Lippencott

Sears, Roebuck & Co.

Chicago, IL

Presidents

1886	Richard W. Sears
1908	Julius Rosenwald
1924	Charles M. Kittle
1928	Robert E. Wood
1939	Thomas J. Carney
1942	Arthur S. Barrows
1946	Fowler B. McConnell

1958	Charles H. Kellstadt
1960	Crowdus Baker
1968	Arthur M. Wood
1973	A. Dean Swift
1981	Edward R. Telling
1982	Archie Boe
1986	Richard M. Jones

Board Chairmen

1924	Julius Rosenwald
1932	Lessing Rosenwald
1939	Robert E. Wood
1954	Theodore V. Houser
1958	Fowler B. McConnell
1960	Charles H. Kellstadt
1962	Austin T. Cushman
1967	Gordon M. Metcalf
1973	Arthur M. Wood
1978	Edward R. Telling
1981	Edward A. Brennan
1982	Edward R. Telling
1986	Edward A. Brennan

Shell Oil Co.

Houston, TX

Presidents

1922	Avery D. Andrews
1922	William H. Allen
1922	Henri W. A. Deterding
1924	J. C. Van Eck
1933	R. G. A. van der Woude
1947	Alexander Fraser
1949	H. S. M. Burns
1961	Monroe E. Spaght
1966	R. C. McCurdy
1970	Denis B. Kemball-Cook
1971	Harry Bridges
1976	John F. Bookout

Board Chairmen

1924	Henri W. A. Deterding
1937	Frederick Godber
1946	George Legh-Jones
1951	Francis Hopwood
1958	John H. Loudon
1965	Vacant
1971	David H. Barran
1972	G. A. Wagner
1977	Dirk De Bruyne
1985	L. C. Van Wachem

Signal Companies, Inc.

La Jolla, CA

(Signal Oil & Gas Co. until 1971.)

Presidents

1928	Samuel B. Mosher
1958	Russell H. Green
1964	Forrest N. Shumway
1980	Daniel W. Derbes
1983	Michael D. Dingman

Board Chairmen

1969	William E. Walkup
1980	Forrest N. Shumway

SmithKline Beckman Corp.

Philadelphia, PA

(Smith, Kline & French Laboratories until 1974; SmithKline Corp. until 1984.)

Presidents

1946	C. Mahlon Kline
1953	Francis Boyer
1959	Walter A. Munns
1967	F. Markoe Rivinus
1968	Thomas M. Rauch
1972	Robert F. Dee
1976	Henry Wendt, III

Board Chairmen

1952	C. Mahlon Kline
1959	Francis Boyer
1967	Walter A. Munns
1972	Lewis E. Harris
1976	Robert F. Dee

Southern California Edison Co.

Rosemead, CA

Presidents

1909	John B. Miller
1918	William A. Brackenridge
1920	John B. Miller
1928	Russell H. Ballard
1932	George C. Ward
1933	Harry J. Bauer
1945	William C. Mullendore
1954	Harold Quinton
1959	Jack K. Horton
1968	Thomas M. McDaniel, Jr.
1978	William R. Gould
1980	Howard P. Allen
1984	H. Frederick Christie

Board Chairmen

1918	John B. Miller
1932	Harry J. Bauer
1959	Harold Quinton
1968	Jack K. Horton
1980	William R. Gould
1984	Howard P. Allen

Southern Pacific Transportation Co.

San Francisco, CA

Presidents

1884	Frank H. Davis
1884	William E. Brown
1885	Leland Stanford
1890	Collis P. Huntington
1900	Charles M. Hays
1901	Edward H. Harriman
1909	Robert S. Lovett
1911	William Sproule
1918	Julius Kruttschnitt
1920	William Sproule
1929	Paul Shoup
1932	A. D. McDonald
1941	Armand T. Mercier

1952	Donald J. Russell
1964	Benjamin F. Biaggini
1976	Denman K. McNear
1982	R. D. Krebs
1983	Denman K. McNear

Board Chairmen

1900	Charles H. Tweed
1929	Henry W. deForest
1932	Hale Holden
1964	Donald J. Russell
1976	Benjamin F. Biaggini
1982	Denman K. McNear

Southern Railway Co.

Norfolk, VA

Presidents

1894	Samuel Spencer
1906	W. W. Finley
1913	Fairfax Harrison
1937	Ernest E. Norris
1952	Harry A. DeButts
1962	D. William Brosnan
1967	W. Graham Claytor, Jr.
1976	L. Stanley Crane
1979	Harold H. Hall
1982	Edward B. Burwell

Board Chairmen

1976	W. Graham Claytor, Jr.
1979	L. Stanley Crane
1982	Robert B. Claytor

Sperry Corp.

New York, NY

(Sperry Rand Corp. until 1980; formed by merger of Sperry Corp. and Remington Rand, Inc. in 1955; became part of Unisys in 1986.)

Presidents

1955	Harry F. Vickers
1965	J. Frank Forster
1971	J. Paul Leyt
1972	Robert E. McDonald
1980	Gerald G. Probst

Board Chairmen

1965	Harry F. Vickers
1967	J. Frank Forster
1972	J. Paul Leyt
1982	Gerald G. Probst

Standard Oil Company Ohio Corp.

Cleveland, OH

Presidents

1870	John D. Rockefeller
1900	Ambrose M. McGregor
1901	Frank Q. Barstow
1908	Henry M. Tilford
1911	Walter C. Teagle
1911	A. Palmer Coombe
1928	Wallace T. Holliday

1949	Clyde T. Foster
1957	Charles E. Spahr
1970	Alton W. Whitehouse, Jr.
1976	Joseph D. Harnett
1980	John R. Miller

Board Chairmen

1949	Wallace T. Holliday
1950	Armstrong A. Stambaugh
1956	Clyde T. Foster
1970	Charles E. Spahr
1978	Alton W. Whitehouse, Jr.

State Mutual Life Assurance Company of America

Worcester, MA

Presidents

1845	John Davis
1854	Isaac Davis
1882	Philip L. Moen
1883	A. George Bullock
1910	Burton H. Wright
1927	Chandler Bullock
1942	George A. White
1951	H. Ladd Plumley
1968	Robert A. Miller
1969	W. Douglas Bell
1980	Frederick Fedeli

Board Chairmen

1960	H. Ladd Plumley
1980	W. Douglas Bell

Sun Co., Inc.

Radnor, PA

(Sun Oil Co. until 1976.)

Presidents

1901	Joseph N. Pew
1912	J. Howard Pew
1947	Robert G. Dunlop
1970	H. Robert Sharbaugh
1976	Theodore A. Burtis
1981	R. McClements, Jr.

Board Chairmen

1947	Joseph N. Pew, Jr.
1963	J. Howard Pew
1970	Robert G. Dunlop
1975	H. Robert Sharbaugh
1979	Theodore A. Burtis

Swift & Co., Inc.

Chicago, IL

(Became part of Beatrice Foods in 1985.)

Presidents

1885	Gustavus F. Swift, Sr.
1903	Louis F. Swift
1931	Gustavus F. Swift, Jr.
1937	John Holmes
1955	Porter M. Jarvis
1964	Robert W. Reneker
1974	Charles C. Olcott

1977	William S. Watchman
1981	Joseph P. Sullivan

Board Chairmen

1931	Louis F. Swift
1937	Gustavus F. Swift, Jr.
1955	John Holmes
1964	Porter M. Jarvis

Teledyne, Inc.

Los Angeles, CA

Presidents

1960	Henry E. Singleton
1967	George A. Roberts

Board Chairmen

1966	Henry E. Singleton

Tenneco, Inc.

Houston, TX

(Tennessee Gas & Transmission Co. until 1962; Tenneco Oil Co. until 1975.)

Presidents

1956	Gardiner Symonds
1962	R. C. Graham
1964	W. E. Scott
1967	Nelson W. Freeman
1969	James E. Ivins
1970	Nelson W. Freeman
1972	R. E. McGee
1974	Wilton E. Scott
1977	James L. Ketelsen
1979	John P. Diesel

Board Chairmen

1960	Gardiner Symonds
1972	Nelson W. Freeman
1977	Wilton E. Scott
1978	James L. Ketelsen

Texaco, Inc.

White Plains, NY

Presidents

1902	Joseph S. Gullinan
1913	Elgood C. Lufkin
1920	Amos L. Beaty
1926	Ralph C. Holmes
1933	W. S. S. Rodgers
1944	Harry T. Klein
1952	J. S. Leach
1953	Augustus C. Long
1956	J. W. Foley
1964	J. Howard Rambin, Jr.
1965	Marion J. Epley, Jr.
1970	Maurice F. Granville
1971	John K. McKinley
1983	Alfred C. Decrane, Jr.

Board Chairmen

1920	Elgood C. Lufkin
1926	Amos L. Beaty
1933	Ralph C. Holmes
1933	Charles B. Ames

1935	Torkild Rieber
1944	W. S. S. Rodgers
1953	J. S. Leach
1956	Augustus C. Long
1965	J. Howard Rambin, Jr.
1970	Marion J. Epley, Jr.
1971	Maurice F. Granville
1980	John K. McKinley

Chief Executive Officers

1965	Augustus C. Long
1971	Maurice F. Granville
1980	John K. McKinley

Texas Instruments, Inc.

Dallas, TX

Presidents

1950	Cecil H. Green
1951	J. E. Jonsson
1958	Patrick E. Haggerty
1967	Mark Shepherd, Jr.
1970	Robert D. Rogers
1975	Mark Shepherd, Jr.
1976	J. Fred Bucy
1986	Jerry R. Junkins

Board Chairmen

1953	Eugene McDermott
1955	Cecil H. Green
1958	J. E. Jonsson
1969	Patrick E. Haggerty
1970	Ralph B. Rogers
1975	Patrick E. Haggerty
1976	Mark Shepherd, Jr.

Textron, Inc.

Providence, RI

(Franklin Rayon Corp. until 1939; Atlantic Rayon Corp. until 1944.)

Presidents

1928	Eugene S. Graves
1930	William A. Traver
1936	Royal Little
1953	Robert L. Huffines, Jr.
1955	Royal Little
1956	Rupert C. Thompson, Jr.
1960	G. William Miller
1974	Joseph B. Collinson
1978	Robert P. Straetz
1980	Beverly F. Dolan

Board Chairmen

1928	Eliot Farley
1930	William A. Traver
1936	Eliot Farley
1953	Royal Little
1960	Rupert C. Thompson, Jr.
1974	G. William Miller
1978	Joseph B. Collinson
1980	Robert P. Straetz

Time, Inc.

New York, NY

Presidents

1923	Henry R. Luce

1939	Roy E. Larsen
1960	James A. Linen
1969	James R. Shepley
1980	J. Richard Munro
1986	N. J. Nicholas, Jr.

Board Chairmen

1923	Henry R. Luce
1943	Maurice T. Moore
1960	Andrew Heiskell
1980	Ralph P. Davidson
1986	J. Richard Munro

Trans World Corp. (TWA)

New York, NY

(Trans World Airlines, Inc. until 1979.)

Presidents

1930	H. M. Hanshue
1931	Richard W. Robbins
1934	Jack Frye
1947	LaMotte T. Cohu
1949	Ralph S. Damon
1956	Carter L. Burgess
1958	Charles S. Thomas
1961	Charles C. Tillinghast, Jr.
1969	Forwood C. Wiser, Jr.
1976	Carl E. Meyer, Jr.
1978	L. Edwin Smart
1983	Carl E. Meyer, Jr.

Board Chairmen

1969	Charles C. Tillinghast, Jr.
1977	L. Edwin Smart

Transcontinental Gas Pipe Line Corp.

Houston, TX

Presidents

1946	Claude A. Williams
1953	Tom P. Walker
1957	E. Clyde McGraw
1967	James B. Henderson
1973	G. Montgomery Mitchell
1974	W. J. Bowen
1981	Kenneth L. Lay
1982	Brian E. O'Neill

Board Chairmen

1957	Tom P. Walker
1967	E. Clyde McGraw
1976	W. J. Bowen

Travelers Insurance Co.

Hartford, CT

(See also Phoenix Insurance Co.)

Presidents

1864	James G. Batterson
1901	Sylvester C. Dunham
1915	Louis F. Butler
1929	L. Edmund Zacher
1945	Jesse W. Randall
1952	J. Doyle DeWitt

1964 Sterling T. Tooker
1969 Roger C. Wilkins
1971 Morrison H. Beach
1976 Edward H. Budd
1981 Alva O. Way
1983 Edward H. Budd

Board Chairmen

1945 Francis W. Cole
1964 J. Doyle DeWitt
1971 Roger C. Wilkins
1974 Morrison H. Beach
1982 Edward H. Budd

TRW, Inc.

Cleveland, OH

(Formed by merger of Ramo-Woolidge Corp. with Thompson Pdts., Inc. in 1958.)

Presidents

1962 Horace A. Shephard
1969 Ruben F. Mettler
1977 Stanley C. Pace
1985 J. T. Gorman

Board Chairmen

1966 John D. Wright
1969 Horace A. Shepard
1977 Ruben F. Mettler

Union Carbide Corp.

Danbury, CT

Presidents

1917 George O. Knapp
1925 Jesse J. Ricks
1941 Benjamin O'Shea
1944 Fred H. Haggerson
1952 Morse G. Dial
1958 Howard S. Bunn
1960 Birny Mason, Jr.
1966 Kenneth Rush
1969 F. Perry Wilson
1971 William S. Sneath
1976 Warren M. Anderson
1982 Alec Flamm

Board Chairmen

1951 Fred H. Haggerson
1958 Morse G. Dial
1966 Birny Mason, Jr.
1971 F. Perry Wilson
1976 William S. Sneath
1982 Warren M. Anderson
1986 Robert D. Kennedy

Union Electric Co.

St. Louis, MO

Presidents

1902 Julius S. Walsh
1905 John I. Beggs
1907 W. V. N. Powelson
1909 Charles W. Wetmore
1910 Alten S. Miller
1911 J. D. Mortimer
1920 Louis H. Egan

1939 William McClellan
1941 James W. McAfee
1966 Charles J. Dougherty
1980 William E. Cornelius

Board Chairmen

1941 William McClellan
1954 Ralph E. Moody
1966 James W. McAfee
1980 Charles J. Dougherty

Union Pacific Railroad Co.

Omaha, NE

Presidents

1862 William B. Ogden
1863 John A. Dix
1866 Oliver Ames
1871 Thomas A. Scott
1872 Horace Clark
1873 John Duff
1874 Sidney Dillon
1884 Charles Francis Adams
1890 Sidney Dillon
1892 S. H. H. Clark
1897 Winslow S. Pierce
     (Acting)
1897 Horace G. Burt
1904 Edward H. Harriman
1909 Robert S. Lovett
1911 A. L. Mohler
1916 Edgar E. Calvin
1918 Charles B. Seger
1919 Robert S. Lovett
1920 Carl R. Gray
1937 William M. Jeffers
1946 George F. Ashby
1949 A. E. Stoddard
1965 Edd H. Bailey
1971 John C. Kenefick
1982 R. G. Flannery

Board Chairmen

1897 Winslow S. Pierce
1898 Edward H. Harriman
1909 Robert S. Lovett
1932 W. Averell Harriman
1946 E. Roland Harriman
1969 Frank E. Barnett
1977 James H. Evans
1982 John C. Kenefick
1985 Andrew L. Lewis, Jr.

Uniroyal, Inc.

Middlebury, CT

(United States Rubber Co. until 1967.)

Presidents

1892 W. L. Trenholm
1892 Robert D. Evans
1893 Joseph Banigan
1896 Robert D. Evans
1897 Frederick M. Shepard
1901 Samuel P. Colt
1918 Charles P. Seger
1929 Francis B. Davis, Jr.
1942 Herbert E. Smith

1949 Harry E. Humphreys, Jr.
1957 John W. McGovern
1960 George R. Vila
1974 David Beretta
1977 Joseph P. Flannery

Board Chairmen

1918 Samuel P. Colt
1921 Charles B. Seger
1929 Francis B. Davis, Jr.
1949 Herbert E. Smith
1951 Harry E. Humphreys, Jr.
1964 George R. Vila
1975 David Beretta
1982 Joseph P. Flannery

United Brands Co.

Chicago, IL

Presidents

1970 John M. Fox
1975 Wallace W. Booth
1977 Seymour Milstein
1981 Paul Milstein
1984 Ronald F. Walker

Board Chairmen

1970 Eli M. Black
1975 Max M. Fisher
1978 Seymour Milstein
1984 Carl H. Lindner

United States National Bank of Oregon

Portland, OR

Presidents

1891 Donald Macleay
1895 Tyler Woodward
1902 John C. Ainsworth
1931 Paul S. Dick
1945 Edward C. Sammons
1960 Edward J. Kolar
1966 LeRoy B. Staver
1971 Earl L. Dresler
1972 John A. Elorriaga
1974 Robert R. Mitchell

Board Chairmen

1960 Edward C. Sammons
1966 Edward J. Kolar
1971 LeRoy B. Staver
1974 John A. Elorriaga

United Technologies Corp.

Hartford, CT

(United Aircraft Corp. until 1976.)

Presidents

1934 Donald L. Brown
1939 Eugene E. Wilson
1943 H. Mansfield Horner
1955 William P. Gwinn

1967 Arthur E. Smith
1971 Harry J. Gray
1979 Alexander M. Haig, Jr.
1982 Harry J. Gray
1984 Robert F. Daniell

Board Chairmen

1935 Frederick B. Rentschler
1955 H. Mansfield Horner
1967 William P. Gwinn
1972 Arthur E. Smith
1974 Harry J. Gray
1986 Robert F. Daniell

United Telecommunications, Inc.

Kansas City, MO

(United Utilities, Inc. until 1973.)

Presidents

1938 Harry S. Berlin
1939 Ralph W. Dockstader
1940 Alden L. Hart
1959 Carl A. Scupin
1964 Paul H. Henson
1973 Raymond M. Alden
1981 Charles W. Battey
1985 W. T. Ersey

Board Chairmen

1966 Paul H. Henson

Unocal Corp.

Los Angeles, CA

(Union Oil Co. of California until 1985.)

Presidents

1890 Thomas R. Bard
1894 D. T. Perkins
1895 Lyman Stewart
1914 William L. Stewart
1930 L. P. St. Clair
1938 Reese H. Taylor
1957 A. C. Rubel
1961 Dudley Tower
1963 A. C. Rubel
1964 Fred L. Hartley
1986 Richard Stegemeier

Board Chairmen

1914 Lyman Stewart
1923 Vacant
1930 E. W. Clark
1939 L. P. St. Clair
1941 Vacant
1957 Reese H. Taylor
1965 A. C. Rubel
1974 Fred L. Hartley

U.S. Industries, Inc.

Stamford, CT

(Pressed Steel Car Co. until 1954.)

Presidents

1902	Frank N. Hoffstot
1934	W. A. Bonitz
1937	J. F. MacEnulty
1946	Ernest Murphy
1948	John I. Snyder
1966	I. John Billera
1970	Charles E. Selecman
1973	I. John Billera
1974	C. Russell Luigs
1978	Gordon A. Walker
1985	David H. Clarke

Board Chairmen

1934	Lester N. Selig
1946	J. F. MacEnulty
1947	John I. Snyder
1966	I. John Billera
1981	Gordon A. Walker

USX Corp.

Pittsburgh, PA

(United States Steel Corp. until 1986.)

Presidents

1901	Charles M. Schwab
1903	William E. Corey
1911	James A. Farrell
1932	William A. Irvin
1938	Benjamin F. Fairless
1953	Clifford F. Hood
1959	Walter F. Munford
1959	Leslie B. Worthington
1967	Edwin H. Gott
1969	Edgar B. Speer
1973	Wilbert A. Walker
1975	David M. Roderick
1979	William R. Roesch
1986	James V. Sidell

Board Chairmen

1903	Elbert H. Gary
1927	J. Pierpont Morgan, Jr.
1932	Myron C. Taylor
1938	Edward R. Stettinius, Jr.
1940	Irving S. Olds
1952	Benjamin F. Fairless
1955	Roger M. Blough
1961	Edwin H. Gott
1973	Edgar B. Speer
1979	David M. Roderick

Chief Executive Officers

1910	Elbert H. Gary
1927	James A. Farrell
1932	Myron C. Taylor
1952	Benjamin F. Fairless
1955	Roger M. Blough
1969	Edwin H. Gott

Virginia Electric & Power Co.

Richmond, VA

Presidents

1909	William Northrop
1912	Thomas S. Wheelwright
1925	Luke C. Bradley
1927	William E. Wood
1929	J. Frank McLaughlin
1929	Jack G. Holtzclaw
1956	Erwin H. Will
1958	Alfred H. McDowell, Jr.
1967	John M. McGurn
1970	T. Justin Moore, Jr.
1978	Stanley Ragone
1980	William W. Berry
1985	Jack H. Ferguson

Board Chairmen

1971	John M. McGurn
1979	T. Justin Moore
1985	William W. Berry

Warner-Lambert Co.

Morris Plains, NJ

(Warner-Lambert Pharmaceutical Co. until 1967.)

Presidents

1958	Alfred E. Driscoll
1966	Stuart K. Hensley
1967	E. Burke Giblin
1973	Robert T. Wieringa
1976	Ward S. Hagan
1979	Joseph D. Williams
1985	Melvin R. Goodes

Board Chairmen

1958	Elmer H. Bobst
1967	Stuart K. Hensley
1973	E. Burke Giblin
1979	Ward S. Hagan
1985	Joseph D. Williams

Wells Fargo Bank

San Francisco, CA

Presidents

1960	Ransom M. Cook
1964	H. Stephens Chase
1966	Richard P. Cooley
1978	Carl E. Reichardt
1984	Paul Hazen

Board Chairmen

1960	I. W. Hellman
1964	Ransom M. Cook
1966	H. Stephens Chase
1968	Ernest C. Arbuckle
1977	James K. Dobey

1978	Richard P. Cooley
1983	Carl E. Reichardt

Western Electric Co., Inc.

New York, NY

(Became part of AT&T after 1984.)

Presidents

1872	Anson Stager
1885	William A. S. Smoot
1886	Enos M. Barton
1908	Harry B. Thayer
1919	Charles G. DuBois
1926	Edgar S. Bloom
1940	Clarence G. Stoll
1947	Stanley Bracken
1954	Frederick R. Kappel
1956	Arthur B. Goetze
1959	Haakon I. Romnes
1964	Paul A. Gorman
1969	Harvey G. Melhouse
1971	Donald E. Procknow

Board Chairmen

1971	Harvey G. Melhouse
1983	James E. Olson

Westinghouse Electric Corp.

Pittsburgh, PA

Presidents

1886	George Westinghouse, Jr.
1910	Edwin F. Atkins
1911	Edwin M. Herr
1929	Frank A. Merrick
1938	George H. Bucher
1946	Gwilym A. Price
1958	Mark W. Cresap, Jr.
1963	Donald C. Burnham

Board Chairmen

1891	Brayton Ives
1909	Robert Mather
1912	Guy E. Tripp
1927	Paul D. Cravath
1929	Andrew W. Robertson
1955	Gwilym A. Price
1969	Donald C. Burnham
1975	Robert E. Kirby
1983	Douglas D. Danforth

Weyerhaeuser Co.

Federal Way, WA

(Weyerhaeuser Steamship Co. until 1946, when Weyerhaeuser Timber Co. was formed; companies were separate until Weyerhaeuser Timber & Steamship Co. was formed around 1961; assumed present name in 1965.)

Presidents

1946	John P. Weyerhaeuser, Jr.
1958	C. H. Ingram (Steamship)
1959	Donald Watson (Steamship)
1958	F. K. Weyerhaeuser (Timber)
1961	Norton Clapp
1966	George H. Weyerhaeuser

Board Chairmen

1946	John P. Weyerhaeuser, Jr.
1949	Laird Bell (Timber)
1956	F. K. Weyerhaeuser (Timber)
1958	Norton Clapp (Timber)
1961	F. K. Weyerhaeuser
1967	Norton Clapp
1976	Robert B. Wilson
1982	Vacant

Whirlpool Corp.

Benton Harbor, MI

(Whirlpool - Seeger Corp. from 1956 to 1958.)

Presidents

1951	Elisha Gray
1956	Elisha Gray, II
1959	Robert E. Brooker
1961	Elisha Gray, II
1962	John H. Platts
1977	Herbert K. Anspach
1984	Jack D. Sparks

Board Chairmen

1951	Louis C. Upton
1953	Vacant
1956	Walter G. Seeger
1959	Elisha Gray, II
1971	John H. Platts
1983	Jack D. Sparks

Xerox Corp.

Stamford, CT

Presidents

1962	Joseph C. Wilson
1966	C. Peter McColough
1971	Archie R. McCardle
1977	David T. Kearns
1986	Paul A. Allaire

Board Chairmen

1962	S. M. Linowitz
1967	Joseph C. Wilson
1971	C. Peter McColough
1985	David T. Kearns

XVII

Labor Leaders

Labor Leaders

Actors' Equity Association

1913 Francis Wilson
1920 John Emerson
1928 Frank Gilmore
1938 Arthur Byron
1940 Bert Lytell
1946 Clarence Derwent
1952 Ralph Bellamy
1964 Frederick O'Neal
1973 Theodore Bikel
1982 Ellen Burstyn
1987 Colleen Dewhurst

Allied Industrial Workers of America, International Union

1935 F. J. Dillon
1936 Homer Martin
1940 Irvan Cary
1943 Lester Washburn
1954 George Grisham
1954 Earl Heaton
1957 Carl W. Griepentrog
1970 Gilbert Jewell
1975 Dominick D'Ambrosio

Aluminum, Brick, and Glass Workers International Union

(Aluminum Workers International Union until 1981.)

1953 Eddie R. Stahl
1967 Henry S. Olsen
1973 Vernon E. Kelly
1977 Lawrence A. Holley
1985 Ernie J. LaBaff

Amalgamated Clothing and Textile Workers Union

(Amalgamated Clothing Workers of America until 1976; merged with the Textile Workers Union of America.)

1914 Sidney Hillman
1946 Jacob S. Potofsky
1972 Murray H. Finley

Amalgamated Meat Cutters and Butcher Workmen

1897 George Byer
1898 Michael Donnelly
1905 Howard W. Potter
1909 John E. Carney
1910 John F. Hart
1921 C. J. Hayes
1923 Patrick E. Gorman
1942 Earl W. Jimerson
1959 Thomas J. Lloyd
1972 Joseph Belsky
1976 Harry Poole

Amalgamated Transit Union

1892 William Law
1893 W. D. Mahon
1946 A. L. Spradling
1959 John M. Elliott
1973 Dan V. Maroney, Jr.
1981 John W. Rowland
1986 James La Sala

American Federation of Government Employees

1932 John A. Shaw
1933 E. Claude Babock
1936 Charles I. Stengle
1939 Cecil E. Custer
1939 James B. Burns
1948 James G. Yaden
1950 Henry Ihler
1951 James A. Campbell
1962 John F. Griner
1972 Clyde M. Webber
1976 Kenneth T. Blaylock

American Federation of Musicians of the United States and Canada

1896 Owen Miller
1900 Joseph N. Weber
1940 James C. Petrillo
1958 Herman Kenin
1970 Hal C. Davis
1978 Victor W. Fuentealba

American Federation of Teachers

1916 Charles B. Stillman
1923 Florence Rood
1925 Mary C. Barker
1931 Henry R. Linville
1934 Raymond E. Lowry
1936 Jerome C. Davis
1939 George S. Counts
1942 John M. Fewkes
1943 Joseph F. Landis
1948 John M. Eklund
1952 Carl J. Megel
1964 Charles Cogen
1968 David Selden
1972 Albert Shanker

American Federation of Television and Radio Artists

1937 Eddie Cantor
1940 Lawrence Tibbett
1946 Kenneth Carpenter
1948 Clayton Collyer
1950 Knox Manning
1952 Alan Bunce
1954 Frank Nelson
1957 Clayton Collyer
1959 Virginia Payne
1961 Art Gilmore
1963 Vicki Vola
1965 Tyler McVey
1967 Mel Brandt
1970 Bill Baldwin
1973 Kenneth Harvey
1976 Joseph Slattery
1979 Bill Hillman
1985 Frank Maxwell

American Postal Workers Union

(United Federation of Postal Clerks until 1971.)

1906 Edward B. Goltra
1910 Oscar F. Nelson
1913 George Pfeiffer
1915 Arthur Honewell
1917 Gilbert E. Hyatt
1923 Leo E. George
1956 J. Cline House
1960 Elroy C. Hallbeck
1969 Francis S. Filbey
1977 Emmet C. Andrews
1980 Morris Biller

Bakery, Confectionery, and Tobacco Workers International Union

(Tobacco Workers International Union until 1978; merged with Bakery and Confectionery Workers Union of America.)

1895 John Fischer
1908 A. McAndrews
1921 W. R. Walden
1925 E. Lewis Evans
1940 W. Warren Smith
1943 Radford G. Powell
1944 John O'Hare
1968 Howard W. Vogt
1970 Rene Rondou
1978 John De Concini

Brotherhood of Locomotive Engineers

1863 W. D. Robinson
1864 Charles Wilson
1874 P. M. Arthur
1903 A. B. Youngson
1903 Warren S. Stone
1924 William B. Prenter
1925 Alvanley Johnston
1950 J. P. Shields
1953 Guy L. Brown
1960 Roy E. Davidson
1964 Perry S. Heath
1969 C. J. Coughlin
1973 B. N. Whitmire
1976 John F. Sytsma
1986 R. E. Delaney

Brotherhood of Maintenance of Way Employes

1887 John T. Wilson
1908 A. B. Lowe
1914 T. H. Gerrey
1914 A. E. Barker
1920 E. F. Grable
1922 F. H. Fljozdal
1940 Elmer E. Milliman
1947 T. C. Carroll
1958 H. C. Crotty
1978 Ole M. Berge
1987 Geoffrey N. Zeh

Brotherhood of Railroad Signalmen

1908 Philip Weller
1908 John Bindscheattel
1909 M. J. Hooper
1910 J. A. Martin
1913 W. J. Pettit
1917 D. W. Helt
1934 A. E. Lyon
1945 Jesse Clark
1967 Charles J. Chamberlain
1977 R. T. Bates

Brotherhood of Railroad Trainmen

(Became part of the United Transportation Union in 1969.)

1883 J. E. Grimes
1885 S. E. Wilkinson
1895 P. H. Morrissey
1909 William G. Lee
1928 A. F. Whitney
1949 W. P. Kennedy
1960 Charles Luna

Glass Bottle Blowers Association of the United States and Canada

(Became part of Glass, Pottery, Plastics, and Allied Workers International Union in 1982.)

1876 Samuel Simpson
1880 Louis Arrington
1894 Joseph D. Troth
1896 Denis A. Hayes
1917 John A. Voll
1924 James Maloney
1946 Lee W. Minton
1971 Newton W. Black

Glass, Pottery, Plastics, and Allied Workers International Union

1971 Newton W. Black
1973 Harry A. Tulley
1976 James E. Hatfield

Industrial Union of Marine and Shipbuilding Workers of America

1933 John Green
1951 John J. Grogan
1968 Andrew A. Pettis
1971 Frank Derwin
1982 Arthur Batson, Jr.

International Association of Bridge, Structural, and Ornamental Iron Workers

1896 Edward J Ryan
1899 John T. Butler
1901 Frank Buchanan
1905 Frank M. Ryan
1914 James E. McClory
1918 P. J. Morrin
1948 John H. Lyons, Sr.
1961 John H. Lyons, Jr.
1987 Juel D. Drake

International Association of Machinists and Aerospace Workers

1888 Thomas W. Talbot
1890 J. J. Creamer
1892 John O'Day
1893 James O'Connell
1911 William H. Johnston
1926 A. O. Wharton
1939 Harvey W. Brown
1949 A. J. Hayes
1965 P. L. Siemiller
1969 Floyd E. Smith
1977 William W. Winpisinger

International Brotherhood of Electrical Workers

1891 Henry Miller
1893 Quinn Jansen
1894 H. W. Sherman
1897 J. A. Maloney
1899 Thomas Wheeler
1901 W. A. Jackson
1903 F. J. McNulty
1919 J. P. Noonan
1929 H. H. Broach
1933 D. W. Tracy
1940 Edward J Brown
1947 D. W. Tracy
1954 J. Scott Milne
1955 Gordon M. Freeman
1968 Charles H. Pillard
1986 John J. Barry

International Brotherhood of Painters and Allied Trades

1887 Joseph Harrold
1888 George A. Thompson
1892 James W. McKinney
1894 John M. Welter
1894 James H. Sullivan
1896 Michael P. Carrick
1897 Robert H. Siekmann
1898 Fred Kneeland
1899 William DeVaux
1901 Joseph Bahlhorn
1909 George F. Hedrick
1928 John M. Finan
1929 Lawrence P. Lindelof
1952 Lawrence M. Raftery
1965 S. Frank Raftery
1984 William A. Duval

International Brotherhood of Paper Makers

(Became part of United Papermakers and Paperworkers in 1957.)

1902 George Mackey
1905 Jeremiah T. Carey
1924 Matthew H. Parker
1926 William R. Smith
1930 Matthew J. Burns
1940 Arthur Huggins
1944 Matthew J. Burns
1948 Paul L. Phillips

International Brotherhood of Pottery and Allied Workers

(Became part of Glass, Pottery, Plastics, and Allied Workers International Union in 1982.)

1890 Harry Layden
1892 A. S. Hughes
1912 Edward Menge
1921 John T. Wood
1927 James M. Duffy
1953 Frank Hull
1956 E. L. Wheatley
1969 Lester H. Null, Sr.

International Brotherhood of Pulp, Sulphite, and Paper Mill Workers

(Became part of United Paperworkers International Union in 1972.)

1906 James E. Fitzgerald
1909 John H. Malin
1917 John P. Burke
1965 William H. Burnell
1965 Joseph P. Tonelli

International Brotherhood of Teamsters, Chauffeurs, Warehousemen and Helpers of America

1899 John Callahan
1900 Jasper Clark
1902 N. W. Evans
1902 Albert Young
1903 Cornelius P. Shea
1907 Daniel J. Tobin
1952 David Beck
1957 James R. Hoffa
1971 Frank Fitzsimmons
1981 Roy L. Williams
1983 Jackie Presser

International Ladies' Garment Workers Union

1900 Herman Grossman
1903 Benjamin Schlesinger
1904 James McCauley
1905 Herman Grossman
1907 Mortimer Julian
1908 Charles Jacobson
1908 Abraham Rosenberg
1914 Benjamin Schlesinger
1923 Salvatore Ninfo
1923 Morris Sigman
1928 Benjamin Schlesinger
1931 Salvatore Ninfo
1932 David Dubinsky
1966 Louis Stulberg
1975 Sol C. Chaikin
1986 Jay Mazur

International Longshoremen's Association

1895 Daniel J. Keefe
1909 T. V. O'Connor
1921 Anthony Chlopek
1927 Joseph P. Ryan
1953 William V. Bradley
1964 Thomas W. Gleason

International Longshoremen's and Warehousemen's Union

1938 Harry Bridges
1977 James R. Herman

International Molders and Allied Workers Union

1859 William C. Rea
1860 Isaac J. Neall
1861 Norman Van Alstyne
1863 William H. Sylvis
1869 F. J. Meyers
1870 William Saffin
1879 P. F. Fitzpatrick
1890 Martin Fox
1903 Joseph F. Valentine
1924 M. J. Keough
1932 Lawrence O'Keefe
1939 Harry Stevenson
1948 Chester A. Sample
1960 William A. Lazzerini
1971 Draper Doyal
1973 Anton J. Trizna
1976 Carl W. Studenroth
1983 Bernard Butsavage

International Typographical Union

1850 J. W. Peregoy
1851 J. L. Gibbons
1852 J. S. Nafew
1853 Gerard Stith
1854 Lewis Graham
1855 Charles F. Town
1856 M. C. Brown
1857 William Cuddy
1858 R. C. Smith
1860 J. M. Farquhar
1863 Eugene Valette
1864 A. M Carver
1865 Robert E. Craig
1866 John H. Oberly
1868 Robert McKechnie

1869 Isaac D. George
1870 W. J. Hammond
1873 W. R. McLean
1874 William H. Bodwell
1875 Walter W. Bell
1876 John McVicar
1877 D. R. Streeter
1878 John Armstrong
1879 Samuel Haldeman
1880 William P. Atkinson
1881 George Clark
1883 M. L. Crawford
1884 R. H. Witter
1886 William Aimison
1888 E. T. Plank
1891 W. B. Prescott
1899 Samuel B. Donnelly
1901 James M. Lynch
1914 James M. Duncan
1915 M. G. Scott
1921 John McParland
1923 Charles P. Howard
1925 James M. Lynch
1927 Charles P. Howard
1938 C. M. Baker
1944 Woodruff Randolph
1958 Elmer Brown
1968 John J. Pilch
1973 A. Sandy Bevis
1978 Joe Bingel
1983 Robert S. McMichen

International Union of Bricklayers and Allied Craftsmen

(Bricklayers, Masons, and Plasterers, International Union of America until 1975.)

1865 John A. White
1867 John S. Frost
1869 Samuel Gaul
1870 John O'Keefe
1871 Meredith Moore
1872 James T. Kirby
1874 Stephen A. Carr
1875 Lewis Carpenter
1877 Charles H. Rihl
1878 Lewis Carpenter
1879 Thomas R. Gockel
1881 E. J. O'Rourk
1882 Henry O. Cole
1884 John Pearson
1885 Thomas R. Gockel
1886 Alex Darragh
1890 Alfred J. McDonald
1891 John Heartz
1894 William Klein
1901 George P. Gubbins
1904 William J. Bowers
1928 George T. Thornton
1936 Harry C. Bates
1960 John J. Murphy
1966 Thomas F. Murphy

International Union of Electronic, Electrical, Technical, Salaried and Machine Workers

(International Union of Electrical, Radio, and Machine Workers until 1983.)

1949 James B. Carey

1965 Paul Jennings
1971 Albert J. Fitzgerald
1978 David J. Fitzmaurice
1982 William H. Bywater

International Union of Operating Engineers

1896 C. J. Delong
1897 Frank Bowker
1898 Frank Pfohl
1898 S. L. Bennett
1899 P. A. Peregrine
1900 Frank B. Monaghan
1901 George Lighthall
1903 Patrick McMahon
1904 John E. Bruner
1905 Matt Comerford
1916 Milton Snelling
1921 Arthur M. Huddell
1931 John Possehl
1940 William E. Maloney
1958 Joseph J. Delaney
1962 Hunter P. Wharton
1975 James C. Turner
1985 Larry Dugan, Jr.

International Union, United Automobile, Aerospace, and Agricultural Implement Workers of America-UAW

1935 Francis J. Dillon
1936 Homer Martin
1939 R. J. Thomas
1946 Walter P. Reuther
1970 Leonard Woodcock
1977 Douglas A. Fraser
1983 Owen F. Bieber

International Woodworkers of America

1937 Harold Pritchett
1940 O. M. Orton
1941 Worth Lowery
1943 Claude Ballard
1944 J. E. Fadling
1951 A. F. Hartung
1967 Roland F. Roley
1973 Keith Johnson

National Association of Postal Supervisors

1908 L. E. Palmer
1910 George A. Gasman
1911 Ernest Green
1916 William Sansom
1917 J. J. Fields
1921 V. C. Burke
1922 H. M. Tittle
1924 Peter Wiggle
1925 Harry Folger
1930 W. Bruce Luna
1931 M. F. O'Connell
1933 Herschel Ressler
1937 M. F. Fitzpatrick

1941 John J. Lane
1946 John McMahon
1950 M. C. Nave
1958 Fred J. O'Dwyer
1970 Donald N. Ledbetter
1986 Rubin Handelman

National Federation of Federal Employees

1917 H. M. McLarin
1918 Luther C. Steward
1955 Michael E. Markwood
1957 Vaux Owen
1964 Nathan T. Wolkomir
1976 James N. Peirce

National Maritime Union of America

1937 Joseph E. Curran
1973 Shannon J. Wall

Newspaper Guild

(American Newspaper Guild until 1972.)

1933 Heywood Broun
1940 Kenneth G. Crawford
1940 Donal M. Sullivan
1941 Milton Murray
1947 Harry Martin
1953 Joseph F. Collis
1959 Arthur Rosenstock
1967 James B. Woods
1969 Charles A. Perlik, Jr.

Office and Professional Employees International Union

1945 Paul Hutchings
1953 Howard Coughlin
1979 John Kelly

Retail, Wholesale, and Department Store Union

1937 Samuel Wolchok
1948 Irving M. Simon
1954 Max Greenberg
1976 Alvin E. Heaps
1986 Lenore Miller

Screen Actors Guild

1933 Ralph Morgan
1933 Eddie Cantor
1935 Robert Montgomery
1938 Ralph Morgan
1940 Edward Arnold
1942 James Cagney
1944 George Murphy
1946 Robert Montgomery
1947 Ronald Reagan
1952 Walter Pidgeon
1957 Leon Ames

1958 Howard Keel
1959 Ronald Reagan
1960 George Chandler
1963 Dana Andrews
1965 Charlton Heston
1971 John Gavin
1974 Dennis Weaver
1975 Kathleen Nolan
1979 William J. Schallert
1981 Edward Asner
1986 Patty Duke

Seafarers International Union of North America

1938 Harry Lundeberg
1957 Paul Hall
1980 Frank Drozak

Service Employees International Union

1940 William L. McFetridge
1960 David Sullivan
1971 George Hardy
1980 John J. Sweeney

Textile Workers Union of America

(Became part of Amalgamated Clothing and Textile Workers Union in 1976.)

1939 Emil Rieve
1956 William Pollock
1973 Sol Stein

Transport Workers Union of America

1934 Michael J. Quill
1966 Matthew Guinan
1982 William G. Lindner
1985 John Lawe

United Association of Journeymen and Apprentices of the Plumbing and Pipe Fitting Industry of the United States and Canada

1889 Patrick J. Quinlan
1891 John A. Lee
1892 Patrick H. Gleason
1893 John A. Lee
1894 M. J. Moran
1896 William P. Redmond
1896 Thomas H. O'Brien
1897 John S. Kelley
1900 William M. Merrick
1906 John R. Alpine
1919 John Coefield
1940 George Masterton
1943 Martin P. Durkin
1955 Peter T. Schoemann
1971 Martin J. Ward

1982   Marvin J. Boede

United Brotherhood of Carpenters and Joiners of America

1881   Gabriel Edmonston
1882   John D. Allen
1883   J. P. McGinley
1884   Joseph P. Billingsley
1886   William J. Shields
1888   D. P. Rowland
1890   W. H. Kliver
1892   Henry H. Trenor
1894   Charles B. Owens
1896   Harry Lloyd
1898   John Williams
1899   William D. Huber
1913   James Kirby
1915   William L. Hutcheson
1952   Maurice A. Hutcheson
1972   William Sidell
1981   William Konyha
1982   Patrick J. Campbell

United Electrical, Radio, and Machine Workers of America

1936   James B. Carey
1941   Albert J. Fitzgerald
1978   Denis Glavin
1981   James M. Kane

United Hatters, Cap and Millinery Workers International Union

(Became the Headwear Division of Amalgamated Clothing and Textile Workers Union in 1983.)

1934   Michael F. Greene
1936   Max Zaritsky
1950   Alex Rose
1975   Nicholas Gyory

United Papermakers and Paperworkers

(Became part of United Paperworkers International Union in 1972.)

1957   Paul L. Phillips
1968   Harry D. Sayre

United Paperworkers International Union

1972   Joseph P. Tonelli
1978   Wayne E. Glenn

United Rubber, Cork, Linoleum, and Plastic Workers of America

1935   Sherman H. Dalrymple
1945   L. S. Buckmaster
1960   George Burdon
1966   Peter Bommarito
1981   Milan Stone

United Shoe Workers of America

(Became part of Amalgamated Clothing and Textile Workers Union in 1979.)

1937   Powers Hapgood
1939   Frank McGrath
1947   Raymond Swansen
1948   Rocco Francheschini
1949   William Thornton
1952   Russell J. Taylor
1956   George O. Fecteau

United Steelworkers of America

1942   Philip Murray
1952   David J. McDonald
1965   I. W. Abel
1977   Lloyd McBride
1983   Lynn Williams

United Transportation Union

1969   Charles Luna
1971   Al H. Chesser
1979   Fred A. Hardin

Upholsterers' International Union of North America

(Became part of United Steelworkers of America in 1985.)

1882   William Gratz
1884   Frank Kreis
1892   Anton J. Engel
1907   James H. Hatch
1921   William Kohn
1931   James H. Hatch
1937   Sal B. Hoffman
1981   Martin L. Garber
1983   John H. Serembes

Utility Workers Union of America

1945   Joseph A. Fisher
1960   William J. Pachler
1970   William R. Munger
1971   Harold T. Rigley
1979   Valentine T. Murphy
1980   James Joy, Jr.

XVIII

Association Executives

Association Executives

A listing of presidents or executive directors of national learned, scientific, technical, professional, and fraternal organizations.

Academy of Motion Picture Arts and Sciences

1927	Douglas Fairbanks
1929	William DeMille
1931	M. C. Levee
1932	Conrad Nagel
1933	J. Theodore Reed
1934	Frank Lloyd
1935	Frank Capra
1939	Walter Wanger
1941	Bette Davis
1941	Walter Wanger
1945	Jean Hersholt
1949	Charles Brackett
1955	George Seaton
1958	George Stevens
1959	Bejamin B. Kahane
1960	Valentine Davies
1961	Wendell Corey
1963	Arthur Freed
1967	Gregory Peck
1971	Daniel Taradash
1975	James M. Roberts (Executive Director)

Academy of Natural Sciences

1812	Gerard Troost
1817	William Maclure
1840	William Hembel
1849	Samuel G. Morton
1851	George Ord
1858	Isaac Lea
1863	Thomas B. Wilson
1864	Robert Bridges
1865	Isaac Hays
1869	William S. W. Ruschenberger
1881	Joseph Leidy
1891	Isaac J. Wistar
1895	Samuel G. Dixon
1918	John Cadwalader
1922	Richard A. F. Penrose
1926	T. Chalkley Palmer
1928	Effingham B. Morris
1937	Charles M. B. Cadwalader
1951	M. Albert Linton
1962	George R. Clark
1963	John W. Bodine
1972	William W. Marvel
1975	Milton H. Wahl (Managing Director)
1977	Thomas Peter Bennett (to 1985)

American Academy of Arts and Letters

1908	William Dean Howells
1920	William Milligan Sloane
1928	Nicholas Murray Butler
1941	Walter Damrosch
1948	Paul Manship
1953	Archibald MacLeish
1956	Mark Van Doren
1959	Douglas Moore
1962	Lewis Mumford
1965	Allan Nevins
1968	George F. Kennan
1971	Aaron Copland
1973	Margaret M. Mills (Executive Director)

American Academy of Arts and Sciences

1780	James Bowdoin
1791	John Adams
1814	Edward A. Holyoke
1820	John Quincy Adams
1829	Nathaniel Bowditch
1838	James Jackson
1839	John Pickering
1846	Jacob Bigelow
1863	Asa Gray
1873	Charles Francis Adams
1880	Joseph Lovering
1892	Josiah P. Cooke
1894	Alexander Agassiz
1903	William W. Goodwin
1908	John Trowbridge
1915	Henry P. Walcott
1917	Charles P. Bowditch
1919	Theodore W. Richards
1921	George F. Moore
1924	Theodore Lyman
1927	Edwin B. Wilson
1931	Jeremiah D. M. Ford
1933	George H. Parker
1935	Roscoe Pound
1937	Dugald C. Jackson
1939	Harlow Shapley
1944	Howard Mumford Jones
1951	Edwin H. Land
1954	John E. Burchard
1957	Kirtley F. Mather
1961	Hudson Hoagland
1964	Paul A. Freund
1967	Talcott Parsons
1971	Harvey Brooks
1972	John Voss (Executive Director)

American Academy of Political and Social Science

1890	Edmund J. James
1901	Samuel M. Lindsay
1902	Leo S. Rowe
1930	Ernest M. Patterson
1953	James C. Charlesworth
1956	Thorsten Sellin
1958	Charles C. Charlesworth (to 1964)
1972	Richard D. Lambert
1977	Marvin E. Wolfgang (to 1985)

American Anthropological Association

1947	Clyde Kluckhohn
1948	Harry L. Shapiro
1949	A. Irving Hallowell
1950	Ralph L. Beals
1951	William W. Howells
1952	Wendell C. Bennett
1953	Fred Eggan
1954	John O. Brew
1955	George P. Murdock
1956	Emil W. Haury
1957	E. Adamson Hoebel
1958	Harry Hoijer
1959	Sol Tax
1960	Margaret Mead
1961	Gordon R. Willey
1962	Sherwood L. Washburn
1963	Marvin K. Opler
1964	Leslie A. White
1965	Alexander Spoehr
1966	John P. Gillin
1967	Frederica De Laguna
1968	Irving Rouse
1969	Cora Du Bois
1970	George M. Foster, Jr.
1971	Charles Wagley
1972	Anthony F. C. Wallace
1973	E. J. Lehman (Executive Director, to 1985)

American Antiquarian Society

1812	Isaiah Thomas
1831	Thomas L. Winthrop
1841	Edward Everett
1853	John Davis
1854	Stephen Salisbury
1884	George F. Hoar
1887	Stephen Salisbury, Jr.
1906	Edward E. Hale
1907	Waldo Lincoln
1927	Charles L. Nichols
1929	Calvin Coolidge
1933	Arthur P. Rugg
1938	Samuel Eliot Morison
1952	Thomas W. Streeter
1955	Clarence S. Brigham
1959	Carleton R. Richmond
1964	Clifton W. Barrett
1966	Clifford K. Shipton (Director)
1969	Marcus A. McCorison (Director)

American Association for the Advancement of Science

1848	William B. Rogers (Acting)
1848	William C. Redfield
1850	Alexander D. Bache
1851	Louis Agassiz
1852	Benjamin Peirce
1854	James D. Dana
1855	John Torrey
1856	James Hall
1857	J. W. Bailey
1857	Alexis Caswell
1858	Jeffries Wyman
1859	Stephen Alexander
1860	Isaac Lea
1866	Frederick A. P. Barnard
1867	J. S. Newberry
1868	Benjamin A. Gould
1869	J. W. Foster
1870	William Chauvenet
1870	T. Sterry Hunt
1871	Asa Gray
1872	J. Lawrence Smith
1873	Joseph Lovering
1874	John L. LeConte
1875	Julius L. Hilgard
1876	William B. Rogers
1877	Simon Newcomb
1878	O. C. Marsh
1879	George F. Barker
1880	Lewis H. Morgan
1881	George J. Brush
1882	J. William Dawson
1883	Charles A. Young
1884	J. P. Lesley
1885	H. A. Newton
1886	Edward S. Morse
1887	S. P. Langley
1888	J. W. Powell
1889	T. C. Mendenhall
1890	George L. Goodale
1891	Albert B. Prescott
1892	Joseph LeConte
1893	William Harkness
1894	Daniel G. Brinton
1895	Edward W. Morley

1896 Edward D. Cope
1896 Theodore Gill
1897 Wolcott Gibbs
1897 W. J. McGee
1898 F. W. Putnam
1899 Edward Orton
1899 Marcus Benjamin
1899 Grove K. Gilbert
1900 R. S. Woodward
1901 Charles S. Minot
1902 Asaph Hall
1902 Ira Remsen
1903 Carroll D. Wright
1904 William G. Farlow
1905 C. M. Woodward
1906 William H. Welch
1907 E. L. Nichols
1908 Thomas C. Chamberlin
1909 David S. Jordan
1910 A. A. Michelson
1911 Charles E. Bessey
1912 E. C. Pickering
1913 Edmund B. Wilson
1914 Charles W. Eliot
1915 William W. Campbell
1916 Charles R. Van Hise
1917 Theodore W. Richards
1918 John M. Coulter
1919 Simon Flexner
1920 Leland O. Howard
1921 Eliakim H. Moore
1922 J. Playfair McMurrich
1923 Charles D. Walcott
1924 J. McKeen Cattell
1925 Michael I. Pupin
1926 Liberty Hyde Bailey
1927 Arthur A. Noyes
1928 Henry F. Osborn
1929 Robert A. Millikan
1930 Thomas H. Morgan
1931 Franz Boas
1932 John J. Abel
1933 Henry N. Russell
1934 Edward L. Thorndike
1935 Karl T. Compton
1936 Edwin G. Conklin
1937 George D. Birkhoff
1938 Wesley C. Mitchell
1939 Walter B. Cannon
1940 Albert F. Blakeslee
1941 Irving Langmuir
1942 Arthur H. Compton
1943 Isaiah Bowman
1944 Anton J. Carlson
1946 Charles F. Kettering
1946 James B. Conant
1947 Harlow Shapley
1948 Edmund W. Sinnott
1949 Elvin C. Stakman
1950 Roger Adams
1951 Kirtley F. Mather
1952 Detlev W. Bronk
1953 Edward U. Condon
1954 Warren Weaver
1955 George W. Beadle
1956 Paul B. Sears
1957 Laurence H. Snyder
1958 Wallace R. Brode
1959 Paul E. Klopsteg
1960 Chauncey D. Leake
1961 Thomas Park
1962 Paul M. Gross
1963 Alan T. Waterman
1964 Laurence M. Gould
1965 Henry Eyring
1966 Alfred S. Romer
1967 Don K. Price
1968 Walter Orr Roberts
1969 H. Bentley Glass
1970 Athelstan Spilhaus
1971 Mina Rees

1972 Glenn T. Seaborg
1973 Leonard M. Reiser
1975 William D. Carey
       (Executive Director)

American Association of Petroleum Geologists

1917 J. Elmer Thomas
1918 Alexander Deussen
1919 I. C. White
1920 Wallace E. Pratt
1921 George C. Matson
1922 William E. Wrather
1923 Max W. Ball
1924 James H. Gardner
1925 E. L. DeGolyer
1926 Alex W. McCoy
1927 George C Gester
1928 R. S. McFarland
1929 J. Y. Snyder
1930 Sidney Powers
1931 L. P. Garrett
1932 Frederic H. Lahee
1933 Frank R. Clark
1934 William B. Heroy
1935 A. I. Levorsen
1936 Ralph D. Reed
1937 Herbert B. Fuqua
1938 Donald C. Barton
1939 Henry A. Ley
1940 Luther C. Snider
1941 Edgar W. Owen
1942 Fritz L. Aurin
1943 Rodger Denison
1944 Ira H. Cram
1945 Monroe G. Cheney
1946 Earl B. Noble
1947 C. E. Dobbin
1948 Paul Weaver
1949 C. W. Tomlinson
1950 Clarence L. Moody
1951 Frank A. Morgan
1952 Morgan J. Davis, Sr.
1953 John E. Adams
1954 Ed. A. Koester
1955 G. Moses Knebel
1956 Theodore A. Link
1957 Graham B. Moody
1958 George S. Buchanan
1959 Lewis G. Weeks
1960 Ben H. Parker
1961 Mason L. Hill
1962 Robert E. Rettger
1963 John C. Sproule
1964 Grover E Murray
1965 Orlo E. Childs
1966 Michel T. Halbouty
1967 J. Ben Carsey
1968 Frank B. Conselman
1969 Kenneth H. Crandall
1970 William H. Curry
1972 Sherman A Wengerd
1977 Fred A. Dix, Jr.
       (Executive Director)

American Association of University Professors

1915 John Dewey
1916 John H. Wigmore
1917 Frank Thilly
1918 John M. Coulter
1919 A. O. Lovejoy
1920 Edward Capps
1921 Vernon L. Kellogg

1921 E. R. A. Seligman
1922 J. V. Denney
1924 A. O. Leuschner
1926 W. T. Semple
1928 Henry Crew
1930 W. B. Munro
1932 Walter C. Cook
1934 S. A. Mitchell
1936 Anton J. Carlson
1938 Mark H. Ingraham
1940 Frederick S. Deibler
1942 W. T. Laprade
1944 Quincy Wrights
1946 Edward C. Kirkland
1948 Ralph H. Lutz
1950 Richard H. Shryock
1952 Fred B. Millett
1954 William E. Britton
1956 Helen C. White
1958 H. Bentley Glass
1960 Ralph F. Fuchs
1962 Fritz Machlup
1964 David Fellman
1966 Clark Byse
1968 Ralph S. Brown
1970 Sanford N. Kadish
1972 Walter Adams
1973 Bertran H. Davis
       (General Secretary)
1975 William W. VanAlstyne

General Secretaries

1976 Joseph Duffey
1977 Jordan E. Kurkland
1978 Morton S. Baratz
1980 Martha Friedman
       (International)
1981 Irving J. Spitzberg
1985 Ernest Benjamin

American Astronautical Society

1953 Hans Behm
1955 Norman V. Petersen
1957 Ross Fleisig
1959 George Arthur
1961 Alfred M. Mayo
1963 William O. Whitson
1964 George W. Morgenthaler
1966 Lewis Larmore
1968 Eugene B. Konecci
1969 Paul Dergarabedian
1972 Paul B. Richards
1975 George E. Cranston
       (Executive Secretary)
1979 George E. Cranston
       (Executive Secretary, to
       1980)
1981 Edward V. B. Stearns
1982 George E. Cranston
       (Executive Secretary, to
       1984)
1985 G. Lynwood May
1987 George E. Cranston
       (Executive Secretary)

American Astronomical Society

1899 Simon Newcomb
1905 Edward C. Pickering
1919 Frank Schlesinger
1922 William W. Campbell
1925 George C. Comstock

1928 Ernest W. Brown
1931 Walter S. Adams
1934 Henry N. Russell
1937 Robert G. Aitken
1940 Joel Stebbins
1943 Harlow Shapley
1946 Otto Struve
1949 Alfred H. Joy
1952 Robert R. McMath
1954 Donald H. Menzel
1956 Paul Merrill
1958 G. M. Clemence
1960 Lyman Spitzer, Jr.
1962 C. S. Beals
1964 Leo Goldberg
1967 A. E. Whitvord
1969 Martin Schwarzschild
1972 Bart J. Bok
1973 H. M. Gurin (Executive
       Officer)
1980 Peter B. Boyce (Executive
       Officer)

American Bankers Association

1875 Charles B. Hall
1878 Alex Mitchell
1881 George S. Coe
1883 Lyman J. Gage
1886 Logan C. Murray
1888 Charles Parsons
1890 Morton McMichael
1892 William H. Rhawn
1893 M. M. White
1894 John J. P. Odell
1895 Eugene H. Pullen
1896 Robert J. Lowry
1897 Joseph C. Hendrix
1898 George H. Russell
1899 Walker Hill
1900 Alvah Trowbridge
1901 Myron T. Herrick
1902 Caldwell Hardy
1904 E. F. Swinney
1905 John L. Hamilton
1906 G. S. Whitson
1907 J. D. Powers
1908 George M. Reynolds
1909 Lewis E. Pierson
1910 F. O. Watts
1911 William Livingstone
1912 Charles H. Huttig
1913 Arthur Reynolds
1914 William A. Law
1915 James K. Lynch
1916 P. W. Goebell
1917 Charles A. Hinsch
1918 Robert F. Maddox
1919 Richard S. Hawes
1920 John S. Drum
1921 Thomas B. McAdams
1922 John H. Puelicher
1923 Walter W. Head
1924 William E. Knox
1925 Oscar Wells
1926 Melvin A. Traylor
1927 Thomas R. Preston
1928 Craig B. Hazlewood
1929 John G. Lonsdale
1930 Rome C. Stephenson
1931 Harry J. Haas
1932 Francis H. Sisson
1933 Francis M. Law
1934 Rudolph S. Hecht
1935 Robert V. Fleming
1936 Tom K. Smith
1937 Orval W. Adams
1938 Philip A. Benson

1939 Robert M. Hanes
1940 P. D. Houston
1941 H. W. Koeneke
1942 W. L. Hemingway
1943 A. L. M. Wiggins
1944 W. Randolph Burgess
1945 Frank C. Rathje
1946 C. W. Bailey
1947 Joseph M. Dodge
1948 Evans Woollen, Jr.
1949 F. Raymond Peterson
1950 James E. Shelton
1951 C. Francis Cocke
1952 W. Harold Brenton
1953 Everett D. Reese
1954 Homer J. Livingston
1955 Fred F. Florence
1956 Erle Cocke, Sr.
1957 J. C. Welman
1958 Lee P. Miller
1959 John W. Remington
1960 Carl A. Bimson
1961 Sam M. Fleming
1962 M. Monroe Kimbrel
1963 William F. Kelly
1964 Reno Odlin
1965 Archie K. Davis
1966 Jack T. Conn
1967 J. Howard Laeri
1968 Willis W. Alexander
1969 Nat S. Rogers
1970 George H. Gustafson
1971 Clifford C. Sommer
1972 Allen P. Stults
1975 Goerge L. Whyel
1976 Willis W. Alexander
    (Executive Vice President,
    to 1983)
1984 Robert J. Wagner
1985 Don Oglivie (Executive
    Vice President)

American Bar Association

1878 James O. Broadhead
1879 Benjamin H. Bristow
1880 Edward J. Phelps
1881 Clarkson N. Potter
1882 Alexander R. Lawton
1883 Cortlandt Parker
1884 John W. Stevenson
1885 William Allen Butler
1886 Thomas J. Semmes
1887 George G. Wright
1888 David Dudley Field
1889 Henry Hitchcock
1890 Simeon E. Baldwin
1891 John F. Dillon
1892 John Randolph Tucker
1893 Thomas M. Cooley
1894 James C. Carter
1895 Moorfield Storey
1896 James M. Woolworth
1897 William Wirt Howe
1898 Joseph H. Choate
1899 Charles F. Manderson
1900 Edmund Wetmore
1901 U. M. Rose
1902 Francis Rawle
1903 James Hagerman
1904 Henry St. George Tucker
1905 George R. Peck
1906 Alton B. Parker
1907 Jacob M. Dickinson
1908 Frederick W. Lehmann
1909 Charles F. Libby
1910 Edgar H. Farrar
1911 Stephen S. Gregory
1912 Frank B. Kellogg

1913 William H. Taft
1914 Peter W. Meldrim
1915 Elihu Root
1916 George Sutherland
1917 Walter George Smith
1918 George T. Page
1919 Hampton L. Carson
1920 William A. Blount
1921 Cordenio A. Severance
1922 John W. Davis
1923 R. E. L. Saner
1924 Charles E. Hughes
1925 Chester I. Long
1926 Charles S. Whitman
1927 Silas H. Strawn
1928 Gurney E. Newlin
1929 Henry Upson Sims
1930 Josiah Marvel
1930 Charles A. Boston
1931 Guy A. Thompson
1932 Clarence E. Martin
1933 Earle W. Evans
1934 Scott M. Loftin
1935 William L. Ransom
1936 Frederick H. Stinchfield
1937 Arthur T. Vanderbilt
1938 Frank J. Hogan
1939 Charles A. Beardsley
1940 Jacob M. Lashly
1941 Walter P. Armstrong
1942 George M. Morris
1943 Joseph W. Henderson
1944 David A. Simmons
1945 Willis Smith
1946 Carl B. Rix
1947 Tappan Gregory
1948 Frank E. Holman
1949 Harold J. Gallagher
1950 Cody Fowler
1951 Howard L. Barkdull
1952 Robert G. Storey
1953 William J. Jameson
1954 Loyd Wright
1955 E. Smythe Gambrell
1956 David F. Maxwell
1957 Charles S. Rhyne
1958 Ross L. Malone
1959 John D. Randall
1960 Whitney North Seymour
1961 John C. Satterfield
1962 Sylvester C. Smith, Jr.
1963 Walter E. Craig
1964 Lewis F. Powell, Jr.
1965 Edward W. Kuhn
1966 Orison S. Marden
1967 Earl F. Morris
1968 William T. Gossett
1969 Bernard G. Segal
1970 Edward L. Wright
1971 Leon Jaworski
1972 Robert W. Meserve
1974 Bert H. Early (Executive
    Director)
1979 Leonard S. Janofsky
1980 William Reece Smith, Jr.
1981 Thomas H. Gonser
    (Executive Director)

American Bible Society

1816 Elias Boudinot
1821 John Jay
1828 Richard Varick
1831 John Cotton Smith
1846 Theodore Frelinghuysen
1862 Luther Bradish
1864 James Lenox
1872 William H. Allen
1881 S. Wells Williams

1884 Frederick T.
    Frelinghuysen
1885 Enoch L. Fancher
1903 Daniel Coit Gilman
1909 Theophilus A. Brouwer
1911 James Wood
1919 Churchill H. Cutting
1924 E. Francis Hyde
1931 J. Frederick Talcott
1934 John T. Manson
1944 Daniel Burke
1962 Everett Smith
1967 Edmund F. Wagner
1969 Laton E. Holmgren
    (General Officer)
1979 John D. Erickson
    (General Secretary)
1980 Alice E. Ball (General
    Secretary)
1986 John Wood

American Cancer Society, Inc.

1913 George C. Clark
1919 Charles A. Powers
1923 Edward Reynolds
1925 Howard C. Taylor
1930 Jonathan M. Wainwright
1932 George H. Bigelow
1934 Burton T. Simpson
1936 Robert B. Greenough
1937 Frederick F. Russell
1938 John J. Morton, Jr.
1942 Herman C. Pitts
1944 Frank E. Adair
1947 Edwin P. Lehman
1948 Clifford C. Nesselrode
1949 Alton Ochsner
1950 Guy Aud
1951 Charles C Lund
1952 Harry M. Nelson
1953 Alfred M. Popma
1954 Howard C. Taylor, Jr.
1955 George V. Brindley
1956 David A. Wood
1957 Lowell T. Coggeshall
1958 Eugene P. Pendergrass
1959 Warren H. Cole
1960 John W. Cline
1961 Thomas Carlile
1962 Isidor S. Ravdin
1963 Wendell G. Scott
1964 Murray M. Copeland
1965 Leonard W. Larson
1966 Ashbel C. Williams
1967 Roger A. Harvey
1968 Sidney Farber
1969 Jonathan E. Rhoads
1970 H. Marvin Pollard
1971 A. Hamblin Letton
1972 Lane W. Adams
    (Executive Vice President,
    to 1984)
1987 G. Robert Gadberry
    (Vice President)

American Chemical Society

1876 John W. Draper
1877 J. Lawrence Smith
1878 Samuel W. Johnson
1879 T. Sterry Hunt
1880 Frederick A. Genth
1881 Charles F. Chandler

1882 John W. Mallet
1883 James C. Booth
1886 Albert B. Prescott
1887 Charles A. Goessmann
1888 T. Sterry Hunt
1889 Charles F. Chandler
1890 Henry B. Nason
1891 George F. Barker
1892 George C. Caldwell
1893 Harvey W. Wiley
1895 Edgar F. Smith
1896 Charles B. Dudley
1898 Charles E. Munroe
1899 Edward W. Morley
1900 William McMurtrie
1901 Frank W. Clarke
1902 Ira Remsen
1903 John H. Long
1904 Arthur A. Noyes
1905 Francis P. Venable
1906 William F. Hillebrand
1907 Marston T. Bogert
1909 Willis R. Whitney
1910 Wilder D. Bancroft
1911 Alexander Smith
1912 Arthur D. Little
1914 Theodore W. Richards
1915 Charles H. Herty
1917 Julius Stieglitz
1918 William H. Nichols
1920 William A. Noyes
1921 Edgar F. Smith
1923 Edward C. Franklin
1924 Leo H. Baekeland
1925 James F. Norris
1927 George D. Rosengarten
1928 Samuel W. Parr
1929 Irving Langmuir
1930 William McPherson
1931 Moses Gomberg
1932 L. V. Redman
1933 Arthur B. Lamb
1934 Charles L. Reese
1935 Roger Adams
1936 Edward Bartow
1937 Edward R. Weidlein
1938 Frank C. Whitmore
1939 Charles A. Kraus
1940 Samuel C. Lind
1941 William Lloyd Evans
1942 Harry N. Holmes
1943 Per K. Frolich
1944 Thomas Midgley, Jr.
1945 Carl S. Marvel
1946 Bradley Dewey
1947 W. Albert Noyes, Jr.
1948 Charles A. Thomas
1949 Linus Pauling
1950 Ernest H. Volwiler
1951 N. Howell Furman
1952 Edgar C. Britton
1953 Farrington Daniels
1954 Harry L. Fisher
1955 Joel H. Hildebrand
1956 J. C. Warner
1957 Roger J. Williams
1958 C. F. Rassweiler
1959 John C. Bailar, Jr.
1960 Albert L. Elder
1961 Arthur C. Cope
1962 Karl Folkers
1963 Henry Eyring
1964 Maurice H. Arveson
1965 Charles C. Price
1966 William J. Sparks
1967 Charles G. Overberger
1968 Robert W. Cairns
1969 Wallace R. Brode
1970 Byron Riegel
1971 Melvin Calvin

Executive Directors

1976 Robert W. Cairns
1978 Raymond P. Mariella
1983 John K. Crum

American College of Surgeons

1913 John M. T. Finney
1916 George W. Crile
1918 William J. Mayo (to 1920)
1921 John B. Deaver
1922 Harvey Cushing
1923 Albert J. Ochsner
1924 Charles H. Mayo
1925 Rudolph Matas (to 1926)
1927 George D. Stewart
1928 Franklin H. Martin
1929 Merritte W. Ireland
1930 C. Jeff Miller
1931 Allen B. Kanavel
1932 J. Bentley Squier
1933 William D. Haggard
1934 Robert B. Greenough
1935 Donald C. Balfour
1936 Eugene H. Pool
1937 Frederic A. Besley
1938 Howard C. Naffziger
1939 George P. Muller
1940 Evarts A. Graham
1942 Vacant
1946 Irvin W. Abell
1947 Arthur W. Allen
1948 Dallas B. Phemister
1949 Frederick A. Coller
1950 Henry W. Cave
1951 Alton Ochsner
1952 Harold L. Foss
1953 Fred W. Rankin
1954 Frank Glenn
1954 Alfred Blalock
1955 Warren H. Cole
1956 Daniel C. Elkin
1957 William L. Estes, Jr. (to 1958)
1959 Owen H. Wangensteen
1960 I. S. Ravdin
1961 Robert M. Zollinger
1962 Loyal Davis
1963 J. Englebert Dunphy
1964 James T. Priestley
1965 Howard A. Patterson (to 1966)
1967 Reed M. Nesbit
1968 Preston A. Wade
1969 Joel Baker
1970 Howard Mahorner
1971 Jonathan E. Rhoads
1971 C. Rollins Hanlon (Director)

American College of Trial Lawyers

1950 Emil Gumpert
1951 C. Ray Robinson
1952 Cody Fowler
1953 E. D. Bronson
1954 Cody Fowler
1955 Wayne E. Stichter
1956 Jesse E. Nichols
1957 Lewis C. Ryan
1958 Albert E. Jenner, Jr.
1959 Samuel P. Sears

1960 Lon Hocker
1961 Leon Jaworski
1962 Grant B. Cooper
1963 Whitney North Seymour
1964 Bernard G. Segal
1965 Edward L. Wright
1966 Frank G. Raichle
1967 Joseph A. Ball
1968 Robert W. Meserve
1969 Lewis F. Powell, Jr.
1970 Barnabas F. Sears
1971 Hicks Epton
1972 L. A. Genter (Executive Secretary)
1973 Richard W. Pruter (Executive Director)
1985 Robert A. Young (Executive Director)

American Correctional Association

1945 Sanford Bates
1946 E. R. Cass
1947 Blanche La Du
1948 Austin H. MacCormick
1949 James V. Bennett
1950 Richard A. McGee
1951 Garrett Heyns
1952 W. Frank Smyth
1953 John C. Burke
1954 Joseph E. Ragen
1955 Walter M. Wallack
1956 Kenyon J. Scudder
1957 Myrl E. Alexander
1958 E. Preston Sharp
1959 Roberts J. Wright
1960 Gervaise Brinkman
1961 Sanger B. Powers
1962 Arthur T. Prasse
1963 Peter P. Lejins
1964 Harry C. Tinsley
1965 Harold V. Langlois
1966 Walter Dunbar
1967 Parker L. Hancock
1968 Ellis C. MacDougall
1969 George Beto
1970 Louie L. Wainwright
1971 Maurice H. Sigler
1972 E. Preston Sharp (General Secretary)
1973 Joseph S. Coughlin
1974 John W. Braithwaite
1975 Anthony P. Trovisono (Executive Director, to 1981)
1982 Amos E. Reed
1983 H. G. "Gus" Moeller
1984 Anthony P. Trovisono (Executive Director)
1985 T. Don Hutto
1986 Su Cunningham
1987 Anthony P. Trovisono (Executive Director)

American Council of Learned Societies

1919 Waldo Leland (Director)
1946 Richard H. Shryock (Acting)
1947 Cornelius Kruse (Exec. Director)
1948 Charles Odegaard (Exec. Director)

1953 Mortimer Graves (Exec. Director)
1957 Frederick Burkhardt
1975 R. M. Lumiansky
1982 John William Ward
1985 R. M. Lumiansky

American Dental Association

1859 William W. Allport
1860 William H. Atkinson
1862 George Watt
1863 William H. Allen
1864 John H. McQuillen
1865 Christopher W. Spalding
1866 Chauncey P. Fitch
1867 Ambrose Lawrence
1868 Jonathan Taft
1869 Homer Judd
1870 William H. Morgan
1871 George H. Cushing
1872 Phineas G. C. Hunt
1873 Thomas L. Buckingham
1874 Mason S. Dean
1875 Aaron L. Northrop
1876 George W. Keely
1877 Frederick H. Rehwinkel
1878 Henry J. McKellops
1879 Luther D. Shepard
1880 Cyrus N. Pierce
1881 H. A. Smith
1882 William H. Goddard
1883 Edwin T. Darby
1884 John N. Crouse
1885 William C. Barrett
1886 William W. Allport
1887 Frank Abbott
1888 Charles R. Butler
1889 Matthew W. Foster
1890 Allison W. Harlan
1891 William W. Walker
1892 John D Patterson
1894 James Y. Crawford
1896 James Truman
1897 Thomas Fillerbrown
1898 Harvey J. Burkhart
1899 B. Holly Smith
1900 Greene V. Black
1901 James A. Libbey
1902 Llewellyn G. Noel
1903 Charles C. Chittenden
1904 Waldo E. Boardman
1905 Mark F. Finley
1906 Adelbert H. Peck
1907 William Carr
1908 Vines E. Turner
1909 Burton L. Thorpe
1910 Edmund S. Gaylord
1911 Arthur R. Melendy
1912 Frank O. Hetrick
1913 Homer C. Brown
1914 Donald M. Gallie
1915 Thomas P. Hinman
1916 Lafayette L. Barber
1917 William H. G. Logan
1918 Clement V. Vignes
1919 John V. Conzett
1920 H. Edmund Friesell
1921 Thomas B. Hartzell
1922 John P. Buckley
1923 William A. Giffen
1924 Charles N. Johnson
1925 Sheppard W. Foster
1926 Henry L. Banzhaf
1927 Roscoe H. Volland
1928 Percy R. Howe
1929 Robert B. Bogle
1930 Robert T. Oliver

1931 Martin Dewey
1932 George W. Dittmar
1933 Arthur C. Wherry
1934 Frank M. Casto
1935 George Ben W. Winter
1936 Leroy M. S. Miner
1937 C. Willard Camalier
1938 Marcus L. Ward
1939 Arthur H. Merritt
1940 Wilfred H. Robinson
1941 Oren A. Oliver
1942 J. Ben Robinson
1943 Charles R. Wells
1944 Walter H. Scherer (to 1946)
1946 Sterling V. Mead
1947 Harvey B. Washburn
1948 Clyde E. Minges
1949 Philip E. Adams
1950 Harold W. Oppice
1951 LeRoy M. Ennis
1952 Otto W. Brandhorst
1953 Leslie M. Fitzgerald
1954 Daniel F. Lynch
1955 Bernerd C. Kingsbury
1956 Harry Lyons
1957 William R. Alstadt
1958 Percy T. Phillips
1959 Paul H. Jeserich
1960 Charles H. Patton
1961 John R. Abel
1962 Gerald D. Timmons
1963 James P. Hollers
1964 Fritz A. Pierson
1965 Maynard K. Hine
1966 William A. Garrett
1967 Floyd D. Ostrander
1968 Hubert A. McGuirl
1969 Harry M. Klenda
1970 John M. Deines
1971 Carl A. Laughlin

Executive Directors

1974 C. Gordon Watson
1979 John M Coady
1986 Thomas J. Ginley

American Dialect Society

1890 F. J. Child
1891 James M. Hart
1893 James M. Garnett
1894 Edward S. Sheldon
1896 Charles H. Grandgent
1897 G. L. Kittredge
1898 O. F. Emerson
1899 Lewis F. Mott
1901 George Hempl
1906 Oliver F. Emerson
1910 Raymond Weeks
1911 Calvin Thomas
1913 William E. Mead
1916 James W. Bright
1946 Kemp Malone
1947 Atcheson L. Hench
1949 Allen W. Read
1951 E. H. Criswell
1953 James B. McMillan
1956 Levette J. Davidson
1958 Frederic G. Cassidy
1960 Thomas Pyles
1962 Albert H. Marckwardt
1964 Allan F. Hubbell
1965 Einar Haugen
1967 Raven I. McDavid
1969 David W. Maurer
1971 Harold B. Allen

Executive Secretaries

1972 A. Hood Roberts
1977 H. Rex Wilson
1981 Allan A. Metcalf

American Economic Association

1886 Francis A. Walker
1893 Charles F. Dunbar
1894 John B. Clark
1896 Henry C. Adams
1898 Arthur T. Hadley
1900 Richard T. Ely
1902 Edwin R. A. Seligman
1904 Frank W. Taussig
1906 Jeremiah W. Jenks
1908 Simon N. Patten
1909 Davis R. Dewey
1910 Edmund J. James
1911 Henry W. Farnam
1912 Frank A. Fetter
1913 David Kinley
1914 John H. Gray
1915 Walter F. Willcox
1916 Thomas N. Carver
1917 John R. Commons
1918 Irving Fisher
1919 Henry B. Gardner
1920 Herbert J. Davenport
1921 Jacob H. Hollander
1922 Henry R. Seager
1923 Carl C. Plehn
1924 Wesley C. Mitchell
1925 Allyn A. Young
1926 Edwin W. Kemmerer
1927 Thomas S. Adams
1928 Fred M. Taylor
1929 Edwin F. Gay
1930 Matthew B. Hammond
1931 Ernest L. Bogart
1932 George E. Barnett
1933 William Z. Ripley
1934 Harry A. Millis
1935 John M. Clark
1936 Alvin S. Johnson
1937 Oliver M. W. Sprague
1938 Alvin H. Hansen
1939 Jacob Viner
1940 Frederick C. Mills
1941 Sumner H. Slichter
1942 Edwin G. Nourse
1943 Albert B. Wolfe
1944 Joseph S. Davis
1945 I. L. Sharfman
1946 Emanuel A. Goldenweiser
1947 Paul H. Douglas
1948 Joseph A. Schumpeter
1949 Howard S. Ellis
1950 Frank H. Knight
1951 John H. Williams
1953 Calvin B. Hoover
1954 Simon Kuznets
1955 John D. Black
1956 Edwin E. Witte
1957 Morris A. Copeland
1958 George W. Stocking
1959 Arthur F. Burns
1960 Theodore W. Schultz
1961 Paul A. Samuelson
1962 Edward S. Mason
1963 Gottfried Haberler
1964 George J. Stigler
1965 Joseph J. Spengler
1966 Fritz Machlup
1967 Milton Friedman
1968 Kenneth E. Boulding
1969 Wassily Leontief

1970 James Tobin
1971 John Kenneth Galbraith
1972 Kenneth J. Arrow
1974 Walter W. Heller
1975 Robert Aaron Gordon
1976 Prof. Rendigs Fels
     (Secretary-Treasurer)
1977 C. Elton Hinshaw
     (Secretary)

American Geographical Society

1852 George Bancroft
1854 Francis L. Hawks
1861 Henry Grinnell
1864 Charles P. Daly
1900 Seth Low
1903 Robert E. Peary
1907 Archer M. Huntington
1916 John Greenough
1925 John H. Finley
1934 Roland L. Redmond
1947 Richard U. Light
1957 Walter A. Wood
1967 Serge A. Korff
1971 Serge A. Korff
1974 Richard H. Nolte
1977 Sarah K. Meyers
     (Director, to 1980)
1985 Mary Lynne Bird
     (Director)

American Geophysical Union

1920 William Bowie
1922 Louis A. Bauer
1924 Harry F. Reid
1926 H. S. Washington
1929 William Bowie
1932 W. J. Humphreys
1935 N. H. Heck
1938 Richard M. Field
1941 W. C. Lowdermilk
1944 Leason H. Asams
1947 O. E. Meinzer
1948 W. H. Bucher
1953 James B. Macelwane
1956 Maurice Ewing
1959 L. V. Berkner
1961 Thomas F. Malone
1964 George P. Woollard
1966 William C. Ackerman
1968 Helmut E. Landsberg
1970 Homer E. Newell
1971 Waldo E. Smith
     (Executive Director)
1972 A. F. Spilhaus (Executive
     Director)

American Heart Association

1924 Lewis A. Connor
1925 Joseph Sailor
1927 James B. Herrick
1929 William H. Robey
1931 Robert H. Halsey
1933 Stewart R. Roberts
1935 John Wyckoff
1937 William J. Kerr
1939 William D. Stroud
1941 Paul D. White

1943 Roy W. Scott
1946 Howard West
1947 Arlie R. Barnes
1948 Tinsley R. Harrison
1949 H. M. Marvin
1950 Howard B. Sprague
1951 Louis N. Katz
1952 Irving S. Wright
1953 Robert L. King
1954 E. Cowles Andrus
1955 Irvine H. Page
1956 Edgar V. Allen
1957 Robert W. Wilkins
1958 Francis L. Chamberlain
1959 A. Carlton Ernestene
1960 Oglesby Paul
1961 J. Scott Butterworth
1962 James W. Warren
1963 John J. Sampson
1964 Carleton B. Chapman
1965 Helen B. Taussig
1966 Lewis E. January
1967 Jesse E. Edwards
1968 Walter B. Frommeyer, Jr.
1969 W. Proctor Harvey
1971 William Glenn
1972 J. Willis Hurst
1973 James M. Hundley
     (Executive Director)
1974 William W. Moore
     (Executive Vice President)
1981 Dudley H. Hafner
     (Executive Vice President)

American Historical Association

1884 Andrew D. White
1885 George Bancroft
1886 Justin Winsor
1887 William F. Poole
1888 Charles K. Adams
1889 John Jay
1890 William W. Henry
1891 James B. Angell
1893 Henry Adams
1895 George F. Hoar
1896 Richard S. Storrs
1897 James Schouler
1898 George P. Fisher
1899 James F. Rhodes
1900 Edward Eggleston
1901 Charles Francis Adam
1902 Alfred T. Mahan
1903 Henry C. Lea
1904 Goldwin Smith
1905 John B. McMaster
1906 Simeon E. Baldwin
1907 J. Franklin Jameson
1908 George B. Adams
1909 Albert B. Hart
1910 Frederick J. Turner
1911 William M. Sloane
1912 Theodore Roosevelt
1913 William A. Dunning
1914 Andrew C. McLaughlin
1915 H. Morse Stephens
1916 George L. Burr
1917 Worthington C. Ford
1918 William R. Thayer
1920 Edward Channing
1922 Charles H. Haskins
1923 Edward P. Cheyney
1924 Woodrow Wilson
1925 Charles M. Andrews
1926 Dana C. Munro
1927 Henry O. Taylor
1928 James H. Breasted
1929 James H. Robinson

1930 Evarts B. Greene
1931 Carl L. Becker
1932 Herbert E. Bolton
1933 Charles A. Beard
1934 William E. Dodd
1936 Charles McIlwain
1937 Guy S. Ford
1938 Laurence M. Larson
1938 Frederic L. Paxson
1939 William S. Ferguson
1940 Max Farrand
1941 James W. Thompson
1942 Arthur M. Schlesinger,
     Sr.
1943 Nellie Neilson
1944 William L. Westermann
1945 Carlton J. H. Hayes
1946 Sidney B. Fay
1947 Thomas J. Wertenbaker
1948 Kenneth S. Latourette
1949 Conyers Read
1950 Samuel Eliot Morison
1951 Robert L. Schuyler
1952 James G. Randall
1953 Louis Gottschalk
1954 Merle Curti
1955 Lynn Thorndike
1956 Dexter Perkins
1957 William Langer
1958 Walter P. Webb
1959 Allan Nevins
1960 Bernadotte E. Schmitt
1961 Samuel F. Bemis
1962 Carl Bridenbaugh
1963 Crane Brinton
1964 Julian P. Boyd
1965 Frederic C. Lane
1966 Roy F. Nichols
1967 Hajo Holborn
1968 John K. Fairbank
1969 C. Vann Woodward
1970 Robert R. Palmer
1971 David M. Potter
1971 Joseph R. Strayer
     (Acting)
1972 Thomas G. Cochran

Executive Directors

1973 Paul L. Ward
1975 Mack Thompson
1982 Samuel R. Gammon

American Institute of Aeronautics and Astronautics

1963 William H. Pickering
1964 Courtland D. Perkins
1965 Richard E. Horner
1966 Raymond L. Bisplinghoff
1967 Harold T. Luskin
1968 Floyd L. Thompson
1969 Robert C. Seamans, Jr.
1970 Ronald Smelt
1971 Martin Goland
1972 James J. Hartford
     (Executive Secretary, to
     1979)
1980 James J. Hartford
     (Executive Director)

American Institute of Architects

1857 Richard Upjohn

1877 Thomas U. Walter
1888 Richard M. Hunt
1892 Edward H. Kendall
1894 Daniel H. Burnham
1896 George B. Post
1899 Henry Van Brunt
1900 Robert S. Peabody
1902 Charles F. McKim
1904 William S. Eames
1906 Frank Miles Day
1908 Cass Gilbert
1910 Irving K. Pond
1912 Walter Cook
1913 R. Clipston Sturgis
1915 John L. Mauran
1918 Thomas R. Kimball
1920 Henry H. Kendall
1922 William B. Faville
1924 Dan Everett Waid
1926 Milton B. Medary
1928 C. Herrick Hammond
1930 Robert D. Kohn
1932 Ernest J. Russell
1935 Stephen F. Voorhees
1937 Charles D. Maginnis
1939 Edwin Bergstrom
1941 R. H. Shreve
1943 Raymond J. Ashton
1945 James R. Edmunds, Jr.
1947 Douglas W. Orr
1949 Ralph Walker
1951 Glenn Stanton
1953 Clair W. Ditchy
1955 George B. Cummings
1956 Leon Chatelain, Jr.
1958 John N. Richards
1960 Philip Will, Jr.
1962 Henry L. Wright
1963 J. Roy Carroll, Jr.
1964 Arthur G. Odell, Jr.
1965 Morris Ketchum, Jr.
1966 Charles M. Nes, Jr.
1967 Robert L. Durham
1968 George E Kassabaum
1969 Rex W. Allen
1970 Robert F. Hastings
1971 Max O. Urbahn
1972 William L. Slayton
     (Executive Vice President)
1978 David Olan Meeker, Jr.
     (Executive Vice President)
1979 Jeanne Butler Hodges
1980 David Olan Meeker, Jr.
     (Executive Vice President)
1985 Louis L. Marines
     (Executive Vice President)
1986 Louis L. Marines (Chief
     Executive Officer)

American Institute of Certified Public Accountants

1949 J. Harold Stewart
1950 T. Coleman Andrews
1951 J. William Hope
1952 Jay A. Phillips
1953 Arthur B. Foye
1954 Maurice H. Stans
1955 John H. Zebley, Jr.
1956 Marquis G. Eaton
1957 Alvin R. Jennings
1958 Louis H. Penney
1959 J. S. Seidman
1960 Louis H. Pilie
1961 John W. Queenan
1962 Robert E. Witschey
1963 Clifford V. Heimbucher

1964 Thomas D. Flynn
1965 Robert M. Trueblood
1966 Hilliard R. Giffen
1967 Marvin L. Stone
1968 Ralph E. Kent
1969 Louis M. Kessler
1970 Marshall S. Armstrong
1971 Walter T. Oliphant
1972 Leonard M. Savoie
     (Executive Vice President)
1974 Wallace E. Olson
     (Executive Vice President)
1981 Philip B. Chenok

American Institute of Chemists

1923 Horace G. Byers
1924 M. L. Crossley
1926 Treat B. Johnson
1928 Frederick E. Breithut
1932 Henry G. Knight
1934 M. L. Crossley
1936 Maximilian Toch
1938 Robert J. Moore
1940 Harry L. Fisher
1942 Gustav Egloff
1946 Foster D. Snell
1948 Lawrence Flett
1952 Lincoln T. Work
1954 Donald B. Keyes
1955 Ray P. Dinsmore
1956 John H. Nair
1957 Henry B. Hass
1958 Emil Ott
1959 Wayne E. Kuhn
1960 MIlton Harris
1961 Johan Bjorksten
1962 C. Harold Fisher
1963 W. George Parks
1964 W. E. Hanford
1965 Lloyd H. Reyerson
1966 John L. Hickson
1967 Emmett B. Carmichael
1969 Emerson Venable
1971 David W. Young

Executive Directors

1972 Paul B. Slawter, Jr.
1974 John L. Hickson
1975 Paul Pierpoint
1977 David A. H. Roethel (to
     1987)

American Institute of Mining, Metallurgical, and Petroleum Engineers

1932 Scott Turner
1941 John R. Suman
1943 Champion H. Mathewson
1947 Clyde Williams
1950 Donald H. McLaughlin
1951 Willis M. Peirce
1952 Michael L. Haider
1953 Andrew Fletcher
1954 Leo F. Reinartz
1956 Carl E. Reistle, Jr.
1957 Grover J. Holt
1958 Augustus B. Kinzel
1959 Howard C. Pyle
1961 Ronald R. McNaughton
1962 Lloyd E. Elkins
1964 Karl L. Fetters
1965 Thomas C. Frick

1966 William B. Stephenson
1967 Walter R. Hibbard, Jr.
1968 John R. McMillan
1969 James Boyd
1970 John C. Kennear, Jr.
1971 John S. Bell
1972 John S. Bell
1973 Dennis L. McElroy

Executive Directors

1974 Joe B. Alford
1983 Edward A. Buckley
1984 Robert H. Marcrum

American Iron and Steel Institute

1908 Elbert H. Gary
1927 Charles M. Schwab
1932 Robert P. Lamont
1934 Eugene G. Grace
1937 Tom M. Girdler
1939 E. T. Weir
1940 Walter S. Tower
1955 Benjamin F. Fairless
1962 Max D. Howell
1963 John P. Roche
1965 John P. Roche
1976 Frederick C. Langenberg
1980 Robert B. Peabody

American Judicature Society

1914 Harry Olson (Chairman)
1929 Charles Evans Hughes
1930 Newton D. Baker
1938 Frank E. Atwood
1938 Arthur T. Vanderbilt
1940 David A. Simmons
1944 Merrill E. Otis
1944 George E. Brand
1953 Albert J. Harno
1956 William J. Jameson
1958 Albert E. Jenner, Jr.
1960 Cecil E. Burney
1962 Sterry R. Waterman
1964 Henry L. Woolfenden
1966 Herbert Brownell
1968 Gerald C. Snyder
1970 Robert H. Hall
1971 Glenn R. Winters
     (Executive Director, to
     1974)
1977 George H. Williams
     (Executive Vice President)

American Law Institute

1923 George W. Wickersham
1935 George Wharton Pepper
1947 Harrison Tweed
1961 Norris Darrell
1963 Herbert Wechsler
     (Director, to 1975)
1976 Norris Darrell
1977 Herbert Wechsler
     (Director, to 1983)
1985 Paul A. Wolkin
     (Executive Vice President)

American Legion

National Commanders

1919 Franklin D'Olier
1920 Frederick W. Galbraith,
     Jr.
1921 John G. Emery
1921 Hanford MacNider
1922 Alvin M. Owsley
1923 John R. Quinn
1924 James A. Drain
1925 John R. McQuigg
1926 Howard P. Savage
1927 Edward P. Spafford
1928 Paul V. McNutt
1929 O. L. Bodenhamer
1930 Ralph T. O'Neill
1931 Henry L. Stevens, Jr.
1932 Louis A. Johnson
1933 Edward A. Hayes
1934 Frank N. Belgrano
1935 Ray Murphy
1936 Harry W. Colmery
1937 Daniel J. Doherty
1938 Stephen F. Chadwick
1939 Raymond J. Kelly
1940 Milo J. Warner
1941 Lynn U. Stambaugh
1942 Roane Waring
1943 Warren H. Atherton
1944 Edward N. Scheiberling
1945 John Stelle
1946 Paul H. Griffith
1947 James F. O'Neil
1948 S. Perry Brown
1949 George N. Craig
1950 Erle Cocke, Jr.
1951 Donald R. Wilson
1952 Lewis K. Gough
1953 Arthur J. Connell
1954 Seaborn P. Collins
1955 J. Addington Wagner
1956 W. C. Daniel
1957 John S. Gleason, Jr.
1958 Preston J. Moore
1959 Martin M. McKneally
1960 William R. Burke
1961 Charles L. Bacon
1962 James E. Powers
1963 Daniel F. Foley
1964 Donald E. Johnson
1965 L. Eldon James
1966 John E. Davis
1967 William E. Galbraith
1968 William C. Doyle
1969 J. Milton Patrick
1970 Alfred P. Chamie
1971 John H. Geiger
1973 William F. Hauck
     (National Adjutant)
1974 James M. Wagonseller
1975 William F. Hauck
     (National Adjutant)
1978 Frank C. Momsen
     (National Adjutant)
1983 Robert W. Spangole
     (National Adjutant)

American Library Association

1876 Justin Winsor
1885 William F. Poole
1887 Charles A. Cutter
1889 Frederick M. Crunden
1890 Melvil Dewey
1891 Samuel S. Green

1891	William I. Fletcher
1892	Melvil Dewey
1893	Josephus N. Larned
1894	Henry M. Utley
1895	John C. Dana
1896	William H. Brett
1897	Justin Winsor
1898	Herbert Putnam
1898	William C. Lane
1899	Reuben G. Thwaites
1900	Henry J. Carr
1901	John S. Billings
1902	James K. Hosmer
1903	Herbert Putnam
1904	Ernest C. Richardson
1905	Frank P. Hill
1906	Clement W. Andrews
1907	Arthur E. Bostwick
1908	Charles H. Gould
1909	Nathaniel D. C. Hodges
1910	James I. Wyer
1911	Theresa West Elmendorf
1912	Henry E. Legler
1913	Edwin H. Anderson
1914	Hiller C. Wellman
1915	Mary W. Plummer
1916	Walter L. Brown
1917	Thomas L. Montgomery
1918	William W. Bishop
1919	Chalmers Hadley
1920	Alice S. Tyler
1921	Azariah S. Root
1922	George B. Utley
1923	Judson T. Jennings
1924	Herman H. B. Meyer
1925	Charles F. D. Belder
1926	George H. Locke
1927	Carl B. Roden
1928	Linda A. Eastman
1929	Andrew Keogh
1930	Adam Strohm
1931	Josephine A. Rathbone
1932	Harry M. Lydenberg
1933	Gratia A. Countryman
1934	Charles H. Compton
1935	Louis R. Wilson
1936	Malcolm G. Wyer
1937	Harrison W. Craver
1938	Milton J. Ferguson
1939	Ralph Munn
1940	Essae M. Culver
1941	Charles H. Brown
1942	Keyes D. Metcalf
1943	Althea H. Warren
1944	Carl Vitz
1945	Ralph A. Ulveling
1946	Mary U. Rothrock
1947	Paul N. Rice
1948	Errett W. McDiarmid
1949	Milton E. Lord
1950	Clarence R. Graham
1951	Loleta Dawson Fyan
1952	Robert B. Downs
1953	Flora B. Ludington
1954	Lewis Q. Mumford
1955	John S. Richards
1956	Ralph R. Shaw
1957	Lucile M. Morsch
1958	Emerson Greenaway
1959	Benjamin E. Powell
1960	Frances L. Spain
1961	Florrinell F. Morton
1962	James E. Bryan
1963	Frederick H. Wagman
1964	Edwin Castagna
1965	Robert Vosper
1966	Mary V. Gaver
1967	Foster E. Mohrhardt
1968	Roger McDonough
1969	William S. Dix

Executive Directors

1972	David H. Clift
1973	Robert Wedgeworth
1986	Thomas J. Galvin

American Management Association

1923	Sam A. Lewisohn
1926	Frank L. Sweetser
1928	Cyrus S. Ching
1930	William J. Graham
1934	Malcolm C. Rorty
1936	Alvin E. Dodd
1948	Lawrence A. Appley
1968	Alexander B. Trowbridge
1970	Don G. Mitchell
1971	Alexander B. Trowbridge (to 1972)
1974	James L. Hayes (to 1981)
1983	Dr. Thomas R. Horton

American Marketing Association

1936	Frank R. Coutant
1938	Fred E. Clark
1939	N. H. Engle
1940	Donald R. G. Cowan
1941	Howard T. Hovde
1942	Vergil D. Reed
1943	Albert Haring
1944	Howard W. Green
1945	Donald M. Hobart
1946	Lyman Hill
1947	Ross M. Cunningham
1948	Wroe Alderson
1949	Harvey W. Huegy
1950	Everett P. Smith
1951	George H. Brown
1952	Gordon A. Hughes
1953	Neil H. Borden
1954	Thomas G. MacGowan
1955	Ira D. Anderson
1956	Charles W. Smith
1957	D. Maynard Phelps
1958	Wendell R. Smith
1959	Reavis Cox
1960	William F. O'Dell
1961	Albert W. Frey
1962	Donald R. Longman
1963	William R. Davidson
1964	Edwin H. Sonnecken
1965	Schuyler F. Otteson
1966	Robert J. Lavidge
1967	Robert J. Holloway
1968	Victor P. Buell
1969	Robert Ferber
1970	Elmer Lotshaw
1971	Earl G. Johnson (Executive Director)
1972	Wayne A. Lemburg (Executive Vice President)

American Mathematical Society

1889	John H. Van Amringe
1891	Emory McClintock
1895	G. W. Hill
1897	Simon Newcomb
1899	Robert S. Woodward
1901	Eliakim H. Moore
1903	Thomas S. Fiske
1905	William F. Osgood
1907	Henry S. White
1909	Maxime Bocher
1911	Henry B. Fine
1913	Edward B. Van Vleck
1915	Ernest W. Brown
1917	Leonard E. Dickson
1919	Frank Morley
1921	Gilbert A. Bliss
1923	Oswald Veblen
1925	George D. Birkhoff
1927	Virgil Snyder
1929	Earle R. Hedrick
1931	Luther P. Eisenhart
1933	Arthur B. Coble
1935	Solomon Lefschetz
1937	Robert L. Moore
1939	Griffith C. Evans
1941	Marston Morse
1943	Marshall H. Stone
1945	Theophil H. Hildebrandt
1947	Einar Hille
1949	Joseph L. Walsh
1951	John von Neumann
1953	Gordon T. Whyburn
1955	Raymond L. Wilder
1957	Richard D. Brauer
1959	Edward J. McShane
1961	Deane Montgomery
1963	Joseph L. Doob
1965	A. Adrian Albert
1967	Charles B. Morrey, Jr.
1969	Oscar Zariski
1971	Nathan Jacobson
1972	Nathan Jacobson
1973	Gordon L. Walker (Executive Director)
1978	Dr. William J. LeVeque (Executive Director)

American Medical Association

1847	Nathaniel Chapman
1848	Alexander H. Stevens
1849	John C. Warren
1850	Reuben D. Mussey
1851	James Moultrie
1852	Beverley R. Wellford
1853	Jonathan Knight
1854	Charles A. Pope
1855	George B. Wood
1856	Zina Pitcher
1857	Paul F. Eve
1858	Harve Lindsly
1859	Henry Miller
1860	Eli Ives
1863	Alden March
1864	Nathan S. Davis
1866	D. Humphreys Storer
1867	Henry F. Askew
1868	Samuel D. Gross
1869	William O. Baldwin
1870	George Mendenhall
1871	Alfred Stille
1872	David W. Yandell
1873	Thomas M. Logan
1874	Joseph M. Toner
1875	William K. Bowling
1876	J. Marion Sims
1877	Henry I. Bowditch
1878	Tobias G. Richardson
1879	Theophilus Parvin
1880	Lewis A. Sayre
1881	John T. Hodgen
1882	Joseph J. Woodward
1883	John L. Atlee
1884	Austin Flint, Sr.
1885	Henry F. Campbell
1886	William Brodie
1887	Elisha H. Gregory
1888	Alexander Y. P. Garnett
1889	William W. Dawson
1890	Edward M. Moore
1891	William T. Briggs
1892	Henry O. Marcy
1893	Hunter McGuire
1894	James F. Hibberd
1895	Donald MacLean
1896	R. Beverly Cole
1897	Nicholas Senn
1898	George M. Sternberg
1899	Joseph M. Mathews
1900	William W. Keen
1901	Charles A. L. Reed
1902	John W. Wyeth
1903	Frank Billings
1904	John H. Musser
1905	Lewis S. McMurty
1906	William J. Mayo
1907	Joseph D. Bryant
1908	Herbert L. Burrell
1909	William C. Gorgas
1910	William H. Welch
1911	John B. Murphy
1912	Abraham Jacobi
1913	John A. Witherspoon
1914	Victor C. Vaughan
1915	William L. Rodman
1916	Rupert Blue
1917	Charles H. Mayo
1918	Arthur D. Bevan
1919	Alexander Lambert
1920	William C. Braisted
1921	Hubert Work
1922	George E. Schweinitz
1923	Ray L. Wilbur
1924	William A. Pusey
1925	William D. Haggard
1926	Wendell C. Phillips
1927	Jabez N. Jackson
1928	William S. Thayer
1929	Malcolm L. Harris
1930	William G. Morgan
1931	E. Starr Judd
1932	Edward H. Cary
1933	Dean D. Lewis
1934	Walter L. Bierring
1935	James S. McLester
1936	James T. Mason
1936	Charles G. Heyd
1937	John H. J. Upham
1938	Irvin W. Abell
1939	Rock Sleyster
1940	Nathan B. Van Etten
1941	Frank H. Lahey
1942	Fred W. Rankin
1943	James E. Paullin
1944	Herman L. Kretschmer
1945	Roger I. Lee
1946	Harrison H. Shoulders
1947	Edward L. Bortz
1948	R. L. Sensenich
1949	Ernest E. Irons
1950	Elmer L. Henderson
1951	John W. Cline
1952	Louis H. Bauer
1953	Edward J. McCormick
1954	Walter B. Martin
1955	Elmer Hess
1956	Dwight H. Murray
1957	David B. Allman
1958	Gunnar Gundersen
1959	Louis M. Orr
1960	E. Vincent Askey
1961	Leonard W. Larson
1962	George M. Fister
1963	Edward R. Annis
1964	Norman A. Welch

1964 Donovan F. Wood
1965 James Z. Appel
1966 Charles L. Hudson
1967 Milford O. Rouse
1968 Dwight L. Wilbur
1969 Gerald D. Dorman
1970 Walter C. Bornemeier
1971 Wesley W. Hall
1972 C. A. Hoffman
1973 Ernest B. Howard
   (Executive Vice President)
1975 James H. Sammons
   (Executive Vice President)
1976 Susan Crawford
   (Director)
1977 James H. Sammons
   (Executive Vice President)

American National Red Cross

1881 Clara Barton
1904 William K. Van Reypen
1906 Robert M. O'Reilly
1906 George W. Davis
1915 William Howard Taft
1919 Livingston Farrand
1921 John Barton Payne
1935 Cary T. Grayson
1938 Norman H. Davis
1944 Basil O'Connor
1949 George C. Marshall
1950 E. Roland Harriman
1954 Ellsworth Bunker
1957 Alfred M. Gruenther
1964 James F. Collins
1970 George M. Elsey
1972 George M. Elsey (to 1980)
1984 Richard F. Schubert

American Neurological Association

1880 Frank T. Miles
1881 Roberts Bartholow
1882 William A. Hammond
1883 Robert T. Edes
1884 Isaac Ott
1885 Burt G. Wilder
1886 Charles K. Mills
1887 Landon C. Gray
1888 James W. Putnam
1889 Edouard C. Seguin
1890 Edward C. Spitzka
1891 Wharton Sinkler
1892 Charles L. Dana
1893 Henry M. Lyman
1894 Bernard Sachs
1895 Philip C. Knapp
1896 Francis X. Dercum
1897 Moses A. Starr
1898 Graeme M. Hammond
1899 James H. Lloyd
1900 Edward D. Fisher
1901 George L. Walton
1902 Joseph Collins
1903 James W. Putnam
1904 Frank R. Fry
1905 William G. Spiller
1906 Henry R. Stedman
1907 Hugh T. Patrick
1908 Charles W. Burr
1909 S. Weir Mitchell
1910 Morton Prince
1911 Henry M. Thomas

1912 William N. Bullard
1913 Pearce Bailey
1914 Henry Hun
1915 George W. Jacoby
1916 Lewellys F. Barker
1917 Edward W. Taylor
1918 Theodore H. Weisenburg
1919 James McBride
1920 J. Ramsey Hunt
1921 Sidney I. Schwab
1922 Adolf Meyer
1923 Harvey Cushing
1924 Charles K. Mills
1925 Frederick Peterson
1926 Frederick Tilney
1927 Peter Bassoe
1928 Charles L. Dana
1929 Charles H. Frazier
1930 Smith E. Jelliffe
1931 James B. Ayer
1932 Bernard Sachs
1933 Daniel J. McCarthy
1934 Israel Strauss
1936 Albert M. Barrett
1937 Henry H. Donaldson
1938 Charles A. Elsberg
1939 Williams B. Cadwalader
1940 Foster Kennedy
1941 H. Douglas Singer
1941 Harry Solomon
1942 Lewis J. Pollock
1943 Ernest Sachs
1944 Edwin G. Zabriskie
1945 Walter F. Schaller
1947 Henry A. Riley
1948 George Wilson
1949 Stanley Cobb
1950 Henry W. Woltman
1952 S. Bernard Wortis
1953 Hans H. F. Reese
1954 Roland P. Mackay
1955 Percival Bailey
1956 Johannes M. Nielsen
1957 H. Houston Merritt
1958 Israel S. Wechsler
1959 Bernard J. Alpers
1960 Dered E. Denny-Brown
1961 Harold G. Wolff
1962 James L. O'Leary
1963 Charles D. Aring
1964 Richard B. Richter
1965 Russell N. DeJong
1966 A. Earl Walker
1967 Raymond D. Adams
1968 Adolph L. Sahs
1969 Augustus S. Rose
1970 Melvin D. Yahr
1971 A. B. Baker
1972 Paul C. Busy
1973 Samuel A. Trufant
   (Secretary-Treasurer)
1976 Peritz Scheinberg
   (Secretary-Treasurer)
1979 James F. Toole
   (Secretary-Treasurer)
1984 Jan W. Kolehmainen
   (Executive Director)

American Nuclear Society

1956 C. Rogers McCullough
1957 Leland J. Haworth
1958 Chauncey Starr
1959 Alvin M. Weinberg
1960 Miles C. Leverett
1961 William B. Lewis
1962 Manson Benedict
1963 Clarke Williams
1964 William E. Shoupp

1965 Norman Hilberry
1966 Sidney Siegel
1967 Raemer Schreiber
1968 Karl P. Cohen
1969 Louis H. Roddis, Jr.
1970 N. Joseph Palladino
1971 John W. Landis
1972 James R. Lilienthal
1973 John W. Simpson
1974 J. Ernest Wilkins, Jr.
1975 Melvin J. Feldman
1976 Vincent S. Boyer
1977 Joseph R. Dietrich
1978 William R. Kimel
1979 Edward J. Hennelly
1980 Harry Lawroski
1981 Corwin L. Rickard
1982 L. Manning Muntzing
1983 Octave J. DuTemple
   (Executive Director)

American Ornithologists' Union

1883 Joel A. Allen
1890 Daniel G. Elliot
1892 Elliott Coues
1895 William Brewster
1898 Robert Ridgway
1900 C. Hart Merriam
1903 Charles B. Cory
1905 Charles F. Batchelder
1908 Edward W. Nelson
1911 Frank M. Chapman
1914 Albert K. Fisher
1917 John H. Sage
1920 Witmer Stone
1923 Jonathan Dwight
1926 Alexander Wetmore
1929 Joseph Grinnell
1932 James H. Fleming
1935 Arthur C. Bent
1937 Herbert Friedmann
1939 James P. Chapin
1942 James L. Peters
1945 Hoyes Lloyd
1948 Robert C. Murphy
1950 Josselyn Van Tyne
1953 Alden H. Miller
1956 Ernst Mayr
1959 George H. Lowery, Jr.
1962 Austin L. Rand
1964 Dean Amadon
1966 Harold F. Mayfield
1968 John W. Aldrich
1971 Robert W. Storer

Secretaries

1972 Richard C. Banks
1974 George E. Watson
1979 Kendall W. Corbin
1982 Dennis M. Power
1985 Stephen M. Russell

American Peace Society

1837 William Ladd
1841 Samuel E. Coues
1846 Theodore Frelinghuysen
1847 Anson G. Phelps
1848 William Jay
1859 Francis Wayland
1861 Howard Malcolm
1873 Edward S. Tobey
1891 Robert Treat Paine
1911 Theodore E. Burton

1916 George W. Kirchwey
1917 James L. Slayden
1920 Andrew J. Montague
1923 Theodore E. Burton
1929 William Fortune
1930 John J. Esch
1938 Mark L. Bristol
1940 Philip M. Brown
1946 Amos J. Peaslee
1949 Ulysses S. Grant, III
1959 Charles W. Lowry
1962 Paul M. A. Linebarger
1964 Charles J. Zinn
1966 Donald Armstrong
1967 Claude E. Hawley
1969 Evron M. Kirkpatrick

American Petroleum Institute

1919 T. A. O'Donnell
1925 J. Edgar Pew
1926 William S. Farish
1927 Edward W. Clark
1929 Edwin B. Reeser
1932 Amos L. Beaty
1933 Charles B. Ames
1934 Axtell J. Byles
1942 William R. Boyd, Jr.
1950 Frank M. Porter
1963 Frank N. Ikard
1965 Frank M. Porter
1966 Frank N. Ikard
1979 Charles J. DiBona

American Pharmaceutical Association

1936 George D. Beal
1937 E. N. Gathercoal
1938 J. Leon Lascoff
1939 Andrew G. DuMez
1940 Charles H. Evans
1941 B. V. Christensen
1942 Roy B. Cook
1943 Ivor Griffith
1944 George A. Moulton
1946 Earl R. Serles
1947 Sylvester H. Dretzka
1948 Ernest Little
1949 Glenn L. Jenkins
1950 Henry H. Gregg
1951 Don E. Francke
1952 R. Q. Richards
1953 F. Royce Franzoni
1954 Newell W. Stewart
1955 John B. Heinz
1956 John A. McCartney
1957 Joseph B. Burt
1958 Louis J. Fischl
1959 Howard C. Newton
1960 Ronald V. Robertson
1961 J. Warren Landsdowne
1962 George F. Archambault
1963 Robert J. Gillespie
1964 J. Curtis Nottingham
1965 Grover C. Bowles
1966 Linwood F. Tice
1967 George W. Grider
1968 Max W. Eggleston
1969 William B. Hennessey
1970 William R. Whitten
1971 Lloyd M. Parks
1972 William S. Apple
1984 John F. Schlegal

American Philological Association

1869 William D. Whitney
1870 Howard Crosby
1871 William W. Goodwin
1872 Asahel C. Kendrick
1873 Francis A. March
1874 James H. Trumbull
1875 Albert Harkness
1876 Samuel S. Haldeman
1877 Basil L. Gildersleeve
1878 Jotham B. Sewall
1879 Crawford H. Toy
1880 Lewis R. Packard
1881 Frederic D. Allen
1882 Milton W. Humphreys
1883 Martin L. D'Ooge
1884 William W. Goodwin
1885 Tracy Peck
1886 Augustus C. Merriam
1887 Isaac H. Hall
1888 Thomas D. Seymour
1889 Charles R. Lanman
1890 Julius Sachs
1891 Samuel Hart
1892 William G. Hale
1893 James M. Garnett
1894 John H. Wright
1895 Francis A. March
1896 Bernadotte Perrin
1897 Minton Warren
1898 Clement L. Smith
1899 Abby Leach
1900 Samuel B. Platner
1901 Andrew F. West
1902 Charles F. Smith
1903 George Hempl
1904 Herbert W. Smyth
1905 Elmer T. Merrill
1906 Francis W. Kelsey
1907 Charles E. Bennett
1908 Basil L. Gildersleeve
1909 Paul Shorey
1910 John C. Rolfe
1911 Thomas D. Goodell
1912 Harold N. Fowler
1913 Edward Capps
1914 Edward P. Morris
1915 Carl D. Buck
1916 Frank G. Moore
1917 Frank F. Abbott
1918 John A. Scott
1919 Clifford H. Moore
1920 Walton B. McDaniel
1921 Francis G. Allinson
1922 Edward K. Rand
1923 Samuel E. Bassett
1926 Frank C. Babbitt
1927 Clarence P. Bill
1928 Tenney Frank
1929 Charles B. Gulick
1930 Henry W. Prescott
1931 Ivan M. Linforth
1932 Campbell Bonner
1933 Elizabeth H. Haight
1934 Berthold L. Ullman
1935 George L. Hendrickson
1936 Henry A. Sanders
1937 William A. Oldfather
1938 Austin M. Harmon
1939 Arthur S. Pease
1940 George M. Calhoun
1941 Lily R. Taylor
1942 Marbury B. Ogle
1943 John G. Winter
1944 George D. Hadzsits
1945 Levi A. Post
1946 Norman W. DeWitt
1947 Cornelia C. Coulter

1948 William H. Alexander
1949 Lucius R. Shero
1950 William C. Greene
1951 Jakob A. O. Larsen
1952 Benjamin D. Meritt
1954 Harry Caplan
1955 George E. Duckworth
1956 Charles B. Welles
1957 Gertrude E. Smith
1960 Robert S. Rogers
1961 Inez S. Ryberg
1962 Howard Comfort
1963 Gerald F. Else
1964 Dorothy M. Robathan
1965 John L. Heller
1966 Phillip H. DeLacy
1967 Frederick M. Combellack
1968 Herbert Bloch
1970 Malcolm F. McGregor
1971 Edward T. Salmon
1972 Agnes K. L. Michels

Secretary-Treasurers

1973 John J. Bateman
1975 Robert W. Carrubba
1978 Harold D. Evjen
1980 Roger S. Bagnall

American Philosophical Society

1769 Benjamin Franklin
1791 David Rittenhouse
1797 Thomas Jefferson
1815 Caspar Wistar
1819 Robert Patterson
1825 William Tilghman
1828 Peter S. Du Ponceau
1845 Robert M. Patterson
1846 Nathaniel Chapman
1849 Robert M. Patterson
1853 Franklin Bache
1855 Alexander D. Bache
1857 John K. Kane
1859 George B. Wood
1880 Frederick Fraley
1902 Isaac J. Wistar
1903 Edgar F. Smith
1908 William W. Keen
1918 William B. Scott
1925 Charles D. Walcott
1927 Francis X. Dercum
1931 Henry N. Russell
1932 Roland S. Morris
1942 Edwin G. Conklin
1945 Thomas S. Gates
1948 Edwin G. Conklin
1952 Owen J. Roberts
1956 William J. Robbins
1959 Henry A. Moe
1970 Leonard Carmichael
1972 George W. Corner
     (Executive Director)
1978 Whitfield J. Bell, Jr.
     (Executive Officer)
1985 Herman H. Goldstine
     (Executive Officer)

American Physical Society

1899 Henry A. Rowland
1901 Albert A. Michelson
1903 Arthur G. Webster
1905 Carl Barus

1907 Edward L. Nichols
1909 Henry Crew
1911 William F. Magie
1913 B. O. Pierce
1914 Ernest Merritt
1916 Robert A. Millikan
1918 Henry A. Bumstead
1919 Joseph S. Ames
1921 Theodore Lyman
1923 Charles E. Mendenhall
1925 Dayton C. Miller
1927 Karl T. Compton
1929 Henry G. Gale
1933 Paul D. Foote
1934 Arthur H. Compton
1935 Robert W. Wood
1936 Floyd K. Richtmyer
1937 Harrison M. Randall
1938 Lyman J. Briggs
1939 John T. Tate
1940 John Zeleny
1941 George B. Pegram
1941 George W. Stewart
1942 Percy W. Bridgman
1943 Albert W. Hull
1944 Arthur J. Dempster
1945 Harvey Fletcher
1946 Edward U. Condon
1947 Lee A. DuBridge
1948 J. Robert Oppenheimer
1949 Francis W. Loomis
1950 Isidor I. Rabi
1951 Charles C. Lauritsen
1952 John H. Van Vleck
1953 Enrico Fermi
1954 Hans A. Bethe
1955 Raymond T. Birge
1956 Eugene P. Wigner
1957 Henry D. Smyth
1958 Jesse W. Beams
1959 George E. Uhlenbeck
1960 Victor F. Weisskopf
1961 Frederick Seitz
1962 William V. Houston
1963 John H. Williams
1964 Robert F. Bacher
1965 Felix Bloch
1966 John A. Wheeler
1967 Charles H. Townes
1968 John Bardeen
1969 Luis W. Alvarez
1970 Edward M. Purcell
1971 Robert Serber
1972 Philip M. Morse
1974 W. W. Havens, Jr.
     (Executive Secretary)

American Physiological Society

1888 Henry P. Bowditch
1889 S. Weir Mitchell
1891 Henry P. Bowditch
1896 Russell H. Chittenden
1905 William H. Howell
1911 Samuel J. Meltzer
1914 Walter B. Cannon
1917 Frederick S. Lee
1919 Warren P. Lombard
1923 Anton J. Carlson
1926 E. Joseph Erlanger
1930 Walter J. Meek
1933 Arno B. Luckhardt
1935 Clarence W. Greene
1936 Frank C. Mann
1938 Walter E. Garrey
1940 Andrew C. Ivy
1942 Phillip Bard
1946 Wallace O. Fenn

1948 Maurice B. Visscher
1949 Carl J. Wiggers
1950 David B. Dill
1951 Ralph W. Gerard
1952 Eugene M. Landis
1953 Edward F. Adolph
1954 Hiram E. Essex
1955 William F. Hamilton
1956 Alan C. Burton
1957 Louis N. Katz
1958 Hallowell Davis
1959 Robert F. Pitts
1960 Julius H. Comroe, Jr.
1961 Horace W. Davenport
1962 Hymen S. Mayerson
1963 Herman Rahn
1964 John R. Pappenheimer
1965 John M. Brookhart
1966 Robert E. Forster
1967 Robert W. Berliner
1968 Loren D. Carlson
1969 C. Ladd Prosser
1970 A. Clifford Barger
1971 John R. Brobeck

Executive Secretary-Treasurers

1972 Ray C. Daggs
1974 Orr E. Reynolds
1986 Martin Frank

American Political Science Association

1904 Frank J. Goodnow
1906 Albert Shaw
1907 Frederick N. Judson
1908 James Bryce
1909 A. Lawrence Lowell
1910 Woodrow Wilson
1911 Simeon E. Baldwin
1912 Albert B. Hart
1913 Westel W. Willoughby
1914 John B. Moore
1915 Ernest Freund
1916 Jesse Macy
1917 Munroe Smith
1918 Henry J. Ford
1920 Paul S. Reinsch
1921 Leo S. Rowe
1922 William A. Dunning
1923 Harry A. Garfield
1924 James W. Garner
1925 Charles E. Merriam
1926 Charles A. Beard
1927 William B. Munro
1928 Jesse S. Reeves
1929 John A. Fairlie
1930 Benjamin F. Shambaugh
1931 Edward S. Corwin
1932 W. F. Willoughby
1933 Isidor Loeb
1934 Walter J. Shepard
1935 Francis W. Coker
1936 Arthur N. Holcombe
1937 Thomas R. Powell
1938 Clarence A. Dykstra
1939 Charles G. Haines
1940 Robert C. Brooks
1941 Frederic A. Ogg
1942 William Anderson
1943 Robert E. Cushman
1944 Leonard D. White
1945 John M. Gaus
1946 Walter F. Dodd
1947 Arthur W. Macmahon
1948 Henry R. Spencer
1949 Quincy Wright
1950 James K. Pollock

1951	Peter H. Odegard
1952	Luther Gulick
1953	Pendleton Herring
1954	Ralph J. Bunche
1955	Charles McKinley
1956	Harold D. Lasswell
1957	E. E. Schattschneider
1958	V. O. Key, Jr.
1959	R. Taylor Cole
1960	Carl B. Swisher
1961	Emmette S. Redford
1962	Charles S. Hyneman
1963	Carl J. Friedrich
1964	C. Herman Pritchett
1965	David B. Truman
1966	Gabriel A. Almond
1967	Robert A. Dahl
1968	Merle Fainsod
1969	David Easton
1970	Karl W. Deutsch
1971	Robert E. Lane
1972	Evron M. Kirkpatrick (Executive Director)
1982	Thomas E. Mann (Executive Director)

American Psychiatric Association

1844	Samuel B. Woodward
1848	William McClay Awl
1851	Luther V. Bell
1855	Isaac Ray
1859	Andrew McFarland
1862	Thomas S. Kirkbride
1870	John S. Butler
1873	Charles H. Nichols
1879	Clement A. Walker
1882	John H. Callender
1883	John P. Gray
1884	Pliny Earle
1885	Orpheus Everts
1886	H. A. Buttolph
1887	Eugene Grissom
1888	John P. Chapin
1889	W. W. Godding
1890	H. P. Stearns (to 1891)
1892	J. B. Andrews
1893	John Curwen
1894	Edward Cowles
1895	Richard Dewey
1896	Theophilus O. Powell (to 1897)
1898	Henry M. Hurd
1899	Joseph G. Rogers
1900	Peter M. Wise
1901	Robert J. Preston
1902	G. Alder Blumer
1903	A. E. Macdonald (to 1904)
1905	C. B. Burr
1906	Charles G. Hill
1907	Charles P. Bancroft
1908	Arthur F. Kilbourne
1909	William F. Drewry
1910	Charles W. Pilgrim
1911	Hubert Work
1912	James T. Searcy
1913	Carlos F. MacDonald
1914	Samuel E. Smith
1915	Edward N. Brush
1916	Charles G. Wagner (to 1917)
1918	Elmer E. Southard
1919	Henry C. Eyman
1920	Owen Copp
1921	Albert M. Barrett
1922	Henry W. Mitchell
1923	Thomas W. Salmon

1924	William A. White
1925	C. Floyd Haviland
1926	George M. Kline
1927	Adolf Meyer
1928	Samuel T. Orton
1929	Earl D. Bond (to 1930)
1931	William L. Russell
1932	James V. May
1933	George H. Kirby
1934	C. Fred Williams
1935	Clarence O. Cheney
1936	C. Macfie Campbell
1937	Ross M. Chapman
1938	Richard H. Hutchings
1939	William C. Sandy
1940	George H. Stevenson
1941	James K. Hall
1942	Arthur H. Ruggles
1943	Edward A. Strecker
1944	Karl M. Bowman
1946	Samuel W. Hamilton
1947	Winfred Overholser
1948	William C. Menninger
1949	George S. Stevenson
1950	John C. Whitehorn
1951	Leo H. Bartemeier (to 1952)
1953	Kenneth E. Appel
1954	Arthur P. Noyes
1955	R. Finley Gayle, Jr.
1956	Francis J. Braceland
1957	Harry C. Solomon
1958	Francis J. Gerty
1959	William Malamud
1960	Robert H. Felix
1961	Walter E. Barton
1962	C. H. Hardin Branch
1963	Jack R. Ewalt
1964	Daniel Blain
1965	Howard P. Rome
1966	Harvey J. Tompkins
1967	Henry W. Brosin
1968	Lawrence C. Kolb
1969	Raymond W. Waggoner
1970	Robert S. Garber
1971	Ewald W. Busse
1972	Walter E. Barton (Medical Director)
1976	Melvin Sabshin (Medical Director)
1978	Jules H. Masserman
1980	Melvin Sabshin (Medical Director)

American Psychological Association

1892	Granville S. Hall
1893	George T. Ladd
1894	William James
1895	J. McKeen Cattell
1896	George S. Fullerton
1897	James M. Baldwin
1898	H. Muensterberg
1899	John Dewey
1900	Joseph Jastrow
1901	Josiah Royce
1902	Edmund C. Sanford
1903	William L. Bryan
1904	William James
1905	Mary W. Calkins
1906	James R. Angell
1907	Henry R. Marshall
1908	George M. Stratton
1909	Charles H. Judd
1910	Walter B. Pillsbury
1911	Carl E. Seashore
1912	Edward L. Thorndike
1913	Howard C. Warren

1914	Robert S. Woodworth
1915	John B. Watson
1916	Raymond Dodge
1917	Robert M. Yerkes
1918	John W. Baird
1919	Walter D. Scott
1920	Shepherd I. Franz
1921	Margaret F. Washburn
1922	Knight Dunlap
1923	Lewis M. Terman
1924	Granville S. Hall
1925	Madison Bentley
1926	Harvey A. Carr
1927	Harry L. Hollingworth
1928	Edwin G. Boring
1929	Karl S. Lashley
1930	Herbert S. Langfeld
1931	Walter S. Hunter
1932	Walter R. Miles
1933	Louis L. Thurstone
1934	Joseph Peterson
1935	Albert T. Poffenberger
1936	Clark L. Hull
1937	Edward C. Tolman
1938	John F. Dashiell
1939	Gordon W. Allport
1940	Leonard Carmichael
1941	Herbert Woodrow
1942	Calvin P. Stone
1943	John E. Anderson
1944	Gardner Murphy
1945	Edwin R. Guthrie
1946	Henry E. Garrett
1947	Carl R. Rogers
1948	Donald G. Marquis
1949	Ernest R. Hilgard
1950	J. Paul Guilford
1951	Robert R. Sears
1952	Joseph M. Hunt
1953	Laurence F. Shaffer
1954	Orral H. Mowrer
1955	Everett L. Kelly
1956	Theodore M. Newcomb
1957	Lee J. Cronbach
1958	Harry F. Harlow
1959	Wolfgang Kohler
1960	Donald O. Hebb
1961	Neal E. Miller
1962	Paul E. Meehl
1963	Charles E. Osgood
1964	Quinn McNemar
1965	Jerome S. Bruner
1966	Nicholas Hobbs
1967	Gardner Lindzey
1968	Abraham H. Maslow
1969	George A. Miller
1970	George W. Albee
1971	Kenneth B. Clark
1972	Leona Tyler
1973	Albert Bandura (to 1974)
1976	Charles Kiesler (Executive Officer)
1980	Michael Pallak (Executive Officer)
1986	Leonard S. Goodstein (Executive Officer)

American Public Health Association

1872	Stephen Smith
1875	Joseph M. Toner
1876	Edwin M. Snow
1877	John Henry Rauch
1878	Elisha Harris
1879	James L. Cabell
1880	John Shaw Billings
1881	Charles B. White
1882	Robert C. Kedzie

1883	Ezra M. Hunt
1884	Albert L. Gihon
1885	James E. Reeves
1886	Henry P. Walcott
1887	George M. Sternberg
1888	Charles N. Hewitt
1889	Hosmer A. Johnson
1890	Henry B. Baker
1892	Felix Formento
1893	Samuel H. Durgin
1895	William Bailey
1897	Henry B. Horlbeck
1898	Charles A. Lindsey
1899	Henry Mitchell
1901	Benjamin Lee
1902	Henry D. Holton
1903	Walter Wyman
1905	Frank F. Wesbrook
1906	Franklin C. Robinson
1908	Richard H. Lewis
1909	Gardner T. Swarts
1910	Charles O. Probst
1912	John N. Hurty
1913	Rudolph Hering
1914	William C. Woodward
1915	William T. Sedgwick
1916	John F. Anderson
1917	William A. Evans
1919	L. K. Frankel
1920	Watson S. Rankin
1921	Mazyck P. Ravenel
1922	Allan J. McLaughlin
1923	Ernest C. Levy
1924	William H. Park
1925	Henry F. Vaughan
1926	Charles-Edward A. Winslow
1927	Charles V. Chapin
1928	Herman H. Bundesen
1929	George W. Fuller
1930	Albert J. Chesley
1931	Hugh S. Cumming
1932	Louis I. Dublin
1933	John A. Ferrell
1934	Haven Emerson
1935	Eugene L. Bishop
1936	Walter H. Brown
1937	Thomas Parran
1938	Arthur T. McCormack
1939	Abel Wolman
1940	Edward S. Godfrey, Jr.
1941	W. S. Leathers
1942	John L. Rice
1943	Allen W. Freeman
1944	Felix J. Underwood
1945	John J. Sippy
1947	Harry S. Mustard
1948	Martha M. Eliot
1949	Charles F. Wilinsky
1950	Lowell J. Reed
1951	William P. Shepard
1952	Gaylord W. Anderson
1953	Wilton L. Halverson
1954	Hugh R. Leavell
1955	Herman E. Hilleboe
1956	Ira V. Hiscock
1957	John W. Knutson
1958	Roy J. Morton
1959	Leona Baumgartner
1960	Malcolm H. Merrill
1961	Marion Sheahan
1962	Charles G. King
1963	John W. R. Norton
1964	John D. Porterfield
1965	Dwight F. Metzler
1966	Ernest L. Stebbins
1967	Milton Terris
1968	John J. Hanlon
1969	Lester Breslow
1970	Paul B. Cornely
1971	P. Walton Purdom

1972 Myron E. Wegman	1878 Ellis S. Chesbrough	1958 Louis R. Howson	1970 Elmer R. Jennings
1973 James R. Kimmey	1879 William M. Roberts	1959 Francis S. Friel	1971 William D. Dolan
(Executive Director)	1880 Albert Fink	1960 Frank A. Marston	1972 Jack M. Layton
1975 William H. McBeath	1881 James B. Francis	1961 Glenn W. Holcomb	1973 Albert G. Boeck
(Executive Director)	1882 Ashbel Welch	1962 George B. Earnest	(Executive Director)
	1883 Charles Paine	1963 Edmund Friedman	1974 George F. Stevenson
	1884 Don Juan Whittemore	1964 Waldo G. Bowman	(Executive Director)
	1885 Frederic Graff	1965 Wallace L. Chadwick	1975 David L. Gilcrest
American Society for	1886 Henry Flad	1966 William J. Hedley	(Executive Director)
Metals	1887 William E. Worthen	1967 Earle T. Andrews	1979 Meryl H. Haber
	1888 Thomas C. Keefer	1968 Richard H. Tatlow	(Executive Vice President)
1920 Albert E. White	1889 Max J. Becker	1969 Frank H. Newnam, Jr.	1984 Robert A. Dietrich
1921 Frank P. Gilligan	1890 William P. Shinn	1970 Thomas M. Niles	(Executive Officer)
1922 Tillman D. Lynch	1891 Octave Chanute	1971 Samuel Baxter	
1923 George K. Burgess	1892 Mendes Cohen	1972 Oscar Bray	
1924 William S. Bidle	1893 William Metcalf	1973 Eugene Zwoyer	
1925 Robert M. Bird	1894 William P. Craighill	(Executive Director)	**American Society of**
1926 J. Fletcher Harper	1895 George S Morison	1975 William M. Sangster	**Composers, Authors, and**
1927 Fredrick G. Hughes	1896 Thomas C. Clarke	1976 Arthur J. Fox, Jr.	**Publishers (ASCAP)**
1928 Zay Jeffries	1897 Benjamin M. Harrod	1977 Leland J. Walker	
1929 Robert G. Guthrie	1898 Alphonse Fteley	1978 Eugene Zwoyer	1914 George Maxwell
1930 James M. Watson	1899 Desmond FitzGerald	(Executive Director)	1925 Gene Buck
1931 Alex. H. D'Arcambal	1900 John F. Wallace	1983 Louis L. Meier	1942 Deems Taylor
1932 William B. Coleman	1901 John J. R. Croes	(Executive Director)	1948 Fred E. Ahlert
1933 William H. Phillips	1902 Robert Moore	1984 Edward O. Pfrang	1950 Otto A. Harbach
1934 Benjamin F. Shepherd	1903 Alfred Noble	(Executive Director)	1953 Stanley Adams
1935 Robert S. Archer	1904 Charles Hermany		1956 Paul Cunningham
1936 Edgar C. Bain	1905 Charles C. Schneider		1959 Stanley Adams
1937 George B. Waterhouse	1906 Frederic P. Stearns		1981 Hal David
1938 William P. Woodside	1907 George H. Benzenberg	**American Society of**	
1939 James P. Gill	1908 Charles Macdonald	**Clinical Pathologists**	
1940 Oscar E. Harder	1909 Onward Bates		**American Society of**
1941 Bradley Stoughton	1910 John A. Bensel	1922 Philip Hillkowitz	**International Law**
1942 Herbert J. French	1911 Mordecai T. Endicott	1923 William C. MacCarty	
1943 Marcus A. Grossman	1912 John A. Ockerson	1924 John A. Kolmer	1907 Elihu Root
1944 Kent. R. Van Horn	1913 George F. Swain	1925 Frederic E. Sondern	1925 Charles Evans Hughes
1945 Charles H. Herty, Jr.	1914 Hunter McDonald	1926 William G. Exton	1930 James B. Scott
1946 A. L. Boegehold	1915 Charles D. Marx	1927 Arthur H. Sanford	1940 Cordell Hull
1947 Francis B. Foley	1916 Elmer L. Corthell	1928 Frank W. Hartman	1943 Frederic R. Coudert
1948 Harold K. Work	1916 Clemens Herschel	1929 James H. Black	1946 Charles C. Hyde
1949 Arthur E. Focke	1917 George H. Pegram	1930 Kenneth M. Lynch	1950 Manley O. Hudson
1950 Walter E. Jominy	1918 Arthur N. Talbot	1931 Harry J. Corper	1953 Edwin D. Dickinson
1951 John Chipman	1919 Fayette S. Curtis	1932 Walter M. Simpson	1954 Charles G. Fenwick
1952 Ralph L. Wilson	1920 Arthur P. Davis	1933 Alvin G. Foord	1955 Philip C. Jessup
1953 James B. Austin	1921 George S. Webster	1934 Frederick H. Lamb	1956 Quincy Wright
1954 George A. Roberts	1922 John R. Freeman	1935 Foster M. Johns	1957 Lester H. Woolsey
1955 Adolph O. Schaefer	1923 Charles F. Loweth	1935 Robert A. Kilduffe	1958 Robert R. Wilson
1956 Donald S. Clark	1924 Carl E. Grunsky	1936 Roy R. Kracke	1959 Myres S. McDougal
1957 G. M. Young	1925 Robert Ridgway	1937 Carl W. Maynard	1960 Herbert W. Briggs
1958 Clarence H. Lorig	1926 George S. Davison	1938 Thomas B. Magath	1961 Charles E. Martin
1959 Walter Crafts	1927 John F. Stevens	1939 Leonard W. Larson	1962 Arthur H. Dean
1960 William Pennington	1928 Lincoln Bush	1940 Armin V. St. George	1963 Hardy C. Dillard
1961 Carl E. Swartz	1929 Anson Marston	1941 John L. Lattimore	1964 James N. Hyde
1962 Robert Raudebaugh	1930 John F. Coleman	1942 Harry Goldblatt	1965 Brunson MacChesney
1963 Merrill A. Scheil	1931 Francis L. Stuart	1943 Walter S. Thomas	1967 John R. Stevenson
1964 John A. Fellows	1932 Herbert S. Crocker	1944 Frank W. Konzelmann	1969 Oscar Schachter
1965 Stewart G. Fletcher	1933 Alonzo J. Hammond	1946 Stanley P. Reimann	1971 Harold D. Lasswell
1966 John Convey	1934 Harrison P. Eddy	1947 Theodore J. Curphey	
1967 Earl Parker	1935 Arthur S. Tuttle	1948 Osborne A. Brines	*Executive Directors*
1968 Carl Samans	1936 Daniel W. Mead	1949 James B. McNaught	
1969 Morris Cohen	1937 Louis C. Hill	1950 F. William Sunderman	1972 Stephen M. Schwebel
1970 Thomas E. Leontis	1938 Henry E. Riggs	1951 Israel Davidsohn	1975 Seymour J. Rubin
1971 Nathan E. Promisel	1939 Donald H. Sawyer	1952 Henry F. Hunt	1986 John Lawrence Hargrove
1973 Allan Ray Putnam	1940 John P. Hogan	1953 John R. Schenken	
(Managing Director)	1941 Frederick H. Fowler	1954 Frank B. Queen	
1975 Edward L. Langer	1942 Ernest B. Black	1955 Emma S. Moss	**American Society of**
(Managing Director)	1943 Ezra B. Whitman	1956 John L. Goforth	**Landscape Architects**
	1944 Malcolm Pirnie	1957 Harry P. Smith	
	1945 John C. Stevens	1958 Edward L. Burns	1899 John C. Olmsted
	1946 Wesley W. Horner	1959 John J. Clemmer	1902 Samuel Parsons, Jr.
	1947 Edgar M. Hastings	1960 John J. Andujar	1903 Nathan F. Barrett
American Society of Civil	1948 Richard E. Dougherty	1961 Merlin L. Trumbull	1904 John C. Olmsted
Engineers	1949 Franklin Thomas	1961 Richard E. Palmer	1906 Samuel Parsons, Jr.
	1950 Ernest E. Howard	1962 Harold D. Palmer	1908 Frederick L. Olmsted, Jr.
1853 James Laurie	1951 Gail A. Hathaway	1963 Robert W. Coon	1910 Charles N. Lowrie
1868 James P. Kirkwood	1952 Carlton S. Proctor	1964 William O. Russell	1912 Harold A. Caparn
1869 William J. McAlpine	1953 Walter L. Huber	1965 Albert L. McQuown	1913 Ossian C. Simonds
1870 Alfred Craven	1954 Daniel V. Terrell	1966 Lall G. Montgomery	1914 Warren H. Manning
1872 Horatio Allen	1955 William R. Glidden	1967 Rosser L. Mainwaring	
1874 Julius W. Adams	1956 Enoch R. Needles	1968 Thomas M. Peery	
1876 George S. Greene	1957 Mason G. Lockwood	1969 Clyde G. Culbertson	

1915 James S. Pray
1919 Frederick L. Olmsted, Jr.
1923 James L. Greenleaf
1927 Arthur A. Shurcliff
1931 Henry V. Hubbard
1935 Albert D. Taylor
1941 S. Herbert Hare
1945 Markley Stevenson
1949 Gilmore D. Clarke
1951 Lawrence G. Linnard
1953 Leon Zach
1957 Norman T. Newton
1961 John I. Rogers
1963 John O. Simonds
1965 Hubert B. Owens
1967 Theodore Osmundson
1969 Campbell E. Miller
1971 Raymond L. Freeman
1973 Robert C. LaGasse
     (Executive Director)
1978 Edward H. Able
     (Executive Vice President)

American Society of Mechanical Engineers

1880 Robert H. Thurston
1883 Erasmus D. Leavitt
1884 John E. Sweet
1885 Josephus F. Holloway
1886 Coleman Sellers
1887 George H. Babcock
1888 Horace See
1889 Henry R. Towne
1890 Oberlin Smith
1891 Robert W. Hunt
1892 Charles H. Loring
1893 Eckley B. Coxe
1895 E. F. C. Davies
1895 Charles E. Billings
1896 John Fritz
1897 Worcester R. Warner
1898 Charles W. Hunt
1899 George W. Melville
1900 Charles H. Morgan
1901 Samuel T. Wellman
1902 Edwin Reynolds
1903 James M. Dodge
1904 Ambrose Swasey
1905 John R. Freeman
1906 Frederick W. Taylor
1907 Frederick R. Hutton
1908 Minard L. Holman
1909 Jesse M. Smith
1910 George Westinghouse
1911 E. D. Meier
1912 Alex C. Humphreys
1913 William F. Goss
1914 James Hartness
1915 John A. Brashear
1916 D. S. Jacobus
1917 Ira N. Hollis
1918 Charles T. Main
1919 Mortimer E. Cooley
1920 Fred J. Miller
1921 Edwin S. Carman
1922 Dexter S. Kimball
1923 John L. Harrington
1924 Fred R. Low
1925 William F. Durand
1926 William L. Abbott
1927 Charles M. Schwab
1928 Alex Dow
1929 Elmer A. Sperry
1930 Charles Piez
1931 Roy V. Wright
1932 Conrad N. Lauer
1933 A. A. Potter
1934 Paul Doty

1935 Ralph E. Flanders
1936 William L. Batt
1937 James H. Herron
1938 Harvey N. Davis
1939 Alexander G. Christie
1940 Warren H. McBryde
1941 William A. Hanley
1942 James W. Parker
1943 Harold V. Coes
1944 Robert M. Gates
1945 Alex D. Bailey
1946 D. Robert Yarnall
1947 Eugene W. O'Brien
1948 Ervin G. Bailey
1949 James M. Todd
1950 James D. Cunningham
1951 J. Calvin Brown
1952 R. J. S. Pigott
1953 Frederick S. Blackall, Jr.
1954 Lewis K. Sillcox
1955 David W. R. Morgan
1956 Joseph W. Barker
1957 William F. Ryan
1958 James N. Landis
1959 Glenn B. Warren
1960 Walker L. Cisler
1961 William H. Byrne
1962 Clifford H. Shumaker
1963 Ronald B. Smith
1964 Elmer O. Bergman
1965 Henry N. Muller
1966 James H. Harlow
1967 Louis N. Rowley
1968 George F. Habach
1969 Donald E. Marlowe
1970 Allen F. Rhodes
1971 Kenneth A. Roe
1972 Kenneth A. Roe
1974 Rogers B. Finch
     (Executive Director, to 1980)
1981 Irma S. Bennett
1983 Paul F. Allmendinger
     (Deputy Executive Director)
1984 Louise LeRoy
1985 Paul F. Allmendinger
     (Director)

American Society of Newspaper Editors

1922 Casper S. Yost
1926 Erie C. Hopwood
1928 Walter M. Harrison
1930 Fred F Shedd
1933 Paul Bellamy
1934 Grove Patterson
1936 Marvin H. Creager
1937 A. H. Kirchhofer
1938 William A. White
1939 Donald J. Sterling
1940 Tom Wallace
1941 Dwight Marvin
1942 W. S. Gilmore
1943 Roy A. Roberts
1944 John S. Knight
1946 Wilbut Forrest
1947 N. R. Howard
1948 Erwin D. Canham
1949 B. M. McKelway
1950 Dwight Young
1951 Alexander F. Jones
1952 Wright Bryan
1953 Basil L. Walters
1954 James S. Pope
1955 Kenneth MacDonald
1956 Jenkin L. Jones
1957 Virginius Dabney

1958 George W. Healy, Jr.
1959 J. R. Wiggins
1960 Turner Catledge
1961 Felix R. McKnight
1962 Lee Hills
1963 Herbert Brucker
1964 Miles H. Wolff
1965 Vermont C. Royster
1966 Robert C. Notson
1967 Michael J. Ogden
1968 Vincent S. Jones
1969 Norman E. Isaacs
1970 Newbold Noyes
1971 Gene Giancarlo
     (Executive Secretary)
1979 Gene Giancarlo
     (Executive Director, to 1983)
1984 Lee Stinnett (Executive Director)

American Society of Zoologists

1914 Clarence E. McClung
1915 William A. Locy
1916 David H. Tennent
1917 M. M. Metcalf
1918 George Lefevre
1919 C. M. Child
1920 Gilman A. Drew
1921 C. A. Kofoid
1922 H. H. Wilder
1923 M. F. Guyer
1924 Ross G. Harrison
1925 Charles R. Stockard
1926 Samuel O. Mast
1927 S. J. Holmes
1928 Caswell Grave
1929 Charles B. Davenport
1930 Herbert V. Neal
1931 Fernandus Payne
1932 W. C. Curtis
1933 Charles Zeleny
1934 A. H. Sturtevant
1935 R. W. Hegner
1936 W. C. Allee
1937 F. L. Hisaw
1938 M. H. Jacobs
1939 J. T. Patterson
1940 Wesley R. Coe
1941 R. E. Coker
1942 L. L. Woodruff
1943 T. S. Painter
1944 Sewall Wright
1945 A. S. Pearse
1946 D. E. Minnich
1947 J. H. Bodine
1948 C. G. Hartman
1949 Robert Chambers
1950 Alfred S. Romer
1951 D. M. Whitaker
1952 Franz Schrader
1953 E. Newton Harvey
1954 J. Walter Wilson
1955 Viktor Hamburger
1956 Tracy M. Sonneborn
1957 Elmer G. Butler
1958 H. Burr Steinbach
1959 Victor C. Twitty
1960 Emil Witschi
1961 C. Ladd Prosser
1962 Curt Stern
1963 Theodosius Dobzhansky
1964 George G. Simpson
1965 Theodore H. Bullock
1966 Clifford Grobstein
1967 Howard A. Bern
1968 Vincent G. Dethier

1969 Clement L. Markert
1970 James D. Ebert
1971 Arthur D. Hasler
1972 John O. Corliss
1973 Mary Wiley (Business Manager)
1984 Mary Wiley (Executive Officer)
1986 Mary Adams-Wiley (Executive Officer)

American Sociological Association

1906 Lester F. Ward
1908 William G. Sumner
1910 Franklin H. Giddings
1912 Albion W. Small
1914 Edward A. Ross
1916 George E. Vincent
1917 George E. Howard
1918 Charles H. Cooley
1919 Frank W. Blackmar
1920 James W. Dealey
1921 Edward C. Hayes
1922 James P. Lichtenberger
1923 Ulysses G. Weatherly
1924 Charles A. Ellwood
1925 Robert E. Park
1926 John L. Gillin
1927 William I. Thomas
1928 John M. Gillette
1929 William F. Ogburn
1930 Howard W. Odum
1931 Emory S. Bogardus
1932 Luther L. Bernard
1933 Edward B. Reuter
1934 Ernest W. Burgess
1935 F. Stuart Chapin
1936 Henry P. Fairchild
1937 Ellsworth Faris
1938 Frank H. Hankins
1939 Edwin H. Sutherland
1940 Robert M. MacIver
1941 Stuart A. Queen
1942 Dwight Sanderson
1943 George A. Lundberg
1944 Rupert B. Vance
1945 Kimball Young
1946 Carl C. Taylor
1947 Louis Wirth
1948 E. Franklin Frazier
1949 Talcott Parsons
1950 Leonard S. Cottrell, Jr.
1951 Robert C. Angell
1952 Dorothy S. Thomas
1953 Samuel A. Stouffer
1954 Florian Znaniecki
1955 Donald Young
1956 Herbert Blumer
1957 Robert K. Merton
1958 Robin M. Williams, Jr.
1959 Kingley Davis
1960 Howard Becker
1961 Robert E. L. Faris
1962 Paul F. Lazarsfeld
1963 Everett C. Hughes
1964 George C. Homans
1965 Pitirim A. Sorokin
1966 Wilbert E. Moore
1967 Charles P. Loomis
1968 Philip M. Hauser
1969 Arnold M. Rose
1969 Ralph H. Turner
1970 Reinhard Bendix
1971 William H. Sewell
1972 William J. Goode
1973 Otto N. Larsen
     (Executive Officer)

1975	Lewis A. Coser
1976	Alfred McClung Lee
1977	Hans O. Mauksch
	(Executive Officer)
1978	Russell R. Dynes
	(Executive Officer)
1983	William V. D'Antonio
	(Executive Officer)

American Watercolor Society

1866	Samuel Colman
1870	William Hart
1872	James D. Smillie
1878	Thomas W. Wood
1887	J. G. Brown
1905	James C. Nicoll
1910	Alex T. Van Laer
1914	William S. Robinson
1920	Eliot Clark
1923	John W. Dunsmore
1930	George P. Ennis
1936	Hobart Nichols
1938	Roy Brown
1949	Frederic Whitaker
1956	William A. Smith
1957	Hans A. Walleen
1960	Mario Cooper
1986	William Gorman

Archaeological Institute of America

1883	Charles E. Norton
1890	Seth Low
1897	John W. White
1904	Thomas D. Seymour
1908	Francis W. Kelsey
1913	Harry L. Wilson
1914	F. W. Shipley
1918	James C. Egbert
1922	Ralph V. D. Magoffin
1932	Louis E. Lord
1936	William B. Dinsmoor
1946	Sterling Dow
1949	Hugh Hencken
1952	Kenneth J. Conant
1953	Henry T. Rowell
1957	George E. Mylonas
1961	Jotham Johnson
1965	Margaret Thompson
1969	Rodney S. Young
1970	Margaret Thompson
1971	Elizabeth Whitehead
	(General Secretary)
1972	Rodney S. Young
1973	Mary Kathleen Brown
	(Executive Director)
1978	Eugene Sterud (Executive Director)
1981	Robert H. Dyson, Jr.
1982	Eugene Sterud (Executive Director)
1984	Raymond A. Liddell (Executive Director)

Authors League of America

1913	Winston Churchill
1917	Rex Beach
1921	Jesse L. Williams
1922	Ellis P. Butler

1924	George B. McCutcheon
1926	Owen Davis
1928	Arthur Train
1929	Arthur Richman
1931	Inez Haynes Irwin
1933	Marc Connelly
1939	Elmer Davis
1941	Howard Lindsay
1943	Russel Crouse
1945	Elmer Rice
1947	Oscar Hammerstein, II
1951	Rex Stout
1955	Moss Hart
1961	Rex Stout
1969	Jerome Weidman
1970	Mills Ten Eyck, Jr. (Executive Secretary)
1976	Kim Tsang Bogart (Administrative Assistant)
1978	Faye W. Glover (Administrative Assistant)
1980	Helen A Stephenson (Administrator)
1985	Mary Louise Lopez (Administrator)
1986	Nancy Weidner (Administrator)

Benevolent and Protective Order of Elks (BPOE)

Grand Exalted Rulers

1871	George J. Green
1871	Charles T. White
1872	Joseph C. Pinckney
1874	James W. Powell
1875	Henry P. O'Neil
1876	Frank Girard
1878	George R. Maguire
1879	Charles E. Davies
1879	Louis C. Waehner
1880	Thomas E. Garrett
1882	John J. Tindale
1883	Edwin A. Perry
1884	Henry S. Sanderson
1885	Daniel A. Kelly
1886	William E. English
1887	Hamilton E. Leach
1889	Simon Quinlin
1891	Edwin B. Hay
1893	Astley Apperly
1894	Edwin B. Hay
1895	William G. Meyers
1896	Meade D. Detweiler
1898	John Galvin
1899	B. M. Allen
1900	Jerome B. Fisher
1901	Charles E. Pickett
1902	George P. Cronk
1903	Joseph T. Fanning
1904	William J. O'Brien, Jr.
1905	Robert W. Brown
1906	Henry A. Melvin
1907	John K. Tener
1908	Rush L. Holland
1909	J. U. Sammis
1910	August Herrmann
1911	John P. Sullivan
1912	Thomas B. Mills
1913	Edward Leach
1914	Raymond Benjamin
1915	James R. Nicholson
1916	Edward Rightor
1917	Fred Harper
1918	Bruce A. Campbell
1919	Frank L. Rain
1920	William M. Abbott
1921	W. W. Mountain

1922	J. E. Masters
1923	James G. McFarland
1924	John G. Price
1925	William H. Atwell
1926	Charles H. Grakelow
1927	John F. Malley
1928	Murray Hulbert
1929	Walter P. Andrews
1930	Lawrence H. Rupp
1931	John R. Coen
1932	Floyd E. Thompson
1933	Walter F. Meier
1934	Michael F. Shannon
1935	James T. Hallinan
1936	David Sholtz
1937	Charles S. Hart
1938	Edward J. McCormick
1939	Henry C. Warner
1940	Joseph G. Buch
1941	John S. McClelland
1942	E. Mark Sullivan
1943	Frank J. Lonergan
1944	Robert S. Barrett
1945	Wade H. Kepner
1946	Charles E. Broughton
1947	L. A. Lewis
1948	George I. Hall
1949	Emmett T. Anderson
1950	Joseph B. Kyle
1951	Howard R. Davis
1952	Sam Stern
1953	Earl E. James
1954	William J. Jernick
1955	John L. Walker
1956	Fred L. Bohn
1957	H. L. Blackledge
1958	H. R. Wisely
1959	W. S. Hawkins
1960	John E. Fenton
1961	William A. Wall
1962	Lee A. Donaldson
1963	Ronald J. Dunn
1964	Robert G. Pruitt
1965	R. Leonard Bush
1966	Raymond C. Dobson
1967	Robert E. Boney
1968	Edward W. McCabe
1969	Frank Hise
1970	Glenn L. Miller
1971	E. Gene Fournace

Grand Secretaries

1972	Homer Huhn, Jr.
1978	Stanley F. Kocur

Botanical Society of America

1907	George F. Atkinson
1908	William F. Ganong
1909	Roland Thaxter
1910	Erwin F. Smith
1911	William G. Farlow
1912	Lewis R. Jones
1913	Douglas H. Campbell
1914	Albert S. Hitchcock
1915	John M. Coulter
1916	Robert A. Harper
1917	F. C. Newcombe
1918	William Trelease
1919	Joseph C. Arthur
1920	Nathaniel L. Britton
1921	Charles E. Allen
1922	Henry C. Cowles
1923	Benjamin M. Duggar
1924	William Crocker
1925	Jacob R. Schramm
1926	Liberty Hyde Bailey

1927	H. H. Bartlett
1928	A. H. R. Buller
1929	Margaret C. Ferguson
1930	L. W. Sharp
1931	C. J. Chamberlain
1932	G. J. Peirce
1933	E. J. Kraus
1934	E. D. Merrill
1935	Aven Nelson
1936	C. Stuart Gager
1937	Edmund W. Sinnott
1938	Arthur J. Eames
1939	Karl M. Weigand
1940	Edgar N. Transeau
1941	John T. Buchholz
1942	Merritt L. Fernald
1943	William J. Robbins
1944	Gilbert M. Smith
1945	I. W. Bailey
1946	Neil E. Stevens
1947	Ralph E. Cleland
1948	Henry A. Gleason
1949	Ivey F. Lewis
1950	Albert F. Blakeslee
1951	Katherine Esau
1952	Edgar Anderson
1953	Ralph H. Wetmore
1954	Adriance S. Foster
1955	Oswald Tippo
1956	Harriet B. Creighton
1957	George S. Avery, Jr.
1958	Frits W. Went
1959	William C. Steere
1960	Kenneth V. Thimann
1961	Vernon I. Cheadle
1962	G. Ledyard Stebbins, Jr.
1963	Constantine J. Alexopoulos
1964	Paul J. Kramer
1965	Aaron J. Sharp
1966	Harold C. Bold
1967	Ralph Emerson
1968	Arthur Galston
1969	Harlan P. Banks
1970	Lincoln Constance
1971	Richard C. Starr
1972	Charles Heimsch

Secretaries

1973	Barbara F. Palser
1975	Patricia K. Holmgren
1980	Carol C. Baskin
1984	David L. Dilcher

Boy Scouts of America

1910	Colin H. Livingstone
1925	James J. Storrow
1926	Milton A. McRae
1926	Walter W. Head
1931	Mortimer L. Schiff
1946	Amory Houghton
1951	John M. Schiff
1956	Kenneth K. Bechtel
1959	Ellsworth H. Augustus
1964	Thomas J. Watson, Jr.
1968	Irving J. Feist
1969	Joseph A. Brunton, Jr. (Chief Executive)
1971	Alden G. Barber (Chief Executive)
1977	Harvey L. Price (Chief Executive)
1979	J. L. Tarr (Chief Executive)
1980	William R. Brickler (National Director)

1981 J. L. Tarr (Chief Executive)
1982 Edward C. Joullian, III
1985 Sanford N. McDonald
1986 Ben H. Love (Chief Executive)

Chamber of Commerce of the United States

1912 Harry A. Wheeler
1914 John H. Fahey
1916 R. G. Rhett
1918 Harry A. Wheeler
1919 Homer L. Ferguson
1920 Joseph H. Defrees
1922 Julius H. Barnes
1924 Richard F. Grant
1925 John W. O'Leary
1927 Lewis E. Pierson
1928 William Butterworth
1931 Silas H. Strawn
1932 Henry I. Harriman
1935 Harper Sibley
1937 George H. Davis
1939 W. Gibson Carey, Jr.
1940 James S. Kemper
1941 Albert W. Hawkes
1942 Eric A. Johnston
1946 William K. Jackson
1947 Earl O. Shreve
1949 Herman W. Steinkraus
1950 Otto A. Seyferth
1951 Dechard A. Hulcy
1952 Laurence F. Lee
1953 Richard L. Bowditch
1954 Clem D. Johnston
1955 A. Boyd Campbell
1956 John C. Coleman
1957 Philip M. Talbott
1958 William A. McDonnell
1959 Erwin D. Canham
1960 Arthur H. Motley
1961 Richard Wagner
1962 H. Ladd Plumley
1963 Edwin P. Neilan
1964 Walter F. Carey
1965 Robert P. Gerholz
1966 M. A. Wright
1967 Allan Shivers
1968 Winton M. Blount
1969 Jenkin L. Jones
1970 F. Ritter Shumway
1971 Archie K. Davis
1972 Arch N. Booth (Executive Vice President)
1975 Richard L. Lesher (to 1986)

Directors Guild of America

(Formerly Screen Directors Guild.)

1936 King Vidor
1938 Frank Capra
1941 George Stevens
1943 Mark Sandrich
1944 John Cromwell
1946 George Stevens
1948 George Marshall
1950 Joseph L. Mankiewicz
1951 George Sidney
1959 Frank Capra
1961 George Sidney
1967 Delbert Mann

1971 Robert Wise
1972 Joseph C. Youngerman (Executive Secretary)
1978 Michael H. Franklin (Executive Director)

Ecological Society of America

1916 V. E. Shelford
1917 Ellsworth Huntington
1918 Henry C. Cowles
1919 Barrington Moore
1921 Stephen A. Forbes
1922 Forest Shreve
1923 Charles C. Adams
1924 E. N. Transeau
1925 A. S. Pearse
1926 J. W. Harshberger
1927 Chancey Juday
1928 H. L. Shantz
1929 W. C. Allee
1930 J. E. Weaver
1931 A. O. Feese
1932 G. E. Nichols
1933 E. B. Powers
1934 George D. Fuller
1935 Walter P. Taylor
1936 William S. Cooper
1937 R. E. Coker
1938 H. C. Hanson
1939 Charles T. Vorhies
1940 Francis Ramaley
1941 Alfred E. Emerson
1942 C. F. Korstian
1943 Orlando Park
1944 Robert F. Griggs
1945 Alfred C. Redfield
1946 John M. Aikman
1947 Aldo Leopold
1948 Paul B. Sears
1949 Z. P. Metcalf
1950 E. Lucy Braun
1951 S. Charles Kendeigh
1952 Frank C. Gates
1953 Lee R. Dice
1954 John E. Potzger
1955 W. J. Hamilton, Jr.
1956 Henry J. Oosting
1957 W. A. Dreyer
1958 Stanley A. Cain
1959 Thomas Park
1960 Charles E. Olmsted
1961 Arthur D. Hasler
1962 Murray F. Buell
1963 W. Frank Blair
1964 John F. Reed
1965 Eugene P. Odum
1966 Bostwick H. Ketchum
1967 Rexford Daubenmire
1968 LaMont C. Cole
1969 John E. Cantlon
1970 Edward S. Deevey
1971 S. I. Auerbach
1972 Robert B. Platt
1973 Frank McCormick (Secretary)
1977 Edward J. Kormondy (Secretary, to 1978)
1980 Paul G. Risser (Secretary)
1983 Robert P. McIntosh (Secretary)
1986 Hazel R. Delcourt (Executive Officer)

Electrochemical Society

1902 Joseph W. Richards
1904 Henry S. Carhart
1905 Wilder D. Bancroft
1906 Carl Hering
1907 Charles F. Burgess
1908 Edward G. Acheson
1909 Leo H. Baekeland
1910 William H. Walker
1911 Willis R. Whitney
1913 Eugene F. Roeber
1914 Frank A. Lidbury
1915 Lawrence Addicks
1916 Francis A. J. Fitzgerald
1917 Colin G. Fink
1918 Frank J. Tone
1919 Wilder D. Bancroft
1920 Walter S. Landis
1921 Acheson Smith
1922 Carl G. Schluederberg
1923 Arthur T. Hinckley
1924 Howard C. Parmelee
1925 Frederick M. Becket
1926 William Blum
1927 Samuel C. Lind
1928 Paul J. Kruesi
1929 Francis C. Frary
1930 Louis Kahlenberg
1931 Bradley Stoughton
1933 John Johnston
1934 Hiram S. Lukens
1935 James H. Critchett
1936 Duncan A. MacInnes
1937 William G. Harvey
1938 Robert L. Baldwin
1939 H. Jermain Creighton
1940 Frank C. Mathers
1941 Raymond R. Ridgway
1942 Edwin M. Baker
1943 Robert M. Burns
1944 Sidney D. Kirkpatrick
1945 William R. Veazey
1946 William C. Moore
1947 George W. Heise
1948 James A. Lee
1949 Albert L. Ferguson
1950 Charles L. Faust
1951 Ralph M. Hunter
1952 John C. Warner
1953 Robert J. Mackay
1954 Marvin J. Udy
1955 Herbert H. Uhlig
1956 Hans Thurnauer
1957 Norman Hackerman
1958 Sherlock Swann, Jr.
1959 William C. Gardiner
1960 Ralph A. Schaefer
1961 Henry B. Linford
1962 Francis L. LaQue
1963 Walter J. Hamer
1964 Lyle I. Gilbertson
1965 Ernest B. Yeager
1966 Harold J. Read
1967 Harry C. Gatos
1968 Ivor E. Campbell
1969 N. Corey Cahoon
1970 Charles W. Tobias
1971 Cecil V. King
1972 Ernest G. Enck (Executive Officer, to 1976)
1978 V. H. Branneky (Executive Secretary)

Electrochemical Society

Electrochemical Society

English-Speaking Union of the United States

1921 William Howard Taft
1930 John W. Davis
1938 James R. Angell
1946 Lewis W. Douglas
1947 William V. Griffin
1957 Arthur A. Houghton, Jr.
1959 J. W. F. Treadwell (Acting)
1961 Charles E. Saltzman
1966 Archbold Van Beuren
1967 John Jay Schieffelin (Executive Director)
1969 William G. Gridley (Executive Director)
1973 John I. B. McCulloch
1974 William G. Gridley (Executive Director)
1975 Charles P. Dennison (Executive Director)
1980 John D. Walker (Executive Director)

Franklin Institute

1824 James Ronaldson
1842 Samuel V. Merrick
1855 John C. Cresson
1864 William Sellers
1867 J. Vaughan Merrick
1870 Coleman Sellers
1875 Robert E. Rogers
1879 William P. Tatham
1886 Charles H. Banes
1887 Joseph M. Wilson
1897 John Birkinbine
1907 Walton Clark
1924 William C. L. Eglin
1929 Nathan Haywood
1937 Philip C. Staples
1941 Charles S. Redding
1946 Richard T. Nalle
1952 S. Wyman Rolph
1958 Wynn L. LePage
1967 Athelstan F. Spilhaus
1970 Bowen C. Dees
1987 Joel Bloom

General Society of Colonial Wars

Governors General

1893 Frederic J. de Peyster
1905 Arthur J. C. Sowdon
1911 Howland Pell
1915 Richard M. Cadwalader
1918 William W. Ladd
1927 Henry G. Sanford
1929 Louis R. Cheney
1930 George de B. Keim
1936 Francis R. Stoddard
1939 Robert M. Boyd, Jr.
1942 Edwin O. Lewis
1945 Alexander G. Brown, Jr.
1948 Philip L. Poe
1951 Daniel M. Bates
1953 Harry P. Cross
1954 Walter M. Pratt
1957 Branton H. Henderson
1960 Robert W. Groves
1963 Anastasio C. M. Azoy
1965 Nathaniel C. Hale
1969 Asa E. Phillips, Jr.

Secretaries General

1970 Edward Holloway, Jr.
1973 Lawson Ewing Whitesides

General Society of Mayflower Descendants

Governors General

1897 Henry E. Howland
1903 Charles Francis Adams
1903 Samuel B. Capen
1909 Howland Davis
1912 Thomas S. Hopkins
1915 Leonard Wood
1921 John P. Tilden
1924 Addison P. Munroe
1930 Robert M. Boyd
1933 Burnham S. Colburn
1939 Francis R. Stoddard
1942 Frederick A. Van Fleet
1948 Walter M. Pratt
1954 Waldo M. Allen
1960 Lewis E. Neff
1963 Tilbee D. Gray, II
1966 Norman J. Greene
1969 Lee D. Van Antwerp
1970 Mrs. Robert M. Sherman (Secretary General)
1979 Mildred Ramos (Secretary General)
1984 Barbara L. Merrick (Historian General)

Geological Society of America

1889 James Hall
1890 James D. Dana
1891 Alexander Winchell
1892 Grove K. Gilbert
1893 J. William Dawson
1894 Thomas C. Chamberlin
1895 N. S. Shaler
1896 Joseph Le Conte
1897 Edward Orton
1898 John V. Stevenson
1899 Benjamin K. Emerson
1900 G. M. Dawson
1901 Charles D. Walcott
1902 Newton H. Winchell
1903 S. F. Emmons
1904 John C. Branner
1905 Raphael Pumpelly
1906 Israel C. Russell
1907 C. R. Van Hise
1908 Samuel Calvin
1909 Grove K. Gilbert
1910 Arnold Hague
1911 William M. Davis
1912 H. L. Fairchild
1913 Eugene A. Smith
1914 George F. Becker
1915 Arthur P. Coleman
1916 John M. Clarke
1917 Frank D. Adams
1918 Whitman Cross
1919 J. C. Merriam
1920 Israel C. White
1921 James F. Kemp
1922 Charles Schuchert
1923 David White
1924 Waldemar Lindgren
1925 William B. Scott
1926 Andrew C. Lawson

1927 Arthur Keith
1928 Bailey Willis
1929 Heinrich Ries
1930 R. A. F. Penrose, Jr.
1931 Alfred C. Lane
1932 Reginald A. Daly
1933 C. K. Leith
1934 W. H. Collins
1935 Nevin M. Fenneman
1936 W. C. Mendenhall
1937 Charles Palache
1938 Arthur L. Day
1939 T. Wayland Vaughan
1940 Eliot Blackwelder
1941 Charles P. Berkey
1942 Douglas Johnson
1943 E. L. Bruce
1944 Adolph Knopf
1945 Edward W. Berry
1946 Norman L. Bowen
1947 A. I. Levorsen
1948 James Gilluly
1949 Chester R. Longwell
1950 William W. Rubey
1951 Chester Stock
1952 Thomas S. Lovering
1953 Wendell P. Woodring
1954 Ernst Cloos
1955 Walter H. Bucher
1956 George S. Hume
1957 Richard J. Russell
1958 Raymond C. Moore
1959 Marland P. Billings
1960 Hollis D. Hedberg
1961 Thomas B. Nolan
1962 M. King Hubbert
1963 Harry H. Hess
1964 Francis Birch
1965 Wilmot H. Bradley
1966 Robert F. Legget
1967 Konrad B. Krauskopf
1968 Ian Campbell
1969 Morgan J. Davis
1970 John Rodgers
1971 Richard E. Jahns
1972 Luna B. Leopold
1973 John Maxwell
1974 Edwin B. Eckel (Executive Secretary)
1975 John C. Frye (Executive Director)
1983 F. Michael Wahl (Executive Director)

Girl Scouts of the United States of America

1915 Mrs. Juliette Low
1920 Mrs. Arthur O. Choate
1922 Mrs. Herbert Hoover
1925 Dean Sarah Louise Arnold
1928 Mrs. William H. Hoffman
1930 Mrs. Frederick Edey
1935 Mrs. Herbert Hoover
1937 Mrs. Frederick H. Brooke
1939 Mrs. Harvey S. Mudd
1941 Mrs. Alan H. Means
1946 Mrs. C. Vaughan Ferguson
1951 Mrs. Roy F. Layton
1957 Mrs. Charles U. Culmer
1963 Mrs. Holton R. Price, Jr.
1969 Mrs. Douglas H. MacNeil

Executive Directors

1970 Louise A. Wood (to 1972)
1974 Cecily C. Selby
1976 Frank Kanis (Acting)
1977 Frances R. Hesselbein

Institute of Electrical and Electronics Engineers, Inc.

(Association of Electrical and Electronic Engineers until 1963.)

1934 J. Allen Johnson
1935 E. B. Meyer
1936 A. M. MacCutcheon
1937 W. H. Harrison
1938 John C. Parker
1939 F. Malcolm Farmer
1940 R. W. Sorensen
1941 David C. Prince
1942 Harold S. Osborne
1943 Nevin E. Funk
1944 C. A. Powel
1945 W. E. Wickenden
1946 J. Elmer Housley
1947 B. D. Hull
1948 Everett S. Lee
1949 James F. Fairman
1950 Titus G. LeClair
1951 F. O. McMillan
1952 Donald A. Quarles
1953 Elgin B. Robertson
1954 A. C. Monteith
1955 M. D. Hooven
1956 M. S. Coover
1957 W. J. Barrett
1958 L. F. Hickernell
1959 J. H. Foote
1960 Clarence H. Linder
1961 W. H. Chase
1962 B. R. Teare, Jr.
1963 Ernst Weber
1964 Clarence H. Linder
1965 Bernard M. Oliver
1966 William G. Shepherd
1967 Walter K. MacAdam
1968 Seymour W. Herwald
1969 F. Karl Willenbrock
1970 J. V. N. Granger
1971 James H. Mulligan, Jr.
1972 Robert H. Tanner
1972 Donald G. Fink (General Manager)
1973 H. A. Schulke, Jr. (Executive Director)
1978 R. M. Emberson (Executive Director, to 1981)
1983 Eric Herz (General Manager)

Izaak Walton League of America

1922 Will H. Dilg
1925 Charles W. Folds
1926 Jacob M. Dickinson
1927 Henry B. Ward
1931 Preston Bradley
1935 George W. Wood
1938 Otto C. Doering
1940 Tappan Gregory
1942 Ivar Hennings

1944 Paul Clement
1946 Tom Wallace
1948 Walter Frye
1950 William B. Holton
1952 John W. Tobin
1953 William H. H. Wertz
1955 L. H. Dunten
1956 William H. Pringle
1958 Robert C. O'Hair
1959 George F. Jackson
1960 Alden J. Erskine
1962 L. C. "Jack" Binford
1963 Burt G. Brickner
1965 Reynolds T. Harnsberger
1967 J. Justin Rogers
1968 Raymond A. Haik
1970 Roy B. Crockett
1971 Raymond C. Hubley, Jr. (Executive Director, to 1975)
1977 Jack Lorenz (Executive Director)

Kiwanis International

1916 George F Hixson
1918 Perry S. Patterson (to 1919)
1920 J. Mercer Barnett
1921 Harry E. Karr (to 1922)
1923 Edmund F. Arras
1924 Victor M. Johnson
1925 John H. Moss
1926 Ralph A. Amerman
1927 Henry C. Heinz
1928 O. Sam Cummings
1929 Horace W. McDavid
1930 Raymond M. Crossman
1931 William O. Harris
1932 Carl E. Endicott
1933 Joshua L. Johns
1934 William J. Carrington
1935 Harper Gatton
1936 A. Copeland Callen (to 1937)
1938 H. G. Hatfield
1939 Bennett O. Knudson
1940 Mark A. Smith
1941 Charles S. Donley (to 1942)
1943 Donald B. Rice
1944 Ben Dean
1945 Hamilton Holt
1946 J. N. Emerson
1947 Charles W. Armstrong
1948 J. Belmont Mosser
1949 J. Hugh Jackson (to 1950)
1951 Claude B. Hellmann
1952 Walter J. L. Ray
1953 Donald T. Forsythe
1954 Don E. Engdahl
1955 J. A. Raney
1956 Reed C. Culp
1957 H. Park Arnold (to 1958)
1959 Albert J. Tully
1960 J. O. Tally, Jr.
1961 I. R. Witthuhn
1962 Merle H. Tucker
1963 Charles A. Swain
1964 Edward B. Moylan, Jr.
1965 Edward C. Keefe
1966 R. Glenn Reed, Jr.
1967 James M. Moler
1968 Harold M. Heimbaugh
1969 Robert F. Weber
1970 T. R. Johnson
1971 Wes H. Bartlett

1972 R. P. Merridew
    (Secretary)
1982 J. W. Kleindorfer
    (International Secretary)
1984 G. H. "Gil" Zitzelberger
    (International Secretary)

Knights of Pythias

Supreme Chancellors

1868 Samuel Reed
1872 Henry C. Berry
1874 Stillman S. Davis
1878 David B. Woodruff
1880 George W. Lindsay
1882 John P. Linton
1884 John Van Valkenberg
1886 Howard Douglass
1888 William Ward
1890 George B. Shaw
1892 William B. Blackwell
1894 Walter B. Ritchie
1896 Philip T. Colgrove
1898 Thomas G. Sample
1900 Ogden H. Fethers
1902 Tracy R. Bangs
1904 Charles E. Shiveley
1906 Charles A. Barnes
1908 Henry P. Brown
1910 George M. Hanson
1912 Thomas J. Carling
1914 Brig S. Young
1916 John J. Brown
1918 Charles S. Davis
1920 William Ladew
1922 George C. Cabell
1924 John Ballantyne
1926 Richard S Witte
1928 Alva S. Lumpkin
1930 Leslie E. Crouch
1932 James Dunn, Jr.
1934 Reno S. Harp
1936 Fred H. Jones
1938 E. Lee Stapp
1940 Roy O. Garber
1942 John Lee Smith
1944 Charles J. Schuck
1946 Willard M. Kent
1948 Fred Ratliff
1950 Earle N. Genzberger
1952 Sheldon M. Roper
1954 Peter S. Ford
1956 Archie B. Jackson
1958 William H. Pierce
1960 Leonard M. Eisenberg
1962 Joseph B. Hacker
1964 James C. Bayley
1966 Otto E. Nobis
1968 Otto R. Shuman
1972 Jule O. Pritchard
    (Supreme Secretary)

Lions International

1917 W. P. Woods
1918 L. H. Lewis
1919 Jesse Robinson
1920 C. C. Reid
1921 Ewen W. Cameron
1922 Ed. S. Vaught
1923 John S. Noel (to 1924)
1925 Benjamin F. Jones
1926 William A. Westfall
1927 Irving L. Camp
1928 Ben A. Ruffin
1929 Ray L. Riley

1930 Earle W. Hodges
1931 Julien C. Hyer
1932 Charles H. Hatton
1933 Roderick Beddow
1934 Vincent C. Hascall
1935 Richard J. Osenbaugh
1936 Edwin R. Kingsley
1937 Frank V. Birch
1938 Walter F. Dexter
1939 Alexander T. Wells
1940 Karl M. Sorrick
1941 George R. Jordan
1942 Edward H. Paine
1943 E. G. Gill
1944 D. A. Skeen (to 1945)
1946 Clifford D. Pierce
1947 Fred W. Smith
1948 Eugene S. Briggs
1949 Walter C. Fisher
1950 Herb C. Petry, Jr.
1951 Harold P. Nutter
1952 Edgar M. Elbert
1953 S. A. Dodge
1954 Monroe L. Nute (to 1955)
1956 John L. Stickley
1957 Edward G. Barry
1958 Dudley L. Simms
1959 Clarence L. Sturm
1960 Finis E. Davis (to 1961)
1962 Curtis D. Lovill
1963 Aubrey D. Green
1964 Claude M. DeVorss
1965 Walter H. Campbell
1966 Edward M. Lindsey (to 1967)
1968 David A. Evans
1969 W. R. Bryan
1970 Robert D McCullough
1971 Robert J. Uplinger

Executive Administrators

1972 John H. Vogt
1974 W. L. Wilson
1978 Roy Schaetzl

Loyal Order of Moose

Governors

1904 Abner C. Jones
1905 Morey M. Dunlap
1906 O. W. Edmunds
1907 Curtis M. Gregg
1908 Ewing B. Marshall
1909 John D. O'Brien
1910 Edmund E. Tanner
1911 Arthur H. Jones
1912 Ralph W. E. Donges
1913 Walter E. Dorn
1914 Mahlon M. Garland
1915 Edward J. Henning
1916 Hyman D. Davis
1917 John W. Ford
1918 Charles A. A. McGee
1919 William F. Broening
1920 Darius A. Brown
1921 James F. Griffin
1922 J. Willis Pierson
1923 Frank J. Monahan
1924 Willard A. Markle
1925 J. Albert Cassedy
1926 Norman G. Heyd
1927 Ethelred M. Stafford
1928 Wallace A. McGowan
1929 Albert H. Ladner, Jr.
1930 Rodney H. Brandon
1931 Frederick N. Zihlman

1932 Henry W. Busch
1933 Albert J. Sartori
1934 William E. Buehler
1935 Walter S. Ruff
1936 William A. Anderson
1937 William J. Egan
1938 Roy H. Williams
1939 Bert W. Johnson
1940 Francis J. Clohessy
1941 Matthew M. Neely
1942 Frank J. LaBell
1943 Mark R. Gray
1944 George E. Gwilliam
1945 Charles W. Bowers
1946 Leo W. Ryan
1947 F. Roy Yoke
1948 Walter Gibson
1949 Willis E. Donley
1950 Oliver S. Twist
1951 James M. Ballard
1952 Fritchof T. Sallness
1953 Willard D. Campbell
1954 Ray V. Gibbens
1955 Paul E McCarville
1956 George W. Young
1957 Ralph A. Villani
1958 Henry F. Wallenwein
1959 Louis K. Thaler
1960 Clayton J. Crooks
1961 H. C. Byrd
1962 Gordon Jeffery
1963 Robert H. Mollohan
1964 Thomas J. Griffin
1965 Elmer E. Harter
1966 Harold D. Ross
1967 George R. Reilly
1969 Cecil Webster
1969 Carl A. Weis
1970 Howard Kline
1971 Edward C. Boyle
1972 Paul P. Schmitz (Director General)
1973 Carl A. Weis (Supreme Secretary)
1984 Donald Ross (Supreme Secretary)

Mediaeval Academy of America

1926 Edward K. Rand
1926 Charles H. Haskins
1927 Edward K. Rand
1929 John M. Manly
1930 Dana C. Munro
1933 Ralph A. Cram
1936 Charles H. Beeson
1939 Jeremiah D. M. Ford
1942 John S. P. Tatlock
1945 George R. Coffman
1948 Fred N. Robinson
1951 William E. Lunt
1954 Austin P. Evans
1957 Ernest H. Wilkins
1960 Berthold L. Ullman
1963 Albert C. Baugh
1966 Joseph R. Strayer
1969 Hamilton M. Smyser
1972 Paul J. Meyvaert
    (Executive Secretary)
1981 Luke Wenger (Executive Director)

Modern Language Association of America

1884 Franklin Carter
1887 James Russell Lowell
1892 Francis A. March
1894 A. Marshall Elliott
1895 James M. Hart
1896 Calvin Thomas
1897 Albert S. Cook
1898 Alcee Fortier
1899 Hans C. C. von Jagemann
1900 Thomas R. Price
1901 Edward S. Sheldon
1902 James W. Bright
1903 George Hempl
1904 George Lyman Kittredge
1905 Francis B. Gummere
1906 Henry A. Todd
1907 Fred N. Scott
1908 Frederick M. Warren
1909 Marion D. Learned
1910 Brander Matthews
1911 Lewis F. Mott
1912 Charles H. Grandgent
1913 Alexander R. Hohlfeld
1914 Felix E. Schelling
1915 Jefferson B. Fletcher
1916 James D. Bruce
1917 Kuno Francke
1918 Edward C. Armstrong
1920 John M. Manly
1921 William G. Howard
1922 Raymond Weeks
1923 Oliver F. Emerson
1924 William A. Neilson
1925 Hermann Collitz
1926 T. Atkinson Jenkins
1927 Ashley H. Thorndike
1928 Hugo K. Schilling
1929 William A. Nitze
1930 Frederick Tupper
1931 George O. Curme
1932 C. Carroll Marden
1933 John L. Lowes
1934 James T. Hatfield
1935 Colbert Searles
1936 Carleton Brown
1937 Eduard Prokosch
1938 John S. P. Tatlock
1939 H. Carrington Lancaster
1940 Karl Young
1941 John A. Walz
1942 Frederick M. Padelford
1943 Rudolph Schevill
1944 Robert H. Fife
1945 Fred N. Robinson
1946 Ernest H. Wilkins
1947 T. Moody Campbell
1948 Percy W. Long
1949 George W. Sherburn
1950 S. Griswold Morley
1951 Archer Taylor
1952 Albert C. Baugh
1953 Hayward Keniston
1954 LeRoy S. Kimball
1955 Louise Paund
1956 Gilbert Chinard
1957 Taylor Starck
1958 James H. Hanford
1959 William R. Parker
1960 Henri M. Peyre
1961 Henry W. Nordmeyer
1962 Kemp Malone
1963 Majorie Nicolson
1964 Morris Bishop
1965 Howard M. Jones
1966 Hermann J. Weigand
1967 George W. Stone, Jr.

1968	Otis W. Green			1934	Eric A. Camman	1913	George Pope
1969	Henry N. Smith			1935	Grant R. Lohnes	1918	Steven Mason
1970	Maynard Mack			1936	F. Richmond Fletcher	1921	John E. Edgerton
1971	Louis Kamps			1937	William F. Marsh	1932	Robert L. Lund
1972	Stuart P. Atkins			1938	J. Hugh Jackson	1934	C. L. Bardo

National Aeronautic Association

Executive Directors

1973 William David Schaefer
1979 Joel Canarroe
1985 Phyllis Franklin

1922	Howard E. Coffin
1923	Frederick B. Patterson
1924	Godfrey L. Cabot
1926	Porter H. Adams
1928	Hiram Bingham
1934	William Gibbs McAdoo
1936	Charles F. Horner
1940	Gill R. Wilson
1944	William R. Enyart
1946	L. Welch Pogue
1947	Arthur I. Boreman
1948	Louis E. Leverone
1951	Donald D. Webster
1951	Joseph T. Geuting, Jr.
1952	Harry K. Coffey
1954	Thomas G. Lanphier, Jr.
1960	Jacqueline Cochran
1962	Martin M. Decker
1963	William A. Ong
1965	Edward C. Sweeny
1966	James F. Nields
1968	Frederick B. Lee
1970	A. S. "Mike" Monroney
1974	J. B. Montgomery
1976	John P. Henebry
1977	John R. Alison
1979	Vic Powell (Executive Director)
1980	Brooke Allen (Executive Vice President)
1982	Clifton F. VonKann
1983	Everett W. Langworthy (Executive Vice President)

Motion Picture Association of America

1922 Will H. Hays
1945 Eric Johnston
1963 Ralph D. Hetzel (Acting)
1966 Jack Valenti

National Academy of Design

1826	Samuel F. B. Morse
1845	Asher B. Durand
1861	Samuel F. B. Morse
1862	Daniel Huntington
1870	Henry P. Gray
1871	William Page
1873	J. Q. A. Ward
1874	Worthington Whittredge
1877	Daniel Huntington
1890	Thomas W. Wood
1900	Frederick Dielman
1909	John W. Alexander
1915	J. Alden Weir
1917	Herbert Adams
1920	Edwin H. Blashfield
1926	Cass Gilbert
1933	Harry W. Watrous
1934	Jonas Lie
1939	Hobart Nichols
1949	DeWitt M. Lockman
1950	Lawrence G. White
1956	Eliot Clark
1959	John F. Harbeson
1962	Edgar I. Williams
1966	Alfred E. Poor
1965	Alice G. Melrose (Director)
1978	John H. Dobkin (Director)

National Association for the Advancement of Colored People (NAACP)

Presidents

1909 Storey Moorfield
1930 Joel E. Spingarn
1939 Arthur B. Spingarn
1966 Kivie Kaplan

Executive Secretaries

1909 Frances Blascoer
1917 Royal Nash
1918 John Shillady
1920 James Weldon Johnson
1929 Walter White
1955 Roy Wilkins
1976 Benjamin L. Hooks

National Academy of Television Arts and Sciences

1957 Ed Sullivan
1958 Harry S. Ackerman
1959 Walter Cronkite
1960 Harry S. Ackerman
1961 Robert F. Lewine
1963 Mort Werner
1964 Rod Serling
1966 Royal E. Blakeman
1968 Seymour Berns
1970 Robert F. Lewine
1977 John Cannon

National Association of Accountants

1919	J. Lee Nicholson
1920	William M. Lybrand
1922	J. P. Jordan
1924	William S. Kemp
1925	Clinton H. Scovell
1926	C. M. Finney
1927	Charles R. Stevenson
1928	Frank L. Sweetser
1929	Addison Boren
1930	Walter S. Gee
1930	V. W. Collins
1931	Thomas H. Sanders
1932	Harry A. Bullis
1933	Arthur H. Carter

1934	Eric A. Camman
1935	Grant R. Lohnes
1936	F. Richmond Fletcher
1937	William F. Marsh
1938	J. Hugh Jackson
1939	C. Howard Knapp
1940	Victor H. Stempf
1941	Harry E. Howell
1942	Wyman P. Fiske
1943	John H. DeVitt
1944	Martin A. Moore
1945	Frank Klein
1946	William J. Carter
1947	Mason Smith
1948	Clinton W. Bennett
1949	Logan Monroe
1950	William B. McCloskey
1951	Herman A. Papenfoth
1952	J. Brooks Heckert
1953	I. Wayne Keller
1954	Alexander J. Lindsay
1955	Charles R. Israel
1956	Philip J. Warner
1957	Harold W. Scott
1958	John B. Inglis
1959	Leslie I. Asher
1960	George A. Hewitt
1961	Donald G. Eder
1962	John B. Bachofer
1963	Merwin P. Cass
1964	Colin A. Stillwagen
1965	Joseph L. Brumit
1966	Firman H. Hass
1967	Thomas L. Morison
1968	James E. Meredith, Jr.
1969	Grant U. Meyers
1970	Ettore Barbatelli
1971	Julius E. Underwood

Executive Directors

1972 J. G. Underwood
1973 William M. Young, Jr.
1981 Robert L. Shultis

National Association of Broadcasters

1923	Eugene F. McDonald, Jr.
1925	Frank W. Elliot
1926	Earle C. Anthony
1928	William S. Hedges
1930	Walter J. Damm
1931	Harry Shaw
1932	Alfred J. McCosker
1934	J. Truman Ward
1935	Leo J. Fitzpatrick
1936	Charles W. Myers
1937	John Elmer
1938	Mark Ethridge
1938	Neville Miller
1944	J. Harold Ryan
1945	Justin Miller
1951	Harold E. Fellows
1961	LeRoy Collins
1965	Vincent T. Wasilewski
1983	Edward O. Fritts

National Association of Manufacturers (NAM)

1895	Thomas Dolan
1896	Theodore C. Search
1902	D. M. Parry
1906	J. W. Van Cleave
1909	John Kirby, Jr.

1913	George Pope
1918	Steven Mason
1921	John E. Edgerton
1932	Robert L. Lund
1934	C. L. Bardo
1936	C. W. Chester
1937	W. B. Warner
1938	Charles R. Hook
1939	Howard Coonley
1940	H. W. Prentis, Jr.
1941	W. D. Fuller
1942	W. P. Witherow
1943	F. C. Crawford
1944	R. M. Gaylord
1945	Ira Mosher
1946	R. R. Wason
1947	Earl Bunting
1948	Morris Sayre
1949	W. F. Bennett
1950	C. A. Putnam
1951	William H. Ruffin
1952	William J. Grede
1953	Charles R. Sligh, Jr.
1954	H. C. McClellan
1955	G. H. Riter, III
1956	C. G. Parker
1957	Ernest G. Swiger
1958	Milton C. Lightner
1959	Stanley C. Hope
1960	R. F. Bannow
1961	John W. McGovern
1962	Donald J. Hardenbrook
1963	W. P. Gullander
1974	E. Douglas Kenna
1977	R. Heath Larry
1980	Alexander B. Trowbridge

National Conference of Christians and Jews

1928 Everett R. Clinchy
1958 Lewis W. Jones
1965 Sterling W. Brown
1973 David Hyatt
1983 Jacqueline G. Wexler

National Education Association

1939	Amy Hinrichs
1942	A. Cline Flora
1944	Frank L. Schlagle
1946	Pearl Wanamaker
1947	Glenn E. Snow
1948	Mabel Studebaker
1949	Andrew D. Holt
1950	Corma A. Mowrey
1951	J. Cloyd Miller
1952	Sarah C. Caldwell
1953	William A. Early
1954	Waurine Walker
1955	John L. Buford
1956	Martha A. Shull
1957	Lyman V. Ginger
1958	Ruth S. Wright
1959	Walter W. Eshelman
1960	Clarice Kline
1961	Ewald Turner
1962	Hazel B. Nielson
1963	Robert H. Wyatt
1964	Lois V. Edinger
1965	Richard D. Batchelder
1966	Irvamae Applegate
1967	Braulio Alonso
1968	Libby Koontz
1969	George D. Fischer

1970 Helen Bain
1971 Donald E. Morrison
1972 Catharine Barrett
1973 Sim M. Lambert
(Executive Secretary)
1974 James A. Harris
1975 Terry E. Herndon
(Executive Director, to
1983)
1985 Don Cameron (Executive
Director)

National Geographic Society

1888 Gardiner G. Hubbard
1898 Alexander Graham Bell
1904 W. J. McGee
1904 Grove K. Gilbert
(Acting)
1905 Willis L. Moore
1910 Henry Gannett
1915 O. H. Tittmann
1919 John E. Pillsbury
1920 Gilbert H. Grosvenor
1954 John O. La Gorce
1957 Melville B. Grosvenor
1967 Melvin M. Payne
1977 Robert E. Doyle
1981 Gilbert M. Grosvenor

National Grange

1868 William Saunders
1874 D. W. Adams
1876 John T. Jones
1878 S. E. Adams
1880 J. J. Woodman
1886 Put Darden
1888 James Draper
1889 J. H. Brigham
1898 Aaron Jones
1906 N. J. Bachelder
1912 Oliver Wilson
1920 S. J. Lowell
1924 L. J. Taber
1942 A. S. Goss
1950 Henry Sherwood
1951 Herschel D. Newsom
1969 John W. Scott
1980 Edward Anderson

National Health Council

1921 Livingston Farrand
1923 L. K. Frankel
1927 William F. Snow
1934 Theodore Roosevelt
1936 Donald B. Armstrong
1938 Ira V. Hiscock
1940 Kendall Emerson
1942 George S. Stevenson
1944 Eleanor Brown Merrill
1946 Philip R. Mather
1950 Ernest L. Stebbins
1952 Mrs. Oswald B. Lord
1953 Robin C. Buerki
1953 A. W. Dent
1955 Hugh R. Leavell
1956 Leona Baumgartner
1957 Basil O'Connor
1958 Norvin C. Kiefer
1959 Ruth B. Freeman
1960 James E. Perkins
1961 James H. Sterner

1962 George Bugbee
1963 Rome A. Betts
1964 Edwin L. Crosby
1965 George James
1966 John W. Knutson
1967 J. Douglas Colman
1968 Leroy E. Burney
1969 Margaret B. Dolan
1970 Hollis S. Ingraham
1971 Richard P. McGrail
1972 Peter G. Meek (Executive
Director)
1974 Robert C. Long
1976 Edward H. Van Ness
(Executive Vice President)

National Institute of Arts and Letters

1899 Charles D. Warner
1901 William Dean Howells
1904 Edmund C. Stedman
1906 William M. Sloane
1909 Henry Van Dyke
1911 John W. Alexander
1912 Brander Matthews
1914 Edwin H. Blashfield
1916 Augustus Thomas
1918 Cass Gilbert
1920 Robert Grant
1923 Maurice F. Egan
1924 John C. Van Dyke
1925 Arthur T. Hadley
1927 Walter Damrosch
1929 William Lyon Phelps
1931 Wilbur L. Cross
1936 Walter Damrosch
1941 Arthur Train
1945 Douglas Moore
1953 Marc Connelly
1956 Malcolm Cowley
1959 Glenway Wescott
1962 Malcolm Cowley
1965 George F. Kennan
1968 Allen Tate
1969 William Maxwell
1972 Jacques Barzun
1973 Margaret M. Mills
(Executive Director)

National Institute of Social Sciences

1912 Hamilton W. Mabie
1916 Nicholas Murray Butler
1917 Irving Fisher
1918 Emory R. Johnson
1922 Austin B. Fletcher
1923 Helen Hartley Jenkins
1924 Chester S. Lord
1926 William C. Redfield
1932 C. Stuart Gager
1935 Henry Fletcher
1937 William E. Hall
1942 Colby M. Chester
1945 Clarence G. Michalis
1950 Hugh Bullock
1953 Walter Hoving
1956 Frank Pace, Jr.
1959 Arthur K. Watson
1962 Frank Pace, Jr.
1978 Susan H. Archdeacon, Jr.
1980 Geraldine Kunstadter
1981 J. Sinclair Armstrong
1985 Robert E. Salisbury (Vice
President)

National Municipal League

1894 James C. Carter
1903 Charles J. Bonaparte
1910 William D. Foulke
1915 Lawson Purdy
1919 Charles Evans Hughes
1921 Henry M. Waite
1923 Frank L. Polk
1927 Richard S. Childs
1931 Murray Seasongood
1934 Harold W. Dodds
1937 Clarence A. Dykstra
1940 John G. Winant
1946 Charles Edison
1950 Henry Bruere
1953 George H. Gallup
1957 Cecil Morgan
1960 William Collins
1963 Alfred E. Driscoll
1970 William W. Scranton
1972 William N. Cassella, Jr.
(Executive Director)
1987 John Parr (Executive
Director)

National Sculpture Society

1893 J. Q. A. Ward
1905 Daniel Chester French
1906 Karl Bitter
1908 Herbert Adams
1910 Hermon A. MacNeil
1912 Herbert Adams
1914 Karl Bitter
1915 Herbert Adams
1917 Paul W. Bartlett
1919 F. G. R. Roth
1920 Robert Aitken
1922 Hermon A. MacNeil
1924 James E. Fraser
1927 Chester Beach
1928 Adolph A. Weinman
1931 Charles Keck
1934 John Gregory
1939 Paul Manship
1942 Edmond Amateis
1944 Cecil Howard
1944 Paul Manship (Acting)
1945 Donald De Lue
1948 Sidney Waugh
1950 Karl H. Gruppe
1951 Wheeler Williams
1954 Leo Friedlander
1957 Adlai S. Hardin
1960 C. Paul Jennewein
1963 Adolph Block
1965 Herbert L. Kammerer
1967 Frank Eliscu
1970 Michael Lantz
1973 Robert A. Weinman
1976 Charles Parks
1979 Granville W. Carter
1980 Claire A. Stein (Executive
Director)

National Society of the Daughters of the American Revolution

Presidents General

1890 Mrs. Benjamin Harrison

1893 Mrs. Adlai E. Stevenson
1895 Mrs. John W. Foster
1896 Mrs. Adlai E. Stevenson
1898 Mrs. Daniel Manning
1901 Mrs. Charles W.
Fairbanks
1905 Mrs. Donald McLean
1909 Mrs. Matthew T. Scott
1913 Mrs. William Cumming
Story
1917 Mrs. George Thacher
Guernsey
1920 Mrs. George Maynard
Minor
1923 Mrs. Anthony Wayne
Cook
1926 Mrs. Grace L. H.
Brosseau
1929 Mrs. Lowell Fletcher
Hobart
1932 Mrs. Russell W. Magna
1935 Mrs. William A. Becker
1938 Mrs. Henry M. Robert,
Jr.
1941 Mrs. William H. Pouch
1944 Mrs. Julius Y. Talmadge
1947 Mrs. Roscoe C. O'Byrne
1950 Mrs. James B. Patton
1953 Gertrude S. Carraway
1956 Mrs. Frederic A. Groves
1959 Mrs. Ashmead White
1962 Mrs. Robert V. H.
Duncan
1965 Mrs. William H. Sullivan,
Jr.
1968 Mrs. Erwin F. Seimes
1971 Mrs. Donald Spicer
1976 Mrs. Waklee Rawson
Smith
1977 Mrs. George Upham
Baylies
1981 Mrs. Richard Denny
Shelby
1982 Patricia W. Shelby
1984 Sarah M. King

National Society of the Sons of the American Revolution

Presidents General

1889 Lucius P. Deming
1890 William S. Webb
1892 Horace Porter
1897 Edwin S. Barrett
1899 Franklin Murphy
1900 J. C. Breckinridge
1901 Walter S. Logan
1902 Edwin Warfield
1903 Edwin S. Greeley
1904 James D. Hancock
1905 Francis H. Appleton
1906 Cornelius A. Pugsley
1907 Nelson A. McClary
1908 Henry Stockbridge
1909 Morris B. Beardsley
1910 William A. Marble
1911 Moses G. Parker
1912 James M. Richardson
1913 R. C. Ballard Thruston
1915 Newell B. Woodworth
1916 Elmer M. Wentworth
1918 Louis A. Ames
1919 Chancellor L. Jenks
1920 James H. Preston
1921 Wallace McCamant
1922 W. I. L. Adams
1923 Arthur P. Sumner

1924	Harrison L. Lewis
1925	Harvey F. Remington
1926	Wilbert H. Barrett
1927	Ernest E. Rogers
1928	Ganson Depew
1929	Howard C. Rowley
1930	Josiah A. Van Orsdel
1931	Benjamin N. Johnson
1932	Frederick W. Millspaugh
1933	Arthur M. McCrillis
1935	Henry F. Baker
1936	Messmore Kendall
1940	Loren E. Souers
1941	G. Ridgely Sappington
1942	Sterling F. Mutz
1943	Smith L. Multer
1946	Allen L. Oliver
1947	A. Herbert Foreman
1948	Charles B. Shaler
1948	Ben H. Powell, III
1949	John W. Finger
1950	Wallace C. Hall
1952	Ray O. Edwards
1953	Arthur A. de la Houssaye
1954	Milton M. Lory
1955	Edgar Williamson, Jr.
1956	Eugene P. Carver, Jr.
1957	George E. Tarbox, Jr.
1958	Walter A. Wentworth
1959	Charles A. Jones
1960	Herschel S. Murphy
1961	Horace Y. Kitchell
1962	Charles A. Anderson
1963	Robert L. Sonfield
1964	Harry T. Burn
1965	Howard E. Coe
1966	Kenneth G. Smith
1967	Len Y. Smith
1968	Walter G. Sterling
1969	James B. Gardiner
1970	Walter R. Martin
1971	Eugene C. McGuire
1972	Warren S. Woodward (Executive Secretary)
1978	Ralph H. Goodell, Jr. (Executive Secretary)
1981	John C. Davis (Executive Director)

National Urban League

1910	George E. Haynes
1917	Eugene K. Jones
1941	Lester B. Granger
1961	Whitney M. Young, Jr.
1971	Vernon E. Jordan, Jr.
1982	John E. Jacobs

National Wildlife Federation

1936	Jay N. Darling
1938	David A. Aylward
1950	Claude D. Kelley
1961	Paul A. Herbert
1963	Ross Leffler
1964	Louis D. McGregor
1967	Donald J. Zinn
1970	James H. Shaeffer
1971	Thomas L. Kimball (Executive Vice President)
1981	Jay D. Hair (Executive Vice President)

Nobles of the Mystic Shrine (Shriners)

Imperial Potentates

1876	Walter M. Fleming
1886	Sam Briggs
1892	William B. Melish
1893	Thomas J. Hudson
1894	William B. Melish
1895	Charles L. Field
1896	Harrison Dingman
1897	Albert B. McGaffey
1898	Ethelbert F. Allen
1899	John H. Atwood
1900	Lou B. Winsor
1901	Philip C. Shaffer
1902	Henry C. Akin
1903	George H. Green
1904	George L. Brown
1905	Henry A. Collins
1906	Alvah P. Clayton
1907	Frank C. Roundy
1908	Edwin I. Alderman
1909	George L. Street
1910	Fred A. Hines
1911	John F. Treat
1912	William J. Cunningham
1913	William W. Irwin
1914	Frederick R. Smith
1915	J. Putnam Stevens
1916	Henry F. Niedringhaus
1917	Charles E. Ovenshire
1918	Elias J. Jacoby
1919	W. Freeland Kendrick
1920	Ellis L. Garretson
1921	Ernest A. Cutts
1922	James S. McCandless
1923	Conrad V. Dykeman
1924	James E. Chandler
1925	James C. Burger
1926	David W. Crosland
1927	Clarence M. Dunbar
1928	Frank C. Jones
1929	Leo V. Youngworth
1930	Esten A. Fletcher
1931	Thomas J. Houston
1932	Earl C. Mills
1933	John N. Sebrell
1934	Dana S. Williams
1935	Leonard P. Steuart
1936	Hugh M. Caldwell
1936	Clyde I. Webster
1937	Walter S. Sugden
1938	A. A. D. Rahn
1939	Walter D. Cline
1940	George F. Olendorf
1941	Thomas C. Law
1942	Albert H. Fiebach
1943	Morley E. Mackenzie
1944	Alfred G. Arvold
1945	William H. Woodfield, Jr.
1946	George H. Rowe
1947	Karl R. Hammers
1948	Galloway Calhoun
1949	Harold Lloyd
1950	Hubert M. Poteat
1951	Robert G. Wilson, Jr.
1952	Harvey A. Beffa
1953	Remmie L. Arnold
1954	Frank S. Land
1955	Walter C. Guy
1956	Gerald D. Crary
1957	Thomas W. Melham
1958	George E. Stringfellow
1959	Clayton F. Andrews
1960	George A. Mattison, Jr.
1961	Marshall M. Porter
1962	George M. Klepper

1963	Harold C. Close
1964	O. Carlyle Brock
1965	Barney W. Collins
1966	Orville F. Rush
1967	Thomas F. Seay
1968	Chester A. Hogan
1969	J. Worth Baker
1972	Booker T. Alexander (Imperial Recorder)
1984	Charles G. Cumpstone, Jr. (Executive Director)

Optical Society of America

1916	P. G. Nutting
1918	F. E. Wright
1920	F. K. Richtmyer
1921	J. P. C. Southall
1922	L. T. Troland
1924	H. E. Ives
1926	W. E. Forsythe
1928	I. G. Priest
1930	L. A. Jones
1932	E. C. Crittenden
1933	W. B. Rayton
1935	Arthur C. Hardy
1937	R. C. Gibbs
1939	K. S. Gibson
1941	A. G. Worthing
1943	A. H. Pfund
1945	G. R. Harrison
1947	Rudolf Kingslake
1949	William F. Meggers
1951	Brian O'Brien
1953	Deane B. Judd
1955	Ralph A. Sawyer
1958	Irvine C. Gardner
1959	John Strong
1960	James G. Baker
1961	Wallace R. Brode
1962	David L. MacAdam
1963	Stanley S. Ballard
1964	Richard C. Lord
1965	S. Q. Duntley
1966	Van Zandt Williams
1967	John A. Sanderson
1968	A. Francis Turner
1969	Karl G. Kessler
1970	W. Lewis Hyde
1971	Bruce H. Billings
1972	Alden B. Meinel
1973	Jarus W. Quinn (Executive Director)

Pilgrim Society

1820	Joshua Thomas
1821	John Watson
1926	Alden Bradford
1841	Nathaniel M. David
1845	Charles H. Warren
1853	Richard Warren
1862	Edward Everett
1865	Edward S. Tobey
1872	William T. Davis
1879	Thomas Russell
1887	John Davis Long
1895	Arthur Lord
1925	Howland Davis
1930	William R. Hedge
1943	Ellis W. Brewster
1965	Horace C. Weston
1970	Ralph C. Weaver
1971	Lawrence D. Geller (Director)

1978	Laurence R. Pizer (Director)

Poetry Society of America

1910	Edward J. Wheeler
1920	Witter Bynner
1922	John Erskine
1924	Charles W. Stork
1925	Arthur Guiterman
1927	Curtis H. Page
1929	William Griffith
1932	Harold T. Pulsifer
1933	Leonora Speyer
1935	Henry G. Leach
1938	Padraic Colum
1940	A. M. Sullivan
1943	Alfred Kreymborg
1945	J. Donald Adams
1947	Carl Carmer
1949	Robert Hillyer
1950	A. M. Sullivan
1952	Robert Hillyer
1954	George N. Shuster
1955	Edward Davison
1957	Clarence R. Decker
1961	Cecil Hemley
1963	Richard V. Lindabury
1963	Loyd Haberly
1969	Charles Angoff
1970	Charles A. Wagner (Executive Secretary)
1976	Richard Eberhart
1977	Charles A. Wagner (Executive Secretary)
1979	Douglas Turnbaugh (Executive Director)
1986	Judith Baumel (Administrative Director)

Rotary International

1910	Paul P. Harris
1912	Glenn C. Mead
1913	Russell F. Greiner
1914	Frank L. Mulholland
1915	Allen D. Albert
1916	Arch C. Klumph
1918	John Poole
1919	Albert S. Adams
1920	Estes Snedecor
1922	Raymond M. Mavens
1923	Guy Gundaker
1924	Everett W. Hill
1925	Donald A. Adams
1926	Harry H. Rogers
1927	Arthur H. Sapp
1929	M. Eugene Newsom
1930	Almon E. Roth
1932	Clinton P. Anderson
1934	Robert S. Lee Hill
1935	Edward R. Johnson
1936	Will R. Manier, Jr.
1938	George C. Hager
1939	Walter D. Head
1941	Tom J. Davis
1943	Charles L. Wheeler
1944	Richard H. Wells
1946	Richard C. Hedke
1947	S. Kendrick Guernsey
1949	Percy Hodgson
1951	Frank E. Spain
1952	H. J. Brunnier
1954	Herbert J. Taylor
1955	A. Z. Baker
1957	Charles G. Tennent

1958 Clifford A. Randall
1960 J. Edd McLaughlin
1961 Joseph A. Abey
1963 Carl P. Miller
1964 Charles W. Pettengill
1966 Richard L. Evans
1967 Luther H. Hodges
1969 James F. Conway
1970 William E. Walk, Jr.
1972 Ernst G. Breitholtz
1972 Harry A. Stewart
     (General Secretary)
1980 Herbert A. Pigman
     (General Secretary)

Society of Motion Picture and Television Engineers

1916 C. Francis Jenkins
1919 H. A. Campe
1922 Lawrence C. Porter
1924 Lloyd A. Jones
1926 Willard B. Cook
1929 Lawrence C. Porter
1930 John I. Crabtree
1932 Alfred N. Goldsmith
1934 Homer G. Tasker
1937 Sidney K. Wolf
1939 E. Allan Williford
1941 Emery Huse
1943 Herbert Griffin
1945 Donald E. Hyndman
1947 Loren L. Ryder
1949 Earl I. Sponable
1951 Peter Mole
1953 Herbert Barnett

1955 John G. Frayne
1957 Barton Kreuzer
1959 Norwood L. Simmons
1961 John W. Servies
1963 Reid H. Ray
1965 Ethan M. Stifle
1967 G. Carleton Hunt
1969 Deane R. White
1971 Wilton R. Holm

Executive Directors

1972 Dennis A. Courtney
1980 Donald F. Breidt
1982 Conrad L. Scheetz
1985 Lynette H. Robinson

Society of the Cincinnati

Presidents General

1783 George Washington
1800 Alexander Hamilton
1805 Charles C. Pinckney
1825 Thomas Pinckney
1829 Aaron Ogden
1839 Morgan Lewis
1844 William Popham
1848 Henry A. S. Dearborn
1854 Hamilton Fish
1896 William Wayne
1902 Winslow Warren
1932 John C. Daves
1939 Bryce Metcalf
1950 Isaac A. Pennypacker
1950 Edgar E. Hume
1952 John F. R. Scott
1953 Richard H. Wilmer
1956 Catesby Jones
1959 Blanchard Randall

1962 Francis W. Hatch
1965 Charles W. Lippitt
1968 Frank A. Chisholm

Secretaries General

1969 Irving Caywood Hanners
1971 Stephen Caldwell Millett
1977 John Absalom Baird
1983 Michael Miller

Veterans of Foreign Wars of the United States

1913 Rice W. Means
1914 Thomas Crago
1915 Gus E. Hartung
1916 Albert Rabing
1917 William E. Ralston
1918 F. Warner Karling
1920 Robert G. Woodside
1922 Tillinghast Huston
1923 Lloyd M. Brett
1924 John H. Dunn
1925 Fred Stover
1926 Theodore Stitt
1927 Frank T. Strayer
1928 Eugene P. Carver
1929 Hezekiah N. Duff
1930 Paul C. Wolman
1931 Darold D. DeCoe
1932 Robert E. Coontz
1933 James E. VanZandt
1936 Bernard W. Kearney
1937 Scott P. Squyers
1938 Eugene I. Van Antwerp

1939 Otis N. Brown
1940 Joseph C. Menendez
1941 Max Singer
1942 Robert T. Merrill
1943 Carl J. Schoeninger
1944 Jean A. Brunner
1945 Joseph M. Stack
1946 Louis E. Starr
1947 Ray H. Brannaman
1948 Lyall T. Beggs
1949 Clyde A. Lewis
1950 Charles C. Ralls
1951 Frank C. Hilton
1952 James W. Cothran
1953 Wayne E. Richards
1954 Merton B. Tice
1955 Timothy J. Murphy
1956 Cooper T. Holt
1957 Richard L. Roudebush
1958 John W. Mahan
1959 Louis G. Feldmann
1960 Ted C. Connell
1961 Robert E. Hansen
1962 Byron B. Gentry
1963 Joseph J. Lombardo
1964 John A. Jenkins
1965 Andy Borg
1966 Leslie M. Fry
1967 Joseph A. Scerra
1968 Richard Homan
1969 Ray Gallagher
1970 Herbert R. Rainwater
1971 Joseph L. Vicites
1972 Julian Dickenson
     (Adjutant General)
1982 Howard E. Vander-Clute,
     Jr. (Adjutant General)

XIX
Laureates

Laureates

A listing of Americans who have been recognized for outstanding achievements in the arts, sciences, and the humanities and for contributions to the betterment of mankind.

Academy of American Poets Fellowship

(Recognizes distinguished poetic achievement.)

1937 Edwin Markham
1946 Edgar Lee Masters
1947 Ridgely Torrence
1948 Percy Mackaye
1950 E. E. Cummings
1952 Padraic Colum
1953 Robert Frost
1954 Louise Townsend Nicholl
1955 Rolfe Humphries
1956 William Carlos Williams
1957 Conrad Aiken
1958 Robinson Jeffers
1959 Leonie Adams
1959 Louis Bogan
1960 Jesse Stuart
1961 Horace Gregory
1962 John Crowe Ransom
1963 Ezra Pound
1963 Allen Tate
1964 Elizabeth Bishop
1965 Marianne Moore
1966 Archibald MacLeish
1966 John Berryman
1967 Mark Van Doren
1968 Stanley Kunitz
1969 Richard Eberhart
1969 Anthony Hecht
1970 Howard Nemerov
1971 James Wright
1972 W. D. Snodgrass
1973 W. S. Merwin
1974 Leonie Adams
1975 Robert Hayden
1976 J. V. Cunningham
1977 Louis O. Coxe
1978 Josephine Miles
1979 Mark Strand
1979 May Swenson
1980 Mona Van Duyn
1981 Richard Hugo
1982 John Frederick Nims
1983 James Schuyler
1984 John Ashbery
1985 Maxine Kumin
1986 Irving Feldman

Edward Goodrich Acheson Medal and Prize

(Awarded every second year by the Electrochemical Society, Inc., for a distinguished contribution to any of the branches fostered by the society.)

1929 Edward G. Acheson
1931 Edwin F. Northrup

1933 Colin G. Fink
1935 Frank J. Tone
1937 Frederick M. Becket
1939 Francis C. Frary
1942 Charles F. Burgess
1944 William Blum
1948 Duncan A. MacInnes
1950 George W. Vinal
1952 John W. Marden
1954 George W. Heise
1956 Robert M. Burns
1958 William J. Kroll
1960 Henry B. Linford
1962 Charles L. Faust
1964 Earl A. Gulbransen
1966 Warren C. Vosburgh
1968 Francis L. LaQue
1970 Samuel Ruben
1972 Charles W. Tobias
1974 C. V. King
1976 N. Bruce Hannay
1978 David A. Vermilyea
1980 Ernest B. Yeager
1982 Harry C. Gatos
1984 Norman Hackerman
1986 Erik M. Pell

Benjamin Altman Prize

(Awarded annually by the National Academy of Design to recognize achievement in painting in oil.)

Figure Painting

1915 Charles W. Hawthorne
1916 Lawton Parker
1917 Daniel Garber
1918 Victor Higgins
1919 Charles C. Curran
1921 Walter Ufer
1921 Ernest L. Blumenschein
1922 Leon Kroll
1923 Louis Betts
1924 Childe Hassam
1926 Karl Anderson
1926 Wayman Adams
1927 Lilian Wescott Hale
1928 J. W. Schlaikjer
1929 Harry W. Watrous
1930 Gifford Beal
1931 Eugene Higgins
1932 Leon Kroll
1935 Jean MacLane
1936 Sidney E. Dickinson
1937 Charles S. Duncan
1939 Abram Poole
1940 Abram Poole
1941 Randall Davey
1942 Eugene Higgins
1943 Paul Clemens
1944 Ivan Albright
1945 Greta Matson
1945 Guy Pene Du Bois

1947 Philip Guston
1948 John Carroll
1949 Fletcher Martin
1951 Robert Philipp
1952 Marion Greenwood
1953 Fred Nagler
1954 John Carroll
1955 Isabel Bishop
1956 Morton Roberts
1957 Nancy Ellen Craig
1958 Ben Kamihira
1959 Joseph Hirsch
1960 Ann Eshner
1961 Jules Kirschenbaum
1962 Ben Kamihira
1963 John W. Reilly
1964 Edward Melcarth
1966 Joseph Hirsch
1967 Isabel Bishop
1968 Barbara Adrian
1969 Burton Silverman
1971 Alice Neel
1972 Gregorio Prestopino
1973 Isabel Bishop
1974 Charles Reid
1975 Jack Levine
1976 Balcomb Greene
1977 Will Barnet
1978 Joseph Hirsch
1979 Robert Gwathmey
1980 Joe Lasker
1981 Lenart Anderson
1983 Alice Neel
1984 Cornelius Ruhtenberg
1985 Jerome Witkin
1986 Rosemarie Beck

Landscape Painting

1916 Charles Rosen
1917 Charles H. Davis
1918 Paul Dougherty
1919 Edward W. Redfield
1920 W. Elmer Schofield
1921 Ernest Lawson
1922 Daniel Garber
1923 Paul King
1924 William L. Lathrop
1925 Hobart Nichols
1926 Childe Hassam
1927 Daniel Garber
1928 Ernest Lawson
1929 William S. Robinson
1930 Theodore Van Soelen
1931 Aldro T. Hibbard
1932 Victor Higgins
1933 W. Granville-Smith
1934 Hobart Nichols
1935 Leon Kroll
1937 Sidney Laufman
1938 Frank Mechau
1940 Chauncey F. Ryder
1941 John F. Folinsbee
1942 Zsissly
1943 Antonio P. Martino

1944 Carl Gaertner
1945 James W. Kerr
1945 Guy Pene Du Bois
1950 John F. Folinsbee
1951 Francis Speight
1952 Carl Gaertner
1953 Walter Stuempfig
1954 William Thon
1955 Furman J. Finck
1956 Ethel Magafan
1957 Edward Betts
1958 Francis Speight
1959 Edward Betts
1960 Seymour Reminick
1961 William Thon
1962 Paul Sample
1963 Karl Knaths
1964 Zsissly
1965 Karl Knaths
1966 Edward Betts
1967 William Thon
1968 Ida Oganoff
1969 Paul W. Zimmerman
1971 Anne Poor
1972 John Hultberg
1973 Ethel Magafan
1974 Reuben Tam
1975 Giovanni Martino
1976 Herman Rose
1977 Reuben Tam
1978 John Day
1979 Sidney Laufman
1980 Ethel Magafan
1981 Karl Schrag
1983 Herman Rose
1984 Carolyn Harris
1985 Gregory Gillespie
1986 Carl Ashby

American Academy of Arts and Letters Award of Merit Medal

(Presented annually to an outstanding person in America, not a member of the institute, representing the following arts: painting, sculpture, novel, poetry, and drama.)

1942 Charles E. Burchfield
1944 Theodore Dreiser
1945 W. H. Auden
1947 Andrew Wyeth
1948 Donal Hord
1951 Sidney Kingsley
1952 Rico Lebrun
1953 Ivan Mestrovic
1954 Ernest Hemingway
1957 Raphael Soyer
1960 Hilda Doolittle

531

1961	Clifford Odets
1962	Charles Sheeler
1963	Chaim Gross
1964	John O'Hara
1967	John E. Heliker
1968	Joseph Cornell
1969	Vladimir Nabokov
1970	Reed H. Whittemore
1972	Clyfford Still
1973	Reuben Nakian
1974	Nelson Algren
1975	Galway Kinnell
1978	Tony Smith
1979	William Gass
1980	Richard Howard
1981	John Guare
1982	Myron Stout
1983	Elizabeth Spencer
1984	Raoul Hague
1985	Richard Stern
1986	Kenneth Koch

American Academy of Arts and Letters Gold Medal

(Awarded to an American citizen, not a member of the academy of National Institute of Arts and Letters, to recognize special distinction in literature, art, or music. Discontinued in order to avoid confusion with the Gold Medal of the Institute, which is presented in the name of the academy.)

1915	Charles W. Eliot
1923	Mariana Griswold
1923	Van Rensselaer
1925	Cecilia Beaux
1929	Edith Wharton
1930	Anna Hyatt Huntington
1942	Ernest Bloch
1948	Bruce Rogers

American Bar Association Medal

(Awarded to a member of the bar in the United States for conspicuous service to the cause of American jurisprudence.)

1929	Samuel Williston
1930	Elihu Root
1931	Oliver Wendell Holmes
1932	John H. Wigmore
1934	George W. Wickersham
1938	Herbert Harley
1939	Edgar B. Tolman
1940	Roscoe Pound
1941	George Wharton Pepper
1942	Charles Evans Hughes
1943	John J. Parker
1944	Hatton W. Sumners
1946	Carl McFarland
1947	William L. Ransom
1948	Arthur T. Vanderbilt
1950	Orie L. Phillips
1951	Reginald H. Smith
1952	Harrison Tweed
1953	Frank E. Holman
1954	George M. Morris
1956	Robert G. Storey
1957	William C. Mason
1958	E. Smythe Gambrell
1959	Grenville Clark
1960	William A. Schnader
1961	Jacob M. Lashly

1962	Tom C. Clark
1963	Felix Frankfurter
1964	Henry S. Drinker
1965	Edmund M. Morgan
1966	Charles S. Rhyne
1967	Roger J. Traynor
1968	J. Edward Lumbard
1969	Walter V. Schaefer
1970	Frank J. Haymond
1971	Whitney North Seymour
1972	Harold J. Gallagher
1973	William J. Jameson
1974	Ross L. Malone
1975	Leon Jaworski
1976	Bernard G. Segal
1977	Edward L. Wright
1978	Erwin N. Griswold
1979	Lewis F. Powell, Jr.
1981	Chesterfield Smith
1982	Earl F. Morris
1984	Robert W. Meserve
1986	Justin A. Stanley

American Heart Association Research Achievement Award

(Conferred annually for outstanding achievement in the field of cardiovascular research.)

1953	Paul Dudley White
1954	Albert Szent-Gyorgyi
1955	Carl J. Wiggers
1956	Louis N. Katz
1957	Isaac Starr
1958	Irvine H. Page
1959	Robert E. Gross
1960	Karl P. Link
1960	Edgar V. Allen
1960	Irving S. Wright
1961	Charles H. Rammelkamp, Jr.
1962	Maurice B. Visscher
1963	Donald E. Gregg
1964	Rebecca C. Lancefield
1965	John H. Gibbon, Jr.
1966	Harry Goldblatt
1967	Wallace O. Fenn
1968	Julius H. Comroe, Jr.
1969	Otto Krayer
1970	Robert W. Berliner
1971	Earl W. Sutherland, Jr.
1972	Eugene Braunwald
1973	Earl H. Wood
1974	Richard J. Bing
1975	Arthur C. Guyton
1976	John W. Kirklin
1977	Brian F. Hoffman
1978	Edward H. Ahrens, Jr.
1979	Robert M. Berne
1980	Jesse E. Edwards
1980	Maurice Lev
1981	Jeremiah Stamler
1982	Lewis Dexter
1983	Murray Rabinowitz
1984	Michael S. Brown
1984	Joseph L. Goldstein
1985	Harold T. Dodge
1986	Edgar Haber

American Institute of Architects Fine Arts Medal

(Awarded annually to honor distinguished achievement in the fine arts, including painting, sculpture, music, and literature; discontinued after 1975.)

1921	Paul Manship
1923	Arthur F. Mathews
1925	John Singer Sargent
1926	Leopold Stokowski
1927	Lee Lawrie
1928	H. Siddons Mowbray
1930	Adolph A. Weinman
1931	Frederick L. Olmsted
1934	James H. Breasted
1936	Robert Edmond Jones
1944	John Taylor Arms
1947	Samuel Chamberlain
1948	John Marin
1949	Louis C. Rosenberg
1950	Edward Steichen
1951	Thomas Church
1952	Marshall M. Fredericks
1953	Donal Hord
1954	Julian H. Harris
1955	Ivan Mestrovic
1956	M. Hidreth Meiere
1957	Mark Tobey
1958	Viktor Schreckengost
1959	Kenneth Hedrich
1960	Thomas Hart Benton
1961	Alexander Calder
1962	Stuart Davis
1963	Isamu Noguchi
1965	Roberto B. Marx
1966	Ben Shahn
1967	Constantino Nivola
1968	Gyorgy Kepes
1970	Richard Lippald
1971	Anthony Smith
1972	George Rickey
1973	Harry Bertoia
1974	Ruth A. Lanier
1975	Josef Albers

American Institute of Architects Gold Medal

(Awarded from time to time to honor distinguished achievement in architecture.)

1909	Charles F. McKim
1911	George B. Post
1923	Henry Bacon
1925	Bertram G. Goodhue
1927	Howard V. Shaw
1929	Milton B. Medary
1938	Paul P. Cret
1944	Louis H. Sullivan
1947	Eliel Saarinen
1948	Charles D. Maginnis
1949	Frank Lloyd Wright
1951	Bernard R. Maybeck
1953	William A. Delano
1956	Clarence S. Stein
1957	Ralph Walker
1957	Louis Skidmore
1958	John W. Root
1959	Walter Gropius
1960	Ludwig Mies van der Rohe
1962	Eero Saarinen
1967	Wallace K. Harrison

1968	Marcel Breuer
1969	William W. Wurster
1970	R. Buckminster Fuller
1971	Louis I. Kahn
1972	Pietro Belluschi
1977	Richard Joseph Neutra
1978	Philip C. Johnson
1979	I. M. Pei
1981	Jose Luis Sert
1982	Romaldo Giurgola
1983	Nathaniel A. Owings
1985	William Caudill
1986	Arthur Erickson

American Institute of Chemists Gold Medal

(Awarded annually to recognize outstanding service to the science of chemistry or to the profession of chemistry in America.)

1926	William Blum
1927	Lafayette B. Mendel
1929	Francis P. Garvan
1929	Mrs. Francis P. Garvan
1930	George Eastman
1931	Andrew W. Mellon
1931	Richard B. Mellon
1932	Charles H. Herty
1933	Henry C. Sherman
1934	James B. Conant
1936	Marston T. Bogert
1937	James F. Norris
1938	Frederick G. Cottrell
1940	Gustav Egloff
1941	Henry G. Knight
1942	William L. Evans
1943	Walter S. Landis
1944	Willard H. Dow
1945	John W. Thomas
1946	Robert P. Russell
1947	M. L. Crossley
1948	Charles A. Thomas
1949	Warren K. Lewis
1950	Walter J. Murphy
1951	Harry N. Holmes
1952	Fred J. Emmerich
1953	J. C. Warner
1954	William J. Sparks
1955	Carl S. Marvel
1956	Raymond Stevens
1957	Roy C. Newton
1958	Lawrence Flett
1959	Crawford H. Greenewalt
1960	Ernest H. Volwiler
1961	Alden H. Emery
1962	W. George Parks
1963	Ralph Connor
1964	Roger Adams
1965	Edwin Cox
1966	John H. Nair
1967	Wayne E. Kuhn
1968	Orville E. May
1969	Henry B. Hass
1970	Willard F. Libby
1971	Emmett B. Carmichael
1972	Harold C. Urey
1973	Glenn T. Seaborg
1974	W. E. 'Butch' Hanford
1975	William O. Baker
1976	Kenneth S. Pitzer
1977	Max Tishler
1978	Norman Hackerman
1979	Melvin Calvin
1980	Arthur M. Bueche
1981	Lewis Sarett
1982	Milton Harris
1983	Mary L. Good

1984 John H. Sinfelt
1985 Herbert C. Brown
1986 N. Bruce Hannay

American Medical Association Distinguished Service Award

(Presented annually to recognize outstanding service in the science and art of medicine.)

1938 Rudolph Matas
1939 James B. Herrick
1940 Chevalier Jackson
1941 James Ewing
1942 Ludvig Hektoen
1943 Elliott P. Joslin
1944 George Dock
1945 George R. Minot
1946 Anton J. Carlson
1947 Henry A. Christian
1948 Isaac A. Abt
1949 Seale Harris
1950 Evarts A. Graham
1951 Allen C. Whipple
1952 Paul Dudley White
1953 Alfred Blalock
1954 W. Wayne Babcock
1955 Donald C. Balfour
1956 Walter L. Bierring
1957 Tom D. Spies
1958 Frank H. Krusen
1959 Michael E. De Bakey
1960 Charles Doan
1961 Walter H. Judd
1962 Russell L. Cecil
1963 Lester R. Dragstedt
1964 Irvine H. Page
1965 Tinsley R. Harrison
1966 Warren H. Cole
1967 Alton Ochsner
1968 Owen H. Wangensteen
1969 Jay Arnold Bargen
1970 Henry L. Bockus
1971 George R. Herrmann
1972 Milton Helpern
1973 George H. Whipple
1974 William F. House
1975 William R. Willard
1976 Claude E. Welch
1977 Franz J. Ingelfinger
1978 William P. Longmire, Jr.
1979 William A. Sodeman, Sr.
1980 Frank H. Mayfield
1981 John W. Kirklin
1982 John E. Dunphy
1983 Merrill O. Hines
1984 William D. Holden
1985 G. Valter Brindley, Jr.
1986 Kenneth M. Brinkhous

American Petroleum Institute Gold Medal for Distinguished Achievement

(Awarded from time to time to recognize contributions to the arts and sciences, particularly befitting the petroleum industry.)

1946 Henry Ford
1947 William M. Burton
1948 Charles F. Kettering
1949 J. Howard Pew
1950 Walter C. Teagle
1951 Ernest O. Thompson
1953 Otto D. Donnell
1954 Wallace E. Pratt
1956 J. Frank Drake
1957 Warren K. Lewis
1958 W. S. S. Rodgers
1960 Eugene Holman
1965 M. J. Rathbone
1966 Albert C. Rubel
1967 Alfred Jacobsen
1968 R. Gwin Follis
1969 Hugo A. Anderson
1969 John E. Warren
1971 Michael L. Haider
1972 Leonard F. McCollum
1973 Albert L. Nickerson
1974 Jake L. Hamon
1975 Robert G. Dunlop
1977 James C. Donnell, II
1979 Frank N. Ikard
1980 Charles E. Spahr
1981 Dean A. McGee
1982 George A. Brown
1983 John E. Swearingen
1984 Jerry McAfee
1985 H. A. True, Jr.
1986 Robert O. Anderson

American Psychiatric Association Distinguished Service Award

(Presented annually to honor meritorious service to American psychiatry.)

1965 Karl Menninger
1966 Franklin Ebaugh, Sr.
1967 Howard Potter
1968 Lister Hill
1969 Nolan D. C. Lewis
1970 Lauren H. Smith
1971 Dana L. Farnsworth
1972 M. Ralph Kaufman
1972 Roy S. Grinker
1973 George Tarjan
1974 Robert Felix
1975 David L. Bazelon
1975 Walter E. Barton
1976 Francis J. Braceland
1976 Anna Freud
1976 Howard Rome
1977 Jack R. Ewalt
1978 Leo H. Bartemeier
1978 Kenneth E. Appel
1979 John Romano
1979 Harry C. Solomon
1980 Daniel Blain
1980 Seymour S. Kety
1981 Milton Greenblatt
1981 Margaret S. Mahler
1982 Lester Shapiro
1983 Viola Bernard
1983 Lawrence Kolb
1984 Hayden Donahue
1984 Francis Gerty
1985 Charles Prudhomme
1985 Fritz Redlich
1986 Melvin Sabshin

American Society of Mechanical Engineers Medal

(Awarded annually for distinguished service in engineering and science. May be presented for service in science having possible application in engineering.)

1921 Hjalmar G. Carlson
1922 Frederick A. Halsey
1923 John R. Freeman
1926 Robert A. Millikan
1927 Wilfred Lewis
1928 Julian Kennedy
1930 William L. Emmett
1931 Albert Kingsbury
1933 Ambrose Swasey
1934 Willis H. Carrier
1935 Charles T. Main
1936 Edward Bausch
1937 Edward P. Bullard, Jr.
1938 Stephen J. Pigott
1939 James E. Gleason
1940 Charles F. Kettering
1941 Theodore von Karman
1942 Ervin G. Bailey
1943 Lewis K. Sillcox
1944 Edward G. Budd
1945 William F. Durand
1946 Morris E. Leeds
1947 Paul W. Kiefer
1948 Frederick G. Keyes
1949 Fred L. Dornbrook
1950 Harvey C. Knowles
1951 Glenn B. Warren
1952 Nevin E. Funk
1953 Crosby Field
1954 E. Burnley Powell
1955 Granville M. Read
1956 Harry F. Vickers
1957 L. M. K. Boelter
1958 Wilbur H. Armacost
1959 Martin Frisch
1960 C. Richard Soderberg
1962 Philip Sporn
1963 Igor I. Sikorsky
1964 Alan Howard
1965 Johannes M. Burgers
1967 Mayo D. Hersey
1968 Samuel C. Collins
1969 Lloyd H. Donnell
1970 Robert R. Gilruth
1971 Horace S. Beattie
1972 Waloddi Weibull
1973 Christopher C. Kraft, Jr.
1974 Nicholas J. Hoff
1975 Maxime A. Faget
1976 Raymond D. Mindlin
1977 Robert W. Mann
1979 Jacob P. DenHartog
1981 Robert S. Hahn
1983 Jack N. Binns, Sr.
1984 Aaron Cohen
1985 Milton C. Shaw
1986 Orlan W. Boston

American Watercolor Society Gold Medal of Honor

(Awarded for the best watercolor painting shown in the society's annual exhibition.)

1948 Ogden Pleissner
1949 John Taylor
1950 Leonard Cutrow
1951 Walter Biggs
1952 Andrew Wyeth
1953 Donald Teague
1954 Ted Kautzky
1955 Emerton Heitland
1956 Ogden Pleissner
1957 William A. Smith
1958 Maurice Logan
1959 Morton Roberts
1960 Morton Grossman
1961 Roy Mason
1962 Claus Hoie
1963 Doris White
1964 Donald Teague
1965 William A. Smith
1966 Chen Chi
1967 Avel de Knight
1968 Hugh Gumpel
1969 Tom Nicholas
1970 William Thon
1971 Richard Schmid
1972 Edwin Dahlberg
1973 Carol Pyle Jones
1974 Mario Cooper
1975 Franklin Jones
1976 Chen Chi
1977 Barbara G. Watts
1978 William Thon
1979 Burt Silverman
1980 Tom Hale
1981 Vladimir Shatalow
1982 Linda Stevens
1983 Serge Hollerbach
1984 Joan Rothermel
1985 Betty Bowes
1986 Al Brouillette

Archaelogical Institute of America Gold Medal

(Awarded annually to recognize distinguished achievement by a professional archaeologist.)

1965 Carl W. Blegen
1966 Hetty Goldman
1967 William F. Albright
1968 Gisela M. A. Richter
1969 Oscar T. Broneer
1969 Rhys Carpenter
1969 William B. Dinsmoor
1970 George E. Mylonas
1971 Robert J. Braidwood
1972 Homer A. Thompson
1973 Gordon R. Willey
1974 Margaret Bieber
1975 Eugene Vanderpool
1976 Lucy S. Meritt
1977 Edith Porada
1978 George M. A. Hanfmann
1979 Dows Dunham
1980 John L. Caskey
1981 William A. McDonald
1982 Peter H. von Blanckenhagen
1983 James B. Pritchard
1984 Margaret Thompson
1985 Gladys D. Weinberg
1985 Saul S. Weinberg

ASM International Gold Medal

(Awarded to recognize outstanding metallurgical knowledge, versatility in the application of science to the metal industry, and the ability to diagnose and solve diversified metallurgical problems. Formerly known as American Society for Metals Gold Medal.)

1943 Zay Jeffries
1945 Earle C. Smith
1947 Champion H. Mathewson
1948 Francis C. Frary
1949 Edgar C. Bain
1951 Paul D. Merica
1952 Robert F. Mehl
1953 George Sachs
1955 A. L. Boegehold
1956 William H. Eisenman
1957 John Chipman
1958 Albert J. Phillips
1959 Matthew A. Hunter
1960 John B. Johnson
1961 Cyril S. Smith
1962 Clarence H. Lorig
1963 Francis B. Foley
1964 Walter Crafts
1965 Joseph D. Hanawalt
1966 Carl E. Swartz
1967 William J. Kroll
1968 Morris Cohen
1970 Kent R. Van Horn
1971 Lawrence S. Darken
1972 Earl R. Parker
1973 Carl Wilhelm Wagner
1974 Clarence M. Zener
1975 F. Denys Richardson
1976 Charles S. Barrett
1977 George A. Roberts
1978 John R. Low, Jr.
1979 Mars G. Fontana
1980 Alan H. Cottrell
1981 Raymond F. Decker
1982 Allen S. Russell
1983 Harold W. Paxton
1984 Lawrence H. Van Vlack
1985 Oleg D. Sherby
1986 Morris E. Fine

Audubon Medal

(Awarded from time to time by the National Audubon Society to honor distinguished service to the conservation of natural resources.)

1947 Hugh H. Bennett
1949 Ira N. Gabrielson
1950 John D. Rockefeller, Jr.
1952 Louis Bromfield
1955 Walt Disney
1956 Ludlow Griscom
1959 Olaus J. Murie
1960 Jay N. Darling
1961 Clarence Cottam
1962 William O. Douglas
1963 Rachel Carson
1964 Laurance S. Rockefeller
1966 A. Starker Leopold
1967 Stewart L. Udall
1968 Fairfield Osborn
1969 Horace M. Albright
1972 Roger Tory Peterson
1973 Barbara Ward
1974 Tom McCall
1975 Maurice Strong

1976 John Oakes
1977 Russell W. Peterson
1978 Charles H. Callison

Bancroft Prize

(Awarded by Columbia University to honor distinguished published works in categories of American history, including biography, American diplomacy, and the international relations of the United States.)

1948 Allan Nevins
1948 Bernard DeVoto
1949 Robert E. Sherwood
1949 Samuel Eliot Morison
1950 Lawrence H. Gipson
1950 Herbert E. Bolton
1951 Arthur N. Holcombe
1951 Henry N. Smith
1952 Merlo J. Pusey
1952 C. Vann Woodward
1953 George Dangerfield
1953 Eric F. Goldman
1954 Clinton Rossiter
1954 William L. Langer
1954 S. Everett Gleason
1955 Paul Horgan
1955 Leonard D. White
1956 Elizabeth Stevenson
1956 James G. Randall
1956 Richard N. Current
1957 George F. Kennan
1957 Arthur S. Link
1958 Arthur M. Schlesinger, Jr.
1958 Frank Luther Mott
1959 Ernest Samuels
1959 Daniel J. Boorstin
1960 Robert R. Palmer
1960 Margaret Leech
1961 Merrill D. Peterson
1961 Arthur S. Link
1962 Lawrence A. Cremin
1962 Felix Gilbert
1962 Martin B. Duberman
1963 Page Smith
1963 Roberta Wohlstetter
1963 John G. Stoessinger
1964 William E. Leuchtenburg
1964 John L. Thomas
1964 Paul Seabury
1965 Bradford Perkins
1965 William B. Willcox
1965 Dorothy Borg
1966 Richard B. Morris
1966 Theodore W. Friend, III
1967 William W. Freehling
1967 Charles C. Sellers
1967 James S. Young
1968 Henry A. Bullock
1968 Richard L. Bushman
1968 Bernard Bailyn
1969 Winthrop Jordan
1969 N. Gordon Levin, Jr.
1969 Rexford Guy Tugwell
1970 Charles C. Sellers
1970 Gordon S. Wood
1970 Dan T. Carter
1971 Erik Barnouw
1971 David M. Kennedy
1971 Joseph F. Wall
1972 Carl N. Degler
1972 Robert Middlekauff
1972 Samuel Eliot Morrison
1973 Frances FitzGerald
1973 John Lewis Gaddis

1973 Louis R. Harlan
1974 Ray Allen Billington
1974 Townsend Hoopes
1974 Stephan Thernstrom
1975 Robert William Fogel
1975 Stanley L. Engerman
1975 Alexander L. George
1975 Richard Smoke
1976 David Brion Davis
1976 R. W. B. Lewis
1977 Alan Dawley
1977 Robert A. Gross
1977 Barry Higman
1978 Alfred D. Chandler, Jr.
1978 Morton J. Horwitz
1979 Christopher Thorne
1979 Anthony F. C. Wallace
1980 Robert Daller
1980 Thomas Dublin
1980 Donald Worster
1981 Ronald Steel
1981 Jean Strouse
1982 Edward Countryman
1982 Mary P. Ryan
1983 John P. Demos
1983 Nick Salvatore
1984 Louis R. Harlan
1984 Paul Starr
1985 Suzanne Lebstock
1985 Kenneth Silverman
1986 Kenneth T. Jackson
1986 Jacqueline Jones

Barnard Medal

(Awarded by Columbia University on the recommendation of the National Academy of Sciences for a notable discovery in physical or astronomical science or a novel application of science to purposes beneficial to the human race over a five-year period.)

1920 Albert Einstein
1935 Edwin P. Hubble
1950 Enrico Fermi
1955 Merle A. Tuve
1960 Isidor I. Rabi
1965 William A. Fowler
1975 Louis P. Hammett
1980 Andre Weil
1985 Benoit Mandelbrot

Bollingen Prize

(Awarded biennially by the Yale University Library to recognize distinguished achievement by an American poet. Given annually, 1949-1963. First award was sponsored by the Library of Congress.)

1949 Ezra Pound
1950 Wallace Stevens
1951 John Crowe Ransom
1952 Archibald MacLeish
1952 William Carlos Williams
1953 Marianne Moore
1954 W. H. Auden
1955 Leonie Adams
1955 Louise Bogan
1956 Conrad Aiken
1957 Allen Tate
1958 E. E. Cummings
1959 Theodore Roethke
1960 Delmore Schwartz
1961 Yvor Winters

1962 Richard Eberhart
1962 John Hall Wheelock
1963 Robert Frost
1965 Horace Gregory
1967 Robert Penn Warren
1969 John Berryman
1969 Karl Shapiro
1971 Mona Van Duyn
1971 Richard Wilbur
1973 James Merrill
1975 A. R. Ammons
1977 David Ignatow
1979 W. S. Merwin
1981 Howard Nemerov
1981 May Swenson
1983 Anthony Hecht
1983 John Hollander
1985 John Ashbery
1985 Fred Chappell

Borden Award

(Presented annually by the American Academy of Pediatrics for contributions in the areas of nutrition and development of infants and children.)

1944 Harry H. Gordon
1944 S. Z. Levine
1945 Edwards A. Park
1946 James L. Gamble
1947 Grover F. Powers
1948 Dorothy Andersen
1949 Alfred Washburn
1950 Josef Warkany
1951 Daniel C. Darrow
1952 Julius Hess
1953 Lawson Wilkins
1954 Paul Gyorgy
1955 L. Emmett Holt, Jr.
1956 A. Ashley Weech
1957 Arild E. Hansen
1958 Charles D. May
1959 Harold C. Stuart
1960 Harold E. Harrison
1961 Clement A. Smith
1962 Nathan B. TAlbot
1963 David Gitlin
1964 Gilbert Forbes
1965 Joseph Dancis
1966 Samuel J. Fomon
1967 Donald B. Cheek
1968 Bruce Mackler
1969 Norman Kretchmer
1970 Albert Dorfman

Brandeis University Creative Arts Award

(Presented annually to recognize outstanding lifetime artistic contributions by artists in several fields.)

Theatre Arts/Film

1957 Hallie Flanagan Davis
1958 Stark Young
1959 George Kelly
1960 Thornton Wilder
1961 Lillian Hellman
1962 S. N. Behrman
1963 Jo Mielziner
1964 Cheryl Crawford
1965 Tennessee Williams
1966 Eva Le Gallienne
1967 Jerome Robbins

1968	Richard Rodgers	1978	Robert Rauschenberg
1969	Boris Aronson	1979	George Rickey
1970	Arthur Miller	1980	Philip Guston
1971	Charles Chaplin	1981	I. M. Pei
1971	Bruce Baille	1981	Henry Cobb
1972	Lynn Fontanne	1981	James Freed
1972	Alfred Lunt	1981	Leonard Jacobson
1973	John Ford	1981	Eason Leonard
1974	Helen Hays	1981	Werner Wandelmaier
1975	King Vidor	1982	Peter Voulkos
1976	Harold Clurman	1983	Al Held
1977	Howard Hawks	1984	John Chamberlain
1978	Hume Cronyn	1985	Cy Twombly
1978	Jessica Tandy	1986	Paul Rudolph
1979	George Cukor		
1980	Lanford Wilson		
1981	Samuel Fuller		
1982	Stephen Sondheim		
1982	Billy Wilder		
1984	Sam Shepard		
1985	Harry Callahan		
1986	John Huston		

Music/Dance

1957	William Schuman
1958	Roger Sessions
1959	Ernest Bloch
1960	Aaron Copland
1961	Wallingford Riegger
1962	Edgard Varese
1963	Walter Piston
1964	Carl Ruggles
1965	Elliott Carter
1966	Stefan Wolpe
1967	Ross Lee Finney
1968	Virgil Thomson
1969	Ernst Krenek
1970	Milton Babbitt
1971	Earl Kim
1972	John Harbison
1972	Merce Cunningham
1973	Roy Harris
1974	Anna Sokolow
1975	Vincent Perischetti
1976	Anthony Tudor
1977	Leon Kirchner
1978	Paul Taylor
1979	George Crumb
1980	Suzanne Farrell
1981	Otto Luening
1982	Trisha Brown
1982	Jennifer Tipton
1983	Lukas Foss
1984	Jerome Robbins
1985	George Rochberg
1986	Agnes de Mille

Literature/Poetry/Nonfiction

1957	William Carlos Williams
1958	John Crowe Ransom
1959	Hilda Doolittle
1960	Yvor Winters
1961	Allen Tate
1962	Louise Bogan
1963	Marianne Moore
1964	Vladimir Nabokov
1965	Stanley Kunitz
1966	Eudora Welty
1967	Conrad Aiken
1968	Lionel Trilling
1969	Leonie Adams
1970	Isaac Bashevis Singer
1971	Richard Wilbur
1971	James Wright
1972	Katherine Anne Porter
1973	Alfred Kazin
1974	Robert Francis
1975	Christopher Isherwood
1976	Irving Howe
1977	Robert Lowell
1978	Saul Bellow
1979	Jeremy Bernstein
1980	Edgar Bowers
1981	Bernard Malamud
1982	C. Vann Woodward
1983	Robert Penn Warren
1984	William Maxwell
1985	James Merrill
1986	Stanley Elkin
1986	George Kennan

Fine Arts

1957	Stuart Davis
1959	Edwin Dickinson
1960	Naum Gabo
1961	Karl Knaths
1962	Alexander Calder
1963	Georgia O'Keefe
1964	David Smith
1965	Mark Rothko
1966	Isamu Noguchi
1967	Ludwig Mies van der Rohe
1968	Joseph Cornell
1969	Jose de Rivera
1970	Barnett Newman
1971	Louise Nevelson
1972	Louis I. Kahn
1973	Willem deKooning
1974	Tony Smith
1975	Isabel Bishop
1976	Philip C. Johnson
1977	Reuben Nakiacio

Brewster Memorial Award

(Presented annually, originally every two years, by the American Ornithologists' Union to the author of an important work relating to the birds of the Western Hemisphere.)

1921	Robert Ridgway
1923	Arthur C. Bent
1925	W. E. Clyde Todd
1925	M. A. Carriker, Jr.
1927	John C. Phillips
1931	Florence Merriam Bailey
1933	Frank M. Chapman
1935	Herbert L. Stoddard
1937	Robert C. Murphy
1938	Thomas S. Roberts
1939	Witmer Stone
1940	James Lee Peters
1941	Donald E. Dickey
1941	Adrian J. Van Rossem
1942	Margaret Morse Nice
1943	Alden H. Miller
1944	Roger Tory Peterson
1950	Alexander Skutch
1951	S. Charles Kendeigh

1952	John T. Zimmer
1953	Hildegarde Howard
1954	James Bond
1956	George H. Lowery, Jr.
1957	Robert Porter Allen
1958	Arlie W. Schorger
1959	Alexander Wetmore
1960	Donald S. Farner
1961	Harold F. Mayfield
1962	Albert Wolfson
1963	Ralph S. Palmer
1964	Herbert Friedmann
1965	Ernst Mayr
1966	George A. Batholomew, Jr.
1967	W. E. Clyde Todd
1968	Wesley E. Lanyon
1972	Barbara K. Snow
1972	David W. Snow
1973	J. D. Goodall
1973	Alfred W. Johnson
1973	Rudolfo Phillipi
1974	James King
1975	Jurgen Haffner
1976	Gordon Orians
1977	R. Meyer de Schauensee
1978	P. Brodkorb
1979	W. Dawson
1980	F. Pitelka
1981	W. T. Keeton
1982	R. E. Ricklefs
1983	P. R. Grant
1984	S. T. Emlen
1985	J. W. Fitzpatrick
1985	G. E. Woolfenden
1986	V. Nolan, Jr.

Bronfman Prize

(Awarded annually by the American Public Health Association in recognition of meritorious achievement leading directly to improved health for large numbers of people; discontinued after 1971.)

1961	James E. Perkins
1961	James Watt
1962	Theodore F. Hatch
1962	Charles E. Smith
1963	Harold D. Chope
1963	Marion B. Folsom
1963	Herman E. Hillboe
1964	Robert H. Felix
1964	Malcolm E. Merrill
1964	George E. Moore
1965	Guillermo Arbona
1965	Alexander D. Langmuir
1965	George James
1966	Bernard G. Greenberg
1966	Emmett M. Hall
1967	Wilbur J. Cohen
1967	Forrest E. Linder
1967	Myron E. Wegman
1968	Moises Behar
1968	James L. Goddard
1968	Abraham L. Lilienfeld
1969	William Haddon, Jr.
1969	Edwin H. Lennette
1970	Karl Evarg
1970	Alan Guttmacher
1970	Edmund S. Muskie
1971	Ruth Freeman
1971	John F. Brotherston
1971	James H. Steele
1971	Herman E. Hilleboe

Franklin L. Burr Prize for Science

(Awarded by the National Geographic Society to leaders of the Society's expeditions and to researchers to recognize meritorious work in the field of geographic science.)

1933	Albert W. Stevens
1936	Albert W. Stevens
1936	Orvil A. Anderson
1936	Randolph P. Williams
1938	William M. Mann
1938	Mrs. William M. Mann
1939	Bradford Washburn
1939	Matthew W. Stirling
1941	Matthew W. Stirling
1941	Mrs. Matthew W. Stirling
1944	Alexander Wetmore
1945	Thomas A. Jaggar
1945	Lyman J. Briggs
1947	George Van Biesbroeck
1948	Edward A. Halbach
1948	Francis J. Heyden
1948	Carl W. Miller
1948	Charles H. Smiley
1948	George Van Biesbroeck
1948	Arthur A. Allen
1950	Frank M. Setzler
1952	Harold E. Edgerton
1953	George Van Biesbroeck
1954	Lyman J. Briggs
1955	Neil M. Judd
1955	Mrs. Robert E. Peary
1955	Marie Peary Stafford
1956	Robert F. Griggs
1957	Matthew W. Stirling
1959	Carl F. Miller
1962	Lyman J. Briggs
1963	Donald B. MacMillan
1963	Neil M. Judd
1963	Barry C. Bishop
1965	Bradford Washburn
1965	Norman G. Dyhrenfurth
1967	Maynard M. Miller
1973	Kenan T. Erim
1973	Dian Fossey
1973	Richard E. Leakey
1979	Jared M. Diamond
1979	Fred A. Urquhart
1979	Norah R. Urquhart
1981	Birute Galdikas

Burroughs Medal

(Awarded at intervals by the John Burroughs Memorial Association, Inc., to the author of a distinguished book in the field of nature writing.)

1926	William Beebe
1927	Ernest Thompson Seton
1929	Frank M. Chapman
1930	Archibald Rutledge
1933	Oliver P. Medsger
1934	W. W. Christman
1936	Charles C. Gorst
1938	Robert C. Murphy
1939	T. Gilbert Pearson
1940	Arthur C. Bent
1941	Louis J. Halle, Jr.
1943	Edwin M. Teale
1945	Rutherford Platt
1946	Francis Lee Jaques
1946	Mrs. Francis Lee Jaques

1948	Theodora Stanwell-Fletcher
1949	Allan D. Cruickshank
1949	Mrs. Allan D. Cruickshank
1950	Roger Tory Peterson
1952	Rachel Carson
1953	Gilbert Klingel
1954	Joseph Wood Krutch
1955	Wallace B. Grange
1956	Guy Murchie
1957	Archie Carr
1958	Robert Porter Allen
1960	John Kieran
1961	Loren Eiseley
1962	George M. Sutton
1963	Adolph Murie
1964	John Hay
1965	Paul Brooks
1966	Louis Darling
1967	Charlton Ogburn
1968	Hal Borland
1969	Louise de Kiriline Lawrence
1970	Victor B. Scheffer
1971	John K. Terres
1972	Robert Arbib
1973	Elizabeth Barlow
1974	Sigurd F. Olson
1976	Ann H. Zwinger
1977	Aldo Leopold
1978	Ruth Kirk
1979	Barry Lopez
1981	Mary Durant
1981	Michael Harwood
1982	Peter Matthiessen
1983	Alexander F. Skutch
1984	David R. Wallace
1985	Delia Owens
1985	Mark Owens
1986	Gary Paul Nabban

Butler Medal

(Awarded by Columbia University to honor a distinguished contribution made during a five-year period to philosophy or to educational theory, practice, or administration.)

1925	Edward L. Thorndike
1930	Alfred North Whitehead
1935	John Dewey
1945	George Santayana
1950	Clarence I. Lewis
1965	Rudolf Carnap
1970	Willard V. Quine
1975	Jean Paul Sartre
1980	Ernest Nagel

Capezio Dance Award

(Presented annually by Capezio, Inc., to focus attention on meritorious work in the field of dance.)

1952	Zachary Solov
1953	Lincoln Kirstein
1954	Doris Humphrey
1955	Louis Horst
1956	Genevieve Oswald
1957	Ted Shawn
1958	Alexandra Danilova
1959	Sol Hurok
1960	Martha Graham
1961	Ruth St. Denis
1962	Barbara Karinska

1963	Donald McKayle
1964	Jose Limon
1965	Maria Tallchief
1966	Agnes DeMille
1967	Paul Taylor
1968	Lucia Chase
1969	John Martin
1970	William Kolodney
1971	Arthur Mitchell
1972	Gladys Laubin
1972	Reginald Laubin
1972	La Meri
1973	Isadora Bennett
1974	Robert Joffrey
1975	Robert Irving
1976	Jerome Robbins
1977	Merce Cunningham
1978	Hanya Holm
1979	Alvin Ailey
1980	Walter Terry
1981	Dorothy Alexander
1982	Alwin Nikolais
1983	Harvey Lichenstein
1984	Harold Christensen
1984	Lew Christensen
1984	William Christensen
1985	Doris Hering
1986	Anthony Tudor

W. A. Clark Prize

(Awarded biennially by the Corcoran Gallery of Art to recognize achievement in oil painting by living American artists; discontinued.)

First Prize

1907	Willard L. Metcalf
1908	Edward W. Redfield
1910	Edmund C. Tarbell
1912	Childe Hassam
1914	J. Alden Weir
1916	Arthur B. Davies
1919	Frank W. Benson
1921	Daniel Garber
1923	George Bellows
1926	Charles W. Hawthorne
1928	Bernard Karfiol
1930	Maurice Sterne
1932	George Luks
1935	Eugene Speicher
1937	Edward Hopper
1939	Franklin C. Watkins
1941	John E. Heliker
1943	Henry Mattson
1945	Reginald Marsh
1947	Sigmund Menkes
1949	Eric Isenburger
1951	Raphael Soyer
1953	Abraham Rattner
1955	John Hultberg
1957	Loren MacIver
1959	Walter Plate
1961	Lee Gatch
1963	Jack Tworkov
1965	Robert Rauschenberg
1967	Jules Olitski

Second Prize

1907	Frank W. Benson
1908	Joseph DeCamp
1910	Gari Melchers
1912	Daniel Garber
1914	Charles H. Woodbury
1916	Ernest Lawson
1919	Charles H. Davis

1921	Burtis Baker
1923	Charles W. Hawthorne
1926	W. Elmer Schofield
1928	Eugene Speicher
1930	Gifford Beal
1932	John R. Grabach
1935	F. C. Frieseke
1937	Guy Pene DuBois
1939	Robert Philipp
1941	Fred Nagler
1943	Aaron Bohrod
1945	Zsissly
1947	Walter Stuempfig
1949	Fred Conway
1951	Philip Evergood
1953	Hobson Pittman
1955	Ivan Albright
1957	Fritz Glarner
1959	Jack Levine
1961	Ben Kamihira
1963	Lee Bontecou
1965	Richard Pousette-Dart
1967	Paul Jenkins

Thomas B. Clarke Prize

(Awarded by the National Academy of Design to recognize outstanding figure composition painted in oil.)

1884	Charles F. Ulrich
1885	Francis C. Jones
1886	Walter Satterlee
1887	Thomas W. Dewing
1888	H. Siddons Mowbray
1889	Irving R. Wiles
1890	Edmund C. Tarbell
1891	Frank W. Benson
1892	William S. Harper
1893	Charles C. Curran
1894	Harry W. Watrous
1895	Henry O. Walker
1896	Robert Reid
1898	Abbott H. Thayer
1899	Edward H. Potthast
1900	Charles Schreyvogel
1901	William F. Kline
1902	Eliott Daingerfield
1903	Lydia Amanda Sewell
1904	Harry M. Walcott
1905	Childe Hassam
1906	Hugo Ballin
1907	Henry Prellwitz
1908	Robert D. Gauley
1909	Lydia F. Emmet
1910	Frederick J. Waugh
1911	Charles W. Hawthorne
1912	Charles Bittinger
1913	Gifford Beal
1914	Ivan G. Olinsky
1915	Richard E. Miller
1916	Frederic E. Church
1917	Max Bohm
1918	Walter Ufer
1919	Jerome Myers
1920	James Hopkins
1921	Leon Kroll
1922	Gertrude Fiske
1923	Eugene F. Savage
1924	Clifford Addams
1925	Gertrude Fiske
1926	Will Foster
1927	John E. Costigan
1928	Alice K. Stoddard
1929	Ettore Caser
1930	Ernest Trubach
1931	Gordon Samstag
1932	Robert Brackman

1933	Jerry Farnsworth
1934	Gerald Leake
1935	Maurice Sterne
1936	Franklin Robbins
1937	Reginald Marsh
1938	Randall Davey
1940	Hugo Ballin
1941	Dan Lutz
1942	Douglas W. Gorsline
1944	Robert Philipp
1945	Eugene Higgins
1945	Raphael Soyer
1947	Louis DiValentin
1948	Raphael Soyer
1949	Eugene Berman
1950	Hazel J. Teyral
1951	Lee Jackson
1952	Doris Rosenthal
1953	Sigmund Menkes
1954	Fletcher Martin
1955	Thomas Yerxa
1956	Adolf Konrad
1957	Morton Roberts
1958	Robert Sivard
1959	Hughie Lee-Smith
1960	Werner Groshans
1961	Aaron Shikler
1962	David Levine
1963	Thomas Yerxa
1964	Moses Soyer
1965	Philip B. White
1966	Bruce Currie
1967	Jack Henderson
1968	Philip B. White
1969	Edward Melcarth
1970	Philip B. White
1971	Charles Alston
1972	Robert C. Baxter
1973	William Gropper
1974	Vincent Smith
1975	Diana A. Marinara
1976	Anne T. Rothe
1977	Cornelius Ruhtenberg
1978	Charles Reid
1979	Selina Trieff
1980	Jeffrey Kronsnoble
1981	Mary Beth McKenzie
1982	Jack M. Kramer
1984	Alan Feltus
1986	Elinor Schnurr

Robert J. Collier Trophy

(Presented annually by the National Aeronautic Association for the greatest achievement in aviation in America, the value of which has been demonstrated by astral use during the preceding year.)

1911	Glenn H. Curtiss
1912	Glenn H. Curtiss
1913	Orville Wright
1914	Elmer A. Sperry
1915	W. Sterling Burgess
1916	Elmer A. Sperry
1921	Grover Loening
1925	S. Albert Reed
1926	E. L. Hoffman
1927	Charles L. Lawrence
1930	Harold Pitcairn
1932	Glenn L. Martin
1933	Frank W. Caldwell
1934	Albert F. Hegenberger
1935	Donald Douglas
1938	Howard Hughes
1940	Sanford Moss
1942	Henry H. Arnold
1943	Luis de Florez

1944	Carl A. Spaatz
1945	Luis W. Alvarez
1946	Lewis A. Rodert
1947	John Stack
1947	Lawrence D. Bell
1947	Charles E. Yeager
1949	William P. Lear
1951	John Stack
1952	Leonard S. Hobbs
1953	James H. Kindelberger
1953	Edward H. Heinemann
1954	Richard T. Whitcomb
1955	William M. Allen
1955	Nathan F. Twining
1956	Charles J. McCarthy
1956	James S. Russell
1957	Edward P. Curtis
1958	Clarence L. Johnson
1958	Neil Burgess
1958	Gerhard Neumann
1958	Howard C. Johnson
1958	Walter W. Irwin
1960	William F. Raborn
1961	Robert M. White
1961	Joseph A. Walker
1961	A. S. Crossfield
1961	Forrest Petersen
1962	M. Scott Carpenter
1962	L. Gordon Cooper
1962	John H. Glenn, Jr.
1962	Virgil I. Grissom
1962	Walter M. Schirra, Jr.
1962	Alan B. Sheppard, Jr.
1962	Donald K. Slayton
1963	Clarence L. Johnson
1964	Curtis E. LeMay
1965	James E. Webb
1965	Hugh L. Dryden
1966	James S. McDonnell
1967	Lawrence A. Hyland
1968	Frank Borman
1968	James A. Lovell, Jr.
1968	William A. Anders
1969	Neil A. Armstrong
1969	Edwin E. Aldrin, Jr.
1969	Michael Collins
1970	William M. Allen
1971	David R. Scott
1971	James B. Irwin
1971	Alfred M. Worden
1971	Robert R. Gilruth
1972	Thomas H. Moorer
1973	William C. Schneider
1974	John F. Clark
1974	Daniel J. Fink
1975	David S. Lewis
1976	David C. Jones
1976	Robert Anderson
1977	Robert J. Dixon
1978	Sam B. Williams
1979	Paul B. MacCready
1980	Edward C. Stone
1981	John W. Young
1981	Robert L. Crippen
1981	Joe H. Engle
1981	Richard H. Truly
1982	T. A. Wilson
1983	Apache Attack Helicopter Team
1984	Bruce McCandless, II
1984	Charles E. Whitsett, Jr.
1984	Walter W. Bollendonk
1985	Russell W. Meyer
1986	Jeana L. Yeager
1986	Richard G. Rutan
1986	Elbert L. Rutan
1986	Bruce Evans

Elliott Cresson Medal

(Awarded by the Franklin Institute to recognize notable discoveries or original research in the arts or sciences, invention or improvement of a useful machine, and new processes or combinations of materials in manufacture.)

1875	William G. A. Bonwill
1875	Benjamin C. Tilghman
1875	Joseph Zentmayer
1877	Plimmon H. Dudley
1878	Henry Bower
1878	Williams F. Goodwin
1881	W. Woodnut Griscom
1886	Patrick B. Delany
1886	Thaddeus S. C. Lowe
1886	Robert H. Ramsay
1887	Charles F. Albert
1887	Eugene H. Cowles
1887	Alfred H. Cowles
1889	Edward A. Cowper
1889	T. Hart Robertson
1889	Ottmar Mergenthaler
1889	G. F. Simonds
1890	James B. Hammond
1891	Stockton Bates
1891	Edwin Shaw
1891	G. M. von Culin
1891	James H. Bevington
1891	Bradley A. Fiske
1892	Philip H. Holmes
1892	Henry M. Howe
1893	Clifford H. Batchellor
1893	Frederic E. Ives
1893	George E. Marks
1894	Nikola Tesla
1895	Henry M. Howe
1895	J. Peckover
1895	Lester A. Pelton
1896	Patrick B. Delany
1896	Tolbert Lanston
1897	Hamilton Y. Castner
1897	Elisha Gray
1898	Wilbur O. Atwater
1898	Edward B. Rosa
1898	Clemens Herschel
1898	Thomas Corscaden
1898	Charles F. Jenkins
1900	Louis E. Levy
1901	John S. Forbes
1901	A. G. Waterhouse
1901	Lewis M. Haupt
1902	Charles E. Acker
1902	Fred W. Taylor
1902	Maunsel White
1903	Guilliam H. Clamer
1903	Joseph L. Ferrell
1903	Frank J. Sprague
1903	Wilson L. Gill
1904	James M. Dodge
1904	Louis E. Levy
1904	Alexander E. Outerbridge, Jr.
1904	John C. Parker
1905	Michael I. Pupin
1906	William J. Hammer
1907	J. Allen Heany
1907	Ferdinand Philips
1907	Edward R. Taylor
1908	Romeyn B. Hough
1909	James Gayley
1909	George O. Squier
1909	Walter V. Turner
1909	H. A. Wise Wood
1910	John A. Brashear
1910	Peter C. Hewitt
1910	John Fritz
1910	Edward Weston

1910	Harvey W. Wiley
1912	Alexander Graham Bell
1912	Albert A. Michelson
1912	Edward W. Morley
1912	Alfred Noble
1912	Samuel W. Stratton
1912	Elihu Thomson
1913	Emile Berliner
1913	Emil Fischer
1913	Isham Randolph
1913	Albert Sauveur
1913	Charles P. Steinmetz
1914	Karl P. G. Linde
1914	Edgar F. Smith
1914	Orville Wright
1915	Michael J. Owens
1916	Byron E. Eldred
1917	Edwin F. Northrup
1918	Isaac N. Lewis
1920	William L. Emmett
1923	Lee de Forest
1923	Raymond D. Johnson
1923	Albert Kingsbury
1925	Francis Hodgkinson
1926	George E. Hale
1926	Charles S. Hastings
1927	Dayton C. Miller
1927	Edward L. Nichols
1928	Gustaf W. Elmen
1928	Henry Ford
1928	Vladimir Karapetoff
1928	Charles L. Lawrance
1929	Chevalier Jackson
1929	Elmer A. Sperry
1930	Norman R. Gibson
1930	Irving E. Moultrop
1931	Clinton J. Davisson
1931	Lester H. Germer
1931	Theodore Lyman
1932	Percy W. Bridgman
1932	Charles L. Fortescue
1932	John B. Whitehead
1934	Stuart Ballantine
1936	George O. Curme, Jr.
1936	Robert J. Van de Graaff
1937	Carl D. Anderson
1937	William Bowie
1937	William F. Giauque
1937	Ernest O. Lawrence
1938	Edwin H. Land
1939	George A. Campbell
1939	John R. Carson
1940	Frederick M. Becket
1940	Robert R. Williams
1942	Claude S. Hudson
1942	Isidor I. Rabi
1943	Charles M. Allen
1944	Roger Adams
1945	Stanford C. Hooper
1945	Lewis F. Moody
1946	Gladeon M. Barnes
1948	Edwin H. Colpitts
1952	Edward C. Molina
1952	H. Birchard Taylor
1953	William Blum
1953	George R. Harrison
1953	William F. Meggers
1957	Willard F. Libby
1957	Reginald J. S. Pigott
1958	Joseph C. Patrick
1958	Stephen P. Timoshenko
1959	John H. Hammond, Jr.
1959	Henry C. Harrison
1959	Irving Wolff
1960	Hugh L. Dryden
1960	Arpad L. Nadai
1960	William F. G. Swann
1961	Donald A. Glaser
1961	Reinhold Rudenberg
1961	James A. Van Allen
1962	Wernher von Braun

1962	James G. Baker
1963	Grote Reber
1964	Waldo L. Semon
1964	Robert R. Wilson
1965	Donald D. Van Slyke
1966	Everitt P. Blizard
1966	Herman F. Mark
1969	Henry Eyring
1969	Peter C. Goldmark
1970	Walter H. Zinn
1971	Paul J. Flory
1971	John H. Van Vleck
1972	William P. Lear
1972	Brian D. Josephson
1973	Allan R. Sandage
1973	John Paul Stapp
1974	Theodore L. Cairns
1974	Robert H. Dicke
1974	Bruno B. Rossi
1974	A. J. Haagen-Smit
1975	Mildred Cohn
1975	Michael J. Lightbill
1976	Leon M. Lederman
1978	Herbert C. Brown
1979	Steven Weinberg
1980	Riccardo Giacconi
1981	M. King Hubbert
1982	Harold P. Eubank
1982	E. Bright Wilson
1983	Elizabeth F. Newfeld
1983	Herbert B. Callen
1985	Robert N. Clayton
1985	Andrei Sakharov
1986	Leo Kadanoff

Cullum Geographical Medal

(Awarded from time to time by the American Geographical Society to honor those who distinguish themselves by geographical discoveries or in the advancement of geographical science.)

1896	Robert E. Peary
1901	Thomas C. Mendenhall
1902	A. Donaldson Smith
1906	Robert Bell
1908	William M. Davis
1914	Ellen C. Semple
1917	George W. Goethals
1918	Frederick H. Newell
1919	Henry Fairfield Osborn
1925	Harvey C. Hayes
1930	Curtis F. Marbut
1931	Mark Jefferson
1935	Douglas Johnson
1938	Louise Arner Boyd
1940	Robert Cushman Murphy
1948	Hugh H. Bennett
1956	J. Russell Smith
1958	Charles W. Thornthwaite
1959	Albert P. Crary
1961	William M. Ewing
1962	Richard J. Russell
1963	Rachel L. Carson
1964	John Leighly
1965	Kirtley F. Mather
1968	Luna B. Leopold
1969	Neil A. Armstrong
1969	Edwin E. Aldrin, Jr.
1969	Michael Collins
1973	Bruce Heezen
1975	Rene Dubos
1985	Chauncy D. Harris

Charles P. Daly Medal

(Awarded intermittently by the American Geographical Society to explorers, writers, and men of science who have contributed to the advancement of geographical knowledge.)

1902 Robert E. Peary
1908 George Davidson
1909 William W. Rockhill
1909 Charles Chaille-Long
1910 Grove K. Gilbert
1913 Alfred H. Brooks
1918 Vilhjalmur Stefansson
1920 George O. Smith
1922 Adolphus W. Greely
1922 Ernest de K. Leffingwell
1924 Claude H. Birdseye
1925 Robert A. Bartlett
1925 David L. Brainard
1930 Nelson H. Darton
1935 Roy Chapman Andrews
1939 Herbert J. Fleure
1940 Carl O. Sauer
1954 John K. Wright
1959 Richard Hartshorne
1962 Osborn M. Miller
1965 William S. Cooper
1967 Marston Bates
1968 O. H. K. Spate
1969 Paul B. Sears
1969 William O. Field
1971 Gilbert F. White
1973 Walter Sullivan
1974 Walter Wood
1978 Roman Drazniowsky
1985 Wolfgang Meckelein
1986 Donald W. Meinig

Melvil Dewey Award

(Awarded annually by the American Library Association to honor creative professional achievement in the fields of library management, training, cataloging, classification, and the tools and techniques of librarianship.)

1953 Ralph R. Shaw
1954 Herman H. Fussler
1955 Maurice F. Tauber
1956 Norah A. MacColl
1957 Wyllis E. Wright
1958 Janet S. Dickson
1959 Benjamin A. Custer
1960 Harriet E. Howe
1961 Julia C. Pressey
1962 Leon Carnovsky
1963 Frank B. Rogers
1964 John W. Cronin
1965 Bertha M. Frick
1966 Lucile Morsch
1967 Walter H. Kaiser
1968 Jesse H. Shera
1969 William S. Dix
1970 Joseph Treyz
1971 William J. Welsh
1972 Jerrold Orne
1973 Virginia Lacy Jones
1974 Robert B. Downs
1976 Louis Round Wilson
1977 Seymour Lubetsky
1978 Frederick C. Kilgour
1979 Russell E. Bidlack
1980 Robert D. Stueart
1981 Henriette Avram

1982 Sarah K. Vann
1983 Edward G. Holley
1984 Warren J. Haas
1985 Joseph H. Howard
1986 Richard DeGennaro

James Douglas Gold Medal

(Awarded annually by the American Institute of Mining, Metallurgical, and Petroleum Engineers to recognize achievement in non-ferrous metallurgy.)

1923 Frederick Laist
1924 Charles W. Merrill
1925 William H. Bassett
1926 John M. Callow
1927 Zay Jeffries
1928 Selwyn G. Blalock
1929 Paul D. Merica
1930 John V. Dorr
1931 William H. Peirce
1932 Champion H. Mathewson
1933 James O. Elton
1935 George C. Stone
1938 Harry W. Hardinge
1940 Louis D. Ricketts
1942 Arthur S. Dwight
1945 Robert F. Mehl
1949 William Wraith
1950 Francis C. Frary
1954 William J. Kroll
1955 E. L. Oliver
1956 Charles R. Kuzell
1957 R. B. Caples
1958 J. R. Gordon
1959 Clyde Williams
1960 Augustus B. Kinzel
1961 Frank H. Spedding
1963 Cyril S. Smith
1964 T. D. Jones
1965 Frank A. Forward
1966 Albert J. Phillips
1967 Walter R. Hibbard, Jr.
1968 Paul Queneau
1969 S. W. K. Morgan
1970 Reinhardt Schuhmann, Jr.
1973 Herbert H. Kellogg
1974 Alan H. Cottrell
1975 Petri B. Bryk
1976 John F. Elliott
1977 Carleton C. Long

Edison Medal

(Awarded annually by the Institute of Electrical and Electronic Engineers to recognize a career of meritorious achievement in electrical science, electrical engineering, or the electrical arts.)

1909 Elihu Thomson
1910 Frank J. Sprague
1911 George Westinghouse
1912 William Stanley
1913 Charles F. Brush
1914 Alexander Graham Bell
1916 Nikola Tesla
1917 John J. Carty
1918 Benjamin G. Lamme
1919 William L. Emmet
1920 Michael I. Pupin
1921 Cummings C. Chesney
1922 Robert A. Millikan

1923 John W. Lieb
1924 John W. Howell
1925 Harris J. Ryan
1927 William D. Coolidge
1928 Frank B. Jewett
1929 Charles F. Scott
1930 Frank Conrad
1931 E. Wilbur Rice, Jr.
1932 Bancroft Gherardi
1933 Arthur E. Kennelly
1934 Willis R. Whitney
1935 Willis B. Stillwell
1936 Alex Dow
1937 Gano S. Dunn
1938 Dugald C. Jackson
1939 Philip Torchio
1940 George A. Campbell
1941 John B. Whitehead
1942 Edwin H. Armstrong
1943 Vannevar Bush
1944 E. F. W. Alexanderson
1945 Philip Sporn
1946 Lee deForest
1947 Joseph Slepian
1948 Morris E. Leeds
1949 Karl B. McEachron
1950 Otto B. Blackwell
1951 Charles F. Wagner
1952 Vladimir K. Zworykin
1953 John F. Peters
1954 Oliver E. Buckley
1956 Comfort A. Adams
1957 John K. Hodnette
1958 Charles F. Kettering
1959 James F. Fairman
1960 Harold S. Osborne
1961 William B. Kouwenhoven
1962 Alexander C. Monteith
1963 John R. Pierce
1965 Walker L. Cisler
1966 Wilmer L. Barrow
1967 George H. Brown
1968 Charles F. Avila
1969 Hendrik W. Bode
1970 Howard H. Aiken
1971 John W. Simpson
1972 William H. Pickering
1973 B. D. H. Tellegen
1974 Jan A. Rajchman
1975 Sidney Darlington
1976 Murray Joslin
1977 Henri G. Busignies
1978 Daniel E. Noble
1979 Albert Rose
1980 Robert Adler
1981 C. Chapin Cutler
1982 Nathan Cohn
1983 Herman Paul Schwan
1984 Eugene I. Gordon
1985 John D. Kraus
1986 James L. Flanagan

Einstein Medal and Award

(Presented by the Institute for Advanced Study, Princeton, NJ, to honor contributions to knowledge in the mathematical and physical sciences.)

1951 Julian Schwinger
1951 Kurt Godel
1954 Richard P. Feynman
1958 Edward Teller
1959 Willard F. Libby
1960 Leo Szilard
1961 Luis W. Alvarez
1962 Shields Warren

1965 John A. Wheeler
1967 Marshall N. Rosenbluth
1972 Eugene P. Wigner

Benjamin F. Fairless Award

(Presented annually by the American Institute of Mining, Metallurgical, and Petroleum Engineers to honor achievement in iron and steel production and ferrous metallurgy.)

1955 Stewart J. Cort
1956 Stephen M. Jenks
1957 Leo F. Reinartz
1958 Hjalmar W. Johnson
1959 James L. Mauthe
1960 Charles M. White
1961 Thomas E. Millsop
1962 Harold M. Griffith
1963 John Chipman
1964 Thomas L. Joseph
1965 Edward J. Hanley
1966 Robert Durrer
1967 Alexander L. Feild
1968 Herbert W. Graham
1969 James B. Austin
1970 Edmund F. Martin
1973 John H. Chesters
1974 Theodore F. Olt
1975 Michael Tenenbaum
1976 David S. Holbrook
1977 Edgar B. Speer

Enrico Fermi Award

(Presented annually by the U.S. Department of Energy to recognize outstanding scientific or technical achievement related to the development, use, or control of nuclear energy.)

1954 Enrico Fermi
1956 John von Neumann
1957 Ernest O. Lawrence
1958 Eugene P. Wigner
1959 Glenn T. Seaborg
1961 Hans A. Bethe
1962 Edward Teller
1963 J. Robert Oppenheimer
1964 Hyman G. Rickover
1966 Otto Hahn
1966 Lise Meitner
1966 Fritz Strassman
1968 John A. Wheeler
1969 Walter H. Zinn
1970 Norris E. Bradbury
1971 Stafford L. Warren
1971 Shields Warren
1972 Manson Benedict
1976 William L. Russell
1978 Harold M Agnew
1978 Wolfgang K. H. Panofsky
1980 Rudolf E. Peirls
1980 Alvin M. Weinberg
1981 W. Bennett Lewis
1982 Herbert Anderson
1982 Seth Nedermeyer
1983 Alexander Hollaender
1983 John Lawrence
1984 Georges Vendryes
1984 Robert R. Wilson
1985 Norman C. Rasmussen
1985 Marshall N. Rosenblath

1986 Ernest D. Courant
1986 M. Stanley Livingston

Henry Johnson Fisher Award

(Presented annually by the Magazine Publishers Association, Inc., to honor outstanding achievement in magazine publishing.)

1964 DeWitt Wallace
1965 Henry R. Luce
1966 Richard E. Berlin
1967 Edward Weeks
1968 Arnold Gingrich
1969 Albert L. Cole
1970 Roy E. Larsen
1970 Maurice R. Robinson
1971 Gibson McCabe
1972 John H. Johnson
1973 Norman Cousins
1974 Laurence W. Lane, Jr.
1974 Melvin B. Lane
1974 Mrs. Laurence W. Lane, Sr.
1975 Richard J. Babcock
1975 Emory O. Cunningham
1976 Stephen E. Kelly
1978 Richard E. Deems
1979 Gerard Piel
1980 George H. Allen
1981 Robert A. Burnett
1982 Andrew Heiskell
1983 Malcolm Forbes
1984 Walter H. Annenberg
1985 S. I. Newhouse, Jr.
1986 Gilbert C. Maurer

Foundations' Fund Prize for Research in Psychiatry

(Presented by the American Psychiatric Association; supersedes the Lester H. Hofheimer Prize.)

1978 Louis A. Gottschalk
1978 Myrna Weissman
1978 Alberto DiMascio
1978 Brigitte Prusoff
1978 Gerald L. Klerman
1978 Eugene S. Paykel
1979 Aaron T. Beck
1979 Arnold J. Mandell
1979 Irvin D. Yalom
1980 Merton M. Gill
1980 Albert J. Stunkard
1980 Mardi J. Horowitz
1981 George K. Aghajanian
1981 Mark S. Gold
1981 Herbert D. Kleber
1981 Donald E. Redmond, Jr.
1982 Eli Robins
1983 Robert Morton Post
1984 George E. Vaillant

Franklin Medal

(Awarded annually by the Franklin Institute to honor physical scientists or technologists who have notably advanced a knowledge of physical science or its application.)

1915 Thomas A. Edison
1916 John J. Carty
1916 Theodore W. Richards
1917 David W. Taylor
1918 Thomas C. Mendenhall
1919 George O. Squier
1921 Frank J. Sprague
1922 Ralph Modjeski
1923 Albert A. Michelson
1924 Edward Weston
1925 Elihu Thomson
1926 Samuel Rea
1927 George E. Hale
1928 Charles F. Brush
1929 Emile Berliner
1930 John F. Stevens
1931 Willis R. Whitney
1932 Ambrose Swasey
1933 Orville Wright
1934 Henry N. Russell
1934 Irving Langmuir
1935 Albert Einstein
1936 Frank B. Jewett
1936 Charles F. Kettering
1937 Robert A. Millikan
1938 William F. Durand
1938 Charles A. Kraus
1939 Edwin P. Hubble
1939 Albert Sauveur
1940 Leo H. Baekeland
1940 Arthur H. Compton
1941 Edwin H. Armstrong
1942 Jerome C. Hunsaker
1942 Paul D. Merica
1943 George W. Pierce
1943 Harold C. Urey
1944 William D. Coolidge
1945 Harlow Shapley
1946 Henry C. Sherman
1947 Enrico Fermi
1948 Wendell M. Stanley
1948 Theodore von Karman
1950 Eugene P. Wigner
1953 William F. Gibbs
1954 C. E. Kenneth Mees
1957 Hugh S. Taylor
1958 Donald W. Douglas
1959 Hans A. Bethe
1960 Roger Adams
1961 Detlev W. Bronk
1963 Glenn T. Seaborg
1964 Gregory Breit
1965 Frederick Seitz
1966 Britton Chance
1967 Murray Gell-Mann
1968 Marshall W. Nirenberg
1969 John A. Wheeler
1970 Wolfgang K. H. Panofsky
1972 George B. Kistiakowsky
1973 Theodosius G. Dobzhansky
1974 Nikolai Bogolyubov
1975 John Bardeen
1976 Mahlon B. Hoagland
1977 Cyril Manton Harris
1978 Elias J. Corey
1979 G. Evelyn Hutchinson
1980 Avram Goldstein
1980 Lyman Spitzer, Jr.
1981 Stephen W. Hawking
1982 Ceasar Milstein
1983 Kenneth G. Wilson

1984 Verner E. Suomi
1985 George C. Pimentel
1986 Benoit Mandelbrot

John Fritz Medal

(Presented annually by the John Fritz Medal Board of Award for notable scientific or industrial achievement in the field of pure or applied science. Sponsored by the American Society of Civil Engineers, American Institute of Electrical and Electronics Engineers, and Institute of Mining, Metallurgical, and Petroleum Engineers, American Society of Mechanical Engineers, and American Institute of Chemical Engineers.)

1902 John Fritz
1906 George Westinghouse
1907 Alexander Graham Bell
1908 Thomas A. Edison
1909 Charles T. Porter
1912 Robert W. Hunt
1914 John E. Sweet
1915 James Douglas
1916 Elihu Thomson
1917 Henry M. Howe
1918 J. Waldo Smith
1919 George W. Goethals
1920 Orville Wright
1924 Ambrose Swasey
1925 John F. Stevens
1926 Edward D. Adams
1927 Elmer A. Sperry
1928 John J. Carty
1929 Herbert Hoover
1930 Ralph Modjeski
1931 David W. Taylor
1932 Michael I. Pupin
1933 Daniel C. Jackling
1934 John R. Freeman
1935 Frank J. Sprague
1936 William F. Durand
1937 Arthur N. Talbot
1938 Paul D. Merica
1939 Frank B. Jewett
1940 Clarence F. Hirshfeld
1941 Ralph Budd
1942 E. L. DeGolyer
1943 Willis R. Whitney
1944 Charles F. Kettering
1945 John L. Savage
1946 Zay Jeffries
1947 Lewis W. Chubb
1948 Theodore von Karman
1949 Charles M. Allen
1950 Walter H. Aldridge
1951 Vannevar Bush
1952 Ervin G. Bailey
1953 Benjamin F. Fairless
1954 William E. Wrather
1955 Harry A. Winne
1956 Philip Sporn
1957 Ben Moreell
1958 John R. Suman
1959 Mervin J. Kelly
1960 Gwilym A. Price
1961 Stephen D. Bechtel
1962 Crawford H. Greenewalt
1963 Hugh L. Dryden
1964 Lucius D. Clay
1965 Frederick R. Kappel
1966 Warren K. Lewis
1967 Walker L. Cisler
1968 Igor I. Sikorsky
1969 Michael L. Haider

1970 Glenn B. Warren
1971 Patrick E. Haggerty
1972 William Webster
1973 Lyman D. Wilbur
1974 H. I. Rumnes
1975 Manson Benedict
1976 Thomas O. Paine
1977 George R. Brown

Gary Memorial Medal

(Awarded from time to time by the American Iron and Steel Institute for outstanding contributions to the iron and steel industry.)

1929 James A. Farrell
1930 Charles M. Schwab
1931 William J. Filblert
1932 Julian Kennedy
1933 Willis L. King
1934 Eugene G. Grace
1935 John B. Tytus
1944 Quincy Bent
1949 Benjamin F. Fairless
1951 Edward L. Ryerson
1952 Walter S. Tower
1954 Elton Hoyt, II
1955 Tom M. Girdler
1955 Charles R. Hook
1955 Ernest T. Weir
1961 Charles M. White
1964 Arthur B. Homer
1965 Thomas F. Patton
1967 Leslie B. Worthington
1968 Roger M. Blough
1969 Edmund F. Martin
1970 Logan T. Johnston
1971 George A. Stinson
1973 Edwin H. Gott
1975 Stewart J. Cort
1976 Roger S. Ahlbrandt
1977 Frederick G. Jaicks
1979 Edgar B. Speer
1980 Lewis W. Foy
1982 William J. De Lancey
1984 David M. Roderick
1985 William T. Hogan
1985 Harry Holiday, Jr.
1986 Donald H. Trautlein

Goddard Astronautics Award

(Presented annually by the American Institute of Aeronautics and Astronautics; successor of the Goddard Award and the Louis W. Hill Space Transportation Award.)

1977 James S. Martin, Jr.
1978 Joseph V. Charyk
1979 Maxime A. Faget
1980 Robert J. Parks
1981 Peter T. Burr
1982 John F. Yardley
1983 George E. Mueller
1984 Krafft Ehricke
1985 Frederic C. E. Oder
1986 George E. Solomon

Goddard Award

(Presented annually by the American Institute of Aeronautics and Astronautics for notable contributions to the engineering science of propulsion or energy; succeeded by Goddard Astronautics Award in 1976.)

1965	Frank Whittle
1966	Hans J. P. von Ohain
1966	A. Wade Blackman
1966	George D. Lewis
1967	Robert O. Bullock
1967	Irving A. Johnsen
1967	Seymour Lieblein
1968	Donald C. Berkey
1968	Ernest C. Simpson
1968	James E. Worsham
1969	Perry W. Pratt
1970	Gerhard Neumann
1972	Howard Shumacher
1972	Bryan Brimelow
1972	Gary Tlourde
1973	Edward S. Taylor
1974	Paul D. Castenholz
1974	Richard Mulready
1974	John Sloop
1975	George Rosen
1975	Gordon Holbrook

Daniel Guggenheim Medal

(Awarded annually by the Daniel Guggenheim Medal Board of Award for outstanding contributions to the promotion of aeronautics, the medal is sponsored by the American Society of Mechanical Engineers, Society of Automotive Engineers, and American Institute of Aeronautics and Astronautics.)

1929	Orville Wright
1933	Jerome C. Hunsaker
1934	William E. Boeing
1935	William F. Durand
1936	George W. Lewis
1939	Donald W. Douglas
1940	Glenn L. Martin
1941	Juan T. Trippe
1942	James H. Doolittle
1944	Lawrence D. Bell
1945	Theodore P. Wright
1947	Lester D. Gardner
1948	Leroy R. Grumman
1949	Edward P. Warner
1950	Hugh L. Dryden
1951	Igor I. Sikorsky
1953	Charles A. Lindbergh
1955	Theodore Von Karman
1956	Frederick B. Rentschler
1957	Arthur E. Raymond
1958	William Littlewood
1960	Grover Loening
1961	Jerome F. Lederer
1962	James H. Kindelberger
1963	James S. McDonnell
1964	Robert H. Goddard
1966	Charles S. Draper
1967	George S. Schairer
1968	H. Mansfield Horner
1969	H. Julian Allen
1972	William C. Mentzer
1973	William McPherson Allen
1974	Floyd L. Thompson
1975	Duane Wallace

1976	Marcel Dassault
1977	Cyrus R. Smith
1978	Edward Heinemann
1979	Gerhard Neumann
1981	Edward C. Wells
1982	Davis S. Lewis
1983	Nicholas Hoff

Hall of Fame for Great Americans

(Administered by New York University, the hall of fame honors notable Americans of the past whose achievements in various fields of endeavor have been of outstanding inspiration. No new elections since 1976.)

1900	John Adams
	John James Audubon
	Henry Ward Beecher
	William Ellery Channing
	Henry Clay
	Peter Cooper
	Jonathan Edwards
	Ralph Waldo Emerson
	David G. Farragut
	Benjamin Franklin
	Robert Fulton
	Ulysses S. Grant
	Asa Gray
	Nathaniel Hawthorne
	Washington Irving
	Thomas Jefferson
	James Kent
	Robert E. Lee
	Abraham Lincoln
	Henry Wadsworth Longfellow
	Horace Mann
	John Marshall
	Samuel F. B. Morse
	George Peabody
	Joseph Story
	Gilbert Stuart
	George Washington
	Daniel Webster
	Eli Whitney
1905	John Quincy Adams
	James Russell Lowell
	Mary Lyon
	James Madison
	Maria Mitchell
	William T. Sherman
	John Greenleaf Whittier
	Emma Willard
1910	George Bancroft
	Phillips Brooks
	William Cullen Bryant
	James Fenimore Cooper
	Oliver Wendell Hoomes
	Andrew Jackson
	John Lothrop Motley
	Edgar Allan Poe
	Harriett Beecher Stowe
	Francis E. Willard
1915	Louis Agassiz
	Daniel Boone
	Rufus Choate
	Charlotte S. Cushman
	Alexander Hamilton
	Joseph Henry
	Mark Hopkins
	Elias Howe
	Francis Parkman
1920	Samuel L. Clemens
	James Buchanan Eads
	Patrick Henry

	William T. G. Morton
	Alice Freeman Palmer
	Augustus Saint-Gaudens
	Roger Williams
1925	Edwin Booth
	John Paul Jones
1930	Matthew F. Maury
	James Monroe
	James A. McNeill Whistler
	Walt Whitman
1935	Grover Cleveland
	Simon Newcomb
	William Penn
1940	Stephen Collins Foster
1945	Sidney Lanier
	Thomas Paine
	Walter Reed
	Booker T. Washington
1950	Susan B. Anthony
	Alexander Graham Bell
	Josiah W. Gibbs
	William C. Gorgas
	Theodore Roosevelt
	Woodrow Wilson
1955	Thomas 'Stonewall' Jackson
	George Westinghouse
	Wilbur Wright
1960	Thomas A. Edison
	Edward A. MacDowell
	Henry David Thoreau
1965	Jane Addams
	Oliver Wendell Holmes, Jr.
	Sylvanus Thayer
	Orville Wright
1970	Lillian D. Wald
	Albert A. Michelson
1973	Louis D. Brandeis
	George Washington Carver
	Franklin Delano Roosevelt
	John Philip Sousa
1976	Clara Barton
	Luther Burbank
	Andrew Carnegie

Hayden Memorial Geological Award

(Awarded every three years, at first annually, by the Academy of Natural Sciences of Philadelphia for the best publication, exploration, discovery or research in the sciences of geology or paleontology; discontinued 1972-1978; reinstituted as biennial award in 1979.)

1890	James Hall
1891	Edward D. Cope
1905	Charles D. Walcott
1908	John M. Clark
1911	John C. Branner
1914	Henry Fairfield Osborn
1917	William M. Davis
1920	Thomas C. Chamberlin
1926	William B. Scott
1929	Charles Schuchert
1932	Reginald A. Daly
1935	Andrew C. Lawson
1941	Amadeus W. Grabau
1944	Joseph A. Cushman
1950	George G. Simpson
1953	Norman L. Bowen
1956	Raymond C. Moore
1959	Carl O. Dunbar

1962	Alfred S. Romer
1965	Norman D. Newell
1968	Elso S. Barghoorn
1971	Wilmot H. Bradley
1979	Daniel I. Axelrod
1982	Stephen Jay Gould
1986	John H. Ostrom

Louis W. Hill Space Transportation Award

(Presented annually by the American Institute of Aeronautics and Astronautics to honor significant contributions to the art and science of space flight; succeeded by the Goddard Astronautics Award in 1976.)

1958	Robert H. Goddard
1959	James A. Van Allen
1960	Samuel K. Hoffman
1960	Thomas F. Dixon
1961	Robert R. Gilruth
1962	Charles S. Draper
1963	Robert J. Parks
1963	Jack M. James
1964	Hugh L. Dryden
1965	Wernher von Braun
1966	W. Randolph Lovelace, II
1967	Abe Silverstein
1968	William H. Pickering
1969	George M. Low
1970	Christopher C. Kraft, Jr.
1971	Hubertus Strughold
1972	David G. Hoag
1972	Richard H. Battin
1973	Kurt H. Debus
1974	Rocco A. Petrone
1975	Glenn Lunney

Sidney Hillman Foundation Award for Meritorious Public Service

(Presented from time to time to outstanding figures in public life who have devoted themselves to community welfare.)

1949	Frank P. Graham
1950	Oscar R. Ewing
1951	Herbert H. Lehman
1952	William O. Douglas
1953	Harry S. Truman
1954	Bernard J. Sheil
1955	Wayne L. Morse
1956	Eleanor Roosevelt
1957	Paul H. Douglas
1958	Robert M. Hutchins
1966	Martin Luther King, Jr.
1966	George C. Higgins
1966	Jacob Weinstein
1968	W. Willard Wirtz
1969	David L. Morse
1978	Andrew Young
1979	E. G. Marshall

Lester H. Hofheimer Prize

(Awarded annually by the American Psychiatric Association to recognize outstanding research accomplishment in psychiatry and mental hygiene; superseded by Foundations' Fund Prize for Research in Psychiatry.)

1949 Benjamin Pasamanick
1951 Jurgen Ruesch
1952 Robert Arnot
1952 Beatrice Talbot
1952 Milton Greenblatt
1953 Thomas H. Holmes
1953 Helen Goodell
1953 Stewart Wolf
1953 Harold G. Wolff
1955 Philip F. D. Seitz
1956 John Money
1956 Joan G. Hampson
1956 John L. Hampson
1957 Christoph M. Heinicke
1958 James Olds
1959 Irving L. Janis
1960 Albert J. Stunkard
1961 Seymour Levine
1962 Ogden R. Lindsley
1962 Joseph D. Matarazzo
1963 Howard E. Freeman
1963 Ozzie G. Simmons
1963 Jerome Kagan
1963 Howard A. Moss
1964 William C. Dement
1965 Jack H. Mendelson
1966 Lyman C. Wynne
1966 Margaret Thaler Singer
1967 Benjamin Pasamanick
1967 Simon Dinitz
1967 Frank Scarpitti
1968 Robert Coles
1969 Jonathan O. Cole
1969 Gerald L. Klerman
1969 Solomon C. Goldberg
1970 Arnold M. Ludwig
1970 Jerome Levine

Holley Medal

(Awarded from time to time by the American Society of Mechanical Engineers to honor an act of genius in engineering that has accomplished a great and timely public benefit.)

1924 Hjalmar G. Carlson
1928 Elmer A. Sperry
1934 Irving Langmuir
1936 Henry Ford
1937 Frederick G. Cottrell
1938 Francis Hodgkinson
1939 Carl E. Johansson
1940 Edwin H. Armstrong
1941 John C. Garand
1942 Ernest O. Lawrence
1943 Vannevar Bush
1944 Carl L. Norden
1945 Sanford A. Moss
1946 Norman R. Gibson
1947 Raymond D. Johnson
1948 Edwin H. Land
1950 Charles G. Curtis
1951 George R. Fink
1952 Sanford L. Cluett
1953 Philip M. McKenna
1954 Walter A. Shewhart

1955 George J. Hood
1957 Charles S. Draper
1959 Maurice J. Fletcher
1961 Thomas E. Moon
1963 William Schockley
1968 Chester F. Carlson
1969 Willis J. Whitfield
1973 Harold E. Edgerton
1973 Kenneth J. Germeshausen
1975 George M. Grover
1976 Emmett N. Leith
1976 Juris Upatnieks
1977 J. David Margerum
1979 David G. Collipp
1979 Douwe deVries
1980 Soichiro Honda
1982 Jack St. Clair Kilby
1985 John V. Atanasoff
1986 Wilson Greatbatch

Hoover Medal

(Awarded to honor distinguished public service by an engineer. Administered by a board of award representing the American Society of Mechanical Engineers, American Society of Civil Engineers, Institute of Electrical and Electronics Engineers, and American Institute of Mining, Metallurgical, and Petroleum Engineers.)

1930 Herbert Hoover
1936 Ambrose Swasey
1938 John F. Stevens
1940 Gano S. Dunn
1941 D. Robert Yarnall
1942 Gerard Swope
1944 Ralph E. Flanders
1945 William Henry Harrison
1946 Vannevar Bush
1948 Malcolm Pirnie
1949 Frank B. Jewett
1950 Karl T. Compton
1951 William L. Batt
1952 Clarence D. Howe
1954 Alfred P. Sloan, Jr.
1955 Charles F. Kettering
1956 Herbert Hoover, Jr.
1957 Scott Turner
1958 Raymond A. Wheeler
1959 Henry T. Heald
1960 Dwight D. Eisenhower
1961 Mervin J. Kelly
1962 Walker L. Cisler
1963 James R. Killian, Jr.
1964 John A. McCone
1966 Lillian M. Gilbreth
1967 Lucius D. Clay
1969 Edgar F. Kaiser
1971 Luis A. Ferre
1972 Frederick R. Kappel
1973 William J. Hedley
1974 David Packard
1975 James Boyd
1976 James B. Fisk
1977 Peter C. Goldmark
1977 Donald C. Burnham
1979 Charles M. Brinckerhoff
1980 Stephen D. Bechtel, Jr.
1981 Arnold O. Beckman
1982 Michel T. Halbouty
1983 Joseph J. Jacobs
1984 Kenneth A. Roe
1985 Robert C. West
1986 Lawrence P. Grayson

Howells Medal

(Awarded once every five years by the American Academy of Arts and Letters to recognize the most distinguished work of American fiction published during that period.)

1925 Mary E. Wilkins Freeman
1930 Willa Cather
1935 Pearl S. Buck
1940 Ellen Glasgow
1945 Booth Tarkington
1950 William Faulkner
1955 Eudora Welty
1960 James Gould Cozzens
1965 John Cheever
1970 William Styron
1975 Thomas Pynchon
1980 William Maxwell

Hubbard Medal

(Presented from time to time by the National Geographic Society to recognize distinction in geographic research, exploration, and discovery.)

1906 Robert E. Peary
1909 Robert A. Bartlett
1909 Grove K. Gilbert
1919 Vilhjalmur Stefansson
1926 Richard E. Byrd, Jr.
1927 Charles A. Lindbergh
1931 Roy Chapman Andrews
1934 Anne Morrow Lindbergh
1935 Albert W. Stevens
1935 Orvil A. Anderson
1936 Lincoln Ellsworth
1945 Henry H. Arnold
1953 Donald B. MacMillan
1958 Paul A. Siple
1962 John H. Glenn, Jr.
1967 Juan T. Trippe
1969 Frank Borman
1969 James A. Lovell, Jr.
1969 William A. Anders
1970 Neil A. Armstrong
1970 Edwin E. Aldrin, Jr.
1970 Michael Collins
1975 Alexander Wetmore
1978 Marie Tharp
1978 Bruce C. Heezen
1979 James E. Webb
1981 Robert L. Crippen
1981 John W. Young

Charles Evans Hughes Award

(Presented annually by the National Conference of Christians and Jews to recognize courageous leadership in governmental service.)

1965 LeRoy Collins
1965 Nelson Rockefeller
1965 Edmund G. Brown
1965 George Romney
1966 Dwight D. Eisenhower
1967 Harry S Truman
1967 Edward W. Brooke
1967 Paul H. Douglas
1968 Lewis L. Strauss

1968 John W. Gardner
1969 Ivan Allen, Jr.
1969 Earl Warren
1970 Constance Baker Motley
1970 Theodore M. Hesburgh
1971 Lucius D. Clay
1971 Tom C. Clark
1971 Walter E. Washington
1972 Jerome H. Holland
1973 Henry A. Kissinger
1974 David Rockefeller
1975 Brooks Hays
1975 Linwood Holton
1975 Robert D. Murphy
1976 John D. deButts
1977 Betty Ford
1977 Gerald Ford
1979 Bob Hope
1980 Alexander M. Haig, Jr.
1981 Walter Cronkite
1982 Ronald Reagan
1983 Jacob K. Javits
1984 Beverly Sills
1985 John Brademas

Institute of Electrical and Electronics Engineers Medal of Honor

(Awarded for outstanding achievement in engineering science and technology.)

1917 Edwin H. Armstrong
1919 E. F. W. Alexanderson
1921 Reginald A. Fessenden
1922 Lee deForest
1924 Michael I. Pupin
1926 Greenleaf W. Pickard
1927 Louis W. Austin
1928 Jonathan Zenneck
1929 George W. Pierce
1930 P. O. Pedersen
1932 Arthur E. Kennelly
1933 John A. Fleming
1934 Stanford C. Hooper
1936 George A. Campbell
1937 Melville Eastham
1938 John H. Dellinger
1940 Lloyd Espenscheid
1941 Alfred N. Goldsmith
1942 A. H. Taylor
1944 Haraden Pratt
1945 Harold H. Beverage
1949 Ralph Bown
1950 Frederick E. Terman
1951 Vladimir K. Zworykin
1954 William L. Everitt
1955 Harald T. Friis
1957 Julius A. Stratton
1958 Albert W. Hull
1959 E. Leon Chaffee
1960 Harry Nyquist
1961 Ernst A. Guillemin
1962 Edward V. Appleton
1963 John H. Hammond, Jr.
1963 George C. Southworth
1964 Harold A. Wheeler
1966 Claude E. Shannon
1967 Charles H. Townes
1968 Gordon K. Teal
1969 Edward L. Ginzton
1971 John Bardeen
1972 Jay W. Forrester
1973 Rudolf Kompfner
1974 Rudolf E. Kalman
1975 John R. Pierce
1977 H. Earle Vaughan
1978 Robert N. Noyce

1979 Richard Bellman
1980 William Shockley
1981 Sidney Darlington
1982 John W. Tukey
1983 Nicolaas Bloembergen
1984 Norman F. Ramsey
1985 John R. Whinnery
1986 Jack St. Clair Kilby

Joseph S. Isidor Medal

(Awarded by the National Academy of Design to recognize achievement in figure painting composition.)

1907 Hugo Ballin
1908 Sergeant Kendall
1909 Frederick B. Williams
1910 Kenyon Cox
1911 E. Irving Couse
1912 Ernest L. Blumenschein
1913 Francis C. Jones
1914 Charles W. Hawthorne
1915 Charles W. Hawthorne
1916 George Bellows
1917 Alice Kent Stoddard
1918 Adolphe W. Blondheim
1919 Ralph McLellan
1921 Howard E. Smith
1921 George L. Nelson
1923 Marie Danforth Page
1924 Eugene F. Savage
1926 F. Martin Hennings
1926 Walter Ufer
1927 Sergeant Kendall
1928 Robert Spencer
1929 Edmund C. Tarbell
1930 John W. Benson
1931 Leopold Seyffert
1932 Paul Sample
1935 Andrew Winter
1936 Jerry Farnsworth
1937 Gerald Leake
1938 Jerome Myers
1940 Herbert M. Stoops
1941 Louis Betts
1953 Colleen Browning
1954 Lou Sardella
1955 Gladys Rockmore Davis
1956 Philip Reisman
1957 Isabel Bishop
1958 John Fenton
1961 Umberto Romano
1962 Leon Kroll
1963 Joseph Floch
1965 William Rose
1967 Burton Silverman
1969 Seymour Pearlstein
1970 Robert Vickrey
1971 Robert Gwathmey
1972 Joe Lasker
1974 May Stevens
1975 Raphael Soyer
1976 David Aaronson
1980 Rudolph Baranik

Thomas Jefferson Memorial Foundation Medal in Architecture

(Awarded by the University of Virginia to honor distinguished achievement in architecture.)

1966 Ludwig Mies van der
      Rohe

1967 Alvar Aalto
1968 Marcel Breuer
1969 John Ely Burchard
1970 Kenzo Tange
1971 Jose Luis Sert
1972 Lewis Mumford
1973 Jean Labatut
1974 Frei Otto
1975 Nikolaus Pevsner
1976 I. M. Pei
1977 Ada Louise Huxtable
1978 Philip Johnson
1979 Lawrence Halprin
1980 Hugh Stubbins
1981 Edward Larrabee Barnes
1982 Vincent Scully
1983 Robert Venturi
1984 Aga Khan
1985 Leon Krier
1986 James Stirling

E. Mead Johnson Award

(Presented by the American Academy of Pediatrics for outstanding research work in the fields of special interest to the academy.)

1940 Robert E. Gross
1940 Lee E. Farr
1941 Rene J. Dubos
1941 Albert B. Sabin
1942 David Bodian
1942 Howard A. Howe
1942 Harold E. Harrison
1942 Helen C. Harrison
1943 Hattie E. Alexander
1943 Philip Levine
1944 Fuller Albright
1944 Josef Warkany
1944 Horace L. Hodes
1946 Paul A. Harper
1947 Helen B. Taussig
1947 Louis K. Diamond
1948 Wolf W. Zuelzer
1948 Benjamin M. Spock
1948 Nathan B. Talbot
1949 Henry L. Barnett
1950 Charles D. May
1950 Harry Shwachman
1950 Gertrude Henle
1950 Werner Henle
1951 William M. Wallace
1951 Victor A. Najjar
1952 Seymour S. Cohen
1952 Orvar Swenson
1952 Edward B. D. Newhauser
1953 Frederick C. Robbins
1953 Thomas H. Weller
1953 Margaret H. D. Smith
1954 Robert E. Cooke
1954 Vincent C. Kelley
1955 Robert A. Good
1956 David Gitlin
1956 Arnall Patz
1957 Alfred M. Bongiovanni
1957 Walter R. Eberlein
1958 William A. Silverman
1958 Norman Kretchmer
1959 C. Henry Kempe
1959 Barton Childs
1960 Robert A. Aldrich
1960 Irving Schulman
1961 Lytt I. Gardner
1961 Donald E. Pickering
1962 Park S. Gerald
1962 Robert L. Vernier
1963 D. Carleton Gajdusek
1963 Richard T. Smith

1964 Robert M. Chanock
1964 Abraham M. Rudolph
1965 David Y. Hsia
1965 L. Stanley James
1966 William H. Tooley
1966 Robert W. Winters
1967 Henry N. Kirkman, Jr.
1967 Harry M. Meyer, Jr.
1967 Paul D. Parkman
1968 Mary Ellen Avery
1969 Frederick C. Battaglia
1969 Gerard P. Odell
1970 Joseph A. Bellanti
1970 Myron Winick
1972 H. H. Sandstead
1973 V. R. Young
1974 J. W. Suttie
1975 H. E. Ganther
1976 L. D. Stegink

Laetare Medal

(Presented annually by the University of Notre Dame to an American Catholic to recognize achievement in the fields of art, science, literature, law, medicine, philosophy, philanthropy, and statesmanship.)

1883 John G. Shea
1884 Patrick C. Keeley
1885 Eliza A. Starr
1886 John Newton
1887 Edward Preuss
1888 Patrick V. Hickey
1889 Anna H. Dorsey
1890 William J. Onahan
1891 Daniel Dougherty
1892 Henry F. Brownson
1893 Patrick Donohue
1894 Augustine Daly
1895 Mary A. Sadlier
1896 William S. Rosecrans
1897 Thomas A. Emmet
1898 Timothy E. Howard
1899 Mary G. Caldwell
1900 John A. Creighton
1901 W. Bourke Cockran
1902 John B. Murphy
1903 Charles J. Bonaparte
1904 Richard C. Kerens
1905 Thomas B. Fitzpatrick
1906 Francis J. Quinlan
1907 Katherine E. Conway
1908 James C. Monaghan
1909 Frances C. F. Tiernan
1910 Maurice F. Egan
1911 Agnes Repplier
1912 Thomas M. Mulry
1913 Charles G. Herbermann
1914 Edward D. White
1915 Mary V. Merrick
1916 James J. Walsh
1917 William S. Benson
1918 Joseph Scott
1919 George L. Duval
1920 Lawrence F. Flick
1921 Elizabeth Nourse
1922 Charles R. Neill
1923 Walter G. Smith
1924 Charles D. Maginnis
1925 Albert F. Zahm
1926 Edward N. Hurley
1927 Margaret Anglin
1928 John J. Spaulding
1929 Alfred E. Smith
1930 Frederick P. Kenkel
1931 James J. Phelan

1932 Stephen J. Maher
1933 John McCormack
1934 Genevieve G. Brady
1935 Francis H. Spearman
1936 Richard Reid
1937 Jeremiah D. M. Ford
1938 Irvin W. Abell
1939 Josephine Van Dyke
      Brownson
1940 Hugh A. Drum
1941 William T. Walsh
1942 Helen C. White
1943 Thomas F. Woodlock
1944 Anne O'Hare McCormick
1945 G. Howland Shaw
1946 Carlton J. H. Hayes
1947 William Cabell Bruce
1948 Frank C. Walker
1949 Irene Dunne
1950 J. Lawton Collins
1951 John H. Phelan
1952 Thomas E. Murray
1953 I. A. O'Shaughnessy
1954 Jefferson Caffery
1955 George Meany
1956 Alfred M. Gruenther
1957 Clare Boothe Luce
1958 Frank M. Folsom
1959 Robert D. Murphy
1960 George M. Shuster
1961 John F. Kennedy
1962 Francis J. Braceland
1963 George W. Anderson, Jr.
1964 Phyllis McGinley
1965 Frederick D. Rossini
1966 Patrick F. Crowley
1966 Mrs. Patrick F. Crowley
1967 J. Peter Grace
1968 R. Sargent Shriver
1969 William J. Brennan, Jr.
1970 William B. Walsh
1971 Walter F. Kerr
1971 Jean Kerr
1972 Dorothy Day
1973 John A. O'Brien
1974 James A. Farley
1975 Ann Ida Gannon
1976 Paul Horgan
1977 Mike Mansfield
1978 John Tracy Ellis
1979 Helen Hays
1980 Thomas P. O'Neill, Jr.
1981 Edmund S. Muskie
1982 John Dearden
1983 Edmund A. Stephan
1983 Evelyn Stephan
1984 John T. Noonan
1985 Guido Calabrese
1986 Mary Elizabeth Charney
1986 Thomas P. Charney

Lamme Medal

(Awarded annually by the Institute of Electrical and Electronic Engineers to recognize meritorious achievement in the development of electrical or electronic apparatus or systems.)

1928 Allan B. Field
1929 Rudolf E. Hellmund
1930 William J. Foster
1931 Giuseppe Faccioli
1932 Edward Weston
1933 Lewis B. Stillwell
1934 Henry E. Warren
1935 Vannevar Bush
1936 Frank Conrad

1937 Robert E. Doherty	1953 George Wald	1954 Robert E. Gross	1928 Henry A. Pilsbry
1938 Marion A. Savage	1954 Edwin P. Astwood	1955 C. Walton Lillehei	1931 William M. Wheeler, Jr.
1939 Norman W. Storer	1954 John F. Enders	1955 Herbert E. Warden	1934 Gerrit S. Miller, Jr.
1940 Comfort A. Adams	1955 Karl P. Link	1955 Richard L. Varco	1937 Edwin Linton
1941 Forrest E. Ricketts	1956 Karl F. Meyer	1955 Edward H. Robitzek	1940 Merritt L. Fernald
1942 Joseph Slepian	1956 Francis O. Schmitt	1955 Irving Selikoff	1943 Chancey Juday
1943 A. H. Kehoe	1958 Peyton Rous	1955 Walsh McDermott	1946 Ernst Mayr
1944 S. H. Mortensen	1958 Theodore Puck	1955 Carl Muschenheim	1949 Warren P. Spencer
1945 David C. Prince	1958 Alfred D. Hershey	1956 Jonas E. Salk	1952 G. Evelyn Hutchinson
1946 John B. MacNeill	1959 Albert H. Coons	1956 V. Everett Kinsey	1955 Herbert Friedmann
1947 Aleck M. MacCutcheon	1959 Jules Freund	1956 Arnall Patz	1958 H. B. Hungerford
1948 Vladimir K. Zworykin	1960 James D. Watson	1957 Nathan S. Kline	1961 Robert E. Snodgrass
1949 C. M. Laffoon	1960 James V. Neel	1957 Robert H. Noce	1964 Carl E. Hubbs
1950 Donald I. Bohn	1960 James Hillier	1957 Heinz E. Lehmann	1967 Donn E. Rosen
1951 Arthur E. Silver	1962 Choh H. Li	1958 Robert W. Wilkins	1970 Arthur Cronquist
1952 I. F. Kinnard	1963 Lyman C. Craig	1959 John H. Dingle	1975 James Bond
1953 F. A. Cowan	1964 Renato Dulbecco	1959 Gilbert Dalldorf	1979 Edward O. Wilson
1954 A. M. deBellis	1964 Harry Rubin	1962 Joseph Smadel	1983 G. Ledyard Stebbins
1955 Clinton R. Hanna	1965 Robert W. Holley	1963 Michael E. De Bakey	1985 Hampton L. Carson
1956 Harold H. Beverage	1966 George E. Palade	1963 Charles B. Huggins	
1957 Harold S. Black	1967 Bernard B. Brodie	1964 Nathan S. Kline	
1958 Philip L. Alger	1968 Marshall W. Nirenberg	1965 Albert B. Sabin	
1958 Sterling Beckwith	1969 F. Gobind Khorana	1966 Sidney Farber	
1959 L. A. Kilgore	1969 William F. Windle	1967 Robert A. Phillips	**Joseph W. Lippincott**
1960 John G. Trump	1969 Bruce Merrifield	1968 John H. Gibbin, Jr.	**Award**
1961 Charles Concordia	1970 Robert A. Good	1969 George C. Cotzias	
1962 E. L. Harder	1970 Earl W. Sutherland, Jr.	1971 Edward D. Fries	(Presented annually by the Ameri-
1963 Loyal V. Bewley	1971 Seymour Benzer	1972 Min Chiu Li	can Library Association to honor
1965 A. Uno Lamm	1971 Charles Yanofsky	1972 Roy Hertz	noteworthy service in the profes-
1967 Warren P. Mason	1971 Sydney Brenner	1972 Denis Burkitt	sion of librarianship.)
1968 Nathan Cohn	1972 Ludwick Gross	1972 Joseph H. Burchenal	
1969 James D. Cobine	1972 Howard E. Skipper	1972 V. Anomah Ngu	1938 Mary U. Rothrock
1970 Harry F. Olson	1972 Sol Spiegelman	1972 John L. Ziegler	1939 Herbert Putnam
1971 Winthrop M. Leeds	1972 Howard M. Temin	1972 Edmund Klein	1948 Carl H. Milam
1972 Yu H. Ku	1975 Roger C. L. Guillemin	1972 Emil Frei, III	1949 Harry M. Lydenberg
1972 Robert H. Park	1975 Andrew V. Schally	1972 Emil J. Freireich	1950 Halsey W. Wilson
1973 Charles S. Draper	1975 Frank J. Dixon	1972 James F. Holland	1951 Helen Haines
1974 Seymour B. Cohn	1975 Henry G. Kunkel	1972 Donald Pinkel	1952 Carl Vitz
1975 Harold B. Law	1976 Rosalyn Yalow	1972 Paul P. Carbone	1953 Marian C. Manley
1976 C. Kumar	1977 K. Sune D. Bergstrom	1972 Vincent T. DeVita, Jr.	1954 Jack Dalton
1976 N. Patel	1977 Bengt Samuelsson	1972 Eugene J. Van Scott	1955 Emerson Greenway
1977 Bernard M. Oliver	1977 John R. Vane	1972 Isaac Djerassi	1956 Ralph A. Ulveling
1978 Harry W. Mergler	1978 Solomon H. Snyder	1972 C. Gordon Zubrod	1957 Flora B. Ludington
1979 James M. Cafferty	1978 Hans W. Kosterlitz	1973 Paul M. Zoll	1958 Carleton B. Joeckel
1980 Eugene C. Starr	1979 Roger Wolcott Sperry	1973 William B. Kouwenhoven	1959 Essae M. Colver
1981 George B. Litchford	1979 Walter Gilbert	1974 John Charnley	1960 Verner W. Clapp
1982 Marvin Chodorow	1979 Frederick Sanger	1975 Godfrey N. Hounsfield	1961 Joseph L. Wheeler
1983 Marion E. Hines	1980 Paul Berg	1975 William Oldendorf	1962 David H. Clift
1984 William C. MacMurray	1980 Stanley N. Cohen	1976 Raymond P. Ahlquist	1963 Frances W. Henne
1985 Loren Frank Stringer	1980 A. Dale Kaiser	1976 J. W. Black	1964 Robert B. Downs
1986 Ingolf Birger Johnson	1980 Herbert W. Boyer	1977 Inge G. Edler	1965 Frances C. Sayers
	1981 Barbara McClintock	1977 C. Helmuth Hertz	1966 Keyes D. Metcalf
	1982 J. Michael Bishop	1978 Robert Austrian	1967 Edmon Low
Albert Lasker Medical	1982 Raymond L. Erickson	1978 Emil C. Gotschlich	1968 Lucile Nix
Research Awards	1982 Robert C. Gallo	1978 Michael Heidelberger	1969 Germaine Krettek
	1982 Hidesaburo Hanafusa	1980 Vincent J. Freda	1970 Paul Howard
(Presented by the Albert and Mary	1982 Harold E. Varmus	1980 John Gorman	1971 William S. Dix
Lasker Foundation, originally	1983 Eric R. Kandel	1980 William Pollack	1972 Guy Lyle
through the American Public	1983 Vernon B. Mountcastle,	1980 Cyril A. Clarke	1973 Jesse H. Shera
Health Association, to honor those	Jr.	1980 Ronald Finn	1974 Jerrold Orne
who have made significant contri-	1984 Georges J. F. Kohler	1981 Louis Sokoloff	1975 Leon Carnovsky
butions to basic or clinical re-	1984 Ceasar Milstein	1982 Roscoe O. Brady	1976 Lester Asheim
search in disabling and fatal dis-	1984 Michael Potter	1982 Elizabeth F. Neufeld	1977 Virginia Lacy Jones
eases.)	1985 Michael S. Brown	1983 F. Mason Sones	1978 Henry T. Drennan
	1985 Joseph L. Goldstein	1984 Paul C. Lauterbur	1979 Helen H. Lyman
Basic Research	1986 Rita Levi-Montalcini	1985 Bernard Fisher	1980 E. J. Josey
	1986 Stanley Cohen	1986 Myron Essex	1981 Eric Moon
1946 Carl F. Cori		1986 Robert C. Gallo	1982 Keith Doms
1947 Oswald T. Avery		1986 Luc Montagnier	1983 Russell Bidlack
1947 Thomas Francis, Jr.	*Clinical Research*		1984 Nettie Barcrott Taylor
1947 Homer W. Smith			1985 Robert G. Vosper
1948 Vincent du Vigneaud	1946 John F. Mahoney	**Leidy Medal**	1986 Elizabeth W. Stone
1948 Selman A. Waksman	1949 Max Theiler		
1948 Rene J. Dubos	1951 Catherine MacFarlane	(Awarded every three years by the	
1949 Andre F. Cournand	1951 William G. Lennox	Academy of Natural Sciences of	
1949 William S. Tillett	1951 Frederic A. Gibbs	Philadelphia for the best publica-	
1950 George W. Beadle	1952 Conrad A. Elvehjem	tion, exploration, discovery, or re-	
1951 Karl F. Meyer	1952 Frederick S. McKay	search in the natural sciences.)	
1953 Michael Heidelberger	1952 H. Trendley Dean		
	1954 Alfred Blalock	1925 Herbert S. Jennings	
	1954 Helen B. Taussig		

Loines Award for Poetry

(Presented periodically by the National Institute of Arts and Letters as administrators of the Russell Loines Memorial Fund to recognize distinguished poetic achievements; discontinued after 1983.)

1931	Robert Frost
1942	Horace Gregory
1948	William Carlos Williams
1951	John Crowe Ransom
1960	Abbie Huston Evans
1962	I. A. Richards
1964	John Berryman
1966	William Meredith
1968	Anthony Hecht
1970	Robert Hayden
1972	William Jay Smith
1974	Philip Larkin
1976	Mona Van Duyn
1981	Ben Belitt
1983	Geoffrey Hill

Edward Longstreth Medal

(Awarded by the Franklin Institute to recognize notable inventions or meritorious improvements and developments in machines and mechanical processes.)

1891	Wallace H. Dodge
1891	Albert J. Pitkin
1891	Henry W. Roby
1891	W. George Schemerhorn
1891	John J. White
1892	Alexander C. Chenoweth
1892	J. R. Jones
1892	J. E. Roeder
1893	W. G. Adams
1893	John S. Forbes
1893	Frederick B. Hill
1893	William M. Mackay
1894	Christian H. Baush
1894	Victor G. Bloede
1894	W. H. Bristol
1894	William H. Clark
1894	Frank W. Collins
1894	W. R. DeVoe
1894	E. Ivins
1894	A. Langstaff Johnston
1894	John F. Lewis
1894	William F. Mattes
1894	Max E. Schmidt
1894	Joseph Sieber
1895	E. G. Bates
1895	Walter L. Cheney
1895	W. S. Cooper
1895	Charles Goodyear
1895	C. C. Taintor
1896	William T. Armstrong
1896	Jacob D. Cox
1896	G. Kroll
1896	George Lodge
1897	Angelo Heilprin
1897	E. B. Marsh
1897	H. C. Regan, Jr.
1897	G. M. Richards
1898	Thomas B. Doolittle
1898	W. B. Hollingshead
1899	Harold P. Brown
1899	Thomas A. Edison
1899	Frederick Frick
1899	G. C. Henning
1899	W. Lewis
1900	Charles Deshler
1900	Edwin J. McAllister

1900	C. N. Fay
1900	Z. G. Sholes
1900	H. Hochklassen
1900	Henry Goldman
1900	Horace G. Hoadley
1900	Eugene C. Lewis
1900	Henry D. Williams
1900	Milton O. Reeves
1900	C. L. Riker
1900	William H. Tucker
1901	Russell Bonnell
1901	Henry J. Schmitt
1901	Arthur Kitson
1902	Willis J. Roussel
1903	Bion J. Arnold
1903	Henry H. Cummings
1903	Henry F. Eberhardt
1903	Frederick L. Ulrich
1903	Frederic E. Ives
1903	W. F. C. Morsell
1903	J. W. von Pittler
1903	Edward W. Scripture
1903	William L. Schellenbach
1903	C. C. Wentworth
1904	C. W. Draper
1904	Henry J. Seitz
1904	H. M. Shaw
1905	John E. Alexander
1905	John J. Carty
1905	Michael Miley
1905	Henry M. Miley
1906	W. I. Follett
1906	George H. Meeker
1906	Charles B. Weidlog
1906	Henry E. Wetherill
1907	Herbert F. Ives
1908	G. Breed
1908	Allerton S. Cushman
1909	Charles A. Bennett
1909	J. A. Pearce Christfield
1909	J. H. Granberry
1909	B. F. Teal
1910	B. D. Reese
1910	Kenneth Rushton
1911	Joseph S. Hepburn
1911	E. P. Hyde
1911	Morton G. Lloyd
1911	Walter V. Turner
1911	Charles Roper
1912	Charles Baskerville
1912	Edwin M. Chance
1912	E. Lathrop
1912	Oswald Schreiner
1912	Edwin F. Northrup
1912	C. G. Thomas
1913	Cleveland Abbe
1913	E. Leon Chaffee
1913	Harry C. Jones
1913	Isaac N. Knapp
1913	John S. Stone
1914	Herbert T. Herr
1914	Hiram H. Hirsch
1914	W. J. Humphreys
1914	J. M. Rusby
1914	George A. Wheeler
1915	Herbert E. Ives
1915	Will G. Lenker
1915	Max von Recklinghausen
1915	Carrington C. Tutwiler
1915	Charles D. Young
1916	Carleton Ellis
1916	George W. Fuller
1916	George F. Stradling
1916	Benjamin G. Waggner
1917	F. H. Achard
1917	Arthur E. Kennelly
1917	A. S. Dana
1917	John T. Austin
1917	John D. Ball
1917	Christopher A. Becker
1917	Max Levy

1917	Dayton C. Miller
1917	George A. Rankin
1917	Albert Ringland
1917	Frank Schoenfuss
1918	H. Jermain Creighton
1918	Levi T. Edwards
1918	John H. Taussig
1918	Charles F. Zeek
1918	John B. Whitehead
1919	Herbert E. Ives
1919	Edwin P. Kingsbury
1919	Enoch Karrer
1919	John W. Ledoux
1919	Richard B. Moore
1919	Frederick J. Schlink
1919	Joshua I. Skinner
1919	Homer C. Snook
1920	Bert H. Hite
1920	William W. Kemp
1920	William H. Van Horn
1920	Gottdank L. Kothny
1920	Robert Suczek
1920	Morris E. Leeds
1920	Matthew Luckiesh
1921	Leason H. Adams
1921	E. D. Williamson
1921	William B. Eddison
1921	James Hartness
1921	Thomas W. Hicks
1921	Jacob M. Spitzglass
1922	Edward J. Brandt
1922	Samuel T. Freas
1922	Joseph F. Keller
1922	A. Herman Pfund
1922	Martin F. Tierman
1922	Charles F. Wallace
1923	Harry S. Parks
1924	William S. Elliott
1924	Thomas C. McBride
1924	Milton R. Sheen
1924	William F. Zimmermann
1925	Thomas M. Chance
1925	William E. Hoke
1925	Daniel H. Meloche
1925	Thomas Midgley, Jr.
1925	Carl P. Nachod
1926	Alonzo G. Kinyon
1927	Harry W. Hardinge
1927	Wilfred Lewis
1927	James F. Smathers
1928	Frank N. Speller
1928	Warren P. Valentine
1929	Edward G. Herbert
1929	Adolph W. Machlet
1929	John F. Peters
1930	Ervin G. Bailey
1930	Charles N. Weyl
1933	Howard L. Ingersoll
1933	Dunlap J. McAdam, Jr.
1934	William E. Sykes
1935	Edmond Bruce
1935	Howard D. Colman
1935	Burt A. Peterson
1935	Peter Davey
1935	Karl B. McEachron
1936	Alfred V. deForest
1936	William R. Hoke
1936	Elmer A. Sperry, Jr.
1937	Emile M. Chamot
1937	Richard T. Erban
1937	John S. Haug
1937	Herbert L. Whittemore
1938	Clarence W. Balke
1938	Frederick Hellweg
1938	Paul Sollenberger
1938	Frederick C. Langenberg
1938	Norman F. S. Russell
1939	Arthur C. Hardy
1939	Jesse E. Stareck
1939	John D. Strong
1939	Robley C. Williams

1940	Leopold Godowsky, Jr.
1940	Leopold Mannes
1940	Games Slayter
1940	Richard L. Templin
1940	Maxwell M. Upson
1941	Benjamin J. Wilson
1942	Ralph E. Flanders
1942	Ernest V. Flanders
1942	Charles M. Kearns
1943	Robert G. De La Mater
1943	William Schwemlein
1944	Frank B. Allen
1944	Edward E. Simmons, Jr.
1944	J. Stogdell Stokes
1945	Sanford L. Cluett
1947	Samuel Berman
1947	Harold J. W. Fay
1948	Nicholas F. Arone
1948	Edwin H. Brink
1948	Raleigh J. Wise
1949	William H. Millspaugh
1949	Arthur M. Young
1951	Howard O. McMahon
1953	Chester F. Carlson
1955	Richard Y. Case
1956	Floyd A. Firestone
1957	John B. Johnson
1958	Price C. McLemore
1958	George S. Crampton
1959	David M. Potter
1959	Jacob Rabinow
1960	W. Edward Chamberlain
1960	John W. Coltman
1960	Frederick A. Keidel
1960	Moulton B. Taylor
1961	Robert L. Alcorn, Jr.
1961	Eugene C. Clark
1961	Henry A. Weyer
1961	Josiah L. Merrill, Jr.
1962	Felix Zandman
1962	Albert L. Genter
1962	Walter O. Snelling
1962	Carlos B. Mirick
1962	Matthew H. Schrenk
1963	Herman Epstein
1963	Norman M. Imbertson
1963	Reinout P. Kroon
1963	Stewart Way
1964	P. R. Bell
1964	Bolton L. Corson
1964	Ernest Wildhaber
1966	Frederick D. Braddon
1967	Raymond C. Goertz
1968	Henry C. Theuerer
1969	Carl J. Frosch
1969	Jean A. Hoerni
1970	Darrell H. Harting
1971	Harold G. Mead
1972	Samuel A. Ruben
1973	Gerhard W. Goetze
1975	Edward S. Bristol
1976	Walter L. Bond
1977	Norris Fitz Dow
1980	Leonard T. Skeggs, Jr.
1982	Erich Peter Ippen-Mit
1982	Charles V. Shank

Elijah Parish Lovejoy Award

(Awarded annually by Colby College to a newswriter who has made an outstanding contribution to the nation's journalistic achievement.)

1952	James S. Pope
1953	Irving Dilliard
1954	James R. Wiggins
1955	Charles A. Sprague

1956 Arthur Hays Sulzberger
1957 Buford Boone
1958 John N. Heiskell
1959 Clark R. Mollenhoff
1960 Ralph McGill
1961 Bernard Kilgore
1962 Thomas M. Storke
1963 Louis M. Lyons
1964 John Hay Whitney
1965 Colbert A. McKnight
1966 Otis Chandler
1967 Edwin A. Lahey
1968 Carl T. Rowan
1969 John S. Knight
1971 Erwin D. Canham
1972 Dolph C. Simons, Jr.
1973 Katharine Graham
1974 Henry Beetle Hough
1975 James Reston
1976 Vermont Royster
1977 Donald F. Bolles
1978 Clayton Kirkpatrick
1979 Katherine Fanning
1980 Roger Tatarian
1981 A. M. Rosenthal
1982 W. E. Chilton, III
1983 Anthony Lewis
1984 Thomas Winship
1985 Mary McGrory

Anthony F. Lucas Gold Medal

(Awarded annually by the American Institute of Mining, Metallurgical, and Petroleum Engineers to honor achievement in improving the technique and practice of finding and producing petroleum.)

1937 J. Edgar Pew
1938 Henry L. Doherty
1940 E. L. DeGolyer
1941 Conrad Schlumberger
1941 Marcel Schlumberger
1943 John R. Suman
1944 Charles Van O. Millikan
1946 James O. Lewis
1947 William N. Lacey
1948 Wallace E. Pratt
1950 William E. Wrather
1953 Morris Muskat
1954 Bruce H. Sage
1956 Stuart E. Buckley
1957 J. E. Brantly
1958 Carl E. Reistle, Jr.
1959 John T. Hayward
1960 Albert C. Rubel
1961 Edwin O. Bennett
1962 John E. Elliott
1963 Lyon F. Terry
1964 William Hurst
1965 Ralph D. Wyckoff
1966 Lloyd E. Elkins
1967 John E. Sherborne
1968 Antonius F. van Everdingen
1969 C. J. Coberly
1970 Henri G. Doll
1972 Albert G. Loomis
1974 William L. Horner
1975 Michel T. Halbouty
1976 J. Clarence Karcher
1977 Marshall B. Standing
1980 R. C. Earlougher

National Book Award

(Presented annually until 1978 by the National Book Committee to honor the authors of books in several categories considered the most distinguished works published by American citizens during the preceding year. Presented by the National Institute of Arts and Letters, 1978-1979. From 1980 to 1987, presented by the Association of American Publishers under the name American Book Award. Returned to National Book Award name under independent sponsorship in 1987.)

1950 Nelson Algren
    Fiction
    Ralph L. Rusk
    Nonfiction
    William Carlos Williams
    Poetry
1951 Newton Arvin
    Nonfiction
    William Faulkner
    Fiction
    Wallace Stevens
    Poetry
1952 Rachel Carson
    Nonfiction
    James Jones
    Fiction
    Marianne Moore
    Poetry
1953 Bernard DeVoto
    Nonfiction
    Ralph Ellison
    Fiction
    Archibald MacLeish
    Poetry
1954 Conrad Aiken
    Poetry
    Saul Bellow
    Fiction
    Bruce Catton
    Nonfiction
1955 William Faulkner
    Fiction
    Joseph Wood Krutch
    Nonfiction
    Wallace Stevens
    Poetry
1956 W. H. Auden
    Poetry
    Herbert Kubly
    Nonfiction
    John O'Hara
    Fiction
1957 George F. Kennan
    Nonfiction
    Wright Morris
    Fiction
    Richard Wilbur
    Poetry
1958 Catherine Drinker Bowen
    Nonficiton
    John Cheever
    Fiction
    Robert Penn Warren
    Poetry
1959 J. Christopher Herold
    Nonfiction
    Bernard Malamud
    Fiction
    Theodore Roethke
    Poetry
1960 Richard Ellmann
    Nonfiction

    Robert Lowell
    Poetry
    Philip Roth
    Fiction
1961 Randall Jarrell
    Poetry
    Conrad Richter
    Fiction
    William L. Shirer
    Nonfiction
1962 Alan Dugan
    Poetry
    Lewis Mumford
    Nonfiction
    Walker Percy
    Fiction
1963 Leon Edel
    Nonfiction
    J. F. Powers
    Fiction
    William Stafford
    Poetry
1964 William H. McNeill
    History and Biography
    Boris Pushkarev
    Science, Philosophy, and Religion
    John Crowe Ransom
    Poetry
    Christopher Tunnard
    Science, Philosophy, and Religion
    John Updike
    Fiction
    Aileen Ward
    Arts and Letters
1965 Saul Bellow
    Fiction
    Eleanor Clark
    Arts and Letters
    Louis Fischer
    History and Biography
    Theodore Roethke
    Poetry
    Norbert Wiener
    Science, Philosophy, and Religion
1966 James Dickey
    Poetry
    Janet Flanner
    Arts and Letters
    Katherine Anne Porter
    Fiction
    Arthur M. Schlesinger, Jr.
    History and Biography
1967 Peter Gay
    History and Biography
    Justin Kaplan
    Arts and Letters
    Oscar Lewis
    Science, Philosophy, and Religion
    Bernard Malamud
    Fiction
    James Merrill
    Poetry
    Gregory Rabassa
    Translation
    Willard Trask
    Translation
1968 Robert Bly
    Poetry
    Edna Hong
    Translation
    Howard Hong
    Translation
    George F. Kennan
    History and Biography

    Jonathan Kozol
    Science, Philosophy, and Religion
    William Troy
    Arts and Letters
    Thornton Wilder
    Fiction
1969 John Berryman
    Poetry
    Meindert Dejong
    Children's Literature
    Winthrop Jordan
    History and Biography
    Jerzy Kosinski
    Fiction
    Robert J. Lifton
    The Sciences
    Norman Mailer
    Arts and Letters
    William Weaver
    Translation
1970 Elizabeth Bishop
    Poetry
    Erik H. Erikson
    Philosophy and Religion
    Lillian Hellman
    Arts and Letters
    Ralph Manheim
    Translation
    Joyce Carol Oates
    Fiction
    Isaac Bashevis Singer
    Children's Literature
    T. Harry Williams
    History and Biography
1971 Lloyd Alexander
    Children's Books
    Saul Bellow
    Fiction
    James McGregor Burns
    History and Biography
    Frank Jones
    Translation
    Edward G. Seidensticker
    Translation
    Raymond P. Stearns
    Science
    Mona Van Duyn
    Poetry
1972 Donald Barthelme
    Children's Books
    Stewart Brand
    Contemporary Affairs
    Joseph P. Lash
    Biography
    Martin E. Marty
    Philosophy and Religion
    Howard Moss
    Poetry
    Allan Nevins
    History
    Flannery O'Connor
    Fiction
    Frank O'Hara
    Poetry
    Charles Rosen
    Arts and Letters
    George L. Small
    Science
    Austryn Wainhouse
    Translation
1973 Sydney E. Ahlstrom
    Philosophy and Religion
    A. R. Ammons
    Poetry
    John Barth
    Fiction

Frances FitzGerald
  Contemporary Affairs
James T. Flexner
  Biography
Ursula LeGuin
  Children's Literature
Allen Mandelbaum
  Translation
Robert M. Myers
  History
George B. Schaller
  The Sciences
Isaiah Trunk
  History
John Williams
  Fiction
Arthur M. Wilson
  Arts and Letters
1974 Karen Brazell
  Translation
Eleanor Cameron
  Children's Literature
John Clive
  History
Douglas Day
  Biography
Allen Ginsburg
  Poetry
Pauline Kael
  Arts and Letters
Murray Kempton
  Contemporary Affairs
Helen R. Lane
  Translation
S. E. Luria
  The Sciences
Jackson Mathews
  Translation
Maurice Natanson
  Philosophy and
  Religion
Thomas Pynchon
  Fiction
Adrienne Rich
  Poetry
Isaac Bashevis Singer
  Fiction
1975 Silvano Arieti
  The Sciences
Bernard Bailyn
  History
Marilyn Hacker
  Poetry
Virginia Hamilton
  Children's Literature
Anthony Kerrigan
  Translation
Robert Nozick
  Philosophy and
  Religion
Theodore Rosengarten
  Contemporary Affairs
Richard B. Sewall
  Biography
Roger Shattuck
  Arts and Letters
Robert Stone
  Fiction
Lewis Thomas
  The Sciences
Thomas Williams
  Fiction
1976 Michael J. Arlen
  Contemporary Affairs
John Ashberg
  Poetry
David Brion Davis
  History
Walter D. Edmonds
  Children's Literature

Paul Fussell
  Arts and Letters
William Gaddis
  Fiction
1977 Bruno Bettelheim
  Contemporary Thought
Li-li Ch'en
  Translation
Richard Eberhart
  Poetry
Alex Haley
  Special History Award
Irving Howe
  History
Katherine W. Paterson
  Children's Literature
Wallace Stegner
  Fiction
W. A. Swanberg
  Biography and
  Autobiography
1978 W. Jackson Bate
  Biography and
  Autobiography
Gloria Emerson
  Contemporary Thought
Herbert Kohl
  Children's Literature
Judith Kohl
  Children's Literature
David McCullough
  History
Howard Nemerov
  Poetry
Mary Lee Settle
  Fiction
Clara Winston
  Translation
Richard Winston
  Translation
1979 Jose Rubia Barcia
  Translation
Richard Beale Davis
  History
Clayton Eshleman
  Translation
James Merrill
  Poetry
Peter Matthiessen
  Contemporary Thought
Tim O'Brien
  Fiction
Katherine W. Paterson
  Children's Literature
Arthur M. Schlesinger,
  Jr.
  Biography and
  Autobiography

American Book Award

1980 Lauren Bacall
  Autobiography
  (hardcover)
A. Scot Berg
  Biography (paperback)
Joan W. Blos
  Children's Books
  (hardcover)
Tim Brooks
  General Reference
  (paperback)
William F. Buckley, Jr.
  Mystery (paperback)
Julia Child
  Current Interest
  (hardcover)

Malcolm Cowley
  Autobiography
  (paperback)
Jane Gary Harris
  Translation
Douglas Hofstadter
  Science (hardcover)
John Irving
  Fiction (paperback)
Henry Kissinger
  History (hardcover)
Louis L'Amour
  Western
Christopher Lasch
  Current Interest
  (paperback)
Madeline L'Engle
  Children's Books
  (paperback)
Philip Levine
  Poetry
Constance Link
  Translation
John D. MacDonald
  Mystery (hardcover)
Earle Marsh
  General Reference
  (paperback)
Peter Matthiessen
  General Nonfiction
  (paperback)
Edmund Morris
  Biography (hardcover)
Elaine Pagels
  Religion/Inspiration
  (hardcover)
Frederik Pohl
  Science Fiction
  (hardcover)
William Styron
  Fiction (hardcover)
Barbara W. Tuchman
  History (paperback)
Sheldon Vanauken
  Religion/Inspiration
  (paperback)
Walter Wangerin, Jr.
  Science Fiction
  (paperback)
William Wharton
  First Novel
Elder Witt
  General Reference
  (hardcover)
Tom Wolfe
  General Nonfiction
  (hardcover)
Gary Zukav
  Science (paperback)

Design Awards

Carol Brightman
  Illustrated Art
  (hardcover collection)
Emily Blair Chewning
  Illustrated Art
  (paperback)
Linda Ferrara
  Jacket Design
Barbara Hennessey
  Illustrated Art
  (hardcover original)
Dana Levy
  Illustrated Art
  (paperback)
Leonard Lubin
  Illustrated Art
  (hardcover original)
Fred Marcellino
  Jacket Design

Frank Metz
  Illustrated Art
  (paperback)
David Myers
  Cover Design
Larry Rivers
  Illustrated Art
  (hardcover collection)
R. D. Scudellari
  Book Design
Ann Spinelli
  Cover Design
Hermann Strohbach
  Illustrated Art
  (hardcover collection)
1981 Ann Arensberg
  First Novel
Deidre Blair
  Autobiography/Biography
  (paperback)
John Boswell
  History (hardcover)
Betsy Byars
  Children's Fiction
  (hardcover)
John Cheever
  Fiction (paperback)
Beverly Cleary
  Children's Fiction
  (paperback)
Stephen Jay Gould
  Science (hardcover)
Alison Cragin Herzig
  Children's Nonfiction
Justin Kaplan
  Autobiography/Biography
  (hardcover)
Maxine Hong Kingston
  General Nonfiction
  (hardcover)
Jane Kramer
  General Nonfiction
  (paperback)
Leon F. Litwack
  History (paperback)
Jane Lawrence Mali
  Children's Nonfiction
Wright Morris
  Fiction (hardcover)
Lisel Mueller
  Poetry
Francis Steegmuller
  Translation
Lewis Thomas
  Science (paperback)
John E. Woods
  Translation

Design Awards

Quist-Couratin
  Cover Design
Richard Hendel
  Book Design
  (typographical)
R. D. Scudellari
  Book Design (pictorial)
R. D. Scudellari
  Jacket Design
Michael Shroyer
  Book Illustration
  (collected or adapted)
1982 Lloyd Alexander
  Children's Fiction
  (hardcover)
Susan Bonners
  Children's Nonfiction
William Bronk
  Poetry
Robert Lyons Danly
  Translation

Robb Forman Dew
  First Novel
Maitland Edey
  Science (hardcover)
Donald Johanson
  Science (hardcover)
Tracy Kidder
  General Nonfiction
  (hardcover)
Ian Hideo Levy
  Translation
William Maxwell
  Fiction (paperback)
David McCullough
  Autobiography/Biography
  (hardcover)
Victor S. Navsky
  General Nonfiction
  (paperback)
Peter John Powell
  History (hardcover)
Quida Sebestyn
  Children's Fiction
  (paperback)
Maurice Sendak
  Children's Picture
  Books (hardcover)
Peter Spier
  Children's Picture
  Books (paperback)
Ronald Steel
  Autobiography/Biography
  (paperback)
Robert Wohl
  History (paperback)
Fred Alan Wolf
  Science (paperback)
John Updike
  Fiction (hardcover)

Design Awards

Betty Anderson
  Book Design
  (typographical)
Milton Charles
  Cover Design (mass
  market paperback)
Bill Katz
  Book Illustration
  (collected art)
Fred Marcellino
  Cover Design (trade
  paperback)
Susan Mitchell
  Book Design (pictorial)
Janet Odgis
  Jacket Design
Deborah Turbeville
  Book Illustration
  (photography)
Chris Van Allsburg
  Book Illustration
  (original art)
1983 Alan Brinkley
  History (hardcover)
Fox Butterfield
  General Nonfiction
  (hardcover)
Barbara Cooney
  Children's Picture
  Books (hardcover)
Philip J. Davis
  Science (paperback)
James Fallows
  General Nonfiction
  (paperback)
Paula Fox
  Children's Ficiton
  (paperback)

Betty Fraser
  Children's Picture
  Books (paperback)
Jean Fritz
  Children's Fiction
  (hardcover)
Lisa Goldstein
  Original Paperback
James Cross Goslin
  Children's Nonfiction
Reuben Hersh
  Science (paperback)
Mary Ann Hoberman
  Children's Picture
  Books (paperback)
Richard Howard
  Translation
Galway Kinnell
  Poetry
Frank E. Manuel
  History (paperback)
Fritzie P. Manuel
  History (paperback)
James R. Mellow
  Autobiography/Biography
  (paperback)
Gloria Naylor
  First Novel
Abraham Pais
  Science (hardcover)
William Steig
  Children's Picture
  Books (hardcover)
Joyce Carol Thomas
  Children's Fiction
  (paperback)
Judith Thurman
  Autobiography/Biography
  (hardcover)
Margot Tomes
  Children's Nonfiction
Alice Walker
  Fiction (hardcover)
Eudora Welty
  Fiction (paperback)
Charles Wright
  Poetry

Design Awards

Eleanor Morris Caponigro
  Book Illustration
  (photography)
Doris Ettlinger
  Cover Design
David Lance Goines
  Book Design
  (typographical)
Erick Ingraham
  Book Illustration
  (original art)
William F. Luckey
  Book Design
  (typographical)
Fred Marcellino
  Jacket Design
Frank Metz
  Jacket Design
Howard Morris
  Book Illustration
  (collected art)
Barry Moser
  Book Design (pictorial)
Steve Renick
  Book Design (pictorial)
Neil Stuart
  Cover Design
1984 Harriet Doerr
  First Fiction
Ellen Gilchrist
  Fiction

     Robert V. Remini
       Nonfiction
1985 Don DeLillo
       Fiction
     J. Anthony Lukas
       Nonfiction
     Bob Shacochis
       First Novel
1986 E. L. Doctorow
       Fiction
     Barry Lopez
       Nonfiction

National Institute of Arts and Letters Award for Distinguished Service to the Arts

(Presented from time to time to an American citizen, not a member of the Institute, who has made outstanding contributions to the arts.)

1941 Robert Moses
1944 Samuel S. McClure
1949 Mrs. Edward MacDowell
1952 Mrs. Simon Guggenheim
1954 J. William Fulbright
1955 Henry A. Moe
1957 Francis Henry Taylor
1958 Lincoln Kirstein
1959 Elizabeth Ames
1962 Paul Mellon
1963 Marie L. Bullock
1965 Frances Steloff
1968 Alfred H. Barr, Jr.
1969 Leopold Stokowski
1970 Martha Graham
1973 Felicia Geffen
1974 Walker Evans
1975 George Balanchine
1977 James Laughlin
1978 John Brademas
1979 Lloyd Goodrich
1981 Joseph Papp
1982 Alfred A. Knopf
1983 Sidney R. Yates
1984 Roger L. Stevens
1985 Claiborne Pell
1985 William Shawn
1986 Brooke Astor

National Institute of Arts and Letters Gold Medal

(Awarded by the Institute in the name of the American Academy of Arts and Letters to recognize achievement in the arts based on the entire work of the recipient.)

1909 Augustus Saint-Gaudens
1910 James Ford Rhodes
1911 James Whitcomb Riley
1912 W. Rutherford Mead
1913 Augustus Thomas
1914 John Singer Sargent
1915 William Dean Howells
1916 John Burroughs
1917 Daniel Chester French
1918 William R. Thayer
1919 Charles M. Loeffler
1921 Cass Gilbert
1922 Eugene O'Neill
1923 Edwin H. Blashfield
1924 Edith Wharton

1925 William C. Brownell
1926 Herbert Adams
1927 William M. Sloane
1928 George W. Chadwick
1929 Edwin Arlington
      Robinson
1930 Charles Adams Platt
1931 William Gillette
1932 Gari Melchers
1933 Booth Tarkington
1935 Agnes Repplier
1936 George G. Barnard
1937 Charles McLean Andrews
1938 Walter Damrosch
1939 Robert Frost
1940 William Adams Delano
1941 Robert E. Sherwood
1942 Cecilia Beaux
1943 Stephen Vincent Benet
1944 Willa Cather
1945 Paul Manship
1946 Van Wyck Brooks
1947 John Alden Carpenter
1948 Charles A. Beard
1949 Frederick Law Olmsted
1950 John Sloan
1950 Henry L. Mencken
1951 James E. Fraser
1951 Igor Stravinsky
1952 Thornton Wilder
1952 Carl Sandburg
1953 Marianne Moore
1953 Frank Lloyd Wright
1954 Maxwell Anderson
1954 Reginald Marsh
1955 Edward Hopper
1955 Ivan Mestrovic
1956 Aaron Copland
1957 John Dos Passos
1957 Allan Nevins
1958 Conrad Aiken
1958 Henry R. Shepley
1959 Arthur Miller
1959 George Grosz
1960 Charles E. Burchfield
1960 E. B. White
1961 William Zorach
1961 Roger Sessions
1962 William Faulkner
1962 Samuel Eliot Morison
1963 William Carlos Williams
1963 Ludwig Mies van der
      Rohe
1964 Lillian Hellman
1964 Ben Shahn
1965 Andrew Wyeth
1965 Walter Lippmann
1966 Virgil Thomson
1967 Katherine Anne Porter
1967 Arthur Schlesinger, Jr.
1968 R. Buckminster Fuller
1968 W. H. Auden
1969 Tennessee Williams
1969 Leonard Baskin
1970 Georgia O'Keefe
1970 Lewis Mumford
1971 Alexander Calder
1971 Elliott Carter
1972 Eudora Welty
1972 Henry Steele Commager
1973 Louis I. Kahn
1973 John Crowe Ransom
1974 Saul Steinberg
1975 Kenneth Burke
1975 Willem deKooning
1976 Leon Edel
1976 Samuel Barber
1977 Isamu Noguchi
1977 Saul Bellow
1978 Barbara Tuchman
1978 Peter Taylor

1979	I. M. Pei
1979	Archibald MacLeish
1980	Edward Albee
1980	Peggy Bacon
1981	Malcolm Cowley
1981	Raphael Soyer
1982	William Schuman
1982	Francis Steegmuller
1983	Bernard Malamud
1983	Louise Nevelson
1984	Gordon Bunshaft
1984	George F. Kennan
1985	Leonard Bernstein
1985	Robert Penn Warren
1986	Jasper Johns
1986	Sidney Kingsley

National Institute of Social Sciences Gold Medal

(Awarded annually for distinguished service to humanity.)

1913	Archer M. Huntington
1913	Samuel L. Parrish
1913	William Howard Taft
1914	Charles W. Eliot
1914	George W. Goethals
1914	Abraham Jacobi
1914	Henry F. Osborn
1915	Luther Burbank
1915	Andrew Carnegie
1916	Robert Bacon
1916	Helen Hartley Jenkins
1916	Adolph Lewisohn
1917	George W. Crile
1917	William C. Gorgas
1917	John P. Mitchell
1917	Michael I. Pupin
1918	Henry P. Davison
1918	Herbert C. Hoover
1918	William J. Mayo
1919	Samuel Gompers
1919	William H. Welch
1920	Alexis Carrel
1920	H. Holbrook Curtis
1920	Harry P. Judson
1921	Charles F. Chandler
1921	Calvin Coolidge
1921	Cleveland H. Dodge
1923	Charles B. Davenport
1923	Emory R. Johnson
1923	John D. Rockefeller, Sr.
1924	Walter Hampden
1924	Charles Evans Hughes
1924	Mrs. C. Lorillard Spencer
1925	Mary W. Harriman
1925	William H. Park
1925	Elihu Root
1926	S. Parkes Cadman
1926	Clarence H. Mackay
1926	Stephen T. Mather
1926	Mary Schenck Woolman
1927	George Pierce Baker
1927	Walter Damrosch
1927	Harry Emerson Fosdick
1927	Adolph S. Ochs
1928	Liberty Hyde Bailey
1928	Robert W. deForest
1928	Willis R. Whitney
1929	Valeria Langeloth
1929	Rose Livingston
1929	John D. Rockefeller, Jr.
1929	James T. Shotwell
1929	Daniel Willard
1930	Anna B. Gallup
1930	George R. Minot
1930	William Lyon Phelps

1930	Nathan Straus
1931	Grace Abbott
1931	Richard C. Cabot
1931	Grace Goodhue Coolidge
1931	Frank B. Kellogg
1932	Edward E. Allen
1932	James H. Post
1932	William C. Redfield
1932	Gerard Swope
1933	Newton D. Baker
1933	Clifford W. Beers
1933	Evangeline Booth
1934	Eleanor Robson Belmont
1934	Walter B. Cannon
1934	Samuel Seabury
1935	Cornelius N. Bliss
1935	Harvey Cushing
1935	Carter Glass
1935	George E. Vincent
1936	Nicholas Murray Butler
1936	Dorothy H. Eustis
1936	William E. Hall
1936	J. Pierpont Morgan
1937	James R. Angell
1937	Mrs. Edward W. Bok
1937	J. Edgar Hoover
1937	Wesley C. Mitchell
1938	John W. Davis
1938	Walter S. Gifford
1938	Dorothy Thompson
1939	Martha Berry
1939	William C. Osborn
1939	George Wharton Pepper
1940	Carrie Chapman Catt
1940	James E. West
1940	Wendell L. Wilkie
1941	Norman H. Davis
1941	Mrs. J. Borden Harriman
1941	Alfred E. Smith
1942	Rufus B. von KleinSmid
1942	Anne O'Hare McCormick
1942	Donald M. Nelson
1943	Edwin G. Conklin
1943	Mildred H. McAffee
1943	Juan T. Trippe
1944	Bernard Baruch
1944	Mrs. Henry Pomeroy Davison
1944	James G. K. McClure
1945	Vannevar Bush
1945	Mrs. John H. Hammond
1945	William M. Lewis
1946	Virginia Crocheron Gildersleeve
1946	Robert Moses
1946	Edward R. Stettinius, Jr.
1947	Katherine F. Lenroot
1947	Edward Johnson
1947	Thomas J. Watson, Sr.
1948	Georgiana F. Sibley
1948	Basil O'Connor
1948	Warren R. Austin
1949	Lillian M. Gilbreth
1949	Alfred P. Sloan, Jr.
1949	George C. Marshall
1950	Henry Bruere
1950	Sarah G. Blanding
1951	Bayard F. Pope
1951	Paul G. Hoffman
1951	John Foster Dulles
1951	Lewis W. Douglas
1951	Douglas MacArthur
1952	Harold R. Medina
1952	Helen Keller
1952	Robert A. Lovett
1952	John J. McCloy
1953	E. Roland Harriman
1953	Oveta Culp Hobby
1953	Charles F. Kettering
1954	Howard A. Rusk
1954	Mrs. Lytle Hull

1954	Walter Bedell Smith
1955	Samuel D. Leidesdorf
1955	Elizabeth Luce Moore
1955	Henry Cabot Lodge, Jr.
1956	Clarence G. Michalis
1956	Mary Pilsbury Lord
1956	Henry T. Heald
1957	William F. Graham, Jr.
1957	Clare Boothe Luce
1957	Alfred M. Gruenther
1958	Marian Anderson
1958	James R. Killian, Jr.
1958	Robert B. Anderson
1958	Herbert Hoover
1959	Helen Hayes
1959	Laurance S. Rockefeller
1959	Jonas E. Salk
1960	Rudolf Bing
1960	Gilbert Darlington
1960	Millicent C. McIntosh
1960	Grayson L. Kirk
1961	Mary L. Bullock
1961	Karl Menninger
1961	William C. Menninger
1961	Edward Durrell Stone
1962	Mary I. Bunting
1962	Ralph J. Bunche
1962	John W. Gardner
1962	Lucius D. Clay
1963	Arthur H. Dean
1963	Katherine E. McBride
1963	Nathan M. Pusey
1963	Frank Stanton
1964	Margaret Chase Smith
1964	Dean Rusk
1964	Frederick R. Kappel
1964	Bob Hope
1965	Dorothy B. Chandler
1965	James A. Perkins
1965	Maxwell D. Taylor
1966	Lady Bird Johnson
1966	Francis Cardinal Spellman
1966	David Sarnoff
1966	G. Keith Funston
1966	Danny Kaye
1967	John D. Rockefeller, III
1967	Nelson A. Rockefeller
1967	Laurance S. Rockefeller
1967	Winthrop Rockefeller
1967	David Rockefeller
1968	Anne Morrow Lindbergh
1968	Ralph W. Sockman
1968	Eugene R. Black
1968	Charles A. Lindbergh
1969	Frank Borman
1969	Theodore M. Hesburgh
1970	William P. Rogers
1970	Katharine Graham
1970	Lauris Norstad
1970	Eric Sevareid
1971	Joan Ganz Cooney
1971	Arthur K. Watson
1971	Thomas J. Watson, Jr.
1971	Charles H. Malik
1972	George Bush
1972	Henry A. Kissinger
1972	Mrs. Laurance Rockefeller
1972	Fulton J. Sheen
1973	John T. Flynn
1973	Jean Kerr
1973	Paul Moore, Jr.
1973	Elliot L. Richardson
1974	Peter M. Dawkins
1974	Golda Meir
1974	George P. Schultz
1974	Roy Wilkins
1975	Nancy Hanks
1975	William E. Simon
1975	Donald K. Slayton

1975	Lowell Thomas
1975	Lowell Thomas, Jr.
1976	Barry M. Goldwater
1976	John J. McCloy
1976	Norman Vincent Peale
1976	Peter J. Peterson
1976	Barbara Walters
1977	Anne Armstrong
1977	Dina Merrill
1977	Cliff Robertson
1977	William Rockefeller
1977	William B. Walsh
1978	Hernrik Beer
1978	Arthur F. Burns
1978	Julia Child
1978	James R. Dumpson
1979	McGeorge Bundy
1979	C. Douglas Dillon
1979	Jane Pickens Hoving
1979	Linus C. Pauling
1980	Alexander M. Haig, Jr.
1980	Henry Labouisse
1980	William McChesney Martin
1980	William J. McGill
1980	Iphigene Ochs Sulzberger

National Medal for Literature

(Conferred annually by the National Book Committee under an endowment of the Guinzburg Fund on a living American writer to honor his total contribution to American letters.)

1965	Thornton Wilder
1966	Edmund Wilson
1967	W. H. Auden
1968	Marianne Moore
1969	Conrad Aiken
1970	Robert Penn Warren
1971	E. B. White
1972	Lewis Mumford
1973	Vladimir Nabokov
1976	Allen Tate
1977	Robert Lowell
1978	Archibald MacLeish
1980	Eudora Welty
1981	Kenneth Burke
1982	John Cheever
1984	Mary McCarthy

National Medal of Science

(Presented by the President of the United States for outstanding achievement in science.)

1962	Theodore von Karman
1963	Luis W. Alvarez
	Vannevar Bush
	John R. Pierce
	Cornelis B. Van Niel
	Norbert Wiener
1964	Roger Adams
	Othmar H. Ammann
	Theodosius Dobzhansky
	Charles S. Draper
	Solomon Lefschetz
	Neal E. Miller
	Marston Morse
	Marshall W. Nirenberg
	Julian Schwinger
	Harold C. Urey

Robert Woodward
1965 John Bardeen
Peter J. W. Debye
Hugh L. Dryden
Clarence L. Johnson
Leon M. Lederman
Warren K. Lewis
Francis P. Rous
William W. Rubey
George G. Simpson
Donald D. Van Slyke
Oscar Zariski
1966 Jacob Bjerknes
Subrahmanyan
   Chandrasekhar
Henry Eyring
Edward F. Knipling
Fritz A. Lipmann
John W. Milnor
William C. Rose
Claude E. Shannon
John H. Van Vleck
Sewall Wright
Vladimir K. Zworykin
1967 Jesse W. Beams
Francis Birch
Gregory Breit
Paul J. Cohen
Kenneth S. Cole
Louis P. Hammett
Harry F. Harlow
Michael Heidelberger
George B. Kistiakowsky
Edwin H. Land
Igor I. Sikorsky
Alfred H. Sturtevant
1968 Horace A. Barker
Paul D. Bartlett
Bernard B. Brodie
Detlev W. Bronk
J. Presper Eckert
Herbert Friedman
Jay L. Lush
Nathan M. Newmark
Jerzy Neyman
Lars Onsager
Burrhus F. Skinner
Eugene P. Wigner
1969 Herbert C. Brown
William Feller
Robert J. Huebner
Jack St. Clair Kilby
Ernst Mayr
Wolfgang Panofsky
1970 Richard D. Brauer
Robert H. Dicke
Barbara McClintock
George E. Mueller
Albert Sabin
Allan R. Sandage
John C. Slater
John A. Wheeler
Saul Winstein
1973 Daniel I. Arnon
Carl Djerassi
Harold E. Edgerton
William Maurice Ewing
Arie J. Haagen-Smit
Vladimir Haensel
Frederick Seitz
Earl W. Sutherland, Jr.
John W. Tukey
Richard Travis Whitcomb
Robert R. Wilson
1974 Nicolaas Bloembergen
Britton Chance
Erwin Chargaff
Paul J. Flory
William A. Fowler
Kurt Godel
Rudolf Kompfner

James V. Neel
Linus Pauling
Ralph B. Peck
K. S. Pitzer
James A. Shannon
Abel Wolman
1975 John Backus
Manson Benedict
Hans A. Bethe
Shiing-Shen Chern
George B. Dantzig
Hallowell Davis
Paul Gyorgy
Sterling B. Hendricks
Joseph O. Hirschfelder
William H. Pickering
Lewis H. Sarett
Frederick E. Terman
Orville A. Vogel
E. Bright Wilson
Chien-Shiung Wu
1976 Morris Cohen
Kurt O. Fredricks
Peter C. Goldmark
Samuel A. Goudsmit
Roger C. L. Guillemin
Herbert S. Gotowsky
Erwin W. Mueller
Keith R. Porter
Efraim Racker
Frederick D. Rossini
Verner E. Soumi
Henry Taube
George E. Valenbeck
Hassler Whitney
Edward O. Wilson
1979 Robert H. Burris
Elizabeth C. Crosby
Joseph L. Doob
Richard P. Feynman
Donald F. Knuth
Arthur Kornberg
Emmett M. Leith
Herman F. Mark
Raymond D. Mindlin
Robert N. Noyce
Servero Ochoa
Earl R. Parker
Edward M. Purcell
Simon Ramo
John H. Sinfelt
Lyman Spitzer, Jr.
Earl R. Stadtman
G. Ledyard Stebbins
Paul A. Weiss
Victor F. Weisskopf
1981 Philip Handler
1982 Philip W. Anderson
Seymour Benzer
Glenn W. Burton
Mildred Cohn
F. Albert Cotton
Edward F. Heinemann
Donald L. Katz
Yoichiro Nambu
Marshall Stone
Gilbert Stork
Edward Teller
Charles H. Townes
1983 Howard L. Bachrach
Paul Berg
E. Margaret Burbidge
Maurice Goldhaber
Herman H. Goldstine
William R. Hewlett
Roald Hoffman
Helmut E. Landsberg
George M. Low
Walter H. Munk
George C. Pimentel
Frederick Reines

Wendell L. Roelofs
Bruno B. Rossi
Berta Scharrer
J. Robert Schrieffer
I. M. Singer
John G. Trump
Richard N. Zare
1986 Solomon J. Buchsbaum
Stanley Cohen
Horace R. Crane
Herman Feschback
Harry B. Gray
Donald A. Henderson
Robert Hofstadter
Peter D. Lax
Yuan Tseh Lee
Hans W. Leipmann
Tung Yen Lin
Carl S. Marvel
Vernon B. Mountcastle,
   Jr.
Bernard M. Oliver
George E. Palade
Herbert A. Simon
Joan A. Steitz
Frank H. Westheimer
Chen Ning Yang
Antoni Zygmund

Nobel Prize—American Winners

(Asterisk—*—denotes the award is shared with a person not a U.S. citizen.)

1906 Theodore Roosevelt
   Peace
1907 Albert A. Michelson
   Physics
1912 Alexis Carrel
   Physiology and
   Medicine
   Elihu Root
   Peace
1914 Theodore W. Richards
   Chemistry
1919 Woodrow Wilson
   Peace
1921 Albert Einstein
   Physics
1922 Otto F. Meyerhof*
   Physiology and
   Medicine
1923 Robert A. Millikan
   Physics
1925 Charles G. Dawes*
   Peace
1927 Albert H. Compton
   Physics
1929 Frank B. Kellogg
   Peace
1930 Karl Landsteiner
   Physiology and
   Medicine
   Sinclair Lewis
   Literature
1931 Jane Addams
   Peace
   Nicholas Murray Butler
   Peace
1932 Irving Langmuir
   Chemistry
1933 Thomas H. Morgan
   Physiology and
   Medicine
1934 George R. Minot*
   Physiology and
   Medicine

William P. Murphy*
   Physiology and
   Medicine
Harold C. Urey
   Chemistry
George H. Whipple*
   Physiology and
   Medicine
1936 Carl D. Anderson*
   Physics
Peter J. W. Debye
   Chemistry
Victor F. Hess*
   Physics
Otto Loewi*
   Physiology and
   Medicine
Eugene O'Neill
   Literature
1937 Clinton J. Davisson*
   Physics
Albert Szent-Gyorgyi
   Physiology and
   Medicine
1938 Pearl S. Buck
   Literature
Enrico Fermi
   Physics
1939 Ernest O. Lawrence
   Physics
1943 Edward A. Doisy*
   Physiology and
   Medicine
Otto Stern
   Physics
1944 E. Joseph Erlanger*
   Physiology and
   Medicine
Herbert S. Gasser*
   Physiology and
   Medicine
Isidor I. Rabi
   Physics
1945 Cordell Hull
   Peace
Wolfgang Pauli
   Physics
1946 Emily Balch*
   Peace
Percy W. Bridgman
   Physics
John R. Mott*
   Peace
Hermann J. Muller
   Physiology and
   Medicine
John H. Northrop
   Chemistry
Wendell M. Stanley
   Chemistry
James B. Sumner
   Chemistry
1947 Carl F. Cori
   Physiology and
   Medicine
Gerty T. Cori
   Physiology and
   Medicine
1949 William F. Giauque
   Chemistry
William Faulkner
   Literature
1950 Ralph J. Bunche
   Peace
Philip S. Hency
   Physiology and
   Medicine
Edward C. Kendall
   Physiology and
   Medicine

1951 Edwin M. McMillan
Chemistry
Glenn T. Seaborg
Chemistry
Max Theiler
Physiology and
Medicine
1952 Felix Bloch
Physics
Edward M. Purcell
Physics
Selman A. Waksman
Physiology and
Medicine
1953 Fritz A. Lipmann
Physiology and
Medicine
George C. Marshall
Peace
1954 John F. Enders*
Physiology and
Medicine
Ernest Hemingway
Literature
Linus C. Pauling
Chemistry
Frederick C. Robbins
Physiology and
Medicine
Thomas H. Weller
Physiology and
Medicine
1955 Polykarp Kusch
Physics
Willis E. Lamb, Jr.
Physics
Vincent du Vigneaud
Chemistry
1956 John Bardeen
Physics
Walter H. Brattain
Physics
Andre F. Cournand
Physiology and
Medicine
D. W. Richards
Physiology and
Medicine
William B. Shockley
Physics
1957 Tsung-Dao Lee
Physics
Chen Ning Yand
Physics
1958 George W. Beadle
Physiology and
Medicine
Joshua Lederberg
Physiology and
Medicine
Edward L. Tatum
Physiology and
Medicine
1959 Owen Chamberlain*
Physics
Arthur Kornberg
Physiology and
Medicine
Servero Ochoa
Physiology and
Medicine
Emilio Segre*
Physics
1960 Donald A. Glaser
Physics
Willard F. Libby
Chemistry
1961 Melvin Calvin
Chemistry
Robert Hofstadter*
Physics

George von Bekesy
Physiology and
Medicine
1962 Linus Pauling
Peace
John Steinbeck
Literature
James D. Watson*
Physiology and
Medicine
1963 Maria Goeppert-Mayer
Physics
Eugene P. Wigner
Physics
1964 Konrad E. Bloch*
Physiology and
Medicine
Martin Luther King, Jr.
Peace
Charles H. Townes
Physics
1965 Richard P. Feynman
Physics
Julian S. Schwinger
Physics
Robert B. Woodward
Chemistry
1966 Charles B. Huggins
Physiology and
Medicine
Robert S. Mulliken
Chemistry
Francis P. Rous
Physiology and
Medicine
1967 Hans A. Bethe
Physics
Haldan K. Hartline
Physiology and
Medicine
George Wald
Physiology and
Medicine
1968 Luis W. Alvarez
Physics
Robert W. Holley
Physiology and
Medicine
F. Gobind Khorana
Physiology and
Medicine
Marshall W. Nirenberg
Physiology and
Medicine
Lars Onsager
Chemistry
1969 Max Delbruck
Physiology and
Medicine
Murray Gell-Mann
Physics
Alfred D. Hershey
Physiology and
Medicine
Salvador E. Luria
Physiology and
Medicine
1970 Julius Axelrod
Physiology and
Medicine
Norman E. Borlaug
Peace
Paul A. Samuelson
Economics
1971 Simon Kuznets
Economics
Earl W. Sutherland, Jr.
Physiology and
Medicine
1972 Christian B. Anfinsen
Chemistry

Kenneth J. Arrow
Economics
John Bardeen
Physics
Leon N. Cooper
Physics
Gerald M. Edelman
Physiology and
Medicine
Stanford Moore
Chemistry
John R. Schrieffer
Physics
William H. Stein
Chemistry
1973 Ivar Giaever*
Physics
Henry A. Kissinger*
Peace
Wassily Leontief
Economics
1974 Albert Claude*
Physiology and
Medicine
Paul J. Flory
Chemistry
1975 David Baltimore
Physiology and
Medicine
Renato Dulbecco
Physiology and
Medicine
Tjalling C. Koopmans*
Economics
James Rainwater*
Physics
Howard M. Temin
Physiology and
Medicine
1976 Saul Bellow
Literature
Baruch S. Blumber
Physiology and
Medicine
Milton Friedman
Economics
D. Carleton Gajdusek
Physiology and
Medicine
William N. Lipscomb
Chemistry
Burton Richter
Physics
Samuel C. C. Ting
Physics
1977 Philip W. Anderson*
Physics
Roger C. L. Guillemin
Physiology and
Medicine
Andrew V. Schally
Physiology and
Medicine
John H. Van Vleck*
Physics
Rosalyn S. Yalow
Physiology and
Medicine
1978 Daniel Nathans*
Physiology and
Medicine
Arno A. Penzias*
Physics
Herbert A. Simon
Economics
Isaac Bashevis Singer
Literature
Hamilton Smith*
Physiology and
Medicine

Robert W. Wilson*
Physics
1979 Herbert C. Brown*
Chemistry
Allan McLeod Cormack*
Physiology and
Medicine
Sheldon L. Glashow*
Physics
Theodore W. Schultz*
Economics
Steven Weinberg*
Physics
1980 Baruj Benacerraf*
Physiology and
Medicine
Paul Berg*
Chemistry
James Cronin
Physics
Val Fitch
Physics
Walter Gilbert*
Chemistry
Lawrence R. Klein
Economics
Czeslaw Milosz
Literature
George Snell*
Physiology and
Medicine
1981 Nicolaas Bloembergen*
Physics
Ronald Hoffman*
Chemistry
David H. Hubel
Physiology and
Medicine
Arthur Schawlow*
Physics
Roger W. Sperry
Physiology and
Medicine
James Tobin
Economics
Torsten N. Wiesel
Physiology and
Medicine
1982 George Stigler
Economics
Kenneth G. Wilson
Physics
1983 Subrahmanyan
Chandrasekhar
Physics
Gerard Debreu
Economics
William A. Fowler
Physics
Barbara McClintock
Physiology and
Medicine
Henry Taube
Chemistry
1984 Robert B. Merrifield
Chemistry
1985 Michael S. Brown
Physiology and
Medicine
Joseph C. Goldstein
Physiology and
Medicine
Herbert A. Hauptman
Chemistry
Jerome Karle
Chemistry
Bernard Lown*
Peace
Franco Modigliani
Economics

1986 James McGill Buchanan
Economics
Stanley Cohen
Physiology and
Medicine
Dudley Herschbach
Chemistry
Yuan T. Lee
Chemistry
Rita Levi-Montalcini
Physiology and
Medicine
Elie Wiesel
Peace

Passano Award

(Presented annually by the Passano Foundation to an American citizen who has made an outstanding contribution to the advancement of medical science, particularly for work having a clinical application.)

1945 Edwin J. Cohn
1946 Ernest W. Goodpasture
1947 Selman A. Waksman
1948 Helen B. Taussig
1948 Alfred Blalock
1949 Oswald T. Avery
1950 Edward C. Kendall
1950 Philip S. Hench
1951 Philip Levine
1951 Alexander S. Wiener
1952 Herbert M. Evans
1953 John F. Enders
1954 Homer W. Smith
1955 Vincent du Vigneaud
1956 George N. Papanicolaou
1957 William M. Clark
1958 George W. Corner
1959 Stanhope Bayne-Jones
1960 Rene J. Dubos
1961 Owen H. Wangensteen
1962 Albert H. Coons
1963 Horace W. Magoun
1964 Keith R. Porter
1964 George E. Palade
1965 Charles B. Huggins
1966 John T. Edsall
1967 Irvine H. Page
1968 John E. Howard
1969 George H. Hitchings
1970 Paul C. Zamecnik
1971 Stephen W. Kuffler
1972 Kimishige Ishizaka
1972 Teruko Ishizaka
1973 Roger W. Sperry
1974 Seymour S. Cohen
1975 Henry G. Kunkel
1976 Roger C. L. Guillemin
1977 Curt P. Richter
1978 Michael S. Brown
1978 Joseph L. Goldstein
1979 Donald F. Steiner
1980 Seymour S. Kelly
1981 Hugh O. McDevitt
1982 Roscoe O. Brady
1982 Elizabeth F. Neufeld
1983 J. Michael Bishop
1983 Harold E. Varmus
1984 Peter C. Nowell
1985 Howard Green
1986 Albert Lester Lehninger
1986 Eugene Patrick Kennedy

Penrose Medal

(Awarded annually by the Geological Society of America to honor achievement marking a decided advance in the science of geology.)

1927 Thomas C. Chamberlin
1931 William M. Davis
1932 Edward O. Ulrich
1933 Waldemar Lindgren
1934 Charles Schuchert
1935 Reginald A. Daly
1938 Andrew C. Lawson
1939 William B. Scott
1940 Nelson H. Darton
1941 Norman L. Bowen
1942 Charles K. Leith
1944 Bailey Willis
1946 T. Wayland Vaughan
1947 Arthur L. Day
1949 Wendell P. Woodring
1952 George G. Simpson
1953 Esper S. Larsen, Jr.
1954 Arthur F. Buddington
1958 James Gilluly
1959 Adolph Knopf
1960 Walter H. Bucher
1962 Alfred S. Romer
1963 William W. Rubey
1964 Donnel F. Hewett
1965 Philip B. King
1966 Harry H. Hess
1969 Francis Birch
1970 Ralph A. Bagnold
1971 Marshall Kay
1972 Wilmot H. Bradley
1973 M. King Hubbert
1974 William M. Ewing
1975 Francis J. Pettijohn
1976 Preston Cloud
1977 Robert P. Sharp
1978 Robert M. Garrels
1979 J. Harlen Bretz
1980 Hollis D. Hedberg
1981 John Rodgers
1982 Aaron C. Waters
1983 G. Arthur Cooper
1984 Donald E. White
1985 Rudolf Trumpy
1986 Laurence L. Sloss

Pittsburgh International Prizes

(Selections made by a jury of award from entries in the Pittsburgh International Exhibition of Contemporary Painting and Sculpture, formerly the Carnegie Institute International Exhibition. After 1964 a new system of equal prizes was instituted.)

First Prize

1898 Dwight W. Tryon
1899 Cecilia Beaux
1901 Alfred Maurer
1903 Frank W. Benson
1904 W. Elmer Schofield
1908 Thomas W. Dewing
1909 Edmund C. Tarbell
1911 John W. Alexander
1914 Edward W. Redfield
1920 Abbott H. Thayer
1921 Ernest Lawson
1922 George W. Bellows
1923 Arthur B. Davies

1931 Franklin C. Watkins
1934 Peter Blume
1936 Leon Kroll
1939 Alexander Brook
1959 Alexander Calder
1961 Mark Tobey
1964 Ellsworth Kelly
1967 Josef Albers

Second Prize

1898 Childe Hassam
1899 Frank W. Benson
1900 Ben Foster
1901 Ellen W. Ahrens
1903 Bryson Burroughs
1904 Edmund C. Tarbell
1905 Edward W. Redfield
1907 Thomas Eakins
1910 Karl Anderson
1912 Paul Dougherty
1921 Howard Giles
1923 Eugene Speicher
1929 William J. Glackens
1930 Alexander Brook
1933 John S. Curry
1935 Charles E. Burchfield
1939 Yasuo Kuniyoshi
1950 Lyonel Feininger
1961 Jules Olitski
1961 George Sugarman

Third Prize

1896 Cecilia Beaux
1897 J. Alden Weir
1900 William S. Kendall
1901 Edmund C. Tarbell
1903 William L. Lathrop
1904 Howard G. Cushing
1905 Childe Hassam
1908 Emil Carlsen
1909 Bruce Crane
1910 Edward F. Rook
1913 Gifford Beal
1914 George W. Bellows
1920 Walter Ufer
1921 Eugene Speicher
1924 Daniel Garber
1925 Charles W. Hawthorne
1926 Robert Spencer
1927 Andrew Dasburg
1928 Glenn O. Coleman
1933 Henry V. Poor
1934 Sidney Laufman
1935 Henry E. Mattson
1938 Arnold Blanch
1950 Priscilla Roberts
1961 Adolph Gottlieb
1961 David Smith

Equal Prizes

1964 Ellsworth Kelly
(Painting)
1967 Josef Albers (Painting)
1985 Richard Serra (Sculpture)

George Polk Memorial Award

(Awarded by the Overseas Press Club for best reporting in any medium requiring exceptional courage and enterprise in other countries; discontinued after 1973.)

1948 Homer W. Bigart

1949 Wayne Richardson
1950 Marguerite Higgins
1951 William Oatis
1952 Homer Bigart
1954 Robert Capa
1955 Gene Symonds
1956 Russell Jones
1957 Herbert Matthews
1958 Joseph Taylor
1960 Henry Taylor
1960 Lionel Durant
1961 Dickey Chapelle
1962 Dana Adams Schmidt
1963 Richard Tregaskis
1964 George Clay
1965 Morley Safer
1966 Ron Nessen
1967 Eric Pace
1968 Peter Rehak
1969 Horst Faas
1969 Peter Arnett
1970 John Laurence
1970 Keith Kay
1970 James Clevenger
1970 Russ Bensley
1970 Ernest Leiser
1971 Nicholas W. Stroh
1973 Leon Dash

Howard N. Potts Medal

(Awarded by the Franklin Institute to honor distinguished work in science or the arts, important development of previous basic discoveries, and inventions or products of superior excellence or utilizing important principles.)

1911 William W. Coblentz
1912 William A. Bone
1913 James A. Bizzell
1913 T. L. Lyon
1914 Ralph Modjeski
1915 W. J. Humphreys
1917 Ulric Dahlgren
1918 Alexander Gray
1918 Arthur B. Kennelly
1919 Reynold Janney
1919 Harvey D. Williams
1919 Clarence P. Landreth
1920 Wendell A. Barker
1920 Edward P. Bullard, Jr.
1921 Elmer V. McCollum
1922 E. G. Coker
1922 Charles R. Downs
1922 J. M. Weiss
1922 Richard B. Moore
1923 Albert W. Hull
1924 John A. Anderson
1924 William Gaertner
1925 Charles T. R. Wilson
1926 William D. Coolidge
1927 George E. Beggs
1927 Marion Eppley
1928 Eugene C. Sullivan
1928 William C. Taylor
1928 Oscar G. Thurlow
1933 Igor I. Sikorsky
1934 Ernst G. Fischer
1937 John C. Hostetter
1938 Lars O. Grondahl
1939 Newcomb K. Chaney
1939 H. Jermain Creighton
1941 Harold E. Edgerton
1942 Jesse W. Beams
1942 Harcourt C. Drake
1943 Paul R. Heyl
1945 Edwin A. Link

1946	Ira S. Bowen
1946	Sanford A. Moss
1947	Robert H. Kent
1947	Vladimir K. Zworykin
1948	David B. Parkinson
1948	Clarence A. Lovell
1948	Eugene J. Houdry
1949	John W. Mauchly
1949	J. Presper Eckert
1949	Clinton R. Hanna
1950	Merle A. Tuve
1951	Clifford M. Foust
1956	Edwin H. Land
1958	William N. Goodwin, Jr.
1958	Emanuel Rosenberg
1959	George W. Morey
1960	Charles S. Draper
1962	Wilbur H. Goss
1964	Erwin H. Mueller
1966	Robert Kunin
1967	John L. Moll
1969	Albert Ghiorso
1969	Charles P. Ginsburg
1971	William D. McElroy
1972	Jacques Ernest Piccard
1973	Howard Vollum
1974	Jay W. Forrester
1975	Legrand G. van Vitert
1976	Stephanie L. Kwolek
1976	Paul W. Morgan
1977	Godfrey N. Hounsfield
1978	Michael Szwarc
1979	Seymour R. Cray
1979	Richard T. Whitcomb
1980	Stanley G. Mason
1981	A. Uno Lamm
1982	Charles G. Overberger
1983	Paul C. Lauterbur
1983	George G. Guilbault
1985	William Cochran
1986	Martin D. Kruskal

Sidney Powers Memorial Medal

(Presented by the American Association of Petroleum Geologists for distinguished contributions to and achievements in the field of special interest to the association.)

1945	Wallace E. Pratt
1947	Alexander Deussen
1948	A. I. Levorsen
1950	E. L. DeGolyer
1952	K. C. Heald
1953	Frederic H. Lahee
1956	William E. Wrather
1957	J. P. D. Hull
1958	Paul Weaver
1959	Raymond C. Moore
1960	Henry V. Howe
1961	Clarence L. Moody
1962	Lewis G. Weeks
1963	Hollis D. Hedberg
1964	Edgar W. Owen
1965	Victor E. Monnett
1966	William B. Heroy
1967	Carey Croneis
1968	Maurice Ewing
1969	Ira H. Cram
1970	Frank R. Clark
1971	Frank A. Morgan
1972	Morgan J. Davis, Sr.
1973	Gordon I. Atwater
1974	G. Moses Knebel
1975	Dean A. McGee
1976	W. Dow Hamm
1977	Michel T. Halbouty

1978	Kenneth H. Crandall
1979	William Hirst Curry, Jr.
1980	Kenneth K. Landes
1981	Mason L. Hill
1982	Daniel A. Busch
1983	Grover E. Murray
1984	Robert J. Weimer
1985	J. Ben Carsey
1986	Merrill W. Haas

Presidential Medal of Freedom

(Known as the Medal of Freedom before 1963 and awarded by the President of the United States to recognize meritorious contributions to the country's security or national interest, to world peace, or to cultural or other significant public or private endeavors.)

1946	George L. Howe
	Gordon T. Jackson
	Richard Mazzarini
	Dennis Puleston
	Chen Sun
	William M. Wheeler, Jr.
1955	Robert B. Anderson
1956	John Von Neumann
1957	Charles E. Wilson
1958	Lewis L. Strauss
1959	John Foster Dulles
	Neil H. McElroy
	Donald A. Quarles
1961	James H. Douglas, Jr.
	Thomas S. Gates, Jr.
	Gordon Gray
	Christian A. Herter
	George B. Kistiakowsky
1963	Marian Anderson
	Ralph J. Bunche
	Ellsworth Bunker
	Genevieve Caulfield
	James B. Conant
	John F. Enders
	Felix Frankfurter
	Karl Holton
	John F. Kennedy
	Robert J. Kiphuth
	Edwin H. Land
	Herbert H. Lehman
	Robert A. Lovett
	John J. McCloy
	J. Clifford MacDonald
	George Meany
	Alexander Meiklejohn
	Luis Munoz-Marin
	Clarence B. Randall
	Rudolph Serkin
	Edward Steichen
	George W. Taylor
	Ludwig Mies van der Rohe
	Alan T. Waterman
	Mark S. Watson
	Annie D. Wauneka
	E. B. White
	Thornton N. Wilder
	Edmund Wilson
	Andrew Wyeth
1964	Dean G. Acheson
	Detlev W. Bronk
	Aaron Copland
	Willem deKooning
	Walt Disney
	J. Frank Dobie
	Lena F. Edwards
	Lynn Fontanne

	John W. Gardner
	Theodore M. Hesburgh
	Clarence L. Johnson
	Frederick R. Kappel
	Helen Keller
	John L. Lewis
	Walter Lippmann
	Alfred Lunt
	Ralph McGill
	Samuel Eliot Morison
	Lewis Mumford
	Edward R. Murrow
	Reinhold Niebuhr
	Leontyne Price
	A. Philip Randolph
	Carl Sandburg
	John Steinbeck
	Helen B. Taussig
	Carl Vinson
	Thomas J. Watson, Jr.
	Paul Dudley White
1968	Ellsworth Bunker
	Robert W. Komer
	Eugene M. Locke
	Robert S. McNamara
	James E. Webb
1969	Edwin E. Aldrin, Jr.
	Neil A. Armstrong
	Eugene R. Black
	McGeorge Bundy
	Clark M. Clifford
	Michael Collins
	Michael E. DeBakey
	David Dubinsky
	Edward (Duke) Ellington
	Ralph Ellison
	Henry Ford II
	W. Averell Harriman
	Bob Hope
	Edgar F. Kaiser
	Mary Lasker
	John W. Macy, Jr.
	Gregory Peck
	Laurance S. Rockefeller
	Walt W. Rostow
	Dean Rusk
	Merriman Smith
	Cyrus R. Vance
	William S. White
	Roy Wilkins
	Whitney M. Young, Jr.
1970	Earl C. Behrens
	Edward T. Folliard
	Fred W. Haise, Jr.
	William M. Henry
	Arthur Krock
	David Lawrence
	George G. Lincoln
	James A. Lovell, Jr.
	Raymond Moley
	Eugene Ormandy
	Adela Rogers St. Johns
	John L. Swigert, Jr.
1971	Manilo Brosio
	Samuel Goldwyn
	William J. Hopkins
	John Paul Vann
1972	DeWitt Wallace
	Lila Wallace
1973	John Ford
	William P. Rogers
1974	Paul G. Hoffman
	Melvin R. Laird
	Charles L. Lowman
1976	David K. E. Bruce
	Martha Graham
	Jesse Owens
	Arthur Rubenstein
1977	I. W. Abel
	John Bardeen
	Irving Berlin

	Norman E. Borlaug
	Omar N. Bradley
	Arleigh Burke
	Alexander Calder
	Bruce Catton
	Joseph P. DiMaggio
	Ariel Durant
	Will Durant
	Arthur Fiedler
	Henry J. Friendly
	Claudia 'Lady Bird' Johnson
	Martin Luther King, Jr.
	Henry A. Kissinger
	Archibald MacLeish
	James Michener
	Georgia O'Keefe
	Nelson Rockefeller
	Donald H. Rumsfeld
	Jonas Salk
	Katherine Felene Shouse
	Lowell Thomas
	James D. Watson
1978	Arthur J. Goldberg
1979	Margaret Mead
1980	Ansel Adams
	Horace M. Albright
	Rachel Carson
	Lucia Chase
	Hubert H. Humphrey
	Archbishop Iakavas
	Lyndon B. Johnson
	Clarence Mitchell
	Roger Tory Peterson
	Hyman Rickover
	Beverly Sills
	Robert Penn Warren
	John Wayne
	Eudora Welty
	Tennessee Williams
1981	Roger Baldwin
	James H. (Eubie) Blake
	Harold Brown
	Zbigniew Brzezinski
	Warren Christopher
	Walter Cronkite
	Kirk Douglas
	Ella T. Grasso
	Bryce N. Harlow
	Walter H. Judd
	Morris T. Leibman
	Margaret Craig McNamara
	Karl Menninger
	Edmund S. Muskie
	Esther Peterson
	Gerard C. Smith
	Robert S. Strauss
	Charles B. Thornton
	Elbert Parr Tuttle
	Earl Warren
	Andrew M. Young
1982	Philip C. Habib
	Kate Smith
1983	George Balanchine
	Paul W. (Bear) Bryant
	James Burnham
	James Cheek
	R. Buckminster Fuller
	Billy Graham
	Eric Hoffer
	Jacob K. Javits
	Clare Boothe Luce
	Dumas Malone
	Mabel Mercer
	Simon Ramo
1984	Howard H. Baker
	James Cagney
	Whittaker Chambers
	Leo Cherne
	Terence Cardinal Cook

Denton A. Cooley
Tennessee Ernie Ford
Hector P. Garcia
Andrew J. Goodpaster
Lincoln Kirstein
Louis L'Amour
Norman Vincent Peale
Carlos P. Romulo
Jack Roosevelt Robinson
Anwar el-Sadat
Eunice Kennedy Shriver
1985 Count Basie
Jacques Yves Cousteau
Jerome Holland
Sidney Hook
Jeane J. Kirkpatrick
George M. Low
Frank Reynolds
S. Dillon Ripley
Frank Sinatra
James Stewart
Mother Teresa
Albert C. Wedemeyer
Charles E. Yeager
1986 Walter H. Annenberg
Earl (Red) Blaik
Barry Goldwater
Helen Hays
Matthew B. Ridgway
Vermont Royster
Albert Sabin

Priestly Medal

(Awarded annually, originally every three years, by the American Chemical Society to honor distinguished service to chemistry.)

1923 Ira Remsen
1926 Edgar F. Smith
1929 Francis P. Garvan
1932 Charles L. Parsons
1935 William A. Noyes
1938 Marston T. Bogert
1941 Thomas Midgley, Jr.
1944 James B. Conant
1946 Roger Adams
1947 Warren K. Lewis
1948 Edward R. Weidlein
1949 Arthur B. Lamb
1950 Charles A. Kraus
1951 E. J. Crane
1952 Samuel C. Lind
1953 Robert Robinson
1954 W. Albert Noyes, Jr.
1955 Charles A. Thomas
1956 Carl S. Marvel
1957 Farrington Daniels
1958 Ernest H. Volwiler
1959 Hermann I. Schlesinger
1960 Wallace R. Brode
1961 Louis P. Hammett
1962 Joel H. Hildebrand
1963 Peter J. W. Debye
1964 John C. Bailar, Jr.
1965 William J. Sparks
1966 William O. Baker
1967 Ralph Connor
1968 William G. Young
1969 Kenneth S. Pitzer
1970 Max Tishler
1971 Frederick D. Rossini
1972 George B. Kistiakowsky
1973 Harold C. Urey
1974 Paul J. Flory
1975 Henry Eyring
1976 George S. Hammond
1977 Henry Gilman

1978 Melvin Calvin
1979 Glenn T. Seaborg
1980 Herbert C. Brown
1981 Bryce Crawford, Jr.
1982 Robert S. Milliken
1983 Linus Pauling
1984 Henry Taube

Pulitzer Prize Winners

(Names are listed alphabetically by year.)

1917 Maude Howe Elliott
Biography
Florence Howe Hall
Biography
Laura E. Richards
Biography
Herbert Bayard Swope
General reporting
1918 William Cabell Bruce
Biography
Henry Beetle Hough
Newspaper history
Minna Lewison
Newspaper history
Harold A. Littledale
General reporting
Ernest Poole
Fiction
James Ford Rhodes
History
Sara Teasdale
Poetry (Poetry Society award)
Jesse Lynch Williams
Drama
1919 Henry Adams
Autobiography
Carl Sandburg
Poetry (Poetry Society award)
Booth Tarkington
Fiction
Margaret Widdemer
Poetry (Poetry Society award)
1920 Albert J. Beveridge
Biography
John J. Leary, Jr.
General reporting
Harvey E. Newbranch
Editorial writing
Eugene O'Neill
Drama
Justin H. Smith
History
1921 Edward Bok
Autobiography
Zona Gale
Drama
Burton J. Hendrick
History
Louis Seibold
General reporting
William S. Sims
History
Edith Wharton
Fiction
1922 James Truslow Adams
History
Hamlin Garland
Biography
Rollin Kirby
Cartoon
Frank M. O'Brien
Editorial writing

Eugene O'Neill
Drama
Edwin Arlington
Robinson
Poetry
Kirke L. Simpson
General reporting
Booth Tarkington
Fiction
1923 Willa Cather
Fiction
Owen Davis
Drama
Burton J. Hendrick
Biography
Alva Johnston
General reporting
Edna St. Vincent Millay
Poetry
Charles Warren
History
William Allen White
Editorial writing
1924 Frank I. Cobb
Editorial writing
Jay N. Darling
Cartoon
Robert Frost
Poetry
Charles H. McIlwain
History
Hatcher Hughes
Drama
Magner White
General reporting
Margaret Wilson
Fiction
1925 Edna Ferber
Fiction
Alvin H. Goldstein
General reporting
Sidney Howard
Drama
Mark A. DeWolfe Howe
Biography
Rollin Kirby
Cartoon
James W. Mulroy
General reporting
Frederic L. Paxson
History
Michael I. Pupin
Autobiography
Edwin Arlington
Robinson
Poetry
1926 Edward Channing
History
Harvey Cushing
Biography
Daniel R. Fitzpatrick
Cartoon
George Kelly
Drama
Edward M. Kingsbury
Editorial writing
Sinclair Lewis
Fiction
Amy Lowell
Poetry
William B. Miller
General reporting
1927 Samuel F. Bemis
History
Louis Bromfield
Fiction
F. Lauriston Bullard
Editorial writing
Paul Green
Drama

Nelson Harding
Cartoon
Emory Holloway
Biography
John T. Rogers
General reporting
Leonora Speyer
Poetry
1928 Grover C. Hall
Editorial writing
Nelson Harding
Cartoon
Eugene O'Neill
Drama
Vernon L. Parrington
History
Edwin Arlington
Robinson
Poetry
Charles E. Russell
Biography
Thornton Wilder
Fiction
1929 Paul Y. Anderson
General reporting
Stephen Vincent Benet
Poetry
Burton J. Hendrick
Biography
Louis I. Jaffe
Editorial writing
Rollin Kirby
Cartoon
Paul Scott Mowrer
General correspondence
Julia Peterkin
Fiction
Elmer L. Rice
Drama
Fred A. Shannon
History
1930 Conrad Aiken
Poetry
Marc Connelly
Drama
Marquis James
Biography
Oliver LaFarge
Fiction
Charles R. Macauley
Cartoon
Russell D. Owen
General reporting
Leland Stowe
General correspondence
Claude H. Van Tyne
History
1931 Margaret Ayer Barnes
Fiction
Edmund Duffy
Cartoon
Robert Frost
Poetry
Susan Glaspell
Drama
Henry James
Biography
H. R. Knickerbocker
General correspondence
A. B. MacDonald
General reporting
Charles S. Ryckman
Editorial writing
Bernadotte E. Schmitt
History
1932 Pearl S. Buck
Fiction
George Dillon
Poetry
Walter Duranty
General correspondence

Ira Gershwin
  Drama
George S. Kaufman
  Drama
John T. McCutcheon
  Cartoon
D. D. Martin
  General reporting
John J. Pershing
  History
J. S. Pooler
  General Reporting
Henry F. Pringle
  Biography
W. C. Richards
  General reporting
Charles G. Ross
  General correspondence
Morrie Ryskind
  Drama
F. D. Webb
  General reporting
1933 Maxwell Anderson
  Drama
Francis A. Jamieson
  General reporting
Archibald MacLeish
  Poetry
Edgar Ansel Mowrer
  General correspondence
Allan Nevins
  Biography
T. S. Stribling
  Fiction
Harold M. Talburt
  Cartoon
Frederick Jackson Turner
  History
1934 Herbert Agar
  History
Frederick T. Birchall
  General correspondence
Royce Brier
  General reporting
E. P. Chase
  Editorial writing
Tyler Dennett
  Biography
Edmund Duffy
  Cartoon
Robert Hillyer
  Poetry
Sidney Kingsley
  Drama
Caroline Miller
  Fiction
1935 Zoe Akins
  Drama
Charles McLean Andrews
  History
Douglas Southhall
  Freeman
  Biography
Josephine Winslow
  Johnson
  Fiction
Arthur Krock
  General correspondence
Ross A. Lewis
  Cartoon
William H. Taylor
  General reporting
Audrey Wurdemann
  Poetry
1936 Wilfred C. Barber
  General correspondence
Robert P. Tristram
  Coffin
  Poetry
H. L. Davis
  Fiction

Lauren D. Lyman
  General reporting
Andrew C. McLaughlin
  History
Felix Morley
  Editorial writing
George B. Parker
  Editorial writing
Ralph B. Perry
  Biography
Robert E. Sherwood
  Drama
1937 Clarence D. Batchelor
  Cartoon
Howard W. Blakeslee
  General reporting
Van Wyck Brooks
  History
David Dietz
  General reporting
Robert Frost
  Poetry
Moss Hart
  Drama
George S. Kaufman
  Drama
Gobind Behari Lal
  General reporting
William L. Laurence
  General reporting
Anne O'Hare McCormick
  General correspondence
Margaret Mitchell
  Fiction
Allan Nevins
  Biography
John J. O'Neill
  General reporting
John W. Owens
  Editorial writing
1938 Paul H. Buck
  History
Marquis James
  Biography
Arthur Krock
  General correspondence
John P. Marquand
  Fiction
Odell Shepard
  Biography
Vaughn Shoemaker
  Cartoon
Raymond Sprigle
  General reporting
W. W. Waymack
  Editorial writing
Thornton Wilder
  Drama
Marya Zaturenska
  Poetry
1939 Ronald G. Callvert
  Editorial writing
John Gould Fletcher
  Poetry
Louis P. Lochner
  General correspondence
Frank Luther Mott
  History
Marjorie Kinnan
  Rawlings
  Fiction
Robert E. Sherwood
  Drama
Thomas L. Stokes
  General reporting
Carl Van Doren
  Biography
Charles G. Werner
  Cartoon
1940 Ray S. Baker
  Biography

Edmund Duffy
  Cartoon
S. Burton Heath
  General reporting
Bart Howard
  Editorial writing
Carl Sandburg
  History
William Saroyan
  Drama (declined)
John Steinbeck
  Fiction
Otto D. Tolischus
  General correspondence
Mark Van Doren
  Poetry
1941 Leonard Bacon
  Poetry
Jacob Burck
  Cartoon
Marcus Lee Hanson
  History
Reuben Maury
  Editorial writing
Westbrook Pegler
  General reporting
Robert E. Sherwood
  Drama
Loa Elizabeth Winslow
  Biography
1942 Laurence E. Allen
  International telegraphic
  reporting
William Rose Benet
  Poetry
Herbert L. Block
  Cartoon
Milton Brooks
  News photography
Stanton Delaplane
  General reporting
Ellen Glasgow
  Fiction
Margaret Leech
  History
Geoffrey Parsons
  Editorial writing
Carlos P. Romulo
  General correspondence
Louis Stark
  National telegraphic
  reporting
Forrest Wilson
  Biography
1943 Hanson W. Baldwin
  General correspondence
Jay N. Darling
  Cartoon
Esther Forbes
  History
Robert Frost
  Poetry
Samuel Eliot Morison
  Biography
Frank Noel
  News photography
William Schuman
  Music
Forrest W. Seymour
  Editorial writing
Upton Sinclair
  Fiction
George Weller
  General reporting
Thornton Wilder
  Drama
Ira Wolpert
  International telegraphic
  reporting
1944 Stephen Vincent Benet
  Poetry

Clifford K. Berryman
  Cartoon
Earle L. Bunker
  News photography
Merle Curti
  History
Daniel De Luce
  International telegraphic
  reporting
Frank Filan
  News photography
Martin Flavin
  Fiction
Dewey L. Fleming
  National telegraphic
  reporting
Oscar Hammerstein, II
  Special citation
Howard Hanson
  Music
Henry J. Haskell
  Editorial writing
Carleton Mabee
  Biography
Byron Price
  Newspaper and radio
  codes
Ernest T. (Ernie) Pyle
  General correspondence
Richard Rodgers
  Special citation
Paul Schoenstein
  General reporting
William Allen White
  Special citation
1945 Stephen Bonsal
  History
Harold V. Boyle
  General correspondence
Mary Chase
  Drama
Aaron Copland
  Music
John Hersey
  Fiction
Jack S. McDowell
  General reporting
William Mauldin
  Cartoon
Russell B. Nye
  Biography
George W. Potter
  Editorial writing
James Reston
  National telegraphic
  reporting
Joe Rosenthal
  News photography
Karl Shapiro
  Poetry
Mark S. Watson
  International telegraphic
  reporting
1946 Homer W. Bigart
  International telegraphic
  reporting
Hodding Carter, Jr.
  Editorial writing
Arnaldo Cortesi
  General correspondence
Russel Crouse
  Drama
Edward A. Harris
  National telegraphic
  reporting
William L. Laurence
  General reporting
Howard Lindsay
  Drama
Bruce A. Russell
  Cartoon

Arthur M. Schlesinger,
Jr.
History
Leo Sowerby
Music
Linnie Marsh Wolfe
Biography
1947 Brooks Atkinson
General correspondence
James P. Baxter, III
History
Edward T. Folliard
National telegraphic
reporting
Eddy Gilmore
International telegraphic
reporting
William H. Grimes
Editorial writing
Arnold Hardy
News photography
Charles Ives
Music
Robert Lowell
Poetry
Vaughn Shoemaker
Cartoon
Robert Penn Warren
Fiction
William Allen White
Autobiography
Frederick Woltman
General reporting
1948 Bert Andrews
National reporting
W. H. Auden
Poetry
Margaret Clapp
Biography
Frank Cushing
News photography
Virginius Dabney
Editorial writing
Bernard DeVoto
History
Frank D. Fackenthal
Special citation
Nat S. Finney
National reporting
Reuben L. Goldberg
Cartoon
George E. Goodwin
General reporting
James A. Michener
Fiction
Walter Piston
Music
Paul W. Ward
International
correspondence
Tennessee Williams
Drama
1949 James Gould Cozzens
Fiction
John H. Crider
Editoral writing
Price Day
International
correspondence
Herbert Elliston
Editoral writing
Nathaniel Fein
News photography
Malcolm Johnson
General reporting
Arthur Miller
Drama
Roy F. Nichols
History
Lute Pease
Cartoon

Robert E. Sherwood
Biography
Virgil Thompson
Music
C. P. Trussel
National reporting
Peter Viereck
Poetry
1950 Samuel F. Bemis
Biography
Meyer Berger
General reporting
James T. Berryman
Cartoon
Gwendolyn Brooks
Poetry
Bill Crouch
News photography
A. B. Guthrie, Jr.
Fiction
Edwin O. Guthman
National reporting
Oscar Hammerstein, II
Drama
Oliver W. Larkin
History
Joshua Logan
Drama
Gian-Carlo Menotti
Music
Richard Rodgers
Drama
Carl M. Saunders
Editorial writing
Edmund Stevens
International
correspondence
1951 Keyes Beech
International
correspondence
Homer W. Bigart
International
correspondence
R. Carlyle Buley
History
Margaret Louise Coit
Biography
Max Desfor
News photography
William H. Fitzpatrick
Editorial writing
Marguerite Higgins
International
correspondence
Reginald W. Manning
Cartoon
Edward S. Montgomery
General reporting
Douglas Moore
Music
Relman Morin
International
correspondence
Conrad Richter
Fiction
Carl Sandburg
Poetry
Fred Sparks
International
correspondence
Cyrus L. Sulzberger
Special citation
Don Whitehead
International
correspondence
1952 George de Carvalho
General reporting
Oscar Handlin
History

John M. Hightower
International
correspondence
Max Kase
Special citation
Joseph Kramm
Drama
Gail Kubick
Music
Louis LaCoss
Editorial writing
Anthony Leviero
National reporting
Marianne Moore
Poetry
Fred L. Packer
Cartoon
Merlo J. Pusey
Biography
John Robinson
News photography
Don Ultany
News photography
Herman Wouk
Fiction
1953 George Dangerfield
History
William M. Gallagher
News photography
Ernest Hemingway
Fiction
William Inge
Drama
Edward D. Kuekes
Cartoon
Archibald MacLeish
Poetry
Donald J. Mays
Biography
Edward J. Mowery
Local reporting
Vermont C. Royster
Editorial writing
Austin Wehrwein
International
correspondence
Don Whitehead
National reporting
1954 Herbert L. Block
Cartoon
Bruce Catton
History
Charles A. Lindbergh
Autobiography
Jim C. Lucas
International
correspondence
Alvin S. McCoy
Local reporting
Don Murray
Editorial writing
John Patrick
Drama
Quincy Porter
Music
Theodore Roethke
Poetry
Mrs. Walter M. Schau
News photography
Richard Wilson
National reporting
1955 Mrs. Caro Brown
Local reporting
William Faulkner
Fiction
Daniel R. Fitzpatrick
Cartoon
John L. Gaunt, Jr.
News photography
Paul Horgan
History

Royce Howes
Editorial writing
Anthony Lewis
National reporting
Gian-Carlo Menotti
Music
Harrison E. Salisbury
International
correspondence
Wallace Stevens
Poetry
Roland K. Towery
Local reporting
William S. White
Biography
Tennessee Williams
Drama
1956 Charles L. Bartlett
National reporting
Elizabeth Bishop
Poetry
Frank Coniff
International
correspondence
Arthur Daley
Local reporting
Frances Goodrich
Drama
Albert Hackett
Drama
Talbot F. Hamlin
Biography
William Randolph Hearst,
Jr.
International
correspondence
Lee Hills
Local reporting, against
deadline
Richard Hofstadter
History
MacKinlay Kantor
Fiction
Kingsbury Smith
International
correspondence
Lauren K. Soth
Editorial writing
Ernest Toch
Music
Robert York
Cartoon
1957 Buford Boone
Editorial writing
Norman Dello Joio
Music
Russell Jones
International
correspondence
George F. Kennan
History
John F. Kennedy
Biography
William Lambert
Local reporting
Tom Little
Cartoon
Eugene O'Neill
Drama
James Reston
National reporting
Kenneth Roberts
Nonfiction
Harry A. Trask
News photography
Wallace Turner
Local reporting
Richard Wilbur
Poetry
1958 James Agee
Fiction

Harry S. Ashmore
Editorial writing
Mary Wells Ashworth
Biography
Samuel Barber
Music
William C. Beall
News photography
George Beveridge
Local reporting
John A. Carroll
Biography
Douglas Southall
Freeman
Biography
Ketti Frings
Drama
Bray Hammond
History
Walter Lippmann
Special citation
Clark R. Mollenhoff
National reporting
Relman Morin
National reporting
Bruce M. Shanks
Cartoon
Robert Penn Warren
Poetry
1959 John H. Brislin
Local reporting
Stanley Kunitz
Poetry
John La Montaine
Music
Ralph McGill
Editorial writing
Archibald MacLeish
Drama
Joseph Martin
International
correspondence
William Mauldin
Cartoon
Philip Santora
International
correspondence
Jean Schneider
History
William Seaman
News photography
Robert Lewis Taylor
Fiction
Howard Van Smith
National reporting
Arthur Walworth
Biography
Mary Lou Werner
Local reporting, against
deadline
Leonard D. White
History
1960 George Abbott
Drama
Jerry Bock
Drama
Elliott Carter
Music
Lenoir Chambers
Editorial writing
Allen Drury
Fiction
Sheldon Harnick
Drama
Margaret Leech
History
Andrew Lopez
News photography
Garrett Mattingly
Nonfiction

Samuel Eliot Morison
Biography
Jack Nelson
Local reporting, against
deadline
Miriam Ottenberg
Local reporting
A. M. Rosenthal
International
correspondence
W. D. Snodgrass
Poetry
Vana Trimble
National reporting
Jerome Weidman
Drama
1961 Edward R. Cony
National reporting
Sanche de Gramont
Local reporting, against
deadline
David Donald
Biography
William J. Dorvillier
Editorial writing
Herbert Feis
History
Lyman Heinzerling
International
correspondence
Harper Lee
Fiction
Phyllis McGinley
Poetry
Edgar May
Local reporting
Tad Mosel
Drama
Carey Orr
Cartoon
Walter Piston
Music
1962 George Bliss
Local reporting
Abe Burrows
Drama
Nathan G. Caldwell
National reporting
Alan Dugan
Poetry
Lawrence H. Gipson
History
Gene S. Graham
National reporting
Walter Lippmann
International
correspondence
Frank Loesser
Drama
Robert D. Mullins
Local reporting, against
deadline
Edwin O'Connor
Fiction
Thomas M. Storke
Editorial writing
Edmund S. Valtman
Cartoon
Paul Vathis
News photography
Robert Ward
Music
Theodore H. White
Nonfiction
1963 Samuel Barber
Music
Leon Edel
Biography
William Faulkner
Fiction

Sylvan Fox
Local reporting, against
deadline
Constance McLaughlin
Green
History
Oscar O. Griffin, Jr.
Local reporting
Ira B. Harkey, Jr.
Editorial writing
Hall Hendrix
International
correspondence
Anthony Lewis
National reporting
William Longgood
Local reporting, against
deadline
Frank Miller
Cartoon
Hector Rondon
News photography
Anthony Shannon
Local reporting, against
deadline
Barbara W. Tuchman
Nonfiction
William Carlos Williams
Poetry
1964 Walter J. Bates
Biography
Malcolm W. Browne
International
correspondence
Paul Conrad
Cartoon
Albert V. Gaudiosi
Local reporting
David Halberstam
International
correspondence
Richard Hofstadter
Nonfiction
Robert Hill Jackson
News photography
James V. Magee
Local reporting
Frederick A. Meyer
Local reporting
Norman C. Miller
Local reporting, against
deadline
Sumner Chilton Powell
History
Louis Simpson
Poetry
Hazel Brannan Smith
Editorial writing
Merriman Smith
National reporting
1965 John Berryman
Poetry
Frank D. Gilroy
Drama
Gene Goltz
Local reporting
Shirley Ann Grau
Fiction
John R. Harrison
Editorial writing
Howard Mumford Jones
Nonfiction
Louis M. Kohlmeier
National reporting
J. A. Livingston
International
correspondence
Melvin H. Ruder
Local reporting, against
deadline

Ernest Samuels
Biography
Irwin Unger
History
1966 Peter Arnett
International
correspondence
Leslie Bassett
Music
John A. Frasca
Local reporting
Haynes Johnson
National reporting
Robert Lasch
Editorial writing
Perry Miller
History
Katherine Anne Porter
Fiction
Arthur M. Schlesinger,
Jr.
Biography
Edwin W. Teale
Nonfiction
Don Wright
Cartoon
1967 Edward Albee
Drama
Robert V. Cox
Local reporting, against
deadline
David B. Davis
Nonfiction
William H. Goetzmann
History
R. John Hughes
International
correspondence
Justin Kaplan
Biography
Monroe W. Karmin
National reporting
Leon Kirchner
Music
Bernard Malamud
Fiction
Gene Miller
Local reporting
Patrick B. Oliphant
Cartoon
Eugene Patterson
Editorial writing
Stanley W. Penn
National reporting
Anne Sexton
Poetry
Jack R. Thornell
News photography
1968 Bernard Bailyn
History
George Crumb
Music
Ariel Durant
Nonfiction
Will Durant
Nonfiction
Alfred Friendly
International
correspondence
Anthony Hecht
Poetry
Howard James
National reporting
Nathan K. Katz
National reporting
George F. Kennan
Autobiography
John S. Knight
Editorial writing
J. Anthony Lukas
Local reporting

Eugene Gray Payne
  Cartoon
William Styron
  Fiction
1969 Edward T. Adams
  News photography
Robert Cahn
  National reporting
Albert L. Delugach
  Local reporting
Rene J. Dubos
  Nonfiction
John Fetterman
  Local reporting, against
  deadline
John Fischetti
  Cartoon
Paul Greenberg
  Editorial writing
Karel Husa
  Music
Leonard W. Levy
  History
Norman Mailer
  Nonfiction
M. Scott Momaday
  Fiction
George Oppen
  Poetry
Benjamin L. Reid
  Biography
Howard Sackler
  Drama
Moneta Sleet, Jr.
  News photography
William Tuohy
  International
  correspondence
Denny Walsh
  Local reporting
1970 Dean G. Acheson
  History
Marquis Childs
  Commentary
Thomas F. Darcy
  Cartoons
William J. Eaton
  National reporting
Erik H. Erikson
  Nonfiction
Thomas Fitzpatrick
  Local reporting, general
Philip L. Geyelin
  Editorial writing
Charles Gordone
  Drama
Seymour M. Hersh
  International reporting
Richard Howard
  Poetry
Ada Louise Huxtable
  Criticism
Dallas Kinney
  Feature photography
Harold E. Martin
  Local reporting, special
Jean Stafford
  Fiction
Steve Starr
  Spot news photography
T. Harry Williams
  Biography
Charles W. Wuorinen
  Music
1971 James McGregor Burns
  History
William A. Caldwell
  Commentary
Paul Conrad
  Editorial cartooning

Mario Davidowsky
  Music
Horace G. Davis, Jr.
  Editorial writing
Jack Dykinga
  Feature photography
John Paul Filo
  Spot news photography
Lucinda Franks
  National reporting
Jimmie Lee Hoagland
  International reporting
William H. Jones
  Special local reporting
William S. Merwin
  Poetry
Thomas Powers
  National reporting
Harold C. Schonberg
  Criticism
Lawrence R. Thompson
  Biography
John Toland
  General nonfiction
Paul Zindel
  Drama
1972 Jack Anderson
  National reporting
Richard Cooper
  Local reporting
Carl N. Degler
  History
Ann DeSantis
  Special local reporting
Jacob Druckman
  Music
Horst Fass
  Spot news photography
Peter R. Kann
  International reporting
David Kennerly
  Feature photography
Stephen A. Kurkjian
  Special local reporting
Michael Laurent
  Spot news photography
Joseph P. Lash
  Biography
Timothy Leland
  Special local reporting
John Machacek
  General local reporting
Jeffrey K. MacNelly
  Editorial cartooning
Gerald M. O'Neill
  Special local reporting
Frank Peters, Jr.
  Music criticism
Mike Royko
  Commentary
Wallace E. Stegner
  Fiction
John Strohmeyer
  Editorial writing
Barbara W. Tuchman
  General nonfiction
James Wright
  Poetry
1973 Robert Boyd
  National reporting
David S. Broder
  Commentary
Elliott Carter
  Music
Robert Coles
  General nonfiction
Frances FitzGerald
  General nonfiction
Max Frankel
  International reporting

Clark Hoyt
  National reporting
Michael Kammen
  History
Maxine Winokur Kumin
  Poetry
Brian Lanker
  Feature photography
Roger B. Linscott
  Editorial writing
Jason Miller
  Drama
Ronald Powers
  Criticism
W. A. Swanberg
  Biography
Huynh Cong Ut
  Spot news photography
Eudora Welty
  Fiction
1974 Ernest Becker
  General nonfiction
Daniel J. Boorstin
  History
Emily Genaver
  Criticism
Hugh F. Hough
  General local reporting
Robert Lowell
  Poetry
Donald Martino
  Music
Arthur M. Petacque
  General local reporting
James R. Polk
  National reporting
Anthony K. Roberts
  Spot news photography
Edwin A. Roberts
  Commentary
Louis Sheaffer
  Biography
William Sherman
  Special local reporting
Henrick Smith
  International reporting
F. Gilman Spencer
  Editorial writing
Paul Szep
  Editorial cartooning
Slava Veder
  Feature photography
Jack White
  National reporting
1975 Edward Albee
  Drama
Dominick Argento
  Music
Donald L. Bartlett
  National reporting
Robert A. Caro
  Biography
Ovie Carter
  International reporting
Annie Dillard
  General nonfiction
Roger Ebert
  Criticism
Gerald H. Gay
  Spot news photography
Matthew Lewis
  Feature photography
Dumas Malone
  History
John Daniell Maurice
  Editorial writing
Mary McGrory
  Commentary
William Mullen
  International reporting

Michael Shaara
  Fiction
Gary Snyder
  Poetry
James B. Steele
  National reporting
Garry Trudeau
  Editorial cartooning
1976 John Ashbery
  Poetry
Tony Auth
  Editorial Cartooning
Saul Bellow
  Fiction
Michael Bennett
  Drama
George Bliss
  Special local reporting
Robert N. Butler
  General nonfiction
Nicholas Dante
  Drama
Stanley Forman
  Spot news photography
Marvin Hamlisch
  Drama
Paul Horgan
  History
Philip P. Kerby
  Editorial writing
James Kirkwood
  Drama
Edward Kleban
  Drama
Alan M. Kriegsman
  Criticism
Richard W. B. Lewis
  Biography
Gene Miller
  General local reporting
James Risser
  National reporting
Ned Rorem
  Music
Sydney Schanberg
  International reporting
Walter 'Red" Smith
  Commentary
1977 Norman F. Cardoza
  Editorial writing
Foster Church
  Editorial writing
Michael Chistofer
  Drama
Stanley Forman
  Spot news photography
Robin Hood
  Feature photography
Margo Huston
  General local reporting
Warren L. Lerude
  Editorial writing
John E. Mack
  Biography
William McPherson
  Criticism
Walter Mears
  National reporting
James Merrill
  Poetry
Acel Moore
  Special local reporting
David M. Potter
  History
Wendell Rawls, Jr.
  Special local reporting
Paul Szep
  Editorial cartooning
Neal Ulevich
  Spot news photography

William W. Warner
General nonfiction
Richard Wernick
Music
George F. Will
Commentary
1978 Walter Jackson Bate
Biography
J. Ross Baughman
Feature photography
John W. Blair
Spot news photography
Alfred D. Chandler, Jr.
History
Donald L. Coburn
Drama
Michael Colgrass
Music
Anthony R. Dolan
Special local reporting
Meg Greenfield
Editorial writing
Henry Kamm
International reporting
Walter Kerr
Criticism
Jeffrey K. MacNelly
Editorial cartooning
William K. Marimow
Public service reporting
James Alan McPherson
Fiction
Howard Nemerov
Poetry
Jonathan Neumann
Public service reporting
William Safire
Commentary
Carl Sagan
General nonfiction
Gaylord Shaw
National reporting
Richard Whitt
General local reporting
1979 Leonard Baker
Biography
Russell Baker
Commentary
Herbert L. Block
Editorial cartooning
John Cheever
Fiction
Richard B. Cramer
International reporting
Don E. Fehrenbacher
History
Jon B. Franklin
Feature writing
Paul Gapp
Criticism
Gilbert M. Gaul
Special local reporting
Elliot G. Jaspin
Special local reporting
Thomas J. Kelly, III
Spot news photography
James Risser
National reporting
Joseph Schwantner
Music
Sam Shepard
Drama
Robert Penn Warren
Poetry
Edwin M. Yodler, Jr.
Editorial writing
1980 Robert L. Bartley
Editorial writing
Madeleine Blais
Feature writing

Joel Brinkley
International reporting
Nils J. Bruzelius
Special local reporting
Ellen H. Goodman
Commentary
Erwin H. Hailer
Feature photography
Alexander B. Hawes, Jr.
Special local reporting
William A. Henry, III
Criticism
Douglas R. Hofstadter
General nonfiction
Donald R. Justice
Poetry
Stephen A. Kurkjian
Special local reporting
Leon F. Litwack
History
Norman Mailer
Fiction
Jay Mather
International reporting
Edmund Morris
Biography
Bette Swenson Orsini
National reporting
Robert Porterfield
Special local reporting
Charles Stafford
National reporting
David del Tredici
Music
Joan Vennochi
Special local reporting
Lanford Wilson
Drama
Don Wright
Editorial cartooning
1981 Dave Anderson
Commentary
Teresa Carpenter
Feature writing
Shirley Christian
International reporting
Lawrence A. Cremin
History
John M. Crewdson
National reporting
Clark Hallas
Special local reporting
Beth Henley
Drama
Robert B. Lowe
Special local reporting
Robert K. Massie
Biography
Mike Peters
Editorial cartooning
Larry Price
Spot news photography
Carl E. Schorske
General nonfiction
James Schuyler
Poetry
John Kennedy Toole
Fiction
Taro M. Yamasaki
Feature photography
Jonathan Yardley
Criticism
1982 Martin Bernheimer
Criticism
Art Buchwald
Commentary
Ron Edmonds
Spot news photography
Charles Fuller
Drama

Paul Henderson
Special local reporting
Tracy Kidder
General nonfiction
William S. McFeely
Biography
Saul Pett
Feature writing
Sylvia Plath
Poetry
Ben Sargent
Editorial cartooning
Roger Sessions
Music
John Updike
Fiction
John H. White
Feature photography
C. Vann Woodward
History
1983 Russell Baker
Biography
James B. Dickman
Feature photography
Bill Foley
Spot news photography
Thomas L. Friedman
International reporting
Manuela Hoelterhoff
Criticism
Rhys L. Isaac
History
Loren Jenkins
International reporting
Galway Kinnell
Poetry
Richard Locker
Editorial cartooning
Marsha Norman
Drama
Nan Robertson
Feature writing
Susan Sheehan
General nonfiction
Claude Sitton
Commentary
Loretta Tofani
Special local reporting
Alice Walker
Fiction
Ellen T. Zwilich
Music
1984 Paul Conrad
Editorial cartooning
Paul Goldberger
Criticism
Stan Grossfeld
Spot news photography
Louis R. Harlan
Biography
Karen Elliott House
International reporting
William Kennedy
Fiction
David Mamet
Drama
Mary Oliver
Poetry
Peter Mark Rinearson
Feature writing
Vermont Royster
Commentary
Albert Scardino
Editorial writing
Paul Starr
General nonfiction
Anthony Suau
Feature photography
John Nobel Wilford
National reporting

1985 Stephen Albert
Music
Richard Aregood
Editorial writing
Dennis Bell
International reporting
Jackie Crosby
Specialized reporting
Jon Franklin
Explanatory journalism
Josh Friedman
International reporting
Stan Grossfeld
Feature photography
Murray Kempton
Commentary
Carolyn Kizer
Poetry
Thomas J. Knudson
National reporting
James Lapine
Drama
Alison Lurie
Fiction
Jeff MacNelly
Editorial cartooning
William K. Marimow
Investigative reporting
Thomas K. McCraw
History
Lucy Morgan
Investigative reporting
Ozier Muhammad
International reporting
Larry C. Price
Feature photography
Jack Reed
Investigative reporting
Howard Rosenberg
Criticism
Randall Savage
Specialized reporting
Kenneth Silverman
Biography
Stephen Sondheim
Drama
Alice Steinbach
Feature writing
Studs Terkel
General nonfiction
Thomas Turcol
General news reporting
1986 Edna Buchanan
General news reporting
Jimmy Breslin
Commentary
John Camp
Feature writing
Pete Carey
International reporting
Michel duCille
Spot news photography
Katherine Ellison
International reporting
Jules Feiffer
Editorial cartooning
Mary Pat Flaherty
Specialized reporting
Craig Flournoy
National reporting
Elizabeth Frank
Biography
Jack Fuller
Editorial writing
Tom Gralish
Feature photography
Carol Guzy
Spot news photography
Donal Henahan
Criticism

Arthur Howe
  National reporting
Joseph Lelyveld
  General nonfiction
J. Anthony Lukas
  General nonfiction
Jeffrey A. Marx
  Investigative reporting
Walter A. McDougall
  History
Larry McMurtry
  Fiction
George Perle
  Music
George Rodrugue
  National reporting
Andrew Schneider
  Specialized reporting
Lewis M. Simons
  International reporting
Henry Taylor
  Poetry
Michael M. York
  Investigative reporting

Isaac Ray Award

(Presented by the American Psychiatric Association for outstanding contributions to forensic phychiatry or to the psychiatric aspects of jurisprudence.)

1952	Winfred Overholser
1953	Gregory Zilboorg
1954	John Biggs, Jr.
1955	Henry Weihofen
1956	Philip Q. Roche
1957	Manfred S. Guttmacher
1960	David L. Bazelon
1961	Sheldon Glueck
1962	Karl Menninger
1963	Morris Ploscowe
1964	Justine Wise Polier
1968	Bernard Diamond
1975	Jay Katz
1976	Jonas Robitscher
1977	Bruno Lonier
1980	Seymour L. Halleck
1982	Alan Stone
1984	Jonas R. Rappeport
1986	Saleem A. Shah

Reed Aeronautics Award

(Presented annually by the American Institute of Aeronautics and Astronautics to honor a contribution to aeronautical engineering design or the aeronautical sciences whose influence is apparent on the development of paractical aeronautics. Known as the Sylvanus Albert Reed Award until 1977.)

1934	C. G. Rossby
1934	H. G. Willett
1935	Frank W. Caldwell
1936	Edward S. Taylor
1937	Eastman N. Jacobs
1938	Alfred V. de Forest
1939	George J. Mead
1940	Hugh L. Dryden
1941	Theodore von Karman
1942	Igor I. Sikorsky
1943	Sanford A. Moss
1944	Fred E. Weick
1945	Charles S. Draper

1946	Robert T. Jones
1947	Galen B. Schubauer
1947	Harold K. Skromstad
1948	George W. Brady
1949	George S. Schairer
1950	Robert R. Gilruth
1951	Edward H. Heinemann
1952	John Stack
1953	Ernest G. Stout
1954	Clark B. Millikan
1955	H. Julian Allen
1956	Clarence L. Johnson
1957	Raymond L. Bisplinghoff
1958	Victor E. Carbonera
1959	Karel J. Bossart
1960	John W. Becker
1961	Alfred J. Eggers, Jr.
1962	Walter C. Williams
1964	Abe Silverstein
1965	Arthur E. Raymond
1966	Clarence L. Johnson
1967	Adolph Busemann
1968	William H. Cook
1969	Rene H. Miller
1970	Richard T. Whitcomb
1971	Ira G. Hedrick
1972	Max M. Munk
1973	I. E. Garrick
1974	Willis Hawkins
1975	Antonio Ferri
1976	George Spangenberg
1977	William C. Dietz
1978	James T. Stewart
1979	Paul B. MacCready
1980	Donald Malvern
1981	William R. Sears
1982	John H. McLucas
1983	Robert Widmer
1984	Frederick T. Rall, Jr.
1985	Thomas V. Jones
1986	Robert J. Patton

Remington Honor Medal

(Awarded by the American Pharmaceutical Association, New York Chapter, for distinguished service to pharmacy in the preceding year or for outstanding achievement during a longer period of activity.)

1919	James J. Beal
1920	John Uri Lloyd
1922	Henry V. Arny
1923	Henry H. Rusby
1924	George M. Beringer
1925	Henry M. Whelpley
1926	H. A. B. Dunning
1928	Charles H. LaWall
1929	Wilbur L. Scoville
1930	Edward Kremers
1931	Ernest F. Cook
1932	Eugene G. Eberle
1933	Evander F. Kelly
1935	Samuel L. Hilton
1936	Edmund N. Gathercoal
1937	J. Leon Lascoff
1938	Henry C. Christensen
1940	Robert L. Swain
1941	George D. Beal
1942	Josiah K. Lilly
1943	Robert P. Fischelis
1944	H. Evert Kendig
1945	Joseph Rosin
1947	Rufus A. Lyman
1948	Andrew G. DuMez
1949	Ernest Little
1950	Edwin L. Newcomb
1951	Hugo H. Schaefer

1952	Patrick H. Costello
1953	Hugh C. Muldoon
1955	Roy B. Cook
1956	Frank W. Moudry
1957	W. Paul Briggs
1958	Eli Lilly
1959	Justin L. Powers
1960	Ivor Griffith
1962	Harry J. Anslinger
1963	Glenn L. Jenkins
1964	Robert A. Hardt
1965	K. K. Chen
1967	William S. Apple
1969	George F. Archambault
1970	Don E. Francke
1971	Linwood F. Tice
1972	Glenn Sonnedecker
1973	Grover C. Bowles
1974	Lloyd M. Parks
1975	Albert Doerr
1976	Melvin W. Green
1978	Eugene V. White
1980	Joseph D. Williams
1983	Tukera Higuchi
1984	William M. Heller
1985	Leonard Blockstein
1986	Irving Rubin

Theodore Roosevelt Distinguished Service Medal

(Awarded annually until 1967 by the Theodore Roosevelt Association for notable contributions in the following domains: public and international law, industrial peace, American literature, outdoor life, national defense, international affairs, administration of public office, conservation of natural resources, advancement of social justice, expression of the pioneer virtues, distinguished public service by a private citizen, and leadership of youth and the development of the American character. Now awarded irregularly.)

1923	Louisa L. Schuyler
1923	Henry Fairfield Osborn
1923	Leonard Wood
1924	Oliver Wendell Holmes
1924	Charles W. Eliot
1924	Elihu Root
1925	Gifford Pinchot
1925	George B. Grinnell
1925	Martha Berry
1926	Daniel C. Beard
1926	William S. Sims
1926	Albert J. Beveridge
1927	John B. Moore
1927	Herbert Hoover
1927	John J. Pershing
1928	Charles Evans Hughes
1928	Frank M. Chapman
1928	Charles A. Lindbergh
1929	Herbert Putnam
1929	Owen Wister
1929	Owen D. Young
1930	Richard E. Byrd
1930	William Green
1930	Hastings H. Hart
1931	Hamlin Garland
1931	Benjamin N. Cardozo
1931	C. Hart Merriam
1932	Robert A. Millikan
1933	Stephen Vincent Benet
1934	William Allen White

1934	Samuel Seabury
1935	William H. Park
1936	Helen Keller
1936	Anne Sullivan Macy
1937	James H. Dillard
1938	Carter Glass
1938	Robert Moses
1939	George Washington Carver
1939	Frank R. McCoy
1939	Carl Sandburg
1940	Grenville Clark
1940	Homer Folks
1940	Chester H. Rowell
1942	Rufus M. Jones
1942	Henry L. Stimson
1942	Booth Tarkington
1943	Eleanor Robson Belmont
1943	Jay N. Darling
1943	Joseph C. Grew
1945	Vannevar Bush
1945	Cordell Hull
1945	George C. Marshall
1946	Irving Berlin
1946	Dwight D. Eisenhower
1946	William F. Halsey
1946	Douglas MacArthur
1946	Chester N. Nimitz
1947	Omar N. Bradley
1947	Learned Hand
1947	Jeremiah Milbank
1947	Arthur Hays Sulzberger
1948	James B. Conant
1948	Millicent C. McIntosh
1948	Arthur H. Vandenberg
1949	Lucius D. Clay
1949	David Hinshaw
1949	J. Edgar Hoover
1950	Warren R. Austin
1950	Bernard M. Baruch
1950	Anne O'Hare McCormick
1951	Frederick M. Davenport
1951	Lewis W. Douglas
1951	Frank C. Laubach
1952	John Foster Dulles
1952	Fairfield Osborn
1953	William Beebe
1953	Van Wyck Brooks
1954	Ralph J. Bunche
1954	Robert Frost
1954	DeWitt Wallace
1954	Mrs. DeWitt Wallace
1955	Arthur H. Compton
1955	Thomas E. Dewey
1956	Herman Hagedorn
1956	Samuel Eliot Morison
1956	Clarence B. Randall
1957	David E. Finley
1957	Helen Rogers Reid
1958	Alfred M. Gruenther
1958	Hyman G. Rickover
1959	Horace M. Albright
1959	Henry Cabot Lodge
1960	Irving S. Olds
1960	Don Walsh
1960	Theodore Roosevelt, Jr.
1961	Erwin D. Canham
1961	John J. McCloy
1961	Alan B. Shepard, Jr.
1962	Arthur H. Dean
1962	John H. Glenn, Jr.
1962	Stanley M. Isaacs
1963	Laurance S. Rockefeller
1964	Louis K. Diamond
1964	Gilbert H. Grosvenor
1964	Harry L. Shapiro
1965	Richard K. Mellon
1965	Robert D. Murphy
1965	Conrad L. Wirth
1966	Wallace K. Harrison
1966	Henry Viscardi, Jr.

1967	Arthur Kantrowitz	1980	Dolores Milmoe
1967	William B. Walsh	1981	Alan Magee
1967	Roy Wilkins	1982	Terry Winters
1973	Leonard W. Hall	1983	Joanne Lowenthal
1977	Ethel Roosevelt Derby	1984	James Brown
1983	Edward L. Beach	1985	David Kapp
1983	Philip H. Habib	1986	Richard Ryan
1983	Harold Schafer		
1983	Sheila Schafer		
1985	Norman Vincent Peale		
1985	Charles E. Yeager		

Richard and Hinda Rosenthal Foundation Awards

(I: Administered by the National Institute of Arts and Letters and presented to the author of a novel published during the preceding 12 months that is judged to be a considerable literary achievement.)

1957	Elizabeth Spencer
1958	Bernard Malamud
1959	Frederick Buechner
1960	John Updike
1961	John H. Knowles
1962	Paule Marshall
1963	William M. Kelley
1964	Ivan Gold
1965	Thomas Berger
1966	Tom Cole
1967	Thomas Pynchon
1968	Joyce Carol Oates
1969	Frederick Exley
1970	Jonathan Strong
1971	Christopher Brookhouse
1972	Thomas McGuane
1973	Thomas Rogers
1974	Alice Walker
1975	William Gaddis
1976	Richard Yates
1977	Spencer Holst
1978	Douglas Day
1979	Diane Johnson
1980	Stanley Elkin
1981	Richard Charyn
1982	Marilynne Robinson
1983	A. G. Majtabai
1984	Danny Santiago
1985	Janet Kauffman
1986	Richard Powers

(II: Administered by the National Institute of Arts and Letters and presented to a young American painter of distinction.)

1960	Ann Steinbrocker
1961	Zubel Kachadoorian
1962	Robert Andrew Parker
1963	Karen Arden
1964	Gregory Gillespie
1965	Marcia Marcus
1966	Howard Hack
1967	Robert D'Arista
1968	Elizabeth Osborn
1969	Nicholas Sperakis
1970	George Schneeman
1971	Donald Perlis
1972	Barkley L. Hendricks
1973	Jim Sullivan
1974	Julie Curtis Reed
1975	Richard Merkin
1976	Carl Nicholas Titolo
1977	Sigrid Burton
1978	Clifford Ross
1979	Nicholas Issak

Rumford Prize

(Awarded by the American Academy of Arts and Sciences to recognize important discoveries or useful improvements in the fields of heat or light.)

1839	Robert Hare
1862	John Ericsson
1865	Daniel Treadwell
1866	Alvan Clark
1869	George H. Corliss
1871	Joseph Harrison, Jr.
1873	Lewis M. Rutherfurd
1875	John W. Draper
1880	Josiah W. Gibbs
1883	Henry A. Rowland
1886	Samuel P. Langley
1888	Albert A. Michelson
1891	Edward C. Pickering
1895	Thomas A. Edison
1898	James E. Keeler
1899	Charles F. Brush
1900	Carl Barus
1901	Elihu Thomson
1902	George E. Hale
1904	Ernest F. Nichols
1907	Edward G. Acheson
1909	Robert W. Wood
1910	Charles G. Curtis
1911	James M. Crafts
1912	Frederic E. Ives
1913	Joel Stebbins
1914	William D. Coolidge
1915	Charles G. Abbot
1917	Percy W. Bridgman
1918	Theodore Lyman
1920	Irving Langmuir
1925	Henry N. Russell
1926	Arthur H. Compton
1928	Edward L. Nichols
1931	Karl T. Compton
1933	Harlow Shapley
1937	William W. Coblentz
1939	George R. Harrison
1941	Vladimir K. Zworykin
1943	C. E. Kenneth Mees
1945	Edwin H. Land
1947	Edmund N. Harvey
1949	Ira S. Bowen
1951	Herbert E. Ives
1953	Enrico Fermi
1953	Willis E. Lamb, Jr.
1953	Lars Onsager
1955	James Franck
1957	Subrahmanyan Chandrasekhar
1959	George Wald
1961	Charles H. Townes
1963	Hans A. Bethe
1965	Samuel C. Collins
1965	William D. McElroy
1967	Robert H. Dicke
1967	Cornelis B. Van Niel
1968	Maarten Schmidt
1971	*MIT Group*
	John A. Ball
	Alan H. Barrett
	Bernard F. Burke
	Joseph C. Carter

	Patricia P. Crowther
	James M. Moran, Jr.
	Alan E. E. Rogers
	Canadian Group
	Norman W. Broten
	R. M. Chisholm
	John A. Galt
	Herbert P. Gush
	Thomas H. Legg
	John L. Locke
	Charles W. McLeish
	Roger S. Richards
	Jui Lin Yen
	NRAO-Cornell Group
	C. C. Baret
	Barry G. Clark
	Marshall H. Cohen
	David L. Jauncey
	Kenneth I. Kellermann
1973	E. Bright Wilson
1976	Bruno Rossi
1980	Robert L. Mills
1980	Gregorio Weber
1980	Chen Ning Yang
1985	Hans Georg Dehmelt
1985	Martin Deutsch
1985	Vernon Willard Hughes
1985	Norman Foster Ramsey
1986	Robert B. Leighton
1986	Frank J. Low
1986	Gerry Neugebauer

Saltus Gold Medal for Merit

(Awarded by the National Academy of Design to recognize outstanding achievement in painting or sculpture.)

1908	Edmund C. Tarbell
1909	George de F. Brush
1910	Douglas Volk
1911	John C. Johansen
1912	Bruce Crane
1913	Gardner Symons
1914	Cecilia Beaux
1915	Abbott H. Thayer
1916	Emil Carlsen
1917	Charles S. Chapman
1918	Joseph T. Pearson, Jr.
1919	Malcolm Parcell
1920	Anna V. Hyatt
1921	Charles H. Davis
1922	Anna V. Hyatt
1923	Eugene F. Savage
1924	Laura G. Fraser
1925	John E. Costigan
1926	Attilio Piccirilli
1927	Edward W. Redfield
1928	Laura G. Fraser
1929	Carl Rungius
1930	Ernest Lawson
1931	Louis Betts
1933	Ruth Nickerson
1934	Harry W. Watrous
1935	Childe Hassam
1936	Jonas Lie
1937	Arthur Lee
1938	Jonas Lie
1940	Charles S. Chapman
1941	Robert Brackman
1942	C. Paul Jennewein
1943	Kenneth H. Miller
1944	Jon Corbino
1945	Stanley Crane
1946	Adlai S. Hardin
1947	Jean de Marco
1948	Gifford Beal

1949	Ben Stahl
1950	Alexander Brook
1951	Charles Hopkinson
1952	Karl H. Gruppe
1953	Hobson Pittman
1954	Everett G. Du Pen
1955	Stephen Etnier
1956	Andrew Winter
1957	Raphael Soyer
1958	Lenard Kester
1959	Umberto Romano
1960	Katharine L. Weems
1961	Aaron Bohrod
1962	John Koch
1963	Paul Manship
1964	Antonio P. Martino
1965	Alan Price
1966	Leon Kroll
1967	Joseph Floch
1968	George Bobritzky
1969	Chen Chi
1970	Gertrude K. Lathrop
1971	Joseph Solman
1972	Gregory Gillespie
1973	George L. K. Morris
1974	Bruno Lucchesi
1975	Ben Kamihira
1976	Avel de Knight
1977	Robert Gwathmey
1980	Eric Isenburger
1982	Jane Piper
1983	Stephen Greene
1984	Len C. Everett
1986	Wolf Kahn

Margaret Sanger Award

(Presented annually by Planned Parenthood - World Population to honor distinguished service in promoting the course of family planning and in advancing social justice.)

1966	William H. Draper, Jr.
1966	Carl G. Hartman
1966	Martin Luther King, Jr.
1966	Lyndon B. Johnson
1967	John D. Rockefeller, III
1968	Ernest Gruening
1970	Joseph Tidings
1971	Louis Hellman
1972	Alan F. Guttmacher
1973	Sarah Lewit
1973	Christopher Tietze
1974	Harriet F. Pilpel
1975	Cass Canfield
1976	John Rock
1977	Bernard Berelson
1978	Julia Henderson
1978	Frederick Jaffee
1978	Edris Rice-Wray
1979	Alfred Moran
1979	Robert Packwood
1980	Mary Calderone
1980	Sarah Weddington
1981	William G. Milliken
1982	Jihan Sadat
1983	Katharine Hepburn
1984	Paul Moore, Jr.
1985	Guadalupe de la Vega
1985	Mechai Viravaidya
1986	Jeannie I. Rosoff

William Lawrence Saunders Gold Medal

(Awarded annually by the American Institute of Mining, Metallurgical, and Petroleum Engineers to recognize achievement in the mining of metals, coal, and other nonmetallic minerals.)

1927 David W. Brunton
1928 Herbert Hoover
1929 John Hays Hammond
1930 Daniel C. Jackling
1931 Francis W. Maclennan
1932 F. W. Bradley
1933 Walter H. Aldridge
1934 Pope Yeatman
1935 James MacNaughton
1936 Clinton H. Crane
1937 Erskine Ramsay
1939 Louis S. Cates
1941 Herman C. Bellinger
1944 George B. Harrington
1946 Fred Searls, Jr.
1947 LeRoy Salsich
1949 Stanly A. Easton
1950 Howard N. Eavenson
1951 Clyde E. Weed
1954 Simeon S. Clarke
1956 Louis Buchman
1958 W. J. Coulter
1959 John B. Knaebel
1960 Robert J. Linney
1961 Marcus D. Banghart
1962 Joseph H. Reid
1963 Edward I. Renouard
1964 Walter C. Lawson
1965 Francis Cameron
1966 Wesley P. Goss
1967 Ralph D. Parker
1968 Charles M. Brinckerhoff
1970 Elmer A. Jones
1972 Stanley M. Jarrett
1974 H. Myles Jacob
1975 Charles Dixon Clarke
1976 Frank Coolbaugh

Sedgwick Memorial Medal

(Awarded annually by the American Public Health Association to honor distinguished service over a long period of time in areas of special interest to the association.)

1929 Charles V. Chapin
1930 Theobald Smith
1931 George W. McCoy
1932 William H. Park
1933 Milton J. Rosenau
1934 Edwin O. Jordan
1935 Haven Emerson
1936 Frederick F. Russell
1938 Wade H. Frost
1939 Thomas Parran
1940 Hans Zinsser
1941 Charles Armstrong
1942 Charles Edward Winslow
1943 James S. Simmons
1944 Ernest W. Goodpasture
1946 Karl F. Meyer
1947 Reginald M. Atwater
1948 Abel Wolman
1949 Henry F. Vaughan
1950 Rolla E. Dyer
1951 Edward S. Godfrey, Jr.

1952 Kenneth F. Maxcy
1953 Carl E. Buck
1954 Wilson G. Smillie
1955 Albert J. Chesley
1956 Frederick W. Jackson
1957 Lowell J. Reed
1958 Martha M. Eliot
1959 Louis I. Dublin
1960 Fred T. Foard
1961 Frank G. Boudreau
1962 Ira V. Hiscock
1963 Gaylord W. Anderson
1964 Leona Baumgartner
1965 Willimina R. Walsh
1966 Fred L. Soper
1967 George Baehr
1968 Herman E. Hilleboe
1969 Marion W. Sheahan
1970 Hugh R. Leavell
1971 Margaret G. Arnstein
1972 Paul B. Cornely
1973 Isidore S. Falk
1974 Myron E. Wegman
1975 Leroy E. Burney
1976 Malcolm H. Merrill
1977 Lester Breslow
1978 M. Allen Pond
1979 Doris E. Roberts
1980 Lorin E. Kerr
1981 Dwight F. Metzler
1982 C. Rufus Rorem
1983 Milton I. Roemer
1984 Milton Terris
1985 Henrik L. Blum
1986 C. Arden Miller

Shelley Memorial Award

(Presented annually by the Poetry Society of America to a living American poet selected on the basis of genius and need.)

1929 Conrad Aiken
1930 Lizette W. Reese
1931 Archibald MacLeish
1932 Stephen Vincent Benet
1933 Lola Ridge
1933 Frances Frost
1934 Lola Ridge
1934 Marya Zaturenska
1935 Josephine Miles
1936 Charlotte Wilder
1936 Ben Belitt
1937 Lincoln Fitzel
1938 Robert Francis
1938 Harry Brown
1939 Herbert Bruncken
1939 Winfield T. Scott
1940 Marianne Moore
1941 Ridgely Torrence
1942 Robert Penn Warren
1942 Percy MacKaye
1943 Edgar Lee Masters
1944 E. E. Cummings
1945 Karl Shapiro
1946 Rolfe Humphries
1947 Janet Lewis
1948 John Berryman
1949 Louis Kent
1950 Jeremy Ingalls
1951 Richard Eberhart
1952 Elizabeth Bishop
1953 Kenneth Patchen
1954 Leonie Adams
1955 Robert Fitzgerald
1956 George Abbe
1957 Kenneth Rexroth
1958 Jose Garcia Villa

1959 Delmore Schwartz
1960 Robinson Jeffers
1961 Theodore Roethke
1962 Eric Barker
1963 William Stafford
1964 Ruth Stone
1965 David Ignatow
1966 Anne Sexton
1967 May Swenson
1968 Ann Stanford
1969 X. J. Kennedy
1969 Mary Oliver
1971 Louise Townsend Nicholl
1971 Adrienne Rich
1972 Galway Kinnell
1973 John Ashbery
1973 Richard Wilbur
1974 W. S. Merwin
1975 Edward Field
1976 Gwendolyn Brooks
1977 Muriel Rukeyser
1978 Jane Cooper
1978 William Everson
1979 Hayden Carruth
1980 Julia Randall
1981 Robert Creeley
1982 Alan Dugan
1983 Leo Connellan
1984 Robert Duncan
1984 Denise Levertov
1985 Etheridge Kent

Elmer A. Sperry Award

(An award presented under the joint sponsorship of several engineering societies in recognition of a distinguished engineering contribution which has advanced the art of transportation.)

1955 William F. Gibbs
1956 Donald W. Douglas
1957 Harold L. Hamilton
1957 Richard M. Dilworth
1957 Eugene W. Kettering
1960 Frederick D. Braddon
1961 Robert G. Letourneau
1962 Lloyd J. Hibbard
1963 Earl A. Thompson
1964 Igor I. Sikorsky
1964 Michael E. Gluhareff
1965 Maynard L. Pennell
1965 Richard L. Rouzie
1965 John E. Steiner
1965 William H. Cook
1965 Richards L. Loesch, Jr.
1967 Edward R. Dye
1967 Hugh DeHaven
1967 Robert A. Wolf
1969 Douglas C. MacMillan
1969 M. Nielsen
1969 Edward L. Teale, Jr.
1970 Charles Stark Draper
1971 George W. Baughman
1971 Sedwig N. Wight
1972 Leonard S. Hobb
1972 Perry W. Pratt
1975 Jerome L. Goldman
1975 James J. Henry
1975 Frank A. Nemec
1977 Clifford L. Eastberg
1977 Hanley Unbach
1978 Roberts Puiseup
1979 Leslie J. Clark
1980 W. M. Allen
1980 Malcolm Stamper
1980 Joseph Sutter
1980 Everette Webb

1981 Edward J. Wasp

Spingarn Medal

(Awarded annually by the National Association for the Advancement of Colored People to recognize the highest achievement by an American Negro in the many fields of human endeavor.)

1915 Ernest E. Just
1916 Charles Young
1917 Harry T. Burleigh
1918 William S. Braithwaite
1919 Archibald H. Grimke
1920 William E. B. DuBois
1921 Charles S. Gilpin
1922 Mary B. Talbert
1923 George Washington Carver
1924 Roland Hayes
1925 James Weldon Johnson
1926 Carter G. Woodson
1927 Anthony Overton
1928 Charles W. Chesnutt
1929 Mordecai W. Johnson
1930 Henry A. Hunt
1931 Richard B. Harrison
1932 Robert R. Moton
1933 Max Yergan
1934 William T. B. Williams
1935 Mary McLeod Bethune
1936 John Hope
1937 Walter White
1939 Marian Anderson
1940 Louis T. Wright
1941 Richard Wright
1942 A. Philip Randolph
1943 William H. Hastie
1944 Charles R. Drew
1945 Paul Robeson
1946 Thurgood Marshall
1947 Percy L. Julian
1948 Channing H. Tobias
1949 Ralph J. Bunche
1950 Charles H. Houston
1951 Mabel Keaton Staupers
1952 Harry T. Moore
1953 Paul R. Williams
1954 Theodore K. Lawless
1955 Carl Murphy
1956 Jack R. Robinson
1957 Martin Luther King, Jr.
1958 Daisy Bates
1959 Edward (Duke) Ellington
1960 Langston Hughes
1961 Kenneth B. Clark
1962 Robert C. Weaver
1963 Medgar W. Evers
1964 Roy Wilkins
1965 Leontyne Price
1966 John H. Johnson
1967 Edward W. Brooke
1968 Sammy Davis, Jr.
1969 Clarence M. Mitchell, Jr.
1970 Jacob Lawrence
1971 Leon H. Sullivan
1972 Gordon Parks
1973 Wilson C. Riles
1974 Damon J. Keith
1975 Henry Aaron
1976 Alvin Ailey
1977 Alex Haley
1978 Andrew M. Young
1979 Rosa L. Parks
1980 Rayford W. Logan
1981 Coleman Young
1982 Benjamin E. Mays

1983	Lena Horne	1961	Mark L. Ireland, Jr.
1984	Thomas Bradley	1962	Charles D. Wheelock
1985	Bill Cosby	1963	Arthur R. Gatewood
1986	Benjamin L. Hooks	1964	Henry A. Schade

Spirit of St. Louis Medal

(Awarded from time to time by the American Society of Mechanical Engineers to recognize meritorious service in the advancement of aeronautics.)

1929	Daniel Guggenheim
1932	Paul Litchfield
1935	Will Rogers
1938	James H. Doolittle
1941	John E. Younger
1944	George W. Lewis
1947	John K. Northrop
1950	Reinout P. Kroon
1954	Arthur E. Raymond
1955	Ralph S. Damon
1958	George S. Schairer
1961	Samuel K. Hoffman
1962	Robert H. Widmer
1963	Frederick C. Crawford
1964	Robert R. Gilruth
1965	William H. Pickering
1966	Christopher C. Craft
1967	Ira G. Hedrick
1968	George S. Moore
1969	G. Merritt Preston
1970	Clarence L. Johnson
1971	Ralph L. Creel
1972	Neil A. Armstrong
1973	John F. Yardley
1974	Abe Silverstein
1977	George D. McLean
1978	Paul B. MacCready
1979	Freddie Laker
1980	Michael Collins
1981	Edgar M. Cortright, Jr.
1982	Frank N. Piasecki
1983	John W. Young
1984	Charles S. Draper
1985	Kurt H. Hohenemser
1986	Bruce McCandless, II

David W. Taylor Medal

(Awarded by the Society of Naval Architects and Marine Engineers for notable achievement in the areas of special interest to the society.)

1936	David W. Taylor
1938	William L. Emmett
1939	Hugo P. Frear
1940	John F. Metten
1942	Samuel M. Robinson
1943	William Hovgaard
1945	Edward L. Cochrane
1946	William F. Gibbs
1947	David Arnott
1948	Earle W. Mills
1949	George G. Sharp
1950	Harold E. Saunders
1951	C. Richard Waller
1953	John E. Burkhardt
1954	Edwin L. Stewart
1955	Kenneth S. M. Davidson
1956	Andrew I. McKee
1957	David P. Brown
1958	John C. Niedermair
1959	Olin J. Stephens
1960	Glenn B. Warren

1965	John P. Comstock
1966	Richard B. Couch
1967	Wilson D. Leggett, Jr.
1968	Matthew G. Forrest
1969	Douglas C. MacMillan
1970	Ludwig C. Hoffman
1971	Phillip Eisenberg
1972	John R. Kane
1973	Jerome L. Goldman
1974	Roger E. M. Brard
1975	James B. Robertson, Jr.
1976	Harry Benford
1977	James J. Henry
1978	John J. Nachtsheim
1979	Philip F. Spaulding
1980	Peter M. Palermo
1981	Erwin Carl Rohde
1982	Jacques B. Hadler
1983	Jens T. Holm
1984	Jan Dirk Van Manen
1985	J. Randolph Paulling, Jr.
1986	Robert N. Herbert

Marjorie Peabody Waite Award

(Presented annually by the National Institute of Arts and Letters to an older person for continuing achievement and integrity in his art and given in rotation to an artist, a composer, and a writer; discontinued in 1985.)

1956	Fred Nagler
1957	Theodore Ward Chanler
1958	Dorothy Parker
1959	Leon Hartl
1960	Louise Talma
1961	Edward McSorley
1962	Abraham Walkowitz
1963	Richard Donovan
1964	Dawn Powell
1965	Paul Burlin
1966	Harry Partch
1967	Stringfellow Barr
1968	Abraham Harriton
1969	Herbert Elwell
1970	Ramon Guthrie
1971	Ben Benn
1972	Vittorio Rieti
1973	A. Hyatt Mayor
1974	Ray Prohaska
1975	Leo Ornstein
1976	Rene Wellek
1977	Kenzo Okada
1978	Dane Rudhyar
1979	James Still
1980	Sidney Laufman
1981	Normand Lockwood
1982	Edouard Roditi
1983	Giorgio Cavallon
1984	Herman Berlinski

John Price Wetherill Medal

(Awarded by the Franklin Institute for discovery or invention in the physical sciences or for new and important combinations of principles or methods already known.)

1926	Frank Twyman
1927	Carl Akeley
1928	Albert S. Howell
1928	Frank E. Ross
1929	Gustave Fast
1929	William H. Mason
1930	Charles S. Chrisman
1930	William N. Jennings
1931	Thomas T. Gray
1931	Arthur J. Mason
1931	Henry M. Sutton
1931	Walter L. Steele
1931	Edwin G. Steele
1931	Edward C. Wente
1932	Halvor O. Hem
1932	Frank Wenner
1933	Henry S. Hulbert
1933	Francis C. McMath
1933	Robert R. McMath
1934	E. Newton Harvey
1934	Alfred L. Loomis
1935	Francis F. Lucas
1935	Robert Naumberg
1935	James E. Shrader
1935	Louis B. Tuckerman
1935	Henry E. Warren
1936	Albert L. Marsh
1939	William A. Hyde
1940	Laurens Hammond
1940	Edward E. Kleinschmidt
1940	Howard L. Krum
1941	Harold S. Black
1943	Robert H. Leach
1944	Willem F. Westendorp
1944	Richard C. du Pont
1946	Lewis A. Rodert
1947	Kenneth S. M. Davidson
1948	Wendell F. Hess
1949	Edgar C. Bain
1949	Thomas L. Fawick
1949	Harlan D. Fowler
1950	Kenneth C. D. Hickman
1950	Donald W. Kerst
1950	Russell H. Varian
1950	Sigurd F. Varian
1951	Samuel C. Collins
1951	Reid B. Gray
1951	Gaylord W. Penney
1952	Harrison P. Hood
1952	Martin E. Nordberg
1952	Albert J. Williams, Jr.
1953	Robert H. Dalton
1953	S. Donald Stookey
1954	William D. Buckingham
1954	Clarence N. Hickman
1954	Edwin T. Lorig
1955	Rene A. Higonnet
1955	Louis M. Moyroud
1957	Warren W. Carpenter
1959	Robert B. Aitchison
1959	Clarence Zener
1960	Walter Juda
1960	Victor Vacquier
1961	Albert E. Hitchcock
1961	Percy W. Zimmerman
1962	S. Donald Stookey
1962	Chien-Shiung Wu
1962	Ernest Ambler
1962	Raymond W. Hayward
1962	Dale D. Hoppes

1962	Ralph P. Hudson
1963	Daryl M. Chapin
1963	Calvin S. Fuller
1963	Gerald L. Pearson
1964	Howard H. Aiken
1964	Bernd T. Matthias
1964	John K. Hulm
1964	John E. Kunzler
1965	Wendell F. Moore
1965	John H. Reynolds
1965	Frederick D. Rossini
1965	Eugene Merle Shoemaker
1965	Edward Ching-Te Chao
1965	Fred N. Spiess
1966	Howard G. Rogers
1967	Ernest O. Wollan
1968	Nathan Cohn
1969	George R. Cowan
1969	John J. Douglass
1969	Arnold H. Holtzman
1970	Paul D. Bartlett
1972	Otto H. Schmitt
1973	A. R. Howell
1974	Aage N. Bohr
1974	Ben Roy Mottelson
1975	Donald N. Langenberg
1975	William H. Parker
1975	Barry N. Taylor
1976	Herbert Blades
1976	James W. Cronin
1976	Val L. Fitch
1978	William Klemperer
1979	Elias Burstein
1980	Ralph A. Alpher
1980	Robert Herman
1981	Frank F. Fang
1981	Alan B. Fowler
1981	Webster E. Howard
1981	Frank Stern
1981	Philip J. Stiles
1982	Lawrence A. Harris
1983	Eugene Garfield
1985	Lynn A. Conway

Woodrow Wilson Award

(Awarded annually by Princeton University to an outstanding alumnus.)

1957	Norman Armour
1958	Allen O. Whipple
1959	Charles L. House
1960	Bayard Dodge
1961	Raymond B. Fosdick
1962	C. Tyler Wood
1963	Adlai E. Stevenson
1964	Henry D. Smyth
1965	Nicholas deB. Katzenbach
1966	William F. Ballard
1967	Eugene Carson Blake
1968	James H. Cleveland
1969	Walsh McDermott
1970	John B. Oakes
1971	George B. Schultz
1972	Ralph Nader
1973	John D. Rockefeller, III
1974	Claiborne Pell
1975	John Doar
1976	George F. Kennan
1977	Thomas Hoving
1978	Henry R. Labouisse
1980	Paul A. Volcker
1981	Lewis Thomas
1982	John McPhee
1983	James A. Baker, III
1984	William D. Ruckelshaus
1985	Donald Rumsfeld

1986 William H. Hudnut

Wright Brothers Memorial Trophy

(Awarded annually by the National Aeronautic Association to honor public service of enduring value to aviation in the United States.)

1948 William F. Durand

1949 Charles A. Lindbergh
1950 Grover Loening
1951 Jerome C. Hunsaker
1952 James H. Doolittle
1953 Carl Hinshaw
1954 Theodore Von Karman
1955 Hugh L. Dryden
1956 Edward P. Warher
1957 Stuart Symington
1958 John F. Victory
1959 William P. MacCracken, Jr.
1960 Frederick C. Crawford

1961 A. S. Mike Monroney
1962 John Stack
1963 Donald W. Douglas
1964 Harry F. Guggenheim
1965 Jerome F. Lederer
1966 Juan T. Trippe
1967 Igor I. Sikorsky
1968 Warren G. Magnuson
1969 William M. Allen
1970 C. R. Smith
1971 Howard W. Cannon
1972 John H. Shaffer
1973 Barry M. Goldwater

1974 Richard T. Whitcomb
1975 Clarance C. Johnson
1976 William Allen Patterson
1977 Ira C. Aker
1978 Jennings Randolph
1979 T. A. Wilson
1980 Olive Ann Beech
1981 Dwane L. Wallace
1982 Willis Hawkins
1983 John Leland Atwood
1984 David S. Lewis
1985 Harry Combs
1986 Joseph F. Sutter

Indexes

Personal Name Index

Allen, Leo E. *194, 197, 200, 204, 207, 210, 213, 217, 220, 223, 226, 229, 232, 236*
Allen, Lew, Jr. *346, 381*
Allen, Louis G. *491*
Allen, Nathaniel *58*
Allen, O. H. *386*
Allen, Orlando *393*
Allen, Oscar K. *299*
Allen, Philip *89, 90, 92, 310*
Allen, Raymond B. *423*
Allen, Rex W. *514*
Allen, Richard *477*
Allen, Richard J. *345*
Allen, Robert *58, 60, 62, 63, 65, 67, 68*
Allen, Robert E. L. *180*
Allen, Robert G. *202, 205*
Allen, Robert H. *331*
Allen, Robert Porter *535, 536*
Allen, Roderick R. *343*
Allen, Roger *307*
Allen, Samuel *5*
Allen, Samuel C. *56, 58, 59, 61, 62, 64*
Allen, Stephen *393*
Allen, Terry *341, 343*
Allen, Thomas *118, 398*
Allen, W. M. *561*
Allen, Waldo M. *523*
Allen, William *70, 73, 75, 77, 79, 81, 82, 94, 96, 307, 308, 395, 404*
Allen, William A. *483*
Allen, William F. *200*
Allen, William H. *414, 496, 511, 512*
Allen, William J. *95, 97*
Allen, William M. *483, 537, 563*
Allen, William McPherson *540*
Allen, William S. *416*
Allen, William V. *134, 136, 139, 142, 145, 303*
Allen, Willis *85, 87*
Allerton, Isaac *1*
Allerton, John *1*
Alley, John B. *94, 96, 98, 100*
Allgood, Miles C. *177, 180, 184, 187, 190, 193*
Allin, J. Maury *459*
Allin, John M. *455*
Alling, Paul H. *367, 369, 374*
Allinson, Francis G. *517*
Allison, Archie *399*
Allison, C. FitzSimons *457, 461*
Allison, James, Jr. *61, 63*
Allison, James B. *332*
Allison, John *86, 90*
Allison, John M. *359, 364, 365*
Allison, Robert *68*
Allison, William B. *97, 99, 101, 104, 108, 110, 113, 115, 118, 120, 122, 125, 127, 130, 133, 136, 138, 141, 144, 147, 150, 153, 297*
Allman, David B. *515*
Allmendinger, Paul F. *520*
Allott, Gordon L. *229, 232, 235, 239, 242, 245, 248, 251, 255, 293*
Allport, Gordon W. *518*
Allport, William W. *512*
Allred, James V. *312*
Allston, Robert F. W. *310*
Allyn, Robert *416*
Allyn, Stanley C. *433, 493*
Allyn, Timothy M. *386*
Almand, Bond *296*

Almon, Edward B. *165, 168, 171, 174, 177, 181, 184, 187, 190, 193*
Almond, Edward M. *343, 344, 351*
Almond, Gabriel A. *518*
Almond, J. Lindsay, Jr. *216, 219, 286, 287, 313*
Alonso, Braulio *525*
Alpers, Bernard J. *516*
Alpher, Ralph A. *562*
Alpine, John R. *505*
Alschuler, Samuel *285*
Alsop, John *4*
Alsop, John T. *385*
Alsop, John T., Jr. *387*
Alstadt, William R. *512*
Alston, Charles *536*
Alston, Joseph *310*
Alston, Lemuel J. *50, 52*
Alston, Philip H., Jr. *355, 368*
Alston, William J. *83*
Alston, Willis *46, 47, 48, 49, 50, 51, 52, 54, 63, 65, 66*
Alter, Chester M. *419*
Alter, Karl J. *464, 469*
Alter, Wilbur M. *293*
Altgeld, John P. *296*
Althoff, Henry *466*
Altimari, Frank X. *284*
Altmann, William *438*
Altmeyer, Arthur J. *382*
Alton, Ralph T. *472*
Alvarez, Luis W. *517, 537, 538, 548, 550*
Alvey, Richard H. *300*
Alvord, Henry E. *414*
Alvord, William *386*
Amadon, Dean *516*
Amat, Thaddeus *465*
Amateis, Edmond *526*
Ambler, Ernest *562*
Ambler, Gordon B. *398*
Ambler, Jacob A. *105, 107*
Ambro, Jerome A., Jr. *262, 266, 269*
Ambrose, Myles J. *382*
Amdahl, Douglas K. *302*
Amerman, A. E. *397*
Amerman, Lemuel *131*
Amerman, Ralph A. *523*
Ames, A. A. *391*
Ames, Adelbert *104, 106, 109, 302, 339*
Ames, Butler *147, 150, 153, 156, 159*
Ames, Charles B. *497, 516*
Ames, Edward R. *471*
Ames, Eli B. *391*
Ames, Elizabeth *547*
Ames, Fisher *41, 42, 43*
Ames, Jesse H. *424*
Ames, Joseph S. *517*
Ames, Jospeh S. *410*
Ames, Leon *505*
Ames, Louis A. *526*
Ames, Oakes *98, 100, 102, 104, 106*
Ames, Oliver *300, 498*
Ames, Samuel *310*
Ames, Winslow *437*
Amlie, Thomas R. *193, 200, 203*
Ammann, Othmar H. *548*
Ammen, Daniel *349*
Ammerman, Joseph S. *266*
Ammons, A. R. *534, 545*
Ammons, Edsel A. *472*
Ammons, Elias M. *293*
Ammons, Teller *293*
Amstutz, Hobart B. *471*

Amyx, Jay S. *388*
Anastos, Rosemary (Park) *404*
Anaya, Toney *306*
Ancona, Sydenham E. *97, 98, 100*
Andeen, G. Kenneth *426*
Anders, Thomas J. *314*
Anders, William A. *369, 381, 537, 541*
Andersen, Dorothy *534*
Andersen, Elmer L. *301*
Andersen, H. Carl *204, 208, 211, 214, 217, 221, 224, 227, 230, 233, 236, 240*
Anderson, Carl D. *549*
Anderson, Philip W. *550*
Anderson, A. Scott *398*
Anderson, Albert B. *285*
Anderson, Albert R. *125*
Anderson, Alexander *75, 312, 396*
Anderson, Alexander E. *342*
Anderson, Alexander J. *423*
Anderson, Andrew *396*
Anderson, Archibald B. *405*
Anderson, Betty *547*
Anderson, C. Arthur *201, 204*
Anderson, C. Elmer *301*
Anderson, Carl C. *157, 160*
Anderson, Carl D. *537*
Anderson, Chapman L. *125, 128*
Anderson, Charles A. *417, 527*
Anderson, Charles M. *124*
Anderson, Charles P. *449, 458*
Anderson, Clifford *321*
Anderson, Clinton P. *30, 36, 208, 211, 215, 221, 224, 227, 230, 234, 237, 240, 243, 247, 250, 253, 256, 306, 527*
Anderson, Craig B. *461*
Anderson, Craig Berry *457*
Anderson, Dave *558*
Anderson, David *376*
Anderson, Douglas S. *417*
Anderson, Edgar *521*
Anderson, Edward C. *526*
Anderson, Edward V. *489*
Anderson, Edwin H. *515*
Anderson, Eileen *388*
Anderson, Eleanor *433*
Anderson, Emmett T. *521*
Anderson, Ernfred *437*
Anderson, Eugenie *357, 360*
Anderson, Forrest H. *303*
Anderson, Galusha *407*
Anderson, Gaylord W. *518, 561*
Anderson, George A. *125, 494*
Anderson, George A. M. *340*
Anderson, George W. *100, 102, 284*
Anderson, George W., Jr. *347, 348, 370, 542*
Anderson, Glenn M. *251, 255, 258, 261, 264, 267, 270, 273, 276*
Anderson, H. Ray *473*
Anderson, Herbert *538*
Anderson, Hugh H. *299*
Anderson, Hugh J. *72, 74*
Anderson, Hugo A. *533*
Anderson, Hurst M. *403, 409*
Anderson, Ira D. *515*
Anderson, Isaac *48, 49*
Anderson, J. Blaine *286*
Anderson, J. Lowrie *474*
Anderson, J. Macfie *396*
Anderson, J. Patton *319, 323, 324*
Anderson, Jack *557*
Anderson, Jerry M. *404*
Anderson, Jesse *417*

Anderson, John *62, 64, 66, 67*
Anderson, John, Jr. *297*
Anderson, John A. *115, 118, 120, 122, 125, 127, 411, 551*
Anderson, John B. *239, 242, 245, 249, 252, 255, 258, 261, 264, 268, 341, 343*
Anderson, John C. *291*
Anderson, John E. *518*
Anderson, John F. *518*
Anderson, John Z. *203, 206, 210, 213, 216, 219, 223*
Anderson, Jonathan W. *341*
Anderson, Joseph *45, 46, 47, 48, 49, 50, 52, 53, 54, 311*
Anderson, Joseph H. *78, 80*
Anderson, Josiah M. *85*
Anderson, Karl *531, 551*
Anderson, L. D. *476*
Anderson, Larz *356*
Anderson, Lenart *531*
Anderson, LeRoy H. *233, 237*
Anderson, Lucien *98*
Anderson, M. D. *431*
Anderson, Marian *548, 552, 561*
Anderson, Martin B. *422*
Anderson, Marvin J. *419*
Anderson, Maxwell *547, 554*
Anderson, O. Kelley *493*
Anderson, Orvil A. *535, 541*
Anderson, Paul F. *467*
Anderson, Paul R. *416*
Anderson, Paul Y. *553*
Anderson, Philip W. *549*
Anderson, Rasmus B. *360*
Anderson, Richard C., Jr. *56, 57, 358*
Anderson, Richard H. *322, 323*
Anderson, Robert *359, 360, 368, 496, 537*
Anderson, Robert B. *30, 34, 327, 548, 552*
Anderson, Robert L., III *285, 286*
Anderson, Robert M. *459*
Anderson, Robert Marshall *456*
Anderson, Robert O. *482, 483, 533*
Anderson, Robert P. *284, 287*
Anderson, Roger E. *486*
Anderson, Ross C. *440*
Anderson, Roy A. *491*
Anderson, S. T. *417*
Anderson, Samuel *65, 406*
Anderson, Samuel E. *346*
Anderson, Sigurd *311*
Anderson, Simeon H. *74*
Anderson, Stephen Hale *286*
Anderson, Sydney *159, 163, 166, 169, 172, 175, 179*
Anderson, Thomas H. *356*
Anderson, Thomas H., Jr. *355, 356*
Anderson, Thomas J. *389*
Anderson, Thomas L. *92, 94*
Anderson, Victor E. *303, 392*
Anderson, W. B. *474*
Anderson, W. F. *404*
Anderson, W. M. *474*
Anderson, W. S. *347*
Anderson, Walker *295*
Anderson, Warren M. *498*
Anderson, Webster *332*
Anderson, Wendell R. *265, 301, 302*
Anderson, William *51, 53, 54, 57, 517*
Anderson, William A. *391, 524*
Anderson, William B. *110*
Anderson, William C. *93, 137, 412, 488*

Anderson, William F. *471*
Anderson, William R. *247, 251, 254, 257*
Anderson, William S. *433, 493*
Andewelt, Roger B. *286*
Andreas, Dwayne O. *482*
Andreas, Lowell W. *482*
Andresen, August H. *182, 185, 188, 191, 198, 201, 204, 208, 211, 214, 217, 221, 224, 227, 230, 233*
Andrew, A. Piatt, Jr. *175, 178, 182, 185, 188, 191, 194, 198*
Andrew, Ike F. *263*
Andrew, James O. *471*
Andrew, John A. *300*
Andrew, John F. *128, 130*
Andrew, Michael A. *276*
Andrew, Samuel *427*
Andrews, Adolphus *349*
Andrews, Avery D. *496*
Andrews, Bert *555*
Andrews, Charles *86, 306*
Andrews, Charles B. *293, 294*
Andrews, Charles M. *513*
Andrews, Charles McLean *547, 554*
Andrews, Charles O. *197, 200, 203, 207, 210, 213, 295*
Andrews, Christopher C. *373*
Andrews, Clayton F. *527*
Andrews, Clement W. *515*
Andrews, Dana *505*
Andrews, Earle T. *519*
Andrews, Edward C., Jr. *423*
Andrews, Edward G. *471*
Andrews, Elisha B. *405, 407, 421*
Andrews, Elizabeth *254*
Andrews, Emmet C. *503*
Andrews, F. M. *330, 340*
Andrews, Frank *393*
Andrews, Frank L. *340*
Andrews, George *254, 330*
Andrews, George R. *84, 367*
Andrews, George W. *210, 213, 216, 219, 222, 226, 229, 232, 235, 238, 242, 245, 248, 251*
Andrews, Glenn *245*
Andrews, Graham H. *394*
Andrews, Henry E. *437*
Andrews, Ike F. *259, 266, 269, 272, 275*
Andrews, Israel W. *412*
Andrews, J. B. *518*
Andrews, John *422*
Andrews, John D. *397*
Andrews, John T. *73*
Andrews, Joseph *390*
Andrews, Landaff W. *74, 76*
Andrews, Lorin *411*
Andrews, Major A. *393*
Andrews, Mark *244, 247, 250, 253, 256, 260, 263, 266, 269, 272, 275, 278, 307*
Andrews, Michael A. *279*
Andrews, Philip *349*
Andrews, R. Carl *398*
Andrews, Reddin *404*
Andrews, Roy Chapman *437, 538, 541*
Andrews, Samuel G. *92*
Andrews, Sherlock J. *77*
Andrews, Stanley *379*
Andrews, T. Coleman *380, 514*
Andrews, Walter G. *192, 195, 198, 202, 205, 208, 211, 215, 218*
Andrews, Walter P. *521*
Andrews, William *397*

Andrews, William E. *136, 172, 176*
Andrews, William N. *172*
Andros, Edmund *5, 6*
Andrus, Cecil D. *31, 36, 296*
Andrus, Clift *330, 341*
Andrus, E. Cowles *513*
Andrus, John E. *151, 154, 157, 160*
Andrus, Reuben *407*
Andujar, John J. *519*
Anfinsen, Christian B. *550*
Anfuso, Victor L. *224, 231, 234, 237, 240*
Angel, Benjamin F. *373*
Angel, William G. *63, 66, 68*
Angell, Homer D. *205, 209, 212, 215, 218, 221, 225, 228*
Angell, James B. *358, 374, 420, 423, 513*
Angell, James R. *427, 431, 518, 522, 548*
Angell, Robert C. *520*
Angellotti, Frank M. *293*
Angier, Nedom L. *387*
Anglin, Margaret *542*
Angoff, Charles *527*
Anheuser, Eberhard *482*
Ankeny, Levi *149, 152, 155, 314*
Annabring, Joseph *470*
Annenberg, Walter H. *362, 431, 539, 553*
Annis, Edward R. *515*
Annunzio, Frank *246, 249, 252, 255, 258, 261, 264, 268, 271, 274, 277*
Ansberry, Timothy T. *154, 157, 160, 163*
Ansel, Martin F. *310*
Anslinger, Harry J. *559*
Ansorge, Martin C. *176*
Anspach, Herbert K. *499*
Anthony, Beryl, Jr. *267, 270, 273, 276*
Anthony, Daniel R., Jr. *153, 156, 159, 162, 165, 168, 172, 175, 178, 181, 184*
Anthony, Earle C. *525*
Anthony, George T. *297*
Anthony, Henry B. *94, 97, 99, 101, 103, 105, 107, 109, 112, 114, 116, 119, 121, 310*
Anthony, Joseph B. *70, 71*
Anthony, Susan B. *540*
Antonelli, Theodore *351*
Antony, Edwin Le Roy *132*
Antoville, S. W. *484*
Apache Attack Helicopter Team, *537*
Aplin, Henry H. *144*
Apodaca, Jerry *306*
Apostol, John C. *390*
Appel, Anthony R. *408*
Appel, Daniel F. *493*
Appel, James Z. *516*
Appel, Kenneth E. *518, 533*
Apperly, Astley *521*
Apple, Henry H. *408*
Apple, Thomas G. *408*
Apple, William S. *516, 559*
Appleby, Stewart H. *182*
Appleby, T. Frank *176*
Applegate, Douglas *266, 269, 272, 275, 278*
Applegate, Irvamae *525*
Appleton, Edward V. *541*
Appleton, Francis H. *439, 526*
Appleton, Janes Means *20*
Appleton, Jesse *404*

Appleton, John *86, 300, 356, 371*
Appleton, John J. *373*
Appleton, Nathan *67, 76*
Appleton, William *86, 88, 96*
Appleton, William H. *416*
Appley, Lawrence A. *515*
Appleyard, Robert *455*
Appleyard, Robert B. *461*
Apsley, Lewis D. *133, 136*
Aquilano, Thomas J. *287*
Aranda, Thomas, Jr. *375*
Arant, Herschel W. *285*
Araskog, Rand V. *490*
Arbib, Robert *536*
Arbona, Guillermo *535*
Arbuckle, Ernest C. *499*
Archambault, George F. *516, 559*
Archbald, Robert W. *284*
Archbold, John D. *487, 491*
Archdale, John *5, 6*
Archdeacon, Susan H., Jr. *526*
Archer, Bill *257, 260*
Archer, Glenn L., Jr. *286*
Archer, John *46, 47, 49*
Archer, Lawrence *386*
Archer, Raymond L. *471*
Archer, Robert S. *519*
Archer, Roy *273*
Archer, S. M. *482*
Archer, Samuel H. *413*
Archer, Stevenson *52, 53, 55, 58, 102, 104, 106, 108, 300*
Archer, William R. *263, 266, 269, 273, 276, 279*
Archer, William S. *59, 60, 62, 63, 65, 67, 68, 70, 77, 79, 81, 314*
Archey, William T. *382*
Arden, Karen *560*
Aregood, Richard *558*
Arends, Leslie C. *197, 200, 204, 207, 210, 213, 217, 220, 223, 226, 229, 232, 236, 239, 242, 246, 249, 252, 255, 258*
Arens, Henry *195*
Arensberg, Ann *546*
Arentz, Samuel S. *176, 182, 185, 188, 192*
Arentzen, Willard P. *347*
Argall, Samuel *6*
Argento, Dominick *557*
Arieti, Silvano *546*
Aring, Charles D. *516*
Ariyoshi, George R. *296*
Arkus, Leon A. *438*
Arlen, Michael J. *546*
Armacost, Michael Hayden *370*
Armacost, Peter H. *475*
Armacost, Samuel H. *483*
Armacost, Wilbur H. *533*
Armenti, Carmen J. *393*
Armey, Richard K. *279*
Armfield, Robert F. *116, 119*
Armistead, W. K. *331*
Armitage, William E. *448, 459*
Armour, Claude A. *396*
Armour, Frank, Jr. *489*
Armour, J. Ogden *482*
Armour, Norman *355, 358, 363, 373, 375, 562*
Armour, Philip D. *482*
Arms, John Taylor *532*
Armsby, George N. *496*
Armstrong, A. H. *392*
Armstrong, Ann Legendre *362*
Armstrong, Anne *548*
Armstrong, Arthur J. *472*
Armstrong, Charles *561*
Armstrong, Charles J. *421*

Armstrong, Charles W. *523*
Armstrong, David H. *113, 303*
Armstrong, Donald *351, 516*
Armstrong, Donald B. *526*
Armstrong, Edward C. *524*
Armstrong, Edwin H. *538, 539, 541*
Armstrong, Francis *397*
Armstrong, Frank C. *323*
Armstrong, George E. *332*
Armstrong, J. Sinclair *381, 526*
Armstrong, James *43*
Armstrong, James F. *473*
Armstrong, James I. *412*
Armstrong, John *4, 14, 23, 34, 46, 47, 48, 306, 335, 505*
Armstrong, Joseph G. *395, 454, 460*
Armstrong, Marshall S. *514*
Armstrong, Neil A. *537, 541, 552, 562*
Armstrong, Orland K. *224*
Armstrong, Robert A. *426*
Armstrong, Robert J. *465*
Armstrong, Samuel T. *390*
Armstrong, Thomas F. *487*
Armstrong, Thomas N. *444*
Armstrong, Walter P. *511*
Armstrong, Warren B. *426*
Armstrong, William *63, 65, 67, 68, 396*
Armstrong, William H. *105*
Armstrong, William L. *258, 261, 264, 267, 270, 273, 277, 293*
Armstrong, William T. *544*
Arn, Edward F. *297*
Arnall, Ellis G. *295*
Arnell, Samuel M. *101, 103, 105*
Arnerich, M. E. *386*
Arnett, Alvin J. *381*
Arnett, Peter *551, 556*
Arnold, Archibald V. *341*
Arnold, B. L. *414*
Arnold, Ben *308*
Arnold, Benedict *6, 66, 335*
Arnold, Bion J. *544*
Arnold, Charles N. *388*
Arnold, Dean Sarah Louise *523*
Arnold, Edward *505*
Arnold, George P. *392*
Arnold, H. Park *523*
Arnold, Henry A. *341*
Arnold, Henry H. *330, 536, 541*
Arnold, Henry J. *386*
Arnold, Isaac N. *95, 97*
Arnold, Jackson D. *349*
Arnold, Jonathan *4*
Arnold, Laurence F. *200, 204, 207*
Arnold, Lemuel H. *81, 310*
Arnold, Leon G. *441*
Arnold, Marshall *131, 133*
Arnold, Morris F. *456*
Arnold, Olney *360*
Arnold, Peleg *4, 310*
Arnold, Remmie L. *527*
Arnold, Richard S. *285*
Arnold, Samuel *91*
Arnold, Samuel G. *97, 310*
Arnold, Samuel W. *211, 214, 217*
Arnold, Thomas *310*
Arnold, Thomas D. *68, 77*
Arnold, Thurman W. *286*
Arnold, Warren O. *126, 129, 137*
Arnold, William C. *137, 140*
Arnold, William H. *334, 342, 343*
Arnold, William R. *331*

Berry, Albert S. *133, 136, 139, 141*
Berry, Burton Y. *364*
Berry, Campbell P. *115, 117*
Berry, Edward W. *523*
Berry, Ellis Y. *225, 228, 231, 234, 238, 241, 244, 247, 250, 254*
Berry, George L. *202, 312*
Berry, Henry C. *524*
Berry, Hiram G. *337*
Berry, James H. *122, 124, 127, 129, 132, 135, 138, 141, 143, 146, 149, 292*
Berry, John *109*
Berry, Joseph F. *471*
Berry, Lampton *358*
Berry, Lucien W. *407*
Berry, Martha *548, 559*
Berry, Nathaniel S. *304*
Berry, Sidney B. *418*
Berry, Theodore M. *394*
Berry, Tom *311*
Berry, William A. *308*
Berry, William W. *499*
Berryman, Clifford K. *554*
Berryman, James T. *555*
Berryman, John *531, 534, 544, 545, 556, 561*
Berthelot, James A. *387*
Bertholf, Ellsworth P. *382*
Bertholf, Lloyd M. *410*
Bertoia, Harry *532*
Bertrand, C. P. *385*
Bertrand, Frederic H. *397, 492*
Bertus, Paul *389*
Beschter, John W. *409*
Beshlin, Earl H. *170*
Besley, Frederic A. *512*
Bess, Elmer A. *412*
Bessey, Charles E. *421, 510*
Best, William R. *437*
Bethe, Hans A. *517, 538, 539, 549, 550, 560*
Bethel, Walter A. *331*
Bethell, W. D. *396*
Bethune, Edwin R., Jr. *267, 270, 273*
Bethune, Lauchlin *68*
Bethune, Marion *103*
Bethune, Mary McLeod *561*
Beto, George *512*
Bettelheim, Bruno *546*
Betton, Silas *48, 49*
Betts, Austin W. *330*
Betts, Edward *531*
Betts, Jackson E. *224, 228, 231, 234, 237, 241, 244, 247, 250, 253, 256*
Betts, Louis *531, 542, 560*
Betts, Rome A. *526*
Betts, Samuel R. *55*
Betts, Thaddeus *74, 294*
Betz, John F. *495*
Beuret, John D. *349*
Beury, Charles E. *416*
Bevan, Arthur D. *515*
Beven, John L. *490*
Beverage, Harold H. *541, 543*
Beveridge, Albert J. *141, 144, 147, 150, 153, 156, 297, 553, 559*
Beveridge, George *556*
Beveridge, John L. *106, 296*
Bevilacqua, Anthony J. *469*
Bevilacqua, Joseph A. *310*
Bevill, Tom *248, 251, 254, 258, 261, 264, 267, 270, 273, 276*
Bevington, James H. *537*
Bevis, A. Sandy *505*
Bevis, Howard L. *414*

Bewkes, Eugene G. *415*
Bewley, Loyal V. *543*
Beyer, Gordon R. *374*
Beyer, Otto S. *380*
Biaggi, Mario *253, 256, 259, 262, 269, 272, 275, 278*
Biaggini, Benjamin F. *496*
Bibb, George M. *24, 25, 33, 52, 53, 65, 67, 69, 298*
Bibb, Thomas *291*
Bibb, Thomas W. *411*
Bibb, William W. *49, 50, 51, 52, 53, 54, 291, 295*
Bibignaus, Thomas M. *86*
Bible, Alan *240, 243, 246, 250, 253, 256, 259*
Bible, Alan H. *227, 230, 233, 237, 304*
Bickett, Thomas W. *307*
Bickley, George H. *471*
Bickmore, Albert S. *437*
Bicknell, Bennett *73*
Bicknell, George A. *113, 115*
Biddle, Anthony J. Drexel, Jr. *356, 359, 362, 368, 369, 370, 373, 376*
Biddle, Charles J. *97*
Biddle, Edward *4*
Biddle, Francis *29, 30, 35, 284*
Biddle, James *391*
Biddle, John *390, 418*
Biddle, Joseph F. *192*
Biddle, Nicholas *442*
Biddle, Richard *73, 75*
Biddle, Thomas *372*
Biddle, William P. *348*
Biddle, William S. *442*
Biden, Joseph R., Jr. *258, 261, 264, 267, 270, 274, 277, 294*
Bidermann, Antoine *487*
Bidgood, Lee *418*
Bidlack, Benjamin A. *79, 358*
Bidlack, Russell *543*
Bidlack, Russell E. *538*
Bidle, William S. *519*
Bidwell, Barnabas *49, 50*
Bidwell, C. H. S. *386*
Bidwell, John *17, 99*
Biebel, Franklin M. *439*
Bieber, Margaret *533*
Bieber, Owen F. *505*
Biebrach, W. L. *386*
Biemiller, Andrew J. *216, 222*
Bieri, Bernard H. *348*
Biermann, Fred *194, 197, 201*
Bierring, Walter L. *515, 533*
Bierwirth, John C. *489*
Bierworth, F. W. *434*
Biery, James S. *109*
Biester, Edward G., Jr. *250, 253, 257, 260, 263*
Bigart, Homer W. *551, 554, 555*
Bigby, John S. *106*
Bigelow, Abijah *51, 52, 53*
Bigelow, Charles *397*
Bigelow, Frederic R. *434*
Bigelow, George H. *511*
Bigelow, George T. *301*
Bigelow, Hardin *386*
Bigelow, Herbert S. *202*
Bigelow, Hobart B. *293*
Bigelow, Horace F. *332*
Bigelow, Jacob *509*
Bigelow, John *361*
Bigelow, John P. *390*
Bigelow, Lewis *59*
Bigger, Samuel *297*
Biggs, Asa *80, 90, 92, 307*
Biggs, Benjamin T. *103, 106, 294*

Biggs, John, Jr. *284, 559*
Biggs, Marion *124, 127*
Biggs, Thomas J. *419*
Biggs, Walter *533*
Bigler, John *292, 358*
Bigler, William *90, 92, 94, 309*
Bigliardi, Matthew P. *456, 460*
Bikel, Theodore *503*
Bilandic, Michael A. *388*
Bilbo, Theodore G. *198, 201, 204, 208, 211, 214, 217, 302*
Bilderback, C. P. *388*
Bilirakis, Michael *274, 277*
Bill, Clarence P. *517*
Billard, Frederick C. *382, 417*
Billard, J. B. *389*
Biller, George, Jr. *450, 461*
Biller, Morris *503*
Billera, I. John *499*
Billinghurst, Charles *93*
Billings, Bruce H. *527*
Billings, Charles E. *520*
Billings, Frank *515*
Billings, Franklin S. *313*
Billings, Franklin S., Jr. *313*
Billings, John S. *515*
Billings, John Shaw *518*
Billings, Marland P. *523*
Billingshurst, Charles *91*
Billingsley, Joseph P. *506*
Billington, John *1*
Billington, Ray Allen *534*
Billman, Howard *418*
Billmeyer, Alexander *145*
Bimeler, Joseph M. *477*
Bimson, Carl A. *511*
Binai, Paul *437*
Binder, Fred H. *391*
Binder, Joseph B. *396*
Binderup, Charles G. *198, 201*
Bindscheattel, John *504*
Bines, Thomas *54*
Binford, L. C. "Jack" *523*
Bing, Richard J. *532*
Bing, Rudolf *548*
Bingaman, Jeff *275, 278, 306*
Bingay, James S. *492*
Bingel, Joe *505*
Binger, James H. *489*
Bingham, Flavel *394*
Bingham, George H. *284*
Bingham, Henry H. *116, 119, 121, 124, 126, 129, 131, 134, 137, 140, 143, 145, 148, 151, 154, 157, 160*
Bingham, Hiram *178, 181, 184, 187, 190, 294, 525*
Bingham, John A. *90, 92, 94, 96, 100, 102, 105, 107, 365*
Bingham, Jonathan B. *247, 250, 253, 256, 259, 262, 266, 269, 272*
Bingham, Kinsley S. *82, 84, 94, 96, 301*
Bingham, Robert W. *362, 389*
Bingham, Walter D. *476*
Bingham, William *4, 43, 44, 45, 46, 309, 395*
Binney, D. B. *337*
Binney, Horace *70*
Binney, Joseph G. S. *408*
Binns, Jack N., Sr. *533*
Binns, Jack R. *364*
Binns, Walter P. *426*
Binsted, Norman S. *452, 460*
Binz, Leo *464*
Birch, Francis *523, 549, 551*
Birch, Frank V. *524*
Birch, Stephen *490*
Birch, Thomas H. *370*
Birch, William F. *169*

Birchall, Frederick T. *554*
Birchard, Matthew *308*
Bird, Augustus A. *398*
Bird, John *46, 47*
Bird, John T. *104, 107*
Bird, Mary Lynne *513*
Bird, Remsen *414*
Bird, Richard E. *175*
Bird, Robert M. *519*
Bird, Rose Elizabeth *293*
Bird, Thompson *388*
Birdsall, Ausburn *82*
Birdsall, Benjamin P. *147, 150, 153*
Birdsall, Carl *486*
Birdsall, James *55*
Birdsall, Samuel *73*
Birdsall, William W. *416*
Birdseye, Claude H. *538*
Birdseye, Victory *55, 77*
Birenbaum, William M. *403*
Birge, Edward A. *423*
Birge, Henry W. *339*
Birge, Raymond T. *517*
Birkenhauer, Henry F. *410*
Birkhoff, George D. *510, 515*
Birkinbine, John *522*
Birney, David B. *337, 338, 459*
Birney, David B., IV *457*
Birney, James *368*
Birney, Lauriss J. *471*
Birnie, Upton, Jr. *331*
Birrell, Don R. *438*
Bisbee, Horatio, Jr. *113, 115, 117, 120*
Bish, Milan D. *355, 356, 360, 371*
Bishop, Albert W. *418*
Bishop, Barry C. *535*
Bishop, Budd Harris *438*
Bishop, Cecil W. *207, 210, 213, 217, 220, 223, 226*
Bishop, Charles *386*
Bishop, Charles E. *418, 419*
Bishop, Charles F. *393*
Bishop, Charles P. *395*
Bishop, Elizabeth *531, 545, 555, 561*
Bishop, Eugene L. *518*
Bishop, Harry *385*
Bishop, Harry G. *331*
Bishop, Isabel *531, 535, 542*
Bishop, J. Michael *543, 551*
Bishop, James *90*
Bishop, James K. *368*
Bishop, Max W. *374*
Bishop, Morris *524*
Bishop, Phanuel *46, 47, 48, 49*
Bishop, Richard M. *307, 394, 476*
Bishop, Robert H. *412*
Bishop, Roswell P. *136, 139, 142, 145, 147, 150*
Bishop, William D. *91, 381*
Bishop, William M. *515*
Biskup, George J. *463, 466*
Bisplinghoff, Raymond L. *513, 559*
Bissell, Clark *293*
Bissell, Clayton L. *329, 340*
Bissell, Jean Galloway *286*
Bissell, William H. *83, 85, 87, 296*
Bissell, William H. A. *448, 461*
Bissell, Wilson S. *27, 36, 416*
Bitter, Karl *526*
Bittinger, Charles *536*
Bittle, David F. *415*
Bixby, William H. *331*
Bixler, Harris J. *176, 180, 183*
Bixler, Julius S. *406*

Bizzell, James A. *551*
Bizzell, William B. *416, 421*
Bjerknes, Jacob *549*
Bjorksten, Johan *514*
Blachford, Samuel *473*
Black, Craig C. *438, 441*
Black, Edward J. *74, 76*
Black, Eli M. *498*
Black, Ernest B. *519*
Black, Eugene *167, 170, 174, 177, 180, 183, 186*
Black, Eugene R. *380, 548, 552*
Black, Francis M. *303*
Black, Frank D. *398*
Black, Frank S. *137, 306*
Black, Frederick *440*
Black, Frederick H. *343*
Black, George D. *403*
Black, George R. *117*
Black, Greene V. *512*
Black, Harold S. *543, 562*
Black, Henry *77*
Black, Hugo L. *184, 187, 190, 193, 197, 200, 283, 291*
Black, J. W. *543*
Black, James *71, 79, 81, 420*
Black, James A. *81, 83*
Black, James C. C. *133, 135*
Black, James D. *298*
Black, James H. *519*
Black, Jeremiah S. *25, 33, 35, 309*
Black, John *67, 69, 71, 73, 302, 399*
Black, John C. *133, 380*
Black, John D. *513*
Black, Loring M., Jr. *179, 182, 185, 189, 192, 195*
Black, Mary *442*
Black, Newton W. *504*
Black, O. B. *397*
Black, Samuel C. *425*
Black, Samuel L. *394*
Black, Shirley Temple *362*
Black, W. F. *405*
Black, William Grant *457*
Black, William M. *331*
Blackall, Frederick S., Jr. *520*
Blackbird, W. H. *308*
Blackburn, Benjamin B. *249, 252, 255, 258*
Blackburn, Edmond *151*
Blackburn, Edmond S. *145*
Blackburn, John C. *390*
Blackburn, Joseph C. S. *111, 113, 115, 118, 120, 123, 125, 127, 130, 133, 136, 144, 147, 150, 298*
Blackburn, Luke P. *298*
Blackburn, Paul P., Jr. *348*
Blackburn, Robert E. Lee *188*
Blackburn, Robert M. *472*
Blackburn, Thomas W. *340*
Blackburn, W. Jasper *102*
Blackburn, William M. *421*
Blackford, Isaac N. *286*
Blackford, William M. *358*
Blackie, William *484*
Blackie, William A. *484*
Blackistone, Nathaniel *5*
Blackledge, H. L. *521*
Blackledge, William *48, 49, 50, 52*
Blackledge, William S. *58, 60*
Blackman, A. Wade *540*
Blackman, William F. *415*
Blackmar, Esbon *82*
Blackmar, Frank W. *520*
Blackmon, Fred L. *158, 161, 165, 171*
Blackmore, James *395*

Blackmun, Harry A. *283*
Blackney, William W. *198, 204, 208, 211, 214, 217, 220, 224*
Blackwelder, Eliot *523*
Blackwell, Arnold W. *346*
Blackwell, Gordon W. *408, 421*
Blackwell, John *6*
Blackwell, Julius W. *75, 79*
Blackwell, Otto B. *538*
Blackwell, Robert E. *415*
Blackwell, William B. *524*
Blackwood, Irbra C. *310*
Bladen, Thomas *5*
Blades, Herbert *562*
Blaik, Earl (Red) *553*
Blain, Daniel *518, 533*
Blaine, James G. *16, 26, 27, 33, 98, 100, 102, 103, 104, 105, 106, 107, 108, 111, 113, 115, 118, 299*
Blaine, John G. *315*
Blaine, John J. *187, 190, 193, 315*
Blair, Austin *102, 104, 106, 301*
Blair, Bernard *77*
Blair, David H. *380*
Blair, Deidre *546*
Blair, Francis P., Jr. *16, 92, 94, 96, 98, 104, 106, 303, 337, 338*
Blair, Henry W. *111, 114, 116, 118, 121, 123, 126, 128, 134, 305*
Blair, Jacob B. *97, 99, 359*
Blair, James *6, 60, 66, 68, 70*
Blair, James G. *106*
Blair, James T. *303*
Blair, James T., Jr. *303, 392*
Blair, John *2, 6, 62, 63, 65, 67, 68, 70, 283*
Blair, John W. *558*
Blair, Montgomery *25, 36*
Blair, Samuel S. *94, 97*
Blair, W. Frank *522*
Blair, William M., Jr. *360, 370*
Blais, Madeleine *558*
Blaisdell, Daniel *51*
Blaisdell, James A. *414*
Blaisdell, Neal S. *388*
Blake, Bruce *314*
Blake, Edgar *471*
Blake, Eugene Carson *562*
Blake, George H. *495*
Blake, George S. *418*
Blake, Gordon A. *381*
Blake, Harrison G. O. *94, 96*
Blake, Henry N. *303*
Blake, James *387*
Blake, James H. (Eubie) *552*
Blake, James Jr. *364*
Blake, John, Jr. *49, 50*
Blake, John L. *116*
Blake, John R. *407*
Blake, Joseph *6*
Blake, Maurice C. *386*
Blake, Maxwell *367*
Blake, Robert O. *367*
Blake, Thomas H. *64*
Blakeley, Harold W. *341*
Blakeley, Henry *396*
Blakeman, Royal E. *525*
Blakeney, Albert A. *144, 175*
Blakeslee, Albert F. *510, 521*
Blakeslee, Howard W. *554*
Blakley, William A. *234, 241, 312*
Blalock, Alfred *512, 533, 543, 551*
Blalock, R. J. *396*
Blalock, Selwyn G. *538*
Blanc, Anthony *464, 467*

Blanch, Arnold *551*
Blanchard, Elizabeth *413*
Blanchard, Ferdinand Q. *475*
Blanchard, George J. *332*
Blanchard, George L. *397*
Blanchard, George W. *196*
Blanchard, James J. *262, 265, 268, 271, 301*
Blanchard, John *81*
Blanchard, Jonathan *3, 411*
Blanchard, Newton C. *118, 120, 123, 125, 128, 130, 133, 136, 299*
Blanchard, Noah F. *495*
Blanchard, Roger W. *454, 461*
Blanchard, William H. *346*
Blanchet, Augustine M. A. *470*
Blanchet, Francis N. *464*
Blanchette, Romeo *466*
Blanchgard, John *83*
Blancke, W. Wendell *358, 362, 369*
Bland, Oscar E. *168, 172, 175, 286, 287*
Bland, Richard *4*
Bland, Richard P. *109, 111, 113, 116, 118, 121, 123, 125, 128, 131, 133, 139*
Bland, Schuyler Otis *171, 174, 177, 180, 183, 187, 190, 193, 196, 199, 203, 206, 209, 212, 216, 219, 222*
Bland, Theodorick *4, 41*
Bland, William T. *172*
Blandford, Mark H. *321*
Blanding, Albert H. *331*
Blanding, Sarah G. *424, 548*
Blandy, William H. P. *348, 349*
Blane, John *358, 371*
Blankenburg, R. *395*
Blankingship, A. H. *453*
Blanton, Joseph P. *419*
Blanton, L. Ray *251, 254, 257*
Blanton, Ray *311*
Blanton, Thomas L. *170, 174, 177, 180, 183, 186, 190, 193, 196, 199*
Blascoer, Frances *525*
Blasdel, Henry G. *304*
Blashfield, Edwin H. *525, 526, 547*
Blatchford, Richard M. *339, 369*
Blatchford, Samuel *283*
Blatnik, John A. *217, 221, 224, 227, 230, 233, 236, 240, 243, 246, 249, 253, 256, 259*
Blattenberger, Raymond *380*
Blauvelt, Howard W. *486*
Blavatsky, Helena P. H. *477*
Blaylock, Kenneth T. *503*
Blaylock, L. *397*
Blazer, Paul G. *483*
Blazer, Rexford S. *483*
Blease, Coleman L. *183, 186, 189, 310, 311*
Blease, Eugene S. *311*
Bleckley, Logan E. *296*
Bledsoe, Albert T. *420*
Bledsoe, Jesse *53, 298*
Bledsoe, Samuel T. *483*
Blee, Robert *394*
Bleecker, Charles E. *393*
Bleecker, Harmanus *52, 368*
Bleecker, Johannes *393*
Bleecker, Johannes, Jr. *393*
Bleecker, Rutger *393*
Blegen, Carl W. *533*
Bleicken, Gerhard D. *490*
Blenk, James H. *464*
Blenkinsop, Peter J. *406*

Blessing, James H. *393*
Blettner, Edward F. *488*
Blieck, John De *411*
Bliley, Thomas J., Jr. *273, 276, 279, 398*
Blinn, C. J. *394*
Blish, John *476*
Bliss, Aaron T. *128, 301*
Bliss, Archibald M. *111, 114, 116, 118, 123, 126*
Bliss, Charles A. *386*
Bliss, Cornelius N. *27, 36, 548*
Bliss, Don C. *361*
Bliss, George *88, 98, 556, 557*
Bliss, George Y. *451*
Bliss, Gilbert A. *515*
Bliss, Philemon *90, 92*
Bliss, Raymond W. *332*
Bliss, Robert W. *355, 373*
Bliss, Tasker H. *329, 351*
Blitch, Iris F. *229, 232, 236, 239*
Blizard, Everitt P. *537*
Bloch, Konrad E. *550*
Bloch, Claude C. *349*
Bloch, Ernest *531, 535*
Bloch, Felix *517, 550*
Bloch, Herbert *517*
Bloch, Milton J. *440*
Block, Adolph *526*
Block, Claude C. *347*
Block, Herbert L. *554, 555, 558*
Block, John R. *32, 37*
Block, Joseph L. *490*
Block, Karl M. *452, 458*
Block, Leigh B. *432*
Block, Leigh E. *490*
Block, Philip D. *490*
Blocksom, Augustus P. *333, 339*
Blockstein, Leonard *559*
Blodgett, Frank D. *403*
Blodgett, Isaac N. *305*
Blodgett, Rufus *126, 128, 131, 305*
Bloede, Victor G. *544*
Bloembergen, Nicolaas *542, 549, 550*
Blomgren, Paul B. *405*
Blomquist, Harry L., Jr. *485*
Blomquist, John E. *495*
Blondheim, Adolphe W. *542*
Blood, Henry H. *312*
Blood, Robert O. *304*
Bloodgood, Francis *393*
Bloodgood, Thomas *485*
Bloodworth, Timothy *4, 41, 44, 45, 46, 307*
Bloom, Edgar S. *499*
Bloom, Isaac *48*
Bloom, Joel *522*
Bloom, Sol *179, 182, 185, 189, 192, 195, 198, 202, 205, 208, 211, 215, 218, 221*
Bloomer, Betty [Elizabeth] *20*
Bloomer, Henry G. *438*
Bloomfield, Joseph *56, 58, 305*
Bloomfield, Richard J. *360, 370*
Blos, Joan W. *546*
Bloss, John M. *414*
Blough, Roger M. *499, 539*
Blouin, Michael T. *262, 265*
Blount, James H. *108, 110, 113, 115, 117, 120, 122, 125, 127, 130, 363*
Blount, Thomas *43, 44, 45, 49, 50, 52*
Blount, William *4, 44, 45, 311*
Blount, William A. *511*
Blount, William G. *56, 57*
Blount, Willie *311*
Blount, Willliam *2*

Brewster, Caroll W. *410*
Brewster, Chauncey B. *449, 458*
Brewster, Daniel B. *236, 239, 243, 246, 249, 300*
Brewster, David P. *75, 77*
Brewster, Ellis W. *527*
Brewster, Henry C. *137, 139*
Brewster, Kingman, Jr. *362, 427*
Brewster, Ralph O. *198, 201, 204, 207, 211, 214, 217, 220, 223, 299, 476*
Brewster, Robert C. *360*
Brewster, William *1, 516*
Breyer, Stephen Gerald *284*
Breyfogel, Sylvanus *472*
Breyfogle, C. W. *386*
Brezzo, Steven L. *443*
Brice, Calvin S. *131, 134, 137, 308*
Brice, James *390*
Brice, John *390*
Brick, Abraham L. *141, 144, 147, 150, 153*
Brickell, Robert C. *291*
Bricker, John W. *18, 218, 221, 224, 228, 231, 234, 308*
Bricker, William H. *486*
Brickhouse, Ben D. *385*
Brickler, William R. *521*
Brickner, Burt G. *523*
Brickner, George H. *129, 132, 135*
Bridenbaugh, Carl *513*
Bridgers, Robert R. *320*
Bridges, Charles H. *330*
Bridges, George W. *97*
Bridges, H. Styles *201, 205, 208, 211, 214, 218, 221, 224, 226, 227, 230, 233, 237, 304, 305*
Bridges, Harry *496, 504*
Bridges, John *7*
Bridges, Peter S. *372*
Bridges, Robert *509*
Bridges, Robert R. *321*
Bridges, Ronald *475*
Bridges, Samuel A. *83, 88, 114*
Bridges, Styles *240*
Bridgford, W. L. *398*
Bridgham, Samuel W. *395*
Bridgman, George H. *409*
Bridgman, George Herbert *357*
Bridgman, Percy W. *517, 537, 549, 560*
Brier, Royce *554*
Briest, John *393*
Briggs, Ansel *297*
Briggs, Clay Stone *174, 177, 180, 183, 186, 190, 193, 196*
Briggs, Ellis O. *357, 359, 360, 363, 370, 371, 375*
Briggs, Eugene S. *524*
Briggs, Everett E. *369*
Briggs, Frank A. *307*
Briggs, Frank O. *154, 157, 160, 305, 393*
Briggs, Frank P. *214, 303*
Briggs, George *84, 86, 94*
Briggs, George N. *67, 69, 71, 73, 74, 76, 300*
Briggs, Herbert W. *519*
Briggs, James E. *394, 417*
Briggs, James F. *114, 116, 118*
Briggs, LeBaron R. *415*
Briggs, Lyman J. *517, 535*
Briggs, M. C. *423*
Briggs, Sam *527*
Briggs, W. Paul *559*
Briggs, William T. *515*
Brigham, Clarence S. *509*

Brigham, Claude E. *331*
Brigham, Elbert S. *183, 186, 190, 492*
Brigham, Elijah *52, 53, 55*
Brigham, J. H. *526*
Brigham, Lewis A. *116*
Brigham, Paul *313*
Brigham, William T. *437*
Bright, J. Fulmer *398*
Bright, James W. *512, 524*
Bright, Jesse D. *80, 82, 83, 85, 87, 89, 91, 93, 95, 297*
Bright, John M. *107, 109, 112, 114, 117*
Bright, Myron H. *285*
Brightman, Carol *546*
Briley, C. Beverly *396*
Brim, Orville G., Jr. *433*
Brimelow, Bryan *540*
Brimhall, George H. *405*
Brimmer, Martin *390*
Brinckerhoff, Charles M. *482, 541, 561*
Brindley, G. Valter, Jr. *533*
Brindley, George V. *511*
Brinegar, Claude S. *31, 38*
Brines, Osborne A. *519*
Bringhurst, William L. *416*
Bringle, William F. *347, 348*
Brink, Edwin H. *544*
Brinker, Howard R. *453, 460*
Brinkerhoff, Jacob *79, 81, 308*
Brinkhous, Kenneth M. *533*
Brinkley, Alan *547*
Brinkley, Jack T. *249, 252, 255, 258, 261, 264, 267, 271*
Brinkley, Joel *558*
Brinkman, Gervaise *512*
Brinkman, John A. *442*
Brinson, Samuel M. *173, 176*
Brinton, Crane *513*
Brinton, Daniel G. *509*
Brisbin, John *85*
Brisbin, John B. *391*
Brisco, M. M. *432*
Brisco, Milo M. *487*
Briscoe, Dolph *312*
Brislin, John H. *556*
Brister, John W. *412*
Bristol, Edward S. *544*
Bristol, Frank M. *471*
Bristol, Henry P. *484*
Bristol, Lee H. *484*
Bristol, Mark L. *516*
Bristol, W. H. *544*
Bristol, William M. *484*
Bristow, Benjamin H. *26, 33, 511*
Bristow, Francis M. *88, 93*
Bristow, Henry *145*
Bristow, Joseph L. *156, 159, 162, 298*
Britt, Albert *411*
Britt, Charles R. *275*
Britt, James J. *166, 170*
Britt, Laurence V. *419*
Brittain, Alfred, III *483*
Brittain, Marion L. *409*
Britten, Fred A. *162, 165, 168, 171, 175, 178, 181, 184, 187, 191, 194*
Britteridge, Richard *1*
Britton, Edgar C. *511*
Britton, James H. *392*
Britton, Nathaniel L. *521*
Britton, Theodore R., Jr. *356, 363*
Britton, William E. *510*
Broach, H. H. *504*
Broaddus, Andrew *389*
Broadfoot, Grover L. *315*

Broadhead, James O. *121, 373, 511*
Broadley, Hugh T. *442*
Broadwell, Norman M. *388*
Brobeck, John R. *517*
Brock, Glen *490*
Brock, Isaac *335*
Brock, Lawrence *237*
Brock, O. Carlyle *527*
Brock, Ray L., Jr. *312*
Brock, William E. *32, 37, 189, 312*
Brock, William E., III *244, 247, 251, 254, 257, 260, 263, 312*
Brockenbrough, John W. *320*
Brockenbrough, William H. *79*
Brockett, Ernest D., Jr. *489*
Brockett, William A. *350*
Brocklesby, John *417*
Brockman, Hubert F. *427*
Brockson, Frank *162*
Brockway, John H. *74, 76*
Brodbeck, Andrew R. *164, 170*
Brode, Wallace R. *510, 511, 527, 553*
Broder, David S. *557*
Broderick, Case *130, 133, 136, 138*
Broderick, David C. *91, 93, 292*
Broderick, Edwin B. *468*
Broderick, Francis L. *420*
Brodeur, Leon R. *488*
Brodhead, J. Davis *154*
Brodhead, John *66, 67*
Brodhead, John C. *68, 73*
Brodhead, Richard *79, 81, 83, 86, 88, 90, 309*
Brodhead, William M. *262, 265, 268, 271*
Brodie, Bernard B. *543, 549*
Brodie, Edward E. *361, 372*
Brodie, H. Keith H. *408*
Brodie, William *515*
Brodkorb, P. *535*
Broening, William F. *390, 524*
Brogan, Thomas J. *305*
Brogden, Curtis H. *114, 307*
Brom, Robert H. *467*
Bromberg, Frederick G. *107*
Bromery, Randolph W. *420*
Bromfield, Louis *534, 553*
Bromwell, Henry P. H. *99, 101*
Bromwell, Jacob H. *134, 137, 140, 142, 145*
Bromwell, James E. *239, 242*
Brondel, John B. *468*
Broneer, Oscar T. *533*
Bronk, Detlev W. *410, 510, 539, 549, 552*
Bronk, William *546*
Bronson, David *76*
Bronson, E. D. *512*
Bronson, Greene C. *306*
Bronson, Isaac H. *73*
Bronson, Sherlock A. *411*
Bronwell, Arthur B. *426*
Broocks, Moses S. *152*
Brook, Alexander *551, 560*
Brooke, David S. *438*
Brooke, Edward W. *249, 252, 256, 259, 262, 265, 301, 541, 561*
Brooke, Francis K. *449, 460*
Brooke, Francis T. *314*
Brooke, Mrs. Frederick H. *523*
Brooke, Robert *313*
Brooke, Walker *86, 302, 319*
Brooker, Robert E. *499*
Brookhart, John M. *517*
Brookhart, Smith W. *175, 178, 181, 184, 188, 191, 297*

Brookhouse, Christopher *560*
Brooks, Alfred H. *538*
Brooks, Bryant B. *315*
Brooks, C. Wayland *204, 207, 210, 213, 217, 296*
Brooks, David *45*
Brooks, Edward H. *329, 333, 341, 343, 344*
Brooks, Edward S. *173, 176*
Brooks, Edwin B. *171, 175*
Brooks, Ernest, Jr. *433*
Brooks, Eugene C. *413*
Brooks, F. H. *489*
Brooks, Franklin E. *146, 149*
Brooks, George M. *104, 106*
Brooks, Gwendolyn *555, 561*
Brooks, Harvey *509*
Brooks, Henry L. *285*
Brooks, J. Twing *196, 199*
Brooks, Jabez *409*
Brooks, Jack *263*
Brooks, Jack B. *228, 231, 235, 238, 241, 244, 247, 251, 254, 257, 260, 266, 269, 273, 276, 279*
Brooks, James *84, 86, 98, 100, 102, 104, 107, 109*
Brooks, John *300, 394*
Brooks, John A. *17*
Brooks, John B. *340*
Brooks, John E. *406*
Brooks, Joseph T. *386*
Brooks, Kendall *411*
Brooks, Micah *55*
Brooks, Milton *554*
Brooks, Overton *201, 204, 207, 211, 214, 217, 220, 223, 227, 230, 233, 236, 239*
Brooks, Paul *536*
Brooks, Peter A. *412*
Brooks, Phillips *449, 459, 540*
Brooks, Preston S. *89, 90*
Brooks, Ralph G. *303*
Brooks, Robert C. *517*
Brooks, Robert N. *471*
Brooks, Samuel P. *404*
Brooks, Stratton D. *421*
Brooks, Tim *546*
Brooks, Van Wyck *547, 554, 559*
Brooks, Walker *319*
Brooks, Wiley G. *410*
Brooks, William P. *420*
Brooks, William T. H. *337*
Brookshire, Elijah V. *127, 130, 133*
Broom, Jacob *2, 90*
Broom, James M. *48, 50*
Broomall, John M. *99, 100, 103*
Broome, James E. *295*
Broomfield, John C. *471*
Broomfield, William S. *233, 236, 240, 243, 246, 249, 252, 256, 259, 262, 265, 268, 271, 274, 278*
Brophy, John C. *219*
Brosin, Henry W. *518*
Brosio, Manlio *552*
Brosius, Marriott *129, 131, 134, 137, 140, 143*
Brosnahan, Timothy *404*
Brosnan, D. William *496*
Brossard, Edgar B. *382*
Brossart, Ferdinand *466*
Brosseau, Mrs. Grace L. H. *526*
Broten, Norman R. *560*
Brotherston, John F. *535*
Brotzman, Donald G. *242, 248, 251, 255, 258*
Brough, Charles H. *292*
Brough, John *307*

Bruce, William Cabell *178, 182, 185, 300, 542, 553*
Bruck, Philip H. *394*
Brucker, Ferdinand *139*
Brucker, Herbert *520*
Brucker, Wilber M. *301, 327*
Bruckner, Henry *163, 166, 170*
Bruere, Henry *526, 548*
Brugginck, Eric *286*
Brumbaugh, Clement L. *163, 167, 170, 173*
Brumbaugh, D. Emmert *212, 215*
Brumbaugh, Martin G. *309*
Brumit, Joseph L. *525*
Brumm, Charles N. *119, 121, 124, 126, 137, 140, 151, 154*
Brumm, George F. *180, 183, 189, 192, 196*
Bruncken, Herbert *561*
Brundage, Percival F. *381*
Brundidge, Stephen, Jr. *138, 141, 143, 146, 149, 152*
Brune, Frederick W. *300*
Brunengo, Aloysius *422*
Bruner, Jerome J. *518*
Bruner, John E. *505*
Brunetti, Melvin *286*
Bruni, Stephen T. *438*
Brunini, Joseph B. *467*
Brunner, David J. *129, 131*
Brunner, Jean A. *528*
Brunner, William F. *189, 192, 195, 198*
Brunnier, H. J. *527*
Bruns, Bernard *391*
Brunsdale, C. Norman *237, 307*
Brunton, David W. *561*
Brunton, Joseph A., Jr. *521*
Brush, Alexander *393*
Brush, Alvin G. *481*
Brush, Charles F. *538, 539, 560*
Brush, David M. *432*
Brush, Edward N. *518*
Brush, George de F. *560*
Brush, George J. *509*
Brush, Gerard M. *395*
Brush, Henry *58*
Brush, Rapp *342*
Brush, Thomas B. *394*
Brute de Remur, Simon G. *466*
Bruyn, Andrew D. W. *73*
Bruynes, Cees *493*
Bruzelius, Nils J. *558*
Bryan, Albert V. *284*
Bryan, B. F. *389*
Bryan, Blackshear M. *332, 333, 344, 418*
Bryan, C. R. *350*
Bryan, Charles P. *356, 357, 365, 370*
Bryan, Charles W. *18, 303, 392*
Bryan, Elmer B. *406, 414*
Bryan, Enoch A. *425*
Bryan, George *1*
Bryan, George D. *396*
Bryan, Guy M. *93*
Bryan, Henry H. *58*
Bryan, Henry S. *492*
Bryan, James E. *515*
Bryan, James W. *164*
Bryan, John A. *370*
Bryan, John H. *63, 65*
Bryan, John S. *406*
Bryan, Joseph *47, 49*
Bryan, Joseph H. *55, 57*
Bryan, Monk *472*
Bryan, Nathan P. *44, 45*
Bryan, Nathan P. *158, 162, 165, 284, 295*
Bryan, R. R. *406*

Bryan, Richard *304*
Bryan, Thomas P., Jr. *398*
Bryan, W. R. *524*
Bryan, William A. *441*
Bryan, William J. *152, 295*
Bryan, William Jennings *17, 28, 33, 131, 134*
Bryan, William L. *410, 518*
Bryan, Wright *520*
Bryant, Andrew J. *386*
Bryant, Farris *295*
Bryant, G. Hyde *386*
Bryant, John *276, 279*
Bryant, Joseph D. *515*
Bryant, Paul W. (Bear) *552*
Bryant, William Cullen *540*
Bryant, William L. *438*
Bryce, James *517*
Bryce, John *396*
Bryce, Lloyd *366, 368*
Bryce, Lloyd S. *126*
Bryk, Petri B. *538*
Bryoade, Henry A. *355, 360*
Bryon, Goodloe E. *259*
Bryson, John *386*
Bryson, Joseph R. *206, 209, 212, 215, 219, 222, 225, 228*
Brzana, Stanislaus *468*
Brzezinski, Zbigniew *552*
Bucahanan, James P. *196*
Buch, Joseph G. *521*
Buchanan, Andrew *71, 73*
Buchanan, Angela *381*
Buchanan, Edna *558*
Buchanan, Frank *159, 162, 165, 215, 218, 222, 504*
Buchanan, Frank B. *225*
Buchanan, Franklin *324, 418*
Buchanan, George S. *510*
Buchanan, Hugh *117, 120*
Buchanan, James *11, 16, 25, 33, 60, 61, 63, 65, 66, 70, 71, 73, 75, 77, 79, 81, 123, 126, 128, 131, 309, 362, 371*
Buchanan, James M. *359*
Buchanan, James McGill *551*
Buchanan, James P. *164, 167, 170, 174, 177, 180, 183, 186, 190, 193, 199, 203*
Buchanan, James S. *421*
Buchanan, Jesse E. *419*
Buchanan, John *300*
Buchanan, John A. *129, 132*
Buchanan, John H., Jr. *245, 248, 251, 254, 258, 261, 264, 267*
Buchanan, John L. *408, 418, 424*
Buchanan, John P. *311*
Buchanan, Thomas C. *380*
Buchanan, Vera D. *225, 228, 231*
Buchanan, Wiley T., Jr. *356, 366*
Buchanan, William I. *355*
Buchanan, William L. *369*
Bucher, George H. *499*
Bucher, J. F. *425*
Bucher, John C. *68*
Bucher, W. H. *513*
Bucher, Walter H. *523, 551*
Buchholz, John T. *521*
Buchman, Frank N. D. *477*
Buchman, Louis *561*
Buchsbaum, Solomon J. *549*
Buchtel, Henry A. *293, 419*
Buchwald, Art *558*
Buck, Alfred E. *103, 365*
Buck, C. Douglass *210, 213, 216, 294*
Buck, Carl D. *517*

Buck, Carl E. *561*
Buck, Charles F. *136*
Buck, Charles W. *370*
Buck, Daniel *44*
Buck, Daniel A. A. *62, 65*
Buck, Daniel W. *391*
Buck, Ellsworth B. *211, 215, 218*
Buck, Frank H. *194, 197, 200, 203, 206*
Buck, Gene *519*
Buck, George S. *393*
Buck, Hugh Q. *431*
Buck, John R. *117, 122*
Buck, Paul H. *554*
Buck, Pearl S. *541, 549, 553*
Buck, Peter H. *437*
Buck, Robert T. *437*
Buck, Robert T., Jr. *437*
Buck, Samuel J. *409*
Buckalew, Charles R. *98, 100, 103, 126, 129, 309, 360*
Buckbee, John T. *184, 187, 191, 194, 197*
Buckham, Matthew H. *423*
Buckingham, George M. *432*
Buckingham, Richard G. *386*
Buckingham, Thomas L. *512*
Buckingham, William A. *103, 105, 108, 293, 294*
Buckingham, William D. *562*
Buckland, Ralph P. *100, 102*
Buckler, Richard T. *198, 201, 204, 208*
Bucklew, Neil S. *421, 426*
Buckley, Charles A. *198, 202, 205, 208, 211, 215, 218, 221, 224, 227, 231, 234, 237, 240, 243*
Buckley, Charles E. *438, 443*
Buckley, Charles W. *101, 103, 105*
Buckley, Edward A. *514*
Buckley, James L. *256, 259, 262, 286, 306*
Buckley, James R. *178*
Buckley, James V. *220*
Buckley, John P. *512*
Buckley, Oliver E. *538*
Buckley, Stuart E. *545*
Buckley, William F., Jr. *546*
Bucklin, John C. *389*
Buckman, Clarence B. *147, 150*
Buckmaster, L. S. *506*
Buckner, Alexander *67, 69, 303*
Buckner, Aylett *82*
Buckner, Aylett H. *109, 111, 113, 116, 118, 121*
Buckner, Benjamin P. *397*
Buckner, George W. *366*
Buckner, R. B. *386*
Buckner, Richard A. *61, 62, 64*
Buckner, Simon B. *17, 298, 323*
Buckson, David P. *294*
Bucy, J. Fred *497*
Budd, Edward B. *494*
Budd, Edward G. *533*
Budd, Edward H. *498*
Budd, James H. *119, 292*
Budd, John M. *484, 489*
Budd, Ralph *485, 489, 539*
Buddington, Arthur F. *551*
Buddy, Charles F. *465*
Budge, Hamer H. *223, 226, 229, 232, 236, 381*
Budig, Gene A. *410, 420, 426*
Budlong, Frederick G. *452, 458*
Bueche, Arthur M. *532*
Bueche, Wendell F. *431*
Buechner, Frederick *560*
Buechner, Thomas S. *437*

Buehler, William E. *524*
Buel, Alexander W. *84*
Buel, David H. *409*
Buell, Alexander H. *86*
Buell, Don Carlos *335, 336*
Buell, George P. *338*
Buell, Murray F. *522*
Buell, Victor P. *515*
Buell, Willis *387*
Buerki, Robin C. *526*
Buetow, Herbert P. *492*
Buffett, Howard H. *211, 214, 218, 224*
Buffington, Adelbert R. *332*
Buffington, Joseph *79, 81, 284*
Buffinton, James *90, 94, 96, 104, 106, 108*
Buffum, Joseph, Jr. *58*
Buffum, Robert E. *476*
Buffum, William B. *366*
Buffunton, James *92*
Buford, John *337*
Buford, John L. *525*
Bugbee, F. *385*
Bugbee, George *526*
Bugbee, Lucius *403*
Bugg, Robert M. *89*
Bugliarello, George *414*
Buher, Stephen *394*
Buhl, Christian H. *391*
Buhl, Frederick *391*
Buley, R. Carlyle *555*
Bulkeley, Eliphalet A. *481, 485*
Bulkeley, Morgan G. *149, 152, 155, 293, 294, 386, 481*
Bulkley, Robert J. *160, 163, 189, 192, 195, 199, 202, 308*
Bull, Harold R. *330, 341, 351*
Bull, Henry *6*
Bull, James G. *394*
Bull, John *4, 69*
Bull, Melville *137, 140, 143, 146*
Bull, Storm *398*
Bull, William *6*
Bullard, Edward P., Jr. *533, 551*
Bullard, F. Lauriston *553*
Bullard, Henry A. *67, 69, 84*
Bullard, Robert L. *333, 339*
Bullard, Samuel *388*
Bullard, Todd H. *404*
Bullard, William N. *516*
Bullen, John *390*
Bullene, Egbert F. *331*
Bullene, Thomas B. *392*
Buller, A. H. R. *521*
Bullington, James R. *357*
Bullions, Peter *473*
Bullis, Harry A. *488, 525*
Bullitt, William C. *361, 375*
Bulloch, Archibald *3, 5*
Bulloch, William B. *53, 295*
Bullock, A. George *497*
Bullock, Alexander H. *300*
Bullock, Chandler *497*
Bullock, David *398*
Bullock, Henry A. *534*
Bullock, Hugh *526*
Bullock, Marie L. *547*
Bullock, Mary L. *548*
Bullock, Robert *127, 130*
Bullock, Robert O. *540*
Bullock, Rufus B. *295*
Bullock, Stephen *44*
Bullock, Theodore H. *520*
Bullock, Wingfield *59*
Bulow, William J. *193, 196, 199, 202, 206, 209, 311*

Bulwinkle, Alfred L. *176, 179, 182, 186, 192, 195, 199, 202, 205, 208, 212, 215, 218, 221*

Bumpers, Dale *261, 264, 267, 270, 273, 276, 292*

Bumpus, Hermon C. *417, 437*

Bumstead, Henry A. *517*

Bunce, Alan *503*

Bunce, J. H. *389*

Bunce, Jonathan B. *494*

Bunch, Samuel *70, 72*

Bunche, Ralph J. *518, 548, 549, 552, 559, 561*

Bundel, Charles M. *351*

Bundesen, Herman H. *518*

Bundlie, Gerhard J. *391*

Bundy, Charles A. *434*

Bundy, Hezekiah S. *100, 109, 134*

Bundy, McGeorge *432, 548, 552*

Bundy, Omar *339*

Bundy, Solomon *114*

Bunker, Arthur H. *431*

Bunker, Berkeley L. *205, 208, 214, 304*

Bunker, Earle L. *554*

Bunker, Ellsworth *355, 364, 365, 368, 375, 516, 552*

Bunker, George M. *491*

Bunn, Benjamin H. *128, 131, 134*

Bunn, Edward B. *409*

Bunn, Henry G. *292*

Bunn, Howard S. *498*

Bunnell, Frank C. *107, 124, 126*

Bunnell, Peter C. *442*

Bunner, Rudolph *64*

Bunshaft, Gordon *548*

Bunting, Earl *525*

Bunting, James W. *414*

Bunting, John R. *488*

Bunting, Josiah, III *409*

Bunting, Mary I. *415, 548*

Bunting, Thomas L. *131*

Bunzel, John H. *405*

Buquor, P. S. *397*

Burbank, Luther *540, 548*

Burbeck, Henry *331*

Burbidge, E. Margaret *549*

Burbridge, J. Q. *387*

Burcaw, Ellis *441*

Burch, Charles S. *450, 460*

Burch, Dean *379*

Burch, James C. *389*

Burch, John C. *93*

Burch, John G. *393*

Burch, Rousseau A. *298*

Burch, Thomas G. *193, 196, 199, 203, 206, 209, 212, 216, 314*

Burchard, Horatio C. *103, 106, 108, 110, 113*

Burchard, John E. *509*

Burchard, John Ely *542*

Burchard, Samuel D. *112*

Burchenal, Joseph H. *543*

Burchfield, Charles E. *532, 547, 551*

Burchill, Thomas F. *211*

Burchinal, David A. *328*

Burck, Jacob *554*

Burd, George *68, 70*

Burden, William A. M. *356*

Burdett, Allen M., Jr. *334*

Burdett, Samuel S. *104, 106*

Burdett, William C. *367, 368*

Burdick, Clark *173, 177, 180, 183, 186, 189, 193*

Burdick, Quentin N. *237, 240, 244, 247, 250, 253, 256, 260, 263, 266, 269, 272, 275, 278, 307*

Burdick, Theodore W. *113*

Burdick, Usher L. *199, 202, 205, 208, 212, 221, 224, 228, 231, 234*

Burdon, George *506*

Burgener, Clair W. *258, 261, 264, 267, 270*

Burger, James C. *527*

Burger, Warren E. *283, 286*

Burgers, Johannes M. *533*

Burges, Dempsey *44, 45*

Burges, Tristam *63, 65, 66, 68, 70, 310*

Burgess, Alexander *448, 461*

Burgess, Carter L. *355, 497*

Burgess, Charles F. *522, 531*

Burgess, Ernest W. *520*

Burgess, Frederick *450, 459*

Burgess, Gavon D. *303*

Burgess, George *447, 459*

Burgess, George F. *146, 149, 152, 155, 158, 161, 164, 167*

Burgess, George K. *519*

Burgess, John M. *455, 459*

Burgess, Neil *537*

Burgess, Otis R. *405*

Burgess, Paul S. *418*

Burgess, Theodore C. *404*

Burgess, Thomas M. *395*

Burgess, W. Randolph *511*

Burgess, W. Sterling *536*

Burgin, William O. *205, 208, 212, 215*

Burgreen, Charles Lee *457*

Burgstahler, Herbert J. *407*

Burk, Frederick L. *405*

Burk, Henry *145, 148*

Burke, Aedanus *41*

Burke, Andrew H. *307*

Burke, Andrew J. *397*

Burke, Arleigh *552*

Burke, Arleigh A. *347*

Burke, Bernard F. *560*

Burke, Charles H. *143, 146, 149, 152, 157, 161, 164*

Burke, Daniel *511*

Burke, Edmond W. *291*

Burke, Edmund *75, 77, 78, 381*

Burke, Edward J. *415*

Burke, Edward R. *195, 198, 201, 205, 304*

Burke, Frank W. *236, 239, 389*

Burke, Haslett P. *293*

Burke, J. Herbert *248, 252, 255, 258, 261, 264*

Burke, James A. *236, 240, 243, 246, 249, 252, 256, 259, 262, 265*

Burke, James D. *443*

Burke, James E. *490*

Burke, James F. *151, 154, 157, 160, 164*

Burke, John *307, 381*

Burke, John C. *512*

Burke, John H. *194*

Burke, John P. *504*

Burke, John R. *363*

Burke, Joseph A. *468*

Burke, Kenneth *547, 548*

Burke, M. J. *386*

Burke, Maurice F. *468, 470*

Burke, Michael E. *161, 164, 168*

Burke, Raymond H. *218*

Burke, Robert E. *140, 143*

Burke, Thomas *4, 6, 394*

Burke, Thomas A. *228, 308*

Burke, Thomas H. *221*

Burke, Thomas M. A. *468*

Burke, V. C. *505*

Burke, William A. *344*

Burke, William J. *173, 176*

Burke, William R. *514*

Burke, Yvonne Brathwaite *258, 261, 264*

Burket, Jacob *308*

Burkett, Elmer J. *142, 145, 148, 151, 154, 157, 303*

Burkhalter, Everett G. *242*

Burkhardt, Frederick *404, 512*

Burkhardt, John E. *562*

Burkhart, Harvey J. *512*

Burkitt, Denis *543*

Burleigh, Edwin C. *139, 142, 144, 147, 150, 153, 156, 162, 165, 299*

Burleigh, Harry T. *561*

Burleigh, Henry G. *121, 123*

Burleigh, John H. *108, 111*

Burleigh, William *61, 62*

Burleson, Albert A. *158*

Burleson, Albert S. *28, 36, 143, 146, 149, 152, 155, 161, 164*

Burleson, Hugh L. *451, 461*

Burleson, Omar T. *219, 222, 225, 228, 231, 235, 238, 241, 244, 247, 251, 254, 257, 260, 263, 266*

Burleson, Rufus C. *404*

Burlin, Paul *562*

Burlingame, Anson *90, 92, 94, 358*

Burlison, Bill D. *253, 256, 259, 262, 265, 268*

Burma, John H. *417*

Burn, Harry T. *527*

Burnaham, Alfred A. *93*

Burnell, Barker *76, 78*

Burnell, William H. *504*

Burnes, James N. *121, 123, 125*

Burnet, D. S. *476*

Burnet, David *380*

Burnet, Isaac G. *394*

Burnet, Jacob *65, 66, 308*

Burnet, William *3, 5*

Burnett, Charles T. *437*

Burnett, Edgar A. *421*

Burnett, Edward *125*

Burnett, Edwin K. *441*

Burnett, Hamilton S. *312*

Burnett, Henry C. *89, 91, 93, 95, 319, 320, 321*

Burnett, Howard J. *425*

Burnett, J. M. *406*

Burnett, John L. *141, 143, 146, 149, 152, 155, 158, 161, 165, 168*

Burnett, Peter H. *292*

Burnett, Robert A. *539*

Burnett, Theodore L. *319, 320*

Burney, Cecil E. *514*

Burney, Dwight W. *303*

Burney, Leroy E. *381, 526, 561*

Burney, William R. *203*

Burnham, Alfred A. *95*

Burnham, Daniel H. *514*

Burnham, Donald C. *499, 541*

Burnham, George *194, 197*

Burnham, Henry E. *145, 148, 151, 154, 157, 160, 305*

Burnham, Hiram *337*

Burnham, James *552*

Burnham, Marion *440*

Burnham, William P. *351*

Burnquist, Joseph A. A. *301*

Burns, Arthur F. *361, 380, 513, 548*

Burns, Charles W. *471*

Burns, Daniel D. *133*

Burns, Dennis F. *427*

Burns, Edward L. *519*

Burns, Findley, Jr. *360, 365*

Burns, Francis *471*

Burns, H. S. M. *496*

Burns, Haydon *295, 387*

Burns, Hobert W. *405*

Burns, James A. *421*

Burns, James B. *503*

Burns, James McGregor *545, 557*

Burns, John A. *296*

Burns, John H. *358, 374*

Burns, John L. *485, 495*

Burns, Joseph *92*

Burns, Matthew J. *504*

Burns, Robert *69, 71*

Burns, Robert E. *423*

Burns, Robert M. *522, 531*

Burns, Robert W. *476*

Burns, Ross *389*

Burns, William W. *337*

Burnside, Ambrose E. *112, 114, 116, 119, 310, 335, 336, 338*

Burnside, Maurice G. *222, 225, 232*

Burnside, Thomas *55*

Burr, Aaron *12, 14, 23, 42, 43, 44, 46, 47, 306, 414*

Burr, Albert G. *101, 103*

Burr, C. B. *518*

Burr, C. C. *392*

Burr, Charles W. *516*

Burr, Ephraim W. *386*

Burr, George L. *513*

Burr, George W. *330*

Burr, Peter *7*

Burr, Peter T. *539*

Burrall, William P. *490*

Burrell, David J. *411*

Burrell, Herbert L. *515*

Burrell, J. E. *433*

Burrell, J. Earl *494*

Burrell, Orlando *135*

Burress, Withers A. *333, 343*

Burrill, G. Francis *454, 458*

Burrill, James, Jr. *57, 58, 310*

Burrill, Thomas J. *420*

Burrill, William G., Jr. *461*

Burrill, William George *457*

Burrington, George *6*

Burris, Robert H. *549*

Burroughs, Bryson *551*

Burroughs, Charles *392*

Burroughs, George S. *425*

Burroughs, John *306, 547*

Burroughs, John A. *367*

Burroughs, Nelson M. *454, 460*

Burroughs, Sherman E. *169, 173, 176*

Burroughs, Silas M. *92, 94*

Burrowes, Alexander J. *411, 412, 415, 427*

Burrowes, Thomas H. *414*

Burrows, Abe *556*

Burrows, Charles R. *364*

Burrows, Daniel *59*

Burrows, Joseph H. *118*

Burrows, Julius C. *108, 116, 118, 123, 125, 128, 130, 133, 136, 139, 142, 144, 147, 150, 153, 156, 301*

Burrows, Lansing *475*

Burrows, Lorenzo *84, 86*

Burrows, William S. *347*

Burruss, Julian A. *424*

Bursley, Herbert S. *364*

Bursom, Holm O. *176*

Burstein, Elias *562*

Burstyn, Ellen *503*

Cannon, Clarence *179, 182, 185, 188, 192, 195, 198, 201, 204, 208, 211, 214, 217, 221, 224, 227, 230, 233, 237, 240, 243*
Cannon, Frank J. *137, 140, 312*
Cannon, Henry W. *484*
Cannon, Howard W. *237, 240, 243, 246, 250, 253, 256, 259, 262, 265, 268, 272, 304, 563*
Cannon, Isabella W. *394*
Cannon, James, Jr. *471*
Cannon, John *525*
Cannon, John K. *346*
Cannon, Joseph G. *108, 110, 113, 115, 117, 120, 122, 125, 127, 133, 135, 138, 141, 144, 146, 147, 149, 150, 152, 153, 155, 156, 159, 165, 168, 171, 175*
Cannon, Marion *132*
Cannon, Newton *54, 56, 58, 60, 311*
Cannon, Raymond J. *196, 200, 203*
Cannon, Robert N. *334*
Cannon, Walter B. *510, 517, 548*
Cannon, William *294*
Cannon, William R. *472*
Cantey, James *324*
Cantlon, John E. *522*
Cantor, Eddie *503, 505*
Cantor, Jacob A. *163*
Cantrell, Stephen, Jr. *396*
Cantrill, James C. *156, 159, 162, 165, 169, 172, 175*
Cantwell, James W. *414*
Cantwell, John J. *463, 465*
Capa, Cornell *440*
Capa, Robert *551*
Caparn, Harold A. *519*
Capdeville, Paul *389*
Capehart, Homer E. *213, 217, 220, 223, 226, 229, 233, 236, 239, 297*
Capehart, James *132, 135*
Capen, Elmer H. *417*
Capen, Samuel B. *523*
Capen, Samuel P. *416*
Capers, Ellison *449, 461*
Capers, John G. *380*
Capers, William *471*
Capers, William T. *451, 462*
Caperton, Allen T. *112, 314, 320, 321*
Caperton, Hugh *54*
Caperton, William *350*
Caplan, Harry *517*
Caples, R. B. *538*
Caples, William G. *411*
Caplin, Mortimer M. *380*
Caponigro, Eleanor Morris *547*
Capozzoli, Louis J. *208, 211*
Capper, Arthur *172, 175, 178, 181, 184, 188, 191, 194, 197, 201, 204, 207, 210, 214, 217, 297, 298*
Capps, Edward *367, 510, 517*
Capps, Edwin M. *386*
Capps, W. L. *349*
Capra, Frank *509, 522*
Capron, Adin B. *140, 143, 146, 149, 151, 154, 157*
Capstick, John H. *166, 169*
Caputo, Bruce F. *266*
Caraway, Hattie W. *190, 193, 197, 200, 203, 206, 210, 292*
Caraway, Thaddeus H. *161, 165, 168, 171, 174, 177, 181, 184, 187, 190, 292*

Carberry, John J. *463, 464, 466, 469*
Carberry, Thomas *387*
Carbone, Paul P. *543*
Carbonera, Victor E. *559*
Cardamone, Richard J. *284*
Carden, Cap R. *194, 197*
Cardenas, Michael *382*
Cardoza, Norman F. *557*
Cardozo, Benjamin N. *283, 306, 559*
Cardwell, James B. *382*
Cardwell, Richard H. *314*
Carew, John F. *163, 166, 170, 173, 176, 179, 182, 185, 189*
Carey, H. Lloyd *390*
Carey, Hugh L. *240, 243, 247, 250, 253, 256, 259, 306*
Carey, J. M. *399*
Carey, James B. *505, 506*
Carey, Jeremiah T. *504*
Carey, John *94*
Carey, Joseph M. *129, 132, 135, 315*
Carey, P. V. *388*
Carey, Pete *558*
Carey, Robert D. *190, 193, 196, 200, 315*
Carey, W. Gibson, Jr. *522*
Carey, Walter F. *522*
Carey, William D. *510*
Cargill, O. A. *394*
Cargo, David F. *306*
Cargo, William I. *368*
Carhart, Henry S. *522*
Carkner, James W. *494*
Carland, John E. *285*
Carle, Robert *366*
Carleton, Alsie H. *472*
Carleton, Ezra C. *120, 123*
Carleton, Peter *50*
Carley, Patrick J. *185, 189, 192, 195*
Carlile, John S. *91, 97, 99, 314*
Carlile, Thomas *511*
Carlin, Charles C. *155, 158, 161, 164, 167, 171*
Carlin, James J. *406*
Carlin, John *298*
Carlin, Paul N. *382*
Carlin, Thomas *296*
Carlin, William P. *338*
Carling, Thomas J. *524*
Carlisle, Floyd L. *486, 496*
Carlisle, James H. *426*
Carlisle, John G. *27, 34, 113, 115, 118, 119, 120, 122, 123, 124, 125, 127, 130, 298*
Carlisle, S. S. *356*
Carlsen, Emil *551, 560*
Carlson, Anton J. *510, 517, 533*
Carlson, Chester F. *541, 544*
Carlson, D. L. *349*
Carlson, Delmar R. *363*
Carlson, Frank *197, 201, 204, 207, 210, 214, 220, 223, 226, 230, 233, 236, 239, 243, 246, 249, 297, 298*
Carlson, George A. *293*
Carlson, Hjalmar G. *533, 541*
Carlson, Loren D. *517*
Carlson, Maxwell *495*
Carlson, Reinhold O. *388*
Carlson, Reynold E. *359*
Carlson, William D. *424*
Carlson, William H. *386*
Carlson, William S. *416, 419, 423*
Carlton, Doyle E. *295*
Carlton, Henry H. *125, 127*
Carlton, Paul K. *346*

Carlton, Richard P. *492*
Carlucci, Frank *381*
Carlucci, Frank C. *327, 370*
Carlyle, F. Ertel *221, 224, 228, 231*
Carlyon, P. H. *398*
Carmack, Edward W. *140, 143, 146, 149, 152, 312*
Carmalt, James W. *380*
Carman, Edwin S. *520*
Carman, Gregory W. *272, 287*
Carman, James W. F. *454, 460*
Carmer, Carl *527*
Carmichael, Archibald H. *193, 197*
Carmichael, D. W. *386*
Carmichael, Emmett B. *514, 532*
Carmichael, Leonard *417, 443, 517, 518*
Carmichael, Oliver C. *418, 424*
Carmichael, Richard B. *69*
Carmichael, William *3, 373*
Carnahan, A. S. J. *372*
Carnahan, Albert S. J. *214, 221, 224, 227, 230, 233, 237*
Carnahan, James *414*
Carnap, Rudolf *536*
Carnegie, Andrew *540, 548*
Carnes, Thomas P. *42*
Carnes, W. D. *423*
Carney, Charles J. *253, 256, 260, 263, 266*
Carney, John E. *503*
Carney, Leonard T. *476*
Carney, Robert B. *347, 348*
Carney, Thomas *297*
Carney, Thomas J. *496*
Carney, William *269, 272, 275, 278*
Carnovsky, Leon *538, 543*
Carns, Edwin H. J. *329*
Caro, Robert A. *557*
Carolan, John M. *397*
Carow, Edith Kermit *20*
Carpenter, Alonzo P. *305*
Carpenter, Arthur S. *348*
Carpenter, Charles C. J. *452, 458*
Carpenter, Cyrus C. *115, 118, 297*
Carpenter, Davis *88*
Carpenter, Edmund M. *490*
Carpenter, Edmund N. *183*
Carpenter, Fred W. *367, 372*
Carpenter, George T. *408*
Carpenter, Homer W. *476*
Carpenter, John Alden *547*
Carpenter, Kenneth *503*
Carpenter, L. L. *476*
Carpenter, Levi D. *78*
Carpenter, Lewis *505*
Carpenter, Lewis C. *109*
Carpenter, M. Scott *537*
Carpenter, Matthew H. *105, 107, 110, 117, 315*
Carpenter, Newton H. *437*
Carpenter, R. B. *387*
Carpenter, Rhys *533*
Carpenter, Teresa *558*
Carpenter, Terry M. *195*
Carpenter, Thomas G. *412*
Carpenter, W. L. *388*
Carpenter, Walter S., Jr. *487*
Carpenter, Warren M. *562*
Carpenter, William R. *194, 197*
Carper, Thomas R. *274, 277*
Carr, Archie *536*
Carr, Caleb *6*
Carr, Clark E. *360*
Carr, Dabney S. *374*

Carr, Elias *307*
Carr, Eugene A. *335, 337*
Carr, Francis *52*
Carr, Harvey A. *518*
Carr, Henry J. *515*
Carr, Irving J. *332, 351*
Carr, James *55*
Carr, John *67, 69, 71, 74*
Carr, Joseph B. *337*
Carr, M. Robert *262, 265, 268, 274, 278*
Carr, Nathan T. *110*
Carr, Ralph L. *293*
Carr, Robert K. *414*
Carr, Stephen A. *505*
Carr, Thomas H. *385*
Carr, W. H. *397*
Carr, Wilbur J. *359*
Carr, William *512*
Carr, William Franklin *457*
Carr, Wooda N. *164*
Carral-Solar, Anselmo *456*
Carraway, Gertrude S. *526*
Carrel, Alexis *548, 549*
Carrel, George P. *394*
Carrell, George A. *415, 426, 466*
Carrick, Michael P. *504*
Carrick, Samuel *423*
Carrico, Harry L. *314*
Carrier, Chester O. *210*
Carrier, Warren P. *424*
Carrier, Wilbur O. *406*
Carrier, Willis H. *533*
Carrigg, Joseph L. *225, 228, 231, 234*
Carriker, M. A., Jr. *535*
Carrington, Edward *4, 398*
Carrington, Walter C. *372*
Carrington, William C. *398*
Carrington, William J. *523*
Carroll, Beryl F. *297*
Carroll, Charles *1, 3, 300*
Carroll, Charles H. *78, 80*
Carroll, Coleman F. *463, 465*
Carroll, Daniel *2, 3, 41*
Carroll, Daniel L. *409*
Carroll, David W. *321*
Carroll, Edward G. *472*
Carroll, George W. *17*
Carroll, Howard A. *469*
Carroll, J. Roy, Jr. *514*
Carroll, James *74*
Carroll, John *464, 467, 531*
Carroll, John A. *216, 220, 232, 235, 239, 293, 556*
Carroll, John E. *398*
Carroll, John L. *300*
Carroll, John M. *107*
Carroll, John P. *468*
Carroll, Julian *298*
Carroll, Mark K. *466*
Carroll, Nicholas *390*
Carroll, Richard S. *442*
Carroll, T. B. *396*
Carroll, T. C. *503*
Carroll, Thomas H. *409*
Carroll, Thomas K. *300*
Carroll, William *311*
Carroll of Carrollton, Charles *41, 42*
Carron, Malcolm *419*
Carrubba, Robert W. *517*
Carruth, Hayden *561*
Carruthers, Garrey *306*
Carruthers, Thomas N. *453, 461*
Carsey, J. Ben *510, 552*
Carson, David W. *473*
Carson, Hampton L. *511, 543*
Carson, Harry R. *451*
Carson, Henderson H. *212, 218*

Childs, Marquis 557
Childs, Orlo E. 510
Childs, Richard S. 526
Childs, Robert A. 133
Childs, Thomas W. 431
Childs, Timothy 66, 71, 73, 77
Chiles, L. F. 391
Chiles, Lawton M., Jr. 255, 258, 261, 264, 267, 270, 274, 277, 295
Chillman, James, Jr. 441
Chilton, C. M. 476
Chilton, Horace 132, 137, 140, 143, 312
Chilton, James 1
Chilton, Samuel 79
Chilton, Samuel B. 455
Chilton, Thomas 64, 65, 69
Chilton, W. E., III 545
Chilton, William E. 161, 164, 167, 315
Chilton, William P. 291, 319, 320, 321
Chinard, Gilbert 524
Chindblom, Carl R. 171, 175, 178, 181, 184, 187, 191
Ching, Cyrus S. 379, 515
Chinn, Joseph W. 68, 70
Chinn, Thomas W. 74, 372
Chinn, William S. 389
Chiperfield, Burnett M. 165, 187, 191
Chiperfield, Robert B. 204, 207, 210, 213, 217, 220, 223, 226, 229, 233, 236, 239
Chipman, Daniel 56
Chipman, J. Logan 125, 128, 130, 133
Chipman, John 519, 534, 538
Chipman, John S. 80
Chipman, Nathaniel 7, 45, 46, 47, 313
Chisholm, Frank A. 528
Chisholm, R. M. 560
Chisholm, Shirley 253, 256, 259, 262, 266, 269, 272
Chism, John Edward 392
Chistofer, Michael 557
Chittenden, Charles C. 512
Chittenden, Martin 48, 49, 50, 52, 53, 313
Chittenden, Russell H. 517
Chittenden, Simeon B. 109, 114, 116
Chittenden, Thomas 6, 313
Chittenden, Thomas C. 75, 77
Chittendin, Simeon B. 111
Chitwood, Robert H. 485
Chlopek, Anthony 504
Chmurny, William W. 424
Choate, Joseph H. 362, 511
Choate, Mrs. Arthur O. 523
Choate, Rufus 67, 69, 74, 76, 78, 301, 540
Choate, Winfield S. 389
Chodorow, Marvin 543
Chollar, Robert G. 432
Chope, Harold D. 535
Choy, Herbert Y. C. 285
Choy, Wilbur W. Y. 472
Chrisman, Charles S. 562
Chrisman, James S. 88, 320
Christ, Benjamin C. 336
Christensen, A. Sherman 287
Christensen, B. V. 516
Christensen, Harold 536
Christensen, Henry C. 559
Christensen, Lew 536
Christensen, P. P. 17
Christensen, Val S. 399
Christensen, Walter 386

Christensen, William 536
Christfield, J. A. Pearce 544
Christgau, Victor 188, 191
Christian, Henry A. 533
Christian, John 389
Christian, Letitia 20
Christian, Shirley 558
Christiancy, Isaac P. 111, 113, 301, 370
Christianson, Theodore 195, 198, 301
Christie, Alexander 464
Christie, Alexander G. 520
Christie, Andrew D. 294
Christie, Gabriel 42, 43, 45
Christie, H. Frederick 496
Christ-Janer, Arland F. 404, 407, 416
Christman, W. W. 535
Christoffersen, Ralph E. 407
Christopher, George 386
Christopher, George H. 221, 230, 233, 237
Christopher, Warren 552
Christopherson, Charles A. 174, 177, 180, 183, 186, 189, 193
Christopherson, Weston R. 493
Christy, Francis T. 493
Christy, John G. 392
Christy, Lloyd B. 385
Christy, Robert W. 405
Chrysler, Walter P. 485
Chubb, Edwin W. 414
Chubb, Lewis W. 539
Chudoff, Earl 222, 225, 228, 231, 234
Church, A. B. 418
Church, Alonzo 419
Church, Benjamin 332
Church, Denver S. 161, 165, 168, 194
Church, Foster 557
Church, Frank 232, 236, 239, 242, 245, 249, 252, 255, 258, 261, 264, 268
Church, Frank F. 296
Church, Frederic E. 536
Church, John H. 344
Church, Marguerite Stitt 223, 226, 229, 233, 236, 239
Church, Ralph E. 197, 200, 204, 210, 213, 217, 220
Church, Samuel 294
Church, Sanford E. 306
Church, Thomas 532
Churchill, Alfred V. 443
Churchill, John C. 102, 104
Churchill, Marlborough 329
Churchill, Neil 394
Churchill, Sylvester 331
Churchill, Thomas J. 292
Churchill, Winston 521
Churchwell, William M. 87, 89
Ciampi, Anthony F. 406
Cianci, Vincent A., Jr. 395
Cicaterri, Felix 422
Cilley, Bradbury 54, 55
Cilley, Jonathan 72
Cilley, Joseph 80, 304
Cilley, Robert Howard 456
Cisler, Walker L. 486, 520, 538, 539, 541
Cisneros, Henry G. 397
Citron, William M. 197, 200
Civiletti, Benjamin R. 31, 35
Cizik, Robert 486
Claflin, William 113, 116, 300
Clagett, Clifton 48, 56, 58
Claggett, John T. 447, 459
Clague, Frank 175, 179, 182, 185, 188, 191

Claiborne, James R. 195, 198
Claiborne, John 49, 51
Claiborne, John F. H. 71, 73
Claiborne, Mrs. Robert W. 443
Claiborne, Nathaniel H. 63, 65, 67, 68, 70, 72
Claiborne, Randolph R., Jr. 454, 458
Claiborne, Thomas 43, 44, 45, 47, 48, 57
Claiborne, William C. C. 45, 46, 56, 298, 299
Clair, James 406
Clair, Matthew W. 471
Clair, Matthew W., Jr. 471
Clamer, Guilliam H. 537
Clancy, Donald D. 241, 244, 247, 250, 253, 256, 260, 263, 394
Clancy, John M. 128, 131, 134
Clancy, John R. 163
Clancy, Robert H. 179, 185, 188, 191
Clap, Thomas 427
Clapham, A. R. 490
Clapp, Almon M. 380
Clapp, Asa W. H. 82
Clapp, Charles H. 421
Clapp, Frederick M. 439
Clapp, Gordon R. 382
Clapp, Henry W. 392
Clapp, J. W. 320
Clapp, Margaret 425, 555
Clapp, Moses E. 142, 145, 147, 150, 153, 156, 159, 163, 166, 302
Clapp, Norton 499
Clapp, Verner W. 543
Clapp, W. L. 396
Clardy, John D. 136, 139
Clardy, Kit F. 227
Clardy, Martin L. 116, 118, 121, 123, 125
Clare, David R. 490
Clarey, Bernard A. 348
Clark, Aaron 393
Clark, Abraham 1, 2, 3, 42, 43
Clark, Addison 417
Clark, Albert P. 417
Clark, Alex M. 388
Clark, Alonzo M. 315
Clark, Alvah A. 114, 116
Clark, Alvan 560
Clark, Ambrose W. 96, 98
Clark, Amos, Jr. 109
Clark, Barry G. 560
Clark, Barzilla W. 296
Clark, Bennett C. 286
Clark, Bennett Champ 192, 195, 198, 201, 204, 208, 211, 303
Clark, Champ 133, 139, 142, 145, 148, 151, 153, 156, 158, 160, 161, 163, 164, 166, 168, 169, 172
Clark, Charles 285, 302, 322
Clark, Charles A. 296
Clark, Charles B. 127, 129
Clark, Charles E. 284
Clark, Charles N. 136
Clark, Christopher 48, 49
Clark, Clarence D. 129, 132, 135, 138, 141, 143, 146, 149, 152, 155, 158, 161, 164, 168, 315
Clark, D. Worth 197, 200, 204, 207, 210, 296
Clark, Daniel 92, 94, 96, 97, 98, 100, 304
Clark, David H. 349
Clark, Davis W. 471
Clark, Donald S. 519

Clark, E. W. 499
Clark, Edward 312
Clark, Edward A. 355
Clark, Edward S. 431
Clark, Edward W. 516
Clark, Eleanor 545
Clark, Eliot 521, 525
Clark, Eugene C. 544
Clark, Ezra, Jr. 89, 91
Clark, Francine J. M. 431
Clark, Frank 150, 152, 155, 158, 162, 165, 168, 171, 175, 178
Clark, Frank M. 231, 234, 237, 241, 244, 247, 250, 254, 257, 260
Clark, Frank R. 510, 552
Clark, Franklin 82
Clark, Fred E. 515
Clark, G. Edward 362, 367, 372
Clark, George 389, 505
Clark, George C. 511
Clark, George H. 386
Clark, George R. 347, 509
Clark, George Rogers 335
Clark, George T. 386
Clark, Georgia Neese 381
Clark, Grenville 532, 559
Clark, Harry C. 386
Clark, Henry A. 170
Clark, Henry S. 80
Clark, Henry T. 307
Clark, Herbert B. 475
Clark, Homer J. 403
Clark, Horace 498
Clark, Horace F. 92, 94
Clark, J. Bayard 189, 192, 195, 199, 202, 205, 208, 212, 215, 218
Clark, J. Reuben, Jr. 367
Clark, James 53, 55, 62, 64, 65, 298, 406, 425
Clark, James G. 426
Clark, James P. 146, 149
Clark, James W. 55
Clark, Jasper 504
Clark, Jesse 504
Clark, Joan M. 367
Clark, John 294, 295, 387, 397
Clark, John B. 92, 94, 96, 320, 321, 473, 513
Clark, John B., Jr. 109, 111, 113, 116, 118
Clark, John C. 64, 73, 75, 77
Clark, John F. 537
Clark, John H. 87
Clark, John S. 513, 540
Clark, Joseph 473
Clark, Joseph J. 348
Clark, Joseph S. 234, 237, 241, 244, 247, 250, 309, 395
Clark, Kenneth B. 518, 561
Clark, Leslie J. 561
Clark, Lewis W. 305
Clark, Lincoln 86
Clark, Linwood L. 188
Clark, Lot 61
Clark, Louise Bennett 440
Clark, Lucius C. 403
Clark, Malcolm E. 418
Clark, Mark W. 333, 334, 339, 341, 344
Clark, Matthew H. 468
Clark, Myron 306
Clark, Paul F. 490
Clark, Ramsey 30, 35
Clark, Raymond M. 411
Clark, Richard 258, 261, 265, 297
Clark, Robert 58
Clark, Robert D. 405, 422

Denver, James W. *89*
Denver, Matthew R. *154, 157, 160*
Denwinski, Edward J. *271*
DePaulis, Palmer *397*
Depew, Chauncey M. *142, 145, 148, 151, 154, 157, 306*
Depew, Ganson *527*
DePeyster, Abraham *7*
dePoix, Vincent P. *348*
DePriest, Oscar *187, 191, 194*
Depue, David A. *305*
Derbes, Daniel W. *496*
Derbigny, Pierre *298*
Derby, Ethel Roosevelt *560*
Derby, Samuel C. *403*
Derby, Wilfred N. *417*
Derbyshire, Arthur *440*
Dercum, Francis X. *516, 517*
Dergarabedian, Paul *510*
Derge, David R. *416*
Dern, George H. *29, 34, 312*
DeRocco, Andrew G. *407*
DeRouen, Rene L. *185, 188, 191, 194, 198, 201, 204*
Derounian, Steven B. *227, 231, 234, 237, 240, 243*
Derrick, Butler *263, 269, 272, 276, 279*
Derrick, Butler C. *266*
Dershem, Frank L. *164*
Derthick, Lawrence G. *381*
DeRussy, Rene E. *418*
Dervall, William *393*
Derwent, Clarence *503*
Derwin, Frank *504*
Derwinski, Edward J. *236, 239, 242, 246, 249, 252, 255, 258, 261, 264, 268*
Des Portes, Fay A. *357, 359, 363*
DeSantis, Ann *557*
deSaussure, Edward H., Jr. *345*
deSaussure, Henry W. *396*
DeSaussure, William F. *87, 311, 396*
Desch, Carl W. *432*
deSchweinitz, Edmund A. *413*
Desfor, Max *555*
Desha, Joseph *50, 51, 52, 53, 55, 56, 298*
Desha, Robert *65, 67*
Deshler, Charles *544*
Desmond, Charles S. *306*
Desmond, Daniel F. *467*
Deterding, Henri W. A. *496*
Dethier, Vincent G. *520*
Detweiler, Meade D. *521*
Deukmejian, George *292*
Deupree, Richard R. *495*
Deussen, Alexander *510, 552*
Deuster, Peter V. *117, 119, 122*
Deutermann, Harold T. *348*
Deutsch, Karl W. *518*
Deutsch, Martin *560*
Devan, R. P. *398*
Devaney, Charles *390*
Devaney, John P. *302*
DeVaux, William *504*
Devens, Charles *26, 35, 337*
Dever, Paul A. *301*
Dever, William E. *388*
Devereaux, Gregory *440*
Devereux, Harry H. *388*
Devereux, James P. S. *223, 227, 230, 233*
Devers, Jacob L. *332, 339, 340*
Devin, William A. *307*
Devin, William F. *398*
Devine, Frank J. *360*
Devine, J. M. *397*

Devine, John M. *343*
Devine, Joseph M. *307*
Devine, Samuel L. *237, 241, 247, 250, 253, 256, 260, 263, 266, 269*
Deviny, John J. *380*
DeVita, Vincent T., Jr. *543*
Devitt, Edward I. *404*
Devitt, Edward J. *217*
Devitt, James E. *492*
DeVitt, John H. *525*
Devlin, William *404*
DeVoe, W. R. *544*
DeVorss, Claude M. *524*
DeVos, Peter J. *363, 371*
DeVos, Peter Jon *368*
DeVoto, Bernard *534, 545, 555*
deVries, Douwe *541*
DeVries, Marion *287*
Dew, Robb Forman *547*
Dew, Thomas R. *406*
DeWald, Ernest T. *442*
Dewalt, Arthur G. *167, 170, 173*
Dewart, Lewis *68*
D'Ewart, Wesley A. *214, 217, 221, 224, 227*
Dewart, William L. *92*
Deweese, John T. *102, 105*
Dewey, Bradley *511*
Dewey, Charles *492*
Dewey, Charles S. *207, 210*
Dewey, Daniel *53*
Dewey, Davis R. *513*
Dewey, George *350*
Dewey, John *510, 518, 536*
Dewey, Julius Y. *492*
Dewey, Martin *512*
Dewey, Melvil *514, 515*
Dewey, Nelson *315*
Dewey, Richard *518*
Dewey, Thomas E. *18, 306, 559*
Dewhurst, Colleen *503*
Dewine, Michael *275, 278*
Dewing, Thomas W. *536, 551*
DeWitt, Charles *4*
DeWitt, Charles G. *66, 361*
DeWitt, J. Doyle *497, 498*
DeWitt, Jesse R. *472*
DeWitt, John H. *334*
DeWitt, John L. *332, 340, 351*
DeWitt, Norman W. *517*
Dewitt, Robert L. *455, 460*
DeWitt, W. H. *320*
DeWolf, James *60, 62, 63*
DeWolfe, Florence (Kling) *20*
DeWolfe, James P. *453, 459*
Dexter, Andrew *385*
Dexter, Gregory *6*
Dexter, Lewis *532*
Dexter, Samuel *23, 33, 34, 43, 46, 301*
Dexter, Walter F. *524*
Dey, J. Ramsey *387*
DeYoung, Russell *489*
Dezendorf, John F. *119*
d'Harnoncourt, Rene *441*
Dhilton, William P. *319*
di Cesnola, Louis Palma *440*
Diak, William N. *37*
Dial, Morse G. *498*
Dial, Nathaniel B. *173, 177, 180, 311*
Diamandopoulos, Peter *403*
Diamond, Bernard *559*
Diamond, Jared M. *535*
Diamond, Louis K. *542, 559*
Diamond, Sidney *381*
Dibble, Samuel *119, 121, 124, 126, 129*
DiBiaggio, John A. *412, 419*

Dibitonto, Sam *392*
DiBona, Charles J. *516*
Dibrell, George G. *112, 114, 117, 119, 121*
DiCarlo, Dominick L. *287*
Dice, Lee R. *522*
Dichman, Ernest *358*
Dick, Charles W. F. *140, 142, 145, 148, 151, 154, 157, 308*
Dick, John *88, 90, 92*
Dick, Paul S. *498*
Dick, Samuel *3*
Dick, Samuel B. *116*
Dick, William W., Jr. *330, 333*
Dicke, Robert H. *537, 549, 560*
Dickens, J. L. *417*
Dickens, Samuel *55*
Dickenson, Julian *528*
Dickenson, Russell E. *380*
Dickerman, Charles H. *148*
Dickerson, Denver S. *304*
Dickerson, George W. *345*
Dickerson, Mahlon *24, 35, 56, 58, 59, 61, 63, 64, 66, 68, 305*
Dickerson, Philemon *69, 71, 75, 305*
Dickerson, William W. *127, 130*
Dickey, Charles A. *473*
Dickey, Charles D., Jr. *496*
Dickey, Donald E. *535*
Dickey, Frank G. *420*
Dickey, Henry L. *114, 116*
Dickey, James *545*
Dickey, James E. *408, 471*
Dickey, Jesse C. *85*
Dickey, John *79, 83*
Dickey, John S. *407*
Dickey, Oliver J. *103, 105, 107*
Dickie, Samuel *403*
Dickinson, Andrew B. *368*
Dickinson, Baxter *473*
Dickinson, Charles M. *357*
Dickinson, Clement C. *156, 160, 163, 166, 169, 172, 179, 182, 185, 192, 195*
Dickinson, Daniel S. *78, 80, 82, 84, 306*
Dickinson, David W. *70, 79*
Dickinson, Don M. *26, 27, 36*
Dickinson, Dwight *374*
Dickinson, Edward *88*
Dickinson, Edward F. *105*
Dickinson, Edwin *535*
Dickinson, Edwin D. *519*
Dickinson, H. C. *398*
Dickinson, J. C., Jr. *439*
Dickinson, Jacob M. *28, 34, 511, 523*
Dickinson, James S. *321*
Dickinson, John *1, 2, 3, 4, 5, 6*
Dickinson, John D. *58, 60, 64, 66*
Dickinson, Jonathan *395, 414*
Dickinson, Lauren D. *301*
Dickinson, Lester J. *172, 175, 178, 181, 184, 188, 191, 194, 197, 297*
Dickinson, Philemon *3, 41, 42, 305, 335*
Dickinson, Rodolphus *82, 84*
Dickinson, Sidney E. *531*
Dickinson, William L. *245, 248, 251, 254, 258, 261, 264, 267, 270, 273, 276*
Dickman, Francois *375*
Dickman, Francois M. *365*
Dickman, Franklin *308*
Dickman, James B. *558*
Dickman, Joseph T. *333, 339*
Dickmann, Bernard F. *392*

Dicks, Norman D. *267, 270, 273, 276, 279*
Dickson, Alex D. *462*
Dickson, Alex D., Jr. *457*
Dickson, David *71*
Dickson, Frank S. *150*
Dickson, Janet S. *538*
Dickson, John *68, 69, 472*
Dickson, Joseph *46*
Dickson, Leonard E. *515*
Dickson, Samuel *90*
Dickson, Thomas H. *391*
Dickson, William *47, 48, 49*
Dickson, William A. *156, 159*
Dickstein, Samuel *179, 182, 186, 189, 192, 195, 198, 202, 205, 208, 211, 215*
Dicus, Richard E. *454*
Diefendorf, Charles H. *491*
Diehl, Conrad *393*
Diehl, Michael *426*
Diehl, Samuel W. B. *347*
Diehl, William J. *395*
Diekema, Gerrit J. *153, 156, 368*
Dielman, Frederick *525*
Dierckes, Albert A. *427*
Dies, Martin *158, 161, 164, 167, 170*
Dies, Martin, Jr. *193, 196, 199, 203, 206, 209, 212, 228, 231, 235*
Diesel, John P. *497*
Dietel, William M. *433*
Dieterich, William *191*
Dieterich, William H. *194, 197, 200, 296*
Dietrich, C. Elmer *199*
Dietrich, Charles H. *145, 148, 303*
Dietrich, Frank S. *285*
Dietrich, Joseph R. *516*
Dietrich, Robert A. *519*
Dietz, David *554*
Dietz, William *63*
Dietz, William C. *559*
DiFederico, Mario A. *488*
Diffenderfer, Robert E. *160, 164*
Digges, Edward *6*
Diggs, Charles C., Jr. *230, 233, 236, 240, 243, 246, 249, 252, 256, 259, 262, 265, 268*
Dilcher, David L. *521*
Dilg, Will H. *523*
Dill, Clarence C. *167, 171, 180, 183, 187, 190, 193, 196, 314*
Dill, David B. *517*
Dill, Franklin G. *423*
Dillard, Annie *557*
Dillard, Hardy C. *519*
Dillard, James H. *559*
Dillery, C. Edward *361, 374*
Dilliard, Irving *544*
Dillin, Harry L. *475*
Dilling, George W. *398*
Dillingham, Paul, Jr. *79, 81, 313*
Dillingham, William P. *143, 146, 149, 152, 155, 158, 161, 164, 167, 171, 174, 177, 313*
Dillon, C. Douglas *30, 34, 361, 548*
Dillon, Charles H. *164, 167, 170*
Dillon, F. J. *503*
Dillon, Francis J. *505*
Dillon, George *553*
Dillon, John F. *511*
Dillon, Joseph E. *391*
Dillon, Patrick *421*
Dillon, Richard C. *305*

Farrand, Livingston *407, 419, 516, 526*
Farrand, Max *439, 513*
Farrar, Donald K. *483*
Farrar, Edgar H. *511*
Farrar, Frank L. *311*
Farrell, Francis D. *411*
Farrell, Francis W. *334*
Farrell, James A. *499, 539*
Farrell, James P. *432*
Farrell, Raymond F. *380*
Farrell, Suzanne *535*
Farrelly, John P. *469*
Farrelly, John W. *83*
Farrelly, Patrick *60, 61, 63*
Farrington, James *73*
Farrington, Valerie *440*
Farris, Jerome *286*
Farrow, James *320, 321*
Farrow, Samuel *54*
Farwell, Charles B. *106, 108, 110, 117, 122, 125, 127, 296*
Farwell, Leonard J. *315*
Farwell, Nathan A. *98, 299*
Farwell, Sewall S. *118*
Fary, John G. *264, 268, 271*
Fascell, Dante B. *229, 232, 236, 239, 242, 245, 248, 252, 255, 258, 261, 264, 267, 270, 274, 277*
Fasi, Frank F. *388*
Fass, Horst *557*
Fassett, J. Sloat *151, 154, 157*
Fast, Gustave *562*
Fatzer, Harold R. *298*
Faubus, Orville *292*
Faulkner, Charles J. *87, 89, 91, 93, 112, 127, 129, 132, 135, 138, 140, 315, 361*
Faulkner, William *541, 545, 547, 549, 555, 556*
Faunce, William H. P. *405*
Fauquier, Francis *6*
Faurer, Lincoln D. *381*
Faust, Charles L. *176, 179, 182, 185, 522, 531*
Faust, Daniel *396*
Faville, William B. *514*
Favrot, George K. *153, 175, 178*
Fawcett, Jacob *304*
Fawcett, M. Edward *450, 461*
Fawcett, Novice G. *414*
Fawell, Harris *277*
Fawick, Thomas L. *562*
Fay, Albert B. *374*
Fay, C. N. *544*
Fay, Eliphaz *406*
Fay, Francis B. *86*
Fay, Harold J. W. *544*
Fay, James H. *205, 211*
Fay, John *58*
Fay, Peter T. *285, 286*
Fay, Sidney B. *513*
Fay, Theodore S. *373*
Fazio, Victor H. *267, 270, 273, 276*
Fearing, Lamar M. *490*
Fearn, J. Walker *362, 371, 372*
Fearn, Thomas M. *319*
Featherston, Winfield S. *82, 84, 324*
Featherstone, Lewis P. *127*
Feazel, William C. *217, 299*
Fechet, James E. *330*
Fechteler, William M. *347, 348*
Fecteau, George O. *506*
Fedeli, Frederick *497*
Federal, Joseph Lennox *470*
Fedigan, John *424*
Fee, James A. *285*

Fee, John G. *404*
Feehan, Daniel F. *467*
Feehan, Patrick A. *463, 469*
Feely, Edward F. *357*
Feely, John J. *144*
Feeney, Al G. *388*
Feeney, Daniel J. *467*
Feese, A. O. *522*
Fehrenbacher, Don E. *558*
Feiffer, Jules *558*
Feighan, Edward F. *275, 278*
Feighan, Michael A. *212, 215, 218, 221, 224, 228, 231, 234, 237, 241, 244, 247, 250, 253*
Feild, Alexander L. *538*
Fein, Nathaniel *555*
Feinberg, Wilfred *284*
Feiner, William *409*
Feininger, Lyonel *551*
Feinstein, Dianne *386*
Feis, Herbert *556*
Feist, Irving J. *521*
Felch, Alpheus *82, 84, 86, 301*
Felder, John M. *68, 70*
Feldman, George J. *366, 367*
Feldman, Harvey J. *369, 372*
Feldman, Herman *332*
Feldman, Irving *531*
Feldman, Melvin J. *516*
Feldmann, Louis G. *528*
Felix, Robert *533*
Felix, Robert H. *518, 535*
Felker, Samuel D. *304*
Fell, D. Newlin *309*
Fell, John *3*
Fell, Thomas *415*
Fell, Thomas B. *420*
Feller, William *549*
Fellman, David *510*
Fellows, Charles A. *389*
Fellows, Frank *207, 211, 214, 217, 220, 223*
Fellows, George E. *420*
Fellows, Harold E. *525*
Fellows, John A. *519*
Fellows, John R. *131, 134*
Fellows, Raymond *300*
Fellows, Samuel M. *407*
Felmley, David *410*
Fels, Prof. Rendigs *513*
Fels, Samuel S. *432*
Fels, William C. *404*
Felt, Harry D. *347, 348*
Felton, Charles N. *122, 124, 130, 292*
Felton, Cornelius C. *409*
Felton, William H. *110, 113, 115*
Feltus, Alan *536*
Fendall, Josias *5*
Fenerty, Clare G. *199*
Fenn, E. Hart *174, 178, 181, 184, 187*
Fenn, Wallace O. *517, 532*
Fenneman, Nevin M. *523*
Fenner, Arthur *310*
Fenner, Goodrich R. *452, 459*
Fenner, James *49, 50, 310*
Fenton, Frank *405*
Fenton, Ivor D. *205, 209, 212, 215, 218, 222, 225, 228, 231, 234, 238, 241*
Fenton, John *542*
Fenton, John E. *521*
Fenton, Lucien J. *137, 140*
Fenton, Reuben E. *88, 94, 96, 98, 104, 107, 109, 306*
Fenton, William *442*
Fentress, Calvin, Jr. *431*
Fenwick, Benedict J. *409, 467*
Fenwick, Charles G. *519*

Fenwick, Edward *469*
Fenwick, Enoch *409*
Fenwick, Millicent H. *262, 265, 269, 272*
Ferber, Edna *553*
Ferber, Robert *515*
Ferch, John A. *364*
Ferdon, John W. *116*
Fergusen, Glenn *419*
Ferguson, Albert L. *522*
Ferguson, Arthur D. *386*
Ferguson, C. Vaughan *366*
Ferguson, Charles B. *441*
Ferguson, Clarence C., Jr. *374*
Ferguson, Francis E. *493*
Ferguson, Franklin L. *414*
Ferguson, Glenn W. *365*
Ferguson, Harley B. *351*
Ferguson, Homer *211, 214, 217, 220, 224, 227, 301, 370*
Ferguson, Homer L. *522*
Ferguson, Jack H. *499*
Ferguson, James *346*
Ferguson, James E. *312*
Ferguson, James L. *488*
Ferguson, James M. *474*
Ferguson, James S. *421*
Ferguson, John *393*
Ferguson, John H. *367*
Ferguson, Margaret C. *521*
Ferguson, Milton J. *515*
Ferguson, Miriam A. *312*
Ferguson, Mrs. C. Vaughan *523*
Ferguson, Phil *199, 202, 205*
Ferguson, R. G. *473*
Ferguson, Samuel D. *449*
Ferguson, Sydney *492*
Ferguson, Thomas B. *373*
Ferguson, Warren J. *286*
Ferguson, William S. *513*
Fergusson, Harvey B. *160, 163*
Ferland, E. James *495*
Ferle, Jacob W. *391*
Fermi, Enrico *517, 534, 538, 539, 549, 560*
Fern, Alan *441*
Fern, Joseph J. *388*
Fernald, Bert M. *165, 169, 172, 175, 178, 181, 299*
Fernald, Merritt C. *420*
Fernald, Merritt L. *521, 543*
Fernandez, Antonio M. *211, 215, 218, 221, 224, 227, 230*
Fernandez, Joachim O. *191, 194, 198, 201, 204*
Fernandez, Louis *492*
Ferrara, Linda *546*
Ferrari, Michael R., Jr. *404, 408*
Ferrario, Joseph A. *466*
Ferraro, Geraldine A. *19, 269, 272, 275*
Ferre, Luis A. *541*
Ferrell, John A. *518*
Ferrell, Joseph L. *537*
Ferrell, Thomas M. *121*
Ferrero, Edward *338*
Ferri, Antonio *559*
Ferris, Charles D. *379*
Ferris, Charles G. *69, 77*
Ferris, David L. *451, 461, 462*
Ferris, Isaac *413*
Ferris, Scott *154, 157, 160, 164, 167, 170, 173*
Ferris, Woodbridge N. *179, 182, 185, 301*
Ferriss, Orange *102, 104*
Ferriter, John P. *360*
Ferry, Elisha P. *314*
Ferry, Frederick C. *409*

Ferry, Orris S. *93, 101, 103, 105, 108, 110, 294*
Ferry, Thomas W. *100, 102, 104, 106, 108, 110, 111, 112, 113, 116, 118, 301*
Ferry, William M. *397*
Ferusson, Frances Daly *424*
Fery, John B. *483, 484*
Feschback, Herman *549*
Fess, Simeon D. *163, 167, 170, 173, 176, 179, 183, 186, 189, 192, 195, 308, 403*
Fessenden, Edson *494*
Fessenden, Reginald A. *541*
Fessenden, Samuel C. *96*
Fessenden, Thomas A. D. *96*
Fessenden, William P. *25, 33, 76, 88, 90, 91, 94, 96, 98, 100, 102, 104, 299*
Festge, Otto *398*
Fetchko, Peter *442*
Fethers, Ogden H. *524*
Fetter, Frank A. *513*
Fetterman, John *557*
Fetterolf, C. Fred *481*
Fetters, Karl L. *514*
Feuerstein, Moses I. *476*
Few, Ignatius A. *408*
Few, William *2, 3, 41, 42, 295, 485*
Few, William P. *408*
Fewkes, John M. *503*
Fey, John T. *423, 424, 487, 492*
Feynman, Richard P. *538, 549, 550*
Fibiger, John A. *493*
Fickel, Jacob E. *340*
Ficken, John F. *396*
Ficklin, Orlando B. *78, 80, 81, 85*
Fiebach, Albert H. *527*
Fiedler, Arthur *552*
Fiedler, Bobbi *270, 273, 276*
Fiedler, William H. F. *121*
Field, Allan B. *542*
Field, Charles L. *527*
Field, Charles W. *323*
Field, Crosby *533*
Field, David Dudley *111, 511*
Field, Edward *561*
Field, F. A. *391*
Field, Fred T. *301*
Field, George R. *424*
Field, James G. *17*
Field, John A., Jr. *284*
Field, Moses W. *108*
Field, Richard M. *513*
Field, Richard S. *96, 305*
Field, Scott *149, 152*
Field, Stanley *486*
Field, Stephen J. *283, 292*
Field, Thomas S. *426*
Field, Walbridge A. *113, 116, 301*
Field, William O. *538*
Fielder, George B. *134*
Fielder, James F. *305*
Fields, Emmet B. *416*
Fields, J. J. *505*
Fields, Jack M., Jr. *273, 276, 279*
Fields, William C. *102*
Fields, William J. *159, 162, 165, 169, 172, 175, 178, 298*
Fiesinger, William L. *192, 195, 199*
Fife, Ray *413*
Fife, Robert H. *524*
Fifer, Joseph W. *296*
Figgins, Jessie D. *439*
Filan, Frank *554*

Filbey, Emery T. *442*
Filbey, Francis S. *503*
Filblert, William J. *539*
Filene, Edward A. *434*
Filer, John H. *481*
Filler, Mervin G. *407*
Fillerbrown, Thomas *512*
Filley, Chauncey I. *392*
Filley, Oliver D. *392*
Fillmore, Charles *477*
Fillmore, Millard *11, 12, 15, 16, 25, 69, 73, 75, 77, 83, 85, 416*
Filo, John Paul *557*
Finan, John M. *504*
Finberg, Barbara D. *433*
Finch, Charles C. *302*
Finch, Herbert I. *487*
Finch, Isaac *66*
Finch, Robert H. *31, 37*
Finch, Rogers B. *520*
Finch, William C. *408*
Finch, William R. *369, 375*
Fincher, John A. *406*
Finck, Furman J. *531*
Finck, William E. *98, 100, 109*
Findlay, James *63, 65, 66, 68*
Findlay, John *60, 61, 63*
Findlay, John V. L. *120*
Findlay, William *60, 61, 63, 309*
Findley, Paul *239, 242, 246, 249, 252, 255, 258, 261, 264, 268, 271*
Findley, William *42, 43, 44, 45, 48, 49, 50, 51, 53, 54, 55*
Fine, Henry B. *515*
Fine, John *75*
Fine, John S. *309*
Fine, Morris E. *534*
Fine, Sidney A. *224, 227, 231*
Finerty, John F. *120*
Finger, H. Ellis, Jr. *472*
Finger, John W. *527*
Fink, Albert *519*
Fink, Colin G. *522, 531*
Fink, Daniel J. *537*
Fink, Donald G. *523*
Fink, George R. *541*
Fink, Michael L. *466*
Finkelnburg, Gustavus A. *104, 106*
Finlay, Kirkman, Jr. *396*
Finlay, Kirkman G. *451, 461*
Finlayson, John D. *423, 426*
Finletter, Thomas K. *327*
Finley, Charles *188, 191*
Finley, Clement A. *332*
Finley, David E. *143, 146, 149, 151, 154, 157, 161, 164, 167, 441, 559*
Finley, Ebenezer B. *114, 116*
Finley, Hugh F. *125, 127*
Finley, James C. *408*
Finley, Jesse J. *110, 113, 117, 396*
Finley, John H. *406, 411, 513*
Finley, Mark F. *512*
Finley, Murray H. *503*
Finley, Robert *419*
Finley, Robert C. *314*
Finley, Samuel *414*
Finley, Thomas D. *343*
Finley, W. A. *414*
Finley, W. W. *496*
Finn, Ronald *543*
Finnegan, Edward R. *239, 242*
Finnegan, George J. *468*
Finnegan, Hugh M. *407*
Finnegan, John G. *348*
Finnegan, Joseph F. *379*

Finnegan, Philip J. *285*
Finney, Benjamin F. *423*
Finney, C. M. *525*
Finney, Charles G. *414*
Finney, Darwin A. *103*
Finney, John M. T. *512*
Finney, Nat S. *555*
Finney, Ross Lee *535*
Fino, Paul A. *227, 231, 234, 237, 240, 243, 247, 250*
Fintel, Norman D. *415*
Fiorenza, Joseph A. *470*
Firestone, Floyd A. *544*
Firestone, Harvey S. *488*
Firestone, Harvey S., Jr. *488*
Firestone, Leonard Kimball *356*
Firestone, Raymond C. *488*
Fischelis, Robert P. *559*
Fischer, Clyde L. *386*
Fischer, David J. *372*
Fischer, Emil *537*
Fischer, Ernst G. *551*
Fischer, Fred *391*
Fischer, George D. *525*
Fischer, Israel F. *137, 139, 287*
Fischer, John *503*
Fischer, John H. *433*
Fischer, John S. *309*
Fischer, Louis *545*
Fischer, Louis E. *489*
Fischetti, John *557*
Fischl, Louis J. *516*
Fish, A. J. *387*
Fish, Bert *360, 370, 372*
Fish, Charles J. *438*
Fish, Frederick P. *482*
Fish, Hamilton *26, 33, 79, 86, 88, 90, 157, 306, 528*
Fish, Hamilton, Jr. *173, 176, 179, 182, 186, 189, 192, 195, 198, 202, 205, 208, 211, 253, 256, 259, 262, 266, 269, 272, 275, 278*
Fish, Nicholas *356, 373*
Fish, Stuyvesant *490*
Fish, William H. *296*
Fishback, William M. *292*
Fishbourn, William *395*
Fishburne, John W. *193*
Fishel, Leslie H., Jr. *410*
Fisher, Albert K. *516*
Fisher, Bernard *543*
Fisher, C. Harold *514*
Fisher, Charles *57, 58, 75*
Fisher, David *82*
Fisher, Edward D. *516*
Fisher, Frederick B. *471*
Fisher, George *66*
Fisher, George P. *95, 513*
Fisher, Harry L. *511, 514*
Fisher, Hendrick *1*
Fisher, Horatio G. *116, 119*
Fisher, Hubert F. *170, 174, 177, 180, 183, 186, 190*
Fisher, Irving *513, 526*
Fisher, Jerome B. *521*
Fisher, John *104*
Fisher, Joseph A. *506*
Fisher, Joseph L. *263, 267, 270, 433*
Fisher, Max M. *498*
Fisher, Michael M. *421, 426*
Fisher, O. Clark *212, 215, 219, 222, 225, 228, 231, 235, 238, 241, 244, 247, 251, 254, 257, 260*
Fisher, Samuel *473*
Fisher, Samuel S. *381*
Fisher, Samuel W. *409, 473*
Fisher, Spencer O. *123, 125*
Fisher, Stephen E. *476*

Fisher, W. C. *396*
Fisher, Walter C. *524*
Fisher, Walter L. *28, 36*
Fisher, William *395*
Fisk, B. F. *261*
Fisk, Clinton B. *16*
Fisk, Dwight *399*
Fisk, Ezra *473*
Fisk, James *49, 50, 53, 54, 57, 313*
Fisk, James B. *541*
Fisk, Jonathan *51, 54, 55*
Fisk, Lewis R. *412*
Fisk, Richmond *415*
Fisk, Wilbur *425*
Fiske, Bradley A. *537*
Fiske, Charles *451, 458*
Fiske, Gertrude *536*
Fiske, Haley *492*
Fiske, Lewis R. *403*
Fiske, Richard S. *441*
Fiske, Thomas S. *515*
Fiske, Wyman P. *525*
Fister, George M. *515*
Fitch, Alvah R. *329*
Fitch, Asa *52*
Fitch, Ashbel P. *126, 128, 131, 134*
Fitch, Aubrey W. *418*
Fitch, Chauncey P. *512*
Fitch, Ebenezer *426*
Fitch, Graham N. *83, 85, 89, 91, 93, 297*
Fitch, Thomas *5, 7, 104*
Fitch, Val *550*
Fitch, Val L. *562*
Fite, Daniel H. *406*
Fite, Dean P. *433*
Fithian, Floyd J. *261, 265, 268, 271*
Fithian, George W. *127, 130, 133*
Fitler, Edwin H. *395*
Fitz, Raymond L. *419*
Fitzel, Lincoln *561*
Fitzgerald, Albert J. *505, 506*
Fitzgerald, C. B. *398*
FitzGerald, Desmond *519*
Fitzgerald, Edmund *493*
Fitzgerald, Edward *465*
Fitzgerald, Edward A. *467*
Fitzgerald, Ernest A. *472*
FitzGerald, Frances *534, 546, 557*
Fitzgerald, Francis A. J. *522*
Fitzgerald, Frank D. *301*
Fitzgerald, James E. *504*
Fitzgerald, James N. *471*
Fitzgerald, John F. *136, 139, 142, 172, 390*
Fitzgerald, John J. *142, 145, 148, 151, 154, 157, 160, 163, 166, 170*
Fitzgerald, Leslie M. *512*
Fitzgerald, Oscar P. *471*
Fitzgerald, Robert *561*
Fitzgerald, Roy G. *176, 179, 183, 186, 189*
Fitzgerald, Rufus H. *422*
Fitzgerald, Thomas *82, 301, 411*
Fitzgerald, Thomas R. *416*
Fitzgerald, Thomas S. *407, 412*
Fitzgerald, William *68*
FitzGerald, William S. *394*
Fitzgerald, William T. *183, 186*
Fitzgibbons, John *195*
FitzHenry, Louis *162, 285*
Fitzhugh, Gilbert W. *492*
Fitzhugh, William *4*
Fitzmaurice, David J. *505*

Fitzmaurice, Edmond J. *465*
Fitzmaurice, John E. *469*
Fitzpatrick, Benjamin *81, 83, 85, 87, 91, 93, 291*
Fitzpatrick, Daniel R. *553, 555*
Fitzpatrick, J. W. *535*
Fitzpatrick, James M. *186, 189, 192, 195, 198, 202, 205, 208, 211*
Fitzpatrick, John *389*
Fitzpatrick, John J. *470*
Fitzpatrick, Leo J. *525*
Fitzpatrick, M. F. *505*
Fitzpatrick, Morgan C. *149*
Fitzpatrick, P. F. *504*
Fitzpatrick, Thomas *557*
Fitzpatrick, Thomas B. *542*
Fitzpatrick, Thomas Y. *139, 141*
Fitzpatrick, William H. *555*
Fitzptrick, Benjamin *89*
Fitzsimmons, Cantidius T. *412*
Fitzsimmons, Frank *504*
Fitzsimmons, Laurence J. *469*
Fitzsimons, George K. *466*
Fitzsimons, Thomas *2, 4, 41, 42, 43*
Fitzwhylson, William H. *398*
Fjare, Orvin B. *230*
Flack, Joseph *357, 359, 370*
Flack, William H. *148, 151*
Flad, Henry *519*
Flager, Thomas T. *88*
Flaget, Benedict J. *466, 467*
Flagg, F. H. *387*
Flagler, Daniel W. *332*
Flagler, Henry M. *487*
Flagler, Thomas T. *90*
Flaherty, Joseph A. *424*
Flaherty, Lawrence J. *181*
Flaherty, Mary Pat *558*
Flaherty, Peter F. *395*
Flaherty, Thomas A. *201, 204, 207*
Flake, Wilson C. *362*
Flamm, Alec *498*
Flanagan, Bernard J. *465, 467*
Flanagan, DeWitt C. *145*
Flanagan, Edward M., Jr. *334*
Flanagan, James L. *538*
Flanagan, James W. *105, 107, 110, 312*
Flanagin, Harris *292*
Flanders, Benjamin F. *96, 299, 389*
Flanders, Ernest V. *544*
Flanders, Ralph E. *216, 219, 222, 225, 228, 232, 235, 313, 520, 541, 544*
Flanders, Walter C. *433*
Flannagan, John W., Jr. *193, 196, 199, 203, 206, 209, 212, 216, 219*
Flanner, Janet *545*
Flannery, J. Harold *202, 205, 209*
Flannery, Joseph P. *498*
Flannery, R. G. *498*
Flannery, Robert G. *492*
Flasch, Kilian C. *470*
Flaum, Joel M. *285*
Flavin, Glennon P. *468*
Flavin, Martin *554*
Flawn, Peter T. *423*
Fleeger, George W. *124*
Fleet, James A. Van *334, 341*
Fleetwood, Frederick G. *180*
Fleger, Anthony A. *202*
Fleischman, Julius *394*
Fleisig, Ross *510*
Fleming, Aretas B. *314*

Fleming, Dewey L. *554*
Fleming, Fenton B. *392*
Fleming, Francis P. *295*
Fleming, J. R. *385*
Fleming, James H. *516*
Fleming, John A. *541*
Fleming, Philip B. *359*
Fleming, Raymond H. *331*
Fleming, Robben W. *420*
Fleming, Robert V. *510*
Fleming, Sam M. *511*
Fleming, Samuel W. *395*
Fleming, Sandford *475*
Fleming, Wallace B. *404*
Fleming, Walter M. *527*
Fleming, William *4*
Fleming, William B. *113*
Fleming, William F. *314*
Fleming, William H. *138, 141, 144*
Fleming, William P. *491*
Flemming, Arthur S. *30, 37, 412, 422*
Flennikan, Robert P. *359*
Flenniken, John C. *425*
Flesh, M. M. *391*
Fletcher, Albert L. *465*
Fletcher, Allen M. *313*
Fletcher, Andrew *514*
Fletcher, Austin B. *526*
Fletcher, Benjamin *5, 6*
Fletcher, Betty B. *286*
Fletcher, Charles K. *216*
Fletcher, Duncan U. *155, 158, 162, 165, 168, 171, 175, 178, 181, 184, 187, 190, 194, 197, 295, 387*
Fletcher, Esten A. *527*
Fletcher, F. Richmond *525*
Fletcher, H. L. *385*
Fletcher, Harvey *517*
Fletcher, Henry *395, 526*
Fletcher, Henry P. *356, 358, 365, 366, 367, 382*
Fletcher, Isaac *74, 75*
Fletcher, James C. *380, 423*
Fletcher, Jefferson B. *524*
Fletcher, Jesse C. *409*
Fletcher, John G. *385*
Fletcher, John Gould *554*
Fletcher, Loren *133, 136, 139, 142, 145, 150*
Fletcher, Maurice J. *541*
Fletcher, Moses *1*
Fletcher, Richard *73, 391*
Fletcher, Ryland *313*
Fletcher, Samuel H. *389*
Fletcher, Stewart G. *519*
Fletcher, Thomas *55, 292*
Fletcher, Thomas B. *183, 186, 195, 199, 202*
Fletcher, Thomas C. *302*
Fletcher, William I. *515*
Flett, Lawrence *514, 532*
Fleure, Herbert J. *538*
Flexner, James T. *546*
Flexner, Simon *510*
Flick, James P. *127, 130*
Flick, Lawrence F. *542*
Flickinger, Daniel *472*
Flinn, Andre *473*
Flint, Austin, Sr. *515*
Flint, Charles L. *420*
Flint, Charles W. *407, 416, 471*
Flint, Edward S. *394*
Flint, Frank P. *149, 152, 155, 292*
Flint, George W. *419*
Flint, Leroy *437*
Flint, Willis H. *392*
Flippin, John R. *396*

Flippo, Ronnie G. *264, 267, 270, 273, 276*
Fliss, Raphael M. *470*
Fljozdal, F. H. *503*
Floch, Joseph *542, 560*
Floersh, John A. *464, 467*
Flood, Daniel J. *215, 222, 225, 231, 234, 238, 241, 244, 247, 250, 254, 257, 260, 263, 266, 269*
Flood, Henry D. *146, 149, 152, 155, 158, 161, 164, 167, 171, 174, 177*
Flood, Joel W. *193*
Flood, Thomas S. *126, 128*
Flora, A. Cline *525*
Florence, Elias *79*
Florence, Fred F. *511*
Florence, Thomas B. *87, 88, 90, 92, 94*
Flores, Patrick F. *464, 470*
Florio, James J. *262, 265, 269, 272, 275, 278*
Florman, Irving *357*
Flory, Paul J. *537, 549, 550, 553*
Flournoy, Craig *558*
Flournoy, Thomas S. *83*
Flower, Ebenezer *386*
Flower, Roswell P. *118, 128, 306*
Flower, Walter C. *389*
Flowerree, Robert E. *489*
Flowers, Robert L. *408*
Flowers, Walter *251, 254, 258, 264*
Floyd, Charles A. *77*
Floyd, Charles M. *304*
Floyd, John *15, 57, 59, 60, 62, 63, 64, 65, 313*
Floyd, John B. *25, 34, 313, 398*
Floyd, John C. *149, 152, 155, 158, 161*
Floyd, John G. *75, 77, 86*
Floyd, William *1, 4, 41*
Fluckey, Eugene B. *347*
Fluno, Francis J. *476*
Fly, James L. *379*
Flye, Edwin *111*
Flynn, Edmund W. *310*
Flynn, Gerald T. *238*
Flynn, J. W. *389*
Flynn, John A. *415*
Flynn, John T. *548*
Flynn, Joseph V. *166, 170*
Flynn, Raymond L. *390*
Flynn, Thomas D. *514*
Flynn, Thomas E. *347*
Flynn, William S. *310*
Flynt, John J., Jr. *229, 236, 239, 242, 245, 249, 252, 255, 258, 261, 264*
Flynt, John James, Jr. *232*
Foard, Fred T. *561*
Focht, Benjamin K. *154, 157, 160, 167, 170, 173, 177, 196, 199, 202*
Focht, John B. *416*
Focke, Arthur E. *519*
Foelker, Otto G. *154, 157*
Foerderer, Robert H. *145*
Foery, Walter A. *468*
Fogarty, John E. *209, 212, 215, 218, 222, 225, 228, 231, 234, 238, 241, 244, 247*
Fogel, Robert William *534*
Fogg, George G. *100, 304, 373*
Fogg, Sanford L. *389*
Fogg, Sanford L., Jr. *389*
Foght, H. W. *426*

Foglietta, Thomas M. *272, 275, 279*
Folds, Charles W. *523*
Foley, B. Charles *412*
Foley, Bill *558*
Foley, Daniel F. *514*
Foley, Eugene P. *382*
Foley, Francis B. *519, 534*
Foley, J. W. *497*
Foley, James B. *91*
Foley, James D. *419*
Foley, John R. *236*
Foley, John S. *467*
Foley, Sylvester R. *348*
Foley, Thomas S. *248, 251, 254, 257, 260, 263, 267, 270, 273, 276, 279*
Folger, Alonzo D. *205, 208*
Folger, Charles J. *26, 34, 306*
Folger, Harry *505*
Folger, John C. *356*
Folger, John H. *208, 212, 215, 218*
Folger, Walter, Jr. *56, 58*
Folger, William M. *349*
Folinsbee, John F. *531*
Folk, Joseph W. *302*
Folkers, Karl *511*
Folks, Homer *559*
Follett, John F. *121*
Follett, W. I. *544*
Folliard, Edward T. *552, 555*
Follis, R. Gwin *485, 533*
Folmar, Emory *385*
Folsom, Frances *20*
Folsom, Frank M. *495, 542*
Folsom, George *368*
Folsom, James E. *291*
Folsom, Marion B. *30, 37, 535*
Folsom, Nathaniel *3*
Folsom, Robert S. *397*
Foltz, J. M. *347*
Folwell, William *456*
Folwell, William H. *458*
Folwell, William W. *420*
Fomon, Samuel J. *534*
Fones, William H. D. *312*
Fong, Hiram L. *236, 239, 242, 245, 249, 252, 255, 258, 261, 296*
Fontana, Mars G. *534*
Fontanne, Lynn *535, 552*
Fontein, Jan *441*
Fonville, R. H. *397*
Foord, Alvin G. *519*
Foot, Solomon *79, 81, 87, 89, 91, 93, 95, 97, 99, 101, 313*
Foote, Andrew H. *350*
Foote, Charles A. *61*
Foote, Edward T., II *420*
Foote, Elisha *381*
Foote, Ellsworth B. *216*
Foote, Henry S. *82, 84, 86, 302, 320, 321*
Foote, J. H. *523*
Foote, Lucius H. *365*
Foote, Norman L. *454, 459*
Foote, Patrick *422*
Foote, Paul D. *517*
Foote, Samuel A. *57, 60, 64, 65, 67, 68, 293*
Foote, Thomas M. *356, 358*
Foote, Wallace T., Jr. *137, 139*
Foote, William A. *486*
Foraker, Joseph B. *140, 142, 145, 148, 151, 154, 307, 308*
Foran, Martin A. *121, 124, 126*
Forand, Aime J. *202, 209, 212, 215, 218, 222, 225, 228, 231, 234, 238*
Forbes, Edward W. *439*

Forbes, Esther *554*
Forbes, Gilbert *534*
Forbes, Harland C. *486*
Forbes, James *3*
Forbes, John F. *416*
Forbes, John M. *355, 485*
Forbes, John S. *537, 544*
Forbes, Malcolm *539*
Forbes, Robert C. *345*
Forbes, Stephen A. *522*
Forbes, W. Cameron *365*
Force, Juliana *444*
Force, Manning F. *338*
Force, Peter *387*
Force, Raymond C. *484*
Force, Roland W. *437, 441*
Forcina, James A. *426*
Ford, Aaron L. *198, 201, 204, 208*
Ford, Betty *541*
Ford, Cornelius *380*
Ford, Edsel *432, 488*
Ford, Edward *494*
Ford, Elbert L. *332*
Ford, Frederick W. *379*
Ford, George *122*
Ford, Gerald *541*
Ford, Gerald R. *11, 12, 19, 31*
Ford, Gerald R., Jr. *220, 224, 227, 230, 233, 236, 240, 243, 246, 249, 252, 256, 259*
Ford, Guy S. *420, 513*
Ford, Harold E. *263, 266, 269, 273, 276, 279*
Ford, Henry *488, 533, 537, 541*
Ford, Henry, II *432, 488, 552*
Ford, Henry J. *517*
Ford, Henry P. *395*
Ford, James *66, 68*
Ford, James R. *387*
Ford, Jeremiah D. M. *509, 524, 542*
Ford, John *535, 552*
Ford, John H. *415*
Ford, John S. *397*
Ford, John W. *524*
Ford, L. H. *319*
Ford, Leland M. *203, 206*
Ford, Melbourne H. *125, 130*
Ford, Morgan *287*
Ford, Nicholas *116, 118*
Ford, Peter S. *524*
Ford, Sam C. *303*
Ford, Seabury *307*
Ford, Stanley H. *329*
Ford, Tennessee Ernie *553*
Ford, Thomas *296*
Ford, Thomas F. *194, 197, 200, 206, 210*
Ford, Wendell H. *262, 265, 268, 271, 274, 277, 298*
Ford, William *493*
Ford, William D. *58, 246, 249, 252, 256, 259, 262, 265, 268, 271, 274, 278*
Ford, Worthington C. *513*
Ford, Y. A. *420*
Fordham, Christopher C., III *421*
Fordney, Joseph W. *142, 145, 147, 150, 153, 156, 159, 163, 166, 169, 172, 175*
Foreman, A. Herbert *527*
Foreman, Edgar F. *253*
Foreman, Thomas M. *319*
Forest, John A. *470*
Forest, Uriah *42*
Forester, John B. *70, 72*
Forgan, James B. *488*
Forker, Samuel C. *107*
Forman, David *335*

Fredendall, Lloyd R. *333, 340, 341*
Frederick, Benjamin T. *120, 122*
Frederick, Robert R. *495*
Frederick, Robert T. *342*
Fredericks, John D. *178, 181*
Fredericks, Marshall M. *532*
Fredricks, Kurt O. *549*
Fredrikson, Roger L. *475*
Free, Arthur M. *174, 178, 181, 184, 187, 190*
Free, Lytle R. *474*
Freed, Arthur *509*
Freed, James *535*
Freedley, John *83, 85*
Freedman, Abraham L. *284*
Freedman, James O. *420*
Freehling, William W. *534*
Freeman, Alice *425*
Freeman, Allen W. *518*
Freeman, Chapman *112, 114*
Freeman, Charles Y. *485*
Freeman, Douglas Southall *556*
Freeman, Douglas Southhall *554*
Freeman, Fulton *359, 367*
Freeman, Gaylord A., Jr. *488*
Freeman, George W. *447, 458*
Freeman, Gordon M. *504*
Freeman, Howard E. *541*
Freeman, James *477*
Freeman, James C. *108*
Freeman, James E. *451, 461*
Freeman, John D. *86*
Freeman, John H. *431*
Freeman, John R. *519, 520, 533, 539*
Freeman, Jonathan *45, 46*
Freeman, Mary E. Wilkins *541*
Freeman, Nathaniel, Jr. *44, 45*
Freeman, Nelson W. *497*
Freeman, Orville L. *30, 31, 36, 301*
Freeman, Paul L., Jr. *332*
Freeman, Raymond L. *520*
Freeman, Richard P. *165, 168, 171, 174, 178, 181, 184, 187, 190*
Freeman, Ruth *535*
Freeman, Ruth B. *526*
Freeman, S. David *382*
Freeman, Thomas W. *320*
Freer, Hamline H. *407*
Freer, Romeo H. *143*
Frei, Emil, III *543*
Freiberg, J. Walter *476*
Freiberg, Julius *476*
Freiberger, I. F. *482*
Freireich, Emil J. *543*
Freking, Frederick W. *466, 470*
Freley, Jasper W. *425*
Frelinghuysen, Frederick *4, 43, 44, 305*
Frelinghuysen, Frederick T. *26, 33, 100, 102, 107, 109, 111, 305, 511*
Frelinghuysen, Joseph S. *169, 173, 176, 305*
Frelinghuysen, Peter H. B., Jr. *227, 230, 234, 237, 240, 243, 247, 250, 253, 256, 259*
Frelinghuysen, Theodore *15, 66, 68, 69, 305, 413, 415, 511, 516*
Fremont, John C. *16, 83, 292, 335*
French, Augustus C. *296*
French, Burton L. *147, 150, 153, 159, 162, 168, 171, 175, 178, 181, 184, 187, 191*
French, C. Clement *425*
French, Calvin H. *415*

French, Carlos *124*
French, Charles J. *392*
French, Daniel Chester *526, 547*
French, Ezra B. *94*
French, Francis H. *339*
French, Herbert J. *519*
French, J. Stewart *408*
French, James H. *397*
French, John R. *102*
French, Jonas H. *389*
French, Philip *393*
French, Richard *71, 78, 82, 386*
French, Samuel G. *324*
French, William H. *336, 337, 473*
French, William M. R. *437*
Frensdorff, Wesley *456, 460*
Frenzel, Bill *256, 259*
Frenzel, William E. *262, 265, 268, 271, 274, 278*
Freret, William *389*
Freud, Anna *533*
Freudenheim, Thomas *437*
Freudenheim, Tom L. *444*
Freund, Ernest *517*
Freund, John F. *345*
Freund, Jules *543*
Freund, Paul A. *509*
Frey, Albert W. *515*
Frey, Fred C. *411*
Frey, Gerard L. *466, 467*
Frey, Louis, Jr. *252, 255, 258, 261, 264*
Frey, Oliver W. *196, 199, 202*
Frey, William C. *455, 458*
Fri, Robert W. *379*
Frick, Bertha M. *538*
Frick, Frederick *544*
Frick, Henry *79*
Frick, Thomas C. *514*
Fricke, Richard I. *492, 493*
Friday, David *412*
Friday, William C. *421*
Fridell, Elmir A. *475*
Friedel, Samuel N. *227, 230, 233, 236, 239, 243, 246, 249, 252*
Frieden, John P. *415, 419, 422*
Friedlander, Leo *526*
Friedman, Daniel M. *286*
Friedman, Daniel Mortimer *287*
Friedman, Edmund *519*
Friedman, Herbert *549*
Friedman, Jeffrey M. *397*
Friedman, Josh *558*
Friedman, Martha *510*
Friedman, Milton *513, 550*
Friedman, Thomas L. *558*
Friedmann, Herbert *441, 516, 535, 543*
Friedrich, Carl J. *518*
Friedrich, Walter G. *424*
Friel, Francis S. *519*
Friend, Theodore W., III *416, 534*
Friend, William B. *467*
Friendly, Alfred *556*
Friendly, Henry J. *284, 552*
Fries, Amos A. *331*
Fries, Edward D. *543*
Fries, Frank W. *200, 204*
Fries, George *81, 82*
Frieseke, F. C. *536*
Friesell, H. Edmund *512*
Frieze, Henry S. *420*
Friis, Harald T. *541*
Friley, Charles E. *410*
Friley, W. C. *409*
Frings, Ketti *556*
Frink, Daniel A. *392*
Frisbee, Edward S. *425*

Frisch, Martin *533*
Fritchey, John A. *395*
Fritchman, Harry K. *388*
Fritts, Edward O. *525*
Fritts, Robert E. *362, 371*
Fritz, Jean *547*
Fritz, John *520, 537, 539*
Fritz, Oscar M. *315*
Fritz, Robert J. *426*
Fritzinger, Noel C. *442*
Froderman, Edward *476*
Froehlich, Harold V. *260*
Froehlke, Robert F. *327, 487*
Frolich, Per K. *511*
Fromentin, Eligius *53, 55, 56, 299*
Frommeyer, Walter B., Jr. *513*
Frosch, Carl J. *544*
Frosch, Robert A. *380*
Frost, Frances *561*
Frost, George *3*
Frost, Joel *61*
Frost, John S. *505*
Frost, Laurence H. *381*
Frost, Lawrence H. *347*
Frost, Martin *269, 273, 276, 279*
Frost, Richard G. *116, 118*
Frost, Robert *531, 534, 544, 547, 553, 554, 559*
Frost, Rufus S. *111*
Frost, Wade H. *561*
Frost, Wesley *369*
Frost, William G. *404*
Frothingham, Louis A. *175, 179, 182, 185*
Frucolo, Foster *220*
Frueauff, Harry D. *432*
Frueauff, Harry D., Jr. *432*
Frueauff, Lena R. *432*
Fry, Charles M. *483*
Fry, Frank R. *516*
Fry, Franklin C. *475, 476*
Fry, Jacob, Jr. *71, 73*
Fry, James C. *342, 344*
Fry, Joseph, Jr. *65, 66*
Fry, Joseph L. *398*
Fry, Leslie M. *528*
Frye, Calvin A. *476*
Frye, Jack *497*
Frye, John C. *523*
Frye, Walter *523*
Frye, William P. *106, 108, 111, 113, 115, 118, 120, 123, 125, 128, 133, 135, 136, 138, 139, 141, 142, 143, 144, 146, 147, 149, 150, 152, 153, 155, 156, 158, 159, 299*
Fteley, Alphonse *519*
Fuchs, Ralph F. *510*
Fuentealba, Victor W. *503*
Fugate, Thomas B. *222, 225*
Fuhrman, Robert A. *491*
Fuhrmann, Louis P. *393*
Fulbright, J. William *210, 213, 216, 219, 222, 226, 229, 232, 235, 238, 242, 245, 248, 251, 254, 258, 292, 418, 547*
Fulbright, James F. *179, 185, 192*
Fulcher, George A. *466*
Fuld, Stanley *306*
Fulkerson, Abram *119*
Fulkerson, Frank B. *151*
Fullam, William F. *418*
Fuller, Albert M. *440*
Fuller, Alvan T. *169, 172, 300*
Fuller, Ben H. *348*
Fuller, Benoni S. *110, 113*
Fuller, Calvin S. *562*
Fuller, Charles *558*

Fuller, Charles E. *147, 150, 153, 156, 159, 165, 168, 172, 175, 178, 181*
Fuller, Claude A. *187, 190, 193, 197, 200*
Fuller, Douglas R. *493*
Fuller, Edward *1*
Fuller, Edward C. *404*
Fuller, George *79*
Fuller, George D. *522*
Fuller, George W. *518, 544*
Fuller, H. Laurence *482*
Fuller, Hadwen C. *211, 215, 218*
Fuller, Henry M. *87, 90*
Fuller, Homer T. *426*
Fuller, Horace H. *342, 351*
Fuller, J. O. *408*
Fuller, Jack *558*
Fuller, John W. *338*
Fuller, Levi K. *313*
Fuller, Marvin D. *331*
Fuller, Melville W. *283*
Fuller, Nathan *397*
Fuller, Philo L. *69, 71*
Fuller, R. Buckminster *532, 547, 552*
Fuller, Richard *475*
Fuller, Richard E. *443*
Fuller, Robert *414*
Fuller, Samuel *1, 411, 535*
Fuller, T. P. *392*
Fuller, Thomas C. *321*
Fuller, Thomas J. D. *84, 86, 88, 90*
Fuller, Timothy *56, 58, 59, 61*
Fuller, W. D. *525*
Fuller, William E. *122, 125*
Fuller, William K. *69, 71*
Fullerton, Baxter P. *473*
Fullerton, David *58*
Fullerton, Gail J. *405*
Fullerton, George S. *518*
Fullerton, Mark A. *314*
Fulmer, Hampton P. *177, 180, 183, 186, 189, 193, 196, 199, 202, 206, 209, 212*
Fulmer, Willa L. *212*
Fulton, Andrew *395*
Fulton, Andrew S. *83*
Fulton, Charles W. *148, 151, 154, 309*
Fulton, Elmer L. *154*
Fulton, James G. *215, 218, 222, 225, 228, 231, 234, 238, 241, 244, 247, 250, 254, 257*
Fulton, John H. *70*
Fulton, Richard *397*
Fulton, Richard H. *244, 247, 251, 254, 257, 260, 263*
Fulton, Robert *540*
Fulton, Robert B. *404, 420*
Fulton, Robert D. *297*
Fulton, Samuel A. *474*
Fulton, William S. *70, 72, 74, 76, 78, 292*
Funderburk, David B. *371*
Funderburk, H. Hanley, Jr. *403*
Funk, Benjamin F. *133*
Funk, Frank H. *175, 178, 181*
Funk, Nevin E. *523, 533*
Funkhouser, Richard *362*
Funsten, David *320, 321*
Funsten, James B. *449, 459, 462*
Funston, Edward H. *120, 123, 125, 127, 130, 133*
Funston, Frederick *333, 351*
Funston, G. Keith *417, 548*
Fuqua, Don *242, 245, 248, 252, 255, 258, 261, 264, 267, 270, 274, 277*

Gesner, Conrad H. *453, 461*
Gessaman, Myron B. *394*
Gessner, James W. *492*
Gest, Joseph H. *438*
Gest, William H. *125, 127*
Gester, George C *510*
Gettell, Richard G. *413*
Getty, George W. *337, 338*
Getty, J. Paul *489*
Gettys, Charles M. *344*
Gettys, Tom S. *247, 250, 254, 257, 260*
Getz, J. Lawrence *103, 105, 107*
Getz, John I. *367*
Geuting, Joseph T., Jr. *525*
Gewin, Walter P. *285, 287*
Geyelin, Philip L. *557*
Geyer, Henry S. *86, 88, 90, 303*
Geyer, John *395*
Geyer, Lee E. *203, 206*
Gezork, Herbert *475*
Ghelston, David *4*
Gherardi, Bancroft *538*
Ghiorso, Albert *552*
Gholson, James H. *70*
Gholson, Samuel J. *71, 73*
Gholson, Thomas, Jr. *51, 52, 53, 54, 56*
Gholson, Thomas S. *321*
Ghormley, Alfred M. *484*
Ghormley, Robert L. *347*
Ghougassian, Joseph *370*
Giacconi, Riccardo *537*
Giaever Ivar *550*
Giaimo, Robert *261*
Giaimo, Robert N. *235, 239, 242, 245, 248, 252, 255, 258, 264, 267*
Giamatti, A. Bartlett *427*
Giancarlo, Gene *520*
Gianera, William C. *422*
Giannini, A. P. *483*
Giannini, Lawrence M. *483*
Giauque, William F. *537, 549*
Gibb, Richard D. *419*
Gibbens, Ray V. *524*
Gibbes, James G. *396*
Gibbes, R. W. *396*
Gibbes, Robert *6*
Gibbes, T. H. *396*
Gibbes, W. H. *396*
Gibbin, John H., Jr. *543*
Gibbins, Henry *332*
Gibbon, John *337, 338*
Gibbon, John H., Jr. *532*
Gibbons, A. S. *423*
Gibbons, Edmund F. *468*
Gibbons, J. L. *504*
Gibbons, James *463, 464, 470*
Gibbons, John H. *418*
Gibbons, John J. *284*
Gibbons, Sam M. *242, 245, 248, 252, 255, 258, 261, 264, 267, 270, 274, 277*
Gibbons, William *3*
Gibbs, Addison C. *309*
Gibbs, Barbara K. *438*
Gibbs, David P. *332*
Gibbs, Florence R. *203*
Gibbs, Frederic A. *543*
Gibbs, George S. *332*
Gibbs, Josiah W. *540, 560*
Gibbs, R. C. *527*
Gibbs, Richard *356, 370*
Gibbs, Thomas F. *387*
Gibbs, W. Benjamin *204*
Gibbs, William C. *310*
Gibbs, William D. *421*
Gibbs, William F. *539, 561, 562*
Gibbs, Wolcott *510*
Giblin, E. Burke *499*

Gibson, A. R. *393*
Gibson, Charles H. *123, 125, 128, 130, 133, 136, 300*
Gibson, Ernest W. *180, 183, 186, 190, 193, 196, 199, 203, 206, 313*
Gibson, Ernest W., Jr. *206, 313*
Gibson, Eustace *122, 124*
Gibson, Floyd R. *285*
Gibson, Foye G. *408*
Gibson, George *332*
Gibson, Henry R. *137, 140, 143, 146, 149*
Gibson, Hugh S. *356, 357, 366, 370, 373*
Gibson, James *392*
Gibson, James King *105*
Gibson, James M. *344*
Gibson, James O. *433*
Gibson, John *395*
Gibson, John B. *309*
Gibson, John R. *285*
Gibson, John S. *207, 210, 213*
Gibson, K. S. *527*
Gibson, Matthew M. *473*
Gibson, Norman R. *537, 541*
Gibson, Paris *145, 148, 303*
Gibson, Phil S. *293*
Gibson, Randall L. *111, 113, 115, 118, 120, 123, 125, 128, 130, 299*
Gibson, Reginald W. *286*
Gibson, Robert A. *449, 461*
Gibson, Robert F. *461*
Gibson, Robert F., Jr. *454*
Gibson, Robert W. *474*
Gibson, Thomas L. *308*
Gibson, Walter *524*
Giddens, Paul H. *409*
Giddings, De Witt C. *107, 110, 114*
Giddings, Franklin H. *520*
Giddings, Joshua R. *73, 75, 77, 79, 81, 82, 84, 86, 88, 90, 92*
Gideonse, Harry D. *405*
Giesy, J. B. *395*
Giffen, Hilliard R. *514*
Giffen, J. Kelly *474*
Giffen, William A. *512*
Gifford, Charles L. *175, 179, 185, 188, 191, 194, 198, 201, 204, 207, 211, 214, 217*
Gifford, Edward W. *440*
Gifford, Oscar S. *129*
Gifford, Walter S. *362, 482, 548*
Gignoux, Edward T. *287*
Gihon, Albert L. *518*
Gilbeau, Francis *397*
Gilbert, Abijah *103, 106, 108, 295*
Gilbert, Cass *514, 525, 526, 547*
Gilbert, Charles B. *411*
Gilbert, Charles K. *452, 460*
Gilbert, Edward *83*
Gilbert, Eliphalet W. *419*
Gilbert, Ezekiel *43, 44*
Gilbert, Felix *534*
Gilbert, George G. *141, 144, 147, 150*
Gilbert, Grove K. *510, 523, 526, 538, 541*
Gilbert, Jacob H. *237, 240, 243, 247, 250, 253*
Gilbert, Mahlon N. *449*
Gilbert, Newton W. *150*
Gilbert, Ralph *175, 178, 181, 185, 191*
Gilbert, Sylvester *56*
Gilbert, Sylvio J. *390*
Gilbert, Walter *543, 550*
Gilbert, William A. *90*

Gilbert, William B. *285*
Gilbertson, Lyle I. *522*
Gilbreth, Lillian M. *541, 548*
Gilchrist, Albert W. *295*
Gilchrist, Ellen *547*
Gilchrist, Fred C. *191, 194, 197, 201, 204, 207, 210*
Gilchrist, Gibb *416*
Gilchrist, Harry L. *331*
Gilchrist, John J. *286, 305*
Gilcrest, David L. *519*
Gildea, James H. *199, 202*
Gildersleeve, Basil L. *517*
Gildersleeve, Virginia Crocheron *404, 548*
Gildred, Theodore *355*
Giles, Barney M. *340*
Giles, Benjamin F. *340*
Giles, Howard *551*
Giles, William B. *41, 42, 43, 44, 45, 47, 48, 49, 51, 52, 53, 54, 313, 314*
Giles, William F. *80*
Giles, William L. *412*
Gilfillan, Calvin W. *105*
Gilfillan, Francis *468*
Gilfillan, Francois A. *414*
Gilfillan, James *302, 381*
Gilfillan, John B. *123*
Gilhams, Clarence C. *150, 153*
Gilkeson, Robert F. *494*
Gill, D. W. *399*
Gill, E. G. *524*
Gill, Hiram C. *398*
Gill, James P. *519*
Gill, John, Jr. *150, 153, 156*
Gill, Joseph J. *142, 145*
Gill, Laura Drake *404*
Gill, Merton M. *539*
Gill, Michael J. *163*
Gill, Patrick F. *156, 160*
Gill, Theodore *510*
Gill, Thomas P. *242*
Gill, Turner A. *392*
Gill, William H. *342, 343*
Gill, Wilson L. *537*
Gillem, Alvan C., Jr. *333, 340, 341, 343*
Gillen, Courtland C. *191*
Gillespie, Charles A., Jr. *359*
Gillespie, Cornelius *415*
Gillespie, Dean M. *210, 213*
Gillespie, Eugene P. *131*
Gillespie, Frank *194*
Gillespie, George DeN. *448, 462*
Gillespie, Gregory *531, 560*
Gillespie, Gwain H. *431*
Gillespie, James *43, 44, 45, 48*
Gillespie, L. *331*
Gillespie, Oscar W. *149, 152, 155, 158*
Gillespie, Robert J. *516*
Gillesple, Robert G. *302*
Gillet, Charles W. *134, 137, 139, 142, 145, 148*
Gillet, Joseph A. *410*
Gillet, Ranson H. *71*
Gillett, Arthur D. S. *424*
Gillett, Frederick H. *133, 136, 139, 142, 144, 147, 150, 153, 156, 159, 162, 166, 169, 171, 172, 174, 175, 177, 179, 182, 185, 188, 301*
Gillett, James N. *146, 292*
Gillett, James S. *149*
Gillett, Ranson H. *69*
Gillette, Edward H. *115*
Gillette, Francis *87, 294*
Gillette, Guy M. *194, 197, 201, 204, 207, 210, 220, 223, 226, 297*

Gillette, John M. *520*
Gillette, Robert S. *492*
Gillette, William *547*
Gillette, Wilson D. *209, 212, 215, 218, 222, 225*
Gilliam, Jackson *455*
Gilliam, Jackson E. *459*
Gillie, George W. *204, 207, 210, 213, 217*
Gilligan, Frank P. *519*
Gilligan, John J. *247, 308, 379*
Gilligan, Michael B. *426*
Gillin, John L. *520*
Gillin, John P. *509*
Gillis, James L. *92*
Gillon, Alexander *43*
Gilluly, James *523, 551*
Gilman, Alfred A. *451*
Gilman, Benjamin A. *259, 262, 266, 269, 272, 275, 278*
Gilman, Charles J. *92*
Gilman, Daniel C. *410, 418*
Gilman, Daniel Coit *511*
Gilman, Henry *553*
Gilman, John T. *304*
Gilman, John Taylor *3*
Gilman, Nicholas *3, 41, 42, 43, 44, 49, 50, 51, 52, 53, 304*
Gilman, Richard C. *414*
Gilmer, Ben S. *482*
Gilmer, George R. *59, 64, 69, 295*
Gilmer, John A. *92, 94, 321*
Gilmer, Thomas E. *409*
Gilmer, Thomas W. *35, 77, 79, 313*
Gilmer, William F. *221*
Gilmore, Albert F. *476*
Gilmore, Alfred *85, 87*
Gilmore, Art *503*
Gilmore, Donald S. *432*
Gilmore, Eddy *555*
Gilmore, Edward *162*
Gilmore, Eugene A. *420*
Gilmore, F. C. *387*
Gilmore, Frank *503*
Gilmore, John *66, 68*
Gilmore, John W. *419*
Gilmore, Joseph A. *304*
Gilmore, Joseph M. *468*
Gilmore, Robert E. *484*
Gilmore, Samuel L. *156*
Gilmore, W. S. *520*
Gilmore, William J. *308*
Gilmour, Richard *469*
Gilpatric, Roswell L. *327*
Gilpin, Charles *395*
Gilpin, Charles S. *561*
Gilpin, Henry D. *24, 34*
Gilroy, Frank D. *556*
Gilroy, Thomas F. *394*
Gilruth, Robert R. *533, 537, 540, 559, 562*
Gilson, Charles P. *455*
Gilstrap, Sam P. *367*
Ginder, P. D. *344*
Ginder, Philip D. *334*
Gindrat, John *385*
Ginger, Lyman V. *525*
Gingery, Don *199, 202*
Gingrich, Arnold *539*
Gingrich, John *349*
Gingrich, Newt *271, 274, 277*
Gingrich, Newton L. *267*
Ginley, Thomas J. *512*
Ginn, Ronald B. *258*
Ginn, Ronald B. (Bo) *261, 264, 267, 271*
Ginn, Rosemary L. *366*
Ginsburg, Allen *546*
Ginsburg, Charles P. *552*

Grant, Frederick D. *356*
Grant, Frederick J. *356*
Grant, George M. *200, 203, 206, 210, 213, 216, 219, 222, 226, 229, 232, 235, 238, 242*
Grant, Heber J. *476*
Grant, Hugh G. *355, 374*
Grant, Hugh J. *394*
Grant, James B. *293*
Grant, Jedediah M. *397*
Grant, John G. *157*
Grant, Leonard T. *408*
Grant, P. R. *535*
Grant, Richard F. *522*
Grant, Robert *526*
Grant, Robert A. *204, 207, 210, 213, 217, 287*
Grant, Ulysses S. *11, 16, 26, 329, 335, 336, 337, 338, 540*
Grant, Ulysses S., III *516*
Grant, Walter S. *351*
Grant, Whit M. *394*
Grant, William T. *432*
Grantland, Seaton *70, 72*
Grant-Smith, Ulysses *355, 375*
Granville, Maurice F. *497*
Granville, William A. *409*
Granville-Smith, W. *531*
Grason, William *300*
Grassi, John A. *409*
Grassky, Charles E. *297*
Grassley, Charles E. *262, 265, 268, 271, 274, 277*
Grasso, Ella T. *255, 258, 293, 552*
Gratiat, Charles *331*
Gratz, Hyman *488*
Gratz, William *506*
Grau, Shirley Ann *556*
Grauer, Gerhard W. *475*
Graustein, Archibald R. *490*
Gravatt, John J. *453, 461*
Gravatt, William L. *449, 462*
Grave, Caswell *520*
Gravel, Mike *251, 254, 258, 261, 264, 267*
Gravel, Mike (Maurice R.) *291*
Gravely, Joseph J. *102*
Gravely, Samuel L., Jr. *348*
Graves, Alexander *121*
Graves, Anson R. *449, 462*
Graves, Benjamin B. *418*
Graves, Charles H. *373*
Graves, David Bibb *291*
Graves, Dixie Bibb *200, 291*
Graves, Ernest *381*
Graves, Eugene S. *497*
Graves, Frank P. *423, 424*
Graves, Frederick R. *449*
Graves, Gerald W. *391*
Graves, Henry L. *404*
Graves, Lawrence P. *467*
Graves, Mortimer *512*
Graves, R. B. *391*
Graves, Samuel *413*
Graves, Thomas A., Jr. *406*
Graves, Thomas Ashley, Jr. *439*
Graves, Waller W. *303*
Graves, William J. *71, 72, 74*
Gray, Albert E. *438*
Gray, Alexander *551*
Gray, Asa *442, 509, 540*
Gray, Bowman *495*
Gray, Bowman, Jr. *495*
Gray, Campbell *452, 460*
Gray, Carl R. *489, 498*
Gray, Charles M. *388*
Gray, Charles O. *417*
Gray, Clifton D. *404*
Gray, Dan W. *386*
Gray, David *364*

Gray, Duncan M. *453, 459*
Gray, Duncan M., Jr. *456, 459*
Gray, E. L. *385*
Gray, Edward M. *421*
Gray, Edward W. *166, 169*
Gray, Edwin *46, 47, 48, 49, 51, 52, 53*
Gray, Edwin J. *379*
Gray, Elisha *499, 537*
Gray, Elisha, II *499*
Gray, Finly H. *159, 162, 165, 194, 197, 200*
Gray, G. W. *395*
Gray, George *122, 125, 127, 130, 132, 135, 138, 284, 294*
Gray, Gordon *327, 421, 552*
Gray, Hanna Holborn *419*
Gray, Harold *404*
Gray, Harold E. *494*
Gray, Harry B. *549*
Gray, Harry J. *498*
Gray, Henry *321*
Gray, Henry P. *525*
Gray, Hiram *73*
Gray, Horace *283, 301*
Gray, Isaac P. *297*
Gray, Issac P. *367*
Gray, James *391*
Gray, James A. *495*
Gray, John C. *59*
Gray, John H. *513*
Gray, John P. *518*
Gray, John R. *485*
Gray, John S. *488*
Gray, Joseph *199, 202*
Gray, Joseph M. M. *403*
Gray, Kenneth J. *229, 233, 236, 239, 242, 246, 249, 252, 255, 258, 277*
Gray, Landon C. *516*
Gray, Mark R. *524*
Gray, Norman B. *315*
Gray, Oscar L. *165, 168*
Gray, Paul E. *412*
Gray, Peter F. *391*
Gray, Peter W. *320*
Gray, Ralph L. *482*
Gray, Reid B. *562*
Gray, Thomas T. *562*
Gray, Tilbee D., II *523*
Gray, W. H., Jr. *408*
Gray, Walter H. *453, 458*
Gray, William C. *449, 461*
Gray, William H., III *269, 272, 275, 279*
Grayson, Cary T. *516*
Grayson, Lawrence P. *541*
Grayson, William *4, 41, 314*
Grayson, William J. *70, 72*
Grazier, Joseph A. *482*
Greason, A. LeRoy, Jr. *404*
Greatbatch, Wilson *541*
Greco, Charles P. *467*
Grede, William J. *525*
Greeley, Edwin S. *526*
Greeley, Horace *16, 82*
Greeley, J. C. *387*
Greely, Adolphus W. *332, 538*
Green, Alan, Jr. *379*
Green, Allen J. *396*
Green, Ashbel *414, 473*
Green, Aubrey D. *524*
Green, Bill *272, 275, 278*
Green, Byram *79*
Green, Cecil H. *497*
Green, Christopher *386*
Green, Clarence W. *411*
Green, Constance McLaughlin *556*
Green, Cordes B. *423*
Green, Dwight H. *296*

Green, Edith *234, 241, 244, 247, 250, 253, 257, 260*
Green, Edith S. *231, 237*
Green, Edward *491*
Green, Ernest *505*
Green, Floyd F. *394*
Green, Francis J. *465*
Green, Fred W. *301*
Green, Frederick W. *86, 88*
Green, George H. *527*
Green, George J. *521*
Green, Grafton *312*
Green, Henry *309*
Green, Henry D. *143, 145*
Green, Henry W. *305*
Green, Howard *551*
Green, Howard W. *515*
Green, Innis *65, 66*
Green, Isaiah L. *49, 50, 52*
Green, James S. *82, 84, 90, 92, 94, 303, 358*
Green, John *504*
Green, John L., Jr. *425*
Green, Joseph *468*
Green, Joseph A. *331, 339*
Green, Joseph C. *365*
Green, Lewis W. *409, 417*
Green, Marshall *355, 364, 368*
Green, Melvin W. *559*
Green, Otis W. *525*
Green, Paul *553*
Green, Richard *390*
Green, Robert A. *181, 184, 187, 190, 194, 197, 200, 203, 207, 210*
Green, Robert S. *123, 305*
Green, Roy M. *407*
Green, Rufus S. *408*
Green, Russell H. *496*
Green, S. William *269*
Green, Samuel A. *390*
Green, Samuel S. *514*
Green, Theodore F. *202, 206, 209, 212, 215, 218, 222, 225, 228, 231, 234, 238, 310*
Green, Thomas *5*
Green, Thomas H. *331*
Green, Traill *411*
Green, W. Henry *473*
Green, Warren E. *311*
Green, Wharton J. *121, 123*
Green, William *389, 395, 559*
Green, William J. *244, 247, 250, 254, 257, 260, 263*
Green, William J., Jr. *215, 222, 225, 228, 231, 234, 238, 241, 244*
Green, William M. *447, 451, 459*
Green, William R. *159, 162, 165, 168, 172, 175, 178, 181, 184, 286*
Green, Willis *74, 76, 78*
Greenaway, Emerson *515*
Greenberg, Bernard G. *535*
Greenberg, Max *505*
Greenberg, Paul *557*
Greenblatt, Milton *533, 541*
Greene, Albert C. *81, 83, 85, 310*
Greene, Balcomb *531*
Greene, Belle Da Costa *440*
Greene, Clarence W. *411, 517*
Greene, Douglass T. *343*
Greene, Eugene H. *476*
Greene, Evarts B. *513*
Greene, Frank L. *161, 164, 167, 171, 174, 177, 180, 183, 186, 190, 313*
Greene, George S. *336, 519*
Greene, George W. *104*

Greene, Henry A. *339, 351*
Greene, Jacob L. *485*
Greene, James F. *380*
Greene, John P. *426*
Greene, Michael F. *506*
Greene, Nathaniel *332, 335*
Greene, Nehemiah *297*
Greene, Norman J. *523*
Greene, R. H. *385*
Greene, Ray *45, 46, 47, 310*
Greene, Richard L. *425*
Greene, Richard W. *310*
Greene, S. H. *408*
Greene, Stephen *560*
Greene, Wallace M., Jr. *348*
Greene, Walter K. *426*
Greene, William *6, 7*
Greene, William C. *517*
Greene, William L. *139*
Greene, William S. *139, 142, 144, 147, 150, 153, 156, 159, 162, 166, 169, 172, 175, 179*
Greenebaum, Robert J. *432*
Greenewalt, Crawford H. *487, 532, 539*
Greenfield, Meg *558*
Greenhalge, Frederic T. *128, 300*
Greenhill, Joe R. *312*
Greenhow, Robert *398*
Greenleaf, Halbert S. *121, 131*
Greenleaf, James L. *520*
Greenlief, Francis F. *331*
Greenly, William L. *301*
Greenman, Edward W. *126*
Greenough, James C. *420*
Greenough, John *513*
Greenough, Robert B. *511, 512*
Greenup, Christopher *42, 43, 298*
Greenway, Emerson *543*
Greenway, G. Lauder *432*
Greenway, Isabella S. *193, 197*
Greenwood, Alfred B. *87, 89, 91*
Greenwood, Arthur H. *178, 181, 184, 188, 191, 194, 197, 200*
Greenwood, Ernest *224*
Greenwood, Marion *531*
Greer, David H. *450, 460*
Greer, Joy L. *476*
Greever, Paul R. *200, 203*
Gregg, Alexander *448, 461*
Gregg, Alexander W. *149, 152, 155, 158, 161, 164, 167, 170*
Gregg, Andrew *42, 43, 44, 45, 46, 47, 48, 49, 50, 51, 53, 309*
Gregg, Arthur J. *330*
Gregg, Clifford C. *439*
Gregg, Curtis H. *160, 524*
Gregg, David L. *363*
Gregg, David M. *337, 338*
Gregg, Donald E. *532*
Gregg, Henry H. *516*
Gregg, Hugh *304*
Gregg, J. A. *426*
Gregg, James *396*
Gregg, James M. *91*
Gregg, John *320*
Gregg, Judd *275*
Gregg, Judd A. *272, 278*
Gregg, Richard N. *440*
Gregory, Clint *396*
Gregory, David T. *472*
Gregory, Dudley S. *82*
Gregory, Edmund B. *332*
Gregory, Elisha H. *515*
Gregory, Eugene J. *386*
Gregory, Herbert E. *437*
Gregory, Horace *531, 534, 544*

Guilfoyle, Merlin J. *465*
Guilfoyle, Richard T. *469*
Guill, Ben H. *222*
Guillemin, Ernst A. *541*
Guillemin, Roger C. L. *543, 549, 550, 551*
Guillotte, J. Valsin *389*
Guinan, Matthew *505*
Guinn, D. Henry *349*
Guion, John I. *302*
Guion, Walter *169, 299*
Guiterman, Arthur *527*
Gulbransen, Earl A. *531*
Gulick, Charles B. *517*
Gulick, John W. *331*
Gulick, Luther *518*
Gulik, W. Lawrence *415*
Gullander, W. P. *525*
Gullinan, Joseph S. *497*
Gullion, Allen W. *331, 332*
Gullion, Edmund A. *359, 375*
Gulliver, John P. *411*
Gum, Walter C. *472*
Gummere, Francis B. *524*
Gummere, John *494*
Gummere, Samuel J. *409*
Gummere, Samuel R. *367*
Gummere, William S. *305*
Gumpel, Hugh *533*
Gumpert, Emil *512*
Gunckel, Lewis B. *109*
Gund, George *482*
Gundaker, Guy *527*
Gundellinger, Andrew *391*
Gundersen, Gunnar *515*
Gundersheimer, Werner *439*
Gunderson, Carl *311*
Gunderson, Steven *273, 276, 279*
Gunn, Calvin *391*
Gunn, Douglas *386*
Gunn, George P. *453, 461*
Gunn, James *41, 42, 43, 44, 45, 138, 295*
Gunn, John E. *467*
Gunnell, Francis M. *347*
Gunness, Robert C. *482*
Gunnison, Almon *415*
Gunter, Gaston *385*
Gunter, Julius C. *293*
Gunter, Thomas M. *108, 110, 112, 115, 117*
Gunter, W. A. *385*
Gunter, William D., Jr. *258*
Gunther, C. Godfrey *393*
Gunther, Franklin M. *360, 371*
Guptill, Nathanael M. *475*
Gupton, William *396*
Gurfein, Murray Irwin *284*
Gurin, H. M. *510*
Gurkin, John A. *398*
Gurley, Fred G. *483*
Gurley, Henry H. *61, 62, 64, 66*
Gurley, John A. *94, 96*
Gurley, Phineas D. *473*
Gurnee, Walter S. *388*
Gurney, Edward J. *242, 245, 248, 252, 255, 258, 295*
Gurney, J. Chandler *206, 209, 212, 215, 219, 222, 311*
Gush, Herbert P. *560*
Guskin, Alan E. *403*
Gustafson, George H. *511*
Gustafson, K. W. *332*
Gustavson, Reuben G. *421, 433*
Gustine, Amos *77*
Guston, Philip *531, 535*
Guth, William W. *409, 423*
Guthe, Carl *442*
Guthman, Edwin O. *555*
Guthrie, A. B., Jr. *555*

Guthrie, Edwin R. *518*
Guthrie, George W. *365, 395*
Guthrie, Hunter *409*
Guthrie, J. B. *395*
Guthrie, James *25, 33, 99, 102, 298, 491*
Guthrie, Ramon *562*
Guthrie, Robert G. *519*
Guthrie, Rodney M. *315*
Guttmacher, Alan *535*
Guttmacher, Alan F. *560*
Guttmacher, Manfred S. *559*
Guy, Ralph B., Jr. *285*
Guy, Walter C. *527*
Guy, William L. *263, 307*
Guyer, M. F. *520*
Guyer, Tennyson *260, 263, 266, 269, 272*
Guyer, Ulysses S. *178, 185, 188, 191, 194, 197, 201, 204, 207, 210*
Guyon, James, Jr. *58*
Guyton, Arthur C. *532*
Guzy, Carol *558*
Guzzetta, Dominic J. *418*
Gwalter, L. Ivimy *476*
Gwathmey, Robert *531, 542, 560*
Gwilliam, George E. *524*
Gwin, William M. *76, 83, 85, 87, 89, 91, 93, 292*
Gwinn, Ralph W. *215, 218, 221, 224, 227, 231, 234*
Gwinn, William P. *498*
Gwinnett, Button *1, 2, 3, 5*
Gwynne, John W. *197, 201, 204, 207, 210, 214, 217*
Gyorgy, Paul *534, 549*
Gyory, Nicholas *506*
Haack, Robert W. *491*
Haagen-Smit, A. J. *537*
Haagen-Smit, Arie J. *549*
Haak, Harold H. *405*
Haakenson, Marlan *394*
Haaland, Gordon A. *421*
Haan, William G. *339*
Haas, Francis J. *467*
Haas, Harry J. *510*
Haas, John A. W. *413*
Haas, John C. *433*
Haas, Leonard *424*
Haas, Merrill W. *552*
Haas, Otto *433*
Haas, Peter E. *433*
Haas, Warren J. *538*
Habach, George F. *520*
Haber, Edgar *532*
Haber, Meryl H. *519*
Haberler, Gottfried *513*
Haberly, Loyd *527*
Habersham, John *3*
Habersham, Joseph *382*
Habersham, Richard W. *74, 76*
Habib, Philip C. *371, 552*
Habib, Philip H. *560*
Hack, Howard *560*
Hacker, Hilary B. *469*
Hacker, Joseph B. *524*
Hacker, Marilyn *546*
Hackerman, Norman *415, 423, 522, 531, 532*
Hackett, Albert *555*
Hackett, Richard C. *396*
Hackett, Richard N. *154*
Hackett, Robert *333*
Hackett, Thomas C. *83*
Hackett, William S. *393*
Hackley, Aaron, Jr. *58*
Hackley, Robert J. *387*
Hackney, F. Sheldon *422*
Hackney, Sheldon *417*

Hackney, Thomas *153*
Hadden, D. P. *396*
Haddock, Charles B. *370*
Haddock, Edward E. *398*
Haddon, William, Jr. *535*
Haden, Clarence R. *454*
Haden, Clarence R., Jr. *460*
Hadler, Jacques B. *562*
Hadley, Arthur T. *427, 513, 526*
Hadley, Chalmers *515*
Hadley, Herbert S. *303, 425*
Hadley, Hiram *413*
Hadley, Hiram E. *314*
Hadley, Joshua *394*
Hadley, Lindley H. *167, 171, 174, 177, 180, 183, 187, 190, 193*
Hadley, Ozro A. *292*
Hadley, Rollin van N. *439*
Hadley, William F. L. *135*
Hadlock, Wendell S. *439*
Hadsel, Fred L. *362, 372*
Hadzsits, George D. *517*
Haehl, John G., Jr. *493*
Haenicke, Diether H. *426*
Haensel, Vladimir *549*
Hafey, William J. *468, 469*
Haffner, Charles C., Jr. *343*
Haffner, Jurgen *535*
Hafner, Dudley H. *513*
Hagaman, Frank L. *297*
Hagan, G. Elliott *239, 242, 245, 249, 252, 255*
Hagan, Harlan F. *226*
Hagan, Ward S. *499*
Hagans, John M. *110*
Hagarty, Frank A. *387*
Hagedorn, Herman *559*
Hagedorn, Thomas M. *262, 265, 268, 271*
Hagemeyer, W. A. *398*
Hagen, Harlan F. *229, 232, 235, 239, 242, 245*
Hagen, Harold C. *211, 214, 217, 221, 224, 227*
Hager, Alva L. *133, 136, 138*
Hager, George C. *527*
Hager, John S. *108, 292*
Hagerman, B. C. *404*
Hagerman, James *511*
Hagerty, William W. *408*
Haggard, William D. *512, 515*
Haggerson, Fred H. *498*
Haggerty, Patrick E. *497, 539*
Haggerty, Robert J. *432*
Haggin, James B. A. *482*
Haggott, Warren A. *152*
Hagood, Johnson *310, 334*
Hague, Arnold *523*
Hague, Raoul *532*
Hague, Wesley M. *351*
Hahn, John *55*
Hahn, Michael *96, 123, 299*
Hahn, Otto *538*
Hahn, Paul M. *481*
Hahn, Robert S. *533*
Hahn, T. Marshall, Jr. *489*
Hahn, Thomas M., Jr. *424*
Hahne, Ernest H. *412*
Haider, M. L. *487*
Haider, Michael L. *487, 514, 533, 539*
Haig, Alexander M., Jr. *31, 33, 498, 541, 548*
Haight, Charles *102, 104*
Haight, Edward *96*
Haight, Elizabeth H. *517*
Haight, Henry H. *292*
Haight, Thomas G. *284*
Haik, Raymond A. *523*

Haile, William *63, 64, 304*
Hailer, Erwin H. *558*
Hainer, Eugene J. *134, 136*
Haines, Charles D. *134, 433*
Haines, Charles G. *517*
Haines, Daniel *305*
Haines, Elwood L. *453, 459*
Haines, Harry L. *192, 196, 199, 202, 209*
Haines, Helen *543*
Haines, John C. *388*
Haines, John M. *296, 388*
Haines, Ralph E., Jr. *332*
Haines, William T. *299*
Hair, Jay D. *527*
Haire, Charles *387*
Hairfield, J. C. *409*
Haise, Fred W., Jr. *552*
Haislip, Wade H. *329, 334, 341, 342*
Hait, James M. *488*
Halaby, Najeeb E. *494*
Halbach, Edward A. *535*
Halberstam, David *556*
Halbouty, Michel T. *510, 541, 545, 552*
Haldeman, Jacob S. *373*
Haldeman, Richard J. *105, 107*
Haldeman, Samuel *505*
Haldeman, Samuel S. *517*
Halderman, J. A. *372*
Hale, Artemas *80, 82*
Hale, Benjamin *410*
Hale, Benjamin E. *494*
Hale, Charles R. *449*
Hale, Edward E. *509*
Hale, Edward J. *359*
Hale, Eugene *104, 106, 108, 111, 113, 118, 120, 123, 125, 128, 130, 133, 136, 139, 142, 144, 147, 150, 153, 156, 299*
Hale, Fletcher *182, 185, 188*
Hale, Frank *314*
Hale, Frederick *169, 172, 175, 178, 181, 185, 188, 191, 194, 198, 201, 204, 299*
Hale, George E. *537, 539, 560*
Hale, Horace M. *419*
Hale, James T. *94, 97, 99*
Hale, John B. *123*
Hale, John P. *78, 84, 86, 90, 92, 94, 96, 98, 304, 373, 398*
Hale, Lilian Wescott *531*
Hale, Nathan W. *152, 155*
Hale, Nathaniel C. *522*
Hale, Robert *211, 214, 217, 220, 223, 227, 230, 233*
Hale, Robert S. *100, 109*
Hale, S. L. *319*
Hale, Salma *56*
Hale, Samuel W. *304*
Hale, Stephen F. *319*
Hale, Tom *533*
Hale, William *51, 54, 55*
Hale, William G. *517*
Hale, Willis H. *340*
Hales, John P. *82*
Haley, Alex *546, 561*
Haley, Elisha *70, 72*
Haley, George W. *390*
Haley, James A. *226, 229, 232, 236, 239, 242, 245, 248, 252, 255, 258, 261*
Haley, James S. *397*
Haley, John L. *493*
Haley, Thomas P. *476*
Hall, A. G. *417*
Hall, A. Oakey *394*
Hall, Albert R. *181, 184, 188*
Hall, Allen A. *356, 375*
Hall, Arnold B. *422*

Hancock, James D. *526*
Hancock, John *1, 2, 3, 5, 14, 107, 110, 112, 121, 300, 335*
Hancock, Lewis *397*
Hancock, Parker L. *512*
Hancock, Winfield S. *16, 336, 337, 338*
Hand, Augustus C. *75*
Hand, Augustus N. *284*
Hand, Edward *4, 330, 335*
Hand, Learned *284, 559*
Hand, T. Millet *214, 218, 221, 224, 227, 230*
Handelman, Rubin *505*
Handler, Evelyn E. *404, 421*
Handler, Philip *549*
Handley, George *5*
Handley, Harold W. *297*
Handley, William A. *105*
Handley, William J. *367, 374*
Handlin, Oscar *555*
Handy, Alexander H. *302*
Handy, Levin I. *138*
Handy, Thomas T. *329, 332, 334*
Handy, W. T., Jr. *472*
Handyside, Holsey G. *367*
Hanes, Robert M. *511*
Haney, Bert E. *285*
Hanfmann, George M. A. *533*
Hanford, Benjamin *17*
Hanford, James H. *524*
Hanford, W. E. *514*
Hanford, W. E. "Butch" *532*
Hanifen, Richard C. *465*
Hankins, Frank H. *520*
Hanks, James M. *105*
Hanks, Nancy *548*
Hanley, Edward J. *538*
Hanley, James M. *247, 250, 253, 256, 259, 262, 266, 269*
Hanley, John W. *492*
Hanley, Thomas B. *321*
Hanley, William A. *520*
Hanlon, C. Rollins *512*
Hanlon, John J. *518*
Hanly, J. Frank *17, 136, 297*
Hanly, Thomas B. *320, 321*
Hanna, Bayless W. *355*
Hanna, Clinton R. *543, 552*
Hanna, Edward J. *463*
Hanna, Ira L. *399*
Hanna, James R. *388*
Hanna, John *113*
Hanna, John A. *45, 46, 47, 48, 49*
Hanna, Katherine *443*
Hanna, Louis B. *157, 160, 307*
Hanna, Marcus A. *140, 142, 145, 148, 308*
Hanna, Matthew E. *363, 368*
Hanna, Richard T. *242, 245, 248, 251, 255, 258*
Hanna, Robert *67, 297*
Hanna, Septimus J. *476*
Hanna, Thomas H. *473*
Hannaford, Jule M. *493*
Hannaford, Mark W. *261, 264*
Hannah, John A. *379, 412*
Hannah, Mary-Emily *424*
Hannan, Jerome D. *469*
Hannan, Philip M. *464*
Hannay, N. Bruce *531, 533*
Hannegan, Edward A. *69, 71, 78, 80, 82, 297, 370*
Hannegan, Robert E. *30, 36, 380*
Hanners, Irving Caywood *528*
Hannett, Arthur T. *305*
Hannifin, Patrick *328*
Hannigan, Judson D. *490*

Hannon, John W., Jr. *483*
Hanold, Terrance *494*
Hanrahan, Edmond M. *381*
Hanrahan, James T. *490*
Hanrahan, Robert P. *258*
Hansberger, R. V. *483*
Hansbroug, Henry C. *137*
Hansbrough, Henry C. *128, 131, 134, 140, 142, 145, 148, 151, 154*
Hanscom, Isaiah *349*
Hanselman, Joseph F. *406*
Hansen, Alvin H. *513*
Hansen, Arild E. *534*
Hansen, Arne R. *438*
Hansen, Arthur G. *409, 415*
Hansen, Clifford P. *251, 254, 257, 261, 264, 267, 315*
Hansen, George *261, 264, 268, 271, 274*
Hansen, George V. *245*
Hansen, George V. F. *249*
Hansen, Hendrick *393*
Hansen, James V. *273, 276, 279*
Hansen, Johannes *393*
Hansen, John R. *246*
Hansen, Julia Butler *241, 245, 248, 251, 254, 257, 260*
Hansen, Orval *252, 255, 258*
Hansen, Robert E. *528*
Hansen, Walter F. *388*
Hansen, William C. *424*
Hansford, Charles R. *385*
Hanshue, H. M. *497*
Hanson, Abraham *366*
Hanson, Alexander C. *53, 55, 56, 58, 300*
Hanson, Anne Coffin *444*
Hanson, C. Arnold *409*
Hanson, George M. *524*
Hanson, H. C. *522*
Hanson, Harold E. *398*
Hanson, Henry W. A. *409*
Hanson, Howard *554*
Hanson, John *2, 3*
Hanson, Marcus Lee *554*
Hanson, Ole *398*
Hanson, Robert A. *486*
Hanson, Thor *328*
Hapgood, Norman *360*
Hapgood, Powers *506*
Haralson, Hugh A. *78, 80, 81, 83*
Haralson, Jeremiah *110*
Haralson, Jonathan *475*
Harbach, Otto A. *519*
Harberger, John S. *484*
Harbeson, John F. *525*
Harbison, Alexander *386*
Harbison, John *535*
Harbord, James G. *495*
Hard, Gideon *69, 71*
Hardcastle, Dennis F. *494*
Hardee, Cary A. *295*
Hardee, William J. *322, 323, 324*
Hardeman, Thomas *120*
Hardeman, Thomas, Jr. *93*
Harden, Cecil M. *220, 223, 226, 229, 233*
Hardenberg, James R. *386*
Hardenbergh, Augustus A. *111, 114, 118*
Hardenbergh, Jacob R. *415*
Hardenbrook, Donald J. *525*
Harder, E. L. *543*
Harder, H. C. *486*
Harder, Oscar E. *519*
Hardin, Adlai S. *526, 560*
Hardin, Benjamin *55, 57, 59, 69, 71*

Hardin, Clarles H. *302*
Hardin, Clifford M. *31, 36, 421*
Hardin, Fred A. *506*
Hardin, J. M. *476*
Hardin, John J. *78*
Hardin, Martin D. *55, 298*
Hardin, Paul *416, 426*
Hardin, Paul, Jr. *472*
Hardine, William M. *29*
Harding, Aaron *96, 98, 99*
Harding, Abner C. *99, 101*
Harding, Alfred *450, 461*
Harding, Arthur M. *418*
Harding, Benjamin F. *96, 98, 309*
Harding, Edwin F. *342*
Harding, J. Eugene *154*
Harding, Nelson *553*
Harding, R. Bertrand *381*
Harding, Ralph R. *239, 242*
Harding, W. P. G. *380*
Harding, Warren G. *11, 17, 28, 167, 170, 173, 308*
Harding, William L. *297*
Hardinge, Harry W. *538, 544*
Hardison, O. B., Jr. *439*
Hardman, Lamartine G. *295*
Hardt, J. William *494*
Hardt, John W. *472*
Hardt, Robert A. *559*
Hardwick, Thomas W. *147, 150, 153, 155, 159, 162, 165, 168, 295*
Hardy, Alan M. *361*
Hardy, Alexander M. *136*
Hardy, Arnold *555*
Hardy, Arthur C. *527, 544*
Hardy, Arthur S. *362, 370, 371, 372, 373*
Hardy, Caldwell *510*
Hardy, Charles *5*
Hardy, Dorcas R. *381*
Hardy, Edward L. *405*
Hardy, George *505*
Hardy, Guy U. *171, 174, 178, 181, 184, 187, 190*
Hardy, H. W. *392*
Hardy, John *118, 121*
Hardy, John C. *412*
Hardy, John S. *351*
Hardy, Josiah *5*
Hardy, Porter, Jr. *219, 222, 225, 228, 232, 235, 238, 241, 244, 248, 251*
Hardy, Rufus *155, 158, 161, 164, 167, 170, 174, 177*
Hardy, Samuel *4*
Hardy, Summers *308*
Hare, Butler B. *183, 186, 189, 193, 206, 209, 212, 215*
Hare, Darius D. *131, 134*
Hare, James B. *222*
Hare, Paul J. *376*
Hare, Raymond A. *360, 366, 372, 374, 375, 376*
Hare, Robert *560*
Hare, S. Herbert *520*
Hare, Silas *126, 129*
Hare, William H. *448, 461*
Harford, Robert L. *403*
Harford, W. G. W. *438*
Hargis, Denver D. *236*
Hargrave, Thomas J. *487*
Hargrave, William L. *455, 461*
Hargrove, James W. *355, 368*
Hargrove, John Lawrence *519*
Hargrove, Robert K. *471*
Hargroves, V. Carney *475*
Haring, Albert *515*
Haring, John *4*
Harison, John Scott *90*

Harithas, James *438*
Harkey, Ira B., Jr. *556*
Harkin, Tom *262, 265, 268, 271, 274, 277, 297*
Harkins, Kenneth R. *286*
Harkins, Matthew *469*
Harkins, Paul D. *330, 344*
Harkness, Albert *517*
Harkness, Edward S. *431*
Harkness, William *509*
Harlan, Aaron *88, 90, 92*
Harlan, Allison W. *512*
Harlan, Andrew J. *83, 87*
Harlan, Byron B. *192, 195, 199, 202*
Harlan, James *26, 36, 71, 72, 89, 91, 93, 95, 97, 99, 101, 104, 106, 297*
Harlan, James E. *407*
Harlan, John M. *283, 284*
Harlan, Joseph G. *409*
Harlan, Louis R. *534, 558*
Harless, Richard F. *210, 213, 216*
Harleston, Bernard W. *406*
Harley, Herbert *532*
Harley, J. E. *310*
Harley, John *408*
Harlfinger, Frederick J. *347*
Harlin, Robert H. *398*
Harllee, John *379*
Harlow, Bryce N. *552*
Harlow, Harry F. *518, 549*
Harlow, James G. *426*
Harlow, James H. *520*
Harmanson, John H. *80, 82, 84*
Harmel, Paul R. *433*
Harmer, Alfred C. *107, 109, 114, 116, 119, 121, 124, 126, 129, 131, 134, 137, 140, 143*
Harmer, Josiah *329*
Harmon, Andrew D. *417, 476*
Harmon, Austin M. *517*
Harmon, Ernest N. *333, 341, 343, 414*
Harmon, Gene L. *433*
Harmon, Henry G. *408*
Harmon, Hubert R. *340, 417*
Harmon, John H. *391*
Harmon, Judson *27, 35, 308*
Harmon, L. L. *385*
Harmon, Nolan B. *472*
Harmon, Randall S. *236*
Harmony, David B. *349*
Harms, Oliver R. *475*
Harned, David B. *403*
Harner, Nevin C. *410*
Harness, Edward G. *495*
Harness, Forest A. *204, 207, 210, 213, 217*
Harnett, Cornelius *2, 4*
Harnett, Joseph D. *497*
Harnett, Thomas F. *272, 276, 279*
Harnett, William *424*
Harnick, Sheldon *556*
Harnish, J. Lester *475*
Harno, Albert J. *514*
Harnsberger, Harry S. *315*
Harnsberger, Reynolds T. *523*
Harnwell, Gaylord P. *422*
Harp, Reno S. *524*
Harper, Alexander *73, 79, 81, 86*
Harper, Arthur C. *386*
Harper, Arthur M. *343*
Harper, Charles M. *485*
Harper, Charles W. *433*
Harper, Francis J. *73*
Harper, Fred *521*
Harper, George H. *419*

Harper, Heber R. *419*
Harper, J. Fletcher *519*
Harper, James *70, 72, 393, 473*
Harper, James C. *107*
Harper, John *386*
Harper, John A. *52*
Harper, John D. *481*
Harper, Joseph M. *67, 69*
Harper, Paul A. *542*
Harper, R. D. *473*
Harper, Robert *46*
Harper, Robert A. *521*
Harper, Robert G. *14, 15, 43, 44, 45, 55, 300*
Harper, William *63, 311*
Harper, William R. *404, 419*
Harper, William S. *536*
Harrar, J. George *433*
Harreld, John W. *173, 176, 180, 183, 308*
Harrell, Ben *333, 334*
Harrell, Costen J. *471*
Harrelson, John W. *413*
Harries, William H. *131*
Harriman, E. Roland *498, 516, 548*
Harriman, Edward H. *496, 498*
Harriman, Florence Jaffray *369*
Harriman, Henry I. *522*
Harriman, Job *17*
Harriman, Mary W. *548*
Harriman, Mrs. J. Borden *548*
Harriman, W. Averell *30, 37, 306, 362, 375, 379, 483, 498, 552*
Harriman, Walter *304*
Harrington, Donald J. *413*
Harrington, Emerson C. *300*
Harrington, Fred H. *424*
Harrington, George *373*
Harrington, George B. *561*
Harrington, Henry H. *416*
Harrington, Henry W. *97*
Harrington, Isaac R. *393*
Harrington, John L. *520*
Harrington, Joseph B. *390*
Harrington, Julian F. *369*
Harrington, Marion T. *416*
Harrington, Mark W. *423*
Harrington, Michael J. *252, 256, 259, 262, 265*
Harrington, Russell C. *380*
Harrington, Samuel M. *294*
Harrington, Timothy J. *467*
Harrington, Vincent F. *201, 204, 207*
Harrington, William W. *294*
Harriott, Don *392*
Harris, Abram W. *413, 420*
Harris, Addison C. *356*
Harris, Alexander L. *392*
Harris, Andrew L. *308*
Harris, Arthur M. *475*
Harris, Basil *382*
Harris, Benjamin G. *98, 100*
Harris, Benjamin W. *108, 111, 113, 116, 118*
Harris, Bessom Smith *439*
Harris, Bravid W. *453*
Harris, Carleton *292*
Harris, Carolyn *531*
Harris, Charles C. *432*
Harris, Charles M. *97*
Harris, Chauncy D. *537*
Harris, Christopher C. *161*
Harris, Cyril Manton *539*
Harris, Dave E. *493*
Harris, Edward A. *554*
Harris, Edwin B. *385*
Harris, Elisha *310, 518*
Harris, Franklin S. *405*

Harris, Fred R. *244, 247, 250, 253, 257, 308*
Harris, Frederic R. *349*
Harris, George *403*
Harris, George B. *485*
Harris, George C. *457, 458*
Harris, George E. *104, 106*
Harris, H. H. *422*
Harris, Henry R. *108, 110, 113, 122*
Harris, Henry S. *118*
Harris, Herbert E., II *263, 267, 270*
Harris, Hugh *332*
Harris, Hugh P. *334*
Harris, Hunter *346*
Harris, Ira *96, 98, 100, 306, 422*
Harris, Isham G. *85, 87, 114, 117, 119, 121, 124, 126, 129, 132, 134, 137, 140, 311, 312*
Harris, J. Morrison *90, 92, 94*
Harris, James A. *526*
Harris, Jane Gary *546*
Harris, Joe F. *295*
Harris, John *50, 348*
Harris, John H. *405*
Harris, John S. *102, 104, 299*
Harris, John T. *95, 107, 110, 112, 114, 117*
Harris, Julian H. *532*
Harris, Lawrence A. *562*
Harris, Leavitt *361, 371*
Harris, Leonard A. *394*
Harris, Lewis E. *496*
Harris, Malcolm L. *515*
Harris, Mark *59*
Harris, Marquis L. *472*
Harris, Merriman C. *471*
Harris, MIlton *514, 532*
Harris, Mitchell *398*
Harris, Nathaniel E. *295*
Harris, Oren *206, 210, 213, 216, 219, 223, 226, 229, 232, 235, 238, 242, 245*
Harris, Patricia R. *366*
Harris, Patricia Roberts *31, 37, 38*
Harris, Paul P. *527*
Harris, Paul S. *443*
Harris, Peter C. *330*
Harris, Robert *61, 63, 485*
Harris, Robert LeR. *451, 460*
Harris, Robert O. *159, 380*
Harris, Rogers Sanders *457*
Harris, Roy *535*
Harris, Rufus C. *412, 417*
Harris, Sampson W. *81, 83, 85, 87, 89*
Harris, Samuel *404*
Harris, Samuel S. *448, 459*
Harris, Seale *533*
Harris, Stephen R. *137*
Harris, Steven R. *386*
Harris, Sue *395*
Harris, Thomas A. *320*
Harris, Thomas H. *396*
Harris, Thomas K. *54*
Harris, Thomas L. *83, 89, 91, 477*
Harris, Thomas R. *404*
Harris, Townsend *365*
Harris, Vincent M. *469*
Harris, Wiley P. *88, 319*
Harris, William *407*
Harris, William A. *77, 133, 138, 141, 144, 298, 355*
Harris, William J. *171, 175, 178, 181, 184, 187, 191, 295*
Harris, William L. *471*
Harris, William O. *523*

Harris, William T. *381*
Harris, Winder R. *209, 212*
Harrison, Albert G. *71, 73, 75*
Harrison, Albertis S., Jr. *313*
Harrison, Benjamin *2, 4, 6, 11, 16, 17, 27, 117, 120, 122, 297*
Harrison, Burr P. *219, 222, 225, 228, 232, 235, 238, 241*
Harrison, Byron P. *302*
Harrison, Carter B. *43, 44, 45*
Harrison, Carter H. *110, 113*
Harrison, Carter H., Jr. *388*
Harrison, Carter H., Sr. *388*
Harrison, Charles C. *422*
Harrison, Earl G. *380*
Harrison, Edwin D. *409*
Harrison, Fairfax *496*
Harrison, Francis B. *148, 154, 157, 160, 163*
Harrison, Frank *275*
Harrison, Frank J. *468*
Harrison, G. R. *527*
Harrison, George M. *314*
Harrison, George P. *132, 135*
Harrison, George R. *537, 560*
Harrison, Gessner *423*
Harrison, Harold E. *534, 542*
Harrison, Helen C. *542*
Harrison, Henry *395*
Harrison, Henry B. *293*
Harrison, Henry C. *537*
Harrison, Horace H. *109*
Harrison, Hugh *391*
Harrison, James F. *423*
Harrison, James L. *380*
Harrison, James T. *303, 319*
Harrison, Jason *391*
Harrison, John B. *308*
Harrison, John R. *556*
Harrison, John Scott *88*
Harrison, Joseph, Jr. *560*
Harrison, Leland *371, 373, 374, 375*
Harrison, Mrs. Benjamin *526*
Harrison, Pat *159, 163, 166, 169, 172, 176, 179, 182, 185, 188, 191, 195, 198, 201, 204, 206, 208*
Harrison, R. W. *419*
Harrison, Richard A. *96*
Harrison, Richard B. *561*
Harrison, Robert D. *224, 227, 230, 233*
Harrison, Robert H. *14*
Harrison, Ross G. *520*
Harrison, Samuel S. *70, 72*
Harrison, Shelby M. *433*
Harrison, T. O. C. *304*
Harrison, Thomas S. *360*
Harrison, Thomas W. *167, 171, 174, 177, 180, 183, 187*
Harrison, Tinsley R. *513, 533*
Harrison, W. *389*
Harrison, W. H. *523*
Harrison, Wallace K. *532, 559*
Harrison, Walter M. *520*
Harrison, William, Jr. *3*
Harrison, William H. *15, 225, 229, 241, 245, 251, 490*
Harrison, William Henry *11, 15, 24, 55, 57, 63, 65, 308, 335, 358, 541*
Harrison, William K., Jr. *341*
Harrison, William S. *389*
Harriton, Abraham *562*
Harrod, Benjamin M. *519*
Harrold, Joseph *504*
Harrold, Thomas L. *344, 351*
Harrop, William C. *363, 365, 372*
Harrow, William *338*

Harry, Joseph E. *419*
Harsha, William H. *263, 266, 269*
Harsha, William H., Jr. *241, 244, 247, 250, 253, 256, 260*
Harshberger, J. W. *522*
Harshe, Robert B. *437*
Harshman, Ralph G. *404*
Hart, Albert B. *513, 517*
Hart, Alden L. *498*
Hart, Alphonso *121*
Hart, Archibald C. *160, 163, 166*
Hart, Charles *490*
Hart, Charles B. *359*
Hart, Charles C. *355, 370*
Hart, Charles E. *333*
Hart, Charles S. *521*
Hart, E. Kirke *114*
Hart, Edward J. *198, 201, 205, 208, 211, 214, 218, 221, 224, 227*
Hart, Emanuel B. *86*
Hart, Ernest *488*
Hart, Gary *261, 264, 267, 270, 273, 277, 293*
Hart, Hastings H. *559*
Hart, James M. *512, 524*
Hart, Jesse C. *292*
Hart, John *1, 4, 5*
Hart, John F. *503*
Hart, Joseph H. *470*
Hart, Joseph J. *137*
Hart, Julian D. *408*
Hart, Loring *414*
Hart, Louis F. *314*
Hart, Michael J. *191, 195*
Hart, Moss *521, 554*
Hart, Oliver J. *453, 460*
Hart, Ossian B. *295*
Hart, Parker T. *365, 372, 374, 376*
Hart, Philip A. *236, 240, 243, 246, 249, 252, 256, 259, 262, 301*
Hart, Robert A. *389*
Hart, Roswell *100*
Hart, Samuel *517*
Hart, Samuel F. *360*
Hart, Thomas B. *388*
Hart, Thomas C. *213, 294, 418*
Hart, Thomas N. *390*
Hart, William *521*
Hart, William H. *332*
Harte, Joseph M. *454, 458*
Hartenbower, J. J. *388*
Harter, Dow W. *195, 199, 202, 205, 208*
Harter, Elmer E. *524*
Harter, George A. *419*
Harter, J. Francis *205*
Harter, Michael D. *131, 134*
Hartford, James J. *513*
Hartigan, John P. *284*
Harting, Darrell H. *544*
Hartke, Vance *236, 239, 242, 246, 249, 252, 255, 258, 261, 297*
Hartl, Leon *562*
Hartle, Russell P. *341, 342*
Hartley, Fred A., Jr. *189, 192, 195, 198, 201, 205, 208, 211, 214, 218*
Hartley, Fred L. *498*
Hartley, James J. *469*
Hartley, Roland H. *314*
Hartley, Thomas *41, 42, 43, 44, 45, 46*
Hartline, Haldan K. *550*
Hartman, A. K. *385*
Hartman, Arthur A. *362, 375*

Hellman, Lillian *534, 545, 547*
Hellman, Louis *560*
Hellmann, Claude B. *523*
Hellmund, Rudolf E. *542*
Hellweg, Frederick *544*
Helm, Harold H. *484*
Helm, Harvey *153, 156, 159, 162, 165, 169*
Helm, James *7*
Helm, John L. *298, 491*
Helm, Joseph C. *293*
Helmick, Eli A. *331*
Helmick, William *94*
Helming, Carlton T. *433*
Helms, Jesse A. *259, 263, 266, 269, 272, 275, 278, 307*
Helms, Richard *364*
Helms, Richard M. *379*
Helms, William *47, 48, 49, 50, 51*
Helmsing, Charles *468*
Helmsing, Charles H. *467*
Helpern, Milton *533*
Helstoski, Henry *247, 250, 253, 256, 259, 262*
Helt, D. W. *504*
Heltne, Paul G. *441*
Heltzer, Harry *492*
Helvering, Guy T. *162, 165, 168*
Helwig, John B. *426*
Hem, Halvor O. *562*
Hembel, William *509*
Hemenway, James A. *136, 138, 141, 144, 147, 150, 153, 297*
Hemingway, Ernest *532, 550, 555*
Hemingway, W. L. *511*
Hemingway, William *391*
Hemley, Cecil *527*
Hempelmann, John *260*
Hemphill, John *95, 97, 312, 320*
Hemphill, John J. *121, 124, 126, 129, 132*
Hemphill, Joseph *47, 58, 60, 61, 63, 66*
Hemphill, Robert W. *234, 238, 241, 244, 287*
Hemphill, William A. *387*
Hempl, George *512, 517, 524*
Hempstead, Clark *494*
Hempstead, Stephen *297*
Hemsley, William *3*
Henahan, Donal *558*
Hench, Atcheson L. *512*
Hench, Philip S. *551*
Henchey, John E. *392*
Hencken, Hugh *521*
Hency, Philip S. *549*
Hendee, George W. *110, 112, 114, 313*
Hendel, Richard *546*
Henderson, Albert J. *286*
Henderson, Albert John *285*
Henderson, Algo D. *403*
Henderson, Archibald *46, 47, 348*
Henderson, Bennett H. *56*
Henderson, Branton H. *522*
Henderson, Charles *291*
Henderson, Charles B. *169, 173, 304*
Henderson, David B. *120, 122, 125, 127, 130, 133, 136, 138, 141, 143, 144*
Henderson, David N. *240, 244, 247, 250, 253, 256, 260, 263*
Henderson, Donald A. *549*
Henderson, Douglas *357*
Henderson, Elmer L. *515*
Henderson, Homer B. *474*

Henderson, J. Pinckney *93*
Henderson, J. T. *406*
Henderson, J. W. *312*
Henderson, Jack *536*
Henderson, James A. *431*
Henderson, James B. *497*
Henderson, James H. *100*
Henderson, James P. *312*
Henderson, John *75, 76, 78, 302*
Henderson, John B. *96, 98, 100, 102, 303*
Henderson, John E. *231, 234, 237*
Henderson, John S. *123, 126, 128, 131, 134*
Henderson, John W. *387, 425*
Henderson, Joseph *70, 72*
Henderson, Joseph W. *511*
Henderson, Julia *560*
Henderson, Junius *443*
Henderson, Leonard *307*
Henderson, Loy W. *364, 368*
Henderson, Oran K. *345*
Henderson, Paul *558*
Henderson, Samuel *54, 388*
Henderson, Theodore S. *471*
Henderson, Thomas *44*
Henderson, Thomas J. *110, 113, 115, 117, 120, 122, 125, 127, 130, 133*
Henderson, William L. *300*
Hendon, William M. *272, 278*
Hendren, H. H. *386*
Hendrick, Archer W. *421*
Hendrick, Burton J. *553*
Hendrick, John K. *136*
Hendrick, John T. *387*
Hendricks, Barkley L. *560*
Hendricks, Joe *200, 203, 207, 210, 213, 216*
Hendricks, Sterling B. *549*
Hendricks, Thomas A. *12, 16, 26, 86, 87, 97, 99, 101, 122, 297*
Hendricks, William *55, 56, 57, 59, 62, 64, 65, 67, 69, 71, 297*
Hendrickson, George L. *517*
Hendrickson, Robert C. *221, 224, 227, 305, 368*
Hendrickson, Waino *385*
Hendrie, Joseph M. *381*
Hendrix, Eugene R. *471*
Hendrix, Hall *556*
Hendrix, Joseph C. *134, 510*
Henebry, John P. *525*
Henkle, Eli J. *111, 113, 115*
Henle, Gertrude *542*
Henle, Robert J. *409*
Henle, Werner *542*
Henley, Barclay *119, 122*
Henley, Beth *558*
Henley, J. Smith *285*
Henley, James W. *472*
Henley, Thomas J. *78, 80, 82*
Henn, Bernhart *86, 88*
Henne, Frances W. *543*
Henneke, Ben G. *423*
Hennelly, Edward J. *516*
Hennemeyer, Robert T. *362*
Hennessey, Barbara *546*
Hennessey, Edward F. *301*
Hennessey, Edward L., Jr. *481*
Hennessey, John J. *334, 345, 466*
Hennessey, William B. *516*
Hennessy, John *463, 466*
Hennessy, John J. *466*
Henney, Charles W. *196*
Henney, Richard B. *432*

Henney, William F. *386*
Henni, John M. *464, 470*
Henniker-Heaton, Raymond *444*
Henning, Edward J. *524*
Henning, G. C. *544*
Henning, John F. *368*
Hennings, F. Martin *542*
Hennings, Ivar *523*
Hennings, Thomas C., Jr. *198, 201, 204, 224, 227, 230, 233, 237, 303*
Henricken, Thomas F. *469*
Henrickson, Albert N. *437*
Henriques, J. A. *417*
Henry, Alexander *395*
Henry, Charles L. *136, 138*
Henry, Daniel M. *113, 115*
Henry, David *425*
Henry, David D. *420*
Henry, E. Stevens *135, 138, 141, 144, 147, 149, 152, 155, 158*
Henry, E. William *379*
Henry, Fred A. *476*
Henry, Gustavus A. *320, 321*
Henry, Guy V. *330*
Henry, J. Addison *473*
Henry, James *4*
Henry, James J. *561, 562*
Henry, John *3, 14, 41, 42, 43, 44, 80, 300*
Henry, John F. *62*
Henry, John W. *303*
Henry, Joseph *443, 540*
Henry, Joseph W. *312*
Henry, Lewis *176*
Henry, Lou *20*
Henry, M. George *462*
Henry, Matthew G. *453*
Henry, Patrick *4, 6, 139, 142, 145, 540*
Henry, Paul *278*
Henry, Robert *422*
Henry, Robert K. *216*
Henry, Robert L. *140, 143, 146, 149, 152, 155, 158, 161, 164, 167*
Henry, Robert P. *61, 62*
Henry, Stephen G. *329, 343*
Henry, Thomas *73, 75, 77*
Henry, W. Laird *133*
Henry, William *4, 83, 85, 391*
Henry, William A., III *558*
Henry, William M. *552*
Henry, William W. *513*
Henselman, Frances *440*
Henshaw, David *25, 35*
Henshaw, John P. K. *447, 461*
Hensley, Stuart K. *499*
Hensley, Walter L. *160, 163, 166, 169*
Henson, Harold *385*
Henson, Paul H. *498*
Henton, Willis R. *456, 460, 462*
Hepburn, A. Barton *484*
Hepburn, A. J. *347*
Hepburn, Andrew D. *407, 412*
Hepburn, Joseph S. *544*
Hepburn, Katharine *560*
Hepburn, William P. *118, 120, 122, 133, 136, 138, 141, 144, 147, 150, 153*
Hepner, Walter R. *405*
Hepner, William H. *395*
Herald, William H. *155*
Herbermann, Charles G. *542*
Herbert, Caleb C. *320, 321*
Herbert, Edward G. *544*
Herbert, F. Edward *239*
Herbert, Hardy *385*

Herbert, Hilary A. *27, 35, 112, 115, 117, 119, 122, 124, 127, 129*
Herbert, John C. *55, 56*
Herbert, Paul A. *527*
Herbert, Philemon T. *89*
Herbert, Robert N. *562*
Herbert, Thomas J. *308*
Herbert, William C. *398*
Herbster, Ben *475*
Hereford, Frank *107, 110, 112, 114, 117, 314*
Hereford, Frank L., Jr. *423*
Herget, John F. *426*
Hering, Carl *522*
Hering, Doris *536*
Hering, Hermann S. *476*
Hering, Rudolph *518*
Herkimer, John *56, 61*
Herkimer, Nicholas *335*
Herlands, William B. *476*
Herlong, Albert S., Jr. *220, 223, 226, 229, 232, 236, 239, 242, 245, 248*
Herman, James R. *504*
Herman, John C. *395*
Herman, Robert *562*
Hermann, Binger *124, 126, 129, 131, 134, 137, 148, 151*
Hermann, Grover M. *491*
Hermany, Charles *519*
Hernandez, Benigno C. *166, 173, 369*
Hernandez, Diego E. *348*
Herndon, Ellen Lewis *20*
Herndon, Terry E. *526*
Herndon, Thomas H. *115, 117*
Herndon, William H. *388*
Herndon, William S. *107, 110*
Hero, Andrew, Jr. *331*
Herod, William *71, 72*
Herold, Henry R. *433*
Herold, J. Christopher *545*
Heron, Alexander R. *405*
Heron, Raymond A. *452*
Heroy, William B. *510, 552*
Herr, Edwin M. *499*
Herr, Herbert T. *544*
Herr, John *477*
Herr, John K. *330*
Herreid, Charles N. *311*
Herren, Thomas W. *333, 342*
Herrick, Anson *98*
Herrick, Clarence L. *421*
Herrick, Ebenezer *59, 61, 62*
Herrick, George M. *425*
Herrick, James B. *513, 533*
Herrick, John W. *422*
Herrick, Joshua *78*
Herrick, Manuel *176*
Herrick, Myron T. *308, 361, 510*
Herrick, P. R. *394*
Herrick, Paul M. *472*
Herrick, Peter *483*
Herrick, Richard P. *80*
Herrick, Samuel *57, 58*
Herring, Clyde L. *201, 204, 207, 297*
Herring, Pendleton *518*
Herrington, John S. *32, 38*
Herrion, John Q. *344*
Herrmann, August *521*
Herrmann, Daniel L. *294*
Herrmann, Edward J. *469*
Herrmann, George R. *533*
Herron, Charles D. *332, 333*
Herron, Francis *473*
Herron, Francis J. *335, 337*
Herron, Helen *20*
Herron, James H. *520*

Hillelson, Jeffrey P. *227*
Hillen, Solomon, Jr. *74, 390*
Hillenbrand, Martin J. *361, 364*
Hiller, William A. *481*
Hillestad, Albert W. *456, 461*
Hillhard, Henry W. *356*
Hillhouse, James *41, 42, 43, 44, 45, 46, 47, 48, 50, 51, 293*
Hillhouse, William *3*
Hilliard, Benjamin C. *165, 168, 293*
Hilliard, Henry W. *79, 81, 83, 357*
Hilliard, William *387*
Hillier, James *543*
Hillinger, Raymond P. *466*
Hillings, Patrick J. *223, 226, 229, 232*
Hillis, Elwood H. *255, 258, 261, 265, 268, 271, 274, 277*
Hillis, Isaac L. *388*
Hillkowitz, Philip *519*
Hillman, Bill *503*
Hillman, James N. *408*
Hillman, Richard L. *390*
Hillman, Sidney *503*
Hillman, Stanley E. G. *490*
Hills, Carla A. *31, 38*
Hills, Charles F. *441*
Hills, Lee *520, 555*
Hills, Roderick M. *381*
Hillsman, Matt *406*
Hillyer, George *387*
Hillyer, Junius *85*
Hillyer, Robert *527, 554*
Hilton, Frank C. *528*
Hilton, James H. *410*
Hilton, Robert B. *320, 321*
Hilton, Samuel L. *559*
Hilyer, Junius *87*
Himes, Joseph H. *176*
Himmel, Joseph J. *409*
Himrod, Charles *388*
Hinckley, Arthur T. *522*
Hinckley, H. D. *417*
Hinckley, Thomas *5*
Hincks, Carroll C. *284*
Hindle, Brooke *441*
Hindman, Joseph A. E. *348*
Hindman, Thomas C. *93, 323*
Hindman, William *3, 42, 43, 44, 45, 46, 300*
Hinds, Asher C. *159, 162, 166*
Hinds, James *101*
Hinds, Thomas *64, 66*
Hine, Maynard K. *512*
Hinebaugh, William H. *162*
Hines, Frank T. *369*
Hines, Fred A. *527*
Hines, John E. *453, 461*
Hines, John L. *329, 339*
Hines, Linnaeus *410*
Hines, Marion E. *543*
Hines, Merrill O. *533*
Hines, Richard *63*
Hines, Vincent J. *465*
Hines, Walter D. *483*
Hines, Wellington T. *349*
Hines, William H. *134*
Hinitt, Frederick W. *425*
Hinkhouse, Forest M. *442*
Hinkle, James F. *305*
Hinkle, John H. *394*
Hinkley, J. William *433*
Hinks, Samuel *390*
Hinman, Clark T. *413*
Hinman, Edward B. *490*
Hinman, George W. *412*
Hinman, Joel *294*
Hinman, John H. *490*
Hinman, Thomas P. *512*

Hinners, Noel W. *441*
Hinrichs, Amy *525*
Hinrichs, John H. *332*
Hinrichsen, William H. *138*
Hinsch, Charles A. *510*
Hinsdale, Burke A. *410*
Hinsdale, Robert G. *410*
Hinshaw, Andrew *261*
Hinshaw, Andrew J. *258*
Hinshaw, C. Elton *513*
Hinshaw, Carl *203, 206, 210, 213, 216, 219, 223, 226, 229, 563*
Hinshaw, David *559*
Hinshaw, Edmund H. *148, 151, 154, 157*
Hinson, Jon *271*
Hinson, Jon C. *268*
Hinton, Deane R. *361, 369, 376*
Hipple, J. E. *396*
Hires, George *123, 126*
Hirsch, Hiram H. *544*
Hirsch, Joseph *531*
Hirsch, Solomon *374*
Hirschfelder, Joseph O. *549*
Hirshfeld, Clarence F. *539*
Hirshson, Louis M. *410*
Hirst, A. C. *423*
Hisaw, F. L. *520*
Hiscock, Frank *114, 116, 118, 121, 123, 126, 128, 131, 306*
Hiscock, Ira V. *518, 526, 561*
Hise, Elijah *100, 363*
Hise, Frank *521*
Hitch, Charles J. *418, 433*
Hitchcock, Albert E. *562*
Hitchcock, Albert S. *521*
Hitchcock, Edward *403*
Hitchcock, Ethan A. *27, 36, 371*
Hitchcock, Frank H. *28, 36*
Hitchcock, Gilbert M. *148, 154, 157, 160, 163, 166, 169, 172, 176, 303*
Hitchcock, Henry *291, 511*
Hitchcock, Henry E. *421*
Hitchcock, Henry L. *426*
Hitchcock, Henry-Russell *443*
Hitchcock, Herbert E. *199, 202, 311*
Hitchcock, Peter *57, 308*
Hitchcock, Phileas W. *109*
Hitchcock, Phineas W. *106, 303*
Hitchings, George H. *551*
Hitchock, Phineas W. *111*
Hite, Bert H. *544*
Hitt, R. S. Reynolds *363, 369*
Hitt, Robert H. *127*
Hitt, Robert R. *117, 120, 122, 125, 130, 133, 135, 138, 141, 144, 147, 150*
Hitz, William *286*
Hixson, Fred W. *403*
Hixson, George F *523*
Hoadley, George *394*
Hoadley, Horace G. *544*
Hoadley, Jeremy *386*
Hoadly, George *307*
Hoag, David G. *540*
Hoag, Ella W. *476*
Hoag, Truman H. *105*
Hoagland, Hudson *509*
Hoagland, Jimmie Lee *557*
Hoagland, Laurance R. *440*
Hoagland, Mahlon B. *539*
Hoagland, Moses *84*
Hoan, Daniel W. *399*
Hoar, Ebenezer R. *26, 35, 108*

Hoar, George F. *104, 106, 108, 111, 113, 116, 118, 120, 123, 125, 128, 130, 133, 136, 139, 142, 144, 147, 301, 509, 513*
Hoar, Leonard *409*
Hoar, Rockwood *150*
Hoar, Samuel *71*
Hoar, Sherman *130*
Hoard, Charles B. *92, 94*
Hoard, William D. *315*
Hoban, Edward F. *466, 469*
Hoban, Michael J. *469*
Hobart, Aaron *58, 59, 61, 62*
Hobart, Donald M. *515*
Hobart, Garret A. *12, 17, 138, 141*
Hobart, Garrett A. *27*
Hobart, John H. *447, 460*
Hobart, John S. *45, 306*
Hobart, Mrs. Lowell Fletcher *526*
Hobb, Leonard S. *561*
Hobbie, Selah R. *64*
Hobbins, James R. *482*
Hobbs, A. I. *476*
Hobbs, Barnabas C. *408*
Hobbs, Herschel H. *475*
Hobbs, Leland S. *342*
Hobbs, Leonard S. *537*
Hobbs, Nathaniel W. *392*
Hobbs, Nicholas *518*
Hobbs, Sam *197, 200, 203, 206, 210, 213, 216, 219*
Hobbs, William D. *495*
Hobbs, William J. *485*
Hobby, Oveta Culp *30, 37, 330, 548*
Hobby, William P. *312*
Hoben, Allan *411*
Hoberman, Mary Ann *547*
Hobgood, Clarence *456*
Hoblitzell, Bruce *389*
Hoblitzell, Fetter S. *118, 120*
Hoblitzell, John D., Jr. *235, 315*
Hobson, Henry W. *452, 461*
Hobson, Kenneth B. *346*
Hobson, Merk *421*
Hobson, Richmond P. *152, 155, 158, 161*
Hoch, Daniel K. *212, 215*
Hoch, Edward W. *297*
Hoch, Homer *172, 175, 178, 181, 185, 188, 191*
Hoch, Lambert A. *469*
Hoch, Orion L. *491*
Hochklassen, H. *544*
Hockenhull, Andy W. *305*
Hocker, Lon *522*
Hodapp, Leroy C. *472*
Hodel, Donald P. *32, 36, 38*
Hodes, Henry I. *332, 334, 344, 351*
Hodes, Horace L. *542*
Hodgdon, Daniel R. *424*
Hodgdon, Samuel *488*
Hodge, Bachman G. *472*
Hodge, Benjamin L. *321*
Hodge, Charles *473*
Hodge, George B. *319, 320*
Hodge, John R. *333, 341, 342, 343*
Hodge, Mrs. Maurice B. *475*
Hodgen, John T. *515*
Hodges, Alpheus P. *385*
Hodges, Arthur *388*
Hodges, Asa *108*
Hodges, Campbell B. *411*
Hodges, Charles D. *91*
Hodges, Courtney H. *331, 333, 340, 341*

Hodges, Earle W. *524*
Hodges, George H. *297*
Hodges, George T. *91*
Hodges, Henry C., Jr. *339*
Hodges, J. C., Jr. *333*
Hodges, James *390*
Hodges, James L. *64, 66, 67*
Hodges, Jeanne Butler *514*
Hodges, Joseph H. *470*
Hodges, Luther H. *30, 37, 307, 528*
Hodges, Nathaniel D. C. *515*
Hodges, Paul V. *293*
Hodges, Ralph B. *308*
Hodges, Silas H. *381*
Hodges, Thomas E. *426*
Hodgkins, Howard L. *409*
Hodgkinson, Francis *537, 541*
Hodgman, Thomas M. *412*
Hodgson, D. B. *417*
Hodgson, James D. *31, 37, 365*
Hodgson, Laurence C. *391*
Hodgson, Percy *527*
Hodgson, Samuel *332*
Hodgson, Telfair *423*
Hodnette, John K. *538*
Hodson, Kenneth J. *331*
Hoebel, E. Adamson *509*
Hoeffer, James F. X. *407, 411, 415*
Hoeg, Halstead H. *387*
Hoegh, Leo A. *297*
Hoelterhoff, Manuela *558*
Hoenemyer, Frank J. *434*
Hoeppel, John H. *194, 197*
Hoerni, Jean A. *544*
Hoes, Hanna *20*
Hoeven, Charles B. *210, 214, 217, 220, 223, 226, 230, 233, 236, 239, 242*
Hoey, Clyde R. *173, 215, 218, 221, 224, 228, 307*
Hof, Samuel *332*
Hoff, Nicholas *540*
Hoff, Nicholas J. *533*
Hoff, Philip H. *313*
Hoffa, James R. *504*
Hoffacker, Lewis *357, 361*
Hoffecker, John H. *141*
Hoffecker, Walter O. *141*
Hoffer, Eric *552*
Hoffman Ronald *550*
Hoffman, Brian F. *532*
Hoffman, C. A. *516*
Hoffman, Carl H. *215*
Hoffman, Clare E. *198, 201, 204, 208, 211, 214, 217, 220, 224, 227, 230, 233, 236, 240*
Hoffman, E. L. *536*
Hoffman, Elmer J. *236, 239, 242*
Hoffman, Harold G. *185, 189, 305*
Hoffman, Henry W. *90*
Hoffman, Hugh F. T. *343, 345*
Hoffman, J. Ogden *73*
Hoffman, James R. *469*
Hoffman, John T. *306, 393*
Hoffman, Joseph *472*
Hoffman, Ludwig C. *562*
Hoffman, Martin R. *327*
Hoffman, Michael *63, 64, 66, 68*
Hoffman, Mrs. William H. *523*
Hoffman, Ogden J. *75*
Hoffman, Paul G. *379, 432, 548, 552*
Hoffman, Philip G. *419*
Hoffman, Richard W. *220, 223, 226, 229*
Hoffman, Roald *549*

Hoffman, Sal B. *506*
Hoffman, Samuel K. *540, 562*
Hoffman, Walter E. *287*
Hoffman, Wickham *360*
Hoffmann, Ralph *443*
Hoffmann, Robert S. *441*
Hoffstot, Frank N. *499*
Hofheinz, Fred *397*
Hofheinz, Roy *397*
Hofmann, Philip B. *490*
Hofstadter Robert *550*
Hofstadter, Douglas *546*
Hofstadter, Douglas R. *558*
Hofstadter, Richard *555, 556*
Hofstadter, Robert *549*
Hofstede, Albert J. *391*
Hogan, Aloysius J. *408*
Hogan, Bartholomew W. *347*
Hogan, Chester A. *527*
Hogan, Earl L. *236*
Hogan, Frank J. *511*
Hogan, Henry H. *496*
Hogan, James J. *469*
Hogan, John *100*
Hogan, John J. *467, 468*
Hogan, John P. *519*
Hogan, Joseph F. *486*
Hogan, Joseph L. *468*
Hogan, Lawrence J. *252, 256, 259*
Hogan, Michael J. *176*
Hogan, William *68*
Hogan, William T. *539*
Hoge, James *473*
Hoge, John *48*
Hoge, John B. *119*
Hoge, Joseph P. *78, 80*
Hoge, Moses *409*
Hoge, Solomon L. *105, 112*
Hoge, William *47, 48, 50*
Hoge, William M. *332, 334, 343, 344*
Hogeboom, James L. *61*
Hogemann, George L. *483*
Hogenson, Roald A. *286*
Hogg, Charles E. *127*
Hogg, David *181, 184, 188, 191*
Hogg, Herschel M. *146, 149*
Hogg, James S. *312*
Hogg, Robert L. *190, 193*
Hogg, Samuel *57*
Hogg, Wilbur E. *458*
Hogg, Wilbur Emory, Jr. *456*
Hogin, P. E. *434*
Hogle, John F. *391*
Hogness, John R. *423*
Hogue, D. P. *387*
Hohenemser, Kurt H. *562*
Hohlfeld, Alexander R. *524*
Hoidale, Einar *195*
Hoie, Claus *533*
Hoijer, Harry *509*
Hoisington, Elizabeth P. *330*
Hoke, R. F. *324*
Hoke, William A. *307*
Hoke, William E. *544*
Hoke, William R. *544*
Holabird, Samuel B. *332*
Holaday, William P. *178, 181, 184, 187, 191*
Holborn, Hajo *513*
Holbrock, Greg J. *208*
Holbrook, David S. *538*
Holbrook, Frederick *313*
Holbrook, Gordon *540*
Holbrook, Lucius R. *351*
Holbrook, Willard A., Jr. *343*
Holbrook, Willard A. *330, 339*
Holcomb, Glenn W. *519*
Holcomb, Marcus H. *293*
Holcomb, Silas A. *303, 304*

Holcomb, Thomas *348, 375*
Holcombe, Arthur N. *517, 534*
Holcombe, George *59, 61, 63, 64*
Holcombe, James P. *320*
Holcombe, John M. *494*
Holcombe, Oscar *397*
Holden, Edward S. *418*
Holden, Hale *485, 496*
Holden, James S. *313*
Holden, Louis E. *407*
Holden, William D. *533*
Holden, William W. *307*
Holder, William D. *320, 321*
Holderman, James B. *422*
Holdridge, John H. *364, 372*
Holgate, Thomas F. *413*
Holiday, Harry *482*
Holiday, Harry, Jr. *539*
Holifield, Chet *210, 213, 216, 219, 223, 226, 229, 232, 235, 239, 242, 245, 248, 251, 255, 258*
Holl, D. E. *489*
Holladay, Alexander Q. *413*
Holladay, Alexander R. *85, 87*
Hollaender, Alexander *538*
Holland, Albert E. *410*
Holland, Arthur J. *393*
Holland, Benjamin L. *494*
Holland, Cornelius *66, 67*
Holland, E. V. *293*
Holland, Edward *393*
Holland, Edward E. *161, 164, 167, 171, 174*
Holland, Elmer J. *209, 231, 234, 238, 241, 244, 247, 250*
Holland, Ernest O. *425*
Holland, F. P. *397*
Holland, Floyd *399*
Holland, James *44, 47, 48, 49, 50, 51*
Holland, James F. *543*
Holland, Jeffrey R. *405*
Holland, Jerome *553*
Holland, Jerome H. *373, 541*
Holland, Kenneth L. *263, 266, 269, 272*
Holland, R. A. *442*
Holland, Rush L. *521*
Holland, Spessard L. *213, 216, 220, 223, 226, 229, 232, 236, 239, 242, 245, 248, 252, 295*
Holland, W. M. *397*
Holland, William J. *422, 438*
Hollander, Jacob H. *513*
Hollander, John *534*
Holleman, Joel *76*
Hollenbeck, Conrad *304*
Hollenbeck, Harold C. *265, 269, 272*
Hollerbach, Serge *533*
Hollers, James P. *512*
Holley, Alexander H. *293*
Holley, Edward G. *538*
Holley, Horace *417*
Holley, James A. *398*
Holley, John M. *82*
Holley, Lawrence A. *503*
Holley, Robert W. *543, 550*
Hollick, Arthur *443*
Holliday, Cal *399*
Holliday, Cyrus K. *389*
Holliday, Elias S. *144, 147, 150, 153*
Holliday, Frederick W. M. *313, 321*
Holliday, J. S. *442*
Holliday, Wallace T. *496, 497*
Holling, Thomas L. *393*

Hollings, Ernest F. *250, 254, 257, 260, 263, 266, 269, 272, 276, 279, 311*
Hollingshead, W. B. *544*
Hollingsworth, David A. *157, 167, 170*
Hollingworth, Harry L. *518*
Hollins, George N. *324*
Hollins, John S. *390*
Hollinsworth, Henry *396*
Hollinsworth, S. N. *396*
Hollis, Harris W. *344*
Hollis, Henry F. *163, 166, 169, 305*
Hollis, Ira N. *426, 520*
Hollis, John H. *385*
Hollis, Orlando J. *422*
Hollis, Pat *393*
Hollis, Robert P. *351*
Hollister, Gideon H. *363*
Hollister, John B. *192, 195, 199, 379*
Hollomon, John H. *421*
Holloran, Patrick J. *416*
Holloway, Anne F. *367*
Holloway, Bruce K. *346*
Holloway, David P. *89, 381*
Holloway, Edward, Jr. *523*
Holloway, Emory *553*
Holloway, Fred G. *472*
Holloway, James L., III *347, 348*
Holloway, James L., Jr. *347, 349, 418*
Holloway, Josephus F. *520*
Holloway, Robert J. *515*
Holloway, William G. *489*
Holloway, William J. *308*
Holloway, William J., Jr. *286*
Hollyday, R. C. *349*
Holm, Hanya *536*
Holm, Jens T. *562*
Holm, Wilton R. *528*
Holman, Eugene *487, 533*
Holman, Frank E. *511, 532*
Holman, Minard L. *520*
Holman, Rufus C. *205, 209, 212, 309*
Holman, William S. *93, 95, 97, 101, 103, 106, 108, 110, 117, 120, 122, 125, 127, 130, 133, 138*
Holmes, Adoniram J. *120, 122, 125*
Holmes, Arthur *408*
Holmes, Benjamin *392*
Holmes, Charles H. *104*
Holmes, D. Brainerd *495*
Holmes, David *45, 46, 47, 48, 49, 51, 58, 59, 61, 63, 302*
Holmes, Edward J. *440*
Holmes, Edwin R. *284*
Holmes, Elias B. *80, 82*
Holmes, Ephraim P. *348*
Holmes, Gabriel *63, 65, 306*
Holmes, George F. *420*
Holmes, H. Allen *370*
Holmes, Hal *212, 216, 219, 222, 225, 228, 232, 235*
Holmes, Harry N. *511, 532*
Holmes, Isaac E. *75, 77, 79, 81, 83, 85*
Holmes, John *56, 58, 59, 61, 62, 64, 66, 67, 299, 497*
Holmes, John B. *396*
Holmes, Julius C. *364, 367*
Holmes, Leslie A. *413*
Holmes, Merrill J. *410*
Holmes, Oliver Wendell *283, 301, 532, 559*
Holmes, Oliver Wendell, Jr. *540*

Holmes, Pehr G. *191, 194, 198, 201, 204, 207, 211, 214*
Holmes, Philip H. *537*
Holmes, Ralph C. *497*
Holmes, Ralston S. *347*
Holmes, Robert D. *309*
Holmes, S. J. *520*
Holmes, Sidney T. *100*
Holmes, Theophilus H. *322*
Holmes, Thomas H. *541*
Holmes, Uriel *56*
Holmes, William H. *441*
Holmes, William J., Jr. *416*
Holmgren, Laton E. *511*
Holmgren, Patricia K. *521*
Holmstedt, Raleigh W. *410*
Holsey, Hopkins *70, 72*
Holshouser, James E. *307*
Holst, Spencer *560*
Holt, Andrew D. *423, 525*
Holt, Cooper T. *528*
Holt, Elmer *303*
Holt, Grover J. *514*
Holt, Hamilton *415, 523*
Holt, Henry W. *314*
Holt, Hines *74, 320*
Holt, Homer A. *314*
Holt, Ivan Lee *471*
Holt, Jack W., Jr. *292*
Holt, Jordan *389*
Holt, Joseph *25, 34, 36, 331, 381*
Holt, Joseph F. *226, 229, 232, 235*
Holt, L. Emmett, Jr. *534*
Holt, Marjorie S. *259, 262, 265, 268, 271, 274, 277*
Holt, O. T. *397*
Holt, Orrin *70, 72*
Holt, Rush D. *200, 203, 206, 315*
Holt, Samuel D. *385*
Holt, Thomas M. *307*
Holt, Victor, Jr. *489*
Holten, Samuel *2, 3, 43*
Holter, Don W. *472*
Holton, Hart B. *120*
Holton, Henry D. *518*
Holton, Karl *552*
Holton, Linwood *313, 541*
Holton, William B. *523*
Holtoner, J. Stanley *351*
Holtzclaw, Jack G. *499*
Holtzman, Arnold H. *562*
Holtzman, Elizabeth *259, 262, 266, 269*
Holtzman, John W. *388*
Holtzman, Lester *227, 231, 237, 240*
Holyoke, Edward *409*
Holyoke, Edward A. *509*
Holzapfel, E. W. *426*
Holzapple, Joseph R. *346*
Holzman, Lester *234*
Homan, Fletcher *426*
Homan, Richard *528*
Homan, W. K. *476*
Homans, George C. *520*
Homer, Arthur B. *483, 539*
Honaman, Earl M. *454, 458*
Honda, Soichiro *541*
Hone, Philip *393*
Hones, Tiberius G. *422*
Honewell, Arthur *503*
Honeyman, Nan Wood *202*
Honeywell, Mark C. *489*
Hong, Edna *545*
Hong, Howard *545*
Hood, Clifford F. *434, 499*
Hood, George E. *166, 170*
Hood, George H. *371*

Hood, George J. *541*
Hood, Graham S. *442*
Hood, Harrison P. *562*
Hood, John B. *322, 323, 324*
Hood, Robin *557*
Hood, Solomon P. *366*
Hoogkamp, Herman F. *393*
Hook, Charles R. *482, 525, 539*
Hook, Enos *75, 77*
Hook, Frank E. *198, 201, 204, 208, 214*
Hook, H. M. *399*
Hook, Sidney *553*
Hook, William C. *285*
Hooker, Charles E. *111, 113, 116, 118, 125, 128, 131, 133, 145*
Hooker, David G. *399*
Hooker, Edward Payson *415*
Hooker, Edward W. *386*
Hooker, Elon H. *433*
Hooker, James M. *177, 180*
Hooker, John *396*
Hooker, Joseph *335, 336, 337, 338*
Hooker, Michael K. *404*
Hooker, Warren B. *131, 134, 137, 139*
Hooks, Benjamin L. *525, 562*
Hooks, Charles *55, 58, 60, 61*
Hoomes, Oliver Wendell *540*
Hooper, Alcaeus *390*
Hooper, Ben W. *311*
Hooper, Benjamin S. *122*
Hooper, Franklin *403*
Hooper, Franklin W. *437*
Hooper, Johnson J. *319*
Hooper, Joseph L. *182, 185, 188, 191, 195*
Hooper, M. J. *504*
Hooper, Robert L. *7*
Hooper, Samuel *96, 98, 100, 102, 104, 106, 108*
Hooper, Stanford C. *537, 541*
Hooper, William *1, 4, 425*
Hooper, William L. *417*
Hoopes, Townsend *534*
Hoopman, Harold D. *491*
Hooven, M. D. *523*
Hoover, Calvin B. *513*
Hoover, Herbert *11, 18, 28, 29, 539, 541, 548, 559, 561*
Hoover, Herbert, Jr. *541*
Hoover, Herbert C. *37, 548*
Hoover, J. Edgar *548, 559*
Hoover, Mrs. Herbert *523*
Hoover, Paul A. *486*
Hoover, William H. *482*
Hope, Bob *541, 548, 552*
Hope, Clifford R. *185, 188, 191, 194, 197, 201, 204, 207, 210, 214, 217, 220, 223, 226, 230*
Hope, J. William *514*
Hope, John *413, 561*
Hope, Stanley C. *525*
Hopkin, Larry J. *277*
Hopkins, Albert C. *131, 134*
Hopkins, Albert J. *122, 125, 127, 130, 133, 135, 138, 141, 144, 147, 150, 153, 296*
Hopkins, Arthur F. *291*
Hopkins, Benjamin F. *103, 105*
Hopkins, David W. *185, 188, 192*
Hopkins, Edward *5, 387*
Hopkins, Ernest M. *407, 492*
Hopkins, Esek *350*
Hopkins, Frank A. *147, 150*
Hopkins, George W. *72, 74, 76, 77, 79, 81, 93, 370*

Hopkins, Harold A., Jr. *457, 460*
Hopkins, Harry L. *29, 37*
Hopkins, Henry *426*
Hopkins, Henry T. *443*
Hopkins, Isaac S. *408, 409*
Hopkins, J. W. *385*
Hopkins, James *536*
Hopkins, James H. *112, 121*
Hopkins, John H. *447, 461*
Hopkins, John Jay *488*
Hopkins, John P. *388*
Hopkins, Larry J. *268, 271, 274*
Hopkins, Louis B. *425*
Hopkins, Mark *426, 540*
Hopkins, Nathan T. *136*
Hopkins, P. S. *441*
Hopkins, Samuel *53*
Hopkins, Samuel I. *126*
Hopkins, Samuel M. *54, 473*
Hopkins, Stephen *1, 2, 4, 6, 7*
Hopkins, Stephen T. *126*
Hopkins, Thomas S. *523*
Hopkins, William H. *409, 415*
Hopkins, William J. *552*
Hopkins, William R. *394*
Hopkinson, Charles *560*
Hopkinson, Francis *1, 2, 4, 442*
Hopkinson, Joseph *55, 57*
Hopper, Edward *536, 547*
Hoppes, Dale D. *562*
Hoppin, William W. *310*
Hopps, Walter *438*
Hopson, W. H. *476*
Hopwood, Erie C. *520*
Hopwood, Francis *496*
Hopwood, Herbert G. *348*
Hopwood, Robert F. *167*
Horan, Harold E. *367*
Horan, Hume A. *357, 361, 373*
Horan, John J. *492*
Horan, Walter F. *212, 216, 219, 222, 225, 228, 232, 235, 238, 241, 245*
Hord, Donal *531*
Horgan, Paul *534, 542, 555, 557*
Horkan, George A. *332*
Horlbeck, Henry B. *518*
Horn, Carl, Jr. *487*
Horn, Charles L. *433*
Horn, Francis H. *414, 422*
Horn, Henry *68*
Horn, Kent R. Van *534*
Horn, Marian Blank *286*
Horn, Nelson P. *404*
Horn, Paul W. *417*
Horn, Raymond E *481*
Horn, Stephen *405*
Horn, William *472*
Horn, Williamson H. *396*
Hornbeak, Samuel L. *417*
Hornbeck, John W. *83*
Hornbeck, Stanley K. *368*
Hornblower, Joseph C. *305*
Hornblower, Josiah *4*
Hornby, Robert A. *493*
Horne, Edmund C. *410*
Horne, John E. *379, 382*
Horne, Lena *562*
Horner, Charles F. *525*
Horner, H. Mansfield *498, 540*
Horner, Henry *296*
Horner, John W. *403*
Horner, Junius M. *449, 462*
Horner, Matina *415*
Horner, Richard E. *513*
Horner, Wesley W. *519*
Horner, William L. *545*
Hornibrook, William H. *355, 359, 364, 370, 372*

Hornig, Donald F. *405*
Hornor, Lynn S. *193, 196*
Horowitz, Mardi J. *539*
Horr, J. C. *398*
Horr, Ralph A. *193*
Horr, Roswell G. *116, 118, 120*
Horrigan, Edward A., Jr. *495*
Horrocks, James *406*
Horry, Elias *396*
Horsey, Outerbridge *51, 52, 53, 54, 56, 57, 294, 359*
Horsford, Jerediah *86*
Horsky, Charles A. *433*
Horsky, Edward *392*
Horsmanden, Daniel *7*
Horst, Louis *536*
Horstick, William W. *453, 458*
Horstmann, Ignatius F. *469*
Horton, Albert H. *298*
Horton, Dr. Thomas R. *515*
Horton, Frank *256, 262, 278*
Horton, Frank E. *422, 424*
Horton, Frank J. *243, 247, 250, 253, 259, 266, 269, 272, 275*
Horton, Frank O. *206*
Horton, Henry H. *311*
Horton, Jack K. *496*
Horton, Loton *491*
Horton, Mildred M. *425*
Horton, Thomas R. *90*
Horton, Valentine B. *90, 92, 96*
Horvitz, Wayne L. *379*
Horwitz, Morton J. *534*
Hosea, Addison *456, 459*
Hoshour, Samuel *405*
Hoskins, Fred *475*
Hoskins, George G. *109, 111*
Hoskins, James D. *423*
Hosmer, Craig *226, 229, 232, 235, 239, 242, 245, 248, 251, 255, 258*
Hosmer, George W. *403*
Hosmer, Hezekiah L. *45*
Hosmer, James K. *515*
Hosmer, Stephen T. *294*
Hosmer, Titus *2, 3*
Hospers, John *19*
Hoss, E. Embree *408, 471*
Hostetler, Abraham J. *115*
Hostetter, Jacob *57, 58*
Hostetter, John C. *551*
Hotchkiss, Elisha *394*
Hotchkiss, Giles W. *98, 100, 104*
Hotchkiss, Julius *101*
Hott, James *472*
Hotz, Henry H., Jr. *442*
Houchin, John M. *494*
Houck, Jacob, Jr. *77*
Houck, William R. *467*
Houdek, Robert G. *374*
Houdry, Eugene J. *552*
Hough, Charles M. *284*
Hough, David *48, 49*
Hough, Henry Beetle *545, 553*
Hough, Henry H. *347*
Hough, Hugh F. *557*
Hough, Lynn H. *413*
Hough, Romeyn B. *537*
Hough, Warwick *303*
Hough, William J. *80*
Houghteling, James L. *380*
Houghton, Alanson B. *173, 176, 362*
Houghton, Amory *361, 493, 521*
Houghton, Arthur A., Jr. *522*
Houghton, Douglas *391*
Houghton, Herbert P. *406, 425*
Houghton, James C. *492*
Houghton, S. O. *386*
Houghton, Sherman O. *105, 108*

Houk, George W. *131, 134*
Houk, John C. *132, 134*
Houk, Leonidas C. *117, 119, 121, 124, 126, 129*
Houlihan, Patrick T. *442*
Hounsfield, Godfrey N. *543, 552*
House, Charles L. *562*
House, Charles S. *294*
House, J. Cline *503*
House, Jay E. *389*
House, John F. *112, 114, 117, 119, 320*
House, Karen Elliott *558*
House, T. W., Sr. *397*
House, William F. *533*
Houseman, Julius *120*
Houser, T. B. *433*
Houser, Theodore V. *496*
Housley, J. Elmer *523*
Houston, Charles H. *561*
Houston, David F. *28, 34, 36, 416, 423, 425, 492*
Houston, Frank K. *484*
Houston, George S. *76, 78, 79, 81, 87, 89, 91, 93, 115, 291*
Houston, George W. *85*
Houston, Henry A. *147*
Houston, J. Michael *388*
Houston, John *3, 5*
Houston, John M. *197, 201, 204, 207*
Houston, John W. *79, 81, 83*
Houston, P. D. *511*
Houston, Robert G. *181, 184, 187, 190*
Houston, Russell *491*
Houston, Sam *62, 63, 81, 83, 85, 87, 89, 91, 93, 311, 312*
Houston, Thomas J. *527*
Houston, Turner *392*
Houston, William *2, 3*
Houston, William C. *2, 4, 152, 155, 158, 161, 164, 167, 170*
Houston, William V. *415, 517*
Houx, Frank L. *315*
Hovde, Frederick L. *415*
Hovde, Howard T. *515*
Hoven, Mathew J. *398*
Hoverter, George A. *395*
Hovey, Alvin P. *125, 297, 337, 338, 370*
Hovgaard, William *562*
Hoving, Jane Pickens *548*
Hoving, Thomas *562*
Hoving, Thomas P. F. *440*
Hoving, Walter *526*
How, John *392*
How, Samuel B. *407*
Howard, Ada *425*
Howard, Alan *533*
Howard, Alfred T. *472*
Howard, Allen B. *390*
Howard, Arthur F. *390*
Howard, Bart *554*
Howard, Benjamin *50, 51*
Howard, Benjamin C. *66, 67, 71, 73*
Howard, Cecil *526*
Howard, Charles *391*
Howard, Charles P. *505*
Howard, Edgar *179, 182, 185, 188, 192, 195*
Howard, Edward D. *464*
Howard, Ernest B. *516*
Howard, Ernest E. *519*
Howard, Everett B. *186*
Howard, Everette B. *173, 180*
Howard, Findley B. *369*
Howard, Francis *6*
Howard, Francis W. *466*

Jensen, Ben F. *204, 207, 210, 214, 217, 220, 223, 226, 230, 233, 236, 239, 242*
Jensen, Erling N. *413*
Jensen, James H. *414*
Jensen, Leslie *311*
Jepsen, Roger W. *268, 271, 274*
Jepson, Roger W. *297*
Jernegan, John D. *364*
Jernick, William J. *521*
Jernigan, John D. *355*
Jerome, David H. *301*
Jerome, J. Hanson *390*
Jerome, William T., III *404*
Jertberg, Gilbert H. *285*
Jeserich, Paul H. *512*
Jesse, R. H. *421*
Jesse, Richard H. *421*
Jessup, Henry H. *473*
Jessup, Morris K. *437*
Jessup, Philip C. *519*
Jessup, Walter A. *420, 431*
Jester, Beauford H. *312*
Jesup, Thomas S. *332*
Jeter, Thomas B. *310*
Jett, Robert C. *451, 461*
Jett, Thomas M. *138, 141, 144*
Jewell, B. Frank *443*
Jewell, Gilbert *503*
Jewell, Marshall *26, 36, 293, 371*
Jewett, Albert G. *370*
Jewett, Charles W. *388*
Jewett, Daniel T. *104, 303*
Jewett, Edgar B. *393*
Jewett, Frank B. *538, 539, 541*
Jewett, Freeborn G. *68, 306*
Jewett, Hugh J. *109*
Jewett, Joshua H. *90, 91*
Jewett, Luther *56*
Jewett, Milo P. *424*
Jimerson, Earl W. *503*
Jinks, J. R. *387*
Jischke, Martin C. *422*
Job, Reuben P. *472*
Jocelyn, George B. *403*
Jocobus, M. W. *473*
Joeckel, Carleton B. *543*
Joelson, Charles S. *240, 243, 247, 250, 253*
Joffrey, Robert *536*
Johannes, Francis *466*
Johansen, August E. *230, 233, 236, 240, 243*
Johansen, Eivind H. *330*
Johansen, John C. *560*
Johanson, Donald *547*
Johansson, Carl E. *541*
John, David C. *409*
John, John P. D. *407*
Johns, Carol J. *425*
Johns, Charley E. *295*
Johns, Foster M. *519*
Johns, Jasper *548*
Johns, John *406, 447, 461*
Johns, John E. *408, 416*
Johns, Joshua L. *206, 209, 523*
Johns, Kensey *294*
Johns, Kensey, Jr. *64, 65, 294*
Johns, Robert *405, 421*
Johns, W. Lloyd *405*
Johnsen, Harvey M. *285*
Johnsen, Irving A. *540*
Johnson, A. W. *347*
Johnson, Adna R. *157*
Johnson, Albert *164, 167, 171, 174, 177, 180, 183, 187, 190, 193*
Johnson, Albert W. *244, 247, 250, 254, 257, 260, 263*
Johnson, Albinus A. *424*

Johnson, Alexander S. *306*
Johnson, Alfred W. *535*
Johnson, Alvin S. *513*
Johnson, Andrew *11, 12, 16, 25, 79, 81, 83, 85, 87, 93, 95, 97, 99, 112, 311, 312*
Johnson, Anton J. *204, 207, 210, 213, 217*
Johnson, Arthur M. *420*
Johnson, Ben *153, 156, 159, 162, 165, 169, 172, 175, 178, 181*
Johnson, Benjamin N. *527*
Johnson, Bert W. *524*
Johnson, Bushrod R. *323*
Johnson, Byron L. *235*
Johnson, C. E. *292*
Johnson, C. Oscar *475*
Johnson, Calvin D. *210*
Johnson, Cave *25, 35, 67, 68, 70, 72, 75, 77, 79*
Johnson, Charles *47*
Johnson, Charles E. *422*
Johnson, Charles F. *159, 162, 165, 284, 299*
Johnson, Charles N. *512*
Johnson, Charles P. *392*
Johnson, Charles W. *441*
Johnson, Clarance C. *563*
Johnson, Clarence B. *484*
Johnson, Clarence L. *537, 549, 552, 559, 562*
Johnson, Clarke H. *310*
Johnson, Claudia "Lady Bird" *552*
Johnson, Davenport *340*
Johnson, David *310*
Johnson, David E. *143*
Johnson, David Elliot *457*
Johnson, Dewey W. *201*
Johnson, Diane *560*
Johnson, Donald E. *514*
Johnson, Donald M. *481*
Johnson, Douglas *523, 537*
Johnson, Earl D. *488*
Johnson, Earl G. *515*
Johnson, Eben S. *471*
Johnson, Ebenezer *393*
Johnson, Edward *323, 324, 390, 548*
Johnson, Edward R. *527*
Johnson, Edwin C. *200, 203, 207, 210, 213, 216, 219, 223, 226, 293*
Johnson, Edwin S. *167, 170, 174, 311*
Johnson, Eldon L. *421*
Johnson, Emory R. *526, 548*
Johnson, Felix *347*
Johnson, Francis *58, 59, 61, 62*
Johnson, Frank B. *391*
Johnson, Frank M., Jr. *285, 286, 287*
Johnson, Franklin W. *406*
Johnson, Fred G. *188*
Johnson, Frederick A. *121, 123*
Johnson, Frederick F. *450, 459, 461*
Johnson, George K. *494*
Johnson, George W. *180, 196, 200, 203, 206, 209*
Johnson, Glen D. *218*
Johnson, Glendon E. *482*
Johnson, Grove L. *135*
Johnson, Hale *17*
Johnson, Hallett *359*
Johnson, Harold K. *329, 351*
Johnson, Harold T. *235, 239, 242, 245, 248, 251, 255, 258, 261, 264, 267*
Johnson, Harry H. *343*

Johnson, Harvey H. *88*
Johnson, Haynes *556*
Johnson, Henry *56, 58, 59, 61, 69, 71, 72, 78, 80, 82, 298, 299, 437*
Johnson, Henry U. *130, 133, 136, 138*
Johnson, Henry V. *386*
Johnson, Herman M. *407*
Johnson, Herrick *473*
Johnson, Herschel V. *16, 81, 295, 320, 321, 357, 373*
Johnson, Hiram W. *17, 168, 171, 174, 178, 181, 184, 187, 190, 193, 197, 200, 203, 206, 210, 213, 292*
Johnson, Hjalmar W. *538*
Johnson, Hosmer A. *518*
Johnson, Howard A. *303*
Johnson, Howard C. *537*
Johnson, Howard W. *412*
Johnson, Ingolf Birger *543*
Johnson, Irving P. *451, 458*
Johnson, Isaac *298*
Johnson, J. Allen *523*
Johnson, J. T. *385*
Johnson, Jacob *164*
Johnson, James *54, 56, 57, 59, 62, 85, 295*
Johnson, James A. *101, 103*
Johnson, James C. *398*
Johnson, James H. *80, 82*
Johnson, James I. *394*
Johnson, James L. *84*
Johnson, James N. *292*
Johnson, James P. *258, 261, 264, 267*
Johnson, James W. *490*
Johnson, James Weldon *525, 561*
Johnson, Janet H. *442*
Johnson, Jed *186, 189, 192, 196, 199, 202, 205, 209, 212, 215, 287*
Johnson, Jed, Jr. *247*
Johnson, Jeromus *63, 64*
Johnson, Jesse *413*
Johnson, John *86, 390, 392, 396*
Johnson, John A. *301*
Johnson, John B. *534, 544*
Johnson, John G. *405*
Johnson, John H. *539, 561*
Johnson, John T. *59, 61, 308*
Johnson, John W. *422*
Johnson, Joseph *62, 63, 68, 72, 74, 76, 81, 313, 396*
Johnson, Joseph B. *313*
Johnson, Joseph E. *324*
Johnson, Joseph H. *449, 459*
Johnson, Joseph L. *366*
Johnson, Joseph T. *146, 149, 151, 154, 157, 161, 164, 167*
Johnson, Joseph W. *386*
Johnson, Josephine Winslow *554*
Johnson, Josiah S. *64, 67*
Johnson, Jotham *521*
Johnson, Keen *298*
Johnson, Keith *505*
Johnson, Kermit D. *331*
Johnson, Lady Bird *548*
Johnson, Leon H. *412*
Johnson, Leroy *210, 213, 216, 219, 223, 226, 229*
Johnson, Lester *382*
Johnson, Lester R. *229, 232, 235, 238, 241, 245*
Johnson, Louis A. *30, 37, 327, 514*
Johnson, Louisa Catherine *20*

Johnson, Luther A. *180, 183, 186, 190, 193, 196, 199, 203, 206, 209, 212, 215, 417*
Johnson, Lyndon B. *11, 12, 19, 30, 203, 206, 209, 212, 215, 219, 222, 225, 228, 231, 235, 238, 242, 312, 552, 560*
Johnson, Magnus *179, 195, 302*
Johnson, Malcolm *555*
Johnson, Maria L. *380*
Johnson, Marilyn P. *374*
Johnson, Martin N. *131, 134, 137, 140, 157, 307*
Johnson, Max S. *351*
Johnson, Mordecai W. *410, 561*
Johnson, N. B. *308*
Johnson, Nancy L. *274, 277*
Johnson, Nathaniel *6*
Johnson, Nels C. *328*
Johnson, Nelson T. *355, 358*
Johnson, Noadiah *69*
Johnson, Noble J. *181, 184, 188, 204, 207, 210, 213, 217, 287*
Johnson, P. G. *483*
Johnson, Paul B. *172, 176, 302*
Johnson, Perley B. *79*
Johnson, Philip *97, 99, 100, 542*
Johnson, Philip C. *532, 535*
Johnson, R. P. *386*
Johnson, Raymond D. *537, 541*
Johnson, Reverdy *25, 35, 80, 82, 84, 98, 100, 102, 300, 362*
Johnson, Richard M. *12, 15, 24, 50, 51, 52, 53, 55, 56, 57, 59, 61, 62, 64, 65, 67, 69, 71, 72, 74, 298*
Johnson, Richard O. *392*
Johnson, Richard W. *337, 338*
Johnson, Robert *6, 320, 321*
Johnson, Robert D. *192*
Johnson, Robert E. *392*
Johnson, Robert L. *416*
Johnson, Robert W. *81, 83, 85, 87, 89, 91, 93, 292, 319, 320, 321, 490*
Johnson, Robert W., Jr. *490*
Johnson, Roy L. *348*
Johnson, Royal C. *167, 170, 174, 177, 180, 183, 186, 189, 193*
Johnson, Samuel *407*
Johnson, Samuel D. *285*
Johnson, Samuel W. *511*
Johnson, Sir William *1*
Johnson, T. R. *523*
Johnson, Thomas *3, 5, 283, 292, 319*
Johnson, Thomas C. *415*
Johnson, Thomas F. *236, 239*
Johnson, Tom L. *131, 134, 394*
Johnson, Treat B. *514*
Johnson, Treby *389*
Johnson, U. Alexis *359, 365, 374*
Johnson, Victor M. *523*
Johnson, W. H. *494*
Johnson, Waldo P. *96, 303, 320, 321*
Johnson, Walter W. *293*
Johnson, Ward *206, 210*
Johnson, Wayne *385*
Johnson, Wendell G. *410*
Johnson, William *283*
Johnson, William B. *475, 490*
Johnson, William Cost *69, 73, 74, 76*
Johnson, William R. *181, 184, 187, 191, 382, 465*
Johnson, William S. *1, 2, 3, 41, 293, 407*

King, William H. *140, 143, 170, 174, 177, 180, 183, 186, 190, 193, 196, 199, 203, 206, 312, 397*
King, William R. *12, 15, 25, 52, 54, 55, 57, 59, 60, 62, 64, 65, 67, 68, 70, 72, 74, 76, 77, 81, 83, 85, 87, 291, 361*
King, William S. *111*
King, Willis J. *471*
King, Willis L. *539*
King, Yelverton P. *358*
Kingham, Herbert *399*
Kingman, Dan C. *331*
Kingman, Eugene *440*
Kingman, Samuel A. *298*
Kingsbury, Albert *533, 537*
Kingsbury, Bernerd C. *512*
Kingsbury, Edward M. *553*
Kingsbury, Edwin P. *544*
Kingsbury, Joseph R. *423*
Kingsbury, Kenneth R. *485*
Kingslake, Rudolf *527*
Kingsland, Ambrose C. *393*
Kingsland, Lawrence C. *381*
Kingsley, Calvin *471*
Kingsley, Edwin R. *524*
Kingsley, J. Gordon *426*
Kingsley, Sidney *531, 548, 554*
Kingsley, William H. *494*
Kingston, Maxine Hong *546*
Kinkaid, Moses P. *148, 151, 154, 157, 160, 163, 166, 169, 172, 176*
Kinkaid, Thomas C. *348*
Kinkead, Eugene F. *157, 160, 163*
Kinkead, John H. *304*
Kinley, David *420, 513*
Kinloch, Francis *4*
Kinna, John *392*
Kinnard, George L. *69, 71*
Kinnard, Harry W. B. *344*
Kinnard, Harry W. O. *333*
Kinnard, I. F. *543*
Kinnel, William *113*
Kinnell, Galway *532, 547, 558, 561*
Kinney, Dallas *557*
Kinney, E. Robert *488*
Kinney, John F. *469*
Kinney, William B. *372*
Kinnickell, Ralph E., Jr. *380*
Kinnison, William A. *426*
Kinsella, George B. *387*
Kinsella, James H. *387*
Kinsella, Richard J. *387*
Kinsella, Thomas *107*
Kinsey, Charles *56, 58*
Kinsey, James *4, 305*
Kinsey, Oliver P. *424*
Kinsey, V. Everett *543*
Kinsey, William M. *128*
Kinsley, Martin *58*
Kinsman, Frederick J. *450, 458*
Kinsolving, Arthur B., II *453, 458*
Kinsolving, Charles J., III *454, 461*
Kinsolving, George H. *449, 461*
Kinsolving, Lucien L. *449*
Kintner, William R. *374*
Kinyon, Alonzo G. *544*
Kinzel, Augustus B. *514, 538*
Kinzer, J. Roland *189, 192, 196, 199, 202, 205, 209, 212, 215*
Kip, William I. *448, 458*
Kiphuth, Robert J. *552*
Kipp, George W. *154, 160*
Kirby, Abner *399*

Kirby, Ellwood *391*
Kirby, George H. *518*
Kirby, Hal P. *438*
Kirby, James *506*
Kirby, James T. *505*
Kirby, John, Jr. *525*
Kirby, Robert E. *499*
Kirby, Rollin *553*
Kirby, William F. *165, 168, 171, 292*
Kirchhofer, A. H. *520*
Kirchhoffer, Richard A. *453, 459*
Kirchner, Leon *535, 556*
Kirchwey, George W. *516*
Kirk, Alan G. *347, 356, 358, 366, 375*
Kirk, Alexander C. *360, 363, 365, 372*
Kirk, Andrew J. *181*
Kirk, Claude R. *295*
Kirk, Grayson *407*
Kirk, Grayson L. *548*
Kirk, Norman T. *332*
Kirk, Raymond V. *408*
Kirk, Robert C. *355, 375*
Kirk, Roger *371, 372*
Kirk, Ruth *536*
Kirkbride, Thomas S. *518*
Kirkendall, James F. *351*
Kirker, Thomas *307*
Kirkes, L. C. *417*
Kirkland, Edward C. *510*
Kirkland, James H. *424*
Kirkland, John T. *409*
Kirkland, Joseph *60*
Kirklin, John W. *532, 533*
Kirkman, Henry N., Jr. *542*
Kirkpatrick, A. F. *474*
Kirkpatrick, Andrew *305*
Kirkpatrick, C. C. *418*
Kirkpatrick, Clayton *545*
Kirkpatrick, Evron M. *516, 518*
Kirkpatrick, G. R. *17*
Kirkpatrick, Jeane J. *553*
Kirkpatrick, John L. *407*
Kirkpatrick, Littleton *78*
Kirkpatrick, Sanford *162*
Kirkpatrick, Sidney D. *522*
Kirkpatrick, Snyder *136*
Kirkpatrick, William *50*
Kirkpatrick, William H. *177*
Kirkpatrick, William S. *140, 411*
Kirksey, James *387*
Kirkwood, Daniel *419*
Kirkwood, James *557*
Kirkwood, James P. *519*
Kirkwood, Samuel J. *26, 36, 99, 113, 115, 118, 297*
Kirman, Richard *304*
Kirsch, Dwight *443*
Kirschenbaum, Jules *531*
Kirstein, Lincoln *536, 547, 553*
Kirtland, Dorrance *56*
Kirwan, Albert D. *420*
Kirwan, Michael J. *202, 205, 208, 212, 215, 218, 221, 225, 228, 231, 234, 237, 241, 244, 247, 250, 253*
Kissel, John *176*
Kissinger, Henry A. *31, 33, 541, 546, 548, 550, 552*
Kistiakowsky, George B. *539, 549, 552, 553*
Kitchel, Harvey D. *412*
Kitchell, Aaron *42, 43, 44, 46, 49, 50, 51, 305*
Kitchell, Horace Y. *527*
Kitchen, Bethuel M. *103*
Kitchen, Lawrence O. *491*

Kitchens, Wade H. *200, 203*
Kitchin, A. Paul *234, 237, 240*
Kitchin, Claude *145, 148, 151, 154, 157, 160, 163, 166, 170, 173, 176*
Kitchin, Thurman D. *425*
Kitchin, William H. *116*
Kitchin, William W. *140, 142, 145, 148, 151, 154, 307*
Kitson, Arthur *544*
Kittera, John W. *42, 43, 44, 45, 46*
Kittera, Thomas *63*
Kittle, Charles M. *496*
Kittleson, I. Milo *398*
Kittredge, Alfred B. *146, 149, 152, 154, 311*
Kittredge, G. L. *512*
Kittredge, George Lyman *524*
Kittredge, George W. *88*
Kittredge, William C. *492*
Kittson, Norman W. *391*
Kivette, Frederick N. *348*
Kizer, Carolyn *558*
Klapper, Paul *415*
Klassen, Edwin T. *382*
Kleban, Edward *557*
Kleber, Herbert D. *539*
Kleberg, Richard M. *193, 196, 199, 203, 206, 209, 212*
Kleberg, Rudolph *137, 140, 143, 146*
Kleczka, Gerald D. *279*
Kleczka, John C. *174, 177*
Kleihauer, Cleveland *476*
Klein, Arthur G. *208, 211, 215, 218, 221, 224, 227, 231*
Klein, Dorothy E. *476*
Klein, Edmund *543*
Klein, Frank *525*
Klein, H. M. J. *408*
Klein, Harry T. *497*
Klein, J. Warren *403*
Klein, John A. *330*
Klein, Lawrence R. *550*
Klein, Walter C. *455, 460*
Klein, William *505*
Kleindienst, Richard G. *31, 35*
Kleindorfer, J. W. *524*
Kleiner, John J. *120, 122*
Kleinpell, Eugene H. *424*
Kleinschmidt, Edward E. *562*
Kleinschmidt, T. H. *392*
KleinSmid, Rufus B. von *423*
Klekotka, John A. *424*
Klemperer, William *562*
Klenda, Harry M. *512*
Kleppe, Thomas S. *31, 36, 250, 253, 382*
Kleppe, Tom *394*
Klepper, Frank B. *151*
Klepper, George M. *527*
Klerman, Gerald L. *539, 541*
Kline, Ardolph L. *176, 394*
Kline, C. Mahlon *496*
Kline, Charles H. *395*
Kline, Clarice *525*
Kline, George M. *518*
Kline, Howard *524*
Kline, I. Clinton *177*
Kline, Marcus C. L. *148, 151*
Kline, Marvin L. *391*
Kline, Nathan S. *543*
Kline, Reamer *404*
Kline, Virginia *385*
Kline, William F. *536*
Klingel, Gilbert *536*
Klingensmith, John, Jr. *72, 73*
Klipstein, Kenneth H. *481*
Kliver, W. H. *506*
Kloeb, Frank L. *195, 199, 202*

Klopfenstein, Philip A. *440*
Klopsteg, Paul E. *510*
Klotsche, J. Martin *424*
Klotz, Robert *116, 119*
Kluckhohn, Clyde *509*
Kluczynski, John C. *223, 226, 229, 233, 236, 239, 242, 246, 249, 252, 255, 258, 261*
Klumph, Arch C. *527*
Klumpp, George L. *386*
Kluttz, Theodore F. *142, 145, 148*
Klutznick, Philip M. *31, 37*
Knabenshue, Paul *364*
Knachel, Philip A. *439*
Knaebel, John B. *561*
Knapp, A. Blair *407*
Knapp, Anthony L. *95, 97*
Knapp, Bliss *476*
Knapp, Bradford *403, 414, 417*
Knapp, C. Howard *525*
Knapp, Charles *104*
Knapp, Charles J. *128*
Knapp, Charles L. *145, 148, 151, 154, 157*
Knapp, Chauncey L. *90, 92*
Knapp, Edward F. *397*
Knapp, George O. *498*
Knapp, Isaac N. *544*
Knapp, Joseph F. *492*
Knapp, Martin A. *284*
Knapp, Philip C. *516*
Knapp, Ralph H. *476*
Knapp, Robert M. *108, 113*
Knapp, S. A. *410*
Knappen, Loyal E. *285*
Knappenmeyer, Henry *410*
Knaths, Karl *531, 535*
Knauss, Francis J. *293*
Knebel, G. Moses *510, 552*
Knebel, John *31, 37*
Kneeland, Fred *504*
Kneeland, George J. *496*
Kneip, Richard F. *311*
Kneller, John W. *405*
Knickerbacker, David B. *449, 459*
Knickerbocker, H. R. *553*
Knickerbocker, Herman *51*
Kniep, Richard F. *372*
Kniffin, Frank C. *192, 195, 199, 202*
Knight, Albion W. *423, 450*
Knight, Austin *350*
Knight, Austin M. *352*
Knight, Avel de *533*
Knight, Charles F. *487*
Knight, Charles L. *176*
Knight, Charles M. *418*
Knight, Cyrus F. *449, 459*
Knight, Douglas M. *408, 411*
Knight, E. W. *392*
Knight, Edward J. *450, 462*
Knight, Erastus *393*
Knight, Frank H. *513*
Knight, Goodwin J. *292*
Knight, Harry E. *329*
Knight, Henry G. *514, 532*
Knight, Jabez C. *395*
Knight, Jesse *315*
Knight, John E. *385*
Knight, John S. *520, 545, 556*
Knight, Jonathan *90, 515*
Knight, Nehemiah *48, 49, 50*
Knight, Nehemiah R. *58, 60, 62, 63, 65, 66, 68, 70, 72, 73, 75, 310*
Knight, Raymond D. *387*
Knight, Ridgway B. *356, 370, 374*
Knight, Samuel *313*

Lea, John M. *396*
Lea, Luke *70, 72, 161, 164, 167, 312*
Lea, Preston *294*
Lea, Pryor *65, 67*
Leach, Abby *517*
Leach, Claude *268*
Leach, DeWitt C. *92, 94*
Leach, Edward *521*
Leach, George E. *331, 391*
Leach, Hamilton E. *521*
Leach, Henry G. *527*
Leach, J. S. *497*
Leach, James A. S. *265, 268, 271, 274, 277*
Leach, James M. *94, 107, 109, 321*
Leach, James T. *321*
Leach, Raymond H. *417*
Leach, Robert H. *562*
Leach, Robert M. *179*
Leadbetter, Daniel P. *73, 75*
Leader, George M. *309*
Leafe, Joseph A. *398*
Leahy, Edward L. *222, 310*
Leahy, Patrick J. *263, 266, 270, 273, 276, 279, 313*
Leahy, William D. *347, 349, 361*
Leake, Chauncey D. *510*
Leake, Eugene W. *154*
Leake, Gerald *536, 542*
Leake, Shelton F. *81, 95*
Leake, Walter *56, 58, 302*
Leakey, Richard E. *535*
Leakin, Sheppard *390*
Leamy, F. A. *417*
Lear, Ben *332, 333, 340*
Lear, William P. *537*
Learned, Amasa *41, 42*
Learned, Marion D. *524*
Learned, Stanley *494*
Learson, T. Vincent *490*
Leary, Cornelius L. L. *96*
Leary, Eugene (Bus) *394*
Leary, Herbert F. *348*
Leary, John *398*
Leary, John J., Jr. *553*
Leas, W. H. *388*
Leath, Marvin *270, 273, 276, 279*
Leathers, W. S. *518*
Leatherwood, Elmer O. *177, 180, 183, 186, 190*
Leavell, Hugh R. *518, 526, 561*
Leavell, James R. *486*
Leavell, William H. *363*
Leavenworth, Elias W. *111*
Leavenworth, M. *386*
Leavenworth, T. M. *386*
Leavey, Edmond H. *490*
Leavitt, Erasmus D. *520*
Leavitt, Humphrey H. *66, 68, 70*
Leavitt, John M. *415*
Leavitt, John McD. *411*
Leavitt, Scott *179, 182, 185, 188, 192*
Leavitt, Thomas W. *443*
Leavy, Charles H. *203, 206, 209*
LeBlanc, Fred S. *389*
LeBlond, Charles H. *468*
LeBourgeois, Julien J. *352*
LeBoutillier, John *272*
Lebrun, Rico *532*
Lebstock, Suzanne *534*
Leche, Richard W. *299*
LeClair, Titus G. *523*
Lecompte, Joseph *62, 64, 65, 67*

LeCompte, Karl M. *204, 207, 210, 214, 217, 220, 223, 226, 230, 233*
LeConte, John L. *418, 509*
LeConte, Joseph *509, 523*
LeCraw, Roy *387*
Ledbetter, Donald N. *505*
Ledden, W. Earl *471*
Ledder, Edward J., Jr. *481*
Lederberg, Joshua *550*
Lederer, Jerome F. *540, 563*
Lederer, Raymond F. *266, 269, 272*
Lederle, John W. *420*
Lederman, Leon M. *537, 549*
Ledoux, John W. *544*
Ledvina, Emmanuel B. *470*
Ledyard, Henry *391*
Lee, Alfred *447, 458*
Lee, Alfred McClung *521*
Lee, Andrew E. *311*
Lee, Ann *477*
Lee, Arthur *4, 560*
Lee, Benjamin *518*
Lee, Benjamin F. *426*
Lee, Blair *162, 166, 300*
Lee, Blair, III *300*
Lee, Charles *23, 34, 335*
Lee, Darryl A. *392*
Lee, Edward W. *393*
Lee, Edwin F. *471*
Lee, Elmo P., Sr. *284*
Lee, Everett S. *523*
Lee, Fitzhugh *313, 323, 351*
Lee, Francis Lightfoot *2, 4*
Lee, Frank H. *195*
Lee, Frederick B. *525*
Lee, Frederick S. *517*
Lee, Gary A. *269, 272*
Lee, George W. C. *425*
Lee, Gideon *71, 393*
Lee, Gordon *150, 153, 155, 159, 162, 165, 168, 171, 175, 178, 181*
Lee, Harold B. *476*
Lee, Harper *556*
Lee, Henry *4, 15, 46, 313*
Lee, Henry W. *448, 459*
Lee, J. Bracken *312, 397*
Lee, J. R. E. *408*
Lee, James A. *522*
Lee, James E. *489*
Lee, James M. *333, 345*
Lee, John *61*
Lee, John A. *505*
Lee, John C. *415*
Lee, John C. H. *340, 341*
Lee, John F. *331*
Lee, John S. *415*
Lee, Joseph W. J. *360, 363*
Lee, Josh *199, 202, 205, 209, 308*
Lee, Joshua *71*
Lee, Kent L. *349*
Lee, Laurence F. *522*
Lee, M. Lindley *94*
Lee, Percy M. *302*
Lee, Peter James *457, 461*
Lee, Raymond E. *329*
Lee, Richard Bland *41, 42, 43*
Lee, Richard Henry *2, 3, 4, 41, 42, 314*
Lee, Robert E. *160, 164, 322, 323, 418, 425, 540*
Lee, Robert G. *475*
Lee, Robert M. *346*
Lee, Robert Q. *190*
Lee, Robert V. *330*
Lee, Roger I. *515*
Lee, Samuel P. *350*
Lee, Sherman E. *438*

Lee, Silas *46, 47*
Lee, Stephen D. *323, 324, 412*
Lee, T. George *482*
Lee, Thomas *6, 69, 71*
Lee, Thomas S. *3, 5, 300*
Lee, Tsung-Dao *550*
Lee, Umphrey *416*
Lee, Wallace H. *411*
Lee, Warren I. *176*
Lee, William *391*
Lee, William B. *441*
Lee, William C. *339, 343*
Lee, William G. *504*
Lee, William H. F. *126, 129, 323*
Lee, William S. *386*
Lee, William S., III *487*
Lee, Yuan T. *551*
Lee, Yuan Tseh *549*
Leebrick, Karl C. *411*
Leech, George L. *469*
Leech, J. Russell *186, 189, 192*
Leech, Margaret *534, 554, 556*
Leedom, John P. *119*
Leeds, Charles J. *389*
Leeds, Morris E. *533, 538, 544*
Leeds, Winthrop M. *543*
Leedy, John W. *297*
Lee-Smith, Hughie *536*
Leet, Isaac *75*
Leete, Frederick D. *471*
Leete, William *5*
LeFante, Joseph A. *265*
Lefavour, Henry *416*
Lefever, Joseph *53*
LeFevre, Benjamin *116, 119, 121*
Lefevre, George *520*
LeFevre, Jay *211, 215, 218, 221*
Lefevre, Peter P. *467*
Lefferts, John *54*
Leffingwell, Ernest de K. *538*
Leffler, Isaac *65*
Leffler, Ross *527*
Leffler, Shepherd *80, 82, 84*
Lefschetz, Solomon *515, 548*
Leftwich, Jabez *60, 62*
Leftwich, John W. *101, 396*
Legare, George S. *149, 151, 154, 157, 161*
Legare, Hugh S. *24, 34, 73, 356*
Legg, Thomas H. *560*
Legge, Alexander *490*
Legget, Robert F. *523*
Leggett, Glenn *409*
Leggett, Mortimer D. *338, 381*
Leggett, Robert L. *242, 245, 248, 251, 255, 258, 261, 264*
Leggett, Wilson D., Jr. *349, 562*
Legh-Jones, George *496*
Legler, Henry E. *515*
LeGrand, John C. *300*
LeGuin, Ursula *546*
Lehlbach, Frederick R. *166, 169, 173, 176, 179, 182, 185, 189, 192, 195, 198*
Lehlbach, Herman *123, 126, 128*
Lehman, Arnold L. *437*
Lehman, E. J. *509*
Lehman, Edwin P. *511*
Lehman, Herbert H. *221, 224, 227, 231, 306, 540, 552*
Lehman, Irving *306*
Lehman, John F., Jr. *327*
Lehman, Raymond G. *343*
Lehman, Richard *273*
Lehman, Richard H. *276*
Lehman, William *258, 261, 264, 267, 270, 274, 277*
Lehman, William E. *97*

Lehmann, Frederick W. *511*
Lehmann, Heinz E. *543*
Lehmann, William F. *406*
Lehninger, Albert Lester *551*
Lehr, John C. *195*
Lehr, Lewis W. *492*
Lehy, John F. *406*
Leib, Michael *46, 47, 48, 49, 50, 51, 53, 54, 309*
Leib, Owen D. *81*
Leibman, Morris T. *552*
Leibold, Paul F. *464, 466*
Leibrecht, John J. *468*
Leidel, Donald C. *356*
Leidesdorf, Samuel D. *548*
Leidig, Daniel G. *408*
Leidy, Joseph *509*
Leidy, Paul *92*
Leigh, Benjamin W. *70, 72, 314*
Leigh, Richard H. *349*
Leigh, Robert D. *404*
Leighly, John *537*
Leighton, David, Sr. *459*
Leighton, David K. *455*
Leighton, Moses R. *389*
Leighton, Robert B. *560*
Leighty, Jacob D. *136*
Lein, Charles D. *422*
Leinhard, Gustav O. *490*
Leiper, George C. *66*
Leipmann, Hans W. *549*
Leipzig, Francis P. *469*
Leisenring, John *137*
Leiser, Ernest *551*
Leiserson, William M. *380*
Leishman, John G. A. *362, 365, 373, 374*
Leisler, Jacob *1, 5*
Leitch, William T. *398*
Leiter, Benjamin F. *90, 92*
Leith, C. K. *523*
Leith, Charles K. *551*
Leith, Emmett N. *541, 549*
Lejeune, John A. *348, 424*
Lejins, Peter P. *512*
Leland, Aaron W. *473*
Leland, George T. *270*
Leland, George T. (Mickey) *273, 276, 279*
Leland, Timothy *557*
Leland, Waldo *512*
Lelyveld, Joseph *559*
LeMaistre, Charles A. *423*
LeMay, Curtis E. *19, 346, 537*
Lemburg, Wayne A. *515*
LeMelle, Wilbert J. *365, 372*
Lemieux, Joseph H. *493*
Lemitzer, Lyman L. *333*
Lemke, William *195, 199, 202, 205, 212, 215, 218, 221*
Lemley, Harry J., Jr. *330, 351*
Lemly, Samuel C. *347*
Lemmon, Clarence E. *476*
Lemmon, Dal M. *285*
Lemmonier, August *421*
Lemnitzer, Lyman L. *328, 329, 333, 334*
Lemp, John *388*
Lenahan, John T. *154*
Leng, Charles W. *443*
L'Engle, Claude *162*
L'Engle, Madeline *546*
Lenhart, A. P. *394*
Lenihan, Mathias C. *468*
Lenihan, Thomas M. *470*
Lenker, Will G. *544*
Lennette, Edwin H. *535*
Lennon, Alton A. *228, 234, 237, 240, 244, 247, 250, 253, 256, 307*
Lennon, Max *406*

Lilly, Thomas J. *180*
Lilly, William *134*
Limon, Jose *536*
Lin, Tung Yen *549*
Lincoln, Abraham *11, 16, 25, 82, 540*
Lincoln, Benjamin *14, 335*
Lincoln, C. S. *330*
Lincoln, David C. *432*
Lincoln, Enoch *56, 58, 59, 61, 62, 299*
Lincoln, Francis H. *329*
Lincoln, Frederic W., Jr. *390*
Lincoln, George G. *552*
Lincoln, John C. *432*
Lincoln, Lawrence J., Jr. *330, 334*
Lincoln, Leroy A. *492*
Lincoln, Levi *23, 34, 46, 47, 69, 73, 74, 300*
Lincoln, Robert T. *26, 34, 362*
Lincoln, Waldo *509*
Lincoln, William S. *102*
Lind, George *392*
Lind, James F. *222, 225*
Lind, John *125, 128, 131, 147, 301*
Lind, Samuel C. *511, 522, 553*
Lindabury, Richard V. *527*
Lindbergh, Anne Morrow *541, 548*
Lindbergh, Charles A. *153, 156, 159, 163, 166, 540, 541, 548, 555, 559, 563*
Linde, Karl P. G. *537*
Lindelof, Lawrence P. *504*
Lindeman, Philip F. *332*
Linden, Charles *438*
Linder, Clarence H. *523*
Linder, Forrest E. *535*
Linder, Harold F. *358, 379*
Lindgren, Waldemar *523, 551*
Lindholm, William L. *482*
Lindley, Ernest H. *420*
Lindley, James J. *88, 90*
Lindley, Walter C. *285, 287*
Lindly, Earnest H. *419*
Lindly, Jacob *414*
Lindner, Carl H. *498*
Lindner, Kenneth E. *424*
Lindner, William G. *505*
Lindquist, Carl *303*
Lindquist, Emory *426*
Lindquist, Francis O. *163*
Lindquist, Kenneth H. *437*
Lindsay, Alexander J. *525*
Lindsay, F. S. P. *392*
Lindsay, G. Carroll *442*
Lindsay, George E. *438*
Lindsay, George H. *145, 148, 151, 154, 157, 160*
Lindsay, George W. *179, 182, 189, 192, 195, 524*
Lindsay, Goerge W. *186*
Lindsay, Howard *521, 554*
Lindsay, John V. *240, 244, 247, 394*
Lindsay, Robert B. *291*
Lindsay, Samuel M. *509*
Lindsay, William *133, 136, 139, 141, 298*
Lindsey, Charles A. *518*
Lindsey, Edward M. *524*
Lindsey, Robert E. *395*
Lindsey, Stephen D. *113, 115, 118*
Lindsey, Washington E. *305*
Lindsley, Henry D. *397*
Lindsley, James G. *123*
Lindsley, Ogden R. *541*
Lindsley, Philip *473*

Lindsley, William D. *88*
Lindsly, Harve *515*
Lindzey, Gardner *518*
Linebarger, Paul M. A. *516*
Lineberger, Walter F. *174, 178, 181*
Linehan, John A., Jr. *372*
Linehan, Neil J. *220*
Linen, James A. *497*
Lines, Edwin S. *450, 460*
Linford, Henry B. *522, 531*
Linforth, Ivan M. *517*
Ling, James J. *491*
Lingle, William L. *407*
Link, Arthur A. *256, 307*
Link, Arthur S. *534*
Link, Constance *546*
Link, Edwin A. *551*
Link, Karl P. *532, 543*
Link, Theodore A. *510*
Link, William W. *213*
Linn, Archibald L. *77*
Linn, Henry W. *407*
Linn, James *46*
Linn, John *56, 58*
Linn, Lewis F. *69, 71, 73, 75, 76, 78, 303*
Linn, William *415*
Linnard, Lawrence G. *520*
Linnell, Frank H. *345*
Linney, Robert J. *561*
Linney, Romulus Z. *137, 140, 142*
Linowitz, S. M. *499*
Linscott, Roger B. *557*
Linsley, Joel H. *412*
Linthicum, J. Charles *159, 162, 166, 169, 172, 175, 178, 182, 185, 188, 191*
Linton, Edwin *543*
Linton, John P. *524*
Linton, M. Albert *495, 509*
Linton, William S. *133, 136*
Linville, Henry R. *503*
Lipinski, William O. *274, 277*
Lipke, William C. *439*
Lipmann, Fritz A. *549, 550*
Lippald, Richard *532*
Lippencott, Philip E. *496*
Lippincott, Joshua A. *420*
Lippitt, Charles W. *310, 528*
Lippitt, Henry *310*
Lippitt, Henry F. *161, 164, 167, 310*
Lippmann, Walter *547, 552, 556*
Lips, Evan *394*
Lipscomb, Abner *291*
Lipscomb, Andrew A. *419*
Lipscomb, Andy A. *345*
Lipscomb, Glenard P. *226, 229, 232, 235, 239, 242, 245, 248, 251*
Lipscomb, Oscar H. *463*
Lipscomb, T. J. *396*
Lipscomb, William N. *550*
Lisensky, Robert *426*
Lisle, Marcus C. *133*
Lispenard, Leonard *1*
List, Robert *304*
Lister, Edward *1*
Lister, Ernest *314*
Litchfield, Edward H. *422*
Litchfield, Elisha *60, 61*
Litchfield, Lawrence, Jr. *481*
Litchfield, Paul *562*
Litchfield, Paul W. *489*
Litchford, George B. *543*
Lithgow, James S. *389*
Littauer, Lucius N. *139, 142, 145, 148, 151*
Littell, Samuel H. *452, 459*

Litterer, William *396*
Little, Arthur D. *511*
Little, Charles *473*
Little, Chauncey B. *181*
Little, Clarence C. *420*
Little, David B. *439*
Little, David M. *390*
Little, Edward C. *168, 172, 175, 178*
Little, Edward H. *485*
Little, Edward P. *86*
Little, Edward S. *358*
Little, Ernest *516, 559*
Little, Feramorz *397*
Little, Ganse *474*
Little, John *124*
Little, John S. *132, 135, 138, 141, 144, 146, 149, 292*
Little, Joseph J. *131*
Little, Peter *52, 55, 56, 58, 59, 61, 62, 64*
Little, Royal *497*
Little, Samuel W. *392*
Little, Tom *555*
Little, William *395*
Littledale, Harold A. *553*
Littlefield, Alfred H. *310*
Littlefield, Charles E. *142, 144, 147, 150, 153*
Littlefield, Henry W. *418*
Littlefield, Nathaniel S. *76, 84*
Littlejohn, Abram N. *448, 459*
Littlejohn, De Witt C. *98*
Littlepage, Adam B. *161, 167, 171*
Littleton, Benjamin H. *286*
Littleton, Martin W. *160*
Littlewood, William *540*
Litton, Jerry *259, 262*
Litty, H. H. *396*
Litwack, Leon F. *546, 558*
Lively, G. W. *397*
Lively, Pierce *285*
Lively, Robert M. *158*
Livermore, Arthur *56, 58, 61, 305*
Livermore, Edward S. *50, 51*
Livermore, Samuel *3, 41, 42, 43, 44, 45, 46, 47, 304*
Livernash, Edward J. *146*
Liversidge, Horace P. *494*
Livesay, Thomas A. *441*
Livesay, William G. *343*
Livesey, William J. *333, 334*
Livesley, T. A. *395*
Livingston, Edward *24, 33, 44, 45, 46, 61, 62, 64, 66, 67, 299, 361, 393*
Livingston, Henry B. *283*
Livingston, Henry W. *48, 49*
Livingston, Homer J. *488, 511*
Livingston, J. A. *556*
Livingston, J. Ed *291*
Livingston, James M. *493*
Livingston, John H. *415*
Livingston, Leonidas F. *130, 133, 135, 138, 141, 144, 147, 150, 153, 155*
Livingston, M. Stanley *539*
Livingston, Philip *1, 4*
Livingston, Robert, Jr. *393*
Livingston, Robert B. *361*
Livingston, Robert L. *51, 52, 265, 268, 271, 274, 277*
Livingston, Robert R. *1, 2, 4*
Livingston, Rose *548*
Livingston, Vanbrugh *360*
Livingston, Walter *4*
Livingston, William *2, 4, 5, 305*
Livingstone, Colin H. *521*
Livingstone, William *510*

Lloyd, Arthur S. *450*
Lloyd, Edward *3, 5, 49, 50, 58, 59, 61, 62, 300*
Lloyd, Frank *509*
Lloyd, Harold *527*
Lloyd, Harry *506*
Lloyd, Henry *300*
Lloyd, Hoyes *516*
Lloyd, James *44, 45, 50, 51, 52, 53, 59, 61, 62, 300, 301*
Lloyd, James F. *261, 264, 267*
Lloyd, James H. *516*
Lloyd, James T. *139, 142, 145, 148, 151, 154, 156, 160, 163, 166*
Lloyd, John H. *492*
Lloyd, John Uri *559*
Lloyd, Marilyn *266, 269, 279*
Lloyd, Morton G. *544*
Lloyd, R. McAllister *432*
Lloyd, Ralph W. *473*
Lloyd, Sherman P. *244, 251, 254, 257*
Lloyd, Thomas *6*
Lloyd, Thomas J. *503*
Lloyd, Wesley *196, 200*
Loan, Benjamin F. *98, 100, 102*
Lobdell, Harrison, Jr. *351*
Lobeck, Charles O. *160, 163, 166, 169*
Locher, Cyrus *186, 308*
Locher, Ralph S. *394*
Lochner, Louis P. *554*
Lochrane, Osborne A. *296*
Locke, Charles E. *471*
Locke, Eugene M. *369, 552*
Locke, G. B. *396*
Locke, George H. *515*
Locke, John *61, 62, 64*
Locke, John L. *560*
Locke, John W. *403*
Locke, Matthew *43, 44, 45*
Locke, Samuel *409*
Locker, Jesse D. *366*
Locker, Richard *558*
Lockhard, Earl T. *411*
Lockhart, Clinton *417*
Lockhart, James *86, 91*
Lockhart, James A. *137*
Lockman, DeWitt M. *525*
Lockweed, Daniel N. *134*
Lockwood, A. A. *397*
Lockwood, A. I. *397*
Lockwood, Benoni *488*
Lockwood, Daniel N. *114, 131*
Lockwood, Francis C. *418*
Lockwood, Henry W. *396*
Lockwood, Mason G. *519*
Lockwood, Normand *562*
Lockwood, Theodore D. *417*
Lockwood, Timothy J. *393*
Locy, William A. *520*
Loder, Dwight H. *472*
Lodge, George *544*
Lodge, Henry Cabot *19, 125, 128, 130, 133, 136, 139, 142, 144, 147, 150, 153, 156, 158, 159, 162, 166, 169, 172, 175, 178, 301, 361, 375, 559*
Lodge, Henry Cabot, Jr. *201, 204, 207, 211, 217, 220, 223, 301, 548*
Lodge, John C. *391*
Lodge, John D. *293, 374*
Lodge, John Davis *216, 220, 355, 373*
Lodge, John E. *439*
Lodwick, Charles *393*
Loeb, Henry, II *396*
Loeb, Henry, III *396*
Loeb, Isidor *421, 517*

Lowell, Amy *553*
Lowell, Francis C. *284*
Lowell, James Russell *362, 373, 524, 540*
Lowell, John *3*
Lowell, Joshua A. *74, 76*
Lowell, Robert *535, 545, 548, 555, 557*
Lowell, S. J. *526*
Lowenstein, Allard K. *253*
Lowenstein, James G. *366*
Lowenthal, Joanne *560*
Lower, Christian *49*
Lowery, Bill *273, 276*
Lowery, George H., Jr. *516, 535*
Lowery, Worth *505*
Lowes, John L. *524*
Loweth, Charles F. *519*
Lowman, Charles L. *552*
Lown, Bernard *550*
Lowndes, Lloyd *300*
Lowndes, Lloyd, Jr. *108*
Lowndes, Rawlins *6, 396*
Lowndes, Thomas *47, 48*
Lowndes, William *53, 54, 55, 57, 58, 60*
Lowrance, V. L. *347*
Lowrey, Bill G. *176, 179, 182, 185*
Lowrey, Mark B. *323*
Lowrie, Charles N. *519*
Lowrie, John C. *473*
Lowrie, Walter *58, 60, 61, 309*
Lowrie, Walter H. *309*
Lowry, Bates *441*
Lowry, Bill *270*
Lowry, Charles W. *516*
Lowry, D. M. *387*
Lowry, Fred N. *387*
Lowry, Howard F. *407*
Lowry, Michael E. *270, 273, 276, 279*
Lowry, Raymond E. *503*
Lowry, Robert *120, 122, 302*
Lowry, Robert J. *510*
Loy, M. *406*
Loyall, George *67, 70, 72*
Loyd, Alexander *388*
Lozano, Ignacio E., Jr. *360*
Lozier, Ralph F. *179, 182, 185, 188, 192, 195*
Lubbock, Francis R. *312*
Lubetsky, Seymour *538*
Lubin, Leonard *546*
Lucas, A. W. *394*
Lucas, Edward *70, 72*
Lucas, Francis F. *562*
Lucas, Frank *315*
Lucas, Frederic A. *437*
Lucas, Harry I. *385*
Lucas, Jim C. *555*
Lucas, John B. C. *48, 49*
Lucas, John P. *334, 341*
Lucas, Mabel E. *476*
Lucas, Robert *307*
Lucas, Robert H. *380*
Lucas, Scott W. *197, 200, 204, 207, 210, 213, 217, 220, 296*
Lucas, William *76, 79*
Lucas, William V. *134*
Lucas, Wingate H. *219, 222, 225, 228*
Lucchesi, Bruno *560*
Luccock, Naphtali *471*
Luce, B. *388*
Luce, Charles F. *486*
Luce, Clare Boothe *210, 213, 365, 542, 548, 552*
Luce, Cyrus G. *301*
Luce, Donald C. *495*

Luce, Henry R. *497, 539*
Luce, Robert *172, 175, 179, 182, 185, 188, 191, 194, 201, 204*
Luce, Stephen B. *351*
Lucey, Patrick J. *315, 367*
Lucey, Robert E. *464, 469*
Lucker, Raymond A. *467*
Luckey, Henry C. *198, 201*
Luckey, William F. *547*
Luckhardt, Arno B. *517*
Luckiesh, Matthew *544*
Lucking, Alfred *147*
Ludden, Patrick A. *468*
Ludeling, John T. *299*
Ludington, Flora B. *515, 543*
Ludington, Harrison *315, 399*
Ludington, Marshall I. *332*
Ludlow, Daniel *484*
Ludlow, George C. *305*
Ludlow, John *422*
Ludlow, Louis *197, 201, 204, 207, 210, 213, 217*
Ludlow, Louis L. *188, 191, 194*
Ludlow, Theodore R. *452*
Ludvigsen, E. L. *487*
Ludwell, Philip *5, 6*
Ludwig, Arnold M. *541*
Luecke, John *201*
Luedecke, Alvin R. *417*
Luedtke, Roland *392*
Luellen, Charles J. *483*
Luening, Otto *535*
Luers, John H. *466*
Luers, William H. *359, 375*
Luerssen, Frank W. *490*
Lufkin, Elgood C. *497*
Lufkin, Willfred W. *169, 172, 175*
Lugar, Richard G. *265, 268, 271, 274, 277, 297, 388*
Lught, Gerrit T. Vander *406*
Luhnow, Harold W. *434*
Luhring, Oscar R. *172, 175*
Luigs, C. Russell *499*
Lujan, Manuel *393*
Lujan, Manuel, Jr. *253, 256, 259, 262, 266, 269, 272, 275, 278*
Lukas, J. Anthony *547, 556, 559*
Luken, Charles J. *394*
Luken, James T. *394*
Luken, Thomas *394*
Luken, Thomas A. *266, 269, 272, 275, 278*
Lukens, Alan W. *369*
Lukens, Donald E. *250, 253*
Lukens, Hiram S. *522*
Luks, George *536*
Lull, Richard S. *442*
Lum, Herman T. F. *296*
Lumbard, J. Edward *284, 532*
Lumiansky, R. M. *512*
Lumpias, Manuel C. *460*
Lumpias, Manuel Capuyan *456*
Lumpkin, Alva S. *524*
Lumpkin, John H. *78, 80, 81, 89*
Lumpkin, Joseph H. *295*
Lumpkin, Wilson *55, 64, 65, 72, 74, 295*
Lumsden, G. Quincy, Jr. *375*
Luna, Charles *504, 506*
Luna, W. Bruce *505*
Lund, Charles C. *511*
Lund, F. Edward *411*
Lund, Robert L. *525*
Lundberg, George A. *520*
Lundborg, Louis B. *483*
Lundeberg, Harry *505*

Lundeen, Ernest *169, 195, 198, 201, 204, 302*
Lundeen, Robert W. *487*
Lundin, Frederick *156*
Lundine, Stanley N. *266, 269, 272, 275, 278*
Lundy, Robert F. *472*
Luneberg, William V. *482*
Lunger, Irvin E. *417*
Lungren, Daniel E. *267, 270, 273, 276*
Lunn, George R. *170*
Lunney, Glenn *540*
Lunt, Alfred *535, 552*
Lunt, William E. *524*
Lupton, Nathaniel T. *418*
Luria, S. E. *546*
Luria, Salvador E. *550*
Lurie, Alison *558*
Lurting, Robert *393*
Lurton, Horace H. *283, 285, 312*
Lush, Jay L. *549*
Lusk, Georgia L. *218*
Lusk, Hall S. *237, 309*
Luskin, Harold T. *513*
Lutes, LeRoy *330, 334*
Luther, Flavel S. *417*
Lutkewitte, Lawrence *392*
Luttgens, Leslie L. *433*
Luttrell, John K. *108, 110, 112*
Lutz, Dan *536*
Lutz, Ralph H. *510*
Lybrand, Archibald *140, 143*
Lybrand, William M. *525*
Lydenberg, Harry M. *515, 543*
Lydman, Jack W. *367*
Lydon, Thomas J. *286*
Lykins, Johnston *392*
Lyle, Aaron *51, 53, 54, 55*
Lyle, Guy *543*
Lyle, John E., Jr. *215, 219, 222, 225, 228*
Lyman, Charles *380*
Lyman, Daniel *310*
Lyman, Helen H. *543*
Lyman, Henry M. *516*
Lyman, Joseph *122, 125*
Lyman, Joseph S. *58*
Lyman, Lauren D. *554*
Lyman, Richard W. *416, 433*
Lyman, Rufus A. *559*
Lyman, Samuel *44, 45, 46*
Lyman, Theodore *120, 509, 517, 537, 560*
Lyman, Theodore, Jr. *390*
Lyman, Theodore B. *448, 460*
Lyman, William *43, 44*
Lynch, Andrew G. *372*
Lynch, Charles *302*
Lynch, Daniel F. *512*
Lynch, Edmund C. *340*
Lynch, Frank W. *493*
Lynch, George A. *331*
Lynch, James K. *510*
Lynch, James M. *505*
Lynch, John *100, 102, 104, 106, 126*
Lynch, John J. *413*
Lynch, John R. *109, 111, 118*
Lynch, Joseph P. *470*
Lynch, Kenneth M. *519*
Lynch, Patrick N. *469*
Lynch, Thomas *1, 132, 135*
Lynch, Thomas, Jr. *1, 4*
Lynch, Thomas, Sr. *4*
Lynch, Tillman D. *519*
Lynch, Walter A. *205, 208, 211, 215, 218, 221*
Lynch, William F. *324*
Lynde, Benjamin *7*

Lynde, William P. *83, 112, 115, 398*
Lyndon, Josias *6*
Lynn, James T. *31, 38, 381, 481*
Lyon, A. E. *504*
Lyon, Alfred E. *492*
Lyon, Asa *56*
Lyon, Caleb *88*
Lyon, Cecil B. *358, 367*
Lyon, Chittenden *64, 65, 67, 69*
Lyon, E. Wilson *414*
Lyon, Ernest *366*
Lyon, Francis L. *320*
Lyon, Francis S. *70, 72, 321*
Lyon, Homer L. *176, 179, 182, 186*
Lyon, Lafayette A. *490*
Lyon, Lucius *73, 78, 301*
Lyon, Mary *540*
Lyon, Matthew *45, 46, 47, 49, 50, 51*
Lyon, T. L. *551*
Lyon, William P. *315*
Lyons, Charles W. *404, 409, 415*
Lyons, Harry *512*
Lyons, Henry *396*
Lyons, Henry A. *292*
Lyons, Hugh *391*
Lyons, J. H. *397*
Lyons, James *321*
Lyons, James J. *422*
Lyons, John A., Jr. *348*
Lyons, John H., Jr. *504*
Lyons, John H., Sr. *504*
Lyons, Louis M. *545*
Lyons, Peter *314*
Lyons, Robert W. *395*
Lyons, William L. *389*
Lytell, Bert *503*
Lytle, Robert T. *70*
Lytle, William P. *474*
Lyttleton, William H. *6*
Maas, Melvin J. *185, 188, 191, 198, 201, 204, 208, 211*
Mabee, Carleton *554*
Mabey, Charles R. *312*
Mabie, Hamilton W. *526*
Mabry, Milton H. *295*
Mabry, Thomas J. *305*
MacAdam, David L. *527*
MacAdam, Walter K. *523*
Macadie, Donald *454*
MacAlister, James *408*
MacArthur, Arthur *315*
MacArthur, Douglas *329, 333, 340, 344, 418, 548, 559*
MacArthur, Douglas, II *356, 364, 365*
Macartney, Clarence E. *473*
Macartney, Thomas B. *417*
Macauley, Charles R. *553*
Macbeth, Charles *396*
MacBriar, Wallace N., Jr. *440*
MacBride, Thomas H. *420*
MacBride, Thomas J. *287*
MacCarty, William C. *519*
MacChesney, Brunson *519*
MacColl, Norah A. *538*
MacCorkle, William A. *314*
MacCormack, Daniel W. *380*
MacCormick, Austin H. *512*
MacCracken, Henry M. *413, 422, 424*
MacCracken, John H. *411, 426*
MacCracken, William P., Jr. *563*
MacCrate, John *173*
MacCready, Paul B. *537, 559, 562*

McCort, John J. *469*
McCosh, James *414*
McCosker, Alfred J. *525*
McCoskry, Samuel A. *447, 459*
McCowen, Edward O. *212, 215, 218*
McCown, E. C. *474*
McCown, John P. *323*
McCoy, Alex W. *510*
McCoy, Alvin S. *555*
McCoy, Charles B. *487*
McCoy, Cornelius J. *422*
McCoy, Frank R. *559*
McCoy, George W. *561*
McCoy, James H. *471*
McCoy, Robert *68*
McCoy, Walter I. *160, 163*
McCoy, Whitley P. *379*
McCoy, William *53, 54, 56, 57, 59, 60, 62, 63, 65, 67, 68*
McCoy, William D. *366*
McCrackan, William D. *476*
McCracken, Charles C. *419*
McCracken, Robert M. *165*
McCrady, Edward *423*
McCrary, George W. *26, 34, 104, 106, 108, 110*
McCrate, John D. *80*
McCraw, Thomas K. *558*
McCray, Warren T. *297*
McCrea, Samuel P. *413*
McCrea, Theodore H. *455*
McCready, James *388*
McCready, William U. *390*
McCreary, George D. *148, 151, 154, 157, 160*
McCreary, James B. *123, 125, 127, 130, 133, 136, 147, 150, 153, 298*
McCreary, John *58*
McCredie, William W. *158*
McCree, Wade H., Jr. *285*
McCreery, Fenton R. *360, 364*
McCreery, John *388*
McCreery, Thomas C. *102, 104, 108, 111, 113, 298*
McCreery, William *47, 49, 50, 66*
McCrillis, Arthur M. *527*
McCrory, James T. *474*
McCue, J. J. *388*
McCuish, John *297*
McCulloch, Edgar A. *292*
McCulloch, George *75*
McCulloch, Hugh *26, 33, 34*
McCulloch, John *88*
McCulloch, John I. B. *522*
McCulloch, Philip D., Jr. *132, 135, 138, 141, 144*
McCulloch, Roscoe C. *167, 170, 173, 189, 308*
McCulloch, W. E. *474*
McCulloch, William M. *218, 221, 225, 228, 231, 234, 237, 241, 244, 247, 250, 253, 257*
McCullogh, Welty *126*
McCullough, C. Rogers *516*
McCullough, David *546, 547*
McCullough, Hiram *100, 102*
McCullough, John G. *313*
McCullough, Robert D *524*
McCullough, Thomas G. *58*
McCumber, Porter J. *142, 145, 148, 151, 154, 157, 160, 163, 167, 170, 173, 176, 307*
McCune, Shannon *423*
McCurdy, Charles J. *356*
McCurdy, Dave *272, 275, 278*
McCurdy, R. C. *496*
McCurdy, Richard A. *492*
McCurdy, Thomas A. *411*

McCurdy, William F. *433*
McCutcheon, George B. *521*
McCutcheon, John T. *554*
McDade, Joseph M. *244, 247, 250, 254, 257, 260, 263, 266, 269, 272, 275, 279*
McDaniel, Dennis K. *437*
McDaniel, Edward H. *331*
McDaniel, George W. *475*
McDaniel, Henry D. *295*
McDaniel, J. R. *387*
McDaniel, Thomas M., Jr. *496*
McDaniel, Walton B. *517*
McDaniel, William *80*
McDannold, John J. *133*
McDavid, Horace W. *523*
McDavid, Joel D. *472*
McDavid, Raven I. *512*
McDearmon, James C. *134, 137*
McDermott, Allan L. *142, 145, 148, 151*
McDermott, Eugene *497*
McDermott, George T. *286*
McDermott, James T. *153, 156, 159, 162, 165*
McDermott, Michael J. *360*
McDermott, Walsh *543, 562*
McDevitt, Hugh O. *551*
McDevitt, Joseph B. *347*
McDevitt, Philip R. *469*
McDiarmid, Errett W. *515*
McDiarmid, Hugh *404*
McDill, Alexander S. *110*
McDill, James W. *108, 110, 118, 297*
McDonald, A. D. *496*
McDonald, Alexander *101, 103, 292, 369*
McDonald, Alfred J. *505*
McDonald, Andrew J. *465*
McDonald, Charles J. *295*
McDonald, David J. *506*
McDonald, David L. *347, 348*
McDonald, Edward F. *131*
McDonald, Eugene F., Jr. *525*
McDonald, F. James *489*
McDonald, Harry A. *381*
McDonald, Howard S. *405*
McDonald, Hunter *519*
McDonald, J. S. *397*
McDonald, Jack H. *249, 252, 256*
McDonald, James G. *364*
McDonald, Jesse F. *293*
McDonald, John *139, 397*
McDonald, Joseph E. *83, 110, 113, 115, 297*
McDonald, Larry P. *261, 264, 267, 271, 274*
McDonald, Lyle *495*
McDonald, Ralph W. *404*
McDonald, Robert E. *496*
McDonald, Sanford N. *522*
McDonald, Wesley L. *348*
McDonald, William A. *533*
McDonald, William C. *305*
McDonald, William J. *406*
McDonnell, Charles E. *468*
McDonnell, James S. *491, 537, 540*
McDonnell, James S., Jr. *491*
McDonnell, John F. *491*
McDonnell, Sanford N. *491*
McDonnell, William A. *522*
McDonough, Gordon L. *213, 216, 219, 223, 226, 229, 232, 235, 239*
McDonough, John J. *391*
McDonough, Joseph P. *345*
McDonough, Roger *515*

McDonough, Thomas J. *464, 466*
McDougal, Myres S. *519*
McDougall, Alexander *4, 335, 483*
McDougall, James A. *87, 95, 97, 99, 292*
McDougall, John *292*
McDougall, Walter A. *559*
McDowell, Abraham J. *394*
McDowell, Alexander *134*
McDowell, Alfred H., Jr. *499*
McDowell, Bert F. *385*
McDowell, C. E. *347*
McDowell, Harris B., Jr. *229, 236, 239, 242, 245*
McDowell, Irvin *336*
McDowell, Jack S. *554*
McDowell, James *81, 83, 85, 313*
McDowell, James F. *97*
McDowell, John *415, 422, 473, 494*
McDowell, John A. *140, 143*
McDowell, John R. *205, 218*
McDowell, Joseph *43, 45*
McDowell, Joseph J. *79, 81*
McDowell, Samuel *70*
McDowell, Thomas D. *320*
McDowell, W. W. *364*
McDowell, William A. *473*
McDowell, William C. *451*
McDowell, William F. *419, 471*
McDowell, William G. *458*
McDuffie, George *60, 62, 63, 65, 66, 68, 70, 77, 79, 81, 310, 311*
McDuffie, John *171, 174, 177, 181, 184, 187, 190, 193, 197*
McDuffie, John V. *127*
McDuffie, William C. *489, 493*
McEachron, Karl B. *538, 544*
McElhiney, Thomas W. *362*
McElhinney, C. F. *419*
McElrath, D. *415*
McElroy, Clarence H. *414*
McElroy, Dennis L. *514*
McElroy, Neil H. *30, 37, 327, 495, 552*
McElroy, T. F. *398*
McElroy, William D. *380, 552, 560*
McElwain, Frank A. *450, 459*
McElwee, John G. *490*
McEnery, Samuel D. *139, 141, 144, 147, 150, 153, 156, 299*
McEnery, Thomas *386*
McEntee, Edward M. *284*
McEntegart, Bryan J. *406, 468*
McEttrick, Michael J. *133*
McEvoy, Christopher *424*
McEwan, James B. *393*
McEwan, Thomas, Jr. *137, 139*
McEwen, Bob *272, 275, 278*
McEwen, John A. *396*
McEwen, Robert C. *247, 250, 253, 256, 259, 263, 266, 269*
McEwen, Robert W. *409*
McFadden, James A. *469*
McFadden, Joseph M. *422*
McFadden, Louis T. *167, 170, 173, 177, 180, 183, 186, 189, 192, 196*
McFadden, P. W. *397*
McFall, Jack *361*
McFall, John J. *232, 235, 239, 242, 245, 248, 251, 255, 258, 261, 264*
McFarlan, Duncan *49*
McFarland, Andrew *518*
McFarland, Carl *421, 532*

McFarland, Ernest W. *206, 210, 213, 216, 219, 222, 291, 292*
McFarland, Francis *473*
McFarland, James G. *521*
McFarland, James P. *488*
McFarland, Norman F. *468*
McFarland, R. S. *510*
McFarland, Robert W. *412*
McFarland, William *112*
McFarlane, William D. *196, 199, 203*
McFaul, James A. *468*
McFeatters, Dale *434*
McFeely, William S. *558*
McFetridge, William L. *505*
McGaffey, Albert B. *527*
McGann, John R. *468*
McGann, Lawrence E. *130, 133, 136*
McGarr, Lionel C. *351*
McGarry, William J. *404*
McGarth, Raymond J. *278*
McGarvey, Robert N. *218*
McGaughey, Edward W. *80, 83*
McGavick, Alexander J. *470*
McGavin, Charles *150, 153*
McGavock, Randal W. *396*
McGavock, Randal *396*
McGee, Charles A. A. *524*
McGee, Dean A. *533, 552*
McGee, Elijah M. *392*
McGee, Gale W. *238, 241, 245, 248, 251, 254, 257, 261, 264, 315*
McGee, James *487*
McGee, R. E. *497*
McGee, Richard A. *512*
McGee, Tom E. *394*
McGee, W. J. *510, 526*
McGehee, Dan R. *198, 201, 204, 208, 211, 214*
McGehee, Francis *385*
McGehee, H. Coleman, Jr. *456, 459*
McGehee, Harvey *302*
McGhee, George C. *361, 374*
McGiffert, John R., II *334*
McGill, Alexander T. *473*
McGill, Andrew R. *301*
McGill, George *188, 191, 194, 197, 201, 298*
McGill, John *391, 470*
McGill, Ralph *545, 552, 556*
McGill, William J. *407, 548*
McGillicuddy, Daniel J. *159, 162, 166*
McGinley, Donald F. *237*
McGinley, J. P. *506*
McGinley, James J. *405*
McGinley, Laurence J. *408*
McGinley, Phyllis *542, 556*
McGinn, Howard J. *487*
McGinty, Bonaventure T. *412*
McGirk, Matthias *303*
McGlachlin, E. F., Jr. *351*
McGlasson, T. N. E. *385*
McGlennon, Cornelius A. *173*
McGlinchey, Herbert J. *215*
McGlothlin, William J. *408, 475*
McGolrick, James *467*
McGonagle, William A. *440*
McGoodwin, Preston *375*
McGovern, Francis E. *315*
McGovern, George *19, 234, 238, 244, 247, 250, 254, 257, 260, 263, 266, 269, 311*
McGovern, John W. *498, 525*
McGovern, Patrick A. *470*
McGovern, R. Gordon *484*
McGovern, Thomas *469*
McGowan, Alexander *397*

Mompesson, Roger *7*
Momsen, Frank C. *514*
Momyer, William W. *346*
Monagan, John S. *235, 239, 242, 245, 248, 252, 255*
Monaghan, Francis J. *468*
Monaghan, Frank B. *505*
Monaghan, James C. *542*
Monaghan, John J. *465*
Monaghan, Joseph P. *195, 198*
Monaghan, Kathleen M. *437*
Monahan, Frank J. *524*
Monahan, James G. *174*
Monahan, Thomas *386*
Monast, Louis *186*
Monat, William R. *413*
Monckton, Robert *5*
Moncure, Richard C. L. *314*
Mondale, Walter F. *13, 19, 31, 246, 249, 253, 256, 259, 262, 264, 267, 302*
Mondell, Frank W. *138, 143, 146, 149, 152, 155, 158, 161, 164, 168, 171, 174, 177*
Monell, Robert *58, 66*
Money, Hernando D. *111, 113, 116, 118, 120, 133, 136, 139, 142, 145, 148, 150, 153, 156, 302*
Money, John *541*
Mongan, Agnes *439*
Monget, Joseph *389*
Monheimer, Richard *442*
Monihan, J. D. *385*
Monihan, J. O. *385*
Monk, Tom B. *386*
Monkiewicz, Boleslaus J. *203, 210*
Monnet, Julien C. *421*
Monnett, Victor E. *552*
Monroe, A. J. *395*
Monroe, Frank A. *299*
Monroe, James *4, 11, 14, 15, 23, 24, 33, 34, 41, 42, 43, 75, 107, 109, 112, 114, 116, 313, 314, 361, 362, 540*
Monroe, John T. *389*
Monroe, Logan *525*
Monroe, Thomas *319*
Monroney, A. S. Mike *205, 209, 212, 215, 218, 221, 225, 228, 231, 234, 237, 241, 244, 247, 250, 308, 525, 563*
Monson, David D. *279*
Montagnier, Luc *543*
Montagu, Charles G. *6*
Montague, Andrew J. *164, 167, 171, 174, 177, 180, 183, 187, 190, 193, 196, 199, 203, 313, 516*
Montague, Andrew P. *408*
Montague, Robert L. *321*
Montague, Theodore *484*
Montague, Theodore G. *484*
Montano, Louis R. *393*
Montanya, James DeLa *75*
Montegut, Joseph E. *389*
Montegut, Joseph E. *389*
Monteith, A. C. *523*
Monteith, Alexander C. *538*
Monteith, Walter E. *397*
Monteith, William J. *411*
Montet, Numa F. *188, 191, 194, 198*
Monteverde, F. L. *396*
Montgomerie, John *5*
Montgomery, Alexander B. *125, 127, 130, 133*
Montgomery, Alfred E. *348*
Montgomery, Charles F. *439*
Montgomery, Daniel, Jr. *50*
Montgomery, Deane *515*

Montgomery, E. Roger *484*
Montgomery, Edward S. *555*
Montgomery, G. V. *265*
Montgomery, George C. *369*
Montgomery, George T. *465*
Montgomery, Gillespie V. *249, 253, 256, 259, 262, 268, 271, 275, 278*
Montgomery, Helen Barrett *475*
Montgomery, Henry *421*
Montgomery, J. B. *525*
Montgomery, J. K. *474*
Montgomery, James W. *455, 458*
Montgomery, John *50, 51, 52, 390, 426*
Montgomery, John F. *364*
Montgomery, John K. *413*
Montgomery, Joseph *4*
Montgomery, Lall G. *519*
Montgomery, Martin V. B. *381*
Montgomery, Richard *335*
Montgomery, Riley B. *476*
Montgomery, Robert *505*
Montgomery, Robert M. *287*
Montgomery, Robert N. *413, 474*
Montgomery, Samuel J. *183*
Montgomery, Thomas *53, 58, 59*
Montgomery, Thomas L. *515*
Montgomery, W. A. *406*
Montgomery, William *43, 71, 73, 75, 92, 94*
Montoya, Joseph M. *234, 237, 240, 243, 247, 250, 253, 256, 259, 262, 306*
Montoya, Nestor *176*
Montrose, Donald W. *465*
Moodey, James R. *457, 460*
Moodie, Thomas H. *307*
Moody, Arthur Blair *224*
Moody, Arthur E. B. *301*
Moody, Clarence L. *510, 552*
Moody, Dan *312*
Moody, Gideon C. *129, 311*
Moody, Graham B. *510*
Moody, James M. *145*
Moody, James P. *276, 279*
Moody, Lewis F. *537*
Moody, Malcolm A. *143, 145*
Moody, Paul D. *412*
Moody, R. G. *386*
Moody, Ralph E. *498*
Moody, Tom *394*
Moody, William H. *27, 35, 136, 139, 142, 144, 283*
Moody, William L., Jr. *482*
Moody, William R. *453, 459*
Moody, Zenas F. *309*
Moon, Eric *543*
Moon, John A. *140, 143, 146, 149, 152, 155, 158, 161, 164, 167, 170, 174*
Moon, John W. *133*
Moon, Reuben O. *148, 151, 154, 157, 160*
Moon, Thomas E. *541*
Mooney, Charles A. *173, 179, 183, 186, 189*
Mooney, Daniel F. *369*
Mooney, Edward A. *463, 464, 468*
Mooney, William C. *167*
Moonlight, Thomas *357*
Moor, F. C. *387*
Moor, Frank D. *387*
Moor, William L. *387*
Moor, Wyman B. S. *82, 299*
Moore, A. Harry *198, 201, 305*
Moore, Acel *557*

Moore, Alexander P. *370, 373*
Moore, Alfred *283*
Moore, Allen F. *175, 178*
Moore, Andrew *41, 42, 43, 44, 48, 49, 51, 314*
Moore, Andrew B. *291*
Moore, Arch A., Jr. *235, 238, 241, 245, 248, 251, 314*
Moore, Arthur J. *471*
Moore, Barrington *522*
Moore, Benjamin *407, 447, 460*
Moore, Bryant E. *342, 344, 418*
Moore, C. Ellis *173, 176, 179, 183, 186, 189, 192*
Moore, C. Robert *357, 361, 367*
Moore, Charles C. *296*
Moore, Charles H. *439*
Moore, Clifford H. *517*
Moore, Constance *438*
Moore, Daniel K. *307*
Moore, David H. *419, 471*
Moore, Douglas *509, 526, 555*
Moore, Edward B. *381*
Moore, Edward H. *212, 215, 218, 308*
Moore, Edward M. *515*
Moore, Eliakim H. *105, 510, 515*
Moore, Elizabeth Luce *548*
Moore, Ely *71, 73*
Moore, Francis, Jr. *397*
Moore, Frank G. *517*
Moore, Frank M. *439*
Moore, Gabriel *59, 60, 62, 64, 67, 68, 70, 291*
Moore, George E. *535*
Moore, George F. *312, 333, 509*
Moore, George S. *485, 562*
Moore, H. Guy *426*
Moore, Harold G. *329*
Moore, Harry T. *451, 458, 561*
Moore, Heman A. *79*
Moore, Henry *5*
Moore, Henry D. *85, 87*
Moore, Henry T. *416*
Moore, Hollis A. *404*
Moore, Horace L. *133*
Moore, J. Hampton *151, 154, 157, 160, 164, 167, 170, 173, 395*
Moore, James *6, 417*
Moore, James E. *329, 351*
Moore, James W. *320, 321*
Moore, Jere A. *417*
Moore, Jeremiah *417*
Moore, Jesse H. *103, 106*
Moore, John *74, 76, 86, 332, 465*
Moore, John B. *517, 559*
Moore, John C. *386*
Moore, John D. J. *364*
Moore, John L., Jr. *379*
Moore, John M. *152, 155, 158, 161, 471*
Moore, John P. *286*
Moore, John W. *181, 185, 188, 191, 392, 415*
Moore, Joseph *408*
Moore, Laban T. *93*
Moore, Lamont *444*
Moore, Leonard P. *284*
Moore, Littleton W. *126, 129, 132*
Moore, Marianne *531, 534, 535, 545, 547, 548, 555, 561*
Moore, Martin A. *525*
Moore, Maurice T. *497*
Moore, Meredith *505*
Moore, Moultrie *458*
Moore, Nathaniel F. *407*

Moore, Nicholas R. *47, 49, 50, 51, 53, 55*
Moore, Noah W. *472*
Moore, Noah W., Jr. *472*
Moore, O. Otto *293*
Moore, Orlando H. *339*
Moore, Orren C. *128*
Moore, Oscar F. *90*
Moore, Paul *386*
Moore, Paul, Jr. *455, 460, 548, 560*
Moore, Paul J. *185*
Moore, Pius *422*
Moore, Preston J. *514*
Moore, R. Lee *178*
Moore, R. Walton *174, 177, 180, 183, 187, 190*
Moore, Raymond C. *523, 540, 552*
Moore, Richard B. *544, 551*
Moore, Richard C. *447, 461*
Moore, Robert *57, 58, 519*
Moore, Robert E. *392*
Moore, Robert J. *514*
Moore, Robert L. *515*
Moore, Robert M. *394*
Moore, Russel J. *440*
Moore, Samuel *57, 58, 60*
Moore, Samuel B. *291*
Moore, Samuel M. *70*
Moore, Stanford *550*
Moore, Sydenham *91, 93*
Moore, T. Justin *499*
Moore, T. Justin, Jr. *499*
Moore, Thomas *47, 48, 49, 50, 52, 53, 55*
Moore, Thomas L. *59, 60*
Moore, Thomas O. *299*
Moore, Thomas P. *61, 62, 64, 358*
Moore, W. F. *312*
Moore, W. Henson *262, 265, 268, 271, 274, 277*
Moore, Wendell F. *562*
Moore, Wilbert E. *520*
Moore, William *6, 102, 104*
Moore, William C. *522*
Moore, William D. *420*
Moore, William E. *473*
Moore, William G. *346*
Moore, William H. *398, 483*
Moore, William M. *455*
Moore, William R. *119*
Moore, William S. *109*
Moore, William W. *513*
Moore, Willis L. *526*
Moore, Zephaniah S. *403, 426*
Moorehead, Tom V. *241*
Moorehead, Warren K. *442*
Moorer, John P. *347*
Moorer, Thomas H. *328, 347, 348, 537*
Moores, John H. *395*
Moores, Merrill *165, 168, 172, 175, 178*
Moorfield, Storey *525*
Moorhead, Carlos J. *258, 261, 264, 267, 270, 273, 276*
Moorhead, James K. *94, 97, 99, 101, 103*
Moorhead, William S. *238, 241, 244, 247, 250, 254, 257, 260, 263, 266, 269*
Moorman, Henry D. *185*
Moorman, Thomas S. *417*
Moos, Malcolm C. *420*
Moose, George E. *356*
Moose, James S., Jr. *372, 373, 374*
Moot, Robert C. *382*
Mooz, R. Peter *437, 443*

Oatis, William *551*
Ober, Edgar B. *492*
Oberholtzer, Edison E. *419*
Oberly, Henry S. *415*
Oberly, John H. *504*
Oberstar, James L. *262, 265, 268, 271, 274, 278*
Obey, David R. *254, 257, 260, 264, 267, 270, 273, 276, 279*
O'Boyle, Francis B. *415*
O'Boyle, Patrick *463*
O'Brady, William *469*
O'Brien, A. J. *495*
O'Brien, Brian *527*
O'Brien, Charles F. X. *176, 179*
O'Brien, Charles M. *386*
O'Brien, Christopher D. *391*
O'Brien, Edward C. *369, 375*
O'Brien, Eugene W. *520*
O'Brien, Frank M. *553*
O'Brien, G. Dennis *422*
O'Brien, George D. *201, 208, 211, 214, 220, 224, 227, 405*
O'Brien, George M. *258, 261, 264, 268, 271, 274, 277*
O'Brien, Henry J. *463, 465*
O'Brien, Henry X. *310*
O'Brien, Hugh *390*
O'Brien, James *116*
O'Brien, James H. *163*
O'Brien, Jeremiah *61, 62, 64*
O'Brien, John *489*
O'Brien, John A. *406, 542*
O'Brien, John D. *524*
O'Brien, John P. *394*
O'Brien, Joseph J. *205, 208, 211*
O'Brien, Lawrence F. *31, 36*
O'Brien, Leo W. *224, 227, 231, 234, 237, 240, 244, 247*
O'Brien, R. G. *398*
O'Brien, Robert L. *382*
O'Brien, Thomas H. *505*
O'Brien, Thomas J. *194, 197, 200, 210, 213, 217, 220, 223, 226, 229, 233, 236, 239, 242, 360, 365, 465*
O'Brien, Tim *546*
O'Brien, William J. *108, 111*
O'Brien, William J., Jr. *521*
O'Brien, William S. *187*
O'Byrne, John J. *413*
O'Byrne, Mrs. Roscoe C. *526*
O'Callaghan, Mike *304*
Ochiltree, David *387*
Ochiltree, Thomas P. *121*
Ochiltree, William B. *320*
Ochoa, Servero *549, 550*
Ochs, Adolph S. *548*
Ochs, Clarence I. *487*
Ochs, Elmer R. *345*
Ochsner, Albert J. *512*
Ochsner, Alton *511, 512, 533*
Ockerson, John A. *519*
O'Connell, Ambrose *287*
O'Connell, Daniel C. *416*
O'Connell, David J. *173, 179, 182, 186, 189*
O'Connell, Denis J. *406, 470*
O'Connell, Eugene *465*
O'Connell, James *504*
O'Connell, James D. *332*
O'Connell, Jeremiah E. *180, 183, 189*
O'Connell, Jerry J. *201*
O'Connell, John J. *284*
O'Connell, John M. *196, 199, 202*
O'Connell, Joseph F. *153, 156*
O'Connell, M. F. *505*
O'Connell, Michael J. *407*

O'Connell, Stephen C. *419*
O'Connell, William H. *463, 464, 467*
O'Connor, Basil *516, 526, 548*
O'Connor, Charles *189*
O'Connor, Dennis P. *387*
O'Connor, Edwin *556*
O'Connor, Flannery *545*
O'Connor, George G. *344*
O'Connor, James *172, 175, 178, 181, 185, 188, 468*
O'Connor, James F. *201, 205, 208, 211, 214*
O'Connor, James J. *485*
O'Connor, Jeremiah *404*
O'Connor, John B. *487*
O'Connor, John J. *179, 182, 186, 189, 192, 195, 198, 202, 463, 464, 468*
O'Connor, Maconda B. *431*
O'Connor, Michael *469*
O'Connor, Michael J. *415, 427*
O'Connor, Michael P. *117, 119*
O'Connor, Paul L. *427*
O'Connor, Sandra Day *283*
O'Connor, T. V. *504*
O'Connor, William A. *466*
O'Connor, William P. *470*
O'Conor, Herbert R. *217, 220, 223, 300*
O'Daniel, John W. *333, 341, 344*
O'Daniel, W. Lee *209, 212, 215, 219, 312*
O'Day, Caroline *198, 202, 205*
O'Day, John *504*
O'Day, Timothy *385*
Oddie, Tasker L. *176, 179, 182, 185, 188, 192, 304*
O'Dea, Edward J. *470*
Odegaard, Charles *512*
Odegaard, Charles E. *423*
Odegard, Peter H. *518*
Odell, Arthur G., Jr. *514*
Odell, Benjamin B., Jr. *137, 139, 306*
Odell, Gerard P. *542*
Odell, John J. P. *510*
Odell, Morgan S. *411*
Odell, Moses F. *96, 98*
Odell, N. Holmes *111*
O'Dell, William F. *515*
Odenheimer, William H. *448, 460*
Oder, Frederic C. E. *539*
Odets, Clifford *532*
Odgers, Merle M. *405*
Odgis, Janet *547*
Odin, Jean Marie *464, 470*
Odlin, Reno *511*
Odom, William E. *329, 381*
O'Donaghue, Denis *467*
O'Donnell, Charles L. *421*
O'Donnell, Cletus P. *470*
O'Donnell, Edward J. *412*
O'Donnell, Emmett, Jr. *346*
O'Donnell, J. Hugh *421*
O'Donnell, James *123, 125, 128, 130*
O'Donnell, T. A. *516*
O'Donohue, Daniel A. *357*
Odum, Eugene P. *522*
Odum, Howard W. *520*
O'Dwyer, Fred J. *505*
O'Dwyer, John P. *424*
O'Dwyer, William *367, 394*
Oelman, Robert S. *433, 493*
O'Farrell, Michael J. *468*
O'Ferrall, Charles T. *122, 124, 126, 129, 132, 135, 313*
Offenhauer, Roy E. *404*

O'Flanagan, Dermot *465*
Ofstie, Ralph A. *348*
Oganoff, Ida *531*
Ogburn, Charlton *536*
Ogburn, William F. *520*
Ogden, Aaron *46, 47, 305, 528*
Ogden, Charles F. *172, 175*
Ogden, David A. *56*
Ogden, David A. D. *331*
Ogden, Henry W. *133, 136, 139*
Ogden, Michael J. *520*
Ogden, Robert *1*
Ogden, Wesley *312*
Ogden, William B. *388, 498*
Ogden, William S. *486*
Ogg, Frederic A. *517*
Ogilby, Lyman C. *454, 460*
Ogilby, Remsen B. *417*
Ogilvie, Richard B. *296*
Oglesby, Richard J. *108, 110, 113, 296*
Oglesby, Woodson R. *163, 166*
Oglethorpe, James E. *5*
Oglivie, Don *511*
O'Gorman, James A. *160, 163, 166, 306*
O'Gorman, Patrick F. *415*
O'Gorman, Thomas *469*
O'Grady, James M. E. *142*
O'Green, Fred W. *491*
O'Hagan, Joseph B. *406*
O'Hair, Frank T. *162*
O'Hair, Robert C. *523*
O'Hara, Barratt *220, 226, 229, 233, 236, 239, 242, 246, 249*
O'Hara, Edwin V. *467, 468*
O'Hara, Frank *545*
O'Hara, Gerald P. *466*
O'Hara, James *332*
O'Hara, James E. *121, 123*
O'Hara, James G. *236, 240, 243, 246, 249, 252, 256, 259, 262*
O'Hara, John *532, 545*
O'Hara, John F. *421, 463, 464, 468*
O'Hara, Joseph P. *208, 211, 214, 217, 221, 224, 227, 230, 233*
O'Hara, William *469*
O'Hare, John *503*
O'Hare, Joseph A. *408*
O'Hern, John F. *468*
Ohliger, Lewis P. *131*
Okada, Kenzo *562*
O'Kane, Michael *406*
O'Keefe, Arthur J. *389*
O'Keefe, Georgia *535, 547, 552*
O'Keefe, Gerald F. *466*
O'Keefe, John *505*
O'Keefe, Lawrence *504*
O'Keefe, Matthias J. *390*
O'Keefe, Vincent T. *408*
O'Kelly, James *477*
Okey, John W. *308*
O'Konski, Alvin E. *213, 216, 219, 222, 225, 229, 232, 235, 238, 241, 245, 248, 251, 254, 257*
Okun, Herbert S. *362*
Olander, William *437*
Olcott, Ben W. *309*
Olcott, Charles C. *497*
Olcott, J. Van Vechten *151, 154, 157*

Olcott, Simeon *47, 48, 304, 305*
Olden, Charles S. *305*
Oldenburg, Richard *441*
Oldendorf, William *543*
Oldfather, William A. *517*
Oldfield, Pearl Peden *184, 187*
Oldfield, William A. *155, 158, 161, 165, 168, 171, 174, 177, 181, 184*
Oldham, George A. *451, 458*
Oldham, John P. *391*
Oldham, William F. *471*
Oldham, William S. *320, 321*
Olds, Edson B. *84, 86, 88*
Olds, George D. *403*
Olds, Glenn A. *411*
Olds, Irving S. *499, 559*
Olds, James *541*
Olds, Leland *380*
Olds, Robert *340*
O'Leary, Arthur A. *409*
O'Leary, Denis *163*
O'Leary, Edward C. *467*
O'Leary, Edward J. *432*
O'Leary, James A. *198, 202, 205, 208, 211*
O'Leary, James L. *516*
O'Leary, John W. *522*
O'Leary, Thomas M. *467*
O'Leary, Vincent I. *416*
Olendorf, George F. *527*
Olgeert, Benjamin H., Jr. *369*
Olin, Abram B. *92, 94, 96*
Olin, Franklin W. *433*
Olin, Gideon *48, 49*
Olin, Henry *62*
Olin, James *276, 279*
Olin, Stephen *415, 425*
Olinsky, Ivan G. *536*
Oliphant, Benjamin R. *472*
Oliphant, Patrick B. *556*
Oliphant, Walter T. *514*
Olitski, Jules *536, 551*
Olivarez, Graciela *381*
Oliver, Allen L. *527*
Oliver, Andrew *88, 90*
Oliver, Bernard M. *523, 543, 549*
Oliver, Covey T. *359*
Oliver, Daniel C. *170*
Oliver, E. L. *538*
Oliver, Frank *179, 182, 186, 189, 192, 195*
Oliver, George T. *157, 160, 164, 167, 309*
Oliver, Henry K. *390*
Oliver, James *347*
Oliver, James A. *437*
Oliver, James C. *201, 204, 207, 236*
Oliver, Lunsford E. *343*
Oliver, Mary *558, 561*
Oliver, Mordecai *88, 90*
Oliver, Oren A. *512*
Oliver, Peter *7*
Oliver, Robert T. *512*
Oliver, Robert W. *420*
Oliver, S. Addison *110, 113*
Oliver, Webster J. *287*
Oliver, William B. *165, 168, 171, 174, 177, 181, 184, 187, 190, 193, 197*
Oliver, William M. *77*
Olmstead, Dawson *332*
Olmstead, Philo H. *394*
Olmsted, Charles E. *522*
Olmsted, Charles S. *450, 458*
Olmsted, Charles T. *450, 458*
Olmsted, David *391*
Olmsted, Frederick L. *532*

Owen, David B. *404*
Owen, Edgar W. *510, 552*
Owen, Emmett M. *194, 197, 200, 204*
Owen, George W. *60, 62, 64*
Owen, James *57*
Owen, James H. *396*
Owen, John *307*
Owen, Richard *415*
Owen, Robert D. *78, 80, 372*
Owen, Robert L. *154, 157, 160, 164, 167, 170, 173, 176, 180, 308*
Owen, Russell D. *553*
Owen, Ruth Bryan *187, 191, 360*
Owen, Selwyn N. *308*
Owen, Thomas H. *308*
Owen, Vaux *505*
Owen, William D. *122, 125, 127*
Owens, Charles B. *506*
Owens, D. Wayne *260*
Owens, Delia *536*
Owens, Frank C. *396*
Owens, George W. *70, 72*
Owens, Hubert B. *520*
Owens, James B. *319*
Owens, James W. *129, 131*
Owens, Jesse *552*
Owens, Jesse N. *392*
Owens, John W. *554*
Owens, L. B. *396*
Owens, Major R. *275, 278*
Owens, Mark *536*
Owens, Michael J. *537*
Owens, Thomas L. *217*
Owens, William C. *136*
Owings, Nathaniel A. *532*
Owsley, Alvin M. *360, 364, 371, 514*
Owsley, Bryan Y. *76*
Owsley, William *298*
Oxley, Michael *275, 278*
Oxnam, G. Bromley *407, 471*
Oxnam, Robert *414*
Paca, William *1, 3, 5*
Pace, Charles N. *409*
Pace, Eric *551*
Pace, Frank *381*
Pace, Frank, Jr. *327, 488, 526*
Pace, Joseph L., *386*
Pace, Stanley C. *488, 498*
Pace, Stephen *200, 204, 207, 210, 213, 216, 220*
Pacheco, Romualdo *112, 115, 117, 292, 363, 364*
Pachler, William J. *506*
Pack, John Paul *476*
Packard, Alpheus S. *442*
Packard, Arthur W. *433*
Packard, C. S. W. *488*
Packard, David *327, 489, 541*
Packard, Jasper *104, 106, 108*
Packard, Lewis R. *517*
Packard, Ron *276*
Packer, Asa *88, 90*
Packer, Fred L. *555*
Packer, Horace B. *140, 143*
Packer, John B. *105, 107, 109, 112*
Packer, William F. *309*
Packwood, Robert *257, 560*
Packwood, Robert W. *253, 260, 263, 266, 269, 272, 275, 278, 309*
Paddock, Algernon S. *111, 113, 116, 126, 128, 131, 303*
Paddock, Benjamin H. *448, 459*
Paddock, F. J. *385*
Paddock, George A. *207*

Paddock, George W. *403*
Paddock, John A. *448, 460*
Paddock, Robert L. *450, 458*
Padelford, Frederick M. *524*
Padelford, Seth *310*
Padgett, Lemuel P. *146, 149, 152, 155, 158, 161, 164, 167, 170, 174, 177*
Paganelli, Robert P. *370, 374*
Page, Addison Franklin *443*
Page, Carroll S. *155, 158, 161, 164, 167, 171, 174, 177, 313*
Page, Charles G. *442*
Page, Charles H. *124, 131, 134*
Page, Curtis H. *527*
Page, Daniel D. *392*
Page, Edward, Jr. *357*
Page, George T. *285, 511*
Page, Henry *130*
Page, Herman *451, 459, 461*
Page, Herman L. *398*
Page, Herman R. *453, 460*
Page, Horace F. *108, 110, 112, 115, 117*
Page, Irvine H. *513, 532, 533, 551*
Page, John *41, 42, 43, 44, 71, 304, 313*
Page, John B. *313*
Page, Mann *4*
Page, Marie Danforth *542*
Page, Richard L. *324*
Page, Robert *46*
Page, Robert N. *148, 151, 154, 157, 160, 163, 166*
Page, Sherman *69, 71*
Page, Thomas N. *365*
Page, Thomas W. *382*
Page, Walter H. *362*
Page, William *525*
Pagels, Elaine *546*
Pahls, John *411*
Pahls, John N. X. *407*
Paige, Calvin D. *162, 166, 169, 172, 175, 179*
Paige, David R. *121*
Paige, Hilliard W. *488*
Paige, John K. *393*
Paine, Charles *313, 519*
Paine, Charles J. *339*
Paine, Edward H. *524*
Paine, Elijah *44, 45, 46, 47, 313*
Paine, Ephraim *4*
Paine, Halbert E. *101, 103, 105, 381*
Paine, Robert *471*
Paine, Robert T. *90*
Paine, Robert Treat *1, 3, 516*
Paine, Rowlett *396*
Paine, Thomas *540*
Paine, Thomas O. *380, 493, 539*
Paine, William W. *103*
Painter, T. S. *520*
Painter, Theophilus S. *423*
Pais, Abraham *547*
Palache, Charles *523*
Palade, George E. *543, 549, 551*
Palamountain, Joseph C., Jr. *416*
Palen, Rufus *75*
Palermo, Peter M. *562*
Palfrey, John G. *82*
Palladino, N. Joseph *516*
Palladino, Ralph A. *332*
Pallak, Michael *518*
Pallidino, Nunzio J. *381*
Palmer, A. Mitchell *28, 35, 157, 160, 164*
Palmer, Albert *390*

Palmer, Albert W. *475*
Palmer, Alice Freeman *540*
Palmer, Anthony *6*
Palmer, Beriah *48*
Palmer, Bruce, Jr. *329, 344*
Palmer, Charles D. *334, 344*
Palmer, Cyrus M. *186*
Palmer, Ely E. *355*
Palmer, Everett W. *472*
Palmer, Frank W. *104, 106, 380*
Palmer, George W. *92, 94*
Palmer, Harold D. *519*
Palmer, Henry L. *493*
Palmer, Henry W. *146, 148, 151, 157*
Palmer, James S. *350*
Palmer, John *57, 73*
Palmer, John M. *16, 17, 130, 133, 296, 337, 338*
Palmer, John McA. *135*
Palmer, John W. *188*
Palmer, Joseph, II *366, 368*
Palmer, Joseph C. *347*
Palmer, L. E. *505*
Palmer, Leigh C. *349*
Palmer, Lester E. *397*
Palmer, Potter *437*
Palmer, Ralph S. *535*
Palmer, Richard E. *519*
Palmer, Robert M. *355*
Palmer, Robert R. *513, 534*
Palmer, Ronald D. *374*
Palmer, Ronald DeWayne *367*
Palmer, Samuel S. *473*
Palmer, T. Chalkley *509*
Palmer, Thomas W. *120, 123, 125, 301*
Palmer, William A. *57, 58, 60, 62, 313*
Palmer, Williston B. *330, 344*
Palmisano, Vincent L. *185, 188, 191, 194, 198, 201*
Palser, Barbara F. *521*
Pamplin, Robert B. *489*
Panetta, Leon E. *264, 267, 270, 273, 277*
Pankow, Steven *393*
Panofsky, Wolfgang *549*
Panofsky, Wolfgang K. H. *538, 539*
Pantzer, Robert T. *421*
Paolino, Joseph, Jr. *395*
Papanicolaou, George N. *551*
Papenfoth, Herman A. *525*
Papp, Joseph *547*
Pappenheimer, John R. *517*
Parcell, Malcolm *560*
Pardee, Don A. *284*
Pardee, George C. *292*
Pardue, Austin *453, 461*
Paret, William *449, 459*
Park, Edwards A. *534*
Park, Frank *162, 165, 168, 171, 175, 178*
Park, Guy B. *303*
Park, John *396*
Park, John D. *294*
Park, Marion Edwards *405*
Park, Orlando *522*
Park, Robert E. *520*
Park, Robert H. *543*
Park, Samuel C. *397*
Park, Thomas *510, 522*
Park, William E. *416*
Park, William H. *518, 548, 559, 561*
Parke, John G. *337, 418*
Parker, Abraham X. *118, 121, 123, 126*
Parker, Albert *389*

Parker, Alton B. *17, 306, 511*
Parker, Amasa J. *73*
Parker, Andrew *87*
Parker, Arthur C. *442*
Parker, B. B. *487*
Parker, Ben H. *510*
Parker, C. G. *525*
Parker, Cola G. *491*
Parker, Cortlandt *341, 511*
Parker, Daniel *330, 331, 379*
Parker, Dorothy *562*
Parker, Earl *519*
Parker, Earl R. *534, 549*
Parker, Edward M. *450, 460*
Parker, Edwin P., Jr. *332, 342*
Parker, Edwin W. *471*
Parker, Emmett N. *314*
Parker, F. A. *418*
Parker, Frank *330*
Parker, Gail T. *404*
Parker, George B. *554*
Parker, George H. *509*
Parker, Glenn *315*
Parker, Harry S., III *438*
Parker, Henry *5*
Parker, Homer C. *191, 194*
Parker, Hosea W. *107, 109*
Parker, Isaac *45, 301*
Parker, Isaac C. *106, 109*
Parker, James *53, 58, 69, 71*
Parker, James E. *340, 341*
Parker, James K. *426*
Parker, James S. *163, 166, 170, 173, 176, 179, 182, 186, 189, 192, 195*
Parker, James W. *486, 520*
Parker, Jay S. *298*
Parker, Joel *305*
Parker, John *4*
Parker, John C. *523, 537*
Parker, John J. *284, 532*
Parker, John M. *90, 92, 299*
Parker, Joseph O. *382*
Parker, Josiah *41, 42, 43, 44, 45, 46*
Parker, Lauris S. *385*
Parker, Lawton *531*
Parker, Linus *471*
Parker, Lutrelle F. *381*
Parker, Matthew H. *504*
Parker, Millard M. *418*
Parker, Moses G. *526*
Parker, Nahum *50, 51, 304*
Parker, Paul *438*
Parker, R. Hunt *307*
Parker, Ralph D. *561*
Parker, Richard *85*
Parker, Richard B. *355, 366, 368*
Parker, Richard E. *72, 74, 314*
Parker, Richard H. *137, 139, 142, 145, 148, 151, 154, 157, 163, 166, 169, 176*
Parker, Robert Andrew *560*
Parker, Robert C. *387*
Parker, Roy H. *331*
Parker, Samuel *447, 459*
Parker, Samuel W. *86, 87*
Parker, Severn E. *59*
Parker, T. Nelson *398*
Parker, Theodore W. *329*
Parker, Torrance *476*
Parker, William H. *154, 562*
Parker, William R. *524*
Parkhill, James W. *414*
Parkhurst, Charles *437*
Parkhurst, Christopher F. *310*
Parkhurst, Frederick H. *299*
Parkhurst, John G. *356*
Parkinson, C. Jay *482*
Parkinson, Daniel B. *416*

Parkinson, David B. *552*
Parkinson, Thomas I. *487*
Parkinson, W. Lynn *285*
Parkman, Francis *540*
Parkman, Paul D. *542*
Parks, Charles *526*
Parks, Charles W. *349*
Parks, Floyd L. *333*
Parks, Gordon *561*
Parks, Gorham *69, 71*
Parks, Harry S. *544*
Parks, Lloyd M. *516, 559*
Parks, Robert J. *539, 540*
Parks, Robert O. *443*
Parks, Rosa L. *561*
Parks, Tilman B. *174, 177, 181, 184, 187, 190, 193, 197*
Parks, W. George *514, 532*
Parks, W. Robert *410*
Parmelee, Howard C. *522*
Parmelee, William *393*
Parmenter, William *73, 74, 76, 78*
Parnell, Harvey *292*
Parr, Albert E. *437, 442*
Parr, John *526*
Parr, Samuel W. *511*
Parran, Thomas *159, 381, 432, 518, 561*
Parrett, Tom *397*
Parrett, William F. *127, 130*
Parrington, Vernon L. *553*
Parris, Albion K. *55, 56, 64, 299*
Parris, Stanford E. *260, 273, 276, 279*
Parris, Virgil D. *73, 74*
Parrish, Edward *416*
Parrish, Isaac *75, 81*
Parrish, Lucian W. *174, 177*
Parrish, Samuel L. *548*
Parrott, John F. *56, 58, 59, 61, 304*
Parry, Charles W. *481*
Parry, D. M. *525*
Parsons, Andrew *301*
Parsons, Archibald L. *349*
Parsons, Charles *510*
Parsons, Charles L. *553*
Parsons, Claude V. *187, 191, 194, 197, 200, 204*
Parsons, Donald J. *461*
Parsons, Donald James *456*
Parsons, Edward L. *451, 458*
Parsons, Edward S. *412*
Parsons, Edward Y. *111*
Parsons, Ernest *385*
Parsons, Frank N. *305*
Parsons, Geoffrey *554*
Parsons, Herbert *151, 154, 157*
Parsons, J. Graham *366, 373*
Parsons, Lewis E. *291*
Parsons, Richard C. *109*
Parsons, Robert W. *432*
Parsons, Robert W., Jr. *432*
Parsons, Samuel *335*
Parsons, Samuel, Jr. *519*
Parsons, Talcott *509, 520*
Parsons, Theophilus *301*
Parsons, William W. *410*
Partain, Edward A. *334*
Partch, Harry *562*
Partridge, Alden *414, 418*
Partridge, Charlotte *440*
Partridge, Earle E. *340, 346*
Partridge, Frank C. *190, 193, 313, 375*
Partridge, George *3, 41*
Partridge, James R. *357, 363, 371, 375*
Partridge, Oliver *1*

Partridge, Richard C. *329*
Partridge, Samuel *77*
Partridge, Sidney C. *449, 461*
Parvin, Theophilus *515*
Pasamanick, Benjamin *541*
Paschal, George *397*
Paschal, Thomas M. *135*
Paschall, Davis Y. *406*
Paschall, H. Franklin *475*
Paschang, John L. *468*
Pasco, Samuel *125, 127, 130, 132, 135, 138, 141, 295*
Pashayan, Charles, Jr. *267, 270, 273, 277*
Passman, Otto E. *217, 220, 223, 227, 230, 233, 236, 239, 243, 246, 249, 252, 255, 259, 262*
Pastore, John O. *222, 225, 228, 231, 234, 238, 241, 244, 247, 250, 254, 257, 260, 263, 310*
Pastoriza, Joseph J. *397*
Patch, Alexander M., Jr. *334, 341, 342, 343*
Patch, Joseph D. *342*
Patchen, Kenneth *561*
Pate, Randolph M. *348*
Patel, N. *543*
Paterson, John *48*
Paterson, Katherine W. *546*
Paterson, William *2, 41, 283, 305*
Patman, William N. *273, 276*
Patman, Wright *190, 193, 196, 199, 203, 206, 209, 212, 215, 219, 222, 225, 228, 231, 235, 238, 241, 244, 247, 251, 254, 257, 260, 263*
Patrick, Edwin D. *341*
Patrick, Hugh T. *516*
Patrick, J. Milton *514*
Patrick, John *555*
Patrick, Joseph C. *537*
Patrick, Luther *200, 203, 206, 213*
Patrick, Mason M. *330*
Patridge, Donald B. *191*
Pattangall, William R. *300*
Patten, Edward J. *243, 247, 250, 253, 256, 259, 262, 265, 269*
Patten, Harold A. *219, 222, 226*
Patten, John *3, 42, 43*
Patten, Simon N. *513*
Patten, Thomas G. *160, 163, 166*
Patterson, Alex E. *492*
Patterson, Boyd C. *425*
Patterson, David T. *101, 103, 312*
Patterson, Donis D. *457, 458*
Patterson, Edward G. *394*
Patterson, Edward W. *197, 201*
Patterson, Ellis L. *213*
Patterson, Ernest M. *509*
Patterson, Eugene *556*
Patterson, Francis F., Jr. *173, 176, 179, 182*
Patterson, Frederick B. *493, 525*
Patterson, Frederick D. *417*
Patterson, G. V. *481*
Patterson, George R. *146, 148, 151*
Patterson, George W. *114*
Patterson, Gilbert B. *148, 151*
Patterson, Grove *520*
Patterson, Herbert P. *484*
Patterson, Howard A. *512*
Patterson, Isaac L. *309*
Patterson, J. T. *520*
Patterson, James K. *420*

Patterson, James O. *151, 154, 157*
Patterson, James T. *216, 220, 223, 226, 229, 232*
Patterson, James W. *98, 100, 102, 104, 106, 304*
Patterson, Jefferson *375*
Patterson, Jerry *264*
Patterson, Jerry M. *261, 267, 270, 273*
Patterson, John *61, 335*
Patterson, John D. *395, 512*
Patterson, John H. *493*
Patterson, John J. *109, 112, 114, 311*
Patterson, John L. *420*
Patterson, John M. *291*
Patterson, Joseph W. *389*
Patterson, Josiah *132, 134, 137*
Patterson, LaFayette L. *184, 187, 190*
Patterson, Malcolm R. *146, 149, 152*
Patterson, Neville *302*
Patterson, Paul L. *309*
Patterson, Perry S. *523*
Patterson, Richard C. *374*
Patterson, Richard C., Jr. *363, 376*
Patterson, Robert *517*
Patterson, Robert M. *423, 517*
Patterson, Robert P. *29, 34, 284*
Patterson, Robert U. *332, 488*
Patterson, Robert W. *473*
Patterson, Roscoe C. *176, 188, 192, 195, 303*
Patterson, Thomas *57, 58, 60, 61*
Patterson, Thomas J. *79*
Patterson, Thomas M. *112, 144, 146, 149, 293*
Patterson, W. *423*
Patterson, Walter *60*
Patterson, William *70, 71, 73, 305, 422*
Patterson, William Allen *563*
Patteson, Okey L. *314*
Pattillo, Manning M., Jr. *414*
Pattison, Edward W. *263, 266*
Pattison, John M. *131, 308*
Pattison, Robert E. *309, 406*
Patton, Alexander *394*
Patton, Carl S. *475*
Patton, Charles E. *160, 164*
Patton, Charles H. *512*
Patton, David H. *130*
Patton, Francis L. *414, 473*
Patton, George S., Jr. *332, 333, 334, 341, 343*
Patton, Henry *425*
Patton, Isaac W. *389*
Patton, John *97, 126, 391*
Patton, John, Jr. *133, 301*
Patton, John D. *121*
Patton, John M. *67, 68, 70, 72, 74*
Patton, Kenneth S. *368*
Patton, Leslie K. *417*
Patton, Mrs. James B. *526*
Patton, Nat *199, 203, 206, 209, 212*
Patton, Robert J. *559*
Patton, Robert M. *291*
Patton, Thomas F. *539*
Patton, William M. *410*
Paty, Raymond R. *418*
Patz, Arnall *542, 543*
Paul, Arloe W. *431*
Paul, David *413, 473*
Paul, Henry N. *488*

Paul, James *488*
Paul, James R. *485*
Paul, John *119, 177*
Paul, John J. *470*
Paul, Oglesby *513*
Paul, Ron *266*
Paul, Ronald E. *270, 273, 276*
Paul, Thomas *477*
Paul, Willard S. *329, 342, 409*
Paulding, James K. *24, 35*
Paulding, William *393*
Paulding, William, Jr. *52*
Paulen, Ben S. *297*
Pauli, Wolfgang *549*
Paulin, Richard C. *443*
Pauling, Linus *511, 548, 549, 550, 553*
Paullin, James E. *515*
Paulling, J. Randolph, Jr. *562*
Pauly, John W. *346*
Paund, Louise *524*
Pawley, William D. *357, 370*
Pawling, Levi *57*
Paxson, Edward M. *309*
Paxson, Frederic L. *513, 553*
Paxton, Harold W. *534*
Paxton, Robert *488*
Paxton, William M. *473*
Paykel, Eugene S. *539*
Payne, D. A. *426*
Payne, Eugene Gray *557*
Payne, Fernandus *520*
Payne, Frederick G. *227, 230, 233, 299, 389*
Payne, Henry B. *112, 123, 126, 128, 308*
Payne, Henry C. *27, 36*
Payne, John *447*
Payne, John B. *28, 36*
Payne, John Barton *516*
Payne, Ladell *415*
Payne, Melvin M. *526*
Payne, Milton J. *392*
Payne, Nathan F. *394*
Payne, Sereno E. *121, 123, 128, 131, 134, 137, 139, 142, 145, 148, 151, 154, 157, 160, 163*
Payne, Virginia *503*
Payne, William M. *76, 78, 79*
Paynter, Lemuel *73, 75*
Paynter, Samuel *294*
Paynter, Thomas H. *127, 130, 133, 153, 156, 159, 298*
Payson, Lewis E. *117, 120, 122, 125, 127*
Payton, Benjamin F. *417*
Payton, Daniel *395*
Payton, Robert L. *357, 410, 432*
Peabody, Charles *492*
Peabody, Charles A. *490*
Peabody, Endicott *301*
Peabody, Francis *439*
Peabody, George *540*
Peabody, James H. *293*
Peabody, Malcolm E. *452, 458*
Peabody, Nathaniel *3*
Peabody, Paul E. *341*
Peabody, Robert B. *514*
Peabody, Robert S. *514*
Peabody, Selim H. *419, 441*
Peace, Roger C. *209, 311*
Peacock, Leslie C. *486*
Peak, John L. *373*
Peake, Alonzo W. *482*
Peale, Norman Vincent *548, 553, 560*
Pearce, Charles C. *387*
Pearce, Charles E. *139, 142*
Pearce, Charles S. *485*

Pierce, Franklin *11, 15, 25, 69, 71, 73, 75, 76, 304*
Pierce, George E. *426*
Pierce, George F. *408, 471*
Pierce, George W. *539, 541*
Pierce, Gilbert A. *128, 307, 370*
Pierce, Henry A. *363*
Pierce, Henry L. *108, 111, 390*
Pierce, Henry N. *448, 458*
Pierce, John L. *343*
Pierce, John R. *538, 541, 548*
Pierce, Joseph *47*
Pierce, Lawrence W. *284*
Pierce, P. E. *330*
Pierce, Ray V. *116*
Pierce, Rice A. *121, 129, 132, 140, 143, 146, 149*
Pierce, Robert B. F. *117*
Pierce, Samuel R., Jr. *32, 38*
Pierce, W. E. *388*
Pierce, Wallace E. *205*
Pierce, Walter M. *196, 199, 202, 205, 209, 309*
Pierce, William *2, 3*
Pierce, William H. *524*
Pierce, Winslow S. *498*
Piercy, George T. *434*
Pierpoint, John *313*
Pierpoint, Paul *514*
Pierpont, Francis H. *313*
Pierrepont, Edwards *26, 35, 362*
Pierson, Abraham *427*
Pierson, Albert *331*
Pierson, Fritz A. *512*
Pierson, Isaac *64, 66*
Pierson, J. Willis *524*
Pierson, Jeremiah H. *60*
Pierson, Job *68, 69*
Pierson, Lewis E. *510, 522*
Pierson, W. W., Jr. *421*
Pierson, Warren L. *379*
Pietenpol, Clarence J. *407*
Piez, Charles *520*
Pifer, Alan *431*
Pigman, Herbert A. *528*
Pigott, James P. *132*
Pigott, R. J. S. *520*
Pigott, Reginald J. S. *537*
Pigott, Stephen J. *533*
Pike, Austin F. *109, 121, 123, 305*
Pike, Frederick A. *96, 98, 100, 102*
Pike, James *90, 92*
Pike, James A. *454, 458*
Pike, James S. *368*
Pike, Jarvis *394*
Pike, Otis G. *240, 244, 247, 250, 253, 256, 259, 263, 266*
Pike, Sumner T. *379*
Pike, Zebulon *335*
Pike, Zebulon M. *330, 331*
Pilarczyk, Daniel E. *464*
Pilch, John J. *505*
Pilcher, John L. *226, 229, 232, 236, 239, 242*
Pilcher, W. S. *389*
Pile, William A. *102, 375*
Piles, Samuel H. *152, 155, 158, 314, 359*
Pilgard, John A. *387*
Pilgrim, Charles W. *518*
Pilie, Louis H. *514*
Pilla, Anthony M. *469*
Pillard, Charles H. *504*
Pilliod, Charles J., Jr. *489*
Pillion, John R. *227, 231, 234, 237, 240, 244*
Pillsbury, George A. *391, 392*
Pillsbury, Gilbert *396*
Pillsbury, John E. *349, 526*

Pillsbury, John S. *301, 494*
Pillsbury, Philip W. *494*
Pillsbury, Walter B. *518*
Pilpel, Harriet F. *560*
Pilsbry, Henry A. *543*
Pilsbury, Edward *389*
Pilsbury, Timothy *81, 83*
Pimentel, George C. *539, 549*
Pimper, James L. *379*
Pina, Hugo Luis *457*
Pinasco, John *422*
Pinchback, P. B. S. *299*
Pinchot, Gifford *309, 559*
Pinckney, Charles *2, 4, 45, 46, 47, 58, 310, 311, 373*
Pinckney, Charles C. *2, 14, 528*
Pinckney, Henry L. *70, 72, 396*
Pinckney, John A. *455, 461*
Pinckney, Joseph C. *521*
Pinckney, Thomas *6, 14, 45, 46, 362, 373, 528*
Pindall, James *57, 59*
Pindall, Xenophon *292*
Pindar, John S. *123, 128*
Pine, James *417*
Pine, William B. *183, 186, 189, 308*
Ping, Charles J. *414, 417*
Pingree, David *390*
Pingree, H. S. *391*
Pingree, Hazen S. *301*
Pingree, Samuel E. *313*
Pinkel, Donald *543*
Pinkerton, Lowell C. *364, 366, 373*
Pinkham, William P. *408*
Pinkney, Robert F. *324*
Pinkney, William *23, 24, 34, 42, 55, 58, 59, 300, 362, 371, 372, 390, 448, 459*
Pinney, J. A. *388*
Pinney, Silas U. *398*
Pinnock, Thomas C. *390*
Pinten, Joseph G. *467, 470*
Pinter, Lawrence J. *443*
Piotrowski, John L. *346*
Piper, James H. *423*
Piper, Jane *560*
Piper, Larry G. *362*
Piper, William *53, 54, 55*
Piper, William A. *110*
Pirce, William A. *124*
Pirie, Robert B. *348*
Pirnie, Alexander *237, 240, 244, 247, 250, 253, 256*
Pirnie, Malcolm *519, 541*
Piskor, Frank P. *415*
Piston, Walter *535, 555, 556*
Pitaval, John B. *464*
Pitblado, John M. *492*
Pitcairn, Harold *536*
Pitcairn, John *494*
Pitcher, James *385*
Pitcher, Nathaniel *58, 60, 68, 306*
Pitcher, Thomas G. *418*
Pitcher, Zina *390, 391, 515*
Pitchford, John H. *308*
Pitelka, F. *535*
Pithan, Athalicio T. *453*
Pitkin, Albert J. *544*
Pitkin, Frederick W. *293*
Pitkin, John R. G. *355*
Pitkin, Timothy *48, 50, 51, 52, 53, 54, 56*
Pitkin, William *1, 5, 7*
Pitman, Charles W. *85*
Pitman-Gelles, Bonnie *443*
Pitney, Mahlon *137, 139, 283*
Pitot, James *389*
Pittenger, Lemuel A. *404, 410*

Pittenger, William A. *188, 191, 198, 204, 208, 211, 214*
Pittman, Beatrice T. *476*
Pittman, Hobson *536, 560*
Pittman, Key *160, 163, 166, 169, 173, 176, 179, 182, 185, 188, 192, 193, 195, 196, 198, 200, 201, 203, 205, 304*
Pittman, Vail M. *304*
Pitts, Herman C. *511*
Pitts, Robert F. *517*
Pitzer, K. S. *549*
Pitzer, Kenneth S. *415, 416, 532, 553*
Pixley, Charles C. *332*
Pizer, Laurence R. *527*
Place, John B. M. *482, 486*
Plagens, Joseph C. *467*
Plaisted, Frederick W. *299, 389*
Plaisted, Harris M. *111, 299*
Plank, E. T. *505*
Plant, David *64*
Plants, Tobias A. *100, 102*
Plantz, Samuel *411*
Plass, Norman *425*
Plassmann, Thomas *415*
Plate, Douglas C. *348*
Plate, Walter *536*
Plater, George *3, 300*
Plater, Thomas *46, 48*
Plath, Sylvia *558*
Platner, Samuel B. *517*
Platt, Charles Adams *547*
Platt, Edmund *163, 166, 170, 173*
Platt, James H., Jr. *105, 107, 110*
Platt, Jonas *46*
Platt, Nicholas *376*
Platt, Orville H. *115, 117, 120, 122, 124, 127, 130, 132, 135, 138, 141, 144, 147, 149, 294*
Platt, Robert B. *522*
Platt, Rutherford *535*
Platt, Thomas C. *109, 111, 139, 142, 145, 148, 151, 154, 306*
Platt, Zephaniah *4*
Platten, Donald C. *484*
Platten, John W. *484*
Platts, John H. *499*
Plauche, Vance *207*
Pleasant, Ruffin G. *299*
Pleasanton, Alfred *337*
Pleasants, James *53, 54, 56, 57, 59, 60, 313, 314*
Pleasants, James J., Jr. *396*
Pleasonton, Alfred *380*
Plehn, Carl C. *513*
Pleissner, Ogden *533*
Plimpton, Calvin H. *403*
Plitt, Edwin A. *367*
Ploeser, Walter C. *208, 211, 214, 217, 359, 369*
Ploscowe, Morris *559*
Plowman, Thomas S. *138*
Plumb, Preston B. *113, 115, 118, 120, 122, 125, 127, 130, 298*
Plumb, Ralph *122, 125*
Plumer, Arnold *73, 77*
Plumer, George *60, 61, 63*
Plumer, William *47, 48, 49, 304*
Plumer, William, Jr. *58, 59, 61*
Plumer, William S. *473*
Plumley, Charles A. *196, 199, 203, 206, 209, 212, 216, 219, 222, 414*
Plumley, Frank *158, 161, 164*
Plumley, H. Ladd *497, 522*
Plummer, Edward H. *339*
Plummer, Franklin E. *67, 69*

Plummer, Mary W. *515*
Plumsted, Clement *395*
Plumsted, William *395*
Plunkett, Robert *409*
Plunkett, Willis H. *385*
Plyler, John P. *408*
Poage, William R. *203, 206, 209, 212, 215, 219, 222, 225, 228, 231, 235, 238, 241, 244, 247, 251, 254, 257, 260, 263, 266*
Podell, Bertram L. *250, 253, 256, 259*
Poe, Bryce, II *346*
Poe, Edgar Allan *540*
Poe, Philip L. *522*
Poehler, Henry *116*
Poelker, John *392*
Poetker, Albert H. *419*
Poff, Richard H. *228, 232, 235, 238, 241, 244, 248, 251, 254, 257*
Poffenberger, Albert T. *518*
Pogue, L. Welch *525*
Pohl, Frederik *546*
Pohl, LaVera *440*
Pohlman, Julius *438*
Poillon, Howard A. *433*
Poindexter, George *56, 66, 67, 68, 69, 302*
Poindexter, Miles *158, 161, 164, 167, 171, 174, 177, 314, 370*
Poinsett, Joel R. *24, 34, 60, 62, 63, 367*
Pointer, Sam C. *287*
Poland, Luke P. *101, 103, 105, 107, 110, 122, 313*
Poland, Reginald *439*
Poland, Reginald R. *438, 443*
Poletti, Charles *306*
Polier, Justine Wise *559*
Poling, Harold A. *488*
Politz, Henry A. *285*
Polk, Albert F. *168*
Polk, Charles *294*
Polk, Frank L. *526*
Polk, James G. *192, 195, 199, 202, 205, 221, 225, 228, 231, 234, 237*
Polk, James H. *332*
Polk, James K. *11, 15, 25, 63, 65, 67, 68, 70, 72, 74, 311*
Polk, James R. *557*
Polk, Leonidas *322, 323, 447, 458, 459*
Polk, Rufus K. *143, 146*
Polk, Sylvanus *396*
Polk, Trusten *92, 94, 96, 302, 303*
Polk, William H. *87, 372*
Pollack, Jerome M. *408*
Pollack, William *543*
Pollard, Charles L. *443*
Pollard, Ernest M. *151, 154*
Pollard, H. Marvin *511*
Pollard, Henry M. *113*
Pollard, John G. *313*
Pollard, Mrs. John Garland *443*
Pollard, Ramsey *475*
Pollard, Richard *358*
Pollock, Howard W. *248, 251*
Pollock, James *79, 81, 83, 309*
Pollock, James K. *517*
Pollock, Lewis J. *516*
Pollock, P. D. *412*
Pollock, Thomas *5, 6*
Pollock, Thomas C. *474*
Pollock, William *505*
Pollock, William P. *170, 311*
Polsgrove, James *389*
Polsley, Daniel H. *103*

Pomerene, Atlee *160, 163, 167, 170, 173, 176, 308*
Pomeroy, Allan *398*
Pomeroy, Charles *104*
Pomeroy, Samuel C. *95, 98, 99, 101, 104, 106, 298*
Pomeroy, Seth *335*
Pomeroy, Theodore M. *96, 98, 100, 101, 102*
Pomfret, John E. *406, 439*
Pond, Benjamin *52*
Pond, Charles H. *293*
Pond, Edward B. *386*
Pond, Irving K. *514*
Pond, M. Allen *561*
Pond, Theodore H. *437, 438*
Ponder, James *294*
Pontius, Clarence I. *423*
Pool, Eugene H. *512*
Pool, Joe R. *244, 247, 251*
Pool, John *102, 105, 107, 307*
Pool, Solomon S. *421*
Pool, Walter F. *121*
Poole, Abram *531*
Poole, Cecil F. *286*
Poole, Ernest *553*
Poole, Harry *503*
Poole, John *527*
Poole, R. F. *406*
Poole, Theodore L. *137*
Poole, William F. *513, 514*
Pooler, J. S. *554*
Poor, Alfred E. *525*
Poor, Anne *531*
Poor, Enoch *335*
Poor, Henry V. *551*
Pope, Arthur *439*
Pope, Bayard F. *548*
Pope, Charles A. *515*
Pope, Clarence C. *459*
Pope, Clarence Cullam, Jr. *457*
Pope, George *525*
Pope, J. P. *388*
Pope, Jack *312*
Pope, Jack M. *488*
Pope, James P. *194, 197, 200, 296*
Pope, James S. *520, 544*
Pope, John *50, 51, 52, 72, 74, 76, 298, 335, 336*
Pope, John A. *439*
Pope, O. C. *409*
Pope, Patrick H. *69*
Pope, W. Kenneth *472*
Pope, Walter L. *285*
Pope, Willia T. *419*
Pope, Young J. *311*
Popejoy, Thomas L. *421*
Popham, William *528*
Popma, Alfred M. *511*
Poppen, Emanuel *476*
Popper, David H. *358, 359*
Poppleton, Earley F. *112*
Porada, Edith *533*
Port, Martin *405*
Porter, A. W. Noel *452, 460*
Porter, Albert G. *93, 95, 297, 365*
Porter, Alexander *69, 71, 299*
Porter, Augustus A. *390*
Porter, Augustus S. *75, 76, 78, 301*
Porter, Charles H. *105, 107*
Porter, Charles O. *234, 237*
Porter, Charles T. *539*
Porter, D. T. *396*
Porter, Daniel R., III *442*
Porter, David *350, 374*
Porter, David D. *349, 350, 418*
Porter, David H. *406*
Porter, David R. *309*

Porter, De Forest *385*
Porter, Dean A. *443*
Porter, Dwight J. *366*
Porter, Fitz-John *336*
Porter, Frank M. *516*
Porter, Gilchrist *86, 90*
Porter, Henry Kirke *148*
Porter, Horace *526*
Porter, James *57*
Porter, James D. *311, 358*
Porter, James M. *24, 34*
Porter, John *49, 50, 51*
Porter, John C. *386*
Porter, John E. *271, 274, 277*
Porter, Joseph E. *490*
Porter, Katherine Anne *535, 545, 547, 556*
Porter, Keith R. *549, 551*
Porter, Lawrence C. *528*
Porter, Lester G. *484*
Porter, Marshall M. *527*
Porter, Noah *427*
Porter, Paul A. *379*
Porter, Peter A. *154*
Porter, Peter B. *24, 34, 51, 52, 55*
Porter, Quincy *555*
Porter, Ray E. *330, 342*
Porter, Robert W., Jr. *333*
Porter, Stephen G. *160, 164, 167, 170, 173, 177, 180, 183, 186, 189*
Porter, Timothy H. *63*
Porter, William H. *484*
Porter, William J. *355, 358, 367, 371, 372*
Porter, William N. *331*
Porterfield, John D. *518*
Porterfield, Robert *558*
Porteus, Morgan *456, 458*
Porth, J. P. *391*
Portier, Michael *465*
Posey, Francis B. *125*
Posey, Thomas *52, 299*
Posner, Richard A. *285*
Pospisilik, Theophilus *415*
Possehl, John *505*
Post, A. M. *304*
Post, Avery *475*
Post, George A. *121*
Post, George B. *514, 532*
Post, James D. *160, 163*
Post, James H. *548*
Post, Jothan, Jr. *54*
Post, Levi A. *517*
Post, Philip S. *125, 127, 130, 133*
Post, Robert Morton *539*
Posvar, Wesley W. *422*
Pote, Harold W. *487*
Pote, Lloyd W. *486*
Poteat, Edwin McN. *408*
Poteat, Hubert M. *527*
Poteat, William L. *425*
Pothier, Aram J. *310*
Potofsky, Jacob S. *503*
Pott, John *6*
Pott, W. S. A. *408*
Potter, A. A. *520*
Potter, Allen *111*
Potter, Alonzo *447, 460*
Potter, Charles E. *217, 220, 224, 227, 230, 233, 301*
Potter, Charles N. *315*
Potter, Clarkson N. *104, 107, 109, 114, 511*
Potter, David M. *513, 544, 557*
Potter, Eliphalet N. *410, 417*
Potter, Elisha R. *44, 45, 52, 53, 54*
Potter, Elisha R., Jr. *79*

Potter, Emery D. *79, 84*
Potter, George W. *554*
Potter, Henry C. *449, 460*
Potter, Horatio *448, 460*
Potter, Howard *533*
Potter, Howard W. *503*
Potter, John F. *93, 95, 97*
Potter, John M. *410*
Potter, Michael *543*
Potter, Orlando B. *121*
Potter, Robert *66, 68*
Potter, Robert B. *337, 338*
Potter, Samuel J. *48, 310*
Potter, William *365*
Potter, William K. *395*
Potter, William P. *349*
Potter, William W. *73*
Potthast, Edward H. *536*
Pottle, Emory B. *92, 94*
Potts, Charles E. *414*
Potts, David, Jr. *68, 70, 72, 73*
Potts, David M. *218*
Potts, Frederick A. *494*
Potts, R. D. *351*
Potts, Richard *3, 42, 43, 300*
Potts, Stacy *392*
Potts, Thomas R. *391*
Potts, William E. *329*
Potzger, John E. *522*
Pou, Edward W. *145, 148, 151, 154, 157, 160, 163, 166, 170, 173, 176, 179, 182, 186, 189, 192, 195*
Pouch, Mrs. William H. *526*
Pough, Frederick H. *443*
Poullada, Leon B. *374*
Poulson, Norris *210, 216, 219, 223, 226, 386*
Poulton, Bruce R. *413, 421*
Pouncey, Peter R. *403*
Pound, Cuthbert W. *306*
Pound, Ezra *531, 534*
Pound, Roscoe *509, 532*
Pound, Thaddeus C. *115, 117, 119*
Pousette-Dart, Richard *536*
Povish, Kenneth *467*
Povish, Kenneth J. *467*
Powel, C. A. *523*
Powel, Samuel *395*
Powell, A. M. *394*
Powell, Adam Clayton *240, 244, 247, 250, 253*
Powell, Adam Clayton, Jr. *215, 218, 221, 224, 227, 231, 234, 237*
Powell, Alfred H. *63*
Powell, Ben H., III *527*
Powell, Benjamin E. *515*
Powell, Chilton *454, 460*
Powell, Cuthbert *77*
Powell, David *259*
Powell, Dawn *562*
Powell, E. Burnley *533*
Powell, E. I. *476*
Powell, Earl A., III *440*
Powell, Herbert B. *332, 333, 368*
Powell, J. W. *509*
Powell, James L. *408, 414*
Powell, James W. *521*
Powell, John W. *380*
Powell, Joseph *112*
Powell, Lazarus W. *93, 95, 98, 298*
Powell, Leonard J. *423*
Powell, Levin *46*
Powell, Lewis F., Jr. *283, 511, 512, 532*
Powell, Lyman P. *410*
Powell, Noble C. *453, 459*

Powell, Paulus *85, 87, 89, 91, 93*
Powell, Peter John *547*
Powell, Radford G. *503*
Powell, Samuel *56*
Powell, Sumner Chilton *556*
Powell, Theophilus O. *518*
Powell, Thomas R. *517*
Powell, Vic *525*
Powell, Walter E. *257, 260*
Powell, Wesley *304*
Powell, William F. *360, 363*
Powelson, W. V. N. *498*
Power, Cornelius M. *464, 470*
Power, Dennis M. *443, 516*
Power, F. D. *476*
Power, J. B. *413*
Power, John J., Jr. *494*
Power, Thomas C. *131, 134, 303*
Power, Thomas S. *346*
Power, W. *408*
Powers, Abigail *20*
Powers, Caleb *159, 162, 165, 169*
Powers, Charles A. *511*
Powers, D. Lane *195, 198, 201, 205, 208, 211, 214*
Powers, E. B. *522*
Powers, George M. *313*
Powers, Gershom *66*
Powers, Grover F. *534*
Powers, H. Henry *132, 135, 137, 140, 143*
Powers, J. D. *510*
Powers, J. F. *545*
Powers, James E. *514*
Powers, James K. *418*
Powers, John J., Jr. *494*
Powers, Joseph N. *420*
Powers, Justin L. *559*
Powers, Llewellyn *113, 144, 147, 150, 153, 299*
Powers, Richard *560*
Powers, Ridgley C. *302*
Powers, Ronald *557*
Powers, Samuel L. *144, 147*
Powers, Sanger B. *512*
Powers, Sidney *510*
Powers, Thomas *557*
Powers, Thomas C. *128*
Powers, Winn *391*
Pownall, Thomas *5*
Pownall, Thomas G. *491*
Poynter, William A. *303*
Pracht, C. Frederick *212*
Prados, John W. *423*
Prall, Anning S. *179, 182, 186, 189, 192, 195, 379*
Prasse, Arthur T. *512*
Prather, William L. *423*
Prator, Ralph *405*
Pratt, Benjamin *7*
Pratt, Charles *414*
Pratt, Charles C. *157*
Pratt, Daniel D. *103, 106, 108, 297, 380*
Pratt, E. Spencer *369*
Pratt, Edmund T. *494*
Pratt, Edmund T., Jr. *494*
Pratt, Eliza Jane *215*
Pratt, Frederick *444*
Pratt, George C. *284*
Pratt, George O., Jr. *443*
Pratt, Haraden *541*
Pratt, Harcourt J. *182, 186, 189, 192*
Pratt, Harry H. *166, 170*
Pratt, Harry N. *438*
Pratt, Henry C. *340*
Pratt, Henry O. *108, 110*

Pratt, Hiram *393*
Pratt, James T. *87*
Pratt, John *330, 407*
Pratt, Joseph M. *212*
Pratt, Le Gage *154*
Pratt, Nathan P. *409*
Pratt, Perry W. *540, 561*
Pratt, Richard T. *379*
Pratt, Richardson, Jr. *414*
Pratt, Robert *391*
Pratt, Ruth S. B. *189,. 192*
Pratt, Thomas G. *84, 86, 88, 90, 300*
Pratt, Wallace E. *510, 533, 545, 552*
Pratt, Walter M. *522, 523*
Pratt, William V. *347, 352*
Pratt, Zadock *73, 79*
Pratte, Bernard *392*
Pray, Charles N. *154, 157, 160*
Pray, James S. *520*
Preble, William P. *368*
Predergast, Edmond F. *464*
Pree, William A. D. *368*
Preeg, Ernest *363*
Pregerson, Harry *286*
Prellwitz, Henry *536*
Prenter, William B. *503*
Prentice, Donald B. *411*
Prentice, Samuel O. *294*
Prentis, H. W., Jr. *525*
Prentis, Robert R. *314*
Prentiss, Benjamin M. *336*
Prentiss, John H. *73, 75*
Prentiss, Samuel *68, 70, 72, 74, 75, 77, 313*
Prentiss, Sergeant S. *73*
Prentiss, William A. *398*
Prescott, Albert B. *509, 511*
Prescott, Benjamin F. *304*
Prescott, Cyrus D. *116, 118*
Prescott, Henry W. *517*
Prescott, Kenneth W. *441*
Prescott, Stedman *300*
Prescott, W. B. *505*
Press, Ernst *475*
Presser, Jackie *504*
Pressey, Julia C. *538*
Pressler, Larry *263, 266, 269, 272, 276, 279, 311*
Pressly, John T. *473*
Preston, Francis *43, 44*
Preston, G. Merritt *562*
Preston, Jacob A. *78*
Preston, James H. *390, 526*
Preston, James P. *313*
Preston, John F. *331*
Preston, Maurice A. *346*
Preston, Miles B. *386*
Preston, Prince H., Jr. *216, 220, 223, 226, 229, 232, 236*
Preston, Robert J. *518*
Preston, Samuel *395*
Preston, Thomas J., Jr. *425*
Preston, Thomas R. *510*
Preston, Walter *320, 321*
Preston, Willard *423*
Preston, William *86, 88, 323, 373*
Preston, William B. *25, 35, 83, 320*
Preston, William C. *70, 72, 73, 75, 77, 311, 396, 422*
Prestopino, Gregorio *531*
Prettyman, Cornelius W. *407*
Prettyman, E. Barrett *286*
Preus, David W. *476*
Preus, Jacob A. O. *301, 475*
Preuss, Edward *542*
Prewitt, Alan M. *312*

Preyer, L. Richardson *253, 256, 260, 263, 266, 269, 431*
Price, Alan *560*
Price, Andrew *128, 130, 133, 136, 495*
Price, Andrew, Jr. *495*
Price, Byron *554*
Price, C. Melvin *255, 258, 261, 264, 268, 271, 274*
Price, Charles C. *511*
Price, Charles H. *362*
Price, Charles H., II *356*
Price, Don K. *434, 510*
Price, Emory H. *210, 213, 216*
Price, Gwilym A. *499, 539*
Price, Harvey L. *521*
Price, Hiram *97, 99, 113, 115*
Price, Hollis F. *475*
Price, Hugh H. *124*
Price, James F. *419*
Price, James H. *313*
Price, James L. *308*
Price, Jesse D. *162, 166, 169*
Price, John G. *521*
Price, Larry *558*
Price, Larry C. *558*
Price, Leontyne *552, 561*
Price, Malcolm *421*
Price, Melvin *213, 217, 220, 223, 226, 229, 233, 236, 239, 242, 246, 249, 252, 277*
Price, Mrs. Holton R., Jr. *523*
Price, Naomi *476*
Price, Robert D. *251, 254, 257, 260*
Price, Robert M. *486*
Price, Robert T. *298*
Price, Rodman M. *86, 305*
Price, Samuel *112, 314*
Price, Sterling *80, 302, 322*
Price, Thomas C. *96, 391*
Price, Thomas R. *524*
Price, William C. *381*
Price, William J. *369*
Price, William P. *103, 106*
Price, William T. *122, 124*
Prichard, Vernon E. *343*
Prickett, Fay B. *342, 343*
Prickett, H. E. *388*
Pride, Alfred M. *348*
Pridemore, Auburn L. *114*
Pridgeon, John, Jr. *391*
Pridmore, Howard J. *431*
Priest, Degory *1*
Priest, I. G. *527*
Priest, Ira A. *418*
Priest, Ivy Baker *381*
Priest, J. Percy *209, 212, 215, 219, 222, 225, 228, 231*
Priest, John W. *388*
Priestley, James T. *512*
Prieur, Denis *389*
Prime, S. Irenaeus *425*
Primeau, Ernest J. *468*
Primm, James N. *410*
Primo, Quintin E., Jr. *456*
Prince, Charles H. *101*
Prince, David C. *523, 543*
Prince, Frederick H. *483*
Prince, Frederick O. *390*
Prince, George W. *136, 138, 141, 144, 147, 150, 153, 156, 159*
Prince, John D. *360, 372, 376*
Prince, John S. *391*
Prince, Morton *516*
Prince, Oliver H. *64, 295*
Prince, Thomas *5*
Prince, Thomas A. *385*
Prince, William *61*
Prince, William Wood *482, 483*

Prindle, Elizur H. *107*
Prine, Margaret *475*
Pringey, Joseph C. *176*
Pringle, Benjamin *88, 90*
Pringle, Edward E. *293*
Pringle, George H. *492*
Pringle, Henry F. *554*
Pringle, James R. *396*
Pringle, Joel R. P. *352*
Pringle, William H. *523*
Prioleau, Samuel *396*
Prior, Frank O. *482*
Prior, Harris K. *440*
Pritchard, George M. *189*
Pritchard, James B. *533*
Pritchard, Jeter C. *134, 137, 140, 142, 145, 284, 307*
Pritchard, Joel *263, 267, 270, 273, 276*
Pritchard, Jule O. *524*
Pritchard, Ross *419*
Pritchard, Stuart *432*
Pritchard, Thomas H. *425*
Pritchett, C. Herman *518*
Pritchett, Harold *505*
Pritchett, Henry S. *412, 431*
Pritzlaff, John C., Jr. *367*
Probst, Charles O. *518*
Probst, Gerald G. *496*
Prochnow, Herbert V. *488*
Procknow, Donald E. *499*
Procter, William A. *495*
Procter, William C. *495*
Proctor, Carlton S. *519*
Proctor, Fletcher D. *313*
Proctor, James M. *286*
Proctor, John R. *380*
Proctor, Mortimer R. *313*
Proctor, Ralph E. *387*
Proctor, Redfield *27, 34, 132, 135, 137, 140, 143, 146, 149, 152, 155, 313*
Proctor, W. Theodore *387*
Proffit, George H. *74, 76, 357*
Proffitt, David W. *473*
Prohaska, Ray *562*
Prokop, Ruth T. *380*
Prokop, Stanley A. *238*
Prokosch, Eduard *524*
Promisel, Nathan E. *519*
Prosser, C. Ladd *517, 520*
Prosser, Sewart *483*
Prosser, William F. *105*
Proudfit, Andrew *398*
Prout, Frank J. *404*
Prouty, George H. *313*
Prouty, Solomon F. *159, 162*
Prouty, Winston L. *225, 228, 232, 235, 238, 241, 244, 248, 251, 254, 257, 313*
Provoost, David *393*
Provoost, Samuel *447, 460*
Provosty, Olivier O. *299*
Proxmire, William *235, 238, 241, 245, 248, 251, 254, 257, 260, 264, 267, 270, 273, 276, 279, 315*
Pruden, Edward H. *475*
Prudhomme, Charles *533*
Prugh, George S. *331*
Pruis, John J. *404*
Pruitt, Robert G. *521*
Prusoff, Brigitte *539*
Prussia, Leland S. *483*
Pruter, Richard W. *512*
Pruyn, John V. L. *98, 102*
Pruyn, Robert H. *365*
Pruyn, Robert L. *389*
Pryer, Thomas M. *472*
Pryor, David *267, 270, 273, 276, 292*

Pryor, David H. *248, 251, 254*
Pryor, Luke *115, 119, 291*
Pryor, Roger A. *95, 320, 321*
Pryor, Samuel B. *397*
Pryor, Thomas M. *472*
Puchta, George *394*
Pucinski, Roman C. *236, 239, 242, 246, 249, 252, 255*
Puck, Theodore *543*
Puelicher, John H. *510*
Pugh, George E. *90, 92, 94, 308*
Pugh, Herbert L. *347*
Pugh, James L. *93, 115, 117, 119, 122, 124, 127, 129, 132, 135, 291, 320, 321*
Pugh, John *49, 50*
Pugh, John H. *114*
Pugh, Robert L. *367*
Pugh, Samuel J. *136, 139, 141*
Pugsley, Cornelius A. *145, 526*
Pugsley, Jacob J. *126, 129*
Puhan, Alfred *364*
Puiseup, Roberts *561*
Pujo, Arsene P. *147, 150, 153, 156, 159*
Puleston, Dennis *552*
Puleston, W. D. *347*
Pulitzer, Joseph *123*
Pullen, Eugene H. *510*
Pulliam, Roscoe *416*
Pulliam, Samuel *398*
Pulliam, Walter B. *475*
Pulsifer, Harold T. *527*
Pumpelly, Raphael *523*
Pupin, Michael I. *510, 537, 538, 539, 541, 548, 553*
Purcell, Clare *471*
Purcell, Dale *426*
Purcell, Edward M. *517, 549, 550*
Purcell, Ganson *381*
Purcell, Graham *241, 244, 248, 251, 254, 257*
Purcell, John B. *426, 464, 469*
Purcell, R. R. *392*
Purcell, William E. *157, 307*
Purcifull, Robert O. *494*
Purdom, P. Walton *518*
Purdom, W. A. *391*
Purdy, Lawson *526*
Purdy, Smith M. *79*
Purinton, Daniel B. *407, 425, 426*
Purman, William J. *108, 110*
Purnell, Benjamin *477*
Purnell, Fred S. *168, 172, 175, 178, 181, 184, 188, 191*
Purnell, William H. *419*
Pursell, Carl D. *265, 268, 271, 274, 278*
Pursley, Leo Aloysius *466*
Purtell, William A. *226, 229, 232, 294*
Purviance, Samuel A. *90, 92*
Purviance, Samuel D. *48*
Puryear, Bennett *422*
Puryear, Charles *416*
Puryear, R. C. *320*
Puryear, Richard C. *88, 90*
Pusey, Merlo J. *534, 555*
Pusey, Nathan M. *409, 411, 432, 548*
Pusey, William A. *515*
Pusey, William H. M. *120*
Pusey, William W., III *425*
Pushkarev, Boris *545*
Pustay, John S. *351*
Putman, Frederick *460*
Putman, Frederick W., Jr. *455*
Putnam, Allan Ray *519*

Putnam, C. A. *525*
Putnam, Daniel *411*
Putnam, Emily James (Smith) *404*
Putnam, F. W. *510*
Putnam, Frederic W. *440, 442*
Putnam, George W., Jr. *344*
Putnam, Harvey *73, 82, 84*
Putnam, Herbert *380, 515, 543, 559*
Putnam, Israel *335*
Putnam, James J. *516*
Putnam, James O. *356, 416*
Putnam, James W. *405, 516*
Putnam, Rufus *331*
Putnam, William L. *284*
Putt, Donald R. *346*
Pye, William S. *352*
Pyle, Ernest T. (Ernie) *554*
Pyle, Gladys *202, 311*
Pyle, Howard *291*
Pyle, Howard C. *514*
Pyles, Thomas *512*
Pynchon, David M. *441*
Pynchon, Thomas *541, 546, 560*
Pynchon, Thomas R. *417*
Pyne, Percy R. *485*
Qua, Stanley E. *301*
Quackenbush, John A. *128, 131*
Quain, Edwin A. *409*
Quainton, Anthony C. *365*
Quainton, Anthony C. E. *358, 368*
Quarles, Donald A. *327, 523, 552*
Quarles, James M. *95*
Quarles, Joseph V. *143, 146, 149, 315*
Quarles, Julian M. *143*
Quarles, Louis *431*
Quarles, Tunstall *56, 58*
Quarry, Robert *6*
Quarter, William *466*
Quarterman, George H. *453, 460*
Quay, Matthew S. *126, 129, 131, 134, 137, 140, 143, 145, 148, 309*
Quayle, Dan *271, 274, 277, 297*
Quayle, J. Danforth *265, 268*
Quayle, John F. *179, 182, 186, 189*
Quayle, William A. *404, 471*
Queen, Frank B. *519*
Queen, Stuart A. *520*
Queenan, John W. *514*
Queeny, Edgar Monsanto *492*
Queeny, John F. *492*
Queneau, Paul *538*
Quenstedt, Walter E. *390*
Quesada, Elwood R. *346*
Quie, Albert H. *233, 236, 240, 243, 246, 249, 253, 256, 259, 262, 265, 302*
Quigg, Donald J. *381*
Quigg, Lemuel E. *134, 137, 139*
Quigley, Donn P. *441*
Quigley, James E. *463, 468*
Quigley, James M. *231, 238*
Quill, Michael J. *505*
Quillen, James H. *244, 247, 251, 254, 257, 260, 266, 269, 273, 276, 279*
Quimby, J. A. *386*
Quimby, J. F. *337*
Quin, C. K. *397*
Quin, Clinton S. *451, 461*
Quin, Percy E. *163, 166, 169, 172, 176, 179, 182, 185, 191*
Quinby, Henry B. *304*
Quinby, William E. *368*

Quincy, Josiah *49, 50, 51, 52, 390, 409*
Quincy, Josiah, Jr. *390*
Quincy, Samuel M. *389*
Quine, Willard V. *536*
Quinette, E. N. *398*
Quinlan, Francis J. *542*
Quinlan, John *465*
Quinlan, Patrick J. *505*
Quinlin, Simon *521*
Quinn, Daniel J. *408*
Quinn, Francis A. *465*
Quinn, Huston *389*
Quinn, J. Herbert *392*
Quinn, James L. *199, 202, 441*
Quinn, Jarus W. *527*
Quinn, John *128*
Quinn, John R. *463, 464, 469, 514*
Quinn, Joseph R. *293*
Quinn, Percy E. *188*
Quinn, Peter A. *215*
Quinn, Robert E. *310*
Quinn, T. Vincent *221, 224*
Quinn, Terence J. *114*
Quinn, William F. *296*
Quinn, William J. *485*
Quinn, William W. *334*
Quintard, Charles T. *423, 448, 461*
Quinton, Cornelia B. Sage *437, 438*
Quinton, Harold *496*
Quisenberry, H. N. *416*
Quist-Couratin, *546*
Quitman, John A. *90, 92, 302*
Quynn, Allen *390*
Raab, G. Kirk *481*
Raab, George *440*
Rabassa, Gregory *545*
Rabaut, Louis C. *198, 201, 204, 208, 211, 214, 220, 224, 227, 230, 233, 236, 240*
Rabb, Maxwell M. *365*
Rabi, Isidor I. *517, 534, 537, 549*
Rabin, Benjamin J. *215, 218*
Rabing, Albert *528*
Rabinow, Jacob *544*
Rabinowitz, Jay A. *291*
Rabinowitz, Murray *532*
Raborn, William F. *537*
Rabun, William *295*
Race, John A. *248*
Racker, Efraim *549*
Radcliff, Jacob *393*
Radcliffe, Amos H. *173, 176*
Radcliffe, George L. *198, 201, 204, 207, 211, 214, 300*
Radcliffe, Wallace *473*
Raddin, Charles S. *441*
Rademacher, Joseph *466, 469*
Rader, Frank *386*
Rader, I. Andrew *431*
Radford, Arthur W. *328, 347, 348*
Radford, William *98, 100*
Radford, William A. *379*
Radwan, Edmund P. *224, 227, 231, 234*
Rae, C. W. *349*
Raffel, Mrs. Alvin *438*
Rafferty, William *415*
Raftery, Lawrence M. *504*
Raftery, S. Frank *504*
Ragen, Joseph E. *512*
Ragon, Heartsill *177, 181, 184, 187, 190, 193*
Ragone, David V. *406*
Ragone, Stanley *499*
Ragsdale, B. A. *387*

Ragsdale, Isaac N. *387*
Ragsdale, J. Willard *164, 167, 170, 173*
Raguet, Condy *488*
Rahall, Nick J., II *267, 270, 273, 276, 279*
Rahn, A. A. D. *527*
Rahn, Herman *517*
Raichle, Frank G. *512*
Railsback, Thomas F. *249, 252, 255, 258, 261, 265, 268, 271*
Rain, Frank L. *521*
Raines, Albert *238*
Raines, John *128, 131*
Raines, Richard C. *471*
Rainey, Henry T. *147, 150, 153, 156, 159, 162, 165, 168, 178, 181, 184, 187, 191, 193, 194*
Rainey, Homer P. *405, 416, 423*
Rainey, John W. *168, 172, 175*
Rainey, Joseph H. *105, 107, 109, 112, 114*
Rainey, Lilius B. *171, 174*
Rainey, Robert M. *308*
Rainie, Herbert W. *392*
Rains, Albert *213, 216, 219, 222, 226, 229, 232, 235, 242*
Rainsford, George N. *411*
Rainwater, James *550*
Rainwater, Herbert R. *528*
Rajchman, Jan A. *538*
Raker, John E. *158, 161, 165, 168, 171, 174, 178*
Rall, Frederick T., Jr. *559*
Ralls, Charles C. *528*
Ralls, John R. *320*
Ralph, John E. *351*
Ralston, Samuel M. *178, 297*
Ralston, William E. *528*
Ramage, Lawson P. *348*
Ramaley, Francis *522*
Rambaut, Thomas *426*
Rambin, J. Howard, Jr. *497*
Ramer, John E. *368*
Ramey, Frank M. *187*
Ramey, Homer A. *212, 215, 218*
Ramey, Kathleen *392*
Ramirez, Ricardo *468*
Rammelkamp, Charles H., Jr. *532*
Ramo, Simon *549, 552*
Ramos, Mildred *523*
Rampton, Calvin L. *312*
Ramsay, David *4*
Ramsay, Erskine *561*
Ramsay, Francis M. *349, 418*
Ramsay, George D. *332*
Ramsay, Nathaniel *3*
Ramsay, Robert H. *537*
Ramsay, Robert L. *196, 200, 203, 209, 225*
Ramsdell, George A. *304*
Ramseur, S. D. *323*
Ramsey, Alexander *26, 34, 79, 81, 98, 100, 102, 104, 106, 109, 301, 302, 391*
Ramsey, Dewitt C. *348*
Ramsey, James G. *321*
Ramsey, John R. *169, 173*
Ramsey, Lloyd B. *332, 344*
Ramsey, Norman F. *542*
Ramsey, Norman Foster *560*
Ramsey, Robert *70, 77*
Ramsey, Robert L. *222*
Ramsey, William *65, 66*
Ramsey, William M. *395*
Ramsey, William S. *75*
Ramseyer, C. William *165, 168, 172, 175, 178, 181, 184, 188, 191*

Ramspeck, Robert *197, 200, 204, 207, 210, 213, 380*
Ramspeck, Robert C. *187, 191, 194*
Rand, A. C. *391*
Rand, Austin L. *516*
Rand, Edward K. *517, 524*
Rand, George F. *491*
Rand, Robert L. *379*
Rand, Sidney Anders *369*
Rand, William McN. *492*
Randall, Alexander *76*
Randall, Alexander W. *26, 36, 315, 369*
Randall, Benjamin *74, 76, 477*
Randall, Blanchard *528*
Randall, Carolyn D. *285*
Randall, Charles H. *165, 168, 171*
Randall, Charles S. *128, 130, 133*
Randall, Clarence B. *490, 552, 559*
Randall, Clifford A. *528*
Randall, Clifford E. *174*
Randall, Edwin J. *453*
Randall, Edwin M. *295*
Randall, George M. *448, 458*
Randall, Harrison M. *517*
Randall, James G. *513, 534*
Randall, James R. *482*
Randall, Jesse W. *497*
Randall, John *390*
Randall, John D. *511*
Randall, Julia *561*
Randall, Richard H., Jr. *443*
Randall, Samuel J. *99, 101, 103, 105, 107, 109, 110, 112, 114, 115, 116, 119, 121, 124, 126, 129*
Randall, William H. *98, 100*
Randall, William J. *237, 240, 243, 246, 249, 253, 256, 259, 262*
Randell, Choice B. *146, 149, 152, 155, 158, 161*
Randolph, A. Philip *552, 561*
Randolph, Alfred M. *449, 461*
Randolph, Beverly *6, 313*
Randolph, Edmund *2, 4, 6, 23, 33, 34*
Randolph, Evan *494*
Randolph, George W. *319*
Randolph, Isham *537*
Randolph, James F. *64, 66, 68*
Randolph, James H. *114*
Randolph, Jennings *196, 200, 203, 206, 209, 213, 216, 235, 238, 241, 245, 248, 251, 254, 257, 260, 264, 267, 270, 273, 276, 315, 563*
Randolph, John *46, 47, 48, 49, 51, 52, 53, 56, 59, 60, 62, 63, 65, 70, 314, 371*
Randolph, Joseph F. *73, 75, 77*
Randolph, Lucretia *20*
Randolph, Peyton *3, 4*
Randolph, Theodore F. *111, 114, 116, 305*
Randolph, Thomas M. *48, 49, 313*
Randolph, Victor M. *324*
Randolph, Wallace F. *330*
Randolph, Woodruff *505*
Raney, George P. *295*
Raney, J. A. *523*
Raney, John H. *136*
Rangel, Charles B. *256, 259, 263, 266, 269, 272, 275, 278*
Rankin, Alan C. *410*

Reese, Charles L. *511*
Reese, David A. *87*
Reese, Everett D. *511*
Reese, Frederick F. *450, 459*
Reese, Hans H. F. *516*
Reese, Jack E. *423*
Reese, Lizette W. *561*
Reese, Manoah B. *304*
Reese, Seaborn *117, 120, 122*
Reese, Theodore I. *450, 461*
Reese, W. S. *385*
Reese, William B. *423*
Reeser, Edwin B. *516*
Reeve, Tapping *294*
Reeves, Albert L., Jr. *217*
Reeves, Charles F. *423*
Reeves, G. Paul *459*
Reeves, George P. *456*
Reeves, Henry A. *104*
Reeves, Ira L. *414*
Reeves, James E. *518*
Reeves, James H. *329*
Reeves, Jesse S. *517*
Reeves, Milton O. *544*
Reeves, Raymond J. *346*
Reeves, Walter *136, 138, 141, 144*
Regan, Donald T. *31, 34*
Regan, H. C., Jr. *544*
Regan, John K. *287*
Regan, Kenneth M. *219, 222, 225, 228*
Register, Benjamin F., Jr. *330*
Regula, Ralph S. *260, 263, 266, 269, 272, 275, 278*
Reh, Francis F. *467, 469*
Rehak, Peter *551*
Rehnquist, William H. *283*
Rehring, George J. *469*
Rehwinkel, Frederick H. *512*
Reich, Otto J. *375*
Reichardt, Carl E. *499*
Reichelderfer, Donald E. *482*
Reichelderfer, Luther H. *387*
Reicher, Louis Joseph *469*
Reid, Benjamin L. *557*
Reid, C. C. *524*
Reid, Charles *531, 536*
Reid, Charles C. *144, 146, 149, 152, 155*
Reid, Charles S. *296*
Reid, Charlotte T. *242, 246, 249, 252, 255*
Reid, David S. *79, 81, 88, 90, 92, 307*
Reid, Frank R. *178, 181, 184, 187, 191, 194*
Reid, Harry *275, 278*
Reid, Harry F. *513*
Reid, Harry M. *304*
Reid, Helen Rogers *559*
Reid, James *412*
Reid, James R. *4*
Reid, James W. *121, 123, 394*
Reid, John W. *96*
Reid, Joseph H. *561*
Reid, Ogden R. *244, 247, 250, 253, 256, 259, 364*
Reid, Richard *542*
Reid, Robert *536*
Reid, Robert R. *56, 57, 59*
Reid, Whitelaw *17, 362*
Reid, William S. *409*
Reid, William T. *418*
Reifel, Benjamin *241, 244, 247, 250, 254*
Reiff, Evan A. *409*
Reifsnider, Charles S. *451*
Reilly, Daniel P. *465*
Reilly, George R. *524*

Reilly, James B. *112, 114, 129, 131, 134*
Reilly, James W. *339*
Reilly, John *112*
Reilly, John W. *531*
Reilly, Michael K. *164, 168, 190, 193, 196, 200, 203*
Reilly, Thomas L. *158, 162*
Reilly, Wilson *92*
Reily, Luther *73*
Reimann, Stanley P. *519*
Reinartz, Leo F. *514, 538*
Reinburg, J. E. *417*
Reinecke, Ed *245, 248*
Reinert, Carl M. *407*
Reinert, Paul C. *416*
Reines, Frederick *549*
Reinhard, Diane L. *426*
Reinhardt, Aurelia H. *412*
Reinhardt, Emil F. *341, 342*
Reinhardt, G. Frederick *365, 375, 376*
Reinhardt, John E. *368, 382*
Reinhardt, Stephen *286*
Reinhart, C. S. *398*
Reinhart, Stanley E. *342*
Reinheimer, Bartel H. *452, 461*
Reinsch, Paul S. *358, 517*
Reischauer, Edwin O. *365*
Reiser, Leonard M. *510*
Reisman, Philip *542*
Reiss, John C. *468*
Reistle, Carl E., Jr. *514, 545*
Reitt, L. M. *319*
Reitz, J. Wayne *419*
Relfe, James H. *78, 80*
Remey, William B. *347*
Remington, Harvey F. *527*
Remington, John W. *511*
Remington, William P. *451, 458*
Remini, Robert V. *547*
Reminick, Seymour *531*
Remmel, Pratt C. *385*
Remsen, Henry *484*
Remsen, Ira *410, 510, 511, 553*
Renchard, George W. *357*
Renchard, William S. *484*
Rencher, Abraham *66, 68, 69, 71, 73, 77, 370*
Reneker, Robert W. *497*
Renick, Steve *547*
Renne, Roland R. *412*
Rennebohm, Oscar *315*
Renneker, George J. *419*
Renner, William B. *481*
Reno, Jesse L. *336*
Renouard, Edward I. *561*
Rensch, Joseph R. *493*
Rensselaer, Maunsell Van *410*
Rensselaer, Van *532*
Rentschler, Frederick B. *498, 540*
Rentschler, Gordon S. *485*
Rentschler, James M. *367*
Renzel, Ernest *386*
Rephlo, Louis S. *391*
Replogle, Luther J. *364*
Repplier, Agnes *542, 547*
Resa, Alexander J. *213*
Rese, Frederick *467*
Resnick, Joseph Y. *247, 250*
Resor, Stanley R. *327*
Ressler, Herschel *505*
Restani, Jane A. *287*
Restarick, Henry B. *450, 459*
Reston, James *545, 554, 555*
Rettger, Robert E. *510*
Reus-Froylan, Francisco *455, 461*

Reuss, Henry S. *232, 235, 238, 241, 245, 248, 251, 254, 257, 260, 264, 267, 270, 273*
Reuter, Edward B. *520*
Reuther, Walter P. *505*
Reutter, J. G. *391*
Reveley, W. Taylor *409*
Revels, Hiram R. *104, 302*
Revercomb, Chapman *213, 216, 219, 232, 235, 315*
Reverman, Theodore M. *470*
Rewak, William J. *422*
Rex, George *308*
Rexford, E. L. *418*
Rexroth, Kenneth *561*
Reybold, Eugene *330, 331*
Reyburn, John E. *129, 131, 134, 137, 151, 395*
Reyburn, William S. *160*
Reyerson, Lloyd H. *514*
Reynolds, A. William *488*
Reynolds, Arthur *486, 510*
Reynolds, Charles R. *332*
Reynolds, David P. *495*
Reynolds, Edward *442, 511*
Reynolds, Edwin *520*
Reynolds, Edwin R. *94*
Reynolds, Fidelis *415*
Reynolds, Frank *553*
Reynolds, George Lazenby *457, 461*
Reynolds, George M. *510*
Reynolds, Gideon *82, 84*
Reynolds, Henry E. *398*
Reynolds, Herbert H. *404*
Reynolds, Ignatius A. *469*
Reynolds, James B. *56, 62*
Reynolds, John *5, 69, 71, 74, 76, 296*
Reynolds, John F. *336, 337*
Reynolds, John H. *94, 562*
Reynolds, John M. *151, 154, 157*
Reynolds, John W. *315*
Reynolds, Joseph *71*
Reynolds, Joseph J. *338*
Reynolds, Orr E. *517*
Reynolds, Powell B. *426*
Reynolds, Richard J. *495*
Reynolds, Richard S., Jr. *495*
Reynolds, Richard S., Sr. *495*
Reynolds, Robert J. *294*
Reynolds, Robert M. *356*
Reynolds, Robert R. *192, 195, 199, 202, 205, 208, 212, 307*
Reynolds, Sam W. *227, 304*
Reynolds, Thomas *296, 302*
Reynolds, Thomas H. *404*
Reynolds, W. E. *417*
Reynolds, W. M. *405*
Reynolds, Walter H. *395*
Reynolds, William E. *382*
Reynolds, William N. *495*
Rhawn, William H. *510*
Rhea, Frank A. *453, 459*
Rhea, John *48, 49, 50, 52, 53, 54, 57, 58, 60*
Rhea, John S. *139, 141, 144, 147*
Rhea, William F. *143, 146*
Rheem, Richard S. *438*
Rhees, Rush *422*
Rhett, John T. *396*
Rhett, R. Barnwell *73, 75, 77, 79, 81, 83, 85, 87, 311*
Rhett, R. Barnwell, Sr. *320*
Rhett, R. G. *522*
Rhett, R. Goodwin *396*
Rhett, Robert B. *319*
Rhetts, Charles E. *366*
Rhinelander, Philip M. *450, 460*

Rhinock, Joseph L. *150, 153, 156*
Rhoades, Edward H., Jr. *475*
Rhoads, James E. *405*
Rhoads, Jonathan E. *511, 512*
Rhoads, Samuel *4, 395*
Rhode, Paul P. *470*
Rhodes, Allen F. *520*
Rhodes, Frank H. T. *407*
Rhodes, George M. *222, 225, 228, 231, 234, 238, 241, 244, 247, 250*
Rhodes, James A. *308, 394*
Rhodes, James F. *513*
Rhodes, James Ford *547, 553*
Rhodes, John J. *226, 229, 232, 235, 238, 242, 245, 248, 251, 254, 258, 261, 264, 267, 270*
Rhodes, Kent *433*
Rhodes, Marion E. *151, 172, 176*
Rhodes, Stephen H. *490*
Rhyne, Charles S. *511, 532*
Ribicoff, Abraham *293, 294*
Ribicoff, Abraham A. *30, 37, 220, 223, 242, 245, 248, 251, 255, 258, 261, 264, 267*
Ricaud, James B. *90, 92*
Riccardo, John J. *485*
Rice, A. D. *397*
Rice, Alexander H. *94, 96, 98, 100, 300, 390*
Rice, Americus V. *112, 114*
Rice, Baldwin *397*
Rice, Benjamin F. *101, 103, 105, 292*
Rice, Benjamin H. *473*
Rice, Caleb *492*
Rice, David B. *411*
Rice, Donald B. *523*
Rice, E. Wilbur, Jr. *538*
Rice, Edmund *125, 391*
Rice, Edward Y. *106*
Rice, Elial J. *403*
Rice, Elliott W. *338*
Rice, Elmer *521*
Rice, Elmer L. *553*
Rice, H. Baldwin *397*
Rice, Harvey M. *412*
Rice, Henry M. *92, 94, 96, 302*
Rice, Hiram P. *101*
Rice, Howard L. *474*
Rice, John B. *108, 119, 388*
Rice, John H. *96, 98, 100, 473*
Rice, John J. *426*
Rice, John L. *518*
Rice, John M. *104, 106*
Rice, John S. *368*
Rice, Joseph J. *470*
Rice, M. C. *387*
Rice, Nathan L. *426, 473*
Rice, Nathaniel *6*
Rice, Norman S. *437*
Rice, Paul N. *515*
Rice, Robert E. *413*
Rice, Samuel F. *291*
Rice, Theron M. *118*
Rice, Thomas *55, 56*
Rice, W. Thomas *491*
Rice, Walter L. *355*
Rice, William *393*
Rice, William W. *113, 116, 118, 120, 123*
Rice-Wray, Edris *560*
Rich, Adrienne *546, 561*
Rich, Bennett M. *425*
Rich, Carl W. *244, 394*
Rich, Charles *54, 57, 59, 60, 62*
Rich, Charles W. G. *333*
Rich, Daniel C. *437, 444*
Rich, Giles S. *286, 287*

Rich, John T. *118, 301*
Rich, Raymond A. *483*
Rich, Robert F. *189, 192, 196, 199, 202, 205, 209, 215, 218, 222*
Richard, Paul *393*
Richards, Arthur L. *361*
Richards, Benjamin W. *395*
Richards, C. *396*
Richards, Charles L. *179*
Richards, Charles R. *411*
Richards, Cyril F. *407*
Richards, D. W. *550*
Richards, David E. *454*
Richards, DeForest *315*
Richards, G. M. *544*
Richards, George W. *475*
Richards, I. A. *544*
Richards, J. H. *388*
Richards, J. Havens *409*
Richards, Jacob *48, 49, 50*
Richards, James *473*
Richards, James A. D. *134*
Richards, James P. *196, 199, 202, 206, 209, 212, 215, 219, 222, 225, 228, 231*
Richards, John *44, 61*
Richards, John G. *310*
Richards, John K. *285*
Richards, John N. *514*
Richards, John S. *515*
Richards, Joseph W. *522*
Richards, Laura E. *553*
Richards, Mark *57, 59*
Richards, Matthias *50, 51*
Richards, Noel J. *424*
Richards, Paul B. *510*
Richards, R. Q. *516*
Richards, Roger S. *560*
Richards, Theodore W. *509, 510, 511, 539, 549*
Richards, W. C. *554*
Richards, Wallace *438*
Richards, Wayne E. *528*
Richards, William A. *315*
Richardson, A. R. *387*
Richardson, Arthur B. *485*
Richardson, Bill *275, 278*
Richardson, David C. *348, 398*
Richardson, David P. *116, 118*
Richardson, Dean E. *491*
Richardson, Edgar P. *439*
Richardson, Elliot L. *31, 35, 37, 327, 362, 548*
Richardson, Ernest C. *515*
Richardson, Ernest G. *471*
Richardson, F. Denys *534*
Richardson, Friend W. *292*
Richardson, George F. *133*
Richardson, H. G. *398*
Richardson, H. Smith, Jr. *433*
Richardson, Harold D. *403*
Richardson, Harry A. *152, 155, 158, 294*
Richardson, Israel B. *336*
Richardson, J. A. *395*
Richardson, J. Milton *461*
Richardson, James A., III *331*
Richardson, James D. *124, 126, 129, 132, 134, 137, 140, 143, 146, 149*
Richardson, James L., Jr. *329*
Richardson, James M. *150, 455, 526*
Richardson, James O. *349*
Richardson, James R. *310*
Richardson, James T., Jr. *334*
Richardson, John *412*
Richardson, John P. *72, 73, 310*
Richardson, John S. *117, 119*
Richardson, John T. *407*

Richardson, Joseph *64, 66*
Richardson, R. Randolph *433*
Richardson, Robert C. *333*
Richardson, Robert C., Jr. *340, 341*
Richardson, Rupert N. *409*
Richardson, Scovel *287*
Richardson, Tobias G. *515*
Richardson, W. R. *476*
Richardson, Wayne *551*
Richardson, William *141, 143, 146, 149, 152, 155, 158, 161, 398*
Richardson, William A. *33, 82, 83, 85, 87, 89, 95, 97, 286, 296*
Richardson, William E. *196, 199*
Richardson, William F. *476*
Richardson, William M. *52, 53, 305*
Richardson, William R. *330, 333, 345*
Richardson, William S. *296*
Richert, William *391*
Richeson, Forrest L. *476*
Richey, Thomas *404*
Richman, Arthur *521*
Richman, John M. *491*
Richmond, Alfred C. *382*
Richmond, Carleton R. *509*
Richmond, Charles A. *417*
Richmond, Frederick W. *263, 266, 269, 272*
Richmond, Hiram L. *109*
Richmond, James B. *117*
Richmond, Jonathan *58*
Richmond, Julius B. *381*
Richmond, Lewis *370*
Richter, Burton *550*
Richter, Conrad *545, 555*
Richter, Curt P. *551*
Richter, Gisela M. A. *533*
Richter, Henry J. *467*
Richter, Richard B. *516*
Richtmyer, F. K. *527*
Richtmyer, Floyd K. *517*
Rickard, Corwin L. *516*
Rickards, George C. *331*
Rickards, John E. *303*
Rickenbacker, Edward V. *487*
Ricketts, Claude V. *348*
Ricketts, Edwin D. *167, 173, 176*
Ricketts, Forrest E. *543*
Ricketts, James B. *336, 338*
Ricketts, Louis D. *538*
Rickey, George *532, 535*
Ricklefs, R. E. *535*
Rickover, Hyman *552*
Rickover, Hyman G. *538, 559*
Ricks, Earl T. *331*
Ricks, Jesse J. *498*
Riddick, Carl W. *172, 176*
Riddick, E. G. *397*
Riddick, Wallace C. *413*
Riddick, Walter G. *285*
Riddle, Albert G. *96*
Riddle, David H. *410, 422, 473*
Riddle, George R. *85, 87, 97, 99, 101, 294*
Riddle, Haywood Y. *112, 114*
Riddle, John W. *355, 360, 371, 372*
Riddleberger, Harrison H. *122, 124, 126, 314*
Riddleberger, James W. *356, 363, 376, 379*
Riddler, John G. *391*
Rider, Ira E. *148*
Rider, R. P. *416*
Ridge, Albert A. *285*

Ridge, Lola *561*
Ridge, Thomas J. *275, 279*
Ridgedale, John *1*
Ridgeley, Henry M. *52, 53, 62, 64*
Ridgely, Charles C. *300*
Ridgely, Edwin R. *138, 141*
Ridgely, Henry M. *294*
Ridgely, Nicholas *294*
Ridgely, Richard *3*
Ridgley, R., Jr. *417*
Ridgway, Joseph *73, 75, 77*
Ridgway, Matthew B. *329, 333, 334, 341, 343, 344, 553*
Ridgway, Raymond R. *522*
Ridgway, Robert *105, 516, 519, 535*
Ridgway, Rozanne L. *361, 362*
Ridley, Clarence S. *341*
Ridley, J. J. *423*
Ridout, Samuel *390*
Rieber, Torkild *497*
Rieck, Edward E. *491*
Riegel, Byron *511*
Riegger, Wallingford *535*
Riegle, Donald W., Jr. *249, 252, 256, 259, 262, 265, 268, 271, 274, 277, 301*
Riehlman, R. Walter *218, 221, 224, 227, 231, 234, 237, 240, 244*
Ries, Heinrich *523*
Rieti, Vittorio *562*
Rieve, Emil *505*
Rife, John W. *129, 131*
Rigby, W. O. *389*
Rigge, Joseph *412*
Riggio, Vincent *481*
Riggs, C. E. *347*
Riggs, Henry E. *519*
Riggs, James M. *120, 122*
Riggs, Jetur R. *94*
Riggs, Lewis *77*
Riggs, Walter M. *406*
Righter, Walter C. *456, 459*
Rightmire, George W. *414*
Rightor, Edward *521*
Rigley, Harold T. *506*
Rigney, Hugh M. *200*
Rihl, Charles H. *505*
Riker, C. L. *544*
Riker, Samuel *48, 50*
Riles, Wilson C. *561*
Riley, Corinne B. *241*
Riley, Fletcher *308*
Riley, Henry A. *516*
Riley, Herbert D. *328*
Riley, James Whitcomb *547*
Riley, John J. *215, 219, 225, 228, 231, 234, 238, 241*
Riley, Joseph P., Jr. *396*
Riley, Ray L. *524*
Riley, Richard A. *488*
Riley, Richard W. *311*
Rinaker, John I. *136*
Rinaldo, Matthew J. *259, 262, 265, 269, 272, 275, 278*
Rincliffe, Roy G. *494*
Rinearson, Peter Mark *558*
Rinehart, Dana *394*
Riner, C. W. *399*
Riner, William A. *315*
Ring, Harold *422*
Ringgold, Samuel *51, 52, 53, 56, 58*
Ringgold, Thomas *1*
Ringland, Adam W. *411*
Ringland, Albert *544*
Ringo, Daniel *292*

Riordan, Daniel J. *142, 151, 154, 157, 160, 163, 166, 170, 173, 176*
Riordan, Joseph W. *422*
Riordan, Patrick W. *463*
Riotte, Charles N. *359, 368*
Ripley, Christopher G. *302*
Ripley, Edward P. *483*
Ripley, Eleazar W. *71, 72*
Ripley, James W. *62, 64, 66, 332*
Ripley, Philip *386*
Ripley, S. Dillon *442, 443, 553*
Ripley, Thomas C. *80*
Ripley, William Z. *513*
Rippel, Julius A. *433*
Ripple, Kenneth F. *285*
Risedorph, Edward *494*
Risenhoover, Theodore M. *263, 266*
Risk, Charles F. *199, 206*
Risley, Elijah *84*
Risley, John E. *360*
Risser, James *557, 558*
Risser, Paul G. *522*
Ritchey, Thomas *82, 88*
Ritchie, Albert C. *300*
Ritchie, Andrew C. *437, 444*
Ritchie, Bryon F. *134*
Ritchie, David *89, 90, 92*
Ritchie, James M. *119*
Ritchie, John *106*
Ritchie, Walter B. *524*
Riter, G. H., III *525*
Ritner, Joseph *309*
Rittenhouse, David *517*
Ritter, Burwell C. *100*
Ritter, Donald L. *269, 272, 275, 279*
Ritter, George *398*
Ritter, John *79, 81*
Ritter, Joseph E. *463, 466*
Ritter, Louis *387*
Ritter, Russell J. *392*
Rittle, R. M. *395*
Rivera, Jose de *535*
Rivera, Victor M. *455, 461*
Rivero, Horacio *373*
Rivers, Eurith D. *295*
Rivers, L. Mendel *209, 212, 215, 219, 222, 225, 228, 231, 234, 238, 241, 244, 247, 250, 254*
Rivers, Larry *546*
Rivers, Ralph J. *235, 238, 242, 245*
Rivers, Thomas *91*
Rivers, William C. *331*
Rives, Francis E. *74, 76*
Rives, Lloyd M. *357*
Rives, Richard T. *284, 286*
Rives, William C. *62, 63, 65, 67, 68, 70, 72, 74, 75, 77, 79, 314, 320, 321, 361*
Rives, Zeno J. *150*
Rivinus, F. Markoe *496*
Rivkin, William R. *362, 366, 372*
Rivlin, Harry N. *406*
Rix, Carl B. *511*
Rixey, John F. *140, 143, 146, 149, 152*
Rixford, Gulian P. *438*
Rixley, Presley M. *347*
Rizley, Ross *209, 212, 215, 218*
Rizzo, Frank J. *395*
Roach, Isaac *395*
Roach, John R. *464*
Roach, Sidney C. *176, 179*
Roach, William N. *134, 137, 140, 307*

Rockwell, Hosea H. *131*
Rockwell, John A. *79, 81*
Rockwell, Julius *78, 80, 82, 84, 88, 301*
Rockwell, Robert F. *207, 210, 213, 216*
Rockwell, Stuart W. *367*
Rockwell, Willard F., Jr. *496*
Roddan, Edward L. *375*
Roddenbery, Seaborn A. *156, 159, 162*
Roddey, Philip D. *323*
Roddis, Louis H., Jr. *486, 516*
Rode, James D. *482*
Rodeck, Hugo G. *443*
Roden, Carl B. *515*
Rodenberg, William A. *141, 147, 150, 153, 156, 159, 165, 168, 172, 175*
Roderick, David M. *434, 499, 539*
Rodert, Lewis A. *537, 562*
Rodes, Harold P. *404*
Rodes, Robert E. *323*
Rodgers, C. R. P. *349, 418*
Rodgers, G. F. *395*
Rodgers, George W. *350*
Rodgers, Joe M. *362*
Rodgers, John *473, 523, 551*
Rodgers, Raymond P. *352*
Rodgers, Richard *535, 554, 555*
Rodgers, Robert L. *205, 209, 212, 215*
Rodgers, W. S. S. *497, 533*
Rodgers, William C. *404*
Rodgers, William L. *352*
Rodimer, Frank J. *468*
Rodino, Peter W., Jr. *221, 224, 227, 230, 234, 237, 240, 243, 247, 250, 253, 256, 259, 262, 265, 269, 272, 275, 278*
Roditi, Edouard *562*
Rodman, Benedict J. *410*
Rodman, Isaac P. *336*
Rodman, William *53*
Rodman, William L. *515*
Rodman, William M. *395*
Rodney, Caesar A. *1, 3, 5, 23, 34, 47, 59, 294, 355*
Rodney, Caleb *294*
Rodney, Daniel *15, 59, 62, 294*
Rodney, George B. *76, 78*
Rodney, Thomas *3*
Rodrigue, George *559*
Roe, Azel *473*
Roe, Dudley G. *214*
Roe, James A. *215*
Roe, Kenneth A. *520, 541*
Roe, Robert A. *253, 256, 259, 262, 265, 269, 272, 275, 278*
Roeber, Eugene F. *522*
Roeder, Bernard F. *348*
Roeder, J. E. *544*
Roelofs, Wendell L. *549*
Roemer, Buddy *271, 274, 277*
Roemer, Milton I. *561*
Roesch, Charles E. *393*
Roesch, Raymond A. *419*
Roesch, William R. *434, 499*
Roessler, John E. *424*
Roethel, David A. H. *514*
Roethke, Theodore *534, 545, 555, 561*
Roffignoc, Joseph *389*
Rogers, Adrian P. *475*
Rogers, Alan E. E. *560*
Rogers, Andrew J. *98, 100*
Rogers, Anthony A. C. *103*
Rogers, Bernard W. *329, 332*
Rogers, Bruce *531*

Rogers, Byron G. *223, 226, 229, 232, 235, 239, 242, 245, 248, 251*
Rogers, C. J. *315*
Rogers, Carl R. *518*
Rogers, Charles *79*
Rogers, Daniel *294*
Rogers, Dwight L. *213, 216, 220, 223, 226*
Rogers, Edith Nourse *182, 185, 188, 191, 194, 198, 201, 204, 207, 211, 214, 217, 220, 224, 227, 230, 233, 236*
Rogers, Edward *75*
Rogers, Ernest E. *527*
Rogers, Felix M. *346*
Rogers, Frank B. *538*
Rogers, George F. *215*
Rogers, H. Gold *372*
Rogers, Harold *271, 274, 277*
Rogers, Harry H. *476, 527*
Rogers, Harry L. *332*
Rogers, Henry S. *414*
Rogers, Henry W. *284, 413*
Rogers, Howard G. *562*
Rogers, J. Justin *523*
Rogers, Jacob S. *491*
Rogers, James *72, 75, 77*
Rogers, Jefferson T. *391*
Rogers, John *3, 107, 409, 476*
Rogers, John H. *119, 122, 124, 127*
Rogers, John I. *520*
Rogers, John Jacob *162, 166, 169, 172, 175, 179*
Rogers, John R. *314*
Rogers, John T. *553*
Rogers, John W. *438*
Rogers, Johnathan C. *419*
Rogers, Joseph G. *518*
Rogers, Leo J. *393*
Rogers, Lorene L. *423*
Rogers, Meyric R. *437, 443*
Rogers, Millard F., Jr. *438*
Rogers, Nat S. *511*
Rogers, Paul G. *229, 232, 236, 239, 242, 245, 248, 252, 255, 258, 261, 264*
Rogers, Platt *386*
Rogers, Ralph B. *497*
Rogers, Robert D. *497*
Rogers, Robert E. *522*
Rogers, Robert S. *517*
Rogers, S. St. George *321*
Rogers, Sion H. *88, 107*
Rogers, Thomas *1, 560*
Rogers, Thomas J. *57, 58, 60, 61*
Rogers, Walter E. *225, 228, 231, 235, 238, 241, 244, 248*
Rogers, Warren L. *452, 460*
Rogers, Will *196, 199, 202, 205, 209, 562*
Rogers, Will, Jr. *210*
Rogers, William *350, 406*
Rogers, William B. *412, 415, 423, 509*
Rogers, William F. *121*
Rogers, William H. *398*
Rogers, William N. *179, 192, 195, 198*
Rogers, William O. *417*
Rogers, William P. *30, 31, 33, 35, 548, 552*
Rogers, Woodall *397*
Rogoff, Fannie *433*
Rogoff, Julius M. *433*
Rohde, Erwin Carl *562*
Rohe, Ludwig Mies van der *535*
Rohlfs, Mrs. Marcus *475*
Rohlman, Henry P. *464, 466*

Rohrbough, Edward G. *213, 219*
Roland, Edwin J. *382*
Roley, Roland F. *505*
Rolfe, John C. *517*
Roll, Lyle C. *490*
Rollins, Edward A. *380*
Rollins, Edward H. *96, 98, 100, 114, 116, 118, 304*
Rollins, Frank W. *304*
Rollins, James S. *96, 98*
Rollins, Lloyd *438*
Rollins, Walter H. *426*
Rolph, James, Jr. *292, 386*
Rolph, S. Wyman *522*
Rolph, Thomas *207, 210*
Rolvaag, Karl F. *301, 364*
Romaine, Henry S. *492*
Roman, Andre B. *298*
Roman, J. Dixon *82*
Romano, Frank O. *397*
Romano, John *533*
Romano, Umberto *542, 560*
Romanoff, Paul *440*
Romberg, Paul F. *405*
Rombouts, Francis *393*
Rome, Howard *533*
Rome, Howard P. *518*
Romeis, Jacob *124, 126*
Romer, Alfred S. *510, 520, 540, 551*
Romer, Roy *293*
Romeyn, John B. *473*
Romjue, Milton A. *169, 172, 179, 182, 185, 188, 192, 195, 198, 201, 205, 208*
Romnes, Haakon I. *482, 499*
Romney, George *301, 541*
Romney, George W. *31, 38, 482*
Romulo, Carlos P. *553, 554*
Ronald, James T. *398*
Ronaldson, James *522*
Ronan, Daniel J. *246, 249, 252*
Roncalio, Teno *248, 257, 261, 264, 267*
Roncallo, Angelo D. *259*
Rondon, Fernando E. *360, 366*
Rondon, Hector *556*
Rondou, Rene *503*
Roney, Paul H. *285, 286*
Ronnebeck, Arnold *438*
Rood, Florence *503*
Rook, Edward F. *551*
Rooks, Lowell W. *343*
Roome, Charles *486*
Rooney, Fred B. *244, 247, 250, 254, 257, 260, 263, 266*
Rooney, John J. *211, 215, 218, 221, 224, 227, 231, 234, 237, 240, 244, 247, 250, 253, 256, 259, 315*
Roop, J. Clawson *381*
Roosevelt, Eleanor *20, 540*
Roosevelt, Franklin D. *11, 18, 29, 306, 540*
Roosevelt, Franklin D., Jr. *221, 224, 227*
Roosevelt, Isaac *483*
Roosevelt, James *229, 232, 235, 239, 242, 245*
Roosevelt, James I. *77*
Roosevelt, Nicholas *364*
Roosevelt, Robert B. *107, 368*
Roosevelt, Theodore *11, 12, 17, 27, 143, 306, 513, 526, 540, 549*
Roosevelt, Theodore, Jr. *559*
Root, Azariah S. *515*
Root, Elihu *27, 33, 34, 157, 160, 163, 306, 511, 519, 532, 548, 549, 559*
Root, Erastus *48, 51, 55, 68*

Root, Jesse *3, 294*
Root, John F. *365*
Root, John G. *386*
Root, John W. *532*
Root, Joseph M. *81, 82, 84*
Root, Joseph P. *358*
Roots, Logan H. *101, 103, 450*
Roper, Albert L. *397*
Roper, Charles *544*
Roper, Daniel C. *29, 37, 358, 380*
Roper, John W. *349*
Roper, Sheldon M. *524*
Roper, Thomas *396*
Rorem, C. Rufus *561*
Rorem, Ned *557*
Rorimer, James J. *440*
Rorty, Malcolm C. *515*
Rosa, Edward B. *537*
Rosati, Joseph *467, 468*
Rose, Albert *538*
Rose, Alex *506*
Rose, Arnold M. *520*
Rose, Augustus S. *516*
Rose, Charles G., III *260, 263, 266, 269, 272, 275, 278*
Rose, David S. *399, 454, 461*
Rose, Frank A. *417, 418*
Rose, Henry R. *386*
Rose, Herman *531*
Rose, John C. *284*
Rose, John M. *170, 173, 177*
Rose, M. Richard *415*
Rose, Maurice *343*
Rose, Merle R. *403*
Rose, Robert J. *467*
Rose, Robert L. *82, 84*
Rose, Robert R., Jr. *315*
Rose, Robert S. *61, 63, 66*
Rose, Rufus E. *351*
Rose, U. M. *511*
Rose, William *542*
Rose, William C. *549*
Rose, William G. *394*
Roseborough, Morgan G. *344*
Rosecrans, Sylvester H. *469*
Rosecrans, William S. *117, 119, 335, 336, 337, 367, 542*
Rosellini, Albert D. *314*
Rosellini, Hugh J. *314*
Rosen, Charles *531, 545*
Rosen, Donn E. *543*
Rosen, George *540*
Rosen, James *284*
Rosenau, Milton J. *561*
Rosenbaum, Allen *442*
Rosenbaum, Joan H. *440*
Rosenberg, Abraham *504*
Rosenberg, Adolph *476*
Rosenberg, Emanuel *552*
Rosenberg, Howard *558*
Rosenberg, Louis C. *532*
Rosenberry, Marvin B. *315*
Rosenblath, Marshall N. *538*
Rosenbloom, Benjamin L. *177, 180*
Rosenblum, Donald E. *333*
Rosenbluth, Marshall N. *538*
Rosenfield, John *439*
Rosengarten, Frederic *492*
Rosengarten, George D. *511*
Rosengarten, Theodore *546*
Rosenhaupt, Hans *434*
Rosenn, Max *284*
Rosenstein, Samuel M. *287*
Rosenstock, Arthur *505*
Rosenthal, A. M. *545, 556*
Rosenthal, Benjamin S. *240, 244, 247, 250, 253, 256, 259, 263, 266, 269, 272, 275*
Rosenthal, Doris *536*

Rosenthal, James D. *363*
Rosenthal, Joe *554*
Rosenwald, Julius *496*
Rosenwald, Lessing *496*
Rosier, Joseph *209, 315*
Rosin, Joseph *559*
Roskens, Ronald W. *421*
Rosoff, Jeannie I. *560*
Rosoff, Bennett B. *403*
Ross, C. Ben *296*
Ross, Charles G. *554*
Ross, Clarence F. *403*
Ross, Claude G. *358, 363, 374*
Ross, Clifford *560*
Ross, David *3*
Ross, Donald *524*
Ross, Donald R. *285*
Ross, Edmund G. *99, 101, 104, 298*
Ross, Edward A. *520*
Ross, Erskine M. *285*
Ross, Frank E. *562*
Ross, George *1, 4*
Ross, Harold D. *524*
Ross, Heck *388*
Ross, Henry H. *63*
Ross, James *14, 43, 44, 45, 46, 47, 309*
Ross, John *51, 55, 57, 390*
Ross, John W. *387*
Ross, Jonathan *140, 143, 313*
Ross, Lawrence S. *312, 416*
Ross, Lewis W. *97, 99, 101*
Ross, Marion C. *333*
Ross, Maurice O. *405*
Ross, Miles *111, 114, 116, 118*
Ross, Morrill *343*
Ross, Nellie T. *315*
Ross, Robert T. *218, 224*
Ross, Sobieski *109, 112*
Ross, Stanford G. *382*
Ross, Thomas *85, 87*
Ross, Thomas R. *58, 60, 61*
Ross, W. W. *389*
Ross, William B. *315*
Ross, William H. H. *294*
Rossby, C. G. *559*
Rossdale, Albert B. *176*
Rossell, William T. *331*
Rossem, Adrian J. Van *535*
Rosser, Richard F. *407*
Rossi, Angelo J. *386*
Rossi, Bruno *560*
Rossi, Bruno B. *537, 549*
Rossin, R. S. *385*
Rossini, Frederick D. *542, 549, 553, 562*
Rossiter, Clinton *534*
Rossiter, Percival S. *347*
Rosson, W. S. *389*
Rosson, William B. *333, 344, 345*
Rostenkowski, Dan *236, 239, 242, 246, 249, 252, 255, 258, 261, 265, 268, 271, 274, 277*
Rostker, Bernard D. *381*
Rostow, Walt W. *552*
Roth, Almon E. *527*
Roth, F. G. R. *526*
Roth, Philip *545*
Roth, Toby *270, 273, 276, 279*
Roth, William G. *482*
Roth, William V., Jr. *248, 252, 255, 258, 261, 264, 267, 270, 274, 277, 294*
Rothe, Anne T. *536*
Rothenburger, William F. *476*
Rothermel, Joan *533*
Rothermel, John H. *154, 157, 160, 164*
Rothko, Mark *535*

Rothrock, Mary U. *515, 543*
Rothschild, Jerome J. *432*
Rothwell, Charles E. *412*
Rothwell, Gideon F. *116*
Rothwell, William R. *426*
Roudebush, Richard L. *239, 242, 246, 249, 252, 528*
Roukema, Marge *272, 275, 278*
Roumfort, Augustus L. *395*
Rounds, Nelson *426*
Rounds, Sterling P. *380*
Roundy, Frank C. *527*
Rountree, William M. *357, 369, 371, 373*
Rourke, Russell A. *327*
Rous, Francis P. *549, 550*
Rous, Peyton *543*
Rouse, Arthur B. *159, 162, 165, 169, 172, 175, 178, 181*
Rouse, Irving *509*
Rouse, Milford O. *516*
Rouse, William *396*
Roush, J. Edward *236, 239, 242, 246, 249, 255, 258, 261*
Rousseau, Lawrence *324*
Rousseau, Lovell H. *100, 337*
Rousseau, Richard J. *363*
Roussel, Willis J. *544*
Rousselot, John *261*
Rousselot, John H. *239, 251, 255, 258, 264, 267, 270*
Routt, John L. *293, 386*
Routzohn, Harry N. *205*
Roux, Jules *389*
Rouzie, Richard L. *561*
Rowan, Carl *382*
Rowan, Carl T. *361, 545*
Rowan, John *50, 62, 64, 65, 298, 372*
Rowan, Joseph *173*
Rowan, Matthew *6*
Rowan, Stephen N. *473*
Rowan, Thomas E. *386*
Rowan, William A. *210, 213*
Rowbottom, Harry E. *181, 184, 188*
Rowcliff, Gilbert J. *347*
Rowden, Marcus A. *381*
Rowden, W. *350*
Rowe, Ed *212*
Rowe, Frederick W. *166, 170, 173*
Rowe, George H. *527*
Rowe, James *434*
Rowe, Leo S. *509, 517*
Rowe, Peter *88*
Rowe, Peter T. *449, 458*
Rowe, Roscoe C. *390*
Rowell, Chester H. *559*
Rowell, Edward M. *357*
Rowell, Henry T. *521*
Rowell, John W. *313*
Rowell, Jonathan H. *120, 122, 125, 127*
Rowell, Lester J., Jr. *495*
Rowell, Lyman S. *423*
Rowland, Alfred *126, 128*
Rowland, Charles H. *167, 170*
Rowland, D. P. *506*
Rowland, David *1*
Rowland, Henry A. *517, 560*
Rowland, J. Roy *274, 277*
Rowland, John G. *277*
Rowland, John W. *503*
Rowland, Raymond E. *495*
Rowley, Howard C. *527*
Rowley, Louis N. *520*
Rowley, Park A. *484*
Rowley, T. A. *337*
Rowlinson, C. C. *410*
Roy, Alphonse *201*

Roy, J. Stapleton *372*
Roy, Richard *274*
Roy, William R. *255, 258*
Royal, John K. *395*
Royall, Kenneth C. *29, 34, 327*
Royar, M. L. *349*
Roybal, Edward R. *242, 245, 248, 251, 255, 258, 261, 264, 267, 270, 273, 277*
Royce, Asa M. *424*
Royce, Homer E. *93, 95, 313*
Royce, Josiah *518*
Royce, Ralph *340*
Royce, Stephen *313*
Royer, Charles T. *398*
Royko, Mike *557*
Roys, Francis W. *426*
Royse, Lemuel W. *136, 138*
Royster, Vermont *545, 553, 558*
Royster, Vermont C. *520, 555*
Royston, Grandison D. *320*
Rubel, Albert C. *498, 533, 545*
Ruben, Samuel *531*
Ruben, Samuel A. *544*
Rubendall, Howard L. *407*
Rubenstein, Arthur *552*
Rubey, Thomas L. *160, 163, 166, 169, 172, 179, 182, 185*
Rubey, William W. *523, 549, 551*
Rubin, Alvin B. *285*
Rubin, Harry *543*
Rubin, Irving *559*
Rubin, Seymour J. *519*
Rublee, Horace *373*
Rubottom, Roy R., Jr. *355*
Ruby, John C. *398*
Ruckelshaus, William D. *379, 562*
Rucker, Atterson W. *155, 158*
Rucker, Daniel H. *332*
Rucker, S. M. *386*
Rucker, Tinsley W. *165*
Rucker, Willaim W. *148*
Rucker, William L. *166*
Rucker, William W. *142, 145, 151, 154, 156, 160, 163, 169, 172, 176*
Ruckman, John W. *339*
Rudd, Eldon *264, 267, 270, 273, 276*
Rudd, Hurley *387*
Rudd, John A., Sr. *387*
Rudd, Stephen A. *192, 195, 198*
Rudd, Thomas B. *409*
Rudder, James E. *416*
Ruddy, Francis S. *361*
Rudenberg, Reinhold *537*
Ruder, Melvin H. *556*
Rudesill, C. E. *398*
Rudhyar, Dane *562*
Rudin, Anna N. *386*
Rudkin, Frank H. *285, 314*
Rudman, Warren *272, 275, 278, 305*
Rudolph, Abraham M. *542*
Rudolph, C. Hugo *387*
Rudolph, Louis C. *422*
Rudolph, Michael *330, 331*
Rudolph, Paul *535*
Rue, Levi L. *494*
Ruehlmann, Eugene P. *394*
Rueppel, Merrill C. *438, 441*
Ruesch, Jurgen *541*
Ruff, Walter S. *524*
Ruffer, David G. *403*
Ruffin, Ben A. *524*
Ruffin, James E. *195*
Ruffin, Thomas *88, 90, 92, 94, 307, 320*

Ruffin, William H. *525*
Ruffner, Clark L. *333, 344*
Ruffner, David L. *344*
Ruffner, Henry *425*
Ruffo, Albert *386*
Ruger, Thomas H. *295, 339, 351, 418*
Ruger, William C. *306*
Rugg, Arthur P. *301, 509*
Ruggiero, Lawrence J. *442*
Ruggles, Arthur H. *518*
Ruggles, Benjamin *55, 57, 58, 60, 61, 63, 65, 66, 68, 308*
Ruggles, Carl *535*
Ruggles, Charles H. *60, 306*
Ruggles, Daniel *322*
Ruggles, G. D. *330*
Ruggles, John *69, 71, 72, 74, 299*
Ruggles, Nathaniel *53, 55, 56*
Ruggles, Timothy *1*
Rugh, William A. *376*
Ruhtenberg, Cornelius *531, 536*
Rukeyser, Muriel *561*
Rulison, Nelson S. *449, 458*
Rumford, Beatrix T. *442*
Rummell, Joseph F. *464, 468*
Rumnes, H. I. *539*
Rumple, John N. W. *144*
Rumsey, Benjamin *3, 7, 300*
Rumsey, David, Jr. *82, 84*
Rumsey, Edward *72*
Rumsey, Julian S. *388*
Rumsfeld, Donald *242, 246, 249, 252, 381, 562*
Rumsfeld, Donald H. *31, 37, 327, 552*
Rungius, Carl *560*
Runk, John *80*
Runkle, John D. *412*
Runnels, Hardin R. *312*
Runnels, Harold *256, 259, 262, 266, 269*
Runnels, Hiram G. *302*
Runyon, Theodore *336, 362*
Runyon, William N. *305*
Rupert, Joseph *389*
Rupley, A. S. *489*
Rupley, Arthur R. *164*
Rupp, George E. *415*
Rupp, Lawrence H. *521*
Ruppe, Philip E. *249, 252, 256, 259, 262, 265*
Ruppert, Jacob, Jr. *142, 145, 148, 151*
Rusack, Robert C. *455, 459*
Rusby, Henry H. *559*
Rusby, J. M. *544*
Ruschenberger, William S. W. *509*
Rush, Benjamin *1, 4*
Rush, Kenneth *327, 361, 498*
Rush, Orville F. *527*
Rush, Richard *15, 24, 33, 34, 361, 362*
Rushton, Kenneth *544*
Rusk, Dean *30, 33, 433, 548, 552*
Rusk, Harry W. *123, 125, 128, 130, 133, 136*
Rusk, Howard A. *548*
Rusk, Jeremiah M. *27, 36, 107, 110, 112, 315*
Rusk, Ralph L. *545*
Rusk, Thomas J. *81, 83, 85, 87, 89, 91, 93, 312*
Russ, John *57, 59*
Russ, Robert D. *346*
Russ, William M. *394*
Russell, Allen S. *534*
Russell, Benjamin E. *133, 135*

Scofield, Glenni W. *99, 101, 103, 105, 107, 109, 286*
Scollan, Thomas P. *386*
Scotes, Thomas J. *376*
Scott, Abram M. *302*
Scott, Angelo C. *414*
Scott, Arthur H. *496*
Scott, Austin *415*
Scott, Byron N. *197, 200*
Scott, Caroline Lavinia *20*
Scott, Charles *298, 335*
Scott, Charles F. *147, 150, 153, 156, 538*
Scott, Charles L. *91, 93, 340, 341, 375*
Scott, David C. *431*
Scott, David R. *537*
Scott, David W. *441*
Scott, Donald *442*
Scott, Elmon *314*
Scott, Frank D. *166, 169, 172, 175, 179, 182*
Scott, Fred N. *524*
Scott, George C. *159, 162, 168*
Scott, George M. *397*
Scott, Gustavus *3*
Scott, Hardie *218, 222, 225*
Scott, Harold W. *525*
Scott, Harvey D. *89*
Scott, Hugh *241, 244, 247, 250, 253, 257, 260, 263*
Scott, Hugh D., Jr. *209, 212, 218, 222, 225, 228, 231, 234, 237, 309*
Scott, Hugh L. *329, 418*
Scott, Isaiah B. *471*
Scott, James B. *519*
Scott, John *59, 61, 63, 66, 105, 107, 109, 309*
Scott, John A. *517*
Scott, John F. *389*
Scott, John F. R. *528*
Scott, John G. *98*
Scott, John M. *395*
Scott, John Morin *4*
Scott, John R. K. *167, 170*
Scott, John Thad, Jr. *380*
Scott, John W. *425, 526*
Scott, Joseph *542*
Scott, Josiah *308*
Scott, L. S. *395*
Scott, Levi *471*
Scott, Lon A. *177*
Scott, M. G. *505*
Scott, Marshal L. *474*
Scott, Mrs. Matthew T. *526*
Scott, Nathan B. *143, 146, 149, 152, 155, 158, 315, 380*
Scott, Orange *477*
Scott, Owen *130*
Scott, Ralph J. *234, 237, 240, 244, 247*
Scott, Richard H. *315*
Scott, Robert E. *320*
Scott, Robert K. *310*
Scott, Robert W. *307*
Scott, Roy W. *513*
Scott, Stanley L. *330*
Scott, Stuart Nash *370*
Scott, Thomas *41, 43, 308*
Scott, Thomas A. *498*
Scott, Thomas F. *448, 460*
Scott, Tully *293*
Scott, Upton *390*
Scott, W. E. *497*
Scott, W. Kerr *228, 231, 234, 307*
Scott, Walter *391*
Scott, Walter D. *413, 518*
Scott, Walter Q. *414*
Scott, Wendell G. *511*

Scott, William *303*
Scott, William A. *473*
Scott, William B. *517, 523, 540, 551*
Scott, William H. *414*
Scott, William L. *124, 126, 251, 254, 257, 260, 263, 267, 314*
Scott, Wilton E. *497*
Scott, Winfield *15, 329, 335*
Scott, Winfield T. *561*
Scott, Winfield W., Jr. *417, 418*
Scotten, Robert M. *359, 360, 368*
Scouller, John C. *473*
Scouller, John Y. *473*
Scoval, Sylvester F. *407*
Scovell, Clinton H. *525*
Scoville, Jonathan *116, 118, 393*
Scoville, Wilbur L. *559*
Scoy, Thomas Van *426*
Scranton, George W. *94, 97*
Scranton, Joseph A. *119, 124, 129, 134, 137*
Scranton, William W. *241, 309, 526*
Screen, Pat *389*
Scribner, A. W. *392*
Scripture, Edward W. *544*
Scriven, George P. *332*
Scrivner, Errett P. *210, 214, 217, 220, 223, 226, 230, 233*
Scrivner, Eugene M. *392*
Scroggy, Thomas E. *151*
Scruggs, William L. *358, 375*
Scrugham, James G. *195, 198, 201, 205, 208, 211, 214, 304*
Scudder, Caleb *388*
Scudder, Henry J. *109*
Scudder, Hubert B. *219, 223, 226, 229, 232*
Scudder, Isaac W. *109*
Scudder, John A. *51*
Scudder, Kenyon J. *512*
Scudder, Nathaniel *2, 4*
Scudder, Samuel H. *441*
Scudder, Townsend *142, 148*
Scudder, Tredwell *57*
Scudder, Zeno *86, 88*
Scudellari, R. D. *546*
Scull, Edward *126, 129, 131*
Scully, Cornelius *395*
Scully, John *408*
Scully, Thomas J. *160, 163, 166, 169, 173*
Scully, Vincent *542*
Scully, William A. *468*
Scupin, Carl A. *498*
Scurry, Richardson *87*
Seaborg, Glenn T. *379, 418, 510, 532, 538, 539, 550, 553*
Seabrook, Whitemarsh B. *310*
Seabury, Paul *534*
Seabury, Samuel *447, 458, 548, 559*
Seager, Henry R. *513*
Sealock, William E. *421*
Seaman, Eugene C. *451, 460*
Seaman, Henry J. *80*
Seaman, Jonathan O. *333, 344*
Seaman, William *556*
Seaman, William H. *285*
Seamans, Robert C., Jr. *327, 513*
Seamster, Lee *292*
Sear, Morey L. *287*
Search, Theodore C. *525*
Searcy, James T. *518*
Searing, Hudson R. *486*
Searing, John A. *92*
Searle, James *4*
Searles, Colbert *524*

Searls, Fred, Jr. *561*
Searls, Niles *293*
Sears, Barnabas F. *512*
Sears, Barnas *405*
Sears, Clinton W. *410*
Sears, Paul B. *510, 522, 538*
Sears, Richard W. *496*
Sears, Robert R. *518*
Sears, Samuel P. *512*
Sears, William J. *165, 168, 171, 175, 178, 181, 184, 194, 197*
Sears, William R. *559*
Sears, Willis G. *179, 182, 185, 188*
Seashore, Carl E. *518*
Seasongood, Murray *394, 526*
Seaton, Frederick A. *30, 36, 224, 304*
Seaton, George *509*
Seaton, John L. *403, 423*
Seaton, Lewis H. *347*
Seaton, William W. *387*
Seaver, Benjamin *390*
Seaver, Ebenezer *48, 49, 50, 51, 52*
Seaver, Esther I. *438*
Seavey, Clyde L. *380*
Seawell, William T. *494*
Seay, Thomas *291*
Seay, Thomas F. *527*
Seay, William A. *356*
Sebald, W. W. *482*
Sebald, William J. *355, 357, 365*
Sebastian, Charles E. *386*
Sebastian, Peter *374*
Sebastian, William K. *81, 83, 85, 87, 89, 91, 93, 95, 292*
Sebelius, Keith G. *252, 255, 258, 262, 265, 268*
Sebestyn, Quida *547*
Sebree, Edmund B. *342, 343*
Sebrell, John N. *527*
Sebring, William H. *387*
Seccombe, James *205*
Secor, Philip *407*
Secrest, Robert T. *195, 199, 202, 205, 208, 221, 225, 228, 244, 247*
Seddon, James A. *81, 85, 319, 320*
Sedgwick, Charles B. *94, 96*
Sedgwick, John *336, 337, 338*
Sedgwick, Samuel H. *304*
Sedgwick, Theodore *3, 41, 42, 43, 44, 45, 46, 301*
Sedgwick, William T. *518*
Sedita, Frank A. *393*
See, Horace *520*
Seebold, Andrew L. *419*
Seeger, Walter G. *499*
Seegers, J. Conrad *413*
Seeley, Elias P. *305*
Seeley, John E. *107*
Seely, Paul S. *476*
Seely-Brown, Horace, Jr. *216, 223, 226, 229, 232, 239*
Seelye, Julius H. *111, 403*
Seelye, Laurens H. *415*
Seelye, Laurenus *416*
Seelye, Talcott W. *374*
Seerley, Homer H. *421*
Seerley, John J. *130*
Sees, John V. *475*
Segal, Bernard G. *511, 512, 532*
Segall, Joel *404*
Segar, Joseph E. *97*
Seger, Charles B. *498*
Seger, Charles P. *498*
Seger, George N. *179, 182, 185, 189, 192, 195, 198, 201, 205*

Seghers, Charles J. *464*
Segnar, Sam F. *489*
Segre, Emilio *550*
Seguin, Edouard C. *516*
Sehon, John L. *386*
Seibels, John J. *356*
Seiberling, Francis *189, 192*
Seiberling, Frank A. *489*
Seiberling, John F. *257, 260, 263, 266, 269, 272, 275, 278*
Seibert, Donald V. *494*
Seibold, Louis *553*
Seidel, Emil *17, 399*
Seidensticker, Edward G. *545*
Seidewitz, Edwin A. *390*
Seidman, J. S. *514*
Seignious, George M., II *328*
Seimes, Mrs. Erwin F. *526*
Seip, Theodore L. *413*
Seitz, Collins J. *284*
Seitz, Frederick *517, 539, 549*
Seitz, Henry J. *544*
Seitz, Philip F. D. *541*
Selby, Cecily C. *523*
Selby, John D. *486*
Selby, Thomas H. *386*
Selby, Thomas J. *144*
Selden, Armistead I., Jr. *226, 229, 232, 235, 238, 242, 245, 248, 361, 376*
Selden, David *503*
Selden, Dudley *69*
Selden, Samuel L. *306*
Selden, William *381*
Seldomridge, Harry H. *162*
Seldon, Armistead I., Jr. *368*
Selecman, Charles C. *416, 471*
Selecman, Charles E. *499*
Selig, Lester N. *499*
Seligman, Arthur *305, 393*
Seligman, E. R. A. *510*
Seligman, Edwin R. A. *513*
Selikoff, Irving *543*
Sella, George J., Jr. *481*
Sellars, Richard B. *490*
Selleck, John K. *421*
Selleck, R. H. *434*
Seller, David F. *347*
Sellers, Charles C. *534*
Sellers, Coleman *520, 522*
Sellers, David F. *418*
Sellers, Robert V. *485*
Sellers, William *522*
Sellery, George C. *423*
Sellin, Thorsten *509*
Sells, Sam R. *161, 164, 167, 170, 174*
Selmon, A. C. *432*
Selton, Robert W. *345*
Selvig, Conrad G. *185, 188, 191*
Selvig, Forrest *437*
Selway, George R. *455, 460*
Selye, Lewis *102*
Semmes, B. J., Jr. *349*
Semmes, Benedict J. *66, 67*
Semmes, Benedict J., Jr. *348, 352*
Semmes, Raphael *324, 437*
Semmes, Thomas J. *320, 321, 511*
Semon, Waldo L. *537*
Semple, Ellen C. *537*
Semple, James *78, 80, 296, 358*
Semple, W. T. *510*
Sena, Jose D. *393*
Sendak, Maurice *547*
Sener, James B. *110*
Seney, George E. *121, 124, 126, 129*
Seney, Joshua *3, 41, 42*
Senn, Nicholas *515*

Smith, Howard W. *193, 196, 199, 203, 206, 209, 212, 216, 219, 222, 225, 228, 232, 235, 238, 241, 244, 248*
Smith, Huldah M. *439*
Smith, Hulett C. *314*
Smith, Isaac *44, 54*
Smith, Israel *42, 43, 44, 47, 48, 49, 50, 313*
Smith, J. A. *324*
Smith, J. Amber *110*
Smith, J. Emil *388*
Smith, J. Frank *473*
Smith, J. Henry *487*
Smith, J. Hyatt *118*
Smith, J. Joseph *197, 200, 203, 207, 284*
Smith, J. L. *397*
Smith, J. Lawrence *509, 511*
Smith, J. Lucian *485*
Smith, J. Millard *412*
Smith, J. Russell *537*
Smith, J. Stanford *490*
Smith, J. W. *395*
Smith, J. Waldo *539*
Smith, James *1, 4*
Smith, James, Jr. *134, 139, 305*
Smith, James F. *286, 287*
Smith, James H., Jr. *379*
Smith, James M. *321, 411*
Smith, James Morton *439*
Smith, James S. *57, 58*
Smith, James V. *250*
Smith, James W. *397, 486*
Smith, James Y. *310, 395*
Smith, Jedediah K. *50*
Smith, Jeffrey G. *333*
Smith, Jeremiah *42, 43, 44, 45, 304, 305*
Smith, Jerome V. C. *390*
Smith, Jesse M. *520*
Smith, Joe F. *398*
Smith, Joe L. *190, 193, 196, 200, 203, 206, 209, 213*
Smith, Joel P. *407*
Smith, John *6, 46, 47, 48, 49, 50, 51, 52, 53, 54, 75, 306, 308*
Smith, John A. *105, 107, 406*
Smith, John B. *304, 409, 417, 473*
Smith, John C. *45, 46, 47, 48, 293, 474*
Smith, John C., Jr. *356*
Smith, John Cotton *511*
Smith, John E. *337, 338*
Smith, John F., Jr. *490*
Smith, John G. *313*
Smith, John Hugh *396*
Smith, John L. *494*
Smith, John Lee *524*
Smith, John M. C. *159, 163, 166, 169, 172, 175*
Smith, John Owen *472*
Smith, John Q. *109*
Smith, John S. *59*
Smith, John T. *79*
Smith, John V. *351*
Smith, John W. *300, 388, 391, 397*
Smith, John Walter *142, 153, 156, 159, 162, 166, 169, 172*
Smith, Jonathan B. *4*
Smith, Jonathan Bayard *2*
Smith, Joseph *346, 349, 476*
Smith, Joseph F. *476*
Smith, Joseph Fielding *476*
Smith, Joseph M. *295*
Smith, Joseph S. *105*
Smith, Joseph T. *473*
Smith, Josiah *47*

Smith, Justin H. *553*
Smith, Kate *552*
Smith, Kenneth G. *527*
Smith, Kingsbury *555*
Smith, L. P. *398*
Smith, Larry *274, 277*
Smith, Lauren H. *533*
Smith, Lawrence H. *209, 213, 216, 219, 222, 225, 229, 232, 235*
Smith, Len Y. *527*
Smith, Leo R. *468*
Smith, Leslie R. *476*
Smith, Loren A. *286*
Smith, Luther M. *408*
Smith, Madison R. *154, 363*
Smith, Malcolm B. *433*
Smith, Marcus A. *158, 161, 165, 168, 171, 292*
Smith, Margaret Chase *204, 207, 211, 214, 217, 220, 223, 227, 230, 233, 236, 239, 243, 246, 249, 252, 255, 299, 548*
Smith, Margaret H. D. *542*
Smith, Margaret Mackall *20*
Smith, Marion *391*
Smith, Mark A. *523*
Smith, Martin F. *196, 200, 203, 206, 209*
Smith, Martin L. *323, 338*
Smith, Mason *525*
Smith, Mathew C. *338*
Smith, Melancthon *4*
Smith, Meriwether *4*
Smith, Merriman *552, 556*
Smith, Milton H. *491*
Smith, Mrs. Waklee Rawson *526*
Smith, Munroe *517*
Smith, Myrtle Holm *476*
Smith, Nathan *68, 70, 294*
Smith, Nathaniel *43, 44*
Smith, Neal *236, 239, 242, 246, 249, 252, 255, 258, 262, 265, 268, 271, 274, 277*
Smith, Nels H. *315*
Smith, Nelson Lee *380*
Smith, Norman M. *349, 422*
Smith, Norvel L. *433*
Smith, Oberlin *520*
Smith, O'Brien *49*
Smith, Olcott D. *481*
Smith, Oliver H. *64, 72, 74, 76, 297*
Smith, Orson *486*
Smith, Osborn L. *408*
Smith, Otis *412*
Smith, Owen L. W. *366*
Smith, Page *534*
Smith, Paul F. *345*
Smith, Paul J. *437*
Smith, Paul T. *330*
Smith, Perry *72, 74, 76, 294*
Smith, Perry M. *351*
Smith, Philip A. *456, 460*
Smith, Philip L. *488*
Smith, Preston *312*
Smith, R. C. *504*
Smith, R. Rundle *442*
Smith, Ralph C. *342, 343*
Smith, Ralph T. *252, 296*
Smith, Reginald H. *532*
Smith, Rhoten A. *413*
Smith, Richard *4*
Smith, Richard T. *542*
Smith, Robert *23, 33, 35, 78, 80, 82, 91, 420, 447, 461, 473*
Smith, Robert A. *391*
Smith, Robert B. *303*
Smith, Robert C. *278*
Smith, Robert H. *319*

Smith, Robert I. *495*
Smith, Robert Montgomery *442*
Smith, Robert P. *362, 366, 367*
Smith, Robert S. *365*
Smith, Roger B. *489*
Smith, Ronald B. *520*
Smith, Rosalynn *20*
Smith, S. S. *397*
Smith, S. Stanhope *409, 414, 473*
Smith, Samuel *42, 43, 44, 45, 46, 47, 48, 49, 50, 51, 52, 53, 54, 55, 56, 58, 59, 61, 62, 64, 65, 66, 67, 300, 390*
Smith, Samuel A. *66, 68, 89, 91, 93*
Smith, Samuel E. *299, 518*
Smith, Samuel F. *494*
Smith, Samuel H. *425*
Smith, Samuel W. *139, 142, 145, 147, 150, 153, 156, 159, 163*
Smith, Seymour A. *416*
Smith, Soloman A. *493*
Smith, Solomon A. *486, 493*
Smith, Stephen *518*
Smith, Sydney *302*
Smith, Sylvester C. *149, 152, 155, 158*
Smith, Sylvester C., Jr. *511*
Smith, Theobald *561*
Smith, Thomas *4, 6, 55, 74, 78, 80, 442*
Smith, Thomas A. *150*
Smith, Thomas B. *395*
Smith, Thomas F. *170, 173*
Smith, Thomas J. *410, 413*
Smith, Thomas L. *485*
Smith, Thomas M. *411*
Smith, Thomas Rhett *396*
Smith, Thomas S. *411*
Smith, Thomas V. *204*
Smith, Thomas W. M. *362, 369*
Smith, Thorowgood *390*
Smith, Tom K. *510*
Smith, Tony *532, 535*
Smith, Truman *74, 76, 79, 81, 83, 85, 87, 294*
Smith, Vincent *536*
Smith, Virginia *262, 265, 268, 272, 275, 278*
Smith, Virginia B. *424*
Smith, W. Angie *471*
Smith, W. Herman *398*
Smith, W. J. *417*
Smith, W. N. H. *320, 321*
Smith, W. Warren *503*
Smith, Waldo E. *513*
Smith, Walter Bedell *333, 375, 379, 548*
Smith, Walter G. *542*
Smith, Walter George *511*
Smith, Walter I. *141, 144, 147, 150, 153, 156, 159, 285*
Smith, Walter L. *408*
Smith, Walter "Red" *557*
Smith, Wendell L. *432*
Smith, Wendell R. *515*
Smith, Willard J. *382*
Smith, William *1, 3, 7, 15, 41, 45, 55, 57, 58, 60, 62, 63, 65, 66, 77, 89, 91, 93, 95, 311, 313, 321, 422, 442*
Smith, William, Jr. *422*
Smith, William A. *109, 298, 415, 521, 533*
Smith, William Alden *136, 139, 142, 145, 147, 150, 153, 156, 159, 163, 166, 169*
Smith, William B. *395*

Smith, William E. *110, 113, 115, 315, 321*
Smith, William F. *284, 336, 337*
Smith, William French *32, 35*
Smith, William H. *291, 412*
Smith, William Henry *484*
Smith, William J. *105*
Smith, William Jay *544*
Smith, William L. *41, 42, 43, 44, 45, 370*
Smith, William N. H. *94, 307*
Smith, William O. *148, 151*
Smith, William R. *85, 87, 89, 149, 152, 155, 158, 161, 164, 167, 320, 321, 333, 418, 504*
Smith, William Reece, Jr. *511*
Smith, William S. *54, 301, 337*
Smith, William S., Jr. *495*
Smith, William W. *415*
Smith, Willis *221, 224, 228, 307, 511*
Smith, Wint *217, 220, 223, 226, 230, 233, 236*
Smith, Worthington *423*
Smith, Worthington C. *103, 105, 107*
Smith, Zachary T., II *431*
Smith 2d, Benjamin A. *240*
Smithburg, William D. *495*
Smithers, Nathaniel B. *97*
Smithwick, John H. *171, 175, 178, 181*
Smoke, Richard *534*
Smoot, Abraham O. *397*
Smoot, Reed *149, 152, 155, 158, 161, 164, 167, 170, 174, 177, 180, 183, 186, 190, 193, 312*
Smoot, William A. S. *499*
Smylie, Robert E. *296*
Smyser, Hamilton M. *524*
Smyser, Martin L. *129, 151*
Smyth, Alexander *57, 59, 60, 62, 65, 67, 331, 335*
Smyth, Constantine J. *286*
Smyth, Frederick *7, 304*
Smyth, George W. *89*
Smyth, Henry D. *517, 562*
Smyth, Herbert W. *517*
Smyth, J. Adger *396*
Smyth, John H. *366*
Smyth, Lindley *488*
Smyth, Timothy C. *466*
Smyth, W. Frank *512*
Smyth, William *104*
Smythe, F. R. *394*
Smythe, George W. *344*
Smythe, Henry M. *360, 363*
Smythe, Hugh H. *367, 374*
Smythe, Mabel M. *357*
Smythe, Mable Murphy *361*
Snapp, Henry *106*
Snapp, Howard M. *147, 150, 153, 156*
Snavely, Guy *411*
Snead, Harold F. *314*
Snead, Thomas L. *321*
Snead, William S. *487*
Sneath, William S. *498*
Snedecor, Estes *527*
Sneed, Joseph T., III *286*
Sneed, Thomas E. *397*
Sneed, William H. *91*
Sneeden, Emory *284*
Sneer, George *388*
Sneider, Richard L. *371*
Snelbaker, David T. *394*
Snell, Bertrand H. *166, 170, 173, 176, 179, 182, 186, 189, 192, 195, 198, 202*
Snell, Earl *309*

Stanton, Robert L. *412, 473*
Stanton, William H. *112*
Stanwell-Fletcher, Theodora *536*
Staples, D. T. *489*
Staples, P. A. *432*
Staples, Philip C. *522*
Staples, Waller R. *320, 321*
Staples, William R. *310*
Stapleton, Benjamin F. *386*
Stapleton, Walter K. *284*
Stapp, E. Lee *524*
Stapp, John Paul *537*
Starbird, George *386*
Starcher, George W. *421*
Starck, Taylor *524*
Stareck, Jesse E. *544*
Stariha, John N. *469*
Starin, John H. *114, 116*
Staring, Merlin H. *347*
Stark, Benjamin *96, 309*
Stark, Dudley S. *454, 461*
Stark, Fortney H. *258, 261, 264, 270, 273, 277*
Stark, Fortney H., Jr. *267*
Stark, Harold R. *347, 349*
Stark, Leland *454, 460*
Stark, Lloyd Crow *303*
Stark, Louis *554*
Stark, Robert *396*
Stark, William L. *139, 142, 145*
Starkey, Frank T. *214*
Starkey, Thomas A. *448, 460*
Starkweather, David A. *75, 81, 358*
Starkweather, George A. *82*
Starkweather, Henry H. *101, 103, 105, 108, 110*
Starkweather, Samuel *394*
Starnes, Joe *197, 200, 203, 206, 210*
Starr, Chauncey *516*
Starr, Eliza A. *542*
Starr, Eugene C. *543*
Starr, Isaac *532*
Starr, John F. *98, 100*
Starr, Kenneth W. *286*
Starr, Louis E. *528*
Starr, M. Kenneth *440*
Starr, Moses A. *516*
Starr, Paul *534, 558*
Starr, Richard C. *521*
Starr, S. Frederick *414*
Starr, Steve *557*
Starr, William G. *415*
Starry, Donn A. *333*
Start, Charles N. *302*
Start, Theodore *396*
Stassen, Harold E. *301, 379, 422, 475*
Staton, David M. (Mick) *273*
Statton, Arthur *472*
Staub, E. Norman *493*
Stauffer, John N. *426*
Stauffer, S. Walter *228, 234*
Staunton, E. W. *398*
Staupers, Mabel Keaton *561*
Staver, LeRoy B. *498*
Stayton, John W. *312*
Steadman, David *442*
Steagall, Henry B. *165, 168, 171, 174, 177, 181, 184, 187, 190, 193, 197, 200, 203, 206, 210*
Stearly, Wilson R. *451, 460*
Stearman, Lloyd *491*
Stearns, Asahel *55*
Stearns, Charles F. *310*
Stearns, Edward V. B. *510*
Stearns, Foster *205, 208, 211*
Stearns, Frederic P. *519*
Stearns, H. P. *518*

Stearns, Jonathan F. *473*
Stearns, Marcellus L. *295*
Stearns, Monteagle *363, 365*
Stearns, Onslow *304*
Stearns, Ozora P. *104, 302*
Stearns, Raymond P. *545*
Stearns, Robert E. C. *438*
Stearns, Robert L. *419*
Stearns, William A. *403*
Stebbins, Ernest L. *518, 526*
Stebbins, G. Ledyard *543, 549*
Stebbins, G. Ledyard, Jr. *521*
Stebbins, Henry E. *368, 374*
Stebbins, Henry G. *98*
Stebbins, Joel *510, 560*
Steck, Amos *386*
Steck, Daniel F. *181, 184, 188, 297*
Stedman, Charles M. *160, 163, 166, 170, 173, 176, 179, 182, 186, 189*
Stedman, Edmund C. *526*
Stedman, Henry R. *516*
Stedman, Seymour *18*
Stedman, William *48, 49, 50, 51*
Stedman, William Perry, Jr. *357*
Steed, Thomas J. *221, 225, 228, 231, 234, 237, 241, 244, 247, 250, 253, 257*
Steed, Tom *260, 263, 266, 269*
Steedman, James B. *338*
Steegmuller, Francis *546, 548*
Steel, George *348*
Steel, Ronald *534, 547*
Steele, Alfred N. *494*
Steele, E. N. *398*
Steele, Edwin G. *562*
Steele, Frederick *337*
Steele, George *481*
Steele, George McK. *411*
Steele, George W. *117, 120, 122, 125, 136, 138, 141, 144*
Steele, Harry L. *331*
Steele, Henry J. *167, 170, 173*
Steele, Holmes *387*
Steele, Isaac N. *375*
Steele, James B. *557*
Steele, James H. *535*
Steele, John *41, 42*
Steele, John B. *96, 98*
Steele, John H. *304*
Steele, John N. *69, 71*
Steele, Leslie J. *184, 187*
Steele, Robert D. *406*
Steele, Robert H. *252, 255, 258*
Steele, Robert W. *293*
Steele, Thomas J. *165*
Steele, W. L. *392*
Steele, Walter L. *114, 116, 562*
Steele, William G. *96, 98*
Steelman, Alan *260, 263*
Steelman, John R. *379*
Steenerson, Halvor *148, 150, 153, 156, 159, 163, 166, 169, 172, 175*
Steenrod, Lewis *76, 77, 79*
Steenwyck, Cornelius *393*
Steere, William C. *521*
Steers, Newton I., Jr. *265*
Steeves, B. L. *395*
Steeves, John M. *355*
Stefan, Karl *198, 201, 205, 208, 211, 214, 218, 221, 224*
Stefansson, Vilhjalmur *538, 541*
Stegemeier, Richard *498*
Stegemeier, Richard J. *498*
Stegemoeller, Harvey A. *406*
Steger, Joseph A. *419*
Stegink, L. D. *542*
Stegner, Wallace *546*
Stegner, Wallace E. *557*

Steichen, Edward *532, 552*
Steig, William *547*
Steiger, Sam *248, 251, 254, 258*
Steiger, William A. *251, 254, 257, 260, 264, 267, 270*
Steigman, Andrew L. *362, 372*
Stein, Claire A. *526*
Stein, Clarence S. *532*
Stein, Robert A. *366*
Stein, Sol *505*
Stein, William H. *550*
Steinbach, Alice *558*
Steinbach, H. Burr *520*
Steinbeck, John *550, 552, 554*
Steinberg, Saul *547*
Steinbrocker, Ann *560*
Steiner, Celestin J. *419, 427*
Steiner, Donald F. *551*
Steiner, John E. *561*
Steinert, William J. *314*
Steinfeld, Jesse L. *381*
Steinhardt, Laurence A. *358, 359, 370, 373, 374, 375*
Steinkraus, Herman W. *522*
Steinman, B. U. *386*
Steinmetz, Charles P. *537*
Steitz, Joan A. *549*
Steiwer, Frederick *186, 189, 192, 196, 199, 202, 309*
Stelger, Sam *261*
Stelle, John *514*
Stelle, John H. *296*
Stellhorn, William F. *406*
Steloff, Frances *547*
Stempf, Victor H. *525*
Stenger, William S. *112, 114*
Stengle, Charles I. *179, 503*
Stenholm, Charles W. *270, 273, 276, 279*
Stennis, John C. *217, 221, 224, 227, 230, 233, 237, 240, 243, 246, 249, 253, 256, 259, 262, 265, 268, 271, 275, 278, 302*
Stenvig, Charles *391*
Stephan, Edmund A. *542*
Stephan, Evelyn *542*
Stephansky, Ben S. *357*
Stephen, Adam *335*
Stephens, Abraham P. *86*
Stephens, Albert Lee *285*
Stephens, Alexander *319*
Stephens, Alexander H. *78, 80, 81, 83, 85, 87, 89, 91, 108, 110, 113, 115, 117, 295, 319*
Stephens, Ambrose E. B. *173, 176, 179, 183*
Stephens, Daniel V. *160, 163, 166, 169*
Stephens, E. W. *475*
Stephens, Frederick *393*
Stephens, H. Morse *513*
Stephens, Harold M. *286*
Stephens, Hubert D. *159, 163, 166, 169, 172, 179, 182, 185, 188, 191, 195, 302*
Stephens, John H. *140, 143, 146, 149, 152, 155, 158, 161, 164, 167*
Stephens, John L. *361*
Stephens, L. L. *396*
Stephens, Lon V. *302*
Stephens, Olin J. *562*
Stephens, Philander *66, 68*
Stephens, Robert G. *239*
Stephens, Robert G., Jr. *242, 245, 249, 252, 255, 258, 261*
Stephens, Samuel *5*
Stephens, Thomas J. *394*
Stephens, William *5*
Stephens, William D. *158, 161, 165, 292, 386*

Stephenson, Andrew *62*
Stephenson, Helen A *521*
Stephenson, Isaac *122, 124, 127, 155, 158, 161, 164, 315*
Stephenson, James *48, 52, 60, 62*
Stephenson, John B. *404*
Stephenson, John G. *380*
Stephenson, Rome C. *510*
Stephenson, Roy Laverne *285*
Stephenson, Samuel M. *128, 130, 133, 136*
Stephenson, William B. *514*
Sterett, James P. *309*
Sterett, Samuel *42*
Sterigere, John B. *65, 66*
Sterling, Ansel *59, 60*
Sterling, Bruce F. *170*
Sterling, Chandler W. *454, 459*
Sterling, Donald J. *520*
Sterling, Frederick A. *357, 361, 364, 366, 373*
Sterling, J. E. Wallace *416, 439*
Sterling, John A. *147, 150, 153, 156, 159, 165, 168*
Sterling, John W. *423*
Sterling, Micah *60*
Sterling, Ross S. *312*
Sterling, Theodore *411*
Sterling, Thomas *164, 167, 170, 174, 177, 180, 311*
Sterling, Walter G. *527*
Stern, Curt *520*
Stern, Frank *562*
Stern, Harold P. *439*
Stern, Horace *309*
Stern, Otto *549*
Stern, Paula *382*
Stern, Richard *532*
Stern, Sam *521*
Sternberg, George M. *332, 515, 518*
Sterne, Bobbie *394*
Sterne, Maurice *536*
Sterner, James H. *526*
Sterner, Michael *375*
Sterrett, Frank W. *451, 458*
Sterud, Eugene *521*
Stetson, Charles *84*
Stetson, Herbert L. *411*
Stetson, John B., Jr. *361, 370*
Stetson, John C. *327*
Stetson, Lemuel *79*
Stettinius, Edward R., Jr. *29, 33, 499, 548*
Steuart, Leonard P. *527*
Steuart, William *390*
Steunenberg, Frank *296*
Stevens, Aaron F. *102, 104*
Stevens, Albert W. *535, 541*
Stevens, Alexander H. *515*
Stevens, Benjamin F. *493*
Stevens, Bradford N. *106*
Stevens, Breese J. *398*
Stevens, Charles A. *108*
Stevens, Daniel *396*
Stevens, Edmund *555*
Stevens, Eugene M. *486*
Stevens, Frederick C. *139, 142, 145, 148, 150, 153, 156, 159, 163*
Stevens, George *509, 522*
Stevens, George W. *443*
Stevens, Henry L., Jr. *514*
Stevens, Hester L. *88*
Stevens, Isaac I. *336*
Stevens, J. Putnam *527*
Stevens, James *57*
Stevens, James H. *397*
Stevens, John *4*
Stevens, John C. *519*

Sturgis, R. Clipston *514*
Sturgis, Samuel D. *336, 337*
Sturgis, Samuel D., Jr. *331*
Sturgiss, George C. *155, 158*
Sturm, Clarence L. *524*
Sturtevant, A. H. *520*
Sturtevant, Alfred H. *549*
Sturtevant, Harwood *452, 459*
Sturtevant, John C. *140*
Stutesman, James F. *357*
Stuyvesant, Peter *5*
Styron, William *541, 546, 557*
Suarez, Miss Rocio *431*
Suau, Anthony *558*
Subblefield, Frank A. *243*
Suczek, Robert *544*
Sugarman, George *551*
Sugden, Walter S. *527*
Suggs, John T. *492*
Sullins, David *408*
Sullivan, A. M. *527*
Sullivan, Barry F. *488*
Sullivan, Christopher D. *170, 173, 176, 179, 182, 186, 189, 192, 195, 198, 202, 205*
Sullivan, David *505*
Sullivan, Denis J. *390*
Sullivan, Donal M. *505*
Sullivan, E. Mark *521*
Sullivan, Ed *525*
Sullivan, Eugene C. *551*
Sullivan, Eugene J. *484*
Sullivan, George *52*
Sullivan, Ignatius A. *386*
Sullivan, J. Stephen *412*
Sullivan, James *3, 300, 392*
Sullivan, James H. *504*
Sullivan, James J. *415*
Sullivan, James L. *475*
Sullivan, James M. *360*
Sullivan, James S. *469*
Sullivan, Jerd F., Jr. *486*
Sullivan, Jerry B. *287*
Sullivan, Jim *560*
Sullivan, John *3, 5, 304, 335*
Sullivan, John A. *147, 150*
Sullivan, John B. *208, 214, 221, 224*
Sullivan, John J. *468*
Sullivan, John L. *304, 327*
Sullivan, John P. *521*
Sullivan, John T. *467*
Sullivan, Joseph P. *497*
Sullivan, Joseph V. *467*
Sullivan, Leon H. *561*
Sullivan, Leonor K. *262*
Sullivan, Leonor Kretzer *227, 230, 233, 237, 240, 243, 246, 249, 253, 256, 259*
Sullivan, Louis H. *532*
Sullivan, Martin E. *442*
Sullivan, Matt I. *293*
Sullivan, Maurice J. *211*
Sullivan, Max W. *442*
Sullivan, Mike *315*
Sullivan, Mortimer A. *424*
Sullivan, Mrs. William H., Jr. *526*
Sullivan, Patrick J. *189, 190, 193, 315*
Sullivan, Peter J. *358*
Sullivan, Reginald H. *388*
Sullivan, Robert *442*
Sullivan, Thomas L. *388*
Sullivan, Timothy D. *148, 151, 163*
Sullivan, Walter *538*
Sullivan, Walter F. *470*
Sullivan, William H. *364, 366, 370*

Sullivan, William V. *139, 142, 302*
Sulloway, Cyrus A. *136, 139, 142, 145, 148, 151, 154, 157, 160, 166, 169*
Sultan, Daniel I. *331, 340, 342*
Sulzberger, Arthur Hays *545, 559*
Sulzberger, Cyrus L. *555*
Sulzberger, Iphigene Ochs *548*
Sulzer, William *137, 139, 142, 145, 148, 151, 154, 157, 160, 306*
Suman, John R. *514, 539, 545*
Summer, James A. *488*
Summerall, Charles P. *329, 333, 339*
Summerfield, Arthur E. *30, 36*
Summerlin, George T. *364, 369, 375*
Summers, A. Burke *366*
Summers, Augustus N. *308*
Summers, Charles *88*
Summers, Frank W. *299*
Summers, George W. *77, 79*
Summers, John W. *174, 177, 180, 183, 187, 190, 193*
Summerskill, John *405*
Summitt, H. C. *387*
Sumner, Arthur P. *526*
Sumner, Charles *86, 90, 92, 94, 96, 98, 100, 102, 104, 106, 108, 301*
Sumner, Charles A. *119*
Sumner, Daniel H. *122*
Sumner, Edwin V. *336*
Sumner, George G. *386*
Sumner, Increase *300*
Sumner, James B. *549*
Sumner, Jessie *204, 207, 210, 213*
Sumner, Jethro *335*
Sumner, Walter T. *451, 460*
Sumner, William G. *520*
Sumners, Hatton W. *164, 167, 170, 174, 177, 180, 183, 186, 190, 193, 196, 199, 203, 206, 209, 212, 215, 532*
Sumter, Thomas *41, 42, 45, 46, 47, 48, 49, 50, 52, 311, 335*
Sumter, Thomas, Jr. *370*
Sumter, Thomas D. *75, 77*
Sumwalt, Robert L. *422*
Sun, Chen *552*
Sund, R. J. *431*
Sunderland, Byron *410*
Sunderman, F. William *519*
Sundquist, Donald K. *279*
Sundstrom, Frank L. *211, 214, 218*
Sunquist, Donald K. *276*
Sununu, John H. *304*
Suomi, Verner E. *539*
Super, Charles W. *414*
Supplee, Henderson, Jr. *483*
Surface, James R. *420*
Surles, Alexander D., Jr. *334*
Surut, L. E. *351*
Sutherland, Archibald H. *331*
Sutherland, Charles *332*
Sutherland, Earl W., Jr. *532, 543, 549, 550*
Sutherland, Edwin H. *520*
Sutherland, George *146, 152, 155, 158, 161, 164, 167, 283, 312, 511*
Sutherland, Howard *164, 167, 171, 174, 177, 315*
Sutherland, Jabez G. *106*
Sutherland, James W., Jr. *344*

Sutherland, Joel B. *65, 66, 68, 70, 72*
Sutherland, Josiah *86*
Sutherland, Peter A. *356*
Sutherland, Roderick D. *139, 142*
Sutphin, William H. *192, 195, 198, 201, 205, 208*
Sutro, Adolph *386*
Sutter, Joseph *561*
Sutter, Joseph F. *563*
Suttie, J. W. *542*
Sutton, George M. *536*
Sutton, Glenn W. *382*
Sutton, Goyn A. *388*
Sutton, Henry M. *562*
Sutton, James P. *222, 225, 228*
Sutton, Joseph L. *410*
Sutton, Leonard B. *293*
Sutton, William J. *332*
Sutton, William S. *423*
Suzzallo, Henry *423*
Svahn, John A. *382*
Swaebe, Geoffrey *356*
Swaim, H. Nathan *285*
Swain, Charles A. *523*
Swain, David G. *331*
Swain, David L. *307, 421*
Swain, Donald C. *420*
Swain, George F. *519*
Swain, Joseph *410, 416*
Swain, Mrs. Leslie E. *475*
Swain, Robert L. *559*
Swain, W. W. *397*
Swainson, John B. *301*
Swales, William E. *491*
Swallow, Silas C. *17*
Swan, John *4*
Swan, Joseph R. *308*
Swan, Samuel *60, 61, 63, 64, 66*
Swan, Thomas W. *284*
Swan, William G. *321*
Swanberg, W. A. *546, 557*
Swank, Emory C. *365*
Swank, Fletcher B. *176, 180, 183, 186, 192, 196*
Swann, Edward *145*
Swann, Richard *390*
Swann, Sherlock, Jr. *522*
Swann, Thomas *104, 106, 108, 111, 113, 300, 390*
Swann, William F. G. *537*
Swansen, Raymond *506*
Swanson, Charles E. *188, 191*
Swanson, Claude A. *29, 35, 135, 137, 140, 143, 146, 149, 152, 158, 161, 164, 167, 171, 174, 177, 180, 183, 187, 190, 193, 313*
Swanson, Clifford A. *347*
Swanson, Ralph A. *398*
Swanwick, John *44, 45*
Swart, Peter *50*
Swarts, Gardner T. *518*
Swartwout, Mary Cooke *440*
Swartwout, Robert *332*
Swartz, Carl E. *519, 534*
Swartz, Joshua W. *183*
Swartz, William J. *483*
Swasey, Ambrose *520, 533, 539, 541*
Swasey, John P. *153, 156*
Swayne, Noah H. *283*
Sweall, Samuel *44*
Swearer, Howard R. *405, 406*
Swearingen, Eugene L. *423*
Swearingen, Henry *73, 75*
Swearingen, Henry C. *473*
Swearingen, John E. *482, 533*
Swearingen, Van C. *387*

Sweat, Lorenzo D. M. *98*
Sweatt, Harold W. *489*
Sweazey, George E. *474*
Sweeney, David McC. *279*
Sweeney, James J. *466*
Sweeney, James Johnson *439, 441*
Sweeney, James P. *405*
Sweeney, John J. *505*
Sweeney, Martin L. *192, 195, 199, 202, 205, 208*
Sweeney, Robert E. *247*
Sweeney, Thomas W. *338*
Sweeney, Walter C., Jr. *346*
Sweeney, William N. *104*
Sweeney, Zachary T. *476*
Sweeny, Edward C. *525*
Sweeny, George *75, 77*
Sweet, Burton E. *165, 168, 172, 175*
Sweet, Edwin F. *159*
Sweet, Frederick A. *442*
Sweet, James R. *397*
Sweet, John E. *520, 539*
Sweet, John H. *205*
Sweet, Philip W. K., Jr. *493*
Sweet, Thaddeus C. *179, 182, 186*
Sweet, William E. *293, 475*
Sweet, William H. *404*
Sweet, Willis *127, 130, 133*
Sweetland, William H. *310*
Sweetser, Charles *84, 86*
Sweetser, Frank L. *515, 525*
Sweney, Joseph H. *127*
Swengel, Uriah *472*
Swenson, Eric P. *485*
Swenson, Harold A. *395*
Swenson, Laurits S. *360, 368, 369, 373*
Swenson, May *531, 534, 561*
Swenson, Orvar *542*
Swensrud, Sidney A. *489*
Swetman, Ralph W. *403*
Swett, Josiah *414*
Swick, J. Howard *186, 189, 193, 196*
Swidler, Joseph C. *380*
Swift, A. Dean *496*
Swift, A. Ervine *454*
Swift, Allan B. *270, 273, 276, 279*
Swift, Benjamin *65, 67, 70, 72, 74, 313*
Swift, C. H. *386*
Swift, Eben *351*
Swift, George B. *388*
Swift, George R. *213, 291*
Swift, Gustavus F., Jr. *497*
Swift, Gustavus F., Sr. *497*
Swift, H. A. *301*
Swift, Innis P. *341, 343*
Swift, John *395*
Swift, Joseph G. *331, 418*
Swift, Louis F. *497*
Swift, Oscar W. *166, 170*
Swift, Willis E. *389*
Swift, Zephaniah *42, 43, 294*
Swiger, Ernest G. *525*
Swigert, Jack *273*
Swigert, John L., Jr. *552*
Swigert, Phillip *389*
Swinburne, John *123, 393*
Swindall, Charles *173*
Swindall, Patrick *277*
Swing, Joseph M. *334, 343, 351, 380*
Swing, Philip D. *174, 178, 181, 184, 187, 190*
Swing, William E. *458*
Swing, William Edwin *457*

Taylor, Frederick W. *449, 461, 520*
Taylor, Gene *259, 262, 265, 268, 271, 275, 278*
Taylor, George *1, 4, 92*
Taylor, George A. *455, 458*
Taylor, George W. *138, 141, 143, 146, 149, 152, 155, 158, 161, 552*
Taylor, Glen *18*
Taylor, Glen H. *213, 216, 220, 296*
Taylor, H. Birchard *537*
Taylor, H. M. *391*
Taylor, Hannis *373*
Taylor, Harold *416*
Taylor, Harry *331*
Taylor, Henry *551, 559*
Taylor, Henry C. *352*
Taylor, Henry Clay *349*
Taylor, Henry J. *374*
Taylor, Henry O. *513*
Taylor, Herbert J. *527*
Taylor, Herbert W. *176, 182*
Taylor, Horace D. *397*
Taylor, Howard C. *511*
Taylor, Howard C., Jr. *511*
Taylor, Hugh S. *434, 539*
Taylor, Isaac H. *124*
Taylor, J. Alfred *180, 183*
Taylor, J. Randolph *474*
Taylor, J. Will *174, 177, 180, 183, 186, 190, 193, 196, 199, 202, 206*
Taylor, J. Winthrop *347*
Taylor, Jack D. *494*
Taylor, James M. *424*
Taylor, John *42, 43, 48, 50, 52, 53, 54, 55, 60, 62, 306, 310, 311, 314, 393, 396, 476, 533*
Taylor, John C. *196, 199, 202*
Taylor, John J. *88*
Taylor, John L. *83, 84, 86, 88, 307*
Taylor, John M. *121, 124, 348, 485*
Taylor, John W. *54, 55, 57, 58, 60, 61, 62, 63, 64, 66, 68, 420*
Taylor, Jonathan *75*
Taylor, Joseph *551*
Taylor, Joseph D. *119, 121, 126, 129, 131*
Taylor, Joshua C. *441*
Taylor, Lady Bird [Claudia Alta] *20*
Taylor, Leon *305*
Taylor, Lily R. *517*
Taylor, Mark P. *394*
Taylor, Maxwell D. *328, 329, 330, 333, 334, 343, 344, 375, 418, 548*
Taylor, Miles *90, 91, 94*
Taylor, Moses *485*
Taylor, Moulton B. *544*
Taylor, Myron C. *499*
Taylor, Nathaniel G. *89, 101*
Taylor, Nelson *100*
Taylor, Nelson F. *421*
Taylor, Nettie Barcrott *543*
Taylor, Paul *535, 536*
Taylor, Peter *547*
Taylor, Prince A., Jr. *472*
Taylor, R. L. *347*
Taylor, Reese H. *498*
Taylor, Richard M. *398*
Taylor, Richard R. *332*
Taylor, Robert *63*
Taylor, Robert F. *295*
Taylor, Robert L. *117, 155, 158, 161, 311, 312*

Taylor, Robert Lewis *556*
Taylor, Roy A. *237, 240, 244, 247, 250, 253, 256, 260, 263*
Taylor, Russell J. *506*
Taylor, S. J. *391*
Taylor, Sam F. *416*
Taylor, Samuel M. *158, 161, 165, 168, 171, 174*
Taylor, Simon *396*
Taylor, Stephen W. *406*
Taylor, Theophilus M. *474*
Taylor, Vincent A. *131*
Taylor, W. R. L. *398*
Taylor, Waller *55, 56, 57, 59, 61, 297*
Taylor, Walter P. *522*
Taylor, Wayne C. *379*
Taylor, William *69, 71, 73, 79, 81, 471*
Taylor, William C. *551*
Taylor, William H. *391, 494, 554*
Taylor, William J. *490*
Taylor, William P. *70*
Taylor, William R. *315*
Taylor, William S. *298*
Taylor, Zachary *11, 15, 25, 124*
Tazewell, Henry *42, 43, 44, 45, 314*
Tazewell, Littleton W. *15, 46, 62, 63, 65, 67, 68, 313, 314*
Teagle, Walter C. *434, 487, 496, 533*
Teague, Charles M. *229, 232, 235, 239, 242, 245, 248, 251, 255, 258*
Teague, Donald *533*
Teague, Olin E. *219, 222, 225, 228, 231, 235, 238, 241, 244, 248, 251, 254, 257, 260, 263, 266*
Teague, Sam E., Jr. *387*
Teague, W. M. *385*
Teal, B. F. *544*
Teal, Gordon K. *541*
Teale, Edward L., Jr. *561*
Teale, Edwin W. *535, 556*
Teare, B. R., Jr. *523*
Teasdale, Joseph P. *303*
Teasdale, Sara *553*
Tebbetts, George P. *386*
Teel, Warren F. *403*
Teese, Frederick H. *111*
Teets, John W. *482, 483*
Teigan, Henry G. *201*
Teitz, Richard S. *439, 444*
Telfair, Edward *2, 3, 5, 14, 295*
Telfair, Thomas *53, 55*
Telford, William C. *388*
Tellegen, B. D. H. *538*
Teller, Edward *538, 549*
Teller, Henry M. *26, 36, 110, 112, 115, 117, 122, 124, 127, 130, 132, 135, 138, 141, 144, 146, 149, 152, 293*
Teller, Isaac *88*
Teller, James H. *293*
Teller, Ludwig *234, 237*
Telles, Raymond *359*
Tellier, Remigius I. *408*
Telling, Edward R. *496*
Temin, Howard M. *543, 550*
Temple, Edward A. *450, 460*
Temple, Gray *455, 461*
Temple, Henry W. *164, 167, 170, 173, 177, 180, 183, 186, 189, 193*
Temple, J. R. *397*
Temple, Jackson *292*
Temple, William *294*
Templeton, B. J. *396*

Templeton, Charles A. *293*
Templeton, Max A. *391*
Templeton, Thomas W. *170*
Templin, Richard L. *544*
Ten Broeck, Abraham *393*
Ten Broeck, Dirck *393*
Ten Eyck, Anthony *363*
Ten Eyck, Egbert *61, 63*
Ten Eyck, Jacob C. *393*
Ten Eyck, John C. *94, 96, 98*
Ten Eyck, Peter G. *163, 176*
Tench, Thomas *5*
Tenenbaum, Michael *490, 538*
Tener, John K. *157, 309, 521*
Tenerowicz, Rudolph G. *204, 208*
Tennant, Georgina *476*
Tennehill, Wilkins *396*
Tennent, Charles G. *527*
Tennent, David H. *520*
Tennent, William M. *473*
Tenney, Henry M. *414*
Tenney, John S. *300*
Tenney, Samuel *46, 47, 48, 49*
Tenzer, Herbert *247, 250*
Teresa, Mother *553*
Terkel, Studs *558*
Terman, Frederick E. *541, 549*
Terman, Lewis M. *518*
Terral, Thomas J. *292*
Terrell, Alexander W. *374*
Terrell, Daniel V. *519*
Terrell, Edwin E. *356*
Terrell, George B. *196*
Terrell, Glenn, Jr. *425*
Terrell, Henry, Jr. *341, 343*
Terrell, James C. *70*
Terrell, Joseph M. *155, 159, 295*
Terrell, William *56, 57*
Terres, John K. *536*
Terris, Milton *518, 561*
Terry, Alfred H. *339*
Terry, Charles L., Jr. *294*
Terry, David D. *193, 197, 200, 203, 206*
Terry, David S. *292*
Terry, John H. *256*
Terry, Luther L. *381*
Terry, Lyon F. *545*
Terry, Nathaniel *56, 386*
Terry, Thomas A. *340*
Terry, Thomas D. *422*
Terry, Walter *536*
Terry, William *107, 112*
Terry, William L. *129, 132, 135, 138, 141*
Terwilliger, Robert Elwin *456*
Teschemacher, Henry F. *386*
Tesla, Nikola *537, 538*
Test, John *61, 62, 65*
Tetzlaff, Joseph *419*
Tewes, Donald E. *235*
Tewksbury, Donald G. *404*
Tewksbury, Howard H. *369*
Teyral, Hazel J. *536*
Thach, Charles C. *403*
Thach, John S. *347*
Thacher, George *3, 41, 42, 43, 44, 45, 46, 420*
Thacher, George H. *393*
Thacher, John B. *393*
Thacher, John B., II *393*
Thacher, John M. *381*
Thacher, Nicholas G. *372*
Thaler, Louis K. *524*
Thalheimer, Walter J. *385*
Tharp, Marie *541*
Tharp, William *294*
Thatcher, George O. *409*
Thatcher, H. M. *395*

Thatcher, Henry C. *293*
Thatcher, Henry K. *350*
Thatcher, Maurice H. *178, 181, 185, 188, 191*
Thatcher, Roscoe W. *420*
Thatcher, Samuel *47, 48*
Thatcher, Thomas C. *162*
Thaxter, Benjamin A. *411*
Thaxter, Roland *521*
Thayer, Abbott H. *536, 551, 560*
Thayer, Amos M. *285*
Thayer, Andrew J. *96*
Thayer, Benjamin B. *482*
Thayer, Edwin B. *455, 458*
Thayer, Eli *92, 94*
Thayer, Harry B. *482, 499*
Thayer, Harry E. T. *372*
Thayer, Harry I. *182*
Thayer, Henry E. *426*
Thayer, John A. *159*
Thayer, John M. *100, 102, 104, 303*
Thayer, John R. *142, 144, 147*
Thayer, M. Russell *99, 101*
Thayer, Robert H. *371*
Thayer, Samuel R. *368*
Thayer, Sylvanus *418, 540*
Thayer, W. Paul *327, 491*
Thayer, William R. *513, 547*
Thayer, William S. *515*
Thayer, William W. *309*
Theaker, Thomas C. *94, 381*
Thebaud, Augustus J. *408*
Thebaud, Hewlett *347*
Theberge, James D. *358, 368*
Theiler, Max *543, 550*
Theis, John B. *405*
Thelen, Max *431*
Thelen, Max, Jr. *431*
Theobald, John J. *415*
Theophilus, Donald R. *419*
Thernstrom, Stephan *534*
Theuerer, Henry C. *544*
Thibodeau, Gary A. *424*
Thibodeaux, Bannon G. *80, 82*
Thiele, Walter G. *298*
Thielepape, W. C. A. *397*
Thieme, Frederick P. *419*
Thill, Frank A. *466*
Thill, Lewis D. *206, 209*
Thilly, Frank *510*
Thimann, Kenneth V. *521*
Thirkfield, Wilbur *410, 471*
Thistlewood, Napoleon B. *153, 156, 159*
Thoburn, James M. *471*
Thom, Cameron E. *386*
Thom, Horace B. *431*
Thom, William R. *195, 199, 202, 208, 215*
Thomas, A. G. *476*
Thomas, Albert *203, 206, 209, 212, 215, 219, 222, 225, 228, 231, 235, 238, 241, 244, 248*
Thomas, Albert S. *452, 461*
Thomas, Allen *375*
Thomas, Augustus *526, 547*
Thomas, Benjamin F. *96*
Thomas, C. G. *544*
Thomas, C. W. *391*
Thomas, Calvin *512, 524*
Thomas, Charles A. *492, 511, 532, 553*
Thomas, Charles B. *345*
Thomas, Charles R. *107, 109, 142, 145, 148, 151, 154, 157*
Thomas, Charles S. *158, 161, 165, 168, 171, 293, 327, 497*
Thomas, Christopher Y. *110*
Thomas, David *47, 48, 49, 50*

Walgren, Doug *269, 272, 275, 279*
Walgren, Douglas *266*
Walk, William E., Jr. *528*
Walker, A. Earl *516*
Walker, Abram J. *291*
Walker, Alice *547, 558, 560*
Walker, Amasa *96*
Walker, Austin A. *388*
Walker, Benjamin *47*
Walker, Buz M. *412*
Walker, Charles C. B. *111*
Walker, Clement A. *518*
Walker, Clifford *295*
Walker, Cranville T. *476*
Walker, D. Ormonde *426*
Walker, Daniel *296*
Walker, David *56, 58, 292*
Walker, David S. *295, 387*
Walker, David S., Jr. *387*
Walker, Donald *405*
Walker, Donald B. *482*
Walker, E. C. *418*
Walker, E. Don *423*
Walker, E. S. Johnny *247, 250*
Walker, Edward B., III *489*
Walker, Emmett H. *332*
Walker, Eric A. *414*
Walker, Felix *57, 58, 60*
Walker, Francis *43*
Walker, Francis A. *412, 513*
Walker, Frank C. *29, 30, 36, 542*
Walker, Fred L. *342*
Walker, Freeman *57, 59, 295*
Walker, George *53, 298*
Walker, George H. *398*
Walker, George W. *387*
Walker, Gilbert C. *112, 114, 313*
Walker, Glenn D. *344*
Walker, Gordon A. *499*
Walker, Gordon L. *515*
Walker, Henderson *5*
Walker, Henry O. *536*
Walker, Howard K. *374*
Walker, Hugh K. *473*
Walker, Isaac P. *83, 85, 87, 89, 315*
Walker, James *409*
Walker, James A. *137, 140*
Walker, James D. *115, 117, 119, 292*
Walker, James J. *394*
Walker, James M. *485*
Walker, James P. *126, 128*
Walker, Jerald C. *404*
Walker, John *41, 314, 441*
Walker, John C. *322*
Walker, John D. *522*
Walker, John D. G. *349*
Walker, John L. *521*
Walker, John M. *453, 458*
Walker, John R. *162, 165, 168*
Walker, John T. *456, 461*
Walker, John W. *57, 59, 291*
Walker, Joseph A. *537*
Walker, Joseph H. *128, 130, 133, 136, 139*
Walker, Joseph M. *298*
Walker, Julius Waring *375*
Walker, Lannon *372*
Walker, Leland J. *519*
Walker, Leroy P. *319*
Walker, Lewis L. *188*
Walker, M. B. *337*
Walker, Paul A. *379*
Walker, Percy *89*
Walker, Pinkney H. *296*
Walker, Prentiss *246*
Walker, R. L. *398*

Walker, R. Lindsay *323*
Walker, Ralph *514, 532*
Walker, Richard L. *371*
Walker, Richard W. *284, 319*
Walker, Robert B. *481*
Walker, Robert F. *303*
Walker, Robert J. *25, 33, 71, 73, 75, 76, 78, 80, 302*
Walker, Robert J. C. *119*
Walker, Robert S. *266, 269, 272, 275, 279*
Walker, Ronald F. *498*
Walker, Ronald H. *380*
Walker, Sam S. *424*
Walker, Samuel *387*
Walker, Shelby *392*
Walker, Stephen L. *405*
Walker, T. J. *349*
Walker, Thomas J. *287*
Walker, Thomas W. *414*
Walker, Tom P. *497*
Walker, Walter *190*
Walker, Walton H. *334, 341, 343, 344*
Walker, Waurine *525*
Walker, Wilbert A. *434, 499*
Walker, William A. *88*
Walker, William B. *488*
Walker, William D. *449, 460, 462*
Walker, William H. *522*
Walker, William H. T. *323*
Walker, William W. *512*
Walker-Taylor, Yvonne *426*
Walkowitz, Abraham *562*
Walkup, William E. *496*
Wall, Garret D. *71, 75, 305*
Wall, Garrett D. *73*
Wall, James W. *96, 305*
Wall, Joseph F. *534*
Wall, Shannon J. *505*
Wall, William *96*
Wall, William A. *521*
Wallace, Alexander S. *105, 107, 109, 112*
Wallace, Anthony F. C. *509, 534*
Wallace, Bess [Elizabeth Virginia] *20*
Wallace, Charles F. *544*
Wallace, D. A. *473*
Wallace, Daniel *83, 85, 87*
Wallace, David *76, 297*
Wallace, David A. *413*
Wallace, David R. *536*
Wallace, DeWitt *433, 539, 552, 559*
Wallace, Duane *540*
Wallace, Dwane L. *563*
Wallace, Fred C. *341*
Wallace, George C. *19, 291*
Wallace, Harry B. *425*
Wallace, Harry R. *388*
Wallace, Henry *29*
Wallace, Henry A. *12, 18, 29, 30, 37, 206, 209*
Wallace, Henry C. *28, 36*
Wallace, Hugh C. *361*
Wallace, J. Clifford *286*
Wallace, James *411*
Wallace, James M. *55, 57, 58*
Wallace, John F. *519*
Wallace, John M. *397*
Wallace, John W. *97, 112*
Wallace, Jonathan H. *121*
Wallace, Leigh Allen *457*
Wallace, Leigh Allen, Jr. *461*
Wallace, Lew *336, 374*
Wallace, Lila *552*
Wallace, Lurleen B. *291*
Wallace, Mrs. DeWitt *559*

Wallace, Nathaniel D. *123*
Wallace, Robert M. *146, 149, 152, 155*
Wallace, Rodney *128*
Wallace, Tom *520, 523*
Wallace, Walter C. *380*
Wallace, William A. *112, 114, 116, 309*
Wallace, William C. *128*
Wallace, William H. L. *336*
Wallace, William J. *284, 388*
Wallace, William M. *542*
Wallach, Richard *387*
Wallack, Walter M. *512*
Wallau, H. J. *391*
Wallber, Emil *399*
Walleen, Hans A. *521*
Wallenwein, Henry F. *524*
Waller, C. Richard *562*
Waller, Curtis L. *284*
Waller, Edwin N. *397*
Waller, Thomas M. *293*
Waller, William L. *302*
Walley, Samuel H. *88*
Wallgren, Mon C. *380*
Wallgren, Monrad C. *196, 200, 203, 206, 209, 212, 314*
Wallhauser, George M. *237, 240, 243*
Wallin, Franklin W. *408*
Wallin, Homer N. *349*
Wallin, Samuel *163*
Wallin, Winston R. *494*
Walling, Ansel T. *112*
Wallis, Severn T. *420*
Wallis, W. Allen *422*
Wallop, Malcolm *267, 270, 273, 276, 279, 315*
Walls, Josiah T. *106, 108, 110*
Walmsley, Arthur E. *458*
Walmsley, Arthur Edward *457*
Walmsley, T. Semmes *389*
Walmsley, Walter N., Jr. *374*
Waln, Robert *45, 46*
Walrath, John F. *481*
Walsh, Allan B. *163*
Walsh, Arthur *211, 305*
Walsh, Charles J. *422*
Walsh, David I. *172, 175, 178, 182, 185, 188, 191, 194, 198, 201, 204, 207, 211, 214, 300, 301*
Walsh, Denny *557*
Walsh, Don *559*
Walsh, Edward J. *413, 415*
Walsh, Emmet M. *469*
Walsh, James J. *137, 542*
Walsh, John P. *365*
Walsh, John R. *220*
Walsh, Joseph *166, 169, 172, 175*
Walsh, Joseph L. *515*
Walsh, Julius S. *498*
Walsh, Louis S. *467*
Walsh, Matthew J. *421*
Walsh, Michael P. *404, 408*
Walsh, Mike *88*
Walsh, Nicolas E. *470*
Walsh, Patrick *133, 295*
Walsh, Redmond J. *415*
Walsh, Robert L. *340*
Walsh, Robert M. *359*
Walsh, Thomas E. *421*
Walsh, Thomas J. *163, 166, 169, 172, 176, 179, 182, 185, 188, 192, 303, 464, 468*
Walsh, Thomas Yates *86*
Walsh, William *111, 113*
Walsh, William B. *542, 548, 560*

Walsh, William F. *259, 263, 266*
Walsh, William T. *542*
Walsh, Willimina R. *561*
Walshe, James J. *419*
Walter, Francis E. *196, 199, 202, 205, 209, 212, 215, 218, 222, 225, 228, 231, 234, 238, 241, 244*
Walter, Paul A. F. *441*
Walter, Thomas U. *514*
Walters, Anderson H. *164, 173, 177, 183*
Walters, Barbara *548*
Walters, Basil L. *520*
Walters, George M. *495*
Walters, Henry *491*
Walters, Herbert S. *244, 312*
Walters, Jack E. *403*
Walters, Johnnie M. *380*
Walters, Raymond *419*
Walters, Robert *393*
Walters, Sumner F. D. *453, 461*
Walters, Vernon A. *379*
Walters, William H. *385*
Walthall, Edward C. *123, 125, 128, 131, 133, 136, 139, 302, 324*
Walther, C. F. W. *475*
Walthour, John B. *454, 458*
Walton, Aubrey G. *472*
Walton, Charles W. *96*
Walton, Clarence C. *406*
Walton, Eliakim P. *93, 95, 97*
Walton, Frank E. *494*
Walton, George *1, 2, 3, 5, 43, 295*
Walton, George L. *516*
Walton, J. C. *394*
Walton, James C. *308*
Walton, Lester A. *366*
Walton, Matthew *47, 49*
Walton, Thomas O. *416*
Walton, William B. *169*
Waltrip, William H. *494*
Walworth, Arthur *556*
Walworth, Reuben H. *60*
Walz, John A. *524*
Wampler, Fred *236*
Wampler, William C. *228, 251, 254, 257, 260, 263, 267, 270, 273*
Wanamaker, John *27, 36*
Wanamaker, Pearl *525*
Wandelmaier, Werner *535*
Wang, Chi P'ing *471*
Wangensteen, Owen H. *512, 533, 551*
Wanger, Irving P. *134, 137, 140, 143, 146, 148, 151, 154, 157*
Wanger, Walter *509*
Wangerin, Walter, Jr. *546*
Wantland, William C. *457, 458*
Wanton, Gideon *6*
Wanton, John *6*
Wanton, Joseph *6*
Wanton, William *6*
Warburg, Felix M. *433*
Warburton, Herbert B. *226*
Warburton, Stanton *161*
Warch, Richard *411*
Ward, Aaron *63, 64, 68, 69, 71, 77*
Ward, Aileen *545*
Ward, Alfred G. *348*
Ward, Andrew H. *100*
Ward, Angus *355*
Ward, Artemas *3, 42, 43, 335*
Ward, Artemas, Jr. *53, 55*
Ward, Barbara *534*

Wherry, Kenneth S. *211, 214, 218, 221, 224, 304*
Whetcroft, Burton *390*
Whetstone, Karl F. *421*
Whidden, Benjamin F. *363*
Whillock, H. Westerman *388*
Whinnery, John R. *542*
Whipple, George H. *549*
Whipple, Allen C. *533*
Whipple, Allen O. *562*
Whipple, Amiel W. *337*
Whipple, George H. *533*
Whipple, Henry B. *448, 459*
Whipple, J. C. *399*
Whipple, Thomas, Jr. *59, 61, 63, 64*
Whipple, William *1, 3*
Whipple, William G. *385*
Whistler, James A. McNeill *540*
Whitacre, John J. *160, 163*
Whitaker, Benjamin P. *417*
Whitaker, D. M. *520*
Whitaker, Frederic *521*
Whitaker, George *426*
Whitaker, H. E. *492*
Whitaker, Jard I. *387*
Whitaker, John A. *217, 220, 223*
Whitaker, John C. *495*
Whitaker, Martin D. *411*
Whitaker, O'Kelley *457, 458*
Whitaker, Ozi W. *448, 458, 460*
Whitaker, Samuel *286*
Whitcomb, Edgar *297*
Whitcomb, James *83, 85, 297*
Whitcomb, Richard T. *537, 552, 559, 563*
Whitcomb, Richard Travis *549*
White, A. C. *397*
White, Addison *86*
White, Albert B. *314*
White, Albert E. *519*
White, Albert S. *72, 74, 76, 78, 95, 297*
White, Alden P. *439*
White, Alexander *41, 42, 85*
White, Alexander C. *124*
White, Allison *92*
White, Alma B. *477*
White, Andrew D. *362, 371, 407, 513*
White, Arthur A. *342*
White, Barbara *412*
White, Bartow *63*
White, Benjamin *78*
White, Byron R. *283*
White, C. Dale *472*
White, Campbell P. *66, 68, 69*
White, Cecil F. *219*
White, Charles *425*
White, Charles B. *518*
White, Charles D. *364, 470*
White, Charles H. *341*
White, Charles L. *406*
White, Charles M. *538, 539*
White, Charles T. *521*
White, Chilton A. *96, 98*
White, Clinton I. *386*
White, Compton I. *194, 197, 200, 204, 207, 210, 213, 220*
White, Compton I., Jr. *242, 245*
White, Daniel A. *439*
White, Daniel P. *319*
White, David *61, 523*
White, Deane R. *528*
White, Donald E. *551*
White, Doris *533*
White, Dudley A. *202, 205*
White, E. B. *547, 548, 552*

White, Edward D. *66, 67, 69, 74, 76, 130, 133, 283, 298, 299, 542*
White, Emerson E. *415*
White, Eugene V. *559*
White, F. Edson *482*
White, Francis *54, 359, 367, 373*
White, Frank *292, 307, 381*
White, Frank S. *161, 291*
White, Frank X. *431*
White, Frederick E. *130*
White, George *160, 164, 170, 308*
White, George A. *497*
White, George B. *349*
White, George E. *136, 138*
White, George H. *140, 142*
White, George W. *423*
White, Gideon *390*
White, Gilbert F. *409, 538*
White, Goodrich C. *408*
White, Gordon *489*
White, H. O. *395*
White, Harry *114, 116, 398*
White, Hays B. *172, 175, 178, 181, 185*
White, Helen C. *510, 542*
White, Henry *361, 365*
White, Henry H. *417*
White, Henry S. *515*
White, Horace *306*
White, Hugh *80, 82, 84, 302*
White, Hugh L. *15, 63, 65, 66, 67, 68, 70, 72, 74, 75, 302, 312*
White, I. C. *510*
White, Ian McKibbin *438, 439*
White, Isaac D. *333, 334, 343, 344*
White, Israel C. *523*
White, Jack *557*
White, James *4, 473*
White, James B. *125, 144*
White, John *71, 72, 74, 76, 78*
White, John A. *505*
White, John B. *425*
White, John C. *363, 367, 451, 461*
White, John Campbell *370, 407*
White, John D. *111, 118, 120*
White, John H. *449, 459, 460, 558*
White, John J. *544*
White, John W. *521*
White, Joseph L. *76*
White, Joseph W. *98*
White, Julius *355*
White, K. Owen *475*
White, Katherine E. *360*
White, Kevin H. *390*
White, Lawrence G. *525*
White, Lee C. *380*
White, Leonard *52*
White, Leonard D. *517, 534, 556*
White, Leslie A. *509*
White, Luther W., III *415*
White, Lynn T., Jr. *412*
White, M. M. *510*
White, Magner *553*
White, Mark, Jr. *312*
White, Mastin G. *286*
White, Maunsel *537*
White, Michael D. *113*
White, Miller G. *329*
White, Milo *120, 123*
White, Mrs. Ashmead *526*
White, Paul D. *513*
White, Paul Dudley *532, 533, 552*

White, Paul W. *304*
White, Philip B. *536*
White, Phillips *3*
White, Philo *360*
White, Phineas *60*
White, R. E. *397*
White, R. N., Sr. *397*
White, Richard C. *248, 251, 254, 257, 260, 263, 266, 270, 273*
White, Robert *395*
White, Robert E. *361, 369*
White, Robert I. *411*
White, Robert M. *537*
White, Roger J. *459*
White, Roger John *457*
White, S. Harrison *184, 293*
White, Samuel *45, 46, 47, 48, 50, 51, 294*
White, Stafford G. *314*
White, Stephen M. *132, 135, 138, 292*
White, Stephen V. *126*
White, Steven A. *349*
White, Theodore H. *556*
White, Thomas D. *340, 346*
White, Thomas W. *386*
White, W. S., Jr. *481*
White, Wallace H., Jr. *169, 172, 175, 178, 182, 185, 188, 191, 194, 198, 201, 204, 207, 211, 214, 217, 299*
White, Walter *525, 561*
White, Walter M. *476*
White, Wilbur M. *192*
White, Wilbur W. *423*
White, William *1, 308, 447, 460*
White, William A. *518, 520*
White, William Allen *553, 554, 555, 559*
White, William H. *89*
White, William J. *134*
White, William R. *404, 409*
White, William S. *433, 552, 555*
White, Woodie W. *472*
Whiteaker, John *116, 309*
Whiteford, William K. *489*
Whitehead, Alfred North *536*
Whitehead, C. Frank *387*
Whitehead, Cortlandt *448, 461*
Whitehead, Don *555*
Whitehead, Elizabeth *521*
Whitehead, Ennis C. *340, 346*
Whitehead, Frank *351*
Whitehead, James L. *443*
Whitehead, John B. *537, 538, 544*
Whitehead, Joseph *183, 187, 190*
Whitehead, Robert F. *381*
Whitehead, Thomas *110*
Whitehill, Alexander R. *426*
Whitehill, James *54*
Whitehill, John *48, 49*
Whitehill, Robert *49, 50, 51, 53, 54*
Whitehorn, John C. *518*
Whitehouse, A. W., Jr. *490*
Whitehouse, Alton W., Jr. *497*
Whitehouse, Charles S. *366, 374*
Whitehouse, Henry J. *447, 458*
Whitehouse, John O. *109, 111*
Whitehouse, Seth C. *389*
Whitehouse, Sheldon *359, 363*
Whitehouse, William P. *300*
Whitehouse, William W. *403*
Whitehurst, G. William *254, 257, 260, 263, 267, 270, 273, 276, 279*
Whitelaw, Robert H. *128*

Whiteley, Richard H. *103, 106, 108*
Whiteley, William G. *91, 93*
Whitener, Basil L. *234, 237, 240, 244, 247, 250*
Whiteside, Jenkin *52, 53, 311*
Whiteside, John *55, 57*
Whitesides, Lawson Ewing *523*
Whitfield, Albert H. *302*
Whitfield, Henry L. *302*
Whitfield, James *302, 464, 470*
Whitfield, James B. *295*
Whitfield, Robert L. *321*
Whitfield, Willis J. *541*
Whitford, Greeley W. *293*
Whiting, Frederic A. *438, 439*
Whiting, Harry H. *494*
Whiting, Justin R. *125, 128, 131, 133, 486*
Whiting, Richard H. *110*
Whiting, William *108, 120, 123, 125*
Whiting, William D. *349*
Whiting, William F. *29, 37*
Whiting, William H., Jr. *409*
Whiting, William H. C. *322*
Whitley, Charles *266*
Whitley, Charles O. *272, 275, 278*
Whitley, James L. *189, 192, 195*
Whitlock, Brand *356*
Whitlock, John J. *440*
Whitlock, Roger H. *416*
Whitly, Charles *269*
Whitman, Benaiah L. *406, 408*
Whitman, Charles S. *306, 511*
Whitman, Ezekiel *51, 56, 58, 59, 300*
Whitman, Ezra B. *519*
Whitman, Frederic B. *433*
Whitman, Lemuel *60*
Whitman, Walt *540*
Whitmarsh, Thomas *397*
Whitmer, George C. *388*
Whitmire, B. N. *503*
Whitmire, Kathryn *397*
Whitmore, Elias *63*
Whitmore, Frank C. *511*
Whitmore, George W. *105*
Whitmore, Kay R. *487*
Whitney, A. F. *504*
Whitney, Cornelius V. *494*
Whitney, Eli *540*
Whitney, George *432*
Whitney, Hassler *549*
Whitney, John D. *409*
Whitney, John Hay *362, 545*
Whitney, Louis B. *385*
Whitney, Thomas R. *90*
Whitney, William C. *26, 27, 35*
Whitney, William D. *517*
Whitney, Willis R. *511, 522, 538, 539, 548*
Whiton, Edward V. *315*
Whitsett, Charles E., Jr. *537*
Whitson, G. S. *510*
Whitson, William O. *510*
Whitt, Richard *558*
Whittaker, Charles E. *283, 285*
Whittaker, Robert R. *268, 271, 274, 277*
Whittemore, B. Frank *103, 105*
Whittemore, Don Juan *519*
Whittemore, Edward W. *481*
Whittemore, Herbert L. *544*
Whittemore, Lewis B. *452*
Whittemore, Reed H. *532*

Wilson, Riley J. *165, 169, 172, 175, 178, 181, 185, 188, 191, 194, 198*
Wilson, Robert *96, 98, 303*
Wilson, Robert B. *499*
Wilson, Robert C. *226, 229, 232, 235, 239, 242, 245, 248, 251, 255, 258, 264, 267*
Wilson, Robert E. *482*
Wilson, Robert G. *414*
Wilson, Robert G., Jr. *527*
Wilson, Robert P. C. *128, 131*
Wilson, Robert R. *519, 537, 538, 549*
Wilson, Russell *394*
Wilson, S. Davis *395*
Wilson, Samuel *413*
Wilson, Samuel B. *302*
Wilson, Samuel J. *425, 473*
Wilson, Samuel K. *411*
Wilson, Scott *284, 300*
Wilson, Simon C. *395*
Wilson, Stanley C. *313*
Wilson, Stanyarne *137, 140, 143*
Wilson, Stephen F. *101, 103*
Wilson, T. A. *537, 563*
Wilson, T. Webber *179, 182, 185*
Wilson, Ted *397*
Wilson, Theodore D. *349*
Wilson, Thomas *53, 54, 55, 125, 302, 398*
Wilson, Thomas B. *509*
Wilson, Thomas M. *364*
Wilson, Thornton A. *483*
Wilson, Val H. *416*
Wilson, W. Bruce *474*
Wilson, W. L. *524*
Wilson, W. T. *319*
Wilson, Walter K. *341*
Wilson, Walter K., Jr. *331*
Wilson, Willard *419*
Wilson, William *55, 57, 61, 63, 65, 296, 387*
Wilson, William A. *363*
Wilson, William B. *28, 37, 154, 157, 160*
Wilson, William E. *178*
Wilson, William H. *199, 474*
Wilson, William L. *27, 36, 122, 124, 127, 129, 132, 135, 425*
Wilson, William S. *320*
Wilson, William W. *147, 150, 153, 156, 159, 165, 168, 172*
Wilson, Winston P. *331*
Wilson, Woodrow *11, 17, 28, 305, 414, 513, 517, 540, 549*
Wilstach, Charles F. *394*
Wilthrow, Gardner R. *222*
Wiltz, Louis A. *299, 389*
Wiman, Charles Deere *486*
Wimberley, Don A. *459*
Wimberly, Don Adger *457*
Wimberly, George E. *385*
Wimberly, W. Carl *424*
Wimer, John M. *392*
Wimpress, Gordon D., Jr. *417*
Winans, Edwin B. *120, 123, 301, 333, 418*
Winans, James J. *105*
Winans, John *122*
Winant, John G. *304, 362, 382, 526*
Winborne, J. Wallace *307*
Winchell, Alexander *416, 523*
Winchell, Newton H. *523*
Winchester, Boyd *104, 106, 373*
Winchester, James R. *450, 458*
Winchester, M. B. *396*
Winder, Levin *300*
Winder, William H. *330, 331*

Winding, Charles A. *491*
Windle, William F. *543*
Windom, William *26, 27, 34, 94, 96, 98, 100, 102, 104, 106, 109, 111, 113, 116, 118, 302*
Wine, J. R., Jr. *392*
Wine, James W. *365, 366*
Winebrenner, John *477*
Winer, Donald A. *440*
Winfield, Charles H. *98, 100*
Wing, Asa S. *495*
Wing, E. Rumsey *360*
Wing, George W. *397*
Wing, John D. *452, 461*
Wing, Leonard F. *342*
Wingate, Joseph F. *64, 66*
Wingate, Paine *3, 41, 42, 43, 304*
Wingate, Washington M. *425*
Wingfield, Clyde J. *404, 413*
Wingfield, Edward M. *6*
Wingfield, J. W. *398*
Wingfield, John H. D. *448, 460*
Wingo, Effiegene (Locke) *187, 190*
Wingo, Otis *161, 165, 168, 171, 174, 177, 181, 184, 187*
Winick, Myron *542*
Winkelmann, Christian H. *466*
Winkenwerder, Hugh *423*
Winkler, Henry R. *419*
Winlock, Herbert E. *440*
Winn, A. M. *386*
Winn, Courtland S. *387*
Winn, Larry, Jr. *249, 252, 255, 258, 262, 265, 268, 271, 274*
Winn, Richard *43, 44, 47, 48, 49, 50, 52, 53*
Winn, Thomas E. *130*
Winne, Harry A. *539*
Winnet, Nochem S. *432*
Winnett, H. J. *392*
Winpisinger, William W. *504*
Winship, Blanton *331*
Winship, North *375*
Winship, Thomas *545*
Winslow, Charles Edward *561*
Winslow, Charles-Edward A. *518*
Winslow, Edward *1, 5*
Winslow, Gilbert *1*
Winslow, John B. *315*
Winslow, Josiah *5*
Winslow, Loa Elizabeth *554*
Winslow, Samuel E. *162, 166, 169, 172, 175, 179*
Winslow, Warren *90, 92, 94, 307*
Winsor, Curtin, Jr. *359*
Winsor, Justin *513, 514, 515*
Winsor, Lou B. *527*
Winstanley, Thomas *396*
Winstead, W. Arthur *211, 214, 217, 221, 224, 227, 230, 233, 237, 240, 243*
Winstein, Saul *549*
Winston, Clara *546*
Winston, Frederick S. *492*
Winston, George T. *413, 421, 423*
Winston, John A. *291*
Winston, Joseph *43, 48, 49*
Winston, Phillip B. *391*
Winston, Richard *546*
Winter, Andrew *542, 560*
Winter, Charles E. *180, 184, 187*
Winter, Edwin W. *493*
Winter, Elisha J. *54*
Winter, George Ben W. *512*

Winter, Harrison L. *284*
Winter, John G. *517*
Winter, Ralph K., Jr. *284*
Winter, T. Z. *393*
Winter, Thomas D. *204, 207, 210, 214*
Winter, William *302*
Winterle, Fred S. *387*
Winters, Glenn R. *514*
Winters, Robert W. *542*
Winters, Terry *560*
Winters, Yvor *534, 535*
Winthrop, Fitz-John *5*
Winthrop, Francis B. *387*
Winthrop, John *5*
Winthrop, John, Jr. *5*
Winthrop, Robert C. *75, 76, 78, 80, 81, 82, 84, 301*
Winthrop, Thomas L. *509*
Winthrop, Waitsill *7*
Wirt, William *15, 24, 34*
Wirth, Conrad L. *380, 559*
Wirth, Louis *520*
Wirth, Timothy E. *261, 264, 267, 270, 273, 277, 293*
Wirtz, W. Willard *30, 31, 37, 540*
Wisdom, John M. *284*
Wise, George D. *119, 122, 124, 126, 129, 132, 135*
Wise, Henry A. *70, 72, 74, 77, 79, 313, 357*
Wise, Henry Augustus *349*
Wise, Henry W. *76*
Wise, James *451, 459*
Wise, James W. *165, 168, 171, 175*
Wise, John S. *122*
Wise, Morgan R. *116, 119*
Wise, Peter M. *518*
Wise, Raleigh J. *544*
Wise, Richard A. *140, 143*
Wise, Robert *522*
Wise, Robert E., Jr. *276, 279*
Wise, Wes *397*
Wisely, H. R. *521*
Wiser, Forwood C., Jr. *494, 497*
Wishart, Charles F. *407, 473*
Wishart, Paul B. *489*
Wishart, W. I. *474*
Wisner, Frank G., II *355, 376*
Wisner, Henry *4*
Wisner, Moses *301*
Wisner, William *473*
Wisner, William C. *473*
Wissemann, Andrew F. *462*
Wissemann, Andrew Frederick *457*
Wisser, John P. *333, 339*
Wistar, Caspar *517*
Wistar, Isaac J. *509, 517*
Wister, Owen *559*
Wiswell, Andrew P. *300*
Witcher, John S. *105*
Witcher, Robert Campbell *456, 459*
Witherell, James *50*
Witherow, W. P. *525*
Withers, Charles D. *371*
Withers, Garrett L. *220, 226, 298*
Withers, Jones M. *322, 323*
Withers, Robert E. *112, 114, 117, 314*
Withers, Thomas J. *319, 320*
Witherspoon, James H. *321*
Witherspoon, James W. *473*
Witherspoon, John *1, 2, 4, 414, 473*
Witherspoon, John A. *515*

Witherspoon, Robert *52*
Witherspoon, Samuel A. *159, 163, 166*
Witherspoon, William W. *329*
Withington, Frederic S. *349*
Withrow, Gardner R. *193, 196, 200, 203, 225, 229, 232, 235, 238*
Withrow, John L. *473*
Withycombe, James *309*
Witkin, Jerome *531*
Witman, William, II *374*
Witmer, C. Paul *432*
Witmer, Percy *392*
Witschey, Robert E. *514*
Witschi, Emil *520*
Witsell, Edward F. *330*
Witt, Elder *546*
Witt, Helen M. *380*
Witte, Edwin E. *513*
Witte, Richard S *524*
Wittemore, Lewis B. *462*
Witter, R. H. *505*
Witthorne, Washington C. *129*
Witthuhn, I. R. *523*
Wittmann, Otto *443*
Woelfle, Arthur W. *491*
Woerner, Frederick F., Jr. *334*
Woffard, Thomas A. *231*
Wofford, Harris L., Jr. *405*
Wofford, Thomas A. *311*
Wogan, John B. *343*
Wohl, Robert *547*
Wohlstetter, Roberta *534*
Wolchok, Samuel *505*
Wolcott, Daniel F. *294*
Wolcott, Edward O. *127, 130, 132, 135, 138, 141, 293*
Wolcott, James L. *294*
Wolcott, Jesse P. *191, 195, 198, 201, 204, 208, 211, 214, 217, 220, 224, 227, 230*
Wolcott, Josiah O. *168, 171, 175, 294*
Wolcott, Oliver *1, 2, 3, 293*
Wolcott, Oliver, Jr. *23, 33, 293*
Wolcott, Roger *1, 5, 7, 300*
Wold, John *254*
Wolf, Frank R. *273, 276, 279*
Wolf, Fred Alan *547*
Wolf, George *61, 63, 65, 309*
Wolf, Harry B. *153*
Wolf, Leonard G. *236*
Wolf, Milton A. *356*
Wolf, Robert A. *561*
Wolf, Sidney K. *528*
Wolf, Stewart *541*
Wolf, William P. *104*
Wolfe, Albert B. *513*
Wolfe, Frederick B. *455, 459*
Wolfe, Linnie Marsh *555*
Wolfe, Simeon K. *108*
Wolfe, Tom *546*
Wolfenden, James *186, 189, 193, 196, 199, 202, 205, 209, 212, 215*
Wolff, Harold G. *516, 541*
Wolff, Herbert E. *333*
Wolff, Irving *537*
Wolff, J. Scott *179*
Wolff, Lester L. *247, 250, 253, 256, 259, 263, 266, 269*
Wolff, Miles H. *520*
Wolfgang, Marvin E. *509*
Wolfolk, Jean *476*
Wolford, Frank L. *120, 123*
Wolfowitz, Paul D. *364*
Wolfrum, William H. *457*
Wolfson, Albert *535*
Wolkin, Paul A. *514*
Wolkomir, Nathan T. *505*

Organization Index

This index cites the institutions, agencies, military commands, states and cities, awards, and other organizations under which personal names are listed in *Notable Americans*.